CONSTITUTIONAL LAW

Fifth Edition

CONSTITUTIONAL LAW

FIFTH EDITION

Norman Redlich
Dean Emeritus and Judge Edward Weinfeld Professor of Law Emeritus
New York University School of Law

John Attanasio
Dean and William Hawley Atwell Professor of Constitutional Law
Dedman School of Law at Southern Methodist University

Joel K. Goldstein
Vincent C. Immel Professor of Law
Saint Louis University School of Law

Library of Congress Cataloging-in-Publication Data

Redlich, Norman.
Constututional law / Norman Redlich, John Attanasio,
Joel K. Goldstein.—5th ed.
p. cm.
Includes index.
ISBN 978–1–4224–1738–6 (hard cover)
1. Constitutional law—United States—Cases. I. Attanasio, John. II. Goldstein, Joel K. (Joel Kramer), 1953–III. Title.
KF4549.R4 2008
342.73–dc22
2008005854

This publication is designed to provide accurate and authoritative information in regard to the subject matter covered. It is sold with the understanding that the publisher is not engaged in rendering legal, accounting, or other professional services. If legal advice or other expert assistance is required, the services of a competent professional should be sought.

LexisNexis, the knowledge burst logo, and Michie are trademarks of Reed Elsevier Properties Inc, used under license. Matthew Bender is a registered trademark of Matthew Bender Properties Inc.

NOTE TO USERS

To ensure that you are using the latest materials available in this area, please be sure to periodically check the LexisNexis Law School web site for downloadable updates and supplements at www.lexisnexis.com/lawschool.

Editorial Offices
744 Broad Street, Newark, NJ 07102 (973) 820-2000
201 Mission St., San Francisco, CA 94105-1831 (415) 908-3200
www.lexisnexis.com

MATTHEW◆BENDER

(2008–Pub.170)

ACKNOWLEDGMENTS

A number of people helped us produce this Fifth Edition of this casebook. We would like to thank Kathleen Spartana for her outstanding editing and administrative help and research assistants Lea Ann Carlisle, John J. Greffet, Merideth Helgeson, Laura Kemp, Nancy McCahan, Mark Murray, Elizabeth Stewart Raines, Susan Southerland, and Heather Stobaugh for their significant contributions, and Mary Dougherty, Tina Brosseau and Rachael Short for their help in organizing and typing the book. As always, we appreciate the institutional support of Dedman School of Law at Southern Methodist University; Saint Louis University School of Law; and Wachtell, Lipton, Rosen & Katz. Pali Chheda of LexisNexis helped edit this Fifth Edition.

Bernard Schwartz co-authored the first three editions of this book. He died on December 23, 1997 and accordingly did not work on subsequent editions. He was a giant among those who follow the Supreme Court's work and who interpret the Constitution, and he is greatly missed.

Joel Goldstein is primarily responsible for the first six chapters. John Attanasio and Norman Redlich prepared chapters 7 to 16.

Norman Redlich

John Attanasio

Joel K. Goldstein

March 2008

PREFACE

This book aims to present Constitutional Law in the grand tradition. More than 200 years after its adoption, the United States Constitution continues to provide the basic framework against which many of our problems are addressed. The enterprise of constitutional interpretation involves government officials in all three branches yet judges play a unique role. The judicial review power distinguishes American judges from those of many other lands. Many other nations have now adopted it.

The power is truly awesome. Six citizens — five members of the Supreme Court and one person challenging a law — can trump the wishes of popular majorities and lead to a rule of constitutional law binding on other branches of government and the nation at large. Constitutional jurisprudence is riveting, too, due to the nature of the questions it routinely addresses. These involve the basic structure of our government and our fundamental values as a society and as a culture. Indeed, we live in an age when the Supreme Court routinely encounters issues that engage deep questions of political morality.

We have tried to provide a book that will acquaint readers with constitutional law primarily as it is practiced in courts. We consciously provide readers with tools to recognize and assess the available types of constitutional arguments made in cases, and those that might have been advanced. The constitutional issues the Court addresses often involve deep questions of ethics or political theory. We have tried to organize this book in a way which would encourage students to explore those questions.

We think, too, that cases are important teaching devices. We have erred on the side of retaining the justices' language rather than editing it out and have included important concurrences and dissents. This approach helps educate students about the Court's thinking by allowing the justices to speak for themselves. It also helps redirect the focus away from narrow holdings and toward the reasoning that drives constitutional adjudication. Retaining more of the case serves several other important functions. We include the logical steps of the Court's analysis so the reader can understand the cases more thoroughly, and more quickly. The cases include more of the reasoning of the justices on issues that grow ever more complex. The inclusion of more dicta from the opinions helps the reader make sense of "the law" when decisions are the product of several opinions. Inclusion of this material also helps to predict future decisions in an era when it is growing more necessary to know the views of individual justices. Inclusion of dissents and concurrences provides a dynamic point of departure for classroom discussion as students have already been exposed to a variety of views in their reading. It also suggests the dynamics of constitutional law as students see that the dissents of one generation command majorities in other days.

The Fifth Edition remains faithful to the scheme of the first four. In order to maintain a manageable length while continuing to give a more complete view of what the justices think, we present many important cases as long notes. These notes quote profusely from the opinions of the justices; they extensively review not only majority opinions but also concurrences and dissents. While the principal cases remain less heavily edited than those of other books, they have been pruned to some extent. We also have added many more references to scholarly works with parentheticals designed not so much to summarize the work as to provoke thoughts and discussion. The ellipse structure is streamlined; for example, we often omit citations without notice.[1]

We have tried to make this book one which a range of readers will find accessible. We hope it allows them to share our passion for, and fascination with, constitutional law. For the reader's convenience, we provide a brief roadmap or overview of where we are going.

II

The book begins by examining the fundamental building block of the course, the power of judicial review. The power of courts to review the constitutionality of decisions of government is fundamental and all but a few of the cases in this book involve exercises of this power. Chapter I reviews the basic organization of the Federal court system and Congress' role in creating Federal courts and in establishing their jurisdiction. Chapter I exposes students to the power of judicial review and the limitations on the judiciary. This includes treatment of the extent to which Congress can limit the jurisdiction of the Supreme Court. Chapter I also explores justiciability, constitutional or prudential reasons why a Federal court may refuse to hear a constitutional or other challenge. Included are basic doctrines involving advisory opinions, mootness, ripeness, standing, and political questions. As with all chapters, we expose students to the types of arguments courts use to shape the doctrine and try to present sufficient material to allow them to shape their views.

The discussion of the court system and the power of judicial review is a fundamental building block for the entire course. At the same time, it also involves the structure of one branch of American government. The Framers intended to disperse power among various government entities. They viewed dispersing governmental authority as an important means of preventing tyranny. In the Federalist Papers, James Madison said:[2]

"[T]he great security against a gradual concentration of the several powers in the same department consists in giving to those who administer each department, the necessary constitutional means and personal motives to resist encroachments of the others. The provision for defense must in this, as in all other cases, be made commensurate to the danger of attack. Ambition must be made to counteract ambition. The interest of the man must be connected with the constitutional rights of the place. It may be a reflection on human nature that such devices should be necessary to control the abuses of government. But what is government itself but the greatest of all reflections on human nature? If men were angels, no government would be necessary. If angels were to govern men, neither external nor internal controls on government would be necessary. In framing a government which is to be administered by men over men, the great difficulty lies in this: you must first enable the government to control the governed; and in the next place oblige it to control itself. A dependence on the people is, no doubt, the primary control on the government; but experience has taught mankind the necessity of auxiliary precautions."

Not vesting sovereignty in a single governmental authority, like a king, presents a complex set of problems. Most important, what are the boundary lines between these various

---

[1] Ellipses frequently depart from bluebook form. When an ellipses appears, it only signifies that some material is omitted. For example, an ellipses at the end of a paragraph may mean that the rest of that paragraph is missing, or only that subsequent paragraphs are missing, or that both the remainder of that paragraph and subsequent paragraphs are missing. Moreover, if a paragraph begins with bracketed material, it indicates that some material in the beginning of the paragraph has been omitted.

[2] Federalist No. 51 *in* THE FEDERALIST 321-22 (C. Rossiter ed., 1961).

governmental entities? Moreover, who sets these boundary lines between various governmental entities? The next few chapters explore the dispersal of power among the three branches of the federal government (the doctrine of separation of powers) and the division of power between the national government and the states (the doctrine of federalism).

Chapter II analyzes the constitutional authority of the United States Congress. After contrasting enumerated and implied powers, the chapter takes up several of Congress' constitutionally enumerated powers. Congressional powers explored include the Commerce Power, the Taxing Power, the Spending Power and Treaty Power. These topics all have implications for separation of powers theory in that they all involve the division of authority between Congress and the other branches of the national government. Still, the cases treating the powers of Congress generally focus on federalism issues; that is, they focus on the division of regulatory authority between Congress and the states.

Emphasizing federalism concerns, Chapter III treats the extent to which the United States Constitution limits the power of Congress to regulate, thereby leaving regulatory power to the States. To a great extent, Chapter III focuses on the Tenth and Eleventh Amendments and structural arguments that have shaped the pertinent doctrine.

Chapter IV continues to focus on federalism issues but turns to examine the extent to which the United States Constitution limits the regulatory powers of the several states. It begins by discussing the fundamental notion that laws and regulations promulgated by the national government are supreme over competing exercises of regulatory power by the states. The chapter proceeds to examine whether there are any limits on the supremacy of the national government itself in the way of directly regulating the states. It then turns to examine intergovernmental tax and regulatory immunities, briefly explores interstate relationships, and concludes by examining the constitutional limits on the ability of the states to regulate interstate commerce. This so-called "dormant commerce clause" jurisprudence is rather extensive and consequently is treated in some detail.

Chapter V returns to separation of powers issues to examine the powers of the executive branch of the national government. The seminal *Youngstown* case is advanced to the beginning of the chapter and presented in greater length because of its centrality. Principal areas examined are authority over domestic and international affairs, and the role as commander-in-chief of the armed forces. In the domestic realm, the chapter explores the President's legislative powers and administrative powers. In connection with the international arena, we explore the foreign affairs power, the power to make executive agreements, and the commander-in-chief authority. The chapter concludes with some fascinating interbranch collisions focused on the Presidency. These include cases dealing with presidential privileges and immunities and cases raising more general themes regarding separation of powers.

The first five Chapters of the book are concerned with structure of government issues revolving around the twin themes of federalism and separation of powers. Chapters VII to XVI focus on individual rights and liberties issues. Chapter VI is the transition to individual rights issues. Specifically, this chapter treats the congressional powers to enforce individual rights using the Thirteenth, Fourteenth, of Fifteenth Amendments to the Constitution — the post-Civil War amendments. These amendments dramatically shifted regulatory power away from the states in favor of the national government. Consequently, the amendments clearly implicate federalism concerns. For example, congressional enforcement of individual rights and liberties stands in some tension with the Supreme Court's role as arbiter of the Constitution, particularly if Congress uses its enforcement power to define the scope of a constitutional right. These congressional enforcement powers thus also raise important separation of power issues.

By combining separation of powers, federalism, and individual rights issues, Chapter VI serves as a natural transition between the first five chapters of the book which focus on structure of government questions and the last ten which focus on individual rights and liberties issues. This transition also nicely illuminates several important larger points about constitutional analysis. For example, it illustrates that notwithstanding the Court's role as arbiter of the Constitution, other branches of government have authority to enforce the document as well. More importantly, the chapter illuminates the artificiality of rigidly distinguishing between issues of government structure, and issues of individual rights and liberties. The Framers certainly did not create any such stringent distinction. Their design contemplated the protection of individual rights through a government structure that divided power among many different persons and entities. Along with judicial enforcement of rights, this structure prevented impairments of individual rights through unchecked abuse of government power. Moreover, many individual rights decisions have deep structure of government implications. For example, many raise questions about the proper scope of the power of the courts in our constitutional scheme. Some cases, involving such issues as busing or election redistricting, have even more direct federalism or separation of powers implications.

Chapter VI also introduces the critical concept of state action. With rare exceptions, the Constitution only applies to the activities of government. While involvement by the government is a prerequisite for nearly all causes of action arising under the Constitution, such involvement is necessarily present in virtually all structure of government cases. Consequently, the concept of state action is not introduced until this point in the book. Without state action of some sort, no constitutional cause of action generally exists.

Chapter VII focuses on the Due Process Clauses of the Fifth and Fourteenth Amendments. These Clauses prohibit the government from depriving persons of "life, liberty, or property without due process of law." These Clauses have been interpreted by the Supreme Court to protect various categories or kinds of rights. Some of these rights have been more oriented toward property or economics; others involve more personal liberties, such as the right of the accused explicitly guaranteed by the Bill of Rights, or in such other areas as childbearing and child rearing. Some of the rights that the Court has grounded in the Due Process Clauses have largely procedural content, while others are substantive. In the course of the chapter, several additional provisions of the Constitution relating to liberty or property rights are also discussed.

Chapter VII begins by overviewing many of the changes promulgated by the post-Civil War amendments from a judicial perspective rather than the primarily legislative focus of Chapter V. The scope of the changes brought by these amendments has been so vast that many commentators refer to their promulgation as the second framing period. The chapter proceeds briefly to review how the construction of the Due Process Clause of the Fourteenth Amendment incorporates against the states select provisions of the Bill of Rights. We will primarily focus on the selective incorporation against the states of the procedural guarantees afforded a person accused of committing a crime. Proceeding to focus on economic or property rights that are overtly substantive, the chapter explores the rise and fall of liberty of contract as guaranteed by the Court through the doctrine of substantive due process. In this section, we also explore modern economic or property rights afforded by the Court using the Contracts Clause of Article 1, Section 10, and the Takings Clause of the Fifth Amendment.

PREFACE

Turning to the modern Court's revival of substantive due process, the chapter examines cases involving such matters as birth control, abortion, homosexuality and termination of life support systems. The chapter concludes by reviewing the constitutional protections for entitlements granted by the government.

The next four chapters deal with the Equal Protection Clause. With the important exception of the prohibition against titles of nobility, the emphasis on equality is of comparatively recent vintage in the American constitutional landscape. Indeed, the original document explicitly recognized slavery. Despite these ignominious beginnings, a rich jurisprudence of equality has evolved. Chapter VIII examines the developments in the area of racial discrimination. The chapter traces the downfall of segregation and continues by exploring busing and other remedies designed to dismantle segregated schools. It then examines some general themes, in particular, purposeful discrimination and suspect classes. Chapter VIII concludes by examining racial discrimination decisions applying these and other principles to such areas as employment, housing and zoning, voting, and the criminal justice system.

Chapter IX takes up a major, and more recent, theme in the Court's equal protection jurisprudence — gender discrimination. The chapter begins by surveying the different attitudes that the Court has exhibited toward gender discrimination over time. In this section, we also review the Court's struggle to settle on an appropriate standard to deal with these cases. The Court analyzes these cases using a "middle tier" level of scrutiny that is less exacting than the strict scrutiny standard used to review discrimination based on race or ethnicity. After treating some general themes in equal protection jurisprudence relating to gender, the chapter devotes separate sections to gender discrimination cases involving employment, government benefits, and pregnancy. Particularly difficult for the Court have been cases involving the constitutionality of allegedly benign discrimination programs, which are designed to compensate for past discrimination but are often criticized for falling prey to the same stereotypes that they are trying to combat.

Chapter X examines affirmative action. Many of the cases reveal the Court's struggle with the powerful ideal that the law should be color blind and gender neutral, and the harsh reality that strict adherence to this ideal hampers efforts to redress the continuing effects of past discrimination. At times the Court has emphasized what might be called the nondiscrimination principle; at other times, it has allowed affirmative action for the historically disadvantaged. Separate sections of Chapter X deal with affirmative action in education and employment. To achieve a broader understanding of the Court's affirmative action jurisprudence, we have included a few cases decided under Title VII of the Civil Rights Act of 1964, the principal statute dealing with racial, gender, and certain other forms of discrimination in employment. These Title VII cases shed additional light on the Court's affirmative action jurisprudence under the Equal Protection Clause.

Concluding the discussion of equal protection, Chapter XI surveys a number of other theories under which litigants have brought, or the Court has granted, equal protection challenges. These theories generally fall into two categories. One concerns extending some form of suspect class status to other groups. The other tack engages a different strand of equal protection jurisprudence involving fundamental rights. This latter theory maintains that certain fundamental rights, such as the right of access to the appellate process, should be distributed equally — primarily irrespective of wealth. Some decisions incorporate both fundamental rights and suspect class analyses. Chapter XI begins by discussing whether the Court should extend some form of heightened scrutiny to such groups as aliens, illegitimates, the aged, the mentally retarded, homosexuals, and the poor. It proceeds to discuss the right to travel, and equality in the political process. This latter subject involves such issues as political gerrymandering. The discussion of the Equal Protection Clause concludes by surveying the overwhelming majority of governmental actions involving economic or social policy questions in which the Court exercises virtually no scrutiny and thus affords wide discretion to governmental decisions.

The last five chapters of the book treat the rich jurisprudence of the First Amendment. Some commentators consider this amendment the capstone of American liberties. The first four chapters treat freedom of expression. Various commentators offer different justifications for stringently protecting freedom of speech, but most agree that safeguarding the free flow of information is essential in a democracy to empower the electorate to be able to make informed decisions. Chapter XII traces the development of free speech jurisprudence and the theory underlying it. This development largely evolved from cases pertaining to political speech and association.

Surprisingly, First Amendment jurisprudence did not really develop until the time of the First World War. From this starting point, Chapter XII recounts the celebrated dissents and concurrences of Justices Holmes and Brandeis that laid the groundwork for strong protection of freedom of speech. The chapter also discusses the stringent protection that the modern Court affords freedom of speech and association. Continuing with the theme of political speech and association, the chapter concludes by discussing the free speech rights of government employees. This section treats such problems as patronage dismissals of government employees, restraints on their political activity, and their ability to criticize the government.

Although it has not been construed differently from the Free Speech Clause, the First Amendment has a separate Press Clause. Chapter XIII treats the extensive body of free speech jurisprudence relating to the print and broadcast media. The chapter treats such varied issues as the doctrine against prior restraints, media access to the government, regulation and taxation of the media, confidentiality of reporters' sources, and defamation. Just as some of the doctrines discussed in Chapter XII have applicability beyond political speech and association, many of the doctrines in Chapter XIII have applicability beyond the media. Examples include constitutional protection for defamatory speech, and constitutional proscription of prior restraints against speech.

Even if one has strong rights to say whatever one chooses, these may be meaningless if one does not have ready means through which to express one's ideas. For those who do not own a newspaper, an auditorium, or another medium of communication, expressing certain unpopular ideas — or any ideas at all — may prove difficult. Chapter XIV treats public forum analysis, the primary means by which First Amendment jurisprudence seeks to afford access to the marketplace of ideas. The notion is that persons have a right to speak on certain government property. Classic public forums include parks, streets, and sidewalks. After tracing the development of public forum theory, the chapter first recounts the testing of that theory during the civil rights movement, and then examines the modern approach to public forum analysis which relates free speech rights to the character of the property where the speech takes place. The chapter also reviews cases discussing certain special candidates for public forum analysis, such as company towns, private shopping centers, and public schools.

Chapter XV discusses some special doctrines in the system of free expression. These are expressive conduct (or symbolic speech), campaign expenditures, government funding of speech activity, commercial speech, and pornography. Extending constitutional protection to these various kinds of behavior poses special dangers and problems for First Amendment jurisprudence. On the other hand, not affording constitutional protection to any of these areas poses dangers of another kind. The Court has sought to reconcile these difficulties by fashioning special doctrines for scrutinizing each of these areas. Generally, these doctrines afford less protection than First Amendment jurisprudence affords other forms of protected expression.

The last chapter of the book explores the other major pillar of the First Amendment, freedom of religion. Treating this topic last in no way reflects its importance in the constitutional scheme. Many people came to this nation seeking to escape religious persecution and secure freedom of conscience. The Constitution enshrined these aspirations in two provisions, the Establishment and the Free Exercise Clauses. The former prohibits the state from establishing religion; the latter prohibits the government from interfering with freedom of conscience and religious worship. As the cases indicate, the Clauses stand in some tension with each other. Specific topics treated in Chapter XVI include aid to religious schools, prayer in the public schools, displays of religious symbols, and Sunday closing laws. The book concludes with cases focusing on the free exercise of religion.

"Human history," says H. G. Wells, "is in essence a history of ideas." The great theme in the history of American Constitutional Law is the concept of law as a check upon public power. That idea has been given practical reality in the decisions of the Supreme Court of the United States. Those decisions are — to paraphrase Holmes — a virtual magic mirror in which we see reflected our whole constitutional development and all that it has meant to the nation. When one thinks on this majestic theme, the eyes dazzle: that is what Constitutional Law is all about. If only part of our feelings are communicated to those who use the book, we will be amply rewarded for our efforts.

Norman Redlich

John Attanasio

Joel K. Goldstein

March 2008

Table of Contents

Table of Contents

Table of Contents

Table of Contents

Table of Contents

Table of Contents

Table of Contents

Table of Contents

Table of Contents

Table of Contents

Table of Contents

Table of Contents

Table of Contents

Table of Contents

Table of Contents

Table of Contents

Table of Contents

Table of Contents

Table of Contents

Chapter I

JUDICIAL REVIEW: ESTABLISHMENT AND OPERATION

§ 1.01 ESTABLISHMENT

MARBURY v. MADISON
5 U.S. (1 Cranch) 137, 2 L. Ed. 60 (1803)

[Editor's Note: At the December, 1801 term of the Supreme Court, William Marbury and others petitioned the Court to order Secretary of State James Madison to show cause why a mandamus should not issue directing him to deliver to petitioners commissions as Justices of the Peace. Affidavits established that a) President John Adams had nominated the petitioners to be Justices of the Peace of the District of Columbia; b) the Senate had advised and consented to the nominations, c) President Adams had signed their commissions appointing them; d) the Secretary of State had affixed the United States seal to the commissions, and e) despite requests, the commissions had not been delivered.]

Mr. Chief Justice Marshall delivered the opinion of the court.

At the last term, on the affidavits then read and filed with the clerk, a rule was granted in this case, requiring the secretary of state to show cause why a mandamus should not issue, directing him to deliver to William Marbury his commission as a justice of the peace for the county of Washington, in the district of Columbia. . . .

In the order in which the court has viewed this subject, the following questions have been considered and decided.

1. Has the applicant a right to the commission he demands? . . .

2. If he has a right, and that right has been violated, do the laws of his country afford him a remedy?

3. If they do afford him a remedy, is it a mandamus issuing from this court?

The first object of enquiry is,

1. Has the applicant a right to the commission he demands?

It is therefore, decidedly, the opinion of the court, that when a commission has been signed by the president, the appointment is made; and that the commission is complete, when the seal of the United States has been affixed to it by the secretary of state.

Where an officer is removable at the will of the executive, the circumstance which completes his appointment is of no concern; because the act is at any time revocable; and the commission may be arrested, if still in the office. But when the officer is not removable at the will of the executive, the appointment is not revocable and cannot be annulled. It has conferred legal rights which cannot be resumed.

The discretion of the executive is to be exercised until the appointment has been made. But having once made the appointment, his power over the office is terminated in all cases, where by law the officer is not removable by him. The right to the office is then in the person appointed, and he has the absolute, unconditional power of accepting or rejecting it.

Mr. Marbury, then, since his commission was signed by the president and sealed by the secretary of state, was appointed; and as the law creating the office, gave the officer a right to hold for five years, independent of the executive, the appointment was not revocable; but vested in the officer legal rights, which are protected by the laws of his country.

To withhold his commission, therefore, is an act deemed by the court not warranted by law, but violative of a vested legal right.

This brings us to the second inquiry; which is,

2. If he has a right, and that right has been violated, do the laws of his country afford him a remedy?

The very essence of civil liberty certainly consists in the right of every individual to claim the protection of the laws, whenever he receives an injury. One of the first duties of government is to afford that protection. In Great Britain the king himself is sued in the respectful form of a petition, and he never fails to comply with the judgment of his court. . . .

The government of the United States has been emphatically termed a government of laws, and not of men. It will certainly cease to deserve this high appellation, if the laws furnish no remedy for the violation of a vested legal right.

If this obloquy is to be cast on the jurisprudence of our country, it must arise from the peculiar character of the case.

It behooves us then to enquire whether there be in its composition any ingredient which shall exempt from legal investigation, or exclude the injured party from legal redress. In pursuing this enquiry the first question which presents itself, is, whether this can be arranged with that class of cases which comes under the description of damnum absque injuria — a loss without an injury.

This description of cases never has been considered, and it is believed never can be considered as comprehending offices of trust, of honour or of profit. The office of justice of peace in the district of Columbia is such an office; it is therefore worthy of the attention and guardianship of the laws. It has received that attention and guardianship. It has been created by special act of congress, and has been secured, so far as the laws can give security to the person appointed to fill it, for five years. It is not then on account of the worthlessness of the thing pursued, that the injured party can be alleged to be without remedy.

Is it in the nature of the transaction? Is the act of delivering or withholding a commission to be considered as a mere political act, belonging to the executive department alone, for the performance of which entire confidence is placed by our constitution in the supreme executive; and for any misconduct respecting which, the injured individual has no remedy.

That there may be such cases is not to be questioned; but that every act of duty, to be performed in any of the great departments of government constitutes such a case, is not to be admitted. . . .

It is not believed that any person whatever would attempt to maintain such a proposition.

It follows then that the question, whether the legality of an act of the head of a department be examinable in a court of justice or not, must always depend on the nature of that act.

If some acts be examinable, and others not, there must be some rule of law to guide the court in the exercise of its jurisdiction.

In some instances there may be difficulty in applying the rule to particular cases; but there cannot, it is believed, be much difficulty in laying down the rule.

By the constitution of the United States, the president is invested with certain important political powers, in the exercise of which he is to use his own discretion, and is accountable only to his country in his political character, and to his own conscience. To aid him in the performance of these duties, he is authorized to appoint certain officers, who act by his authority and in conformity with his orders.

In such cases, their acts are his acts; and whatever opinion may be entertained of the manner in which executive discretion may be used, still there exists, and can exist, no power to control that discretion. The subjects are political. They respect the nation, not individual rights, and being entrusted to the executive, the decision of the executive is conclusive. The application of this remark will be perceived by adverting to the act of congress for establishing the department of foreign affairs. This officer, as his duties were prescribed by that act, is to conform precisely to the will of the president. He is the mere organ by whom that will is communicated. The acts of such an officer, as an officer, can never be examinable by the courts.

But when the legislature proceeds to impose on that officer other duties; when he is directed peremptorily to perform certain acts; when the rights of individuals are dependent on the performance of those acts; he is so far the officer of the law; is amenable to the laws for his conduct; and cannot at his discretion sport away the vested rights of others.

The conclusion from this reasoning is, that where the heads of departments are the political or confidential agents of the executive, merely to execute the will of the president, or rather to act in cases in which the executive possesses a constitutional or legal discretion, nothing can be more perfectly clear than that their acts are only politically examinable. But where a specific duty is assigned by law, and individual rights depend upon the performance of that duty, it seems equally clear that the individual who considers himself injured, has a right to resort to the laws of his country for a remedy.

If this be the rule, let us inquire how it applies to the case under the consideration of the court.

The power of nominating to the senate, and the power of appointing the person nominated, are political powers, to be exercised by the president according to his own discretion. When he has made an appointment, he has exercised his whole power, and his discretion has been completely applied to the case. If, by law, the officer be removable at the will of the president, then a new appointment may be immediately made, and the rights of the officer are terminated. But as a fact which has existed cannot be made never to have existed, the appointment cannot be annihilated; and consequently if the officer is by law not removable at the will of the president, the rights he has acquired are protected by the law, and are not resumable by the president. They cannot be extinguished by executive authority, and he has the privilege of asserting them in like manner as if they had been derived from any other source.

The question whether a right has vested or not, is, in its nature, judicial, and must be tried by the judicial authority, If, for example, Mr. Marbury had taken the oaths of a magistrate, and proceeded to act as one; in consequence of which a suit had been instituted against him, in which his defence had depended on his being a magistrate; the validity of his appointment must have been determined by judicial authority.

So, if he conceives that, by virtue of his appointment he has a legal right either to the commission which has been made out for him, or to a copy of that commission, it is equally a question examinable in a court, and the decision of the court upon it must depend on the opinion entertained of his appointment.

That question has been discussed, and the opinion is, that the latest point of time which can be taken as that at which the appointment was complete, and evidenced, was when, after the signature of the president, the seal of the United States was affixed to the commission.

It is then the opinion of the court,

1. That by signing the commission of Mr. Marbury, the president of the United States appointed him a justice of peace for the county of Washington in the district of Columbia; and that the seal of the United States, affixed thereto by the secretary of state, is conclusive testimony of the verity of the signature, and of the completion of the appointment; and that the appointment conferred on him a legal right to the office for the space of five years.

2. That, having this legal title to the office, he has a consequent right to the commission; a refusal to deliver which is a plain violation of that right, for which the laws of his country afford him a remedy.

It remains to be enquired whether,

3. He is entitled to the remedy for which he applies. . . .

This, then, is a plain case for a mandamus, either to deliver the commission, or a copy of it from the record; and it only remains to be enquired,

Whether it can issue from this court.

The act to establish the judicial courts of the United States authorizes the Supreme Court "to issue writs of mandamus, in cases warranted by the principles and usages of law, to any courts appointed, or persons holding office, under the authority of the United States."

The secretary of state, being a person holding an office under the authority of the United States, is precisely within the letter of the description; and if this court is not authorized to issue a writ of mandamus to such an officer, it must be because the law is unconstitutional, and therefore absolutely incapable of conferring the authority, and assigning the duties which its words purport to confer and assign.

The constitution vests the whole judicial power of the United States in one Supreme Court, and such inferior courts as congress shall, from time to time, ordain and establish. This power is expressly extended to all cases arising under the laws of the United States; and consequently, in some form, may be exercised over the present case; because the right claimed is given by a law of the United States.

In the distribution of this power it is declared that "the Supreme Court shall have original jurisdiction in all cases affecting ambassadors, other public ministers and consuls, and those in which a state shall be a party. In all other cases, the Supreme Court shall have appellate jurisdiction."

It has been insisted, at the bar, that as the original grant of jurisdiction to the supreme and inferior courts is general, and the clause, assigning original jurisdiction to the Supreme Court, contains no negative or restrictive words; the power remains to the legislature, to assign original jurisdiction to that court in other cases than those specified in the article which has been recited; provided those cases belong to the judicial power of the United States.

If it had been intended to leave it in the discretion of the legislature to apportion the judicial power between the supreme and inferior courts according to the will of that body, it would certainly have been useless to have proceeded further than to have defined the judicial power, and the tribunals in which it should be vested. The subsequent part of the section is mere surplusage, is entirely without meaning, if such is to be the construction. If congress remains at liberty to give this court appellate jurisdiction, where the constitution has declared their jurisdiction shall be original; and original jurisdiction where the constitution has declared it shall be appellate; the distribution of jurisdiction made in the constitution, is form without substance. . . .

When an instrument organizing fundamentally a judicial system, divides it into one supreme, and so many inferior courts as the legislature may ordain and establish; then enumerates its powers, and proceeds so far to distribute them, as to define the jurisdiction of the Supreme Court by declaring the cases in which it shall take original jurisdiction, and that in others it shall take appellate jurisdiction; the plain import of the words seems to be, that in one class of cases its jurisdiction is original, and not appellate; in the other it is appellate, and not original. If any other construction would render the clause inoperative, that is an additional reason for rejecting such other construction, and for adhering to their obvious meaning.

To enable this court then to issue a mandamus, it must be shown to be an exercise of appellate jurisdiction, or to be necessary to enable them to exercise appellate jurisdiction.

It has been stated at the bar that the appellate jurisdiction may be exercised in a variety of forms, and that if it be the will of the legislature that a mandamus should be used for that purpose, that will must be obeyed. This is true; yet the jurisdiction must be appellate, not original.

It is the essential criterion of appellate jurisdiction, that it revises and corrects the proceedings in a cause already instituted, and does not create that cause. Although, therefore, a mandamus may be directed to courts, yet to issue such a writ to an officer for the delivery of a paper, is in effect the same as to sustain an original action for that paper, and therefore seems not to belong to appellate, but to original jurisdiction. Neither is it necessary in such a case as this, to enable the court to exercise its appellate jurisdiction.

The authority, therefore, given to the Supreme Court, by the act establishing the judicial courts of the United States, to issue writs of mandamus to public officers, appears not to be warranted by the constitution; and it becomes necessary to inquire whether a jurisdiction, so conferred, can be exercised.

The question, whether an act, repugnant to the constitution, can become the law of the land, is a question deeply interesting to the United States; but, happily, not of an intricacy proportioned to its interest. It seems only necessary to recognize certain principles, supposed to have been long and well established, to decide it.

That the people have an original right to establish, for their future government, such principles as, in their opinion, shall most conduce to their own happiness, is the basis on which the whole American fabric has been erected. The exercise of this original right is a very great exertion; nor can it nor ought it to be frequently repeated. The principles, therefore, so established, are deemed fundamental. And as the authority, from which they proceed, is supreme, and can seldom act, they are designed to be permanent.

This original and supreme will organizes the government, and assigns to different departments their respective powers. It may either stop here; or establish certain limits not to be transcended by those departments.

The government of the United States is of the latter description. The powers of the legislature are defined and limited; and that those limits may not be mistaken or forgotten, the constitution is written. To what purpose are powers limited, and to what purpose is that limitation committed to writing, if these limits may, at any time, be passed by those intended to be restrained? The distinction, between a government with limited and unlimited powers is abolished, if those limits do not confine the persons on whom they are imposed, and if acts prohibited and acts allowed, are of equal obligation. It is a proposition too plain to be contested, that the constitution controls any legislative act repugnant to it; or, that the legislature may alter the constitution by an ordinary act.

Between these alternatives there is no middle ground. The constitution is either a superior, paramount law, unchangeable by ordinary means, or it is on a level with ordinary legislative acts, and like other acts, is alterable when the legislature shall please to alter it.

If the former part of the alternative be true, then a legislative act contrary to the constitution is not law: if the latter part be true, then written constitutions are absurd attempts, on the part of the people, to limit a power in its own nature illimitable.

Certainly all those who have framed written constitutions contemplate them as forming the fundamental and paramount law of the nation, and consequently the theory of every such government must be, that an act of the legislature, repugnant to the constitution is void.

This theory is essentially attached to a written constitution, and is consequently to be considered, by this court, as one of the fundamental principles of our society. It is not therefore to be lost sight of in the further consideration of this subject.

If an act of the legislature, repugnant to the constitution, is void, does it, notwithstanding its invalidity, bind the courts and oblige them to give it effect? Or, in other words, though it be not law, does it constitute a rule as operative as if it was a law? This would be to overthrow in fact what was established in theory; and would seem, at first view, an absurdity too gross to be insisted on. It shall, however, receive a more attentive consideration.

It is emphatically the province and duty of the judicial department to say what the law is. Those who apply the rule to particular cases, must of necessity expound and interpret that rule. If two laws conflict with each other, the courts must decide on the operation of each.

So if a law be in opposition to the constitution: if both the law and the constitution apply to a particular case, so that the court must either decide that case conformably to the law, disregarding the constitution; or conformably to the constitution, disregarding the law: the court must determine which of these conflicting rules governs the case. This is of the very essence of judicial duty.

If then the courts are to regard the constitution; and the constitution is superior to any ordinary act of the legislature; the constitution, and not such ordinary act, must govern the case to which they both apply.

Those then who controvert the principle that the constitution is to be considered, in court, as a paramount law, are reduced to the necessity of maintaining that courts must close their eyes on the constitution, and see only the law.

This doctrine would subvert the very foundation of all written constitutions. It would declare that an act, which, according to the principles and theory of our government, is entirely void; is yet, in practice, completely obligatory. It would declare, that if the legislature shall do what is expressly forbidden, such act, notwithstanding the express prohibition, is in reality effectual. It would be giving to the legislature a practical and real omnipotence with the same breath which professes to restrict their powers within narrow limits. It is prescribing limits, and declaring that those limits may be passed at pleasure.

That it thus reduces to nothing what we have deemed the greatest improvement on political institutions — a written constitution, would of itself be sufficient, in America, where written constitutions have been viewed with so much reverence, for rejecting the construction. But the peculiar expressions of the constitution of the United States furnish additional arguments in favour of its rejection.

The judicial power of the United States is extended to all cases arising under the constitution. Could it be the intention of those who gave this power, to say that, in using it, the constitution should not be looked into? That a case arising under the constitution should be decided without examining the instrument under which it arises?

This is too extravagant to be maintained.

In some cases then, the constitution must be looked into by the judges. And if they can open it at all, what part of it are they forbidden to read, or to obey?

There are many other parts of the constitution which serve to illustrate this subject.

It is declared that "no tax or duty shall be laid on articles exported from any state." Suppose a duty on the export of cotton, of tobacco, or of flour; and a suit instituted to recover it. Ought judgment to be rendered in such a case? Ought the judges to close their eyes on the constitution, and only see the law?

The constitution declares that "no bill of attainder or ex post facto law shall be passed."

If, however, such a bill should be passed and a person should be prosecuted under it; must the court condemn to death those victims whom the constitution endeavours to preserve?

"No person," says the constitution, "shall be convicted of treason unless on the testimony of two witnesses to the same overt act, or on confession in open court."

Here the language of the constitution is addressed especially to the courts. It prescribes, directly for them, a rule of evidence not to be departed from. If the legislature should change that rule, and declare one witness, or a confession out of court, sufficient for conviction, must the constitutional principle yield to the legislative act?

From these, and many other selections which might be made, it is apparent, that the framers of the constitution contemplated that instrument as a rule for the government of courts, as well as of the legislature.

Why otherwise does it direct the judges to take an oath to support it? This oath certainly applies, in an especial manner, to their conduct in their official character. How immoral to impose it on them, if they were to be used as the instruments, and the knowing instruments, for violating what they swear to support!

The oath of office, too, imposed by the legislature, is completely demonstrative of the legislative opinion on this subject. It is in these words: "I do solemnly swear that I will administer justice without respect to persons, and do equal right to the poor and to the rich; and that I will faithfully and impartially discharge all the duties incumbent on me as according to the best of my abilities and understanding, agreeably to the constitution and the laws of the United States."

Why does a judge swear to discharge his duties agreeably to the constitution of the United States, if that constitution forms no rule for his government? if it is closed upon him and cannot be inspected by him?

If such be the real state of things, this is worse than solemn mockery. To prescribe, or to take this oath, becomes equally a crime.

It is also not entirely unworthy of observation, that in declaring what shall be the supreme law of the land, the constitution itself is first mentioned; and not the laws of the United States generally, but those only which shall be made in pursuance of the constitution, have that rank.

Thus, the particular phraseology of the constitution of the United States confirms and strengthens the principle, supposed to be essential to all written constitutions, that a law repugnant to the constitution is void; and that courts, as well as other departments, are bound by that instrument.

The rule must be discharged. . . .

NOTE ON HISTORICAL CONTEXT OF *MARBURY*

In late 1800, following bitter campaigns, Republicans, led by Vice President Thomas Jefferson, captured the presidency from Federalist President John Adams (although it was not immediately clear that Jefferson rather than Aaron Burr was the President, it was clear that one of the two Republicans had displaced Adams) and won majorities in the House of Representatives and Senate. The Federalists, the party of George Washington, John Adams, and Alexander Hamilton, had controlled the Presidency and Congress since 1789. The impending change was significant — "[t]he mainstays of the Federalist Party were the propertied and commercial classes, men who valued order and stability, the security of property, and opportunities for trade." Jefferson's Republicans, however, consisted of "farmers, frontiersmen, and debtor classes, joined in Virginia and to the south by plantation aristocrats." ARCHIBALD COX, THE COURT AND THE CONSTITUTION 45-46 (1987). The differences between the parties were not only geographic (New England vs. the South and frontier) and economic but ideological as well; the Federalists found the French Revolution and its celebration of popular sovereignty troubling whereas the Republicans were committed to democratic political processes and sought to control the growth of the national government.

Prior to ratification of the Twentieth Amendment in 1933, the terms of the President and Congressmen continued until March of the following year. Accordingly, President Adams and the Federalist majorities in the House and Senate remained in office until then despite the party's electoral repudiation. During the interval, several significant events occurred.

First, in December, 1800, Chief Justice Oliver Ellsworth resigned due to poor health. After John Jay (who had been an author of essays published in THE FEDERALIST PAPERS along with Hamilton and James Madison and the first Chief Justice until he resigned to run for Governor of New York) declined the appointment, Adams nominated Secretary of State John Marshall to be Chief Justice. Marshall was confirmed by the Federalist Senate. Marshall continued as Secretary of State until almost the end of Adams' tenure, even after being commissioned as the new Chief Justice. (Jay and Ellsworth, two of Marshall's predecessors, had also undertaken executive responsibilities while Chief Justice).

Second, on February 13, 1801, less than three weeks before Adams' term ended, the Federalist Congress passed, and President Adams signed into law, the Circuit Court Act or Judiciary Act of 1801. The Act ended the requirement that Supreme Court justices ride circuit, i.e., travel to sit as part of Courts of Appeals, a requirement unpopular with the justices due to the difficulty of travel and the fact that the justices were then potentially placed in the untenable position of having to review their own decisions. The Act also created six new Circuits with 16 new judges, a change that provided manpower for the judiciary to fulfill some of the circuit work the Supreme Court justices would no longer perform, but also provided jobs for ousted Federalist politicians and an opportunity for the party to establish a foothold in at least one branch of government. Finally, the Act provided that on the next retirement, death, or resignation, the Supreme Court would shrink from six justices to five. Although Federalists claimed that the Court would have less work because its members would no longer ride circuit, the change also delayed Jefferson's first appointment to the Court.

Two weeks later, Congress passed legislation creating courts in the District of Columbia. Adams nominated 42 persons as justices of the peace for the District of Columbia on March 2 and the Senate confirmed them the following day. President

Adams signed the requisite commissions and Secretary of State Marshall had the United States seal affixed to them, but Marshall never delivered them. When Jefferson became President, he ordered that the commissions not be delivered. Instead, he determined that only 30 justices of the peace were needed and proceeded to have commissions delivered to 25 of the Adams appointees and to five that he nominated. William Marbury was among the Adams appointees to whom Jefferson decided not to deliver commissions.

Jefferson was inaugurated on March 4, 1801. Chief Justice Marshall administered the oath of office after which Jefferson delivered a conciliatory address ("But every difference of opinion is not a difference of principle. We have called by different names brethren of the same principle. We are all republicans: we are all federalists.") But the spirit of these remarks quickly disappeared.

On January 6, 1802, Jeffersonians introduced in the Senate a resolution calling for the repeal of the Judiciary Act of 1801. When Federalists argued that the proposed law was unconstitutional, some Republicans denied that a court could review the constitutionality of an act of Congress. In any event, the Senate approved the measure on February 3 by a vote of 16 to 15; the House approved the bill the following month by a large majority. Jefferson signed it into law. The repealing act abolished the 16 new federal judgeships and required the justices again to ride circuit (although the Republicans' legislation eased the burden by assigning each justice one circuit and reducing the Supreme Court to a single February session each year by eliminating its summer session and the December session).

In early 1802, Jeffersonians in the House initiated proceedings to impeach Federal District Judge John Pickering, a Federalist. Pickering was probably incompetent by reasons of temperament to serve as a judge and the proceedings signaled that the Republicans might be willing to use impeachment to remove other Federalist judges.

In December, 1801, William Marbury and the others similarly situated petitioned in the Supreme Court for a writ of mandamus to issue directing Secretary of State James Madison to deliver the commissions to them. Two days later, the Court ordered Madison to appear and show cause why a mandamus should not issue. The Court's directive to Madison, the President's closest advisor, had constitutional and political ramifications; no doubt it encouraged the Republicans to take some of the steps sketched above. In any event, the order to Madison was not returnable until the Court's next session which, once Congress abolished the summer and December sessions, did not occur until February 1803, more than one year later. The case was heard for two days. Jefferson's Attorney General, Levi Lincoln, appeared reluctantly and initially refused to answer questions. Ultimately, he said he did not know whether the commissions were ever possessed by Madison (who was not Secretary of State when the commissions were withheld) or whether there was a commission for Marbury or the other petitioners. Marbury's attorney, Charles Lee, who had been Adams' Attorney General, then submitted an affidavit from James Marshall, brother of Chief Justice John Marshall, who was to have delivered commissions to some of the Adams' appointees in the waning hours of his tenure. He testified that he had picked up commissions for various persons living in the Alexandria area, that he could not carry all so had returned some, and that he thought he had been given commissions for at least two of the petitioners.

Sources for this discussion include: LEONARD BAKER, JOHN MARSHALL: A LIFE IN LAW (1974); ARCHIBALD COX, THE COURT AND THE CONSTITUTION (1987); PETER IRONS, A PEOPLE'S HISTORY OF THE SUPREME COURT (1999); DUMAS MALONE, JEFFERSON THE PRESIDENT (1970); WILLIAM E. NELSON, MARBURY V. MADISON: THE ORIGINS AND LEGACY OF JUDICIAL REVIEW (2000); WILLIAM REHNQUIST, THE SUPREME COURT: HOW IT WAS, HOW IT

Is (1987); BERNARD SCHWARTZ, A HISTORY OF THE SUPREME COURT (1993).

NOTES ON *MARBURY*

(1) *Marbury* held that the Court lacked jurisdiction over Marbury's claim because the statute conferring jurisdiction, Section 13 of the Judiciary Act of 1789, was unconstitutional. Before stating that holding, Chief Justice Marshall concluded that Marbury had the right to the commission and that the Court could issue writs of mandamus to executive officials in appropriate situations. If the Court lacked jurisdiction over the case, why did Marshall not simply say so and dismiss the case without discussing the merits? After all, a court lacking subject matter jurisdiction lacks authority to proceed to the merits.

(2) The holding in *Marbury* rested on two basic propositions the case articulated — the Constitution is paramount law and the Court has the power to review legislation to determine if it complies with the Constitution. The Constitution does not articulate either explicitly. Does the textual silence on these points impeach *Marbury*'s holding? Are there other constitutional arguments to support *Marbury*'s conclusions?

(3) Considerable evidence suggests the framers of the Constitution intended some power of judicial review. Professor Bernard Schwartz argued that "*Marbury* merely confirmed a doctrine that was part of the American legal tradition of the time." BERNARD SCHWARTZ, A HISTORY OF THE SUPREME COURT 41 (1993). Various state courts had exercised the power frequently. In THE FEDERALIST PAPERS, a collection of essays published to urge ratification of the Constitution, Alexander Hamilton argued that the judiciary would and should have some power of judicial review under the Constitution. He rejected the idea that Congress could police its own exercise of powers. In Federalist No. 78, he wrote:

> The interpretation of the laws is the proper and peculiar province of the courts. A constitution is in fact and must be, regarded by the judges as a fundamental law. It therefore belongs to them to ascertain its meaning as well as the meaning of any particular act proceeding from the legislative body. If there should happen to be an irreconcilable variance between the two, that which has the superior obligation and validity ought of course to be preferred; or in other words, the constitution ought to be preferred to the statute, the intention of the people to the intention of their agents.

THE FEDERALIST No. 78, at 525 (Alexander Hamilton) (Clinton Rossiter ed., 1961).

(4) Marshall's argument in *Marbury* closely paralleled Hamilton's. Why did he not invoke the framers' intent to support his argument? Relying on the intent of the framers is, after all, a common mode of constitutional argument; Hamilton's argument that the Constitution assumed judicial review not only offered evidence of one important framer's intent but also presumably influenced many of those who voted to ratify the Constitution.

Was intent of the framers something of a double-edged sword in *Marbury*? Although Federalist No. 78 suggested the framers intended judicial review, the fact that the First Congress adopted the Judiciary Act of 1789 including § 13, the section *Marbury* declared unconstitutional, provides some argument to suggest that § 13 was constitutional. After all, that body included many framers and ratifiers who presumably understood what they had intended in the Constitution.

(5) Although *Marbury* provided the first occasion for the Court to hold that the judiciary could declare a legislative act unconstitutional, earlier cases at least implicitly recognized the power of judicial review. *See, e.g., Hayburn's Case*, 2 U.S. (2 Dall.) 408 (1792) (Justices, as circuit Justices, agreeing Congress could not require federal courts

to render advisory opinions); *Hylton v. United States*, 3 U.S. (3 Dall.) 171 (1796) (Court considers whether Congress enacted unconstitutional tax but avoids constitutional issue); *Calder v. Bull*, 3 U.S. (3 Dall.) 386 (1798) (state law challenged as unconstitutional). Marshall did not rely on these precedents to support his conclusion.

(6) Would invocation of the framers' intent or judicial precedent have convinced an early 19th century audience? Modern jurists rely on those modes of argument in part to demonstrate that their conclusion is faithful to law. They need not convince the American people of the essential merit of constitutional government. Marshall, however, faced a different challenge. The jury was still out on whether constitutional government would benefit the public. The Court needed to demonstrate the merit of this arrangement as Professor Christopher L. Eisgruber argues: "The early judiciary's claim to speak for the American People was contested, but so too were the claims of Congress and the state legislatures. Marshall accordingly approached the legitimacy of judicial review from a different perspective than the one adopted by modern judges: rather than trying to convince people that the judiciary posed no threat to majoritarian institutions, Marshall tried to convince people that national institutions, including the federal judiciary, would govern well." Eisgruber, *John Marshall's Judicial Rhetoric*, 1996 Sup. Ct. Rev. 439, 440-441.

(7) If Marshall did not rely primarily on the Constitution's text or its framers' presumed intent, what type of arguments did he rely on?

(8) Marshall construed § 13 of the Judiciary Act of 1789 as conferring original jurisdiction on the Court in cases where a writ of mandamus was sought. Is this a fair construction of § 13? Are other interpretations possible? Preferable? Section 13 read as follows:

JUDICIARY ACT OF 1789 § 13

And be it further enacted, That the Supreme Court shall have exclusive jurisdiction of all controversies of a civil nature, where a state is a party, except between a state and its citizens; and except also between a state and citizens of other states, or aliens, in which latter case it shall have original but not exclusive jurisdiction. And shall have exclusively all such jurisdiction of suits or proceedings against ambassadors, or other public ministers, or their domestics, or domestic servants, as a court of law can have or exercise consistently with the law of nations; and original, but not exclusive jurisdiction of all suits brought by ambassadors, or other public ministers, or in which a consul, or vice consul, shall be a party. And the trial of issues of fact in the Supreme Court, in all actions at law against citizens of the United States, shall be by jury. *The Supreme Court shall also have appellate jurisdiction from the circuit courts and courts of the several states, in the cases herein after specially provided for; and shall have power to issue* writs of prohibition to the district courts, when proceeding as courts of admiralty and maritime jurisdiction, and *writs of mandamus, in cases warranted by the principles and usages of law, to any courts appointed, or persons holding office, under the authority of the United States.* [Emphasis added.]

(9) The claim that the federal courts may declare an act of Congress unconstitutional is far more modest than claiming it is the only or final constitutional interpreter. For a more recent interpretation by the Court of *Marbury*, see *Cooper v. Aaron*, 358 U.S. 1, 17-18 (1958):

What has been said, in the light of the facts developed, is enough to dispose of the case. However, we should answer the premise of the actions of the Governor and Legislature that they are not bound by our holding in the *Brown* case [*infra* § 8.02[1]]. It is necessary only to recall some basic constitutional propositions which are settled doctrine.

Article VI of the Constitution makes the Constitution the "supreme Law of the Land." In 1803, Chief Justice Marshall, speaking for a unanimous Court, referring to the Constitution as "the fundamental and paramount law of the nation," declared in the notable case of *Marbury v. Madison*, . . . that "it is emphatically the province and duty of the judicial department to say what the law is." This decision declared the basic principle that the federal judiciary is supreme in the exposition of the law of the Constitution, and that principle has ever since been respected by this Court and the Country as a permanent and indispensable feature of our constitutional system. It follows that the interpretation of the Fourteenth Amendment enunciated by this Court in the Brown case is the supreme law of the land, and Art. VI of the Constitution makes it of binding effect on the States "any Thing in the Constitution or Laws of any State to the Contrary notwithstanding." Every state legislator and executive and judicial officer is solemnly committed by oath taken pursuant to Art. VI, ¶ 3 "to support this Constitution."

Of course, *Cooper v. Aaron* might be distinguished on the grounds that it involved claims by state officials to be authorized to interpret the Constitution contrary to the Court's views. But the Court has made similar assertions vis-á-vis Congress (*see Powell v. McCormack*, 395 U.S. 486 (1969)) and vis-á-vis the Executive (*see United States v. Nixon*, 418 U.S. 683 (1974)).

(10) Some have criticized the notion of judicial supremacy as judicial usurpation. In 1832, President Andrew Jackson vetoed the bill to renew the charter of the Second Bank of the United States which the Court had held constitutional. The veto argued for power in the President to review a constitutional question already decided by the Supreme Court. He stated:

> The Congress, the Executive, and the Court must each for itself be guided by its own opinion of the Constitution. Each public officer who takes an oath to support the Constitution swears that he will support it as he understands it, and not as it is understood by others. It is as much the duty of the House of Representatives, of the Senate, and of the President to decide upon the constitutionality of any bill or resolution which may be presented to them for passage or approval as it is of the supreme judges when it may be brought before Congress than the opinion of Congress has over the judges, and on that point the President is independent of both. The authority of the Supreme Court must not, therefore, be permitted to control the Congress or the Executive when acting in their legislative capacities, but to have only such influence as the force of their reasoning may deserve.

Andrew Jackson Veto Message, 2 RICHARDSON, MESSAGES AND PAPERS OF THE PRESIDENTS 1789-1897, at 581-582 (1901).

In his First Inaugural Address, Abraham Lincoln made a related argument:

> I do not forget the position assumed by some that constitutional questions are to be decided by the Supreme Court, nor do I deny that such decisions must be binding in any case upon the parties to a suit as to the object of that suit, while they are also entitled to very high respect and consideration in all parallel cases by all other departments of the Government. And while it is obviously possible that such decision may be erroneous in any given case, still the evil effect following it, being limited to that particular case, with the chance that it may be overruled and never become a precedent for other cases, can better be borne than could the evils of a different practice. At the same time, the candid

citizen must confess that if the policy of the Government upon vital questions affecting the whole people is to be irrevocably fixed by decisions of the Supreme Court, the instant they are made in ordinary litigation between parties in personal actions the people will have ceased to be their own rulers, having to that extent practically resigned their Government into the hands of that eminent tribunal. Nor is there in this view any assault upon the court or the judges. It is a duty from which they may not shrink to decide cases properly brought before them, and it is no fault of theirs if others seek to turn their decisions to political purposes.

Abraham Lincoln, *1861 Inaugural Address*, 6 RICHARDSON, *supra*, at 9-10.

(11) In *United States v. Butler*, 297 U.S. 1, 62 (1936), Justice Roberts wrote that when the validity of a statute was challenged, the judiciary's duty was simply "to lay the article of the Constitution which is invoked beside the statute which is challenged and to decide whether the latter squares with the former." Yet *Marbury* suggests constitutional adjudication is not so simple a task; it involves interpretation, not mechanical comparison. How can one justify the practice of judicial review which results in unelected judges declaring unconstitutional the acts of the people's representatives?

Some argue that the Constitution represents a higher expression of democracy than normally reflected in legislation. Thus, enforcement of the Constitution over statutes is democratic, not countermajoritarian. *See* Susan Rose-Ackerman, *The Storr's Lectures: Discovering the Constitution*, 93 YALE L.J. 1013 (1984). Others argue that judicial review is necessary, and most appropriately exercised, to protect those rights necessary for democracy to survive and to protect certain minorities who may be disadvantaged by majorities and whose rights might be jeopardized by majoritarian politics. *See, e.g.*, JOHN HART ELY, DEMOCRACY AND DISTRUST: A THEORY OF JUDICIAL Review (1980). Some suggest that some institution must be empowered to determine if legislative acts are constitutional; the Court, as the least dangerous branch, possessed control of neither the purse nor the sword, is best suited for that task. Because federal judges have life tenure and certain insulations from congressional control, they need not be subservient to popular opinion. Their institutional weakness gives reason to proceed cautiously. *See* ALEXANDER BICKEL, THE LEAST DANGEROUS BRANCH: THE SUPREME COURT AT THE BAR OF POLITICS 1-33 (1962). As Hamilton wrote in THE FEDERALIST 78, the judiciary, lacking "influence over either the sword or the purse" has "neither FORCE nor WILL but merely judgment." Accordingly, it posed the least threat to "the general liberty of the people."

(12) In *Bush v. Gore*, 531 U.S. 98 (2000), the Supreme Court held that the recount of Florida votes in the 2000 presidential election which the Florida Supreme Court had ordered violated requirements of the Equal Protection clause of the Fourteenth Amendment. The case furnished a contemporary reminder of the power of the federal judiciary. For the first time in American history, the Court decided a case which may have decided a presidential election.

The Per Curiam opinion, which five justices joined, concluded

None are more conscious of the vital limits on judicial authority than are the Members of this Court, and none stand more in admiration of the Constitution's design to leave the selection of the President to the people, through their legislatures, and to the political sphere. When contending parties invoke the process of the courts, however, it becomes our unsought responsibility to resolve the federal and constitutional issues the judicial system has been forced to confront.

Id. at 111.

Is the Court's formulation consistent with *Marbury*'s notion of judicial review? Did

Marbury "resolve the federal and constitutional issues the judicial system has been forced to confront?" Did *Marbury* suggest that federal courts should resolve any constitutional issue placed before them?

Those in dissent viewed the Court's intervention and opinion differently from the sentiments quoted above. Justice Stevens concluded his dissent (which Justices Ginsburg and Breyer joined):

> Although we may never know with complete certainty the identity of the winner of this year's Presidential election, the identity of the loser is perfectly clear. It is the Nation's confidence in the judge as an impartial guardian of the rule of law.

Id. at 128-29.

The Supreme Court did not hold that the Florida Supreme Court erred in deeming a recount required under Florida law but rather concluded "that the recount cannot be conducted in compliance with the requirements of equal protection and due process without substantial additional work." *Id.* at 110. The Court did not believe sufficient time remained to structure and conduct a proper recount under the electoral calendar. Although Justices Souter and Breyer agreed with those joining the Per Curiam that the Florida recount raised constitutional problems under the Fourteenth Amendment, they, unlike the five signers of the Per Curiam, thought the Florida courts should be given an opportunity to fashion an appropriate remedy. *Marbury* stated that the government of the United States would forfeit its distinction as "a government of laws, and not of men" if "the laws furnish no remedy for the violation of a vested legal right." If Vice President Gore had a right to contest the Florida vote, was he entitled to a remedy? The four dissenters thought an "appropriate remedy" would remand the case to the Florida Supreme Court for a recount of all under counted votes in Florida.

§ 1.02   REVIEW OF STATE LAW

MARTIN v. HUNTER'S LESSEE
14 U.S. (1 Wheat.) 304, 4 L. Ed. 97 (1816)

[Editors' Note: *Martin v. Hunter's Lessee* arose out of a land dispute in Virginia. King Charles II had granted Lord Fairfax a substantial estate in Virginia during the colonial period. Lord Fairfax left his estate to his nephew and fellow British subject, Denny Martin. During the Revolutionary War, Virginia seized land of British subjects. In 1782, after Fairfax died, it barred aliens from inheriting Virginia real estate. Virginia granted some 800 acres of the Fairfax estate to one David Hunter at some point between 1777 and 1782. Martin's brother, Thomas, a Virginia citizen, chased Hunter off the land, relying on a confusing 1779 Virginia law. Moreover, the Jay Treaty of 1783 recommended that states return property to British loyalists. Long before the matter came to the court, John Marshall and his brother bought Denny Martin's claim to the Fairfax estate of some 300,000 acres.

The highest court of Virginia ruled in Hunter's favor in 1810. After Martin appealed, the Supreme Court in 1813 ruled in Martin's favor (Marshall recused himself) and ordered the Virginia Court to enter judgment in favor of Martin's devisees. The Virginia Court refused. In an opinion by Spencer Roane, Marshall's long-time adversary, the Virginia Court made the points contained in the first paragraph below. The matter came back to the Supreme Court, again with Marshall having sidelined himself. *See* PETER IRONS, A PEOPLE'S HISTORY OF THE SUPREME COURT 116-118 (1999).]

STORY, J., delivered the opinion of the court:

This is a writ of error from the Court of Appeals of Virginia, founded upon the refusal of that court to obey the mandate of this court, requiring the judgment rendered in this very cause, at February term, 1813, to be carried into due execution. The following is the judgment of the Court of appeals rendered on the mandate: "The court is unanimously of opinion, that the appellate power of the Supreme Court of the United States does not extend to this court, under a sound construction of the constitution of the United States; that so much of the 25th section of the act of congress to establish the judicial courts of the United States, as extends the appellate jurisdiction of the Supreme Court to this court, is not in pursuance of the constitution of the United States; that the writ of error, in this cause, was improvidently allowed under the authority of that act; that the proceedings thereon in the Supreme Court were, *coram non judice*, in relation to this court, and that obedience to its mandate be declined by the court."

The questions involved in this judgment are of great importance and delicacy. Perhaps it is not too much to affirm, that, upon their right decision, rest some of the most solid principles which have hitherto been supposed to sustain and protect the constitution itself. . . .

The third article of the constitution is that which must principally attract our attention. The 1st section declares, "the judicial power of the United States shall be vested in one Supreme Court, and in such other inferior courts as the Congress may, from time to time, ordain and establish." The 2nd section declares, that "the judicial power shall extend to all cases in law or equity, arising under this constitution, the laws of the United States, and the treaties made, or which shall be made, under their authority; to all cases affecting ambassadors, other public ministers and consuls; to all cases of admiralty and maritime jurisdiction; to controversies to which the United States shall be a party; to controversies between two or more states; between a state and citizens of another state; between citizens of different states; between citizens of the same state, claiming lands under the grants of different states; and between a state or the citizens thereof, and foreign states, citizens, or subjects." It then proceeds to declare, that "in all cases affecting ambassadors, other public ministers and consuls, and those in which a state shall be a party, the Supreme Court shall have original jurisdiction. In all the other cases before mentioned the Supreme Court shall have appellate jurisdiction, both as to law and fact, with such exceptions, and under such regulations, as the congress shall make." . . . Let this article be carefully weighed and considered. The language of the article throughout is manifestly designed to be mandatory upon the legislature. Its obligatory force is so imperative that congress could not, without a violation of its duty, have refused to carry it into operation. . . .

The object of the constitution was to establish three great departments of government; the legislative, the executive and the judicial departments. The first was to pass laws, the second to approve and execute them, and the third to expound and enforce them. Without the latter it would be impossible to carry into effect some of the express provisions of the constitution. How, otherwise, could crimes against the United States be tried and punished? How could causes between two states be heard and determined? The judicial power must, therefore, be vested in some court, by congress; and to suppose that it was not an obligation binding on them, but might, at their pleasure, be omitted or declined, is to suppose that, under the sanction of the constitution, they might defeat the constitution itself; a construction which would lead to such a result cannot be sound. . . .

This leads us to the consideration of the great question as to the nature and extent of the appellate jurisdiction of the United States. . . .

As, then, by the terms of the constitution, the appellate jurisdiction is not limited as to the Supreme Court, and as to this court it may be exercised in all other cases than those of which it has original cognizance, what is there to restrain its exercise over state tribunals in the enumerated cases? The appellate power is not limited by the terms of the third article to any particular courts. The words are, "the judicial power (which includes appellate power) shall extend to all cases," and "in all other cases before mentioned the Supreme Court shall have appellate jurisdiction." It is the case, then, and not the court, that gives the jurisdiction. If the judicial power extends to the case, it will be in vain to search in the letter of the constitution for any qualification as to the tribunal where it depends. . . .

On the other hand, if, as has been contended, a discretion be vested in congress to establish, or not to establish, inferior courts at their own pleasure, and congress should not establish such courts, the appellate jurisdiction of the Supreme Court would have nothing to act upon, unless it could act upon cases pending in the state courts. Under such circumstances it must be held that the appellate power would extend to state courts; for the constitution is peremptory that it shall extend to certain enumerated cases, which cases could exist in no other courts. Any other construction, upon this supposition, would involve this strange contradiction, that a discretionary power vested in congress, and which they might rightfully omit to exercise, would defeat the absolute injunctions of the constitution in relation to the whole appellate power.

But it is plain that the framers of the constitution did contemplate that cases within the judicial cognizance of the United States not only might but would arise in the state courts, in the exercise of their ordinary jurisdiction. With this view the sixth article declares that "this constitution, and the laws of the United States which shall be made in pursuance thereof, and all treaties made, or which shall be made, under the authority of the United States, shall be the supreme law of the land, and the judges in every state shall be bound thereby, anything in the constitution or laws of any state to the contrary notwithstanding." It is obvious that this obligation is imperative upon the state judges in their official, and not merely in their private, capacities. From the very nature of their judicial duties they would be called upon to pronounce the law applicable to the case in judgment. They were not to decide merely according to the laws or constitution of the state, but according to the constitution, laws and treaties of the United States — "the supreme law of the land." . . .

It must, therefore, be conceded that the constitution not only contemplated, but meant to provide for cases within the scope of the judicial power of the United States, which might yet depend before state tribunals. It was foreseen that in the exercise of their ordinary jurisdiction, state courts would incidentally take cognizance of cases arising under the constitution, the laws and treaties of the United States. Yet to all these cases the judicial power, by the very terms of the constitution, is to extend. It cannot extend by original jurisdiction if that was already rightfully and exclusively attached in the state courts, which (as has been already shown) may occur; it must, therefore, extend by appellate jurisdiction, or not at all. It would seem to follow that the appellate power of the United States must, in such cases, extend to state tribunals; and if in such cases, there is no reason why it should not equally attach upon all others within the purview of the constitution.

It has been argued that such an appellate jurisdiction over state courts is inconsistent with the genius of our governments, and the spirit of the constitution. That the latter was never designed to act upon state sovereignties, but only upon the people, and that if the power exists, it will materially impair the sovereignty of the states, and the independence of their courts. We cannot yield to the force of this reasoning; it assumes principles which we cannot admit, and draws conclusions to which we do not yield our assent.

It is a mistake that the constitution was not designed to operate upon states in their corporate capacities. It is crowded with provisions which restrain or annul the sovereignty of the states in some of the highest branches of their prerogatives. . . .

When, therefore, the states are stripped of some of the highest attributes of sovereignty, and the same are given to the United States; when the legislatures of the states are, in some respects, under the control of congress, and in every case are, under the constitution, bound by the paramount authority of the United States; it is certainly difficult to support the argument that the appellate power over the decisions of state courts is contrary to the genius of our institutions. The courts of the United States can, without question, revise the proceedings of the executive and legislative authorities of the states, and if they are found to be contrary to the constitution, may declare them to be of no legal validity. Surely the exercise of the same right over judicial tribunals is not a higher or more dangerous act of sovereign power.

Nor can such a right be deemed to impair the independence of state judges. It is assuming the very ground in controversy to assert that they possess an absolute independence of the United States. In respect to the powers granted to the United States, they are not independent; they are expressly bound to obedience by the letter of the constitution; and if they should unintentionally transcend their authority, or misconstrue the constitution, there is no more reason for giving their judgments an absolute and irresistible force, than for giving it to the acts of the other co-ordinate departments of state sovereignty. . . .

This is not all. A motive of another kind, perfectly compatible with the most sincere respect for state tribunals, might induce the grant of appellate power over their decisions. That motive is the importance, and even necessity of uniformity of decisions throughout the whole United States, upon all subjects within the purview of the constitution. Judges of equal learning and integrity, in different states, might differently interpret a statute, or a treaty of the United States, or even the constitution itself. If there were no revising authority to control these jarring and discordant judgments, and harmonize them into uniformity, the laws, the treaties, and the constitution of the United States would be different in different states, and might, perhaps, never have precisely the same construction, obligation, or efficacy, in any two states. The public mischiefs that would attend such a state of things would be truly deplorable; and it cannot be believed that they could have escaped the enlightened convention which formed the constitution. What, indeed, might then have been only prophecy, has now become fact; and the appellate jurisdiction must continue to be the only adequate remedy for such evils. . . .

On the whole, the court are of opinion, that the appellate power of the United States does extend to cases pending in the state courts; and that the 25th section of the judiciary act, which authorizes the exercise of this jurisdiction in the specified cases, by a writ of error, is supported by the letter and spirit of the constitution. We find no clause in that instrument which limits this power; and we dare not interpose a limitation where the people have not been disposed to create one. . . .

The next question which has been argued, is, whether the case at bar be within the purview of the 25th section of the judiciary act, so that this court may rightfully sustain the present writ of error. This section, stripped of passages unimportant in this inquiry, enacts, in substance, that a final judgment or decree in any suit in the highest court of law or equity of a state, where is drawn in question the validity of a treaty or statute of or an authority exercised under, the United States, and the decision is against their validity; or where is drawn in question the validity of a statute of, or an authority exercised under, any state, on the ground of their being repugnant to the constitution, treaties, or laws, of the United States, and the decision is in favor of such their validity; or of the constitution, or of a treaty or statute of or commission held under, the United

States, and the decision is against the title, right, privilege, or exemption, specially set up or claimed by either party under such clause of the said constitution, treaty, statute, or commission, may be re-examined and reversed or affirmed in the Supreme Court of the United States, upon a writ of error, in the same manner, and under the same regulations, and the writ shall have the same effect, as if the judgment or decree complained of had been rendered or passed in a circuit court, and the proceeding upon the reversal shall also be the same, except that the Supreme Court, instead of remanding the cause for a final decision, as before provided, may, at their discretion, if the cause shall have been once remanded before, proceed to a final decision of the same, and award execution. But no other error shall be assigned or regarded as a ground of reversal in any such case as aforesaid, than such as appears upon the face of the record, and immediately respects the before-mentioned question of validity or construction of the said constitution, treaties, statutes, commissions, or authorities in dispute.

That the present writ of error is founded upon a judgment of the court below, which drew in question and denied the validity of a statute of the United States, is incontrovertible, for it is apparent upon the face of the record. That this judgment is final upon the rights of the parties is equally true; for if well founded, the former judgment of that court was of conclusive authority, and the former judgment of this court utterly void. The decision was, therefore, equivalent to a perpetual stay of proceedings upon the mandate, and a perpetual denial of all the rights acquired under it. The case, then, falls directly within the terms of the act. It is a final judgment in a suit in a state court, denying the validity of a statute of the United States; and unless a distinction can be made between proceedings under a mandate, and proceedings in an original suit, a writ of error is the proper remedy to revise that judgment. In our opinion no legal distinction exists between the cases. . . .

We have not thought it incumbent on us to give any opinion upon the question, whether this court have authority to issue a writ of mandamus to the court of appeals to enforce the former judgments, as we do not think it necessarily involved in the decision of this cause.

It is the opinion of the whole, court that the judgment of the court of appeals of Virginia, rendered on the mandate in this cause, be reversed, and the judgment of the district court, held at Winchester, be, and the same is hereby affirmed.

NOTES ON *MARTIN v. HUNTER'S LESSEE*

A. Supreme Court Review of State Legislation

(1) "I do not think," Justice Oliver Wendell Holmes once asserted, "the United States would come to an end if we lost our power to declare an Act of Congress void. I do think the Union would be imperilled if we could not make that declaration as to the laws of the several states. For one in my place sees how often a local policy prevails with those who are not trained to national views and how often action is taken that embodies what the [Constitution] was meant to end." Is power to pass on the validity of state legislation necessary to maintain the Constitution as supreme law throughout the land?

(2) The Supreme Court first held a state law unconstitutional in *Fletcher v. Peck*, 10 U.S. (6 Cranch) 87 (1810). In ruling that a Georgia statute violated the Contract Clause of Article I, Sec. 10, of the Constitution, Marshall, for the Court, declared that Georgia was not a wholly autonomous sovereign subject only to restrictions in her own constitution. On the contrary, Georgia is part of the Union, "and that Union has a constitution the supremacy of which all acknowledge, and which imposes limits to the legislatures of the several states, which none claim a right to pass." Georgia, therefore, could not pass laws impairing contractual obligation in violation of the contract clause.

(3) *Fletcher v. Peck* laid a second cornerstone in the structure of American constitutional law, the power of judicial review of state legislation. Yet it alone was not adequate to enable the Court to maintain the Supremacy of the Constitution. As Archibald Cox pointed out, "if state court decisions were final, state judges would be permitted up to the limits of their judicial consciences to nullify within their State's boundaries federal laws and constitutional guarantees." Cox, THE COURT AND THE CONSTITUTION 65 (1987). Review power over state court judgments is also necessary to enable the Court to maintain the supremacy of federal law over conflicting state law or when challenged by state authority.

B. Supreme Court Review of State Court Decisions

(4) In Section 25 of the Judiciary Act of 1789, Congress empowered the Supreme Court to review state court decisions which (a) invalidated a statute or treaty of the United States or act of a federal official; (b) upheld a state statute or act of a state official against a claim that it was contrary to the Constitution, treaties, or laws of the United States; or (c) denied a "title, right, privilege or exemption specially set up or claimed by either party" under the Constitution, or any treaty or statute of, or commission held under, the United States. Not until later did Congress empower the Court to hear appeals from state court decisions *upholding* federal law against state law claims. Does this suggest that § 25 was animated primarily by concerns for supremacy of federal law rather than uniformity of federal law? The Court's power to review state court decisions no longer depends upon the highest state court decision being adverse to the federal interest. *See* 28 U.S.C. § 1257 (1993).

(5) The Virginia judges argued in part that the Constitution failed to designate the Court as an umpire of such disputes and that this textual silence supported the inference that the framers did not intend the Court to have such a role. Is this argument convincing? Professor Charles L. Black, Jr. wrote that "there is nothing in our entire governmental structure which has a more leak-proof claim to legitimacy then the function of the courts in reviewing state acts for federal constitutionality." BLACK, STRUCTURE AND RELATIONSHIP IN CONSTITUTIONAL LAW 74 (1969).

(6) *Cohens v. Virginia.* Despite Justice Story's unqualified assertion, in *Martin v. Hunter's Lessee,* the question of the constitutionality of federal review over state court decisions arose again only five years later in *Cohens v. Virginia,* 19 U.S. (6 Wheat.) 264 (1821). Defendants had been convicted in a Virginia court of violating the state law prohibiting sale of lottery tickets. They claimed the protection of an Act of Congress, which authorized the District of Columbia to conduct lotteries. After the state court conviction, the case came to the Supreme Court by a writ of error. Defendants claimed that, because Congress authorized the lottery tickets, any state law prohibiting their sale conflicted with federal law.

(7) In *Cohens v. Virginia,* Marshall was able to lend his reasoning and prestige to the opinion. The Virginia argument against Supreme Court jurisdiction, Marshall declared, was contrary to the Constitution. The states were not independent sovereignties but members of one great nation — a nation endowed with a government competent to attain all national objects. "In a government so constituted," Marshall asked rhetorically, "is it unreasonable that the judicial power should be competent to give efficacy to the constitutional laws of the legislature? . . . Is it unreasonable that it should also be empowered to decide on the judgment of a state tribunal enforcing such unconstitutional law?" As Marshall expressed it, "The exercise of the appellate power over those judgments of the State tribunals which may contravene the constitution or laws of the United States, is, we believe, essential to the attainment of those objects."

§ 1.03 SUPREME COURT ORGANIZATION AND JURISDICTION

[1] Supreme Court Organization

NOTES

(1) Although *Marbury* confirmed the Court's power to review the constitutionality of legislative acts, the federal judiciary remains dependent on Congress. Article III provides: "The judicial Power of the United States shall be vested in one Supreme Court, and in such inferior Courts as the Congress may from time to time ordain and establish." Article III provides for "one Supreme Court." Did Article III impose upon Congress the duty of creating the Supreme Court? "Could Congress have lawfully refused to create a supreme court . . . ? But one answer can be given . . . it must be in the negative." *Martin v. Hunter's Lessee, supra* § 1.02.

(2) The Constitution does not fix the composition of the Court. Its membership has varied from six (at its creation) to five, to seven, to nine, to ten, to seven again, and finally to the present membership of nine. President Franklin D. Roosevelt's Court-Packing Plan of 1937, as explained by FDR provided that "whenever a . . . Justice has reached the age of seventy and does not avail himself of the opportunity to retire on a pension, a new member shall be appointed by the President." If passed by Congress, the proposal could have given Roosevelt the authority to appoint as many as six new Justices. Was the Court-Packing Plan constitutional? Is there any limit on Congressional power to fix the number of Justices? May Congress deprive a President of the opportunity to fill vacancies by providing that no vacancy on the Supreme Court is to be filled until the Court is reduced to seven members? *See* 14 Stat. 210 (1866). When a new President is elected, may Congress then enact a statute raising the number of Justices to nine and authorizing the President to make the necessary appointments? *See* 16 Stat. 44 (1869).

(3) Can Congress control the internal functioning of the Supreme Court? Can it fix the time of the Court's sessions? Can it prevent the Court from sitting to delay a particular decision? When the Republicans took control of the White House, House of Representatives, and Senate in 1801 they promptly repealed the Federalists' Judiciary Act of 1801 which had created new federal judgeships. In order to postpone a decision on the constitutional question it raised (Whether Congress' action violated the constitutional guarantee of life tenure to federal judges?) Congress passed a bill abolishing the Court's June and December Terms but restoring the old February Term. This left the Court adjourned from December 1801 to February 1803. *See* 1 WARREN, THE SUPREME COURT IN UNITED STATES HISTORY 222-223 (1924).

(4) Can Congress abolish the Supreme Court? Alternatively, could Congress retain the Court but render it no longer "Supreme" by providing for appeals from it to a higher court? The International Prize Court Convention, concluded at the Second Hague Conference of 1907, allowed an appeal to an international tribunal from national court decisions. If the United States had ratified this Convention, could Congress have provided for appeals to the international tribunal from the Supreme Court?

[2] Supreme Court Original Jurisdiction

NOTES

(1) Article III distinguishes between the original and appellate jurisdiction of the Supreme Court. It expressly specifies that original jurisdiction extends to "all Cases affecting Ambassadors, other public Ministers and Consuls, and those in which a State shall be Party." Could the Court exercise the original jurisdiction specified in Article III even if Congress had not provided for it in the Judicial Code? *See California v. Arizona*, 440 U.S. 59 (1979) (Supreme Court's original jurisdiction conferred by the Constitution, not Congress).

(2) In *Marbury*, the Court held that its original jurisdiction was limited to "all cases affecting Ambassadors, other public Ministers and Consuls, and those in which a state shall be a party." That language operated as a ceiling (i.e., no additional cases could be brought within the Court's original jurisdiction) not as a floor.

Can Congress restrict the Court's original jurisdiction? Justice Stewart in *California v. Arizona*, 440 U.S. 59, 66 (1979) stated: "Congress has broad powers over the jurisdiction of the federal courts, . . . but it is extremely doubtful that they include the power to limit in this manner the original jurisdiction conferred upon this Court by the Constitution."

(3) Congress has assumed that the Supreme Court's original jurisdiction is not exclusive. *See* 28 U.S.C. § 1251 (2000) (Supreme Court vested with "original and exclusive" jurisdiction of all controversies between two or more states, while other cases in which a state is a party can be heard either by Supreme Court or inferior federal courts); 28 U.S.C. § 1351 (2000) (district courts given jurisdiction "of all actions and proceedings against consuls or vice consuls of the foreign states"). *See Bors v. Preston*, 111 U.S. 252 (1884), (upholding concurrent original jurisdiction in Supreme Court and the lower federal court).

[3] Supreme Court Appellate Jurisdiction

EX PARTE McCARDLE
74 U.S. (7 Wall.) 506, 19 L. Ed. 264 (1868)

[Editors' Note: McCardle, having published newspaper articles critical of Reconstruction, was charged with libel, inciting disorder and other offenses and held in custody by military authority then controlling Mississippi under the national plan of Reconstruction that Congress had adopted. McCardle petitioned for a writ of habeas corpus in the United States District Court for the Southern District of Mississippi challenging as unconstitutional the system of military government. The military commander appeared, admitted custody of McCardle, but denied that it was illegal. After the lower court upheld the custody, McCardle appealed under the 1867 Habeas Corpus Act. The Court denied a motion to dismiss the appeal, heard argument on the merits of McCardle's appeal, and took the case under advisement. Congress, fearing the case might jeopardize its Reconstruction plan, passed a statute repealing the 1867 Act. President Andrew Johnson, shortly before his impeachment trial in the Senate was to begin, vetoed the measure. Congress overrode his veto by the requisite constitutional two-thirds majority in each house of Congress.

The 2d section of the 1868 Act was as follows:

> And be it further enacted, that so much of the Act approved February 5, 1867, entitled "An Act to Amend an Act to Establish the Judicial Courts of the United States," approved September 24, 1789, as authorized an appeal from the

judgment of the circuit court to the Supreme Court of the United States, for the exercise of any such jurisdiction by said Supreme Court on appeals which have been or may hereafter be taken, be, and the same is hereby repealed. . . .]

THE CHIEF JUSTICE [CHASE] delivered the opinion of the court:

The first question necessarily is that of jurisdiction; for, if the Act of March, 1868, takes away the jurisdiction defined by the Act of February, 1867, it is useless, if not improper, to enter into any discussion of other questions.

It is quite true, as was argued by the counsel for the petitioner, that the appellate jurisdiction of this court is not derived from acts of Congress. It is, strictly speaking, conferred by the Constitution. But it is conferred "with such exceptions and under such regulations as Congress shall make."

It is unnecessary to consider whether, if Congress had made no exceptions and no regulations, this court might not have exercised general appellate jurisdiction under rules prescribed by itself. For among the earliest acts of the first Congress, at its first session, was the act of September 24th, 1789, to establish the judicial courts of the United States. That act provided for the organization of this court, and prescribed regulations for the exercise of its jurisdiction.

The source of that jurisdiction, and the limitations of it by the Constitution and by statute, have been on several occasions subjects of consideration here. In the case of *Durousseau v. The United States*, . . . particularly, the whole matter was carefully examined, and the court held, that while "the appellate powers of this court are not given by the judicial act, but Constitution," they are, nevertheless, "limited and regulated by that act, and by such other acts as have been passed on the subject." The court said, further, that the judicial act was an exercise of the power given by the Constitution to Congress "of making exceptions to the appellate jurisdiction of the Supreme Court." "They have described affirmatively," said the court, "its jurisdiction, and this affirmative description has been understood to imply a negation of the exercise of such appellate power as is not comprehended within it."

The principle that the affirmation of appellate jurisdiction implies the negation of all such jurisdiction not affirmed having been thus established, it was an almost necessary consequence that acts of Congress, providing for the exercise of jurisdiction, should come to be spoken of as acts granting jurisdiction, and not as acts making exceptions to the constitutional grant of it.

The exception to appellate jurisdiction in the case before us, however, is not an inference from the affirmation of other appellate jurisdiction. It is made in terms.

The provision of the act of 1867, affirming the appellate jurisdiction of this court in cases of habeas corpus, is expressly repealed. It is hardly possible to imagine a plainer instance of positive exception.

We are not at liberty to inquire into the motives of the legislature. We can only examine into its power under the Constitution; and the power to make exceptions to the appellate jurisdiction of this court is given by express words.

What, then, is the effect of the repealing act upon the case before us? We cannot doubt as to this. Without jurisdiction the court cannot proceed at all in any cause. Jurisdiction is power to declare the law, and when it ceases to exist, the only function remaining to the court is that of announcing the fact and dismissing the cause. And this is not less clear upon authority than upon principle. . . .

It is quite clear, therefore, that this court cannot proceed to pronounce judgment in this case, for it has no longer jurisdiction of the appeal; and judicial duty is not less fitly performed by declining ungranted jurisdiction than in exercising firmly that which the Constitution and the laws confer.

Counsel seem to have supposed, if effect be given to the repealing act in question, that the whole appellate power of the court, in cases of habeas corpus, is denied. But this is an error. The Act of 1868 does not except from that jurisdiction any cases but appeals from Circuit Courts under the act of 1867. It does not affect the jurisdiction which was previously exercised.

The appeal of the petitioner in this case must be *Dismissed For Want of Jurisdiction.*

NOTES ON THE SUPREME COURT'S APPELLATE JURISDICTION

(1) John Marshall once proclaimed, "The appellate powers of this court are not given by the judicial act. They are given by the constitution." *Durousseau v. United States*, 10 U.S. (6 Cranch) 307, 314 (1810).

(2) What authority does Congress receive under the Exceptions Clause? From time to time, the Court's controversial decisions on, for instance, school prayer, abortion, or school desegregation, provoke proposals to strip the Court of jurisdiction to hear cases in those fields. Would such acts be constitutional? Could Congress remove all of the Court's appellate jurisdiction or almost all of it?

What arguments can be made from the text of the Exceptions Clause on this issue? Some argue, for instance, that the Clause allowed Congress to limit the Court's appellate jurisdiction to consider questions of fact but not of law. *See* RAOUL BERGER, CONGRESS V. THE SUPREME COURT 285-296 (1969). For an opposing view, see Gerald Gunther, *Congressional Power to Curtail Federal Court Jurisdiction: An Opinionated Guide to the Ongoing Debate*, 36 STAN. L. REV. 895 (1984). Does the power to make "exceptions" confer broad power to carve away the Court's appellate jurisdiction or only narrow authority?

(3) Does judicial precedent, like *Ex Parte McCardle*, suggest a broad power to restrict the Court's appellate jurisdiction? Justice Felix Frankfurter thought so. Relying on *Ex Parte McCardle*, in his dissent in *National Mut. Ins. Co. v. Tidewater Transfer Co.*, 337 U.S. 582, 655 (1949), he wrote, "Congress need not give this Court any appellate power; it may withdraw appellate jurisdiction once conferred and it may do so even while a case is sub judice." Referring to *McCardle*, Justice Owen Roberts asked: "What is there to prevent Congress taking away, bit by bit, all the appellate jurisdiction of the Supreme Court?" Roberts, *Now Is The Time: Fortifying the Court's Independence*, 35 A.B.A. J. 1, 4 (1949). Does *Ex Parte McCardle* truly confer on Congress such unrestrained power over the Court's appellate jurisdiction? Would the last paragraph of the opinion be useful in fashioning a contrary argument? In *Ex Parte Yerger*, 75 U.S. (8 Wall.) 85 (1869) decided shortly after *Ex Parte McCardle*, the Court decided it could still review lower court decisions via a habeas petition under § 14 of the 1789 Judiciary Act as suggested in the last paragraph of *Ex parte McCardle*.

(4) In *Felker v. Turpin*, 518 U.S. 651 (1996), the Court relied on that rationale to uphold Title I of the Antiterrorism and Effective Death Penalty Act, which required dismissal of a claim presented in a state prisoner's second or successive federal habeas application if the claim was previously presented unless a court of appeals panel grants leave to file a second or successive habeas application in the district court. The Act also provided that the grant or denial of authorization to file "shall not be appealable and shall not be the subject of a petition for . . . writ of certiorari." In upholding Title I, Chief Justice Rehnquist wrote:

> Turning to the present case, we conclude that Title I of the Act has not repealed our authority to entertain original habeas petitions, for reasons similar to those stated in *Yerger*. No provision of Title I mentions our authority to entertain original habeas petitions. . . . As we declined to find a repeal of §14 of the Judiciary Act of 1789 as applied to this Court by implication then, we

decline to find a similar repeal of §2241 of Title 28 — its descendant by implication now. . . .

This conclusion obviates one of the constitutional challenges raised. The critical language of Article III, §2, of the Constitution provides that, apart from several classes of cases specifically enumerated in this Court's original jurisdiction, "[i]n all the other Cases . . . the supreme Court shall have appellate Jurisdiction, both as to Law and Fact, with such Exceptions, and under such Regulations as the Congress shall make." Previous decisions construing this clause have said that while our appellate powers "are given by the constitution," "they are limited and regulated by the [Judiciary Act of 1789], and by such other acts as have been passed on the subject." The Act does remove our authority to entertain an appeal or a petition for a writ of certiorari to review a decision of a court of appeals exercising its "gatekeeping" function over a second petition. But since it does not repeal our authority to entertain a petition for habeas corpus, there can be no plausible argument that the Act has deprived this Court of appellate jurisdiction in violation of Article III, §2.

(5) Just as some cite *Ex Parte McCardle* to support broad congressional power to limit the Court's appellate jurisdiction, others invoke *United States v. Klein*, 80 U.S. (13 Wall.) 128 (1872) to argue that Congress cannot manipulate jurisdiction to dictate substantive outcomes. The statutes at issue in *Klein* made proof of loyalty necessary to recover property the Government seized during the Civil War. A Supreme Court decision, *United States v. Padelford*, 76 U.S. (9 Wall.) 531 (1869), had held that a presidential pardon demonstrated loyalty; but Congress here made such pardons inadmissible in support of such claims. Moreover, the statute provided that proof of such a pardon would oust the court of jurisdiction. The Court held the statute invalid. Rather than constituting an exercise of congressional power under the Exceptions Clause, Congress was attempting to dictate rules of decision to the judiciary in pending cases. *See also Glidden Co. v. Zdanok*, 370 U.S. 530 (1962) (describing *Klein* as involving "an unconstitutional attempt to invade the judicial province by prescribing a rule of decision in a pending case").

Accordingly, some argue *Klein* prohibits jurisdiction stripping to prescribe outcomes in controversial cases. The Court has more recently held that *Klein* precludes Congress from telling courts how to apply antecedent law to pending cases. *See Robertson v. Seattle Audubon Society*, 503 U.S. 429 (1992). Alternatively, others argue that the vice in *Klein* was that Congress violated other constitutional provisions, i.e., by interfering with the President's pardon power or by constituting a taking without just compensation. They view *Klein* as holding only that Congress cannot limit the Supreme Court's jurisdiction in a way that otherwise violates the constitution. Is *Klein* consistent with *McCardle*? Note that Chief Justice Chase delivered both opinions.

(6) Do any principles regarding the Constitution's structure shed light on these issues? Some suggest that Congress' power to restrict judicial intervention is necessary in order to make judicial review acceptable in a democratic society. Under this view, some ability to remove the Court's appellate jurisdiction helps keep courts in check and makes it tolerable to allow unelected judges to strike down acts passed by the people's representatives. But can one reconcile an unlimited right to restrict the Court's appellate jurisdiction with *Marbury*? If *Marbury* stands for the proposition that the rule of law requires some robust power of judicial review of legislation, is that principle undermined if Congress has broad power to limit the Court's appellate jurisdiction? Some suggest that stripping the Court of appellate jurisdiction in controversial areas would prevent the Court from discharging its "essential functions" of giving law uniform meaning throughout the nation and of protecting the supremacy of federal law. *See*

generally Ratner, *Congressional Power Over the Appellate Jurisdiction of the Supreme Court*, 109 U. PA. L. REV. 157 (1960).

§ 1.04 LOWER FEDERAL COURTS ORGANIZATION AND JURISDICTION

NOTES

(1) The vesting clause of Article III lodges "the judicial Power" in the Supreme Court "and in such inferior Courts as the Congress may from time to time ordain and establish." Does this language obligate Congress to create lower federal courts? Professor Paul Bator argued that such a conclusion upset the terms of the Madisonian Compromise whereby the Constitution created a Supreme Court but left the decision whether or not to create lower federal courts as "a matter of political and legislative judgment, to be made from time to time in the light of particular circumstances." Bator, *Congressional Power over the Jurisdiction of the Federal Courts*, 27 VILL. L. REV. 1030, 1031 (1982).

(2) In *Martin v. Hunter's Lessee, supra* § 1.02, Justice Story reasoned that Article III was mandatory. He concluded: "It would seem, therefore, to follow that congress are bound to create some inferior courts, in which to vest all that jurisdiction which, under the constitution, is exclusively vested in the United States, and of which the Supreme Court cannot take original cognizance." In *Palmore v. United States*, 411 U.S. 389 (1973), *infra* § 1.05, however, Justice White said Congress had discretion regarding the creation and jurisdiction of lower courts.

(3) Congress has never extended lower court jurisdiction to the full limits of Article III. Although the judicial power extends to controversies between citizens of different states, i.e., diversity jurisdiction, Congress has never allowed all such cases in federal court but has imposed amount in controversy requirements which mean that some diversity cases do not qualify for federal jurisdiction. The Judiciary Act of 1789 not only limited diversity jurisdiction but conferred no original federal question jurisdiction on lower courts. The Court held in *Sheldon v. Sill*, 49 U.S. (8 How.) 441 (1850) that Congress has discretion whether to confer all, or only some, of the judicial power Article III authorizes.

(4) In *Tarble's Case*, 80 U.S. (13 Wall.) 397 (1871), the Court held that state courts cannot grant habeas corpus relief to federal prisoners. Absent lower federal courts to hear such claims, no judicial tribunal could decide them because a) they would not be within the Supreme Court's original jurisdiction and b) they could not arise initially in the nonexistent lower federal courts or in the forbidden state courts. Would such a state of affairs constitute an improper suspension of the writ of habeas corpus in violation of Art. I, § 9, cl. 2 of the Constitution? In *Swain v. Pressley*, 430 U.S. 372 (1977), the Court held that Congress could, without violating the Suspension Clause, substitute for the habeas corpus petition a different collateral remedy which was "neither inadequate nor ineffective to test the legality of a person's detention."

(5) What if Congress bars any court, federal or state, from taking jurisdiction or granting a remedy in a particular case? Faced with such statutes, courts frequently construe the applicable statutes to avoid the constitutional issue. For instance in *Webster v. Doe*, 486 U.S. 592 (1988), the Court held that § 102(c) of the National Security Act of 1947 did not preclude judicial review in a district court over constitutional claims arising from the discharge of a CIA employee because of his homosexuality. The Court's decision was made "in part to avoid the 'serious constitutional question' that would arise if a federal statute were construed to deny any

judicial forum for a colorable constitutional claim." Justice Scalia, dissenting, took strong issue with what he called "the Court's ominous warning." According to him, it is settled "(1) that not all constitutional claims require a judicial remedy, and (2) that the identification of those that do not can, even if only within narrow limits, be determined by Congress." Hence, he asserted, "it is clear that the 'serious constitutional question' feared by the Court is an illusion."

Justice Scalia further wrote, "The first response to the Court's grave doubt about the constitutionality of denying all judicial review to a 'colorable constitutional claim' is that the denial of all judicial review is not at issue here, but merely the denial of review in United States district courts. As to that, the law is, and has long been, clear. Article III, § 2 of the Constitution extends the judicial power to 'all Cases . . . arising under this Constitution.' But Article III, § 1 provides that the judicial power shall be vested 'in one supreme Court, and in such inferior Courts as the Congress may from time to time ordain and establish' (emphasis added). We long ago held that the power not to create any lower federal courts at all includes the power to invest them with less than all of the judicial power. . . . Thus, if there is any truth to the proposition that judicial cognizance of constitutional claims cannot be eliminated, it is, at most, that they cannot be eliminated from state courts, and from this Court's appellate jurisdiction over cases from state courts (or cases from federal courts, should there be any) involving such claims." *Id.* at 611.

Despite Justice Scalia's statement, *Tarble's Case* might suggest that state courts lack jurisdiction to review federal agency action. Denial of federal court jurisdiction here would leave a party remediless. Would such a state of affairs violate the principle from *Marbury* that the essence of law requires some judicial remedy to vindicate any legal right?

(6) In *Plaut v. Spendthrift Farm, Inc.*, 514 U.S. 211 (1995), the Court held that Congress violated separation of powers principles by invading the judiciary's province when it passed a law requiring federal courts to reopen final judicial decisions disposing of private civil litigation. In ordering reinstatement of cases courts had dismissed as filed outside the statute of limitations, Congress had violated a "deeply rooted" "postulate of Article III," Justice Scalia wrote for the majority. *Marbury* "said it was the Court's province and duty . . . to say what the law is" in particular cases and controversies; that role carried with it the power to resolve those cases finally, subject only to judicial review by a higher court. Justice Scalia wrote:

> The record of history shows that the Framers crafted this charter of the judicial department with an expressed understanding that it gives the Federal Judiciary the power, not merely to rule on cases, but to decide them, subject to review only by superior courts in the Article III hierarchy — with an understanding, in short, that "a judgment conclusively resolves the case" because "a 'judicial Power' is one to render dispositive judgments." By retroactively commanding the federal courts to reopen final judgments, Congress has violated this fundamental principle.

§ 1.05   NON-ARTICLE III COURTS

PALMORE v. UNITED STATES
411 U.S. 389, 93 S. Ct. 1670, 36 L. Ed. 2d 342 (1973)

Mr. Justice White delivered the opinion of the Court.

. . . [T]his case requires us to decide whether a defendant charged with a felony under the District of Columbia Code may be tried by a judge who does not have protection with respect to tenure and salary under Art. III of the Constitution. We hold that under its Art. I, § 8, cl. 17, power to legislate for the District Columbia, Congress may provide for trying local criminal cases before judges who, in accordance with the District of Columbia Code, are not accorded life tenure and protection against reduction in salary. In this respect, the position of the District of Columbia defendant is similar to that of the citizen of any of the 50 States when charged with violation of a state criminal law: Neither has a federal constitutional right to be tried before judges with tenure and salary guarantees. . . .

III

Art. I, § 8, cl. 17, of the Constitution provides that Congress shall have power "[t]o exercise exclusive Legislation in all Cases whatsoever, over" the District of Columbia. The power is plenary. Not only may statutes of Congress of otherwise nationwide application be applied to the District of Columbia, but Congress may also exercise all the police and regulatory powers which a state legislature or municipal government would have in legislating for state or local purposes. . . .

The conviction was clearly within the authority granted Congress by Art. I, § 8, cl. 17, unless, as Palmore contends, Art. III of the Constitution requires that prosecutions for District of Columbia felonies must be presided over by a judge having the tenure and salary protections provided by Art. III.

[Palmore's] position ultimately rests on the proposition that an Art. III judge must preside over every proceeding in which a charge, claim, or defense is based on an Act of Congress or a law made under its authority. At the very least, it asserts that criminal offenses under the laws passed by Congress may not be prosecuted except in courts established pursuant to Art. III. In our view, however, there is no support for this view in either constitutional text or in constitutional history and practice.

Article III describes the judicial power as extending to all cases, among others, arising under the laws of the United States; but, aside from this Court, the power is vested "in such inferior Courts as the Congress may from time to time ordain and establish." The decision with respect to inferior federal courts, as well as the task of defining their jurisdiction, was left to the discretion of Congress. That body was not constitutionally required to create inferior Art. III courts to hear and decide cases within the judicial power of the United States, including those criminal cases arising under the laws of the United States. Nor, if inferior federal courts were created, was it required to invest them with all the jurisdiction it was authorized to bestow under Art. III. . . .

Congress plainly understood this, for until 1875 Congress refrained from providing the lower federal courts with general federal-question jurisdiction. Until that time, the state courts provided the only forum for vindicating many important federal claims. . . .

It is also true that throughout our history, Congress has exercised its power under Art. IV to "make all needful Rules and Regulations respecting the Territory or other Property belonging to the United States" by creating territorial courts and manning them with judges appointed for a term of years. These courts have not been deemed subject to the strictures of Art. III, even though they characteristically enforced not only the civil and criminal laws of Congress applicable throughout the United States, but also the laws applicable only within the boundaries of the particular territory. . . .

V

It is apparent that neither this Court nor Congress has read the Constitution as requiring every federal question arising under the federal law, or even every criminal prosecution for violating an Act of Congress, to be tried in an Art. III court before a judge enjoying lifetime tenure and protection against salary reduction. Rather, both Congress and this Court have recognized that state courts are appropriate forums in which federal questions and federal crimes may at times be tried; and that the requirements of Art. III, which are applicable where laws of national applicability and affairs of national concern are at stake, must in proper circumstances give way to accommodate plenary grants of power to Congress to legislate with respect to specialized areas having particularized needs and warranting distinctive treatment. Here, Congress reorganized the court system in the District of Columbia and established one set of courts in the District with Art. III characteristics and devoted to matters of national concern. It also created a wholly separate court system designed primarily to concern itself with local law and to serve as a local court system for a large metropolitan area.

Furthermore, Congress, after careful consideration, determined that it preferred, and had the power to utilize, a local court system staffed by judges without lifetime tenure. . . . Congress made a deliberate choice to create judgeships with terms of 15 years, D.C. Code Ann. § 11-1502 (Supp. V, 1972), and to subject judges in those positions to removal or suspension by a judicial commission under certain established circumstances. *Id.* §§ 11-1502, 11-1521 et seq. It was thought that such a system would be more workable and efficient in administering and discharging the work of a multifaceted metropolitan court system.

In providing for fixed terms of office, Congress was cognizant of the fact that "virtually no State has provided" for tenure during good behavior, . . . the District of Columbia Court of Appeals noting that 46 of the 50 States have not provided life tenure for trial judges who hear felony cases, 290 A.2d, at 578 n. 12, and the provisions of the Act, with respect to court administration and to judicial removal and suspension, were considered by some as a model for the States. . . .

We do not discount the importance attached to the tenure and salary provisions of Art. III, but we conclude that Congress was not required to provide an Art. III court for the trial of criminal cases arising under its laws applicable only within the District of Columbia. Palmore's trial in the Superior Court was authorized by Congress' Art. I power to legislate for the District in all cases whatsoever. Palmore was no more disadvantaged and no more entitled to an Art. III judge than any other citizen of any of the 50 States who is tried for a strictly local crime. Nor did his trial by a nontenured judge deprive him of due process of law under the Fifth Amendment any more than the trial of the citizens of the various States for local crimes by judges without protection as to tenure deprives them of due process of law under the Fourteenth Amendment.

The judgment of the District of Columbia Court of Appeals is affirmed.

MR. JUSTICE DOUGLAS, dissenting. . . .

The judges of the court that convicted [appellant]

— hold office for a term of fifteen years, not for life as do Art. III judges;
— unlike Art. III judges, their salaries are not protected from diminishment during their continuance in office;
— unlike Art. III judges, they can be removed from office by a five-member Commission through less formidable means of procedure than impeachment. While two of the five members must be lawyers (one a member of the District Bar in active practice for at least five of the ten years prior to his appointment and one an active or retired federal judge serving in the District) the other three may be laymen. One of the three must be a layman. D.C. Code Ann. § 11-1522 (Supp. V, 1972).

In other words, these Superior Court judges are not members of the independent judiciary which has been one of our proudest boasts, by reason of Art. III. The safeguards accorded Art. III judges were designed to protect litigants with unpopular or minority causes or litigants who belong to despised or suspect classes. The safeguards surround the judge and give him a measure of protection against the hostile press, the leftist or rightist demands of the party in power, the glowering looks of those in the top echelon in whose hands rest the power of reappointment. . . .

Manipulated judiciaries are common across the world, especially in communist and fascist nations. The faith in freedom which we profess and which is opposed to those ideologies assumes today an ominous cast. . . . Those who hold the gun at the heads of Superior Court judges can retaliate against those who respect the spirit of the Fourth Amendment and the Fifth Amendment and who stand firmly against the ancient practice of using the third degree to get confessions and who fervently believe that the end does not justify the means.

I would reverse the judgment below.

NOTES ON NON-ARTICLE III COURTS

(1) Article III, § 1 provides that "[t]he Judges, both of the supreme and inferior Courts, shall hold their Offices during good Behavior, and shall, at stated Times, receive for their Services a Compensation, which shall not be diminished during their Continuance in Office."

(2) *Palmore* provides that Congress can, pursuant to Art. I, § 8, cl. 17, proscribe crimes applicable in the District of Columbia which can be tried in local courts "staffed by judges without lifetime tenure" or salary protection. Does not *Palmore* make the District of Columbia judges dependent on the Congressional will alone for their tenure and salaries? Note Justice Douglas' list of Article III safeguards that do not extend to non-Article III judges. If the power exercised is "judicial power" as defined in Article III, should the Article III safeguards of an independent judiciary govern?

(3) The exercise of Article III power by non-Article III judges (sometimes called Article I judges) extends beyond the facts of *Palmore* involving as it did, the District of Columbia, the functional equivalent of a state. According to *Thomas v. Union Carbide Agric. Prod. Co.*, 473 U.S. 568, 585 (1985), the Constitution "permit[s] . . . three clearly defined exceptions to the rule of Article III adjudication: military tribunals, territorial courts, and decisions involving public as opposed to private rights." Classic public rights issues generally involve a dispute between government and an individual.

(4) Courts have struggled to find the right lines to separate permissible from impermissible delegations of judicial power to non-Article III courts. The late Professor Paul Bator suggested that delegations were appropriate if the arrangement was a necessary and proper means of achieving the ends of a legitimate federal program, due process was provided, and an Article III court could ultimately review the legality of the asserted powers. Bator, *The Constitution as Architecture: Legislative and Administrative Courts Under Article III*, 65 IND. L.J. 233, 267-68 (1990). In *Thomas*, the court held that Congress could create an arbitration system within a governmental agency (i.e., non-Article III tribunal) to adjudicate certain disputes between private parties which were "closely integrated into a public regulatory scheme" even though very limited judicial review was allowed. The court noted the "public" nature of the regulatory scheme and that some review by an Article III court was allowed. Courts must look to substance, not formal categories, Justice O'Connor wrote for the Court.

The following year, in *Commodity Futures Trading Commission v. Schor*, 478 U.S. 833 (1986), the Court upheld a statute empowering an administrative agency to decide state law counterclaims against a broker in the context of an administrative reparations action against the broker. Although classic private rights seemed to be implicated, the Court rejected an approach looking to formal legal categories. Instead, it balanced a number of factors, none of which were alone dispositive, "with an eye to the practical effect that the Congressional action will have on the constitutionally assigned role of the federal judiciary." *Id.* at 851. The balanced factors included the extent to which essential attributes of judicial power are reserved to Article III courts, the extent to which non-Article III tribunals are given power typically exercised by Article III courts, the nature of the rights adjudicated, and the reasons Congress chose to delegate power to a non-Article III body.

In 1989, however, the Court appeared to reinvigorate the public-private rights distinction in *Granfinanciera S.A. v. Nordberg*, 492 U.S. 33 (1989). For the majority, Justice Brennan, who had generally advocated a more categorical approach than had Justice O'Connor, wrote that Congress could not empower a non-Article III tribunal to adjudicate a cause of action involving private rights.

§ 1.06   CASES AND CONTROVERSIES; JUSTICIABILITY DOCTRINE

[1]   Introduction

NOTES

(1) "The right to declare a law unconstitutional arises because an act of Congress relied upon by one or the other of such parties in determining their rights is in conflict with the fundamental law. The exercise of this, the most important and delicate duty of this court, is not given to it as a body with revisory power over the action of Congress, but because the rights of the litigants in justiciable controversies require the court to choose between the fundamental law and a law purporting to be enacted within constitutional authority, but in fact beyond the power delegated to the legislative branch of the government." *Muskrat v. United States*, 219 U.S. 346, 361 (1911).

(2) Relying largely on the "Case" or "Controversy" requirement of Article III, the Court has articulated a number of doctrines identifying the conditions under which the federal courts may exercise the subject matter jurisdiction the Constitution and Congress have given them. Those concepts, known as justiciability doctrines, generally perform two functions — they limit the federal courts to issues that arise in an adversary context and which are susceptible to judicial resolution and they prevent the judiciary from invading the turf of the executive or legislative branches. *See Flast v. Cohen*, 392 U.S. 83, 94-95 (1968). Although these doctrines derive, in part, from constitutional text (the "Case" or "Controversy" requirement) and constitutional structure (separation of powers), they also reflect, to some extent, prudential considerations. At times, courts fashion and deploy justiciability doctrine to avoid reaching matters that are within federal judicial power. Is it proper for federal courts not to use the judicial power the Constitution and the Congress have given them?

(3) The justiciability doctrines limit the ability of the federal court to hear and decide certain disputes. Whatever their constitutional moorings, these doctrines are not explicitly mentioned in the Constitution. Instead, courts have recognized these doctrines. What conclusions do you draw from the fact that the Court has identified and enforced limitations on its power?

[2] Advisory Opinions

NOTES ON ADVISORY OPINIONS

(1) From the beginning, the Supreme Court has construed the "Case" or "Controversy" requirement as precluding federal courts from acting as advisers to the other departments. Indeed, the very first Court declined to provide President George Washington an advisory opinion on questions regarding which Washington was anxious to have judicial illumination. Acting through Secretary of State Jefferson, the President had sent the Supreme Court a letter asking its advice on pressing questions of international law. The Justices replied to the President as follows:

Philadelphia, 8th August, 1793.

Sir:

We have considered the previous question stated in a letter written by your direction to us by the Secretary of State on the 18th of last month, [regarding] the lines of separation drawn by the Constitution between the three departments of the government. These being in certain respects checks upon each other, and our being judges of a court in the last resort, are considerations which afford strong arguments against the propriety of our extra-judicially deciding the questions alluded to, especially as the power given by the Constitution to the President, of calling on the heads of departments for opinions, seems to have been *purposely* as well as expressly united to the *executive* departments.

We exceedingly regret every event that may cause embarrassment to your administration, but we derive consolation from the reflection that your judgment will discern what is right, and that your usual prudence, decision, and firmness will surmount every obstacle to the preservation of the rights, peace, and dignity of the United States.

We have the honour to be, with perfect respect, sir, your most obedient and most humble servants.

(2) In *Chicago & Southern Air Lines, Inc. v. Waterman S.S. Corp. Civil Aeronautics Bd.*, 333 U.S. 103 (1948), the Court held that federal courts could not exercise judicial review over orders of the Civil Aeronautics Board which were thereafter subject to presidential review under a regulatory scheme Congress had devised. For the Court, Justice Jackson wrote:

The court below considered that after it reviewed the Board's order its judgment would be submitted to the President, that his power to disapprove would apply after as well as before the court acts, and hence that there would be no chance of a deadlock and no conflict of function. But if the President may completely disregard the judgment of the court, it would be only because it is one the courts were not authorized to render. Judgments within the powers vested in courts by the Judiciary Article of the Constitution may not lawfully be revised, overturned or refused faith and credit by another Department of Government.

To revise or review an administrative decision which has only the force of a recommendation to the President, would be to render an advisory opinion in its most obnoxious form — advice that the President has not asked, tendered at the demand of a private litigant, on a subject concededly within the President's exclusive, ultimate control. This Court early and wisely determined that it would not give advisory opinions even when asked by the Chief Executive. It has also been the firm and unvarying practice of Constitutional Courts to render no judgments not binding and conclusive on the parties and none that are subject to later review or alteration by administrative action.

(3) In *Nashville, C. & St. L. Ry. v. Wallace*, 288 U.S. 249 (1933), a case dealing with the constitutionality of a state declaratory judgment act, the Court held that seeking coercive relief is not an essential element of an Article III "Case or Controversy?" Thereafter, Congress passed the Federal Declaratory Judgment Act, which the Court unanimously upheld, in *Aetna Life Ins. Co. v. Haworth*, 300 U.S. 227 (1937), a case in which an insurance company sought a declaration that the defendant's policies had lapsed. Chief Justice Hughes noted that the lawsuit involved a true dispute between adverse parties regarding legal rights and obligations flowing from contracts. The controversy was "definite and concrete, not hypothetical or abstract."

(4) A minority of states allow their courts to render advisory opinions, at least in certain circumstances. Why are these permissible in some states but not in federal courts?

(5) The remaining justiciability doctrines involve questions of *who* may bring a lawsuit (standing), *when* may a suit be brought (ripeness, mootness) and *what* may be the subject of a lawsuit (political question).

§ 1.07 STANDING

MASSACHUSETTS v. ENVIRONMENTAL PROTECTION AGENCY
127 S. Ct. 1438, 167 L. Ed. 2d 248 (2007)

JUSTICE STEVENS delivered the opinion of the Court. . . .

Calling global warming "the most pressing environmental challenge of our time," a group of States, local governments, and private organizations, alleged in a petition for certiorari that the Environmental Protection Agency (EPA) has abdicated its responsibility under the Clean Air Act to regulate the emissions of four greenhouse gases, including carbon dioxide. Specifically, petitioners asked us to answer two questions concerning the meaning of § 202(a)(1) of the Act: whether EPA has the statutory authority to regulate greenhouse gas emissions from new motor vehicles; and if so, whether its stated reasons for refusing to do so are consistent with the statute. . . .

I.

Section 202(a)(1) of the Clean Air Act, . . . provides:

The [EPA] Administrator shall by regulation prescribe (and from time to time revise) in accordance with the provisions of this section, standards applicable to the emission of any air pollutant from any class or classes of new motor vehicles or new motor vehicle engines, which in his judgment cause, or contribute to, air pollution which may reasonably be anticipated to endanger public health or welfare. . . .

II.

On October 20, 1999, a group of 19 private organizations filed a rulemaking petition asking EPA to regulate "greenhouse gas emissions from new motor vehicles under § 202 of the Clean Air Act." Petitioners maintained that 1998 was the "warmest year on record"; that carbon dioxide, methane, nitrous oxide, and hydrofluorocarbons are "heat trapping greenhouse gases"; that greenhouse gas emissions have significantly accelerated climate change; and that the IPCC's 1995 report warned that "carbon dioxide remains the most important contributor to [man-made] forcing of climate change." The petition further alleged that climate change will have serious adverse effects on human health and the environment. As to EPA's statutory authority, the petition observed that the agency itself had already confirmed that it had the power to regulate carbon dioxide. . . .

On September 8, 2003, EPA entered an order denying the rulemaking petition. The agency gave two reasons for its decision: (1) that contrary to the opinions of its former general counsels, the Clean Air Act does not authorize EPA to issue mandatory regulations to address global climate change, and (2) that even if the agency had the authority to set greenhouse gas emission standards, it would be unwise to do so at this time.

III.

Petitioners, now joined by intervenor States and local governments, sought review of EPA's order in the United States Court of Appeals for the District of Columbia Circuit. Although each of the three judges on the panel wrote a separate opinion, two judges agreed "that the EPA Administrator properly exercised his discretion under § 202(a)(1) in denying the petition for rule making." 415 F.3d 50, 58 (2005). The court therefore denied the petition for review. . . .

IV.

Article III of the Constitution limits federal-court jurisdiction to "Cases" and "Controversies." Those two words confine "the business of federal courts to questions presented in an adversary context and in a form historically viewed as capable of resolution through the judicial process." *Flast v. Cohen*, 392 U.S. 83, 95. . . .

The parties' dispute turns on the proper construction of a congressional statute, a question eminently suitable to resolution in federal court. Congress has moreover authorized this type of challenge to EPA action That authorization is of critical importance to the standing inquiry: "Congress has the power to define injuries and articulate chains of causation that will give rise to a case or controversy where none existed before." *Lujan*, 504 U.S. at 580 (Kennedy, J., concurring in part and concurring in judgment). "In exercising this power, however, Congress must at the very least identify the injury it seeks to vindicate and relate the injury to the class of persons entitled to bring suit." *Id.* We will not, therefore, "entertain citizen suits to vindicate the public's nonconcrete interest in the proper administration of the laws." *Id.* at 581.

EPA maintains that because greenhouse gas emissions inflict widespread harm, the doctrine of standing presents an insuperable jurisdictional obstacle. We do not agree. At bottom, "the gist of the question of standing" is whether petitioners have "such a personal stake in the outcome of the controversy as to assure that concrete adverseness which sharpens the presentation of issues upon which the court so largely depends for illumination." *Baker v. Carr*, 369 U.S. 186, 204 (1962). As Justice Kennedy explained in his *Lujan* concurrence:

> While it does not matter how many persons have been injured by the challenged action, the party bringing suit must show that the action injures him in a concrete and personal way. This requirement is not just an empty formality. It preserves the vitality of the adversarial process by assuring both that the parties before the court have an actual, as opposed to professed, stake in the outcome, and that the legal questions presented . . . will be resolved, not in the rarified atmosphere of a debating society, but in a concrete factual context conducive to a realistic appreciation of the consequences of judicial action.

To ensure the proper adversarial presentation, *Lujan* holds that a litigant must demonstrate that it has suffered a concrete and particularized injury that is either actual or imminent, that the injury is fairly traceable to the defendant, and that it is likely that a favorable decision will redress that injury. However, a litigant to whom Congress has "accorded a procedural right to protect his concrete interests," here, the right to challenge agency action unlawfully withheld, "can assert that right without meeting all the normal standards for redressability and immediacy." When a litigant is vested with a procedural right, that litigant has standing if there is some possibility that the requested relief will prompt the injury-causing party to reconsider the decision that allegedly harmed the litigant. . . .

Only one of the petitioners needs to have standing to permit us to consider the petition for review. . . . We stress here . . . the special position and interest of Massachusetts. It is of considerable relevance that the party seeking review here is a sovereign State and not, as it was in *Lujan* a private individual.

Well before the creation of the modern administrative state, we recognized that States are not normal litigants for the purposes of invoking federal jurisdiction. . . . That Massachusetts does in fact own a great deal of the "territory alleged to be affected" only reinforces the conclusion that its stake in the outcome of this case is sufficiently concrete to warrant the exercise of federal judicial power.

When a State enters the Union, it surrenders certain sovereign prerogatives. Massachusetts cannot invade Rhode Island to force reductions in greenhouse gas emissions, it cannot negotiate an emissions treaty with China or India, and in some circumstances the exercise of its police powers to reduce in-state motor-vehicle emissions might well be pre-empted. . . .

These sovereign prerogatives are now lodged in the Federal Government, and Congress has ordered EPA to protect Massachusetts (among others) by prescribing standards applicable to the "emission of any air pollutant from any class or classes of new motor vehicle engines, which in [the Administrator's] judgment cause, or contribute to, air pollution which may reasonably be anticipated to endanger public health or welfare." 42 U.S.C. § 7521(a)(1). Congress has moreover recognized a concomitant procedural right to challenge the rejection of its rulemaking petition as arbitrary and capricious. § 7607(b)(1). Given that procedural right and Massachusetts' stake in protecting its quasi-sovereign interests, the Commonwealth is entitled to special solicitude in our standing analysis.

With that in mind, it is clear that petitioners' submissions as they pertain to Massachusetts have satisfied the most demanding standards of the adversarial process. EPA's steadfast refusal to regulate greenhouse gas emissions presents a risk of harm to Massachusetts that is both "actual" and "imminent." *Lujan*, 504 U.S., at 560 (internal quotation marks omitted). There is, moreover, a "substantial likelihood that the judicial relief requested" will prompt EPA to take steps to reduce that risk. *Duke Power Co. v. Carolina Environmental Study Group, Inc.*, 438 U.S. 59, 79 (1978).

The Injury

The harms associated with climate change are serious and well recognized. . . . That these climate-change risks are "widely shared" does not minimize Massachusetts' interest in the outcome of this litigation. . . .

Causation

EPA does not dispute the existence of a causal connection between man-made greenhouse gas emissions and global warming. At a minimum, therefore, EPA's refusal to regulate such emissions "contributes" to Massachusetts' injuries.

EPA nevertheless maintains that its decision not to regulate greenhouse gas emissions from new motor vehicles contributes so insignificantly to petitioners' injuries that the agency cannot be haled into federal court to answer for them. For the same reason, EPA does not believe that any realistic possibility exists that the relief petitioners seek would mitigate global climate change and remedy their injuries. . . . But EPA overstates its case. Its argument rests on the erroneous assumption that a small incremental step, because it is incremental, can never be attacked in a federal judicial forum. Yet accepting that premise would doom most challenges to regulatory action. . . . That a first step might be tentative does not by itself support the notion that federal courts lack jurisdiction to determine whether that step conforms to law. Judged by any standard, U.S. motor-vehicle emissions make a meaningful contribution to greenhouse gas concentrations and hence, according to petitioners, to global warming.

The Remedy

While it may be true that regulating motor-vehicle emissions will not by itself reverse global warming, it by no means follows that we lack jurisdiction to decide whether EPA has a duty to take steps to slow or reduce it. . . .

In sum-at least according to petitioners' uncontested affidavits-the rise in sea levels associated with global warming has already harmed and will continue to harm Massachusetts. The risk of catastrophic harm, though remote, is nevertheless real. That risk would be reduced to some extent if petitioners received the relief they seek. We therefore hold that petitioners have standing to challenge the EPA's denial of their rulemaking petition.

CHIEF JUSTICE ROBERTS, with whom JUSTICE SCALIA, JUSTICE THOMAS, and JUSTICE ALITO join, dissenting. . . .

I would reject these challenges as nonjusticiable. Such a conclusion involves no judgment on whether global warming exists, what causes it, or the extent of the problem. Nor does it render petitioners without recourse. This Court's standing jurisprudence simply recognizes that redress of grievances of the sort at issue here "is the function of Congress and the Chief Executive," not the federal courts. *Lujan v. Defenders of Wildlife*, 504 U.S. 555, 576 (1992). I would vacate the judgment below and remand for dismissal of the petitions for review.

I.

. . . Relaxing Article III standing requirements because asserted injuries are pressed by a State, however, has no basis in our jurisprudence, and support for any such "special solicitude" is conspicuously absent from the Court's opinion. The general judicial review provision cited by the Court, affords States no special rights or status. The Court states that "Congress has ordered EPA to protect Massachusetts (among others)" through the statutory provision at issue, and that "Congress has . . . recognized a concomitant procedural right to challenge the rejection of its rulemaking petition as arbitrary and capricious." The reader might think from this unfortunate phrasing that Congress said something about the rights of States in this particular provision of the statute. Congress knows how to do that when it wants to, . . . but it has done nothing of the sort here. Under the law on which petitioners rely, Congress treated public and private litigants exactly the same. . . .

A claim of *parens patriae* standing is distinct from an allegation of direct injury. *See Wyoming v. Oklahoma*, 502 U.S. 437, 448-449, 451 (1992). Far from being a substitute for Article III injury, *parens patriae* actions raise an additional hurdle for a state litigant: the articulation of a "quasi-sovereign interest" "apart from the interests of particular private parties." *Alfred L. Snapp & Son, Inc. v. Puerto Rico ex rel. Barez*, 458 U.S. 592, 607 (1982). Just as an association suing on behalf of its members must show not only that it represents the members but that at least one satisfies Article III requirements, so too a State asserting quasi-sovereign interests as *parens patriae* must still show that its citizens satisfy Article III. Focusing on Massachusetts's interests as quasi-sovereign makes the required showing here harder, not easier. The Court, in effect, takes what has always been regarded as a necessary condition for *parens patriae* standing-a quasi-sovereign interest-and converts it into a sufficient showing for purposes of Article III.

What is more, the Court's reasoning falters on its own terms. The Court asserts that Massachusetts is entitled to "special solicitude" due to its "quasi-sovereign interests," but then applies our Article III standing test to the asserted injury of the State's loss of coastal property (concluding that Massachusetts "has alleged a particularized injury *in its capacity as a landowner*" (emphasis added)). In the context of *parens patriae* standing, however, we have characterized state ownership of land as a "nonsovereign interes[t]" because a State "is likely to have the same interests as other similarly situated proprietors." *Alfred L. Snapp & Son, supra.* . . .

II.

It is not at all clear how the Court's "special solicitude" for Massachusetts plays out in the standing analysis, except as an implicit concession that petitioners cannot establish standing on traditional terms. But the status of Massachusetts as a State cannot compensate for petitioners' failure to demonstrate injury in fact, causation, and redressability. . . .

The very concept of global warming seems inconsistent with this particularization requirement. Global warming is a phenomenon "harmful to humanity at large," and the redress petitioners seek is focused no more on them than on the public generally — it is literally to change the atmosphere around the world. If petitioners' particularized injury is loss of coastal land, it is also that injury that must be "actual or imminent, not conjectural or hypothetical, *Defenders of Wildlife*. . . .

III.

Petitioners' reliance on Massachusetts's loss of coastal land as their injury in fact for standing purposes creates insurmountable problems for them with respect to causation and redressability. To establish standing, petitioners must show a causal connection between that specific injury and the lack of new motor vehicle greenhouse gas emission standards, and that the promulgation of such standards would likely redress that injury. As is often the case, the questions of causation and redressability overlap. . . . And importantly, when a party is challenging the Government's allegedly unlawful regulation, or lack of regulation, of a third party, satisfying the causation and redressability requirements becomes "substantially more difficult." . . .

Petitioners are never able to trace their alleged injuries back through this complex web to the fractional amount of global emissions that might have been limited with EPA standards. In light of the bit-part domestic new motor vehicle greenhouse gas emissions have played in what petitioners describe as a 150-year global phenomenon, and the myriad additional factors bearing on petitioners' alleged injury-the loss of Massachusetts coastal land-the connection is far too speculative to establish causation.

IV.

Redressability is even more problematic. To the tenuous link between petitioners' alleged injury and the indeterminate fractional domestic emissions at issue here, add the fact that petitioners cannot meaningfully predict what will come of the 80 percent of global greenhouse gas emissions that originate outside the United States. . . .

The Court's sleight-of-hand is in failing to link up the different elements of the three-part standing test. What must be *likely* to be redressed is the particular injury in fact. The injury the Court looks to is the asserted loss of land. The Court contends that regulating domestic motor vehicle emissions will reduce carbon dioxide in the atmosphere, *and therefore* redress Massachusetts's injury. But even if regulation does reduce emissions-to some indeterminate degree, given events elsewhere in the world-the Court never explains why that makes it *likely* that the injury in fact-the loss of land-will be redressed. . . . The realities make it pure conjecture to suppose that EPA regulation of new automobile emissions will *likely* prevent the loss of Massachusetts coastal land.

V.

. . . The limitation of the judicial power to cases and controversies "is crucial in maintaining the tripartite allocation of power set forth in the Constitution."

. . . The good news is that the Court's "special solicitude" for Massachusetts limits the future applicability of the diluted standing requirements applied in this case. The bad news is that the Court's self-professed relaxation of those Article III requirements has caused us to transgress "the proper-and properly limited-role of the courts in a democratic society." *Allen*, 468 U.S. at 750.

NOTES

A. Basic Elements of Standing

(1) In *Lujan v. Defenders of Wildlife*, 504 U.S. 555 (1992), the Court held that various organizations dedicated to wildlife conservation lacked standing to challenge a rule promulgated by the Secretary of Interior that limited the applicability of portions of the Endangered Species Act of 1973 (ESA) to actions in the United States and on the high seas. Various members of the organization alleged that they had previously traveled abroad to observe certain exotic and endangered species like the Nile crocodile and Asian elephant and leopard and intended to do so again. The Secretary's rule increased the likelihood that these species would not be observable when they returned. Although the Court held that "purely ascetic purposes" may support standing, "'some day intentions' — without any description of concrete plans" were insufficient to show actual or imminent injury which is one of the constitutional requirements for standing. In *Lujan*, the Court identified the irreducible constitutional minimum of standing as requiring an "injury in fact" which is "fairly . . . trace[able] to the challenged action of the defendant" (i.e., causation) which is "likely" to be "redressed by a favorable decision." Plaintiff must prove all three elements to establish standing. In his majority opinion in *Lujan*, Justice Scalia wrote that a plaintiff's burden to establish standing may vary depending on whether or not he/she is "an object of the action (or foreign action) at issue." He wrote:

> When the suit is one challenging the legality of government action or inaction, the nature and extent of facts that must be averred (at the summary judgment stage) or proved (at the trial stage) in order to establish standing depends considerably upon whether the plaintiff is himself an object of the action (or forgone action) at issue. If he is, there is ordinarily little question that the action or inaction has caused him injury, and that a judgment preventing or

requiring the action will redress it. When, however, as in this case, a plaintiff's asserted injury arises from the government's allegedly unlawful regulation (or lack of regulation) of someone else, much more is needed. In that circumstance, causation and redressability ordinarily hinge on the response of the regulated (or regulable) third party to the government action or inaction — and perhaps on the response of others as well. The existence of one or more of the essential elements of standing "depends on the unfettered choices made by independent actors not before the courts and whose exercise of broad and legitimate discretion the courts cannot presume either to control or to predict." . . . and it becomes the burden of the plaintiff to adduce facts showing that those choices have been or will be made in such manner as to produce causation and permit redressability of injury. . . . Thus, when the plaintiff is not himself the object of the government action or inaction he challenges, standing is not precluded, but it is ordinarily "substantially more difficult" to establish. . . .

(2) *Harm.* In *Sierra Club v. Morton*, 405 U.S. 727 (1972) the Court found plaintiff Sierra Club lacked standing to litigate to stop construction of a ski resort in Mineral King Valley, California because it did not allege that any of its members used Mineral King Valley. "Why didn't the Sierra Club have one goddamn member walk through the park and then there would have been standing to sue?," Justice White reportedly exclaimed. *See* WOODWARD & ARMSTRONG, THE BRETHREN 164 (1974). A plaintiff seeking injunctive relief must show the likelihood of future harm. Thus, in *City of Los Angeles v. Lyons*, 461 U.S. 95 (1983), an African-American plaintiff lacked standing to enjoin the local police department from using chokeholds in non-threatening situations. After being stopped for having a burnt out light, Lyons had been placed in a chokehold until he passed out. Six other chokehold victims had died. The Court said Lyons did not have standing to seek injunctive relief because he could not establish he was likely to receive a chokehold again.

(3) *Causation*, too, must be established. In *Simon v. Kentucky Welfare Rights*, 426 U.S. 26 (1976) indigent plaintiffs who had been denied medical care challenged a revised Internal Revenue Ruling that relaxed prior requirements that tax-exempt hospitals provide free care. Plaintiffs had been harmed but could not show that the harm was caused by IRS's action.

(4) *Redressability.* In *Steel Co. v. Citizens for a Better Environment*, 523 U.S. 83 (1998), an environmental group lacked standing because it failed to establish redressability, i.e., the Court deemed the relief sought could not redress any injury to plaintiff. Plaintiffs sought declaratory and other relief for the failure of a steel company to file required reports on time. The company had filed the reports, but too late. Plaintiff's request for a declaration that the delay violated the Emergency Planning and Community Right to Know Act of 1986 (EPCRA) was deemed "worthless" to plaintiffs and "to all the world" because there was no controversy regarding the company's failure to file reports as required. The civil penalties plaintiff sought were not redress because they went to the United States Treasury, not to plaintiff. The litigation costs sought could not establish redressability because "a plaintiff cannot achieve standing to litigate a substantive issue by bringing suit for the cost of bringing suit." Allowing plaintiff to inspect the company's records was injunctive relief that would only address a future harm. But plaintiff had not alleged that any future harm was likely.

(5) *Laidlaw.* In *Friends of the Earth, Inc. v. Laidlaw Environmental Services (TOC), Inc.*, 528 U.S. 167 (2000), the Court held that plaintiff demonstrated standing by submitting affidavits which contained more than "general averments" and "conclusory allegations" of their "recreational, aesthetic, and economic interests." Although plaintiffs could not demonstrate injury to the environment by defendant's discharge in violation of their permit, these allegations regarding plaintiff's concerns about the

effects of the discharge were sufficient to show injury to the plaintiff for standing purposes. Dissenting, Justice Scalia found the allegations insufficient to demonstrate harm, because they were "vague, contradictory and unsubstantiated." The Court, said Justice Scalia, made the "injury-in-fact requirement a sham" and its handling of redressability was "equally cavalier."

B. Standing in Specific Applications

(6) *Citizen Standing.* The Court has not recognized standing of citizens to sue to force government to enforce the law. Thus, in *Schlesinger v. Reservists Comm. to Stop the War*, 418 U.S. 208 (1934), the Court held citizens lacked standing to sue to prevent members of Congress from holding military commissions as a violation of the Incompatibility Clause, U.S. Const. Art I. § 6. The Court held that only "the generalized interest of all citizens in constitutional governance" was implicated and that was too "abstract" to be a "concrete" harm. *Id.* at 217. "[S]tanding to sue may not be predicated upon an interest of the kind alleged here which is held in common by all members of the public, because of the necessarily abstract nature of the injury all citizens share." *Id.* at 220. Allowing citizen standing would violate principles of separation of powers. Similarly, in *United States v. Richardson,* 418 U.S. 166 (1974), the Court rejected a citizen's attempted judicial challenge that the Central Intelligence Agency Act violated the Statement and Accounts Clause of Article I, § 9 by protesting the secrecy of certain CIA expenditures. Plaintiff had only a generalized grievance he shared with his fellow citizens. The Court was untroubled by the fact that there might not be a plaintiff who would be able to litigate the issue if citizen standing were not recognized. That fact suggested the issue "is committed to the surveillance of Congress, and ultimately to the political process." *Id.* at 179. Conversely, if citizen standing was allowed, what would remain of the standing requirement?

(7) *Taxpayer standing.* Does a taxpayer's interest in ensuring that public funds are not spent illegally give the taxpayer standing? In *Frothingham v. Mellon*, 262 U.S. 447 (1923), plaintiff, a taxpayer of the United States, sued to enjoin on constitutional grounds a federal statute that provided for appropriations to be apportioned among the states to reduce maternal and infant mortality. Plaintiff claimed standing based on the contention that the appropriations would increase future taxation. The Court dismissed the action, holding that a federal taxpayer lacks standing to challenge a Congressional enactment because the federal taxpayer's interest was too remote and the federal taxpayer had no personal interest in the challenged statute. Should the small size of the taxpayer's interest be a determinative factor? In fiscal year 1958, for example, with federal expenditures at roughly $72 billion, the American Telephone and Telegraph Company paid some $915 million in federal income taxes. It clearly had more than a "minute" interest in federal expenditures. Did AT&T have standing, while Mrs. Frothingham did not?

The second reason given in *Frothingham* rests on a floodgates argument. "If one taxpayer may champion and litigate such a case, then every other taxpayer may do the same," the Court said. To permit constitutional issues to be raised by those with no unique personal interest but only an interest common to the taxpaying public, might open the floodgate of constitutional law litigation. "So much by way of limitation seems necessary to prevent . . . mass appeals by the industry at large, with resulting hopeless clogging of the [governmental] process by judicial review." *Federal Communications Comm'n. v. National Broadcasting Co.*, 319 U.S. 239, 260 (1943) (Frankfurter, J., dissenting).

(8) *Frothingham* left some invalid legislation immune from constitutional attack. If a taxpayer lacks standing, as a practical matter, Congressional appropriations cannot be challenged in court. Thus, even if Congress provided for grants to church-related

schools in violation of the First Amendment (*see infra* § 16.02), *Frothingham* would insulate such action from judicial scrutiny. To avoid that result, the Court modified the *Frothingham* doctrine in *Flast v. Cohen*, 392 U.S. 83 (1968), where it upheld the standing of a federal taxpayer to challenge Congressional expenditures on the ground that they violated the Establishment Clause of the First Amendment. Of course, *Flast* does not hold that a federal taxpayer always has standing. As Chief Justice Rehnquist has pointed out, for standing to exist under *Flast*, "a two-part test" must be met: (1) the taxpayer must attack an expenditure under the Taxing and Spending Clause (not simply an incidental expenditure of tax funds in administrating an essentially regulatory statute); and (2) the taxpayer must show that the challenged expenditure exceeds a specific constitutional limitation (such as that of the Establishment Clause) upon the taxing and spending power. In practice, the *Flast* criteria have allowed limited taxpayer standing. In *Valley Forge Christian College v. Americans United*, 454 U.S. 464 (1982), the Court held a taxpayer lacked standing to challenge the Department of Health, Education and Welfare's gift of 77 acres of land containing an Army hospital to a religious school for use to advance its sectarian work. The Court held *Flast* inapplicable since the gift was made by an executive agency, not by Congress, under the Disbursement of Property Clause of Art. IV, § 3, cl. 2, not under the Spending Clause of Art. I, § 8.

In *Hein v. Freedom From Religion Foundation, Inc.*, 127 S. Ct. 2553 (2007), the Court, in a plurality opinion by Justice Alito, concluded that the *Flast* exception to the rule against taxpayer standing only applies when a party challenges a specific congressional action or appropriation or asks the Court to invalidate an enactment or legislatively created program. Respondents challenged a 2001 executive order which created the White House Office of Faith-Based and Community Initiatives on the grounds that it violated the Establishment Clause. Justice Alito, joined by Chief Justice Roberts and Justice Kennedy, concluded that the *Flast* two-part test had not been satisfied because the challenge was not directed at an exercise of congressional power and thus lacked the required nexus between taxpayer status and the legislative enactment attacked. The agency was established using general Executive Branch appropriations. The plurality reasoned that "[b]ecause almost all Executive Branch activity is ultimately funded by some congressional appropriation, extending the *Flast* exception to purely executive expenditures would effectively subject every federal action . . . to Establishment Clause challenge by any taxpayer in federal court." Justices Scalia and Thomas agreed that respondent lacked standing but reached that conclusion because they viewed *Flast* as "irreconcilable" with Article III. They would overrule, not distinguish, *Flast*. The four dissenters thought the *Flast* exception should apply when a taxpayer challenges the expenditure by an executive agency of identifiable sums of tax dollars for religious purposes.

(9) *Voter Standing*. The *Flast* two-part test does not apply when a litigant asserts standing as a voter, not a taxpayer. In *Federal Election Comm'n v. Akins*, 524 U.S. 11 (1998), a group of citizens with views often adverse to the American Israel Public Affairs Committee (AIPAC) brought suit to compel the Federal Election Commission (FEC) to require AIPAC to disclose certain information regarding membership, contributions, and expenditures. The FEC had determined such disclosure requirements did not apply to AIPAC. The voters claimed the information would help them (and others with whom they shared it) assess candidates for public office.

In a 6-3 decision, the Court, speaking through Justice Breyer, rejected the government's claim that the voters failed to meet the Court's prudential standing requirements. Congress had included a generous citizen-suit provision in the Federal Election Campaign Act (FECA) (authorizing "[a]ny person" who believes the FECA has been violated to file an FEC complaint and authorizing "[a]ny party aggrieved" by an FEC order dismissing that party's complaint to file a lawsuit in federal court) which reflected a "congressional intent to cast the standing net broadly" and overrode any prudential standing requirements.

The Court also rejected the government's claim that constitutional standing requirements were not met. The denial of the information constituted "injury in fact." The Court found the causation and redressability requirements satisfied, too, even though FEC had discretion to exempt AIPAC from disclosure requirements even if the plaintiffs' view of the law was correct. The *Flast* "logical nexus" test was inapplicable since "there is no constitutional provision requiring the demonstration of the 'nexus' the Court believed must be shown . . . in *Flast*"; instead Congress had passed a statute seeking "to protect individuals [like Akins] from the kind of harm [asserted]."

Although the Court viewed the FEC's "strongest argument" against standing as "its contention that this lawsuit involves only a generalized grievance," (because the inability to obtain information about AIPAC was equally shared by most) it did not view that argument as persuasive. In most cases where standing had failed due to the alleged harm being a "generalized grievance" the Court said, the harm had been "not only widely shared" but "also of an abstract and indefinite nature." The "informational injury" alleged in *Akins*, however, "directly related to voting, the most basic of political rights," and was "sufficiently concrete and specific."

In dissent, Justice Scalia (joined by Justice O'Connor and Justice Thomas) relied heavily on *Richardson* and argued that Akins' injury was not "particularized" but was "undifferentiated and common" to all. Justice Scalia reiterated the concern he expressed in *Lujan v. Defenders of Wildlife*, that low Article III standing barriers and permissive citizen action provisions raised separation of powers concerns. He wrote:

> A system in which the citizenry at large could sue to compel Executive compliance with the law would be a system in which the courts, rather than of the President, are given the primary responsibility to "take Care that the Laws be faithfully executed," Art. II, § 3. We do not have such a system because the common understanding of the interest necessary to sustain suit has included the requirement, . . . that the complained-of injury be particularlized and differentiated, rather than common to all the electorate.

(10) *Congressional standing*. In *Raines v. Byrd*, 521 U.S. 811 (1997), six members of Congress who had voted against the Line Item Veto Act (LIVA) challenged the Act's constitutionality alleging that it diluted their Article I voting power. They did so under a provision in LIVA authorizing "[a]ny Member of Congress or any individual adversely affected by [LIVA]" to "bring an action" for declaratory and injunctive relief on the grounds that it violates the Constitution. The district court found the case justiciable and ruled LIVA unconstitutional. On expedited appeal as allowed by LIVA, the Supreme Court speaking through Chief Justice Rehnquist "put aside the natural urge to proceed directly to the merits of this important dispute" to consider the jurisdictional standing issue, an inquiry which becomes "especially rigorous when reaching the merits . . . would force us to decide whether an action taken by one of the other two branches . . . was unconstitutional." *Id.* at 820.

The Court held that the legislators lacked standing. Their claim of dilution of institutional legislative power was insufficient to show particular personal harm to them individually since any grievance they had was shared by all legislators equally. Moreover, the litigants complained of loss of political power, not loss of some "private right." The Court, therefore, found Byrd distinguishable from *Powell v. McCormack*, *infra* § 1.09, Note (5) after *Nixon*, which held that Representative Adam Clayton Powell had standing to challenge his exclusion from the House of Representatives (and consequent loss of salary); he had sustained personal injury. The Court also distinguished *Byrd* from *Coleman v. Miller*, 307 U.S. 433 (1939), which had upheld standing for Kansas legislators. In *Coleman*, 20 Kansas state senators who had voted against ratification of the proposed "Child Labor Amendment" to the Constitution and several colleagues sought a writ of mandamus to compel Kansas officials to recognize that the Kansas state Senate had not voted to ratify the proposed constitutional amendment. The Court held that the Kansas legislators had standing since, if correct in their substantive claim (that the Lieutenant Governor had illegally cast a deciding vote), their votes could have defeated the measure. *Coleman*, said the *Byrd* Court, stands at most "for the proposition that legislators whose votes would have been sufficient to defeat (or enact) a specific legislative act have standing to sue if that legislative action goes into effect (or does not go into effect), on the ground that their votes have been completely nullified." *Raines*, 521 U.S. at 823.

In dissent, Justice Stevens argued that LIVA, if valid, injured Congressmen by depriving them of the right to vote on "the precise text that will ultimately become law." Justice Breyer argued that the line between "personal" and "official" harm was not so stark as the majority suggested. He saw *Coleman*, as a weaker, not more compelling, case for standing. In *Coleman*, 26 states had already rejected the proposed amendment making remote any chance of passage and accordingly making the Kansas votes insignificant. But the legislators in *Byrd* complained of the LIVA procedure that would affect many of their future votes.

(11) *Standing in the state courts.* State courts are not subject to the "Case" or "Controversy" requirement of Article III and accordingly are not restricted by federal law on taxpayer standing. Virtually all states have rejected the *Frothingham v. Mellon* denial of taxpayer standing. This may create anomalous situations if a plaintiff who lacks federal standing brings a lawsuit involving a federal question, and the state court's decision on the federal issue is appealed to the Supreme Court. If the plaintiff lacks standing under the relevant federal cases, what should the Supreme Court do? In *Doremus v. Board of Educ.*, 342 U.S. 429 (1952), plaintiff as taxpayer challenged a New Jersey statute which provided for reading of Old Testament verses at the beginning of each public school day as violating the Constitution. The highest New Jersey court upheld plaintiff's capacity to sue and upheld the statute on the merits. The Supreme Court dismissed the appeal for lack of standing. Though the state courts may decide federal questions under circumstances which do not constitute a true "Case" or "Controversy," the Supreme Court, bound as it is by Article III, may not accept any such state decision for review. Is the *Doremus* approach sound? What does it do to the policy underlying *Martin v. Hunter's Lessee*, *supra* § 1.02, which requires one national tribunal as the supreme expounder of the U.S. Constitution?

(12) *State standing.* A case may also raise the question of whether a state has standing to bring an action challenging a federal statute. In *Massachusetts v. Mellon*, 262 U.S. 447 (1923), Massachusetts challenged the constitutionality of the statute at issue in *Frothingham*, its companion case. That law, it will be recalled, provided for federal appropriations to be allocated among the states to reduce maternal and infant mortality. The allotment to each state was conditional upon acceptance by the state of the terms of the statute. Massachusetts claimed the statute usurped power the Tenth Amendment reserved to the states. The Court ruled that a state does not have standing as a state to challenge the constitutionality of a federal statute in order to vindicate its citizens rights against the federal government. "Nor does a State have standing as the parent of its citizens to invoke these constitutional provisions against the Federal Government, the ultimate *parens patriae* of every American citizen." *South Carolina v. Katzenbach*, 383 U.S. 301, 324 (1966).

A state may, however, sue to protect its own interests. Compare *Maryland v. Louisiana*, 451 U.S. 725 (1981) (state may bring action where the injury alleged affects state's economic interest in substantial way); *Alfred L. Snapp & Son v. Puerto Rico, Inc.*, 458 U.S. 592 (1982) (state may have standing as parens patriae when it asserts an injury to a "quasi-sovereign" interest — e.g., Puerto Rico's interest in protecting its citizens from discrimination in favor of foreign workers in violation of federal statutes).

(13) A litigant normally lacks standing to vindicate the rights of others. In *Whitmore v. Arkansas*, 495 U.S. 149 (1990), defendant, sentenced to death for murder, had waived his right to appeal. Plaintiff, another death row inmate who had exhausted his own appellate remedies, sought to intervene as "next friend." The Court held that he lacked standing. One may not have "next friend" standing without a showing that the real party in interest is unable to litigate his own cause due to mental incapacity, lack of access to court, or other similar disability. Otherwise, plaintiff lacks standing unless he can show that he has suffered a concrete "injury in fact." Nor can plaintiff validly contend that, as an Arkansas citizen, he is entitled to invoke the Court's jurisdiction to insure that the State does not carry out an execution without mandatory appellate review in violation of the Eighth Amendment. That raises only the generalized interest of all citizens in constitutional governance, an inadequate basis for standing.

(14) In *Campbell v. Louisiana*, 523 U.S. 392 (1998), the Court held that a white criminal defendant had third-party standing to assert the rights of black persons discriminated against in grand jury selections. Following its decision in *Powers v. Ohio*, 499 U.S. 400 (1991) (white defendant had standing to assert third party rights of blacks discriminated against in use of peremptory challenges), the Court found three tests for third party standing satisfied:

(1)   the defendant suffered an "injury in fact";
(2)   the defendant had a "close relationship" to the excluded jurors;
(3)   there was some hindrance to the excluded jurors asserting their own rights.

Racial discrimination in the selection of even one grand juror harmed a white criminal defendant by questioning the integrity of the criminal justice process. The defendant had the requisite relationship with the excluded grand jurors because both shared an interest in eradicating discrimination in the grand jury selection process. Economic disincentives might dissuade excluded black grand jurors from asserting their rights.

§ 1.08   RIPENESS; MOOTNESS

NOTES

(1) Ripeness relates to when a lawsuit may be brought. The requirement of ripeness bars the courts from considering constitutional issues prematurely. A constitutional question is ripe for judicial review only when the governmental act in question has direct adverse effect upon the individual making the challenge. Absent such actual adverse effect, when the challenge is only to the hypothetical operation of a government act no real "Case" or "Controversy" exists.

(2) When is a governmental act ripe for constitutional challenge? The issue typically arises when a party seeks to challenge a statute before the government has applied it to that party. Ripeness involves "the fitness of the issue for judicial decision and the hardship to the parties of withholding court consideration." *Abbott Lab. v. Gardner*, 387 U.S. 136, 144 (1967). That determination often involves balancing factors including the hardship to plaintiff of postponing review and the need for further factual development to facilitate judicial decision. Thus, an environmental challenge to a general plan for managing a national forest was premature since no rights or duties were created or imposed. Deferring litigation would allow further agency definition of its plans and provide a factual context for disputes. Litigation efficiencies to the plaintiff were

deemed insufficient to justify early review. *Ohio Forestry Ass'n, v. Sierra Club*, 523 U.S. 726 (1998).

(3) Criminal statutes are often ripe for judicial review even in advance of prosecution for violation. In *Ex parte Young*, 209 U.S. 123, 165 (1908), the Court permitted an injunction suit to be brought against enforcement of a state statute containing criminal penalties, prior to its application: "To await proceedings against the company in a state court, grounded upon a disobedience of the act, and then, if necessary, obtain a review in this court by writ of error to the highest state court, would place the company in peril of large loss and its agents in great risk of fines and imprisonment if it should be finally determined that the act was valid. This risk the company ought not to be required to take."

(4) In *United Public Workers v. Mitchell*, 330 U.S. 75 (1947), where government employees challenged the Hatch Act for limiting in an unconstitutional manner their future political activities, the Court ruled that, except for one plaintiff who had already violated the statute's prohibition, there was no Article III "Case" or "Controversy." The other plaintiffs alleged only their desire to participate in specified political activities and had not as yet committed any acts in violation of the statute; therefore their suit was premature. With regard to those plaintiffs, the challenged statute was not ripe for review because, in advance of any violation, only a "hypothetical threat" to the rights of plaintiffs was presented: "No threat of interference . . . with rights of appellants appears beyond that implied by the existence of the law." But in *Civil Serv. Comm'n v. Letter Carriers*, 413 U.S. 548 (1973), the Court reached the merits of a challenge to the Hatch Act without even mentioning the ripeness issue where plaintiffs alleged they wanted to run for local office, write letters on political subjects to newspapers, participate in political party activity, and campaign for candidates. Which case reaches the better result on ripeness — *Mitchell* or *Letter Carriers*?

(5) *Desuetude and Ripeness.* In *Poe v. Ullman*, 367 U.S. 497, 507 (1961), a sharply divided Court ruled that "the mere existence of a state penal statute would constitute insufficient grounds to support a federal court's adjudication of its constitutionality in proceedings brought against the State's prosecuting officials if real threat of enforcement is wanting." The decision was rendered in an action brought for a declaratory judgment that a state statute prohibiting use of contraceptives and containing criminal penalties was unconstitutional. The highest state court upheld the statute on the merits. The Supreme Court affirmed without reaching the merits, ruling instead that the statute was not ripe for review. The Court noted that although the challenged law had been on the books for more than three quarters of a century and although contraceptives were commonly and notoriously sold in the state, only one prosecution (a "test case") had been initiated under its provisions. Accordingly the case was too hypothetical to adjudicate. By contrast, *Epperson v. Arkansas*, 393 U.S. 97 (1968), involved a declaratory judgment challenge to the constitutionality of an Arkansas law prohibiting the teaching of evolution. The statute at issue was similar to the one in the celebrated 1925 "Great Monkey Trial" in Tennessee, in which a young teacher, John T. Scopes, was prosecuted. There had been no similar prosecutions since the *Scopes* case, and there was no record of any prosecution under the Arkansas statute. Though the *Epperson* Court characterized the statute as "presently more of a curiosity than a vital fact of life," it decided the constitutional issues presented. That a criminal statute has slumbered on the books as though dead for 40 years does not mean it is not ripe for review. Which case takes the better approach to ripeness — *Poe v. Ullman* or *Epperson v. Arkansas*?

(6) *Moot Cases.* Mootness, like ripeness, involves a timing question. Whereas ripeness focuses on whether litigation should be deferred since premature, mootness asks whether events have essentially resolved a controversy that once existed.

Mootness asks whether the plaintiff, who may have had a case or controversy at the time the complaint was filed, still has a live one at the time a court reviews the case. Cases may become moot because the parties have settled their dispute or because events outside the parties control resolved the matter.

(7) In *DeFunis v. Odegaard*, 416 U.S. 312 (1974), petitioner challenged the admission criteria of a state university law school as invidiously discriminatory against him on account of his race. By the time the case was argued in the Supreme Court, petitioner was in the final quarter of his last law school year, and the university stated that it would not cancel his registration regardless of the outcome of the litigation. The case was deemed moot since petitioner would complete law school regardless of the Court's decision on the merits. The constitutional issue raised in *DeFunis* would not inevitably be moot by the time a case presenting it reached the Supreme Court. *See, e.g., Regents of University of California Regents v. Bakke*, 438 U.S. 265 (1978), *infra* § 10.01. What happens, however, when a case raising a constitutional issue must always be moot because of the time that elapses between filing of the original complaint and consideration of the case by the Supreme Court?

(8) In *Roe v. Wade*, 410 U.S. 113 (1973), *infra* § 7.04[1], an unwed pregnant woman challenged the constitutionality of a state abortion law. The case was challenged as moot because plaintiff, though pregnant when the complaint was filed in 1970, was no longer so when the Supreme Court decided the case almost three years later. The argument was rejected. Pregnancy comes to term before the usual appellate process is complete. If that makes a case moot, Supreme Court review will be effectively denied in pregnancy litigation. Pregnancy thus provides a classic justification for a conclusion of nonmootness. It is plainly capable of repetition; but a rigid concept of mootness would mean it could always evade review. The Court may exercise jurisdiction in a case otherwise moot as to the plaintiff concerned, if the underlying dispute between the parties is "capable of repetition, yet evading review . . . since otherwise there may well never be a definitive resolution of the constitutional claim on the merits by this Court." *Kremens v. Bartley*, 431 U.S. 119, 133 (1977). This doctrine applies generally only when the challenged action is too short to allow full litigation and a reasonable expectation exists of a recurrence involving the same plaintiff, a requirement subject to some relaxation in the contest of class actions.

(9) *Voluntary Cessation.* A defendant's voluntary cessation of a practice does not render a pending case moot unless "subsequent events make it absolutely clear that the allegedly wrongful behavior could not reasonably be expected to recur." The party asserting mootness bears a "heavy burden" of persuasion. *See Friends of the Earth, Inc. v. Laidlaw Environmental Services (TOC), Inc.*, 528 U.S. 167 (2000).

(10) In *City of Erie v. Pap's A.M., TDBA "Kandyland,"* 529 U.S. 277 (2000), Pap's A.M. (Pap's), the owner of "Kandyland," a nude dancing establishment, challenged in state court as unconstitutional Erie's anti-nudity ordinance and ultimately prevailed in Pennsylvania's state courts. The City of Erie petitioned for certiorari to the U.S. Supreme Court challenging the Pennsylvania court's interpretation of the Constitution. Before the certiorari petition was filed, Pap's sold the "Kandyland" property and ceased its nude dancing operations. The Court granted certiorari, at which point, Pap's filed a motion to dismiss the case as moot.

The Court held the cessation of Pap's nude dancing activities did not moot the case since Pap's was still incorporated in Pennsylvania and could resume operations after the decision. Pap's did not raise its mootness defense in opposing the petition for certiorari despite having already ceased nude dancing operations. The Court also recognized that dismissal of the appeal would leave the state judgment as law. Based on Pap's voluntary termination of its nude dancing activities, Justice Scalia thought the case should have been declared moot, because, "there is 'no reasonable *expectation*,' only a theoretical possibility, that Pap's will resume nude dancing operations in the future." The majority thought the "reasonable expectation" standard met. Had the Court dismissed the case as moot the state court decision invalidating the anti-nudity statute, which Pap's obtained before going out of business, would have stood. As with *Doremus v. Board of Education, supra* § 1.07, Note (11), the workings of the justiciability doctrines would insulate a state court constitutional interpretation from review. How big a problem does this pose? Justice Scalia compared it to the Court's decision to deny certiorari in such a case. Is that really an apt comparison? When the Court denies certiorari, it has at least made a determination that the constitutional issues at stake are not sufficiently pressing or developed for its review. Failure to reach a case on grounds of mootness involves no necessary judgment regarding the magnitude of the substantive constitutional issues at stake. Should the Court's mootness determination vary depending on whether the party obtaining the state court decision produced the facts that supported the mootness argument?

In *City News and Novelty, Inc. v. City of Waukesha*, 531 U.S. 278 (2001), the Court indicated that this factor is significant. Waukesha's decision not to renew City News' license was upheld in state court proceedings against First Amendment challenge. City News petitioned for certiorari but then ceased operation. The Court thereupon granted Waukesha's motion to dismiss the case as moot. The Court was not persuaded by City News' suggestion that it might resume operation, a fact the Court had cited a year earlier in *Pap's* in holding that case still ripe. That "speculation" alone was insufficient the Court now explained. The more prominent fact in *Pap's*, the Court said, was that the prevailing party there had sought to insulate its state court judgment from federal constitutional review by raising the mootness argument. Here, however, City News, the party opposing mootness, "left the fray as a loser, not a winner." Whereas Erie would have been saddled with an adverse state court judgment against its ordinance, Waukesha would incur no such burden. *City News*, 531 U.S. at 284.

The Court also suggested that the "good faith" of the moving party might be relevant. In *Pap's*, Kandyland "arguably would have prevailed in an 'attemp[t] to manipulate the Court's jurisdiction to insulate a favorable decision from review.'" *City News*, 531 U.S. at 284 (quoting *Pap's*). Here a mootness dismissal would not "reward an arguable manipulation of our jurisdiction." *Id.* Should "good faith" be relevant? Does that standard commit the courts to a fact intensive approach? What advantages or disadvantages does a fact intensive approach carry? Does the Court in *Pap's* and *City News* judge the good or bad faith simply from the consequences of the parties' cessation and mootness argument?

The "reasonable expectation" standard itself is fact sensitive. Should mootness decisions allow the Court some flexibility to reach pressing constitutional issues but allow it to dodge others?

(11) Is the mootness doctrine based upon Article III, or is it a prudential doctrine? *See* Chief Justice Rehnquist, concurring, in *Honig v. Doe*, 484 U.S. 305, 330-31 (1988):

> The Court implies in its opinion, and the dissent expressly states, that the mootness doctrine is based upon Art. III of the Constitution. There is no doubt that our recent cases have taken that position. . . . But it seems very doubtful that the earliest case I have found discussing mootness, *Mills v. Green*, 159 U.S. 651 (1895), was premised on constitutional constraints; Justice Gray's opinion in that case nowhere mentions Art. III.

> If it were indeed Art. III which — by reason of its requirement of a case or controversy for the exercise of federal judicial power — underlies the mootness doctrine, the "capable of repetition, yet evading review" exception relied upon

by the court in this case would be incomprehensible. Article III extends the judicial power of the United States only to cases and controversies; it does not except from this requirement other lawsuits which are "capable of repetition, yet evading review." If our mootness doctrine were forced upon us by the case or controversy requirement of Art. III itself, we would have no more power to decide lawsuits which are "moot" but which also raise questions which are capable of repetition but evading review than we would to decide cases which are "moot" but raise no such questions. . . . The logical conclusion to be drawn from these cases, and from the historical development of the principle of mootness, is that while an unwillingness to decide moot cases may be connected to the case or controversy requirement of Art. III, it is an attenuated connection that may be overridden where there are strong reasons to override it. The "capable of repetition, yet evading review" exception is an example.

Compare Justice Scalia's dissent, *Id.* at 339:

The Chief Justice joins the majority opinion on the ground not that this case is not moot, but that where the events giving rise to the mootness have occurred after we have granted certiorari we may disregard them, since mootness is only a prudential doctrine and not part of the "case or controversy" requirement of Art. III. I do not see how that can be. There is no more reason to intuit that mootness is merely a prudential doctrine than to intuit that initial standing is. Both doctrines have equivalently deep roots in the common-law understanding, and hence the constitutional understanding, of what makes a matter appropriate for judicial disposition. . . .

In sum, I cannot believe that it is only our prudence, and nothing inherent in the understood nature of "The judicial Power," U.S. Const., Art. III, § 1, that restrains us from pronouncing judgment in a case that the parties have settled, or a case involving a nonsurviving claim where the plaintiff has died, or a case where the law has been changed so that the basis of the dispute no longer exists, or a case where conduct sought to be enjoined has ceased and will not recur. . . ."

§ 1.09 POLITICAL QUESTIONS

GOLDWATER v. CARTER
444 U.S. 996, 100 S. Ct. 533, 62 L. Ed. 2d 428 (1979)

The petition for a writ of certiorari is granted. The judgment of the Court of Appeals is vacated and the case is remanded to the District Court with directions to dismiss the complaint.

MR. JUSTICE MARSHALL concurs in the result.

MR. JUSTICE POWELL, concurring in the judgment.

Although I agree with the result reached by the Court, I would dismiss the complaint as not ripe for judicial review.

This Court has recognized that an issue should not be decided if it is not ripe for judicial review. . . . Prudential considerations persuade me that a dispute between Congress and the President is not ready for judicial review unless and until each branch has taken action asserting its constitutional authority. Differences between the President and the Congress are commonplace under our system. The differences should, and almost invariably do, turn on political rather than legal considerations. The Judicial Branch should not decide issues affecting the allocation of power between the President and Congress until the political branches reach a constitutional impasse.

Otherwise, we would encourage small groups or even individual Members of Congress to seek judicial resolution of issues before the normal political process has the opportunity to resolve the conflict.

In this case, a few Members of Congress claim that the President's action in terminating the treaty with Taiwan has deprived them of their constitutional role with respect to a change in the supreme law of the land. Congress has taken no official action.

In the present posture of this case, we do not know whether there ever will be an actual confrontation between the Legislative and Executive Branches. Although the Senate has considered a resolution declaring that Senate approval is necessary for the termination of any mutual defense treaty . . . , no final vote has been taken on the resolution. . . . It cannot be said that either the Senate or the House has rejected the President's claim. If the Congress chooses not to confront the President, it is not our task to do so. I therefore concur in the dismissal of this case.

II

Mr. Justice Rehnquist suggests, however, that the issue presented by this case is a nonjusticiable political question which can never be considered by this Court. I cannot agree. In my view, reliance upon the political-question doctrine is inconsistent with our precedents. As set forth in the seminal case of *Baker v. Carr*, 369 U.S. 186, 217 (1962), the doctrine incorporates three inquiries: (i) Does the issue involve resolution of questions committed by the text of the Constitution to a coordinate branch of government? (ii) Would resolution of the question demand that a court move beyond areas of judicial expertise? (iii) Do prudential considerations counsel against judicial intervention? In my opinion the answer to each of these inquiries would require us to decide this case if it were ready for review.

First, the existence of "a textually demonstrable constitutional commitment of the issue to a coordinate political branch," *id.*, turns on an examination of the constitutional provisions governing the exercise of the power in question. . . . No constitutional provision explicitly confers upon the President the power to terminate treaties. Further, Art. II, § 2, of the Constitution authorizes the President to make treaties with the advice and consent of the Senate. Article VI provides that treaties shall be a part of the supreme law of the land. These provisions add support to the view that the text of the Constitution does not unquestionably commit the power to terminate treaties to the President alone. . . .

Second, there is no "lack of judicially discoverable and manageable standards for resolving" this case; nor is a decision impossible "without an initial policy determination of a kind clearly for nonjudicial discretion." *Baker v. Carr,* 369 U.S., at 217. We are asked to decide whether the President may terminate a treaty under the Constitution without congressional approval. Resolution of the question may not be easy, but it only requires us to apply normal principles of interpretation to the constitutional provisions at issue. . . . The present case involves neither review of the President's activities as Commander in Chief nor impermissible interference in the field of foreign affairs. Such a case would arise if we were asked to decide, for example, whether a treaty required the President to order troops into a foreign country. But "it is error to suppose that every case or controversy which touches foreign relations lies beyond judicial cognizance." *Baker v. Carr, supra.* This case "touches" foreign relations, but the question presented to us concerns only the constitutional division of power between Congress and the President.

A simple hypothetical demonstrates the confusion that I find inherent in Mr. Justice Rehnquist's opinion concurring in the judgment. Assume that the President signed a mutual defense treaty with a foreign country and announced that it would go into effect despite its rejection by the Senate. Under Justice Rehnquist's analysis that situation would present a political question even though Art. II, § 2, clearly would resolve the dispute. Although the answer to the hypothetical case seems self-evident because it demands textual rather than interstitial analysis, the nature of the legal issue presented is no different from the issue presented in the case before us. In both cases, the Court would interpret the Constitution to decide whether congressional approval is necessary to give a Presidential decision on the validity of a treaty the force of law. Such an inquiry demands no special competence or information beyond the reach of the Judiciary. . . .

Finally, the political-question doctrine rests in part on prudential concerns calling for mutual respect among the three branches of Government. Thus, the Judicial Branch should avoid "the potentiality of embarrassment [that would result] from multifarious pronouncements by various departments on one question." Similarly, the doctrine restrains judicial action where there is an "unusual need for unquestioning adherence to a political decision already made." *Baker v. Carr, supra.*

If this case were ripe for judicial review, see Part I *supra*, none of these prudential considerations would be present. Interpretation of the Constitution does not imply lack of respect for a coordinate branch. *Powell v. McCormack, supra.* If the President and the Congress had reached irreconcilable positions, final disposition of the question presented by this case would eliminate, rather than create, multiple constitutional interpretations. The specter of the Federal Government brought to a halt because of the mutual intransigence of the President and the Congress would require this Court to provide a resolution pursuant to our duty "to say what the law is." *United States v. Nixon*, quoting *Marbury v. Madison.*

III

In my view, the suggestion that this case presents a political question is incompatible with this Court's willingness on previous occasions to decide whether one branch of our government has impinged upon the power of another. *See Buckley v. Valeo*; *United States v. Nixon, supra*; *The Pocket Veto Case*, 279 U.S. 655, 676-678 (1929); *Myers v. United States*, 272 U.S. 52 (1926). Under the criteria enunciated in *Baker v. Carr*, we have the responsibility to decide whether both the Executive and Legislative Branches have constitutional roles to play in termination of a treaty. If the Congress, by appropriate formal action, had challenged the President's authority to terminate the treaty with Taiwan, the resulting uncertainty could have serious consequences for our country. In that situation, it would be the duty of this Court to resolve the issue.

Mr. Justice Rehnquist, with whom The Chief Justice, Mr. Justice Stewart, and Mr. Justice Stevens join, concurring in the judgment.

I am of the view that the basic question presented by the petitioners in this case is "political" and therefore nonjusticiable because it involves the authority of the President in the conduct of our country's foreign relations and the extent to which the Senate or the Congress is authorized to negate the action of the President. In *Coleman v. Miller*, 307 U.S. 433 (1939), a case in which members of the Kansas Legislature brought an action attacking a vote of the State Senate in favor of the ratification of the Child Labor Amendment. Mr. Chief Justice Hughes wrote in what is referred to as the "Opinion of the Court":

> We think that . . . the question of the efficacy of ratifications by state legislatures, in the light of previous rejection or attempted withdrawal, should be regarded as a political question pertaining to the political departments, with the ultimate authority in the Congress in the exercise of its control over the

promulgation of the adoption of the Amendment.

The precise question as now raised is whether, when the legislature of the State, as we have found, has actually ratified the proposed Amendment, the Court should restrain the State officers from certifying the ratification to the Secretary of State, because of an earlier rejection, and thus prevent the question from coming before the political departments. We find no basis in either Constitution or statute for such judicial action. Article V, speaking solely of ratification, contains no provision as to rejection. . . .

Thus, Mr. Chief Justice Hughes' opinion concluded that "Congress in controlling the promulgation of the adoption of a constitutional amendment has the final determination of the question whether by lapse of time its proposal of the amendment had lost its vitality prior to the required ratifications."

I believe it follows *a fortiori* from *Coleman* that the controversy in the instant case is a nonjusticiable political dispute that should be left for resolution by the Executive and Legislative Branches of the Government. Here, while the Constitution is express as to the manner in which the Senate shall participate in the ratification of a treaty, it is silent as to that body's participation in the abrogation of a treaty. In this respect the case is directly analogous to *Coleman*. . . . In light of the absence of any constitutional provision governing the termination of a Treaty, and the fact that different termination procedures may be appropriate for different treaties, the instant case in my view also "must surely be controlled by political standards."

I think that the justifications for concluding that the question here is political in nature are even more compelling than in *Coleman* because it involves foreign relations — specifically a treaty commitment to use military force in the defense of a foreign government if attacked. . . .

The present case differs in several important respects from *Youngstown Sheet & Tube Co. v. Sawyer*, 343 U.S. 579 (1952), cited by petitioners as authority both for reaching the merits of this dispute and for reversing the Court of Appeals. In *Youngstown*, private litigants brought a suit contesting the President's authority under his war powers to seize the Nation's steel industry, an action of profound and demonstrable domestic impact. Here, by contrast, we are asked to settle a dispute between coequal branches of our Government, each of which has resources available to protect and assert its interests, resources not available to private litigants outside the judicial forum. Moreover, . . . the effect of this action, as far as we can tell, is "entirely external to the United States, and [falls] within the category of foreign affairs." Finally, as already noted, the situation presented here is closely akin to that presented in Coleman, where the Constitution spoke only to the procedure for ratification of an amendment, not to its rejection. . . .

Mr. Justice BLACKMUN, with whom Mr. Justice WHITE joins, dissenting in part.

In my view, the time factor and its importance are illusory; if the President does not have the power to terminate the treaty (a substantial issue that we should address only after briefing and oral argument), the notice of intention to terminate surely has no legal effect. It is also indefensible, without further study, to pass on the issue of justiciability or on the issues of standing or ripeness. While I therefore join in the grant of the petition for certiorari, I would set the case for oral argument and give it the plenary consideration it so obviously deserves.

Mr. Justice BRENNAN, dissenting.

In stating that this case presents a nonjusticiable "political question," Mr. Justice Rehnquist, profoundly misapprehends the political-question principle as it applies to matters of foreign relations. Properly understood, the political question doctrine restrains courts from reviewing an exercise of foreign policy judgment by the coordinate political branch to which authority to make that judgment has been "constitutional[ly] commit[ted]." *Baker v. Carr*, 369 U.S. 186, 211-213, 217 (1962). But the doctrine does not pertain when a court is faced with the antecedent question whether a particular branch has been constitutionally designated as the repository of political decisionmaking power. . . . The issue of decisionmaking authority must be resolved as a matter of constitutional law, not political discretion; accordingly, it falls within the competence of the courts.

The constitutional question raised here is prudently answered in narrow terms. Abrogation of the defense treaty with Taiwan was a necessary incident to Executive recognition of the Peking Government, because the defense treaty was predicated upon the now-abandoned view that the Taiwan Government was the only legitimate political authority in China. Our cases firmly establish that the Constitution commits to the President alone the power to recognize, and withdraw recognition from, foreign regimes. . . . That mandate being clear, our judicial inquiry into the treaty rupture can go no further. . . .

NOTES

(1) Like so much of American constitutional law, the political question doctrine was first suggested by John Marshall. In *Marbury v. Madison*, he drew a distinction between cases in which the President and those acting as his agents exercise purely political powers and those in which they exercise duties the law assigned upon which the rights of individuals depend. In the latter case the officer concerned is amenable to the laws for his conduct. Where "the President is invested with certain important political powers, in the exercise of which he is to use his own discretion, [he] is accountable only to his country in his political character and to his own conscience." But though Chief Justice Marshall stated that political questions were not within judicial competence, he did not indicate what made a question political within the meaning of the rule. According to *Elrod v. Burns*, 427 U.S. 347, 351 (1976), "A question presented to this Court for decision is properly deemed political when its resolution is committed by the Constitution to a branch of the Federal Government other than this Court."

(2) The leading case on political questions relating to internal affairs is *Baker v. Carr*, 369 U.S. 186 (1962). Before *Baker v. Carr*, the validity of legislative apportionment laws constituted a political question beyond judicial cognizance. In *Baker v. Carr*, Tennessee voters challenged a state 1901 statute apportioning the seats in the state legislature as contrary to the Equal Protection Clause. In the years since that law was enacted, there had been no new apportionment, though the population of the state had completely altered. A vote from the most populous county had only a fraction of the weight of one from the least populous county. The population ratio for the most and least populous districts was more than nineteen to one. The lower court had dismissed the complaint, relying upon the political question doctrine. The Supreme Court reversed, holding that a justiciable controversy was presented.

Baker v. Carr signaled that cases involving apportionments of voting power can no longer be considered as political questions beyond the competence of the courts. "Of course," in the language of *Baker v. Carr*, "the mere fact that the suit seeks protection of a political right does not mean it presents a political question. Such an objection 'is little more than a play upon words.' "

In *Baker v. Carr*, Justice Brennan summarized the political question doctrine as follows:

> Prominent on the surface of any case held to involve a political question is found a textually demonstrable constitutional commitment of the issue to a

coordinate political department; or a lack of judicially discoverable and manageable standards for resolving it; or the impossibility of deciding without an initial policy determination of a kind clearly for nonjudicial discretion; or the impossibility of a court's undertaking independent resolution without expressing lack of the respect due coordinate branches of government; or an unusual need for unquestioning adherence to a political decision already made; or the potentiality of embarrassment from multifarious pronouncements by various departments on one question.

Does the doctrine seek to assure fidelity to the constitutional text, to limit the judiciary to areas most susceptible to judicial decision, or to protect the judiciary from getting into hot water? Or do different strands reflect different objectives? Justice Scalia has more recently argued that the six *Baker v. Carr* tests "are probably listed in descending order of both importance and certainty." *Vieth v. Jubelirer*, 541 U.S. 267, 278 (2004) (plurality opinion).

(3) When courts invoke the political question doctrine do they violate their responsibility under *Marbury* to interpret the constitution to state what the law is? Or can they sometimes defend their action by claiming rather to be interpreting the Constitution to assign the case to another branch of the federal government?

Professor Alexander M. Bickel described the political question doctrine as "the Court's sense of lack of capacity, compounded in unequal parts of (a) the strangeness of the issue and its intractibility to principled resolution; (b) the sheer momentousness of it, which tends to unbalance judicial judgment; (c) the anxiety, not so much that the judicial judgment will be ignored, as that perhaps it should but will not be; (d) finally ("in a mature democracy"), the inner vulnerability, the self-doubt of an institution which is electorally irresponsible and has no earth to draw strength from." *See* ALEXANDER M. BICKEL, THE LEAST DANGEROUS BRANCH 184 (1962).

(4) The political question doctrine has its broadest scope regarding foreign affairs. Perhaps the strongest statement of the doctrine of judicial abstention in the field of foreign affairs was made in the *Chicago & Southern Airlines* case, 333 U.S. 103, 111 (1948):

> The President, both as Commander-in-Chief and as the Nation's organ for foreign affairs, has available intelligence services whose reports neither are nor ought to be published to the world. It would be intolerable that courts, without the relevant information, should review and perhaps nullify actions of the Executive taken on information properly held secret. Nor can courts sit in camera in order to be taken into executive confidences. But even if courts could require full disclosure, the very nature of executive decisions as to foreign policy is political, not judicial. Such decisions are wholly confided by our Constitution to the political departments of the government, Executive and Legislative. They are delicate, complex and involve large elements of prophecy. They are and should be undertaken only by those directly responsible to the people whose welfare they advance or imperil. They are decisions of a kind for which the Judiciary has neither aptitude, facilities nor responsibility and have long been held to belong in the domain of political power not subject to judicial intrusion or inquiry.

(5) Do the same considerations apply to questions involving employment of the armed forces abroad? The Vietnam conflict, in particular, gave rise to a number of constitutional challenges. The Supreme Court denied review in each case, presumably on the ground that use of the armed forces in Vietnam, even without any declaration of war, presented only a political question beyond judicial competence. *See, e.g., Mora v.*

McNamara, 389 U.S. 934 (1967); *Massachusetts v. Laird*, 400 U.S. 886 (1970); *DaCosta v. Laird*, 405 U.S. 979 (1972).

NIXON v. UNITED STATES
506 U.S. 224, 113 S. Ct. 732, 122 L. Ed. 2d 1 (1993)

CHIEF JUSTICE REHNQUIST delivered the opinion of the Court.

Petitioner Walter L. Nixon, Jr., asks this court to decide whether Senate Rule XI, which allows a committee of Senators to hear evidence against an individual who has been impeached and to report that evidence to the full Senate, violates the Impeachment Trial Clause, Art. I, § 3, cl. 6. That Clause provides that the "Senate shall have the sole Power to try all Impeachments." But before we reach the merits of such a claim, we must decide whether it is "justiciable," that is, whether it is a claim that may be resolved by the courts. We conclude that it is not.

Nixon, a former Chief Judge of the United States District Court for the Southern District of Mississippi, was convicted by a jury of two counts of making false statements before a federal grand jury and sentenced to prison. . . . The grand jury investigation stemmed from reports that Nixon had accepted a gratuity from a Mississippi businessman in exchange for asking a local district attorney to halt the prosecution of the businessman's son. . . .

On May 10, 1989, the House of Representatives adopted three articles of impeachment for high crimes and misdemeanors. The first two articles charged Nixon with giving false testimony before the grand jury and the third article charged him with bringing disrepute on the Federal Judiciary.

After the House presented the articles to the Senate, the Senate voted to invoke its own Impeachment Rule XI, under which the presiding officer appoints a committee of Senators to "receive evidence and take testimony." . . . The Senate committee held four days of hearings, during which 10 witnesses, including Nixon, testified. . . . Pursuant to Rule XI, the committee presented the full Senate with a complete transcript of the proceeding and a report stating the uncontested facts and summarizing the evidence on the contested facts. Nixon and the House impeachment managers submitted extensive final briefs to the full Senate and delivered arguments from the Senate floor during the three hours set aside for oral argument in front of that body. Nixon himself gave a personal appeal, and several Senators posed questions directly to both parties. The Senate voted by more than the constitutionally required two-thirds majority to convict Nixon on the first two articles. The presiding officer then entered judgment removing Nixon from his office as United States District Judge.

Nixon thereafter commenced the present suit, arguing that Senate Rule XI violates the constitutional grant of authority to the Senate to "try" all impeachments because it prohibits the whole Senate from taking part in the evidentiary hearings. See Art. I, § 3, cl. 6. Nixon sought a declaratory judgment that his impeachment conviction was void and that his judicial salary and privileges should be reinstated. The District Court held that his claim was nonjusticiable, and the Court of Appeals for the District of Columbia Circuit agreed. . . .

A controversy is nonjusticiable — i.e., involves a political question — where there is "a textually demonstrable constitutional commitment of the issue to a coordinate political department; or a lack of judicially discoverable and manageable standards for resolving it. . . ." *Baker v. Carr*, 369 U.S. 186, 217 (1962). But the courts must, in the first instance, interpret the text in question and determine whether and to what extent the issue is textually committed. . . . As the discussion that follows makes clear, the concept of a textual commitment to a coordinate political department is not completely separate from the concept of a lack of judicially discoverable and manageable standards for resolving it; the lack of judicially manageable standards may strengthen the conclusion that there is a textually demonstrable commitment to a coordinate branch.

In this case, we must examine Art. I, § 3, cl. 6, to determine the scope of authority conferred upon the Senate by the Framers regarding impeachment. It provides:

> The Senate shall have the sole Power to try all Impeachments. When sitting for that Purpose, they shall be on Oath or Affirmation. When the President of the United States is tried, the Chief Justice shall preside: And no Person shall be convicted without the Concurrence of two thirds of the Members present.

The first sentence is a grant of authority to the Senate, and the word "sole" indicates that this authority is reposed in the Senate and nowhere else. . . .

Petitioner argues that the word "try" in the first sentence imposes by implication an additional requirement on the Senate in that the proceedings must be in the nature of a judicial trial. From there petitioner goes on to argue that this limitation precludes the Senate from delegating to a select committee the task of hearing the testimony of witnesses. . . . Petitioner concludes from this that courts may review whether or not the Senate "tried" him before convicting him.

There are several difficulties with this position which lead us ultimately to reject it. The word "try" . . . has considerably broader meanings than those to which petitioner would limit it. . . . For example, try can mean "to examine or investigate judicially," "to conduct the trial of," or "to put to the test by experiment, investigation, or trial." Webster's Third New International Dictionary 2457 (1971). . . . Based on the variety of definitions, however, we cannot say that the Framers used the word "try" as an implied limitation on the method by which the Senate might proceed in trying impeachments. . . .

The conclusion that the use of the word "try" in the first sentence of the Impeachment Trial Clause lacks sufficient precision to afford any judicially manageable standard of review of the Senate's actions is fortified by the existence of the three very specific requirements that the Constitution does impose on the Senate when trying impeachments: The Members must be under oath, a two-thirds vote is required to convict, and the Chief Justice presides when the President is tried. These limitations are quite precise, and their nature suggests that the Framers did not intend to impose additional limitations on the form of the Senate proceedings by the use of the word "try" in the first sentence.

As noted above, [clause 6] provides that "[t]he Senate shall have the sole Power to try all Impeachments." We think that the word "sole" is of considerable significance. Indeed, the word "sole" appears only one other time in the Constitution — with respect to the House of Representatives' "sole Power of Impeachment." Art. I, § 2, cl. 5 (emphasis added). The commonsense meaning of the word "sole" is that the Senate alone shall have authority to determine whether an individual should be acquitted or convicted. The dictionary definition bears this out. "Sole" is defined as "having no companion," "solitary," "being the only one," and "functioning . . . independently and without assistance or interference." Webster's Third New International Dictionary 2168 (1971). If the courts may review the actions of the Senate in order to determine whether that body "tried" an impeached official, it is difficult to see how the Senate would be "functioning . . . independently and without assistance or interference." . . .

Petitioner finally argues that even if significance be attributed to the word "sole" in the first sentence of the clause, the authority granted is to the Senate, and this means that "the Senate — not the courts, not a lay jury, not a Senate Committee — shall try impeachments." It would be possible to read the first sentence of the Clause this way, but it is not a natural reading. Petitioner's interpretation would bring into judicial purview not merely the sort of claim made by petitioner, but other similar claims based on the conclusion that the word "Senate" has imposed by implication limitations on procedures which the Senate might adopt. Such limitations would be inconsistent with the construction of the Clause as a whole, which, as we have noted, sets out three express limitations in separate sentences.

The history and contemporary understanding of the impeachment provisions support our reading of the constitutional language. The parties do not offer evidence of a single word in the history of the Constitutional Convention or in contemporary commentary that even alludes to the possibility of judicial review in the context of the impeachment powers.

. . . This silence is quite meaningful in light of the several explicit references to the availability of judicial review as a check on the Legislature's power with respect to bills of attainder, ex post facto laws, and statutes. . . .

There are two additional reasons why the Judiciary, and the Supreme Court in particular, were not chosen to have any role in impeachments. First, the Framers recognized that most likely there would be two sets of proceedings for individuals who commit impeachable offenses — the impeachment trial and a separate criminal trial. . . . The Framers deliberately separated the two forums to avoid raising the specter of bias and to ensure independent judgments. . . .

Second, judicial review would be inconsistent with the Framers' insistence that our system be one of checks and balances. In our constitutional system, impeachment was designed to be the only check on the Judicial Branch by the Legislature. . . . Judicial involvement in impeachment proceedings, even if only for purposes of judicial review, is counterintuitive because it would eviscerate the "important constitutional check" placed on the Judiciary by the Framers. Nixon's argument would place final reviewing authority with respect to impeachments in the hands of the same body that the impeachment process is meant to regulate.

Nevertheless, Nixon argues that judicial review is necessary in order to place a check on the Legislature. Nixon fears that if the Senate is given unreviewable authority to interpret the Impeachment Trial Clause, there is a grave risk that the Senate will usurp judicial power. The Framers anticipated this objection and created two constitutional safeguards to keep the Senate in check. The first safeguard is that the whole of the impeachment power is divided between the two legislative bodies, with the House given the right to accuse and the Senate given the right to judge. . . . The second safeguard is the two-thirds supermajority vote requirement. Hamilton explained that "[a]s the concurrence of two-thirds of the senate will be requisite to a condemnation, the security to innocence, from this additional circumstance, will be as complete as itself can desire."

In addition to the textual commitment argument, we are persuaded that the lack of finality and the difficulty of fashioning relief counsel against justiciability. . . . We agree with the Court of Appeals that opening the door of judicial review to the procedures used by the Senate in trying impeachments would "expose the political life of the country to months, or perhaps years, of chaos." This lack of finality would manifest itself most dramatically if the President were impeached. The legitimacy of any successor, and hence his effectiveness, would be impaired severely, not merely while the judicial process was running its course, but during any retrial that a differently constituted Senate might conduct if its first judgment of conviction were invalidated. Equally uncertain is the question of what relief a court may give other than simply setting aside the judgment of conviction. Could it order the reinstatement of a convicted federal judge, or order Congress to create an additional judgeship if the seat had been filled in the interim?

Petitioner finally contends that a holding of nonjusticiability cannot be reconciled with our opinion in *Powell v. McCormack*, 395 U.S. 486. The relevant issue in Powell was whether courts could review the House of Representatives' conclusion that Powell was "unqualified" to sit as a Member because he had been accused of misappropriating public funds and abusing the process of the New York courts. We stated that the question of justiciability turned on whether the Constitution committed authority to the House to judge its Members' qualifications, and if so, the extent of that commitment. . . . Art. I, § 2 specifies three requirements for membership in the House: The candidate must be at least 25 years of age, a citizen of the United States for no less than seven years, and an inhabitant of the State he is chosen to represent. . . .

Our conclusion in *Powell* was based on the fixed meaning of "[q]ualifications]" set forth in Art. I, § 2. The claim by the House that its power to "be the Judge of the Elections, Returns and Qualifications of its own Members" was a textual commitment of unreviewable authority was defeated by the existence of this separate provision specifying the only qualifications which might be imposed for House membership. The decision as to whether a Member satisfied these qualifications was placed with the House, but the decision as to what these qualifications consisted of was not.

In the case before us, there is no separate provision of the Constitution which could be defeated by allowing the Senate final authority to determine the meaning of the word "try" in the Impeachment Trial Clause. We agree with Nixon that courts possess power to review either legislative or executive action that transgresses identifiable textual limits. . . . But we conclude, after exercising that delicate responsibility, that the word "try" in the Impeachment Clause does not provide an identifiable textual limit on the authority which is committed to the Senate.

For the foregoing reasons, the judgment of the Court of Appeals is

Affirmed.

NOTES

(1) Compare Justice Souter, concurring in the judgment:

I agree with the Court that this case presents a nonjusticiable political question. . . .

One can, nevertheless, envision different and unusual circumstances that might justify a more searching review of impeachment proceedings. If the Senate were to act in a manner seriously threatening the integrity of its results, convicting, say, upon a coin-toss, or upon a summary determination that an officer of the United States was simply "a bad guy," judicial interference might well be appropriate. In such circumstances, the Senate's action might be so far beyond the scope of its constitutional authority, and the consequent impact on the Republic so great, as to merit a judicial response despite the prudential concerns that would ordinarily counsel silence. . . ."

Would the Court refuse to intervene in the extreme hypotheticals posited by Justice Souter?

Nixon v. United States reveals that the political question doctrine is not confined to cases involving foreign affairs and use of the armed forces abroad. Other examples exist.

(2) *Luther v. Borden*, 48 U.S. (7 How.) 1 (1849), arose out of the so-called Dorr Rebellion in Rhode Island in 1841. That state was still operating under the royal charter of 1663, which provided for a very limited suffrage and contained no procedure for amendments. An elected convention drafted a new constitution which provided for universal suffrage. Elections were held, and Dorr was elected the governor. These acts were unauthorized by the existing charter government, which declared martial law and

sent the militia to repel the threatened attack. In addition, the charter government appealed to the federal government for aid. President Tyler recognized the charter government and declared that he would use armed force if necessary. The announcement of the President's determination caused Dorr's Rebellion to fade. *Luther v. Borden*, decided several years later, was its constitutional legacy.

When a charter government agent broke into the house of, and arrested, a Dorr supporter, the latter brought a trespass action. Defendant justified his action under the authority of the legal state government. Plaintiff contended that the charter government was not republican in form, as required by the Constitution; thus that government had no valid legal existence and the acts of its agents were not justified in law. He claimed the action of the charter government violated his constitutional right to live under a republican government and that that claim was cognizable in a court.

The Supreme Court rejected the claim, concluding it lacked judicial competence to apply the constitutional guaranty. On the contrary, the enforcement of the guaranty is solely for Congress. Under Article IV, section 4, declared the opinion of Chief Justice Taney, "it rests with Congress to decide what government is the established one in a State . . . , as well as its republican character." Moreover, the Congressional decision in the matter is not subject to any judicial scrutiny: "its decision is binding on every other department of the government, and could not be questioned in a judicial tribunal."

(3) Should enforcement of the Guaranty Clause be beyond judicial competence? In *Luther v. Borden*, enforcement ultimately involved the presidential threat to use force. After such action by the President, asked Chief Justice Taney, "is a circuit court of the United States authorized to inquire whether his decision was right? Could the Court, while the parties were actually contending in arms for the possession of the government, call witnesses before it and inquire which party represented a majority of the people?"

Even if Chief Justice Taney was right in *Luther v. Borden*, does it justify judicial refusal to rule on whether the Article IV guaranty has been violated in other cases? In the century after *Luther v. Borden*, its "holding metamorphosed into the sweeping assertion that '[v]iolation of the great guaranty of a republican form of government in States cannot be challenged in the courts.'" *New York v. United States*, 505 U.S. 144, 184-85 (1992). "More recently, the Court has suggested that perhaps not all claims under the Guarantee Clause present nonjusticiable political questions."

(4) The Court has held other questions relating to internal affairs political questions. *See, e.g., O'Brien v. Brown*, 409 U.S. 1 (1972) (questions relating to the deliberative processes of a national political convention); *Coleman v. Miller*, 307 U.S. 433 (1939) (whether constitutional amendments validly adopted); *United States v. Ballin*, 144 U.S. 1 (1892) (questions concerning the organization and procedure of the legislature); *Field v. Clark*, 143 U.S. 649 (1892) (questions relating to whether statutes have been validly enacted).

(5) Determination of qualifications for legislative membership had been ruled within the sole authority of the legislature under the political question doctrine. In *Powell v. McCormack*, 395 U.S. 486 (1969), the House of Representatives refused to seat Adam Clayton Powell who had been elected to it. Powell met the age, citizenship, and residence requirements of Article I, section 2, but was not permitted to take his seat pursuant to a House resolution, after a select committee had found that he had committed certain improper acts. The Court interpreted Article I as leaving "the House without authority to exclude any person, duly elected by his constituents, who meets all the requirements for membership expressly prescribed in the Constitution."

The Court disposed of the political question contention as follows:

Respondents' alternate contention is that the case presents a political question because judicial resolution of petitioners' claim would produce a "potentially embarrassing confrontation between coordinate branches" of the Federal Government. But, as our interpretation of Art. I, § 5 discloses, a determination of petitioner Powell's right to sit would require no more than an interpretation of the Constitution. Such a determination falls within the traditional role accorded courts to interpret the law, and does not involve a "lack of the respect due [a] coordinate [branch] of government," nor does it involve an "initial policy determination of a kind clearly for nonjudicial discretion." *Baker v. Carr*. . . . Our system of government requires that federal courts on occasion interpret the Constitution in a manner at variance with the construction given the document by another branch. The alleged conflict that such an adjudication may cause cannot justify the courts' avoiding their constitutional responsibility. . . . Nor are any of the other formulations of a political question "inextricable from the case at bar." . . . Petitioners seek a determination . . . for which clearly there are "judicially manageable standards." Finally, a judicial resolution of petitioners' claim will not result in "multifarious pronouncements by various departments on one question." For, as we noted in *Baker v. Carr* . . . , it is the responsibility of this Court to act as the ultimate interpreter of the Constitution."

Id. at 548.

(6) In *Bush v. Gore*, 531 U.S. 98 (2000), the Court granted certiorari and held that the recount ordered by the Florida Supreme Court violated the Fourteenth Amendment.

The Twelfth Amendment provides, in pertinent part, that after the states transmit certified lists of electoral votes, "[t]he President of the Senate shall, in the presence of the Senate and House of Representatives, open all the certificates and the votes shall then be counted." Does the power to count electoral votes imply the power to determine whether pertinent electoral votes are properly cast? If so, does the text commit that power to Congress? If so, should the Court have considered the matter a political question constitutionally delegated to Congress?

The five justice majority thought the Court had the "unsought responsibility to resolve the federal and constitutional issues" presented. The dissenters disagreed. Justice Breyer wrote: "Of course, the selection of the President is of fundamental national importance. But that importance is political, not legal." *Bush*, 531 U.S. at 153.

The Constitution and federal statutes empower state courts and ultimately Congress to resolve presidential election disputes, Justice Breyer wrote. Federal courts were consigned to the sidelines by the Twelfth Amendment and the Electoral Count Act of 1887. Moreover, "in this highly politicized matter, the appearance of a split decision runs the risk of undermining the public confidence in the Court itself." *Id.* at 157.

Chapter II
CONGRESSIONAL POWERS

§ 2.01 ENUMERATED AND IMPLIED POWERS

McCULLOCH v. MARYLAND
17 U.S. (4 Wheat.) 316, 4 L. Ed. 579 (1819)

[Editors' Note: Congress chartered the Second Bank of the United States in 1816. It was authorized to print bank notes and to hold federal funds. The Bank established branches in many states. Maryland enacted a statute regulating banking activity in state, including notes that could be issued, and imposing taxes on banks. Violations of the regulations were punishable by fine. Maryland brought an action to recover the statutory penalty against James McCulloch, cashier of the Baltimore branch of the Bank of the United States. An agreed statement of facts admitted that the Bank did business in Baltimore without authority from the state and that McCulloch had issued banknotes without complying with the Maryland law. The highest state court affirmed a judgment for Maryland and the case was brought to the Supreme Court by writ of error. *See generally* MARK R. KILLENBECK, M'CULLOCH v. MARYLAND: SECURING A NATION (2006).]

MARSHALL, C.J. delivered the opinion of the court:

In the case now to be determined, the defendant, a sovereign state, denies the obligation of a law enacted by the legislature of the Union, and the plaintiff, on his part, contests the validity of an act which has been passed by the legislature of that state. The constitution of our country, in its most interesting and vital parts, is to be considered; the conflicting powers of the government of the Union and of its members, as marked in that constitution, are to be discussed; and an opinion given, which may essentially influence the great operations of the government. No tribunal can approach such a question without a deep sense of its importance, and of the awful responsibility involved in its decision. But it must be decided peacefully, or remain a source of hostile legislation, perhaps of hostility of a still more serious nature; and if it is to be so decided, by this tribunal alone can the decision be made. On the Supreme Court of the United States has the constitution of our country devolved this important duty.

The first question made in the cause is, has Congress power to incorporate a bank?

It has been truly said, that this can scarcely be considered as an open question, entirely unprejudiced by the former proceedings of the nation respecting it. The principle now contested was introduced at a very early period of our history, has been recognized by many successive legislatures, and has been acted upon by the judicial department, in cases of peculiar delicacy, as a law of undoubted obligation.

It will not be denied, that a bold and daring usurpation might be resisted, after an acquiescence still longer and more complete than this. But it is conceived, that a doubtful question, one on which human reason may pause, and the human judgment be suspended, in the decision of which the great principles of liberty are not concerned, but the respective powers of those who are equally the representatives of the people, are to be adjusted; if not put at rest by the practice of the government, ought to receive a considerable impression from that practice. An exposition of the constitution, deliberately established by legislative acts, on the faith of which an immense property has been advanced, ought not to be lightly disregarded.

The power now contested was exercised by the first congress elected under the present constitution. The bill for incorporating the Bank of the United States did not steal upon an unsuspecting legislature, and pass unobserved. Its principle was completely understood, and was opposed with equal zeal and ability. After being resisted, first, in the fair and open field of debate, and afterwards, in the executive cabinet, with as much persevering talent as any measure has ever experienced, and being supported by arguments which convinced minds as pure and as intelligent as this country can boast, it became a law. The original act was permitted to expire; but a short experience of the embarrassments to which the refusal to revive it exposed the government, convinced those who were most prejudiced against the measure of its necessity, and induced the passage of the present law. It would require no ordinary share of intrepidity, to assert that a measure adopted under these circumstances, was a bold and plain usurpation, to which the constitution gave no countenance. These observations belong to the cause; but they are not made under the impression, that, were the question entirely new, the law would be found irreconcilable with the constitution.

In discussing this question, the counsel for the state of Maryland have deemed it of some importance, in the construction of the constitution, to consider that instrument, not as emanating from the people, but as the act of sovereign and independent states. The powers of the general government, it has been said, are delegated by the states, who alone are truly sovereign; and must be exercised in subordination to the states, who alone possess supreme dominion.

It would be difficult to sustain this proposition. The convention which framed the constitution was indeed elected by the state legislatures. But the instrument, when it came from their hands, was a mere proposal, without obligation, or pretensions to it. It was reported to the then existing Congress of the United States, with a request that it might "be submitted to a convention of delegates, chosen in each state by the people thereof, under the recommendation of its legislature, for their assent and ratification." This mode of proceeding was adopted; and by the convention, by Congress, and by the state legislatures, the instrument was submitted to the people. They acted upon it in the only manner in which they can act safely, effectively, and wisely, on such a subject, by assembling in convention. It is true, they assembled in their several states and where else should they have assembled? No political dreamer was ever wild enough to think of breaking down the lines which separate the states, and of compounding the American people into one common mass. Of consequence, when they act, they act in their states. But the measures they adopt do not, on that account, cease to be the measures of the people themselves, or become the measures of the state governments.

From these conventions the constitution derives its whole authority. The government proceeds directly from the people; is 'ordained and established' in the name of the people; and is declared to be ordained, 'in order to form a more perfect union, establish justice, insure domestic tranquillity, and secure the blessings of liberty to themselves and to their posterity.' The assent of the states, in their sovereign capacity, is implied in calling a convention, and thus submitting that instrument to the people. But the people were at perfect liberty to accept or reject it; and their act was final. It required not the affirmance, and could not be negatived, by the state governments. The constitution, when thus adopted, was of complete obligation, and bound the state sovereignties.

It has been said, that the people had already surrendered all their powers to the state sovereignties, and had nothing more to give. But, surely, the question whether they may resume and modify the powers granted to government, does not remain to be settled in this country. Much more might the legitimacy of the general government be doubted, had it been created by the states. The powers delegated to the state sovereignties were to be exercised by themselves, not by a distinct and independent sovereignty, created by themselves. To the formation of a league, such as was the confederation, the state sovereignties were certainly competent. But when, "in order to form a more perfect union," it was deemed necessary to change this alliance into an effective government, possessing great and sovereign powers, and acting directly on the people, the necessity of referring it to the people, and of deriving its powers directly from them, was felt and acknowledged by all.

The government of the Union, then (whatever may be the influence of this fact on the case), is, emphatically, and truly, a government of the people. In form and in substance it emanates from them. Its powers are granted by them, and are to be exercised directly on them, and for their benefit.

This government is acknowledged by all to be one of enumerated powers. The principle, that it can exercise only the powers granted to it, would seem too apparent to have required to be enforced by all those arguments, which its enlightened friends, while it was depending before the people, found it necessary to urge; that principle is now universally admitted. But the question respecting the extent of the powers actually granted, is perpetually arising, and will probably continue to arise, as long as our system shall exist.

In discussing these questions, the conflicting powers of the general and state governments must be brought into view, and the supremacy of their respective laws, when they are in opposition, must be settled.

If any one proposition could command the universal assent of mankind, we might expect it would be this — that the government of the Union, though limited in its powers, is supreme within its sphere of action. This would seem to result, necessarily, from its nature. It is the government of all; its powers are delegated by all; it represents all, and acts for all. Though any one state may be willing to control its operations, no state is willing to allow others to control them. The nation, on those subjects on which it can act, must necessarily bind its component parts. But this question is not left to mere reason; the people have, in express terms, decided it by saying, "this constitution, and the laws of the United States, which shall be made in pursuance thereof," "shall be the supreme law of the land," and by requiring that the members of the state legislatures, and the officers of the executive and judicial departments of the states, shall take the oath of fidelity to it.

The government of the United States, then, though limited in its powers, is supreme; and its laws, when made in pursuance of the constitution, form the supreme law of the land, "anything in the constitution or laws of any state to the contrary notwithstanding."

Among the enumerated powers, we do not find that of establishing a bank or creating a corporation. But there is no phrase in the instrument which, like the articles of confederation, excludes incidental or implied powers; and which requires that everything granted shall be expressly and minutely described. Even the 10th amendment, which was framed for the purpose of quieting the excessive jealousies which had been excited, omits the word 'expressly,' and declares only, that the powers 'not delegated to the United States, nor prohibited to the states, are reserved to the states or to the people;' thus leaving the question, whether the particular power which may become the subject of contest, has been delegated to the one government, or prohibited to the other, to depend on a fair construction of the whole instrument. The men who drew and adopted this amendment had experienced the embarrassments resulting from the insertion of this word in the articles of confederation, and probably omitted it, to avoid those embarrassments. A constitution, to contain an accurate detail of all the subdivisions of which its great powers will admit, and of all the means by which they may be carried into execution, would partake of the prolixity of a legal code, and could scarcely be embraced by the human mind. It would, probably, never be understood by the public. Its nature, therefore, requires that only its great outlines should be marked, its important objects designated, and the minor ingredients which compose those objects, be deduced from the nature of the objects themselves. That this idea was entertained by the framers of the American constitution, is not only to be inferred from the nature of the instrument, but from the language. Why else were some of the limitations, found in the 9th section of the 1st article, introduced? It is also, in some degree, warranted, by their having omitted to use any restrictive term which might prevent its receiving a fair and just interpretation. In considering this question, then, we must never forget that it is a constitution we are expounding.

Although, among the enumerated powers of government, we do not find the word "bank" or "incorporation," we find the great powers to lay and collect taxes; to borrow money; to regulate commerce; to declare and conduct a war; and to raise and support armies and navies. The sword and the purse, all the external relations, and no inconsiderable portion of the industry of the nation, are entrusted to its government. It can never be pretended that these vast powers draw after them others of inferior importance, merely because they are inferior. Such an idea can never be advanced. But it may with great reason be contended, that a government, entrusted with such ample powers, on the due execution of which the happiness and prosperity of the nation so vitally depends, must also be entrusted with ample means for their execution. The power being given, it is the interest of the nation to facilitate its execution. It can never be their interest, and cannot be presumed to have been their intention, to clog and embarrass its execution by withholding the most appropriate means. Throughout this vast republic, from the St. Croix to the Gulf of Mexico, from the Atlantic to the Pacific, revenue is to be collected and expended, armies are to be marched and supported. The exigencies of the nation may require, that the treasure raised in the north should be transported to the south, that raised in the east, conveyed to the west, or that this order should be reversed. Is that construction of the constitution to be preferred, which would render these operations difficult, hazardous and expensive? Can we adopt that construction (unless the words imperiously require it), which would impute to the framers of that instrument, when granting these powers for the public good, the intention of impeding their exercise by withholding a choice of means? If, indeed, such be the mandate of the constitution, we have only to obey; but that instrument does not profess to enumerate the means by which the powers it confers may be executed; nor does it prohibit the creation of a corporation, if the existence of such a being be essential, to the beneficial exercise of those powers. It is, then, the subject of fair inquiry, how far such means may be employed.

It is not denied, that the powers given to the government imply the ordinary means of execution. That, for example, of raising revenue, and applying it to national purposes, is admitted to imply the power of conveying money from place to place, as the exigencies of the nation may require, and of employing the usual means of conveyance. But it is denied, that the government has its choice of means; or, that it may employ the most convenient means, if, to employ them, it be necessary to erect a corporation.

On what foundation does this argument rest? On this alone: the power of creating a corporation, is one appertaining to sovereignty, and is not expressly conferred on congress. This is true. But all legislative powers appertain to sovereignty. The original power of giving the law on any subject whatever, is a sovereign power; and if the government of the Union is restrained from creating a corporation, as a means for performing its functions, on the single reason that the creation of a corporation is an act of sovereignty; if the sufficiency of this reason be acknowledged, there would be some difficulty in sustaining the authority of congress to pass other laws for the accomplishment of the same objects. The government which has a right to do an act, and has imposed on it, the duty of performing that act, must, according to the dictates of reason, be allowed to select the means; and those who contend that it may not select any appropriate means, that one particular mode of effecting the object is excepted, take upon themselves the burden of establishing that exception. . . .

The power of creating a corporation, though appertaining to sovereignty, is not, like the power of making war, or levying taxes, or of regulating commerce, a great substantive and independent power, which cannot be implied as incidental to other powers, or used as a means of executing them. It is never the end for which other powers are exercised, but a means by which other objects are accomplished. . . . The power of creating a corporation is never used for its own sake, but for the purpose of effecting something else. No sufficient reason is, therefore, perceived, why it may not pass as incidental to those powers which are expressly given, if it be a direct mode of executing them.

But the constitution of the United States has not left the right of Congress to employ the necessary means, for the execution of the powers conferred on the government, to general reasoning. To its enumeration of powers is added, that of making "all laws which shall be necessary and proper, for carrying into execution the foregoing powers, and all other powers vested by this constitution, in the government of the United States, or in any department thereof." . . .

[T]he argument on which most reliance is placed, is drawn from that peculiar language of this clause. Congress is not empowered by it to make all laws, which may have relation to the powers conferred on the government, but such only as may be 'necessary and proper' for carrying them into execution. The word 'necessary' is considered as controlling the whole sentence, and as limiting the right to pass laws for the execution of the granted powers, to such as are indispensable, and without which the power would be nugatory. That it excludes the choice of means, and leaves to Congress, in each case, that only which is most direct and simple.

Is it true, that this is the sense in which the word "necessary" is always used? Does it always import an absolute physical necessity, so strong, that one thing to which another may be termed necessary, cannot exist without that other? We think it does not. If reference be had to its use, in the common affairs of the world, or in approved authors, we find that it frequently imports no more than that one thing is convenient, or useful, or essential to another. To employ the means necessary to an end, is generally understood as employing any means calculated to produce the end, and not as being confined to those single means, without which the end would be entirely unattainable. . . .

A thing may be necessary, very necessary, absolutely or indispensably necessary. To no mind would the same idea be conveyed by these several phrases. This comment on the word is well illustrated by the passage cited at the bar, from the 10th section of the 1st article of the constitution. It is, we think, impossible to compare the sentence which prohibits a state from laying "imposts or duties on imports or exports, except what may be absolutely necessary for executing its inspection laws," with that which authorizes Congress "to make all laws which shall be necessary and proper for carrying into execution" the powers of the general government, without feeling a conviction that the convention understood itself to change materially the meaning of the word "necessary," by prefixing the word "absolutely." This word, then, like others, is used in various senses; and, in its construction, the subject, the context, the intention of the person using them, are all to be taken into view.

Let this be done in the case under consideration. The subject is the execution of those great powers on which the welfare of a nation essentially depends. It must have been the intention of those who gave these powers, to insure, as far as human prudence could insure, their beneficial execution. This could not be done by confiding the choice of means to such narrow limits as not to leave it in the power of Congress to adopt any which might be appropriate, and which were conducive to the end. This provision is made in a constitution intended to endure for ages to come, and, consequently, to be adapted to the various crises of human affairs. To have prescribed the means by which government should, in all future time, execute its powers, would have been to change, entirely, the character of the instrument, and give it the properties of a legal code. It would have been an unwise attempt to provide, by immutable rules, for exigencies which, if foreseen at all, must have been seen dimly, and which can be best provided for as they occur. To have declared that the best means shall not be used, but those alone, without which the power given would be nugatory, would have been to deprive the legislature of the capacity to avail itself of experience, to exercise its reason, and to accommodate its legislation to circumstances. . . .

Take, for example, the power "to establish post-offices and post-roads." This power is executed, by the single act of making the establishment. But, from this has been inferred the power and duty of carrying the mail along the post-road, from one post-office to another. And from this implied power, has again been inferred the right to punish those who steal letters from the post-office, or rob the mail. It may be said, with some plausibility, that the right to carry the mail, and to punish those who rob it, is not indispensably necessary to the establishment of a post-office and post-road. This right is indeed essential to the beneficial exercise of the power, but not indispensably necessary to its existence. So, of the punishment of the crimes of stealing or falsifying a record or process of a court of the United States, or of perjury in such court. To punish these offences, is certainly conducive to the due administration of justice. But courts may exist, and may decide the causes brought before them, though such crimes escape punishment. . . .

If this limited construction of the word "necessary" must be abandoned, in order to punish, whence is derived the rule which would reinstate it, when the government would carry its powers into execution, by means not vindictive in their nature? If the word "necessary" means "needful," "requisite," "essential," "conducive to," in order to let in the power of punishment for the infraction of law; why is it not equally comprehensive, when required to authorize the use of means which facilitate the execution of the powers of government, without the infliction of punishment?

In ascertaining the sense in which the word "necessary" is used in this clause of the constitution, we may derive some aid from that with which it is associated. Congress shall have power "to make all laws which shall be necessary and proper to carry into execution" the powers of the government. If the word "necessary" was used in that strict and rigorous sense for which the counsel for the state of Maryland contend, it would be an extraordinary departure from the usual course of the human mind, as exhibited in composition, to add a word, the only possible effect of which is, to qualify that strict and rigorous meaning; to present to the mind the idea of some choice of means of legislation, not strained and compressed within the narrow limits for which gentlemen contend.

But the argument which most conclusively demonstrates the error of the construction contended for by the counsel for the state of Maryland, is founded on the intention of the convention, as manifested in the whole clause. To waste time and argument in proving that, without it, congress might carry its powers into execution, would be not much less idle, than to hold a lighted taper to the sun. As little can it be required to prove, that in the absence of this clause, congress would have some choice of means. That it might employ those which, in its judgment, would most advantageously effect the object to be accomplished. That any means adapted to the end, any means which tended directly to the execution of the constitutional powers of the government, were in themselves constitutional. This clause, as construed by the state of Maryland, would abridge, and almost annihilate, this useful and necessary right of the legislature to select its means. That this could not be intended, is, we should think, had it not been already controverted, too apparent for controversy.

We think so for the following reasons: 1st. The clause is placed among the powers of congress, not among the limitations on those powers. 2d. Its terms purport to enlarge, not to diminish the powers vested in the government. It purports to be an additional power, not a restriction on those already granted. No reason has been, or can be assigned, for thus concealing an intention to narrow the discretion of the national legislature, under words which purport to enlarge it. The framers of the constitution wished its adoption, and well knew that it would be endangered by its strength, not by its weakness. Had they been capable of using language which would convey to the eye one idea, and, after deep reflection, impress on the mind, another, they would rather have disguised the grant of power, than its limitation. If, then, their intention had been, by this clause, to restrain the free use of means which might otherwise have been implied, that intention would have been inserted in another place, and would have been expressed in terms resembling these. "In carrying into execution the foregoing powers, and all others," "no laws shall be passed but such as are necessary and proper." Had the intention been to make this clause restrictive, it would unquestionably have been so in form as well as in effect.

The result of the most careful and attentive consideration bestowed upon this clause is, that if it does not enlarge, it cannot be construed to restrain the powers of Congress, or to impair the right of the legislature to exercise its best judgment in the selection of measures to carry into execution the constitutional powers of the government. If no other motive for its insertion can be suggested, a sufficient one is found in the desire to remove all doubts respecting the right to legislate on that vast mass of incidental powers which must be involved in the constitution, if that instrument be not a splendid bauble.

We admit, as all must admit, that the powers of the government are limited, and that its limits are not to be transcended. But we think the sound construction of the constitution must allow to the national legislature that discretion, with respect to the means by which the powers it confers are to be carried into execution, which will enable that body to perform the high duties assigned to it, in the manner most beneficial to the people. Let the end be legitimate, let it be within the scope of the constitution, and all means which are appropriate which are plainly adapted to that end, which are not prohibited, but consist with the letter and spirit of the constitution, are constitutional. . . .

If a corporation may be employed indiscriminately with other means to carry into execution the powers of the government, no particular reason can be assigned for excluding the use of a bank, if required for its fiscal operation. To use one, must be within the discretion of Congress, if it be an appropriate mode of executing the powers of government. That it is a convenient, a useful, and essential instrument in the prosecution of its fiscal operations, is not now a subject of controversy. . . .

But were its necessity less apparent, none can deny its being an appropriate measure; and if it is, the decree of its necessity, as has been very justly observed, is to be discussed in another place. Should Congress, in the execution of its powers, adopt measures which are prohibited by the constitution; or should Congress, under the pretext of executing its powers, pass laws for the accomplishment of objects not intrusted to the government; it would become the painful duty of this tribunal, should a case requiring such a decision come before it, to say, that such an act was not the law of the land. But where the law is not prohibited, and is really calculated to effect any of the objects intrusted to the government, to undertake here to inquire into the decree of its necessity, would be to pass the line which circumscribes the judicial department, and to tread on legislative ground. This court disclaims all pretensions to such a power. . . .

After the most deliberate consideration, it is the unanimous and decided opinion of this court that the act to incorporate the Bank of the United States is a law made in pursuance of the constitution, and is a part of the supreme law of the land. . . .

[For additional portions of Marshall's opinion, see *infra* § 4.01.]

NOTES

(1) On behalf of *McCulloch*, Daniel Webster had argued that past practice of the Executive and Congress in recognizing the Bank made it presumptively constitutional.

> The executive government has acted upon it; and the courts of law have acted upon it. Many of those who doubted or denied the existence of the power, when first attempted to be exercised, have yielded to the first decision, and acquiesced in it, as a settled question. When all branches of the government have thus been acting on the existence of this power nearly thirty years, it would seem almost too late to call it in question, unless its repugnancy with the constitution were plain and manifest.

McCulloch, 17 U.S. (4 Wheat.) 316, 323 (1819).

Similarly, William Pinkney argued that the constitutionality of the Bank was "no longer an open question" having been "settled by decisions of the most revered authority, legislative, executive, and judicial." *McCulloch*, 17 U.S. at 378. The Congress which created the first Bank included many framers who "must have understood their own work." *McCulloch*, 17 U.S. at 379. See also KILLENBECK, M'CULLOCH v. MARYLAND 105-09 for a summary of Pinkney's argument which prompted Justice Joseph Story to proclaim, "I never, in my whole life, heard a greater speech; . . . . "

(2) In 1791, James Madison had argued that Congress lacked power to create a bank.

> Mark the reasoning on which the validity of the bill depends. To borrow money is made the *end* and the accumulation of capitals, *implied* as the *means*. The accumulation of capitals is then the *end*, and a bank *implied* as the *means*. The bank is then the *end*, and a charter of incorporation, a monopoly, capital punishments, &c. *implied* as the *means*.
>
> If implications, thus remote and thus multiplied, can be linked together, a chain may be formed that will reach every object of legislation, every object within the whole compass of political economy.

The Bank was not "necessary" but was at most "convenient." 13 THE PAPERS OF JAMES MADISON 377-78 (Hobson & Rutland eds., 1981). Similarly, Thomas Jefferson thought immaterial the argument that a Bank would be "convenient."

> [T]he constitution allows only the means which are "necessary" not those which are merely "convenient" for effecting the enumerated powers. If such a latitude of construction be allowed to this phrase as to give any non-enumerated power, it will go to every one, for [there] is no one which ingenuity may not torture into a *convenience, in some way or other*, to *some one* of so long a list of enumerated powers. It would swallow up all the delegated powers, and reduce the whole to one phrase as before observed. Therefore it was that the constitution restrained them to the *necessary* means, that is to say, to those means without which the grant of the power would be nugatory.

19 THOMAS JEFFERSON, THE PAPERS OF THOMAS JEFFERSON 278 (Boyd ed., 1974).

Alexander Hamilton disagreed, and his opinion carried the day. He wrote:

> [T]his *general principle* is *inherent* in the very *definition* of *Government* and

essential to every step of the progress to be made by that of the United States, namely-that every power vested in a Government is in its nature *sovereign*, and includes by *force* of the *term*, a right to employ all the *means* requisite, and fairly *applicable* to the attainment of the *ends* of such power; and which are not precluded by restrictions and exceptions specified in the constitution, or not immoral, or not contrary to the essentials ends of political society.

8 ALEXANDER HAMILTON, THE PAPERS OF ALEXANDER HAMILTON 98 (Syrett ed., 1965).

Hamilton argued that implied powers were "delegated equally with express ones." Hamilton thought:

the powers contained in a constitution of government, especially those which concern the general administration of the affairs of a country, its finances, trade, defence etc. ought to be construed liberally, in advancement of the public good.

Id. at 105.

The constitutional criterion was:

If the end be clearly comprehended within any of the specified powers, & if the measure have an obvious relation to that end, and is not forbidden by any particular provision of the constitution-it may safely be deemed to come within the compass of the national authority.

Id. at 107.

(3) Webster also argued in part:

It is not enough to say, that it does not appear that a bank was in the contemplation of the framers of the constitution. It was not their intention, in these cases, to enumerate particulars. The true view of the subject is, that if it be a fit instrument to an authorized purpose, it may be used, not being specially prohibited. Congress is authorized to pass all laws "necessary and proper" to carry into execution the powers conferred on it. These words, "necessary and proper," in such an instrument, are probably to be considered as synonimous. *Necessary* powers must here intend such powers as are *suitable* and *fitted* to the object; such as are *best* and *most useful* in relation to the end proposed. If this be not so, and if Congress could use no means but such as were *absolutely indispensable* to the existence of a granted power, the government would hardly exist; at least, it would be wholly inadequate to the purposes of its formation. It is not for this Court to decide whether a *bank*, or *such a bank* as this, be the *best* possible means to aid these purposes of government. Such topics must be left to that discussion which belongs to them in the two houses of Congress. Here, the only question is, whether a bank, in its known and ordinary operations, is capable of being so connected with the finances and revenues of the government, as to be fairly within the discretion of Congress, when selecting means and instruments to execute its powers and perform its duties. Corporations are but means. They are not ends and objects of government. No government exists for the purpose of creating corporations as one of the ends of its being. They are institution established to effect certain beneficial purposes; and, as means, take their character generally from their end and object. (emphasis in original)

McCulloch, 17 U.S. (4 Wheat) at 324–326.

Moreover, Pinkney argued that:

> The power of erecting corporations is not an end of any government; it is a necessary means of accomplishing the ends of all governments. It is an authority inherent in, and incident to, all sovereignty.

McCulloch, 17 U.S. at 383.

One would not have expected the framers to itemize the means government might pursue, Pinckney argued.

> It was impossible for the framers of the constitution to specify, prospectively, all these means, both because it would have involved an immense variety of details, and because it would have been impossible for them to foresee the infinite variety of circumstances, in such an unexampled state of political society as ours, for ever changing and for ever improving. How unwise would it have been, to legislate immutably for exigencies which had not then occurred, and which must have been foreseen but dimly and imperfectly!

McCulloch, 17 U.S. at 385.

(4) In THE FEDERALIST NO. 44, James Madison wrote that even without the Necessary and Proper Clause, "there can be no doubt that all the particular powers requisite as means of executing the general powers would have resulted to the government, by unavoidable implication. No axiom is more clearly established in law, or in reason, than that whenever the end is required, the means are authorized; wherever general power to do a thing is given, every particular power necessary for doing it is included." Similarly, in FEDERALIST NO. 33, Alexander Hamilton suggested that the Necessary and Proper Clause was superfluous — "declaratory of a truth which would have resulted by necessary and unavoidable implication from the very act of constituting a federal government, and vesting it with certain specified powers." Marshall makes a similar argument but does not rely upon the Federalist Papers, to show that his interpretation accurately captures the framers' intent. Why not?

(5) Professor Charles Black, Jr. has argued that *McCulloch* is the classic example of structural constitutional argument — basing arguments not so much on the explicit text but on the structures the Constitution creates and their relationships. He wrote: "I am inclined to think well of the method of reasoning from structure and relation. I think well of it, above all, because to succeed it has to make sense — current, practical sense. The textual-explication method, operating on general language, may often — perhaps more often than not — be made to make sense, by legitimate enough devices of interpretation. But it contains within itself no guarantee that it will make sense, for a court may always present itself or even see itself as being bound by the stated intent, however nonsensical, of somebody else." CHARLES BLACK JR, STRUCTURE AND RELATIONSHIP IN CONSTITUTIONAL LAW 22 (1969).

(6) What does Chief Justice Marshall mean when he declares that "we must never forget that it is a constitution we are expounding"? Justice Frankfurter thought this statement "the single most important utterance in the literature of constitutional law." Felix Frankfurter, *John Marshall and the Judicial Function*, 69 HARV. L. REV. 217, 219 (1955). Is Marshall suggesting that the manner in which we interpret a constitution, and our expectations of it, differ from the way in which we interpret a statute? Is he suggesting that a constitution must be flexible enough to adapt to changing historical contexts?

(7) Is the Necessary and Proper Clause limited to the powers of Congress listed in Article I, section 8? Although the Necessary and Proper Clause is contained at the end of Article I, section 8, it expressly gives Congress the power "[T]o make all Laws which shall be necessary and proper" not only "for carrying into Execution the foregoing

Powers" (i.e., those enumerated in Article I, section 8), but also "all other Powers vested by this Constitution in the Government of the United States, or any Department or Officer thereof."

The Necessary and Proper Clause has been used to expand many powers of the National Government. According to *The Thomas Barlum*, 293 U.S. 21 (1934), the Necessary and Proper Clause gives Congress the power to revise and amend the maritime law that existed at the time the Constitution was adopted. That power is an appropriate means to carry into execution the admiralty and maritime jurisdiction conferred upon the federal courts by Article III. *See also Neely v. Henkel*, 180 U.S. 109 (1901) (Necessary and Proper Clause confers power to enact laws to carry out treaties); *Kohl v. United States*, 91 U.S. 367 (1875) (power to acquire property by eminent domain); *Legal Tender Cases*, 79 U.S. (12 Wall.) 457 (1870) (power to make paper money legal tender); *Murray v. Hoboken Land & Improvement Co.*, 59 U.S. (18 How.) 272 (1855) (power to seize property to secure collections of taxes).

(8) Chief Justice Marshall had previously previewed some of the prominent ideas he expressed in *McCulloch*. *See, e.g., Bank of the United States v. Deveaux*, 9 U.S. (5 Cranch) 61, 87 (1809). ("A constitution, from its nature, deals in generals, not in detail. Its framers cannot perceive minute distinctions which arise in the progress of the nation, and therefore confine it to the establishment of broad and general principles"); *United States v. Fisher*, 6 U.S. (2 Cranch) 358, 396 (1805):

> In construing the Necessary and Proper Clause it would be incorrect and would produce endless difficulties, if the opinion should be maintained that no law was authorized which was not indispensably necessary to give effect to a specified power.

> Where various systems might be adopted for that purpose, it might be said with respect to each, that it was not necessary because the end might be obtained by other means. Congress must possess the choice of means, and must be empowered to use any means which are in fact conducive to the exercise of a power granted by the constitution.

(9) In another famous formulation in *McCulloch*, Marshall suggested that Congress could constitutionally employ all appropriate means plainly adapted to achieve legitimate ends consistent with the Constitution. Some critically suggest Marshall's means-ends language gave Congress carte blanche to do whatever it wanted to do. *See* Yoo, *McCulloch v. Maryland, in* Constitutional Stupidities, Constitutional Tragedies 245 (Eskridge and Levinson eds., 1998). Professor David P. Currie points out that Marshall had previously construed the Necessary and Proper Clause in *United States v. Fisher*, 6 U.S. (2 Cranch) 358 (1805), to empower Congress "to use any means which are in fact conducive to the exercise of a power granted by the Constitution." Is this interpretation broader than that of *McCulloch*, as Professor Currie argues? Does the *McCulloch* formulation limit Congress in any way? Professor Currie finds it "remarkably careful and hard to improve upon in the light of a century and a half of experience." Currie, *The Constitution in the Supreme Court: State and Congressional Powers, 1801-1835*, 49 U. Chi. L. Rev. 887, 930 (1982).

§ 2.02 THE COMMERCE POWER

GIBBONS v. OGDEN
22 U.S. (9 Wheat.) 1, 6 L. Ed. 23 (1824)

[Editors' Note: New York granted Robert Fulton and Robert Livingston the exclusive right to operate steam-powered vessels in the State's territorial waters. Fulton and Livingston thereafter assigned to Aaron Ogden the right to navigate steamboats between Elizabethtown Point, N.J., and New York City. In violation of Ogden's submonopoly, one Thomas Gibbons began operating two passenger ferries. Gibbons' steamboats had been enrolled and granted "license . . . to be employed in carrying on the coasting trade" under the Federal Enrollment and Licensing Act.

At Ogden's request, the New York courts issued an injunction restraining Gibbons from operating ferries in New York waters. New York Courts rejected Gibbons' preemption claim based upon his federal licenses. They found the sole purpose of the license was to establish the vessels as an American ship, not to oust the State's power to regulate the use of chattels. The highest state court affirmed. It ruled that "the only effect" of the license was "to determine [the vessel's] national character, and the rate of duties which she is to pay." 17 Johns. 488, 509 (1820). Gibbons appealed to the Supreme Court.]

CHIEF JUSTICE MARSHALL delivered the opinion of the Court. . . .

The appellant contends that this decree is erroneous, because the laws which purport to give the exclusive privilege it sustains, are repugnant to the constitution and laws of the United States.

They are said to be repugnant:

1st. To that clause in the constitution which authorizes Congress to regulate commerce. . . .

This instrument contains an enumeration of powers expressly granted by the people to their government. It has been said, that these powers ought to be construed strictly. But why ought they to be so construed? Is there one sentence in the constitution which gives countenance to this rule? In the last of the enumerated powers, that which grants, expressly, the means for carrying all others into execution, Congress is authorized "to make all laws which shall be necessary and proper" for the purpose. But this limitation on the means which may be used, is not extended to the powers which are conferred. . . .

The words are: "Congress shall have power to regulate commerce with foreign nations, and among the several States, and with the Indian tribes."

The subject to be regulated is commerce; and . . . to ascertain the extent of the power it becomes necessary to settle the meaning of the word. The counsel for the appellee would limit it to traffic, to buying and selling, or the interchange of commodities, and do not admit that it comprehends navigation. This would restrict a general term, applicable to many objects, to one of its significations. Commerce, undoubtedly, is traffic, but it is something more: it is intercourse. It describes the commercial intercourse between nations, and parts of nations, in all its branches, and is regulated by prescribing rules for carrying on that intercourse. The mind can scarcely conceive a system for regulating commerce between nations, which shall exclude all laws concerning navigation, which shall be silent on the admission of the vessels of the one nation into the ports of the other, and be confined to prescribing rules for the conduct of individuals, in the actual employment of buying and selling, or of barter. . . .

All America understands, and has uniformly understood, the word "commerce" to comprehend navigation. It was so understood, and must have been so understood, when the constitution was framed. The power over commerce, including navigation, was one of the primary objects for which the people of America adopted their government, and must have been contemplated in forming it. The convention must have used the word in that sense, because all have understood it in that sense; and the attempt to restrict it comes too late. . . .

The word used in the constitution, then, comprehends, and has been always understood to comprehend, navigation within its meaning; and a power to regulate navigation is as expressly granted as if that term had been added to the word "commerce."

To what commerce does this power extend? The constitution informs us, to commerce "with foreign nations, and among the several States, and with the Indian tribes."

It has, we believe, been universally admitted that these words comprehend every species of commercial intercourse between the United States and foreign nations. No sort of trade can be carried on between this country and any other, to which this power does not extend. . . .

The subject to which the power is next applied, is to commerce "among the several states." The word "among" means intermingled with. A thing which is among others, is intermingled with them. Commerce among the States, cannot stop at the external boundary line of each State, but may be introduced into the interior.

It is not intended to say that these words comprehend that commerce which is completely internal, which is carried on between man and man in a State, or between different parts of the same State, and which does not extend to or affect other States. Such a power would be inconvenient, and is certainly unnecessary.

Comprehensive as the word "among" is, it may very properly be restricted to that commerce which concerns more States than one. The phrase is not one which would probably have been selected to indicate the completely interior traffic of a State, because it is not an apt phrase for that purpose; and the enumeration of the particular classes of commerce, to which the power was to be extended, would not have been made, had the intention been to extend the power to every description. The enumeration presupposes something not enumerated; and that something, if we regard the language or the subject of the sentence, must be the exclusively internal commerce of a State. The genius and character of the whole government seem to be, that its action is to be applied to all the external concerns of the nation, and to those internal concerns which affect the States generally; but not to those which are completely within a particular State, which do not affect other States, and with which it is not necessary to interfere, for the purpose of executing some of the general powers of the government. The completely internal commerce of a State, then, may be considered as reserved for the State itself.

But, in regulating commerce with foreign nations, the power of Congress does not stop at the jurisdictional lines of the several States. It would be a very useless power, if it could not pass those lines. The commerce of the United States with foreign nations, is that of the whole United States. Every district has a right to participate in it. The deep streams which penetrate our country in every direction, pass through the interior of almost every State in the Union, and furnish the means of exercising this right. If Congress has the power to regulate it, that power must be exercised whenever the subject exists. If it exists within the States, if a foreign voyage may commence or terminate at a port within a State, then the power of Congress may be exercised within a State.

This principle is, if possible, still more clear, when applied to commerce "among the several States." They either join each other, in which case they are separated by a mathematical line, or they are remote from each other, in which case other States lie between them. What is commerce "among" them; and how is it to be conducted? Can a trading expedition between two adjoining States, commence and terminate outside of each? And if the trading intercourse be between two States remote from each other, must it not commence in one, terminate in the other, and probably pass through a third? Commerce among the States must, of necessity, be commerce with the States. In the regulation of trade with the Indian tribes, the action of the law, especially when the constitution was made, was chiefly within a State. The power of Congress, then, whatever it may be, must be exercised within the territorial jurisdiction of the several States. The sense of the nation on this subject, is unequivocally manifested by the provisions made in the laws for transporting goods, by land, between Baltimore and Providence, between New York and Philadelphia, and between Philadelphia and Baltimore.

We are now arrived at the inquiry. What is this power?

It is the power to regulate; that is, to prescribe the rule by which commerce is to be governed. This power, like all others vested in Congress, is complete in itself, may be exercised to its utmost extent, and acknowledges no limitations, other than are prescribed in the constitution. These are expressed in plain terms, and do not affect the questions which arise in this case, or which have been discussed at the bar. If, as has always been understood, the sovereignty of Congress, though limited to specified objects, is plenary as to those objects, the power over commerce with foreign nations, and among the several States, is vested in Congress as absolutely as it would be in a single government, having in its constitution the same restrictions on the exercise of the power as are found in the constitution of the United States. The wisdom and the discretion of Congress, their identity with the people, and the influence which their constituents possess at elections, are, in this, as in many other instances, as that, for example, of declaring war, the sole restraints on which they have relied, to secure them from its abuse. They are the restraints on which the people must often rely solely, in all representative governments. . . .

In our complex system, presenting the rare and difficult scheme of one general government, whose action extends over the whole, but which possesses only certain enumerated powers; and of numerous State governments, which retain and exercise all powers not delegated to the Union, contests respecting power must arise. Were it even otherwise, the measures taken by the respective governments to execute their acknowledged powers, would often be of the same description, and might sometimes, interfere. This, however, does not prove that the one is exercising, or has a right to exercise, the powers of the other. . . . .

It has been contended by the counsel for the appellant, that, as the word "to regulate" implies in its nature, full power over the thing to be regulated, it excludes, necessarily, the action of all others that would perform the same operation on the same thing. That regulation is designed for the entire result, applying to those parts which remain as they were, as well as to those which are altered. It produces a uniform whole, which is as much disturbed and deranged by changing what the regulating power designs to leave untouched, as that on which it has operated.

There is great force in this argument, and the court is not satisfied that it has been refuted.

Since, however, in exercising the power of regulating their own purely internal affairs, whether of trading or police, the states may sometimes enact laws, the validity of which depends on their interfering with, and being contrary to, an act of Congress passed in pursuance of the constitution, the court will enter upon the inquiry, whether the laws of New York, as expounded by the highest tribunal of that state, have, in their application to this case, come into collision with an act of Congress, and deprived a citizen of a right to which that act entitles him. Should this collision exist, it will be immaterial whether those laws were passed in virtue of a concurrent power "to regulate commerce with foreign nations and among the several States," or, in virtue of a power to regulate their domestic trade and police. In one case and the other, the acts of New York must yield to the law of Congress; and the decision sustaining the privilege they confer, against a right given by law of the Union, must be erroneous. . . .

. . . The nullity of any act, inconsistent with the constitution, is produced by the declaration that the constitution is the supreme law. The appropriate application of that part of the clause which confers the same supremacy on laws and treaties, is to such acts of the State Legislatures as do not transcend their powers, but, though enacted in the execution of acknowledged State powers, interfere with, or are contrary to the laws of Congress, made in pursuance of the constitution, or some treaty made under the authority of the United States. In every such case, the act of Congress, or the treaty, is supreme; and the law of the State, though enacted in the exercise of powers not controverted, must yield to it. . . .

[The Court held that the Act of Congress of 1793 referred to in the statement of facts gave the possessors of licenses under it the right to engage in navigation between states and the New York law at issue conflicted with the rights of licensees under the federal statute.]

This act demonstrates the opinion of Congress, that steam boats may be enrolled and licensed, in common with vessels using sails. They are, of course, entitled to the same privileges, and can no more be restrained from navigating waters, and entering ports which are free to such vessels, than if they were wafted on their voyage by the winds, instead of being propelled by the agency of fire. The one element may be as legitimately used as the other, for every commercial purpose authorized by the laws of the Union; and the act of a State inhibiting the use of either to any vessel having a license under the act of Congress, comes, we think, in direct collision with that act. . . .

[The New York decree was reversed and the bill for an injunction was ordered dismissed.]

NOTES

(1) *Gibbons v. Ogden* is important in part for its interpretation of the Supremacy Clause. *See infra* § 4.01, Note (2). The New York monopoly law was invalid because it conflicted with the federal licensing law. The conflict occurred, however, only if the federal licensing law was valid under the Commerce Clause. Accordingly, the case afforded Marshall an opportunity for his classic discussion of the Congressional Commerce Power, which Professor Bernard Schwartz described as "the most important substantive power vested in the Federal Government in time of peace." SCHWARTZ, A HISTORY OF THE SUPREME COURT 47 (1993).

(2) Ogden's counsel argued that commerce did not include transportation of passengers but entailed "the transportation and sale of commodities" and was limited to "the exchange of one thing for another; the interchange of commodities; trade or traffic." Daniel Webster, who argued for Gibbons, denied that the Commerce Clause was thus limited. "Nothing" urged Webster, "was more complex than commerce; and in such an age as this, no words embraced a wider field than commercial regulation. Almost all the business and intercourse of life may be connected, incidentally, more or less, with commercial regulations." *Gibbons*, 22 U.S. 1, 9-10.

(3) In *Gibbons v. Ogden*, Marshall did not claim for Congress a power over all

commerce carried on within a state. "It is not," he conceded, "intended to say that these words comprehend that commerce which is completely internal." But Marshall avoided drawing any rigid line between the commerce over which Congress had authority and the "internal" commerce of the states. Marshall's concept was more flexible. As he stated it in *Gibbons*, the word "among" in the Commerce Clause "may very properly be restricted to that commerce which concerns more States than one." As Justice Felix Frankfurter wrote, Marshall "had an organic conception of commerce." FRANKFURTER, THE COMMERCE CLAUSE UNDER MARSHALL, TANEY AND WAITE 42 (1937). The test, in Marshall's conception, was not mere movement across state lines, but whether the particular commerce affected more than one state.

(4) Marshall's recognition of the "completely internal" commerce of a state was, however, later exploited to establish a rigid dichotomy between interstate and intrastate commerce. Under the post-Marshall approach, the criterion became the physical crossing of state lines. Only commerce that moved across state boundaries was subject to federal regulation. Congressional power came to turn upon whether particular commerce crossed state lines. The state never surrendered its power until its boundaries were crossed. "All commercial action within the limits of a State, and which does not extend to any other state or foreign country, is exclusively under State regulation. Congress have no more power to control this than a State has to regulate [interstate] commerce." McLean, J., in *Passenger Cases*, 48 U.S. (7 How.) 283, 400 (1849).

(5) For much of the nineteenth century, Congress passed little legislation under the Commerce Clause. During the late nineteenth and early twentieth centuries, the Court used a variety of techniques to narrow the possible reach of the Commerce Clause. These techniques are considered in the following section.

§ 2.03 COMMERCE POWER 1895-1936

[1] Productive Industries

UNITED STATES v. E.C. KNIGHT CO.
156 U.S. 1, 15 S. Ct. 249, 39 L. Ed. 325 (1895)

CHIEF JUSTICE FULLER . . . delivered the opinion of the court.

By the purchase of the stock of the four Philadelphia refineries with shares of its own stock the American Sugar Refining Company acquired nearly complete control of the manufacture of refined sugar within the United States. The bill charged that the contracts under which these purchases were made constituted combinations in restraint of trade, and that in entering into them the defendants combined and conspired to restrain the trade and commerce in refined sugar among the several states and with foreign nations, contrary to the act of Congress of July 2, 1890.

The relief sought was the cancellation of the agreements under which the stock was transferred, the redelivery of the stock to the parties respectively, and an injunction against the further performance of the agreements and further violations of the act. . . .

The argument is that the power to control the manufacture of refined sugar is a monopoly over a necessary of life, to the enjoyment of which by a large part of the population of the United States interstate commerce is indispensable, and that, therefore, the general government, in the exercise of the power to regulate commerce may repress such monopoly directly, and set aside the instruments which have created it. . . . Doubtless the power to control the manufacture of a given thing involves, in a certain sense, the control of its disposition, but this is a secondary, and not the primary, sense; and although the exercise of that power may result in bringing the operation of commerce into play, it does not control it, and affects it only incidentally and indirectly. Commerce succeeds to manufacture, and is not a part of it. The power to regulate commerce is the power to prescribe the rule by which commerce shall be governed, and is a power independent of the power to suppress monopoly. But it may operate in repression of monopoly whenever that comes within the rules by which commerce is governed, or whenever the transaction is itself a monopoly of commerce. . . .

It will be perceived how far-reaching the proposition is that the power of dealing with a monopoly directly may be exercised by the general government whenever interstate or international commerce may be ultimately affected. The regulation of commerce applies to the subjects of commerce, and not to matters of internal police. Contracts to buy, sell, or exchange goods to be transported among the several states, the transportation and its instrumentalities, and articles bought, sold, or exchanged for the purposes of such transit among the States, or put in the way of transit, may be regulated; but this is because they form part of interstate trade or commerce. The fact that an article is manufactured for export to another state does not of itself make it an article of interstate commerce, and the intent of the manufacturer does not determine the time when the article or product passes from the control of the State and belongs to commerce. . . .

. . . [I]n *Kidd v. Pearson*, 128 U.S. 1, 20, 24, where the question was discussed whether the right of a State to enact a statute prohibiting within its limits the manufacture of intoxicating liquors, except for certain purposes, could be overthrown by the fact that the manufacturer intended to export the liquors when made, it was held that the intent of the manufacturer did not determine the time when the article or product passed from the control of the state and belonged to commerce, and that, therefore, the statute, in omitting to except from its operation the manufacture of intoxicating liquors within the limits of the state for export, did not constitute an unauthorized interference with the right of Congress to regulate commerce. And Justice Lamar remarked:

> No distinction is more popular to the common mind, or more clearly expressed in economic and political literature, than that between manufacture and commerce. Manufacture is transformation — the fashioning of raw materials into a change of form for use. The functions of commerce are different. The buying and selling, and the transportation incidental thereto, constitute commerce; and the regulation of commerce in the constitutional sense embraces the regulation at least of such transportation. . . . If it be held that the term includes the regulation of all such manufactures as are intended to be the subject of commercial transactions in the future, it is impossible to deny that it would also include all productive industries that contemplate the same thing. The result would be that Congress would be invested, to the exclusion of the states, with the power to regulate, not only manufactures, but also agriculture, horticulture, stock raising, domestic fisheries, mining-in short, every branch of human industry. For is there one of them that does not contemplate, more or less clearly, an interstate or foreign market? Does not the wheat grower of the Northwest, and the cotton planter of the South, plant, cultivate, and harvest his crop with an eye on the prices at Liverpool, New York, and Chicago? The power being vested in Congress and denied to the states, it would follow as an inevitable result that the duty would devolve on Congress to regulate all of these delicate, multiform and vital interests — interests which in their nature are, and must be, local in all the details of their successful management. . . .

Slight reflection will show that, if the national power extends to all contracts and combinations in manufacture, agriculture, mining, and other productive industries, whose ultimate result may affect external commerce, comparatively little of business operations and affairs would be left for state control.

It was in the light of well-settled principles that the act of July 2, 1890, was framed. . . . [W]hat the law struck at was combinations, contracts, and conspiracies to monopolize trade and commerce among the several states or with foreign nations; but the contracts and acts of the defendants related exclusively to the acquisition of the Philadelphia refineries and the business of sugar refining in Pennsylvania, and bore no direct relation to commerce between the states or with foreign nations. The object was manifestly private gain in the manufacture of the commodity, but not through the control of interstate or foreign commerce. . . .

The circuit court declined, upon the pleadings and proofs, to grant the relief prayed, and dismissed the bill, and we are of opinion that the Circuit Court of Appeals did not err in affirming that decree.

Decree affirmed.

Mr. Justice Harlan, dissenting.

[Editor's Note: In stating the facts, Justice Harlan noted American Sugar's purpose to control sugar refining and sales. He thought it regrettable if the Constitution did not confer power on the national government to control such impulses. Justice Harlan quoted *Gibbons* extensively to support a broad definition of commerce. Commerce was not limited to "transportation simply" but "includes the purchase and sale of articles that are intended to be transported from one state to another — every species of commercial intercourse among the states and with foreign nations." Numerous state courts had addressed illegal restraints of trades and had held combinations like American Sugar to violate public policy. His opinion then continued:]

. . . [I]t will not be doubted that it would be competent for a state, under the power to regulate its domestic commerce, and for the purpose of protecting its people against fraud and injustice, to make it a public offense, punishable by fine and imprisonment, for individuals or corporations to make contracts, form combinations, or engage in conspiracies, which unduly restrain trade or commerce carried on within its limits, and also to authorize the institution of proceedings for the purpose of annulling contracts of that character, as well as of preventing or restraining such combinations and conspiracies.

But there is a trade among the several states which is distinct from that carried on within the territorial limits of a state. The regulation and control of the former is committed by the national Constitution to Congress. . . . The jurisdiction of the general government extends over every foot of territory within the United States. Under the power with which it is invested, Congress may remove unlawful obstructions, of whatever kind, to the free course of trade among the states. In so doing it would not interfere with the "autonomy of the states," because the power thus to protect interstate commerce is expressly given by the people of all the States. . . .

. . . Any combination, therefore, that disturbs or unreasonably obstructs freedom in buying and selling articles manufactured to be sold to persons in other states, or to be carried to other states, — a freedom that cannot exist if the right to buy and sell is fettered by unlawful restraints that crush out competition, — affects, not incidentally, but directly, the people of all the states; and the remedy for such an evil is found only in the exercise of powers confided to a government which, this court has said, was the government of all, exercising powers delegated by all, representing all, acting for all. . . .

It may be admitted that an act which did nothing more than forbid, and which had no other object than to forbid, the mere refining of sugar in any State, would be in excess of any power granted to Congress. But the act of 1890 is not of that character. It does not strike at the manufacture simply of articles that are legitimate or recognized subjects of commerce, but at combinations that unduly restrain, because they monopolize, the buying and selling of articles which are to go into interstate commerce. . . .

In committing to congress the control of commerce with foreign nations and among the several states, the constitution did not define the means that may be employed to protect the freedom of commercial intercourse and traffic established for the benefit of all the people of the Union. It wisely forbore to impose any limitations upon the exercise of that power except those arising from the general nature of the government, or such as are embodied in the fundamental guaranties of liberty and property. It gives to Congress, in express words, authority to enact all laws necessary and proper for carrying into execution the power to regulate commerce; and whether an act of Congress, passed to accomplish an object to which the general government is competent, is within the power granted, must be determined by the rule announced [in *McCulloch*]. . . The end proposed to be accomplished by the act of 1890 is the protection of trade and commerce among the States against unlawful restraints. Who can say that that end is not legitimate, or is not within the scope of the Constitution? The means employed are the suppression, by legal proceedings, of combinations, conspiracies, and monopolies which, by their inevitable and admitted tendency, improperly restrain trade and commerce among the States. Who can say that such means are not appropriate to attain the end of freeing commercial intercourse among the States from burdens and exactions imposed upon it by combinations which, under principles long recognized in this country, as well as at the common law, are illegal and dangerous to the public welfare? What clause of the constitution can be referred to which prohibits the means thus prescribed in the act of Congress?

. . . I find it impossible to refuse my assent to this proposition: Whatever a State may do to protect its completely interior traffic or trade against unlawful restraints, the general government is empowered to do for the protection of the people of all the states — for this purpose, one people — against unlawful restraints imposed upon interstate traffic or trade in articles that are to enter into commerce among the several states. . . . Each state can reach and suppress combinations so far as they unlawfully restrain its interior trade, while the national government may reach and suppress them so far as they unlawfully restrain trade among the states. . . .

. . . The common government of all the people is the only one that can adequately deal with a matter which directly and injuriously affects the entire commerce of the country, which concerns equally all the people of the Union, and which, it must be confessed, cannot be adequately controlled by any one state. Its authority should not be so weakened by construction that it cannot reach and eradicate evils that, beyond all question, tend to defeat an object which that government is entitled, by the constitution, to accomplish. . . .

NOTES

(1) *E.C. Knight* — popularly called the *Sugar Trust Case* — involved the first important prosecution under the Sherman Anti-Trust Act. Although some have criticized the government's presentation of the *Knight* case, Professor Charles W. McCurdy argues that the government's mistake was its decision to file the lawsuit in the first place. The government "hardly could have chosen a weaker case," he wrote. American Sugar Refining was engaged simply in production; independent entities distributed its products. Does *E.C. Knight* contain language suggesting Congress could

reach a monopoly of both distribution *and* production? *See generally* McCurdy, *The Knight Sugar Decision of 1895 and the Modernization of American Corporation Law, 1869-1903*, 53 BUS. HIST. REV. 304, 328-29 (1979).

(2) *E.C. Knight* asserts that "Commerce succeeds to manufacture, and is not a part of it." Justice Harlan, who dissented, thought *Knight* defeated the main object of the Sherman Act. Compare the Court's statement in *Mandeville Island Farms, Inc. v. American Crystal Sugar Co.*, 334 U.S. 219, 230 (1948):

> The *Knight* decision made the statute a dead letter . . . and, had its full force remained unmodified, the Act today would be a weak instrument, as would also the power of Congress, to reach evils in all the vast operations of our gigantic national industrial system antecedent to interstate sale and transportation of manufactured products.

The court did, however, uphold the Sherman Act when applied to interstate rail companies. *See, e.g.*, Cushman, *Formalism and Realism in Commerce Clause Jurisprudence*, 67 CHI. L. REV. 1089, 1094-95 (2000).

(3) The Court found that the "object" of the contract was simply gain in the manufacture of sugar, not its interstate trade. Had the Court discerned a different intent would the case have been decided differently? *See Standard Oil Co. v. United States*, 221 U.S. 1, 74-77 (1911) (intent to control oil market); *United States v. American Tobacco Co.*, 221 U.S. 106, 181-83 (1911) (intent to monopolize tobacco market). Cushman, *Formalism, supra* at 1095-96.

(4) In addition to the production-commerce dichotomy, what other device does the Court use to limit the Commerce Clause? The *E.C. Knight* approach illustrates the doctrine of dual federalism. As Chief Justice Fuller wrote: "That which belongs to commerce is within the jurisdiction of the United States, but that which does not belong to commerce is within the jurisdiction of the police power of the state." *See also Hopkins v. United States*, 171 U.S. 578 (1898) (using dual federalism to restrict commerce power).

(5) *E.C. Knight* is often regarded as "a great victory for laissez-faire conservatism." *See* ARNOLD M. PAUL, CONSERVATIVE CRISIS AND THE RULE OF LAW 181 (1976). But the formalistic restrictions *E.C. Knight* imposed did not mean that the Court was trying to shield vast economic power from regulation. Professor Charles W. McCurdy has demonstrated that "[t]he states . . . were indeed armed with an impressive array of legal devices for controlling the concentration of industrial power." State statutory law of corporations allowed states to control the size, scope, and activities of commercial entities and to exclude foreign corporations (other than common carriers, i.e., railroads, telegraphs, express companies) from conducting intrastate activities. *See* McCurdy, *The Knight Sugar Decision of 1895 and The Modernization of American Corporation Law, 1869-1903*, 53 BUS. HIST. REV. 304, 305-06 (1979). Contrary to the Court's expectations, Professor McCurdy argues that states failed to address manufacturing concentration.

(6) Commerce Clause jurisprudence was not, of course, formulated in isolation from other concepts the Court developed. Professor Barry Cushman points out that dual federalism, which constrained federal power under the Commerce Clause, existed alongside the due process doctrine limiting government regulation of business to those affected with a public interest. *See* BARRY CUSHMAN, RETHINKING THE NEW DEAL COURT 143 (1998); *see also Chas. Wolff Packing Co. v. Court of Indust. Relations*, 262 U.S. 522, 535-36 (1923).

(7) Along with the dual federalism doctrine typified by *E.C. Knight*, two other doctrines developed that were potentially subversive of dual federalism.

In *Swift & Co. v. United States*, 196 U.S. 375 (1905), Justice Holmes articulated the current of commerce, or stream of commerce, doctrine. Defendants, stockyard firms in

Chicago and elsewhere, were charged with violating the Sherman Anti-Trust Act by conspiring to monopolize the sale and distribution of fresh meat in the nation's stockyards. Defendants urged that the buying and selling of livestock in a stockyard was not "commerce among the states." Holmes and the Court rejected this claim. Holmes wrote that commerce was "not a technical legal conception, but a practical one, drawn from the course of business." *Id.* at 398. The local activities involved were part of an integrated commercial whole: "When cattle are sent for sale from a place in one state, with the expectation that they will end their transit, after purchase, in another, and when in effect they do so, with only the interruption necessary to find a purchaser at the stockyards, and when this is a typical, constantly recurring course, the current thus existing is a current of commerce among the states, and the purchase of the cattle is a part and incident of such commerce." *Id.* at 398-99.

Although the current of commerce doctrine potentially posed some threat to dual federalism, Professor Cushman points out, the current of commerce doctrine was limited by the public/private distinction. "[T]he current of commerce came to be understood as a sequence of interstate business activities connected by intrastate business activities affected with a public interest. Because the category of business affected with a public interest promised to remain small and select, the current of commerce promised to cut a narrow channel." CUSHMAN, RETHINKING THE NEW DEAL COURT, *supra* at 146.

In *Houston, East & West Texas Ry. Co. v. United States*, 234 U.S. 342 (1914), the *Shreveport Rate Case*, the Court upheld an order of the Interstate Commerce Commission fixing intrastate railroad rates to prevent a railroad from charging less for an intrastate trip than for an interstate trip of the same distance. The Court concluded that Congress could prevent discriminations against interstate commerce even where the discrimination arose from intrastate rates. "Wherever the interstate and intrastate transactions of carriers are so related that the government of the one involves the control of the other, it is Congress, and not the state, that is entitled to prescribe the final and dominant rule, for otherwise Congress would be denied the exercise of its constitutional authority, and the state, and not the nation, would be supreme within the national field." *Id.* at 351-52. Although some have characterized the *Shreveport* doctrine as a competitor to the dual federalism of the time, Professor Cushman points out the doctrine "was always limited to the paradigmatic business affected with a public interest: rail carriage." CUSHMAN, RETHINKING THE NEW DEAL COURT, *supra* at 193.

[2] Regulation versus Prohibition

CHAMPION v. AMES [LOTTERY CASE]
188 U.S. 321, 23 S. Ct. 321, 47 L. Ed. 492 (1903)

JUSTICE HARLAN delivered the opinion of the court:

The general question arising upon this appeal involves the constitutionality of the 1st section of the act of Congress of March 2d, 1895, 191, entitled "An Act for the Suppression of Lottery Traffic through National and Interstate Commerce and the Postal Service, Subject to the Jurisdiction and Laws of the United States." 28 Stat. at L. 963, U.S. Comp. Stat. 1901, p. 3178. . . .

The First section of the act of 1895, upon which the indictment was based, is as follows: "§ 1. That any person who shall cause to be brought within the United States from abroad, for the purpose of disposing of the same, or deposited in or carried by the mails of the United States, or carried from one state to another in the United States, any paper, certificate, or instrument purporting to be or represent a ticket, chance, share, or interest in or dependent upon the event of a lottery, so-called gift concert, or similar enterprise, offering prizes dependent upon lot or chance, or shall cause any advertisement of such lottery, so-called gift concert, or similar enterprise, offering prizes dependent upon lot or chance, to be brought into the United States, or deposited in or carried by the mails of the United States, or transferred from one state to another in the same, shall be punishable [for] the first offense by imprisonment for not more than two years, or by a fine of not more than $1,000, or both, and in the second and after offenses by such imprisonment only." 28 Stat. at L. 963 (U.S. Comp. Stat. 1901, p. 3178.

. . . .

We are of opinion that lottery tickets are subjects of traffic, and therefore are subjects of commerce, and the regulation of the carriage of such tickets from state to state, at least by independent carriers, is a regulation of commerce among the several states.

But it is said that the statute in question does not regulate the carrying of lottery tickets from state to state, but by punishing those who cause them to be so carried Congress in effect prohibits such carrying; that in respect of the carrying from one state to another of articles or things that are, in fact, or according to usage in business, the subjects of commerce, the authority given Congress was not to prohibit, but only to regulate. This view was earnestly pressed at the bar by learned counsel, and must be examined.

It is to be remarked that the Constitution does not define what is to be deemed a legitimate regulation of interstate commerce. In *Gibbons v. Ogden*, [*supra* § 2.02] it was said that the power to regulate such commerce is the power to prescribe the rule by which it is to be governed. But this general observation leaves it to be determined, when the question comes before the court, whether Congress, in prescribing a particular rule, has exceeded its power under the Constitution. . . .

We have said that the carrying from state to state of lottery tickets constitutes interstate commerce, and that the regulation of such commerce is within the power of Congress under the Constitution. Are we prepared to say that a provision which is, in effect, a prohibition of the carriage of such articles from state to state is not a fit or appropriate mode for the regulation of that particular kind of commerce? If lottery traffic, carried on through interstate commerce, is a matter of which Congress may take cognizance and over which its power may be exerted, can it be possible that it must tolerate the traffic, and simply regulate the manner in which it may be carried on? Or may not Congress, for the protection of the people of all the states, and under the power to regulate interstate commerce, devise such means, within the scope of the Constitution, and not prohibited by it, as will drive that traffic out of commerce among the states? . . .

If a state, when considering legislation for the suppression of lotteries within its own limits, may properly take into view the evils that inhere in the raising of money, in that mode, why may not Congress, invested with the power to regulate commerce among the several states, provide that such commerce shall not be polluted by the carrying of lottery tickets from one state to another? In this connection it must not be forgotten that the power of Congress to regulate commerce among the states is plenary, is complete in itself, and is subject to no limitations except such as may be found in the Constitution. What provision in that instrument can be regarded as limiting the exercise of the power granted? What clause can be cited which, in any degree, countenances the suggestion that one may, of right, carry or cause to be carried from one state to another that which will harm the public morals? . . . [The Court considered, and rejected, an argument that prohibiting carriage of lottery tickets between states is inconsistent with the Tenth Amendment. Furthermore, the Court discussed several other statutes, prohibiting certain activities, which had been upheld by the Court, as valid exertions of Congress' commerce clause power.]

We decide nothing more in the present case than that lottery tickets are subjects of traffic among those who choose to sell or buy them; that the carriage of such tickets by independent carriers from one state to another is therefore interstate commerce; that under its power to regulate commerce among the several states Congress — subject to the limitations imposed by the Constitution upon the exercise of the powers granted — has plenary authority over such commerce, and may prohibit the carriage of such tickets from state to state; and that legislation to that end, and of that character, is not inconsistent with any limitation or restriction imposed upon the exercise of the powers granted to Congress.

The judgment is affirmed.

[CHIEF JUSTICE FULLER and JUSTICES BREWER, SHIRAS, and PECKHAM dissented.]

NOTES

(1) The *Lottery Case* holding has been applied to federal laws closing the channels of commerce to commodities themselves dangerous or harmful or that have an adverse effect upon the public. "Congress is free to exclude from interstate commerce articles whose use in the states for which they are destined it may reasonably conceive to be injurious to the public health, morals, or welfare." *United States v. Carolene Prod. Co.*, 304 U.S. 144, 147 (1938). The anticipated evil may proceed from something inherent in the commodity itself in the purpose of the transportation, such as lottery tickets. *See James Clark Distilling Co. v. Western Maryland Ry. Co.*, 242 U.S. 311 (1917) (intoxicating liquors); *see also Brooks v. United States*, 267 U.S. 432 (1925) (stolen motor vehicles); *Hoke v. United States*, 227 U.S. 308 (1913) (women transported for immoral purposes); *Hipolite Egg Co. v. United States*, 220 U.S. 45 (1911) (adulterated and misbranded articles); *Reid v. Colorado*, 187 U.S. 137 (1902) (diseased livestock). In these cases, prevention of harm to the public becomes a proper end of the commerce power, even though the harm does not affect commerce. The commerce power includes authority to bar the shipment in commerce of articles, not only to render interstate transportation more efficient and safe, but also to prevent a social, economic, or moral result disapproved of by Congress.

(2) In his dissent in the *Lottery Case*, Chief Justice Fuller warned that the majority's decision gave Congress a "general police power" and made "everything . . . an article of commerce the moment it is taken to be transported from place to place, and of interstate commerce if from State to State." *Lottery Case*, 188 U.S. at 371. He argued that "[a]n invitation to dine, or to take a drive, or a note of introduction" deposited with a delivery service would fall within Congress' regulating power. *Id.*

(3) "Congress can certainly regulate interstate commerce to the extent of forbidding and punishing the use of such commerce as an agency to promote immorality, dishonesty, or the spread of any evil or harm to the people of other states from the state of origin. In doing this it is merely exercising the police power, for the benefit of the public, within the field of interstate commerce." *Brooks v. United States*, 267 U.S. 432, 436-37 (1925). Congress may exert its prohibitory authority to reach commerce it may reasonably deem injurious to public health, safety, morals, or welfare.

HAMMER v. DAGENHART [CHILD LABOR CASE]
247 U.S. 251, 38 S. Ct. 529, 62 L.Ed. 1101 (1918)

JUSTICE DAY delivered the opinion of the Court.

A bill was filed in the United States District Court for the Western District of North Carolina by a father in his own behalf and as next friend of his two minor sons, one under the age of fourteen years and the other between the ages of fourteen and sixteen years, employe[e]s in a cotton mill at Charlotte, North Carolina, to enjoin the enforcement of the act of Congress intended to prevent interstate commerce in the products of child labor. . . .

The District Court held the act unconstitutional and entered a decree enjoining its enforcement. This appeal brings the case here. . . .

Is it within the authority of Congress in regulating commerce among the states to prohibit the transportation in interstate commerce of manufactured goods, the product of a factory in which, within thirty days prior to their removal therefrom, children under the age of fourteen have been employed or permitted to work, or children between the ages of fourteen and sixteen years have been employed or permitted to work more than eight hours in any day, or more than six days in any week, or after the hour of seven o'clock P.M., or before the hour of 6 o'clock A.M.?

The power essential to the passage of this act, the government contends, is found in the commerce clause of the Constitution which authorizes Congress to regulate commerce with foreign nations and among the States.

In *Gibbons v. Ogden,* . . . Chief Justice Marshall, speaking for this court, and defining the extent and nature of the commerce power, said, "It is the power to regulate; that is, to prescribe the rule by which commerce is to be governed." In other words, the power is one to control the means by which commerce is carried on, which is directly the contrary of the assumed right to forbid commerce from moving and thus destroying it as to particular commodities. But it is insisted that adjudged cases in this court establish the doctrine that the power to regulate given to Congress incidentally includes the authority to prohibit the movement of ordinary commodities and therefore that the subject is not open for discussion. The cases demonstrate the contrary. They rest upon the character of the particular subjects dealt with and the fact that the scope of governmental authority, state or national, possessed over them is such that the authority to prohibit is as to them but the exertion of the power to regulate.

[The Court discussed cases in which the power of Congress to prohibit interstate transportation of goods had been upheld, including *Champion v. Ames, supra* § 2.03[2].]

In each of these instances the use of interstate transportation was necessary to the accomplishment of harmful results. In other words, although the power over interstate transportation was to regulate, that could only be accomplished by prohibiting the use of the facilities of interstate commerce to effect the evil intended.

This element is wanting in the present case. The thing intended to be accomplished by this statute is the denial of the facilities of interstate commerce to those manufacturers in the States who employ children within the prohibited ages. The act in its effect does not regulate transportation among the States, but aims to standardize the ages at which children may be employed in mining and manufacturing within the States. The goods shipped are of themselves harmless. The act permits them to be freely shipped after thirty days from the time of their removal from the factory. When offered for shipment, and before transportation begins, the labor of their production is over, and the mere fact that they were intended for interstate commerce transportation does not make their production subject to federal control under the commerce power.

Commerce consists of intercourse and traffic . . . and includes the transportation of persons and property, as well as the purchase, sale and exchange of commodities. The making of goods and the mining of coal are not commerce, nor does the fact that these things are to be afterwards shipped, or used in interstate commerce, make their production a part thereof. . . .

Over interstate transportation, or its incidents, the regulatory power of Congress is ample, but the production of articles, intended for interstate commerce, is a matter of local regulation. . . . If it were otherwise, all manufacture intended for interstate shipment would be brought under federal control to the practical exclusion of the authority of the States, a result certainly not contemplated by the framers of the Constitution when they vested in Congress the authority to regulate commerce among the States. . . .

It may be desirable that [child labor] laws be uniform, but our federal government is one of enumerated powers. . . . A statute must be judged by its natural and reasonable effect. . . . The maintenance of the authority of the States over matters purely local is as essential to the preservation of our institutions as is the conservation of the supremacy of the federal power in all matters entrusted to the Nation by the Federal Constitution. . . .

To sustain this statute would not be in our judgment a recognition of the lawful exertion of congressional authority over interstate commerce, but would sanction an invasion by the federal power of the control of a matter purely local in its character, and over which no authority has been delegated to Congress in conferring the power to regulate commerce among the States.

We have neither authority nor disposition to question the motives of Congress in enacting this legislation. The purposes intended must be attained consistently with constitutional limitations and not by an invasion of the powers of the States. This court has no more important function than that which devolves upon it the obligation to preserve inviolate the constitutional limitations upon the exercise of authority federal and state to the end that each may continue to discharge, harmoniously with the other, the duties entrusted to it by the Constitution.

In our view the necessary effect of this act is, by means of a prohibition against the movement in interstate commerce of ordinary commercial commodities, to regulate the hours of labor of children in factories and mines within the States, a purely state authority. Thus the act in a two-fold sense is repugnant to the Constitution. It not only transcends the authority delegated to Congress over commerce but also exerts a power as to a purely local matter to which the federal authority does not extend. The far reaching result of upholding the act cannot be more plainly indicated than by pointing out that if Congress can thus regulate matters entrusted to local authority by prohibition of the movement of commodities in interstate commerce, all freedom of commerce will be at an end, and the power of the States over local matters may be eliminated, and thus our system of government be practically destroyed.

For these reasons we hold that this law exceeds the constitutional authority of Congress. It follows that the decree of the District Court must be

Affirmed.

JUSTICE HOLMES, dissenting. . . .

The first step in my argument is to make plain what no one is likely to dispute — that the statute in question is within the power expressly given to Congress if considered only as to its immediate effects and that if invalid it is so only upon some collateral ground. The statute confines itself to prohibiting the carriage of certain goods in interstate or foreign commerce. Congress is given power to regulate such commerce in unqualified terms. It would not be argued today that the power to regulate does not include the power to prohibit. Regulation means the prohibition of something, and when interstate commerce is the matter to be regulated I cannot doubt that the regulation may prohibit any part of such commerce that Congress sees fit to forbid. At all events it is established by the *Lottery Case* and others that have followed it that a law is not beyond the regulative power of Congress merely because it prohibits certain transportation out and out. So I repeat that this statute in its immediate operation is clearly within the Congress's constitutional power.

The question then is narrowed to whether the exercise of its otherwise constitutional power by Congress can be pronounced unconstitutional because of its possible reaction upon the conduct of the States in a matter upon which I have admitted that they are free from direct control. I should have thought that that matter had been disposed of so fully as to leave no room for doubt. I should have thought that the most conspicuous decisions of this Court had made it clear that the power to regulate commerce and other constitutional powers could not be cut down or qualified by the fact that it might interfere with the carrying out of the domestic policy of any State. . . .

The notion that prohibition is any less prohibition when applied to things now thought evil I do not understand. But if there is any matter upon which civilized countries have agreed — far more unanimously than they have with regard to intoxicants and some other matters over which this country is now emotionally aroused — it is the evil of premature and excessive child labor. I should have thought that if we were to introduce our own moral conceptions where in my opinion they do not belong, this was preeminently a case for upholding the exercise of all its powers by the United States.

But I had thought that the propriety of the exercise of a power admitted to exist in some cases was for the consideration of Congress alone and that this Court always had disavowed the right to intrude its judgment upon questions of policy or morals. It is not for this Court to pronounce when prohibition is necessary to regulation if it ever may be necessary — to say that it is permissible as against strong drink but not as against the product of ruined lives.

The Act does not meddle with anything belonging to the States. They may regulate their internal affairs and their domestic commerce as they like. But when they seek to send their products across the State line they are no longer within their rights. If there were no Constitution and no Congress their power to cross the line would depend upon their neighbors. Under the Constitution such commerce belongs not to the States but to Congress to regulate. It may carry out its views of public policy whatever indirect effect they may have upon the activities of the States. . . . The national welfare as understood by Congress may require a different attitude within its sphere from that of some self-seeking State. It seems to me entirely constitutional for Congress to enforce its understanding by all the means at its command.

JUSTICE MCKENNA, JUSTICE BRANDEIS, and JUSTICE CLARKE concur in this opinion.

NOTES

(1) In *E.C. Knight*, the Court deemed irrelevant empirical evidence of the effect of the regulated activity on commerce, focusing instead simply on the formalities of whether the activity was commerce or something else. In *Champion*, the Court emphasized the formal fact that the statute regulated movement from state A to state B, rather than the reality that the statute had a moral, not economic, motivation. *E.C. Knight* and *Champion* might be viewed as formalistic opinions that emphasized the statutes' compliance with, or violation of, formal requirements, not their real world

purpose or effect. Does the majority take a formalistic or realistic approach in *Hammer*? How would you classify Justice Holmes' *Hammer* approach?

(2) Even if regulation of local production was Congress' real purpose, should that invalidate a transportation regulation? When an act of Congress regulates what is plainly interstate commerce, the movement of economic goods from state A to state B, should it be invalidated on some collateral ground? What was the practical result of the Court's decision? Under it, was effective regulation of child labor in this country possible?

(3) Is Justice Day correct in suggesting that in *Hammer*, regulation of commerce is not needed to prevent a harm in state B from goods manufactured in state A? If state A is free to allow industry to use child labor in the manufacture of goods, and to ship those goods interstate, what effect will that have on the price of those goods? On conduct in state B? Should market demoralization suffice to empower Congress to reach such practices as a regulation of commerce?

(4) Did the Framers include the Commerce Clause to address measures like the anti-lottery statute upheld in *Champion* or the anti-child labor statute the Court struck down in *Hammer*?

[3] Striking Down New Deal Legislation

CARTER v. CARTER COAL CO.
298 U.S. 238, 56 S. Ct. 855, 80 L. Ed. 1160 (1936)

JUSTICE SUTHERLAND delivered the opinion of the Court.

The purposes of the "Bituminous Coal Conservation Act of 1935," involved in [this suit], as declared by the title, are to stabilize the bituminous coal-mining industry and promote its interstate commerce; to provide for co-operative marketing of bituminous coal; to levy a tax on such coal and provide for a drawback under certain conditions; to declare the production, distribution, and use of such coal to be affected with a national public interest; to conserve the national resources of such coal; to provide for the general welfare, and for other purposes. . . . The constitutional validity of the act is challenged in each of the suits.

[These suits] are cross-writs of certiorari in a stockholder's suit, brought in the Supreme Court of the District of Columbia by Carter against the Carter Coal Company and some of its officers . . . to enjoin the coal company and its officers named from filing an acceptance of the code provided for in said act, from paying any tax imposed upon the coal company under the authority of the act, and from complying with its provisions or the provisions of the code. . . .

Without repeating the long and involved provisions with regard to the fixing of minimum prices, it is enough to say that the act confers the power to fix the minimum price of coal at each and every coal mine in the United States, with such price variations as the board may deem necessary and proper. There is also a provision authorizing the commission, when deemed necessary in the public interest, to establish maximum prices in order to protect the consumer against unreasonably high prices. . . .

The labor provisions of the code, . . . require that in order to effectuate the purposes of the act the district boards and code members shall accept specified conditions contained in the code, among which are the following:

> Employees to be given the right to organize and bargain collectively, through representatives of their own choosing, free from interference, restraint, or coercion of employers or their agents in respect of their concerted activities. . . .

The [lower] court conclude[d] as a matter of law that the bringing of the suit was not premature; that the plaintiff was without legal remedy, and rightly invoked relief in equity; that the labor provisions of the act and code were unconstitutional for reasons stated, but the price-fixing provisions were valid and constitutional; that the labor provisions are separable; and, since the provisions with respect to price-fixing . . . are valid, . . . the act could stand. Therefore, . . . the court denied the relief sought, and dismissed the bill. . . .

[In an omitted portion, the Court described as fallacious the argument that Congress possessed some unenumerated power to legislate in the "national interest" to affect "the health and comfort of the people and the general welfare of the Nation"; instead the federal government was limited to its "specifically enumerated" powers and "such implied powers as are necessary and proper to carry into effect the enumerated powers." The Court rejected the idea that Congress had inherent power to deal with problems affecting the nation as a whole with which the States would not deal.

The Court discussed *Kidd v. Pearson* and *United States v. E.C. Knight Co.*, *supra* § 2.03[1] to illustrate the "distinction between manufacture and commerce."]

That commodities produced or manufactured within a state are intended to be sold or transported outside the state does not render their production or manufacture subject to federal regulation under the commerce clause. . . .

One who produces or manufactures a commodity, subsequently sold and shipped by him in interstate commerce, whether such sale and shipment were originally intended or not, has engaged in two distinct and separate activities. So far as he produces or manufactures a commodity, his business is purely local. So far as he sells and ships, or contracts to sell and ship, the commodity to customers in another state, he engages in interstate commerce. In respect of the former, he is subject only to regulation by the state; in respect of the latter, to regulation only by the federal government. . . . Production is not commerce; but a step in preparation for commerce. . . .

[T]he word "commerce" is the equivalent of the phrase "intercourse for the purposes of trade." Plainly, the incidents leading up to and culminating in the mining of coal do not constitute such intercourse. The employment of men, the fixing of their wages, hours of labor, and working conditions, the bargaining in respect of these things — whether carried on separately or collectively — each and all constitute intercourse for the purposes of production, not of trade. The latter is a thing apart from the relation of employer and employee, which in all producing occupations is purely local in character. Extraction of coal from the mine is the aim and the completed result of local activities. Commerce in the coal mined is not brought into being by force of these activities, but by negotiations, agreements and circumstances entirely apart from production. Mining brings the subject-matter of commerce into existence. Commerce disposes of it.

A consideration of the foregoing, and of many cases which might be added to those already cited, renders inescapable the conclusion that the effect of the labor provisions of the act, including those in respect of minimum wages, wage agreements, collective bargaining, and the Labor Board and its powers, primarily falls upon production and not upon commerce; and confirms the further resulting conclusion that production is a purely local activity. It follows that none of these essential antecedents of production constitutes a transaction in or forms any part of interstate commerce. . . .

That the production of every commodity intended for interstate sale and transportation has some effect upon interstate commerce may be, if it has not already been, freely granted; and we are brought to the final and decisive inquiry, whether here that effect is direct, as the "Preamble" recites, or indirect. . . . The distinction between a direct and an indirect effect turns, not upon the magnitude of either the cause or the effect, but entirely upon the manner in which the effect has been brought about. If the production by one man of a single ton of coal intended for interstate sale and shipment, and actually so sold and shipped, affects interstate commerce indirectly, the effect does not become direct by multiplying the tonnage, or increasing the number of men employed, or adding to the expense or complexities of the business, or by all combined. It is quite true that rules of law are sometimes qualified by considerations of degree, as the government argues. But the matter of degree has no bearing upon the question here, since that question is not — What is the extent of the local activity or condition, or the extent of the effect produced upon interstate commerce? but — What is the relation between the activity or condition and the effect?

Much stress is put upon the evils which come from the struggle between employers and employees over the matter of wages, working conditions, the right of collective bargaining, etc., and the resulting strikes, curtailment, and irregularity of production and effect on prices; and it is insisted that interstate commerce is greatly affected thereby. But, in addition to what has just been said, the conclusive answer is that the evils are all local evils over which the federal government has no legislative control. The relation of employer and employee is a local relation. At common law it is one of the domestic relations. The wages are paid for the doing of local work. Working conditions are obviously local conditions. The employees are not engaged in or about commerce, but exclusively in producing a commodity. And the controversies and evils, which it is the object of the act to regulate and minimize, are local controversies and evils affecting local work undertaken to accomplish that local result. Such effect as they may have upon commerce, however extensive it may be, is secondary and indirect. An increase in the greatness of the effect adds to its importance. It does not alter its character.

The government's contentions in defense of the labor provisions are really disposed of adversely by our decision in the *Schechter Case*. The only perceptible difference between that case and this is that in the *Schechter Case* the federal power was asserted with respect to commodities which had come to rest after their interstate transportation; while here, the case deals with commodities at rest before interstate commerce has begun. That difference is without significance. The federal regulatory power ceases when interstate commercial intercourse ends; and, correlatively, the power does not attach until interstate commercial intercourse begins. There is no basis in law or reason for applying different rules to the two situations. . . . The opinion [in *Schechter*] . . . [called] attention to the fact that if the commerce clause could be construed to reach transactions having an indirect effect upon interstate commerce, the federal authority would embrace practically all the activities of the people, and the authority of the state over its domestic concerns would exist only by sufferance of the federal government. . . . A reading of [*Schechter*] makes clear, what we now declare, that the want of power on the part of the federal government is the same whether the wages, hours of service, and working conditions, and the bargaining about them, are related to production before interstate commerce has begun, or to sale and distribution after it has ended.

[The Court found that the price-fixing provisions of the act and code were not separable from the labor provisions and could not stand independently. It, therefore, held that] [t]he decrees . . . must be reversed and the causes remanded for further consideration in conformity with this opinion. . . .

[CHIEF JUSTICE HUGHES filed a separate opinion concurring with the majority in striking down the regulations of wages as "production . . . which precedes commerce" and "is not itself commerce" and on other grounds. He dissented from the Court's decision insofar as it struck down the price regulations.]

[JUSTICE CARDOZO, joined by JUSTICES BRANDEIS and STONE, dissented.] . . .

First. I am satisfied that the act is within the power of the central government in so far as it provides for minimum and maximum prices upon sales of bituminous coal in the transactions of interstate commerce and in those of intrastate commerce where interstate commerce is directly or intimately affected. . . .

Regulation of prices being an exercise of the commerce power in respect of interstate transactions, the question remains whether it comes within that power as applied to intrastate sales where interstate prices are directly or intimately affected. Mining and agriculture and manufacture are not interstate commerce considered by themselves, yet their relation to that commerce may be such that for the protection of the one there is need to regulate the other. *Schechter Poultry.* . . Sometimes it is said that the relation must be "direct" to bring that power into play. In many circumstances such a description will be sufficiently precise to meet the needs of the occasion. But a great principle of constitutional law is not susceptible of comprehensive statement in an adjective. The underlying thought is merely this, that "the law is not indifferent to considerations of degree." *Schechter Poultry,* concurring opinion, . . . It cannot be indifferent to them without an expansion of the commerce clause that would absorb or imperil the reserved powers of the states. At times, as in the case cited, the waves of causation will have radiated so far that their undulatory motion, if discernible at all, will be too faint or obscure, too broken by cross-currents, to be heeded by the law. In such circumstances the holding is not directed at prices or wages considered in the abstract, but at prices or wages in particular conditions. The relation may be tenuous or the opposite according to the facts. Always the setting of the facts is to be viewed if one would know the closeness of the tie. Perhaps, if one group of adjectives is to be chosen in preference to another, "intimate" and "remote" will be found to be as good as any. At all events, "direct" and "indirect," even if accepted as sufficient must not be read too narrowly. *Cf.* Stone, J., in *Di Santo v. Pennsylvania.* . . . A survey of the cases shows that the words have been interpreted with suppleness of adaptation and flexibility of meaning. The power is as broad as the need that evokes it.

One of the most common and typical instances of a relation characterized as direct has been that between interstate and intrastate rates for carriers by rail where the local rates are so low as to divert business unreasonably from interstate competitors. In such circumstances Congress has the power to protect the business of its carriers against disintegrating encroachments. . . . To be sure, the relation even then may be characterized as indirect if one is nice or over-literal in the choice of words. Strictly speaking, the intrastate rates have a primary effect upon the intrastate traffic and not upon any other, though the repercussions of the competitive system may lead to secondary consequences affecting interstate traffic also. . . . What the cases really mean is that the causal relation in such circumstances is so close and intimate and obvious as to permit it to be called direct without subjecting the word to an unfair or excessive strain. There is a like immediacy here. Within rulings the most orthodox, the prices for intrastate sales of coal have so inescapable a relation to those for interstate sales that a system of regulation for transactions of the one class is necessary to give adequate protection to the system of regulation adopted for the other. The argument is strongly pressed by intervening counsel that this may not be true in all communities or in exceptional conditions. If so, the operators unlawfully affected may show that the act to that extent is invalid as to them. . . .

NOTES

(1) *Carter Coal* represented the culmination of the restricted conception of the commerce power. Along with earlier decisions, it nullified the most important measures of President Franklin D. Roosevelt's New Deal. Earlier decisions had invalidated the National Industrial Recovery Act and the Agricultural Adjustment Act. In *Schechter Poultry Corp. v. United States*, 295 U.S. 495 (1935), referred to by both the majority

and dissenting opinions, the NIRA was held beyond Congressional power as applied to small wholesale poultry dealers in Brooklyn. Their business was held purely local even though the poultry they handled came from outside the state. It did not matter that the business had some effect upon interstate commerce. "The mere fact that there may be a constant flow of commodities into a state does not mean that the flow continues after the property has arrived and has become commingled with the mass of property within the state and is there held solely for local disposition and use. So far as the poultry here in question is concerned, the flow in interstate commerce had ceased. The poultry had come to a permanent rest within the state." *Id.* at 543. *See also United States v. Butler*, 297 U.S. 1 (1936) (agriculture not commerce so immune from federal control).

(2) Critics of *Carter* asserted that this decision left government powerless against the greatest economic catastrophe in our history. Is such an assertion fair to the Supreme Court of the mid-thirties? Did this decision affect the power of the states over productive industries within their own boundaries? Under *Carter*, the economic crisis facing the country was irrelevant. If mining did not constitute commerce, its regulation was not within federal power, unless there was "direct" effect upon interstate commerce. Here, in the Court's view, there was no such "direct" effect. The evils at which the federal statute was aimed were all local evils. The "direct" effect was thus upon the local process of production, not upon commerce.

(3) In *Schechter*, the Court sought to explain the difference between direct effects on commerce (which Congress could reach) and indirect effects (which it could not).

> In determining how far the federal government may go in controlling intrastate transactions upon the ground that they "affect" interstate commerce, there is a necessary and well-established distinction between direct and indirect effects. The precise line can be drawn only as individual cases arise, but the distinction is clear in principle. Direct effects are illustrated by the railroad cases we have cited, as e.g., the effect of failure to use prescribed safety appliances on railroads which are the highways of both interstate and intrastate commerce, injury to an employee engaged in interstate transportation by the negligence of an employee engaged in an intrastate movement, the fixing of rates for intrastate transportation which unjustly discriminate against interstate commerce. But where the effect of intrastate transactions upon interstate commerce is merely indirect, such transactions remain within the domain of state power. If the commerce clause were construed to reach all enterprises and transactions which could be said to have an indirect effect upon interstate commerce, the federal authority would embrace practically all the activities of the people, and the authority of the state over its domestic concerns would exist only by sufferance of the federal government. Indeed, on such a theory, even the development of the state's commercial facilities would be subject to federal control.

Schecter, 295 U.S. at 546. Is the distinction convincing? What purpose does it serve?

(4) At the time, President Roosevelt said the implications of *Schechter* "are much more important than any decision probably since the *Dred Scott* case. . . . The big issue is this. Does this decision mean that the United States Government has no control over any national economic problem?" Frank Freidel, *The Sick Chicken Case, in* QUARRELS THAT HAVE SHAPED THE CONSTITUTION 207 (John A. Garrity ed., 1964).

§ 2.04   COMMERCE POWER: MODERN APPROACHES

[1]   "The Court Retreats to the Constitution"[1]

NATIONAL LABOR RELATIONS BD. v. JONES & LAUGHLIN STEEL CORP.
301 U.S. 1, 57 S. Ct. 615, 81 L. Ed. 893 (1937)

CHIEF JUSTICE HUGHES delivered the opinion of the Court.

In a proceeding under the National Labor Relations Act of 1935, the National Labor Relations Board found that the respondent, Jones & Laughlin Steel Corporation, had violated the Act by engaging in unfair labor practices affecting commerce. The proceeding was instituted by . . . a labor organization. The unfair labor practices charged were that the corporation was discriminating against members of the union with regard to hire and tenure of employment, and was coercing and intimidating its employees in order to interfere with their self-organization. The discriminatory and coercive action alleged was the discharge of certain employees.

The National Labor Relations Board, sustaining the charge, ordered the corporation to cease and desist from such discrimination and coercion, to offer reinstatement to ten of the employees named, to make good their losses in pay, and to post for thirty days notices that the corporation would not discharge or discriminate against members, or those desiring to become members, of the labor union. As the corporation failed to comply, the Board petitioned the Circuit Court of Appeals to enforce the order. The court denied the petition, holding that the order lay beyond the range of federal power. We granted certiorari. . . .

Contesting the ruling of the Board, the respondent argues (1) that the act is in reality a regulation of labor relations and not of interstate commerce; (2) that the act can have no application to the respondent's relations with its production employees because they are not subject to regulation by the federal government. . . .

The facts as to the nature and scope of the business of the Jones & Laughlin Steel Corporation have been found by the Labor Board, and, so far as they are essential to the determination of this controversy, they are not in dispute. The Labor Board has found: The corporation is organized under the laws of Pennsylvania and has its principal office at Pittsburgh. It is engaged in the business of manufacturing iron and steel in plants situated in Pittsburgh and nearby Aliquippa, Pa. It manufactures and distributes a widely diversified line of steel and pig iron, being the fourth largest producer of steel in the United States. With its subsidiaries — nineteen in number — it is a completely integrated enterprise, owning and operating ore, coal and limestone properties, lake and river transportation facilities and terminal railroads located at its manufacturing plants. It owns or controls mines in Michigan and Minnesota. It operates four ore steamships on the Great Lakes, used in the transportation of ore to its factories. It owns coal mines in Pennsylvania. It operates towboats and steam barges used in carrying coal to its factories. It owns limestone properties in various places in Pennsylvania and West Virginia. It owns the Monongahela connecting railroad which connects the plants of the Pittsburgh works and forms an interconnection with the Pennsylvania, New York Central and Baltimore & Ohio Railroad systems. It owns the Aliquippa & Southern Railroad Company which connects the Aliquippa works with the Pittsburgh & Lake Erie, part of the New York Central system. Much of its product is

---

[1] *See* Note (1) after *Jones & Laughlin.*

shipped to its warehouses in Chicago, Detroit, Cincinnati and Memphis — to the last two places by means of its own barges and transportation equipment. In Long Island City, New York, and in New Orleans it operates structural steel fabricating shops in connection with the warehousing of semi-finished materials sent from its works. Through one of its wholly-owned subsidiaries it owns, leases and operates stores, warehouses and yards for the distribution of equipment and supplies for drilling and operating oil and gas wells and for pipe lines, refineries and pumping stations. It has sales offices in twenty cities in the United States and a wholly-owned subsidiary which is devoted exclusively to distributing its product in Canada. Approximately 75 per cent of its product is shipped out of Pennsylvania.

Summarizing these operations, the Labor Board concluded that the works in Pittsburgh and Aliquippa "might be likened to the heart of a self-contained, highly integrated body. They draw in the raw materials from Michigan, Minnesota, West Virginia, Pennsylvania in part through arteries and by means controlled by the respondent; they transform the materials and then pump them out to all parts of the nation through the vast mechanism which the respondent has elaborated."

To carry on the activities of the entire steel industry, 33,000 men mine ore, 44,000 men mine coal, 4,000 men quarry limestone, 16,000 men manufacture coke, 343,000 men manufacture steel, and 83,000 men transport its product. Respondent has about 10,000 employees in its Aliquippa plant, which is located in a community of about 30,000 persons. . . .

We think it clear that the National Labor Relations Act may be construed so as to operate within the sphere of constitutional authority. The jurisdiction conferred upon the Board, and invoked in this instance, is found in § 10(a), which provides:

> Sec. 10(a). The Board is empowered, as hereinafter provided, to prevent any person from engaging in any unfair labor practice . . . affecting commerce.

The critical words of this provision, prescribing the limits of the Board's authority in dealing with the labor practices, are "affecting commerce." The Act specifically defines the "commerce" to which it refers (§ 2(6)):

> The term "commerce" means trade, traffic, commerce, transportation, or communication among the several States, or between the District of Columbia or any Territory of the United States and any State or other Territory, or between any foreign country and any State, Territory, or the District of Columbia, or within the District of Columbia or any Territory, or between points in the same State but through any other State or any Territory or the District of Columbia or any foreign country.

There can be no question that the commerce thus contemplated by the act (aside from that within a Territory or the District of Columbia) is interstate and foreign commerce in the constitutional sense. The act also defines the term "affecting commerce" (§ 2(7)):

> The term "affecting commerce" means in commerce, or burdening or obstructing commerce or the free flow of commerce, or having led or tending to lead to a labor dispute burdening or obstructing commerce or the free flow of commerce.

This definition is one of exclusion as well as inclusion. The grant of authority to the Board does not purport to extend to the relationship between all industrial employees and employers. Its terms do not impose collective bargaining upon all industry regardless of effects upon interstate or foreign commerce. It purports to reach only what may be deemed to burden or obstruct that commerce and, thus qualified, it must be construed as contemplating the exercise of control within constitutional bounds. It is a familiar principle that acts which directly burden or obstruct interstate or foreign commerce, or its free flow, are within the reach of the congressional power. Acts having that effect are not rendered immune because they grow out of labor disputes. . . . It is the effect upon commerce, not the source of the injury, which is the criterion. . . . Whether or not particular action does affect commerce in such a close and intimate fashion as to be subject to federal control, and hence to lie within the authority conferred upon the Board, is left by the statute to be determined as individual cases arise. We are thus to inquire whether in the instant case the constitutional boundary has been passed. . . .

Third. The application of the Act to employees engaged in production. — The principle involved. — Respondent says that, whatever may be said of employees engaged in interstate commerce, the industrial relations and activities in the manufacturing department of respondent's enterprise are not subject to federal regulation. The argument rests upon the proposition that manufacturing in itself is not commerce. *Kidd v. Pearson, Schechter* . . . .

The government distinguishes these cases. The various parts of respondent's enterprise are described as interdependent and as thus involving "a great movement of iron ore, coal and limestone along well-defined paths to the steel mills, thence through them, and thence in the form of steel products into the consuming centers of the country — a definite and well-understood course of business." It is urged that these activities constitute a "stream" or "flow" of commerce, of which the Aliquippa manufacturing plant is the focal point, and that industrial strife at that point would cripple the entire movement. . . .

We do not find it necessary to determine . . . the asserted analogy to the "stream of commerce" cases. The instances in which that metaphor has been used are but particular, and not exclusive, illustrations of the protective power which the Government invokes in support of the present act. The congressional authority to protect interstate commerce from burdens and obstructions is not limited to transactions which can be deemed to be an essential part of a "flow" of interstate or foreign commerce. . . . Although activities may be intrastate in character when separately considered, if they have such a close and substantial relation to interstate commerce that their control is essential or appropriate to protect that commerce from burdens and obstructions, Congress cannot be denied the power to exercise that control.

Undoubtedly the scope of this power must be considered in the light of our dual system of government and may not be extended so as to embrace effects upon interstate commerce so indirect and remote that to embrace them, in view of our complex society, would effectually obliterate the distinction between what is national and what is local and create a completely centralized government. . . . The question is necessarily one of degree. . . .

That intrastate activities, by reason of close and intimate relation to interstate commerce, may fall within federal control is demonstrated in the case of carriers who are engaged in both interstate and intrastate transportation. There federal control has been found essential to secure the freedom of interstate traffic from interference or unjust discrimination and to promote the efficiency of the interstate service. . . .

The close and intimate effect which brings the subject within the reach of federal power may be due to activities in relation to productive industry although the industry when separately viewed is local. . . .

It is thus apparent that the fact that the employees here concerned were engaged in production is not determinative. The question remains as to the effect upon interstate commerce of the labor practice involved. In the *Schechter* case, [*supra* § 2.03[3], Note (1)], we found that the effect there was so remote as to be beyond the federal power. To find "immediacy or directness" there was to find it "almost everywhere," a result inconsistent with the maintenance of our federal system. In the *Carter* case, [*supra* § 2.03[3]], the Court was of the opinion that the provisions of the statute relating to production were invalid upon several grounds, — that there was improper delegation of legislative power, and that the requirements not only went beyond any sustainable measure of protection of interstate commerce but were also inconsistent with due process. These cases are not controlling here.

Fourth. Effects of the unfair labor practice in respondent's enterprise. Giving full weight to respondent's contention with respect to a break in the complete continuity of the "stream of commerce" by reason of respondent's manufacturing operations, the fact remains that the stoppage of those operations by industrial strife would have a most serious effect upon interstate commerce. In view of respondent's far-flung activities, it is idle to say that the effect would be indirect or remote. It is obvious that it would be immediate and might be catastrophic. We are asked to shut our eyes to the plainest facts of our national life and to deal with the question of direct and indirect effects in an intellectual vacuum. Because there may be but indirect and remote effects upon interstate commerce in connection with a host of local enterprises throughout the country, it does not follow that other industrial activities do not have such a close and intimate relation to interstate commerce as to make the presence of industrial strife a matter of the most urgent national concern. When industries organize themselves on a national scale, making their relation to interstate commerce the dominant factor in their activities, how can it be maintained that their industrial labor relations constitute a forbidden field into which Congress may not enter when it is necessary to protect interstate commerce from the paralyzing consequences of industrial war? We have often said that interstate commerce itself is a practical conception. It is equally true that interferences with that commerce must be appraised by a judgment that does not ignore actual experience.

Experience has abundantly demonstrated that the recognition of the right of employees to self-organization and to have representatives of their own choosing for the purpose of collective bargaining is often an essential condition of industrial peace. Refusal to confer and negotiate has been one of the most prolific causes of strife. This is such an outstanding fact in the history of labor disturbances that it is a proper subject of judicial notice and requires no citation of instances. . . .

It is not necessary again to detail the facts as to respondent's enterprise. Instead of being beyond the pale, we think that it presents in a most striking way the close and intimate relation which a manufacturing industry may have to interstate commerce and we have no doubt that Congress had constitutional authority to safeguard the right of respondent's employees to self-organization and freedom in the choice of representatives for collective bargaining. . . .

Our conclusion is that the order of the Board was within its competency and that the act is valid as here applied. The judgment of the Circuit Court of Appeals is reversed and the cause is remanded for further proceedings in conformity with this opinion.

Reversed.

JUSTICE McREYNOLDS delivered the following dissenting opinion [joined by JUSTICES VAN DEVANTER, SUTHERLAND and BUTLER] . . .

Any effect on interstate commerce by the discharge of employees shown here would be indirect and remote in the highest degree, as consideration of the facts will show. In [one of the cases under consideration] ten men out of ten thousand were discharged; in the other cases only a few. The immediate effect in the factor may be to create discontent among all those employed and a strike may follow, which, in turn, may result in reducing production, which ultimately may reduce the volume of goods moving in interstate commerce. By this chain of indirect and progressively remote events we finally reach the evil with which it is said the legislation under consideration undertakes to deal. A more remote and indirect interference with interstate commerce or a more definite invasion of the powers reserved to the states is difficult, if not impossible, to imagine.

The Constitution still recognizes the existence of states with indestructible powers; the Tenth Amendment was supposed to put them beyond controversy.

We are told that Congress may protect the "stream of commerce" and that one who buys raw material without the state, manufactures it therein, and ships the output to another state is in that stream. Therefore it is said he may be prevented from doing anything which may interfere with its flow.

This, too, goes beyond the constitutional limitations heretofore enforced. If a man raises cattle and regularly delivers them to a carrier for interstate shipment, may Congress prescribe the conditions under which he may employ or discharge helpers on the ranch? The products of a mine pass daily into interstate commerce; many things are brought to it from other states. Are the owners and the miners within the power of Congress in respect of the latter's tenure and discharge? May a mill owner be prohibited from closing his factory or discontinuing his business because so to do would stop the flow of products to and from his plant in interstate commerce? May employees in a factory be restrained from quitting work in a body because this will close the factory and thereby stop the flow of commerce? May arson of a factory be made a federal offense whenever this would interfere with such flow? If the business cannot continue with the existing wage scale, may Congress command a reduction? If the ruling of the Court just announced is adhered to, these questions suggest some of the problems certain to arise.

And if this theory of a continuous "stream of commerce" as now defined is correct, will it become the duty of the federal government hereafter to suppress every strike which by possibility it may cause a blockade in that stream? . . . Moreover, since Congress has intervened, are labor relations between most manufacturers and their employees removed from all control by the state? . . .

Whatever effect any cause of discontent may ultimately have upon commerce is far too indirect to justify congressional regulation. Almost anything — marriage, birth, death — may in some fashion affect commerce.

That Congress has power by appropriate means, not prohibited by the Constitution, to prevent direct and material interference with the conduct of interstate commerce is settled doctrine. But the interference struck at must be direct and material, not some mere possibility contingent on wholly uncertain events; and there must be no impairment of rights guaranteed. A state by taxation on property may indirectly but seriously affect the cost of transportation; it may not lay a direct tax upon the receipts from interstate transportation. The first is an indirect effect, the other direct.

NOTES

(1) The title of this subsection is taken from Justice Jackson's book, THE STRUGGLE FOR JUDICIAL SUPREMACY (1941), specifically from the title Jackson gave to the chapter describing *Jones & Laughlin*. In his book, Justice Jackson termed *Jones & Laughlin* "the most far-reaching victory ever won on behalf of labor in the Supreme Court." JACKSON, THE STRUGGLE FOR JUDICIAL SUPREMACY 214 (1941). The National Labor Relations Act of 1935 was a comprehensive enactment regulating labor relations throughout the economy. It guaranteed the right of workers to organize collectively in

unions and made it unlawful for employers to interfere with that right or to refuse to bargain collectively with the representatives chosen by their employees. In *Jones & Laughlin*, the Labor Act was applied to protect the rights of workers producing iron and steel products.

(2) Government attorneys presented *Jones & Laughlin* and its companion cases in part as current of commerce cases in which materials flow into a state, are transformed, and then transported to purchasers in other states. *See* Peter H. Irons, The New Deal Lawyers 272-89 (1982). Could *Jones & Laughlin* have been decided on this basis?

(3) The conventional historical account depicts Justice Roberts' "switch in time" in *Jones & Laughlin*, and in contemporary cases upholding other New Deal measures, as motivated by President Roosevelt's court-packing plan. In essence, in February, 1937, three months after his landslide reelection, Roosevelt proposed that Congress permit the President to appoint to the Court an additional Justice for each member of the court who had not retired within six months after turning seventy. The provision could have allowed FDR to add six members to the Court, thereby securing a comfortable majority on it. Although the proposal engendered such opposition that its defeat became inevitable, many historians have concluded that it bullied the Court into submission, in part by achieving Roberts' shift. Professor Barry Cushman's historical research and reasoning have cast significant doubt on the conventional account. Professor Cushman points out that; a) some of Roberts' "switches" occurred in votes the Court took before Roosevelt's plan was known; b) despite the Democrats' huge majority in the Senate, it was never clear that a majority supported the court-packing plan; c) the plan's supporters lacked the 2/3 support needed to stop a Senate filibuster against the plan; d) the plan angered some Justices, and induced Justices Sutherland and Van Devanter to defer retirement, and thus might have been expected to cause other Justices to fight rather than switch; and e) if the Court was so sensitive to the plan in deciding its cases, rather than to doctrinal consideration, it might have adopted different judicial strategies like 1) deciding *Jones & Laughlin* on the narrower current of commerce doctrine; 2) ruling for the government on some, but not all, of the NLRA cases; or 3) deferring these cases until the plan was defeated. *See* Cushman, Rethinking the New Deal Court 11-32 (1998).

(4) In *Jones & Laughlin*, Chief Justice Hughes states that the "constitutional boundary" of the commerce power turns on whether the regulated action affects commerce "in such a close and intimate fashion." 301 U.S. at 31-32. Where does the Court find this test? Does this new test suggest that the court majority had become convinced that the direct/indirect approach was unworkable?

(5) Professor Cushman pointed out that in *Jones & Laughlin* and its companion cases, Chief Justice Hughes placed the manufacturing enterprise involved within "a current of interstate commerce and then proceeded to characterize the enterprise or the industry of which it was a part in the broad language of a business affected with a public interest." Cushman, Rethinking the New Deal Court 173 (1998). Why does the Court include so much current of commerce imagery if the decision of the case ultimately turns on the "close and intimate" test?

(6) How does the shift from the direct/indirect doctrine of the dual federalism approach, to the "close and intimate" approach affect the judicial role in overseeing commerce clause cases? Notice how much attention Chief Justice Hughes pays to developing the factual background in the case. Does the new approach commit the Court to fact-intensive, case by case adjudication?

(7) *Jones & Laughlin* made clear that manufacturing was not necessarily excluded from the reach of the commerce power. But the Court did not immediately hold that Congress could reach all productive activity. In *Mulford v. Smith*, 307 U.S. 38 (1939),

the Court upheld the Agricultural Adjustment Act of 1938, which allowed the Secretary of Agriculture to set marketing quotes for certain crops. "The statute does not purport to control production," wrote Justice Roberts. Rather, the statute addressed *marketing* at the marketing warehouse, "the throat" where the crop entered the current of commerce. *Id.* at 47.

(8) Along with *Jones & Laughlin*, the Court decided *National Labor Relations Bd. v. Friedman-Harry Marks Clothing Co.*, 301 U.S. 58 (1937). The clothing company there was "a typical small manufacturing concern which produce[d] less than one-half of one per cent of the men's clothing produced in the United States and employ[ed] 800 of the 150,000 workmen engaged therein." *Jones & Laughlin*, 301 U.S. at 87 (McReynolds, J., dissenting). Although the interruption of such a business would hardly cripple interstate commerce, Marks' plant was within a current of interstate commerce and clothing was a significant industry. "The business of the Company," asserted a dissenting Justice, "is so small that to close its factory would have no direct or material effect upon the volume of interstate commerce in clothing." *Id.* at 94. The Court ruled that *Jones & Laughlin* justified federal regulation.

(9) In *National Labor Relations Bd. v. Fainblatt*, 306 U.S. 601 (1939), the Court stated expressly that the operation of the Commerce Clause does not depend on any particular volume of commerce affected. The company there was an even smaller clothing manufacturer, employing from 60 to 200 employees. The Court held that the smallness of the volume of commerce affected is without significance: "[C]ommerce may be affected in the same manner and to the same extent in proportion to its volume, whether it be great or small." *Id.* at 607. According to the *Fainblatt* dissent, "[i]f the plant presently employed only one woman who stitched one skirt during each week . . ., Congressional power would extend to the enterprise, according to the logic of the Court's opinion." *Id.* at 610 (McReynolds, J., dissenting). Note that the Court characterized *Fainblatt*, too, as within a stream of interstate commerce.

[2]   The Commerce Clause from the 1940s: *Darby* and *Wickard*

UNITED STATES v. DARBY
312 U.S. 100, 61 S. Ct. 451, 85 L. Ed. 609 (1941)

JUSTICE STONE delivered the opinion of the Court.

The two principal questions raised by the record in this case are, first, whether Congress has constitutional power to prohibit the shipment in interstate commerce of lumber manufactured by employees whose wages are less than a prescribed minimum or whose weekly hours of labor at that wage are greater than a prescribed maximum, and, second, whether it has power to prohibit the employment of workmen in the production of goods "for interstate commerce" at other than prescribed wages and hours. . . .

The Fair Labor Standards Act set up a comprehensive legislative scheme for preventing the shipment in interstate commerce of certain products and commodities produced in the United States under labor conditions as respects wages and hours which fail to conform to standards set up by the Act. . . .

The indictment charges that appellee is engaged, in the state of Georgia, in the business of acquiring raw materials, which he manufactures into finished lumber with the intent, when manufactured, to ship it in interstate commerce to customers outside the state, and that he does in fact so ship a large part of the lumber so produced. There are numerous counts charging appellee with the shipment in interstate commerce from Georgia to points outside the state of lumber in the production of which, for interstate commerce, appellee has employed workmen at less than the prescribed minimum wage or more than the prescribed maximum hours without payment to them of any wage for overtime. Other counts charge the employment by appellee of workmen in the production of lumber for interstate commerce at wages of less than 25 cents an hour or for more than the maximum hours per week without payment to them of the prescribed overtime wage. . . .

The demurrer, so far as now relevant to the appeal, challenged the validity of the Fair Labor Standards Act under the Commerce Clause. . . .

The prohibition of shipment of the proscribed goods in interstate commerce. Section 15(a)(1) prohibits, and the indictment charges, the shipment in interstate commerce, of goods produced for interstate commerce by employees whose wages and hours of employment do not conform to the requirements of the Act. Since this section is not violated unless the commodity shipped has been produced under labor conditions prohibited by § 6 and § 7, the only question arising under the commerce clause with respect to such shipments is whether Congress has the constitutional power to prohibit them.

While manufacture is not of itself interstate commerce the shipment of manufactured goods interstate is such commerce and the prohibition of such shipment by Congress is indubitably a regulation of the commerce. The power to regulate commerce is the power "to prescribe the rule by which commerce is to be governed." *Gibbons v. Ogden,* [*supra* § 2.02]. It extends not only to those regulations which aid, foster, and protect the commerce, but embraces those which prohibit it. . . . It is conceded that the power of Congress to prohibit transportation in interstate commerce includes noxious articles, . . . stolen articles, . . . kidnapped persons . . . and articles such as intoxicating liquor or convict made goods, traffic in which is forbidden or restricted by the laws of the state of destination. . . .

But it is said that the present prohibition falls within the scope of none of these categories; that while the prohibition is nominally a regulation of the commerce its motive or purpose is regulation of wages and hours of persons engaged in manufacture, the control of which has been reserved to the states and upon which Georgia and some of the states of destination have placed no restriction; that the effect of the present statute is not to exclude the prescribed articles from interstate commerce in aid of state regulation . . . but instead, under the guise of a regulation of interstate commerce, it undertakes to regulate wages and hours within the state contrary to the policy of the state which has elected to leave them unregulated.

The power of Congress over interstate commerce "is complete in itself, may be exercised to its utmost extent, and acknowledges no limitations, other than are prescribed by the Constitution." *Gibbons v. Ogden, supra.* . . . That power can neither be enlarged nor diminished by the exercise or non-exercise of state power. . . . Congress, following its own conception of public policy concerning the restrictions which may appropriately be imposed on interstate commerce, is free to exclude from the commerce articles whose use in the states for which they are destined it may conceive to be injurious to the public health, morals, or welfare, even though the State has not sought to regulate their use. . . .

Such regulation is not a forbidden invasion of state power merely because either its motive or its consequence is to restrict the use of articles of commerce within the States of destination and is not prohibited unless by other Constitutional provisions. It is no objection to the assertion of the power to regulate interstate commerce that its exercise is attended by the same incidents which attend the exercise of the police power of the states. . . .

The motive and purpose of the present regulation is plainly to make effective the

Congressional conception of public policy that interstate commerce should not be made the instrument of competition in the distribution of goods produced under substandard labor conditions, which competition is injurious to the commerce and to the states from and to which the commerce flows. The motive and purpose of a regulation of interstate commerce are matters for the legislative judgment upon the exercise of which the Constitution places no restriction and over which the courts are given no control. . . . Whatever their motive and purpose, regulations of commerce which do not infringe some constitutional prohibition are within the plenary power conferred on Congress by the Commerce Clause. Subject only to that limitation, presently to be considered, we conclude that the prohibition of the shipment interstate of goods produced under the forbidden substandard labor conditions is within the constitutional authority of Congress.

In the more than a century which has elapsed since the decision of *Gibbons v. Ogden*, these principles of constitutional interpretation have been so long and repeatedly recognized by this Court as applicable to the Commerce Clause, that there would be little occasion for repeating them now were it not for the decision of this Court twenty-two years ago in *Hammer v. Dagenhart*, [*supra* § 2.03[2]]. In that case it was held by a bare majority of the Court over the powerful and now classic dissent of Justice Holmes setting forth the fundamental issues involved, that Congress was without power to exclude the products of child labor from interstate commerce. The reasoning and conclusion of the Court's opinion there cannot be reconciled with the conclusion which we have reached, that the power of Congress under the Commerce Clause is plenary to exclude any article from interstate commerce subject only to the specific prohibitions of the Constitution.

Hammer v. Dagenhart has not been followed. The distinction on which the decision was rested that Congressional power to prohibit interstate commerce is limited to articles which in themselves have some harmful or deleterious property — a distinction which was novel when made and unsupported by any provision of the Constitution — has long since been abandoned. The thesis of the opinion that the motive of the prohibition or its effect to control in some measure the use or production within the states of the article thus excluded from the commerce can operate to deprive the regulation of its constitutional authority has long since ceased to have force. . . .

The conclusion is inescapable that *Hammer v. Dagenhart* was a departure from the principles which have prevailed in the interpretation of the commerce clause both before and since the decision and that such vitality, as a precedent, as it then had has long since been exhausted. It should be and now is overruled.

Validity of the wage and hour requirements. Section 15(a)(2) and § § 6 and 7 require employers to conform to the wage and hour provisions with respect to all employees engaged in the production of goods for interstate commerce. As appellee's employees are not alleged to be "engaged in interstate commerce" the validity of the prohibition turns on the question whether the employment, under other than the prescribed labor standards, of employees engaged in the production of goods for interstate commerce is so related to the commerce and so affects it as to be within the reach of the power of Congress to regulate it. . . .

The power of Congress over interstate commerce is not confined to the regulation of commerce among the states. It extends to those activities intrastate which so affect interstate commerce or the exercise of the power of Congress over it as to make regulation of them appropriate means to the attainment of a legitimate end, the exercise of the granted power of Congress to regulate interstate commerce. . . .

A recent example is the National Labor Relations Act, 29 U.S.C.A. § 151 *et seq.*, for the regulation of employer and employee relations in industries in which strikes, induced by unfair labor practices named in the Act, tend to disturb or obstruct interstate commerce. *See National Labor Relations Board v. Jones & Laughlin Steel Corp*, [*supra* § 2.04[1]].

But long before the adoption of the National Labor Relations Act, this Court had many times held that the power of Congress to regulate interstate commerce extends to the regulation through legislative action of activities intrastate which have a substantial effect on the commerce or the exercise of the Congressional power over it. . . .

Congress, having by the present Act adopted the policy of excluding from interstate commerce all goods produced for the commerce which do not conform to the specified labor standards, it may choose the means reasonably adapted to the attainment of the permitted end, even though they involve control of intrastate activities. Such legislation has often been sustained with respect to powers, other than the commerce power granted to the national government, when the means chosen, although not themselves within the granted power, were nevertheless deemed appropriate aids to the accomplishment of some purpose within an admitted power of the national government. . . .

We think also that § 15(a)(2), now under consideration, is sustainable independently of § 15(a)(1), which prohibits shipment or transportation of the proscribed goods. As we have said the evils aimed at by the Act are the spread of substandard labor conditions through the use of the facilities of interstate commerce for competition by the goods so produced with those produced under the prescribed or better labor conditions; and the consequent dislocation of the commerce itself caused by the impairment or destruction of local businesses by competition made effective through interstate commerce. The Act is thus directed at the suppression of a method or kind of competition in interstate commerce which it has in effect condemned as "unfair", as the Clayton Act, 38 Stat. 730, has condemned other "unfair methods of competition" made effective through interstate commerce. . . .

The means adopted by § 15(a)(2) for the protection of interstate commerce by the suppression of the production of the condemned goods for interstate commerce is so related to the commerce and so affects it as to be within the reach of the commerce power. . . . Congress, to attain its objective in the suppression of nationwide competition in interstate commerce by goods produced under substandard labor conditions, has made no distinction as to the volume or amount of shipments in the commerce or of production for commerce by any particular shipper or producer. It recognized that in present day industry, competition by a small part may affect the whole and that the total effect of the competition of many small producers may be great. . . .

Our conclusion is unaffected by the Tenth Amendment which provides: "The powers not delegated to the United States by the Constitution, nor prohibited by it to the States, are reserved to the States respectively, or to the people." The amendment states but a truism that all is retained which has not been surrendered. There is nothing in the history of its adoption to suggest that it was more than declaratory of the relationship between the national and state governments as it had been established by the Constitution before the amendment or that its purpose was other than to allay fears that the new national government might seek to exercise powers not granted, and that the states might not be able to exercise fully their reserved powers. . . .

From the beginning and for many years the amendment has been construed as not depriving the national government of authority to resort to all means for the exercise of a granted power which are appropriate and plainly adapted to the permitted end. . . .

Reversed.

NOTES

(1) *Darby* returned to Marshall's conception of the power to regulate. Justice Stone invokes Marshall's definition of the power as that "to prescribe the rule by which commerce is governed." Under that definition, can the judiciary probe legislative motive? Justice Joseph Story, a leading member of the Marshall Court, wrote on the commerce power: "Now, the motive of the grant of the power is not even alluded to in the constitution." JOSEPH STORY, COMMENTARIES ON THE CONSTITUTION OF THE UNITED STATES § 1089 (2d ed. 1851). May Congress exercise its commerce power for any reason? Consider Marshall's famous statement: "This power . . . is complete in itself, may be exercised to its utmost extent, and acknowledges no limitations, other than are prescribed in the constitution." *Gibbons v. Ogden, supra* § 2.02.

(2) *Darby* connects the two key words in the Commerce Clause: the noun "commerce" and the verb "regulate." The prohibition of interstate shipments was a valid regulation of commerce (i.e., it prescribed the rule by which commerce was to be governed) even though Congress passed the measure to control wages and hours in production. The Court also upheld the statute's requirement that employees engaged in production of goods for interstate commerce conform to the federal wages and hours standards.

In part, the Court says that the commerce power extends to activities the regulation of which are "appropriate means to the attainment of a legitimate end, the exercise of the granted power of Congress to regulate interstate commerce." *Darby*, 312 U.S. at 118. Does the Court need to find this power in the commerce clause? Could it find it elsewhere in Article I? Does the Court's reasoning support federal regulation of all local activities where their products can be brought within the commerce-prohibiting technique?

(3) *Perez v. United States*, 402 U.S. 146 (1971), well illustrates the *Darby* commerce-prohibiting technique. Perez, a loan shark, was convicted of violating a federal law prohibiting "extortionate credit transactions" even though he conducted his business entirely in Brooklyn, N.Y. Perez claimed his loan sharking was "a traditionally local activity." According to the Court, however, "[e]xtortionate credit transactions, though purely intrastate, may in the judgment of Congress affect interstate commerce. . . . [L]oan sharking in its national setting is one way organized interstate crime holds its guns to the heads of the poor and the rich alike and syphons funds from numerous localities to finance its national operations." *Id.* at 154, 157. The *Perez* key "may be found in the difficulty of proving in each individual case that the loan shark had an interstate connection even when it existed." In such a case, the *Darby* commerce-prohibiting technique permits Congress to prohibit all loan sharking (including purely intrastate loan sharking) as "a means reasonably adapted to the attainment of the permitted end" of prohibiting interstate loan sharking. *See* Robert Stern, *The Commerce Clause Revisited — The Federalization of Intrastate Crime*, 15 ARIZ. L. REV. 271, 278-79 (1973).

(4) Chief Justice Hughes began the Court's consideration of *Darby* at conference with a long discussion of the case. Before the Chief Justice concluded his lengthy presentation, Justice Murphy recorded in his notes "McReynolds is sound asleep, mouth open — and Stone is dozing away!" Although Justice McReynolds passed immediately after the Chief Justice finished, Justice Stone apparently awoke sufficiently to articulate much of the basic rationale which later found its way into his

opinion for the Court. *See* THE COURT IN CONFERENCE (1940-1985), at 219 (Del Dickson ed., 2001).

(5) In *Kirschbaum v. Walling*, 316 U.S. 517 (1942), the Court held that the FLSA included employees engaged in the maintenance and operation of a building in which goods for interstate commerce were produced. The Court deemed such employees necessary for the production of goods for commerce: "Without light and heat and power the tenants could not engage, as they do, in the production of goods for interstate commerce. The maintenance of a safe, habitable building is indispensable to that activity." *Id.* at 524. The Fair Labor Standards Act has been held applicable to employees of a window-cleaning company, the greater part of whose work was done on the windows of people engaged in interstate commerce, *Martino v. Michigan Window Cleaning Co.*, 327 U.S. 173 (1946); employees putting in standby time in the auxiliary fire-fighting service of an employer engaged in interstate commerce, *Armour & Co. v. Wantock*, 323 U.S. 126 (1944); and members of a rotary drilling crew, employed within a state by an independent contractor in partially drilling oil wells, some of whose product "ultimately found its way into interstate commerce," *Warren-Bradshaw Drilling Co. v. Hall*, 317 U.S. 88, 91 (1942).

(6) The Court that decided *Darby* differed in composition from that which decided *Jones & Laughlin*. The four dissenters had died or retired to be replaced by younger Justices educated at a later time who had been associated with the New Deal.

WICKARD v. FILBURN
317 U.S. 111, 63 S. Ct. 82, 87 L. Ed. 122 (1942)

JUSTICE JACKSON delivered the opinion of the Court.

The appellee filed his complaint against the Secretary of Agriculture of the United States, three members of the County Agricultural Conservation Committee for Montgomery County, Ohio, and a member of the State Agricultural Conservation Committee for Ohio. He sought to enjoin enforcement against himself of the marketing penalty imposed by the amendment of May 26, 1941, to the Agricultural Adjustment Act of 1938, upon that part of his 1941 wheat crop which was available for marketing in excess of the marketing quota established for his farm. He also sought a declaratory judgment that the wheat marketing quota provisions of the Act as amended and applicable to him were unconstitutional because not sustainable under the Commerce Clause. . . .

The appellee for many years past has owned and operated a small farm in Montgomery County, Ohio, maintaining a herd of dairy cattle, selling milk, raising poultry, and selling poultry and eggs. It has been his practice to raise a small acreage of winter wheat, sown in the Fall and harvested in the following July; . . . to feed part to poultry and livestock on the farm, some of which is sold; to use some in making flour for home consumption; and to keep the rest for the following seeding. The intended disposition of the crop here involved has not been expressly stated.

In July of 1940, pursuant to the Agricultural Adjustment Act of 1938, as then amended, there were established for the appellee's 1941 crop a wheat acreage allotment of 11.1 acres and a normal yield of 20.1 bushels of wheat an acre. He was given notice of such allotment in July of 1940 before the Fall planting of his 1941 crop of wheat, and again in July of 1941, before it was harvested. He sowed, however, 23 acres, and harvested from his 11.9 acres of excess acreage 239 bushels, which under the terms of the Act as amended on May 26, 1941, constituted farm marketing excess, subject to a penalty of 49 cents a bushel, or $117.11 in all. . . .

The court below . . . permanently enjoined appellants from collecting a marketing penalty of more than 15 cents a bushel on the farm marketing excess of appellee's 1941 wheat crop, from subjecting appellee's entire 1941 crop to a lien for the payment of the penalty, and from collecting a 15-cent penalty except in accordance with the provisions of § 339 of the Act as that section stood prior to the amendment of May 26, 1941. The Secretary and his co-defendants have appealed. . . .

It is urged that under the Commerce Clause of the Constitution, Article I, § 8, clause 3, Congress does not possess the power it has in this instance sought to exercise. The question would merit little consideration since our decision in *United States v. Darby*, 312 U.S. 100 [*supra* § 2.04[2]], sustaining the federal power to regulate production of goods for commerce except for the fact that this Act extends federal regulation to production not intended in any part for commerce but wholly for consumption on the farm. The Act includes a definition of "market" and its derivatives so that as related to wheat in addition to its conventional meaning it also means to dispose of "by feeding (in any form) to poultry or livestock which, or the products of which, are sold, bartered, or exchanged, or to be so disposed of." Hence, marketing quotas not only embrace all that may be sold without penalty but also what may be consumed on the premises. Wheat produced on excess acreage is designated as "available for marketing" as so defined and the penalty is imposed thereon. Penalties do not depend upon whether any part of the wheat either within or without the quota is sold or intended to be sold. . . .

At the beginning Chief Justice Marshall described the federal commerce power with a breadth never yet exceeded. *Gibbons v. Ogden*, [*supra* § 2.02]. He made emphatic the embracing and penetrating nature of this power by warning that effective restraints on its exercise must proceed from political rather than from judicial processes.

For nearly a century, however, decisions of this Court under the Commerce Clause dealt rarely with questions of what Congress might do in the exercise of its granted power under the Clause and almost entirely with the permissibility of state activity which it was claimed discriminated against or burdened interstate commerce. During this period there was perhaps little occasion for the affirmative exercise of the commerce power, and the influence of the Clause on American life and law was a negative one, resulting almost wholly from its operation as a restraint upon the powers of the states. In discussion and decision the point of reference instead of being what was "necessary and proper" to the exercise by Congress of its granted power, was often some concept of sovereignty thought to be implicit in the status of statehood. Certain activities such as "production," "manufacturing," and "mining" were occasionally said to be within the province of state governments and beyond the power of Congress under the Commerce Clause. . . .

The Court's recognition of the relevance of the economic effects in the application of the Commerce Clause . . . has made the mechanical application of legal formulas no longer feasible. Once an economic measure of the reach of the power granted to Congress in the Commerce Clause is accepted, questions of federal power cannot be decided simply by finding the activity in question to be "production" nor can consideration of its economic effects be foreclosed by calling them "indirect." . . .

Whether the subject of the regulation in question was "production," "consumption," or "marketing" is, therefore, not material for purposes of deciding the question of federal power before us. That an activity is of local character may help in a doubtful case to determine whether Congress intended to reach it. The same consideration might help in determining whether in the absence of Congressional action it would be permissible for the state to exert its power on the subject matter, even though in so doing it to some degree affected interstate commerce. But even if appellee's activity be local and though it may not be regarded as commerce, it may still, whatever its nature, be reached by Congress if it exerts a substantial economic effect on interstate commerce and this irrespective of whether such effect is what might at some earlier time have been defined as "direct" or "indirect.". . .

The effect of consumption of homegrown wheat on interstate commerce is due to the fact that it constitutes the most variable factor in the disappearance of the wheat crop. Consumption on the farm where grown appears to vary in an amount greater than 20 per cent of average production. The total amount of wheat consumed as food varies but relatively little, and use as seed is relatively constant.

The maintenance by government regulation of a price for wheat undoubtedly can be accomplished as effectively by sustaining or increasing the demand as by limiting the supply. The effect of the statute before us is to restrict the amount which may be produced for market and the extent as well to which one may forestall resort to the market by producing to meet his own needs. That appellee's own contribution to the demand for wheat may be trivial by itself is not enough to remove him from the scope of federal regulation where, as here, his contribution, taken together with that of many others similarly situated, is far from trivial. . . .

It is well established by decisions of this Court that the power to regulate commerce includes the power to regulate the prices at which commodities in that commerce are dealt in and practices affecting such prices. One of the primary purposes of the Act in question was to increase the market price of wheat and to that end to limit the volume thereof that could affect the market. It can hardly be denied that a factor of such volume and variability as home-consumed wheat would have a substantial influence on price and market conditions. This may arise because being in marketable condition such wheat overhangs the market and if induced by rising prices tends to flow into the market and check price increases. But if we assume that it is never marketed, it supplies a need of the man who grew it which would otherwise be reflected by purchases in the open market. Homegrown wheat in this sense competes with wheat in commerce. The stimulation of commerce is a use of the regulatory function quite as definitely as prohibitions or restrictions thereon. This record leaves us in no doubt that Congress may properly have considered that wheat consumed on the farm where grown if wholly outside the scheme of regulation would have a substantial effect in defeating and obstructing its purpose to stimulate trade therein at increased prices. . . .

Reversed.

NOTES

(1) *Wickard* is often portrayed as following naturally from *Jones & Laughlin. See, e.g.,* David P. Currie, *The Constitution in the Supreme Court: The New Deal, 1931-1940,* 54 U. Chi. L. Rev. 504, 545-46 (1987) (*Wickard* "was only to write the epitaph; constitutional federalism had died in 1937"). Is this view persuasive? Is *Wickard* really consistent with cases like *Jones & Laughlin* or does it mark a new doctrinal departure? Did the Court cast *Wickard* in the current of interstate commerce language it deployed in *Jones & Laughlin*? What inference should be drawn from the fact that Justice Jackson's opinion does not cite *Jones & Laughlin*?

(2) Compare the doctrinal test used in *Wickard* with that used five years earlier in *Jones & Laughlin.* What impact does this new test have on the judicial role in commerce clause cases? Note that Justice Jackson credits Chief Justice Marshall as warning "that effective restraints" on the commerce power "must proceed from political rather than from judicial processes."

(3) Professor Barry Cushman's research suggests that *Wickard* did not follow

inevitably from *Jones & Laughlin*. Justice Jackson's early opinion drafts remanded the case to the federal district court for further factual findings to determine whether the regulated home consumption of wheat substantially affected interstate commerce. This treatment assumed the judiciary would ultimately decide the issue; not surprisingly, the drafts cited *Jones & Laughlin*. After further reflection, the Court decided to set *Wickard* for reargument the following term regarding the scope of commerce power rather than remanding it. Over the summer, Justice Jackson considered three alternative approaches to determine whether the commerce clause allowed the regulation under consideration in *Wickard*. The Court could: (a) find production for home consumption within the exclusive control of the state á la *E.C. Knight*; (b) find such activity within state control unless the Court found federal regulation necessary to protect the commerce power; or (c) find it within state control unless Congress decided to regulate it. Professor Cushman writes, the "history of failure to frame an adequate standard caused Jackson to despair of the enterprise" and ultimately, with the unanimous agreement of his colleagues, to reject *Jones & Laughlin* and adopt the third approach in *Wickard*. See CUSHMAN, RETHINKING THE NEW DEAL COURT 208-225 (1998).

(4) Shortly before *Wickard v. Filburn*, the Court decided *United States v. Wrightwood Dairy Co.*, 315 U.S. 110 (1942), which involved the constitutionality of federal regulation of the price of milk produced and sold interstate in Illinois. The Supreme Court upheld the regulation since intrastate milk competed with milk transported from outside the state. The power to regulate interstate milk confers authority to regulate local milk because the latter competes with the former. Is *Wrightwood* justified by the *Shreveport* doctrine, *supra* § 2.03[1], Note (7)? Did *Wrightwood* compel *Wickard* or are they distinguishable?

(5) In *Mabee v. White Plains Publ'g Co.*, 327 U.S. 178 (1946), the employer was a newspaper with a circulation of about 10,000 copies, of which only about of 1 per cent, (a mere 45 copies) circulated out-of-state. The Supreme Court held the paper subject to the FLSA. Justice Murphy, in dissent asserted: "In my opinion, a company that produces 99-1/2% of its products for local commerce is essentially and realistically a local business." *Id.* at 186. Is Justice Murphy correct? Would the paper affect interstate commerce even if it had no out-of-state circulation? Why?

(6) Other post *Darby* and *Wickard* cases marked the expansion of commerce power. In *United States v. Sullivan*, 332 U.S. 689 (1948), the Court affirmed the conviction of a small localized pharmacist who had improperly sold a few pills without a label. The pharmacist was subject to a federal statute predicated on the commerce power because the pills had crossed a state line in coming to the wholesaler, who later sold them to the pharmacist. Similarly, in *Scarborough v. United States*, 431 U.S. 563 (1977) the Court upheld a federal prohibition of possession by a convicted felon of a gun which had at some prior time been in or affected commerce.

(7) The difficulty of formulating judicial standards under the Commerce Clause and faith in the political process to protect states, are arguments used in support of deferential review in Comerce Clause cases. On the other hand, some question Congress' ability to restrain itself and believe treating the Commerce Clause as a political question conflicts with the concept of judicial review announced in *Marbury*. See Grant S. Nelson & Robert J. Pushaw, Jr., *Rethinking the Commerce Clause: Applying First Principles to Uphold Federal Commercial Regulations but Preserve State Control Over Social Issues*, 85 IOWA L. REV. 1, 103-05 (1999).

(8) Two children, Rachel and Josh, set up a neighborhood lemonade stand. After *Wickard*, could Congress regulate their prices? Does it matter that their stand has, at most, a trivial effect on the economy?

[3]   Commerce and Civil Rights

HEART OF ATLANTA MOTEL, INC. v. UNITED STATES
379 U.S. 241, 85 S. Ct. 348, 13 L. Ed. 2d 258 (1964)

MR. JUSTICE CLARK delivered the opinion of the Court.

This is a declaratory judgment action, 28 U.S.C. § 2201 and § 2202 (1958 ed.) attacking the constitutionality of Title II of the Civil Rights Act of 1964, 78 Stat. 241, 241. In addition to declaratory relief the complaint sought an injunction restraining the enforcement of the Act and damages against appellees based on allegedly resulting injury in the event compliance was required. Appellees counterclaimed for enforcement under § 206(a) of the Act and asked for a three-judge district court under § 206(b). A three-judge court, empaneled under § 206(b) as well as 28 U.S.C. § 2282 (1958 ed.) sustained the validity of the Act and issued a permanent injunction on appellees' counterclaim restraining appellant from continuing to violate the Act. . . . We affirm the judgment.

1. The Factual Background and Contentions of the Parties.

The case comes here on admissions and stipulated facts. Appellant owns and operates the Heart of Atlanta Motel which has 216 rooms available to transient guests. The motel is located on Courtland Street, two blocks from downtown Peachtree Street. It is readily accessible to interstate highways 75 and 85 and state highways 23 and 41. Appellant solicits patronage from outside the State of Georgia through various national advertising media, including magazines of national circulation; it maintains over 50 billboards and highway signs within the State, soliciting patronage for the motel; it accepts convention trade from outside Georgia and approximately 75% of its registered guests are from out of State. Prior to passage of the Act the motel had followed a practice of refusing to rent rooms to Negroes, and it alleged that it intended to continue to do so. In an effort to perpetuate that policy this suit was filed. . . .

3. Title II of the Act.

This Title is divided into seven sections beginning with § 201(a) which provides that:

> All persons shall be entitled to the full and equal enjoyment of the goods, services, facilities, privileges, advantages, and accommodations of any place of public accommodation, as defined in this section, without discrimination or segregation on the ground of race, color, religion, or national origin.

There are listed in § 201(b) four classes of business establishments, each of which "serves the public" and "is a place of public accommodation" within the meaning of § 201(a) "if its operations affect commerce, or if discrimination or segregation by it is supported by State action." The covered establishments are:

> (1) any inn, hotel, motel, or other establishment which provides lodging to transient guests, other than an establishment located within a building which contains not more than five rooms for rent or hire and which is actually occupied by the proprietor of such establishment as his residence;

> (2) any restaurant, cafeteria . . . (not here involved);

> (3) any motion picture house . . . (not here involved);

> (4) any establishment . . . which is physically located within the premises of any establishment otherwise covered by this subsection, or . . . within the premises of which is physically located any such covered establishment- . . . [not here involved].

Section 201(c) defines the phrase "affect commerce" as applied to the above establishments. It first declares that "any inn, hotel, motel, or other establishment which provides lodging to transient guests" affects commerce per se. . . . Restaurants . . . affect commerce only if they serve or offer to serve interstate travelers or if a substantial portion of the food which they serve or products which they sell have "moved in commerce.". . .

4. Application of Title II to Heart of Atlanta Motel.

It is admitted that the operation of the motel brings it within the provisions of § 201(a) of the Act and that appellant refused to provide lodging for transient Negroes because of their race or color and that it intends to continue that policy unless restrained.

The sole question posed is, therefore, the constitutionality of the Civil Rights Act of 1964 as applied to these facts. . . .

The Senate Commerce Committee made it quite clear that the fundamental object of Title II was to vindicate "the deprivation of personal dignity that surely accompanies denials of equal access to public establishments." At the same time, however, it noted that such an objective has been and could be readily achieved "by congressional action based on the commerce power of the Constitution." S. Rep. No. 872, *supra*, at 16-17. Our study of the legislative record, made in the light of prior cases, has brought us to the conclusion that Congress possessed ample power in this regard, and we have therefore not considered the other grounds relied upon. This is not to say that the remaining authority upon which it acted was not adequate, a question upon which we do not pass, but merely that since the commerce power is sufficient for our decision here we have considered it alone. Nor is § 201(d) or § 202, having to do with state action, involved here and we do not pass upon either of those sections.

5. The Civil Rights Cases, 109 U.S. 3 (1883) and their Application.

In light of our ground for decision, it might be well at the outset to discuss the *Civil Rights Cases*, *supra*, which declared provisions of the Civil Rights Act of 1875 unconstitutional. 18 Stat. 335, 336. We think that decision inapposite, and without precedential value in determining the constitutionality of the present Act. Unlike Title II of the present legislation, the 1875 Act broadly proscribed discrimination in "inns, public conveyances on land or water, theaters, and other places of public amusement," without limiting the categories of affected businesses to those impinging upon interstate commerce. In contrast, the applicability of Title II is carefully limited to enterprises having a direct and substantial relation to the interstate flow of goods and people, except where state action is involved. Further, the fact that certain kinds of businesses may not in 1875 have been sufficiently involved in interstate commerce to warrant bringing them within the ambit of the commerce power is not necessarily dispositive of the same question today. Our populace had not reached its present mobility, nor were facilities, goods and services circulating as readily in interstate commerce as they are today. Although the principles which we apply today are those first formulated by Chief Justice Marshall in *Gibbons v. Ogden*, [*supra* § 2.02], the conditions of transportation and commerce have changed dramatically, and we must apply those principles to the present state of commerce. The sheer increase in volume of interstate traffic alone would give discriminatory practices which inhibit travel a far larger impact upon the Nation's commerce than such practices had on the economy of another day. . . . We, therefore, conclude that the *Civil Rights Cases* have no relevance to the basis of decision here where the Act explicitly relies upon the commerce power, and where the record is filled with testimony of obstructions and restraints resulting from the discriminations found to be existing. We now pass to that phase of the case.

6. The Basis of Congressional Action.

While the Act as adopted carried no congressional findings the record of its passage through each house is replete with evidence of the burdens that discrimination by race or color places upon interstate commerce. . . . This testimony included the fact that our people have become increasingly mobile with millions of people of all races traveling from State to State; that Negroes in particular have been the subject of discrimination in transient accommodations, having to travel great distances to secure the same; that often they have been unable to obtain accommodations and have had to call upon friends to put them up overnight, . . . and that these conditions had become so acute as to require the listing of available lodging for Negroes in a special guidebook which was itself "dramatic testimony to the difficulties" Negroes encounter in travel. . . . We shall not burden this opinion with further details since the voluminous testimony presents overwhelming evidence that discrimination by hotels and motels impedes interstate travel.

7. The Power of Congress Over Interstate Travel.

The power of Congress to deal with these obstructions depends on the meaning of the Commerce Clause. . . . [T]he determinative test of the exercise of power by the Congress under the Commerce Clause is simply whether the activity sought to be regulated is "commerce which concerns more States than one" and has a real and substantial relation to the national interest. Let us now turn to this facet of the problem.

That the "intercourse" of which the Chief Justice spoke included the movement of persons through more States than one was settled as early as 1849, in the *Passenger Cases (Smith v. Turner)*, 7 How. 283, 12 L. Ed. 702, where Justice McLean stated: "That the transportation of passengers is a part of commerce is not now an open question." Again in 1913 Justice McKenna, speaking for the Court, said: "Commerce among the states, we have said, consists of intercourse and traffic between their citizens, and includes the transportation of persons and property." *Hoke v. United States*, 227 U.S. 308, 320. . . .

That Congress was legislating against moral wrongs in many of these areas rendered its enactments no less valid. In framing Title II of this Act Congress was also dealing with what it considered a moral problem. But that fact does not detract from the overwhelming evidence of the disruptive effect that racial discrimination has had on commercial intercourse. It was this burden which empowered Congress to enact appropriate legislation, and, given this basis for the exercise of its power, Congress was not restricted by the fact that the particular obstruction to interstate commerce with which it was dealing was also deemed a moral and social wrong.

It is said that the operation of the motel here is of a purely local character. But, assuming this to be true, "[i]f it is interstate commerce that feels the pinch, it does not matter how local the operation which applies the squeeze." *United States v. Women's Sportswear Mfg. Ass'n*, 336 U.S. 460, 464 (1949). . . . Thus the power of Congress to promote interstate commerce also includes the power to regulate the local incidents thereof, including local activities in both the States of origin and destination, which might have a substantial and harmful effect upon that commerce. One need only examine the evidence which we have discussed above to see that Congress may — as it has — prohibit racial discrimination by motels serving travelers, however "local" their operations may appear. . . .

We, therefore, conclude that the action of the Congress in the adoption of the Act as applied here to a motel which concededly serves interstate travelers is within the power granted it by the Commerce Clause of the Constitution, as interpreted by this Court for 140 years. It may be argued that Congress could have pursued other methods to eliminate the obstructions it found in interstate commerce caused by racial discrimination. But this is a matter of policy that rests entirely with the Congress not with the courts. How obstructions in commerce may be removed — what means are to be employed — is within the sound and exclusive discretion of the Congress. It is subject only to one caveat — that the means chosen by it must be reasonably adapted to the end permitted by the Constitution. We cannot say that its choice here was not so adapted. The Constitution requires no more.

Affirmed.

NOTES

(1) The Court's decision in *The Civil Rights Cases*, 109 U.S. 3 (1883), was an obstacle to passage of the Civil Rights Act of 1964. The Court had held unconstitutional an 1875 regulation passed under the Fourteenth Amendment on the grounds that the necessary state action was lacking. Rather than confront that precedent, Congress based the 1964 Act on the Commerce Clause. Congress relied upon an opinion of the eminent constitutional scholar, Professor Paul Freund of Harvard Law School who wrote: "The commerce power is clearly adequate and appropriate. No impropriety need be felt in using the commerce clause as a response to a deep moral concern." S. Rep. No. 88-872 (1964).

(2) A companion case, *Katzenbach v. McClung*, 379 U.S. 294, 296 (1964), upheld the Civil Rights Act as applied to a restaurant which the Court described as follows:

> Ollie's Barbecue is a family-owned restaurant in Birmingham, Alabama, specializing in barbecued meats and homemade pies, with a seating capacity of 220 customers. It is located on a state highway 11 blocks from an interstate one and a somewhat greater distance from railroad and bus stations. The restaurant caters to a family and white-collar trade with a take-out service for Negroes. It employs 36 persons, two-thirds of whom are Negroes.

> In the 12 months preceding the passage of the Act, the restaurant purchased locally approximately $150,000 worth of food, $69,683 or 46% of which was meat that it bought from a local supplier who had procured it from outside the State.

(3) As Congress addressed the Civil Rights legislation in 1963 and 1964, the Supreme Court considered *Bell v. Maryland*, 378 U.S. 226 (1964) which raised the issue of whether the Equal Protection Clause prohibited a private restaurant owner from discriminating based on race. Some justices believed the Equal Protection Clause alone did not preclude use of state trespass laws to enforce a private entrepreneur's discriminatory choice. Others worried that such a ruling would prejudice congressional consideration of Title II. Ultimately, the Court decided *Bell* on narrow, nonconstitutional grounds. Several of the opinions in the case signaled a willingness to defer to Congress. Ten days after the Court decided *Bell*, Congress passed the Civil Rights Act of 1964. *See* Joel K. Goldstein, *Constitutional Dialogue and the Civil Rights Act of 1964*, 49 SAINT LOUIS U. L.J. 1095, 1134-38 (2005).

(4) In his concurrence, Justice Black wrote that the Necessary and Proper Clause, along with the Commerce Clause, allowed Congress "to protect interstate commerce from the injuries bound to befall it from . . . discriminatory practices." *Heart of Atlanta*, 379 U.S. at 276.

§ 2.05   THE COMMERCE CLAUSE: A NEW TURNING POINT?

UNITED STATES v. LOPEZ
514 U.S. 549, 115 S. Ct. 1624, 131 L. Ed. 2d 626 (1995)

CHIEF JUSTICE REHNQUIST delivered the opinion of the Court.

In the Gun-Free School Zones Act of 1990, Congress made it a federal offence "for any individual knowingly to possess a firearm at a place that the individual knows, or has reasonable cause to believe, is a school zone." 18 U.S.C. § 922(9)(1)(A) (1988 ed., Supp. V). The Act neither regulates a commercial activity nor contains a requirement that the possession be connected in any way to interstate commerce. We hold that the Act exceeds the authority of Congress "[t]o regulate Commerce . . . among the several States. . . ." U.S. Const., Art. I, § 8, cl. 3.

On March 10, 1992, respondent, who was then a 12th-grade student, arrived at Edison High School in San Antonio, Texas, carrying a concealed .38 caliber handgun and five bullets. . . . He was arrested and charged . . . with violating the Gun-Free School Zones Act. . . .

The District Court conducted a bench trial, found him guilty of violating § 922(q), and sentenced him to six months' imprisonment and two years' supervised release. . . . The Court of Appeals for the Fifth Circuit . . . reversed respondent's conviction . . . and we now affirm.

We start with first principles. The Constitution creates a Federal Government of enumerated powers. . . . [In a historical summary, the Court noted that after *Gibbons*, cases for almost a century dealt "almost entirely with the Commerce Clause as a limit on state legislation that discriminated against interstate commerce." In those cases the Court located production activities within the province of state government and outside of Congress' powers. This approach was imported into later cases addressing federal legislation. The Court then discussed how this approach was changed by the *Jones and Laughlin, Darby*, and *Wickard* cases, *supra*.]

Jones and Laughlin Steel, Darby, and *Wickard* ushered in an era of Commerce Clause jurisprudence that greatly expanded the previously defined authority of Congress under that Clause. In part, this was a recognition of the great changes that had occurred in the way business was carried on in this country. Enterprises that had once been local or at most regional in nature had become national in scope. But the doctrinal change also reflected a view that earlier Commerce Clause cases artificially had constrained the authority of Congress to regulate interstate commerce.

But even these modern-era precedents which have expanded congressional power under the Commerce Clause confirm that this power is subject to outer limits. In *Jones & Laughlin Steel*, the Court warned that the scope of the interstate commerce power "must be considered in the light of our dual system of government and may not be extended so as to embrace effects upon interstate commerce so indirect and remote that to embrace them, in view of our complex society, would effectually obliterate the distinction between what is national and what is local and create a completely centralized government." . . . See also *Darby*. . . (Congress may regulate intrastate activity that has a "substantial effect" on interstate commerce); *Wickard* . . . (Congress may regulate activity that "exerts a substantial economic effect on interstate commerce"). Since that time, the Court has heeded that warning and undertaken to decide whether a rational basis existed for concluding that a regulated activity sufficiently affected interstate commerce. . . .

Consistent with this structure, we have identified three broad categories of activity that Congress may regulate under its commerce power. . . . First, Congress may regulate the use of the channels of interstate commerce. . . . Second, Congress is empowered to regulate and protect the instrumentalities of interstate commerce, or persons or things in interstate commerce, even though the threat may come only from intrastate activities. . . . Finally, Congress' commerce authority includes the power to regulate those activities having a substantial relation to interstate commerce, . . . those activities that substantially affect interstate commerce. . . .

Within this final category, admittedly, our case law has not been clear whether an activity must "affect" or "substantially affect" interstate commerce in order to be within Congress' power to regulate it under the Commerce Clause. . . . We conclude, consistent with the great weight of our case law, that the proper test requires an analysis of whether the regulated activity "substantially affects" interstate commerce.

We now turn to consider the power of Congress, in light of this framework, to enact § 922(q). The first two categories of authority may be quickly disposed of: § 922(q) is not a regulation of the use of the channels of interstate commerce, nor is it an attempt to prohibit the interstate transportation of a commodity through the channels of commerce; nor can § 922(q) be justified as a regulation by which Congress has sought to protect an instrumentality of interstate commerce or a thing in interstate commerce. Thus, if § 922(q) is to be sustained, it must be under the third category as a regulation of an activity that substantially affects interstate commerce.

First, we have upheld a wide variety of congressional Acts regulating intrastate economic activity where we have concluded that the activity substantially affected interstate commerce. Examples include the regulation of intrastate coal mining, intrastate extortionate credit transactions, restaurants utilizing substantial interstate supplies, inns and hotels catering to interstate guests, and production and consumption of home-grown wheat. These examples are by no means exhaustive, but the pattern is clear. Where economic activity substantially affects interstate commerce, legislation regulating that activity will be sustained.

Even *Wickard*, which is perhaps the most far reaching example of Commerce Clause authority over intrastate activity, involved economic activity in a way that the possession of a gun in a school zone does not. Roscoe Filburn operated a small farm in Ohio, on which, in the year involved, he raised 23 acres of wheat. It was his practice to sow winter wheat in the fall, and after harvesting it in July to sell a portion of the crop, to feed part of it to poultry and livestock on the farm, to use some in making flour for home consumption, and to keep the remainder for seeding future crops. The Secretary of Agriculture assessed a penalty against him under the Agricultural Adjustment Act of 1938 because he harvested about 12 acres more wheat than his allotment under the Act permitted. The Act was designed to regulate the volume of wheat moving in interstate and foreign commerce in order to avoid surpluses and shortages, and concomitant fluctuation in wheat prices, which had previously obtained. The Court said, in an opinion sustaining the application of the Act to Filburn's activity:

> One of the primary purposes of the Act in question was to increase the market price of wheat and to that end to limit the volume thereof that could affect the market. It can hardly be denied that a factor of such volume and variability as home-consumed wheat would have a substantial influence on price and market conditions. This may arise because being in marketable condition such wheat overhangs the market and, if induced by rising prices, tends to flow into the market and check price increases. But if we assume that it is never marketed, it supplies a need of the man who grew it which would otherwise be

reflected by purchases in the open market. Home-grown wheat in this sense competes with wheat in commerce. . . .

Section 922(q) is a criminal statute that by its terms has nothing to do with "commerce" or any sort of economic enterprise, however broadly one might define those terms. Section 922(q) is not an essential part of a larger regulation of economic activity, in which the regulatory scheme could be undercut unless the intrastate activity were regulated. It cannot, therefore, be sustained under our cases upholding regulations of activities that arise out of or are connected with a commercial transaction, which viewed in the aggregate, substantially affects interstate commerce.

Second, § 922(q) contains no jurisdictional element which would ensure, through case-by-case inquiry, that the firearm possession in question affects interstate commerce. For example, in *United States v. Bass*, . . . the Court interpreted former 18 U.S.C. § 1202(a), which made it a crime for a felon to "receiv[e], posses[s], or transpor[t] in commerce or affecting commerce . . . any firearm." . . . The Court interpreted the possession component of § 1202(a) to require an additional nexus to interstate commerce both because the statute was ambiguous and because "unless Congress conveys its purpose clearly, it will not be deemed to have significantly changed the federal-state balance." *Id.*, at 349. . . . The *Bass* Court set aside the conviction because, although the Government had demonstrated that Bass had possessed a firearm, it had failed "to show the requisite nexus with interstate commerce." *Id.* at 347, ... Unlike the statute in *Bass*, § 922(q) has no express jurisdictional element which might limit its reach to a discrete set of firearm possessions that additionally have an explicit connection with or effect on interstate commerce.

Although as part of our independent evaluation of constitutionality under the Commerce Clause we of course consider legislative findings, and indeed even congressional committee findings, regarding effect on interstate commerce, . . . the Government concedes that "[n]either the statute nor its legislative history contain[s] express congressional findings regarding the effects upon interstate commerce of gun possession in a school zone." Brief for United States 5-6. We agree with the Government that Congress normally is not required to make formal findings as to the substantial burdens that an activity has on interstate commerce. . . . But to the extent that congressional findings would enable us to evaluate the legislative judgment that the activity in question substantially affected interstate commerce, even though no such substantial effect was visible to the naked eye, they are lacking here. . . .

The Government's essential contention, *in fine*, is that we may determine here that § 922(q) is valid because possession of a firearm in a local school zone does indeed substantially affect interstate commerce. . . . The Government argues that possession of a firearm in a school zone may result in violent crime and that violent crime can be expected to affect the functioning of the national economy in two ways. First, the costs of violent crime are substantial, and, through the mechanism of insurance, those costs are spread throughout the population. . . . Second, violent crime reduces the willingness of individuals to travel to areas within the country that are perceived to be unsafe. The Government also argues that the presence of guns in schools poses a substantial threat to the educational process by threatening the learning environment. A handicapped educational process, in turn, will result in a less productive citizenry. That, in turn, would have an adverse effect on the Nation's economic well-being. As a result the Government argues that Congress could rationally have concluded that § 922(q) substantially affects interstate commerce. . . . [Discussion of *Gibbons* omitted].

We pause to consider the implications of the Government's arguments. The Government admits, under its "costs of crime" reasoning, that Congress could regulate not only all violent crime, but all activities that might lead to violent crime, regardless of how tenuously they relate to interstate commerce. . . . Similarly, under the Government's "national productivity" reasoning, Congress could regulate any activity that it found was related to the economic productivity of individual citizens: family law (including marriage, divorce, and child custody), for example. Under the theories that the Government presents in support of § 922(q), it is difficult to perceive any limitation on federal power, even in areas such as criminal law enforcement or education where States historically have been sovereign. Thus, if we were to accept the Government's arguments, we are hard-pressed to posit any activity by an individual that Congress is without power to regulate. . . .

For instance, if Congress can, pursuant to its Commerce Clause power, regulate activities that adversely affect the learning environment, then, *a fortiori*, it also can regulate the educational process directly. Congress could determine that a school's curriculum has a "significant" effect on the extent of classroom learning. As a result, Congress could mandate a federal curriculum for local elementary and secondary schools because what is taught in local schools has a significant "effect on classroom learning," . . . and that, in turn, has a substantial effect on interstate commerce.

Justice Breyer rejects our reading of precedent and argues that "Congress . . . could rationally conclude that schools fall on the commercial side of the line." Again, Justice Breyer's rationale lacks any real limits because, depending on the level of generality, any activity can be looked upon as commercial. Under the dissent's rationale, Congress could just as easily look at child rearing as "fall[ing] on the commercial side of the line" because it provides a "valuable service — namely, to equip [children] with the skills they need to survive in life and, more specifically, in the workplace." We do not doubt that Congress has authority under the Commerce Clause to regulate numerous commercial activities that substantially affect interstate commerce and also affect the educational process. That authority, though broad, does not include the authority to regulate each and every aspect of local schools.

Admittedly, a determination whether an intrastate activity is commercial or noncommercial may in some cases result in legal uncertainty. But, so long as Congress' authority is limited to those powers enumerated in the Constitution, and so long as those enumerated powers are interpreted as having judicially enforceable outer limits, congressional legislation under the Commerce Clause always will engender "legal uncertainty." . . .

The Constitution mandates this uncertainty by withholding from Congress a plenary police power that would authorize enactment of every type of legislation. . . . Congress has operated within this framework of legal uncertainty ever since this Court determined that it was the Judiciary's duty "to say what the law is." . . . Any possible benefit from eliminating this "legal uncertainty" would be at the expense of the Constitution's system of enumerated powers. . . . In *Jones & Laughlin Steel*, . . . we held that the question of congressional power under the Commerce Clause "is necessarily one of degree." . . .

These are not precise formulations, and in the nature of things they cannot be. But we think they point the way to a correct decision of this case. The possession of a gun in a local school zone is in no sense an economic activity that might, through repetition elsewhere, substantially affect any sort of interstate commerce. Respondent was a local student at a local school; there is no indication that he had recently moved in interstate commerce, and there is no requirement that his possession of the firearm have any concrete tie to interstate commerce.

To uphold the Government's contentions here, we would have to pile inference upon inference in a manner that would bid fair to convert congressional authority under the Commerce Clause to a general police power of the sort retained by the States.

Admittedly, some of our prior cases have taken long steps down that road, giving great deference to congressional action. . . . The broad language in these opinions has suggested the possibility of additional expansion, but we decline here to proceed any further. To do so would require us to conclude that the Constitution's enumeration of powers does not presuppose something not enumerated, . . . and that there never will be a distinction between what is truly national and what is truly local. . . . This we are unwilling to do.

For the foregoing reasons the judgment of the Court of Appeals is

Affirmed.

JUSTICE KENNEDY, with whom JUSTICE O'CONNOR joins, concurring.

The history of the judicial struggle to interpret the Commerce Clause during the transition from the economic system the Founders knew to the single, national market still emergent in our own era counsels great restraint before the Court determines that the Clause is insufficient to support an exercise of the national power. That history gives me some pause about today's decision, but I join the Court's opinion with these observations on what I conceive to be its necessary though limited holding. . . .

The history of our Commerce Clause decisions contains at least two lessons of relevance to this case. The first . . . is the imprecision of content-based boundaries used without more to define the limits of the Commerce Clause. The second, related to the first but of even greater consequence, is that the Court as an institution and the legal system as a whole have an immense stake in the stability of our Commerce Clause jurisprudence as it has evolved to this point. Stare decisis operates with great force in counseling us not to call in question the essential principles now in place respecting the congressional power to regulate transactions of a commercial nature. That fundamental restraint on our power forecloses us from reverting to an understanding of commerce that would serve only an 18th-century economy, dependent then upon production and trading practices that had changed but little over the preceding centuries; it also mandates against returning to the time when congressional authority to regulate undoubted commercial activities was limited by a judicial determination that those matters had an insufficient connection to an interstate system. Congress can regulate in the commercial sphere on the assumption that we have a single market and a unified purpose to build a stable national economy. . . .

Of the various structural elements in the Constitution, separation of powers, checks and balances, judicial review, and federalism, only concerning the last does there seem to be much uncertainty respecting the existence, and the content, of standards that allow the judiciary to play a significant role in maintaining the design contemplated by the Framers. Although the resolution of specific cases has proved difficult, we have derived from the Constitution workable standards to assist in preserving separation of powers and checks and balances. . . . These standards are by now well accepted. Judicial review is also established beyond question. . . . Our role in preserving the federal balance seems more tenuous.

There is irony in this, because of the four structural elements in the Constitution just mentioned, federalism was the unique contribution of the Framers to political science and political theory. . . . Though on the surface the idea may seem counterintuitive, it was the insight of the Framers that freedom was enhanced by the creation of two governments, not one. . . .

The theory that two governments accord more liberty than one requires for its realization two distinct and discernable lines of political accountability: one between the citizens and the Federal Government; the second between the citizens and the

States. . . . Were the Federal Government to take over the regulation of entire areas of traditional state concern, areas having nothing to do with the regulation of commercial activities, the boundaries between the spheres of federal and state authority would blur and political responsibility would become illusory. . . . The resultant inability to hold either branch of government answerable to the citizens is more dangerous even than devolving too much authority to the remote central power. . . .

The statute before us upsets the federal balance to a degree that renders it an unconstitutional assertion of the commerce power, and our intervention is required. As the Chief Justice explains, unlike the earlier cases to come before the Court here neither the actors nor their conduct have a commercial character, and neither the purposes nor the design of the statute have an evident commercial nexus. . . . The statute makes the simple possession of a gun within 1,000 feet of the grounds of the school a criminal offence. . . . If Congress attempts that extension, then at the least we must inquire whether the exercise of national power seeks to intrude upon an area of traditional state concern.

An interference of these dimensions occurs here, for it is well established that education is a traditional concern of the States. . . . The proximity to schools, including of course schools owned and operated by the States or their subdivisions, is the very premise for making the conduct criminal. In these circumstances, we have a particular duty to insure that the federal-state balance is not destroyed. . . .

While it is doubtful that any State, or indeed any reasonable person, would argue that it is wise policy to allow students to carry guns on school premises, considerable disagreement exists about how best to accomplish that goal. In this circumstance, the theory and utility of our federalism are revealed, for the States may perform their role as laboratories for experimentation to devise various solutions where the best solution is far from clear. . . .

If a State or municipality determines that harsh criminal sanctions are necessary and wise to deter students from carrying guns on school premises, the reserved powers of the States are sufficient to enact those measures. Indeed, over 40 States already have criminal laws outlawing the possession of firearms on or near school grounds. . . .

The statute now before us forecloses the States from experimenting and exercising their own judgment in an area to which States lay claim by right of history and expertise, and it does so by regulating an activity beyond the realm of commerce in the ordinary and usual sense of that term. The tendency of this statute to displace state regulation in areas of traditional state concern is evident from its territorial operation. . . .

While the intrusion on state sovereignty may not be as severe in this instance as in some of our recent Tenth Amendment cases, the intrusion is nonetheless significant. Absent a stronger connection or identification with commercial concerns that are central to the Commerce Clause, that inference contradicts the federal balance the Framers designed and that this Court is obliged to enforce.

For these reasons, I join in the opinion and judgment of the Court.

JUSTICE THOMAS, concurring.

. . . Although I join the majority, I write separately to observe that our case law has drifted far from the original understanding of the Commerce Clause. In a future case, we ought to temper our Commerce Clause jurisprudence in a manner that both makes sense of our more recent case law and is more faithful to the original understanding of that Clause.

We have said that Congress may regulate not only "Commerce . . . among the several States," U.S. Const., Art. I, § 8, cl. 3, but also anything that has a "substantial effect" on such commerce. This test, if taken to its logical extreme, would give Congress a "police power" over all aspects of American life. . . . Indeed, on this crucial point, the majority and Justice Breyer agree in principle: The Federal Government has nothing approaching a police power. . . .

But it seems to me that the power to regulate "commerce" can by no means encompass authority over mere gun possession, any more than it empowers the Federal Government to regulate marriage, littering, or cruelty to animals, throughout the 50 States. Our Constitution quite properly leaves such matters to the individual States, notwithstanding these activities' effects on interstate commerce. Any interpretation of the Commerce Clause that even suggests that Congress could regulate such matters is in need of reexamination.

In an appropriate case, I believe that we must further reconsider our "substantial effects" test with an eye toward constructing a standard that reflects the text and history of the Commerce Clause without totally rejecting our more recent Commerce Clause jurisprudence. . . .

At the time the original Constitution was ratified, "commerce" consisted of selling, buying, and bartering, as well as transporting for these purposes. . . . As one would expect, the term "commerce" was used in contradistinction to productive activities such as manufacturing and agriculture. . . . Moreover, interjecting a modern sense of commerce into the Constitution generates significant textual and structural problems. . . .

The Constitution not only uses the word "commerce" in a narrower sense than our case law might suggest, it also does not support the proposition that Congress has authority over all activities that "substantially affect" interstate commerce. The Commerce Clause does not state that Congress may "regulate matters that substantially affect commerce with foreign Nations, and among the several States, and with the Indian Tribes." . . .

In addition to its powers under the Commerce Clause, Congress has the authority to enact such laws as are "necessary and proper" to carry into execution its power to regulate commerce among the several States. U.S. Const., Art. I, § 8, cl. 18. But on this Court's understanding of congressional power under these two Clauses, many of Congress' other enumerated powers under Art. I, § 8, are wholly superfluous. After all, if Congress may regulate all matters that substantially affect commerce, there is no need for the Constitution to specify that Congress may enact bankruptcy laws, cl. 4, or coin money and fix the standard of weights and measures, cl. 5, or punish counterfeiters of United States coin and securities, cl. 6. Likewise, Congress would not need the separate authority to establish post offices and post roads, cl. 7, or to grant patents and copyrights, cl. 8, or to "punish Piracies and Felonies committed on the high Seas," cl. 10. It might not even need the power to raise and support an Army and Navy, cls. 12 and 13, for fewer people would engage in commercial shipping if they thought that a foreign power could expropriate their property with ease. Indeed, if Congress could regulate matters that substantially affect interstate commerce, there would have been no need to specify that Congress can regulate international trade and commerce with the Indians. As the Framers surely understood, these other branches of trade substantially affect interstate commerce.

Put simply, much if not all of Art. I, § 8 (including portions of the Commerce Clause itself), would be surplusage if Congress had been given authority over matters that substantially affect interstate commerce. An interpretation of cl. 3 that makes the rest of § 8 superfluous simply cannot be correct. Yet this Court's Commerce Clause jurisprudence has endorsed just such an interpretation: The power we have accorded Congress has swallowed Art. I, § 8. . . .

The exchanges during the ratification campaign reveal the relatively limited reach of the Commerce Clause and of federal power generally. The Founding Fathers confirmed that most areas of life (even many matters that would have substantial effects on commerce) would remain outside the reach of the Federal Government. Such affairs would continue to be under the exclusive control of the States. . . . [Historical discussion omitted.]

These cases all establish a simple point: From the time of the ratification of the Constitution to the mid-1930's, it was widely understood that the Constitution granted Congress only limited powers, notwithstanding the Commerce Clause. Moreover, there was no question that activities wholly separated from business, such as gun possession, were beyond the reach of the commerce power. If anything, the "wrong turn" was the Court's dramatic departure in the 1930's from a century and a half of precedent.

Apart from its recent vintage and its corresponding lack of any grounding in the original understanding of the Constitution, the substantial effects test suffers from the further flaw that it appears to grant Congress a police power over the Nation. . . .

This extended discussion of the original understanding and our first century and a half of case law does not necessarily require a wholesale abandonment of our more recent opinions. It simply reveals that our substantial effects test is far removed from both the Constitution and from our early case law and that the Court's opinion should not be viewed as "radical" or another "wrong turn" that must be corrected in the future. The analysis also suggests that we ought to temper our Commerce Clause jurisprudence.

JUSTICE SOUTER, dissenting.

In reviewing congressional legislation under the Commerce Clause, we defer to what is often a merely implicit congressional judgment that its regulation addresses a subject substantially affecting interstate commerce "if there is any rational basis for such a finding." *Hodel v. Virginia Surface Mining & Reclamation Assn., Inc.* . . . If that congressional determination is within the realm of reason, "the only remaining question for judicial inquiry is whether 'the means chosen by Congress [are] reasonably adapted to the end permitted by the Constitution.' " . . .

The practice of deferring to rationally based legislative judgments "is a paradigm of judicial restraint." . . . In judicial review under the Commerce Clause, it reflects our respect for the institutional competence of the Congress on a subject expressly assigned to it by the Constitution and our appreciation of the legitimacy that comes from Congress's political accountability in dealing with matters open to a wide range of possible choices.

It was not ever thus, however, as even a brief overview of Commerce Clause history during the past century reminds us. The modern respect for the competence and primacy of Congress in matters affecting commerce developed only after one of this Court's most chastening experiences, when it perforce repudiated an earlier and untenably expansive conception of judicial review in derogation of congressional commerce power. A look at history's sequence will serve to show how today's decision tugs the Court off course, leading it to suggest opportunities for further developments that would be at odds with the rule of restraint to which the Court still wisely states adherence. . . .

These restrictive views of commerce subject to congressional power complemented the Court's activism in limiting the enforceable scope of state economic regulation. It is most familiar history that during this same period the Court routinely invalidated state social and economic legislation under an expansive conception of Fourteenth Amendment substantive due process. . . . The fulcrums of judicial review in these cases were the notions of liberty and property characteristic of laissez-faire economics, whereas the

Commerce Clause cases turned on what was ostensibly a structural limit of federal power, but under each conception of judicial review the Court's character for the first third of the century showed itself in exacting judicial scrutiny of a legislature's choice of economic ends and of the legislative means selected to reach them.

It was not merely coincidental, then, that sea changes in the Court's conceptions of its authority under the Due Process and Commerce Clauses occurred virtually together, in 1937, with *West Coast Hotel Co. v. Parrish*, . . . and *NLRB v. Jones & Laughlin Steel Corp.* . . . In the years following these decisions, deference to legislative policy judgments on commercial regulation became the powerful theme under both the Due Process and Commerce Clauses, see *United States v. Carolene Products Co.* . . .

There is today, however, a backward glance at both the old pitfalls, as the Court treats deference under the rationality rule as subject to gradation according to the commercial or noncommercial nature of the immediate subject of the challenged regulation. . . . The distinction between what is patently commercial and what is not looks much like the old distinction between what directly affects commerce and what touches it only indirectly. And the act of calibrating the level of deference by drawing a line between what is patently commercial and what is less purely so will probably resemble the process of deciding how much interference with contractual freedom was fatal. Thus, it seems fair to ask whether the step taken by the Court today does anything but portend a return to the untenable jurisprudence from which the Court extricated itself almost 60 years ago. . . .

Further glosses on rationality review, moreover, may be in the offing. Although this case turns on commercial character, the Court gestures toward two other considerations that it might sometime entertain in applying rational basis scrutiny (apart from a statutory obligation to supply independent proof of a jurisdictional element): Does the congressional statute deal with subjects of traditional state regulation, and does the statute contain explicit factual findings supporting the otherwise implicit determination that the regulated activity substantially affects interstate commerce? Once again, any appeal these considerations may have depends on ignoring the painful lesson learned in 1937, for neither of the Court's suggestions would square with rational basis scrutiny. . . .

JUSTICE BREYER, with whom JUSTICE STEVENS, JUSTICE SOUTER, and JUSTICE GINSBURG join, dissenting.

The issue in this case is whether the Commerce Clause authorizes Congress to enact a statute that makes it a crime to possess a gun in, or near, a school. In my view, the statute falls well within the scope of the commerce power as this Court has understood that power over the last half century.

I

In reaching this conclusion, I apply three basic principles of Commerce Clause interpretation. First, the power to "regulate Commerce . . . among the several States" . . . encompasses the power to regulate local activities insofar as they significantly affect interstate commerce. . . . As the majority points out, the Court, in describing how much of an effect the Clause requires, sometimes has used the word "substantial" and sometimes has not. . . . I use the word "significant" because the word "substantial" implies a somewhat narrower power than recent precedent suggests. . . . But, to speak of "substantial effect" rather than "significant effect" would make no difference in this case.

Second, in determining whether a local activity will likely have a significant effect upon interstate commerce, a court must consider, not the effect of an individual act (a single instance of gun possession), but rather the cumulative effect of all similar instance (i.e., the effect of all guns possessed in or near schools). . . .

Third, the Constitution requires us to judge the connection between a regulated activity and interstate commerce, not directly, but at one remove. Courts must give Congress a degree of leeway in determining the existence of a significant factual connection between the regulated activity and interstate commerce — both because the Constitution delegates the commerce power directly to Congress and because the determination requires an empirical judgment of a kind that a legislature is more likely than a court to make with accuracy. The traditional words "rational basis" capture this leeway. . . . Thus, the specific question before us, as the Court recognizes, is not whether the "regulated activity sufficiently affected interstate commerce," but, rather, whether Congress could have had "a rational basis" for so concluding. . . .

II

Applying these principles to the case at hand, we must ask whether Congress could have had a rational basis for finding a significant (or substantial) connection between gun-related school violence and interstate commerce. Or, to put the question in the language of the explicit finding that Congress made when it amended this law in 1994: Could Congress rationally have found that "violent crime in school zones," through its effect on the "quality of education," significantly (or substantially) affects "interstate" or "foreign commerce"? . . . As long as one views the commerce connection, not as a "technical legal conception," but as "a practical one," . . . the answer to this question must be yes. Numerous reports and studies — generated both inside and outside government — make clear that Congress could reasonably have found the empirical connection that its law, implicitly or explicitly, asserts.

For one thing, reports, hearings, and other readily available literature make clear that the problem of guns in and around schools is widespread and extremely serious. These materials report, . . . that this widespread violence in schools throughout the Nation significantly interferes with the quality of education in those schools. . . . Based on reports such as these, Congress obviously could have thought that guns and learning are mutually exclusive. . . . And, Congress could therefore have found a substantial educational problem — teachers unable to teach, students unable to learn — and concluded that guns near schools contribute substantially to the size and scope of that problem.

Having found that guns in schools significantly undermine the quality of education in our Nation's classrooms, Congress could also have found, given the effect of education upon interstate and foreign commerce, that gun-related violence in and around schools is a commercial, as well as a human, problem. Education, although far more than a matter of economics, has long been inextricably intertwined with the Nation's economy. . . .

In recent years the link between secondary education and business has strengthened, becoming both more direct and more important. [Evidence omitted] . . . Increasing global competition also has made primary and secondary education economically more important. [Evidence omitted] . . . Finally, there is evidence that, today more than ever, many firms base their location decisions upon the presence, or absence, of a work force with a basic education. [Evidence omitted] . . .

The economic links I have just sketched seem fairly obvious. Why then is it not equally obvious, in light of those links, that a widespread, serious, and substantial physical threat to teaching and learning also substantially threatens the commerce to which that teaching and learning is inextricably tied? . . . At the very least, Congress could rationally have concluded that the links are "substantial." . . .

In sum, a holding that the particular statute before us falls within the commerce power would not expand the scope of that Clause. Rather, it simply would apply preexisting law to changing economic circumstances. . . . It would recognize that, in today's economic world, gun-related violence near the classroom makes a significant difference to our economic, as well as social, well-being. In accordance with precedent, such a holding would permit Congress "to act in terms of economic . . . realities," would interpret the commerce power as "an affirmative power commensurate with the national needs," and would acknowledge that the "commerce clause does not operate so as to render the nation powerless to defend itself against economic forces that Congress decrees inimical or destructive of the national economy." . . .

III

The majority's holding — that § 922 falls outside the scope of the Commerce Clause — creates three serious legal problems. First, the majority's holding runs contrary to modern Supreme Court cases that have upheld congressional actions despite connections to interstate or foreign commerce that are less significant than the effect of school violence. . . .

The second legal problem the Court creates comes from its apparent belief that it can reconcile its holding with earlier cases by making a critical distinction between "commercial" and noncommercial "transaction[s]." . . . That is to say, the court believes the Constitution would distinguish between two local activities, each of which has an identical effect upon interstate commerce, if one, but not the other, is "commercial" in nature. . . .

. . . The majority's test is not consistent with what the Court saw as the point of the cases that the majority now characterizes. Although the majority today attempts to categorize *Perez*, *McClung*, and *Wickard* as involving intrastate "economic activity," . . . the Courts that decided each of those cases did not focus upon the economic nature of the activity regulated. Rather, they focused upon whether that activity affected interstate or foreign commerce. In fact, the *Wickard* Court expressly held that Filburn's consumption of home grown wheat, "though it may not be regarded as commerce," could nevertheless be regulated — "whatever its nature" — so long as "it exerts a substantial economic effect on interstate commerce." . . .

Regardless, if there is a principled distinction that could work both here and in future cases, Congress (even in the absence of vocational classes, industry involvement, and private management) could rationally conclude that schools fall on the commercial side of the line. . . . Why could Congress, for Commerce Clause purposes, not consider schools as roughly analogous to commercial investments from which the Nation derives the benefit of an educated work force?

The third legal problem created by the Court's holding is that it threatens legal uncertainty in an area of law that, until this case, seemed reasonably well settled. Congress has enacted many statutes (more than 100 sections of the United States Code), including criminal statues (at least 25 sections), that use the words "affecting commerce" to define their scope. . . .

. . . .

IV

In sum, to find this legislation within the scope of the Commerce Clause would permit "Congress . . . to act in terms of economic . . . realities." It would interpret the Clause as this Court has traditionally interpreted it, with the exception of one wrong turn subsequently corrected. . . . Upholding this legislation would do no more than simply recognize that Congress had a "rational basis" for finding a significant connection between guns in or near schools and (through their effect on education) the interstate and foreign commerce they threaten. For these reasons, I would reverse the judgment of the Court of Appeals. Respectfully, I dissent.

NOTES

(1) Does *Lopez* have more in common with the deferential approach of *Wickard* or that of *Jones & Laughlin*, which envisions more judicial scrutiny? Note the Court's citations to *Jones & Laughlin*. Why did the Court not overturn *Wickard*?

(2) Would the Framers have intended Congress to use the Commerce Clause as a means to outlaw guns in schools? Even if this use of the clause would be inconsistent with original intent, should this dispose of the constitutional issue? The national (and world) economy are much more interdependent than when the Framers wrote, so that local events, which once had little, if any, impact on other states, now have national significance. Does this justify recognizing a more robust commerce power than did the Framers? *See* Lawrence Lessig, *Translating Federalism:* United States v. Lopez, 1995 SUP. CT. REV. 125.

(3) What state interest did the Gun Free School Zones Act infringe? Professor Lawrence Lessig asks rhetorically, "Was there really a state that wanted to permit gun possession within 1,000 feet of a school, but which was disallowed by Congress' statute?" *See* Lessig, *Translating Federalism:* United States v. Lopez, *supra*, at 125, 209.

(4) Professor Donald H. Regan criticizes all of the opinions in *Lopez* for talking "past one another" since "none of them is discussing the right question — whether there is any reason why gun possession in school zones is better regulated by the federal government than by the states." Regan, *How to Think About the Federal Commerce Power and Incidentally Rewrite* United States v. Lopez, 94 MICH L. REV. 554, 563 (1995). Professor Steven G. Calabresi, however, has defended the majority opinion in *Lopez* for allowing "room for doctrinal movement toward the restoration of federalism without any socially disturbing disruption of legitimate expectations." Calabresi, *"A Government of Limited and Enumerated Powers": In Defense of* United Sates v. Lopez, 94 MICH. L. REV. 752, 827 (1995).

(5) *United States v. Morrison*, 528 U.S. 598 (2000). In its first major post *Lopez* decision on the Commerce Clause per se, the Court, in a 5-4 decision, held that Congress exceeded its Commerce Clause powers in passing the Violence Against Women Act, 42 U.S.C. § 13981 which provided a federal civil remedy for victims of gender motivated violence. Chief Justice Rehnquist, for the same five Justices who made up the *Lopez* majority, relied heavily on *Lopez* but further explained that decision. *Lopez* turned on four considerations — the statute in question (a) had nothing to do with an economic or commercial activity, (b) lacked a jurisdictional link to commerce, (c) had no legislative findings regarding the effect on commerce of the prohibited activity, and (d) rested on an attenuated link between the challenged activity (gun possession) and commerce. The VAWA, too, contained no jurisdictional link and rested on attenuated reasoning. Moreover, VAWA also did not address economic activity. The Chief Justice wrote: "Gender-motivated crimes of violence are not, in any sense of the phrase, economic activity. While we need not adopt a categorical rule against aggregating the effects of any noneconomic activity in order to decide these cases, thus far in our Nation's history our cases have upheld Commerce Clause regulation of intrastate activity only where that activity is economic in nature. . . ." Why did the Court decline to characterize the "economic activity" criteria as a categorical rule?

Unlike *Lopez*, VAWA did rest on substantial legislative findings. The Court said these were insufficient alone to uphold the measure.

The majority stated that the Constitution "requires a distinction between what is truly national and what is truly local." How does one decide what is truly national and what is truly local? Should it make a difference that the Attorney Generals, of more than 70% of the states argued that VAWA was constitutional and that a national approach to the problem was needed?

GONZALES v. RAICH
545 U.S. 1, 125 S. Ct. 2195, 162 L. Ed. 2d 1 (2005)

JUSTICE STEVENS delivered the opinion of the Court.

California is one of at least nine States that authorize the use of marijuana for medicinal purposes. The question presented in this case is whether the power vested in Congress by Article I, § 8, of the Constitution "[t]o make all Laws which shall be necessary and proper for carrying into Execution" its authority to "regulate Commerce with foreign Nations, and among the several States" includes the power to prohibit the local cultivation and use of marijuana in compliance with California law.

I

. . . In 1996, California voters passed Proposition 215, now codified as the Compassionate Use Act of 1996. The proposition was designed to ensure that "seriously ill" residents of the State have access to marijuana for medical purposes, and to encourage Federal and State Governments to take steps towards ensuring the safe and affordable distribution of the drug to patients in need. The Act creates an exemption from criminal prosecution for physicians, as well as for patients and primary caregivers who possess or cultivate marijuana for medicinal purposes with the recommendation or approval of a physician. . . .

Respondents Angel Raich and Diane Monson are California residents who suffer from a variety of serious medical conditions and have sought to avail themselves of medical marijuana pursuant to the terms of the Compassionate Use Act. . . . Both women have been using marijuana as a medication for several years pursuant to their doctors' recommendation, and both rely heavily on cannabis to function on a daily basis. Indeed, Raich's physician believes that forgoing cannabis treatments would certainly cause Raich excruciating pain and could very well prove fatal. . . .

[After federal drug agents seized and destroyed Monson's cannabis plants] Respondents . . . brought this action against the Attorney General of the United States and the head of the DEA seeking injunctive and declaratory relief prohibiting the enforcement of the federal Controlled Substances Act (CSA), to the extent it prevents them from possessing, obtaining, or manufacturing cannabis for their personal medical use. . . .

The District Court denied respondents' motion for a preliminary injunction. *Raich v. Ashcroft*, 248 F. Supp. 2d 918 (N.D.Cal. 2003). . . .

A divided panel of the Court of Appeals for the Ninth Circuit reversed and ordered the District Court to enter a preliminary injunction. *Raich v. Ashcroft*, 352 F.3d 1222 (2003). . . .

The obvious importance of the case prompted our grant of certiorari. 542 U.S. 936 (2004). The case is made difficult by respondents' strong arguments that they will suffer irreparable harm because, despite a congressional finding to the contrary, marijuana does have valid therapeutic purposes. The question before us, however, is not whether it is wise to enforce the statute in these circumstances; rather, it is whether Congress' power to regulate interstate markets for medicinal substances encompasses the portions of those markets that are supplied with drugs produced and consumed locally. Well-settled law controls our answer. The CSA is a valid exercise of federal power, even as applied to the troubling facts of this case. We accordingly vacate the judgment of the Court of Appeals.

II

[President Nixon's "war on drugs"] culminated in the passage of the Comprehensive Drug Abuse Prevention and Control Act of 1970 [(CSA)]. The main objectives of the CSA were to conquer drug abuse and to control the legitimate and illegitimate traffic in controlled substances. Congress was particularly concerned with the need to prevent the diversion of drugs from legitimate to illicit channels. To effectuate these goals, Congress devised a closed regulatory system making it unlawful to manufacture, distribute, dispense, or possess any controlled substance except in a manner authorized by the CSA. . . .

III

Respondents in this case do not dispute that passage of the CSA, as part of the Comprehensive Drug Abuse Prevention and Control Act, was well within Congress' commerce power. . . . Nor do they contend that any provision or section of the CSA amounts to an unconstitutional exercise of congressional authority. Rather, respondents' challenge is actually quite limited; they argue that the CSA's categorical prohibition of the manufacture and possession of marijuana as applied to the intrastate manufacture and possession of marijuana for medical purposes pursuant to California law exceeds Congress' authority under the Commerce Clause.

In assessing the validity of congressional regulation, none of our Commerce Clause cases can be viewed in isolation. As charted in considerable detail in *United States v. Lopez*, our understanding of the reach of the Commerce Clause, as well as Congress' assertion of authority thereunder, has evolved over time. The Commerce Clause emerged as the Framers' response to the central problem giving rise to the Constitution itself: the absence of any federal commerce power under the Articles of Confederation. For the first century of our history, the primary use of the Clause was to preclude the kind of discriminatory state legislation that had once been permissible. Then, in response to rapid industrial development and an increasingly interdependent national economy, Congress "ushered in a new era of federal regulation under the commerce power," [in the late nineteenth century].

Cases decided during that "new era," which now spans more than a century, have identified three general categories of regulation in which Congress is authorized to engage under its commerce power. First, Congress can regulate the channels of interstate commerce. Second, Congress has authority to regulate and protect the instrumentalities of interstate commerce, and persons or things in interstate commerce. Third, Congress has the power to regulate activities that substantially affect interstate commerce. Only the third category is implicated in the case at hand.

Our case law firmly establishes Congress' power to regulate purely local activities that are part of an economic "class of activities" that have a substantial effect on interstate commerce. *See, e.g., Perez,*. . .; *Wickard v. Filburn*, 317 U.S. 111, 128-129, (1942). As we stated in *Wickard*, "even if appellee's activity be local and though it may not be regarded as commerce, it may still, whatever its nature, be reached by Congress if it exerts a substantial economic effect on interstate commerce." *Id.* at 125. We have never required Congress to legislate with scientific exactitude. When Congress decides that the " 'total incidence' " of a practice poses a threat to a national market, it may regulate the entire class. *See Perez*, 402 U.S. at 154-155, . . . In this vein, we have reiterated that when " 'a general regulatory statute bears a substantial relation to commerce, the *de minimis* character of individual instances arising under that statute is of no consequence.' " *E.g., Lopez*, 514 U.S. at 558, (emphasis deleted).

Our decision in *Wickard*, 317 U.S. 111, is of particular relevance . . . *Wickard* . . . establishes that Congress can regulate purely intrastate activity that is not itself "commercial," in that it is not produced for sale, if it concludes that failure to regulate that class of activity would undercut the regulation of the interstate market in that commodity.

The similarities between this case and *Wickard* are striking. Like the farmer in *Wickard*, respondents are cultivating, for home consumption, a fungible commodity for which there is an established, albeit illegal, interstate market. Just as the Agricultural Adjustment Act was designed "to control the volume [of wheat] moving in interstate and foreign commerce in order to avoid surpluses . . ." and consequently control the market price . . . [A] primary purpose of the CSA is to control the supply and demand of controlled substances in both lawful and unlawful drug markets. [. . .] In *Wickard*, we had no difficulty concluding that Congress had a rational basis for believing that, when viewed in the aggregate, leaving home-consumed wheat outside the regulatory scheme would have a substantial influence on price and market conditions. Here too, Congress had a rational basis for concluding that leaving home-consumed marijuana outside federal control would similarly affect price and market conditions.

More concretely, one concern prompting inclusion of wheat grown for home consumption in the 1938 Act was that rising market prices could draw such wheat into the interstate market, resulting in lower market prices. . . . The parallel concern making it appropriate to include marijuana grown for home consumption in the CSA is the likelihood that the high demand in the interstate market will draw such marijuana into that market. . . . In both cases, the regulation is squarely within Congress' commerce power because production of the commodity meant for home consumption, be it wheat or marijuana, has a substantial effect on supply and demand in the national market for that commodity.

Nonetheless, respondents suggest that *Wickard* differs from this case in three respects: (1) the Agricultural Adjustment Act, unlike the CSA, exempted small farming operations; (2) *Wickard* involved a "quintessential economic activity" — a commercial farm — whereas respondents do not sell marijuana; and (3) the *Wickard* record made it clear that the aggregate production of wheat for use on farms had a significant impact on market prices. Those differences, though factually accurate, do not diminish the precedential force of this Court's reasoning.

The fact that Filburn's own impact on the market was "trivial by itself" was not a sufficient reason for removing him from the scope of federal regulation. . . . That the Secretary of Agriculture elected to exempt even smaller farms from regulation does not speak to his power to regulate all those whose aggregated production was significant, nor did that fact play any role in the Court's analysis. Moreover, even though Filburn was indeed a commercial farmer, the activity he was engaged in — the cultivation of wheat for home consumption — was not treated by the Court as part of his commercial farming operation. And while it is true that the record in the *Wickard* case itself established the causal connection between the production for local use and the national market, we have before us findings by Congress to the same effect. . . .

In assessing the scope of Congress' authority under the Commerce Clause, we stress that the task before us is a modest one. We need not determine whether respondents' activities, taken in the aggregate, substantially affect interstate commerce in fact, but

only whether a "rational basis" exists for so concluding. *Lopez*, 514 U.S. at 557. . . .
Given the enforcement difficulties that attend distinguishing between marijuana
cultivated locally and marijuana grown elsewhere. . . , and concerns about diversion
into illicit channels, we have no difficulty concluding that Congress had a rational basis
for believing that failure to regulate the intrastate manufacture and possession of
marijuana would leave a gaping hole in the CSA. . . .

IV

To support their contrary submission, respondents rely heavily on two of our more
recent Commerce Clause cases. In their myopic focus, they overlook the larger context
of modern-era Commerce Clause jurisprudence preserved by those cases. Moreover,
even in the narrow prism of respondents' creation, they read those cases far too
broadly.

Those two cases, of course, are *Lopez*, . . . and [*United States v.*]
Morrison, . . . As an initial matter, the statutory challenges at issue in those cases
were markedly different from the challenge respondents pursue in the case at hand.
Here, respondents ask us to excise individual applications of a concededly valid
statutory scheme. In contrast, in both *Lopez* and *Morrison*, the parties asserted that a
particular statute or provision fell outside Congress' commerce power in its entirety.
This distinction is pivotal for we have often reiterated that "[w]here the class of
activities is regulated and that class is within the reach of federal power, the courts
have no power 'to excise, as trivial, individual instances' of the class." *Perez*, 402 U.S. at
154, (emphasis deleted) (quoting *Wirtz*, 392 U.S. at 193); *see also Hodel*, 452 U.S. at 308.

At issue in *Lopez*, . . . was the validity of the Gun-Free School Zones Act of 1990,
which was a brief, single-subject statute making it a crime for an individual to possess
a gun in a school zone. . . . The Act did not regulate any economic activity and did not
contain any requirement that the possession of a gun have any connection to past
interstate activity or a predictable impact on future commercial activity. . . . The
statutory scheme that the Government is defending in this litigation is at the opposite
end of the regulatory spectrum. [T]he CSA . . . was a lengthy and detailed statute
creating a comprehensive framework for regulating the production, distribution, and
possession of five classes of "controlled substances." . . .

Nor does this Court's holding in *Morrison*, 529 U.S. 598 [cast doubt on CSA.] The
Violence Against Women Act of 1994 . . . created a federal civil remedy for the victims
of gender-motivated crimes of violence. The remedy was enforceable in both state and
federal courts, and generally depended on proof of the violation of a state law. Despite
congressional findings that such crimes had an adverse impact on interstate commerce,
we held the statute unconstitutional because, like the statute in *Lopez*, it did not
regulate economic activity. . . .

Unlike those at issue in *Lopez* and *Morrison*, the activities regulated by the CSA are
quintessentially economic. "Economics" refers to "the production, distribution, and
consumption of commodities." Webster's Third New International Dictionary 720
(1966). The CSA is a statute that regulates the production, distribution, and
consumption of commodities for which there is an established, and lucrative, interstate
market. Prohibiting the intrastate possession or manufacture of an article of commerce
is a rational (and commonly utilized) means of regulating commerce in that
product. . . . Because the CSA is a statute that directly regulates economic,
commercial activity, our opinion in *Morrison* casts no doubt on its constitutionality.

The Court of Appeals was able to conclude otherwise only by isolating a "separate
and distinct" class of activities that it held to be beyond the reach of federal power,
defined as "the intrastate, noncommercial cultivation, possession and use of marijuana

for personal medical purposes on the advice of a physician and in accordance with state law." 352 F.3d at 1229. . . . The question, however, is whether Congress' contrary policy judgment, i.e., its decision to include this narrower "class of activities" within the larger regulatory scheme, was constitutionally deficient. We have no difficulty concluding that Congress acted rationally in determining that none of the characteristics making up the purported class, whether viewed individually or in the aggregate, compelled an exemption from the CSA; rather, the subdivided class of activities defined by the Court of Appeals was an essential part of the larger regulatory scheme. . . .

[L]imiting the activity to marijuana possession and cultivation "in accordance with state law" cannot serve to place respondents' activities beyond congressional reach. The Supremacy Clause unambiguously provides that if there is any conflict between federal and state law, federal law shall prevail. . . .

Respondents acknowledge this proposition, but nonetheless contend that their activities were not "an essential part of a larger regulatory scheme" because they had been "isolated by the State of California, and [are] policed by the State of California," and thus remain "entirely separated from the market." . . .

So, from the "separate and distinct" class of activities identified by the Court of Appeals (and adopted by the dissenters), we are left with "the intrastate, noncommercial cultivation, possession and use of marijuana." . . . Thus the case for the exemption comes down to the claim that a locally cultivated product that is used domestically rather than sold on the open market is not subject to federal regulation. Given the findings in the CSA and the undisputed magnitude of the commercial market for marijuana, our decisions in *Wickard v. Filburn* and the later cases endorsing its reasoning foreclose that claim.

V

[P]erhaps even more important than . . . legal avenues is the democratic process, in which the voices of voters allied with these respondents may one day be heard in the halls of Congress. Under the present state of the law, however, the judgment of the Court of Appeals must be vacated. The case is remanded for further proceedings consistent with this opinion.

It is so ordered.

JUSTICE SCALIA, concurring in the judgment.

I agree with the Court's holding that the Controlled Substances Act (CSA) may validly be applied to respondents' cultivation, distribution, and possession of marijuana for personal, medicinal use. I write separately because my understanding of the doctrinal foundation on which that holding rests is, if not inconsistent with that of the Court, at least more nuanced.

Since *Perez v. United States*, 402 U.S. 146, (1971), our cases have mechanically recited that the Commerce Clause permits congressional regulation of three categories: (1) the channels of interstate commerce; (2) the instrumentalities of interstate commerce, and persons or things in interstate commerce; and (3) activities that "substantially affect" interstate commerce. . . . The first two categories are self-evident, since they are the ingredients of interstate commerce itself. . . . The third category, however, is different in kind, and its recitation without explanation is misleading and incomplete.

It is *misleading* because, unlike the channels, instrumentalities, and agents of interstate commerce, activities that substantially affect interstate commerce are not themselves part of interstate commerce, and thus the power to regulate them cannot come from the Commerce Clause alone. Rather, as this Court has acknowledged since at least *United States v. Coombs*, 12 Pet. 72, (1838), Congress's regulatory authority over intrastate activities that are not themselves part of interstate commerce (including activities that have a substantial effect on interstate commerce) derives from the Necessary and Proper Clause. . . . And the category of "activities that substantially affect interstate commerce," *Lopez*, . . . is *incomplete* because the authority to enact laws necessary and proper for the regulation of interstate commerce is not limited to laws governing intrastate activities that substantially affect interstate commerce. Where necessary to make a regulation of interstate commerce effective, Congress may regulate even those intrastate activities that do not themselves substantially affect interstate commerce.

I

Our cases show that the regulation of intrastate activities may be necessary to and proper for the regulation of interstate commerce in two general circumstances. Most directly, the commerce power permits Congress not only to devise rules for the governance of commerce between States but also to facilitate interstate commerce by eliminating potential obstructions, and to restrict it by eliminating potential stimulants. *See NLRB v. Jones & Laughlin Steel Corp.*, 301 U.S. 1, 36-37, (1937). That is why the Court has repeatedly sustained congressional legislation on the ground that the regulated activities had a substantial effect on interstate commerce. . . . *Lopez* and *Morrison* recognized the expansive scope of Congress's authority in this regard: "[T]he pattern is clear. Where economic activity substantially affects interstate commerce, legislation regulating that activity will be sustained." . . .

As we implicitly acknowledged in *Lopez*, however, Congress's authority to enact laws necessary and proper for the regulation of interstate commerce is not limited to laws directed against economic activities that have a substantial effect on interstate commerce. Though the conduct in *Lopez* was not economic, the Court nevertheless recognized that it could be regulated as "an essential part of a larger regulation of economic activity, in which the regulatory scheme could be undercut unless the intrastate activity were regulated." . . . This statement referred to those cases permitting the regulation of intrastate activities "which in a substantial way interfere with or obstruct the exercise of the granted power." *Wrightwood Dairy Co.*, 315 U.S. at 119. . . . As the Court put it in *Wrightwood Dairy*, where Congress has the authority to enact a regulation of interstate commerce, "it possesses every power needed to make that regulation effective." . . .

Although this power "to make . . . regulation effective" commonly overlaps with the authority to regulate economic activities that substantially affect interstate commerce, and may in some cases have been confused with that authority, the two are distinct. The regulation of an intrastate activity may be essential to a comprehensive regulation of interstate commerce even though the intrastate activity does not itself "substantially affect" interstate commerce. Moreover, as the passage from *Lopez* quoted above suggests, Congress may regulate even noneconomic local activity if that regulation is a necessary part of a more general regulation of interstate commerce. . . . The relevant question is simply whether the means chosen are "reasonably adapted" to the attainment of a legitimate end under the commerce power. *See Darby, supra* at 121.

. . . .

II

Today's principal dissent objects that, by permitting Congress to regulate activities necessary to effective interstate regulation, the Court reduces *Lopez* and *Morrison* to "little more than a drafting guide." . . . I think that criticism unjustified. Unlike the power to regulate activities that have a substantial effect on interstate commerce, the power to enact laws enabling effective regulation of interstate commerce can only be exercised in conjunction with congressional regulation of an interstate market, and it extends only to those measures necessary to make the interstate regulation effective. As *Lopez* itself states, and the Court affirms today, Congress may regulate noneconomic intrastate activities only where the failure to do so "could . . . undercut" its regulation of interstate commerce. . . . This is not a power that threatens to obliterate the line between "what is truly national and what is truly local." . . .

Lopez and *Morrison* affirm that Congress may not regulate certain "purely local" activity within the States based solely on the attenuated effect that such activity may have in the interstate market. But those decisions do not declare noneconomic intrastate activities to be categorically beyond the reach of the Federal Government. Neither case involved the power of Congress to exert control over intrastate activities in connection with a more comprehensive scheme of regulation; *Lopez* expressly disclaimed that it was such a case, . . . and *Morrison* did not even discuss the possibility that it was. . . . To dismiss this distinction as "superficial and formalistic," . . . (O'Connor, J., dissenting), is to misunderstand the nature of the Necessary and Proper Clause, which empowers Congress to enact laws in effectuation of its enumerated powers that are not within its authority to enact in isolation. *See McCulloch v. Maryland*, 4 Wheat. 316, 421-422 (1819).

And there are other restraints upon the Necessary and Proper Clause authority. As Chief Justice Marshall wrote in *McCulloch v. Maryland*, even when the end is constitutional and legitimate, the means must be "appropriate" and "plainly adapted" to that end. . . . Moreover, they may not be otherwise "prohibited" and must be "consistent with the letter and spirit of the constitution." *Id.* These phrases are not merely hortatory. For example, cases such as *Printz v. United States*, 521 U.S. 898 (1997), and *New York v. United States*, 505 U.S. 144 (1992), affirm that a law is not "'*proper* for carrying into Execution the Commerce Clause'" "[w]hen [it] violates [a constitutional] principle of state sovereignty." . . .

III

The application of these principles to the case before us is straightforward. In the CSA, Congress has undertaken to extinguish the interstate market in Schedule I controlled substances, including marijuana. The Commerce Clause unquestionably permits this. The power to regulate interstate commerce "extends not only to those regulations which aid, foster and protect the commerce, but embraces those which prohibit it." . . . To effectuate its objective, Congress has prohibited almost all intrastate activities related to Schedule I substances — both economic activities (manufacture, distribution, possession with the intent to distribute) and noneconomic activities (simple possession). . . . That simple possession is a noneconomic activity is immaterial to whether it can be prohibited as a necessary part of a larger regulation. Rather, Congress's authority to enact all of these prohibitions of intrastate controlled-substance activities depends only upon whether they are appropriate means of achieving the legitimate end of eradicating Schedule I substances from interstate commerce.

By this measure, I think the regulation must be sustained. Not only is it impossible to distinguish "controlled substances manufactured and distributed intrastate" from "controlled substances manufactured and distributed interstate," but it hardly makes sense to speak in such terms. Drugs like marijuana are fungible commodities. As the Court explains, marijuana that is grown at home and possessed for personal use is never more than an instant from the interstate market — and this is so whether or not the possession is for medicinal use or lawful use under the laws of a particular State. . . .

*   *   *

I thus agree with the Court that, however the class of regulated activities is subdivided, Congress could reasonably conclude that its objective of prohibiting marijuana from the interstate market "could be undercut" if those activities were excepted from its general scheme of regulation. *See Lopez*, 514 U.S. at 561. That is sufficient to authorize the application of the CSA to respondents.

JUSTICE O'CONNOR, with whom THE CHIEF JUSTICE and JUSTICE THOMAS join as to all but Part III, dissenting.

We enforce the "outer limits" of Congress' Commerce Clause authority not for their own sake, but to protect historic spheres of state sovereignty from excessive federal encroachment and thereby to maintain the distribution of power fundamental to our federalist system of government. *United States v. Lopez*, 514 U.S. 549, 557 (1995); *NLRB v. Jones & Laughlin Steel Corp.*, 301 U.S. 1, 37 (1937). One of federalism's chief virtues, of course, is that it promotes innovation by allowing for the possibility that "a single courageous State may, if its citizens choose, serve as a laboratory; and try novel social and economic experiments without risk to the rest of the country." . . .

This case exemplifies the role of States as laboratories. The States' core police powers have always included authority to define criminal law and to protect the health, safety, and welfare of their citizens. . . . Exercising those powers, California . . . has come to its own conclusion about the difficult and sensitive question of whether marijuana should be available to relieve severe pain and suffering. Today the Court sanctions an application of the federal Controlled Substances Act that extinguishes that experiment, without any proof that the personal cultivation, possession, and use of marijuana for medicinal purposes, if economic activity in the first place, has a substantial effect on interstate commerce and is therefore an appropriate subject of federal regulation. In so doing, the Court announces a rule that gives Congress a perverse incentive to legislate broadly pursuant to the Commerce Clause — nestling questionable assertions of its authority into comprehensive regulatory schemes — rather than with precision. That rule and the result it produces in this case are irreconcilable with our decisions in *Lopez, supra*, and *United States v. Morrison*, 529 U.S. 598 (2000). Accordingly I dissent.

I

In *Lopez*, we . . . explained that "Congress' commerce authority includes the power to regulate those activities having a substantial relation to interstate commerce . . ., *i.e.*, those activities that substantially affect interstate commerce." 514 U.S. at 558-559 (citation omitted). This power derives from the conjunction of the Commerce Clause and the Necessary and Proper Clause. . . . We held in *Lopez* that the Gun-Free School Zones Act could not be sustained as an exercise of that power. [Summary of four *Lopez* factors omitted] In my view, the case before us is materially indistinguishable from *Lopez* and *Morrison* when the same considerations are taken into account.

II

A

. . . Today's decision suggests that the federal regulation of local activity is immune to Commerce Clause challenge because Congress chose to act with an ambitious, all-encompassing statute, rather than piecemeal. In my view, allowing Congress to set the terms of the constitutional debate in this way, *i.e.*, by packaging regulation of local activity in broader schemes, is tantamount to removing meaningful limits on the Commerce Clause.

The Court's principal means of distinguishing *Lopez* from this case is to observe that the Gun-Free School Zones Act of 1990 was a "brief, single-subject statute," . . . whereas the CSA is "a lengthy and detailed statute creating a comprehensive framework for regulating the production, distribution, and possession of five classes of 'controlled substances,'" . . . Thus, according to the Court, it was possible in *Lopez* to evaluate in isolation the constitutionality of criminalizing local activity (there gun possession in school zones), whereas the local activity that the CSA targets (in this case cultivation and possession of marijuana for personal medicinal use) cannot be separated from the general drug control scheme of which it is a part.

Today's decision allows Congress to regulate intrastate activity without check, so long as there is some implication by legislative design that regulating intrastate activity is essential (and the Court appears to equate "essential" with "necessary") to the interstate regulatory scheme. . . . [T]he Court appears to reason that the placement of local activity in a comprehensive scheme confirms that it is essential to that scheme. If the Court is right, then *Lopez* stands for nothing more than a drafting guide: Congress should have described the relevant crime as "transfer or possession of a firearm anywhere in the nation" — thus including commercial and noncommercial activity, and clearly encompassing some activity with assuredly substantial effect on interstate commerce. Had it done so, the majority hints, we would have sustained its authority to regulate possession of firearms in school zones. Furthermore, today's decision suggests we would readily sustain a congressional decision to attach the regulation of intrastate activity to a pre-existing comprehensive (or even not-so-comprehensive) scheme. If so, the Court invites increased federal regulation of local activity even if, as it suggests, Congress would not enact a *new* interstate scheme exclusively for the sake of reaching intrastate activity. . . .

I cannot agree that our decision in *Lopez* contemplated such evasive or overbroad legislative strategies with approval. Until today, such arguments have been made only in dissent. . . . *Lopez* and *Morrison* did not indicate that the constitutionality of federal regulation depends on superficial and formalistic distinctions. Likewise I did not understand our discussion of the role of courts in enforcing outer limits of the Commerce Clause for the sake of maintaining the federalist balance our Constitution requires, see *Lopez*, 514 U.S. at 557; *id.* at 578 (Kennedy, J., concurring), as a signal to Congress to enact legislation that is more extensive and more intrusive into the domain of state power. If the Court always defers to Congress as it does today, little may be left to the notion of enumerated powers.

The hard work for courts, then, is to identify objective markers for confining the analysis in Commerce Clause cases. Here, respondents challenge the constitutionality of the CSA as applied to them and those similarly situated. I agree with the Court that we must look beyond respondents' own activities. Otherwise, individual litigants could always exempt themselves from Commerce Clause regulation merely by pointing to the obvious — that their personal activities do not have a substantial effect on interstate commerce. . . . The task is to identify a mode of analysis that allows Congress to regulate more than nothing (by declining to reduce each case to its litigants) and less than everything (by declining to let Congress set the terms of analysis). The analysis may not be the same in every case, for it depends on the regulatory scheme at issue and the federalism concerns implicated.

A number of objective markers are available to confine the scope of constitutional review here. Both federal and state legislation — including the CSA itself, the California Compassionate Use Act, and other state medical marijuana legislation — recognize that medical and nonmedical (i.e., recreational) uses of drugs are realistically distinct and can be segregated, and regulate them differently. . . . Moreover, because fundamental structural concerns about dual sovereignty animate our Commerce Clause cases, it is relevant that this case involves the interplay of federal and state regulation in areas of criminal law and social policy, where "States lay claim by right of history and expertise." *Lopez, supra* at 583, . . . (Kennedy, J., concurring); . . . California, like other States, has drawn on its reserved powers to distinguish the regulation of medicinal marijuana. To ascertain whether Congress' encroachment is constitutionally justified in this case, then, I would focus here on the personal cultivation, possession, and use of marijuana for medicinal purposes.

B

Having thus defined the relevant conduct, we must determine whether, under our precedents, the conduct is economic and, in the aggregate, substantially affects interstate commerce. Even if intrastate cultivation and possession of marijuana for one's own medicinal use can properly be characterized as economic, and I question whether it can, it has not been shown that such activity substantially affects interstate commerce. Similarly, it is neither self-evident nor demonstrated that regulating such activity is necessary to the interstate drug control scheme.

The Court's definition of economic activity is breathtaking. It defines as economic any activity involving the production, distribution, and consumption of commodities. And it appears to reason that when an interstate market for a commodity exists, regulating the intrastate manufacture or possession of that commodity is constitutional either because that intrastate activity is itself economic, or because regulating it is a rational part of regulating its market. Putting to one side the problem endemic to the Court's opinion — the shift in focus from the activity at issue in this case to the entirety of what the CSA regulates, . . . — the Court's definition of economic activity for purposes of Commerce Clause jurisprudence threatens to sweep all of productive human activity into federal regulatory reach.

The Court uses a dictionary definition of economics to skirt the real problem of drawing a meaningful line between "what is national and what is local," *Jones & Laughlin Steel*, 301 U.S. at 37. It will not do to say that Congress may regulate noncommercial activity simply because it may have an effect on the demand for commercial goods, or because the noncommercial endeavor can, in some sense, substitute for commercial activity. Most commercial goods or services have some sort of privately producible analogue. Home care substitutes for daycare. Charades games substitute for movie tickets. Backyard or windowsill gardening substitutes for going to the supermarket. To draw the line wherever private activity affects the demand for market goods is to draw no line at all, and to declare everything economic. We have already rejected the result that would follow — a federal police power. *Lopez, supra* at 564.

In *Lopez* and *Morrison*, we suggested that economic activity usually relates directly to commercial activity. . . . The homegrown cultivation and personal possession and use of marijuana for medicinal purposes has no apparent commercial character. Everyone agrees that the marijuana at issue in this case was never in the stream of commerce, and neither were the supplies for growing it. . . .

The Court suggests that *Wickard*, which we have identified as "perhaps the most far reaching example of Commerce Clause authority over intrastate activity," *Lopez, supra* at 560, established federal regulatory power over any home consumption of a commodity for which a national market exists. I disagree. . . . The AAA itself confirmed that Congress made an explicit choice not to reach — and thus the Court could not possibly have approved of federal control over — small-scale, noncommercial wheat farming. . . . *Wickard*, then, did not extend Commerce Clause authority to something as modest as the home cook's herb garden. This is not to say that Congress may never regulate small quantities of commodities possessed or produced for personal use, or to deny that it sometimes needs to enact a zero tolerance regime for such commodities. It is merely to say that *Wickard* did not hold or imply that small-scale production of commodities is always economic, and automatically within Congress' reach.

Even assuming that economic activity is at issue in this case, the Government has made no showing in fact that the possession and use of homegrown marijuana for medical purposes, in California or elsewhere, has a substantial effect on interstate commerce. Similarly, the Government has not shown that regulating such activity is necessary to an interstate regulatory scheme. . . .

That is why characterizing this as a case about the Necessary and Proper Clause does not change the analysis significantly. Congress must exercise its authority under the Necessary and Proper Clause in a manner consistent with basic constitutional principles. . . . As Justice Scalia recognizes, . . . Congress cannot use its authority under the Clause to contravene the principle of state sovereignty embodied in the Tenth Amendment. . . . Likewise, that authority must be used in a manner consistent with the notion of enumerated powers — a structural principle that is as much part of the Constitution as the Tenth Amendment's explicit textual command. Accordingly, something more than mere assertion is required when Congress purports to have power over local activity whose connection to an intrastate market is not self-evident. Otherwise, the Necessary and Proper Clause will always be a back door for unconstitutional federal regulation. *Cf. Printz v. United States*, 521 U.S. 898, 923 (1997) (the Necessary and Proper Clause is "the last, best hope of those who defend ultra vires congressional action"). Indeed, if it were enough in "substantial effects" cases for the Court to supply conceivable justifications for intrastate regulation related to an interstate market, then we could have surmised in *Lopez* that guns in school zones are "never more than an instant from the interstate market" in guns already subject to extensive federal regulation, . . . recast *Lopez* as a Necessary and Proper Clause case, and thereby upheld the Gun-Free School Zones Act of 1990. . . .

There is simply no evidence that homegrown medicinal marijuana users constitute, in the aggregate, a sizable enough class to have a discernable, let alone substantial, impact on the national illicit drug market — or otherwise to threaten the CSA regime. . . .

Relying on Congress' abstract assertions, the Court has endorsed making it a federal crime to grow small amounts of marijuana in one's own home for one's own medicinal use. This overreaching stifles an express choice by some States, concerned for the lives and liberties of their people, to regulate medical marijuana differently. If I were a California citizen, I would not have voted for the medical marijuana ballot initiative; if I were a California legislator I would not have supported the Compassionate Use Act. But whatever the wisdom of California's experiment with medical marijuana, the federalism principles that have driven our Commerce Clause cases require that room for experiment be protected in this case. For these reasons I dissent.

JUSTICE THOMAS, dissenting.

Respondents Diane Monson and Angel Raich use marijuana that has never been bought or sold, that has never crossed state lines, and that has had no demonstrable effect on the national market for marijuana. If Congress can regulate this under the Commerce Clause, then it can regulate virtually anything — and the Federal Government is no longer one of limited and enumerated powers.

I

Respondents' local cultivation and consumption of marijuana is not "Commerce . . . among the several States." U.S. Const., Art. I, § 8, cl. 3. . . . Regulating respondents' conduct, however, is not "necessary and proper for carrying into Execution" Congress' restrictions on the interstate drug trade. Art. I, § 8, cl. 18. Thus, neither the Commerce Clause nor the Necessary and Proper Clause grants Congress the power to regulate respondents' conduct.

A

. . . The [Commerce] Clause's text, structure, and history all indicate that, at the time of the founding, the term " 'commerce' consisted of selling, buying, and bartering, as well as transporting for these purposes." . . . Commerce, or trade, stood in contrast to productive activities like manufacturing and agriculture. . . .

Even the majority does not argue that respondents' conduct is itself "Commerce among the several States." Art. I, § 8, cl. 3. . . . Respondents are correct that the CSA exceeds Congress' commerce power as applied to their conduct, which is purely intrastate and noncommercial.

B

More difficult, however, is whether the CSA is a valid exercise of Congress' power to enact laws that are "necessary and proper for carrying into Execution" its power to regulate interstate commerce. Art. I, § 8, cl. 18. The Necessary and Proper Clause is not a warrant to Congress to enact any law that bears some conceivable connection to the exercise of an enumerated power. Nor is it, however, a command to Congress to enact only laws that are absolutely indispensable to the exercise of an enumerated power.

In *McCulloch v. Maryland*, 4 Wheat. 316, this Court, speaking through Chief Justice Marshall, set forth a test for determining when an Act of Congress is permissible under the Necessary and Proper Clause:

"Let the end be legitimate, let it be within the scope of the constitution, and all means which are appropriate, which are plainly adapted to that end, which are not prohibited, but consist with the letter and spirit of the constitution, are constitutional.". . .

To act under the Necessary and Proper Clause, then, Congress must select a means that is "appropriate" and "plainly adapted" to executing an enumerated power; the means cannot be otherwise "prohibited" by the Constitution; and the means cannot be inconsistent with "the letter and spirit of the [C]onstitution." . . . The CSA, as applied to respondents' conduct, is not a valid exercise of Congress' power under the Necessary and Proper Clause.

1

Congress has exercised its power over interstate commerce to criminalize trafficking in marijuana across state lines. The Government contends that banning Monson and Raich's intrastate drug activity is "necessary and proper for carrying into Execution" its regulation of interstate drug trafficking. Art. I, § 8, cl. 18. *See* 21 U.S.C. § 801(6). However, in order to be "necessary," the intrastate ban must be more than "a reasonable means [of] effectuat[ing] the regulation of interstate commerce." . . . It must be "plainly adapted" to regulating interstate marijuana trafficking — in other words, there must be an "obvious, simple, and direct relation" between the intrastate ban and the regulation of interstate commerce. . . .

On its face, a ban on the intrastate cultivation, possession, and distribution of marijuana may be plainly adapted to stopping the interstate flow of marijuana. Unregulated local growers and users could swell both the supply and the demand sides of the interstate marijuana market, making the market more difficult to regulate. . . [R]espondents do not challenge the CSA on its face. Instead, they challenge it as applied to their conduct. The question is thus whether the intrastate ban is "necessary and proper" as applied to medical marijuana users like respondents. . . .

But even assuming that States' controls allow some seepage of medical marijuana into the illicit drug market, there is a multibillion-dollar interstate market for marijuana. . . . It is difficult to see how this vast market could be affected by diverted medical cannabis, let alone in a way that makes regulating intrastate medical marijuana obviously essential to controlling the interstate drug market.

. . . .

In sum, neither in enacting the CSA nor in defending its application to respondents has the Government offered any obvious reason why banning medical marijuana use is necessary to stem the tide of interstate drug trafficking. Congress' goal of curtailing the interstate drug trade would not plainly be thwarted if it could not apply the CSA to patients like Monson and Raich. That is, unless Congress' aim is really to exercise police power of the sort reserved to the States in order to eliminate even the intrastate possession and use of marijuana.

2

Even assuming the CSA's ban on locally cultivated and consumed marijuana is "necessary," that does not mean it is also "proper." The means selected by Congress to regulate interstate commerce cannot be "prohibited" by, or inconsistent with the "letter and spirit" of, the Constitution. *McCulloch*, 4 Wheat. at 421. . . .

II

A

The majority's treatment of the substantial effects test is rootless, because it is not tethered to either the Commerce Clause or the Necessary and Proper Clause. Under the Commerce Clause, Congress may regulate interstate commerce, not activities that substantially affect interstate commerce — any more than Congress may regulate activities that do not fall within, but that affect, the subjects of its other Article I powers. Whatever additional latitude the Necessary and Proper Clause affords, . . . the question is whether Congress' legislation is essential to the regulation of interstate commerce itself — not whether the legislation extends only to economic activities that substantially affect interstate commerce. . . .

Moreover, even a Court interested more in the modern than the original understanding of the Constitution ought to resolve cases based on the meaning of words that are actually in the document. Congress is authorized to regulate "Commerce," and respondents' conduct does not qualify under any definition of that term. The majority's opinion only illustrates the steady drift away from the text of the Commerce Clause. There is an inexorable expansion from " 'commerce,' " . . . to "commercial" and "economic" activity, . . . and finally to all "production, distribution, and consumption" of goods or services for which there is an "established . . . interstate market,". . . . Federal power expands, but never contracts, with each new locution. The majority is not interpreting the Commerce Clause, but rewriting it.

The majority's rewriting of the Commerce Clause seems to be rooted in the belief that, unless the Commerce Clause covers the entire web of human activity, Congress will be left powerless to regulate the national economy effectively. . . . The interconnectedness of economic activity is not a modern phenomenon unfamiliar to the Framers. . . . Moreover, the Framers understood what the majority does not appear to fully appreciate: There is a danger to concentrating too much, as well as too little, power in the Federal Government. This Court has carefully avoided stripping Congress of its ability to regulate *inter*state commerce, but it has casually allowed the Federal Government to strip States of their ability to regulate *intra*state commerce — not to mention a host of local activities, like mere drug possession, that are not commercial.

One searches the Court's opinion in vain for any hint of what aspect of American life is reserved to the States. Yet this Court knows that " '[t]he Constitution created a Federal Government of limited powers.' " . . . That is why today's decision will add no measure of stability to our Commerce Clause jurisprudence: This Court is willing neither to enforce limits on federal power, nor to declare the Tenth Amendment a dead letter. If stability is possible, it is only by discarding the stand-alone substantial effects test and revisiting our definition of "Commerce among the several States." Congress may regulate interstate commerce — not things that affect it, even when summed together, unless truly "necessary and proper" to regulating interstate commerce.

. . . .

NOTES

(1) *Gonzales v. Raich* represented the third significant Commerce Clause case the Supreme Court decided in a decade following *Lopez* and *Morrison*. Professor Thomas W. Merrill suggested in 2003 that Justice Scalia had never been as committed to the Rehnquist Court's federalism agenda as had some of his colleagues in the Rehnquist-O'Connor-Kennedy-Thomas bloc. Professor Merrill argued Justice Scalia had joined with them in *Lopez, Morrison*, and other cases due to strategic considerations. *See* Thomas W. Merrill, *The Making of the Second Rehnquist Court: A Preliminary Analysis*, 47 SAINT LOUIS U. L.J. 569, 604-20 (2003).

(2) In a more recent article, Professor Merrill argued that the Rehnquist Court's federalism jurisprudence initially was characterized by a clear statement approach before shifting its focus in the mid 1990s to the imposition of prohibitory rules. Thomas W. Merrill, *Paper Symposium: Federalism after Gonzales v. Raich; Symposium Article: Rescuing Federalism after* Raich; *The Case for Clear Statement Rules*, 9 LEWIS & CLARK L. REV. 823, 824-25 (2005).

Professor Merrill argued that the requirement of a clear statement is preferable to the imposition of prohibitive limitations where, as in the Commerce Clause context, the interpretational question involves the need to accommodate stability and change in the balance between federal and state powers, the meaning of the constitutional provision is not well settled, and interpretation requires the determination of legislative facts rather than adjudicative facts. *Id.* at 828-30. The prohibitory approach is better suited to areas where stability, not change, is needed or where the meaning of the constitutional provision is clear. Professor Merrill concluded that returning to a clear statement approach and applying it to Commerce Clause cases would be consistent with the outcome of the *Lopez* era cases, including *Raich*, and would best protect federalism. *Id.* at 851.

§ 2.06 TAXING POWER

NOTES

(1) *General Welfare Clause.* Article I, section 8, cl. 1 provides: "The Congress shall have Power To lay and collect Taxes, Duties, Imposts and Excises, to pay the Debts and provide for the common Defence and general Welfare of the United States." What does the power to provide for the general welfare include? Is the General Welfare Clause a distinctive source of power or merely a modification of the power of taxation? On this issue, Thomas Jefferson's view has prevailed — the General Welfare Clause qualifies the taxing power rather than constitutes an independent grant of power.

(2) What is the scope of the taxing power? Can Congress only tax for purposes suggested elsewhere in Article I? Or does the General Welfare Clause confer a broader license? Madison and Hamilton disagreed. Madison contended that the power must be confined to the enumerated fields committed to Congress. Hamilton maintained that the General Welfare Clause confers a power distinct from those enumerated and is not limited by the direct grants of legislative power in Article I. In *United States v. Butler,* 297 U.S. 1 (1936), the Supreme Court endorsed Hamilton's position. According to *Butler,* under Madison's approach, the "general welfare" phrase is "mere tautology." Hamilton's interpretation, is more consistent with the constitutional text. As *Butler* put it, "While, therefore, the power to tax is not unlimited, its confines are set in the clause which confers it, and not in those of section 8 which bestow and define the legislative powers of the Congress. It results that the power of Congress to authorize expenditure of public moneys for public purposes is not limited by the direct grants of legislative power found in the Constitution." *Id.* at 66. Congress' power to tax is thus limited only by the requirement that it be exercised to provide for the general welfare of the United States. Although the General Welfare Clause is only a qualification of the taxing power, not an independent source of authority, it confers tremendous powers. The breadth of the term means Congress' taxing authority is practically unlimited.

(3) *Purpose of taxation.* Justice Joseph Story posed the key question: "whether the government has a right to lay taxes for any other purpose, than to raise revenue, however much that purpose may be for the common defence, or general welfare." STORY, COMMENTARIES ON THE CONSTITUTION OF THE UNITED STATES § 958 (2d ed. 1851). A tax is primarily a means of raising revenue. But, read Marshall's celebrated statement in *McCulloch v. Maryland, infra* § 4.01, "the power to tax involves the power to destroy." It may also involve the power to regulate. May Congress flex its taxing power to suppress an activity it deems harmful?

(4) In *Veazie Bank v. Fenno,* 75 U.S. (8 Wall.) 533 (1869), an 1866 federal statute had imposed a 10 per cent tax on state bank notes circulated as currency to drive state bank notes out of circulation. According to John Kenneth Galbraith, the 1866 law "was perhaps the most directly impressive evidence in the nation's history that the power to tax is, indeed, the power to destroy." GALBRAITH, MONEY, WHENCE IT CAME, WHERE IT WENT 90 (1975). Since the purpose of Congress was destruction, rather than revenue, the statute was attacked as an invalid exercise of the taxing power. The Court rejected

the contention that because the law sought to destroy the subject of the tax it was invalid.

Veazie Bank emphasized that Congress could eliminate state bank notes by a law based upon Congress' Article I power to provide for a national currency. What happens, however, when power to tax is used to destroy an activity which Congress cannot suppress directly?

(5) *Bailey v. Drexel Furniture Co. (Child Labor Tax Cases)* 259 U.S. 20 (1922). Plaintiff Drexel Furniture Co. challenged an assessment against it of federal taxes of $6312.79 under the Child Labor Tax law. The law taxed employers 10 percent of profits if they employed children under certain ages or more than specified hours. Drexel Furniture argued that the Tenth Amendment reserved child employment to the states; IRS collector Bailey defended the tax under Art. I § 8.

The Court, speaking through Chief Justice Taft, held the Child Labor Tax unconstitutional. "Its prohibitory and regulatory effect and purpose are palpable." Although the Court had upheld other taxing acts even where a regulatory motive was suspected, here the "proof of the [regulatory motive] is found on the very face of [the statute]." To allow the federal government to regulate child labor through the tax power would "break down all constitutional limitation of the powers of Congress and completely wipe out the sovereignty of the States." The case was indistinguishable from *Hammer v. Dagenhart, supra* § 2.03[2]. The Court distinguished earlier cases in which regulatory taxes were upheld as either not regulatory on their face or regulating within another enumerated power of Congress. The substantial expansion of Congress' commerce power since *Hammer* was decided, has, to a great extent, lessened the importance of the question *Bailey* raised. If Congress could reach an array of activities under the Commerce Clause, it could also reach them under its taxing power even if the power to tax was limited by the powers and purposes of Article I. Moreover, since Congress could regulate an activity under the Commerce Clause, its dependence on the taxing power was considerably lessened. Although *Bailey* has not been overruled, it has only been applied once since 1922 to strike down a federal tax, during the period when the Court took a restrictive view of the Commerce Power. *See United States v. Constantine*, 296 U.S. 287 (1935) (invalidating higher federal tax on certain liquor businesses). Since *Constantine*, the Court has repeatedly rejected challenges to federal taxes based on a regulatory purpose beyond Congress' power.

(6) *United States v. Kahriger*, 345 U.S. 22 (1953), for instance, involved a challenge to the constitutionality of certain provisions of the Revenue Act of 1951, which taxed persons in the business of accepting wagers, and required them to register with the Collector of Internal Revenue. The tax was challenged on the grounds "that Congress, under the pretense of exercising its power to tax has attempted to penalize illegal intrastate gambling through the regulatory features of the Act, . . . and has thus infringed the police power which is reserved to the states . . . [and] that the registration provisions of the tax violate the privilege against self-incrimination and are arbitrary and vague, contrary to the guarantees of the Fifth Amendment." *Id.* at 24. The taxpayer argued that contrary to the Tenth Amendment "Congress has chosen to tax a specified business which is not within its power to regulate." For the majority Justice Reed wrote in part:

> Appellee would have us say that because there is legislative history indicating a congressional motive to suppress wagering, this tax is not a proper exercise of such taxing power. . . . The intent to curtail and hinder, as well as tax, was also manifest in the following cases, and in each of them the tax was upheld: *Veazie Bank v. Fenno*, 8 Wall. 533 (tax on paper money issued by state banks): *McCray v. United States*, 195 U.S. 27, 59 (tax on colored oleomargarine); *United States*

v. Doremus, 249 U.S. 86, and *Nigro v. United States*, 276 U.S. 332 (tax on narcotics); *Sonzinsky v. United States*, 300 U.S. 506 (tax on firearms); *United States v. Sanchez*, 340 U.S. 42 (tax on marijuana).

It is conceded that a federal excise tax does not cease to be valid merely because it discourages or deters the activities taxed. Nor is the tax invalid because the revenue obtained is negligible. Appellee, however, argues that the sole purpose of the statute is to penalize only illegal gambling in the states through the guise of a tax measure. As with the above excise taxes which we have held to be valid, the instant tax has a regulatory effect. But regardless of its regulatory effect, the wagering tax produces revenue. As such it surpasses both the narcotics and firearms taxes which we have found valid.

It is axiomatic that the power of Congress to tax is extensive and sometimes falls with crushing effect on businesses deemed unessential or inimical to the public welfare, or where, as in dealings with narcotics, the collection of the tax also is difficult. As is well known, the constitutional restraints on taxing are few. . . . The difficulty of saying when the power to lay uniform taxes is curtailed, because its use brings a result beyond the direct legislative power of Congress, has given rise to diverse decisions. In that area of abstract ideas, a final definition of the line between state and federal power has baffled judges and legislators. . . .

It is hard to understand why the power to tax should raise more doubts because of indirect effects than other federal powers. . . . Unless there are provisions, extraneous to any tax need, courts are without authority to limit the exercise of the taxing power. All the provisions of this excise are adapted to the collection of a valid tax."

Id. at 27-29, 31.

The Court also upheld the registration requirements regarding the filing of names, addresses, and places of business, as "directly and intimately related to the collection of the tax and [as] 'obviously supportable as in aid of a revenue purpose.' The registration provisions make the tax simpler to collect."

In dissent, Justice Frankfurter wrote, in part, that legislative motive was not subject to judicial scrutiny "provided only that the ulterior purpose is not expressed in ways which negative what the revenue words on their face express and, which do not seek enforcement of the formal revenue purpose through means that offend those standards of decency in our civilization against which due process is a barrier." He thought the formal revenue measure was really "an effort to check if not to stamp out professional gambling."

§ 2.07 SPENDING POWER

UNITED STATES v. BUTLER
297 U.S. 1, 56 S. Ct. 312, 80 L. Ed. 477 (1936)

Mr. Justice Roberts delivered the opinion of the Court.

In this case we must determine whether certain provisions of the Agricultural Adjustment Act, 1933, conflict with the Federal Constitution.

[Editor's note: In part, the Act declared an economic emergency due to the collapse of agricultural commodities. It authorized the Secretary of Agriculture to enter into voluntary agreements "for rental or benefit payments" with farmers "for reduction in the acreage or reduction in the production for market, or both, of any basic agricultural commodity." The Secretary's determination to institute rental or benefit payments regarding a product gave rise to a processing tax on that commodity to finance, along with an appropriation, the program. In July, 1933, the Secretary made the requisite determination regarding cotton.]

. . . .

The government asserts that even if the respondents may question the propriety of the appropriation embodied in the statute, their attack must fail because article 1, § 8 of the Constitution, authorizes the contemplated expenditure of the funds raised by the tax. This contention presents the great and the controlling question in the case. . . .

Article 1, § 8, of the Constitution, vests sundry powers in the Congress. . . .

The clause thought to authorize the legislation, the first, confers upon the Congress power "to lay and collect Taxes, Duties, Imposts and Excises, to pay the Debts and provide for the common Defence and general Welfare of the United States. . . ." The view that the clause grants power to provide for the general welfare, independently of the taxing power, has never been authoritatively accepted. . . . The true construction undoubtedly is that the only thing granted is the power to tax for the purpose of providing funds for payment of the nation's debts and making provision for the general welfare.

Nevertheless, the government asserts that warrant is found in this clause for the adoption of the Agricultural Adjustment Act. The argument is that Congress may appropriate and authorize the spending of moneys for the "general welfare"; that the phrase should be liberally construed to cover anything conducive to national welfare; that decision as to what will promote such welfare rests with Congress alone, and the courts may not review its determination; and, finally, that the appropriation under attack was in fact for the general welfare of the United States.

The Congress is expressly empowered to lay taxes to provide for the general welfare . . . These words cannot be meaningless, else they would not have been used. The conclusion must be that they were intended to limit and define the granted power to raise and to expend money. How shall they be construed to effectuate the intent of the instrument? . . .

We are not now required to ascertain the scope of the phrase "general welfare of the United States" or to determine whether an appropriation in aid of agriculture falls within it. Wholly apart from that question, another principle embedded in our Constitution prohibits the enforcement of the Agricultural Adjustment Act. The act invades the reserved rights of the states. It is a statutory plan to regulate and control agricultural production, a matter beyond the powers delegated to the federal government. The tax, the appropriation of the funds raised, and the direction for their disbursement, are but parts of the plan. They are but means to an unconstitutional end. . . .

It is an established principle that the attainment of a prohibited end may not be accomplished under the pretext of the exertion of powers which are granted. . . .

If the taxing power may not be used as the instrument to enforce a regulation of matters of state concern with respect to which the Congress has no authority to interfere, may it, as in the present case, be employed to raise the money necessary to purchase a compliance which the Congress is powerless to command? The government asserts that whatever might be said against the validity of the plan, if compulsory, it is constitutionally sound because the end is accomplished by voluntary co-operation. There are two sufficient answers to the contention. The regulation is not in fact voluntary. The farmer, of course, may refuse to comply, but the price of such refusal is the loss of benefits. The amount offered is intended to be sufficient to exert pressure on him to agree to the proposed regulation. The power to confer or withhold unlimited benefits is the power to coerce or destroy. . . .

But if the plan were one for purely voluntary co-operation it would stand no better so far as federal power is concerned. At best, it is a scheme for purchasing with federal funds submission to federal regulation of a subject reserved to the states. . . .

Congress has no power to enforce its commands on the farmer to the ends sought by the Agricultural Adjustment Act. It must follow that it may not indirectly accomplish those ends by taxing and spending to purchase compliance. The Constitution and the entire plan of our government negative any such use of the power to tax and to spend as the act undertakes to authorize. It does not help to declare that local conditions throughout the nation have created a situation of national concern; for this is but to say that whenever there is a widespread similarity of local conditions, Congress may ignore constitutional limitations upon its own powers and usurp those reserved to the states. If in lieu of compulsory regulation of subjects within the states' reserved jurisdiction, which is prohibited, the Congress could invoke the taxing and spending power as a means to accomplish the same end, clause 1 of section 8 of article 1 would become the instrument for total subversion of the governmental powers reserved to the individual states. . . .

The judgment is affirmed.

Mr. Justice Stone dissenting.

. . . It is upon the contention that state power is infringed by purchased regulation of agricultural production that chief reliance is placed. It is insisted that, while the Constitution gives to Congress, in specific and unambiguous terms, the power to tax and spend, the power is subject to limitations which do not find their origin in any express provision of the Constitution and to which other expressly delegated powers are not subject.

The Constitution requires that public funds shall be spent for a defined purpose, the promotion of the general welfare. Their expenditure usually involves payment on terms which will insure use by the selected recipients within the limits of the constitutional purpose. Expenditures would fail of their purpose and thus lose their constitutional sanction if the terms of payment were not such that by their influence on the action of the recipients the permitted end would be attained. The power of Congress to spend is inseparable from persuasion to action over which Congress has no legislative control. . . . It makes no difference that there is a promise to do an act which the condition is calculated to induce. Condition and promise are alike valid since both are in furtherance of the national purpose for which the money is appropriated. . . .

It is a contradiction in terms to say that there is power to spend for the national welfare, while rejecting any power to impose conditions reasonably adapted to the attainment of the end which alone would justify the expenditure.

The limitation now sanctioned must lead to absurd consequences. The government may give seeds to farmers, but may not condition the gift upon their being planted in places where they are most needed or even planted at all. The government may give money to the unemployed, but may not ask that those who get it shall give labor in return, or even use it to support their families. It may give money to sufferers from earthquake, fire, tornado, pestilence, or flood, but may not impose conditions, health precautions, designed to prevent the spread of disease, or induce the movement of population to safer or more sanitary areas. All that, because it is purchased regulation infringing state powers, must be left for the states, who are unable or unwilling to supply the necessary relief. . . .

MR. JUSTICE BRANDEIS and MR. JUSTICE CARDOZO join in this opinion.

NOTE

In a portion of his dissent not reproduced, Justice Stone noted, "That the governmental power of the purse is a great one is not now for the first time announced. Every student of the history of government and economics is aware of its magnitude and of its existence in every civilized government." *Butler*, 297 U.S. at 86. The power of the purse, in its broadest sense, is comprehended in the grant to Congress of taxing authority. The power to tax includes the power to spend, and the latter is at least as broad as the tax power itself. This means that public funds may be appropriated "to provide for the general welfare." Can the disbursement of federal funds be attacked on the ground that it is motivated by an invalid purpose? How does the *Butler* Court's answer compare to that given in the *Child Labor Tax Case, supra* § 2.03[2]? Despite its disclaimer, did the *Butler* Court really adopt Madison's interpretation of the General Welfare Clause, as discussed *supra* § 2.06, Note (1)?

SOUTH DAKOTA v. DOLE
483 U.S. 203, 107 S. Ct. 2793, 97 L. Ed. 2d 171 (1987)

CHIEF JUSTICE RREHNQUIST delivered the opinion of the Court.

Petitioner South Dakota permits persons 19 years of age or older to purchase beer containing up to 3.2% alcohol. S.D. Codified Laws § 35-6-27 (1986). In 1984 Congress enacted 23 U.S.C. § 158 (1982 ed., Supp. III) ("§ 158"), which directs the Secretary of Transportation to withhold a percentage of federal highway funds otherwise allocable from States "in which the purchase or possession of any alcoholic beverage by a person who is less than twenty-one years of age is lawful." The State sued in United States District Court seeking declaratory judgment that § 158 violates the constitutional limitations on congressional exercise of the spending power and violates the Twenty-first Amendment to the United States Constitution. The District Court rejected the State's claims, and the Court of Appeals for the Eighth Circuit affirmed. . . .

The Constitution empowers Congress to "lay and collect Taxes, Duties, Imposts, and Excises, to pay the Debts and provide for the common Defence and general Welfare of the United States." Art. I, § 8, cl. 1. Incident to this power, Congress may attach conditions on the receipt of federal funds, and has repeatedly employed the power "to further broad policy objectives by conditioning receipt of federal moneys upon compliance by the recipient with federal statutory and administrative directives." . . . The breadth of this power was made clear in *United States v. Butler*, where the Court, resolving a longstanding debate over the scope of the Spending Clause, determined that "the power of Congress to authorize expenditure of public moneys for public purposes is not limited by the direct grants of legislative power found in the Constitution." Thus, objectives not thought to be within Article I's "enumerated legislative fields" . . . may nevertheless be attained through the use of the spending power and the conditional grant of federal funds.

The spending power is of course not unlimited, . . . but is instead subject to several general restrictions articulated in our cases. The first of these limitations is derived from the language of the Constitution itself: the exercise of the spending power must be in pursuit of "the general welfare." . . . In considering whether a particular expenditure is intended to serve general public purposes, courts should defer substantially to the judgment of Congress. . . . Second, we have required that if Congress desires to condition the States' receipt of federal funds, it "must do so unambiguously . . . , enabl[ing] the States to exercise their choice knowingly, cognizant of the consequences of their participation.". . . Third, our cases have suggested (without significant elaboration) that conditions on federal grants might be illegitimate if they are unrelated "to the federal interest in particular national projects or programs." . . . Finally, we have noted that other constitutional provisions may provide an independent bar to the conditional grant of federal funds. . . .

South Dakota does not seriously claim that § 158 is inconsistent with any of the first three restrictions mentioned above. We can readily conclude that the provision is designed to serve the general welfare . . . . The means it chose to address this dangerous situation were reasonably calculated to advance the general welfare. The conditions upon which States receive the funds, moreover, could not be more clearly stated by Congress. . . . Indeed, the condition imposed by Congress is directly related to one of the main purposes for which highway funds are expended — safe interstate travel. This goal of the interstate highway system had been frustrated by varying drinking ages among the States. . . . By enacting § 158, Congress conditioned the receipt of federal funds in a way reasonably calculated to address this particular impediment to a purpose for which the funds are expended.

The remaining question about the validity of § 158 — and the basic point of disagreement between the parties — is whether the Twenty-first Amendment constitutes an "independent constitutional bar" to the conditional grant of federal funds. . . . Petitioner, relying on its view that the Twenty-first Amendment prohibits direct regulation of drinking ages by Congress, asserts that "Congress may not use the spending power to regulate that which it is prohibited from regulating directly under the Twenty-first Amendment." But our cases show that this "independent constitutional bar" limitation on the spending power is not of the kind petitioner suggests. *United States v. Butler*, . . . for example, established that the constitutional limitations on Congress when exercising its spending power are less exacting than those on its authority to regulate directly.

We have also held that a perceived Tenth Amendment limitation on congressional regulation of state affairs did not concomitantly limit the range of conditions legitimately placed on federal grants. . . . [Our] cases establish that the "independent constitutional bar" limitation on the spending power is not, as petitioner suggests, a prohibition on the indirect achievement of objectives which Congress is not empowered to achieve directly. Instead, we think that the language in our earlier opinions stands for the unexceptionable proposition that the power may not be used to induce the States to engage in activities that would themselves be unconstitutional. Thus, for example, a grant of federal funds conditioned on invidiously discriminatory state action or the infliction of cruel and unusual punishment would be an illegitimate exercise of the Congress' broad spending power. But no such claim can be or is made here. Were South Dakota to succumb to the blandishments offered by Congress and raise its drinking age to 21, the State's action in so doing would not violate the constitutional rights of anyone.

Our decisions have recognized that in some circumstances the financial inducement offered by Congress might be so coercive as to pass the point at which "pressure turns into compulsion." . . . Here, however, Congress has directed only that a State desiring to establish a minimum drinking age lower than 21 lose a relatively small percentage of certain federal highway funds. Petitioner contends that the coercive nature of this program is evident from the degree of success it has achieved. We cannot conclude, however, that a conditional grant of federal money of this sort is unconstitutional simply by reason of its success in achieving the congressional objective.

When we consider, for a moment, that all South Dakota would lose if she adheres to her chosen course as to a suitable minimum drinking age is 5% of the funds otherwise obtainable under specified highway grant programs, the argument as to coercion is shown to be more rhetoric than fact. As we said a half century ago in *Steward Machine Co. v. Davis*:

> [E]very rebate from a tax when conditioned upon conduct is in some measure a temptation. But to hold that motive or temptation is equivalent to coercion is to plunge the law in endless difficulties. The outcome of such a doctrine is the acceptance of a philosophical determinism by which choice becomes impossible. Till now the law has been guided by a robust common sense which assumes the freedom of the will as a working hypothesis in the solution of its problems. . . .

Here Congress has offered relatively mild encouragement to the States to enact higher minimum drinking ages than they would otherwise choose. But the enactment of such laws remains the prerogative of the States not merely in theory but in fact. Even if Congress might lack the power to impose a national minimum drinking age directly, we conclude that encouragement to state action found in § 158 is a valid use of the spending power. Accordingly, the judgment of the Court of Appeals is *Affirmed*.

NOTES

(1) *Conditional-grants-in-aid.* The grant of federal subventions to the states is not a new practice. During the early days of the Republic, the federal government gave vast amounts of public lands to the states for the development of schools, universities, roads, canals and railroads and for reclamation purposes. In 1837, a $28 million surplus in the federal treasury was given to the states in proportion to their representation in Congress. These early cases involved simple grants without conditions: there was no attempt to regulate the manner in which the federal subventions might be used.

(2) Note how the *South Dakota v. Dole* approach fits in with the post-*Jones & Laughlin* Commerce Clause cases, *supra* § 2.04[1] and *Kahriger, supra* § 2.06. If the Court will not look behind a law regulating commerce or a tax law to see that it was not motivated by an improper purpose, should the same be true where spending of federal funds is concerned? Should the Court condemn federal disbursements to promote what Congress deems the general welfare because the money is spent to induce action that Congress may not be able to control directly?

(3) In *Oklahoma v. United States Civil Service Commission*, 330 U.S. 127 (1947), discussed in an omitted part of *South Dakota v. Dole*, the state protested enforcement of a federal statute which conditioned its right to receive federal highway funds upon its removal from office of a member of the State Highway Commission who was active in politics. Does Congress have any power to regulate the political activities of state employees? Can it use the power of the purse to accomplish the desired end of a politically neutral state government service? According to the *Oklahoma* opinion, "[W]hile the United States is not concerned and has no power to regulate local political activities as such of state officials, it does have the power to fix the terms upon which its money allotments to states shall be disbursed." *Id.* at 143. How far does the *Oklahoma* rationale go? May the spending power be used without limit to secure "purchased compliance" by the states with any and all Congressional policies?

(4) *Rust v. Sullivan*, 500 U.S. 173 (1991), upheld regulations of the Department of Health and Human Services that placed conditions on the grant of federal funds to projects providing services under Title X of the Public Health Services Act. Specifically, Title X prohibited projects from providing "counseling concerning the use of abortion as a method of family planning." If a pregnant woman requested counseling or referral, the regulations suggested that a permissible response would be that "the project does not consider abortion an appropriate method of family planning and therefore does not counsel or refer for abortion." Other conditions prohibited Title X projects from engaging in activities that "encourage, promote or advocate abortion as a method of

family planning" and "require that Title X projects be organized so that they are 'physically and financially separate' " from prohibited abortion activities.

Among the constitutional challenges to the regulations was the contention that they imposed unconstitutional conditions on the expenditure of federal funds. The regulations were upheld, with Chief Justice Rehnquist writing the majority opinion in which Justices White, Kennedy, Scalia, and Souter joined. Justices Blackmun, Marshall, Stevens, and O'Connor dissented.

(5) After the decision in *United States v. Lopez*, *supra* § 2.05, President Clinton indicated how he thought Congress could achieve the result sought under the Gun-Free School Zones Act:

> Congress could encourage states to ban guns from school zones by linking federal funds to enactment of school zone gun bans.

President's Radio Address, I PUBLIC PAPERS OF PRESIDENT'S WILLIAM JEFFERSON CLINTON 610 (April 29, 1995).

Could Congress thus, as the President's speech put it, "reverse the practical impact of the Court's [*Lopez*] decision?" Is there a difference between Congress acting under the Commerce Clause and the spending power? Might Congress prefer to regulate through the commerce power rather than through conditional grants?

(6) In *Sabri v. United States*, 541 U.S. 600 (2004), the Court held that under Article I of the Constitution, Congress could criminalize bribery of state and local officials of entities receiving federal funds even absent any connection between the forbidden conduct and the federal funds. Sabri was indicted for violating 18 U.S.C. § 666(a)(2) which proscribed attempting to bribe, with anything of at least $5,000 value, a state, local or tribal official with an entity that received more than $10,000 in federal benefits. Sabri challenged the law as facially invalid because it failed to require a connection between the bribe and federal funds. In a unanimous decision, the Court rejected Sabri's argument. Under the Spending Clause, Congress could appropriate money to promote the general welfare, and under the Necessary and Proper Clause, it could take action to make certain that federal funds were not diverted from the general welfare to corrupt applications. *Id.* at 605. Congress was not limited to legislating with respect to bribes traceable to federal programs since the federal interest encompassed having any untrustworthy officials in possession of federal funds. *Id.*

The Court distinguished *Sabri* from the statutes at issue in *United States v. Lopez*, 514 U.S. 549 (1995), and *United States v. Morrison*, 529 U.S. 598 (2000), which the Court held were beyond Congress' commerce power since the relationship between the legislation and commerce was too attenuated. "No piling [of inference upon inference] is needed here to show that Congress was within its prerogative to protect spending objects from the menace of local administrators on the take," wrote Justice Souter for eight justices. *Lopez*, 541 U.S. at 608.

§ 2.08 TREATY POWER

NOTES

(1) The Supremacy Clause of Article VI expressly makes treaties (along with the Constitution and federal laws) "the supreme Law of the Land." In American law, a treaty is more than an international compact or agreement; it must "be regarded in courts of justice as equivalent to an act of the legislature, whenever it operates of itself without the aid of any legislative provision." *Foster v. Neilson*, 27 U.S. (2 Pet.) 253, 314 (1829). In other words, unless a treaty is not self-executing, it takes effect of itself as part of our law, like an Act of Congress. "A treaty, then, is a law of the land as an act

of Congress is, whenever its provisions prescribe a rule by which the rights of the private citizen or subject may be determined." *Head Money Cases*, 112 U.S. 580, 598-99 (1884)A court may resort to a treaty for a rule of decision as it would to a statute. A part of "the supreme Law of the Land," a treaty must override all conflicting state laws. What happens if a treaty conflicts with a federal law? Article VI provides that both treaties and "Laws of the United States . . . shall be the supreme Law of the Land." This means that a treaty has the same status as a federal statute. Where treaties and federal statutes conflict, the later in date will control.

(2) Should an act of our Congress override an international obligation of the United States? In the *Head Money Cases*, the Court upheld a federal statute which imposed a head tax on immigrants entering this country, despite earlier treaties guaranteeing their free admission: . . ."we are of opinion that, so far as a treaty made by the United States with any foreign nation can become the subject of judicial cognizance in the courts of this country, it is subject to such acts as Congress may pass for its enforcement, modification, or repeal." *Id.* at 599. Good faith toward the other contracting nation might require Congress to refrain from making any change, "but if it does act, its enactment becomes the controlling law in this country. The other nation may have ground for complaint, but every person is bound to obey the law." *Rainey v. United States*, 232 U.S. 310, 316-317 (1914).

MISSOURI v. HOLLAND
252 U.S. 416, 40 S. Ct. 382, 64 L.E d. 641 (1920)

MR. JUSTICE HOLMES delivered the opinion of the Court.

This is a bill in equity brought by the State of Missouri to prevent a game warden of the United States from attempting to enforce the Migratory Bird Treaty Act of July 3, 1918. . . . The ground of the bill is that the statute is an unconstitutional interference with the rights reserved to the States by the Tenth Amendment. . . . A motion to dismiss was sustained by the District Court on the ground that the Act of Congress is constitutional. . . . The State appeals.

On December 8, 1916, a treaty between the United States and Great Britain was proclaimed by the President. It recited that many species of birds in their annual migrations traversed many parts of the United States and of Canada, that they were of great value as a source of food and in destroying insects injurious to vegetation, but were in danger of extermination through lack of adequate protection. It therefore provided for specified closed seasons and protection in other forms, and agreed that the two powers would take or propose to their lawmaking bodies the necessary measures for carrying the treaty out. . . . The above mentioned act of July 3, 1918, entitled an act to give effect to the convention, prohibited the killing, capturing or selling any of the migratory birds included in the terms of the treaty except as permitted by regulations compatible with those terms, to be made by the Secretary of Agriculture. . . . It is unnecessary to go into any details, because, as we have said, the question raised is the general one whether the treaty and statute are void as an interference with the rights reserved to the States.

To answer this question it is not enough to refer to the Tenth Amendment, reserving the powers not delegated to the United States, because by Article 2, Section 2, the power to make treaties is delegated expressly, and by Article 6 treaties made under the authority of the United States, along with the Constitution and laws of the United States made in pursuance thereof, are declared the supreme law of the land. If the treaty is valid there can be no dispute about the validity of the statute under Article 1, Section 8, as a necessary and proper means to execute the powers of the Government. The language of the Constitution as to the supremacy of treaties being general, the question before us is narrowed to an inquiry into the ground upon which the present supposed exception is placed.

It is said that a treaty cannot be valid if it infringes the Constitution, that there are limits, therefore, to the treaty-making power, and that one such limit is that what an act of Congress could not do unaided, in derogation of the powers reserved to the States, a treaty cannot do. An earlier act of Congress that attempted by itself and not in pursuance of a treaty to regulate the killing of migratory birds within the States had been held bad in the District Court. *United States v. Shauver*, 214 Fed. 154. *United States v. McCullagh*, 221 Fed. 288. Those decisions were supported by arguments that migratory birds were owned by the States in their sovereign capacity for the benefit of their people, and that . . . this control was one that Congress had no power to displace. The same argument is supposed to apply now with equal force.

Whether the two cases cited were decided rightly or not they cannot be accepted as a test of the treaty power. Acts of Congress are the supreme law of the land only when made in pursuance of the Constitution, while treaties are declared to be so when made under the authority of the United States. It is open to question whether the authority of the United States means more than the formal acts prescribed to make the convention. We do not mean to imply that there are no qualifications to the treaty-making power; but they must be ascertained in a different way. It is obvious that there may be matters of the sharpest exigency for the national well being that an act of Congress could not deal with but that a treaty followed by such an act could, and it is not lightly to be assumed that, in matters requiring national action, "a power which must belong to and somewhere reside in every civilized government" is not to be found. *Andrews v. Andrews*, 188 U.S. 14, 33. What was said in that case with regard to the powers of the States applies with equal force to the powers of the nation in cases where the States individually are incompetent to act. We are not yet discussing the particular case before us but only are considering the validity of the test proposed. With regard to that we may add that when we are dealing with words that also are a constituent act, like the Constitution of the United States, we must realize that they have called into life a being the development of which could not have been foreseen completely by the most gifted of its begetters. It was enough for them to realize or to hope that they had created an organism; it has taken a century and has cost their successors much sweat and blood to prove that they created a nation. The case before us must be considered in the light of our whole experience and not merely in that of what was said a hundred years ago. The treaty in question does not contravene any prohibitory words to be found in the Constitution. The only question is whether it is forbidden by some invisible radiation from the general terms of the Tenth Amendment. We must consider what this country has become in deciding what that amendment has reserved. . . .

Here a national interest of very nearly the first magnitude is involved. It can be protected only by national action in concert with that of another power. The subject matter is only transitorily within the State and has no permanent habitat therein. But for the treaty and the statute there soon might be no birds for any powers to deal with.

We see nothing in the Constitution that compels the Government to sit by while a food supply is cut off and the protectors of our forests and our crops are destroyed. It is not sufficient to rely upon the States. The reliance is vain, and were it otherwise, the question is whether the United States is forbidden to act. We are of opinion that the treaty and statute must be upheld. . . .

Decree affirmed.

Justice Van Devanter and Justice Pitner dissent.

NOTES

(1) Before *Missouri v. Holland*, no one doubted that the governing rule was stated in *The Cherokee Tobacco*, 78 U.S. (11 Wall.) 616, 620-21 (1870): "It need hardly be said that a treaty cannot change the Constitution or be held valid if it be in violation of that instrument. This results from the nature and fundamental principles of our government." Does *Missouri v. Holland* change this rule? What are the implications of Justice Holmes' opinion?

(2) Two years prior to *Missouri v. Holland, Hammer v. Dagenhart, supra* § 2.03[2], had held that Congress could not prohibit child labor in production under its commerce power. Under *Missouri v. Holland*, could child labor be subjected to Congressional power by the making of a treaty on the subject with another country?

(3) In *Missouri v. Holland*, the Court noted that whereas congressional acts "are the supreme law of the land only when made in pursuance of the Constitution, . . . treaties are declared to be so when made under the authority of the United States." Does this mean a treaty, made by the President with the advise and consent of two-thirds of the Senate, can violate other constitutional provisions? If so, is a treaty more supreme than the Constitution? Does the Amendment Clause of the Constitution, which requires a more onerous mechanism for constitutional amendment, impeach any argument that a treaty can violate the Constitution?

(4) In *Reid v. Covert*, 354 U.S. 1 (1957), Mrs. Clarice Covert killed her husband, an Air Force sergeant, at an airbase in England. Mrs. Covert, a civilian, was tried by a court-martial for murder under Article 118 of the Uniform Code of Military Justice (UCMJ). Jurisdiction was asserted over Mrs. Covert under an executive agreement between the United States and Great Britain that permitted American military courts to exercise exclusive jurisdiction over offenses committed in Great Britain by American servicemen or their dependents.

A court-martial did not afford Mrs. Covert trial by jury and other Bill of Rights protections. The Court, in a plurality opinion by Justice Black, held Mrs. Covert entitled to the protection of the Bill of Rights notwithstanding the international agreement. "The obvious and decisive answer . . . of course, is that no agreement with a foreign nation can confer power on the Congress, or on any branch of Government, which is free from the restraints of the Constitution." *Id.* at 16.

According to Justice Black, the Supremacy Clause does not intimate

> that treaties and laws enacted pursuant to them do not have to comply with the provisions of the Constitution. Nor is there anything in the debates which accompanied the drafting and ratification of the Constitution which even suggests such a result. These debates as well as the history that surrounds the adoption of the treaty provision in Article VI make it clear that the reason treaties were not limited to those made in "pursuance" of the Constitution was so that agreements made by the United States under the Articles of Confederation, including the important peace treaties which concluded the Revolutionary War, would remain in effect. It would be manifestly contrary to the objectives of those who created the Constitution, as well as those who were responsible for the Bill of Rights — let alone alien to our entire constitutional history and tradition — to construe Article VI as permitting the United States to exercise power under an international agreement without observing constitutional prohibitions. In effect, such construction would permit amendment of

that document in a manner not sanctioned by Article V. The prohibitions of the Constitution were designed to apply to all branches of the National government and they cannot be nullified by the Executive or by the Executive and the Senate combined.

Id. at 16-17.

(5) A few years before *Reid v. Covert*, Secretary of State, John Foster Dulles said treaties are "more supreme than ordinary laws, for congressional laws are invalid if they do not conform to the Constitution, whereas treaty law can override the Constitution." Treaties and Executive Agreements, *Hearings before a Subcommittee of the Senate Committee on the Judiciary*, 83d Cong., 1st Sess. 862 (1953). Is the Dulles statement consistent with *Reid v. Covert*? Would Justice Black's reasoning apply to a treaty as well as the executive agreements with Britain upon which the government relied?

(6) Who has the power to terminate treaties? Note that under the Constitution, both the President and the Senate participate in the making of treaties. Does the President have the power to terminate treaties without any Congressional or Senatorial participation? *See Goldwater v. Carter, supra* § 1.09.

(7) During the 1950s, Senator John Bricker of Ohio spearheaded a move to overturn *Holland* by a constitutional amendment. The move died out for a variety of reasons, including the fact that *Reid* addressed some of the concerns animating Senator Bricker's effort.

(8) *Missouri v. Holland*, of course, suggests that the treaty power is not subject to federalism constraints. Professor Curtis A. Bradley has written:

> The treaty power in this country is a power to make supreme federal law. For much of our history, courts, commentators, and government officials have assumed that this power is limited by subject matter, states' rights, or both. In recent years, however, conventional wisdom has denied any such limitations. The result of this view is that the treaty makers have essentially unlimited power vis-á-vis the states. Such unlimited power, however, is inconsistent with a central principle of American federalism — that the national government's powers are limited and enumerated. This inconsistency is particularly significant today, in light of the rapidly expanding nature of this country's treaty commitments.

See Bradley, *The Treaty Power and American Federalism*, 97 MICH. L. REV. 390, 461 (1998). Must the judiciary vindicate federalism by reviewing treaties to detect any intrusions on state prerogatives? Does the political process offer any safeguards? Does the fact that the senate must approve a treaty by a two-thirds vote protect the states?

Chapter III
LIMITS ON NATIONAL POWER OVER THE STATES

§ 3.01 RESERVED POWERS

U.S. TERM LIMITS INC. v. THORNTON
514 U.S. 779, 115 S. Ct. 1842, 131 L. Ed. 2d. 881 (1995)

[Editor's Note: In 1992, Arkansas voters approved Amendment 73 to the state constitution. In part, it imposed term limits on Arkansas' members of the United States Senate and House of Representatives. Various Arkansas citizens and associations sought a declaration in state court that the measure was unconstitutional. A state circuit court held it violated Article I of the Constitution. The state supreme court affirmed. The State of Arkansas petitioned for certiorari.]

JUSTICE STEVENS delivered the opinion of the Court.

The Constitution sets forth qualifications for membership in the Congress of the United States. Article I, § 2, cl. 2, which applies to the House of Representatives, provides:

> No Person shall be a Representative who shall not have attained to the Age of twenty five Years, and been seven Years a Citizen of the United States, and who shall not, when elected, be an Inhabitant of that State in which he shall be chosen.

Article I, § 3, cl. 3, which applies to the Senate, similarly provides:

> No Person shall be a Senator who shall not have attained to the Age of thirty Years, and been nine Years a Citizen of the United States, and who shall not, when elected, be an Inhabitant of that State for which he shall be chosen.

Today's cases present a challenge to an amendment to the Arkansas State Constitution that prohibits the name of an otherwise-eligible candidate for Congress from appearing on the general election ballot if that candidate has already served three terms in the House of Representatives or two terms in the Senate. . . . Such a state-imposed restriction is contrary to the "fundamental principle of our representative democracy," embodied in the Constitution, that "the people should choose whom they please to govern them." . . . Allowing individual States to adopt their own qualifications for congressional service would be inconsistent with the Framers' vision of a uniform National Legislature representing the people of the United States. If the qualifications set forth in the text of the Constitution are to be changed, that text must be amended. . . . [T]he constitutionality of Amendment 73 depends critically on . . . whether the Constitution forbids States from adding to or altering the qualifications specifically enumerated in the Constitution. . . . Our resolution of these issues draws upon our prior resolution of a related but distinct issue: whether Congress has the power to add to or alter the qualifications of its Members.

Twenty-six years ago, in *Powell v. McCormack*, 395 U.S. 486 (1969) [*supra* § 1.09, Note (5) after *Nixon*] we reviewed the history and text of the Qualifications Clauses in a case involving an attempted exclusion of a duly elected Member of Congress [Adam Clayton Powell, Jr.]. The principal issue was whether the power granted to each House in Art. I, § 5, to judge the "Qualifications of its own Members" includes the power to impose qualifications other than those set forth in the text of the Constitution. In an opinion by Chief Justice Warren . . . we held that it does not. . . .

Powell's Reliance on Democratic Principles

In *Powell*, of course, we did not rely solely on an analysis of the historical evidence, but instead complemented that analysis with "an examination of the basic principles of our democratic system." We noted that allowing Congress to impose additional qualifications would violate that "fundamental principle of our representative democracy . . . 'that the people should choose whom they please to govern them.' "

Our opinion made clear that this broad principle incorporated at least two fundamental ideas. First, we emphasized the egalitarian concept that the opportunity to be elected was open to all. . . . Second, we recognized the critical postulate that sovereignty is vested in the people, and that sovereignty confers on the people the right to choose freely their representatives to the National Government. . . . *Powell* thus establishes two important propositions: first, . . . that, at least with respect to qualifications imposed by Congress, the Framers intended the qualifications listed in the Constitution to be exclusive; and second, that that conclusion is equally compelled by an understanding of the "fundamental principle of our representative democracy . . . 'that the people should choose whom they please to govern them.' " . . .

III

Our reaffirmation of *Powell*, does not necessarily resolve the specific questions presented in these cases. For petitioners argue that whatever the constitutionality of additional qualifications for membership imposed by Congress, the historical and textual materials discussed in *Powell* do not support the conclusion that the Constitution prohibits additional qualifications imposed by States. In the absence of such a constitutional prohibition, petitioners argue, the Tenth Amendment and the principle of reserved powers require that States be allowed to add such qualifications. . . .

Petitioners argue that the Constitution contains no express prohibition against state-added qualifications, and that Amendment 73 is therefore an appropriate exercise of a State's reserved power to place additional restrictions on the choices that its own voters may make. We disagree for two independent reasons. First, we conclude that the power to add qualifications is not within the "original powers" of the States, and thus is not reserved to the States by the Tenth Amendment. Second, even if States possessed some original power in this area, we conclude that the Framers intended the Constitution to be the exclusive source of qualifications for members of Congress, and that the Framers thereby "divested" States of any power to add qualifications. . . .

Source of the Power

Contrary to petitioners' assertions, the power to add qualifications is not part of the original powers of sovereignty that the Tenth Amendment reserved to the States. Petitioners' Tenth Amendment argument misconceives the nature of the right at issue because that Amendment could only "reserve" that which existed before. As Justice Story recognized, "the states can exercise no powers whatsoever, which exclusively spring out of the existence of the national government, which the constitution does not delegate to them. . . . No state can say, that it has reserved, what it never possessed." . . .

With respect to setting qualifications for service in Congress, no such right existed before the Constitution was ratified. The contrary argument overlooks the revolutionary character of the government that the Framers conceived. . . . [T]he Framers envisioned a uniform national system, rejecting the notion that the Nation was a collection of States, and instead creating a direct link between the National Government and the people of the United States. . . . In that National Government, representatives owe primary allegiance not to the people of a State, but to the people of the Nation. . . . Representatives and Senators are as much officers of the entire union as is the

President. States thus "have just as much right, and no more, to prescribe new qualifications for a representative, as they have for a president. . . . It is no original prerogative of state power to appoint a representative, a senator, or president for the union." . . .

We believe that the Constitution reflects the Framers' general agreement with the approach later articulated by Justice Story. For example, Art. I, § 5, cl. 1, provides: "Each House shall be the Judge of the Elections, Returns and Qualifications of its own Members." The text of the Constitution thus gives the representatives of all the people the final say in judging the qualifications of the representatives of any one State. For this reason, the dissent falters when it states that "the people of Georgia have no say over whom the people of Massachusetts select to represent them in Congress.". . .

Two other sections of the Constitution further support our view of the Framers' vision. First, consistent with Story's view, the Constitution provides that the salaries of representatives should "be ascertained by Law, and paid out of the Treasury of the United States," Art. I, § 6, rather than by individual States. The salary provisions reflect the view that representatives owe their allegiance to the people, and not to the States. Second, the provisions governing elections reveal the Framers' understanding that powers over the election of federal officers had to be delegated to, rather than reserved by, the States. It is surely no coincidence that the context of federal elections provides one of the few areas in which the Constitution expressly requires action by the States, namely that "[t]he Times, Places and Manner of holding Elections for Senators and Representatives, shall be prescribed in each State by the Legislature thereof." Art. I, § 4, cl. 1. This duty parallels the duty under Article II that "Each State shall appoint, in such Manner as the Legislature thereof may direct, a Number of Electors." Art. II, § 1, cl. 2. These Clauses are express delegations of power to the States to act with respect to federal elections. . . .

In short, . . . electing representatives to the National Legislature was a new right, arising from the Constitution itself. The Tenth Amendment thus provides no basis for concluding that the States possess reserved power to add qualifications to those that are fixed in the Constitution. Instead, any state power to set the qualifications for membership in Congress must derive not from the reserved powers of state sovereignty, but rather from the delegated powers of national sovereignty. In the absence of any constitutional delegation to the States of power to add qualifications to those enumerated in the Constitution, such a power does not exist. . . .

Democratic Principles

Our conclusion that States lack the power to impose qualifications vindicates the same "fundamental principle of our representative democracy" that we recognized in *Powell*, namely that "the people should choose whom they please to govern them."

. . . [T]he *Powell* Court recognized that an egalitarian ideal — that election to the National Legislature should be open to all people of merit — provided a critical foundation for the Constitutional structure. This egalitarian theme echoes throughout the constitutional debates. . . .

Similarly, we believe that state-imposed qualifications, as much as congressionally imposed qualifications, would undermine the second critical idea recognized in *Powell*: that an aspect of sovereignty is the right of the people to vote for whom they wish. Again, the source of the qualification is of little moment in assessing the qualification's restrictive impact.

Finally, state-imposed restrictions, unlike the congressionally imposed restrictions at issue in *Powell*, violate a third area central to the basic principle: that the right to choose representatives belongs not to the States, but to the people. . . . [T]he Framers, in perhaps their most important contribution, conceived of a Federal Government directly responsible to the people, possessed of direct power over the people, and chosen directly, not by States, but by the people. The Framers implemented this ideal most clearly in the provision, extant from the beginning of the Republic, that calls for the Members of the House of Representatives to be "chosen every second Year by the People, of the several States." Art. I, § 2, cl. 1. Following the adoption of the 17th Amendment in 1913, this ideal was extended to elections for the Senate. The Congress of the United States, therefore, is not a confederation of nations in which separate sovereigns are represented by appointed delegates, but is instead a body composed of representatives of the people. . . . Ours is a "government of the people, by the people, for the people." . . .

Consistent with these views, the constitutional structure provides for a uniform salary to be paid from the national treasury, allows the States but a limited role in federal elections, and maintains strict checks on state interference with the federal election process. The Constitution also provides that the qualifications of the representatives of each State will be judged by the representatives of the entire Nation. The Constitution thus creates a uniform national body representing the interests of a single people.

Permitting individual States to formulate diverse qualifications for their representatives would result in a patchwork of state qualifications, undermining the uniformity and the national character that the Framers envisioned and sought to ensure. . . . Such a patchwork would also sever the direct link that the Framers found so critical between the National Government and the people of the United States. . . .

In sum, the available historical and textual evidence, read in light of the basic principles of democracy underlying the Constitution and recognized by this Court in *Powell*, reveal the Framers' intent that neither Congress nor the States should possess the power to supplement the exclusive qualifications set forth in the text of the Constitution.

[Lengthy discussion omitted regarding Arkansas' claim that Amendment 73 is exercise of state power to regulate time, place and manner of holding elections].

V

The merits of term limits, or "rotation," have been the subject of debate since the formation of our Constitution, when the Framers unanimously rejected a proposal to add such limits to the Constitution. . . .

We are, however, firmly convinced that allowing the several States to adopt term limits for congressional service would effect a fundamental change in the constitutional framework. Any such change must come not by legislation adopted either by Congress or by an individual State, but rather — as have other important changes in the electoral process — through the Amendment procedures set forth in Article V. . . .

The judgment is affirmed.

Justice Kennedy, concurring.

I join the opinion of the Court.

The majority and dissenting opinions demonstrate the intricacy of the question whether or not the Qualifications Clauses are exclusive. In my view, however, it is well settled that the whole people of the United States asserted their political identity and unity of purpose when they created the federal system. The dissent's course of reasoning suggesting otherwise might be construed to disparage the republican character of the National Government, and it seems appropriate to add these few remarks to explain why that course of argumentation runs counter to fundamental principles of federalism.

Federalism was our Nation's own discovery. The Framers split the atom of sovereignty. It was the genius of their idea that our citizens would have two political capacities, one state and one federal, each protected from incursion by the other. The resulting Constitution created a legal system unprecedented in form and design, establishing two orders of government, each with its own direct relationship, its own privity, its own set of mutual rights and obligations to the people who sustain it and are governed by it. It is appropriate to recall these origins, which instruct us as to the nature of the two different governments created and confirmed by the Constitution.

A distinctive character of the National Government, the mark of its legitimacy, is that it owes its existence to the act of the whole people who created it. . . . It denies the dual character of the Federal Government which is its very foundation to assert that the people of the United States do not have a political identity as well, one independent of, though consistent with, their identity as citizens of the State of their residence. It must be recognized that " '[f]or all the great purposes for which the Federal government was formed, we are one people, with one common country.' " . . .

The political identity of the entire people of the Union is reinforced by the proposition, which I take to be beyond dispute, that, though limited as to its objects, the National Government is and must be controlled by the people without collateral interference by the States. *McCulloch* affirmed this proposition as well, when the Court rejected the suggestion that States could interfere with federal powers. . . .

It is maintained . . . that the State of Arkansas seeks nothing more than to grant its people surer control over the National Government, a control, it is said, that will be enhanced by the law at issue here. The arguments for term limitations (or ballot restrictions having the same effect) are not lacking in force; but the issue, as all of us must acknowledge, is not the efficacy of those measures but whether they have a legitimate source, given their origin in the enactments of a single State. There can be no doubt, if we are to respect the republican origins of the Nation and preserve its federal character, that there exists a federal right of citizenship, a relationship between the people of the Nation and their National Government, with which the States may not interfere. Because the Arkansas enactment intrudes upon this federal domain, it exceeds the boundaries of the Constitution.

JUSTICE THOMAS, with whom THE CHIEF JUSTICE, JUSTICE O'CONNOR, and JUSTICE SCALIA join, dissenting.

It is ironic that the Court bases today's decision on the right of the people to "choose whom they please to govern them.". . . Under our Constitution, there is only one State whose people have the right to "choose whom they please" to represent Arkansas in Congress. The Court holds, however, that neither the elected legislature of that State nor the people themselves (acting by ballot initiative) may prescribe any qualifications for those representatives. The majority therefore defends the right of the people of Arkansas to "choose whom they please to govern them" by invalidating a provision that won nearly 60% of the votes cast in a direct election and that carried every congressional district in the State.

I dissent. Nothing in the Constitution deprives the people of each State of the power to prescribe eligibility requirements for the candidates who seek to represent them in Congress. The Constitution is simply silent on this question. And where the Constitution is silent, it raises no bar to action by the States or the people.

I

Because the majority fundamentally misunderstands the notion of "reserved" powers, I start with some first principles. Contrary to the majority's suggestion, the people of the States need not point to any affirmative grant of power in the Constitution in order to prescribe qualifications for their representatives in Congress, or to authorize their elected state legislators to do so.

A

Our system of government rests on one overriding principle: all power stems from the consent of the people. To phrase the principle in this way, however, is to be imprecise about something important to the notion of "reserved" powers. The ultimate source of the Constitution's authority is the consent of the people of each individual State, not the consent of the undifferentiated people of the Nation as a whole. . . .

When they adopted the Federal Constitution, of course, the people of each State surrendered some of their authority to the United States (and hence to entities accountable to the people of other States as well as to themselves). . . .

In each State, the remainder of the people's powers . . . are either delegated to the state government or retained by the people. The Federal Constitution does not specify which of these two possibilities obtains; it is up to the various state constitutions to declare which powers the people of each State have delegated to their state government. As far as the Federal Constitution is concerned, then, the States can exercise all powers that the Constitution does not withhold from them. The Federal Government and the States thus face different default rules: where the Constitution is silent about the exercise of a particular power — that is, where the Constitution does not speak either expressly or by necessary implication — the Federal Government lacks that power and the States enjoy it.

These basic principles are enshrined in the Tenth Amendment, which declares that all powers neither delegated to the Federal Government nor prohibited to the States "are reserved to the States respectively, or to the people." . . .

B

. . . .

1

The majority begins by announcing an enormous and untenable limitation on the principle expressed by the Tenth Amendment. According to the majority, the States possess only those powers that the Constitution affirmatively grants to them or that they enjoyed before the Constitution was adopted; the Tenth Amendment "could only 'reserve' that which existed before." . . . From the fact that the States had not previously enjoyed any powers over the particular institutions of the Federal Government established by the Constitution, the majority derives a rule precisely opposite to the one that the Amendment actually prescribes: " '[T]he states can exercise no powers whatsoever, which exclusively spring out of the existence of the national government, which the constitution does not delegate to them.' ". . .

The majority's essential logic is that the state governments could not "reserve" any powers that they did not control at the time the Constitution was drafted. But it was not the state governments that were doing the reserving. The Constitution derives its authority instead from the consent of the people of the States. Given the fundamental principle that all governmental powers stem from the people of the States, it would simply be incoherent to assert that the people of the States could not reserve any powers that they had not previously controlled.

The Tenth Amendment's use of the word "reserved" does not help the majority's position. If someone says that the power to use a particular facility is reserved to some group, he is not saying anything about whether that group has previously used the facility. He is merely saying that the people who control the facility have designated that group as the entity with authority to use it. The Tenth Amendment is similar: the people of the States, from whom all governmental powers stem, have specified that all powers not prohibited to the States by the Federal Constitution are reserved "to the States respectively, or to the people."

. . . .

The question raised by the present case . . . is not whether any principle of state sovereignty implicit in the Tenth Amendment bars congressional action that Article I appears to authorize, but rather whether Article I bars state action that it does not appear to forbid. The principle necessary to answer this question is express on the Tenth Amendment's face: unless the Federal Constitution affirmatively prohibits an action by the States or the people, it raises no bar to such action. . . .

[Discussion of *McCulloch* and Justice Story omitted].

. . . [W]hile the majority is correct that the Framers expected the selection process to create a "direct link" between Members of the House of Representatives and the people, . . . the link was between the Representatives from each State and the people of that State; the people of Georgia have no say over whom the people of Massachusetts select to represent them in Congress. This arrangement must baffle the majority, whose understanding of Congress would surely fit more comfortably within a system of nationwide elections. But the fact remains that when it comes to the selection of Members of Congress, the people of each State have retained their independent political identity. As a result, there is absolutely nothing strange about the notion that the people of the States or their state legislatures possess "reserved" powers in this area. . . .

II

I take it to be established, then, that the people of Arkansas do enjoy "reserved" powers over the selection of their representatives in Congress. Purporting to exercise those reserved powers, they have agreed among themselves that the candidates covered by § 3 of Amendment 73 — those whom they have already elected to three or more terms in the House of Representatives or to two or more terms in the Senate — should not be eligible to appear on the ballot for reelection, but should nonetheless be returned to Congress if enough voters are sufficiently enthusiastic about their candidacy to write in their names. Whatever one might think of the wisdom of this arrangement, we may not override the decision of the people of Arkansas unless something in the Federal Constitution deprives them of the power to enact such measures.

The majority settles on "the Qualifications Clauses" as the constitutional provisions that Amendment 73 violates. . . . [T]he Qualifications Clauses are merely straightforward recitations of the minimum eligibility requirements that the Framers thought it essential for every Member of Congress to meet. They restrict state power only in that they prevent the States from abolishing all eligibility requirements for membership in Congress. . . .

A

. . . At least on their face, . . . the Qualifications Clauses do nothing to prohibit the people of a State from establishing additional eligibility requirements for their own representatives. [It is argued that] such a prohibition was nonetheless implicit in the constitutional list of qualifications, because "[f]rom the very nature of such a provision, the affirmation of these qualifications would seem to imply a negative of all others." This argument rests on the maxim *expressio unius est exclusio alterius*. When the Framers decided which qualifications to include in the Constitution, they also decided not to include any other qualifications in the Constitution. [It is claimed that] it would conflict with this latter decision for the people of the individual States to decide, as a matter of state law, that they would like their own representatives in Congress to meet additional eligibility requirements.

To spell out the logic underlying this argument is to expose its weakness. Even if one were willing to ignore the distinction between requirements enshrined in the Constitution and other requirements that the Framers were content to leave within the reach of ordinary law, [such] application of the *expressio unius* maxim takes no account of federalism. At most, the specification of certain nationwide disqualifications in the Constitution implies the negation of other nationwide disqualifications; it does not imply that individual States or their people are barred from adopting their own disqualifications on a state-by-state basis. . . . The Qualifications Clauses do prevent the individual States from abolishing all eligibility requirements for Congress. This restriction on state power reflects the fact that when the people of one State send immature, disloyal, or unknowledgeable representatives to Congress, they jeopardize not only their own interests but also the interests of the people of other States. Because Congress wields power over all the States, the people of each State need some guarantee that the legislators elected by the people of other States will meet minimum standards of competence. The Qualifications Clauses provide that guarantee: they list the requirements that the Framers considered essential to protect the competence of the National Legislature. If the people of a State decide that they would like their representatives to possess additional qualifications, however, they have done nothing to frustrate the policy behind the Qualifications Clauses. . . .

As for the majority's related assertion that the Framers intended qualification requirements to be uniform, this is a conclusion, not an argument. Indeed, it is a conclusion that the Qualifications Clauses themselves contradict. At the time of the framing, and for some years thereafter, the Clauses' citizenship requirements incorporated laws that varied from State to State. Thus, the Qualifications Clauses themselves made it possible that a person would be qualified to represent State A in Congress even though a similarly situated person would not be qualified to represent State B. . . .

B

. . . .

I agree with the majority that Congress has no power to prescribe qualifications for its own Members. This fact, however, does not show that the Qualifications Clauses contain a hidden exclusivity provision. The reason for Congress' incapacity is not that the Qualifications Clauses deprive Congress of the authority to set qualifications, but rather that nothing in the Constitution grants Congress this power. In the absence of such a grant, Congress may not act. But deciding whether the Constitution denies the qualification-setting power to the States and the people of the States requires a fundamentally different legal analysis. . . .

The fact that the Framers did not grant a qualification-setting power to Congress does not imply that they wanted to bar its exercise at the state level. . . . Congressional power over qualifications would have enabled the representatives from some States, acting collectively in the National Legislature, to prevent the people of another State from electing their preferred candidates. . . . Americans . . . might well have wanted to prevent the National Legislature from fettering the choices of the people of any individual State (for the House of Representatives) or their state legislators (for the Senate).

. . . .

The majority appears to believe that restrictions on eligibility for office are inherently undemocratic. But the Qualifications Clauses themselves prove that the Framers did not share this view; eligibility requirements to which the people of the States consent are perfectly consistent with the Framers' scheme. . . . When the people of a State themselves decide to restrict the field of candidates whom they are willing to send to Washington as their representatives, they simply have not violated the principle that "the people should choose whom they please to govern them."

. . . .

III

It is radical enough for the majority to hold that the Constitution implicitly precludes the people of the States from prescribing any eligibility requirements for the congressional candidates who seek their votes. This holding, after all, does not stop with negating the term limits that many States have seen fit to impose on their Senators and Representatives. Today's decision also means that no State may disqualify congressional candidates whom a court has found to be mentally incompetent, . . . who are currently in prison, or who have past vote-fraud convictions[.] . . .

The majority's opinion . . . does not itself suggest any principled stopping point. No matter how narrowly construed, however, today's decision reads the Qualifications Clauses to impose substantial implicit prohibitions on the States and the people of the States. I would not draw such an expansive negative inference from the fact that the Constitution requires Members of Congress to be a certain age, to be inhabitants of the States that they represent, and to have been United States citizens for a specified period. Rather, I would read the Qualifications Clauses to do no more than what they say. I respectfully dissent.

NOTES

(1) The majority argues that the Qualifications Clauses impose three qualifications but do not impose term limits; accordingly term limits are precluded. But if the designated qualifications were meant to be exclusive, why did the framers include the prohibition on religious tests for public office in Art. VI, cl. 3? After all, that clause would be superfluous regarding members of Congress if only qualifications regarding age, citizenship, and residency were allowed. On the other hand, if Justice Thomas' approach to the Qualifications Clauses of Article I is followed, what becomes of the maxim, *expressio unius est exclusio alterius*, the constitutional doctrine that the expression of one thing implies the exclusion of all others? Does Justice Thomas adequately answer this question? Recall that *Marbury v. Madison* argued that the listing in Article III of two classes of cases within the Supreme Court's original jurisdiction precluded Congress from adding additional types of cases to its original jurisdiction cases. In *Nixon v. United States*, Chief Justice Rehnquist deemed the constitutional requirements in the Impeachment Clause to be exclusive. How does one decide when a constitutional clause states exclusive criteria?

(2) Dean Kathleen Sullivan argues that *U.S. Term Limits* pitted a formalist majority against a formalist dissent. Formalism, she suggests, involves belief in a strict separation between national and state powers policed relatively vigorously by the courts generally using rules; the Constitution's limits cannot be waived. By contrast,

functional approaches are "pragmatic and evolutionary in method"; they allow experimentation and blending of power and rely on the checks and balances of the system to prevent aggrandizement of power. The majority resisted any encroachment on the processes of federal government by deploying a strict rule — no additional state-imposed qualification on Congressional membership — rather than evaluating separately the impact of different qualifications. The dissent articulated an opposing formalist approach that constitutional silence permits additional state-imposed qualifications. *See* Kathleen Sullivan, *Dueling Sovereignties:* U.S. Term Limits, Inc. v. Thornton, 109 HARV. L. REV. 78 (1995).

(3) Prior to the Nineteenth Amendment, the states limited the right to run for office (as well as that to vote) to males. Were those limitations, enforced without question during most of our history, all unconstitutional as applied to Congressional candidates (even absent any arguments which the Fourteenth Amendment might provide)?

(4) In a portion of his dissent here omitted, Justice Thomas dismissed the majority's reliance on Justice Story. He wrote: "Justice Story was a brilliant and accomplished man, and one cannot casually dismiss his views. On the other hand, he was not a member of the Founding generation, and his Commentaries on the Constitution were written a half century after the framing. Rather than representing the original understanding of the Constitution, they represent only his own understanding." Can Justice Story's interpretations be dismissed on that basis or are they entitled to weight based on any other type of constitutional argument?

(5) The majority relies on *McCulloch* for the proposition that the Constitution was the creation of the people of the United States; since the "national" people, not the states, was the sovereign that created the Constitution in a constitutional "big bang" the states could not retain any control other than that they previously had and that delegated back to them. The dissent challenges this precept of *McCulloch*; it claims that the Constitution came from the people of the states; the states were the sovereign and therefore reserved all that was not specifically or implicitly granted. What weight should judicial doctrine from *McCulloch* be given? In other words, even if one could argue, as Justice Thomas does, as a matter of original intent that *McCulloch* was wrong, should we defer to doctrine from *McCulloch* and Marshall based on the fact that it comes from *McCulloch* and Marshall?

§ 3.02 THE STATES AND GENERALLY APPLICABLE LAWS

GARCIA v. SAN ANTONIO METROPOLITAN TRANSIT AUTHORITY [SAMTA]
469 U.S. 528, 105 S. Ct. 1005, 83 L. Ed. 2d. 1016 (1985)

JUSTICE BLACKMUN delivered the opinion of the Court.

We revisit in these cases an issue raised in *National League of Cities v. Usery* [*infra* § 3.02, Note (1)]. In that litigation, this Court, by a sharply divided vote, ruled that the Commerce Clause does not empower Congress to enforce the minimum-wage and overtime provisions of the Fair Labor Standards Act (FLSA) against the States "in areas of traditional governmental functions." Although *National League of Cities* supplied some examples of "traditional governmental functions," it did not offer a general explanation of how a "traditional" function is to be distinguished from a "nontraditional" one. Since then, federal and state courts have struggled with the task, thus imposed, of identifying a traditional function for purposes of state immunity under the Commerce Clause.

In the present cases, a Federal District Court concluded that municipal ownership and operation of a mass-transit system is a traditional governmental function and thus, under *National League of Cities*, is exempt from the obligations imposed by the FLSA. Faced with the identical question, three Federal Courts of Appeals and one state appellate court have reached the opposite conclusion.

Our examination of this "function" standard applied in these and other cases over the last eight years now persuades us that the attempt to draw the boundaries of state regulatory immunity in terms of "traditional governmental function" is not only unworkable but is inconsistent with established principles of federalism and, indeed, with those very federalism principles on which *National League of Cities* purported to rest. That case, accordingly, is overruled. . . . .

[U]nder *National League of Cities* four conditions must be satisfied before a state activity may be deemed immune from a particular federal regulation under the Commerce Clause. First, it is said that the federal statute at issue must regulate "the 'States as States.'" Second, the statute must "address matters that are indisputably 'attribute[s] of state sovereignty.'" Third, state compliance with the federal obligation must "directly impair [the States'] ability 'to structure integral operations in areas of traditional governmental functions.'" Finally, the relation of state and federal interests must not be such that "the nature of the federal interest . . . justifies state submission."

The controversy in the present cases has focused on the . . . requirement . . . that the challenged federal statute trench on "traditional governmental functions." The District Court voiced a common concern: "Despite the abundance of adjectives, identifying which particular state functions are immune remains difficult.". . . . Just how troublesome the task has been is revealed by the results reached in other federal cases.

Thus far, this Court itself has made little headway in defining the scope of the governmental functions deemed protected under *National League of Cities*. In that case the Court set forth examples of protected and unprotected functions, but provided no explanation of how these examples were identified. . . .

Many constitutional standards involve "undoubte[d] . . . gray areas," and, despite the difficulties that this Court and other courts have encountered so far, it normally might be fair to venture the assumption that case-by-case development would lead to a workable standard for determining whether a particular governmental function should be immune from federal regulation under the Commerce Clause. A further cautionary note is sounded, however, by the Court's experience in the related field of state immunity from federal taxation. . . .

If [the] tax immunity cases had any common thread, it was in the attempt to distinguish between "governmental" and "proprietary" functions. To say that the distinction between — "governmental" and "proprietary" proved to be stable, however, would be something of an overstatement. . . .

The distinction the Court discarded as unworkable in the field of tax immunity has proved no more fruitful in the field of regulatory immunity under the Commerce Clause. Neither do any of the alternative standards that might be employed to distinguish between protected and unprotected governmental functions appear manageable. We rejected the possibility of making immunity turn on a purely historical standard of "tradition" . . . and properly so. The most obvious defect of a historical approach to state immunity is that it prevents a court from accommodating changes in the historical functions of States, changes that have resulted in a number of once-private functions like education being assumed by the States and their subdivisions. . . . [T]he only apparent virtue of a rigorous historical standard, namely, its promise of a reasonably objective measure for state immunity, is illusory. Reliance on history as an organizing principle results in line drawing of the most arbitrary sort; the genesis of state governmental functions stretches over a historical continuum from before the Revolution to the present, and courts would have to decide by fiat precisely how longstanding a pattern of state involvement had to be for federal regulatory authority to be defeated.

A nonhistorical standard for selecting immune governmental functions is likely to be just as unworkable as is a historical standard. The goal of identifying "uniquely" governmental functions, for example, has been rejected by the Court in the field of governmental tort liability in part because the notion of a "uniquely" governmental function is unmanageable. . . . Another possibility would be to confine immunity to "necessary" governmental services, that is, services that would be provided inadequately or not at all unless the government provided them. . . . The set of services that fits into this category, however, may well be negligible. The fact that an unregulated market produces less of some service than a State deems desirable does not mean that the State itself must provide the service; in most if not all cases, the State can "contract out" by hiring private firms to provide the service or simply by providing subsidies to existing suppliers. It also is open to question how well equipped courts are to make this kind of determination about the workings of economic markets.

We believe, however, that there is a more fundamental problem at work here, a problem that explains why the Court was never able to provide a basis for the governmental/proprietary distinction in the intergovernmental tax-immunity cases and why an attempt to draw similar distinctions with respect to federal regulatory authority under *National League of Cities* is unlikely to succeed regardless of how the distinctions are phrased. The problem is that neither the governmental/proprietary distinction nor any other that purports to separate out important governmental functions can be faithful to the role of federalism in a democratic society. The essence of our federal system is that within the realm of authority left open to them under the Constitution, the States must be equally free to engage in any activity that their citizens choose for the common weal, no matter how unorthodox or unnecessary anyone else — including the judiciary — deems state involvement to be. Any rule of state immunity that looks to the "traditional," "integral," or "necessary" nature of governmental functions inevitably invites an unelected federal judiciary to make decisions about which state policies it favors and which ones it dislikes. "The science of government . . . is the science of experiment,". . . and the States cannot serve as laboratories for social and economic experiment, . . . if they must pay an added price when they meet the changing needs of their citizenry by taking up functions that an earlier day and a different society left in private hands. . . .

We therefore now reject, as unsound in principle and unworkable in practice, a rule of state immunity from federal regulation that turns on a judicial appraisal of whether a particular governmental function is "integral" or "traditional." Any such rule leads to inconsistent results at the same time that it disserves principles of democratic self-governance, and it breeds inconsistency precisely because it is divorced from those principles. If there are to be limits on the Federal Government's power to interfere with state functions — as undoubtedly there are — we must look elsewhere to find them. We accordingly return to the underlying issue that confronted this Court in *National League of Cities* — the manner in which the Constitution insulates States from the reach of Congress' power under the Commerce Clause.

The central theme of *National League of Cities* was that the States occupy a special position in our constitutional system and that the scope of Congress' authority under the Commerce Clause must reflect that position. . . . What has proved problematic is not the perception that the Constitution's federal structure imposes limitations on the Commerce Clause, but rather the nature and content of those limitations. . . .

One approach to defining the limits on Congress' authority to regulate the States under the Commerce Clause is to identify certain underlying elements of political sovereignty that are deemed essential to the States' "separate and independent existence." . . . In *National League of Cities* itself, for example, the Court concluded that decisions by a State concerning the wages and hours of its employees are an "undoubted attribute of state sovereignty." The opinion did not explain what aspects of such decisions made them such an "undoubted attribute," and the Court since then has remarked on the uncertain scope of the concept. . . .

We doubt that courts ultimately can identify principled constitutional limitations on the scope of Congress' Commerce Clause powers over the States merely by relying on *a priori* definitions of state sovereignty. . . .

In part, this is because of the elusiveness of objective criteria for "fundamental" elements of state sovereignty, a problem we have witnessed in the search for "traditional governmental functions." There is, however, a more fundamental reason: the sovereignty of the States is limited by the Constitution itself. A variety of sovereign powers, for example, are withdrawn from the States by Article I, § 10. Section 8 of the same Article works an equally sharp contraction of state sovereignty by authorizing Congress to exercise a wide range of legislative powers and (in conjunction with the Supremacy Clause of Article VI) to displace contrary state legislation. By providing for final review of questions of federal law in this Court, Article III curtails the sovereign power of the States' judiciaries to make authoritative determinations of law. Finally, the developed application, through the Fourteenth Amendment, of the greater part of the Bill of Rights to the States limits the sovereign authority that States otherwise would possess to legislate with respect to their citizens and to conduct their own affairs.

. . . The power of the Federal Government is a "power to be respected" as well, and the fact that the States remain sovereign as to all powers not vested in Congress or denied them by the Constitution offers no guidance about where the frontier between state and federal power lies. In short, we have no license to employ freestanding conceptions of state sovereignty when measuring congressional authority under the Commerce Clause.

When we look for the States' "residuary and inviolable sovereignty" . . . in the shape of the constitutional scheme rather than in predetermined notions of sovereign power, a different measure of state sovereignty emerges. Apart from the limitation on federal authority inherent in the delegated nature of Congress' Article I powers, the principal means chosen by the Framers to ensure the role of the States in the federal system lies in the structure of the Federal Government itself. It is no novelty to observe that the composition of the Federal Government was designed in large part to protect the States from overreaching by Congress. The Framers thus gave the States a role in the selection both of the Executive and the Legislative Branches of the Federal Government. The States were vested with indirect influence over the House of Representatives and the Presidency by their control of electoral qualifications and their role in Presidential elections, U.S. Const., Art. I, § 2 and Art. II, § 1. They were given more direct influence in the Senate where each State received equal representation and each Senator was to be selected by the legislature of his State. Art. I, § 3. . . .

. . . [T]he Framers chose to rely on a federal system in which special restraints on federal power over the States inhered principally in the workings of the National Government itself, rather than in discrete limitations on the objects of federal authority. State sovereign interests, then, are more properly protected by procedural safeguards inherent in the structure of the federal system than by judicially created limitations on federal power.

The effectiveness of the federal political process in preserving the States' interests is apparent even today in the course of federal legislation. On the one hand, the States have been able to direct a substantial proportion of federal revenues into their own treasuries in the form of general and program-specific grants in aid. . . . In the past quarter-century alone, federal grants to States and localities have grown from $7 billion to $96 billion. As a result, federal grants now account for about one-fifth of state and local government expenditures. The States have obtained federal funding for such services as police and fire protection, education, public health and hospitals, parks and recreation, and sanitation. . . .

We realize that changes in the structure of the Federal Government have taken place since 1789, not the least of which has been the substitution of popular election of Senators by the adoption of the Seventeenth Amendment in 1913, and that these changes may work to alter the influence of the States in the federal political process. Nonetheless, against this background, we are convinced that the fundamental limitation that the constitutional scheme imposes on the Commerce Clause to protect the "States as States" is one of process rather than one of result. Any substantive restraint on the exercise of Commerce Clause powers must find its justification in the procedural nature of this basic limitation, and it must be tailored to compensate for possible failings in the national political process rather than to dictate a "sacred province of state autonomy." . . .

Insofar as the present cases are concerned, then, we need go no further than to state that we perceive nothing in the overtime and minimum-wage requirements of the FLSA, as applied to SAMTA, that is destructive of state sovereignty or violative of any constitutional provision. SAMTA faces nothing more than the same minimum-wage and overtime obligations that hundreds of thousands of other employers, public as well as private, have to meet. . . .

Of course, we continue to recognize that the States occupy a special and specific position in our constitutional system and that the scope of Congress' authority under the Commerce Clause must reflect that position. But the principal and basic limit on the federal commerce power is that inherent in all congressional action — the built-in restraints that our system provides through state participation in federal governmental action. The political process ensures that laws that unduly burden the States will not be promulgated. In the factual setting of these cases the internal safeguards of the political process have performed as intended. . . .

Though the separate concurrence providing the fifth vote in *National League of Cities* was "not untroubled by certain possible implications" of the decision, the Court in that case attempted to articulate affirmative limits on the Commerce Clause power in terms of core governmental functions and fundamental attributes of state sovereignty. But the model of democratic decision-making the Court there identified underestimated, in our view, the solicitude of the national political process for the continued vitality of the States. Attempts by other courts since then to draw guidance from this model have proved it both impracticable and doctrinally barren. In sum, in *National League of Cities* the Court tried to repair what did not need repair.

We do not lightly overrule recent precedent. We have not hesitated, however, when it has become apparent that a prior decision has departed from a proper understanding of congressional power under the Commerce Clause. . . . Due respect for the reach of congressional power within the federal system mandates that we do so now.

National League of Cities v. Usery . . . is overruled. The judgment of the District Court is reversed, and these cases are remanded to that court for further proceedings consistent with this opinion.

JUSTICE POWELL, with whom THE CHIEF JUSTICE, JUSTICE REHNQUIST, and JUSTICE O'CONNOR join, dissenting.

The Court today, in its 5-4 decision, overrules *National League of Cities v. Usery*, . . . a case in which we held that Congress lacked authority to impose the requirements of the Fair Labor Standards Act on state and local governments. Because I believe this discussion substantially alters the federal system embodied in the Constitution, I dissent. . . .

Although the doctrine is not rigidly applied to constitutional questions, "any departure from the doctrine of stare decisis demands special justification."

In the present case, the five Justices who compose the majority today participated in *National League of Cities* and the cases reaffirming it. The stability of judicial decision, and with it respect for the authority of this Court, are not served by the precipitous overruling of multiple precedents that we witness in these cases.

Whatever effect the Court's decision may have in weakening the application of *stare decisis* it is likely to be less important than what the Court has done to the Constitution itself. A unique feature of the United States is the federal system of government guaranteed by the Constitution and implicit in the very name of our country. Despite some genuflecting in the Court's opinion to the concept of federalism, today's decision effectively reduces the Tenth Amendment to meaningless rhetoric when Congress acts pursuant to the Commerce Clause. . . .

To leave no doubt about its intention, the Court renounces its decision in *National League of Cities* because it "inevitably invites an unelected federal judiciary to make decisions about which state policies it favors and which ones it dislikes." In other words, the extent to which the States may exercise their authority, when Congress purports to act under the Commerce Clause, henceforth is to be determined from time to time by political decisions made by members of the federal government, decisions the Court says will not be subject to judicial review. I note that it does not seem to have occurred to the Court that it — an unelected majority of five Justices — today rejects almost 200 years of the understanding of the constitutional status of federalism. In doing so, there is only a single passing reference to the Tenth Amendment. Nor is so much as a dictum of any court cited in support of the view that the role of the States in the federal system may depend upon the grace of elected federal officials, rather than on the Constitution as interpreted by this Court. . . .

The Court finds that the test of state immunity approved in *National League of Cities* and its progeny is unworkable and unsound in principle. In finding the test to be unworkable, the Court begins by mischaracterizing *National League of Cities* and subsequent cases. In concluding that efforts to define state immunity are unsound in principle, the Court radically departs from long- settled constitutional values and ignores the role of judicial review in our system of government.

A

Much of the Court's opinion is devoted to arguing that it is difficult to define a priori "traditional governmental functions." *National League of Cities* neither engaged in, nor required, such a task. The Court discusses and condemns as standards "traditional governmental functions," "purely historical" functions, " 'uniquely' governmental functions," and " 'necessary' governmental services." . . . But nowhere does it mention that *National League of Cities* adopted a familiar type of balancing test for determining whether Commerce Clause enactments transgress constitutional limitations imposed by the federal nature of our system of government. This omission is noteworthy, since the author of today's opinion joined *National League of Cities* and concurred separately to point out that the Court's opinion in that case "adopt[s] a balancing approach [that] does not outlaw federal power in areas . . . where the federal interest is demonstrably greater and where state . . . compliance with imposed federal standards would be essential."

Today's opinion does not explain how the States' role in the electoral process guarantees that particular exercises of the Commerce Clause power will not infringe on residual state sovereignty. Members of Congress are elected from the various States, but once in office they are Members of the Federal Government. Although the States participate in the Electoral College, this is hardly a reason to view the President as a representative of the States' interest against federal encroachment. . . .

The Court apparently thinks that the State's success at obtaining federal funds for various projects and exemptions from the obligations of some federal statutes is indicative of the "effectiveness of the federal political process in preserving the States' interests. . . ." But such political success is not relevant to the question whether the political processes are the proper means of enforcing constitutional limitations. The fact that Congress generally does not transgress constitutional limits on its power to reach State activities does not make judicial review any less necessary to rectify the cases in which it does do so. The States' role in our system of government is a matter of constitutional law, not of legislative grace. . . .

More troubling than the logical infirmities in the Court's reasoning is the result of its holding, i.e., that federal political officials, invoking the Commerce Clause, are the sole judges of the limits of their own power. This result is inconsistent with the fundamental principles of our constitutional system. . . . At least since *Marbury v. Madison* [*supra* § 1.01] . . . it has been the settled province of the federal judiciary "to say what the law is" with respect to the constitutionality of acts of Congress. In rejecting the role of the judiciary in protecting the States from federal overreaching, the Court's opinion offers no explanation for ignoring the teaching of the most famous case in our history. . . .

The Court maintains that the standard approved in *National League of Cities* "disserves principles of democratic self-goverance.". . . . In reaching this conclusion, the Court looks myopically only to persons elected to positions in the Federal Government. It disregards entirely the far more effective role of democratic self-government at the state and local levels. One must compare realistically the operation of the state and local governments with that of the Federal Government. Federal legislation is drafted primarily by the staffs of the congressional committees. In view of the hundreds of bills introduced at each session of Congress and the complexity of many of them, it is virtually impossible for even the most conscientious legislators to be truly familiar with many of the statutes enacted. Federal departments and agencies customarily are authorized to write regulations. Often these are more important than the text of the statutes. As is true of the original legislation, these are drafted largely by staff personnel. The administration and enforcement of federal laws and regulations necessarily are largely in the hands of staff and civil service employees. These employees may have little or no knowledge of the States and localities that will be affected by the statutes and regulations for which they are responsible. In any case, they hardly are as accessible and responsive as those who occupy analogous positions in state and local governments.

In drawing this contrast, I imply no criticism of these federal employees or the officials who are ultimately in charge. The great majority are conscientious and faithful to their duties. My point is simply that members of the immense federal bureaucracy are not elected, know less about the services traditionally rendered by States and localities, and are inevitably less responsive to recipients of such services, than are state legislatures, city councils, boards of supervisors, and state and local commissions, boards, and agencies. It is at these state and local levels — not in Washington as the Court so mistakenly thinks — that "democratic self-government" is best exemplified.

The Court emphasizes that municipal operation of an intracity mass transit system is relatively new in the life of our country. It nevertheless is a classic example of the type of service traditionally provided by local government. It is local by definition. It is indistinguishable in principle from the traditional services of providing and maintaining streets, public lighting, traffic control, water, and sewerage systems. . . . State and local officials of course must be intimately familiar with these services and sensitive to their quality as well as cost. Such officials also know that their constituents and the press respond to the adequacy, fair distribution, and cost of these services. It is this kind of state and local control and accountability that the Framers understood would insure the vitality and preservation of the federal system that the Constitution explicitly requires. . . . Although the Court's opinion purports to recognize that the States retain some sovereign power, it does not identify even a single aspect of state authority that would remain when the Commerce Clause is invoked to justify federal regulation. . . .

As I view the Court's decision today as rejecting the basic precepts of our federal system and limiting the constitutional role of judicial review, I dissent.

Justice Rehnquist, dissenting.

. . . [T]he judgment in these cases should be affirmed, and I do not think it incumbent on those of us in dissent to spell out further the fine points of a principle that will, I am confident, in time again command the support of a majority of this Court.

Justice O'Connor, with whom Justice Powell and Justice Rehnqust join, dissenting.

The Court today surveys the battle scene of federalism and sounds a retreat. Like Justice Powell, I would prefer to hold the field and, at the very least, render a little aid to the wounded. . . .

In my view, federalism cannot be reduced to the weak "essence" distilled by the majority today. There is more to federalism than the nature of the constraints that can be imposed on the States in "the realm of authority left open to them by the Constitution." The central issue of federalism, of course, is whether any realm is left open to the States by the Constitution — whether any area remains in which a State may act free of federal interference. . . . The true "essence" of federalism is that the States as States have legitimate interests which the National Government is bound to respect even though its laws are supreme. . . . If federalism so conceived and so carefully cultivated by the Framers of our Constitution is to remain meaningful, this Court cannot abdicate its constitutional responsibility to oversee the Federal Government's compliance with its duty to respect the legitimate interests of the States. . . .

Due to the emergence of an integrated and industrialized national economy, this Court has been required to examine and review a breathtaking expansion of the powers of Congress. In doing so the Court correctly perceived that the Framers of our Constitution intended Congress to have sufficient power to address national problems. But the Framers were not single-minded. The Constitution is animated by an array of intentions. . . . Just as surely as the Framers envisioned a National Government capable of solving national problems, they also envisioned a republic whose vitality was assured by the diffusion of power not only among the branches of the Federal Government, but also between the Federal Government and the States. . . . In the 18th century these intentions did not conflict because technology had not yet converted every local problem into a national one. A conflict has now emerged, and the Court today retreats rather than reconcile the Constitution's dual concerns for federalism and an effective commerce power.

The problems of federalism in an integrated national economy are capable of more responsible resolution than holding that the States as States retain no status apart from that which Congress chooses to let them retain. The proper resolution, I suggest, lies in weighing state autonomy as a factor in the balance when interpreting the means by which Congress can exercise its authority on the States as States. It is insufficient, in assessing the validity of congressional regulation of a State pursuant to the commerce power, to ask only whether the same regulation would be valid if enforced against a private party. That reasoning, embodied in the majority opinion, is inconsistent with the spirit of our Constitution. It remains relevant that a State is being regulated, as *National League of Cities* and every recent case have recognized. . . .

It has been difficult for this Court to craft bright lines defining the scope of the state autonomy protected by *National League of Cities*. Such difficulty is to be expected whenever constitutional concerns as important as federalism and the effectiveness of the commerce power come into conflict. Regardless of the difficulty, it is and will remain the duty of this Court to reconcile these concerns in the final instance. That the Court shuns the task today by appealing to the "essence of federalism" can provide scant comfort to those who believe our federal system requires something more than a unitary, centralized government. I would not shirk the duty acknowledged by *National League of Cities* and its progeny, and I share Justice Rehnquist's belief that this Court will in time again assume its constitutional responsibility.

I respectfully dissent.

NOTES

(1) In *National League of Cities v. Usery*, 426 U.S. 833 (1976), the Court in a 5-4 decision, ruled that Congress could not subject the states to wage and hour requirements previously imposed on private employers. In so doing, the Court overruled *Maryland v. Wirtz*, 392 U.S. 183 (1968), a 5-4 decision upholding application of the Fair Labor Standards Act (FLSA) to state employees. The Court distinguished federal regulation of private, from public, employment and noted that decisions establishing the breadth of Congressional authority under the Commerce Clause had involved laws regulating private parties. The Court imposed additional restraints when Congress seeks to exercise the commerce power in a manner infringing on the states' existence as essential elements of the federal system. Prior to *National League of Cities*, the Tenth Amendment was regarded as simply stating "a truism that all is retained which has not been surrendered." *United States v. Darby*, 312 U.S. 100, 124 (1941). From 1937 until 1992, *National League of Cities* was the only case to strike down a federal law based on the Tenth Amendment.

(2) Between *National League of Cities* and *Garcia*, the Court heard a handful of cases which afforded the opportunity to develop its *National League of Cities* jurisprudence. In each, the Court distinguished *National League of Cities* and upheld the federal statutes under attack. *See Equal Employment Opportunity Comm'n v. Wyoming*, 460 U.S. 226 (1983); *United Transportation Union v. Long Island R.R. Co.*, 455 U.S. 678 (1982); *Federal Energy Regulatory Comm'n (FERC) v. Mississippi*, 456 U.S. 742 (1982); *Hodel v. Virginia Surface Mining & Reclamation Ass'n*, 452 U.S. 264 (1981). Justice Blackmun was in the majority in each case the first two of which were divided on 5–4 divisions.

(3) Why did *National League of Cities* not survive? Professor Martha A. Field mentions a number of factors that may have contributed to its demise: it was a 5-4

decision, it lacked any unequivocal textual roots, its proponents failed to agree on an underlying rationale, its standards were vague and subject to manipulation, and it subjected the Court to the charge that it was substituting its judgments regarding the merits of legislation for that of Congress. *See* Martha A. Field, Garcia v. San Antonio Metropolitan Transit Authority: *The Demise of a Misguided Doctrine*, 99 HARV. L. REV. 84 (1985).

(4) Notwithstanding the demise of *National League of Cities*, does federalism have value as an important structural constraint on federal power? "Perhaps the most frequently mentioned function of the federal system is . . . the protection of the citizen against governmental oppression," writes Professor Andrew Rapaczynski. He also suggests the states, as smaller units, may better reflect their constituents' interests. *See* Andrew Rapaczynski, *From Sovereignty to Process: The Jurisprudence of Federalism after Garcia*, 1985 SUP. CT. REV. 341, 380, 391.

On the other hand, some question these arguments. Professor David Shapiro wonders, for instance, whether a state like California is really much closer to the citizenry and therefore in a position to mirror their views. *See* DAVID SAPIRO, FEDERALISM: A DIALOGUE 93 (1995). While diffusion of power may constrain national power, states, as smaller units, may be more susceptible to falling under the control of a faction which could abuse non-members.

(5) How does one conduct the sort of balancing test Justice Powell and Justice O'Connor advocate? Justice Powell wrote in a footnote omitted above: "In undertaking such balancing, we have considered, on the one hand, the strength of the federal interest in the challenged legislation and the impact of exempting the States from its reach. Central to our inquiry into the federal interest is how closely the challenged action implicates the central concerns of the Commerce Clause, *viz.*, the promotion of a national economy and free trade among the States."

(6) The majority leaves to the political process protections for states. Justice Powell complained in a footnote: "One can hardly imagine this Court saying that because Congress is composed of individuals, individual rights guaranteed by the Bill of Rights are amply protected by the political process. Yet, the position adopted today is indistinguishable in principle. The Tenth Amendment also is an essential part of the Bill of Rights. . . ." Is this convincing? The Bill of Rights removes certain issues from the reach of political majorities to protect minorities who cannot prevail in Congress. Does the same rationale apply to the states?

(7) Can the political process safeguard states' interests? In an influential article, Professor Herbert Wechsler wrote in 1954 that the Court stood on its "weakest ground when it opposes its interpretation of the Constitution to that of Congress in the interest of the states, whose representatives control the legislative process and, by hypothesis, have broadly acquiesced in sanctioning the challenged Act of Congress." Herbert Wechsler, *The Political Safeguards of Federalism: The Role of the States in the Composition and Selection of the National Government*, 54 COLUM. L. REV. 543, 559 (1954). Justice Powell argued that developments had eroded the ability of the political process to protect the states. He wrote: "The adoption of the Seventeenth Amendment (providing for direct election of Senators), the weakening of political parties on the local level, and the rise of national media, among other things, have made Congress increasingly less representative of state and local interests, and more likely to be responsive to the demands of various national constituencies." Is the majority relying on a normative or ideal vision of how Senators and Representatives should operate? Is Justice Powell relying on a descriptive account of how they do behave? Which approach is appropriate?

(8) When the Court first discussed *Garcia* in conference, Justice Blackmun voted to

affirm the lower court decision, thereby agreeing with Chief Justice Burger and Justices Powell, Rehnquist, and O'Connor. At conference, he said that "a good opinion can be written either way. I come down on the side that this is local. . . ." Justice Powell agreed that "[o]ne can write a principled decision either way" but reasoned that transporting people to and from work was an "essential" service. Chief Justice Burger assigned Justice Blackmun to write the majority opinion, hoping that the assignment would strengthen the commitment to that position of the most uncertain member of the majority. Instead, Justice Blackmun found himself unable to write a principled opinion to affirm and switched his vote to create a 5-4 majority to reverse and abandon *National League of Cities. See* THE SUPREME COURT IN CONFERENCE (1940-1985), at 231-32 (Del Dickson ed., 2001)

(9) *Garcia* seems to admit the possibility of judicial intervention to protect states from certain "horrible possibilities." What might these be? Suppose Congress tried to create a new state within the boundaries of an existing state or deprive a state of one or both of its Senators? *See* U.S. Const. art. IV, sec. 3; art. V. Suppose Congress tried to relocate a state capital? *See Coyle v. Oklahoma*, 221 U.S. 559, 565 (1961) (calling power to locate and move seat of state government, "essentially and peculiarly state powers").

(10) In *U.S. Term Limits* the majority opinion, written by Justice Stevens, viewed members of Congress as national representatives whereas the dissent treated them as representing their states. In *Garcia*, the majority, including Justice Stevens, treated members of Congress as representing states whereas the dissent (including Chief Justice Rehnquist and Justice O'Connor from the *U.S. Term Limits* dissent) viewed members of Congress as national officials. Are both sides inconsistent?

(11) Note also the statements by Justices Rehnquist and O'Connor that *Garcia* itself will one day be overruled and *National League of Cities* again be followed. Is that likely? Would it be desirable? Are their complaints that the Court in *Garcia* paid insufficient homage to stare decisis undermined by the fact that in 1976 *Usery* overruled *Maryland v. Wirtz*, itself a recent precedent?

§ 3.03 COMMANDEERING THE STATES

NEW YORK v. UNITED STATES
505 U.S. 144, 112 S. Ct. 2408, 120 L. Ed. 2d 120 (1992)

JUSTICE O'CONNOR delivered the opinion of the Court.

These cases implicate one of our Nation's newest problems of public policy and perhaps our oldest question of constitutional law. The public policy issue involves the disposal of radioactive waste: In this case, we address the constitutionality of three provisions of the Low-Level Radioactive Waste Policy Amendments Act of 1985, Pub. L. 99-240, 99 Stat. 1842, 42 U.S.C. § 2021b *et seq.* The constitutional question is as old as the Constitution: It consists of discerning the proper division of authority between the Federal Government and the States. We conclude that while Congress has substantial power under the Constitution to encourage the States to provide for the disposal of the radioactive waste generated within their borders, the Constitution does not confer upon Congress the ability simply to compel the States to do so. We therefore find that only two of the Act's three provisions at issue are consistent with the Constitution's allocation of power to the Federal Government.

I

. . . .

Faced with the possibility that the Nation would be left with no disposal sites for low-level radioactive waste, Congress responded by enacting the Low-Level Radioactive Waste Policy Act, Pub. L. 96-573, 94 Stat. 3347. . . . Congress declared a federal policy of holding each State "responsible for providing for the availability of capacity either within or outside the State for the disposal of low-level radioactive waste generated within its borders," and found that such waste could be disposed of "most safely and efficiently . . . on a regional basis." § 4(a)(1), 94 Stat. 3348. The 1980 Act authorized States to enter into regional compacts that, once ratified by Congress, would have the authority beginning in 1986 to restrict the use of their disposal facilities to waste generated within member States. § 4(a)(2)(B), 94 Stat. 3348. The 1980 Act included no penalties for States that failed to participate in this plan. By 1985, only three approved regional compacts had operational disposal facilities . . . and the remaining 31 states would have had no assured outlet for their low level radioactive waste.

With this prospect looming, Congress once again took up the issue of waste disposal. The result was the legislation challenged here, the Low-Level Radioactive Waste Policy Amendments Act of 1985. . . .

The Act provides three types of incentives to encourage the States to comply with their statutory obligation to provide for the disposal of waste generated within their borders.

1. Monetary incentives. One quarter of the surcharges collected by the sited States must be transferred to an escrow account held by the Secretary of Energy. § 2021e(d)(2)(A). The Secretary then makes payments from this account to each State that has complied with a series of deadlines. . . . Each State that has not met the 1993 deadline must either take title to the waste generated within its borders or forfeit to the waste generators the incentive payments it has received. § 2021e(d)(2)(C).

2. Access incentives. The second type of incentive involves the denial of access to disposal sites. States that fail to meet the July 1986 deadline may be charged twice the ordinary surcharge . . . and may be denied access to disposal facilities thereafter. . . .

3. The take title provision. The third type of incentive is the most severe. The Act provides: "if a State (or, where applicable, a compact region) in which low-level radioactive waste is generated is unable to provide for the disposal of all such waste generated within such State or compact region by January 1, 1996, each State in which such waste is generated, upon the request of the generator or owner of the waste, shall take title to the waste, be obligated to take possession of the waste, and shall be liable for all damages directly or indirectly incurred by such generator or owner as a consequence of the failure of the State to take possession of the waste as soon after January 1, 1996, as the generator or owner notifies the State that the waste is available for shipment." § 2021e(d)(2)(C). These three incentives are the focus of petitioners' constitutional challenge. . . .

Petitioners — the State of New York and . . . two counties — filed this suit against the United States in 1990. . . . [P]etitioners claim . . . that the Act is inconsistent with the Tenth Amendment. . . .

II

A

While no one disputes the proposition that "[t]he Constitution created a Federal Government of limited powers" . . . and while the Tenth Amendment makes explicit that "[t]he powers not delegated to the United States by the Constitution, nor prohibited by it to the States, are reserved to the States respectively, or to the people"; the task of ascertaining the constitutional line between federal and state power has given rise to many of the Court's most difficult and celebrated cases. . . .

These questions can be viewed in either of two ways. In some cases the Court has inquired whether an Act of Congress is authorized by one of the powers delegated to Congress in Article I of the Constitution. In other cases the Court has sought to determine whether an Act of Congress invades the province of state sovereignty reserved by the Tenth Amendment. . . . In a case like this one, involving the division of authority between federal and state governments, the two inquiries are mirror images of each other. If a power is delegated to Congress in the Constitution, the Tenth Amendment expressly disclaims any reservation of that power to the States; if a power is an attribute of state sovereignty reserved by the Tenth Amendment, it is necessarily a power the Constitution has not conferred on Congress. . . .

It is in this sense that the Tenth Amendment "states but a truism that all is retained which has not been surrendered." *United States v. Darby*, [*supra* § 2.04[2]]. As Justice Story put it, "[t]his amendment is a mere affirmation of what, upon any just reasoning, is a necessary rule of interpreting the constitution. Being an instrument of limited and enumerated powers, it follows irresistibly, that what is not conferred, is withheld, and belongs to the state authorities." . . .

Congress exercises its conferred powers subject to the limitations contained in the Constitution. Thus, for example, under the Commerce Clause Congress may regulate publishers engaged in interstate commerce, but Congress is constrained in the exercise of that power by the First Amendment. The Tenth Amendment likewise restrains the power of Congress, but this limit is not derived from the text of the Tenth Amendment itself, which, as we have discussed, is essentially a tautology. Instead, the Tenth Amendment confirms that the power of the Federal Government is subject to limits that may, in a given instance, reserve power to the States. The Tenth Amendment thus directs us to determine, as in this case, whether an incident of state sovereignty is protected by a limitation on an Article I power. . . .

This framework has been sufficiently flexible over the past two centuries to allow for enormous changes in the nature of government. The Federal Government undertakes activities today that would have been unimaginable to the Framers in two senses; first, because the Framers would not have conceived that any government would conduct such activities; and second, because the Framers would not have believed that the Federal Government, rather than the States, would assume such responsibilities. Yet the powers conferred upon the Federal Government by the Constitution were phrased in language broad enough to allow for the expansion of the Federal Government's role. Among the provisions of the Constitution that have been particularly important in this regard, three concern us here.

First, the Constitution allocates to Congress the power "[t]o regulate Commerce . . . among the several States." Art. I, § 8, cl. 3. Interstate commerce was an established feature of life in the late 18th century. . . . The volume of interstate commerce and the range of commonly accepted objects of government regulation have, however, expanded considerably in the last 200 years, and the regulatory authority of Congress has expanded along with them. As interstate commerce has become ubiquitous, activities once considered purely local have come to have effects on the national economy, and have accordingly come within the scope of Congress' commerce power. . . .

Second, the Constitution authorizes Congress "to pay the Debts and provide for the . . . general Welfare of the United States." Art. I, § 8, cl. 1. As conventional notions of the proper objects of government spending have changed over the years, so has the ability of Congress to "fix the terms on which it shall disburse federal money to the States. . . ."

The Court's broad construction of Congress' power under the Commerce and

Spending Clauses has of course been guided, as it has with respect to Congress' power generally, by the Constitution's Necessary and Proper Clause, which authorizes Congress "[t]o make all Laws which shall be necessary and proper for carrying into Execution the foregoing Powers. . . ."

Finally, the Constitution provides that "the Laws of the United States . . . shall be the supreme Law of the Land . . . any Thing in the Constitution or Laws of any State to the Contrary notwithstanding." U.S. Const., Art. VI, cl. 2. As the Federal Government's willingness to exercise power within the confines of the Constitution has grown, the authority of the States has correspondingly diminished to the extent that federal and state policies have conflicted. . . . We have observed that the Supremacy Clause gives the Federal Government "a decided advantage in th[e] delicate balance" the Constitution strikes between State and Federal power. . . .

The actual scope of the Federal Government's authority with respect to the States has changed over the years, therefore, but the constitutional structure underlying and limiting that authority has not. In the end, just as a cup may be half empty or half full, it makes no difference whether one views the question at issue in this case as one of ascertaining the limits of the power delegated to the Federal Government under the affirmative provisions of the Constitution or one of discerning the core of sovereignty retained by the States under the Tenth Amendment. Either way, we must determine whether any of the three challenged provisions of the Low-Level Radioactive Waste Policy Amendments Act of 1985 oversteps the boundary between federal and state authority.

B

Petitioners do not contend that Congress lacks the power to regulate the disposal of low level radioactive waste. Space in radioactive waste disposal sites is frequently sold by residents of one State to residents of another. Regulation of the resulting interstate market in waste disposal is therefore well within Congress' authority under the Commerce Clause. . . . Petitioners likewise do not dispute that under the Supremacy Clause Congress could, if it wished, pre-empt state radioactive waste regulation. Petitioners contend only that the Tenth Amendment limits the power of Congress to regulate in the way it has chosen. Rather than addressing the problem of waste disposal by directly regulating the generators and disposers of waste, petitioners argue, Congress has impermissibly directed the States to regulate in this field.

Most of our recent cases interpreting the Tenth Amendment have concerned the authority of Congress to subject state governments to generally applicable laws. The Court's jurisprudence in this area has traveled an unsteady path. *See Maryland v. Wirtz*, 392 U.S. 183 (1968) (state schools and hospitals are subject to Fair Labor Standards Act); *National League of Cities v. Usery*, [*supra* § 3.02, Note (1)] (overruling *Wirtz*) (state employers are not subject to Fair Labor Standards Act); *Garcia v. San Antonio Metropolitan Transit Authority*, [*supra* § 3.02] (overruling *National League of Cities*) (state employers are once again subject to Fair Labor Standards Act). . . . This litigation presents no occasion to apply or revisit the holdings of any of these cases, as this is not a case in which Congress has subjected a State to the same legislation applicable to private parties. . . .

This litigation instead concerns the circumstances under which Congress may use the States as implements of regulation; that is, whether Congress may direct or otherwise motivate the States to regulate in a particular field or a particular way. Our cases have established a few principles that guide our resolution of the issue.

1

As an initial matter, Congress may not simply "commandee[r] the legislative processes of the States by directly compelling them to enact and enforce a federal regulatory program." *Hodel v. Virginia Surface Mining & Reclamation Ass'n, Inc.*, 452 U.S. 264, 288 (1981).

While Congress has substantial powers to govern the Nation directly, including in areas of intimate concern to the States, the Constitution has never been understood to confer upon Congress the ability to require the States to govern according to Congress' instructions. . . .

Indeed, the question whether the Constitution should permit Congress to employ state governments as regulatory agencies was a topic of lively debate among the Framers. Under the Articles of Confederation, Congress lacked the authority in most respects to govern the people directly. The Convention generated a great number of proposals for the structure of the new Government. . . . In providing for a stronger central government, . . . the Framers explicitly chose a Constitution that confers upon Congress the power to regulate individuals, not States. As we have seen, the Court has consistently respected this choice. We have always understood that even where Congress has the authority under the Constitution to pass laws requiring or prohibiting certain acts, it lacks the power directly to compel the States to require or prohibit those acts. . . .

2

This is not to say that Congress lacks the ability to encourage a State to regulate in a particular way, or that Congress may not hold out incentives to the States as a method of influencing a State's policy choices. Our cases have identified a variety of methods, short of outright coercion, by which Congress may urge a State to adopt a legislative program consistent with federal interests. Two of these methods are of particular relevance here.

First, under Congress' spending power, "Congress may attach conditions on the receipt of federal funds." *South Dakota v. Dole*, [*supra* § 2.07]. Such conditions must (among other requirements) bear some relationship to the purpose of the federal spending; otherwise, of course, the spending power could render academic the Constitution's other grants and limits of federal authority. Where the recipient of federal funds is a State, as is not unusual today, the conditions attached to the funds by Congress may influence a State's legislative choices. . . .

Second, where Congress has the authority to regulate private activity under the Commerce Clause, we have recognized Congress' power to offer States the choice of regulating that activity according to federal standards or having state law pre-empted by federal regulation. . . . This arrangement, which has been termed "a program of cooperative federalism," . . . is replicated in numerous federal statutory schemes. . . .

By either of these two methods, as by any other permissible method of encouraging a State to conform to federal policy choices, the residents of the State retain the ultimate decision as to whether or not the State will comply. If a State's citizens view federal policy as sufficiently contrary to local interests, they may elect to decline a federal grant. If state residents would prefer their government to devote its attention and resources to problems other than those deemed important by Congress, they may choose to have the Federal Government rather than the State bear the expense of a federally mandated regulatory program, and they may continue to supplement that program to the extent state law is not preempted. Where Congress encourages state regulation rather than compelling it, state governments remain responsive to the local electorate's preferences; state officials remain accountable to the people. By contrast, where the Federal Government compels States to regulate, the accountability of both state and federal officials is diminished. If the citizens of New York, for example, do not consider that making provision for the disposal of radioactive waste is in their best interest, they may elect state officials who share their view. That view can always be preempted under the Supremacy Clause if it is contrary to the national view, but in such a case it is the Federal Government that makes the decision in full view of the public, and it will be federal officials that suffer the consequences if the decision turns out to be detrimental or unpopular. But where the Federal Government directs the States to regulate, it may be state officials who will bear the brunt of public disapproval, while the federal officials who devised the regulatory program may remain insulated from the electoral ramifications of their decision. Accountability is thus diminished when, due to federal coercion, elected state officials cannot regulate in accordance with the views of the local electorate in matters not pre-empted by federal regulation. . . .

With these principles in mind, we turn to the three challenged provisions of the Low-Level Radioactive Waste Policy Amendments Act of 1985.

III

. . . .

A

The first set of incentives works in three steps. First, Congress has authorized States with disposal sites to impose a surcharge on radioactive waste received from other States. Second, the Secretary of Energy collects a portion of this surcharge and places the money in an escrow account. Third, States achieving a series of milestones receive portions of this fund.

The first of these steps is an unexceptionable exercise of Congress' power to authorize the States to burden interstate commerce. While the Commerce Clause has long been understood to limit the States' ability to discriminate against interstate commerce . . . that limit may be lifted, as it has been here, by an expression of the "unambiguous intent" of Congress. . . . Whether or not the States would be permitted to burden the interstate transport of low level radioactive waste in the absence of Congress' approval, the States can clearly do so with Congress' approval, which is what the Act gives them.

The second step, the Secretary's collection of a percentage of the surcharge, is no more than a federal tax on interstate commerce, which petitioners do not claim to be an invalid exercise of either Congress' commerce or taxing power. . . . The third step is a conditional exercise of Congress' authority under the Spending Clause: Congress has placed conditions — the achievement of the milestones — on the receipt of federal funds. Petitioners do not contend that Congress has exceeded its authority in any of the four respects our cases have identified. . . . The expenditure is for the general welfare, . . . the States are required to use the money they receive for the purpose of assuring the safe disposal of radioactive waste. 42 U.S.C. § 2021e(d)(2)(E). The conditions imposed are unambiguous . . . the Act informs the States exactly what they must do and by when they must do it in order to obtain a share of the escrow account. The conditions imposed are reasonably related to the purpose of the expenditure, . . . both the conditions and the payments embody Congress' efforts to address the pressing problem of radioactive waste disposal. Finally, petitioners do not claim that the conditions imposed by the Act violate any independent constitutional prohibition. . . .

The Act's first set of incentives, in which Congress has conditioned grants to the

States upon the States' attainment of a series of milestones, is thus well within the authority of Congress under the Commerce and Spending Clauses. Because the first set of incentives is supported by affirmative constitutional grants of power to Congress, it is not inconsistent with the Tenth Amendment.

B

In the second set of incentives, Congress has authorized States and regional compacts with disposal sites gradually to increase the cost of access to the sites, and then to deny access altogether, to radioactive waste generated in States that do not meet federal deadlines. As a simple regulation, this provision would be within the power of Congress to authorize the States to discriminate against interstate commerce. . . . Where federal regulation of private activity is within the scope of the Commerce Clause, we have recognized the ability of Congress to offer states the choice of regulating that activity according to federal standards or having state law pre-empted by federal regulation. . . .

This is the choice presented to nonsited States by the Act's second set of incentives: States may either regulate the disposal of radioactive waste according to federal standards by attaining local or regional self-sufficiency, or their residents who produce radioactive waste will be subject to federal regulation authorizing sited States and regions to deny access to their disposal sites. The affected States are not compelled by Congress to regulate, because any burden caused by a State's refusal to regulate will fall on those who generate waste and find no outlet for its disposal, rather than on the State as a sovereign. A State whose citizens do not wish it to attain the Act's milestones may devote its attention and its resources to issues its citizens deem more worthy; the choice remains at all times with the residents of the State, not with Congress. The State need not expend any funds, or participate in any federal program, if local residents do not view such expenditures or participation as worthwhile. . . . Nor must the State abandon the field if it does not accede to federal direction; the State may continue to regulate the generation and disposal of radioactive waste in any manner its citizens see fit.

The Act's second set of incentives thus represents a conditional exercise of Congress' commerce power, along the lines of those we have held to be within Congress' authority. As a result, the second set of incentives does not intrude on the sovereignty reserved to the States by the Tenth Amendment.

C

The take title provision is of a different character. This third so-called "incentive" offers States, as an alternative to regulating pursuant to Congress' direction, the option of taking title to and possession of the low level radioactive waste generated within their borders and becoming liable for all damages waste generators suffer as a result of the States' failure to do so promptly. In this provision, Congress has crossed the line distinguishing encouragement from coercion. . . .

The take title provision offers state governments a "choice" of either accepting ownership of waste or regulating according to the instructions of Congress. Respondents do not claim that the Constitution would authorize Congress to impose either option as a freestanding requirement. On one hand, the Constitution would not permit Congress simply to transfer radioactive waste from generators to state governments. Such a forced transfer, standing alone, would in principle be no different than a congressionally compelled subsidy from state governments to radioactive waste producers. The same is true of the provision requiring the States to become liable for the generators' damages. Standing alone, this provision would be indistinguishable from an Act of Congress directing the States to assume the liabilities of certain state residents. Either type of federal action would "commandeer" state governments into the service of federal regulatory purposes, and would for this reason be inconsistent with the Constitution's division of authority between federal and state governments. On the other hand, the second alternative held out to state governments — regulating pursuant to Congress' direction — would, standing alone, present a simple command to state governments to implement legislation enacted by Congress. As we have seen, the Constitution does not empower Congress to subject state governments to this type of instruction.

Because an instruction to state governments to take title to waste, standing alone, would be beyond the authority of Congress, and because a direct order to regulate, standing alone, would also be beyond the authority of Congress, it follows that Congress lacks the power to offer the States a choice between the two. Unlike the first two sets of incentives, the take title incentive does not represent the conditional exercise of any congressional power enumerated in the Constitution. In this provision, Congress has not held out the threat of exercising its spending power or its commerce power; it has instead held out the threat, should the States not regulate according to one federal instruction, of simply forcing the States to submit to another federal instruction. A choice between two unconstitutionally coercive regulatory techniques is no choice at all. Either way, "the Act commandeers the legislative processes of the States by directly compelling them to enact and enforce a federal regulatory program," . . . an outcome that has never been understood to lie within the authority conferred upon Congress by the Constitution. . . .

IV

. . . .

B

The sited state respondents focus their attention on the process by which the Act was formulated. They correctly observe that public officials representing the State of New York lent their support to the Act's enactment. . . . Respondents note that the Act embodies a bargain among the sited and unsited States, a compromise to which New York was a willing participant and from which New York has reaped much benefit. Respondents then pose what appears at first to be a troubling question: How can a federal statute be found an unconstitutional infringement of state sovereignty when state officials consented to the statute's enactment?

The answer follows from an understanding of the fundamental purpose served by our Government's federal structure. The Constitution does not protect the sovereignty of States for the benefit of the States or state governments as abstract political entities, or even for the benefit of the public officials governing the States. To the contrary, the Constitution divides authority between federal and state governments for the protection of individuals. State sovereignty is not just an end in itself: "Rather, federalism secures to citizens the liberties that derive from the diffusion of sovereign power." . . . The constitutional authority of Congress cannot be expanded by the "consent" of the governmental unit whose domain is thereby narrowed, whether that unit is the Executive Branch or the States.

State officials thus cannot consent to the enlargement of the powers of Congress beyond those enumerated in the Constitution. Indeed, the facts of these cases raise the possibility that powerful incentives might lead both federal and state officials to view departures from the federal structure to be in their personal interests. Most citizens recognize the need for radioactive waste disposal sites, but few want sites near their homes. As a result, while it would be well within the authority of either federal or state officials to choose where the disposal sites will be, it is likely to be in the political interest of each individual official to avoid being held accountable to the voters for the choice of location. If a federal official is faced with the alternatives of choosing a location or directing the States to do it, the official may well prefer the latter, as a means of shifting responsibility for the eventual decision. If a state official is faced with the same set of alternatives — choosing a location or having Congress direct the choice of a location — the state official may also prefer the latter, as it may permit the avoidance of personal responsibility. The interests of public officials thus may not coincide with the Constitution's intergovernmental allocation of authority. Where state officials purport to submit to the direction of Congress in this manner, federalism is hardly being advanced. . . .

VII

Some truths are so basic that, like the air around us, they are easily overlooked. Much of the Constitution is concerned with setting forth the form of our government, and the courts have traditionally invalidated measures deviating from that form. The result may appear "formalistic" in a given case to partisans of the measure at issue, because such measures are typically the product of the era's perceived necessity. But the Constitution protects us from our own best intentions: it divides power among sovereigns and among branches of government precisely so that we may resist the temptation to concentrate power in one location as an expedient solution to the crisis of the day. The shortage of disposal sites for radioactive waste is a pressing national problem, but a judiciary that licensed extra-constitutional government with each issue of comparable gravity would, in the long run, be far worse.

States are not mere political subdivisions of the United States. State governments are neither regional offices nor administrative agencies of the Federal Government. The positions occupied by state officials appear nowhere on the Federal Government's most detailed organizational chart. The Constitution instead "leaves to the several States a residuary and inviolable sovereignty," reserved explicitly to the States by the Tenth Amendment.

Whatever the outer limits of that sovereignty may be, one thing is clear: the Federal Government may not compel the States to enact or administer a federal regulatory program. The Constitution permits both the Federal Government and the States to enact legislation regarding the disposal of low level radioactive waste. The Constitution enables the Federal Government to pre-empt state regulation contrary to federal interests, and it permits the Federal Government to hold out incentives to the States as a means of encouraging them to adopt suggested regulatory schemes. It does not, however, authorize Congress simply to direct the States to provide for the disposal of the radioactive waste generated within their borders. While there may be many constitutional methods of achieving regional self-sufficiency in radioactive waste disposal, the method Congress has chosen is not one of them. The judgment of the Court of Appeals is accordingly affirmed in part and reversed in part.

JUSTICE WHITE, with whom JUSTICE BLACKMUN and JUSTICE STEVENS join, concurring in part and dissenting in part.

. . . My disagreement with the Court's analysis begins at the basic descriptive level of how the legislation at issue in these cases came to be enacted. The Court goes some way toward setting out the bare facts, but its omissions cast the statutory context of the take title provision in the wrong light. To read the Court's version of events, . . . one would think that Congress was the sole proponent of a solution to the Nation's low-level radioactive waste problem. Not so. The Low-Level Radioactive Waste Policy Act of 1980, and its amendatory 1985 Act, resulted from the efforts of state leaders to achieve a state-based set of remedies to the waste problem. They sought not federal pre-emption or intervention, but rather congressional sanction of interstate compromises they had reached. . . . The imminence of a crisis in low-level radioactive waste management cannot be overstated. . . . In sum, the 1985 Act was very much the product of cooperative federalism, in which the States bargained among themselves to achieve compromises for Congress to sanction. . . .

. . . It does, however, seem critical to emphasize . . . the assumption by Congress of "the role of arbiter of disputes among the several States." Unlike legislation that directs action from the Federal Government to the States, the 1980 and 1985 Acts reflected hard-fought agreements among States as refereed by Congress. The distinction is key, and the Court's failure properly to characterize this legislation ultimately affects its analysis of the take title provision's constitutionality. . . .

. . . Curiously absent from the Court's analysis is any effort to place the take title provision within the overall context of the legislation. . . . Congress could have pre-empted the field by directly regulating the disposal of this waste pursuant to its powers under the Commerce and Spending Clauses, but instead it unanimously assented to the States' request for congressional ratification of agreements to which they had acceded. . . .

. . . In my view, New York's actions subsequent to enactment of the 1980 and 1985 Acts fairly indicate its approval of the interstate agreement process embodied in those laws within the meaning of Art. I, § 10, cl. 3, of the Constitution, which provides that "[n]o State shall, without the Consent of Congress, . . . enter into any Agreement or Compact with another State." First, the States — including New York — worked through their Governors to petition Congress for the 1980 and 1985 Acts. As I have attempted to demonstrate, these statutes are best understood as the products of collective state action, rather than as impositions placed on States by the Federal Government. Second, New York acted in compliance with the requisites of both statutes in key respects, thus signifying its assent to the agreement achieved among the States as codified in these laws. . . . New York continued to take full advantage of the import concession made by the sited States, by exporting its low-level radioactive waste for the full 7-year extension period provided in the 1985 Act. By gaining these benefits and complying with certain of the 1985 Act's deadlines, therefore, New York fairly evidenced its acceptance of the federal-state arrangement — including the take title provision. . . .

. . . The State should be estopped from asserting the unconstitutionality of a provision that seeks merely to ensure that, after deriving substantial advantages from the 1985 Act, New York in fact must live up to its bargain by establishing an in-state low-level radioactive waste facility or assuming liability for its failure to act. . . .

. . . Finally, to say, as the Court does, that the incursion on state sovereignty "cannot be ratified by the 'consent' of state officials," . . . is flatly wrong. . . . Hard public policy choices sometimes require strong measures, and the Court's holding, while not irremediable, essentially misunderstands that the 1985 take title provision was part of a complex interstate agreement about which New York should not now be permitted to complain.

The Court announces that it has no occasion to revisit such decisions as . . . *Garcia v. San Antonio Metropolitan Transit Authority,* . . . and *National League of Cities v. Usery,* . . . because "this is not a case in which Congress has subjected a State to the same legislation applicable to private parties." *Id.* Although this statement sends the welcome signal that the Court does not intend to cut a wide swath through our recent Tenth Amendment precedents, it nevertheless is unpersuasive. . . .

. . . The Court's distinction between a federal statute's regulation of States and private parties for general purposes, as opposed to a regulation solely on the activities of States, is unsupported by our recent Tenth Amendment cases. In no case has the Court rested its holding on such a distinction. Moreover, the Court makes no effort to explain why this purported distinction should affect the analysis of Congress' power under general principles of federalism and the Tenth Amendment. . . . An incursion on state sovereignty hardly seems more constitutionally acceptable if the federal statute that "commands" specific action also applies to private parties. The alleged diminution in state authority over its own affairs is not any less because the federal mandate restricts the activities of private parties. . . .

. . . I would also submit, in this connection, that the Court's attempt to carve out a doctrinal distinction for statutes that purport solely to regulate state activities is especially unpersuasive after *Garcia*. . . . In *Garcia*, we stated the proper inquiry: "[W]e are convinced that the fundamental limitation that the constitutional scheme imposes on the Commerce Clause to protect the 'States as States' is one of process rather than one of result. Any substantive restraint on the exercise of Commerce Clause powers must find its justification in the procedural nature of this basic limitation, and it must be tailored to compensate for possible failings in the national political process rather than to dictate a 'sacred province of state autonomy.' " . . .

. . . Ultimately, I suppose, the entire structure of our federal constitutional government can be traced to an interest in establishing checks and balances to prevent the exercise of tyranny against individuals. But these fears seem extremely far distant to me in a situation such as this. We face a crisis of national proportions in the disposal of low-level radioactive waste, and Congress has acceded to the wishes of the States by permitting local decisionmaking rather than imposing a solution from Washington. New York itself participated and supported passage of this legislation at both the gubernatorial and federal representative levels, and then enacted state laws specifically to comply with the deadlines and timetables agreed upon by the States in the 1985 Act. For me, the Court's civics lecture has a decidedly hollow ring at a time when action, rather than rhetoric, is needed to solve a national problem. . . .

. . . The ultimate irony of the decision today is that in its formalistically rigid obeisance to "federalism," the Court gives Congress fewer incentives to defer to the wishes of state officials in achieving local solutions to local problems. This legislation was a classic example of Congress acting as arbiter among the States in their attempts to accept responsibility for managing a problem of grave import. The States urged the National Legislature not to impose from Washington a solution to the country's low-level radioactive waste management problems. Instead, they sought a reasonable level of local and regional autonomy consistent with Art. I, § 10, cl. 3, of the Constitution. By invalidating the measure designed to ensure compliance for recalcitrant States, such as New York, the Court upsets the delicate compromise achieved among the States and forces Congress to erect several additional formalistic hurdles to clear before achieving exactly the same objective. Because the Court's justifications for undertaking this step are unpersuasive to me, I respectfully dissent. . . .

NOTES

(1) Why did the Court strike down the take title regulation? What was wrong with the options Congress offered the states — taking title to waste or regulating as Congress instructed? Professor Laurence Tribe writes that "[i]nstead of offering New York an exit to a world that Congress would have been free simply to impose . . . this

statute offered New York a choice between two exits *each* of which lead to a world Congress lacked authority to mandate." 1 LAURENCE TRIBE, AMERICAN CONSTITUTIONAL LAW 879 (3d ed. 1999).

(2) Did Congress have available, alternative legislative approaches to accomplish its purpose to induce the states, to provide for the disposal of low-level radioactive waste by January 1, 1996? Could Congress provide under the Commerce Clause that low-level radioactive waste could not be shipped out of a state that failed to meet a federal deadline to achieve a means of waste disposal and which had not taken title to its waste?

Could Congress refuse to disburse funds for low-level radioactive disposal to any state that had made no such provisions? Justice White wrote that:

> the spending power offers a means of enacting a take title provision under the Court's standards. Congress could, in other words, condition the payment of funds on the State's willingness to take title if it has not already provided a waste disposal facility. Under the scheme upheld in this case, for example, monies collected in the surcharge provision might be withheld or disbursed depending on a State's willingness to take title to or otherwise accept responsibility for the low-level radioactive waste generated in state after the statutory deadline for establishing its own waste disposal facility has passed.

If Justice White is correct, has the Court enhanced state power or simply made it more difficult to solve some national problems? Is the Court a better umpire of these disputes than Congress?

(3) The Court has often held that where Congress regulates states it must express its intent to regulate states in a clear statement. *See Gregory v. Ashcroft*, 501 U.S. 452 (1991). According to Professor Ernest A. Young, "[t]he purpose of such rules is to make sure that the 'political safeguards' of federalism are fully operational. . . . By demanding that the intent to infringe on state interests be clear and obvious, in other words, the Court ensures that the State's representatives in Congress have focused on the federalism issue in the course of enacting the legislation in question." Ernest Young, *State Sovereign Immunity and the Future of Federalism*, 1999 SUP. CT. REV. 1 (1999).

PRINTZ v. UNITED STATES, 521 U.S. 898 (1997). Five years after *New York v. United States*, the Court again considered the extent to which the federal government could impose duties upon state government in pursuance of federal objectives. *Printz v. United States* involved a constitutional challenge to the Brady Handgun Violence Prevention Act which required state and local law enforcement officers to perform background checks on prospective purchasers of handguns within five days. The state officials could, but need not, report their findings to the dealer. State officials were to discharge this duty only during an interim period pending creation of a national checking system. In a 5-4 decision, the Court held the provision unconstitutional.

Writing for the majority, Justice Scalia conceded that "there is no constitutional text speaking to this precise question" and found the evidence of original intent inconclusive. He concluded that arguments based on the Constitution's structure and precedent controlled the case. The Constitution established a system of dual sovereignty which would be compromised if the federal government could "impress into its service . . . at no cost to itself" state and local police. Moreover, the law offended the constitutional separation of powers by allocating part of the President's duty to "take care that the law be faithfully executed" to the states.

The Court's precedents were most persuasive, Justice Scalia suggested. "[O]pinions of ours have made clear that the Federal Government may not compel the states to implement, by legislation or executive action, federal regulatory programs." "We held in *New York* that Congress cannot compel the States to enact or enforce a federal regulatory program. Today we hold that Congress cannot circumvent that prohibition by conscripting the State's officers directly. The Federal Government may neither issue directives requiring the States to address particular problems, nor command the States' officers, or those of their political subdivisions, to administer or enforce a federal regulatory program. It matters not whether policymaking is involved, and no case-by-case weighing of the burdens or benefits is necessary; such commands are fundamentally incompatible with our constitutional system of dual sovereignty."

Justice Stevens (for himself and Justices Souter, Ginsberg, and Breyer) dissented. He found the Commerce Clause, supplemented by the Necessary and Proper Clause, an "affirmative delegation of power" which provided "ample authority" for the provision at issue. (Justice Scalia was unpersuaded. He derided the dissent's "resort to the last, best hope of those who defend *ultra vires* congressional action, the Necessary and Proper Clause." The Brady Law was not a "proper" law so was not within the power Article I delegated to Congress.) In addition to this textual argument, Justice Stevens found "the historical materials strongly suggest that the Founders intended to enhance the capacity of the federal government by empowering it — as a part of the new authority to make demands directly on individual citizens — to act through local officials. Hamilton made clear that the new Constitution, 'by extending the authority of the federal head to the individual citizens of the several States, will enable the government to employ the ordinary magistracy of each, in the execution of its laws.' The Federalist No. 27." Moreover, early Congresses required that "state judges and their clerks perform various executive duties." Justice Stevens was unpersuaded by the Court's structural arguments. The role of the states in the federal government protected state interests and was not threatened by such occasional "modest burdens on state officials." *New York* was inapposite since it involved commandeering state legislative bodies.

In a separate dissent, Justice Breyer invoked the comparative experience of other federal systems (i.e., Switzerland, Germany, the European Union) which rely on states rather than federal bureaucracies to implement federal law. "Of course, we are interpreting our own Constitution, not those of other nations, and there may be relevant political and structural differences between their systems and our own. . . . But their experience may nonetheless cast an empirical light on the consequences of different solutions to a common legal problem — in this case the problem of reconciling central authority with the need to preserve the liberty-enhancing autonomy of a smaller constituent governmental entity. . . ." Justice Scalia thought comparative analysis relevant in writing, but not in interpreting, a constitution.

NOTES

(1) Do the states have a constitutional obligation to lend their officials to the execution of federal statutes? The government and the dissent argued that such a principle found support in *Testa v. Katt*, 330 U.S. 386 (1947) and *Federal Energy Regulatory Comm'n v. Mississippi*, 456 U.S. 742 (1982). In *Testa*, the Court (according to Justice Stevens), held that Congress could require state courts to hear federal cases and decide them according to federal law regardless of the condition of state court dockets from state law matters. Justice Scalia asserts that *Testa* is irrelevant to the issue in *Printz* and stands for the more limited proposition that the Supremacy Clause mandates that state courts cannot refuse to apply federal law.

(2) Does *Printz* preclude the federal government from imposing any information — gathering or reporting assignments on state officials? Justice O'Connor, one of the five who formed the majority, suggested *Printz* may not be fatal to all such legislation. She wrote in her concurrence:

. . . [T]he Court appropriately refrains from deciding whether other purely ministerial reporting requirements imposed by Congress on state and local authorities pursuant to its Commerce Clause powers are similarly invalid. *See, e.g.,* 42 U.S.C. § 5779(a) (requiring state and local law enforcement agencies to report cases of missing children to the Department of Justice). The provisions invalidated here, however, which directly compel state officials to administer a federal regulatory program, utterly fail to adhere to the design and structure of our constitutional scheme.

(3) Could Congress have enlisted the assistance of state officials to enforce the Brady Act in other ways? Suppose Congress had simply required the dealer to report the sale to a Chief Law Enforcement Officer (CLEO) but had not required the CLEO to investigate? Could Congress have used the spending power to offer grants to states conditioned on performing background checks on gun purchasers? Would such an approach still have been an impermissible transfer of executive power to the states in violation of the Take Care Clause? Would states be better protected if Congress empowered a federal bureaucracy to correct information and conduct background checks?

Although Justice Thomas joined with the majority in concluding that the Brady Act violated the Tenth Amendment in compelling state law enforcement officials to help administer the federal scheme, he reiterated the view expressed in his concurrence in *United States v. Lopez*, 514 U.S. 549 (1995), that the Commerce Clause does not give Congress power to regulate intrastate sales of firearms. Accordingly, he apparently would have ruled the Brady Act generally beyond Congress' power to the extent it reached intrastate sales. Even under the majority's reasoning, however, which did not accept his view, he suggested Congress' regulation might still be barred by the Second Amendment to the Constitution.

(4) *New York* and *Printz* do not mean that claims that a federal statute commandeers the states will always prevail. In *Reno v. Condon*, 528 U.S. 141 (2000), the Court unanimously rejected South Carolina's claim that the Driver's Privacy Protection Act of 1994 (DPPA) unconstitutionally commandeered the states by requiring expenditure of time and effort by state officials. DPPA restricted the freedom of states to disclose a driver's personal information. The Court accepted South Carolina's complaint that DPPA would cause states to commit state resources to learning and applying the statutory regime. This was not the sort of commandeering the Constitution proscribes, however, since "the DPPA does not require the states in their sovereign capacity to regulate their own citizens." Moreover, DPPA "does not require the [state] to enact any laws or regulations, . . . and it does not require state officials to assist in the enforcement of federal statutes regulating private individuals." *Id.* at 151.

The Court drew an analogy to *South Carlina v. Baker*, 485 U.S. 505 (1988) where it held that a federal law barring states from issuing unregistered bonds did not constitute impermissible commandeering although the states had to amend various state statutes to comply. In *Condon*, Chief Justice Rehnquist quoted with approval the language Justice Brennan wrote for the Court in *Baker*. "Such 'commandeering' is, however, an inevitable consequence of regulating a state activity. Any federal regulation demands compliance. That a State wishing to engage in certain activity must take administrative and sometimes legislative action to comply with federal standards regulating that activity is a commonplace that presents no constitutional defect." *Condon*, 528 U.S. at 150-51.

§ 3.04   IMMUNITY FROM SUIT

SEMINOLE TRIBE OF FLORIDA v. FLORIDA
517 U.S. 44, 116 S. Ct. 1114, 134 L. Ed. 2d 252 (1996)

CHIEF JUSTICE REHNQUIST delivered the opinion of the Court.

The Indian Gaming Regulatory Act provides that an Indian tribe may conduct certain gaming activities only in conformance with a valid compact between the tribe and the State in which the gaming activities are located. 25 U.S.C. § 2710(d)(1)(C). The Act, passed by Congress under the Indian Commerce Clause, imposes upon the States a duty to negotiate in good faith with an Indian tribe toward the formation of a compact and authorizes a tribe to bring suit in federal court against a State in order to compel performance of that duty. We hold that notwithstanding Congress' clear intent to abrogate the States' sovereign immunity, the Indian Commerce Clause does not grant Congress that power, and therefore § 2710(d)(7) cannot grant jurisdiction over a State that does not consent to be sued. We further hold that the doctrine of *Ex parte Young*, 209 U.S. 123 (1908), may not be used to enforce § 2710(d)(3) against a state official. . . .

In September 1991, the Seminole Tribe of Indians, petitioner, sued the State of Florida and its Governor, Lawton Chiles, respondents. . . . petitioner alleged that respondents had "refused to enter into any negotiation for inclusion of [certain gaming activities] in a tribal-state compact" thereby violating the "requirement of good faith negotiation" contained in § 2710(d)(3). . . . The Court of Appeals [held] that the Eleventh Amendment barred petitioner's suit against respondents. . . . The Eleventh Amendment provides:

> The Judicial power of the United States shall not be construed to extend to any suit in law or equity, commenced or prosecuted against one of the United States by Citizens of another State, or by Citizens or Subject of any Foreign State.

Although the text of the Amendment would appear to restrict only the Article III diversity jurisdiction of the federal courts, "we have understood the Eleventh Amendment to stand not so much for what it says, but for the presupposition . . . which it confirms." That presupposition, first observed over a century ago has two parts: first, that each State is a sovereign entity in our federal system; and second, that " '[i]t is inherent in the nature of sovereignty not to be amenable to the suit of an individual without its consent.' " For over a century we have reaffirmed that federal jurisdiction over suits against unconsenting States "was not contemplated by the Constitution when establishing the judicial power of the United States."

Here, petitioner has sued the State of Florida and it is undisputed that Florida has not consented to the suit. Petitioner nevertheless contends that its suit is not barred by state sovereign immunity. First, it argues that Congress through the Act abrogated the States' sovereign immunity. Alternatively, petitioner maintains that its suit against the Governor may go forward under *Ex parte Young*, *supra*. We consider each of those arguments in turn.

Petitioner argues that Congress through the Act abrogated the States' immunity from suit. In order to determine whether Congress has abrogated the States' sovereign immunity, we ask two questions: first, whether Congress has "unequivocally expresse[d] its intent to abrogate the immunity," . . .and second, whether Congress has acted "pursuant to a valid exercise of power.". . .

Here we agree . . . that Congress has in § 2710(d)(7) provided an "unmistakably clear" statement of its intent to abrogate. . . . Having concluded that Congress clearly intended to abrogate the States' sovereign immunity through § 2710(d)(7), we turn now to consider whether the Act was passed "pursuant to a valid exercise of power." . . .

Petitioner suggests that one consideration weighing in favor of finding the power to abrogate here is that the Act authorizes only prospective injunctive relief rather than retroactive monetary relief. But we have often made it clear that the relief sought by a plaintiff suing a State is irrelevant to the question whether the suit is barred by the Eleventh Amendment. . . . We think it follows *a fortiori* from this proposition that the type of relief sought is irrelevant to whether Congress has power to abrogate States' immunity. . . .

Thus our inquiry into whether Congress has the power to abrogate unilaterally the States' immunity from suit is narrowly focused on one question: Was the Act in question passed pursuant to a constitutional provision granting Congress the power to abrogate? Previously, in conducting that inquiry we have found authority to abrogate only two provisions of the Constitution. In *Fitzpatrick [v. Bitzer*, 427 U.S. 445 (1976)] we . . . held that through the Fourteenth Amendment, federal power extended to intrude upon the province of the Eleventh Amendment and therefore that § 5 of the Fourteenth Amendment allowed Congress to abrogate the immunity from suit guaranteed by that Amendment.

In only one other case has congressional abrogation of the States' Eleventh Amendment immunity been upheld. In *Pennsylvania v. Union Gas Co.*, 491 U.S. 1 (1989), a plurality of the Court found that the Interstate Commerce Clause, Art. I, § 8, cl. 3, granted Congress the power to abrogate state sovereign immunity, stating that the power to regulate interstate commerce would be "incomplete without the authority to render States liable in damages." . . .

Both parties make their arguments from the plurality decision in *Union Gas*, and we, too, begin there. We think it clear that Justice Brennan's opinion finds Congress' power to abrogate under the Interstate Commerce Clause from the States' cession of their sovereignty when they gave Congress plenary power to regulate interstate commerce. . . . While the plurality decision states that Congress' power under the Interstate Commerce Clause would be incomplete without the power to abrogate, that statement is made solely in order to emphasize the broad scope of Congress' authority over interstate commerce. . . . Indeed, it was in those circumstances where Congress exercised complete authority that Justice Brennan thought the power to abrogate most necessary. . . .

Following the rationale of the *Union Gas* plurality, our inquiry is limited to determining whether the Indian Commerce Clause, like the Interstate Commerce Clause, is a grant of authority to the Federal Government at the expense of the states. The answer to that question is obvious. If anything, the Indian Commerce Clause accomplishes a greater transfer of power from the States to the Federal Government than does the Interstate Commerce Clause. This is clear enough from the fact that the States still exercise some authority over interstate trade but have been divested of virtually all authority over Indian commerce and Indian tribes. Under the rationale of *Union Gas*, if the States' partial cession of authority over a particular area includes cession of the immunity from suit, then their virtually total cession of authority over a different area must also include cession of the immunity from suit. . . . [T]he plurality opinion in *Union Gas* allows no principled distinction in favor of the States to be drawn between the Indian Commerce Clause and the Interstate Commerce Clause.

Respondents argue, however, that we need not conclude that the Indian Commerce Clause grants the power to abrogate the States' sovereign immunity. Instead, they contend that if we find the rationale of the *Union Gas* plurality to extend to the Indian Commerce Clause, then "*Union Gas* should be reconsidered and overruled." Generally, the principle of *stare decisis*, and the interests that it serves, *viz.*, "the evenhanded, predictable, and consistent development of legal principles, . . . reliance on judicial decisions, and . . . the actual and perceived integrity of the judicial process," counsel strongly against reconsideration of our precedent. Nevertheless, we always have treated *stare decisis* as a "principle of policy," and not as an "inexorable command." "[W]hen governing decisions are unworkable or are badly reasoned, 'this Court has never felt constrained to follow precedent.' " . . . Our willingness to reconsider our earlier decisions has been "particularly true in constitutional cases, because in such cases 'correction through legislative action is practically impossible.' "

The Court in *Union Gas* reached a result without an expressed rationale agreed upon by a majority of the Court. . . . Since it was issued, *Union Gas* has created confusion among the lower courts that have sought to understand and apply the deeply fractured decision. . . .

The plurality's rationale also deviated sharply from our established federalism jurisprudence. . . . It was well established in 1989 when *Union Gas* was decided that the Eleventh Amendment stood for the constitutional principle that state sovereign immunity limited the federal courts' jurisdiction under Article III. The text of the Amendment itself is clear enough on this point: "The Judicial power of the United States shall not be construed to extend to any suit." . . . [T]he plurality's conclusion that Congress could under Article I expand the scope of the federal courts' jurisdiction under Article III "contradict[ed] our unvarying approach to Article III as setting forth the *exclusive* catalog of permissible federal court jurisdiction."

Never before the decision in *Union Gas* had we suggested that the bounds of Article III could be expanded by Congress operating pursuant to any constitutional provision other than the Fourteenth Amendment. Indeed, it had seemed fundamental that Congress could not expand the jurisdiction of the federal courts beyond the bounds of Article III. *Marbury v. Madison*, [*supra* § 1.01]. . . .

The plurality's extended reliance upon our decision in *Fitzpatrick v. Bitzer*, . . . that Congress could under the Fourteenth Amendment abrogate the States' sovereign immunity was also, we believe, misplaced. *Fitzpatrick* was based upon a rationale wholly inapplicable to the Interstate Commerce Clause, *viz.*, that the Fourteenth Amendment, adopted well after the adoption of the Eleventh Amendment and the ratification of the Constitution, operated to alter the pre-existing balance between state and federal power achieved by Article III and the Eleventh Amendment. . . . *Fitzpatrick* cannot be read to justify "limitation of the principle embodied in the Eleventh Amendment through appeal to antecedent provisions of the Constitution."

In the five years since it was decided, *Union Gas* has proven to be a solitary departure from established law. Reconsidering the decision in *Union Gas*, we conclude that none of the policies underlying *stare decisis* require our continuing adherence to its holding. The decision has, since its issuance, been of questionable precedential value, largely because a majority of the Court expressly disagreed with the rationale of the plurality. . . . The case involved the interpretation of the Constitution and therefore may be altered only by constitutional amendment or revision by this Court. Finally, both the result in *Union Gas* and the plurality's rationale depart from our established understanding of the Eleventh Amendment and undermine the accepted function of Article III. We feel bound to conclude that *Union Gas* was wrongly decided and that it should be, and now is, overruled. . . .

For over a century, we have grounded our decisions in the oft repeated understanding of state sovereign immunity as an essential part of the Eleventh Amendment. . . .

It is true that we have not had occasion previously to apply established Eleventh Amendment principles to the question whether Congress has the power to abrogate state sovereign immunity (save in *Union Gas*). But consideration of that question must proceed with fidelity to this century-old doctrine. . . .

In overruling *Union Gas* today, we reconfirm that the background principle of state sovereign immunity embodied in the Eleventh Amendment is not so ephemeral as to dissipate when the subject of the suit is an area, like the regulation of Indian commerce, that is under the exclusive control of the Federal Government. Even when the Constitution vests in Congress complete lawmaking authority over a particular area, the Eleventh Amendment prevents congressional authorization of suits by private parties against unconsenting States. The Eleventh Amendment restricts the judicial power under Article III, and Article I cannot be used to circumvent the constitutional limitations placed upon federal jurisdiction. Petitioner's suit against the State of Florida must be dismissed for a lack of jurisdiction.

Petitioner argues that we may exercise jurisdiction over its suit to enforce § 2710(d)(3) against the Governor notwithstanding the jurisdictional bar of the Eleventh Amendment. Petitioner notes that since our decision in *Ex parte Young*, 209 U.S. 123 (1908), we often have found federal jurisdiction over a suit against a state official when that suit seeks only prospective injunctive relief in order to "end a continuing violation of federal law." The situation presented here, however, is sufficiently different from that giving rise to the traditional *Ex parte Young* action so as to preclude the availability of that doctrine.

Here, the "continuing violation of federal law" alleged by petitioner is the Governor's failure to bring the State into compliance with § 2710(d)(3). But the duty to negotiate imposed upon the State by that statutory provision does not stand alone. Rather, . . . Congress passed § 2710(d)(3) in conjunction with the carefully crafted and intricate remedial scheme set forth in § 2710(d)(7).

Where Congress has created a remedial scheme for the enforcement of a particular federal right, we have, in suits against federal officers, refused to supplement that scheme with one created by the judiciary. . . . Here, of course, the question is not whether a remedy should be created, but instead is whether the Eleventh Amendment bar should be lifted, as it was in *Ex parte Young*, in order to allow a suit against a state officer. Nevertheless, we think that the same general principle applies: therefore, where Congress has prescribed a detailed remedial scheme for the enforcement against a State of a statutorily created right, a court should hesitate before casting aside those limitations and permitting an action against a state officer based upon *Ex parte Young*.

Here, Congress intended § 2710(d)(3) to be enforced against the State in an action brought under § 2710(d)(7); the intricate procedures set forth in that provision show that Congress intended therein not only to define, but also significantly to limit, the duty imposed by § 2710(d)(3). . . . By contrast with this quite modest set of sanctions, an action brought against a state official under *Ex parte Young* would expose that official to the full remedial powers of a federal court, including, presumably, contempt sanctions. If § 2710(d)(3) could be enforced in a suit under *Ex parte Young*, § 2710(d)(7) would have been superfluous; it is difficult to see why an Indian tribe would suffer through the intricate scheme of § 2710(d)(7) when more complete and more immediate relief would be available under *Ex parte Young*.

Here, of course, we have found that Congress does not have authority under the Constitution to make the State suable in federal court under § 2710(d)(7). Nevertheless, the fact that Congress chose to impose upon the State a liability which is significantly more limited than would be the liability imposed upon the state officer under *Ex parte Young* strongly indicates that Congress had no wish to create the latter under § 2710(d)(3). Nor are we free to rewrite the statutory scheme in order to approximate what we think Congress might have wanted had it known that § 2710(d)(7) was beyond its authority. If that effort is to be made, it should be made by Congress, and not by the federal courts. We hold that *Ex parte Young* is inapplicable to petitioner's suit against the Governor of Florida, and therefore that suit is barred by the Eleventh Amendment and must be dismissed for a lack of jurisdiction.

The Eleventh Amendment prohibits Congress from making the State of Florida capable of being sued in federal court. The narrow exception to the Eleventh Amendment provided by the *Ex parte Young* doctrine cannot be used to enforce § 2710(d)(3) because Congress enacted a remedial scheme, § 2710(d)(7), specifically designed for the enforcement of that right. The Eleventh Circuit's dismissal of petitioner's suit is hereby affirmed.

It is so ordered.

[JUSTICES STEVENS, SOUTER, GINSBURG, and BREYER dissented.]

NOTE ON DISSENTS

Justice Souter filed a lengthy dissent which Justice Ginsburg and Justice Breyer joined; Justice Stevens filed a separate dissent while relying, too, on the reasons set forth in Justice Souter's dissent.

Justice Souter's dissent contains extensive historical and doctrinal argument which does not lend itself to easy summary. Justice Souter separated three questions:

> (1) whether the States enjoyed sovereign immunity if sued in their own courts in the period prior to ratification of the National Constitution; (2) if so, whether after ratification the States were entitled to claim some such immunity when sued in a federal court exercising jurisdiction either because the suit was between a State and a non-state litigant who was not its citizen, or because the issue in the case raised a federal question; and (3) whether any state sovereign immunity recognized in federal court may be abrogated by Congress.

He concluded that the answer to the first question was unclear, that *Hans v. Louisiana*, 134 U.S. 1 (1890), had addressed the second in an unpersuasive fashion, and that the *Seminole Tribe* majority had answered the third question "at odds with the Founders' view that common law, when it was received into the new American legal systems, was always subject to legislative amendment."

The text of the original constitution did not support an argument that state sovereign immunity had achieved constitutional status. *Chisholm v. Georgia*, 2 U.S. (2 Dall.) 419, (1793), abrogated any such immunity in federal court. The Eleventh Amendment "repudiated *Chisholm*." But its "history and structure . . . convincingly show that it reaches only to suits subject to federal jurisdiction exclusively under the Citizen-State Diversity Clauses." Weighty commentary, including judicial opinions by Chief Justice John Marshall, articulated this understanding.

Justice Souter suggested that the Court erred in *Hans* when it "invoked a principle of sovereign immunity to cure what it took to be the Eleventh Amendment's anomaly of barring only those state suits brought by noncitizen plaintiffs." Still, *Hans* did not conclude that sovereign immunity was a constitutional principle and *Hans* did not suggest that Congress could not abrogate any such immunity in federal questions cases, a question it did not even consider.

Hans, Justice Souter argued, was seriously flawed for misreading the Eleventh Amendment and misunderstanding historical conditions regarding the status of common law doctrines and the nature of state sovereignty. Much of Justice Souter's opinion is devoted to developing these points to critique *Hans*. In any event, Justice Souter viewed *Hans* as stating simply a common law principle which Congress could override. The

Court's contrary holding in *Seminole Tribe* is inconsistent with the Founders' "abhorrence" of the notion that common law rules would be impervious to legislative revision, he argued.

Justice Souter also rejected the Court's further conclusion that *Ex parte Young* did not here authorize a suit for prospective relief against a state official.

Justice Stevens, too, argued that neither the Eleventh Amendment nor *Hans* imposed a constitutional doctrine of sovereign immunity here applicable. The Eleventh Amendment barred simply diversity or foreigner suits according to its text; any other sovereign immunity simply reflected prudential concern subject to congressional override.

NOTES

A. The History of the Eleventh Amendment

(1) *Chisholm v. Georgia*, 2 U.S. (2 Dall.) 419 (1793), held the Court had original jurisdiction to decide a case in which South Carolina citizens sued Georgia to recover a debt. All five members of the Court had helped frame the Constitution. The four justices in the majority wrote separate opinions, thereby obscuring somewhat the Court's rationale. In essence, however, they denied the immunity of the states. They could draw support from the text of Article III which extended federal judicial power to "controversies . . . between a state and citizens of another state," a virtual description of the South Carolinian *Chisholm*'s suit against Georgia. Justice James Wilson, the framer who helped draft Article III, wrote a lengthy opinion rejecting Georgia's claim to immunity. Only Justice James Iredell dissented, largely on the ground that Congress had not specifically authorized a writ of assumpsit in the Judiciary Act of 1789; the thrust of his opinion did not deny that the Constitution would allow Congress to authorize such an action against a state, a question he largely reserved.

In any event, the Court's decision in *Chisholm* provoked a furious response from the states. Congress proposed the Eleventh Amendment in 1794 and it was ratified four years later. It provides: "The Judicial power of the United States shall not be construed to extend to any suit in law or equity, commenced or prosecuted against any one of the United States by citizens of another state, or by citizens or subjects of any foreign state." Professor Laurence Tribe points out that the text of the Eleventh Amendment might be read to preclude federal jurisdiction over a) any suit against a state brought by a diverse or foreign citizen or b) any such suit where jurisdiction is predicated on diversity. 1 TRIBE, AMERICAN CONSTITUTIONAL LAW 522 (3d ed. 1999). Either reading would not foreclose federal question cases or admiralty cases, for instance, (except perhaps those by diverse or foreign citizens if the first reading were followed). But, as Professor Tribe points out, "according to the prevailing view of the Supreme Court, the Eleventh Amendment goes far beyond *either* of these readings." *Id.*

(2) In *Hans v. Louisiana*, 134 U.S. 1 (1890), the Court held that some principle of sovereign immunity precludes suits against states in federal courts even when based upon federal constitutional or statutory law. *Hans* involved a suit in federal court which was outside the language of the Eleventh Amendment. Hans, a citizen of Louisiana, sued his own state for acting to reduce the return on certain state bonds in violation of the constitutional ban on impairing the obligation of contracts set forth in the Contracts Clause. Chief Justice Bradley rejected Hans' contention that the Eleventh Amendment barred only diversity actions, a view he thought made no sense. Article III had not intended to strip the states of sovereign immunity; the Eleventh Amendment simply corrected the Court's error in *Chisholm*. The Court found a structural principle of sovereign immunity robust enough to bar Hans' claim.

B. Limits to Eleventh Amendment

(3) Prior to *Seminole Tribe*, the Court had recognized limits on, and exceptions to, the Eleventh Amendment and doctrine of sovereign immunity recognized in *Hans*. These boundaries generally related to the identity of the plaintiff (in a suit against a state), the identity of the defendant, the remedy sought, whether the federal government had abrogated a state's immunity, or whether a state had consented to be sued.

(4) *Identity of Plaintiff.* Neither the Eleventh Amendment nor sovereign immunity bars a suit against a state in federal court by the United States, see, e.g., *United States v. Mississippi*, 380 U.S. 128, 140-41 (1965); *United States v. Texas*, 143 U.S. 621 (1892) or by a state, *North Dakota v. Minnesota*, 263 U.S. 365, 372-73 (1923); *Kansas v. Colorado*, 206 U.S. 46 (1907), although the Eleventh Amendment is a bar where a state, though nominally the plaintiff, is actually acting on behalf of individuals, see, e.g., *New Hampshire v. Louisiana*, 108 U.S. 76 (1883). Presumably, the states relinquished any immunity *vis á vis* the United States and each other when they approved the Constitution. What problems, if any, would follow if the federal government could not sue a state? If a state could not sue another state?

(5) *Identity of Defendant.* The Eleventh Amendment does not preclude suits against subdivisions of states, such as cities or counties, see, e.g., *Lincoln County v. Luning*, 133 U.S. 529 (1890), or against multi-state entities, *Hess v. Port Auth.*, 513 U.S. 30 (1994). It also does not preclude suits against state officers, rather than the state itself, provided that the remedy sought is either money damages from the officer personally, not from the state treasury, or injunctive relief as explained below.

(6) *The Remedy Sought.* The most significant exception stems from the Court's seminal opinion in *Ex parte Young*, 209 U.S. 123 (1908). Railroad shareholders sued Minnesota's attorney general to enjoin enforcement of state freight rates as violating the Due Process Clause of the Fourteenth Amendment. The Court rejected defendant's Eleventh Amendment defense since the action named a state officer, not the state. Meeting that pleading requirement allowed plaintiffs to circumvent the bar of the Eleventh Amendment. *Ex parte Young* has provided an important vehicle for federal judicial relief from action by state officials which allegedly violates constitutional rights of citizens. The *Ex parte Young*, action has, however, been limited to requests for prospective injunctive relief.

(7) *Federal Abrogation of Immunity.* As noted in *Seminole Tribe*, the Court had upheld congressional action subjecting states to suit under the Commerce Clause, *Pennsylvania v. Union Gas Co.*, 490 U.S. 1 (1989), and under the Fourteenth Amendment, *Fitzpatrick v. Bitzer*, 427 U.S. 445 (1976). The Court had held that Congress must clearly state its intention to abrogate a state's immunity. *See, e.g., Atascadora State Hospital v. Scanlon*, 473 U.S. 234 (1985); *Quern v. Jordan*, 440 U.S. 332 (1979).

(8) *State Consent.* A state can consent to suit by a clear legislative statement to that effect. *See, e.g., Port Authority v. Feeney*, 495 U.S. 299 (1990).

(9) In *Central Virginia Community College v. Katz*, 546 U.S. 356 (2006), the Court, in a 5-4 decision, recognized at least one instance in which Congress could abrogate a state's sovereign immunity under an Article I power in holding state sovereign immunity under the Eleventh Amendment subordinate to the Article I, § 8, cl. 4 Bankruptcy Power. After "[c]areful study and reflection" the Court concluded it was not bound to follow dicta from *Seminole Tribe* where the issue was not fully debated. *Id.* at 363. The majority consisted of the four justices who dissented in *Seminole Tribe* and *Alden v. Maine* plus Justice O'Connor.

Relying largely on originalist arguments, the Court found that the Bankruptcy Clause was not intended simply to grant legislative power but also to limit state sovereignty in the bankruptcy arena. "The ineluctable conclusion, then, is that States agreed in the plan of the Convention not to assert any sovereign immunity defense they might have had in proceedings brought pursuant to 'Laws on the subject of Bankruptcies." *Id.* at 377.

The majority deemed the scope of the states' consent to be limited since bankruptcy, which largely involves *in rem* proceedings, "does not implicate state sovereignty to nearly the same degree as other kinds of jurisdiction." Still, "[i]n ratifying the Bankruptcy Clause, the States acquiesced in a subordination of whatever sovereign immunity they might otherwise have asserted in proceedings necessary to effectuate the *in rem* jurisdiction of the bankruptcy courts." *Id.* at 378. The dissent read the founders' intent differently; it concluded that the framers conferred legislative power without waiving "the states' sovereign immunity against suit." *Id.* at 380.

Does the decision signal that Congress can abrogate state sovereign immunity under any other Article I power? The Court denied that "the state sovereign immunity implications of the Bankruptcy Clause necessarily mirror those of the Commerce Clause." Moreover, it emphasized the Bankruptcy Clause's unique history, combined with the singular nature of bankruptcy's courts' jurisdiction in explaining its decision. *Id.* at 369. Justice O'Connor's subsequent departure from the Court may still create some uncertainty regarding the breadth, indeed the vitality, of the decision.

ALDEN v. MAINE, 527 U.S. 706 (1999). Some scholars thought *Seminole Tribe* applied only to cases in federal court so that Congress still could subject states to suit for monetary relief in state courts under an Article I power. In *Alden v. Maine*, the Court, in a 5-4 decision, held that Congress could not, under Article I, "subject nonconsenting States to private suits for damages in state courts."

In *Alden*, a group of probation officers sued their employer, the State of Maine, for money damages in the United States District Court for the District of Maine for allegedly violating the overtime provisions of the Fair Labor Standards Act of 1938 (FLSA). After the Court decided *Seminole Tribe*, the District Court dismissed petitioners' action, and the Court of Appeals affirmed. Petitioners re-filed the case in state court which dismissed the suit based on sovereign immunity, and the Maine Supreme Judicial Court affirmed. The Court granted certiorari due to the importance of the issue and a conflict between courts, and affirmed the lower court decision dismissing the case.

Speaking through Justice Kennedy, a five justice majority found that, based on the Constitution's structure, history and judicial doctrine "the states' immunity from suit is a fundamental aspect" of their sovereignty except to the extent altered by the Constitution. Justice Kennedy reasoned that the Eleventh Amendment was neither the source of, nor a limit on, the states' sovereign immunity. Instead, he looked to the Tenth Amendment "to allay lingering concerns" about state sovereignty.

The founders had "considered immunity from private suits central to sovereign dignity." In *Chisholm v. Georgia*, the Court incorrectly construed the Constitution in holding that Article III allowed a citizen of one state to sue another without its consent. The Eleventh Amendment served to restore the original understanding. Prior decisions upholding state assertions of sovereign immunity "reflect a settled doctrinal understanding, consistent with the views of the leading advocates of the Constitution's ratification, that sovereign immunity derives not from the Eleventh Amendment but from the structure of the original Constitution itself."

Accordingly, "the fact that the Eleventh Amendment by its terms limits only [t]he Judicial power of the United States does not" support the conclusion that by application of *expressio unius* Congress could subject the states to suit in state court. The majority rejected this "historical literalism" because, in addition to the Eleventh Amendment, the structural principle of federalism protected the states. Sovereign immunity was not, as the dissent argued, simply a common law principle but one which the Constitution's "structure and history" gave constitutional status.

Although the Court considered the question "whether Congress has authority under Article I to abrogate a State's immunity from suit in its own courts . . . a question of first impression" it concluded that the "history, practice, precedent, and the structure of the Constitution" demonstrated Congress' lack of power. Neither the founders nor early Congresses had thought Congress could "authorize private suits against the States in their own courts." Early judicial decisions "described the States' immunity in sweeping terms, without reference to whether the suit was prosecuted in state or federal court." Finally, structural considerations, namely "the essential principles of federalism" require "that Congress treat the States in a manner consistent with their status as residuary sovereigns and joint participants in the governance of the Nation."

Authorizing private suits against nonconsenting states would offend this principle. A state would be "subject to the power of private citizens to levy on its treasury." The power to press state courts into federal service would "turn the state against itself" and "commandeer the entire political machinery of the state." The federal government was immune from suit; the states deserved "reciprocal" treatment. Finally, states could not govern in accordance with their citizens' preferences if the federal government could authorize such private litigation.

Although the Court found states immune from private suit in their own courts, they were not free to "disregard the Constitution or valid federal law." Moreover, courts still retained some power to review state compliance with federal law. States consented to some suits by state legislation. Under the Constitution, states essentially consented that the United States and other states could sue a state. Congress could authorize private suits against states under § 5 of the Fourteenth Amendment. Finally, sovereign immunity did not preclude suits against subunits of states, injunctive actions, or suits against an officer personally.

In dissent, Justice Souter (for himself and Justices Stevens, Ginsburg, and Breyer) criticized the Court's rationale. If the Court was correct in tracing sovereign immunity to the Tenth Amendment the Eleventh Amendment was unnecessary, he suggested.

The Court's reliance on original intent was unpersuasive because sovereign immunity was a common law, not constitutional, principle which Congress could abrogate under an Article I power. The framers did not regard it as a fundamental principle.

Nor did the dissenters find the Court's structural argument persuasive. The Constitution split "the atom of sovereignty"; the federal government, not Maine, was sovereign regarding FLSA which Congress could extend to the states under *Garcia v. San Antonio Metropolitan Transit Authority* which remained law. *Garcia* settled that Congress could, under the Commerce Clause, bind states without intruding on state sovereignty.

The Supremacy Clause required Maine to enforce federal law in its courts. The majority's emphasis on state dignity was "inimical to the republican conception." In its concern for protecting the will of a state, the majority forgot that that will deserved no respect when it violated federal law.

NOTES

(1) In *Alden*, the majority compared the doctrine of sovereign immunity to the right to a jury trial and the ban on unreasonable searches and seizures, other "rights and principles" which "derive from the common law." Justice Kennedy argued that the "common-law lineage of these rights does not mean they are defeasible by statute or remain mere common-law rights, however. They are, rather, constitutional rights, and form the fundamental law of the land." Is there a difference between sovereign immunity and these other rights? The Seventh Amendment protects the jury right and the Fourth Amendment prevents unreasonable searches and seizures. Justice Kennedy acknowledges that the text does not specify sovereign immunity. Does the majority's treatment of sovereign immunity as a constitutional right comparable to the right to jury trial and the prohibition of unreasonable searches and seizures, both of which, Justice Souter points out, are specifically included in the Constitution's text, imply that textual guarantees have no greater status than those based on structural or originalist arguments?

(2) Should the fact that the federal government retains immunity from suit support a like immunity for state government as the Court argues? If so, should the fact that Congress can consent to suits against the federal government also support a power to abrogate state sovereign immunity?

(3) In *Garcia v. San Antonio Metropolitan Transit Authority*, Justices Rehnquist and O'Connor in dissent, predicted that the Supreme Court would eventually impose limits on Congress' ability to subject states to generally applicable laws. *Garcia* was not directly addressed in *Alden v. Maine*, and, as Justice Souter argues, remains law. What impact does the Court's opinion have on the continued significance of *Garcia* to the extent it allowed Congress to apply a generally applicable law to the states? Has the Court found a way to drain *Garcia* of significance without overruling it?

(4) Does the Court's opinion violate the precept of the Rule of Law that John Marshall invoked in *Marbury v. Madison*, that insists that judicial remedies be available to vindicate rights? Or does the possibility of suit by the federal government or an *Ex parte Young* action afford sufficient remedial options?

(5) After *Seminole Tribe* and *Alden* what tools are available to the federal government to enforce federal rights against states? Could Congress condition grants to states on their consent to lawsuit in federal and/or state court? Could Congress proscribe certain areas of state activity unless a state consents to be sued?

(6) After *Seminole Tribe* and *Alden*, Congress can still abrogate state's sovereign immunity under § 5 of the Fourteenth Amendment provided it expresses such an intent in a clear statement, but the Court has narrowed Congress' § 5 power. On the same day it announced *Alden v. Maine*, the Court in two other 5-4 decisions limited Congress' ability to use § 5 of the Fourteenth Amendment to abrogate state's immunity from suit in federal court under the 11th Amendment. In *College Savings Bank v. Florida Prepaid Postsecondary Education Expense Board*, 527 U.S. 666 (1999), the Court held that Congress could not rely on § 5 to abrogate state sovereign immunity against suit for false advertising under the Lanham Act. That statute does not involve property rights subject to the due process clause. Similarly in *Florida Prepaid Postsecondary Education Expense Board v. College Savings Bank*, 527 U.S. 627 (1999), the Court held § 5 of the Fourteenth Amendment provided no basis for Congress to abrogate state sovereign immunity from patent infringement suits.

More recently, in *Kimel v. Florida Board of Regents*, 528 U.S. 62 (2000), the Court continued the trend of narrowing § 5. It held that Congress exceeded its § 5 authority in abrogating the state's sovereign immunity in the Age Discrimination in Employment Act of 1967 (ADEA). The ADEA's substantive requirements were disproportionate to conduct Congress could address under § 5.

In 2001, the Court held in a 5-4 decision that Congress could not, under § 5 of the Fourteenth Amendment, subject states to suit by private individuals seeking damages under the Americans with Disabilities Act. *Board of Trustees of the University of Alabama v. Garrett*, 531 U.S. 356 (2001). The Court found insufficient evidence that States, as opposed to society generally, had discriminated against disabled Americans.

During the 2002 term, however, the Court held Congress did have power under § 5 to create a private right of action for monetary relief against states for violating the Family and Medical Leave Act of 1993. *Nevada Department of Human Resources v. Hibbs*, 538 U.S. 721 (2003). In his majority opinion, Chief Justice Rehnquist found the remedy congruent and proportional to the injury and concluded that Congress had ample evidence of state discrimination regarding family leave, often based on general stereotypes.

Similarly, during the October 2003 term, the Court in a 5-4 decision in*Tennessee v. Lane*, 541 U.S. 509 (2004), held Congress properly exercised its power under § 5 of the Fourteenth Amendment to abrogate the States' Eleventh Amendment immunity under Title II of the Americans with Disabilities Act of 1990. The case arose from a complaint by two paraplegics that the Tennessee state courthouses denied them access to the state judicial system. Tennessee moved to dismiss based on the Eleventh Amendment. Congress had clearly expressed its intent to abrogate the State's immunity ("A State shall not be immune under the eleventh amendment to the Constitution of the United States from an action in Federal or State court of competent jurisdiction for a violation of this chapter." 42 U.S.C. § 12202). The Court had power under § 5 since the legislation in question satisfied the congruence and proportionality test.

(7) Aside from the constitutional merits of *Seminole Tribe* and *Alden*, a subject on which the Court is badly split, does the Court's current emphasis on sovereign immunity make sense as a strategy for promoting federalism? Professor Ernest A. Young, who describes himself as a "federalism hawk," criticizes the Court for the extent to which it has used sovereign immunity to protect states. He points out that the Court has increasingly used this concept to insulate states from private suits. Moreover, the Court has limited the ability of the federal judiciary to reexamine state court criminal convictions via the writ of habeas corpus, thereby insulating state court decisions from federal review in another class of cases. Immunity from private suits may provide a pyrrhic victory since the states remain subject to suit by the federal government. Such suits could prove more intrusive than private actions. Moreover, if states are immune from suit, Congress may be reluctant to delegate to state governments the authority to administer certain federal programs. Professor Young suggests that reliance primarily on the political process, not immunity doctrine, is likely to best protect states interests. Moreover, process federalism might present a way to unify the Court's current factions to develop doctrine able to command broader support. On the contrary, immunity doctrine may imperil the state's ability to fashion alliances with powerful private interests by causing their interests to diverge. *See* Ernest Young, *State Sovereign Immunity and the Future of Federalism*, 1999 SUP. CT. REV. 1 (1999).

(8) In *Federal Maritime Commission v. South Carolina State Ports Authority*, 535 U.S. 743 (2002), the Court held that state sovereign immunity prohibits executive administrative agencies from adjudicating the claims of private parties against unconsenting states. After its requests to berth a ship were denied by South Carolina State Ports Authority (SCSPA), South Carolina Maritime Services, Inc. (Maritime

Services) filed a complaint with the Federal Maritime Commission (FMC) seeking compensatory and injunctive relief. Justice Thomas, for a five justice majority, reaffirmed that "the sovereign immunity enjoyed by the States extends beyond the literal text of the Eleventh Amendment." *Id.* at 754. The Framers did not intend the States to be subject to proceedings which were " 'anomalous and unheard of when the Constitution was adopted.' " *Id.* at 755. Observing the "strong similarities between FMC proceedings and civil litigation," the Court concluded that "[t]he affront to a State's dignity does not lesson when an adjudication takes place in an administrative tribunal as opposed to an Article III court." *Id.* at 760.

Justice Breyer wrote a dissent which Justices Stevens, Souter, and Ginsburg joined. Though reasserting that *Seminole Tribe* and *Alden* were wrongly decided the dissenters argued that the Court's decision could not even stand on those precedents. Administrative proceedings typically involve Executive Branch agencies exercising Executive Branch powers to determine whether a state agency violated federal law. Such a paradigm stands outside the language or concerns of the Eleventh and Tenth Amendments. The decision "threatens to deny the Executive and Legislative Branches of Government the structural flexibility that the Constitution permits and which modern government demands." *Id.* at 786. It "set loose an interpretative principle that restricts far too severely the authority of the Federal Government to regulate innumerable relationships between State and citizen." *Id.* at 788.

Chapter IV
FEDERALISM AND STATE REGULATORY POWER

§ 4.01 FEDERAL SUPREMACY

McCULLOCH v. MARYLAND
17 U.S. (4 Wheat.) 316, 4 L. Ed. 579 (1819)

[For the facts of this case, see *supra* § 2.01]

. . . It being the opinion of the court, that the act incorporating the bank is constitutional; and that the power of establishing a branch in the state of Maryland might be properly exercised by the bank itself, we proceed to inquire —

2. Whether the state of Maryland may, without violating the constitution, tax that branch?

That the power of taxation is one of vital importance; that it is retained by the states; that it is not abridged by the grant of a similar power to the government of the Union; that it is to be concurrently exercised by the two governments are truths which have never been denied. But such is the paramount character of the constitution, that its capacity to withdraw any subject from the action of even this power, is admitted. The states are expressly forbidden to lay any duties on imports or exports, except what may be absolutely necessary for executing their inspection laws. If the obligation of this prohibition must be conceded . . . the same paramount character would seem to restrain, as it certainly may restrain a state from such other exercise of this power, as is in its nature incompatible with, and repugnant to, the constitutional laws of the Union. . . .

There is no express provision for the case, but the claim has been sustained on a principle which so entirely pervades the constitution, is so intermixed with the materials which compose it, so interwoven with its web, so blended with its texture, as to be incapable of being separated from it, without rending it into shreds. This great principle is, that the constitution and the laws made in pursuance thereof are supreme; that they control the constitution and laws of the respective states, and cannot be controlled by them. From this, which may be almost termed an axiom, other propositions are deduced as corollaries, on the truth or error of which, and on their application to this case, the cause has been supposed to depend. These are, 1st. That a power to create implies a power to preserve: 2d. That a power to destroy, if wielded by a different hand, is hostile to, and incompatible with these powers to create and to preserve: 3d. That where this repugnancy exists, that authority which is supreme must control, not yield to that over which it is supreme. . . .

The power of congress to create, and of course, to continue, the bank, was the subject of the preceding part of this opinion; and is no longer to be considered as questionable. That the power of taxing it by the states may be exercised so as to destroy it, is too obvious to be denied. But taxation is said to be an absolute power, which acknowledges no other limits than those expressly prescribed in the constitution, and like sovereign power of every other description, is intrusted to the discretion of those who use it. But the very terms of this argument admit, that the sovereignty of the state, in the article of taxation itself, is subordinate to, and may be controlled by the constitution of the United States. How far it has been controlled by that instrument, must be a question of construction. In making this construction, no principle, not declared, can be admissible, which would defeat the legitimate operations of a supreme government. It is of the very essence of supremacy, to remove all obstacles to its action within its own sphere, and so to modify every power vested in subordinate governments, as to exempt its own operations from their own influence. This effect need not be stated in terms. It is so involved in the declaration of supremacy, so necessarily implied in it, that the expression of it could not make it more certain. We must, therefore, keep it in view, while construing the constitution.

The argument on the part of the state of Maryland, is, not that the states may directly resist a law of congress, but that they may exercise their acknowledged powers upon it, and that the constitution leaves them this right, in the confidence that they will not abuse it. Before we proceed to examine this argument, and to subject it to test of the constitution, we must be permitted to bestow a few considerations on the nature and extent of this original right of taxation, which is acknowledged to remain with the states. It is admitted, that the power of taxing the people and their property, is essential to the very existence of government, and may be legitimately exercised on the objects to which it is applicable, to the utmost extent to which the government may choose to carry it. The only security against the abuse of this power, is found in the structure of the government itself. In imposing a tax, the legislature acts upon its constituents. This is, in general, a sufficient security against erroneous and oppressive taxation.

The people of a state, therefore, give to their government a right of taxing themselves and their property, and as the exigencies of government cannot be limited, they prescribe no limits to the exercise of this right, resting confidently on the interest of the legislator, and on the influence of the constituent over their representative, to guard them against its abuse. But the means employed by the government of the Union have no such security, nor is the right of a state to tax them sustained by the same theory. Those means are not given by the people of a particular state, not given by the constituents of the legislature, which claim the right to tax them, but by the people of all the states. They are given by all, for the benefit of all — and upon theory, should be subjected to that government only which belongs to all.

. . . That the power to tax involves the power to destroy; that the power to destroy may defeat and render useless the power to create; that there is a plain repugnance in conferring on one government a power to control the constitutional measure of another, which other, with respect to those very measures, is declared to be supreme over that which exerts the control, are propositions not to be denied. But all inconsistencies are to be reconciled by the magic of the word confidence. Taxation, it is said, does not necessarily and unavoidably destroy. To carry it to the excess of destruction, would be an abuse, to presume which, would banish that confidence which is essential to all government.

But is this a case of confidence? Would the people of any one state trust those of another with a power to control the most insignificant operations of their state government? We know they would not. Why, then, should we suppose that the people of any one state should be willing to trust those of another with a power to control the operations of a government to which they have confided the most important and most valuable interests? In the legislature of the Union alone, are all represented. The legislature of the Union alone, therefore, can be trusted by the people with the power of controlling measures which concern all, in the confidence that it will not be abused. This, then, is not a case of confidence, and we must consider it as it really is.

If we apply the principle for which the state of Maryland contends, to the constitution, generally, we shall find it capable of changing totally the character of that instrument. We shall find it capable of arresting all the measures of the government, and of prostrating it at the foot of the states. The American people have declared their constitution and the laws made in pursuance thereof, to be supreme; but this principle would transfer the supremacy, in fact, to the states.

If the states may tax one instrument, employed by the government in the execution of its powers, they may tax any and every other instrument. They may tax the mail; they may tax the mint; they may tax patent-rights: they may tax the papers of the custom-house; they may tax judicial process; they may tax all the means employed by the government, to an excess which would defeat all the ends of government. This was not intended by the American people. They did not design to make their government dependent on the states. . . .

If the controlling power of the states be established; if their supremacy as to taxation be acknowledged; what is to restrain their exercising this control in any shape they may please to give it? Their sovereignty is not confined to taxation; that is not the only mode in which it might be displayed. The question is, in truth, a question of supremacy; and if the right of the states to tax the means employed by the general government be conceded, the declaration that the constitution, and the laws made in pursuance thereof, shall be the supreme law of the land, is empty and unmeaning declamation. . . .

It has also been insisted, that, as the power of taxation in the general and state governments is acknowledged to be concurrent, every argument which would sustain the right of the general government to tax banks chartered by the states, will equally sustain the right of the states to tax banks chartered by the general government.

But the two cases are not on the same reason. The people of all the states have created the general government, and have conferred upon it the general power of taxation. The people of the states, and the states themselves, are represented in congress, and, by their representatives, exercise this power. When they tax the chartered institutions of the states, they tax their constituents; and these taxes must be uniform. But when a state taxes the operations of the government of the United States, it acts upon institutions created, not by their own constituents, but by people over whom they claim no control. It acts upon the measures of a government created by others as well as themselves, for the benefit of others in common with themselves. The difference is that which always exists, and always must exist, between the action of the whole on a part, and the action of a part on the whole — between the laws of a government declared to be supreme, and those of a government which, when in opposition to those laws, is not supreme. . . .

The court has bestowed on this subject its most deliberate consideration. The result is a conviction that the states have no power, by taxation or otherwise, to retard, impede, burden, or in any manner control the operations of the constitutional laws enacted by Congress to carry into execution the powers vested in the general government. This is, we think, the unavoidable consequence of that supremacy which the constitution has declared.

We are unanimously of opinion that the law passed by the legislature of Maryland, imposing a tax on the Bank of the United States, is unconstitutional and void. . . .

It is, therefore, adjudged and ordered, that the said judgment of the said Court of Appeals of the State of Maryland in this case, be, and the same hereby is, reversed and annulled. And this court, proceeding to render such judgment as the said Court of Appeals should have rendered; it is further adjudged and ordered, that the judgment of the said Baltimore County Court be reversed and annulled, and that judgment be entered in the said Baltimore County Court for the said James W. McCulloch.

NOTES

(1) *McCulloch* illustrates that in a federal system inevitably cases arise which pit "the conflicting powers of the government of the Union and of its members." Whether Maryland could tax the national bank "touched the most sensitive nerve in the young Republic. Which was sovereign, the federal union or the States? The isssue split the political parties and geographical sections for three quarters of a century." ARCHIBALD COX, THE COURT AND THE CONSTITUTION 78 (1987). How are such conflicts to be resolved? For Chief Justice Marshall, the Supremacy Clause provided much of the answer. He thought the clause essentially meant that: (1) the states may not interfere in any manner with the functioning of the federal government; and (2) federal action (whether in the form of a statute, a treaty, a court decision, or an administrative act), if itself constitutional, must prevail over inconsistent state action. *McCulloch v. Maryland* articulated the first meaning. The supremacy declared by the Constitution meant that the states may not "retard, impede, burden, or in any manner control the operations of the federal government." A different approach would make the states supreme.

(2) *Gibbons v. Ogden*, 22 U.S. (9 Wheat.) 1 (1824), *supra* § 2.02, developed the second meaning of the Supremacy Clause. The Court held invalid certain New York statutes granting an exclusive license to use steam navigation on the state's waters so far as they applied to vessels licensed under federal statutes to engage in coastwise trade. The question, according to Chief Justice Marshall's opinion, was

> whether the laws of New York, as expounded by the highest tribunal of that state, have, in their application to this case, come into collision with an act of Congress, and deprived a citizen of a right to which that act entitles him. Should this collision exist, it will be immaterial whether those laws were passed in virtue of a concurrent power "to regulate commerce with foreign nations and among the several States," or, in virtue of a power to regulate their domestic trade and police. In one case and the other, the acts of New York must yield to the law of Congress; and the decision sustaining the privilege they confer, against a right given by a law of the Union, must be erroneous.

> This opinion has been frequently expressed in this court, and is founded, as well on the nature of the government as on the words of the constitution. In argument, however, it has been contended that if a law, passed by a state in the exercise of its acknowledged sovereignty, comes into conflict with a law passed by Congress in pursuance of the constitution, they affect the subject, and each other, like equal opposing powers.

> But the framers of our constitution foresaw this state of things, and provided for it, by declaring the supremacy not only of itself, but of the laws made in pursuance of it. The nullity of any act . . . inconsistent with the constitution, is produced by the declaration, that the constitution is the supreme law. The appropriate application of that part of the clause which confers the same supremacy on laws and treaties, is to such acts of the State Legislatures as do not transcend their powers, but, though enacted in the execution of acknowledged State powers, interfere with, or are contrary to the laws of Congress, made in pursuance of the constitution, or some treaty made under the authority of the United States. In every such case, the act of Congress, or the treaty, is supreme; and the law of the State, though enacted in the exercise of powers not controverted, must yield to it. *Id.* at 210-11.

(3) In *McCulloch*, Chief Justice Marshall qualified the prohibition against Maryland taxing a federal bank. "This opinion . . . does not extend to a tax paid by the real

property of the bank, in common with the other real property within the state, nor to a tax imposed on the interest which the citizens of Maryland may hold in this institution, in common with other property of the same description throughout the state." *McCulloch*, 17 U.S. at 436. Why would not the power to impose these taxes constitute the power to destroy too? Professor John Hart Ely explained that the "unity of interest with all Maryland property owners assured by this insistence on equal treatment would protect the Bank from serious disablement by taxes of this sort." To be sure, the power to tax is the power to destroy regardless of the item being taxed. But outsiders, sued as the national bank, derive protection from being abused by a tax when they are treated no worse than those imposing the levy. As Professor Ely put it, "people aren't lemmings, and while they may agree to disadvantage themselves somewhat in the service of some overriding social good, they aren't in the habit of destroying themselves en masse." JOHN HART ELY, DEMOCRACY AND DISTRUST: A THEORY OF JUDICIAL REVIEW 85 (1980).

(4) Professor Edward S. Corwin wrote:

> Federalism in the United States embraces the following elements: (1) as in all federations, the union of several autonomous political entities, or "States," for common purposes; (2) the division of legislative powers between a "National Government," on the one hand, and constituent "States," on the other, which division is governed by the rule that the former is "a government of enumerated powers" while the latter are governments of "residual powers"; (3) the direct operation, for the most part, of each of these centers of government, within its assigned sphere, upon all persons and property within its territorial limits; (4) the provision of each center with the complete apparatus of law enforcement, both executive and judicial; (5) the supremacy of the "National Government" within its assigned sphere over any conflicting assertion of "state" power; (6) dual citizenship.

See EDWARD S. CORWIN, THE CONSTITUTION OF THE UNITEDSTATES OF AMERICA: ANALYSIS AND INTERPRETATION, at xi-xii (1953).

§ 4.02   FEDERAL REGULATORY IMMUNITY

NOTES

(1) The existence of two governments regulating persons and property necessarily occasions conflicts, especially where one government seeks to regulate another. Congress can specifically make federal instrumentalities immune from, or subject to, state regulation or taxation. *See, e.g., Carson v. Roane-Anderson Co.*, 342 U.S. 232 (1952) (upholding Congressionally granted immunity from sales tax for federal contractor); *City of Cleveland v. United States*, 323 U.S. 329 (1945). Where Congress is silent, however, the Constitutional principle recognized in *McCulloch* makes federal instrumentalities presumptively immune.

(2) Other cases also stand for an implicit federal immunity from state regulation. For instance, in *Ohio v. Thomas*, 173 U.S. 276 (1899), the Court held that J.B. Thomas, the federal officer in charge of a branch of a federal home for disabled soldiers, was immune from conviction for serving oleomargarine without posting a conspicuous notice that "Oleomargarine Sold and Used Here" as Ohio required. Thomas was not subject to Ohio's direction when acting as a federal officer within his authority. In *Arizona v. California*, 283 U.S. 423 (1931), the Court held that Secretary of Interior Wilbur need not comply with an Arizona law that required the state engineer approve plans for constructing a dam. For an 8-1 majority, Justice Brandeis wrote: "The United States may perform its functions without conforming to the police regulations of a state. . . . If Congress has power to authorize the construction of the dam and reservoir, Wilbur is

under no obligation to submit the plans and specifications to the state engineer for approval." *Id.* at 451-52. Similarly, in *Mayo v. United States*, 319 U.S. 441 (1943), the Court held that the United States distributing fertilizer, under a soil conservation program, was immune from Florida's inspection law.

(3) These cases do not establish federal immunity from all regulation. In *Johnson v. Maryland*, 254 U.S. 51 (1920), Justice Holmes distinguished the case of "general rules that might affect incidentally the mode of carrying out the employment — as, for instance, a statute or ordinance regulating the mode of turning at the corners of streets." In such cases, Holmes suggested a federal employee "does not secure a general immunity from state law while acting in the course of his employment." *Johnson*, 254 U.S. at 56. Holmes cited the early case of *United States v. Hart*, 26 F. Cas. 193 (Pa. C.C. 1817), where the driver of a mail stage was held bound by an ordinance prohibiting the driving of a carriage on runners, without sleigh bells on the horses.

§ 4.03 INTERGOVERNMENTAL TAX IMMUNITIES: FEDERAL IMMUNITY

UNITED STATES v. NEW MEXICO, 455 U.S. 720 (1982). In *United States v. Mexico*, the Court held that private contractors managing government atomic laboratories were not exempt from New Mexico taxes on gross receipts, sales, and use. Writing for the Court, Justice Blackmun began with Chief Justice Marshall's famous declaration that "the power to tax involves the power to destroy." Marshall thought federal immunity did not extend to situations in which private local property was taxed along with federal property. Subsequent decisions through the 1920s had ignored this qualification in granting broad immunity from state taxes. More recent cases, see, e.g., *James v. Dravo Contracting Co.*, 302 U.S. 134 (1937); *Alabama v. King & Boozer*, 314 U.S. 1 (1981) (upheld state taxes on federal contractors but failed to chart doctrine on "an entirely unwavering line.").

Accordingly, Justice Blackmun found that "the confusing nature of our precedents counsels a return to the underlying constitutional principle" i.e., a state cannot directly tax the United States. This "rule" was subject to "significant" limits. Federal immunity did not exist simply because a) the tax affected the United States, b) the government bore the tax burden, c) a contractor purchased property for the United States, d) the tax fell on a contractor's earnings, e) a tax fell on government property held by the contractor, f) government funds paid the tax. The cases suggested the rule "that tax immunity is appropriate in only one circumstance: when the levy falls on the United States itself, or on an agency or instrumentality so closely connected to the Government that the two cannot realistically be viewed as separate entities, at least insofar as the activity being taxed is concerned." In essence, a private contractor enjoys tax immunity only if it "stand[s] in the Government's shoes."

The government contentions here failed that test. They were not "constituent parts" of the government but had a relationship "for limited and carefully defined purposes," thereby justifying the use and gross receipts taxes. The sales tax presented a closer question; *Kern-Limerick, Inc. v. Scurlock*, 347 U.S. 110 (1954) extended immunity to a contractor where, under a federal statutory scheme, a purchasing agent bought goods for the government with title passing to the government with each sale based on specific government approval and with the government (not the contractor) liable for the invoices. The Court implicitly narrowed *Kern-Limerick* to its facts; here, however, most of the *Kern-Limerick* facts were missing. Accordingly, the Court held the contractors "not protected by the Constitution's guarantee of federal supremacy." It left open the possibility that Congress would confer broader immunity if "political or economic considerations" so warranted.

NOTES

(1) As Justice Blackmun observed, *McCulloch v. Maryland, supra* § 4.01, provides the starting point for the doctrine of intergovernmental tax immunities. If the power to tax involves the power to destroy, to permit the states to tax federal agencies would empower them to nullify federal operations. But did Chief Justice Marshall overstate the case? Justice Holmes thought so. His reference to Marshall's famous "tax-destroy" equation as "certain dicta" is suggestive. He continued:

> In those days it was not recognized as it is today that most of the distinctions of the law are distinctions of degree. If the States had any power, it was assumed that they had all power, and that the necessary alternative was to deny it altogether. But this Court which so often has defeated the attempt to tax in ceratin ways can defeat an attempt to discriminate or otherwise go too far without wholly abolishing the power to tax. The power to tax is not the power to destroy while this Court sits. The power to fix rates is the power to destroy if unlimited, but this Court while it endeavors to prevent confiscation does not prevent the fixing of rates. A tax is not an unconstitutional regulation in every case where an absolute prohibition of sales would be one.

Panhandle Oil Co. v. Knox, 277 U.S. 218, 223 (1928) (Holmes, J. dissenting).

Professor Paul A. Freund suggested that Marshall's per se rule that "the power to tax involves the power to destroy" was doctrine which went "beyond the necessities of the case or the problem" and "plagued constitutional law for a long time, because [it] could not contain the counter pressure from state interests that had been slighted. . . . The general direction of Marshall was characteristically wise, but the momentum of doctrine shot beyond its mark, and other generations were obliged to retrace some giant steps in order to follow a viable course." Paul A. Freund, *New Vistas in Constitutional Law*, 112 U. Pa. L. Rev. 631 (1964).

(2) *McCulloch* was long read to forbid taxes on those contracting with the federal government or its instrumentalities, whenever the effect of the tax was to increase the cost of performing the pertinent federal functions. Under this principle, the Court created a whole range of private tax immunities for those employed by, or dealing with, the federal government.

More recently, the Court has departed from that interpretation of *McCulloch v. Maryland. Alabama v. King & Boozer*, 314 U.S. 1, 8-9 (1941) ("So far as such a nondiscriminatory state tax upon the contractor enters into the cost of the materials to the Government, that is but a normal incident of the organization within the same territory of two independent taxing sovereignties. The asserted right of the one to be free of taxation by the other does not spell immunity from paying the added costs, attributable to the taxation of those who furnish supplies to the Government and who have been granted no tax immunity."). *United States v. Fresno*, 429 U.S. 452, 460 (1977) ("[s]o long as the tax is not directly laid on the Federal Government, it is valid if nondiscriminatory . . . or until Congress declares otherwise.").

(3) The key question becomes whether the legal incidence of a state tax lands on a federal function or instrumentality. A state tax assessed directly on a federal agency is, of course, invalid. In this sense, an agency of the United States is any authority within the Federal Government (whether called a department, bureau, division, commission, board, or some other name, and regardless of where located in the tripartite governmental structure) or owned by the Government. Such a state tax falling directly upon a federal agency is invalid regardless of the nature of the functions the particular agency

performed, whether proprietary (e.g., operation of a railroad) or more traditional type of governmental function. All lawful activities of the national government enjoy state tax immunity, even though private business traditionally conducts the particular activity.

But the legal incidence test reduces the scope of the tax immunity formerly recognized. The federal government no longer escapes the effect of all state taxes. Rather, "[t]ax immunity is 'appropriate in only one circumstance: when the levy falls on the United States itself, or on an agency or instrumentality so closely connected to the government that the two cannot realistically be viewed as separate entities.'" *United States v. California*, 507 U.S. 746, 753 (1993).

(4) Justice Blackmun indicated that Congress may change the rules of federal immunity. It could revive the private immunities which recent decisions have eliminated. Congress not only has the authority to empower the performance of governmental functions; it also has the power to protect and preserve the operations thus validly authorized. To safeguard those operations, tax immunity wider than that implied from the Constitution alone, may be conferred.

§ 4.04   STATE TAX IMMUNITY

SOUTH CAROLINA v. BAKER, 485 U.S. 505 (1988). The Tax Equity and Fiscal Responsibility Act of 1982 (TEFRA) removed the federal income tax exemption for interest on state and local government bonds unless issued in registered (ownership and transfer based on central list) rather than bearer (ownership presumed from possession) form.

The case arose in the Court's original jurisdiction to consider whether TEFRA either (1) violated the Tenth Amendment and principles of federalism by compelling issuance of state bonds in registered form or (2) violated intergovernmental tax immunity by taxing the interest earned on unregistered state bonds. The section of TEFRA at issue was designed to facilitate IRS collections since bearer bonds leave no trail.

Relying on *Garcia v. San Antonio Metropolitan Transit Authority* [*supra* § 3.02], the Court rejected the Tenth Amendment claim. *Garcia* held that Tenth Amendment "limits are structural, not substantive — i.e., that States must find their protection from congressional regulation through the national political process, not through judicially defined spheres of unregulable state activity."

The Court rejected South Carolina's claims that the political process failed either because Congress was uninformed or chose a bad remedy. South Carolina did not allege "that it was deprived of any right to participate in the national political process or that it was singled out in a way that left it politically isolated and powerless. . . . But nothing in *Garcia* or the Tenth Amendment authorizes courts to second-guess the substantive basis for congressional legislation. . . . Where, as here, the national political *process* did not operate in a defective manner, the Tenth Amendment is not implicated. . . ."

Nor did TEFRA unconstitutionally violate the doctrine of intergovernmental tax immunity by taxing interest on a state bond. *Pollock v. Farmers' Loan & Trust Co.*, 157 U.S. 429 (1895), had held that any interest earned on a state bond was exempt from federal tax. But *Pollock* had been thoroughly repudiated. It had "represented one application of the more general rule that neither the federal nor the state governments could tax income an individual directly derived from *any* contract with another government."

That rule rested on the rationale that "any tax on income a party received under a contract with the government was a tax on the contract and thus a tax 'on' the government because it burdened the government's power to enter into the contract."

Modern caselaw had repudiated the "rationale underlying *Pollock* and the general immunity for government contract income" by rejecting the "burden" theory that a tax on income was a tax on its source.

Summarizing, Justice Brennan wrote that "under current intergovernmental tax immunity doctrine the States can never tax the United States directly but can tax any private parties with whom it does business, even though the financial burden falls on the United States, as long as the tax does not discriminate against the United States or those with whom it deals. . . . The rule with respect to state tax immunity is essentially the same, . . . except that at least some nondiscriminatory federal taxes can be collected directly from the States even though a parallel state tax could not be collected directly from the Federal Government."

TEFRA did not tax states directly nor did it discriminate against states. The Constitution did not require treating differently those who receive state bond interest from those who receive other income from state contracts.

Accordingly, the Court upheld the statute in imposing a bond registration requirement as a condition of tax exemption.

NOTES

(1) *McCulloch v. Maryland* was long thought to imply a reciprocal doctrine of intergovernmental immunity which protected the states and federal government. *Collector v. Day*, 78 U.S. (11 Wall.) 113 (1870), was the leading case articulating the tax immunity of the states. In *Collector*, the Court held the salary of a state judge immune from federal taxation. The Court treated tax on income as a tax on its source. The state government was accorded the same rights in this respect as the federal government. If the operation of the federal government would be impaired if the state could tax the salaries of its officers: "why are not those of the States depending upon their reserved powers, for like reasons, equally exempt from Federal taxation?" *Id.* at 127. The same holding was reached with regard to federal taxation of state and local bonds and the interest thereon, *Pollock v. Farmers Loan & Trust Co.*, 157 U.S. 429 (1895); of sales by private contractors to state and local agencies, *Indian Motorcycle Co. v. United States*, 283 U.S. 570 (1931); and of income derived by the lessees of state-owned lands, *Burnet v. Coronado Oil & Gas Co.*, 285 U.S. 393 (1932). In these cases, the Court recognized areas of tax immunity for those dealing with state government comparable to immunity which sheltered those with financial dealings with the Federal Government.

(2) With the abandonment of the theory that a tax on income is a tax on its source, it was only natural that *Collector v. Day* and its progeny, too, should be overruled. In *Helvering v. Gerhardt*, 304 U.S. 405 (1938), the Court held that employees of the Port of New York Authority were subject to federal income tax. *Collector* was limited, for the time being, to a protection for a state judge engaged in a traditional state governmental function essential to its existence. The Court thought the Constitution should rarely be read to limit by implication Congress' taxing power. Echoing *McCulloch*, Justice Stone wrote "that the people of all the states have created the national government and are represented in Congress. Through that representation they exercise the national taxing power. The very fact that when they are exercising it they are taxing themselves serves to guard against its abuse through the possibility of resort to the unusual processes of political action which provides a readier and more adaptable means than any which courts can afford, for securing accommodation of the competing demands for national revenue, on the one hand, and for reasonable scope for the independence of state action, on the other." *Id.* at 416. *See also Graves v. New York ex rel. O'Keefe*, 306 U.S. 466 (1939); *Helvering v. Mountain Producers Corp.*, 303 U.S. 376 (1938).

(3) More recent decisions have rejected the *Collector v. Day* assumption of

equivalence in intergovernmental tax immunities. National and state immunities do not stand upon an equal constitutional plane. The rule of federal immunity rests on the Supremacy Clause. State immunity does not rest upon a categorical constitutional command like the Supremacy Clause, but upon implications from the States' role in the constitutional scheme.

> In recognizing that implication for the first time, the Court was concerned with the continued existence of the states as governmental entities, and their preservation from destruction by the national taxing power. The immunity which it implied was sustained only because it was one deemed necessary to protect the states from destruction by the federal taxation of those governmental functions which they were exercising when the Constitution was adopted and which were essential to their continued existence.

Helvering v. Gerhardt, 304 U.S. 405, 414 (1938).

§ 4.05 COOPERATIVE FEDERALISM[1]

UNITED STATES STEEL CORP. v. MULTISTATE TAX COMM'N, 434 U.S. 452 (1978). Under the Compact Clause of the Constitution: "No State shall, without the Consent of Congress, . . . enter into any Agreement or Compact with another State, or with a foreign Power. . . ." Art. 1 § 10 cl. 3. In *United States Steel Corp.*, the Court held that the Multistate Tax Compact, which established the Multistate Tax Commission, was valid even though it had not received congressional approval.

The Multistate Tax Compact which had 21 states as members by 1972 was created in "recognition that, as applied to multistate businesses, traditional state tax administration was inefficient and costly to both State and taxpayer." The Compact sought to devise ways to make state taxation of multistate taxpayers more fair and efficient. A Multistate Tax Commission was created to pursue these purposes and given some administrative power. The Compact empowered states to decide to authorize the Commission to conduct an audit for it. Any state could withdraw from the Compact by state legislation.

Various multistate taxpayers who were threatened with audits challenged the Compact as invalid since Congress had not approved it. The Court, speaking through Justice Powell, found that "[r]ead literally, the Compact Clause would require the States to obtain congressional approval before entering into any agreement among themselves, irrespective of form, subject, duration, or interest to the United States."

The Court had rejected a literal interpretation in *Virginia v. Tennessee*, 148 U.S. 503 (1893) and *New Hampshire v. Maine*, 426 U.S. 363 (1976) and adhered to those precedents since it was "reluctant to accept this invitation to circumscribe modes of interstate cooperation that do not enhance state power to the detriment of federal supremacy. . . ."

In view of the breadth of the term "compact" or "agreement" the Court concluded that it was not intended to reach all interstate agreements. Instead, "it was necessary to construe the terms of the Compact Clause by reference to the object of the entire section in which it appears."

In *New Hampshire v. Maine*, the Court had reaffirmed its earlier view that the "application of the Compact Clause is limited to agreements that are 'directed to the formation of any combination tending to the increase of political power in the States, which may encroach upon or interfere with the just supremacy of the United States.' " *Id.* at 369, . . . quoting *Virginia v. Tennessee*, 148 U.S., at 519. The Court thought this

---

[1] The term is used in *New York v. United States*, 505 U.S. 144 (1992).

rule properly balanced federal and state interests even where multiple states were involved.

The Multistate Tax Compact did not "enhance the political power of the member States in a way that encroaches upon the supremacy of the United States." States were given no new powers nor was any state sovereignty surrendered to the Compact since each state could withdraw at any time. The Court rejected the taxpayers' claim that the Compact invaded federal supremacy regarding interstate commerce since, in essence, the Commission did nothing each state could not do.

§ 4.06 STATE REGULATION OF COMMERCE; THE DORMANT COMMERCE CLAUSE

> Though phrased as a grant of regulatory power to Congress, the [Commerce] Clause has long been understood to have a "negative" aspect that denies the States the power unjustifiably to discriminate against or burden the interstate flow of articles of commerce. . . . The Framers granted Congress plenary authority over interstate commerce in "the conviction that in order to succeed, the new Union would have to avoid the tendencies toward economic Balkanization that had plagued relations among the Colonies and later among the States under the Articles of Confederation." . . . "This principle that our economic unit is the Nation, which alone has the gamut of powers necessary to control of the economy, . . . has as its corollary that the states are not separable economic units."

Oregon Waste Systems, Inc. v. Department of Envtl. Quality, 511 U.S. 93, 98 (1994).

[1] Historical Development

COOLEY v. BOARD OF WARDENS OF THE PORT OF PHILADELPHIA
53 U.S. (12 How.) 299, 13 L. Ed. 996 (1851)

[Editor's note: A Pennsylvania statute required "every ship or vessel arriving from or bound to any foreign port or place, and every ship or vessel of the burden of seventy-five tons or more, sailing from or bound to any port not within the River Delaware," to take on a local pilot. Penalties were assessed for failing to take on a pilot or failing to report his name, the proceeds of which went to a fund for retired local pilots. Cooley challenged the constitutionality of the state statute in an action against him to collect the fees. From an adverse decision of the highest court of Pennsylvania, he appealed.]

Mr. Justice Curtis delivered the opinion of the court.

. . . [W]e are brought directly and unavoidably to the consideration of the question, whether the grant of the commercial power to Congress, did per se deprive the States of all power to regulate pilots. This question has never been decided by this court, nor, in our judgment, has any case depending upon all the considerations which must govern this one, come before this court. The grant of commercial power to Congress does not contain any terms which expressly exclude the states from exercising an authority over its subject-matter. If they are excluded it must be because the nature of the power, thus granted to Congress, requires that a similar authority should not exist in the states. If it were conceded on the one side, that the nature of this power, like that to legislate for the District of Columbia, is absolutely and totally repugnant to the existence of similar power in the states, probably no one would deny that the grant of the power to Congress, as effectually and perfectly excludes the states from all future legislation on the subject, as if express words had been used to exclude them. And on the other hand, if it were admitted that the existence of this power in Congress, like the power of taxation, is compatible with the existence of a similar power in the states, then it would be in conformity with the contemporary exposition of the Constitution (Federalist, No. 32), and with the judicial construction, given from time to time by this court, after the most deliberate consideration, to hold that the mere grant of such a power to Congress, did not imply a prohibition on the states to exercise the same power; that it is not the mere existence of such a power, but its exercise by Congress, which may be incompatible with the exercise of the same power by the States, and that the States may legislate in the absence of congressional regulations. . . .

The diversities of opinion, therefore, which have existed on this subject, have arisen from the different views taken of the nature of this power. But when the nature of a power like this is spoken of, when it is said that the nature of the power requires that it should be exercised exclusively by Congress, it must be intended to refer to the subjects of that power, and to say they are of such a nature as to require exclusive legislation by Congress. Now, the power to regulate commerce, embraces a vast field, containing not only many, but exceedingly various subjects, quite unlike in their nature; some imperatively demanding a single uniform rule, operating equally on the commerce of the United States in every port; and some, like the subject now in question, as imperatively demanding that diversity, which alone can meet the local necessities of navigation.

Either absolutely to affirm, or deny that the nature of this power requires exclusive legislation by Congress, is to lose sight of the nature of the subjects of this power, and to assert concerning all of them, what is really applicable but to a part. Whatever subjects of this power are in their nature national, or admit only of one uniform system, or plan of regulation, may justly be said to be of such a nature as to require exclusive legislation by Congress. That this cannot be affirmed of laws for the regulation of pilots and pilotage is plain. . . . [T]he nature of this subject is such, that until Congress should find it necessary to exert its power, it should be left to the legislation of the States; that it is local and not national; that it is likely to be the best provided for, not by one system, or plan of regulations, but by as many as the legislative discretion of the several States should deem applicable to the local peculiarities of the ports within their limits. . . .

. . . [T]he nature of this subject is not such as to require . . . [Congress'] exclusive legislation. The practice of the States, and of the national government, has been in conformity with this . . . from the origin of the national government to this time; and the nature of the subject, when examined, is such as to leave no doubt of the superior fitness and propriety, not to say the absolute necessity, of different systems of regulation, drawn from local knowledge and experience, and conformed to local wants. How then can we say, that by the mere grant of power to regulate commerce, the States are deprived of all the power to legislate on this subject, because from the nature of the power the legislation of Congress must be exclusive . . . .

We are of opinion that this State law was enacted by virtue of a power, residing in the State to legislate; that it is not in conflict with any law of Congress; that it does not interfere with any system which Congress has established by making regulations, or by intentionally leaving individuals to their own unrestricted action; that this law is therefore valid, and the judgment of the Supreme Court of Pennsylvania in each case must be affirmed.

[JUSTICES McLEAN and WAYNE dissented.]

NOTES

A. The Constitutional Basis of the Dormant Commerce Clause

(1) The Commerce Clause, Justice Wiley Rutledge wrote, is "a two-edged sword, cutting both ways." WILEY RUTLEDGE, A DECLARATION OF LEGAL FAITH 33 (1947). It cuts an area in which it empowers Congress to exercise national power. It is, therefore, perhaps the most important source of domestic power for the national government. The Commerce Clause also "cuts down state power by implied or inferential negation." *Id.* As such, it limits state power even when Congress has not spoken.

Chapter 2 presented cases and materials which considered Congress' affirmative exercise of its commerce power. *Cooley* and the following materials address the negative or dormant commerce clause, the extent to which the clause constrains state regulations which affect commerce even when Congress has not acted.

What is the basis of this negative or dormant Commerce Clause? The text of the Commerce Clause does grant power to Congress to regulate commerce among the states. It does not say that states can regulate where Congress has not acted. But neither does it say states *cannot* then regulate. Historically, the Court has treated the clause as a constraint on the states.

(2) How strong is the textual argument for a dormant Commerce Clause? By empowering Congress to regulate commerce does the Constitution imply the states must stay out? Are there other instances where the Constitution specifically expresses constraints on states? *See, e.g.*, U.S. CONST. art. I, § 10, cl. 1 (imposing limits on states) and art. I, § 10, cl. 2 and 3 (imposing limits on states subject to removal by Congress). Might these clauses suggest that when the Constitution wants to limit state power it does so expressly? Or do they simply show that in these instances the Constitution is specific in limiting state power without showing that the Constitution always limits state power specifically?

(3) The dormant Commerce Clause has evolved from the Court's interpretations of the Constitution's silence. As Justice Jackson put it, "Perhaps even more than by interpretation of its written word, this Court has advanced the solidarity and prosperity of this Nation by the meaning it has given to these great silences of the Constitution." *H.P. Hood & Sons, Inc. v. Du Mond*, 336 U.S. 525, 535 (1949).

(4) Do structural arguments support the dormant Commerce Clause? Justice Cardozo (for a unanimous court) thought tolerating economic protectionism by the states "would be to invite a speedy end of our national solidarity. The Constitution was framed under the dominion of a political philosophy less parochial in range. It was framed upon the theory that the peoples of the several states must sink or swim together, and that in the long run prosperity and salvation are in union and not division." *Baldwin v. G.A.F. Seelig, Inc.*, 294 U.S. 511, 523 (1935). The Court continues to invoke the sink or swim metaphor as its political vision of the dormant Commerce Clause.

A second, slightly different, structural argument supports a dormant Commerce Clause. Left to their own devices, states would, wherever possible, externalize costs and internalize benefits. Since out-of-staters would lack representation in state legislatures, they would bear a disproportionate share of burdens.

Although the political rationale behind the dormant Commerce Clause has been dominant, the Court has also sometimes subscribed to an economic rationale. As Justice Jackson wrote:

This principle that our economic unit is the Nation, which alone has the gamut of powers necessary to control of the economy, including the vital power of erecting custom barriers against foreign competition, has as its corollary that the states are not separable economic units. . . . Our system, fostered by the Commerce Clause, is that every farmer and every craftsman shall be encouraged to produce by the certainty that he will have free access to every market in the Nation. . . .

H.P. Hood & Sons, Inc. v. Du Mond, 336 U.S. 525, 537-59 (1949).

(5) *Gibbons v. Ogden.* In representing Gibbons, Daniel Webster "guardedly" argued that Congress' power to regulate commerce was "to a certain extent, necessarily exclusive." Webster "did not mean to say that all regulations which might, in their operation, affect commerce, were exclusively in the power of Congress; but that such power as had been exercised in this case, did not remain with the States." *Gibbons*, 22 U.S. at 9. The Constitution did not intend to allow the states to confer monopolies over trade or navigation. The records relating to the ratification of the Constitution reveal no one advocating for the states retaining a concurrent power over domestic trade. The "commerce of the United States" was to be regulated only by Congress. Since Congress had exclusive power regarding "the great branches" of commerce, the monopoly New York had conferred was void even without any conflict with Gibbon's federal coastwise license.

In *Gibbons v. Ogden*, Chief Justice Marshall noted counsel's argument that the Commerce Clause implied that the nation was to have "full power over the things to be regulated" which would exclude "the action of all others that would perform the same operation in the same thing." Marshall thought "[t]here is great force in this argument, and the court is not satisfied that it has been refuted" suggesting perhaps that Marshall found persuasive the argument for exclusive federal power over commerce. *Id.* at 209. Because the Court held the New York monopoly conflicted with a federal law it did not need to decide whether the Constitution gave Congress a monopoly on commercial regulation. But Marshall sent somewhat mixed signals. Although he suggested that a state could not regulate interstate commerce since that was "the very power that is granted to Congress," he thought states could pass inspection laws, for instance, although they might "have a remote and considerable influence on commerce." *Id.* at 203. Such laws were "a portion of that immense mass of legislation, which embraces everything within the territory of a state, not surrendered to the general government; all of which can be most advantageously exercised by the States themselves." *Id.* In addition to inspection laws, that mass included quarantine laws, health laws, and laws relating to internal commerce of a state.

Justice Johnson, in his concurrence, went further. The Constitution was formed largely to remedy the chaos that emerged after the revolutionary war when each state imposed commercial regulations. The states had transferred full power over commerce to the nation. The unconstitutionality of the New York monopoly did not depend on the coastwise license or the Supremacy Clause. New York simply had no power to enact a law so regulating interstate commerce. Justice Johnson thought the distinction between federal and state power turned on the "different purposes" of its laws.

Professor Norman R. Williams argues that Chief Justice Marshall decided to rest *Gibbons* on the Supremacy Clause rather than the Dormant Commerce Clause to minimize criticism of judicial review "by asserting that it was Congress, not the Court, which chose to displace New York's authority to create the steamboat monopoly." Norman R. Williams, *Gibbons*, 79 N.Y.U. L. Rev. 1398, 1402 (2004).

(6) *Wilson v. Black Bird Creek Marsh Co.*, 27 U.S. (2 Pet.) 245 (1829). Five years later, the Court and Marshall had another opportunity to consider whether a state could legislate in an area within Congress' Commerce power. Delaware passed a law

authorizing a dam to be built in a small creek which flowed into the Delaware River. In conclusory fashion, Marshall wrote simply that the Delaware statute was not "under all the circumstances of the case . . . repugnant to the power to regulate commerce in its dormant state. . . ." *Id.* at 252. How might Marshall have reconciled this decision with his discussion in *Gibbons*?

(7) *Mayor, Aldermen and Commonalty of New York v. Miln*, 36 U.S. (11 Pet.) 102 (1837). The Court distinguished between state laws passed pursuant to the state's police power (which were constitutional) and those regulating commerce (which were not). A state law requiring a passenger list for arriving ships rested on the police power. Justice Story dissented since he regarded the state law as an intrusion on the commerce power.

(8) *Cooley v. Board of Wardens*. Justice Curtis avoided a categorical answer to the question of whether the Commerce Clause vests an exclusive power in Congress to regulate interstate commerce. Instead of answering "Yes" or "No," Justice Curtis answered; "Yes and No" or, more accurately, "Sometimes Yes and sometimes No." *See* THOMAS REED POWELL, VAGARIES AND VARIETIES IN CONSTITUTIONAL INTERPRETATION 152 (1956). *Cooley* refused to interpret the Commerce Clause as conferring exclusive power on the federal government in all instances when commerce was affected. It also rejected the opposing polar position, that when Congress did not exercise its commerce power states were unconstrained in regulating in the empty space. *Cooley* adopted an intermediate position. This "selective exclusiveness" approach recognizes that whether Congressional power is exclusive turns on the circumstances of particular cases, the nature of the subject being regulated. But that leads to a demand for criteria to determine when states can regulate and when they are precluded from regulation.

(9) What criteria does Justice Curtis offer to answer these questions? When, according to him, does the nature of the regulated subject require it to be considered as exclusively vested in Congress? When does it permit state regulation? Are there problems with the *Cooley* approach? What criteria distinguish between those national subjects which required uniform regulations and those local subjects which permitted diverse treatment? Could a state impose protectionist measures within the local subjects?

(10) Dormant Commerce Clause cases no longer follow *Cooley* by focusing on the subjects being regulated and asking whether a national or local approach is in order. Still, *Cooley* has had a continuing impact in that modern dormant Commerce Clause analysis has adopted an intermediate approach. Like *Cooley*, the modern Court has resisted the impulse to find that when Congress is silent the Commerce Clause always prohibits, or automatically allows, all state regulation. Instead, it has upheld some, but not all, state regulations.

B. Transportation Cases

(11) *Railroad Rates*. The *Cooley* test was applied frequently to assess state regulations of transportation, often railroads. *Munn v. Illinois*, 94 U.S. 113 (1876), upheld the authority of the states to prescribe railroad rates, but left open whether state rate control was valid for transportation in interstate commerce. In *Wabash, S. L. & P. Ry. Co. v. Illinois*, 118 U.S. 557 (1886), the Court considered the validity of a state statute regulating railroad rates for transportation whose origin or destination was beyond the state. The Court relied on *Cooley* to strike down the state law. Interstate rate regulation required uniformity which must come from Washington. *Wabash* led to the Interstate Commerce Act of 1887 — the first great regulatory law enacted under the federal commerce power. It empowered the Interstate Commerce Commission to regulate interstate rail rates, though states retained authority over purely intrastate rates.

(12) *Railroad Safety*. The Court allowed greater diversity in railroad safety. It upheld

state regulations of interstate trains which required locomotive engineers be licensed, *Smith v. Alabama*, 124 U.S. 465 (1888); required locomotive headlights of a specified minimum capacity, *Atchison, T. & S.F. Ry. Co. v. Railroad Comm'n.*, 283 U.S. 380 (1931); required trains to reduce speed at crossings, *Southern Ry. Co. v. King*, 217 U.S. 524 (1910); or otherwise addressed speed, *Erb v. Morasch*, 177 U.S. 584 (1900). But the Court struck down a state law which made an interstate train slow at crossings where the effect would have been to cause 124 stops over 123 miles, significantly extending the time of the journey. *Seaboard Air Line Ry. Co. v. Blackwell*, 244 U.S. 310 (1917).

(13) *Direct v. Indirect Regulations.* The state regulations often were justified as simply affecting commerce indirectly, not directly. For instance, in *Smith v. Alabama*, the Court concluded that Alabama's license requirement for railroad engineers "so far as it affects transactions of commerce among the states, . . . does so only indirectly, incidentally, and remotely." 124 U.S. at 482. *See also Southern Ry Co. v. King*, 217 U.S. 524 (1910) (Commerce Clause precludes state from regulating commerce directly).

In *Di Santo v. Pennsylvania*, 273 U.S. 34 (1927), the Court struck down as violative of the Commerce Clause a Pennsylvania law requiring licensing of vendors of steamship tickets to or from foreign countries. Justice Butler, in an opinion for the Court, held that the state statute constituted "a direct burden" on foreign commerce which only Congress could regulate. Justice Brandeis, for himself and Justice Holmes, dissented, arguing that the statute was "an exertion of the police power" of Pennsylvania which "neither obstructs, discriminates against, or directly burdens the commerce." *Id.* at 37-39. Justice Stone wrote a separate dissent (which Justice Brandeis and Holmes joined). He criticized the direct-indirect distinction, which all other members of the Court had invoked as "too mechanical, too uncertain in its application, and too remote from actualities, to be of value." *Id.* at 44. The use of the direct-indirect language was entirely conclusory, he suggested. Instead, the Court must, upon review of all circumstances including the "actual effect on the flow of commerce" determine whether a state regulation "concerns interests peculiarly local and does not infringe the national interest" in free flowing interstate commerce. *Id.*

(14) In *South Carolina State Highway Dept. v. Barnwell Bros. Inc.*, 303 U.S. 177 (1938), the Court essentially applied the *Cooley* local-national dichotomy to uphold a South Carolina statute limiting widths of trucks on its highways to 90 inches. Congress could have, but had not, regulated the issue. "The commerce clause by its own force, prohibits discrimination against interstate commerce, whatever its form or method, and the decisions of this Court have recognized that there is scope for its like operation when state legislation nominally of local concern is in point of fact aimed at interstate commerce, or by its necessary operation is a means of gaining a local benefit by throwing the attendant burdens on those without the state." *Id.* at 185-86. The vice in such discriminatory state measures was "that when the regulation is of such a character that its burden falls principally upon those without the state, legislative action is not likely to be subjected to those political restraints which are normally exerted on legislation where it affects adversely some interests within the state." *Id.* at n.2.

Barnwell posed no such problem, Justice Stone wrote for a 7-0 court. Absent national legislation, South Carolina " 'may rightly prescribe uniform regulations adapted to promote safety upon its highways and the conservation of their use, applicable alike to vehicles moving in interstate commerce and those of its own citizens.' " *Id.* at 189. Justice Stone reasoned that the use of state highways were "peculiarly of local concern." State highways, unlike railroads, "are built, owned, and maintained by state," and states have a strong interest in "their safe and economical administration." *Id.* at 187.

Legislatures, not courts, were suited to assess the merits of safety regulations.

Legislative judgments presumptively enjoyed factual support and were reviewed under a forgiving rational basis standard.

(15) Seven years later, in *Southern Pac. Co. v. Arizona ex rel. Sullivan*, 325 U.S. 761 (1945), the Court struck down an Arizona law limiting rail trains to 14 passenger or 70 freight cars. Although the Court continued to deploy some of the *Cooley* language ("There has thus been left to the states wide scope for the regulation of matters of local state concern, even though it in some measure affects the commerce, provided it does not materially restrict the free flow of commerce across state lines, or interfere with it in matters with respect to which uniformity of regulation is of predominant national concern"), its approach reflected change. Unlike *Barnwell*, the Court was not disposed to defer to state legislatures. Absent Congressional action, "this Court, and not the state legislature, is under the commerce clause the final arbiter of the competing demands of state and national interests." *Id.* at 769.

The Court would arbitrate under a balancing test. "Hence the matters for ultimate determination here are the nature and extent of the burden which the state regulation of interstate trains, adopted as a safety measure, imposes on interstate commerce, and whether the relative weights of the state and national interests involved are such as to make inapplicable the rule, generally observed, that the free flow of interstate commerce and its freedom from local restraints in matters requiring uniformity of regulation are interests safeguarded by the commerce clause from state interference." *Id.* at 770-71.

Whereas the uniqueness of South Carolina's width requirement in *Barnwell* was deemed not relevant, the Court was impressed by the fact that the national norm allowed longer trains than Arizona permitted. Arizona's regulation went "beyond what is plainly essential for safety since it does not appear that it will lessen rather than increase the danger of accident." *Barnwell* was distinguishable since it dealt with highways. Justice Black, in dissent, accused the Court of "acting as a super legislature.'" *Id.* at 788. Legislators, not judges, should balance the claims of safety and efficiency.

(16) In *Bibb v. Navajo Freight Lines, Inc.*, 359 U.S. 520 (1959), the Court held that an Illinois statute requiring a contour type of rear fender mudguard on trucks conflicted with the Commerce Clause. The statute made the conventional or straight mudflap, which was (legal in at least forty-five states), illegal in Illinois; taken with a rule of the Arkansas Commerce Commission requiring straight mudflaps, the Illinois law made the use of the same motor vehicle equipment in both states impossible. The Supreme Court affirmed a lower court decision that the challenged statute unduly and unreasonably burdened commerce.

Although Justice Douglas wrote that such "safety measures carry a strong presumption of validity," he, and the Court, viewed *Bibb* as "one of those cases few in number where local safety measures that are nondiscriminatory place an unconstitutional burden on interstate commerce." *Id.* at 529. States which pursue policies at odds with their neighbors "may sometimes place a great burden of delay and inconvenience" on interstate commerce. "We deal not with absolutes but with questions of degree." *Id.* at 530. Do cases like *Bibb* offer clear rules to guide state legislators and entrepreneurs? What judicial role does *Bibb* envision?

(17) *Kassel v. Consolidated Freightways Corp.*, 450 U.S. 662 (1981). *Kassel* considered whether an Iowa statute prohibiting use of certain large trucks in Iowa unconstitutionally burdened interstate commerce. Iowa, unlike other states in the West and Midwest, outlawed 65-foot double trucks, restricting most trucks to 55 feet. Its statute allowed a few exceptions, generally favoring an apparently small group of Iowa citizens. Consolidated Freightways Corporation of Delaware (Consolidated), one of the nation's largest common carriers, filed suit in federal court to challenge Iowa's scheme under the dormant Commerce Clause. Iowa defended its law as a measure which promoted safety

and reduced road wear by diverting traffic elsewhere. After trial, the District Court found the larger trucks Iowa prohibited as safe as the smaller ones it allowed and ruled the state law unconstitutional. The Court of Appeals affirmed.

Justice Powell, in his plurality opinion, noted that courts normally uphold genuine safety statutes. Still "the incantation of a purpose to promote the public health or safety does not insulate a state law from Commerce Clause attack. Regulations designed for that salutary purpose nevertheless may further the purpose so marginally, and interfere with commerce so substantially, as to be invalid under the Commerce Clause." *Id.* at 670. Here, the State failed to show the larger trucks were more dangerous. "Moreover, Iowa's law is now out of step with the laws of all other midwestern and western States. Iowa thus substantially burdens the interstate flow of goods by truck. In the absence of congressional action to set uniform standards, some burdens associated with state safety regulations must be tolerated. But where, as here, the State's safety interest has been found to be illusory, and its regulations impair significantly the federal interest in efficient and safe interstate transportation, the state law cannot be harmonized with the Commerce Clause." *Id.* at 671.

Justice Brennan, concurring, criticized Justice Powell (and Justice Rehnquist in dissent) for focusing on the litigation justifications, not the legislature's purpose. For Justice Brennan,

> analysis of Commerce Clause challenges to state regulations must consider three principles: (1) The courts are not empowered to second-guess the empirical judgments of lawmakers concerning the utility of legislation. (2) The burdens imposed on commerce must be balanced against the local benefits actually sought to be achieved by the State's lawmakers, and not against those suggested after the fact by counsel. (3) Protectionist legislation is unconstitutional under the Commerce Clause, even if the burdens and benefits are related to safety rather than economics.

Id. at 679-80. He criticized Justices Powell and Rehnquist for focusing on Iowa's litigation rationale rather than its actual protectionist purpose of deflecting traffic elsewhere.

> . . . Iowa may not shunt off its fair share of the burden of maintaining interstate truck routes, nor may it create increased hazards on the highways of neighboring States in order to decrease the hazards on Iowa highways. Such an attempt has all the hallmarks of the "simple . . . protectionism" this Court has condemned in the economic area. . . . Just as a State's attempt to avoid interstate competition in economic goods may damage the prosperity of the Nation as a whole, so Iowa's attempt to deflect interstate truck traffic has been found to make the Nation's highways as a whole more hazardous. That attempt should therefore be subject to "a virtually per se rule of invalidity."

Kassel, 450 U.S. at 686.

Justice Rehnquist, along with Chief Justice Burger and Justice Stewart, dissented. They thought the search for state legislative purpose futile.

> How, for example, would a court adhering to the views expressed in the concurring opinion approach a statute, the legislative history of which indicated that 10 votes were based on safety considerations, 10 votes were based on protectionism, and the statute passed by a vote of 40-20? What would the actual purpose of the legislature have been in that case? . . .

> Whenever a State enacts more stringent safety measures than its neighbors, in an area which affects commerce, the safety law will have the incidental effect of deflecting interstate commerce to the neighboring States. Indeed, the safety

and protectionist motives cannot be separated: The whole purpose of safety regulation of vehicles is to protect the State from unsafe vehicles. If a neighboring State chooses not to protect its citizens from the danger discerned by the enacting State, that is its business, but the enacting State should not be penalized when the vehicles it considers unsafe travel through the neighboring State. . . .

Id. at 703-706.

[2] Protectionism

PHILADELPHIA v. NEW JERSEY
437 U.S. 617, 98 S. Ct. 2531, 57 L. Ed. 2d 475 (1978)

Mr. Justice Stewart delivered the opinion of the Court.

A New Jersey law prohibits the importation of most "solid or liquid waste which originated or was collected outside the territorial limits of the State . . . ." In this case we are required to decide whether this statutory prohibition violates the Commerce Clause of the United States Constitution.

I

The statutory provision in question is ch. 363 of 1973 N.J. Laws, which took effect in early 1974. In pertinent part it provides:

No person shall bring into this State any solid or liquid waste which originated or was collected outside the territorial limits of the State, except garbage to be fed to swine in the State of New Jersey, until the commissioner [of the State Department of Environmental Protection] shall determine that such action can be permitted without endangering the public health, safety and welfare and has promulgated regulations permitting and regulating the treatment and disposal of such waste in this State.

N.J. Stat. Ann. § 13:1I-10 (West Supp. 1978).

As authorized by ch. 363, the Commissioner promulgated regulations permitting four categories of waste to enter the State. Apart from these narrow exceptions, however, New Jersey closed its borders to all waste from other States. . . .

[Operators of New Jersey landfills and various nonresident clients sued New Jersey and its relevant agency in state court. Although the trial court found ch. 363 unconstitutional under dormant Commerce Clause analysis, the New Jersey Supreme Court reversed, viewing the law as a valid exercise of the police power with little impact on commerce. Plaintiffs appealed to the Supreme Court.

[The dispositive question, therefore, is whether the law is constitutionally permissible in light of the Commerce Clause of the Constitution. . . . [The Court ruled that the interstate movement of waste was commerce, thereby implicating the Commerce Clause.]

III

A

Although the Constitution gives Congress the power to regulate commerce among the States, many subjects of potential federal regulation under that power inevitably escape congressional attention "because of their local character and their number and diversity." . . . In the absence of federal legislation, these subjects are open to control by the States so long as they act within the restraints imposed by the Commerce Clause itself. . . . The bounds of these restraints appear nowhere in the words of the Commerce Clause, but have emerged gradually in the decisions of this Court giving effect to its basic purpose. . . .

The opinions of the Court through the years have reflected an alertness to the evils of "economic isolation" and protectionism, while at the same time recognizing that incidental burdens on interstate commerce may be unavoidable when a State legislates to safeguard the health and safety of its people. Thus, where simple economic protectionism is effected by state legislation, a virtually per se rule of invalidity has been erected. . . . The clearest example of such legislation is a law that overtly blocks the flow of interstate commerce at a State's borders. . . . But where other legislative objectives are credibly advanced and there is no patent discrimination against interstate trade, the Court has adopted a much more flexible approach, the general contours of which were outlined in *Pike v. Bruce Church, Inc.*, 397 U.S. 137, 142: . . .

> Where the statute regulates evenhandedly to effectuate a legitimate local public interest, and its effects on interstate commerce are only incidental, it will be upheld unless the burden imposed on such commerce is clearly excessive in relation to the putative local benefits. . . . If a legitimate local purpose is found, then the question becomes one of degree. And the extent of the burden that will be tolerated will of course depend on the nature of the local interest involved, and on whether it could be promoted as well with a lesser impact on interstate activities. . . .

The crucial inquiry, therefore, must be directed to determining whether ch. 363 is basically a protectionist measure, or whether it can fairly be viewed as a law directed to legitimate local concerns, with effects upon interstate commerce that are only incidental.

B

The purpose of ch. 363 is set out in the statute itself as follows:

> The Legislature finds and determines that . . . the volume of solid and liquid waste continues to rapidly increase, that the treatment and disposal of these wastes continues to pose an even greater threat to the quality of the environment of New Jersey, that the available and appropriate land fill sites within the State are being diminished, that the environment continues to be threatened by the treatment and disposal of waste which originated or was collected outside the State, and that the public health, safety and welfare require that the treatment and disposal within this State of all wastes generated outside of the State be prohibited.

The New Jersey Supreme Court accepted this statement of the state legislature's purpose. . . . [Additionally, it found the state's landfill sites would soon be full, and that excluding out of state waste would help extend their service and protect New Jersey's environment. The court concluded that ch. 363 was designed to protect, not the State's economy, but its environment, and that its substantial benefits outweigh its "slight" burden on interstate commerce.]

The appellants strenuously contend that ch. 363, "while outwardly cloaked 'in the currently fashionable garb of environmental protection,' . . . is actually no more than a legislative effort to suppress competition and stabilize the cost of solid waste disposal for New Jersey residents. . . ."

The appellees, on the other hand, deny that ch. 363 was motivated by financial concerns or economic protectionism. In the words of their brief, "[n]o New Jersey commercial interests stand to gain advantage over competitors from outside the state as a result of the ban on dumping out-of-state waste." Noting that New Jersey landfill operators are among the plaintiffs, the appellee's brief argues that "[t]he complaint is not that New Jersey has forged an economic preference for its own commercial interests, but rather that it has denied a small group of its entrepreneurs an economic opportunity to traffic in waste in order to protect the health, safety and welfare of the citizenry at large."

This dispute about ultimate legislative purpose need not be resolved, because its resolution would not be relevant to the constitutional issue to be decided in this case. Contrary to the evident assumption of the state court and the parties, the evil of protectionism can reside in legislative means as well as legislative ends. . . . [W]hatever New Jersey's ultimate purpose, it may not be accomplished by discriminating against articles of commerce coming from outside the State unless there is some reason, apart from their origin, to treat them differently. Both on its face and in its plain effect, ch. 363 violates this principle of nondiscrimination.

The Court has consistently found parochial legislation of this kind to be constitutionally invalid, whether the ultimate aim of the legislation was to assure a steady supply of milk by erecting barriers to allegedly ruinous outside competition, . . .or to create jobs by keeping industry within the State, . . . or to preserve the State's financial resources from depletion by fencing out indigent immigrants. . . . In each of these cases, a presumably legitimate goal was sought to be achieved by the illegitimate means of isolating the State from the national economy.

Also relevant here are the Court's decisions holding that a State may not accord its own inhabitants a preferred right of access over consumers in other States to natural resources located within its borders. . . .

The New Jersey law at issue in this case falls squarely within the area that the Commerce Clause puts off limits to state regulation. On its face, it imposes on out-of-state commercial interests the full burden of conserving the State's remaining landfill space. It is true that in our previous cases the scarce natural resource was itself the article of commerce, whereas here the scarce resource and the article of commerce are distinct. But that difference is without consequence. In both instances, the State has overtly moved to slow or freeze the flow of commerce for protectionist reasons. It does not matter that the State has shut the article of commerce inside the State in one case and outside the State in the other. What is crucial is the attempt by one State to isolate itself from a problem common to many by erecting a barrier against the movement of interstate trade.

The appellees argue that not all laws which facially discriminate against out-of-state commerce are forbidden protectionist regulations. In particular, they point to quarantine laws, which this Court has repeatedly upheld even though they appear to single out interstate commerce for special treatment. . . .

It is true that certain quarantine laws have not been considered forbidden protectionist measures, even though they were directed against out-of-state commerce. . . . But those quarantine laws banned the importation of articles such as diseased livestock that required destruction as soon as possible because their very movement risked contagion and other evils. Those laws thus did not discriminate against interstate commerce as such, but simply prevented traffic in noxious articles, whatever their origin.

The New Jersey statute is not such a quarantine law. There has been no claim here that the very movement of waste into or through New Jersey endangers health, or that waste must be disposed of as soon and as close to its point of generation as possible. The harms caused by waste are said to arise after its disposal in landfill sites, and at that point, as New Jersey concedes, there is no basis to distinguish out-of-state waste from domestic waste. If one is inherently harmful, so is the other. Yet New Jersey has banned the former while leaving its landfill sites open to the latter. The New Jersey law blocks the importation of waste in an obvious effort to saddle those outside the State with the entire burden of slowing the flow of refuse into New Jersey's remaining landfill sites. That legislative effort is clearly impermissible under the Commerce Clause of the Constitution.

Today, cities in Pennsylvania and New York find it expedient or necessary to send their waste into New Jersey for disposal, and New Jersey claims the right to close its borders to such traffic. Tomorrow, cities in New Jersey may find it expedient or necessary to send their waste into Pennsylvania or New York for disposal, and those States might then claim the right to close their borders. The Commerce Clause will protect New Jersey in the future, just as it protects her neighbors now, from efforts by one State to isolate itself in the stream of interstate commerce from a problem shared by all. The judgment is

Reversed.

MR. JUSTICE REHNQUIST, with whom THE CHIEF JUSTICE joins, dissenting.

. . . The health and safety hazards associated with landfills present appellees with a currently unsolvable dilemma. Other, hopefully safer, methods of disposing of solid wastes are still in the development stage. . . . But appellees obviously cannot completely stop the tide of solid waste that its citizens will produce in the interim. For the moment, therefore, appellees must continue to use sanitary landfills to dispose of New Jersey's own solid waste despite the critical environmental problems thereby created.

The question presented in this case is whether New Jersey must also continue to receive and dispose of solid waste from neighboring States, even though these will inexorably increase the health problems discussed above. The Court answers this question in the affirmative. . . .

In my opinion, these [quarantine] cases are dispositive of the present one. Under them, New Jersey may require germ-infected rags or diseased meat to be disposed of as best as possible within the State, but at the same time prohibit the importation of such items for disposal at the facilities that are set up within New Jersey for disposal of such material generated within the State. The physical fact of life that New Jersey must somehow dispose of its own noxious items does not mean that it must serve as a depository for those of every other State. Similarly, New Jersey should be free under our past precedents to prohibit the importation of solid waste because of the health and safety problems that such waste poses to its citizens. The fact that New Jersey continues to, and indeed must continue to, dispose of its own solid waste does not mean that New Jersey may not prohibit the importation of even more solid waste into the State. I simply see no way to distinguish solid waste, on the record of this case, from germ-infected rags, diseased meat, and other noxious items.

The Court's effort to distinguish these prior cases is unconvincing. It first asserts that the quarantine laws which have previously been upheld "banned the importation of articles such as diseased livestock that required destruction as soon as possible because their very movement risked contagion and other evils." . . . According to the Court, the New Jersey law is distinguishable from these other laws, and invalid, because the concern of New Jersey is not with the movement of solid waste but with the present inability to safely dispose of it once it reaches its destination. But I think it far from clear that the State's law has as limited a focus as the Court imputes to it: Solid waste which is a health hazard when it reaches its destination may in all likelihood be an equally great health hazard in transit.

Even if the Court is correct in its characterization of New Jersey's concerns, I do not see why a State may ban the importation of items whose movement risks contagion, but cannot ban the importation of items which, although they may be transported into the State without undue hazard, will then simply pile up in an ever increasing danger to the public's health and safety. The Commerce Clause was not drawn with a view to having the validity of state laws turn on such pointless distinctions.

Second, the Court implies that the challenged laws must be invalidated because New Jersey has left its landfills open to domestic waste. . . . New Jersey must out of sheer necessity treat and dispose of its solid waste in some fashion, just as it must treat New Jersey cattle suffering from hoof-and-mouth disease. It does not follow that New Jersey must, under the Commerce Clause, accept solid waste or diseased cattle from outside its borders and thereby exacerbate its problems.

The Supreme Court of New Jersey expressly found that ch. 363 was passed "to preserve the health of New Jersey residents by keeping their exposure to solid waste and landfill areas to a minimum." . . . The Court points to absolutely no evidence that would contradict this finding by the New Jersey Supreme Court. Because I find no basis for distinguishing the laws under challenge here from our past cases upholding state laws that prohibit the importation of items that could endanger the population of the State, I dissent.

NOTES

(1) As the Court acknowledged, it has upheld certain quarantine measures. Under their quarantine power, the states may enact laws designed to exclude diseased livestock or other articles which may harm public health. *See, e.g., Mintz v. Baldwin*, 289 U.S. 346 (1933) (upholding New York statute prohibiting import of cattle unless certified free of infectious disease by official in state of origin).

(2) *Fort Gratiot Sanitary Landfill v. Michigan Dep't of Natural Resources*, 504 U.S. 353 (1992). In *Fort Gratiot* the Court applied *Philadelphia v. New Jersey* to strike down a Michigan statute which prohibited private landfill operators "from accepting solid waste that originate outside the county in which their facilities are located."

The Court rejected Michigan's attempt to distinguish *Fort Gratiot* on the grounds that it treated interstate waste no differently than waste from other Michigan counties. "[O]ur prior cases teach that a State (or one of its political subdivisions) may not avoid the strictures of the Commerce Clause by curtailing the movement of articles of commerce through subdivisions of the State, rather than through the State itself. . . ." *Id.* In this respect *Fort Gratiot* resembled *Dean Milk Co. v. Madison*, 340 U.S. 349 (1951) in which the Court struck down a Madison, Wisconsin ordinance requiring milk be pasteurized within five miles of the city even though Wisconsin milk producers located at distances from Madison were also disadvantaged.

"Of course, our conclusion would be different if the imported waste raised health or other concerns not presented by Michigan waste. . . . In this case, . . . the lower courts did not find and respondents have not provided any legitimate reason for allowing petitioner to accept waste from inside the county but not waste from outside the county." *Fort Gratiot Sanitary Landfill*, 504 U.S. at 367.

(3) *C & A Carbone, Inc. v. Clarkstown, N.Y.*, 511 U.S. 383 (1994). Clarkstown passed an ordinance requiring all nonhazardous solid waste in Clarkstown to be deposited at a local transfer station. C & A Carbone sought to transport such solid waste to disposal sites in other states. In a 6-3 decision, the Court held that the ordinance violated the Dormant Commerce Clause. Justice Kennedy wrote that the ordinance regulated interstate commerce by, among other things, depriving out-of-state entrepreneurs of access to Clarkstown's solid waste. The ordinance discriminated against out-of-state

processors by favoring a single local business; it was "no less discriminatory because in-state or in-town processors [were] also covered by the prohibition." Justice Kennedy wrote:

> Discrimination against interstate commerce in favor of local business or investment is *per se* invalid, save in a narrow class of cases in which the municipality can demonstrate, under rigorous scrutiny, that it has no other means to advance a legitimate local interest. . . . The Commerce Clause presumes a national market free from local legislation that discriminates in favor of local interests. Here Clarkstown has any number of nondiscriminatory alternatives for addressing the health and environmental problems alleged to justify the ordinance in question. The most obvious would be uniform safety regulations enacted without the object to discriminate. These regulations would ensure that competitors like Carbone do not underprice the market by cutting corners on environmental safety.

Id. at 392-93.

(4) *Maine v. Taylor*, 472 U.S. 131 (1986), is the lone instance in which a state statute survived the strict scrutiny test. Taylor allegedly violated a Maine statute which prohibited importation of live baitfish. He argued that the statute unconstitutionally burdened commerce. Since the statute discriminated against commerce on its face, the Court subjected the statute to strict scrutiny, thereby requiring Maine "to demonstrate both that the statute 'serves a legitimate local purpose,' and that the purpose could not be served as well by available nondiscriminatory means." *Id.* at 138. A legitimate purpose (protecting Maine's fragile marine ecology from parasites common in out-of-state baitfish) animated the statute even if the degree of risk was uncertain. The District Court did not commit clear error in finding that no means existed to inspect baitfish at the border to screen those carrying the harmful parasites. The "abstract possibility" of developing a test in the future did not constitute an available nondiscriminatory alternative. Should such a test emerge in the future as a less discriminatory alternative, Maine's statute might lose its justification. Although "[a] state must make reasonable efforts to avoid restraining the free flow of commerce across its borders . . . it is not required to develop new and unproven means of protection at an uncertain cost." *Id.* at 147.

The Court would not have tolerated "simple economic protectionism," but the Court saw no reason to regard Maine's justifications as a phoney after-the-fact rationalization, even though Justice Stevens, in dissent, found "something fishy about this case," since only Maine banned out-of-state baitfish. *Id.* at 152.

(5) Justice Stevens apparently overcame his misgivings about the fishiness of *Maine v. Taylor* six years later when he cited it for the proposition that an import prohibition might survive if based on genuine health concerns. *Fort Gratiot Sanitary Landfill, Inc. v. Michigan Dep't of Natural Resources*, 504 U.S. 353, 367 (1992).

(6) Under the strict scrutiny test, a state statute will not survive simply because it serves a legitimate purpose. In *Hughes v. Oklahoma*, 441 U.S. 322 (1979), the Court struck down an Oklahoma statute which prohibited taking minnows out of state to sell them, even though Oklahoma could point to a legitimate purpose, maintaining ecological balance. The statute was far from the "least discriminatory alternative." Oklahoma's conservation program included no provisions to limit in-staters' access to the precious minnows. Conservation efforts seemed directed to out-of-state consumption.

(7) States have devised numerous ways to discriminate against out of state interests. Not all cases involve waste or fish; some involve milk. In *Dean Milk Co. v. City of Madison, Wis.*, 340 U.S. 349 (1951), the Court struck down a Madison ordinance forbidding the sale of milk in Madison unless pasteurized within five miles from

Madison. The legitimacy of the avowed purpose did not insulate the statute from strict scrutiny since in "erecting an economic barrier protecting a major local industry" from interstate competition, "Madison plainly discriminates against interstate commerce. This it cannot do, even in the exercise of its unquestioned power to protect the health and safety of its people, if reasonable nondiscriminatory alternatives, adequate to conserve legitimate local interests, are available." *Id.* at 354. Madison could have relied on other official inspectors or sent its own inspectors to check other facilities while charging reasonable costs to the importers.

(8) Protectionism may take forms other than a prohibition on out-of-state products. In *Baldwin v. G.A.F. Seelig*, 294 U.S. 511 (1935), the Court considered a New York statute which set minimum prices at which milk dealers could purchase milk to be sold in New York. New York sought to apply its statute to Seelig, who bought milk in Vermont below the price floor, and deny Seelig a license to sell milk. The Court held that New York could not seek to protect its dairy farmers from competition from the more attractive rates of Vermont milk by raising barriers to sale of Vermont milk. "If New York, in order to promote the economic welfare of her framers, may guard them against competition with the cheaper prices of Vermont, the door has been opened to rivalries and reprisals that were meant to be averted by subjecting commerce between the states to the power of the nation." *Id.* at 522.

(9) What harm flows from measures discriminating against imports? In *Dean Milk Co.*, the Court warned that such measures "would invite a multiplication of preferential trade areas destructive of the very purpose of the Commerce Clause." *Dean Milk*, 340 U.S. at 356.

(10) *Camps Newfound/Owatonna, Inc. v. Town of Harrison, Maine*, 520 U.S. 564 (1997). A Maine statute violated the Dormant Commerce Clause by exempting from generally applicable state taxes charitable organizations serving residents, but giving less favorable treatment to those serving nonresidents. Five members of the Court thought the statute facially discriminatory and accordingly subject to the *per se* rule. Maine failed to offer evidence to meet its heavy burden. Four dissenters thought Maine could overcome the burden strict scrutiny imposed. They thought state legislation favoring domestic charities should not offend the Commerce Clause.

(11) *Oregon Waste Systems, Inc. v. Department of Environmental Quality*, 511 U.S. 93 (1994). Oregon imposed a $2.25 per ton surcharge on disposal of out-of-state waste compared to $0.85 per ton for in-state waste. "Because the Oregon surcharge is discriminatory, the virtually *per se* rule of invalidity provides the proper legal standard here . . . " wrote Justice Thomas for a seven Justice majority. "As a result, the surcharge must be invalidated unless respondents can 'sho[w] that it advances a legitimate local purpose that cannot be adequately served by reasonable nondiscriminatory alternatives.' " *Id.* at 100-01. Oregon's proffered justification was that the higher surcharge for out-of-state waste was a "compensatory tax" to make interstate commerce pay its way. That argument might justify a discriminatory tax if the state a) identified the intrastate burden; b) demonstrated that the interstate tax was approximately the same; and c) showed that the waste being taxed are "substantially equivalent" as in the case, for instance, with sales taxes and use taxes. Oregon failed to meet its burden regarding the compensatory tax and accordingly could not demonstrate the legitimate state purpose and lack of nondiscriminatory alternatives needed to save the discriminatory statute. Chief Justice Rehnquist and Justice Blackmun dissented.

[3]   Facially Neutral Statutes

HUNT v. WASHINGTON STATE APPLE ADVERTISING COMM'N
432 U.S. 333, 97 S. Ct. 2434, 53 L. Ed. 2d 383 (1977)

MR. CHIEF JUSTICE BURGER delivered the opinion of the Court.

In 1973, North Carolina enacted a statute which required, inter alia, all closed containers of apples sold, offered for sale, or shipped into the State to bear "no grade other than the applicable U.S. grade or standard." . . . In an action brought by the Washington State Apple Advertising Commission, a three-judge Federal District Court invalidated the statute insofar as it prohibited the display of Washington State apple grades on the ground that it unconstitutionally discriminated against interstate commerce.

The specific questio[n] presented on appeal [is] . . . whether the challenged North Carolina statute constitutes an unconstitutional burden on interstate commerce.

(1)

Washington State is the Nation's largest producer of apples, its crops accounting for approximately 30% of all apples grown domestically and nearly half of all apples shipped in closed containers in interstate commerce. . . . [T]he production and sale of apples on this scale is a multimillion dollar enterprise which plays a significant role in Washington's economy. Because of the importance of the apple industry to the State, its legislature has undertaken to protect and enhance the reputation of Washington apples by establishing a stringent, mandatory inspection program, administered by the State's Department of Agriculture, which requires all apples shipped in interstate commerce to be tested under strict quality standards and graded accordingly. In all cases, the Washington State grades, which have gained substantial acceptance in the trade, are the equivalent of, or superior to, the comparable grades and standards adopted by the United States Department of Agriculture (USDA). Compliance with the Washington inspection scheme costs the State's growers approximately $1 million each year. . . .

In 1972, the North Carolina Board of Agriculture adopted an administrative regulation, unique in the 50 States, which in effect required all closed containers of apples shipped into or sold in the State to display either the applicable USDA grade or none at all. State grades were expressly prohibited. In addition to its obvious consequence prohibiting the display of Washington State apple grades on containers of apples shipped into North Carolina, the regulation presented the Washington apple industry with a marketing problem of potentially nationwide significance. . . . [C]ompliance with North Carolina's unique regulation would have required Washington growers to obliterate the printed labels on containers shipped to North Carolina, thus giving their product a damaged appearance. Alternatively, they could have changed their marketing practices to accommodate the needs of the North Carolina market, i.e., repack apples to be shipped to North Carolina in containers bearing only the USDA grade, and/or store the estimated portion of the harvest destined for that market in such special containers. As a last resort, they could discontinue the use of the preprinted containers entirely. None of these costly and less efficient options was very attractive to the industry. Moreover, in the event a number of other States followed North Carolina's lead, the resultant inability to display the Washington grades could force the Washington growers to abandon the State's expensive inspection and grading system which their customers had come to know and rely on over the 60-odd years of its existence. . . .

(4)

We turn finally to the appellants' claim that the District Court erred in holding that the North Carolina statute violated the Commerce Clause . . . . [T]hey maintain that any such burdens on the interstate sale of Washington apples were far outweighed by the local benefits flowing from what they contend was a valid exercise of North Carolina's inherent police powers designed to protect its citizenry from fraud and deception in the marketing of apples. . . .

The North Carolina statute, appellants claim, was enacted to eliminate . . . deception and confusion by replacing the numerous state grades with a single uniform standard. Moreover, it is contended that North Carolina sought to accomplish this goal of uniformity in an evenhanded manner as evidenced by the fact that its statute applies to all apples sold in closed containers in the State without regard to their point of origin. . . .

[N]ot every exercise of state authority imposing some burden on the free flow of commerce is invalid. By the same token, however, a finding that state legislation furthers matters of legitimate local concern, even in the health and consumer protection areas, does not end the inquiry. . . . Rather, when such state legislation comes into conflict with the Commerce Clause's overriding requirement of a national "common market," we are confronted with the task of effecting an accommodation of the competing national and local interests. . . .

As the District Court correctly found, the challenged statute has the practical effect of not only burdening interstate sales of Washington apples, but also discriminating against them. This discrimination takes various forms. The first, and most obvious, is the statute's consequence of raising the costs of doing business in the North Carolina market for Washington apple growers and dealers, while leaving those of their North Carolina counterparts unaffected. . . . Second, the statute has the effect of stripping away from the Washington apple industry the competitive and economic advantages it has earned for itself through its expensive inspection and grading system. . . . Third, by prohibiting Washington growers and dealers from marketing apples under their State's grades, the statute has a leveling effect which insidiously operates to the advantage of local apple producers. As noted earlier, the Washington State grades are equal or superior to the USDA grades in all corresponding categories. . . . Such "downgrading" offers the North Carolina apple industry the very sort of protection against competing out-of-state products that the Commerce Clause was designed to prohibit. At worst, it will have the effect of an embargo against those Washington apples in the superior grades as Washington dealers withhold them from the North Carolina market. At best, it will deprive Washington sellers of the market premium that such apples would otherwise command.

Despite the statute's facial neutrality, the Commission suggests that its discriminatory impact on interstate commerce was not an unintended byproduct and there are some indications in the record to that effect. The most glaring is the response of the North Carolina Agriculture Commissioner to the Commission's request for an exemption following the statue's passage in which he indicated that before he could support such an exemption, he would "want to have the sentiment from our apple producers since they were mainly responsible for this legislation being passed. . . ." Moreover, we find it somewhat suspect that North Carolina singled out only closed containers of apples, the very means by which apples are transported in commerce, to effectuate the statute's ostensible consumer protection purpose when apples are not generally sold at retail in their shipping containers. However, we need not ascribe an economic protection motive to the North Carolina Legislature to resolve this case; we conclude that the challenged statute cannot stand insofar as it prohibits the display of

Washington State grades even if enacted for the declared purpose of protecting consumers from deception and fraud in the marketplace.

When discrimination against commerce of the type we have found is demonstrated, the burden falls on the State to justify it both in terms of the local benefits flowing from the statute and the unavailability of nondiscriminatory alternatives adequate to preserve the local interests at stake. . . .

The several States unquestionably possess a substantial interest in protecting their citizens from confusion and deception in the marketing of foodstuffs, but the challenged statute does remarkably little to further that laudable goal at least with respect to Washington apples and grades. The statute, as already noted, permits the marketing of closed containers of apples under no grades at all. Such a result can hardly be thought to eliminate the problems of deception and confusion created by the multiplicity of differing state grades; indeed, it magnifies them by depriving purchasers of all information concerning the quality of the contents of closed apple containers. Moreover, although the statute is ostensibly a consumer protection measure, it directs its primary efforts, not at the consuming public at large, but at apple wholesalers and brokers who are the principal purchasers of closed containers of apples. And those individuals are presumably the most knowledgeable individuals in this area. Since the statute does nothing at all to purify the flow of information at the retail level, it does little to protect consumers against the problems it was designed to eliminate. Finally, we note that any potential for confusion and deception created by the Washington grades was not of the type that led to the statute's enactment. Since Washington grades are in all cases equal or superior to their USDA counterparts, they could only "deceive" or "confuse" a consumer to his benefit, hardly a harmful result.

In addition, it appears that nondiscrimnatory alternatives to the outright ban of Washington State grades are readily available. For example, North Carolina could effectuate its goal by permitting out-of-state growers to utilize state grades only if they also marked their shipments with the applicable USDA label. In that case, the USDA grade would serve as a benchmark against which the consumer could evaluate the quality of the various state grades. If this alternative was for some reason inadequate to eradicate problems caused by state grades inferior to those adopted by the USDA, North Carolina might consider banning those state grades which, unlike Washington's could not be demonstrated to be equal or superior to the corresponding USDA categories. Concededly, even in this latter instance, some potential for "confusion" might persist. However, it is the type of "confusion" that the national interest in the free flow of goods between the States demands be tolerated. . . .

Affirmed.

EXXON, CORP. v. GOVERNOR OF MARYLAND
437 U.S. 117, 98 S. Ct. 2207, 57 L. Ed. 2d 91 (1978)

Mr. Justice Stevens delivered the opinion of the Court.

A Maryland statute provides that a producer or refiner of petroleum products (1) may not operate any retail service station within the State, and (2) must extend all "voluntary allowances" uniformly to all service stations it supplies. The questio[n] presented [is] whether the statute violates either the Commerce or the Due Process Clause of the Constitution of the United States.

I

The Maryland statute is an outgrowth of the 1973 shortage of petroleum. In response to complaints about inequitable distribution of gasoline among retail stations, [Maryland conducted a market survey which] indicated that gasoline stations operated by producers or refiners had received preferential treatment during the period of short supply. [The state adopted] legislation which, according to the Court of Appeals, was "designed to correct the inequities in the distribution and pricing of gasoline reflected by the survey." . . . Exxon Corp. filed a declaratory judgment action challenging the statute in [state] Circuit Court. . . .

The essential facts alleged in the complaint are not in dispute. All of the gasoline sold by Exxon in Maryland is transported into the State from refineries located elsewhere. Although Exxon sells the bulk of this gas to wholesalers and independent retailers, it also sells directly to the consuming public through 36 company-operated stations. Exxon uses these stations to test innovative marketing concepts or products. Focusing primarily on the Act's requirement that it discontinue its operation of these 36 retail stations, Exxon's complaint challenged the validity of the statute on both constitutional and federal statutory grounds. . . .

As brought out during the trial, the salient characteristics of the Maryland retail gasoline market are as follows: Approximately 3,800 retail service stations in Maryland sell over 20 different brands of gasoline. However, no petroleum products are produced or refined in Maryland, and the number of stations actually operated by a refiner or an affiliate is relatively small, representing about 5% of the total number of Maryland retailers. . . .

[After the Maryland Court of Appeals upheld the statute, Exxon appealed to the Supreme Court.] [Discussion of due process claim omitted.]

III

Appellants argue that the divestiture provisions of the Maryland statute violate the Commerce Clause in three ways: (1) by discriminating against interstate commerce; (2) by unduly burdening interstate commerce; and (3) by imposing controls on a commercial activity of such an essentially interstate character that it is not amenable to state regulation.

Plainly, the Maryland statute does not discriminate against interstate goods, nor does it favor local producers and refiners. Since Maryland's entire gasoline supply flows in interstate commerce and since there are no local producers or refiners, such claims of disparate treatment between interstate and local commerce would be meritless. Appellants, however, focus on the retail market arguing that the effect of the statute is to protect in-state independent dealers from out-of-state competition. They contend that the divestiture provisions "create a protected enclave for Maryland independent dealers. . . ." As support for this proposition, they rely on the fact that the burden of the divestiture requirements falls solely on interstate companies. But this fact does not lead, either logically or as a practical matter, to a conclusion that the State is discriminating against interstate commerce at the retail level.

As the record shows, there are several major interstate marketers of petroleum that own and operate their own retail gasoline stations. These interstate dealers, who compete directly with the Maryland independent dealers, are not affected by the Act because they do not refine or produce gasoline. In fact, the Act creates no barriers whatsoever against interstate independent dealers; it does not prohibit the flow of interstate goods, place added costs upon them, or distinguish between in-state and out-of-state companies in the retail market. The absence of any of these factors fully distinguishes this case from those in which a State has been found to have discriminated against interstate commerce. *See, e.g., Hunt v. Washington Apple Advertising Comm'n.,* . . . *Dean Milk Co. v. Madison.* . . . For instance, the Court in *Hunt* noted that the challenged state statute raised the cost of doing business for out-of-state dealers, and, in various other ways, favored the in-state dealer in the local market. . . . No comparable claim can be made here. While the refiners will no longer enjoy their same status in the Maryland market, in-state independent dealers will have no competitive advantage over out-of-state dealers. The fact that the burden of a state regulation falls on some interstate companies does not, by itself, establish a claim of discrimination against interstate commerce.

Appellants argue, however, that this fact does show that the Maryland statute impermissibly burdens interstate commerce. They point to evidence in the record which indicates that, because of the divestiture requirements, at least three refiners will stop selling in Maryland, and which also supports their claim that the elimination of company-operated stations will deprive the consumer of certain special services. Even if we assume the truth of both assertions, neither warrants a finding that the statute impermissibly burdens interstate commerce.

Some refiners may choose to withdraw entirely from the Maryland market, but there is no reason to assume that their share of the entire supply will not be promptly replaced by other interstate refiners. The source of the consumers' supply may switch from company-operated stations to independent dealers, but interstate commerce is not subjected to an impermissible burden simply because an otherwise valid regulation causes some business to shift from one interstate supplier to another.

The crux of appellants' claim is that, regardless of whether the State has interfered with the movement of goods in interstate commerce, it has interfered "with the natural functioning of the interstate market either through prohibition or through burdensome regulation." . . . We cannot, however, accept appellants' underlying notion that the Commerce Clause protects the particular structure or methods of operation in a retail market. . . . [T]he Clause protects the interstate market, not particular interstate firms, from prohibitive or burdensome regulations. It may be true that the consuming public will be injured by the loss of the high-volume, low-priced stations operated by the independent refiners, but again that argument relates to the wisdom of the statute, not to its burden on commerce.

The judgment is affirmed.

Mr. Justice Blackmun, concurring in part and dissenting in part.

. . . I dissent from Part III of the Court's opinion because it fails to condemn impermissible discrimination against interstate commerce in retail gasoline marketing. The divestiture provisions . . . preclude out-of-state competitors from retailing gasoline within Maryland. The effect is to protect in-state retail service station dealers from the competition of the out-of-state businesses. This protectionist discrimination is not justified by any legitimate state interest that cannot be vindicated by more evenhanded regulation. . . .

. . . [T]he unconstitutional discrimination in the Maryland statute [is] apparent. No facial inequality exists; [the statute] preclude[s] all refiners and producers from marketing gasoline at the retail level. But given the structure of the retail gasoline market in Maryland, the effect . . . is to exclude a class of predominantly out-of-state gasoline retailers while providing protection from competition to a class of nonintegrated retailers that is overwhelmingly composed of local businessmen. . . . Similar hardship is not imposed upon the local service station dealers by the divestiture provisions. Indeed, rather than restricting their ability to compete, the Maryland Act effectively and perhaps intentionally improves their competitive position by insulating them from competition by out-of-state integrated producers and refiners. . . .

With discrimination proved against interstate commerce, the burden falls upon the State to justify the distinction with legitimate state interests that cannot be vindicated with more evenhanded regulation. On the record before the Court, the State fails to carry its burden. . . .

NOTES

(1) *Hunt* and *Exxon* were decided by the same Court within less than a year of one another. Why does the Court strike down the facially neutral statute in *Hunt* yet uphold the facially neutral measure in *Exxon*? Justice Blackmun thought the Court inconsistent but his colleagues disagreed. Does the Court subject each statute to the same strict scrutiny standard of review to which it subjects discriminatory legislation?

(2) If the Court applied a different level of scrutiny in the two cases, the better question becomes why did it do so? After all, the level of scrutiny the Court applies in dormant Commerce Clause cases become crucial, almost outcome-determinative. *Maine v. Taylor* aside, state statutes usually fail strict scrutiny. Was it because Maryland could offer a plausible rationale for its statute eliminating the long gas lines whereas North Carolina could not? Was it because Maryland's statute harmed all vertically integrated oil companies where North Carolina's burdened only Washington apple producers? Was it because all of those hurt by North Carolina's statute were located in Washington? Would that fact implicate Justice Cardozo's political rationale for the domestic commerce clause, the "sink or swim together" rationale?

(3) Holding a state statute unconstitutional simply because it hurt an out-of-state interest would be problematic since many state statutes may harm some outsider; Justice Blackmun did not suggest to the contrary. He wrote, however, that "when the burden is significant, when it falls on the most numerous and effective group of out-of-state competitors, when a similar burden does not fall on the class of protected in-state businessmen, and when the State cannot justify the resulting disparity by showing that its legislative interests cannot be vindicated by more evenhanded regulation, unconstitutional discrimination exists." *Exxon*, 437 U.S. at 148.

(4) In *Pike v. Bruce Church, Inc.*, 397 U.S. 137 (1970), the Court articulated a balancing test.

> Where the statute regulates even-handedly to effectuate a legitimate local public interest, and its effects on interstate commerce are only incidental, it will be upheld unless the burden imposed on such commerce is clearly excessive in relation to the putative local benefits. . . . If a legitimate local purpose is found, then the question becomes one of degree. And the extent of the burden that will be tolerated will of course depend on the nature of the local interest involved, and on whether it could be promoted as well with a lesser impact on interstate activities.

(5) In *Pike*, Bruce Church Co. grew cantaloupes at its Arizona facility but performed its processing and packing operations at its nearby Blythe, California site. In 1968, Pike, the responsible Arizona official, pursuant to an Arizona statute requiring Arizona cantaloupes be packed in an approved manner in closed standard containers, prohibited Bruce Church from moving its cantaloupes unpacked to Blythe. The order jeopardized Bruce Church's crop worth about $700,000. Accordingly, Bruce Church sought, and received, an injunction against the order.

The Court distinguished cases where a state had regulated "to protect and enhance the reputation of growers within the State." *Id.* at 143. But Bruce Church's high quality cantaloupes posed no peril to the reputation of Arizona cantaloupes. On the contrary, Pike's order "would forbid [Bruce Church] to pack its cantaloupes outside Arizona, not for the purpose of keeping the reputation of [Arizona's] growers unsullied, but to enhance their reputation through the reflected good will of [Bruce Church's] superior produce." *Id.* at 144. Arizona's interest was outweighed by the burden on commerce as measured by the unneeded expense to which its order would subject Bruce Church.

(6) *Minnesota v. Clover Leaf Creamery Co.*, 449 U.S. 456 (1981). Three years after it decided *Exxon*, the Court upheld under the Dormant Commerce Clause a Minnesota statute banning retail sale of milk in plastic nonreturnable, nonrefillable containers, but allowing such commerce in other nonreturnable, nonrefillable containers. Minnesota justified the statute as advancing environment objectives. Plaintiffs (and skeptics) suggested the measure was intended to protect Minnesota's pulpwood industry from competition from nonresident manufacturers of plastic containers.

The Court rejected any claim of protectionism or discrimination since the statute " 'regulate[d] evenhandedly' by prohibiting all milk retailers from selling their products in plastic, nonreturnable milk containers, without regard to whether the milk, the containers, or the sellers are from outside the state." *Id.* at 471-72. Accordingly, the Court assessed the statute under the forgiving *Pike* balancing test. The burden on interstate commerce was slight. Milk would continue to come into the state at slight inconvenience to dairies forced to conform to Minnesota's unique requirements. Minnesota businesses would "shift from manufacturers of plastic nonreturnable containers to producers of paperboard cartons, refillable bottles and plastic pouches, but there is no reason to suspect" the gains would go to Minnesota firms and the losses to out-of-staters. *Id.* at 472-73. The Court thought plaintiffs exaggerated the burden on out-of-state interests since out-of-state plastic could still be used in some types of milk containers and out-of-state pulpwood could provide some containers. To the extent out-of-state plastic was burdened, the hardship was not "clearly excessive" given the benefits. Any alternative approach would be more burdensome or less effective.

The Court may have taken comfort in the fact that the plaintiffs included several Minnesota firms the statute harmed. "The existence of major in-state interests adversely affected by the Act is a powerful safeguard against legislative abuse," wrote Justice Brennan for the majority. *Id.* at 473 n.17. Presumably, in-staters who are harmed will represent the political interests of out-state losers.

How much stock should the Court put on this concept of surrogate representation? Are there any hard and fast rules which the Court might apply to this issue? Could a state legislature insulate a state statute from attack by making sure it hurt some in-state interest? Should some weight be given to how many in-state losers there are and how much political power they have (obviously not enough clout, or will, to defeat the measure)? In some instances, the Court has not been swayed by the fact that some in-staters suffered. *See, e.g., Dean Milk, Fort Gratiot, C&A Carbone*.

(7) *West Lynn Creamery, Inc. v. Healy*, 512 U.S. 186 (1994). Massachusetts assessed a monthly premium on all fluid milk dealers sold to Massachusetts retailers. Out-of-staters produced two-thirds of the milk. Massachusetts distributed the revenue generated to its dairy farmers. West Lynn Creamery, a Massachusetts dealer who purchased almost all of its milk outside the state, claimed the pricing order discriminated against commerce. The Court struck down the order, 7-2.

The majority opinion, which Justice Stevens wrote for himself and Justices O'Connor, Kennedy, Souter, and Ginsburg, likened the Massachusetts law to the "paradigmatic example of a law discriminating against interstate commerce," a "protective tariff or customs duty" on imports from other states in order to give interstaters a competitive advantage. *Id.* at 193. The "avowed purpose and . . . undisputed effect" of the Massachusetts pricing order was to promote Massachusetts dairy farmers. Although they, like their out-of-state competitors, paid the premium, they received a subsidy from the state since the fund from the assessments was distributed to them, more than reimbursing them for their share of the tax. Since Massachusetts dairy farmers, in effect, received a rebate of their assessment plus a share from the out-of-state moneys they could sell at more competitive prices than their out-of-state rivals. *Id.* at 194-96.

The majority rejected the argument the responsible state official made that since each component of the program — a discriminatory tax and a subsidy — was legal the entire program had to be valid. Although the Court stopped short of endorsing all subsidies, it suggested that two rights may make a wrong. Since Massachusetts funded the subsidy primarily from out-of-state sources, the pricing order burdened commerce.

Moreover, the subsidy eroded the political check that would otherwise exist. "Nondiscriminatory measures, like the evenhanded tax at issue here, are generally upheld, in spite of any adverse effects on interstate commerce, in part because '[t]he existence of major in-state interests adversely affected . . . is a powerful safeguard against legislative abuse.'

"However, when a nondiscriminatory tax is coupled with a subsidy to one of the groups hurt by the tax, a State's political processes can no longer be relied upon to prevent legislative abuse, because one of the in-state interests which would otherwise lobby against the tax has been molllified by the subsidy." *Id.* at 200.

The Court invoked both Justice Cardozo's "sink or swim" political vision and Justice Jackson's national free market economic vision.

Justice Scalia and Thomas concurred in the judgment but not in the majority's opinion which they deemed too expansive. They regarded the Dormant Commerce Clause unsupported by the Constitutional text or "historical record." Still, based on *stare decisis* grounds (i.e., the "vast numbers" of laws "engendering considerable reliance interests") they would "enforce a self-executing 'negative' Commerce Clause in two situations: (1) against a state law that facially discriminates against interstate commerce, and (2) against a state law that is indistinguishable from a type of law previously held unconstitutional by this Court." The statute was discriminatory and was like laws previously invalidated. *Id.* at 209-10.

Chief Justice Rehnquist and Justice Blackmun dissented, stating that Massachusetts could seek to help a local industry, and holding the subsidy constitutional.

More recently, in *United Haulers Ass'n, Inc. v. Oneida-Herkimer Solid Waste Management Authority*, 127 S. Ct. 1786 (2007). Justice Thomas abandoned his prior recognition of a limited Dormant Commerce Clause which he had based on stare decisis grounds. Justice Thomas opined that "application of the negative Commerce Clause turns solely on policy considerations, not on the Constitution." *Id.* at 1799. The Supreme Court "has no policy role in regulating interstate commerce" and accordingly its negative Commerce Clause jurisprudence should be discarded. *Id.*

[4]   Market Participant Exception

REEVES, INC. v. STAKE
447 U.S. 429, 100 S. Ct. 2271, 65 L. Ed. 2d 244 (1980)

Justice Blackmun delivered the opinion of the Court.

The issue in this case is whether, consistent with the Commerce Clause, U.S. Const., Art. I, § 8, cl. 3, the State of South Dakota, in a time of shortage, may confine the sale of the cement it produces solely to its residents.

I

In 1919, South Dakota undertook plans to build a cement plant. . . . The plant, however, located at Rapid City, soon produced more cement than South Dakotans could use. Over the years, buyers in no less than nine nearby States purchased cement from the State's plant. . . .

The plant's list of out-of-state cement buyers included petitioner Reeves, Inc. Reeves is a ready-mix concrete distributor organized under Wyoming law and with facilities in Buffalo, Gillette, and Sheridan, Wyo. From the beginning of its operations in 1958, and until 1978, Reeves purchased about 95% of its cement from the South Dakota plant. . . .

As the 1978 construction season approached, difficulties at the plant slowed production. Meanwhile, a booming construction industry spurred demand for cement both regionally and nationally. The plant found itself unable to meet all orders. Faced with the same type of "serious cement shortage" that inspired the plant's construction, the Commission "reaffirmed its policy of supplying all South Dakota customers first and to honor all contract commitments, with the remaining volume allocated on a first come, first served basis."

Reeves, which had no pre-existing long-term supply contract, was hit hard and quickly by this development. On June 30, 1978, the plant informed Reeves that it could not continue to fill Reeves' orders, and on July 5, it turned away a Reeves truck. Unable to find another supplier, Reeves was forced to cut production by 76% in mid-July.

On July 19, Reeves brought this suit against the Commission, challenging the plant's policy of preferring South Dakota buyers, and seeking injunctive relief. After conducting a hearing and receiving briefs and affidavits, the District Court found no substantial issue of material fact and permanently enjoined the Commission's practice. The court reasoned that South Dakota's "hoarding" was inimical to the national free market envisioned by the Commerce Clause.

The United States Court of Appeals for the Eighth Circuit reversed. It concluded that the State had "simply acted in a proprietary capacity," as permitted by *Hughes v. Alexandria Scrap Corp.*, 426 U.S. 794 (1976). . . . We granted Reeves' petition for certiorari to consider once again the impact of the Commerce Clause on state proprietary activity. . . .

II

A

Alexandria Scrap concerned a Maryland program designed to remove abandoned automobiles from the State's roadways and junkyards. To encourage recycling, a "bounty" was offered for every Maryland-titled junk car converted into scrap. Processors located both in and outside Maryland were eligible to collect these subsidies. The legislation, as initially enacted in 1969, required a processor seeking a bounty to present documentation evidencing ownership of the wrecked car. This requirement however, did not apply to "hulks," inoperable automobiles over eight years old. In 1974, the statute was amended to extend documentation requirements to hulks, which comprised a large majority of the junk cars being processed. Departing from prior practice, the new law imposed more exacting documentation requirements on out-of-state than in-state processors. By making it less remunerative for suppliers to transfer vehicles outside Maryland, the reform triggered a "precipitate decline in the number of bounty-eligible hulks supplied to appellee's [Virginia] plant from Maryland sources."

Indeed, "[t]he practical effect was substantially the same as if Maryland had withdrawn altogether the availability of bounties on hulks delivered by unlicensed suppliers to licensed non-Maryland processors.". . . Invoking the Commerce Clause, a three-judge District Court struck down the legislation. . . .

This Court reversed. It recognized the persuasiveness of the lower court's analysis if the inherent restrictions of the Commerce Clause were deemed applicable. In the Court's view, however, *Alexandria Scrap* did not involve "the kind of action with which the Commerce Clause is concerned." Unlike prior cases voiding state laws inhibiting interstate trade, "Maryland has not sought to prohibit the flow of hulks, or to regulate the conditions under which it may occur. Instead, it has entered into the market itself to bid up their price,". . . "as a purchaser, in effect, of a potential article of interstate commerce," and has restricted "its trade to its own citizens or businesses within the State."

Having characterized Maryland as a market participant, rather than as a market regulator, the Court found no reason to "believe the Commerce Clause was intended to require independent justification for [the State's] action." The Court couched its holding in unmistakably broad terms. "Nothing in the purposes animating the Commerce Clause prohibits a State, in the absence of congressional action, from participating in the market and exercising the right to favor its own citizens over others."

B

The basic distinction drawn in *Alexandria Scrap* between States as market participants and States as market regulators makes good sense and sound law. As that case explains, the Commerce Clause responds principally to state taxes and regulatory measures impeding free private trade in the national marketplace. . . .

Restraint in this area is also counseled by considerations of state sovereignty, the role of each State "as the guardian and trustee for its people," . . . and "the long recognized right of trader or manufacturer, engaged in an entirely private business, freely to exercise his own independent discretion as to parties with whom he will deal.". . . Moreover, state proprietary activities may be, and often are, burdened with the same restrictions imposed on private market participants. Evenhandedness suggests that, when acting as proprietors, States should similarly share existing freedoms from federal constraints, including the inherent limits of the Commerce Clause. . . . Finally, as this case illustrates, the competing considerations in cases involving state proprietary action often will be subtle, complex, politically charged, and difficult to assess under traditional Commerce Clause analysis. Given these factors, *Alexandria Scrap* wisely recognizes that, as a rule, the adjustment of interests in this context is a task better suited for Congress than this Court.

III

South Dakota, as a seller of cement, unquestionably fits the "market participant" label more comfortably than a State acting to subsidize local scrap processors. Thus, the general rule of *Alexandria Scrap* plainly applies here. . . .

[P]etitioner protests that South Dakota's preference for its residents responds solely to the "non-governmental objectiv[e]" of protectionism. Therefore, petitioner argues, the policy is per se invalid. . . .

We find the label "protectionism" of little help in this context. The State's refusal to sell to buyers other than South Dakotans is "protectionist" only in the sense that it limits benefits generated by a state program to those who fund the state treasury and whom the State was created to serve. Petitioner's argument apparently also would characterize as "protectionist" rules restricting to state residents the enjoyment of state educational institutions, energy generated by a state-run plant, police and fire protection, and agricultural improvement and business development programs. Such policies, while perhaps "protectionist" in a loose sense, reflect the essential and patently unobjectionable purpose of state government to serve the citizens of the State.

Second, petitioner echoes the District Court's warning:

> If a state in this union, were allowed to hoard its commodities or resources for the use of their own residents only, a drastic situation might evolve. For example, Pennsylvania or Wyoming might keep their coal, the northwest its timber, and the mining states their minerals. The result being that embargo may be retaliated by embargo and commerce would be halted at state lines. . . .

This argument, although rooted in the core purpose of the Commerce Clause, does not fit the present facts. Cement is not a natural resource, like coal, timber, wild game, or minerals. . . . It is the end product of a complex process whereby a costly physical plant and human labor act on raw materials. South Dakota has not sought to limit access to the State's limestone or other materials used to make cement. Nor has it restricted the ability of private firms or sister States to set up plants within its borders. Moreover, petitioner has not suggested that South Dakota possesses unique access to the materials needed to produce cement. Whatever limits might exist on a State's ability to invoke the *Alexandria Scrap* exemption to hoard resources which by happenstance are found there, those limits do not apply here.

We conclude, then, that the arguments for invalidating South Dakota's resident-preference program are weak at best. Whatever residual force inheres in them is more than offset by countervailing considerations of policy and fairness. Reversal would discourage similar state projects, even though this project demonstrably has served the needs of state residents and has helped the entire region for more than a half century. Reversal also would rob South Dakota of the intended benefit of its foresight, risk, and industry. Under these circumstances, there is no reason to depart from the general rule of *Alexandria Scrap*.

The judgment of the United States Court of Appeals is affirmed.

[Justice Powell, joined by Justices Brennan, White and Stevens, dissented.]

NOTES

(1) Why is the South Dakota policy not an invalid discrimination against interstate commerce? Should Commerce Clause restrictions not apply when the state participates in, rather than regulates, the market? Will this exclude a growing area of commerce in an era of increasing state entry into the commercial arena? Or is there a fundamental difference between the state as regulator and the state as buyer or seller of goods?

(2) *Reeves* and *Alexandria Scrap* were followed by *White v. Massachusetts Council of Construction Employers*, 460 U.S. 204 (1983), which upheld a requirement that all construction projects funded by city funds be performed by a work force at least half of whom were *bona fide* residents of the city.

(3) In *United Building and Construction Trades Council v. Mayor of Camden, N.J.*, 465 U.S. 208 (1984), the Court explained *White* as follows: "The Commerce Clause acts as an implied restraint upon state regulatory powers. Such powers must give way before the superior authority of Congress to legislate on (or leave unregulated) matters involving interstate commerce. When the State acts solely as a market participant, no conflict between state regulation and federal regulatory authority can arise." *Id.* at 220.

Thus, "the market regulator-market participant distinction" is the crucial one under the Commerce Clause.

(4) *South-Central Timber Development Inc. v. Wunnicke*, 467 U.S. 82 (1984). An Alaska law requiring that timber taken from state lands be processed within the state prior to export was invalidated. The market-participant doctrine allows a state to impose burdens on commerce within the market in which it is a participant, but allows it to go no further. The state may not attach restrictions on dispositions subsequent to the goods coming to vest in private hands. At that stage the state is no longer a market participant, but a market regulator. "In my view," Justice Rehnquist, dissenting, declared, "the line of distinction drawn . . . between the State as market participant and the State as market regulator is both artificial and unconvincing." *Id*. at 101-02. Do you agree?

(5) In *Camps Newfound/Owatonna, Inc. v. Town of Harrison, Maine*, 520 U.S. 564 (1997), the Court rejected the Town's argument that its real estate tax exemption was protected from invalidation because the State was acting within its proprietary capacity as a market participant. Maine limited tax exemptions of charities, like camps, which did not principally service Maine residents. The Court explained that "[a] tax exemption is not the sort of direct state involvement in the market that falls within the market-participation doctrine." *Id*. at 593. Unlike the Court's other decisions granting market participant status, which the Court said involved "discrete activity" within a "narrow scope," Maine's exemption "which sweeps to cover broad swathes of the nonprofit sector . . . must be viewed as action taken in the State's sovereign capacity rather than a proprietary decision to make an entry into all of the markets in which the exempted charities function." The Court concluded that the suggested expansion of the market participant exception "would swallow the rule against discriminatory tax schemes." *Id*. at 594.

(6) In *West Lynn Creamery, Inc. v. Healy*, 512 U.S. 186 (1997), the Court observed that "We have never squarely confronted the constitutionality of subsidies, and we need not do so now. We have, however, noted that '[d]irect subsidization of domestic industry does not ordinarily run afoul' of the negative Commerce Clause." *Id*. at 199 n.15. In *Camps Newfound/Owatonna, Inc.*, the Court again avoided discussing the constitutionality of subsidies generally and concluded that even if a direct subsidy of charities oriented locally were constitutional, precedent did not support the same conclusion regarding a tax exemption.

(7) In his dissent in *Camps Newfound/Owatonna, Inc.*, Justice Scalia (joined by Chief Justice Rehnquist and Justices Thomas and Ginsburg) advocated creating a "domestic charities exception" as another exception to the dormant Commerce Clause. "The 'subsidy' and 'market participant' exceptions do not exhaust the realm of state actions that we should abstain from scrutinizing under the Commerce Clause." *Camps Newfound/Owatonna, Inc.*, 520 U.S. at 607. Rather, Justice Scalia suggested, a state, without raising dormant Commerce Clause concerns, may provide "forms of social welfare" to its residents directly, or through means such as the tax exemption at issue, to organizations that relieve the state of carrying out its own duties. The tax exemption at issue, according to Justice Scalia and the other dissenters, is outside the realm of economic protectionism and should therefore be beyond scrutiny.

[5] Congressional Action

NOTES

(1) The cases in this chapter up to now dealt with state power to regulate commerce where Congress has been silent so there were no federal laws on the subject. When Congress does speak with regard to a particular subject of regulation, three basic situations arise:

(a) Congressional conflict: Congress speaks in a manner which conflicts with state regulation;

(b) Congressional consent: Congress speaks in support of state regulation;

(c) Congressional preemption: Congress speaks so as to silence the states.

Congress may preempt state legislation expressly or by implication. In either case, the touchstone is congressional intent. Courts sometimes distinguish between conflict preemption (where compliance with both federal and state law is impossible) and field preemption (where a pervasive federal scheme suggests its exclusivity).

In *Ray v. Atlantic Richfield Co.*, 435 U.S. 151 (1978) the Court articulated basic preemption principles in a case considering whether Washington's Tanker Law conflicted with federal legislation. Justice White wrote for the Court:

The Court's prior cases indicate that when a State's exercise of its police power is challenged under the Supremacy Clause, "we start with the assumption that the historic police powers of the States were not to be superseded by the Federal Act unless that was the clear and manifest purpose of Congress." . . . Under the relevant cases, one of the legitimate inquiries is whether Congress has either explicitly or implicitly declared that the States are prohibited from regulating the various aspects of oil-tanker operations and design with which the Tanker Law is concerned. . . .

Even if Congress has not completely foreclosed state legislation in a particular area, a state statute is void to the extent that it actually conflicts with a valid federal statute. A conflict will be found "where compliance with both federal and state regulations is a physical impossibility. . . . " or where the state "law stands as an obstacle to the accomplishment and execution of the full purposes and objectives of Congress."

The Court proceeded to find that some features of the Tanker Law were in direct conflict with federal law, others were preempted by "the evident congressional intent to establish a uniform federal regime," while others were compatible with the federal rules.

(2) *Congressional Conflict.* Since *Gibbons v. Ogden, supra* § 2.02, a congressional regulation within the commerce power nullifies any inconsistent local one. The only questions are 1) whether the federal regulation is within the commerce power, and 2) whether the two measures conflict. If so, the local regulation must fail.

(3) *Congressional Consent.* Can Congress authorize state action that would otherwise be invalid under the Commerce Clause? In *Cooley,* the Court suggested that Congress could not consent to the states regulating commerce to the extent the Constitution forbade it.

Later cases have allowed Congress to authorize state action that would otherwise be held invalid under the Commerce Clause. In *Leisy v. Hardin,* 135 U.S. 100, 125 (1890), the Court declared states may not exclude sale of interstate liquor in the original package "in the absence of Congressional permission." Congress took advantage of the dictum by enacting legislation to permit state prohibition laws to apply to sales of imported liquors still in their original packages "to the same extent as though such . . . liquors had been produced in such state." *See Wilkerson v. Rahrer*, 140 U.S. 545, 549 (1891) (upholding legislation).

(4) But what of the logical objection raised in *Cooley* against a power of Congress to permit the states to exercise powers forbidden them by the Constitution? "If the commerce clause itself forbids state action 'by its own force,' how is it that Congress by expressly consenting can give that action validity?" WILEY RUTLEDGE, A DECLARATION OF LEGAL FAITH 64 (1947).

(5) The Supreme Court confronted this question in *Prudential Insurance Co. v. Benjamin*, 328 U.S. 408 (1946). In *United States v. South-Eastern Underwriters Ass'n*, 322 U.S. 533 (1944), the Court held that insurance was commerce subject to federal regulatory power. Thereafter, Congress enacted legislation subjecting insurance to state regulatory laws. This law was challenged by Prudential Insurance on the ground that Congress could not extend state power to regulate commerce. Rejecting the challenge, the Court stated in *Prudential*: "[W]henever Congress' judgment has been uttered affirmatively to contradict the Court's previously expressed view that specific action taken by the states in Congress' silence was forbidden by the commerce clause, this body has accommodated its previous judgment to Congress' expressed approval." *Prudential*, 328 U.S. at 425.

As the Court has more recently put it, "While the Commerce Clause has been understood to limit the States' ability to discriminate against interstate commerce . . . that limit may be lifted . . . by an expression of the 'unambiguous intent' of Congress. . . . Whether or not the States would be permitted to burden the interstate transport of low-level radioactive waste in the absence of Congress' approval, the States can clearly do so with Congress' approval." *New York v. United States*, 505 U.S. 144, 171 (1992). *See also Northeast Bancorp, Inc. v. Board of Governors*, 472 U.S. 159, 174 (1985) ("[w]hen Congress so chooses, state actions which it plainly authorizes are invulnerable to constitutional attack under the Commerce Clause").

But see *Metropolitan Life Insurance Co. v. Ward*, 470 U.S. 869 (1985), where the Court held that an Alabama law which imposed a substantially lower gross premiums tax rate on domestic insurance companies than on out-of-state insurance companies violated the equal protection guaranty. The law was not saved by the federal statute which subjected insurance to state regulatory laws. "Although the [Congressional] Act exempts the insurance industry from Commerce Clause restrictions, it does not purport to limit in any way the applicability of the Equal Protection Clause." *Id.* at 880.

(6) *Congressional Preemption.*

The ways in which federal law may pre-empt state law are well established and in the first instance turn on congressional intent. . . . Congress' intent to supplant state authority in a particular field may be expressed in the terms of the statute. . . . Absent explicit pre-emptive language, Congress' intent to supersede state law in a given area may nonetheless be implicit if a scheme of federal regulation is "so pervasive as to make reasonable the inference that Congress left no room for the States to supplement it," if "the Act of Congress . . . touch[es] a field in which the federal interest is so dominant that the federal system will be assumed to preclude enforcement of state laws on the same subject," or if the goals "sought to be obtained" and the "obligations imposed" reveal a purpose to preclude state authority.

Wisconsin Public Intervenor v. Mortier, 501 U.S. 597, 604-05 (1991).

Where Congress acts with its intent to occupy the entire field of regulation, its action bars any state regulation in that field, even if the particular state rule is not covered by any federal regulation.

(7) In *Crosby v. National Foreign Trade Council*, 530 U.S. 363 (2000), the Court held that federal legislation preempted a Massachusetts law regulating state contracts with Burma. The state Burma law was invalid as an obstacle to accomplishment of Congress' objectives as expressed in the federal legislation. Congress had conferred extensive discretion on the President which would be compromised by enforcing state regulations. Congress' failure to provide explicitly for preemption was irrelevant. The Court reasoned that Congress may have relied upon the Court's willingness to apply implied preemption doctrine.

§ 4.07 PRIVILEGES AND IMMUNITIES

SUPREME COURT OF VIRGINIA v. FRIEDMAN
487 U.S. 59, 108 S. Ct. 2260, 101 L. Ed. 2d 56 (1988)

JUSTICE KENNEDY delivered the opinion of the Court.

Qualified lawyers admitted to practice in other States may be admitted to the Virginia bar "on motion," that is, without taking the bar examination which Virginia otherwise requires. The State conditions such admission on a showing, among other matters, that the applicant is a permanent resident of Virginia. The question for decision is whether this residency requirement violates the Privileges and Immunities Clause of the United States Constitution, Art. IV, § 2. We hold that it does.

Myrna E. Friedman was admitted to the Illinois bar by examination in 1977 and to the District of Columbia bar by reciprocity in 1980. From 1977 to 1981, she was employed by the Department of the Navy in Arlington, Virginia, as a civilian attorney, and from 1982 until 1986, she was an attorney in private practice in Washington, D.C. In January 1986, she became associate general counsel for ERC International, Inc., a Delaware corporation. Friedman practices and maintains her offices at the company's principal place of business in Vienna, Virginia. Her duties at ERC International include drafting contracts and advising her employer and its subsidiaries on matters of Virginia law.

From 1977 to early 1986, Friedman lived in Virginia. In February 1986, however, she married and moved to her husband's home in Cheverly, Maryland. In June 1986, Friedman applied for admission to the Virginia bar on motion.

The applicable rule, promulgated by the Supreme Court of Virginia pursuant to statute, is Rule 1A: 1. The Rule permits admission on motion of attorneys who are licensed to practice in another jurisdiction, provided the other jurisdiction admits Virginia attorneys without examination. The applicant must have been licensed for at least five years and the Virginia Supreme Court must determine that the applicant:

(a) Is a proper person to practice law.

(b) Has made such progress in the practice of law that it would be unreasonable to require him to take an examination.

(c) Has become a permanent resident of the commonwealth.

(d) Intends to practice full time as a member of the Virginia bar.

In a letter accompanying her application, Friedman alerted the Clerk of the Virginia Supreme Court to her change of residence, but argued that her application should nevertheless be granted. Friedman gave assurance that she would be engaged full-time in the practice of law in Virginia, that she would be available for service of process and court appearances, and that she would keep informed of local rules. She also asserted "that there appears to be no reason to discriminate against my petition as a nonresident for admission to the Bar on motion," that her circumstances fit within the purview of this Court's decision in *Supreme Court of New Hampshire v. Piper*, 470 U.S. 274 (1985), and that accordingly she was entitled to admission under the Privileges and Immunities Clause of the Constitution, Art. IV, § 2.

The Clerk wrote Friedman that her request had been denied. He explained that because Friedman was no longer a permanent resident of the Commonwealth of Virginia, she was not eligible for admission to the Virginia bar pursuant to Rule 1A:1. . . .

Friedman then commenced this action. . . . She alleged that the residency requirement of Rule 1A:1 violated the Privileges and Immunities Clause. . . .

II

Article IV, § 2, cl. 1, of the Constitution provides that the "Citizens of each State shall be entitled to all Privileges and Immunities of Citizens in the several States." The provision was designed "to place the citizens of each State upon the same footing with citizens of other States, so far as the advantages resulting from citizenship in those States are concerned.". . . The Clause "thus establishes a norm of comity without specifying the particular subjects as to which citizens of one State coming within the jurisdiction of another are guaranteed equality of treatment.". . .

While the Privileges and Immunities Clause cites the term "Citizens," for analytic purposes citizenship and residency are essentially interchangeable. . . . When examining claims that a citizenship or residency classification offends privileges and immunities protections, we undertake a two-step inquiry. First, the activity in question must be " 'sufficiently basic to the livelihood of the Nation' as to fall within the purview of the Privileges and Immunities Clause. . . ." For it is "[o]nly with respect to those 'privileges' and 'immunities' bearing on the vitality of the Nation as 'a single entity' that a State must accord residents and nonresidents equal treatment.". . . Second, if the challenged restriction deprives nonresidents of a protected privilege, we will invalidate it only if we conclude that the restriction is not closely related to the advancement of a substantial state interest. . . . Appellants assert that the residency requirement offends neither part of this test. We disagree.

A

Appellants concede, as they must, that our decision in *Piper* establishes that a nonresident who takes and passes an examination prescribed by the State, and who otherwise is qualified for the practice of law, has an interest in practicing law that is protected by the Privileges and Immunities Clause. Appellants contend, however, that the discretionary admission provided for by Rule 1A:1 is not a privilege protected by the Clause for two reasons. First, appellants argue that the bar examination "serves as an adequate, alternative means of gaining admission to the bar." In appellants' view, "[s]o long as any applicant may gain admission to a State's bar, without regard to residence, by passing the bar examination," the State cannot be said to have discriminated against nonresidents "as a matter of fundamental concern." Second, appellants argue that the right to admission on motion is not within the purview of the Clause because, without offense to the Constitution, the State could require all bar applicants to pass an examination. Neither argument is persuasive.

We cannot accept appellants' first theory because it is quite inconsistent with our precedents. We reaffirmed in *Piper* the well-settled principle that " 'one of the privileges which the Clause guarantees to citizens of State A is that of doing business in State B on terms of substantial equality with the citizens of that State.' " . . . After reviewing our precedents, we explicitly held that the practice of law, like other occupations considered in those cases, is sufficiently basic to the national economy to be deemed a privilege protected by the Clause. . . . The clear import of *Piper* is that the Clause is implicated whenever, as is the case here, a State does not permit qualified nonresidents to practice law within its borders on terms of substantial equality with its own residents.

Nothing in our precedents, moreover, supports the contention that the Privileges and Immunities Clause does not reach a State's discrimination against nonresidents when such discrimination does not result in their total exclusion from the State. . . .

Further, we find appellants' second theory — that Virginia could constitutionally require that all applicants to its bar take and pass an examination — quite irrelevant to the question whether the Clause is applicable in the circumstances of this case. A State's abstract authority to require from resident and nonresident alike that which it has chosen to demand from the nonresident alone has never been held to shield the discriminatory distinction from the reach of the Privileges and Immunities Clause. . . . The issue instead is whether the State has burdened the right to practice law, a privilege protected by the Privileges and Immunities Clause, by discriminating among otherwise equally qualified applicants solely on the basis of citizenship or residency. We conclude it has.

B

Our conclusion that the residence requirement burdens a privilege protected by the Privileges and Immunities Clause does not conclude the matter, of course; for we repeatedly have recognized that the Clause, like other constitutional provisions, is not an absolute. . . . The Clause does not preclude disparity in treatment where substantial reasons exist for the discrimination and the degree of discrimination bears a close relation to such reasons. . . . In deciding whether the degree of discrimination bears a sufficiently close relation to the reasons proffered by the State, the Court has considered whether, within the full panoply of legislative choices otherwise available to the State, there exist alternative means of furthering the State's purpose without implicating constitutional concerns. . . .

The question . . . is whether lawyers who are admitted in other States and seek admission in Virginia are less likely to respect the bar and further its interests solely because they are nonresidents. We cannot say that this is the case. . . . [W]e see no reason to assume that nonresident attorneys who, like Friedman, seek admission to the Virginia bar on motion will lack adequate incentives to remain abreast of changes in the law or to fulfill their civic duties. . . .

We also reject appellants' attempt to justify the residency restriction as a necessary aid to the enforcement of the full-time practice requirement of Rule 1A:1. Virginia already requires, pursuant to the full-time practice restriction of Rule 1A:1, that attorneys admitted on motion maintain an office for the practice of law in Virginia . . . . The office requirement furnishes an alternative to the residency requirement that is not only less restrictive, but also is fully adequate to protect whatever interest the State might have in the full-time practice restriction.

III

We hold that Virginia's residency requirement for admission to the State's bar without examination violates the Privileges and Immunities Clause. The nonresident's interest in practicing law on terms of substantial equality with those enjoyed by residents is a privilege protected by the Clause. A State may not discriminate against nonresidents unless it shows that such discrimination bears a close relation to the achievement of substantial State objectives. Virginia has failed to make this showing. Accordingly, the judgment of the Court of Appeals is affirmed.

[CHIEF JUSTICE REHNQUIST and JUSTICE SCALIA dissented.]

NOTES

(1) The Privileges and Immunities Clause appears in Article IV — the so-called States' Relations Article. The most important clause in that article is the Full Faith and Credit Clause, which has spawned a multitude of cases as its progeny. Full faith and credit cases are dealt with in the conflict of laws course and are not considered here. Article IV's Privileges and Immunities Clause, which is also relevant to the subject of interstate relationships, comes from the longer version in the Articles of Confederation — the only provision in the Articles protecting individual rights. Its purpose was not to create "privileges and immunities" of citizens in the states but "to declare to the several States, that whatever those rights, as you grant or establish them to your own citizens, or as you limit or qualify, or impose restrictions on their exercise, the same, neither more nor less, shall be the measure of the rights of citizens of other States within your jurisdiction." *Slaughterhouse Cases*, 83 U.S. (16 Wall) 36, 77 (1872). "The primary purpose of this clause, like the clauses between which it is located — those relating to full faith and credit and to interstate extradition of fugitives from justice — was to help fuse into one Nation a collection of independent, sovereign States. It was designed to insure to a citizen of State A who ventures into State B the same privileges which the citizens of State B enjoy." *Toomer v. Witsell*, 334 U.S. 385, 395 (1948).

(2) The Privileges and Immunities Clause overlaps with the dormant Commerce Clause in that both protect against state laws discriminating against out-of-staters. But the Privileges and Immunities Clause only protects individuals who are citizens of the United States. Whereas the dormant Commerce Clause also considers challenges to nondiscriminatory, but burdensome state legislation (i.e., the *Pike* test), the Privileges and Immunities Clause does not. Finally, the exceptions to the dormant Commerce Clause (e.g., market participant, congressional consent) do not apply. For a discussion of the relationship between the Article IV Privileges and Immunities Clause and the Dormant Commerce Clause, see Brannon P. Denning, *Why the Privileges and Immunities Clause of Article IV Cannot Replace the Dormant Commerce Clause Doctrine*, 88 MINN. L. REV. 384 (2003-04).

(3) *United Building and Construction Trades Council v. Mayor of Camden, N.J.*, 465 U.S. 208 (1984), invalidated a resident hiring preference law. An ordinance required at least 40% of the employees of contractors and subcontractors working on city construction contracts to be city residents. According to the Court, the Privileges and Immunities Clause applied to laws that discriminate on the basis of municipal residency as well as to laws that discriminate on the basis of state citizenship. The market participant exception, which had insulated a similar provision from challenge under the dormant Commerce Clause in *White v. Massachusetts Council of Construction Employers, Inc.*, 460 U.S. 204 (1983), did not apply.

The Court drew a distinction between challenges to such a law based upon the Commerce Clause and those based upon the Privileges and Immunities Clause. As shown by the *White* case, a city acting as a market participant does not violate the Commerce Clause by a resident-preference requirement on city construction contracts. But the discrimination against out-of-state residents may trigger the Privileges and Immunities Clause. The fact that the city is merely setting conditions for its expenditure for goods and services in the market place may make a difference to the validity of its action under the Commerce Clause. It does not preclude the possibility that those conditions may violate the Privileges and Immunities Clause.

(4) In *Saenz v. Roe*, 526 U.S. 489 (1999), the Court noted that the Privileges and Immunities Clause of Article IV provides some textual basis for the Constitutional right to travel to the extent it includes "the right [of an out-of-stater] to be treated as a welcome visitor rather than as an unfriendly alien when temporarily present" in another state.

Chapter V

THE PRESIDENCY AND SEPARATION OF POWERS

§ 5.01 INHERENT POWER

YOUNGSTOWN SHEET & TUBE CO. v. SAWYER
343 U.S. 579, 72 S. Ct. 863, 96 L. Ed. 1153 (1952)

Justice Black delivered the opinion of the Court.

We are asked to decide whether the President was acting within his constitutional power when he issued an order directing the Secretary of Commerce to take possession of and operate most of the Nation's steel mills. The mill owners argue that the President's order amounts to lawmaking, a legislative function which the Constitution has expressly confided to the Congress and not to the President. The Government's position is that the order was made on findings of the President that his action was necessary to avert a national catastrophe which would inevitably result from a stoppage of steel production, and that in meeting this grave emergency the President was acting within the aggregate of his constitutional powers as the Nation's Chief Executive and the Commander in Chief of the Armed Forces of the United States. The issue emerges here from the following series of events:

In the latter part of 1951, a dispute arose between the steel companies and their employees over terms and conditions that should be included in new collective bargaining agreements. Long-continued conferences failed to resolve the dispute. On December 18, 1951, the employees' representative, United Steelworkers of America, C.I.O., gave notice of an intention to strike when the existing bargaining agreements expired on December 31. The Federal Mediation and Conciliation Service then intervened in an effort to get labor and management to agree. This failing, the President on December 22, 1951, referred the dispute to the Federal Wage Stabilization Board to investigate and make recommendations for fair and equitable terms of settlement. This Board's report resulted in no settlement. On April 4, 1952, the Union gave notice of a nation-wide strike called to begin at 12:01 a.m. April 9. The indispensability of steel as a component of substantially all weapons and other war materials led the President to believe that the proposed work stoppage would immediately jeopardize our national defense and that governmental seizure of the steel mills was necessary in order to assure the continued availability of steel. Reciting these considerations for his action, the President, a few hours before the strike was to begin, . . . directed the Secretary of Commerce to take possession of most of the steel mills and keep them running. The Secretary immediately issued his own possessory orders, calling upon the presidents of the various seized companies to serve as operating managers for the United States. They were directed to carry on their activities in accordance with regulations and directions of the Secretary. The next morning the President sent a message to Congress reporting his action. . . . Congress has taken no action.

Obeying the Secretary's orders under protest, the companies brought proceedings against him in the District Court. Their complaints charged that the seizure was not authorized by an act of Congress or by any constitutional provisions. The District Court was asked to declare the orders of the President and the Secretary invalid and to issue preliminary and permanent injunctions restraining their enforcement. Opposing the motion for preliminary injunction, the United States asserted that a strike disrupting steel production for even a brief period would so endanger the wellbeing and safety of the Nation that the President had "inherent power" to do what he had done — power "supported by the Constitution, by historical precedent, and by court decisions." The Government also contended that in any event no preliminary injunction should be issued because the companies had made no showing that their available legal remedies were inadequate or that their injuries from seizure would be irreparable. Holding against the Government on all points, the District Court on April 30 issued a preliminary injunction restraining the Secretary from "continuing the seizure and possession of the plant . . . and from acting under the purported authority of Executive Order No. 10340." . . . On the same day the Court of Appeals stayed the District Court's injunction. Deeming it best that the issues raised be promptly decided by this Court, we granted certiorari on May 3 and set the cause for argument on May 12. . . .

The President's power, if any, to issue the order must stem either from an act of Congress or from the Constitution itself. There is no statute that expressly authorizes the President to take possession of property as he did here. Nor is there any act of Congress to which our attention has been directed from which such a power can fairly be implied. Indeed, we do not understand the Government to rely on statutory authorization for this seizure. . . .

Moreover, the use of the seizure technique to solve labor disputes in order to prevent work stoppages was not only unauthorized by any congressional enactment; prior to this controversy, Congress had refused to adopt that method of settling labor disputes. When the Taft-Hartley Act was under consideration in 1947, Congress rejected an amendment which would have authorized such governmental seizures in cases of emergency. Apparently it was thought that the technique of seizure, like that of compulsory arbitration, would interfere with the process of collective bargaining. Consequently, the plan Congress adopted in that Act did not provide for seizure under any circumstances. Instead, the plan sought to bring about settlements by use of the customary devices of mediation, conciliation, investigation by boards of inquiry, and public reports. In some instances temporary injunctions were authorized to provide cooling-off periods. All this failing, unions were left free to strike after a secret vote by employees as to whether they wished to accept their employer's final settlement offer.

It is clear that if the President had authority to issue the order he did, it must be found in some provisions of the Constitution. And it is not claimed that express constitutional language grants this power to the President. The contention is that presidential power should be implied from the aggregate of his powers under the Constitution. Particular reliance is placed on provisions in Article II which say that "the executive Power shall be vested in a President . . ."; that "he shall take Care that the Laws be faithfully executed"; and that he "shall be Commander in Chief. . . ."

The order cannot properly be sustained as an exercise of the President's military power as Commander in Chief of the Armed Forces. The Government attempts to do so by citing a number of cases upholding broad powers in military commanders engaged in day-to-day fighting in a theater of war. Such cases need not concern us here. Even though "theater of war" be an expanding concept, we cannot with faithfulness to our constitutional system hold that the Commander in Chief of the Armed Forces has the ultimate power as such to take possession of private property in order to keep labor disputes from stopping production. This is a job for the Nation's lawmakers, not for its military authorities.

Nor can the seizure order be sustained because of the several constitutional provisions that grant executive power to the President. In the framework of our Constitution, the President's power to see that the laws are faithfully executed refutes the idea that he is to be a lawmaker. The Constitution limits his functions in the lawmaking process to the recommending of laws he thinks wise and the vetoing of laws he thinks bad. And the Constitution is neither silent nor equivocal about who shall make laws which the President is to execute. The first section of the first article says that "All legislative Powers herein granted shall be vested in a Congress of the United States. . . ." After granting many powers to the Congress, Article I goes on to provide that Congress may "make all Laws which shall be necessary and proper for carrying into Execution the foregoing Powers and all other Powers vested by this Constitution in the Government of the United States, or in any Department or Officer thereof."

The President's order does not direct that a congressional policy be executed in a manner prescribed by Congress — it directs that a presidential policy be executed in a manner prescribed by the President. The preamble of the order itself, like that of many statutes, sets out reasons why the President believes certain policies should be adopted, proclaims these policies as rules of conduct to be followed, and again, like a statute, authorizes a government official to promulgate additional rules and regulations consistent with the policy proclaimed and needed to carry that policy into execution. The power of Congress to adopt such public policies as those proclaimed by the order is beyond question. It can authorize the taking of private property for public use. It can make laws regulating the relationships between employers and employees, prescribing rules designed to settle labor disputes, and fixing wages and working conditions in certain fields of our economy. The Constitution did not subject this law-making power of Congress to presidential or military supervision or control.

It is said that other Presidents without congressional authority have taken possession of private business enterprises in order to settle labor disputes. But even if this be true, Congress has not thereby lost its exclusive constitutional authority to make laws necessary and proper to carry out the powers vested by the Constitution "in the Government of the United States, or in any Department or Officer thereof."

The Founders of this Nation entrusted the law-making power to the Congress alone in both good and bad times. It would do no good to recall the historical events, the fears of power and the hopes for freedom that lay behind their choice. Such a review would but confirm our holding that this seizure order cannot stand.

The judgment of the District Court is affirmed.

Justice Frankfurter, concurring.

. . . The issue before us can be met, and therefore should be, without attempting to define the President's powers comprehensively. I shall not attempt to delineate what belongs to him by virtue of his office beyond the power even of Congress to contract; what authority belongs to him until Congress acts; what kind of problems may be dealt with either by the Congress or by the President or by both . . . what power must be exercised by the Congress and cannot be delegated to the President. . . . We must therefore put to one side consideration of what powers the President would have had if there had been no legislation whatever bearing on the authority asserted by the seizure, or if the seizure had been only for a short, explicitly temporary period, to be terminated automatically unless Congressional approval were given. . . .

In any event, nothing can be plainer than that Congress made a conscious choice of policy in a field full of perplexity and peculiarly within legislative responsibility for choice. In formulating legislation for dealing with industrial conflicts, Congress could not more clearly and emphatically have withheld authority than it did in 1947. Perhaps as much so as is true of any piece of modern legislation, Congress acted with full consciousness of what it was doing and in the light of much recent history. Previous seizure legislation had subjected the powers granted to the President to restrictions of varying degrees of stringency.

Instead of giving him even limited powers, Congress in 1947 deemed it wise to require the President, upon failure of attempts to reach a voluntary settlement, to report to Congress if he deemed the power of seizure a needed shot for his locker. The President could not ignore the specific limitations of prior seizure statutes. No more could he act in disregard of the limitation put upon seizure by the 1947 Act.

It cannot be contended that the President would have had power to issue this order had Congress explicitly negated such authority in formal legislation. Congress has expressed its will to withhold this power from the President as though it had said so in so many words. The authoritatively expressed purpose of Congress to disallow such power to the President and to require him, when in his mind the occasion arose for such a seizure, to put the matter to Congress and ask for specific authority from it could not be more decisive if it had been written into . . . the Labor Management Relations Act of 1947. . . .

By the Labor Management Relations Act of 1947, Congress said to the President, "You may not seize. Please report to us and ask for seizure power if you think it is needed in a specific situation." This of course calls for a report on the unsuccessful efforts to reach a voluntary settlement, as a basis for discharge by Congress of its responsibility — which it has unequivocally reserved — to fashion further remedies than it provided. . . .

To be sure, the content of the three authorities of government is not to be derived from an abstract analysis. The areas are partly interacting, not wholly disjointed. The Constitution is a framework for government. Therefore the way the framework has consistently operated fairly establishes that it has operated according to its true nature. Deeply embedded traditional ways of conducting government cannot supplant the Constitution or legislation, but they give meaning to the words of a text or supply them. It is an inadmissibly narrow conception of American constitutional law to confine it to the words of the Constitution and to disregard the gloss which life has written upon them. In short, a systematic, unbroken, executive practice, long pursued to the knowledge of the Congress and never before questioned, engaged in by Presidents who have also sworn to uphold the Constitution, making as it were such exercise of power part of the structure of our government, may be treated as a gloss on "executive Power" vested in the President by § 1 of Art. II. . . .

Down to the World War II period . . . the record is barren of instances comparable to the one before us. Of twelve seizures by President Roosevelt prior to the enactment of the War Labor Disputes Act in June, 1943, three were sanctioned by existing law, and six others were effected after Congress, on December 8, 1941, had declared the existence of a state of war. In this case, reliance on the powers that flow from declared war has been commendably disclaimed by the Solicitor General. Thus the list of executive assertions of the power of seizure in circumstances comparable to the present reduces to three in the six-month period from June to December of 1941. We need not split hairs in comparing those actions to the one before us, though much might be said by way of differentiation. Without passing on their validity, as we are not called upon to do, it suffices to say that these three isolated instances do not add up, either in number, scope, duration or contemporaneous legal justification, to the kind of executive construction of the Constitution revealed in the Midwest Oil case. Nor do they come to us sanctioned by long-continued acquiescence of Congress giving decisive weight to a construction by the Executive of its powers. . . .

JUSTICE DOUGLAS, concurring.

There can be no doubt that the emergency which caused the President to seize these steel plants was one that bore heavily on the country. But the emergency did not create power; it merely marked an occasion when power should be exercised. And the fact that it was necessary that measures be taken to keep steel in production does not mean that the President, rather than the Congress, had the constitutional authority to act. The Congress, as well as the President, is trustee of the national welfare. The President can act more quickly than the Congress. The President with the armed services at his disposal can move with force as well as with speed. All executive power — from the reign of ancient kings to the rule of modern dictators — has the outward appearance of efficiency.

Legislative power, by contrast, is slower to exercise. There must be delay while the ponderous machinery of committees, hearings, and debates is put into motion. That takes time; and while the Congress slowly moves into action, the emergency may take its toll in wages, consumer goods, war production, the standard of living of the people, and perhaps even lives. Legislative action may indeed often be cumbersome, time-consuming, and apparently inefficient. But as Mr. Justice Brandeis stated in his dissent in *Myers v. United States*, 272 U.S. 52, 293, 47 S. Ct. 21, 85, 71 L. Ed. 160:

> The doctrine of the separation of powers was adopted by the Convention of 1787 not to promote efficiency but to preclude the exercise of arbitrary power. The purpose was not to avoid friction, but, by means of the inevitable friction incident to the distribution of the governmental powers among three departments, to save the people from autocracy.

We therefore cannot decide this case by determining which branch of government can deal most expeditiously with the present crisis. The answer must depend on the allocation of powers under the Constitution. That in turn requires an analysis of the conditions giving rise to the seizure and of the seizure itself. . . .

The legislative nature of the action taken by the President seems to me to be clear. When the United States takes over an industrial plant to settle a labor controversy, it is condemning property. The seizure of the plant is a taking in the constitutional sense. . . .

But until and unless Congress acted, no condemnation would be lawful. The branch of government that has the power to pay compensation for a seizure is the only one able to authorize a seizure or make lawful one that the President had effected. That seems to me to be the necessary result of the condemnation provision in the Fifth Amendment. It squares with the theory of checks and balances expounded by . . . Justice Black in the opinion of the Court in which I join. . . .

We pay a price for our system of checks and balances, for the distribution of power among the three branches of government. It is a price that today may seem exorbitant to many. Today a kindly President uses the seizure power to effect a wage increase and to keep the steel furnaces in production. Yet tomorrow another President might use the same power to prevent a wage increase, to curb trade unionists, to regiment labor as oppressively as industry thinks it has been regimented by this seizure.

JUSTICE JACKSON, concurring in the judgment and opinion of the Court. . . .

A judge, like an executive adviser, may be surprised at the poverty of really useful and unambiguous authority applicable to concrete problems of executive power as they actually present themselves. Just what our forefathers did envision, or would have envisioned had they foreseen modern conditions, must be divined from materials almost as enigmatic as the dreams Joseph was called upon to interpret for Pharaoh. A century and a half of partisan debate and scholarly speculation yields no net result but only supplies more or less apt quotations from respected sources on each side of any question. They largely cancel each other. And court decisions are indecisive because of the judicial practice of dealing with the largest questions in the most narrow way.

The actual art of governing under our Constitution does not and cannot conform to judicial definitions of the power of any of its branches based on isolated clauses or even single Articles torn from context. While the Constitution diffuses power the better to secure liberty, it also contemplates that practice will integrate the dispersed powers into a workable government. It enjoins upon its branches separateness but interdependence, autonomy but reciprocity. Presidential powers are not fixed but fluctuate, depending upon their disjunction or conjunction with those of Congress. We may well begin by a somewhat over-simplified grouping of practical situations in which a President may doubt, or others may challenge, his powers, and by distinguishing roughly the legal consequences of this factor of relativity.

1. When the President acts pursuant to an express or implied authorization of Congress, his authority is at its maximum, for it includes all that he possesses in his own right plus all that Congress can delegate. In these circumstances, and in these only, may he be said (for what it may be worth), to personify the federal sovereignty. If his act is held unconstitutional under these circumstances, it usually means that the Federal Government as an undivided whole lacks power. A seizure executed by the President pursuant to an Act of Congress would be supported by the strongest of presumptions and the widest latitude of judicial interpretation, and the burden of persuasion would rest heavily upon any who might attack it.

2. When the President acts in absence of either a congressional grant or denial of authority he can only rely upon his own independent powers, but there is a zone of twilight in which he and Congress may have concurrent authority, or in which its distribution is uncertain. Therefore, congressional inertia, indifference or quiescence may sometimes, at least as a practical matter, enable, if not invite, measures on independent presidential responsibility. In this area, any actual test of power is likely to depend on the imperatives of events and contemporary imponderables rather than on abstract theories of law.

3. When the President takes measures incompatible with the expressed or implied will of Congress, his power is at its lowest ebb, for then he can rely only upon his own constitutional powers minus any constitutional powers of Congress over the matter. Courts can sustain exclusive Presidential control in such a case only by disabling the Congress from acting upon the subject. Presidential claim to a power at once so conclusive and preclusive must be scrutinized with caution, for what is at stake is the equilibrium established by our constitutional system.

Into which of these classifications does this executive seizure of the steel industry fit? It is eliminated from the first by admission, for it is conceded that no congressional authorization exists for this seizure. That takes away also the support of the many precedents and declarations which were made in relation, and must be confined, to this category.

Can it then be defended under flexible tests available to the second category? It seems clearly eliminated from that class because Congress has not left seizure of private property an open field but has covered it by . . . statutory policies inconsistent with this seizure. . . .

This leaves the current seizure to be justified only by the severe tests under the third grouping, where it can be supported only by any remainder of executive power after subtraction of such powers as Congress may have over the subject. In short, we can sustain the President only by holding that seizure of such strike-bound industries is within his domain and beyond control by Congress. Thus, this Court's first review of such seizures occurs under circumstances which leave Presidential power most vulnerable to attack and in the least favorable of possible constitutional postures.

I did not suppose, and I am not persuaded, that history leaves it open to question, at least in the courts, that the executive branch, like the Federal Government as a whole, possesses only delegated powers. The purpose of the Constitution was not only to grant power, but to keep it from getting out of hand. . . .

The Solicitor General seeks the power of seizure in three clauses of the Executive Article, the first reading, "The executive Power shall be vested in a President of the United States of America." Lest I be thought to exaggerate, I quote the interpretation which his brief puts upon it: "In our view, this clause constitutes a grant of all the executive powers of which the Government is capable." If that be true, it is difficult to see why the forefathers bothered to add several specific items, including some trifling ones. . . .

. . . I cannot accept the view that this clause is a grant in bulk of all conceivable executive power but regard it as an allocation to the presidential office of the generic powers thereafter stated.

The clause on which the Government next relies is that "The President shall be Commander in Chief of the Army and Navy of the United States. . . ." These cryptic words have given rise to some of the most persistent controversies in our constitutional history. Of course, they imply something more than an empty title. But just what authority goes with the name has plagued Presidential advisers who would not waive or narrow it by nonassertion yet cannot say where it begins or ends. It undoubtedly puts the Nation's armed forces under Presidential command. Hence, this loose appellation is sometimes advanced as support for any Presidential action, internal or external, involving use of force, the idea being that it vests power to do anything, anywhere, that can be done with an army or navy.

That seems to be the logic of an argument tendered at our bar — that the President having, on his own responsibility, sent American troops abroad derives from that act "affirmative power" to seize the means of producing a supply of steel for them. . . .

Nothing in our Constitution is plainer than that declaration of a war is entrusted only to Congress. Of course, a state of war may in fact exist without a formal declaration. But no doctrine that the Court could promulgate would seem to me more sinister and alarming than that a President whose conduct of foreign affairs is so largely uncontrolled, and often even is unknown, can vastly enlarge his mastery over the internal affairs of the country by his own commitment of the Nation's armed forces to some foreign venture. . . .

Assuming that we are in a war *de facto*, whether it is or is not a war *de jure*, does that empower the Commander-in-Chief to seize industries he thinks necessary to supply our army? The Constitution expressly places in Congress power "to raise and *support* Armies" and "to *provide* and *maintain* a Navy." (Emphasis supplied.) This certainly lays upon Congress primary responsibility for supplying the armed forces. Congress alone controls the raising of revenues and their appropriation and may determine in what manner and by what means they shall be spent for military and naval procurement. I suppose no one would doubt that Congress can take over war supply as a Government enterprise. On the other hand, if Congress sees fit to rely on free private enterprise collectively bargaining with free labor for support and maintenance of our armed forces can the Executive because of lawful disagreements incidental to that process, seize the facility for operation upon Government-imposed terms?

There are indications that the Constitution did not contemplate that the title Commander-in-Chief of the Army and Navy will constitute him also Commander-in-Chief of the country, its industries and its inhabitants. He has no monopoly of "war powers," whatever they are. While Congress cannot deprive the President of the command of the army and navy, only Congress can provide him an army or navy to command. It is also empowered to make rules for the "Government and Regulation of land and naval forces," by which it may to some unknown extent impinge upon even command functions. . . .

We should not use this occasion to circumscribe, much less to contract, the lawful role of the President as Commander-in-Chief. I should indulge the widest latitude of interpretation to sustain his exclusive function to command the instruments of national force, at least when turned against the outside world for the security of our society. But, when it is turned inward, not because of rebellion but because of a lawful economic struggle between industry and labor, it should have no such indulgence. His command power is not such an absolute as might be implied from that office in a militaristic system but is subject to limitations consistent with a constitutional Republic whose law and policy-making branch is a representative Congress. . . .

The third clause in which the Solicitor General finds seizure powers is that "he shall take Care that the Laws be faithfully executed. . . ." That authority must be matched against words of the Fifth Amendment that "No person shall be . . . deprived of life, liberty, or property, without due process of law. . . ." One gives a governmental authority that reaches so far as there is law, the other gives a private right that authority shall go no farther. These signify about all there is of the principle that ours is a government of laws, not of men, and that we submit ourselves to rulers only if under rules.

The Solicitor General lastly grounds support of the seizure upon nebulous, inherent powers never expressly granted but said to have accrued to the office from the customs and claims of preceding administrations. The plea is for a resulting power to deal with a crisis or an emergency according to the necessities of the case, the unarticulated assumption being that necessity knows no law.

Loose and irresponsible use of adjectives colors all non-legal and much legal discussion of presidential powers. "Inherent" powers, "implied" powers, "incidental" powers, "plenary" powers, "war" powers and "emergency" powers are used, often interchangeably and without fixed or ascertainable meanings.

The vagueness and generality of the clauses that set forth presidential powers afford a plausible basis for pressures within and without an administration for presidential action beyond that supported by those whose responsibility it is to defend his actions in court. The claim of inherent and unrestricted presidential powers has long been a persuasive dialectical weapon in political controversy. While it is not surprising that counsel should grasp support from such unadjudicated claims of power, a judge cannot accept self-serving press statements of the attorney for one of the interested parties as authority in answering a constitutional question, even if the advocate was himself. But prudence has counseled that actual reliance on such nebulous claims stop short of provoking a judicial test. . . .

In the practical working of our Government we already have evolved a technique within the framework of the Constitution by which normal executive powers may be considerably expanded to meet an emergency. Congress may and has granted extraordinary authorities which lie dormant in normal times but may be called into play by the Executive in war or upon proclamation of a national emergency. In 1939, upon congressional request, the Attorney General listed ninety-nine such separate statutory grants by Congress of emergency or war-time executive powers. They were invoked from time to time as need appeared. Under this procedure we retain Government by law — special, temporary law, perhaps, but law nonetheless. The public may know the extent and limitations of the powers that can be asserted, and persons affected may be informed from the statute of their rights and duties.

In view of the ease, expedition and safety with which Congress can grant and has granted large emergency powers, certainly ample to embrace this crisis, I am quite unimpressed with the argument that we should affirm possession of them without statute. Such power either has no beginning or it has no end. If it exists, it need submit to no legal restraint. I am not alarmed that it would plunge us straightway into dictatorship, but it is at least a step in that wrong direction.

As to whether there is imperative necessity for such powers, it is relevant to note the gap that exists between the President's paper powers and his real powers. The Constitution does not disclose the measure of the actual controls wielded by the modern presidential office. That instrument must be understood as an Eighteenth-Century sketch of a government hoped for, not as a blueprint of the Government that is. Vast accretions of federal power, eroded from that reserved by the States, have magnified the scope of presidential activity. Subtle shifts take place in the centers of real power that do not show on the face of the Constitution.

Executive power has the advantage of concentration in a single head in whose choice the whole Nation has a part, making him the focus of public hopes and expectations. In drama, magnitude and finality his decisions so far overshadow any others that almost alone he fills the public eye and ear. No othe personality in public life can begin to compete with him in access to the public mind through modern methods of communications. By his prestige as head of state and his influence upon public opinion he exerts a leverage upon those who are supposed to check and balance his power which often cancels their effectiveness.

Moreover, rise of the party system has made a significant extraconstitutional supplement to real executive power. No appraisal of his necessities is realistic which overlooks that he heads a political system as well as a legal system. Party loyalties and interests, sometimes more binding than law, extend his effective control into branches of government other than his own and he often may win, as a political leader, what he cannot command under the Constitution. Indeed, Woodrow Wilson, commenting on the President as leader both of his party and of the Nation, observed, "If he rightly interpret the national thought and boldly insist upon it, he is irresistible. His office is anything he has the sagacity and force to make it." I cannot be brought to believe that this country will suffer if the Court refuses further to aggrandize the presidential office, already so potent and so relatively immune from judicial review, at the expense of Congress.

But I have no illusion that any decision by this Court can keep power in the hands of Congress if it is not wise and timely in meeting its problems. A crisis that challenges the President equally, or perhaps primarily, challenges Congress. If not good law, there was worldly wisdom in the maxim attributed to Napoleon that "The tools belong to the man who can use them." We may say that power to legislate for emergencies belongs in the hands of Congress, but only Congress itself can prevent power from slipping through its fingers. . . .

JUSTICE BURTON, concurring in both the opinion and judgment of the Court. . . .

The Constitution has delegated to Congress power to authorize action to meet a national emergency of the kind we face. Aware of this responsibility, Congress has responded to it. It has provided . . . procedures for the use of the President. . . .

For the purposes of this case the most significant feature of the [Taft-Hartley] Act is its omission of authority to seize an affected industry. The debate preceding its passage demonstrated the significance of that omission. Collective bargaining, rather than governmental seizure, was to be relied upon. Seizure was not to be resorted to without specific congressional authority. Congress reserved to itself the opportunity to authorize seizure to meet particular emergencies.

The President, however, chose not to use the Taft-Hartley procedure. . . .

The foregoing circumstances distinguish this emergency from one in which Congress takes no action and outlines no governmental policy. In the case before us, Congress authorized a procedure which the President declined to follow. . . .

This brings us to a further crucial question. Does the President, in such a situation, have inherent constitutional power to seize private property which makes congressional action in relation thereto unnecessary? We find no such power available to him under the present circumstances. The present situation is not comparable to that of an imminent invasion or threatened attack. We do not face the issue of what might be the President's constitutional power to meet such catastrophic situations. Nor is it claimed that the current seizure is in the nature of a military command addressed by the President, as Commander-in-Chief, to a mobilized nation waging, or imminently threatened with, total war.

The controlling fact here is that Congress, within its constitutionally delegated power, has prescribed for the President specific procedures, exclusive of seizure, for his use in meeting the present type of emergency. Congress has reserved to itself the right to determine where and when to authorize the seizure of property in meeting such an emergency. Under these circumstances, the President's order of April 8 invaded the jurisdiction of Congress. It violated the essence of the principle of the separation of governmental powers. Accordingly, the injunction against its effectiveness should be sustained.

JUSTICE CLARK, concurring in the judgment of the Court. . . .

I conclude that where Congress has laid down specific procedures to deal with the type of crisis confronting the President, he must follow those procedures in meeting the crisis; but that in the absence of such action by Congress, the President's independent power to act depends upon the gravity of the situation confronting the nation. I cannot sustain the seizure in question because here . . . .Congress had prescribed methods to be followed by the President in meeting the emergency at hand. . . .

CHIEF JUSTICE VINSON, with whom JUSTICE REED and JUSTICE MINTON join, dissenting.

. . . Those who suggest that this is a case involving extraordinary powers should be mindful that these are extraordinary times. A world not yet recovered from the devastation of World War II has been forced to face the threat of another and more terrifying global conflict. . . .

Admitting that the Government could seize the mills, plaintiffs claim that the implied power of eminent domain can be exercised only under an Act of Congress; under no circumstances, they say, can that power be exercised by the President unless he can point to an express provision in enabling legislation. This was the view adopted by the District Judge when he granted the preliminary injunction. Without an answer, without hearing evidence, he determined the issue on the basis of his "fixed conclusion . . . that defendant's acts are illegal" because the President's only course in the face of an emergency is to present the matter to Congress and await the final passage of legislation which will enable the Government to cope with threatened disaster.

Under this view, the President is left powerless at the very moment when the need for action may be most pressing and when no one, other than he, is immediately capable of action. Under this view, he is left powerless because a power not expressly given to Congress is nevertheless found to rest exclusively with Congress. . . .

A review of executive action demonstrates that our Presidents have on many occasions exhibited the leadership contemplated by the Framers when they made the President Commander in Chief, and imposed upon him the trust to "take Care that the Laws be faithfully executed." With or without explicit statutory authorization, Presidents have at such times dealt with national emergencies by acting promptly and resolutely to enforce legislative programs, at least to save those programs until Congress could act. Congress and the courts have responded to such executive initiative with consistent approval. [Historical examples omitted] . . . .

History bears out the genius of the Founding Fathers, who created a Government subject to law but not left subject to inertia when vigor and initiative are required.

Focusing now on the situation confronting the President on the night of April 8, 1952, we cannot but conclude that the President was performing his duty under the Constitution to "take Care that the Laws be faithfully executed" — a duty described by President Benjamin Harrison as "the central idea of the office." Harrison, This Country of Ours (1897), 98. . . .

Much of the argument in this case has been directed at straw men. We do not now have before us the case of a President acting solely on the basis of his own notions of the public welfare. Nor is there any question of unlimited executive power in this case. The President himself closed the door to any such claim when he sent his Message to Congress stating his purpose to abide by any action of Congress, whether approving or disapproving his seizure action. Here, the President immediately made sure that Congress was fully informed of the temporary action he had taken only to preserve the legislative programs from destruction until Congress could act.

The absence of a specific statute authorizing seizure of the steel mills as a mode of executing the laws — both the military procurement program and the anti-inflation program — has not until today been thought to prevent the President from executing the laws. Unlike an administrative commission confined to the enforcement of the statute under which it was created, or the head of a department when administering a particular statute, the President is a constitutional officer charged with taking care that a "mass of legislation" be executed. Flexibility as to mode of execution to meet critical situations is a matter of practical necessity. . . .

The diversity of views expressed in the six opinions of the majority, the lack of reference to authoritative precedent, the repeated reliance upon prior dissenting opinions, the complete disregard of the uncontroverted facts showing the gravity of the emergency and the temporary nature of the taking all serve to demonstrate how far afield one must go to affirm the order of the District Court.

The broad executive power granted by Article II to an officer on duty 365 days a year cannot, it is said, be invoked to avert disaster. Instead, the President must confine himself to sending a message to Congress recommending action. Under this messenger-boy concept of the Office, the President cannot even act to preserve legislative programs from destruction so that Congress will have something left to act upon. . . .

NOTES

A. Presidential Power Theories

(1) Alexander Hamilton urged a broad theory of Presidential power in 1793. Defending President Washington's Proclamation of Neutrality, he relied on the difference between the language of Article I conferring "All legislative Powers herein granted" upon Congress and that of Article II vesting "The Executive Power" in the President. The different modes of expression imply that the authority vested in the President is not limited to the specific cases of executive power delineated in Article II: "The general doctrine of our Constitution then is, that the *Executive Power* of the nation is vested in the President; subject only to the exceptions and qualifications which are expressed in the instrument." 7 THE WORKS OF ALEXANDER HAMILTON 81 (1851).

(2) Theodore Roosevelt embraced the broad Hamiltonian view in his "Stewardship Theory." Roosevelt thought that "[the President] was a steward of the people bound actively and affirmatively to do all he could for the people. . . . [I]t was not only his right but his duty to do anything that the needs of the Nation demanded unless such

action was forbidden by the Constitution or by the laws." THEODORE ROOSEVELT, AN AUTOBIOGRAPHY 357 (1920).

(3) Theodore Roosevelt's conception of the Presidency influenced some of his successors — especially Wilson, the second Roosevelt, Truman, and Kennedy. But T.R.'s own successor and one time protégé, William Howard Taft, condemned it. In lectures on the Presidency delivered after he had left the White House, Taft denied that the President possessed any "undefined residuum of power." "The true view of the Executive functions," he declared, "is, as I conceive it, that the President can exercise no power which cannot be fairly and reasonably traced to some specific grant of power or justly implied and included within such express grant as proper and necessary to its exercise." WILLIAM HOWARD TAFT, THE PRESIDENT AND HIS POWERS 139-40 (1967 ed.).

(4) The Theodore Roosevelt and Taft views exemplify two principal conflicting interpretations of executive power that have contended with each other from the founding of the Republic. As Justice Jackson put it in his opinion in the *Steel Seizure Case*, "A century and a half of partisan debate and scholarly speculation yields no net result but only supplies more or less apt quotations from respected sources on each side of any question. They largely cancel each other." In striking down the Truman steel-seizure order, did the Court decide that Taft was right and Theodore Roosevelt wrong? Did the opinion of Justice Black so decide?

(5) Could any President (including President Taft himself) limit himself to the Taft concept of Presidential power? Note that Taft's lectures refer to "the landing of marines and quite a campaign" during his Presidency to put an end to an insurrection which threatened American interests in Nicaragua — all without any "specific grant of power" to the President. TAFT, *supra* Note (3), at 96. President Truman thought the Taft view obsolete. Truman wrote in his memoirs:

> Whatever the six justices of the Supreme Court meant by their differing opinions about the constitutional powers of the President, he must always act in a national emergency. It is not very realistic for the justices to say that comprehensive powers shall be available to the President only when a war has been declared or when the country has been invaded. We live in an age when hostilities begin without polite exchanges of diplomatic notes. There are no longer sharp distinctions between combatants and noncombatants, between military targets and the sanctuary of civilian areas. Nor can we separate the economic facts from the problems of defense and security.
>
> In this day and age the defense of the nation means more than building an army, navy, and air force. It is a job for the entire resources of the nation. The President, who is Commander in Chief and who represents the interest of all the people, must be able to act at all times to meet any sudden threat to the nation's security. A wise President will always work with Congress, but when Congress fails to act or is unable to act in a crisis, the President, under the Constitution, must use his powers to safeguard the nation.

HARRY S. TRUMAN, 2 YEARS OF TRIAL AND HOPE 478 (1956).

B. The Government's Argument

(6) President Truman might reasonably have expected the Court to acquiesce in his order. American forces were engaged in the Korean War and arguably depended on the continuous availability of steel. Prior opinions contained language supporting broad presidential power. President Roosevelt and Truman had appointed all nine Justices. Justice Jackson had authored opinions as a Justice and Attorney General, supporting broad presidential powers. *See* HAROLD HONGJU KOH, THE NATIONAL SECURITY CONSTITU-

TION 106 (1990). Chief Justice Vinson had reportedly advised President Truman that the seizure was within his powers.

(7) In the United States District Court for the District of Columbia, the following exchange occurred between Judge Alexander Holtzoff and Assistant Attorney General Holmes Baldridge:

> *Mr. Baldridge:* . . .
>
> Section 1, Article II, of the Constitution reposes all of the executive power in the Chief Executive.
>
> I think that the distinction that the Constitution itself makes between the powers of the Executive and the powers of the legislative branch of the Government are significant and important.
>
> In so far as the Executive is concerned, all executive power is vested in the President.
>
> In so far as legislative powers are concerned, the Congress has only those powers that are specifically delegated to it, plus the implied power to carry out the powers specifically enumerated.
>
> *The Court*: So, when the sovereign people adopted the Constitution, it enumerated the powers set up in the Constitution . . . limited the powers of the Congress and limited the powers of the judiciary, but it did not limit the powers of the Executive.
>
> Is that what you say?
>
> *Mr. Baldridge*: That is the way we read Article II of the Constitution.
>
> The Court: I see. . . .

ALAN F. WESTIN, THE ANATOMY OF A CONSTITUTIONAL LAW CASE 64 (1958).

C. Textual Provisions

(8) The Vesting Clause in Art. II provides that "[t]he Executive Power shall be vested in a President of the United States of America." What is the purpose of this clause? Does it vest in the President "the executive power"? Alexander Hamilton thought the clause was a "general grant of [executive] power"; he regarded the more specific provisions elsewhere in Art. II as simply specifying its principal aspects. Accordingly, he thought the Vesting Clause a fount of broad presidential powers. Others attribute less significance to it. Professor Edward S. Corwin thought the clause simply established a unitary executive with the title President. Edward S. Corwin, *The Steel Seizure Case: A Judicial Brick Without Straw*, 53 COLUM. L. REV. 53 (1953).

If the Vesting Clause itself confers broad executive powers, why are the particular provisions of Section 2 and 3 of Art. II included? Under such a view, are they redundant as grants of power? Or do they, as some suggest, impose duties, not powers? Or, do they limit the President's powers?

In an elaborate argument, Professors Calabresi and Prakash argue that the Vesting Clause confers the "executive power." The Article II Vesting Clause resembles that in Article III; the Article III Vesting Clause must confer "the judicial power" for nowhere else is it granted. Thus, the Article II Clause must achieve a similar purpose. Significantly, the President's powers are not limited, as are those of Congress to those "herein granted." Moreover, the language used is instructive; "shall" is mandatory, not permissive, "vest" means "to place in possession of." Professor Calabresi and Prakash are unimpressed by the "avoidance of redundancy" argument. Repetition may be used deliberately to emphasize. Moreover, the provisions in Article II Section 2 can be viewed as limits. Thus, the President's pardon power is limited to offenses against the United States; the power to require a written opinion is limited to certain officers and subjects, and so forth. *See* Steven G. Calabresi & Saikrishna B. Prakash, *The President's Power to Execute the Laws*, 104 YALE L.J. 541 (1994).

D. Judicial Doctrine

(9) Three Supreme Court decisions provided some support for President Truman's claims.

(a) *In re Neagle*, 135 U.S. 1 (1890), upheld the power of the President, under the Take Care Clause, to take necessary steps to protect Supreme Court Justice Field even without statutory warrant. Neagle, a deputy U.S. Marshall, was charged with killing one Judge Terry who assaulted Justice Field and whom Neagle reasonably believed was preparing to brandish a gun. Neagle claimed he was acting under federal law, but no statute authorized his conduct. The Court found that "any obligation fairly and properly inferable" from the Constitution was a "law" the President must take care to enforce. The President had "power . . . to take measures for the protection" of Justice Field. Neagle was therefore performing his federal duty and could not be subject to criminal prosecution under California law.

(b) *In Re Debs*, 158 U.S. 564 (1895), which arose from the Pullman Strikes of 1894, upheld the inherent power of the Executive Branch to petition the courts to enjoin labor leader Eugene Debs from communicating with railway employees regarding the strike, even though Congress had not authorized such an action. Since the Constitution empowered Congress to regulate interstate commerce, the Executive had power to use the military "to compel obedience to its laws" and to protect commerce and the mails. Accordingly, it also could resort to the lesser remedy of judicial action.

(c) *United States v. Midwest Oil Co.*, 236 U.S. 459 (1915). An 1897 Congressional statute made public lands containing petroleum or mineral deposits open for public exploration. Concerned that exploration would create shortages, President Taft withdrew certain lands from public exploration. Thereafter, Midwest Oil's predecessor in interest discovered oil on some withdrawn land. The United States sought to recover the land and other relief.

The Court upheld the President's order "in the light of the legal consequences flowing from a long continued practice to make orders like the one here involved." Presidents had issued hundreds of Executive Orders affecting public lands. "The President was in a position to know when the public interest required particular portion of the people's lands to be withdrawn from entry or location; his action inflicted no wrong upon any private citizen, and being subject to disaffirmance by Congress, could occasion no harm to the interest of the public at large. Congress did not repudiate the power claimed or the withdrawal orders made. On the contrary it uniformly and repeatedly acquiesced in the practice. . . . "

E. The Steel Seizure Opinions

(10) Did the *Steel Seizure* Court deny all inherent power in the President to deal with emergencies? Consider the statement of Justice Burton, in his concurring opinion: "The present situation is not comparable to that of an imminent invasion or threatened attack. We do not face the issue of what might be the President's constitutional power to meet such catastrophic situations."

Professor Henry Monaghan argued that *"Steel Seizure* represents the bedrock principle of the constitutional order: except perhaps when acting pursuant to some 'specific' constitutional power, the President has no inherent power to invade private rights; the President not only cannot act *contra legen*, he or she must point to affirmative legislative authorization when so acting." Henry P. Monaghan, *The Protective Power of the Presidency*, 93 COLUM. L. REV. 1, 10 (1993).

(11) Although the Framers sought to constrain the Presidency so it did not exhibit the

dangers of a monarchy, they also believed the Presidency needed to be free to act forcefully in some instances. In THE FEDERALIST No. 70, Hamilton wrote: "Energy in the Executive is a leading character in the definition of good government. It is essential to the protection of the community against foreign attacks; it is not less essential to the steady administration of the laws; to the protection of property against those irregular and high-handed combinations which sometimes interrupt the ordinary course of justice; to the security of liberty against the enterprises and assaults of ambition, of faction, and of anarchy." Executive energy would come from a mix of ingredients, including unity (i.e., locating responsibility in an individual, not a collective body), duration (a four-year fixed term), support and "competent powers."

F. Emergency Powers

(12) What are the scope of the President's emergency powers? May the President exercise extra constitutional powers in times of emergency? Some of our greatest Presidents have claimed that right. After he left office, Thomas Jefferson wrote:

> Sir, . . . The question you propose, whether circumstances do not sometimes occur, which make it a duty in officers of high trust, to assume authorities beyond the law, is easy of solution in principle, but sometimes embarrassing in practice. A strict observance of the written laws is doubtless *one* of the high duties of a good citizen, but is not *the highest*. The laws of necessity, of self-preservation, of saving our country when in danger, are of higher obligation.

Letter from Thomas Jefferson to John B. Colvin (Sept. 20, 1810), *in* 9 THE WRITINGS OF THOMAS JEFFERSON 279 (Paul L. Ford ed., 1898).

Abraham Lincoln agreed. He wrote:

> I did understand, however, that my oath to preserve the Constitution to the best of my ability, imposed upon me the duty of preserving, by every indispensable means, that government — that nation — of which that Constitution was the organic law. Was it possible to lose the nation, and yet preserve the Constitution? By general law life *and* limb must be protected; yet often a limb must be amputated to save a life; but a life is never wisely given to save a limb. I felt that measures, otherwise unconstitutional, might become lawful, by becoming indispensable to the preservation of the Constitution, through the preservation of the nation. Right or wrong, I assumed this ground, and now avow it.

Letter to Albert G. Hodges (Apr. 4, 1864) *in* 7 COLLECTED WORKS 281 (Ray P. Basler ed., 1953).

President Franklin D. Roosevelt challenged Congress to repeal a provision of the Emergency Price Control Act which he believed impeded his fight against inflation. "In the event that the Congress should fail to act, and act adequately, I shall accept the responsibility, and I will act." 88 CONG. REC. 7044 (1942).

(13) During a televised discussion with interviewer David Frost several years after he resigned as President, Richard Nixon made sweeping claims regarding presidential power in national security matters.

> FROST: So, what, in a sense, you're saying is that there are certain situations, . . .where the President can decide that it's in the best interest of the nation or something, and do something illegal.
>
> NIXON: Well, when the President does it, that means that it is not illegal.
>
> FROST: By definition.
>
> NIXON: Exactly. Exactly. If the President, for example, approves something

because of the national security, or in this case because of a threat to internal peace and order of significant magnitude, then the President's decision in that instance is one that enables those who carry it out, to carry it out without violating a law. Otherwise they're in an impossible position.

See Excerpts from Interview with Nixon About Domestic Effects of Indochina War, N.Y. TIMES, May 20, 1977, at A16.

§ 5.02   LEGISLATIVE POWERS OF THE EXECUTIVE

[1]   Legislative Veto

IMMIGRATION AND NATURALIZATION SERVICE v. CHADHA
462 U.S. 919, 103 S. Ct. 2764, 77 L. Ed.2d 317 (1983)

CHIEF JUSTICE BURGER delivered the opinion of the Court. . . .

[This case] presents a challenge to the constitutionality of the provision in § 244(c)(2) of the Immigration and Nationality Act, 8 U.S.C. § 1254(c)(2), authorizing one House of Congress, by resolution, to invalidate the decision of the Executive Branch, pursuant to authority delegated by Congress to the Attorney General of the United States, to allow a particular deportable alien to remain in the United States. [Chadha overstayed his student visa. Although deportable, the Attorney General recommended suspending Chadha's deportation and transmitted his recommendation to Congress. Section 244(c)(2) provided in part that if "either the Senate or the House of Representatives passes a resolution stating in substance that it does not favor the suspension of such deportation, the Attorney General shall thereupon deport such alien." The House passed a resolution opposing a grant of permanent residence to Chadha.]

[The Court rejected challenges to its jurisdiction based on various justiceability doctrines.]

III

A

We turn now to the question whether action of one House of Congress under § 244(c)(2) violates strictures of the Constitution. We begin, of course, with the presumption that the challenged statute is valid. Its wisdom is not the concern of the courts; if a challenged action does not violate the Constitution, it must be sustained. . . .

By the same token, the fact that a given law or procedure is efficient, convenient, and useful in facilitating functions of government, standing alone, will not save it if it is contrary to the Constitution. Convenience and efficiency are not the primary objectives — or the hallmarks of democratic government and our inquiry is sharpened rather than blunted by the fact that Congressional veto provisions are appearing with increasing frequency in statutes which delegate authority to executive and independent agencies. . . .

Explicit and unambiguous provisions of the Constitution prescribe and define the respective functions of the Congress and of the Executive in the legislative process. Since the precise terms of those familiar provisions are critical to the resolution of this case, we set them out verbatim. Art. I provides:

"All legislative Powers herein granted shall be vested in a Congress of the

United States, which shall consist of a Senate *and* a House of Representatives." Art. I, § 1. (Emphasis added).

"Every Bill which shall have passed the House of Representatives and the Senate, *shall*, before it becomes a Law, be presented to the President of the United States . . ." Art. I, § 7, cl. 2. (Emphasis added).

"Every Order, Resolution, or Vote to which the Concurrence of the Senate and House of Representatives may be necessary (except on a question of Adjournment) *shall be* presented to the President of the United States; and before the Same shall take Effect, *shall be* approved by him, or being disapproved by him, *shall be* repassed by two thirds of the Senate and House of Representatives, according to the Rules and Limitations prescribed in the Case of a Bill." Art. I, § 7, cl. 3. (Emphasis added).

These provisions of Art. I are integral parts of the constitutional design for the separation of powers. . . .

B

The Presentment Clauses

The records of the Constitutional Convention reveal that the requirement that all legislation be presented to the President before becoming law was uniformly accepted by the Framers. Presentment to the President and the Presidential veto were considered so imperative that the draftsmen took special pains to assure that these requirements could not be circumvented. During the final debate on Art. I, § 7, cl. 2, James Madison expressed concern that it might easily be evaded by the simple expedient of calling a proposed law a "resolution" or "vote" rather than a "bill." . . . As a consequence, Art. I, § 7, cl. 3 was added. . . .

The decision to provide the President with a limited and qualified power to nullify proposed legislation by veto was based on the profound conviction of the Framers that the powers conferred on Congress were the powers to be most carefully circumscribed. It is beyond doubt that lawmaking was a power to be shared by both Houses and the President. . . .

C

Bicameralism

The bicameral requirement of Art. I, §§ 1, 7 was of scarcely less concern to the Framers than was the Presidential veto and indeed the two concepts are interdependent. By providing that no law could take effect without the concurrence of the prescribed majority of the Members of both Houses, the Framers reemphasized their belief, already remarked upon in connection with the Presentment Clauses, that legislation should not be enacted unless it has been carefully and fully considered by the Nation's elected officials. . . .

We see therefore that the Framers were acutely conscious that the bicameral requirement and the Presentment Clauses would serve essential constitutional functions. The President's participation in the legislative process was to protect the Executive Branch from Congress and to protect the whole people from improvident laws. The division of the Congress into two distinctive bodies assures that the legislative power would be exercised only after opportunity for full study and debate in separate settings. The President's unilateral veto power, in turn, was limited by the power of two thirds of both Houses of Congress to overrule a veto thereby precluding final arbitrary action of one person . . . It emerges clearly that the prescription for legislative action in Art. I, §§ 1, 7 represents the Framers' decision that the legislative power of the Federal government be exercised in accord with a single, finely wrought and exhaustively considered, procedure.

IV

The Constitution sought to divide the delegated powers of the new federal government into three defined categories, legislative, executive and judicial, to assure, as nearly as possible, that each Branch of government would confine itself to its assigned responsibility. The hydraulic pressure inherent within each of the separate Branches to exceed the outer limits of its power, even to accomplish desirable objectives, must be resisted.

Although not "hermetically" sealed from one another, *Buckley v. Valeo*, [*infra* § 15.02] . . . the powers delegated to the three Branches are functionally identifiable. When any Branch acts, it is presumptively exercising the power the Constitution has delegated to it. When the Executive acts, it presumptively acts in an executive or administrative capacity as defined in Art. II. And when, as here, one House of Congress purports to act, it is presumptively acting within its assigned sphere.

Beginning with this presumption, we must nevertheless establish that the challenged action under § 244(c)(2) is of the kind to which the procedural requirements of Art. I, § 7 apply. Not every action taken by either House is subject to the bicameralism and presentment requirements of Art. I. . . . Whether actions taken by either House are, in law and fact, an exercise of legislative power depends not on their form but upon "whether they contain matter which is properly to be regarded as legislative in its character and effect." . . .

Examination of the action taken here by one House pursuant to § 244(c)(2) reveals that it was essentially legislative in purpose and effect. In purporting to exercise power defined in Art. I, § 8, cl. 4 to "establish an uniform Rule of Naturalization," the House took action that had the purpose and effect of altering the legal rights, duties, and relations of persons, including the Attorney General, Executive Branch officials and Chadha, all outside the legislative branch. Section 244(c)(2) purports to authorize one House of Congress to require the Attorney General to deport an individual alien whose deportation otherwise would be cancelled under § 244. The one-House veto operated in this case to overrule the Attorney General and mandate Chadha's deportation; absent the House action, Chadha would remain in the United States. Congress has acted and its action has altered Chadha's status.

. . . [W]hen the Draftsmen sought to confer special powers on one House, independent of the other House, or of the President, they did so in explicit, unambiguous terms. These carefully defined exceptions from presentment and bicameralism underscore the difference between the legislative functions of Congress and other unilateral but important and binding one-House acts provided for in the Constitution. These exceptions are narrow, explicit, and separately justified; none of them authorize the action challenged here. On the contrary, they provide further support for the conclusion that Congressional authority is not to be implied and for the conclusion that the veto provided for in § 244(c)(2) is not authorized by the constitutional design of the powers of the Legislative Branch.

Since it is clear that the action by the House under § 244(c)(2) was not within any of the express constitutional exceptions authorizing one House to act alone, and equally clear that it was an exercise of legislative power, that action was subject to the standards prescribed in Article I. The bicameral requirement, the Presentment Clauses, the

President's veto, and Congress' power to override a veto were intended to erect enduring checks on each Branch and to protect the people from the improvident exercise of power by mandating certain prescribed steps. To preserve those checks, and maintain the separation of powers, the carefully defined limits on the power of each Branch must not be eroded. To accomplish what has been attempted by one House of Congress in this case requires action in conformity with the express procedures of the Constitution's prescription for legislative action: passage by a majority of both Houses and presentment to the President. . . .

The choices we discern as having been made in the Constitutional Convention impose burdens on governmental processes that often seem clumsy, inefficient, even unworkable, but those hard choices were consciously made by men who had lived under a form of government that permitted arbitrary governmental acts to go unchecked. There is no support in the Constitution or decisions of this Court for the proposition that the cumbersomeness and delays often encountered in complying with explicit Constitutional standards may be avoided, either by the Congress or by the President. *See Youngstown Sheet & Tube Co. v. Sawyer,* [*supra* § 5.01] . . . With all the obvious flaws of delay, untidiness, and potential for abuse, we have not yet found a better way to preserve freedom than by making the exercise of power subject to the carefully crafted restraints spelled out in the Constitution. (Emphasis added).

V

We hold that the Congressional veto provision in § 244(c)(2) is . . . unconstitutional. Accordingly, the judgment of the Court of Appeals is

Affirmed.

JUSTICE POWELL, concurring in the judgment.

The Court's decision, based on the Presentment Clauses, Art. I, § 7, cls. 2 and 3, apparently will invalidate every use of the legislative veto. The breadth of this holding gives one pause. Congress has included the veto in literally hundreds of statutes, dating back to the 1930s. Congress clearly views this procedure as essential to controlling the delegation of power to administrative agencies. One reasonably may disagree with Congress' assessment of the veto's utility, but the respect due its judgment as a coordinate branch of Government cautions that our holding should be no more extensive than necessary to decide this case. In my view, the case may be decided on a narrower ground. When Congress finds that a particular person does not satisfy the statutory criteria for permanent residence in this country it has assumed a judicial function in violation of the principle of separation of powers. Accordingly, I concur only in the judgment. . . .

JUSTICE WHITE dissenting.

Today the Court not only invalidates § 244(c)(2) of the Immigration and Nationality Act, but also sounds the death knell for nearly 200 other statutory provisions in which Congress has reserved a "legislative veto." For this reason, the Court's decision is of surpassing importance. . . .

The prominence of the legislative veto mechanism in our contemporary political system and its importance to Congress can hardly be overstated. It has become a central means by which Congress secures the accountability of executive and independent agencies. Without the legislative veto, Congress is faced with a Hobson's choice: either to refrain from delegating the necessary authority, leaving itself with a hopeless task of writing laws with the requisite specificity to cover endless special circumstances across the entire policy landscape, or in the alternative, to abdicate its law-making function to the executive branch and independent agencies. To choose the former leaves major national problems unresolved; to opt for the latter risks unaccountable policymaking by those not elected to fill that role. Accordingly, over the past five decades, the legislative veto has been placed in nearly 200 statutes. The device is known in every field of governmental concern: reorganization, budgets, foreign affairs, war powers, and regulation of trade, safety, energy, the environment and the economy. . .

I

[Discussion of history of legislative veto omitted]

Even this brief review suffices to demonstrate that the legislative veto is more than "efficient, convenient, and useful." . . . It is an important if not indispensable political invention that allows the President and Congress to resolve major constitutional and policy differences, assures the accountability of independent regulatory agencies, and preserves Congress' control over lawmaking. Perhaps there are other means of accommodation and accountability, but the increasing reliance of Congress upon the legislative veto suggests that the alternatives to which Congress must now turn are not entirely satisfactory.

The history of the legislative veto also makes clear that it has not been a sword with which Congress has struck out to aggrandize itself at the expense of the other branches — the concerns of Madison and Hamilton. Rather, the veto has been a means of defense, a reservation of ultimate authority necessary if Congress is to fulfill its designated role under Article I as the nation's lawmaker. While the President has often objected to particular legislative vetoes, generally those left in the hands of congressional committees, the Executive has more often agreed to legislative review as the price for a broad delegation of authority. To be sure, the President may have preferred unrestricted power, but that could be precisely why Congress thought it essential to retain a check on the exercise of delegated authority.

II

For all these reasons, the apparent sweep of the Court's decision today is regretable. The Court's Article I analysis appears to invalidate all legislative vetoes irrespective of form or subject. Because the legislative veto is commonly found as a check upon rulemaking by administrative agencies and upon broad-based policy decisions of the Executive Branch, it is particularly unfortunate that the Court reaches its decision in a case involving the exercise of a veto over deportation decisions regarding particular individuals. Courts should always be wary of striking statutes as unconstitutional; to strike an entire class of statutes based on consideration of a somewhat atypical and more-readily indictable exemplar of the class is irresponsible. . . .

III

The Court holds that the disapproval of a suspension of deportation by the resolution of one House of Congress is an exercise of legislative power without compliance with the prerequisites for lawmaking set forth in Art. I of the Constitution. Specifically, the Court maintains that the provisions of § 244(c)(2) are inconsistent with the requirement of bicameral approval, implicit in Art. I, § 1, and the requirement that all bills and resolutions that require the concurrence of both Houses be presented to the President, Art. I, § 7, cl. 2 and 3.

I do not dispute the Court's truismatic exposition of these clauses. . . . It does not, however, answer the constitutional question before us. The power to exercise a legislative veto is not the power to write new law without bicameral approval or presidential consideration. The veto must be authorized by statute and may only negative what an Executive department or independent agency has proposed. On its face, the legislative veto no more allows one House of Congress to make law than does the presidential veto confer such power upon the President. . . . The Court's holding today that all legislative-type action must be enacted through the lawmaking process ignores that legislative authority is routinely delegated to the Executive branch, to the independent regulatory agencies, and to private individuals and groups. . . .

If Congress may delegate lawmaking power to independent and executive agencies, it is most difficult to understand Article I as forbidding Congress from also reserving a check on legislative power for itself. Absent the veto, the agencies receiving delegations of legislative or quasi- legislative power may issue regulations having the force of law without bicameral approval and without the President's signature. It is thus not apparent why the reservation of a veto over the exercise of that legislative power must be subject to a more exacting test. In both cases, it is enough that the initial statutory authorizations comply with the Article I requirements.

. . . Under the Court's analysis, the Executive Branch and the independent agencies may make rules with the effect of law while Congress, in whom the Framers confided the legislative power, Art. I, § 1, may not exercise a veto which precludes such rules from having operative force. If the effective functioning of a complex modern government requires the delegation of vast authority which, by virtue of its breadth, is legislative or "quasi-legislative" in character, I cannot accept that Article I — which is, after all, the source of the non-delegation doctrine — should forbid Congress from qualifying the grant with a legislative veto.

The Court also takes no account of perhaps the most relevant consideration: However resolutions of disapproval under § 244(c)(2) are formally characterized, in reality, a departure from the status quo occurs only upon the concurrence of opinion among the House, Senate, and President. Reservations of legislative authority to be exercised by Congress should be upheld if the exercise of such reserved authority is consistent with the distribution of and limits upon legislative power that Article I provides. . . .

Today's decision strikes down in one fell swoop provisions in more laws enacted by Congress than the Court has cumulatively invalidated in its history. I fear it will now be more difficult "to insure that the fundamental policy decisions in our society will be made not by an appointed official but by the body immediately responsible to the people," . . . I must dissent.

[JUSTICE RREHNQUIST also dissented.]

NOTES

(1) *Veto Power*. The veto is essentially a legislative power that permits the President to participate directly in the process of enacting laws. As Justice White put it, the "President's veto power, which gives him an important role in the legislative process, was obviously not considered an inherently executive function." *Buckley v. Valeo*, 424 U.S. 1, 285 (1976) (White, J., concurring). Woodrow Wilson called the veto the President's "most formidable prerogative." In exercising it, "the President acts not as the executive but as a third branch of the legislature." WOODROW WILSON, CONGRESSIONAL GOVERNMENT 52 (1885).

"Veto" is not used in the Constitution. The power comes from the President's option to return a bill to Congress with objections. Indeed, the procedure is discussed in the Presentment Clause in Art. I, § 7, not in Article II. The veto is not, of course, the sole power that implicates the President in legislation. The Constitution, for instance, provides that the President "shall from time to time give to the Congress Information of the State of the Union, and recommend to their Consideration such Measures as he shall judge necessary and expedient." *See* U.S. CONST. art. II, § 3.

(2) May the President veto on any grounds or only to prevent unconstitutional legislation? Hamilton justified the veto primarily as necessary to allow the President to defend against the legislature's incursions into his powers. Lacking it, "[h]e might gradually be stripped of his authorities by successive resolutions or annihilated by a single vote." The veto afforded the President "a constitutional and effectual power of self defence." THE FEDERALIST No. 73 at 494-95 (Jacob E. Cooke ed., 1961).

Hamilton justified the veto as not simply "a shield to the executive." Secondarily, it afforded "additional security against the enaction of improper laws" which might threaten the "public good." *Id.* at 495. Repeated historical practice has made clear that the veto may be used for any reason. Although the first six Presidents vetoed less than ten bills between them, most by James Madison, President Andrew Jackson vetoed a dozen bills, most on constitutional grounds. President John Tyler vetoed "pretty freely" and on policy grounds which caused some irate Congressmen to propose his impeachment. His successors have consistently followed that practice. For instance, Grover Cleveland vetoed more than 300 bills. *See* Charles L. Black, Jr., *Some Thoughts on the Veto*, 40 L. & CONTEMP. PROB. 87, 90-92 (1976).

(3) *Legislative Veto. Chadha* considered whether Congress could give itself a veto power. Before *Chadha*, Congress often included legislative vetoes in statutes beginning with those giving the President authority to reorganize the executive branch, like the Reorganization Act of 1939. Under these statutes, Congress could disapprove Presidential reorganization plans. The veto technique was also widely used outside the reorganization field. As Justice White points out, nearly 200 statutes provided for disapproval of specified executive and administrative acts by resolution of either or both Houses. These statutes covered a range of executive and administrative action — from Presidential employment of the armed forces abroad (*infra* § 5.05), to promulgation of administrative regulations (such as those prescribing motor vehicle safety standards), to plans issued for improving Pennsylvania Avenue between the White House and the Capitol. In the view of the breadth of the decision, does *Chadha* leave any room for use of the legislative veto technique?

[2]   Line Item Veto

CLINTON v. CITY OF NEW YORK
524 U.S. 417, 188 S. Ct. 2091, 141 L. Ed. 2d 393 (1998)

JUSTICE STEVENS delivered the opinion of the Court.

[Editor's Note: The Line Item Veto Act (LIVA) became effective January 1, 1997. In *Raines v. Byrd*, [*supra* § 1.07, Note (10)], the Court held that members of Congress lacked standing to challenge the Act. Thereafter President Clinton, under LIVA, cancelled a provision of the Balanced Budget Act of 1997 which would have allowed New York to retain more than $1 billion for which the United States Department of Health and Human Services had claimed a refund. He also canceled provisions of the Taxpayer Relief Act of 1997 which gave tax benefits to certain food processors and refineries which sold stock to various farmers' cooperatives. The City of New York and other parties challenged the first cancellation; in a separate lawsuit, Snake River Potato Growers, Inc., an Idaho farmers' cooperative and an individual Idaho farmer challenged the second. The cases were consolidated in the United States District Court which held that the cancellations, on the merits, violated the Constitution. The Supreme Court expedited its review as provided under LIVA; after concluding that plaintiffs had standing and the case was justiciable, the Court addressed the merits.]

IV

The Line Item Veto Act gives the President the power to "cancel in whole" three types of provisions that have been signed into law: "(1) any dollar amount of discretionary budget authority; (2) any item of new direct spending; or (3) any limited tax benefit.". . . It is undisputed that the New York case involves an "item of new direct spending" and that the Snake River case involves a "limited tax benefit" as those terms are defined in the Act. It is also undisputed that each of those provisions had been signed into law pursuant to Article I, § 7, of the Constitution before it was canceled.

The Act requires the President to adhere to precise procedures whenever he exercises his cancellation authority. . . . It is undisputed that the President meticulously followed these procedures in these cases.

A cancellation takes effect upon receipt by Congress of the special message from the President. . . . If, however, a "disapproval bill" pertaining to a special message is enacted into law, the cancellations set forth in that message become "null and void." . . . The Act sets forth a detailed expedited procedure for the consideration of a "disapproval bill,". . . . but no such bill was passed for either of the cancellations involved in these cases. A majority vote of both Houses is sufficient to enact a disapproval bill. The Act does not grant the President the authority to cancel a disapproval bill, . . . but he does, of course, retain his constitutional authority to veto such a bill. . . .

With respect to both an item of new direct spending and a limited tax benefit, the cancellation prevents the item "from having legal force or effect." . . . Thus, under the plain text of the statute, the two actions of the President that are challenged in these cases prevented one section of the Balanced Budget Act of 1997 and one section of the Taxpayer Relief Act of 1997 "from having legal force or effect." The remaining provisions of those statutes . . . continue to have the same force and effect as they had when signed into law.

In both legal and practical effect, the President has amended two Acts of Congress by repealing a portion of each. . . . There is no provision in the Constitution that authorizes the President to enact, to amend, or to repeal statutes. Both Article I and Article II assign responsibilities to the President that directly relate to the lawmaking process, but neither addresses the issue presented by these cases. . . .

There are important differences between the President's "return" of a bill pursuant to Article I, § 7, and the exercise of the President's cancellation authority pursuant to the Line Item Veto Act. The constitutional return takes place *before* the bill becomes law; the statutory cancellation occurs *after* the bill becomes law. The constitutional return is of the entire bill; the statutory cancellation is of only a part. Although the Constitution expressly authorizes the President to play a role in the process of enacting statutes, it is silent on the subject of unilateral Presidential action that either repeals or amends parts of duly enacted statutes.

There are powerful reasons for construing constitutional silence on this profoundly important issue as equivalent to an express prohibition. The procedures governing the enactment of statutes set forth in the text of Article I were the product of the great debates and compromises that produced the Constitution itself. Familiar historical materials provide abundant support for the conclusion that the power to enact statutes may only "be exercised in accord with a single, finely wrought and exhaustively considered, procedure." *Chadha*, [*supra*, § 5.02[1]]. Our first President understood the text of the Presentment Clause as requiring that he either "approve all the parts of a

Bill, or reject it in toto."[1] What has emerged in these cases from the President's exercise of his statutory cancellation powers, however, are truncated versions of two bills that passed both Houses of Congress. They are not the product of the "finely wrought" procedure that the Framers designed. . . .

V

The Government advances two related arguments to support its position that despite the unambiguous provisions of the Act, cancellations do not amend or repeal properly enacted statutes in violation of the Presentment Clause. First, relying primarily on *Field v. Clark*, 143 U.S. 649, 12 S. Ct. 495, 36 L.Ed. 294 (1892), the Government contends that the cancellations were merely exercises of discretionary authority granted to the President by the Balanced Budget Act and the Taxpayer Relief Act read in light of the previously enacted Line Item Veto Act. Second, the Government submits that the substance of the authority to cancel tax and spending items "is, in practical effect, no more and no less than the power to 'decline to spend' specified sums of money, or to 'decline to implement' specified tax measures." . . . Neither argument is persuasive.

In *Field v. Clark*, the Court upheld the constitutionality of the Tariff Act of 1890 . . . [which] exempted from import duties [almost 300 specific articles] "unless otherwise specially provided for in this act." . . . Section 3 was a special provision that directed the President to suspend that exemption for sugar, molasses, coffee, tea, and hides "whenever, and so often" as he should be satisfied that any country producing and exporting those products imposed duties on the agricultural products of the United States that he deemed to be "reciprocally unequal and unreasonable . . . " The section then specified the duties to be imposed on those products during any such suspension. The Court . . . [concluded] that § 3 had not delegated legislative power to the President [because]:

> "Nothing involving the expediency or the just operation of such legislation was left to the determination of the President. . . . [W]hen he ascertained the fact that duties and exactions, reciprocally unequal and unreasonable, were imposed upon the agricultural or other products of the United States by a country producing and exporting sugar, molasses, coffee, tea or hides, it became his duty to issue a proclamation declaring the suspension, as to that country, which Congress had determined should occur. He had no discretion in the premises except in respect to the duration of the suspension so ordered. But that related only to the enforcement of the policy established by Congress. . . . "

[There are] three critical differences between the power to suspend the exemption from import duties and the power to cancel portions of a duly enacted statute. First, the exercise of the suspension power was contingent upon a condition that did not exist when the Tariff Act was passed: the imposition of "reciprocally unequal and unreasonable" import duties by other countries. In contrast, the exercise of the cancellation power within five days after the enactment of the Balanced Budget and Tax Reform Acts necessarily was based on the same conditions that Congress evaluated when it passed those statutes. Second, under the Tariff Act, when the President determined that the

---

[1] [Court's Footnote 30] 33 *Writings of George Washington* 96 (J. Fitzpatrick ed., 1940); *see also* W. Taft, *The Presidency: Its Duties, Its Powers, Its Opportunities and Its Limitations* 11 (1916) (stating that the President "has no power to veto part of a bill and let the rest become a law"); *cf.* 1 W. Blackstone, *Commentaries* *154 ("The crown cannot begin of itself any alterations in the present established law; but it may approve or disapprove of the alterations suggested and consented to by the two houses").

contingency had arisen, he had a duty to suspend; in contrast, while it is true that the President was required by the Act to make three determinations before he canceled a provision, . . . those determinations did not qualify his discretion to cancel or not to cancel. Finally, whenever the President suspended an exemption under the Tariff Act, he was executing the policy that Congress had embodied in the statute. In contrast, whenever the President cancels an item of new direct spending or a limited tax benefit he is rejecting the policy judgment made by Congress and relying on his own policy judgment. Thus, the conclusion in *Field v. Clark* . . . does not undermine our opinion that cancellations pursuant to the Line Item Veto Act are the functional equivalent of partial repeals of Acts of Congress that fail to satisfy Article I, § 7. . . .

The Line Item Veto Act authorizes the President himself to effect the repeal of laws, for his own policy reasons, without observing the procedures set out in Article I, § 7. The fact that Congress intended such a result is of no moment. Although Congress presumably anticipated that the President might cancel some of the items in the Balanced Budget Act and in the Taxpayer Relief Act, Congress cannot alter the procedures set out in Article I, § 7, without amending the Constitution.

Neither are we persuaded by the Government's contention that the President's authority to cancel new direct spending and tax benefit items is no greater than his traditional authority to decline to spend appropriated funds. . . . The critical difference between this statute and all of its predecessors, however, is that unlike any of them, this Act gives the President the unilateral power to change the text of duly enacted statutes. None of the Act's predecessors could even arguably have been construed to authorize such a change.

VI

. . . If there is to be a new procedure in which the President will play a different role in determining the final text of what may "become a law," such change must come not by legislation but through the amendment procedures set forth in Article V of the Constitution. . . .

The judgment of the District Court is affirmed.

JUSTICE KENNEDY, concurring. . . .

I write to respond to my colleague Justice Breyer, who observes that the statute does not threaten the liberties of individual citizens, a point on which I disagree. . . . Liberty is always at stake when one or more of the branches seek to transgress the separation of powers. Separation of powers was designed to implement a fundamental insight: Concentration of power in the hands of a single branch is a threat to liberty. . . .

It is no answer, of course, to say that Congress surrendered its authority by its own hand; nor does it suffice to point out that a new statute, signed by the President or enacted over his veto, could restore to Congress the power it now seeks to relinquish. That a congressional cession of power is voluntary does not make it innocuous. The Constitution is a compact enduring for more than our time, and one Congress cannot yield up its own powers, much less those of other Congresses to follow. . . .

The Constitution is not bereft of controls over improvident spending. Federalism is one safeguard, for political accountability is easier to enforce within the States than nationwide. The other principal mechanism, of course, is control of the political branches by an informed and responsible electorate. . . . The fact that these mechanisms, plus the proper functioning of the separation of powers itself, are not employed, or that they prove insufficient, cannot validate an otherwise unconstitutional device. With these observations, I join the opinion of the Court.

JUSTICE SCALIA, with whom JUSTICE O'CONNOR joins, and with whom JUSTICE BREYER joins as to Part III, concurring in part and dissenting in part.

[In the first part of his opinion, Justice Scalia, joined by Justice O'Connor, concluded that the Idaho plaintiffs lacked standing. Joined by Justices O'Connor and Breyer, he concluded that the New York plaintiffs had standing.]

III

. . . Unlike the Court, . . . I do not believe that Executive cancellation of this item of direct spending violates the Presentment Clause.

The Presentment Clause requires, in relevant part, that "[e]very Bill which shall have passed the House of Representatives and the Senate, shall, before it becomes a Law, be presented to the President of the United States; If he approve he shall sign it, but if not he shall return it," U.S. Const., Art. I, § 7, cl. 2. There is no question that enactment of the Balanced Budget Act complied with these requirements: the House and Senate passed the bill, and the President signed it into law. It was only after the requirements of the Presentment Clause had been satisfied that the President exercised his authority under the Line Item Veto Act to cancel the spending item. Thus, the Court's problem with the Act is not that it authorizes the President to veto parts of a bill and sign others into law, but rather that it authorizes him to "cancel" — prevent from "having legal force or effect" — certain parts of duly enacted statutes.

Article I, § 7 of the Constitution obviously prevents the President from cancelling a law that Congress has not authorized him to cancel. . . . But that is not this case. It was certainly arguable, as an original matter, that Art. I, § 7 also prevents the President from cancelling a law which itself authorizes the President to cancel it. But as the Court acknowledges, that argument has long since been made and rejected . . . in *Field v. Clark.* . . .

I turn, then, to the crux of the matter: whether Congress's authorizing the President to cancel an item of spending gives him a power that our history and traditions show must reside exclusively in the Legislative Branch. I may note, to begin with, that the Line Item Veto Act is not the first statute to authorize the President to "cancel" spending items. . . . The President's discretion under the Line Item Veto Act is . . . no broader than the discretion traditionally granted the President in his execution of spending laws . . . Insofar as the degree of political, "law-making" power conferred upon the Executive is concerned, there is not a dime's worth of difference between Congress's authorizing the President to cancel a spending item, and Congress's authorizing money to be spent on a particular item at the President's discretion. And the latter has been done since the Founding of the Nation. From 1789-1791, the First Congress made lump-sum appropriations for the entire Government — "sum[s] not exceeding" specified amounts for broad purposes. . . . Certain Presidents have claimed Executive authority to withhold appropriated funds even absent an express conferral of discretion to do so. . . .

The short of the matter is this: Had the Line Item Veto Act authorized the President to "decline to spend" any item of spending contained in the Balanced Budget Act of 1997, there is not the slightest doubt that authorization would have been constitutional. What the Line Item Veto Act does instead — authorizing the President to "cancel" an item of spending — is technically different. But the technical difference does not relate to the technicalities of the Presentment Clause, which have been fully complied with; and the doctrine of unconstitutional delegation, which is at issue here, is preeminently not a doctrine of technicalities. The title of the Line Item Veto Act, which was perhaps designed to simplify for public comprehension, or perhaps merely to comply with the terms of a campaign pledge, has succeeded in faking out the Supreme Court. The President's action it authorizes in fact is not a line-item veto and thus does not offend

Art. I, § 7; and insofar as the substance of that action is concerned, it is no different from what Congress has permitted the President to do since the formation of the Union. . . .

For the foregoing reasons, I respectfully dissent.

JUSTICE BREYER, with whom JUSTICE O'CONNOR and JUSTICE SCALIA join as to Part III, dissenting.

I

I agree with the Court that the parties have standing, but I do not agree with its ultimate conclusion. In my view the Line Item Veto Act does not violate any specific textual constitutional command, nor does it violate any implicit Separation of Powers principle. Consequently, I believe that the Act is constitutional. . . .

. . . .

III

The Court believes that the Act violates the literal text of the Constitution. A simple syllogism captures its basic reasoning:

> Major Premise: The Constitution sets forth an exclusive method for enacting, repealing, or amending laws. . . .

> Minor Premise: The Act authorizes the President to "repea[l] or amen[d]" laws in a different way, namely by announcing a cancellation of a portion of a previously enacted law. . . .

> Conclusion: The Act is inconsistent with the Constitution. . . .

I find this syllogism unconvincing, however, because its Minor Premise is faulty. When the President "canceled" the two appropriation measures now before us, he did not repeal any law nor did he amend any law. He simply *followed* the law, leaving the statutes, as they are literally written, intact.

To understand why one cannot say, *literally speaking*, that the President has repealed or amended any law, imagine how the provisions of law before us might have been, but were not, written. Imagine that the canceled New York health care tax provision at issue here, . . . had instead said the following:

> Section One. Taxes that were collected by the State of New York from a health care provider before June 1, 1997 and for which a waiver of provisions [requiring payment] have been sought . . . are deemed to be permissible health care related taxes . . . *provided however that the President may prevent the just-mentioned provision from having legal force or effect if he determines x, y and z.* (Assume x, y and z to be the same determinations required by the Line Item Veto Act).

Whatever a person might say, or think, about the constitutionality of this imaginary law, there is one thing the English language would prevent one from saying. One could not say that a President who "prevent[s]" the deeming language from "having legal force or effect,". . . has either *repealed* or *amended* this particular hypothetical statute. Rather, the President has *followed* that law to the letter. He has exercised the power it explicitly delegates to him. He has executed the law, not repealed it.

It could make no significant difference to this linguistic point were the italicized proviso to appear, not as part of what I have called Section One, but, instead, at the bottom of the statute page, say referenced by an asterisk, with a statement that it applies to every spending provision in the act next to which a similar asterisk appears. And that being so, it could make no difference if that proviso appeared, instead, in a different, earlier-enacted law, along with legal language that makes it applicable to every future spending provision picked out according to a specified formula. . . .

But, of course, this last-mentioned possibility is this very case. The earlier law, namely, the Line Item Veto Act, says that "the President may prevent such [future] budget authority from having legal force or effect.". . . For that reason, one cannot dispose of this case through a purely literal analysis as the majority does. Literally speaking, the President has not "repealed" or "amended" anything. He has simply executed a power conferred upon him by Congress, which power is contained in laws that were enacted in compliance with the exclusive method set forth in the Constitution. . . .

. . . [T]he Act contains a "lockbox" feature, which gives legal significance to the enactment of a particular appropriations item even if, and even after, the President has rendered it without "force or effect.". . . That is . . . why it seems fair to say that, despite the Act's use of the word "cancel," the Act does not delegate to the President the power truly to *cancel* a line item expenditure (returning the legal status quo to one in which the item had never been enacted). Rather, it delegates to the President the power to decide *how* to spend the money to which the line item refers — either for the specific purpose mentioned the item, or for general deficit reduction via the "lockbox" feature.

These features of the law . . . mean that it is not, and it is not just like, the repeal or amendment of a law, or, for that matter, a true line item veto (despite the Act's title). Because one cannot say that the President's exercise of the power the Act grants is, literally speaking, a "repeal" or "amendment," the fact that the Act's procedures differ from the Constitution's exclusive procedures for enacting (or repealing) legislation is beside the point. The Act *itself* was enacted in accordance with these procedures, and its failure to require the President to satisfy those procedures does not make the Act unconstitutional.

IV

Because I disagree with the Court's holding of literal violation, I must consider whether the Act nonetheless violates Separation of Powers principles — principles that arise out of the Constitution's vesting of the "executive Power" in "a President," U.S. Const., Art. II, § 1, and "[a]ll legislative Powers" in "a Congress," Art. I, § 1. There are three relevant Separation of Powers questions here: (1) Has Congress given the President the wrong kind of power, *i.e.*, "non-Executive" power? (2) Has Congress given the President the power to "encroach" upon Congress' own constitutionally reserved territory? (3) Has Congress given the President too much power, violating the doctrine of "nondelegation?" These three limitations help assure "adequate control by the citizen's representatives in Congress," upon which Justice Kennedy properly insists . . . . And with respect to *this* Act, the answer to all these questions is "no."

A

Viewed conceptually, the power the Act conveys is the right kind of power. It is "executive." As explained above, an exercise of that power "executes" the Act. Conceptually speaking, it closely resembles the kind of delegated authority — to spend or not to spend appropriations, to change or not to change tariff rates — that Congress has frequently granted the President, any differences being differences in degree, not kind. . . .

B

The Act does not undermine what this Court has often described as the principal function of the Separation of Powers, which is to maintain the tripartite structure of the Federal Government — and thereby protect individual liberty — by providing a "safeguard against the encroachment or aggrandizement of one branch at the expense of the other." . . .

[O]ne cannot say that the Act "encroaches" upon Congress' power, when Congress retained the power to insert, by simple majority, into any future appropriations bill, into any section of any such bill, or into any phrase of any section, a provision that says the Act will not apply. . . .

Nor can one say that the Act's basic substantive objective is constitutionally improper, for the earliest Congresses could . . . and often did, confer on the President this sort of discretionary authority over spending. . . .

Nor can one say the Act's grant of power "aggrandizes" the Presidential office. The grant is limited to the context of the budget. It is limited to the power to spend, or not to spend, particular appropriated items, and the power to permit, or not to permit, specific limited exemptions from generally applicable tax law from taking effect. These powers, . . . resemble those the President has exercised in the past on other occasions. . . .

C

[Justice Breyer also concluded that LIVA did not violate the "nondelegation" doctrine.]

NOTE ON SIGNING STATEMENTS

Presidential uses of signing statements, though dating to the nineteenth century, have become more controversial in recent years. Some uses of signing statements have long historical roots and are not controversial. For instance, Presidents have issued signing statements to express their views on legislation or to interpret ambiguous portions of statutes. President Ronald Reagan and George H.W. Bush began to use signing statements more frequently to articulate their views that certain provisions were unconstitutional and that they would decline to enforce them. The American Bar Association Task Force on Presidential Signing Statements and the Separation of Powers Doctrine reported that President Reagan challenged 71 provisions of laws whereas President George H.W. Bush challenged 232 such provisions. President Clinton issued fewer signing statements than did President Bush but more than did President Reagan, primarily in legislation relating to foreign policy. President Clinton indicated that he would abide by any Court decision.

President George W. Bush issued more challenges to bills he signed than all of his predecessors combined. He used the signing statement to declare unconstitutional various provisions requiring reports to Congress and to claim the power to waive the McLain Amendment forbidding the use of torture on prisoners.

The ABA Task Force recommended that Presidents veto legislation they deem unconstitutional. It criticized, "as contrary to the rule of law and our constitutional system of separation of powers" using signing statements to "claim the authority or state the intention to disregard or decline to enforce all or part of a law the President has signed, or to interpret such a law in a manner inconsistent with the clear intent of Congress."

§ 5.03 ADMINISTRATIVE CHIEF

MORRISON v. OLSON
487 U.S. 654, 108 S. Ct. 2597, 101 L. Ed. 2d 569 (1988)

CHIEF JUSTICE REHNQUIST delivered the opinion of the Court.

This case presents us with a challenge to the independent counsel provisions of the Ethics in Government Act of 1978, 28 U.S.C. §§ 49, 591 *et seq.* (1982 ed., Supp. V). We hold today that these provisions of the Act do not violate the Appointments Clause of the Constitution, Art. II, § 2, cl. 2, or the limitations of Article III, nor do they impermissibly interfere with the President's authority under Article II in violation of the constitutional principle of separation of powers.

I

Briefly stated, Title VI of the Ethics of Government Act (Title VI of the Act) . . . allows for the appointment of an "independent counsel" to investigate and, if appropriate, prosecute certain high ranking Government officials for violations of federal criminal laws. The Act requires the Attorney General, upon receipt of information that he determines is "sufficient to constitute grounds to investigate whether any person [covered by the Act] may have violated any Federal criminal law," to conduct a preliminary investigation of the matter. When the Attorney General has completed this investigation, or 90 days has elapsed, he is required to report to a special court (the Special Division) created by the Act "for the purpose of appointing independent counsels." . . . If . . . the Attorney General has determined that there are "reasonable grounds to believe that further investigation or prosecution is warranted," then he "shall apply to the division of the court for the appointment of an independent counsel." The Attorney General's application to the court "shall contain sufficient information to assist the [court] in selecting an independent counsel and in defining that independent counsel's prosecutorial jurisdiction." . . . Upon receiving this application, the Special Division "shall appoint an appropriate independent counsel and shall define that independent counsel's prosecutorial jurisdiction." . . .

With respect to all matters within the independent counsel's jurisdiction, the Act grants the counsel "full power and independent authority to exercise all investigative and prosecutorial functions and powers of the Department of Justice, the Attorney General, and any other officer or employee of the Department of Justice." . . .

Two statutory provisions govern the length of an independent counsel's tenure in office. The first defines the procedure for removing an independent counsel. Section 596(a)(1) provides:

> An independent counsel appointed under this chapter may be removed from office, other than by impeachment and conviction, only by the personal action of the Attorney General and only for good cause, physical disability, mental incapacity, or any other condition that substantially impairs the performance of such independent counsel's duties.

If an independent counsel is removed pursuant to this section, the Attorney General is required to submit a report to both the Special Division and the Judiciary Committees of the Senate and House "specifying the facts found and the ultimate grounds for such removal." . . . Under the current version of the Act, an independent counsel can obtain judicial review of the Attorney General's action by filing a civil action in the United States District Court for the District of Columbia. Members of the Special Division "may not hear or determine any such civil action or any appeal of a decision in any such civil action." The reviewing court is authorized to grant reinstatement or "other appropriate relief." . . .

The other provision governing the tenure of the independent counsel defines the procedures for "terminating" the counsel's office. Under § 596(b)(1), the office of an independent counsel terminates when he or she notifies the Attorney General that he or she has completed or substantially completed any investigations or prosecutions undertaken pursuant to the Act. In addition, the Special Division, acting either on its own or on the suggestion of the Attorney General, may terminate the office of an independent counsel at any time if it finds that "the investigation of all matters within the prosecutorial jurisdiction of such independent counsel . . . have been completed or so substantially completed that it would be appropriate for the Department of Justice to complete such investigations and prosecutions." . . .

[I]n May and June 1987, appellant [independent counsel] caused a grand jury to issue and serve subpoenas *ad testificandum* and *duces tecum* on appellees. All three appellees moved to quash the subpoenas, claiming, among other things, that the independent counsel provisions of the Act were unconstitutional and that appellant accordingly had no authority to proceed. . . . The [court of appeals] ruled first that an independent counsel is not an "inferior Officer" of the United States for purposes of the Appointments Clause. Accordingly, the court found the Act invalid because it does not provide for the independent counsel to be nominated by the President and confirmed by the Senate, as the Clause requires for "principal" officers. The court then went on to consider several alternative grounds for its conclusion that the statute was unconstitutional. In the majority's view, the Act also violates the Appointments Clause insofar as it empowers a court of law to appoint an "inferior" officer who performs core executive functions; . . .the Act's restrictions on the Attorney General's power to remove an independent counsel violate the separation of powers; and finally. the Act interferes with the Executive Branch's prerogative to "take care that the Laws be faithfully executed," Art. II, § 3. . . .

III

The Appointments Clause of Article II reads as follows:

[The President] shall nominate, and by and with the Advice and Consent of the Senate, shall appoint Ambassadors, other public Ministers and Consuls, Judges of the supreme Court, and all other Officers of the United States, whose Appointments are not herein otherwise provided for, and which shall be established by Law: but the Congress may by Law vest the Appointment of such inferior Officers, as they think proper, in the President alone, in the Courts of Law, or in the Heads of Departments." U.S. Const., Art. II, § 2 cl. 2. . . .

The line between "inferior" and "principal" officers is one that is far from clear. . . . We need not attempt here to decide exactly where the line falls between the two types of officers, because in our view appellant clearly falls on the "inferior officer" side of that line. Several factors lead to this conclusion.

First, appellant is subject to removal by a higher Executive Branch official. Although appellant may not be "subordinate" to the Attorney General (and the President) insofar as she possesses a degree of independent discretion to exercise the powers delegated to her under the Act, the fact that she can be removed by the Attorney General indicates that she is to some degree "inferior" in rank and authority. Second, appellant is empowered by the Act to perform only certain, limited duties. An independent counsel's role is restricted primarily to investigation and, if appropriate, prosecution for certain federal crimes. . . .

Third, appellant's office is limited in jurisdiction. Not only is the Act itself restricted in applicability to certain federal officials suspected of certain serious federal crimes, but an independent counsel can only act within the scope of the jurisdiction that has been granted by the Special Division pursuant to a request by the Attorney General. Finally, appellant's office is limited in tenure. There is concededly no time limit on the appointment of a particular counsel. Nonetheless, the office of independent counsel is "temporary" in the sense that an independent counsel is appointed essentially to accomplish a single task, and when that task is over the office is terminated, either by the counsel herself or by action of the Special Division. Unlike other prosecutors, appellant has no ongoing responsibilities that extend beyond the accomplishment of the mission that she was appointed for and authorized by the Special Division to undertake. In our view, these factors relating to the "ideas of tenure, duration . . . and duties" of the independent counsel. . . , are sufficient to establish that appellant is an "inferior" officer in the constitutional sense. . . .

This does not, however, end our inquiry under the Appointments Clause. Appellees argue that even if appellant is an "inferior" officer, the Clause does not empower Congress to place the power to appoint such an officer outside the Executive Branch. They contend that the Clause does not contemplate congressional authorization of "interbranch appointments," in which an officer of one branch is appointed by officers of another branch. The relevant language of the Appointments Clause is worth repeating. It reads: ". . . but the Congress may by Law vest the Appointment of such inferior Officers, as they think proper, in the President alone, in the courts of Law, or in the Heads of Departments." On its face, the language of this "excepting clause" admits of no limitation on interbranch appointments. Indeed, the inclusion of "as they think proper" seems clearly to give Congress significant discretion to determine whether it is "proper" to vest the appointment of, for example, executive officials in the "courts of Law". . . .

We do not mean to say that Congress' power to provide for interbranch appointments of "inferior officers" is unlimited. In addition to separation of powers concerns, which would arise if such provisions for appointment had the potential to impair the constitutional functions assigned to one of the branches, . . . Congress' decision to vest the appointment power in the courts would be improper if there was some "incongruity" between the functions normally performed by the courts and the performance of their duty to appoint. . . . In this case, however, we do not think it impermissible for Congress to vest the power to appoint independent counsel in a specially created federal court. We thus disagree with the Court of Appeals' conclusion that there is an inherent incongruity about a court having the power to appoint prosecutorial officers. . . .

V

We now turn to consider whether the Act is invalid under the constitutional principle of separation of powers. Two related issues must be addressed: The first is whether the provision of the Act restricting the Attorney General's power to remove the independent counsel to only those instances in which he can show "good cause," taken by itself, impermissibly interferes with the President's exercise of his constitutionally appointed functions. The second is whether, taken as a whole, the Act violates the separation of powers by reducing the President's ability to control the prosecutorial powers wielded by the independent counsel.

A

Two Terms ago we had occasion to consider whether it was consistent with the separation of powers for Congress to pass a statute that authorized a government official who is removable only by Congress to participate in what we found to be "executive powers." *Bowsher v. Synar*, 478 U.S. 714, 730 (1986). We held in *Bowsher* that "Congress cannot reserve for itself the power of removal of an officer charged with the execution of the laws except by impeachment." . . . A primary antecedent for this ruling was our 1926 decision in *Myers v. United States*, 272 U.S. 52. *Myers* had considered the propriety of a federal statute by which certain postmasters of the United States could be removed by the President only "by and with the advice and consent of the Senate." There too, Congress' attempt to involve itself in the removal of an executive official was found to be sufficient grounds to render the statute invalid. As we observed in *Bowsher*, the essence of the decision in *Myers* was the judgment that the Constitution prevents Congress from "draw[ing] to itself . . . the power to remove or the right to participate in the exercise of that power. To do this would be to go beyond the words and implications of the [Appointments Clause] and to infringe the constitutional principle of the separation of governmental powers." . . .

Unlike both *Bowsher* and *Myers*, this case does not involve an attempt by Congress itself to gain a role in the removal of executive officials other than its established powers of impeachment and conviction. The Act instead puts the removal power squarely in the hands of the Executive Branch; an independent counsel may be removed from office, "only by the personal action of the Attorney General, and only for good cause." . . . In our view, the removal provisions of the Act make this case more analogous to *Humphrey's Executor v. United States*, 295 U.S. 602 (1935), and *Wiener v. United States*, 357 US 349 (1958), than to *Myers* or *Bowsher*.

In *Humphrey's Executor*, the issue was whether a statute restricting the President's power to remove the Commissioners of the Federal Trade Commission (FTC) only for "inefficiency, neglect of duty, or malfeasance in office" was consistent with the Constitution. . . . We stated that whether Congress can "condition the [President's power of removal] by fixing a definite term and precluding a removal except for cause, will depend upon the character of the office." . . . In *Humphrey's Executor*, we found it "plain" that the Constitution did not give the President "illimitable power of removal" over the officers of independent agencies. . . . Were the President to have the power to remove FTC Commissioners at will, the "coercive influence" of the removal power would "threate[n] the independence of [the] commission." . . .

Similarly, in *Wiener* we considered whether the President had unfettered discretion to remove a member of the War Claims Commission, which had been established by Congress in the War Claims Act of 1948. . . . As in *Humphrey's Executor*, however, the Commissioners were entrusted by Congress with adjudicatory powers that were to be exercised free from executive control. . . . Accordingly, we rejected the President's attempt to remove a Commissioner "merely because he wanted his own appointees on [the] Commission", stating that "no such power is given to the President directly by the Constitution, and none is impliedly conferred upon him by statute." . . .

Appellees contend that *Humphrey's Executor* and *Wiener* are distinguishable from this case because they did not involve officials who performed a "core executive function." They argue that our decision in *Humphrey's Executor* rests on a distinction between "purely executive" officials and officials who exercise "quasi-legislative" and "quasi-judicial" powers. In their view, when a "purely executive" official is involved, the governing precedent is *Myers*, not *Humphrey's Executor*. . . . And, under *Myers*, the President must have absolute discretion to discharge "purely" executive officials at will. . . .

We undoubtedly did rely on the terms "quasi-legislative" and "quasi-judicial" to distinguish the officials involved in *Humphrey's Executor* and *Wiener* from those in *Myers*, but our present considered view is that the determination of whether the Constitution allows Congress to impose a "good cause"-type restriction on the President's power to remove an official cannot be made to turn on whether or not that official is classified as "purely executive." The analysis contained in our removal cases is designed not to define rigid categories of those officials who may or may not be removed at will by the President, but to ensure that Congress does not interfere with the President's exercise of the "executive power" and his constitutionally appointed duty to "take care that the laws be faithfully executed" under Article II. *Myers* was undoubtedly correct in its holding, and in its broader suggestion that there are some "purely executive" officials who must be removable by the President at will if he is to be able to accomplish his constitutional role. . . . At the other end of the spectrum from *Myers*, the characterization of the agencies in *Humphrey's Executor* and *Wiener* as "quasi-legislative" and "quasi-judicial" in large part reflected our judgment that it was not essential to the President's proper execution of his Article II powers that these agencies be headed up by individuals who were removable at will. We do not mean to suggest that an analysis of the functions served by the officials at issue is irrelevant. But the real question is whether the removal restrictions are of such a nature that they impede the President's ability to perform his constitutional duty, and the functions of the officials in question must be analyzed in that light.

Considering for the moment the "good cause" removal provision in isolation from the other parts of the Act at issue in this case, we cannot say that the imposition of a "good cause" standard for removal by itself unduly trammels on executive authority. There is no real dispute that the functions performed by the independent counsel are "executive" in the sense that they are law enforcement functions that typically have been undertaken by officials within the Executive Branch. As we noted above, however, the independent counsel is an inferior officer under the Appointments Clause, with limited jurisdiction and tenure and lacking policymaking or significant administrative authority. Although the counsel exercises no small amount of discretion and judgment in deciding how to carry out his or her duties under the Act, we simply do not see how the President's need to control the exercise of that discretion is so central to the function of the Executive Branch as to require as a matter of constitutional law that the counsel be terminable at will by the President.

Nor do we think that the "good cause" removal provision at issue here impermissibly burdens the President's power to control or supervise the independent counsel, as an executive official, in the execution of his or her duties under the Act. This is not a case in which the power to remove an executive official has been completely stripped from the President, thus providing no means for the President to ensure the "faithful execution" of the laws. Rather, because the independent counsel may be terminated for "good cause," the Executive, through the Attorney General, retains ample authority to assure that the counsel is competently performing his or her statutory responsibilities in a manner that comports with the provisions of the Act. Although we need not decide in this case exactly what is encompassed within the term "good cause" under the Act, the legislative history of the removal provision also makes clear that the Attorney General may remove an independent counsel for "misconduct." . . . Here, as with the provision of the Act conferring the appointment authority of the independent counsel on the special court, the congressional determination to limit the removal power of the Attorney General was essential, in the view of Congress, to establish the necessary independence of the office. We do not think that this limitation as it presently stands sufficiently deprives the President of control over the independent counsel to interfere impermissibly with his constitutional obligation to ensure the faithful execution of the laws.

B

The final question to be addressed is whether the Act, taken as a whole, violates the principle of separation of powers by unduly interfering with the role of the Executive Branch. Time and again we have reaffirmed the importance in our constitutional scheme of the separation of governmental powers into the three coordinate branches. . . .

We observe first that this case does not involve an attempt by Congress to increase its own powers at the expense of the Executive Branch. . . .

Similarly, we do not think that the Act works any *judicial* usurpation of properly executive functions. As should be apparent from our discussion of the Appointments Clause above, the power to appoint inferior officers such as independent counsels is not in itself an "executive" function in the constitutional sense, at least when Congress has exercised its power to vest the appointment of an inferior office in the "courts of Law." We note nonetheless that under the Act the Special Division has no power to appoint an independent counsel *sua sponte*; it may only do so upon the specific request of the Attorney General, and the courts are specifically prevented from reviewing the Attorney General's decision not to seek appointment. . . .

Finally, we do not think that the Act "impermissibly undermine[s]" the powers of the Executive Branch . . . or "disrupts the proper balance between the coordinate branches [by] prevent[ing] the Executive Branch from accomplishing its constitutionally assigned functions." . . . It is undeniable that the Act reduces the amount of control or supervision that the Attorney General and, through him, the President exercises over the investigation and prosecution of a certain class of alleged criminal activity. The Attorney General is not allowed to appoint the individual of his choice; he does not determine the counsel's jurisdiction; and his power to remove a counsel is limited. Nonetheless, the Act does give the Attorney General several means of supervising or controlling the prosecutorial powers that may be wielded by an independent counsel. Most importantly, the Attorney General retains the power to remove the counsel for "good cause," a power that we have already concluded provides the Executive with substantial ability to ensure that the laws are "faithfully executed" by an independent counsel. No independent counsel may be appointed without a specific request by the Attorney General, and the Attorney General's decision not to request appointment if he finds "no reasonable grounds to believe that further investigation is warranted" is committed to his unreviewable discretion. The Act thus gives the Executive a degree of control over the power to initiate an investigation by the independent counsel. In addition, the jurisdiction of the independent counsel is defined with reference to the facts submitted by the Attorney General, and once a counsel is appointed, the Act requires that the counsel abide by Justice Department policy unless it is not "possible" to do so. Notwithstanding the fact that the counsel is to some degree "independent" and free from executive supervision to a greater extent than other federal prosecutors, in our view these features of the Act give the Executive Branch sufficient control over the independent counsel to ensure that the President is able to perform his constitutionally assigned duties.

VI

In sum, we conclude today that it does not violate the Appointments Clause for Congress to vest the appointment of independent counsels in the Special Division; that the powers exercised by the Special Division under the Act do not violate Article III; and that the Act does not violate the separation-of-powers principle by impermissibly interfering with the functions of the Executive Branch. The decision of the Court of Appeals is therefore *Reversed*.

JUSTICE SCALIA dissenting.

It is the proud boast of our democracy that we have "a government of laws and not of men." . . .

The Framers of the Federal Constitution similarly viewed the principle of separation of powers as the absolutely central guarantee of a just Government. In No. 47 of The Federalist, Madison wrote that "[n]o political truth is certainly of greater intrinsic value, or is stamped with the authority of more enlightened patrons of liberty.". . . Without a secure structure of separated powers, our Bill of Rights would be worthless, as are the bills of rights of many nations of the world that have adopted, or even improved upon, the mere words of ours.

The principle of separation of powers is expressed in our Constitution in the first section of each of the first three Articles. Article I, § 1, provides that "[a]ll legislative Powers herein granted shall be vested in a Congress of the United States, which shall consist of a Senate and House of Representatives." Article III, § 1, provides that "[t]he judicial Power of the United States, shall be vested in one supreme Court, and in such inferior Courts as the Congress may from time to time ordain and establish." And the provision at issue here, Art. II, § 1, cl. 1, provides that "[t]he executive Power shall be vested in a President of the United States of America."

But just as the mere words of a Bill of Rights are not self-effectuating, the Framers recognized "[t]he insufficiency of a mere parchment delineation of the boundaries" to achieve the separation of powers. . . . "[T]he great security," wrote Madison, "against a gradual concentration of the several powers in the same department consists in giving to those who administer each department the necessary constitutional means and personal motives to resist encroachments of the others. The provision for defense must in this, as in all other cases, be made commensurate to the danger of attack." . . .

The major "fortification" provided [the executive], of course, was the veto power. But in addition to providing fortification, the Founders conspicuously and very consciously declined to sap the Executive's strength in the same way they had weakened the Legislature: by dividing the executive power. Proposals to have multiple executives, or a council of advisers with separate authority were rejected. . . . Thus, while "[a]ll legislative Powers herein granted shall be vested in a Congress of the United States, which shall consist of a Senate *and* House of Representatives," U.S. Const., Art. I, § 1 (emphasis added), "[t]he executive Power shall be vested in *a President of the United States*," Art. II, § 1, cl. 1 (emphasis added).

That is what this suit is about. Power. The allocation of power among Congress, the President, and the courts in such fashion as to preserve the equilibrium the Constitution sought to establish — so that "a gradual concentration of the several powers in the same department," . . . can effectively be resisted. Frequently an issue of this sort will come before the Court clad, so to speak, in sheep's clothing: the potential of the asserted principle to effect important change in the equilibrium of power is not immediately evident, and must be discerned by a careful and perceptive analysis. But this wolf comes as a wolf. . . .

If to describe this case is not to decide it, the concept of a government of separate and coordinate powers no longer has meaning. The Court devotes most of its attention to such relatively technical details as the Appointments Clause and the removal power, addressing briefly and only at the end of its opinion the separation of powers. As my prologue suggests, I think that has it backwards. Our opinions are full of the recognition that it is the principle of separation of powers, and the inseparable corollary that each department's "defense must . . . be made commensurate to the danger of attack." Federalist No. 51, p. 322 (Madison). . . .

To repeat, Article II, § 1, cl. 1, of the Constitution provides:

The executive Power shall be vested in a President of the United States.

As I described at the outset of this opinion, this does not mean *some* of the executive power, but *all* of the executive power. It seems to me, therefore, that the decision of the Court of Appeals invalidating the present statute must be upheld on fundamental separation-of-powers principles if the following two questions are answered affirmatively: (1) Is the conduct of a criminal prosecution (and of an investigation to decide whether to prosecute) the exercise of purely executive power? (2) Does the statute deprive the President of the United States of exclusive control over the exercise of that power? Surprising to say, the Court appears to concede an affirmative answer to both questions, but seeks to avoid the inevitable conclusion that since the statute vests some purely executive power in a person who is not the President of the United States it is void. . . .

As I have said, however, it is ultimately irrelevant *how much* the statute reduces Presidential control. The case is over when the Court acknowledges, as it must, that "[i]t is undeniable that the Act reduces the amount of control or supervision that the Attorney General and, through him, the President exercises over the investigation and prosecution of a certain class of alleged criminal activity." . . . It effects a revolution in our constitutional jurisprudence for the Court, once it has determined that (1) purely executive functions are at issue here, and (2) those functions have been given to a person whose actions are not fully within the supervision and control of the President, nonetheless to proceed further to sit in judgment of whether "the President's need to control the exercise of [the independent counsel's] discretion is *so central* to the functioning of the Executive Branch" as to require complete control, . . . (emphasis added), whether the conferral of his powers upon someone else "*sufficiently* deprives the President of control over the independent counsel to interfere impermissibly with [his] constitutional obligation to ensure the faithful execution of the laws," . . . (emphasis added), and whether "the Act give[s] the Executive Branch *sufficient* control over the independent counsel to ensure that the President is able to perform his constitutionally assigned duties," . . . (emphasis added). It is not for us to determine, and we have never presumed to determine, how much of the purely executive powers of government must be within the full control of the President. The Constitution prescribes that they *all* are. . . .

Is it unthinkable that the President should have such exclusive power, even when alleged crimes by him or his close associates are at issue? No more so than that Congress should have the exclusive power of legislation, even when what is at issue is its own exemption from the burdens of certain laws. *See* Civil Rights Act of 1964, Title VII, 42 U. S. C. 696. § 2000e *et seq.* (prohibiting "employers," not defined to include the United States, from discriminating on the basis of race, color, religion, sex, or national origin). No more so than that this Court should have the exclusive power to pronounce the final decision on justiciable cases and controversies, even those pertaining to the constitutionality of a statute reducing the salaries of the Justices. *See United States v. Will*, 449 U.S. 200, 211-217 (1980). . . . A system of separate and coordinate powers necessarily involves an acceptance of exclusive power that can theoretically be abused. As we reiterate this very day, "[i]t is a truism that constitutional protections have costs." *Coy v. Iowa*, 87 U.S. 1012, 1020 (1988). . . . While the separation of powers may prevent us from righting every wrong, it does so in order to ensure that we do not lose liberty. The checks against any branch's abuse of *its* exclusive powers are twofold: First, retaliation by one of the other branch's use of *its* exclusive powers: Congress, for example, can impeach the executive who willfully fails to enforce the laws; the executive can decline to prosecute under unconstitutional statutes, *cf. United States v. Lovett*, 328 U.S. 303 (1946); and the courts can dismiss malicious prosecutions. Second, and ultimately, there is the political check that the people will replace those in the political branches (the branches more "dangerous to the political rights of the Constitution," Federalist No. 78, p. 465) who are guilty of abuse. Political pressures produced special prosecutors — for Teapot Dome and for Watergate, for example — long before this statute created the independent counsel. . . .

The Court has, nonetheless, replaced the clear constitutional prescription that the executive power belongs to the President with a "balancing test." What are the standards to determine how the balance is to be struck, that is, how much removal of Presidential power is too much? Many countries of the world get along with an executive that is much weaker than ours — in fact, entirely dependent upon the continued support of the legislature. Once we depart from the text of the Constitution, just where short of that do we stop? The most amazing feature of the Court's opinion is that it does not even purport to give an answer. It simply *announces*, with no analysis, that the ability to control the decision whether to investigate and prosecute the President's closest advisers, and indeed the President himself, is not "so central to the functioning of the Executive Branch" as to be constitutionally required to be within the President's control. Apparently that is so because we say it is so. Having abandoned as the basis for our decisionmaking the text of Article II that "the executive Power" must be vested in the President, the Court does not even attempt to craft a *substitute* criterion . . ., however remote from the Constitution — that today governs, and in the future will govern, the decision of such questions. Evidently, the governing standard is to be what might be called the unfettered wisdom of a majority of this Court, revealed to an obedient people on a case-by-case basis. This is not only not the government of laws that the Constitution established; it is not a government of laws at all.

In my view, moreover, even as an ad hoc, standardless judgment the Court's conclusion must be wrong. Before this statute was passed, the President, in taking action disagreeable to the Congress, or an executive officer giving advice to the President or testifying before Congress concerning one of those many matters on which the two branches are from time to time at odds, could be assured that his acts and motives would be adjudged — insofar as the decision whether to conduct a criminal investigation and to prosecute is concerned — in the Executive Branch, that is, in a forum attuned to the interests and the policies of the Presidency. That was one of the natural advantages the Constitution gave to the Presidency, just as it gave Members of Congress (and their staffs) the advantage of not being prosecutable for anything said or done in their legislative capacities. It is the very object of this legislation to eliminate that assurance of a sympathetic forum. Unless it can honestly be said that there are "no reasonable grounds to believe" that further investigation is warranted, further investigation must ensue; and the conduct of the investigation, and determination of whether to prosecute, will be given to a person neither selected by nor subject to the control of the President — who will in turn assemble a staff by finding out, presumably, who is willing to put aside whatever else they are doing, for an indeterminate period of time, in order to investigate and prosecute the President or a particular named individual in his administration. The prospect is frightening (as I will discuss at some greater length at the conclusion of this opinion) even outside the context of a bitter, interbranch political dispute. Perhaps the boldness of the President himself will not be affected — though I am not even sure of that. (How much easier it is for Congress, instead of accepting the political damage attendant to the commencement of impeachment proceedings against the President on trivial grounds — or, for that matter, how easy it is for one of the President's political foes outside of Congress — simply to trigger a debilitating criminal investigation of the Chief Executive under this law.) But as for the President's high-level assistants, who typically have no political base of support, it is as utterly unrealistic to think that they will not be intimidated by this prospect, and that their advice to him and their advocacy of his interests before a hostile Congress will not be affected, as it would be to think that the Members of Congress and their staffs would be unaffected by replacing the Speech or Debate Clause with a similar provision. It deeply wounds the President, by substantially reducing the President's ability to protect himself and his staff. That is the whole object of the law, of course, and I cannot imagine why the Court believes it does not succeed.

Besides weakening the Presidency by reducing the zeal of his staff, it must also be obvious that the institution of the independent counsel enfeebles him more directly in his constant confrontations with Congress, by eroding his public support. Nothing is so politically effective as the ability to charge that one's opponent and his associates are not merely wrongheaded, naive, ineffective, but, in all probability, "crooks." And nothing so effectively gives an appearance of validity to such charges as a Justice Department investigation and, even better, prosecution. The present statute provides ample means for that sort of attack, assuring that massive and lengthy investigations will occur, not merely when the Justice Department in the application of its usual standards believes they are called for, but whenever it cannot be said that there are "no reasonable grounds to believe" they are called for. The statute's highly visible procedures assure, moreover, that unlike most investigations these will be widely known and prominently displayed. . . .

In sum, this statute does deprive the President of substantial control over the prosecutory functions performed by the independent counsel, and it does substantially affect the balance of powers. That the Court could possibly conclude otherwise demonstrates both the wisdom of our former constitutional system, in which the degree of reduced control and political impairment were irrelevant, since *all* purely executive power had to be in the President; and the folly of the new system of standardless judicial allocation of powers we adopt today. . . .

IV

There is, of course, no provision in the Constitution stating who may remove executive officers, except the provisions for removal by impeachment. Before the present decision it was established, however, (1) that the President's power to remove principal officers who exercise purely executive powers could not be restricted, *see Myers v. United States*, 272 U.S. 52, 127 (1926), and (2) that his power to remove inferior officers who exercise purely executive powers, and whose appointment Congress had removed from the usual procedure of Presidential appointment with Senate consent, could be restricted, at least where the appointment had been made by an officer of the Executive Branch . . . .

Since our 1935 decision in *Humphrey's Executor v. United States*, 295 U.S. 602 — which was considered by many at the time the product of an activist, anti-New Deal Court bent on reducing the power of President Franklin Roosevelt — it has been established that the line of permissible restriction upon removal of principal officers lies at the point at which the powers exercised by those officers are no longer purely executive. Thus, removal restrictions have been generally regarded as lawful for so-called "independent regulatory agencies," such as the Federal Trade Commission, the Interstate Commerce Commission, and the Consumer Product Safety Commission, which engage substantially in what has been called the "quasi-legislative activity" of rulemaking, and for members of Article I courts, such as the Court of Military Appeals, who engage in the "quasi-judicial" function of adjudication. . . .

As far as I can discern from the Court's opinion, it is now open season upon the President's removal power for all executive officers, with not even the superficially principled restriction of *Humphrey's Executor* as cover. The Court essentially says to the President: "Trust us. We will make sure that you are able to accomplish your constitutional role." I think the Constitution gives the President — and the people — more protection than that.

V

The purpose of the separation and equilibration of powers in general, and of the unitary Executive in particular, was not merely to assure effective government but to preserve individual freedom. Those who hold or have held offices covered by the Ethics in Government Act are entitled to that protection as much as the rest of us, and I conclude my discussion by considering the effect of the Act upon the fairness of the process they receive.

Only someone who has worked in the field of law enforcement can fully appreciate the vast power and the immense discretion that are placed in the hands of a prosecutor with respect to the objects of his investigation. . . .

Under our system of government, the primary check against prosecutorial abuse is a political one. The prosecutors who exercise this awesome discretion are selected and can be removed by a President, whom the people have trusted enough to elect. Moreover, when crimes are not investigated and prosecuted fairly, nonselectively, with a reasonable sense of proportion, the President pays the cost in political damage to his administration. . . .

That is the system of justice the rest of us are entitled to, but what of that select class consisting of present or former high-level Executive Branch officials? If an allegation is made against them of any violation of any federal criminal law (except Class B or C misdemeanors or infractions) the Attorney General must give it his attention. That in itself is not objectionable. But if, after a 90-day investigation without the benefit of normal investigatory tools, the Attorney General is unable to say that there are "no reasonable grounds to believe" that further investigation is warranted, a process is set in motion that is *not* in the full control of persons "dependent on the people," and whose flaws cannot be blamed on the President. An independent counsel is selected, and the scope of his or her authority prescribed, by a panel of judges. What if they are politically partisan, as judges have been known to be, and select a prosecutor antagonistic to the administration, or even to the particular individual who has been selected for this special treatment? There is no remedy for that, not even a political one. Judges, after all, have life tenure, and appointing a surefire enthusiastic prosecutor could hardly be considered an impeachable offense. So if there is anything wrong with the selection, there is effectively no one to blame. The independent counsel thus selected proceeds to assemble a staff. As I observed earlier, in the nature of things this has to be done by finding lawyers who are willing to lay aside their current careers for an indeterminate amount of time, to take on a job that has no prospect of permanence and little prospect for promotion. One thing is certain, however: it involves investigating and perhaps prosecuting a particular individual. Can one imagine a less equitable manner of fulfilling the executive responsibility to investigate and prosecute? . . . But even if it were entirely evident that unfairness was in fact the result — the judges hostile to the administration, the independent counsel an old foe of the President, the staff refugees from the recently defeated administration — *there would be no one accountable to the public to whom the blame could be assigned.*

I do not mean to suggest that anything of this sort (other than the inevitable self-selection of the prosecutory staff) occurred in the present case. I know and have the highest regard for the judges on the Special Division, and the independent counsel herself is a woman of accomplishment, impartiality, and integrity. But the fairness of a process must be adjudged on the basis of what it permits to happen, not what it produced in a particular case. It is true, of course, that a similar list of horribles could be attributed to an ordinary Justice Department prosecution — a vindictive prosecutor, an antagonistic staff, etc. But the difference is the difference that the Founders envisioned when they established a single Chief Executive accountable to the people: the blame can be assigned to someone who can be punished. . . .

It is, in other words, an additional advantage of the unitary Executive that it can achieve a more uniform application of the law. Perhaps that is not always achieved, but the mechanism to achieve it is there. The mini-Executive that is the independent counsel, however, operating in an area where so little is law and so much is discretion, is intentionally cut off from the unifying influence of the Justice Department, and from the perspective that multiple responsibilities provide. What would normally be regarded as a technical violation (there are no rules defining such things), may in his or her small world assume the proportions of an indictable offense. What would normally be regarded as an investigation that has reached the level of pursuing such picayune matters that it should be concluded, may to him or her be an investigation that ought to go on for another year. How frightening it must be to have your own independent counsel and staff appointed, with nothing else to do but to investigate you until investigation is no longer worthwhile — with whether it is worthwhile not depending upon what such judgments usually hinge on, competing responsibilities. And to have that counsel and staff decide, with no basis for comparison, whether what you have done is bad enough, willful enough, and provable enough, to warrant an indictment. How admirable the constitutional system that provides the means to avoid such a distortion. And how unfortunate the judicial decision that has permitted it.

The notion that every violation of law should be prosecuted, including — indeed, *especially* — every violation by those in high places, is an attractive one, and it would be risky to argue in an election campaign that that is not an absolutely overriding value. *Fiat justitia, ruat coelum.* Let justice be done, though the heavens may fall. The reality is, however, that it is not an absolutely overriding value, and it was with the hope that we would be able to acknowledge and apply such realities that the Constitution spared us, by life tenure, the necessity of election campaigns. . . .

Worse than what [the Court] has done, however, is the manner in which it has done it. A government of laws means a government of rules. Today's decision on the basic issue of fragmentation of executive power is ungoverned by rule, and hence ungoverned by law. It extends into the very heart of our most significant constitutional function the "totality of the circumstances" mode of analysis that this Court has in recent years become fond of. Taking all things into account, we conclude that the power taken away from the President here is not really *too* much. The next time executive power is assigned to someone other than the President we may conclude, taking all things into account, that it *is* too much. That opinion, like this one, will not be confined by any rule. We will describe, as we have today (though I hope more accurately) the effects of the provision in question, and will authoritatively announce: "The President's need to control the exercise of the [subject officer's] discretion *is* so central to the functioning of the Executive Branch as to require complete control." This is not analysis; it is ad hoc judgment. And it fails to explain why it is not true that — as the text of the Constitution seems to require, as the Founders seemed to expect, and as our past cases have uniformly assumed — all purely executive power must be under the control of the President.

The ad hoc approach to constitutional adjudication has real attraction, even apart from its work-saving potential. It is guaranteed to produce a result, in every case, that will make a majority of the Court happy with the law. The law is, by definition, precisely what the majority thinks, taking all things into account, it *ought* to be. I prefer to rely upon the judgment of the wise men who constructed our system, and of the people who approved it, and of two centuries of history that have shown it to be sound. Like it or not, that judgment says, quite plainly, that "[t]he executive Power shall be vested in a President of the United States."

NOTES

A. Appointing Power

(1) The President's position as administrative chief rests on his power to appoint and remove executive officers. The Appointments Clause of Article II prescribes the mode of appointing executive officers. Nonetheless, many employees of the Executive Branch hold civil serivce positions which are largely insulated from presidential control.

(2) Congress may not itself appoint executive officers. In *Buckley v. Valeo*, 424 U.S. 1 (1976), the Court held that appointment of four members of the Federal Election Commission by leaders of Congress, rather than the President, violated the Appointments Clause. The Appointments Clause is "a bulwark against one branch aggrandizing its power at the expense of another branch." *Ryder v. United States*, 515 U.S. 177, 182 (1995).

(3) Still, Congress is not powerless regarding the organization of the executive branch. The Senate has power to advise and consent to presidential appointments to office. Congress holds power to create offices. Congress also may prescribe qualifications for appointees. Common statutory restrictions proscribe citizenship, residence, age, and industrial and regional affiliations. Some laws require appointees to have stated political affiliations, possess professional attainments or occupational experience, or pass certain examinations. The entire civil service system has been based upon Congressional prescription of qualifications for federal positions.

(4) Congress may oversee administration of executive departments. The Senate's power to advise and consent to presidential appointments enables it to interrogate and often obtain concessions from cabinet nominees during confirmation hearings. Congress' ability to appropriate money for executive departments also allows the House and Senate to exercise oversight.

(5) *Freytag v. Commissioner of Internal Revenue*, 501 U.S. 868 (1991). The Court held Congress could grant the chief judge of the United States Tax Court authority to appoint special trial judges without violating the Appointments Clause. The Court agreed with the Tax Court and the Second Circuit that a special trial judge is an "inferior Officer" whose appointment, under the Appointments Clause, must be made by the President, a department head or court of law. Although the Tax Court was an Article I body, the Court held that the phrase "courts of law" as used in the Appointments Clause was not limited to Article III courts. Relying on constitutional text, doctrine, and historical practice, the Court held that Congress could allow the Chief Judge of the Tax Court to appoint such an inferior officer. Justice Scalia (joined by Justices O'Connor, Kennedy, and Souter) concurred in part. They, too, saw a special trial judge as an "inferior officer" but thought the Tax Court was a "Department" and not a "Court of Law" as provided by the Appointments Clause. It referred to "*The* Courts of Law"; the article "the" limited the eligible class to Article III courts the Constitution contemplated. The Tax Court was, however, "a free-standing, self-contained entity in the Executive Branch, whose Chief Judge is removable by the President." "Department" was not limited to those agencies headed by a member of the President's Cabinet.

(6) *Inferior Officer*. Like *Freytag*, *Morrison* involved the issue of who is an inferior officer. Does *Morrison* articulate any definite test to answer that question or does it simply identify some factors to consider? In *Edmond v. United States*, 520 U.S. 651, 662-63 (1997) the Court, in an opinion eight justices joined, stated:

Generally speaking, the term "inferior officer" connotes a relationship with some higher ranking officer or officers below the President: whether one is an "inferior" officer depends on whether he has a superior. It is not enough that other officers may be identified who formally maintain a higher rank, or possess responsibilities of a greater magnitude. If that were the intention, the Constitution might have used the phrase "lesser officer." Rather, in the context of a clause designed to preserve political accountability relative to important government assignments, we think it evident that "inferior officers" are officers whose work is directed and supervised at some level by others who were appointed by presidential nomination with the advise and consent of the Senate.

Would the independent counsel be an "inferior officer" under the *Edmond*'s approach? In view of the operation of the independent counsel statute under Kenneth Starr, should *Morrison* be reconsidered?

B. Removal Power

(7) The President's position as administrative chief depends largely on the power to remove officers of the executive branch. If the Chief Executive can remove from office at pleasure, it is impossible for office holders effectively to resist his will. "For it is quite evident that one who holds his office only during the pleasure of another, cannot be depended upon to maintain an attitude of independence against the latter's will." *Humphrey's Executor v. United States*, 295 U.S. 602, 629 (1935).

(8) The Constitution does not specifically confer a power to remove officers of the Executive Branch. The Constitution does require Senate confirmation for appointment and provides for removal by impeachment. These facts might lead a textualist to conclude that the President was not to have a removal power. Yet *Myers v. United States*, 272 U.S. 52 (1926), suggested that an executive officer appointed by the President may be removed by the President alone. Congress has created numerous agencies outside the executive departments, with important judicial-type functions. *Humphrey's Executor v. United States*, 295 U.S 602 (1935), and *Wiener v. United States*, 357 U.S. 349 (1958), held that the members of these agencies could not be removed by the President at will. As the *Humphrey* opinion put it, "The authority of Congress in creating quasi-legislative or quasi-judicial agencies, to require them to act in discharge of their duties independently of executive control cannot well be doubted; and that authority includes, as an appropriate incident, power to fix the period during which they shall continue in office, and to forbid their removal except for cause in the meantime." *Humphrey's Executor*, 295 U.S. at 629. *Morrison* allowed Congress to limit the President's power to remove executive officers by a "good cause" restriction. Does this suggest that *Myers* has a narrower reading than establishing an unfettered right of the President to remove those discharging executive duties?

(9) In *Bowsher v. Synar*, 478 U.S. 714 (1986), the Court held that the assignment to the Comptroller General of certain functions under the Gramm-Rudman Act was invalid. The Comptroller General is appointed by the President, but may be removed from office by a joint resolution of Congress. Gramm-Rudman gave the Comptroller General power to order specified spending reductions to reach targeted deficit levels. The Court ruled this provision an unconstitutional violation of the separation of powers. By placing the responsibility for execution of the statute in an officer subject to its removal power, "Congress in effect has retained control over the execution of the Act and has intruded into the executive function. The Constitution does not permit such intrusion." *Bowsher*, 478 U.S. at 734. Under *Bowsher*, once Congress legislates its role ends. Congress can thereafter control the execution of its law only by passing new legislation. It cannot control the responsible officer. In *Bowsher*, because the responsibility for execution of the statute was placed in an officer subject to its removal power, the constitutional

command that Congress play no direct role in the execution of the laws was directly violated.

C. Law Enforcement

(10) The Constitution also vests the President with responsibilities for law enforcement. He has the duty to "take care that the laws be faithfully executed." Art. II, § 3. "This is the widest power he has," wrote William Howard Taft. TAFT, THE PRESIDENCY 63 (1916). The "Take Care" duty includes the power of the Executive Branch to prosecute those who violate federal law. Did the independent counsel statute at issue in *Morrison* compromise the President's ability to discharge this function, as Justice Scalia suggested?

(11) The President's power to enforce the law includes the Constitution as well as statutes. In *In re Neagle*, 135 U.S. 1, 59 (1890), the Court held that "any obligation fairly and properly inferrible" from the Constitution was a "law" the President was empowered to enforce.

(12) The President's power "to grant Reprieves and Pardons for Offenses against the United States, except in Cases of Impeachment," Art. II, § 2, cl. 2, also helps shape his law enforcement role. What limits does the text of the Pardon Power impose on the President? Do other limits exist? Could a President pardon himself? What constitutional arguments might be made against such a self-pardon? *See* Brian Kalt, *"Pardon Me?: The Constitutional Case Against Presidential Self-Pardons*, 106 YALE L.J. 779 (1996). President Gerald R. Ford pardoned his predecessor, Richard M. Nixon, in 1974 shortly after Nixon's resignation and Ford's succession. Ford was defeated for a term of his own in 1976. In December 1992, after losing his re-election bid, President George H.W. Bush pardoned former defense secretary Casper Weinberger less than two weeks before he was to be tried for participating in a coverup of the Iran-Contra scandal. In the closing hours of his administration, President Clinton issued dozens of pardons, including to relatives and political supporters. Do any of these pardons raise constitutional problems? Were remedies of a sort available in either situation to hold Presidents Ford, Bush, or Clinton accountable?

D. The President's Power to Interpret the Law

(13) Does the President have constitutional power to interpret the Constitution? Just as courts must interpret the law, including the Constitution, so, too, must the President make constitutional judgments. *See* David A. Strauss, *Presidential Interpretation of the Constitution*, 15 CARDOZO L. REV. 113 (1993). Presidents construe the Constitution in public statements, in taking stands before courts, and in vetoing legislation. Constitutional considerations may affect decisions not to prosecute certain persons. President Thomas Jefferson pardoned some convicted under the Alien and Sedition Acts since he thought them unconstitutional. *See generally* Joel K. Goldstein, *The Presidency and the Rule of Law: Some Preliminary Explorations* 43 ST. LOUIS U. L.J. 791, 826-33 (1999).

The more difficult question is whether the President can interpret the Constitution in a manner at odds with the judiciary. Professor Michael Stokes Paulsen argues that the "Supreme Court's interpretations of treaties, federal statutes or the Constitution do not bind the President any more than the President's or Congress's interpretations bind the courts." Michael Stokes Paulsen, *The Most Dangerous Branch: Executive Power to Say What the Law Is*, 83 GEO. L.J. 217, 221-22 (1994). Professor Paulsen's claim presents a direct challenge to the notion that the Court is the ultimate constitutional interpreter. Although the Court upheld the Independent Counsel statute in *Morrison v. Olsen*, could a President veto a reenactment of the law on the grounds that he was persuaded by Justice Scalia's lonely dissent? Could the Chief Executive refuse to enforce a judicial judgment on the grounds that he thought it unconstitutional? Could he depart from judicial doctrine on the same basis? Professor Thomas Merrill argues for substantial executive autonomy but suggests that Presidents must enforce judicial judgments but not opinions. Thomas W. Merrill, *Judicial Opinions as Binding Law and as Explanations for Judgments*, 15 CARDOZO L. REV. 43 (1993). *See also* Christopher L. Eisgruber, *The Most Competent Branches: A Response to Professor Paulsen*, 83 GEO. L.J. 347 (1994); Richard H. Fallon, Jr., *Executive Power and the Political Constitution*, 2007 UTAH L. REV. 1; and David S. Strauss, *Presidential Interpretation of the Constitution*, 15 CARDOZO L. REV. 113 (1993).

§ 5.04   FOREIGN AFFAIRS

[1]   The Scope of Presidential Power

UNITED STATES v. CURTISS-WRIGHT EXPORT CORP.
299 U.S. 304, 57 S. Ct. 216, 81 L. Ed. 255 (1936)

MR. JUSTICE SUTHERLAND delivered the opinion of the Court.

[Editor's Note: An indictment charged that appellees conspired to sell fifteen machine guns to Bolivia, a country then at war in the Chaco, in violation of a Joint Resolution of Congress of May 28, 1934, and a presidential proclamation pursuant to the resolution. . . . The Joint Resolution (c. 365, 48 Stat. 811) provided:

Resolved by the Senate and House of Representatives of the United States of America in Congress assembled, That if the President finds that the prohibition of the sale of arms and munitions of war in the United States to those countries now engaged in armed conflict in the Chaco may contribute to the reestablishment of peace between those countries, and if after consultation with the governments of other American Republics and with their cooperation, as well as that of such other governments as he may deem necessary, he makes proclamation to that effect, it shall be unlawful to sell, except under such limitations and exceptions as the President prescribes, any arms or munitions of war in any place in the United States to the countries now engaged in that armed conflict, or to any person, company, or association acting in the interest of either country, until otherwise ordered by the President or by Congress.

Sec. 2. Whoever sells any arms or munitions of war in violation of section 1 shall, on conviction, be punished by a fine not exceeding $10,000 or by imprisonment not exceeding two years or both. . . .

President Franklin Roosevelt, "acting under and by virtue of the authority conferred in me by the said joint restriction of Congress" admonished American citizens not to provide weapons to parties involved in the conflict. Appellees challenged the first count of the indictment as an invalid delegation of legislative power to the executive. The lower court sustained the objection. The government appealed.] . . .

First. It is contended that by the Joint Resolution, the going into effect and continued operation of the resolution was conditioned (a) upon the President's judgment as to its beneficial effect upon the reestablishment of peace between the countries engaged in armed conflict in the Chaco; (b) upon the making of a proclamation, which was left to his unfettered discretion, thus constituting an attempted substitution of the President's will for that of Congress; (c) upon the making of a proclamation putting an end to the operation of the resolution, which again was left to the President's unfettered discretion; and (d) further, that the extent of its operation in particular cases was subject to limitation and exception by the President, controlled by no standard. In each of these particulars, appellees urge that Congress abdicated its essential functions and delegated them to the Executive.

Whether, if the Joint Resolution had related solely to internal affairs it would be open to the challenge that it constituted an unlawful delegation of legislative power to the Executive, we find it unnecessary to determine. The whole aim of the resolution is to affect a situation entirely external to the United States, and falling within the category of foreign affairs. The determination which we are called to make, therefore, is whether the Joint Resolution, as applied to that situation, is vulnerable to attack under the rule that forbids a delegation of the law-making power. In other words, assuming (but not deciding) that the challenged delegation, if it were confined to internal affairs, would be invalid, may it nevertheless be sustained on the ground that its exclusive aim is to afford a remedy for a hurtful condition within foreign territory?

It will contribute to the elucidation of the question if we first consider the differences between the powers of the federal government in respect of foreign or external affairs and those in respect of domestic or internal affairs. That there are differences between them, and that these differences are fundamental, may not be doubted.

The two classes of powers are different, both in respect of their origin and their nature. The broad statement that the federal government can exercise no powers except those specifically enumerated in the Constitution, and such implied powers as are necessary and proper to carry into effect the enumerated powers, is categorically true only in respect of our internal affairs. . . .

The Union existed before the Constitution, which was ordained and established among other things to form "a more perfect Union." Prior to that event, it is clear that the Union, declared by the Articles of Confederation to be "perpetual," was the sole possessor of external sovereignty and in the Union it remained without change save in so far as the Constitution in express terms qualified its exercise. The Framers' Convention was called and exerted its powers upon the irrefutable postulate that though the states were several their people in respect of foreign affairs were one. . . .

It results that the investment of the federal government with the powers of external sovereignty did not depend upon the affirmative grants of the Constitution. The powers to declare and wage war, to conclude peace, to make treaties, to maintain diplomatic relations with other sovereignties, if they had never been mentioned in the Constitution, would have vested in the federal government as necessary concomitants of national- ity. . . . As a member of the family of nations, the right and power of the United States in that field are equal to the right and power of the other members of the international family. Otherwise, the United States is not completely sovereign. The power to acquire territory by discovery and occupation . . . the power to expel undesirable aliens . . . the power to make such international agreements as do not constitute treaties in the constitutional sense . . . none of which is expressly affirmed by the Constitution, nevertheless exist as inherently inseparable from the conception of nationality. This the court recognized, and in each of the cases cited found the warrant for its conclusions not in the provisions of the Constitution, but in the law of nations. . . .

Not only, as we have shown, is the federal power over external affairs in origin and essential character different from that over internal affairs, but participation in the exercise of the power is significantly limited. In this vast external realm, with its important, complicated, delicate and manifold problems, the President alone has the power to speak or listen as a representative of the nation. He makes treaties with the advice and consent of the Senate; but he alone negotiates. Into the field of negotiation the Senate cannot intrude; and Congress itself is powerless to invade it. As Marshall said in his great argument of March 7, 1800, in the House of Representatives, "The President is the sole organ of the nation in its external relations, and its sole representative with foreign nations." . . .

It is important to bear in mind that we are here dealing not alone with an authority vested in the President by an exertion of legislative power, but with such an authority plus the very delicate, plenary and exclusive power of the President as the sole organ of the federal government in the field of international relations — a power which does not require as a basis for its exercise an act of Congress, but which, of course, like every other governmental power, must be exercised in subordination to the applicable provisions of the Constitution. It is quite apparent that if, in the maintenance of our international relations, embarrassment — perhaps serious embarrassment — is to be avoided and success for our aims achieved, congressional legislation which is to be made effective through negotiation and inquiry within the international field must often accord to the President a degree of discretion and freedom from statutory restriction which would not be admissible were domestic affairs alone involved. Moreover, he, not Congress, has the better opportunity of knowing the conditions which prevail in foreign countries, and especially is this true in time of war. He has his confidential sources of information. He has his agents in the form of diplomatic, consular and other officials. Secrecy in respect of information gathered by them may be highly necessary, and the premature disclosure of it productive of harmful results. . . .

When the President is to be authorized by legislation to act in respect of a matter intended to affect a situation in foreign territory, the legislator properly bears in mind the important consideration that the form of the President's action — or, indeed, whether he shall act at all — may well depend, among other things, upon the nature of the confidential information which he has or may thereafter receive, or upon the effect which his action may have upon our foreign relations. This consideration, in connection with what we have already said on the subject, discloses the unwisdom of requiring Congress in this field of governmental power to lay down narrowly definite standards by which the President is to be governed. . . .

In the light of the foregoing observations, it is evident that this court should not be in haste to apply a general rule which will have the effect of condemning legislation like that under review as constituting an unlawful delegation of legislative power. The principles which justify such legislation find overwhelming support in the unbroken legislative practice which has prevailed almost from the inception of the national government to the present day. . . .

Practically every volume of the United States Statutes contains one or more acts or joint resolutions of Congress authorizing action by the President in respect of subjects affecting foreign relations, which either leave the exercise of the power to his unrestricted judgment, or provide a standard far more general than that which has always been considered requisite with regard to domestic affairs. [Discussion of such acts omitted]. . . .

The uniform, long-continued and undisputed legislative practice . . .rests upon an admissible view of the Constitution which, even if the practice found far less support in principle than we think it does, we should not feel at liberty at this late day to disturb.

We deem it unnecessary to consider, seriatim, the several clauses which are said to evidence the unconstitutionality of the Joint Resolution as involving an unlawful delegation of legislative power. It is enough to summarize by saying that, both upon principle and in accordance with precedent, we conclude there is sufficient warrant for the broad discretion vested in the President to determine whether the enforcement of the statute will have a beneficial effect upon the reestablishment of peace in the affected countries; whether he shall make proclamation to bring the resolution into operation; whether and when the resolution shall cease to operate and to make proclamation accordingly; and to prescribe limitations and exceptions to which the enforcement of the resolution shall be subject. . . .

The judgment of the court below must be reversed and the cause remanded for further proceedings in accordance with the foregoing opinion.

It is so ordered.

Mr. Justice McReynolds does not agree. He is of opinion that the court below reached the right conclusion and its judgment ought to be affirmed.

NOTES

(1) The *Steel Seizure Case, supra* § 5.01, might be viewed as one in which Government power turned inward, as Justice Jackson put it in his concurring opinion, not because of rebellion, but because of an economic struggle between industry and labor. A different situation arises where governmental authority is turned against the outside world. *Curtiss-Wright* argues that federal power over external affairs is different, in origin and essential character, from that over internal affairs. What is the essential constitutional difference between the power over foreign affairs and that over domestic affairs? How does Justice Sutherland answer this question?

(2) Did Justice Sutherland need to write as sweeping a defense of presidential power in foreign affairs matters as he did? After all, Congress had passed a Joint Resolution authorizing the President to prohibit supplying arms to those involved in the Chaco conflict. The President had so acted, but defendants had provided arms nonetheless. Since the case raised the question of the propriety of the Congressional delegation, did the Court need to defend presidential action absent legislative authorization? If *Curtiss-Wright* were analyzed according to Justice Jackson's three categories, where would it fall?

(3) *Diplomacy and Recognition.* Article II gives the President the power to "appoint Ambassadors, other public Ministers and Consuls"; in addition, "he shall receive Ambassadors and other public Ministers." These provisions allow the President to conduct negotiations and diplomatic intercourse with foreign nations. As Thomas Jefferson put it, "[The President] being the only channel of communication between this country and foreign nations, it is from him alone that foreign nations or their agents are to learn what is or has been the will of the nation; and whatever he communicates as such, they have the right, and are bound to consider, as the expression of the nation." Richard M. Pious, The American Presidency 334 (1979).

(4) The constitutional power to "receive Ambassadors" authorizes the President to determine what governments to recognize. These decisions can impact external relations and domestic politics as the more controversial cases involving Cuba, Mexico, the former Soviet Union, Israel, and China indicate.

(5) Professor Pious claims that the executive's foreign affairs' power has expanded because "[t]he president claims the silences of the Constitution. He finds a general 'power to conduct foreign relations' for the nation. Then he assumes that whatever has not been expressly assigned to Congress is to be exercised by the executive." Pious, The American Presidency 333.

(6) Dean Harold Hongju Koh argues that the broad language in *Curtiss-Wright* was inconsistent with prior practice. To be sure, the President has controlled diplomatic communications but elsewhere foreign affairs decisions were made in consultation with Congress. *See* Harold Hongju Koh, The National Security Constitution 93-95 (1990).

(7) From time to time, Congress asserts its power to influence foreign policy. In 1986, Congress authorized aid to the Nicaraguan contras subject to conditions including a prohibition on American personnel entering or going near the border of Nicaragua to render aid to the contras. The Reagan Administration blatantly violated these conditions which produced the Iran-Contra scandal and cover-up. Congressional

investigations explored the extent of the abuses and a lengthy independent counsel inquiry resulted in eleven criminal convictions.

[2] Executive Agreements

DAMES & MOORE v. REGAN
453 U.S. 654, 101 S. Ct. 2972, 69 L. Ed. 2d 918 (1981)

JUSTICE REHNQUIST delivered the opinion of the Court. . . .

On November 4, 1979, the American Embassy in Tehran was seized and our diplomatic personnel were captured and held hostage. In response to that crisis, President Carter, acting pursuant to the International Emergency Economic Powers Act, 91 Stat. 1626, 50 U.S.C. §§ 1701-1706. (1976 ed., Supp. III) (hereinafter IEEPA), declared a national emergency on November 14, 1979, and blocked the removal or transfer of "all property and interests in property of the Government of Iran, its instrumentalities and controlled entities and the Central Bank of Iran which are or become subject to the jurisdiction of the United States. . . . "

On November 26, 1979, the President granted a general license authorizing certain judicial proceedings against Iran but which did not allow the "entry of any judgment or of any decree or order of similar or analogous effect. . . . " On December 19, 1979, a clarifying regulation was issued stating that "the general authorization for judicial proceedings contained in § 535.504(a) includes pre-judgment attachment." . . .

On December 19, 1979, petitioner Dames & Moore filed suit in . . . United States District Court . . . against the Government of Iran, the Atomic Energy Organization of Iran, and a number of Iranian banks [alleging damages for defendants' breach of contract in the amount of] $3,436,694.30 plus interest for services performed under the contract prior to the date of termination. The District Court issued orders of attachment directed against property of the defendants, and the property of certain Iranian banks was then attached to secure any judgment that might be entered against them.

On January 20, 1981, the Americans held hostage were released by Iran pursuant to an Agreement . . . [which] stated that "[i]t is the purpose of [the United States and Iran] . . . to terminate all litigation as between the Government of each party and the nationals of the other, and to bring about the settlement and termination of all such claims through binding arbitration." . . . In furtherance of this goal, the Agreement called for the establishment of an Iran-United States Claims Tribunal which would arbitrate any claims not settled within six months. Awards of the Claims Tribunal are to be "final and binding" and "enforceable . . . in the courts of any nation in accordance with its laws." . . . Under the Agreement, the United States is obligated

> to terminate all legal proceedings in United States courts involving claims of United States persons and institutions against Iran and its state enterprises, to nullify all attachments and judgments obtained therein, to prohibit all further litigation based on such claims, and to bring about the termination of such claims through binding arbitration. . . .

In addition, the United States must "act to bring about the transfer" by July 19, 1981, of all Iranian assets held in this country by American banks. . . . One billion dollars of these assets will be deposited in a security account in the Bank of England, to the account of the Algerian Central Bank, and used to satisfy awards rendered against Iran by the Claims Tribunal. . . . President Carter issued a series of Executive Orders implementing the terms of the agreement. . . . These Orders revoked all licenses permitting the exercise of "any right, power, or privilege" with regard to Iranian funds, securities, or deposits; "nullified" all non-Iranian interests in such assets acquired subsequent to the blocking order of November 14, 1979; and required those banks holding Iranian assets to transfer them "to the Federal Reserve Bank of New York, to be held or transferred as directed by the Secretary of the Treasury." . . .

Meanwhile on January 27, 1981, petitioner moved for summary judgment in the District Court against the Government of Iran and the Atomic Energy Organization, but not against the Iranian banks. The District Court granted petitioner's motion and awarded petitioner the amount claimed under the contract plus interest. . . .

On April 28, 1981, petitioner filed this action in the District Court for declaratory and injunctive relief against the United States and the Secretary of the Treasury, seeking to prevent enforcement of the Executive Orders and Treasury Department regulations implementing the Agreement with Iran. In its complaint, petitioner alleged that the actions of the President and the Secretary of the Treasury implementing the Agreement with Iran were beyond their statutory and constitutional powers and, in any event, were unconstitutional to the extent they adversely affect petitioner's final judgment against the Government of Iran and the Atomic Energy Organization, its execution of that judgment in the State of Washington, its prejudgment attachments, and its ability to continue to litigate against the Iranian banks. . . .

The parties and the lower courts, confronted with the instant questions, have all agreed that much relevant analysis is contained in *Youngstown Sheet & Tube Co. v. Sawyer*, 343 U.S. 579 (1952). Justice Black's opinion for the Court in that case, involving the validity of President Truman's effort to seize the country's steel mills in the wake of a nationwide strike, recognized that "[t]he President's power, if any, to issue the order must stem either from an act of Congress or from the Constitution itself." *Id.* at 585. Justice Jackson's concurring opinion elaborated in a general way the consequences of different types of interaction between the two democratic branches in assessing Presidential authority to act in any given case . . . [summarizing Justice Jackson's formulation].

Although we have in the past found and do today find Justice Jackson's classification of executive actions into three general categories analytically useful, . . . Justice Jackson himself recognized that his three categories represented "a somewhat over-simplified grouping," 343 U.S. at 635, and it is doubtless the case that executive action in any particular instance falls, not neatly in one of three pigeonholes, but rather at some point along a spectrum running from explicit congressional authorization to explicit congressional prohibition. This is particularly true as respects cases such as the one before us, involving responses to international crises the nature of which Congress can hardly have been expected to anticipate in any detail. [The Court found that President Carter's action in nullifying post November 14, 1979 attachments and directing the transfer of Iranian funds to the Federal Reserve was authorized by the International Emergency Economic Powers Act (IEEPA).]

Because the President's action in nullifying the attachments and ordering the transfer of the assets was taken pursuant to specific congressional authorization, it is "supported by the strongest of presumptions and the widest latitude of judicial interpretation, and the burden of persuasion would rest heavily upon any who might attack it." *Youngstown*, 343 U.S., at 637 (Jackson, J., concurring). Under the circumstances of this case, we cannot say that petitioner has sustained that heavy burden. A contrary ruling would mean that the Federal Government as a whole lacked the power exerised by the President, see *id.*, at 636-37, and that we are not prepared to say.

[The Court found that neither the IEEPA nor the Hostage Act authorized President Carter to suspend claims in American courts. The "general tenor" of such legislation might relate to whether presidential conduct enjoyed congressional acquiescence.]

As we have noted, Congress cannot anticipate and legislate with regard to every possible action the President may find it necessary to take or every possible situation in which he might act. Such failure of Congress specifically to delegate authority does not, "especially . . . in the areas of foreign policy and national security," imply "congressional disapproval" of action taken by the Executive. *Haig v. Agee*, . . . On the contrary, the enactment of legislation closely related to the question of the President's authority in a particular case which evinces legislative intent to accord the President broad discretion may be considered to "invite" "measures on independent presidential responsibility," *Youngstown*, 343 U.S., at 637 (Jackson, J., concurring). At least this is so where there is no contrary indication of legislative intent and when, as here, there is a history of congressional acquiescence in conduct of the sort engaged in by the President. It is to that history which we now turn.

Not infrequently in affairs between nations, outstanding claims by nationals of one country against the government of another country are "sources of friction" between the two sovereigns. *United States v. Pink*, 315 U.S. 203, 225 (1942). To resolve these difficulties, nations have often entered into agreements settling the claims of their respective nationals. As one treatise writer puts it, international agreements settling claims by nationals of one state against the government of another "are established international practice reflecting traditional international theory." L. Henkin, Foreign Affairs and the Constitution 262 (1972). Consistent with that principle, the United States has repeatedly exercised its sovereign authority to settle the claims of its nationals against foreign countries. Though those settlements have sometimes been made by treaty, there has also been a longstanding practice of settling such claims by executive agreement without the advice and consent of the Senate. Under such agreements, the President has agreed to renounce or extinguish claims of United States nationals against foreign governments in return for lump sum payments or the establishment of arbitration procedures. To be sure, many of these settlements were encouraged by the United States claimants themselves, since a claimant's only hope of obtaining any payment at all might lie in having his government negotiate a diplomatic settlement on his behalf. But it is also undisputed that the "United States has sometimes disposed of the claims of citizens without their consent, or even without consultation with them, usually without exclusive regard for their interests, as distinguished from those of the nation as a whole." . . . It is clear that the practice of settling claims continues today. Since 1952, the President has entered into at least 10 binding settlements with foreign nations, including an $80 million settlement with the People's Republic of China.

Crucial to our decision today is the conclusion that Congress has implicitly approved the practice of claim settlement by executive agreement. This is best demonstrated by Congress' enactment of the International Claims Settlement Act of 1949, 64 Stat. 13, as amended, 22 U.S.C. § 1621 *et seq.*, (1976 ed. 2d Supp. IV). The Act had two purposes: (1) to allocate to United States nationals funds received in the course of an executive claims settlement with Yugoslavia, and (2) to provide a procedure whereby funds resulting from future settlements could be distributed. To achieve these ends Congress created the International Claims Commission, now the Foreign Claims Settlement Commission, and gave it jurisdiction to make final and binding decisions with respect to claims by United States nationals against settlement funds. . . . By creating a procedure to implement future settlement agreements, Congress placed its stamp of approval on such agreements. Indeed, the legislative history of the Act observed that the United States was seeking settlements with countries other than Yugoslavia and stated that the bill contemplated settlements of a similar nature in the future. . . .

. . . [T]he legislative history of the IEEPA further reveals that Congress has accepted the authority of the Executive to enter into settlement agreements. Though the IEEPA was enacted to provide some limitation on the President's emergency powers,

Congress stressed that "[n]othing in this act is intended . . . to interfere with the authority of the President to [block assets], or to impede the settlement of claims of U.S. citizens against foreign countries." . . .

In addition to congressional acquiescence in the President's power to settle claims, prior cases of this Court have also recognized that the President does have some measure of power to enter into executive agreements without obtaining the advice and consent of the Senate. In *United States v. Pink*, 315 U.S. 203 (1942), for example, the Court upheld the validity of the Litvinov Assignment, which was part of an Executive Agreement whereby the Soviet Union assigned to the United States amounts owed to it by American nationals so that outstanding claims of other American nationals could be paid. The Court explained that the resolution of such claims was integrally connected with normalizing United States' relations with a foreign state:

> Power to remove such obstacles to full recognition as settlement of claims of our nationals . . . certainly is a modest implied power of the President. . . . No such obstacle can be placed in the way of rehabilitation of relations between this country and another nation, unless the historic conception of the powers and responsibilities . . . is to be drastically revised. . . .

In light of all of the foregoing — the inferences to be drawn from the character of the legislation Congress has enacted in the area, such as the IEEPA and the Hostage Act, and from the history of acquiescence in executive claims settlement — we conclude that the President was authorized to suspend pending claims pursuant to Executive Order No. 12294. As Justice Frankfurter pointed out in *Youngstown*, 343 U.S. at 610-611, "a systematic, unbroken, executive practice, long pursued to the knowledge of Congress and never before questioned . . . may be treated as a gloss on 'Executive Power' vested in the President by § 1 of Art. II." Past practice does not, by itself, create power, but "long-continued practice, known to and acquiesced in by Congress, would raise a presumption that the [action] has been [taken] in pursuance of its consent. . . . " . . . Such practice is present here and such a presumption is also appropriate. In light of the fact that Congress may be considered to have consented to the President's action in suspending claims, we cannot say that action exceeded the President's powers.

Our conclusion is buttressed by the fact that the means chosen by the President to settle the claims of American nationals provided an alternate forum, the Claims Tribunal, which is capable of providing meaningful relief. . . . The fact that the President has provided such a forum here means that the claimants are receiving something in return for the suspension of their claims, namely, access to an international tribunal before which they may well recover something on their claims. Because there does appear to be a real "settlement" here, this case is more easily analogized to the more traditional claim settlement cases of the past.

Just as importantly, Congress has not disapproved of the action taken here. Though Congress has held hearings on the Iranian Agreement itself, Congress has not enacted legislation, or even passed a resolution, indicating its displeasure with the Agreement. Quite the contrary, the relevant Senate Committee has stated that the establishment of the Tribunal is "of vital importance to the United States." . . . We are thus clearly not confronted with a situation in which Congress has in some way resisted the exercise of Presidential authority.

Finally, we re-emphasize the narrowness of our decision. We do not decide that the President possesses plenary power to settle claims, even as against foreign governmental entities. . . . But where, as here, the settlement of claims has been determined to be a necessary incident to the resolution of a major foreign policy dispute between our country and another, and where, as here, we can conclude that Congress acquiesced in the President's action, we are not prepared to say that the President lacks the power to settle such claims. . . .

The judgment of the District Court is accordingly affirmed, and the mandate shall issue forthwith.

NOTES

(1) Presidents from President Washington on have used executive agreements. Washington's Postmaster General concluded an agreement for mail service with the Deputy Postmaster General of Canada in 1792. Hundreds of international postal agreements have followed.

During the middle of the nineteenth century, the executive agreement began to rival treaties as an instrument for conduct of external relations. In 1940, the State Department estimated that approximately twelve hundred executive agreements had been entered into by the United States since the adoption of the Constitution. Since then, the number has increased tremendously: 12,968 executive agreements were concluded between 1946 and 1994 (during the same period only 732 treaties were entered into by the United States).

Many executive agreements concern commerce and navigation, including reciprocal arrangements for reduction or suspension of duties. The most noteworthy of these have been the Reciprocal Trade Agreements pursuant to the Trade Agreements Act of 1934.

(2) A treaty negotiated by the President with the advice and consent of 2/3 of the Senate is part of the Supreme Law of the land under the Supremacy Clause. A treaty is the equivalent of a statute such that whichever is later in time controls in case of a conflict. *Choi Chan Ping v. United States*, 130 U.S. 581 (1889). A treaty also overrides any contrary state law *Ware v. Hylton*, 3 U.S. (3 Dall.) 199 (1796). Do executive agreements have the same legal effect as treaties? Is an executive agreement, like a treaty, not only an international agreement, but also part of the Law of the Land, which must be given effect by our courts under the Supremacy Clause? An executive agreement can override state law since the national government exercises full foreign affairs powers unchecked by state law. *See American Insurance Association v. Garamendi*, 539 U.S. 396 (2003) (holding California statute preempted by executive agreement with Germany regarding Holocaust reparations); *United States v. Belmont*, 301 U.S. 324 (1937). An executive agreement cannot override a federal statute. *See United States v. Guy W. Capps, Inc.*, 204 F.2d 655 (4th Cir. 1953), *aff'd on other grounds*, 348 U.S. 296 (1955).

(3) Why was the Court so intent on characterizing its decision as a narrow one? At the outset of the opinion, Justice Rehnquist stated: "We attempt to lay down no general 'guidelines' covering other situations not involved here, and attempt to confine the opinion only to the very question necessary to decision of the case."

§ 5.05 COMMANDER-IN-CHIEF

PRIZE CASES
67 U.S. (2 Black) 635, 17 L. Ed. 59 (1862)

These were cases in which the vessels named, together with their cargoes, were severally captured and brought in as prizes by public ships of the United States. The libels were filed by the proper District Attorneys, on behalf of the United States and on behalf of the officers and crews of the ships, by which the captures were respectively made. In each case the District Court pronounced a decree of condemnation, from which the claimants took an appeal. . . .

MR. JUSTICE GRIER. There are certain propositions of law which must necessarily affect the ultimate decision of these cases, and many others, which it will be proper to discuss and decide before we notice the special facts peculiar to each.

They are, 1st. Had the President a right to institute a blockade of ports in possession of persons in armed rebellion against the Government, on the principles of international law, as known, and acknowledged among civilized States? . . .

That a blockade *de facto* actually existed, and was formally declared and notified by the President on the 27th and 30th of April, 1861, is an admitted fact in these cases.

That the President, as the Executive Chief of the Government and Commander-in-chief of the Army and Navy, was the proper person to make such notification, has not been, and cannot be disputed. . . .

Let us enquire whether, at the time this blockade was instituted, a state of war existed which would justify a resort to these means of subduing the hostile force. . . .

By the Constitution, Congress alone has the power to declare a national or foreign war. It cannot declare war against a State, or any number of States, by virtue of any clause in the Constitution. The Constitution confers on the President the whole Executive power. He is bound to take care that the laws be faithfully executed. He is Commander-in-chief of the Army and Navy of the United States, and of the militia of the several States when called into the actual service of the United States. He has no power to initiate or declare a war either against a foreign nation or a domestic State. But by the Acts of Congress of February 28th, 1795, and 3d of March, 1807, he is authorized to call out the militia and use the military and naval forces of the United States in case of invasion by foreign nations, and to suppress insurrection against the government of a State or of the United States.

If a war be made by invasion of a foreign nation, the President is not only authorized but bound to resist force by force. He does not initiate the war, but is bound to accept the challenge without waiting for any special legislative authority. And whether the hostile party be a foreign invader, or States organized in rebellion, it is none the less a war, although the declaration of it be "*unilateral.*" . . .

This greatest of civil wars was not gradually developed by popular commotion, tumultuous assemblies, or local unorganized insurrections. However long may have been its previous conception, it nevertheless sprung forth suddenly from the parent brain, a Minerva in the full panoply of *war*. The President was bound to meet it in the shape it presented itself, without waiting for Congress to baptize it with a name; and no name given to it by him or them could change the fact. . . .

Whether the President in fulfilling his duties, as Commander-in-chief, in suppressing an insurrection, has met with such armed hostile resistance, and a civil war of such alarming proportions as will compel him to accord to them the character of belligerents, is a question to be decided *by him*, and this Court must be governed by the decisions and acts of the political department of the Government to which this power was entrusted. "He must determine what degree of force the crisis demands." The proclamation of blockade is itself official and conclusive evidence to the Court that a state of war existed which demanded and authorized a recourse to such a measure, under the circumstances peculiar to the case. . . .

. . . [T]herefore we are of the opinion that the president had a right, *jure belli*, to institute a blockade of ports in possession of the States in rebellion, which neutrals are bound to regard. . . .

The decree below is affirmed with costs. . . .

NOTES

(1) Article II declares that "The President shall be Commander-in-Chief of the Army and Navy of the United States." Does this vest the President with an empty title? Does it confer power on the President or limit his power? In THE FEDERALIST No. 69, Alexander Hamilton compared the President's Commander-in-Chief power to that of the King of England. But the President's authority would amount "to nothing more than the supreme command and direction of the military and naval forces" whereas the King's power "extends to the declaring of war and to the raising and regulating of fleets and armies."

(2) An early draft of the Constitution gave Congress the power "to make war." James Madison and Eldbridge Gerry moved to replace "make" war with "declare" war, leaving the Executive power to repel attacks. Their motion carried, resulting in the present language empowering Congress "To declare War."

(3) For most of our history, Congress declared or authorized major military actions. *See* Louis Fisher, *Congressional Abdication: War and Spending Powers*, 43 ST. LOUIS U. L.J. 931, 940 (1999). The United States joined the United Nations only after officials of the Truman Administration assured Congress that it would seek Congressional approval of any commitment of troops to the United Nations. President Truman ignored such procedures in committing troops to Korea.

(4) Do the *Prize Cases* require a declaration of war before the nation can be at war? How far does its reasoning extend? If the President can take belligerent measures to crush civil rebellion, why not for a hostile invasion? If the *Prize Cases* authorize defensive war, must the President wait until the first blow has been struck? Can he order belligerent acts whenever necessary to defend the country's interest?

(5) In *Durand v. Hollins*, 8 F. Cas. 111 (S.D.N.Y. 1860), the American Navy attacked a Nicaraguan town in response to violence by local citizens against American property. Justice Nelson deemed the issue a political question committed to the President's discretion.

(6) The War Powers Resolution of 1973, 87 Stat. 555, provides in part:

SHORT TITLE

SEC. 1. This joint resolution may be cited as the "War Powers Resolution."

PURPOSE AND POLICY

SEC. 2. (a) It is the purpose of this joint resolution to fulfill the intent of the framers of the Constitution of the United States and insure that the collective judgment of both the Congress and the President will apply to the introduction of United States Armed Forces into hostilities, or into situations where imminent involvement in hostilities is clearly indicated by the circumstances, and to the continued use of such forces in hostilities or in such situations.

(b) Under article I, section 8, of the Constitution, it is specifically provided that the Congress shall have the power to make all laws necessary and proper for carrying into execution, not only its own powers but also all other powers vested by the Constitution in the Government of the United States, or in any department or officer thereof.

(c) The constitutional powers of the President as Commander-in-Chief to introduce United States Armed Forces into hostilities, or into situations where imminent involvement in hostilities is clearly indicated by the circumstances, are exercised only pursuant to (1) a declaration of war, (2) specific statutory authorization, or (3) a national emergency created by attack upon the United

States, its territories or possessions, or its armed forces.

CONSULTATION

SEC. 3. The President in every possible instance shall consult with Congress before introducing United States Armed Forces into hostilities or into situations where imminent involvement in hostilities is clearly indicated by the circumstances, and after every such introduction shall consult regularly with the Congress until United States Armed Forces are no longer engaged in hostilities or have been removed from such situations.

REPORTING

SEC. 4. (a) In the absence of a declaration of war, in any case in which United States Armed Forces are introduced —

(1) into hostilities or into situations where imminent involvement in hostilities is clearly indicated by the circumstances;

(2) into the territory, airspace or waters of a foreign nation, while equipped for combat, except for deployments which relate solely to supply, replacement, repair, or training of such forces; or

(3) in numbers which substantially enlarge United States Armed Forces equipped for combat already located in a foreign nation; the President shall submit within 48 hours to the Speaker of the House of Representatives and to the President pro tempore of the Senate a report, in writing, setting forth —

(A) the circumstances necessitating the introduction of United States Armed Forces;

(B) the constitutional and legislative authority under which such introduction took place; and

(C) the estimated scope and duration of the hostilities or involvement. . . .

CONGRESSIONAL ACTION

. . . .

SEC. 5.(b) Within sixty calendar days after a report is submitted or is required to be submitted pursuant to section 4(a)(1), whichever is earlier, the President shall terminate any use of United States Armed Forces with respect to which such report was submitted (or required to be submitted), unless the Congress (1) has declared war or has enacted a specific authorization for such use of United States Armed Forces, (2) has extended by law such sixty-day period, or (3) is physically unable to meet as a result of an armed attack upon the United States. Such sixty-day period shall be extended for not more than an additional thirty days if the President determines and certifies to the Congress in writing that unavoidable military necessity respecting the safety of United States Armed Forces requires the continued use of such armed forces in the course of bringing about a prompt removal of such forces.

(c) Notwithstanding subsection (b), at any time that United States Armed Forces are engaged in hostilities outside the territory of the United States, its possessions and territories without a declaration of war or specific statutory authorization, such forces shall be removed by the President if the Congress so directs by concurrent resolution. . . .

(7) The War Powers Resolution was enacted as a substantive law over President Nixon's veto. It uses the legislative-veto technique. Does *Chadha* pose any problems? In vetoing the War Powers Resolution, President Nixon asserted that the resolution was unconstitutional: "House Joint Resolution 542 would attempt to take away, by a mere legislative act, authorities which the President has properly exercised under the

Constitution for almost 200 years." Was Nixon correct that the War Powers Resolution is unconstitutional for intruding on the President's power? Or, is the War Powers Resolution unconstitutional for giving the President power to wage war without a congressional declaration, for a limited period? That was the view of Senator Thomas F. Eagleton. Though a co-author of the Senate version of the legislation, he voted against the bill which emerged from conference because he thought Congress had abdicated its constitutional powers to the President. *See* 119 CONG. REC. 33,555-33,557 (1973).

(8) Can the War Powers Resolution be controlled judicially or does it raise political questions? *See Ange v. Bush*, 752 F. Supp. 509 (D.D.C. 1990) (action claiming that President violated War Powers Resolution in deploying armed forces in Persian Gulf barred by political question doctrine).

HAMDI v. RUMSFELD
542 U.S. 507, 124 S. Ct. 2633, 159 L. Ed. 2d 578 (2004)

JUSTICE O'CONNOR announced the judgment of the Court and delivered an opinion, in which THE CHIEF JUSTICE, JUSTICE KENNEDY, and JUSTICE BREYER join.

At this difficult time in our Nation's history, we are called upon to consider the legality of the Government's detention of a United States citizen on United States soil as an "enemy combatant" and to address the process that is constitutionally owed to one who seeks to challenge his classification as such. The United States Court of Appeals for the Fourth Circuit held that petitioner's detention was legally authorized and that he was entitled to no further opportunity to challenge his enemy-combatant label. We now vacate and remand. We hold that although Congress authorized the detention of combatants in the narrow circumstances alleged here, due process demands that a citizen held in the United States as an enemy combatant be given a meaningful opportunity to contest the factual basis for that detention before a neutral decisionmaker.

I

On September 11, 2001, the al Qaeda terrorist network used hijacked commercial airliners to attack prominent targets in the United States. Approximately 3,000 people were killed in those attacks. One week later, in response to these "acts of treacherous violence," Congress passed a resolution authorizing the President to "use all necessary and appropriate force against those nations, organizations, or persons he determines planned, authorized, committed, or aided the terrorist attacks" or "harbored such organizations or persons, in order to prevent any future acts of international terrorism against the United States by such nations, organizations or persons." Authorization for Use of Military Force ("the AUMF"), 115 Stat. 224. Soon thereafter, the President ordered United States Armed Forces to Afghanistan, with a mission to subdue al Qaeda and quell the Taliban regime that was known to support it.

This case arises out of the detention of a man whom the Government alleges took up arms with the Taliban during this conflict. His name is Yaser Esam Hamdi. Born an American citizen in Louisiana in 1980, Hamdi moved with his family to Saudi Arabia as a child. By 2001, the parties agree, he resided in Afghanistan. At some point that year, he was seized by members of the Northern Alliance, a coalition of military groups opposed to the Taliban government, and eventually was turned over to the United States military. The Government asserts that it initially detained and interrogated Hamdi in Afghanistan before transferring him to the United States Naval Base in Guantanamo Bay in January 2002. In April 2002, upon learning that Hamdi is an American citizen, authorities transferred him to a naval brig in Norfolk, Virginia, where he remained until a recent transfer to a brig in Charleston, South Carolina. The

Government contends that Hamdi is an "enemy combatant," and that this status justifies holding him in the United States indefinitely — without formal charges or proceedings — unless and until it makes the determination that access to counsel or further process is warranted.

[Hamdi's father petitioned for a writ of habeas corpus under 28 U.S.C. § 2241 in the Eastern District of Virginia, naming as petitioners his son and himself as next friend. The elder Hamdi alleged that the Government had illegally held his son "without access to legal counsel or notice of any charges pending against him," and that his son's constitutional rights as an American citizen had been violated. He asked the court to appoint counsel for Hamdi, declare that he is being held in violation of the Fifth and Fourteenth Amendments, schedule an evidentiary hearing, and order him released from his "unlawful custody." Hamdi's father asserted that his son went to Afghanistan to do "relief work," and that he had been in that country less than two months before September 11, 2001, and could not have received military training.]

The District Court found that Hamdi's father was a proper next friend, appointed the federal public defender as counsel for the petitioners, and ordered that counsel be given access to Hamdi. The United States Court of Appeals for the Fourth Circuit reversed that order, holding that the District Court had failed to extend appropriate deference to the Government's security and intelligence interests. 296 F.3d 278, 279, 283 (2002). It directed the District Court to consider "the most cautious procedures first," and to conduct a deferential inquiry into Hamdi's status, It opined that "if Hamdi is indeed an 'enemy combatant' who was captured during hostilities in Afghanistan, the government's present detention of him is a lawful one."

On remand, the Government filed a response and a motion to dismiss the petition. It attached to its response a declaration from one Michael Mobbs (hereinafter "Mobbs Declaration"), who identified himself as Special Advisor to the Under Secretary of Defense for Policy. . . . Mobbs [declared] that Hamdi "traveled to Afghanistan" in July or August 2001, and that he thereafter "affiliated with a Taliban military unit and received weapons training." . . . that Hamdi "remained with his Taliban unit following the attacks of September 11" and that, during the time when Northern Alliance forces were "engaged in battle with the Taliban," "Hamdi's Taliban unit surrendered" to those forces, after which he "surrender[ed] his Kalishnikov assault rifle" to them. The Mobbs Declaration also states that, because al Qaeda and the Taliban "were and are hostile forces engaged in armed conflict with the armed forces of the United States," "individuals associated with" those groups "were and continue to be enemy combatants."

After the Government submitted this declaration, the Fourth Circuit directed the District Court to proceed in accordance with its earlier ruling and, specifically, to " 'consider the sufficiency of the Mobbs Declaration as an independent matter before proceeding further.' " 316 F.3d at 450, 462 (C.A.4 2003). The District Court found that the Mobbs Declaration fell "far short" of supporting Hamdi's detention. . . . The Fourth Circuit reversed [stating] because it was "undisputed that Hamdi was captured in a zone of active combat in a foreign theater of conflict," no factual inquiry or evidentiary hearing allowing Hamdi to be heard or to rebut the Government's assertions was necessary or proper. Concluding that the factual averments in the Mobbs Declaration, "if accurate," provided a sufficient basis upon which to conclude that the President had constitutionally detained Hamdi pursuant to the President's war powers, it ordered the habeas petition dismissed. The Fourth Circuit emphasized that the "vital purposes" of the detention of uncharged enemy combatants — preventing those combatants from rejoining the enemy while relieving the military of the burden of litigating the circumstances of wartime captures halfway around the globe — were interests "directly derived from the war powers of Articles I and II." In that court's view, because "Article III contains nothing analogous to the specific powers of war so carefully enumerated in Articles I and II," separation of powers principles prohibited a federal court from "delv[ing] further into Hamdi's status and capture," Accordingly, the District Court's more vigorous inquiry "went far beyond the acceptable scope of review." . . .

II

The threshold question before us is whether the Executive has the authority to detain citizens who qualify as "enemy combatants." There is some debate as to the proper scope of this term, and the Government has never provided any court with the full criteria that it uses in classifying individuals as such. It has made clear, however, that, for purposes of this case, the "enemy combatant" that it is seeking to detain is an individual who, it alleges, was " 'part of or supporting forces hostile to the United States or coalition partners' " in Afghanistan and who " 'engaged in an armed conflict against the United States' " there. We therefore answer only the narrow question before us: whether the detention of citizens falling within that definition is authorized.

The Government maintains that no explicit congressional authorization is required, because the Executive possesses plenary authority to detain pursuant to Article II of the Constitution. We do not reach the question whether Article II provides such authority, however, because we agree with the Government's alternative position, that Congress has in fact authorized Hamdi's detention, through the AUMF.

Our analysis on that point, set forth below, substantially overlaps with our analysis of Hamdi's principal argument for the illegality of his detention. He posits that his detention is forbidden by 18 U.S.C. § 4001(a) [which] states that "[n]o citizen shall be imprisoned or otherwise detained by the United States except pursuant to an Act of Congress." . . . [W]e conclude that the AUMF is explicit congressional authorization for the detention of individuals in the narrow category we describe (assuming, without deciding, that such authorization is required), and that the AUMF satisfied § 4001(a)'s requirement that a detention be "pursuant to an Act of Congress" (assuming, without deciding, that § 4001(a) applies to military detentions).

The AUMF authorizes the President to use "all necessary and appropriate force" against "nations, organizations, or persons" associated with the September 11, 2001, terrorist attacks. There can be no doubt that individuals who fought against the United States in Afghanistan as part of the Taliban, an organization known to have supported the al Qaeda terrorist network responsible for those attacks, are individuals Congress sought to target in passing the AUMF. We conclude that detention of individuals falling into the limited category we are considering, for the duration of the particular conflict in which they were captured, is so fundamental and accepted an incident to war as to be an exercise of the "necessary and appropriate force" Congress has authorized the President to use.

The capture and detention of lawful combatants and the capture, detention, and trial of unlawful combatants, by "universal agreement and practice," are "important incident[s] of war." *Ex parte Quirin*, 317 U.S. [1] [(1942)]. The purpose of detention is to prevent captured individuals from returning to the field of battle and taking up arms once again. There is no bar to this Nation's holding one of its own citizens as an enemy combatant. In *Quirin*, one of the detainees, Haupt, alleged that he was a naturalized United States citizen. We held that "[c]itizens who associate themselves with the military arm of the enemy government, and with its aid, guidance and direction enter this country bent on hostile acts, are enemy belligerents within the meaning of . . . the law of war." While Haupt was tried for violations of the law of war, nothing in *Quirin* suggests that his citizenship would have precluded his mere detention for the duration of the relevant hostilities. Nor can we see any reason for drawing such a line here. A citizen, no less than an alien, can be "part of or supporting forces hostile to the United States or coalition partners" and "engaged in an armed conflict against the United States," such a citizen, if released, would pose the same threat of returning to the front during the ongoing conflict.

In light of these principles, it is of no moment that the AUMF does not use specific language of detention. Because detention to prevent a combatant's return to the battlefield is a fundamental incident of waging war, in permitting the use of "necessary and appropriate force," Congress has clearly and unmistakably authorized detention in the narrow circumstances considered here.

Hamdi objects, nevertheless, that Congress has not authorized the *indefinite* detention to which he is now subject. The Government responds that "the detention of enemy combatants during World War II was just as 'indefinite' while that war was being fought." We take Hamdi's objection to be not to the lack of certainty regarding the date on which the conflict will end, but to the substantial prospect of perpetual detention. We recognize that the national security underpinnings of the "war on terror," although crucially important, are broad and malleable. As the Government concedes, "given its unconventional nature, the current conflict is unlikely to end with a formal cease-fire agreement." The prospect Hamdi raises is therefore not far-fetched. If the Government does not consider this unconventional war won for two generations, and if it maintains during that time that Hamdi might, if released, rejoin forces fighting against the United States, then the position it has taken throughout the litigation of this case suggests that Hamdi's detention could last for the rest of his life.

Hamdi contends that the AUMF does not authorize indefinite or perpetual detention. Certainly, we agree that indefinite detention for the purpose of interrogation is not authorized. Further, we understand Congress' grant of authority for the use of "necessary and appropriate force" to include the authority to detain for the duration of the relevant conflict, and our understanding is based on longstanding law-of-war principles. If the practical circumstances of a given conflict are entirely unlike those of the conflicts that informed the development of the law of war, that understanding may unravel. But that is not the situation we face as of this date. Active combat operations against Taliban fighters apparently are ongoing in Afghanistan. The United States may detain, for the duration of these hostilities, individuals legitimately determined to be Taliban combatants who "engaged in an armed conflict against the United States." . . .

Ex parte Milligan, [71 U.S.] (4 Wall.) 2, 125 (1866), does not undermine our holding about the Government's authority to seize enemy combatants, as we define that term today. In that case, the Court made repeated reference to the fact that its inquiry into whether the military tribunal had jurisdiction to try and punish Milligan turned in large part on the fact that Milligan was not a prisoner of war, but a resident of Indiana arrested while at home there. . . . Had Milligan been captured while he was assisting Confederate soldiers by carrying a rifle against Union troops on a Confederate battlefield, the holding of the Court might well have been different. . . . *Quirin* was a unanimous opinion. It both postdates and clarifies *Milligan*, providing us with the most apposite precedent that we have on the question of whether citizens may be detained in such circumstances. Brushing aside such precedent — particularly when doing so gives rise to a host of new questions never dealt with by this Court — is unjustified and unwise.

. . . To be clear, our opinion only finds legislative authority to detain under the AUMF once it is sufficiently clear that the individual is, in fact, an enemy combatant; whether that is established by concession or by some other process that verifies this fact with sufficient certainty seems beside the point. . . .

III

Even in cases in which the detention of enemy combatants is legally authorized, there remains the question of what process is constitutionally due to a citizen who disputes his enemy-combatant status. . . . Though they reach radically different conclusions on the process that ought to attend the present proceeding, the parties begin on common ground. All agree that, absent suspension, the writ of habeas corpus remains available to every individual detained within the United States. U.S. Const., Art. I, § 9, cl. 2 ("The Privilege of the Writ of Habeas Corpus shall not be suspended, unless when in Cases of Rebellion or Invasion the public Safety may require it"). Only in the rarest of circumstances has Congress seen fit to suspend the writ. At all other times, it has remained a critical check on the Executive, ensuring that it does not detain individuals except in accordance with law. All agree suspension of the writ has not occurred here. Thus, it is undisputed that Hamdi was properly before an Article III court to challenge his detention under 28 U.S.C. § 2241. Further, all agree that § 2241 and its companion provisions provide at least a skeletal outline of the procedures to be afforded a petitioner in federal habeas review. Most notably, § 2243 provides that "the person detained may, under oath, deny any of the facts set forth in the return or allege any other material facts," and § 2246 allows the taking of evidence in habeas proceedings by deposition, affidavit, or interrogatories.

The simple outline of § 2241 makes clear both that Congress envisioned that habeas petitioners would have some opportunity to present and rebut facts and that courts in cases like this retain some ability to vary the ways in which they do so as mandated by due process. The Government recognizes the basic procedural protections required by the habeas statute, but asks us to hold that, given both the flexibility of the habeas mechanism and the circumstances presented in this case, the presentation of the Mobbs Declaration to the habeas court completed the required factual development. It suggests two separate reasons for its position that no further process is due.

[The Court rejected the Government's argument that the habeas determination can be made as a matter of law, with no further hearing or fact finding necessary since Hamdi was seized in a combat zone; the Court found the facts were not undisputed].

The Government's second argument requires closer consideration. This is the argument that further factual exploration is unwarranted and inappropriate in light of the extraordinary constitutional interests at stake. . . . At most, the Government argues, courts should review its determination that a citizen is an enemy combatant under a very deferential "some evidence" standard. Under this review, a court would assume the accuracy of the Government's articulated basis for Hamdi's detention, as set forth in the Mobbs Declaration, and assess only whether that articulated basis was a legitimate one. In response, Hamdi emphasizes that this Court consistently has recognized that an individual challenging his detention may not be held at the will of the Executive without recourse to some proceeding before a neutral tribunal to determine whether the Executive's asserted justifications for that detention have basis in fact and warrant in law. . . .

Both of these positions highlight legitimate concerns. And both emphasize the tension that often exists between the autonomy that the Government asserts is necessary in order to pursue effectively a particular goal and the process that a citizen contends he is due before he is deprived of a constitutional right. . . . It is beyond question that substantial interests lie on both sides of the scale in this case. Hamdi's "private interest . . . affected by the official action," is the most elemental of liberty interests — the interest in being free from physical detention by one's own government. "In our society liberty is the norm," and detention without trial "is the carefully limited exception." . . . Nor is the weight on this side of the . . . scale offset by the circumstances of war or the accusation of treasonous behavior, for "[i]t is clear that commitment for *any* purpose constitutes a significant deprivation of liberty that requires due process protection." . . . Moreover, as critical as the Government's interest may be in detaining those who actually pose an immediate threat to the national security of the United States during ongoing international conflict, history and common sense teach us that an unchecked system of detention carries the potential to become a means for oppression and abuse of others who do not present that sort of threat. . . . We reaffirm today the fundamental nature of a citizen's right to be free from involuntary confinement by his own government without due process of law, and we weigh the opposing governmental interests against the curtailment of liberty that such confinement entails.

On the other side of the scale are the weighty and sensitive governmental interests in ensuring that those who have in fact fought with the enemy during a war do not return to battle against the United States. As discussed above, the law of war and the realities of combat may render such detentions both necessary and appropriate, and our due process analysis need not blink at those realities. Without doubt, our Constitution recognizes that core strategic matters of warmaking belong in the hands of those who are best positioned and most politically accountable for making them. . . .

Striking the proper constitutional balance here is of great importance to the Nation during this period of ongoing combat. But it is equally vital that our calculus not give short shrift to the values that this country holds dear or to the privilege that is American citizenship. It is during our most challenging and uncertain moments that our Nation's commitment to due process is most severely tested; and it is in those times that we must preserve our commitment at home to the principles for which we fight abroad. . . .

We therefore hold that a citizen-detainee seeking to challenge his classification as an enemy combatant must receive notice of the factual basis for his classification, and a fair opportunity to rebut the Government's factual assertions before a neutral decisionmaker. . . . These essential constitutional promises may not be eroded. At the same time, the exigencies of the circumstances may demand that, aside from these core elements, enemy combatant proceedings may be tailored to alleviate their uncommon potential to burden the Executive at a time of ongoing military conflict. Hearsay, for example, may need to be accepted as the most reliable available evidence from the Government in such a proceeding. Likewise, the Constitution would not be offended by a presumption in favor of the Government's evidence, so long as that presumption remained a rebuttable one and fair opportunity for rebuttal were provided. Thus, once the Government puts forth credible evidence that the habeas petitioner meets the enemy-combatant criteria, the onus could shift to the petitioner to rebut that evidence with more persuasive evidence that he falls outside the criteria. . . .

We think it unlikely that this basic process will have the dire impact on the central functions of warmaking that the Government forecasts. The parties agree that initial captures on the battlefield need not receive the process we have discussed here; that process is due only when the determination is made to *continue* to hold those who have been seized. . . . While we accord the greatest respect and consideration to the judgments of military authorities in matters relating to the actual prosecution of a war, and recognize that the scope of that discretion necessarily is wide, it does not infringe on the core role of the military for the courts to exercise their own time-honored and constitutionally mandated roles of reviewing and resolving claims like those presented here.

In sum, while the full protections that accompany challenges to detentions in other settings may prove unworkable and inappropriate in the enemy-combatant setting, the threats to military operations posed by a basic system of independent review are not so weighty as to trump a citizen's core rights to challenge meaningfully the Government's case and to be heard by an impartial adjudicator.

In so holding, we necessarily reject the Government's assertion that separation of powers principles mandate a heavily circumscribed role for the courts in such circumstances. . . . We have long since made clear that a state of war is not a blank check for the President when it comes to the rights of the Nation's citizens. *Youngstown Sheet & Tube*, 343 U.S. [579,] 587 [1952]. Whatever power the United States Constitution envisions for the Executive in its exchanges with other nations or with enemy organizations in times of conflict, it most assuredly envisions a role for all three branches when individual liberties are at stake. . . . Thus, while we do not question that our due process assessment must pay keen attention to the particular burdens faced by the Executive in the context of military action, it would turn our system of checks and balances on its head to suggest that a citizen could not make his way to court with a challenge to the factual basis for his detention by his government, simply because the Executive opposes making available such a challenge. Absent suspension of the writ by Congress, a citizen detained as an enemy combatant is entitled to this process.

Because we conclude that due process demands some system for a citizen detainee to refute his classification, the proposed "some evidence" standard is inadequate. Any process in which the Executive's factual assertions go wholly unchallenged or are simply presumed correct without any opportunity for the alleged combatant to demonstrate otherwise falls constitutionally short. . . . This standard therefore is ill suited to the situation in which a habeas petitioner has received no prior proceedings before any tribunal and had no prior opportunity to rebut the Executive's factual assertions before a neutral decisionmaker. . . . Plainly, the "process" Hamdi has received is not that to which he is entitled under the Due Process Clause.

There remains the possibility that the standards we have articulated could be met by an appropriately authorized and properly constituted military tribunal. . . . In the absence of such process, however, a court that receives a petition for a writ of habeas corpus from an alleged enemy combatant must itself ensure that the minimum requirements of due process are achieved. . . . As we have discussed, a habeas court in a case such as this may accept affidavit evidence like that contained in the Mobbs Declaration, so long as it also permits the alleged combatant to present his own factual case to rebut the Government's return. We anticipate that a District Court would proceed with the caution that we have indicated is necessary in this setting, engaging in a factfinding process that is both prudent and incremental. We have no reason to doubt that courts faced with these sensitive matters will pay proper heed both to the matters of national security that might arise in an individual case and to the constitutional limitations safeguarding essential liberties that remain vibrant even in times of security concerns. . . .

The judgment of the United States Court of Appeals for the Fourth Circuit is vacated, and the case is remanded for further proceedings.

It is so ordered.

Justice Souter, with whom Justice Ginsberg joins, concurring in part, dissenting in part, and concurring in the judgment.

. . . The plurality rejects any such limit on the exercise of habeas jurisdiction and so far I agree with its opinion. The plurality does, however, accept the Government's position that if Hamdi's designation as an enemy combatant is correct, his detention (at least as to some period) is authorized by [AUMF]. Here, I disagree and respectfully dissent. . . .

The threshold issue is how broadly or narrowly to read the Non-Detention Act, the tone of which is severe: "No citizen shall be imprisoned or otherwise detained by the United States except pursuant to an Act of Congress." Should the severity of the Act be relieved when the Government's stated factual justification for incommunicado detention is a war on terrorism, so that the Government may be said to act "pursuant" to congressional terms that fall short of explicit authority to imprison individuals? With one possible though important qualification, the answer has to be no. For a number of reasons, the prohibition within § 4001(a) has to be read broadly to accord the statute a long reach and to impose a burden of justification on the Government.

First, the circumstances in which the Act was adopted point the way to this interpretation. The provision superseded a cold-war statute . . . which had authorized the Attorney General, in time of emergency, to detain anyone reasonably thought likely to engage in espionage or sabotage. That statute was repealed in 1971 out of fear that it could authorize a repetition of the World War II internment of citizens of Japanese ancestry; Congress meant to preclude another episode like the one described in *Korematsu v. United States*, 323 U.S. 214 (1944). . . . The fact that Congress intended to guard against a repetition of the World War II internments when it repealed the 1950 statute and gave us § 4001(a) provides a powerful reason to think that § 4001(a) was meant to require clear congressional authorization before any citizen can be placed in a cell . . .*Korematsu*, it intended to preclude reliance on vague congressional authority (for example, providing "accommodations" for those subject to removal) as authority for detention or imprisonment at the discretion of the Executive (maintaining detention camps of American citizens, for example). In requiring that any Executive detention be "pursuant to an Act of Congress," then, Congress necessarily meant to require a congressional enactment that clearly authorized detention or imprisonment.

Finally, . . . [t]he defining character of American constitutional government is its constant tension between security and liberty, serving both by partial helpings of each. In a government of separated powers, deciding finally on what is a reasonable degree of guaranteed liberty whether in peace or war (or some condition in between) is not well entrusted to the Executive Branch of Government, whose particular responsibility is to maintain security. For reasons of inescapable human nature, the branch of the Government asked to counter a serious threat is not the branch on which to rest the Nation's entire reliance in striking the balance between the will to win and the cost in liberty on the way to victory; the responsibility for security will naturally amplify the claim that security legitimately raises. A reasonable balance is more likely to be reached on the judgment of a different branch, just as Madison said in remarking that "the constant aim is to divide and arrange the several offices in such a manner as that each may be a check on the other — that the private interest of every individual may be a sentinel over the public rights." The Federalist No. 51. Hence the need for an assessment by Congress before citizens are subject to lockup, and likewise the need for a clearly expressed congressional resolution of the competing claims.

Under this principle of reading § 4001(a) robustly to require a clear statement of authorization to detain, none of the Government's arguments suffices to justify Hamdi's detention. . . .

Because I find Hamdi's detention forbidden by § 4001(a) and unauthorized by the [AUMF] I would not reach any questions of what process he may be due in litigating disputed issues in a proceeding under the habeas statute or prior to the habeas enquiry itself. . . . Since this disposition does not command a majority of the Court, however, the need to give practical effect to the conclusions of eight members of the Court rejecting the Government's position calls for me to join with the plurality in ordering remand on terms closest to those I would impose. Although I think litigation of Hamdi's status as an enemy combatant is unnecessary, the terms of the plurality's remand will allow Hamdi to offer evidence that he is not an enemy combatant, and he should at the least have the benefit of that opportunity. . . .

JUSTICE SCALIA, with whom JUSTICE STEVENS joins, dissenting.

. . . This case brings into conflict the competing demands of national security and our citizens' constitutional right to personal liberty. Although I share the Court's evident unease as it seeks to reconcile the two, I do not agree with its resolution.

Where the Government accuses a citizen of waging war against it, our constitutional tradition has been to prosecute him in federal court for treason or some other crime. Where the exigencies of war prevent that, the Constitution's Suspension Clause, Art. I, § 9, cl. 2, allows Congress to relax the usual protections temporarily. Absent suspension, however, the Executive's assertion of military exigency has not been thought sufficient to permit detention without charge. No one contends that the congressional Authorization for Use of Military Force, on which the Government relies to justify its actions here, is an implementation of the Suspension Clause. Accordingly, I would reverse the decision below. . . .

The gist of the Due Process Clause, as understood at the founding and since, was to force the Government to follow those common-law procedures traditionally deemed necessary before depriving a person of life, liberty, or property. When a citizen was deprived of liberty because of alleged criminal conduct, those procedures typically required committal by a magistrate followed by indictment and trial. . . . It is unthinkable that the Executive could render otherwise criminal grounds for detention noncriminal merely by disclaiming an intent to prosecute, or by asserting that it was incapacitating dangerous offenders rather than punishing wrongdoing. These due process rights have historically been vindicated by the writ of habeas corpus. [Historical discussion omitted]

The writ of habeas corpus was preserved in the Constitution — the only common-law writ to be explicitly mentioned. *See* Art. I, § 9, cl. 2. Hamilton lauded "the establishment of the writ of *habeas corpus*" in his Federalist defense as a means to protect against "the practice of arbitrary imprisonments . . . in all ages, [one of] the favourite and most formidable instruments of tyranny." The Federalist No. 84, *supra*, at 444. Indeed, availability of the writ under the new Constitution (along with the requirement of trial by jury in criminal cases, see Art. III, § 2, cl. 3) was his basis for arguing that additional, explicit procedural protections were unnecessary. *See* The Federalist No. 83, at 433.

The allegations here, of course, are no ordinary accusations of criminal activity. Yaser Esam Hamdi has been imprisoned because the Government believes he participated in the waging of war against the United States. The relevant question, then, is whether there is a different, special procedure for imprisonment of a citizen accused of wrongdoing *by aiding the enemy in wartime.*

Justice O'Connor, writing for a plurality of this Court, asserts that captured enemy combatants (other than those suspected of war crimes) have traditionally been detained until the cessation of hostilities and then released. That is probably an accurate description of wartime practice with respect to enemy *aliens.* The tradition with respect to American citizens, however, has been quite different. Citizens aiding the enemy have been treated as traitors subject to the criminal process. [Historical discussion omitted]

In more recent times, too, citizens have been charged and tried in Article III courts for acts of war against the United States, even when their noncitizen co-conspirators were not. For example, two American citizens alleged to have participated during World War I in a spying conspiracy on behalf of Germany were tried in federal court. A German member of the same conspiracy was subjected to military process. During World War II, the famous German saboteurs of *Ex parte Quirin*, 317 U.S. 1 (1942) received military process, but the citizens who associated with them (with the exception of one citizen-saboteur, discussed below) were punished under the criminal process.

There are times when military exigency renders resort to the traditional criminal process impracticable. English law accommodated such exigencies by allowing legislative suspension of the writ of habeas corpus for brief periods. . . . Where the Executive has not pursued the usual course of charge, committal, and conviction, it has historically secured the Legislature's explicit approval of a suspension. . . .

Writings from the founding generation also suggest that, without exception, the only constitutional alternatives are to charge the crime or suspend the writ. In 1788, Thomas Jefferson wrote to James Madison questioning the need for a Suspension Clause in cases of rebellion in the proposed Constitution. His letter illustrates the constraints under which the Founders understood themselves to operate:

> Why suspend the Hab. corp. in insurrections and rebellions? The parties who may be arrested may be charged instantly with a well defined crime. Of course the judge will remand them. If the publick safety requires that the government should have a man imprisoned on less probable testimony in those than in other emergencies; let him be taken and tried, retaken and retried, while the necessity continues, only giving him redress against the government for damages.

13 Papers of Thomas Jefferson 442 (July 31, 1788) (J. Boyd ed., 1956).

A similar view was reflected in the 1807 House debates over suspension during the armed uprising that came to be known as Burr's conspiracy[.] . . . The absence of military authority to imprison citizens indefinitely in wartime — whether or not a probability of treason had been established by means less than jury trial — was confirmed by three cases decided during and immediately after the War of 1812. . . . President Lincoln, when he purported to suspend habeas corpus without congressional authorization during the Civil War, apparently did not doubt that suspension was required if the prisoner was to be held without criminal trial. . . . Further evidence comes from this Court's decision in *Ex parte Milligan, supra*. . . . The Court rejected in no uncertain terms the Government's assertion that military jurisdiction was proper "under the 'laws and usages of war[.]' " . . .

Milligan responded to the argument, repeated by the Government in this case, that it is dangerous to leave suspected traitors at large in time of war:

> If it was dangerous, in the distracted condition of affairs, to leave Milligan unrestrained of his liberty, because he 'conspired against the government, afforded aid and comfort to rebels, and incited the people to insurrection,' the *law* said arrest him, confine him closely, render him powerless to do further mischief; and then present his case to the grand jury of the district, with proofs of his guilt, and, if indicted, try him according to the course of the common law. If this had been done, the Constitution would have been vindicated, the law of 1863 enforced, and the securities for personal liberty preserved and defended. . . .

The proposition that the Executive lacks indefinite wartime detention authority over citizens is consistent with the Founders' general mistrust of military power permanently at the Executive's disposal. In the Founders' view, the "blessings of liberty" were threatened by "those military establishments which must gradually poison its very fountain." The Federalist No. 45, p. 238 (J. Madison). No fewer than 10 issues of the Federalist were devoted in whole or part to allaying fears of oppression from the proposed Constitution's authorization of standing armies in peacetime. Many safeguards in the Constitution reflect these concerns. . . . As Hamilton explained, the President's military authority would be "much inferior" to that of the British King[.] . . .

The Government argues that our more recent jurisprudence ratifies its indefinite imprisonment of a citizen within the territorial jurisdiction of federal courts. It places primary reliance upon *Ex parte Quirin*, 317 U.S. 1 (1942), . . . The case was not this Court's finest hour. The Court upheld the commission and denied relief in a brief *per curiam* issued the day after oral argument concluded, a week later the Government carried out the commission's death sentence upon six saboteurs, including Haupt. The Court eventually explained its reasoning in a written opinion issued several months later. Only three paragraphs of the Court's lengthy opinion dealt with the particular circumstances of Haupt's case. . . .

In my view [*Quirin*] seeks to revise *Milligan* rather than describe it. . . . *Milligan* . . . was in accord with the traditional law of habeas corpus I have described: Though treason often occurred in wartime, there was, absent provision for special treatment in a congressional suspension of the writ, no exception to the right to trial by jury for citizens who could be called "belligerents" or "prisoners of war."

But even if *Quirin* gave a correct description of *Milligan*, or made an irrevocable revision of it, *Quirin* would still not justify denial of the writ here. In *Quirin* it was uncontested that the petitioners were members of enemy forces. They were "*admitted* enemy invaders," and it was "undisputed" that they had landed in the United States in service of German forces. The specific holding of the Court was only that, "upon the *conceded* facts," the petitioners were "plainly within [the] boundaries" of military jurisdiction. But where those jurisdictional facts are *not* conceded — where the petitioner insists that he is *not* a belligerent — *Quirin* left the pre-existing law in place: Absent suspension of the writ, a citizen held where the courts are open is entitled either to criminal trial or to a judicial decree requiring his release.

It follows from what I have said that Hamdi is entitled to a habeas decree requiring his release unless (1) criminal proceedings are promptly brought, or (2) Congress has suspended the writ of habeas corpus. A suspension of the writ could, of course, lay down conditions for continued detention, similar to those that today's opinion prescribes under the Due Process Clause. But there is a world of difference between the people's representatives' determining the need for that suspension (and prescribing the conditions for it), and this Court's doing so.

The plurality finds justification for Hamdi's imprisonment in [AUMF] . . . . This is not remotely a congressional suspension of the writ, and no one claims that it is. Contrary to the plurality's view, I do not think this statute even authorizes detention of a citizen with the clarity necessary to satisfy the interpretive canon that statutes should be construed so as to avoid grave constitutional concerns, or with the clarity necessary to overcome the statutory prescription [in] 18 U.S.C. § 4001(a). But even if it did, I would not permit it to overcome Hamdi's entitlement to habeas corpus relief. The Suspension Clause of the Constitution, which carefully circumscribes the conditions under which the writ can be withheld, would be a sham if it could be evaded by congressional prescription of requirements *other than the common-law requirement of committal for criminal prosecution* that render the writ, though available, unavailing. If the Suspension Clause does not guarantee the citizen that he will either be tried or released, unless the conditions for suspending the writ exist and the grave action of suspending the writ has been taken; if it merely guarantees the citizen that he will not be detained unless

Congress by ordinary legislation says he can be detained; it guarantees him very little indeed.

It should not be thought, however, that the plurality's evisceration of the Suspension Clause augments, principally, the power of Congress. As usual, the major effect of its constitutional improvisation is to increase the power of the Court. Having found a congressional authorization for detention of citizens where none clearly exists; and having discarded the categorical procedural protection of the Suspension Clause; the plurality then proceeds, under the guise of the Due Process Clause, to prescribe what procedural protections *it* thinks appropriate. It "weigh[s] the private interest . . . against the Government's asserted interest," and — just as though writing a new Constitution — comes up with an unheard-of system in which the citizen rather than the Government bears the burden of proof, testimony is by hearsay rather than live witnesses, and the presiding officer may well be a "neutral" military officer rather than judge and jury. . . . Whatever the merits of this technique when newly recognized property rights are at issue (and even there they are questionable), it has no place where the Constitution and the common law already supply an answer.

Having distorted the Suspension Clause, the plurality finishes up by transmogrifying the Great Writ — disposing of the present habeas petition by remanding for the District Court to "engag[e] in a factfinding process that is both prudent and incremental." "In the absence of [the Executive's prior provision of procedures that satisfy due process], . . . a court that receives a petition for a writ of habeas corpus from an alleged enemy combatant must itself ensure that the minimum requirements of due process are achieved." This judicial remediation of executive default is unheard of. The role of habeas corpus is to determine the legality of executive detention, not to supply the omitted process necessary to make it legal. It is not the habeas court's function to make illegal detention legal by supplying a process that the Government could have provided, but chose not to. If Hamdi is being imprisoned in violation of the Constitution (because without due process of law), then his habeas petition should be granted; the Executive may then hand him over to the criminal authorities, whose detention for the purpose of prosecution will be lawful, or else must release him.

There is a certain harmony of approach in the plurality's making up for Congress's failure to invoke the Suspension Clause and its making up for the Executive's failure to apply what it says are needed procedures — an approach that reflects what might be called a Mr. Fix-it Mentality. The plurality seems to view it as its mission to Make Everything Come Out Right, rather than merely to decree the consequences, as far as individual rights are concerned, of the other two branches' actions and omissions. Has the Legislature failed to suspend the writ in the current dire emergency? Well, we will remedy that failure by prescribing the reasonable conditions that a suspension should have included. And has the Executive failed to live up to those reasonable conditions? Well, we will ourselves make that failure good, so that this dangerous fellow (if he is dangerous) need not be set free. The problem with this approach is not only that it steps out of the courts' modest and limited role in a democratic society; but that by repeatedly doing what it thinks the political branches ought to do it encourages their lassitude and saps the vitality of government by the people.

Several limitations give my views in this matter a relatively narrow compass. They apply only to citizens, accused of being enemy combatants, who are detained within the territorial jurisdiction of a federal court. This is not likely to be a numerous group; currently we know of only two, Hamdi and Jose Padilla. Where the citizen is captured outside and held outside the United States, the constitutional requirements may be different. Cf. *Johnson v. Eisentrager*, 339 U.S. 763, 769-771 (1950); Moreover, even within the United States, the accused citizen-enemy combatant may lawfully be detained once prosecution is in progress or in contemplation. The Government has been notably successful in securing conviction, and hence long-term custody or execution, of those who have waged war against the state.

I frankly do not know whether these tools are sufficient to meet the Government's security needs, including the need to obtain intelligence through interrogation. It is far beyond my competence, or the Court's competence, to determine that. But it is not beyond Congress's. If the situation demands it, the Executive can ask Congress to authorize suspension of the writ — which can be made subject to whatever conditions Congress deems appropriate, including even the procedural novelties invented by the plurality today. To be sure, suspension is limited by the Constitution to cases of rebellion or invasion. But whether the attacks of September 11, 2001, constitute an "invasion," and whether those attacks still justify suspension several years later, are questions for Congress rather than this Court. If civil rights are to be curtailed during wartime, it must be done openly and democratically, as the Constitution requires, rather than by silent erosion through an opinion of this Court.

The Founders well understood the difficult tradeoff between safety and freedom. . . . The Founders warned us about the risk, and equipped us with a Constitution designed to deal with it. Many think it not only inevitable but entirely proper that liberty give way to security in times of national crisis — that, at the extremes of military exigency, *inter arma silent leges.* Whatever the general merits of the view that war silences law or modulates its voice, that view has no place in the interpretation and application of a Constitution designed precisely to confront war and, in a manner that accords with democratic principles, to accommodate it. Because the Court has proceeded to meet the current emergency in a manner the Constitution does not envision, I respectfully dissent.

JUSTICE THOMAS, dissenting.

The Executive Branch, acting pursuant to the powers vested in the President by the Constitution and with explicit congressional approval, has determined that Yaser Hamdi is an enemy combatant and should be detained. This detention falls squarely within the Federal Government's war powers, and we lack the expertise and capacity to second-guess that decision. As such, petitioners' habeas challenge should fail, and there is no reason to remand the case. The plurality reaches a contrary conclusion by failing adequately to consider basic principles of the constitutional structure as it relates to national security and foreign affairs and by using [a] balancing scheme. . . . I do not think that the Federal Government's war powers can be balanced away by this Court. Arguably, Congress could provide for additional procedural protections, but until it does, we have no right to insist upon them. But even if I were to agree with the general approach the plurality takes, I could not accept the particulars. The plurality utterly fails to account for the Government's compelling interests and for our own institutional inability to weigh competing concerns correctly. I respectfully dissent. . . .

The Founders intended that the President have primary responsibility — along with the necessary power — to protect the national security and to conduct the Nation's foreign relations. They did so principally because the structural advantages of a unitary Executive are essential in these domains. "Energy in the executive is a leading character in the definition of good government. It is essential to the protection of the community against foreign attacks." The Federalist No. 70, p. 471 (A. Hamilton). . . . These structural advantages are most important in the national-security and foreign-affairs contexts. . . . This Court has long recognized these features and has accordingly held that the President has *constitutional* authority to protect the national security and that this authority carries with it broad discretion. . . .

Congress, to be sure, has a substantial and essential role in both foreign affairs and national security. But it is crucial to recognize that *judicial* interference in these domains destroys the purpose of vesting primary responsibility in a unitary Executive. . . .

For these institutional reasons and because "Congress cannot anticipate and legislate with regard to every possible action the President may find it necessary to take or every possible situation in which he might act," it should come as no surprise that "[s]uch failure of Congress . . . does not, 'especially . . . in the areas of foreign policy and national security,' imply 'congressional disapproval' of action taken by the Executive." *Dames & Moore v. Regan*, 453 U.S. 654, 678 (1981). Rather, in these domains, the fact that Congress has provided the President with broad authorities does not imply — and the Judicial Branch should not infer — that Congress intended to deprive him of particular powers not specifically enumerated. . . .

Finally, and again for the same reasons, where "the President acts pursuant to an express or implied authorization from Congress, he exercises not only his powers but also those delegated by Congress[, and i]n such a case the executive action 'would be supported by the strongest of presumptions and the widest latitude of judicial interpretation, and the burden of persuasion would rest heavily upon any who might attack it.' " That is why the Court has explained, in a case analogous to this one, that "the detention[,] ordered by the President in the declared exercise of his powers as Commander in Chief of the Army in time of war and of grave public danger[, is] not to be set aside by the courts without the clear conviction that [it is] in conflict with the Constitution or laws of Congress constitutionally enacted." *Ex parte Quirin*, 317 U.S. 1, 25, 63 (1942). . . .

I acknowledge that the question whether Hamdi's executive detention is lawful is a question properly resolved by the Judicial Branch, though the question comes to the Court with the strongest presumptions in favor of the Government. The plurality agrees that Hamdi's detention is lawful if he is an enemy combatant. But the question whether Hamdi is actually an enemy combatant is "of a kind for which the Judiciary has neither aptitude, facilities nor responsibility and which has long been held to belong in the domain of political power not subject to judicial intrusion or inquiry." . . . That is, although it is appropriate for the Court to determine the judicial question whether the President has the asserted authority, we lack the information and expertise to question whether Hamdi is actually an enemy combatant, a question the resolution of which is committed to other branches. . . .

Although the President very well may have inherent authority to detain those arrayed against our troops, I agree with the plurality that we need not decide that question because Congress has authorized the President to do so [in the AUMF]. . . . Accordingly, the President's action here is "supported by the strongest of presumptions and the widest latitude of judicial interpretation." *Dames & Moore*, 453 U.S., at 668. The question becomes whether the Federal Government (rather than the President acting alone) has power to detain Hamdi as an enemy combatant. More precisely, we must determine whether the Government may detain Hamdi given the procedures that were used. I agree with the plurality that the Federal Government has power to detain those that the Executive Branch determines to be enemy combatants. But I do not think that the plurality has adequately explained the breadth of the President's authority to detain enemy combatants, an authority that includes making virtually conclusive factual findings. In my view, the structural considerations discussed above, as recognized in our precedent, demonstrate that we lack the capacity and responsibility to second-guess this determination.

This makes complete sense once the process that is due Hamdi is made clear. As an initial matter, it is possible that the Due Process Clause requires only "that our Government must proceed according to the 'law of the land' — that is, according to written constitutional and statutory provisions." I need not go this far today because the Court has already explained the nature of due process in this context. . . . In this context, due process requires nothing more than a good-faith executive determination. To be clear: The Court has held that an executive, acting pursuant to statutory and constitutional authority may, consistent with the Due Process Clause, unilaterally decide to detain an individual if the executive deems this necessary for the public safety *even if he is mistaken.* . . .

The Government's asserted authority to detain an individual that the President has determined to be an enemy combatant, at least while hostilities continue, comports with the Due Process Clause. As the[. . .] cases also show, the Executive's decision that a detention is necessary to protect the public need not and should not be subjected to judicial second-guessing. Indeed, at least in the context of enemy-combatant determinations, this would defeat the unity, secrecy, and dispatch that the Founders believed to be so important to the warmaking function. . . .

Justice Scalia . . . finds support in a letter Thomas Jefferson wrote to James Madison. I agree that this provides some evidence for his position. But I think this plainly insufficient to rebut the authorities upon which I have relied. In any event, I do not believe that Justice Scalia's evidence leads to the necessary "clear conviction that [the detention is] in conflict with the Constitution or laws of Congress constitutionally enacted," *Quirin, supra,* at 25, to justify nullifying the President's wartime action.

Finally, Justice Scalia's position raises an additional concern. Justice Scalia apparently does not disagree that the Federal Government has all power necessary to protect the Nation. If criminal processes do not suffice, however, Justice Scalia would require Congress to suspend the writ. But the fact that the writ may not be suspended "unless when in Cases of Rebellion or Invasion the public Safety may require it," Art. I, § 9, cl. 2, poses two related problems. First, this condition might not obtain here or during many other emergencies during which this detention authority might be necessary. Congress would then have to choose between acting unconstitutionally and depriving the President of the tools he needs to protect the Nation. Second, I do not see how suspension would make constitutional otherwise unconstitutional detentions ordered by the President. It simply removes a remedy. Justice Scalia's position might therefore require one or both of the political branches to act unconstitutionally in order to protect the Nation. But the power to protect the Nation must be the power to do so lawfully.

Accordingly, I conclude that the Government's detention of Hamdi as an enemy combatant does not violate the Constitution. By detaining Hamdi, the President, in the prosecution of a war and authorized by Congress, has acted well within his authority. Hamdi thereby received all the process to which he was due under the circumstances. I therefore believe that this is no occasion to balance the competing interests, as the plurality unconvincingly attempts to do. . . .

Undeniably, Hamdi has been deprived of a serious interest, one actually protected by the Due Process Clause. Against this, however, is the Government's overriding interest in protecting the Nation. If a deprivation of liberty can be justified by the need to protect a town, the protection of the Nation, *a fortiori,* justifies it. . . .

For these reasons, I would affirm the judgment of the Court of Appeals.

NOTES

(1) Can the President suspend the writ of habeas corpus? The Suspension Clause ("The Privilege of the court of habeas corpus shall not be suspended, unless when in cases of rebellion or invasion the public safety require it") appears in Article I (Art. I § 9 cl. 2) of the Constitution, not in Article II. In *Ex parte Merryman*, 17 F. Cas. 144 (1861), Chief Justice Taney emphatically held that the President lacked power to

suspend the writ. The President "does not faithfully execute the laws, if he takes upon himself legislative power, by suspending the writ of habeas corpus, and the judicial power also, by arresting and imprisoning a person without due process." *Id.* at 149. Proclaiming that he had "exercised all the power with the constitution and laws confer upon me, but that power has been resisted by a force too strong for me to overcome," Chief Justice Taney directed that his order be sent to President Lincoln for his consideration.

(2) Various opinions in *Hamdi* discuss *Ex parte Milligan*, 71 U.S. (4 Wall.) 2 (1867) in which Lambdin P. Milligan petitioned the United States Circuit Court for the District of Indiana, to be discharged from an alleged unlawful imprisonment. He claimed he was a United States citizen who had lived for twenty years in Indiana who had never been in the United States military. He was arrested on October 5, 1864 and confined by order of General Alvin P. Hovey, commanding the military district of Indiana. A few weeks later, he was tried before a military commission at Indianapolis on certain charges, found guilty, and sentenced to be hanged on May 19, 1865. In January, 1865 a grand jury was empanelled by the United States Circuit Court for Indiana but returned no indictment or presentment against Milligan. Milligan argued that the military commission lacked jurisdiction to try him because he was a citizen of the United States and of Indiana, and had not been a resident of a confederate state and that the right of trial by jury was guaranteed to him by the Constitution of the United States. The Court held that Milligan's military trial was unlawful. Justice Davis began his majority opinion:

> During the late wicked Rebellion, the temper of the times did not allow that calmness in deliberation and discussion so necessary to a correct conclusion of a purely judicial question. *Then*, considerations of safety were mingled with the exercise of power; and feelings and interests prevailed which are happily terminated. *Now*, that the public safety is assured, this question, as well as all others, can be discussed and decided without passion or the admixture of any element not required to form a legal judgment. We approach the investigation of this case, fully sensible of the magnitude of the inquiry and the necessity of full and cautious deliberation. . . .

> No graver question was ever considered by this court, nor one which more nearly concerns the rights of the whole people; for it is the birthright of every American citizen when charged with crime, to be tried and punished according to law.

The Court held that laws and wages of war "can never be applied to citizens in states which have upheld the authority of the government, and where the courts are open and their process unobstructed." The federal courts in Indiana were available to hear criminal cases and accordingly "[o]ne of the plainest constitutional provisions" was infringed when Milligan was denied trial by an Article II court and trial by jury.

(3) Justice Davis suggested in dicta that where "the courts are actually closed" due to foreign invasion or civil war" military tribunals might, of necessity, replace civil authority "until the law can have their free course." Does this dicta suggest that the Constitution may be suspended due to emergency? The Constitution does not so provide in its text and Article III and various provisions of the Bill of Rights might support a contrary inference since they generally make no exception for emergency. How should this constitutional silence be construed? Professor David Currie criticizes Justice Davis' dicta for undermining the "earlier ringing statements" in his opinion. He suggests Justice Davis might have better avoided the question "whether the Framers meant to do away with traditional military powers to govern either military personnel or conquered territories" by observing that it was "unnecessary to the decision of the case at hand."

David P. Currie, The Constitution in the Supreme Court: The First Hundred Years 1789-1888, at 290 (1985).

(4) Justice Davis' opinion reasoned that Congress lacked power to pass a law providing for trial of defendants like Milligan before a military commission. Should the Court have addressed this issue? Chief Justice Rehnquist argued that since Congress had not enacted such a law, Justice Davis should not have reached the issue. Indeed, in addressing the issue, Chief Justice Rehnquist argued, the Court violated a cardinal principle of avoiding unnecessary constitutional pronouncements. The concurring justices argued in portions of their opinion not reproduced herein that the Habeas Corpus Act of 1863 required discharging Milligan since it allowed his detention only until a grand jury met to consider indicting him. Chief Justice Rehnquist argued that the majority could reasonably have interpreted the statute to apply only to those detained for trial in civil courts. Under that interpretation, the statute would not have reached Milligan leaving the Court with the issue of whether the President could unilaterally authorize wartime trial of civilians by military commissions. William H. Rehnquist, All the Law But One: Civil Liberties in Wartime 128-37 (1998).

Justice Davis did seem to create a bright line rule that military tribunals could not be used to try "citizens in states which have upheld the authority of the government, and where the courts are open and their process unobstructed."

(5) President Abraham Lincoln took extensive emergency action during the Civil War, blockading southern ports without Congress' authorization, raising the size of the military beyond statutory ceilings, spending funds for purposes not authorized and suspending the write of habeas corpus. See generally David Herbert Donald, Lincoln 302-04 (1995). Lincoln's justification, in part, is suggested at supra § 5.01, Note (12). "[A]re all the laws, but one, to go unexecuted, and the government itself go to pieces, lest that one be violated?" he asked rhetorically. Congress was not in session when Lincoln took office on march 4, 1861. Does that put Lincoln's actions in a different light? In his Special Session Message of July 4, 1861, Lincoln justified these steps "whether strictly legal or not" due to "popular demand," "public necessity," his belief they were within Congress' power (Congress being out of session), and his belief Congress would ratify his actions. See Lincoln, Special Session Message, in 7 Messages and Papers of the Presidents 3221, 3225, 3226 (James Richardson ed., 1897).

(6) During the Civil War, the Court avoided the question Ex parte Milligan raised regarding the constitutionality of military trial of a civilian. See Ex parte Vallandigham, 68 U.S. (1Wall.) 243 (1864) (no jurisdiction for direct review of military commission). Ex parte Milligan was decided after the conflict ended.

(7) As opinions in Hamdi point out, in Ex parte Quirin, 317 U.S. 1 (1942), the Court upheld the trial by a military tribunal of a group of Nazi saboteurs, including one American citizen, who had travelled clandestinely by submarine to the United States during World War II to carry out various acts of war. The group abandoned their military uniforms and were wearing civilian dress when apprehended. The Court concluded that the saboteurs were unlawful enemy combatants not entitled to protections accorded prisoners of war. "By a long course of practical administrative construction by its military authorities, our Government" had viewed such unlawful combatants as subject to military trial. American citizenship of an enemy belligerent did not accord greater rights. Ex parte Milligan did not apply because Milligan was not an enemy belligerent.

§ 5.06   PRESIDENTIAL ACCOUNTABILITY

[1]   Privilege

UNITED STATES v. NIXON

418 U.S. 683, 94 S. Ct. 3090, 41 L. Ed. 2d 1039 (1974)

Mr. Chief Justice Burger delivered the opinion of the Court.

[Editor's Note: This case arose out of a federal subpoena issued to President Richard M. Nixon for tape recordings and other documents pertinent to conversations he had with various advisers. The evidence was sought by the Watergate Special Prosecutor for use in a criminal trial against former associates of President Nixon charged with various federal offenses including conspiracy to defraud the United States and obstruction of justice related to the Watergate Scandal. President Nixon moved to quash the subpoena *duces tecum* by challenging the District Court's jurisdiction and by claiming executive privilege.

The District Court denied the motion to quash. It held that the judiciary, not the President, was the final arbiter of a claim of executive privilege. The court concluded that, under the circumstances of this case, any presumptive privilege was overcome by the Special Prosecutor's prima facie "demonstration of need sufficiently compelling to warrant judicial examination in chambers." The President appealed and petitioned for certiorari which the Court granted.

The Court held that it had jurisdiction. Although the appealed District Court order denying a motion to quash and ordering production of evidence was not final, the normal requirement that the party submit to contempt was sometimes relaxed and should be "due to the unique setting" involving as it did the President of the United States. The issues were justiciable although they involved an "intra-branch dispute." In reality, a real controversy existed between the President and the Special Prosecutor dealing with production of evidence. The Court noted such issues are "traditionally justiciable" and again noted "the uniqueness of the setting." The requirements for a pretrial return of the subpoena were also satisfied.]

IV

The Claim of Privilege

A

[W]e turn to the claim that the subpoena should be quashed because it demands "confidential conversations between a President and his close advisors that it would be inconsistent with the public interest to produce." . . . The first contention is a broad claim that the separation of powers doctrine precludes judicial review of a President's claim of privilege. The second contention is that if he does not prevail on the claim of absolute privilege, the court should hold as a matter of constitutional law that the privilege prevails over the subpoena duces tecum.

In the performance of assigned constitutional duties each branch of the Government must initially interpret the Constitution, and the interpretation of its powers by any branch is due great respect from the others. The President's counsel, as we have noted, reads the Constitution as providing an absolute privilege of confidentiality for all Presidential communications. Many decisions of this Court, however, have unequivocally reaffirmed the holding of *Marbury v. Madison*, . . . that "[i]t is emphatically the province and duty of the judicial department to say what the law is." . . .

No holding of the Court has defined the scope of judicial power specifically relating to the enforcement of a subpoena for confidential Presidential communications for use in a criminal prosecution, but other exercises of power by the Executive Branch and the Legislative Branch have been found invalid as in conflict with the Constitution. *Powell v. McCormack*, . . . [*supra* § 1.09, Note (5) after *Nixon*]; *Youngstown Sheet & Tube Co. v. Sawyer*, . . . [*supra* § 5.01]. . . .

Our system of government "requires that federal courts on occasion interpret the Constitution in a manner at variance with the construction given the document by another branch." . . . Notwithstanding the deference each branch must accord the others, the "judicial Power of the United States" vested in the federal courts by Art. III, § 1, of the Constitution can no more be shared with the Executive Branch than the Chief Executive, for example, can share with the Judiciary the veto power, or the Congress share with the Judiciary the power to override a Presidential veto. Any other conclusion would be contrary to the basic concept of separation of powers and checks and balances that flow from the scheme of a tripartite government. . . . We therefore reaffirm that it is the province and duty of this Court "to say what the law is" with respect to the claim of privilege presented in this case.

B

In support of his claim of absolute privilege, the President's counsel urges two grounds one of which is common to all governments and one of which is peculiar to our system of separation of powers. The first ground is the valid need for protection of communications between high Government officials and those who advise and assist them in the performance of their manifold duties; the importance of this confidentiality is too plain to require further discussion. Human experience teaches that those who expect public dissemination of their remarks may well temper candor with a concern for appearances and for their own interests to the detriment of the decision-making process. Whatever the nature of the privilege of confidentiality of Presidential communications in the exercise of Art. II powers, the privilege can be said to derive from the supremacy of each branch within its own assigned area of constitutional duties. Certain powers and privileges flow from the nature of enumerated powers; the protection of the confidentiality of Presidential communications has similar constitutional underpinnings.

The second ground asserted by the President's counsel in support of the claim of absolute privilege rests on the doctrine of separation of powers. Here it is argued that the independence of the Executive Branch within its own sphere . . .insulates a President from a judicial subpoena in an ongoing criminal prosecution, and thereby protects confidential Presidential communications.

However, neither the doctrine of separation of powers, nor the need for confidentiality of high-level communications, without more, can sustain an absolute, unqualified Presidential privilege of immunity from judicial process under all circumstances. The President's need for complete candor and objectivity from advisers calls for great deference from the courts. However, when the privilege depends solely on the broad, undifferentiated claim of public interest in the confidentiality of such conversations, a confrontation with other values arises. Absent a claim of need to protect military, diplomatic, or sensitive national security secrets, we find it difficult to accept the argument that even the very important interest in confidentiality of Presidential communications is significantly diminished by production of such material for in camera inspection with all the protection that a district court will be obliged to provide.

The impediment that an absolute, unqualified privilege would place in the way of the primary constitutional duty of the Judicial Branch to do justice in criminal prosecutions would plainly conflict with the function of the courts under Art. III. In designing the structure of our Government and dividing and allocating the sovereign power among three co-equal branches, the Framers of the Constitution sought to provide a comprehensive system, but the separate powers were not intended to operate with absolute independence. . . . To read the Art. II powers of the President as providing an absolute privilege as against a subpoena essential to enforcement of criminal statutes on no more than a generalized claim of the public interest in confidentiality of nonmilitary and nondiplomatic discussions would upset the constitutional balance of "a workable government" and gravely impair the role of the courts under Art. III.

C

Since we conclude that the legitimate needs of the judicial process may outweigh Presidential privilege, it is necessary to resolve those competing interests in a manner that preserves the essential functions of each branch. The right and indeed the duty to resolve that question does not free the Judiciary from according high respect to the representations made on behalf of the President. . . .

The expectation of a President to the confidentiality of his conversations and correspondence, like the claim of confidentiality of judicial deliberations, for example, has all the values to which we accord deference for the privacy of all citizens and, added to those values, is the necessity for protection of the public interest in candid, objective, and even blunt or harsh opinions in Presidential decision-making. A President and those who assist him must be free to explore alternatives in the process of shaping policies and making decisions and to do so in a way many would be unwilling to express except privately. These are the considerations justifying a presumptive privilege for Presidential communications. The privilege is fundamental to the operation of Government and inextricably rooted in the separation of powers under the Constitution. . . .

But this presumptive privilege must be considered in light of our historic commitment to the rule of law. This is nowhere more profoundly manifest than in our view that "the twofold aim [of criminal justice] is that guilt shall not escape or innocence suffer." . . . The ends of criminal justice would be defeated if judgments were to be founded on a partial or speculative presentation of the facts. The very integrity of the judicial system and public confidence in the system depend on full disclosure of all the facts, within the framework of the rules of evidence. To ensure that justice is done, it is imperative to the function of courts that compulsory process be available for the production of evidence needed either by the prosecution or by the defense.

Only recently the Court restated the ancient proposition of law, albeit in the context of a grand jury inquiry rather than a trial,

> that "the public . . . has a right to every man's evidence," except for those persons protected by a constitutional, common-law, or statutory privilege. . . .

In this case the President challenges a subpoena served on him as a third party requiring the production of materials for use in a criminal prosecution; he does so on the claim that he has a privilege against disclosure of confidential communications. He does not place his claim of privilege on the ground they are military or diplomatic secrets. As to these areas of Art. II duties the courts have traditionally shown the utmost deference to Presidential responsibilities. . . . No case of the Court, however, has extended this high degree of deference to a President's generalized interest in confidentiality. Nowhere in the Constitution, as we have noted earlier, is there any explicit reference to a privilege of confidentiality, yet to the extent this interest relates to the effective discharge of a President's powers, it is constitutionally based. . . .

In this case we must weigh the importance of the general privilege of confidentiality of Presidential communications in performance of the President's responsibilities against the inroads of such a privilege on the fair administration of criminal justice. The interest in preserving confidentiality is weighty indeed and entitled to great respect. However, we cannot conclude that advisers will be moved to temper the candor of their remarks by the infrequent occasions of disclosure because of the possibility that such conversations will be called for in the context of a criminal prosecution.

On the other hand, the allowance of the privilege to withhold evidence that is demonstrably relevant in a criminal trial would cut deeply into the guarantee of due process of law and gravely impair the basic function of the courts. A President's acknowledged need for confidentiality in the communications of his office is general in nature, whereas the constitutional need for production of relevant evidence in a criminal proceeding is specific and central to the fair adjudication of a particular criminal case in the administration of justice. . . .

We conclude that when the ground for asserting privilege as to subpoenaed materials sought for use in a criminal trial is based only on the generalized interest in confidentiality, it cannot prevail over the fundamental demands of due process of law in the fair administration of criminal justice. The generalized assertion of privilege must yield to the demonstrated, specific need for evidence in a pending criminal trial.

D

We have earlier determined that the District Court did not err in authorizing the issuance of the subpoena. If a President concludes that compliance with a subpoena would be injurious to the public interest he may properly, as was done here, invoke a claim of privilege on the return of the subpoena. Upon receiving a claim of privilege from the Chief Executive, it became the further duty of the District Court to treat the subpoenaed material as presumptively privileged and to require the Special Prosecutor to demonstrate that the Presidential material was "essential to the justice of the [pending criminal] case.". . . Here the District Court treated the material as presumptively privileged, proceeded to find that the Special Prosecutor had made a sufficient showing to rebut the presumption, and ordered an in camera examination of the subpoenaed material. On the basis of our examination of the record we are unable to conclude that the District Court erred in ordering the inspection. Accordingly we affirm the order of the District Court that subpoenaed materials be transmitted to that court. . . .

Affirmed.

NOTES

(1) The *Nixon* case addresses two issues of great importance to the law on presidential power: (1) is the President subject to judicial process, and (2) executive privilege.

(2) Does subjecting the President to a lawsuit violate the separation of powers? Thomas Jefferson once asked, "would the Executive be independent of the judiciary if he were subject to the *commands* of the latter?" 9 PAUL LEICESTER FORD, THE WRITINGS OF THOMAS JEFFERSON 60 (1898) (letter to Mr. George Hay, June 20, 1807).

(3) *Mississippi v. Johnson*, 71 U.S. (4 Wall.) 475 (1866), involved an action against President Andrew Johnson to enjoin him from enforcing the Reconstruction Acts on the ground that they were unconstitutional. Based on the separation of powers doctrine, the Court held that such an action could not be maintained. "The Congress is the legislative department of the government; the President is the executive department. Neither can be restrained in its action by the judicial department."

(4) In *Franklin v. Massachusetts*, 505 U.S. 788 (1992), the Supreme Court reversed a district court order to the President. Justice Scalia, concurring, wrote:

> It is a commentary upon the level to which judicial understanding — indeed, even judicial awareness — of the doctrine of separation of powers has fallen, that the District Court entered this order against the President without blinking an eye. I think it clear that no court has authority to direct the President to take an official act. A court may not require [the President] to exercise the "executive Power" in a judicially prescribed fashion. . . . The apparently unbroken historical tradition supports the view, which I think implicit in the separation of powers established by the Constitution, that the principals in whom the executive and legislative powers are ultimately vested — viz., the President and the Congress (as opposed to their agents) — may not be ordered to perform particular executive or legislative acts at the behest of the Judiciary.

> For similar reasons, I think we cannot issue a declaratory judgment against the President. It is incompatible with his constitutional position that he be compelled personally to defend his executive actions before a court.

According to Justice Scalia's *Franklin* opinion, the rule barring injunctive or declaratory relief against the President "in [no] way suggests that Presidential action is *unreviewable*. Review of the legality of Presidential action can ordinarily be obtained in a suit seeking to enjoin the officers who attempt to enforce the President's directive."

The Court reviewed President Truman's steel-seizure order in the *Steel Seizure Case*, *supra* § 5.01. in this manner. Under *Mississippi v. Johnson*, the steel companies could not sue President Truman directly. Secretary of Commerce Sawyer, who was the instrument for the execution of the President's order, had no direct immunity. An action against Secretary Sawyer allowed the court to determine if the order was legal. The court could direct its order to the Secretary without any need formally to summon the President. The District Court reasoned that Secretary Sawyer, not the President, was the defendant and "the Supreme Court has held on many occasions that officers of the Executive Branch of the Government may be enjoined when their conduct is unauthorized by statute." The Supreme Court affirmed, without discussion.

The *Nixon* case was a rare case in which the President was an indispensable party, since he alone had custody of the subpoenaed tapes. In such a case, the Court holds that the President may be sued in a federal court.

(5) *United States v. Nixon* stands as a metaphor to a central component of the rule of law ideal, the idea that no one is above the law. Unlike many other important decisions involving executive power, i.e., *Marbury v. Madison, Youngstown v. Sawyer*, here the President was the defendant in a case brought by the United States. The very style of the case thus conveys powerful symbolism.

(6) But if the Constitution vests executive power in a President of the United States, how can the executive branch proceed against the head of that branch? The Court relied on a regulation issued by the Attorney General authorizing the Special Prosecutor to control the investigation and litigation of the matters relating to abuses of the Nixon 1972 re-election campaign. The Court recognized Nixon could have rescinded that

regulation and fired Special Prosecutor Leon Jaworski as he had done with Jaworski's predecessor, Archibald Cox. Until he did, the Court argued the regulation was law to which Nixon was subject. But Professor Akhil Reed Amar asks: "Why were the Justices insisting that Nixon first rescind, and only then countermand Jaworski? Why wasn't it enough that in their very courtroom, the President was clearly saying that he disagreed with his inferior about the proper discharge of executive-branch business?"

Professor Amar answers his own question:

> The best answer is one the Court never stated forthrightly: Richard Nixon was a crook, using the Oval Office as a hub of a massive ongoing criminal conspiracy to obstruct justice, and the Court already had evidence under seal that proved this. If Nixon wanted to fire or countermand Jaworski, he would not get a finger of support from the Justices; he would have to do it himself (twice) at high noon on main street, for all to see.

Akhil Reed Amar, *Nixon's Shadow*, 83 MINN. L. REV. 1405, 1407 (1999).

(7) Did the legal system need to allow Nixon to be sued in court over the tapes and other evidence under subpoena in order to hold Nixon accountable? Was there another method of obtaining that information and/or holding Nixon accountable? Impeachment proceedings were underway in the House of Representatives at the time the Court issued its decision. *See* Steven G. Calabresi, *Caesarism, Departmentalism, and Professor Paulsen*, 83 MINN. L. REV. 1421, 1423-24 (1999).

(8) Could the Court have dodged a constitutional confrontation with the President as Marshall did in *Marbury*, by finding no real justiciable controversy existed and accordingly dismissing it for lack of jurisdiction? "Whereas the Court in *Marbury*, danced away from a confrontation with the President in part by making more timid claims regarding its power over the Executive, the Court, in *United States v. Nixon*, boldly advanced across the ring." Joel K. Goldstein, *The Presidency and the Rule of Law: Some Preliminary Explorations*, 43 ST. LOUIS L.J. 791, 824 (1999). Why did the Court act in this manner? Was it because the Court's prestige had grown over the 170 years since *Marbury*? Because Nixon, unlike Jefferson, was a weakened President? Because Nixon was a crook? Because it wanted Nixon to understand that he could not continue to defy the American political and legal systems?

(9) The Special Prosecutor was seeking the tapes in part as evidence in connection with a pending criminal trial against some of Nixon's closest associates. Chief Justice Burger analogized the subpoena to *United States v. Burr*, 25 F. Cas. 30 (C.C.D. Va. 1807) (No. 14,692d) in which Chief Justice Marshall, riding circuit, upheld a subpoena against Thomas Jefferson for documents defendant (and former Vice President) Aaron Burr, sought. Was *Burr* really analogous to *United States v. Nixon*? In *Burr*, a defendant sought evidence to exonerate himself from the government which was prosecuting him. The government should not be able to prosecute someone but withhold evidence that might help establish a defense. In *Nixon*, however, the prosecution (Jaworski) sought the evidence. *See* Amar, *Nixon's Shadow*, at 1408. Was *Burr* an even stronger case?

(10) In a footnote, the Court stated: "We are not here concerned with the balance between the President's generalized interest in confidentiality and the need for relevant evidence in civil litigation, nor with that between the confidentiality interest and congressional demands for information, nor with the President's interest in preserving state secrets. We address only the conflict between the President's assertion of a generalized privilege of confidentiality and the constitutional need for relevant evidence in criminal trials." *Nixon*, 418 U.S. at 712 n.19.

(11) The Court distinguished between privilege based on the "claim of public interest

in the confidentiality" of presidential communications and that based on the need "to protect military, diplomatic, or sensitive national security secrets." In *Nixon v. Administrator of General Services*, 433 U.S. 425 (1977), the Court referred to "the more particularized and less qualified privilege relating to the need 'to protect military, diplomatic, or sensitive national security secrets. . . . '" Is the privilege relating to national security and foreign affairs subject to "judicial control"? Or is it less subject to judicial scrutiny? In either event, what will prevent Presidents from invoking security or diplomatic considerations to prevent disclosures that have nothing to do with security or foreign affairs? Suppose Nixon had asserted his claim of privilege based upon a claimed need to protect national security, rather than the more generalized need to protect the confidentiality of Presidential communications?

[2] Immunities

NIXON v. FITZGERALD
457 U.S. 731, 102 S. Ct. 2690, 73 L. Ed. 2d (1982)

JUSTICE POWELL delivered the opinion of the Court.

The plaintiff in this lawsuit seeks relief in civil damages from a former President of the United States. The claim rests on actions allegedly taken in the former President's official capacity during his tenure in office. The issue before us is the scope of the immunity possessed by the President of the United States. . . .

[Plaintiff A. Ernest Fitzgerald, sued President Nixon and other executive branch officials claiming that he was dismissed from his job in the Department of the Air Force in retaliation for testimony he gave to Congress regarding embarrassing cost over-runs. The Court granted certiorari to consider the scope of immunity of a President of the United States.]

. . . .

This case now presents the claim that the President of the United States is shielded by absolute immunity from civil damages liability. In the case of the President the inquiries into history and policy, though mandated independently by our cases, tend to converge. Because the Presidency did not exist through most of the development of common law, any historical analysis must draw its evidence primarily from our constitutional heritage and structure. Historical inquiry thus merges almost at its inception with the kind of "public policy" analysis appropriately undertaken by a federal court. This inquiry involves policies and principles that may be considered implicit in the nature of the President's office in a system structured to achieve effective government under a constitutionally mandated separation of powers. . . .

The President occupies a unique position in the constitutional scheme. . . . Because of the singular importance of the President's duties, diversion of his energies by concern with private lawsuits would raise unique risks to the effective functioning of government. As is the case with prosecutors and judges — for whom absolute immunity now is established — a President must concern himself with matters likely to "arouse the most intense feelings." *Pierson v. Ray*, 386 U.S. at 554. Yet, as our decisions have recognized, it is in precisely such cases that there exists the greatest public interest in providing an official "the maximum ability to deal fearlessly and impartially with" the duties of his office. *Ferri v. Ackerman*, 444 U.S. 193, 203 (1979). This concern is compelling where the officeholder must make the most sensitive and far-reaching decisions entrusted to any official under our constitutional system. Nor can the sheer prominence of the President's office be ignored. In view of the visibility of his office and the effect of his actions on countless people, the President would be an easily identifiable target for suits for civil damages. Cognizance of this personal vulnerability frequently could distract a President from his public duties, to the detriment of not only the President and his office but also the Nation that the Presidency was designed to serve. . . .

In defining the scope of an official's absolute privilege, this Court has recognized that the sphere of protected action must be related closely to the immunity's justifying purposes. Frequently our decisions have held that an official's absolute immunity should extend only to acts in performance of particular functions of his office. . . . In view of the special nature of the President's constitutional office and functions, we think it appropriate to recognize absolute Presidential immunity from damages liability for acts within the "outer perimeter" of his official responsibility.

Under the Constitution and laws of the United States the President has discretionary responsibilities in a broad variety of areas, many of them highly sensitive. In many cases it would be difficult to determine which of the President's innumerable "functions" encompassed a particular action. . . .

A rule of absolute immunity for the President will not leave the Nation without sufficient protection against misconduct on the part of the Chief Executive. There remains the constitutional remedy of impeachment. In addition, there are formal and informal checks on Presidential action that do not apply with equal force to other executive officials. The President is subjected to constant scrutiny by the press. Vigilant oversight by Congress also may serve to deter Presidential abuses of office, as well as to make credible the threat of impeachment. Other incentives to avoid misconduct may include a desire to earn reelection, the need to maintain prestige as an element of Presidential influence, and a President's traditional concern for his historical stature.

The existence of alternative remedies and deterrents establishes that absolute immunity will not place the President "above the law." For the President, as for judges and prosecutors, absolute immunity merely precludes a particular private remedy for alleged misconduct in order to advance compelling public ends. . . .

JUSTICE WHITE, with whom JUSTICE BRENNAN, JUSTICE MARSHALL, and JUSTICE BLACKMUN join, dissenting.

. . .The Court now applies the [following view] to the Office of the President: A President, acting within the outer boundaries of what Presidents normally do, may, without liability, deliberately cause serious injury to any number of citizens even though he knows his conduct violates a statute or tramples on the constitutional rights of those who are injured. Even if the President in this case ordered Fitzgerald fired by means of a trumped-up reduction in force, knowing that such a discharge was contrary to the civil service laws, he would be absolutely immune from suit. By the same token, if a President, without following the statutory procedures which he knows apply to himself as well as to other federal officials, orders his subordinates to wiretap or break into a home for the purpose of installing a listening device, and the officers comply with his request, the President would be absolutely immune from suit. He would be immune regardless of the damage he inflicts, regardless of how violative of the statute and of the Constitution he knew his conduct to be, and regardless of his purpose.

The Court intimates that its decision is grounded in the Constitution. If that is the case, Congress cannot provide a remedy against Presidential misconduct and the criminal laws of the United States are wholly inapplicable to the President. I find this approach completely unacceptable. I do not agree that if the Office of President is to operate effectively, the holder of that Office must be permitted, without fear of liability and regardless of the function he is performing, deliberately to inflict injury on others by conduct that he knows violates the law. We have not taken such a scatter-gun approach in other cases. . . .

Attaching absolute immunity to the Office of the President, rather than to particular activities that the President might perform, places the President above the law. It is a reversion to the old notion that the King can do no wrong. Until now, this concept had survived in this country only in the form of sovereign immunity. That doctrine forecloses suit against the Government itself and against Government officials, but only when the suit against the latter actually seeks relief against the sovereign. *Larson v. Domestic & Foreign Commerce Corp.*, 337 U.S. 682, 687 (1949). Suit against an officer, however, may be maintained where it seeks specific relief against him for conduct contrary to his statutory authority or to the Constitution. *Id.*, at 698. Now, however, the Court clothes the Office of the President with sovereign immunity, placing it beyond the law. . . .

The Speech or Debate Clause, Art. I, § 6, guarantees absolute immunity to Members of Congress; nowhere, however, does the Constitution directly address the issue of Presidential immunity. . . .

[The dissenters dismissed originalist arguments for absolute presidential immunity].

No bright line can be drawn between arguments for absolute immunity based on the constitutional principle of separation of powers and arguments based on what the Court refers to as "public policy." This necessarily follows from the Court's functional interpretation of the separation-of-powers doctrine:

> "[I]n determining whether the Act disrupts the proper balance between the coordinate branches, the proper inquiry focuses on the extent to which it prevents the Executive Branch from accomplishing its constitutionally assigned functions." *Nixon v. Administrator of General Services*, 433 U.S. 425, 443 (1977). . . .

Taken at face value, the Court's position that as a matter of constitutional law the President is absolutely immune should mean that he is immune not only from damages actions but also from suits for injunctive relief, criminal prosecutions and, indeed, from any kind of judicial process. But there is no contention that the President is immune from criminal prosecution in the courts under the criminal laws enacted by Congress or by the States for that matter. Nor would such a claim be credible. The Constitution itself provides that impeachment shall not bar "Indictment, Trial, Judgment and Punishment, according to Law." Art. I, § 3, cl. 7. Similarly, our cases indicate that immunity from damages actions carries no protection from criminal prosecution. . . .

Focusing on the actual arguments the majority offers for its holding of absolute immunity for the President, one finds surprisingly little. As I read the relevant section of the Court's opinion, I find just three contentions from which the majority draws this conclusion. Each of them is little more than a makeweight; together they hardly suffice to justify the wholesale disregard of our traditional approach to immunity questions.

First, the majority informs us that the President occupies a "unique position in the constitutional scheme," including responsibilities for the administration of justice, foreign affairs, and management of the Executive Branch. . . . True as this may be, it says nothing about why a "unique" rule of immunity should apply to the President. . . .

Second, the majority contends that because the President's "visibility" makes him particularly vulnerable to suits for civil damages, . . .a rule of absolute immunity is required. The force of this argument is surely undercut by the majority's admission that "there is no historical record of numerous suits against the President." . . . Even if judicial procedures were found not to be sufficient, Congress remains free to address this problem if and when it develops.

Finally, the Court suggests that potential liability "frequently could distract a

President from his public duties." . . . Unless one assumes that the President himself makes the countless high-level executive decisions required in the administration of government, this rule will not do much to insulate such decisions from the threat of liability. The logic of the proposition cannot be limited to the President; its extension, however, has been uniformly rejected by this Court. . . . Furthermore, in no instance have we previously held legal accountability in itself to be an unjustifiable cost. The availability of the courts to vindicate constitutional and statutory wrongs has been perceived and protected as one of the virtues of our system of delegated and limited powers. . . .

NOTES

(1) In *Harlow v. Fitzgerald*, 457 U.S. 800 (1982), a companion case, the Court denied that presidential aides enjoyed absolute immunity. They could claim absolute immunity only upon demonstrating that they were discharging official duties of such sensitivity to warrant such protection. Otherwise, their immunity was qualified upon a showing that the official had a reasonable basis to believe his action was legal.

(2) In *Clinton v. Jones*, 520 U.S. 681 (1997), the Court rejected President Clinton's claim that a private damage suit against him based on alleged actions before his term must be deferred until he left office. The immunity recognized in *Nixon v. Fitzgerald* rested primarily on the need to allow the President to discharge official duties without fear of personal liability; it did not rest on the need to protect his calendar. The Court reasoned that the judiciary could schedule court appearances in a manner that would not interfere with the President's conduct of his office.

[3] Impeachment

NOTES

(1) The Constitution provides that "The President, Vice President, and all Civil Officers of the United States, shall be removed from Office on Impeachment for, and conviction of, Treason, Bribes, or other high crimes and misdemeanors." U.S. CONST. art. II § 4. The Constitution gives the House "the sole Power of Impeachment", U.S. CONST. art. I, § 2 cl. 5, and the Senate "the sole Power to try all impeachments." U.S. CONST. art. I, § 3, cl. 6. Impeachment requires a majority of the House, conviction, two-thirds of the Senate.

(2) President Andrew Johnson and President William Jefferson Clinton were both impeached by the House of Representatives but acquitted by the Senate. President Richard M. Nixon resigned after being advised by his party's Congressional leadership that his impeachment and conviction were inevitable.

(3) What qualifies as grounds for impeachment? Must the defendant have committed an indictable crime? Raoul Berger argued that "high crimes and misdemeanors" was a term of art from England that included some non-criminal misconduct. RAOUL BERGER, IMPEACHMENT: THE CONSTITUTIONAL PROBLEMS 70-71 (1973). Opponents of the efforts to impeach Presidents Johnson and Nixon argued that an indictable crime is required. For a discussion, see Richard M. Pious, *Impeaching the President: The Intersection of Constitutional and Popular Law*, 43 ST. LOUIS U. L.J. 859, 866-76 (1999).

Could the President properly be impeached for: (a) departing on a four year vacation to Camp David; (b) refusing to report to Congress on the State of the Union; (c) refusing to fill a vice-presidential vacancy under § 2 of the Twenty-fifth Amendment? "[I]t is inconceivable that Congress could not remove a President who drank himself into insensibility by lunchtime on a daily basis," wrote two scholars. Frank O. Bowman

III & Stephen L. Sepinuck, *"High Crimes and Misdemeanors": Defining the Constitutional Limits on Presidential Impeachment*, 72 S. CAL. L. REV. 1517, 1526 (1999). *See also* CHARLES L. BLACK, JR., IMPEACHMENT: A HANDBOOK 33 (1974); RICHARD A. POSNER, AN AFFAIR OF STATE: THE INVESTIGATION IMPEACHMENT AND TRIAL OF PRESIDENT CLINTON 99 (1999).

(4) Does any felony constitute "a high crime or misdemeanor" sufficient to support impeachment? The House Judiciary Committee voted against impeaching President Nixon based on possible criminal income tax fraud. Many of President Clinton's supporters argued that even if he perjured himself in a private civil lawsuit, such perjury was not grounds for impeachment and conviction. Does the text of the Constitution provide any guidance? Does the association of "other high crimes and misdemeanors" with Treason and Bribery imply that impeachable offenses must be public (rather than private) offenses? The House Judiciary Committee argued in 1974 that "[i]mpeachment is a constitutional remedy addressed to serious offenses against the system of government." H.R. Rep. No. 93-1305, at 6 (1974). *See also* Bowman & Sepinuck, *"High Crimes and Misdemeanors": Defining the Constitutional Limits on Presidential Impeachment*, *supra* Note (3), at 1533 ("presidents are to be impeached only for 'great' transgressions that present danger to the constitutional order"). Michael J. Gerhardt has found that the Senate's seven decisions to convict various officers "have in common the judgment that impeachable offenses consist of serious breaches of the public trust or misconduct that are so incompatible with the office that conviction and removal by the Senate are required." Michael J. Gerhardt, *Putting the Law of Impeachment in Perspective*, 43 ST. LOUIS U. L.J. 905, 920 (1999).

(5) During the House of Representative's consideration of articles of impeachment against President Clinton, Representative Rick Boucher (D. Va.) argued that "only that presidential misconduct which is seriously incompatible with either the constitutional form and principles of our government or the proper performance of the constitutional duties of the office of the presidency will justify impeachment." 144 CONG. REC. 41,1781 (daily ed. Dec. 18, 1998). Representative Charles T. Canady (R. Fla.), argued that "[t]here is nothing in the text, structure, or history of the Constitution, which suggests that Presidents are subject to impeachment only for official misconduct." 144 CONG. REC. 41, 1827 (daily ed., Dec. 18, 1998). Who is right? Who decides what constitutes a high crime and misdemeanor?

(6) Is the standard the same for the House in deciding whether to impeach as it is for the Senate in deciding whether to convict? Professor John Hart Ely suggested that in the Clinton case "impeachment without conviction may have been about right[.]" Ely, *The Apparent Inevitability of Mixed Government*, 16 CONST. COMMENT. 283, 288 n.27 (1999). Was the House correct to impeach President Clinton and the Senate right in deciding not to convict him?

(7) The Constitution provides that when the President is tried in the Senate upon impeachment, the Chief Justice of the United States Supreme Court shall preside. U.S. CONST. art. I, § 3, cl. 6. Why does the Constitution so provide, instead of, say, the Vice President, who is President of the Senate U.S. CONST. art. I, § 3, cl. 4? The Constitution does not provide for the Chief Justice to preside if the Vice President is tried upon impeachment. Is it reasonable to infer that the Vice President could preside over his own impeachment trial? *See* Stephen L. Carter, *The Political Aspects of Judicial Power: Some Notes on the Presidential Immunity Decision*, 131 U. PA. L. REV. 1341, 1357 n.72 (1983) (arguing Vice President could preside); Michael Stokes Paulsen, *Someone Should Have Told Spiro Agnew*, 14 CONST. COMMENT. 245 (1997) (same). *But see* Joel K. Goldstein, *Can the Vice President Preside at His Own Impeachment Trial: A Critique of Bare Textualism*, 44 ST. LOUIS U. L.J. 849 (2000) (Vice President could not preside).

(8) Can a sitting President be indicted? The Constitution provides that a party convicted on impeachment "shall nevertheless be liable and subject to Indictment, Trial, Judgment, and Punishment according to Law." U.S. Const. art. I, § 3, cl. 7. Does this provision imply that impeachment must precede indictment? If so, it would seem to apply to all offices subject to impeachment, yet others have been indicted before being impeached and convicted (including Vice Presidents Aaron Burr and Spiro T. Agnew). Is it more likely that the clause simply makes clear that criminal trial following impeachment does not constitute double jeopardy? Does the unique status of the President as the repository of the Executive Power provide a convincing structural argument against indicting a sitting President? *See* Akhil Reed Amar & Brian Kalt, *The Presidential Privilege Against Prosecution*, 2 Nexus J. Op. 11 (1997).

That argument is weakened somewhat if *Morrison v. Olson* is good law since it suggests that someone independent of the President can constitutionally prosecute the President. But even if *Morrison* remains valid, might one still make an exception for the President?

[4] Presidential Succession and Inability

NOTES

(1) Constitutional provisions regarding presidential succession and inability are set forth in Art. II, § 1, cl. 6, the Twentieth and Twenty-fifth Amendment. Section one of the Twenty-fifth Amendment provides that the Vice President becomes President if the President dies, resigns or is removed. Section two creates a means to fill a vice-presidential vacancy by presidential nomination and congressional confirmation. Compare that procedure to the method for appointing federal judges or cabinet officials. That procedure has been used twice — in 1973 when President Nixon nominated Representative Gerald R. Ford to be the Vice President after Agnew's resignation and the following year when Ford chose Nelson A. Rockefeller to be his Vice President. *See* John D. Feerick, The Twenty-Fifth Amendment: Its Complete History and Application 117-90 (1992); Joel K. Goldstein, The Modern American Vice Presidency: The Transformation of a Political Institution 228-48 (1982).

(2) Sections 3 and 4 provide procedures to transfer presidential powers to the Vice President if the President is "unable to discharge the powers and duties of his office." *See* Feerick, *supra* Note (1); Managing Crisis: Presidential Disability and the 25th Amendment (Robert E. Gilbert ed., 2000).

§ 5.07 SEPARATION OF POWERS

MISTRETTA v. UNITED STATES
488 U.S. 361, 109 S. Ct. 647, 102 L. Ed. 2d 714 (1989)

[Editor's Note: The Sentencing Reform Act of 1984 established the Sentencing Commission, with authority to promulgate mandatory guidelines to be used for sentencing in federal criminal cases. The Commission was also obligated to "review and revise" the guidelines. The Commission was "an independent commission in the judicial branch of the United States" consisting of seven members appointed by the President "by and with the advice and consent of the Senate." At least three members are federal judges selected from a list of six judges recommended to the President by the Judicial Conference of the United States. The members of the Commission are subject to removal by the President "only for neglect of duty or malfeasance in office or for other good cause shown." Petitioner, who was indicted in a federal court, moved to have the guidelines promulgated by the Commission ruled unconstitutional on the grounds that the Sentencing Commission was constituted in violation of the doctrine of separation of powers and that Congress delegated excessive authority to the Commission to structure the guidelines.]

JUSTICE BLACKMUN delivered the opinion of the Court.

[The opinion first held that excessive legislative discretion had not been delegated, since adequate criteria had been provided by Congress to guide the Commission.]

IV. Separation of Powers

Having determined that Congress has set forth sufficient standards for the exercise of the Commission's delegated authority, we turn to Mistretta's claim that the Act violates the constitutional principle of separation of powers. . . .

In applying the principle of separated powers in our jurisprudence, we have sought to give life to Madison's view of the appropriate relationship among the three coequal Branches. Accordingly, we have recognized, as Madison admonished at the founding, that while our Constitution mandates that "each of the three general departments of government [must remain] entirely free from the control or coercive influence, direct or indirect, of either of the others," . . . the Framers did not require — and indeed rejected — the notion that the three Branches must be entirely separate and distinct. . . .

In adopting this flexible understanding of separation of powers, we simply have recognized Madison's teaching that the greatest security against tyranny — the accumulation of excessive authority in a single branch — lies not in a hermetic division between the Branches, but in a carefully crafted system of checked and balanced power within each Branch. . . . Accordingly, as we have noted many times, the Framers "built into the tripartite Federal Government . . . a self-executing safeguard against the encroachment or aggrandizement of one branch at the expense of the other." . . .

It is this concern of encroachment and aggrandizement that has animated our separation-of-powers jurisprudence and aroused our vigilance against the "hydraulic pressure inherent within each of the separate Branches to exceed the outer limits of its power." . . . In cases specifically involving the Judicial Branch, we have expressed our vigilance against two dangers: first, that the Judicial Branch neither be assigned nor allowed "tasks that are more appropriately accomplished by [other] branches," . . . and, second, that no provision of law "impermissibly threatens the institutional integrity of the Judicial Branch." . . .

Mistretta argues that the Act suffers from each of these constitutional infirmities. He argues that Congress, in constituting the Commission as it did, effected an unconstitutional accumulation of power within the Judicial Branch while at the same time undermining the Judiciary's independence and integrity. Specifically, petitioner claims that in delegating to an independent agency within the Judicial Branch the power to promulgate sentencing guidelines, Congress unconstitutionally has required the Branch, and individual Article III judges, to exercise not only their judicial authority but legislative authority — the making of sentencing policy — as well. Such rulemaking authority, petitioner contends, may be exercised by Congress, or delegated by Congress to the Executive, but may not be delegated to or exercised by the Judiciary. . . .

At the same time, petitioner asserts, Congress unconstitutionally eroded the integrity and independence of the Judiciary by requiring Article III judges to sit on the Commission, by requiring that those judges share their rulemaking authority with nonjudges, and by subjecting the Commission's members to appointment and removal by the President. . . . Although the unique composition and responsibilities of the

Sentencing Commission give rise to serious concerns about a disruption of the appropriate balance of governmental power among the coordinate Branches, we conclude, upon close inspection, that petitioner's fears for the fundamental structural protections of the Constitution prove, at least in this case, to be "more smoke than fire," and do not compel us to invalidate Congress' considered scheme for resolving the seemingly intractable dilemma of excessive disparity in criminal sentencing.

A

Location of the Commission

The Sentencing Commission unquestionably is a peculiar institution within the framework of our Government. Although placed by the Act in the Judicial Branch, it is not a court and does not exercise judicial power. Rather, the Commission is an "independent" body comprised of seven voting members including at least three federal judges, entrusted by Congress with the primary task of promulgating sentencing guidelines. . . . Our constitutional principles of separated powers are not violated, however, by mere anomaly or innovation. . . . Congress' decision to create an independent rulemaking body to promulgate sentencing guidelines and to locate that body within the Judicial Branch is not unconstitutional unless Congress has vested in the Commission powers that are more appropriately performed by the other Branches or that undermine the integrity of the Judiciary. . . . [W]e have recognized significant exceptions to this general rule and have approved the assumption of some nonadjudicatory activities by the Judicial Branch. In keeping with Justice Jackson's *Youngstown* admonition that the separation of powers contemplates the integration of dispersed powers into a workable government, we have recognized the constitutionality of a "twilight area" in which the activities of the separate Branches merge. . . .

That judicial rulemaking, at least with respect to some subjects, falls within this twilight area is no longer an issue for dispute. . . . Pursuant to this power to delegate rulemaking authority to the Judicial Branch, Congress expressly has authorized this Court to establish rules for the conduct of its own business and to prescribe rules of procedure for lower federal courts in bankruptcy cases, in other civil cases, and in criminal cases, and to revise the Federal Rules of Evidence. . . .

In light of this precedent and practice, we can discern no separation-of-powers impediment to the placement of the Sentencing Commission within the Judicial Branch. As we described at the outset, the sentencing function long has been a peculiarly shared responsibility among the Branches of Government and has never been thought of as the exclusive constitutional province of any one Branch. . . . For more than a century, federal judges have enjoyed wide discretion to determine the appropriate sentence in individual cases and have exercised special authority to determine the sentencing factors to be applied in any given case. Indeed, the legislative history of the Act makes clear that Congress' decision to place the Commission within the Judicial Branch reflected Congress' "strong feeling" that sentencing has been and should remain "primarily a judicial function." . . . That Congress should vest such rulemaking in the Judicial Branch, far from being "incongruous" or vesting within the Judiciary responsibilities that more appropriately belong to another Branch, simply acknowledges the role that the Judiciary always has played, and continues to play, in sentencing.

Given the consistent responsibility of federal judges to pronounce sentence within the statutory range established by Congress, we find that the role of the Commission in promulgating guidelines for the exercise of that judicial function bears considerable similarity to the role of this Court in establishing rules of procedure under the various enabling Acts. Such guidelines, like the Federal Rules of Criminal and Civil Procedure, are court rules — rules . . .for carrying into execution judgments that the Judiciary has the power to pronounce. Just as the rules of procedure bind judges and courts in the proper management of the case before them, so the Guidelines bind judges and courts in the exercise of their uncontested responsibility to pass sentence in criminal cases. In other words, the Commission's functions, like this Court's function in promulgating procedural rules, are clearly attendant to a central element of the historically acknowledged mission of the Judicial Branch. . . . In this case, the "practical consequences" of locating the Commission within the Judicial Branch pose no threat of undermining the integrity of the Judicial Branch or of expanding the powers of the Judiciary beyond constitutional bounds by uniting within the Branch the political or quasi-legislative power of the Commission with the judicial power of the courts.

First, although the Commission is located in the Judicial Branch, its powers are not united with the powers of the Judiciary in a way that has meaning for separation-of-powers analysis. Whatever constitutional problems might arise if the powers of the Commission were vested in a court, the Commission is not a court, does not exercise judicial power, and is not controlled by or accountable to members of the Judicial Branch. . . .

Second, although the Commission wields rulemaking power and not the adjudicatory power exercised by individual judges when passing sentence, the placement of the Sentencing Commission in the Judicial Branch has not increased the Branch's authority. Prior to the passage of the Act, the Judicial Branch, as an aggregate, decided precisely the questions assigned to the Commission: what sentence is appropriate to what criminal conduct under what circumstances. It was the everyday business of judges, taken collectively, to evaluate and weigh the various aims of sentencing and to apply those aims to the individual cases that came before them. The Sentencing Commission does no more than this, albeit basically through the methodology of sentencing guidelines, rather than entirely individualized sentencing determinations. Accordingly, in placing the Commission in the Judicial Branch, Congress cannot be said to have aggrandized the authority of that Branch or to have deprived the Executive Branch of a power it once possessed. . . .

In sum, since substantive judgment in the field of sentencing has been and remains appropriate to the Judicial Branch, and the methodology of rulemaking has been and remains appropriate to that Branch, Congress' considered decision to combine these functions in an independent Sentencing Commission and to locate that Commission within the Judicial Branch does not violate the principle of separation of powers.

B

Composition of the Commission

We now turn to Petitioner's claim that Congress' decision to require at least three federal judges to serve on the Commission and to require those judges to share their authority with nonjudges undermines the integrity of the Judicial Branch. . . .

The text of the Constitution contains no prohibition against the service of active federal judges on independent commissions such as that established by the Act. The Constitution does include an Incompatibility Clause applicable to national legislators:

> No Senator or Representative shall, during the Time for which he was elected, be appointed to any civil Office under the Authority of the United States, which shall have been created, or the Emoluments whereof shall have been increased during such time; and no Person holding any Office under the

United States, shall be a Member of either House during his Continuance in Office. U.S. CONST., Art. I, § 6, cl. 2.

No comparable restriction applies to judges, and we find it at least inferentially meaningful that at the Constitutional Convention two prohibitions against plural officeholding by members of the Judiciary were proposed, but did not reach the floor of the Convention for a vote.

Our inferential reading that the Constitution does not prohibit Article III judges from undertaking extrajudicial duties finds support in . . . historical practice. . . .

[H]istory . . . reveals a frequent and continuing, albeit controversial, practice of extrajudicial service. [The Court noted that Chief Justices John Jay, Oliver Ellsworth and John Marshall undertook significant executive branch duties. Five Justices served on the Election Commission to resolve the Presidential election of 1876. Justices Nelson, Fuller, Brewer, Hughes, Day, Roberts, Van Devanter and Warren served on various commissions. Justice Jackson was a prosecutor at the Nuremberg trials. Lower court federal judges have also so served]. . . . Our 200-year tradition of extrajudicial service is additional evidence that the doctrine of separated powers does not prohibit judicial participation in certain extrajudicial activity. . . .

In light of the foregoing history and precedent, we conclude that the principle of separation of powers does not absolutely prohibit Article III judges from serving on commissions such as that created by the Act. The judges serve on the Sentencing Commission not pursuant to their status and authority as Article III judges, but solely because of their appointment by the President as the Act directs. Such Power as these judges wield as Commissioners is not judicial Power; it is administrative power derived from the enabling legislation. Just as the nonjudicial members of the Commission act as administrators, bringing their experience and wisdom to bear on the problems of sentencing disparity, so too the judges, uniquely qualified on the subject of sentencing, assume a wholly administrative role upon entering into the deliberations of the Commission. In other words, the Constitution, at least as a *per se* matter, does not forbid judges to wear two hats; it merely forbids them to wear both hats at the same time.

This is not to suggest, of course, that every kind of extrajudicial service under every circumstance necessarily accords with the Constitution. That the Constitution does not absolutely prohibit a federal judge from assuming extrajudicial duties does not mean that every extrajudicial service would be compatible with, or appropriate to, continuing service on the bench; nor does it mean that Congress may require a federal judge to assume extrajudicial duties as long as the judge is assigned those duties in an individual, not judicial, capacity. The ultimate inquiry remains whether a particular extrajudicial assignment undermines the integrity of the Judicial Branch. . . .

C

Presidential Control

The Act empowers the President to appoint all seven members of the Commission with the advice and consent of the Senate. The Act further provides that the President shall make his choice of judicial appointees to the Commission after considering a list of six judges recommended by the Judicial Conference of the United States. The Act also grants the President authority to remove members of the Commission although "only for neglect of duty or malfeasance in office or for other good cause shown." . . .

The notion that the President's power to appoint federal judges to the Commission somehow gives him influence over the Judicial Branch or prevents, even potentially, the

Judicial Branch from performing its constitutionally assigned functions is fanciful. . . . The mere fact that the President within his appointment portfolio has positions that may be attractive to federal judges does not, of itself, corrupt the integrity of the Judiciary. Were the impartiality of the Judicial Branch so easily subverted, our constitutional system of tripartite government would have failed long ago. . . .

The President's removal power over Commission members poses a similarly negligible threat to judicial independence. The Act does not, and could not under the Constitution, authorize the President to remove, or in any way diminish the status of Article III judges, as judges. Even if removed from the Commission, a federal judge appointed to the Commission would continue, absent impeachment, to enjoy tenure "during good Behaviour" and a full judicial salary. . . . Also, the President's removal power under the Act is limited. In order to safeguard the independence of the Commission from executive control, Congress specified in the Act that the President may remove the Commission members only for good cause. Such congressional limitation on the President's removal power, like the removal provisions upheld in *Morrison v. Olson*, [*supra* § 5.03], . . .is specifically crafted to prevent the President from exercising "coercive influence" over independent agencies. . . .

We conclude that in creating the Sentencing Commission — an unusual hybrid in structure and authority — Congress neither delegated excessive legislative power nor upset the constitutionally mandated balance of powers among the coordinate Branches. The Constitution's structural protections do not prohibit Congress from delegating to an expert body located within the Judicial Branch the intricate task of formulating sentencing guidelines consistent with such significant statutory direction as is present here. Nor does our system of checked and balanced authority prohibit Congress from calling upon the accumulated wisdom and experience of the Judicial Branch in creating policy on a matter uniquely within the ken of judges. Accordingly, we hold that the Act is constitutional.

The judgment of the United States District Court for the Western District of Missouri is affirmed.

[JUSTICE SCALIA dissented.]

NOTES

(1) In his dissent, Justice Scalia wrote, in part:

Today's decision follows the regrettable tendency of our recent separation-of-powers jurisprudence, . . .to treat the Constitution as though it were no more than a generalized prescription that the functions of the Branches should not be commingled too much-how much is too much to be determined, case-by-case, by this Court. The Constitution is not that. Rather, as its name suggests, it is a prescribed structure, a framework, for the conduct of government. In designing that structure, the Framers *themselves* considered how much commingling was, in the generality of things, acceptable, and set forth their conclusions in the document.

(2) In *Metropolitan Washington Airports Authority v. Citizens for the Abatement of Aircraft Noise*, 501 U.S. 252 (1991), the Court struck down an Act of Congress which transferred control of two major airports from the federal government to the Metropolitan Washington Airports Authority (MWAA). The Act conditioned the transfer on the creation by MWAA of a "Board of Review" composed of nine members of Congress and given veto power over decisions of MWAA's Board of Directors. In a 6-3 decision, the Court held that the power delegated to the Board of Review, whether executive or legislative in nature, was constitutionally impermissible. If executive, it would be improper for agents of Congress to exercise it; if legislative, the exercise of the power

must conform to the bicameralism and presentment requirements consistent with *Chadha*. Because the Board of Review's composition and function did not comport with either of these constitutional principles, it was unconstitutional on separation-of-powers grounds.

In dissent, Justice White, joined by Chief Justice Rehnquist and Justice Marshall, argued that the Court had, for the first time, used separation-of-powers doctrine to invalidate a body created under state law. The dissent noted that neither the Executive nor Congress opposed the arrangement which it saw as "another innovative and otherwise lawful governmental experiment."

Chapter VI
CONGRESSIONAL PROTECTION OF CIVIL RIGHTS

§ 6.01 INTRODUCTION

This chapter provides something of a transition between the first five chapters which address the allocation of powers of government (federal and state) under the United States Constitution, and the remaining chapters, which concern individual rights. To be sure, that familiar dichotomy is somewhat artificial. Structural features like federalism and separation of powers were designed, in large part, to protect liberty and such structural considerations are often invoked in cases dealing with individual rights. In any event, this chapter combines the two, concerning as it does Congressional power to protect individual rights. That power rests largely on the authority to enforce the post-Civil War amendments to the Constitution.

The Bill of Rights and the States

The Bill of Rights contains the principal guaranties of individual rights in the U.S. Constitution. It consists of the first ten amendments and was ratified in 1791. The Bill of Rights restrains government power to abridge individual rights. As such, it binds only the federal government. The Marshall Court so held in *Barron v. Mayor of Baltimore*, 32 U.S. (7 Pet.) 243 (1833). Plaintiff sued the City of Baltimore for compensation because the city had rendered his wharf useless. He invoked the Fifth Amendment's prohibition against taking private property for public use without just compensation which he claimed restrained state, as well as national, power. Chief Justice Marshall thought the issue of great importance but "not of much difficulty." When the Constitution sought to limit state power it did so expressly, stating that "No state shall . . . ." *See* U.S. Const. art. I, § 10. The Bill of Rights contained no such language. The Bill of Rights was enacted to provide "security against the apprehended encroachments of the general government — not against those of local governments." The Fifth Amendment's Just Compensation Clause "is intended solely as a limitation on the exercise of power by the government of the United States, and is not applicable to the . . . states." The same conclusion applied to all provisions of the Bill of Rights. The original Constitution addressed state infringements of individual rights only in its relatively minor limitations upon state power contained in Article I, section 10. *Barron* probably captured the best reading of the text and reflected correctly the original understanding. *See* Akhil Reed Amar, The Bill of Rights 140-62 (1998); John Hart Ely, Democracy and Distrust 196 n.58 (1980). *Barron* settled the issue until after the Civil War.

§ 6.02 POST-CIVIL WAR AMENDMENTS

The Civil War marked a watershed in American development. It had significant constitutional effects, the most important of which was the inclusion in the Constitution of the guaranties contained in the three post-Civil War amendments. The Civil War amendments called upon the federal government to protect the citizens of a state against the state itself.

§ 6.03   STATE ACTION

SHELLEY v. KRAEMER
334 U.S. 1, 68 S. Ct. 836, 92 L. Ed. 1161 (1948)

CHIEF JUSTICE VINSON delivered the opinion of the Court.

These cases present for our consideration questions relating to the validity of court enforcement of private agreements, generally described as restrictive covenants, which have as their purpose the exclusion of persons of designated race or color from the ownership or occupancy of real property. Basic constitutional issues of obvious importance have been raised. . . .

On February 16, 1911, thirty out of a total of thirty-nine owners of property fronting both sides of Labadie Avenue between Taylor Avenue and Cora Avenue in the city of St. Louis, signed an agreement, which was subsequently recorded, providing in part:

> . . . the said property is hereby restricted to the use and occupancy for the term of Fifty (50) years from this date, so that it shall be a condition all the time and whether recited and referred to as [sic] not in subsequent conveyances and shall attach to the land, as a condition precedent to the sale of the same, that hereafter no part of said property or any portion thereof shall be, for said term of Fifty-years, occupied by any person not of the Caucasian race, it being intended hereby to restrict the use of said property for said period of time against the occupancy as owners or tenants of any portion of said property for resident or other purpose by people of the Negro or Mongolian Race.

The entire district described in the agreement included fifty-seven parcels of land. The thirty owners who signed the agreement held title to forty-seven parcels, including the particular parcel involved in this case. . . .

On August 11, 1945, pursuant to a contract of sale, petitioners Shelley, who are Negroes, for valuable consideration received from one Fitzgerald a warranty deed to the parcel in question. The trial court found that petitioners had no actual knowledge of the restrictive agreement at the time of the purchase.

On October 9, 1945, respondents, as owners of other property subject to the terms of the restrictive covenant, brought suit in the Circuit Court of the city of St. Louis praying that petitioners Shelley be restrained from taking possession of the property and that judgment be entered divesting title out of petitioners Shelley and revesting title in the immediate grantor or in such other person as the court should direct. . . .

The Supreme Court of Missouri . . . held the agreement effective and concluded that enforcement of its provisions violated no rights guaranteed to petitioners by the Federal Constitution. . . .

I

. . . .

It cannot be doubted that among the civil rights intended to be protected from discriminatory state action by the Fourteenth Amendment are the rights to acquire, enjoy, own and dispose of property. Equality in the enjoyment of property rights was regarded by the framers of that Amendment as an essential pre-condition to the realization of other basic civil rights and liberties which the Amendment was intended to guarantee. . . .

Since the decision of this Court in the *Civil Rights Cases*, 109 U.S. 3 (1883), the principle has become firmly embedded in our constitutional law that the action inhibited by the first section of the Fourteenth Amendment is only such action as may fairly be said to be that of the States. That Amendment erects no shield against merely private conduct, however discriminatory or wrongful.

We conclude, therefore, that the restrictive agreements standing alone cannot be regarded as a violation of any rights guaranteed to petitioners by the Fourteenth Amendment. So long as the purposes of those agreements are effectuated by voluntary adherence to their terms, it would appear that there has been no action by the State and the provisions of the Amendment have not been violated. . . .

But here there was more. These are cases in which the purposes of the agreements were secured only by judicial enforcement by state courts of the restrictive terms of the agreements. The respondents urge that judicial enforcement of private agreements does not amount to state action; or, in any event, the participation of the State is so attenuated in character as not to amount to state action within the meaning of the Fourteenth Amendment. Finally, it is suggested, even if the States in these cases may be deemed to have acted in the constitutional sense, their action did not deprive petitioners of rights guaranteed by the Fourteenth Amendment. We move to a consideration of these matters.

II

That the action of state courts and judicial officers in their official capacities is to be regarded as action of the State within the meaning of the Fourteenth Amendment, is a proposition which has long been established by decisions of this Court. That principle was given expression in the earliest cases involving the construction of the terms of the Fourteenth Amendment. . . . In the *Civil Rights Cases*, this Court pointed out that the Amendment makes void "state action of every kind" which is inconsistent with the guaranties therein contained, and extends to manifestations of "state authority in the shape of laws, customs, or judicial or executive proceedings." Language to like effect is employed no less than eighteen times during the course of that opinion. . . .

The short of the matter is that from the time of the adoption of the Fourteenth Amendment until the present, it has been the consistent ruling of this Court that the action of the States to which the Amendment has reference includes action of state courts and state judicial officials. Although, in construing the terms of the Fourteenth Amendment, differences have from time to time been expressed as to whether particular types of state action may be said to offend the Amendment's prohibitory provisions, it has never been suggested that state court action is immunized from the operation of those provisions simply because the act is that of the judicial branch of the state government.

III

Against this background of judicial construction, extending over a period of some three-quarters of a century, we are called upon to consider whether enforcement by state courts of the restrictive agreements in [this case] may be deemed to be the acts of those States; and, if so, whether that action has denied these petitioners the equal protection of the laws which the Amendment was intended to insure.

We have no doubt that there has been state action in these cases in the full and complete sense of the phrase. The undisputed facts disclose that petitioners were willing purchasers of properties upon which they desired to establish homes. The owners of the properties were willing sellers; and contracts of sale were accordingly consummated. It is clear that but for the active intervention of the state courts, supported by the full panoply of state power, petitioners would have been free to occupy the properties in question without restraint. . . .

We hold that in granting judicial enforcement of the restrictive agreements in [this case], the [State has] denied petitioners the equal protection of the laws and that, therefore, the action of the state courts cannot stand. We have noted that freedom from discrimination by the States in the enjoyment of property rights was among the basic objectives sought to be effectuated by the framers of the Fourteenth Amendment. That such discrimination has occurred in these cases is clear. Because of the race or color of these petitioners they have been denied rights of ownership or occupancy enjoyed as a matter of course by other citizens of different race or color. . . .

For the reasons stated, the judgment of the Supreme Court of Missouri . . . must be reversed.

NOTES

(1) The Fourteenth Amendment, in part, prohibited any state from depriving "any person of life, liberty, or property, without due process of law" or denying "any person . . . the equal protection of the laws." These self-executing prohibitions have generated volumes of cases brought directly under the Fourteenth Amendment.

(2) As *Shelley v. Kraemer* shows, the Amendment's prohibition against deprivation of due process and denial of equal protection applies exclusively to state action. In the *Civil Rights Cases*, 109 U.S. 3 (1883), the Court struck down the prohibition in the Civil Rights Act of 1875 against racial discrimination in inns, public conveyances, and places of amusement on the ground that it addressed purely private discriminatory action outside the Fourteenth Amendment. "Can the act of a mere individual," asked the Court, "the owner of the inn, the public conveyance, or place of amusement, refusing the accommodation, be justly regarded as imposing any badge of slavery or servitude upon the applicant, or only as inflicting an ordinary civil injury, properly cognizable by the laws of the state, and presumably subject to redress by those laws until the contrary appears?" *Id.* at 24. The Court asserted that "[i]ndividual invasion of individual rights is not the subject-matter of the amendment." *Id.* at 11.

During the reaction against Reconstruction, the Court adopted a restrictive attitude toward the civil rights statutes. In *United States v. Harris*, 106 U.S. 629 (1883), the provision of the 1871 statute establishing criminal penalties was held unconstitutional. According to the Court, the Congressional power to enforce the Fourteenth Amendment was limited to legislation aimed at "state action," the approach the Court had followed in the *Civil Rights Cases*.

A century later, in *United States v. Guest*, 383 U.S. 745 (1966), six justices suggested that the Fourteenth Amendment allowed Congress to regulate some private behavior. The six justices who reached this conclusion signed two separate opinions. At issue were the indictments of six defendants for criminal conspiracy to deny blacks constitutional rights in violation of 18 U.S. C. § 241. Justice Clark, joined by Justices Black and Fortas, wrote that "there can now be no doubt that the specific language of § 5 empowers the Congress to enact laws punishing all conspiracies — with or without state action — that interfere with Fourteenth Amendment rights." *Id.* at 762. Justice Brennan, joined by Chief Justice Warren and Justice Douglas, thought § 5 allowed Congress to reach private actions based on an argument akin to *McCulloch*'s treatment of the Necessary and Proper Clause. He wrote:

> Rather, § 5 authorizes Congress to make laws that it concludes are reason-
> ably necessary to protect a right created by and arising under that Amendment;
> and Congress is thus fully empowered to determine that punishment of private

conspiracies interfering with the exercise of such a right is necessary to its full protection. *Id.* at 782.

In recognizing the power of Congress to reach some private conduct, *Guest* appeared to qualify the *Court Rights Cases* and *Harris.*

In *United States v. Morrison*, 529 U.S. 598 (2000), the Court reaffirmed the *Civil Rights Cases* and *Harris.* Chief Justice Rehnquist wrote for the Court:

> The force of the doctrine of *stare decisis* behind these decisions stems not only from the length of time they have been on the books, but also from the insight attributable to the Members of the Court at that time. Every Member had been appointed by Presidents Lincoln, Grant, Hayes, Garfield, or Arthur — and each of their judicial appointees obviously had intimate knowledge and familiarity with the events surrounding the adoption of the Fourteenth Amendment.

The Court denied that *Guest* had signified a change in doctrine. The observations of the six justices in *Guest* were dicta. Although Justice Brennan's opinion provided a "reasoned explanation" for his view that the *Civil Rights Cases* were wrongly decided, Justice Clark's opinion "gave no explanation whatever" for his conclusion.

> This is simply not the way that reasoned constitutional adjudication proceeds. We accordingly have no hesitation in saying that it would take more than the naked dicta contained in Justice Clark's opinion, when added to Justice Brennan's opinion, to case any doubt upon the enduring vitality of the *Civil Rights Cases* and *Harris.* . . .

The Violence Against Women Act (VAWA) was beyond Congress' § 5 power because it addressed private, not state, action.

(3) The "essential dichotomy," is "between deprivation by the State, subject to scrutiny under its provisions, and private conduct, however discriminatory or wrongful, against which the Fourteenth Amendment offers no shield." *Jackson v. Metropolitan Edison Co.*, 419 U.S. 345, 349 (1974).

(4) When the challenged action is legislative, whether a statute, ordinance, or other legislative act, there can be no doubt that state action is involved. "State action, for purposes of the Equal Protection Clause, may [also] emanate from rulings of administrative and regulatory agencies, as well as from legislative or judicial action." *Moose Lodge No. 107 v. Irvis*, 407 U.S. 163, 179 (1972). *Shelley v. Kraemer* shows that judicial action also comes within "state action." Is the holding limited to injunctive action directly enforcing the restrictive covenant? Does it also apply to a lawsuit for damages for breach of the covenant? *See Barrows v. Jackson*, 346 U.S. 249 (1953) (answering in the affirmative).

(5) The State action doctrine has proven controversial. Professor Charles L. Black, Jr. described "state action" as a doctrine "without shape or line" and as "a conceptual disaster area." "The whole thing has the flavor of a torchless search for a way out of a damp, echoing cave." Charles L. Black, Jr., *Foreword: "State Action," Equal Protection, and California's Proposition 14*, 81 HARV. L. REV. 69, 95 (1967).

Are there costs to the state action requirement? Can private conduct also infringe basic rights? "The congressional debates concerning the Fourteenth Amendment indicate that there were three general goals of the Amendment's proponents. First, the amendment, in section 1, was to create a national minimum set of civil rights that could be judicially enforced. Second, the legal status of minority race persons, specifically Afro-American persons who had recently been freed from slavery, was to be upgraded by the Fourteenth Amendment. Third, Congress would now clearly have the power to define and protect civil liberties." John E. Nowak, *Federalism and the Civil War*

Amendments, 23 Ohio N.U. L. Rev. 1209, 1214 (1997).

GEORGIA v. McCOLLUM
505 U.S. 42, 112 S. Ct. 2348, 120 L. Ed. 2d 33 (1992)

Justice Blackmun delivered the opinion of the Court.

For more than a century, this Court consistently and repeatedly has reaffirmed that racial discrimination by the State in jury selection offends the Equal Protection Clause. . . . Last Term this Court held that racial discrimination in a civil litigant's exercise of peremptory challenges also violates the Equal Protection Clause. See *Edmonson v. Leesville Concrete Co.*, 500 U.S. 614 (1991). Today, we are asked to decide whether the Constitution prohibits a *criminal defendant* from engaging in purposeful racial discrimination in the exercise of peremptory challenges.

I

[Georgia indicted defendants, white people, for assault and battery against an African-American couple. The trial court denied the state's motion to prohibit defendants from using preemptory challenges in a racially discriminatory manner. The Georgia Supreme Court affirmed, distinguishing *Edmonson* as involving a civil, not criminal case.]

III

. . . .

Racial discrimination, although repugnant in all contexts, violates the Constitution only when it is attributable to state action. . . . Thus, the . . . question that must be answered is whether a criminal defendant's exercise of a peremptory challenge constitutes state action for purposes of the Equal Protection Clause.

Until *Edmonson*, the cases decided by this Court that presented the problem of racially discriminatory peremptory challenges involved assertions of discrimination by a prosecutor, a quintessential state actor. In *Edmonson*, by contrast, the contested peremptory challenges were exercised by a private defendant in a civil action. In order to determine whether state action was present in that setting, the Court in *Edmonson* used the analytical framework summarized in *Lugar v. Edmondson Oil Co.*, 457 U.S. 922 (1982).

The first inquiry is "whether the claimed [constitutional] deprivation has resulted from the exercise of a right or privilege having its source in state authority." "There can be no question" that peremptory challenges satisfy this first requirement, as they "are permitted only when the government, by statute or decisional law, deems it appropriate to allow parties to exclude a given number of persons who otherwise would satisfy the requirements for service on the petit jury." As in *Edmonson*, a Georgia defendant's right to exercise peremptory challenges and the scope of that right are established by a provision of state law. Ga. Code Ann. § 15-12-165 (1990).

The second inquiry is whether the private party charged with the deprivation can be described as a state actor. In resolving that issue, the Court in *Edmonson* found it useful to apply three principles: (1) "the extent to which the actor relies on governmental assistance and benefits"; (2) "whether the actor is performing a traditional governmental function"; and (3) "whether the injury caused is aggravated in a unique way by the incidents of governmental authority." . . .

As to the first principle, the *Edmonson* Court found that the peremptory challenge system, as well as the jury system as a whole, "simply could not exist" without the "overt and significant participation of the government.". . . . Georgia provides for the compilation of jury lists by the board of jury commissioners in each county and establishes the general criteria for service and the sources for creating a pool of qualified jurors representing a fair cross section of the community. . . . State law further provides that jurors are to be selected by a specified process; they are to be summoned to court under the authority of the State; and they are to be paid an expense allowance by the State whether or not they serve on a jury. At court, potential jurors are placed in panels in order to facilitate examination by counsel; they are administered an oath; they are questioned on voir dire to determine whether they are impartial; and they are subject to challenge for cause.

In light of these procedures, the defendant in a Georgia criminal case relies on "governmental assistance and benefits" that are equivalent to those found in the civil context in *Edmonson*. "By enforcing a discriminatory peremptory challenge, the Court 'has . . . elected to place its power, property and prestige behind the [alleged] discrimination.' ". . . .

In regard to the second principle, the Court in *Edmonson* found that peremptory challenges perform a traditional function of the government: "Their sole purpose is to permit litigants to assist the government in the selection of an impartial trier of fact." And, as the *Edmonson* Court recognized, the jury system in turn "performs the critical governmental functions of guarding the rights of litigants and 'ensur[ing] continued acceptance of the laws by all of the people.' " These same conclusions apply with even greater force in the criminal context because the selection of a jury in a criminal case fulfills a unique and constitutionally compelled governmental function. . . . The State cannot avoid its constitutional responsibilities by delegating a public function to private parties. *Cf. Terry v. Adams*, 345 U.S. 461 (1953) (private political party's determination of qualifications for primary voters held to constitute state action).

Finally, the *Edmonson* Court indicated that the courtroom setting in which the peremptory challenge is exercised intensifies the harmful effects of the private litigant's discriminatory act and contributes to its characterization as state action. These concerns are equally present in the context of a criminal trial. Regardless of who precipitated the jurors' removal, the perception and the reality in a criminal trial will be that the court has excused jurors based on race, an outcome that will be attributed to the State.

Respondents nonetheless contend that the adversarial relationship between the defendant and the prosecution negates the governmental character of the peremptory challenge. . . .

The exercise of a peremptory challenge differs significantly from other actions taken in support of a defendant's defense. In exercising a peremptory challenge, a criminal defendant is wielding the power to choose a quintessential governmental body — indeed, the institution of government on which our judicial system depends. Thus, as we held in *Edmonson*, when "a government confers on a private body the power to choose the government's employees or officials, the private body will be bound by the constitutional mandate of race neutrality.". . . .

Lastly, the fact that a defendant exercises a peremptory challenge to further his interest in acquittal does not conflict with a finding of state action. Whenever a private actor's conduct is deemed "fairly attributable" to the government, it is likely that private motives will have animated the actor's decision. Indeed, in *Edmonson*, the Court recognized that the private party's exercise of peremptory challenges constituted state action, even though the motive underlying the exercise of the peremptory challenge may be to protect a private interest. . . .

The judgment of the Supreme Court of Georgia is reversed. . . .

CHIEF JUSTICE REHNQUIST, concurring.

I was in dissent in *Edmondson v. Leesville Concrete Co.*, . . . and continue to believe that case to have been wrongly decided. But so long as it remains the law, I believe that it controls the disposition of this case on the issue of "state action" under the Fourteenth Amendment. I therefore join the opinion of the Court.

JUSTICE O'CONNOR, dissenting.

The Court reaches the remarkable conclusion that criminal defendants being prosecuted by the State act on behalf of their adversary when they exercise peremptory challenges during jury selection. The Court purports merely to follow precedents, but our cases do not compel this perverse result. To the contrary, our decisions specifically establish that criminal defendants and their lawyers are not government actors when they perform traditional trial functions.

I

. . . In *Lugar v. Edmondson Oil Co.* . . . , the Court developed a two-step approach to identifying state action in cases such as this. First, the Court will ask "whether the claimed deprivation has resulted from the exercise of a right or privilege having its source in state authority." . . . Next, it will decide whether, on the particular facts at issue, the parties who allegedly caused the deprivation of a federal right can "appropriately" and "in all fairness" be characterized as state actors. . . . The Court's determination in this case that the peremptory challenge is a creation of state authority . . . breaks no new ground. . . . But disposing of this threshold matter leaves the Court with the task of showing that criminal defendants who exercise peremptories should be deemed governmental actors. What our cases require, and what the Court neglects, is a realistic appraisal of the relationship between defendants and the government that has brought them to trial. . . .

Even aside from our prior rejection of it, the Court's functional theory fails. "[A] State normally can be held responsible for a private decision only when it has exercised coercive power or has provided such significant encouragement . . . that the choice must in law be deemed to be that of the State." Thus, a private party's exercise of choice allowed by state law does not amount to state action for purposes of the Fourteenth Amendment so long as "the initiative comes from [the private party] and not from the State." . . . The government in no way influences the defense's decision to use a peremptory challenge to strike a particular juror. Our adversarial system of criminal justice and the traditions of the peremptory challenge vest the decision to strike a juror entirely with the accused. A defendant "may, if he chooses, peremptorily challenge 'on his own dislike, without showing any cause;' he may exercise that right without reason or for no reason, arbitrarily and capriciously." . . . "The essential nature of the peremptory challenge is that it is one exercised without a reason stated, without inquiry and without being subject to the court's control." . . .

That the Constitution does not give federal judges the reach to wipe all marks of racism from every courtroom in the land is frustrating, to be sure. But such limitations are the necessary and intended consequence of the Fourteenth Amendment's state action requirement. Because I cannot accept the Court's conclusion that government is responsible for decisions criminal defendants make while fighting state prosecution, I respectfully dissent.

NOTES

(1) In his dissent (which is not provided above), Justice Scalia argued that the *McCollum* decision was a "reduction to the terminally absurd: A criminal defendant, in the process of defending himself against the state, is held to be acting on behalf of the state." Indeed, declared Justice Scalia, the

> decision gives the lie once again to the belief that an activist, "evolutionary" constitutional jurisprudence always evolves in the direction of greater individual rights. In the interest of promoting the supposedly greater good of race relations in the society as a whole (make no mistake that that is what underlies all of this), we use the Constitution to destroy the ages-old right of criminal defendants to exercise peremptory challenges as they wish, to secure a jury that they consider fair.

(2) In her *Edmonson v. Leesville Concrete Co.* dissent, Justice O'Connor had asserted:

> Peremptory challenges are not a traditional government function; the "tradition" is one of unguided private choice. . . . The peremptory challenge forms no part of the *government's* responsibility in selecting a jury. . . .

> Trials in this country are adversarial proceedings. Attorneys for private litigants do not act on behalf of the government, or even the public as a whole; attorneys represent their clients. An attorney's job is to "advanc[e] the 'undivided interests of his client.' This is essentially a private function . . . for which state office and authority are not needed."

Edmondson, 500 U.S. at 639, 641-42 (O'Connor, J., dissenting). "The alleged state action here is a far cry from that . . . in *Shelley v. Kraemer*." *Id.* at 635.

(3) *Public Function Exception.* "While the principle that private action is immune from the restrictions of the Fourteenth Amendment is well established and easily stated, the question whether particular conduct is, 'private,' on the one hand, or 'state action,' on the other, frequently admits of no easy answer." . . . "We . . . found state action present in the exercise by a private entity of powers traditionally exclusively reserved to the State." *Jackson v. Metropolitan Edison Co.*, 419 U.S. 345, 349, 352 (1974).

The starting point for this "governmental function" doctrine is *Smith v. Allwright*, 321 U.S. 649 (1944), the white primary case, where a primary election conducted by a political party was held to involve invalid state action, since the party, though not a state entity as such, was performing the public function of conducting the election. Where an activity, such as conduct of an election, is a governmental function, any organization controlling the election procedure must be deemed an agency of the state for purposes of the Fourteenth and Fifteenth Amendments: "That is to say, when private individuals or groups are endowed by the State with powers or functions governmental in nature, they become agencies or instrumentalities of the State and subject to its constitutional limitations." *Evans v. Newton*, 382 U.S. 296, 299 (1966).

In *Marsh v. Alabama*, 326 U.S. 501 (1946), the Court reversed a conviction of a Jehovah's Witness for distributing religious literature in a company town contrary to its owner's wishes. Neither a state nor a municipality could have absolutely barred distribution. The state may not escape the constitutional bar by permitting a private corporation to conduct a governmental function of running a city. The Court balanced the private owner's property rights against the people's rights of press and religion in resolving the state action inquiry.

In *Evans v. Newton*, 382 U.S. 296 (1966), the Court extended the governmental function doctrine to a private park. The case involved a testamentary devise of land to Macon, Georgia, for use as a park by whites only. The city operated the park as trustee, but after it became clear that no governmental agency might operate a segregated park, it withdrew and private trustees were appointed to operate the park on a segregated basis. The Supreme Court ruled that in such circumstances running the park was a public function subject to review under the Equal Protection Clause.

The Court said its decision was "buttressed by the nature of the service rendered the community by a park. The service rendered even by a private park of this character is municipal in nature." *Id.* at 301. Operating a park is traditionally a governmental function.

Justice Harlan, dissenting, thought applying the "governmental function" concept to operation of a park involved "a novel state action theory." If operation of a park is a public function, why, Harlan asked, is not operation of schools? He thought the same logic "might be spun out to reach privately owned orphanages, libraries, garbage collection companies, detective agencies, and a host of other functions commonly regarded as nongovernmental though paralleling fields of governmental activity." . . . *Id.* at 322.

(4) *State Inaction.* Can a state's failure to act to protect constitutional rights constitute state action for Fourteenth Amendment purposes? *DeShaney v. Winnebago County Dept. of Social Services*, 489 U.S. 189, 195-96 (1989), involved a claim that a state's failure to remove a child from his father's custody involved state action. State officials had received reports of child abuse but had failed to act. Eventually the child was severely beaten and injured. The Court found no state action. The harm was inflicted by a private actor, the father, not the state. Chief Justice Rehnquist wrote for the Court:

> [N]othing in the language of the Due Process Clause itself requires the State to protect the life, liberty, and property of its citizens against invasion by private actors. The Clause is phrased as a limitation on the State's power to act, not as a guarantee of certain minimal levels of safety and security. It forbids the State itself to deprive individuals of life, liberty, or property without "due process of law," but its language cannot fairly be extended to impose an affirmative obligation on the State to ensure that those interests do not come to harm through other means. . . . Its purpose was to protect the people from the State, not to ensure that the State protected them from each other.

MOOSE LODGE NO. 107 v. IRVIS
407 U.S. 163, 92 S. Ct. 1965. 32 L. Ed. 2d 627 (1972)

JUSTICE REHNQUIST delivered the opinion of the Court.

Appellee Irvis, a Negro (hereafter appellee), was refused service by appellant Moose Lodge, a local branch of the national fraternal organization located in Harrisburg, Pennsylvania. Appellee then brought this action under 42 U.S.C. § 1983 for injunctive relief in the United States District Court for the Middle District of Pennsylvania. He claimed that because the Pennsylvania liquor board had issued appellant Moose Lodge a private club license that authorized the sale of alcoholic beverages on its premises, the refusal of service to him was "state action" for the purposes of the Equal Protection Clause of the Fourteenth Amendment. He named both Moose Lodge and the Pennsylvania Liquor Authority as defendants, seeking injunctive relief that would have required the defendant liquor board to revoke Moose Lodge's license so long as it continued its discriminatory practices. Appellee sought no damages. A three-judge district court . . . entered a decree declaring invalid the liquor license issued to Moose

Lodge "as long as it follows a policy of racial discrimination in its membership or operating policies or practices." Moose Lodge alone appealed from the decree. . . .

. . . .

Moose Lodge is a private club in the ordinary meaning of that term. It is a local chapter of a national fraternal organization having well-defined requirements for membership. It conducts all of its activities in a building that is owned by it. It is not publicly funded. Only members and guests are permitted in any lodge of the order; one may become a guest only by invitation of a member or upon invitation of the house committee.

Appellee, while conceding the right of private clubs to choose members upon a discriminatory basis, asserts that the licensing of Moose Lodge to serve liquor by the Pennsylvania Liquor Control Board amounts to such state involvement with the club's activities as to make its discriminatory practices forbidden by the Equal Protection Clause of the Fourteenth Amendment. . . . We conclude that Moose Lodge's refusal to serve food and beverages to a guest by reason of the fact that he was a Negro does not, under the circumstances here presented, violate the Fourteenth Amendment. . . .

While the principle is easily stated, the question of whether particular discriminatory conduct is private, on the one hand, or amounts to "state action," on the other hand, frequently admits of no easy answer. "Only by sifting facts and weighing circumstances can the non-obvious involvement of the State in private conduct be attributed its true significance." *Burton v. Wilmington Parking Authority.* . . .

Our cases make clear that the impetus for the forbidden discrimination need not originate with the State if it is state action that enforces privately originated discrimination. *Shelley v. Kraemer*, [*supra* § 6.03]. The Court held in *Burton v. Wilmington Parking Authority, supra*, that a private restaurant owner who refused service because of a customer's race violated the Fourteenth Amendment, where the restaurant was located in a building owned by a state-created parking authority and leased from the authority. The Court, after a comprehensive review of the relationship between the lessee and the parking authority concluded that the latter had "so far insinuated itself into a position of interdependence with Eagle (the restaurant owner) that it must be recognized as a joint participant in the challenged activity, which, on that account, cannot be considered to have been so 'purely private' as to fall without the scope of the Fourteenth Amendment." . . .

The Court has never held, of course, that discrimination by an otherwise private entity would be violative of the Equal Protection Clause if the private entity receives any sort of benefit or service at all from the State, or if it is subject to state regulation in any degree whatever. Since state-furnished services include such necessities of life as electricity, water, and police and fire protection, such a holding would utterly emasculate the distinction between private as distinguished from state conduct set forth in *The Civil Rights Cases*, [*supra* § 6.03, Note (2) after *Shelley*], and adhered to in subsequent decisions. Our holdings indicate that where the impetus for the discrimination is private, the State must have "significantly involved itself with invidious discriminations, . . ." in order for the discriminatory action to fall within the ambit of the constitutional prohibition. . . .

Here there is nothing approaching the symbiotic relationship between lessor and lessee that was present in *Burton*, where the private lessee obtained the benefit of locating in a building owned by the state-created parking authority, and the parking authority was enabled to carry out its primary public purpose of furnishing parking space by advantageously leasing portions of the building constructed for that purpose to commercial lessees such as the owner of the Eagle Restaurant. Unlike *Burton*, the

Moose Lodge building is located on land owned by it, not by any public authority. Far from apparently holding itself out as a place of public accommodation, Moose Lodge quite ostentatiously proclaims the fact that it is not open to the public at large. Nor is it located and operated in such surroundings that although private in name, it discharges a function or performs a service that would otherwise in all likelihood be performed by the State. In short, while Eagle was a public restaurant in a public building, Moose Lodge is a private social club in a private building. . . .

The District Court was at pains to point out in its opinion what it considered to be the "pervasive" nature of the regulation of private clubs by the Pennsylvania Liquor Control Board. As that court noted, an applicant for a club license must make such physical alterations in its premises as the board may require, must file a list of the names and addresses of its members and employees, and must keep extensive financial records. The board is granted the right to inspect the licensed premises at any time when patrons, guests, or members are present.

However detailed this type of regulation may be in some particulars, it cannot be said to in any way foster or encourage racial discrimination. Nor can it be said to make the State in any realistic sense a partner or even a joint venturer in the club's enterprise. The limited effect of the prohibition against obtaining additional club licenses when the maximum number of retail licenses allotted to a municipality has been issued, when considered together with the availability of liquor from hotel, restaurant, and retail licensees, falls far short of conferring upon club licensees a monopoly in the dispensing of liquor in any given municipality or in the State as a whole. We therefore hold that . . . the operation of the regulatory scheme enforced by the Pennsylvania Liquor Control Board does not sufficiently implicate the State in the discriminatory guest policies of Moose Lodge to make the latter "state action" within the ambit of the Equal Protection Clause of the Fourteenth Amendment. . . .

. . . The judgment of the District Court is reversed, and the cause remanded with instructions to enter a decree in conformity with this opinion.

[JUSTICES DOUGLAS, MARSHALL, and BRENNAN dissented].

NOTES

(1) *Moose Lodge* shows that the holding of the *Civil Rights Cases* is still followed — i.e., purely private action lies beyond the reach of the Fourteenth Amendment. In cases involving private action, the extent of state involvement is crucial: "the inquiry must be whether there is a sufficiently close nexus between the State and the challenged action of the regulated entity so that the action of the latter may be fairly treated as that of the State itself." *Jackson v. Metropolitan Edison Co.*, 419 U.S. 345, 351 (1974).

(2) *Moose Lodge* points out that state action includes conduct that does not originate with the state if state action makes the private action feasible. *See, e.g., Burton v. Wilmington Parking Authority*, 365 U.S. 715 (1961) (state action where private restaurant on public-owned place discriminates against African-Americans). In *Burton*, the Court found that Delaware had "so far insinuated itself into a position of interdependence with [the private entrepreneur] that it must be recognized as a joint participant in the challenged activity." . . . *Id.* at 725. The restaurant was on the state's property, paid its rent, and benefitted from the fact that its customers used the state's parking lot. *See also Gilmore v. Montgomery*, 417 U.S. 556 (1974) (grant of exclusive use of city recreational facilities by private segregated schools constituted improper state action).

(3) *Entanglement Exception.* These cases illustrate the entanglement exception to the state action doctrine, which provide instances when private conduct is treated as that of the state and therefore subject to Fourteenth Amendment scrutiny. How far

should the entanglement exception be pushed? States issue corporate charters but presumably this and other regulation does not make corporate acts state action.

In his *Moose Lodge* dissent, Justice Douglas argued that the discriminatory action of any licensed business should fall within the state action concept. This argument has not prevailed. *See Jackson v. Metropolitan Edison Co.*, 419 U.S. 345 (1974); (termination of electric service by a privately owned utility company without notice and hearing not state action, even though utility operated under state license and was subject to extensive state regulation); *Columbia Broadcasting System v. Democratic National Committee*, 412 U.S. 94 (1973) (broadcaster's receipt of FCC licenses held not to make their refusal of political advertising governmental action subject to constitutional free speech requirements).

(4) The Court narrowed the entanglement exception in *American Manufacturers Mutual Insurance Co. v. Sullivan*, 526 U.S. 40 (1999). In *Sullivan* the Court predicated state action based on the entanglement exception on two conditions.

> [S]tate action requires *both* an alleged constitutional deprivation "caused by the exercise of some right or privilege created by the State or by a rule of conduct imposed by the State or by a person for whom the State is responsible", *and* that "the party charged with the deprivation must be a person who may fairly be said to be a state actor.'

Id. at 50.

In *Sullivan*, the Court held that "a *private insurer's* decision to withhold payment for disputed medical treatment" was not state action since the state neither compelled nor was directly involved in the disputed decision. *Id.* at 51-52. That the state allowed insurers this option pending review was at most "subtle encouragement" which did not rise to the level of state action. *Id.* at 53

(5) A nonprofit association's "regulatory activity may and should be treated as state action owing to the pervasive entwinement of state school officials in the structure of the association" absent some "offsetting reason." *Brentwood Academy v. Tennessee Secondary School Athletic Association*, 531 U.S. 288 (2001). The association, which was incorporated to regulate interscholastic sports competition among public and private high schools, had placed Brentwood Academy on probation for recruiting violations. The case involved the issue whether action of the association could constitute state action. The Court, in a 5-4 decision, concluded that identifying state action was "a matter of normative judgment" based on criteria which "lack rigid simplicity."

> From the range of circumstances that could point toward the State behind an individual face, no one fact can function as a necessary condition across the board for finding state action; nor is any set of circumstances absolutely sufficient, for there may be some countervailing reason against attributing activity to the government. 531 U.S. at 295-96.

Entwinement of the "private" action with government policies or government "management or control" was among the criteria that could lead to a finding of state action. Here, the

> nominally private character of the Association is overborne by the pervasive entwinement of public institutions and public officials in its composition and workings, and there is no substantial reason to claim unfairness in applying constitutional standards to it. *Id.* at 298.

In dissent, Justice Thomas (joined by Chief Justice Rehnquist, Justice Scalia and Justice Kennedy) argued that the Court has "never found state action based upon mere 'entwinement,'" but had previously considered a private organization's actions as state action only if it performed a public function, "was created, coerced or encouraged by the government; or acted in a symbiotic relationship with the government." *Id.* at 305. Justice Souter, writing for the majority, rejected this claim. None of these criterion must necessarily be met for state action to exist. Where "the relevant facts show pervasive entwinement to the point of largely overlapping identity" state action may exist unless "outweighed in the name of some value at odds with finding public accountability in the circumstances." *Id.* at 303.

(6) *Subsidies.* In some cases, the Court has found state action where the government provided subsidies to a private school that discriminated against racial minorities. *See, e.g., Gilmore v. City of Montgomery*, 417 U.S. 556 (1974) (city barred from giving segregated private schools sole use of recreational facilities); *Norwood v. Harrison*, 413 U.S. 455 (1973) (subsidy for textbooks to segregated private schools constituted state action). The Court has limited the extent to which subsidies constitute state action, however.

In *Blum v. Yaretsky*, 457 U.S. 991, 1004-05 (1982), the Court held that the fact that the state bore most of the medical cost for medicaid patients did not make the care decisions of private facilities state action.

> First, although it is apparent that nursing homes in New York are extensively regulated, "[t]he mere fact that a business is subject to state regulation does not by itself convert its action into that of the State for purposes of the Fourteenth Amendment." *Jackson v. Metropolitan Edison Co.*, 419 U.S. 348 (1974). The complaining party must also show that "there is a sufficiently close nexus between the State and the challenged action of the regulated entity so that the action of the latter may be fairly treated as that of the State itself." The purpose of this requirement is to assure that constitutional standards are invoked only when it can be said that the State is responsible for the specific conduct of which the plaintiff complains. The importance of this assurance is evident when, as in this case, the complaining party seeks to hold the State liable for the actions of private parties.
>
> Second, although the factual Setting of each case will be significant, our precedents indicate that a State normally can be held responsible for a private decision only when it has exercised coercive power or has provided such significant encouragement, either overt or covert, that the choice must in law be deemed to be that of the State. . . . Mere approval of or acquiescence in the initiatives of a private party is not sufficient to justify holding the State responsible for those initiatives under the terms of the Fourteenth Amendment. . . .
>
> Third, the required nexus may be present if the private entity has exercised powers that are "traditionally the exclusive prerogative of the State." . . .

§ 6.04 POST-BELLUM CIVIL RIGHTS STATUTES

The post Civil-War amendments, as already pointed out, contain self-executing prohibitions protecting civil rights. These lay down rules of decision for judicial enforcement. The Thirteenth Amendment outlaws all forms of slavery and involuntary servitude; the Fourteenth Amendment strikes down all "state action" which denies due process or equal protection; the Fifteenth Amendment ends all state attempts to restrict the franchise on racial grounds. It is the self-executing aspect of the amendments that has made possible the many cases brought directly under them.

These amendments also provide for legislative enforcement. Each amendment expressly grants Congress authority to enforce its provisions "by appropriate legislation." The amendments sought to empower the federal government to protect civil rights in order to overcome the deficient prior approach which entrusted those rights to state protection. They expanded federal power at the expense of state sovereignty. These clauses have been the constitutional source of many civil rights statutes from Reconstruction to our own time.

The Reconstruction statutes, like the post-Civil War amendments, sought to ensure enforcement of the Fifteenth Amendment since equal rights were contingent upon protection of the right to vote. Criminal prohibitions and independent federal enforcement machinery were designed to secure black voting. These laws also provided sanctions to deter violations of other civil rights and provided for equality in public accommodations.

§ 6.05   CONGRESSIONAL ENFORCEMENT POWER: FOURTEENTH AMENDMENT

KATZENBACH v. MORGAN
384 U.S. 641, 86 S. Ct. 1717, 16 L. Ed. 2d 828 (1966)

JUSTICE BRENNAN delivered the opinion of the Court.

These cases concern the constitutionality of § 4(e) of the Voting Rights Act of 1965. That law, in the respects pertinent in these cases, provides that no person who has successfully completed the sixth primary grade in a public school in, or a private school accredited by, the Commonwealth of Puerto Rico in which the language of instruction was other than English shall be denied the right to vote in any election because of his inability to read or write English. Appellees, registered voters in New York City, brought this suit to challenge the constitutionality of § 4(e) insofar as it pro tanto prohibits the enforcement of the election laws of New York requiring an ability to read and write English as a condition of voting. . . . We hold that, in the application challenged in these cases, § 4(e) is a proper exercise of the powers granted to Congress by § 5 of the Fourteenth Amendment and that by force of the Supremacy Clause, Article VI, the New York English literacy requirement cannot be enforced to the extent that it is inconsistent with § 4(e).

Under the distribution of powers effected by the Constitution, the States establish qualifications for voting for state officers, and the qualifications established by the States for voting for members of the most numerous branch of the state legislature also determine who may vote for United States Representatives and Senators. . . . But, of course, the States have no power to grant or withhold the franchise on conditions that are forbidden by the Fourteenth Amendment, or any other provision of the Constitution. Such exercises of state power are no more immune to the limitations of the Fourteenth Amendment than any other state action. The Equal Protection Clause itself has been held to forbid some state laws that restrict the right to vote.

The Attorney General of the State of New York argues that an exercise of congressional power under § 5 of the Fourteenth Amendment that prohibits enforcement of a state law can only be sustained if the judicial branch determines that the state law is prohibited by the provisions of the Amendment that Congress sought to enforce. More specifically, he urges that § 4(e) cannot be sustained as appropriate legislation to enforce the Equal Protection Clause unless the judiciary decides — even with the guidance of a congressional judgment — that the application of the English literacy requirement prohibited by § 4(e) is forbidden by the Equal Protection Clause itself. We disagree. Neither the language nor the history of § 5 supports such a construction. . . . A construction of § 5 that would require a judicial determination that the enforcement of the state law precluded by Congress violated the Amendment, as a condition of sustaining the congressional enactment, would depreciate both congressional resourcefulness and congressional responsibility for implementing the Amendment. It would confine the legislative power in this context to the insignificant role of abrogating only those state laws that the judicial branch was prepared to adjudge unconstitutional, or of merely informing the judgment of the judiciary by particularizing the "majestic generalities" of § 1 of the Amendment. . . .

Thus our task in this case is not to determine whether the New York English literacy requirement as applied to deny the right to vote to a person who successfully completed the sixth grade in a Puerto Rican school violates the Equal Protection Clause. . . . Without regard to whether the judiciary would find that the Equal Protection Clause itself nullifies New York's English literacy requirement as so applied, could Congress prohibit the enforcement of the state law by legislating under § 5 of the Fourteenth Amendment? In answering this question, our task is limited to determining whether such legislation is, as required by § 5, appropriate legislation to enforce the Equal Protection Clause.

By including § 5 the draftsmen sought to grant to Congress, by a specific provision applicable to the Fourteenth Amendment, the same broad powers expressed in the Necessary and Proper Clause, Art. I, § 8, cl. 18. The classic formulation of the reach of those powers was established by Chief Justice Marshall in *McCulloch v. Maryland.* . . .

> Let the end be legitimate, let it be within the scope of the constitution, and all means which are appropriate, which are plainly adapted to that end, which are not prohibited, but consist with the letter and spirit of the constitution, are constitutional. . . .

[T]he *McCulloch v. Maryland* standard is the measure of what constitutes "appropriate legislation" under § 5 of the Fourteenth Amendment. Correctly viewed, § 5 is a positive grant of legislative power authorizing Congress to exercise its discretion in determining whether and what legislation is needed to secure the guarantees of the Fourteenth Amendment. . . .

There can be no doubt that § 4(e) may be regarded as an enactment to enforce the Equal Protection Clause. Congress explicitly declared that it enacted § 4(e) "to secure the rights under the fourteenth amendment of persons educated in American-flag schools in which the predominant classroom language was other than English." The persons referred to include those who have migrated from the Commonwealth of Puerto Rico to New York and who have been denied the right to vote because of their inability to read and write English, and the Fourteenth-Amendment rights referred to include those emanating from the Equal Protection Clause. More specifically, § 4(e) may be viewed as a measure to secure for the Puerto Rican community residing in New York nondiscriminatory treatment by government — both in the imposition of voting qualifications and the provision or administration of governmental services, such as public schools, public housing and law enforcement.

Section 4(e) may be readily seen as "plainly adapted" to furthering these aims of the Equal Protection Clause. The practical effect of § 4(e) is to prohibit New York from denying the right to vote to large segments of its Puerto Rican community. Congress has thus prohibited the State from denying to that community the right that is "preservative of all rights." . . . This enhanced political power will be helpful in gaining nondiscriminatory treatment in public services for the entire Puerto Rican community. Section 4(e) thereby enables the Puerto Rican minority better to obtain "perfect equality of civil rights and the equal protection of the laws." It was well within congressional authority to say that this need of the Puerto Rican minority for the vote warranted federal intrusion upon any state interests served by the English literacy requirement. It was for Congress, as the branch that made this judgment, to assess and weigh the various conflicting considerations — the risk or pervasiveness of the discrimination in governmental services, the effectiveness of eliminating the state restriction on the right to vote as a means of dealing with the evil, the adequacy or availability of alternative remedies, and the nature and significance of the state interests that would be affected by the nullification of the English literacy requirement as applied to residents who have successfully completed the sixth grade in a Puerto Rican school. It is not for us to review the congressional resolution of these factors. It is enough that we be able to perceive a basis upon which the Congress might resolve the conflict as it did. There plainly was such a basis to support § 4(e) in the application in question in this case. Any contrary conclusion would require us to be blind to the realities familiar to the legislators.

The result is no different if we confine our inquiry to the question whether § 4(e) was merely legislation aimed at the elimination of an invidious discrimination in establishing voter qualifications. We are told that New York's English literacy requirement originated in the desire to provide an incentive for non-English speaking immigrants to learn the English language and in order to assure the intelligent exercise of the franchise. Yet Congress might well have questioned, in light of the many exemptions provided, and some evidence suggesting that prejudice played a prominent role in the enactment of the requirement, whether these were actually the interests being served. Congress might have also questioned whether denial of a right deemed so precious and fundamental in our society was a necessary or appropriate means of encouraging persons to learn English, or of furthering the goal of an intelligent exercise of the franchise. Finally, Congress might well have concluded that as a means of furthering the intelligent exercise of the franchise, an ability to read or understand Spanish is as effective as an ability to read English for those to whom Spanish-language newspapers and Spanish language radio and television programs are available to inform them of election issues and governmental affairs. Since Congress undertook to legislate so as to preclude the enforcement of the state law, and did so in the context of a general appraisal of literacy requirements for voting, . . . to which it brought a specially informed legislative competence, it was Congress' prerogative to weigh these competing considerations. Here again, it is enough that we perceive a basis upon which Congress might predicate a judgment that the application of New York's English literacy requirement to deny the right to vote to a person with a sixth grade education in Puerto Rican schools in which the language of instruction was other than English constituted an invidious discrimination in violation of the Equal Protection Clause. . . .

We therefore conclude that § 4(e), in the application challenged in this case, is appropriate legislation to enforce the Equal Protection Clause and that the judgment of the District Court must be and hereby is reversed.

JUSTICE HARLAN, whom JUSTICE STEWART joins, dissenting.

Worthy as its purposes may be thought by many, I do not see how § 4(e) of the Voting Rights Act of 1965 . . . can be sustained except at the sacrifice of fundamentals in the American constitutional system — the separation between the legislative and judicial function and the boundaries between federal and state political authority. By the same token I think that the validity of New York's literacy test, a question which the Court considers only in the context of the federal statute, must be upheld. . . .

The pivotal question in this instance is what effect the added factor of a congressional enactment has on the straight equal protection argument. . . . The Court declares that since § 5 of the Fourteenth Amendment gives to the Congress power to "enforce" the prohibitions of the Amendment by "appropriate" legislation, the test for judicial review of any congressional determination in this area is simply one of rationality; that is in effect was Congress acting rationally in declaring that the New York statute is irrational? Although § 5 most certainly does give to the Congress wide powers in the field of devising remedial legislation to effectuate the Amendment's prohibition on arbitrary state action. . . . I believe the Court has confused the issue of how much enforcement power Congress possesses under § 5 with the distinct issue of what questions are appropriate for congressional determination and what questions are essentially judicial in nature.

When recognized state violations of federal constitutional standards have occurred, Congress is of course empowered by § 5 to take appropriate remedial measures to redress and prevent the wrongs. . . . But it is a judicial question whether the condition with which Congress has thus sought to deal is in truth an infringement of the Constitution, something that is the necessary prerequisite to bringing the § 5 power into play at all. . . .

. . . The question here is not whether the statute is appropriate remedial legislation to cure an established violation of a constitutional command, but whether there has in fact been an infringement of that constitutional command, that is, whether a particular state practice or, as here, a statute is so arbitrary or irrational as to offend the command of the Equal Protection Clause of the Fourteenth Amendment. That question is one for the judicial branch ultimately to determine. Were the rule otherwise, Congress would be able to qualify this Court's constitutional decisions under the Fourteenth and Fifteenth Amendments, let alone those under other provisions of the Constitution, by resorting to congressional power under the Necessary and Proper Clause. . . . In effect the Court reads § 5 of the Fourteenth Amendment as giving Congress the power to define the substantive scope of the Amendment. If that indeed be the true reach of § 5, then I do not see why Congress should not be able as well to exercise its § 5 "discretion" by enacting statutes so as in effect to dilute equal protection and due process decisions of this Court. In all such cases there is room for reasonable men to differ as to whether or not a denial of equal protection or due process has occurred, and the final decision is one of judgment. Until today this judgment has always been one for the judiciary to resolve. . . .

To deny the effectiveness of this congressional enactment is not of course to disparage Congress' exertion of authority in the field of civil rights; it is simply to recognize that the Legislative Branch like the other branches of federal authority is subject to the governmental boundaries set by the Constitution. To hold, on this record, that § 4(e) overrides the New York literacy requirement seems to me tantamount to allowing the Fourteenth Amendment to swallow the State's constitutionally ordained primary authority in this field. For if Congress by what, as here, amounts to mere *ipse dixit* can set that otherwise permissible requirement partially at naught, I see no reason why it could not also substitute its judgment for that of the States in other fields of their exclusive primary competence as well.

I would affirm the judgments in each of these cases.

NOTES

(1) The substantive provisions of the post-Civil War amendments are self-executing; they lay down rules of decision enforceable by the courts, which "could strike down state laws found directly to violate the dictates of any of the Amendments." In addition, "Congress might affirmatively legislate under § 5 of the Fourteenth Amendment to carry out the purposes of that Amendment." *Trimble v. Gordon*, 430 U.S. 762, 778 (1977) (Rehnquist, J., dissenting).

(2) How can Congress enact § 4(e) as "legislation aimed at the elimination of an invidious discrimination in establishing voter qualifications," when absent § 4(e), New York's English literacy requirement would not fall as an invidious discrimination? In

Katzenbach v. Morgan, the Court said the enforcement clause of the Fourteenth Amendment was intended to grant Congress, regarding the amendment, the same broad powers expressed in the Necessary and Proper Clause of Article I; "Correctly viewed, § 5 is a positive grant of legislative power authorizing Congress to exercise its discretion in determining whether and what legislation is needed to secure the guarantees of the Fourteenth Amendment." *Katzenbach*, 384 U.S. at 651.

(3) Under these enforcement provisions, Congress has discretion regarding mode of enforcement. It may determine whether to provide for enforcement by prohibition (as by prohibiting state officers from excluding citizens from jury service because of race), by declaration (as by declaring that all persons are entitled to enjoyment of public accommodations without discrimination), by procedural mechanism (as by authorizing removal of cases involving acts violating equal protection from state to federal courts), or even by provision for federal officers to vindicate equality (as has been done in the field of voting rights). Congress also has discretion to decide what sanctions to provide for enforcement. It may limit the remedies provided to civil actions for preventive or other relief, or may provide a criminal sanction, with violation of the statutory provisions entailing the traditional criminal penalties of fine and/or imprisonment. The very language of the enforcement section of the Fourteenth Amendment indicates that, though the enforcement authority granted is limited to the types of cases specified, "within its limits it is complete." *Ex parte Virginia*, 100 U.S. 339, 348 (1880).

(4) In *Oregon v. Mitchell*, 400 U.S. 472 (1970), the Court upheld Congress' action in the Voting Rights Act Amendments of 1970 in lowering the minimum age of voters to 18 in federal elections, in barring the use of literacy tests in all elections for five years and in forbidding states from disqualifying voters in elections to choose presidential and vice-presidential electors on the grounds that they have not met state residency requirements. By a 5-4 margin, the Court held that Congress could not lower the voting age for state and local elections.

Justice Black announced the Court's decision in an opinion which did not command majority assent. He argued that the Civil War Amendments authorized Congress to "enforce" those Amendments with "appropriate legislation." He argued that the Civil War Amendments sought to address racial discrimination; although decisions had recognized other claims under the Equal Protection Clause of the Fourteenth Amendment.

> The Fourteenth Amendment was surely not intended to make every discrimination between groups of people a constitutional denial of equal protection. Nor was the Enforcement Clause of the Fourteenth Amendment intended to permit Congress to prohibit every discrimination between groups of people. On the other hand, the Civil War Amendments were unquestionably designed to condemn and forbid every distinction, however trifling, on account of race.

Justice Black found three limitations in Congress' enforcement power regarding the three Civil War Amendments.

> First, Congress may not by legislation repeal other provisions of the Constitution. Second, the power granted to Congress was not intended to strip the States of their power to govern themselves or to convert our national government of enumerated powers into a central government of unrestrained authority over every inch of the whole Nation. Third, Congress may only "enforce" the provisions of the amendments and may do so only by "appropriate legislation." Congress has no power under the enforcement sections to undercut the amendments' guarantee of personal equality and freedom from discrimination, see *Katzenback v. Morgan*, 384 U.S. 641, 651 n.10, (1966), or to undermine those protections of the Bill of Rights which we have held the Fourteenth

Amendment made applicable to the States. . . .

Justice Stewart (joined by Chief Justice Burger and Justice Blackmun) joined Justice Black in concluding that Congress lacked power to lower the voting age in state elections. The state statutes the Voting Rights Act 1970 Amendments invalidated did not "invidiously discriminate against any discrete and insular minority." Those Amendments could be valid

> only if Congress has the power not only to provide the means of eradicating situations that amount to a violation of the Equal Protection Clause, but also to determine as a matter of substantive constitutional law what situation fall within the ambit of the clause, and what state interests are "compelling."

Justice Stewart thought *Morgan* did not go so far.

Subsequently, the Twenty sixth Amendment superceded *Oregon v. Mitchell* in part, insofar as it lowered the voting age to 18.

(5) *See also City of Rome v. United States*, 446 U.S. 156, 211-13 (1980) (Rehnquist, J., dissenting):

> If the enforcement power is construed as a "remedial" grant of authority, it is this Court's duty to ensure that a challenged congressional Act does no more than "enforce" the limitations on state power established in the Fourteenth and Fifteenth Amendments. . . . While [the] Amendments prohibit only purposeful discrimination, the decisions of this Court have recognized that in some circumstances, congressional prohibition of state or local action which is not purposefully discriminatory may nevertheless be appropriate remedial legislation. . . . [C]ongressional prohibition of some conduct which may not itself violate the Constitution is "appropriate" legislation "to enforce" [the] Amendments if that prohibition is necessary to remedy prior constitutional violations by the governmental unit, or if necessary to effectively prevent purposeful discrimination by a governmental unit. In both circumstances, Congress would still be legislating in response to the incidence of state action violative of [the] Amendments. These precedents are carefully formulated around a historic tenet of the law that in order to invoke a remedy, there must be a wrong — and under a remedial construction of congressional power to enforce [the] Amendments, that wrong must amount to a constitutional violation.

CITY OF BOERNE v. FLORES
521 U.S. 507, 117 S. Ct. 2157, 138 L. Ed. 2d 624 (1997)

JUSTICE KENNEDY delivered the opinion of the Court.

A decision by local zoning authorities to deny a church a building permit was challenged under the Religious Freedom Restoration Act of 1993 (RFRA). . . . The case calls into question the authority of Congress to enact RFRA. We conclude the statute exceeds Congress' power.

I

[The City of Boerne denied St. Peter Catholic Church a building permit to enlarge its structure. The Church challenged the decision based, in part, on RFRA.]

II

Congress enacted RFRA in direct response to the Court's decision in *Employment Div., Dept. of Human Resources of Oregon v. Smith*, [*infra* § 16.05]. . . . *Smith* held that neutral, generally applicable laws may be applied to religious practices even when not supported by a compelling governmental interest. . . . Members of Congress . . . criticized the Court's reasoning, and this disagreement resulted in the passage of RFRA. . . .

The Act's stated purposes are:

(1) to restore the compelling interest test as set forth in *Sherbert v. Verner* . . . and to guarantee its application in all cases where free exercise of religion is substantially burdened; and

(2) to provide a claim or defense to persons whose religious exercise is substantially burdened by government. . . .

RFRA prohibits "[g]overnment" from "substantially burden[ing]" a person's exercise of religion even if the burden results from a rule of general applicability unless the government can demonstrate the burden "(1) is in furtherance of a compelling governmental interest; and (2) is the least restrictive means of furthering that compelling governmental interest." . . .

III

A

. . . .

Congress relied on its Fourteenth Amendment enforcement power in enacting [RFRA]. . . . The parties disagree over whether RFRA is a proper exercise of Congress' § 5 power "to enforce" by "appropriate legislation" the constitutional guarantee that no State shall deprive any person of "life, liberty, or property, without due process of law" nor deny any person "equal protection of the laws."

In defense of the Act respondent contends, with support from the United States [as *amicus*], that RFRA is permissible enforcement legislation. Congress, it is said, is only protecting by legislation one of the liberties guaranteed by the Fourteenth Amendment's Due Process Clause, the free exercise of religion, beyond what is necessary under *Smith*. It is said the congressional decision to dispense with proof of deliberate or overt discrimination and instead concentrate on a law's effects accords with the settled understanding that § 5 includes the power to enact legislation designed to prevent, as well as remedy, constitutional violations. It is further contended that Congress' § 5 power is not limited to remedial or preventive legislation.

All must acknowledge that § 5 is "a positive grant of legislative power" to Congress. . . . It is also true, however, that "[a]s broad as the congressional enforcement power is, it is not unlimited." . . . In assessing the breadth of § 5's enforcement power, we begin with its text. Congress has been given the power "to enforce" the "provisions of this article." We agree . . . that Congress can enact legislation under § 5 enforcing the constitutional right to the free exercise of religion. The "provisions of this article," to which § 5 refers, include the Due Process Clause of the Fourteenth Amendment [and] Congress' power to enforce the Free Exercise Clause. . . .

Congress' power under § 5, however, extends only to "enforc[ing]" the provisions of the Fourteenth Amendment. The Court has described this power as "remedial." . . . The design of the Amendment and the text of § 5 are inconsistent with the suggestion that Congress has the power to decree the substance of the Fourteenth Amendment's restrictions on the States. Legislation which alters the meaning of the Free Exercise Clause cannot be said to be enforcing the Clause. Congress does not enforce a constitutional right by changing what the right is. It has been given the power "to enforce," not the power to determine what constitutes a constitutional violation.

Were it not so, what Congress would be enforcing would no longer be, in any meaningful sense, the "provisions of [the Fourteenth Amendment]."

While the line between measures that remedy or prevent unconstitutional actions and measures that make a substantive change in the governing law is not easy to discern, and Congress must have wide latitude in determining where it lies, the distinction exists and must be observed. There must be a congruence and proportionality between the injury to be prevented or remedied and the means adopted to that end. Lacking such a connection, legislation may become substantive in operation and effect. History and our case law support drawing the distinction, one apparent from the text of the Amendment. . . .

The design of the Fourteenth Amendment has proved significant . . . in maintaining the traditional separation of powers between Congress and the Judiciary. The first eight Amendments to the Constitution set forth self-executing prohibitions on governmental action, and this Court has had primary authority to interpret those prohibitions . . . . As enacted, the Fourteenth Amendment confers substantive rights against the States which, like the provisions of the Bill of Rights, are self-executing. . . . The power to interpret the Constitution in a case or controversy remains in the Judiciary.

The remedial and preventive nature of Congress' enforcement power, and the limitation inherent in the power, were confirmed in our . . . cases on the Fourteenth Amendment. . . .

Any suggestion that Congress has a substantive, non-remedial power under the Fourteenth Amendment is not supported by our case law. In *Oregon v. Mitchell*, [*supra*, § 6.05, Note (4), after *Katzenbach*], a majority of the Court concluded Congress had exceeded its enforcement powers by enacting legislation lowering the minimum age of voters from 21 to 18 in state and local elections. The five Members of the Court who reached this conclusion explained that the legislation intruded into an area reserved by the Constitution to the States. . . .

There is language in our opinion in *Katzenbach v. Morgan*, which could be interpreted as acknowledging a power in Congress to enact legislation that expands the rights contained in § 1 of the Fourteenth Amendment. This is not a necessary interpretation, however, or even the best one. . . . The Court provided two related rationales for its conclusion that § 4(e) could "be viewed as a measure to secure for the Puerto Rican community residing in New York nondiscriminatory treatment by government." . . . Under the first rationale, Congress could prohibit New York from denying the right to vote to large segments of its Puerto Rican community, in order to give Puerto Ricans "enhanced political power" that would be "helpful in gaining non-discriminatory treatment in public services for the entire Puerto Rican community." . . . Section 4(e) thus could be justified as a remedial measure to deal with "discrimination in governmental services." . . . The second rationale, an alternative holding, did not address discrimination in the provision of public services but "discrimination in establishing voter qualifications." . . . The Court perceived a factual basis on which Congress could have concluded that New York's literacy requirement "constituted an invidious discrimination in violation of the Equal Protection Clause." . . . Both rationales for upholding § 4(e) rested on unconstitutional discrimination by New York and Congress' reasonable attempt to combat it. As Justice Stewart explained in *Oregon v. Mitchell*, interpreting *Morgan* to give Congress the power to interpret the Constitution "would require an enormous extension of that decision's rationale."

If Congress could define its own powers by altering the Fourteenth Amendment's meaning, no longer would the Constitution be "superior paramount law, unchangeable by ordinary means." It would be "on a level with ordinary legislative acts, and, like other acts, . . . alterable when the legislature shall please to alter it." *Marbury v. Madison*, [*supra* § 1.01]. Under this approach, it is difficult to conceive of a principle that would limit congressional power. . . . Shifting legislative majorities could change the Constitution and effectively circumvent the difficult and detailed amendment process contained in Article V.

We now turn to consider whether RFRA can be considered enforcement legislation under § 5 of the Fourteenth Amendment.

B

Respondent contends that RFRA is a proper exercise of Congress' remedial or preventive power. The Act, it is said, is a reasonable means of protecting the free exercise of religion as defined by *Smith*. It prevents and remedies laws which are enacted with the unconstitutional object of targeting religious beliefs and practices. . . . To avoid the difficulty of proving such violations, it is said, Congress can simply invalidate any law which imposes a substantial burden on a religious practice unless it is justified by a compelling interest and is the least restrictive means of accomplishing that interest. If Congress can prohibit laws with discriminatory effects in order to prevent racial discrimination in violation of the Equal Protection Clause . . . then it can do the same, respondent argues, to promote religious liberty.

While preventive rules are sometimes appropriate remedial measures, there must be a congruence between the means used and the ends to be achieved. The appropriateness of remedial measures must be considered in light of the evil presented. . . . Strong measures appropriate to address one harm may be an unwarranted response to another, lesser one. . . .

A comparison between RFRA and the Voting Rights Act is instructive. In contrast to the record which confronted Congress and the judiciary in the voting rights cases, RFRA's legislative record lacks examples of modern instances of generally applicable laws passed because of religious bigotry. The history of persecution in this country detailed in the hearings mentions no episodes occurring in the past 40 years. . . . The absence of more recent episodes stems from the fact that, as one witness testified "deliberate persecution is not the usual problem in this country." . . . Rather, the emphasis of the hearings was on laws of general applicability which place incidental burdens on religion. Much of the discussion centered upon anecdotal evidence. . . . It is difficult to maintain that [the examples given] of legislation enacted or enforced due to animus or hostility to the burdened religious practices or that they indicate some widespread pattern of religious discrimination in this country. Congress' concern was with the incidental burdens imposed, not the object or purpose of the legislation- . . . . This lack of support in the legislative record, however, is not RFRA's most serious shortcoming. Judicial deference, in most cases, is based not on the state of the legislative record Congress compiles but "on due regard for the decision of the body constitutionally appointed to decide." . . . As a general matter, it is for Congress to determine the method by which it will reach a decision.

Regardless of the state of the legislative record, RFRA cannot be considered remedial, preventive legislation, if those terms are to have any meaning. RFRA is so out of proportion to a supposed remedial or preventive object that it cannot be understood as responsive to, or designed to prevent, unconstitutional behavior. It appears, instead, to attempt a substantive change in constitutional protections. Preventive measures prohibiting certain types of laws may be appropriate when there is reason to believe that many of the laws affected by the congressional enactment have a significant likelihood of being unconstitutional. . . . Remedial legislation under § 5 "should be adapted to the mischief and wrong which the [Fourteenth] Amendment was intended to provide against." . . .

RFRA is not so confined. Sweeping coverage ensures its intrusion at every level of government, displacing laws and prohibiting official actions of almost every description and regardless of subject matter. RFRA's restrictions apply to every agency and official of the Federal, State, and local Governments. . . . RFRA applies to all federal and state law, statutory or otherwise, whether adopted before or after its enactment. . . . RFRA has no termination date or termination mechanism. Any law is subject to challenge at any time by any individual who alleges a substantial burden on his or her free exercise of religion.

The reach and scope of RFRA distinguish it from other measures passed under Congress' enforcement power, even in the area of voting rights. . . . This is not to say, of course, that § 5 legislation requires termination dates, geographic restrictions or egregious predicates. Where, however, a congressional enactment pervasively prohibits constitutional state action in an effort to remedy or to prevent unconstitutional state action, limitations of this kind tend to ensure Congress' means are proportionate to ends legitimate under § 5.

The stringent test RFRA demands of state laws reflects a lack of proportionality or congruence between the means adopted and the legitimate end to be achieved. If an objector can show a substantial burden on his free exercise, the State must demonstrate a compelling governmental interest and show that the law is the least restrictive means of furthering its interest. Claims that a law substantially burdens someone's exercise of religion will often be difficult to contest. . . . Requiring a State to demonstrate a compelling interest and show that it has adopted the least restrictive means of achieving that interest is the most demanding test known to constitutional law. If " 'compelling interest' really means what it says . . . many laws will not meet the test. . . . [The test] would open the prospect of constitutionally required religious exemptions from civic obligations of almost every conceivable kind." . . . Laws valid under *Smith* would fall under RFRA without regard to whether they had the object of stifling or punishing free exercise. We make these observations not to reargue the position of the majority in *Smith* but to illustrate the substantive alteration of its holding attempted by RFRA. Even assuming RFRA would be interpreted in effect to mandate some lesser test, say, one equivalent to intermediate scrutiny, the statute nevertheless would require searching judicial scrutiny of state law with the attendant likelihood of invalidation. This is a considerable congressional intrusion into the States' traditional prerogatives and general authority to regulate for the health and welfare of their citizens. . . .

Our national experience teaches that the Constitution is preserved best when each part of the government respects both the Constitution and the proper actions and determinations of the other branches. When the Court has interpreted the Constitution, it has acted within the province of the Judicial Branch, which embraces the duty to say what the law is. *Marbury v. Madison* [*supra* § 1.01]. When the political branches of the Government act against the background of a judicial interpretation of the Constitution already issued, it must be understood that in later cases and controversies the Court will treat its precedents with the respect due them under settled principles, including *stare decisis*, and contrary expectations must be disappointed. RFRA was designed to control cases and controversies, such as the one before us; but as the provisions of the federal statute here invoked are beyond congressional authority, it is this Court's precedent, not RFRA, which must control.

It is for Congress in the first instance to "determin[e] whether and what legislation is needed to secure the guarantees of the Fourteenth Amendment," and its conclusions are entitled to much deference. . . . Congress' discretion is not unlimited, however, and the courts retain the power, as they have since *Marbury v. Madison*, to determine if Congress has exceeded its authority under the Constitution. Broad as the power of Congress is under the Enforcement Clause of the Fourteenth Amendment, RFRA contradicts vital principles necessary to maintain separation of powers and the federal balance. The judgment of the Court of Appeals sustaining the Act's constitutionality is reversed.

It is so ordered.

[JUSTICES STEVENS and SCALIA concurred, and JUSTICES O'CONNOR, SOUTER, and BREYER dissented.]

NOTES

(1) Does *Boerne* adopt the reasoning of Justice Harlan's dissent in *Katzenbach v. Morgan*?

(2) Near the beginning of her dissent, Justice O'Connor wrote:

I agree with much of the reasoning set forth in Part III-A of the Court's opinion. Indeed, if I agreed with the Court's standard in *Smith*, I would join the opinion. As the Court's careful and thorough historical analysis shows, Congress lacks the "power to decree the substance of the Fourteenth Amendment's restrictions on the States." Rather, its power under § 5 of the Fourteenth Amendment extends only to enforcing the Amendment's provisions. In short, Congress lacks the ability independently to define or expand the scope of constitutional rights by statute. Accordingly, whether Congress has exceeded its § 5 powers turns on whether there is a "congruence and proportionality between the injury to be prevented or remedied and the means adopted to that end."

Boerne, 521 U.S. at 545 (O'Connor, J., dissenting).

(3) *Boerne* has engendered much controversy. Steven A. Engel "argues that the *Boerne* Court, like many modern constitutional scholars, went astray in focusing upon the judicial branch as the ultimate interpreter of the Fourteenth Amendment. While the Court may retain the last word, the judicial reading obscures the Framers' conviction that it would be Congress, and not the courts, that would be the first reader, and primary enforcer, of the Fourteenth Amendment. The amendment speaks in open generalities not because the Framers naively believed the judiciary might ascertain a definite meaning behind those words, but because they were interested in granting to the national government broad discretion to protect civil liberties against state infringement. Rather than seeking to codify a definite set of rights, the Framers undertook to grant future Congresses the discretion to protect civil liberties, as they might understand them, against state infringement." Steven A. Engel, *The McCulloch Theory of the Fourteenth Amendment:* City of Boerne v. Flores *and the Original Understanding of Section 5*, 109 YALE L.J. 115, 117 (1999).

Simarly, Judge Michael W. McConnell writes:

In *Boerne*, the Court erred in assuming that congressional interpretation of the Fourteenth Amendment is illegitimate. The historical record shows that the framers of the Amendment expected Congress, not the Court, to be the primary agent of its enforcement, and that Congress would not necessarily consider itself bound by Court precedents in executing that function. That does not mean that the Court is required to follow Congress's interpretation, any more than Congress is required to follow the Court's. But it does mean that the Court should give respectful attention — and probably the presumption of constitutionality — to the interpretive judgments of Congress. For the Court simply to assume the correctness of its own prior interpretations, and fail to take the contrary opinion of Congress into consideration, was unjustifiable.

Michael W. McConnell, *Institutions and Interpretation: A Critique of* City of Boerne v. Flores, 111 HARV. L. REV. 153, 194-95 (1997).

(4) Section 5 of the Fourteenth Amendment offers Congress certain advantages over some other sources of power. Congress can abrogate the state's Eleventh Amendment immunity under § 5 (unlike under the Commerce Clause) and it can regulate without opening the federal purse (unlike the Spending Clause) or subjecting the public to tax. *See, e.g.*, Ronald D. Rotunda, *The Powers of Congress Under Section 5 of the Fourteenth Amendment After* City of Boerne v. Flores, 32 IND. L. REV. 163, 169-70 (1998).

(5) In *Seminole Tribe of Florida v. Florida*, 517 U.S. 44 (1996), the Court limited Congress' ability to abrogate state sovereign immunity in federal court to situations in which Congress acted pursuant to § 5 of the Fourteenth Amendment. In a series of later cases, the Court limited Congress' ability to abrogate state sovereign immunity under § 5 of the Fourteenth Amendment. *See* § 3.04, Note 6 after *Alden*.

(6) In *Kimel v. Florida Board of Regents*, 528 U.S. 62 (2000), the Court held that although Congress clearly intended to abrogate the states' sovereign immunity in the Age Discrimination in Employment Act of 1967 (ADEA), it lacked that authority under § 5 because ADEA failed the "congruence and proportionality" test.

Justice O'Connor wrote, in part:

> Applying the same "congruence and proportionality" test in these cases, we conclude that the ADEA is not "appropriate legislation" under § 5 of the Fourteenth Amendment. Initially, the substantive requirements the ADEA imposes on state and local governments are disproportionate to any unconstitutional conduct that conceivably could be targeted by the Act. . . .
>
> States may discriminate on the basis of age without offending the Fourteenth Amendment if the age classification in question is rationally related to a legitimate state interest. . . . Judged against the backdrop of [this Court's] equal protection jurisprudence, it is clear that the ADEA is "so out of proportion to a supposed remedial or preventive object that it cannot be understood as responsive to, or designed to prevent, unconstitutional behavior." . . .
>
> That the ADEA prohibits very little conduct likely to be held unconstitutional, while significant, does not alone provide the answer to the § 5 inquiry. Difficult and intractable problems often require powerful remedies, and we have never held that § 5 precludes Congress from enacting reasonably prophylactic legislation. Our task is to determine whether the ADEA is in fact just such an appropriate remedy or, instead, merely an attempt to substantively redefine the States' legal obligations with respect to age discrimination. One means by which we have made such a determination in the past is by examining the legislative record containing the reasons for Congress' action. . . .
>
> Our examination of the ADEA's legislative record confirms that Congress' 1974 extension of the Act to the States was an unwarranted response to a perhaps inconsequential problem. Congress never identified any pattern of age discrimination by the States, much less any discrimination whatsoever that rose to the level of constitutional violation. The evidence compiled by petitioners to demonstrate such attention by Congress to age discrimination by the States falls well short of the mark. That evidence consists almost entirely of isolated sentences clipped from floor debates and legislative reports. . . .
>
> A review of the ADEA's legislative record as a whole, then, reveals that Congress had virtually no reason to believe that state and local governments were unconstitutionally discriminating against their employees on the basis of age. Although the lack of support is not determinative of the § 5 inquiry-

. . . Congress' failure to uncover any significant pattern of unconstitutional discrimination here confirms that Congress had no reason to believe that broad prophylactic legislation was necessary in this field. In light of the indiscriminate scope of the Act's substantive requirements, and the lack of evidence of widespread and unconstitutional age discrimination by the States, we hold that the ADEA is not a valid exercise of Congress' power under § 5 of the Fourteenth Amendment. The ADEA's purported abrogation of the States' sovereign immunity is accordingly invalid.

Kimel, 528 U.S. at 82-92.

(7) *Board of Trustees of the University of Alabama v. Garrett*, 531 U.S. 356 (2001). The Court further narrowed the utility of § 5 to subject states to suits for money damages in *Garrett*. Alabama state employees ought money damages for the state's alleged failure to comply with Title I of the Americans with Disabilities Act of 1990 (ADA) specifically by failing to accommodate their disabilities.

In a 5-4 decision, the Court held that Congress lacked power to subject states to suits for monetary relief under ADA because it had failed to demonstrate a pattern of discrimination against the disabled by the states and that Congress' remedy was "congruent and proportional to the targeted violation."

Although Congress had found that society had discriminated against the disabled, the Court concluded that relatively few of the documented incidents involved the states. Thus, Congress had failed to support its legislation with adequate fact-finding.

Justice Kennedy wrote, for himself and Justice O'Connor, in a concurrence representing the views of two of the five justices in the majority, "The predicate for money damages against an unconsenting State in suits brought by private persons must be a federal statute enacted upon the documentation of patterns of constitutional violations committed by the State in its official capacity. That predicate, for reasons discussed here and in the decision of the Court, has not been established."

In dissent, Justice Breyer argued that " Congress reasonably could have concluded that the remedy before [the Court] constitutes an 'appropriate' way to enforce this basic equal protection requirement." The majority's scrutiny of Congress' fact finding was unprecedented and unwarranted. Congress was better situated to make the sort of fact finding involved and the record assembled supported its conclusions. "The Court's harsh review of Congress' use of its § 5 power is reminiscent of the similar (now-discredited) limitation that it once imposed upon Congress' Commerce Clause power," wrote Justice Breyer. The Court had usurped a power assigned Congress and had deprived § 5 of force.

(8) In *Nevada Department of Human Resources v. Hibbs*, 538 U.S. 721 (2003), the Court held that Congress properly abrogated the states' sovereign immunity in the Family and Medical Leave Act (FMLA) which allowed eligible employees to take up to 12 work weeks of unpaid leave for various reasons, including a serious family illness. For a 6-3 majority, Chief Justice Rehnquist wrote:

Two provisions of the Fourteenth Amendment are relevant here: Section 5 grants Congress the power "to enforce" the substantive guarantees of § 1 — among them, equal protection of the laws — by enacting "appropriate legislation. Congress may, in the exercise of its § 5 power, do more than simply proscribe conduct that we have held unconstitutional. " 'Congress' power "to enforce" the Amendment includes the authority both to remedy and to deter violation of rights guaranteed thereunder by prohibiting a somewhat broader swath of conduct, including that which is not itself forbidden by the Amendment's text.' " . . . In other words, Congress may enact so-called prophylactic legislation that proscribes facially constitutional conduct, in order to prevent and deter unconstitutional conduct.

City of Boerne also confirmed, however, that it falls to this Court, not Congress, to define the substance of constitutional guarantees. . . . "The ultimate interpretation and determination of the Fourteenth Amendment's substantive meaning remains the province of the Judicial Branch. . . . Section 5 legislation reaching beyond the scope of § 1's actual guarantees must be an appropriate remedy for identified constitutional violations, not "an attempt to substantively redefine the States' legal obligations.". . . We distinguish appropriate prophylactic legislation from "substantive redefinition of the Fourteenth Amendment right at issue,". . .by applying the test set forth in *City of Boerne*: Valid § 5 legislation must exhibit "congruence and proportionality between the injury to be prevented or remedied and the means adopted to that end.". . .

FMLA, the Chief Justice pointed out, "aims to protect the right to be free from gender-based discrimination in the workplace." Gender classifications receive "heightened scrutiny." Congress had evidence that "states continue to rely on invalid gender stereotypes in the employment context" and had applied state programs in a discriminatory fashion. Because gender-based classifications are subject to heightened judicial review Congress could more easily find "a pattern of state constitutional violations" than it could when assessing classifications subject to rational basis review.

The author of *Boerne*, Justice Kennedy, dissented (joined by Justices Scalia and Thomas). He wrote:

The Court is unable to show that States have engaged in a pattern of unlawful conduct which warrants the remedy of opening state treasuries to private suits. The inability to adduce evidence of alleged discrimination, coupled with the inescapable fact that the federal scheme is not a remedy but a benefit program, demonstrates the lack of the requisite link between any problem Congress has identified and the program it mandated. . . .

Justice Kennedy insisted that the "evidence to substantiate" a charge of widespread gender discrimination regarding family leave "must be far more specific . . . than a simple recitation of a general history of employment discrimination against women."

Justice Scalia wrote a separate dissent in which he argued that the relevant question was not whether states had discriminated but whether Nevada had.

(9) The Court followed its decision in *Hibbs* the next term by holding in *Tennessee v. Lane*, 541 U.S. 509 (2004), that Congress had properly abrogated the States' Eleventh Amendment immunity under Title II of the Americans with Disabilities Act of 1990 (ADA), which precluded denying a "qualified individual with a disability" "benefits of the services, programs or activities of a public entity." 42 U.S.C. § 12132. The question resolved in *Lane* had been left open in *Garrett*, 531 U.S. at 360 n.1. *Lane* arose when two paraplegics complained that they were effectively denied access to Tennessee's state courthouses.

Congress had clearly stated its intent to abrogate the States' immunity ("A State shall not be immune under the eleventh amendment to the Constitution of the United States from an action in Federal or State court of competent jurisdiction for a violation of this chapter." 42 U.S.C. § 12202). Writing for a five justice majority, Justice Stevens concluded that Title II was the sort of "prophylactic legislation" that was within the § 5 power because it proscribed practices which were "discriminatory in effect, if not in intent, to carry out the basic objectives of the Equal Protection Clause." *Lane*, 541 U.S. at 520. Title II sought to protect a range of basic constitutional rights including, but not limited to, those involving access to the courts which the Due Process Clause of the

Fourteenth Amendment protected. Congressional proceedings had disclosed that many individuals were denied access to courts due to disabilities. The basic rights at issue called for "a standard of judicial review at least as searching, and in some cases more searching, than the standard that applies to sex-based classifications" at issue in *Hibbs*. *Id.* at 529. The Court need not consider whether Title II was "appropriately tailored to serve its objectives" in all of its potential applications (e.g., seating at state-owned hockey arenas), but need ask only whether it met the congruence and proportionality test with respect to the issue in question relating to access to the judicial system. *Id.* at 529-34. To that application, Title II "unquestionably is valid" § 5 legislation. *Id.* at 531. The "considerable evidence of the shortcomings of previous legislative responses" justified Congress in concluding that additional prophylactic legislation was needed and that when adopted, was a limited remedy appropriate in its scope. *Id.*

In dissent, Chief Justice Rehnquist (joined by Justices Kennedy and Thomas) argued that the Court had misapplied the congruence and proportionality test by considering evidence unrelated to access to courts issues and which involved "discrimination by nonstate governments." *Id.* at 542. Moreover, the dissent criticized the majority's "as applied" approach, arguing instead that the Court should have "measured the full breadth of the statute . . . that Congress enacted against the scope of the constitutional right it purported to enforce." *Id.* at 551-52.

Justice Scalia also dissented, but in doing so suggested a new doctrinal approach. He had joined the congruence and proportionality test in the past with misgivings. He now "yield[ed] to the lessons of experience" and concluded that it, "like all such flabby tests, is a standing invitation to judicial arbitrariness and policy-driven decisionmaking." *Id.* at 557-58. Moreover, the test made the Court Congress' "taskmaster" and required it to "regularly check Congress's homework." *Id.* at 558. The Court should not perform judicial review of congressional acts based only on a test "that has no demonstrable basis in the text of the Constitution and cannot objectively be shown to have been met or failed." *Id.* Justice Scalia would require that § 5 legislation "enforce, by appropriate legislation" the provisions of the Fourteenth Amendment; it should not serve as the basis for prophylactic measures "prohibiting primary conduct that is itself not forbidden by the Fourteenth Amendment." *Id.* at 560. Justice Scalia distinguished the cases authorizing a broader approach (except *Hibbs*) as involving racial discrimination which, he pointed out, was the Fourteenth Amendment's principal target. *Id.* at 561.

§ 6.06   THIRTEENTH AND FIFTEENTH AMENDMENTS

SOUTH CAROLINA v. KATZENBACH
383 U.S. 301, 86 S. Ct. 803, 15 L. Ed. 2d 769 (1966)

CHIEF JUSTICE WARREN delivered the opinion of the Court.

By leave of the Court, . . . South Carolina has filed a bill of complaint seeking a declaration that selected provisions of the Voting Rights Act of 1965 violate the Federal Constitution, and asking for an injunction against enforcement of these provisions by the Attorney General. Original jurisdiction is founded on the presence of a controversy between a State and a citizen of another State under Art. III, § 2, of the Constitution. . . .

The Voting Rights Act was designed by Congress to banish the blight of racial discrimination in voting, which has infected the electoral process in parts of our country for nearly a century. The Act creates stringent new remedies for voting discrimination where it persists on a pervasive scale, and in addition the statute strengthens existing remedies for pockets of voting discrimination elsewhere in the country. Congress assumed the power to prescribe these remedies from § 2 of the Fifteenth Amendment, which authorizes the National Legislature to effectuate by "appropriate" measures the constitutional prohibition against racial discrimination in voting. We hold that the sections of the Act which are properly before us are an appropriate means for carrying out Congress' constitutional responsibilities and are consonant with all other provisions of the Constitution. We therefore deny South Carolina's request that enforcement of these sections of the Act be enjoined. . . .

II

The Voting Rights Act of 1965 reflects Congress' firm intention to rid the country of racial discrimination in voting. The heart of the Act is a complex scheme of stringent remedies aimed at areas where voting discrimination has been most flagrant. . . . [The Act applied to any state or political subdivision which, as of November 1, 1964, maintained a literacy or other test or device as a prerequisite to voting and in which less than 50% were registered or had voted in November, 1964. South Carolina was found subject to the Act in 1965. As such, it was precluded from enforcing its literacy test and was subject to scrutiny by federal voting examiners.]

III

These provisions of the Voting Rights Act of 1965 are challenged on the fundamental ground that they exceed the powers of Congress and encroach on an area reserved to the States by the Constitution. . . .

The objections to the Act which are raised under these provisions may therefore be considered as additional aspects of the basic question presented by the case: Has Congress exercised its powers under the Fifteenth Amendment in an appropriate manner with relation to the States?

The ground rules for resolving this question are clear. The language and purpose of the Fifteenth Amendment, the prior decisions construing its several provisions, and the general doctrines of constitutional interpretation, all point to one fundamental principle. As against the reserved powers of the States, Congress may use any rational means to effectuate the constitutional prohibition of racial discrimination in voting. . . . We turn now to a more detailed description of the standards which govern our review of the Act.

Section 1 of the Fifteenth Amendment declares that "[t]he right of citizens of the United States to vote shall not be denied or abridged by the United States or by any State on account of race, color, or previous condition of servitude." This declaration has always been treated as self-executing and has repeatedly been construed, without further legislative specification, to invalidate state voting qualifications or procedures which are discriminatory on their face or in practice. . . .

South Carolina contends that [there] are precedents only for the authority of the judiciary to strike down state statutes and procedures — that to allow an exercise of this authority by Congress would be to rob the courts of their rightful constitutional role. On the contrary, § 2 of the Fifteenth Amendment expressly declares that "Congress shall have power to enforce this article by appropriate legislation." By adding this authorization, the Framers indicated that Congress was to be chiefly responsible for implementing the rights created in § 1. "It is the power of Congress which has been enlarged. Congress is authorized to enforce the prohibitions by appropriate legislation. Some legislation is contemplated to make the [Civil War] amendments fully effective." *Ex parte Virginia*. . . . Accordingly, in addition to the courts, Congress has full remedial powers to effectuate the constitutional prohibition against racial discrimination in voting. . . .

The basic test to be applied in a case involving § 2 of the Fifteenth Amendment is the same as in all cases concerning the express powers of Congress with relation to the reserved powers of the States. Chief Justice Marshall laid down the classic formulation, 50 years before the Fifteenth Amendment was ratified:

> Let the end be legitimate, let it be within the scope of the constitution, and all means which are appropriate, which are plainly adapted to that end, which are not prohibited, but consist with the letter and spirit of the constitution, are constitutional. . . .

We therefore reject South Carolina's argument that Congress may appropriately do no more than to forbid violations of the Fifteenth Amendment in general terms — that the task of fashioning specific remedies or of applying them to particular localities must necessarily be left entirely to the courts. Congress is not circumscribed by any such artificial rules under § 2 of the Fifteenth Amendment. In the oft-repeated words of Chief Justice Marshall, referring to another specific legislative authorization in the Constitution, "This power, like all others vested in Congress is complete in itself, may be exercised to its utmost extent, and acknowledges no limitations, other than are prescribed in the constitution." *Gibbons v. Ogden*, [*supra* § 2.02]. . . .

IV

Congress exercised its authority under the Fifteenth Amendment in an inventive manner when it enacted the Voting Rights Act of 1965. First: The measure prescribes remedies for voting discrimination which go into effect without any need for prior adjudication. This was clearly a legitimate response to the problem, for which there is ample precedent under other constitutional provisions. . . . Congress has found that case-by-case litigation was inadequate to combat widespread and persistent discrimination in voting, because of the inordinate amount of time and energy required to overcome the obstructionist tactics invariably encountered in these lawsuits. After enduring nearly a century of systematic resistance to the Fifteenth Amendment, Congress might well decide to shift the advantage of time and inertia from the perpetrators of the evil to its victims. The question remains, of course, whether the specific remedies prescribed in the Act were an appropriate means of combating the evil, and to this question we shall presently address ourselves.

Second: The Act intentionally confines these remedies to a small number of States and political subdivisions which in most instances were familiar to Congress by name. This, too, was a permissible method of dealing with the problem. Congress had learned that substantial voting discrimination presently occurs in certain sections of the country, and it knew no way of accurately forecasting whether the evil might spread elsewhere in the future. In acceptable legislative fashion, Congress chose to limit its attention to the geographic areas where immediate action seemed necessary. . . .

We now consider the related question of whether the specific States and political subdivisions within § 4(b) of the Act were an appropriate target for the new remedies. South Carolina contends that the coverage formula is awkwardly designed in a number of respects and that it disregards various local conditions which have nothing to do with racial discrimination. These arguments, however, are largely beside the point. Congress began work with reliable evidence of actual voting discrimination in a great majority of the States and political subdivisions affected by the new remedies of the Act. The formula eventually evolved to describe these areas was relevant to the problem of voting discrimination, and Congress was therefore entitled to infer a significant danger of the evil in the few remaining States and political subdivisions covered by § 4(b) of the Act. No more was required to justify the application to these areas of Congress' express powers under the Fifteenth Amendment. . . .

We now arrive at consideration of the specific remedies prescribed by the Act for areas included within the coverage formula. . . . The record shows that in most of the States covered by the Act, including South Carolina, various tests and devices have been instituted with the purpose of disenfranchising Negroes, have been framed in such a way as to facilitate this aim, and have been administered in a discriminatory fashion for many years. . . .

The Act suspends literacy tests and similar devices for a period of five years from the last occurrence of substantial voting discrimination. This was a legitimate response to the problem, for which there is ample precedent in Fifteenth Amendment cases. . . .

The Act authorizes the appointment of federal examiners to list qualified applicants who are thereafter entitled to vote, subject to an expeditious challenge procedure. This was clearly an appropriate response to the problem. . . . In many of the political subdivisions covered by § 4(b) of the Act, voting officials have persistently employed a variety of procedural tactics to deny Negroes the franchise, often in direct defiance or evasion of federal court decrees. Congress realized that merely to suspend voting rules which have been misused or are subject to misuse might leave this localized evil undisturbed. As for the briskness of the challenge procedure, Congress knew that in some of the areas affected, challenges had been persistently employed to harass registered Negroes. It chose to forestall this abuse, at the same time providing alternative ways for removing persons listed through error or fraud. . . .

In recognition of the fact that there were political subdivisions covered by § 4(b) of the Act in which the appointment of federal examiners might be unnecessary, Congress assigned the Attorney General the task of determining the localities to which examiners should be sent. There is no warrant for the claim . . . that the Attorney General is free to use this power in an arbitrary fashion, without regard to the purposes of the Act. Section 6(b) sets adequate standards to guide the exercise of his discretion, by directing him to calculate the registration ratio of non-whites to whites, and to weigh evidence of good faith efforts to avoid possible voting discrimination. At the same time, the special termination procedures of § 13(a) provide indirect judicial review for the political subdivisions affected, assuring the withdrawal of federal examiners from areas where they are clearly not needed. . . .

After enduring nearly a century of widespread resistance to the Fifteenth Amendment, Congress has marshaled an array of potent weapons against the evil, with authority in the Attorney General to employ them effectively. . . . We here hold that the portions of the Voting Rights Act properly before us are a valid means for carrying out the commands of the Fifteenth Amendment. Hopefully, millions of non-white Americans will now be able to participate for the first time on an equal basis in the government under which they live. We may finally look forward to the day when truly "[t]he right of citizens of the United States to vote shall not be denied or abridged by the United States or by any State on account of race, color, or previous condition of servitude."

The bill of complaint is dismissed.

[JUSTICE BLACK dissented in part].

NOTES

(1) The Fifteenth Amendment contains a self-executing provision which the courts enforce directly and an Enforcement Clause empowering Congressional action in the area of voting rights. Congress' enforcement power has been important. Judicial action alone could not eliminate voting discrimination.

(2) The Voting Rights Act of 1965, the key Congressional statute protecting voting rights, was upheld in *South Carolina v. Katzenbach*. The Enforcement Clause

resembled the Necessary and Proper Clause of Article I, § 8, in its sweep.

(3) The 1965 Voting Rights Act by its terms, was to continue for ten years. Its provisions were, however, extended for another seven years in 1975, 89 Stat. 400 (1975), and for another twenty-five years in 1982, 96 Stat. 131 (1982).

(4) *City of Rome v. United States*, 446 U.S. 156 (1980), addressed the contention that since § 1 of the Fifteenth Amendment prohibits only purposeful racial discrimination in voting, Congress, in enforcing that provision pursuant to § 2, could not prohibit voting practices lacking discriminatory intent even if they were discriminatory in effect. The Court held that,

> even if § 1 of the Amendment prohibits only purposeful discrimination, the prior decisions of this Court foreclose any argument that Congress may not, pursuant to § 2, outlaw voting practices that discriminatory in effect. . . . It is clear, then, that under § 2 of the Fifteenth Amendment Congress may prohibit practices that in and of themselves do not violate § 1 of the Amendment, so long as the prohibitions attacking racial discrimination in voting are "appropriate." . . . In the present case, we hold that the Act's ban on electoral changes that are discriminatory in effect is an appropriate method of promoting the purposes of the Fifteenth Amendment, even if it is assumed that § 1 of the Amendment prohibits only intentional discrimination in voting. Congress could rationally have concluded that, because electoral changes by jurisdictions with a demonstrable history of intentional racial discrimination in voting create the risk of purposeful discrimination, it was proper to prohibit changes that have a discriminatory impact.

Id. at 173, 177.

JONES v. ALFRED H. MAYER CO.
392 U.S. 409, 88 S. Ct. 2186. 20 L. Ed.2d 1189 (1968)

JUSTICE STEWART delivered the opinion of the Court.

In this case we are called upon to determine the scope and constitutionality of an Act of Congress, 42 U.S.C. § 1982, which provides that:

> All citizens of the United States shall have the same right, in every State and Territory, as is enjoyed by white citizens thereof to inherit, purchase, lease, sell, hold, and convey real and personal property.

On September 2, 1965, the petitioners filed a complaint in the District Court for the Eastern District of Missouri, alleging that the respondents had refused to sell them a home in the Paddock Woods community of St. Louis County for the sole reason that petitioner Joseph Lee Jones is a Negro. Relying in part upon § 1982, the petitioners sought injunctive and other relief. The District Court sustained the respondents' motion to dismiss the complaint, and the Court of Appeals for the Eighth Circuit affirmed, concluding that § 1982 applies only to state action and does not reach private refusals to sell. We granted certiorari to consider the questions thus presented. For the reasons that follow, we reverse the judgment of the Court of Appeals. We hold that § 1982 bars all racial discrimination, private as well as public, in the sale or rental of property, and that the statute, thus construed, is a valid exercise of the power of Congress to enforce the Thirteenth Amendment. . . .

We begin with the language of the statute itself. In plain and unambiguous terms, § 1982 grants to all citizens, without regard to race or color, "the same right" to purchase and lease property "as is enjoyed by white citizens." As the Court of Appeals in this case evidently recognized, that right can be impaired as effectively by "those who place property on the market" as by the State itself. For, even if the State and its agents lend no support to those who wish to exclude persons from their communities on racial grounds, the fact remains that, whenever property "is placed on the market for whites only, whites have a right denied to Negroes." So long as a Negro citizen who wants to buy or rent a home can be turned away simply because he is not white, he cannot be said to enjoy "the *same* right . . . as is enjoyed by white citizens . . . to . . . purchase [and] lease . . . real and personal property." 42 U.S.C. § 1982. (Emphasis added.)

On its face, therefore, § 1982 appears to prohibit all discrimination against Negroes in the sale or rental of property — discrimination by private owners as well as discrimination by public authorities. Indeed, even the respondents seem to concede that, if § 1982 "means what it says" — to use the words of the respondents' brief — then it must encompass every racially motivated refusal to sell or rent and cannot be confined to officially sanctioned segregation in housing. Stressing what they consider to be the revolutionary implications of so literal a reading of § 1982, the respondents argue that Congress cannot possibly have intended any such result. Our examination of the relevant history, however, persuades us that Congress meant exactly what it said.

In its original form, 42 U.S.C. § 1982 was part of § 1 of the Civil Rights Act of 1866. . . . The crucial language for our purposes was that which guaranteed all citizens "the same right, in every State and Territory in the United States, . . . to inherit, purchase, lease, sell, hold, and convey real and personal property . . . as is enjoyed by white citizens. . . . " To the Congress that passed the Civil Rights Act of 1866, it was clear that the right to do these things might be infringed not only by "State or local law" but also by "custom, or prejudice." Thus, when Congress provided in § 1 of the Civil Rights Act that the right to purchase and lease property was to be enjoyed equally throughout the United States by Negro and white citizens alike, it plainly meant to secure that right against interference from any source whatever, whether governmental or private. . . .

In light of the concerns that led Congress to adopt it and the contents of the debates that preceded its passage, it is clear that the Act was designed to do just what its terms suggest: to prohibit all racial discrimination, whether or not under color of law, with respect to the rights enumerated therein — including the right to purchase or lease property. . . .

The remaining question is whether Congress has power under the Constitution to do what § 1982 purports to do: to prohibit all racial discrimination, private and public, in the sale and rental of property. Our starting point is the Thirteenth Amendment, for it was pursuant to that constitutional provision that Congress originally enacted what is now § 1982. The Amendment consists of two parts. Section 1 states:

> Neither slavery nor involuntary servitude, except as a punishment for crime whereby the party shall have been duly convicted, shall exist within the United States, or any place subject to their jurisdiction.

Section 2 provides:

> Congress shall have power to enforce this article by appropriate legislation.

As its text reveals, the Thirteenth Amendment "is not a mere prohibition of state laws establishing or upholding slavery, but an absolute declaration that slavery or involuntary servitude shall not exist in any part of the United States." *Civil Rights Cases* [*supra* § 6.03, Note (2), after *Shelley*]. It has never been doubted, therefore, "that the power vested in Congress to enforce the article by appropriate legislation," includes the power to enact laws "direct and primary, operating upon the acts of individuals, whether sanctioned by state legislation or not.". . .

Thus, the fact that § 1982 operates upon the unofficial acts of private individuals, whether or not sanctioned by state law, presents no constitutional problem. If Congress has power under the Thirteenth Amendment to eradicate conditions that prevent Negroes from buying and renting property because of their race or color, then no federal statute calculated to achieve that objective can be thought to exceed the constitutional power of Congress simply because it reaches beyond state action to regulate the conduct of private individuals. The constitutional question in this case, therefore, comes to this: Does the authority of Congress to enforce the Thirteenth Amendment "by appropriate legislation" include the power to eliminate all racial barriers to the acquisition of real and personal property? We think the answer to that question is plainly yes.

"By its own unaided force and effect," the Thirteenth Amendment "abolished slavery, and established universal freedom." *Civil Rights Cases.* . . . Whether or not the Amendment *itself* did any more than that — a question not involved in this case — it is at least clear that the Enabling Clause of that Amendment empowered Congress to do much more. For that clause clothed "Congress with power to pass *all laws necessary and proper for abolishing all badges and incidents of slavery in the United States.*" *Id.* (Emphasis added.)

Those who opposed passage of the Civil Rights Act of 1866 argued in effect that the Thirteenth Amendment merely authorized Congress to dissolve the legal bond by which the Negro slave was held to his master. Yet many had earlier opposed the Thirteenth Amendment on the very ground that it would give Congress virtually unlimited power to enact laws for the protection of Negroes in every state. And the majority leaders in Congress — who were, after all, the authors of the Thirteenth Amendment — had no doubt that its Enabling Clause contemplated the sort of positive legislation that was embodied in the 1866 Civil Rights Act. . . .

. . . Surely Congress has the power under the Thirteenth Amendment rationally to determine what are the badges and the incidents of slavery, and the authority to translate that determination into effective legislation. Nor can we say that the determination Congress has made is an irrational one. For this Court recognized long ago that, whatever else they may have encompassed, the badges and incidents of slavery — its "burdens and disabilities" — included restraints upon "those fundamental rights which are the essence of civil freedom, namely, the same right . . . to inherit, purchase, lease, sell and convey property, as is enjoyed by white citizens." *Civil Rights Cases.* . . . Just as the Black Codes, enacted after the Civil War to restrict the free exercise of those rights, were substitutes for the slave system, so the exclusion of Negroes from white communities became a substitute for the Black Codes. And when racial discrimination herds men into ghettos and makes their ability to buy property turn on the color of their skin, then it too is a relic of slavery.

Negro citizens, North and South, who saw in the Thirteenth Amendment a promise of freedom — freedom to "go and come at pleasure" and to "buy and sell when they please" — would be left with "a mere paper guarantee" if Congress were powerless to assure that a dollar in the hands of a Negro will purchase the same thing as a dollar in the hands of a white man. At the very least, the freedom that Congress is empowered to secure under the Thirteenth Amendment includes the freedom to buy whatever a white man can buy, the right to live wherever a white man can live. If Congress cannot say that being a free man means at least this much, then the Thirteenth Amendment made a promise the Nation cannot keep. . . .

. . . The judgment is reversed.

[JUSTICES HARLAN and WHITE dissented.]

NOTE

Jones v. Alfred H. Mayer Co. shows that the Thirteenth Amendment not only outlaws slavery and forced labor, but also gives Congress power to enforce its ban by legislating against all incidents of slavery. The Supreme Court, in effect, adopts the view of the first Justice Harlan in his dissent in the *1883 Civil Rights Cases*, 109 U.S. 3, 35-6:

> That there are burdens and disabilities which constitute badges of slavery and servitude, and that the express power delegated to congress to enforce, by appropriate legislation, the thirteenth amendment, may be exerted by legislation of a direct and primary character, for the eradication, not simply of the institution, but of its badges and incidents, are propositions which ought to be deemed indisputable. . . . [S]lavery, as the court has repeatedly declared, was the moving or principal cause of the adoption of that amendment, and since that institution rested wholly upon the inferiority, as a race, of those held in bondage, their freedom necessarily involved immunity from, and protection against, all discrimination against them, because of their race, in respect of such civil rights as belong to freemen of other races. Congress, therefore, under its express power to enforce that amendment, by appropriate legislation, may enact laws to protect that people against the deprivation, *on account of their race*, of any civil rights enjoyed by other freemen in the same state. (Emphasis in original.)

RUNYON v. McCRARY
427 U.S. 160, 96 S. Ct. 2586, 49 L. Ed. 2d 415 (1976)

JUSTICE STEWART delivered the opinion of the Court.

The principal issue presented by these consolidated cases is whether a federal law, namely, 42 U.S.C. § 1981, prohibits private schools from excluding qualified children solely because they are Negroes.

I

The respondents . . . are Negro children. By their parents, they filed a class action against the petitioners . . . , who are the proprietors of Bobbe's Private School in Arlington, Va. Their complaint alleged that they had been prevented from attending the school because of the petitioners' policy of denying admission to Negroes, in violation of 42 U.S.C. § 1981[1]. . . . They sought declaratory and injunctive relief and damages. . . .

The suits were consolidated for trial. The findings of the District Court, which were left undisturbed by the Court of Appeals, were as follows. Bobbe's School opened in 1958 and grew from an initial enrollment of five students to 200 in 1972. A day camp was begun in 1967 and has averaged 100 children per year. . . .

---

[1] [Court's footnote 1] 42 U.S.C. § 1981 provides:

> All persons within the jurisdiction of the United States shall have the same right in every State and Territory to make and enforce contracts, to sue, be parties, give evidence, and to the full and equal benefit of all laws and proceedings for the security of persons and property as is enjoyed by white citizens, and shall be subject to like punishment, pains, penalties, taxes, licenses, and exactions of every kind, and to no other.

. . . In August 1972, Mrs. McCrary telephoned Bobbe's School in response to an advertisement in the telephone book. She inquired about nursery school facilities for her son, Michael. She also asked if the School was integrated. The answer was no.

Upon these facts, the District Court found. . . that Bobbe's School had denied admission on racial grounds. The Court held that 42 U.S.C. § 1981 makes illegal the school's racially discriminatory admissions policies. It therefore enjoined . . . Bobbe's School . . . from discriminating against applicants for admission on the basis of race. . . .

The Court of Appeals for the Fourth Circuit, sitting en banc, affirmed. . . . On the basic issue of law, the Court agreed that 42 U.S.C. § 1981 is a "limitation upon private discrimination, and its enforcement in the context of this case is not a deprivation of any right of free association or of privacy of the defendants, of the intervenor, or their pupils or patrons." . . . The relationship the parents had sought to enter into with the schools was in the court's view undeniably contractual in nature, within the meaning of § 1981, and the court rejected the schools' claim that § 1981 confers no right of action unless the contractual relationship denied to Negroes is available to all whites. Finally, the appellate court rejected the schools' contention that their racially discriminatory policies are protected by any constitutional right of privacy. . . .

II

It is worth noting at the outset some of the questions that these cases do not present. They do not present any question of the right of a private social organization to limit its membership on racial or any other grounds. They do not present any question of the right of a private school to limit its student body to boys, girls, or to adherents of a particular religious faith, since 42 U.S.C. § 1981 is in no way addressed to such categories of selectivity. They do not even present the application of § 1981 to private sectarian schools that practice *racial* exclusion on religious grounds. Rather, these cases present only two basic questions: whether § 1981 prohibits private, commercially operated, non-sectarian schools from denying admission to prospective students because they are Negroes, and, if so, whether that federal law is constitutional as so applied.

A. Applicability of § 1981

It is now well established that § 1 of the Civil Rights Act of 1866, 42 U.S.C. § 1981, prohibits racial discrimination in the making and enforcement of private contracts. . . .

As the Court indicated in *Jones*, . . . that holding necessarily implied that the portion of § 1 of the 1866 Act presently codified as 42 U.S.C. § 1981 likewise reaches purely private actions of racial discrimination. The statutory holding in *Jones* was that the "[1866] Act was designed to do just what its terms suggest: to prohibit all racial discrimination, whether or not under color of law, with respect to the rights enumerated therein — including the right to purchase or lease property." . . . One of the "rights enumerated" in § 1 is "the same right . . . to make and enforce contracts as is enjoyed by white citizens. . . . " Just as in *Jones* a Negro's § 1 right to purchase property on equal terms with whites was violated when a private person refused to sell to the prospective purchaser solely because he was a Negro, so also a Negro's § 1 right to "make and enforce contracts" is violated if a private offeror refuses to extend to a Negro, solely because he is a Negro, the same opportunity to enter into contracts as he extends to white offerees. . . .

It is apparent that the racial exclusion practiced by . . . Bobbe's Private School amounts to a classic violation of § 1981. The parents of . . . Michael McCrary sought to enter into contractual relationships with Bobbe's Private School for educational services. . . . Under those contractual relationships, the schools would have received payments for services rendered, and the prospective students would have received instruction in return for those payments. The educational services of Bobbe's Private School . . . were advertised and offered to members of the general public. . . .

The petitioning schools and school association argue principally that § 1981 does not reach private acts of racial discrimination. That view is wholly inconsistent with *Jones'* interpretation of the legislative history of § 1 of the Civil Rights Act of 1866, and . . . this consistent interpretation of the law necessarily requires the conclusion that § 1981, like § 1982, reaches private conduct. . . .

The question remains whether § 1981, as applied, violates constitutionally protected rights of free association and privacy, or a parent's right to direct the education of his children.

. . . [I]t may be assumed that parents have a First Amendment right to send their children to educational institutions that promote the belief that racial segregation is desirable, and that the children have an equal right to attend such institutions. But it does not follow that the practice of excluding racial minorities from such institutions is also protected by the same principle. . . .

. . . .

It is clear that the present application of § 1981 infringes no parental right recognized in [prior cases]. No challenge is made to the petitioner's right to operate their private schools or the right of parents to send their children to a particular private school rather than a public school. Nor do these cases involve a challenge to the subject matter which is taught at any private school. Thus, . . . Bobbe's Private School and members of the intervenor association remain presumptively free to inculcate whatever values and standards they deem desirable. [Our earliest cases] entitle them to no more.

. . . .

While the application of § 1981 to the conduct at issue here — a private school's adherence to a racially discriminatory admissions policy — does not represent governmental intrusion into the privacy of the home or a similarly intimate setting, it does implicate parental interests. . . . A person's decision whether to bear a child and a parent's decision concerning the manner in which his child is to be educated may fairly be characterized as exercises of familial rights and responsibilities. But it does not follow that because government is largely or even entirely precluded from regulating the child-bearing decision, it is similarly restricted by the Constitution from regulating the implementation of parental decisions concerning a child's education.

The Court has repeatedly stressed that while parents have a constitutional right to send their children to private schools and a constitutional right to select private schools that offer specialized instruction, they have no constitutional right to provide their children with private school education unfettered by reasonable government regulation. . . .

The prohibition of racial discrimination that interferes with the making and enforcement of contracts for private educational services furthers goals closely analogous to those served by § 1981's elimination of racial discrimination in the making of private employment contracts and, more generally, by § 1982's guarantee that "a dollar in the hands of a Negro will purchase the same thing as a dollar in the hands of a white man." . . .

For the reasons stated in this opinion, the judgment of the Court of Appeals is in all respects affirmed.

[JUSTICES WHITE and REHNQUIST dissented.]

NOTES

(1) Does the Court's decision, as Justice White contended in dissent, "establish a general prohibition against a private individual or institution refusing to enter into a contract with another person because of that person's race"? Would the decision apply, as Justice White asserts, to "Social clubs . . . and associations designed to further the interests of blacks or whites"? What about sectarian schools that practice racial exclusion on religious grounds?

(2) 42 U.S.C. § 1981 affords private employees a right of action based on racial discrimination in employment. *McDonald v. Santa Fe Trail Transp. Co.*, 427 U.S. 273 (1976). *McDonald* construed § 1981 to protect white persons as well as nonwhites. The decision implicitly confirmed Congressional power under the Thirteenth Amendment to bar discrimination against whites.

(3) How can inability to contract be an incident of slavery which the Thirteenth Amendment can reach, where the enforcement power is used to benefit members of a race who were not enslaved?

(4) Justice Rehnquist thought the Court's decision in *Runyun* was wrong. In an April 7, 1987, letter to Justice White, Chief Justice Rehnquist also "question[ed] the soundness of our opinion in *Jones v. Alfred H. Mayer Co.*, . . . which held that this class was protected not merely against state action but against action by other private individuals." Justice Powell wrote Justice White two days later indicating that he "share[d] the reservation expressed by the Chief Justice. . . . In retrospect, I think our cases following *Jones v. Alfred H. Mayer Co.*, misconstrued §§ 1981 and 1982. As you persuasively wrote in *Runyon v. McCrary*, Congress did not intend these statutes to apply in the absence of state action." Justice Powell wrote that "John [Stevens] . . . also stated that he thought these precedents were 'incorrectly decided.'" Justice O'Connor wrote to Justice White as well: "I also share your reservations about the Court's construction of legislative intent with respect to §§ 1981 and 1982."

In *Patterson v. McLean Credit Union*, 491 U.S. 164 (1988), the Court scheduled argument on "[w]hether or not the interpretation of . . . § 1981 in *Runyon v. McCrary* . . . should be reconsidered" but unanimously refused to overrule *Runyon*, saying "that no special justification has been shown for overruling *Runyon*." *Id.* at 171, 173. Why did the Justices who agreed that *Runyon* had been wrongly decided refuse to overrule that case? In his already-quoted letter, Justice Powell wrote "that it was 'too late' to reexamine the prior precedents" and that Justice Stevens also "concluded that it would be inadvisable to overrule *Jones* and its progeny." *See* BERNARD SCHWARTZ, THE UNPUBLISHED OPINIONS OF THE REHNQUIST COURT 198-99 (1996).

Chapter VII

LIBERTY AND PROPERTY RIGHTS IN THE DUE PROCESS, TAKING, AND CONTRACT CLAUSES

Introductory Note. While this Chapter comprehends a number of provisions of the Constitution, the focus is clearly on the multifaceted concept of due process. The Due Process Clauses of the Fifth and Fourteenth Amendments to the Constitution have been invoked in a variety of distinct categories of rights. Although it has limits, one simple classification that has occasionally been used describes some of the rights protected by the Clauses as property rights and others as personal rights. Another classifying principle for rights guaranteed by the Due Process Clauses is the distinction between substantive and procedural rights. As some cases in the last section of this Chapter indicate, even this distinction may have limits. Nevertheless, using these Clauses to guarantee overtly substantive rights has caused considerable scholarly debate and controversy.

The Chapter begins with some introductory materials focusing on whether the Due Process Clause of the Fourteenth Amendment incorporates provisions of the Bill of Rights and makes particular amendments applicable against the states. The rich *Slaughter-House Cases* go beyond the question of incorporation to discuss the extent to which rights provided by the federal Constitution limit the power of state governments. Section 7.02 treats the selective incorporation of the guarantees of the Bill of Rights as against the states, focusing on the rights of the accused.

Section 7.03 considers a spectrum of property rights protected by the Constitution. The first subsection reviews the Court's unsuccessful and controversial endeavors to guarantee property rights using the doctrine of substantive due process. The second and third subsections turn to consider the modern Court's efforts to guarantee property rights using the Contracts Clause of Article I, § 10, and the Takings Clause of the Fifth Amendment.

Section 7.04 combines some of the themes discussed in the preceding two sections, focusing on rights that are both personal and substantive. Specifically, the section treats the use of the Due Process Clause and, less frequently, the Ninth Amendment to guarantee substantive rights of a personal nature. The focus is on procreative liberty and the abortion issue. Various subsections examine the Court's responses to claims for other substantive personal rights involving such areas as birth control, marriage, homosexual relationships, and the right to die.

Finally, the cases included in Section 7.05 blur the two classifying principles discussed in this Note. Entitled "Personal Property Rights: New Forms of Protection for New Property Interests," the Section treats property rights that involve employment and subsistence. The cases considered contrast with the decidedly commercial thrust of the cases dealt with in Section 7.03. Moreover, the cases combine procedural and substantive elements.

§ 7.01 INTRODUCTION TO THE INCORPORATION CONTROVERSY AND THE BILL OF RIGHTS

The Incorporation Controversy historically involves the determination of which specific protections in the Bill of Rights are guaranteed against state infringement by the federal government through the Fourteenth Amendment. Prior to the adoption of the Fourteenth Amendment, the Supreme Court held that the guarantees of the Bill of Rights did not apply against the States. In *Barron v. The Mayor and City Council of*

Baltimore, 7 Pet. 243 (1833), the Court, in an opinion by Chief Justice Marshall, held "that the provision in the fifth amendment to the Constitution, declaring that private property shall not be taken for public use without just compensation, is intended solely as a limitation on the exercise of power by the government of the United States, and is not applicable to the legislation of the States."

Chief Justice Marshall buttressed his conclusion with a discussion of the nature of the federal system:

The Constitution was ordained and established by the people of the United States for themselves, for their own government, and not for the government of the individual States. Each State established a constitution for itself, and in that constitution provided such limitations and restrictions on the powers of its particular government as its judgment dictated.

For example, Chief Justice Marshall pointed to the tenth section of the first article of the Constitution, which explicitly prohibited a variety of actions by the States, such as passing bills of attainder or ex post facto laws. The Chief Justice noted that the Constitution specifically states that " 'no State shall . . .' " in this limited area where the Constitution restricts state action.

In almost every convention by which the Constitution was adopted, amendments to guard against the lapse of power were recommended. These amendments demanded security against apprehended encroachments of the general government not against those of the local governments.

SLAUGHTER-HOUSE CASES
83 U.S. 36, 21 L. Ed. 394 (1873)

JUSTICE MILLER . . . delivered the opinion of the court.

[Butchers from New Orleans brought the cases to the Supreme Court, appealing decisions of the Supreme Court of Louisiana in favor of the Slaughter-House Company. In 1869, the Louisiana legislature passed a statute designed to protect the health of the residents of New Orleans by limiting the locations of stock-landings and slaughterhouses. The act created the Crescent City Live-Stock Landing and Slaughter-House Company and granted it the exclusive right to conduct the business of livestock landing and slaughtering of animals for food in the New Orleans city limits. Although all butchers were allowed to do their own slaughtering in the Company's slaughterhouses for a fee, New Orleans butchers challenged the statute as "creating a monopoly" and depriving the butchers of the "right to exercise their trade." Moreover, the butchers asserted that "the unrestricted exercise of the business of butchering is necessary to the daily subsistence of the population of the city." The butchers argued that the statute was unconstitutional, alleging that it violated the Thirteenth Amendment by creating an involuntary servitude, and the Privileges and Immunities, Due Process and Equal Protection Clauses of the Fourteenth Amendment.]

. . . It is not, and cannot be successfully controverted, that it is both the right and the duty of the legislative body the supreme power of the State or municipality to prescribe and determine the localities where the business of slaughtering for a great city may be conducted. . . .

The statute under consideration defines these localities and forbids slaughtering in any other. It does not, as has been asserted, prevent the butcher from doing his own slaughtering. On the contrary, the Slaughter-House Company is required, under a heavy penalty, to permit any person who wishes to do so, to slaughter in their houses. . . . The butcher then is still permitted to slaughter, to prepare, and to sell his own meats; but he is required to slaughter at a specified place and to pay a reasonable compensation for the use of the accommodations furnished him at that place. . . .

. . . The prices or charges to be made by the company are limited by the statute, and we are not advised that they are on the whole exorbitant or unjust.

The proposition is, therefore, reduced to these terms: Can any exclusive privileges be granted to any of its citizens, or to a corporation, by the legislature of a State? . . .

The plaintiffs in error . . . allege that the statute is a violation of the Constitution of the United States in these several particulars:

> That it creates an involuntary servitude forbidden by the thirteenth article of amendment;

> That it abridges the privileges and immunities of citizens of the United States;

> That it denies to the plaintiffs the equal protection of the laws; and,

> That it deprives them of their property without due process of law; contrary to the provisions of the first section of the fourteenth article of the amendment. . . .

The most cursory glance at these articles discloses a unity of purpose, when taken in connection with the history of the times, which cannot fail to have an important bearing on any question of doubt concerning their true meaning. . . .

The institution of African slavery, as it existed in about half the States of the Union, and the contests pervading the public mind for many years, between those who desired its curtailment and ultimate extinction and those who desired additional safeguards for its security and perpetuation, culminated in the effort, on the part of most of the States in which slavery existed, to separate from the Federal government, and to resist its authority. This constituted the war of the rebellion, and whatever auxiliary causes may have contributed to bring about this war, undoubtedly the overshadowing and efficient cause was African slavery.

In that struggle slavery, as a legalized social relation, perished. . . . The proclamation of President Lincoln expressed an accomplished fact as to a large portion of the insurrectionary districts, when he declared slavery abolished in them all. But the war being over, those who had succeeded in re-establishing the authority of the Federal government were not content to permit this great act of emancipation to rest on the actual results of the contest or the proclamation of the Executive, both of which might have been questioned in after times, and they determined to place this main and most valuable result in the Constitution of the restored Union as one of its fundamental articles. Hence the thirteenth article of amendment of that instrument. Its two short sections seem hardly to admit of construction, so vigorous is their expression and so appropriate to the purpose we have indicated.

> 1. Neither slavery nor involuntary servitude, except as a punishment for crime, whereof the party shall have been duly convicted, shall exist within the United States or any place subject to their jurisdiction.

> 2. Congress shall have power to enforce this article by appropriate legislation. . . .

. . . The word servitude is of larger meaning than slavery, as the latter is popularly understood in this country, and the obvious purpose was to forbid all shades and conditions of African slavery. . . .

. . . Among the first acts of legislation adopted by several of the States in the legislative bodies which claimed to be in their normal relations with the Federal government, were laws which imposed upon the colored race onerous disabilities and burdens, and curtailed their rights in the pursuit of life, liberty, and property to such an extent that their freedom was of little value. . . .

They were in some States forbidden to appear in the towns in any other character than menial servants. They were required to reside on and cultivate the soil without the right to purchase or own it. They were excluded from many occupations of gain, and were not permitted to give testimony in the courts in any case where a white man was a party. . . .

. . . [T]he statesmen who had conducted the Federal government in safety through the crisis of the rebellion . . . accordingly passed through Congress the proposition for the fourteenth amendment, and they declined to treat as restored to their full participation in the government of the Union the States which had been in insurrection, until they ratified that article by a formal vote of their legislative bodies.

. . . A few years' experience satisfied the thoughtful men who had been the authors of the other two amendments that . . . a race of men distinctively marked as was the negro, living in the midst of another and dominant race, could never be fully secured in their person and their property without the right of suffrage.

Hence the fifteenth amendment, which declares that "the right of a citizen of the United States to vote shall not be denied or abridged by any State on account of race, color, or previous condition of servitude." The negro having, by the fourteenth amendment, been declared to be a citizen of the United States, is thus made a voter in every State of the Union.

. . . [O]n the most casual examination of the language of these amendments, no one can fail to be impressed with the one pervading purpose found in them all . . . we mean the freedom of the slave race, the security and firm establishment of that freedom, and the protection of the newly-made freeman and citizen from the oppressions of those who had formerly exercised unlimited dominion over him. It is true that only the fifteenth amendment, in terms, mentions the negro by speaking of his color and his slavery. But it is just as true that each of the other articles was addressed to the grievances of that race, and designed to remedy them as the fifteenth.

. . . Undoubtedly while negro slavery alone was in the mind of the Congress which proposed the thirteenth article, it forbids any other kind of slavery, now or hereafter. If Mexican peonage or the Chinese coolie labor system shall develop slavery of the Mexican or Chinese race within our territory, this amendment may safely be trusted to make it void. And so if other rights are assailed by the States which properly and necessarily fall within the protection of these articles, that protection will apply, though the party interested may not be of African descent. . . .

The first section of the fourteenth article, to which our attention is more specially invited, opens with a definition of citizenship not only citizenship of the United States, but citizenship of the States. . . . [I]t had been held by this court, in the celebrated *Dred Scott* case, only a few years before the outbreak of the civil war, that a man of African descent, whether a slave or not, was not and could not be a citizen of a State or of the United States. This decision, while it met the condemnation of some of the ablest statesmen and constitutional lawyers of the country, had never been overruled; and if it was to be accepted as a constitutional limitation of the right of citizenship, then all the negro race who had recently been made freemen, were still, not only not citizens, but were incapable of becoming so by anything short of an amendment to the Constitution.

To remove this difficulty primarily, and to establish a clear and comprehensive definition of citizenship which would declare what should constitute citizenship of the United States, and also citizenship of a State, the first clause of the first section was framed.

"All persons born or naturalized in the United States, and subject to the jurisdiction thereof, are citizens of the United States and of the States wherein they reside."

[T]his clause . . . declares that persons may be citizens of the United States without regard to their citizenship of a particular State, and it overturns the *Dred Scott* decision by making all persons born within the United States and subject to its jurisdiction citizens of the United States. That its main purpose was to establish the citizenship of the negro can admit of no doubt. . . .

[T]he distinction between citizenship of the United States and citizenship of a State is clearly recognized and established. Not only may a man be a citizen of the United States without being a citizen of a State, but an important element is necessary to convert the former into the latter. He must reside within the State to make him a citizen of it, but it is only necessary that he should be born or naturalized in the United States to be a citizen of the Union. . . .

We think this distinction and its explicit recognition in this amendment of great weight in this argument, because the next paragraph of this same section, which is the one mainly relied on by the plaintiffs in error, speaks only of privileges and immunities of citizens of the United States, and does not speak of those of citizens of the several States. . . .

The language is, "No State shall make or enforce any law which shall abridge the privileges or immunities of citizens of the United States." It is a little remarkable, if this clause was intended as a protection to the citizen of a State against the legislative power of his own State, that the word citizen of the State should be left out when it is so carefully used, and used in contradistinction to citizens of the United States, in the very sentence which precedes it. . . .

[T]he corresponding provision is found in section two of the fourth article, in the following words: "The citizens of each State shall be entitled to all the privileges and immunities of citizens of the several States."

There can be but little question that the purpose of both these provisions is the same, and that the privileges and immunities intended are the same in each. . . .

. . . The first and the leading case on the subject is that of *Corfield v. Coryell*, decided by Justice Washington in the Circuit Court for the District of Pennsylvania in [4 Washington Circuit Court, 371] 1823.

"The inquiry," he says, "is, what are the privileges and immunities of citizens of the several States? We feel no hesitation in confining these expressions to those privileges and immunities which are fundamental; which belong of right to the citizens of all free governments, and which have at all times been enjoyed by citizens of the several States which compose this Union, from the time of their becoming free, independent, and sovereign. What these fundamental principles are, it would be more tedious than difficult to enumerate. They may all, however, be comprehended under the following heads: protection by the government, with the right to acquire and possess property of every kind, and to pursue and obtain happiness and safety, subject, nevertheless, to such restraints as the government may prescribe for the general good of the whole."

This definition of the privileges and immunities of citizens of the States . . . embraces nearly every civil right for the establishment and protection of which organized government is instituted. They are, in the language of Judge Washington, those rights which are fundamental. Throughout his opinion, they are spoken of as rights belonging to the individual as a citizen of a State. . . .

In the case of *Paul v. Virginia*, [12 Wallace, 430,] the court, in expounding this clause of the Constitution, says that "the privileges and immunities secured to citizens of each State in the several States, by the provision in question, are those privileges and immunities which are common to the citizens in the latter States under their constitution and laws by virtue of their being citizens." . . .

Its sole purpose was to declare to the several States, that whatever those rights, as you grant or establish them to your own citizens, or as you limit or qualify, or impose restrictions on their exercise, the same, neither more nor less, shall be the measure of the rights of citizens of other States within your jurisdiction.

It would be the vainest show of learning to attempt to prove by citations of authority, that up to the adoption of the recent amendments, no claim or pretense was set up that those rights depended on the Federal government for their existence or protection, beyond the very few express limitations which the Federal Constitution imposed upon the States such, for instance, as the prohibition against ex post facto laws, bills of attainder, and laws impairing the obligation of contracts. But with the exception of these and a few other restrictions, the entire domain of the privileges, and immunities of citizens of the States, as above defined, lay within the constitutional and legislative power of the States, and without that of the Federal government. Was it the purpose of the fourteenth amendment, by the simple declaration that no State should make or enforce any law which shall abridge the privileges and immunities of citizens of the United States, to transfer the security and protection of all the civil rights which we have mentioned, from the States to the Federal government? And where it is declared that Congress shall have the power to enforce that article, was it intended to bring within the power of Congress the entire domain of civil rights heretofore belonging exclusively to the States?

All this and more must follow, if the proposition of the plaintiffs in error be sound. For not only are these rights subject to the control of Congress whenever in its discretion any of them are supposed to be abridged by State legislation, but that body may also pass laws in advance, limiting and restricting the exercise of legislative power by the States, in their most ordinary and usual functions. . . . And still further, such a construction followed by the reversal of the judgments of the Supreme Court of Louisiana in these cases, would constitute this court a perpetual censor upon all legislation of the States, on the civil rights of their own citizens, with authority to nullify such as it did not approve as consistent with those rights, as they existed at the time of the adoption of this amendment. The argument we admit is not always the most conclusive which is drawn from the consequences urged against the adoption of a particular construction of an instrument. But when, as in the case before us, these consequences are so serious, so far-reaching and pervading, so great a departure from the structure and spirit of our institutions; when the effect is to fetter and degrade the State governments by subjecting them to the control of Congress, in the exercise of powers heretofore universally conceded to them of the most ordinary and fundamental character; when in fact it radically changes the whole theory of the relations of the State and Federal governments to each other and of both these governments to the people; the argument has a force that is irresistible, in the absence of language which expresses such a purpose too clearly to admit of doubt.

We are convinced that no such results were intended by the Congress which proposed these amendments, nor by the legislatures of the States which ratified them.

Having shown that the privileges and immunities relied on in the argument are those which belong to citizens of the States as such, and that they are left to the State governments for security and protection . . . we may hold ourselves from defining the privileges and immunities of citizens of the United States which no State can abridge, until some case involving those privileges may make it necessary to do so.

But lest it should be said that no such privileges and immunities are to be found if those we have been considering are excluded, we venture to suggest some which owe their existence to the Federal government, its National character, its Constitution, or its laws.

One of these is well described in the case of *Crandall v. Nevada*, [6 Wallace, 36]. It is said to be the right of the citizen of this great country, protected by implied guarantees of its Constitution, "to come to the seat of government to assert any claim he may have upon that government, to transact any business he may have with it, to seek its protection, to share its offices, to engage in administering its functions. He has the right of free access to its seaports, through which all operations of foreign commerce are conducted, to the sub-treasuries, land offices, and courts of justice in the several States." And quoting from the language of Chief Justice Taney in another case, it is said "that for all the great purposes for which the Federal government was established, we are one people, with one common country, we are all citizens of the United States;" and it is, as such citizens, that their rights are supported in this court in *Crandall v. Nevada*.

Another privilege of a citizen of the United States is to demand the care and protection of the Federal government over his life, liberty, and property when on the high seas or within the jurisdiction of a foreign government. . . . The right to peaceably assemble and petition for redress of grievances, the privilege of the writ of habeas corpus, are rights of the citizen guaranteed by the Federal Constitution. The right to use the navigable waters of the United States, however they may penetrate the territory of the several States, all rights secured to our citizens by treaties with foreign nations, are dependent upon citizenship of the United States, and not citizenship of a State. One of these privileges is conferred by the very article under consideration. It is that a citizen of the United States can, of his own volition, become a citizen of any State of the Union by a bona fide residence therein, with the same rights as other citizens of that State. To these may be added the rights secured by the thirteenth and fifteenth articles of amendment, and by the other clause of the fourteenth, next to be considered.

. . . [T]he rights claimed by these plaintiffs in error, if they have any existence, are not privileges and immunities of citizens of the United States. . . .

The argument has not been much pressed in these cases that the defendant's charter deprives the plaintiffs of their property without due process of law, or that it denies to them the equal protection of the law. The first of these paragraphs has been in the Constitution since the adoption of the Fifth Amendment, as a restraint upon the Federal power. It is also to be found in some form of expression in the constitutions of nearly all the States, as a restraint upon the power of the States. . . .

We are not without judicial interpretation, therefore, both State and National, of the meaning of this clause. And it is sufficient to say that under no construction of that provision that we have ever seen, or that we deem admissible, can the restraint imposed by the State of Louisiana upon the exercise of their trade by the butchers of New Orleans be held to be a deprivation of property within the meaning of that provision.

"Nor shall any State deny to any person within its jurisdiction the equal protection of the laws."

. . . The existence of laws in the States where the newly emancipated negroes resided, which discriminated with gross injustice and hardship against them as a class, was the evil to be remedied by this clause, and by it such laws are forbidden.

If, however, the States did not conform their laws to its requirements, then by the fifth section of the article of amendment Congress was authorized to enforce it by suitable legislation. We doubt very much whether any action of a State not directed by way of discrimination against the negroes as a class, or on account of their race, will ever be held to come within the purview of this provision. It is so clearly a provision for that race and that emergency, that a strong case would be necessary for its application to any other. But as it is a State that is to be dealt with, and not alone the validity of its laws, we may safely leave that matter until Congress shall have exercised its power, or some case of State oppression, by denial of equal justice in its courts, shall have claimed a decision at our hands. . . .

In the early history of the organization of the government, its statesmen seem to have divided on the line which should separate the powers of the National government from those of the State governments, and though this line has never been very well defined in public opinion, such a division has continued from that day to this.

The adoption of the first eleven amendments to the Constitution so soon after the original instrument was accepted, shows a prevailing sense of danger at that time from the Federal power. And it cannot be denied that such a jealousy continued to exist with many patriotic men until the breaking out of the late civil war. It was then discovered that the true danger to the perpetuity of the Union was in the capacity of the State organizations to combine and concentrate all the powers of the State, and of contiguous States, for a determined resistance to the General Government.

Unquestionably, this has given great force to the argument, and added largely to the number of those who believe in the necessity of a strong National government.

But, however pervading this sentiment, and however it may have contributed to the adoption of the amendments we have been considering, we do not see in those amendments any purpose to destroy the main features of the general system. Under the pressure of all the excited feeling growing out of the war, our statesmen have still believed that the existence of the States with powers for domestic and local government, including the regulation of civil rights the rights of person and of property was essential to the perfect working of our complex form of government, though they have thought proper to impose additional limitations on the States, and to confer additional power on that of the Nation. . . .

JUSTICE FIELD, dissenting. . .

It is contended in justification for the act in question that it was adopted in the interest of the city, to promote its cleanliness and protect its health, and was the legitimate exercise of what is termed the police power of the State. That power undoubtedly extends to all regulations affecting the health, good order, morals, peace, and safety of society, and is exercised on a great variety of subjects, and in almost numberless ways. But under the pretense of prescribing a police regulation the State cannot be permitted to encroach upon any of the just rights of the citizen, which the Constitution intended to secure against abridgement.

In the law in question there are only two provisions which can properly be called police regulations — the one which requires the landing and slaughtering of animals below the city of New Orleans, and the other which requires the inspection of the animals before they are slaughtered. When these requirements are complied with, the sanitary purposes of the act are accomplished. . . . It is plain that if the corporation can, without endangering the health of the public, carry on the business of landing, keeping, and slaughtering cattle within a district below the city embracing an area of over a thousand square miles, it would not endanger the public health if other persons were also permitted to carry on the same business within the same district under similar conditions as to the inspection of the animals. . . . The pretense of sanitary regulations for the grant of the exclusive privileges is a shallow one, which merits only this passing notice. . . .

. . . A person allowed to pursue only one trade or calling, and only in one locality of the country, would not be, in the strict sense of the term, in a condition of slavery, but probably none would deny that he would be in a condition of servitude. He certainly would not possess the liberties nor enjoy the privileges of a freeman. The compulsion which would force him to labor even for his own benefit only in one direction, or in one place, would be almost as oppressive and nearly as great an invasion of his liberty as the compulsion which would force him to labor for the benefit or pleasure of another, and would equally constitute an element of servitude. . . .

It is not necessary, however, . . . to rest my objections to the act in question upon the terms and meaning of the thirteenth amendment. The provisions of the fourteenth amendment, which is properly a supplement to the thirteenth, cover, in my judgment, the case before us, and inhibit any legislation which confers special and exclusive privileges like these under consideration. . . .

The first clause of this amendment determines who are citizens of the United States, and how their citizenship is created. . . .

. . . A citizen of a State is now only a citizen of the United States residing in that State. The fundamental rights, privileges, and immunities which belong to him as a free man and a free citizen, now belong to him as a citizen of the United States, and are not dependent upon his citizenship of any State. . . .

What, then, are the privileges and immunities which are secured against abridgment by State legislation?

In the first section of the Civil Rights Act Congress has given its interpretation to these terms, or at least has stated some of the rights which, in its judgment, these terms include; it has there declared that they include the right "to make and enforce contracts, to sue, be parties and give evidence, to inherit, purchase, lease, sell, hold, and convey real and personal property, and to full and equal benefit of all laws and proceedings for the security of person and property." . . .

. . . All monopolies in any known trade or manufacture are an invasion of these privileges. . . .

. . . All such grants relating to any known trade or manufacture have been held by all the judges of England, whenever they have come up for consideration, to be void at common law as destroying the freedom of trade, discouraging labor and industry, restraining persons from getting an honest livelihood, and putting it into the power of the grantees to enhance the price of commodities. . . .

This equality of right, with exemption from all disparaging and partial enactments, in the lawful pursuit of life, throughout the whole country, is the distinguishing privilege of citizens of the United States. To them, everywhere, all pursuits, all professions, all avocations are open without other restrictions than such as are imposed equally upon all others of the same age, sex, and condition. The State may prescribe such regulations for every pursuit and calling of life as will promote the public health, secure the good order and advance the general prosperity of society. . . .

I am authorized by the CHIEF JUSTICE, JUSTICE SWAYNE, and JUSTICE BRADLEY, to state that they concur with me in this dissenting opinion.

JUSTICE BRADLEY, also dissenting:

. . . The question is now settled by the fourteenth amendment itself, that citizenship of the United States is the primary citizenship in this country; and that State citizenship is secondary and derivative, depending upon citizenship of the United States and the citizen's place of residence. . . .

[I]n my judgment, the right of any citizen to follow whatever lawful employment he chooses to adopt (submitting himself to all lawful regulations) is one of his most valuable rights, and one which the legislature of a State cannot invade, whether restrained by its own constitution or not. . . .

[A]ny law which establishes a sheer monopoly, depriving a large class of citizens of the privilege of pursuing a lawful employment, does abridge the privileges of those citizens.

The amendment also prohibits any State from depriving any person (citizen or otherwise) of life, liberty, or property, without due process of law.

. . . Their right of choice is a portion of their liberty; their occupation is their property. Such a law also deprives those citizens of the equal protection of the laws, contrary to the last clause of the section. . . .

It is futile to argue that none but persons of the African race are intended to be benefited by this amendment. They may have been the primary cause of the amendment, but its language is so general, embracing all citizens. . . .

The mischief to be remedied was not merely slavery and its incidents and consequences; but that spirit of insubordination and disloyalty to the National government which had troubled the country for so many years in some of the States, and that intolerance of free speech and free discussion which often rendered life and property insecure, and led to much unequal legislation. . . .

But great fears are expressed that this construction of the amendment will lead to enactments by Congress interfering with the internal affairs of the States, and establishing therein civil and criminal codes of law for the government of the citizens, and thus abolishing the State governments in everything but name; or else, that it will lead the Federal court to draw to their cognizance the supervision of State tribunals on every subject of judicial inquiry, on the plea of ascertaining whether the privileges and immunities of citizens have not been abridged. . . .

In my judgment no such practical inconveniences would arise. . . . As the privileges and immunities protected are only those fundamental ones which belong to every citizen, they would soon become so far defined as to cause but a slight accumulation of business in the Federal courts. . . . But even if the business of the National courts should be increased, Congress could easily supply the remedy by increasing their number and efficiency. . . .

[JUSTICE SWAYNE, also wrote a dissent.]

[The case immediately following *Slaughter-House* in the Reports was *Bradwell v. Illinois*, 16 Wall. 130 (1873), which was decided only one day later. In *Bradwell*, the Court (8-1) upheld an Illinois law that restricted the practice of law to males. Three of the *Slaughter-House* dissenters (Bradley, Swayne, and Field) voted with the *Slaughter-House* majority to uphold a male monopoly that prevented a woman from pursuing her chosen career. Of the *Slaughter-House* dissenters, only Chief Justice Chase was consistent. He voted to invalidate both laws.]

NOTES

(1) The holding in *Barron v. Baltimore* that the Bill of Rights does not apply to the states, and the narrow interpretation of the Fourteenth Amendment's Privileges and Immunities Clause in the *Slaughter-House Cases*, remain undisturbed, although there have been occasional efforts to breathe life into the phrase "privileges and immunities of citizens of the United States." *See Twining v. New Jersey*, 211 U.S. 78 (1908) ("Thus among the rights and privileges of National citizenship recognized by this court are the right to pass freely from State to State, . . . the right to petition Congress for a redress of grievances, . . . the right to vote for National officers, . . . the right to enter the public lands, . . . the right to be protected against violence while in the lawful custody of a United States Marshall, . . . and the right to inform United States authorities of violations of its laws."); *see also Hague v. C.I.O.*, 307 U.S. 496 (1939).

But history has overtaken both cases. *Gitlow v. New York*, 268 U.S. 652 (1925), held that the Due Process Clause of the Fourteenth Amendment incorporated the free expression protections of the First Amendment. The religion clauses have been similarly incorporated. While the Court, in *Gitlow* and similar cases, split sharply over the scope of these rights, there was no disagreement that the substantive values of the First Amendment were included within the word "liberty" and cloaked with whatever protection the Court chose to provide through the Due Process Clause.

The so-called procedural provisions have been similarly made applicable to the states. In 1897, the Court held that the Due Process Clause prevented states from taking property without just compensation, thus imposing on the states a restriction found in the Fifth Amendment. *See Chicago, B. & Q.R. Co. v. Chicago*, 166 U.S. 226 (1897). The next section of this chapter will trace the developments whereby most of the procedural provisions in the Bill of Rights have been held applicable to the states. This was accomplished, not by enlarging the Privileges and Immunities Clause, but by the Due Process Clause. This is what is meant by "procedural due process."

In the area of substantive rights, First Amendment freedoms were not the only values to work their way into the Fourteenth Amendment. The *Slaughter-House Cases* failed to deter the Court from erecting other constitutional barriers against state regulations of business. Here again, the Due Process Clause, which was accorded scant attention in Justice Miller's opinion, was the vehicle as the Court read into it the substantive values of a free enterprise economic system, thereby invalidating a wide range of regulatory legislation. Not until the New Deal constitutional crisis of the mid-1930s did the Court finally stop using the Fourteenth Amendment as a shield against government regulation of business. *See Slaughter-House Cases, supra.*

The demise of one form of "substantive due process" in the 1930s, however, has been followed in recent years by the recognition of important new areas of constitutionally protected rights. Much of this chapter will be devoted to these developments, as we will observe how the Court has reinterpreted provisions of the Bill of Rights (now applicable to the states), or has evolved new constitutional approaches such as the Ninth Amendment, or has recognized new rights within the meaning of the Fourteenth Amendment's prohibition against the taking of "liberty or property without due process of law." "Substantive due process," thought to have died in the 1930s, has shown telling recuperative powers.

Finally, it is interesting to compare the limited role that Justice Miller predicted for the Equal Protection Clause with the burgeoning equal protection developments of recent years. We will see (Chapters VIII and X) how the Clause has provided a constitutional basis for attacking laws discriminating on the basis of gender, alienage, illegitimacy, poverty, and other characteristics. Equal protection analysis has also provided doctrinal support for protecting several substantive rights. As in the preceding chapter, we will encounter this use of equal protection again in cases dealing with other substantive rights.

(2) For an account of the deep historical roots of the tension in the Fourteenth Amendment between protecting individual rights and preserving local autonomy, see W. NELSON, THE FOURTEENTH AMENDMENT: FROM POLITICAL PRINCIPLE TO JUDICIAL DOCTRINE (1988). Professor Nelson "identifies equality as the master concept that best gives effect both to individual rights and to legislative freedom." *Id.* at 11.

(3) The Privileges and Immunities Clause of the Fourteenth Amendment has been used in *Saenz v. Roe*, 526 U.S. 489 (1999).

§ 7.02 THE RIGHTS OF THE ACCUSED: THE "INCORPORATION CONTROVERSY"

NOTES

(1) *"Traditions and Conscience of Our People."* In *Palko v. Connecticut*, 302 U.S. 319 (1937), the Court upheld a Connecticut statute allowing the State to appeal in criminal cases, rejecting defendant's double jeopardy challenge under the Fifth Amendment. During his second trial, appellant argued that the State's right to appeal in criminal cases placed him in double jeopardy in violation of the Due Process Clause of the Fourteenth Amendment which, he argued, incorporated the Fifth Amendment protection against double jeopardy. The appellant also argued that the Fourteenth Amendment fully incorporated the Bill of Rights.

Rejecting both arguments, Justice Cardozo pointed out that the Court had not even applied all the Fifth Amendment provisions to the states. Those portions of the Bill of Rights not "absorbed" into the Fourteenth Amendment, such as the right to be free of double jeopardy, "are not of the very essence of a scheme of ordered liberty. To abolish them is not to violate a 'principle of justice so rooted in the traditions and conscience of our people as to be ranked as fundamental.' Few would be so narrow and provincial as to maintain that a fair and enlightened system of justice would be impossible without them."

(2) *Selective or Total Incorporation.* In *Adamson v California*, 332 U.S. 46 (1947), the Court held that the Fifth Amendment guarantee against self-incrimination was not applicable to the states through the Fourteenth Amendment. The appellant (defendant) argued first that the Fifth Amendment privilege against compulsory self-incrimination is a fundamental natural privilege or immunity protected under the Fourteenth Amendment against state infringement and second, that the California procedure violated his Fourteenth Amendment due process rights.

Writing for a majority of six, Justice Reed rejected both arguments. Justice Frankfurter wrote a concurring opinion that criticized both the "selective incorporation" view urged by the defendant and the total incorporation view of Justice Black's dissent. He criticized selective incorporation for lacking principles to guide the incorporation of certain amendments and for leaving others out. For Justice Frankfurter, the Due Process Clauses of the Fifth and Fourteenth Amendments carry the same meaning. The framers of the Fifth Amendment did not intend the Clause as "merely a shorthand statement of other clauses in the same amendment" like the prohibition against double jeopardy. Neither did the framers of the Due Process Clause of the Fourteenth Amendment. Selective or total incorporation, according to Justice Frankfurter, would unduly restrict the states' freedom to define their own systems of individual rights and governmental powers and "would tear up by the roots much of the fabric of the law in the several States."

Justice Black wrote a famous dissenting opinion in support of total incorporation of the Bill of Rights into the Fourteenth Amendment. For Justice Black, the Court's approach rested on the personal predilections of individual Justices: "this decision reasserts a constitutional theory spelled out in *Twining v. New Jersey*, 211 U.S. 78 (1908), that this Court is endowed by the Constitution with boundless power under 'natural law' periodically to expand and contract constitutional standards to conform to the Court's conception of what at a particular time constitutes 'civilized decency' and 'fundamental principles of liberty and justice.'" Justice Black attached to the dissent a detailed appendix of his research supporting his belief that "the language of the first section of the Fourteenth Amendment, taken as a whole, was thought by those responsible for its submission to the people, and by those who opposed its submission, sufficiently explicit to guarantee that thereafter no state could deprive its citizens of the privileges and protections of the Bill of Rights."

Justice Black believed that the Court's "natural law" method was dangerous. "To hold that this Court can determine what, if any, provisions of the Bill of Rights will be enforced, and if so to what degree, is to frustrate the great design of the written Constitution." Nonetheless, Justice Black said that in a choice between selective incorporation and incorporating none of the amendments, he would support selective incorporation, which he did in *Duncan v. Louisiana.*

Justices Murphy and Rutledge dissented. Although they agreed with Justice Black that the Bill of Rights should be totally incorporated into the Fourteenth Amendment, they were unwilling to limit the Fourteenth Amendment to only those provisions embodied in the Bill of Rights: "Occasions may arise where a proceeding falls so far short of conforming to fundamental standards of procedure as to warrant a constitutional condemnation in terms of a lack of due process despite the absence of a specific provision in the Bill of Rights."

DUNCAN v. LOUISIANA, 391 U.S. 145 (1968). In *Duncan*, the Court dealt with the issue of whether or not the Sixth Amendment right to a jury trial was incorporated into state law by the Fourteenth Amendment. The appellant, Duncan, was sentenced to 60 days in a parish prison after being convicted of battery by the trial court judge in Louisiana, where only those accused of crimes carrying the punishments of hard labor or capital punishment are entitled to a jury trial.

Justice White, delivering the opinion of the Court, first listed those of the Bill of Rights that are incorporated into the states by the Due Process Clause of the Fourteenth Amendment. The clause protects "the right to compensation for property taken by the State; the rights of speech, press, and religion covered by the First Amendment; the Fourth Amendment rights to be free from unreasonable searches and seizures and to have excluded from criminal trials any evidence illegally seized; the right guaranteed by the Fifth Amendment to be free of compelled self-incrimination; and the Sixth Amendment rights to counsel, to a speedy and public trial, to confrontation of opposing witnesses, and to compulsory process for obtaining witnesses."

Continuing, Justice White stated that the test for incorporation was whether or not the right in question was a fundamental principle of justice basic to the American jurisprudential scheme. He concluded: "Because we believe that trial by jury in criminal cases is fundamental to the American scheme of justice, we hold that the Fourteenth Amendment guarantees a right of jury trial in all criminal cases which — were they to be tried in a federal court — would come within the Sixth Amendment's guarantee."

Tracing the development of the jury trial back to the Magna Carta, Justice White claimed that those who set up the American system of government knew from experience that juries were an important safeguard to prevent mob rule and judicial tyranny. "Providing an accused with the right to be tried by a jury of his peers gave him an inestimable safeguard against the corrupt or overzealous prosecutor and against the compliant, biased, or eccentric judge."

The Court next addressed Louisiana's argument that this was a petty offense that resulted in only a 60-day sentence. Louisiana noted that the Court had recognized in *Cheff v. Schnackenberg*, 384 U.S. 373 (1966), that petty offenses do not require trials by jury. This was a common law practice that had been adapted to the American States. The benefit of a trial by jury in cases where petty offenses resulted was thought to be outweighed by judicial expediency in non-jury trials. The standard for petty offenses, however, was unclear.

Justice White refused to lay down a bright line test for what was and was not a petty offense. He wrote that it was "sufficient for our purposes to hold that a crime punishable by two years in prison is, based on past and contemporary standards in this country, a serious crime and not a petty offense." His conclusion was that the defendant deserved a trial by jury and it was an error to deny this.

Justice Black, joined by Justice Douglas, concurred. Justice Black noted that he was happy to support the selective incorporation of the Sixth Amendment in the cases decided by the Court since *Adamson*. He critiqued Justice Harlan's dissent in *Duncan*, writing:

> My Brother Harlan's objections to my *Adamson* dissent history, like that of most of the objectors, relies most heavily on a criticism written by Professor Charles Fairman and published in the Stanford Law Review. 2 STAN. L. REV. 5 (1949). I have read and studied this article extensively, including the historical references, but am compelled to add that in my view it has completely failed to refute the inferences and arguments that I suggested in my *Adamson* dissent.

Justice Black, a former U.S. Senator from Alabama, criticized the article for not relying more on the legislative experience and beliefs of the Amendment's sponsors, Congressman Bingham and Senator Howard.

Justice Black argued that under Justice Harlan's view of due process, the term would have no particular meaning, only a definition that shifted from era to era. Justice Harlan's fundamental fairness test was highly individualized varying from court to court and judge to judge.

While Justice Black generally supported a balanced federal system, he had "never believed that under the guise of federalism the States should be able to experiment with the protections afforded our citizens through the Bill of Rights." Finally, Justice Black pointed out that he still believed in the theory of total incorporation of the Bill of Rights through the Fourteenth Amendment. He was, however, "willing to support the selective incorporation doctrine . . . as an alternative, although perhaps less historically supportable than complete incorporation." Selective incorporation had "already worked to make most of the Bill of Rights' protections applicable to the States."

Justice Harlan, joined by Justice Stewart, dissented. Justice Harlan noted that while each States' criminal justice system had to conform to the national constitution, the due process clause "does not . . . impose or encourage nationwide uniformity for its own sake . . . and it does not impose on the States the rules that may be in force in the federal courts except where such rules are also found to be essential to basic fairness."

In a footnote, he attacked Justice Black's opinion by relying on Professor Fairman's article, which turned up little support for total incorporation in "hundreds of pages of legislative discussion." The article also criticized the words used in the Fourteenth Amendment, arguing that if it was trying to suggest incorporation of the Bill of Rights, the words used were unclear.

Instead, Justice Harlan argued that the "Bill of Rights is evidence, at various points, of the content Americans find in the term 'liberty' and of American standards of fundamental fairness." For Justice Harlan, the critical issue was not that elements of fundamental fairness were found in the Bill of Rights but "were deemed, in the context of American legal history, to be fundamental. . . . " In applying this standard, Justice Harlan, relying on *Palko*, found that a fundamental fairness interpretation of the Due Process Clause required in this instance a fair trial, but not a jury trial.

Finally, Justice Harlan celebrated the diversity of views and important experimentation supplied by the States in the federal system of government. He agreed with Justice Brandeis' language in *New State Ice Co. v. Liebman*, 285 U.S. 280, 311 (dissenting opinion) " 'one of the happy incidents of the federal system that a single courageous State may, if its citizens choose, serve as a laboratory.' "

NOTES

(1) *Scope of Incorporation.* As the opinions in *Duncan* indicate, by the end of the 1960s all of the specific procedural guarantees of the Fourth, Fifth, Sixth, Seventh, and Eighth Amendments had been incorporated in the Fourteenth Amendment's Due Process Clause, except for the Fifth Amendment's requirement of a grand jury indictment and the Seventh Amendment's guarantee of a jury trial in all civil cases where the amount in controversy exceeds twenty dollars. Despite the misgivings of some of the Justices, a majority has adhered to the position that these procedural protections should be as fully applicable against the states as against the federal government. For additional discussion of the scope of selective incorporation, see Israel, *Selective Incorporation Revisited*, 71 Geo. L.J. 253 (1982). The Second and Third Amendments also have not been incorporated. For the classic critique of incorporation based on the original intent of the Fourteenth Amendment, see Fairman, *Does the Fourteenth Amendment Incorporate the Bill of Rights?*, 2 Stan. L. Rev. 5 (1949).

For further discussion, see Ackerman, *Constitutional Politics/Constitutional Law*, 99 Yale L.J. 453, 460 (1989) ("From its first encounter with these questions in the *Slaughter-house Cases* of 1873, the Court has self-consciously struggled with the synthetic problems involved in integrating Founding (time one) and Reconstruction (time two) into a principled doctrinal whole. Perhaps the most famous modern synthetic problem is raised by Hugo Black's claim that the Fourteenth Amendment (time two) made the Bill of Rights (time one) binding on the states.").

(2) *Tying state and federal standards.* In the line of cases from *Adamson* to *Duncan*, set forth in the footnotes at the start of Justice White's opinion in *Duncan*, each incorporation of a provision of the Bill of Rights into the Fourteenth Amendment involved a raising of state standards to a stricter national standard of procedural protection for criminal defendants. Recent developments suggest that the pattern is not necessarily inevitable.

For example, the rule excluding the use of unconstitutionally obtained evidence was first adopted as a federal standard in 1914 in *Weeks v. United States*, 232 U.S. 383 (1914); it was extended to the states in 1961 in *Mapp v. Ohio*, 367 U.S. 643 (1961). In *United States v. Leon*, 468 U.S. 897 (1984), the Court (6-3) created a "good-faith" exception to the rule: "In the absence of an allegation that the magistrate abandoned his detached and neutral role, suppression [of evidence] is appropriate only if the officers were dishonest or reckless in preparing their affidavit or could not have harbored an objectively reasonable belief in the existence of probable cause."

§ 7.03 REGULATION OF BUSINESS AND OTHER PROPERTY INTERESTS

[1] Liberty of Contract Under the Due Process Clauses

LOCHNER v. NEW YORK
198 U.S. 45, 25 S. Ct. 539, 49 L. Ed. 2d 937 (1905)

JUSTICE PECKHAM . . . delivered the opinion of the court:

The indictment, it will be seen, charges that the plaintiff in error violated the 110th section of article 8, chapter 415, of the Laws of 1897,[1] known as the labor law of the state of New York, in that he wrongfully and unlawfully required and permitted an employee working for him to work more than sixty hours in one week. . . .

The statute necessarily interferes with the right of contract between the employer and employees, concerning the number of hours in which the latter may labor in the bakery of the employer. The general right to make a contract in relation to his business is part of the liberty of the individual protected by the 14th Amendment of the Federal Constitution. *Allgeyer v. Louisiana*, 165 U.S. 578. Under that provision no state can deprive any person of life, liberty, or property without due process of law. . . . There are, however, certain powers, existing in the sovereignty of each state in the Union, somewhat vaguely termed police powers, the exact description and limitation of which have not been attempted by the courts. Those powers, broadly stated, and without, at present, any attempt at a more specific limitation, relate to the safety, health, morals, and general welfare of the public. . . .

. . . Contracts in violation of a statute, either of the Federal or state government, or a contract to let one's property for immoral purposes, or to do any other unlawful act, could obtain no protection from the Federal Constitution, as coming under the liberty of person or of free contract. . . .

This court has recognized the existence and upheld the exercise of the police powers of the states in many cases which might fairly be considered as border ones. . . . Among the later cases where the state law has been upheld by this court is that of *Holden v. Hardy*, 169 U.S. 366. A provision in the act of the legislature of Utah was there under consideration, the act limiting the employment of workmen in all underground mines or workings, to eight hours per day, "except in cases of emergency, where life or property is in imminent danger." It also limited the hours of labor in smelting and other institutions for the reduction or refining of ores or metals to eight hours per day, except in like cases of emergency. . . . It was held that the kind of employment, mining, smelting, etc., and the character of the employees in such kinds of labor, were such as to make it reasonable and proper for the state to interfere to prevent the employees from being constrained by the rules laid down by the proprietors in regard to labor. . . .

The latest case decided by this court, involving the police power, is that of *Jacobson v. Massachusetts*, decided at this term and reported in 197 U.S. 11. It related to compulsory vaccination, and the law was held valid as a proper exercise of the police

---

[1] § 110. Hours of labor in bakeries and confectionery establishments.—No employee shall be required or permitted to work in a biscuit, bread, or cake bakery or confectionery establishment more than sixty hours in any one week, or more than ten hours in any one day, unless for the purpose of making a shorter work day on the last day of the week; nor more hours in any one week than will make an average of ten hours per day for the number of days during such week in which such employee shall work.

powers with reference to the public health. . . .

. . . Of course the liberty of contract relating to labor includes both parties to it. The one has as much right to purchase as the other to sell labor.

This is not a question of substituting the judgment of the court for that of the legislature. If the act be within the power of the state it is valid, although the judgment of the court might be totally opposed to the enactment of such a law. . . .

The question whether this act is valid as a labor law, pure and simple, may be dismissed in a few words. There is no reasonable ground for interfering with the liberty of person or the right of free contract, by determining the hours of labor, in the occupation of a baker. There is no contention that bakers as a class are not equal in intelligence and capacity to men in other trades or manual occupations, or that they are not able to assert their rights and care for themselves without the protecting arm of the state, interfering with their independence of judgment and of action. They are in no sense wards of the state. Viewed in the light of a purely labor law, with no reference whatever to the question of health, we think that a law like the one before us involves neither the safety, the morals, nor the welfare, of the public, and that the interest of the public is not in the slightest degree affected by such an act. . . . Clean and wholesome bread does not depend upon whether the baker works but ten hours per day or only sixty hours a week. . . .

. . . The mere assertion that the subject relates, though but in a remote degree, to the public health, does not necessarily render the enactment valid. The act must have a more direct relation, as a means to an end, and the end itself must be appropriate and legitimate, before an act can be held to be valid which interferes with the general right of an individual to be free in his person and in his power to contract in relation to his own labor. . . .

We think the limit of the police power has been reached and passed in this case. There is, in our judgment, no reasonable foundation for holding this to be necessary or appropriate as a health law to safeguard the public health, or the health of the individuals who are following the trade of a baker. If this statute be valid, and if, therefore, a proper case is made out in which to deny the right of an individual, *sui juris*, as employer or employee, to make contracts for the labor of the latter under the protection of the provisions of the Federal Constitution, there would seem to be no length to which legislation of this nature might not go. . . .

. . . In looking through statistics regarding all trades and occupations, it may be true that the trade of a baker does not appear to be as healthy as some other trades, and is also vastly more healthy than still others. . . . It might be safely affirmed that almost all occupations more or less affect the health. There must be more than the mere fact of the possible existence of some small amount of unhealthiness to warrant legislative interference with liberty. It is unfortunately true that labor, even in any department, may possibly carry with it the seeds of unhealthiness. But are we all, on that account, at the mercy of legislative majorities? . . . No trade, no occupation, no mode of earning one's living, could escape this all-pervading power, and the acts of the legislature in limiting the hours of labor in all employments would be valid, although such limitation might seriously cripple the ability of the laborer to support himself and his family. . . .

It was further urged on the argument that restricting the hours of labor in the case of bakers was valid because it tended to cleanliness on the part of the workers, as a man was more apt to be cleanly when not overworked, and if cleanly then his "output" was also more likely to be so. . . . The state in that case would assume the position of a supervisor, or *pater familiae*, over every act of the individual. . . . In our judgment it is not possible in fact to discover the connection between the number of hours a baker may work in the bakery and the healthful quality of the bread made by the workman. . . .

This interference on the part of the legislatures of the several states with the ordinary trades and occupations of the people seems to be on the increase. . . .

It is manifest to us that the limitation of the hours of labor as provided for in this section of the statute under which the indictment was found, and the plaintiff in error convicted, has no such direct relation to, and no such substantial effect upon, the health of the employee, as to justify us in regarding the section as really a health law. It seems to us that the real object and purpose were simply to regulate the hours of labor between the master and his employees (all being men, *sui juris*), in a private business, not dangerous in any degree to morals, or in any real and substantial degree to the health of the employees. Under such circumstances the freedom of master and employee to contract with each other in relation to their employment, and in defining the same, cannot be prohibited or interfered with, without violating the Federal Constitution. . . .

JUSTICE HOLMES dissenting:

. . . This case is decided upon an economic theory which a large part of the country does not entertain. If it were a question whether I agreed with that theory, I should desire to study it further and long before making up my mind. But I do not conceive that to be my duty, because I strongly believe that my agreement or disagreement has nothing to do with the right of a majority to embody their opinions in law. . . . The liberty of the citizen to do as he likes so long as he does not interfere with the liberty of others to do the same, which has been a shibboleth for some well-known writers, is interfered with by school laws, by the Post Office, by every state or municipal institution which takes his money for purposes thought desirable, whether he likes it or not. The 14th Amendment does not enact Mr. Herbert Spencer's Social Statics. . . . United States and state statutes and decisions cutting down the liberty to contract by way of combination are familiar to this court. *Northern Securities Co. v. United States*, 193 U.S. 197. . . . The decision sustaining an eight-hour law for miners is still recent. *Holden v. Hardy*, 169 U.S. 366. Some of these laws embody convictions or prejudices which judges are likely to share. Some may not. But a Constitution is not intended to embody a particular economic theory, whether of paternalism and the organic relation of the citizen to the state or of *laissez faire*. It is made for people of fundamentally differing views. . . .

I think that the word "liberty," in the 14th Amendment, is perverted when it is held to prevent the natural outcome of a dominant opinion, unless it can be said that a rational and fair man necessarily would admit that the statute proposed would infringe fundamental principles as they have been understood by the traditions of our people and our law. It does not need research to show that no such sweeping condemnation can be passed upon the statute before us. A reasonable man might think it a proper measure on the score of health. Men whom I certainly could not pronounce unreasonable would uphold it as a first installment of a general regulation of the hours of work. . . .

JUSTICE HARLAN (with whom JUSTICE WHITE and JUSTICE DAY concurred) dissenting. . . .

[T]he rule is universal that a legislative enactment, Federal or state, is never to be disregarded or held invalid unless it be, beyond question, plainly and palpably in excess of legislative power. . . . If the end which the legislature seeks to accomplish be one to which its power extends, and if the means employed to that end, although not the wisest or best, are yet not plainly and palpably unauthorized by law, then the court cannot interfere. . . .

. . . Under our systems . . . of government the courts are not concerned with the wisdom or policy of legislation. . . . I find it impossible, in view of common experience, to say that there is here no real or substantial relation between the means employed by the state and the end sought to be accomplished by its legislation. . . . Nor can I say that the statute has no appropriate or direct connection with that protection to health which each state owes to her citizens . . . or that it is not promotive of the health of the employees in question . . . or that the regulation prescribed by the state is utterly unreasonable and extravagant or wholly arbitrary. . . . Still less can I say that the statute is, beyond question, a plain, palpable invasion of rights secured by the fundamental law. . . .

A decision that the New York statute is void under the 14th Amendment will, in my opinion, involve consequences of a far-reaching and mischievous character; for such a decision would seriously cripple the inherent power of the states to care for the lives, health, and well-being of their citizens. . . .

NOTE: The Development of Liberty of Contract and the Court-Packing Crisis

The restrictive construction of the Due Process Clause in the *Slaughter-House Cases*, *supra* § 7.01, in matters of economic regulation prevailed for some time despite the narrow majority and the strong dissents. Ultimately, however, the decision served as only a temporary barrier to the use of the Fourteenth Amendment in checking state economic regulation. A combination of pressures caused the Court to adopt substantive due process as a tool for judicial intervention in economic regulation. The growth of industrialization and urbanization created new socio-economic problems and prompted increased legislative responses. Proponents of current economic and social theories, such as Adam Smith's economic laissez-faire and social Darwinism, opposed these increased governmental regulations. Arguments that property and economic interests were fundamental rights entitled to judicial protection found an increasingly receptive audience among members of the Court. *Allgeyer v. Louisiana*, 165 U.S. 578 (1897), was an early use of substantive due process to invalidate a state regulatory statute. The case involved a state law that prohibited anyone from obtaining insurance on property located within the state from any insurance company failing to comply with Louisiana law. The defendant had contracted for an insurance policy with an insurer who was not licensed to do business in Louisiana. In striking down the statute as a violation of due process, the Court, per Justice Peckham, gave an expansive reading to the concept of "liberty" protected by the Fourteenth Amendment. This broad construction of "liberty" was to become a characteristic component of the Court's later decisions striking down state attempts to regulate individual economic arrangements.

The *Lochner* case represented a high point of judicial intervention in economic regulation. Over the next 30 years, the Court used due process to strike down laws regulating prices, maximum hours, minimum wages, labor relations, conditions for entry into business, and other types of economic regulations. The pattern was not uniform, however, as large numbers of regulatory laws were upheld during this period. Just three years after *Lochner*, the Court sustained an Oregon law that prescribed a ten-hour maximum work day for women employed in any factory or laundry. *See Muller v. Oregon*, 208 U.S. 412 (1908). The Court's opinion stressed that liberty of contract was not absolute and that the state could validly legislate such protection in the public interest. Nine years later, the Court again sustained a statute establishing a maximum ten-hour day for factory workers in *Bunting v. Oregon*, 243 U.S. 426 (1917).

Though willing to uphold the regulation of work hours, the Court held that regulation of wages violated due process. In *Adkins v. Children's Hospital*, 261 U.S.

525 (1923), the Court invalidated a District of Columbia law setting minimum wages for women. Justice Holmes' dissent pointed out the inconsistency of invalidating minimum wage legislation while sustaining maximum hours regulations. Nonetheless, the Court adhered to the *Adkins* decision until 1937, when it was overruled in *West Coast Hotel v. Parrish*, 300 U.S. 379 (1937). *See infra* Note: The New Deal, Constitutional Crisis, Economic Regulation, and Property Rights. In the intervening period, the Court continued its checkered career of close judicial scrutiny of economic legislation. For additional discussion, see Ackerman, *Constitutional Politics/Constitutional Law*, 99 YALE L.J. 453, 457–58 (1989) ("The period between Reconstruction and New Deal can then be viewed as a (complex) story about the fall from grace wherein most of the Justices (not Holmes, of course) strayed from the path of righteousness and imposed their antidemocratic laissez-faire philosophy on the nation through the pretext of constitutional interpretation. Predictably, these acts of judicial usurpation set the judges at odds with more democratic institutions, which acutely perceived the failure of laissez-faire to do justice to an increasingly complex and interdependent world."); Bewig, *Lochner v. the Journeymen Bakers of New York: The Journeymen Bakers, Their Hours of Labor, and the Constitution*, 38 AM. J. LEGAL HIST. 413, 419 (1994) ("Unlike liberals, the journeymen bakers believed that the Constitution did have something to say about economic rights; unlike the libertarians, the bakers believed that what the Constitution said was that the civic community had substantive economic rights and thus could defend its members and its institutions by regulating the hours of labor."); Currie, *The Constitution in the Supreme Court: The Protection of Economic Interests, 1889–1910*, 52 U. CHI. L. REV. 867 (1985); Currie, *The Constitution in the Supreme Court, 1910–1921*, 1985 DUKE L.J. 1111; Currie, *The Constitution in the Supreme Court: 1921–1930* , 1986 DUKE L.J. 65.

NEBBIA v. NEW YORK, 291 U.S. 502 (1934). *Nebbia* signaled the decline in the Court's use of substantive due process and a return to giving deference to state economic and social legislation. *Nebbia* involved a New York statute passed to regulate the troubled dairy industry. Milk prices were falling and dairy farmers were unable to recoup their production costs. Accordingly, the State established a Milk Control Board to set prices on milk and stabilize the industry.

Justice Roberts delivered the opinion of the Court and denied Nebbia's arguments that the New York law violated the Due Process and Equal Protection Clauses of the Fourteenth Amendment. "[S]o far as the requirement of due process is concerned, and in the absence of other constitutional restriction, a state is free to adopt whatever economic policy may reasonably be deemed to promote public welfare, and to enforce that policy by legislation adapted to its purpose."

According to Justice Roberts, the appropriate standard of review was "[i]f the laws passed are seen to have a reasonable relation to a proper legislative purpose, and are neither arbitrary nor discriminatory, the requirements of due process are satisfied." Justice Roberts emphasized that the Court's proper role is not to judge the wisdom of the legislation.

Justice McReynolds dissented, joined by Justices VanDevanter, Sutherland, and Butler. The statute "is not regulation, but management, control, dictation — it amounts to the deprivation of the fundamental right which one has to conduct his own affairs honestly and along customary lines."

NOTE: The New Deal, Constitutional Crisis, Economic Regulation, and Property Rights

Starting with his inauguration in March 1933, President Franklin D. Roosevelt moved quickly to cope with the Great Depression that had gripped the country during the final three years of the Hoover Administration. *Nebbia v. New York* might have been seen as an indication that the Supreme Court, faced with a national economic emergency, would be willing to sustain much-needed state and federal regulation against claims that Congress had exceeded its enumerated powers and that the states were infringing rights guaranteed by the Fourteenth Amendment. *Nebbia* turned out, however, to be a false spring, as the winter of discontent and controversy between the popular New Deal President and the "Nine Old Men" reached crisis proportions in 1935 and 1936 when the Court struck down the National Industrial Recovery Act, *Schechter Poultry Corp. v. United States*, 295 U.S. 495 (1935), the Agricultural Adjustment Act, *United States v. Butler*, 297 U.S. 1 (1936), the Bituminous Coal Conservation Act, *Carter v. Carter Coal Co.*, 298 U.S. 238 (1936), and New York's minimum wage law for women, *Morehead v. People of State of New York ex rel. Tipaldo*, 298 U.S. 587 (1936). These cases are discussed in Chapter II.

These decisions provoked the New Deal Constitutional Crisis as President Roosevelt, following his overwhelming re-election victory in 1936, proposed a "court packing" plan whereby the President could appoint a new Supreme Court justice for every incumbent who was seventy-years old and had served on the Court for ten years. The plan sparked a furor of controversy, with many of Roosevelt's staunchest supporters balking at this attempt to overturn unpopular Court decisions by increasing the number of justices. During a critical period in the spring of 1937, the Supreme Court made the famous "switch-in-time-that-saved-nine," upholding key federal and state legislation, through the shifting votes of Chief Justice Hughes and Justice Roberts. Upheld were the National Labor Relations Act, *National Labor Relations Board v. Jones & Laughlin Steel Corp.*, 301 U.S. 1 (1937), the Social Security Act, involving old-age and unemployment benefits, *Steward Machine Co. v. Davis*, 301 U.S. 48 (1937), and *Helvering v. Davis*, 301 U.S. 619 (1937) (*see* § 2.04). *Cf.* Cushman, *Doctrinal Synergies and Liberal Dilemmas: The Case of the Yellow Dog Contract*, 1992 SUP. CT. REV. 235; Cushman, *A Stream of Legal Consciousness: The Current of the Commerce Doctrine from Swift to Jones & Laughlin*, 61 FORDHAM L. REV. 105 (1992) (describing a much more gradual transition in the Court's views on economic regulation).

These cases, discussed in Chapter II, upheld these statutes against Commerce Clause challenges. Of particular importance in the area of substantive due process jurisprudence is *West Coast Hotel v. Parrish*, 300 U.S. 379 (1937). In that case, the Court upheld the constitutionality of a Washington minimum wage law for women against a due process challenge. *West Coast Hotel* is particularly significant because, only one year earlier, the Court had invalidated New York's minimum wage law for women in *New York ex rel. Tipaldo*.

The above cases marked the end of the crisis. Although Congress rejected the court-packing plan, it remains a matter of conjecture as to what would have happened if the Court, in the spring of 1937, had not defused the crisis by its decisions that were handed down before President Roosevelt appointed his first Justice in the summer of 1937. For additional discussion of the court-packing controversy see, e.g., R. JACKSON, THE STRUGGLE FOR JUDICIAL SUPREMACY (1941); Currie, *The Constitution in the Supreme Court: The New Deal, 1931–1940*, 54 U. CHI. L. REV. 504 (1987); Leuchtenbert, *The Origins of Franklin D. Roosevelt's "Court-Packing" Plan*, 1966 SUP. CT. REV. 347.

While the Court, in 1937, adopted a policy of extreme judicial deference with regard to government regulation of business activity, a few months later, in a famous footnote, Justice Stone outlined three areas in which the newly adopted position of judicial deference would not be appropriate. The case, *United States v. Carolene Products*, 304 U.S. 144 (1938), involved Commerce Clause, due process, and equal protection challenges to a federal statute prohibiting the interstate shipment of a product — "filled milk" — which combined skimmed milk with a butterfat substitute.

UNITED STATES v. CAROLENE PRODUCTS CO.
304 U.S. 144, 58 S. Ct. 778, 82 L. Ed. 1234 (1938)

JUSTICE STONE delivered the opinion of the Court.

The question for decision is whether the "Filled Milk Act" of Congress of . . . 1923 which prohibits the shipment in interstate commerce of skimmed milk compounded with any fat or oil other than milk fat, so as to resemble milk or cream, transcends the power of Congress to regulate interstate commerce or infringes the Fifth Amendment. . . .

Appellee assails the statute as beyond the power of Congress over interstate commerce, and hence an invasion of a field of action said to be reserved to the states by the Tenth Amendment. Appellee also complains that the statute denies to it equal protection of the laws, and in violation of the Fifth Amendment, deprives it of its property without due process of law, particularly in that the statute purports to make binding and conclusive upon appellee the legislative declaration that appellee's product "is an adulterated article of food, injurious to the public health, and its sale constitutes a fraud on the public."

First. The power to regulate commerce is the power "to prescribe the rule by which commerce is to be governed," . . . The power "is complete in itself, may be exercised to its utmost extent, and acknowledges no limitations, other than are prescribed in the Constitution." . . . Hence Congress is free to exclude from interstate commerce articles whose use in the states for which they are destined it may reasonably conceive to be injurious to the public health, morals or welfare. . . .

Second. The prohibition of shipment of appellee's product in interstate commerce does not infringe the Fifth Amendment. Twenty years ago this Court, in *Hebe Co. v. Shaw*, 248 U.S. 297, . . . held that a state law which forbids the manufacture and sale of a product assumed to be wholesome and nutritive, made of condensed skimmed milk, compounded with coconut oil, is not forbidden by the Fourteenth Amendment. . . .

We see no persuasive reason for departing from that ruling here, where the Fifth Amendment is concerned; and since none is suggested, we might rest decision wholly on the presumption of constitutionality. But affirmative evidence also sustains the statute. In twenty years evidence has steadily accumulated of the danger to the public health from the general consumption of foods which have been stripped of elements essential to the maintenance of health. The Filled Milk Act was adopted by Congress after committee hearings, in the course of which eminent scientists and health experts testified. . . .

. . . Whether in such circumstances the public would be adequately protected by the prohibition of false labels and false branding imposed by the Pure Food and Drugs Act, . . . or whether it was necessary to go farther and prohibit a substitute food product thought to be injurious to health if used as a substitute when the two are not distinguishable, was a matter for the legislative judgment and not that of courts. . . .

Appellee raises no valid objection to the present statute by arguing that its prohibition has not been extended to oleomargarine or other butter substitutes in which vegetable fats or oils are substituted for butter fat. The Fifth Amendment has no equal protection clause, and even that of the Fourteenth, applicable only to the states, does not compel their Legislatures to prohibit all like evils, or none. A Legislature may hit at an abuse which it has found, even though it has failed to strike at another. . . .

Third. . . .

[T]he existence of facts supporting the legislative judgment is to be presumed, for regulatory legislation affecting ordinary commercial transactions is not to be pronounced unconstitutional unless in the light of the facts made known or generally assumed it is of such a character as to preclude the assumption that it rests upon some rational basis within the knowledge and experience of the legislators. . . . [2]

. . . [B]y their very nature . . . inquiries, where the legislative judgment is drawn in question, must be restricted to the issue whether any state of facts either known or which could reasonably be assumed affords support for it. . . .

. . . As the statute is not unconstitutional on its face, the demurrer should have been overruled and the judgment will be reserved.

JUSTICE BLACK concurs in the result and in all of the opinion, except the part marked "*Third.*"

JUSTICE McREYNOLDS thinks that the judgment should be affirmed.

JUSTICE CARDOZO and JUSTICE REED took no part in the consideration or decision of this case.

JUSTICE BUTLER [concurs].

NOTES

(1) *Deference and Rationality Review.* In the years since 1937, the Court has generally followed the judicial philosophy toward state economic regulation articulated in *West Coast Hotel v. Parrish and United States v. Carolene Products*. It has rejected due process claims with language emphasizing great deference to legislative judgment. *See, e.g., Ferguson v. Skrupa*, 372 U.S. 726 (1963); *Day-Brite Lighting, Inc. v. Missouri*, 342 U.S. 421 (1952); and *Olsen v. Nebraska*, 313 U.S. 236 (1941).

Some of these challenges to state laws were framed in equal protection terms, and, here again, the Court declined to intervene. *See Williamson v. Lee Optical of Oklahoma*, 348 U.S. 483 (1955) and *Kotch v. Board of River Port Pilot Comm'rs*, 330 U.S. 552 (1947). In *Williamson*, an unanimous Court upheld a law regulating the business of making, fitting, and selling lenses and eyeglasses, rejecting due process and

---

[2] [Court's footnote 4] There may be narrower scope for operation of the presumption of constitutionality when legislation appears on its face to be within a specific prohibition of the Constitution, such as those of the first ten Amendments, which are deemed equally specific when held to be embraced within the Fourteenth. *See Stromberg v. California*, 283 U.S. 359, 369, 370; *Lovell v. Griffin*, 303 U.S. 444, decided March 28, 1938.

It is unnecessary to consider now whether legislation which restricts those political processes which can ordinarily be expected to bring about repeal of undesirable legislation, is to be subjected to more exacting judicial scrutiny under the general prohibitions of the Fourteenth Amendment than are most other types of legislation. On restrictions upon the right to vote, *see Nixon v. Herndon*, 273 U.S. 536; *Nixon v. Condon*, 286 U.S. 73; on restraints upon the dissemination of information, *see Near v. Minnesota*, 283 U.S. 697, 718–714, 718–720, 722; *Grosjean v. American Press Co.*, 297 U.S. 233; *Lovell v. Griffin, infra*; on interferences with political organizations, *see Stromberg v. California, infra*, 283 U.S. 359, 369; *Fiske v. Kansas*, 274 U.S. 380; *Whitney v. California*, 274 U.S. 357, 373–378; *Herndon v. Lowry*, 301 U.S. 242; and *see* Holmes, J., in *Gitlow v. New York*, 268 U.S. 652, 673; as to prohibition of peaceable assembly, *see De Jonge v. Oregon*, 269 U.S. 358, 365.

Nor need we inquire whether similar considerations enter into the review of statutes directed at particular religious, *Pierce v. Society of Sisters*, 268 U.S. 510, or national, *Meyer v. Nebraska*, 262 U.S. 390; *Bartels v. Iowa*, 262 U.S. 404; *Farrington v. Tokushige*, 273 U. S. 284, or racial minorities. *Nixon v. Herndon, infra*; *Nixon v. Condon, infra*; whether prejudice against discrete and insular minorities may be a special condition, which tends seriously to curtail the operation of those political processes ordinarily to be relied upon to protect minorities, and which may call for a correspondingly more searching judicial inquiry. Compare *McCulloch v. Maryland*, 4 Wheat. 316, 428; *South Carolina State Highway Department v. Barnwell Bros.*, 303 U.S. 177, decided February 14, 1938, note 2. and cases cited.

equal protection arguments. The Court wrote:

> [T]he law need not be in every respect logically consistent with its aims to be constitutional. It is enough that there is an evil at hand for correction, and that it might be thought that the particular legislative measure was a rational way to correct it. The day is gone when this Court uses the Due Process Clause of the Fourteenth Amendment to strike down state laws, regulatory of business and industrial conditions, because they may be unwise, improvident, or out of harmony with a particular school of thought. . . . The problem of legislative classification is a perennial one, admitting of no doctrinaire definition. Evils in the same field may be of different dimensions and proportions, requiring different remedies. Or so the legislature may think. . . . Or the reform may take one step at a time, addressing itself to the phase of the problem which seems most acute to the legislative mind. . . . The legislature may select one phase of the field and apply a remedy there, neglecting the others. . . . The prohibition of the Equal Protection Clause goes no further than the invidious discrimination.

Id. at 487-89. *See also McGowan v. Maryland, infra* § 16.05, Note (2)(a) after *Sherbert.*

The rise of the so-called "new equal protection" in the 1960s and 1970s, with its promise of judicial intervention to protect such economic interests as housing and subsistence for poorer segments of the population, suggested the possibility of a return to a pre-1937 judicial approach to some types of social and economic regulatory laws. This has not happened. *See Conn v. Gabbert*, 526 U.S. 286 (1999) (due process right to practice one's profession subject to reasonable government regulations, which is not violated by brief interruptions in daily work routine as opposed to complete deprivation of one's job).

For additional commentary, see Friedman, *Dialogue and Judicial Review*, 91 MICH. L. REV. 577, 582 (1993) (rejecting the basic notion that courts are countermajoritarian: "courts are seen as promoters of, and participants in, a national dialogue about the meaning of the Constitution"); Eskridge & Frickey, *Foreword: Law as Equilibrium*, 108 HARV. L. REV. 26, 27 (1994) ("With the confirmation of Justice Stephen Breyer to the United States Supreme Court, the legal process school has quietly attained what every Supreme Court litigator seeks: a majority on the Court. Along with Justice Breyer, Justices Scalia, Kennedy, Souter, and Ginsburg are all alumni of Henry Hart's and Albert Sacks's Harvard Law School courses on 'The Legal Process.' As such, they have been schooled in the legal process's emphasis on the creation of law by interacting institutions, the purposiveness of law and these institutions, and the mediating role of procedure.").

(2) The celebrated footnote 4 in *Carolene Products* is far more important than the decision itself. It has functioned as a kind of blueprint, guiding a large part of the work of the modern Court. For additional discussion of footnote 4, see J. ELY, DEMOCRACY AND DISTRUST (1980); L. LUSKY, BY WHAT RIGHT? (1975); Lusky, *Footnote Redux: A Carolene Products Reminiscence*, 82 COLUM. L. REV. 1093 (1982); Powell, *Carolene Products Revisited*, 82 COLUM. L. REV. 1087 (1982). *See also* Ackerman, *Beyond Carolene Products*, 98 HARV. L. REV. 713 (1985); Attanasio, *Everyman's Constitutional Law: A Theory of the Power of Judicial Review*, 72 GEO. L.J. 1665 (1984). For a listing of some of the various writings about the footnote, see Note, *Don't Cry Over Filled Milk: The Neglected Footnote Three to Carolene Products*, 136 U. PA. L. REV. 1553, 1553 n.3 (1988).

For an analysis tracing deep historical roots in the basic *Carolene Products* distinction between personal and economic or property rights, see Nelson, *The Eighteenth Century Constitution as a Basis for Protecting Personal Liberty, in* LIBERTY AND COMMUNITY: CONSTITUTIONAL RIGHTS IN THE EARLY AMERICAN REPUBLIC 18 (1987)

("[E]ighteenth-century history has its greatest utility as a device for illuminating the deep-seated political structures and values that continue to underlie American constitutionalism today and that help to account for the *Carolene Products* dichotomy between economic and moral regulation.").

[2] Limiting Punitive Damages Under the Due Process Clause

Although due process and equal protection challenges to economic regulation have generally not evoked judicial protection, § 7.03[3] detects some judicial rumblings that possibly herald stricter scrutiny of state economic regulation through the use of the "taking" clause of the Fifth Amendment (as made applicable to the states through the Fourteenth Amendment). The modern revival of substantive due process has largely been confined to personal rights in the areas of contraception and abortion (§ 7.04). Moreover, there has been some judicial willingness to expand the definition of "liberty" and "property" to include "personal property rights," such as a right to continued welfare benefits, and to protect these rights through procedural safeguards. These cases, which are discussed in the concluding section of this Chapter (§ 7.05), indicate that the line between "personal rights" and "property rights" is far less clear today than it was when the Court decided cases like *Lochner, Nebbia,* and *Carolene Products.* Before turning to these various topics, the remainder of this section explores one area of apparent revival of economic substantive due process — punitive damages. For a time, the Court hesitated to set aside punitive awards based on due process challenges to the procedures followed or the amounts of the awards. Of late, the Court has taken a more expansive approach to constitutional review of punitive awards under the Due Process Clause.

BMW OF NORTH AMERICA v. GORE, 517 U.S. 559 (1996). In *Gore,* the Court invalidated a $2 million punitive damages award under the Due Process Clause, finding that the award was "grossly excessive," in light of the $4,000 compensatory damages award. Dr. Ira Gore brought suit against BMW of North America claiming that an authorized Alabama BMW dealership fraudulently failed to disclose that the new car that Dr. Gore purchased had been repainted. "At trial, BMW acknowledged that it had adopted a nationwide policy" of not informing dealers or customers of damaged cars when "the repair cost did not exceed 3 percent of the suggested retail price." As the "$601.37 cost of repainting Dr. Gore's car was only 1.5 percent of its suggested retail price," it was subject to this policy.

Relying on a former BMW dealer's estimate "that the value of a repainted BMW was approximately 10 percent less than" that of a new one, the jury awarded Gore $4,000 in compensatory damages. The jury also awarded plaintiff $4 million in punitive damages based on his argument that BMW had sold "approximately 1,000" refinished cars nationwide with a diminished value of $4,000 each. Before the verdict, BMW had altered its policy to stop selling refinished cars in Alabama and two other states. After the verdict, "BMW promptly instituted a nationwide policy of full disclosure of all repairs, no matter how minor." The trial judge denied BMW's post-trial motion to set aside the punitive damages award despite BMW's showing that its "nondisclosure policy was consistent" with the disclosure laws of approximately 25 other states, and its "policy had never been adjudged unlawful before this action was filed."

The Alabama Supreme Court reduced the punitive damages award to $2 million because the jury had "improperly computed the amount of punitive damages by multiplying Dr. Gore's compensatory damages by the number of" refinished cars sold by BMW in other jurisdictions. Holding that the punitive damages should be based solely on BMW's conduct in Alabama, the court predicated the $2 million amount on a

" 'comparative analysis' that considered Alabama cases, 'along with cases from other jurisdictions, involving' " juries awarding purchasers punitive damages for fraudulent vehicle sales.

Writing for a 5-4 majority, Justice Stevens first discussed Alabama's interest in imposing the punitive damages award. The states' "legitimate interests" in "punishing" and "deterring" unlawful conduct afford them "considerable flexibility" in determining the appropriate amounts of punitive damages "in different classes of cases or in any particular case." Nevertheless, to avoid "infringing on the policy choices of other States," Alabama's legislative and judicial economic penalties must advance its "interest in protecting its own consumers and its own economy."[3]

As a result, Alabama could require BMW to comply with a disclosure policy in its own state, but could not "punish BMW for conduct that was lawful" in other states "and that had no impact on Alabama or its residents." In a criminal proceeding, the "sentencing judge may even consider past criminal behavior which did not result in a conviction and lawful conduct that bears on the defendant's character and prospects for rehabilitation." (In the criminal area, the Court has upheld habitual offender statutes that "permit the sentencing court to enhance a defendant's punishment for a crime in light of prior convictions, including convictions in foreign jurisdictions.") However, the Court has not allowed a sentencing court to punish lawful conduct as Alabama seeks to do in punishing nondisclosure that was lawful in other states.[4]

While it was improper for Alabama to compute punitive damages by multiplying sales in other jurisdictions, evidence of out-of-state conduct is relevant in determining "the degree of reprehensibility of the defendant's conduct."

Basic constitutional notions of fairness require "that a person receive fair notice not only of the conduct that will subject him to punishment but also of the severity of the penalty that a State may impose. Three guideposts" suggest "that BMW did not receive adequate notice of the magnitude of the sanction that Alabama might impose," and consequently that the $2 million punitive damages award was "grossly excessive."

The first and perhaps the most important guidepost "of the reasonableness of a punitive damages award is the degree of reprehensibility of the defendant's conduct."[5]

Crimes involving violence, intentional malice and trickery or deceit are more reprehensible than those that do not involve violence or are merely negligent. "The presale refinishing of the car had no effect on its performance or safety features, or even its appearance for at least nine months after his [Gore's] purchase. BMW's conduct evinced no indifference to or reckless disregard for the health and safety of others."[6]

Justice Stevens also rejected plaintiff's argument that BMW's actions were "particularly reprehensible" because it knowingly engaged in a "nationwide pattern of tortious conduct." First, while no state court had determined whether Alabama's disclosure laws provided "a safe harbor for nondisclosure of presumptively minor

---

[3] "State power may be exercised as much by a jury's application of a state rule of law in a civil lawsuit as by a statute."

[4] Because the jury verdict was based partly on conduct outside Alabama that was lawful where it occurred, Justice Stevens declined to consider whether a "State may properly attempt to change a tortfeasors' unlawful conduct in another State."

[5] "The principle that punishment should fit the crime 'is deeply rooted and frequently repeated in common-law jurisprudence.' "

[6] Certainly, the "infliction of economic injury, especially when done intentionally through affirmative acts of misconduct, or when the target is financially vulnerable, can warrant a substantial penalty."

repairs," BMW could have reasonably assumed that Alabama's disclosure statutes provided such a "safe harbor." Indeed, "BMW's decision to follow a disclosure policy that coincided with the strictest extant state statute" would not justify the $2 million punitive award.

Second, the Court rejected the argument that BMW should have anticipated that some or all jurisdictions would have considered its behavior fraudulent. Justice Stevens reasoned that "fraud requires a material misrepresentation or omission." Minor flaws in a new car's finish do not materially affect the car's value and "BMW could reasonably rely on state disclosure statutes" to draw the line between major and minor damages.

Lastly, BMW's actions were not "particularly reprehensible" because "the record in this case discloses no deliberate false statements, acts of affirmative misconduct, or concealment of evidence of improper motive, such as were present in *Pacific Mutual Life Ins. Co. v. Haslip*, 499 U.S. 1 (1991), or *TXO Production Corp. v. Alliance Resources Corp.*, 509 U.S. 443 (1993). We accept, of course, the jury's finding" that under Alabama law BMW was required to inform customers of the repainted condition of the cars. "But the omission of a material fact may be less reprehensible than a deliberate false statement, particularly when there is a good-faith basis for believing that no duty to disclose exists."

"The second and perhaps most commonly cited" guidepost signaling "an unreasonable or excessive punitive damages award is its ratio to the actual harm inflicted on the plaintiff." In *Haslip*, the Court found that "a punitive damages award of 'more than 4 times the amount of compensatory damages,' might be close to the line." Following *Haslip*, the Court, in *TXO*, upheld a $10 million award because "the difference between that figure and the harm to the victim that would have ensued if the tortious plan had succeeded" did not exceed "10 to 1." In contrast, plaintiff's $2 million punitive damages award was "500 times the amount of his actual harm as determined by the jury."[7]

The Court has "consistently rejected the notion that the constitutional line is marked by a simple mathematical formula, even one that compares actual and potential damages to the punitive award. *TXO*. Indeed, low awards of compensatory damages may properly support a higher ratio than high compensatory awards, if, for example, a particularly egregious act has resulted in only a small amount of economic damages. A higher ratio may also be justified in cases in which the injury is hard to detect or the monetary value of noneconomic harm might have been difficult to determine." While a "'mathematical bright line'" could not be drawn, a 500 to 1 ratio was "breathtaking" enough to "'raise a suspicious judicial eyebrow.'"

The third guidepost indicating excessiveness compares "the punitive damages award and the civil or criminal penalties that could be imposed for comparable misconduct." The maximum civil penalty under Alabama's Deceptive Trade Practices Act is $2,000; "other States authorize more severe sanctions, with the maxima ranging from $5,000 to $10,000." Not one of these statutes provided an "out-of-state distributor with fair notice that the first violation or, indeed the first 14 violations of its provisions might subject an offender to a multimillion dollar penalty. Moreover, at the time BMW's policy was first challenged, there does not appear to have been any judicial decision in Alabama or elsewhere indicating that application of that policy might give rise to such severe punishment." Even though the award prompted a change in BMW's policy, one could not assume that "a lesser deterrent would have adequately protected the interests of Alabama consumers." The argument that a severe penalty was needed to deter "future

---

[7] Even if a repainted BMW diminishes in value by $4,000, "the award is 35 times greater than the total damages of all 14 Alabama consumers who purchased repainted BMW's."

misconduct" was not convincing because BMW did not have "a history of noncompliance with known statutory requirements."

Justice Stevens pointed out that BMW's status as a large corporation "does not diminish its entitlement to fair notice of the demands that the several States impose on the conduct of its business." BMW's active involvement "in the national economy implicates the federal interest in preventing individual States from imposing undue burdens on interstate commerce." The Court was "fully convinced that the grossly excessive award imposed in this case transcends the constitutional limit."

Justice Breyer, joined by Justices O'Connor and Souter, concurred in the judgment. Alabama courts applied standards that "are vague and open-ended to the point where they risk arbitrary results." While such vagueness does "not, by itself, violate due process, it does invite the kind of scrutiny the Court has given the particular verdict before us." Justice Breyer found that "the award in this case was both (a) the product of a system of standards that did not significantly constrain a court's, and hence a jury's, discretion in making the award; and (b) was grossly excessive in light of the State's legitimate punitive damages objectives." These reasons overcame the " 'strong presumption of validity' " to which damage awards are normally entitled.

Justice Scalia wrote a dissenting opinion, in which Justice Thomas joined. As the Constitution afforded the Court no authority to scrutinize the constitutionality of excessive punitive damage awards, the decision was "an unjustified incursion" in state matters. The Due Process Clause is not a "secret repository of substantive guarantees against 'unfairness.' . . . What the Fourteenth Amendment's procedural guarantee assures is an opportunity to contest the reasonableness of a damages judgment in state court." Moreover, the Court's new rule was "constrained by no principle other than the Justices' subjective assessment of the 'reasonableness' of the award in relation to the conduct for which it was assessed."

Justice Scalia also said that the "three federal 'guideposts' can be overridden if 'necessary to deter future misconduct' a loophole that will encourage state reviewing courts to uphold awards as necessary for the 'adequate protection' of state consumers." If the Court is correct in asserting that all unreasonably excessive punitive damages awards are unconstitutional, so are unreasonably excessive awards of compensatory damages. "By today's logic, every dispute as to evidentiary sufficiency in a state civil suit poses a question of constitutional moment."

Justice Ginsburg, joined by Chief Justice Rehnquist, also dissented. Justice Ginsburg maintained that the Court "unnecessarily and unwisely ventures into territory traditionally within the States' domain, and does so in the face of reform measures recently adopted or currently under consideration in legislative arenas."

The Court has " 'no mathematical formula,' " or the like, to address the excessiveness of an award, but rather, "has only a vague concept of substantive due process, a 'raised eyebrow' test as its ultimate guide." The Court will work in this area unaided by the federal district courts and the federal courts of appeals. Previously, the Court was even reluctant to review the punitive damages awards of lower federal courts.

NOTES

(1) *De Novo Review.* In *Cooper Industries, Inc. v. Leatherman Tool Group, Inc.*, 523 U.S. 424 (2001), the Court held that a de novo standard of review should be applied to cases on appeal to determine whether punitive damages awards are excessive under the Eighth and Fourteenth Amendments. Leatherman Tool Group filed suit against Cooper Industries, alleging that Cooper engaged in unfair competition through false advertising and selling an " 'imitation' " of Leatherman's Pocket Survival Tool (PST). After trial, a jury found Cooper guilty of unfair competition and awarded Leatherman

$50,000 in compensatory damages and $4.5 million in punitive damages. The District Court upheld the award, and the Court of Appeals applied an abuse-of-discretion standard in affirming the judgment. In an 8-1 decision, the Supreme Court vacated and remanded the case, instructing the Court of Appeals to review the case de novo.

Writing for the majority, Justice Stevens noted that punitive damages have been described as " 'quasi-criminal,' " operating as " 'private fines' " that punish and deter. The Eighth Amendment prohibits excessive fines and cruel and unusual punishment, and the Court has applied it against the states to prohibit " 'grossly excessive' punishment on a tortfeasor." *BMW of North America, Inc. v. Gore, quoting TXO Production Corp. v. Alliance Resources.*

The Court has overturned excessive punishments in various cases from capital punishment to forfeiture. For example, in *United States v. Bajakajian*, 524 U.S. 321 (1998), the Court held that "punitive forfeiture of $357,144" due to an attempt to illegally transport those funds was " 'grossly disproportional' to the gravity of the offense." *Bajakajian* expressly states that "courts of appeals must review the proportionality determination 'de novo,' " and not by an abuse-of-discretion standard. First, "the precise meaning of concepts like 'reasonable suspicion' and 'probable cause' cannot be articulated with precision." Second, " 'the legal rules for probable cause and reasonable suspicion acquire content only through application,' " making independent review necessary for "appellate courts . . . to maintain control of, and to clarify, the legal principles." Third, " 'de novo review tends to unify precedent' and 'stabilize the law,' " which facilitates " 'the uniform treatment' " of individuals.

Rejecting the argument that de novo review violates the Seventh Amendment guarantee to a civil jury trial, the Court reasoned that punitive damage awards, unlike actual damages, do not "constitute a finding of 'fact.' " Indeed, appellate judges may be better positioned than trial judges to make determinations about the constitutionality of punitive damage awards. *Gore* sets forth three criteria for assessing the constitutionality of punitive awards: "(1) the degree or reprehensibility of the defendant's misconduct, (2) the disparity between the harm (or potential harm) suffered by the plaintiff and the punitive damages award, and (3) the difference between the punitive damages awarded by the jury and the civil penalties authorized or imposed in comparable cases." While the trial court can better analyze the first factor, both trial courts and appellate courts appear "equally capable of analyzing the second factor." However, appellate courts seem "more suited" to determine "the third *Gore* criterion, which calls for a broad legal comparison."

Justice Thomas concurred with the majority opinion that de novo review was appropriate but continued to think that *BMW* should be overruled because "the Constitution does not constrain the size of punitive damages awards." In a separate concurrence, Justice Scalia agreed with the Court's holding in light of its prior decisions but also thought *BMW* was wrongly decided.

Dissenting, Justice Ginsburg would apply an abuse-of-discretion standard: "One million dollars' worth of pain and suffering does not exist as a 'fact' in the world any more or less than one million dollars' worth of moral outrage. Both derive their meaning from a set of underlying facts as determined by a jury." (*See also Honda Motor Co. Ltd. v. Oberg*, 512 U.S. 415 (1994) (held that Oregon's constitutional prohibition against judicial review of jury-awarded punitive damages violated procedural due process)).

(2) *Excessive Fines Clause.* (a) In *Browning-Ferris Industries of Vermont, Inc. v. Kelco Disposal, Inc.*, 492 U.S. 257 (1989), the Court held that the Excessive Fines Clause of the Eighth Amendment does not apply to punitive damages awards in cases between private parties.

Writing for a 7-2 majority, Justice Blackmun stated that the Framers had not intended that the Eighth Amendment would apply to punitive damages awards. "Whatever the outer confines of the [Excessive Fines] Clause's reach may be, we now decide only that it does not constrain an award of money damages in a civil suit when the government neither has prosecuted the action nor has any right to receive a share of the damages awarded. . . . [T]he Eighth Amendment places limits on the steps a government may take against an individual." The Clause simply did not apply in cases "between private parties."

(b) *Forfeiture as an Excessive Fine*. In *United States v. Bajakajian*, 524 U.S. 321 (1998), Bajakajian attempted to leave the United States with $357,144 in U.S. currency in violation of a federal law requiring persons to report the transportation of more than $10,000 in currency. Federal law also provides that those failing to report "shall forfeit to the government 'any property . . . involved in such offense.'" Writing for the Court, Justice Thomas invalidated the forfeiture of the $357,144 under the Excessive Fines Clause of the Eighth Amendment.

Generally, a statutory forfeiture is considered a "'fine' for Eighth Amendment purposes if it constitutes punishment, even in part, regardless of whether the proceeding is styled in rem or in personam." Because the government proceeded against Bajakajian in personam and not against the currency in rem, the currency was not an instrumentality of the crime. In any event, the currency is not an instrumentality as cash did not "facilitate the commission of that crime" in the way that an automobile conceals and transports goods to facilitate the crime of tax avoidance.

As the forfeiture is punitive, the Court assesses whether the forfeiture is excessive by determining whether it is "grossly disproportional to the gravity of defendant's offense."

The District Court found that Bajakajian's crime was isolated, that the money was to be used to repay a debt, and that Bajakajian was not in the class that the forfeiture statute primarily targets — money launderers, drug traffickers and tax evaders. The harm caused was minimal and there was no evidence of fraud or "loss to the public fisc." The forfeiture was "larger than the $5,000 fine imposed by the District Court by many orders of magnitude, and it bears no articulable correlation to any injury suffered by the Government." Moreover, the procedure was civil, not criminal.

Justice Kennedy dissented, joined by the Chief Justice and Justices O'Connor and Scalia. The dissent noted that the majority's decision is the first that invalidated a fine as excessive. The cash was an instrumentality of the crime, as "cash is not just incidentally related to the offense of cash smuggling." The behavior at issue was serious and suspicious: "The drug trade, money laundering, and tax evasion all depend in part on smuggled and unreported cash." Defendant hid over $300,000 in cash "in a case with a false bottom." He also lied about the source of the money. The "fine permitted by the majority would be a modest cost of doing business in the world of drugs and crime."

(c) *Forfeiture by an innocent owner*. In *Bennis v. Michigan*, 516 U.S. 442 (1996), the Court denied a due process challenge to a court-ordered forfeiture of an innocent owner's interest in property. Defendant was the joint owner of an automobile that her husband used to engage in sexual activity with a prostitute. The state court declared defendant's vehicle a public nuisance and ordered its forfeiture and sale.

Writing for a 5-4 majority, Chief Justice Rehnquist held that the Due Process Clause does not protect a defendant against government forfeiture, even though she did not know that her car would be used in an illegal activity. Defendant argued that the forfeiture was excessive, as she had not engaged in wrongdoing. Chief Justice Rehnquist stated that this nuisance abatement was an equitable action, not a punitive one. Distinct from any punitive purpose, forfeiture serves a deterrent purpose by exacting an economic penalty and preventing the risk of further criminal use of the property.

Justices Thomas and Ginsburg concurred. Justice Stevens dissented joined by Justices Souter and Breyer. Justice Kennedy filed a separate dissenting opinion.

STATE FARM MUT. AUTO. INS. CO. v. CAMPBELL, 538 U.S. 408 (2003). In *State Farm*, the Court held that punitive damages which are 145 times the amount of compensatory damages violate due process. Campbell tried to pass 6 vans on a two-lane highway. Crossing into the lane of oncoming traffic, he caused an accident which killed one driver and left another permanently disabled. Campbell's insurance company, State Farm, declined settlement offers for the policy limit of $50,000 ($25,000 per claimant). State Farm took the case to trial and assured the Campbells that " 'their assets were safe, that they had no liability for the accident, that [State Farm] would represent their interests and that they did not need to procure separate counsel.' " The jury handed down a judgment for $185,849.

Originally, State Farm refused to cover the $135,849 in excess of the policy limit. Counsel for State Farm suggested to the Campbells that they might consider selling their house to cover the judgment. When State Farm would not appeal, Campbell contracted with the two original plaintiffs "not to seek satisfaction of their claims against the Campbells." The attorney for the plaintiffs would then represent Campbell in a bad faith action against State Farm. Both plaintiffs had to approve of any settlement reached with State Farm, and they would receive 90% of any award against State Farm.

Although State Farm eventually paid the entire judgment, the Campbells pursued their claims of bad faith, fraud, and intentional infliction of emotional distress. The jury awarded the Campbells $2.6 million in compensatory damages and $145 million in punitive damages. The trial court reduced this award to $1 million in compensatory damages and $25 million in punitive damages. The Utah Supreme Court, however, reinstated the $145 million in punitive damages.

Relying on *BMW of North America, Inc. v. Gore, supra* § 7.03[2], Justice Kennedy concluded that this case "is neither close nor difficult." *Gore* stated that " '[t]he most important indicium of the reasonableness of a punitive damages award is the degree of reprehensibility of the defendant's conduct.' "

In the instant case, punitive damages were used "as a platform to expose, and punish, the perceived deficiencies of State Farm's operations throughout the country." The Utah Supreme Court condemned State Farm for its "nationwide policies rather than for the conduct direct[ed] toward the Campbells." A state may not punish one for "conduct that may have been lawful where it occurred." Nor may a state punish "unlawful acts committed outside of the State's jurisdiction" with punitive damages. However, "[l]awful out-of-state conduct may be probative when it demonstrates the deliberateness and culpability of the defendant's action in the State where it is tortious, but that conduct must have a nexus to the specific harm suffered by the plaintiff." When so used, a jury must be instructed that "it may not use evidence of out-of-state conduct to punish a defendant for action that was lawful in the jurisdiction where it occurred." Central to the concept of federalism is the idea "that each State may make its own reasoned judgment about what conduct is permitted or proscribed within its borders, and each State alone can determine what measure of punishment, if any, to impose on a defendant who acts within its jurisdiction."

More fundamentally, the Utah courts attempted "to punish and deter conduct that bore no relation to the Campbells' harm." Punishment should be for "the conduct that harmed the plaintiff, not for being an unsavory individual or business."[8] The award cannot be based on classifying defendant as a "recidivist. Although 'our holdings that a recidivist may be punished more severely than a first offender recognize that repeat misconduct is more reprehensible than an individual instance of malfeasance,' in the context of civil actions courts must ensure the conduct in question replicates the prior transgressions." This "reprehensibility guidepost does not permit courts to expand the scope of the case so that a defendant may be punished for any malfeasance which in this case extended for a 20-year period."

Moving "to the second *Gore* guidepost," the Court has "been reluctant to identify concrete constitutional limits on the ratio between harm, or potential harm, to the plaintiff and the punitive damages award." *Pac. Mut. Life Ins. Co. v. Haslip*, 499 U.S. 1 (1991), concluded that an award of more than four times the amount of compensatory damages "might be close to the line of constitutional impropriety." The Court "cited that 4-to-1 ratio again in *Gore*." The *Gore* Court "further referenced a long legislative history, dating back over 700 years and going forward to today, providing for sanctions of double, treble, or quadruple damages to deter and punish. While these ratios are not binding, they are instructive. They demonstrate what should be obvious. Single-digit multipliers are more likely to comport with due process." While "there are no rigid benchmarks" for punitive damages, "ratios greater than those we have previously upheld may comport with due process where 'a particularly egregious act has resulted in only a small amount of economic damages.' " However, for substantial compensatory awards, "then a lesser ratio, perhaps only equal to compensatory damages" might be higher than due process would allow. The precise award in any case is, of course, dependent on "the facts and circumstances of the defendant's conduct and the harm to the plaintiff." Punitive awards must be "both reasonable and proportionate to the amount of harm to the plaintiff and to the general damages recovered."

In this case, the Court found a presumption against an award with a 145-to-1 ratio. "The compensatory award in this case was substantial; the Campbells were awarded $1 million for a year and a half of emotional distress. This was complete compensation." An unconstitutional punitive damages award cannot be justified simply because the defendant is wealthy.

"The third guidepost in *Gore* is the disparity between the punitive damages award and the 'civil penalties authorized or imposed in comparable cases.' " This Court has, in the past, looked "to criminal penalties that could be imposed." In Utah, the most relevant civil sanction appears to be a $10,000 fine for fraud.

Justice Kennedy concluded that the $145 million punitive damages award was "neither reasonable nor proportionate to the wrong committed, and it was an irrational and arbitrary deprivation of the property of the defendant."

Justices Scalia, Thomas, and Ginsburg each filed separate dissenting opinions. For Justice Scalia, the Due Process Clause does not provide substantive protection against " 'excessive' or 'unreasonable' awards of punitive damages." Such scrutiny of punitive awards is "insusceptible of principled application." Consequently, *Gore* should not have stare decisis effect.

Justice Thomas also maintained that the Constitution does not constrain the size of punitive damages.

In dissent, Justice Ginsburg maintained that "the Court 'works at this business [of checking state courts] alone,' unaided by the participation of federal district courts and

---

[8] Punishment based on reprehensibility "creates the possibility of multiple punitive damages awards for the same conduct; for in the usual case nonparties are not bound by the judgment some other plaintiff obtains."

courts of appeals." The majority account of the evidence is "abbreviated." For example, the claims-adjustment process " 'has functioned, and continues to function, as an unlawful scheme . . . to deny benefits owed consumers by paying out less than fair value in order to meet preset, arbitrary payout targets designed to enhance corporate profits.' "

Moreover, "State Farm made 'systematic' efforts to destroy internal company documents that might reveal its scheme."[9] Justice Ginsburg concludes that the "numerical controls" that this decision establishes seem "boldly out of order." Gore's "flexible guides" are being transformed "into instructions that begin to resemble marching orders."

NOTE

Punitives for Nonparties. In *Philip Morris USA v. Williams*, 127 S. Ct. 1057 (2007), the Court held that the Due Process Clause does not allow a jury to consider harm to nonparties of a lawsuit when determining its award for punitive damages. Writing for the Court, Justice Breyer stated such recovery "would amount to a taking of 'property' from the defendant without due process." The jury awarded the plaintiff $821,000 in compensatory damages and $79.5 million in punitive damages. The trial judge subsequently reduced the punitive damages award to $32 million. Philip Morris appealed the award arguing that the trial court erred first because the trial court did not use its proposed instruction which stated "the jury could not seek to punish Philip Morris for injury to other persons not before the court." Second, Philip Morris complained that the court did not follow the rule set out in *State Farm*, of setting punitive damages usually at "two, three or four times the size of compensatory damages." The Supreme Court considered only the first ground of appeal.

The Due Process Clause provides that an individual must have " 'an opportunity to present every available defense,' " which a defendant cannot do against allegedly injured nonparties. Questions about nonparties, such as, how seriously they were injured, and under what circumstances the injury occurred, are not answered at trial. Since the jury will have to speculate about the harm caused to the nonparties, the fundamental due process concerns to which our punitive damages cases refer — right of arbitrariness, uncertainty, and lack of notice — will be magnified. The jury may consider the harm the defendant could have caused; however, the court may only consider the harm the defendant could have caused to *the plaintiff*. Additionally, the court does allow the jury to consider the harm caused by the defendant's conduct in order to determine the reprehensibility of the defendant's act, one of the three *Gore* guideposts. *See supra* § 7.03[2]. In order to protect defendants from being punished for harm they caused to nonparties, states must institute procedures to direct juries only to consider harm to others when determining the reprehensibility of a defendant's conduct.

In his dissent, Justice Stevens warned about the expansion of substantive due process " 'because guideposts for responsible decisionmaking in this unchartered area are scarce and open-ended.' " Justice Thomas also dissented, maintaining that the " 'Constitution does not constrain the size of punitive damages awards.' " Finally, Justice Ginsburg stated that the line between not considering harm to nonparties and using such harm to assess reprehensibility "slips from my grasp" and confuses the jury.

---

[9] The majority acknowledges that evidence of out-of-state conduct "may be 'probative [even if the conduct is lawful in the state where it occurred]' when it demonstrated the deliberateness and culpability of the defendant's action in the State where it is tortious."

[3] Economic Regulation and the Contract Clause of Article I, Section 10

ENERGY RESERVES GROUP, INC. v. KANSAS POWER AND LIGHT CO.
459 U.S. 400, 103 S. Ct. 697, 74 L. Ed. 2d. 569 (1983)

JUSTICE BLACKMUN delivered the opinion of the Court.

I

[In 1975, Kansas Power and Light Co. (KPL) entered into two intrastate natural gas supply contracts with Clinton Oil Co., the predecessor-in-interest of Energy Reserves Group (ERG). KPL agreed to purchase natural gas from ERG. Both contracts contained two clauses called "indefinite price escalator clauses." The first was a governmental price escalator clause. This clause allowed for an increase in the contract price of gas to meet a higher price level set by a government authority. The second clause was a price redetermination clause which gave ERG the option to increase the contract price, no more than once every two years.

After either price escalator was implemented, KPL agreed, within a specified time period, to petition the Kansas Corporation Commission (Commission) for approval to pass the increase through to consumers. If the Commission refused to approve the pass-through, and KPL decided not to pay the increase, then ERG could terminate the contracts.

Both contracts specified that the sole purpose of the price escalator clauses was to compensate ERG for "anticipated" increases in its operating costs and in the value of its gas. Furthermore, the contracts provided that either party's failure to perform under the contracts due to any "relevant present or future state and federal laws" would not be considered a default.

In 1978, the Natural Gas Policy Act (Act) became effective, superseding previous federal price regulation of natural gas. The Act established slowly increasing price ceilings for various categories of natural gas.

While part of the National Act set maximum prices for gas produced and held intrastate, the National Act also authorized a State to enforce maximum price levels for such gas which were lower than the federal ceilings. Pursuant to this provision of the National Act, the Kansas legislature passed the Kansas Natural Gas Price Protection Act (Kansas Act). The Kansas Act set lower maximum prices for gas produced and sold intrastate. It applied to gas contracts executed before April 20, 1977, and controlled prices until December 31, 1984. The Kansas Act prohibited parties from considering either federal price ceilings or prices paid in Kansas under other natural gas contracts when applying their own price escalator clauses.

On November 20, 1978, ERG sought to implement the government price escalator clause to increase the price of gas to the ceiling permitted by the National Act. KPL failed to request the pass-through approval from the Commission and refused to pay the increased price. ERG notified KPL that it would terminate the contracts in thirty days and KPL replied that the Kansas Act prevented the National Act from triggering the governmental price escalator clause, and thus KPL was under no duty to petition the Commission. ERG filed suit in Kansas district court seeking declaratory judgment that it had the right to terminate the contracts. Subsequently, ERG requested a price increase pursuant to the price redetermination clause. KPL replied that the Kansas Act relieved it of its obligation to comply with ERG's request since the Kansas Act prohibited reference to government price ceilings in the application of price redetermination clauses.

On cross motions for summary judgment, the trial court held that the National Act's regulation of intrastate price ceilings did not trigger the government price escalator clause and that the Kansas Act did not violate the Contract Clause. The Kansas Supreme Court affirmed.]

II

. . . The constitutional issue is whether the Kansas Act impairs ERG's contracts with KPL in violation of the Contract Clause, U.S. Const., Art. I, § 10, cl. 1. . . .

A

Although the language of the Contract Clause is facially absolute, its prohibition must be accommodated to the inherent police power of the State "to safeguard the vital interests of its people." *Home Bldg. & Loan Ass'n. v. Blaisdell*, 290 U.S. 398, 434 (1934). . . .

. . . In *United States Trust Co. v. New Jersey*, 431 U.S. 1 (1977), the Court held that New Jersey could not retroactively alter a statutory bond covenant relied upon by bond purchasers. One year later, in *Allied Structural Steel Co. v. Spannaus*, 438 U.S. 234 (1978), the Court invalidated a Minnesota statute that required an employer who closed its office in the State to pay a "pension funding charge" if its pension fund at the time was insufficient to provide full benefits for all employees with at least 10 years' seniority. . . .

The inquiry is "whether the state law has, in fact, operated as a substantial impairment of a contractual relationship." *Allied Structural Steel Co.*, 438 U.S. at 244. *See United States Trust Co.*, 431 U.S., at 17. The severity of the impairment is said to increase the level of scrutiny to which the legislation will be subjected. *Allied Structural Steel Co.*, 438 U.S., at 245. Total destruction of contractual expectations is not necessary for a finding of substantial impairment. *United States Trust Co.*, 431 U.S., at 26–27. On the other hand, state regulation that restricts a party to gains it reasonably expected from the contract does not necessarily constitute a substantial impairment. *Id.*, at 31. In determining the extent of the impairment, we are to consider whether the industry the complaining party has entered has been regulated in the past. *Allied Structural Steel Co.*, 438 U.S., at 242, n. 13. . . .

If the state regulation constitutes a substantial impairment, the State, in justification, must have a significant and legitimate public purpose behind the regulation, *United States Trust Co.*, 431 U.S., at 22, such as the remedying of a broad and general social or economic problem. *Allied Structural Steel Co.*, 438 U.S. at 247, 249. Furthermore, since *Blaisdell*, the Court has indicated that the public purpose need not be addressed to an emergency or temporary situation. . . . The requirement of a legitimate public purpose guarantees that the State is exercising its police power, rather than providing a benefit to special interests.[10]

Once a legitimate public purpose has been identified, the next inquiry is whether the adjustment of "the rights and responsibilities of contracting parties [is based] upon reasonable conditions and [is] of a character appropriate to the public purpose

---

[10] [Court's footnote 13] In *Allied Structural Steel Co. v. Spannaus*, . . . [t]he State had not acted to meet an important general social problem. The pension statute had a very narrow focus: it was aimed at specific employers. Indeed, it even may have been directed at one particular employer planning to terminate its pension plan when its collective-bargaining agreement expired.

justifying [the legislation's] adoption." *United States Trust Co.*, 431 U.S., at 22. Unless the State itself is a contracting party,[11] "[a]s is customary in reviewing economic and social regulation, . . . courts properly defer to legislative judgment as to the necessity and reasonableness of a particular measure." *Id.*, at 22–23.

B

The threshold determination is whether the Kansas Act has impaired substantially ERG's contractual rights. Significant here is the fact that the parties are operating in a heavily regulated industry. At the time of the execution of these contracts, Kansas did not regulate natural gas prices specifically, but its supervision of the industry was extensive and intrusive. Moreover, under the authority of § 5(a) of the 1938 Natural Gas Act, the Federal Power Commission (FPC) set "just and reasonable" rates for prices of gas both at the wellhead and in pipelines. . . .

. . . In drafting each of the contracts, the parties included a statement of intent, which made clear that the escalator clause was designed to guarantee price increases consistent with *anticipated* increases in the value of ERG's gas. . . . The very existence of the governmental price escalator clause and the price redetermination clause indicates that the contracts were structured against the background of regulated gas prices. . . . [12]

Moreover, the contracts expressly recognize the existence of extensive regulation by providing that any contractual terms are subject to relevant present and future state and federal law. This latter provision could be interpreted to incorporate all future state price regulation, and thus dispose of the Contract Clause claim. . . . Price regulation existed and was foreseeable as the type of law that would alter contract obligations. . . . In short, ERG's reasonable expectations have not been impaired by the Kansas Act.

C

To the extent, if any, the Kansas Act impairs ERG's contractual interests, the Kansas Act rests on, and is prompted by, significant and legitimate state interests. Kansas has exercised its police power to protect consumers from the escalation of natural gas prices caused by deregulation. The State reasonably could find that higher gas prices have caused and will cause hardship among those who use gas heat but must exist on limited fixed incomes.

The State also has a legitimate interest in correcting the imbalance between the interstate and intrastate markets. . . . By slowly deregulating interstate prices, the Act took the cap off intrastate prices as well. The Kansas Act attempts to coordinate the intrastate and interstate prices by supplementing the federal Act's regulation of intrastate gas. . . . [13]

---

[11] [Court's footnote 14] . . . In *United States Trust Co.*, but not in *Allied Structural Steel Co.*, the State was one of the contracting parties. . . . In almost every case, the Court has held a governmental unit to its contractual obligations when it enters financial or other markets. When the State is a party to the contract, "complete deference to a legislative assessment of reasonableness and necessity is not appropriate because the State's self-interest is at stake." *United States Trust Co.*, 431 U.S. at 26.

[12] [Court's footnote 21] Absent deregulation, the existing interstate price would have continued to act as a brake on increases ERG could obtain under the price redetermination clause . . . . There is no reason to believe that, by operation of either escalator clause under the old regulatory structure, ERG's prices ever would have reached the Act's [National] levels.

[13] [Court's footnote 25] ERG claims that the legislation was designed to benefit KPL. Unlike *Allied*

Nor are the means chosen to implement these purposes deficient, particularly in light of the deference to which the Kansas Legislature's judgment is entitled. . . .

Finally, the Act is a temporary measure that expires when federal price regulation of certain categories of gas terminates. The Kansas statute completes the regulation of the gas market by imposing gradual escalation mechanisms on the intrastate market, consistent with the new national policy toward gas regulation.

We, thus, resolve the constitutional issue against ERG.

Justice Powell, with whom The Chief Justice and Justice Rehnquist join, concurring in part.

. . . The Court concludes . . . that there has been no substantial impairment of ERG's contractual rights. . . . This conclusion is dispositive, and it is unnecessary for the Court to address the question of whether, if there were an impairment of contractual rights, it would constitute a violation of the Contract Clause.

The Court concludes . . . that even if ERG's "contractual interests" were impaired, the Act furthers "significant and legitimate state interests" and is a valid exercise of the State's police power. I do not necessarily disagree with this conclusion, particularly in the context of the pervasive regulation of public utilities. I decline to join [in it], however, because it addresses a substantial question and our discussion of the [substantial impairment] issue . . . disposes of this case.

NOTES

(1) *Tax Pass Through.* In *Exxon Corp. v. Eagerton*, 462 U.S. 176 (1983), the Court upheld an Alabama law that imposed a 2% severance tax increase on oil and gas production. The statute also "prohibited producers from passing the tax increase through to consumers." Appellants were "parties to sale contracts that required the purchasers to reimburse them for any and all severance taxes on the oil or gas." The parties had entered into these contracts "before the pass-through prohibition was enacted and their terms extended through the period during which the prohibition was in effect." Appellants challenged the Alabama statute under the Contract Clause of the Constitution.

Writing for the Court, Justice Marshall stated that restrictions on, or complete prohibitions of, contractual obligations alone did not violate the Contract Clause. Relying on *United States Trust Co. v. New Jersey*, Justice Marshall acknowledged that the "Contract Clause does not deprive the States of their 'broad power to adopt general regulatory measures without being concerned that private contracts will be impaired, or even destroyed, as a result.'" The pass-through prohibition at issue was not directed at altering private contracts, but "instead imposed a generally applicable rule of conduct designed to advance a 'broad societal interest,' protecting consumers from excessive prices." Justice Marshall contrasted the Alabama statute with statutes at issue in *United States Trust Co. v. New Jersey* and *Allied Structural Steel Co. v.*

Structural Steel Co. v. Spannaus, there is little or nothing in the record here to support the contention that the Kansas Act is special interest legislation. Given the nature of the industry sales to public utilities it is impossible for any regulation not to have a major effect on a small number of participants. This differs from the statute under challenge in *Allied Structural Steel Co.*, where a small number of employers were singled out from the larger group. The fact that there was a close vote at the committee stage, and that some of the committee dissenters expressed the view that the Kansas Act was special interest legislation, bears little if any resemblance to the circumstantial evidence present in *Allied Structural Steel Co.* Nor is there any indication that the Kansas political process had broken down. . . . In addition, the automatic price pass-through adjustment indicates that KPL will not benefit significantly from the statute. Although ERG is correct that the Commission could revoke the pass-through, it has given no indication that it will do so.

Spannaus. In *United States Trust Co.*, the Court struck down statutes whose only effect was to nullify a contract between the New York and New Jersey Port Authority and bond holders. In *Allied Structural Steel Co.*, the Court invalidated a statute because it "applied only to employers that had entered into pension agreements, its sole effect was to alter contractual duties."

As the Contract Clause allows a state to regulate the price of commodities, it also allows a state to require "that sellers absorb a tax increase themselves rather than pass it through to their customers."

(2) *Changes in Regulation of Government-Created Entities.* The Court rejected a Contract Clause claim in *National Railroad Passenger Corp. v. A.T. & S.F. Railway Co*, 470 U.S. 451 (1985). Justice Marshall's unanimous opinion (Justice Powell did not participate) upheld a Congressional statute altering the reimbursement scheme whereby the railroads were compelled to reimburse Amtrak for the cost of providing pass privileges to the railroad's employees. The railroads had argued that Congress violated the agreements whereby the railroads had turned their passenger service over to Amtrak. Although these agreements were made pursuant to a federal statute, the Court held that they did not constitute a contractual agreement between the United States and the railroads. Nor was there any contractual right created either by the 1970 statute establishing Amtrak or by a 1972 act creating the reimbursement formula that was altered again in 1979. Congress had not bargained away its Commerce Clause power to alter the reimbursement formula. The Court also rejected the claim that a private contractual right had been impaired in violation of the Due Process Clause of the Fifth Amendment. To meet the Due Process standard, Congress need show only that it acted rationally in spreading the costs of employees' passenger travel among the various parties. *Cf. United States v. Sperry Corporation*, 493 U.S. 52 (1989) (upholding a retroactive user fee assessing successful litigants in a special arbitration tribunal a percentage of their winnings).

(3) Several commentators have suggested heightened scrutiny under the Contracts Clause. *See* Epstein, *Toward a Revitalization of the Contract Clause*, 51 U. Chi. L. Rev. 703 (1984); Kmiec & McGinnis, *The Contracts Clause: A Return to the Original Understanding*, 14 Hastings Const. L.Q. 525 (1987); Note, *Takings Law and the Contract Clause: A Takings Law Approach to Legislative Modifications of Public Contracts*, 36 Stan. L. Rev. 1447 (1984).

[4]   Government Takings of Property Requiring Just Compensation

(a)   General Principles

KEYSTONE BITUMINOUS COAL ASSOCIATION v. DEBENEDICTIS
480 U.S. 470, 107 S. Ct. 1232, 94 L. Ed. 2d 472 (1987)

[In *Pennsylvania Coal Co. v. Mahon*, 260 U.S. 393 (1922), the Court reviewed the constitutionality of a Pennsylvania statute that admittedly destroyed "previously existing rights of property and contract." Writing for the Court, Justice Holmes explained:

> Government hardly could go on if to some extent values incident to property could not be diminished without paying for every such change in the general law. As long recognized, some values are enjoyed under an implied limitation and must yield to the police power. But obviously the implied limitation must have its limits, or the contract and due process clauses are gone. One fact for

consideration in determining such limits is the extent of the diminution. When it reaches a certain magnitude, in most if not in all cases there must be an exercise of eminent domain and compensation to sustain the act. So the question depends upon the particular facts.

Id. In that case, the "particular facts" led the Court to hold that the Pennsylvania Legislature had gone beyond its constitutional powers when it enacted a statute prohibiting the mining of anthracite coal in a manner that would cause the subsidence of land on which certain structures were located.]

Now, 65 years later, we address a different set of "particular facts," involving the Pennsylvania Legislature's 1966 conclusion that the Commonwealth's existing mine subsidence legislation had failed to protect the public interest in safety, land conservation, preservation of affected municipalities' tax bases, and land development in the Commonwealth. Based on detailed findings, the legislature enacted the Bituminous Mine Subsidence and Land Conservation Act (the "Subsidence Act" or the "Act"). . . . Petitioners contend, relying heavily on our decision in *Pennsylvania Coal*, that § 4 and § 6 of the Subsidence Act and certain implementing regulations violate the Takings Clause . . . of the Federal Constitution. The District Court and the Court of Appeals concluded that *Pennsylvania Coal* does not control for several reasons and that our subsequent cases make it clear that neither § 4 nor § 6 is unconstitutional on its face. We agree.

I

Coal mine subsidence is the lowering of strata overlying a coal mine, including the land surface, caused by the extraction of underground coal. This lowering of the strata can cause devastating effects. . . .

[M]ining companies have long been required by various Pennsylvania laws and regulations, the legitimacy of which is not challenged here, to leave coal in certain areas for public safety reasons. Since 1966, Pennsylvania has placed an additional set of restrictions on the amount of coal that may be extracted. . . .

. . . Section 4 of the Subsidence Act prohibits mining that causes subsidence damage to three categories of structures that were in place on April 17, 1966: public buildings and noncommercial buildings generally used by the public; dwellings used for human habitation; and cemeteries. Since 1966 the DER has applied a formula that generally required 50% of the coal beneath structures protected by § 4 to be kept in place as a means of providing surface support. Section 6 of the Subsidence Act . . . authorizes the DER to revoke a mining permit if the removal of coal causes damages to a structure or area protected by § 4 and the operator has not within six months either repaired the damage, satisfied any claim arising therefrom, or deposited a sum equal to the reasonable cost of repair with the DER as security.

II

. . . The complaint alleges that Pennsylvania recognizes three separate estates in land: The mineral estate; the surface estate; and the "support estate." Beginning well over 100 years ago, land owners began severing title to underground coal and the right of surface support while retaining or conveying away ownership of the surface estate. . . . When acquiring or retaining the mineral estate, petitioners or their predecessors typically acquired or retained certain additional rights that would enable them to extract and remove the coal. [T]hey typically acquired a waiver of any claims for damages that might result from the removal of coal.

In the portions of the complaint that are relevant to us, petitioners alleged that both § 4 of the Subsidence Act, as implemented by the 50% rule, and § 6 of the Subsidence Act, constitute a taking of their private property without compensation in violation of the Fifth and Fourteenth Amendments. . . .

III

Petitioners assert that disposition of the takings claim calls for no more than a straightforward application of the Court's decision in *Pennsylvania Coal Co. v. Mahon.*

. . . The Mahons filed a bill in equity seeking to enjoin the coal company from removing any coal that would cause "the caving in, collapse or subsidence" of their dwelling. The bill acknowledged that the Mahons owned only "the surface or right of soil" in the lot, and that the Coal Company had reserved the right to remove the coal without any liability to the owner of the surface estate. Nonetheless, the Mahons asserted that Pennsylvania's then recently enacted Kohler Act of 1921, . . . which prohibited mining that caused subsidence under certain structures, entitled them to an injunction. . . .

Justice Holmes first characteristically decided the specific case at hand in a single, terse paragraph:

> This is the case of a single private house. The extent of the public interest is shown by the statute to be limited, since the statute ordinarily does not apply to land when the surface is owned by the owner of the coal. Furthermore, it is not justified as a protection of personal safety. That could be provided for by notice. . . . On the other hand the extent of the taking is great. It purports to abolish what is recognized in Pennsylvania as an estate in land a very valuable estate and what is declared by the Court below to be a contract hitherto binding the plaintiffs. If we were called upon to deal with the plaintiffs' position alone, we should think it clear that the statute does not disclose a public interest sufficient to warrant so extensive a destruction of the defendant's constitutionally protected rights.

260 U.S., at 413–414.

Then uncharacteristically Justice Holmes provided the parties with an advisory opinion discussing "the general validity of the Act." In the advisory portion of the Court's opinion, Justice Holmes rested on two propositions, both critical to the Court's decision. First, because it served only private interests, not health and safety, the Kohler Act could not be "sustained as an exercise of the police power." *Id.*, at 414. Second, the statute made it "commercially impracticable" to mine "certain coal" in the areas affected by the Kohler Act.

. . . The two factors that the Court considered relevant, have become integral parts of our takings analysis. We have held that land use regulation can effect a taking if it "does not substantially advance legitimate state interests, . . . or denies an owner economically viable use of his land." *Agins v. Tiburon*, 447 U.S. 255, 260 (1980). Application of these tests to petitioners' challenge demonstrates that they have not satisfied their burden of showing that the Subsidence Act constitutes a taking. First, unlike the Kohler Act, the character of the governmental action involved here leans heavily against finding a taking; the Commonwealth of Pennsylvania has acted to arrest what it perceives to be a significant threat to the common welfare. Second, there is no record in this case to support a finding, similar to the one the Court made in *Pennsylvania Coal*, that the Subsidence Act makes it impossible for petitioners to profitably engage in their business, or that there has been undue interference with their investment-backed expectations.

The Public Purpose

. . . The Pennsylvania Legislature specifically found that important public interests are served by enforcing a policy that is designed to minimize subsidence in certain areas. . . .

None of the indicia of a statute enacted solely for the benefit of private parties identified in Justice Holmes' opinion are present here. First, Justice Holmes explained that the Kohler Act was a "private benefit" statute since it "ordinarily does not apply to land when the surface is owned by the owner of the coal." 260 U.S., at 414. The Subsidence Act, by contrast, has no such exception. The current surface owner may only waive the protection of the Act if the DER consents. . . . Moreover, the Court was forced to reject the Commonwealth's safety justification for the Kohler Act because it found that the Commonwealth's interest in safety could as easily have been accomplished through a notice requirement to landowners. The Subsidence Act, by contrast, is designated to accomplish a number of widely varying interests, with reference to which petitioners have not suggested alternative methods through which the Commonwealth could proceed.

. . . With regard to the Kohler Act, the Court believed that the Commonwealth had acted only to ensure against damage to some private landowners' homes. . . . Here, by contract, the Commonwealth is acting to protect the public interest in health, the environment, and the fiscal integrity of the area. . . .

In *Pennsylvania Coal*, the Court recognized that the nature of the State's interest in the regulation is a critical factor in determining whether a taking has occurred, and thus whether compensation is required. . . . [14]

Just five years after the *Pennsylvania Coal* decision, Justice Holmes joined the Court's unanimous decision in *Miller v. Schoene*, 276 U.S. 272 (1928), holding that the Takings Clause did not require the State of Virginia to compensate the owners of cedar trees for the value of the trees that the State had ordered destroyed. The trees needed to be destroyed to prevent a disease from spreading to nearby apple orchards, which represented a far more valuable resource. . . .

The Court's hesitance to find a taking when the state merely restrains uses of property that are tantamount to public nuisances is consistent with the notion of "reciprocity of advantage" that Justice Holmes referred to in Pennsylvania Coal.[15]

Under our system of government, one of the state's primary ways of preserving the public weal is restricting the uses individuals can make of their property. . . . Long ago it was recognized that "all property in this country is held under the implied obligation that the owner's use of it shall not be injurious to the community. . . ."[16] In

---

[14] [Court's footnote 18] Of course, the type of taking alleged is also an often critical factor. It is well settled that a "taking" may more readily be found when the interference with property can be characterized as a physical invasion by government, . . . than when interference arises from some public program adjusting the benefits and burdens of economic life to promote the common good." *Penn Central Transportation Co. v. New York City*, 438 U.S. 104, 124 (1978). . . .

[15] [Court's footnote 20] The special status of this type of state action can also be understood on the simple theory that since no individual has a right to use his property so as to create a nuisance or otherwise harm others, the state has not "taken" anything when it asserts its power to enjoin the nuisance-like activity. *Cf.* Sax, *Takings, Private Property and Public Rights*, 81 Yale L.J. 149, 155–161 (1971); Michelman, *Property, Utility and Fairness; Comments on the Ethical Foundations of "Just Compensation" Law*, 80 Harv. L. Rev. 1165, 1235–1237 (1967).

[16] [Court's footnote 22] Courts have consistently held that a State need not provide compensation when it diminishes or destroys the value of property by stopping illegal activity or abating a public nuisance. . . .

Agins v. Tiburon, we explained that the "determination that governmental action constitutes a taking, is, in essence, a determination that the public at large, rather than a single owner, must bear the burden of an exercise of state power in the public interest," and we recognized that this question "necessarily requires a weighing of private and public interests." 447 U.S., at 260–261. As the cases discussed above demonstrate, the public interest in preventing activities similar to public nuisances is a substantial one, which in many instances has not required compensation. The Subsidence Act, unlike the Kohler Act, plainly seeks to further such an interest. Nonetheless, we need not rest our decision on this factor alone, because petitioners have also failed to make a showing of diminution of value sufficient to satisfy the test set forth in *Pennsylvania Coal* and our other regulatory takings cases.

Diminution of Investment and Investment-Backed Expectations

The second factor that distinguishes this case from *Pennsylvania Coal* is the finding in that case that the Kohler Act made mining of "certain coal" commercially impracticable. In this case, by contrast, petitioners have not shown any deprivation significant enough to satisfy the heavy burden placed upon one alleging a regulatory taking. For this reason, their takings claim must fail.

In addressing petitioners' claim we must not disregard the posture in which this case comes before us. The District Court granted summary judgment to respondents only on the facial challenge to the Subsidence Act. . . .

Just last Term, we reaffirmed that this court has generally "been unable to develop any 'set formula' for determining when 'justice and fairness' require that economic injuries caused by public action be compensated by the government, rather than remain disproportionately concentrated on a few persons." Rather, it has examined the "taking" question by engaging in essentially ad hoc, factual inquiries that have identified several factors such as the economic impact of the regulation, its interference with reasonable investment backed expectations, and the character of the government action that have particular significance. . . .

These "ad hoc, factual inquires" must be conducted with respect to specific property, and the particular estimates of economic impact and ultimate valuation relevant in the unique circumstances. . . .

Petitioners thus face an uphill battle in making a facial attack on the Act as a taking.

. . . Petitioners described the effect that the Subsidence Act had from 1966–1982 on 13 mines that the various companies operate, and claimed that they have been required to leave a bit less than 27 million tons of coal in place to support § 4 areas. The total coal in those 13 mines amounts to over 1.46 billion tons. Thus § 4 requires them to leave less than 2% of their coal in place. But, as we have indicated, nowhere near all of the underground coal is extractable even aside from the Subsidence Act. The categories of coal that must be left for § 4 purposes and other purposes are not necessarily distinct sets, and there is no information in the record as to how much coal is actually left in the ground solely because of § 4. We do know, however, that petitioners have never claimed that their mining operations, or even any specific mines, have been unprofitable since the Subsidence Act was passed. Nor is there evidence that mining in any specific location affected by the 50% rule has been unprofitable. . . .

Because our test for regulatory taking requires us to compare the value that has been taken from the property with the value that remains in the property, one of the critical questions is determining how to define the unit of property "whose value is to furnish the denominator of the fraction." Michelman, *Property, Utility, and Fairness: Comments on the Ethical Foundations of "Just Compensation" Law*, 80 HARV. L. REV. 1165, 1192 (1967). . . .

[I]n *Andrus v. Allard*, 444 U.S. 51 (1979), we held that "where an owner possesses a full 'bundle' of property rights, the destruction of one 'strand' of the bundle is not a taking because the aggregate must be viewed in its entirety." *Id.*, at 65–66. . . .

The Coal in Place

. . . Many zoning ordinances place limits on the property owner's right to make profitable use of some segments of his property. . . .   There is no basis for treating the less than 2% of petitioners' coal as a separate parcel of property. . . .

When the coal that must remain beneath the ground is viewed in the context of any reasonable unit of petitioners' coal mining operations and financial-backed expectations, it is plain that the petitioners have not come close to satisfying their burden of proving that they have been denied the economically viable use of that property. The record indicates that only about 75% of petitioners' underground coal can be profitably mined in any event, and there is no showing that petitioners' reasonable "investment-backed expectations" have been materially affected by the additional duty to retain the small percentage that must be used to support the structures protected by § 4.[17]

The Support Estate

Pennsylvania property law is apparently unique in regarding the support estate as a separate interest in land that can be conveyed apart from either the mineral estate or the surface estate. . . .   It is clear, however, that our takings jurisprudence forecloses reliance on such legalistic distinctions within a bundle of property rights. For example, in *Penn Central*, the Court rejected the argument that the "air rights" above the terminal constituted a separate segment of property for Takings Clause purposes. 438 U.S., at 130. Likewise, in *Andrus v. Allard*, we viewed the right to sell property as just one element of the owner's property interest. 444 U.S., at 65–66. . . .

But even if we were to accept petitioners' invitation to view the support estate as a distinct segment of property for "takings" purposes, they have not satisfied their heavy burden of sustaining a facial challenge to the Act. . . .   The record is devoid of any evidence on what percentage of the purchased support estates, either in the aggregate or with respect to any individual estate, has been affected by the Act. . . .

CHIEF JUSTICE REHNQUIST, with whom JUSTICE POWELL, JUSTICE O'CONNOR, and JUSTICE SCALIA join, dissenting. . . .

II

The Court first determines that this case is different from *Pennsylvania Coal* because "the Commonwealth of Pennsylvania has acted to arrest what it perceives to be a significant threat to the common welfare." In my view, reliance on this factor represents both a misreading of *Pennsylvania Coal* and a misunderstanding of our precedents.

---

[17] [Court's footnote 27] We do not suggest that the State may physically appropriate relatively small amounts of private property for its own use without paying just compensation. The question here is whether there has been any taking at all when no coal has been physically appropriated, and the regulatory program places a burden on the use of only a small fraction of the property that is subjected to regulation.

A

. . . A review of the Kohler Act shows that . . . [t]he Pennsylvania legislature passed the statute "as remedial legislation, designed to cure existing evils and abuses." 274 Pa., at 495, . . . (quoting the Act). These were public "evils and abuses," identified in the preamble as "wrecked and dangerous streets and highways, collapsed public buildings, churches, schools, factories, streets, and private dwellings, broken gas, water and sewer systems, the loss of human life. . . . " *Id.*, at 497. . .

. . . The public purposes in this case are not sufficient to distinguish it from *Pennsylvania Coal.*

B

. . . This statute is not the type of regulation that our precedents have held to be within the "nuisance exception" to takings analysis. . . .

[T]hough nuisance regulations have been sustained despite a substantial reduction in value, we have not accepted the proposition that the State may completely extinguish a property interest or prohibit all use without providing compensation. . . .

Here, petitioners' interests in particular coal deposits have been completely destroyed. . . .

Though suggesting that the purposes alone are sufficient to uphold the Act, the Court avoids reliance on the nuisance exception by finding that the Subsidence Act does not impair petitioners' investment backed expectations or ability to profitably operate their businesses. This conclusion follows mainly from the Court's broad definition of the "relevant mass of property." . . .

III

A

. . . In this case, enforcement of the Subsidence Act and its regulations will require petitioners to leave approximately 27 million tons of coal in place. . . . From the relevant perspective that of the property owners this interest has been destroyed every bit as much as if the government had proceeded to mine the coal for its own use. The regulation, then, does not merely inhibit one strand in the bundle, . . . but instead destroys completely any interest in a segment of property. . . .

B

Petitioners also claim that the Subsidence Act effects a taking of their support estate. . . .

I see no reason for refusing to evaluate the impact of the Subsidence Act on the support estate alone, for Pennsylvania has clearly defined it as a separate estate in property. . . .

IV

In sum, . . . the Act works to extinguish petitioners' interest in at least 27 million tons of coal by requiring that coal to be left in the ground, and destroys their purchased support estates by returning to them financial liability for subsidence. . . .

NOTES

These notes focus on the question of what constitutes a compensable taking. The question of what amounts to just compensation — often in dispute — is a complex one that is beyond the scope of this book. Generally, courts will try to determine the fair market value of the property taken.

(1) *Just Compensation.* The Fifth Amendment's guarantee against taking without just compensation was one of the earliest constitutional protections of economic rights incorporated into the Fourteenth Amendment. *See Chicago, Burlington and Quincy R.R. Co. v. Chicago,* 166 U.S. 226 (1897).

(2) *Taking.* (a) *Eminent domain.* Straightforward government condemnation of private property entitles the owner to just compensation. The governmental obligation to pay was clear when the state or federal government exercised its power of eminent domain. For example, the Court sustained a taking claim in *Kaiser Aetna v. United States,* 444 U.S. 164 (1979), when the Army Corps of Engineers declared a pond to be a navigable water of the United States and demanded a free right of access for the public.

(b) *Regulatory taking.* A more difficult problem arose, however, when government did not formally assume title to property but, rather, regulated its use in such a way as to affect its values, as in the *Keystone Bituminous* case, *supra.* Although the "taking" challenge succeeded in limited instances, such as *Pennsylvania Coal,* the Court has made little use of the Fifth Amendment (and Fourteenth) in invalidating economic regulations. Substantive due process was a more favored technique. For example, as early as 1887 the Court sustained a law prohibiting a liquor business and rejected a "taking" challenge. *Mugler v. Kansas,* 123 U.S. 623 (1887).

(c) *Forfeiture action.* In *Bennis v. Michigan,* 516 U.S. 442 (1996), the Court held that the Takings Clause of the Fifth Amendment does not apply when the government lawfully acquires property by an equitable forfeiture action. In that case, an automobile seized under a public nuisance abatement statute was not a "taking" requiring just compensation when the forfeiture proceeding did not violate the Fourteenth Amendment. For additional discussion of this case, see *supra* § 7.03[2], Note (2)(c).

(3) *Real Property.* Although takings claims often involve real property, they need not occur in that context. (a) *Personalty.* In *Andrus v. Allard,* 444 U.S. 51 (1979), the Court upheld the Eagle Protection Act and the Migratory Bird Treaty Act, which prohibited commercial dealing in parts of birds that were legally killed before the Acts became effective. The appellees traded in Indian artifacts that contained parts of birds that are now covered by the Acts, but were killed before the effective dates of the Acts. Appellees were prosecuted for selling their artifacts after the Acts took effect. In response, they contended that the Acts violated their Fifth Amendment property rights in the artifacts by wholly depriving them of the opportunity to profit from them.

Writing for the Court, Justice Brennan explained that property comprehends a "bundle" of rights. ". . . [A]t least where an owner possesses a full 'bundle' of property rights, the destruction of one 'strand' of the bundle is not a taking, because the aggregate must be viewed in its entirety. . . . In this case, it is crucial that appellees retain the rights to possess and transport their property, and to donate or devise the protected birds." Justice Brennan further observed that "it is not clear that appellees will be unable to derive economic benefit from the artifacts; for example, they might exhibit the artifacts for an admissions charge. At any rate, loss of future profits unaccompanied by any physical property restriction provides a slender reed upon which to rest a takings claim. Prediction of profitability is essentially a matter of reasoned speculation that courts are not especially competent to perform."

(b) *Intellectual property.* In *Ruckelshaus v. Monsanto Co.*, 467 U.S. 986 (1984), the Court reviewed whether the government had taken Monsanto's trade secrets. Under the authority of the Federal Insecticide, Fungicide, Rodenticide and Act (FIFRA), the Environmental Protection Agency (EPA) required Monsanto and other pesticide companies to submit information about products to be registered. The EPA monitored the veracity of the labeling and the possible environmental problems that the chemical could create.

In 1972, Congress amended the FIFRA and allowed a company that submitted data to specify the information that it believed to be trade secrets. The EPA could not publicly disclose such information without first obtaining a declaratory judgment rejecting its characterization as a trade secret. In addition, the 1972 amendments contained a data-consideration provision that allowed the EPA to use data submitted in evaluating a different subsequent applicant, provided that the subsequent applicant offered to compensate the original submitter. However, the information designated as trade secrets could not be used by EPA in these subsequent evaluations. Congress again amended FIFRA in 1978. The 1978 amendments gave an original submitter a 10-year period of exclusive use of data submitted after September 30, 1978. All other data could be used in consideration of other applicants and for a 15-year period the original submitter must be compensated by the applicant for his data. After the 15-year period, however, the original submitter was no longer entitled to compensation. Lastly, the 1978 amendments allowed the EPA to disclose health, safety and environmental information to the general public even if it comprised a trade secret. Monsanto challenged the data-consideration and data-disclosure provisions of FIFRA.

In delivering the opinion of the Court, Justice Blackmun announced an expansive interpretation of property rights, which included trade secrets and other intangibles.

During the post-1978 period, "as long as Monsanto is aware of the conditions under which the data are submitted, and the conditions are rationally related to a legitimate government interest, a voluntary submission of data by an applicant in exchange for the economic advantages of a registration can hardly be called a taking."

In the pre-1972 period, Justice Blackmun found irrelevant the fact that the FIFRA did not afford the EPA authority to disclose trade secrets submitted by applicants like Monsanto. For him, absent an express promise, Monsanto had "no reasonable investment-backed expectation that its information would remain inviolate in the hands of the EPA. In an industry that long has been the focus of great public concern and significant government regulation, the possibility was substantial that the Federal Government which had thus far taken no position on disclosure of health, safety and environmental data concerning pesticides, would find disclosure to be in the public interest."

For the 1972-1978 period, "the Federal Government had explicitly guaranteed to Monsanto and other registrants an extensive measure of confidentiality and exclusive use. This governmental guarantee formed the basis of a reasonable investment-backed expectation." Consequently, the EPA could not now disclose data submitted between 1972 and 1978 without compensation.

(c) *Pension plans.* In *Concrete Pipe & Products of California, Inc. v. Construction Laborers Pension Trust for Southern California*, 508 U.S. 602 (1993), the Court denied a takings challenge for employer withdrawal liability from a multiemployer pension plan program. The imposition of such liability withstood a facial challenge in *Connolly v. Pension Benefit Guaranty Corp.*, 475 U.S. 211 (1986). Under the Multiemployer Pension Plan Amendments Act of 1980, an employer withdrawing from an employee pension plan incurs "withdrawal liability" based on "its proportionate share of the plan's unfunded vested benefits."

Writing for a unanimous Court on the taking issue, Justice Souter analyzed three factors derived from prior takings analysis. First, withdrawal liability does not constitute a physical invasion or permanent appropriation of an employer's assets. The Court also refused to characterize the government's action as a physical invasion or a permanent appropriation that amounts to the property being "taken in its entirety." The government did not take all of the property but "only a portion of the parcel in question." Second, the Court considered the severity of the economic impact of the plan and determined that Concrete Pipe's liability was not "out of proportion to its experience with the plan." Citing cases in which the value of property diminished 75 percent and 92.5 percent, the Court stated that diminution in value alone does not constitute a taking. Third, Concrete Pipe's withdrawal liability did not interfere with its reasonable investment-backed expectations. When plaintiff began investing in the plan, a withdrawing employer could be liable for up to 30 percent of its net worth; the employer in this case was liable for 46 percent. Nevertheless, since pension plans had long been the subject of federal regulation, businesses with regulated plans could not reasonably have expected that Congress would never increase their liability for withdrawal.

(d) *User fees.* In *United States v. Sperry Corp.* 493 U.S. 52 (1989), the Court upheld § 502 of the Foreign Relations Authorization Act against a Takings Clause challenge. As part of the settlement of the Iranian seizure of the American Embassy in Tehran, the United States and Iran entered into the Algiers Accords, which established the Iran-United States Claims Tribunal to arbitrate American claims against Iran. The Accords, along with a series of Executive Orders, placed $1 billion of Iranian assets in an English bank to cover Tribunal awards, specified that all pending claims against the Iranian government should be adjudicated only through the Tribunal, terminated all such claims already being tried in the American courts, and declared all Tribunal awards to be final. *Cf. Dames & Moore v. Regan, supra* § 5.04[2] (upholding the President's power to use Executive Order to revoke these claims pending in the American courts).

Prior to the establishment of the Tribunal, the Sperry Corporation had been adjudicating a claim against the Iranian government. The Executive Orders forced Sperry to drop the suit and file a claim with the Tribunal. Sperry and Iran reached an agreement and filed a joint settlement application with the Tribunal. The Tribunal awarded Sperry $2.8 million, but deducted 1.5 percent from Sperry's award. Sperry challenged only this deduction.

Justice White, writing for a unanimous Court, upheld § 502 against a takings challenge. The deduction was not a taking but a "user fee." The user fee was constitutional because the amount was reasonable and Sperry benefited from the Tribunal. The Court would not compel the government to calibrate its user fees with actual costs. In this case, the costs were "not so clearly excessive as to belie their purported character as user fees." The amount was reasonable because 1.5 percent was a "fair approximation of the cost of the benefits supplied."

(4) *Physical invasion.* (a) *Cable.* In *Loretto v. Teleprompter Manhattan CATV Corp.*, 458 U.S. 419 (1982), the Court held that a New York law that gave cable television companies the right to install their cables and related facilities on rental property was a "taking." The physical invasion of the apartment house consisted of cables less than 1/2 inch in diameter, screws, bolts, nails, and roof cables to permit cross-overs from one apartment building to another. The law had been passed to facilitate the wiring of urban areas. Writing for the majority (6-3), Justice Marshall said

that when the governmental action has the character of "a permanent physical invasion of property, our cases uniformly have found a taking to the extent of the occupation, without regard to whether the action achieves an important public benefit or has only minimal economic impact on the owner." Justice Blackmun's dissent, joined by Justices Brennan and White, objected to the Court's adoption of a "per se" rule based on "outmoded distinctions between physical and nonphysical intrusions."

(b) *Rent control.* In *Yee v. City of Escondido*, 503 U.S. 519 (1992), the Court rejected the argument made by mobile home park owners that a municipal rent control ordinance, when considered along with California's Mobilehome Residency Law, violates the Takings Clause. Writing for the Court, Justice O'Connor held that while a physical occupation generally requires compensation, a regulatory taking requires compensation "only if considerations such as the purpose of the regulation or the extent to which it deprives the owner of the economic use of the property suggest that the regulation has unfairly singled out the property owner to bear a burden that should be borne by the public as a whole." This determination "necessarily entails complex factual assessments of the purposes and economic effects of government actions."

Park owners argued that the rent ceilings and the limits on their power to exclude tenants effectively decreased the value of their property and correspondingly increased the property value of individual mobile homes, which rarely move from the plots on which they are initially located. Taken together, the ordinance, read in light of the state law, transferred from the park owners to their tenants the right to occupy the park owners' land indefinitely at submarket rents. While the park owners raised both "physical" and "regulatory" Takings Clause concerns below, Justice O'Connor limited the analysis to the physical occupation question because that was the only issue set forth in the petition for certiorari.

The Court held that the alleged value shift caused by the combined effect of these statutes did not affect a physical taking. This only occurs when government *"requires the landowner to submit to the physical occupation of his land."* The Court recognized the property rights of the park owners but found that the ordinance did provide a means to increase rents, and the state statute permitted park owners to evict tenants upon the nonpayment of rent or upon the park owners' decision to change the use of the land. Justice O'Connor acknowledged the "right to exclude" as "one of the most essential sticks in the bundle" of property rights, but refused to analyze the alleged impairment of the right in the context of this facial challenge.

While this government-regulated relationship may transfer wealth from the park owners to incumbent mobile home owners, the existence of the transfer alone did not convert the regulation into a physical invasion. "Traditional zoning regulations can transfer wealth from those whose activities are prohibited to their neighbors." The wealth transfer effect might bear on whether a regulatory taking has occurred, "as it may shed some light on whether there is a sufficient nexus between the effect of the ordinance and the objectives it is supposed to advance." *See Nollan v. California Coastal Commission, infra* § 7.03[4](d), Note after *Dolan.* Justices Blackmun and Souter wrote separate opinions concurring in the judgment.

(5) *Other Land Use Regulation.* (a) *Zoning.* Perhaps the most common government regulation of real property is zoning. Generally, the Court affords zoning measures substantial deference. *See Goldblatt v. Hempstead*, 369 U.S. 590 (1962) (denied "taking" challenge to a zoning ordinance which put plaintiff out of the sand and gravel mining business by prohibiting, for safety reasons, excavations below the water table); *Hadacheck v. Sebastian*, 239 U.S. 394 (1915) (rejecting a "taking" challenge to a law prohibiting operation of a brickyard because it was inconsistent with neighboring uses). *Cf. Euclid v. Ambler Realty Co.*, 272 U.S. 365 (1927) (rejecting equal protection and

substantive due process challenges to a comprehensive zoning regulation).

(b) *Landmark preservation.* In *Penn Central Transportation Co. v. New York*, 438 U.S. 104 (1978), the Court rejected a "taking" challenge to a New York statute that restricted the plaintiff's development rights associated with Grand Central Station. New York City passed the Landmarks Preservation Law in 1965, which preserved historic state buildings and sites designated as landmarks by the Landmarks Preservation Commission. Once the Commission specified a building or site as a landmark, this decision went before New York City's Board of Estimate, which could alter or reject the Commission's designation. The landowner could seek judicial review of the Board's final decision.

The landmark status required that the owner keep the site "in good repair" and required that the landowner apply for the Commission's advance approval before altering or adding onto the landmark site. The landmark status also grants the owner Transfer Development Rights (TDRs). TDRs allow an owner to transfer to other property under his ownership those development rights on the landmark sites that are rendered unusable by the Act's restrictions, thereby allowing the owner to develop the transferee property beyond its applicable zoning limitations.

Penn Central owned New York's Grand Central Station, which was designated a landmark in 1967. In 1968, the Commission rejected Penn Central's plan to construct a multistory office building above the Terminal.

In an opinion by Justice Brennan, the Court held "that the application of New York City's Landmark Preservation Law [did] not [effect] a 'taking' of appellant's property. The restrictions imposed were substantially related to the promotion of the general welfare. They not only permitted reasonable beneficial use of the landmark site but afford appellants opportunities further to enhance not only the Terminal site proper but also other properties."

The Court listed several factors that helped to determine whether a taking had occurred: "The economic impact of the regulation [and] particularly, the extent to which the regulation has interfered with distinct investment backed expectations are, of course, relevant. So, too, is the character of the governmental action. Furthermore a 'taking' may more readily be found when the interference with the property can be characterized as a physical invasion . . . than when interference arises from some public program adjusting the benefits and burdens of economic life to promote the common good."

The Court rejected the broad contention that all such historical landmark zoning effected a taking. " '[T]aking' jurisprudence does not divide a single parcel into discrete segments and attempt to determine whether rights in a particular segment have been entirely abrogated. In deciding whether a particular governmental action has effected a taking, this Court focuses rather both on the character of the action and on the nature and extent of the interference with rights in the parcel as a whole — here, the city block designated as the 'landmark site.' " Justice Brennan analogized such historical designation to a particularized form of zoning that applied to selected parcels.

Having rejected a general attack against New York's scheme, Justice Brennan proceeded to examine its application to Grand Central Station. In rejecting this "as applied" attack, Justice Brennan stressed that Penn Central could still obtain a " 'reasonable return' on its investment." Moreover, the Commission had not prohibited all building, or use of air rights, above the Terminal; it had only rejected the plan Penn Central had submitted. Thus, the Commission might approve another design.

Transfer Development Rights also lessened the Act's impact: "While these rights may well not have constituted 'just compensation' if a 'taking' had occurred, the rights, nevertheless, undoubtedly mitigate whatever financial burden the law has imposed and, for that reason, are to be taken into account in considering the impact of the regulation."

Justice Rehnquist dissented, joined by Chief Justice Burger and Justice Stevens. "[W]here the government prohibits a noninjurious use, the Court has ruled that a taking does not take place if the prohibition applies over a broad cross section of land and thereby '[secures] an average reciprocity of advantage.' " In this case, the Commission had focused a substantial burden on the owners of some 500 New York landmarks, which comprise less than one percent of the buildings in New York.

(c) *Transferable Development Rights.* In *Suitum v. Tahoe Regional Planning Agency*, 520 U.S. 725 (1997), the Court established that the prudential ripeness principles do not forbid judicial review when the owner of a development right has not attempted to sell that right. Suitum bought undeveloped property and requested permission to construct a house. The Tahoe Regional Planning Agency determined that her property lay within a Stream Environment Zone (SEZ), an undeveloped parcel carrying run-off into the watershed, and denied permission to build. As an owner of undeveloped land and of SEZ property, Suitum received certain Transferable Development Rights (TDRs), which she could sell to owners of property suitable for development. Without attempting to sell her TDRs, Suitum brought suit, claiming a regulatory taking of her land.

In an effort to prevent a low estimation of market value, the agency claimed that Suitum must attempt to sell the TDRs to establish valuation. However, in a 9-0 decision delivered by Justice Souter, the Court held that the matter was ripe for adjudication even if market value is difficult to determine. No question existed that the entire property lay within the SEZ which would prohibit any construction on it. Justice Scalia wrote a concurring opinion, joined by Justice O'Connor and Justice Thomas.

(6) *De Minimis Expropriations.* (a) *Fractional land interests.* In *Babbitt v. Youpee*, 519 U.S. 234 (1997), the Court struck down a law requiring certain fractional interests of devised Indian land to escheat to the tribe. Youpee's will devised to the plaintiffs (his children and potential heirs) his several undivided interests in congressionally-allotted trust lands. Together, these lands were worth $1,239. To avoid the fractionalization caused by passing each interest to a single descendant, amended § 207 escheated Youpee's interests to the appropriate tribal governments.

The law served " 'to completely abolish one of the sticks in the bundle of rights [constituting property] for a class of Indian landowners.' " The value of the land, unlike the land's income generating capabilities, could not be properly thought of as " 'de minimis.' "

In dissent, Justice Stevens argued that the Court had "repeatedly 'upheld the power of the State to condition the retention of a property right upon the performance of an act within a limited period of time,' " in this case, six years.

(b) *Small amounts of money.* In *Phillips v. Washington Legal Foundation*, 524 U.S. 156 (1998), Texas and 48 other states adopted an Interest on Lawyers Trust Account (IOLTA) program that required attorneys who were entrusted with nominal funds or short-term funds to place the funds in an IOLTA account. Funds were invested in IOLTA accounts only if they could not earn net interest, that is, interest sufficient "to offset the 'cost of establishing and maintaining the account.' " Texas then used the interest on these funds to help fund legal services for low-income individuals. The Court held that the interest earned on an IOLTA account was " 'private property.' "

Writing for the majority, Chief Justice Rehnquist stated that since the U.S. Constitution only protects property rights, the Court would turn to other sources, such as state law, to determine the existence of such rights. Texas followed the English common law rule established since the mid-1700s that " 'interest follows principal.' " A state has some control over the use of property, but where confiscatory regulations are involved, "a State may not sidestep the Takings Clause by disavowing traditional property interests long recognized under state law."

Moreover, "a physical item is not 'property' simply because it lacks a positive economic or market value." *See Lorretto v. Teleprompter Manhattan CATV Corp.*, 458 U.S. 419 (1982) (holding that although a property right infringement increased the value of the property, there was still a taking of that property right).

The Court stated that "property is more than economic value"; it also includes the " 'right to possess, use and dispose of it.' " The Chief Justice left the issues of whether there was a taking and whether there was just compensation to the appellate court on remand.

Justice Souter dissented, joined by Justices Stevens, Ginsburg and Breyer. The client's "inability to earn net interest outside IOLTA, due to the unchallenged federal and state regulations" also impairs any claim for just compensation. The federal government's failure to remit to a taxpayer interest earned on tax withheld does not constitute a taking.

Justice Breyer also dissented, joined by Justices Stevens, Souter and Ginsburg. Without IOLTA, there could be no "expectation of receiving interest" on the principal in an IOLTA trust.

(c) *Net Interest.* In *Brown v. Legal Found. of Washington*, 538 U.S. 216 (2003), the Court held that a law requiring that funds that cannot earn interest for a client be deposited in an IOLTA account does not amount to a regulatory taking. However, a law that requires this interest to be transferred to another for a legitimate public use could be construed as a per se taking, which would require just compensation to the client. The state used interest on lawyers' trust accounts (IOLTA) to pay for legal services for the poor.

The aggregate value of contributions derived from IOLTA accounts exceeded $200 million. The funds that are subject to the IOLTA program are " 'only those funds that *cannot, under any circumstances, earn net* interest (after deducting transaction and administrative costs and bank fees) for the client.' " The record shows that "without IOLTA those funds would not have produced any net interest for either" of these plaintiffs.

Writing for a 5-4 Court, Justice Stevens referred to *Phillips v. Washington Legal Foundation, supra* Note 6(b), which held that interest generated by IOLTA accounts was the property of the clients who owned the principal. The Court did not address in *Phillips* "whether the income had been 'taken' by the State," nor did it address the amount of just compensation the respondents were due.

Plaintiffs were not owed just compensation, which "is measured by the property owner's loss rather than the government's gain." If plaintiff's net loss was zero, the compensation that is due is also zero. "Because that compensation is measured by the owner's pecuniary loss — which is zero whenever the Washington law is obeyed — there has been no violation of the *Just Compensation Clause of the Fifth Amendment* in this case." However, " 'as cost effective subaccounting services become available, making it possible to earn net interest for clients on increasingly smaller amounts held for increasingly shorter periods of time, more trust money will have to be invested for the clients' benefit under the new rule.' "

Justice Scalia dissented, joined by the Chief Justice Rehnquist and Justices Kennedy and Thomas. Justice Scalia maintained that "the Court creates a novel exception to our oft-repeated rule that the just compensation owed to former owners of confiscated property is the fair market value of the property taken." IOLTA's pooling is irrelevant. "[J]ust compensation is not to be measured by what would have happened in a hypothetical world in which the State's IOLTA program did not exist."

Justice Kennedy filed a separate dissent.

(b) Public Use

KELO v. CITY OF NEW LONDON, 545 U.S. 469 (2005). In *Kelo*, a 5-4 Court held that a city's taking property for economic development did not violate the public use requirement of the Takings Clause. New London targeted for economic revitalization an area known as Fort Trumbull, and enlisted a non-profit group called New London Development Corporation (NLDC) to create "an integrated development plan focused on 90 acres of the Fort Trumbull area." Pfizer Inc. was planning to build a "$300 million research facility" near Fort Trumbull which the city hoped would further "the area's rejuvenation." The Fort Trumbull area encompasses "approximately 115 privately owned properties." Plaintiffs own property located in parcels 3 and 4A of the development plan. Parcel 3 "will contain at least 90,000 square feet of research and development office space" and 4A will support either the nearby state park or marina with visitor parking or retail.

Writing for the majority, Justice Stevens said: "it has long been accepted that the sovereign may not take the property of A for the sole purpose of transferring it to another private party B, even though A is paid just compensation. On the other hand, it is equally clear that a State may transfer property from one private party to another if future 'use by the public' is the purpose of the taking."[18]

Justice Stevens rejected the argument that "using eminent domain for economic development impermissibly blurs the boundary between public and private takings." Instead, "the government's pursuit of a public purpose will often benefit individual private parties." The Court deferred to the legislature regarding the plan's effectiveness and the lands necessary to carry it out. Of course, "many States already impose 'public use' requirements that are stricter than the federal baseline."

Justice Kennedy concurred. *Hawaii Housing Authority v. Midkiff, infra* § 7.03[4](b), Note, permitted a taking "as long as it is "rationally related to a conceivable public purpose.' " Still, the public use requirement may forbid "transfers intended to confer benefits on particular, favored private entities, and with only incidental or pretextual public benefits." Moreover, private transfers involved in a taking may entail a "risk of undetected impermissible favoritism of private parties" so great as to create "a presumption (rebuttable or otherwise) of invalidity." However, this case does not "justify a more demanding standard" as the "taking occurred in the context of a comprehensive development plan meant to address a serious city-wide depression" and "the identity of most of the private beneficiaries were unknown at the time the city formulated its plans."

Justice O'Connor dissented, joined by Chief Justice Rehnquist, and Justices Scalia and Thomas. "To reason, as the Court does, that the incidental public benefits resulting from the subsequent ordinary use of private property render economic development

---

[18] The record below establishes that the takings entailed "a 'carefully considered' development plan" that "was not intended to serve the interests of Pfizer, Inc., or any other private entity, but rather, to revitalize the local economy." Although a private developer will be involved, who will lease space to other private parties, "the identities of those private parties were not known when the plan was adopted." Consequently, it is "difficult to accuse the government of having taken A's property to benefit the private interests of B when the identity of B was unknown."

takings 'for public use' is to wash out any distinction between private and public use of property — and thereby effectively to delete the words 'for public use' from the Takings Clause of the Fifth Amendment." Consequently, private property is "vulnerable to being taken and transferred to another private owner, so long as it might be upgraded."

There are "three categories of takings that comply with the public use requirement." One is "public ownership — such as for a road," another is "use-by-the-public," many times involving common carriers, and the third is designed "to meet certain exigencies" and allows certain takings "even if the property is destined for subsequent private use." Economic development takings are invalid for want of a valid public purpose. To satisfy this requirement, "the targeted property" must impose "affirmative harm on society" as was the case "in *Berman* [*v. Parker*, 348 U.S. 26 (1954),] through blight resulting from extreme poverty and in *Midkiff* through oligopoly." With the present case, the Court moves "away from our decisions sanctioning the condemnation of harmful property use" and "significantly expands the meaning of public use. It holds that the sovereign may take private property currently put to ordinary private use, and give it over for new, ordinary private use, so long as the new use is predicted to generate some secondary benefit for the public — such as increased tax revenue, more jobs, maybe even aesthetic pleasure." The rule adopted by the majority contains no mechanism to "prohibit property transfers generated with less care . . . whose only projected advantage is the incidence of higher taxes," or the transformation of "an already prosperous city into an even more prosperous one." The likely beneficiaries of this rule would be "citizens with disproportionate influence and power in the political process, including large corporations and development firms."

In a separate dissent, Justice Thomas argued that the originalist understanding of the Public Use Clause is "a meaningful limit on the government's eminent domain power." He would reconsider the "deferential conception of 'public use' " from *Hawaii Housing Authority v. Midkiff*, 467 U.S. 229 (1984). Upholding " 'urban renewal' programs" and "extending the concept of public purpose to encompass any economically beneficial goal guarantees" a disproportionate impact on the poor, due to their lack of political influence and the fact that their land is likely not being used in the "highest and best social" manner. "Urban renewal projects have long been associated with the displacement of blacks." In this case, "over 97 percent of the individuals forcibly removed from their homes by the 'slum-clearance' project upheld by this Court in *Berman* were black."

NOTE

Public Use Requirement. In *Hawaii Housing Authority v. Midkiff*, 467 U.S. 299 (1984), the Court construed the public use requirement.

Much of the fee simple title to real property in Hawaii was concentrated in a small number of landowners. Under the Land Reform Act, once a sufficient number of tenants within a development tract requested the option to buy their land, the State could condemn the property, compensate the landowner, and sell title to the tenant.

In a unanimous opinion, Justice O'Connor said: "Deference to the legislature's 'public purpose' determination is required 'until it is shown to involve an impossibility.' " The Court only required that the "legislature *rationally could have believed* that the [Act] would promote its objective. . . . Redistribution of ownership to correct a land oligopoly is a rational exercise of the eminent domain power."

(c) Temporary Takings

LUCAS v. SOUTH CAROLINA COASTAL COUNCIL, 505 U.S. 1003 (1992). In *Lucas*, the Court examined whether a regulation depriving a landowner of all "economically viable use of his land" without compensation may be justified on the grounds that it prevents "harmful or noxious uses."

In 1986, plaintiff David Lucas paid $975,000 for two residential lots on a South Carolina barrier island. He planned to erect single-family homes, as had already been done on similar adjacent lots. When Lucas purchased the parcel in 1986, no law prohibited such development. In 1988, South Carolina enacted the Beachfront Management Act (the Act), which established a perimeter, "based on the landward-most 'point[s] of erosion . . . during the past forty years.' " The Act prohibited all improvements outside this perimeter. It effectively barred Lucas from building on his land, located seaward of the perimeter in the "coastal zone." Lucas challenged the law for failing to compensate him for rendering his property "valueless."[19]

Justice Scalia wrote for the majority. *Pennsylvania Coal v. Mahon,* 260 U.S. 393 (1922), distinguished between permissible regulation and a compensable taking, but the decision failed to clarify "when, and under what circumstances, a given regulation would be seen as going 'too far' for purposes of the Fifth Amendment. In 70-odd years of succeeding 'regulatory takings' jurisprudence, we have generally eschewed any 'set formula' for determining how far is too far." He added that the Court has "however, described at least two discrete categories of regulatory action as compensable without case-specific inquiry into the public interest advanced in support of the restraint." In addition to the "physical invasion" line of cases, "we have found categorical treatment appropriate . . . where regulation denies all economically beneficial or productive use of land."

Justice Scalia reasoned that " 'harmful or noxious uses' " could not be the "basis for departing from our categorical rule that total regulatory takings must be compensated." When "the State seeks to sustain regulation that deprives land of all economically beneficial use, we think it may resist compensation only if the logically antecedent inquiry into the nature of the owner's estate shows that the proscribed use interests were not part of his title to begin with."

Justice Scalia said that "the property owner necessarily expects the uses of his property to be restricted, from time to time, by various measures newly enacted by the State in the legitimate exercise of its police powers. . . . When, however, a regulation that declares 'off-limits' all economically productive or beneficial uses of land goes beyond what the relevant background principles would dictate, compensation must be paid to sustain it." Justice Scalia clarified "relevant background principles" through reference to nuisance law. "The fact that a particular use has long been engaged in by similarly situated owners ordinarily imports a lack of any common-law prohibition (though changed circumstances or new knowledge may make what was previously permissible no longer so, see Restatement of Torts (Second), § 827, comment g). So also does the fact that other landowners, similarly situated, are permitted to continue in the use denied to the claimant."

On remand, "South Carolina must identify background principles of nuisance and

---

[19] After the parties had submitted arguments to the South Carolina Supreme Court, but before it issued an opinion, South Carolina amended the Act to allow the South Carolina Coastal Council to grant "special permits" for development in the coastal zone. Because the amendment came after Lucas presented his case to the South Carolina Supreme Court and the decision of the South Carolina Supreme Court was so categorically against this being a taking, Justice Scalia opted not to dispose of the case on prudential ripeness grounds.

property law that prohibit the uses [Lucas] now intends in the circumstances in which the property is presently found. Only on this showing can the State fairly claim that, in proscribing all such beneficial uses, the Beachfront Management Act is taking nothing."

Justice Kennedy concurred in the judgment. He emphasized that the Court has not decided "whether a temporary taking has occurred in this case. The facts necessary to the determination have not been developed in the record. Among the matters to be considered on remand must be whether petitioner had the intent and capacity to develop the property and failed to do so in the interim because the State prevented him."

When the alleged taking involves "regulations which deprive property of all value, the test must be whether the deprivation is contrary to reasonable, investment-backed expectations." This analysis was inherently circular. Specifically, "if the owner's reasonable expectations are shaped by what courts allow as a proper exercise of governmental authority, property tends to become what courts say it is."

Justice Blackmun dissented. "Nothing in the record undermines the General Assembly's assessment that prohibitions on building in front of the setback line are necessary to protect people from storms, high tides, and beach erosion." Justice Blackmun also criticized the majority for formulating a new "categorical rule" that regulations that deprive property of all economic value are a taking "unless they prohibit a background common-law nuisance or property principle." Finally, the trial court's finding that the regulation caused Lucas's property to lose "all economic value . . . is almost certainly erroneous. Petitioner still can enjoy other attributes of ownership, such as the right to exclude others, 'one of the most essential sticks in the bundle of rights that are commonly characterized as property.' Petitioner can picnic, swim, camp in a tent, or live on the property in a movable trailer. State courts frequently have recognized that land has economic value where the only residual uses are recreation and camping."

Justice Stevens also dissented. He questioned the majority's finding of injury-in-fact from Lucas's temporary deprivation. "If we assume that petitioner is now able to build on the lot, . . . the record does not tell us whether his building plans were even temporarily frustrated by the enactment of the statute."

Justice Stevens further warned that the majority's approach to the nuisance law exception contradicted *Mugler v. Kansas, supra* § 7.03[4](a), Note (2)(b). "Under our reasoning in *Mugler*, a state's decision to prohibit or to regulate certain uses of property is not a compensable taking just because the particular uses were previously lawful. Under the Court's opinion today, however, if a state should decide to prohibit the manufacture of asbestos, cigarettes, or concealable firearms, for example, it must be prepared to pay for the adverse economic consequences of its decision."

Finally, Justice Stevens suggested that the Court has, "in our takings law frequently looked to the generality of a regulation of property." In this case, the Beachfront Management Act "does not target particular landowners, but rather regulates the use of the coastline of the entire state."

Justice Souter would "dismiss the instant writ and await an opportunity to face the total deprivation question squarely."

TAHOE-SIERRA PRESERVATION COUNCIL, INC. v. TAHOE REGIONAL PLANNING AGENCY, 535 U.S. 302 (2002). In *Tahoe-Sierra*, the Court considered "whether a moratorium on development imposed during the process of devising a comprehensive land-use plan constitutes a *per se* taking of property requiring compensation." While studying the "impact of development on Lake Tahoe and designing a strategy for environmentally sound growth," the Tahoe Regional Planning

Agency (TRPA) ordered two moratoria, Ordinance 81-5 and Resolution 83-21, which, in combination, "effectively prohibited all construction on sensitive lands in California and on all SEZ lands [" 'Stream Environment Zones' "] in the entire Basin for 32 months, and on sensitive lands in Nevada (other than SEZ lands) for eight months." Although another plan, the 1984 regional plan had been subjected to protracted litigation in the lower courts, the challenge to it was not before the Supreme Court "because both the District Court and the Court of Appeals held that it was the federal injunction against implementing that plan, rather than the plan itself, that caused the post-1984 injuries that petitioners allegedly suffered, and those rulings are not encompassed within our limited grant of certiorari." Thus, the Court limited its "discussion to the lower courts' disposition of the claims based on the 2-year moratorium (Ordinance 81-5) and the ensuing 8-month moratorium (Resolution 83-21)."

Writing for the majority, Justice Stevens concluded that no *per se* taking had occurred, and that "the circumstances in this case are best analyzed within the *Penn Central* framework." While the Court's "jurisprudence involving condemnations and physical takings. . . for the most part, involves the straightforward application of *per se* rules," Justice Stevens indicated that its regulatory takings jurisprudence, as in this case, "is characterized by 'essentially ad hoc, factual inquires,' " carefully weighing all the circumstances. "Land-use regulations are ubiquitous and most of them impact property values in some tangential way — often in completely unanticipated ways. Treating them all as *per se* takings would transform government regulation into a luxury few governments could afford." The *Penn Central* framework eschews set formulas. "In deciding whether a particular governmental action has effected a taking, this Court focuses both on the character of the action and on the nature and extent of the interference with rights in the parcel as a whole."

In *First English Evangelical Church of Glendale v. County of Los Angeles*, 482 U.S. 304 (1987), the California Courts had decided that a taking had occurred, and that the Supreme Court only decided the question of remedy. Indeed, *First English* gave two reasons "why a regulation temporarily denying an owner all use of her property might not constitute a taking." First, "the county might avoid the conclusion that a compensable taking had occurred by establishing that the denial of all use was insulated as a part of the State's authority to enact safety regulations." Second, the *First English* Court recognized "the quite different questions that would arise in the case of normal delays in obtaining building permits, changes in zoning ordinances, variances, and the like which [were] not before us." The taking in *Lucas v. South Carolina Coastal Council, supra* § 7.03[4](c), "was unconditional and permanent." The Court's holding "was limited to the 'extraordinary circumstance when no productive or economically beneficial use of land is permitted.' "

A court should begin by asking "whether there was a total taking of the entire parcel; if not, then *Penn Central* was the proper framework." To avoid that fact-driven inquiry, there must be "complete elimination of value," or a "total loss."

Justice Stevens rejected petitioners' broad *per se* rule because it "would apply to numerous 'normal delays in obtaining building permits, changes in zoning ordinances, variances and the like,' as well as to orders temporarily prohibiting access to crime scenes, businesses that violate health codes, fire-damaged buildings," in addition to other traditional exercises of the police power. "[T]he extreme categorical rule that any deprivation of all economic use, no matter how brief, constitutes a compensable taking surely cannot be sustained." However, "we do not hold that the temporary nature of a land-use restriction precludes finding that it effects a taking; we simply recognize that it should not be given exclusive significance one way or the other." The Court would have created perverse incentives had it held "that landowners must wait for a taking claim to ripen so that planners can make well-reasoned decisions while, at the same time, holding that those planners must compensate landowners for the delay." A government's interest in well-reasoned decisions becomes "even stronger when an agency is developing a regional plan than when it is considering a permit for a single parcel." The two moratoria at issue in this case, for example, "enabled TRPA to obtain the benefit of comments and criticisms from interested parties, such as the petitioners, during its deliberations." Moreover, "property values throughout the Basin can be expected to reflect the added assurance that Lake Tahoe will remain in its pristine state."

Chief Justice Rehnquist dissented, joined by Justices Scalia and Thomas. Unlike the majority, Chief Justice Rehnquist concluded that "the 'temporary' denial of all viable use of land for six years is a taking." In contrast, the taking in *Lucas* lasted less than two years. Public and private nuisances can still be abated without effecting a taking. Similarly, "short-term delays attendant to zoning and permit regimes are a longstanding feature of state property law and part of a landowner's reasonable investment-backed expectations." Common "moratoria thus prohibit only certain categories of development, such as fast-food restaurants," rather than "deprive landowners of all economically beneficial use."

Justice Thomas dissented, joined by Justice Scalia. He maintained that *First English* "held that temporary and permanent takings 'are not different in kind' when a landowner is deprived of all beneficial use of his land." For Justice Thomas, "potential future value bears on the amount of compensation due and has nothing to do with the question whether there was a taking."

(d) Court Decisions

Land Use. In *First English Evangelical Lutheran Church of Glendale v. County of Los Angeles*, 482 U.S. 304 (1987), the Court required compensation for " 'temporary' regulatory takings." The temporary taking occurred between the time that the ordinance was enacted and the time that the court determined that the regulation effected a "taking" of property.

The First Evangelical Lutheran Church owned acreage along the banks of the Middle Fork of Mill Creek in the Los Angeles National Forest on which they operated a retreat called "Lutherglen." In 1978, after a severe storm, major flooding destroyed Lutherglen. As an emergency measure, the County of Los Angeles passed an "Interim Ordinance" prohibiting building or rebuilding in the Mill Creek Canyon. One month after the effective date of the ordinance, the Church filed a complaint claiming that the ordinance had deprived them of all use of Lutherglen.

Writing for the Court, Chief Justice Rehnquist said that " 'temporary' takings which, as here, . . . deny a landowner all use of his property, are not different in kind from permanent takings." He distinguished the "different questions that would arise in the case of normal delays in obtaining building permits, changes in zoning ordinances, variances, and the like," and concluded that since the Los Angeles County ordinances have "denied appellant all use of its property for a considerable period of years," the appellant was entitled to just compensation.

Justice Stevens, with whom Justices Blackmun and O'Connor partially joined, dissented. "Regulations are three dimensional; they have depth, width, and length. As for depth, regulations define the extent to which the owner may not use the property in question. With respect to width, regulations define the amount of property encompassed by the restrictions. Finally, and for purposes of this case, essentially, regulations set forth the duration of the restrictions." The interval required for a court to make a taking determination was a normal delay that rarely, if ever, could amount to a taking. Allowing damages for temporary takings would have an unfortunate chilling effect on land-use regulation: "Cautious local officials and land-use planners may avoid taking any action that might later be challenged and thus give rise to a damages action."

(e) Nexus Requirement

DOLAN v. CITY OF TIGARD, 512 U.S. 374 (1994). In *Dolan*, a 5-4 majority invalidated a zoning commission's conditioning a building permit on the dedication of some property for public use, because "rough proportionality" did not exist between the conditions and the improvement's impact. Plaintiff Florence Dolan challenged the City of Tigard's permit condition requiring her to dedicate a part of her property for flood control and traffic alleviation. The case analyzed "what is the required degree of connection between the exactions imposed by the city and the projected impacts of the proposed development."

Dolan, the owner of a hardware store on Fanno Creek in Tigard's business district, applied to the city for permission to nearly double the size of her building to 17,600 square feet and pave a 39-space parking lot. The City Planning Commission granted the permit, but "required that petitioner dedicate the portion of her property lying within the 100-year floodplain for improvement of a [public] storm drainage system along Fanno Creek and that she dedicate an additional 15-foot strip of land adjacent to the floodplain as a pedestrian/bicycle pathway" designed to alleviate traffic. These conditions would exact 7,000 square feet, or 10 percent, of Dolan's property and were adopted pursuant to the city's Master Drainage Plan and the Community Development Code. The City's Community Development Code was enacted to comply with an Oregon state land use law requiring 15 percent of all business district property to remain open space. The Planning Commission denied Dolan's application for a variance.

The Supreme Court invalidated the Commission's conditions. Writing for the Court, Chief Justice Rehnquist saw Dolan's case as falling between a straightforward taking and a permissible land use regulation. On the one hand, it would surely have been a taking had the city simply required Dolan to dedicate her land to public use, rather than making the dedication conditional. On the other hand, "land use regulation does not effect a taking if it 'substantially advance[s] legitimate state interests' and does not 'den[y] an owner economically viable use of his land.'" The Chief Justice explained that what set this case apart from zoning and other land use regulations was: (1) the specific, adjudicative nature of the conditions and, (2) the fact that the conditions did not simply regulate Dolan's use of her property, but required her to surrender part of her property to public access. As such, the case invoked the "unconstitutional conditions" doctrine. Specifically, "the government may not require a person to give up a constitutional right — here the right to receive just compensation when property is taken for a public use — in exchange for a discretionary benefit conferred by the government where the property sought has little or no relationship to the benefit."

To evaluate the constitutionality of the permit conditions, the Court employed a two-pronged approach: (1) does the "essential nexus," required by *Nollan v. California*, *infra* § 7.03[4](d), Note after *Dolan*, exist between the conditions and the "legitimate state interests" that the city seeks to advance by them and, (2) does a sufficient connection exist between the conditions and the *impact* of the new development? The Chief Justice explained that the absence of an "essential nexus" rendered the zoning commission's regulation in *Nollan* "'an out-and-out plan of extortion.'" In contrast, no "such gimmicks are associated with the permit conditions imposed by the city in this case." Theoretically, the dedication of land for a public drainage system could advance the city's interest in flood control, and the provision for a pathway could reduce traffic congestion. Thus, both conditions satisfied the "essential nexus" prong.

Turning to the second prong, *Nollan* did not clarify the closeness of the nexus required to justify a land use regulation, because the conditions at issue in that case bore no relationship to the goals of the permit scheme involved. State courts have filled this gap by requiring a "reasonable relationship" between the conditions and the proposed use of the property. The Court reformulated the latter requirement into a "rough proportionality" test: To clear the second prong "the city must make some sort of individualized determination that the required dedication is related both in nature and extent to the impact of the proposed development."

In applying the second prong to the dedication of floodplain land for the public drainage system, the Court emphasized that the "city has never said why a public greenway, as opposed to a private one, was required in the interest of flood control." A public greenway deprived Dolan of her right to exclude others. This right is "one of the most essential sticks in the bundle of rights that are commonly characterized as property." The commercial character of her property did not lessen Dolan's interest in excluding the public. Depriving Dolan of her right to decide when and where the public would enter her property was not proportional to her development's potential impact on drainage into the creek. Had Dolan's development threatened existing greenway, the city could have required alternative greenway on her property or elsewhere.

The bicycle pathway dedication condition likewise encroached on Dolan's right to exclude. Although the city had, in fact, calculated that Dolan's new development would generate an additional 435 trips to the business district, "[t]he findings of fact that the bicycle pathway system" *could* " 'offset some of the traffic demand' is a far cry from a finding that the bicycle pathway system *will*, or is *likely to*, 'offset some of the traffic demand.' " While the Court did not require a "precise mathematical calculation," the city had to "make some effort to quantify its findings in support of the dedication for the pedestrian/bicycle pathway beyond the conclusory statement that it could offset some of the traffic demand generated."

Justice Stevens dissented, joined by Justices Blackmun and Ginsburg. Undoubtedly, the impact of Dolan's development would justify denying her permit entirely. However, this fact did not give the city free rein to impose arbitrary conditions in lieu of a permit denial. Nevertheless, the Court's new "rough proportionality" test, and its application of it, departed from traditional takings doctrine. Once the city had demonstrated a rational and impartial basis for the conditions, the Court should not require "individualized determinations" to show proportionality

Courts should "venture beyond considerations of a condition's nature or germaneness only if the developer establishes that a concededly germane condition is so grossly disproportionate to the proposed development's adverse effects that it manifests motives other than land use regulation on the part of the city." Through its expansion of "regulatory takings" doctrine, the Court was resurrecting the kind of substantive due process logic exemplified by the notorious *Lochner* case, *supra* § 7.03[1]. "Besides having similar ancestry, both doctrines are potentially open-ended sources of judicial power to invalidate state economic regulations that Members of this Court view as unwise or unfair." When "the government can demonstrate that the conditions it has imposed in a land-use permit are rational, impartial and conducive to fulfilling the aims of a valid land-use plan, a strong presumption of validity should attach to those conditions."

Justice Souter dissented separately, arguing that the city had established the *Nollan* nexus by calculating the increased traffic flow of 435 trips and submitting studies correlating decreased traffic congestion with alternative means of transportation.

NOTE

Beachfront Easement. In *Nollan v. California Coastal Commision*, 483 U.S. 825 (1987), the Court held that conditioning a building permit on a landowner granting the government a public easement across his land constituted a "taking." The Nollans applied for a permit from the California Coastal Commission to build a new house on their property. The Commission granted the permit subject to the Nollans' providing an easement to allow the public to traverse an area approximately 10 feet wide along the beachfront. The Commission contended that the easement furthered legitimate public purposes such as "protecting the public's ability to see the beach, assisting the public in overcoming the 'psychological barrier' to using the beach created by a developed shorefront, and preventing congestion on the public beaches."

In an opinion by Justice Scalia, the Court found the access condition violated the Taking Clause. For Justice Scalia, the Taking Clause requires "the condition for abridgement of property rights through the police power as a 'substantial advancing' of a legitimate State interest." He found no nexus between the legitimate governmental end of maintaining public access to the beach and the means of conditioning the building permit on the Nollans' granting an access easement. "[O]btaining of an easement to serve some valid governmental purpose, but without payment of compensation" is outside the limits of " 'legitimate state interest,'. . . unless the permit condition serves the same governmental purpose as the development ban." Here the easement did not further interests advanced by California, because it did not reduce any obstacles to viewing the beach, did not lower any "psychological barrier" to using public beaches, and did not remedy beach congestion. Therefore, "the Commission's imposition of the permit condition cannot be treated as an exercise of its land use power for any of these purposes."

Justice Brennan dissented, joined by Justice Marshall. "It is also by now commonplace that this Court's review of the rationality of a State's exercise of its police power demands only that the State *'could rationally have decided'* that the measure adopted might achieve the State's objective."

Justice Brennan contended that the State action did not substantially interfere with the Nollans' investment-backed expectations. It only allowed the public to pass along 10 extra feet of a beach that they could already traverse a bit closer to the shoreline.

Justice Blackmun filed a separate dissenting opinion, arguing that the nexus requirement will impair creative land use regulation.

LINGLE v. CHEVRON U.S.A., INC., 544 U.S. 528 (2005). In *Lingle*, a unanimous Court held that the "substantially advances" test of *Agins v. City of Tiburon*, 447 U.S. 255 (1980), is not appropriate to apply in deciding whether a regulation of how much Chevron can charge lessee-dealers for rent on its gas stations constitutes a taking. Chevron challenged the rent cap provision as facially invalid under the Takings Clause.

Government appropriation of property always comprised a taking. *Pennsylvania Coal Co. v. Mahon*, 260 U.S. 393 (1922), first recognized regulatory takings. As Justice Holmes noted, "while property may be regulated to a certain extent, if regulation goes too far it will be recognized as a taking." However, government regulation inherently "involves the adjustment of rights for the public good." Indeed, "[g]overnment hardly could go on if to some extent values incident to property could not be diminished without paying for every such change in the general law."

Justice O'Connor outlined several recognized types of regulatory takings. First, a permanent physical invasion of property — however minor — is a *per se* taking. A second categorical rule applies to regulations that completely deprive an owner of 'all economically beneficial use' of her property." *Penn Central Transportation Co. v. New York City*, *supra* § 7.03[4](a), Note(5)(b), identifies several factors that courts should consider in finding regulatory takings. "Primary among those factors are 'the economic impact of the regulation on the claimant and, particularly, the extent to which the regulation has interfered with distinct investment-backed expectations.' Another relevant factor may be the 'character of the governmental action' — for instance whether it amounts to a physical invasion or instead merely affects property interests through 'some public program adjusting the benefits and burdens of economic life to promote the common good.' "

Courts have also used the "substantially advances" test of *Agins v. City of Tiburon*, 447 U.S. 255 (1980), to determine whether a regulatory taking has occurred. Such a means-ends test is inappropriate for takings analysis, as it does not help to determine whether property has been taken. "An inquiry of this nature has some logic in the context of a due process challenge, for a regulation that fails to serve any legitimate governmental objective may be so arbitrary or irrational that it runs afoul of the Due Process Clause. But such a test is not a valid method of discerning whether private property has been 'taken' for purposes of the *Fifth Amendment*. The 'substantially advances' inquiry reveals nothing about the *magnitude or character of the burden* a particular regulation imposes upon private property rights," and "is tethered neither to the text of the Takings Clause" nor to the basic rationale for regulatory takings. "A test that tells us nothing about the actual burden imposed on property rights, or how that burden is allocated cannot tell us when justice might require that the burden be spread among taxpayers through the payment of compensation. The owner of a property subject to a regulation that effectively serves a legitimate state interest may be just as singled out and just as burdened as the owner of a property subject to an ineffective regulation."

In the case at bar, Hawaii's legislation will cause Chevron to lose $207,000 in rental income per year. However, the parties stipulated that Chevron "expects to receive a return on its investment in these stations that satisfies any constitutional standard." Chevron could regain this lost income through increasing gas prices. Therefore, Hawaii's law will not cause Chevron to suffer any regulatory burden, and the Takings Clause should not apply.

Besides being doctrinally ineffective, the "substantially advances" test also creates serious practical problems in its application. "The *Agins* formula can be read to demand heightened means-ends review of virtually any regulation of private property. If so interpreted, it would require courts to scrutinize the efficacy of a vast array of state and federal regulations" — a task for which elected legislatures and expert agencies are better suited than courts.

The Court was careful to state that its holding in Lingle does not "disturb any of our prior holdings," in particular *Nollan v. California Coastal Commission* and *Dolan v. City of Tigard*. Although both of those opinions rely on *Agins*, "the rule those decisions established is entirely distinct from the 'substantially advances' test we address today. Whereas, the 'substantially advances' inquiry before us now is unconcerned with the degree or type of burden a regulation places upon property, *Nollan* and *Dolan* both involved dedications of property so onerous that, outside the exactions context, they would be deemed per se physical takings. In neither case did the Court question whether the exaction would substantially advance some legitimate state interest. Rather, the issue was whether the exactions substantially advanced the same interests that land-use authorities asserted would allow them to deny the permit altogether."

In his brief concurring opinion, Justice Kennedy emphasized that "today's decision does not foreclose the possibility that a regulation might be so arbitrary or irrational as to violate due process."

NOTE

Related Issues. For further discussion of issues relating to the Takings Clause, see, e.g., B. ACKERMAN, PRIVATE PROPERTY AND THE CONSTITUTION (1977) (differentiating between governmental takings of property and government regulation); R. EPSTEIN, TAKINGS: PRIVATE PROPERTY AND THE POWER OF EMINENT DOMAIN (1985) (favoring a more active judicial role in limiting wealth-related infringements by government); Symposium, *The Jurisprudence of Takings*, 88 COLUM. L. REV. 1581 (1988); Baker, *Property and its Relation to Constitutionally Protected Liberty*, 134 U. PA. L. REV. 741 (1986) (discussing how the unrestricted use of property can restrict personal liberty); Michaelman, *Property as a Constitutional Right*, 38 WASH. & LEE L. REV. 1097 (1981) (emphasizing the right to participate in the political process which determines the distribution of property); Michaelman, *Property, Utility, and Fairness: Comments on the Ethical Foundations of Just Compensation Theory*, 80 HARV. L. REV. 1165 (1967) (discussing the philosophical underpinnings of takings jurisprudence); Sax, *Takings and the Police Power*, 74 YALE L.J. 36, 67 (1964) ("when an individual or limited group in society sustains a detriment to legally acquired existing economic value of some governmental enterprise, then the act is a taking and compensation is constitutionally required; but when the challenged act is an improvement of the public condition through resolution of conflict within the private sector of the society, compensation is not constitutionally required"). For historical background on the origins of the Takings Clause, see Note, *The Origins and Original Significance of the Just Compensation Clause of the Fifth Amendment*, 94 YALE L.J. 694 (1985).

PALAZZOLO v. RHODE ISLAND, 121 U.S. 2448 (2001). In *Palazzolo*, the Court established that subsequent property owners who acquire land already subject to certain governmental regulations are not necessarily barred from bringing a regulatory takings claim. From 1959 to 1978, Shore Gardens, Inc. (SGI) unsuccessfully sought approval from the appropriate regulatory bodies to develop the corporation's land, most of which was "salt marsh subject to tidal flooding." In 1971, Rhode Island passed legislation establishing the Council which promulgated new regulations protecting coastal wetlands. In 1978, SGI lost its corporate status, and the title to the property passed to its sole shareholder, Palazzolo. Since all of Palazzolo's proposals to develop the land entailed filling some portion of the protected wetlands, the Council repeatedly denied his applications. Palazzolo filed an inverse condemnation action.

Writing for a 6-3 majority, Justice Kennedy explained that a regulation that " 'denies all economically beneficial or productive use of land' " effects a taking. Absent such a total depravation, a regulation may still constitute a taking, "depending on a complex of factors including the regulation's economic effect on the landowner, the extent to which the regulation interferes with reasonable investment-backed expectations, and the character of the government action. *Penn Central* [*Transp. Co. v. New York*, 439 U.S. 883 (1978)]."

Such a regulatory takings claim "is not ripe unless 'the government entity charged with implementing the regulations has reached a final decision regarding the application of the regulations to the property at issue.' " The Council's repeated denials of Palazzolo's applications represented a "final decision," from which "federal ripeness rules do not require the submission of further and futile applications with other agencies."

Palazzolo also had the right to assert a takings claim even though the regulations at issue were already in force when he acquired the title from the corporation. "In a direct condemnation action or when a State has physically invaded the property without filing suit, the fact and extent of the taking are known." In that case, "any award goes to the owner at the time of the taking," and "the right to compensation is not passed to a subsequent purchaser." However, a "post-enactment transfer of ownership" does not bar a regulatory takings claim when "the steps necessary to make the claim ripe were not taken, or could not have been taken, by a previous owner."

The Court also observed that "a regulation that otherwise would be unconstitutional absent compensation is not transformed into a background principle of the State's law by mere virtue of the passage of title." In this connection, "a regulation or common-law rule cannot be a background principle for some owners but not for others. The determination whether an existing, general law can limit all economic use of property must turn on objective factors, such as the nature of the land use proscribed," and " 'the degree of harm to public lands and resources.' "

The majority rejected the claim that the wetlands regulations constituted "a deprivation of all economic value," since the undisputed evidence showed that the upland portion of the parcel retained "significant worth for construction of a residence." Even though Palazzolo failed to establish a total deprivation, the Court remanded the case to ascertain whether his claim was viable under the *Penn Central* analysis.

Justice O'Connor's concurrence noted that "interference with investment-backed expectations" is only one of several factors a court must consider. Specifically, "the regulatory regime in place at the time the claimant acquires the property at issue helps to shape the reasonableness of those expectations."

Concurring, Justice Scalia disagreed with Justice O'Connor's concurrence. "In my view, the fact that a restriction existed at the time the purchaser took title (other than a restriction forming part of the 'background principles of the State's law of property and nuisance') should have no bearing upon the determination of whether the restriction is so substantial as to constitute a taking."

Justice Ginsburg dissented, joined by Justices Souter and Breyer. Palazzolo's claim was not a ripe "final decision." All Palazzolo's applications to develop his land concerned "the wetlands portion of the property. None aimed to develop only the uplands."

Also dissenting, Justice Breyer agreed with Justice O'Connor that transferring property ownership "does not always and automatically bar a takings claim." Specifically, "much depends upon whether, or how, the timing and circumstances of a change of ownership affect whatever reasonable investment-backed expectations might otherwise exist. Ordinarily, such expectations will diminish in force and significance — rapidly and dramatically — as property continues to change hands over time."

Concurring in part and dissenting in part, Justice Stevens argued that Palazzolo lacked standing to bring his claim. "If those early regulations changed the character of [Palazzolo's] title to the property, thereby diminishing its value, [he] acquired only the net value that remained after that diminishment occurred."

§ 7.04 LIBERTY IN PROCREATION AND OTHER PERSONAL MATTERS

[1] The Childbearing Decision: Contraception and Abortion

SKINNER v. OKLAHOMA, 316 U.S. 535 (1942). Oklahoma's Habitual Criminal Sterilization Act allowed the state to sterilize habitual criminals. The statute defined a "habitual criminal" as one who had been convicted three or more times of "felonies involving moral turpitude." The Act exempted from this definition "violation[s] of the prohibitory laws, revenue acts, embezzlement, or political offenses." The defendant in *Skinner* was convicted once of stealing chickens and twice of robbery with firearms.

A unanimous Court, in an opinion by Justice Douglas, struck down the statute as unconstitutional because of "its failure to meet the requirements of the equal protection clause of the Fourteenth Amendment." Justice Douglas pointed to the unequal treatment that the law applied to similar criminals: "A person who enters a chicken coop and steals chickens commits a felony, and he may be sterilized if he is thrice convicted. If, however, he is a bailee of the property and fraudulently appropriates it, he is an embezzler. Hence no matter how habitual his proclivities for embezzlement are and no matter how often his conviction, he may not be sterilized." Justice Douglas was careful to admit that a state is free to set its own criminal classifications and punishments. Nevertheless, "strict scrutiny of the classification which a state makes in a sterilization law is essential, lest unwittingly or otherwise, invidious discriminations are made against groups or types of individuals in violation of the constitutional guarantee of just and equal laws."

In fashioning the equal protection rationale for the decision, Justice Douglas emphasized the "fundamental" nature of the individual right affected by the statute as justification for the Court's strict scrutiny: "We are dealing here with legislation which involves one of the basic civil rights of man. Marriage and procreation are fundamental to the very existence and survival of the race."

Chief Justice Stone concurred in the judgment, but based his opinion on due process rather than equal protection grounds: "[W]hile the state may protect itself from demonstrably inheritable tendencies of the individual which are injurious to society, the most elementary notions of due process would seem to require it to take appropriate steps to safeguard the liberty of the individual by affording him, before he is condemned to an irreparable injury in his person, some opportunity to show that he is without such inheritable tendencies."

Justice Jackson also concurred and supported both the equal protection and due process arguments: "There are limits to the extent to which a legislatively represented majority may conduct biological experiments at the expense of the dignity and personality and natural powers of a minority even those who have been guilty of what the majority define as crimes."

NOTE

Although *Skinner v. Oklahoma* raised some of the same issues posed by the next group of cases — the extent to which the Constitution protected an individual's childbearing decision — the Court was able to decide the case on traditional equal protection grounds because of the apparent irrationality of the classifications created by the Oklahoma Habitual Criminal Sterilization Act. When the Court next confronted these issues in a group of cases involving a Connecticut law that made it unlawful for a person to use contraceptives, the *Lochner* approach to the Due Process Clause had been replaced by the extremely deferential hands-off attitude, typified by *West Coast Hotel v. Parrish* and other cases discussed *supra*.

GRISWOLD v. CONNECTICUT
381 U.S. 479, 85 S. Ct. 1678, 14 L. Ed. 2d 510 (1965)

Justice Douglas delivered the opinion of the Court.

Appellant Griswold is Executive Director of the Planned Parenthood League of Connecticut. Appellant Buxton is a licensed physician and a professor at the Yale Medical School who served as Medical Director for the League at its Center in New

Haven . . . when appellants were arrested.

They gave information, instruction, and medical advice to married persons as to the means of preventing conception. . . .

. . . [Section] 53-32 of the General Statutes of Connecticut (1958 rev.) . . . provides:

> Any person who uses any drug, medicinal article, or instrument for the purpose of preventing conception shall be fined not less than fifty dollars or imprisoned not less than sixty days nor more than one year or be both fined and imprisoned.

Section 54-196 provides: Any person who assists, abets, counsels, causes, hires, or commands another to commit any offense may be prosecuted and punished as if he were the principal offender.

The appellants were found guilty as accessories and fined $100 each. . . .

[W]e are met with a wide range of questions that implicate the Due Process Clause of the Fourteenth Amendment. Overtones of some arguments suggest that *Lochner v. State of New* York, 198 U.S. 45, should be our guide. But we decline that invitation as we did in *West Coast Hotel Co. v. Parrish*, 300 U.S. 379; *Williamson v. Lee Optical Co.*, 348 U.S. 483. We do not sit as a super-legislature to determine the wisdom, need, and propriety of laws that touch economic problems, business affairs, or social conditions. This law, however, operates directly on an intimate relation of husband and wife and their physician's role in one aspect of that relation. . . .

The association of people is not mentioned in the Constitution or in the Bill of Rights. The right to educate a child in a school of the parents' choice whether public or private or parochial is also not mentioned. Nor is the right to study any particular subject or any foreign language. Yet the First Amendment has been construed to include certain of those rights.

By *Pierce v. Society of Sisters*, [268 U.S. 510], the right to educate one's children as one chooses is made applicable to the States by the force of the First and Fourteenth Amendments. By *Meyer v. State of Nebraska*, [262 U.S. 390], the same dignity is given the right to study the German language in a private school. . . .

In *NAACP v. State of Alabama*, 357 U.S. 449, 462, we protected the "freedom to associate and privacy in one's associations," noting that freedom of association was a peripheral First Amendment right . . . In other words, the First Amendment has a penumbra where privacy is protected from governmental intrusion. In like context, we have protected forms of "association" that are not political in the customary sense but pertain to the social, legal, and economic benefit of the members. *NAACP v. Button*, 371 U.S. 415, 430–431. . . .

The foregoing cases suggest that specific guarantees in the Bill of Rights have penumbras, formed by emanations from those guarantees that help give them life and substance. . . . Various guarantees create zones of privacy. The right of association contained in the penumbra of the First Amendment is one, as we have seen. The Third Amendment in its prohibition against the quartering of soldiers "in any house" in time of peace without consent of the owner is another facet of that privacy. The Fourth Amendment explicitly affirms the "right of the people to be secure in their persons, houses, papers, and effects, against unreasonable searches and seizures." The Fifth Amendment in its Self-Incrimination Clause enables the citizens to create a zone of privacy which government may not force him to surrender to his detriment. The Ninth Amendment provides: "The enumeration in the Constitution, of certain rights, shall not be construed to deny or disparage others retained by the people.". . .

The present case, then, concerns a relationship lying within the zone of privacy created by several fundamental constitutional guarantees. And it concerns a law which, in forbidding the use of contraceptives rather than regulating their manufacture or sale, seeks to achieve its goals by means having a maximum destructive impact upon that relationship. Such a law cannot stand in light of the familiar principle, so often applied by this Court, that a "governmental purpose to control or prevent activities constitutionally subject to state regulation may not be achieved by means which sweep unnecessarily broadly and thereby invade the area of protected freedoms." *NAACP v. Alabama*, 377 U.S. 288, 307. Would we allow the police to search the sacred precincts of marital bedrooms for telltale signs of the use of contraceptives? The very idea is repulsive to the notions of privacy surrounding the marriage relationship.

We deal with the right of privacy older than the Bill of Rights. . . . Marriage is a coming together . . . to the degree of being sacred. It is an association . . . as noble a purpose as any involved in our prior decisions.

Reversed.

JUSTICE GOLDBERG, whom THE CHIEF JUSTICE and JUSTICE BRENNAN join, concurring.

I agree with the Court that Connecticut's birth-control law unconstitutionally intrudes upon the right of marital privacy, and I join in its opinion and judgment. Although I have not accepted the view that "due process" as used in the Fourteenth Amendment includes all of the first eight Amendments. . . . I do agree that the concept of liberty protects those personal rights that are fundamental, and is not confined to the specific terms of the Bill of Rights. My conclusion that the concept of liberty is not so restricted and that it embraces the right of marital privacy though that right is not mentioned explicitly in the Constitution is supported both by numerous decisions of this Court, referred to in the Court's opinion, and by the language and history of the Ninth Amendment. . . .

The Ninth Amendment . . . was introduced in Congress by him [*James Madison*] and passed the House and Senate with little or no debate and virtually no change in language. It was proffered to quiet expressed fears that a bill of specifically enumerated rights could not be sufficiently broad to cover all essential rights and that the specific mention of certain rights would be interpreted as a denial that others were protected.[20]

. . .

While this Court has had little occasion to interpret the Ninth Amendment,[21] "[i]t cannot be presumed that any clause in the constitution is intended to be without effect." *Marbury v. Madison*, 1 Cranch 137, 174. . . . To hold that a right so basic and fundamental and so deep-rooted in our society as the right of privacy in marriage may be infringed because that right is not guaranteed in so many words by the first eight amendments to the Constitution . . . would violate the Ninth Amendment, which specifically states that "[t]he enumeration in the Constitution, of certain rights shall not be *construed* to deny or disparage others retained by the people." (emphasis added.)

. . . I do not mean to imply that the Ninth Amendment is applied against the States

---

[20] [Court's footnote 4] Alexander Hamilton was opposed to a bill of rights on the ground that it was unnecessary because the Federal Government was a government of delegated powers and it was not granted the power to intrude upon fundamental personal rights. The Federalist, No. 84 (Cooke ed. 1961), at 578–579. . . .

The Ninth Amendment and the Tenth Amendment, which provides, "The powers not delegated to the United States by the Constitution, nor prohibited by it to the States, are reserved to the States respectively, or to the people," were apparently also designed in part to meet the above-quoted argument of Hamilton.

[21] [Court's footnote 6] This Amendment has been referred to as "The Forgotten Ninth Amendment," in a book with that title by Bennet B. Patterson (1955). Other commentary on the Ninth Amendment includes Redlich, *Are there "Certain Rights . . . Retained by the People"?* 37 N.Y.U. L. REV. 787 (1962), and Kelsey, *The Ninth Amendment of the Federal Constitution*, 11 IND. L.J. 309 (1936). . . .

by the Fourteenth. Nor do I mean to state that the Ninth Amendment constitutes an independent source of rights protected from infringement by either the States or the Federal Government. Rather, the Ninth Amendment shows a belief of the Constitution's authors that fundamental rights exist that are not expressly enumerated in the first eight amendments and, an intent that the list of rights included there not be deemed exhaustive. . . .

Nor am I turning somersaults with history in arguing that the Ninth Amendment is relevant in a case dealing with a State's infringement of a fundamental right. While the Ninth Amendment and indeed the entire Bill of Rights originally concerned restrictions upon federal power, the subsequently enacted Fourteenth Amendment prohibits the States as well from abridging fundamental personal liberties. And, the Ninth Amendment, in indicating that not all such liberties are specifically mentioned in the first eight amendments, is surely relevant in showing the existence of other fundamental personal rights, now protected from state, as well as federal, infringement. In sum, the Ninth Amendment simply lends strong support to the view that the "liberty" protected by the Fifth and Fourteenth Amendments from infringement by the Federal Government or the States is not restricted to rights specifically mentioned in the first eight amendments. . . .

In determining which rights are fundamental, judges are not left at large to decide cases in light of their personal and private notions. Rather, they must look to the "traditions and [collective] conscience of our people" to determine whether a principle is "so rooted [there] . . . as to be ranked as fundamental." *Snyder v. Com. of Massachusetts*, 291 U.S. 97, 105. The inquiry is whether a right involved "is of such a character that it cannot be denied without violating those 'fundamental principles of liberty and justice which lie at the base of all our civil and political institutions'. . . . " *Powell v. State of Alabama*, 287 U.S. 45, 67. "Liberty" also "gains content from the emanations of- . . . specific [constitutional] guarantees" and "from experience with the requirements of a free society." *Poe v. Ullman*, 367 U.S. 497, 517. . . .

The entire fabric of the Constitution and the purposes that clearly underlie its specific guarantees demonstrate that the rights to marital privacy and to marry and raise a family are of similar order and magnitude as the fundamental rights specifically protected. . . .

The logic of the dissents would sanction federal or state legislation that seems to me even more plainly unconstitutional than the statute before us. Surely the Government, absent a showing of a compelling subordinating state interest, could not decree that all husbands and wives must be sterilized after two children have been born to them. . . .

The State, at most, argues that there is some rational relation between this statute and what is admittedly a legitimate subject of state concern the discouraging of extra-marital relations. It says that preventing the use of birth-control devices by married persons helps prevent the indulgence by some in such extra-marital relations. The rationality of this justification is dubious, particularly in light of the admitted widespread availability to all persons in the State of Connecticut, unmarried as well as married, of birth-control devices for the prevention of disease, as distinguished from the prevention of conception. . . . The State of Connecticut does have some statutes, the constitutionality of which is beyond doubt, which prohibit adultery and fornication. These statutes demonstrate that means for achieving the same basic purpose of protecting marital fidelity are available to Connecticut without the need to "invade the area of protected freedoms." *NAACP v. State of Alabama, supra,* 377 U.S. at 307.

Finally, it should be said of the Court's holding today that it in no way interferes with a State's proper regulation of sexual promiscuity or misconduct. As my Brother Harlan so well stated in his dissenting opinion in *Poe v. Ullman, supra,* 367 U.S. at 553[:]

Adultery, homosexuality and the like are sexual intimacies which the State forbids . . . but the intimacy of husband and wife is necessarily an essential and accepted feature of the institution of marriage, an institution which the State not only must allow, but which always and in every age it has fostered and protected. It is one thing when the State exerts its power either to forbid extra-marital sexuality . . . or to say who may marry, but it is quite another when, having acknowledged a marriage and the intimacies inherent in it, it undertakes to regulate by means of the criminal law the details of that intimacy. . . .

JUSTICE HARLAN, concurring in the judgment.

. . . [T]he Court's opinion . . . seems to me to evince an approach to this case very much like that taken by my Brothers Black and Stewart in dissent, namely: the Due Process Clause of the Fourteenth Amendment does not touch this Connecticut statute unless the enactment is found to violate some right assured by the letter or penumbra of the Bill of Rights.

In other words, what I find implicit in the Court's opinion is that the "incorporation" doctrine may be used to restrict the reach of the Fourteenth Amendment Due Process. . . .

In my view, the proper constitutional inquiry in this case is whether this Connecticut statute infringes the Due Process Clause of the Fourteenth Amendment because the enactment violates basic values "implicit in the concept of ordered liberty," *Palko v. State of Connecticut*, 302 U.S. 319, 325. . . . I believe that it does. While the relevant inquiry may be aided by resort to one or more of the provisions of the Bill of Rights, it is not dependent on them or any of their radiations. The Due Process Clause of the Fourteenth Amendment stands, in my opinion, on its own bottom.

. . . [M]y Brothers Black and Stewart "incorporation" approach to this case . . . does not rest on historical reasons, which are, of course, wholly lacking (see Fairman, *Does the Fourteenth Amendment Incorporate the Bill of Rights? The Original Understanding*, 2 STAN. L. REV. 5 (1949)), but on the thesis that by limiting the content of the Due Process Clause of the Fourteenth Amendment to the protection of rights which can be found elsewhere in the Constitution, in this instance in the Bill of Rights, judges will thus be confined to "interpretation" of specific constitutional provisions, and will thereby be restrained from introducing their own notions of constitutional right and wrong into the "vague contours of the Due Process Clause." *Rochin v. People of State of California*, 342 U.S. 165, 170.

. . . "Specific" provisions of the Constitution, no less than "due process," lend themselves as readily to "personal" interpretations by judges. . . .

Judicial self-restraint will not, I suggest, be brought about in the "due process" area by the historically unfounded incorporation formula . . . [but] only by continual insistence upon respect for the teachings of history, solid recognition of the basic values that underlie our society, and wise appreciation of the great roles that the doctrines of federalism and separation of powers have played in establishing and preserving American freedoms. . . .

JUSTICE WHITE, concurring in the judgment.

. . . [T]he right invoked in this case, to be free of regulation of the intimacies of the marriage relationship, "come[s] to this Court with a momentum for respect lacking when appeal is made to liberties which derive merely from shifting economic arrangements." *Kovacs v. Cooper*, 336 U.S. 77, 95 (opinion of Frankfurter, J.).

The Connecticut anti-contraceptive statute . . . bears a substantial burden of justification when attacked under the Fourteenth Amendment. . . .

. . . I wholly fail to see how a ban on the use of contraceptives by married couples in any way reinforces the State's ban on illicit sexual relationships. . . . Connecticut does not bar the importation or possession of contraceptive devices. . . .

. . . A statute limiting its prohibition on use to persons engaging in the prohibited relationship would serve the end posited by Connecticut in the same way, and with the same effectiveness, or ineffectiveness, as the broad anti-use statute under attack in this case. . . .

JUSTICE BLACK, with whom JUSTICE STEWART joins, dissenting.

[T]he law is every bit as offensive to me as it is my Brethren. . . .

. . . The Court talks about a constitutional "right of privacy" as though there is some constitutional provision or provisions forbidding any law ever to be passed which might abridge the "privacy" of individuals. But there is not. . . .

. . . "Privacy" is a broad, abstract and ambiguous concept which can easily be shrunken in meaning but which can also, on the other hand, easily be interpreted as a constitutional ban against many things other than searches and seizures. . . .

The due process argument which my Brothers Harlan and White adopt here is based, as their opinions indicate, on the premise that this Court is vested with power to invalidate all state laws that it considers to be arbitrary, capricious, unreasonable, or oppressive. . . . If these formulas based on "natural justice," or others which mean the same thing, are to prevail, they require judges to determine what is or is not constitutional on the basis of their own appraisal of what laws are unwise or unnecessary. . . . Such an appraisal of the wisdom of legislation is an attribute of the power to make laws, not of the power to interpret them. . . .

My Brother Goldberg has adopted the recent discovery[22] that the Ninth Amendment, as well as the Due Process Clause, can be used by this Court as authority to strike down all state legislation which this Court thinks violates "fundamental principles of liberty and justice," or is contrary to the "traditions and [collective] conscience of our people." . . . Our Court certainly has no machinery with which to take a Gallup Poll. . . . Moreover, one would certainly have to look far beyond the language of the Ninth Amendment to find that the Framers vested in this Court any such awesome veto powers over lawmaking, either by the States or by the Congress. . . . The whole history of the adoption of the Constitution and Bill of Rights points the other way. . . . [F]or a period of a century and a half no serious suggestion was ever made that the Ninth Amendment, enacted to protect state powers against federal invasion, could be used as a weapon of federal power to prevent state legislatures from passing laws they consider appropriate to govern local affairs. Use of any such broad, unbounded judicial authority would make of this Court's members a day-to-day constitutional convention. . . .

. . . The Due Process Clause with an "arbitrary and capricious" or "shocking to the conscience" formula was liberally used by this Court to strike down economic legislation

---

[22] [Court's footnote 12] . . . In Redlich, *Are There "Certain Rights . . . Retained by the People"?*, 37 N.Y.U. L. REV. 787, Professor Redlich, in advocating reliance on the Ninth and Tenth Amendments to invalidate the Connecticut law before us, frankly states:

> But for one who feels that the marriage relationship should be beyond the reach of a state law forbidding the use of contraceptives, the birth control case poses a troublesome and challenging problem of constitutional interpretation. He may find himself saying, "The law is unconstitutional but why?" There are two possible paths to travel in finding the answer. One is to revert to a frankly flexible due process concept even on matters that do not involve specific constitutional prohibitions. The other is to attempt to evolve a new constitutional framework within which to meet this and similar problems which are likely to arise. *Id.*, at 798.

in the early decades of this century, threatening, many people thought, the tranquility and stability of the Nation. *See, e.g., Lochner v. State of New York*, 198 U.S. 45. That formula, based on subjective considerations of "natural justice," is no less dangerous when used to enforce this Court's views about personal rights than those about economic rights. . . .

JUSTICE STEWART, whom JUSTICE BLACK joins, dissenting.

Since 1879, Connecticut has had on its books a law which forbids the use of contraceptives by anyone. I think this is an uncommonly silly law. As a practical matter, the law is obviously unenforceable, except in the oblique context of the present case. . . .

. . . There is no claim that this law, duly enacted by the Connecticut Legislature, is unconstitutionally vague. There is no claim that the appellants were denied any of the elements of procedural due process at their trial. . . .

. . . [T]o say that the Ninth Amendment has anything to do with this case is to turn somersaults with history. The Ninth Amendment, like its companion the Tenth, which this Court held "states but a truism that all is retained which has not been surrendered," *United States v. Darby*, 312 U.S. 100, was . . . adopted by the States simply to make clear that the adoption of the Bill of Rights did not alter the plan that the Federal Government was a government of express and limited powers, and that all rights and powers not delegated to it were retained by the people and the individual States. Until today no member of this Court has ever suggested that the Ninth Amendment meant anything else, and the idea that a federal court could ever use the Ninth Amendment to annul a law passed by the elected representatives of the people of the State of Connecticut would have caused James Madison no little wonder. . . .

. . . If, as I should surely hope, the law before us does not reflect the standards of the people of Connecticut, the people of Connecticut can freely exercise their true Ninth and Tenth Amendment rights to persuade their elected representatives to repeal it. . . .

NOTES

(1) Justice Goldberg's key concurring opinion in *Griswold* relied in part on the Ninth Amendment. The precise meaning and effect of the Ninth Amendment has been a point of some controversy. For additional discussion of this previously little used Amendment, see, e.g., J. ELY, DEMOCRACY AND DISTRUST (1981); *Symposium on Interpreting the Ninth Amendment*, 64 CHI.-KENT L. REV. 1 (1988); Attanasio, *Everyman's Constitutional Law: A Theory of the Power of Judicial Review*, 72 GEO. L.J. 1665 (1984); Berger, *The Ninth Amendment*, 66 CORNELL L. REV. 1 (1980); Caplan, *The History and Meaning of the Ninth Amendment*, 69 VA. L. REV. 223 (1983); Kelly, *Clio and the Court: An Illicit Love Affair*, 1965 SUP. CT. REV. 119; Redlich, *Are There "Certain Rights . . . Retained by the People?"*, 37 N.Y.U. L. REV. 787 (1962).

(2) *Unmarried Individuals*. Subsequent decisions by the Court extended *Griswold's* rationale from its narrow application to married couples to cover unmarried individuals as well. In *Eisenstadt v. Baird*, 405 U.S. 438 (1972), the Court struck down a Massachusetts statute that prohibited the distribution of contraceptives to single persons. Appellee Baird was convicted under the statute for giving a young woman a contraceptive sample at the close of his lecture on contraception techniques. Holding that Baird had standing to assert the constitutional rights of unmarried persons, the Court, per Justice Brennan, invalidated the statute using the Equal Protection Clause. Justice Brennan concluded that the statute's distinction between married and unmarried persons could not rationally further any discernible state purpose. In examining the possible state objectives, Justice Brennan found that the statute could not reasonably serve the purpose of deterring fornication or protecting public health.

He avoided deciding the validity of a flat ban on contraception by stating that whatever an individual's rights to access to contraceptives, those rights must be the same for the unmarried and married alike.

Justice Brennan also made some important comments on the *Griswold* decision. "If the right of privacy means anything, it is the right of the individual, married or single, to be free from unwarranted governmental intrusion into matters so fundamentally affecting a person as the decision whether to bear or beget a child." *Eisenstadt*, 405 U.S. at 453.

(3) For further discussion of *Eisenstadt*, see Dolgin, *The Family in Transition: From Griswold to Eisenstadt and Beyond*, 82 GEO. L.J. 1519, 1571 (1994) ("These changes are represented dramatically in a comparison of *Griswold*, the first case in which the Supreme Court expressly recognized a constitutional right to privacy, and *Eisenstadt*, in which the Court transformed the familial privacy apparently protected in *Griswold* into an individual right.").

(4) *Minors.* In *Carey v. Population Services International*, 431 U.S. 678 (1977), the Court held invalid a New York statute that made it a crime for anyone to sell or distribute contraceptives to persons under 16 (except by a physician to married females between 14 and 16), for anyone other than a licensed pharmacist to distribute contraceptives to persons over 16, and for anyone to advertise or display contraceptives. Justice Brennan's opinion for the Court concluded that the statute violated the due process right of privacy because its ban on the sale or distribution of contraceptives to persons over 16, except by a licensed pharmacist, imposed significant burdens on an individual's right to use contraceptives and served no compelling state interest. Justice Brennan utilized strict scrutiny "not because there is an independent fundamental right of access to contraceptives, but because such access is essential to exercise of the decision in matters of childbearing." The provision prohibiting all displays or advertisements of contraceptives violated the First Amendment by suppressing commercial speech without any legitimate state justification.

Although their rationales differed, seven members of the Court also agreed that the total ban on the distribution of contraceptives to minors under 16 violated the right to privacy under the Due Process Clause. Justice Brennan, joined in this part of the opinion by Justices Stewart, Marshall, and Blackmun, concluded that this provision was constitutionally impermissible because the right to privacy in making procreation decisions extended to minors as well as adults. These four Justices found that such a blanket prohibition on providing minors with contraceptives was foreclosed by the Court's decisions invalidating similar restraints on a minor's access to abortions. *See Planned Parenthood v. Danforth*, 428 U.S. 52 (1976), discussed *infra*. Moreover, Justice Brennan expressed substantial doubt that limiting access to contraceptives would discourage sexual activity among the young. In separate concurrences, Justices White, Powell, and Stevens would afford states broad latitude to control their children's access to contraception.

Chief Justice Burger dissented without opinion. Justice Rehnquist dissented on the grounds that nothing in the Bill of Rights or the Civil War Amendments, both made possible by the "blood of brave men," could impute to the Constitution "the right of commercial vendors of contraceptives to peddle them to unmarried minors through such means as window displays and vending machines located in the men's rooms of truck stops."

ROE v. WADE
410 U.S. 113, 93 S. Ct. 705, 35 L. Ed. 2d 147 (1973)

JUSTICE BLACKMUN delivered the opinion of the Court.

This Texas federal appeal and its Georgia companion, *Doe v. Bolton*, 410 U.S. 179, present constitutional challenges to state criminal abortion legislation. The Texas statutes under attack here are typical of those that have been in effect in many States for approximately a century. The Georgia statutes, in contrast, have a modern cast and are a legislative product that, to an extent at least, obviously reflects the influences of recent attitudinal change, of advancing medical knowledge and techniques, and of new thinking about an old issue.

We forthwith acknowledge our awareness of the sensitive and emotional nature of the abortion controversy, of the vigorous opposing views, even among physicians, and of the deep and seemingly absolute convictions that the subject inspires. One's philosophy, one's experiences, one's exposure to the raw edges of human existence, one's religious training, one's attitudes toward life and family and their values, and the moral standards one establishes and seeks to observe, are all likely to influence and to color one's thinking and conclusions about abortion.

In addition, population growth, pollution, poverty, and racial overtones tend to complicate and not to simplify the problem.

Our task, of course, is to resolve the issue by constitutional measurement, free of emotion and of predilection. We seek earnestly to do this, and, because we do, we have inquired into, and in this opinion place some emphasis upon, medical and medical-legal history and what that history reveals about man's attitudes toward the abortion procedure over the centuries. . . .

The Texas statutes that concern us here . . . make it a crime to "procure an abortion," as therein defined, or to attempt one, except with respect to "an abortion procured or attempted by medical advice for the purpose of saving the life of the mother." Similar statutes are in existence in a majority of the States. . . .

Jane Roe, a single woman who was residing in Dallas County, Texas, instituted this federal action in March 1970 against the District Attorney of the county. She sought a declaratory judgment that the Texas criminal abortion statutes were unconstitutional on their face, and an injunction restraining the defendant from enforcing the statutes.

Roe alleged that she was unmarried and pregnant; that she wished to terminate her pregnancy by an abortion "performed by a competent, licensed physician, under safe, clinical conditions"; that she was unable to get a "legal" abortion in Texas because her life did not appear to be threatened by the continuation of her pregnancy; and that she could not afford to travel to another jurisdiction in order to secure a legal abortion under safe conditions. . . .

We . . . agree with the District Court that . . . the termination of her 1970 pregnancy has not rendered her case moot.[23] . . .

. . . Those laws, generally proscribing abortion or its attempt at any time during pregnancy except when necessary to preserve the pregnant woman's life, are not of ancient or even of common-law origin. Instead, they derive from statutory changes effected, for the most part, in the latter half of the 19th century.

[Justice Blackmun traced Greek, Roman, and English statutory and common law attitudes toward abortion.] . . .

. . . It was not until after the War Between the States that legislation began

---

[23] For discussion of the Court's mootness determination, see *supra*.

generally to replace the common law. Most of these initial statutes dealt severely with abortion after quickening but were lenient with it before quickening. Most punished attempts equally with completed abortions. While many statutes included the exception for an abortion thought by one or more physicians to be necessary to save the mother's life, that provision soon disappeared and the typical law required that the procedure actually be necessary for that purpose.

Gradually, in the middle and late 19th century the quickening distinction disappeared from the statutory law of most States and the degree of the offense and the penalties were increased. By the end of the 1950s, a large majority of the jurisdictions banned abortion, however and whenever performed, unless done to save or preserve the life of the mother. . . .   In the past several years, however, a trend toward liberalization of abortion statutes has resulted in adoption, by about one-third of the States, of less stringent laws, most of them patterned after the ALI Model Penal Code, § 230.3. . . .

. . . When most criminal abortion laws were first enacted, the procedure was a hazardous one for the woman. . . .

. . . Mortality rates for women undergoing early abortions, where the procedure is legal, appear to be as low as or lower than the rates for normal childbirth. . . .   The State has a legitimate interest in seeing to it that abortion, like any other medical procedure, is performed under circumstances that insure maximum safety for the patient. . . .   The prevalence of high mortality rates at illegal "abortion mills" strengthens, rather than weakens, the State's interest in regulating the conditions under which abortions are performed. Moreover, the risk to the woman increases as her pregnancy continues. Thus, the State retains a definite interest in protecting the woman's own health and safety when an abortion is proposed at a late stage of pregnancy.

. . . The State [also has an] interest — some phrase it in terms of duty — in protecting prenatal life. Some of the argument for this justification rests on the theory that a new human life is present from the moment of conception. . . .   Only when the life of the pregnant mother herself is at stake, balanced against the life she carries within her, should the interest of the embryo or fetus not prevail. Logically, of course, a legitimate state interest in this area need not stand or fall on acceptance of the belief that life begins at conception or at some other point prior to live birth. In assessing the State's interest, recognition may be given to the less rigid claim that as long as at least potential life is involved, the State may assert interests beyond the protection of the pregnant woman alone.

Parties challenging state abortion laws . . . claim that adoption of the "quickening" distinction through received common law and state statutes tacitly recognizes the greater health hazards inherent in the late abortion and impliedly repudiates the theory that life begins at conception. . . .

The Constitution does not explicitly mention any right of privacy. In a line of decisions, however, going back perhaps as far as *Union Pacific R. Co. v. Botsford*, 141 U.S. 250 (1891), the Court has recognized that a right of personal privacy, or a guarantee of certain areas or zones of privacy, does exist under the Constitution. In varying contexts, the Court or individual Justices have, indeed, found at least the roots of that right in the First Amendment, *Stanley v. Georgia*, 394 U.S. 557 (1969); in the Fourth and Fifth Amendment, *Terry v. Ohio*, 392 U.S. 1, 8-9 (1968), *Katz v. United States* , 389 U.S. 347, 350 (1967), *Boyd v. United* States, 116 U.S. 616 (1886); in the penumbras of the Bill of Rights, *Griswold v. Connecticut*, 381 U.S. at 484–485, in the Ninth Amendment, *id.*, at 486, (Goldberg, J., concurring); or in the concept of liberty guaranteed by the first section of the Fourteenth Amendment, *see Meyer v. Nebraska*,

262 U.S. 390, 399 (1923). These decisions make it clear that only personal rights that can be deemed "fundamental" or "implicit in the concept of ordered liberty," *Palko v. Connecticut*, 302 U.S. 319, 325 (1937), are included in this guarantee of personal privacy. They also make it clear that the right has some extension to activities relating to marriage, *Loving v. Virginia*, 388 U.S. 1, 12 (1967); procreation, *Skinner v. Oklahoma*, 316 U.S. 535, 541–542 (1942); contraception, *Eisenstadt v. Baird*, 405 U.S. at 453–454; family relationships, *Prince v. Massachusetts*, 321 U.S. 158, 166 (1944); and child rearing and education, *Pierce v. Society of Sisters*, 268 U.S. 510, 535 (1925), *Meyer v. Nebraska, supra.*

This right of privacy, whether it be found in the Fourteenth Amendment's concept of personal liberty and restrictions upon state action, as we feel it is, or, as the District Court determined, in the Ninth Amendment's reservation of rights to the people, is broad enough to encompass a woman's decision whether or not to terminate her pregnancy. The detriment that the State would impose upon the pregnant woman by denying this choice altogether is apparent. Specific and direct harm medically diagnosable even in early pregnancy may be involved. Maternity, or additional offspring, may force upon the woman a distressful life and future. Psychological harm may be imminent. Mental and physical health may be taxed by child care. There is also the distress, for all concerned, associated with the unwanted child, and there is the problem of bringing a child into a family already unable, psychologically and otherwise, to care for it. In other cases, as in this one, the additional difficulties and continuing stigma of unwed motherhood may be involved. . . .

On the basis of elements such as these, appellant and some amici argue that the woman's right is absolute and that she is entitled to terminate her pregnancy at whatever time, in whatever way, and for whatever reason she alone chooses. With this we do not agree. . . .

Where certain "fundamental rights" are involved, the Court has held that regulation limiting these rights may be justified only by a "compelling state interest," *Kramer v. Union Free School District*, 395 U.S. 621, 627. . . . and that legislative enactments must be narrowly drawn to express only the legitimate state interests at stake. *Griswold v. Connecticut*, 381 U.S. at 485. . . .

The [State] and certain amici argue that the fetus is a "person" within the language and meaning of the Fourteenth Amendment. In support of this, they outline at length and in detail the well-known facts of fetal development. . . .

The Constitution does not define "person" in so many words. Section 1 of the Fourteenth Amendment contains three references to "person." The first, in defining "citizens," speaks of "persons born or naturalized in the United States." The word also appears both in the Due Process Clause and in the Equal Protection Clause. "Person" is used in other places in the Constitution: in the listing of qualifications for Representatives and Senators, Art. I, § 2, cl. 2, and § 3, cl. 3; in the Apportionment Clause, Art. I, § 2, cl. 3; in the Migration and Importation provision, Art. I, § 9, cl. 1; in the Emolument Clause, Art. I, § 9, cl. 8; in the Electors provisions, Art. II, § 1, cl. 2, and the superseded cl. 3; in the provision outlining qualifications for the office of President, Art. II, § 1, cl. 5; in the Extradition provisions, Art. IV, § 2, cl. 2, and the superseded Fugitive Slave Clause 3; and in the Fifth, Twelfth, and Twenty-second Amendments, as well as in §§ 2 and 3 of the Fourteenth Amendment. But in nearly all these instances, the use of the word is such that it has application only postnatally. . . .

All this, together with our observation, that throughout the major portion of the 19th century prevailing legal abortion practices were far freer than they are today, persuades us that the word "person," as used in the Fourteenth Amendment, does not include the unborn. . . .

This conclusion, however, does not of itself fully answer the contentions raised by Texas. . . .

The pregnant woman cannot be isolated in her privacy. She carries an embryo and, later, a fetus. . . . The situation, therefore, is inherently different from marital intimacy, or bedroom possession of obscene material, or marriage, or procreation, or education, . . . becomes significantly involved. . . .

Texas urges that, apart from the Fourteenth Amendment, life begins at conception and is present throughout pregnancy, and that, therefore, the State has a compelling interest in protecting that life from and after conception. We need not resolve the difficult question of when life begins. When those trained in the respective disciplines of medicine, philosophy, and theology are unable to arrive at any consensus, the judiciary, at this point in the development of man's knowledge, is not in a position to speculate as to the answer. . . .

Physicians . . . have regarded [quickening] with less interest and have tended to focus either upon conception, upon live birth, or upon the interim point at which the fetus becomes "viable," that is, potentially able to live outside the mother's womb, albeit with artificial aid. Viability is usually placed at about seven months (28 weeks) but may occur earlier, even at 24 weeks. . . . [N]ew embryological data . . . purport to indicate that conception is a "process" over time, rather than an event. . . .

In view of all this, we do not agree that, by adopting one theory of life, Texas may override the rights of the pregnant woman that are at stake. We repeat, however, that the State does have an important and legitimate interest in preserving and protecting the health of the pregnant woman, . . . and that it has still another important and legitimate interest in protecting the potentiality of human life. These interests are separate and distinct. Each grows in substantiality as the woman approaches term and at a point during pregnancy, each becomes "compelling."

With respect to the State's important and legitimate interest in the health of the mother, the "compelling" point, in the light of present medical knowledge, is at approximately the end of the first trimester. This is so because of the now-established medical fact . . . that until the end of the first trimester mortality in abortion may be less than mortality in normal childbirth. It follows that, from and after this point, a State may regulate the abortion procedure to the extent that the regulation reasonably relates to the preservation and protection of maternal health. Examples of permissible state regulation in this area are requirements as to the qualifications of the person who is to perform the abortion; as to the licensure of that person; as to the facility in which the procedure is to be performed, that is, whether it must be a hospital or may be a clinic or some other place of less-than-hospital status; as to the licensing of the facility; and the like.

This means, on the other hand, that, for the period of pregnancy prior to this "compelling" point, the attending physician, in consultation with his patient, is free to determine, without regulation by the State that, in his medical judgment, the patient's pregnancy should be terminated. . . .

With respect to the State's important and legitimate interest in potential life, the "compelling" point is at viability. This is so because the fetus then presumably has the capability of meaningful life outside the mother's womb. . . . If the State is interested in protecting fetal life after viability, it may go so far as to proscribe abortion during that period, except when it is necessary to preserve the life or health of the mother.

Measured against these standards, Art. 1196 of the Texas Penal Code, in restricting legal abortions to those "procured or attempted by medical advice for the purpose of saving the life of the mother," sweeps too broadly. . . .

. . . The decision vindicates the right of the physician to administer medical treatment according to his professional judgment up to the points where important state interests provide compelling justifications for intervention. Up to those points, the abortion decision in all its aspects is inherently, and primarily, a medical decision, and basic responsibility for it must rest with the physician. . . .

[CHIEF JUSTICE BURGER wrote a brief concurring opinion.]

JUSTICE DOUGLAS, concurring.

. . . Elaborate argument is hardly necessary to demonstrate that childbirth may deprive a woman of her preferred lifestyle and force upon her a radically different and undesired future. . . . to endure the discomforts of pregnancy; to incur the pain, higher mortality rate, and aftereffects of childbirth; to abandon educational plans; to sustain loss of income; to forgo the satisfactions of careers; to tax further mental and physical health in providing child care; and, in some cases, to bear the lifelong stigma of unwed motherhood, a badge which may haunt, if not deter, later legitimate family relationships. . . .

JUSTICE STEWART, concurring.

In 1963, this Court, in *Ferguson v. Skrupa*, 372 U.S. 726, purported to sound the death knell for the doctrine of substantive due process. . . .

Barely two years later, in *Griswold v. Connecticut*, 381 U.S. 479, the Court held a Connecticut birth control law unconstitutional. . . . *Griswold* stands as one in a long line of pre-*Skrupa* cases decided under the doctrine of substantive due process, and I now accept it as such. . . .

JUSTICE WHITE, with whom JUSTICE REHNQUIST joins, dissenting.

At the heart of the controversy . . . are those recurring pregnancies that pose no danger whatsoever to the life or health of the mother but are, nevertheless, unwanted for any one or more of a variety of reasons convenience, family planning, economics, dislike of children, the embarrassment of illegitimacy, etc. The common claim before us is that for any one of such reasons, or for no reason at all, and without asserting or claiming any threat to life or health, any woman is entitled to an abortion at her request if she is able to find a medical advisor willing to undertake the procedure.

. . . I find nothing in the language or history of the Constitution to support the Court's judgment. . . . As an exercise of raw judicial power, the Court perhaps has authority to do what it does today; but in my view its judgment is an improvident and extravagant exercise of the power of judicial review. . . .

. . . This issue, for the most part, should be left with the people and to the political processes the people have devised to govern their affairs. . . .

JUSTICE REHNQUIST, dissenting.

. . . [T]he "liberty" against deprivation of which without due process the Fourteenth Amendment protects, embraces . . . only . . . deprivation without due process of law. The test traditionally applied in the area of social and economic legislation is whether or not a law such as that challenged has a rational relation to a valid state objective. *Williamson v. Lee Optical Co.* The Due Process Clause of the Fourteenth Amendment undoubtedly does place a limit, albeit a broad one, on legislative power to enact laws such as this. If the Texas statute were to prohibit an abortion even where the mother's life is in jeopardy, I would have little doubt that such a statute would lack a rational relation to a valid state objective under the test stated in *Williamson, supra*. But the Court's sweeping invalidation of any restrictions on abortion during the first trimester is impossible to justify under that standard, and the conscious weighing of competing factors that the Court's opinion apparently substitutes for the established test is far more appropriate to a legislative judgment than to a judicial one. . . .

As in *Lochner* [*v. New York*] and similar cases applying substantive due process standards to economic and social welfare legislation, the adoption of the compelling state interest standard will inevitably require this Court to examine the legislative policies and pass on the wisdom of these policies. . . .   The decision here to break pregnancy into three distinct terms and to outline the permissible restrictions the State may impose in each one, for example, partakes more of judicial legislation than it does of a determination of the intent of the drafters of the Fourteenth Amendment.

The fact that a majority of the States reflecting, after all, the majority sentiment in those States, have had restrictions on abortions for at least a century is a strong indication, it seems to me, that the asserted right to an abortion is not "so rooted in the traditions and conscience of our people as to be ranked as fundamental," *Snyder v. Massachusetts*, 291 U.S. 97, 105, (1934). . . .

To reach its result the Court necessarily has had to find within the scope of the Fourteenth Amendment a right that was apparently completely unknown to the drafters of the Amendment. . . .

There apparently was no question concerning the validity of this provision or of any of the other state statutes when the Fourteenth Amendment was adopted. . . .

NOTES

(1) *Abortion Restrictions.* State legislatures have passed regulations limiting the right to choose an abortion in many different ways. Until its decisions in *Webster v. Reproductive Health Services*, *infra*, and *Planned Parenthood of Southeastern Pennsylvania v. Casey*, *infra*, the Court struck nearly all such state regulations of the right to choose an abortion.

(2) *Husband and Parental Consent, Saline Abortions, Viability, Record Keeping.* In *Planned Parenthood of Missouri v. Danforth*, 428 U.S. 52 (1976), writing for the Court, Justice Blackmun invalidated most of a Missouri statute's restrictions on access to abortion.

The Missouri statute also barred a married woman from obtaining an abortion in most instances without her husband's written consent. Although he recognized the husband's interest in a wife's pregnancy, the woman's interest outweighed her husband's interest, as she was more directly and immediately affected by pregnancy.

The majority also invalidated a provision that prohibited saline amniocentesis abortions — the majority concluded that the regulation was unreasonably designed to inhibit and actually did inhibit second trimester abortions.

The Court sustained only a record keeping requirement. Except for inspection by health officials, the records on places performing abortions were confidential, kept only for statistical purposes, and used to advance medical knowledge about preserving maternal health.

The Court also upheld the statute's definition of viability as "that state of fetal development when the life of the unborn child may be continued indefinitely outside the womb by natural or artificial life-supportive systems." This definition closely reflected that offered by the Court in *Roe*: "the point at which the fetus is potentially able to live outside the mother's womb, albeit with artificial aid, and presumably capable of 'meaningful life outside the mother's womb.'" The statute preserved viability as a flexible concept within the sound judgment of the physician that need not be statutorily tied to a specified number of weeks.

(3) *Supporters and Critics of Roe. Roe v. Wade* has generated much scholarly

writing. A number of commentators have defended the decision on various grounds. D. RICHARDS, TOLERATION AND THE CONSTITUTION (1986) ("The moral arguments for the prohibition of abortion cluster around certain traditional conceptions of the natural processes of sexuality and gender. On this view, an abortion is an immoral revolt against this natural order of sexuality and gender roles." The principle that a potential person is entitled to protection "is not a neutral argument for protecting a general good, as it proclaims to be, but the enforcement at large of the requirements of a now controversial, powerfully sectarian ideology about proper sexuality and gender roles."); Law, *Rethinking Sex and the Constitution*, 132 U. PA. L. REV. 955 (1984) ("The law is a social creation that produced the legal structure that made biology destiny and enforced the subjugation of women. In the 1970s we began the divergent movements to create a different social construct of sex equality and reproductive freedom. We can, if we choose, move toward a more unified understanding of the ways in which the law perpetuates sex-based restraints on human equality and liberty."); Regan, *Rewriting Roe v. Wade*, 77 MICH. L. REV. 1569 (1979) (arguing that the fetus is an unwanted intruder in the mother's body and the law does not impose any duty to be a "good Samaritan" in accommodating the fetus); Rubenfeld, *The Right of Privacy*, 102 HARV. L. REV. 737 (1989) (arguing that laws prohibiting abortion are totalitarian in nature as they profoundly constrict a woman's life).

Many arguments have been made against *Roe*. *See, e.g.*, J. NOONAN, A PRIVATE CHOICE: ABORTION IN AMERICA IN THE SEVENTIES (1979) (broadranging critique of the abortion decisions arguing that they are constitutionally illegitimate "raw exercises of judicial power"; are based on "multiple errors in history, medicine, constitutional law, political psychology, and biology"; and have had "disquieting ethical consequences for the nation's respect for life, family, and other important societal values"); Ely, *The Wages of Crying Wolf: A Comment on* Roe v. Wade, 82 YALE L.J. 920 (1973) (arguing that *Roe* has no connection with the "special values" contained in the text of the Constitution; "it is not constitutional law and gives almost no sense of any obligation to try to be"); Finnis, *The Rights and Wrongs of Abortion: A Reply to Judith Thomson*, 2 PHIL. & PUB. AFF. 144 (1973) (arguing that no coherent line of what is or is not a person can be drawn after conception: "Two sex cells, each with only twenty-three chromosomes, unite and more or less immediately fuse to become a new cell with forty-six chromosomes providing a unique genetic composition (not the father's, not the mother's, and not a mere juxtaposition of the parents') which thenceforth throughout its life, however long, will substantially determine the individual's makeup. The new cell is the first stage in a dynamic integrated system that has nothing much in common with individual male and female sex cells, save that it sprang from the pair of them and will in time produce new sets of them."); Van Alstyne, *Closing the Circle of Constitutional Review from Griswold v. Connecticut to Roe v. Wade: An Outline of a Decision Merely Overruling Roe*, 1989 DUKE L.J. 1677, 1688 ("There is no such thing as a personal, freestanding, fundamental right embedded in the Constitution of the United States to kill gestating life.").

Cf. Lupu, *Book Review: When Cultures Collide*, 103 HARV. L. REV. 951, 961 (1990) ("At the time of the decision in *Roe v. Wade*, no state in the union had abortion laws as permissive as the trimester framework *Roe* created. The statutes ranged from New York's then-recent liberalization, which allowed abortions without special justification until the twenty-fourth week of pregnancy, to the far more common and restrictive approach represented by the Texas law condemned in *Roe*.").

For an interesting perspective on the scope of the Roe decision articulated by Justice Ginsburg, see Ginsburg, *Speaking in a Judicial Voice*, 67 N.Y.U. L. REV. 1185, 1199 (1992) ("A less encompassing *Roe*, one that merely struck down the extreme Texas law and went no further on that day, I believe and will summarize why, might have served to reduce rather than to fuel controversy.").

Guido Calabresi has described what he perceives to be a clash of ideals, with each side in the debate ignoring the deeply felt claims of the other. G. CALABRESI, IDEAS, BELIEFS, ATTITUDES, AND THE LAW (1985) (arguing that the abortion controversy is founded on a profound collision between the egalitarian rights of sexual equality of the mother and the claim for legal recognition of the fetus that has prevailed in many other areas of the law).

(4) *Theories of Constitutional Interpretation.* Many commentators have criticized *Roe* as not being grounded in the Constitution and consequently being an illegitimate exercise of the power of judicial review. These criticisms have sparked intense debate on theories of constitutional interpretation. The participants in the debate cluster around three different camps. First, there are the interpretivists, or the originalists as they are often now called. Generally, they confine legitimate exercises of judicial review to interpreting the values embodied in the text of the Constitution as illuminated by the intention of the Framers. Many argue that judicial adventures in invoking values beyond the text rest on the personal predilections of unelected Justices and undermine democracy. *See generally* W. BERNS, TAKING THE CONSTITUTION SERIOUSLY (1987); Berger, *New Theories of "Interpretation": The Activist Flight from the Constitution*, 47 OHIO ST. L.J. 1 (1986); Bork, *Neutral Principles and Some First Amendment Problems*, 47 IND. L.J. 1 (1971); Graglia, *Constitutional Mysticism: The Aspirational Defense of Judicial Review*, 98 HARV. L. REV. 1331 (1985); Kay, *Adherence to the Original Intentions in Constitutional Adjudication: Three Objections and Responses*, 82 NW. U. L. REV. 226 (1988); MacArthur, *Abandoning the Constitution: The New Wave in Constitutional Theory*, 59 TUL. L. REV. 280 (1984). *See also* Justice Department Office of Legal Policy, *Original Meaning Jurisprudence: A Sourcebook* (1987).

Another group of commentators have used a variety of different arguments to maintain that constitutional jurisprudence can quite legitimately proceed to assert a variety of values beyond the text and legislative history of the document. These scholars are often referred to as noninterpretivists. Many argue that the text of the Constitution is itself "open-textured" and was intended to be so by the Framers. *See, e.g.*, R. DWORKIN, A MATTER OF PRINCIPLE (1985); M. PERRY, THE CONSTITUTION, THE COURTS AND HUMAN RIGHTS (1982); Barber, *Judicial Review and The Federalist*, 55 U. CHI. L. REV. 836 (1988); Brest, *The Misconceived Quest for the Original Understanding*, 60 B.U. L. REV. 204 (1980); Grey, *Do We Have an Unwritten Constitution?*, 27 STAN. L. REV. 703 (1975); Tushnet, *Following the Rules Laid Down: A Critique of Interpretivism and Neutral Principles*, 96 HARV. L. REV. 781 (1983); *see also* Eisgruber, *Justice and the Text: Rethinking the Constitutional Relation Between Principle and Prudence*, 43 DUKE L.J. 1, 2 (1993) ("The resulting theory traces constitutional authority to the substantive goodness of constitutional norms, rather than to the process that created them.").

A third group of authors have sought to carve out intermediate positions. *See, e.g.*, Carter, *Constitutional Adjudication and the Indeterminate Text: A Preliminary Defense of an Imperfect Muddle*, 94 YALE L.J. 821 (1985); and Monaghan, *Stare Decisis and Constitutional Adjudication*, 88 COLUM. L. REV. 723 (1988). Perhaps the most discussed of these intermediate positions is that of John Ely. He has argued that certain parts of the Constitution are open-textured but that these must be construed in light of the basic values expressed in the structure of the document itself. For Professor Ely, the document itself reveals a "representation-reinforcing orientation" and most Supreme Court decisions can be justified as advancing this fundamental orientation. *See* J. ELY, DEMOCRACY AND DISTRUST (1980); *see also* Ely, *Foreword: On Discovering Fundamental Values*, 92 HARV. L. REV. 5 (1978); Ely, *Constitutional Interpretivism: Its Allure and Impossibility*, 53 IND. L.J. 399 (1978); Ely, *The Wages of Crying Wolf: A*

Comment on Roe v. Wade, 82 YALE L.J. 920 (1973); *Symposium on Democracy and Distrust: Ten Years After*, 77 Va. L. REV. 631 (1991).

For some contrasting opinions on this issue by members of the Supreme Court, see Brennan, *The Constitution of the United States: Contemporary Ratification*, 27 So. TEX. L. REV. 433 (1986); Rehnquist, *The Notion of a Living Constitution*, 54 TEX. L. REV. 693 (1976). For sources attempting to overview the debate, see, e.g., E. CHERMINSKY, INTERPRETING THE CONSTITUTION (1987); Symposium, *Constitutional Adjudication and Democratic Theory*, 56 N.Y.U. L. REV. 259 (1981). *See also* Symposium: *Constitutional Interpretation*, 15 N. KY. L. REV. 437 (1988); *Interpretation Symposium*, 58 S. CAL. L. REV 1 (1985). For a discussion of how the interpretivism debate relates to the question of judicial power, see Attanasio, *Everyman's Constitutional Law: A Theory of the Power of Judicial Review*, 72 GEO. L.J. 1665 (1984).

For additional perspectives on the originalism debate, see Bittker, *The Bicentennial of the Jurisprudence of Original Intent: The Recent Past*, 77 CAL. L. REV. 235 (1989); Kahn, *Reason and Will in the Origins of the American Constitution*, 98 YALE L.J. 449 (1989); *Essays*, 57 U. CIN. L. REV. 847 (1989) (essays by Antonin Scalia, Louis Pollak, and Orrin Hatch).

HARRIS v. McRAE, 448 U.S. 297 (1980). In *Harris*, the Court (5-4) upheld the constitutionality of a federal Medicaid program for the needy that funded childbirth but excluded the cost for most abortions. The law provided compensation only when the mother's life was put in jeopardy by carrying the fetus to term, or abortion was necessary for rape or incest victims and the rape or incest had been properly and promptly reported to officials.

Writing for the majority, Justice Stewart first addressed whether the Hyde Amendment violated the Due Process Clause of the Fifth Amendment by denying a woman the right to terminate a pregnancy. In *Maher v. Roe*, 432 U.S. 464 (1977), the Court held constitutional a Connecticut statute that reimbursed Medicaid recipients for medical costs associated with childbirth and withheld reimbursement for nontherapeutic abortions. The state could constitutionally make a " 'value judgment favoring childbirth over abortion.' " While the statute may have influenced a woman's decision or made the choice of abortion economically impractical, the statute did not impose any "restriction on access to abortions that was not already there."

While indigents were particularly unable to take advantage of these protected choices, this failure was not due to any governmental imposition but rather to the indigence itself. The fact that Congress chose to reimburse certain medically necessary services and not others, like abortion, "leaves an indigent woman with at least the same range of choice in deciding whether to obtain a medically necessary abortion as she would have had if Congress had chosen to subsidize no health care costs at all." To hold otherwise would mandate that because *Griswold v. Connecticut, supra*, prohibited government from denying the use of contraceptives, and *Pierce v. Society of Sisters*, 268 U.S. 510 (1925), required government to allow parents to send their children to private schools, government must now provide the funding for persons to acquire contraception and enroll their children in private schools.

The Court also rejected the Establishment Clause challenge to the Hyde Amendment. Plaintiffs asserted that the Hyde Amendment violated the Establishment Clause of the First Amendment because it "incorporates into law the doctrines of the Roman Catholic Church concerning the sinfulness of abortion and the time at which life commences." It also restricts the freedom of women of Protestant and Jewish beliefs from obtaining a medically necessary abortion, possibly "a product of [their] religious beliefs." While government cannot constitutionally enact laws favoring or promoting one, or all, religions, a law is not unconstitutional because it "happens to coincide or harmonize with the tenets of some or all religions."

Justice Stewart also rejected the Fifth Amendment equal protection challenge, as the Hyde Amendment did not invidiously discriminate on the basis of suspect classifications.

Relying on *Roe v. Wade*, the Court stated that government has "an important and legitimate interest in protecting the potentiality of human life." This interest grows as the pregnancy proceeds to term. Justice Stewart concluded that by affording Medicaid recipients' reimbursements for the medical expenses of term pregnancies and not the expenses of abortion, Congress has made childbirth "a more attractive alternative than abortion," which is directly related to Congress's interest in protecting potential life.

Dissenting, Justice Brennan, joined by Justices Marshall and Blackmun, argued that denying funding for medically necessary abortions violated a pregnant woman's constitutionally protected right to choose abortion. Rather than protecting a woman's choice, the Hyde Amendment's coercive nature encouraged "indigent pregnant women to bear children that they would otherwise elect not to have."[24]

The government's discriminatory distribution of Medicaid benefits "can discourage the exercise of fundamental liberties just as effectively as can outright denial of those rights through criminal and regulatory sanctions."

Dissenting, Justice Marshall predicted that the Hyde Amendment's denial of funding for necessary medical treatment would produce an increase in the death or suffering due to medical complications in poor women.

Justice Marshall distinguished this case from *Maher* because the Hyde Amendment denied funding even if a normal childbirth would not result. Finally, Justice Marshall criticized the Court's differentiation between a " 'limitation on governmental power' and 'an affirmative funding obligation.' " A poor person prohibited from exercising her constitutionally protected right to choose abortion could not understand this difference.

Justice Stevens also dissented. While he recognized the reasonable exclusion of certain costly procedures in order to provide Medicaid funding to the greatest number of recipients, he also noted the relative inexpensiveness of abortion in relation to the costs associated with childbirth. Over time, denying funding for medically necessary abortions would drain Medicaid funds that would be required to compensate for the possible serious, long-term health complications resulting from childbirth.

NOTES

(1) *Decisions on State Funding.* The Court's decision in *McRae* was foreshadowed by the 1977 decisions in three companion cases, *Beal v. Doe*, 432 U.S. 348, *Maher v. Roe*, 432 U.S. 464, and *Poelker v. Doe*, 432 U.S. 519. The Court split 6-3 in all three cases and concluded that neither the Constitution nor any federal legislation required the states to fund nontherapeutic abortions for indigent women.

The Pennsylvania Medicaid plan upheld in *Beal* limited assistance for abortions to those certified as medically necessary. In the eyes of two physicians, in addition to the mother's attending physician, examine her and concur in writing that the abortion was medically necessary. Justice Powell, writing for the majority, touched on constitutional issues but decided the case on statutory interpretation grounds. He concluded that

---

[24] By providing for medically necessary operations except abortions, the Amendment was irrational both as "a means of allocating health-care resources or otherwise serving legitimate social welfare goals." These disparities illustrated the Amendment's contrived attempt to dissuade a woman's exercise of her constitutionally protected right to choose abortion.

Title XIX did not compel a participating state to fund elective abortions. Each state was given broad discretion to determine the extent of medical assistance that was "reasonable" and consistent with Title XIX's objectives. Given the state's strong interest, recognized in *Roe*, in protecting potential human life, he found nothing unreasonable in a state's furthering that interest in encouraging childbirth by refusing to fund medically unnecessary abortions.

The Connecticut Medicaid Plan involved in *Maher* was similar to the Pennsylvania plan in *Beal*. It, too, limited public funding to medically necessary abortions, although it did provide assistance for childbirth costs. In analyzing the equal protection challenge, Justice Powell, again writing for the majority, rejected the argument that a strict standard of scrutiny was required. Neither a suspect class nor a fundamental right was involved. The fundamental right to abortion articulated in *Roe* did not limit the state's authority "to make a value judgment favoring childbirth over abortion and to implement that judgment by the allocation of public funds." The mother's indigence rather than state law served to inhibit the exercise of her constitutional right.

Relying on *Maher*, the Court's per curiam opinion in *Poelker* rejected the constitutional attack on St. Louis' policy of providing publicly financed hospital services for childbirth but refusing to provide corresponding services for nontherapeutic abortions in city-owned hospitals.

Justices Brennan, Marshall and Blackmun dissented in all three decisions. Justice Brennan insisted that all three funding schemes unduly burdened the fundamental right to have an abortion by coercing only indigent women to bear unwanted children. Justice Blackmun also wrote a separate dissenting opinion.

(2) Justice Powell's majority opinion in *Harris* rests on a distinction between positive and negative rights. *See generally* I. BERLIN, FOUR ESSAYS ON LIBERTY (1969); Currie, *Positive and Negative Constitutional Rights*, 53 U. CHI. L. REV. 864 (1986) (arguing that the Constitution is a charter of negative rather than positive rights); Kreimer, *Allocative Sanctions: The Problem of Negative Rights in a Positive State*, 132 U. PA. L. REV. 1293 (1984) (arguing that the distinction between positive and negative rights is "gossamer" in a welfare state that is increasingly involved in people's lives and that holds the power to constrict liberty by doling out or withholding largess).

Michael Perry criticized *Harris* and the other abortion funding decisions. He argues that the Hyde amendment upheld in *Harris* was based on an illicit legislative motive that "abortion is morally objectionable." It thus goes squarely against *Roe*. Perry also took issue with the positive versus negative rights distinction upon which the decision rests. "For while *Roe* quite plainly does not forbid all governmental actions that might have the effect of making a woman prefer childbirth to abortion, *Roe* does require that government take no action, including the selective withholding of Medicaid funds, predicated on the view that abortion is per se morally objectionable." *See* Perry, *Why the Supreme Court Was Plainly Wrong in the Hyde Amendment Case: A Brief Comment on* Harris v. McRae, 32 STAN. L. REV. 1113, 1122 (1980).

Richard Epstein defended the abortion funding decisions in part by invoking freedom of conscience claims: "Some substantial fraction of taxpayers object to abortions on religious grounds." He also takes exception to the illicit motive argument. "If the foes of abortion were able to exclude both abortion funding and all pregnancy and neonatal care from Medicaid solely for religious reasons, would federal funding of abortion (and other pregnancy and neonatal care) then be required because of the motive behind its opposition, even with the entire issue of differential incentives no longer in the case? . . . In the end, therefore, it seems quite difficult to protect the free exercise rights of opponents of abortion under a system that involves any affirmative government support of abortions. In this context, the funding of abortions through charitable contributions has at least the modest advantage of keeping the government from the middle of the abortion battle." Epstein, *Foreword: Unconstitutional Conditions, State Power, and the Limits of Consent*, 102 HARV. L. REV. 4 (1988).

Laurence Tribe has argued that the remedy of requiring government to fund abortions is not susceptible of judicially manageable standards: "it is difficult to contemplate any court knowing when such an open-ended duty to invest has been faithfully discharged." Nevertheless, the decisions do not relieve the elected branches of government of a duty to "protect the interests of the fetus as well as those of the woman. . . . Government has many options for acting to minimize the conflict in a manner consistent with a woman's right, under *Roe*, to terminate a pregnancy prior to viability. Initially, it can save many women from the tragic fate of being forced to choose between abortion and unwanted pregnancy by providing sex education and more widely available contraception. It can also help make those unplanned pregnancies that do occur easier for women to want or at least to tolerate by providing improved prenatal care, better financial support for women with infants, and expanded adoption opportunities. Finally, when all else fails and the conflict remains intractable, government can invest in better technology to advance the line of fetal viability to a point ever closer to conception. With such a technology, after all, it would become possible, at an ever earlier point, for government simultaneously to facilitate the woman's termination of a pregnancy that she does not choose to continue and to provide for the survival of the fetus." Tribe, *The Abortion Funding Conundrum: Inalienable Rights, Affirmative Duties, and the Dilemma of Dependence*, 99 HARV. L. REV. 330, 341 (1985). *Cf.* Hirt, *Why the Government is not Required to Subsidize Abortion Funding and Referral*, 101 HARV. L. REV. 1895 (1988).

(3) *Abortion Counseling.* In *Rust v. Sullivan*, 500 U.S. 173 (1991), the Court upheld Department of Health and Human Services regulations that limit the ability of Title X fund recipients to counsel abortion as a method of family planning. Title X of the Public Health Services Act provides federal funding for family-planning services. None of the funds, however, may be used in programs where abortion is a method of family planning.

The regulations prohibit grantees from providing counseling concerning the use of, or referral for, abortion as a method of family planning. They also prohibit Title X projects from encompassing "activities that encourage, promote, or advocate abortion as a method of family planning." Moreover, the projects must be organized so that they are "physically and financially separate from prohibited abortion activities." The Court held that the regulations are a permissible construction of Title X and, relying heavily on *McRae*, that they do not violate either the First or Fifth Amendments. The *Rust* case is reproduced at § 15.03.

(4) In *City of Akron v. Akron Center for Reproductive Health, Inc.*, 462 U.S. 416 (1983), the Court invalidated several regulations placed on the right to choose an abortion.

Writing for the 6-3 majority, Justice Powell struck down the requirement that a second trimester abortion be performed in a hospital rather than an outpatient facility. This requirement heavily and unnecessarily burdened a woman's right to an abortion, as second trimester abortions could be performed safely and less expensively in outpatient clinics. The Court also struck down as an arbitrary incursion on medical judgment a 24-hour waiting period after any decision to abort has been made. Finally, Justice Powell invalidated as vague the requirement that a fetus be " 'disposed of in a humane and sanitary way.' "

Justice O'Connor dissented, joined by Justices White and Rehnquist. She began her dissent by asserting that advancing medical technology is undercutting the bright-line trimester approach. "Just as improvements in medical technology inevitably will move forward the point at which the State may regulate for reasons of maternal health, different technological improvements will move backward the point of viability at which the State may proscribe abortions except when necessary to preserve the life and health of the mother."

Justice O'Connor contended that the state's interest in protecting potential life exists throughout the pregnancy. Moreover, she asserted that designating viability as the time that the state's interest in potential life becomes compelling is arbitrary. To attract strict scrutiny, state regulation of abortion must "infringe substantially" or " 'heavily burden' " a woman's choice. If such substantial interference does not exist, rational basis review is appropriate.

(5) *Second Physician; Pathology Reports.* In *Planned Parenthood Association of Kansas City v. Ashcroft*, 462 U.S. 476 (1983), Justice Powell sustained Missouri's requirement of a second physician during abortions performed after viability. The Court relied on the statement in *Roe v. Wade* that the state has a compelling interest in potential human life during the third trimester of pregnancy. "The first physician's primary concern will be the life and health of the woman," he wrote. "A second physician, in situations where Missouri permits third-trimester abortions, may be of assistance to the woman's physician in preserving the health and life of the child."

Only Chief Justice Burger concurred in this portion of Justice Powell's opinion. Justice O'Connor, joined by Justices Rehnquist and White, agreed that the state has a compelling interest in protecting and preserving fetal life "extant throughout pregnancy."

The same division in the Court upheld the requirement in the same Missouri law that for all abortions the tissue removed must be submitted to a pathologist who must then "file a copy of the tissue report with the State Division of Health." Justice Powell disagreed with the dissenting Justices over the question of whether accepted medical practice required reports by a pathologist, as distinct from the performing physician, and whether it was appropriate for the state to single out abortions as the only procedure performed in clinics for which such reports were required. Justice Powell concluded that the requirement was a relatively insignificant burden on the abortion decision, a point challenged by Justice Blackmun's dissent, which emphasized that the procedure could increase cost of an abortion by as much as $40.

Finally, Justice Powell, again joined only by the Chief Justice, upheld a parental or judicial consent requirement for abortions on immature minors. Missouri juvenile court could deny permission to a minor for any "good cause," but such denial was not permitted "unless it first found after having received the required evidence that the minor was not mature enough to make her own decision." In a footnote, Justice Powell said that "the Court need not consider whether a qualified and independent non-judicial decision-maker would be appropriate." Justice O'Connor, joined by Justices White and Rehnquist, concurred. Justice Blackmun, again joined by Justices Brennan, Marshall and Stevens, dissented.

(6) *Licensed Outpatient Clinics. Simopoulos v. Virginia*, 462 U.S. 506 (1983), upheld, 8-1, a Virginia statute requiring second-trimester abortions to be performed in a "hospital," including an outpatient licensed surgical hospital. Virginia regulations "appear to be generally compatible with accepted medical standards governing outpatient second-trimester abortions," requiring that these facilities meet the same standards as those provided for other surgical procedures.

Justice O'Connor concurred, joined by Justices White and Rehnquist. Justice Stevens dissented.

(7) *Scientific Developments*. For responses to Justice O'Connor's criticisms in *Akron* that the *Roe* trimester scheme is being undermined by advancing scientific developments, see Rhode, *Trimesters and Technology: Revamping Roe v. Wade*, 95 YALE L.J. 639 (1986) ("'Late gestation' can be designated explicitly and it can stay still."); Comment, *Technology Advances and Roe v. Wade: The Need to Rethink Abortion Law*, 29 U.C.L.A. L. REV. 1194 (1982) (arguing that the viability test be abandoned in favor of a "standard for deciding when life begins based on fetal brain development").

For further discussion of how other dramatic scientific developments in human genetic engineering and other areas impact the right to procreative liberty, see, e.g., Attanasio, *The Genetic Revolution: What Lawyers Don't Know*, 63 N.Y.U. L. REV. 662 (1988) (examining the integral relationship between the right to choose an abortion, and present and future developments in human genetic engineering); Attanasio, *The Constitutionality of Regulating Human Genetic Engineering: Where Procreative Liberty and Equal Opportunity Collide*, 53 U. CHI. L. REV. 1274 (1986) (noting that the right to procreative liberty established in the abortion cases may lead to a right to engage in human genetic engineering).

(8) In *Webster v. Reproductive Health Services*, 492 U.S. 490 (1989), the Court addressed four sections of a Missouri Act: (1) the preamble, which contained "findings" by the state legislature that " '[t]he life of each human being begins at conception,' and that 'unborn children have protectable interests in life, health, and well-being' "; (2) the prohibition on the use of public facilities or employees to perform abortions; (3) the prohibition on public funding of abortion counseling; and (4) the requirement that physicians conduct viability tests prior to performing abortions "on any woman whom a physician has reason to believe is 20 or more weeks pregnant."

Chief Justice Rehnquist, writing for the Court, began by addressing the preamble of the Act. The State contended that the preamble was "precatory" and did not by its terms regulate abortion or any other aspect of appellees' medical practice.[25] Only Missouri courts can decide the extent to which the abstract preamble may be used to interpret other state statutes. The federal courts will be able "to address the meaning of the preamble should it be applied to restrict the activities of appellees in some concrete way."

The Court next addressed Missouri's prohibition on using public facilities or employees within the scope of their duties to perform abortions that are unnecessary to save the mother's life.[26]

"Missouri's refusal to allow public employees to perform abortions in public hospitals leaves a pregnant woman with the same choices as if the State had chosen not to operate any public hospitals at all." Moreover, private physicians and their patients do not have a constitutional right of access to facilities for the performance of abortions. Relying on *Harris v. McRae*, the Court reasoned that if a State may favor childbirth over abortion and allocate public funds accordingly, it may use the same value preference to allocate "other public resources, such as hospitals and medical staff."[27]

---

[25] *Maher v. Roe* emphasizes that *Roe* allows the " 'State to make a value judgment favoring childbirth over abortion.' " *Roe* also allows state tort and probate law to protect "unborn children."

[26] The statute defines " 'public employee' " as " 'any person employed by this state or any agency or political subdivision thereof.' " It defines " 'public facility' " as " 'any public institution, public facility, public equipment, or any physical asset owned, leased, or controlled by this state or any agency or political subdivisions thereof.' "

[27] The Court suggested that it might analyze the case differently if a "State had socialized medicine and all of its hospitals and physicians were publicly funded. This case might also be different if the State barred

The Court also upheld Missouri's prohibition on public funding to encourage or counsel "a woman to have an abortion not necessary to save her life."

The Court accepted, for purposes of this decision, Missouri's claim that these provisions were not "directed at the conduct of any physician or health care provider, private or public," but were "directed solely at those persons responsible for expending public funds." So interpreted, Appellees conceded that this provision did not adversely affect them and, therefore, no case or controversy remained before the Court.

Fourth, the Court addressed the requirement that physicians conduct viability tests prior to performing an abortion on any woman whom the physician has reason to believe is 20 or more weeks pregnant. Specifically, the Act provided: " 'In making this determination of viability, the physician shall perform or cause to be performed such medical examinations and tests as are necessary to make a finding of the gestational age, weight, and lung maturity of the unborn child and shall enter such findings and determinations of viability in the medical record of the mother.' "

Chief Justice Rehnquist, writing only for himself and Justices White and Kennedy, stated that the District Court found that uncontradicted evidence established " 'that a 20-week old fetus is *not* viable' " and that no reasonable possibility for viability exists before 23 1/2 weeks. "But it also found that there may be a 4-week error in estimating gestational age, which supports testing at 20 weeks."

Plaintiffs challenged the constitutionality of this provision on two grounds. First, as the Court stated in *Colautti v. Franklin*, reaffirming its statement in *Planned Parenthood of Central Missouri v. Danforth*, "the determination of whether a particular fetus is viable is, and must be, a matter for the judgment of the responsible attending physician." The plurality stated that insofar as the Missouri Act "regulates the method for determining viability, it undoubtedly does superimpose state regulation on the medical determination of whether a particular fetus is viable." Second, to the extent that the viability tests increase the cost of what are in fact second-trimester abortions, "their validity may also be questioned under *Akron*, where the Court held that a requirement that second-trimester abortions must be performed in hospitals was invalid because it substantially increased the expense of those procedures."

The plurality rejected these challenges as being predicated on *Roe's* "rigid trimester analysis," which "has resulted in subsequent cases like *Colautti* and *Akron* making constitutional law in this area a virtual Procrustean bed." The plurality would abandon the *Roe* trimester framework as a "web of legal rules that have become increasingly intricate, resembling a code of regulations rather than a body of constitutional doctrine." The plurality stated that the text of the Constitution did not support the key elements of *Roe* trimesters and viability. Moreover, the plurality did not see "why the State's interest in protecting potential human life should come into existence only at the point of viability, and that there should therefore be a rigid line allowing state regulation after viability but prohibiting it before viability."

Conceding that viability tests would both increase the expense of abortion and regulate the discretion of the physician in determining viability, the plurality was satisfied "that the requirement of these tests permissibly furthers the State's interest in protecting potential human life" and was, therefore, constitutional. The plurality also stated that its holding would allow more governmental regulation of abortion than the Court's previous holdings in *Colautti* and *Akron*. Finally, the plurality was not overruling *Roe v. Wade*; however, their opinion indicated ways in which they "would modify and narrow *Roe* and succeeding cases."

Justice O'Connor concurred in the Court's opinion on the preamble, on the

---

doctors who performed abortions in private facilities from the use of public facilities for any purpose."

prohibition on the use of public facilities or employees, and on public funding of abortion counseling. Additionally, she concurred in the judgment as to the requirement that physicians conduct a viability test prior to performing abortions. Justice O'Connor agreed that the preamble presented no case or controversy before the Court, as all of the "intimations of unconstitutionality are simply too hypothetical." Additionally, Justice O'Connor believed that the constitutionality of Missouri's ban on the utilization of public facilities and the participation of public employees in the performance of abortions not necessary to save the mother's life followed directly from the Court's previous decisions in *Harris v. McRae, Maher v. Roe,* and *Poelker v. Doe.* Upholding the testing requirements, she opined that requiring the performance of examinations and tests useful to determining when a fetus is viable, when viability is possible and when it would not be medically imprudent to do so, does not impose an undue burden on a woman's decision.

Unlike the plurality, however, Justice O'Connor did not believe that the viability testing requirements conflicted with any of the Court's past decisions concerning state regulation of abortion. She maintained that the State's invitation to reexamine the constitutional validity of *Roe v. Wade* was unnecessary. The viability testing provision only requires, "when not imprudent, the performance of 'those tests that are useful to making subsidiary findings as to viability.'" This provision "would only marginally, if at all, increase the cost of an abortion."

Justice Scalia concurred with all parts of the Court's opinion, except the viability testing provisions of § 188.029. As to these provisions, Justice Scalia stated that the plurality's opinion would effectively overrule *Roe,* which he stated should be done "more explicitly." By "our [the Court's] retaining control, through *Roe,* of what I believe to be, and many of our citizens recognize to be, a political issue, continuously distorts the public perception of the role of this Court. We can now look forward to at least another Term with carts full of mail from the public, and streets full of demonstrators, urging us their unelected and life-tenured judges who have been awarded those extraordinary, undemocratic characteristics precisely in order that we might follow the law despite the popular will to follow the popular will." This plurality's approach would disassemble *Roe* incrementally rather than flatly overrule it.[28]

Justice Blackmun, joined by Justices Brennan and Marshall, concurred in part and dissented in part. In a footnote, Justice Blackmun criticized the preamble as not being "'abortion neutral'" as the Court maintained. Moreover, because the public facility prohibition extended to private hospitals located on public, leased property, it interfered with private abortions.

Justice Blackmun was particularly concerned with the plurality's discussion of the Act's viability testing provision. The plurality misconstrued the plain language of § 188.029 as requiring that the physician perform tests only in order to determine *viability.* In contrast, the Act's explicit language required that the physician undertake "whatever tests are necessary to determine gestational age, weight, and lung maturity, regardless of whether these tests are necessary to a finding of viability, and regardless of whether the tests subject the pregnant woman or the fetus to additional health risks or add substantially to the cost of an abortion." Properly read, this provision does not even pass "a rational-basis standard."

Finally, the plurality's "permissibly furthers" standard effectively overrules *Roe.* The test is "nothing more than a dressed-up version of rational-basis review."

Justice Stevens concurred in part and dissented in part. He agreed with the plurality

---

[28] In a footnote, Justice Scalia criticized Justice O'Connor's undue burden standard as vague.

about the constitutionality of the abortion counseling provision. He would have struck down the other portions of the Act.

PLANNED PARENTHOOD OF SOUTHEASTERN PA. v. CASEY
505 U.S. 833, 112 S. Ct. 2791, 120 L. Ed. 2d 674 (1992)

JUSTICE O'CONNOR, JUSTICE KENNEDY, and JUSTICE SOUTERannounced the judgment of the Court and delivered the opinion of the Court with respect to Parts I, II, III, V-A, V-C, and VI, an opinion with respect to Part V-E, in which JUSTICE STEVENS joins, and an opinion with respect to Parts IV, V-B, and V-D.

I

Liberty finds no refuge in a jurisprudence of doubt. Yet 19 years after our holding that the Constitution protects a woman's right to terminate her pregnancy in its early stages, *Roe v. Wade*, that definition of liberty is still questioned. Joining the respondents as amicus curiae, the United States, as it has done in five other cases in the last decade, again asks us to overrule *Roe*.

. . . [T]he Pennsylvania Abortion Control Act . . . requires that a woman seeking an abortion give her informed consent prior to the abortion procedure, and specifies that she be provided with certain information at least 24 hours before the abortion is performed. § 3205. For a minor to obtain an abortion, the Act requires the informed consent of one of her parents, but provides for a judicial bypass option if the minor does not wish to or cannot obtain a parent's consent. § 3206. Another provision of the Act requires that, unless certain exceptions apply, a married woman seeking an abortion must sign a statement indicating that she has notified her husband of her intended abortion. § 3209. The Act exempts compliance with these three requirements in the event of a "medical emergency," which is defined in § 3203 of the Act. In addition to the above provisions regulating the performance of abortions, the Act imposes certain reporting requirements on facilities that provide abortion services.

Before any of these provisions took effect, the petitioners . . . brought this suit seeking declaratory and injunctive relief. Each provision was challenged as unconstitutional on its face. . . .

After considering the fundamental constitutional questions resolved by *Roe*, principles of institutional integrity, and the rule of *stare decisis*, we are led to conclude this: the essential holding of *Roe v. Wade* should be retained and once again reaffirmed.

. . . *Roe's* essential holding . . . has three parts. First is a recognition of the right of the woman to choose to have an abortion before viability and to obtain it without undue interference from the State. Before viability, the State's interests are not strong enough to support a prohibition of abortion or the imposition of a substantial obstacle to the woman's effective right to elect the procedure. Second is a confirmation of the State's power to restrict abortions after fetal viability, if the law contains exceptions for pregnancies which endanger a woman's life or health. And third is the principle that the State has legitimate interests from the outset of the pregnancy in protecting the health of the woman and the life of the fetus that may become a child. . . .

II

Constitutional protection of the woman's decision to terminate her pregnancy derives from the Due Process Clause of the Fourteenth Amendment. . . . Although a literal reading of the Clause might suggest that it governs only the procedures by which a State may deprive persons of liberty, . . . the Clause has been understood to contain a substantive component as well, one "barring certain government actions regardless of the fairness of the procedures used to implement them." *Daniels v. Williams*, 474 U.S. 327, 331 (1986). . . .

The most familiar of the substantive liberties protected by the Fourteenth Amendment are those recognized by the Bill of Rights. . . .

Neither the Bill of Rights nor the specific practices of States at the time of the adoption of the Fourteenth Amendment marks the outer limits of the substantive sphere of liberty which the Fourteenth Amendment protects. *See* U.S. Const., Amend. 9. . . .

. . . As Justice Harlan observed:

> Due process has not been reduced to any formula . . . The best that can be said is that through the course of this Court's decisions it has represented the balance which our Nation . . . has struck between that liberty and the demands of organized society. . . . The balance of which I speak is the balance struck by this country, having regard to what history teaches are the traditions from which it developed as well as the traditions from which it broke. That tradition is a living thing. A decision of this Court which radically departs from it could not long survive, while a decision which builds on what has survived is likely to be sound. . . . *Poe v. Ullman*, 367 U.S. 542 (Harlan, J., dissenting from dismissal on jurisdictional grounds). . . .

Some of us as individuals find abortion offensive to our most basic principles of morality, but that cannot control our decision. Our obligation is to define the liberty of all, not to mandate our own moral code. . . .

Our law affords constitutional protection to personal decisions relating to marriage, procreation, contraception, family relationships, child rearing, and education. These matters, involving the most intimate and personal choices a person may make in a lifetime, choices central to personal dignity and autonomy, are central to the liberty protected by the Fourteenth Amendment. At the heart of liberty is the right to define one's own concept of existence, of meaning, of the universe, and of the mystery of human life. . . .

Abortion is a unique act. It is an act fraught with consequences for others: for the woman who must live with the implications of her decision; for the persons who perform and assist in the procedure; for the spouse, family, and society which must confront the knowledge that these procedures exist, procedures some deem nothing short of an act of violence against innocent human life; and, depending on one's beliefs, for the life or potential life that is aborted. . . . [T]he liberty of the woman is at stake in a sense unique to the human condition and so unique to the law. The mother who carries a child to full term is subject to anxieties, to physical constraints, to pain that only she must bear. . . . Her suffering is too intimate and personal for the State to insist, without more, upon its own vision of the woman's role. . . .

. . . [T]he reservations any of us may have in reaffirming the central holding of *Roe* are outweighed by the explication of individual liberty we have given combined with the force of *stare decisis*. We turn now to that doctrine. . . .

III

A

. . . When this Court reexamines a prior holding, its judgment is customarily informed by a series of prudential and pragmatic considerations designed to test the consistency of overruling a prior decision with the ideal of the rule of law, and to gauge the respective costs of reaffirming and overruling a prior case. Thus, for example, we may ask whether the rule has proved to be intolerable simply in defying practical workability; whether the rule is subject to a kind of reliance that would lend a special hardship to the consequences of overruling and add inequity to the cost of repudiation; whether related principles of law have so far developed as to have left the old rule no more than a remnant of abandoned doctrine; or whether facts have so changed or come to be seen so differently, as to have robbed the old rule of significant application or justification. . . .

1

Although *Roe* has engendered opposition, it has in no sense proven "unworkable," *see Garcia v. San Antonio Metropolitan Transit Authority*, 469 U.S. 528, 546 (1985), representing as it does a simple limitation beyond which a state law is unenforceable. . . . The required determination falls within judicial competence.

2

The inquiry into reliance counts the cost of a rule's repudiation as it would fall on those who have relied reasonably on the rule's continued application. . . . For two decades of economic and social developments, people have organized intimate relationships and made choices that define their views of themselves and their places in society, in reliance on the availability of abortion in the event that contraception should fail. The ability of women to participate equally in the economic and social life of the Nation has been facilitated by their ability to control their reproductive lives. . . .

3

No evolution of legal principle has left *Roe's* doctrinal footings weaker than they were in 1973. . . .

If indeed the woman's interest in deciding whether to bear and beget a child had not been recognized as in *Roe*, the State might as readily restrict a woman's right to choose to carry a pregnancy to term as to terminate it, to further asserted state interests in population control, or eugenics, for example. . . . In any event, because *Roe's* scope is confined by the fact of its concern with postconception potential life, a concern otherwise likely to be implicated only by some forms of contraception protected independently under *Griswold* and later cases, any error in *Roe* is unlikely to have serious ramifications in future cases.

4

We have seen how time has overtaken some of *Roe's* factual assumptions: advances in maternal health care allow for abortions safe to the mother later in pregnancy than was true in 1973 and advances in neonatal care have advanced viability to a point somewhat earlier. . . . [D]ivergences from the factual premises of 1973 have no bearing on the validity of *Roe's* central holding, that viability marks the earliest point at which the State's interest in fetal life is constitutionally adequate to justify a legislative ban on nontherapeutic abortions. The soundness or unsoundness of that constitutional judgment in no sense turns on whether viability occurs at approximately 28 weeks, as was usual at the time of *Roe*, at 23 to 24 weeks, as it sometimes does today, or at some moment even slightly earlier in pregnancy, as it may if fetal respiratory capacity can somehow be enhanced in the future. . . .

5

. . . Within the bounds of normal *stare decisis* analysis, then, and subject to the considerations on which it customarily turns, the stronger argument is for affirming *Roe's* central holding, with whatever degree of personal reluctance any of us may have, not for overruling it.

B

In a less significant case, *stare decisis* analysis could, and would, stop at the point we have reached. But the sustained and widespread debate *Roe* has provoked calls for some comparison between that case and others of comparable dimension that have responded to national controversies and taken on the impress of the controversies addressed. . . .

The first example is that line of cases identified with *Lochner v. New York*, . . . adopting, in Justice Holmes' view, the theory of *laissez-faire*. . . . Of course, it was true that the Court lost something by its misperception, or its lack of prescience, and the Court-packing crisis only magnified the loss; but the clear demonstration that the facts of economic life were different from those previously assumed warranted the repudiation of the old law.

The second comparison that 20th century history invites is with the cases employing the separate-but-equal rule for applying the Fourteenth Amendment's equal protection guarantee. They began with *Plessy v. Ferguson*. . . .

. . . [W]hatever may have been the understanding in *Plessy's* time of the power of segregation to stigmatize those who were segregated with a "badge of inferiority," it was clear by 1954 that legally sanctioned segregation had just such an effect. . . . [W]e must also recognize that the *Plessy* Court's explanation for its decision was so clearly at odds with the facts apparent to the Court in 1954. . . .

. . . [A] decision to overrule should rest on some special reason over and above the belief that a prior case was wrongly decided. *See, e.g., Mitchell v. Grant*, 416 U.S. 600, 636 (1974) (Stewart, J., dissenting) ("A basic change in the law upon a ground no firmer than a change in our membership invites the popular misconception that this institution is little different from the two political branches of the Government. No misconception could do more lasting injury to this Court . . . ").

C

. . . [O]verruling *Roe's* central holding would not only reach an unjustifiable result under principles of *stare decisis*, but would seriously weaken the Court's capacity to exercise the judicial power. . . .

The Court's power lies in its legitimacy. . . .

. . . The Court must take care to speak and act in ways that allow people to accept its decisions on the terms the Court claims for them, as grounded truly in principle, not as compromises with social and political pressures. . . .

In two circumstances the Court would almost certainly fail to receive the benefit of the doubt in overruling prior cases. . . .

That first circumstance can be described as hypothetical; the second is to the point here and now. Where, in the performance of its judicial duties, the Court decides a case in such a way as to resolve the sort of intensely divisive controversy reflected in *Roe* and those rare, comparable cases, its decision has a dimension that the resolution of the normal case does not carry. It is the dimension present whenever the Court's interpretation of the Constitution calls the contending sides of a national controversy to end their national division by accepting a common mandate rooted in the Constitution.

The Court is not asked to do this very often, having thus addressed the Nation only twice in our lifetime, in the decisions of *Brown* and *Roe*. But when the Court does act in this way, its decision requires an equally rare precedential force to counter the inevitable efforts to overturn it and to thwart its implementation. . . . [O]nly the most convincing justification under accepted standards of precedent could suffice to demonstrate that a later decision overruling the first was anything but a surrender to political pressure. . . . So to overrule under fire in the absence of the most compelling reason to reexamine a watershed decision would subvert the Court's legitimacy. . . .

IV

. . . We conclude that the basic decision in *Roe* was based on a constitutional analysis which we cannot now repudiate. The woman's liberty is not so unlimited, however, that from the outset the State cannot show its concern for the life of the unborn, and at a later point in fetal development the State's interest in life has sufficient force so that the right of the woman to terminate the pregnancy can be restricted. . . .

We conclude the line should be drawn at viability, so that before that time the woman has a right to choose to terminate her pregnancy. We adhere to this principle for two reasons. First, as we have said, is the doctrine of *stare decisis*. . . .

The second reason is that the concept of viability, as we noted in *Roe*, is the time at which there is a realistic possibility of maintaining and nourishing a life outside the womb, so that the independent existence of the second life can in reason and all fairness be the object of state protection that now overrides the rights of the woman. . . . [T]here is no line other than viability which is more workable. . . . [T]here may be some medical developments that affect the precise point of viability. . . . The viability line also has, as a practical matter, an element of fairness. In some broad sense it might be said that a woman who fails to act before viability has consented to the States intervention on behalf of the developing child.

The woman's right to terminate her pregnancy before viability is the most central principle of *Roe v. Wade*.

On the other side of the equation is the interest of the State in the protection of potential life. . . . We do not need to say whether each of us, had we been Members of the Court when the valuation of the State interest came before it as an original matter, would have concluded, as the *Roe* Court did, that its weight is insufficient to justify a ban on abortions prior to viability even when it is subject to certain exceptions. . . .

Yet it must be remembered that *Roe v. Wade* speaks with clarity in establishing not only the woman's liberty but also the State's "important and legitimate interest in potential life." That portion of the decision in *Roe* has been given too little acknowledgment and implementation by the Court in its subsequent cases. . . .

Though the woman has a right to choose to terminate or continue her pregnancy before viability, it does not at all follow that the State is prohibited from taking steps to ensure that this choice is thoughtful and informed. Even in the earliest stages of pregnancy, the State may enact rules and regulations designed to encourage her to know that there are philosophic and social arguments of great weight that can be brought to bear in favor of continuing the pregnancy to full term and that there are procedures and institutions to allow adoption of unwanted children as well as a certain degree of state assistance if the mother chooses to raise the child herself. . . .

We reject the trimester framework, which we do not consider to be part of the essential holding of *Roe*. . . . The trimester framework suffers from these basic flaws: in its formulation it misconceives the nature of the pregnant woman's interest; and in practice it undervalues the State's interest in potential life, as recognized in *Roe*. . . .

. . . Numerous forms of state regulation might have the incidental effect of increasing the cost or decreasing the availability of medical care, whether for abortion or any other medical procedure. The fact that a law which serves a valid purpose, one not designed to strike at the right itself, has the incidental effect of making it more difficult or more expensive to procure an abortion cannot be enough to invalidate it. Only where state regulation imposes an undue burden on a woman's ability to make this decision does the power of the State reach into the heart of the liberty protected by the Due Process Clause. . . .

. . . [T]he Court's experience applying the trimester framework has led to the striking down of some abortion regulations which in no real sense deprived women of the ultimate decision. . . . [T]hat brings us to the other basic flaw in the trimester framework. . .

Before viability, *Roe* and subsequent cases treat all governmental attempts to influence a woman's decision on behalf of the potential life within her as unwarranted. This treatment is, in our judgment, incompatible with the recognition that there is a substantial state interest in potential life throughout pregnancy. . . .

Some guiding principles should emerge. What is at stake is the woman's right to make the ultimate decision, not a right to be insulated from all others in doing so. Regulations which do no more than create a structural mechanism by which the State, or the parent or guardian of a minor, may express profound respect for the life of the unborn are permitted, if they are not a substantial obstacle to the woman's exercise of the right to choose. Unless it has that effect on her right of choice, a state measure designed to persuade her to choose childbirth over abortion will be upheld if reasonably related to that goal. Regulations designed to foster the health of a woman seeking an abortion are valid if they do not constitute an undue burden.

Even when jurists reason from shared premises, some disagreement is inevitable. . . . We do not expect it to be otherwise with respect to the undue burden standard. We give this summary:

(a) . . . An undue burden exists, and therefore a provision of law is invalid, if its purpose or effect is to place a substantial obstacle in the path of a woman seeking an abortion before the fetus attains viability.

(b) We reject the rigid trimester framework of *Roe v. Wade*. To promote the State's profound interest in potential life, throughout pregnancy the State may take measures to ensure that the woman's choice is informed, and measures designed to advance this interest will not be invalidated as long as their purpose is to persuade the woman to choose childbirth over abortion. . . .

(c) As with any medical procedure, the State may enact regulations to further the health or safety of a woman seeking an abortion. Unnecessary health regulations that have the purpose or effect of presenting a substantial obstacle to a woman seeking an abortion impose an undue burden on the right.

(d) Our adoption of the undue burden analysis does not disturb the central holding of *Roe v. Wade*, and we reaffirm that holding. . . . [A] State may not prohibit any woman from making the ultimate decision to terminate her pregnancy before viability.

(e) We also reaffirm *Roe's* holding that "subsequent to viability, the State in promoting its interest in the potentiality of human life may, if it chooses, regulate, and even proscribe, abortion except where it is necessary, in appropriate medical judgment, for the preservation of the life or health of the mother." *Roe v. Wade*, 410 U.S., at 164–165.

These principles control our assessment of the Pennsylvania statute. . . .

V

A

Because it is central to the operation of various other requirements, we begin with the statute's definition of medical emergency. Under the statute, a medical emergency is "that condition which, on the basis of the physician's good faith clinical judgment, so complicates the medical condition of a pregnant woman as to necessitate the immediate abortion of her pregnancy to avert her death or for which a delay will create serious risk of substantial and irreversible impairment of a major bodily function."

Petitioners argue that the definition is too narrow, contending that it forecloses the possibility of an immediate abortion despite some significant health risks. If the contention were correct, we would be required to invalidate the restrictive operation of the provision, for the essential holding of *Roe* forbids a State from interfering with a woman's choice to undergo an abortion procedure if continuing her pregnancy would constitute a threat to her health.

. . . [T]he Court of Appeals construed the phrase "serious risk . . . to assure that compliance with its abortion regulations would not in any way pose a significant threat to the life or health of a woman. . . . " We . . . conclude that, as construed by the Court of Appeals, the medical emergency definition imposes no undue burden on a woman's abortion right.

B

We next consider the informed consent requirement. Except in a medical emergency, the statute requires that at least 24 hours before performing an abortion a physician inform the woman of the nature of the procedure, the health risks of the abortion and of childbirth, and the "probable gestational age of the unborn child." The physician or a qualified nonphysician must inform the woman of the availability of printed materials published by the State describing the fetus and providing information about medical assistance for childbirth, information about child support from the father, and a list of agencies which provide adoption and other services as alternatives to abortion. An abortion may not be performed unless the woman certifies in writing that she has been informed of the availability of these printed materials and has been provided them if she chooses to view them. . . .

To the extent *Akron I* and *Thornburgh v. American College of Obstetricians and Gynecologists* find a constitutional violation when the government requires, as it does here, the giving of truthful, nonmisleading information about the nature of the procedure, the attendant health risks and those of childbirth, and the "probable gestational age" of the fetus, those cases go too far, are inconsistent with *Roe's* acknowledgment of an important interest in potential life, and are overruled. . . . It cannot be questioned that psychological well-being is a facet of health. Nor can it be doubted that most women considering an abortion would deem the impact on the fetus relevant, if not dispositive, to the decision. In attempting to ensure that a woman apprehend the full consequences of her decision, the State furthers the legitimate purpose of reducing the risk that a woman may elect an abortion, only to discover later, with devastating psychological consequences, that her decision was not fully informed. If the information the State requires to be made available to the woman is truthful and not misleading, the requirement may be permissible.

. . . This requirement cannot be considered a substantial obstacle to obtaining an abortion, and, it follows, there is no undue burden.

[T]he statute now before us does not require a physician to comply with the informed consent provisions "if he or she can demonstrate by a preponderance of the evidence, that he or she reasonably believed that furnishing the information would have resulted in a severely adverse effect on the physical or mental health of the patient." . . .

. . . The doctor-patient relation does not underlie or override the two more general rights under which the abortion right is justified: the right to make family decisions and the right to physical autonomy. . . . Thus, a requirement that a doctor give a woman certain information as part of obtaining her consent to an abortion is, for constitutional purposes, no different from a requirement that a doctor give certain specific information about any medical procedure. . . .

. . . Our cases reflect the fact that the Constitution gives the States broad latitude to decide that particular functions may be performed only by licensed professionals, even if an objective assessment might suggest that those same tasks could be performed by others. *See Williamson v. Lee Optical of Oklahoma, Inc.* Thus, we uphold the provision as a reasonable means to insure that the woman's consent is informed.

. . . Pennsylvania's 24-hour waiting period . . . does not strike us as unreasonable, particularly where the statute directs that important information become part of the background of the decision. The statute, as construed by the Court of Appeals, permits avoidance of the waiting period in the event of a medical emergency and the record evidence shows that in the vast majority of cases, a 24-hour delay does not create any appreciable health risk. In theory, at least, the waiting period is a reasonable measure to implement the State's interest in protecting the life of the unborn, a measure that does not amount to an undue burden.

Whether the mandatory 24-hour waiting period is nonetheless invalid because in practice it is a substantial obstacle to a woman's choice to terminate her pregnancy is a closer question. The findings of fact by the District Court indicate that because of the distances many women must travel to reach an abortion provider, the practical effect will often be a delay of much more than a day because the waiting period requires that a woman seeking an abortion make at least two visits to the doctor. The District Court also found that in many instances this will increase the exposure of women seeking abortions to "the harassment and hostility of anti-abortion protestors demonstrating outside a clinic." As a result, the District Court found that for those women who have the fewest financial resources, those who must travel long distances, and those who have difficulty explaining their whereabouts to husbands, employers, or others, the 24-hour waiting period will be "particularly burdensome."

These findings are troubling in some respects, but they do not demonstrate that the waiting period constitutes an undue burden. . . .

. . . Whether a burden falls on a particular group is a distinct inquiry from whether it is a substantial obstacle even as to the women in that group. . . .

Section 3209 of Pennsylvania's abortion law provides, except in cases of medical emergency, that no physician shall perform an abortion on a married woman without receiving a signed statement from the woman that she has notified her spouse that she is about to undergo an abortion. The woman has the option of providing an alternative signed statement certifying that her husband is not the man who impregnated her; that her husband could not be located; that the pregnancy is the result of spousal sexual assault which she has reported; or that the woman believes that notifying her husband will cause him or someone else to inflict bodily injury upon her. A physician who performs an abortion on a married woman without receiving the appropriate signed statement will have his or her license revoked, and is liable to the husband for damages. . . .

. . . In well-functioning marriages, spouses discuss important intimate decisions such as whether to bear a child. But there are millions of women in this country who are the victims of regular physical and psychological abuse at the hands of their husbands. Should these women become pregnant, they may have very good reasons for not wishing to inform their husbands of their decision to obtain an abortion. . . .

The spousal notification requirement is thus likely to prevent a significant number of women from obtaining an abortion. It does not merely make abortions a little more difficult or expensive to obtain; for many women, it will impose a substantial obstacle. . . .

We recognize that a husband has a "deep and proper concern and interest . . . in his wife's pregnancy and in the growth and development of the fetus she is carrying." *Danforth, supra,* at 69. . . . If this case concerned a State's ability to require the mother to notify the father before taking some action with respect to a living child raised by both, therefore, it would be reasonable to conclude as a general matter that the father's interest in the welfare of the child and the mother's interest are equal.

Before birth, however, . . . state regulation with respect to the child a woman is carrying will have a far greater impact on the mother's liberty than on the father's. . . .

D

We next consider the parental consent provision. Except in a medical emergency, an unemancipated young woman under 18 may not obtain an abortion unless she and one of her parents (or guardian) provides informed consent as defined above. If neither a parent nor a guardian provides consent, a court may authorize the performance of an abortion upon a determination that the young woman is mature and capable of giving informed consent and has in fact given her informed consent, or that an abortion would be in her best interests. . . .

Our cases establish, and we reaffirm today, that a State may require a minor seeking an abortion to obtain the consent of a parent or guardian, provided that there is an adequate judicial bypass procedure. . . .

[S]ome of the provisions regarding informed consent have particular force with respect to minors: the waiting period, for example, may provide the parent or parents of a pregnant young woman the opportunity to consult with her in private, and to discuss the consequences of her decision in the context of the values and moral or religious principles of their family.

E

Under the record keeping and reporting requirements of the statute, every facility which performs abortions is required to file a report stating its name and address as well as the name and address of any related entity, such as a controlling or subsidiary organization. In the case of state-funded institutions, the information becomes public.

For each abortion performed, a report must be filed identifying: the physician (and the second physician where required); the facility; the referring physician or agency; the woman's age; the number of prior pregnancies and prior abortions she has had; gestational age; the type of abortion procedure; the date of the abortion; whether there were any pre-existing medical conditions which would complicate pregnancy; medical complications with the abortion; where applicable, the basis for the determination that the abortion was medically necessary; the weight of the aborted fetus; and whether the woman was married, and if so, whether notice was provided or the basis for the failure to give notice. Every abortion facility must also file quarterly reports showing the number of abortions performed broken down by trimester. In all events, the identity of each woman who has had an abortion remains confidential.

In *Danforth*, we held that record keeping and reporting provisions "that are reasonably directed to the preservation of maternal health and that properly respect a patient's confidentiality and privacy are permissible." We think that under this standard, all the provisions at issue here except that relating to spousal notice are constitutional. Although they do not relate to the State's interest in informing the woman's choice, they do relate to health. The collection of information with respect to actual patients is a vital element of medical research, and so it cannot be said that the requirements serve no purpose other than to make abortions more difficult. Nor do we find that the requirements impose a substantial obstacle to a woman's choice. At most they might increase the cost of some abortions by a slight amount. While at some point increased cost could become a substantial obstacle, there is no such showing on the record before us.

Subsection (12) of the reporting provision requires the reporting of, among other things, a married woman's "reason for failure to provide notice" to her husband. . . . Like the spousal notice requirement itself, this provision places an undue burden on a woman's choice, and must be invalidated for that reason. . . .

The case is remanded for proceedings consistent with this opinion, including consideration of the question of severability.

JUSTICE BLACKMUN, concurring in part, concurring in the judgment in part, and dissenting in part.

I join parts I, II, III, V-A, V-C, and VI of the joint opinion of JUSTICE O'CONNOR, KENNEDY, and SOUTER. . . .

I

. . . In contrast to previous decisions in which Justices O'Connor and Kennedy postponed reconsideration of *Roe v. Wade*, the authors of the joint opinion today join Justice Stevens and me in concluding that "the essential holding of *Roe* should be retained and once again reaffirmed . . ." [and]

[I]n striking down the Pennsylvania statute's spousal notification requirement, . . .

. . . I believe that the joint opinion errs in failing to invalidate the other regulations, . . .[t]he joint opinion makes clear that its specific holdings are based on the insufficiency of the record before it. . . .

II

. . . Our precedents and the joint opinion's principles require us to subject all non-*de minimis* abortion regulations to strict scrutiny. . . .

C

Application of the strict scrutiny standard results in the invalidation of all the challenged provisions. Indeed, as this Court has invalidated virtually identical provisions in prior cases, stare decisis requires that we again strike them down. . . .

III

. . . If there is much reason to applaud the advances made by the joint opinion today, there is far more to fear from The Chief Justice's opinion.

The Chief Justice's criticism of *Roe* follows from his stunted conception of individual liberty. . . .

JUSTICE STEVENS, concurring in part and dissenting in part.

. . . .

I

. . . The central holding of *Roe v. Wade* has been a "part of our law" for almost two decades. . . . The societal costs of overruling *Roe* at this late date would be enormous. *Roe* is an integral part of a correct understanding of both the concept of liberty and the basic equality of men and women. . . .

. . . [A]s a matter of federal constitutional law, a developing organism that is not yet a "person" does not have what is sometimes described as a "right to life. . . . "

II

. . . In my opinion, the principles established in. . . *Akron* (and followed by the Court just six years ago in *Thornburgh*) should govern our decision today. . . .

Accordingly, while I disagree with Parts IV, V-B, and V-D of the joint opinion, I join the remainder of the Court's opinion.

CHIEF JUSTICE REHNQUIST, with whom JUSTICE WHITE, JUSTICE SCALIA, and JUSTICE THOMAS join, concurring in the judgment in part and dissenting in part.

The joint opinion, following its newly-minted variation on *stare decisis*, retains the outer shell of *Roe v. Wade*, but beats a wholesale retreat from the substance of that case. We believe that *Roe* was wrongly decided, and that it can and should be *overruled*, consistently with our traditional approach to *stare decisis* in constitutional cases. We would . . . uphold the challenged provisions of the Pennsylvania statute in their entirety.

I

. . . Although they reject the trimester framework that formed the underpinning of *Roe*, Justices O'Connor, Kennedy, and Souter adopt a revised undue burden standard to analyze the challenged regulations. We conclude, however, that such an outcome is an unjustified constitutional compromise, one which leaves the Court in a position to closely scrutinize all types of abortion regulations despite the fact that it lacks the power to do so under the Constitution. . . .

Although *Roe* allowed state regulation after the point of viability to protect the potential life of the fetus, the Court subsequently rejected attempts to regulate in this manner. . . .

Nor do the historical traditions of the American people support the view that the right to terminate one's pregnancy is "fundamental." The common law which we inherited from England made abortion after "quickening" an offense. At the time of the adoption of the Fourteenth Amendment, statutory prohibitions or restrictions on abortion were commonplace; in 1868, at least 28 of the then-37 States and 8 Territories had statutes banning or limiting abortion. J. Mohr, *Abortion in America* 200 (1978). By the turn of the century virtually every State had a law prohibiting or restricting abortion on its books. By the middle of the present century, a liberalization trend had set in. But 21 of the restrictive abortion laws in effect in 1868 were still in effect in 1973 when *Roe* was decided, and an overwhelming majority of the States prohibited abortion unless necessary to preserve the life or health of the mother. . . .

II

The joint opinion of Justices O'Connor, Kennedy, and Souter cannot bring itself to say that *Roe* was correct as an original matter, but the authors are of the view that "the immediate question is not the soundness of *Roe's* resolution of the issue, but the precedential force that must be accorded to its holding. . . . " This discussion of the principle of *stare decisis* appears to be almost entirely dicta, because the joint opinion does not apply that principle in dealing with *Roe*. *Roe* decided that a woman had a fundamental right to an abortion. The joint opinion rejects that view. *Roe* decided that abortion regulations were to be subjected to "strict scrutiny" and could be justified only in the light of "compelling state interests." The joint opinion rejects that view. *Roe* analyzed abortion regulation under a rigid trimester framework, a framework which has guided this Court's decisionmaking for 19 years. The joint opinion rejects that framework.

. . . While purporting to adhere to precedent, the joint opinion instead revises it. *Roe* continues to exist, but only in the way a storefront on a western movie set exists: a mere facade to give the illusion of reality. Decisions following *Roe*, such as *Akron v. Akron Center for Reproductive Health, Inc.*, and *Thornburgh v. American College of Obstetricians and Gynecologists*, are frankly *overruled*. . . .

The joint opinion discusses several *stare decisis* factors which, it asserts, point toward retaining a portion of *Roe*. . . . [S]urely there is no requirement, in considering whether to depart from *stare decisis* in a constitutional case, that a decision be more wrong now than it was at the time it was rendered. . . .

. . . The "separate but equal" doctrine lasted 58 years after *Plessy*, and *Lochner's* protection of contractual freedom lasted 32 years. . . .

Apparently realizing that conventional *stare decisis* principles do not support its position, the joint opinion advances a belief that retaining a portion of *Roe* is necessary to protect the "legitimacy" of this Court. . . .

. . . Over the past 21 years, ... the Court has *overruled*, in whole or in part 34 of its previous constitutional decisions. . . .

. . . The joint opinion acknowledges that the Court improved its stature by overruling *Plessy* in *Brown* on a deeply divisive issue. And our decision in *West Coast Hotel*, which overruled *Adkins v. Children's Hospital, supra,* and *Lochner*, was rendered at a time when Congress was considering President Franklin Roosevelt's proposal to "reorganize" this Court and enable him to name six additional Justices in the event that any member of the Court over the age of 70 did not elect to retire. It is difficult to imagine a situation in which the Court would face more intense opposition to a prior ruling than it did at that time, and, under the general principle proclaimed in the joint opinion, the Court seemingly should have responded to this opposition by stubbornly refusing to reexamine the *Lochner* rationale, lest it lose legitimacy by appearing to "overrule under fire." . . .

For example, the opinion asserts that the Court could justifiably overrule its decision in *Lochner* only because the Depression had convinced "most people" that constitutional protection of contractual freedom contributed to an economy that failed to protect the welfare of all. . . .

There is . . . a suggestion in the joint opinion that the propriety of overruling a "divisive" decision depends in part on whether "most people" would now agree that it should be overruled. . . . The Judicial Branch derives its legitimacy, not from following public opinion, but from deciding by its best lights whether legislative enactments of the popular branches of Government comport with the Constitution. . . .

The end result of the joint opinion's paeans of praise for legitimacy is the enunciation of a brand new standard for evaluating state regulation of a woman's right to abortion the "undue burden" standard. . . . It is a standard which even today does not command the support of a majority of this Court. . . .

. . . Because the undue burden standard is plucked from nowhere, the question of what is a "substantial obstacle" to abortion will undoubtedly engender a variety of conflicting views. . . .

[W]e think that the correct analysis is that set forth by the plurality opinion in *Webster*. A woman's interest in having an abortion is a form of liberty protected by the Due Process Clause, but States may regulate abortion procedures in ways rationally related to a legitimate state interest. *Williamson v. Lee Optical of Okla., Inc.*, 348 U.S. 483, 491 (1955). With this rule in mind, we examine each of the challenged provisions.

III

A

. . . This Court has held that it is certainly within the province of the States to require a woman's voluntary and informed consent to an abortion. . . .

B

In addition to providing her own informed consent, before an unemancipated woman under the age of 18 may obtain an abortion she must either furnish the consent of one of her parents, or must opt for the judicial procedure that allows her to bypass the consent requirement. . . .

. . . In our view, it is entirely "rational and fair for the State to conclude that, in most instances, the family will strive to give a lonely or even terrified minor advice that is both compassionate and mature." *Ohio v. Akron Center for Reproductive Health*, 497 U.S., at 520. . . .

C

Section 3209 of the Act contains the spousal notification provision. . . .

. . . First, a husband's interests in procreation within marriage and in the potential life of his unborn child are certainly substantial ones. . . . The State itself has legitimate interests both in protecting these interests of the father and in protecting the potential life of the fetus, and the spousal notification requirement is reasonably related to advancing those state interests. . . .

The State also has a legitimate interest in promoting "the integrity of the marital relationship." 18 Pa. Cons. Stat. § 3209(a) (1990). . . . In our view, the spousal notice requirement is a rational attempt by the State to improve truthful communication between spouses and encourage collaborative decisionmaking, and thereby fosters marital integrity. . . .

D

The Act also imposes various reporting requirements. . . . These reporting requirements rationally further legitimate state interest.

E

Finally, . . . medical emergency exempts compliance with the Act's informed consent, parental consent, and spousal notice requirements. . . .

We find that the interpretation of the Court of Appeals in this case is eminently reasonable, and that the provision thus should be upheld. When a woman is faced with any condition that poses a "significant threat to [her] life or health," she is exempted from the Act's consent and notice requirements and may proceed immediately with her abortion. . . .

JUSTICE SCALIA, with whom the CHIEF JUSTICE, JUSTICE WHITE, and JUSTICE THOMAS join, concurring in the judgment in part and dissenting in part.

. . . [A]pplying the rational basis test, I would uphold the Pennsylvania statute in its entirety. . . .

The authors of the joint opinion, of course, do not squarely contend that *Roe v. Wade* was a correct application of "reasoned judgment." . . . But in their exhaustive discussion of all the factors that go into the determination of when *stare decisis* should be observed and when disregarded, they never mention "how wrong was the decision on its face?". . .

The emptiness of the "reasoned judgment" that produced *Roe* is displayed in plain view by the fact that, after more than 19 years of effort by some of the brightest (and most determined) legal minds in the country, . . . the best the Court can do to explain how it is that the word "liberty" must be thought to include the right to destroy human fetuses is to rattle off a collection of adjectives that simply decorate a value judgment and conceal a political choice. . . . Those adjectives might be applied, for example, to homosexual sodomy, polygamy, adult incest, and suicide, all of which are equally "intimate" and "deeply personal" decisions involving "personal autonomy and bodily integrity" and all of which can constitutionally be proscribed because it is our unquestionable constitutional tradition that they are proscribable. It is not reasoned judgment that supports the Court's decision; only personal predilection. . . .

The joint opinion frankly concedes that the amorphous concept of "undue burden" has been inconsistently applied by the Members of this Court. . . .

. . . Not only did *Roe* not, as the Court suggests, resolve the deeply divisive issue of abortion; it did more than anything else to nourish it, by elevating it to the national level where it is infinitely more difficult to resolve. . . . As with many other issues, the division of sentiment within each State was not as closely balanced as it was among the population of the Nation as a whole. . . .

. . . At the same time, *Roe* created a vast new class of abortion consumers and abortion proponents by eliminating the moral opprobrium that had attached to the act. ("If the Constitution guarantees abortion, how can it be bad?" not an accurate line of thought, but a natural one.) . . .

The Imperial Judiciary lives. . . .

[T]he American people love democracy and the American people are not fools. As long as this Court thought (and the people thought) that we Justices were doing essentially lawyers' work up here reading text and discerning our society's traditional understanding of that text the public pretty much left us alone. . . . But if in reality our process of constitutional adjudication consists primarily of making value judgments, then a free and intelligent people's attitude towards us can be expected to be (ought to be) quite different. . . .

There comes vividly to mind a portrait by Emanuel Leutze that hangs in the Harvard Law School: Roger Brooke Taney, painted in 1859, the 82nd year of his life, the 24th of his Chief Justiceship, the second after his opinion in *Dred Scott*. . . . There seems to be on his face, and in his deep-set eyes, an expression of profound sadness and disillusionment. . . . I expect that two years earlier he, too, had thought himself "calling the contending sides of national controversy to end their national division by accepting a common mandate rooted in the Constitution." . . .

STENBERG v. CARHART, 530 U.S. 914 (2000). In a declaratory judgment action, the *Stenberg* Court invalidated Nebraska's " 'partial birth abortion' " statute because it placed an undue burden on a women's right to choose an abortion. The statute at issue made it a felony carrying a prison term of up to 20 years and a fine of up to $25,000 for a doctor to perform a " 'partial birth abortion' " — " 'an abortion procedure in which the person performing the abortion partially delivers vaginally a living unborn child before killing the unborn child and completing the delivery.' " It further defined " 'partially delivers vaginally a living unborn child before killing the unborn child' " to mean " 'deliberately and intentionally delivering into the vagina a living unborn child, or substantial portion thereof, for the purpose of performing a procedure that the person performing such procedure knows will kill the unborn child and does kill the unborn child.' "

That the Nebraska statute "applies both pre- and postviability aggravates the constitutional problem presented" because the state's regulatory interest is "considerably weaker" previability. The Nebraska statute "regulates only a *method* of performing abortion."

However, "a State cannot subject women's health to significant risks" posed by the "pregnancy *itself*" or by "state regulations [that] force women to use riskier methods of abortion." Justice Breyer noted that based on the District Court's finding that "alternatives, such as D&E and induced labor, are safe . . . but D&X method was significantly *safer* in certain circumstances," a division of opinion among some medical experts over whether D&X is generally safer,[29] and an "absence of controlled medical studies that would help answer these medical questions," "the law requires a health exception."

By no means must a state grant physicians unfettered discretion in their selection of abortion methods. But where substantial medical authority supports the proposition that banning a particular abortion procedure could endanger women's health, *Casey* requires the statute to include a health exception when the procedure is " 'necessary, in appropriate medical judgment, for the preservation of the life or health of the mother.' "

The statute failed to distinguish between "D&E (where a foot or arm is drawn through the cervix) and D&X (where the body up to the head is drawn through the cervix)." Even if Nebraska primarily intended the statute to ban D&X, "its language makes clear that it also covers a much broader category of procedures. The language does not track the medical differences between D&E and D&X."

Justice Stevens concurred, joined by Justice Ginsburg. Justice Stevens stated that a doctor should not have "to follow any procedure other than the one that he or she reasonably believes will best protect the woman in her exercise of this constitutional liberty."

Justice O'Connor concurred emphasizing that since "even a postviability proscription of abortion" requires a health exception, it follows that "previability partial-birth abortions, under the circumstances presented here, must include a health exception as

---

[29] " 'The AMA recommends that the procedure not be used *unless alternative procedures pose materially greater risk to the woman.*' "

well." This statute only allows for an exception " 'necessary to save the life of the mother.' "

Justice O'Connor held the statute "unconstitutional on the alternative and independent ground that it imposes an undue burden on a woman's right to choose to terminate her pregnancy before viability." The ban covers not just D&X but also D&E, " 'the most commonly used method for performing previability second trimester abortions,' " thus creating a " 'substantial obstacle to a woman seeking an abortion' " and imposing an "undue burden on a woman's right to terminate her pregnancy prior to viability." "[I]t is unlikely that prohibiting the D&X procedure alone would 'amount in practical terms to a substantial obstacle to a woman seeking an abortion.' "

Justice Ginsburg concurred, joined by Justice Stevens. Justice Ginsburg noted that, "this law does not save any fetus from destruction, for it targets only a *method* of performing abortion. Nor does the statute seek to protect the lives or health of a pregnant woman." Moreover, "the most common method of performing previability second trimester abortions is no less distressing or susceptible to gruesome description."

Chief Justice Rehnquist wrote a brief dissent. He joined the dissents of Justices Kennedy and Thomas because they correctly apply *Casey's* principles.

Justice Scalia dissented. "The method of killing a human child — one cannot even accurately say an entirely unborn human child — proscribed by this statute is so horrible that the most clinical description of it evokes a shudder of revulsion." Moreover, to demand "a 'health exemption' — which requires the abortionist to assure himself that, in his expert medical judgment, this method is, in the case at hand, marginally safer than others (how can one prove the contrary beyond a reasonable doubt?) — is to give live-birth abortion free rein."

Justice Kennedy wrote a dissenting opinion joined by the Chief Justice. In D&E, "traction between the uterus and the vagina is essential to the procedure" The "fetus, in many cases, dies just as a human adult or child would: It bleeds to death as it is torn from limb from limb." All that is left, quoting Dr. Carhart, is " 'a tray full of pieces.' "

The majority "contradicts *Casey's* assurance that the State's constitutional position in the realm of promoting respect for life is more than marginal." Further misconstruing *Casey*, "the Court holds the ban on the D&X procedure fails because it does not include an exception permitting an abortionist to perform a D&X whenever he believes it will best preserve the health of the woman. Casting aside the views of distinguished physicians and the statements of leading medical organizations, the Court awards each physician a veto power."

Justice Thomas dissented, joined by the Chief Justice and Justice Scalia. In *Casey*, "seven Members of that Court, including six Members sitting today, acknowledged that States have a legitimate role in regulating abortion and recognized the States' interest in respecting fetal life at all stages of development."

Justice Thomas noted "numerous medical authorities have equated 'partial birth abortion' with D&X." For example, the American Medical Association "has recognized that this procedure is ethically different from the other destructive abortion techniques because the fetus, normally twenty weeks or longer in gestation, is killed *outside* the womb. The "partial birth" gives the fetus an autonomy which separates it from the right of the woman to choose treatments for her own body.[30]

---

[30] The testimony of a nurse was as follows: " 'The baby's little fingers were clasping and unclasping, and his little feet were kicking. Then the doctor stuck the scissors in to the back of his head, and the baby's arms jerked out, like a startle reaction, like a flinch, like a baby does when he thinks he is going to fall' "

While *Roe* and *Casey* protect abortion procedures " 'necessary' " to protect the mother's health, the majority allows any procedure that "has any comparative health benefits." This "health exception requirement eviscerates *Casey's* undue burden standard and imposes unfettered abortion-on-demand. The exception entirely swallows the rule."[31]

NOTES

(1) For further examination of *Casey*, see Clark, *Abortion and the Pied Piper of Compromise*, 68 N.Y.U. L. REV. 265, 268 (1993) ("Immediately following the release of the opinion, representatives of both the pro-choice and pro-life movements labeled *Casey* a defeat for their respective positions."); Devins, *The Countermajoritarian Paradox*, 93 MICH. L. REV. 1433, 1455 (1995) ("*Planned Parenthood v. Casey* is a culmination of these interchanges between the Court and elected government. After five abortion-dominated Supreme Court confirmation hearings and hundreds of thousands of abortion protesters marching each year at its steps, the Court formally reconsidered and moderated *Roe*."); Devins, *Book Review Essay: Through the Looking Glass: What Abortion Teaches Us About American Politics*, 94 COLUM. L. REV. 293, 329–30 (1994) ("*Roe* nationalized abortion rights at a time when state reform efforts, while on the rise, could not guarantee success. Twenty-one years later, as reflected in the failure of statutory and constitutional amendment repeal efforts as well as *Casey's* utilization of stare decisis to reaffirm *Roe*, the durability of the central holding of *Roe* seems assured. The Court, however, has given way to elected branch counter-initiatives. Abortion funding restrictions have been upheld, some parental rights have been recognized, and the Court has left the development of administrative regulations to the political process. Furthermore, while rejecting Reagan and Bush administration efforts to overturn *Roe*, the undue burden test advocated by Solicitor General Rex Lee in *City of Akron v. Akron Center for Reproductive Health, Inc.* seems the governing standard in state regulation cases."); Hanigsberg, *Homologizing Pregnancy and Motherhood: A Consideration of Abortion*, 94 MICH. L. REV. 371, 381 (1995) ("I also interrogate the meaning of intrauterine life within a feminist pro-choice framework and show that part of the difficulty in discussing abortion as both a political and legal matter is that it is perceived as a particularly egregious form of bad mothering. As a result, abortion becomes enmeshed in a complex set of beliefs and practices that stem from the ideology of motherhood."); Horwitz, *The Constitution of Change: Legal Fundamentality Without Fundamentalism*, 107 HARV. L. REV. 30, 35-36, 40 (1993) ("Justices O'Connor, Kennedy, and Souter, the architects of *Casey's* joint opinion, were part of a generation that had arrived at legal maturity haunted by Chief Justice Charles Evans Hughes's well-known warning that, in 'three notable instances' during the nineteenth century the *Dred Scott* case being the most notorious the Supreme Court 'ha[d] suffered severely from self-inflicted wounds.' The Chief Justice's warning, delivered in 1928, although it did not mention *Lochner v. New York* or what came to be known as the *Lochner* era, was widely understood after 1937 to have forecast the disastrous consequences that would befall any Court that became inattentive to the bases of its own legitimacy.").

For a discussion of the seemingly contradictory positions in *Casey* that reaffirmed

---

The " 'doctor opened up the scissors, stuck a high powered suction tube into the opening, and sucked the baby's brains out. Now the baby went completely limp.' "

[31] The "majority does not indicate whether an exception for physical health only is required, or whether the exception would have to account for 'all factors — physical, emotional, psychological, familial, and the woman's age — relevant to the well being of the patient.' "

the "essential holding" in *Roe v. Wade* that abortions prior to viability may not be "criminalized," while upholding "several other Pennsylvania provisions making abortion more difficult to obtain as a practical matter" see Sullivan, *The Justices of Rules and Standards*, 106 HARV. L. REV. 22, 27–8 (1992). Professor Sullivan posits that this "split result" was a result of the Court steering between two poles. "In the moral and political debate about abortion, one polar position holds that human life begins at conception and therefore abortion is murder in every case. The other pole holds that decisions about continuing or ending a pregnancy should be made solely by the pregnant woman (there being no life interest on the other side prior to birth), either as a matter of liberty or of gender equality."

(2) *Severability.* In *Leavitt v. Jane L.*, 518 U.S. 137 (1996), the Court reversed a Tenth Circuit Court of Appeals decision invalidating a provision of a Utah abortion regulation on the basis that the provision was not severable from another provision which had been struck down as unconstitutional.

The provision which had been found unconstitutional allowed abortions during the first 20 weeks of pregnancy if: (1) it " 'is necessary to save the pregnant woman's life' "; (2) " 'the pregnancy is the result of rape' "; (3) " 'the pregnancy is the result of incest' "; (4) it is necessary " 'to prevent grave damage to the pregnant woman's medical health' "; or (5) the child " 'would be born with grave defects.' " The second provision permitted abortions after 20 weeks gestational age only when necessary to save the life of the pregnant woman or to prevent serious damage to her health, or if the child would have serious birth defects. The District Court found this second provision to be severable from the first, and constitutional. The Court of Appeals did not address the constitutionality of the second provision, but held that it was not severable from the first provision.

In a 5-4 per curiam decision, the Court found that the Utah Legislature intended that the regulations be severable, as evidenced by a clearly worded severability clause. Moreover, the Court found that the two provisions were not so "interrelated" as to prohibit the severing of one provision from the other. The second provision could "function effectively without the invalidated provision."

In his dissent, Justice Stevens, joined by Justices Souter, Ginsburg, and Breyer, stated that the Court commonly did not grant certiorari to review a federal court of appeals ruling on a state-law question.

(3) *Physician Performance Requirement.* In *Mazurek v. Armstrong*, 520 U.S. 968 (1997), the majority upheld a Montana statute that allowed only licensed physicians to perform abortions. In a per curiam opinion, the Court relied on *Planned Parenthood v. Casey*, which had upheld a law allowing only physicians to provide information to patients considering abortions.

The majority rejected the dissent's claim that " 'the sole purpose of the statute was to target a particular licensed professional (respondent Susan Cahill).' " Similar laws already existed in forty states and there was no evidence suggesting this was an unconstitutional bill of attainder. Without deciding whether tainted legislative motive would invalidate a law, such a motive "did not exist here." The Court stressed that the States had discretion to decide who qualified for performing particular professional functions even if those duties could be performed by others.

Moreover, the fact that the statute affected a single practitioner contradicted any conclusion that the legislature intended to impose a substantial obstacle against abortion. Even before the law, physician-assistants "could only perform abortions with a licensed physician (who also performed abortions) present." *Connecticut v. Menillo*, 423 U.S. 9 (1975), allows States to define the term "physician" narrowly to ensure the safety of abortion procedures.

Justice Stevens dissented, joined by Justices Ginsburg and Breyer. Justice Stevens found evidence supporting the bill of attainder argument and maintained that the predominant legislative purpose "was to make abortions more difficult."

HODGSON v. MINNESOTA, 497 U.S. 417 (1990). In *Hodgson*, one majority of the Court (Justices Brennan, Marshall, Blackmun, Stevens, and O'Connor) struck down a Minnesota statute that provided that an abortion cannot be performed on an unemancipated minor "under 18 years of age until at least 48 hours after both of her parents have been notified." The only exceptions to the Minnesota statute's notice requirements were if an immediate abortion was needed to save the woman's life, if both parents had given written consent, or if the woman was "a victim of parental abuse or neglect." However, the Minnesota legislature provided a back-up provision that retained the notice requirement, but included the additional option that a woman may obtain a court order for the abortion to proceed without notification to either parent. A different majority (Chief Justice Rehnquist and Justices White, O'Connor, Scalia, and Kennedy) upheld the two-parent notification requirement with the proviso that a minor woman may "bypass" parental notice with a court order.

Justice Stevens, writing for the Court, invalidated the simple two-parent notification requirement. A two-parent notification requirement serves no useful purpose in the ideal family where notice to one parent would normally constitute notice to both. In many families, however, the parent notified by the child would not notify the other parent. For example, 50 percent of Minnesota's minors live with only one biological parent. Moreover, the Court found that the two-parent requirement "disserves" minors in "dysfunctional" or "abusive" families.

Nevertheless, a different majority upheld the two-parent notification requirement in conjunction with the judicial bypass option. The Kennedy plurality would even have upheld the two-parent notification requirement standing alone, as the law generally required minors to exercise their rights "through and with parental consent." The State cannot intrude on how the family unit handles this notice.

Justice O'Connor provided the crucial swing vote for striking down the simple two-parent notification requirement, but upholding the requirement with a judicial bypass option.

Justice Marshall, joined by Justices Brennan and Blackmun, wrote a separate opinion concurring in part, concurring in the judgment in part, and dissenting in part. Justice Marshall argued that "compelled notification is unlikely to result in productive consultation in families in which a daughter does not feel comfortable consulting her parents about intimate or sexual matters." Justice Marshall also believed that the judicial bypass itself was unconstitutional, as it does not provide judges with adequate standards to determine whether the minor is "mature" and "capable" to make the decision on her own.

NOTES

(a) *Judicial Bypass to Parental Notice.* In *Ohio v. Akron Center for Reproductive Health*, 497 U.S. 502 (1990), the Court upheld an Ohio statute that made it a crime for a physician to perform an abortion on an unmarried, unemancipated minor woman without having met one of four conditions. First, the physician must give one parent 24 hours notice or notify certain relatives who then, along with the minor, must each file an affidavit expressing fear of "physical, sexual or severe emotional abuse." Second, the physician may have written consent from one parent. Third, a court order may authorize the abortion. Fourth, an action by the juvenile court or the court of appeals may give "constructive authority" for the abortion.

To obtain a court order bypassing the notice requirements, the minor must file a complaint alleging not only her desire to have an abortion without notifying her parents, but "that she has sufficient maturity and information to make an intelligent decision," or that she has been subjected to a "pattern of physical, sexual, or emotional abuse" by a parent, or that "notice is not in her best interests." The minor must prove one of these three circumstances by "clear and convincing evidence." Moreover, if the court rejects the minor's petition, she has the right to appeal. If either the trial court or the appellate court fails to act within mandatory time frames, the minor is granted "constructive authority" for the abortion.

Justice Kennedy, writing for the 6-3 majority, noted that, "although our cases have required bypass procedures for parental consent statutes, we have not decided whether parental notice statutes must contain such procedures." Moreover, the Court continued to leave this question open as the Ohio bypass procedures met the requirements for judicial bypasses in consent statutes. The Ohio statute allowed the minor to show that she was sufficiently mature to make the decision, or if not, to show that abortion was in her best interest. It also ensured anonymity even though it required the minor to put her name on a form thus permitting unauthorized disclosure. Finally, the procedure was expeditious. The possibility that the statute could permit a 22-day delay was insufficient to sustain a facial challenge.

Justices Stevens and Scalia each filed concurring opinions. Justice Blackmun dissented, joined by Justices Brennan and Marshall.

(b) In *Ayotte v. Planned Parenthood of N. New England*, 546 U.S. 320 (2006), the Court refused to facially invalidate New Hampshire's parental notification statute. Writing for a unanimous Court, Justice O'Connor stated that facial invalidation was not warranted simply because the statute did not contain a medical emergency exception. Justice O'Connor outlined established propositions, the first two legal and the third factual. First, states may require parental involvement in a minor's decision to terminate a pregnancy. Second, states may not restrict abortions that are necessary to preserve the life or health of the mother. Third, minors, like adults, may need immediate abortions to avoid serious health problems.

To remedy the statute's failure to provide a medical emergency exception, courts may either enjoin unconstitutional applications of the statute or sever that part of the statute. Courts should avoid invalidating any more of the statute than necessary. Moreover, courts may not rewrite statutes to remedy constitutional problems. Lastly, courts must determine whether a legislature would prefer to retain the remaining constitutional portion of the statute or to have the entire statute invalidated. The New Hampshire statute was only invalid in a few applications. Although the Act contains a severability clause, the Court remanded the case to determine whether the legislature would have intended total invalidation if the unconstitutional applications were enjoined.

GONZALES v. CARHART
127 S. Ct. 1610, 167 L. Ed. 2d 480 (2007)

JUSTICE KENNEDY delivered the opinion of the Court.

These cases require us to consider the validity of the Partial-Birth Abortion Ban Act of 2003 (Act), 18 U.S.C. § 1531 (2000 ed., Supp. IV), a federal statute regulating abortion procedures. In recitations preceding its operative provisions the Act refers to the Court's opinion in *Stenberg v. Carhart*, 530 U.S. 914 (2000), which also addressed the subject of abortion procedures used in the later stages of pregnancy. Compared to the state statute at issue in *Stenberg*, the Act is more specific concerning the instances to which it applies and in this respect more precise in its coverage. We conclude the Act should be sustained against the objections lodged by the broad, facial attack brought against it.[32] . . .

I

A

The Act proscribes a particular manner of ending fetal life, so it is necessary here, as it was in *Stenberg*, to discuss abortion procedures in some detail. . . . We refer to the District Courts' exhaustive opinions in our own discussion of abortion procedures.

Abortion methods vary depending to some extent on the preferences of the physician and, of course, on the term of the pregnancy and the resulting stage of the unborn child's development. Between 85 and 90 percent of the approximately 1.3 million abortions performed each year in the United States take place in the first three months of pregnancy, which is to say in the first trimester. The most common first-trimester abortion method is vacuum aspiration (otherwise known as suction curettage) in which the physician vacuums out the embryonic tissue. Early in this trimester an alternative is to use medication, such as mifepristone (commonly known as RU-486), to terminate the pregnancy. The Act does not regulate these procedures.

Of the remaining abortions that take place each year, most occur in the second trimester. The surgical procedure referred to as "dilation and evacuation" or "D&E" is the usual abortion method in this trimester. Although individual techniques for performing D&E differ, the general steps are the same.

A doctor must first dilate the cervix at least to the extent needed to insert surgical instruments into the uterus and to maneuver them to evacuate the fetus. . . . Some may keep dilators in the cervix for two days, while others use dilators for a day or less.

After sufficient dilation the surgical operation can commence. The woman is placed under general anesthesia or conscious sedation. The doctor, often guided by ultrasound, inserts grasping forceps through the woman's cervix and into the uterus to grab the fetus. The doctor grips a fetal part with the forceps and pulls it back through the cervix and vagina, continuing to pull even after meeting resistance from the cervix. The friction causes the fetus to tear apart. For example, a leg might be ripped off the fetus as it is pulled through the cervix and out of the woman. The process of evacuating the fetus piece by piece continues until it has been completely removed. A doctor may make 10 to 15 passes with the forceps to evacuate the fetus in its entirety, though sometimes removal is completed with fewer passes. Once the fetus has been evacuated, the placenta and any remaining fetal material are suctioned or scraped out of the uterus. The doctor examines the different parts to ensure the entire fetal body has been removed.

Some doctors, especially later in the second trimester, may kill the fetus a day or two before performing the surgical evacuation. They inject digoxin or potassium chloride into the fetus, the umbilical cord, or the amniotic fluid. Fetal demise may cause contractions and make greater dilation possible. Once dead, moreover, the fetus' body will soften, and its removal will be easier. Other doctors refrain from injecting chemical agents, believing it adds risk with little or no medical benefit.

The abortion procedure that was the impetus for the numerous bans on "partial-birth abortion," including the Act, is a variation of this standard D&E. The medical

---

[32] The Second, Eighth, and Ninth Circuits had struck down the Act. Only the decisions of the Eighth and Ninth Circuits were at issue in this case.

community has not reached unanimity on the appropriate name for this D&E variation. It has been referred to as "intact D&E," "dilation and extraction" (D&X), and "intact D&X." . . . For discussion purposes this D&E variation will be referred to as intact D&E. The main difference between the two procedures is that in intact D&E a doctor extracts the fetus intact or largely intact with only a few passes. . . .

Intact D&E, like regular D&E, begins with dilation of the cervix. Sufficient dilation is essential for the procedure. To achieve intact extraction some doctors thus may attempt to dilate the cervix to a greater degree. . . .

In an intact D&E procedure the doctor extracts the fetus in a way conducive to pulling out its entire body, instead of ripping it apart. One doctor, for example, testified:

> If I know I have good dilation and I reach in and the fetus starts to come out and I think I can accomplish it, the abortion with an intact delivery, then I use my forceps a little bit differently. I don't close them quite so much, and I just gently draw the tissue out attempting to have an intact delivery, if possible.

Rotating the fetus as it is being pulled decreases the odds of dismemberment. A doctor also "may use forceps to grasp a fetal part, pull it down, and re-grasp the fetus at a higher level — sometimes using both his hand and a forceps — to exert traction to retrieve the fetus intact until the head is lodged in the [cervix]."

Intact D&E gained public notoriety when, in 1992, Dr. Martin Haskell gave a presentation describing his method of performing the operation. In the usual intact D&E the fetus' head lodges in the cervix, and dilation is insufficient to allow it to pass. Haskell explained the next step as follows:

> At this point, the right-handed surgeon slides the fingers of the left [hand] along the back of the fetus and "hooks" the shoulders of the fetus with the index and ring fingers (palm down).

> While maintaining this tension, lifting the cervix and applying traction to the shoulders with the fingers of the left hand, the surgeon takes a pair of blunt curved Metzenbaum scissors in the right hand. He carefully advances the tip, curved down, along the spine and under his middle finger until he feels it contact the base of the skull under the tip of his middle finger.

> The surgeon then forces the scissors into the base of the skull or into the foramen magnum. Having safely entered the skull, he spreads the scissors to enlarge the opening.

> The surgeon removes the scissors and introduces a suction catheter into this hole and evacuates the skull contents. With the catheter still in place, he applies traction to the fetus, removing it completely from the patient.

This is an abortion doctor's clinical description. Here is another description from a nurse who witnessed the same method performed on a 26-week fetus and who testified before the Senate Judiciary Committee:

> Dr. Haskell went in with forceps and grabbed the baby's legs and pulled them down into the birth canal. Then he delivered the baby's body and the arms — everything but the head. The doctor kept the head right inside the uterus. . . .

> The baby's little fingers were clasping and unclasping, and his little feet were kicking. Then the doctor stuck the scissors in the back of his head, and the baby's arms jerked out, like a startle reaction, like a flinch, like a baby does when he thinks he is going to fall.

> The doctor opened up the scissors, stuck a high-powered suction tube into the opening, and sucked the baby's brains out. Now the baby went completely limp. . . .

He cut the umbilical cord and delivered the placenta. He threw the baby in a pan, along with the placenta and the instruments he had just used.

Dr. Haskell's approach is not the only method of killing the fetus once its head lodges in the cervix, and "the process has evolved" since his presentation. Another doctor, for example, squeezes the skull after it has been pierced "so that enough brain tissue exudes to allow the head to pass through." Still other physicians reach into the cervix with their forceps and crush the fetus' skull. Others continue to pull the fetus out of the woman until it disarticulates at the neck, in effect decapitating it. These doctors then grasp the head with forceps, crush it, and remove it.

Some doctors performing an intact D&E attempt to remove the fetus without collapsing the skull. Yet one doctor would not allow delivery of a live fetus younger than 24 weeks because "the objective of [his] procedure is to perform an abortion," not a birth. The doctor thus answered in the affirmative when asked whether he would "hold the fetus' head on the internal side of the [cervix] in order to collapse the skull" and kill the fetus before it is born. Another doctor testified he crushes a fetus' skull not only to reduce its size but also to ensure the fetus is dead before it is removed. For the staff to have to deal with a fetus that has "some viability to it, some movement of limbs," according to this doctor, "[is] always a difficult situation."

D&E and intact D&E are not the only second-trimester abortion methods. Doctors also may abort a fetus through medical induction. The doctor medicates the woman to induce labor, and contractions occur to deliver the fetus. Induction, which unlike D&E should occur in a hospital, can last as little as 6 hours but can take longer than 48. It accounts for about five percent of second-trimester abortions before 20 weeks of gestation and 15 percent of those after 20 weeks. Doctors turn to two other methods of second-trimester abortion, hysterotomy and hysterectomy, only in emergency situations because they carry increased risk of complications. In a hysterotomy, as in a cesarean section, the doctor removes the fetus by making an incision through the abdomen and uterine wall to gain access to the uterine cavity. A hysterectomy requires the removal of the entire uterus. These two procedures represent about .07% of second-trimester abortions.

B

After Dr. Haskell's procedure received public attention, with ensuing and increasing public concern, bans on " 'partial birth abortion' " proliferated. By the time of the *Stenberg* decision, about 30 States had enacted bans designed to prohibit the procedure. In 1996, Congress also acted to ban partial-birth abortion. President Clinton vetoed the congressional legislation, and the Senate failed to override the veto. Congress approved another bill banning the procedure in 1997, but President Clinton again vetoed it. In 2003, after this Court's decision in *Stenberg*, Congress passed the Act at issue here. On November 5, 2003, President Bush signed the Act into law. . . .

The Act responded to *Stenberg* in two ways. First, Congress made factual findings. Congress determined that this Court in *Stenberg* "was required to accept the very questionable findings issued by the district court judge," but that Congress was "not bound to accept the same factual findings." Congress found, among other things, that "[a] moral, medical, and ethical consensus exists that the practice of performing a partial-birth abortion . . . is a gruesome and inhumane procedure that is never medically necessary and should be prohibited."

Second, and more relevant here, the Act's language differs from that of the Nebraska statute struck down in *Stenberg*. . . .

II

. . . *Casey* [*Planned Parenthood of Southeastern Pa. v. Casey*, 505 U.S. 833 (1992)] involved a challenge to *Roe v. Wade*, 410 U.S. 113 (1973). The opinion contains this summary:

> It must be stated at the outset and with clarity that *Roe's* essential holding, the holding we reaffirm, has three parts. First is a recognition of the right of the woman to choose to have an abortion before viability and to obtain it without undue interference from the State. Before viability, the State's interests are not strong enough to support a prohibition of abortion or the imposition of a substantial obstacle to the woman's effective right to elect the procedure. Second is a confirmation of the State's power to restrict abortions after fetal viability, if the law contains exceptions for pregnancies which endanger the woman's life or health. And third is the principle that the State has legitimate interests from the outset of the pregnancy in protecting the health of the woman and the life of the fetus that may become a child. These principles do not contradict one another; and we adhere to each.

. . . [W]e must determine whether the Act furthers the legitimate interest of the Government in protecting the life of the fetus that may become a child.

To implement its holding, *Casey* rejected both *Roe's* rigid trimester framework and the interpretation of *Roe* that considered all previability regulations of abortion unwarranted. . . .

We assume the following principles for the purposes of this opinion. Before viability . . . "regulations which do no more than create a structural mechanism by which the State, or the parent or guardian of a minor, may express profound respect for the life of the unborn are permitted, if they are not a substantial obstacle to the woman's exercise of the right to choose." *Casey*, in short, struck a balance. The balance was central to its holding. . . .

III

We begin with a determination of the Act's operation and effect. A straightforward reading of the Act's text demonstrates its purpose and the scope of its provisions: It regulates and proscribes, with exceptions or qualifications to be discussed, performing the intact D&E procedure.

Respondents agree the Act encompasses intact D&E, but they contend its additional reach is both unclear and excessive. Respondents assert that, at the least, the Act is void for vagueness because its scope is indefinite. In the alternative, respondents argue the Act's text proscribes all D&Es. Because D&E is the most common second-trimester abortion method, respondents suggest the Act imposes an undue burden. In this litigation the Attorney General does not dispute that the Act would impose an undue burden if it covered standard D&E.

We conclude that the Act is not void for vagueness, does not impose an undue burden from any overbreadth, and is not invalid on its face.

A

The Act punishes "knowingly performing" a "partial-birth abortion." It defines the unlawful abortion in explicit terms.

First, the person performing the abortion must "vaginally deliver a living fetus." The Act does not restrict an abortion procedure involving the delivery of an expired fetus.

The Act, furthermore, is inapplicable to abortions that do not involve vaginal delivery (for instance, hysterotomy or hysterectomy). The Act does apply both previability and postviability because, by common understanding and scientific terminology, a fetus is a living organism while within the womb, whether or not it is viable outside the womb. We do not understand this point to be contested by the parties.

Second, the Act's definition of partial-birth abortion requires the fetus to be delivered "until, in the case of a head-first presentation, the entire fetal head is outside the body of the mother, or, in the case of breech presentation, any part of the fetal trunk past the navel is outside the body of the mother." The Attorney General concedes, and we agree, that if an abortion procedure does not involve the delivery of a living fetus to one of these "anatomical 'landmarks' " — where, depending on the presentation, either the fetal head or the fetal trunk past the navel is outside the body of the mother — the prohibitions of the Act do not apply.

Third, to fall within the Act, a doctor must perform an "overt act, other than completion of delivery, that kills the partially delivered living fetus." For purposes of criminal liability, the overt act causing the fetus' death must be separate from delivery. And the overt act must occur after the delivery to an anatomical landmark. . . .

Fourth, the Act contains scienter requirements concerning all the actions involved in the prohibited abortion. To begin with, the physician must have "deliberately and intentionally" delivered the fetus to one of the Act's anatomical landmarks. If a living fetus is delivered past the critical point by accident or inadvertence, the Act is inapplicable. In addition, the fetus must have been delivered "for the purpose of performing an overt act that the [doctor] knows will kill [it]." If either intent is absent, no crime has occurred. . . .

B

. . . "As generally stated, the void-for-vagueness doctrine requires that a penal statute define the criminal offense with sufficient definiteness that ordinary people can understand what conduct is prohibited and in a manner that does not encourage arbitrary and discriminatory enforcement." *Kolender v. Lawson*, 461 U.S. 352, 357 (1983); *Posters 'N' Things, Ltd. v. United States*, 511 U.S. 513, 525 (1994). The Act satisfies both requirements.

The Act provides doctors "of ordinary intelligence a reasonable opportunity to know what is prohibited." *Grayned v. City of Rockford*, 408 U.S. 104 (1972). Indeed, it sets forth "relatively clear guidelines as to prohibited conduct" and provides "objective criteria" to evaluate whether a doctor has performed a prohibited procedure. *Posters 'N' Things, supra*, at 525-526. Unlike the statutory language in *Stenberg* that prohibited the delivery of a " 'substantial portion' " of the fetus — where a doctor might question how much of the fetus is a substantial portion — the Act defines the line between potentially criminal conduct on the one hand and lawful abortion on the other. *Stenberg*, 530 U.S., at 922. Doctors performing D&E will know that if they do not deliver a living fetus to an anatomical landmark they will not face criminal liability.

This conclusion is buttressed by the intent that must be proved to impose liability. The Court has made clear that scienter requirements alleviate vagueness concerns. . . . The Act requires the doctor deliberately to have delivered the fetus to an anatomical landmark. Because a doctor performing a D&E will not face criminal liability if he or she delivers a fetus beyond the prohibited point by mistake, the Act cannot be described as "a trap for those who act in good faith." *Colautti [v. Franklin*, 439 U.S. 379, 395 (1979)].

Respondents likewise have failed to show that the Act should be invalidated on its face because it encourages arbitrary or discriminatory enforcement. Just as the Act's anatomical landmarks provide doctors with objective standards, they also "establish minimal guidelines to govern law enforcement." *Smith v. Goguen*, 415 U.S. 566, 574 (1974). The scienter requirements narrow the scope of the Act's prohibition and limit prosecutorial discretion. . . . Respondents' arguments concerning arbitrary enforcement, furthermore, are somewhat speculative. This is a preenforcement challenge, where "no evidence has been, or could be, introduced to indicate whether the [Act] has been enforced in a discriminatory manner or with the aim of inhibiting [constitutionally protected conduct]." *Hoffman Estates v. Flipside, Hoffman Estates, Inc.*, 455 U.S. 489 (1982). The Act is not vague.

C

We next determine whether the Act imposes an undue burden, as a facial matter, because its restrictions on second-trimester abortions are too broad. A review of the statutory text discloses the limits of its reach. The Act prohibits intact D&E; and, notwithstanding respondents' arguments, it does not prohibit the D&E procedure in which the fetus is removed in parts.

1

The Act prohibits a doctor from intentionally performing an intact D&E. The dual prohibitions of the Act, both of which are necessary for criminal liability, correspond with the steps generally undertaken during this type of procedure. First, a doctor delivers the fetus until its head lodges in the cervix, which is usually past the anatomical landmark for a breech presentation. Second, the doctor proceeds to pierce the fetal skull with scissors or crush it with forceps. This step satisfies the overt-act requirement because it kills the fetus and is distinct from delivery. The Act's intent requirements, however, limit its reach to those physicians who carry out the intact D&E after intending to undertake both steps at the outset.

The Act excludes most D&Es in which the fetus is removed in pieces, not intact. If the doctor intends to remove the fetus in parts from the outset, the doctor will not have the requisite intent to incur criminal liability. A doctor performing a standard D&E procedure can often "take about 10-15 'passes' through the uterus to remove the entire fetus." Removing the fetus in this manner does not violate the Act because the doctor will not have delivered the living fetus to one of the anatomical landmarks or committed an additional overt act that kills the fetus after partial delivery.

A comparison of the Act with the Nebraska statute struck down in *Stenberg* confirms this point. The statute in *Stenberg* prohibited " 'deliberately and intentionally delivering into the vagina a living unborn child, or a substantial portion thereof, for the purpose of performing a procedure that the person performing such procedure knows will kill the unborn child and does kill the unborn child.' " The Court concluded that this statute encompassed D&E because "D&E will often involve a physician pulling a 'substantial portion' of a still living fetus, say, an arm or leg, into the vagina prior to the death of the fetus." . . .

Congress, it is apparent, responded to these concerns because the Act departs in material ways from the statute in *Stenberg*. It adopts the phrase "delivers a living fetus," instead of " 'delivering . . . a living unborn child, or a substantial portion thereof.' " The Act's language, unlike the statute in *Stenberg*, expresses the usual meaning of "deliver" when used in connection with "fetus," namely, extraction of an entire fetus rather than removal of fetal pieces. . . . The Act thus displaces the interpretation of "delivering" dictated by the Nebraska statute's reference to a "substantial portion" of the fetus. . . . D&E does not involve the delivery of a fetus because it requires the removal of fetal parts that are ripped from the fetus as they are pulled through the cervix.

The identification of specific anatomical landmarks to which the fetus must be partially delivered also differentiates the Act from the statute at issue in *Stenberg*. The Court in *Stenberg* interpreted " 'substantial portion' " of the fetus to include an arm or a leg. The Act's anatomical landmarks, by contrast, clarify that the removal of a small portion of the fetus is not prohibited. The landmarks also require the fetus to be delivered so that it is partially "outside the body of the mother." To come within the ambit of the Nebraska statute, on the other hand, a substantial portion of the fetus only had to be delivered into the vagina; no part of the fetus had to be outside the body of the mother before a doctor could face criminal sanctions.

By adding an overt-act requirement Congress sought further to meet the Court's objections to the state statute considered in *Stenberg*. . . . The fatal overt act must occur after delivery to an anatomical landmark, and it must be something "other than [the] completion of delivery." This distinction matters because, unlike intact D&E, standard D&E does not involve a delivery followed by a fatal act.

The canon of constitutional avoidance, finally, extinguishes any lingering doubt as to whether the Act covers the prototypical D&E procedure. " 'The elementary rule is that every reasonable construction must be resorted to, in order to save a statute from unconstitutionality.' " *Edward J. DeBartolo Corp. v. Florida Gulf Coast Building & Constr. Trades Council*, 485 U.S. 568, 575 (1988) (quoting *Hooper v. California*, 155 U.S. 648, 657 (1895)). It is true this longstanding maxim of statutory interpretation has, in the past, fallen by the wayside when the Court confronted a statute regulating abortion. The Court at times employed an antagonistic " 'canon of construction under which in cases involving abortion, a permissible reading of a statute [was] to be avoided at all costs.' " *Casey* put this novel statutory approach to rest. In *Stenberg* the Court found the statute covered D&E. . . . Here, by contrast, interpreting the Act so that it does not prohibit standard D&E is the most reasonable reading and understanding of its terms.

2

. . . Respondents . . . contend — relying on the testimony of numerous abortion doctors — that D&E may result in the delivery of a living fetus beyond the Act's anatomical landmarks in a significant fraction of cases. . . .

This reasoning, however, does not take account of the Act's intent requirements, which preclude liability from attaching to an accidental intact D&E. . . .

The evidence also supports a legislative determination that an intact delivery is almost always a conscious choice rather than a happenstance. . . .

IV

Under the principles accepted as controlling here, the Act, as we have interpreted it, would be unconstitutional "if its purpose or effect is to place a substantial obstacle in the path of a woman seeking an abortion before the fetus attains viability." The abortions affected by the Act's regulations take place both previability and postviability; so the quoted language and the undue burden analysis it relies upon are applicable. The question is whether the Act, measured by its text in this facial attack, imposes a substantial obstacle to late-term, but previability, abortions. The Act does not on its face impose a substantial obstacle, and we reject this further facial challenge to its validity.

A

. . . The Act proscribes a method of abortion in which a fetus is killed just inches before completion of the birth process. Congress stated as follows: "Implicitly approving such a brutal and inhumane procedure by choosing not to prohibit it will further coarsen society to the humanity of not only newborns, but all vulnerable and innocent human life, making it increasingly difficult to protect such life." The Act expresses respect for the dignity of human life.

Congress was concerned, furthermore, with the effects on the medical community and on its reputation caused by the practice of partial-birth abortion. The findings in the Act explain:

> Partial-birth abortion . . . confuses the medical, legal, and ethical duties of physicians to preserve and promote life, as the physician acts directly against the physical life of a child, whom he or she had just delivered, all but the head, out of the womb, in order to end that life.

There can be no doubt the government "has an interest in protecting the integrity and ethics of the medical profession." *Washington v. Glucksberg*, 521 U.S. 702, 731 (1997). . . . Under our precedents it is clear the State has a significant role to play in regulating the medical profession.

Casey reaffirmed these governmental objectives. The government may use its voice and its regulatory authority to show its profound respect for the life within the woman. A central premise of the opinion was that the Court's precedents after *Roe* had "undervalued the State's interest in potential life." The plurality opinion indicated "the fact that a law which serves a valid purpose, one not designed to strike at the right itself, has the incidental effect of making it more difficult or more expensive to procure an abortion cannot be enough to invalidate it." This was not an idle assertion. The three premises of *Casey* must coexist. The third premise, that the State, from the inception of the pregnancy, maintains its own regulatory interest in protecting the life of the fetus that may become a child, cannot be set at naught by interpreting *Casey's* requirement of a health exception so it becomes tantamount to allowing a doctor to choose the abortion method he or she might prefer. Where it has a rational basis to act, and it does not impose an undue burden, the State may use its regulatory power to bar certain procedures and substitute others, all in furtherance of its legitimate interests in regulating the medical profession in order to promote respect for life, including life of the unborn.

The Act's ban on abortions that involve partial delivery of a living fetus furthers the Government's objectives. No one would dispute that, for many, D&E is a procedure itself laden with the power to devalue human life. Congress could nonetheless conclude that the type of abortion proscribed by the Act requires specific regulation because it implicates additional ethical and moral concerns that justify a special prohibition. Congress determined that the abortion methods it proscribed had a "disturbing similarity to the killing of a newborn infant," and thus it was concerned with "drawing a bright line that clearly distinguishes abortion and infanticide." The Court has in the past confirmed the validity of drawing boundaries to prevent certain practices that extinguish life and are close to actions that are condemned. *Glucksberg* found reasonable the State's "fear that permitting assisted suicide will start it down the path to voluntary and perhaps even involuntary euthanasia."

Respect for human life finds an ultimate expression in the bond of love the mother has for her child. The Act recognizes this reality as well. Whether to have an abortion requires a difficult and painful moral decision. While we find no reliable data to measure the phenomenon, it seems unexceptionable to conclude some women come to regret their choice to abort the infant life they once created and sustained. Severe depression and loss of esteem can follow.

In a decision so fraught with emotional consequence some doctors may prefer not to disclose precise details of the means that will be used, confining themselves to the required statement of risks the procedure entails. . . . *See, e.g., Nat. Abortion Federation* [*v. Ashcroft*], 330 F. Supp. 2d 436, 466, n.22 (2004) ("Most of [the plaintiffs'] experts acknowledged that they do not describe to their patients what [the D&E and intact D&E] procedures entail in clear and precise terms"); *see also id.*, at 479.

It is, however, precisely this lack of information concerning the way in which the fetus will be killed that is of legitimate concern to the State. *Casey, supra,* at 873 (plurality opinion) ("States are free to enact laws to provide a reasonable framework for a woman to make a decision that has such profound and lasting meaning"). The State has an interest in ensuring so grave a choice is well informed. It is self-evident that a mother who comes to regret her choice to abort must struggle with grief more anguished and sorrow more profound when she learns, only after the event, what she once did not know that she allowed a doctor to pierce the skull and vacuum the fast-developing brain of her unborn child, a child assuming the human form.

It is a reasonable inference that a necessary effect of the regulation and the knowledge it conveys will be to encourage some women to carry the infant to full term, thus reducing the absolute number of late-term abortions. The medical profession, furthermore, may find different and less shocking methods to abort the fetus in the second trimester, thereby accommodating legislative demand. The State's interest in respect for life is advanced by the dialogue that better informs the political and legal systems, the medical profession, expectant mothers, and society as a whole of the consequences that follow from a decision to elect a late-term abortion.

It is objected that the standard D&E is in some respects as brutal, if not more, than the intact D&E, so that the legislation accomplishes little. . . . It was reasonable for Congress to think that partial-birth abortion, more than standard D&E, "undermines the public's perception of the appropriate role of a physician during the delivery process, and perverts a process during which life is brought into the world." There would be a flaw in this Court's logic, and an irony in its jurisprudence, were we first to conclude a ban on both D&E and intact D&E was overbroad and then to say it is irrational to ban only intact D&E because that does not proscribe both procedures. In sum, we reject the contention that the congressional purpose of the Act was "to place a substantial obstacle in the path of a woman seeking an abortion."

B

The Act's furtherance of legitimate government interests bears upon, but does not resolve, the next question: whether the Act has the effect of imposing an unconstitutional burden on the abortion right because it does not allow use of the barred procedure where " 'necessary, in appropriate medical judgment, for [the] preservation of the . . . health of the mother.' " *Ayotte v. Planned Parenthood of Northern New England*, 546 U.S. 320, 327-328 (2006) (quoting *Casey, supra,* at 879 (plurality opinion)). The prohibition in the Act would be unconstitutional, under precedents we here assume to be controlling, if it "subjected [women] to significant health risks." . . . [W]hether the Act creates significant health risks for women has been a contested factual question. The evidence presented in the trial courts and before Congress demonstrates both sides have medical support for their position.

Respondents presented evidence that intact D&E may be the safest method of abortion, for reasons similar to those adduced in *Stenberg*. Abortion doctors testified, for example, that intact D&E decreases the risk of cervical laceration or uterine perforation because it requires fewer passes into the uterus with surgical instruments and does not require the removal of bony fragments of the dismembered fetus, fragments that may be sharp. Respondents also presented evidence that intact D&E was safer both because it reduces the risks that fetal parts will remain in the uterus and because it takes less time to complete. Respondents, in addition, proffered evidence that intact D&E was safer for women with certain medical conditions or women with fetuses that had certain anomalies.

These contentions were contradicted by other doctors who testified in the District Courts and before Congress. They concluded that the alleged health advantages were based on speculation without scientific studies to support them. They considered D&E always to be a safe alternative.

There is documented medical disagreement whether the Act's prohibition would ever impose significant health risks on women. *See, e.g., Planned Parenthood*, 320 F. Supp. 2d, at 1033 ("There continues to be a division of opinion among highly qualified experts regarding the necessity or safety of intact D & E"). The three District Courts that considered the Act's constitutionality appeared to be in some disagreement on this central factual question. . . .

The question becomes whether the Act can stand when this medical uncertainty persists. The Court's precedents instruct that the Act can survive this facial attack. The Court has given state and federal legislatures wide discretion to pass legislation in areas where there is medical and scientific uncertainty. *See . . . Marshall v. United States*, 414 U.S. 417, 427 (1974) ("When Congress undertakes to act in areas fraught with medical and scientific uncertainties, legislative options must be especially broad").

This traditional rule is consistent with *Casey*, which confirms the State's interest in promoting respect for human life at all stages in the pregnancy. Physicians are not entitled to ignore regulations that direct them to use reasonable alternative procedures. The law need not give abortion doctors unfettered choice in the course of their medical practice, nor should it elevate their status above other physicians in the medical community. In *Casey* the controlling opinion held an informed-consent requirement in the abortion context was "no different from a requirement that a doctor give certain specific information about any medical procedure." The opinion stated "the doctor-patient relation here is entitled to the same solicitude it receives in other contexts."

Medical uncertainty does not foreclose the exercise of legislative power in the abortion context any more than it does in other contexts. The medical uncertainty over whether the Act's prohibition creates significant health risks provides a sufficient basis to conclude in this facial attack that the Act does not impose an undue burden.

The conclusion that the Act does not impose an undue burden is supported by other considerations. Alternatives are available to the prohibited procedure. As we have noted, the Act does not proscribe D&E. One District Court found D&E to have extremely low rates of medical complications. Another indicated D&E was "generally the safest method of abortion during the second trimester." *Carhart [v. Ashcroft]*, 331 F. Supp. 2d 805, 1031 (2004); *see also Nat. Abortion Federation, supra*, at 467-468 (explaining that "experts testifying for both sides" agreed D&E was safe). In addition the Act's prohibition only applies to the delivery of "a living fetus." If the intact D&E procedure is truly necessary in some circumstances, it appears likely an injection that kills the fetus is an alternative under the Act that allows the doctor to perform the procedure. . . .

In reaching the conclusion the Act does not require a health exception we reject certain arguments made by the parties on both sides of these cases. On the one hand, the Attorney General urges us to uphold the Act on the basis of the congressional findings alone. Although we review congressional factfinding under a deferential standard, we do not in the circumstances here place dispositive weight on Congress' findings. The Court retains an independent constitutional duty to review factual findings where constitutional rights are at stake. . . .

Uncritical deference to Congress' factual findings in these cases is inappropriate.

On the other hand, relying on the Court's opinion in *Stenberg*, respondents contend that an abortion regulation must contain a health exception "if 'substantial medical authority supports the proposition that banning a particular procedure could endanger women's health.' " As illustrated by respondents' arguments and the decisions of the Courts of Appeals, *Stenberg* has been interpreted to leave no margin of error for legislatures to act in the face of medical uncertainty. . . .

A zero tolerance policy would strike down legitimate abortion regulations, like the present one, if some part of the medical community were disinclined to follow the proscription. This is too exacting a standard to impose on the legislative power, exercised in this instance under the Commerce Clause, to regulate the medical profession. Considerations of marginal safety, including the balance of risks, are within the legislative competence when the regulation is rational and in pursuit of legitimate ends. When standard medical options are available, mere convenience does not suffice to displace them; and if some procedures have different risks than others, it does not follow that the State is altogether barred from imposing reasonable regulations. The Act is not invalid on its face where there is uncertainty over whether the barred procedure is ever necessary to preserve a woman's health, given the availability of other abortion procedures that are considered to be safe alternatives.

V

The considerations we have discussed support our further determination that these facial attacks should not have been entertained in the first instance. In these circumstances the proper means to consider exceptions is by as-applied challenge. This is the proper manner to protect the health of the woman if it can be shown that in discrete and well-defined instances a particular condition has or is likely to occur in which the procedure prohibited by the Act must be used. In an as-applied challenge the nature of the medical risk can be better quantified and balanced than in a facial attack.

The latitude given facial challenges in the First Amendment context is inapplicable here. Broad challenges of this type impose "a heavy burden" upon the parties maintaining the suit. *Rust v. Sullivan*, 500 U.S. 173, 183 (1991). What that burden consists of in the specific context of abortion statutes has been a subject of some question. *Compare Ohio v. Akron Center for Reproductive Health*, 497 U.S. 502, 514 (1990) ("Because appellees are making a facial challenge to a statute, they must show that no set of circumstances exists under which the Act would be valid"), *with Casey*, 505 U.S., at 895 (opinion of the Court) (indicating a spousal-notification statute would impose an undue burden "in a large fraction of the cases in which [it] is relevant" and holding the statutory provision facially invalid). We need not resolve that debate.

As the previous sections of this opinion explain, respondents have not demonstrated that the Act would be unconstitutional in a large fraction of relevant cases.

The Act is open to a proper as-applied challenge in a discrete case. No as-applied challenge need be brought if the prohibition in the Act threatens a woman's life because the Act already contains a life exception.

Respondents have not demonstrated that the Act, as a facial matter, is void for vagueness, or that it imposes an undue burden on a woman's right to abortion based on its overbreadth or lack of a health exception. . . .

JUSTICE THOMAS, with whom JUSTICE SCALIA joins, concurring.

I join the Court's opinion because it accurately applies current jurisprudence, including *Planned Parenthood of Southeastern Pa. v. Casey*, I write separately to reiterate my view that the Court's abortion jurisprudence, including *Casey* and *Roe v. Wade*, has no basis in the Constitution. I also note that whether the Act constitutes a permissible exercise of Congress' power under the Commerce Clause is not before the Court. The parties did not raise or brief that issue; it is outside the question presented; and the lower courts did not address it.

JUSTICE GINSBURG, with whom JUSTICE STEVENS, JUSTICE SOUTER, and JUSTICE BREYER join, dissenting.

In *Planned Parenthood of Southeastern Pa. v. Casey*, the Court declared that "liberty finds no refuge in a jurisprudence of doubt.". . .

Of signal importance here, the *Casey* Court stated with unmistakable clarity that state regulation of access to abortion procedures, even after viability, must protect "the health of the woman."

Today's decision is alarming. It refuses to take *Casey* and *Stenberg* seriously. It tolerates, indeed applauds, federal intervention to ban nationwide a procedure found necessary and proper in certain cases by the American College of Obstetricians and Gynecologists (ACOG). It blurs the line, firmly drawn in *Casey*, between previability and postviability abortions. And, for the first time since *Roe*, the Court blesses a prohibition with no exception safeguarding a woman's health.

[T]he Court upholds an Act that surely would not survive under the close scrutiny that previously attended state-decreed limitations on a woman's reproductive choices.

I

A

As *Casey* comprehended, at stake in cases challenging abortion restrictions is a woman's "control over her [own] destiny." *See also id.* at 852 (majority opinion). "There was a time, not so long ago," when women were "regarded as the center of home and family life, with attendant special responsibilities that precluded full and independent legal status under the Constitution.". . .   Thus, legal challenges to undue restrictions on abortion procedures do not seek to vindicate some generalized notion of privacy; rather, they center on a woman's autonomy to determine her life's course, and thus to enjoy equal citizenship stature.

Planned Parenthood of Southeastern Pa. v. Casey, described more precisely than did *Roe v. Wade*, the impact of abortion restrictions on women's liberty. *Roe's* focus was in considerable measure on "vindicating the right of the physician to administer medical treatment according to his professional judgment."

We have thus ruled that a State must avoid subjecting women to health risks not only where the pregnancy itself creates danger, but also where state regulation forces women to resort to less safe methods of abortion. . . .

Dilation and evacuation (D&E) is the most frequently used abortion procedure during the second trimester of pregnancy; intact D&E is a variant of the D&E procedure. . . . Between 85 and 90 percent of all abortions performed in the United States take place during the first three months of pregnancy. . . .

Minors may be unaware they are pregnant until relatively late in pregnancy, while poor women's financial constraints are an obstacle to timely receipt of services. . . . Severe fetal anomalies and health problems confronting the pregnant woman are also causes of second-trimester abortions; many such conditions cannot be diagnosed or do not develop until the second trimester. . . .

In *Stenberg*, . . . we made clear that as long as "substantial medical authority supports the proposition that banning a particular abortion procedure could endanger women's health," a health exception is required. We explained: "The word 'necessary' in *Casey's* phrase 'necessary, in appropriate medical judgment, for the preservation of the life or health of the [pregnant woman],' cannot refer to an absolute necessity or to absolute proof. Medical treatments and procedures are often considered appropriate (or inappropriate) in light of estimated comparative health risks (and health benefits) in particular cases. . . *Casey's* words 'appropriate medical judgment' must embody the judicial need to tolerate responsible differences of medical opinion. . . . "

Thus, we reasoned, division in medical opinion "at most means uncertainty, a factor that signals the presence of risk, not its absence." "[A] statute that altogether forbids [intact D&E] . . . consequently must contain a health exception."

B

. . . Congress claimed there was a medical consensus that the banned procedure is never necessary. But the evidence "very clearly demonstrated the opposite."

Similarly, Congress found that "there is no credible medical evidence that partial-birth abortions are safe or are safer than other abortion procedures." But the congressional record includes letters from numerous individual physicians stating that pregnant women's health would be jeopardized under the Act, as well as statements from nine professional associations, including ACOG, the American Public Health Association, and the California Medical Association, attesting that intact D&E carries meaningful safety advantages over other methods. . . . No comparable medical groups supported the ban. . . .

C

. . . During the District Court trials, "numerous" "extraordinarily accomplished" and "very experienced" medical experts explained that, in certain circumstances and for certain women, intact D&E is safer than alternative procedures and necessary to protect women's health. . . .

According to the expert testimony plaintiffs introduced, the safety advantages of intact D&E are marked for women with certain medical conditions, for example, uterine scarring, bleeding disorders, heart disease, or compromised immune systems. Further, plaintiffs' experts testified that intact D&E is significantly safer for women with certain pregnancy-related conditions, such as placenta previa and accreta, and for women carrying fetuses with certain abnormalities, such as severe hydrocephalus.

Intact D&E, plaintiffs' experts explained, provides safety benefits over D&E by dismemberment for several reasons: First, intact D&E minimizes the number of times a physician must insert instruments through the cervix and into the uterus, and thereby reduces the risk of trauma to, and perforation of, the cervix and uterus — the most serious complication associated with nonintact D&E. Second, removing the fetus intact, instead of dismembering it in utero, decreases the likelihood that fetal tissue will be retained in the uterus, a condition that can cause infection, hemorrhage, and infertility. Third, intact D&E diminishes the chances of exposing the patient's tissues to sharp bony fragments sometimes resulting from dismemberment of the fetus. Fourth, intact D&E takes less operating time than D&E by dismemberment, and thus may reduce bleeding, the risk of infection, and complications relating to anesthesia.

Based on thoroughgoing review of the trial evidence and the congressional record, each of the District Courts to consider the issue rejected Congress' findings as unreasonable and not supported by the evidence. . . .

The District Courts' findings merit this Court's respect. Nevertheless, despite the District Courts' appraisal of the weight of the evidence, and in undisguised conflict with *Stenberg*, the Court asserts that the Partial-Birth Abortion Ban Act can survive "when . . . medical uncertainty persists." This assertion is bewildering. Not only does it defy the Court's longstanding precedent affirming the necessity of a health exception, with no carve-out for circumstances of medical uncertainty; it gives short shrift to the records before us, carefully canvassed by the District Courts. . . .

II

A

. . . Today's ruling, the Court declares, advances "a premise central to [*Casey's*] conclusion" — i.e., the Government's "legitimate and substantial interest in preserving and promoting fetal life.". . . But the Act scarcely furthers that interest: The law saves not a single fetus from destruction, for it targets only a *method* of performing abortion. . . .

Nonintact D&E could equally be characterized as "brutal," *ante*, at 26, involving as it does "tearing [a fetus] apart" and "ripping off" its limbs. . . .

Delivery of an intact, albeit nonviable, fetus warrants special condemnation, the Court maintains, because a fetus that is not dismembered resembles an infant. *Ante*, at 28. But so, too, does a fetus delivered intact after it is terminated by injection a day or two before the surgical evacuation or a fetus delivered through medical induction or cesarean. . . .

Ultimately, the Court admits that "moral concerns" are at work, concerns that could yield prohibitions on any abortion. . . .

Revealing in this regard, the Court invokes an antiabortion shibboleth for which it concededly has no reliable evidence: Women who have abortions come to regret their choices, and consequently suffer from "severe depression and loss of esteem."[33]

This way of thinking reflects ancient notions about women's place in the family and under the Constitution — ideas that have long since been discredited. . . .

B

In cases on a "woman's liberty to determine whether to [continue] her pregnancy," this Court has identified viability as a critical consideration. . . .

Today, the Court blurs that line, maintaining that "the Act [legitimately] applies both previability and postviability because . . . a fetus is a living organism while within the womb, whether or not it is viable outside the womb." Instead of drawing the line at viability, the Court refers to Congress' purpose to differentiate "abortion and infanti-

---

[33] [Court's footnote 9] . . . When safe abortion procedures cease to be an option, many women seek other means to end unwanted or coerced pregnancies. *See*, e.g., World Health Organization, Unsafe Abortion: Global and Regional Estimates of the Incidence of Unsafe Abortion and Associated Mortality in 2000, pp. 3, 16 (4th ed. 2004) ("Restrictive legislation is associated with a high incidence of unsafe abortion" worldwide; unsafe abortion represents 13% of all "maternal" deaths); . . . H. Boonstra, R. Gold, C. Richards, & L. Finer, Abortion in Women's Lives 13, and fig. 2.2 (2006) ("as late as 1965, illegal abortion still accounted for an estimated . . . 17% of all officially reported pregnancy-related deaths"; "deaths from abortion declined dramatically after legalization").

cide" based not on whether a fetus can survive outside the womb, but on where a fetus is anatomically located when a particular medical procedure is performed. . . .

The Court's hostility to the right *Roe* and *Casey* secured is not concealed. Throughout, the opinion refers to obstetrician-gynecologists and surgeons who perform abortions not by the titles of their medical specialties, but by the pejorative label "abortion doctor." A fetus is described as an "unborn child," and as a "baby," second-trimester, previability abortions are referred to as "late-term," and the reasoned medical judgments of highly trained doctors are dismissed as "preferences" motivated by "mere convenience." Instead of the heightened scrutiny we have previously applied, the Court determines that a "rational" ground is enough to uphold the Act. And, most troubling, *Casey's* principles, confirming the continuing vitality of "the essential holding of *Roe*," are merely "assumed" for the moment, rather than "retained" or "reaffirmed."

III

A

The Court further confuses our jurisprudence when it declares that "facial attacks" are not permissible in "these circumstances," i.e., where medical uncertainty exists. . . .

Without attempting to distinguish *Stenberg* and earlier decisions, the majority asserts that the Act survives review because respondents have not shown that the ban on intact D&E would be unconstitutional "in a large fraction of relevant cases.". . . [A] provision restricting access to abortion, "must be judged by reference to those [women] for whom it is an actual rather than an irrelevant restriction." . . . It makes no sense to conclude that this facial challenge fails because respondents have not shown that a health exception is necessary for a large fraction of second-trimester abortions, including those for which a health exception is unnecessary: The very purpose of a health *exception* is to protect women in *exceptional* cases.

B

If there is anything at all redemptive to be said of today's opinion, it is that the Court is not willing to foreclose entirely a constitutional challenge to the Act. . . .

But it should not escape notice that the record already includes hundreds and hundreds of pages of testimony identifying "discrete and well-defined instances" in which recourse to an intact D&E would better protect the health of women with particular conditions. . . .

The Court's allowance only of an "as-applied challenge in a discrete case," jeopardizes women's health and places doctors in an untenable position. Even if courts were able to carve-out exceptions through piecemeal litigation for "discrete and well-defined instances," women whose circumstances have not been anticipated by prior litigation could well be left unprotected. In treating those women, physicians would risk criminal prosecution, conviction, and imprisonment if they exercise their best judgment as to the safest medical procedure for their patients. . . .

IV

. . ."The very concept of the rule of law underlying our own Constitution requires such continuity over time that a respect for precedent is, by definition, indispensable." . . .

Though today's opinion does not go so far as to discard *Roe* or *Casey*, the Court, differently composed than it was when we last considered a restrictive abortion regulation, is hardly faithful to our earlier invocations of "the rule of law" and the "principles of *stare decisis.*". . .

In sum, the notion that the Partial-Birth Abortion Ban Act furthers any legitimate governmental interest is, quite simply, irrational. . . . In candor, the Act, and the Court's defense of it, cannot be understood as anything other than an effort to chip away at a right declared again and again by this Court — and with increasing comprehension of its centrality to women's lives. . . .

NOTE

Comparative Perspectives. The question of legalized abortion is one that many other countries also have faced. For interesting comparative perspectives examining the issue of legalized abortion in other countries, see M. GLENDON, ABORTION AND DIVORCE IN WESTERN LAW (1987) (asserting that American abortion law is less protective of the fetus than the laws of Western European countries); Note, *The Law of Abortion in the Union of Soviet Socialist Republics and the People's Republic of China: Women's Rights in Two Socialist Countries*, 40 STAN. L. REV. 1027 (1988). In the former U.S.S.R., abortion was elective for the first 12 weeks and permitted for medical reasons thereafter. In the absence of contraception, it was the primary form of birth control. In the Russian republic itself, the ratio of abortions to births reached 2:1. In China, the state uses abortion as a form of population control and many women have been compelled to have abortions against their wills.

[2] The Family Relationship

ZABLOCKI v. REDHAIL, 434 U.S. 374 (1978). In *Zablocki*, the Court found unconstitutional a Wisconsin statute that enabled the State to prevent a person from marrying. The statute applied to a parent who was under an obligation to support his minor child even though the child was not in his custody. The State would only grant such a parent a marriage license if the parent could show compliance with the support obligation and demonstrate that the child would not become a charge of the State. The appellee had an illegitimate child for which a court had ordered that he pay $109 a month in support. Appellee was indigent and had not fulfilled the support obligation. Two years after the court order, appellee filed for a marriage license and was denied because he had not obtained a court order, pursuant to the statute, permitting him to marry.

The Court held that the law violated the Equal Protection Clause. Justice Marshall's opinion found the decision to marry to be fundamentally within a person's right to privacy: "It is not surprising that the decision to marry has been on the same level of importance as decisions relating to procreation, childbirth, child rearing, and family relationships. . . . [I]t would make little sense to recognize a right to privacy with respect to other matters of family life and not with respect to the decision to enter the relationship that is the foundation of the family in our society." Preventing a person from marrying did not advance the State's proposed goals of enforcing financial obligations and advancing the well-being of minors.

Chief Justice Burger wrote a brief concurring opinion. Justice Stewart also concurred. Justice Stewart thought that the case was properly examined using substantive due process rather than equal protection analysis. "I think that the Wisconsin statute is unconstitutional because it exceeds the bounds of permissible state regulation of marriage, and invades the sphere of liberty protected by the Due Process Clause of the Fourteenth Amendment." The State employed an "irrational means" of achieving its objective.

Justice Rehnquist dissented. He argued that the law passed the rationality test required by both the Due Process and Equal Protection Clauses.

TROXEL v. GRANVILLE, 530 U.S. 57 (2000). In *Troxel*, the Court invalidated a court order granting visitation rights to grandparents against a parent's will. Tommie Granville and Brad Troxel had a relationship that produced two daughters. They never married and their relationship ended in June of 1991. After the separation, Brad lived with his parents, Jenifer and Gary Troxel, until Brad committed suicide in 1993.

Under a Washington statute, the Troxels went to court and "requested two weekends of overnight visitation per month and two weeks of visitation each summer" with their granddaughters. The mother was willing to grant the grandparents "one day of visitation per month with no overnight stay." The trial court granted the Troxels "one weekend per month, one week during the summer, and four hours on both of the petitioning Grandparent's birthdays."

Writing for a plurality of four, Justice O'Connor noted the need for "nationwide enactment of nonparental visitation statutes."[34] The one at issue affects the liberty "interest of parents in the care, custody, and control of their children." Justice O'Connor noted that this interest is "perhaps the oldest of the fundamental liberty interests recognized by this Court," discussing *Meyer v. Nebraska*, 262 U.S. 390 (1923) and *Pierce v. Society of Sisters*, 268 U.S. 510 (1925). The Washington statute's "breathtakingly broad" language stated: " '[a]*ny person* may petition the court for visitation rights *at any time*,' and the court may grant such visitation rights whenever visitation may serve *the best interest of the child*."

No one alleged that Granville was an unfit parent. "The decisional framework employed by the Superior Court directly contravened the traditional presumption that a fit parent will act in the best interest of his or her child."[35] Moreover, the parent never "sought to cut off visitation entirely."

The plurality described the case as "nothing more than a simple disagreement between the Washington Superior Court and Granville concerning her children's best interests." The plurality found the statute unconstitutional as applied. "We do not, and need not, define today the precise scope of the parental due process right in the visitation context." Eschewing a broad test, the plurality said "any standard for awarding visitation turns on the specific manner in which the standard is applied." Justice O'Connor did not remand the case back to the Washington Supreme Court because cost of litigation was "already substantial" and it is "apparent that the entry of the visitation order in this case violated the Constitution."

Concurring in the judgment, Justice Souter would affirm the decision of the Supreme Court of Washington that invalidated the non-parental visitation statute on its face, as it authorized "courts to grant visitation rights to any person at any time." Justice Souter emphasized the parent's "interest in controlling a child's associates is as obvious as the influence of personal associations on the development of the child's social and moral character."

Concurring in the judgment, Justice Thomas stated that "recognition of a fundamental right of parents to direct the upbringing of their children resolves this

---

[34] Justice O'Connor noted " 'all 50 States have statutes that provide for grandparent visitation of some form.' "

[35] Indeed, "if a fit parent's decision of the kind at issue here becomes subject to judicial review, the court must accord at least some special weight to the parent's own determination."

case" based on *Pierce v. Society of Sisters*.[36] He would apply "strict scrutiny to infringements of fundamental rights."

Justice Stevens dissented, disagreeing with in the Washington Supreme Court decision that the "statute is invalid in all its applications."[37] The statute covered a "number of cases — indeed, one suspects, the most common to arise — in which the 'person' among 'any' seeking visitation is a once-custodial caregiver, an intimate relation, or even a genetic parent." Further, "constitutional protection against arbitrary state interference with parental rights should not be extended to prevent the States from protecting children against the arbitrary exercise of parental authority" not in fact motivated by the child's welfare.[38] States should assess conflicting interests in cases like this one, not "a federal court employing a national standard."

Nation-wide "state custody and visitation laws [reveal] fully 698 separate references to the best interest of the child' standard." The Court should "pause before it upholds a decision implying that those words, on their face, may be too boundless to pass muster under the Federal Constitution."

Justice Scalia dissented arguing that the range of opinions given by the Justices shows "the theory of unenumerated parental rights underlying these three cases has small claim to *stare decisis* protection."[39] Justice Scalia did not suggest that these cases be overruled, just that they not be extended. State legislature should regulate this area because they "have the great advantages of doing harm in a more circumscribed area, of being able to correct their mistakes in a flash, and of being removable by the people."

In dissent, Justice Kennedy rejected "the concept that the conventional nuclear family ought to establish the visitation standard for every domestic relations case" as this structure does not prevail in many households. *See, e.g. Moore v. East Cleveland*.[40] Considering "the inconclusive historical record and case law, as well as the almost universal adoption of the best interests standard for visitation disputes, I would be hard pressed to conclude the right to be free of such review in all cases is itself 'implicit in the concept of ordered liberty.' "[41]

MICHAEL H. v. GERALD D., 491 U.S. 110 (1989). In *Michael H.*, the Court upheld a California statute against substantive and procedural due process challenges. California Evidence Code § 621 "conclusively presumed" that the child of a wife who was living with her husband was a child of that marriage. Michael H. brought suit seeking paternity and visitation rights to Victoria D., whose blood tests showed with 98.07 percent probability that Michael was her father. At the time of Victoria's conception, Carole D. was living with her husband Gerald D., who was not "impotent or sterile," and thus was "conclusively presumed" to be Victoria's father under the California law. The California courts rejected Michael's challenge to the

---

[36] As no Privileges and Immunities challenge presented, the case "does not present an opportunity to reevaluate the meaning of that Clause."

[37] Also rejecting an as-applied challenge, Justice Stevens stated the "task or reviewing a trial court's application of a state statute to the particular facts of a case is one that should be performed in the first instance by the state appellate courts."

[38] Justice Stevens noted for "the purpose of a facial challenge like this, I think it safe to assume that trial judges usually give great deference to parents' wishes, and I am not persuaded otherwise here."

[39] The three cases being *Meyer v. Nebraska*, *Pierce v. Society of Sisters*, and *Wisconsin v. Yoder*.

[40] For example, "a third party, by acting in a care giving role over a significant period of time, has developed a relationship with a child which is not necessarily subject to absolute parental veto."

[41] All 50 states have a third-party visitation statute and all but one permit "a court order to issue in certain cases if visitation is found to be in the best interests of the child."

constitutionality of § 621. They also denied Michael's motion for visitation rights under California Civil Code § 4601, which gave courts the discretion to grant visitation to anyone "having an interest in the welfare of the child."

Justice Scalia wrote the opinion for a plurality of four that only Chief Justice Rehnquist joined in its entirety. Justice Scalia rejected Michael's claim that § 621 violated his procedural due process rights. He said that the statute involved the "implementation of a substantive rule of law" rather than a simply procedural restriction. In this connection, Justice Scalia viewed conclusive presumptions foreclosing particularized determinations as no different from any "legal rule that establishes a general classification, whether framed in terms of a presumption or not."

Justice Scalia also rejected Michael's claim that § 621 violated his substantive due process rights by depriving him of his relationship with Victoria. Justice Scalia stated that, to be constitutionally protected, a liberty interest must be "an interest traditionally protected by our society." Taking issue with Justice Brennan's dissenting opinion, he found the notion of tradition to have a limiting effect on the jurisprudence of the Due Process Clause. "Its purpose is to prevent future generations from lightly casting aside important traditional values — not to enable this Court to invent new ones." Justice Scalia found no such traditionally protected interest in this case. "What counts is whether the States in fact award substantive parental rights to the natural father of a child conceived within and born into an extant marital union that wishes to embrace a child. We are not aware of a single case, old or new, that has done so."

In a footnote, Justice Scalia defended his focus on the "rights of an adulterous natural father rather than" the dissent's focus on traditions involving the rights of "parenthood." He described his method of identifying constitutionally relevant traditions accordingly: "We refer to the most specific level at which a relevant tradition protecting, or denying protection to, the asserted right can be identified. If, for example, there was no societal tradition, either way, regarding the rights of the natural father of a child adulterously conceived, we would have to consult, and (if possible) reason from, the traditions regarding natural fathers in general. But there is such a more specific tradition, and it unqualifiedly denies protection to such a parent." Justice Scalia concluded the opinion by rejecting a due process challenge on the child's behalf based on the same "traditions" analysis.

Justice O'Connor, joined by Justice Kennedy, wrote an opinion concurring in all of Justice Scalia's opinion except his footnote outlining how to ascertain relevant traditions under the Due Process Clause. "On occasion the Court has characterized relevant traditions protecting asserted rights at levels of generality that might not be 'the most specific level available.'" Justice O'Connor would not confine the Court in advance to "a single mode of historical analysis."

Justice Stevens concurred in the judgment. Even assuming that Michael's interest qualified for due process protection, Justice Stevens thought that § 4601's visitation provision gave Michael a "fair opportunity to show he is Victoria's natural father, that he had developed a relationship with her, and that her interests would be served by granting him visitation rights." Essentially, he found that the trial judge followed California law in making an independent determination of visitation rights that took paternity into account.

Justice Brennan wrote a dissenting opinion, in which Justices Marshall and Blackmun joined. Justice Brennan criticized the specificity with which Justice Scalia described constitutionally relevant traditions. He also criticized excessive reliance on notions of tradition "in interpreting the Constitution's deliberately capacious language." By concentrating on "historical practice," the concept of tradition can transform the Constitution from a "living charter" into a "stagnant, archaic hidebound document steeped in the prejudices and superstitions of a time long past." For Justice Brennan, this narrow, past-oriented emphasis on tradition resulted in the plurality's "rhapsody on the 'unitary family.' "

Justice White filed a separate dissenting opinion in which Justice Brennan joined. Disagreeing with Justice Stevens, he maintained that Michael "was precluded at the very outset from introducing evidence which would support his assertion of paternity" and "has never been afforded an opportunity to present his case in any meaningful manner."

NOTES

(1) *The Family Relationship.* The Court has sometimes viewed critically state laws that unduly interfere with the maintenance of the family unit or with individual rights exercised within the family context. Cases involving the family have posed such problems as parent-child relationships, the education of children, procreative rights, rights involved in divorce and child custody, and state regulations of marriage. In resolving conflicts among the interests of spouses, parents, children, and the state, the Court has relied on a number of constitutional sources. In *Wisconsin v. Yoder, infra* § 16.05, the Court invoked the First Amendment's free exercise of religion clause to invalidate the state's application of its compulsory education law to Amish children whose parents objected to their continuing past the eighth grade. The Court drew on the Fourteenth Amendment's Equal Protection Clause to invalidate a state law that discriminated on the basis of sex by denying a father the right to bar adoption of his illegitimate children while permitting a mother to do so. *See Caban v. Mohammed,* 441 U.S. 380 (1979). State laws that draw distinctions between legitimate and illegitimate children have also been invalidated on equal protection grounds. *See* § 11.01[2] on illegitimates.

(2) *Depriving Parents of Custody over their Children.* In *Santosky v. Kramer,* 455 U.S. 745 (1982), the Court struck down, as violative of due process, New York's procedure for termination of parental care and custody rights of their natural children. Under the New York law, if the state established that the child is "permanently neglected by 'a fair preponderance of the evidence,' " the Family Court could permanently terminate the natural parents' rights in the child. The majority opinion (5-4) of Justice Brennan argued that the "fundamental 'liberty' interest of natural parents in the care, custody, and management of their child . . . does not evaporate simply because they have not been model parents or have lost temporary custody of their child to the State." Applying the criteria in *Mathews v. Eldridge, infra* § 7.05, Note (1) after *Loudermill,* the Court concluded that a "clear and convincing evidence" standard of proof was required. Justice Rehnquist dissented, joined by Chief Justice Burger, and Justices White and O'Connor.

(3) *Extramarital Relationships.* The Court has been less willing to extend constitutional protection for certain privacy claims asserted outside the family unit. Twice the Court has denied certiorari in cases involving extramarital relationships. In *Hollenbaugh v. Carnegie Free Library,* 439 U.S. 1052 (1978), the Court refused to review a decision sustaining the discharge of two public library employees who were living together in adultery. The Eighth Circuit Court of Appeals rejected the challenge of a public school teacher who was fired for living with her male friend. *Sullivan v. Meade Co.,* 530 F.2d 799 (1976).

(4) *The Family Unit.* In *Moore v. City of East Cleveland,* 431 U.S. 494 (1977), the Court struck down a city housing ordinance that limited the occupancy of a dwelling unit to members of a single "family," defined as a group of related individuals. Mrs. Moore lived with her son and two grandsons who were first cousins rather than

brothers. Writing for the Court, Justice Powell ruled that the ordinance violated the Due Process Clause of the Fourteenth Amendment, as it interfered with the freedom of personal choice in matters of marriage and family life.

The City sought to defend its action based on the Court's ruling in *Village of Belle Terre v. Boraas*, 416 U.S. 1 (1974), which upheld a similar restrictive ordinance. Writing for the majority, Justice Powell stated that the ordinance at issue in Belle Terre affected only unrelated individuals. By contrast, the East Cleveland ordinance sliced "deeply into the family itself."

The City contended that any constitutional right to live together extends only to the nuclear family — essentially a couple and its dependent children. Rejecting this contention, the Court said that the tradition of this country has not been limited to a nuclear family. Close relatives often share the duties, pleasures and responsibilities of a common household. Decisions such as *Wisconsin v. Yoder, infra* § 16.05, *Meyer v. Nebraska*, 262 U.S. 390 (1923), and *Pierce v. Society of Sisters* , 268 U.S. 510 (1925), recognize constitutional protection for child-rearing and family life. "[T]he Constitution prevents East Cleveland from standardizing its children — and its adults — by forcing all to live in certain narrowly defined family patterns."

Justice Brennan concurred, joined by Justice Marshall. Justice Brennan stated that "the prominence of other than nuclear families among ethnic and racial minority groups, including our black citizens, surely demonstrates that the 'extended family' pattern remains a vital tenet of our society." By "prohibiting this pattern of family living," the City chose "a device which deeply intrudes into family associational rights."

Justice Stewart filed a dissenting opinion in which Justice Rehnquist joined, arguing that the ordinance did not violate any constitutional right. Justice White also dissented. "The Judiciary, including this Court, is most vulnerable and comes nearest to illegitimacy when it deals with judge-made constitutional law having little or no cognizable roots in the language or even the design of the Constitution." The Court should be reluctant to breathe still further substantive content into the Due Process Clause.

(5) For a generally approving review of the Court's approach in constitutional family law, see *Developments, The Constitution and the Family*, 93 Harv. L. Rev. 1156 (1980). For a more critical view of the Court's handling of family law cases, see Burt, *The Constitution of the Family*, 1979 Sup. Ct. Rev. 329. With specific regard to the *East Cleveland* case, Professor Robert Burt has noted that the community was predominantly black, with a black "City Manager and City Commission." *See* Burt, *supra*, at 389 (quoting from the concurring opinion of Justice Stewart). Moreover, according to Professor Burt, "the purpose of the ordinance was quite straightforward: to exclude from a middle-class, predominantly black community, that saw itself as socially and economically upwardly mobile, other black families most characteristic of lower-class ghetto life." For Burt, the Court's failure to address these realities evidenced " 'a depressing insensitivity toward the economic and emotional needs' of the majority of residents of East Cleveland." *See also* Ely, *On Discovering Fundamental Values*, 92 Harv. L. Rev. 5 (1978); Richards, *The Individual, the Family and the Constitution: A Jurisprudential Perspective*, 55 N.Y.U. L. Rev. 1 (1980).

[3] Homosexuality

LAWRENCE v. TEXAS
539 U.S. 558, 123 S. Ct. 2472, 156 L. Ed. 2d 508 (2003)

JUSTICE KENNEDY delivered the opinion of the Court.

Liberty protects the person from unwarranted government intrusions into a dwelling or other private places. . . .   Freedom extends beyond spatial bounds. Liberty presumes an autonomy of self that includes freedom of thought, belief, expression, and certain intimate conduct. The instant case involves liberty of the person both in its spatial and more transcendent dimensions.

I

The question before the Court is the validity of a Texas statute making it a crime for two persons of the same sex to engage in certain intimate sexual conduct.

In Houston, Texas, officers of the Harris County Police Department were dispatched to a private residence in response to a reported weapons disturbance. They entered an apartment where one of the petitioners, John Geddes Lawrence, resided. The right of the police to enter does not seem to have been questioned. The officers observed Lawrence and another man, Tyron Garner, engaging in a sexual act. The two petitioners were arrested, held in custody over night, and charged and convicted before a Justice of the Peace.

The complaints described their crime as "deviate sexual intercourse, namely anal sex, with a member of the same sex (man)." . . . Tex. Penal Code Ann. § 21.06(a) (2003) provides: "A person commits an offense if he engages in deviate sexual intercourse with another individual of the same sex." The statute defines "deviate sexual intercourse" as follows: " '(A) any contact between any part of the genitals of one person and the mouth or anus of another person; or (B) the penetration of the genitals or the anus of another person with an object.' § 21.01(1)."

. . . The petitioners were each fined $ 200 and assessed court costs of $ 141.25. . . .

II

We conclude the case should be resolved by determining whether the petitioners were free as adults to engage in the private conduct in the exercise of their liberty under the Due Process Clause of the Fourteenth Amendment to the Constitution. . . .

In *Griswold* [*v. Connecticut*, 381 U.S. 479 (1965)], the . . . Court described the protected interest as a right to privacy and placed emphasis on the marriage relation and the protected space of the marital bedroom.

. . . In *Eisenstadt v. Baird*, 405 U.S. 438 (1972), the Court invalidated a law prohibiting the distribution of contraceptives to unmarried persons. . . .

. . . "If the right of privacy means anything, it is the right of the *individual*, married or single, to be free from unwarranted governmental intrusion into matters so fundamentally affecting a person as the decision whether to bear or beget a child." *Id.* at 453.

. . . *Roe* [*v. Wade*, 410 U.S. 113 (1973)] recognized the right of a woman to make certain fundamental decisions affecting her destiny. . . .

In *Carey v. Population Services Int'l*, 431 U.S. 678 (1977), the Court confronted a New York law forbidding sale or distribution of contraceptive devices to persons under 16 years of age. . . .   Both *Eisenstadt* and *Carey*, as well as the holding and rationale in *Roe*, confirmed that the reasoning of *Griswold* could not be confined to the protection of rights of married adults. This was the state of the law with respect to some of the most relevant cases when the Court considered *Bowers v. Hardwick*.

The facts in *Bowers* had some similarities to the instant case. . . . One difference between the two cases is that the Georgia statute prohibited the conduct whether or not the participants were of the same sex, while the Texas statute, as we have seen, applies only to participants of the same sex. Hardwick was not prosecuted, but he brought an action in federal court to declare the state statute invalid. He alleged he was a practicing homosexual and that the criminal prohibition violated rights guaranteed to him by the Constitution. The Court, in an opinion by Justice White, sustained the Georgia law. . . .

The Court began its substantive discussion in *Bowers* as follows: "The issue presented is whether the Federal Constitution confers a fundamental right upon homosexuals to engage in sodomy and hence invalidates the laws of the many States that still make such conduct illegal and have done so for a very long time." . . . To say that the issue in *Bowers* was simply the right to engage in certain sexual conduct demeans the claim the individual put forward, just as it would demean a married couple were it to be said marriage is simply about the right to have sexual intercourse. The laws involved in *Bowers* and here . . . [touch] upon the most private human conduct, sexual behavior, and in the most private of places, the home. The statutes do seek to control a personal relationship that, whether or not entitled to formal recognition in the law, is within the liberty of persons to choose without being punished as criminals.

. . . [A]dults may choose to enter upon this relationship in the confines of their homes and their own private lives and still retain their dignity as free persons. When sexuality finds overt expression in intimate conduct with another person, the conduct can be but one element in a personal bond that is more enduring. The liberty protected by the Constitution allows homosexual persons the right to make this choice.

Having misapprehended the claim of liberty there presented to it, and thus stating the claim to be whether there is a fundamental right to engage in consensual sodomy, the *Bowers* Court said: "Proscriptions against that conduct have ancient roots." In academic writings, and in many of the scholarly *amicus* briefs filed to assist the Court in this case, there are fundamental criticisms of the historical premises relied upon by the majority and concurring opinions in *Bowers*. We need not enter this debate in the attempt to reach a definitive historical judgment, but the following considerations counsel against adopting the definitive conclusions upon which *Bowers* placed such reliance.

At the outset it should be noted that there is no longstanding history in this country of laws directed at homosexual conduct as a distinct matter. Beginning in colonial times there were prohibitions of sodomy derived from the English criminal laws passed in the first instance by the Reformation Parliament of 1533. The English prohibition was understood to include relations between men and women as well as relations between men and men. . . . Nineteenth-century commentators similarly read American sodomy, buggery, and crime-against-nature statutes as criminalizing certain relations between men and women and between men and men. . . . Thus early American sodomy laws were not directed at homosexuals as such but instead sought to prohibit nonprocreative sexual activity more generally. This does not suggest approval of homosexual conduct. It does tend to show that this particular form of conduct was not thought of as a separate category from like conduct between heterosexual persons.

Laws prohibiting sodomy do not seem to have been enforced against consenting adults acting in private. A substantial number of sodomy prosecutions and convictions for which there are surviving records were for predatory acts against those who could not or did not consent, as in the case of a minor or the victim of an assault. As to these, one purpose for the prohibitions was to ensure there would be no lack of coverage if a predator committed a sexual assault that did not constitute rape as defined by the criminal law. . . . Instead of targeting relations between consenting adults in private, 19th-century sodomy prosecutions typically involved relations between men and minor girls or minor boys, relations between adults involving force, relations between adults implicating disparity in status, or relations between men and animals.

. . . The longstanding criminal prohibition of homosexual sodomy upon which the *Bowers* decision placed such reliance is as consistent with a general condemnation of nonprocreative sex as it is with an established tradition of prosecuting acts because of their homosexual character.

. . . American laws targeting same-sex couples did not develop until the last third of the 20th century. The reported decisions concerning the prosecution of consensual, homosexual sodomy between adults for the years 1880-1995 are not always clear in the details, but a significant number involved conduct in a public place.

It was not until the 1970s that any State singled out same-sex relations for criminal prosecution, and only nine States have done so. . . . Post-*Bowers* even some of these States did not adhere to the policy of suppressing homosexual conduct. Over the course of the last decades, States with same-sex prohibitions have moved toward abolishing them. . . .

It must be acknowledged, of course, that the Court in *Bowers* was making the broader point that for centuries there have been powerful voices to condemn homosexual conduct as immoral. . . . These considerations do not answer the question before us, however. . . . "Our obligation is to define the liberty of all, not to mandate our own moral code." *Planned Parenthood of Southeastern Pa. v. Casey.*

Chief Justice Burger joined the opinion for the Court in *Bowers* and further explained his views as follows: "Decisions of individuals relating to homosexual conduct have been subject to state intervention throughout the history of Western civilization. Condemnation of those practices is firmly rooted in Judeo-Christian moral and ethical standards." As with Justice White's assumptions about history, scholarship casts some doubt on the sweeping nature of the statement by Chief Justice Burger as it pertains to private homosexual conduct between consenting adults. In all events we think that our laws and traditions in the past half century are of most relevance here. These references show an emerging awareness that liberty gives substantial protection to adult persons in deciding how to conduct their private lives in matters pertaining to sex. "History and tradition are the starting point but not in all cases the ending point of the substantive due process inquiry." *County of Sacramento v. Lewis*, 523 U.S. 833 (1998) (Kennedy, J., concurring).

This emerging recognition should have been apparent when *Bowers* was decided. In 1955 the American Law Institute promulgated the Model Penal Code and made clear that it did not recommend or provide for "criminal penalties for consensual sexual relations conducted in private." . . . In *Bowers* the Court referred to the fact that before 1961 all 50 States had outlawed sodomy, and that at the time of the Court's decision 24 States and the District of Columbia had sodomy laws. Justice Powell pointed out that these prohibitions often were being ignored, however. Georgia, for instance, had not sought to enforce its law for decades. . . .

The sweeping references by Chief Justice Burger to the history of Western civilization and to Judeo-Christian moral and ethical standards did not take account of other authorities pointing in an opposite direction. A committee advising the British Parliament recommended in 1957 repeal of laws punishing homosexual conduct. Parliament enacted the substance of those recommendations 10 years later.

Of even more importance, almost five years before *Bowers* was decided the European Court of Human Rights considered a case with parallels to *Bowers* and to today's case. An adult male resident in Northern Ireland alleged he was a practicing homosexual who desired to engage in consensual homosexual conduct. . . . The court held that the laws proscribing the conduct were invalid under the European Convention on Human Rights. Authoritative in all countries that are members of the Council of Europe (21 nations then, 45 nations now), the decision is at odds with the premise in *Bowers* that the claim put forward was insubstantial in our Western civilization.

In our own constitutional system the deficiencies in *Bowers* became even more apparent in the years following its announcement. The 25 States with laws prohibiting the relevant conduct referenced in the *Bowers* decision are reduced now to 13, of which 4 enforce their laws only against homosexual conduct. In those States where sodomy is still proscribed, whether for same-sex or heterosexual conduct, there is a pattern of nonenforcement with respect to consenting adults acting in private. The State of Texas admitted in 1994 that as of that date it had not prosecuted anyone under those circumstances.

Two principal cases decided after *Bowers* cast its holding into even more doubt. . . . *Planned Parenthood of Southeastern Pa. v. Casey*, . . . again confirmed that our laws and tradition afford constitutional protection to personal decisions relating to marriage, procreation, contraception, family relationships, child rearing, and education.

The second post-*Bowers* case of principal relevance is *Romer v. Evans*, 517 U.S. 620, (1996). . . .

As an alternative argument in this case, counsel for the petitioners and some *amici* contend that *Romer* provides the basis for declaring the Texas statute invalid under the Equal Protection Clause. That is a tenable argument, but we conclude the instant case requires us to address whether *Bowers* itself has continuing validity. Were we to hold the statute invalid under the Equal Protection Clause some might question whether a prohibition would be valid if drawn differently, say, to prohibit the conduct both between same-sex and different-sex participants.

. . . The central holding of *Bowers* . . . demeans the lives of homosexual persons.

The stigma this criminal statute imposes, moreover, is not trivial. The offense, to be sure, is but a class C misdemeanor. . . . Still, it remains a criminal offense with all that imports for the dignity of the persons charged. The petitioners will bear on their record the history of their criminal convictions. . . . We are advised that if Texas convicted an adult for private, consensual homosexual conduct under the statute here in question the convicted person would come within the registration laws of a least four States were he or she to be subject to their jurisdiction. . . . Furthermore, the Texas criminal conviction carries with it the other collateral consequences always following a conviction, such as notations on job application forms. . . .

The foundations of *Bowers* have sustained serious erosion from our recent decisions in *Casey* and *Romer*. When our precedent has been thus weakened, criticism from other sources is of greater significance. In the United States criticism of *Bowers* has been substantial and continuing, disapproving of its reasoning in all respects, not just as to its historical assumptions. The courts of five different States have declined to follow it in interpreting provisions in their own state constitutions parallel to the Due Process Clause of the Fourteenth Amendment.

To the extent *Bowers* relied on values we share with a wider civilization, it should be noted that the reasoning and holding in *Bowers* have been rejected elsewhere. The European Court of Human Rights has followed not *Bowers* but its own decision in

Dudgeon v. United Kingdom. Other nations, too, have taken action consistent with an affirmation of the protected right of homosexual adults to engage in intimate, consensual conduct. . . .   There has been no showing that in this country the governmental interest in circumscribing personal choice is somehow more legitimate or urgent.

The doctrine of *stare decisis* is essential to the respect accorded to the judgments of the Court and to the stability of the law. It is not, however, an inexorable command. . . .   In *Casey* we noted that when a Court is asked to overrule a precedent recognizing a constitutional liberty interest, individual or societal reliance on the existence of that liberty cautions with particular strength against reversing course. . . .   [T]here has been no individual or societal reliance on *Bowers* of the sort that could counsel against overturning its holding once there are compelling reasons to do so. *Bowers* itself causes uncertainty, for the precedents before and after its issuance contradicts its central holding. . . .

Bowers was not correct when it was decided, . . . and now is overruled.

The present case does not involve minors. It does not involve persons who might be injured or coerced or who are situated in relationships where consent might not easily be refused. It does not involve public conduct or prostitution. It does not involve whether the government must give formal recognition to any relationship that homosexual persons seek to enter. The case does involve two adults who, with full and mutual consent from each other, engaged in sexual practices common to a homosexual lifestyle. The petitioners are entitled to respect for their private lives. The State cannot demean their existence or control their destiny by making their private sexual conduct a crime. Their right to liberty under the Due Process Clause gives them the full right to engage in their conduct without intervention of the government. . . .   The Texas statute furthers no legitimate state interest which can justify its intrusion into the personal and private life of the individual. . . .

JUSTICE O'CONNOR, concurring in the judgment.

The Court today overrules *Bowers v. Hardwick*, 478 U.S. 186 (1986). I joined *Bowers*, and do not join the Court in overruling it. Nevertheless, I agree with the Court that Texas' statute banning same-sex sodomy is unconstitutional. Rather than relying on the substantive component of the Fourteenth Amendment's Due Process Clause, as the Court does, I base my conclusion on the Fourteenth Amendment's Equal Protection Clause.

. . . Under our rational basis standard of review, "legislation is presumed to be valid and will be sustained if the classification drawn by the statute is rationally related to a legitimate state interest."

Laws such as economic or tax legislation that are scrutinized under rational basis review normally pass constitutional muster, since "the Constitution presumes that even improvident decisions will eventually be rectified by the democratic processes." We have consistently held, however, that some objectives, such as "a bare . . . desire to harm a politically unpopular group," are not legitimate state interests. When a law exhibits such a desire to harm a politically unpopular group, we have applied a more searching form of rational basis review to strike down such laws under the Equal Protection Clause.

We have been most likely to apply rational basis review to hold a law unconstitutional under the Equal Protection Clause where, as here, the challenged legislation inhibits personal relationships. . . .

. . . Sodomy between opposite-sex partners . . . is not a crime in Texas. . . .

The Texas statute makes homosexuals unequal in the eyes of the law by making particular conduct — and only that conduct — subject to criminal sanction. . . . And while the penalty imposed on petitioners in this case was relatively minor, the consequences of conviction are not. As the Court notes, petitioners' convictions, if upheld, would disqualify them from or restrict their ability to engage in a variety of professions, including medicine, athletic training, and interior design. . . .

. . . Texas itself has previously asknoweldged the collateral effects of the law, stimpulating in a prior challenge to this action that the law "legally sanctions discrimination against [homosexuals] in a variety of ways unrelated to the criminal law," including in the areas of "employment, family issues, and housing."

. . . *Bowers* did not hold that moral disapproval of a group is a rational basis under the Equal Protection Clause to criminalize homosexual sodomy when heterosexual sodomy is not punished.

. . . Moral disapproval of this group, like a bare desire to harm the group, is an interest that is insufficient to satisfy rational basis review under the Equal Protection Clause. . . .

Texas argues, however, . . . the law discriminates only against homosexual conduct. . . . "[T]here can hardly be more palpable discrimination against a class than making the conduct that defines the class criminal." . . .

. . . In *Romer v. Evans*, we refused to sanction a law that singled out homosexuals "for disfavored legal status." The same is true here. . . .

That this law as applied to private, consensual conduct is unconstitutional under the Equal Protection Clause does not mean that other laws distinguishing between heterosexuals and homosexuals would similarly fail under rational basis review. Texas cannot assert any legitimate state interest here, such as national security or preserving the traditional institution of marriage. Unlike the moral disapproval of same-sex relations — the asserted state interest in this case — other reasons exist to promote the institution of marriage beyond mere moral disapproval of an excluded group. . . .

JUSTICE SCALIA, with whom THE CHIEF JUSTICE and JUSTICE THOMAS join, dissenting.

"Liberty finds no refuge in a jurisprudence of doubt." *Planned Parenthood of Southeastern Pa. v. Casey*. That was the Court's sententious response, barely more than a decade ago, to those seeking to overrule *Roe v. Wade*. The Court's response today, to those who have engaged in a 17-year crusade to overrule *Bowers v. Hardwick* is very different. . . .

[N]owhere does the Court's opinion declare that homosexual sodomy is a "fundamental right" under the Due Process Clause; nor does it subject the Texas law to the standard of review that would be appropriate (strict scrutiny) if homosexual sodomy *were* a "fundamental right." Thus, while overruling the *outcome of Bowers*, the Court leaves strangely untouched its central legal conclusion: "Respondent would have us announce . . . a fundamental right to engage in homosexual sodomy. This we are quite unwilling to do." Instead the Court simply describes petitioners' conduct as "an exercise of their liberty" — which it undoubtedly is — and proceeds to apply an unheard-of form of rational-basis review that will have far-reaching implications beyond this case.

I

. . . I do not myself believe in rigid adherence to *stare decisis* in constitutional cases; . . . invoking the doctrine. Today's opinions in support of reversal do not bother to distinguish — or indeed, even bother to mention — the paean to *stare decisis* coauthored by three Members of today's majority in *Planned Parenthood v. Casey*.

There, when *stare decisis* meant preservation of judicially invented abortion rights, the widespread criticism of *Roe* was strong reason to *reaffirm* it. . . .

Today, however, the widespread opposition to *Bowers*, a decision resolving an issue as "intensely divisive" as the issue in *Roe*, is offered as a reason in favor of *overruling* it. Gone, too, is any "enquiry" (of the sort conducted in *Casey*) into whether the decision sought to be overruled has "proven 'unworkable.' "

Today's approach to *stare decisis* invites us to overrule an erroneously decided precedent (including an "intensely divisive" decision) *if*: (1) its foundations have been "eroded" by subsequent decisions; (2) it has been subject to "substantial and continuing" criticism; and (3) it has not induced "individual or societal reliance" that counsels against overturning. The problem is that *Roe* itself . . . satisfies these conditions to at least the same degree as *Bowers*.

(1) A preliminary digressive observation with regard to the first factor: The Court's claim that *Planned Parenthood v. Casey*, "casts some doubt" upon the holding in *Bowers* (or any other case, for that matter) does not withstand analysis. . . . *Casey* provided a *less* expansive right to abortion than did *Roe*, which was already on the books when *Bowers* was decided. And if the Court is referring . . . to the dictum of its famed sweet-mystery-of-life passage. . . . [I]f the passage calls into question the government's power to regulate *actions based on* one's self-defined "concept of existence, etc.," it is the passage that ate the rule of law.

I do not quarrel with the Court's claim that *Romer v. Evans*, "eroded" the "foundations" of *Bowers*' rational-basis holding. But *Roe* and *Casey* have been equally "eroded" by *Washington v. Glucksberg*, 521 U.S. 702, 721, (1997), which held that *only* fundamental rights which are " 'deeply rooted in this Nation's history and tradition' " qualify for anything other than rational basis scrutiny under the doctrine of "substantive due process." . . .

(2) *Bowers*, the Court says, has been subject to "substantial and continuing [criticism], disapproving of its reasoning in all respects, not just as to its historical assumptions." . . .

(3) That leaves, to distinguish the rock-solid, unamendable disposition of *Roe* from the readily overrulable *Bowers*, only the third factor. "There has been," the Court says, "no individual or societal reliance on *Bowers* of the sort that could counsel against overturning its holding. . . . " It seems to me that the "societal reliance" on the principles confirmed in *Bowers* and discarded today has been overwhelming. Countless judicial decisions and legislative enactments have relied on the ancient proposition that a governing majority's belief that certain sexual behavior is "immoral and unacceptable" constitutes a rational basis for regulation. *See, e.g., Williams v. Pryor*, 240 F.3d 944, 949 (CA11 2001) (citing *Bowers* in upholding Alabama's prohibition on the sale of sex toys on the ground that "the crafting and safeguarding of public morality . . . indisputably is a legitimate government interest under rational basis scrutiny"); *Milner v. Apfel*, 148 F.3d 812, 814 (CA7 1998) (citing *Bowers* for the proposition that "legislatures are permitted to legislate with regard to morality . . . rather than confined to preventing demonstrable harms"); *Holmes v. California Army National Guard*, 124 F.3d 1126, 1136 (CA9 1997) (relying on *Bowers* in upholding the federal statute and regulations banning from military service those who engage in homosexual conduct); *Owens v. State*, 352 Md. 663, 683, 724 A.2d 43, 53 (1999) (relying on *Bowers* in holding that "a person has no constitutional right to engage in sexual intercourse, at least outside of marriage"); *Sherman v. Henry*, 928 S.W.2d 464, 469-473 (Tex. 1996) (relying on *Bowers* in rejecting a claimed constitutional right to commit adultery). We ourselves relied extensively on *Bowers* when we concluded, in *Barnes v. Glen Theatre, Inc.*, 501 U.S. 560, 569 (1991), that Indiana's

public indecency statute furthered "a substantial government interest in protecting order and morality." State laws against bigamy, same-sex marriage, adult incest, prostitution, masturbation, adultery, fornication, bestiality, and obscenity are likewise sustainable only in light of *Bowers'* validation of laws based on moral choices. Every single one of these laws is called into question by today's decision . . . The impossibility of distinguishing homosexuality from other traditional "morals" offenses is precisely why *Bowers* rejected the rational-basis challenge. "The law," it said, "is constantly based on notions of morality." . . .

What a massive disruption of the current social order, therefore, the overruling of *Bowers* entails. Not so the overruling of *Roe*, which would simply have restored the regime that existed for centuries before 1973, in which the permissibility of and restrictions upon abortion were determined legislatively State-by-State. . . . [42]

II

. . . Texas Penal Code Ann. § 21.06(a) (2003) undoubtedly imposes constraints on liberty. So do laws prohibiting prostitution, recreational use of heroin, and, for that matter, working more than 60 hours per week in a bakery. But there is no right to "liberty" under the Due Process Clause . . . The Fourteenth Amendment *expressly allows* States to deprive their citizens of "liberty," *so long as "due process of law"* is provided.

. . . We have held repeatedly, in cases the Court today does not overrule, that *only* fundamental rights qualify for this so called "heightened scrutiny" protection — *Washington v. Glucksberg.* . . . [43]

. . . Noting that "proscriptions against that conduct have ancient roots," that "sodomy was a criminal offense at common law and was forbidden by the laws of the original 13 States when they ratified the Bill of Rights," and that many States had retained their bans on sodomy, *Bowers* concluded that a right to engage in homosexual sodomy was not " 'deeply rooted in this Nation's history and tradition.' "

. . . [T]he Court concludes that the application of Texas's statute to petitioners' conduct fails the rational-basis test, and overrules Bowers' holding to the contrary. . . .

III

. . . [O]ur Nation has a longstanding history of laws prohibiting *sodomy in general* — regardless of whether it was performed by same-sex or opposite-sex couples:

. . . "*Sodomy* was a criminal offense at common law and was forbidden by the laws of the original 13 States when they ratified the Bill of Rights. In 1868, when the Fourteenth Amendment was ratified, all but 5 of the 37 States in the Union had *criminal sodomy laws.* In fact, until 1961, all 50 States outlawed *sodomy*, and today, 24 States and the District of Columbia continue to provide criminal penalties for *sodomy*

[42] [Court's footnote 3] . . . An asserted "fundamental liberty interest" must not only be "deeply rooted in this Nation's history and tradition," but it must also be "implicit in the concept of ordered liberty," so that "neither liberty nor justice would exist if [it] were sacrificed," *id.*

[43] [Court's footnote 3] . . . An asserted "fundamental liberty interest" must not only be "deeply rooted in this Nation's history and tradition," but it must also be "implicit in the concept of ordered liberty," so that "neither liberty nor justice would exist if [it] were sacrificed." Moreover, liberty interests unsupported by history and tradition, though not deserving of "heightened scrutiny," are still protected from state laws that are not rationally related to any legitimate state interest. As I proceed to discuss, it is this latter principle that the Court applies in the present case.

performed in private and between consenting adults. Against this background, to claim that a right to engage in such conduct is 'deeply rooted in this Nation's history and tradition' or 'implicit in the concept of ordered liberty' is, at best, facetious." (citations and footnotes omitted; emphasis added). . . .

Realizing that fact, the Court instead says: "We think that our laws and traditions in the past half century are of most relevance here. These references show *an emerging awareness* that liberty gives substantial protection to adult persons in deciding how to conduct their private lives *in matters pertaining to sex*." (emphasis added). Apart from the fact that such an "emerging awareness" does not establish a "fundamental right," the statement is factually false. States continue to prosecute all sorts of crimes by adults "in matters pertaining to sex": prostitution, adult incest, adultery, obscenity, and child pornography. Sodomy laws, too, have been enforced "in the past half century," in which there have been 134 reported cases involving prosecutions for consensual, adult, homosexual sodomy. In relying, for evidence of an "emerging recognition," upon the American Law Institute's 1955 recommendation not to criminalize " 'consensual sexual relations conducted in private,' " the Court ignores the fact that this recommendation was "a point of resistance in most of the states that considered adopting the Model Penal Code."

In any event, an "emerging awareness" is by definition not "deeply rooted in this Nation's history and traditions," as we have said "fundamental right" status requires. . . .

IV

I turn now to the ground on which the Court squarely rests its holding: the contention that there is no rational basis for the law here under attack. This proposition is so out of accord with our jurisprudence — indeed, with the jurisprudence of *any* society we know — that it requires little discussion.

The Texas statute undeniably seeks to further the belief of its citizens that certain forms of sexual behavior are "immoral and unacceptable," — the same interest furthered by criminal laws against fornication, bigamy, adultery, adult incest, bestiality, and obscenity. . . . If, as the Court asserts, the promotion of majoritarian sexual morality is not even a *legitimate* state interest, none of the above-mentioned laws can survive rational-basis review.

V

Finally, I turn to petitioners' equal-protection challenge. . . .

. . . Even if the Texas law *does* deny equal protection to "homosexuals as a class," that denial *still* does not need to be justified by anything more than a rational basis, which our cases show is satisfied by the enforcement of traditional notions of sexual morality.

. . . [T]he Court has taken sides in the culture war, departing from its role of assuring, as neutral observer, that the democratic rules of engagement are observed. Many Americans do not want persons who openly engage in homosexual conduct as partners in their business, as scoutmasters for their children, as teachers in their children's schools, or as boarders in their home. They view this as protecting themselves and their families from a lifestyle that they believe to be immoral and destructive. The Court views it as "discrimination" which it is the function of our judgments to deter. . . . [T]he Court . . . is seemingly unaware that the attitudes of that culture are not obviously "mainstream"; that in most States what the Court calls "discrimination" against those who engage in homosexual acts is perfectly legal; that proposals to ban such "discrimination" under Title VII have repeatedly been rejected by Congress, that in some cases such "discrimination" is *mandated* by federal statute, and that in some cases such "discrimination" is a constitutional right.

Let me be clear that I have nothing against homosexuals, or any other group, promoting their agenda through normal democratic means. Social perceptions of sexual and other morality change over time, and every group has the right to persuade its fellow citizens that its view of such matters is the best. That homosexuals have achieved some success in that enterprise is attested to by the fact that Texas is one of the few remaining States that criminalize private, consensual homosexual acts. . . . I would no more *require* a State to criminalize homosexual acts — or, for that matter, display *any* moral disapprobation of them — than I would *forbid* it to do so. . . .

Justice Thomas, dissenting.

I join Justice Scalia's dissenting opinion. I write separately to note that the law before the Court today "is . . . uncommonly silly." *Griswold v. Connecticut*, 381 U.S. 479, 527 (1965) (Stewart, J., dissenting). If I were a member of the Texas Legislature, I would vote to repeal it. Punishing someone for expressing his sexual preference through noncommercial consensual conduct with another adult does not appear to be a worthy way to expend valuable law enforcement resources.

. . . And, just like Justice Stewart, I "can find [neither in the Bill of Rights nor any other part of the Constitution a] general right of privacy," [*id.* at 530] or as the Court terms it today, the "liberty of the person both in its spatial and more transcendent dimensions."

[4] Right to Die

CRUZAN v. DIRECTOR, MISSOURI DEPARTMENT OF HEALTH
497 U.S. 261, 110 S. Ct. 2841, 111 L. Ed. 2d 224 (1990)

Chief Justice Rehnquist delivered the opinion of the Court.

Petitioner Nancy Beth Cruzan was rendered incompetent as a result of severe injuries sustained during an automobile accident. Co-petitioners Lester and Joyce Cruzan, Nancy's parents and co-guardians, sought a court order directing the withdrawal of their daughter's artificial feeding and hydration equipment after it became apparent that she had virtually no chance of recovering her cognitive faculties. The Supreme Court of Missouri held that because there was no clear and convincing evidence of Nancy's desire to have life-sustaining treatment withdrawn under such circumstances, her parents lacked authority to effectuate such a request. We granted certiorari, and now affirm.

. . . Nancy Cruzan . . . lies in a Missouri state hospital in what is commonly referred to as a persistent vegetative state: generally, a condition in which a person exhibits motor reflexes but evinces no indications of significant cognitive function.[44] The State of Missouri is bearing the cost of her care.

After it had become apparent that Nancy Cruzan had virtually no chance of regaining her mental faculties her parents asked hospital employees to terminate the artificial nutrition and hydration procedures. . . . The employees refused to honor the request without court approval. The parents then sought and received authorization

---

[44] The State Supreme Court, adopting much of the trial court's findings, described Nancy Cruzan's medical condition as follows . . . "In sum, Nancy is diagnosed as in a persistent vegetative state. She is not dead. She is not terminally ill. Medical experts testified that she could live another thirty years." *Cruzan v. Harmon*, 760 S.W.2d 408, 411 (Mo. 1989) (en banc) . . . .

from the state trial court for termination. . . .

The Supreme Court of Missouri reversed by a divided vote. . . . It rejected the argument that Cruzan's parents were entitled to order the termination of her medical treatment, concluding that "no person can assume that choice for an incompetent in the absence of the formalities required under Missouri's Living Will statutes or the clear and convincing, inherently reliable evidence absent here." *Id.*, at 425. . . .

At common law, even the touching of one person by another without consent and without legal justification was a battery. Before the turn of the century, this Court observed that "[n]o right is held more sacred, or is more carefully guarded, by the common law, than the right of every individual to the possession and control of his own person, free from all restraint or interference of others, unless by clear and unquestionable authority of law." *Union Pacific R. Co. v. Botsford*, 141 U.S. 250, 251 (1891). . . .

. . . [The Court examined a number of state court cases on the right to terminate treatment.]

As these cases demonstrate, the common-law doctrine of informed consent is viewed as generally encompassing the right of a competent individual to refuse medical treatment. Beyond that, these decisions demonstrate both similarity and diversity in their approach of what all agree is a perplexing question with unusually strong moral and ethical overtones. State courts have available to them for decision a number of sources — state constitutions, statutes, and common law — which are not available to us. In this Court, the question is simply and starkly whether the United States Constitution prohibits Missouri from choosing the rule of decision which it did. This is the first case in which we have been squarely presented with the issue of whether the United States Constitution grants what is in common parlance referred to as a "right to die.". . .

. . . The principle that a competent person has a constitutionally protected liberty interest in refusing unwanted medical treatment may be inferred from our prior decisions. In *Jacobson v. Massachusetts*, 197 U.S. 11, 24–30 (1905), for instance, the Court balanced an individual's liberty interest in declining an unwanted smallpox vaccine against the State's interest in preventing disease. . . .

. . . [F]or purposes of this case, we assume that the United States Constitution would grant a competent person a constitutionally protected right to refuse lifesaving hydration and nutrition.

Petitioners go on to assert that an incompetent person should possess the same right in this respect as is possessed by a competent person. . . .

. . . Here, Missouri has in effect recognized that under certain circumstances a surrogate may act for the patient in electing to have hydration and nutrition withdrawn in such a way as to cause death, but it has established a procedural safeguard to assure that the action of the surrogate conforms as best it may to the wishes expressed by the patient while competent. Missouri requires that evidence of the incompetent's wishes as to the withdrawal of treatment be proved by clear and convincing evidence. . . .

. . . Missouri relies on its interest in the protection and preservation of human life, and there can be no gainsaying this interest. As a general matter, the States — indeed, all civilized nations — demonstrate their commitment to life by treating homicide as serious crime. Moreover, the majority of States in this country have laws imposing criminal penalties on one who assists another to commit suicide. We do not think a State is required to remain neutral in the face of an informed and voluntary decision by a physically-able adult to starve to death.

. . . The choice . . . [w]e believe Missouri may legitimately seek to safeguard is the personal element of [the choice between life and death] through the imposition of heightened evidentiary requirements. It cannot be disputed that the Due Process Clause protects an interest in life as well as an interest in refusing life-sustaining medical treatment. Not all incompetent patients will have loved ones available to serve as surrogate decisionmakers. And even where family members are present, "[t]here will, of course, be some unfortunate situations in which family members will not act to protect a patient." *In re Jobes*, 108 N.J. 394, 419 (1987). A State is entitled to guard against potential abuses in such situations. Similarly, a State is entitled to consider that a judicial proceeding to make a determination regarding an incompetent's wishes may very well not be an adversarial one, with the added guarantee of accurate factfinding that the adversary process brings with it. Finally, we think a State may properly decline to make judgments about the "quality" of life that a particular individual may enjoy, and simply assert an unqualified interest in the preservation of human life to be weighed against the constitutionally protected interests of the individual.

In our view, Missouri has permissibly sought to advance these interests through the adoption of a "clear and convincing" standard of proof to govern such proceedings. . . .

[N]ot only does the standard of proof reflect the importance of a particular adjudication, it also serves as "a societal judgment about how the risk of error should be distributed between the litigants." *Santosky [v. Kramer]*, 455 U.S. at 755. . . . We believe that Missouri may permissibly place an increased risk of an erroneous decision on those seeking to terminate an incompetent individual's life-sustaining treatment. An erroneous decision not to terminate results in a maintenance of the status quo; the possibility of subsequent developments such as advancements in medical science, the discovery of new evidence regarding the patient's intent, changes in the law, or simply the unexpected death of the patient despite the administration of life-sustaining treatment, at least create the potential that a wrong decision will eventually be corrected or its impact mitigated. An erroneous decision to withdraw life-sustaining treatment, however, is not susceptible of correction. . . .

It is also worth noting that most, if not all, States simply forbid oral testimony entirely in determining the wishes of parties in transactions which, while important, simply do not have the consequences that a decision to terminate a person's life does. . . . There is no doubt that statutes requiring wills to be in writing, and statutes of frauds which require that a contract to make a will be in writing, on occasion frustrate the effectuation of the intent of a particular decedent, just as Missouri's requirement of proof in this case may have frustrated the effectuation of the not-fully-expressed desires of Nancy Cruzan. . . .

In sum, we conclude that a State may apply a clear and convincing evidence standard in proceedings where a guardian seeks to discontinue nutrition and hydration of a person diagnosed to be in a persistent vegetative state. . . .

The Supreme Court of Missouri held that in this case the testimony adduced at trial did not amount to clear and convincing proof of the patient's desire to have hydration and nutrition withdrawn. . . . The testimony adduced at trial consisted primarily of Nancy Cruzan's statements made to a housemate about a year before her accident that she would not want to live should she face life as a "vegetable," and other observations to the same effect. The observations did not deal in terms with withdrawal of medical treatment or of hydration and nutrition. We cannot say that the Supreme Court of Missouri committed constitutional error in reaching the conclusion that it did.[45]

---

[45] [Court's footnote 11] The clear and convincing standard of proof has been variously defined in this context as "proof sufficient to persuade the trier of fact that the patient held a firm and settled commitment

Petitioners alternatively contend that Missouri must accept the "substituted judgment" of close family members even in the absence of substantial proof that their views reflect the views of the patient. . . .

[W]e do not think the Due Process Clause requires the State to repose judgment on these matters with anyone but the patient herself. . . . But there is no automatic assurance that the view of close family members will necessarily be the same as the patient's would have been had she been confronted with the prospect of her situation while competent. All of the reasons previously discussed for allowing Missouri to require clear and convincing evidence of the patient's wishes lead us to conclude that the State may choose to defer only to those wishes, rather than confide the decision to close family members.[46]

JUSTICE O'CONNOR, concurring.

. . . A seriously ill or dying patient whose wishes are not honored may feel a captive of the machinery required for life-sustaining measures or other medical interventions. . . .

. . . A gastrostomy tube (as was used to provide food and water to Nancy Cruzan) or jejunostomy tube must be surgically implanted into the stomach or small intestine. . . . Accordingly, the liberty guaranteed by the Due Process Clause must protect, if it protects anything, an individual's deeply personal decision to reject medical treatment, including the artificial delivery of food and water.

I also write separately to emphasize that the Court does not today decide the issue whether a State must also give effect to the decisions of a surrogate decisionmaker. In my view, such a duty may well be constitutionally required to protect the patient's liberty interest in refusing medical treatment. Few individuals provide explicit oral or written instructions regarding their intent to refuse medical treatment should they become incompetent.

States which decline to consider any evidence other than such instructions may frequently fail to honor a patient's intent. Such failures might be avoided if the State considered an equally probative source of evidence: the patient's appointment of a proxy to make health care decisions on her behalf. . . . Several States have recognized the practical wisdom of such a procedure by enacting durable power of attorney statutes that specifically authorize an individual to appoint a surrogate to make medical treatment decisions. Some state courts have suggested that an agent appointed pursuant to a general durable power of attorney statute would also be empowered to make health care decisions on behalf of the patient. . . . Other States allow an individual to designate a proxy to carry out the intent of a living will. These procedures for surrogate decisionmaking, which appear to be rapidly gaining in acceptance, may be a valuable additional safeguard of the patient's interest in directing his medical care. . . .

JUSTICE SCALIA, concurring.

The various opinions in this case portray quite clearly the difficult, indeed agonizing,

---

to the termination of life supports under the circumstances like those presented," *In re Westchester County Medical Center on behalf of O'Connor*, 72 N.Y.2d 517 (1988), and as evidence which "produces in the mind of the trier of fact a firm belief or conviction as to the truth of the allegations sought to be established, evidence so clear, direct and weighty and convincing as to enable [the factfinder] to come to a clear conviction, without hesitancy, of the truth of the precise facts in issue." *In re Jobes*, 108 N. J., at 407–408 . . . .

[46] [Court's footnote 12] We are not faced in this case with the question of whether a State might be required to defer to the decision of a surrogate if competent and probative evidence established that the patient herself had expressed a desire that the decision to terminate life-sustaining treatment be made for her by that individual . . . .

questions that are presented by the constantly increasing power of science to keep the human body alive for longer than any reasonable person would want to inhabit it. The States have begun to grapple with these problems through legislation. I am concerned, from the tenor of today's opinions, that we are poised to confuse that enterprise as successfully as we have confused the enterprise of legislating concerning abortion. . . .

While I agree with the Court's analysis today, and therefore join in its opinion, I would have preferred that we announce, clearly and promptly, that the federal courts have no business in this field; that American law has always accorded the State the power to prevent, by force if necessary, suicide — including suicide by refusing to take appropriate measures necessary to preserve one's life; that the point at which life becomes "worthless," and the point at which the means necessary to preserve it become "extraordinary" or "inappropriate," are neither set forth in the Constitution nor known to the nine Justices of this Court any better than they are known to nine people picked at random from the Kansas City telephone directory; and hence, that even when it is demonstrated by clear and convincing evidence that a patient no longer wishes certain measures to be taken to preserve her life, it is up to the citizens of Missouri to decide, through their elected representatives, whether that wish will be honored. . . .

The text of the Due Process Clause does not protect individuals against deprivations of liberty simpliciter. It protects them against deprivations of liberty "without due process of law." . . . It is at least true that no "substantive due process" claim can be maintained unless the claimant demonstrates that the State has deprived him of a right historically and traditionally protected against State interference (plurality opinion). That cannot possibly be established here.

. . . And most States that did not explicitly prohibit assisted suicide in 1868 recognized, when the issue arose in the 50 years following the Fourteenth Amendment's ratification, that assisted and (in some cases) attempted suicide were unlawful. . . .

". . . It seems to me, . . . that Justice Brennan's position ultimately rests upon the proposition that it is none of the State's business if a person wants to commit suicide. Justice Stevens is explicit on the point. . . . This . . . is not a view imposed by our constitutional traditions, in which the power of the State to prohibit suicide is unquestionable.

. . . [W]hat protects us, for example, from being assessed a tax of 100% of our income above the subsistence level, from being forbidden to drive cars, or from being required to send our children to school for 10 hours a day, none of which horribles is categorically prohibited by the Constitution. Our salvation is the Equal Protection Clause, which requires the democratic majority to accept for themselves and their loved ones what they impose on you and me. This Court need not, and has no authority to, inject itself into every field of human activity where irrationality and oppression may theoretically occur, and if it tries to do so it will destroy itself.

Justice Brennan, with whom Justice Marshall and Justice Blackmun join, dissenting.

I

B

Artificial delivery of food and water is regarded as medical treatment by the medical profession and the Federal Government. . . .

II

The only state interest asserted here is a general interest in the preservation of life. But the State has no legitimate general interest in someone's life, completely abstracted from the interest of the person living that life that could outweigh the person's choice to avoid medical treatment. . . .

III

. . . As the majority recognizes, Missouri has a *parens patriae* interest in providing Nancy Cruzan, now incompetent, with as accurate as possible a determination of how she would exercise her rights under these circumstances. . . .

Accuracy, therefore, must be our touchstone. Missouri may constitutionally impose only those procedural requirements that serve to enhance the accuracy of a determination of Nancy Cruzan's wishes or are at least consistent with an accurate determination. . . . Missouri's rule of decision imposes a markedly asymmetrical evidentiary burden. Only evidence of specific statements of treatment choice made by the patient when competent is admissible to support a finding that the patient, now in a persistent vegetative state, would wish to avoid further medical treatment. Moreover, this evidence must be clear and convincing. No proof is required to support a finding that the incompetent person would wish to continue treatment.

A

. . . Just as a State may not override Nancy's choice directly, it may not do so indirectly through the imposition of a procedural rule.

. . . Missouri's heightened evidentiary standard attempts to achieve balance by discounting evidence; the guardian ad litem technique achieves balance by probing for additional evidence. Where, as here, the family members, friends, doctors and guardian ad litem agree, it is not because the process has failed, as the majority suggests. It is because there is no genuine dispute as to Nancy's preference.

. . . [T]he Missouri court imposed a clear and convincing standard as an obstacle to the exercise of a fundamental right.

. . . An erroneous decision to terminate life-support is irrevocable, says the majority, while an erroneous decision not to terminate "results in a maintenance of the status quo." But, from the point of view of the patient, an erroneous decision in either direction is irrevocable. . . . The majority also misconceives the relevance of the possibility of "advancements in medical science," by treating it as a reason to force someone to continue medical treatment against his will. The possibility of a medical miracle is indeed part of the calculus, but it is a part of the patient's calculus. . . .

B

Even more than its heightened evidentiary standard, the Missouri court's categorical exclusion of relevant evidence dispenses with any semblance of accurate factfinding. The court adverted to no evidence supporting its decision, but held that no clear and convincing, inherently reliable evidence had been presented to show that Nancy would want to avoid further treatment. In doing so, the court failed to consider statements Nancy had made to family members and a close friend.[47] The court also failed to

---

[47] [Court's footnote 19] The trial court had relied on the testimony of Athena Comer, a long-time friend, co-worker and a housemate for several months, as sufficient to show that Nancy Cruzan would wish to be free

consider testimony from Nancy's mother and sister that they were certain that Nancy would want to discontinue artificial nutrition and hydration,[48] even after the court found that Nancy's family was loving and without malignant motive. . . . The court also failed to consider the conclusions of the guardian ad litem, appointed by the trial court, that there was clear and convincing evidence that Nancy would want to discontinue medical treatment and that this was in her best interests. . . . The court did not specifically define what kind of evidence it would consider clear and convincing, but its general discussion suggests that only a living will or equivalently formal directive from the patient when competent would meet this standard.

Too few people execute living wills or equivalently formal directives for such an evidentiary rule to ensure adequately that the wishes of incompetent persons will be honored. . . . Often legal help would be necessary. . . .

C

[N]othing in the Constitution prevents States from reviewing the advisability of a family decision, by requiring a court proceeding or by appointing an impartial guardian *ad litem*. . . .

D

Finally, I cannot agree with the majority that where it is not possible to determine what choice an incompetent patient would make, a State's role as *parens patriae* permits the State automatically to make that choice itself. . . .

[A] State may exclude from consideration anyone having improper motives. But a State generally must either repose the choice with the person whom the patient himself would most likely have chosen as proxy or leave the decision to the patient's family.

---

of medical treatment under her present circumstances. Ms. Comer described a conversation she and Nancy had while living together, concerning Ms. Comer's sister who had become ill suddenly and died during the night. The Comer family had been told that if she had lived through the night, she would have been in a vegetative state. Nancy had lost a grandmother a few months before. Ms. Comer testified that: "Nancy said she would never want to live [in a vegetative state] because if she couldn't be normal or even, you know, like half way, and do things for yourself, because Nancy always did, that she didn't want to live . . . and we talked about it a lot." She said "several times" that "she wouldn't want to live that way because if she was going to live, she wanted to be able to live, not to just lay in a bed and not be able to move because you can't do anything for yourself." *Id.*, at 390, 396. "[S]he said that she hoped that [all the] people in her family knew that she wouldn't want to live [as a vegetable] because she knew it was usually up to the family whether you lived that way or not." *Id.*, at 399.

. . . Nancy's sister Christy, to whom she was very close, testified that she and Nancy had had two very serious conversations about a year and a half before the accident. A day or two after their niece was stillborn (but would have been badly damaged if she had lived), Nancy had said that maybe it was part of a "greater plan" that the baby had been stillborn and did not have to face "the possible life of mere existence." A month later, after their grandmother had died after a long battle with heart problems, Nancy said that "it was better for my grandmother not to be kind of brought back and forth [by] medical [treatment], brought back from a critical near point of death . . . . "

[48] [Court's footnote 20] Nancy's sister Christy, Nancy's mother, and another of Nancy's friends testified that Nancy would want to discontinue the hydration and nutrition. Christy said that "Nancy would be horrified at the state she is in." *Id.*, at 535. She would also "want to take that burden away from [her family]." *Id.*, at 544 . . . .

IV

As many as 10,000 patients are being maintained in persistent vegetative states in the United States, and the number is expected to increase significantly in the near future. . . .

Justice Stevens, dissenting . . .

III

. . . Even laws against suicide presuppose that those inclined to take their own lives have some interest in living, and, indeed, that the depressed people whose lives are preserved may later be thankful for the State's intervention. . . . It is not within the province of secular government to circumscribe the liberties of the people by regulations designed wholly for the purpose of establishing a sectarian definition of life.

My disagreement with the Court is thus unrelated to its endorsement of the clear and convincing standard of proof for cases of this kind. Indeed, I agree that the controlling facts must be established with unmistakable clarity. The critical question, however, is not how to prove the controlling facts but rather what proven facts should be controlling. In my view, the constitutional answer is clear: the best interests of the individual, especially when buttressed by the interests of all related third parties, must prevail over any general state policy that simply ignores those interests. . . . A State's procedures must guard against the risk that the survivors' interests are not mistaken for the patient's. Yet, the appointment of the neutral guardian ad litem, coupled with the searching inquiry conducted by the trial judge and the imposition of the clear and convincing standard of proof, all effectively avoided that risk in this case. . . .

WASHINGTON v. GLUCKSBERG
521 U.S. 702, 117 S. Ct. 2258, 138 L. Ed. 2d 772 (1997)

Chief Justice Rehnquist delivered the opinion of the Court.

The question presented in this case is whether Washington's prohibition against "causing" or "aiding" a suicide offends the Fourteenth Amendment to the United States Constitution. We hold that it does not.

It has always been a crime to assist a suicide in the State of Washington. . . . Today, Washington law provides: "A person is guilty of promoting a suicide attempt when he knowingly causes or aids another person to attempt suicide." Wash. Rev. Code 9A.36.060(1) (1994). "Promoting a suicide attempt" is a felony, punishable by up to five years' imprisonment and up to a $ 10,000 fine. . . . At the same time, Washington's Natural Death Act, enacted in 1979, states that the "withholding or withdrawal of life-sustaining treatment" at a patient's direction "shall not, for any purpose, constitute a suicide." Wash. Rev. Code § 70.122.070(1).[49]

. . . Respondents . . . are physicians who practice in Washington. These doctors occasionally treat terminally ill, suffering patients, and declare that they would assist these patients in ending their lives if not for Washington's assisted-suicide ban. . . .

---

[49] . . . In Washington, "any adult person may execute a directive directing the withholding or withdrawal of life-sustaining treatment in a terminal condition or permanent unconscious condition," § 70.122.030, and a physician who, in accordance with such a directive, participates in the withholding or withdrawal of life-sustaining treatment is immune from civil, criminal, or professional liability.

I

We begin, as we do in all due-process cases, by examining our Nation's history, legal traditions, and practices. . . . In almost every State indeed, in almost every western democracy it is a crime to assist a suicide . . . [S]ee *Stanford v. Kentucky*, 492 U.S. 361, 373 (1989) ("The primary and most reliable indication of [a national] consensus is . . . the pattern of enacted laws"). . . .

[F]or over 700 years, the Anglo-American common-law tradition has punished or otherwise disapproved of both suicide and assisting suicide. . . . In the 13th century, Henry de Bracton, one of the first legal-treatise writers, observed that "just as a man may commit felony by slaying another so may he do so by slaying himself." 2 Bracton on Laws and Customs of England 423 (f. 150) (G. Woodbine ed., S. Thorne transl., 1968). . . . Blackstone emphasized that "the law has . . . ranked [suicide] among the highest crimes," [4 W. Blackstone, Commentaries * 189]. . . . [50]

For the most part, the early American colonies adopted the common-law approach. . . .

Over time, however, the American colonies abolished these harsh common-law penalties. . . .

That suicide remained a grievous, though nonfelonious, wrong is confirmed by the fact that colonial and early state legislatures and courts did not retreat from prohibiting assisting suicide. . . . And the prohibitions against assisting suicide never contained exceptions for those who were near death. . . .

. . . Many States . . . now permit "living wills," surrogate health-care decisionmaking, and the withdrawal or refusal of life-sustaining medical treatment. At the same time, however, voters and legislators continue for the most part to reaffirm their States' prohibitions on assisting suicide.

. . . In 1991, Washington voters rejected a ballot initiative which, had it passed, would have permitted a form of physician-assisted suicide. . . .

. . . [I]n 1994, voters in Oregon enacted, also through ballot initiative, that State's "Death With Dignity Act," which legalized physician-assisted suicide for competent, terminally ill adults. Since the Oregon vote, many proposals to legalize assisted-suicide have been and continue to be introduced in the States' legislatures, but none has been enacted. . . . Also, on April 30, 1997, President Clinton signed the Federal Assisted Suicide Funding Restriction Act of 1997, which prohibits the use of federal funds in support of physician-assisted suicide. . . . [51]

. . . [N]ew York State's Task Force on Life and the Law . . . [u]nanimously

---

[50] [Court's footnote 10] . . . Coke regarded suicide as a category of murder, and agreed with Bracton that the goods and chattels but not, for Coke, the lands of a sane suicide were forfeit. 3 E. Coke, Institutes * 54 . . . .

[51] [Court's footnote 16] Other countries are embroiled in similar debates: The Supreme Court of Canada recently rejected a claim that the Canadian Charter of Rights and Freedoms establishes a fundamental right to assisted suicide, *Rodriguez v. British Columbia* (Attorney General), 107 D. L. R. (4th) 342 (1993); the British House of Lords Select Committee on Medical Ethics refused to recommend any change in Great Britain's assisted-suicide prohibition, House of Lords, Session 1993–94 Report of the Select Committee on Medical Ethics, 12 Issues in Law & Med. 193, 202 (1996) ("We identify no circumstances in which assisted suicide should be permitted"); New Zealand's Parliament rejected a proposed "Death With Dignity Bill" that would have legalized physician-assisted suicide in August 1995, Graeme, MPs Throw out Euthanasia Bill, The Dominion (Wellington), Aug. 17, 1995, p. 1. . . . On the other hand, on May 20, 1997, Colombia's Constitutional Court legalized voluntary euthanasia for terminally ill people. Sentencia No. C-239/97 (Corte Constitucional, Mayo 20, 1997); . . .

concluded that "legalizing assisted suicide and euthanasia would pose profound risks to many individuals who are ill and vulnerable. . . . "

. . . Against this backdrop of history, tradition, and practice, we now turn to respondents' constitutional claim.

II

. . . In a long line of cases, we have held that, in addition to the specific freedoms protected by the Bill of Rights, the "liberty" specially protected by the Due Process Clause includes the rights to marry, *Loving v. Virginia*, 388 U.S. 1 (1967); to have children, *Skinner v. Oklahoma ex rel. Williamson*, 316 U.S. 535 (1942); to direct the education and upbringing of one's children, *Meyer v. Nebraska*, 262 U.S. 390 (1923); *Pierce v. Society of Sisters*, 268 U.S. 510 (1925); to marital privacy, *Griswold v. Connecticut*, 381 U.S. 479 (1965); to use contraception, *id.*; *Eisenstadt v. Baird*, 405 U.S. 438 (1972); to bodily integrity, *Rochin v. California*, 342 U.S. 165 (1952), and to abortion, *Casey, supra*. We have also assumed, and strongly suggested, that the Due Process Clause protects the traditional right to refuse unwanted lifesaving medical treatment. *Cruzan*, 497 U.S. at 278–279.

But we "have always been reluctant to expand the concept of substantive due process because guideposts for responsible decisionmaking in this unchartered area are scarce and open-ended." *Collins*, 503 U.S. at 125. . . . We must therefore "exercise the utmost care whenever we are asked to break new ground in this field," *id.*, lest the liberty protected by the Due Process Clause be subtly transformed into the policy preferences of the members of this Court, *Moore*, 431 U.S. at 502 (plurality opinion).

Our established method of substantive-due-process analysis has two primary features: First, we have regularly observed that the Due Process Clause specially protects those fundamental rights and liberties which are, objectively, "deeply rooted in this Nation's history and tradition," *id.*, at 503 (plurality opinion); . . . and "implicit in the concept of ordered liberty," such that "neither liberty nor justice would exist if they were sacrificed," *Palko v. Connecticut*, 302 U.S. 319, 325, 326 (1937). Second, we have required in substantive-due-process cases a "careful description" of the asserted fundamental liberty interest. Our Nation's history, legal traditions, and practices thus provide the crucial "guideposts for responsible decisionmaking," that direct and restrain our exposition of the Due Process Clause. As we stated recently in *Flores*, the Fourteenth Amendment "forbids the government to infringe . . . 'fundamental' liberty interests at all, no matter what process is provided, unless the infringement is narrowly tailored to serve a compelling state interest." 507 U.S. at 302.

Justice Souter, relying on Justice Harlan's dissenting opinion in *Poe v. Ullman*, would largely abandon this restrained methodology, and instead ask "whether [Washington's] statute sets up one of those 'arbitrary impositions' or 'purposeless restraints' at odds with the Due Process Clause of the Fourteenth Amendment," (quoting *Poe*, 367 U.S. 497, 543 (1961) (Harlan, J., dissenting)). In our view, however, the development of this Court's substantive-due-process jurisprudence has been a process whereby the outlines of the "liberty" specially protected by the Fourteenth Amendment never fully clarified, to be sure, and perhaps not capable of being fully clarified have at least been carefully refined by concrete examples involving fundamental rights found to be deeply rooted in our legal tradition. This approach tends to rein in the subjective elements that are necessarily present in due-process judicial review. In addition, by establishing a threshold requirement that a challenged state action implicate a fundamental right before requiring more than a reasonable relation to a legitimate state interest to justify the action, it avoids the need for complex balancing of competing interests in every case.

. . . As noted above, we have a tradition of carefully formulating the interest at stake in substantive-due-process cases. For example, although *Cruzan* is often described as a "right to die" case, . . . we were, in fact, more precise: we assumed that the Constitution granted competent persons a "constitutionally protected right to refuse lifesaving hydration and nutrition." *Cruzan*, 497 U.S. at 279. . . . [T]he question before us is whether the "liberty" specially protected by the Due Process Clause includes a right to commit suicide which itself includes a right to assistance in doing so. . . .

The right assumed in *Cruzan*, however, was not simply deduced from abstract concepts of personal autonomy. Given the common-law rule that forced medication was a battery, and the long legal tradition protecting the decision to refuse unwanted medical treatment, our assumption was entirely consistent with this Nation's history and constitutional traditions. The decision to commit suicide with the assistance of another may be just as personal and profound as the decision to refuse unwanted medical treatment, but it has never enjoyed similar legal protection. . . .

. . . The history of the law's treatment of assisted suicide in this country has been and continues to be one of the rejections of nearly all efforts to permit it. That being the case, our decisions lead us to conclude that the asserted "right" to assistance in committing suicide is not a fundamental liberty interest protected by the Due Process Clause. The Constitution also requires, however, that Washington's assisted-suicide ban be rationally related to legitimate government interests. This requirement is unquestionably met here. As the court below recognized, Washington's assisted-suicide ban implicates a number of state interests.

First, Washington has an "unqualified interest in the preservation of human life." *Cruzan*, 497 U.S. at 282. . . .

Those who attempt suicide terminally ill or not often suffer from depression or other mental disorders. *See* New York Task Force 13–22, 126–128 (more than 95% of those who commit suicide had a major psychiatric illness at the time of death; among the terminally ill, uncontrolled pain is a "risk factor" because it contributes to depression). . . . Research indicates, however, that many people who request physician-assisted suicide withdraw that request if their depression and pain are treated. . . .

The State also has an interest in protecting the integrity and ethics of the medical profession. . . . And physician-assisted suicide could, it is argued, undermine the trust that is essential to the doctor-patient relationship by blurring the time-honored line between healing and harming. . . .

Next, the State has an interest in protecting vulnerable groups including the poor, the elderly, and disabled persons from abuse, neglect, and mistakes. . . . We have recognized . . . the real risk of subtle coercion and undue influence in end-of-life situations. *Cruzan*. . . . If physician-assisted suicide were permitted, many might resort to it to spare their families the substantial financial burden of end-of-life health-care costs.

. . . The State's assisted-suicide ban reflects and reinforces its policy that the lives of terminally ill, disabled, and elderly people must be no less valued than the lives of the young and healthy. . . .

Finally, the State may fear that permitting assisted suicide will start it down the path to voluntary and perhaps even involuntary euthanasia. . . . [N]ot only physicians, but also family members and loved ones, will inevitably participate in assisting suicide. Thus, it turns out that what is couched as a limited right to "physician-assisted suicide" is likely, in effect, a much broader license, which could prove extremely difficult to police and contain.

. . . The Dutch government's own study revealed that in 1990, there were 2,300 cases of voluntary euthanasia (defined as "the deliberate termination of another's life at his request"), 400 cases of assisted suicide, and more than 1,000 cases of euthanasia without an explicit request. In addition to these latter 1,000 cases, the study found an additional 4,941 cases where physicians administered lethal morphine overdoses without the patients' explicit consent. . . .

We need not weigh exactingly the relative strengths of these various interests. They are unquestionably important and legitimate, and Washington's ban on assisted suicide is at least reasonably related to their promotion and protection. We therefore hold that Wash. Rev. Code § 9A.36.060(1) (1994) does not violate the Fourteenth Amendment, either on its face or "as applied to competent, terminally ill adults who wish to hasten their deaths by obtaining medication prescribed by their doctors." 79 F.3d, at 838.[52]

Throughout the Nation, Americans are engaged in an earnest and profound debate about the morality, legality, and practicality of physician-assisted suicide. Our holding permits this debate to continue, as it should in a democratic society. . . .

It is so ordered.

JUSTICE O'CONNOR, concurring.

Death will be different for each of us. For many, the last days will be spent in physical pain and perhaps the despair that accompanies physical deterioration and a loss of control of basic bodily and mental functions. Some will seek medication to alleviate that pain and other symptoms. . . .

. . . [T]here is no need to address the question whether suffering patients have a constitutionally cognizable interest in obtaining relief from the suffering that they may experience in the last days of their lives. There is no dispute that dying patients in Washington and New York can obtain palliative care, even when doing so would hasten their deaths. The difficulty in defining terminal illness and the risk that a dying patient's request for assistance in ending his or her life might not be truly voluntary justifies the prohibitions on assisted suicide we uphold here.

JUSTICE STEVENS, concurring in the judgments. . . .

I

. . . Much more than the State's paternalistic interest in protecting the individual from the irrevocable consequences of an ill-advised decision motivated by temporary concerns is at stake.. . . The State has an interest in preserving and fostering the benefits that every human being may provide to the community. . . . The value to others of a person's life is far too precious to allow the individual to claim a constitutional entitlement to complete autonomy in making a decision to end that life. . . .

---

[52] [Court's footnote 24] . . . We emphasize that we today reject the Court of Appeals' specific holding that the statute is unconstitutional "as applied" to a particular class. Justice Stevens agrees with this holding but would not "foreclose the possibility that an individual plaintiff seeking to hasten her death, or a doctor whose assistance was sought, could prevail in a more particularized challenge," *id.* Our opinion does not absolutely foreclose such a claim. However, given our holding that the Due Process Clause of the Fourteenth Amendment does not provide heightened protection to the asserted liberty interest in ending one's life with a physician's assistance, such a claim would have to be quite different from the ones advanced by respondents here.

II

. . . As Justice Brennan pointed out in his *Cruzan* dissent, we have upheld legislation imposing punishment on persons refusing to be vaccinated, 497 U.S. at 312, n. 12, citing *Jacobson v. Massachusetts*, 197 U.S. 11, 26–27 (1905), and as Justice Scalia pointed out in his concurrence, the State ordinarily has the right to interfere with an attempt to commit suicide by, for example, forcibly placing a bandage on a self-inflicted wound to stop the flow of blood. In most cases, the individual's constitutionally protected interest in his or her own physical autonomy, including the right to refuse unwanted medical treatment, will give way to the State's interest in preserving human life. . . .

. . . The now-deceased plaintiffs in this action may in fact have had a liberty interest even stronger than Nancy Cruzan's because, not only were they terminally ill, they were suffering constant and severe pain. . . .

III

. . . Although as a general matter the State's interest in the contributions each person may make to society outweighs the person's interest in ending her life, this interest does not have the same force for a terminally ill patient faced not with the choice of whether to live, only of how to die. . . .

Similarly, the State's legitimate interests in preventing suicide, protecting the vulnerable from coercion and abuse, and preventing euthanasia are less significant in this context. . . .

. . . Encouraging the development and ensuring the availability of adequate pain treatment is of utmost importance; palliative care, however, cannot alleviate all pain and suffering. . . .

. . . [T]here is in fact significant tension between the traditional view of the physician's role and the actual practice in a growing number of cases.[53]

I do not . . . foreclose the possibility that an individual plaintiff seeking to hasten her death, or a doctor whose assistance was sought, could prevail in a more particularized challenge. . . .

JUSTICE SOUTER, concurring in the judgment . . .

. . . [T]hat the terminally sick might be pressured into suicide decisions by close friends and family members. . . . is possible, not only because the costs of care might be more than family members could bear but simply because they might naturally wish to see an end of suffering for someone they love. . . .

The State, however, goes further, to argue that dependence on the vigilance of

---

[53] [Court's footnote 12] I note that there is evidence that a significant number of physicians support the practice of hastening death in particular situations. A survey published in the New England Journal of Medicine, found that 56% of responding doctors in Michigan preferred legalizing assisted suicide to an explicit ban. In a survey of Oregon doctors, 60% of the responding doctors supported legalizing assisted suicide for terminally ill patients. Another study showed that 12% of physicians polled in Washington State reported that they had been asked by their terminally ill patients for prescriptions to hasten death, and that, in the year prior to the study, 24% of those physicians had complied with such requests. [S]ee also Doukas, Waterhouse, Gorenflo, & Seld, *Attitudes and Behaviors on Physician-Assisted Death: A Study of Michigan Oncologists*, 13 J. Clinical Oncology 1055 (1995) (reporting that 18% of responding Michigan oncologists reported active participation in assisted suicide); Slome, Moulton, Huffine, Gorter, & Abrams, *Physicians' Attitudes Toward Assisted Suicide in AIDS*, 5 J. Acquired Immune Deficiency Syndromes 712 (1992) (reporting that 24% of responding physicians who treat AIDS patients would likely grant a patient's request for assistance in hastening death).

physicians will not be enough. First, the lines proposed here (particularly the requirement of a knowing and voluntary decision by the patient) would be more difficult to draw than the lines that have limited other recently recognized due process rights. . . . [T]he trimester measurements of *Roe* and the viability determination of *Casey* were easy to make with a real degree of certainty. But the knowing and responsible mind is harder to assess. . . . Physicians, and their hospitals, have their own financial incentives, too, in this new age of managed care.

Respondents propose an answer to all this, the answer of state regulation with teeth. Legislation proposed in several States, for example, would authorize physician-assisted suicide but require two qualified physicians to confirm the patient's diagnosis, prognosis, and competence; and would mandate that the patient make repeated requests witnessed by at least two others over a specified time span; and would impose reporting requirements and criminal penalties for various acts of coercion.

. . . Respondents' proposals, as it turns out, sound much like the guidelines now in place in the Netherlands. . . . Some commentators marshall evidence that the Dutch guidelines have in practice failed to protect patients from involuntary euthanasia and have been violated with impunity. . . .

. . . While I do not decide for all time that respondents' claim should not be recognized, I acknowledge the legislative institutional competence as the better one to deal with that claim at this time.

Justice Ginsburg, concurring in the judgments.

I concur in the Court's judgments in these cases substantially for the reasons stated by Justice O'connor in her concurring opinion.

Justice Breyer, concurring in the judgments.

. . . I do not agree . . . with the Court's formulation of [the] claimed "liberty" interest. The Court describes it as a "right to commit suicide with another's assistance." But . . . a different formulation. . . . would use words roughly like a "right to die with dignity." But irrespective of the exact words used, at its core would lie personal control over the manner of death, professional medical assistance, and the avoidance of unnecessary and severe physical suffering combined.

I do not believe, however, that this Court need or now should decide whether or a not such a right is "fundamental." That is because, in my view, the avoidance of severe physical pain (connected with death) would have to comprise an essential part of any successful claim and because, as Justice O'Connor points out, the laws before us do not force a dying person to undergo that kind of pain. . . . The Court also rejected another equal protection claim against these statutes in *Vacco v. Quill*, 512 U.S. 793 (1997).

[5] Other Autonomy Issues

WHALEN v. ROE, 429 U.S. 589 (1977). In *Whalen*, the Court upheld the New York State Controlled Substances Act of 1972, which required recording, "in a centralized computer file, the names and addresses of all persons who have obtained, pursuant to a doctor's prescription, certain drugs for which there is both a lawful and an unlawful market."

Based on the findings of a special commission, New York was concerned that drugs prescribed for legitimate medical purposes were being used illegally. The Act categorized "potentially harmful drugs in five schedules." The Court limited its concern to "Schedule II, which includes the most dangerous of the legitimate drugs." These drugs include "opium and opium derivatives, cocaine, methadone, amphetamines, and methaqualone" and have been prescribed to treat "epilepsy, narcolepsy, hyperkinesia, schizo-affective disorders, and migraine headaches." The Act limited prescriptions to a 30-day supply and prohibited them from being refilled. The Act also required physicians to prepare all prescription forms in triplicate. A completed official form for the prescriptions "identifies the prescribing physician; the dispensing pharmacy; the drug and dosage; and the name, address and age of the patient." The physician and pharmacist each keep a copy of the form for five years and then destroy them. The third copy was delivered each month to a "receiving room" in the Department of Health in Albany where they were processed as computer data, retained in a vault for five years, and then destroyed.

"The receiving room is surrounded by a locked wire fence and protected by an alarm system." Once the forms were processed onto computer files, the files were stored in a locked cabinet. When the computer files are "used, the computers run 'off-line,' which means that no terminal outside of the computer room can read or record any information." A Department of Health regulation prohibited public disclosure of patient identities and provided that any "willful violation of these prohibitions is a crime punishable by up to one year in prison and a $2,000 fine." When this Act was challenged, "there were 17 Department of Health employees with access to the files; in addition there were 24 investigators with authority to investigate cases of overdispensing which might be identified by the computer. Twenty months after the effective date of the Act, the computerized data had only been used in two investigations involving alleged overuse by specific patients."

Justice Stevens wrote for a unanimous Court. "There surely was nothing unreasonable in the assumption that the patient-identification requirement might aid in the enforcement of laws designed to minimize the misuse of dangerous drugs. For the requirement could reasonably be expected to have a deterrent effect on potential violators as well as aid in the detection or investigation of specific instances of apparent abuse. At the very least, it would seem clear that the State's vital interest in controlling the distribution of dangerous drugs would support a decision to experiment with new techniques for control." Responding to the argument that the Act invaded the challengers' "constitutionally protected 'zone of privacy,'" Justice Stevens distinguished two types of interests usually involved in the privacy cases. "One is the individual interest in avoiding disclosure of personal matters, and another is the interest in independence in making certain kinds of important decisions." He noted that "disclosures of private medical information" to medical personnel have become "an essential part of modern medical practice even when the disclosure may reflect unfavorably on the character of the patient." Justice Stevens compared the requirements at issue to "statutory reporting requirements relating to venereal disease, child abuse, injuries caused by deadly weapons, and certifications of fetal death." The patient-identification requirements did not invade patient reputation or independence in violation of the Fourteenth Amendment.

"We are not unaware of the threat to privacy implicit in the accumulation of vast amounts of personal information in computerized data banks or other massive governmental files. The collection of taxes, the distribution of welfare and social security benefits, the supervision of public health, the direction of our Armed Forces and the enforcement of the criminal laws all require the orderly preservation of great quantities of information, much of which is personal in character and potentially embarrassing or harmful if disclosed. The right to collect and use such data for public purposes is typically accompanied by a concomitant statutory or regulatory duty to avoid unwarranted disclosures. Recognizing that in some circumstances that duty arguably has roots in the Constitution, nevertheless New York's statutory scheme, and it's implementing administrative procedures, evidence a proper concern with, and protection of, the individual's interest in privacy. We therefore need not, and do not, decide any questions which might be presented by the unwarranted disclosure of accumulated private data — whether intentional or unintentional — or by a system that did not contain comparable security provisions. We simply hold that this record does not establish an invasion of any right or liberty protected by the Fourteenth Amendment."

JUSTICES BRENNAN and STEWART filed concurring opinions.

NOTES

(1) *Sexual Conduct.* The privacy issues that the Court dealt with in *Whalen* have been arising in a variety of contexts, such as adult consensual sex, cohabitation, adultery, parietal rules for college students, personal appearance and lifestyle choices, use of marijuana, use of laetrile, and the right to die. In *State v. Saunder*, 75 N.J. 200 (1977), the New Jersey Supreme Court struck down New Jersey's antifornication statute as violative of the right to privacy that is implicitly guaranteed by both the New Jersey and United States Constitutions.

The right to privacy claims in both *Sullivan v. Meade Co.* (cohabitation) and *Hollenbaugh v. Carnegie Free Library* (adultery), were rejected by the lower courts and the Supreme Court denied certiorari. For a fuller discussion of sexual conduct and privacy issues, see Richards, *Sexual Autonomy and Constitutional Right of Privacy: A Case Study in Human Rights and the Unwritten Constitution*, 30 HAST. L.J. 957 (1979), and Note, *Fornication, Cohabitation and the Constitution*, 77 MICH. L. REV. 252 (1978).

(2) *Personal Appearance.* The courts have similarly upheld state regulations on personal appearance when justified by some legitimate state objective. In *Kelley v. Johnson*, 425 U.S. 238 (1976), the Court rejected a police officer's challenge of a police department regulation specifying the style and length of a patrolman's hair. The officer claimed that the grooming regulations violated his freedom of expression under the First Amendment and his equal protection and due process rights under the Fourteenth Amendment. Justice Rehnquist deferred largely to the State's legislative decision: "Choice of organization, dress, and equipment for law enforcement personnel is a decision entitled to the same sort of presumption of legislative validity as are state choices designed to promote other aims within the cognizance of the State's police power."

In dissent, Justice Marshall argued that "the right in one's personal appearance is inextricably bound up with the historically recognized right of 'every individual to the possession and control of his own person.' "

(3) *Private Organizations.* (a) *National civic groups.* In *Roberts v. United States Jaycees*, 468 U.S. 609 (1984), the Jaycees, an all-male civic organization, raised two constitutional defenses against Minnesota's effort to enforce its Human Rights Act against the group's exclusionary membership policies. Both were rejected in a unanimous (7-0) opinion; see § 12.05 for the Court's rejection of a freedom of association claim derived from the First Amendment. The Court also rejected a different association claim based on the concept of personal liberty in the Due Process Clause of the Fourteenth Amendment. This claim of intimate association derives from a line of cases in which "the Court has concluded that choices to enter into and maintain certain intimate personal relationships must be secured against undue intrusion by the State because of the role of such relationships in safeguarding individual freedom that is central to our constitutional scheme." Justice Brennan, in rejecting this argument, wrote: "The personal affiliations that exemplify these considerations . . . are those that attend the creation and sustenance of a family . . . marriage . . . childbirth . . . the raising and education of children . . . and cohabitation with one's relatives. Family

relationships . . . are distinguished by such attributes as relative smallness, a high degree of selectivity in decisions to begin and maintain the affiliation, and seclusion from others in critical aspects of the relationship. . . . Several features of the Jaycees place the organization outside of the category of relationships worthy of this kind of constitutional protection." In reaching this conclusion, the opinion relied on the Jaycees' size, the routine recruiting of members with no regard for individual qualifications and the participation by women in many activities of the Jaycees, thereby undermining the argument that the exclusion of women from membership was an essential part of the associational relationship.

A similar claim was reached in *Board of Directors of Rotary International v. Rotary Club of Duarte*, 481 U.S. 537 (1987). A unanimous Court (Justices O'Connor and Blackmun not participating) upheld a California civil rights law on grounds that Rotary Club membership did not involve "the kind of intimate or private relation that warrants constitutional protection." A First Amendment "expressive conduct" challenge to the law was also rejected. See § 12.05 for further discussion of this case.

(b) *Private clubs.* In *New York State Club Ass'n, Inc. v. City of New York*, 487 U.S. 1 (1988), the Court unanimously upheld a New York ordinance that barred discrimination in certain private clubs that have over 400 members. The primary opposition to the law was by clubs that barred women from membership. In rejecting a facial challenge to the law, the Court held that it could certainly be applied "at least to some of the large clubs." Justice White's majority opinion recognized that there might conceivably be some smaller clubs covered by the law that might be able to assert claims of "intimate" or "expressive" association. See § 12.05 for additional discussion of this case.

(4) For arguments that rights of privacy should be expanded into some of the areas treated in this note, see, e.g., D. RICHARDS, TOLERATION AND THE CONSTITUTION (1986); D. RICHARDS, SEX, DRUGS, DEATH, AND THE LAW (1982). For an argument that the power of new computers requires greater sensitivity to privacy rights, see Tremper & Small, *Privacy Regulation of Computer-Assisted Testing and Instruction*, 63 WASH. L. REV. 841 (1988).

One commentator has asserted that "[a] national health information policy that encourages the collection of vast amounts of electronic data while creating uniform rules for handling these data may be the best way of reconciling equally compelling public and private claims. Yet it remains far from perfect. To be sure, such a policy defeats legitimate privacy claims: it permits innumerable access by authorized professionals and organizations for treatment, reimbursement, regulation, research, and public health and fails to tightly circumscribe the scope of permissible disclosures or redisclosures for 'compatible' or 'routine' purposes." *See* Gostin, *Health Information Privacy*, 80 CORNELL L. REV. 451, 527 (1995).

§ 7.05 PERSONAL PROPERTY RIGHTS: NEW FORMS OF PROTECTION FOR NEW PROPERTY INTERESTS

Section Note. As the Court expanded the scope of personal rights (*see* § 7.04 *supra*) and showed signs of moving away from its "hands off" approach to claims of protection for property rights (*see* § 7.03 *supra*), it is not surprising that during this same period protection was also accorded to new rights that hugged the line between "personal" and "property" rights. These cases, which can best be described as involving "personal property" rights, contained a blend of substantive and procedural due process analysis. Since the "right" being asserted was less tangible than the traditional right to the ownership or use of physical property, or a contractual relationship, the Court first had to determine whether the "right" was entitled to some form of constitutional protection.

Only such recognition would enable the claimant to enter the door of the Due Process Clause and allow the Court to consider what procedure would meet the requirements of the Clause. Earlier cases, such as *Mullane v. Central Hanover Bank and Trust Co.*, 139 U.S. 306 (1950), considered such procedural issues as the degree of notice that was required to affect a property interest. In contrast, *Goldberg v. Kelly*, 397 U.S. 154 (1970), launched a new wave of cases in which the Court was asked to limit the extent and manner of the government's ability to deprive individuals of certain interests. While these interests lacked the tangible qualities of traditional property interests, they were still sufficiently important to warrant constitutional protection.

GOLDBERG v. KELLY, 397 U.S. 254 (1970). In *Goldberg*, the Court held that due process requires the state to provide an evidentiary hearing before it can terminate welfare benefits. Under the New York City procedure at issue, a caseworker who believed that a recipient was no longer eligible for welfare would talk to the recipient. A caseworker who still believed the recipient was ineligible would notify a supervisor who would, in turn, write a letter to the welfare recipient. The letter would indicate the reasons for ineligibility and notify that the recipient may request an appeal of the determination within seven days to a higher official. In that appeal, the recipient could submit a written statement prepared personally or with the help of an attorney. If the reviewing official affirmed the caseworker's conclusion, then the recipient's benefits were terminated immediately. The recipient could then seek review of the official's decision by an independent state official and then through the judicial system.

The Court, in an opinion by Justice Brennan, found that "when welfare is discontinued, only a pre-termination evidentiary hearing provides the recipient with procedural due process." The Court emphasized the devastating effect that a wrongful termination of benefits would have on the life of an eligible recipient. "[T]he crucial factor in this context — a factor not present in the case of the blacklisted government contractor, the discharged government employee, the taxpayer denied a tax exemption, or virtually anyone else whose governmental entitlements are ended — is that termination of aid pending resolution of a controversy over eligibility may deprive an eligible recipient of the very means by which to live while he waits [for a decision]. Since he lacks independent resources, his situation becomes immediately desperate. His need to concentrate upon finding the means of daily subsistence, in turn, adversely affects his ability to seek redress from the welfare bureaucracy."

Justice Brennan said that welfare helps to "foster the dignity and well-being of all persons . . . the same government interests that counsel the provision of welfare, counsel as well its uninterrupted provision to those eligible to receive it; pre-termination evidentiary hearings are indispensable to that end." The Court also recognized the opposing state interest in conserving fiscal resources. "Summary adjudication protects the public fisc by stopping payments upon discovery of reason to believe that a recipient is no longer eligible. Since most terminations are accepted without challenge, summary adjudication also conserves both the fisc and administrative time and energy by reducing the number of evidentiary hearings actually held." Nevertheless, Justice Brennan concluded that "the interest of the eligible recipient in uninterrupted receipt of public assistance, coupled with the State's interest that his payments not be erroneously terminated, clearly outweighs the State's competing concern to prevent any increase in its fiscal and administrative burdens."

The requisite pre-termination hearing "need not take the form of a judicial or quasi-judicial trial." Rather, the hearing's form is shaped by its function of producing "an initial determination of the validity of the welfare department's grounds for discontinuance of payments in order to protect a recipient against an erroneous termination of his benefits. . . . Thus, a complete record and a comprehensive opinion, which would serve primarily to facilitate judicial review and to guide future decisions, need not be provided at the pre-termination stage." The procedure should afford a recipient "timely and adequate notice detailing the reasons for a proposed termination, and an effective opportunity to defend by confronting any adverse witnesses and by presenting his own arguments and evidence orally." The proceedings may be "informal" without "a particular order of proof or model of offering evidence." The recipient may have the assistance of an attorney, but one need not be provided by the state. The decision-maker "should state the reasons for his determination and indicate the evidence relied on . . . though his statement need not amount to a full opinion or even formal findings of fact or conclusions at law." Lastly, Justice Brennan noted "an impartial decision maker is essential. . . . [P]rior involvement in some aspects of a case will not necessarily bar a welfare official from acting as a decision maker. He should not, however, have participated in making the determination under review."

Justice Black dissented. He argued that the Court was using substantive due process and moving toward "a constitution designed to be no more and no less than what the judges of a particular social and economic philosophy declare on the one hand to be fair or on the other hand to be shocking and unconscionable." The proper remedy for this situation is legislative.

Justice Black predicted that the Court's procedure for taking people off the rolls would hurt welfare recipients by deterring the state from extending benefits to those whose eligibility is questionable.

PAUL v. DAVIS, 424 U.S. 693 (1976). To combat the increase in shoplifting that occurs around the holiday season, two local police departments compiled a flyer warning local merchants of shoplifters and attached a list of names and photographs of "persons [who] . . . have been active in various criminal fields in high density shopping areas." Each page of the flyer was titled "active shoplifters." The local police distributed the flyers to approximately 800 merchants in the Louisville, Kentucky area. Respondent's name and photograph appeared on the flyer because he had previously been picked up on a shoplifting charge in Louisville. He had pleaded not guilty to the charge and, at the time the flyer was circulated, he had not been tried. A Louisville judge later dropped the charge. Respondent's employer saw the flyer and called him in to discuss the matter. Respondent was not fired, but the employer told him he "had best not find himself in a similar situation" in the future.

Respondent brought suit in federal court against the police, seeking damages, declaratory and injunctive relief in a 1983 action claiming that the police had deprived him of his "liberty" in violation of the Fourteenth Amendment.

In an opinion by Justice Rehnquist, the Court held "that the interest in reputation asserted in this case is neither 'liberty' nor 'property' guaranteed against state deprivation without due process of law." For defamation to be recognized as "liberty" it must be accompanied by the deprivation of a right recognized by state law: "[Our] cases [do] not establish the proposition that reputation alone, apart from some more tangible interests such as employment, is either 'liberty' or 'property' by itself sufficient to invoke the procedural protection of the Due Process Clause." Instead, state tort law provides the remedy for damage to reputation. Consequently, to have a valid due process claim, a right or status recognized by the state must be either altered or extinguished, not solely damage one's reputation.

Justice Brennan dissented, joined by Justice Marshall and joined in part by Justice White. Justice Brennan argued that "a person's interest in his good name and reputation falls within the broad term 'liberty' and clearly require[s] that the government afford procedural protections before infringing that name and reputation by branding a person a criminal." The decision renders due process "concerns *never* applicable to the official stigmatization, however arbitrary, of an individual."

NOTES

(1) *Constitutional vs. Statutory Claims. Goldberg v. Kelly* and *Paul v. Davis* highlight the two approaches taken by the Court in recent years when confronted with the claim that a government has deprived an individual of a liberty or property interest without adequate procedural protection. In *Goldberg*, there appeared to be little question that the property interest — the termination of welfare benefits — was entitled to some procedural protection, and the question that the Court decided was "how much?" In *Paul v. Davis* the Court asked the threshold question: "Was there a 'property' or 'liberty' interest that was infringed?" A negative answer to the second question, of course, precludes consideration of the first.

Cases other than *Paul v. Davis* have raised this definitional barrier to consideration of the procedural issue invoked in *Goldberg v. Kelly. See Bishop v. Wood*, 426 U.S. 341 (1976) (dismissed policeman did not have property interests); *Board of Regents v. Roth*, 408 U.S. 564 (1972), and *Perry v. Sindermann*, 408 U.S. 593 (1972) (non-tenured teachers generally do not have "property" interest sufficient to require hearing on a decision not to renew contract); *Leis v. Flynt*, 439 U.S. 438 (1979) (the right of an out-of-state attorney to appear *pro hac vice* is not protected by the Due Process Clause); and *Meachum v. Fano*, 437 U.S. 215 (1976) (transfer of a state prisoner to a more restrictive facility does not trigger due process review).

Despite *Paul v. Davis* and its progeny, the Court has continued to recognize a wide range of personal "liberty" or "property" interests, thereby deciding the extent of procedural protection that the asserted interest requires under the Fourteenth Amendment. As might be expected, the person asserting the right does not always succeed, but the Court, under this approach, reaches the procedural issue. *See, e.g., Ingraham v. Wright*, 430 U.S. 651 (1977) ("liberty" interest is involved where a school child is subjected to corporal punishment, although no hearing is required). *Compare Goss v. Lopez*, 419 U.S. 565 (1975), *with Board of Curators v. Horowitz*, 435 U.S. 78 (1978) (hearing required before suspension of a student but not where student is dismissed from medical school for academic reasons); *Memphis Light, Gas & Water Div. v. Kraft*, 436 U.S. 1 (1978) (utility may not cut off services without giving customer opportunity to settle billing dispute through a meeting); *Youngberg v. Romeo*, 457 U.S. 307 (1982) (an involuntarily committed mentally retarded person has a constitutionally protected "liberty" interest in safety, freedom from bodily restraint and "minimally adequate or reasonable training to ensure safety and freedom from undue restraint."); *Logan v. Zimmerman Brush Co.*, 455 U.S. 422 (1982) (the right to use a state-created adjudicatory procedure for the hearing of complaints under a state fair employment practices act is a protected "property" interest); *Foucha v. Louisiana*, 504 U.S. 71 (1992) (involuntary confinement in a mental institution requires adversarial civil commitment proceeding to determine current mental health, and the state has the burden of proving dangerousness); and *City of Los Angeles v. David*, 538 U.S. 715 (2003) (a 30-day delay in a hearing regarding a $134.50 fine for a towed car is "no more than a routine delay substantially required by administrative needs").

(2) *Reference Letter.* In *Siegert v. Gilley*, 500 U.S. 226 (1991), the employment of a clinical psychologist in federal government hospitals was terminated. Siegert experienced a general inability to find comparable work because Gilley, his former supervisor at a previous government hospital, allegedly defamed Siegert in a recommendation letter. Writing for the Court, Chief Justice Rehnquist held that the plaintiff's allegation of defamation, even if accepted as true, did not state a claim for infringement of his "liberty interests" under the Due Process Clause. The alleged

defamation was not uttered incident to the termination of Siegert's employment at the previous hospital, since Siegert had already voluntarily resigned from that facility. Under the "stigma plus" test of *Paul v. Davis*, the interest in reputation, without more, is afforded no constitutional protection.

The existence of a valid due process claim under the Fourteenth Amendment requires that a right or status recognized by the state be either altered or extinguished, along with the damage to one's reputation. The Court also suggested that reputational injury deprives a person of liberty only when combined with loss of present employment, not future employment. Justices Marshall, Blackmun and Stevens dissented.

(3) *Sexual Offenders. See Conn. Dep't of Pub. Safety v. Doe*, 538 U.S. 1 (2003) (registration requirement as a convicted sexual offender does not require a hearing of current dangerousness when the state explicitly disclaims that it is not holding out registrants as currently dangerous).

CLEVELAND BOARD OF EDUCATION v. LOUDERMILL, 470 U.S. 532 (1985). In *Loudermill*, the Court struck down an Ohio statute that defined the pretermination process of a public employee being discharged for cause. The opinion actually addressed two separate disputes. In the first, Loudermill, an employee of the Cleveland Board of Education, was terminated for not indicating on his employment application that he had been convicted of a felony. In the second, Richard Donnelly, a mechanic for the Parma Board of Education, was discharged for failing an eye exam. Both plaintiffs appealed their terminations to the Civil Service Commission pursuant to Ohio law. Plaintiffs then appealed to the Federal District Court on the theory that they were deprived of their due process rights because they were not able to respond to the charges against them before their termination. The plaintiffs also challenged the Ohio statute because the posttermination hearings took too long.

Justice White, delivering the majority opinion, stated that the validity of the plaintiffs' "claim depends on their having had a property right in continued employment." Property interests are not created by the Constitution but by separate legal sources such as the Ohio statute in question. The Parma Board argued that any property right that was created was itself limited by the legislature's choice of procedures for its deprivation. Any additional procedures would impermissibly expand the scope of the property interest.

The Court disagreed with the Parma Board's argument, which inextricably entangled procedural and substantive due process rights. The legislature may choose whether to create a property interest, but it cannot choose to strip such interest, once conferred, without proper procedure.

Having found a property interest, the Court next addressed whether Ohio complied with due process in depriving terminated employees of that interest. A balance of competing interests suggested the need for a pretermination hearing. The government's interests in prompt termination of unsatisfactory employees and administrative convenience did not outweigh the private interests in retaining employment and the risk of a mistaken termination. The administrative costs and normal delays were not unduly burdensome. Government also has an interest in keeping its citizens employed and off welfare.

While these interests require a pretermination proceeding, that proceeding need not be elaborate, particularly as Ohio provided for a posttermination hearing and judicial review. The core requirements of due process "are notice and an opportunity to respond." Under Ohio law, the "tenured public employee is entitled to oral or written notice of the charges against him, an explanation of the employer's evidence, and an opportunity to present his side of the story."

Justice White quickly dispensed with the plaintiffs' complaint that the posttermination hearings took too long. He stated that the requirement of a hearing "at a meaningful time" is not per se violated by Loudermill's nine-month adjudication. The chronology of the proceedings, along with Loudermill's contention that nine months was too long, did not state a constitutional violation.

The majority concluded that due process was satisfied "by a pretermination opportunity to respond, coupled with posttermination administrative procedures as provided by the Ohio statute."

Justice Marshall concurred in part and concurred in the judgment. He argued that the Court did not grant the plaintiffs sufficient due process rights. In addition to notice and the opportunity to respond, the Constitution guaranteed a right to confront and cross-examine adverse witnesses.

Justice Marshall also disagreed that Loudermill's nine-month adjudication was within "a meaningful time." The hardship resulting from the termination of wages was so great, and the likelihood that such an employee would be made economically whole was so low, that a hearing should have been guaranteed within a few days.

Justice Brennan concurred in part and dissented in part. He thought that the pretermination procedure upheld by the Court was sufficient in a case like this one where the discharged employees did not dispute the facts. In Justice Brennan's view, the Court did not foreclose greater procedural rights when the facts were in dispute. This might include a predischarge opportunity to present records or testimony or to "confront an accuser in front of the decisionmaker."

In Justice Brennan's view, the Court also did not foreclose holding that a nine-month delay was too long; it simply said that the plaintiff had not alleged sufficient facts to establish a constitutional violation.

Justice Rehnquist dissented. He argued that the state as employer should be given deference in prescribing procedures by which employment can be terminated. He also criticized the Court's balancing as "an ad hoc weighing which depends to a great extent upon how the Court subjectively views the underlying interests at stake." Moreover, the vagueness of balancing tests would generate difficult litigation.

NOTES

(1) *Disability Benefits. Loudermill* is one of a group of cases, spawned by *Goldberg v. Kelly* and *Paul v. Davis*, that have broadened the definition of "liberty or property" interests whose deprivation might trigger the procedural due process requirements of the Fourteenth Amendment. *See supra* § 7.05, Note (1), after *Paul. Loudermill* also addressed the type of hearing required by the Due Process Clause. The Court gave important guidance on the scope of the hearing right in *Mathews v. Eldridge*, 424 U.S. 319 (1976). In *Mathews*, the Court (Justice Powell for the majority) held that evidentiary hearings (of the *Goldberg v. Kelly* variety) were not required before termination of disability benefits. Justice Powell's opinion set forth three factors that the Court considered in deciding whether the state had complied with the requirements of due process: "First, the private interest that will be affected by the official action; second, the risk of erroneous deprivation of such interest through the procedures used, and the probable value, if any, of additional or substitute safeguards; and finally, the government's interest, including the function involved and the fiscal and administrative burdens that the additional or substitute procedural requirement would entail."

(2) *Administrative Judiciary.* For further discussion, see Schwartz, *Recent Administrative Law Issues and Trends*, 3 Admin. L.J. 543, 569 (1989/1990) ("If we look at recent administrative law developments, perhaps the most striking is the creation of

an administrative judiciary to deal with the plethora of cases that has been a direct result of the *Goldberg v. Kelly* revolution").

(3) *Pre-suspension Hearings.* In *Gilbert v. Homar*, 520 U.S. 924 (1997), the Court held that a tenured employee suspended after being arrested for a felony has no due process right to a pre-suspension hearing. In this case, a public university suspended a police officer without pay who had been arrested for the felony of "criminal conspiracy to violate the controlled substance law." Writing for a unanimous Court, Justice Scalia noted that *Loudermill* requires a very limited pre-termination hearing for a public employee who may be fired only for cause. Just as a grand jury indictment suggests that a suspension may be justified, an arrest and formal felony charges support a suspension. Like an indictment, an arrest with charges by an independent entity shows that the suspension is not arbitrary, and the charges are an objective factor that will usually arouse serious public concern. Under these circumstances a pre-suspension hearing may not advance the employee's interest in avoiding a suspension decision made without adequate consideration. However, in this case, a post-suspension hearing did not occur until 17 days after the charges against the employee were dropped. Because the risk of erroneous deprivation significantly increased after the charges were dropped, a prompt hearing was advisable. Justice Scalia remanded the case to determine whether the post-suspension hearing was "sufficiently prompt."

DESHANEY v. WINNEBAGO COUNTY DEP'T OF SOCIAL SERVICES, 489 U.S. 189 (1989). In *DeShaney*, the Supreme Court ruled that the failure of the Department of Social Services (DSS) to provide adequate protection to a child from a parent whom the Department knew was physically abusive did not violate the child's substantive rights under the Due Process Clause of the Fourteenth Amendment.

Joshua DeShaney was born in 1979. In 1980, his parents divorced and his father, Randy DeShaney, was granted custody of Joshua. Father and son moved from Wyoming to Winnebago County, Wisconsin, where Randy DeShaney remarried. The first contact that the DSS had with the DeShaneys was in January of 1982 when the father's second wife reported to the police that he had "hit the boy causing marks and [was] a prime case for child abuse." The DSS interviewed Randy, but dropped the matter when he denied the charges. In January 1983, after Joshua was hospitalized with multiple bruises and abrasions, the examining doctor informed the DSS that he suspected child abuse. Immediately, the DSS obtained a court order placing Joshua in the temporary custody of the hospital. "Three days later, the county convened an ad hoc 'Child Protection Team' — consisting of a pediatrician, a psychologist, a police detective, the county's lawyer, several DSS caseworkers, and various hospital personnel." On the panel's recommendation, the court dismissed the child protection case for insufficient evidence. Nevertheless, the panel secured an agreement from Randy on protective measures, which included providing Randy with counseling and enrolling Joshua in preschool. One month later, emergency room personnel informed the assigned caseworker that Joshua had again received "suspicious injuries." During the next six months, this same caseworker observed numerous suspicious injuries to Joshua during her monthly visits to the DeShaney home. The caseworker noted in her files that the preventive measures that had been agreed upon had not been carried out. She also recorded "her continuing suspicions that someone in the home was abusing Joshua." By now, Randy DeShaney had divorced again and was living with a girlfriend. In November 1983, emergency room personnel again informed the DSS that Joshua had been treated for injuries indicating child abuse. In addition, on her next two visits to the DeShaney household, the caseworker failed to see Joshua, having been told that he was "too ill to see her." No action was taken by the DSS.

In March 1984, Randy DeShaney beat his four-year-old son into a life-threatening coma. "Emergency brain surgery revealed a series of hemorrhages caused by traumatic injuries to the head inflicted over a long period of time." The injuries to Joshua caused profound retardation necessitating institutionalization for life.

After Randy DeShaney was convicted of child abuse, Joshua and his mother filed suit under 42 U.S.C. § 1983, alleging that Winnebago County, the DSS, and certain DSS employees deprived Joshua of his liberty without due process of law. The claim rested on the DSS's failure to protect the child from the risk of abuse about which they knew or should have known. The District Court granted summary judgment for respondents, which was affirmed by the Court of Appeals.

Chief Justice Rehnquist's majority (6-3) opinion described the claim as "one invoking the substantive rather than procedural component of the Due Process Clause."[54] In rejecting this claim, the Court construed the Due Process Clause as a "limitation on the State's power to act, not as a guarantee of certain minimal levels of safety and security." Distinguishing between negative rights and "affirmative obligations," the Court stated that the purpose of the Clause "was to protect the people from the State, not to ensure that the State protected them from each other."

The Chief Justice turned to consider whether there was a "special relationship" between the DSS and Joshua that might impose affirmative duties on the DSS. Petitioners based this argument on *Estelle v. Gamble*, 429 U.S. 97 (1976) and *Youngberg v. Romeo*, 457 U.S. 307 (1982). In *Estelle*, the injured individual was a prisoner and in *Youngberg*, he was an involuntarily committed mental patient. The majority argued that the State's affirmative duty in these cases arose "from the limitation which it has imposed on his freedom to act on his own behalf."

Thus, while DSS "may have been aware of the dangers Joshua faced in the free world, it played no part in their creation, nor did it do anything to render him any more vulnerable to them. That the State once took temporary custody of Joshua does not alter the analysis," as "the State does not become the permanent guarantor of an individual's safety by having once offered him shelter."

While Joshua might still have redress under state tort law; the Due Process Clause "does not transform every tort committed by a state actor into a constitutional violation." Indeed, had state officials "moved too soon to take custody of the son away from the father, they would likely have been met with charges of improperly intruding into the parent-child relationship, charges based on the same Due Process Clause that forms the basis for the present charge of failure to provide adequate protection."

Justice Brennan wrote a dissent in which Justices Marshall and Blackmun joined. The plaintiffs were not asserting that the Constitution generally "safeguards positive as well as negative liberties." The dissent focused on the action followed by the inaction taken by the State of Wisconsin.

The Court failed "to see that inaction can be every bit as abusive of power as action, that oppression can result when a State undertakes a vital duty and then ignores it. Today's opinion construes the Due Process Clause to permit a State to displace private sources of protection and then, at the critical moment, to shrug its shoulders and turn away from the harm that it has promised to try to prevent."

Justice Blackmun filed a separate dissent, criticizing the majority's "sterile

---

[54] Joshua and his mother also argued "that the Wisconsin child protection statutes gave Joshua an 'entitlement' to receive protective services in accordance with the terms of the statute, an entitlement that would enjoy due process protection against state deprivation under our decision in *Board of Regents v. Roth*." As this argument had not been made in either of the lower courts, the Chief Justice declined to consider it.

formalism" that "attempts to draw a sharp and rigid line between action and inaction."

NOTES

(1) For an interesting perspective on *DeShaney*, see Oren, *The State's Failure to Protect Children and Substantive Due Process: DeShaney in Context*, 68 N.C. L. REV. 659, 731 (1990) ("Having set the trap, through its monopolization of child protection in the hands of a social service agency and through its toleration and even endorsement of the physical power parents may exercise over their children, that state may not be excused from constitutional accountability on the pretext that the abusive parent formally retained custody and therefore sprung the trap by himself."); Lupu, *Mediating Institutions: Beyond the Public/Private Distinction: The Separation of Powers and the Protection of Children*, 61 U. CHI. L. REV. 1317, 1372 (1994) ("[T]he Court held that the federal Constitution imposed no duty of care upon child protection agencies to remove allegedly abused children from harm's way.").

(2) *Enforcement of Restraining Orders.* In *Town of Castle Rock, Colorado v. Gonzales*, 545 U.S. 748 (2005), the Court held that lack of enforcement of a restraining order did not give rise to an action under the Due Process Clause. A father took his three children in violation of a restraining order and murdered them. The mother called the police about her husband having taken the children several times that evening, but the police failed to take action, telling her to wait a few hours in hopes that her husband would return the children. Writing for a 7-2 majority, Justice Scalia held that the Colorado statute did not specify a statutory entitlement as it did not make enforcement of the restraining order mandatory. "A well established tradition of police discretion has long coexisted with apparently mandatory arrest statutes." Under this case and *DeShaney v. Winnebago County Department of Social Services, supra*, "the benefit that a third party may receive from having someone else arrested" seldom triggers either the procedural or substantive protection under the Due Process Clause. The Court has been reluctant "to treat the Fourteenth Amendment as 'a font of tort law.'" State law is the appropriate source of such a cause of action.

Justice Souter concurred, joined by Justice Breyer. Finding a statutory entitlement in this case "would federalize every mandatory state-law direction to executive officers." Justice Stevens dissented, joined by Justice Ginsburg. The majority did not sufficiently defer to the Court of Appeals' "eminently reasonable" conclusion that the Colorado legislature intended to remove police discretion in the enforcement of domestic restraining orders.

Chapter VIII
RACIAL EQUALITY

§ 8.01 OVERVIEW

Introductory Note. While there has been considerable debate over the intended scope of the Thirteenth, Fourteenth, and Fifteenth Amendments [see introduction to Chapter VI], there is no doubt that a dominant force behind the Amendments was the desire to secure equal rights for the newly-freed slaves. The Thirteenth and Fifteenth Amendments directly address slavery and racial equality. The Fourteenth Amendment, while far broader in its language and in its subsequent interpretation, emerged in large part from doubts about Congressional power to protect individuals against state violation of civil rights — particularly those infringements which were based on race or which constituted the perpetuation of slavery. As the legacy of slavery remains, questions of racial equality will continue to shape the interpretation of the great Amendments which enshrined in law the military result of the Civil War. *See* Derrick Bell, *Foreword: The Civil Rights Chronicles*, 99 HARV. L. REV. 4 (1985) (examining the path of the civil rights movement and some of the deep problems and "myths" that still beset the achievement of racial justice). Cases concerning racial equality involve primarily the Equal Protection Clause of the Fourteenth Amendment. Of course that Clause has also been the basis of constitutional claims by other individuals and groups, representing interests that cut across all segments of American society. Equality is, after all, a recurring theme in American constitutional law, and the principles governing the interpretation of the Equal Protection Clause overlap from one area to another. Since racial equality cases have provided the forum for the fashioning of the most significant equal protection concepts, we consider these cases to be the appropriate starting point for tracing the development of equality in modern American constitutional law. *See generally* Joseph Tussman & Jacobus tenBroek, *The Equal Protection of Laws*, 37 CAL. L. REV. 341 (1949) (classic treatment of the principles underlying the Equal Protection Clause). Section 8.01 reviews the demise of the system of segregation. The discussion begins with *Plessy v. Ferguson*, 163 U.S. 537 (1896) and *Brown v. Board of Education*, 347 U.S. 483 (1954). Amplifying the specific concern of *Brown*, the remainder of the section considers judicial efforts to effect school desegregation. Section 8.02 begins with some basic principles in the evolution of equal protection jurisprudence in questions of race and ethnicity. These focus on such concepts as purposeful discrimination, suspect class, and strict scrutiny. Subsequent subsections specifically treat racial discrimination in employment, housing, the right to vote, and the criminal justice system. However, before proceeding to specific sections, the Chapter begins with the case of *Dred Scott v. Sandford*, 60 U.S. 393 (1857), which sheds the sobering historical perspective on a system of constitutionalized slavery.

DRED SCOTT v. SANDFORD,[1] 60 U.S. 393 (1857). The plaintiff Dred Scott was a slave owned by Dr. John Emerson, an Army surgeon. In 1834, Dr. Emerson and Dred Scott moved from Missouri, a state where slavery was legal, to a military post at Rock Island in Illinois, a state where slavery was illegal. Two years later they went to Fort Snelling, a military post located in the free territory of Wisconsin north of the latitude line of 36° 30'.[2] While he was at Ft. Snelling, Dr. Emerson purchased another slave,

---

[1] The spelling of the appellee's name in the U.S. Reports is inaccurate. The proper spelling is "Sanford." Apparently John Sanford in Dred Scott was mistaken with a "John F.A. Sandford" in another case argued during the December 1855 Term. *See* John S. Vishneski, III, *What the Court Decided in* Dred Scott v. Sandford, 32 AM. J. LEGAL HIST. 373 (1988).

[2] The Missouri Compromise, a Congressional act passed in 1820, mandated that slavery was illegal in all

Harriet. Dred Scott married Harriet in 1836. The Scotts were still above the northern border of Missouri when their daughter Eliza was born. Dr. Emerson and the Scott family returned to Missouri in 1838; the Scotts' second daughter was born in Missouri.

Dr. Emerson died after his return to Missouri. He left his slaves and property to his wife Irene Emerson. Dred Scott sued Mrs. Emerson in state court in order to obtain his freedom. He contended that he was free because he had resided in a free state, Illinois, and in territory that was free under the Missouri Compromise. The trial court ruled against Dred Scott, but it granted his motion for a new trial. Mrs. Emerson appealed the grant of a new trial to the Missouri Supreme Court. The Missouri Supreme Court refused to review the decision. The second trial court ruled in favor of Dred Scott. On the second appeal, the Missouri Supreme Court held that neither Illinois law nor federal laws applicable only to the territories were pertinent; it reversed the trial court decision.

Dred Scott then sued in the Circuit Court of the United States for the District of Missouri. The suit claimed that John Sanford, the brother of Mrs. Emerson and the alleged owner of Dred Scott[3] had illegally assaulted and imprisoned the Scott family. The suit stated that Sanford was a citizen of New York and that Scott was a citizen of Missouri; therefore, the basis of federal jurisdiction was diversity. Sanford filed a plea in abatement,[4] claiming that the Court did not have jurisdiction over the case because there was no diversity between the parties. The plea asserted that since Dred Scott was a descendant of African slaves, he was not a citizen of Missouri. Scott filed a demurrer to the plea in abatement, and the Circuit Court sustained it. In the trial on the merits, however, the Circuit Court ruled in favor of Sanford. Dred Scott appealed his case to the Supreme Court.

An opinion written by Chief Justice Taney identified two questions that the record presented:

1. Had the Circuit Court of the United States jurisdiction to hear and determine the case between these parties? and,

2. If it had jurisdiction, is the judgment it has given erroneous or not? The first question presented the issue of whether a black person who descended from African slaves could be a United States citizen. If a black person is a citizen, the Chief Justice noted, he would have the privilege of suing in a federal court. The opinion offered the following definition of those who were United States citizens: "It is true, every person, and every class and description of persons, who were at the time of the adoption of the Constitution recognized as citizens in the several States, became also citizens of this new political body, but none other; it was formed by them, and for them and their posterity, but for no one else. And the personal rights and privileges guaranteed to citizens of this new sovereignty were intended to embrace those only who were then members of the several state communities, or who should afterwards, by birthright or otherwise, become

---

territories and any state above the 36° 30' line of latitude. Any of the states below that line could choose to make slavery legal. Moreover, slavery could exist in the territories below the 36° 30' line; when a territory decided to enter the Union as a state, it would choose whether it would be a slave state.

[3] Although the agreed statement of facts in the case maintains that Dr. Emerson had sold Dred Scott to Sanford shortly before the federal suit, there is some doubt as to whether this was actually true. Dr. Emerson had been dead for years before the federal suit began. The ownership issue was important because Sanford could have ended the suit by showing that he did not own Dred Scott. See WALTER EHRLICH, THEY HAVE NO RIGHTS: DRED SCOTT'S STRUGGLE FOR FREEDOM 76–78 (1979).

[4] A plea in abatement was a form of common law pleading, which did not question the merits of a plaintiff's claim but objected to the time, place, or manner of the claim. Although the plea in abatement still exists in some states, it has been abolished by the Federal Rules of Civil Procedure and replaced with the motion to dismiss. See, e.g., FED. R. CIV. P. 12 (b).

members." Chief Justice Taney then asserted that history, legislation pertaining to blacks, and the Declaration of Independence all indicated that neither slaves nor their descendants — "whether they had become free or not" — were intended to be United States citizens. "They had for more than a century before been regarded as beings of an inferior order; and altogether unfit to associate with the white race, either in social or political relations; and so far inferior, that they had no rights which the white man was bound to respect; and that the negro might justly and lawfully be reduced to slavery for his benefit. He was bought and sold, and treated as an ordinary article of merchandise and traffic, whenever a profit could be made by it. This opinion was at that time fixed and universal in the civilized portion of the white race. It was regarded as an axiom in morals as well as in politics, which no one thought of disputing, or supposed to be open to dispute."

Chief Justice Taney relied on specific language in the Constitution for holding erroneous the denial of the plea in abatement. He looked to the fact that the Constitution allowed for the importation of slaves and had required the return of fugitive slaves. Relying on these provisions, the Chief Justice found that the Framers did not intend to confer constitutional rights on blacks or their descendants.

On the first issue, the Court concluded: "Dred Scott was not a citizen of Missouri within the meaning of the Constitution of the United States, and not entitled as such to sue in its courts."

After finding the Circuit Court erred in dismissing the plea in abatement, Chief Justice Taney proceeded to discuss the other errors he had found. He reasoned that the Court was justified in doing so and that the discussion of the merits of the case was not mere dicta. "In a writ of error to a circuit court of the United States, the whole record is before this court for examination and decision; and if the sum in controversy is large enough to give jurisdiction, it is not only the right, but it is the judicial duty of the court, to examine the whole case as presented by the record; and if it appears upon its face that any material error or errors have been committed by the court below, it is the duty of this court to reverse the judgment, and remand the case."

The discussion of the merits focused on two questions: (1) whether the Scotts were free because they had resided in the Wisconsin Territory above the 36° 30' line; (2) whether Dred Scott was free because he had lived in the free state of Illinois. The answer to the first question was dependent on whether the Constitution gave Congress the power to enact the Missouri Compromise which banned slavery above the 36° 30' line of latitude.

Chief Justice Taney stated that with regard to the regulation of the territories, Congress was controlled by the Constitution. He found that the Missouri Compromise was an unconstitutional exercise of Congressional power that violated the Due Process Clause of the Fifth Amendment. "[A]n Act of Congress which deprives a citizen of the United States of his liberty or property, merely because he came himself or brought his property into a particular Territory of the United States, and who had committed no offense against the laws, could hardly be dignified with the name of due process of law."

Chief Justice Taney dismissed the idea that slaves were a special category of property and that different rules applied to them. "[I]f the Constitution recognizes the right of property of the master in a slave, and makes no distinction between that description of property and other property owned by a citizen, no tribunal, acting under the authority of the United States, whether it be legislative, executive, or judicial, has a right to draw such a distinction, or deny to it the benefit of the provisions and guarantees which have been provided for the protection of private property against the encroachments of the governments."

"[T]he right of property in a slave is distinctly and expressly affirmed in the

Constitution. The right to traffic in it, like an ordinary article of merchandise and property, was guaranteed to the citizens of the United States, in every State that might desire it, for twenty years. And the government in express terms is pledged to protect it in all future time, if the slave escapes from his owner. . . . And no word can be found in the Constitution which gives Congress a greater power over slave property, or which entitles property of that kind to less protection than property of any other description."

On the first issue the Court held that "the Act of Congress which prohibited a citizen from holding and owning property of this kind in the territory of the United States north of the line therein mentioned, is not warranted by the Constitution, and is therefore void; and that neither Dred Scott himself, nor any of his family, were made free by being carried into this territory; even if they had been carried there by the owner, with the intention of becoming a permanent resident."

The opinion gave a brief answer on the second issue, holding that "as Scott was a slave when taken into the State of Illinois by his owner, and was there held as such, and brought back in that character, his status, as free or slave, depended on the laws of Missouri, and not of Illinois." The Chief Justice concluded his opinion by restating that Dred Scott was not a citizen of the United States. He ordered the Circuit Court to reverse the judgment in favor of Sanford and then to dismiss the case for lack of jurisdiction.

Six concurring opinions (Justices Wayne, Nelson, Grier, Campbell, Daniel, and Catron) and two dissents (Justices McLean and Curtis) were filed in the case. Because no four other Justices explicitly agreed with Chief Justice Taney's decision to consider the plea in abatement, it is not clear that he spoke for a majority of the Justices on that issue. One analysis suggests that a majority of the Court, Chief Justice Taney and Justices Wayne, Daniel, Curtis, and Grier, supported the Court's authority to examine the plea in abatement.[5] (However, of these five, only three, the Chief Justice and Justices Wayne and Daniel explicitly decided the issue against Dred Scott; Justices Grier and Curtis decided in his favor.)

On the merits of Dred Scott's claim, Justices Wayne, Grier, Daniel, Campbell, and Catron agreed with Chief Justice Taney's finding that Dred Scott was not free by virtue of his stay in the Wisconsin territory because the Missouri Compromise was unconstitutional. Justice Nelson did not pass on the constitutionality of the Missouri Compromise. On the issue of whether the stay in Illinois freed Dred Scott, Justices Wayne, Nelson, Grier, Daniel, and Catron agreed with the Chief Justice that Missouri's law, not Illinois' determined his status.

Justice McLean dissented. He contended that the Framers thought slavery was "emphatically a state institution," and did not intend to classify slaves as property. "[W]e know as a historical fact, that James Madison, that great and good man, a leading member in the Federal Convention, was solicitous to guard the language of that instrument so as not to convey the idea that there could be property in man." He also argued that Congress did have the power to regulate the introduction of slavery in the territories. Moreover, a slave who, with his or her master's consent, goes into a free state or territory becomes free. "[W]here the law does not confer this power, it cannot be exercised." Justice McLean appealed to precedents in slave states, including Missouri (before *Dred Scott v. Irene Emerson*) which supported the proposition that "where the master, by a residence with his slave in a State or Territory where slavery is prohibited, the slave was entitled to his freedom everywhere."

Justice Curtis' dissent maintained that the Court could address the issue of

---

[5] Vishneski, *supra* Footnote 1.

jurisdiction. He found that the Circuit Court correctly rejected the plea in abatement. On the merits of the case, Justice Curtis argued that in accordance with the Missouri Compromise — which he found to be constitutional — Dred Scott was free when he resided in the Wisconsin Territory; his status did not change when he returned to Missouri. Justice Curtis justified his position by referring to rules of international law. He argued that Missouri did have the power to change Scott's status back to slave, but it must do so through some positive law.

§ 8.02 SEGREGATION IN PUBLIC FACILITIES

[1] The Rise and Fall of "Separate but Equal"

PLESSY v. FERGUSON, 163 U.S. 537 (1896). In *Plessy v. Ferguson*, Justice Brown upheld a Louisiana statute requiring separate railway coaches for white and black passengers. The plaintiff was an American citizen residing in Louisiana. Although he did not appear black, he had a mixed heritage and was seven eighths Caucasian and one eighth black. When the plaintiff seated himself in a railway coach reserved for white passengers, the conductor demanded that he move to the coach reserved for non-white passengers. Because he did not comply, the plaintiff was forcibly removed from the railway coach and imprisoned for violating the statute, which provided in pertinent part that railway companies "shall provide equal but separate accommodations for the white, and colored races, by providing two or more passenger coaches for each passenger train, or by dividing the passenger coaches by a partition." A violation of the statute carried a twenty-five dollar fine or a prison term of not more than twenty days.

First, the Court addressed whether the statute violated the Thirteenth Amendment. In the *Slaughter-House Cases*, 83 U.S. 36 (1872), the Court decided that the Amendment was "intended primarily to abolish slavery, as it had been previously known in this country, . . . and that the use of the word 'servitude' was intended to prohibit the use of all forms of involuntary slavery, of whatever class or name." As the statute merely recognized a distinction between races and did not seek to undermine the legal equality of either race, the Court found no Thirteenth Amendment violation.

Considering whether a Fourteenth Amendment violation existed, the Court acknowledged that the Fourteenth Amendment was intended to protect the legal equality of the races. However, the Amendment "could not have been intended to abolish distinctions based upon color, or to enforce social, as distinguished from political equality, or a commingling of the two races upon terms unsatisfactory to either." Indeed, laws allowing or requiring segregation of the races did not suggest the inferiority of either race and had long been recognized as a legitimate exercise of state police power. For example, even courts that had historically championed black rights, such as those in Boston and the District of Columbia, approved of racially segregated schools. In addition, although laws prohibiting intermarriage between the races may technically impair the freedom to contract, they continued to be viewed as valid exercises of police power.

The Court emphasized that it had recognized a distinction between laws that endangered the political equality of blacks and laws that required separation of the races in "schools, theatres and railway carriages." For instance, in *Strauder v. West Virginia*, 100 U.S. 303 (1879), the Court struck down a law that limited juries to white males who were twenty-one years old and citizens of the state; this law openly discriminated against blacks, suggesting a "legal inferiority" and "reducing them to a condition of servility."

But the plaintiff argued that under the Court's logic, legislatures could also require railways to provide separate coaches for individuals with a particular hair color, aliens, and some nationalities or could enact laws that required blacks and whites to walk on different sides of the street and to paint their houses, vehicles, and business signs different colors, based on the theory that one side of the street was no better or worse than the other and that one paint color was no better or worse than the other. The Court responded that the legislature could only enact reasonable laws "in good faith for the promotion for the public good, and not for the annoyance or oppression of a particular class." Following this reasoning, the Court held, "[W]e cannot say that a law which authorizes or even requires the separation of the two races in public conveyances is unreasonable."

Consequently, the Court concluded that to achieve social equality, the races must voluntarily learn to appreciate "each other's merits." The legislature is "powerless to eradicate racial instincts or to abolish distinctions based upon physical differences, and the attempt to do so can only result in accentuating the difficulties of the present situation." Thus, the Constitution can ensure equality only in civil and political rights and cannot enforce social equality.

In a powerful dissent, Justice Harlan disclaimed the Court's decision as one that would "prove to be quite as pernicious as the decision . . . in the *Dred Scott* Case." Justice Harlan argued that the legislature cannot dole out civil rights based on race and contended that the statute at issue was "inconsistent not only with that equality of rights which pertains to citizenship, National and State, but with the personal liberty enjoyed by every one within the United States." The Thirteenth, Fourteenth, and Fifteenth Amendments require " 'that the law in the states shall be the same for the black as for the white; that all persons, whether colored or white, shall stand equal before the laws of the states; in regard to the colored race, for whose protection the amendment was primarily designed, that no discrimination shall be made against them by law because of their color.' "

Justice Harlan further argued that the statute was not nondiscriminatory because its purpose was to exclude blacks from the white railway coaches and not to exclude whites from the black coaches. If the state could regulate in this manner, it could also confine blacks to one side of the street or the courtroom, punish blacks and whites who rode in vehicles together on the street, or outlaw the commingling of the races in public assemblies where political questions were discussed. The state could even segregate public transportation by nationality or religion.

While white citizens may possess more wealth and power, Justice Harlan denied that the Constitution tolerates unequal treatment of the races: "But in view of the Constitution, in the eye of the law, there is in this country no superior, dominant, ruling class of citizens. There is no caste here. Our Constitution is color-blind, and neither knows nor tolerates classes among citizens. In respect of civil rights, all citizens are equal before the law." Justice Harlan concluded that legislation that reinforces the idea that blacks are inferior only exacerbates racial tensions and hostilities, despite the overwhelming need for the races to coexist peacefully.

NOTE

For a critical perspective on the color-blind approach, *see* Neil Gotanda, *A Critique of "Our Constitution Is Color-Blind,"* 44 STAN. L. REV. 1, 2 (1991) (contending that "the United States Supreme Court's use of color-blind constitutionalism — a collection of legal themes functioning as a racial ideology — fosters white racial domination").

BROWN v. BOARD OF EDUCATION OF TOPEKA
347 U.S. 483, 74 S. Ct. 686, 98 L. Ed. 873 (1954)

CHIEF JUSTICE WARREN delivered the opinion of the Court.

These cases come to us from the States of Kansas, South Carolina, Virginia, and Delaware. They are premised on different facts and different local conditions, but a common legal question justifies their consideration together in this consolidated opinion.

In each of the cases, minors of the Negro race, through their legal representatives, seek the aid of the courts in obtaining admission to the public schools of their community on a nonsegregated basis. In each instance, they have been denied admission to schools attended by white children under laws requiring or permitting segregation according to race. This segregation was alleged to deprive the plaintiffs of the equal protection of the laws under the Fourteenth Amendment. In each of the cases other than the Delaware case, a three-judge federal district court denied relief to the plaintiffs on the so-called "separate but equal" doctrine announced by this Court in *Plessy v. Ferguson*, 163 U.S. 537 (1896). Under that doctrine, equality of treatment is accorded when the races are provided substantially equal facilities, even though these facilities be separate. In the Delaware case, the Supreme Court of Delaware adhered to that doctrine, but ordered that the plaintiffs be admitted to the white schools because of their superiority to the Negro schools.

The plaintiffs contend that segregated public schools are not "equal" and cannot be made "equal," and that hence they are deprived of the equal protection of the laws. Because of the obvious importance of the question presented, the Court took jurisdiction. Argument was heard in the 1952 Term, and reargument was heard this Term on certain questions propounded by the Court.

Reargument was largely devoted to the circumstances surrounding the adoption of the Fourteenth Amendment in 1868. It covered exhaustively consideration of the Amendment in Congress, ratification by the states, then existing practices in racial segregation, and the views of proponents and opponents of the Amendment. This discussion and our own investigation convince us that, although these sources cast some light, it is not enough to resolve the problem with which we are faced. At best, they are inconclusive. The most avid proponents of the post-War Amendments undoubtedly intended them to remove all legal distinctions among "all persons born or naturalized in the United States." Their opponents, just as certainly, were antagonistic to both the letter and the spirit of the Amendments and wished them to have the most limited effect. What others in Congress and the state legislatures had in mind cannot be determined with any degree of certainty.

An additional reason for the inconclusive nature of the Amendment's history, with respect to segregated schools, is the status of public education at that time. In the South, the movement toward free common schools, supported by general taxation, had not yet taken hold. Education of white children was largely in the hands of private groups. Education of Negroes was almost nonexistent, and practically all of the race were illiterate. In fact, any education of Negroes was forbidden by law in some states. Today, in contrast, many Negroes have achieved outstanding success in the arts and sciences as well as in the business and professional world. It is true that public school education at the time of the Amendment had advanced further in the North, but the effect of the Amendment on Northern States was generally ignored in the congressional debates. Even in the North, the conditions of public education did not approximate those existing today. The curriculum was usually rudimentary; ungraded schools were common in rural areas; the school term was but three months a year in many states; and compulsory school attendance was virtually unknown. . . .

In the first cases in this Court construing the Fourteenth Amendment, decided shortly after its adoption, the Court interpreted it as proscribing all state-imposed discriminations against the Negro race.[6] The doctrine of "separate but equal" did not make its appearance in this Court until 1896 in the case of *Plessy v. Ferguson*, involving not education but transportation.[7] American courts have since labored with the doctrine for over half a century. In this Court, there have been six cases involving the "separate but equal" doctrine in the field of public education. In *Cumming v. Board of Education of Richmond County*, 175 U.S. 528 [(1899)], and *Gong Lum v. Rice*, 275 U.S. 78 [(1927)], the validity of the doctrine itself was not challenged. In more recent cases, all on the graduate school level, inequality was found in that specific benefits enjoyed by white students were denied to Negro students of the same educational qualifications. *State of Missouri ex rel. Gaines v. Canada*, 305 U.S. 337 [(1938)]; *Sipuel v. Board of Regents of University of Oklahoma*, 332 U.S. 631 [(1948)]; *Sweatt v. Painter*, 339 U.S. 629 [(1950)]; *McLaurin v. Oklahoma State Regents*, 339 U.S. 637 [(1950)]. In none of these cases was it necessary to re-examine the doctrine to grant relief to the Negro plaintiff. And in *Sweatt v. Painter*, the Court expressly reserved decision on the question whether *Plessy v. Ferguson* should be held inapplicable to public education.

In the instant cases, that question is directly presented. Here, unlike *Sweatt v. Painter*, there are findings below that the Negro and white schools involved have been equalized, or are being equalized, with respect to buildings, curricula, qualifications and salaries of teachers, and other "tangible" factors. Our decision, therefore, cannot turn on merely a comparison of these tangible factors in the Negro and white schools involved in each of the cases. We must look instead to the effect of segregation itself on public education.

In approaching this problem, we cannot turn the clock back to 1868 when the Amendment was adopted, or even to 1896 when *Plessy v. Ferguson* was written. We must consider public education in the light of its full development and its present place in American life throughout the Nation. . . .

Today, education is perhaps the most important function of state and local governments. Compulsory school attendance laws and the great expenditures for education both demonstrate our recognition of the importance of education to our democratic society. It is required in the performance of our most basic public responsibilities, even service in the armed forces. It is the very foundation of good citizenship. Today it is a principal instrument in awakening the child to cultural values, in preparing him for later professional training, and in helping him to adjust normally to his environment. In these days, it is doubtful that any child may reasonably be expected to succeed in life if he is denied the opportunity of an education. Such an opportunity, where the state has undertaken to provide it, is a right which must be made available to all on equal terms.

We come then to the question presented: Does segregation of children in public schools solely on the basis of race, even though the physical facilities and other "tangible" factors may be equal, deprive the children of the minority group of equal educational opportunities? We believe that it does.

---

[6] [Court's footnote 5] In re *Slaughter-House Cases*, [111 U.S. 746 (1884)]; *Strauder v. West Virginia*, [100 U.S. 303 (1879)]. . . .

[7] [Court's footnote 6] The doctrine apparently originated in *Roberts v. City of Boston*, 1850, 5 Cush. 198, 59 Mass. 198, 206, upholding school segregation against attack as being violative of a state constitutional guarantee of equality. Segregation in Boston public schools was eliminated in 1855. Mass. Acts 1855, c. 256. But elsewhere in the North segregation in public education has persisted in some communities until recent years. It is apparent that such segregation has long been a nationwide problem, not merely one of sectional concern.

In *Sweatt v. Painter*, in finding that a segregated law school for Negroes could not provide them equal educational opportunities, this Court relied in large part on "those qualities which are incapable of objective measurement but which make for greatness in a law school." In *McLaurin v. Oklahoma State Regents*, the Court, in requiring that a Negro admitted to a white graduate school be treated like all other students, again resorted to the intangible considerations: ". . . his ability to study, to engage in discussions and exchange views with other students and, in general learn his profession." Such considerations apply with added force to children in grade and high schools. To separate them from others of similar age and qualifications solely because of their race generates a feeling of inferiority as to their status in the community that may affect their hearts and minds in a way unlikely ever to be undone. The effect of this separation on their educational opportunities was well stated by a finding in the *Kansas* case by a court which nevertheless felt compelled to rule against the Negro plaintiffs:

> Segregation of white and colored children in public schools has a detrimental effect upon the colored children. The impact is greater when it has the sanction of the law; for the policy of separating the races is usually interpreted as denoting the inferiority of the Negro group. A sense of inferiority affects the motivation of a child to learn. Segregation with the sanction of law, therefore, has a tendency to [retard] the educational and mental development of Negro children and to deprive them of some of the benefits they would receive in a racial[ly] integrated school system.

Whatever may have been the extent of psychological knowledge at the time of *Plessy v. Ferguson*, this finding is amply supported by modern authority.[8] Any language in *Plessy v. Ferguson* contrary to this finding is rejected.

We conclude that in the field of public education the doctrine of "separate but equal" has no place. Separate educational facilities are inherently unequal. Therefore, we hold that the plaintiffs and others similarly situated for whom the actions have been brought are, by reason of the segregation complained of, deprived of the equal protection of the laws guaranteed by the Fourteenth Amendment. This disposition makes unnecessary any discussion whether such segregation also violates the Due Process Clause of the Fourteenth Amendment.

Because these are class actions, because of the wide applicability of this decision, and because of the great variety of local conditions, the formulation of decrees in these cases presents problems of considerable complexity. On reargument, the consideration of appropriate relief was necessarily subordinated to the primary question — the constitutionality of segregation in public education. We have now announced that such segregation is a denial of the equal protection of the laws. In order that we may have the full assistance of the parties in formulating decrees, the cases will be restored to the docket, and the parties are requested to present further argument on Questions 4 and 5 previously propounded by the Court for the reargument this Term.[9] The Attorney

---

[8] [Court's footnote 11] K. B. Clark, *Effect of Prejudice and Discrimination on Personality Development* (Midcentury White House Conference on Children and Youth, 1950); WITMER AND KOTINSKY, PERSONALITY IN THE MAKING (1952), c. VI; Deutscher and Chein, *The Psychological Effects of Enforced Segregation: A Survey of Social Science Opinion*, 26 J. PSYCHOL. 259 (1948); Chein, *What are the Psychological Effects of Segregation Under Conditions of Equal Facilities?*, 3 INT. J. OPINION AND ATTITUDE RES. 229 (1949); BRAMELD, EDUCATIONAL COSTS, IN DISCRIMINATION AND NATIONAL WELFARE (MacIver, ed., 1949), 44–48; FRAZIER, THE NEGRO IN THE UNITED STATES (1949), 674–681. And *see generally* Myrdal, AN AMERICAN DILEMMA (1944).

[9] [Court's footnote 13] "4. Assuming it is decided that segregation in public schools violates the Fourteenth Amendment

"(a) would a decree necessarily follow providing that, within the limits set by normal geographic school

General of the United States is again invited to participate. The Attorneys General of the states requiring or permitting segregation in public education will also be permitted to appear as *amici curiae* upon request to do so by September 15, 1954, and submission of briefs by October 1, 1954.

NOTES

(1) *Equal Protection and the Federal Government.* In the companion case of *Bolling v. Sharpe*, 347 U.S. 497 (1954), the Court held that segregated schools in the District of Columbia violated the Due Process Clause of the Fifth Amendment. Although the Fifth Amendment does not contain an Equal Protection Clause, Chief Justice Warren wrote:

> The concepts of equal protection and due process, both stemming from our American ideal of fairness, are not mutually exclusive. The "equal protection of the laws" is a more explicit safeguard of prohibited unfairness than "due process of law," and, therefore, we do not imply that the two are always interchangeable phrases. But, as this Court has recognized, discrimination may be so unjustifiable as to be violative of due process. Classifications based solely upon race must be scrutinized with particular care, since they are contrary to our traditions and hence constitutionally suspect. . . . Segregation in public education is not reasonably related to any proper governmental objective, and thus it imposes on Negro children of the District of Columbia a burden that constitutes an arbitrary deprivation of their liberty in violation of the Due Process Clause.

While generally parallel, the Due Process Clause of the Fifth Amendment occasionally embodies a standard of equal protection different from that applicable to the states through the Fourteenth Amendment. *See Hampton v. Mow Sun Wong*, 426 U.S. 88 (1976).

(2) *Social Science Data.* Perhaps because the *Brown* case was purposefully devoid of equal protection doctrine which (in later years) has accompanied Supreme Court pronouncements in this area, (e.g., there was no reference in *Brown* to "suspect classes" or "strict scrutiny" or "fundamental rights"), there has been considerable debate concerning the legitimacy of the opinion. This controversy was fueled by the references, in a famous footnote, to social science data, leading to the oft-repeated assertion that the court "relied" on such data. Also, the result could hardly be justified on historical grounds, as the opinion itself makes clear. For an argument that the law of race relations in the late nineteenth and early twentieth centuries was partly driven by social scientific theories of a very different and racist kind, see Herbert Hovenkamp, *Social Science and Segregation Before* Brown, 1985 DUKE L.J. 624 (1985). The most extensive treatment of *Brown* is found in Richard Kluger's excellent book, SIMPLE JUSTICE (1976). For

---

districting, Negro children should forthwith be admitted to schools of their choice, or

"(b) may this Court, in the exercise of its equity powers, permit an effective gradual adjustment to be brought about from existing segregated systems to a system not based on color distinctions?

"5. On the assumption on which questions 4(a) and (b) are based, and assuming further that this Court will exercise its equity powers to the end described in questions 4(b),

"(a) should this Court formulate detailed decrees in these cases;

"(b) if so, what specific issues should the decrees reach;

"(c) should this Court appoint a special master to hear evidence with a view to recommending specific terms for such decrees;

"(d) should this Court remand to the courts of first instance with directions to frame decrees in these cases, and if so what general directions should the decrees of this Court include and what procedures should the courts of first instance follow in arriving at the specific terms of more detailed decrees?"

contemporary discussion taking different views of the decision, see, e.g., Alexander Bickel, *The Original Understanding and the Segregation Decision*, 69 HARV. L. REV. 1 (1955); Charles L. Black, Jr., *The Lawfulness of the Segregation Decisions*, 69 YALE L.J. 421 (1960); Robert McKay, *Segregation and Public Recreation*, 40 VA. L. REV. 697 (1959); Louis Pollak, *Racial Discrimination and Judicial Integrity*, 108 U. PA. L. REV. 1 (1959); Herbert Wechsler, *Toward Neutral Principles of Constitutional Law*, 73 HARV. L. REV. 1 (1959). For an assessment of impact of *Brown* in the path toward the achievement of racial justice, see William Taylor, Brown, *Equal Protection, and the Isolation of the Poor*, 95 YALE L.J. 1700 (1986). Taylor claims that *Brown* was a "resounding success" but that problems of racial segregation and caste have proven more intransigent than some might have expected. He particularly suggests a need to focus on the problems of the poor.

(3) *A Moral Judgment*. In two penetrating articles, Professor Edmond Cahn took sharp issue with the claim that *Brown* was based neither on the testimony of social scientists (which was ignored by the Supreme Court, although part of the lower court record) nor on the works cited in the footnote. *See* Edmond Cahn, *Jurisprudence*, 30 N.Y.U. L. REV. 150 (1955), and Edmond Cahn, *Jurisprudence*, 31 N.Y.U. L. REV. 182 (1956). On at least one public occasion, the dedication of the Edmond Cahn Room at the New York University School of Law on October 21, 1967, Chief Justice Warren stated that he had not relied on the social science material in reaching the conclusion that segregated education was a violation of the Equal Protection Clause. This is confirmed by Kluger in SIMPLE JUSTICE, at 706.

If the decision was not based on history, or the "evidence" of social scientists, or persuasive legal analysis, what was it based on? Edmond Cahn, in the articles cited above, states that *Brown* was essentially a moral judgment. Is this a valid justification? For an argument that *Brown* is based on history, see Michael W. McConnell, *Originalism and the Desegregation Decisions*, 81 VA. L. REV. 947, 1140 (1995) ("Most commentators have assumed that the ahistorical quality of *Brown* was unavoidable, because an historical approach to the question would have produced a morally unacceptable answer. . . [T]o the contrary . . . school segregation was understood during Reconstruction to violate the principles of equality of the Fourteenth Amendment."). *But see* Michael J. Klarman, *Brown, Originalism, and Constitutional Theory: A Response to Professor McConnell*, 81 VA. L. REV. 1881, 1934–35 (1995) (". . . [L]egal scholars have overwhelmingly portrayed *Brown* as the principal cause of the civil rights revolution, rather than seeing the decision itself as the product of deep social and political forces impelling the nation gradually but ineluctably toward greater racial equality — forces such as the Great Migration, the increasing urbanization of the black population, the decline of Southern agriculture, the increasing potency of the Northern black vote, the burgeoning black middle class, increasing black literacy rates, the egalitarian ideology of World War II, the Cold War imperative for racial change, and the growing social and economic integration of the nation.").

For discussion of the process of drafting *Brown*, see Michael S. Paulsen & Daniel N. Rosen, Brown, Casey-*Style: The Shocking First Draft of the Segregation Opinion*, 69 N.Y.U. L. REV. 1287, 1287–8 (1994) ("Recent historical work on the *Brown* case suggests that it is entirely plausible that a 'middle bloc' of Justices, consisting of Felix Frankfurter, Robert Jackson, and Tom Clark, opposed segregation on policy grounds but were troubled by the legal position of those on the Court (Hugo Black, William Douglas, Harold Burton, and Sherman Minton) who thought that *Plessy* should be forthrightly and flatly overruled. Moreover, it is now recognized that Chief Justice Fred Vinson and Associate Justice Stanley Reed were, at least at first, most unlikely to join the position of the firm anti-*Plessy* bloc. The partial draft 'compromise' opinion reproduced here seems most concerned with the damage to the Court's institutional prestige and credibility, and the possibility that the Court's decree would be disregarded or occasion violence in the South, if a closely divided Court were to overrule *Plessy* in the face of a heated dissenting opinion.").

(4) *Extensions of* Brown. In the first few years after *Brown*, the Court summarily extended its scope to other public facilities, including buses, beaches, libraries, parks and other recreational facilities, casting serious doubt on whether the *Brown* decision was based on the special circumstances surrounding segregated education. See cases cited in Justice White's dissent in *Palmer v. Thompson*, 403 U.S. 217, 244–46 (1971).

The effects of *Brown* were far-reaching: "By winning in court and forcing segregationists to go outside the law to maintain their power, the Movement's litigators helped to erode the facade of inevitability that surrounded the segregation regime and to create the perception of a gap between right and reality, authority and force. Here it is useful to recall the speech with which King launched the boycott in Montgomery. 'We are not wrong,' he told his listeners. For 'if we are wrong, then the Supreme Court of this Nation is wrong.' " *See* Randall Kennedy, *Martin Luther King's Constitution: A Legal History of the Montgomery Bus Boycott*, 98 YALE L.J. 999, 1065 (1989).

(5) *Closing Facilities.* Can a state avoid the constitutional obligation to desegregate public facilities by discontinuing the facility entirely? *Compare Griffin v. County School Board of Prince Edward County*, 377 U.S. 218 (1964) (closing of public schools with county providing public funds to assist children to attend private schools held unconstitutional) *with Palmer v. Thompson*, 403 U.S. 217 (1971) (closing of municipal swimming pool upheld in absence of showing that city was continuing to operate segregated pools; motive of city officials held immaterial).

[2] Enforcing *Brown*: The Fashioning of Judicial Relief

Section Note. Over fifty years after *Brown II, infra* § 8.02[2], which directed the federal courts to implement *Brown I* with all deliberate speed, the task of implementation remains difficult to define and accomplish. At first the challenge was to overcome the resistance in those states where segregated schools were ensconced in law, i.e., *de jure* segregation. Then there was the task of remedying the consequences of these legally-imposed dual school systems. These were primarily the problems of the South. Outside the South, however, segregated school systems existed which were becoming more segregated than those in those states where *de jure* segregation had existed. As the cases in this section demonstrate, the Supreme Court first authorized broad implementation remedies in the Southern states and then extended its reasoning to cases of Northern school desegregation by requiring, as a basis for remedies, proof of a governmental intent to segregate, instead of the existence of a legally imposed dual school system such as had been involved in the *Brown* cases.

The earlier cases in the school desegregation area are concerned with questions of how to establish discriminatory intent and what should be the scope of the remedy. More recent cases often focus on when the desegregation remedy must end.

BROWN v. BOARD OF EDUCATION (BROWN II)
349 U.S., 294, 75 S. Ct. 753, 99 L. Ed. 1083 (1955)

CHIEF JUSTICE WARREN delivered the opinion of the Court.

These cases [*Brown I*] were decided on May 17, 1954. . . .

. . . [W]e requested further argument on the question of relief. In view of the nationwide importance of the decision, we invited the Attorney General of the United States and the Attorneys General of all states requiring or permitting racial discrimination in public education to present their views on that question. . . .

Full implementation of these constitutional principles may require solution of varied local school problems. School authorities have the primary responsibility for elucidating, assessing, and solving these problems; courts will have to consider whether the action of school authorities constitutes good faith implementation of the governing constitutional principles. Because of their proximity to local conditions and the possible need for further hearings, the courts which originally heard these cases can best perform this judicial appraisal. Accordingly, we believe it appropriate to remand the cases to those courts.

In fashioning and effectuating the decrees, the courts will be guided by equitable principles. Traditionally, equity has been characterized by a practical flexibility in shaping its remedies and by a facility for adjusting and reconciling public and private needs. These cases call for the exercise of these traditional attributes of equity power. . . .

While giving weight to these public and private considerations, the courts will require that the defendants make a prompt and reasonable start toward full compliance with our May 17, 1954, ruling. Once such a start has been made, the courts may find that additional time is necessary to carry out the ruling in an effective manner. The burden rests upon the defendants to establish that such time is necessary in the public interest and is consistent with good faith compliance at the earliest practicable date. To that end, the courts may consider problems related to administration, arising from the physical condition of the school plant, the school transportation system, personnel, revision of school districts and attendance areas into compact units to achieve a system of determining admission to the public schools on a nonracial basis, and revision of local laws and regulations which may be necessary in solving the foregoing problems. They will also consider the adequacy of any plans the defendants may propose to meet these problems and to effectuate a transition to a racially nondiscriminatory school system. During this period of transition, the courts will retain jurisdiction of these cases.

The judgments below, except that in the *Delaware* case, are accordingly reversed and the cases are remanded to the District Courts to take such proceedings and enter such orders and decrees consistent with this opinion as are necessary and proper to admit to public schools on a racially nondiscriminatory basis with all deliberate speed the parties to these cases. The judgment in the *Delaware* case — ordering the immediate admission of the plaintiffs to schools previously attended only by white children — is affirmed on the basis of the principles stated in our May 17, 1954, opinion, but the case is remanded to the Supreme Court of Delaware for such further proceedings as that Court may deem necessary in light of this opinion.

NOTES: STATE REACTION TO *BROWN*

(1) *"Massive Resistance."* In *Cooper v. Aaron*, 358 U.S. 1 (1958), the Court reacted to official state resistance to the *Brown* decisions. Arkansas amended its state constitution to command the state legislature to oppose school desegregation. In accordance with this amendment, Arkansas passed a law allowing school students to choose not to attend integrated schools.

The Little Rock District School Board, however, agreed to comply with *Brown* and implemented a desegregation plan for Central High School. The day before the first black students were to attend classes, Governor Orvil Faubus dispatched the Arkansas National Guard to the school and placed it off limits to black students. When nine black students tried to attend Central High, National Guardsmen forcibly prevented them from entering. Eventually, a Federal District Court issued a preliminary injunction enjoining the Governor and the Guard from obstructing the integration plan. When the black students came to the school, however, large demonstrations began outside the building. As a result, President Eisenhower ordered federal troops to the school to protect the black students.

These problems prompted the School Board to seek a stay of the integration plan. The District Court allowed the Board to delay the integration plan and to send the black students back to segregated schools. The Court of Appeals for the Eighth Circuit reversed the District Court decision but stayed its decision pending the Board's petition for certiorari to the Supreme Court. In order to decide the issues in time to allow the parties to make arrangements for the school year, the Supreme Court convened in Special Term on September 11, 1958. To make the school board aware of its obligation to integrate by the commencement of classes on September 15, the Court issued a September 12 judgment, without opinion, unanimously affirming the decision of the Eighth Circuit. On September 29, 1958, the Court issued an unprecedented opinion, signed by all nine Justices, explaining its previous judgment.

The Justices began: "As this case reaches us it raises questions of the highest importance to the maintenance of our federal system of government." The Court acknowledged that the School Board had attempted in good faith to integrate the schools. However, the acts of other state instrumentalities compelled the Court to reject the Board's position. "The constitutional rights of respondents are not to be sacrificed or yielded to the violence and disorder which have followed upon the actions of the Governor and Legislature. . . . [L]aw and order are not here to be preserved by depriving Negro children of their constitutional rights."

In reply to the claims by the Governor and the Legislature of Arkansas that they were not bound by *Brown*, the Court invoked the doctrine of *Marbury v. Madison*. "[*Marbury*] declared the basic principle that the federal judiciary is supreme in the exposition of the law of the Constitution, and that principle has ever since been respected by this Court and the Country as a permanent and indispensable feature of our constitutional system. It follows that the interpretation of the Fourteenth Amendment enunciated by this Court in the *Brown* Case is the supreme law of the land, and Art. 6 of the Constitution makes it of binding effect on the States 'any Thing in the Constitution or Laws of any State to the Contrary notwithstanding.' Every state legislator and executive and judicial officer is solemnly committed by oath taken pursuant to Art. 6, cl.3, 'to support this Constitution.'" For further discussion of *Cooper*, see Daniel Farber, *The Supreme Court and the Rule of Law: Cooper v. Aaron Revisited*, 1980 U. ILL. L. REV. 387.

(2) *"Freedom of Choice" Plans*. In *Green v. County School Board*, 391 U.S. 430 (1968), the Court decided that a school board's adoption of a "freedom of choice" plan was not enough to comply with *Brown*. The plan permitted students to choose which of the two schools in the county they wished to attend.

The Court considered relevant that the fact the Board did not attempt to dismantle its segregated system until ten years after *Brown II*. The Court did not hold that "freedom of choice" plans were unconstitutional or could not be part of desegregation plan. "[A]ll we decide today is that in desegregating a dual system a plan utilizing 'freedom of choice' is not an end in itself."

Although the Court acknowledged that "freedom of choice" plans tended to be an ineffective means of desegregation, it left open the possibility that they could aid in desegregation. However, "if there are reasonably available other ways, such for illustration as zoning, promising speedier and more effective conversion to a unitary, nonracial school system, 'freedom of choice' must be held unacceptable." After three years under the New Kent Board's "freedom of choice" plan not one white child had opted to attend the previously all-black school and 85% of the black children still attended that school.

SWANN v. CHARLOTTE-MECKLENBURG BOARD OF EDUCATION, 402 U.S. 1 (1971). During the 1968-1969 school year, the Charlotte-Mecklenburg school district in North Carolina, which covered an area of 550 square miles, maintained 107 schools with 84,000 students. The ratio of white to black students was 71% to 29% and approximately 14,000 out of the 21,000 black students attending schools in the city of Charlotte were enrolled in schools comprised of either all or 99% black students. This was the result of a District Court desegregation plan featuring "geographic zoning with a free-transfer provision." The District Court ordered extensive, more dramatic remedies to ameliorate this situation. Reacting to the order of the District Court, the Supreme Court amplified guidelines for appropriate remedies to be undertaken by school authorities and courts. Writing for the Court, Chief Justice Burger attributed some of the difficulties of eliminating the "state-enforced discrimination of racially separate school systems" to demographic changes. These included "changes since 1954 in the structure and patterns of communities, the growth of student population, movement of families, and other changes" which sometimes had the effect of "neutralizing or negating remedial action before it was fully implemented." Rural areas could adapt to an implemented system of bus transportation more easily than urban areas with dense and shifting populations, more schools, and considerable traffic. When school districts failed to desegregate on their own, district courts had broad equitable powers to fashion remedies commensurate with the scope of the constitutional violation. The remedy should avoid future construction or abandonment of schools that perpetuated or furthered segregation.

The Chief Justice discussed student assignment in four main areas. First, the Court considered to what extent courts could impose racial quotas to remedy segregation. School officials argued that the District Court's order required all schools within the system to maintain a 79% to 21% ratio. The District Court could not impose a rigid "racial balance or mixing" as a "matter of substantive constitutional right." Each individual school need not "reflect the racial composition" of the entire school district. Instead, in this case, the District Court correctly used the mathematical ratio as a "starting point in the process of shaping a remedy."

Second, the Chief Justice examined whether desegregation required that all one-race schools be abolished. A few one-race or virtually one-race schools would not characterize a system as dual because high minority concentrations in certain, often urban, areas may delay desegregation "until new schools can be provided or neighborhood patterns change." If a school system has a history of segregation, a presumption arises against "schools that are substantially disproportionate in their racial composition." School officials can rebut this presumption by showing that their present or past discriminatory action did not cause the racial imbalance in these schools.

Third, the Court then considered gerrymandering or grouping student attendance zones to advance desegregation. School officials and courts sometimes drastically gerrymandered school districts and attendance zones to dismantle the dual system. They have also paired, clustered, or grouped schools transferring black students to formerly segregated white schools and vice-versa. "More often than not, these zones are neither compact nor contiguous; indeed they may be on opposite ends of the city. As an interim corrective measure, this cannot be said to be beyond the broad remedial powers of a court." Nevertheless, Chief Justice Burger did note that "all things being equal, with no history of discrimination, it might well be desirable to assign pupils to schools nearest their homes." The Court allowed great deference to the district courts in fashioning and implementing these assignment plans. Courts could not rely solely on maps as noncontiguous zones could exact less travel time depending on traffic and highway patterns. Variations in local conditions undercut the utility of rigid rules.

Finally, the Court considered the extent to which officials could use transportation to facilitate desegregation. The Court declined to prescribe inflexible rules that would constrict the variety of responses necessitated by thousands of local situations. "Transportation has been an integral part of the public education system for years."[10] The District Court's attendance plan would only require students to travel not more than seven miles or 35 minutes each way, a substantial improvement on the previous transportation plan in Charlotte that forced many children to travel more than fifteen miles, which took over an hour each way. Travel time or distance may be objectionable if it impairs the children's health or the educational process. While travel time will vary with many factors, the most important factor was the age of the children. The Court concluded that the District Court plan was "reasonable, feasible and workable." In time, schools would completely comply with the *Brown* decisions. Communities served by unitary systems would not remain stable, considering the inevitable changing patterns of neighborhoods. Absent further violations, annual reapportionment of the racial compositions in individual schools would be unnecessary "once the affirmative duty to desegregate has been accomplished and racial discrimination through official action is eliminated from the system."

NOTES

(1) For an illuminating account of *Swann* and the decision to pursue the remedy of court-ordered busing, see BERNARD SCHWARTZ, SWANN'S WAY: THE SCHOOL BUSING CASE AND THE SUPREME COURT (1986).

(2) *Geographic Presumption.* In *Keyes v. School District No. 1, Denver, Colo.*, 413 U.S. 189 (1973), the Court first considered the applicability of *Brown* to a northern school system, which had "never . . . operated under a constitutional or statutory provision mandating or permitting racial segregation." The District Court found that by constructing a new school in a predominantly black community and gerrymandering attendance zones, the school board had engaged in an "unconstitutional policy of deliberate racial segregation with respect to the Park Hill schools."

Writing for the Court, Justice Brennan noted that plaintiffs had proven that the school board had, for over a decade, promoted unconstitutional segregation. Indeed, defendant school board had followed a deliberate segregation policy at schools attended in 1969 by 37.69% of Denver's total black school population.

Official segregation affecting a substantial portion of the students provides a basis for finding a dual school system. Occasionally, there may be a case "in which the geographical structure of, or the natural boundaries within, a school district may have the effect of dividing the district into separate, identifiable and unrelated units." Absent such rare conditions "a finding of intentionally segregative school board actions in a meaningful portion of a school system, as in this case, creates a presumption" of intentional segregation in other schools in the system. Such evidence creates a *prima facie* case of district-wide unlawful segregation and shifts to school authorities the burden of proving that other segregated schools within the system were not the product of intentional racial segregation. This burden shift occurs even if different areas of the school system are independent of one another. When a segregative policy infects "a meaningful or significant" part of a school system, "it is both fair and reasonable to require that the school authorities bear the burden of showing that their actions as to other segregated schools within the system were not also motivated by segregative intent." To satisfy their burden, school authorities must produce sufficient evidence to support a finding that segregative intent was not a motivating factor. Even

---

[10] In 1969-1970, approximately 39% of 18 million public school children all over the country were bused.

segregative intent that antedated *Brown* was relevant. Segregative intent that was remote in time could only be rebutted if "past segregative acts did not create or contribute to the current segregated condition of the core city schools."

On remand, the District Court must first allow the school board "to prove its contention that the Park Hill area is a separate, identifiable and unrelated section of the school district that should be treated as isolated from the rest of the district." Second, if the school board fails to establish such separateness, the District Court will next determine whether the board's policies of deliberate racial segregation in Park Hill for almost ten years following 1960 establishes the entire district as a dual system. Third, even if the court finds that the board's actions in Park Hill did not cause a dual system, the board must still rebut plaintiff's *prima facie* case of intentional segregation in the core city schools raised by the finding of intentional discrimination in the Park Hill schools. If the board fails to rebut the *prima facie* case, the District Court must order desegregation throughout the entire district.

Justice Powell concurred in part and dissented in part. He noted that a 1971 Department of Health, Education and Welfare study indicated that 43.9% of black students attended majority white schools in the South as opposed to 27.8% in the North and West. Fifty-seven percent of all black students in the North and West attended schools with over 80% minority population as compared with 32.2% in the South. Rather than require plaintiffs to prove *de jure* segregation or intentional segregation, Justice Powell would simply focus on the discriminatory effect.

Justice Powell also took issue with the remedy of "large-scale or long-distance" busing of students. Not only does a constitutional requirement of extensive student transportation infringe on community goals and personal rights, but it also channels resources away from quality education — the most important goal of any school system. The requirement causes serious financial strains on public education, and more significantly, imposes an impairment of liberty and privacy on every affected student. Finally, a transportation requirement may cause students to transfer from public to private schools with only the disadvantaged of both races remaining in public schools. It may prompt a mass exodus to the suburbs causing further geographic separation of the races.

Justice Rehnquist also dissented, arguing that gerrymandering a single attendance zone in a large city could put an entire school district in a federal receivership.

(3) *De jure/de facto.* The Court's adherence to the *de jure/de facto* distinction, and its insistence on linking any remedy to a finding of segregative intent, has its parallel in employment cases such as *Washington v. Davis*, 426 U.S. 229 (1976), and *Massachusetts v. Feeney*, 442 U.S. 256 (1979), *infra* § 9.02, where the Court insisted that discriminatory effect, in the absence of proof of purposeful intent to discriminate, could not sustain an equal protection claim. Justices Powell and Douglas, in their opinions in *Keyes*, urge an abandonment of this concept in school desegregation cases and the adoption of a rule that would create a *prima facie* violation of a constitutional right whenever significant segregated conditions exist in the operation of public school systems. What is the justification, if any, for a different rule in school desegregation cases from that in employment discrimination cases such as *Davis* and *Feeney*?

Decisions of the Court in non-school cases, such as *Arlington Heights v. Metropolitan Housing Corp.*, *infra* § 8.03[3], still require that the plaintiff show some evidence of intent, e.g., the legislative history of decisions, or the absence of a reasonable explanation (other than discrimination) for the government's actions.

(4) *Temporal Presumption.* (a) In *Columbus Board of Education v. Penick*, 443 U.S. 449 (1979), the Court agreed with the District Court that the Columbus Board of Education had operated a segregated school system in violation of the Fourteenth

Amendment. In 1976, almost one-third of the students in the district were black. About 70% of all students attended schools that were at least 80% black or 80% white; half of the schools were 90% black or 90% white. Justice White's majority opinion emphasized that "the District Court found that the 'Columbus Public Schools were *officially* segregated by race in 1954' . . . . " Justice White noted that Chief Justice Burger's opinion in *Swann* recognized that *Brown II* and *Green* imposed a continuing "affirmative duty to desegregate" upon the Board and at the time of the trial the Board had not discharged that duty. "The Board 'never actively set out to dismantle this dual system,'" which the Board's own "past intentionally segregative policies" had produced. If anything the Board's policies since 1954 advanced rather than ameliorated its past segregation.

The Court cited the District Court's finding that since 1954 the Board had engaged in a number of practices that "could not 'reasonably be explained without reference to racial concerns,' and that 'intentionally aggravated, rather than alleviated,' racial separation in schools. These matters included the general practice of assigning black teachers only to those schools with substantial black student populations, a practice that was terminated only in 1974 as the result of a conciliation agreement with the Ohio Civil Rights Commission; the intentionally segregative use of optional attendance zones, discontiguous attendance areas, and boundary changes; and the selection of sites for new school construction that had the foreseeable and anticipated effect of maintaining the racial separation of the schools."

Justice White rejected the Board's contention that the District Court based its findings of an equal protection violation on a showing of disparate impact. While the Court rejected any notion that it was imposing a disparate impact test, "actions having foreseeable and anticipated disparate impact are relevant evidence to prove the ultimate fact, forbidden purpose."

Chief Justice Burger and Justice Stewart concurred in the result and filed separate opinions. Justices Powell and Rehnquist dissented, in separate opinions.

(b) In *Dayton Board of Education v. Brinkman*, 443 U.S. 526 (1979), a companion case to *Columbus*, the Court upheld system-wide desegregation remedies (including busing) in Dayton, Ohio, relying, as in the *Columbus* case, on: (1) the existence of a dual system at the time of *Brown I*, (2) the failure of the Dayton Board of Education to eliminate the effects of that system, (3) the segregative intent of actions taken by the Board between *Brown I* and the time of the trial, and (4) the failure of the Board to rebut the presumption established in *Keyes* and re-stated in the *Columbus* case, i.e., that purposeful segregative actions in a substantial portion of a school district create a *prima facie* case which, unless rebutted, permits a finding that there was system-wide segregative intent and that segregation in the rest of the system was the result of the intentionally segregative actions. Justice White, writing for the majority, noted that the Court of Appeals was quite justified in "utilizing the board's total failure to fulfill its affirmative duty — and indeed its conduct resulting in increased segregation — to trace the current, systemwide segregation back to the purposefully dual system of the 1950s and to the subsequent acts of intentional discrimination." As viewed by the majority, there was little difference in the two cases.

Justice Stewart, in an opinion joined by Chief Justice Burger, dissented in *Dayton* (having concurred in *Columbus*.) Although the Court of Appeals in the Columbus case had also relied on the existence of a pre-1954 dual school system, evidence of recent discriminatory intent, so lacking in the *Dayton* case, was relatively strong in *Columbus*.

In a separate opinion, Chief Justice Burger criticized the Court's reliance on the pre-1954 policies of the Board which imposed a previously "unknown and unforeseeable affirmative duty to desegregate their schools for the past 25 years."

Justice Rehnquist dissented in both cases. By relying on the 1954 date, said Justice Rehnquist, "the question is apparently whether the pre-1954 acts contributed in some unspecified manner to segregated conditions that existed in 1954. If the answer is yes, then the only question is whether the school board has exploited all integrative opportunities that presented themselves in the subsequent 25 years."

In a separate dissent Justice Powell objected to the use of "fictions and presumptions" in order to "prescribe system-wide remedies." Like Justice Rehnquist, he contended that the majority substituted a "foreseeable effects" test for the intent requirement.

[3]   Limiting the Remedies

MILLIKEN v. BRADLEY
418 U.S. 717, 94 S. Ct. 3112, 41 L. Ed. 2d 1069 (1974)

CHIEF JUSTICE BURGER delivered the opinion of the Court.

We granted certiorari in these consolidated cases to determine whether a federal court may impose a multi-district, area-wide remedy to a single district *de jure* segregation problem absent any finding that the other included school districts have failed to operate unitary school systems within their districts, absent any claim or finding that the boundary lines of any affected school district were established with the purpose of fostering racial segregation in public schools, absent any finding that the included districts committed acts which effected segregation within the other districts, and absent a meaningful opportunity for the included neighboring school districts to present evidence or be heard on the propriety of a multi-district remedy or on the question of constitutional violations by those neighboring districts. . . .

I

. . . The trial of the issue of segregation in the Detroit school system . . . consum[ed] some 41 trial days. On September 27, 1971, the District Court issued its findings . . . that "[g]overnmental actions and inaction at all levels, federal, state and local, have combined, with those of private organizations, such as loaning institutions and real estate associations and brokerage firms, to establish and to maintain the pattern of residential segregation throughout the Detroit metropolitan area." . . .

The District Court also found that the State of Michigan had committed several constitutional violations with respect to the exercise of its general responsibility for, and supervision of, public education.[11] The State, for example, was found to have failed, until the 1971 Session of the Michigan Legislature, to provide authorization or funds for the transportation of pupils within Detroit regardless of their poverty or distance from the school to which they were assigned; during this same period the State provided many neighboring, mostly white, suburban districts the full range of state-supported transportation.

The District Court found that the State, through Act 48, acted to "impede, delay and minimize racial integration in Detroit schools." . . . § 12 of Act 48 . . . . sought to prescribe for each school in the eight districts criteria of "free choice" and "neighborhood schools," which, the District Court found, "had as their purpose and effect the maintenance of segregation." 338 F. Supp. at 589.

---

[11] [Court's footnote 5] School districts in the State of Michigan are instrumentalities of the State and subordinate to its State Board of Education and legislature. Constitution of the State of Michigan, Art 8, § 2. . . .

The District Court also held that the acts of the Detroit Board of Education, as a subordinate entity of the State, were attributable to the State of Michigan, thus creating a vicarious liability on the part of the State. . . .

Turning to the question of an appropriate remedy for these several constitutional violations, the District Court . . . proceeded to order the Detroit Board of Education to submit desegregation plans limited to the segregation problems found to be existing within the city of Detroit. At the same time, however, the state defendants were directed to submit desegregation plans encompassing the three-county metropolitan area despite the fact that the 85 outlying school districts of these three counties were not parties to the action and despite the fact that there had been no claim that these outlying districts had committed constitutional violations. . . .

It found that the best of the three [Detroit-only] plans "would make the Detroit school system more identifiably Black . . . thereby increasing the flight of Whites from the city and the system." . . . Accordingly, the District Court held that it "must look beyond the limits of the Detroit school district for a solution to the problem. . . . "

[T]he court designated 53 of the 85 suburban school districts plus Detroit as the "desegregation area" and appointed a panel to prepare and submit "an effective desegregation plan". . . . The plan was to be based on 15 clusters, each containing part of the Detroit system and two or more suburban districts. . . .

The Court of Appeals agreed with the District Court that "any less comprehensive a solution than a metropolitan area plan would result in an all black school system immediately surrounded by practically all white suburban school systems, with an overwhelmingly white majority population in the total metropolitan area." . . .

Viewing the record as a whole, it seems clear that the District Court and the Court of Appeals shifted the primary focus from a Detroit remedy to the metropolitan area only because of their conclusion that total desegregation of Detroit would not produce the racial balance which they perceived as desirable. . . .

. . . Boundary lines may be bridged where there has been a constitutional violation calling for interdistrict relief, but the notion that school district lines may be casually ignored or treated as a mere administrative convenience is contrary to the history of public education in our country. . . .

The Michigan educational structure involved in this case, in common with most States, provides for a large measure of local control[12]. . . . The metropolitan remedy would require, in effect, consolidation of 54 independent school districts historically administered as separate units into a vast new super school district. . . . Entirely apart from the logistical and other serious problems attending large-scale transportation of students, the consolidation would give rise to an array of other problems in financing and operating this new school system. Some of the more obvious questions would be: What would be the status and authority of the present popularly elected school boards? Would the children of Detroit be within the jurisdiction and operating control of a school board elected by the parents and residents of other districts? What board or boards would levy taxes for school operations in these 54 districts constituting the consolidated metropolitan area? What provisions could be made for assuring substantial equality in tax levies among the 54 districts, if this were deemed requisite? What provisions would be made for financing? Would the validity of long-term bonds be jeopardized unless approved by all of the component districts as

---

[12] [Court's footnote 20] Under the Michigan School Code of 1955, the local school district is an autonomous political body corporate, operating through a Board of Education popularly elected. As such, the day-to-day affairs of the school district are determined at the local level . . . .

well as the State? What body would determine that portion of the curricula now left to the discretion of local school boards? Who would establish attendance zones, purchase school equipment, locate and construct new schools, and indeed attend to all the myriad day-to-day decisions that are necessary to school operations affecting potentially more than three-quarters of a million pupils? . . .

. . . Before the boundaries of separate and autonomous school districts may be set aside by consolidating the separate units for remedial purposes or by imposing a cross-district remedy, it must first be shown that there has been a constitutional violation within one district that produces a significant segregative effect in another district. Specifically, it must be shown that racially discriminatory acts of the state or local school districts, or of a single school district have been a substantial cause of interdistrict segregation. Thus an inter-district remedy might be in order where the racially discriminatory acts of one or more school districts caused racial segregation in an adjacent district, or where district lines have been deliberately drawn on the basis of race . . . . [W]ithout an interdistrict violation and interdistrict effect, there is no constitutional wrong calling for an interdistrict remedy.

The record before us, voluminous as it is, contains evidence of *de jure* segregated conditions only in the Detroit schools. . . .

In dissent, Justice White and Justice Marshall undertake to demonstrate that agencies having statewide authority participated in maintaining the dual school system found to exist in Detroit. They are apparently of the view that once such participation is shown, the District Court should have a relatively free hand to reconstruct school districts outside of Detroit in fashioning relief. Our assumption, *arguendo*, . . . that state agencies did participate in the maintenance of the Detroit system, should make it clear that it is not on this point that we part company. . . .

The constitutional right of the Negro respondents residing in Detroit is to attend a unitary school system in that district . . . .

III

. . . With a single exception, . . . there has been no showing that either the State or any of the 85 outlying districts engaged in activity that had a cross-district effect. The boundaries of the Detroit School District, which are coterminous with the boundaries of the city of Detroit, were established over a century ago by neutral legislation when the city was incorporated. . . .

. . . [T]here was no evidence suggesting that the State's activities with respect to either school construction or site acquisition within Detroit affected the racial composition of the school population outside Detroit or, conversely, that the State's school construction and site acquisition activities within the outlying districts affected the racial composition of the schools within Detroit. . . .

[Justice Stewart wrote a brief concurring opinion.]

Justice White, with whom Justice Douglas, Justice Brennan, and Justice Marshall join, dissenting. . . .

. . . [D]istrict . . . courts must keep in mind that they are dealing with a process of educating the young, including the very young. The task is. . . . to desegregate an educational system in which the races have been kept apart, without, at the same time, losing sight of the central educational function of the schools. . . .

This Court. . . . does not question the District Court's findings that *any* feasible Detroit-only plan would leave many schools 75 to 90 percent black and that the district would become progressively more black as whites left the city. . . . [T]he Court leaves unchallenged the District Court's conclusion that a plan including the suburbs would be physically easier and more practical and feasible than a Detroit-only plan. Whereas the most promising Detroit-only plan, for example, would have entailed the purchase of 900 buses, the metropolitan plan would involve the acquisition of no more than 350 new vehicles. . . .

I am surprised that the Court, sitting at this distance from the State of Michigan, claims better insight than the Court of Appeals and the District Court. . . .

I am even more mystified as to how the Court can ignore the legal reality that the constitutional violations, even if occurring locally, were committed by governmental entities for which the State is responsible. . . .

JUSTICE MARSHALL, with whom JUSTICE DOUGLAS, JUSTICE BRENNAN, and JUSTICE WHITE join, dissenting. . . .

I

. . . [T]he District Court . . . concluded that responsibility for the segregation . . . rested not only with the Detroit Board of Education, but belonged to the State of Michigan itself. . . . [T]his conclusion . . . was . . . based on three considerations. First, the evidence at trial showed that the State itself had taken actions contributing to the segregation within the Detroit schools. Second, . . . the Detroit Board of Education was an agency of the State of Michigan. . . . Finally, the District Court found that under Michigan law and practice, the system of education was in fact a state school system, characterized by relatively little local control and a large degree of centralized state regulation, with respect to both educational policy and the structure and operation of school districts. . . .

II

. . . The State's control over education is reflected in the fact that, contrary to the Court's implication, there is little or no relationship between school districts and local political units . . . .

. . . The State's power over the purse can be and is in fact used to enforce the State's powers over local districts. . . .

Most significantly for present purposes, the State has wide-ranging powers to consolidate and merge school districts, even without the consent of the districts themselves or of the local citizenry. . . .

. . . [T]he most essential finding [of the District Court] was that Negro children in Detroit had been confined by intentional acts of segregation to a growing core of Negro schools surrounded by a receding ring of white schools. . . . This increase in the proportion of Negro students was the highest of any major Northern city. . . .

Under our decisions, it was clearly proper for the District Court to take into account the so-called "white flight" from the city schools which would be forthcoming from any Detroit-only decree. . . .

Under a Detroit-only decree. . . . [s]chools with 65% and more Negro students will stand in sharp and obvious contrast to schools in neighboring districts with less than 2% Negro enrollment. . . .

III

. . . [G]iven the 1,000 or so consolidations of school districts which have taken place in the past, it is hard to believe that the State has not already devised means of solving most, if not all, of the practical problems which the Court suggests consolidation would entail.

Furthermore, the majority ignores long-established Michigan procedures under which school districts may enter into contractual agreements to educate their pupils in other districts using state or local funds to finance nonresident education. Such agreements could form an easily administrable framework for interdistrict relief short of outright consolidation of the school districts. . . .

. . . [T]he metropolitan plan would not involve the busing of substantially more students than already ride buses. . . .

As far as economics are concerned, a metropolitan remedy would actually be more sensible than a Detroit-only remedy. . . . [including] the possibility of pairing up Negro schools near Detroit's boundary with nearby white schools on the other side of the present school district line. . . .

. . . Today's holding, I fear, is more a reflection of a perceived public mood that we have gone far enough in enforcing the Constitution's guarantee of equal justice . . . . In the short run, it may seem to be the easier course to allow our great metropolitan areas to be divided up each into two cities — one white, the other black — but it is a course, I predict, our people will ultimately regret . . . .

NOTES

(1) *The Aftermath.* Inter-district remedies have been ordered by lower courts since *Milliken. See, e.g., Evans v. Buchanan,* 416 F. Supp. 328 (D. Del. 1976), *aff'd,* 555 F.2d 373 (3d Cir.), *cert. denied,* 434 U.S. 944 (1977) (Wilmington, Delaware); *United States v. Missouri,* 515 F.2d 1365 (8th Cir. 1975), *cert. denied,* 423 U.S. 951 (1975) (St. Louis County, Missouri).

(2) *Legislative Restrictions.* Since the *Swann* case approved busing as a desegregation remedy, there were various proposals in Congress to restrict the authority of federal agencies or federal courts to seek or issue busing orders.

FREEMAN v. PITTS
503 U.S. 467, 112 S. Ct. 1430, 118 L. Ed. 2d 108 (1992)

JUSTICE KENNEDY delivered the opinion of the Court.

. . . This case involves a court-ordered desegregation decree for the DeKalb County School System (DCSS). . . .

DCSS has been subject to the supervision and jurisdiction of the United States District Court for the Northern District of Georgia since 1969, when it was ordered to dismantle its dual school system. In 1986, petitioners filed a motion for final dismissal. . . . In its order the District Court relinquished remedial control as to those aspects of the system in which unitary status had been achieved, and retained supervisory authority only for those aspects of the school system in which the district was not in full compliance. The Court of Appeals for the Eleventh Circuit reversed, 887 F.2d 1439 (1989), holding that a District Court should retain full remedial authority over a school system until it achieves unitary status in six categories at the same time for several years. We now reverse the judgment of the Court of Appeals and remand, holding that a District Court is permitted to withdraw judicial supervision with respect to discrete categories in which the school district has achieved compliance with a court-ordered desegregation plan. A District Court need not retain active control over every aspect of school administration until a school district has demonstrated unitary status in all facets of its system.

I

A

. . . The District Court found. . . . that DCSS is a unitary system with regard to student assignments, transportation, physical facilities, and extracurricular activities, and ruled that it would order no further relief in those areas. The District Court stopped short of dismissing the case, however, because it found . . . that vestiges of the dual system remain in the areas of teacher and principal assignments, resource allocation, and quality of education. . . .

B

. . . [A] critical beginning point is the degree of racial imbalance in the school district, that is to say a comparison of the proportion of majority to minority students in individual schools with the proportions of the races in the district as a whole. . . .

The school system that the District Court ordered desegregated in 1969 had 5.6% black students; by 1986 the percentage of black students was 47%.

. . . The District Court found that "as the result of these demographic shifts, the population of the northern half of DeKalb County is now predominantly white and the southern half of DeKalb County is predominantly black."

. . . During the relevant period, the black population in the southern portion of the county experienced tremendous growth while the white population did not, and the white population in the northern part of the county experienced tremendous growth while the black population did not. . . .

Concerned with racial imbalance in the various schools of the district, respondents presented evidence that during the 1986-1987 school year DCSS had the following features: (1) 47% of the students attending DCSS were black; (2) 50% of the black students attended schools that were over 90% black; (3) 62% of all black students attended schools that had more than 20% more blacks than the systemwide average; (4) 27% of white students attended schools that were more than 90% white; (5) 59% of the white students attended schools that had more than 20% more whites than the systemwide average; (6) of the 22 DCSS high schools, five had student populations that were more than 90% black, while five other schools had student populations that were more than 80% white; and (7) of the 74 elementary schools in DCSS, 18 are over 90% black, while 10 are over 90% white. . . .

. . . The District Court made these findings:

"[The actions of DCSS] achieved maximum practical desegregation from 1969 to 1986. The rapid population shifts in DeKalb County were not caused by any action on the part of the DCSS. . . . There is no evidence that the school system's previous unconstitutional conduct may have contributed to this segregation. This court is convinced that any further actions taken by defendants, while the actions might have made marginal adjustments in the population trends, would not have offset the factors that were described above and the same racial segregation would have occurred at approximately the same speed."

. . .

Having found no constitutional violation with respect to student assignment, the District Court next considered the other . . . factors [in *Green v. County School Board of New Kent County, VA*, 391 U.S. 430 (1968)] beginning with faculty and staff assignments. The District Court first found that DCSS had fulfilled its constitutional obligation with respect to hiring and retaining minority teachers and administrators.

DCSS has taken active steps to recruit qualified black applicants and has hired them in significant numbers, employing a greater percentage of black teachers than the statewide average. The District Court also noted that DCSS has an "equally exemplary record" in retention of black teachers and administrators. Nevertheless, the District Court found that DCSS had not achieved or maintained a ratio of black to white teachers and administrators in each school to approximate the ratio of black to white teachers and administrators throughout the system. . . .

The District Court found the crux of the problem to be that DCSS has relied on the replacement process to attain a racial balance in teachers and other staff and has avoided using mandatory reassignment. . . . In fact, because teachers prefer to work close to their homes, DCSS has a voluntary transfer program in which teachers who have taught at the same school for a period of three years may ask for a transfer. Because most teachers request to be transferred to schools near their homes, this program makes compliance with the objective of racial balance in faculty and staff more difficult. . . .

Addressing the more ineffable category of quality of education, the District Court rejected most of respondents' contentions that there was racial disparity in the provision of certain educational resources (e.g., teachers with advanced degrees, teachers with more experience, library books). . . . concerning achievement of black students in DCSS. . . . : "the court cannot find, as plaintiffs urge, that the DCSS has been negligent in its duties to implement programs to assist black students. . . . "

Despite its finding that there was no intentional violation, the District Court found that DCSS had not achieved unitary status with respect to quality of education because teachers in schools with disproportionately high percentages of white students tended to be better educated and have more experience than their counterparts in schools with disproportionately high percentages of black students, and because per pupil expenditures in majority white schools exceeded per pupil expenditures in majority black schools. From these findings, the District Court ordered DCSS to equalize spending and remedy the other problems.

The final *Green* factors considered by the District Court were: (1) physical facilities, (2) transportation, and (3) extracurricular activities. The District Court noted that . . . respondents . . . in effect conceded that DCSS has achieved unitary status with respect to physical facilities.

In accordance with its fact-finding, the District Court held that it would order no further relief in the areas of student assignment, transportation, physical facilities and extra-curricular activities. The District Court, however, did order DCSS to establish a system to balance teacher and principal assignments and to equalize per pupil expenditures throughout DCSS. . . .

II

A

. . . We . . . identified various parts of the school system which, in addition to student attendance patterns, must be free from racial discrimination before the mandate of *Brown* is met: faculty, staff, transportation, extracurricular activities and facilities. The *Green* factors are a measure of the racial identifiability of schools in a system that is not in compliance with *Brown*. . . .

. . . But . . . the term "unitary" is not a precise concept:

". . . Courts have used the term 'dual' to denote a school system which has engaged in intentional segregation of students by race, and 'unitary' to describe a school system which has been brought into compliance with the command of the Constitution. . . . "

. . . Equitable remedies must be flexible. . . .

. . . A federal court in a school desegregation case has the discretion to order an incremental or partial withdrawal of its supervision and control. . . .

. . . Returning schools to the control of local authorities at the earliest practicable date is essential to restore their true accountability in our governmental system. . . . discrimination and racial hostility . . . may emerge in new and subtle forms after the effects of *de jure* desegregation have been eliminated. It is the duty of the State and its subdivisions to ensure that such forces do not shape or control the policies of its school systems. Where control lies, so too does responsibility.

We hold that, in the course of supervising desegregation plans, federal courts have the authority to relinquish supervision and control of school districts in incremental stages, before full compliance has been achieved in every area of school operations. While retaining jurisdiction over the case, the court may determine that it will not order further remedies in areas where the school district is in compliance with the decree. . . . In particular, the district court may determine that it will not order further remedies in the area of student assignments where racial imbalance is not traceable, in a proximate way, to constitutional violations.

. . . Among the factors which must inform the sound discretion of the court in ordering partial withdrawal are the following: whether there has been full and satisfactory compliance with the decree in those aspects of the system where supervision is to be withdrawn; whether retention of judicial control is necessary or practicable to achieve compliance with the decree in other facets of the school system; and whether the school district has demonstrated, to the public and to the parents and students of the once disfavored race, its good faith commitment to the whole of the court's decree and to those provisions of the law and the constitution that were the predicate for judicial intervention in the first instance.

In considering these factors a court should give particular attention to the school system's record of compliance. A school system is better positioned to demonstrate its good-faith commitment to a constitutional course of action when its policies form a consistent pattern of lawful conduct directed to eliminating earlier violations. . . .

B

. . . The District Court's approach illustrates . . . the uses of equitable discretion. By withdrawing control over areas where judicial supervision is no longer needed, a district court can concentrate both its own resources and those of the school district on the areas where the effects of *de jure* discrimination have not been eliminated. . . .

. . . The desegregation decree was designed to achieve maximum practicable desegregation. Its central remedy was the closing of black schools and the reassignment of pupils to neighborhood schools, with attendance zones that achieved racial balance. The plan accomplished its objective in the first year of operation, before dramatic demographic changes altered residential patterns. . . .

. . . Once the racial imbalance due to the *de jure* violation has been remedied, the school district is under no duty to remedy imbalance that is caused by demographic factors. . . . The school district bears the burden of showing that any current imbalance is not traceable, in a proximate way, to the prior violation.

The findings of the District Court that the population changes which occurred in DeKalb County were not caused by the policies of the school district, but rather by independent factors, are consistent with the mobility that is a distinct characteristic of our society. . . . Studies show a high correlation between residential segregation and school segregation. . . . The District Court in this case heard evidence tending to show that racially stable neighborhoods are not likely to emerge because whites prefer a racial mix of 80% white and 20% black, while blacks prefer a 50%-50% mix.

. . . It is beyond the authority and beyond the practical ability of the federal courts to try to counteract these kinds of continuous and massive demographic shifts. . . .

As the *de jure* violation becomes more remote in time and these demographic changes intervene, it becomes less likely that a current racial imbalance in a school district is a vestige of the prior *de jure* system. The causal link between current conditions and the prior violation is even more attenuated if the school district has demonstrated its good faith. . . .

. . . Racial balancing in elementary and secondary school student assignments may be a legitimate remedial device to correct other fundamental inequities that were themselves caused by the constitutional violation. . . .

There was no showing that racial balancing was an appropriate mechanism to cure other deficiencies in this case. . . .

The requirement that the school district show its good faith commitment to the entirety of a desegregation plan so that parents, students and the public have assurance against further injuries or stigma also should be a subject for more specific findings. . . . A history of good-faith compliance is evidence that any current racial imbalance is not the product of a new *de jure* violation. . . .

. . . With respect to those areas where compliance had not been achieved, the District Court did not find that DCSS had acted in bad faith or engaged in further acts of discrimination since the desegregation plan went into effect. This, though, may not be the equivalent of a finding that the school district has an affirmative commitment to comply in good faith with the entirety of a desegregation plan, and further proceedings are appropriate for this purpose as well. . . .

Justice Thomas took no part in the consideration or decision of this case.

Justice Scalia, concurring. . . .

Our decision. . . . will have little effect . . . upon the many other school districts throughout the country that are still being supervised by federal judges, since it turns upon the extraordinarily rare circumstance of a finding that no portion of the current racial imbalance is a remnant of prior *de jure* discrimination. . . .

. . . We have never sought to describe how one identifies a condition as the effluent of a violation, or how a "vestige" or a "remnant" of past discrimination is to be recognized. . . .

Our post-*Green* cases provide that, once state-enforced school segregation is shown to have existed in a jurisdiction in 1954, there arises a presumption, effectively irrebuttable (because the school district cannot prove the negative), that any current racial imbalance is the product of that violation, at least if the imbalance has continuously existed, *see, e.g., Swann, supra,* at 26; *Keyes,* 413 U.S., at 209–210.

But granting the merits of this approach at the time of *Green,* it is now 25 years later. "From the very first, federal supervision of local school systems was intended as a temporary measure to remedy past discrimination." *Dowell,* 498 U.S. at 247. . . . [T]he rational basis for the extraordinary presumption of causation simply must dissipate as the *de jure* system and the school boards who produced it recede further into the past. . . .

We must soon revert to the ordinary principles of our law, . . . that plaintiffs alleging Equal Protection violations must prove intent and causation and not merely the existence of racial disparity, *see Washington v. Davis*, 426 U.S. 229, 245 (1976). . . .

JUSTICE SOUTER, concurring.

. . . We recognize that although demographic changes influencing the composition of a school's student population may well have no causal link to prior *de jure* segregation, judicial control of student assignments may still be necessary to remedy persisting vestiges of the unconstitutional dual system, such as remaining imbalance in faculty assignments. . . .

Even after attaining compliance as to student composition, other factors such as racial composition of the faculty, quality of the physical plant, or per-pupil expenditures may leave schools racially identifiable. . . . Before a district court ends its supervision of student assignments, then, it should make a finding that there is no immediate threat of unremedied *Green*-type factors causing population or student enrollment changes that in turn may imbalance student composition in this way. . . .

JUSTICE BLACKMUN, with whom JUSTICE STEVENS and JUSTICE O'CONNOR join, concurring in the judgment. . . .

I

. . . It makes little sense, it seems to me, for the court to disarm itself by renouncing jurisdiction in one aspect of a school system, while violations of the Equal Protection Clause persist in other aspects of the same system. It would seem especially misguided to place unqualified reliance on the school board's promises in this case, because the two areas of the school system the District Court found still in violation of the Constitution — expenditures and teacher assignments — are two of the *Green* factors over which DCSS exercises the greatest control. . . .

Whether a district court must maintain active supervision over student assignment, and order new remedial actions depends on two factors. As the Court discusses, the district court must order changes in student assignment if it "is necessary or practicable to achieve compliance in other facets of the school system." The district court also must order affirmative action in school attendance if the school district's conduct was a "contributing cause" of the racially identifiable schools. . . . It is the application of this latter causation requirement that I now examine in more detail.

II

A

DCSS claims that it need not remedy the segregation in DeKalb County schools because it was caused by demographic changes for which DCSS has no responsibility. It is not enough, however, for DCSS to establish that demographics exacerbated the problem; it must prove that its own policies did not contribute.

Such contribution can occur in at least two ways: DCSS may have contributed to the demographic changes themselves, or it may have contributed directly to the racial imbalance in the schools. . . .

. . . [M]any families are concerned about the racial composition of a prospective school and will make residential decisions accordingly. . . .

Actions taken by a school district can aggravate or eliminate school segregation independent of residential segregation. School board policies concerning placement of new schools and closure of old schools and programs such as magnet classrooms and majority-to-minority (M to M) transfer policies affect the racial composition of the schools. . . .

B

The District Court's opinion suggests that it did not examine DCSS' actions in light of the foregoing principles. The court did note that the migration farther into the suburbs was accelerated by "white flight" from black schools and the "blockbusting" of former white neighborhoods. It did not examine, however, whether DCSS might have encouraged that flight by assigning faculty and principals so as to identify some schools as intended respectively for black students or white students. Nor did the court consider how the placement of schools, the attendance zone boundaries, or the use of mobile classrooms might have affected residential movement. . . .

Nor did the District Court correctly analyze whether DCSS' past actions had contributed to the school segregation independent of residential segregation. . . .

Virtually all the demographic changes that DCSS claims caused the school segregation occurred after 1975. . . .

A review of the record suggests that from 1969 until 1975, DCSS failed to desegregate its schools. . . .

NOTES

(1) For further discussion of *Freeman*, see James S. Liebman, *Desegregating Politics: "All-Out" School Desegregation Explained*, 90 COLUM. L. REV. 1463, 1467 (1990) ("Since meaningful desegregation began in the early 1970s, there has been a powerful nationwide trend away from isolating black students in black schools: In the 125 school districts studied, the percentage of black students attending virtually all-minority schools fell from 62 to 30, while the proportion attending schools that are 26 to 75 percent white climbed from 17 to 44 percent."); *see also* Pamela J. Smith, *Our Children's Burden: The Many-Headed Hydra of the Educational Disenfranchisement of Black Children*, 42 HOWARD L.J. 133, 231 (1999). ("As a group, Black children's 'hearts and minds' are still being scarred by racial discrimination, albeit a different method of racial discrimination than they faced under historical *de jure* and *de facto* segregation. Currently, however, the racial scarring does not result from physical distance from white children; rather it results from proximity to white children and primarily white educators.").

(2) In *Board of Education of Oklahoma City v. Dowell*, 498 U.S. 237 (1991), the Court remanded a lower court decision to dissolve a desegregation plan in order to determine whether the school district at issue had complied in good faith with the plan and whether vestiges of past discrimination had been eliminated to the "extent practicable."

With a desegregation decree entered in 1972, the District Court found in 1977 that the district had achieved a "unitary" status. In 1984, the school board ended busing for grades K-4 and adopted a Student Reassignment Plan (SRP) under which students were allowed to transfer from schools in which they comprised a racial majority to ones in which they were a racial minority. This plan would result in 11 schools with more than 90% black enrollment, 22 with more than 90% white enrollment, and 22 racially mixed schools. In 1985, the District Court dissolved the decree.

"Dissolving a desegregation decree after the local authorities have operated in compliance with it for a reasonable period of time properly recognizes that 'necessary concern for the important values of local control of public school systems dictates that a federal court's regulatory control of such systems not extend beyond the time required to remedy the effects of past intentional discrimination.' " The Chief Justice also emphasized the importance of compliance. With previous court orders in the present case, the court found *de jure* segregation in 1961; the court entered a decree in

1972; and the Board made a good faith compliance with this decree until 1985.

The Court remanded the case for a determination of "whether the Board made a sufficient showing of constitutional compliance as of 1985, when the SRP was adopted, to allow the injunction to be dissolved." On remand, the District Court was required to consider whether the Board has complied in good faith with the desegregation decree and "whether the vestiges of past discrimination had been eliminated to the extent practicable." Moreover, the District Court should determine the validity of the SRP under the Equal Protection Clause.

Justice Marshall, joined by Justices Blackmun and Stevens, dissented. He would require that "formerly *de jure* segregated school districts take all feasible steps to *eliminate* racially identifiable schools" and that "desegregation be fully completed."

(3) *Scope of Remedy.* In *Missouri v. Jenkins* (*Jenkins II*), 515 U.S. 70 (1995), a closely divided (5-4) Court reversed a District Court order commanding the State to fund salary increases and remedial " 'quality education' " programs for the Kansas City, Missouri, School District (KCMSD). In 1977, a Federal District Court found the State and the KCMSD liable for intradistrict violations for operating a segregated school system within the KCMSD.

In 1986, the District Court, in an effort to desegregate the KCMSD, "approved a comprehensive magnet school and capital improvements plan and held the State and the KCMSD jointly and severally liable for its funding." The District Court's desegregation "plan has been described as the most ambitious and expensive remedial program in the history of school desegregation." It included $540 million in capital improvements ordered, a salary increase to faculty and staff costing more than $200 million since 1987, and annual costs of nearly $200 million. KCMSD's annual per pupil costs far exceeded those of any other school district in Missouri.

Writing for the majority, Chief Justice Rehnquist, relying on *Board of Ed. of Oklahoma City v. Dowell*, 498 U.S. 237 (1991), stated that appropriate inquiry into the District Court's remedies must evaluate "their serving as proper means to the end of restoring the victims of discriminatory conduct to the position they would have occupied in the absence of that conduct." The District Court "has all but made the KCMSD into a magnet district." The purpose was not only to improve students' test scores but also to attract nonminority students from outside the KCMSD. The Chief Justice said that magnet schools are a proper remedy when used in an intradistrict way. However, the District Court's plan used magnet schools in order to attract students from suburban school districts (SSDs) outside the KCMSD. The District Court cannot use this magnet school remedy to circumvent the requirement in *Milliken v. Bradley* of an interdistrict violation for an interdistrict remedy.

The District Court's findings, that *de jure* segregation caused "white flight" rather than its desegregation remedy, were inconsistent with the evidence. Indeed, the District Court itself had specifically found that the requirements for an interdistrict remedy, laid out in *Milliken v. Bradley*, had not been met.

The "desegregative attractiveness" rationale, under which spending is increased to bring whites into the KCMSD, has no objective limitations in amount spent or in duration. Finally, Chief Justice Rehnquist rejected the District Court's order that indefinite funding continue until student achievement scores reach national norms. The District Court issued this order without any findings rejecting the State's request for a declaration of partial unitary status of the quality of education. "The basic task of the District Court is to decide whether the reduction in achievement by minority students attributable to prior *de jure* segregation has been remedied to the extent practicable." The District Court should also consider the impact of its prior orders on the quality of education. "On remand, the District Court must bear in mind that its end purpose is not only 'to remedy the violation' to the extent practicable, but also 'to restore state and local authorities to the control of a school system that is operating in compliance with the Constitution.'"

Justice O'Connor concurred in the judgment. Interdistrict violations can be redressed by interdistrict remedies. However, in the case at bar, the District Court held that the State's and the KCMSD's constitutional violation was not interdistrict, nor did it have significant interdistrict effects. Interdistrict *de facto* segregation should not be redressed through a district court's interdistrict remedy.

Justice Thomas concurred in the judgment. Any supposition that black students necessarily suffer "an unspecified psychological harm from segregation that retards their mental and educational development" rests on a principle of "black inferiority." This notion intimated that black persons must be in the company of whites to achieve success. Justice Thomas questioned the sociological studies propounding this notion relied on in *Brown v. Board of Education*.

The "unlimited equitable powers" exercised by federal courts in desegregation cases infringed on federalism and separation of powers. Justice Thomas recommended that any remedy for *de jure* segregation pass strict scrutiny and be limited to students in school or alive at the time of the violation.

Justice Souter dissented, joined by Justices Stevens, Ginsburg, and Breyer. He suggested that "the Court is on shaky grounds when it assumes that prior segregation and later desegregation are separable in fact as causes of 'white flight.'" Justice Souter also disagreed with the Court's reading of *Milliken I* to forbid an interdistrict remedy, in spite of segregative interdistrict intent, unless the violation has a segregative interdistrict effect.

Justice Ginsburg also filed a separate dissenting opinion. She objected to the Court mandating an end to the practice of attracting nonminority students to the KCMSD, a district which is 68.3% black.

PARENTS INVOLVED IN COMMUNITY SCHOOLS v. SEATTLE SCHOOL DISTRICT
127 S. Ct. 2738, 168 L. Ed. 2d 508 (2007)

CHIEF JUSTICE ROBERTS announced the judgment of the Court, and delivered the opinion of the Court with respect to Parts I, II, III-A, and III-C, and an opinion with respect to Parts III-B and IV, in which JUSTICES SCALIA, THOMAS, and ALITO join.

The school districts in these cases voluntarily adopted student assignment plans that rely upon race to determine which public schools certain children may attend. The Seattle school district classifies children as white or nonwhite; the Jefferson County school district as black or "other." In Seattle, this racial classification is used to allocate slots in oversubscribed high schools. In Jefferson County, it is used to make certain elementary school assignments and to rule on transfer requests. In each case, the school district relies upon an individual student's race in assigning that student to a particular school, so that the racial balance at the school falls within a predetermined range based on the racial composition of the school district as a whole. Parents of students denied assignment to particular schools under these plans solely because of their race brought suit. . . .

I

Both cases present the same underlying legal question — whether a public school that had not operated legally segregated schools or has been found to be unitary may choose to classify students by race and rely upon that classification in making school assignments. Although we examine the plans under the same legal framework, the specifics of the two plans, and the circumstances surrounding their adoption, are in some respects quite different.

A

Seattle School District . . . allows incoming ninth graders to choose from among any of the district's high schools, ranking however many schools they wish in order of preference.

. . . If too many students list the same school as their first choice, the district employs a series of "tiebreakers.". . . The first tiebreaker selects for admission students who have a sibling currently enrolled in the chosen school. The next tiebreaker depends upon the racial composition of the particular school and the race of the individual student. In the district's public schools approximately 41 percent of enrolled students are white; the remaining 59 percent, comprising all other racial groups, are classified by Seattle for assignment purposes as nonwhite.[13] If an oversubscribed school is not within 10 percentage points of the district's overall white/nonwhite racial balance, it is what the district calls "integration positive," and the district employs a tiebreaker that selects for assignment students whose race "will serve to bring the school into balance." If it is still necessary to select students for the school after using the racial tiebreaker, the next tiebreaker is the geographic proximity of the school to the student's residence.

Seattle has never operated segregated schools — legally separate schools for students of different races — nor has it ever been subject to court-ordered desegregation. . . . Most white students live in the northern part of Seattle, most students of other racial backgrounds in the southern part. . . .

For the 2000-2001 school year, five of these schools were oversubscribed . . . so much so that 82 percent of incoming ninth graders ranked one of these schools as their first choice. Three of the oversubscribed schools were "integration positive" because the school's white enrollment the previous school year was greater than 51 percent. . . . Franklin was "integration positive" because its nonwhite enrollment the previous school year was greater than 69 percent; 89 more white students were assigned to Franklin by operation of the racial tiebreaker in the 2000-2001 school year than otherwise would have been. . . .

B

Jefferson County Public Schools operates the public school system in metropolitan Louisville, Kentucky. In 1973 a federal court found that Jefferson County had maintained a segregated school system, and in 1975 the District Court entered a desegregation decree. Jefferson County operated under this decree until 2000, when the District Court dissolved the decree after finding that the district had achieved unitary status by eliminating "to the greatest extent practicable" the vestiges of its prior policy of segregation.

In 2001, after the decree had been dissolved, Jefferson County adopted the voluntary student assignment plan at issue in this case. Approximately 34 percent of the district's 97,000 students are black; most of the remaining 66 percent are white. The plan requires all nonmagnet schools to maintain a minimum black enrollment of 15 percent, and a maximum black enrollment of 50 percent.

---

[13] [Court's footnote 2] The racial breakdown of this nonwhite group is approximately 23.8 percent Asian-American, 23.1 percent African-American, 10.3 percent Latino, and 2.8 percent Native-American.

. . . Parents of kindergartners, first-graders, and students new to the district may submit an application indicating a first and second choice among the schools within their cluster; students who do not submit such an application are assigned within the cluster by the district. "Decisions to assign students to schools within each cluster are based on available space within the schools and the racial guidelines in the District's current student assignment plan." If a school has reached the "extremes of the racial guidelines," a student whose race would contribute to the school's racial imbalance will not be assigned there. After assignment, students at all grade levels are permitted to apply to transfer between nonmagnet schools in the district. Transfers may be requested for any number of reasons, and may be denied because of lack of available space or on the basis of the racial guidelines. . . .

III

A

It is well established that when the government distributes burdens or benefits on the basis of individual racial classifications, that action is reviewed under strict scrutiny. . . . In order to satisfy this searching standard of review, the school districts must demonstrate that the use of individual racial classifications in the assignment plans here under review is "narrowly tailored" to achieve a "compelling" government interest. *Adarand Constructors, Inc. v. Pena*, 515 U.S. 211, 227 (1995).

Without attempting in these cases to set forth all the interests a school district might assert, it suffices to note that our prior cases, in evaluating the use of racial classifications in the school context, have recognized two interests that qualify as compelling. The first is the compelling interest of remedying the effects of past intentional discrimination. *See Freeman v. Pitts*, 503 U.S. 467, 494 (1992). Yet the Seattle public schools have not shown that they were ever segregated by law, and were not subject to court-ordered desegregation decrees. The Jefferson County public schools were previously segregated by law and were subject to a desegregation decree entered in 1975. In 2000, the District Court that entered that decree dissolved it, finding that Jefferson County had "eliminated the vestiges associated with the former policy of segregation and its pernicious effects," and thus had achieved "unitary" status. . . .

We have emphasized that the harm being remedied by mandatory desegregation plans is the harm that is traceable to segregation, and that "the Constitution is not violated by racial imbalance in the schools, without more." *Milliken v. Bradley*, 433 U.S. 267, 280, n. 14 (1977). *See also Freeman, supra*, at 495-496; *Board of Ed. of Oklahoma City Public Schools v. Dowell*, 498 U.S. 237, 248 (1991); *Milliken v. Bradley*, 418 U.S. 717, 746 (1974). Once Jefferson County achieved unitary status, it had remedied the constitutional wrong that allowed race-based assignments. Any continued use of race must be justified on some other basis.

The second government interest we have recognized as compelling for purposes of strict scrutiny is the interest in diversity in higher education upheld in *Grutter v. Bollinger*, 539 U.S. 306, 328 (2003). The specific interest found compelling in *Grutter* was student body diversity "in the context of higher education." *Ibid.* The diversity interest was not focused on race alone but encompassed "all factors that may contribute to student body diversity." *Id.*, at 337. We described the various types of diversity that the law school sought. . . .

The Court quoted the articulation of diversity from Justice Powell's opinion in *Regents of the University of California v. Bakke*, 438 U.S. 265 (1978), noting that "it is not an interest in simple ethnic diversity, in which a specified percentage of the student body is in effect guaranteed to be members of selected ethnic groups, that can justify the use of race." *Grutter, supra,* at 324-325 (citing and quoting *Bakke, supra,* at 314-315 (opinion of Powell, J.). Instead, what was upheld in *Grutter* was consideration of "a far broader array of qualifications and characteristics of which racial or ethnic origin is but a single though important element." 539 U.S., at 325 (quoting *Bakke, supra,* at 315 (opinion of Powell, J.).

The entire gist of the analysis in *Grutter* was that the admissions program at issue there focused on each applicant as an individual, and not simply as a member of a particular racial group. The classification of applicants by race upheld in *Grutter* was only as part of a "highly individualized, holistic review," 539 U.S., at 337. . . . The point of the narrow tailoring analysis in which the *Grutter* Court engaged was to ensure that the use of racial classifications was indeed part of a broader assessment of diversity, and not simply an effort to achieve racial balance, which the Court explained would be "patently unconstitutional." *Id.,* at 330.

In the present cases, by contrast, race is not considered as part of a broader effort to achieve "exposure to widely diverse people, cultures, ideas, and viewpoints," *ibid.;* race, for some students, is determinative standing alone. The districts argue that other factors, such as student preferences, affect assignment decisions under their plans, but under each plan when race comes into play, it is decisive by itself. It is not simply one factor weighed with others in reaching a decision, as in *Grutter*; it is *the* factor. Like the University of Michigan undergraduate plan struck down in *Gratz v. Bollinger,* 539 U.S. 244, 275 (2003), the plans here "do not provide for a meaningful individualized review of applicants" but instead rely on racial classifications in a "nonindividualized, mechanical" way. *Id.,* at 276, 280 (O'Connor, J., concurring).

. . . The Court in *Grutter* expressly articulated key limitations on its holding — defining a specific type of broad-based diversity and noting the unique context of higher education — but these limitations were largely disregarded by the lower courts in extending *Grutter* to uphold race-based assignments in elementary and secondary schools. The present cases are not governed by *Grutter.*

B

Perhaps recognizing that reliance on *Grutter* cannot sustain their plans, both school districts assert additional interests, distinct from the interest upheld in *Grutter,* to justify their race-based assignments. . . . Each school district argues that educational and broader socialization benefits flow from a racially diverse learning environment, and each contends that because the diversity they seek is racial diversity — not the broader diversity at issue in *Grutter* — it makes sense to promote that interest directly by relying on race alone.

. . . It is clear that the racial classifications employed by the districts are not narrowly tailored to the goal of achieving the educational and social benefits asserted to flow from racial diversity. In design and operation, the plans are directed only to racial balance, pure and simple, an objective this Court has repeatedly condemned as illegitimate.

The plans are tied to each district's specific racial demographics, rather than to any pedagogic concept of the level of diversity needed to obtain the asserted educational benefits. In Seattle, the district seeks white enrollment of between 31 and 51 percent (within 10 percent of "the district white average" of 41 percent), and nonwhite enrollment of between 49 and 69 percent (within 10 percent of "the district minority average" of 59 percent). In Jefferson County, by contrast, the district seeks black enrollment of no less than 15 or more than 50 percent, a range designed to be "equally above and below Black student enrollment systemwide,". . . based on the objective of achieving at "all schools . . . an African-American enrollment equivalent to the average district-wide African-American enrollment" of 34 percent. . . . The plans here are not tailored to achieving a degree of diversity necessary to realize the asserted educational benefits; instead the plans are tailored, in the words of Seattle's Manager of Enrollment Planning, Technical Support, and Demographics, to "the goal established by the school board of attaining a level of diversity within the schools that approximates the district's overall demographics.". . .

In fact, in each case the extreme measure of relying on race in assignments is unnecessary to achieve the stated goals, even as defined by the districts. For example, at Franklin High School in Seattle, the racial tiebreaker was applied because nonwhite enrollment exceeded 69 percent, and resulted in an incoming ninth-grade class in 2000-2001 that was 30.3 percent Asian-American, 21.9 percent African-American, 6.8 percent Latino, 0.5 percent Native-American, and 40.5 percent Caucasian. Without the racial tiebreaker, the class would have been 39.6 percent Asian-American, 30.2 percent African-American, 8.3 percent Latino, 1.1 percent Native-American, and 20.8 percent Caucasian. . . . When the actual racial breakdown is considered, enrolling students without regard to their race yields a substantially diverse student body under any definition of diversity.[14]

In *Grutter*, the number of minority students the school sought to admit was an undefined "meaningful number" necessary to achieve a genuinely diverse student body. . . .

Grutter itself reiterated that "outright racial balancing" is "patently unconstitutional." 539 U.S., at 330.

Accepting racial balancing as a compelling state interest would justify the imposition of racial proportionality throughout American society, contrary to our repeated recognition that "at the heart of the Constitution's guarantee of equal protection lies the simple command that the Government must treat citizens as individuals, not as simply components of a racial, religious, sexual or national class." *Miller v. Johnson*, 515 U.S. 900, 911 (1995). . . .

The validity of our concern that racial balancing has "no logical stopping point," [*Richmond v. J. A. Croson, Co.*, 488 U.S. 469, 498 (1989)] is demonstrated here by the degree to which the districts tie their racial guidelines to their demographics. As the districts' demographics shift, so too will their definition of racial diversity. . . .

C

The districts assert, as they must, that the way in which they have employed individual racial classifications is necessary to achieve their stated ends. The minimal effect these classifications have on student assignments, however, suggests that other means would be effective. . . .

[T]he minimal impact of the districts' racial classifications on school enrollment casts doubt on the necessity of using racial classifications. In *Grutter*, the consideration of race was viewed as indispensable in more than tripling minority representation at the law school — from 4 to 14.5 percent. . . .

The districts have also failed to show that they considered methods other than explicit racial classifications to achieve their stated goals. Narrow tailoring requires "serious, good faith consideration of workable race-neutral alternatives," *Grutter*, *supra*, at 339. . . .

---

[14] [Court's footnote 13] Data for the Seattle schools in the several years since this litigation was commenced further demonstrate the minimal role that the racial tiebreaker in fact played. . . .

IV

. . . Justice Breyer seeks to justify the plans at issue under our precedents recognizing the compelling interest in remedying past intentional discrimination. . . . The dissent elides this distinction between *de jure* and *de facto* segregation. . . . [15]

Justice Breyer's dissent candidly dismisses the significance of this Court's repeated *holdings* that all racial classifications must be reviewed under strict scrutiny, arguing that a different standard of review should be applied because the districts use race for beneficent rather than malicious purposes. . . .

Accepting Justice Breyer's approach would "do no more than move us from 'separate but equal' to 'unequal but benign.' " *Metro Broadcasting, Inc. v. FCC*, 497 U.S. 547, 638 (1990). (Kennedy, J., dissenting).

Justice Breyer speaks of bringing "the races" together (putting aside the purely black-and-white nature of the plans), as the justification for excluding individuals on the basis of their race. Again, this approach to racial classifications is fundamentally at odds with our precedent, which makes clear that the Equal Protection Clause "protects *persons*, not *groups*," *Adarand*, 515 U.S., at 227. . . .

Justice Breyer's position comes down to a familiar claim: The end justifies the means. He admits that "there is a cost in applying 'a state-mandated racial label,' " but he is confident that the cost is worth paying. Our established strict scrutiny test for racial classifications, however, insists on "detailed examination, both as to ends *and* as to means." *Adarand, supra*, at 236. . . . [16]

Justice Breyer also suggests that other means for achieving greater racial diversity in schools are necessarily unconstitutional if the racial classifications at issue in these cases cannot survive strict scrutiny. These other means — e.g., where to construct new schools, how to allocate resources among schools, and which academic offerings to provide to attract students to certain schools — implicate different considerations than the explicit racial classifications at issue in these cases, and we express no opinion on their validity — not even in dicta. . . .

Before *Brown*, schoolchildren were told where they could and could not go to school based on the color of their skin. The school districts in these cases have not carried the heavy burden of demonstrating that we should allow this once again — even for very different reasons. . . . The way to stop discrimination on the basis of race is to stop discriminating on the basis of race. . . .

Justice Thomas, concurring.

Today, the Court holds that state entities may not experiment with race-based means to achieve ends they deem socially desirable. . . . Contrary to the dissent's

---

[15] [Court's footnote 15] Justice Breyer makes much of the fact that in 1978 Seattle "settled" an NAACP complaint alleging illegal segregation with the federal Office for Civil Rights (OCR). The memorandum of agreement between Seattle and OCR, of course, contains no admission by Seattle that such segregation ever existed or was ongoing at the time of the agreement, and simply reflects a "desire to avoid the inconvenience [sic] and expense of a formal OCR investigation," which OCR was obligated under law to initiate upon the filing of such a complaint. . . .

[16] [Court's footnote 17] Justice Breyer also tries to downplay the impact of the racial assignments by stating that in Seattle "students can decide voluntarily to transfer to a preferred district high school (without any consideration of race-conscious criteria)." This presumably refers to the district's decision to cease, for 2001-2002 school year assignments, applying the racial tiebreaker to students seeking to transfer to a different school after ninth grade. There are obvious disincentives for students to transfer to a different school after a full quarter of their high school experience has passed, and the record sheds no light on how transfers to the oversubscribed high schools are handled.

arguments, resegregation is not occurring in Seattle or Louisville; these school boards have no present interest in remedying past segregation; and these race-based student-assignment programs do not serve any compelling state interest. . . .   Disfavoring a color-blind interpretation of the Constitution, the dissent would give school boards a free hand to make decisions on the basis of race — an approach reminiscent of that advocated by the segregationists in *Brown I*. This approach is just as wrong today as it was a half-century ago. . . .

A

. . . Racial imbalance is not segregation. . . .

[R]acial imbalance without intentional state action to separate the races does not amount to segregation. . . . [17]

B

. . . [T]his Court has authorized the use of race-based measures for remedial purposes in two narrowly defined circumstances. First, in schools that were formerly segregated by law, race-based measures are sometimes constitutionally compelled to remedy prior school segregation. Second, in *Croson*, the Court appeared willing to authorize a government unit to remedy past discrimination for which it was responsible. *Richmond v. J. A. Croson Co.*, 488 U.S. 469, 504 (1989). . . .

3

. . . [F]or a government unit to remedy past discrimination for which it was responsible, . . . requires proper findings regarding the extent of the government unit's past racial discrimination. . . .   For Seattle, the dissent . . . advert[s] to allegations made in past complaints filed against the Seattle school district. However, allegations in complaints cannot substitute for specific findings of prior discrimination – even when those allegations lead to settlements with complaining parties. . . .

C

. . . [T]he further we get from the era of state-sponsored racial separation, the less likely it is that racial imbalance has a traceable connection to any prior segregation. . . .

II

A

. . . [E]xclusion, solely on the basis of race, is precisely the sort of government action that pits the races against one another. . . .

---

[17] [Concurrence of Justice Thomas, Footnote 3] The dissent's assertion that these plans are necessary for the school districts to maintain their "hard-won gains" reveals its conflation of segregation and racial imbalance. . . .   Nothing but an interest in classroom aesthetics and a hypersensitivity to elite sensibilities justifies the school districts' racial balancing programs. . . .

B

1

. . . Moreover, the school boards have no interest in remedying the sundry consequences of prior segregation unrelated to schooling, such as "housing patterns, employment practices, economic conditions, and social attitudes." . . . [R]emedial measures geared toward such broad and unrelated societal ills have " 'no logical stopping point,' " [*Croson*, 488 U.S. at 498], and threaten to become "ageless in their reach into the past, and timeless in their ability to affect the future." *Wygant* [*v. Jackson Bd. of Ed.*, 476 U.S. 267, 276 (1986)] (plurality opinion). . . .

2

Next, the dissent argues that the interest in integration has an educational element. . . .

Scholars have differing opinions as to whether educational benefits arise from racial balancing. . . .

Add to the inconclusive social science the fact of black achievement in "racially isolated" environments. . . . There is also evidence that black students attending historically black colleges achieve better academic results than those attending predominantly white colleges.

The Seattle school board itself must believe that racial mixing is not necessary to black achievement. Seattle operates a K-8 "African-American Academy," which has a "nonwhite" enrollment of 99%. . . . This racially imbalanced environment has reportedly produced test scores "higher across all grade levels in reading, writing and math.". . .

3

Finally, the dissent asserts a "democratic element" to the integration interest. It defines the "democratic element" as "an interest in producing an educational environment that reflects the 'pluralistic society' in which our children will live.". . .

. . . Simply putting students together under the same roof does not necessarily mean that the students will learn together or even interact.

Furthermore, it is unclear whether increased interracial contact improves racial attitudes and relations. . . .

Given our case law and the paucity of evidence supporting the dissent's belief that these plans improve race relations, no democratic element can support the integration interest. . . .

III

. . . My view of the Constitution is Justice Harlan's view in *Plessy*: "Our Constitution is color-blind, and neither knows nor tolerates classes among citizens." *Plessy v. Ferguson*, 163 U.S. 537, 559 (1896) (dissenting opinion). And my view was the rallying cry for the lawyers who litigated *Brown*. . . .

The segregationists in *Brown* embraced the arguments the Court endorsed in *Plessy*. Though *Brown* decisively rejected those arguments, today's dissent replicates them to a distressing extent. . . .

. . . Like the dissent, the segregationists repeatedly cautioned the Court to consider practicalities and not to embrace too theoretical a view of the Fourteenth Amendment. . . .

JUSTICE KENNEDY, concurring in part and concurring in the judgment.

The Nation's schools strive to teach that our strength comes from people of different races, creeds, and cultures uniting in commitment to the freedom of all. In these cases two school districts in different parts of the country seek to teach that principle by having classrooms that reflect the racial makeup of the surrounding community. That the school districts consider these plans to be necessary should remind us our highest aspirations are yet unfulfilled. But the solutions mandated by these school districts must themselves be lawful. To make race matter now so that it might not matter later may entrench the very prejudices we seek to overcome. In my view the state-mandated racial classifications at issue, official labels proclaiming the race of all persons in a broad class of citizens — elementary school students in one case, high school students in another — are unconstitutional as the cases now come to us.

I . . . join Parts I and II of the Court's opinion. I also join Parts III-A and III-C. . . . My views do not allow me to join the balance of the opinion by the Chief Justice, which seems to me to be inconsistent in both its approach and its implications with the history, meaning, and reach of the Equal Protection Clause. Justice Breyer's dissenting opinion, on the other hand, rests on what in my respectful submission is a misuse and mistaken interpretation of our precedents. This leads it to advance propositions that, in my view, are both erroneous and in fundamental conflict with basic equal protection principles. . . .

I

. . . Justice Breyer's dissent finds that the school districts have identified a compelling interest in increasing diversity, including for the purpose of avoiding racial isolation. The plurality, by contrast, does not acknowledge that the school districts have identified a compelling interest here. For this reason, among others, I do not join Parts III-B and IV. Diversity, depending on its meaning and definition, is a compelling educational goal a school district may pursue. . . .

. . . Jefferson County in its briefing has explained how and when it employs these classifications only in terms so broad and imprecise that they cannot withstand strict scrutiny. While it acknowledges that racial classifications are used to make certain assignment decisions, it fails to make clear, for example, who makes the decisions; what if any oversight is employed; the precise circumstances in which an assignment decision will or will not be made on the basis of race; or how it is determined which of two similarly situated children will be subjected to a given race-based decision. . . .

. . . When a court subjects governmental action to strict scrutiny, it cannot construe ambiguities in favor of the State.

As for the Seattle case, the school district has gone further in describing the methods and criteria used to determine assignment decisions on the basis of individual racial classifications. . . .

The district has identified its purposes as follows: "(1) to promote the educational benefits of diverse school enrollments; (2) to reduce the potentially harmful effects of racial isolation by allowing students the opportunity to opt out of racially isolated schools; and (3) to make sure that racially segregated housing patterns did not prevent non-white students from having equitable access to the most popular over-subscribed schools." Yet the school district does not explain how, in the context of its diverse student population, a blunt distinction between "white" and "non-white" furthers these goals. As the Court explains, "a school with 50 percent Asian-American students and 50 percent white students but no African-American, Native-American, or Latino students would qualify as balanced, while a school with 30 percent Asian-American, 25 percent African-American, 25 percent Latino, and 20 percent white students would not." Far from being narrowly tailored to its purposes, this system threatens to defeat its own ends. . . .   Other problems are evident in Seattle's system, but there is no need to address them now. . . .

II

. . . The enduring hope is that race should not matter; the reality is that too often it does.

. . . The plurality opinion is at least open to the interpretation that the Constitution requires school districts to ignore the problem of *de facto* resegregation in schooling. I cannot endorse that conclusion. To the extent the plurality opinion suggests the Constitution mandates that state and local school authorities must accept the status quo of racial isolation in schools, it is, in my view, profoundly mistaken.

The statement by Justice Harlan that "our Constitution is color-blind" was most certainly justified in the context of his dissent in *Plessy v. Ferguson.* . . .   In the real world, it is regrettable to say, it cannot be a universal constitutional principle.

In the administration of public schools by the state and local authorities it is permissible to consider the racial makeup of schools and to adopt general policies to encourage a diverse student body, one aspect of which is its racial composition. *Cf. Grutter*; *id.*, at 387-388. If school authorities are concerned that the student-body compositions of certain schools interfere with the objective of offering an equal educational opportunity to all of their students, they are free to devise race-conscious measures to address the problem in a general way and without treating each student in different fashion solely on the basis of a systematic, individual typing by race.

School boards may pursue the goal of bringing together students of diverse backgrounds and races through other means, including strategic site selection of new schools; drawing attendance zones with general recognition of the demographics of neighborhoods; allocating resources for special programs; recruiting students and faculty in a targeted fashion; and tracking enrollments, performance, and other statistics by race. These mechanisms are race conscious but do not lead to different treatment based on a classification that tells each student he or she is to be defined by race, so it is unlikely any of them would demand strict scrutiny to be found permissible. . . .   Assigning to each student a personal designation according to a crude system of individual racial classifications is quite a different matter; and the legal analysis changes accordingly.

. . . [I]ndividual racial classifications employed in this manner may be considered legitimate only if they are a last resort to achieve a compelling interest.

In the cases before us it is noteworthy that the number of students whose assignment depends on express racial classifications is limited. I join Part III-C of the Court's opinion because I agree that in the context of these plans, the small number of assignments affected suggests that the schools could have achieved their stated ends through different means. These include the facially race-neutral means set forth above or, if necessary, a more nuanced, individual evaluation of school needs and student characteristics that might include race as a component. The latter approach would be informed by *Grutter*, though of course the criteria relevant to student placement would differ based on the age of the students, the needs of the parents, and the role of the schools.

III

The dissent rests on the assumptions that these sweeping race-based classifications of persons are permitted by existing precedents; that its confident endorsement of race categories for each child in a large segment of the community presents no danger to individual freedom in other, prospective realms of governmental regulation; and that the racial classifications used here cause no hurt or anger of the type the Constitution prevents. Each of these premises is, in my respectful view, incorrect.

A

The dissent's reliance on this Court's precedents to justify the explicit, sweeping, classwide racial classifications at issue here is a misreading of our authorities that, it appears to me, tends to undermine well-accepted principles needed to guard our freedom. And in his critique of that analysis, I am in many respects in agreement with the Chief Justice. The conclusions he has set forth in Part III-A of the Court's opinion are correct, in my view, because the compelling interests implicated in the cases before us are distinct from the interests the Court has recognized in remedying the effects of past intentional discrimination and in increasing diversity in higher education. As the Court notes, we recognized the compelling nature of the interest in remedying past intentional discrimination in *Freeman*, and of the interest in diversity in higher education in *Grutter*. At the same time, these compelling interests, in my view, do help inform the present inquiry. And to the extent the plurality opinion can be interpreted to foreclose consideration of these interests, I disagree with that reasoning.

As to the dissent, the general conclusions upon which it relies have no principled limit and would result in the broad acceptance of governmental racial classifications in areas far afield from schooling. The dissent's permissive strict scrutiny (which bears more than a passing resemblance to rational-basis review) could invite widespread governmental deployment of racial classifications. . . .

[T]he dissent's reliance on the Court's opinions in *Gratz* and *Grutter* . . . is, with all respect, simply baffling. . . .

B

To uphold these programs the Court is asked to brush aside two concepts of central importance for determining the validity of laws and decrees designed to alleviate the hurt and adverse consequences resulting from race discrimination. The first is the difference between *de jure* and *de facto* segregation; the second, the presumptive invalidity of a State's use of racial classifications to differentiate its treatment of individuals.

In the immediate aftermath of *Brown* the Court addressed other instances where laws and practices enforced *de jure* segregation. . . .

. . . [L]ike so many other legal categories that can overlap in some instances, the constitutional distinction between *de jure* and *de facto* segregation has been thought to be an important one. . . . [T]he distinction serves as a limit on the exercise of a power that reaches to the very verge of constitutional authority. . . .

Notwithstanding these concerns, . . . [t]he Court has allowed school districts to remedy their prior *de jure* segregation by classifying individual students based on their race. . . .

. . . [W]hen *de facto* discrimination is at issue . . . [t]he State must seek alternatives to the classification and differential treatment of individuals by race, at least absent some extraordinary showing not present here.

C

. . . Governmental classifications that command people to march in different directions based on racial typologies can cause a new divisiveness. The practice can lead to corrosive discourse. . . .

The idea that if race is the problem, race is the instrument with which to solve it cannot be accepted as an analytical leap forward. . . .

. . . A compelling interest exists in avoiding racial isolation, an interest that a school district, in its discretion and expertise, may choose to pursue. Likewise, a district may consider it a compelling interest to achieve a diverse student population. Race may be one component of that diversity, but other demographic factors, plus special talents and needs, should also be considered. What the government is not permitted to do, absent a showing of necessity not made here, is to classify every student on the basis of race and to assign each of them to schools based on that classification. Crude measures of this sort threaten to reduce children to racial chits valued and traded according to one school's supply and another's demand. . . .

JUSTICE STEVENS, dissenting.

. . . There is a cruel irony in the Chief Justice's reliance on our decision in *Brown v. Board of Education*, 349 U.S. 294 (1955). The first sentence in the concluding paragraph of his opinion states: "Before *Brown*, schoolchildren were told where they could and could not go to school based on the color of their skin.". . . The Chief Justice fails to note that it was only black schoolchildren who were so ordered; indeed, the history books do not tell stories of white children struggling to attend black schools. . . .

The Chief Justice rejects the conclusion that the racial classifications at issue here should be viewed differently than others, because they do not impose burdens on one race alone and do not stigmatize or exclude. . . .

JUSTICE BREYER, with whom JUSTICE STEVENS, JUSTICE SOUTER, and JUSTICE GINSBURG join, dissenting.

. . . The school board plans before us resemble many others adopted in the last 50 years by primary and secondary schools throughout the Nation. . . . [T]o bring about the kind of racially integrated education that *Brown v. Board of Education*, 347 U.S. 483 (1954), long ago promised — efforts that this Court has repeatedly required, permitted, and encouraged local authorities to undertake. This Court has recognized that the public interests at stake in such cases are "compelling." We have approved of "narrowly tailored" plans that are no less race-conscious than the plans before us. And we have understood that the Constitution *permits* local communities to adopt desegregation plans even where it does not *require* them to do so.

The plurality pays inadequate attention to this law, to past opinions' rationales, their language, and the contexts in which they arise. . . . [W]ith the growing resegregation of public schools, [the plurality] threatens to substitute for present calm a disruptive round of race-related litigation, and it undermines *Brown's* promise of integrated primary and secondary education that local communities have sought to make a reality. . . .

I

Facts

. . . School authorities are traditionally charged with broad power to formulate and implement educational policy and might well conclude, for example, that in order to prepare students to live in a pluralistic society each school should have a prescribed ratio of Negro to white students reflecting the proportion for the district as a whole. *To do this as an educational policy is within the broad discretionary powers of school authorities.*

Swann v. Charlotte-Mecklenburg Bd. of Ed., 402 U.S. 1, 16 (1971). . . .

Overall these efforts brought about considerable racial integration. More recently, however, progress has stalled. . . . Today, more than one in six black children attend a school that is 99-100% minority. In light of the evident risk of a return to school systems that are in fact (though not in law) resegregated, many school districts have felt a need to maintain or to extend their integration efforts. . . .

In both Seattle and Louisville, the local school districts began with schools that were highly segregated in fact. In both cities plaintiffs filed lawsuits claiming unconstitutional segregation. In Louisville, a federal district court found that school segregation reflected pre-*Brown* state laws separating the races. In Seattle, the plaintiffs alleged that school segregation unconstitutionally reflected not only generalized societal discrimination and residential housing patterns, but also *school board policies and actions* that had helped to create, maintain, and aggravate racial segregation. In Louisville, a federal court entered a remedial decree. In Seattle, the parties settled after the school district pledged to undertake a desegregation plan. In both cities, the school boards adopted plans designed to achieve integration by bringing about more racially diverse schools. In each city the school board modified its plan several times in light of, for example, hostility to busing, the threat of resegregation, and the desirability of introducing greater student choice. And in each city, the school boards' plans have evolved over time in ways that progressively *diminish* the plans' use of explicit race-conscious criteria.

The histories that follow set forth these basic facts. . . .

A

Seattle

. . . The Seattle Plan achieved the school integration that it sought. Just prior to the plan's implementation, for example, 4 of Seattle's 11 high schools were "imbalanced," i.e., almost exclusively "black" or almost exclusively "white." By 1979, only two were out of "balance." By 1980 only [one] remained out of "balance" (as the board defined it) and that by a mere two students.

Nonetheless, the Seattle Plan, due to its busing, provoked serious opposition within the State. *See generally Washington v. Seattle School Dist. No. 1*, 458 U.S. 457, 461-466 (1982). Thus, Washington state voters enacted an initiative that amended state law to require students to be assigned to the schools closest to their homes. The Seattle School Board challenged the constitutionality of the initiative. This Court then held that the initiative — which would have prevented the Seattle Plan from taking effect — violated the Fourteenth Amendment.

6. *Student Choice, 1988 to 1998.* By 1988, many white families had left the school district, and many Asian families had moved in. The public school population had fallen

from about 100,000 to less than 50,000. The racial makeup of the school population amounted to 43% white, 24% black, and 23% Asian or Pacific Islander, with Hispanics and Native Americans making up the rest. The cost of busing, the harm that members of all racial communities feared that the Seattle Plan caused, the desire to attract white families back to the public schools, and the interest in providing greater school choice led the board to abandon busing and to substitute a new student assignment policy that resembles the plan now before us.

The new plan permitted each student to choose the school he or she wished to attend, subject to race-based constraints. . . .

7. *The Current Plan, 1999 to the Present.* . . . [T]he present plan . . . sought to deemphasize the use of racial criteria and to increase the likelihood that a student would receive an assignment at his first or second choice high school. The district retained a racial tiebreaker for oversubscribed schools, which takes effect only if the school's minority or majority enrollment falls outside of a 30% range centered on the minority/majority population ratio within the district. At the same time, all students were free subsequently to transfer . . . without regard to race. Thus, at worst, a student would have to spend one year at a high school he did not pick as a first or second choice.

. . . During the period the tiebreaker applied, it typically affected about 300 students per year. Between 80% and 90% of all students received their first choice assignment; between 89% and 97% received their first or second choice assignment. . . .

B

Louisville

. . . 4. *The Current Plan: Project Renaissance Modified, 1996 to 2003.* . . . [T]he district's public school population was approximately 30% black. The plan . . . redrew the racial "guidelines," setting the boundaries at 15% to 50% black for *all* schools. It again redrew school assignment boundaries. And it expanded the transfer opportunities available to elementary and middle school pupils. The plan forbade transfers, however, if the transfer would lead to a school population outside the guideline range, i.e., if it would create a school where fewer than 15% or more than 50% of the students were black. . . .

C

. . . In both cases the efforts were in part remedial. Louisville began its integration efforts in earnest when a federal court in 1975 entered a school desegregation order. Seattle undertook its integration efforts in response to the filing of a federal lawsuit and as a result of its settlement of a segregation complaint filed with the federal OCR. . . .

A court finding of *de jure* segregation cannot be the crucial variable. After all, a number of school districts in the South that the Government or private plaintiffs challenged as segregated *by law* voluntarily desegregated their schools *without a court order* — just as Seattle did. . . .

Moreover, Louisville's history makes clear that a community under a court order to desegregate might submit a race-conscious remedial plan *before* the court dissolved the order, but with every intention of following that plan even *after* dissolution. How could such a plan be lawful the day before dissolution but then become unlawful the very next day? . . .

Because the Constitution emphatically does not forbid the use of race-conscious measures by districts in the South that voluntarily desegregated their schools, on what basis does the plurality claim that the law forbids Seattle to do the same? . . .

[T]he law often leaves legislatures, city councils, school boards, and voters with a broad range of choice. . . .

II

The Legal Standard

. . . This context is *not* a context that involves the use of race to decide who will receive goods or services that are normally distributed on the basis of merit and which are in short supply. . . . The context here is one of racial limits that seek, not to keep the races apart, but to bring them together. . . .

The view that a more lenient standard than "strict scrutiny" should apply in the present context would not imply abandonment of judicial efforts carefully to determine the need for race-conscious criteria and the criteria's tailoring in light of the need. . . .

But unlike the plurality, such a judge would also be aware that a legislature or school administrators, ultimately accountable to the electorate, could *nonetheless* properly conclude that a racial classification sometimes serves a purpose important enough to overcome the risks they mention, for example, helping to end racial isolation or to achieve a diverse student body in public schools. Where that is so, the judge would carefully examine the program's details to determine whether the use of race-conscious criteria is proportionate to the important ends it serves. . . .

Nonetheless, in light of *Grutter* and other precedents, *see, e.g., Bakke*, I shall . . . apply the version of strict scrutiny that those cases embody. I shall consequently ask whether the school boards in Seattle and Louisville adopted these plans to serve a "compelling governmental interest" and, if so, whether the plans are "narrowly tailored" to achieve that interest. . . . Hence, I conclude that the plans before us pass both parts of the strict scrutiny test. . . .

III

Applying the Legal Standard

A

Compelling Interest

The principal interest advanced in these cases to justify the use of race-based criteria goes by various names. . . . I have used more general terms to signify that interest, describing it, for example, as an interest in promoting or preserving greater racial "integration" of public schools. . . .

[T]he interest at stake possesses three essential elements. First, there is a historical and remedial element: an interest in setting right the consequences of prior conditions of segregation. . . .

Second, there is an educational element: an interest in overcoming the adverse educational effects produced by and associated with highly segregated schools. . . .

[T]he evidence supporting an educational interest in racially integrated schools is well established and strong enough to permit a democratically elected school board reasonably to determine that this interest is a compelling one.

Research suggests, for example, that black children from segregated educational environments significantly increase their achievement levels once they are placed in a more integrated setting. . . .

One commentator, reviewing dozens of studies of the educational benefits of desegregated schooling, found that the studies have provided "remarkably consistent" results, showing that: (1) black students' educational achievement is improved in integrated schools as compared to racially isolated schools, (2) black students' educational achievement is improved in integrated classes, and (3) the earlier that black students are removed from racial isolation, the better their educational outcomes. Multiple studies also indicate that black alumni of integrated schools are more likely to move into occupations traditionally closed to African-Americans, and to earn more money in those fields. . . .

Third, there is a democratic element: an interest in producing an educational environment that reflects the "pluralistic society" in which our children will live. . . .

How do the educational and civic interests differ in kind from those that underlie and justify the racial "diversity" that the law school sought in *Grutter*, where this Court found a compelling interest?

The plurality tries to draw a distinction by reference to the well-established conceptual difference between *de jure* segregation ("segregation by state action") and *de facto* segregation ("racial imbalance caused by other factors"). But that distinction concerns what the Constitution *requires* school boards to do, not what it *permits* them to do. . . .

B

Narrow Tailoring

. . . Several factors, taken together, nonetheless lead me to conclude that the boards' use of race-conscious criteria in these plans passes even the strictest "tailoring" test.

First, the race-conscious criteria at issue only help set the outer bounds of *broad ranges.* . . .

In fact, the defining feature of both plans is greater emphasis upon student choice. In Seattle, for example, in more than 80% of all cases, that choice alone determines which high schools Seattle's ninth graders will attend. After ninth grade, students can decide voluntarily to transfer to a preferred district high school (without any consideration of race-conscious criteria). . . .

Indeed, the race-conscious ranges at issue in these cases often have no effect, either because the particular school is not oversubscribed in the year in question, or because the racial makeup of the school falls within the broad range, or because the student is a transfer applicant or has a sibling at the school. In these respects, the broad ranges are less like a quota and more like the kinds of "useful starting points" that this Court has consistently found permissible. . . .

Second, broad-range limits on voluntary school choice plans are less burdensome, and hence more narrowly tailored, *see Grutter, supra,* at 341, than other race-conscious restrictions this Court has previously approved. *See, e.g., Swann, supra,* at 26-27. Indeed, the plans before us are *more narrowly tailored* than the race-conscious admission plans that this Court approved in *Grutter.* . . . Disappointed students are not rejected from a State's flagship graduate program; they simply attend a different one of the district's many public schools, which in aspiration and in fact are substantially equal. And, in Seattle, the disadvantaged student loses at most one year at the high school of his choice. . . .

Third, the manner in which the school boards developed these plans itself reflects "narrow tailoring." Each plan was devised to overcome a history of segregated public schools. Each plan embodies the results of local experience and community consultation. Each plan is the product of a process that has sought to enhance student choice, while diminishing the need for mandatory busing. And each plan's use of race-conscious elements is *diminished* compared to the use of race in preceding integration plans.

The school boards' widespread consultation, their experimentation with numerous other plans, indeed, the 40-year history that Part I sets forth, make clear that plans that are less explicitly race-based are unlikely to achieve the board's "compelling" objectives. The history of each school system reveals highly segregated schools, followed by remedial plans that involved forced busing, followed by efforts to attract or retain students through the use of plans that abandoned busing and replaced it with greater student choice. Both cities once tried to achieve more integrated schools by relying solely upon measures such as redrawn district boundaries, new school building construction, and unrestricted voluntary transfers. In neither city did these prior attempts prove sufficient to achieve the city's integration goals.

Moreover, giving some degree of weight to a local school board's knowledge, expertise, and concerns in these particular matters is not inconsistent with rigorous judicial scrutiny. It simply recognizes that judges are not well suited to act as school administrators. . . .

Experience in Seattle and Louisville is consistent with experience elsewhere. In 1987, the U.S. Commission on Civil Rights studied 125 large school districts seeking integration. It reported that most districts – 92 of them, in fact – adopted desegregation policies that combined two or more highly race-conscious strategies, for example, rezoning or pairing. . . .

Nor could the school districts have accomplished their desired aims (e.g., avoiding forced busing, countering white flight, maintaining racial diversity) by other means. . . .

Finally, I recognize that the Court seeks to distinguish *Grutter* . . . by claiming that *Grutter* arose in " 'the context of higher education.' " But that is not a meaningful legal distinction. . . . The context here does not involve admission by merit; a child's academic, artistic, and athletic "merits" are not at all relevant to the child's placement. These are not affirmative action plans, and hence "individualized scrutiny" is simply beside the point. . . .

IV

Direct Precedent

. . . No one claims that (the relevant portion of) Louisville's plan was unlawful in 1996 when Louisville adopted it. To the contrary, there is every reason to believe that it represented part of an effort to implement the 1978 desegregation order. But if the plan was lawful when it was first adopted and if it was lawful the day before the District Court dissolved its order, how can the plurality now suggest that it became *unlawful* the following day? . . .

Second, *Seattle School Dist. No. 1*, 458 U.S. 457, is directly on point. That case involves the original Seattle Plan, a *more heavily race-conscious predecessor* of the very plan now before us. In *Seattle School Dist. No. 1*, this Court struck down a state referendum that effectively barred implementation of Seattle's desegregation plan and "burdened all future attempts to integrate Washington schools in districts throughout the State." *Id.*, at 462-463, 483. . . .

V

Consequences

. . . [C]onsider the effect of the plurality's views on the parties before us and on similar school districts throughout the Nation. . . .

A majority of [local school board's] desegregation techniques explicitly considered a student's race. . . .

. . . Hundreds of state and federal statutes and regulations use racial classifications for educational or other purposes. . . .

VI

Conclusions

. . . *First*, the histories of Louisville and Seattle reveal complex circumstances and a long tradition of conscientious efforts by local school boards to resist racial segregation in public schools. . . . For decades now, these school boards have considered and adopted and revised assignment plans that sought to rely less upon race, to emphasize greater student choice, and to improve the conditions of all schools for all students, no matter the color of their skin, no matter where they happen to reside. . . .

Second, since this Court's decision in *Brown*, the law has consistently and unequivocally approved of both voluntary and compulsory race-conscious measures to combat segregated schools. . . .

Third, the plans before us, subjected to rigorous judicial review, are supported by compelling state interests and are narrowly tailored to accomplish those goals. . . . These plans are *more* "narrowly tailored" than the race-conscious law school admissions criteria at issue in *Grutter*. . . .

Fourth, the plurality's approach risks serious harm to the law and for the Nation. Its view of the law rests either upon a denial of the distinction between exclusionary and inclusive use of race-conscious criteria. . . .

The last half-century has witnessed great strides toward racial equality, but we have not yet realized the promise of *Brown*. To invalidate the plans under review is to threaten the promise of *Brown*. . . .

UNITED STATES v. FORDICE, 505 U.S. 717 (1992). In *United States v. Fordice*, the Court decided what standards to apply in determining whether a State "has met its affirmative obligation to dismantle its prior *de jure* segregated system" in its colleges and universities. Mississippi had 5 all-white institutions of higher education and three all-black institutions. "Mississippi's policy of *de jure* segregation continued" beyond *Brown I* and *Brown II*. By court order, the first black student was admitted to UM in 1962. In the 1980s, 99% of Mississippi's white students were still enrolled at the five schools with 80–91% white students. "Seventy-one percent of the State's black students attended" the institutions with 92–99% black students. After years of negotiations, the parties went to trial in 1987, presenting "voluminous evidence."

The Supreme Court reversed and remanded. Justice White first noted that "a State does not discharge its constitutional obligations until it eradicates policies and practices traceable to its prior *de jure* dual system that continues to foster segregation." The test is whether "the State perpetuates policies and practices traceable to its prior system that continue to have segregative effects — whether by influencing student enrollment decisions or by fostering segregation in other facets of the university system — and such policies are without sound educational justification and can be practicably eliminated."

Justice White proceeded to identify four "surviving aspects of Mississippi's prior dual system which are constitutionally suspect;" that, though facially race-neutral, "restrict a person' choice of which institution to enter" and "contribute to the racial identifiability of the eight public universities." The four policies were admission standards, program duplication, institutional mission assignments, and continued operation of all eight public universities.

First, Mississippi's present admission standards, which are traceable to the *de jure* system, were originally adopted for a discriminatory purpose, and have present discriminatory effects. Although the Court did not disturb the lower court's findings of "no discriminatory purpose," it restated that no intent is needed to prove a constitutional violation through "perpetuation of policies traceable to the prior de jure segregative regime which have continuing discriminatory effects." For example, the three "comprehensive" exclusively white schools enacted policies in 1963, which required scores of 15 on the American College Testing Program (ACT) for admittance. At that time, the average ACT score for white students was 18; the average for black students was 7. Because, for example in 1985, "72 percent of Mississippi's white high school seniors scored 15 or better, while less than 30 percent of black high school seniors earned that score," a proportionally larger number of blacks are excluded from the five predominantly white universities.

Several factors make these automatic admission requirements more "suspect." First, universities with the same "mission" have dissimilar requirements. For example, the two predominantly white "regional" universities had a required minimum entrance score of 15 — the two predominantly black "regional" universities had a required minimum entrance score of 13. Because the different standards were remnants of the past *de jure* segregation, however, the Court found the justifications offered by the Board and the lower courts inadequate. These justifications were that students with lower scores were not prepared for the historically white institutions and that regional universities have a "more modest" function. Further "justification in terms of sound educational policy" was required.

Finally, the Court found problematic the universities' policy of denying automatic admission to applicants based on their ACT scores, "without also resorting to the applicant's high school grades as an additional factor in predicting college performance."

The Court pointed out that the record "indicated that the disparity between black and white students' high school grade averages was much narrower than the gap between their average ACT scores." The Board argued that it was "concerned with grade inflation and the lack of comparability in grading practices and course offerings among the State's diverse high schools." The Court responded that "the State has so far failed to show that the 'ACT-only' admission standard is not susceptible to elimination without eroding sound educational policy."

Second, the Court found that "widespread duplication of programs" also "necessitates further inquiry." Segregated dual systems required duplication and the "present unnecessary duplication is a continuation of that practice." The District Court erred in failing "to consider the combined effects of unnecessary program duplication with other policies, such as differential admissions standards, in evaluating whether the State had met its duty to dismantle" its dual system.

Third, Justice White asked whether Mississippi's mission classifications "perpetuates the State's formerly *de jure* dual system." On remand, the District Court should "inquire whether it would be practicable and consistent with sound educational practices to eliminate any such discriminatory effects of the State's present policy of mission assignments."

Fourth, Justice White criticized the State's "continuing to maintain and operate all eight higher educational institutions." The District Court found "[e]limination of program duplication and revision of admissions criteria may make institutional closure unnecessary. However, on remand . . . whether retention of all eight institution-s . . . perpetuates the segregated higher education system, whether maintenance of each of the universities is educationally justifiable, and whether one or more of them can be practicably closed or merged with other existing institutions."

At bottom, "the State may not leave in place policies rooted in its prior officially-segregated system that serve to maintain the racial identifiability of its universities if those policies can practicably be eliminated without eroding sound educational policies." Finally, the Court refused to order the upgrading of the historically black colleges. It reasoned that the "State provides these facilities for all its citizens" and cannot perpetuate "a separate, but 'more equal' " system. The Court, however, acknowledged that "such an increase in funding" might be "necessary to achieve a full dismantlement under the standards" it had outlined, and reserved this issue for the lower courts on remand.

Concurring, Justice O'Connor stated "that if the State shows that maintenance of certain remnants of its prior system is essential to accomplish its legitimate goals, then it still must prove that it has counteracted and minimized the segregative impact of such policies to the extent possible."

Justice Thomas also concurred. Because the standard adopted by the Court "does not compel the elimination of all observed racial imbalance, it portends neither the destruction of historically black colleges nor the severing of those institutions from their distinctive histories and traditions."

Black colleges "are both a source of pride to blacks who have attended them and a source of hope to black families who want the benefits of higher learning for their children." It would be ironic "if the institutions that sustained blacks during segregation were themselves destroyed in an effort to combat its vestiges."

Justice Scalia concurred in part and dissented in part. He agreed that Mississippi must remedy funding disparities and dispense with discriminatory ACT requirements, but he argued that the majority's test lacked clarity. "What the Court means by 'substantially restricting a person's choice of which institution to enter' is not clear." The Court varies the definition of this concept from "strong coercion," to "middling pressure," to "slight inducement." Justice Scalia thought that the opinion posed a considerable threat to historically black institutions by giving lower courts "virtually standardless discretion."

§ 8.03 OTHER FORMS OF RACIAL DISCRIMINATION

[1] General Principles: Purposeful Discrimination and Suspect Classes

Section Note. The school desegregation cases emphasized one important principle which is applicable generally in cases involving claims of discrimination under the Equal Protection Clause: the discriminatory governmental action must be purposeful, i.e., one must prove an intent to discriminate. Actions which have a discriminatory effect, or impact, will not, absent some showing of purposeful discrimination, sustain an equal protection claim. This principle assumes particular importance in cases involving claims of discrimination in employment, housing, zoning, and voting where laws, which are usually neutral on their face, have a demonstrably uneven impact on different racial groups. Further consideration of how the Court has developed the requirement of purposeful discrimination and the significance of that requirement on equal protection law, will be deferred until the sections dealing with discrimination in employment, housing, zoning, voting, and the criminal justice system.

In this section, we consider some of the other principles which have been developed by the Court in dealing with racial discrimination claims. These concepts are applicable not only in racial discrimination cases, but also in cases involving gender discrimination, discrimination against aliens, illegitimates, and similarly situated groups.

In the segregation cases, once the Court overruled *Plessy v. Ferguson* and recognized that segregation of public facilities was a denial of equal protection, the principal constitutional issues revolved around the two related questions of (1) defining the nature of the governmental action which would constitute a denial of equal protection, and (2) tailoring a judicial remedy to correct the violation.

In other equal protection areas, however, courts have grappled with questions which either do not arise in the segregation cases, or have been implicitly answered by the finding that segregation was unconstitutional. For example, the holding in *Brown* involved a conclusion that there can be no constitutional justification for the segregation of public schools. But, in other areas of the law, governments attempt to justify the classifications by arguing that they are "reasonable" or "necessary" and the courts have had to develop standards by which to evaluate these classifications. Involved in such cases may be the further questions of whether there should be different standards for different types of classifications, i.e., racial classifications, as against classifications which distinguish between different types of businesses. Also, racial segregation obviously involves racial classifications. In other contexts, a classification may be basically neutral, e.g., a zoning ordinance, or an ordinance that contains a racial classification which appears to apply to all races equally, e.g., a law forbidding interracial marriages. The following cases illustrate the principles which have evolved from these equal protection issues.

KOREMATSU v. UNITED STATES, 323 U.S. 214 (1944). In *Korematsu*, the Court upheld a lower court conviction for violation of an order issued after the United States was at war with Japan. "The petitioner, an American citizen of Japanese descent, was convicted in a federal district court for remaining in San Leandro, California, a 'Military Area,' contrary to Civilian Exclusion Order No. 34 of the Commanding General of the Western Command, U.S. Army, which directed that after May 9, 1942, all persons of Japanese ancestry should be excluded from that area. No question was raised as to the petitioner's loyalty to the United States."

Writing for the Court, Justice Black began by declaring that "all legal restrictions which curtail the civil rights of a single racial group are immediately suspect. That is not to say that all such restrictions are unconstitutional. It is to say that courts must subject them to the most rigid scrutiny. Pressing public necessity may sometimes justify the existence of such restrictions; racial antagonism never can."

Defendant was prosecuted for a violation of an Act of Congress of March 21, 1942, which provided:

> [W]hoever shall enter, remain in, leave, or commit any act in any military area or military zone prescribed, under the authority of an Executive order of the President, by the Secretary of War, or by any military commander designated by the Secretary of War, contrary to the restrictions applicable to any such area or zone or contrary to the order of the Secretary of War or any such military commander, shall, if it appears that he knew or should have known of the

existence and extent of the restrictions or order and that his act was in violation thereof, be guilty of a misdemeanor and upon conviction shall be liable to a fine of not to exceed $5,000 or to imprisonment for not more than one year, or both, for each offense.

The Court relied in part on its decision in *Hirabayashi v. United States*, 320 U.S. 81 (1943), where it construed the same order. In *Haribayashi*, the Court upheld a curfew order against a citizen of Japanese ancestry on grounds that the order was a reasonable exercise of the war power. The Court opined that:

> [E]xclusion from the area in which one's home is located [in *Korematsu*] is a far greater deprivation that the constant confinement to the home from 8 p.m. to 6 a.m. [in *Hirabayashi*]. Nothing short of apprehension by the proper military authorities of the gravest danger to public safety can justify either. But, exclusion from a threatened area, no less than curfew, has a definite and close relationship to the prevention of espionage and sabotage. . . . Here, as in the *Hirabayashi* case, "we cannot reject as unfounded the judgement of the military authorities and of Congress that there were disloyal members of that population, whose number and strength could not be precisely and quickly ascertained. We cannot say that the war-making branches of the Government did not have ground for believing that in a critical hour such persons could not readily be isolated and separately dealt with, and constituted a menace to the national defense and safety, which demanded prompt and adequate answers be taken to guard against it."

> Like curfew, exclusion of those of Japanese origin was deemed necessary because of the presence of an unascertained number of disloyal members of the group, most of whom we have no doubt were loyal to this country. It was because we could not reject finding of the military authorities that it was impossible to bring about segregation of the disloyal from the loyal that we sustained the validity of the curfew order as applying to the whole group. In the instant case, temporary exclusion of the entire group was rested by the military in the same ground. The judgment that exclusion of the whole group was for the same reason a military imperative answers the contention that the exclusion was in the nature of group punishment based on antagonism to those of Japanese origin. That there were members of the group who retained loyalties to Japan have been confirmed by investigations made subsequent to the exclusion. Approximately five thousand American citizens of Japanese ancestry refused to swear unqualified allegiance to the United States and to renounce allegiance to the Japanese Emperor, and several thousand evacuees requested repatriation to Japan.[18]

Justice Black concluded that "Korematsu was not excluded from the military area because of hostility to him or his race. He was excluded because we are at war with the Japanese Empire, because the properly constituted military authorities feared an invasion of our West Coast and felt constrained to take proper security measures with congressional authorization. There was evidence of disloyalty on the part of some, and

---

[18] In addition to the exclusion order, there were standing orders commanding each excluded person to an assembly center and, thereafter, to remain in a relocation center. Some who did report to an assembly center were not sent to relocation centers, but were released upon the condition that they remain outside of the prohibited zones. In *Ex Parte Mitsuye Endo*, 323 U.S. 283 (1943), the Court granted Endo her freedom, noting that the statutory provision authorizing relocation cited the necessity of "protection against either espionage or sabotage." Since the statute was silent on the matter of detention, the Court concluded that "detention could only occur when there was a threat of espionage or sabotage." Thus, "the authority to detain a citizen . . . is exhausted when his loyalty is conceded."

military authorities considered that the need for action was great, and the time was short. We cannot — by availing ourselves of the calm perspective of hindsight — now say that at that time these actions were unjustified."

Justice Frankfurter concurred. "To find that the Constitution does not forbid the military measure now complained of does not carry with it approval of that which Congress and the Executive did. That is their business, not ours."

Dissenting, Justice Roberts concluded that the facts "show that the exclusion was but a part of an over-all plan for forcible detention." Justice Roberts asserted that Korematsu could only avoid punishment by submitting himself to military custody and that the term "Assembly Center was a euphemism for a prison."

Justice Murphy filed a harsh dissent. He argued that "no reasonable relation to an 'immediate, imminent, and impending' public danger is evident to support this racial restriction which is one of the most sweeping and complete deprivations of constitutional rights in the history of this nation in the absence of martial law." The exclusion order is invalid because it "necessarily must rely for its reasonableness upon the assumption that *all* persons of Japanese ancestry may have a dangerous tendency to commit sabotage or espionage."

Justice Jackson also dissented, noting that similar restrictions were not imposed on those of German or Italian ancestry. He further maintained that "a judicial construction of the due process clause that will sustain this order is a far more subtle blow to liberty than the promulgation of the order itself." Such a precedent is a "loaded weapon" waiting to be used again in the future. "A military commander may overstep the bounds of constitutionality, and it is an incident. But if we review and approve, that passing becomes the doctrine of the Constitution." The majority's opinion illustrates the "generative powers" of the *Hirabayashi* decision. "I do not suggest that the courts should have attempted to interfere with the Army in carrying out its task. But I do not think they may be asked to execute a military expedient that has no place in law under the Constitution."

NOTES

(1) *Heightened Scrutiny.* As far back as the very first case to interpret the Fourteenth Amendment (*Slaughter-House Cases*, 111 U.S. 746 (1884), *supra* § 7.01), the Supreme Court has indicated that protecting the rights of African Americans was a pervading purpose of the post-Civil War Amendments, particularly the Equal Protection Clause. Other cases before the Japanese Exclusion cases had struck down laws which discriminated on the basis of race, e.g., *Strauder v. West Virginia*, 100 U.S. 303 (1879) (exclusion of Blacks from juries). *Korematsu* was apparently the first Supreme Court case to articulate the concept that a classification which curtails the rights of a racial group is "suspect" and, therefore, must be subjected to "most rigid scrutiny" — justified only if there is "pressing public necessity." *Korematsu* may also have been the only case involving discrimination against a minority race in which this test was applied, and the law was upheld. *See* Eugene V. Rostow, *The Japanese American Cases — A Disaster*, 54 YALE L.J. 489 (1945). Two decades later, in commenting on these cases in his Madison Lecture at New York University Law School, Chief Justice Warren, who was California Attorney General when the orders were issued, wrote "the fact that the Court rules in a case like *Hirabayashi* that a given program is constitutional, does not necessarily answer the question whether, in a broader sense, it actually is." Earl Warren, *The Bill of Rights and the Military, in* THE GREAT RIGHTS (Edmond Cahn ed., 1963).

(2) *Two-tiered Analysis.* The "suspect class" concept has become firmly embedded in equal protection analysis, and has become one aspect of the so-called "two-tier"

standard of equal protection review which was articulated during the later years of the Warren Court. Under this standard, laws which affect "fundamental interests" or "suspect classes" are upheld only if necessary to promote a "compelling state interest." Laws which do not affect such interests or classes are sustained if they bear a reasonable to a legitimate state end. As the reach of the Equal Protection Clause expanded to forbid forms of discrimination other than race, the Court has fashioned middle-tiers of scrutiny to address such areas as gender discrimination.

(3) *Carolene Products.* An early attempt to define "suspect classes" and to explain a stricter standard of judicial review for "suspect class" legislation is found in Justice Stone's famous *Carolene Products* footnote. *Compare United States v. Carolene Products*, 304 U.S. 144 (1938), *supra* § 7.03[1].

In part of the famous footnote 4 of the opinion in *United States v. Carolene Products*, Justice Stone said "[I]t is unnecessary to consider now whether legislation which restricts those political processes which can ordinarily be expected to bring about repeal of undesirable legislation, is to be subjected to more exacting scrutiny under the general prohibitions of the Fourteenth Amendment than are most other types of legislation. . . . Nor need we enquire whether similar considerations enter into the review of statutes directed at particular religious . . . or national . . . or racial minorities . . .; whether prejudice against discrete and insular minorities may be a special condition, which tends seriously to curtail the operation of those political processes ordinarily to be relied upon to protect minorities, and which may call for a correspondingly more searching judicial inquiry."

Although phrased as a tentative hypothesis which, in the context of *Carolene Products*, was unnecessary for the Court to resolve, Justice Stone's formulation has had considerable influence as courts were faced with claims that classifications discriminating against aliens, women, illegitimates, the aged, the mentally retarded, and poor people, among others, should receive heightened review. These issues will be discussed in later sections.

(4) *Discriminatory Administration of Neutral Laws.* In *Yick Wo v. Hopkins*, 18 U.S. 356 (1886), the petitioners challenged their convictions for violations of a San Francisco ordinance prohibiting the operation of laundries in wooden buildings without permission from the county board of supervisors. While 200 Chinese applicants were not permitted to operate wooden laundries, about 80 non-Chinese were allowed to operate such wooden laundries. The Court overturned the conviction in an opinion by Justice Matthews which held that the Equal Protection Clause does not apply exclusively to citizens. While the ordinance was not invalid on its face, the Court determined that the board of supervisors had abused its discretion by discriminating against Chinese laundry owners.

(5) *Equally Applied Racial Classifications.* (a) *Interracial marriage.* The Court has also invalidated statutes which were applied equally but were based on racial classifications. *Loving v. Virginia*, 388 U.S. 1 (1967), involved an equal protection challenge to Virginia's anti-miscegenation statutes. The appellants, Richard Loving, a white man, and Mildred Jeter, a black woman, were residents of Virginia. In 1958, they were legally married in the District of Columbia and returned to Virginia. The next year the Lovings were convicted of violating Virginia's prohibition of interracial marriages and sentenced to a year in jail. The trial judge suspended the sentence for 25 years, provided that the Lovings leave Virginia and not return together for 25 years. He opined: " 'Almighty God created the races white, black, yellow, malay, and red, and he placed them on separate continents. . . . The fact he separated the races shows that he did not intend for the races to mix.' "

Virginia argued that blacks and whites both were punished equally under the statutes. Chief Justice Warren responded: This case "deals with statutes containing racial classifications, and the fact of equal application does not immunize the statute" from strict scrutiny.

The Court held that there was no legitimate overriding purpose for the racial classifications. The statutes did not outlaw all interracial marriages, but only those involving white persons, thereby evincing an intent to maintain White Supremacy. Consequently, the statutes were held unconstitutional because they used racial classifications to restrict the freedom to marry. The Court also held that the statutes violated the Due Process Clause of the Fourteenth Amendment for restricting the freedom to marry.

(b) *Racial designations on the ballot.* Not only does the Equal Protection Clause prohibit state-imposed racial discrimination, but states cannot foster private acts of racial discrimination. In *Anderson v. Martin*, 375 U.S. 399 (1964), the Court invalidated a Louisiana statute which required that in any election a candidate's race must appear on the ballot. Justice Clark's opinion stated that "by directing the citizen's attention to the single consideration of race or color, the State indicates that a candidate's race or color is an important — perhaps paramount — consideration in the citizen's choice, which may decisively influence the citizen to cast his ballot along racial lines. . . . The State's racial classification induces racial prejudice at the polls."

(6) *Discriminatory Purpose.* In *Hunter v. Underwood*, 471 U.S. 222 (1985), the Court (8-0) struck down Art. VIII, § 182 of the Alabama Constitution, a facially neutral provision that denied voting rights to persons convicted of crimes involving felonies and moral turpitude misdemeanors. "Without deciding whether § 182 would be valid if enacted today without any impermissible motivation, we simply observe that its original enactment was motivated by a desire to discriminate against blacks on account of race and the section continues to this day to have that effect." Justice Rehnquist rejected the contention that intentional disenfranchisement of poor whites was a permissible motive which countered any proof of an impermissible motive. Any "additional purpose to discriminate against poor whites would not render nugatory the purpose to discriminate against all blacks, and it is beyond peradventure that the latter was a 'but-for' motivation for the enactment of § 182."

(7) *Tax Exemptions for Racially Discriminatory Schools.* In *Bob Jones University v. United States*, 461 U.S. 574 (1983), and *Goldsboro Christian Schools, Inc. v. United States*, 461 U.S. 574 (1983), the Court upheld the determination of the Internal Revenue Service that denied charitable tax exemptions to two educational institutions, Bob Jones University and Goldsboro Christian Schools, because of their racially discriminatory practices. Goldsboro denied admission to blacks, and Bob Jones admitted blacks but imposed a disciplinary code that forbade inter-racial dating. Both schools based their policies on religious beliefs which lower courts found "genuine," and the Court did not question these findings. In a unanimous judgment (Justice Powell wrote a concurring opinion), the Court concluded that "an educational institution engaging in practices affirmatively at odds with this declared position of the whole government [condemning racial discrimination] . . . is not 'charitable' within the meaning of § 170 and § 501(c)(3)." Although the case is essentially one of statutory interpretation and scope of delegation of legislative authority, it was a further expression by the Court of the overwhelmingly strong national policy against racial discrimination. The Court also readily disposed of the claim that the racially discriminatory policies of the schools were protected by the Free Exercise Clause of the First Amendment. For a discussion of this aspect of the case, see § 16.05, Note (1).

(8) *Valid Racial Classifications.* Not all racial classifications are invalid. In *Lee v. Washington*, 390 U.S. 33 (1968), the Court's *per curiam* opinion, although upholding a

lower court order to desegregate Alabama's jails, left open the possibility that prison security and discipline might justify segregation. Government may also require the designation of individuals by race for certain statistical purposes, such as the national census, or gathering health data. For a discussion of affirmative action programs, see Chapter 11.

(9) *Private prejudice.* In *Palmore v. Sidoti*, 466 U.S. 429 (1984), the Court examined the place personal prejudice has in judicial decision-making. When Linda Sidoti Palmore and Anthony J. Sidoti, both Caucasians, divorced in 1980, Palmore was granted custody of their daughter, Melanie. In 1981, Anthony Sidoti petitioned the court to modify the custody arrangement because of changed conditions, as Linda Palmore had married Clarence Palmore, Jr. an African-American. The lower court found that "there [was] no issue as to either party's devotion to the child, adequacy of housing facilities, or respectability of the new spouse of either parent." A counselor recommended that custody be changed because the wife chose for herself and her child a life-style unacceptable to the father and to society, resulting in environmental pressures on Melanie that would lead to "social stigmatization." The lower court endorsed this recommendation as "being in the best interest of the child" and awarded custody to Anthony Sidoti. The Supreme Court rejected consideration of private biases and the possible resultant injury in determining custody. Writing for the Court, Chief Justice Burger concluded that although the Constitution cannot control private prejudices, it cannot tolerate them. "Private biases may be outside the reach of the law, but the law cannot, directly or indirectly, give them effect."

Cf. Watson v. Memphis, 373 U.S. 526, 535 (1963) (rejecting city officials' claims that desegregation of city parks had to proceed slowly to prevent violence, as such claims were "based on personal speculations or vague disquietudes.").

(10) *Adoption and Race.* For additional discussion of adoption and race, see Elizabeth Bartholet, *Where Do Black Children Belong? The Politics of Race Matching in Adoption*, 139 U. Pa. L. Rev. 1163, 1172 (1991) (arguing that "current racial matching policies [in adoptions] represent a coming together of powerful and related ideologies — old-fashioned white racism, modern-day black nationalism, and what I will call 'biologism' — the idea that what is 'natural' in the context of the biological family is what is normal and desirable in the context of adoption").

[2] Racial Discrimination in Employment

WASHINGTON v. DAVIS, 426 U.S. 229 (1976). In *Washington*, the Court rejected an equal protection challenge to a Washington Police Department requirement that applicants "receive a grade of at least 40 out of 80 on 'Test 21.' " The test was developed by the Federal Civil Service Commission to evaluate " 'verbal ability, vocabulary, reading and comprehension,' " and was generally used throughout the federal service. Two black applicants who failed the test brought suit challenging its validity.

The District Court found that: " '(a) The number of black police officers, while substantial, is not proportionate to the population mix of the city. (b) A higher percentage of blacks fail the Test than whites. (c) The Test has not been validated to establish its reliability for measuring subsequent job performance.' " Nevertheless, the trial court upheld Test 21. An important basis for the District Court was that "[s]ince August 1969, 44% of new police force recruits had been black" which "was roughly equivalent to 20- to 29-year-old blacks in the 50-mile radius" of the Police Department. The District Court also noted that the Department "systematically and affirmatively sought to enroll black officers, many of whom passed the test but failed to report for duty."

Finding lack of discriminatory intent irrelevant, the Court of Appeals invalidated

Test 21 based on its racially discriminatory impact, as four times more blacks than whites failed the test.

Writing for the majority, Justice White required plaintiffs to show discriminatory intent in addition to discriminatory impact to establish an Equal Protection violation.[19] A law or other official act could not be unconstitutional "*solely* because it has a racially disproportionate impact."

Justice White cited cases in which the Court required more than statistics to prove that invidious discrimination caused the exclusion of black jurors. In the 1880 case of *Strauder v. West Virginia*, 100 U.S. 303 (1879), the Court invalidated the racially discriminatory exclusion of blacks from grand and petit juries in criminal proceedings. That "a series of juries does not statistically reflect the racial composition of the community is not enough." The Court has also required intentional or purposeful discrimination in the school desegregation and voting rights cases.

Justice White emphasized that discriminatory purpose need not be express or appear on the face of a statute or act. Disproportionate impact is relevant in determining discriminatory intent. Moreover, in *Yick Wo v. Hopkins* 110 U.S 356 (1886), the Court concluded: "A statute, otherwise neutral on its face, must not be applied so as invidiously to discriminate on the basis of race."

Justice White discussed a number of ways in which unconstitutional racial discrimination manifests itself. First, "an invidious discriminatory purpose may often be inferred from the totality of the relevant facts, including the fact, if it is true, that the law bears more heavily on one race than another." Second, discriminatory impact is sometimes unexplainable on nonracial grounds, such as when black citizens are disproportionately excluded from jury venires. "Nevertheless, we have not held that a law, neutral on its face and serving ends otherwise within the power of government to pursue is invalid under the Equal Protection Clause simply because it may affect a greater proportion of one race than another. Disproportionate impact is not irrelevant, but it is not the sole touchstone of an invidious racial discrimination forbidden by the Constitution."

Verbal skill is a racially neutral employment criterion and "it is untenable that the Constitution prevents the Government from seeking modestly to upgrade the communicative abilities of its employees." While the differential racial effect of Test 21 merited further inquiry, the trial court correctly found that "the affirmative efforts of the Metropolitan Police Department to recruit black officers, the changing racial composition of the recruit classes and of the force in general, and the relationship of the test to the training program negated any inference that the Department discriminated on the basis of race."

A pure discriminatory impact "would raise serious questions about, and perhaps invalidate, a whole range of tax, welfare, public service, regulatory, and licensing statutes that may be more burdensome to the poor and to the average black than to the more affluent white."[20] The extension of such a rule to areas beyond those where it

---

[19] While "the 1972 amendments extending the Title to reach Government employees were adopted prior to the District Court's judgment, the complaint was not amended to state a claim under that Title, nor did the case thereafter proceed as a Title VII case."

[20] *See* Frank I. Goodman, *De Facto School Segregation: A Constitutional and Empirical Analysis*, 60 CALIF. L. REV. 275, 300 (1972) (suggesting that disproportionate-impact analysis might invalidate "tests and qualifications for voting, draft deferment, public employment, jury service, and other government-conferred benefits and opportunities. . ., [s]ales taxes, bail schedules, utility rates, bridge tolls, license fees, and other state-imposed charges." It has also been argued that minimum wage and usury laws as well as professional licensing requirements would require major modifications in light of the unequal-impact rule.); William

already applies — such as employment law — is a matter for the legislature. The Court reversed the decision of the Court of Appeals stating that any potential Title VII challenge could be addressed in a future proceeding.

Justice Stevens concurred, stating that cases relied on by the majority as underpinning a discriminatory intent requirement included "criminal convictions which were set aside because blacks were excluded from the grand jury, a reapportionment case in which political boundaries were obviously influenced to some extent by racial considerations, a school desegregation case, and a case involving the unique administration of an ordinance purporting to prohibit the operation of laundries in frame buildings. Although it may be proper to use the same language to describe the constitutional claim in each of these contexts, the burden of proving the *prima facie* case may well involve differing evidentiary considerations. The extent of deference that one pays to the trial court's determination of the factual issue, and indeed, the extent to which one characterizes the intent issue as a question of fact or a question of law will vary in different contexts."

"Frequently, the most probative evidence of intent will be objective evidence of what actually happened rather than evidence describing the subjective state of mind of the actor. For normally the actor is presumed to have intended the natural consequences of his deeds. This is particularly true in the case of governmental action which is frequently the product of compromise of collective decisionmaking and of mixed motivation. It is unrealistic, on the one hand, to require the victim of alleged discrimination to uncover the actual subjective intent of the decisionmaker or, conversely, to invalidate otherwise legitimate action simply because an improper motive affected the deliberation of a participant in the decisional process."

Justice Stevens asserted that the line between discriminatory purpose and discriminatory impact is not always clear, as demonstrated by such cases as *Gomillion v. Lightfoot*, 364 U.S. 339 (1960), and *Yick Wo v. Hopkins*. When the disproportionate impact is as dramatic as it was in those cases, "it really does not matter whether the standard is phrased in terms of purpose or effect."

Justice Brennan's dissent, joined by Justice Marshall, was not based on constitutional grounds.

NOTES

(1) *Discriminatory Impact.* Under *Washington v. Davis*, the plaintiff must demonstrate discriminatory intent, in addition to establishing that the examination has a discriminatory impact. Presumably, however, a trier of fact might be free to infer intent from the use of an examination which is not related to job performance. What then is the difference between the two standards?

(2) For additional discussion, see Theodore Eisenberg & Sheri Lynn Johnson, *The Effects of Intent: Do We Know How Legal Standards Work?*, 76 CORNELL L. REV. 1151, 1153 (1991) ("Intent claimants' success rate is not markedly different from that of the other civil rights claimants. The more striking finding is the low volume of intent litigation. The Supreme Court's standard takes its toll not through an unusually high loss rate for those plaintiffs reaching trial or appeal, but by deterring victims from even filing claims."); Daniel Ortiz, *The Myth of Intent in Equal Protection*, 41 STAN. L. REV. 1105, 1107, 1150 (1989) ("[I]n my view, intent allocates burdens differently in different contexts in order to 'balance' individual and societal interests consistently with the ideology of traditional liberalism. Where (as in housing and employment) this ideology

Silverman, *Equal Protection, Economic Legislation, and Racial Discrimination*, 25 VAND. L. REV. 1183 (1972).

either relegates decisionmaking to markets or allows the state much leeway in allocating goods, intent makes judicial supervision of decisionmaking difficult. On the other hand, where liberal ideology insists on particular types of nonmarket allocation (as in voting, jury selection, and sometimes education), intent makes judical intervention more likely. . . . Through its allocation of burdens of proof in particular kinds of cases, the intent doctrine makes many of the ultimate value choices implicit in equal protection."); and David A. Strauss, *Discriminatory Intent and the Taming of Brown*, 56 U. CHI. L. REV. 935, 1015 (1989) ("*Washington v. Davis* was a wrong turn not because it recognized the usefulness of the notion of discriminatory intent but because it mistakenly adopted the discriminatory intent standard as a comprehensive account of discrimination. Notions like subordination, stigma, and second-class citizenship must play a role in the law of the Equal Protection Clause.").

[3] Housing and Zoning

ARLINGTON HEIGHTS v. METROPOLITAN HOUSING DEVELOPMENT CORP.
429 U.S. 252, 97 S. Ct. 555, 50 L. Ed. 2d 450 (1977)

JUSTICE POWELL delivered the opinion of the Court.

In 1971, respondent Metropolitan Housing Development Corporation (MHDC) applied to petitioner, the Village of Arlington Heights, Ill., for the rezoning of a 15-acre parcel from single-family to multiple-family classification. Using federal financial assistance, MHDC planned to build 190 clustered townhouse units for low- and moderate-income tenants. The Village denied the rezoning request. MHDC, joined by other plaintiffs who are also respondents here . . . . alleged that the denial was racially discriminatory and that it violated, inter alia, the Fourteenth Amendment and the Fair Housing Act, 82 Stat. 81, 42 U.S.C. §§ 3601 *et seq.* . . .

Arlington Heights is a suburb of Chicago, located about 26 miles northwest of the downtown Loop area. Most of the land in Arlington Heights is zoned for detached single-family homes, and this is in fact the prevailing land use. The Village experienced substantial growth during the 1960s, but, like other communities in northwest Cook County, its population of racial minority groups remained quite low. According to the 1970 census, only 27 of the Village's 64,000 residents were black.

The Clerics of St. Viator, a religious order (the Order), own an 80-acre parcel just east of the center of Arlington Heights. . . .

The Order decided in 1970 to devote some of its land to low- and moderate-income housing. . . .

After some negotiation, MHDC and the Order entered into a 99-year lease and an accompanying agreement of sale covering a 15-acre site. . . .

The planned development [Lincoln Green] did not conform to the Village's zoning ordinance and could not be built unless Arlington Heights rezoned the parcel to R-5, its multiple-family housing classification. Accordingly, MHDC filed with the Village Plan Commission a petition for rezoning. . . .

During the spring of 1971, the Plan Commission considered the proposal at a series of three public meetings, which drew large crowds. . . . Some of the comments, both from opponents and supporters, addressed what was referred to as the "social issue" — the desirability or undesirability of introducing at this location in Arlington Heights low-and moderate-income housing, housing that would probably be racially integrated.

Many of the opponents, however, focused on the zoning aspects of the petition, stressing two arguments. First, the area always had been zoned single-family, and. . . . [r]ezoning threatened to cause a measurable drop in property value. . . . Second, the Village's apartment policy, adopted by the Village Board in 1962 and amended in 1970, called for R-5 zoning primarily to serve as a buffer between single-family development and land uses thought incompatible, such as commercial or manufacturing districts. Lincoln Green did not meet this requirement, as it adjoined no commercial or manufacturing district.

. . . After a public hearing, the Board denied the rezoning by a 6-1 vote. . . .

Our decision last Term in *Washington v. Davis*, 426 U.S. 229 (1976), made it clear that official action will not be held unconstitutional solely because it results in a racially disproportionate impact. . . .

Davis does not require a plaintiff to prove that the challenged action rested solely on racially discriminatory purposes. Rarely can it be said that a legislature or administrative body operating under a broad mandate made a decision motivated solely by a single concern, or even that a particular purpose was the "dominant" or "primary" one. In fact, it is because legislators and administrators are properly concerned with balancing numerous competing considerations that courts refrain from reviewing the merits of their decisions, absent a showing of arbitrariness or irrationality. But racial discrimination is not just another competing consideration. When there is a proof that a discriminatory purpose has been a motivating factor in the decision, this judicial deference is no longer justified.

Determining whether invidious discriminatory purpose was a motivating factor demands a sensitive inquiry into such circumstantial and direct evidence of intent as may be available. The impact of the official action — whether it "bears more heavily on one race than another," *Washington v. Davis* — may provide an important starting point. Sometimes a clear pattern, unexplainable on grounds other than race, emerges from the effect of the state action even when the governing legislation appears neutral on its face. *Yick Wo v. Hopkins*, 118 U.S. 356 [(1886)]; *Gomillion v. Lightfoot*, 364 U.S. 339 [(1960)]. The evidentiary inquiry is then relatively easy. But such cases are rare. Absent a pattern as stark as that in *Gomillion* or *Yick Wo*, impact alone is not determinative, and the Court must look to other evidence.

The historical background of the decision is one evidentiary source, particularly if it reveals a series of official actions taken for invidious purposes. . . . The specific sequence of events leading up to the challenged decision also may shed some light on the decision-maker's purposes. *Reitman v. Mulkey*, 387 U.S. 369 [(1967)]. For example, if the property involved here always had been zoned R-5 but suddenly was changed to R-3 when the town learned of MHDC's plans to erect integrated housing, we would have a far different case. Departures from the normal procedural sequence also might afford evidence that improper purposes are playing a role. Substantive departures too may be relevant, particularly if the factors usually considered important by the decisionmaker strongly favor a decision contrary to the one reached.

The legislative or administrative history may be highly relevant, especially where there are contemporary statements by members of the decisionmaking body, minutes of its meetings, or reports. In some extraordinary instances the members might be called to the stand at trial to testify concerning the purpose of the official action, although even then such testimony frequently will be barred by privilege. . . .

The foregoing summary identifies, without purporting to be exhaustive, subjects of proper inquiry in determining whether racially discriminatory intent existed. With these in mind, we now address the case before us. . . .

We also have reviewed the evidence. The impact of the Village's decision does arguably bear more heavily on racial minorities. Minorities constitute 18% of the

Chicago area population, and 40% of the income groups said to be eligible for Lincoln Green. But there is little about the sequence of events leading up to the decision that would spark suspicion. The area around the Viatorian property has been zoned R-3 since 1959, the year when Arlington Heights first adopted a zoning map. . . . and the Village is undeniably committed to single-family homes as its dominant residential land use. The rezoning request progressed according to the usual procedures. The Plan Commission even scheduled two additional hearings, at least in part to accommodate MHDC. . . .

The statements by the Plan Commission and Village Board members, as reflected in the official minutes, focused almost exclusively on the zoning aspects of the MHDC petition, and the zoning factors on which they relied are not novel criteria in the Village's rezoning decisions . . . . The Village originally adopted its buffer policy long before MHDC entered the picture and has applied the policy too consistently for us to infer discriminatory purpose from its application in this case. Finally, MHDC called one member of the Village Board to the stand at trial. Nothing in her testimony supports an inference of invidious purpose.

In sum, the evidence does not warrant overturning the concurrent findings of both courts below. Respondents simply failed to carry their burden of proving that discriminatory purpose was a motivating factor in the Village's decision.[21] This conclusion ends the constitutional inquiry. The Court of Appeals further finding that the Village's decision carried a discriminatory "ultimate effect" is without independent constitutional significance. . . .

Reserved and remanded.

Justice Stevens took no part in the consideration or decision of this case.

Justice Marshall, with whom Justice Brennan joins, concurring in part and dissenting in part.

. . . I believe the proper result would be to remand this entire case to the Court of Appeals for further proceedings consistent with *Washington v. Davis*, and today's opinion. The Court of Appeals is better situated than this Court both to reassess the significance of the evidence developed below in light of the standards we have set forth. . . .

Justice White, dissenting.

. . . [T]he Court of Appeals rendered its decision in this case before *Washington v. Davis* was handed down. . . .

The Court gives no reason for its failure to follow our usual practice in this situation of vacating the judgment below and remanding in order to permit the lower court to reconsider its ruling in light of our intervening decision. . . .

NOTES

(1) *Statutory Provisions.* With the passage of the 1968 Fair Housing Act, 42 U.S.C. § 3601 *et seq.*, and the decision in *Jones v. Mayer*, 392 U.S. 409 (1968), *see* § 6.05, holding that private racial discrimination in the sale or leasing of housing was

---

[21] [Court's footnote 21] Proof that the decision by the Village was motivated in part by a racially discriminatory purpose would not necessarily have required invalidation of the challenged decision. Such proof, would, however, have shifted to the Village the burden of establishing that the same decision would have resulted even had the impermissible purpose not been considered. If this was established, the complaining party in a case of this kind no longer fairly could attribute the injury complained of to improper consideration of a discriminatory purpose . . . .

actionable under federal civil rights laws, few constitutional barriers remained in dealing with overt racial discrimination in housing, either by governments or private parties, although problems of proof, and of statutory interpretation, can present difficulties. Of major importance are the racially neutral land use decisions of government, such as zoning, the location of housing projects, the granting of variances, etc., which may have a discriminatory impact.

(2) *Poor Persons.* Restrictive zoning is not necessarily racial in its exclusionary impact. It can affect poor persons and unpopular groups. *See generally* Lawrence Gene Sager, *Insular Majorities Unabated*, 91 HARV. L. REV. 1373 (1978), and *Developments in the Law-Zoning*, 91 HARV. L. REV. 1427 (1978).

(3) *Discriminatory Intent.* In *Cuyahoga Falls v. Buckeye Cmty. Hope Found.*, 538 U.S. 188 (2003), the Court held evidence of discriminatory intent was not enough for plaintiffs' equal protection action to survive summary judgment. Plaintiffs brought an action against city officials claiming that a referendum repealing a city affordable housing ordinance violated the Equal Protection Clause. The District Court granted plaintiffs' summary judgment motion. The Court of Appeals reversed, finding that genuine issues of material fact existed as to whether city officials having permitted a referendum against an affordable housing plan to go forward "gave effect to the racial bias reflected in the public's opposition to the project." A unanimous Supreme Court reversed. Defendants followed the "facially neutral petitioning procedure of the City Charter in submitting the referendum petition to the voters." During a "citizen-driven petition drive," a private individual can make statements that "while sometimes relevant to equal protection analysis, do not, in and of themselves, constitute state action for the purposes of the *Fourteenth Amendment.*" In contrast, "statements made by decisionmakers or referendum sponsors during deliberation over a referendum, may constitute relevant evidence of discriminatory intent." In the present case, the plaintiffs have not shown that "city officials exercised any power over voters' decisionmaking during the drive, much less the kind of 'coercive power' either 'overt or covert' that would render the voters' actions and statements, for all intents and purposes, state action." Justice Scalia filed a concurring opinion joined by Justice Thomas.

[4] Voting

ROGERS v. LODGE, 458 U.S. 613 (1982). In *Rogers*, the Court struck down an at-large system of elections in Burke County, Georgia,[22] "for diluting the voting power of black citizens."

To be nominated or elected as one of the five Burke County Board of Commissioners, "a candidate must receive a majority of the votes cast in the primary or general election, and a runoff must be held if no candidate receives a majority in the first primary or general election. Each candidate must run for a specific seat on the Board and a voter may vote only once for any candidate." No black person has even been elected to the Board. The District Court found that while the at-large districting system was " 'racially neutral when adopted, [it] is being *maintained* for invidious purposes.' "

Justice White wrote for a 6-3 majority. Although "multimember districts have been challenged for 'their winner-take-all aspects, their tendency to submerge minorities and to overrepresent the winning party,' " these districts "are not unconstitutional per se." As with other types of Equal Protection violations, such districts are unconstitutional when they are drawn for a discriminatory purpose. To establish an invidious purpose

---

[22] "[W]hites constitute a slight majority of the voting age population. As of 1978, 6,373 persons were registered to vote in Burke County, of whom 38% were black."

for multimember districting, the District Court relied heavily, but not exclusively, on the factors set out in *Zimmer v. McKeithen*, 485 F.2d 1297 (5th Cir. 1973).

Agreeing with the Court of Appeals, Justice White did not think that he "should disturb the District Court's finding that the at-large system in Burke County was being maintained for the invidious purpose of diluting the voting strength of the black population."

In this connection, the District Court found that no black had ever been elected in Burke County. This failure was "important evidence of purposeful exclusion," particularly as blacks comprised a "substantial majority" of the population of Burke County and there was "overwhelming evidence of bloc voting along racial lines." Nevertheless, "such facts are insufficient in themselves to prove purposeful discrimination absent other evidence as proof that blacks have less opportunity to participate in the political process and to elect candidates of their choice."

The District Court found "that historical discrimination had restricted the present opportunity of blacks effectively to participate in the political process." Until the Voting Rights Act of 1965, such practices as literacy tests, poll taxes, and white primaries had rendered black suffrage "virtually non-existent." Even after the Voting Rights Act, only 38% of eligible black voters registered. Other factors limiting the "ability of blacks to participate effectively in the political process" included segregated schools until 1969, prevention "from effectively participating in Democratic Party affairs and primary elections,"[23] and property ownership requirements that made it difficult for blacks to serve as chief registrar in the county. "There had been discrimination in the selection of grand jurors, the hiring of county employees, and in the appointments to boards and committees which oversee county government." Such "historical discrimination is relevant to drawing an inference of purposeful discrimination, particularly in cases such as this one where the evidence shows that discriminatory practices were commonly utilized, that they were abandoned when enjoined by courts or made illegal by civil rights legislation, and that they were replaced by laws and practices which, though neutral on their face, serve to maintain the status quo."

The Court noted the District Court finding "that elected officials of Burke County have been unresponsive and insensitive to the needs of the black community." The "evidence ranged from the effects of past discrimination, which still haunt the county courthouse to the infrequent appointment of blacks to county boards and committees; the overtly discriminatory pattern of paving roads; the reluctance of the county to remedy black complaints, which forced blacks to take legal action to obtain school and grand jury desegregation; and the role played by the County Commissioners in the incorporation of an all-white private school."

Based on the above findings the trial court found Burke County's representatives to the state legislature " 'have retained a system which has minimized the ability of Burke County Blacks to participate in the political system.' "

Aggravating "the tendency of multimember districts to minimize the voting strength of racial minorities," the District Court found "as a matter of law," that the County's size of nearly two-thirds the State of Rhode Island, increases transportation travel time to the polls which further impairs access by black persons. Moreover, "the requirement that candidates run for specific seats enhances respondent's lack of access because it prevents a cohesive political group from concentrating on a single candidate." Indeed, as the seats include residency requirements, theoretically all candidates could come from white neighborhoods in the county. "None of the District Court's findings

---

[23] "Until this lawsuit was filed, there had never been a black member of the County Executive Committee of the Democratic Party."

underlying its ultimate finding of intentional discrimination appears to us to be clearly erroneous."

Justice Powell dissented, joined by Justice Rehnquist. Justice Powell found evidence presented in this case virtually indistinguishable from the evidence found insufficient in *Mobile v. Bolden, infra* § 8.03[4], Note (1) after *Rogers*. Agreeing with Justice Stevens, Justice Powell criticized the standardless devolution of these voter dilution cases to federal district courts.

Justice Stevens also dissented. "Whenever identifiable groups in our society are disadvantaged, they will share common political interests and tend to vote as a 'bloc.' In this respect, racial groups are like other political groups. A permanent constitutional rule that treated them differently would, in my opinion, itself tend to perpetuate race a feature distinct from all others."

NOTES

(1) *Finding of Discriminatory Intent.* In *Mobile v. Bolden*, 446 U.S. 55 (1980), the Court upheld a District Court finding that Mobile, Alabama's at-large electoral system violated neither the Fifteenth nor the Fourteenth Amendment. In a plurality opinion written by Justice Stewart, and joined by Chief Justice Burger and Justices Powell and Rehnquist, the Court stated that "[t]he Fifteenth Amendment. . . . prohibits only purposefully discriminatory denial or abridgment by government of the freedom to vote 'on account of race, color, or previous condition of servitude.' " As blacks had not been hindered from registering or from voting, the Fifteenth Amendment was not violated.

As to the Fourteenth Amendment, that Court stated that an equal protection violation is established only if there is proof that the State intended that the at-large system discriminates against black persons. Disproportionate impact can provide evidence of discriminatory purpose, "[b]ut where the character of a law is readily explainable on grounds apart from race. . . disproportionate impact alone cannot be decisive, and courts must look to other evidence to support a finding of discriminatory purpose." The Court was unconvinced by the fact that no black had been elected to the Mobile City Commission, stating that "that fact alone does not work a constitutional deprivation." Moreover, Alabama's history of past official discrimination could not, "condemn governmental action that is not itself unlawful."

Justice Blackmun concurred in the judgment. Justice Stevens also concurred in the judgment. He proposed a test which focused "on the objective effects of the political decision rather than the subjective motivation of the decisionmaker." Justices Brennan, White and Marshall each wrote dissenting opinions.

(2) *The Voting Rights Act. Rogers v. Lodge* established that the Supreme Court was willing to accept lower courts' findings of intentional discrimination from objective facts. During the two-year interval between *Bolden* and *Rogers*, a vigorous Congressional debate ensued, sparked by the impending expiration of the 1965 Voting Rights Act in 1982. Critics of *Bolden* argued that "intent" could rarely be proved and that an "effects" test was required. Supporters of the *Bolden* result fought the adoption of the "effects" test on grounds that it would require proportionate racial representation, a claim sharply disputed by the other side. A compromise amendment to Section 2 was overwhelmingly passed by Congress and signed by the President on June 29, 1982. It follows:

> No voting qualification or prerequisite to voting or standard practice or procedure shall be imposed or applied by any State or political subdivision in a manner which results in a denial or abridgement of the right of any citizen of the United States to vote on account of race or color. . . . A violation . . . is established if, based on the totality of circumstances, it is shown that the

political processes leading to nomination or election in the state or political subdivision are not equally open to participation by members of a class of citizens protected [by the act] in that its members have less opportunity than other members of the electorate to participate in the political process and to elect representatives of their choice. The extent to which members of a protected class have been elected to office in the state or political subdivision is one 'circumstance' which may be considered, provided that nothing in this section establishes a right to have members of a protected class elected in numbers equal to their proportion in the population.

(3) In *League of United Latin Am. Citizens v. Perry*, 548 U.S. 399 (2006), the fourth part of Justice Kennedy's opinion rejected a claim that District 24 diluted the votes of African-Americans based on the fact that African-Americans "constituted 64% of the voters in the Democratic primary." While only the Chief Justice and Justice Alito joined this part of Justice Kennedy's opinion, Justices Scalia and Thomas concurred in the judgment of this part of the opinion. "If § 2 were interpreted to protect this kind of influence, it would unnecessarily infuse race into virtually every redistricting, raising serious constitutional questions."[24]

For further discussion of the case, see § 11.03.

SHAW v. RENO
509 U.S. 630, 113 S. Ct. 2816, 125 L. Ed. 2d. 511 (1993)

JUSTICE O'CONNOR delivered the opinion of the Court.

This case involves . . . the meaning of the constitutional "right" to vote, and the propriety of race-based state legislation designed to benefit members of historically disadvantaged racial minority groups. As a result of the 1990 census, North Carolina became entitled to a twelfth seat in the United States House of Representatives. The General Assembly enacted a reapportionment plan that included one majority-black congressional district. After the Attorney General of the United States objected to the plan pursuant to § 5 of the Voting Rights Act, the General Assembly passed new legislation creating a second majority-black district. Appellants allege that the revised plan, which contains district boundary lines of dramatically irregular shape, constitutes an unconstitutional racial gerrymander. . . .

I

The voting age population of North Carolina is approximately 78% white, 20% black, . . . blacks constitute a majority of the general population in only 5 of the State's 100 counties . . . . The General Assembly's first redistricting plan contained one majority-black district centered in that area of the State.

Forty of North Carolina's one hundred counties are covered by § 5 of the Voting Rights Act of 1965, 42 U.S.C. § 1973c, which prohibits a jurisdiction subject to its provisions from implementing changes in a "standard, practice, or procedure with respect to voting" without federal authorization. . . . The State chose to submit its plan to the Attorney General for preclearance.

. . . In the Attorney General's view, the General Assembly could have created a second majority-minority district. . . .

. . . [T]he General Assembly enacted a revised redistricting plan, that included a second majority-black district. . . .

---

[24] This argument fails to "demonstrate clear error" because there has not been a "contested Democratic primary in District 24 over the last 20 years."

The first of the two majority-black districts contained in the revised plan, District 1, is somewhat hook shaped. Centered in the northeast portion of the State, it moves southward until it tapers to a narrow band; then, with finger-like extensions, it reaches far into the southern-most part of the State near the South Carolina border. . . .

The second majority-black district, District 12, is even more unusually shaped. It is approximately 160 miles long and, for much of its length, no wider than the I-85 corridor. It winds in snake-like fashion through tobacco country, financial centers, and manufacturing areas "until it gobbles in enough enclaves of black neighborhoods." *Shaw v. Barr*, 808 F. Supp. 461, 476–477 (E.D.NC 1992) (Voorhees, C. J., concurring in part and dissenting in part). . . . Of the 10 counties through which District 12 passes, five are cut into three different districts; even towns are divided. . . .

II

B

. . . It is unsettling how closely the North Carolina plan resembles the most egregious racial gerrymanders of the past. . . .

III

A

. . . No inquiry into legislative purpose is necessary when the racial classification appears on the face of the statute. . . . Accordingly, we have held that the Fourteenth Amendment requires state legislation that expressly distinguishes among citizens because of their race to be narrowly tailored to further a compelling governmental interest.

These principles apply not only to legislation that contains explicit racial distinctions, but also to those "rare" statutes that, although race-neutral, are, on their face, "unexplainable on grounds other than race." *Arlington Heights v. Metropolitan Housing Development Corp.* [429 U.S. 252 (1977)] . . .

B

Appellants contend that redistricting legislation that is so bizarre on its face that it is "unexplainable on grounds other than race," *Arlington Heights, supra,* at 266. . . .

The Court applied the same reasoning to the "uncouth twenty-eight-sided" municipal boundary line at issue in *Gomillion v. Lightfoot*, 364 U.S. 339 (1960). . . .

. . . In some exceptional cases, a reapportionment plan may be so highly irregular that, on its face, it rationally cannot be understood as anything other than an effort to "segregate . . . voters" on the basis of race. *Gomillion, supra,* at 341. *Gomillion,* in which a tortured municipal boundary line was drawn to exclude black voters, was such a case. So, too, would be a case in which a State concentrated a dispersed minority population in a single district by disregarding traditional districting principles such as compactness, contiguity, and respect for political subdivisions. We emphasize that these criteria are important not because they are constitutionally required — they are not. . . — but because they are objective factors that may serve to defeat a claim that a district has been gerrymandered on racial lines. . . .

Put differently, we believe that reapportionment is one area in which appearances do matter. A reapportionment plan that includes in one district individuals who belong to the same race, but who are otherwise widely separated by geographical and political boundaries, and who may have little in common with one another but the color of their skin, bears an uncomfortable resemblance to political apartheid . . . .

. . . [P]laintiffs have stated a claim sufficient to defeat the state appellees' motion to dismiss.

C

. . . Justice Souter apparently believes that racial gerrymandering is harmless unless it dilutes a racial group's voting strength. . . . As we have explained, however, reapportionment legislation that cannot be understood as anything other than an effort to classify and separate voters by race injures voters in other ways. It reinforces racial stereotypes and threatens to undermine our system of representative democracy by signaling to elected officials that they represent a particular racial group rather than their constituency as a whole. . . .

. . . Justice Stevens argues that racial gerrymandering poses no constitutional difficulties when district lines are drawn to favor the minority, rather than the majority. We have made clear, however, that equal protection analysis "is not dependent on the race of those burdened or benefitted by a particular classification." *Richmond v. J. A. Croson Co.*, 488 U.S. 469, 494 (1989) (plurality opinion). . . .

IV

. . . [T]he very reason that the Equal Protection Clause demands strict scrutiny of all racial classifications is because without it, a court cannot determine whether or not the discrimination truly is "benign." Thus, if appellants' allegations of a racial gerrymander are not contradicted on remand, the District Court must determine whether the General Assembly's reapportionment plan satisfies strict scrutiny. We therefore consider what that level of scrutiny requires in the reapportionment context.

The state appellees suggest that a covered jurisdiction may have a compelling interest in creating majority-minority districts in order to comply with the Voting Rights Act. . . .

For example, on remand North Carolina might claim that it adopted the revised plan in order to comply with the § 5 "nonretrogression" principle. Under that principle, a proposed voting change cannot be precleared if it will lead to "a retrogression in the position of racial minorities with respect to their effective exercise of the electoral franchise." *Beer v. United States*, 425 U.S. 130, 141 (1976). . . .

. . . A reapportionment plan would not be narrowly tailored to the goal of avoiding retrogression if the State went beyond what was reasonably necessary to avoid retrogression. . . .

Before us, the state appellees contend that the General Assembly's revised plan was necessary . . . to avoid dilution of black voting strength in violation of § 2, as construed in *Thornburg v. Gingles*, 478 U.S. 30 (1986). In *Gingles* the Court . . . held that members of a racial minority group claiming § 2 vote dilution through the use of multimember districts must prove three threshold conditions: that the minority group "is sufficiently large and geographically compact to constitute a majority in a single-member district," that the minority group is "politically cohesive," and that "the white majority votes sufficiently as a bloc to enable it . . . usually to defeat the minority's preferred candidate." *Id.*, at 50–51. We have indicated that similar preconditions apply in § 2 challenges to single-member districts.

Appellants maintain that the General Assembly's revised plan could not have been required by § 2. They contend that the State's black population is too dispersed to support two geographically compact majority-black districts, as the bizarre shape of District 12 demonstrates, and that there is no evidence of black political cohesion. They also contend that recent black electoral successes demonstrate the willingness of white voters in North Carolina to vote for black candidates. Appellants point out that blacks currently hold the positions of State Auditor, Speaker of the North Carolina House of Representatives, and chair of the North Carolina State Board of Elections. They also point out that in 1990 a black candidate defeated a white opponent in the Democratic Party run-off for a United States Senate seat before being defeated narrowly by the Republican incumbent in the general election. Appellants further argue that if § 2 did require adoption of North Carolina's revised plan, § 2 is to that extent unconstitutional. These arguments were not developed below, and the issues remain open for consideration on remand.

The state appellees alternatively argue that the General Assembly's plan advanced a compelling interest entirely distinct from the Voting Rights Act. We previously have recognized a significant state interest in eradicating the effects of past racial discrimination. . . .

. . . This question also need not be decided at this stage of the litigation. . . .

V

Racial classifications of any sort pose the risk of lasting harm to our society . . . . Racial classifications with respect to voting carry particular dangers. Racial gerrymandering, even for remedial purposes, may balkanize us into competing racial factions; it threatens to carry us further from the goal of a political system in which race no longer matters — a goal that the Fourteenth and Fifteenth Amendments embody. . . .

. . . Today we hold only that appellants have stated a claim under the Equal Protection Clause by alleging that the North Carolina General Assembly adopted a reapportionment scheme so irrational on its face that it can be understood only as an effort to segregate voters into separate voting districts because of their race, and that the separation lacks sufficient justification. If the allegation of racial gerrymandering remains uncontradicted, the District Court further must determine whether the North Carolina plan is narrowly tailored to further a compelling governmental interest.

JUSTICE WHITE, with whom JUSTICE BLACKMUN and JUSTICE STEVENS join, dissenting. . . .

I

A

. . . To date, we have held that only two types of state voting practices could give rise to a constitutional claim. The first involves direct and outright deprivation of the right to vote, for example by means of a poll tax or literacy test. Plainly, this variety is not implicated by appellants' allegations and need not detain us further. The second type of unconstitutional practice is that which "affects the political strength of various groups," *Mobile v. Bolden*, 446 U.S. 55, 83 (1980) (Stevens, J., concurring in judgment), in violation of the Equal Protection Clause. As for this latter category, we have insisted that members of the political or racial group demonstrate that the challenged action have the intent and effect of unduly diminishing their influence on the political process.[25] Although this severe burden has limited the number of successful suits, it was adopted for sound reasons. . . .

. . . "[A]n equal protection violation may be found only where the electoral system *substantially disadvantages* certain voters in their opportunity to influence the political process effectively." [*Davis v. Bandemer*, 478 U.S. 109, 133 (1986)]. . . . *Id.*, at 142.

B

. . . [I]t strains credulity to suggest that North Carolina's purpose in creating a second majority-minority district was to discriminate against members of the majority group by "impairing or burden[ing their] opportunity . . . to participate in the political process." [*United Jewish Organizations of Williamsburgh, Inc. v. Carey*, 430 U.S. 144, 179 (1977)] (Stewart, J., concurring in judgment). The State has made no mystery of its intent, which was to respond to the Attorney General's objections, by improving the minority group's prospects of electing a candidate of its choice. I doubt that this constitutes a discriminatory purpose as defined in the Court's equal protection cases. . . . But even assuming that it does, there is no question that appellants have not alleged the requisite discriminatory effects. Whites constitute roughly 76 percent of the total population and 79 percent of the voting age population in North Carolina. Yet, under the State's plan, they still constitute a voting majority in 10 (or 83 percent) of the 12 congressional districts. . . .

JUSTICE BLACKMUN, dissenting.

. . . It is particularly ironic that the case in which today's majority chooses to abandon settled law and to recognize for the first time this "analytically distinct" constitutional claim, is a challenge by white voters to the plan under which North Carolina has sent black representatives to Congress for the first time since Reconstruction. I dissent.

JUSTICE STEVENS, dissenting.

. . . The duty to govern impartially is abused when a group with power over the electoral process defines electoral boundaries solely to enhance its own political strength at the expense of any weaker group. That duty, however, is not violated when the majority acts to facilitate the election of a member of a group that lacks such power because it remains underrepresented in the state legislature. . . .

. . . If it is permissible to draw boundaries to provide adequate representation for rural voters, for union members, for Hasidic Jews, for Polish Americans, or for Republicans, it necessarily follows that it is permissible to do the same thing for members of the very minority group whose history in the United States gave birth to the Equal Protection Clause. . . .

JUSTICE SOUTER, dissenting.

. . . [T]he Court creates a new "analytically distinct" *ibid.*, cause of action, the principal element of which is that a districting plan be "so bizarre on its face," that it "rationally cannot be understood as anything other than an effort to segregate citizens

---

[25] [Court's footnote 1] It has been argued that the required showing of discriminatory effect should be lessened once a plaintiff successfully demonstrates intentional discrimination. *See Garza v. County of Los Angeles*, 918 F.2d 763, 771 (CA9 1990). Although I would leave this question for another day, I would note that even then courts have insisted on "some showing of injury . . . to assure that the district court can impose a meaningful remedy." *Id.*

into separate voting districts on the basis of race without sufficient justification. . . . "

NOTE

For more on *Shaw*, see T. Alexander Aleinikoff & Samuel Issacharoff, *Race and Redistricting: Drawing Constitutional Lines After* Shaw v. Reno, 92 MICH. L. REV. 588, 592 (1993) ("*Shaw* is as important for what it does not say as for what it does: its inconclusive resolution of the ultimate issue whether race may ever be justifiably relied upon in redistricting reaffirms the messy jurisprudence of compromise that has guided the center of the Court since *Regents of the University of California v. Bakke*. The heart of this jurisprudence is a never quite satisfactory accommodation between deeply individualistic notions of appropriate treatment and a politically charged conception of the representational legitimacy of principal institutions in our society.").

MILLER v. JOHNSON, 515 U.S. 900 (1995). *Miller* rejected a voter district designed predominantly with racial motivations. In 1990, because of an increase in population, Georgia was entitled to an eleventh congressional seat. In redrawing the voting districts to include an eleventh district, the Georgia General Assembly had to obtain preclearance from the U.S. Attorney General under § 5 of the Voting Rights Act. This section requires that the changes "not have the purpose" and "the effect of denying or abridging the right to vote on account of race or color." The Georgia General Assembly twice submitted proposals to the Attorney General for preclearance. Neither proposal was given preclearance because each contained only two majority-minority districts.

The only redistricting plan that the Justice Department appeared willing to accept was the "max-black" plan developed by the ACLU which would create three majority-minority districts. Finally the Georgia General Assembly submitted a third proposal utilizing the "max-black" plan.

The redrawn Eleventh District split 26 counties and 23 existing congressional districts; it connected some neighborhoods 260 miles apart with narrow land bridges and covered 6,784.2 square miles. This plan was precleared by the Attorney General. Subsequently, elections in which a black representative prevailed took place and five white voters from the Eleventh District filed this action.

Justice Kennedy, writing for the (5-4) majority, stated that a bizarrely drawn district may provide "persuasive circumstantial evidence" that drawing race-based lines was the dominant legislative intent. As a general matter, equal protection requires strict scrutiny when statutes contain "explicit racial classifications" or when a racial purpose motivates a statute that is facially neutral. A pattern "unexplainable on grounds other than race" renders the evidentiary inquiry "relatively easy."

Plaintiffs must "show, either through circumstantial evidence of a district's shape and demographics or more direct evidence going to legislative purpose, that race was the predominant factor motivating the legislature's decision to place a significant number of voters within or without a particular district. To make this showing, a plaintiff must prove that the legislature subordinated traditional race-neutral districting principles, including but not limited to compactness, contiguity, respect for political subdivisions or communities defined by actual shared interests, to racial considerations. Where these or other race-neutral considerations are the basis for redistricting legislation, and are not subordinated to race, a state can defeat a claim that a district has been gerrymandered on racial lines."

In this case, the District Court's finding that race was the predominant factor motivating the drawing of the Eleventh District was not clearly erroneous. During preclearance proceedings, " 'it became obvious' " that the Justice Department "would accept nothing less than abject surrender to its maximization agenda." A redistricting plan that features race as the predominant factor must be subjected to strict scrutiny. The State must show that its actions are "narrowly tailored to achieve a compelling interest." In assuming race-based political views, the State was invoking the Voting Rights Act "to demand the very racial stereotyping the Fourteenth Amendment forbids."

Justice O'Connor briefly concurred. This case, like *Shaw*, only applied to "extreme instances of race-based gerrymandering."

Justice Stevens dissented. He protested "the Court's equation of traditional gerrymanders, designed to maintain or enhance a dominant group's power, with a dominant group's decision to share its power with a previously underrepresented group."

Justice Ginsburg dissented, joined by Justices Stevens, Souter, and Breyer.

Justice Ginsburg divided the voter redistricting cases into four groups: one-person-one-vote under *Reynolds v. Sims, infra* § 11.03; minority voter dilution under *Gomillion v. Lightfoot*, 364 U.S. 339 (1960), *supra* § 8.03; *Shaw* which only demands strict scrutiny for race-based lines drawn with " 'extreme irregularity' "; and the instant case. Georgia's Eleventh District is not " 'extremely irregular' " when compared to the district in *Shaw*; instead the redistricting reflected " 'traditional districting factors.' " In contrast to the " 'extreme irregularity' " required by *Shaw*, the majority allows a constitutional claim "whenever plaintiffs plausibly allege that other factors carried less weight than race."

Under the Equal Protection Clause, the history of discrimination justifies "vigilant judicial inspection to protect minority voters — circumstances that do not apply to majority voters." The Voting Rights Act was created "to make once-subordinated people free and equal citizens," not to protect majority voters who can safeguard their interests through the political process.

BUSH v. VERA, 517 U.S. 952 (1996). In *Bush*, the Court (3-2-4) invalidated three Texas congressional districts as racial gerrymanders. Pursuant to the 1990 census, which showed an increase in population allowing Texas three new congressional seats, the Texas Legislature created a new majority-African-American district (District 30), a new majority-Hispanic district (District 29), and reconfigured an existing district as a majority-African-American district (District 18).

Justice O'Connor wrote a plurality opinion in which Chief Justice Rehnquist and Justice Kennedy joined. The plurality stated that strict scrutiny applies when "other, legitimate districting principles were 'subordinated' to race." This meant "that race must be 'the predominant factor motivating the legislature's [redistricting] decision.' "

Taken together, "[t]hese findings — that the State substantially neglected traditional districting criteria such as compactness, that it was committed from the outset to creating majority-minority districts, and that it manipulated district lines to exploit unprecedentedly detailed racial data — together weigh in favor of the application of strict scrutiny. We do not hold that any one of these factors is independently sufficient to require strict scrutiny." The plurality continued: "the direct evidence of racial considerations, coupled with the fact that the computer program used was significantly more sophisticated with respect to race than with respect to other demographic data, provides substantial evidence that it was race that led to the neglect of traditional districting criteria here. We must therefore consider what role other factors played in order to determine whether race predominated."

The plurality first looked at District 30, which is "50% African-American and 17.1% Hispanic" with 50% of its population living "in a compact, albeit irregularly shaped, core in south Dallas, which is 69% African-American. But the remainder of the District consists of narrow and bizarrely shaped tentacles" precisely tailored to cross political subdivisions and reach into other minority neighborhoods. While the plurality agreed with Texas' argument that district lines had some correlation with transportation modes, common media sources, and consistent urban character, these correlations were insufficient to displace the District Court's finding that race predominated over these factors particularly as information about these factors was not " 'available to the Legislature in any organized fashion.' "

A State may use "political data" such as precinct primary and general election voting patterns and legislators' experience, when its goal is "constitutional political gerrymandering," even if this occurs in a majority-minority district or with awareness of "racial implications." However, "the objective evidence provided by the district plans and demographic maps suggests strongly the predominance of race." For example, the computer program the legislature used in creating District 30 "provided only racial data at the block-by-block level."[26]

Turning to Districts 18 and 29, the plurality noted that, according to a leading study, "they are two of the three least regular districts in the country." District 18 is 51% African-American and 15% Hispanic. Its " 'many narrow corridors, wings or fingers . . . reach out to enclose black voters, while excluding nearby Hispanic residents.' " District 29 is 61% Hispanic and 10% African-American, resembling the shape of " 'a sacred Mayan bird.' " In addition to the "bizarre" shapes of the two districts, they both "exhibit utter disregard of city limits, local election precincts, and voter tabulation district lines."

"[T]he State's efforts to maximize racial divisions" far outweighed its efforts to protect incumbents, as evidenced by the early legislative support for " 'creating a new Hispanic safe seat' " while at the same time " 'preserving the safe African-American seat in District 18.' " The lines of Districts 18 and 29 "correlate almost perfectly with race while both districts are similarly solidly Democratic."

The plurality next considered "whether the racial classifications embodied in any of the three districts [were] narrowly tailored to further a compelling state interest." Notably, the Court stated that the district may "avoid strict scrutiny altogether" if the State respects the results test in majority-minority districts.

Assuming without deciding that a State's interest in avoiding liability under § 2 of the Voting Rights Act is compelling, the State must show first, "that [the minority group] is sufficiently large and geographically compact to constitute a majority in a single member district;" second, "that it is politically cohesive;" and third, "that the white majority votes sufficiently as a bloc to enable it . . . usually to defeat the minority's preferred candidate." The district "must not subordinate traditional districting principles to race substantially more than is 'reasonably necessary' to avoid § 2 liability." Assuming without deciding that the districts met the second and third conditions, none met the first as all three were "bizarrely shaped and far from compact." Moreover, "the bizarre shaping of Districts 18 and 29, cutting across pre-existing precinct lines and natural or traditional divisions, is not merely evidentially significant; it is part of the constitutional problem insofar as it disrupts nonracial bases of political identity and thus intensifies the emphasis on race."

The plurality also rejected as compelling the interest in " 'ameliorating the effects of racially polarized voting attributable to past and present racial discrimination.' " To be compelling, "[f]irst, the discrimination that the State seeks to remedy must be specific, 'identified discrimination' "; second, the State "must have had a 'strong basis in

---

[26] The plurality criticized the dissent for "second-guessing" the District Court's factual findings.

evidence' to conclude that remedial action was necessary, 'before it embarks on an affirmative action program.'" *Shaw v. Hunt (Shaw II), infra* § 8.03[4], Note (2) after *Bush v. Vera*. Again relying on *Shaw II*, the plurality found that "vote dilution as a consequence of racial bloc voting," does not "justify race-based districting unless 'the State employs sound districting principles, and . . . the affected racial group's residential patterns afford the opportunity of creating districts in which they will be in the majority.'"

Finally, the plurality rejected Texas' claim that District 18 was justified by a compelling state interest of complying with VRA § 5. Rather than maintain the same percentage of African-American population, Texas had increased that percentage and had not supported this increase by showing it was "necessary to insure nonretrogression" in the voting rights of the minority group.

Justice O'Connor also wrote a separate concurring opinion stating that "compliance with the results test of § 2 of the Voting Rights Act (VRA) is a compelling state interest."

The *Bush* and *Shaw II* decisions, combined with the recognition that compliance with the § 2 results test comprises a compelling state interest, provide "a workable framework" for voter redistricting.

First, if States do not subordinate districting criteria to the use of race for its own sake or as a proxy, a State "may intentionally create majority-minority districts, and may otherwise take race into consideration, without coming under strict scrutiny." "Only if traditional districting criteria are neglected and that neglect is predominantly due to the misuse of race does strict scrutiny apply."

Second, for racially polarized districts, § 2(b) "prohibits States from adopting districting schemes that would have the effect that minority voters 'have less opportunity than other members of the electorate to . . . elect representatives of their choice.' That principle may require a State to create a majority-minority district where the three *Gingles* factors are present — viz., (i) the minority group 'is sufficiently large and geographically compact to constitute a majority in a single-member district,' (ii) 'it is politically cohesive,' and (iii) 'the white majority votes sufficiently as a bloc to enable it . . . usually to defeat the minority's preferred candidate,'" *Thornburg v. Gingles*, 478 U.S. 30, 50–51 (1986).

"Third, the state interest in avoiding liability under VRA § 2 is compelling. If a State has a strong basis in evidence for concluding that the *Gingles* factors are present, it may create a majority-minority district without awaiting judicial findings."

Fourth, if the district created "does not deviate substantially from a hypothetical court-drawn § 2 district for predominantly racial reasons," the State's "districting plan will be deemed narrowly tailored."

Finally, "districts that are bizarrely shaped and non-compact, and that otherwise neglect traditional districting principles and deviate substantially from the hypothetical court-drawn district, for predominantly racial reasons, are unconstitutional."

Justice Kennedy joined the plurality opinion, but wrote a concurring opinion to express his disagreement with the inclusion of the plurality's "dicta" that strict scrutiny does not apply "to all cases of intentional creation of majority-minority districts." Justice Kennedy explained that since the Court "would no doubt apply strict scrutiny if a State decreed that certain districts had to be at least 50 percent white" the "analysis should be no different if the State so favors minority races."

Justice Thomas, concurring in the judgment and joined by Justice Scalia, also disagreed with Justice O'Connor that "strict scrutiny is not invoked by the intentional creation of majority-minority districts." While *Shaw I* reserved this question, *Adarand*

Constructors, Inc. v. Pena, 515 U.S. 211 (1995), stated that "all governmental racial classifications must be strictly scrutinized." Moreover, *Miller v. Johnson, supra* § 8.03[4], determined that the intentional creation of majority-minority districts was "sufficient to show that race was a predominant, motivating factor." Finally, Justice Thomas agreed with the plurality that Texas' "districting attempts were not narrowly tailored to achieve its asserted interest."

Justice Stevens dissented, joined by Justices Ginsburg and Breyer. According to the 1990 census, "Texas' population had grown, over the past decade, almost twice as fast as the population of the country as a whole." The resultant political battles over new districts resulted in "some of the most oddly shaped congressional districts in the United States." In applying strict scrutiny, the plurality "improperly ignores the 'complex interplay' of political and geographical considerations that went into the creation" of the three districts. In this connection, Justice Stevens viewed all of Texas' new districts as political rather than racial gerrymanders. As Justice Stevens maintained that "political gerrymanders are more objectionable than the 'racial gerrymanders' perceived by the Court in recent cases," he was "not entirely unsympathetic to the Court's holding." Nevertheless, "the evils of political gerrymandering should be confronted directly, rather than through the race-specific approach that the Court has taken in recent years."

Justice Stevens would have upheld all three of Texas' new districts, "even if strict scrutiny applies." Each district "considers race only to the extent necessary to comply with the State's responsibilities under the Voting Rights Act while achieving other race-neutral political and geographical requirements."

The 1992 elections reveal Texas' true motives. Specifically, "more than two-thirds of the Districts" in Texas elected Democrats to Congress that year "even though Texas voters are arguably more likely to vote Republican than Democrat." Moreover, "each of the three new districts elected a state legislator who had essentially acted as an incumbent in the districting process, giving 'incumbents' a 97 percent success rate." Computers were partly responsible for the "dramatic increase in bizarrely shaped districts after 1990" because they "allowed legislators to achieve their political goals geographically in a manner far more precise than heretofore possible."

The districting also considered race, as minority groups accounted for nearly all of Texas' increase in population. Justice Stevens also noted that three majority-white districts in Texas also rank among the most oddly shaped in the nation.

The District Court and the plurality did both recognize that "the creation of 'safe' districts for incumbents was intimately related to the bizarre shape of district lines throughout the State." Texas was "neither irrational, nor invidious" in assuming "that a black resident of a particular community is a Democrat if reliable statistical evidence discloses that 97% of the blacks in that community vote in Democratic primary elections."

Justice Souter also wrote a dissenting opinion, joined by Justices Ginsburg and Breyer. Justice Souter noted that "'prior to the latest round of redistricting after the 1990 Census . . . blacks, who constitute 11.1% of the nation's voting age population, made up only 4.9% of the members of Congress.'" In the South, "'the probability of a district's electing a Black representative was less than 1% regardless of a district's median family income, its percentage of high school graduates; its proportion of residents who were elderly, urban, foreign-born, or who had been residents of the state for more than five years; or the region of the country in which the district was located.'" Improvements in this area are attributable to the Voting Rights Act and to the Court's "willingness to allow race-conscious districting in certain situations." The Court has never determined "how much is too much" when racial considerations are used in the districting process, but instead "adopted a 'predominant purpose' test." Courts cannot determine with confidence what the predominant factor was in creating a districting plan. Not only does a court have difficulty isolating the predominant motive in a districting decision, but numerous "traditional districting principles cannot be applied without taking race into account and are thus, as a practical matter, inseparable from the supposedly illegitimate racial considerations."

Shaw I failed to set out a "test for distinguishing a 'predominant' racial consideration from the application of traditional districting principles." The States "'now find themselves walking a tightrope: if they draw majority-black districts they face lawsuits under the equal protection clause; if they do not, they face both objections under section 5 of the Voting Rights Act and lawsuits under section 2.'" In this case and in *Shaw II*, the Court assumes that compliance with the Voting Rights Act is a compelling state interest, confirming "the view that the intentional creation of majority-minority districts is not necessarily a violation of *Shaw I*."

Shaw II suggests that a State "seeking to avoid violating § 2 of the Voting Rights Act may draw the district that the Voting Rights Act compels, and this district alone." After *Shaw* and *Miller*, the Court seemed to be heading toward "imposing a principle of color blindness in the name of the Fourteenth Amendment," which ironically "would be submerging the votes of those whom the Fourteenth and Fifteenth Amendments were adopted to protect, precisely the problem that necessitated our recognition of vote dilution as a constitutional violation in the first place."

NOTES

(1) *District Court Plan.* In *Abrams v. Johnson*, 521 U.S. 74 (1997), the Court upheld a redistricting plan for Georgia's congressional districts. This appeal arose after the Court's remand in *Miller v. Johnson*, *supra* § 8.03[4]. In *Miller*, the Court held that the Eleventh Congressional District was unconstitutional because race was "a predominant factor in drawing the district lines." When the Georgia legislature could not agree upon a new redistricting plan, the three-judge District Court crafted its own plan, under which the 1996 general elections occurred. The District Court's plan included only one majority-black district. Appellants argued that Georgia should have two or three majority-minority congressional districts.

Writing for a 5-4 majority, Justice Kennedy examined the background of the District Court's plan. The District Court's plan placed the new Eleventh District near Atlanta in an area of substantial population growth, in order to displace the fewest counties. It then considered Georgia's traditional redistricting principles which included maintaining political subdivisions such as counties and cities. The District Court also attempted to protect incumbents from contests with each other; however, the court subordinated this interest due to its more political nature. The District Court found that Georgia did not have a sufficiently concentrated black population to justify adding a second majority-black district. Had the District Court found such a population, it would have added a second majority-black district, honoring the intentions of Georgia's legislature. The District Court's plan did not split any counties outside the Atlanta area.

First, the evidence of predominant racial motives in the design of the proposed redistricting plans which advocated two or three majority-black districts invalidated these plans. Therefore, "the trial court acted well within its discretion" in determining that it could not develop a redistricting plan containing two majority-black districts without engaging in racial gerrymandering. Second, the trial court's plan did not violate § 2 of the Voting Rights Act because the absence of a second majority-black district did not result in impermissible vote dilution. Third, the District Court's plan did not violate the retrogression principle of § 5 of the Voting Rights Act. While § 5 generally requires administrative preclearance, the Court has made an exception for plans designed by the federal district courts themselves.

Justice Breyer, joined by Justices Stevens, Souter, and Ginsburg, dissented. Justice Breyer began by observing that African-Americans comprise 27% of Georgia's voting age population. "Until 1972, Georgia had not elected any African-American Members of Congress since Reconstruction," and since 1972, it has elected only four. Those four members initially represented minority-majority districts. However, Georgia recently re-elected two of the members as incumbents after district line changes established white majorities in their districts. The record presented " 'a strong basis in the evidence' " for concluding that § 2 or § 5 required two majority-black districts.

Unlike other decisions which use the phrase " 'predominant racial motive,' " the majority did not consider other factors, such as "discriminatory intent, or vote dilution, or even a district's bizarre geographical shape," in interpreting, or limiting the scope of, these words. As a result, legislators cannot judge when they can intentionally locate racial minorities in a district.

(2) *"Dominant and Controlling."* In *Shaw v. Hunt*, 517 U.S. 899 (1996), the Court held that the North Carolina redistricting plan at issue in *Shaw v. Reno, supra* § 8.03[4], violated the Equal Protection Clause because it was "not narrowly tailored to serve a compelling state interest." Chief Justice Rehnquist, writing for the (5-4) majority, stated that legislators "may be conscious of the voters' races without using race as a basis for assigning voters to districts. The constitutional wrong occurs when race becomes 'the dominant and controlling' consideration." The Chief Justice did not dispute the dissent's claim that District 12 advanced the State's interest "in creating one rural and one urban district, and that partisan politicking was actively at work in the districting process." However, "respecting communities of interest and protecting Democratic incumbents came into play only after the race-based decision had been made."

"Accordingly, an effort to alleviate the effects of societal discrimination is not a compelling interest." Second, before the State implements any plan, the racial discrimination claim must be backed by a " 'strong basis in evidence' " establishing that the "action was necessary." The District Court's finding indicated that North Carolina failed to meet these criteria. The court "found that an interest in ameliorating past discrimination did not actually precipitate the use of race in the redistricting plan."

Justice Stevens filed a dissenting opinion joined in part by Justices Ginsburg and Breyer. "If strict scrutiny applies even when a State draws a majority-minority district that respects traditional districting principles, then I do not see how a State can ever create a majority-minority district in order to fulfill its obligations under the Voting Rights Act without inviting constitutional suspicion." A constitutional jurisprudence that allows the state to "draw unsightly lines to favor farmers or city dwellers," but prohibits it from creating "districts that benefit the very group whose history inspired the Amendment that the Voting Rights Act was designed to implement."

Justice Souter filed a separate dissenting opinion which Justices Ginsburg and Breyer joined.

(3) *Clearly Erroneous Findings.* In *Hunt v. Cromartie*, 532 U.S. 234 (2001) (*Cromartie II*), the Court addressed the constitutionality of the districting plan for North Carolina's Congressional District 12 for the fourth time. Writing for a 5-4 majority, Justice Breyer reaffirmed that a party alleging that a legislature has improperly used race in determining a district's boundaries has to show that race was the predominate factor in the legislature's districting decision. However, the Court held clearly erroneous the finding of the three-judge District Court that race was the predominant factor in this case. While the Supreme Court will not " 'lightly overturn' "

the concurrent findings of two lower courts, the Court was the only court to review the three-judge District Court in this case.

Because "racial identification is highly correlated with political affiliation in North Carolina," *Bush v. Vera*, setting aside a district required more than evidence of its "shape, its splitting of towns and counties, and its high African-American voting population."

First, the District Court had primarily relied on "evidence of voting registration, not voting behavior," which the Supreme Court had previously rejected in this case. *Hunt v. Cromartie.* "[R]egistration figures do not accurately predict preference at the polls. . . . In part this is because white voters registered as Democrats 'cross-over' to vote for a Republican candidate more often than do African-Americans."

Second, the District Court relied on expert testimony and witness statements that "simply do not provide significant additional support" for its conclusion.

Third, the Court said that the District Court could not reject the factual data provided by the State's primary expert, Dr. Peterson. His unrefuted statistics showed that "registration was a poor indicator of party preference and that African-Americans are much more reliably Democratic voters."

Fourth, the plaintiffs' own maps indicated that the boundaries "in general placed more-reliably Democratic voters inside the district, while placing less-reliably Democratic voters outside the district," further indicating that the State's primary motivation was political, not racial.

In summary, "where majority-minority districts (or the approximate equivalent) are at issue and where racial identification correlates highly with political affiliation," plaintiff first must show "that the legislature could have achieved its legitimate political objectives in alternative ways that are comparably consistent with traditional districting principles." Second, plaintiff must show "that those districting alternatives would have brought about significantly greater racial balance."

Justice Thomas dissented, joined by Chief Justice Rehnquist, and Justices Scalia and Kennedy. Justice Thomas said that the Court's "incantations" of the clearly erroneous standard mask its actual approach of " 'extensive review.' " "[I]f considerations such as the length of the trial were relevant in deciding how to review factual findings, an assumption about which I have my doubts, these considerations would not counsel against deference in this action." The Court has "never held that factual findings based on documentary evidence and expert testimony justify 'extensive review.' " Finally, the District Court "permissibly could have accorded great weight" to the e-mail of the redistricting staff person as "direct evidence of a racial motive."

(4) *Standing.* In *United States v. Hays*, 515 U.S. 737 (1995), the Court held that residents of one district lack standing to challenge a racial gerrymander in another district in the state. Rejecting the citizens' claim that "anybody in the state" can raise a Fourteenth Amendment challenge to a racial gerrymander, the Court held that to bring a claim, a citizen must show personal injury from the racial classification.

(5) For additional discussion of *Shaw* and *Miller*, see Lani Guinier, *No Two Seats: The Elusive Quest for Political Equality*, 77 Va. L. Rev. 1413, 1513 (1991) ("Instead of emphasizing arbitrary territorial boundaries, which waste the votes of both minority and majority groups, interest representation favors allowing voters of the same interests to join together in voting for candidates of choice, regardless of where the voters live in the jurisdiction. . . . In this fashion, interest representation strives to ensure that groups that are politically cohesive, sufficiently numerous, and strategically mobilized will be able to elect a representative to the legislative body.") *See also* Melissa L. Saunders, *Equal Protection, Class Legislation, and Colorblindness*, 96

MICH. L. REV. 245, 333–34 (1997) ("[T]he Court lost its bearings a bit, losing sight of the fact that the Equal Protection Clause was actually designed to prevent the states from singling out certain classes of people for special benefits or burdens without sufficient justification, not to prevent it from dealing with people on the basis of race, gender, or other immutable personal characteristics. The peculiar vision of the Equal Protection Clause embraced in the racial gerrymandering cases of the 1990s is but the logical conclusion of that earlier misstep. . . . The Court . . . has yet to declare explicitly that a showing of discriminatory effect, as traditionally understood, is no longer an essential element of an equal protection claim. Indeed, the Court does not appear to recognize that this is the logical implication of its decisions in the racial gerrymandering cases."); *see also* Stephen A. Siegel, *The Federal Government's Power To Enact Color-Conscious Laws: An Originalist Inquiry*, 92 Nw. U. L. REV. 477, 590 (1998) ("From an originalist perspective, then, there are strong arguments that the Constitution, as adopted in 1789 and amended in 1791 and 1865-1870, allows the federal government near plenary power to enact invidious, as well as benign, color-conscious laws.").

[5]   The Criminal Justice System

BATSON v. KENTUCKY, 476 U.S. 79 (1986). Batson, a black person, was indicted on charges of second-degree burglary and receiving stolen goods. After the voir dire examination, the prosecutor used all his peremptory challenges to strike all blacks on the venire. The defense counsel alleged that the prosecutor's use of his peremptory challenges violated Batson's Sixth and Fourteenth Amendment rights, and moved to discharge the jury before it was sworn. The trial judge rejected the motion, and the all-white jury proceeded to convict Batson on both counts. The Supreme Court of Kentucky affirmed the conviction.

In a 6-3 decision, the Supreme Court, per Justice Powell, reversed the state court decision and remanded the case for a determination of purposeful discrimination. "The harm from discriminatory jury selection extends beyond that inflicted on the defendant and the excluded juror to touch the entire community. Selection procedures that purposefully exclude black persons from juries undermine public confidence in the fairness of our system of justice."

"While decisions of this court have been concerned largely with discrimination during selection of the venire, the principles announced there also forbid discrimination on account of race in selection of the petit jury."

Justice Powell provided the following elements of a *prima facie* case of racially discriminatory use of peremptories: "the defendant must first show that he is a member of a cognizable racial group, and that the prosecutor has exercised peremptory challenges to remove from the venire members of the defendant's race. Second, the defendant is entitled to rely on the fact, as to which there can be no dispute, that peremptory challenges constitute a jury selection practice that permits 'those to discriminate who are of a mind to discriminate.' Finally, the defendant must show that these facts and any other relevant circumstances raise an inference that the prosecutor used that practice to exclude the veniremen from the petit jury on account of their race. This combination of factors in the empaneling of the petit jury, as in the selection of the venire raises the necessary inference of purposeful discrimination."

Once the defendant makes a *prima facie* showing, the burden shifts to the State to give a racially neutral explanation for challenging black jurors. "Though this requirement imposes a limitation in some cases on the full peremptory character of the historic challenge, we emphasize that the prosecutor's explanation need not rise to the level justifying exercise of a challenge for cause. But the prosecutor may not rebut the defendant's *prima facie* case of discrimination by stating merely that he challenged jurors of the defendant's race on the assumption — or his intuitive judgment — that they would be partial to the defendant because of their shared race. Just as the Equal Protection Clause forbids the State to exclude black persons from the venire on the assumption that blacks as a group are unqualified to serve as jurors, so it forbids the State to strike black veniremen on the assumption that they will be biased in a particular case simply because the defendant is black."

Justice Marshall concurred, stating that the racially discriminatory use of peremptories can be ended only by completely eliminating peremptories. He contended that the majority permits a defendant to establish a *prima facie* case only if the prosecutor blatantly discriminates in jury selection. Moreover, even when a defendant establishes a *prima facie* case, the prosecutor can easily give a neutral explanation in order to hide his discriminatory intent.

Chief Justice Burger, joined by Justice Rehnquist, dissented. Chief Justice Burger argued that the Court slighted the history and importance of the peremptory challenge. In addition, the Court had expressly limited its holding to a prosecutor's use of peremptories, yet he predicted that the Court would extend the holding to a defense attorney's use of them.

The Chief Justice also stated that the decision created a middle ground between peremptory challenges and challenges for cause. "To rebut a *prima facie* case, the Court requires a 'neutral explanation' for the challenge, but is at pains to 'emphasize' that the 'explanation need not rise to the level justifying exercise of a challenge for cause.' " Trial judges would experience considerable difficulty in applying the Court's standard.

Justice Rehnquist, joined by the Chief Justice, filed a separate dissent. Justice Rehnquist asserted that it was not unequal for the State to use peremptories to strike blacks from the jury in cases involving black defendants, as long as the State also uses peremptories to exclude a member of any racial group from a case involving members of that group. "Such use of peremptories is at best based upon seat-of-the-pants instincts, which are undoubtedly crudely stereotypical and may in many cases be hopelessly mistaken. But as long as they are applied across the board to jurors of all races and nationalities, I do not see — and the Court most certainly has not explained — how their use violates the Equal Protection Clause."

Justice Rehnquist did not think that the prosecution's use of peremptory challenges was unusual. "The use of group affiliations such as age, race, or occupation as a 'proxy' for potential juror partiality, based on the assumption or belief that members of one group are more likely to favor defendants who belong to the same group, has long been accepted as a legitimate basis for the State's exercise of peremptory challenges."

NOTES

(1) *Retroactive Application.* In *Griffith v. Kentucky*, 479 U.S. 314 (1987), the Court held that *Batson* applied retroactively to all cases, state and federal, pending on direct review or not yet final. The Court discarded its prior rule whereby retroactivity would be denied in cases where the new rule constituted a "clear break" with past decisions. Justice Blackmun wrote the Court's opinion; Chief Justice Rehnquist, and Justices White and O'Connor dissented.

(2) *Standing to Challenge Exclusions of Jurors Not of Defendant's Race.* In *Powers v. Ohio*, 499 U.S. 400 (1991), the Court held that a criminal defendant has standing to object to the State's "race-based exclusions of jurors through peremptory challenges whether or not the defendant and the excluded jurors share the same race." Defendant Powers, a white man, was indicted on two counts of aggravated murder and one count of attempted aggravated murder. During jury selection, Powers objected each time the

State used seven peremptory challenge to strike black veniremen.

Justice Kennedy wrote for the Court (7-2). The State argued that since Powers is white, he had no standing to object to the exclusion of prospective black jurors. This position comported with neither "accepted rules of standing" nor "with the substantive guarantees of the Equal Protection Clause."

The Court found that while a defendant does not have a right to be tried by a jury composed of members of his or her own race, "he or she does have the right to be tried by a jury whose members are selected by nondiscriminatory criteria." Excluding jurors based on their race also harms the excluded juror who is being stigmatized because of race, and undermines our entire legal system as participation on a jury is one of the most significant ways in which citizens can "participate in the democratic process." While an individual citizen does not have the right to sit on any particular jury, "he or she does possess the right not to be excluded from one on account of race."

Finally, the Court considered whether "a criminal defendant has standing to raise the equal protection rights of a juror excluded from service in violation of these principles."

The Court outlined the three criteria for third-party standing: "the litigant must have suffered an 'injury-in-fact,' thus giving him or her a sufficiently 'concrete interest' in the outcome of the issue in dispute; the litigant must have a close relation to the third party; and there must exist some hindrance to the third party's ability to protect his or her own interests."

First, the prosecution's discriminatory use of peremptory challenges "causes a criminal defendant cognizable injury" because it places in doubt both the fairness of the trial and the "integrity of the judicial process." Second, "the excluded juror and the defendant have a common interest in eliminating racial discrimination in the courtroom." Third, while excluded jurors have the right to bring suit on their behalf, economic and other barriers to such suits are so great that they are rarely brought to court.

Thus, a *Batson* challenge does not hinge on the juror and the defendant sharing the same race. Nevertheless, whether the criminal defendant and the excluded venireman are of the same race remains relevant to establishing bias on the part of the prosecutor making race-based exclusions. Justice Scalia filed a dissenting opinion in which the Chief Justice joined.

Challenger's prima facie case. In *Johnson v. California*, 545 U.S. 162 (2005), the Court issued an 8-1 decision that invalidated California's application of the "more likely than not" standard to the first step of the defendant's *prima facie* case. In *Batson v. Kentucky*, *supra*, the Court "did not intend the first step to be so onerous that a defendant would have to persuade the judge — on the basis of all the facts, some of which are impossible for the defendant to know with certainty — that the challenge was more likely than not the product of purposeful discrimination." At this early stage of the proceeding, a defendant need only produce "evidence sufficient to permit the trial judge to draw an inference that discrimination has occurred." While the defendant must ultimately persuade the court that the prosecutor discriminated in selecting jury members, the defendant bears this burden only after the prosecution has offered a reason for excluding the specific veniremen. A prosecutor's refusal to offer a reason supports the defendant's "inference of discrimination." In the case at bar, the prosecutor used peremptory challenges to remove all three black prospective jurors, prompting the trial judge and the California Supreme Court to note the possibility of discrimination. "Those inferences that discrimination may have occurred," not that discrimination "more likely than not" occurred, established the defendant's *prima facie* case.

Justice Breyer concurred. Justice Thomas dissented.

Batson affords states broad discretion to construct their own method of implementing *Batson's prima facie* case.

(3) *Batson Challenges in Civil Suits.* The Court (6-3) extended a *Batson* challenge to a private civil suit. In *Edmonson v. Leesville*, 500 U.S. 614 (1991), the Court held that a private litigant in a civil case may not use peremptory challenges to exclude jurors based on their race.

Writing for the Court, Justice Kennedy found the private litigant to be a state actor in selecting a jury because statutory law is the source of many jury selection procedures including peremptory challenges, and because the private litigant made extensive use of governmental procedures with the overt, significant assistance of the government — specifically, the judge. Moreover, jury selection involves a traditional governmental function that the government delegates to private litigants, and is "aggravated in a unique way by the incidents of governmental authority" since it takes place in a courtroom. The injury to excluded jurors would be the direct result of governmental delegation and participation." The Court also afforded third-party standing to private litigants to assert constitutional violations suffered by excluded jurors.

Justice O'Connor wrote a dissenting opinion joined by Chief Justice Rehnquist and Justice Scalia, arguing lack of state action. Justice Scalia also filed a separate dissenting opinion.

(4) *Criminal Defendant.* In *Georgia v. McCollum*, 505 U.S. 42 (1992), the Court (5-1-2) held that the Equal Protection Clause prohibits a criminal defendant from purposefully discriminating against jurors by using peremptory challenges to strike them on the basis of race. Defendants, who are white, were indicted for assaulting a black couple. Before trial, respondents' counsel indicated that they intended to use their peremptory strikes to eliminate African-American jurors.

Writing for the Court, Justice Blackmun concluded that a criminal defendant's exercise of peremptory challenges in a racially discriminatory manner implicated *Batson* concerns. *Batson* not only protects criminal defendants by prohibiting prosecutors from exercising their peremptory challenges in a discriminatory manner, but it also protects the "dignity" of the stricken jurors and the "integrity of the courts."

The two-part inquiry in *Edmonson v. Leesville* established state action. Peremptory challenges have their "source in state authority." Government permits them and specifies how they are to be exercised through statute or caselaw. Moreover, the criminal defendant was a "state actor."

Justice Blackmun found that the "governmental assistance and benefits" received by the Georgia criminal defendant are equivalent to those received by the civil litigants in *Edmonson*. In both instances the trial court must enforce the discriminatory peremptory challenge. Again following *Edmonson*, the Court found that litigants exercising peremptory challenges perform a "traditional government function" by assisting government in selecting the trier of fact. Third, government authority "intensifies the harmful effects of the private litigant's discriminatory act and contributes to its characterization as state action."

Finally, limiting defendant's ability to exercise peremptory challenges did not violate his Sixth Amendment rights to a fair trial, an impartial jury, or to counsel. Rights to peremptory challenges may be withheld altogether without offending the Constitution. While criminal defendants have the right to impartial juries absent "racial animus," there is a difference "between exercising a peremptory challenge to discriminate invidiously against jurors on account of race and exercising a peremptory challenge to remove an individual juror who harbors racial prejudice . . . It is an affront to justice to argue that a fair trial includes the right to discriminate against a group of citizens based on their race." Moreover, defense counsel is capable of explaining the reasons for peremptory challenges "without revealing anything about trial strategy or any confidential client communications."

Chief Justice Rehnquist filed a separate concurring opinion, and Justice Thomas filed a separate opinion concurring in the judgment. Justice O'Connor filed a dissenting opinion in which Justice Scalia joined, and Justice Scalia filed a separate dissent. All four Justices expressed reservations regarding the presence of state action. "A criminal defendant, in the process of defending himself against the state, is held to be acting on behalf of the state."

(5) *Trial Court Discretion.* (a) *Exclusion of Spanish-speaking jurors.* In *Hernandez v. New York*, 500 U.S. 352 (1991), the Court referred to a state trial court's determination that the prosecutor did not discriminate on the basis of ethnicity in excluding Latino jurors. Justice Kennedy wrote for a plurality of four. The trial judge did not commit clear error in accepting the prosecutor's claim that the exclusions were race-neutral. The plurality focused on the prosecutor's intent — the best evidence of which is his demeanor. The prosecutor excluded jurors based on whether they might have difficulty in accepting the translator's rendition of Spanish-language testimony. The trial judge found this explanation race-neutral despite the fact that it might have resulted in the disproportionate removal of prospective Latino and bilingual jurors, and despite the availability of a less drastic alternative than exclusion. Justice Kennedy noted that the prosecutor based these claims on observations made during *voir dire* rather than on mere assumptions.

Moreover, the prosecutor insisted that he did not exclude Latino jurors to gain an advantage in prosecuting a Latino defendant given that the victims were also Latino. For the plurality, the fact that the prosecutor's challenges fell with disproportionate impact on members of one ethnic group did not rise to the level of a *Batson* challenge. The plurality noted, however, that "a policy of striking all who speak a given language, without regard to the particular circumstances of the trial or the individual responses of the jurors, may be found by the trial judge to be a pretext for racial discrimination."

Justice O'Connor, joined by Justice Scalia, concurred in the judgment. She said that the absence of discriminatory intent, by itself, extinguishes any cause of action for an equal protection violation. Consequently, courts need not determine that the exercise of peremptory challenges is unrelated to race. Justices Stevens, Blackmun, and Marshall dissented.

(b) *Exclusion for hair length and facial hair.* In *Purkett v. Elem* 514 U.S. 765 (1995), the Court denied a habeas corpus challenge to a prosecutor's using two of six peremptory challenges to strike jurors who were black, because of hair length and facial hair. In state trial court, the prosecutor explained that both jurors had mustaches and goatees, which looked "suspicious" to him. He also did not "like the way they looked, the way their hair [was] cut, both of them." Moreover, as one juror had had a sawed off shotgun pointed at him during a supermarket robbery, he might think that the crime of robbery necessitates having a gun which defendant did not have in this case. The trial court overruled, without explanation, defendant's *Batson* challenges to these peremptory strikes. After being convicted and exhausting his state appeals, defendant filed a federal habeas corpus challenge based on *Batson*. Relying on *Hernandez*, the Court in a *per curiam* opinion stated: "Under our *Batson* jurisprudence, once the opponent of a peremptory challenge has made out a *prima facie* case of racial discrimination (step 1), the burden of production shifts to the proponent of the strike to come forward with a race-neutral explanation (step 2). If a race-neutral explanation is tendered, the trial court must then decide (step 3) whether the opponent of the strike has proved purposeful racial discrimination." Step 2 requires the adjudicator to accept any race-neutral rebuttal given by the prosecutor, "no matter how implausible or fantastic," even if it is "silly, or superstitious." The adjudicator must then proceed under step 3 to decide "that the prosecutor was not motivated by discriminatory intent."

In federal habeas proceedings, the federal court can set aside the factual findings of the state courts (absent procedural error), "only if they are not fairly supported by the record." In this case, the Court of Appeals for the Eighth Circuit "gave no proper basis for overturning the state court's finding of no racial motive, which turns primarily on an assessment of credibility."

Justice Stevens dissented, joined by Justice Breyer. *Batson* required that the prosecutor's race-neutral explanation had to be related to the particular case to be tried, and the hair rationales were unrelated to this case.

(c) *Voir dire questions and other techniques.* In *Miller-El v. Dretke*, 545 U.S. 231 (2005), the Court reversed a Court of Appeals' determination that Miller-El was not entitled to habeas relief for discrimination in jury selection. The evidence established that the prosecutor had exercised peremptory challenges to remove black venire panel members based on their race. Of the 20 black persons on the original 108-person venire, the prosecution struck nine for cause. The prosecution used its peremptory challenges to strike 10 of the 11 black jurors who survived. The one surviving black venireman was the sole black person on the resulting 12-person jury. Writing for a 6-3 majority, Justice Souter stated that more compelling than statistical evidence is that a prosecutor dismisses a black panelist for a reason that also applies to "an otherwise-similar nonblack" panelist allowed to serve on the jury. While the prosecutor in the case at bar did accept a black member towards the end of jury selection, this action did not "neutralize the early-stage decision to challenge a comparable venireman." *Batson v. Kentucky, supra*, permits "the prosecutor to give the reason for striking the juror and it requires the judge to assess the plausibility of that reason in light of all evidence with a bearing on it."

In addition to the above evidence, the trial court granted two of the three jury shuffles requested by the prosecution. Under Texas criminal procedure, these shuffles allowed a reordering of the questioning of jurors so that those toward the back are frequently never reached for questioning but simply excused. All three times the prosecution requested a shuffle, black jurors were among the first to be questioned on the panel. Moreover, among venire panel members who expressed doubt about the death penalty, the prosecution subjected 3-4 times as many black panel members to tough *voir dire* questioning. The Court noted evidence of an old policy at the District Attorney's office of excluding black jury members which had not been countermanded. Finally, the prosecution's "race-neutral reasons" for using peremptory strikes against black panel members "are so far at odds with the evidence that pretext is the fair conclusion."

Justice Breyer concurred, noting the practical difficulties in applying *Batson* and suggesting that the entire system of peremptory challenges should be reconsidered. Justice Thomas dissented, joined by Chief Justice Rehnquist and Justice Scalia. The majority findings violate the Antiterrorism and Effective Death Penalty Act of 1996 (AEDPA), which require that federal courts in habeas corpus matters consider only evidence that was presented in state court. Moreover, under *Batson*, a "strong presumption of validity attaches to a trial court's factual finding," which is even stronger in habeas proceedings.

(d) In *Rice v. Collins*, 546 U.S. 333 (2006), the Court, in a habeas challenge, rejected a *Batson* challenge to a prosecutor's use of a preemptory challenge to remove a young black woman from the jury venire where the prosecutor supported the challenge by stating that the juror had "rolled her eyes in response to a question from the court," and was young and lacked ties to the community, which might make the juror too tolerant of drug dealing. State court credibility determinations in *Batson* challenges are generally reviewed for clear error and state court factual findings are presumed correct unless rebutted by clear and convincing evidence. Although "[r]easonable minds" may "disagree about the prosecutor's credibility, . . . on habeas review that does not suffice to supersede the trial court's credibility determinations."

(6) *Gender discrimination.* In *J.E.B. v. Alabama*, 511 U.S. 127 (1994), the Court held that the Equal Protection Clause forbids exercising peremptory challenges based on gender. In "jury service, African-Americans and women share a history of total exclusion." Allowing gender-based peremptory challenges would serve to "ratify and perpetuate invidious, archaic, and overbroad stereotypes about the relative abilities of men and women." For further discussion of *J.E.B.*, see § 9.01.

McCLESKEY v. KEMP, 481 U.S. 279 (1987). *McCleskey* addressed the question of whether the results of a statistical study proved that the petitioner's death sentence for murder was unconstitutional under the Eighth or Fourteenth Amendment. Warren McCleskey, a black person, was convicted of armed robbery and murder.

One of McCleskey's habeas claims was that Georgia administered its capital sentencing process in a racially discriminatory manner which violated the Eighth and Fourteenth Amendments. McCleskey supported this claim with an extensive statistical report, the Baldus study. The study alleged that defendants who murdered whites were more likely to receive the death sentence than those who murdered blacks. It also alleged that black defendants were more likely to receive the death penalty. Finally, the Baldus study claimed that black defendants, such as McCleskey, who kill whites were most likely to be sentenced to death.[27] The District Court dismissed McCleskey's petition.

The Supreme Court affirmed, with Justice Powell writing for a majority of five.[28] Justice Powell stated that McCleskey presented no evidence indicating a discriminatory purpose in his sentencing. Instead, he contended that the Baldus study supported an inference from its general statistics to the specific conclusion that his sentencing was racially biased.

Justice Powell recognized that the Court had accepted statistics as proof of discriminatory intent in venire-selection and in Title VII cases. However, he distinguished the proposed analogies to venire-selection and Title VII cases on three grounds. First, each petit jury in a death penalty case is unique in its composition and

---

[27] The Baldus study examined over 2,000 murders that occurred in Georgia in the 1970s and accounted for 230 variables that could have given a non-racial explanation for the disparities. "The raw numbers collected by Professor Baldus indicate that defendants charged with killing white persons received the death penalty in 11% of the cases, but defendants charged with killing blacks received the death penalty in only 1% of the cases . . . . Baldus also divided the cases according to the combination of the race of the defendant and the race of the victim. He found that the death penalty was assessed in 22% of the cases involving black defendants and white victims; 8% of the cases involving white defendants and white victims; 1% of the cases involving black defendants and black victims; and 3% of the cases involving white defendants and black victims. Similarly, Baldus found that prosecutors sought the death penalty in 70% of the cases involving black defendants and white victims; 32% of the cases involving white defendants and white victims; 15% of the cases involving black defendants and black victims; and 19% of the cases involving white defendants and black victims."

[28] Much of Justice Powell's opinion dealt with the Eighth Amendment challenge to Georgia's capital sentencing system. This note deals with the equal protection arguments only.

bases its decisions on consideration of innumerable factors which can vary from case to case.

Second, policy considerations suggest that jurors not be called to testify about how they reached a verdict. Other policy considerations advise against requiring prosecutors to explain why they sought the death penalty in cases occurring years ago. Because of these problems, the State "has no practical opportunity to rebut the Baldus study."

Third, as "discretion is essential to the criminal justice process, we would demand exceptionally clear proof before we would infer that the discretion has been abused."

The Court also rejected McCleskey's contention that the Baldus study proved that the State as a whole had acted with discriminatory purpose. "For this claim to prevail, McCleskey would have to prove that the Georgia Legislature enacted or maintained the death penalty statute *because of* an anticipated racially discriminatory effect."

Justice Brennan, joined by Justice Marshall and joined in part by Justices Blackmun and Stevens, dissented. His dissent was based on McCleskey's Eighth Amendment claim. After restating his general opposition to the death penalty on Eighth Amendment grounds, Justice Brennan argued that the statistics and historical evidence indicated the Georgia capital sentencing system was capricious and arbitrary.

"The Court . . . states that its unwillingness to regard the petitioner's evidence as sufficient is based in part on the fear that recognition of McCleskey's claim would open the door to widespread challenges to all aspects of criminal sentencing. Taken on its face, such a statement seems to suggest a fear of too much justice." Justice Brennan considered the statistical evidence against the backdrop of a history of racial discrimination.

Justice Blackmun, joined by Justices Marshall and Stevens and joined in part by Justice Brennan, also wrote a dissent. Justice Blackmun argued that under the three-factor standard established in *Batson*, McCleskey had made a *prima facie* case of racial discrimination. He also took issue with the majority's assertion that statistics involved more variables in capital sentencing decisions than in jury selection and Title VII cases.

Justice Stevens dissented separately, disputing the majority's assertion that acceptance of McCleskey's claim would end Georgia's capital punishment system. Instead, a ruling in McCleskey's favor would only entail a restructuring of the sentencing procedure to a system that is not as likely to discriminate.

NOTES

(1) *Selective Prosecution*. In *United States v. Armstrong*, 517 U.S. 456 (1996), the Court rejected two black defendants' requests for discovery on a selective prosecution claim because defendants failed to show governmental refusal to prosecute similarly situated whites. Defendants, indicted on charges of distributing crack cocaine, filed a motion for discovery or dismissal on the grounds they were selected for prosecution because of their race. The only evidence that defendants offered to support their motion was an affidavit from a " 'Paralegal Specialist' " in the Public Defender's Office that all of the 24 crack cocaine cases closed by the Office in 1991 involved black defendants.

Writing for the Court (8-1), Chief Justice Rehnquist noted that selective prosecution claims require courts to exert power over the prosecutorial function. Ordinarily, this is a " 'special province' of the Executive" over which it exercises broad discretion. Of course, equal protection and other constitutional constraints limit prosecutorial discretion. "A defendant may demonstrate that the administration of a criminal law is 'directed so exclusively against a particular class of persons' " as in *Yick Wo v. Hopkins*.

"In order to dispel the presumption that a prosecutor has not violated equal protection," defendant must show "clear evidence" of discriminatory purpose and effect. As discovery "will divert prosecutors' resources and may disclose the Government's prosecutorial strategy," obtaining it requires a similarly rigorous standard to that for a selective prosecution claim. In accordance with the vast majority of Courts of Appeals, the Chief Justice required "the defendant to produce some evidence that similarly situated defendants of other races could have been prosecuted, but were not."

Over "90% of the persons sentenced in 1994 for crack cocaine trafficking were black; 93.4% of convicted LSD dealers were white; and 91% of those convicted for pornography or prostitution were white."

Justices Souter and Ginsburg each filed concurring opinions, and Justice Breyer filed an opinion concurring in part and concurring in the judgment. All concurred on statutory grounds.

Justice Stevens dissented. He maintained that the District Court did not abuse its discretion in demanding some governmental response to defendant's showing. Eighty-eight percent of crack defendants were black, and blacks received sentences that were forty percent longer than whites.

(2) For one critical perspective on *McCleskey*, see Randall L. Kennedy, McCleskey v. Kemp: *Race, Capital Punishment, and the Supreme Court*, 101 HARV. L. REV. 1388 (1988) ("There is, in the end, no satisfying way to address from a community-oriented perspective the race-of-the-victim equal protection problem in *McCleskey*. Of all the available alternatives, however, the Supreme Court chose the very worst: the pretense that no problem of constitutional magnitude even exists.").

Chapter IX
EQUAL RIGHTS FOR THE SEXES

Introductory Note. The Women's Movement has compelled a reevaluation not only of the role of women in American society, but also of long-accepted attitudes toward both men and women. These roles and attitudes have been embodied into law, often in forms more subtle than in the area of race. They were found in laws seemingly designed to "protect" women, or to reflect the accepted stereotypical views of women. Section 9.01 explores the changing attitudes of the Court toward these gender-based classifications. The emphasis is on the modern cases and the Court's efforts to fashion a middle-tier standard of scrutiny in gender cases.

The remainder of the chapter examines several specific areas upon which many of the cases have focused. Section 9.02 considers the question of employment discrimination based on gender. Section 9.03 treats gender-based classifications in government benefit programs such as social security. Finally, Section 9.04 turns to discrimination relating to pregnancy.

§ 9.01 CHANGING ATTITUDES TOWARD GENDER-BASED CLASSIFICATIONS

GOESAERT v. CLEARY
335 U.S. 464, 69 S. Ct. 198, 93 L. Ed. 2d 163 (1948)

Justice Frankfurter delivered the opinion of the Court.

As part of the Michigan system for controlling the sale of liquor, bartenders are required to be licensed in all cities having a population of 50,000, or more, but no female may be so licensed unless she be "the wife or daughter of the male owner" of a licensed liquor establishment. The claim is that Michigan cannot forbid females generally from being barmaids and at the same time make an exception in favor of the wives and daughters of the owners of liquor establishments.

We are, to be sure, dealing with a historic calling. We meet the alewife, sprightly and ribald, in Shakespeare, but centuries before him she played a role in the social life of England. The Fourteenth Amendment did not tear history up by the roots, and the regulation of the liquor traffic is one of the oldest and most untrammeled of legislative powers. Michigan could, beyond question, forbid all women from working behind a bar. This is so despite the vast changes in the social and legal position of women. The fact that women may now have achieved the virtues that men have long claimed as their prerogatives and now indulge in vices that men have long practiced, does not preclude the States from drawing a sharp line between the sexes, certainly, in such matters as the regulation of the liquor traffic. . . . The Constitution does not require legislatures to reflect sociological insight, or shifting social standards, any more than it requires them to keep abreast of the latest scientific standards.

While Michigan may deny to all women opportunities for bartending, Michigan cannot play favorites among women without rhyme or reason. Since bartending by women may, in the allowable legislative judgment, give rise to moral and social problems against which it may devise preventive measures, the legislature need not go to the full length of prohibition if it believes that as to a defined group of females other factors are operating which either eliminate or reduce the moral and social problems otherwise calling for prohibition. Michigan evidently believes that the oversight assured through ownership of a bar by a barmaid's husband or father minimizes hazards that may confront a barmaid without such protecting oversight. . . . Since the line they have drawn is not without a basis in reason, we cannot give ear to the suggestion that the real impulse behind this legislature was an unchivalrous desire of male bartenders to try to monopolize the calling.

JUSTICE RUTLEDGE, with whom JUSTICE DOUGLAS and JUSTICE MURPHY join, dissenting. . . .

The statute arbitrarily discriminates between male and female owners of liquor establishments. A male owner, although he himself is always absent from his bar, may employ his wife and daughter as barmaids. A female owner may neither work as a barmaid herself nor employ her daughter in that position, even if a man is always present in the establishment to keep order. . . .

NOTES

(1) For an earlier example of a similar attitude, see *Bradwell v. State*, 16 Wall. 130 (1873), which upheld a state law barring women from the practice of law. In a concurring opinion, Justice Bradley wrote, "The paramount destiny and mission of woman is to fulfill the noble and benign offices of wife and mother."

(2) Laws like the one involved in *Goesaert v. Cleary* derived in part from reform-minded legislation intended to protect women and children from sweat-shop working conditions. At a time when the Supreme Court was striking down minimum wage and maximum hour laws as unconstitutional abridgments of "freedom of contract" (*See Lochner v. New York*, 198 U.S. 45 (1905), *supra* § 7.03 [1]), the Court appeared more willing to approve statutes aimed at protecting the working conditions of women. The "Brandeis Brief," which brought detailed economic and social data to the Court's attention, had its origin in one such case, *Muller v. Oregon*, 208 U.S. 412 (1908), which upheld an Oregon law setting maximum hours for female factory workers. While such laws reflected an attitude toward women that modern cases have rejected, it should be remembered that *Muller v. Oregon*, in its time, was an exception to the prevailing laissez-faire attitude of the Court with regard to state regulation of business. The continuing validity of laws that allegedly protect women as a class against certain conditions of employment or that compensate them for past discrimination, will be explored in this chapter. For a discussion of gender stereotyping and constitutional jurisprudence, see Kenneth L. Karst, *Woman's Constitution*, 1984 DUKE L.J. 447.

(3) *Estate Administrators.* Years after *Goesaert*, the Court began dramatically to change its approach to gender discrimination. In *Reed v. Reed*, 404 U.S. 71 (1971), the Court struck down a statute that preferred males over females in appointing estate administrators. Chief Justice Burger, writing for the majority, outlined the demands of equal protection: "classification must be reasonable, not arbitrary, and must rest upon some ground or difference having a fair and substantial relation to the object of the legislation so that persons similarly circumstanced would be treated alike." In this case, the question was whether the gender classification bore a "rational relationship" to the objective of the statute. Idaho's objective of reducing the workload of probate courts had some legitimacy. Nevertheless, "a mandatory preference to members of either sex over members of the other, merely to accomplish the elimination of hearings on the merits, is . . . the very kind of arbitrary legislative choice forbidden by the Equal Protection Clause."

(4) *Age of Majority. Stanton v. Stanton*, 421 U.S. 7 (1975), invalidated a Utah statute that designated different ages of majority for males and females when child support payments were to cease. Utah argued that females mature into adults more quickly and that males need support while they prepare to enter the marketplace. The Court reasoned that if child support payments end at age 18 for females and at age 21 for males, then females do not have the same opportunity to educate themselves and the

stereotype that women do not belong in the marketplace becomes "self-serving."

(5) *Rationales for Heightened Scrutiny.* In *Frontiero v. Richardson*, 411 U.S. 677 (1973), the Court invalidated a federal statute restricting access by husbands of servicewomen to housing and medical benefits. Regardless of the amount of support a serviceman provided for his wife, he could claim her as a "dependent." On the other hand, a servicewoman could not make such a claim unless she proved that her husband actually received over half of his support from her.

Justice Brennan, in a plurality opinion joined by Justices Douglas, White, and Marshall, ruled that classifications based upon sex "are inherently suspect and must therefore be subjected to close judicial scrutiny." To support strict scrutiny, Justice Brennan first noted the "history of discrimination against women." In "much of the 19th century the position of women in our society was, in many respects, comparable to that of blacks under the pre-Civil War slave codes. Neither slaves nor women could hold office, serve on juries, or bring suit in their own names, and married women traditionally were denied the legal capacity to hold or convey property or to serve as legal guardians of their own children." Second, "sex, like race and national origin, is an immutable characteristic determined solely by the accident of birth . . . bearing no relation to ability to perform or contribute to society." Statutory distinctions based on gender have often relegated women "to inferior legal status without regard to the actual capabilities of its individual members." Third, relying on Title VII, the Equal Pay Act and the Equal Rights Amendment, the plurality noted that "Congress itself has concluded that classifications based upon sex are inherently invidious."

The Court rejected "administrative convenience" as a rationale for the disparate treatment at issue. Individual determinations of dependency on servicemen may not be expensive, as dependency determinations for servicewomen were based on affidavits, not hearings.

Justice Powell concurred in the judgment, joined by Chief Justice Burger and Justice Blackmun. Justice Powell stated that *Reed* did not add gender to the list of suspect classifications. Extending strict scrutiny to gender classifications would weaken the democratic process, as Congress had already sent the Equal Rights Amendment to the states for ratification. Justice Stewart concurred in the judgment and Justice Rehnquist dissented.

CRAIG v. BOREN, 429 U.S. 190 (1976). In *Craig*, Justice Brennan, writing for the majority, held that an Oklahoma statute that prohibited the sale of "nonintoxicating" 3.2 percent beer to males under the age of 21 and to females under the age of 18 was a gender-based differential that constituted "a denial to males 18–20 years of age of the equal protection of the laws." Citing *Reed v. Reed, supra* § 9.01, Note (3) after *Goesaert*, Justice Brennan opined that gender classifications are constitutional only if they "serve important governmental objectives and [are] substantially related to achievement of those objectives." Statistical evidence failed to establish that the statute's gender-based distinction was substantially related to the achievement of this important objective.

"The appellees introduced a variety of statistical surveys. First, an analysis of arrest statistics for 1973 demonstrated that 18–20-year-old male arrests for 'driving under the influence' and 'drunkenness' substantially exceeded female arrests for that same age period. Similarly, youths aged 17–21 were found to be overrepresented among those killed or injured in traffic accidents, with males again numerically exceeding females in this regard. Third, a random roadside survey in Oklahoma City revealed that young males were more inclined to drive and drink beer than were their female counterparts. Fourth, Federal Bureau of Investigation nationwide statistics exhibited a notable increase in arrests for 'driving under the influence.' Finally, statistical evidence gathered in other jurisdictions, particularly Minnesota and Michigan, was offered to corroborate Oklahoma's experience by indicating the pervasiveness of youthful participation in motor vehicle accidents following the imbibing of alcohol."

The majority concluded that the statistical data was insufficient to justify the gender-based distinctions in the statute. The "most focused and relevant of the statistical surveys, arrests of 18–20-year-olds for alcohol-related driving offenses, exemplifie[d] the ultimate unpersuasiveness" of the data. The statistical surveys "broadly establish[ed] that .18% of females and 2% of males in that age group were arrested for that offense." Justice Brennan asserted that "if maleness is to serve as a proxy for drinking and driving, a correlation of 2% must be considered an unduly tenuous 'fit.'" At bottom, "proving broad sociological propositions by statistics is a dubious business, and one that inevitably is in tension with the normative philosophy that underlies the Equal Protection Clause."

Justices Powell and Stevens concurred although stressing that the case should not be read so broadly as the majority's language may imply. For Justice Powell, the statute's "gender-based classification" did "not bear a fair and substantial relation to the object of the legislation." Justice Powell was not convinced that the statistical data justified a "classification based on a three-year age differential between the sexes, and especially one that it so easily circumvented as to be virtually meaningless." Justice Stevens expressed his dismay as to analyzing Equal Protection claims under the two-tiered approach and emphasized the importance of looking to the motivating factors underlying particular Equal Protection decisions in order to better understand the Court's approach to this area of the law. Justice Stevens found the law to be in violation of the Equal Protection Clause because the statute "is a mere remnant of the now almost universally rejected tradition of discriminating against males in this age bracket, and because to the extent it reflects any physical difference between males and females, it is actually perverse." Furthermore, it was "difficult to believe that the statute was actually intended to cope with the problem of traffic safety,"[1] and even assuming some slight benefit, it would be improper to punish all of the men of the state for the sins of only two percent of the male population.

Justice Rehnquist dissented on two grounds. First was the majority's "conclusion that *men* challenging a gender-based statute which treats them less favorably than women may invoke a more stringent standard of judicial review than pertains to most other types of classifications." Second he found without precedent the "majority's standard classifications by gender must serve important governmental objectives and must be substantially related to achievement of those objectives." Furthermore, males in this age group are not "peculiarly disadvantaged, subject to systematic discriminatory treatment, or otherwise in need of special solicitude from the courts."

ROSTKER v. GOLDBERG, 453 U.S. 57 (1981). In *Rostker*, the Court upheld, against a Fifth Amendment challenge, the Military Selective Service Act (MSSA), which permitted the president to compel the registration of men and not women. The function of this registration was to facilitate any eventual conscription. Writing for the majority, Justice Rehnquist held that, "Not only is the scope of Congress' constitutional power in this area broad, but the lack of competence on the part of the courts is marked."

Under *Craig v. Boren*, "the Government's interest in raising and supporting armies

---

[1] Justice Stevens stated that "[t]here is no legislative history to indicate that this was the purpose, and several features of the statutory scheme indicate the contrary. . . .

"There is, of course, no way of knowing what actually motivated this discrimination, but I would not be surprised if it represented nothing more than the perpetuation of a stereotyped attitude about the relative maturity of the members of the two sexes in this age bracket."

is an 'important governmental interest.' " Congress deliberated whether to register only males for possible conscription or to register both sexes. Congress decided to register only males.

Justice Rehnquist stated that the courts should afford great deference to Congress when it legislates pursuant to its power to raise and support armies.[2] Congress had determined that the purpose behind registration was eventually to draft combat troops. As women, unlike men, were not eligible for combat, requiring the registration of women was useless. "Men and women, because of the combat restrictions on women, are simply not similarly situated for purposes of a draft or registration for a draft." Moreover, Congress' exemption of women from registration was "not only sufficiently but closely related to Congress' purpose in authorizing registration."

Congress concluded that registering and drafting women to fill a small number of noncombat positions was inefficient. Any need for women in noncombat roles could be filled by volunteers. Congress also concluded that placing women in noncombatant positions during mobilization would be detrimental to military flexibility.

Justice White dissented, joined by Justice Brennan.[3] He maintained that a large number of women could be used in the military without forfeiting combat readiness. Administrative convenience cannot be used to justify such starkly disparate treatment of men and women.

Justice Marshall dissented, joined by Justice Brennan. He argued that the Court excluded "women from a fundamental civic obligation." Even if such a limitation was justified with regard to conscription, its application to registration was not, as registration merely ascertained potential fighting strength. As "eligibility for combat is not a requirement for some of the positions," the government under *Craig v. Boren* must show that excluding women from a draft to fill those "positions substantially furthers an important governmental objective." The Senate Report relied upon by the majority simply said that drafting very large numbers of women or equal numbers of men and women would impair military flexibility. The report, however, did not conclude that drafting "a limited number of women would adversely affect military flexibility."

NOTES

(1) *Alimony. Orr v. Orr*, 440 U.S. 268 (1979), invalidated an Alabama statute which provided that, upon divorce, a husband but not a wife may be required to pay alimony. Justice Brennan's majority (6-3) opinion concluded that, even if the institution of marriage had discriminated against women, and even if gender were generally a reliable indicator of need, the Alabama statute already provided for hearings to determine the financial circumstances of the parties. Since the state's purpose could be served by a gender-neutral classification, rather than by one that carries "the baggage of sexual stereotypes," the state cannot be permitted to classify on the basis of gender.

Justice Rehnquist dissented, joined by Chief Justice Burger. Justice Powell filed a separate dissent.

(2) *Statutory Rape.* In *Michael M. v. Superior Court of Sonoma County*, 450 U.S. 464 (1981), the Court upheld a California statutory rape law that imposed criminal liability only on males who had had sexual intercourse with a female under the age of 18 years. Petitioner, a 17 1/2 year-old male charged with violation of the statute, challenged the constitutionality of the statute on equal protection grounds. The Court

---

[2] Nevertheless, "deference does not mean abdication."

[3] Justice White assumed that barring women from combat did not violate the Constitution, as their exclusion from combat was not contested.

(5-4) upheld the statute, asserting that gender-based classifications are not "inherently suspect," subject only to the traditional minimum rationality test applied with "a sharper focus when gender classifications are challenged."

Justice Rehnquist's opinion concluded that the classification was "sufficiently related to the State's objectives." He wrote, "young men and young women are not similarly situated with respect to the problems and risks of sexual intercourse. Only women can become pregnant and they suffer disproportionately the profound physical, emotional, and psychological consequences of sexual activity." By imposing criminal sanctions on men alone, the statute provided "an additional deterrent for men (since the risk of pregnancy itself constitutes a substantial deterrent for young females). The age of the man is irrelevant, since young men are as capable as older men of inflicting the harm sought to be prevented." Justice Blackmun concurred in the judgment. Justices Brennan, Marshall, and Stevens dissented.

(3) *Parentage.* In *Nguyen v. INS*, 533 U.S. 53 (2001), the Court upheld a federal statute requiring a father who is a U.S. citizen to follow more complex procedures than a mother who is a U.S. citizen to establish the U.S. citizenship of a nonmarital child. Nguyen and his father claimed that 8 U.S.C. § 1409(a) impermissibly discriminated against fathers.

Writing for a 5-4 majority, Justice Kennedy explained that § 1409(a)(4) requires a citizen father to take "one of three affirmative steps" in conferring citizenship on a nonmarital child by his 18th birthday: "legitimation; a declaration of paternity under oath by the father; or a court order of paternity." In contrast, when the child's mother is a U.S. citizen at the time of the birth, the child automatically receives her nationality if she has previously lived in the United States for a year. "[U]nlike the unmarried mother, the unmarried father as a general rule cannot control where the child will be born."

The classification served " 'important governmental objectives.' " Consequently, the Court did not decide whether it should apply a more deferential standard to review Congress' immigration and naturalization power. The first important government interest involved assuring the existence of a blood relationship between the citizen parent and child. Cost, reliability, and availability of DNA tests may have been factors in deciding not to require such tests. Congress drew a "reasonable conclusion" by specifying several alternatives to establish paternity. As birth establishes motherhood, "it is unremarkable that Congress did not require the same affirmative steps of mothers." To require gender neutral terms to ensure a biological relationship "would be to insist on a hollow neutrality."

The second important government interest involved ensuring that "the real, everyday ties" exist "between child and citizen parent and, in turn, the United States." While birth allows the mother to develop such a relationship naturally, the father may not even know the child exists. A DNA test does not establish such a relationship. "There is nothing irrational or improper in the recognition that at the moment of birth . . . the mother's knowledge of the child and the fact of parenthood have been established in a way not guaranteed in the case of the unwed father. This is not a stereotype."

Congress' means must be evaluated in light of the vast number of people who seek U.S. citizenship. "The fit between the means and the important end is 'exceedingly persuasive,' " a test which requires "showing at least that the classification serves 'important governmental objectives and that the discriminatory means employed' are 'substantially related to the achievement of those objectives.' " The additional requirements imposed on fathers were not onerous and could be completed within 18 years. For instance, a father could establish his child's citizenship by simply acknowledging his paternity in writing and under oath, "hardly a substantial burden." At bottom, the law simply acknowledged "basic biological differences" between men and women in the birth process.

Justice Scalia filed a concurring opinion, joined by Justice Thomas.

Justice O'Connor dissented, joined by Justices Souter, Ginsburg, and Breyer. Requiring "both mothers and fathers to prove parenthood" by DNA testing within a specified time after birth was a gender neutral alternative to the statute. The majority seemed to apply the rational basis test rather than the heightened level of scrutiny applied to gender-based discrimination claims. The statute and the majority assume "that mothers are significantly more likely than fathers . . . to develop caring relationships with their children." In contrast "to this stereotype," Nguyen's father has raised him, and he "apparently has lacked a relationship with his mother."

MISSISSIPPI UNIVERSITY FOR WOMEN v. HOGAN
458 U.S. 718, 102 S. Ct. 3331, 73 L. Ed. 2d 1090 (1982)

JUSTICE O'CONNOR delivered the opinion of the Court.

This case presents the narrow issue of whether a state statute that excludes males from enrolling in a state-supported professional nursing school violates the Equal Protection Clause of the Fourteenth Amendment.

I

The facts are not in dispute. . . . Mississippi University for Women (MUW), has from its inception limited its enrollment to women.[4]

In 1971, MUW established a School of Nursing. . . .

Respondent, Joe Hogan, is a registered nurse but does not hold a baccalaureate degree in nursing. . . . In 1979, Hogan applied for admission to the MUW School of Nursing's baccalaureate program. Although he was otherwise qualified, he was denied admission to the School of Nursing solely because of his sex. . . .

II

. . . Because the challenged policy expressly discriminates among applicants on the basis of gender, it is subject to scrutiny under the Equal Protection Clause of the Fourteenth Amendment. . . . That this statute discriminates against males rather than against females does not exempt it from scrutiny or reduce the standard of review. *Caban v. Mohammed*; *Orr v. Orr*. Our decisions also establish that the party seeking to uphold a statute that classifies individuals on the basis of their gender must carry the burden of showing an "exceedingly persuasive justification" for the classification. . . . The burden is met only by showing at least that the classification serves "important governmental objectives and that the discriminatory means employed" are "substantially related to the achievement of those objectives." . . .

. . . Care must be taken in ascertaining whether the statutory objective itself reflects archaic and stereotypic notions. Thus, if the statutory objective is to exclude or "protect" members of one gender because they are presumed to suffer from an inherent handicap or to be innately inferior, the objective itself is illegitimate. . . .

If the State's objective is legitimate and important, we next determine whether the

---

[4] [Court's footnote 1] . . . Mississippi maintains no other single-sex public university or college. Thus, we are not faced with the question of whether States can provide "separate but equal" undergraduate institutions for males and females.

requisite direct, substantial relationship between objective and means is present. The purpose of requiring that close relationship is to assure that the validity of a classification is determined through reasoned analysis rather than through the mechanical application of traditional, often inaccurate, assumptions about the proper roles of men and women. . . . [5]

III

A

The State's primary justification for maintaining the single-sex admissions policy of MUW's School of Nursing is that it compensates for discrimination against women and, therefore, constitutes educational affirmative action.[6] As applied to the School of Nursing, we find the State's argument unpersuasive.

In limited circumstances, a gender-based classification favoring one sex can be justified if it intentionally and directly assists members of the sex that is disproportionately burdened. *See Schlesinger v. Ballard.* However, we consistently have emphasized that "the mere recitation of a benign, compensatory purpose is not an automatic shield which protects against any inquiry into the actual purposes underlying a statutory scheme." *Weinberger v. Wiesenfeld.* The same searching analysis must be made, regardless of whether the State's objective is to eliminate family controversy, *Reed v. Reed,* to achieve administrative efficiency, *Frontiero v. Richardson,* or to balance the burdens borne by males and females.

It is readily apparent that a State can evoke a compensatory purpose to justify an otherwise discriminatory classification only if members of the gender benefited by the classification actually suffer a disadvantage related to the classification. We considered such a situation in *Califano v. Webster,* which involved a challenge to a statutory classification that allowed women to eliminate more low-earning years than men for purposes of computing Social Security retirement benefits. Although the effect of the classification was to allow women higher monthly benefits than were available to men with the same earning history, we upheld the statutory scheme, noting that it took into account that women "as such have been unfairly hindered from earning as much as men" and "work[ed] directly to remedy" the resulting economic disparity. . . .

A similar pattern of discrimination against women influenced our decision in *Schlesinger v. Ballard.* There, we considered a federal statute that granted female Naval officers a 13-year tenure of commissioned service before mandatory discharge, but accorded male officers only a nine-year tenure. We recognized that, because women

---

[5] [Court's footnote 12] *See, e.g., Kirchberg v. Feenstra,* 450 U.S. 455 (1981) (statute granted only husbands the right to manage and dispose of jointly owned property without the spouse's consent); *Wengler v. Druggists Mutual Insurance Co.* (statute required a widower, but not a widow, to show he was incapacitated from earning to recover benefits for a spouse's death under workers' compensation laws); *Orr v. Orr* (only men could be ordered to pay alimony following divorce); *Craig v. Boren* (women could purchase "nonintoxicating" beer at a younger age than could men); *Stanton v. Stanton, supra* (women reached majority at an earlier age than did men); *Weinberger v. Wiesenfeld* (widows, but not widowers, could collect survivors' benefits under the Social Security Act); *Frontiero v. Richardson* (determination of spouse's dependency based upon gender of member of armed forces claiming dependency benefits); *Reed v. Reed* (statute preferred men to women as administrators of estates).

[6] [Court's footnote 13] . . . Apparently, the impetus for founding MUW came not from a desire to provide women with advantages superior to those offered men, but rather from a desire to provide white women in Mississippi access to state-supported higher learning. . . .

were barred from combat duty, they had had fewer opportunities for promotion than had their male counterparts. . . .

In sharp contrast, Mississippi has made no showing that women lacked opportunities to obtain training in the field of nursing. . . . In fact, in 1970, the year before the School of Nursing's first class enrolled, women earned 94 percent of the nursing baccalaureate degrees conferred in Mississippi and 98.6 percent of the degrees earned nationwide. . . .

Rather than compensate for discriminatory barriers faced by women, MUW's policy of excluding males from admission to the School of Nursing tends to perpetuate the stereotyped view of nursing as an exclusively woman's job. . . . Thus, we conclude that, although the State recited a "benign, compensatory purpose," it failed to establish that the alleged objective is the actual purpose underlying the discriminatory classification.

The policy is invalid also because it fails the second part of the equal protection test, for the State has made no showing that the gender-based classification is substantially and directly related to its proposed compensatory objective. To the contrary, MUW's policy of permitting men to attend classes as auditors fatally undermines its claim that women, at least those in the School of Nursing, are adversely affected by the presence of men.

. . . The uncontroverted record reveals that admitting men to nursing classes does not affect teaching style, . . . that the presence of men in the classroom would not affect the performance of the female nursing students. . . . In sum, the record in this case is flatly inconsistent with the claim that excluding men from the School of Nursing is necessary to reach any of MUW's educational goals.

Thus, considering both the asserted interest and the relationship between the interest and the methods used by the State, we conclude that the State has fallen far short of establishing the "exceedingly persuasive justification" needed to sustain the gender-based classification. Accordingly, we hold that MUW's policy of denying males the right to enroll for credit in its School of Nursing violates the Equal Protection Clause of the Fourteenth Amendment.

B

In an additional attempt to justify its exclusion of men from MUW's School of Nursing, the State contends that MUW is the direct beneficiary "of specific congressional legislation which, on its face, permits the institution to exist as it has in the past." . . . The argument is based upon the language of § 901(a) in Title IX of the Education Amendments of 1972, 20 U.S.C. § 1681(a). Although § 901(a) prohibits gender discrimination in education programs that receive federal financial assistance, subsection 5 exempts the admissions policies of undergraduate institutions "that traditionally and continually from [their] establishment [have] had a policy of admitting only students of one sex" from the general prohibition. . . .

Even if Congress envisioned a constitutional exemption, the State's argument would fail. Section 5 of the Fourteenth Amendment gives Congress broad power indeed to enforce the command of the Amendment . . . Congress' power under § 5, however, "is limited to adopting measures to enforce the guarantees of the Amendment; § 5 grants Congress no power to restrict, abrogate, or dilute these guarantees." *Katzenbach v. Morgan*, 384 U.S. 641, 651 n.10 (1966). Although we give deference to congressional decisions and classifications, neither Congress nor a State can validate a law that denies the rights guaranteed by the Fourteenth Amendment. . . .

CHIEF JUSTICE BURGER, dissenting.

. . . Since the Court's opinion relies heavily on its finding that women have traditionally dominated the nursing profession, . . . it suggests that a State might well be justified in maintaining, for example, the option of an all-women's business school or liberal arts program.

JUSTICE BLACKMUN, dissenting.

[R]espondent Hogan "wants in" at this particular location in his home city of Columbus. It is not enough that his state of Mississippi offers baccalaureate programs in nursing open to males at Jackson and at Hattiesburg. Mississippi thus has not closed the doors of its educational system to males like Hogan. . . .

While the Court purports to write narrowly, . . . the Court's ruling today . . . places in constitutional jeopardy any state-supported educational institution that confines its student body in any area to members of one sex, even though the State elsewhere provides an equivalent program to the complaining applicant. . . .

I hope that we do not lose all values that some think are worthwhile (and are not based on differences of race or religion) and relegate ourselves to needless conformity. . . .

JUSTICE POWELL, with whom JUSTICE REHNQUIST joins, dissenting.

The Court's opinion bows deeply to conformity. Left without honor — indeed, held unconstitutional — is an element of diversity that has characterized much of American education and enriched much of American life. The Court in effect holds today that no State now may provide even a single institution of higher learning open only to women students. . . .

Coeducation, historically, is a novel educational theory. From grade school through high school, college, and graduate and professional training, much of the nation's population during much of our history has been educated in sexually segregated classrooms. At the college level, for instance, until recently some of the most prestigious colleges and universities — including most of the Ivy League — had long histories of single-sex education. . . .

The sexual segregation of students has been a reflection of, rather than an imposition upon, the preference of those subject to the policy. It cannot be disputed, for example, that the highly qualified women attending the leading women's colleges could have earned admission to virtually any college of their choice. . . .

. . . In my view, the Court errs seriously by assuming — without argument or discussion — that the equal protection standard generally applicable to sex discrimination is appropriate here. That standard was designed to free women from "archaic and overbroad generalizations. . . . " *Schlesinger v. Ballard*, 419 U.S. 498, 508 (1975). In no previous case have we applied it to invalidate state efforts to *expand* women's choices. Nor are there prior sex discrimination decisions by this Court in which a male plaintiff, as in this case, had the choice of an equal benefit. . . . [7]

. . . The record in this case reflects that MUW has a historic position in the State's educational system dating back to 1884. . . .

. . . [A]s the Court itself acknowledges, MUW's School of Nursing was not created until 1971 — about 90 years after the single-sex campus itself was founded. This hardly

---

[7] [Court's footnote 9] . . . Sexual segregation in education differs from the tradition, typified by the decision in *Plessy v. Ferguson*, of "separate but equal" *racial* segregation. It was characteristic of racial segregation that segregated facilities were offered, not as alternatives to increase the choices available to blacks, but as the *sole* alternative. . . .

supports a link between nursing as a woman's profession and MUW's single-sex admission policy. . . . The School of Nursing makes up only one part — a relatively small part — of MUW's diverse modern university campus and curriculum. . . .

A distinctive feature of America's tradition has been respect for diversity. . . . A constitutional case is held to exist solely because one man found it inconvenient to travel to any of the other institutions made available to him by the State of Mississippi. . . .

NOTES

(1) *All-male Organizations.* In *Roberts v. United States Jaycees*, 468 U.S. 609 (1984), a unanimous Court (Chief Justice Burger and Justice Blackmun not participating) rejected a "freedom of association" defense by the United States Jaycees, an all-male private organization, against the application of a Minnesota human rights law to the organization's discriminatory admission practices. Justice Brennan concluded that the state's interest in eradicating discrimination against women was sufficiently compelling to justify intrusion on the male members' constitutionally-based right of freedom of association. In *Board of Directors of Rotary International v. Rotary Club of Duarte*, 481 U.S. 537 (1987), a unanimous Court (Justices Blackmun and O'Connor not participating) rejected constitutional challenges to the application to a local Rotary Club of a California statute that barred gender discrimination "in all business establishments whatsoever." Membership in a Rotary Club did not involve the type of intimate association that is an element of "liberty" protected by the Fourteenth Amendment. In *Roberts* and *Duarte*, whatever rights of expressive association that may be protected by the First Amendment were overcome by the State's compelling interest in assuring equal access to women "in the acquisition of leadership skills and business contacts." For further discussion of these cases, see § 12.05.

(2) *All-male Clubs.* In *New York State Club Association v. City of New York*, 487 U.S. 1 (1988), the Court unanimously rejected a facial challenge to a New York City law that prohibits discrimination in certain private clubs. A club is subject to the law if it has more than 400 members, provides regular meal service, and receives payment for dues, the use of its facilities, or for meals and beverages "for or on behalf of nonmembers for the furtherance of trade or business." Although this provision was part of the City's overall Human Rights Law and was, therefore, applicable to discrimination against minorities as well as women, the principal focus of opposition to the law came from clubs that barred women from membership.

Relying on the *Rotary* and *Roberts* decisions, the Court held that a facial challenge could not be sustained since the law "certainly could be constitutionally applied at least to some of the large clubs." Justice White's majority opinion recognized that there might conceivably be some clubs with the characteristics specified in the law that might be able to assert claims of "intimate" or "expressive" association, but many of the large clubs covered by the law "are not of this kind. We could hardly hold otherwise on the record before us, which contains no specific evidence on the characteristics of any club covered by the Law." Justices O'Connor, Kennedy, and Scalia concurred.

(3) *Middle-tier Analysis.* Some commentators have criticized the application of middle-tier analysis to gender discrimination cases. *See, e.g.,* Sager, *Some Observations About Race, Sex, and Equal Protection*, 59 TUL. L. REV. 928, 956–57 (1985) ("Middle-tier analysis can be seen as the means by which the Court contends with classifications that materially benefit women but retard their progress toward categorical equality by lending symbolic support to the framework of belief and value that has denied them equality. The status of these classifications is complicated both by the Court's failure to reach an enduring consensus that their symbolic impact is a matter of constitutional concern and by the possibility that some laws materially benefiting women may do more

good than harm to the ultimate goal of categorical equality.").

J.E.B. v. ALABAMA, 511 U.S. 127 (1994). In *J.E.B.*, the Court held that the Equal Protection Clause forbids exercising peremptory challenges based on gender. In a paternity suit, the jury pool consisted of 12 males and 24 females. Of these prospective jurors, two males and one female were excused by the Court for cause. Alabama then used nine of its ten premptory challenges to strike men, while J.E.B. used ten of its eleven challenges to strike women. The resulting jury was entirely female.

Justice Blackmun wrote for a 6-3 majority. Blackstone said that women should be excluded from juries under "the doctrine of *propter defectum secus*, literally, the 'defect of the sex.'" Early on, our courts thought that women were "too fragile and virginal to withstand the polluted courtroom atmosphere."[8]

In *Taylor v. Louisiana*, 419 U.S. 522, 530 (1975), the Court invalidated a system that required men to serve on juries, while only allowing women to volunteer. The diverse and representative character of the jury must be maintained. *Taylor* was a Sixth Amendment case.

The plaintiff, attempting to distinguish *Batson v. Kentucky*, § 8.03[5], which prohibited race-based peremptory challenges in civil actions, argued that gender discrimination had never been as severe as racial discrimination had. Justice Blackmun responded that "with respect to jury service, African-Americans and women share a history of total exclusion, a history which came to an end for women many years after the embarrassing chapter in our history came to an end for African-Americans. We need not determine, however, whether women or racial minorities have suffered more at the hands of discriminatory state actors."

When the state makes a gender-based classification, the only question is "whether discrimination on the basis of gender in jury selection substantially furthers the State's legitimate interest in achieving a fair and impartial trial." In this case, Alabama attempted to justify its selection of a female jury on its historically based perception that female jurors might be more responsive to the mother in a paternity suit. This argument, Blackmun stated, assumes that stereotypes "that would be deemed impermissible if made on the basis of race are somehow permissible when made on the basis of gender."

Race- or gender-based discrimination in jury selection harms "the litigants, the community, and the individual jurors who are wrongfully excluded from participation in the judicial process." Moreover, when state actors strike jurors based on gender stereotypes, the prejudicial views about the respective abilities of men and women are perpetuated.

Parties still may exercise their peremptory challenges to remove any group or class of individuals normally subject to "rational basis" review. Moreover, peremptory challenges based on characteristics that are "disproportionately associated with one gender could be appropriate, absent a showing of pretext." For example, challenging all persons who have had military experience would disproportionately affect men at this time, while challenging all persons employed as nurses would disproportionately affect women.

"As with race-based *Batson* claims, a party alleging gender discrimination must make a *prima facie* showing of intentional discrimination before the party exercising the challenge is required to explain the basis for the strike. When an explanation is required, it need not rise to the level of a 'for cause' challenge; rather, it must merely be

---

[8] In 1946, the Supreme Court in *Ballard v. United States*, 329 U.S. 187 (1946), "first questioned the fundamental fairness of denying women the right to serve on juries."

based on a juror characteristic other than gender, and the proffered explanation may not be pretextual."

Justice O'Connor's concurring opinion sought to limit the reach of the holding solely to the government's use of gender-based peremptory strikes, although she predicted that her view would not prevail. Justice O'Connor feared that this case will further increase the number of cases in which "jury selection — once a sideshow — will become part of the main event." Additionally, more biased persons may be allowed onto the juries due to the difficulty of articulating a "gender-neutral explanation." Peremptory challenges, an important and ancient tool used by lawyers to protect their clients, are becoming more like challenges for cause. "[I]n certain cases a person's gender and resulting life experience will be relevant to his or her view of the case."

Justice Kennedy concurred in the judgment. While there is no doubt that the Equal Protection Clause prohibits peremptory challenges based solely on sex, it is also important to recognize that "a juror sits not as a representative of a racial or sexual group but as an individual citizen."

Chief Justice Rehnquist dissented. As reflected in the different levels of scrutiny for race and gender discrimination, racial groups comprise a numerical minority, whereas the population is nearly equally divided between men and women. "The two sexes differ, both biologically and, to a diminishing extent, in experience. It is not 'merely stereotyping' to say that these differences may produce a difference in outlook which is brought to the jury room. Accordingly, use of peremptory challenges on the basis of sex is generally not the sort of derogatory and invidious act which peremptory challenges directed at black jurors may be."

Justice Scalia, joined by Chief Justice Rehnquist and Justice Thomas, dissented. Justice Scalia felt that the Court should place more emphasis on "the perceptions of experienced litigators" than the lack of statistical evidence of sex as a predictive factor. Moreover, as peremptory challenges extend to all groups, no one group is denied equal protection. "This case is a perfect example of how the system as a whole is even-handed." While the government struck all men and one woman, defendant struck all women and one man. This pattern "displays not a systemic sex-based animus but each side's desire to get a jury favorably disposed to its case." Women are struck from juries not because of their lack of competence, but rather because of "doubt that they are well disposed to the striking party's case." This practice contrasts with the discrimination and dishonor "that infects race-based peremptory strikes." Considerable damage has been done to the peremptory challenge system, "which loses its whole character when 'reasons' for strikes must be given."

NOTE

For an interesting perspective on the jury selection process, see Vikram David Amar, *Jury Service as Political Participation Akin to Voting*, 80 Cornell L. Rev, 203, 259 (1995). ("Rights of political participation are logically and historically distinct from, and in some ways more basic than, individual freedoms from government intrusion. The criteria by which a person or group may be excluded legitimately from partaking in the '[second] most significant opportunity to participate in the democratic process' are thus of obvious importance to our constitutional democracy. Yet we lack a coherent theory about which groups count and why.").

UNITED STATES v. VIRGINIA, 518 U.S. 515 (1996). In *Virginia*, the Court prohibited the State of "Virginia from reserving exclusively to men the unique educational opportunities" that the Virginia Military Institute (VMI) afforded. VMI's "distinctive mission is to produce 'citizen-soldiers,' men prepared for leadership in civilian life and in military service." Assigning prime place to character development,

VMI uses an 'adversative method' modeled on English public schools," and strives to "instill physical and mental discipline" and a "strong moral code" in its cadets. "VMI has notably succeeded in its mission to produce leaders; among its alumni are military generals, Members of Congress, and business executives." Its alumni are successful and intensely loyal to the School.[9]

"Neither the goal of producing citizen-soldiers nor VMI's implementing methodology is inherently unsuitable to women."

"VMI's program is directed at preparation for both 'military and civilian life'; 'only about 15% of VMI cadets enter career military service.'" VMI's "'citizen-soldiers'" are produced "through an 'adversative, or doubting, model of education' which features 'physical rigor, mental stress, absolute equality of treatment, absence of privacy, minute regulation of behavior, and indoctrination in desirable values.'"

Due to the constant surveillance of barracks, cadets have no privacy; "they wear uniforms, eat together in the mess hall, and regularly participate in drills." Freshman are "exposed to the rat line, 'an extreme form of the adversative model,' comparable in intensity to Marine Corps boot camp. Tormenting and punishing, the rat line bonds" VMI freshman together with each other and with upperclassmates.[10] "'Women have no opportunity anywhere to gain the benefits of [the system of education at VMI].'"

In 1990, a female high-school student's failure to gain admission caused the United States to sue "Virginia and VMI, alleging that VMI's exclusively male admission policy violated the Equal Protection Clause." The District Court found that in the two years prior to this lawsuit, VMI failed to respond to 347 inquiries by females. "VMI could 'achieve at least 10% female enrollment a sufficient "critical mass" to provide the female cadets with a positive educational experience.'" The District Court also "established that 'some women are capable of all of the individual activities required of VMI cadets.' In addition, experts agreed that if VMI admitted women, the VMI ROTC experience would become a better training program from the perspective of the armed forces, because it would provide training in dealing with 'a mixed gender army.'" Despite these findings the "District Court ruled in favor of VMI" based on the idea "that education in 'a single-gender environment, be it male or female,' yields substantial benefits."

The Fourth Circuit Court of Appeals reversed and remanded on the issue of remedy. The Court of Appeals "accepted the District Court's finding that 'at least these three aspects of VMI's program physical training, the absence of privacy, and the adversative approach would be materially affected by coeducation.'" The Court of Appeals suggested that the State: "[a]dmit women to VMI; establish parallel institutions or programs; or abandon state support, leaving VMI free to pursue its policies as a private institution." The Supreme Court denied certiorari.

Virginia pursued the Fourth Circuit's second suggestion and "proposed a parallel program for women: Virginia Women's Institute for Leadership (VWIL). The 4-year, state-sponsored undergraduate program would be located at Mary Baldwin College, a private liberal arts school for women, and would be open, initially, to about 25 to 30 students. Although VWIL would share VMI's mission to produce 'citizen-soldiers' the VWIL program would differ, as does Mary Baldwin College, from VMI in academic offerings, methods of education, and financial resources."[11]

---

[9] "VMI has the largest per-student endowment of all undergraduate institutions in the Nation."

[10] There is a "hierarchical 'class system' of privileges and responsibilities, a 'dyke system' for assigning a senior class mentor to each entering class 'rat.'"

[11] "The average combined SAT score of entrants at Mary Baldwin is about 100 points lower than the score for VMI freshman. Mary Baldwin's faculty holds 'significantly fewer Ph.D.'s than the faculty at VMI,' and

The VMIL program was designed by a Task Force, composed of experts in the field of female college education. These experts "determined that a military model would be 'wholly inappropriate' for VWIL." Students attending VMIL "would participate in ROTC programs and a newly established, 'largely ceremonial' Virginia Corps of Cadets, but the VWIL House would not have a military format, and VWIL would not require its students to eat meals together or to wear uniforms during the school day. In lieu of VMI's adversative method, the VWIL Task Force favored 'a cooperative method which reinforces self-esteem.' "

"Virginia represented that it will provide equal financial support for in-state VWIL students and VMI cadets, and the VMI foundation agreed to supply a $5.4625 million endowment for the VWIL program. Mary Baldwin's own endowment is about $19 million; VMI's is $ 131 million. Mary Baldwin will add $35 million to its endowment based on future commitments; VMI will add $220 million.

The District Court "decided the plan met the requirements of the Equal Protection Clause." A divided Court of Appeals affirmed. The Court of Appeals noted that "the adversative method vital to a VMI education 'has never been tolerated in a sexually heterogeneous environment.' "

Writing for a 7-1 majority, Justice Ginsburg stated that the case involved two issues. "First, does Virginia's exclusion of women from the educational opportunities provided by VMI extraordinary opportunities for military training and civilian leadership development deny to women 'capable of all the individual activities required of VMI cadets,' the equal protection of the laws . . . ? Second, if VMI's 'unique' situation as Virginia's sole single-sex public institution of higher education offends the Constitution's equal protection principle, what is the remedial requirement?"

"[T]he reviewing court must determine whether the [state's] justification [for gender discrimination] is 'exceedingly persuasive.' The State must show 'at least that the [challenged] classification serves important governmental objectives and that the discriminatory means employed' are 'substantially related to the achievement of those objectives.' The justification must be genuine, not hypothesized or invented post hoc in response to litigation. And it must not rely on overbroad generalizations about the different talents, capacities, or preferences of males and females."

"Supposed 'inherent differences' are no longer accepted as a ground for race or national origin classifications. *See Loving v. Virginia*, 388 U.S. 1 (1967). Physical differences between men and women, however, are enduring: 'The two sexes are not fungible; a community made up exclusively of one [sex] is different from a community composed of both'. . . . Sex classifications may be used to compensate women 'for particular economic disabilities [they have] suffered,' to 'promote equal employment opportunity,' to advance full development of the talent and capacities of our Nation's people.[12] But such classifications may not be used, as they once were, to create or perpetuate the legal, social, and economic inferiority of women."

Virginia "asserts two justifications in defense of VMI's exclusion of women: 'single-sex education provides important educational benefits and promotes diversity in

---

receives significantly lower salaries." In contrast to VMI's "degrees in liberal arts, the sciences, and engineering, Mary Baldwin, at the time of trial, offered only bachelor of arts degrees.". . . "A VWIL student seeking to earn an engineering degree could gain one, without public support, by attending Washington University in St. Louis, Missouri, for two years, paying the required private tuition."

[12] Justice Ginsburg acknowledged that "the mission of some single-sex schools 'to dissipate, rather than perpetuate, traditional gender classifications.' We do not question the State's prerogative evenhandedly to support diverse educational opportunities. We address specifically and only an educational opportunity available only at Virginia's premier military institute, the State's sole single sex public university or college."

educational approaches;' and 'the unique VMI method of character development and leadership training,' the school's adversative approach, would have to be modified were VMI to admit women."

Justice Ginsburg acknowledged that single-sex education could be beneficial to some students and diverse educational approaches "can serve the public good."[13]

However, " '[b]enign' " justifications for gender-based discrimination must reflect actual governmental purposes rather than post hoc rationalizations. "Neither recent nor distant history bears out Virginia's alleged pursuit of diversity through single-sex educational options." During the time period in which VMI was established, higher educational opportunities for women were "scarcely contemplated."[14] VMI followed the no women policy initially installed by the University of Virginia.

Justice Ginsburg also found Virginia's second justification unacceptable. The State asserts that coeducation would "transform, indeed 'destroy,' " VMI's adversative method. "The District Court forecast from expert witness testimony, and the Court of Appeals accepted, that coeducation would materially affect 'at least these three aspects of VMI's program — physical training, the absence of privacy, and the adversative approach.' " It was uncontested that "accommodations, primarily in arranging housing assignments and physical training programs for female cadets," would be needed. It is also undisputed, however, that " 'the VMI methodology could be used to educate women.' " Likewise, expert testimony established that some women " 'are capable of all of the individual activities required of VMI cadets.' " As the Court of Appeals summarized, " 'neither the goal of producing citizen soldiers, VMI's raison d'etre, nor VMI's implementing methodology is inherently unsuitable to women.' "

States cannot "exclude qualified individuals based on 'fixed notions concerning the roles and abilities of males and females.' " While it may be assumed that the majority of "women would not choose VMI's adversative method," it is also likely "that 'many men would not want to be educated in such an environment' " either.

Justice Ginsburg found that "[t]he notion that admission of women would downgrade VMI's stature, destroy the adversative system and, with it, even the school, is a judgment hardly proved, a prediction hardly different from other 'self-fulfilling prophecies' once routinely used to deny rights or opportunities. When women first sought admission to the bar and access to legal education, concerns of the same order were expressed."[15] Women's success and participation in the nation's federal military academies and forces "indicate that Virginia's fears for the future of VMI may not be solidly grounded."[16]

---

[13] The District Court noted that the benefits of single-sex education apparently are greater for women than men. " 'The pluralistic argument for preserving all-male colleges is uncomfortably similar to the pluralistic argument for preserving all-white colleges . . . The all-male college would be relatively easy to defend if it emerged from a world in which women were established as fully equal to men. But it does not. It is therefore likely to be a witting or unwitting device for preserving tacit assumptions of male superiority.' "

[14] *See* E. Clarke, Sex in Education (1873), ('identical education of the two sexes is a crime before God and humanity, that physiology protests against, and that experience weeps over'); C. Meigs, Females and Their Diseases (1848) (after five or six weeks of "mental and educational discipline," a healthy woman would "lose the habit of menstruation" and suffer numerous ills as a result of depriving her body for the sake of her mind).

[15] Historically, the same argument Virginia asserted has been made on behalf of federal military academies. Likewise, the notion of "men and women as partners in the study of medicine" was previously resisted. "More recently, women seeking careers in policing encountered resistance based on fears that their presence would 'undermine male solidarity.' "

[16] [Court's footnote 13] "Women cadets have graduated at the top of their class at every federal military academy."

The State's justification for excluding all women from 'citizen-soldier' training for which some are qualified, in any event, cannot rank as 'exceedingly persuasive,' as we have explained and applied the standard."

Turning to the remedy fashioned by Virginia, Justice Ginsburg held that "the Mary Baldwin VMIL program" failed to "cure the constitutional violation." To cure the constitutional violation, this proposal "must be shaped to place persons unconstitutionally denied an opportunity or advantage in the position they would have occupied in the absence of [discrimination]". The U.S. Code required the same academic and other standards for the Military, Naval, and Air Force Academies, " 'except for those minimum essential adjustments' " that physiological differences require. "Virginia, in sum, while maintaining VMI for men only, has failed to provide any 'comparable single-gender women's institution.' Instead, the Commonwealth has created a VWIL program fairly appraised as a 'pale shadow' of VMI in terms of the range of curricular choices and faculty stature, funding, prestige, alumni support and influence."

The proposed "VWIL solution is reminiscent of the remedy Texas proposed 50 years ago . . . *See Sweatt v. Painter*, 339 U.S. 629 (1950). Reluctant to admit African Americans to its flagship University of Texas Law School, the State set up a separate school." Because of "marked differences" between the institutions, the Court unanimously required Texas to "admit African Americans to the University of Texas Law School."

In conclusion, "Virginia's remedy does not match the constitutional violation; the State has shown no 'exceedingly persuasive justification' for" depriving women of a VMI education.

Chief Justice Rehnquist concurred in the judgment. Stating the applicable standard for gender classifications, *Craig v. Boren*, requires that they " 'must serve important governmental objectives and must be substantially related to the achievement of those objectives.' . . . While the majority adheres to this test today, it also says that the State must demonstrate an 'exceedingly persuasive justification' to support a gender-based classification. It is unfortunate that the Court thereby introduces an element of uncertainty respecting the appropriate test."

"While terms like 'important governmental objective' and 'substantially related' are hardly models of precision, they have more content and specificity than does the phrase 'exceedingly persuasive justification.' That phrase is best confined, as it was first used, as an observation on the difficulty of meeting the applicable test, not as a formulation of the test itself."

The Chief Justice maintained that the State could have exercised more options than the Court implied to avoid an equal protection violation. "The Court cites, without expressly approving it, a statement from the opinion of the dissenting judge in the Court of Appeals, to the effect that the State could have 'simultaneously opened single-gender undergraduate institutions having substantially comparable curricular and extra-curricular programs, funding, physical plant, administration and support services, and faculty and library resources.' If this statement is thought to exclude other possibilities, it is too stringent a requirement.

"Had Virginia made a genuine effort to devote comparable public resources to a facility for women, and followed through on such a plan, it might have avoided an equal protection violation." Moreover, had "the State provided the kind of support for the private women's schools that it provides for VMI, this may have been a very different case."

Lastly, the Chief Justice noted that Virginia did not violate the Equal Protection

Clause merely by excluding women, but rather, by maintaining "an all-men school without providing any much less a comparable institution for women." For this reason, "the remedy should not necessarily require either the admission of women to VMI, or the creation of a VMI clone for women." The remedy would be sufficient "if the two institutions offered the same quality of education and were of the same overall calibre."

Justice Scalia dissented. "Today the Court shuts down an institution that has served the people of the Commonwealth of Virginia with pride and distinction for over a century and a half." The Court "rejects the finding that there exist 'gender-based developmental differences' supporting Virginia's restriction of the 'adversative' method to only a men's institution, and the finding that the all-male composition of the Virginia Military Institute (VMI) is essential to that institution's character."

For Justice Scalia, " 'when a practice not expressly prohibited by the text of the Bill of Rights bears the endorsement of a long tradition of open, widespread, and unchallenged use that dates back to the beginning of the Republic, we have no proper basis for striking it down.' " The single-sex policy of VMI reflects the traditions of many other government-funded "military colleges." Moreover, from " 'grade school through high school, college, and graduate and professional training, much of the Nation's population during much of our history has been educated in sexually segregated classrooms.' "

The Court also failed to apply the established standard for sex-based classifications of whether law is " 'substantially related to an important governmental objective.' " Instead, it asks whether Virginia had an " 'exceedingly persuasive justification' "

Indeed, *United States v. Carolene Products Co.*, § 7.03, would apply a rationality test to such classifications. Justice Scalia noted that "[i]t is hard to consider women a 'discrete and insular minority' unable to employ the 'political processes ordinarily to be relied upon,' when they constitute a majority of the electorate. And the suggestion that they are incapable of exerting that political power smacks of the same paternalism that the Court so roundly condemns."

Applying traditional middle-tier scrutiny in this case, "Virginia has an important state interest in providing effective college education for its citizens. . . . 'One empirical study in evidence, not questioned by any expert, demonstrates that single-sex colleges provide better educational experiences than coeducational institutions.' "

Justice Scalia continued: the "Court . . . never says that a single finding of the District Court is clearly erroneous in favor of the Justices' own view of the world." The findings of the "two courts below" suggest that the Court errs in concluding that admitting women would not fundamentally change VMI. "It is worth noting that none of the United States' own experts in the remedial phase of this case was willing to testify that VMI's adversative method was an appropriate methodology for educating women."

Justice Scalia found that the Court's decision effectively holds that "single-sex public education is unconstitutional."

NOTE

For some interesting perspectives on the VMI decision, see Mary Anne Case, "*The Very Stereotype the Law Condemns*": *Constitutional Sex Discrimination Law as a Quest for Perfect Proxies*, 85 CORNELL L. REV. 1447, 1448-99 (2000) ("VMI . . . marks yet another application of the rule that has governed constitutional sex discrimination cases since the early 1970s. . . . To determine whether there is unconstitutional sex discrimination, one need generally ask only two questions: 1) Is the rule or practice at issue sex-respecting, that is to say, does it distinguish on its face between males and females? and 2) Does the sex-respecting rule rely on a stereotype?").

§ 9.02   EMPLOYMENT DISCRIMINATION BASED ON GENDER

Section Note. Some of the cases in the preceding section, particularly *Frontiero v. Richardson*, relate to matters of employment discrimination. This section will consider some of the developments in the employment discrimination area since *Frontiero.*

MASSACHUSETTS v. FEENEY, 442 U.S. 256 (1979). In *Feeney,* the Court upheld the Massachusetts Veterans Preference Statute mandating that "all veterans who qualify for state civil service positions must be considered for appointment ahead of any qualifying nonveterans." Helen Feeney, a non-veteran, challenged the constitutionality of the Preference Statute, claiming that it unconstitutionally denied women equal protection by excluding them from Massachusetts civil service jobs.

While most states and the federal government offered veterans hiring preferences, the Massachusetts " 'absolute lifetime' preference, is among the most generous. It applies to all positions in the State's classified civil service, which constitute approximately 60% of the public jobs in the State." Veterans who qualify for a particular civil service job could "exercise the preference at any time and as many times as they wish."

While the preference statute "does not guarantee that a veteran will be appointed, it is obvious that the preference gives to veterans who achieve passing scores a well-nigh absolute advantage." Feeney was a public employee with 12-year tenure. During this time, Feeney took numerous civil service examinations, including one from which she received the second highest score for a position with the Board of Dental Examiners. Because of the Preference Statute, however, Feeney "was ranked sixth behind five male veterans on the Dental Examiner list; she was not certified, and a lower scoring veteran was eventually appointed." Feeney's high scores on other examinations were similarly placed behind often lower scores of veterans.

When Feeney brought this claim, "over 98% of the veterans in Massachusetts were male; only 1.8% were female. And over one-quarter of the Massachusetts population were veterans." Moreover, of 47,005 positions available in official service jobs, "43% of those hired were women, and, 57% were men. Of the women appointed, 1.8% were veterans, while 54% of the men had veteran status. A large unspecified percentage of the female employees were serving in lower paying positions for which males traditionally had not applied."

Writing for the Court, Justice Stewart noted that a statute might overtly or covertly discriminate on the basis of gender. If the classification is not gender-based, a court must determine if "the adverse effect reflects invidious gender-based discrimination." Discriminatory impact can be a useful starting point in proving the requisite purposeful discrimination.

Plaintiff challenged only the absolute lifetime preference. The District Court found that the guaranteed lifetime preference was not enacted to discriminate against women. Although few in number, female veterans also benefited from the preference. Nevertheless, the District Court found that the discriminatory impact of the preference was "too inevitable to have been unintended."

Justice Stewart rejected the presumption "that the State, by favoring veterans, intentionally incorporated into its public employment policies the panoply of sex-based and assertedly discriminatory federal laws that have prevented all but a handful of women from becoming veterans." Massachusetts had not enacted the preference to discriminate against women. While the law overtly granted veterans a preference and was thus not neutral, the preference gave a "group — perceived to be particularly deserving — a competitive head start."[17]

Finally, plaintiff argued that the State must have been aware of the discriminatory effect of the statute, under the presumption that "a person intends the natural and foreseeable consequences of his voluntary actions." Justice Stewart found that a " 'discriminatory purpose' however, implies more than intent as volition or intent as awareness of consequences."[18] This assertion implies that the State pursued a course of action " 'because of,' not merely 'in spite of,' its adverse effects upon an identifiable group."[19] Justice Stewart could find nothing in the record, however, to demonstrate a "collateral goal of keeping women in a stereotypic and predefined place in the Massachusetts Civil Service."

Justice Stevens, joined by Justice White, concurred. Justice Stevens found that the State had not intended to disadvantage women, as the veterans' preference disadvantaged large numbers of both men and women.

Justice Marshall dissented, joined by Justice Brennan. "Where the foreseeable impact of a facially neutral policy is so disproportionate, the burden should rest on the State to establish that sex-based considerations played no part in the choice of the particular legislative scheme." The legislative history of the preference statute demonstrated the State's knowledge of the statute's impact upon women and the State's "desire to mitigate that impact only with respect to certain traditionally female occupations."

NOTE

Height and Weight Requirements. Would a minimum height and weight requirement for police officers, which excluded far more women than men from eligibility, violate the Equal Protection Clause? Would such a requirement violate § 703(a)(1) of Title VII of the 1964 Civil Rights Act (the same provision involved in *Los Angeles v. Manhart*, 435 U.S. 702 (1978))? What about a rule barring the hiring of women as guards in "contact" positions in male prisons? *See Dothard v. Rawlinson*, 433 U.S. 321 (1977), and *Phillips v. Marietta Corp.*, 400 U.S. 542 (1971).

§ 9.03 GENDER DISCRIMINATION IN GOVERNMENT BENEFIT PROGRAMS

WEINBERGER v. WIESENFELD
420 U.S. 636, 95 S. Ct. 1225, 43 L. Ed. 2d 514 (1975)

JUSTICE BRENNAN delivered the opinion of the Court.

Social Security Act benefits based on the earnings of a deceased husband and father covered by the Act are payable, with some limitations, both to the widow and to the couple's minor children in her care. § 202(g) of the Social Security Act as amended, 42 U.S.C. § 402(g). Such benefits are payable on the basis of the earnings of a deceased wife and mother covered by the Act, however, only to the minor children and not to the

---

[17] Although "the enlistment policies of the armed services may well have discriminated on the basis of sex," that was "not on trial in this case."

[18] The discriminatory purpose inquiry must rely on objective factors. Governmental motives may prove themselves to be discriminatory "from the results its actions achieve, or the results they avoid."

[19] Foreseeability of consequences can help to prove discriminatory intent: foreseeable or inevitable adverse effects upon an identifiable group may imply that the adverse effects were desired. Here, however, the statute's legitimacy and history contradict any inference that may have arisen.

widower. The question in this case is whether this gender-based distinction violates the Due Process Clause of the Fifth Amendment. . . .

I

Appellee Stephen C. Wiesenfeld and Paula Polatschek were married on November 15, 1970. Paula, who worked as a teacher for five years before her marriage, continued teaching after her marriage. Each year she worked maximum social security contributions were deducted from her salary. Paula's earnings were the couple's principal source of support during the marriage, being substantially larger than those of appellee.

On June 5, 1972, Paula died in childbirth. Appellee was left with the sole responsibility for the care of their infant son, Jason Paul. Shortly after his wife's death, Stephen Wiesenfeld applied at the Social Security office in New Brunswick, N.J., for Social Security survivors' benefits for himself and his son. He did obtain benefits for his son. . . . However, appellee was told that he was not eligible for benefits for himself, because § 402(g) benefits were available only to women. If he had been a woman, he would have received the same amount as his son as long as he was not working . . . and, if working, that amount reduced by $1 for every $2 earned annually above $2,400. . . .

II

The gender-based distinction made by § 402(g) is indistinguishable from that invalidated in *Frontiero v. Richardson*. *Frontiero* involved statutes which provided the wife of a male serviceman with dependents' benefits but not the husband of a servicewoman unless she proved that she supplied more than one-half of her husband's support. . . . A virtually identical "archaic and overbroad" generalization . . . underlies the distinction drawn by § 402(g), namely, that male workers' earnings are vital to the support of their families, while the earnings of female wage earners do not significantly contribute to their families' support.

Section 402(g) was added to the Social Security Act in 1939 as one of a large number of amendments designed to "afford more adequate protection to the family as a unit." . . .

Underlying the 1939 scheme was the principle that "[u]nder a social-insurance plan the primary purpose is to pay benefits in accordance with the *probable needs* of the beneficiaries . . . in keeping with the principle of social insurance. . . . " [T]he framers of the Act legislated on the "then generally accepted presumption that a man is responsible for the support of his wife and children.". . .

Obviously, the notion that men are more likely than women to be the primary supporters of their spouses and children is not entirely without empirical support. But such a gender-based generalization cannot suffice to justify the denigration of the efforts of women who do work and whose earnings contribute significantly to their families' support.

. . . First, . . . Stephen Wiesenfeld was not given the opportunity to show, as may well have been the case, that he was dependent upon his wife for his support, or that, had his wife lived, she would have remained at work while he took over care of the child. Second, in this case social security taxes were deducted from Paula's salary during the years in which she worked. Thus, she not only failed to receive for her family the same protection which a similarly situated male worker would have received, but she also was deprived of a portion of her own earnings in order to contribute to the fund out of which benefits would be paid to others. . . . [T]he Constitution forbids the gender-based differentiation premised upon assumptions as to dependency . . . [T]he Constitution also forbids the gender-based differentiation that results in the efforts of female workers required to pay social security taxes producing less protection for their families than is produced by the efforts of men.

III

The Government . . . contends that § 402(g) was "reasonably designed to offset the adverse economic situation of women by providing a widow with financial assistance to supplement or substitute for her own efforts in the marketplace" . . .

. . . [T]he mere recitation of a benign, compensatory purpose is not an automatic shield which protects against any inquiry into the actual purposes underlying a statutory scheme. Here, it is apparent both from the statutory scheme itself and from the legislative history of § 402(g) that Congress' purpose in providing benefits to young widows with children was not to provide an income to women who were, because of economic discrimination, unable to provide for themselves. Rather, § 402(g), linked as it is directly to responsibility for minor children, was intended to permit women to elect not to work and to devote themselves to the care of children. Since this purpose in no way is premised upon any special disadvantages of women, it cannot serve to justify a gender-based distinction which diminishes the protection afforded to women who do work.

. . . The Advisory Council on Social Security, which developed the 1939 amendments, said explicitly that "[s]uch payments [under § 402(g)] are intended as supplements to the orphans' benefits *with the purpose of enabling the widow to remain at home and care for the children*." . . . In 1971, a new Advisory Council . . . reiterated this understanding . . . In the Council's judgment, it is desirable to allow a woman who is left with the care of the children the choice of whether to stay at home to care for the children or to work." . . .

The whole structure of survivors' benefits conforms to this articulated purpose. . . . If Congress were concerned with providing women with benefits because of economic discrimination, it would be entirely irrational to except those women who had spent many years at home rearing children, since those women are most likely to be without the skills required to succeed in the job market. . . . Congress was not concerned in § 402(g) with the employment problems of women generally but with the principle that children of covered employees are entitled to the personal attention of the surviving parent if that parent chooses not to work.

Given the purpose of enabling the surviving parent to remain at home to care for a child, the gender-based distinction of § 402(g) is entirely irrational. The classification discriminates among surviving children solely on the basis of the sex of the surviving parent. . . . It is no less important for a child to be cared for by its sole surviving parent when that parent is male rather than female. And a father, no less than a mother, has a constitutionally protected right to the "companionship, care, custody, and management" of "the children he has sired and raised". . . . *Stanley v. Illinois*, 405 U.S. 645, 651 (1972). Further, to the extent that women who work when they have sole responsibility for children encounter special problems, it would seem that men with sole responsibility for children will encounter the same child-care related problems. Stephen Wiesenfeld, for example, found that providing adequate care for his infant son impeded his ability to work. . . .

Finally, . . . [b]enefits under § 402(g) decrease with increased earnings. . . . According to the Government, "the bulk of male workers would receive no benefits in any event" . . . because they earn too much. Thus, the gender-based distinction is gratuitous; without it, the statutory scheme would only provide benefits to those men who are in fact similarly situated to the women the statute aids. . . .

JUSTICE DOUGLAS took no part in the consideration or decision of this case.

JUSTICE POWELL, with whom THE CHIEF JUSTICE joins, concurring.

. . . I would identify the impermissible discrimination effected by § 402(g) somewhat more narrowly than the Court does. . . .

The statutory scheme . . . impermissibly discriminates against a female wage earner because it provides her family less protection than it provides that of a male wage earner. . . .

JUSTICE REHNQUIST, concurring in the result. . . .

. . . [T]he restriction of § 402(g) benefits to surviving mothers does not rationally serve any valid legislative purpose . . . it is irrational to distinguish between mothers and fathers when the sole question is whether a child of a deceased contributing worker should have the opportunity to receive the full-time attention of the only parent remaining to it. . . .

NOTES

(1) *Unemployed Parents.* In *Califano v. Wescott*, 443 U.S. 76 (1979), the Court held unconstitutional § 407 of the Social Security Act, a provision of the program of Aid to Families with Dependent Children (AFDC). The challenged section extended benefits to families whose dependent children were deprived of paternal support because of the unemployment of the father, but did not provide similar support if the mother became unemployed. The government argued that, while the classification was "gender-based," it was not "gender-biased," in part because the section was designed to deal with the problem of unemployed fathers who deserted their families in order to qualify for the program. The Court relied on *Frontiero v. Richarson*, § 9.01, Note (5) and *Weinberger v. Wiesenfeld* in holding that benefits accruing to a family could not be dependent on whether the wage earner was the mother or father. On the constitutional claim, the Court, per Justice Blackmun, was unanimous, although three Justices (Chief Justice Burger, Powell, and Rehnquist), disagreed on the Court's remedy. The majority ordered the extension of benefits to all families where the mother became unemployed, whereas the partial dissenters would have enjoined any further payment of benefits.

(2) *Survivors' Benefits.* In *Califano v. Goldfarb*, 430 U.S. 199 (1977), the Court (5-4) relied on *Weinberger v. Wiesenfeld* and *Frontiero v. Richardson* to invalidate § 402(f)(1)(D) of the Social Security Act. This section provided that survivors' benefits — based on the earnings of a deceased husband — were to be paid to his widow. Similar benefits based on the earnings of a deceased wife, however, would be payable to her surviving husband only if she had been providing at least half of her husband's support. Justice Brennan's opinion concluded that § 402(f)(1)(D) discriminated against female workers because their earnings produced less protection for their surviving spouses than was produced "by the efforts of men." Justice Brennan's opinion argued that Congress had defined its purpose not in terms of the need of the survivor but rather in terms of "dependency." The statute in *Schlesinger v. Ballard*, 419 U.S. 498 (1975), on the other hand, was "justified because the only discernible purpose . . . was the permissible one of redressing our society's long-standing disparate treatment of women." [Note that Justice Brennan dissented in *Ballard*.] Justice Stevens wrote a concurring opinion.

In dissent, Justice Rehnquist (joined by Chief Justice Burger and Justices Stewart and Blackmun) argued that the benefit has been extended to the surviving wife because of past job discrimination. This made it more likely that she was in need.

(3) One commentator has sought to explain the gender cases by reference to a

principle of "equality of respect." *See* C. Edwin Baker, *Neutrality, Process, and Rationality: Flawed Interpretations of Equal Protection*, 58 TEX. L. REV. 1029, 1094 (1980) ("[E]qual protection bars the government practice if, and only if, the gender distinction embodies a negative or stereotyped judgment about the capacities or qualities of either sex, or if the law purposefully contributes to the subordination of a sexual group. . . . [T]he cases suggest that, in allocating benefits and burdens, the state cannot purposefully distinguish between man and woman unless that purpose is to move toward greater equality in the conditions of the two groups or to serve the emancipated interests of both groups.").

§ 9.04 DISCRIMINATION INVOLVING PREGNANCY

GEDULDIG v. AIELLO
417 U.S. 484, 94 S. Ct. 2485, 41 L. Ed. 2d 256 (1974)

JUSTICE STEWART delivered the opinion of the Court.

For almost 30 years California has administered a disability insurance system that pays benefits to persons in private employment who are temporarily unable to work because of disability not covered by workmen's compensation. The appellees brought this action to challenge the constitutionality of a provision of the California program that, in defining "disability," excludes from coverage certain disabilities resulting from pregnancy. . . .

I

California's disability insurance system is funded entirely from contributions deducted from the wages of participating employees. Participation in the program is mandatory unless the employees are protected by a voluntary private plan approved by the State. . . .

In return for his one-percent contribution to the Disability Fund, the individual employee is insured against the risk of disability stemming from a substantial number of "mental or physical illness[es] and mental or physical injur[ies]." Cal. Unemp. Ins. Code § 2626. It is not every disabling condition, however, that triggers the obligation to pay benefits under the program. . . . [A]ny disability of less than eight days' duration is not compensable, except when the employee is hospitalized. Conversely, no benefits are payable for any single disability beyond 26 weeks. Further, disability is not compensable if it results from the individual's court commitment as a dipsomaniac [person with an irresistible, insatiable craving for alcohol], drug addict, or sexual psychopath. Finally, § 2626 of the Unemployment Insurance Code excludes from coverage certain disabilities that are attributable to pregnancy. It is this provision that is at issue in the present case. . . .

[T]he California Court of Appeal, in a suit brought by a woman who suffered an ectopic pregnancy, held that § 2626 does not bar the payment of benefits on account of disability that results from medical complications arising during pregnancy. . . .

II

It is clear that California intended to establish this benefit system as an insurance program that was to function essentially in accordance with insurance concepts. Since the program was instituted in 1946, it has been totally self-supporting. . . .

. . . The State has sought to provide the broadest possible disability protection that would be affordable by all employees, including those with very low incomes. Because any larger percentage or any flat dollar-amount rate of contribution would impose an increasingly regressive levy bearing most heavily upon those with the lowest incomes, the State has resisted any attempt to change the required contribution from the one-percent level. . . .

In ordering the State to pay benefits for disability accompanying normal pregnancy and delivery, the District Court acknowledged the State's contention "that coverage of these disabilities is so extraordinarily expensive that it would be impossible to maintain a program supported by employee contributions if these disabilities are included." . . . There is considerable disagreement between the parties with respect to how great the increased costs would actually be, but they would clearly be substantial.[20] For purposes of analysis the District Court accepted the State's estimate, which was in excess of $100 million annually, and stated: "[I]t is clear that including these disabilities would not destroy the program. The increased costs could be accommodated quite easily by making reasonable changes in the contribution rate, the maximum benefits allowable, and the other variables affecting the solvency of the program." . . .

Each of these "variables" — the benefit level deemed appropriate to compensate employee disability, the risks selected to be insured under the program, and the contribution rate chosen to maintain the solvency of the program and at the same time to permit low-income employees to participate with minimal personal sacrifice — represents a policy determination by the State. The essential issue in this case is whether the Equal Protection Clause requires such policies to be sacrificed or compromised in order to finance the payment of benefits to those whose disability is attributable to normal pregnancy and delivery.

We cannot agree that the exclusion of this disability from coverage amounts to invidious discrimination under the Equal Protection Clause. California does not discriminate with respect to the persons or groups which are eligible for disability insurance protection under the program. The classification challenged in this case relates to the asserted underinclusiveness of the set of risks that the State has selected to insure. Although California has created a program to insure most risks of employment disability, it has not chosen to insure all such risks. . . . This Court has held that, consistently with the Equal Protection Clause. . . "[t]he legislature may select one phase of one field and apply a remedy there, neglecting the others. . . . " *Williamson v. Lee Optical Co.*, 348 U.S. 483, 489. . . . Particularly with respect to social welfare programs, so long as the line drawn by the State is rationally supportable, the courts will not interpose their judgment as to the appropriate stopping point. . . .

The District Court suggested that moderate alterations in what it regarded as "variables" of the disability insurance program could be made to accommodate the substantial expense required to include normal pregnancy within the program's protection. The same can be said, however, with respect to the other expensive class of disabilities that are excluded from coverage — short-term disabilities. If the Equal Protection Clause were thought to compel disability payments for normal pregnancy, it is hard to perceive why it would not also compel payments for short-term disabilities suffered by participating employees. . . .

The State has a legitimate interest in maintaining the self-supporting nature of its

---

[20] [Court's footnote 18] Appellant's estimate of the increased cost of including normal pregnancy within the insured risks has varied between $120.2 million and $131 million annually, or between a 33% or 36% increase in the present amount of benefits paid under the program. On the other hand, appellee contends that the increased cost would be $48.9 million annually, or a 12% increase over present expenditures.

insurance program. Similarly, it has an interest in distributing the available resources in such a way as to keep benefit payments at an adequate level for disabilities that are covered, rather than to cover all disabilities inadequately. Finally, California has a legitimate concern in maintaining the contribution rate at a level that will not unduly burden participating employees, particularly low-income employees who may be most in need of the disability insurance.

These policies provide an objective and wholly noninvidious basis for the State's decision not to create a more comprehensive insurance program than it has. There is no evidence in the record that the selection of the risks insured by the program worked to discriminate against any definable group or class in terms of the aggregate risk protection derived by that group or class from the program.[21] There is no risk from which men are protected and women are not. Likewise, there is no risk from which women are protected and men are not.[22]

JUSTICE BRENNAN, with whom JUSTICE DOUGLAS and JUSTICE MARSHALL join, dissenting.

. . . Because I believe that *Reed v. Reed*, and *Frontiero v. Richardson*, mandate a stricter standard of scrutiny which the State's classification fails to satisfy, I respectfully dissent. . . .

. . . [W]orkers are compensated for costly disabilities such as heart attacks, voluntary disabilities such as cosmetic surgery or sterilization, disabilities unique to sex or race such as prostatectomies or sickle-cell anemia, pre-existing conditions inevitably resulting in disability such as degenerative arthritis or cataracts, and "normal" disabilities such as removal of irritating wisdom teeth or other orthodontia. . . .

In my view, by singling out for less favorable treatment a gender-linked disability peculiar to women, the State has created a double standard for disability compensation: a limitation is imposed upon the disabilities for which women workers may recover, while men receive full compensation for all disabilities suffered, including those that affect only or primarily their sex, such as prostatectomies, circumcision, hemophilia, and gout. In effect, one set of rules is applied to females and another to males. . . .

. . . The essence of the State's justification for excluding disabilities caused by a normal pregnancy from its disability compensation scheme is that covering such disabilities would be too costly. . . . [W]hen a statutory classification is subject to strict judicial scrutiny, the State "must do more than show that denying [benefits to the

---

[21] [Court's footnote 20] . . . The California insurance program does not exclude anyone from benefit eligibility because of gender but merely removes one physical condition — pregnancy — from the list of compensable disabilities. While it is true that only women can become pregnant it does not follow that every legislative classification concerning pregnancy is a sex-based classification. . . . Normal pregnancy is an objectively identifiable physical condition with unique characteristics. Absent a showing that distinctions involving pregnancy are mere pretexts designed to effect an invidious discrimination against the members of one sex or the other, lawmakers are constitutionally free to include or exclude pregnancy from the coverage of legislation such as this on any reasonable basis, just as with respect to any other physical condition.

The lack of identity between the excluded disability and gender as such under this insurance program becomes clear upon the most cursory analysis. The program divides potential recipients into two groups — pregnant women and nonpregnant persons. While the first group is exclusively female, the second includes members of both sexes. The fiscal and actuarial benefits of the program thus accrue to members of both sexes.

[22] [Court's footnote 21] Indeed, the appellant submitted to the District Court data that indicated that both the annual claim rate and annual claim cost are greater for women than for men. As the District Court acknowledged, "women contribute about 28 percent of the total disability insurance fund and receive back about 38 percent of the fund in benefits." . . . Several amici curiae have represented to the Court that they have had a similar experience under private disability insurance programs.

excluded class] saves money." *Memorial Hospital v. Maricopa County*, 415 U.S. 250, 263. . . .

Moreover, California's legitimate interest in fiscal integrity could easily have been achieved through a variety of less drastic, sexually neutral means. As the District Court observed:

. . . [T]he entire cost increase estimated by defendant could be met by requiring workers to contribute an additional amount of approximately .364 percent of their salary and increasing the maximum annual contribution to about $119. . . .

NOTES

(1) *Pregnancy Discrimination Act.* Although *Geduldig v. Aiello* retains its force as a constitutional decision, Title VII has been amended to prohibit discrimination on the basis of pregnancy. In 1978, the Pregnancy Discrimination Act amended Title VII by defining the terms relating to discrimination "because of sex" or "on the basis of sex" to include discrimination "because of or on the basis of pregnancy, childbirth, or related medical conditions." For additional discussion of gender discrimination in relation to pregnancy, see, e.g., Finley, *Transcending Equality Theory: A Way Out of the Maternity and the Workplace Debate*, 86 COLUM. L. REV. 1118 (1986); Strimling, *The Constitutionality of State Laws Providing Employment Leave for Pregnancy: Rethinking* Geduldig *After Cal. Fed*, 77 CAL. L. REV. 171, 172 (1989) ("If equal treatment is defined as identical treatment without regard to biological difference, laws that compel different treatment of women and men based on biological difference perpetuate inequality by reinforcing the stereotype that women's capacity to give birth makes them less serious, less dependable workers. However, if the measure of equality is equal outcome, employment leave for pregnancy helps restructure the workplace to accommodate women as well as men."); *see also Pregnancy and Equality: A Precarious Alliance*, 60 S. CAL. L. REV. 1345 (1987).

(2) For additional discussion of gender equality issues, see, e.g., D. KIRP, M. YUDOF & M. FRANKS, GENDER JUSTICE (1986) (arguing for laws that are blind to gender differences and that emphasize freedom of choice for both men and women); Freedman, *Sex Equality, Sex Differences, and the Supreme Court*, 92 YALE L.J. 913, 960 (1983) (the "Rehnquist-Stewart and Brennan-Marshall approaches simultaneously acknowledge and deny the need for significant changes in sex roles and sex-based hierarchy"); Littleton, *Reconstructing Sexual Equality*, 85 CAL. L. REV. 1279 (1987) (rejecting a "symmetrical" form of equality in the gender area, in favor of a more realistic form of equality that takes relevant differences between men and women into account); *see also Sex, Discrimination and the Fourteenth Amendment: Lost History*, 97 YALE L.J. 1153 (1988) (reviewing the debate as to whether the Framers of the Fourteenth Amendment intended it to cover gender discrimination).

CONCLUDING NOTE

The proposed Equal Rights Amendment provided as follows:

Section 1. Equality of rights under the law shall not be denied or abridged by the United States or by any State on account of sex.

Section 2. The Congress shall have the power to enforce, by appropriate legislation, the provisions of this article.

Section 3. The Amendment shall take effect two years after the date of ratification.

In March of 1978, the original time limit for ratification by the states was extended to June 30, 1982, but on that date the Amendment fell three votes short of the requisite 38.

Query: If the Amendment had been in effect, which, if any, cases in this Chapter would have been decided differently?

Chapter X
AFFIRMATIVE ACTION

But in view of the Constitution, in the eye of the law, there is in this country no superior, dominant, ruling class of citizens. There is no caste here. Our Constitution is color blind, and neither knows nor tolerates classes among citizens.

Justice Harlan, dissenting in *Plessy v. Ferguson* 163 U.S. 537 (1896), *supra* § 8.02[1].

It is because of a legacy of unequal treatment that we now must permit the institutions of this society to give consideration to race in making decisions about who will hold positions of influence, affluence and prestige in America. For far too long, the doors to those positions have been shut to Negroes. If we are ever to become a fully integrated society, one in which the color of a person's skin will not determine the opportunities available to him or her, we must be willing to take steps to open those doors. I do not believe that anyone can truly look into America's past and still find that a remedy for the effects of that past is impermissible.

Justice Marshall's dissenting opinion in *Regents of University of California v. Bakke*, 438 U.S. 265 (1978), *infra*.

Introductory Note. One of the critical problems of justice in any society is the distribution of goods and resources. *See, e.g.*, R. Nozick, Anarchy, State, and Utopia (1974); J. Rawls, A Theory of Justice (1971); M. Waltzer, Spheres of Justice (1983); Dworkin, *What Is Equality? Part I: Equality of Welfare*, 10 Phil. & Pub. Affairs 185 (1981); Dworkin, *What Is Equality? Part II: Equality of Resources*, 10 Phil. & Pub. Affairs 284 (1981); Posner, *Utilitarianism, Economics, and Legal Theory*, 8 J. Legal Stud. 103 (1979). Certainly in a free enterprise system, two of the most important such resources are education and employment. Affirmative action is a race or gender premised method devised for redressing inequality resulting from specific or societal discrimination. As the above quotes indicate, this method of redressing discrimination engenders profound questions regarding distributive and corrective justice, as well as regarding our conception of equality itself. Critics argue that this method utilizes race and gender lines that the law has proscribed in other contexts. Proponents argue that these lines are justified, and indeed necessary, to redress the history of discrimination against minorities and women.

Section 10.01 of this chapter focuses on constitutional issues involving affirmative action in admission to colleges and universities. Section 10.02 treats affirmative action in the employment context. Some of the cases in both sections treat the legality of affirmative action plans under statutes such as Title VII of the Civil Rights Act of 1964, which can shed light on the Court's constitutional thinking in the area.

§ 10.01 EDUCATION

REGENTS OF UNIVERSITY OF CALIFORNIA v. BAKKE
438 U.S. 265, 98 S. Ct. 2733, 57 L. Ed. 2d 750 (1978)

Justice Powell announced the judgment of the Court.

This case presents a challenge to the special admissions program of the petitioner, the Medical School of the University of California at Davis, which is designed to assure the admission of a specified number of students from certain minority groups. . . .

For the reasons stated in the following opinion, I believe that so much of the judgment of the California court as holds petitioner's special admissions program unlawful and directs that respondent be admitted to the Medical School must be affirmed. For the reasons expressed in a separate opinion, my Brothers the Chief Justice, Justice Stewart, Justice Rehnquist and Justice Stevens concur in this judgment.

I also conclude for the reasons stated in the following opinion that the portion of the court's judgment enjoining petitioner from according any consideration to race in its admissions process must be reversed. For reasons expressed in separate opinions, my Brothers Justice Brennan, Justice White, Justice Marshall, and Justice Blackmun concur in this judgment. . . .

I[1]

The Medical School of the University of California at Davis opened in 1968 with an entering class of 50 students. In 1971, the size of the entering class was increased to 100 students, a level at which it remains. No admissions program for disadvantaged or minority students existed when the school opened, and the first class contained three Asians but no blacks, no Mexican-Americans, and no American Indians. Over the next two years, the faculty devised a special admissions program to increase the representation of "disadvantaged" students in each medical school class. The special program consisted of a separate admissions system operating in coordination with the regular admissions process.

Under the regular admissions procedure,[2] . . . the admissions committee screened each one to select candidates for further consideration. Candidates whose overall undergraduate grade point averages fell below 2.5 on a scale of 4.0 were summarily rejected. About one out of six applicants was invited for a personal interview. Following the interviews, each candidate was rated on a scale of 1 to 100 by his interviewers and four other members of the admissions committee. The rating embraced the interviewers' summaries, the candidate's overall grade point average, grade point average in science courses, and scores on the Medical College Admissions Test (MCAT), letters of recommendation, extracurricular activities, and other biographical data. The ratings were added together to arrive at each candidate's "benchmark" score. Since five committee members rated each candidate in 1973, a perfect score was 500; in 1974, six members rated each candidate, so that a perfect score was 600. The full committee then reviewed the file and scores of each applicant and made offers of admission on a "rolling" basis. The chairman was responsible for placing names on the waiting list. They were not placed in strict numerical order; instead the chairman had discretion to include persons with "special skills."

The special admissions program operated with a separate committee, a majority of whom were members of minority groups. On the 1973 application form, candidates were asked to indicate whether they wished to be considered as "economically and/or educationally disadvantaged" applicants; on the 1974 form the question was whether they wished to be considered as members of a "minority group," which the medical school apparently viewed as "Blacks," "Chicanos," "Asians," and "American Indians." If these questions were answered affirmatively, the application was forwarded to the special admissions committee. . . . Having passed this initial hurdle, the applications then were rated by the special committee in a fashion similar to that used by the

---

[1] Justice Brennan, Justice White, Justice Marshall, and Justice Blackmun join Parts I and V-C of this opinion. Justice White also joins part III-A of this opinion.

[2] [Court's footnote 2] For the 1973 entering class of 100 seats, the Davis medical school received 2,464 applications. For the 1974 entering class, 3,737 applications were submitted.

general admissions committee, except that special candidates did not have to meet the 2.5 grade point average cut-off applied to regular applicants. About one-fifth of the total number of special applicants were invited for interviews in 1973 and 1974.[3]

Following each interview, the special committee assigned each special applicant a benchmark score. The special committee then presented its top choices to the general admissions committee. The latter did not rate or compare the special candidates against the general applicants, but could reject recommended special candidates for failure to meet course requirements or other specific deficiencies. The special committee continued to recommend special applicants until a number prescribed by faculty vote were admitted. While the overall class size was still 50, the prescribed number was eight; in 1973 and 1974, when the class size had doubled to 100, the prescribed number of special admissions also doubled, to 16.

From the year of the increase in class size 1971 through 1974, the special program resulted in the admission of 21 black students, 30 Mexican-Americans, and 12 Asians, for a total of 63 minority students. Over the same period, the regular admissions program produced one black, six Mexican-Americans, and 37 Asians, for a total of 44 minority students. Although disadvantaged whites applied to the special program in large numbers, none received an offer of admission through that process. Indeed, in 1974, at least, the special committee explicitly considered only "disadvantaged" special applicants who were members of one of the designated minority groups.

Allan Bakke is a white male who applied to the Davis Medical School in both 1973 and 1974. In both years Bakke's application was considered by the general admissions program, and he received an interview. . . . Despite a strong benchmark score of 468 out of 500, Bakke was rejected. His application had come late in the year, and no applicants in the general admissions process with scores below 470 were accepted after Bakke's application was completed. There were four special admissions slots unfilled at that time however, for which Bakke was not considered. After his 1973 rejection, Bakke wrote to Dr. George H. Lowrey, Associate Dean and Chairman of the Admissions Committee, protesting that the special admissions program operated as a racial and ethnic quota.

Bakke's 1974 application was completed early in the year. . . . [H]is total was 549 out of 600. Again, Bakke's application was rejected. . . . In both years, applicants were admitted under the special program with grade point averages, MCAT scores, and benchmark scores significantly lower than Bakke's. . . .

II

. . . The language of § 601, like that of the Equal Protection Clause, is majestic in its sweep:

No person in the United States shall, on the ground of race, color, or national origin, be excluded from participation in, be denied the benefits of, or be subjected to discrimination under any program or activity receiving Federal financial assistance.

. . . Examination of the voluminous legislative history of Title VI reveals a congressional intent to halt federal funding of entities that violate a prohibition of racial discrimination similar to that of the Constitution. . . .

In view of the clear legislative intent, Title VI must be held to proscribe only those racial classifications that would violate the Equal Protection Clause or the Fifth Amendment.

---

[3] [Court's footnote 5] For the class entering in 1973 the total number of special applicants was 297, of whom 73 were white. In 1974, 628 persons applied to the special committee, of whom 172 were white.

III

A

. . . [T]he parties fight a sharp preliminary action over the proper characterization of the special admissions program. Petitioner prefers to view it as establishing a "goal" of minority representation in the medical school. Respondent, echoing the courts below, labels it a racial quota.[4]

. . . [W]hite applicants could compete only for 84 seats in the entering class, rather than the 100 open to minority applicants. Whether this limitation is described as a quota or a goal, it is a line drawn on the basis of race and ethnic status.

The guarantees of the Fourteenth Amendment extend to persons. Its language is explicit: "No state shall . . . deny to any person within its jurisdiction the equal protection of the laws." . . . The guarantee of equal protection cannot mean one thing when applied to one individual and something else when applied to a person of another color. . . .

Nevertheless, petitioner argues that the court below erred in applying strict scrutiny to the special admissions programs because white males, such as respondent, are not a "discrete and insular minority" requiring extraordinary protection from the majoritarian political process. [*United States v. Carolene Products Co.*, 304 U.S. 144 (1938)]. . . . These characteristics may be relevant in deciding whether or not to add new types of classifications to the list of "suspect" categories. . . . Racial and ethnic distinctions of any sort are inherently suspect and thus call for the most exacting judicial examination.

B

. . . Petitioner urges us to . . . hold that discrimination against members of the white "majority" cannot be suspect if its purpose can be characterized as "benign."[5]

It is far too late to argue that the guarantee of equal protection to all persons permits the recognition of special wards entitled to a degree of protection greater than that accorded others.[6] . . . [T]he white "majority" itself is composed of various minority

---

[4] [Court's footnote 26] . . . Petitioner declares that . . . completely unqualified students will not be admitted simply to meet a "quota." Neither is there a "ceiling," since an unlimited number could be admitted through the general admissions process. . . .

The court below found and petitioner does not deny that white applicants could not compete for the 16 places reserved solely for the special admissions program. Both courts below characterized this as a "quota" system.

[5] [Court's footnote 34] In the view of Justice Brennan, Justice White, Justice Marshall, and Justice Blackmun, the pliable notion of "stigma" is the crucial element in analyzing racial classifications. The Equal Protection Clause is not framed in terms of "stigma." Certainly the word . . . reflects a subjective judgment that is standardless. *All* state-imposed classifications that rearrange burdens and benefits on the basis of race are likely to be viewed with deep resentment by the individuals burdened. . . . Moreover, Justice Brennan, Justice White, Justice Marshall, and Justice Blackmun offer no principle for deciding whether preferential classifications reflect a benign remedial purpose or a malevolent stigmatic classification, since they are willing in this case to accept mere *post hoc* declarations by an isolated state entity a medical school faculty unadorned by particularized findings of past discrimination, to establish such a remedial purpose.

[6] [Court's footnote 35] Professor Bickel noted the self-contradiction of that view:

. . . [D]iscrimination on the basis of race is illegal, immoral, unconstitutional, inherently wrong, and destructive of democratic society. Now this is to be unlearned and we are told that this is not a matter of fundamental principle but only a matter of whose ox is gored. Those for whom racial equality was demanded

groups, most of which can lay claim to a history of prior discrimination at the hands of the state and private individuals. Not all of these groups can receive preferential treatment and corresponding judicial tolerance of distinctions drawn in terms of race and nationality, for then the only "majority" left would be a new minority of White Anglo-Saxon Protestants. . . .

Courts would be asked to evaluate the extent of the prejudice and consequent harm suffered by various minority groups. Those whose societal injury is thought to exceed some arbitrary level of tolerability then would be entitled to preferential classifications at the expense of individuals belonging to other groups. . . . As these preferences began to have their desired effect, and the consequences of past discrimination were undone, new judicial rankings would be necessary. The kind of variable sociological and political analysis necessary to produce such rankings simply does not lie within the judicial competence. . . .

Moreover, there are serious problems of justice connected with the idea of preference itself. First, it may not always be clear that a so-called preference is in fact benign. Courts may be asked to validate burdens imposed upon individual members of particular groups in order to advance the group's general interest. . . . Second, preferential programs may only reinforce common stereotypes holding that certain groups are unable to achieve success without special protection based on a factor having no relationship to individual worth. . . . Third, there is a measure of inequity in forcing innocent persons in respondent's position to bear the burdens of redressing grievances not of their making.

By hitching the meaning of the Equal Protection Clause to these transitory considerations, we would be holding, as a constitutional principle, that judicial scrutiny of classifications touching on racial and ethnic background may vary with the ebb and flow of political forces. Disparate constitutional tolerance of such classifications well may serve to exacerbate racial and ethnic antagonisms rather than alleviate them. . . . Also, the mutability of a constitutional principle, based upon shifting political and social judgments, undermines the chances for consistent application of the Constitution from one generation to the next. . . .

If it is the individual who is entitled to judicial protection against classifications based upon his racial or ethnic background because such distinctions impinge upon personal rights, rather than the individual only because of his membership in a particular group, then constitutional standards may be applied consistently. . . .

C

Petitioner contends that on several occasions this Court has approved preferential classifications without applying the most exacting scrutiny. Most of the cases upon which petitioner relies are drawn from three areas: school desegregation, employment discrimination, and sex discrimination. . . .

The school desegregation cases are inapposite. Each involved remedies for clearly determined constitutional violations. . . .

. . . Such preferences also have been upheld where a legislative or administrative body charged with the responsibility made determinations of past discrimination by the industries affected, and fashioned remedies deemed appropriate to rectify the discrimination.

---

are to be more equal than others. Having found support in the Constitution for equality, they now claim support for inequality under the same Constitution.

A. Bickel, The Morality of Consent 133 (1975).

. . . But we have never approved preferential classifications in the absence of proven constitutional or statutory violations.

. . . With respect to gender there are only two possible classifications. . . . More importantly, the perception of racial classifications as inherently odious stems from a lengthy and tragic history that gender-based classifications do not share. . . .

In this case . . . there has been no determination by the legislature or a responsible administrative agency that the University engaged in a discriminatory practice requiring remedial efforts. . . . [P]etitioner's special admissions program . . . prefers the designated minority groups at the expense of other individuals who are totally foreclosed from competition for the 16 special admissions seats in every medical school class. . . . When a classification denies an individual opportunities or benefits enjoyed by others solely because of his race or ethnic background, it must be regarded as suspect. . . .

IV

We have held that in "order to justify the use of a suspect classification, a State must show that its purpose or interest is both constitutionally permissible and substantial, and that its use of the classification is 'necessary . . . to the accomplishment' of its purpose or the safeguarding of its interest." The special admissions program purports to serve the purposes of: (i) "reducing the historic deficit of traditionally disfavored minorities in medical schools and the medical profession," (ii) countering the effects of societal discrimination; (iii) increasing the number of physicians who will practice in communities currently underserved; and (iv) obtaining the educational benefits that flow from an ethnically diverse student body. . . .

A

If petitioner's purpose is to assure within its student body some specified percentage of a particular group merely because of its race or ethnic origin, such a preferential purpose must be rejected not as insubstantial but as facially invalid. . . .

B

. . . We have never approved a classification that aids persons perceived as members of relatively victimized groups at the expense of other innocent individuals in the absence of judicial, legislative, or administrative findings of constitutional or statutory violations. . . . In such a case, the extent of the injury and the consequent remedy will have been judicially, legislatively, or administratively defined. Also, the remedial action usually remains subject to continuing oversight to assure that it will work the least harm possible to other innocent persons competing for the benefit. . . .

Petitioner does not purport to have made, and is in no position to make, such findings. Its broad mission is education. . . .

Hence, the purpose of helping certain groups whom the faculty of the Davis Medical School perceived as victims of "societal discrimination" does not justify a classification that imposes disadvantages upon persons like respondent, who bear no responsibility for whatever harm the beneficiaries of the special admissions program are thought to have suffered. . . .

C

Petitioner identifies, as another purpose of its program, improving the delivery of health care services to communities currently underserved. It may be assumed that in some situations a State's interest in facilitating the health care of its citizens is sufficiently compelling to support the use of a suspect classification. But there is virtually no evidence in the record indicating that petitioner's special admissions program is either needed or geared to promote that goal. . . .

D

The fourth goal asserted by petitioner is the attainment of a diverse student body. This clearly is a constitutionally permissible goal for an institution of higher education. Academic freedom, though not a specifically enumerated constitutional right, long has been viewed as a special concern of the First Amendment. The freedom of a university to make its own judgments as to education includes the selection of its student body. . . .

. . . The atmosphere of "speculation, experiment and creation" so essential to the quality of higher education is widely believed to be promoted by a diverse student body. . . . [I]t is not too much to say that the "nation's future depends upon leaders trained through wide exposure" to the ideas and mores of students as diverse as this Nation of many peoples.

Thus, in arguing that its universities must be accorded the right to select those students who will contribute the most to the "robust exchange of ideas," petitioner invokes a countervailing constitutional interest, that of the First Amendment. . . .

. . . As the interest of diversity is compelling in the context of a university's admissions program, the question remains whether the program's racial classification is necessary to promote this interest. . . .

V

A

. . . The diversity that furthers a compelling state interest encompasses a far broader array of qualifications and characteristics of which racial or ethnic origin is but a single though important element. Petitioner's special admissions program, focused solely on ethnic diversity, would hinder rather than further attainment of genuine diversity. . . .

The experience of other university admissions programs, which take race into account in achieving the educational diversity valued by the First Amendment, demonstrates that the assignment of a fixed number of places to a minority group is not a necessary means toward that end. An illuminating example is found in the Harvard College program:

In recent years Harvard College has expanded the concept of diversity to include students from disadvantaged economic, racial and ethnic groups. Harvard College now recruits not only Californians or Louisianans but also blacks and Chicanos and other minority students.

In practice, this new definition of diversity has meant that race has been a factor in some admission decisions. When the Committee on Admissions reviews the large middle group of applicants who are "admissible" and deemed capable of doing good work in their courses, the race of an applicant may tip the balance in his favor just as geographic origin or a life spent on a farm may tip the balance in other candidates' cases. A farm boy from Idaho can bring something to Harvard College that a Bostonian cannot offer. Similarly, a black student can usually bring something that a white person cannot offer. . . .

In such an admissions program, race or ethnic background may be deemed a "plus" in a particular applicant's file, yet it does not insulate the individual from comparison with all other candidates for the available seats. The file of a particular black applicant may be examined for his potential contribution to diversity without the factor of race being decisive when compared, for example, with that of an applicant identified as an Italian-American if the latter is thought to exhibit qualities more likely to promote beneficial educational pluralism. Such qualities could include exceptional personal talents, unique work or service experience, leadership potential, maturity, demonstrated compassion, a history of overcoming disadvantage, ability to communicate with the poor, or other qualifications deemed important. In short, an admissions program operated in this way is flexible enough to consider all pertinent elements of diversity in light of the particular qualifications of each applicant, and to place them on the same footing for consideration, although not necessarily according them the same weight. Indeed, the weight attributed to a particular quality may vary from year to year depending upon the "mix" both of the student body and the applicants for the incoming class.

This kind of program treats each applicant as an individual in the admissions process. The applicant who loses out on the last available seat to another candidate receiving a "plus" on the basis of ethnic background will not have been foreclosed from all consideration for that seat simply because he was not the right color or had the wrong surname. It would mean only that his combined qualifications, which may have included similar nonobjective factors, did not outweigh those of the other applicant. . . .

. . . [G]ood faith would be presumed in the absence of a showing to the contrary in the manner permitted by our cases. *See, e.g., Arlington Heights v. Metropolitan Housing Development Corp.* [429 U.S. 252 (1977)]; *Washington v. Davis* [426 U.S. 229 (1976)].[7]

B

. . . [W]hen a State's distribution of benefits or imposition of burdens hinges on the color of a person's skin or ancestry, that individual is entitled to a demonstration that the challenged classification is necessary to promote a substantial state interest. Petitioner has failed to carry this burden. For this reason, that portion of the California court's judgment holding petitioner's special admissions program invalid under the Fourteenth Amendment must be affirmed.

C

. . . [T]he State has a substantial interest that legitimately may be served by a properly devised admissions program involving the competitive consideration of a race and ethnic origin. For this reason, so much of the California court's judgment as enjoins petitioner from any consideration of the race of any applicant must be reversed.

VI

With respect to respondent's entitlement to an injunction directing his admission to the Medical School, petitioner has conceded that it could not carry its burden of proving that, but for the existence of its unlawful special admissions program, respondent still

---

[7] [Court's footnote 53] . . . If an applicant can establish that the institution does not adhere to a policy of individual comparisons, or can show that a systematic exclusion of certain groups results, the presumption of legality might be overcome, creating the necessity of proving legitimate educational purpose.

would not have been admitted. Hence, respondent is entitled to the injunction, and that portion of the judgment must be affirmed. . . .

Opinion of JUSTICE BRENNAN, JUSTICE WHITE, JUSTICE MARSHALL, and JUSTICE BLACKMUN, concurring in the judgment in part and dissenting. . . .

We agree with Justice Powell that, as applied to the case before us, Title VI goes no further in prohibiting the use of race than the Equal Protection Clause of the Fourteenth Amendment itself. . . . Since we conclude that the affirmative admissions program at the Davis Medical School is constitutional, we would reverse the judgment below in all respects. Justice Powell agrees that some uses of race in university admissions are permissible and, therefore, he joins with us to make five votes reversing the judgment below insofar as it prohibits the University from establishing race-conscious programs in the future. . . .

III

. . . Unquestionably we have held that a government practice or statute which restricts "fundamental rights" or which contains "suspect classifications" is to be subjected to "strict scrutiny" and can be justified only if it furthers a compelling government purpose and, even then, only if no less restrictive alternative is available. But no fundamental right is involved here. Nor do whites as a class have any of the "traditional indicia of suspectness: the class is not saddled with such disabilities, or subjected to such a history of purposeful unequal treatment, or relegated to such a position of political powerlessness as to command extraordinary protection from the majoritarian political process." *San Antonio School District v. Rodriguez*, 411 U.S. 1, 28 (1973); *see United States v. Carolene Products Co.* . . .

. . . [A] number of considerations developed in gender discrimination cases but which carry even more force when applied to racial classifications lead us to conclude that racial classifications designed to further remedial purposes "must serve important governmental objectives and must be substantially related to achievement of those objectives." *Califano v. Webster, supra,* quoting *Craig v. Boren.* . . .

In sum, because of the significant risk that racial classifications established for ostensibly benign purposes can be misused, causing effects not unlike those created by invidious classifications, it is inappropriate to inquire only whether there is any conceivable basis that might sustain such a classification. Instead, to justify such a classification an important and articulated purpose for its use must be shown. In addition, any statute must be stricken that stigmatizes any group or that singles out those least well represented in the political process to bear the brunt of a benign program. . . .

IV

. . . .

A

. . . *Swann v. Charlotte-Mecklenburg Board of Ed.*, 402 U.S. 1 (1971), and its companion cases . . . reiterated that racially neutral remedies for past discrimination were inadequate where consequences of past discriminatory acts influence or control present decisions. . . . Moreover, we stated that school boards, even in the absence of a judicial finding of past discrimination, could voluntarily adopt plans which assigned students with the end of creating racial pluralism by establishing fixed ratios of black and white students in each school. . . . *Charlotte-Mecklenburg.* . . .

B

. . . [A] state government may adopt race-conscious programs if the purpose of such programs is to remove the disparate racial impact its actions might otherwise have and if there is reason to believe that the disparate impact is itself the product of past discrimination, whether its own or that of society at large. There is no question that Davis' program is valid under this test.

. . . In 1950 . . . while Negroes comprised 10% of the total population, Negro physicians constituted only 2.2% of the total number of physicians. The overwhelming majority of these, moreover, were educated in two predominantly Negro medical schools, Howard and Meharry. By 1970, . . . [t]he number of Negroes employed in medicine remained frozen at 2.2% while the Negro population had increased to 11.1%. The number of Negro admittees to predominantly white medical schools, moreover, had declined in absolute numbers during the years 1955 to 1964. . . .

. . . Under slavery, penal sanctions were imposed upon anyone attempting to educate Negroes. After enactment of the Fourteenth Amendment the States continued to deny Negroes equal educational opportunity, enforcing a strict policy of segregation. . . .

C

The second prong of our test — whether the Davis program stigmatizes any discrete group or individual and whether race is reasonably used in light of the program's objectives — is clearly satisfied by the Davis program.

It is not even claimed that Davis' program in any way operates to stigmatize or single out any discrete and insular, or even any identifiable, nonminority group. . . .

D

. . . [T]here are no practical means by which it could achieve its ends in the foreseeable future without the use of race-conscious measures. With respect to any factor (such as poverty or family educational background) that may be used as a substitute for race as an indicator of past discrimination, whites . . . far outnumber minorities in absolute terms at every socio-economic level. For example, of a class of recent medical school applicants from families with less than $10,000 income, at least 71% were white. Of all 1970 families headed by a person not a high school graduate which included related children under 18.80% were white and 20% were racial minorities. Moreover, while race is positively correlated with differences in GPA and MCAT scores, economic disadvantage is not. . . .

E

. . . That the Harvard approach does not also make public the extent of the preference and the precise workings of the system while the Davis program employs a specific, openly stated number, does not condemn the latter plan for purposes of Fourteenth Amendment adjudication. . . .

IV

Accordingly, we would reverse the judgment of the Supreme Court of California holding the Medical School's special admissions program unconstitutional and directing respondent's admission, as well as that portion of the judgment enjoining the Medical School from according any consideration to race in the admissions process.

Separate opinion of JUSTICE WHITE.

[Justice White concluded that Congress did not intend to create a private cause of action under Title VI.]

Because each of my colleagues either has a different view or assumes a private cause of action, however, the merits of the Title VI issue must be addressed. My views in that regard, as well as my views with respect to the equal protection issue, are included in the joint opinion that my Brothers Brennan, Marshall, and Blackmun and I have filed.[8]

JUSTICE MARSHALL.

I agree with the judgment of the Court insofar as it permits a university to consider the race of an applicant in making admissions decisions. I do not agree that petitioner's admissions program violates the Constitution. For it must be remembered that, during most of the past 200 years, the Constitution as interpreted by this Court did not prohibit the most ingenious and pervasive forms of discrimination against the Negro. Now, when a State acts to remedy the effects of that legacy of discrimination, I cannot believe that this same Constitution stands as a barrier.

I

A

Three hundred and fifty years ago, the Negro was dragged to this country in chains to be sold into slavery. Uprooted from his homeland and thrust into bondage for forced labor, the slave was deprived of all legal rights. It was unlawful to teach him to read; he could be sold away from his family and friends at the whim of his master; and killing or maiming him was not a crime. . . .

[T]he Constitution . . . treated a slave as being equivalent to three-fifths of a person for purposes of apportioning representatives and taxes among the States. Art. I, § 2. The Constitution also contained a clause ensuring that the "migration or importation" of slaves into the existing States would be legal until at least 1808, Art. I, § 9, and a fugitive slave clause requiring that when a slave escaped to another State, he must be returned on the claim of the master, Art. IV, § 2. . . .

. . . The position of the Negro slave as mere property was confirmed by this Court in *Dred Scott v. Sandford* [60 U.S. 393 (1856)], holding that the Missouri Compromise which prohibited slavery in the portion of the Louisiana Purchase Territory north of Missouri was unconstitutional because it deprived slave owners of their property without due process. . . .

B

. . . The combined actions and inactions of the State and Federal Government maintained Negroes in a position of legal inferiority for another century after the Civil War.

The Southern States took the first steps to re-enslave the Negroes. Immediately following the end of the Civil War, many of the provisional legislatures passed Black Codes, similar to the Slave Codes, which, among other things, limited the rights of Negroes to own or rent property and permitted imprisonment for breach of employment contracts. Over the next several decades, the South managed to disenfranchise the Negroes in spite of the Fifteenth Amendment by various techniques,

---

[8] [Court's footnote 7] I also join Parts I, III-A, and V-C of Justice Powell's opinion.

including poll taxes, deliberately complicated balloting processes, property and literacy qualifications, and finally the white primary. . . .

The Court's ultimate blow to the Civil War Amendments and to the equality of Negroes came in *Plessy v. Ferguson*. . . .

. . . In the wake of *Plessy*, many States expanded their Jim Crow laws, which had up until that time been limited primarily to passenger trains and schools. The segregation of the races was extended to residential areas, parks, hospitals, theaters, waiting rooms and bathrooms. . . .

. . . In many of the Northern States, the Negro was denied the right to vote, prevented from serving on juries and excluded from theaters, restaurants, hotels, and inns. Under President Wilson, the Federal Government began to require segregation in Government buildings; desks of Negro employees were curtained off; separate bathrooms and separate tables in the cafeterias were provided; and even the galleries of the Congress were segregated. . . .

II

. . . A Negro child today has a life expectancy which is shorter by more than five years than that of a white child. The Negro child's mother is over three times more likely to die of complications in childbirth, and the infant mortality rate for Negroes is nearly twice that for whites. The median income of the Negro family is only 60% that of the median of a white family, and the percentage of Negroes who live in families with incomes below the poverty line is nearly four times greater than that of whites.

. . . For Negro adults, the unemployment rate is twice that of whites, and the unemployment rate for Negro teenagers is nearly three times that of white teenagers. . . . Although Negroes represent 11.5% of the population, they are only 1.2% of the lawyers, and judges, 2% of the physicians, 2.3% of the dentists, 1.1% of the engineers and 2.6% of the college and university professors. . . .

. . . [B]ringing the Negro into the mainstream of American life should be a state interest of the highest order. To fail to do so is to ensure that America will forever remain a divided society. . . .

IV

. . . The dream of America as the great melting pot has not been realized for the Negro; because of his skin color he never even made it into the pot. . . .

I fear that we have come full circle. After the Civil War our government started several "affirmative action" programs. This Court in the *Civil Rights Cases and Plessy v. Ferguson* destroyed the movement toward complete equality. For almost a century no action was taken, and this nonaction was with the tacit approval of the courts. Then we had *Brown v. Board of Education* [347 U.S. 483 (1954)] and the Civil Rights Acts of Congress, followed by numerous affirmative action programs. *Now*, we have this Court again stepping in, this time to stop affirmative action programs of the type used by the University of California.

JUSTICE BLACKMUN. . . .

I yield to no one in my earnest hope that the time will come when an "affirmative action" program is unnecessary and is, in truth, only a relic of the past. I would hope that we could reach this stage within a decade at the most. But the story of *Brown v. Board of Education*, decided almost a quarter of a century ago, suggests that that hope is a slim one. At some time, however, beyond any period of what some would claim is only transitional inequality, the United States must and will reach a stage of maturity where action along this line is no longer necessary. . . .

Programs of admission to institutions of higher learning are basically a responsibility for academicians and for administrators and the specialists they employ. . . . [I]nterference by the judiciary must be the rare exception and not the rule.

. . . [T]he Davis program, for me, is within constitutional bounds, though perhaps barely so. . . .

. . . In order to get beyond racism, we must first take account of race. There is no other way. . . . We cannot — we dare not — let the Equal Protection Clause perpetuate racial supremacy. . . .

JUSTICE STEVENS, with whom THE CHIEF JUSTICE, JUSTICE STEWART, JUSTICE REHNQUIST join, concurring in the judgment in part and dissenting in part.

I

. . . The California Supreme Court, in a holding that is not challenged, ruled that the trial court incorrectly placed the burden on Bakke of showing that he would have been admitted in the absence of discrimination. The University then conceded "that it [could] not meet the burden of proving that the special admission program did not result in Bakke's exclusion." Accordingly, the California Supreme Court directed the trial court to enter judgment ordering Bakke's admission. Whether the judgment of the state court is affirmed or reversed, in whole or in part, there is no outstanding injunction forbidding any consideration of racial criteria in processing applications.

It is, therefore, perfectly clear that the question whether race can ever be used as a factor in an admissions decision is not an issue in this case, and that discussion of that issue is inappropriate.

II

Both petitioner and respondent have asked us to determine the legality of the University's special admissions program by reference to the Constitution. Our settled practice, however, is to avoid the decision of a constitutional issue if a case can be fairly decided on a statutory ground. . . .

III

Section 601 of the Civil Rights Act of 1964 provides:

No person in the United States shall, on the ground of race, color, or national origin, be excluded from participation in, be denied the benefits of, or be subjected to discrimination under any program or activity receiving Federal financial assistance.

The University, through its special admissions policy, excluded Bakke from participation in its program of medical education because of his race. The University also acknowledges that it was, and still is, receiving federal financial assistance. The plain language of the statute therefore requires affirmance of the judgment below. . . .

The legislative history reinforces this reading. . . . In response, the proponents of the legislation gave repeated assurances that the Act would be "colorblind" in its application. . . .

Accordingly, I concur in the Court's judgment insofar as it affirms the judgment of the Supreme Court of California. To the extent that it purports to do anything else, I respectfully dissent.

NOTE

Theories of Equality. As indicated by the quotes of Justices Harlan and Marshall at the beginning of this Chapter, affirmative action implicates deep questions about differing conceptions of equality. Should a "right" conception be race neutral or should it take into account race lines to remedy the societal inequalities wrought by past discrimination? *Compare* Fiss, *Groups and the Equal Protection Clause*, 5 PHIL. & PUB. AFF. 107, 136 (1976) ("One shortcoming of the antidiscrimination principle relates to the problem of preferential treatment for blacks. This is a difficult issue, but the antidiscrimination principle makes it more difficult than it is: the permissibility of preferential treatment is tied to the permissibility of hostile treatment against blacks. The antidiscrimination principle does not formally acknowledge social groups, such as blacks; nor does it offer any special dispensation for conduct that benefits a disadvantaged group.") *with* A. BICKEL, THE MORALITY OF CONSENT 133 (1975) ("The lesson of the great decisions of the Supreme Court and the lesson of contemporary history have been the same for at least a generation: discrimination on the basis of race is illegal, immoral, inherently wrong, and destructive of democratic society. Now this is to be unlearned and we are told that this is not a matter of fundamental principle but only a matter of whose ox is gored."). Did the *Bakke* decision embrace either one of these paradigms?

A number of other arguments were advanced in supporting or criticizing affirmative action. One that was particularly influential was that made by Professor John Ely. Professor Ely argued: "regardless of whether it is wise or unwise, it is not 'suspect' in a constitutional sense for a majority, any majority, to discriminate against itself." Ely, *The Constitutionality of Reverse Racial Discrimination*, 41 U. CHI. L. REV. 723, 727 (1974). Many other commentators have also made important contributions to the debate on this issue. *See, e.g.,* EQUALITY AND PREFERENTIAL TREATMENT (R. Dworkin ed., 1977); Greenawalt, *Judicial Scrutiny of "Benign" Racial Preferences in Law School Admissions*, 75 COLUM. L. REV. 559 (1975); Karst & Horowitz, *Affirmative Action and Equal Protection*, 60 VA. L. REV. 955 (1974); Posner, *The Bakke Case and the Future of Affirmative Action*, 67 CAL. L. REV. 171 (1979); Posner, *The DeFunis Case and the Constitutionality of Preferential Treatment of Racial Minorities*, 1974 SUP. CT. REV. l; Sandalow, *Racial Preferences in Higher Education: Political Responsibility and the Judicial Role*, 42 U. CHI. L. REV. 653 (1975).

GRUTTER v. BOLLINGER
539 U.S. 306, 123 S. Ct. 2325, 156 L. Ed. 2d 304 (2003)

JUSTICE O'CONNOR delivered the opinion of the Court.

This case requires us to decide whether the use of race as a factor in student admissions by the University of Michigan Law School (Law School) is unlawful.

I

A

The Law School ranks among the Nation's top law schools. It receives more than 3,500 applications each year for a class of around 350 students. Seeking to "admit a group of students who individually and collectively are among the most capable," the Law School looks for individuals with "substantial promise for success in law school" and "a strong likelihood of succeeding in the practice of law and contributing in diverse ways to the well-being of others." More broadly, the Law School seeks "a mix of students with varying backgrounds and experiences who will respect and learn from each other." In 1992, the dean of the Law School charged a faculty committee with crafting a written admissions policy to implement these goals. In particular, the Law School sought to ensure that its efforts to achieve student body diversity complied with this Court's most recent ruling on the use of race in university admissions. *See Regents of Univ. of Cal. v. Bakke*, 438 U.S. 265 (1978). Upon the unanimous adoption of the committee's report by the Law School faculty, it became the Law School's official admissions policy.

The hallmark of that policy is its focus on academic ability coupled with a flexible assessment of applicants' talents, experiences, and potential "to contribute to the learning of those around them." The policy requires admissions officials to evaluate each applicant based on all the information available in the file, including a personal statement, letters of recommendation, and an essay describing the ways in which the applicant will contribute to the life and diversity of the Law School. In reviewing an applicant's file, admissions officials must consider the applicant's undergraduate grade point average (GPA) and Law School Admissions Test (LSAT) score because they are important (if imperfect) predictors of academic success in law school. The policy stresses that "no applicant should be admitted unless we expect that applicant to do well enough to graduate with no serious academic problems."

The policy makes clear, however, that even the highest possible score does not guarantee admission to the Law School. Nor does a low score automatically disqualify an applicant. Rather, the policy requires admissions officials to look beyond grades and test scores to other criteria that are important to the Law School's educational objectives. So-called " 'soft' variables" such as "the enthusiasm of recommenders, the quality of the undergraduate institution, the quality of the applicant's essay, and the areas and difficulty of undergraduate course selection" are all brought to bear in assessing an "applicant's likely contributions to the intellectual and social life of the institution."

The policy aspires to "achieve that diversity which has the potential to enrich everyone's education. . . ." The policy does not restrict the types of diversity contributions eligible for "substantial weight" in the admissions process, but instead recognizes "many possible bases for diversity admissions." The policy does, however, reaffirm the Law School's longstanding commitment to "one particular type of diversity," that is, "racial and ethnic diversity with special reference to the inclusion of students from groups which have been historically discriminated against, like African-Americans, Hispanics and Native Americans, who without this commitment might not be represented in our student body in meaningful numbers." By enrolling a " 'critical mass' of [underrepresented] minority students," the Law School seeks to "ensure their ability to make unique contributions to the character of the Law School."

The policy does not define diversity "solely in terms of racial and ethnic status." . . . Rather, the policy seeks to guide admissions officers in "producing classes both diverse and academically outstanding, classes made up of students who promise to continue the tradition of outstanding contribution by Michigan Graduates to the legal profession."

B

Petitioner Barbara Grutter is a white Michigan resident who applied to the Law School in 1996 with a 3.8 grade point average and 161 LSAT score. The Law School initially placed petitioner on a waiting list, but subsequently rejected her application. . . .

. . . Dennis Shields, Director of Admissions when petitioner applied to the Law School, testified that he did not direct his staff to admit a particular percentage or number of minority students, but rather to consider an applicant's race along with all other factors. . . .

Erica Munzel, who succeeded Shields as Director of Admissions, testified that " 'critical mass' " means " 'meaningful numbers' " or " 'meaningful representation,' " which she understood to mean a number that encourages underrepresented minority students to participate in the classroom and not feel isolated. Munzel stated there is no number, percentage, or range of numbers or percentages that constitute critical mass. Munzel also asserted that she must consider the race of applicants because a critical mass of underrepresented minority students could not be enrolled if admissions decisions were based primarily on undergraduate GPAs and LSAT scores.

The current Dean of the Law School, Jeffrey Lehman, also testified. Like the other Law School witnesses, Lehman did not quantify critical mass in terms of numbers or percentages. He indicated that critical mass means numbers such that underrepresented minority students do not feel isolated or like spokespersons for their race. When asked about the extent to which race is considered in admissions, Lehman testified that it varies from one applicant to another. In some cases, according to Lehman's testimony, an applicant's race may play no role, while in others it may be a " 'determinative' " factor.

The District Court heard extensive testimony from Professor Richard Lempert, who chaired the faculty committee that drafted the 1992 policy. Lempert emphasized that the Law School seeks students with diverse interests and backgrounds to enhance classroom discussion and the educational experience both inside and outside the classroom. When asked about the policy's " 'commitment to racial and ethnic diversity with special reference to the inclusion of students from groups which have been historically discriminated against,' " Lempert explained that this language did not purport to remedy past discrimination, but rather to include students who may bring to the Law School a perspective different from that of members of groups which have not been the victims of such discrimination. Lempert acknowledged that other groups, such as Asians and Jews, have experienced discrimination, but explained they were not mentioned in the policy because individuals who are members of those groups were already being admitted to the Law School in significant numbers.

Kent . . . Syverud was a professor at the Law School when the 1992 admissions policy was adopted and is now Dean of Vanderbilt Law School. In addition to his testimony at trial, Syverud submitted several expert reports on the educational benefits of diversity. Syverud's testimony indicated that when a critical mass of underrepresented minority students is present, racial stereotypes lose their force because nonminority students learn there is no " 'minority viewpoint' " but rather a variety of viewpoints among minority students.

. . . Relying on data obtained from the Law School, petitioner's expert, Dr. Kinley Larntz, generated and analyzed "admissions grids" for the years in question (1995-2000). These grids show the number of applicants and the number of admittees for all combinations of GPAs and LSAT scores. . . . He concluded that membership in certain minority groups " 'is an extremely strong factor in the decision for acceptance,' " and that applicants from these minority groups " 'are given an extremely large allowance for admission' " as compared to applicants who are members of nonfavored groups. Dr. Larntz conceded, however, that race is not the predominant factor in the Law School's admissions calculus.

Dr. Stephen Raudenbush, the Law School's expert, . . . predicted . . . a race-blind admissions system would have a " 'very dramatic,' " negative effect on underrepresented minority admissions. He testified that in 2000, 35 percent of underrepresented minority applicants were admitted. Dr. Raudenbush predicted that if race were not considered, only 10 percent of those applicants would have been admitted. Under this scenario, underrepresented minority students would have comprised 4 percent of the entering class in 2000 instead of the actual figure of 14.5 percent.

. . . [T]he District Court concluded that the Law School's use of race as a factor in admissions decisions was unlawful. . . .

Sitting en banc, the Court of Appeals reversed the District Court's judgment. . . .

We granted certiorari to resolve the disagreement among the Courts of Appeals on a question of national importance. . . .

II

A

. . . Since this Court's splintered decision in *Bakke*, Justice Powell's opinion announcing the judgment of the Court has served as the touchstone for constitutional analysis of race-conscious admissions policies. . . .

Justice Powell began by stating that "the guarantee of equal protection cannot mean one thing when applied to one individual and something else when applied to a person of another color. . . . *Bakke*, 438 U.S. at 289-290. In Justice Powell's view, when governmental decisions "touch upon an individual's race or ethnic background, he is entitled to a judicial determination that the burden he is asked to bear on that basis is precisely tailored to serve a compelling governmental interest." *Id.* at 299. . . .

First, Justice Powell rejected an interest in " 'reducing the historic deficit of traditionally disfavored minorities in medical schools and in the medical profession' " as an unlawful interest in racial balancing. *Id.* at 306-307. Second, Justice Powell rejected an interest in remedying societal discrimination because such measures would risk placing unnecessary burdens on innocent third parties "who bear no responsibility for whatever harm the beneficiaries of the special admissions program are thought to have suffered." *Id.* at 310. Third, Justice Powell rejected an interest in "increasing the number of physicians who will practice in communities currently underserved," concluding that even if such an interest could be compelling in some circumstances the program under review was not "geared to promote that goal." *Id.* at 306, 310.

Justice Powell approved the university's use of race to further only one interest: "the attainment of a diverse student body." *Id.* at 311. With the important proviso that "constitutional limitations protecting individual rights may not be disregarded," Justice Powell grounded his analysis in the academic freedom that "long has been viewed as a special concern of the First Amendment." *Id.* at 312, 314. Justice Powell emphasized that nothing less than the " 'nation's future depends upon leaders trained through wide exposure' to the ideas and mores of students as diverse as this Nation of many peoples." *Id.* at 313 (quoting *Keyishian v. Board of Regents of Univ. of State of N. Y.*, 385 U.S. 589, 603 (1967)). In seeking the "right to select those students who will contribute the most to the 'robust exchange of ideas,' " a university seeks "to achieve a goal that is of paramount importance in the fulfillment of its mission." 438 U.S. at 313. . . .

Justice Powell was, however, careful to emphasize that . . . "the diversity that furthers a compelling state interest encompasses a far broader array of qualifications and characteristics of which racial or ethnic origin is but a single though important element." *Id.*

In the wake of our fractured decision in *Bakke*, courts have struggled to discern whether Justice Powell's diversity rationale, set forth in part of the opinion joined by no other Justice, is nonetheless binding precedent under *Marks*. In that case, we explained that "when a fragmented Court decides a case and no single rationale explaining the result enjoys the assent of five Justices, the holding of the Court may be viewed as that position taken by those Members who concurred in the judgments on the narrowest grounds." 430 U.S. at 193. . . .

We do not find it necessary to decide whether Justice Powell's opinion is binding under *Marks*. . . . [F]or the reasons set out below, today we endorse Justice Powell's view that student body diversity is a compelling state interest that can justify the use of race in university admissions.

B

. . . Because the Fourteenth Amendment "protects *persons*, not *groups*," all "governmental action based on race — a *group* classification long recognized as in most circumstances irrelevant and therefore prohibited — should be subjected to detailed judicial inquiry to ensure that the *personal* right to equal protection of the laws has not been infringed." *Adarand Constructors, Inc. v. Pena*, 515 U.S. 200, 227 (1995). . . .

We have held that all racial classifications imposed by government "must be analyzed by a reviewing court under strict scrutiny." *Id.* This means that such classifications are constitutional only if they are narrowly tailored to further compelling governmental interests. . . .

Strict scrutiny is not "strict in theory, but fatal in fact." *Adarand Constructors, Inc. v. Pena, supra*, at 237. . . . When race-based action is necessary to further a compelling governmental interest, such action does not violate the constitutional guarantee of equal protection so long as the narrow-tailoring requirement is also satisfied.

Context matters. . . . *See Gomillion v. Lightfoot*, 364 U.S. 339, 343-344 (1960). . . . [S]trict scrutiny is designed to provide a framework for carefully examining the importance and the sincerity of the reasons advanced by the governmental decisionmaker for the use of race in that particular context.

III

A

. . . [T]he Law School asks us to recognize, in the context of higher education, a compelling state interest in student body diversity.

. . . [W]e have never held that the only governmental use of race that can survive strict scrutiny is remedying past discrimination. . . . Today, we hold that the Law School has a compelling interest in attaining a diverse student body.

. . . The Law School's assessment that diversity will, in fact, yield educational benefits is substantiated by respondents and their *amici*. Our scrutiny of the interest asserted by the Law School is no less strict for taking into account complex educational judgments in an area that lies primarily within the expertise of the university. Our holding today is in keeping with our tradition of giving a degree of deference to a university's academic decisions, within constitutionally prescribed limits.

We have long recognized that, given the important purpose of public education and the expansive freedoms of speech and thought associated with the university environment, universities occupy a special niche in our constitutional tradition. . . .

"The freedom of a university to make its own judgments as to education includes the selection of its student body." *Bakke, supra*, at 312. . . . "[T]he right to select those students who will contribute the most to the 'robust exchange of ideas' . . . is of paramount importance in the fulfillment of its mission." 438 U.S. at 313. Our conclusion that the Law School has a compelling interest in a diverse student body is informed by our view that attaining a diverse student body is at the heart of the Law School's proper institutional mission, and that "good faith" on the part of a university is "presumed" absent "a showing to the contrary." 438 U.S. at 318-319.

. . . The Law School's interest is not simply "to assure within its student body some specified percentage of a particular group merely because of its race or ethnic origin." *Bakke*, 438 U.S. at 307 (opinion of Powell, J.). That would amount to outright racial balancing, which is patently unconstitutional. . . . Rather, the Law School's concept of critical mass is defined by reference to the educational benefits that diversity is designed to produce.

These benefits are substantial. As the District Court emphasized, the Law School's admissions policy promotes "cross-racial understanding," helps to break down racial stereotypes, and "enables [students] to better understand persons of different races." These benefits are "important and laudable," because "classroom discussion is livelier, more spirited, and simply more enlightening and interesting" when the students have "the greatest possible variety of backgrounds." *Id.* at 246a, 244a.

. . . [N]umerous studies show that student body diversity promotes learning outcomes, and "better prepares students for an increasingly diverse workforce and society, and better prepares them as professionals." Brief for American Educational Research Association et al. as *Amici Curiae* 3.

These benefits are not theoretical but real, as major American businesses have made clear that the skills needed in today's increasingly global marketplace can only be developed through exposure to widely diverse people, cultures, ideas, and viewpoints. Brief for 3M et al. as *Amici Curiae* 5; Brief for General Motors Corp. as *Amicus Curiae* 3-4. What is more, high-ranking retired officers and civilian leaders of the United States military assert that, "based on [their] decades of experience," a "highly qualified, racially diverse officer corps . . . is essential to the military's ability to fulfill its principle mission to provide national security." Brief for Julius W. Becton, Jr. et al. as *Amici Curiae* 27. The primary sources for the Nation's officer corps are the service academies and the Reserve Officers Training Corps (ROTC), the latter comprising students already admitted to participating colleges and universities. At present, "the military cannot achieve an officer corps that is both highly qualified and racially diverse unless the service academies and the ROTC used limited race-conscious recruiting and admissions policies." [*Id.* at 5]. . . .

We have repeatedly acknowledged the overriding importance of preparing students for work and citizenship, describing education as pivotal to "sustaining our political and cultural heritage" with a fundamental role in maintaining the fabric of society. *Plyler v. Doe*, 457 U.S. 202, 221 (1982). This Court has long recognized that "education . . . is the very foundation of good citizenship." *Brown v. Board of Education*, 347 U.S. 483, 493 (1954). For this reason, the diffusion of knowledge and opportunity through public institutions of higher education must be accessible to all individuals regardless of race or ethnicity. . . .

Moreover, universities, and in particular, law schools, represent the training ground for a large number of our Nation's leaders. *Sweatt v. Painter*, 339 U.S. 629, 634 (1950). . . . Individuals with law degrees occupy roughly half the state governorships, more than half the seats in the United States Senate, and more than a third of the seats in the United States House of Representatives. The pattern is even more striking when it comes to highly selective law schools. A handful of these schools accounts for 25 of the 100 United States Senators, 74 United States Courts of Appeals judges, and nearly 200 of the more than 600 United States District Court judges.

In order to cultivate a set of leaders with legitimacy in the eyes of the citizenry, it is necessary that the path to leadership be visibly open to talented and qualified individuals of every race and ethnicity. All members of our heterogeneous society must have confidence in the openness and integrity of the educational institutions that provide this training. . . . Access to legal education (and thus the legal profession) must be inclusive of talented and qualified individuals of every race and ethnicity, so that all members of our heterogeneous society may participate in the educational institutions that provide the training and education necessary to succeed in America.

The Law School does not premise its need for critical mass on "any belief that minority students always (or even consistently) express some characteristic minority viewpoint on any issue." To the contrary, diminishing the force of such stereotypes is both a crucial part of the Law School's mission, and one that it cannot accomplish with only token numbers of minority students. Just as growing up in a particular region or having particular professional experiences is likely to affect an individual's views, so too is one's own, unique experience of being a racial minority in a society, like our own, in which race unfortunately still matters. The Law School has determined, based on its experience and expertise, that a "critical mass" of underrepresented minorities is necessary to further its compelling interest in securing the educational benefits of a diverse student body.

B

. . . To be narrowly tailored, a race-conscious admissions program cannot use a quota system. . . .

We find that the Law School's admissions program bears the hallmarks of a narrowly tailored plan. As Justice Powell made clear in *Bakke*, truly individualized consideration demands that race be used in a flexible, nonmechanical way. It follows from this mandate that universities cannot establish quotas for members of certain racial groups or put members of those groups on separate admissions tracks. [*See Bakke, supra,* at 315-316.] Nor can universities insulate applicants who belong to certain racial or ethnic groups from the competition for admission. Universities can, however, consider race or ethnicity more flexibly as a "plus" factor in the context of individualized consideration of each and every applicant. [*Id.* at 315-316.]

We are satisfied that the Law School's admissions program, like the Harvard plan described by Justice Powell, does not operate as a quota. Properly understood, a "quota" is a program in which a certain fixed number or proportion of opportunities are "reserved exclusively for certain minority groups." *Richmond v. J.A. Croson Co., supra,* at 496 (plurality opinion). Quotas " 'impose a fixed number or percentage which must be attained, or which cannot be exceeded,' " *Sheet Metal Workers v. EEOC,* 478 U.S. 421, 495 (1986) (O'Connor, J., concurring in part and dissenting in part), and "insulate the individual from comparison with all other candidates for the available seats." *Bakke, supra,* at 317 (opinion of Powell, J.). In contrast, "a permissible goal . . . requires only a good-faith effort . . . to come within a range demarcated by the goal itself," *Sheet Metal Workers v. EEOC, supra,* at 495, and permits consideration of race as a "plus" factor in any given case while still ensuring that each candidate "competes with all other qualified applicants," *Johnson v. Transportation Agency, Santa Clara Cty.,* 480 U.S. 616, 638 (1987). Justice Powell's distinction between the medical school's rigid 16-seat quota and Harvard's flexible use of race as a "plus" factor is instructive. Harvard certainly had minimum goals for minority enrollment, even if it had no specific number firmly in mind. . . .

The Law School's goal of attaining a critical mass of underrepresented minority students does not transform its program into a quota. As the Harvard plan described by Justice Powell recognized, there is of course "some relationship between numbers and achieving the benefits to be derived from a diverse student body, and between numbers and providing a reasonable environment for those students admitted." [438 U.S. at] 323. . . . Nor, as Justice Kennedy posits, does the Law School's consultation of the "daily reports," which keep track of the racial and ethnic composition of the class (as well as of residency and gender), "suggest there was no further attempt at individual review save for race itself" during the final stages of the admissions process. To the contrary, the Law School's admissions officers testified without contradiction that they never gave race any more or less weight based on the information contained in these reports. Moreover, as Justice Kennedy concedes, between 1993 and 2000, the number of African-American, Latino, and Native-American students in each class at the Law School varied from 13.5 to 20.1 percent, a range inconsistent with a quota.

The Chief Justice believes that the Law School's policy conceals an attempt to achieve racial balancing, and cites admissions data to contend that the Law School discriminates among different groups within the critical mass. But, as The Chief Justice concedes, the number of underrepresented minority students who ultimately enroll in the Law School differs substantially from their representation in the applicant pool and varies considerably for each group from year to year. That a race-conscious admissions program does not operate as a quota does not, by itself, satisfy the requirement of individualized consideration. When using race as a "plus" factor in university admissions, a university's admissions program must remain flexible enough to ensure that each applicant is evaluated as an individual and not in a way that makes an applicant's race or ethnicity the defining feature of his or her application. The importance of this individualized consideration in the context of a race-conscious admissions program is paramount. . . . Here, the Law School engages in a highly individualized, holistic review of each applicant's file, giving serious consideration to all the ways an applicant might contribute to a diverse educational environment. The Law School affords this individualized consideration to applicants of all races. There is no policy, either *de jure or de facto*, of automatic acceptance or rejection based on any single "soft" variable. Unlike the program at issue in *Gratz v. Bollinger*, the Law School awards no mechanical, predetermined diversity "bonuses" based on race or ethnicity. . . . Like the Harvard plan, the Law School's admissions policy "is flexible enough to consider all pertinent elements of diversity in light of the particular qualifications of each applicant, and to place them on the same footing for consideration, although not necessarily according them the same weight." *Bakke, supra*, at 317 (opinion of Powell, J.).

We also find that, like the Harvard plan Justice Powell referenced in *Bakke*, the Law School's race-conscious admissions program adequately ensures that all factors that may contribute to student body diversity are meaningfully considered alongside race in admissions decisions. With respect to the use of race itself, all underrepresented minority students admitted by the Law School have been deemed qualified. By virtue of our Nation's struggle with racial inequality, such students are both likely to have experiences of particular importance to the Law School's mission, and less likely to be admitted in meaningful numbers on criteria that ignore those experiences.

. . . [T]he 1992 policy makes clear "there are many possible bases for diversity admissions," and provides examples of admittees who have lived or traveled widely abroad, are fluent in several languages, have overcome personal adversity and family hardship, have exceptional records of extensive community service, and have had successful careers in other fields. The Law School seriously considers each "applicant's promise of making a notable contribution to the class by way of a particular strength, attainment, or characteristic — e.g., an unusual intellectual achievement, employment experience, nonacademic performance, or personal background." All applicants have the opportunity to highlight their own potential diversity contributions through the submission of a personal statement, letters of recommendation, and an essay describing the ways in which the applicant will contribute to the life and diversity of the Law School.

What is more, the Law School actually gives substantial weight to diversity factors besides race. The Law School frequently accepts nonminority applicants with grades and test scores lower than underrepresented minority applicants (and other nonminority applicants) who are rejected. This shows that the Law School seriously weighs many other diversity factors besides race that can make a real and dispositive difference for nonminority applicants as well. . . . Justice Kennedy speculates that "race is likely outcome determinative for many members of minority groups" who do not fall within the upper range of LSAT scores and grades. But the same could be said of the Harvard plan discussed approvingly by Justice Powell in *Bakke*, and indeed of any plan that uses race as one of many factors. . . .

. . . Narrow tailoring does not require exhaustion of every conceivable race-neutral alternative. Nor does it require a university to choose between maintaining a reputation for excellence or fulfilling a commitment to provide educational opportunities to members of all racial groups. *See Wygant v. Jackson Bd. of Ed.*, 476 U.S. 267, 280, n.6 (1986) (alternatives must serve the interest " 'about as well' "). . . . Narrow tailoring does, however, require serious, good faith consideration of workable race-neutral alternatives that will achieve the diversity the university seeks. . . .

. . . The District Court took the Law School to task for failing to consider race-neutral alternatives such as "using a lottery system" or "decreasing the emphasis for all applicants on undergraduate GPA and LSAT scores." But these alternatives would require a dramatic sacrifice of diversity, the academic quality of all admitted students, or both.

. . . Because a lottery would make that kind of nuanced judgment impossible, it would effectively sacrifice all other educational values, not to mention every other kind of diversity. So too with the suggestion that the Law School simply lower admissions standards for all students, a drastic remedy that would require the Law School to become a much different institution and sacrifice a vital component of its educational mission. The United States advocates "percentage plans," recently adopted by public undergraduate institutions in Texas, Florida, and California to guarantee admission to all students above a certain class-rank threshold in every high school in the State. The United States does not, however, explain how such plans could work for graduate and professional schools. Moreover, even assuming such plans are race-neutral, they may preclude the university from conducting the individualized assessments necessary to assemble a student body that is not just racially diverse, but diverse along all the qualities valued by the university. We are satisfied that the Law School adequately considered race-neutral alternatives currently capable of producing a critical mass without forcing the Law School to abandon the academic selectivity that is the cornerstone of its educational mission.

We acknowledge that "there are serious problems of justice connected with the idea of preference itself." *Bakke*, 438 U.S. at 298 (opinion of Powell, J.). . . . Even remedial race-based governmental action generally "remains subject to continuing oversight to assure that it will work the least harm possible to other innocent persons competing for the benefit." *Id.* at 308. To be narrowly tailored, a race-conscious admissions program must not "unduly burden individuals who are not members of the favored racial and ethnic groups." *Metro Broadcasting, Inc. v. FCC*, 497 U.S. 547, 630 (1990) (O'Connor, J., dissenting).

We are satisfied that the Law School's admissions program does not. Because the Law School considers "all pertinent elements of diversity," it can (and does) select nonminority applicants who have greater potential to enhance student body diversity over underrepresented minority applicants. *See Bakke, supra*, at 317 (opinion of Powell, J.). . . .

We are mindful, however, that "[a] core purpose of the Fourteenth Amendment was to do away with all governmentally imposed discrimination based on race." *Palmore v. Sidoti*, 466 U.S. 429, 432 (1984). Accordingly, race-conscious admissions policies must be limited in time. This requirement reflects that racial classifications, however compelling their goals, are potentially so dangerous that they may be employed no more broadly than the interest demands. Enshrining a permanent justification for racial preferences would offend this fundamental equal protection principle. . . .

In the context of higher education, the durational requirement can be met by sunset provisions in race-conscious admissions policies and periodic reviews to determine whether racial preferences are still necessary to achieve student body diversity. Universities in California, Florida, and Washington State, where racial preferences in admissions are prohibited by state law, are currently engaged in experimenting with a wide variety of alternative approaches. Universities in other States can and should draw on the most promising aspects of these race-neutral alternatives as they develop. . . .

The requirement that all race-conscious admissions programs have a termination point "assures all citizens that the deviation from the norm of equal treatment of all racial and ethnic groups is a temporary matter, a measure taken in the service of the goal of equality itself." *Richmond v. J.A. Croson Co.*, 488 U.S. at 510 (plurality opinion). . . .

We take the Law School at its word that it would "like nothing better than to find a race-neutral admissions formula" and will terminate its race-conscious admissions program as soon as practicable. . . . It has been 25 years since Justice Powell first approved the use of race to further an interest in student body diversity in the context of public higher education. Since that time, the number of minority applicants with high grades and test scores has indeed increased. We expect that 25 years from now, the use of racial preferences will no longer be necessary to further the interest approved today.

IV

In summary, the Equal Protection Clause does not prohibit the Law School's narrowly tailored use of race in admissions decisions to further a compelling interest in obtaining the educational benefits that flow from a diverse student body. Consequently, petitioner's statutory claims based on Title VI and 42 U.S.C. § 1981 also fail. *See Bakke, supra*, at 287 (opinion of Powell, J.) ("Title VI . . . proscribes only those racial classifications that would violate the Equal Protection Clause or the Fifth Amendment"); *General Building Contractors Assn., Inc. v. Pennsylvania*, 458 U.S. 375, 389-391 (1982) (the prohibition against discrimination in § 1981 is co-extensive with the Equal Protection Clause). . . .

Justice Ginsburg, with whom Justice Breyer joins, concurring.

The Court's observation that race-conscious programs "must have a logical end point," accords with the international understanding of the office of affirmative action. The International Convention on the Elimination of All Forms of Racial Discrimination, ratified by the United States in 1994 endorses "special and concrete measures to ensure the adequate development and protection of certain racial groups or individuals belonging to them, for the purpose of guaranteeing them the full and equal enjoyment of human rights and fundamental freedoms." Annex to G. A. Res. 2106, 20 U. N. GAOR Res. Supp. (No. 14) 47, U. N. Doc. A/6014, Art. 2(2) (1965). But such measures, the Convention instructs, "shall in no case entail as a consequence the maintenance of unequal or separate rights for different racial groups after the objectives for which they were taken have been achieved." *Id*; *see also* Art. 1(4) (similarly providing for temporally limited affirmative action); Convention on the Elimination of All Forms of Discrimination against Women, Annex to G. A. Res. 34/180, 34 U. N. GAOR Res. Supp. (No. 46) 194, U. N. Doc. A/34/46, Art. 4(1) (1979) (authorizing "temporary special measures aimed at accelerating *de facto* equality" that "shall be discontinued when the objectives of equality of opportunity and treatment have been achieved").

The Court further observes that "it has been 25 years since Justice Powell [in *Regents of Univ. of Cal. v. Bakke*, 438 U.S. 265 (1978)] first approved the use of race to further an interest in student body diversity in the context of public higher education." For at least part of that time, however, the law could not fairly be described as "settled," and in some regions of the Nation, overtly race-conscious admissions policies have been proscribed. *See Hopwood v. Texas*, 78 F.3d 932 (CA5 1996). Moreover, it was only 25 years before *Bakke* that this Court declared public school segregation unconstitutional, a declaration that, after prolonged resistance, yielded an end to a law-enforced racial caste system, itself the legacy of centuries of slavery.

It is well documented that conscious and unconscious race bias, even rank discrimination based on race, remain alive in our land, impeding realization of our highest values and ideals. As to public education, data for the years 2000-2001 show that 71.6% of African-American children and 76.3% of Hispanic children attended a school in which minorities made up a majority of the student body. . . .

However strong the public's desire for improved education systems may be, . . . it remains the current reality that many minority students encounter markedly inadequate and unequal educational opportunities. Despite these inequalities, some minority students are able to meet the high threshold requirements set for admission to the country's finest undergraduate and graduate educational institutions. As lower school education in minority communities improves, an increase in the number of such students may be anticipated. From today's vantage point, one may hope, but not firmly forecast, that over the next generation's span, progress toward nondiscrimination and genuinely equal opportunity will make it safe to sunset affirmative action.

Chief Justice Rehnquist, with whom Justice Scalia, Justice Kennedy, and Justice Thomas join, dissenting.

. . . I do not believe . . . that the University of Michigan Law School's (Law School) means are narrowly tailored to the interest it asserts. . . . Stripped of its "critical mass" veil, the Law School's program is revealed as a naked effort to achieve racial balancing.

. . . [R]espondents must demonstrate that their methods of using race " 'fit' " a compelling state interest "with greater precision than any alternative means." *Regents of Univ. of Cal. v. Bakke*, 438 U.S. 265, 299 (1978) (opinion of Powell, J.). . . .

Before the Court's decision today, we consistently applied the same strict scrutiny analysis regardless of the government's purported reason for using race and regardless of the setting in which race was being used. . . . [E]ven in the specific context of higher education, we emphasized that "constitutional limitations protecting individual rights may not be disregarded." *Bakke*, *supra*, at 314.

Although the Court recites the language of our strict scrutiny analysis, its application of that review is unprecedented in its deference. . . .

In practice, the Law School's program bears little or no relation to its asserted goal of achieving "critical mass.". . .

. . . In order for this pattern of admission to be consistent with the Law School's explanation of "critical mass," one would have to believe that the objectives of "critical mass" offered by respondents are achieved with only half the number of Hispanics and one-sixth the number of Native Americans as compared to African-Americans. . . .

. . . [T]he Law School states that "sixty-nine minority applicants were rejected between 1995 and 2000 with at least a 3.5 [Grade Point Average (GPA)] and a [score of] 159 or higher on the [Law School Admissions Test (LSAT)]" while a number of Caucasian and Asian-American applicants with similar or lower scores were admitted.

Review of the record reveals only 67 such individuals. Of these 67 individuals, 56 were Hispanic, while only 6 were African-American, and only 5 were Native American. This discrepancy reflects a consistent practice. For example, in 2000, 12 Hispanics who scored between a 159-160 on the LSAT and earned a GPA of 3.00 or higher applied for admission and only 2 were admitted. Meanwhile, 12 African-Americans in the same range of qualifications applied for admission and all 12 were admitted. Likewise, that same year, 16 Hispanics who scored between a 151-153 on the LSAT and earned a 3.00 or higher applied for admission and only 1 of those applicants was admitted. Twenty-three similarly qualified African-Americans applied for admission and 14 were admitted.

. . . [T]he Law School's disparate admissions practices with respect to these minority groups demonstrate that its alleged goal of "critical mass" is simply a sham. . . .

. . . [F]rom 1995 through 2000 the percentage of admitted applicants who were members of these minority groups closely tracked the percentage of individuals in the school's applicant pool who were from the same groups.

For example, in 1995, when 9.7% of the applicant pool was African-American, 9.4% of the admitted class was African-American. By 2000, only 7.5% of the applicant pool was African-American, and 7.3% of the admitted class was African-American. . . .

. . .[T]he ostensibly flexible nature of the Law School's admissions program that the Court finds appealing appears to be, in practice, a carefully managed program designed to ensure proportionate representation of applicants from selected minority groups.

. . . [T]his is precisely the type of racial balancing that the Court itself calls "patently unconstitutional."

Finally, I believe that the Law School's program fails strict scrutiny because it is devoid of any reasonably precise time limit on the Law School's use of race in admissions. . . .

. . . Our previous cases have required some limit on the duration of programs such as this because discrimination on the basis of race is invidious.

The Court suggests a possible 25-year limitation on the Law School's current program. Respondents, on the other hand, remain more ambiguous, explaining that "the Law School of course recognizes that race-conscious programs must have reasonable durational limits. . . .

[T]he flaw . . . is not merely a question of "fit" between ends and means. Here the means actually used are forbidden by the Equal Protection Clause of the Constitution.

JUSTICE KENNEDY, dissenting.

The separate opinion by Justice Powell in *Regents of Univ. of Cal. v. Bakke* is based on the principle that a university admissions program may take account of race as one, nonpredominant factor in a system designed to consider each applicant as an individual, provided the program can meet the test of strict scrutiny by the judiciary. . . . The opinion by Justice Powell, in my view, states the correct rule for resolving this case. . . .

Justice Powell's approval of the use of race in university admissions reflected a tradition, grounded in the First Amendment, of acknowledging a university's conception of its educational mission. . . .

. . . Preferment by race, when resorted to by the State, can be the most divisive of all policies, containing within it the potential to destroy confidence in the Constitution and in the idea of equality. The majority today refuses to be faithful to the settled principle of strict review designed to reflect these concerns.

. . . The dissenting opinion by The Chief Justice, which I join in full, demonstrates beyond question why the concept of critical mass is a delusion used by the Law School to mask its attempt to make race an automatic factor in most instances and to achieve numerical goals indistinguishable from quotas. . . .

About 80 to 85 percent of the places in the entering class are given to applicants in the upper range of Law School Admissions Test scores and grades. An applicant with these credentials likely will be admitted without consideration of race or ethnicity. With respect to the remaining 15 to 20 percent of the seats, race is likely outcome determinative for many members of minority groups. . . .

. . . There was little deviation among admitted minority students during the years from 1995 to 1998. The percentage of enrolled minorities fluctuated only by 0.3%, from 13.5% to 13.8%. The number of minority students to whom offers were extended varied by just a slightly greater magnitude of 2.2%, from the high of 15.6% in 1995 to the low of 13.4% in 1998.

. . . Admittedly, there were greater fluctuations among enrolled minorities in the preceding years, 1987-1994, by as much as 5 or 6%. . . . The data would be consistent with an inference that the Law School modified its target only twice, in 1991 (from 13% to 19%), and then again in 1995 (back from 20% to 13%). . . .

. . . Whether the objective of critical mass "is described as a quota or a goal, it is a line drawn on the basis of race and ethnic status," and so risks compromising individual assessment. *Bakke*, 438 U.S. at 289 (opinion of Powell, J.). In this respect the Law School program compares unfavorably with the experience of Little Ivy League colleges. *Amicus* Amherst College, for example, informs us that the offers it extended to students of African-American background during the period from 1993 to 2002 ranged between 81 and 125 out of 950 offers total, resulting in a fluctuation from 24 to 49 matriculated students in a class of about 425. The Law School insisted upon a much smaller fluctuation, both in the offers extended and in the students who eventually enrolled, despite having a comparable class size. . . .

The obvious tension between the pursuit of critical mass and the requirement of individual review increased by the end of the admissions season. Most of the decisions where race may decide the outcome are made during this period. . . .

The consultation of daily reports during the last stages in the admissions process suggests there was no further attempt at individual review save for race itself. The admissions officers could use the reports to recalibrate the plus factor given to race depending on how close they were to achieving the Law School's goal of critical mass. The bonus factor of race would then become divorced from individual review; it would be premised instead on the numerical objective set by the Law School. . . .

To be constitutional, a university's compelling interest in a diverse student body must be achieved by a system where individual assessment is safeguarded through the entire process. There is no constitutional objection to the goal of considering race as one modest factor among many others to achieve diversity, but an educational institution must ensure, through sufficient procedures, that each applicant receives individual consideration and that race does not become a predominant factor in the admissions decisionmaking. . . .

. . . Deference is antithetical to strict scrutiny, not consistent with it.

. . . Were the courts to apply a searching standard to race-based admissions schemes, that would force educational institutions to seriously explore race-neutral alternatives. The Court, by contrast, is willing to be satisfied by the Law School's profession of its own good faith.

For these reasons, though I reiterate my approval of giving appropriate consideration to race in this one context, I must dissent in the present case.

JUSTICE SCALIA, with whom JUSTICE THOMAS joins, concurring in part and dissenting in part. . . . [9] Unlike a clear constitutional holding that racial preferences in state educational institutions are impermissible, or even a clear anticonstitutional holding that racial preferences in state educational institutions are OK, today's *Grutter-Gratz* split double header seems perversely designed to prolong the controversy and the litigation. Some future lawsuits will presumably focus on whether the discriminatory scheme in question contains enough evaluation of the applicant "as an individual," and sufficiently avoids "separate admissions tracks" to fall under *Grutter* rather than *Gratz.* Some will focus on whether a university has gone beyond the bounds of a " 'good faith effort' " and has so zealously pursued its "critical mass" as to make it an unconstitutional *de facto* quota system, rather than merely " 'a permissible goal.' " Other lawsuits may focus on whether, in the particular setting at issue, any educational benefits flow from racial diversity. (That issue was not contested in *Grutter*; and while the opinion accords "a degree of deference to a university's academic decisions," "deference does not imply abandonment or abdication of judicial review," *Miller-El v. Cockrell,* 537 U.S. 322, 340 (2003).) Still other suits may challenge the bona fides of the institution's expressed commitment to the educational benefits of diversity that immunize the discriminatory scheme in *Grutter.* (Tempting targets, one would suppose, will be those universities that talk the talk of multiculturalism and racial diversity in the courts but walk the walk of tribalism and racial segregation on their campuses — through minority-only student organizations, separate minority housing opportunities, separate minority student centers, even separate minority-only graduation ceremonies.) And still other suits may claim that the institution's racial preferences have gone below or above the mystical *Grutter*-approved "critical mass." Finally, litigation can be expected on behalf of minority groups intentionally short changed in the institution's composition of its generic minority "critical mass." . . .

JUSTICE THOMAS, with whom JUSTICE SCALIA joins as to Parts I-VII, concurring in part and dissenting in part.

Frederick Douglass, speaking to a group of abolitionists almost 140 years ago, delivered a message lost on today's majority:

"In regard to the colored people, there is always more that is benevolent, I perceive, than just, manifested towards us. What I ask for the negro is not benevolence, not pity, not sympathy, but simply *justice.* The American people have always been anxious to know what they shall do with us. . . . I have had but one answer from the beginning. Do nothing with us! Your doing with us has already played the mischief with us. Do

[9] [Court's footnote *] Part VII of Justice Thomas's opinion describes those portions of the Court's opinion in which I concur. *See post,* at 2363-2365 (opinion concurring in part and dissenting in part).

nothing with us! If the apples will not remain on the tree of their own strength, if they are worm-eaten at the core, if they are early ripe and disposed to fall, let them fall! . . . And if the negro cannot stand on his own legs, let him fall also. All I ask is, give him a chance to stand on his own legs! Let him alone! . . . Your interference is doing him positive injury." What the Black Man Wants: An Address Delivered in Boston, Massachusetts, on 26 January 1865, reprinted in 4 The Frederick Douglass Papers 59, 68 (J. Blassingame & J. McKivigan eds. 1991) (emphasis in original).

Like Douglass, I believe blacks can achieve in every avenue of American life without the meddling of university administrators. . . .

No one would argue that a university could set up a lower general admission standard and then impose heightened requirements only on black applicants. . . .

The majority upholds the Law School's racial discrimination not by interpreting the people's Constitution, but by responding to a faddish slogan of the cognoscenti. Nevertheless, I concur in part in the Court's opinion. First, I agree with the Court insofar as its decision, which approves of only one racial classification, confirms that further use of race in admissions remains unlawful. Second, I agree with the Court's holding that racial discrimination in higher education admissions will be illegal in 25 years. . . .

II

. . . Attaining "diversity," whatever it means,[10] is the mechanism by which the Law School obtains educational benefits, not an end of itself. The Law School, however, apparently believes that only a racially mixed student body can lead to the educational benefits it seeks. How, then, is the Law School's interest in these allegedly unique educational "benefits" *not* simply the forbidden interest in "racial balancing," that the majority expressly rejects?

I also use the term "aesthetic" because I believe it underlines the ineffectiveness of racially discriminatory admissions in actually helping those who are truly underprivileged. . . . It must be remembered that the Law School's racial discrimination does nothing for those too poor or uneducated to participate in elite higher education and therefore presents only an illusory solution to the challenges facing our Nation.

. . . It is the *educational benefits* that are the end, or allegedly compelling state interest, not "diversity." . . .

. . . Instead the Court upholds the use of racial discrimination as a tool to advance the Law School's interest in offering a marginally superior education while maintaining an elite institution. Unless each constituent part of this state interest is of pressing public necessity, the Law School's use of race is unconstitutional. I find each of them to fall far short of this standard.

III

B

Under the proper standard, there is no pressing public necessity in maintaining a public law school at all and, it follows, certainly not an elite law school. Likewise,

---

[10] [Court's footnote 3] . . . I refer to the Law School's interest as an "aesthetic." That is, the Law School wants to have a certain appearance, from the shape of the desks and tables in its classrooms to the color of the students sitting at them.

marginal improvements in legal education do not qualify as a compelling state interest. . . .

2

. . . Michigan has no compelling interest in having a law school at all, much less an elite one. Still, even assuming that a State may, under appropriate circumstances, demonstrate a cognizable interest in having an elite law school, Michigan has failed to do so here.

. . . The only interests that can satisfy the Equal Protection Clause's demands are those found within a State's jurisdiction.

The only cognizable state interests vindicated by operating a public law school are, therefore, the education of that State's citizens and the training of that State's lawyers. . . .   Less than 16% of the Law School's graduating class elects to stay in Michigan after law school. . . .

[T]he fact that few States choose to maintain elite law schools raises a strong inference that there is nothing compelling about elite status. . . .

IV

. . . [T]he Law School should be forced to choose between its classroom aesthetic and its exclusionary admissions system — it cannot have it both ways.

With the adoption of different admissions methods, such as accepting all students who meet minimum qualifications, the Law School could achieve its vision of the racially aesthetic student body without the use of racial discrimination. The Law School concedes this. . . .   First, under strict scrutiny, the Law School's assessment of the benefits of racial discrimination and devotion to the admissions status quo are not entitled to any sort of deference, grounded in the First Amendment or anywhere else. Second, even if its "academic selectivity" must be maintained at all costs along with racial discrimination, the Court ignores the fact that other top law schools have succeeded in meeting their aesthetic demands without racial discrimination.

A

. . . The only source for the Court's conclusion that public universities are entitled to deference even within the confines of strict scrutiny is Justice Powell's opinion in *Bakke*. . . .

B

1

. . . The Court relies heavily on social science evidence to justify its deference. [B]*ut see also* Rothman, Lipset, & Nevitte, Racial Diversity Reconsidered, 151 Public Interest 25 (2003) (finding that the racial mix of a student body produced by racial discrimination of the type practiced by the Law School in fact hinders students' perception of academic quality). The Court never acknowledges, however, the growing evidence that racial (and other sorts) of heterogeneity actually impairs learning among black students. *See, e.g.*, Flowers & Pascarella, *Cognitive Effects of College Racial Composition on African American Students After 3 Years of College*, 40 J. OF COLLEGE STUDENT DEVELOPMENT 669, 674 (1999) (concluding that black students experience superior cognitive development at Historically Black Colleges (HBCs) and that, even among blacks, "a substantial diversity moderates the cognitive effects of attending an HBC"); Allen, *The Color of Success: African-American College Student Outcomes at Predominantly White and Historically Black Public Colleges and Universities*, 62 HARV. EDUC. REV. 26, 35 (1992) (finding that black students attending HBCs report higher academic achievement than those attending predominantly white colleges). . . .

2

[I]n *United States v. Virginia*, 518 U.S. 515 (1996), . . . a majority of the Court, without a word about academic freedom, accepted the all-male Virginia Military Institute's (VMI) representation that some changes in its "adversative" method of education would be required with the admission of women, *id.* at 540, but did not defer to VMI's judgment that these changes would be too great. . . . Apparently where the status quo being defended is that of the elite establishment — here the Law School — rather than a less fashionable Southern military institution, the Court will defer without serious inquiry and without regard to the applicable legal standard.

C

. . . The sky has not fallen at Boalt Hall at the University of California, Berkeley, for example. Prior to Proposition 209's adoption of Cal. Const., Art. 1, § 31(a), which bars the State from "granting preferential treatment . . . on the basis of race . . . in the operation of . . . public education," Boalt Hall enrolled 20 blacks and 28 Hispanics in its first-year class for 1996. In 2002, without deploying express racial discrimination in admissions, Boalt's entering class enrolled 14 blacks and 36 Hispanics. . . . Total underrepresented minority student enrollment at Boalt Hall now exceeds 1996 levels. . . .

V

. . . Since its inception, selective admissions have been the vehicle for racial, ethnic, and religious tinkering and experimentation by university administrators. . . .

. . . Columbia employed intelligence tests precisely because Jewish applicants, who were predominantly immigrants, scored worse on such tests. . . .

Similarly no modern law school can claim ignorance of the poor performance of blacks, relatively speaking, on the Law School Admissions Test (LSAT). Nevertheless, law schools continue to use the test and then attempt to "correct" for black underperformance by using racial discrimination in admissions so as to obtain their aesthetic student body. The Law School's continued adherence to measures it knows produce racially skewed results is not entitled to deference by this Court. The Law School itself admits that the test is imperfect, as it must, given that it regularly admits students who score at or below 150 (the national median) on the test. *See* App. 156-203 (showing that, between 1995 and 2000, the Law School admitted 37 students — 27 of whom were black; 31 of whom were "underrepresented minorities" — with LSAT scores of 150 or lower). And the Law School's *amici* cannot seem to agree on the fundamental question whether the test itself is useful. Compare Brief for Law School Admission Council as *Amicus Curiae* 12 ("LSAT scores . . . are an effective predictor of students' performance in law school") with Brief for Harvard Black Law Students Association et al. as *Amici Curiae* 27 ("Whether [the LSAT] measures objective merit . . . is certainly questionable").

Having decided to use the LSAT, the Law School must accept the constitutional burdens that come with this decision. . . .

VI

. . . [N]owhere in any of the filings in this Court is any evidence that the purported "beneficiaries" of this racial discrimination prove themselves by performing at (or even near) the same level as those students who receive no preferences. *Cf.* Thernstrom & Thernstrom, Reflections on the Shape of the River, 46 UCLA L. REV. 1583, 1605-1608 (1999) (discussing the failure of defenders of racial discrimination in admissions to consider the fact that its "beneficiaries" are underperforming in the classroom). . . .

The Law School tantalizes unprepared students with the promise of a University of Michigan degree and all of the opportunities that it offers. These overmatched students take the bait, only to find that they cannot succeed in the cauldron of competition. And this mismatch crisis is not restricted to elite institutions. *See* T. Sowell, Race and Culture 176-177 (1994) ("Even if most minority students are able to meet the normal standards at the 'average' range of colleges and universities, the systematic mismatching of minority students begun at the top can mean that such students are generally overmatched throughout all levels of higher education"). Indeed, to cover the tracks of the aestheticists, this cruel farce of racial discrimination must continue — in selection for the Michigan Law Review, . . . and in hiring at law firms and for judicial clerkships — until the "beneficiaries" are no longer tolerated. While these students may graduate with law degrees, there is no evidence that they have received a qualitatively better legal education (or become better lawyers) than if they had gone to a less "elite" law school for which they were better prepared. And the aestheticists will never address the real problems facing "underrepresented minorities," instead continuing their social experiments on other people's children. . . .

It is uncontested that each year, the Law School admits a handful of blacks who would be admitted in the absence of racial discrimination. Who can differentiate between those who belong and those who do not? The majority of blacks are admitted to the Law School because of discrimination, and because of this policy all are tarred as undeserving. . . . When blacks take positions in the highest places of government, industry, or academia, it is an open question today whether their skin color played a part in their advancement. The question itself is the stigma. . . .

Finally, the Court's disturbing reference to the importance of the country's law schools as training grounds meant to cultivate "a set of leaders with legitimacy in the eyes of the citizenry," through the use of racial discrimination deserves discussion. As noted earlier, the Court has soundly rejected the remedying of societal discrimination as a justification for governmental use of race. . . .

VII

As the foregoing makes clear, I believe the Court's opinion to be, in most respects, erroneous. I do, however, find two points on which I agree.

A

First, . . .I join the Court's opinion insofar as it confirms that this type of racial discrimination remains unlawful. Under today's decision, it is still the case that racial discrimination that does not help a university to enroll an unspecified number, or "critical mass," of underrepresented minority students is unconstitutional. Thus, the Law School may not discriminate in admissions between similarly situated blacks and Hispanics, or between whites and Asians. This is so because preferring black to Hispanic applicants, for instance, does nothing to further the interest recognized by the majority today. Indeed, the majority describes such racial balancing as "patently unconstitutional." Like the Court, I express no opinion as to whether the Law School's current admissions program runs afoul of this prohibition.

B

. . . While I agree that in 25 years the practices of the Law School will be illegal, they are, for the reasons I have given, illegal now. The majority does not and cannot rest its time limitation on any evidence that the gap in credentials between black and white students is shrinking or will be gone in that timeframe. In recent years there has been virtually no change, for example, in the proportion of law school applicants with LSAT scores of 165 and higher who are black.[11] In 1993 blacks constituted 1.1% of law school applicants in that score range, though they represented 11.1% of all applicants. Law School Admission Council, National Statistical Report (1994) (hereinafter LSAC Statistical Report). In 2000 the comparable numbers were 1.0% and 11.3%. LSAC Statistical Report (2001). No one can seriously contend, and the Court does not, that the racial gap in academic credentials will disappear in 25 years.[12] . . .

Indeed, the very existence of racial discrimination of the type practiced by the Law School may impede the narrowing of the LSAT testing gap. An applicant's LSAT score can improve dramatically with preparation, but such preparation is a cost, and there must be sufficient benefits attached to an improved score to justify additional study. Whites scoring between 163 and 167 on the LSAT are routinely rejected by the Law School, and thus whites aspiring to admission at the Law School have every incentive to improve their score to levels above that range. See App. 199 (showing that in 2000, 209 out of 422 white applicants were rejected in this scoring range). Blacks, on the other hand, are nearly guaranteed admission if they score above 155. Id. at 198 (showing that 63 out of 77 black applicants are accepted with LSAT scores above 155). As admission prospects approach certainty, there is no incentive for the black applicant to continue to prepare for the LSAT once he is reasonably assured of achieving the requisite score. . . . [13]

[T]he possibility remains that this racial discrimination will help fulfill the bigot's prophecy about black underperformance — just as it confirms the conspiracy theorist's belief that "institutional racism" is at fault for every racial disparity in our society. . . .

GRATZ v. BOLLINGER, 539 U.S. 244 (2003). In *Gratz*, Chief Justice Rehnquist, writing for a 6-3 Court, invalidated the University of Michigan's policy that allocated one-fifth of the required points for admission to a student based solely on her race. Petitioners Gratz and Hamacher were Caucasian applicants that were both rejected from the University's College of Literature, Science, and the Arts even though the College determined that Gratz was "well qualified," and that Hamacher's "academic credentials [were] in the qualified range." They claimed that the University's admission policy violated the Equal Protection Clause, Title VI, and 42 U.S.C. § 1981.

The Court rejected a standing argument based on Hamacher's never having applied

---

[11] [Court's footnote 14] I use a score of 165 as the benchmark here because the Law School feels it is the relevant score range for applicant consideration (absent race discrimination). . . .

[12] [Court's footnote 15] The majority's non sequitur observation that since 1978 the number having of blacks that have scored in these upper ranges on the LSAT has grown, says nothing about current trends. . . . In 1992, 63 black applicants to law school had LSAT scores above 165. In 2000, that number was 65. See LSAC Statistical Reports (1992 and 2000).

[13] [Court's footnote 16] I use the LSAT as an example, but the same incentive structure is in place for any admissions criteria, including undergraduate grades, on which minorities are consistently admitted at thresholds significantly lower than whites.

for admittance as a transfer student. The Chief Justice held that not only had he been denied admission as an undergraduate but he stood ready to transfer.

Respondents argued that their admission program closely followed both the guidelines that Justice Powell outlined in *Regents of Univ. of Cal. v. Bakke*, 438 U.S. 265 (1978), *supra*, and the Harvard College program that Justice Powell endorsed. Disagreeing, the Court subjected all racial classifications to strict scrutiny, regardless of "the race of those burdened or benefited by a particular classification." Based on the University's undergraduate admission policy, an applicant must have received 100 points in order to be guaranteed admission. An applicant that fell into the category of an " 'underrepresented minority' " would automatically receive 20 points based solely on his race. A policy that granted one-fifth of the points needed to be guaranteed admission to an applicant based entirely on the applicant's race "is not narrowly tailored to achieve the interest in educational diversity." Justice Powell's opinion in *Bakke* stressed that a university should consider "each particular applicant as an individual, assessing all of the qualities that individual possesses, and in turn, evaluating that individual's ability to contribute to the unique setting of higher education." Justice Powell required that each characteristic of an applicant be considered based on his entire application. By distributing 20 points to an applicant based on his race, Michigan made race a decisive factor "for virtually every minimally qualified underrepresented minority applicant."

Even if an applicant's " 'extraordinary artistic talent' rivaled that of Monet or Picasso, the applicant would receive, at most, five points," for artistic talent whereas an underrepresented minority applicant "would automatically receive 20 points for submitting an application." The University noted that its undergraduate admissions program allows an applicant's file to be "flagged for individualized consideration." Although a review committee could look at a flagged applicant individually and dismiss the point system, this did not satisfy strict scrutiny. While it is not clear how often applicants were flagged, flagging was "the exception and not the rule" in the University's policy. Such "individualized review is only provided after admissions counselors automatically distribute the University's version of a 'plus' that makes race a decisive factor for virtually every minimally qualified underrepresented minority applicant." The University maintained that using its Law School's admission policy that the Court upheld in *Grutter v. Bollinger*, 539 U.S. 306 (2003), *supra*, was impractical due to " 'the volume of applications and the presentation of applicant information[.]' "

The University's undergraduate admissions policy was not narrowly tailored and thus violated the Equal Protection Clause of the Fourteenth Amendment. Violations of the Clause "committed by an institution that accepts federal funds also constitutes a violation of Title VI. Likewise, with respect to § 1981," the Court stated that "the provision was 'meant, by its broad terms, to proscribe discrimination in the making or enforcement of contracts against, or in favor of, any race.' " A contract that applied to "educational services is a 'contract' for purposes of § 1981." Moreover, purposeful discrimination under the Equal Protection Clause also violated § 1981.

Justice O'Connor's concurring opinion distinguished the University's undergraduate admissions policy from Michigan Law School's policy upheld in *Grutter* by stating that the College's policy did "not provide for a meaningful individualized review of applicants." The undergraduate program used a Selection Index Worksheet to distribute points to calculate an individual's score. Once an applicant received 100 points on a 150 point scale, he was automatically admitted. Candidates in the 95-99 range were classified as " 'admit or postpone,' " while 90-94 points put an applicant into the " 'postponed or admitted' " category. If an applicant scored between 75 and 89 points, he was " 'delayed or postponed.' " Finally, candidates with 74 points or less were " 'delayed or rejected.' " An undergraduate admissions counselor awarded points for various factors to calculate each applicant's selection index score. "Up to 110 points can be assigned for academic performance, and up to 40 points can be assigned for the other, nonacademic factors. Michigan residents, for example, receive 10 points, and children of alumni receive 4. Counselors may assign an outstanding essay up to 3 points and may award up to 5 points for an applicant's personal achievement, leadership, or public service. Most importantly for this case, an applicant automatically receives a 20 point bonus if he or she possesses any one of the following 'miscellaneous' factors: membership in an underrepresented minority group; attendance at a predominantly minority or disadvantaged high school; or recruitment for athletics." The counselor may flag an application if he "is academically prepared, has a selection index score of at least 75 (for non-Michigan residents) or 80 (for Michigan residents), and possesses one of several qualities valued by the University. These qualities include 'high class rank, unique life experiences, challenges, circumstances, interests or talents, socioeconomic disadvantage, and under-represented race, ethnicity, or geography.'" Although the program did assign 20 points to some "'soft' variables other than race, the points available for other diversity contributions, such as leadership and service, personal achievement, and geographic diversity, are capped at much lower levels." For example, an impressive high school leader could not receive more than five points for her achievements.

The record offered little information about how individualized review occured. The information offered depicted the review committee as an "afterthought." The record did not indicate whether the committee reviewed a meaningful percentage of candidates. In sum, the University's undergraduate admissions program was a "nonindividualized, mechanical one."

Concurring, Justice Thomas said that "a State's use of racial discrimination in higher education admissions is categorically prohibited by the Equal Protection Clause." Justice Breyer concurred in the judgment. He joined Justice O'Connor's concurring opinion except the part that joined the Court's opinion. Justice Breyer also joined Part I of Justice Ginsburg's dissent agreeing with her that "in implementing the Constitution's equality instruction, government decisionmakers may properly distinguish between policies of inclusion and exclusion[.]" Policies of inclusion are "more likely to prove consistent with the basic constitutional obligation that the law respect each individual equally."

Justice Stevens filed a dissenting opinion, which Justice Souter joined. Justice Stevens stated that because neither petitioner was reapplying to the University at the time the suit was filed nor had done so since, neither had standing. The transfer policy was not at issue in this case and was not addressed by the District Court. Justice Souter dissented, joined by Justice Ginsburg. The admission of "'virtually every qualified under-represented minority applicant,' may reflect nothing more than the likelihood that very few qualified minority applicants apply, as well as the possibility that self-selection results in a strong minority applicant pool." Justice Souter would not require the University to adopt a percentage system similar to those used at public universities in California, Florida, and Texas that would guarantee admission to a "fixed percentage of the top students from each high school in Michigan."

Justice Ginsburg dissented, joined by Justice Souter and by Justice Breyer in Part I of her opinion. There are large disparities between the races in this country. "Unemployment, poverty, and access to health care vary disproportionately by race. Neighborhoods and schools remain racially divided. African-American and Hispanic children are all too often educated in poverty-stricken and underperforming institutions. Adult African-Americans and Hispanics generally earn less than whites with equivalent levels of education. Equally credentialed job applicants receive different receptions depending on their race. Irrational prejudice is still encountered in real estate markets and consumer transactions." Justice Ginsburg continued: "Actions designed to burden groups long denied full citizenship stature are not sensibly ranked with measures taken to hasten the day when entrenched discrimination and its after effects have been extirpated."[14]

She distinguished between race-conscious laws that aimed to increase inequality and those that aimed to eliminate it. "Contemporary human rights documents draw just this line; they distinguish between policies of oppression and measures designed to accelerate *de facto* equality." She cited United Nations-initiated Conventions that sought to eliminate racial and gender discrimination.

As non-minority applicants greatly outnumber minority applicants, even substantial race-based preferences will not significantly diminish admissions opportunities for applicants who do not receive them.[15] If universities are not permitted to use race in the admissions process, they may "resort to camouflage" in a quest to achieve "similar numbers through winks, nods, and disguises."

§ 10.02   EMPLOYMENT

Section Note. Title VII of the Civil Rights Act of 1964 is the principal federal statute dealing with discrimination in employment based on race, gender, and certain other impermissible criteria. This subsection treats the legality of affirmative action in employment for both public and private employees under Title VII and the Equal Protection Clause.

NOTES

(1) *Layoffs.* In *Wygant v. Jackson Board of Education*, 476 U.S. 267 (1986), the Court invalidated a layoff provision designed to protect minorities by laying off some nonminority teachers with greater seniority before laying off minority teachers with less seniority. This provision required that layoffs not reduce the percentage of minority instructors at the time of the layoff.

Several years later, when layoffs became necessary within the district, adherence to the layoff provision would have resulted in dismissing a number of tenured nonminority teachers while retaining minority teachers on probation. Rather than follow the policy, the Board retained the tenured teachers and laid off the probationary minority teachers. The Union, joined by the dismissed minority teachers, filed suit.

Justice Powell, joined by only Chief Justice Burger and Justices Rehnquist and O'Connor, noted that the level of scrutiny does not vary simply "because the challenged classification operates against a group that historically has not been subject to governmental discrimination." In essence, the ends "must be justified by a compelling governmental interest" and the means chosen to effectuate such ends must be "narrowly tailored to the achievement of that goal."

The plurality said that societal discrimination alone was insufficient to justify racial

---

[14] Quoting Professor Stephen Carter, "To say that two centuries of struggle for the most basic of civil rights have been mostly about freedom from racial categorization rather than freedom from racial oppression is to trivialize the lives and deaths of those who have suffered under racism." To equate *Bakke* and *Brown v. Board of Education*, "'is to pretend that history never happened and that the present doesn't exist." *See Carter, When Victims Happen to Be Black*, 97 YALE L.J. 420, 433-34 (1988).

[15] Admitting the top high school students based on high school grades will yield "significant minority enrollment in universities only if the majority-minority high school population is large enough to guarantee that, in many schools, most of the students in the top 10 or 20% are minorities. However, these plans create "perverse incentives" for parents to enroll their children in "low-performing segregated schools."

discrimination. Justice Powell also rejected the rationale that the layoff provision served the goal of providing minority students with role models. With "no logical stopping point," the theory that minority students are better served by minority teachers could lead to a system rejected by the Court in *Brown v. Board of Education*, *supra* § 8.02[1].

In a portion of his opinion joined only by Chief Justice Burger and Justice Rehnquist, Justice Powell criticized the layoff context of this case. "While hiring goals impose a diffuse burden, often foreclosing only one of several opportunities, layoffs impose the entire burden of achieving racial equality on particular individuals, often resulting in serious disruption of their lives."

Justice O'Connor concurred in part and concurred in the judgment. The hiring goal that prompted the layoff provision corresponded to the percentage of minority students in the district rather than to the qualified minority teachers.

Justice White, concurring in the judgment, stated that the Court has never upheld such a layoff program.

Justice Marshall dissented, joined by Justices Brennan and Blackmun. Justice Marshall maintained that a *per se* rule against race conscious layoffs affords seniority absolute protection.

Justice Stevens dissented. An ethnically diverse faculty could better inculcate the diversity of the nation as a whole.

(2) *One Factor.* In *Johnson v. Transportation Agency*, 480 U.S. 616 (1987), a male employee brought suit against his employer, the Santa Clara County, California County Transit Agency, which had implemented an affirmative action program in 1978. Johnson claimed that the promotion of a female employee, Diane Joyce, instead of him was gender discrimination in violation of Title VII.

Justice Brennan, writing for the Court, pointed out that "none of the 238 Skilled Craft Worker positions [at issue] was held by a woman." The Agency stated that, as a goal, it sought to employ a workforce whose makeup reflected the makeup of the community at large. While this was a long-term goal, the Agency also set up short-term standards to meet.

In 1979, Johnson, Joyce and others applied to fill an opening in the position of road dispatcher. Johnson scored higher than Joyce on the preliminary interviews. After secondary interviews, three supervisors recommended that Johnson receive the job. The Affirmative Action Coordinator for the program recommended that Joyce be given the job.

The final decision took into consideration such things as the applicants' backgrounds, expertise, test scores, and affirmative action status. Both Joyce "and Johnson were rated as "well-qualified" as "Johnson scored 75 and Joyce 73" on their interviews.

Justice Brennan focused on consideration of applicants' sex and whether this was justified by "a 'manifest imbalance' that reflected underrepresentation of women in 'traditionally segregated job categories.' " He refused to use the test suggested by Justice O'Connor, which would require that the evidence show a prima facie case against the employer as this standard would deter employers from initiating affirmative action plans. Like the Harvard Plan described in *Bakke*, the plan at issue merely asked that gender be considered in hiring decisions. All applicants for the position applied for had to be qualified.

Justice Stevens concurred based on Supreme Court precedents construing Title VII to allow preferential minority hiring, even though these decisions went against his "understanding of the actual intent of the authors of the legislation."

Justice O'Connor concurred in the judgment. While approximately five percent of the local labor force who could handle the requisite duties were women, none were employed by the Agency. The Agency looked " 'at the whole picture' " rather than focusing on gender as the determinative factor in hiring.

Justice White dissented. Justice Scalia, joined by Chief Justice Rehnquist and Justice White, also dissented. The District Court found that " '*the determinative factor*' " in the selection of Joyce's promotion was her gender. The result would not necessarily be that the best person for the job received the job, but someone who at least met the minimum qualifications would receive the job. Contrary to the language and legislative history of Title VII, the Court construed the statute to allow discrimination. While the Court decided this case exclusively under Title VII, the Court was not likely to construe Title VII in an unconstitutional manner, particularly in a case involving a public actor.

(3) *Challenges to consent decrees.* In *Martin v. Wilks*, 490 U.S. 755 (1989), the Court, in a 5-4 decision, allowed nonminority employees to challenge an affirmative action consent decree involving minority employees. The fact that the nonminority employees could have intervened in the first suit as a matter of right under Federal Rule of Civil Procedure 24 did not affect their right to bring this subsequent lawsuit. While Rule 24 had afforded these nonminority employees the right to intervene in the previous suit, it imposed no duty on them to intervene.

CITY OF RICHMOND v. J.A. CROSON COMPANY
488 U.S. 469, 109 S. Ct. 706, 102 L. Ed. 2d 854 (1989)

JUSTICE O'CONNOR announced the judgment of the Court and delivered the opinion of the Court with respect to Parts I, III-B, and IV, an opinion with respect to Part II, in which THE CHIEF JUSTICE and JUSTICE WHITE join, and an opinion with respect to Parts III-A and V, in which THE CHIEF JUSTICE, JUSTICE WHITE and JUSTICE KENNEDY join. . . .

I

On April 11, 1983, the Richmond City Council adopted the Minority Business Utilization Plan (the Plan). The Plan required prime contractors to whom the city awarded construction contracts to subcontract at least 30% of the dollar amount of the contract to one or more Minority Business Enterprises (MBEs). . . . The 30% set-aside did not apply to city contracts awarded to minority-owned prime contractors.

The Plan defined an MBE as "[a] business at least fifty-one (51) percent of which is owned and controlled . . . by minority group members." "Minority group members" were defined as "[c]itizens of the United States who are Blacks, Spanish-speaking, Orientals, Indians, Eskimos, or Aleuts." There was no geographic limit to the Plan; an otherwise qualified MBE from anywhere in the United States could avail itself of the 30% set-aside. . . . The Plan expired on June 30, 1988, and was in effect for approximately five years.[16]

The Plan authorized the Director of the Department of General Services to promulgate rules which "shall allow waivers in those individual situations where a contractor can prove to the satisfaction of the director that the requirements herein cannot be achieved." . . . Section D of these rules provided:

---

[16] The expiration of the ordinance has not rendered the controversy between the city and Croson moot. There remains a live controversy between the parties over whether Richmond's refusal to award Croson a contract pursuant to the ordinance was unlawful and thus entitles Croson to damages.

No partial or complete waiver of the foregoing (30% set-aside) requirement shall be granted by the city other than in exceptional circumstances. To justify a waiver, it must be shown that every feasible attempt has been made to comply, and it must be demonstrated that sufficient, relevant, qualified Minority Business Enterprises . . . are unavailable or unwilling to participate in the contract to enable meeting the 30% MBE goal.

. . . The Director of General Services made the final determination on compliance with the set-aside provisions or the propriety of granting a waiver. His discretion in this regard appears to have been plenary. There was no direct administrative appeal from the Director's denial of a waiver. Once a contract had been awarded to another firm a bidder denied an award for failure to comply with the MBE requirements had a general right of protest under Richmond procurement policies.

. . . Proponents of the set-aside provision relied on a study which indicated that, while the general population of Richmond was 50% black, only .67% of the city's prime construction contracts had been awarded to minority businesses in the 5-year period from 1978 to 1983. . . .

There was no direct evidence of race discrimination on the part of the city in letting contracts or any evidence that the city's prime contractors had discriminated against minority-owned subcontractors. . . .

On September 6, 1983, the city of Richmond issued an invitation to bid on a project for the provision and installation of certain plumbing fixtures at the city jail. On September 30, 1983, Eugene Bonn, the regional manager of J.A. Croson Company (Croson), a mechanical plumbing and heating contractor, received the bid forms. . . . Bonn determined that to meet the 30% set-aside requirement, a minority contractor would have to supply the fixtures. The provision of the fixtures amounted to 75% of the total contract price.

On September 30, Bonn contacted five or six MBEs that were potential suppliers of the fixtures, after contacting three local and state agencies that maintained lists of MBEs. No MBE expressed interest in the project or tendered a quote. On October 12, 1983, the day the bids were due, Bonn again telephoned a group of MBEs. This time, Melvin Brown, president of Continental Metal Hose (Continental), a local MBE, indicated that he wished to participate in the project. . . .

On October 13, 1983, the sealed bids were opened. Croson turned out to be the only bidder, with a bid of $126,530. . . .

By October 19, 1983, Croson had still not received a bid from Continental. On that date it submitted a request for a waiver of the 30% set-aside. Croson's waiver request indicated that Continental was "unqualified" and that the other MBEs contacted had been unresponsive or unable to quote. Upon learning of Croson's waiver request, Brown contacted an agent of Acorn, the other fixture manufacturer specified by the city. Based upon his discussions with Acorn, Brown subsequently submitted a bid on the fixtures to Croson. Continental's bid was $6,183.29 higher than the price Croson had included for the fixtures in its bid to the city. This constituted a 7% increase over the market price for the fixtures. With added bonding and insurance, using Continental would have raised the cost of the project by $7,663.16. . . .

Croson wrote the city on November 8, 1983. In the letter, Bonn indicated that Continental was not an authorized supplier for either Acorn or Bradley fixtures. He also noted that Acorn's quotation to Brown was subject to credit approval and in any case was substantially higher than any other quotation Croson had received. Finally, Bonn noted that Continental's bid had been submitted some 21 days after the prime bids were due. In a second letter, Croson laid out the additional costs that using Continental to supply the fixtures would entail, and asked that it be allowed to raise the overall contract price accordingly. The city denied both Croson's request for a waiver and its suggestion that the contract price be raised. The city informed Croson that it had decided to rebid the project. On December 9, 1983, counsel for Croson wrote the city asking for a review of the waiver denial. The city's attorney responded that the city had elected to rebid the project, and that there is no appeal of such a decision. Shortly thereafter Croson brought this action under 42 U.S.C. section 1983, . . . arguing that the Richmond ordinance was unconstitutional on its face and as applied in this case. . . .

II

. . . In *Fullilove* [*v. Klutznick*, 448 U.S. 448 (1980)], we upheld the minority set-aside contained in section 103(f)(2) of the Public Works Employment Act of 1977. . . .

The principal opinion in *Fullilove*, written by Chief Justice Burger, did not employ "strict scrutiny" or any other traditional standard of equal protection review. The Chief Justice noted at the outset that although racial classifications call for close examination, the Court was at the same time, "bound to approach [its] task with appropriate deference to the Congress. . . . "

That Congress may identify and redress the effects of society-wide discrimination does not mean that, a *fortiori*, the States and their political subdivisions are free to decide that such remedies are appropriate. Section 1 of the Fourteenth Amendment is an explicit *constraint* on state power, and the States must undertake any remedial efforts in accordance with that provision. . . .

. . . [S]ection 1 of the Fourteenth Amendment stemmed from a distrust of state legislative enactments based on race. . . .

[I]f the city could show that it had essentially become a "passive participant" in a system of racial exclusion practiced by elements of the local construction industry, we think it clear that the city could take affirmative steps to dismantle such a system. . . .

III

A

. . . The Richmond Plan denies certain citizens the opportunity to compete for a fixed percentage of public contracts based solely upon their race. . . .

. . . [T]he purpose of strict scrutiny is to "smoke out" illegitimate uses of race by assuring that the legislative body is pursuing a goal important enough to warrant use of a highly suspect tool. The test also ensures that the means chosen "fit" this compelling goal so closely that there is little or no possibility that the motive for the classification was illegitimate racial prejudice or stereotype.

Classifications based on race carry a danger of stigmatic harm. Unless they are strictly reserved for remedial settings, they may in fact promote notions of racial inferiority and lead to a politics of racial hostility. . . . We thus reaffirm the view expressed by the plurality in *Wygant* that the standard of review under the Equal Protection Clause is not dependent on the race of those burdened or benefited by a particular classification. . . .

. . . [O]ur interpretation of section 1 stems from our agreement with the view expressed by Justice Powell in *Bakke*, that "[t]he guarantee of equal protection cannot mean one thing when applied to one individual and something else when applied to a person of another color." *Bakke*, *supra*, at 289–290.

. . . The dissent's watered-down version of equal protection review effectively assures that race will always be relevant in American life. . . .

. . . One of the central arguments for applying a less exacting standard to "benign" racial classifications is that such measures essentially involve a choice made by dominant racial groups to disadvantage themselves. If one aspect of the judiciary's role under the Equal Protection Clause is to protect "discrete and insular minorities" from majoritarian prejudice or indifference, *see United States v. Carolene Products Co.*, 304 U.S. 144, 153, n. 4 (1938), some maintain that these concerns are not implicated when the "white majority" places burdens upon itself. *See* J. Ely, Democracy and Distrust 170 (1980).

In this case, blacks comprise approximately 50% of the population of the city of Richmond. Five of the nine seats on the City Council are held by blacks. The concern that a political majority will more easily act to the disadvantage of a minority based on unwarranted assumptions or incomplete facts would seem to militate for, not against, the application of heightened judicial scrutiny in this case. *See* Ely, *The Constitutionality of Reverse Racial Discrimination*, 41 U. CHI. L. REV. 723, 739, n. 58 (1974) ("Of course it works both ways: a law that favors Blacks over Whites would be suspect if it were enacted by a predominantly Black legislature.") . . .

[In *Bakke*] Justice Powell's opinion . . . indicated that for the governmental interest in remedying past discrimination to be triggered "judicial, legislative, or administrative findings of constitutional or statutory violations" must be made. Only then does the Government have a compelling interest in favoring one race over another.

In *Wygant*, four Members of the Court applied heightened scrutiny to a race-based system of employee layoffs. Justice Powell, writing for the plurality, again drew the distinction between "societal discrimination" which is an inadequate basis for race-conscious classifications, and the type of identified discrimination that can support and define the scope of race-based relief. . . .

B

. . . It is sheer speculation how many minority firms there would be in Richmond absent past societal discrimination. . . .

. . . The 30% quota cannot in any realistic sense be tied to any injury suffered by anyone. The District Court relied upon five predicate "facts" in reaching its conclusion that there was an adequate basis for the 30% quota: (1) the ordinance declares itself to be remedial; (2) several proponents of the measure stated their views that there had been past discrimination in the construction industry; (3) minority businesses received .67% of prime contracts from the city while minorities constituted 50% of the city's population; (4) there were very few minority contractors in local and state contractors' associations; and (5) in 1977, Congress made a determination that the effects of past discrimination had stifled minority participation in the construction industry nationally.

None of these "findings," singly or together, provide the city of Richmond with a "strong basis in evidence for its conclusion that remedial action was necessary." *Wygant*, 276 U.S., at 277 (plurality opinion). There is nothing approaching a prima facie case of a constitutional or statutory violation by anyone in the Richmond construction industry. . . .

In the employment context, we have recognized that for certain entry level positions or positions requiring minimal training, statistical comparisons of the racial composition of an employer's workforce to the racial composition of the relevant population may be probative of a pattern of discrimination. But where special qualifications are necessary, the relevant statistical pool for purposes of demonstrating discriminatory exclusion must be the number of minorities qualified to undertake the particular task. . . .

In this case, the city does not even know how many MBEs in the relevant market are qualified to undertake prime or subcontracting work in public construction projects. Nor does the city know what percentage of total city construction dollars minority firms now receive as subcontractors on prime contracts let by the city.

To a large extent, the set-aside of subcontracting dollars seems to rest on the unsupported assumption that white prime contractors simply will not hire minority firms. Indeed, there is evidence in this record that overall minority participation in city contracts in Richmond is seven to eight percent, and that minority contractor participation in Community Block Development Grant *construction* projects is 17% to 22%. . . .

The city and the District Court also relied on evidence that MBE membership in local contractors' associations was extremely low. Again, standing alone this evidence is not probative of any discrimination in the local construction industry. . . .

For low minority membership in these associations to be relevant, the city would have to link it to the number of local MBEs eligible for membership. If the statistical disparity between eligible MBEs and MBE membership were great enough, an inference of discriminatory exclusion could arise. . . .

In sum, none of the evidence presented by the city points to any identified discrimination in the Richmond construction industry. We, therefore, hold that the city has failed to demonstrate a compelling interest in apportioning public contracting opportunities on the basis of race. To accept Richmond's claim that past societal discrimination alone can serve as the basis for rigid racial preferences would be to open the door to competing claims for "remedial relief" for every disadvantaged group. The dream of a Nation of equal citizens in a society where race is irrelevant to personal opportunity and achievement would be lost in a mosaic of shifting preferences based on inherently unmeasurable claims of past wrongs. . . .

The foregoing analysis applies only to the inclusion of blacks within the Richmond set-aside program. There is absolutely no evidence of past discrimination against Spanish-speaking, Oriental, Indian, Eskimo, or Aleut persons in any aspect of the Richmond construction industry. . . . It may well be that Richmond has never had an Aleut or Eskimo citizen. . . .

. . . The gross overinclusiveness of Richmond's racial preference strongly impugns the city's claim of remedial motivation.

IV

As noted by the court below, it is almost impossible to assess whether the Richmond Plan is narrowly tailored to remedy prior discrimination since it is not linked to identified discrimination in any way. We limit ourselves to two observations in this regard.

First, there does not appear to have been any consideration of the use of race-neutral means to increase minority business participation in city contracting. . . . If MBEs disproportionately lack capital or cannot meet bonding requirements, a race-neutral program of city financing for small firms would, *a fortiori*, lead to greater minority participation. . . .

Second, the 30% quota . . . rests upon the "completely unrealistic" assumption that minorities will choose a particular trade in lockstep proportion to their representation in the local population.

. . . As noted above, the congressional scheme upheld in *Fullilove* allowed for a waiver of the set-aside provision where an MBE's higher price was not attributable to the effects of past discrimination. . . . Unlike the program upheld in *Fullilove*, the

Richmond Plan's waiver system focuses solely on the availability of MBEs; there is no inquiry into whether or not the particular MBE seeking a racial preference has suffered from the effects of past discrimination by the city or prime contractors.

. . . Under Richmond's scheme, a successful black, Hispanic, or Oriental entrepreneur from anywhere in the country enjoys an absolute preference over other citizens based solely on their race. . . .

V

. . . Where there is a significant statistical disparity between the number of qualified minority contractors willing and able to perform a particular service and the number of such contractors actually engaged by the locality or the locality's prime contractors, an inference of discriminatory exclusion could arise. *See Bazemore v. Friday*, 478 U.S., at 398; *Teamsters v. United States*, 431 U.S., at 337–339. Under such circumstances, the city could act to dismantle the closed business system by taking appropriate measures against those who discriminate on the basis of race or other illegitimate criteria. *See, e.g., New York State Club Assn. v. New York City*, [47 U.S. 1 (1988)]. In the extreme case, some form of narrowly tailored racial preference might be necessary to break down patterns of deliberate exclusion.

Nor is local government powerless to deal with individual instances of racially motivated refusals to employ minority contractors. Where such discrimination occurs, a city would be justified in penalizing the discriminator and providing appropriate relief to the victim of such discrimination. *See generally McDonnell Douglas Corp. v. Green*, 411 U.S. 792, 802–803 (1973). Moreover, evidence of a pattern of individual discriminatory acts can, if supported by appropriate statistical proof, lend support to a local government's determination that broader remedial relief is justified. [*See Teamsters*, 431 U.S., at 338.]

Even in the absence of evidence of discrimination, the city has at its disposal a whole array of race-neutral devices to increase the accessibility of city contracting opportunities to small entrepreneurs of all races. Simplification of bidding procedures, relaxation of bonding requirements, and training and financial aid for disadvantaged entrepreneurs of all races would open the public contracting market to all those who have suffered the effects of past societal discrimination or neglect. . . .

In the case at hand, the city has not ascertained how many minority enterprises are present in the local construction market nor the level of their participation in city construction projects. The city points to no evidence that qualified minority contractors have been passed over for city contracts or subcontracts, either as a group or in any individual case. . . .

Proper findings in this regard are necessary to define both the scope of the injury and the extent of the remedy necessary to cure its effects. Such findings also serve to assure all citizens that the deviation from the norm of equal treatment of all racial and ethnic groups is a temporary matter, a measure taken in the service of the goal of equality itself. Absent such findings, there is a danger that a racial classification is merely the product of unthinking stereotypes or a form of racial politics. "[I]f there is no duty to attempt either to measure the recovery by the wrong or to distribute that recovery within the injured class in an evenhanded way, our history will adequately support a legislative preference for almost any ethnic, religious, or racial group with the political strength to negotiate 'a piece of the action' for its members." *Fullilove*, 448 U.S., at 539 (Stevens, J., dissenting). . . .

JUSTICE STEVENS, concurring in part and concurring in the judgment.

. . . I . . . do not agree with the premise that seems to underlie today's decision, as well as the decision in *Wygant v. Jackson Board of Education*, 476 U.S. 267 (1986), that a governmental decision that rests on a racial classification is never permissible except as a remedy for a past wrong. I do, however, agree with the Court's explanation of why the Richmond ordinance cannot be justified as a remedy for past discrimination, and therefore join Parts I, III-B, and IV of its opinion. . . .

First, . . . [t]his case is . . . completely unlike *Wygant*, in which I thought it quite obvious that the School Board had reasonably concluded that an integrated faculty could provide educational benefits to the entire student body that could not be provided by an all-white, or nearly all-white faculty. . . .

Second, this litigation involves an attempt by a legislative body, rather than a court, to fashion a remedy for a past wrong. Legislatures are primarily policymaking bodies that promulgate rules to govern future conduct. . . . [I]n cases involving the review of judicial remedies imposed against persons who have been proved guilty of violations of law, I would allow the courts in racial discrimination cases the same discretion that chancellors enjoy in other areas of the law. *See Swann v. Charlotte-Mecklenburg Board of Education*, 402 U.S. 1, 15–16 (1971). . . .

. . . The class of persons benefited by the ordinance is not . . . limited to victims of . . . discrimination — it encompasses persons who have never been in business in Richmond as well as minority contractors who may have been guilty of discriminating against members of other minority groups. . . .

. . . [T]he composition of the disadvantaged class of white contractors presumably includes some who have been guilty of unlawful discrimination, some who practiced discrimination before it was forbidden by law, and some who have never discriminated against anyone on the basis of race. . . .

JUSTICE KENNEDY, concurring in part and concurring in the judgment.

I join all but Part II of Justice O'Connor's opinion and give this further explanation. . . .

The moral imperative of racial neutrality is the driving force of the Equal Protection Clause. Justice Scalia's opinion underscores that proposition, quite properly in my view. . . .

Nevertheless, given that a rule of automatic invalidity for racial preferences in almost every case would be a significant break with our precedents that require a case-by-case test, I am not convinced we need adopt it at this point. On the assumption that it will vindicate the principle of race neutrality found in the Equal Protection Clause, I accept the less absolute rule contained in Justice O'Connor's opinion, a rule based on the proposition that any racial preference must face the most rigorous scrutiny by the courts. . . .

JUSTICE SCALIA, concurring in the judgment. . . .

In my view there is only one circumstance in which the States may act *by race* to "undo the effects of past discrimination": where that is necessary to eliminate their own maintenance of a system of unlawful racial classification. . . . This distinction explains our school desegregation cases, in which we have made plain that States and localities sometimes have an obligation to adopt race-conscious remedies. . . .

In his final book, Professor Bickel wrote:

> [A] racial quota derogates the human dignity and individuality of all to whom it is applied. . . . [A] quota is a divider of society, a creator of castes, and it is all the worse for its racial base, especially in a society desperately striving for an equality that will make race irrelevant. Bickel, The Morality of Consent, at 133. . . .

JUSTICE MARSHALL, with whom JUSTICE BRENNAN and JUSTICE BLACKMUN join, dissenting.

It is a welcome symbol of racial progress when the former capital of the Confederacy acts forthrightly to confront the effects of racial discrimination in its midst. . . .

A majority of this Court holds today, however, that the Equal Protection Clause of the Fourteenth Amendment blocks Richmond's initiative. . . . [T]he Richmond City Council has supported its determination that minorities have been wrongly excluded from local construction contracting. Its proof includes statistics showing that minority-owned businesses have received virtually no city contracting dollars and rarely if ever belonged to area trade associations; testimony by municipal officials that discrimination has been widespread in the local construction industry; and the same exhaustive and widely publicized federal studies relied on in *Fullilove*, studies which showed that pervasive discrimination in the Nation's tight-knit construction industry had operated to exclude minorities from public contracting. These are precisely the types of statistical and testimonial evidence which, until today, this Court had credited in cases approving of race-conscious measures designed to remedy past discrimination.

More fundamentally, today's decision marks a deliberate and giant step backward in this Court's affirmative action jurisprudence. . . . [T]he majority launches a grapeshot attack on race-conscious remedies in general. . . .

I

. . . A 1975 report by the House Committee on Small Business concluded:

> . . . While minority persons comprise about 16 percent of the Nation's population, of the 13 million businesses in the United States, only 382,000, or approximately 3.0 percent, are owned by minority individuals. The most recent data from the Department of Commerce also indicates that the gross receipts of all businesses in this country totals about $2,540.8 billion, and of this amount only $16.6 billion, or about 0.65 percent was realized by minority business concerns. . . .

Congress further found that minorities seeking initial public contracting assignments often faced immense entry barriers which did not confront experienced nonminority contractors. . . .

The members of the Richmond City Council were well aware of these exhaustive congressional findings, a point the majority, tellingly, elides. . . .

The City Council's members also heard testimony that, although minority groups made up half of the city's population, only .67% of the $24.6 million which Richmond had dispensed in construction contracts during the five years ending in March 1983 had gone to minority-owned prime contractors. . . . As the District Court noted, not a single person who testified before the City Council denied that discrimination in Richmond's construction industry had been widespread. . . .

II

A

1

. . . Richmond has two powerful interests in setting aside a portion of public contracting funds for minority-owned enterprises. The first is the city's interest in eradicating the effects of past racial discrimination. . . .

Richmond has a second compelling interest in . . . preventing the city's own spending decisions from reinforcing and perpetuating the exclusionary effects of past discrimination. *See Fullilove.* . . .

2

The remaining question with respect to the "governmental interest" prong of equal protection analysis is whether Richmond has proffered satisfactory proof of past racial discrimination to support its twin interests in remediation and in governmental nonperpetuation. . . .

Richmond's reliance on localized, industry-specific findings is a far cry from the reliance on generalized "societal discrimination" which the majority decries as a basis for remedial action. . . . The majority also takes the disingenuous approach of disaggregating Richmond's local evidence, attacking it piecemeal. . . .

. . . There are roughly equal numbers of minorities and nonminorities in Richmond yet minority-owned businesses receive one seventy-fifth the public contracting funds that other businesses receive.

. . . [M]ore fundamentally, where the issue is not present discrimination but rather whether *past* discrimination has resulted in the continuing exclusion of minorities from an historically tight-knit industry, a contrast between population and work force is entirely appropriate to help gauge the degree of the exclusion. . . .

B

. . . [T]he majority overlooks the fact that since 1975, Richmond has barred both discrimination by the city in awarding public contracts and discrimination by public contractors. . . .

As for Richmond's 30% target, . . . the majority ignores the fact that Richmond's 30% figure was patterned directly on the *Fullilove* precedent. Congress' 10% figure fell "roughly halfway between the present percentage of minority contractors and the percentage of minority group members in the Nation." *Fullilove, supra,* at 513–514 (Powell, J., concurring). The Richmond City Council's 30% figure similarly falls roughly halfway between the present percentage of Richmond-based minority contractors (almost zero) and the percentage of minorities in Richmond (50%).

III

A

Today, for the first time, a majority of this Court has adopted strict scrutiny as its standard of Equal Protection Clause review of race-conscious remedial measures. . . .

In concluding that remedial classifications warrant no different standard of review under the Constitution than the most brute and repugnant forms of state-sponsored racism, a majority of this Court signals that it regards racial discrimination as largely a phenomenon of the past, and that government bodies need no longer preoccupy themselves with rectifying racial injustice. . . .

B

I am also troubled by the majority's assertion that, even if it did not believe generally in strict scrutiny of race-based remedial measures, "the circumstances of this case" require this Court to look upon the Richmond City Council's measure with the strictest scrutiny. . . . [T]he majority observes that "blacks comprise approximately 50% of the population of the city of Richmond" and that "[f]ive of the nine seats on the City Council are held by blacks.". . .

It cannot seriously be suggested that nonminorities in Richmond have any "history of purposeful unequal treatment." . . . [T]he numerical and political dominance of non-minorities within the State of Virginia and the Nation as a whole provide an enormous political check against the "simple racial politics" at the municipal level which the majority fears. . . .

JUSTICE BLACKMUN, with whom JUSTICE BRENNAN joins, dissenting. . . .

I never thought that I would live to see the day when the city of Richmond, Virginia, the cradle of the Old Confederacy, sought on its own, within a narrow confine, to lessen the stark impact of persistent discrimination. But Richmond, to its great credit, acted. Yet this Court, the supposed bastion of equality, strikes down Richmond's efforts as though discrimination had never existed or was not demonstrated in this particular litigation. . . .

NOTES

(1) For some contrasting points of view on affirmative action, see, e.g., R. DWORKIN, A MATTER OF PRINCIPLE 5 (1985) (affirmative action "programs are best justified not on arguments of principle, about the rights of the particular people they benefit but rather on arguments of policy, about the general benefit they secure for the society as a whole"); T. SOWELL, OF CULTURAL DETERMINISM AND THE LIMITS OF LAW (1984) (broad-ranging attack on affirmative action, arguing that it is racially polarizing and that it primarily benefits middle-class rather than poor blacks); L. TRIBE, CONSTITUTIONAL CHOICES 231 (1985) ("[T]he individualized admissions process to which Justice Powell's vote in *Bakke* might lead seems not only 'more acceptable to the public' than a fifth vote for the Brennan wing would in all likelihood have been; it is surely also more reflective of a deep national aversion to explicit quotas to benefit racial minorities, and more responsive to a sense that if such quotas are imposed at all, they should be imposed in a more deliberate and cautious manner and by a more broadly accountable body than was the case in *Bakke*."); Abram, *Affirmative Action: Fair Shakes and Social Engineers*, 99 HARV. L. REV. 1312 (1986) (arguing that race and gender neutral methods be designed to help the "truly needy" in society); Colker, *Anti-Subordination Above All: Sex, Race, and Equal Protection*, 61 N.Y.U. L. REV. 1003 (1986) (arguing that affirmative action for minorities and women is consistent with equal protection as that concept stresses "anti-subordination," rather than "anti-differentiation"); Crenshaw, *Race, Reform, and Retrenchment: Transformation and Legitimation in Antidiscrimination Law*, 101 HARV. L. REV. 1331, 1380 (1988) (notions of "white supremacy" reinforce "whites' sense that American society is really meritocratic and thus helps prevent them from questioning the basic legitimacy of the free market"); Fox-Genovese, *Women's Rights, Affirmative Action, and the Myth of Individualism*, 54 GEO. WASH. L. REV. 338 (1986) (arguing that much of the opposition to affirmative action comes from a male-proprogated value of individual merit: "Like it or not, we are embarking on an age of distributive justice and social rights, in contrast to innately individual rights."); Rosenfeld, *Decoding Richmond: Affirmative Action and the Elusive Meaning of Constitutional Equity*, 87 MICH. L. REV. 1729, 1789 (1989) ("The intent behind racial discrimination is exclusionary while [the intent] behind compensatory affirmative action is inclusionary, as it seeks to integrate the victims of racism into the mainstream of society. Furthermore, the effects of failure in the competition for scarce public goods are not likely to be the same for blacks and whites.

Such a failure by a white is unlikely to lead to his being treated as a second-class citizen. A similar failure by a black, however, is likely to perpetuate the stigma of racial stereotypes."); Schnapper, *Perpetuation of Past Discrimination*, 96 HARV. L. REV. 828 (1983) (arguing that the Constitution should provide a present remedy for past discrimination); Schnapper, *Affirmative Action and the Legislative History of the Fourteenth Amendment*, 71 VA. L. REV. 753 (1985) (arguing that the Framers of the Fourteenth Amendment did intend to allow for affirmative action).

(2) For additional discussion examining *Bakke* and *Croson*, see Paulsen, *Reverse Discrimination and Law School Faculty Hiring: The Undiscovered Opinion*, 71 TEX. L. REV. 993, 999 (1993) ("*Croson's* ban on racial set-asides (absent extraordinary remedial justification) necessarily suggests that any racial preference imposed by a state government is unconstitutional if it has the effect of altering the distribution of benefits or burdens that otherwise would result from a nondiscriminatory, race-neutral government policy. In short, if a race-based preference counts in any meaningful way, it is to that extent a racial set-aside or entitlement, forbidden by the Constitution. If there is anything left of *Bakke*, then, it is that race may be taken into account only if doing so does not result in a decision in which race is the determining factor. To the extent race tips the balance, it is an illegitimate factor. This guts the supposed principle of *Bakke*.").

(3) *Broadcast Ownership*. In *Metro Broadcasting, Inc. v. Federal Communications Commission*, 497 U.S. 547 (1990), the Court (5-4) upheld against challenges to the Fifth Amendment's equal protection guarantee two FCC programs giving preference in broadcast licenses to minorities. The FCC gave preference to minorities competing for broadcast licenses by awarding them a "plus" in reviewing their applications based on their minority status. The "distress-sale" programs of the FCC provided that an existing broadcaster "whose license has been designated for a revocation hearing, or whose renewal application has been designated for hearing," could give the license to an FCC-approved minority.

Writing for the Court, Justice Brennan deferred to "Congress's institutional competence as the national legislature." The Court declined to extend to congressionally mandated affirmative action programs the strict scrutiny that it afforded municipal affirmative action programs in *City of Richmond v. J.A. Croson Company*. The Court found that the FCC has an important interest in promoting program diversity. *Red Lion Broadcasting Co. v. FCC*, 395 U.S. 367 (1969). The Court analogized the First Amendment interests at stake in this case to those relied on by Justice Powell's opinion in *Regents of University of California v. Bakke, supra* § 10.01. The programs not only benefitted the minority groups who received the licenses, but also the public gained "access to a wider diversity of information sources."

The Court also found that the race-preference programs were "substantially related to the goal of promoting broadcast diversity." Congress only assumes that increased minority ownership would, "in the aggregate, result in greater broadcast diversity."

Justice Stevens concurred, calling this an "extremely rare" case in which racial classifications may be used to achieve "future benefit" rather than simply to remedy a past wrong.

Justice O'Connor dissented, joined by Chief Justice Rehnquist and Justices Scalia and Kennedy. Justice O'Connor stated that constitutional equal protection commands "that the Government must treat citizens 'as *individuals*,' not 'as simply components of a racial, religious, sexual or national class.' " She asserted that all racial classifications, whether federally or state-mandated, should be reviewed under the same level of strict scrutiny, i.e., "necessary and narrowly tailored to achieve a compelling state interest."

The program links race to viewpoint in an unrealistic and stereotypical way.

Awarding minority applicants a "plus" afforded them a great advantage over nonminority applicants. Similarly, the "distress-sale" program was virtually a "100% set-aside, substantially burdening nonminorities."

Justice Kennedy filed a separate dissent, joined by Chief Justice Rehnquist and Justice Scalia. Justice Kennedy criticized the "stigma, animosity and discontent," that racial classifications imposed on both classes. "I regret that after a century of judicial opinions we interpret the Constitution to do no more than move us from 'separate but equal' to 'unequal but benign.' "

ADARAND CONSTRUCTORS, INC. v. PENA, 515 U.S. 200 (1995). In *Adarand*, the Court extended strict scrutiny to a race-based federal affirmative action program. In 1989, plaintiff and Gonzales Construction Company each submitted a bid for a subcontract to a prime contractor that had been awarded a federal highway construction project. Though Adarand submitted the low bid, Gonzales was awarded the contract. In the contract with the federal government, a provision allowed the prime contractor to receive "additional compensation if it hired subcontractors certified as small businesses controlled by 'socially and economically disadvantaged individuals.' "

The Small Business Act contains programs that sought to award at least five percent of federal prime and subcontracts to " 'socially and economically disadvantaged businesses.' " To qualify as disadvantaged under the Act, "a business must be 'small,' " and "it must be 51% owned by individuals who qualify as 'socially and economically disadvantaged.' " Under the Act, "Black, Hispanic, Asian Pacific, Subcontinent Asian, and Native Americans, as well as 'members of other groups designated from time to time by SBA' " enjoyed a presumption of at least social, and perhaps economic, disadvantage.[17]

Anyone "not a member of a listed group [may] prove social disadvantage 'on the basis of clear and convincing evidence.' " Such an applicant must also prove economic disadvantage. A third party, however, could rebut any presumption of social or economic disadvantage.

Justice O'Connor wrote for the (5-4) majority. Adarand asserted that the Act violated the Fifth Amendment. While the Court has "accorded varying degrees of significance to the difference in the language of those two Clauses," Justice O'Connor concluded that "all racial classifications, imposed by whatever federal, state, local governmental actor, must be analyzed by a reviewing court under strict scrutiny."

In *Metro Broadcasting, Inc. v. Federal Communications Commission*, 497 U.S. 547 (1990), the Court applied "intermediate scrutiny" to uphold congressionally mandated minority preference programs in FCC distribution of broadcast licenses. Justice O'Connor explained that this adoption of an intermediate scrutiny for federal racial classifications in *Metro Broadcasting* was inconsistent with precedent. *Metro Broadcasting* failed to recognize the explanation in *Richmond v. J.A. Croson Co.*, "of why strict scrutiny of all governmental racial classifications is essential." In adopting a middle-tier standard, *Metro Broadcasting* rejected "congruence between the standards applicable to federal and state racial classifications." This rejection undermined both "skepticism of all racial classifications, and consistency of treatment irrespective of the race of the burdened or benefitted group." These three concepts—congruence, skepticism and consistency — "all derive from the basic principle that the Fifth and Fourteenth Amendments to the Constitution protect persons, not groups." Justice O'Connor held that racial classifications "are constitutional only if they are narrowly

---

[17] Whether the presumption extended to economic disadvantage was unclear under the Act itself. However, regulations promulgated under the Act afford presumptions of social and economic disadvantage to members of certain racial groups, and women. . . .

tailored measures that further compelling governmental interests. To the extent that *Metro Broadcasting* is inconsistent with that holding, it is overruled." While Justices of the Court "have taken different views of the authority § 5 of the Fourteenth Amendment confers upon Congress to deal with the problem of racial discrimination, and the extent to which courts should defer to Congress' exercise of that authority," Justice O'Connor stated that the Court would not confront those differences in this decision. *Cf. City of Boerne v. P.F. Flores*, 521 U.S. 507 (1997), *infra* § 16.05.

In a portion of her opinion joined only by Justice Kennedy, Justice O'Connor stated " 'any departure from the doctrine of *stare decisis* demands special justification.' " Quoting Justice Frankfurter, Justice O'Connor noted that " '*stare decisis* is a principle of policy and not a mechanical formula of adherence to the latest decision, however recent and questionable, when such adherence involves collision with a prior doctrine more embracing in its scope, intrinsically sounder, and verified by experience.' " Because *Metro Broadcasting* was inconsistent with " 'intrinsically sounder' " doctrine established in the prior cases, following it would "simply compound the recent error." Citing *Planned Parenthood of Southeastern Pa. v. Casey*, *supra* § 7.04. Justice O'Connor said that the Court was not overruling "a long-established precedent that has become integrated into the fabric of the law." In "refusing to follow *Metro Broadcasting*, then, we do not depart from the fabric of the law; we restore it."

Again writing for a majority, Justice O'Connor said that "to the extent (if any) that *Fullilove* held racial classifications to be subject to 'a less rigorous standard than strict scrutiny, it is no longer controlling. But we need not decide today whether the program upheld in *Fullilove* would survive strict scrutiny as our more recent cases have defined it.' "

Finally, the Court dispelled the myth that strict scrutiny is "strict in theory, but fatal in fact." The Court refused to assume that all race-based action would be struck down as unconstitutional under this heightened scrutiny. Instead, the Court was confident that when governmental action "is necessary to further a compelling interest, such action is within constitutional constraints if it satisfies the 'narrow tailoring' test." Because the Court of Appeals did not determine whether the interests furthered by the Act were "compelling" or "narrowly tailored," but upheld the Act under intermediate scrutiny, the Court remanded for further consideration under the strict scrutiny test. Under that test, the lower courts should consider, for example, whether the government had considered race-neutral means of expanding minority participation and whether the program would end when the discriminatory effects that it sought to remedy were eliminated. Moreover, because the Act's provisions were unclear, the courts should address on remand what sorts of individualized showings of disadvantage that the Act may require.

Justice Scalia concurred in the judgment. He joined the opinion of the Court, except the discussion of *stare decisis*, and "except insofar as it may be inconsistent with the following: In my view, government can never have a 'compelling interest' in discriminating on the basis of race in order to 'make up' for past racial discrimination in the opposite direction."

Justice Thomas also concurred in part and concurred in the judgment. "Government cannot make us equal; it can only recognize, respect, and protect us as equal before the law." For him, "the paternalism that appears to lie at the heart of this program is at war with the principle of inherent equality that underlies and infuses our Constitution." Federal programs designed to benefit a race, or " 'benign' discrimination," have the effect of promoting the notion that minorities are incapable of competing on equal ground without assistance from the government. These programs foster attitudes of "superiority" or even "provoke resentment among those who believe that they have been wronged by the government's use of race." Justice Thomas asserted that these types of programs "stamp minorities with a badge of inferiority and may cause them to develop dependencies or to adopt an attitude that they are 'entitled' to preferences." He concluded that "government-sponsored racial discrimination based on benign prejudice is just as noxious as discrimination inspired by malicious prejudice."

Justice Stevens wrote a dissenting opinion joined by Justice Ginsburg. Justice Stevens asserted that the Court departed from precedent. Addressing the Court's principle of consistency, he stated that the differences between a program that is "designed to perpetuate a caste system and one that seeks to eradicate racial subordination" accounts for different levels of scrutiny.

He suggested that the Court's concept of consistency will produce another "anomalous result:" Government action to "remedy discrimination against women" will be maintained under the intermediate scrutiny afforded gender classifications while action to remedy discrimination against minorities will be found unconstitutional "even though the primary purpose of the Equal Protection Clause was to end discrimination against the former slaves." Responding to Justice Thomas' concurrence, Justice Stevens did not believe that "the psychological damage brought on by affirmative action is as severe as that engendered by racial subordination. That, in any event, is a judgment the political branches can be trusted to make."

Moreover, the Court's principle of "congruence ignores important practical and legal differences between federal and state or local decisionmakers." In the programs at issue, Congress "draws its power directly from § 5 of the Fourteenth Amendment," which empowers Congress " 'to enforce, by appropriate legislation, the provisions of this article.' "

Justice Stevens also disagreed with Justice O'Connor's treatment of *stare decisis*. He did not view *Metro Broadcasting* as inconsistent with *Croson*. *Metro Broadcasting* involved federally mandated programs, while the programs at issue in *Croson* were locally prescribed. Moreover, unlike *Croson*, *Metro Broadcasting* was not simply a remedial program addressing past discrimination but rather "intended to achieve future benefits in the form of broadcast diversity." Because the Court did not address this aspect of *Metro Broadcasting*, Justice Stevens did not understand the Court's holding to "diminish that aspect" of the *Metro Broadcasting* decision.

Justice Stevens also would have upheld the program under the holding in *Fullilove*, which, in his opinion, was considerably more objectionable than the program at issue. Unlike the Act at issue in *Fullilove*, the statutes here do not make race "the sole criterion of eligibility for participation in the program."

Justice Souter also filed a dissenting opinion joined by Justices Ginsburg and Breyer. This opinion did not resolve what effect Congress' power under § 5 of the Fourteenth Amendment should have in satisfying strict scrutiny. He thought that § 5 should supply a sufficiently important interest for the national government that would satisfy strict scrutiny.

Justice Ginsburg also wrote a dissenting opinion joined by Justice Breyer. Justice Ginsburg wrote "separately to underscore not the differences the several opinions in this case display, but the considerable field of agreement the common understandings and concerns revealed in opinions that together speak for a majority of the Court." She maintained that a majority of the Court acknowledged "Congress's authority to act affirmatively, not only to end discrimination, but also to counteract discrimination's lingering effects." The Court must ensure that "catch-up mechanisms designed to cope with the lingering effects of entrenched racial subjugation" do not "trammel unduly upon the opportunities of others or interfere too harshly with legitimate expectations of persons in once-preferred groups." Justice Ginsburg would uphold the programs at issue and "leave their improvement to the political branches."

NOTES

(1) *Standing to Challenge Set-Aside Programs.* In *Northeastern Florida Chapter of the Associated General Contractors of America v. City of Jacksonville*, 508 U.S. 656 (1993), the Court relaxed the standing requirements for a party disadvantaged by a government set-aside program that advantaged women and minorities. To establish the "injury in fact" necessary for standing, the disadvantaged group did not have to prove that it would have received the contract absent the racial or gender "barrier," but only that it was "able and ready to bid on contracts and that a discriminatory policy prevents it from doing so on an equal basis."

(2) For further discussion, see Klarman, *An Interpretive History of Modern Equal Protection*, 90 MICH. L. REV. 213, 317–318 (1991) ("Notwithstanding recent creative efforts to the contrary, judicial review cannot easily escape the countermajoritarian difficulty inherent in unelected, relatively unaccountable judges invalidating the policy choices of the more majoritarian branches of government. Political process theory seeks to ameliorate the problem by putting judicial review in the service of democracy, policing the political process for systemic flaws. Thus, for example, the Court's embrace of a presumptive ban against racial classifications disadvantaging minority groups was readily justifiable on the ground that southern blacks were largely disfranchised until the 1960s. But how can the Court justify its close scrutiny of gender classifications given that women (and like-minded men) are entirely capable of pressuring the political process into rejecting outmoded gender stereotypes? Even more problematic is the Court's recent hostility towards affirmative action. Since neither political process theory nor the conservative Justices' favored constitutional theory of strict constructionism condemns affirmative action, one is left wondering why minority racial preferences today are presumptively unconstitutional."); Sunstein, *The Anticaste Principle*, 92 MICH. L. REV. 2410, 2454 (1994) (". . . many defenses of affirmative action programs are hard to offer in public. Often the nature of affirmative action programs is not discussed publicly because to do so would be humiliating to the supposed beneficiaries or intolerable to the public at large."); Kahlenberg, *Class-Based Affirmative Action*, 84 CAL. L. REV. 1037, 1037-38 (1996) ("This approach would provide preferences in education, employment, and government contracting based on class or socio-economic status, rather than race or gender — implicitly addressing the current-day legacy of past discrimination without resorting to the toxic remedy of biological preference.").

For additional discussion of *Metro Broadcasting*, see Fried, *Metro Broadcasting, Inc. v. FCC: Two Concepts of Equality*, 104 HARV. L. REV. 107, 110 (1990) ("The conflict between the liberal, individualistic conception and the collectivist, group-rights conception of equal protection plays out in doctrinal terms through the debate over the proper standard of review for race-based governmental action. The issue is whether government needs a 'compelling' justification, one that would overcome 'strict scrutiny,' whenever it classifies persons by race, or whether a more relaxed standard is appropriate, at least when government favors members of groups seen or designated as disadvantaged. The level of scrutiny is an entirely appropriate, even inevitable doctrinal entailment of these contrasting visions. To the individualist, who believes that the equal protection clause requires the government to craft its laws to treat people equally, regardless of race, the government must make a showing of compelling need in order to legislate along racial lines. To the collectivist, for whom equal protection is a command to secure substantive aggregate equality for disadvantaged groups, legislation undertaken in that spirit need not be scrutinized as carefully."); Spitzer, *Justifying Minority Preferences in Broadcasting*, 64 S. CAL. L. REV. 293, 360 (1991) ("The simplest theory that minority and white owners both maximize the profit potential of a given market suggests that they behave the same way. Other theories, based either on the value to owners of programming for their own group or on the values of minority principal/minority agent cost savings, suggest that minorities and whites may program differently. This is particularly likely in markets with large numbers of minorities in the audience, where there are large numbers of broadcasting stations, and where none of the stations are yet serving minority audiences. In markets that do not satisfy one or more of these conditions, the theoretical chance that a minority owner will program differently from a white owner declines.").

See also Rosenfeld, *Metro Broadcasting, Inc. v. FCC: Affirmative Action at the Crossroads of Constitutional Liberty and Equality*, 38 UCLA L. REV. 583, 635 (1991) ("[E]qual opportunity . . . can be used as a suitable constitutional mediating principle instead of the discredited antidiscrimination principle. Not only would adopting equal opportunity as a mediating principle increase the cogency and determinacy of equal protection jurisprudence, it could also help demystify affirmative action. Indeed, under the equal opportunity principle, affirmative action is but a limited tool, the only legitimate function of which is to promote equality of opportunity. If that notion becomes widely accepted, then one can hope that there will be much less hostility toward and much less debate about duly circumscribed, legitimate uses of affirmative action.").

(3) *Voting Districts.* In several cases, the Court has treated the constitutionality of using voter districting to increase the chances of minority representation in legislative bodies. These cases are discussed in Chapter VIII.

Chapter XI
EQUAL PROTECTION FOR OTHER GROUPS AND INTERESTS

Introductory Note. As previous chapters have demonstrated, the Equal Protection Clause of the Fourteenth Amendment, and the equal protection right that the Court has interpreted into the Fifth Amendment's Due Process Clause, have provided the constitutional tools for achieving legal equality among the races and for combating sex discrimination. Sections 11.01 and 11.02 of this chapter explore the use of equal protection to scrutinize legislative classifications affecting some other classes of persons who have claimed that they should receive heightened protection. Specifically, these are aliens, illegitimate children, the aged, the mentally retarded, and the poor. Only the first two groups have received an appreciable amount of heightened protection.

The Court has applied the discrete and insular minority analysis differently in different contexts. *See generally* Minow, *Foreword: Justice Engineering*, 101 HARV. L. REV. 10 (1986) (examining the question of what kinds of distinctions or classifications the law should tolerate). For example, with respect to women, a demographic majority, the Court has emphasized the history of discrimination and stereotypes that have encumbered their opportunities. With respect to the poor, many of the cases affording protection — in, for example, voting or appellate review — reflect a strand of equal protection analysis separate from the discrete and insular minority approach. The fundamental rights strand of equal protection analysis identifies fundamental rights in much the same way as substantive due process analysis, but proceeds to afford the resultant rights less protection. The Court does not ensure that the government permits the exercise of a fundamental right, as it does in its contraception and abortion cases, but only that the fundamental right is distributed equally.

During the 1960s and early 1970s, the Court moved toward using the Equal Protection Clause to afford special protection for certain rights that the Court has deemed "fundamental." Under this so-called "new equal protection" analysis, laws that did not discriminate against "suspect classes" could still be subjected to stricter judicial scrutiny if they affected a fundamental right, like the right to education, vote, judicial access, or travel. Some of the cases in Section 11.02 discuss whether there is a right to education. Section 11.03 treats rights to vote and access to the judicial process and Section 11.04 focuses on the right to travel. Beyond the few relatively discrete areas treated in the book, this fundamental rights strand of equal protection analysis has been largely dormant for many years and the Court has not indicated a willingness to expand it.

Most government legislation, however, does not purposely prejudice classifications that the Court has declared suspect or rights that the Court has declared fundamental. Instead, government acts for the most part through economic and social legislation that may affect some groups favorably but others adversely. Minimum wage and maximum hour laws, professional licensing requirements, and myriad business regulations and government programs all involve classifications that adversely affected groups may wish to challenge. As has already been discussed in Chapter VI, at one point in our constitutional history many of these laws were successfully challenged as deprivations of "liberty or property without due process of law." This period ended in 1937. Nevertheless, the Equal Protection Clause remains as an ever-present reminder to government that there are limits on its power to draw distinctions between people. Section 11.05 discusses the use of equal protection to limit the power of government in the general areas of economic and social regulation.

§ 11.01   DISCRETE AND INSULAR MINORITIES

[1]   Aliens

BERNAL v. FAINTER

467 U.S. 216, 104 S. Ct. 2312, 81 L. Ed. 2d 175 (1984)

JUSTICE MARSHALL delivered the opinion of the Court.

The question posed by this case is whether a statute of the State of Texas violates the Equal Protection Clause of the Fourteenth Amendment of the United States Constitution by denying aliens the opportunity to become notaries public. The Court of Appeals for the Fifth Circuit held that the statute does not offend the Equal Protection Clause. We granted certiorari and now reverse.

I

Petitioner, a native of Mexico, is a resident alien who has lived in the United States since 1961. He works as a paralegal for Texas Rural Legal Aid, Inc., helping migrant farm-workers on employment and civil rights matters. In order to administer oaths to these workers and to notarize their statements for use in civil litigation, petitioner applied in 1978 to become a notary public. . . . The Texas Secretary of State denied petitioner's application because he failed to satisfy the statutory requirement that a notary public be a citizen of the United States. Tex. Rev. Civ. Stat. Ann., Art. 5949(2) (Vernon Supp. 1984) (hereafter Article 5949(2)). . . .

II

As a general matter, a state law that discriminates on the basis of alienage can be sustained only if it can withstand strict judicial scrutiny. In order to withstand strict scrutiny, the law must advance a compelling state interest by the least restrictive means available. Applying this principle, we have invalidated an array of state statutes that denied aliens the right to pursue various occupations. In *Sugarman v. Dougall*, 413 U.S. 634 (1973), we struck down a state statute barring aliens from employment in permanent positions in the competitive class of the state civil service. In *In re Griffiths*, 413 U.S. 717 (1973), we nullified a state law excluding aliens from eligibility for membership in the State Bar. . . .

We have, however, developed a narrow exception to the rule that discrimination based on alienage triggers strict scrutiny. This exception has been labeled the "political function" exception and applies to laws that exclude aliens from positions intimately related to the process of democratic self-government. . . . In *Foley v. Connelie*, 435 U.S. 291 (1978), we held that a State may require police to be citizens because, in performing a fundamental obligation of government, police "are clothed with authority to exercise an almost infinite variety of discretionary powers" often involving the most sensitive areas of daily life. . . . In *Ambach v. Norwick*, 441 U.S. 68 (1979), we held that a State may bar aliens who have not declared their intent to become citizens from teaching in the public schools because teachers, like police, possess a high degree of responsibility and discretion in the fulfillment of a basic governmental obligation. They have direct, day-to-day contact with students, exercise unsupervised discretion over them, act as role models, and influence their students about the government and the political process. . . . Finally, in *Cabell v. Chavez-Salido*, 454 U.S. 432 (1982), we held that a State may bar aliens from positions as probation officers because they, like police and teachers, routinely exercise discretionary power, involving a basic governmental function, that places them in a position of directed authority over other individuals.

The rationale behind the political-function exception is that within broad boundaries a State may establish its own form of government and limit the right to govern to those who are full-fledged members of the political community. Some public positions are so closely bound up with the formulation and implementation of self-government that the State is permitted to exclude from those positions persons outside the political community. . . .

. . . Self-government, whether direct or through representatives, begins by defining the scope of the community of the governed and thus of the governors as well: Aliens are by definition those outside of this community." *Id.* at 439–440.

. . . "While not retreating from the position that restrictions on lawfully resident aliens that primarily affect economic interests are subject to heightened judicial scrutiny . . . we have concluded that strict scrutiny is out of place when the restriction primarily serves a political function. . . . " *Cabell v. Chavez-Salido, supra,* 454 U.S., at 439.

To determine whether a restriction based on alienage fits within the narrow political-function exception, we devised in *Cabell* a two-part test. "First, the specificity of the classification will be examined: a classification that is substantially overinclusive or underinclusive tends to undercut the governmental claim that the classification serves legitimate political ends. . . . Second, even if the classification is sufficiently tailored, it may be applied in the particular case only to 'persons holding state elective or important nonelective executive, legislative, and judicial positions,' those officers who 'participate directly in the formulation, execution, or review of broad public policy' and hence 'perform functions that go to the heart of representative government.' " 454 U.S., at 440 (quoting *Sugarman v. Dougall, supra,* 413 U.S., at 647).[1]

III

. . . Unlike the statute invalidated in *Sugarman,* Article 5949(2) does not indiscriminately sweep within its ambit a wide range of offices and occupations but specifies only one particular post with respect to which the State asserts a right to exclude aliens. Clearly, then, the statute is not overinclusive. . . . Less clear is whether Article 5949(2) is fatally underinclusive. Texas does not require court reporters to be United States citizens even though they perform some of the same services as notaries.[2] Nor does Texas require that its Secretary of State be a citizen, even though he holds the highest appointive position in the State and performs many important functions, including supervision of the licensing of all notaries public. We need not decide this issue, however, because of our decision with respect to the second prong of the *Cabell* test.

. . . This Court . . . has never deemed the *source* of a position — whether it derives from a State's statute or its Constitution — as the dispositive factor in determining whether a State may entrust the position only to citizens. Rather, this Court has always looked to the actual *function* of the position as the dispositive factor. The focus of our inquiry has been whether a position was such that the officeholder would necessarily exercise broad discretionary power over the formulation or execution of public policies importantly affecting the citizen population — power of the sort that

[1] [Court's footnote 7] We emphasize, as we have in the past, that the political-function exception must be narrowly construed; otherwise the exception will swallow the rule. . . .

[2] [Court's footnote 8] Like notaries public, court reporters are authorized to administer oaths and take depositions. Tex. Rev. Civ. Stat. Ann., Art. 2324a(1) (Vernon 1971).

a self-governing community could properly entrust only to full-fledged members of that community. As the Court noted in *Cabell*, . . . "the Court will look to the importance of the function as a factor giving substance to the concept of democratic self-government." 454 U.S., at 441, n. 7.

. . . [A] notary's duties, important as they are, hardly implicate responsibilities that go to the heart of representative government. Rather, these duties are essentially clerical and ministerial. In contrast to state troopers, . . . notaries do not routinely exercise the State's monopoly of legitimate coercive force. Nor do notaries routinely exercise the wide discretion typically enjoyed by public school teachers when they present materials that educate youth respecting the information and values necessary for the maintenance of a democratic political system. . . . To be sure, considerable damage could result from the negligent or dishonest performance of a notary's duties. But the same could be said for the duties performed by cashiers, building inspectors, the janitors who clean up the offices of public officials, and numerous other categories of personnel upon whom we depend for careful, honest service. What distinguishes such personnel from those to whom the political-function exception is properly applied is that the latter are invested either with policymaking responsibility or broad discretion in the execution of public policy that requires the routine exercise of authority over individuals. . . .

The inappropriateness of applying the political-function exception to Texas notaries is further underlined by our decision in *In re Griffiths*, in which we subjected to strict scrutiny a Connecticut statute that prohibited noncitizens from becoming members of the State Bar. Along with the usual powers and privileges accorded to members of the bar, Connecticut gave to members of its Bar additional authority that encompasses the very duties performed by Texas notaries — authority to "sign writs and subpoenas, take recognizances, administer oaths and take depositions and acknowledgments of deeds. . . . "

IV

To satisfy strict scrutiny, the State must show that Article 5949(2) furthers a compelling state interest by the least restrictive means practically available. Respondents maintain that Article 5949(2) serves its "legitimate concern that notaries be reasonably familiar with state law and institutions" and "that notaries may be called upon years later to testify to acts they have performed. . . . " However, both of these asserted justifications utterly fail to meet the stringent requirements of strict scrutiny. There is nothing in the record that indicates that resident aliens, as a class, are so incapable of familiarizing themselves with Texas law as to justify the State's absolute and classwide exclusion. The possibility that some resident aliens are unsuitable for the position cannot justify a wholesale ban against all resident aliens. . . . Similarly inadequate is the State's purported interest in insuring the later availability of notaries' testimony. This justification fails because the State fails to advance a factual showing that the unavailability of notaries' testimony presents a real, as opposed to a merely speculative, problem to the State. . . .

JUSTICE REHNQUIST, dissenting.

I dissent for the reasons stated in my dissenting opinion in *Sugarman v. Dougall*, 413 U.S. 634 (1973).

NOTES

(1) *Bar Applications.* In *In re Griffiths*, 413 U.S. 717 (1973), the Supreme Court invalidated a Connecticut court rule that completely excluded aliens from the legal profession. Griffiths, a citizen of the Netherlands, married to a U.S. citizen, applied to take the Connecticut bar examination after her graduation from an American law school. Although she was qualified in every other respect, the County Bar Association rejected her application solely because she was not a U.S. citizen. Writing for the Court, Justice Powell asserted that "classifications based on alienage, like those based on nationality or race, are inherently suspect and subject to close judicial scrutiny." To sustain such a classification, a state must demonstrate that the classification is necessary to accomplish a constitutionally permissible and substantial interest. While the Court found that the State's interest in ensuring that an applicant possesses the character and general fitness for the bar was substantial, the alienage classification was not necessary to achieve that interest. The State did not reject Griffiths for deficiencies in her character or general fitness. Moreover, the Court found that the responsibilities and powers of a lawyer "hardly involve matters of state policy or acts of such unique responsibility as to entrust them only to citizens." The State could still make individualized determinations of a bar applicant's fitness and character and could continue to punish unprofessional behavior after a lawyer is barred. Connecticut already required bar applicants to take an examination and an oath of allegiance to the United States. Chief Justice Burger, joined by Justice Rehnquist, dissented.

(2) *Civil Service.* In *Sugarman v. Dougall*, 413 U.S. 634 (1973), the Court invalidated a New York statute that barred aliens from the competitive classified civil service, a category encompassing the vast majority of government positions, "from the menial to the policy-making." Justice Blackmun's majority (8-1) opinion stressed, however, that citizenship might be a valid requirement for certain positions. Justice Rehnquist dissented in *Sugarman* and in *Griffiths*. He argued that the Equal Protection Clause was not designed to afford special protection to any "discrete and insular" group other than a racial minority.

(3) *National Regulation.* Does the national government have greater power to regulate aliens than does a state? In *Hampton v. Mow Sun Wong*, 426 U.S. 88 (1976), the Court declined to apply the rationale of *Sugarman v. Dougall* to a federal regulation barring aliens from the federal competitive civil service. While recognizing that the federal government, pursuant to its power over immigration and naturalization, might wish to encourage naturalization by barring aliens from positions in the competitive civil service, the Court concluded that this national interest was within the peculiar domain of Congress and the President, rather than the Civil Service Commission. Since neither the President nor the Congress had imposed the ban, Justice Stevens concluded that it was lacking in the "structural due process" that is required whenever a discrete group is subjected to a discriminatory deprivation of liberty that would have triggered equal protection concerns if promulgated by a state. As for the Civil Service Commission, Justice Stevens concluded that there was nothing in the record to indicate that it had made any considered analysis of the relative merits of a blanket exclusion of all aliens as against a narrower exclusion with regard to positions where citizenship would be a valid qualification. While this was an interest that was within the peculiar competence of the Civil Service Commission, the Commission had not made the requisite analysis and findings to satisfy the due process requirement that the majority found necessary to justify this type of restriction. Justice Rehnquist, joined by Chief Justice Burger and Justices White and Blackmun,

dissented, relying on Congress' broad powers with regard to aliens and criticizing the majority for creating a "structural due process" limitation on the traditional power of Congress to delegate authority to a regulatory agency.

See also Mathews v. Diaz, 426 U.S. 67 (1976), holding unanimously that Congress could require five years of continuous residency and admission to the country for permanent residency as conditions for an alien's eligibility for Medicare benefits.

(4) *Public School Teachers*. In *Ambach v. Norwick*, 441 U.S. 68 (1979), the Court upheld a New York statute prohibiting the certification of a noncitizen as a public school teacher. The appellees, Norwick and Dachinger, were resident aliens who met all requirements for certification, except the citizenship requirement of New York Education Law § 3001(3). That section prohibited the certification of anyone who is not a U.S. citizen, unless that person showed that she or he intended to apply for citizenship.

In upholding the restriction, Justice Powell applied the government function exception, asserting that "principles inherent in the Constitution" were the basis for this exception. "The distinction between citizens and aliens, though ordinarily irrelevant to private activity, is fundamental to the definition and government of a State. The Constitution itself refers to the distinction no less than 11 times."

As public school teaching fell within the "governmental function" exception, the State only had to show that "a citizenship requirement applicable to teaching in the public schools bears a rational relationship to a legitimate state interest." The Court held that the restriction was rationally related to the State's interest in furthering the goal of educating students to be good citizens. "The restriction is carefully framed to serve its purpose, as it bars from teaching only those aliens who have demonstrated their unwillingness to obtain United States citizenship. Appellees, and aliens similarly situated, in effect have chosen to classify themselves. They prefer to retain citizenship in a foreign country with the obligations it entails of primary duty and loyalty."

Justice Blackmun filed a dissenting opinion in which Justices Brennan, Marshall, and Stevens joined. Justice Blackmun disagreed "that in these lower levels of public education a Frenchman may not teach French or, indeed, an Englishwoman may not teach the grammar of the English language." This was particularly true as the teachers in this case were willing "to subscribe to an oath to support the Constitutions of the United States and of New York."

(5) *Peace Officers*. In *Cabell v. Chavez-Salido*, 454 U.S. 432 (1982), the Court upheld a California requirement that "peace officers" must be citizens. The majority opinion of Justice White first rejected the argument that the "peace officer" classification was overinclusive, even though it included over 70 positions, ranging from police officers to toll takers and various types of government inspectors. All of the positions involved a "law enforcement" function and the general category of "peace officer" was, in the majority's view, "sufficiently tailored" to ensure the State's interest that the essential functions of representative government be exercised by those who are part of the political community, i.e., citizens. Thus, a facial challenge was rejected. The positions actually involved in the case — probation officers — were held to "sufficiently partake of the sovereign's power to exercise coercive force over the individual that they may be limited to citizens. Although the range of individuals over whom probationary officers exercise supervisory authority is limited, the powers of the probation officer are broad with respect to those over whom they exercise that authority."

Justice Blackmun dissented, joined by Justices Brennan, Marshall, and Stevens. The position of probation officer involves little discretionary power making them comparable to "prison guards, bailiffs, court clerks, and the myriad other functionaries who execute a State's judicial policy."

(6) *Preemption*. Most of the cases imposing burdens on noncitizens have been decided under the Equal Protection Clause. Because of the Federal Government's dominant role in immigration and naturalization legislation, it has been suggested that federal preemption under the Supremacy Clause might be a preferable rationale for decision. *See* Note, *The Equal Treatment of Aliens: Preemption or Equal Protection?*, 31 STAN. L. REV. 1069 (1979).

In *Toll v. Moreno*, 458 U.S. 1 (1982), the Court voided, on preemption grounds, a University of Maryland rule that denied in-state preferential tuition status to nonimmigrant domiciled aliens holding "G-4" visas. These visas were "issued to nonimmigrant aliens who are officers or employees of certain international organizations, and to members of their immediate families." Justice Brennan's majority opinion concluded that the Maryland rule was a "burden not contemplated by Congress" in admitting the G-4 aliens into the country. *See also Graham v. Richardson*, 403 U.S. 365 (1971), which held that a state could not deny welfare benefits to aliens. Justice Blackmun relied on equal protection and preemption.

(7) *Education for Children of Illegal Aliens*. In *Plyler v. Doe*, 457 U.S. 202 (1982), the Court held that Texas could not constitutionally deny free public education to school-age children of illegal aliens. Writing for a plurality of two, Justice Brennan found that this denial only disabled minor children who were not responsible for their presence in the United States or illegal status. While undocumented aliens are not a suspect class and education is not a fundamental right, Texas could not burden this class of innocent children with a lifetime "stigma of illiteracy without a substantial state interest."

Justices Marshall, Blackmun, and Powell each filed concurring opinions. Justice Marshall asserted that education is a fundamental right whose distribution should be protected under the Equal Protection Clause. Justice Blackmun emphasized that the Texas law effected an absolute deprivation of education to certain children. Justice Powell feared "the creation of an underclass of future citizens."

Chief Justice Burger, joined by Justices White, Rehnquist and O'Connor, dissented. The Chief Justice noted that Federal law also denied many social welfare benefits to illegal aliens, including children.

Because a major element in *Plyler* is the importance the Court attaches to the "right" of free public education, the case triggers a comparison with *San Antonio v. Rodriguez*, 411 U.S. 1 (1973), *infra* § 11.02[1], which upheld public school financing through local property taxes, despite the resulting inequalities among school districts.

(8) *Residency Requirement*. In *Martinez v. Bynum*, 461 U.S. 321 (1983), the Court upheld another provision of the same statute that was at issue in *Plyler*. The statute denied free tuition to a minor who lived apart from his or her parent or guardian and whose presence in the school district was "for the primary purpose of attending the public free schools." Justice Powell's majority (8-1) decision concluded that the Texas law requiring an intention to remain in the state indefinitely was a bona fide residency requirement and, therefore, did not burden the right to interstate travel. Justice Brennan concurred. Justice Marshall dissented.

(9) For more general accounts of the constitutional rights of aliens including, but ranging beyond, equal protection, see E. HULL, WITHOUT JUSTICE FOR ALL: THE CONSTITUTIONAL RIGHTS OF ALIENS (1985); Symposium, *Strangers to the Constitution: Immigrants in American Law*, 44 U. PITT. L. REV. 163 (1983).

[2]   Illegitimate Children

TRIMBLE v. GORDON, 430 U.S. 762 (1977). In *Trimble*, the Court struck down under the Equal Protection Clause an Illinois statute that allowed an illegitimate child to inherit by intestate succession from his mother but not from the alleged father. Justice Powell's majority opinion refused to subject that statute to a strict scrutiny analysis — a level of analysis utilized only on traditionally "suspect" classes. "Despite the conclusion that the classifications based on illegitimacy fall in a 'realm of less than strictest scrutiny,' . . . the scrutiny 'is not a toothless one.' "

The state first asserted that the law promoted legitimate family relationships. Although recognizing the importance of this interest, Justice Powell replied that "imposing disabilities on the illegitimate child is contrary to the basic concept of our system that legal burdens should bear some relationship to individual responsibility or wrongdoing. Obviously, no child is responsible for his birth and penalizing the illegitimate child is an ineffectual as well as an unjust way of deterring the parent." The state also claimed an interest in establishing an accurate and efficient system of disposition of property. The Court responded that problems of proof "might justify a more demanding standard for illegitimate children claiming under their fathers' estates than that required either for illegitimate children claiming under their mothers' estates or for legitimate children generally." The State, however, failed to consider alternatives between complete exclusion and case-by-case determination. As the statute was not "carefully tuned to alternative considerations," it violated the Equal Protection Clause.

Chief Justice Burger dissented, joined by Justices Stewart, Blackmun and Rehnquist. Justice Rehnquist also dissented separately. He argued that the Equal Protection Clause is inherently indeterminant. If the Court did not work to limit the realm of Equal Protection jurisprudence to comport with the intentions of the framers of the clause, its reach would be bounded only by the predilections of the Court.

LALLI v. LALLI, 439 U.S. 259 (1978). In *Lalli*, the Court upheld a New York intestate succession law that imposed greater proof requirements on illegitimate children to inherit from the child's father. Specifically, the law required that eligibility for intestate succession required "during the lifetime of the father, an order of filiation declaring paternity in a proceeding instituted during the pregnancy of the mother or within two years from the birth of the child." Legitimate children were not subjected to the same requirement. Applying this law, New York had denied intestate inheritance to an illegitimate son who presented a notarized document consenting to his son's marriage in which his father referred to him as "my son." Several persons also submitted affidavits stating that the father had acknowledged paternity "openly and often."

In contrast to the law struck down in *Trimble v. Gordon*, *supra*, the statute in this case was only an evidentiary requirement. Also unlike *Trimble*, the New York law did not have the purpose of "encouraging legitimate family relationships"; instead, the primary goal "provided for the just and orderly disposition of property at death." The law was recommended by a commission "to protect 'innocent adults and those rightfully interested in their estates from fraudulent claims of heirship and harassing litigation instituted by those seeking to establish themselves as legitimate heirs.' "

Finding the State's interests to be "substantial," the Court considered that fraudulent claims could be more easily dealt with while the putative father was still alive and able to respond. The Court concluded that the evidentiary requirement was rational. It substantially related to the important state interests that the statute is intended to promote.

Concurring in the judgment, Justice Blackmun found this case difficult to distinguish from *Trimble*. Either *Trimble* now carries little weight or the law in this area will be hopelessly confused. Justice Blackmun would overrule *Trimble*. In a separate concurring opinion, Justice Stewart found persuasive the arguments that the majority made distinguishing *Trimble*.

Justice Brennan dissented, joined by Justices White, Marshall, and Stevens. Justice Brennan found it difficult "to imagine an instance in which an illegitimate child, acknowledged and voluntarily supported by his father, would ever inherit intestate under the New York scheme." As a practical matter, social welfare agencies, the illegitimate children themselves, and their mothers were unlikely to bring proceedings against a father who supports his children.[3]

[3] The Aged

MASSACHUSETTS BOARD OF RETIREMENT v. MURGIA
427 U.S. 307, 96 S. Ct. 2562, 49 L. Ed. 2d 520 (1976)

PER CURIAM.

This case presents the question whether the provision of Mass. Gen. Laws Ann. c. 32, § 26(3)(a) (1966), that a uniformed state police officer "shall be retired . . . upon his attaining age fifty," denies appellee police officer equal protection of the laws in violation of the Fourteenth Amendment.

Appellee Robert Murgia was an officer in the Uniformed Branch of the Massachusetts State Police. The Massachusetts Board of Retirement retired him upon his 50th birthday. . . .

. . . [U]niformed officers participate in controlling prison and civil disorders, respond to emergencies and natural disasters, patrol highways in marked cruisers, investigate crime, apprehend criminal suspects, and provide backup support for local law enforcement personnel . . . . Thus, "even [appellee's] experts concede that there is a general relationship between advancing age and decreasing physical ability to respond to the demands of the job."

These considerations prompt the requirement that uniformed state officers pass a comprehensive physical examination biennially until age 40. After that, until mandatory retirement at age 50, uniformed officers must pass annually a more rigorous examination, including an electrocardiogram and tests for gastro-intestinal bleeding. Appellee Murgia had passed such an examination four months before he was retired, and there is no dispute that, when he retired, his excellent physical and mental health still rendered him capable of performing the duties of a uniformed officer.

. . . [T]he testimony of three physicians . . . clearly established that the risk of physical failure, particularly in the cardiovascular system, increases with age, and that the number of individuals in a given age group incapable of performing stress functions increases with the age of the group. The testimony also recognized that particular individuals over 50 could be capable of safely performing the functions of uniformed officers. The associate professor of medicine, who was a witness for the appellee, further testified that evaluating the risk of cardiovascular failure in a given individual would require a number of detailed studies. . . .

---

[3] Nor would a father who had not even taken time to write a will, likely bring such a filiation proceeding.

I

. . . *San Antonio School District v. Rodriguez*, 411 U.S. 1, reaffirmed that equal protection analysis requires strict scrutiny of a legislative classification only when the classification impermissibly interferes with the exercise of a fundamental right or operates to the peculiar disadvantage of a suspect class.

This Court's decisions give no support to the proposition that a right of governmental employment per se is fundamental. . . .

Nor does the class of uniformed state police officers over 50 constitute a suspect class for purposes of equal protection analysis. *Rodriguez* observed that a suspect class is one "saddled with such disabilities, or subjected to such a history of purposeful unequal treatment, or relegated to such a position of political powerlessness as to command extraordinary protection from the majoritarian political process." While the treatment of the aged in this Nation has not been wholly free of discrimination, such persons, unlike, say, those who have been discriminated against on the basis of race or national origin, have not experienced a "history of purposeful unequal treatment" or been subjected to unique disabilities on the basis of stereotyped characteristics not truly indicative of their abilities. The class subject to the compulsory retirement feature of the Massachusetts statute consists of uniformed state police officers over the age of 50. It cannot be said to discriminate only against the elderly. Rather, it draws the line at a certain age in middle life. But even old age does not define a "discrete and insular" group . . . in need of "extraordinary protection from the majoritarian political process." Instead, it marks a stage that each of us will reach if we live out our normal span. . . .

II

. . . [T]he State's classification rationally furthers the purpose identified by the State. Through mandatory retirement at age 50, the legislature seeks to protect the public by assuring physical preparedness of its uniformed police. There is no indication that § 26(3)(a) has the effect of excluding from service so few officers who are in fact unqualified as to render age 50 a criterion wholly unrelated to the objective of the statute. . . .

JUSTICE STEVENS took no part in the consideration or decision of this case.

JUSTICE MARSHALL, dissenting.

. . . [T]he Court finds that the right to work is not a fundamental right. And . . . the Court holds that the elderly are not a suspect class. Accordingly, the Court undertakes the scrutiny mandated by the bottom tier of its two-tier equal protection framework, finds the challenged legislation not to be "wholly unrelated" to its objective, and holds, therefore, that it survives equal protection attack. . . .

I

Although there are signs that its grasp on the law is weakening, the rigid two-tier model still holds sway as the Court's articulated description of the equal protection test. . . . Again, I must object to its perpetuation . . . [i]n equal protection cases. . . . [T]he inquiry has been much more sophisticated . . . focus[ing] upon the character of the classification in question, the relative importance to individuals in the class discriminated against of the governmental benefits that they do not receive, and the state interests asserted in support of the classification. . . .

Although the Court outwardly adheres to the two-tier model, it has apparently lost interest in recognizing further "fundamental" rights and "suspect" classes. . . . In my view, this result is the natural consequence of the limitations of the Court's traditional equal protection analysis. . . . It should be no surprise . . . that the Court is hesitant to expand the number of categories or rights and classes subject to strict scrutiny, when each expansion involves the invalidation of virtually every classification bearing upon a newly covered category.[4]

But however understandable the Court's hesitancy to invoke strict scrutiny, all remaining legislation should not drop into the bottom tier, and be measured by the mere rationality test. For that test, too, when applied as articulated, leaves little doubt about the outcome; the challenged legislation is always upheld. . . .

II

. . . There is simply no reason why a statute that tells able-bodied police officers, ready and willing to work, that they no longer have the right to earn a living in their chosen profession merely because they are 50 years old should be judged by the same minimal standards of rationality that we use to test economic legislation that discriminates against business interests. . . . Analysis of the three factors I have identified above — the importance of the governmental benefits denied, the character of the class, and the asserted state interests — demonstrates the Court's error. . . .

While depriving any government employee of his job is a significant deprivation, it is particularly burdensome when the person deprived is an older citizen. Once terminated, the elderly cannot readily find alternative employment. . . .

. . . Whether older workers constitute a "suspect" class or not, it cannot be disputed that they constitute a class subject to repeated and arbitrary discrimination in employment. . . .

[4] The Mentally Retarded

CLEBURNE v. CLEBURNE LIVING CENTER
473 U.S. 432, 105 S. Ct. 3249, 87 L. Ed. 2d 313 (1985)

JUSTICE WHITE delivered the opinion of the Court.

A Texas city denied a special use permit for the operation of a group home for the mentally retarded, acting pursuant to a municipal zoning ordinance requiring permits for such homes. The Court of Appeals for the Fifth Circuit held that mental retardation is a "quasi-suspect" classification and that the ordinance violated the Equal Protection Clause because it did not substantially further an important governmental purpose. We hold that a lesser standard of scrutiny is appropriate, but conclude that under that standard the ordinance is invalid as applied in this case.

I

In July, 1980, respondent Jan Hannah purchased a building at 201 Featherston Street in . . . Cleburne, Texas, with the intention of leasing it to Cleburne Living Centers, Inc. (CLC), for the operation of a group home for the mentally retarded. It was anticipated that the home would house 13 retarded men and women, who would be under the constant supervision of CLC staff members. . . .

The city informed CLC that . . . under the zoning regulations applicable to the site,

[4] Of course, the traditional suspect classes and fundamental rights would still rank at the top of the list of protected categories, so that in cases involving those categories analysis would be functionally equivalent to strict scrutiny. . . .

a special use permit, renewable annually, was required for the construction of "[h]ospitals for the insane or feeble-minded, or alcoholic [sic] or drug addicts, or penal or correctional institutions." The city had determined that the proposed group home should be classified as a "hospital for the feeble-minded." After holding a public hearing on CLC's application, the city council voted three to one to deny a special use permit. . . .

II

. . . The general rule is that legislation is presumed to be valid and will be sustained if the classification drawn by the statute is rationally related to a legitimate state interest. . . . When social or economic legislation is at issue, the Equal Protection Clause allows the states wide latitude, and the Constitution presumes that even improvident decisions will eventually be rectified by the democratic processes.

The general rule gives way, however, when a statute classifies by race, alienage or national origin. These factors are so seldom relevant to the achievement of any legitimate state interest that laws grounded in such considerations are deemed to reflect prejudice and antipathy. . . . For these reasons and because such discrimination is unlikely to be soon rectified by legislative means, these laws are subjected to strict scrutiny and will be sustained only if they are suitably tailored to serve a compelling state interest. Similar oversight by the courts is due when state laws impinge on personal rights protected by the Constitution. *Kramer v. Union Free School District No. 15*, 395 U.S. 621 (1969); *Shapiro v. Thompson*, 394 U.S. 618 (1969); *Skinner v. Oklahoma ex rel. Williamson*, 316 U.S. 535 (1942).

Legislative classifications based on gender also call for a heightened standard of review. . . . Rather than resting on meaningful considerations, statutes distributing benefits and burdens between the sexes in different ways very likely reflect outmoded notions of the relative capabilities of men and women.

A gender classification fails unless it is substantially related to a sufficiently important governmental interest. *Mississippi University for Women v. Hogan*; *Craig v. Boren*. Because illegitimacy is beyond the individual's control and bears "no relation to the individual's ability to participate in and contribute to society," *Matthews v. Lucas*, 427 U.S. 495, 505 (1976), official discriminations resting on that characteristic are also subject to somewhat heightened review. Those restrictions "will survive equal protection scrutiny to the extent they are substantially related to a legitimate state interest." *Mills v. Habluetzel*, 456 U.S. 91, 99 (1982).

We have declined, however, to extend heightened review to differential treatment based on age. . . .

The lesson of *Murgia* is that where individuals in the group affected by a law have distinguishing characteristics relevant to interests the state has the authority to implement, the courts have been very reluctant, as they should be in our federal system and with our respect for the separation of powers, to closely scrutinize legislative choices as to whether, how and to what extent those interests should be pursued. In such cases, the Equal Protection Clause requires only a rational means to serve a legitimate end.

III

Against this background, we conclude for several reasons that the Court of Appeals erred in holding mental retardation a quasi-suspect classification calling for a more exacting standard of judicial review than is normally accorded economic and social legislation. First, it is undeniable, and it is not argued otherwise here, that those who are mentally retarded have a reduced ability to cope with and function in the everyday world. Nor are they all cut from the same pattern: as the testimony in this record indicates, they range from those whose disability is not immediately evident to those who must be constantly cared for.[5]

They are thus different, immutably so, in relevant respects, and the states' interest in dealing with and providing for them is plainly a legitimate one. How this large and diversified group is to be treated under the law is a difficult and often a technical matter, very much a task for legislators guided by qualified professionals and not by the perhaps ill-informed opinions of the judiciary. . . .

Second, the distinctive legislative response, both national and state, to the plight of those who are mentally retarded demonstrates not only that they have unique problems, but also that the lawmakers have been addressing their difficulties in a manner that belies a continuing antipathy or prejudice and a corresponding need for more intrusive oversight by the judiciary. . . . The State of Texas has similarly enacted legislation that acknowledges the special status of the mentally retarded by conferring certain rights upon them, such as "the right to live in the least restrictive setting appropriate to [their] individual needs and abilities," including "the right to live . . . in a group home."

. . . Even assuming that many of these laws could be shown to be substantially related to an important governmental purpose, merely requiring the legislature to justify its efforts in these terms may lead it to refrain from acting at all. Much recent legislation intended to benefit the retarded also assumes the need for measures that might be perceived to disadvantage them . . . . Especially given the wide variation in the abilities and needs of the retarded themselves, governmental bodies must have a certain amount of flexibility and freedom from judicial oversight in shaping and limiting their remedial efforts.

Third, the legislative response . . . negates any claim that the mentally retarded are politically powerless in the sense that they have no ability to attract the attention of the lawmakers.

Fourth, if the large and amorphous class of the mentally retarded were deemed quasi-suspect for the reasons given by the Court of Appeals, it would be difficult to find a principled way to distinguish a variety of other groups who have perhaps immutable disabilities setting them off from others, who cannot themselves mandate the desired legislative responses, and who can claim some degree of prejudice from at least part of the public at large. One need mention in this respect only the aging, the disabled, the mentally ill, and the infirm. . . .

Our refusal to recognize the retarded as a quasi-suspect class does not leave them entirely unprotected from invidious discrimination. To withstand equal protection

---

[5] [Court's footnote 9] Mentally retarded individuals fall into four distinct categories. The vast majority — approximately 89% — are classified as "mildly" retarded, meaning that their IQ is between 50 and 70. Approximately 6% are "moderately" retarded, with IQs between 35 and 50. The remaining two categories are "severe" (IQs of 20 to 35) and "profound" (IQs below 20). These last two categories together account for about 5% of the mentally retarded population.

Mental retardation is not defined by reference to intelligence or IQ alone, however. The American Association on Mental Deficiency (AAMD) has defined mental retardation as "significantly subaverage general intellectual functioning existing concurrently with deficits in adaptive behavior and manifested during the developmental period." "Deficits in adaptive behavior" are limitations on general ability to meet the standards of maturation, learning, personal independence, and social responsibility expected for an individual's age level and cultural group. Mental retardation is caused by a variety of factors, some genetic, some environmental, and some unknown.

review, legislation that distinguishes between the mentally retarded and others must be rationally related to a legitimate governmental purpose. . . . The State may not rely on a classification whose relationship to an asserted goal is so attenuated as to render the distinction arbitrary or irrational. Furthermore, some objectives — such as "a bare . . . desire to harm a politically unpopular group" . . . are not legitimate state interests. . . .

IV

. . . The City does not require a special use permit in an R-3 zone for apartment houses, multiple dwellings, boarding and lodging houses, fraternity or sorority houses, dormitories, apartment hotels, hospitals, sanitariums, nursing homes for convalescents or the aged (other than for the insane or feeble-minded or alcoholics or drug addicts), private clubs or fraternal orders, and other specified uses. It does, however, insist on a special permit for the Featherston home, and it does so, as the District Court found, because it would be a facility for the mentally retarded.

. . . Because in our view the record does not reveal any rational basis for believing that the Featherston home would pose any special threat to the city's legitimate interests, we affirm the judgment below insofar as it holds the ordinance invalid as applied in this case.

The District Court found that the City Council's insistence on the permit rested on several factors. First, the Council was concerned with the negative attitude of the majority of property owners located within 200 feet of the Featherston facility, as well as with the fears of elderly residents of the neighborhood. But mere negative attitudes, or fear, unsubstantiated by factors which are properly cognizable in a zoning proceeding, are not permissible bases for treating a home for the mentally retarded differently. . . .

Second, the Council had two objections to the location of the facility. It was concerned that the facility was across the street from a junior high school, and it feared that the students might harass the occupants of the Featherston home. But the school itself is attended by about 30 mentally retarded students, and denying a permit based on such vague, undifferentiated fears is again permitting some portion of the community to validate what would otherwise be an equal protection violation. The other objection to the home's location was that it was located on "a five hundred year flood plain." This concern with the possibility of a flood, however, can hardly be based on a distinction between the Featherston home and, for example, nursing homes, homes for convalescents or the aged, or sanitariums or hospitals, any of which could be located on the Featherston site without obtaining a special use permit. . . .

Fourth, the Council was concerned with the size of the home and the number of people that would occupy it. The District Court found, and the Court of Appeals repeated, that "[i]f the potential residents of the Featherston Street home were not mentally retarded, but the home was the same in all other respects, its use would be permitted under the city's zoning ordinance. " . . . [T]here is no dispute that the home would meet the federal square-footage-per-resident requirement for facilities of this type. . . .

The short of it is that requiring the permit in this case appears to us to rest on an irrational prejudice against the mentally retarded. . . .

The judgment of the Court of Appeals is affirmed insofar as it invalidates the zoning ordinance as applied to the Featherston home. The judgment is otherwise vacated.

JUSTICE STEVENS, with whom THE CHIEF JUSTICE joins, concurring.

. . . [O]ur cases reflect a continuum of judgmental responses to differing classifications which have been explained in opinions by terms ranging from "strict scrutiny" at one extreme to "rational basis" at the other. I have never been persuaded that these so called "standards" adequately explain the decisional process. . . . In my own approach to these cases, I have always asked myself whether I could find a "rational basis" for the classification at issue. . . .

In every equal protection case, we have to ask certain basic questions. What class is harmed by the legislation, and has it been subjected to a "tradition of disfavor" by our laws?

What is the public purpose that is being served by the law? What is the characteristic of the disadvantaged class that justifies the disparate treatment? In most cases the answer to these questions will tell us whether the statute has a "rational basis." The answers will result in the virtually automatic invalidation of racial classifications and in the validation of most economic classifications, but they will provide differing results in cases involving classifications based on alienage, gender, or illegitimacy. But that is not because we apply an "intermediate standard of review" in these cases; rather it is because the characteristics of these groups are sometimes relevant and sometimes irrelevant to a valid public purpose. . . .

Every law that places the mentally retarded in a special class is not presumptively irrational. The differences between mentally retarded persons and those with greater mental capacity are obviously relevant to certain legislative decisions. . . .

JUSTICE MARSHALL, with whom JUSTICE BRENNAN and JUSTICE BLACKMUN join, concurring in the judgment in part and dissenting in part. . . .

. . . Cleburne's ordinance surely would be valid under the traditional rational basis test applicable to economic and commercial regulation. In my view, it is important to articulate, as the Court does not, the facts and principles that justify subjecting this zoning ordinance to the searching review — the heightened scrutiny — that actually leads to its invalidation. Moreover, in invalidating Cleburne's exclusion of the "feebleminded" only as applied to respondents, rather than on its face, the Court radically departs from our equal protection precedents. . . . I cannot accept the Court's disclaimer that no "more exacting standard" than ordinary rational basis review is being applied. . . .

I

. . . The suggestion that the traditional rational basis test allows this sort of searching inquiry creates precedent for this Court and lower courts to subject economic and commercial classifications to similar and searching "ordinary" rational basis review — a small and regrettable step back toward the days of *Lochner v. New York*, [198 U.S. 45 (1905)]. Moreover, by failing to articulate the factors that justify today's "second order" rational basis review, the Court provides no principled foundation for determining when more searching inquiry is to be invoked. . . .

II

I have long believed the level of scrutiny employed in an equal protection case should vary with "the constitutional and societal importance of the interest adversely affected and the recognized invidiousness of the basis upon which the particular classification is drawn." *San Antonio Independent School District v. Rodriguez*, 411 U.S. 1, 99 (1973) (Marshall, J., dissenting). . . .

First, the interest of the retarded in establishing group homes is substantial. . . . [G]roup homes have become the primary means by which retarded adults can enter life in the community. . . .

Second, the mentally retarded have been subject to a "lengthy and tragic history" of segregation and discrimination . . . that in its virulence and bigotry rivaled, and indeed paralleled, the worst excesses of Jim Crow. Massive custodial institutions were built to warehouse the retarded for life. . . .

. . . 29 states enacted compulsory eugenic sterilization laws between 1907 and 1931.

. . . As of 1979, most states still categorically disqualified "idiots" from voting, without regard to individual capacity and with discretion to exclude left in the hands of low-level election officials . . .

III

. . .The government must establish that the classification is substantially related to important and legitimate objectives, see, e.g., *Craig v. Boren*, 429 U.S. 190 (1976). . . .

IV

. . . The Court's as-applied remedy relegates future retarded applicants to the standardless discretion of low-level officials. . . .

Invalidating on its face the ordinance's special treatment of the "feebleminded," in contrast, would place the responsibility for tailoring and updating Cleburne's unconstitutional ordinance where it belongs: with the legislative arm of the City of Cleburne. . . .

[5]   Sexual Orientation

ROMER v. EVANS
517 U.S. 620, 116 S. Ct. 1620, 134 L. Ed. 2d 855 (1996)

JUSTICE KENNEDY delivered the opinion of the Court.

One century ago, the first Justice Harlan admonished this Court that the Constitution "neither knows nor tolerates classes among citizens." *Plessy v. Ferguson*, 163 U.S. 537, 559 (1896) (dissenting opinion). Unheeded then, those words now are understood to state a commitment to the law's neutrality where the rights of persons are at stake. . . .

I

The enactment challenged in this case is an amendment to the Constitution of the State of Colorado, adopted in a 1992 statewide referendum[,] . . . "Amendment 2." . . . The impetus for the amendment and the contentious campaign that preceded its adoption came in large part from ordinances that had been passed in various Colorado municipalities. For example, the cities of Aspen and Boulder and the City and County of Denver each had enacted ordinances which banned discrimination in many transactions and activities, including housing, employment, education, public accommodations, and health and welfare services. What gave rise to the statewide controversy was the protection the ordinances afforded to persons discriminated against by reason of their sexual orientation. *See* Boulder Rev. Code § 12-1-1 (defining "sexual orientation" as "the choice of sexual partners, i.e., bisexual, homosexual or heterosexual"). . . . Amendment 2 repeals these ordinances to the extent they prohibit discrimination on the basis of "homosexual, lesbian or bisexual orientation, conduct, practices or relationships." Colo. Const., Art. II, § 30b.

Yet Amendment 2, in explicit terms, does more than repeal or rescind these provisions. It prohibits all legislative, executive or judicial action at any level of state or local government designed to protect the named class, a class we shall refer to as homosexual persons or gays and lesbians. . . .

II

The State's principal argument in defense of Amendment 2 is that it puts gays and lesbians in the same position as all other persons. So, the State says, the measure does no more than deny homosexuals special rights. This reading of the amendment's language is implausible. We rely . . . upon the authoritative construction of Colorado's Supreme Court. The state court, deeming it unnecessary to determine the full extent of the amendment's reach, found it invalid even on a modest reading of its implications. The critical discussion of the amendment . . . is as follows: "The immediate objective of Amendment 2 is, at a minimum, to repeal existing statutes, regulations, ordinances, and policies of state and local entities that barred discrimination based on sexual orientation at state colleges."

"The 'ultimate effect' of Amendment 2 is to prohibit any governmental entity from adopting similar, or more protective statutes, regulations, ordinances, or policies in the future unless the state constitution is first amended to permit such measures." 854 P.2d at 1284–1285.

Sweeping and comprehensive is the change in legal status effected by this law . . . . The amendment withdraws from homosexuals, but no others, specific legal protection from the injuries caused by discrimination, and it forbids reinstatement of these laws and policies.

The change that Amendment 2 works in the legal status of gays and lesbians in the private sphere is far-reaching, both on its own terms and when considered in light of the structure and operation of modern anti-discrimination laws. That structure is well illustrated by contemporary statutes and ordinances prohibiting discrimination by providers of public accommodations. "At common law, innkeepers, smiths, and others who 'made profession of a public employment,' were prohibited from refusing, without good reason, to serve a customer" . . . .

. . . Colorado's state and municipal laws typify this emerging tradition of statutory protection and follow a consistent pattern. The laws first enumerate the persons or entities subject to a duty not to discriminate. The list goes well beyond the entities covered by the common law. The Boulder ordinance, for example, has a comprehensive definition of entities deemed places of "public accommodation." They include "any place of business engaged in any sales to the general public and any place that offers services, facilities, privileges, or advantages to the general public or that receives financial support through solicitation of the general public or through governmental subsidy of any kind." Boulder Rev. Code § 12-1-1(j) (1987). The Denver ordinance is of similar breadth, applying, for example, to hotels, restaurants, hospitals, dental clinics, theaters, banks, common carriers, travel and insurance agencies, and "shops and stores dealing with goods or services of any kind," Denver Rev. Municipal Code, Art. IV, § 28-92.

. . . Colorado's state and local governments have not limited anti-discrimination laws to groups that have so far been given the protection of heightened equal protection scrutiny under our cases. Rather, they set forth an extensive catalogue of traits which cannot be the basis for discrimination, including age, military status, marital status, pregnancy, parenthood, custody of a minor child, political affiliation, physical or mental disability of an individual or of his or her associates and, in recent times, sexual orientation.

. . . Amendment 2, in addition, nullifies specific legal protections for this targeted class in all transactions in housing, sale of real estate, insurance, health and welfare services, private education, and employment.

Not confined to the private sphere, Amendment 2 also operates to repeal and forbid all laws or policies providing specific protection for gays or lesbians from discrimination by every level of Colorado government. The State Supreme Court cited two examples of protections in the governmental sphere that are now rescinded and may not be reintroduced. The first is Colorado Executive Order D0035 (1990), which forbids employment discrimination against " 'all state employees, classified and exempt' on the basis of sexual orientation." 854 P.2d at 1284. Also repealed, and now forbidden, are "various provisions prohibiting discrimination based on sexual orientation at state colleges." *Id.* at 1284, 1285. . . .

Amendment 2's reach may not be limited to specific laws passed for the benefit of gays and lesbians. It is a fair, if not necessary, inference from the broad language of the amendment that it deprives gays and lesbians even of the protection of general laws and policies that prohibit arbitrary discrimination in governmental and private settings. . . . At some point in the systematic administration of these laws, an official must determine whether homosexuality is an arbitrary and thus forbidden basis for decision. Yet a decision to that effect would itself amount to a policy prohibiting discrimination on the basis of homosexuality. . . .

If this consequence follows from Amendment 2, as its broad language suggests, it would compound the constitutional difficulties the law creates. The state court did not decide whether the amendment has this effect, however, and neither need we. . . . [W]e cannot accept the view that Amendment 2's prohibition on specific legal protections does no more than deprive homosexuals of special rights. To the contrary, the amendment imposes a special disability upon those persons alone. . . . [T]hese are protections against exclusion from an almost limitless number of transactions and endeavors that constitute ordinary civic life in a free society.

III

The Fourteenth Amendment's promise that no person shall be denied the equal protection of the laws must co-exist with the practical necessity that most legislation classifies for one purpose or another, with resulting disadvantage to various groups or persons. We have attempted to reconcile the principle with the reality by stating that, if a law neither burdens a fundamental right nor targets a suspect class, we will uphold the legislative classification so long as it bears a rational relation to some legitimate end.

Amendment 2 fails, indeed defies, even this conventional inquiry. First, the amendment has the peculiar property of imposing a broad and undifferentiated disability on a single named group, an exceptional and, as we shall explain, invalid form of legislation. Second, its sheer breadth is so discontinuous with the reasons offered for it that the amendment seems inexplicable by anything but animus toward the class that it affects; it lacks a rational relationship to legitimate state interests.

Taking the first point, even in the ordinary equal protection case calling for the most deferential of standards, we insist on knowing the relation between the classification adopted and the object to be attained. . . . In the ordinary case, a law will be sustained if it can be said to advance a legitimate government interest, even if the law seems unwise or works to the disadvantage of a particular group, or if the rationale for it seems tenuous. . . . "[W]e ensure that classifications are not drawn for the purpose of disadvantaging the group burdened by the law."

Amendment 2 confounds this normal process of judicial review. It is at once too narrow and too broad. It identifies persons by a single trait and then denies them protection across the board. The resulting disqualification of a class of persons from the right to seek specific protection from the law is unprecedented in our jurisprudence. . . .

. . . Central both to the idea of the rule of law and to our own Constitution's guarantee of equal protection is the principle that government and each of its parts remain open on impartial terms to all who seek its assistance. . . . A law declaring that in general it shall be more difficult for one group of citizens than for all others to seek aid from the government is itself a denial of equal protection of the laws in the most literal sense. . . .

. . . "If the constitutional conception of 'equal protection of the laws' means anything, it must at the very least mean that a bare . . . desire to harm a politically unpopular group cannot constitute a legitimate governmental interest." *Department of Agriculture v. Moreno*, 413 U.S. 528, 534 (1973).

The primary rationale the State offers for Amendment 2 is respect for other citizens' freedom of association, and in particular the liberties of landlords or employers who have personal or religious objections to homosexuality. Colorado also cites its interest in conserving resources to fight discrimination against other groups. The breadth of the Amendment is so far removed from these particular justifications that we find it impossible to credit them. We cannot say that Amendment 2 is directed to any identifiable legitimate purpose or discrete objective. It is a status-based enactment divorced from any factual context from which we could discern a relationship to legitimate state interests; it is a classification of persons undertaken for its own sake, something the Equal Protection Clause does not permit. . . .

We must conclude that Amendment 2 classifies homosexuals not to further a proper legislative end but to make them unequal to everyone else. This Colorado cannot do. A State cannot so deem a class of persons a stranger to its laws. . . .

JUSTICE SCALIA, with whom THE CHIEF JUSTICE and JUSTICE THOMAS join, dissenting.

. . . The constitutional amendment before us here is not the manifestation of a "'bare . . . desire to harm'" homosexuals, but is rather a modest attempt by seemingly tolerant Coloradans to preserve traditional sexual mores against the efforts of a politically powerful minority to revise those mores through use of the laws. That objective, and the means chosen to achieve it, are not only unimpeachable under any constitutional doctrine hitherto pronounced (hence the opinion's heavy reliance upon principles of righteousness rather than judicial holdings); they have been specifically approved by the Congress of the United States and by this Court.

In holding that homosexuality cannot be singled out for disfavorable treatment, the Court contradicts a decision, unchallenged here, pronounced only 10 years ago, *see Bowers v. Hardwick*, 478 U.S. 186 (1986), and places the prestige of this institution behind the proposition that opposition to homosexuality is as reprehensible as racial or religious bias. . . . Since the Constitution of the United States says nothing about this subject, it is left to be resolved by normal democratic means. . . .

I

. . . The amendment prohibits special treatment of homosexuals, and nothing more. . . . Thus, homosexuals could not be denied coverage, or charged a greater premium, with respect to auto collision insurance; but neither the State nor any municipality could require that distinctive health insurance risks associated with homosexuality (if there are any) be ignored.

. . . The only denial of equal treatment [the Court] contends homosexuals have suffered is this: They may not obtain preferential treatment without amending the state constitution. . . .

The central thesis of the Court's reasoning is that any group is denied equal protection when, to obtain advantage (or, presumably, to avoid disadvantage), it must have recourse to a more general and hence more difficult level of political decisionmaking than others. The world has never heard of such a principle, which is why the Court's opinion is so long on emotive utterance and so short on relevant legal citation. . . .

II

I turn next to whether there was a legitimate rational basis for the substance of the constitutional amendment — for the prohibition of special protection for homosexuals.[6] . . .

III

. . . What [Colorado] has done is not only unprohibited, but eminently reasonable. . . .

. . . Of course it is our moral heritage that one should not hate any human being or class of human beings. But I had thought that one could consider certain conduct reprehensible — murder, for example, or polygamy, or cruelty to animals — and could exhibit even "animus" toward such conduct. . . .

. . . The Court's portrayal of Coloradans as a society fallen victim to pointless, hate-filled "gay-bashing" is so false as to be comical. Colorado not only is one of the 25 States that have repealed their antisodomy laws, but was among the first to do so. . . .

There is a problem, however . . . it is evident in many cities of the country, and occasionally bubbles to the surface of the news, in heated political disputes over such matters as the introduction into local schools of books teaching that homosexuality is an optional and fully acceptable "alternate life style." The problem (a problem, that is, for those who wish to retain social disapprobation of homosexuality) is that, because those who engage in homosexual conduct tend to reside in disproportionate numbers in certain communities, have high disposable income, and of course care about homosexual-rights issues much more ardently than the public at large, they possess political power much greater than their numbers, both locally and statewide. Quite understandably, they devote this political power to achieving not merely a grudging social toleration, but full social acceptance, of homosexuality. . . .

. . . Three Colorado cities — Aspen, Boulder, and Denver — had enacted ordinances that listed "sexual orientation" as an impermissible ground for discrimination. . . . I do not mean to be critical of these legislative successes; homosexuals are as entitled to use the legal system for reinforcement of their moral sentiments as are the rest of society. But they are subject to being countered by lawful, democratic countermeasures as well.

. . . The constitutions of the States of Arizona, Idaho, New Mexico, Oklahoma, and Utah to this day contain provisions stating that polygamy is "forever

---

[6] [Court's footnote 1] The Court evidently agrees that "rational basis" — the normal test for compliance with the Equal Protection Clause — is the governing standard. . . . *See Evans v. Romer*, 882 P.2d 1335, 1341, n. 3 (1994). And the Court implicitly rejects the Supreme Court of Colorado's holding, *see Evans v. Romer*, 854 P.2d 1270, 1282 (1993), that Amendment 2 infringes upon a "fundamental right" of "independently identifiable classes" to "participate equally in the political process."

prohibited." . . . The Court's disposition today suggests that these provisions are unconstitutional, and that polygamy must be permitted in these States on a state-legislated, or perhaps even local-option, basis — unless, of course, polygamists for some reason have fewer constitutional rights than homosexuals. . . .

IV

. . . When the Court takes sides in the culture wars, it tends to be with the knights rather than the villeins — and more specifically with the Templars, reflecting the views and values of the lawyer class from which the Court's Members are drawn. . . .

Today's opinion has no foundation in American constitutional law, and barely pretends to. The people of Colorado have adopted an entirely reasonable provision which does not even disfavor homosexuals in any substantive sense, but merely denies them preferential treatment. Amendment 2 is designed to prevent piecemeal deterioration of the sexual morality favored by a majority of Coloradans, and is not only an appropriate means to that legitimate end, but a means that Americans have employed before. Striking it down is an act, not of judicial judgment, but of political will. . . .

NOTE

For additional discussion, see Toni M. Massaro, *Gay Rights, Thick and Thin*, 49 STAN. L. REV. 45, 47 (1996) ("The lesson of *Evans* is that, when advancing arguments for gay rights, advocates should avoid thick doctrinal arguments that alter existing legal categories, extend the upper echelon tiers of review, or construct gay rights as such. Rather, they should emphasize thin doctrinal arguments that merely say that homosexuality cannot and should not be a basis for official discrimination.").

§ 11.02   EQUAL PROTECTION FOR THE POOR

Section Note. As we have seen the "strict scrutiny" standard of review, which generally results in disapproval of the classification, has been generally confined by the Court to purposeful discrimination on grounds of race and national origin. The Court, however, has used equal protection analysis, in varying degrees, to protect other groups against governmental discrimination. The *Murgia* case, *supra*, was a rejection by the Court of the claim that discrimination based on age should be subject to heightened scrutiny.

The most potentially far-reaching equal protection claim to emerge during this period centered around laws and regulations that allegedly discriminated against the indigent, or possibly the less affluent, segments of the population. Obviously, if the Court extended to the indigent some of the judicial protection made available to racial groups, aliens, gender classifications, or illegitimates, a very wide range of economic and social legislation would have been subjected to a higher level of judicial scrutiny than is usually accorded to such laws.

Claims of indigents to special protection under the Equal Protection Clause were usually merged with another strand of equal protection analysis that emerged during this period — that governmental classifications which abridged "fundamental rights" should be subject to "strict scrutiny." Some of these rights — like the right to a fair trial, the right to participation in the electoral process, or the right to travel — had been previously recognized by the Court. The claims of persons not to be denied these rights because of lack of money contributed to a significant expansion of these rights.

But the indigent, or less affluent, also asserted rights that were often defined in terms that related closely to the economic and social status of the claimants. The right to the "necessities of life," or to equality of educational opportunity, or to adequate housing, for example, may have been phrased in universal terms, but the litigants were essentially asking the courts, primarily through the Equal Protection Clause, to require governments to make some important public programs and benefits available on a more equitable basis to the less affluent segments of the population.

The cases below indicate the Supreme Court's response. They focus first on the question of whether classifications based on wealth should be viewed as suspect, or at least whether there should be fundamental rights to certain necessities. Then the section considers cases dealing with the effect of poverty on a person's access to the processes of government, specifically, the electoral process and the justice system.

[1]   Wealth as a Suspect Classification; Fundamental Rights to Necessities

SAN ANTONIO SCHOOL DISTRICT v. RODRIGUEZ, 411 U.S. 1 (1973). In 1968, Mexican-American parents living in the Edgewood Independent School District (Edgewood) brought a class action against Texas education officials on behalf of minority and poor school children living in districts that had a low property-tax base. The parents alleged that the finance system was unconstitutional under the Equal Protection Clause of the Fourteenth Amendment. To finance its educational system, Texas implemented the Texas Minimum Foundation School Program, which increased state funding "to help offset disparities in local spending. . . . " Under the Foundation Program, the State "finances approximately 80% of the Program, and the school districts are responsible — as a unit — for providing the remaining 20%." School districts raised the funds by imposing property taxes. This system had "an equalizing influence on expenditure levels between school districts by placing the heaviest burden on the school districts most capable of paying." The State funds were then "apportioned among the school districts under a formula designed to reflect each district's relative taxpaying ability."

Residents of Edgewood, a primarily Mexican-American district, had the lowest property value per pupil and the lowest median family income. While the district's "equalized tax rate of $1.05 per $100 assessed property" was the highest in the area, the district could only contribute an extra $26 per pupil in addition to $222 contributed by the Foundation Program. With federal funding of an additional $108, the total expenditure per pupil in Edgewood was $356. Plaintiffs compared Edgewood to the most affluent district in the area, Alamo Heights, a primarily white district with a property-based tax rate that generated $333 beyond the Foundation Program share of $225. Although federal funds only allocated $36 per pupil to Alamo Heights, in all, the district spent $594 per student. The Foundation Program did lower the economic disparity between the districts from a ratio of 13:1 during the 1967–68 school year to a little more than 2:1 in 1970–71.

A three-judge District Court held that wealth was a suspect classification. The Supreme Court rejected classifying wealth as a suspect classification and education as a fundamental right.

Justice Powell wrote for the majority. "[A]t least where wealth is involved, the Equal Protection Clause does not require absolute equality or precisely equal advantages." Because many factors affect the quality of an education, no system could guarantee absolute equality among school districts. Justice Powell concluded that the claimants could not be identified as a traditional disadvantaged class. Had the State required each student to pay a specified tuition, then "a clearly defined class of poor" people — definable in terms of their inability to pay the prescribed sum — who would be absolutely precluded from receiving an education could be identified. Here, however, the State not only provided all children with an education, but "attempted, though imperfectly, to ameliorate by state funding and by the local assessment program the disparities in local tax resources."

Justice Powell characterized a school district as a "large, diverse, and amorphous class, unified only by the common factor of residence in districts that happen to have less taxable wealth than other districts." A school district could not qualify as a suspect class because it was not "subjected to such a history of purposeful unequal treatment, or relegated to such a position of political powerlessness as to command extraordinary protection from the majoritarian political process."

Recognizing that the Supreme Court has never found that wealth discrimination alone could attract strict scrutiny, the parents also asserted that the state's educational finance system interfered with a "fundamental" right to education. Justice Powell found that the Constitution neither explicitly or implicitly protects education. He also rejected plaintiffs' claim that education is a "fundamental personal right because it is essential to the effective exercise of First Amendment freedoms and to intelligent utilization of the right to vote." The Court stressed that it had "never presumed to possess either the ability or the authority to guarantee to the citizenry the most *effective* speech or the most *informed* electoral choice." Even if the Constitution required a certain degree of education for the enjoyment of either the right to free speech or voting, no evidence suggested that the education provided by Texas was insufficient. Once again, the Court stated that the argument could be stronger if the state had absolutely denied certain children of all educational opportunities.[7]

The Court lacked the knowledge of local problems to effectively make any decisions about raising or distributing public funds for education. This lack of expertise deterred the Court from ordering a state to change its funding system.[8]

Moreover, the Court did not want "inflexible constitutional restraints to chill state experimentation in seeking to solve educational problems," or attempts "to tailor local programs to local needs." If the challenged educational financing system was unconstitutional, local funds for other services such as police protection or public utilities might also be found unconstitutional. Finally, invalidating the funding system at issue would have prompted "an unprecedented upheaval in public education."

Justice Stewart filed a concurring opinion. Justice White dissented, joined by Justices Douglas and Brennan. Justice White maintained that the property taxes failed to maximize local initiative and discretion. In districts of low property-tax bases, there was "little if any opportunity for interested parents, rich or poor, to augment school district revenues." He also thought that the parents and children of the Edgewood district who asserted relative deprivation in educational opportunity comprised an identifiable suspect class.

Justice Marshall also wrote a dissenting opinion which Justice Douglas joined. One study found that the 10 wealthiest school districts in Texas, each with "more than $100,000 in taxable property per pupil, raised through local effort an average of $610 per pupil." The four poorest districts, however, each with "less than $10,000 in taxable property per pupil, were able to raise only an average of $63 per pupil." Justice

---

[7] Justice Powell also noted that it would be difficult to distinguish a personal interest in education from those interests in food and housing. Obviously, studies could "buttress an assumption that the ill-fed, ill-clothed, and ill-housed are among the most ineffective participants in the political process, and that they derive the least enjoyment from the benefits of the First Amendment."

[8] Plaintiffs did not suggest alternatives to the Texas educational finance system. The Court noted that the likely result would be funding from property taxes or sales and income taxes redistributed among the districts by the State.

Marshall asserted that the burden was on the state to prove that the funding disparities did not affect the quality of the education in the poorer districts.

Justice Marshall said that precedents did not protect the rights of indigents per se but only wealth classifications affecting fundamental rights. The quality of education affects the ability of children to enjoy their First Amendment rights both in understanding and conveying information and ideas. The impact of education on the exercise of the vote even more important.

Wealth classifications need not absolutely deprive a fundamental right to attract strict scrutiny. Wealth classifications alone have not been afforded the same scrutiny as other suspect classifications because the "poor" have not been viewed as politically powerless as other minority groups; poverty is not a permanent condition such as race or ethnicity; and "personal wealth may not necessarily share the general irrelevance as a basis for legislative action that race or nationality is recognized to have." In this case, the constitutional importance of the interest in education and the invidiousness of the wealth classification "dictate close judicial scrutiny."

NOTES

(1) *State Reform of Educational Financing.* In the aftermath of the *Rodriguez* case, reform efforts shifted to the states. *See* Sunstein, *Three Civil Rights Fallacies*, 79 CAL. L. REV. 751, 773 (1991) (The term " 'anti-caste principle' . . . suggests that a system with sufficient opportunities for education, training, or employment, without race- and sex-related violence, and without incentives for teenage childbearing or participation in crime, is a principal goal of civil rights policy. It suggests, finally, that the elaboration and implementation of the relevant policies should be undertaken, at least in the first instance, by legislative and executive bodies and not by the courts.").

Some states held that their systems of public school financing violated provisions of their respective state constitutions. Several commentators have remarked that judicial remedies in these cases have proven difficult to fashion. *See, e.g.,* J. GUTHRIE, SCHOOL FINANCE POLICIES AND PRACTICES (1980); Note, *Strategies for School Finance Reform Litigation in the Post-Rodriguez Era*, 21 NEW ENG. L.J. 817 (1986). For a discussion of the effects of legislative reform, some prompted by judicial action, see S. CARROLL & R. PARK, THE SEARCH FOR EQUITY IN SCHOOL FINANCE (1983); Note, *To Render Them Safe: The Analysis of State Constitutional Provisions in Public School Finance Reform Litigation*, 75 VA. L. REV. 1639, 1642 (1989).

Cf. James E. Ryan, *Schools, Race, and Money*, 109 YALE L.J. 249, 315 (1999). ("School finance reform litigation has not proven, as its advocates had hoped, to be an adequate substitute for school desegregation.")

(2) *Complete Deprivation.* In *San Antonio v. Rodriguez*, the majority seemed to be confining the "fundamental rights" strand of "new" equal protection analysis to rights that are implicit or explicit in the Constitution. They rejected the "right to education" as a justification for strict scrutiny of education financing laws of Texas. Nevertheless, in *Plyler v. Doe*, 457 U.S. 202 (1982), *supra* § 11.01[1], Note (7), the Court (5-4) invalidated a Texas law that completely denied free public education to children who were not legally admitted into the United States. The Court relied in part on the importance of education in "maintaining our basic institutions, and the lasting impact of its deprivation on the life of the child."

The Court cited *San Antonio v. Rodriguez* approvingly for the proposition that public education is not a right. Nevertheless, it noted that "neither is it merely some governmental 'benefit' . . . . Both the importance of education in maintaining our basic institutions, and the lasting impact of deprivation on the life of the child, made the distinction." While *Rodriguez* involved disparate levels of expenditures on education, the *Plyler* statute resulted in a complete denial of public educational benefits. Indeed, the *Rodriguez* Court itself stated that absolute deprivation of educational benefits "would present a far more compelling case."

For discussion of what the contours of a right to education might be, see Bitensky, *Theoretical Foundations for a Right to Education Under the U.S. Constitution: A Beginning to the End of the National Education Crisis*, 86 Nw. U. L. Rev. 550, 552 (1992) ("Were education to be recognized as an affirmative right under the Constitution, those doing battle against the crisis would be armed with a potent pedagogical message — that education is a national priority of the first magnitude and that, as such, children, parents, teachers, administrators, and policymakers must treat their respective responsibilities vis-á-vis education with commensurate dedication and activity. Besides acting as an agent of moral suasion, the right would also have the singular effect of making the federal government the ultimate guarantor of education for school-age children holding the right."); Sherry, *Responsible Republicanism: Educating for Citizenship*, 62 U. Chi. L. Rev. 131 (1995) (arguing that "because the Court has left open the question whether there might be a constitutional right to a minimally adequate education, scholarly commentary has speculated for at least the last decade on possible constitutional bases for such a right. No one, however, has much explored the possible content of a right to education. In particular, there has been little examination of the concrete relationship between education and citizenship. What are the appropriate contours of an education for citizenship?").

(3) *School Finance Litigation.* One commentator has argued that:

> [f]rustrated by the apparent stagnation of efforts to reduce spending disparities and the theoretical and practical problems associated with the equity decisions, school finance reformers now embrace adequacy arguments that demand a meaningful opportunity for all students to benefit from whatever education a state constitution promises. As a tool to reform school finance systems, adequacy arguments are comparatively less threatening and more firmly rooted in a constitutional base. Moreover, court decisions [focusing on adequacy] raise important questions about judicial capacity, the separation of powers and political question doctrines, and the efficacy of litigation as a device to influence public policies.

Heise, *State Constitutions, School Finance Litigation, and the "Third Wave": From Equity to Adequacy*, 68 Temple L. Rev. 1151, 1176 (1995); *see also* Heise, *State Constitutional Litigation, Educational Finance, and Legal Impact: An Empirical Analysis*, 63 U. Cinn. L. Rev. 1735, 1765 (1995) (presenting data assessing the impact of court decisions attempting to reform school finance systems, suggesting "that an interaction of an array of factors, rather than a single discrete event such as a court decision invalidating a state's school finance system, influences educational spending").

(4) *AFDC.* In *Dandridge v. Williams*, 397 U.S. 471 (1970), the Court declined to extend heightened scrutiny to the distribution of welfare benefits to the poor. Maryland imposed a maximum amount on its federal Aid to Families With Dependent Children (AFDC). Different states administered the program in different ways. Some, unlike Maryland, did not impose an absolute cap on the amount a particular family might receive, but distributed according to need relative to family size. In addition to disputing Maryland's distributional scheme on various statutory grounds, the plaintiffs contended "that the maximum grant limitations operate to discriminate against them merely because of the size of their families, in violation of the Equal Protection Clause."

Rejecting this contention, Justice Stewart treated this law like any other in the "area of economics and social welfare." He said that the law rationally advanced the state's interest in "encouraging employment and in avoiding discrimination between welfare families and families of the working poor." While the Constitution may impose certain procedural safeguards upon systems of welfare administration, it "does not empower this Court to second guess state officials charged with the difficult responsibility of allocating limited public welfare funds among the myriad of potential recipients."

Justice Harlan concurred and Justice Douglas dissented on statutory grounds. Justice Marshall dissented, joined by Justice Brennan. Justice Marshall stated that the deprivation was severe and the distinction upon which the benefits were denied was not very compelling. *See Shapiro v. Thompson*, 394 U.S. 618 (1968) (invalidating AFDC residency requirement).

[2] Access to the Justice System

DOUGLAS v. CALIFORNIA, 372 U.S. 353 (1963). In *Douglas*, the Court held that the Fourteenth Amendment required states to provide counsel to indigent criminal defendants on first appeal as a matter of right. The petitioners, W. Douglas and B. Meyers, were jointly tried and convicted on an information charging them with 13 felonies. A single public defender was appointed to defend them. Their attorney complained that, due to the complexity of the case, conflicts of interests between the defendants, etc., one lawyer could not adequately represent both of them.

Relying on *Griffin v. Illinois*, 351 U.S. 12 (1956) (indigent criminal defendant must be provided trial transcript if necessary for appeal, *see infra* § 11.02[2], Note (1)), Justice Douglas stated that "a State may not grant appellate review in such a way as to discriminate against some convicted defendants on account of their poverty." The Court found that the California procedure discriminated against the poor. Persons who could afford counsel presented the merits of their cases with written briefs and oral arguments. "The indigent, where the record is unclear or the errors are hidden, has only the right to a meaningless ritual, where the rich man has a meaningful appeal." Justice Douglas limited the issue to first appeals granted as a matter of right from criminal convictions.

Justice Clark dissented. He considered California's procedure to be an adequate alternative to providing counsel in all cases involving indigents. Justice Clark also complained that "[w]ith this fetish for indigency the Court piles an intolerable burden on the State's judicial machinery."

Justice Harlan dissented, joined by Justice Stewart. He stated that the Court's holding appeared to rely on both the Equal Protection and Due Process Clauses of the Fourteenth Amendment. The Equal Protection Clause, however, did not apply because California did not deny the poor the right to appeal. "[T]he Equal Protection Clause does not impose on the States 'an affirmative duty to lift the handicaps flowing from differences in economic circumstances.' To so construe it would be to read into the Constitution a philosophy of leveling that would be foreign to many of our basic concepts of the proper relations between government and society."

NOTE

Counsel in Discretionary Appeals. In *Ross v. Moffitt*, 417 U.S. 600 (1974), the Court declined to extend *Douglas* to require counsel for discretionary state appeals and for applications for review in the Supreme Court of the United States. Writing for the majority, Justice Rehnquist rejected the equal protection challenge to North Carolina's appellate procedure. Despite the State's failure to provide counsel, an indigent still had a meaningful appeal to the North Carolina Supreme Court. The trial record, the defendant's brief in the Court of Appeals, and often the Court of Appeals' opinion were enough to provide the State Supreme Court an adequate basis for deciding whether to grant review. Moreover, the critical issue in the North Carolina Supreme Court's decision to take a case was not whether the case was decided correctly. Instead, the issue on review was "whether 'the subject matter of the appeal has a significant public interest.' "

Applying a similar analysis, the Court held that the brief prepared for the appeal, along with the lower court opinions, was a sufficient basis upon which to judge whether it should grant certiorari.

Justice Douglas, joined by Justices Brennan and Marshall, dissented. Under the *Douglas* case, "there can be no equal justice where the kind of appeal a man enjoys 'depends on the amount of money he has.' "

UNITED STATES v. KRAS, 409 U.S. 434 (1973). In *Kras*, the Court dealt with the issue of equal access to bankruptcy court. In 1971 the appellee, Robert Kras, wanted to file a voluntary petition in bankruptcy court in the District Court for the Eastern District of New York. Kras sought a discharge from over $6,000 in debts; his total assets were $50 in clothing and household goods. Due to his poverty[9] Kras moved for leave to file and proceed in bankruptcy without paying $50 in filing fees that were a condition precedent to discharge.

The Supreme Court held (5-4) that the filing fee did not violate Kras's constitutional rights. Justice Blackmun's majority opinion distinguished *Boddie v. Connecticut*, 401 U.S. 371 (1971). *Boddie* held that, under the Due Process Clause of the Fourteenth Amendment, a State could not require the indigent to pay court fees as a condition for obtaining a judicial divorce. "*Boddie* was based on the notion that a State cannot deny access, simply because of one's poverty, to a 'judicial proceedings [that is] the only effective means of resolving the dispute at hand.' "

Justice Blackmun stated that in *Boddie* the Court emphasized the fundamental associational interests that marriage involved. "Kras' alleged interest in the elimination of his debt burden, and in obtaining his desired new start in life, although important and so recognized by the enactment of the Bankruptcy Act, does not rise to the same constitutional level. . . . We see no fundamental interest that is gained or lost depending on the availability of a discharge in bankruptcy." Another distinction was that the government's control over the dissolution of debts was not as exclusive as its control over divorces. Kras could have negotiated with his creditors or the debts could dissolve with the passing of the statute of limitations.

The Court also held that requiring Kras to pay the filing fee did not deny him the equal protection of the laws. "Bankruptcy is hardly akin to free speech or marriage 'or other fundamental rights.' " Instead, bankruptcy legislation was in the "area of economics and social welfare." Applying the rational basis test, Justice Blackmun said that charging those who file for a discharge was related to Congress' goal of making the system "self-sustaining and paid for by those who use it rather than by tax revenues drawn from the public at large." Moreover, Kras could pay the fee in installments. The resultant average installment of $1.28 per week "should be within his able-bodied reach."

Chief Justice Burger wrote a short concurring opinion asserting that Congress should make the reforms championed in Justice Stewart's opinion.

---

[9] In 1969, the insurance company Kras worked for fired him when premiums were stolen from him and he could not pay the amount himself. As a result, Kras could not find a steady job because he received bad references. He had to support his wife, two children and two other dependents. His eight-month-old son was in the hospital for treatment of cystic fibrosis. The $366 per month in public assistance he was allotted was spent on rent and necessities.

Justice Stewart wrote a dissent in which Justices Douglas, Brennan and Marshall joined. Justice Stewart contended that *Boddie* did apply. A debtor-creditor relationship is like a marriage in that the Government enforces the obligation. Kras was bankrupt because "the State stands ready to exact all of his debts through garnishment, attachment, and the panoply of other creditor remedies. [Kras] can be pursued and harassed by his creditors since they hold his legally enforceable debts." Moreover, as in *Boddie*, there are no "recognized, effective alternatives for the indigent bankrupt." Justice Stewart rejected the argument that the filing fee was necessary to make the bankruptcy system self-sufficient. The Court is allowing Congress to say that "some poor are too poor even to go bankrupt."

NOTES

(1) *Divorce.* Each side in *Kras* labored either to distinguish, or rely upon, *Boddie v. Connecticut*, 401 U.S. 371 (1971). *Boddie* held (8-1) that the state could not condition access to the courts, for purposes of obtaining a divorce, on a person's ability to pay court costs and fees. *Boddie* could be viewed as an extension of *Griffin v. Illinois*, 351 U.S. 12 (1956). *Griffin* constitutionally required free transcripts for criminal appeals in situations where the transcript was viewed as an essential element of the criminal appellate process.

(2) *Welfare Benefits.* In *Ortwein v. Schwab*, 410 U.S. 656 (1973), the Court upheld a $25 filing fee imposed by Oregon as a condition for court review of denials of welfare benefits.

(3) *Paternity Suits.* In *Little v. Streater*, 452 U.S. 1 (1981), the Court, in a unanimous opinion by Chief Justice Burger, struck down a Connecticut statute that "provides that in paternity actions the cost of blood grouping tests is to be borne by the party requesting them." The Court emphasized the circumstance of Connecticut law whereby the "constant" testimony of the mother created a prima facie case which the defendant could not overcome by testimony alone. The State "in effect forecloses what is potentially a conclusive means for an indigent defendant to surmount that disparity and exonerate himself. Such a practice is irreconcilable with the Due Process Clause." In a footnote, the Court commented: "Because appellant has no choice of an alternative forum and his interests, as well as those of the child, are constitutionally significant, this case is comparable to *Boddie* rather than to *Kras* or *Ortwein*."

(4) *Paternity Rights.* In *M.L.B. v. S.L.J.*, 519 U.S. 102 (1996), the Court held that just as a state may not impede an indigent petty offender's access to an appeal granted to others, see *Mayer v. Chicago*, 404 U.S. 189, 195–96 (1971), poverty may not prevent appellate review of a parental termination decree. At the request of the biological father (S.L.J.), a Mississippi Chancery Court terminated the parental rights of the biological mother (M.L.B.) to her two minor children. M.L.B. filed a timely appeal and paid the $100 filing fee. However, Mississippi further required advance payment of record preparation fees approximating $2,352.36. The Supreme Court of Mississippi denied M.L.B.'s request for leave to appeal *in forma pauperis* and dismissed her appeal.

Writing for a 6-3 majority, Justice Ginsburg acknowledged a narrow category of civil cases that require a state to provide access to its judicial processes, regardless of the party's ability to pay court fees. *See Boddie v. Connecticut, supra.* However, the Equal Protection Clause does not require waiving court fees in civil cases unless the case involves a fundamental right. Thus, the Court upheld a fee required for a discharge in bankruptcy in *United States v. Kras, supra*, and sustained a fee required to appeal the denial of welfare benefits in *Ortwein v. Schwab, supra*.

As choices concerning marriage, family life, and the upbringing of children are fundamental rights involving due process and equal protection concerns, the Court held that a parental termination appeal should be treated like the petty offense appeal in *Mayer*. Parental status termination severs the parent-child bond and irrevocably destroys the family relationship. M.L.B. sought to defend against the state's destruction of her bonds with her children and to avoid being labeled an unfit parent.

Justice Kennedy concurred in the judgment, stating that due process was a sufficient basis for the Court's holding.

Justice Thomas wrote a dissenting opinion, in which Chief Justice Rehnquist and Justice Scalia joined. Justice Thomas doubted that the right to free transcripts in civil appeals could be restricted to this case. In any event, the Due Process Clause does not support M.L.B.'s position because it does not require an appeal, even for a criminal conviction. The Equal Protection Clause only protects against intentional governmental discrimination, not against social and economic inequities.

(5) *Inability to Pay Restitutionary Fines.* In *Beardon v. Georgia*, 461 U.S. 660 (1983), a unanimous Court invalidated a state procedure that required imprisonment as an alternative for inability to pay a fine. Justice O'Connor's opinion relied on both equal protection and due process analyses. She eschewed "easy slogans or pigeonhole analysis" in favor of an examination of the defendant's interests, the extent to which state action affects these interests, the "rationality of the connection between legislative means and purpose," and the availability of alternative means to achieve the state's purposes.

The Court relied on its earlier decisions in *Williams v. Illinois*, 399 U.S. 235 (1970), and *Tate v. Short*, 402 U.S. 395 (1971). In *Williams*, the Court invalidated the state's application of two statutes that forced an indigent prisoner, sentenced to both a prison term and the payment of a fine, to "work off" the fine by remaining in prison for 101 days beyond his original sentence. *Tate* invalidated the conversion of a fine into a prison sentence when the defendant demonstrated an inability to pay. A state could not convert a fine into a prison sentence simply due to inability, as against unwillingness, to pay. Moreover, imprisoning a defendant for failure to pay a fine did not further a state's interest in securing restitution and rehabilitation. Less onerous alternatives, such as lengthening the time to pay or requiring some form of public service or labor, could also further the state's interests. A state could impose imprisonment as an alternative to paying a fine only if Georgia courts determine that the defendant "did not make sufficient bona fide efforts to pay his fine, or determine that alternate punishment is not adequate to meet the State's interest in punishment and deterrence." Justice White wrote a concurring opinion joined by Chief Justice Burger and Justices Powell and Rehnquist.

§ 11.03   EQUALITY IN THE POLITICAL PROCESS

[1]   Distinctions Based on Wealth

Section Note. This section of the Chapter involves a range of classifications that pose barriers to participation in the political process. In Chapter VII, we dealt with racial classifications. Many of the barriers we consider here are based on wealth, such as laws that limit suffrage to property owners or those who can pay a poll tax. Other laws dilute the vote through malapportionment, or barriers to minority party access to the ballot. Because of the importance of the right to vote or to gain access to the ballot, all of these classifications have been subjected to searching scrutiny. Thus, this section demonstrates how the nature of the classification (wealth) and the importance of the right (access to the political process) trigger a more intense judicial inquiry under the Equal Protection Clause.

KRAMER v. UNION FREE SCHOOL DISTRICT, 395 U.S. 621 (1969). In *Kramer*, the Court struck down a New York statute that limited the right to vote in school district elections. The statute granted the right to vote only to those residents who were otherwise qualified to vote and were: (1) owners or lessors of real taxable property in the district, (2) spouses of persons owning or leasing qualifying property, or (3) parents or guardians of a child who was enrolled in the district the previous year. New York claimed that the purpose of the restrictions was to limit the vote to citizens who were primarily interested in school affairs. The appellant, a bachelor who neither owned nor leased property, countered that the voting exclusion denied him equal protection of the laws.

Chief Justice Warren stated, "Thus state apportionment statutes, which may *dilute* the effectiveness of some citizens' votes receive close scrutiny from this Court. *Reynolds v. Sims* [*infra* § 11.03[2]]. . . . Statutes granting the franchise on a selective basis always pose the danger of denying some citizens any effective voice in the governmental affairs which substantially affect their lives. Therefore, if a challenged state statute grants the right to vote to some bona fide residents of requisite age and citizenship and denies the franchise to others, the Court must determine whether the exclusions are necessary to promote a compelling state interest."

Chief Justice Warren rejected the argument that because the elected board members lacked "general" legislative powers the strict scrutiny standard did not apply.

In applying the compelling state interest test, the majority did not decide the issue of whether a State may limit the right to vote to those primarily interested in or affected by a particular government unit. The majority held that the classifications were not necessary to accomplish the State's interest since they permitted "inclusion of many persons who have, at best, a remote and indirect interest, in school affairs and on the other hand, exclud[ed] others who have a distinct and direct interest in the school meeting decisions." For example, the law included an uninterested, unemployed lessee who did not pay taxes but lived with his parents. Appellees also did not "offer any justification for the exclusion of seemingly interested and informed residents."

Justice Stewart, joined by Justices Black and Harlan, dissented. Justice Stewart insisted that States have broad powers to determine voting qualifications unless they discriminate in a way the Constitution condemns.

NOTE

Landowner Voting Rights. In *Salyer Land Co. v. Tulare Water District*, 410 U.S. 719 (1973), landowners, lessees, and residents of the water district challenged provisions of the California Water Code, which assessed charges according to the benefits their land received. Under the provisions, only landowners were allowed to vote for the board of directors of the district. For each $100 of the assessed value of their land, landowners received one vote. These provisions excluded 77 residents in the district from voting, while one landowner was allotted 37,825 votes.

Writing for the Court, Justice Rehnquist upheld the provisions. Unlike the Alabama legislature in *Reynolds v. Sims, infra* § 11.03[2], which established the "one-person-one-vote" rule, the water district only had relatively limited governmental powers. Its main purpose was to manage the area's water supply. The district did not provide any "other general public services such as schools, housing, transportation, utilities, roads, or anything else of the type ordinarily financed by a municipal body." Because landowners bore the water costs of the district, California "could rationally conclude" that the landowners should be responsible for water management decisions of the district.

The Court also upheld the provision that assigned voting rights according to the assessed value of a landowner's land; the landowner who retained 37,825 votes was also responsible for paying $817,865 of a $2,500,000 project, while some landowners had only contributed $46. The Court could not say that these proportions were not "rationally based."

Justice Douglas, joined by Justices Brennan and Marshall, dissented. Justice Douglas argued that the tremendous impact of irrigation, water storage and flood control on all residents in the district required application of the "one-person-one-vote rule."

[2]　Other Barriers to Political Participation: Apportionment, Ballot Access for Minority Parties, Gerrymandering

REYNOLDS v. SIMS, 377 U.S. 533 (1964). In *Reynolds v. Sims*, the plaintiffs, who were "residents, taxpayers and voters of Jefferson County," challenged the apportionment of the Alabama Legislature. They contended that the last apportionment was made according to the 1900 federal census, although the State Constitution mandated decennial reapportionment. They argued that the apportionment discriminated against them because the population of Alabama had changed between 1900 and 1960. Under the 1960 census figures, only 25.1 percent of the population lived in districts represented by a majority of the members of the Senate, and only 25.7 percent lived in counties able to elect a majority in the House of Representatives. "Population-variance ratios of up to 41-to-1 existed in the Senate, and up to about 16-to-1 in the House."

Chief Justice Warren first set forth the test for the constitutionality of apportionment plans, established in *Wesberry v. Sanders*, 376 U.S. 1 (1964), as "one of substantial equality of population among the various districts established by a state legislature for the election of members of the Federal House of Representatives." In that case, the Court determined that in a congressional election all votes should be of equal weight and value. Otherwise, "[i]t would defeat the principle solemnly embodied in the Great Compromise — equal representation in the House for equal numbers of people." The Court recognized that the right to vote is a fundamental element of democracy that must be scrupulously protected. The state could not permit some voters to vote multiple times for their legislators while restricting other voters to just one vote. For "[o]verweighting and overvaluation of the votes of those living here has the certain effect of dilution and undervaluation of the votes of those living there." Based on these observations, the Court concluded that "as a basic constitutional standard, the Equal Protection Clause requires that the seats in both houses of a bicameral state legislature must be apportioned on a population basis."

Looking at the plans, the Court found that one of the plans approximated the state representation in the Federal Congress. For, just as each of the 50 states receives two Senate seats, each of Alabama's 67 counties had only one Senate seat apiece. The Court, however, rejected this analogy, stating that the federal system of representation was "conceived out of compromise and concession indispensable to the establishment of our federal republic." In this capacity, it stemmed from "unique historical circumstances" that required previously autonomous states to form one federal government.

The Constitution does not require that states apportion their legislatures with mathematical exactitude according to the population. A state may validly pursue an attempt to "maintain the integrity of various political subdivisions" or create "compact districts of contiguous territory." In fact, "[i]ndiscriminate districting, without any regard for political subdivision or natural or historical boundary lines, may be little more than an open invitation to partisan gerrymandering." Some states may need single member districts; on the other hand, others require the flexibility of multimember districts. "Whatever the means of accomplishment, the overriding objective must be substantial equality of population among the various districts, so that the vote of any citizen is approximately equal in weight to that of any other citizen in the State." A state may deviate from a "strict population standard" if it does so to effect a rational state interest. It may not, however, create such deviations merely because of geography; modern technology in transportation and communication refute such geographical concerns.

When a court finds an apportionment plan unconstitutional, it must prevent any more elections from occurring under the plan unless equitable considerations require less than immediate relief in situations such as when the state's election process has already been set into motion in an ensuing election. But in considering whether to withhold immediate relief, the court must evaluate "the proximity of a forthcoming election and the mechanics and complexities of the state election laws" and should look to "general equitable principles." In choosing the proper time for remedial action, the court can attempt to avoid impediments to the election process and "unreasonable or embarrassing demands on a State."

Justice Harlan dissented, taking the majority to task for ignoring § 2 of the Fourteenth Amendment, which permits the states to abridge its citizens' right to vote for the state legislators. Contrary to the Court's decision, in 1961, 80 percent of the State Constitutions "recognized bases of apportionment other than geographic spread of population, and to some extent favored sparsely populated areas by a variety of devices." To Justice Harlan's dismay, the Court concluded that a state may only consider political subdivisions in apportionment and even this consideration is unconstitutional if "population is submerged as the controlling consideration."

NOTES

Remedying race-based lines. In *Abrams v. Johnson*, 521 U.S. 74 (1997), the Court upheld a congressional redistricting plan for Georgia. Since the Georgia legislature could not agree to a redistricting plan, the district court designed its own plan, consisting of one majority-black district. Appellants contended that the trial court's redistricting plan should have contained two and possibly three majority-black districts, as most proposals did. One of the reasons for this contention was that the redistricting plan violated the one-person, one-vote guarantee of Article I, § 2.

Writing for the 5-4 majority, Justice Kennedy stated that court-ordered redistricting plans must attain higher levels of population equality than legislative plans. Court-ordered plans may contain " 'little more than de minimis variation' " among the populations of congressional districts. The overall population deviation consists of the difference in population between the two districts with the largest disparity. The average population deviation consists of the average of all districts' deviation from the standard one-person, one-vote rule. Justice Kennedy found that the District Court's plan had an overall population deviation of 0.35% and an average deviation of 0.11%. These deviations were lower than other plans submitted to the court.

Georgia's small counties each represent a community of interest to an unusually great degree. Its 159 counties provide " 'ample building blocks for acceptable voting districts without chopping any of these blocks in half.' " Moreover, correcting any violation of the one-person, one-vote rule should require readjusting district boundary lines rather than creating a second black-majority district.

In addition, appellants' one-person, one-vote objections were "increasingly futile." The last census, taken six years ago, showed that the difference between the court plan's average deviation (0.11%) and the Justice Department's "Illustrative Plan" (0.07%) was 0.04%, representing "328 people out of the perfect district population of

588,928." The rapidly growing population of Georgia continues to grow, shift, and change throughout the state. The dissenting opinions did not discuss one-person, one-vote issues.

BUSH v. PALM BEACH COUNTY CANVASSING BOARD *(Bush I)*, 531 U.S. 70 (2000). In *Bush I*, the Court vacated the Supreme Court of Florida's decision that gave 4 counties a 12-day extension to file amended election returns. The Court remanded the case for further proceedings consistent with its ruling. The day after the 2000 Presidential election, the Florida Division of Elections announced that Governor George Bush won the State's electoral votes over Vice President Al Gore by a margin of 1,784 votes. Under Florida law, an automatic machine recount took place since Governor Bush's margin of victory was narrow. The machine recount reflected an even narrower margin of victory, prompting Vice President Gore to request manual recounts in 4 counties.

Under the Florida Election Code, the deadline for submitting county election returns to the Florida Department of State was 7 days following the election. Arguing that a manual recount could not be conducted within that time frame, the involved counties on November 14 requested that the Florida Secretary of State (Secretary) extend the deadline. The Secretary ordered the counties to "submit a written statement of the facts and circumstances justifying a later filing" by 2 p.m. on November 15. The counties submitted such statements, but the Secretary "determined that none justified an extension."

The Supreme Court of Florida said, " '[B]ecause of our reluctance to rewrite the Florida Election Code, we conclude that we must invoke the equitable powers of this Court to fashion a remedy.' " One provision of the Florida Election Code said that the Secretary of State " 'may . . . ignore' " late election returns and another said the Secretary " 'shall . . . ignore' " late election returns. The Florida Court then held that the " 'may . . . ignore' " provision governed and "imposed a deadline of November 26, at 5 p.m.," extending the 7-day statutory deadline by 12 days and ordering the Secretary to accept late returns until that date.

In a unanimous *per curiam* opinion, the Supreme Court stated " 'that there is considerable uncertainty as to the precise grounds for the [Florida Supreme Court's] decision.' " Article II, § 1, cl. 2 of the United States Constitution requires: " 'Each State shall appoint, in such Manner as the Legislature thereof may direct,' " its electors. In addition, 3 U.S.C. § 5 "creates a 'safe harbor' for a State insofar as congressional consideration of its electoral votes is concerned." Under § 5, where "the state legislature has provided for final determination of contests or controversies" pursuant to a state law enacted prior to election day, "that determination shall be conclusive if made at least six days prior to said time of meeting of the electors."

Portions of the opinion of the Florida Supreme Court seem to indicate it "construed the Florida Election Code without regard to the extent to which the Florida Constitution could, consistent with Art. II. § 1, cl. 2, 'circumscribe the legislative power.' " For example, the Florida Supreme Court stated that even though the legislature has the power to pass laws regulating the electoral process, those laws will not be upheld if they impose " ' "unreasonable or unnecessary" restraints on the right of suffrage' guaranteed by the state constitution."

In conclusion, "we are unclear as to the extent to which the Florida Supreme Court saw the Florida Constitution as circumscribing the legislature's authority under Art. II, § 1, cl. 2. We are also unclear as to the consideration the Florida Supreme Court accorded to 3 U.S.C. § 5." Accordingly, the Court vacated the decision and remanded the case.

BUSH v. GORE
531 U.S. 98, 121 S. Ct. 525, 148 L. Ed. 2d. 388 (2000)

PER CURIAM.

I

On December 8, 2000, the Supreme Court of Florida ordered that the Circuit Court of Leon County tabulate by hand 9,000 ballots in Miami-Dade County. It also ordered the inclusion in the certified vote totals of 215 votes identified in Palm Beach County and 168 votes identified in Miami-Dade County for Vice President Al Gore, Jr., and Senator Joseph Lieberman, Democratic Candidates for President and Vice President. The Supreme Court noted that petitioner, Governor George W. Bush asserted that the net gain for Vice President Gore in Palm Beach County was 176 votes, and directed the Circuit Court to resolve that dispute on remand. The court further held that relief would require manual recounts in all Florida counties where so-called "undervotes" had not been subject to manual tabulation. The court ordered all manual recounts to begin at once. Governor Bush and Richard Cheney, Republican Candidates for the Presidency and Vice Presidency, filed an emergency application for a stay of this mandate. On December 9, we granted the application, treated the application as a petition for a writ of certiorari, and granted certiorari.

The proceedings leading to the present controversy are discussed in some detail in our opinion in *Bush v. Palm Beach County Canvassing Bd.*, (per curiam) (*Bush I* . . . . A dispute arose concerning the deadline for local county canvassing boards to submit their returns to the Secretary of State (Secretary). The Secretary declined to waive the November 14 deadline imposed by statute. The Florida Supreme Court, however, set the deadline at November 26. We granted certiorari and vacated the Florida Supreme Court's decision, finding considerable uncertainty as to the grounds on which it was based. *Bush I*. On December 11, the Florida Supreme Court issued a decision on remand reinstating that date.

On November 26, the Florida Elections Canvassing Commission certified the results of the election and declared Governor Bush the winner of Florida's 25 electoral votes. On November 27, Vice President Gore, pursuant to Florida's contest provisions, filed a complaint in Leon County Circuit Court contesting the certification. Fla. Stat. § 102.168 (2000). He sought relief pursuant to § 102.168(3)(c), which provides that "receipt of a number of illegal votes or rejection of a number of legal votes sufficient to change or place in doubt the result of the election" shall be grounds for a contest. The Circuit Court denied relief, stating that Vice President Gore failed to meet his burden of proof. He appealed to the First District Court of Appeal, which certified the matter to the Florida Supreme Court.

Accepting jurisdiction, the Florida Supreme Court affirmed in part and reversed in part. The court held that the Circuit Court had been correct to reject Vice President Gore's challenge to the results certified in Nassau County and his challenge to the Palm Beach County Canvassing Board's determination that 3,300 ballots cast in that county were not, in the statutory phrase, "legal votes." The Supreme Court held that Vice President Gore had satisfied his burden of proof under § 102.168(3)(c) with respect to his challenge to Miami-Dade County's failure to tabulate, by manual count, 9,000 ballots on which the machines had failed to detect a vote for President ("undervotes"). Noting the closeness of the election, the Court explained that "on this record, there can be no question that there are legal votes within the 9,000 uncounted votes sufficient to place the results of this election in doubt." A "legal vote," as determined by the Supreme Court, is "one in which there is a 'clear indication of the intent of the voter.' " The court therefore ordered a hand recount of the 9,000 ballots in Miami-Dade County. Observing that the contest provisions vest broad discretion in the circuit judge to "provide any relief appropriate under such circumstances," Fla. Stat. § 102.168(8) (2000), the Supreme Court further held that the Circuit Court could order "the Supervisor of Elections and the Canvassing Boards, as well as the necessary public officials, in all counties that have not conducted a manual recount or tabulation of the undervotes . . . to do so forthwith, said tabulation to take place in the individual counties where the ballots are located."

The Supreme Court also determined that both Palm Beach County and Miami-Dade County, in their earlier manual recounts, had identified a net gain of 215 and 168 legal votes for Vice President Gore. Rejecting the Circuit Court's conclusion that Palm Beach County lacked the authority to include the 215 net votes submitted past the November 26 deadline, the Supreme Court explained that the deadline was not intended to exclude votes identified after that date through ongoing manual recounts. As to Miami-Dade County, the Court concluded that although the 168 votes identified were the result of a partial recount, they were "legal votes [that] could change the outcome of the election." The Supreme Court therefore directed the Circuit Court to include those totals in the certified results, subject to resolution of the actual vote total from the Miami-Dade partial recount. The petition presents the following questions: whether the Florida Supreme Court established new standards for resolving Presidential election contests, thereby violating Art. II, § 1, cl. 2, of the United States Constitution and failing to comply with 3 U.S.C. § 5, and whether the use of standardless manual recounts violates the Equal Protection and Due Process Clauses. With respect to the equal protection question, we find a violation of the Equal Protection Clause.

II

A

. . . Nationwide statistics reveal that an estimated 2% of ballots cast do not register a vote for President for whatever reason, including deliberately choosing no candidate at all or some voter error, such as voting for two candidates or insufficiently marking a ballot. . . . In certifying election results, the votes eligible for inclusion in the certification are the votes meeting the properly established legal requirements.

This case has shown that punch card balloting machines can produce an unfortunate number of ballots which are not punched in a clean, complete way by the voter. After the current counting, it is likely legislative bodies nationwide will examine ways to improve the mechanisms and machinery for voting.

B

The individual citizen has no federal constitutional right to vote for electors for the President of the United States unless and until the state legislature chooses a statewide election as the means to implement its power to appoint members of the Electoral College. U.S. Const., Art. II, § 1. . . . [T]he State legislature's power to select the manner for appointing electors is plenary; it may, if it so chooses, select the electors itself, which indeed was the manner used by State legislatures in several States for many years after the Framing of our Constitution. History has now favored the voter, and in each of the several States the citizens themselves vote for Presidential electors. When the state legislature vests the right to vote for President in its people, the right to vote as the legislature has prescribed is fundamental; and one source of its fundamental nature lies in the equal weight accorded to each vote and the equal dignity owed to each voter. . . .

The right to vote is protected in more than the initial allocation of the franchise. Equal protection applies as well to the manner of its exercise. Having once granted the right to vote on equal terms, the State may not, by later arbitrary and disparate treatment, value one person's vote over that of another. *See, e.g., Harper v. Virginia Bd. of Elections*, 383 U.S. 663, 665 (1966). . . . It must be remembered that "the right of suffrage can be denied by a debasement or dilution of the weight of a citizen's vote just as effectively as by wholly prohibiting the free exercise of the franchise." *Reynolds v. Sims*, 377 U.S. 533 (1964).

. . . The question before us . . . is whether the recount procedures the Florida Supreme Court has adopted are consistent with its obligation to avoid arbitrary and disparate treatment of the members of its electorate.

Much of the controversy seems to revolve around ballot cards designed to be perforated by a stylus but which, either through error or deliberate omission, have not been perforated with sufficient precision for a machine to count them. In some cases a piece of the card — a chad — is hanging, say by two corners. In other cases there is no separation at all, just an indentation.

The Florida Supreme Court has ordered that the intent of the voter be discerned from such ballots. . . . The recount mechanisms implemented in response to the decisions of the Florida Supreme Court do not satisfy the minimum requirement for non-arbitrary treatment of voters necessary to secure the fundamental right. Florida's basic command for the count of legally cast votes is to consider the "intent of the voter." This is unobjectionable as an abstract proposition and a starting principle. The problem inheres in the absence of specific standards to ensure its equal application. The formulation of uniform rules to determine intent based on these recurring circumstances is practicable and, we conclude, necessary.

The law does not refrain from searching for the intent of the actor in a multitude of circumstances; and in some cases the general command to ascertain intent is not susceptible to much further refinement. In this instance, however, the question is not whether to believe a witness but how to interpret the marks or holes or scratches on an inanimate object, a piece of cardboard or paper which, it is said, might not have registered as a vote during the machine count. The factfinder confronts a thing, not a person. The search for intent can be confined by specific rules designed to ensure uniform treatment. The want of those rules here has led to unequal evaluation of ballots in various respects. *See Gore v. Harris* (Wells, J., dissenting) ("Should a county canvassing board count or not count a 'dimpled chad' where the voter is able to successfully dislodge the chad in every other contest on that ballot? Here, the county canvassing boards disagree"). As seems to have been acknowledged at oral argument, the standards for accepting or rejecting contested ballots might vary not only from county to county but indeed within a single county from one recount team to another.

The record provides some examples. A monitor in Miami-Dade County testified at trial that he observed that three members of the county canvassing board applied different standards in defining a legal vote. And testimony at trial also revealed that at least one county changed its evaluative standards during the counting process. Palm Beach County, for example, began the process with a 1990 guideline which precluded counting completely attached chads, switched to a rule that considered a vote to be legal if any light could be seen through a chad, changed back to the 1990 rule, and then abandoned any pretense of a *per se* rule, only to have a court order that the county consider dimpled chads legal. . . . An early case in our one person, one vote jurisprudence arose when a State accorded arbitrary and disparate treatment to voters in its different counties. *Gray v. Sanders*, 372 U.S. 368. The Court found a constitutional violation. We relied on these principles in the context of the Presidential selection process in *Moore v. Ogilvie*, 394 U.S. 814, where we invalidated a county-based procedure that diluted the influence of citizens in larger counties in the nominating process. There we observed that "the idea that one group can be granted greater voting strength than another is hostile to the one man, one vote basis of our representative government." 394 U.S. at 819.

The State Supreme Court ratified this uneven treatment. It mandated that the recount totals from two counties, Miami-Dade and Palm Beach, be included in the certified total. The court also appeared to hold *sub silentio* that the recount totals from Broward County, which were not completed until after the original November 14 certification by the Secretary of State, were to be considered part of the new certified vote totals even though the county certification was not contested by Vice President Gore. Yet each of the counties used varying standards to determine what was a legal vote. Broward County used a more forgiving standard than Palm Beach County, and uncovered almost three times as many new votes, a result markedly disproportionate to the difference in population between the counties.

In addition, the recounts in these three counties were not limited to so-called undervotes but extended to all of the ballots. The distinction has real consequences. A manual recount of all ballots identifies not only those ballots which show no vote but also those which contain more than one, the so-called overvotes. Neither category will be counted by the machine. This is not a trivial concern. At oral argument, respondents estimated there are as many as 110,000 overvotes statewide. As a result, the citizen whose ballot was not read by a machine because he failed to vote for a candidate in a way readable by a machine may still have his vote counted in a manual recount; on the other hand, the citizen who marks two candidates in a way discernable by the machine will not have the same opportunity to have his vote count, even if a manual examination of the ballot would reveal the requisite indicia of intent. Furthermore, the citizen who marks two candidates, only one of which is discernable by the machine, will have his vote counted even though it should have been read as an invalid ballot. The State Supreme Court's inclusion of vote counts based on these variant standards exemplifies concerns with the remedial processes that were under way. That brings the analysis to yet a further equal protection problem. The votes certified by the court included a partial total from one county, Miami-Dade. The Florida Supreme Court's decision thus gives no assurance that the recounts included in a final certification must be complete. Indeed, it is respondent's submission that it would be consistent with the rules of the recount procedures to include whatever partial counts are done by the time of final certification, and we interpret the Florida Supreme Court's decision to permit this. . . . This accommodation no doubt results from the truncated contest period established by the Florida Supreme Court in *Bush I*, at respondents' own urging. The press of time does not diminish the constitutional concern. . . . In addition to these difficulties the actual process by which the votes were to be counted under the Florida Supreme Court's decision raises further concerns. That order did not specify who would recount the ballots. The county canvassing boards were forced to pull together ad hoc teams comprised of judges from various Circuits who had no previous training in handling and interpreting ballots. Furthermore, while others were permitted to observe, they were prohibited from objecting during the recount.

The recount process, in its features here described, is inconsistent with the minimum procedures necessary to protect the fundamental right of each voter in the special instance of a statewide recount under the authority of a single state judicial officer. Our consideration is limited to the present circumstances, for the problem of equal protection in election processes generally presents many complexities.

The question before the Court is not whether local entities, in the exercise of their expertise, may develop different systems for implementing elections. Instead, we are presented with a situation where a state court with the power to assure uniformity has ordered a statewide recount with minimal procedural safeguards. When a court orders a statewide remedy, there must be at least some assurance that the rudimentary requirements of equal treatment and fundamental fairness are satisfied.

. . . The contest provision, as it was mandated by the State Supreme Court, is not well calculated to sustain the confidence that all citizens must have in the outcome of elections. . . . Upon due consideration of the difficulties identified to this point, it is obvious that the recount cannot be conducted in compliance with the requirements of equal protection and due process without substantial additional work. It would require not only the adoption (after opportunity for argument) of adequate statewide standards for determining what is a legal vote, and practicable procedures to implement them, but also orderly judicial review of any disputed matters that might arise. In addition, the Secretary of State has advised that the recount of only a portion of the ballots requires that the vote tabulation equipment be used to screen out undervotes, a function for which the machines were not designed. If a recount of overvotes were also required, perhaps even a second screening would be necessary. Use of the equipment for this purpose, and any new software developed for it, would have to be evaluated for accuracy by the Secretary of State, as required by Fla. Stat. § 101.015 (2000).

The Supreme Court of Florida has said that the legislature intended the State's electors to "participate fully in the federal electoral process," as provided in *3 U.S.C. § 5*. That statute, in turn, requires that any controversy or contest that is designed to lead to a conclusive selection of electors be completed by December 12. That date is upon us, and there is no recount procedure in place under the State Supreme Court's order that comports with minimal constitutional standards. Because it is evident that any recount seeking to meet the December 12 date will be unconstitutional for the reasons we have discussed, we reverse the judgment of the Supreme Court of Florida ordering a recount to proceed.

Seven Justices of the Court agree that there are constitutional problems with the recount ordered by the Florida Supreme Court that demand a remedy. *See* (Souter, J., dissenting); (Breyer, J., dissenting). The only disagreement is as to the remedy. Because the Florida Supreme Court has said that the Florida Legislature intended to obtain the safe-harbor benefits of 3 U.S.C. § 5, Justice Breyer's proposed remedy — remanding to the Florida Supreme Court for its ordering of a constitutionally proper contest until December 18 — contemplates action in violation of the Florida election code, and hence could not be part of an "appropriate" order authorized by Fla. Stat. § 102.168(8) (2000).

None are more conscious of the vital limits on judicial authority than are the members of this Court, and none stand more in admiration of the Constitution's design to leave the selection of the President to the people, through their legislatures, and to the political sphere. When contending parties invoke the process of the courts, however, it becomes our unsought responsibility to resolve the federal and constitutional issues the judicial system has been forced to confront.

The judgment of the Supreme Court of Florida is reversed, and the case is remanded for further proceedings not inconsistent with this opinion. . . .

CHIEF JUSTICE REHNQUIST, with whom JUSTICE SCALIA and JUSTICE THOMAS join, concurring.

We join the *per curiam* opinion. We write separately because we believe there are additional grounds that require us to reverse the Florida Supreme Court's decision.

I

We deal here not with an ordinary election, but with an election for the President of the United States. . . .

. . . Article II, § 1, cl. 2, provides that "each State shall appoint, in such Manner as the Legislature thereof may direct," electors for President and Vice President. . . .

In *McPherson v. Blacker*, 146 U.S. 1 (1892) we explained that Art. II, § 1, cl. 2, "conveys the broadest power of determination" and "leaves it to the legislature exclusively to define the method" of appointment. *Id.* at 27 . . . .

3 U.S.C. § 5 informs our application of Art. II, § 1, cl. 2. . . . Section 5 provides that the State's selection of electors "shall be conclusive, and shall govern in the counting of the electoral votes" if the electors are chosen under laws enacted prior to election day, and if the selection process is completed six days prior to the meeting of the electoral college. . . . *Bush v. Palm Beach County Canvassing Bd.*, [531 U.S. 70 (2000)]. . . .

If we are to respect the legislature's Article II powers, therefore, we must ensure that postelection state-court actions do not frustrate the legislative desire to attain the "safe harbor" provided by § 5.

In Florida, the legislature . . . has delegated the authority to run the elections and to oversee election disputes to the Secretary of State (Secretary), Fla. Stat. § 97.012(1) (2000), and to state circuit courts, §§ 102.168(1), 102.168(8). . . . [W]ith respect to a Presidential election, the court must be both mindful of the legislature's role under Article II in choosing the manner of appointing electors and deferential to those bodies expressly empowered by the legislature to carry out its constitutional mandate.

In order to determine whether a state court has infringed upon the legislature's authority, we necessarily must examine the law of the State as it existed prior to the action of the court. Though we generally defer to state courts on the interpretation of state law — see, e.g., *Mullaney v. Wilbur*, 421 U.S. 684 (1975) — there are of course areas in which the Constitution requires this Court to undertake an independent, if still deferential, analysis of state law.

For example, in *NAACP v. Alabama ex rel. Patterson*, 357 U.S. 449 (1958), it was argued that we were without jurisdiction because the petitioner had not pursued the correct appellate remedy in Alabama's state courts. Petitioners had sought a state-law writ of certiorari in the Alabama Supreme Court when a writ of mandamus, according to that court, was proper. We found this state-law ground inadequate to defeat our jurisdiction because we were "unable to reconcile the procedural holding of the Alabama Supreme Court" with prior Alabama precedent. 357 U.S. at 456. . . .

Six years later we decided *Bouie v. City of Columbia*, 378 U.S. 347 (1964), in which the state court had held, contrary to precedent, that the state trespass law applied to black sit-in demonstrators who had consent to enter private property but were then asked to leave. Relying upon *NAACP*, we concluded that the South Carolina Supreme Court's interpretation of a state penal statute had impermissibly broadened the scope of that statute beyond what a fair reading provided, in violation of due process. What we would do in the present case is precisely parallel: Hold that the Florida Supreme Court's interpretation of the Florida election laws impermissibly distorted them beyond what a fair reading required, in violation of Article II. . . .

This inquiry does not imply a disrespect for state *courts* but rather a respect for the constitutionally prescribed role of state *legislatures*. . . .

II

Acting pursuant to its constitutional grant of authority, the Florida Legislature has created a detailed, if not perfectly crafted, statutory scheme that provides for appointment of Presidential electors by direct election. . . . The legislature has designated the Secretary of State as the "chief election officer," with the responsibility to "obtain and maintain uniformity in the application, operation, and interpretation of the election laws." § 97.012. . . .

The state legislature has also provided mechanisms both for protesting election returns and for contesting certified election results. . . .

In its first decision, *Palm Beach Canvassing Bd. v. Harris* (Nov. 21, 2000) *(Harris I)*, the Florida Supreme Court extended the 7-day statutory certification deadline established by the legislature.[10] This modification of the code, by lengthening the protest period, necessarily shortened the contest period for Presidential elections. Underlying the extension of the certification deadline and the shortchanging of the contest period was, presumably, the clear implication that certification was a matter of significance: The certified winner would enjoy presumptive validity, making a contest proceeding by the losing candidate an uphill battle. In its latest opinion, however, the court empties certification of virtually all legal consequence during the contest, and in doing so departs from the provisions enacted by the Florida Legislature.

The court determined that canvassing boards' decisions regarding whether to recount ballots past the certification deadline (even the certification deadline established by *Harris I*) are to be reviewed *de novo*, although the election code clearly vests discretion whether to recount in the boards, and sets strict deadlines subject to the Secretary's rejection of late tallies and monetary fines for tardiness. Moreover, the Florida court held that all late vote tallies arriving during the contest period should be automatically included in the certification regardless of the certification deadline (even the certification deadline established by *Harris I*), thus virtually eliminating both the deadline and the Secretary's discretion to disregard recounts that violate it.

Moreover, the court's interpretation of "legal vote," and hence its decision to order a contest-period recount, plainly departed from the legislative scheme. Florida statutory law cannot reasonably be thought to *require* the counting of improperly marked ballots. Each Florida precinct before election day provides instructions on how properly to cast a vote, § 101.46; each polling place on election day contains a working model of the voting machine it uses, § 101.5611; and each voting booth contains a sample ballot, § 101.46. In precincts using punch-card ballots, voters are instructed to punch out the ballot cleanly:

AFTER VOTING, CHECK YOUR BALLOT CARD TO BE SURE YOUR VOTING SELECTIONS ARE CLEARLY AND CLEANLY PUNCHED AND THERE ARE NO CHIPS LEFT HANGING ON THE BACK OF THE CARD.

Instructions to Voters, quoted in *Touchston v. McDermott*. No reasonable person would call it "an error in the vote tabulation," Fla. Stat. § 102.166(5), or a "rejection of legal votes," Fla. Stat. § 102.168(3)(c), when electronic or electromechanical equipment performs precisely in the manner designed, and fails to count those ballots that are not marked in the manner that these voting instructions explicitly and prominently specify. The scheme that the Florida Supreme Court's opinion attributes to the legislature is one in which machines are *required* to be "capable of correctly counting votes," § 101.5606(4), but which nonetheless regularly produces elections in which legal votes

---

[10] [Court's footnote 2] We vacated that decision and remanded that case; the Florida Supreme Court reissued the same judgment with a new opinion on December 11, 2000.

are predictably *not* tabulated, so that in close elections manual recounts are regularly required. This is of course absurd. The Secretary of State, who is authorized by law to issue binding interpretations of the election code, §§ 97.012, 106.23, rejected this peculiar reading of the statutes. The Florida Supreme Court, although it must defer to the Secretary's interpretations, rejected her reasonable interpretation and embraced the peculiar one. *See Palm Beach County Canvassing Board v. Harris* (Dec. 11, 2000) (*Harris III*).

But as we indicated in our remand of the earlier case, in a Presidential election the clearly expressed intent of the legislature must prevail. And there is no basis for reading the Florida statutes as requiring the counting of improperly marked ballots. . . . The State's Attorney General (who was supporting the Gore challenge) confirmed in oral argument here that never before the present election had a manual recount been conducted on the basis of the contention that "undervotes" should have been examined to determine voter intent. *Cf. Broward County Canvassing Board v. Hogan*, 607 So. 2d 508, 509 (Fla. Ct. App. 1992) (denial of recount for failure to count ballots with "hanging paper chads"). . . .

III

The scope and nature of the remedy ordered by the Florida Supreme Court jeopardizes the "legislative wish" to take advantage of the safe harbor provided by 3 U.S.C. § 5. December 12, 2000, is the last date for a final determination of the Florida electors that will satisfy § 5. Yet in the late afternoon of December 8th — four days before this deadline — the Supreme Court of Florida ordered recounts of tens of thousands of so-called "undervotes" spread through 64 of the State's 67 counties. This was done in a search for elusive — perhaps delusive — certainty as to the exact count of 6 million votes. . . .

Surely when the Florida Legislature empowered the courts of the State to grant "appropriate" relief, it must have meant relief that would have become final by the cut-off date of 3 U.S.C. § 5. In light of the inevitable legal challenges and ensuing appeals to the Supreme Court of Florida and petitions for certiorari to this Court, the entire recounting process could not possibly be completed by that date. Whereas the majority in the Supreme Court of Florida stated its confidence that "the remaining undervotes in these counties can be [counted] within the required time frame," it made no assertion that the seemingly inevitable appeals could be disposed of in that time. Although the Florida Supreme Court has on occasion taken over a year to resolve disputes over local elections, see, e.g., *Beckstrom v. Volusia County Canvassing Bd.*, 707 So. 2d 720 (1998) (resolving contest of sheriff's race 16 months after the election), it has heard and decided the appeals in the present case with great promptness. But the federal deadlines for the Presidential election simply do not permit even such a shortened process. . . .

JUSTICE STEVENS, with whom JUSTICE GINSBURG and JUSTICE BREYER join, dissenting.

The Constitution assigns to the States the primary responsibility for determining the manner of selecting the Presidential electors. *See* Art. II, § 1, cl. 2. When questions arise about the meaning of state laws, including election laws, it is our settled practice to accept the opinions of the highest courts of the States as providing the final answers. On rare occasions, however, either federal statutes or the Federal Constitution may require federal judicial intervention in state elections. This is not such an occasion.

The federal questions that ultimately emerged in this case are not substantial. Article II provides that "each *State* shall appoint, in such Manner as the Legislature *thereof* may direct, a Number of Electors." *Ibid.* (emphasis added). It does not create state legislatures out of whole cloth, but rather takes them as they come — as creatures born of, and constrained by, their state constitutions. . . . [T]he Florida Legislature's own decision to employ a unitary code for all elections indicates that it intended the Florida Supreme Court to play the same role in Presidential elections that it has historically played in resolving electoral disputes. The Florida Supreme Court's exercise of appellate jurisdiction therefore was wholly consistent with, and indeed contemplated by, the grant of authority in Article II. . . .

Neither § 5 nor Article II grants federal judges any special authority to substitute their views for those of the state judiciary on matters of state law.

Nor are petitioners correct in asserting that the failure of the Florida Supreme Court to specify in detail the precise manner in which the "intent of the voter," is to be determined rises to the level of a constitutional violation.[11] We found such a violation when individual votes within the same State were weighted unequally, see, e.g., *Reynolds v. Sims*, 377 U.S. 533, 568 (1964), but we have never before called into question the substantive standard by which a State determines that a vote has been legally cast. . . .

Admittedly, the use of differing substandards for determining voter intent in different counties employing similar voting systems may raise serious concerns. Those concerns are alleviated — if not eliminated — by the fact that a single impartial magistrate will ultimately adjudicate all objections arising from the recount process. Of course, as a general matter, "the interpretation of constitutional principles must not be too literal. We must remember that the machinery of government would not work if it were not allowed a little play in its joints." *Bain Peanut Co. of Tex. v. Pinson*, 282 U.S. 499, 501 (1931) (Holmes, J.). If it were otherwise, Florida's decision to leave to each county the determination of what balloting system to employ — despite enormous differences in accuracy — might run afoul of equal protection. So, too, might the similar decisions of the vast majority of state legislatures to delegate to local authorities certain decisions with respect to voting systems and ballot design.

Even assuming that aspects of the remedial scheme might ultimately be found to violate the Equal Protection Clause, I could not subscribe to the majority's disposition of the case. As the majority explicitly holds, once a state legislature determines to select electors through a popular vote, the right to have one's vote counted is of constitutional stature. As the majority further acknowledges, Florida law holds that all ballots that reveal the intent of the voter constitute valid votes. Recognizing these principles, the majority nonetheless orders the termination of the contest proceeding before all such votes have been tabulated. Under their own reasoning, the appropriate course of action would be to remand to allow more specific procedures for implementing the legislature's uniform general standard to be established.

In the interest of finality, however, the majority effectively orders the disenfranchisement of an unknown number of voters whose ballots reveal their intent — and are therefore legal votes under state law. . . .

What must underlie petitioners' entire federal assault on the Florida election procedures is an unstated lack of confidence in the impartiality and capacity of the state judges who would make the critical decisions if the vote count were to proceed. . . . Time will one day heal the wound to that confidence that will be inflicted by today's decision. One thing, however, is certain. Although we may never know with complete certainty the identity of the winner of this year's Presidential election, the identity of

---

[11] [Court's footnote 2] The Florida statutory standard is consistent with the practice of the majority of States, which apply either an "intent of the voter" standard or an "impossible to determine the elector's choice" standard in ballot recounts. . . .

the loser is perfectly clear. It is the Nation's confidence in the judge as an impartial guardian of the rule of law. . . .

JUSTICE SOUTER, with whom JUSTICE BREYER joins and with whom JUSTICE STEVENS and JUSTICE GINSBURG join with regard to all but Part C, dissenting.

The Court should not have reviewed either *Bush v. Palm Beach County Canvassing Bd.* (*per curiam*), or this case, and should not have stopped Florida's attempt to recount all undervote ballots by issuing a stay of the Florida Supreme Court's orders during the period of this review. If this Court had allowed the State to follow the course indicated by the opinions of its own Supreme Court, it is entirely possible that there would ultimately have been no issue requiring our review, and political tension could have worked itself out in the Congress following the procedure provided in 3 U.S.C. § 15. . . .

A

The 3 U.S.C. § 5 issue is not serious. . . . [N]o State is required to conform to § 5 if it cannot do that (for whatever reason); the sanction for failing to satisfy the conditions of § 5 is simply loss of what has been called its "safe harbor." And even that determination is to be made, if made anywhere, in the Congress.

B

The second matter here goes to the State Supreme Court's interpretation of certain terms in the state statute governing election "contests," Fla. Stat. § 102.168 (2000). . . . that the interpretation of § 102.168 was so unreasonable as to transcend the accepted bounds of statutory interpretation, to the point of being a nonjudicial act and producing new law untethered to the legislative act in question. . . .

None of the state court's interpretations is unreasonable to the point of displacing the legislative enactment quoted. . . . [T]he majority view is in each instance within the bounds of reasonable interpretation, and the law as declared is consistent with Article II. . . .

C

It is only on the third issue before us that there is a meritorious argument for relief, as this Court's *Per Curiam* opinion recognizes. It is an issue that might well have been dealt with adequately by the Florida courts if the state proceedings had not been interrupted, and if not disposed of at the state level it could have been considered by the Congress in any electoral vote dispute. But because the course of state proceedings has been interrupted, time is short, and the issue is before us. . . .

Petitioners have raised an equal protection claim (or, alternatively, a due process claim) . . . in the charge that unjustifiably disparate standards are applied in different electoral jurisdictions to otherwise identical facts. It is true that the Equal Protection Clause does not forbid the use of a variety of voting mechanisms within a jurisdiction, even though different mechanisms will have different levels of effectiveness in recording voters' intentions; local variety can be justified by concerns about cost, the potential value of innovation, and so on. But evidence in the record here suggests that a different order of disparity obtains under rules for determining a voter's intent that have been applied (and could continue to be applied) to identical types of ballots used in identical brands of machines and exhibiting identical physical characteristics (such as "hanging" or "dimpled" chads). . . . I can conceive of no legitimate state interest served by these differing treatments of the expressions of voters' fundamental rights. The differences appear wholly arbitrary.

In deciding what to do about this, we should take account of the fact that electoral votes are due to be cast in six days. I would therefore remand the case to the courts of Florida with instructions to establish uniform standards for evaluating the several types of ballots that have prompted differing treatments, to be applied within and among counties when passing on such identical ballots in any further recounting (or successive recounting) that the courts might order.

Unlike the majority, I see no warrant for this Court to assume that Florida could not possibly comply with this requirement before the date set for the meeting of electors, December 18. Although one of the dissenting justices of the State Supreme Court estimated that disparate standards potentially affected 170,000 votes, the number at issue is significantly smaller. The 170,000 figure apparently represents all uncounted votes, both undervotes (those for which no Presidential choice was recorded by a machine) and overvotes (those rejected because of votes for more than one candidate). But as Justice Breyer has pointed out, no showing has been made of legal overvotes uncounted, and counsel for Gore made an uncontradicted representation to the Court that the statewide total of undervotes is about 60,000. To recount these manually would be a tall order, but before this Court stayed the effort to do that the courts of Florida were ready to do their best to get that job done. . . .

JUSTICE GINSBURG, with whom JUSTICE STEVENS joins, and with whom JUSTICE SOUTER and JUSTICE BREYER join as to Part I, dissenting.

I

. . . [D]isagreement with the Florida court's interpretation of its own State's law does not warrant the conclusion that the justices of that court have legislated. . . .

This Court more than occasionally affirms statutory, and even constitutional, interpretations with which it disagrees. For example, when reviewing challenges to administrative agencies' interpretations of laws they implement, we defer to the agencies unless their interpretation violates "the unambiguously expressed intent of Congress." *Chevron U.S.A. Inc. v. Natural Resources Defense Council, Inc.*, 467 U.S. 837, 843 (1984). . . . And not uncommonly, we let stand state-court interpretations of federal law with which we might disagree. Notably, in the habeas context, the Court adheres to the view that "there is 'no intrinsic reason why the fact that a man is a federal judge should make him more competent, or conscientious, or learned with respect to [federal law] than his neighbor in the state courthouse.'" *Stone v. Powell*, 428 U.S. 465, 494, n. 35 (1976). . . .

Notwithstanding our authority to decide issues of state law underlying federal claims, we have used the certification devise to afford state high courts an opportunity to inform us on matters of their own State's law because such restraint "helps build a cooperative judicial federalism." *Lehman Brothers*, 416 U.S. [386, 391 (1974)]. . . .

Rarely has this Court rejected outright an interpretation of state law by a state high court. *Fairfax's Devisee v. Hunter's Lessee*, 11 U.S. 603 (1813), *NAACP v. Alabama ex rel. Patterson*, 357 U.S. 449 (1958), and *Bouie v. City of Columbia*, 378 U.S. 347 (1964), cited by the Chief Justice, are three such rare instances. . . . *Fairfax's Devisee*, which held that the Virginia Court of Appeals had misconstrued its own forfeiture laws to deprive a British subject of lands secured to him by federal treaties, occurred amidst vociferous States' rights attacks on the Marshall Court. The Virginia court refused to obey this Court's *Fairfax's Devisee* mandate to enter judgment for the British subject's successor in interest. That refusal led to the Court's pathmarking decision in *Martin v.*

Hunter's Lessee, 14 U.S. 304 (1816). *Patterson*, a case decided three months after *Cooper v. Aaron*, 358 U.S. 1 (1958), in the face of Southern resistance to the civil rights movement, held that the Alabama Supreme Court had irregularly applied its own procedural rules to deny review of a contempt order against the NAACP arising from its refusal to disclose membership lists. We said that "our jurisdiction is not defeated if the nonfederal ground relied on by the state court is without any fair or substantial support." 357 U.S. at 455. *Bouie*, stemming from a lunch counter "sit-in" at the height of the civil rights movement, held that the South Carolina Supreme Court's construction of its trespass laws — criminalizing conduct not covered by the text of an otherwise clear statute — was "unforeseeable" and thus violated due process when applied retroactively to the petitioners. . . .

. . . Were the other members of this Court as mindful as they generally are of our system of dual sovereignty, they would affirm the judgment of the Florida Supreme Court.

II

. . . [T]he Florida Supreme Court has produced two substantial opinions within 29 hours of oral argument. . . . [T]he Court's conclusion that a constitutionally adequate recount is impractical is a prophecy the Court's own judgment will not allow to be tested. Such an untested prophecy should not decide the Presidency of the United States. . . .

JUSTICE BREYER, with whom JUSTICE STEVENS and JUSTICE GINSBURG join except as to Part I-A-1, and with whom JUSTICE SOUTER joins as to Part I, dissenting.

The Court was wrong to take this case. It was wrong to grant a stay. It should now vacate that stay and permit the Florida Supreme Court to decide whether the recount should resume.

I

The political implications of this case for the country are momentous. But the federal legal questions presented, with one exception, are insubstantial.

A

1

The majority raises three Equal Protection problems with the Florida Supreme Court's recount order: first, the failure to include overvotes in the manual recount; second, the fact that all ballots, rather than simply the undervotes, were recounted in some, but not all, counties; and third, the absence of a uniform, specific standard to guide the recounts. As far as the first issue is concerned, petitioners presented no evidence, to this Court or to any Florida court, that a manual recount of overvotes would identify additional legal votes. The same is true of the second. . . .

The majority's third concern does implicate principles of fundamental fairness. The majority concludes that the Equal Protection Clause requires that a manual recount be governed not only by the uniform general standard of the "clear intent of the voter," but also by uniform subsidiary standards (for example, a uniform determination whether indented, but not perforated, "undervotes" should count). The opinion points out that the Florida Supreme Court ordered the inclusion of Broward County's undercounted "legal votes" even though those votes included ballots that were not perforated but simply "dimpled," while newly recounted ballots from other counties will likely include only votes determined to be "legal" on the basis of a stricter standard. In light of our previous remand, the Florida Supreme Court may have been reluctant to adopt a more specific standard than that provided for by the legislature for fear of exceeding its authority under Article II. However, since the use of different standards could favor one or the other of the candidates, since time was, and is, too short to permit the lower courts to iron out significant differences through ordinary judicial review, and since the relevant distinction was embodied in the order of the State's highest court, I agree that, in these very special circumstances, basic principles of fairness may well have counseled the adoption of a uniform standard to address the problem. In light of the majority's disposition, I need not decide whether, or the extent to which, as a remedial matter, the Constitution would place limits upon the content of the uniform standard.

2

Nonetheless, there is no justification for the majority's remedy, which is simply to reverse the lower court and halt the recount entirely. An appropriate remedy would be, instead, to remand this case with instructions that, even at this late date, would permit the Florida Supreme Court to require recounting *all* undercounted votes in Florida, including those from Broward, Volusia, Palm Beach, and Miami-Dade Counties, whether or not previously recounted prior to the end of the protest period, and to do so in accordance with a single-uniform substandard.

The majority justifies stopping the recount entirely on the ground that there is no more time. In particular, the majority relies on the lack of time for the Secretary to review and approve equipment needed to separate undervotes. But the majority reaches this conclusion in the absence of *any* record evidence that the recount could not have been completed in the time allowed by the Florida Supreme Court. The majority finds facts outside of the record on matters that state courts are in a far better position to address. Of course, it is too late for any such recount to take place by December 12, the date by which election disputes must be decided if a State is to take advantage of the safe harbor provisions of 3 U.S.C. § 5. Whether there is time to conduct a recount prior to December 18, when the electors are scheduled to meet, is a matter for the state courts to determine. And whether, under Florida law, Florida could or could not take further action is obviously a matter for Florida courts, not this Court, to decide. . . .

[I]n a system that allows counties to use different types of voting systems, voters already arrive at the polls with an unequal chance that their votes will be counted. . . .

B

. . . [T]he concurrence . . . says that "the Florida Supreme Court's interpretation of the Florida election laws impermissibly distorted them beyond what a fair reading required, in violation of Article II." But what precisely is the distortion? Apparently, it has three elements. First, the Florida court, in its earlier opinion, changed the election certification date from November 14 to November 26. Second, the Florida court ordered a manual recount of "undercounted" ballots that could not have been fully completed by the December 12 "safe harbor" deadline. Third, the Florida court, in the opinion now under review, failed to give adequate deference to the determinations of canvassing boards and the Secretary.

To characterize the first element as a "distortion," however, requires the concurrence to second-guess the way in which the state court resolved a plain conflict in the language of different statutes. . . .

To characterize the second element as a "distortion" requires the concurrence to overlook the fact that the inability of the Florida courts to conduct the recount on time is, in significant part, a problem of the Court's own making. . . . This Court improvidently entered a stay. As a result, we will never know whether the recount could have been completed.

. . . Nor can one say that the Court's ultimate determination is so unreasonable as to amount to a constitutionally "impermissible distortion" of Florida law.

. . . Since only a few hundred votes separated the candidates, and since the "undercounted" ballots numbered tens of thousands, it is difficult to see how anyone could find this conclusion unreasonable-however strict the standard used to measure the voter's "clear intent." . . .

The statute goes on to provide the Florida circuit judge with authority to "fashion such orders as he or she deems necessary to ensure that each allegation . . . is *investigated, examined, or checked* . . . and to provide any relief appropriate." The Florida Supreme Court did just that. . . . Indeed, other state courts have interpreted roughly similar state statutes in similar ways. . . .

II

. . . Neither side claims electoral fraud, dishonesty, or the like. And the more fundamental equal protection claim might have been left to the state court to resolve if and when it was discovered to have mattered. It could still be resolved through a remand conditioned upon issuance of a uniform standard; it does not require reversing the Florida Supreme Court. . . .

. . . [T]he Twelfth Amendment commits to Congress the authority and responsibility to count electoral votes. A federal statute, the Electoral Count Act, enacted after the close 1876 Hayes-Tilden Presidential election, specifies that, after States have tried to resolve disputes (through "judicial" or other means), Congress is the body primarily authorized to resolve remaining disputes. *See* Electoral Count Act of 1887, 3 U.S.C. §§ 5, 6, and 15. . . .

However awkward or difficult it may be for Congress to resolve difficult electoral disputes, Congress, being a political body, expresses the people's will far more accurately than does an unelected Court. And the people's will is what elections are about.

Moreover, Congress was fully aware of the danger that would arise should it ask judges, unarmed with appropriate legal standards, to resolve a hotly contested Presidential election contest. Just after the 1876 Presidential election, Florida, South Carolina, and Louisiana each sent two slates of electors to Washington. Without these States, Tilden, the Democrat, had 184 electoral votes, one short of the number required to win the Presidency. With those States, Hayes, his Republican opponent, would have had 185. In order to choose between the two slates of electors, Congress decided to appoint an electoral commission composed of five Senators, five Representatives, and five Supreme Court Justices. . . .

The Commission divided along partisan lines, and the responsibility to cast the deciding vote fell to Justice Bradley. He decided to accept the votes by the Republican electors, and thereby awarded the Presidency to Hayes.

Justice Bradley immediately became the subject of vociferous attacks. Bradley was accused of accepting bribes. . . . Many years later, Professor Bickel concluded that Bradley was honest and impartial. . . .

For present purposes, the relevance of this history lies in the fact that the participation in the work of the electoral commission by five Justices, including Justice Bradley, did not lend that process legitimacy. . . . And the Congress that later enacted the Electoral Count Act knew it.

. . . [A]bove all, in this highly politicized matter, the appearance of a split decision runs the risk of undermining the public's confidence in the Court itself. That confidence is a public treasure. It has been built slowly over many years, some of which were marked by a Civil War and the tragedy of segregation. It is a vitally necessary ingredient of any successful effort to protect basic liberty and, indeed, the rule of law itself. . . . [W]e do risk a self-inflicted wound — a wound that may harm not just the Court, but the Nation. . . .

. . . What it does today, the Court should have left undone. I would repair the damage done as best we now can, by permitting the Florida recount to continue under uniform standards. . . .

NOTES

(1) *Companion Cases.* The Court invalidated legislative apportionments in states around the country. For further discussion of reapportionment, see Symposium, *Comments on the Reapportionment Controversy*, 63 MICH. L. REV. 209 (1969).

(2) *Permissible Deviations from "One-Person-One-Vote."* Subsequent cases have permitted greater flexibility from the "one-person-one-vote" standard than *Reynolds v. Sims* might appear to contemplate. *See Mahan v. Howell*, 410 U.S. 315 (1973) (Virginia legislative apportionment upheld with one district overrepresented by 9.6 percent), and *Abate v. Mundt*, 403 U.S. 182 (1971) (upholding plan for a county governing board permitting almost 12 percent maximum deviation caused by provision for at least one member from each of five towns in the county).

(3) *Congressional Districts.* The Court has required relatively strict adherence to "one-person-one-vote" in Congressional districting. *White v. Weiser*, 412 U.S. 783 (1973). In *Karcher v. Daggett*, 462 U.S. 725 (1983), the Court invalidated Congressional districting where the difference between the largest and smallest district in New Jersey was only 0.6984 percent of the average district, less than the predictable undercount in available census data. Nevertheless, a narrow (5-4) majority held that the standard of Article 1, § 2, which controls Congressional districting, requires a good faith effort on the part of the state to achieve population equality. Since greater population equality could have been achieved with relative ease, the plaintiffs met their burden of showing that the disparities could have been reduced or eliminated altogether. The burden was then placed upon the State to justify the population disparities among the districts. The Court rejected the State's assertion that the districts were needed to preserve the voting strength of racial minority groups. "The State must . . . show with some specificity that a particular objective required the specific deviation in its plan, rather than simply relying on general assertions." *Cf. Department of Commerce v. Montana*, 503 U.S. 442 (1992) (afforded Congress broader discretion to choose an appropriate method of interstate apportionment of the House of Representatives than it permits States when exercising their rights of intrastate apportionment).

DAVIS v. BANDEMER, 478 U.S. 109 (1986). The Court upheld an Indiana legislative apportionment plan against a challenge that it denied equal protection to members of the Democratic Party. When the state apportionment plan was adopted in 1981, the Republicans controlled both Houses of the legislature and the Governor was Republican. Although the new districts were roughly equal in population, they were irregular in shape. In addition, there was a mix of single-member and multi-member districts and district boundaries that did not consistently follow political subdivision boundaries.

In the first election under the new plan, the percentage of seats that the Democrats won was significantly less than the percentage of the vote that Democratic candidates received.

Justice White delivered the opinion. In addition to Justice White, five other members joined in Part II of the opinion. Justice White held that the nonracial gerrymandering issue in this case presented a justiciable controversy rather than a nonjustifiable political question: "Disposition of this question does not involve us in a matter more properly decided by a coequal branch of our Government. There is no risk of foreign or domestic disturbance and in light of our cases since *Baker* we are not persuaded that there are no judicially discernible and manageable standards by which political gerrymander cases are to be decided."

Only a plurality of Justices (White, Brennan, Marshall, Blackmun) agreed on the merits of the equal protection claim. Writing for the plurality, Justice White held that the appellees had to prove intentional discrimination against an identifiable political group and a discriminatory effect on that group. The plurality did not question the District Court's finding of discriminatory intent.

The plurality felt that the District Court erred because it had based the equal protection violation on a showing that the percentage of Democratic winners was less than the percentage of Democratic votes. "Our cases clearly foreclose any claim that the Constitution requires proportional representation or that legislatures in reapportioning must draw district lines to come as near as possible to allocating seats to the contending parties in proportion to what their anticipated statewide vote will be." The plurality claimed that even if a sizable minority party fails to win any legislative seat because of the apportionment plan, the plan is constitutional. Such a result is "inherent in the winner-take-all, district-based elections."

Even though a group may not get the candidate it wants in office, the group could still influence the winning candidates. There must be proof that a system "will consistently degrade a voter's or a group of voters' influence on the political process as a whole."

The inquiry involves effective denial of influence in the political process. "In a challenge to an individual district, this inquiry focuses on the opportunity of members of the group to participate in party deliberations in the slating and nomination of candidates, their opportunity to register and vote, and hence their chance to directly influence the election returns and to secure the attention of the winning candidate. Statewide, however, the inquiry centers on the voters' direct or indirect influence on the elections of the state legislature as a whole. And, as in individual district cases, an equal protection violation may be found only where the electoral system substantially disadvantages certain voters in their opportunity to influence the political process effectively. In this context, such a finding of unconstitutionality must be supported by evidence of continued frustration of the will of a majority of the voters or effective denial to a minority of voters of a fair chance to influence the political process."

"Based on these views," Justice White asserted, "we would reject the District Court's apparent holding that any interference with an opportunity to elect a representative of one's choice would be sufficient to allege or make out an equal protection violation. In the complex context of a political gerrymandering claim, the plurality required "allegations and proof that the challenged legislative plan has had or will have effects that are sufficiently serious to require intervention by the federal courts in state reapportionment decisions."

The District Court's findings did not make out a cause of action. "Relying on a single election to prove unconstitutional discrimination is unsatisfactory. The District Court observed, and the parties do not disagree, that Indiana is a swing State. Voters sometimes prefer Democratic candidates, and sometimes Republican. The District Court did not find that because of the 1981 Act the Democrats could not in one of the next few elections secure a sufficient vote to take control of the assembly. Indeed, the District Court declined to hold that the 1982 election results were the predictable consequences of the 1981 Act and expressly refused to hold that those results were a reliable prediction of future ones. Nor was there any finding that the 1981 reapportionment would consign the Democrats to a minority status in the Assembly throughout the 1980s or that the Democrats would have no hope of doing any better in the reapportionment that would occur after the 1990 census.

Drawing on the experience of the racially discriminatory vote dilution, Justice White afforded additional guidance for establishing a case of political gerrymandering: "In the individual multi-member district cases, we have found equal protection violations only where a history of disproportionate results appeared in conjunction with strong indicia of lack of political power and the denial of fair representation. In those cases, the racial minorities asserting the successful equal protection claims had essentially been shut out of the political process. In the statewide political gerrymandering context, these prior cases lead to the analogous conclusion that equal protection violations may be found only where a history (actual or projected) of disproportionate results appears in conjunction with similar indicia. The mere lack of control of the General Assembly after a single election does not rise to the requisite level."

Chief Justice Burger concurred in the judgment. He argued that the courts should not decide political gerrymandering cases. He asserted that the framers intended that the people correct such flaws by influencing elected representatives.

Justice O'Connor, joined by the Chief Justice and Justice Rehnquist, also concurred in the judgment. The majority's approach would force the federal courts "to attempt to recreate the complex process of legislative apportionment in the context of adversary litigation in order to reconcile the competing claims of political, religious, ethnic, racial, occupational, and socioeconomic groups." Applying equal protection to political gerrymandering would lead toward a requirement of proportional representation.

Unlike racial minorities, "political parties are the dominant groups, and the Court has offered no reason to believe that they are incapable of fending for themselves through the political process." The gerrymandering claims of major political parties were nonjusticiable political questions.

Justice Powell, joined by Justice Stevens, concurred in the justiciability judgment but dissented from the remainder of the Court's opinion. The Court reversed the District Court without concluding that any of its findings was clearly erroneous. Moreover, the plurality's standard failed to provide proper guidance to legislatures and courts. He asserted that the following factors establish a prima facie case of unconstitutional political gerrymandering: "The most important of these factors are the shapes of voting districts and adherence to established political boundaries. Other relevant considerations include the nature of the legislative procedures by which the apportionment law was adopted and legislative history reflecting contemporaneous legislative goals. To make out a case of unconstitutional partisan gerrymandering, the plaintiff should be required to offer proof concerning these factors, which bear directly on the fairness of a redistricting plan, as well as evidence concerning population disparities and statistics tending to show vote dilution." Justice Powell thought that since the District Court's findings met these criteria, it was justified in invalidating the 1981 Act.

VIETH v. JUBELIRER, 541 U.S. 267 (2004). In *Vieth v. Jubelirer*, petitioner Vieth challenged a Pennsylvania redistricting scheme on the grounds that "the districting constitutes an unconstitutional political gerrymander." Five Justices, for different reasons, held the issue of political gerrymandering non-justiciable. Writing for the four-justice plurality, Justice Scalia found political gerrymanders non-justiciable due to a lack of any discoverable or manageable standard of review. "Political gerrymanders are not new to the American scene"; however, "the Framers provided a remedy for such practices in the Constitution. Article I, § 4, while leaving in state legislatures the initial power to draw districts for federal elections, permitted Congress to 'make or alter' those districts if it wished." Congress has exercised this power "to regulate elections, and in particular to restrain the practice of political gerrymandering." The plurality refused to base a remedy in this case on *Davis v. Bandemer, supra*. After reviewing the eighteen years of case law since *Bandemer*, Justice Scalia observed that *Bandemer* and its progeny have failed to provide "judicially discernible and manageable standards for adjudicating political gerrymandering claims." Consequently, *Bandemer* was wrongly decided.

Bandemer and the comparatively few lower court cases decided under it compare unfavorably with the racial gerrymandering cases. "The Constitution clearly contemplates districting by political entities." In "contrast, the purpose of segregating voters on the basis of race" is unlawful. In drawing this separation, one of the determining factors for the Court is "the fact that partisan districting is a lawful and common practice means that there is almost always room for an election-impeding lawsuit contending that partisan advantage was the predominant motivation; not so for claims of racial gerrymandering." While "courts might be justified in accepting a modest degree of unmanageability to enforce a constitutional command which (like the *Fourteenth Amendment* obligation to refrain from racial discrimination) is clear," no such obligation exists to enforce a standard "which is both dubious and severely unmanageable."

Ultimately, the *Bandemer* "standard rests upon the principle that groups (or at least political-action groups) have a right to proportional representation. But the Constitution contains no such principle. It guarantees equal protection of the law to persons, not equal representation in government to equivalently sized groups. It nowhere says that farmers or urban dwellers, Christian fundamentalists or Jews, Republicans or Democrats, must be accorded political strength proportionate to their numbers." The one-person, one-vote principle flowing out of *Reynolds v. Sims, supra* § 11.03[2], requires that each individual, not each group, has equal say in electing representatives. Moreover, that standard is easy to administer by simply making the number of representatives proportional to the population.

The three potential standards proposed in the dissenting opinions further illustrate that there is no single "constitutionally discernible standard." In addressing Justice Stevens' concerns that political gerrymanders are undemocratic, the plurality commented that "the issue we have discussed is not whether severe partisan gerrymanders violate the Constitution, but whether it is for the courts to say when a violation has occurred, and to design a remedy." Although Justice Scalia noted that Justice Kennedy's concurrence left open the possibility that *Bandemer* claims may someday be justiciable, for the present his is "a reluctant fifth vote against justiciability at district and statewide levels." For the plurality, "[e]ighteen years of essentially pointless litigation have persuaded us that *Bandemer* is incapable of principled application."

Concurring in the judgment, Justice Kennedy agreed that "[a] decision ordering the correction of all election district lines drawn for partisan reasons would commit federal and state courts to unprecedented intervention in the American political process."

Justice Kennedy also agreed with the plurality's position that there are currently no judicially manageable standards for political gerrymandering cases. However, he would not shut the door on such challenges forever, pointing out that "new technologies may produce new methods of analysis that make more evident the precise nature of the burdens gerrymanders impose on the representational rights of voters and parties." He continued by noting that "[w]here it is alleged that a gerrymander had the purpose and effect of imposing burdens on a disfavored party and its voters, the *First Amendment* may offer a sounder and more prudential basis for intervention than does the Equal Protection Clause." Ultimately, Justice Kennedy agreed with the plurality that "[t]he failings of the many proposed standards for measuring the burden a gerrymander imposes on representational rights make our intervention improper. If workable standards do emerge to measure these burdens, however, courts should be prepared to order relief."

In dissent, Justice Stevens began by observing that five members of the Court felt that the plurality's holding that political gerrymandering claims were non justiciable was "erroneous," regardless of whether they believed the plaintiffs in this case should prevail. For him, "the critical issue in both racial and political gerrymandering cases is the same:" when "the only possible explanation for a district's bizarre shape is a naked desire to increase partisan strength, then no rational basis exists to save the district from an equal protection challenge."

In a dissent joined by Justice Ginsburg, Justice Souter "would preserve *Davis*'s holding that political gerrymandering is a justiciable issue, but otherwise start anew. I would adopt a political gerrymandering test analogous to the summary judgment standard . . . [requiring] a plaintiff to satisfy elements of a prima facie cause of action, at which point the State would have the opportunity not only to rebut the evidence supporting the plaintiff's case, but to offer an affirmative justification for the districting choices." Agreeing with Justice Stevens, Justice Souter would focus "as much as possible on suspect characteristics of individual districts instead of state-wide patterns." In his dissent, Justice Breyer argued that "gerrymandering that leads to entrenchment violates the *Constitution's Equal Protection Clause*." The Court should be able to separate out the harm caused by "one important gerrymandering evil, the unjustified entrenching in power of a political party that voters have rejected" and "design a remedy for extreme cases."

LEAGUE OF UNITED LATIN AM. CITIZENS v. PERRY, 548 U.S. 399 (2006). In *Perry*, the Court upheld most of a legislated redistricting plan against political gerrymandering claims, but struck down one district and validated another based on racial voter dilution claims under § 2 of the Voting Rights Act. A majority of the Court joined most of the opinion. While only a plurality joined the last part of the opinion, a majority concurred in the judgment.

Justice Kennedy first recounted Texas' recent redistricting history. In 2000, although the Republican Party carried "59% of the vote in statewide elections," they "only won 13 congressional seats to the Democrats' 17." Under the "court-drawn" plan based on " 'neutral' redistricting standards" created out of the *Balderas* litigation, "the 2002 congressional elections resulted in a 17-to-15 Democratic majority in the Texas delegation, compared to a 59% to 40% Republican majority in votes for statewide office in 2000." When the Republicans gained control of both state houses, "the legislature enacted a new congressional districting map in October 2003," Plan 1374C, despite a "protracted partisan struggle." The new district map led to the Republicans winning "21 seats to the Democrats' 11" in "[t]he 2004 congressional elections" in which Republicans obtained "58% of the vote in statewide races against the Democrats' 41%."

In Part II-A, Justice Kennedy, joined by Justices Stevens, Souter, Ginsburg, and

Breyer, addressed the plaintiff's claim "that Plan 1374C should be invalidated as an unconstitutional partisan gerrymander." Their argument invoked "two similar theories that address the mid-decade character of the 2003 redistricting." *Davis v. Bandemer, supra*, held that "an equal protection challenge to a political gerrymander presents a justiciable case." While a plurality in the subsequent decision, *Vieth v. Jubelirer, supra*, "would have held such challenges to be nonjusticiable political questions, . . . a majority declined to do so." After declining to "revisit the justiciability holding," the majority proceeded "to examine whether appellants' claims offer the Court a manageable, reliable measure of fairness for determining whether a partisan gerrymander violates the Constitution."

Turning to the merits of plaintiff's political redistricting claim, the Court said "[a]s the Constitution vests redistricting responsibilities foremost in the legislatures of the States and in Congress, a lawful, legislatively enacted plan should be preferable to one drawn by the courts." Nevertheless, this preference "cannot justify legislative reliance on improper criteria for districting determinations."[12]

While the Texas Legislature plan replaced a court-ordered plan, the Court has "assumed that state legislatures are free to replace court-mandated remedial plans" with their own. Nor is it unconstitutional for legislatures to redistrict mid-decade. "[A] congressional plan that more closely reflects the distribution of state party power seems a less likely vehicle for partisan discrimination than one that entrenches an electoral minority."

In the third part of the majority opinion, Justice Kennedy, joined by Justices Stevens, Souter, Ginsburg, and Breyer, invalidated the redrawing of District 23 as violating § 2 of the Voting Rights Act by diluting the Latino vote.

The creation of another majority-minority district (District 25) did not negate the § 2 violation. States may "use one majority-minority district to compensate for the absence of another only when the racial group in each area had a § 2 right and both could not be accommodated." Moreover, "the creation of a noncompact district does not compensate for the dismantling of a compact opportunity district." Within "the equal protection context, compactness focuses on the contours of district lines to determine whether race was the predominant factor in drawing those lines. Under § 2, by contrast, the injury is vote dilution, so the compactness inquiry embraces different considerations. 'The first . . . condition refers to the compactness of the minority population, not to the compactness of the contested district.' "

The rearrangement of "District 23 undermined the progress of a racial group that has been subject to significant voting-related discrimination and that was becoming increasingly politically active and cohesive." Courts have recognized that " 'Texas has a long, well-documented history of discrimination that has touched upon the rights of African-Americans and Hispanics to register, to vote, or to participate otherwise in the electoral process.' " By redrawing the district lines, "the State took away the Latinos' opportunity because Latinos were about to exercise it. This bears the mark of intentional discrimination that could give rise to an equal protection violation."

The Court did not address appellants' equal protection claim involving the drawing of Districts 23 and 25.

The fourth part of Justice Kennedy's opinion rejected a claim that District 24 diluted

---

[12] Section 2 of Article I states that members of the House of Representatives are elected "every second Year" and Section 4 declares that state legislatures establish "[t]he Times, Places and Manner of holding Elections" for members of the House but that "Congress may at any time by Law make or alter such Regulations. . . . "

the votes of African-Americans based on the fact that African-Americans "constituted 64% of the voters in the Democratic primary." While only the Chief Justice and Justice Alito joined this part of Justice Kennedy's opinion, Justices Scalia and Thomas concurred in the judgment of this part of the opinion. "If § 2 were interpreted to protect this kind of influence, it would unnecessarily infuse race into virtually every redistricting, raising serious constitutional questions."[13]

Justice Stevens concurred in part and dissented in part. In a part of the opinion joined by Justice Breyer, Justice Stevens argued that the Texas Legislature plan "is entirely invalid." He would "reinstate" the "neutral plan fashioned by the three-judge court in *Balderas*." A legislature's "decision to redraw district boundaries-like any other state action that affects the electoral process-must, at the very least, serve some legitimate governmental purpose. A purely partisan desire 'to minimize or cancel out the voting strength of racial *or political* elements of the population,' is not such a purpose." Justice Stevens would have endorsed the plan if "Republicans had adopted a new plan in order to remove the excessively partisan Democratic gerrymander of the 1990s." Rather, "Texas Republicans abandoned a neutral apportionment map for the sole purpose of manipulating district boundaries to maximize their electoral advantage and thus create their own impermissible stranglehold on political power." On these facts, "a straightforward application of settled constitutional law leads to the inescapable conclusion that the State may not decide to redistrict if its sole motivation is 'to minimize or cancel out the voting strength of racial or *political* elements of the voting population.' "

Justice Stevens, not joined in the rest of the opinion by Justice Breyer, would also invalidate rearranging District 24. Although redistricting will always involve partisanship, "in *Vieth*, five Members of this Court explicitly recognized that extreme partisan gerrymandering violates the Constitution."[14]

Justice Souter, joined by Justice Ginsburg, concurred in part and dissented in part because he did not "share Justice Kennedy's seemingly flat rejection of any test of gerrymander turning on the process followed in redistricting." Nor did Justice Souter "rule out the utility of a criterion of symmetry as a test." Justice Souter concurred in invalidating District 23 but dissented from the Court's rejection of appellants' District 24 claim.

Chief Justice Roberts, joined by Justice Alito, concurred in part, concurred in the judgment in part, and dissented in part. Chief Justice Roberts "agree[d] with the determination that appellants have not provided 'a reliable standard for identifying unconstitutional political gerrymanders.' As the justiciability of political gerrymandering had not been argued in these cases, the Chief Justice took "no position on that question."

Justice Breyer wrote a separate opinion concurring in part and dissenting in part. The plan is purely motivated by partisan concerns and "will likely have seriously harmful electoral consequences." Thus, "the plan in its entirety violates the Equal Protection Clause."

Again joined by Justice Alito, the Chief Justice dissented from the third part of the majority opinion invalidating District 25, as *"Latino voters make up 55% of the citizen voting age population in the district and vote as a bloc."* This is the first time that a court has "struck down a State's redistricting plan under § 2, on the ground that the

---

[13] This argument fails to "demonstrate clear error" because there has not been a "contested Democratic primary in District 24 over the last 20 years."

[14] "The other four Justices in Vieth stated that they did not disagree with that conclusion."

plan achieves the maximum number of possible majority-minority districts, but loses on style points, in that the minority voters in one of those districts are not as 'compact' as the minority voters would be in another district were the lines drawn differently."

Chief Justice Roberts concluded: "[i]t is a sordid business, this divvying us up by race. When a State's plan already provides the maximum possible number of majority-minority effective opportunity districts, and the minority enjoys effective political power in the area well in *excess* of its proportion of the population, I would conclude that the courts have no further role to play in rejiggering the district lines under § 2."

Justice Scalia, joined by Justice Thomas, concurred in the judgment in part and dissented in part because "claims of unconstitutional partisan gerrymandering do not present a justiciable case or controversy." The majority "conclud[ed] that the appellants have failed to state a claim as to political gerrymandering, without ever articulating what the elements of such a claim consist of." Rather than dismissing the claim as "nonjusticiable," the Court "again dispose[s] of this claim in a way that provides no guidance to the lower-court judges." In a part of the opinion joined by Justice Thomas, Justice Scalia rejected the challenge to District 23 under § 2 of the Voting Rights Act.

The remainder of Justice Scalia's opinion was joined by the Chief Justice, Justice Thomas, and Justice Alito. Unlike "a *Shaw I* claim, appellants contend, in a vote dilution claim the plaintiff need not show that the racially discriminatory motivation *predominated*, but only that the invidious purpose was a motivating factor." Moreover, "the District Court found that the State's purpose was to protect" the incumbent, "and not just to create a safe Republican district." The key "inquiry, as in all cases under the Equal Protection Clause, goes to the State's purpose, not simply to the effect of state action."

Justice Scalia disagreed with the District Court's approach "with respect to District 25." Critically, "when a legislature intentionally creates a majority-minority district, race is necessarily its predominant motivation and strict scrutiny is therefore triggered." The Court has "in the past left undecided whether compliance with federal antidiscrimination laws can be a compelling state interest." Justice Scalia "would hold that compliance with § 5 of the Voting Rights Act can be such an interest." However, "a State cannot use racial considerations to achieve results beyond those that are required to comply with the statute. Section 5 forbids a State to take action that would worsen minorities' electoral opportunities; it does not require action that would improve them." The Chief Justice and Justices Stevens, Souter, Thomas, Ginsburg, Breyer, and Alito all agreed with Justice Scalia's conclusion that compliance with § 5 of the Voting Rights Act may comprise a compelling state interest.

NOTE

For additional discussion of the question of partisan gerrymandering, see, e.g., Symposium, *Gerrymandering and the Courts*, 33 UCLA L. REV. 1 (1985); Gottlieb, *Fashioning a Test for Gerrymandering*, 15 J. LEGIS. 1 (1988); Schuck, *The Thickest Thicket: Partisan Gerrymandering and Judicial Regulation of Politics*, 87 COLUM. L. REV. 1325 (1987).

§ 11.04 THE RIGHT TO TRAVEL

SAENZ v. ROE, 526 U.S. 489 (1999). In *Saenz*, the Supreme Court addressed the constitutionality of a California statute that denied new residents the same level of welfare benefits available to those who had been California citizens for more than 12 months. The Court's precedents have established that the right to travel contains at least three components: the right of a citizen of one State to enter and leave another State, the right to be treated as a welcome visitor rather than an unfriendly alien when temporarily present in the second State, and, for those travelers who elect to become permanent residents, the right to be treated like other citizens of that State.

The California statute at issue provided that, during the first 12 months of California residency, the State would limit new residents to the amount of welfare benefits that they would have received in their previous home state. Thus, the statute treated new residents who were welfare beneficiaries differently than other California citizens who were welfare beneficiaries, contrary to the third aspect of the right to travel.

Writing for a majority of seven, Justice Stevens recognized that California provides among the "most generous" welfare benefits in the country. The law at issue was part of an effort to reduce its enormous welfare budget.

Justice Stevens briefly discussed the first meaning of the right to travel, as the California statute did not directly limit the freedom to enter and leave the State. " '[F]ree ingress and regress to and from' neighboring States, which was expressly mentioned in the text of the Articles of Confederation, may simply have been 'conceived from the beginning to be a necessary concomitant of the stronger Union the Constitution created.' " *United States v. Guest*, 383 U.S. 745, 758 (1966).

The majority opinion then turned to the second component of the right to travel, which is protected by the express language of the Privileges and Immunities Clause of Article IV, § 2: "The Citizens of each State shall be entitled to all Privileges and Immunities of Citizens in the several States." This clause confers on U.S. citizens freedom from most forms of discrimination when visiting other states. The Court has validated some discrimination between residents and nonresidents when factors beyond citizenship are present. "There may be a substantial reason for requiring the nonresident to pay more than a resident for a hunting license, or to enroll in the state university, but our cases have not identified any acceptable reason for qualifying the protection afforded by the Clause for 'the citizen of State A who ventures into State B to settle there and establish a home.' "

Justice Stevens focused on "the third aspect of the right to travel-the right of the newly arrived citizen to the same privileges and immunities enjoyed by other citizens of the same State." Justice Miller's majority opinion in the *Slaughter-House Cases* stated that one of the privileges conferred by the Privileges and Immunities Clause " 'is that a citizen of the United States can, of his own volition, become a citizen of any State of the Union by a bona fide residence therein with the same rights as other citizens of that State.' " The majority said that discrimination among citizens who receive welfare benefits was not an acceptable means for accomplishing the state's asserted fiscal purpose of reducing its welfare spending. The Citizenship Clause of the Fourteenth Amendment " 'does not provide for, and does not allow for, degrees of citizenship based on length of residence.' " The statute at issue resulted in a "hierarchy of 45 subclasses of similarly situated citizens based on the location of their prior residence."

Finally, congressional approval of durational residence requirements did not render them constitutional. The Court has "consistently held that Congress may not authorize the States to violate the Fourteenth Amendment." The Citizenship Clause of the Fourteenth Amendment limited "the powers of the National Government as well as the States." Justice Cardozo stated that the Fourteenth Amendment was " 'framed upon the theory that the peoples of the several states must sink or swim together, and that in the long run, prosperity and salvation are in union and not division.' " Thus, under the Fourteenth Amendment's Privileges and Immunities and Citizenship Clauses, California could not regulate the amount that it spends on welfare assistance by dividing its citizens into classes based upon length of residence.

Chief Justice Rehnquist and Justice Thomas joined each other in separate dissents. The Chief Justice objected to the majority's use of "any provision of the Constitution — and surely not a provision relied upon for only the second time since its enactment 130 years ago" — to strike down a " 'good-faith residency requirement.' " The majority rejected the Court's own precedents, particularly the analysis in *Shapiro v. Thompson*, which invalidated a statute that denied all welfare benefits during the first year of residence. Contrary to *Shapiro*, the majority does not turn on the right to travel, but "is only about respondents' right to immediately enjoy all the privileges of being a California citizen in relation to that State's ability to test the good-faith assertion of this right." The majority separates "the right to travel and Article IV rights from the right to become a citizen under the Privileges and Immunities Clause," and tests "the residence requirement here against this latter right." There was no difference between California's one-year limitation and one-year residence requirements previously upheld by the Court for in-state tuition benefits, divorce, and voting in primary elections.

Justice Thomas said that the Privileges and Immunities Clause did not establish "the right of the newly arrived citizen to the same privileges and immunities enjoyed by other citizens of the same state." Instead, when the United States was founded, the terms "privileges and immunities" referred "to those fundamental rights and liberties specifically enjoyed by English citizens, and more broadly, by all persons." For Justice Thomas, "the demise of the Privileges and Immunities Clause has contributed in no small part to the current disarray of our Fourteenth Amendment jurisprudence." In an appropriate case, the Court might reevaluate its Privileges and Immunities Clause jurisprudence and decide whether it "should displace, rather than augment, portions of our equal protection and substantive due process jurisprudence."

NOTES

(1) *Welfare Benefits.* In *Shapiro v. Thompson*, 394 U.S. 618 (1969), the Court invalidated regulations of two states and the District of Columbia denying all welfare assistance to persons who had not resided in that governmental entity for one year. The Court stated that "the purpose of inhibiting migration by needy persons into the State is constitutionally impermissible." Justice Brennan invalidated such state regulations as a violation of the right to travel in *United States v. Guest*, 383 U.S. 745 (1966), which has been "repeatedly recognized. [The] right finds no explicit mention in the Constitution. The reason, it has been suggested, is that a right so elementary was conceived from the beginning to be a necessary concomitant of the stronger Union the Constitution created. Some have grounded the right to travel in the Privileges and Immunities Clause of Article IV, § 2."

Justice Brennan also rejected the attempt to justify the regulation as a valid attempt "to distinguish between new and old residents on the basis of the contribution they have made to the community through the payment of taxes." It is unlikely that long-term indigent residents make a larger contribution to the tax base than indigent newcomers. Moreover, this reasoning could permit a state to refuse new residents access to schools, parks, libraries, and police and fire protection.

To pass constitutional scrutiny, the regulations and their professed objectives had "to be necessary to promote a compelling governmental interest." The records in these three cases contained no evidence that the one-year residency requirement was used in budgetary planning. While states have an interest in preventing receipt of welfare from more than one state, states can combat fraud through cooperation among their welfare departments. "We imply no view of the validity of waiting-period or residence requirements determining eligibility to vote, eligibility for tuition-free education, to obtain a license to practice a profession, to hunt or fish, and so forth. Such requirements may promote compelling state interests on the one hand, or, on the other, may not be penalties upon the exercise of the constitutional right of interstate travel."

Justice Stewart concurred in the judgment.

Chief Justice Warren dissented, joined by Justice Black, arguing that Congress could, using its commerce power, authorize states to impose a welfare residence requirement. The Chief Justice predicted that this decision would cause problems with current residency requirements imposed on "eligibility to vote, to engage in certain professions or occupations or the right to attend a state-supported university."

Justice Harlan also dissented. He said that construing the Equal Protection Clause to protect fundamental rights "carries the seeds of more judicial interference with the state and federal legislative process, much more indeed than does the judicial application of 'due process' according to traditional concepts."

(2) *Other Residency Requirements.* In a series of cases after *Shapiro*, it has become apparent that the Court will not simply strike down all durational residency requirements. Some durational residency requirements have been upheld and others rejected, as the Court appears to have considered the importance of the state interest, the extent to which the requirement actually deters a person from migrating, and the need for the requirement in accomplishing the State's purposes.

(3) *Voting.* In *Dunn v. Blumstein*, 405 U.S. 330 (1972), Tennessee's one-year state residency test for voting (three months in a county) was held invalid because it impaired both the right to travel and the right to vote. Chief Justice Burger dissented. The Court later upheld 50-day requirements in *Marston v. Lewis*, 410 U.S. 679 (1973), and *Burns v. Forston*, 410 U.S. 686 (1973).

(4) *Nonemergency Medical Care.* Two years after *Dunn*, the Court (8-1) relied on *Shapiro* in striking down an Arizona law requiring an indigent to reside in a county for one year as a condition for receiving nonemergency medical care or hospitalization in a public hospital. *Memorial Hospital v. Maricopa County*, 415 U.S. 250 (1974). While recognizing that not all durational residency requirements were invalid, Justice Marshall's opinion concluded that the denial of benefits was so great a burden on new arrivals as to constitute a "penalty" on the right to migrate. Consequently, the "penalty" designation triggered the "compelling state interest" test. Justice Rehnquist dissented.

(5) *Divorce Proceedings.* Justice Rehnquist wrote for the Court in *Sosna v. Iowa*, 419 U.S. 393 (1975), upholding a one-year durational residency requirement imposed by Iowa as a condition for instituting a divorce action against a nonresident. The opinion emphasized the traditional state interest in family law matters, in protecting the validity of a State's divorce decree, and in confining the use of State courts, for important family law matters, to those with an attachment to the State. Moreover, this case did not involve as significant a hardship as was involved in the *Shapiro* and *Maricopa County* cases. Justices Marshall and Brennan dissented.

(6) *In-state Tuition.* The Court appears to have accepted the concept that a State may require a year's residency as a condition for obtaining the benefit of reduced tuition at state universities. A district court decision upholding Minnesota's requirement was summarily affirmed by the Supreme Court. *See Starns v. Malkerson*, 326 F. Supp. 234, *aff'd*, 401 U.S. 985 (1971). *But see Vlandis v. Kline*, 412 U.S. 441 (1973), where Connecticut's in-state tuition preference was held invalid because the State had created an "irrebuttable presumption" that individuals in certain categories could never establish that they were bona fide residents. In light of the Court's subsequent virtual abandonment of the "irrebuttable presumption" doctrine, the continued vitality of *Vlandis v. Kline* is in doubt. *See Weinberger v. Salfi*, 422 U.S. 749

(1975), and *Elkins v. Moreno*, 435 U.S. 647 (1978). *See also* Note, *Durational Residence Requirements from Shapiro Through Sosna: The Right to Travel Takes a New Turn*, 50 N.Y.U. L. REV. 622 (1975).

(7) *Tourist and Business Travel to Cuba.* In *Regan v. Wald*, 468 U.S. 222 (1984), the Court upheld regulations barring most travel related economic transactions thereby effectively precluding general tourist and business travel to Cuba. "In the opinion of the State Department, Cuba, with the political, economic, and military backing of the Soviet Union, has provided widespread support for armed violence and terrorism in the Western Hemisphere. Cuba also maintains close to 40,000 troops in various countries in Africa and the Middle East in support of objectives inimical to United States foreign policy interests. . . . Given the traditional deference to executive judgment '[i]n this vast external realm,' *United States v. Curtiss-Wright Export Corp.*, 299 U.S. 304, 319 (1936), we think there is an adequate basis under the Due Process Clause of the Fifth Amendment to sustain the President's decision to curtail the flow of hard currency to Cuba currency that could then be used in support of Cuban adventurism by restricting travel." Justice Blackmun dissented on statutory grounds joined by Justices Brennan, Marshall, and Powell.

(8) *International Travel.* The Court has been less protective of international travel than domestic travel. (a) *Communist beliefs.* In *Kent v. Dulles*, 357 U.S. 116 (1958), the Court narrowly stated that "[t]he right to travel is part of the liberty which cannot be deprived without due process of law under the Fifth Amendment." The Court invalidated the denial of passports to two persons because of their alleged Communist beliefs and their associations with the Communist Party. The Court held that the Passport Act did not allow the Secretary of State to deny passports on these grounds.

(b) *Communist organization.* Under the Congressional statute at issue in *Aptheker v. Secretary of State*, 378 U.S. 500 (1964), it was unlawful for any members of a Communist organization to apply for passports to travel abroad. The Court struck down the statute on First Amendment grounds, see § 12.03, but also noted that the Fifth Amendment right to travel was being restricted in a way inconsistent with the First Amendment.

(c) *Cuban Missile Crisis.* In *Zemel v. Rusk*, 381 U.S. 1 (1965), the Court upheld the denial by the Secretary of State of travel to Cuba during the Cuban missile crisis, noting that the Secretary was justified in seeking to avert international incidents.

(d) *Former CIA employees seeking to subvert the agency.* In *Haig v. Agee*, 453 U.S. 280 (1981), the Court upheld, against a right to travel claim, the Secretary's revocation of the passport to a former CIA agent who had traveled extensively to other countries to expose CIA agents. Chief Justice Burger readily dismissed Agee's First Amendment claims. Even assuming, *arguendo*, that "First Amendment protections reach beyond our national boundaries," disclosures obstructing our security services were not protected. Justice Marshall wrote a dissenting opinion, primarily on statutory grounds, in which Justice Brennan joined. Justice Marshall also asserted that the Court had *sub silentio* overruled *Zemel* and *Kent*.

§ 11.05 "ECONOMIC AND SOCIAL LEGISLATION"

RAILWAY EXPRESS v. NEW YORK
336 U.S. 106, 69 S. Ct. 463, 93 L. Ed. 533 (1949)

JUSTICE DOUGLAS delivered the opinion of the Court.

Section 124 of the Traffic Regulations of the City of New York promulgated by the Police Commissioner provides: "No person shall operate, or cause to be operated, in or upon any street an advertising vehicle; provided that nothing herein contained shall prevent the putting of business notices upon business delivery vehicles, so long as such vehicles are engaged in the usual business or regular work of the owner and not used merely or mainly for advertising."

Appellant is engaged in a nation-wide express business. It operates about 1,900 trucks in New York City and sells the space on the exterior sides of these trucks for advertising. That advertising is for the most part unconnected with its own business.[15]

It was convicted in the magistrate's court and fined. The judgment of conviction was sustained in the Court of Special Sessions. . . . The Court of Appeals affirmed without opinion by a divided vote. . . .

The Court of Special Sessions concluded that advertising on vehicles using the streets of New York City constitutes a distraction to vehicle drivers and to pedestrians alike and therefore affects the safety of the public in the use of the streets. We do not sit to weigh evidence on the due process issue in order to determine whether the regulation is sound or appropriate; nor is it our function to pass judgment on its wisdom. . . .

The question of equal protection of the laws is pressed more strenuously on us. It is pointed out that the regulation draws the line between advertisements of products sold by the owner of the truck and general advertisements. . . . It is therefore contended that the classification which the regulation makes has no relation to the traffic problem since a violation turns not on what kind of advertisements are carried on trucks but on whose trucks they are carried.

That, however, is a superficial way of analyzing the problem, even if we assume that it is premised on the correct construction of the regulation. The local authorities may well have concluded that those who advertise their own wares on their trucks do not present the same traffic problem in view of the nature or extent of the advertising which they use. . . .

We cannot say that that judgment is not an allowable one. Yet if it is, the classification has relation to the purpose for which it is made and does not contain the kind of discrimination against which the Equal Protection Clause affords protection. . . . And the fact that New York City sees fit to eliminate from traffic this kind of distraction but does not touch what may be even greater ones in a different category, such as the vivid displays on Times Square, is immaterial. It is no requirement of equal protection that all evils of the same genus be eradicated or none at all. . . .

It is finally contended that the regulation is a burden on interstate commerce in violation of Art. I, § 8 of the Constitution. Many of these trucks are engaged in delivering goods in interstate commerce from New Jersey to New York. Where traffic control and the use of highways are involved and where there is no conflicting federal regulation, great leeway is allowed local authorities, even though the local regulation materially interferes with interstate commerce. The case in that posture is controlled by *S.C. Hwy. Dept. v. Barnwell Bros.*, 303 U.S. 177, 187 *et seq.* . . .

Justice Rutledge acquiesces in the Court's opinion and judgment, dubitante on the question of equal protection of the laws.

Justice Jackson, concurring.

. . . The burden should rest heavily upon one who would persuade us to use the due

---

[15] [Court's footnote 1] The advertisements for which appellant was convicted consisted of posters from three by seven feet to four by ten feet portraying Camel Cigarettes, Ringling Brothers and Barnum & Bailey Circus, and radio station WOR. . . .

process clause to strike down a substantive law or ordinance. Even its provident use against municipal regulations frequently disables all government — state, municipal and federal — from dealing with the conduct in question. . . . Invalidation of a statute or an ordinance on due process grounds leaves ungoverned and ungovernable conduct which many people find objectionable.

Invocation of the equal protection clause, on the other hand, does not disable any governmental body from dealing with the subject at hand. It merely means that the prohibition or regulation must have a broader impact. . . . The framers of the Constitution knew, and we should not forget today, that there is no more effective practical guaranty against arbitrary and unreasonable government than to require that the principles of law which officials would impose upon a minority must be imposed generally. Conversely, nothing opens the door to arbitrary action so effectively as to allow those officials to pick and choose only a few to whom they will apply legislation and thus to escape the political retribution that might be visited upon them if larger numbers were affected. . . .

This case affords an illustration. Even casual observations from the sidewalks of New York will show that an ordinance which would forbid all advertising on vehicles would run into conflict with many interests, including some, if not all, of the great metropolitan newspapers, which use that advertising extensively. Their blandishment of the latest sensations is not less a cause of diverted attention and traffic hazard than the commonplace cigarette advertisement which this truck-owner is forbidden to display. But any regulation applicable to all such advertising would require much clearer justification in local conditions to enable its enactment than does some regulation applicable to a few. I do not mention this to criticize the motives of those who enacted this ordinance, but it dramatizes the point that we are much more likely to find arbitrariness in the regulation of the few than of the many. Hence, for my part, I am more receptive to attack on local ordinances for denial of equal protection than for denial of due process, while the Court has more often used the latter clause.

In this case, if the City of New York should assume that display of any advertising on vehicles tends and intends to distract the attention of persons using the highways and to increase the dangers of its traffic, I should think it fully within its constitutional powers to forbid it all. . . . Instead of such general regulation of advertising, however, the City seeks to reduce the hazard only by saying that while some may, others may not exhibit such appeals. . . .

. . . There is not even a pretense here that the traffic hazard created by the advertising which is forbidden is in any manner or degree more hazardous than that which is permitted. . . .

The question in my mind comes to this. Where individuals contribute to an evil or danger in the same way and to the same degree, may those who do so for hire be prohibited, while those who do so for their own commercial ends but not for hire be allowed to continue? I think the answer has to be that the hireling may be put in a class by himself and may be dealt with differently than those who act on their own. . . .

NOTES

(1) *Scrutiny of "Economic and Social Regulation."* Despite the expanded use of the Equal Protection Clause in cases involving suspect classes and fundamental rights, the Court has rather consistently maintained a "hands off" policy with regard to equal protection review of economic regulation. One exception was *Morey v. Doud*, 354 U.S. 457 (1957) (holding invalid a state law regulating money order firms, but exempting the American Express Company).

Morey, however, was overruled in *New Orleans v. Dukes*, 427 U.S. 298 (1976). In

Dukes a "pushcart" vendor selling foodstuffs challenged a New Orleans ordinance banning her business from the French Quarter, except during Mardi Gras. The ordinance contained a "grandfather" exception for vendors who had operated in the French Quarter continuously for eight years or more.

Dukes challenged this ordinance as a violation of equal protection. In a per curiam opinion, the Court unanimously rejected her challenge: "We cannot say that these judgments so lack rationality that they constitute a constitutionally impermissible denial of equal protection." *See also McGowan v. Maryland*, 366 U.S. 420 (1961) (upholding Sunday Closing or Blue Laws against equal protection challenge despite the existence of myriad exceptions favoring certain types of vendors, and vendors located in particular counties).

As indicated in Chapter VII, the Due Process Clause of the Fourteenth Amendment was historically the most favored vehicle for invalidating state economic legislation, and such judicial intervention was the source of intense criticisms leveled at the Court during the first third of this Century. Since 1937, the Due Process Clause has been interpreted so as to permit leeway to legislatures in matters of economic and social regulation.

(2) *Out-of-state Persons or Businesses.* State taxes and regulations that discriminate against out-of-state businesses or persons are generally challenged under the Commerce Clause (Ch. IV) or the Privileges and Immunities Clause of Article IV (Ch. II). This is because the Equal Protection Clause, with its limited standard of review for economic legislation, provides scant additional protection for those alleging such discrimination. Occasionally, however, the court has used the equal protection clause to strike down tax laws and the regulations discriminating against out-of-staters.

(3) *In-state Insurance Companies.* An Alabama law imposed a substantially lower gross premium tax on domestic insurance companies. A federal statute, the McCarran-Ferguson Act, exempted the insurance industry from the restrictions on state laws imposed by the Commerce Clause, but did not limit the applicability of the Equal Protection Clause. In *Metropolitan Life Insurance Company v. Ward*, 470 U.S. 865 (1985), a 5-4 majority rejected as a valid purpose the promotion of local business "by discriminating against nonresident competitors." It was apparent that the Court majority, when faced with a state law that would undoubtedly have been invalid under the Commerce Clause, used a heightened level of equal protection analysis to fill the breach left by Congress' action in taking away Commerce Clause protection from the insurance industry.

A strong dissent by Justice O'Connor, joined by Justices Brennan, Marshall, and Rehnquist, sharply criticized the majority for departing from the deferential standard of review set forth in *New Orleans v. Dukes*, 427 U.S. 298 (1976), which was particularly inappropriate in tax legislation. Moreover, state benefits to local businesses should be viewed as constitutionally permissible "where Congress itself has affirmatively authorized the States to promote local business concerns free of Commerce Clause restrictions."

(4) *Use Tax.* In *Williams v. Vermont*, 472 U.S. 14 (1985), a provision of the Vermont use tax that appeared to discriminate against nonresidents was held invalid under the Equal Protection Clause. Vermont residents who purchase a car in another State receive credit against Vermont's use tax in the amount of the sales tax paid to another State when the resident registers the car in Vermont. If a nonresident purchases a car in another State and then registers the car in Vermont, the credit against the Vermont use tax is not allowed. The majority (Justice White, joined by Chief Justice Burger and Justices Brennan, Marshall, and Stevens) held that "to provide a credit only to those who were residents at the time they paid the sales tax to another State is an arbitrary

distinction that violates the Equal Protection Clause." Justice Brennan wrote a separate concurrence. Justice Blackmun dissented, joined by Justices Rehnquist and O'Connor. Justice Powell did not participate.

(5) *Establishing and Acquiring Banks.* In *Northeast Bancorp, Inc. v. Board of Governors of the Federal Reserve System*, 472 U.S. 159 (1985), a unanimous Court (Justice Powell not participating) rejected an equal protection challenge to the reciprocal laws of Connecticut and Massachusetts which provided that an out-of-state bank with its principal place of business in one of the other New England States may acquire or establish a bank in Massachusetts or Connecticut. These laws were passed pursuant to a federal law prohibiting a bank from acquiring a bank in another State unless the State of the bank to be acquired authorized such acquisitions by legislation. Having found that the State laws were authorized by an act of Congress, the majority concluded that "state actions which . . . [Congress] plainly authorizes are invulnerable to constitutional attack under the Commerce Clause."

Turning to the Equal Protection Clause, Justice Rehnquist, who dissented in *Metropolitan Life*, distinguished that case: "Here the States in question — Massachusetts and Connecticut — are not favoring local corporations at the expense of out-of-state corporations. They are favoring out-of-state corporations domiciled within the New England region over out-of-state corporations from other parts of the country, and to this extent the laws may be said to discriminate against the latter." But the preference for regional banking was rational as it "favored widely dispersed control of banking." The "acquisition of Connecticut banks by holding companies headquartered outside the New England region would threaten the independence of local banking institutions."

Justice O'Connor, in a concurring opinion, found the statute at issue indistinguishable from that invalidated in *Metropolitan Life Insurance Company v. Ward.*

(6) *Tax Exemption.* In *Hooper v. Bernalillo County Assessor*, 472 U.S. 612 (1985), the Court held invalid a provision of the New Mexico Constitution that granted a real property tax exemption to honorably discharged Vietnam veterans who had served for more than 90 days and who were New Mexico residents before May 8, 1976. Chief Justice Burger's majority (5-3) opinion relied heavily on *Zobel v. Williams*, 457 U.S. 55 (1982). *Zobel* had struck down an Alaskan law that drew "fixed, permanent distinctions between . . . classes of concededly bona fide residents" based on when they arrived in the State. The law had given a state dividend distribution to Alaskan residents of $50 for every year of their residency.

Like the Alaska law, the Court held that the New Mexico statute failed even a rationality test. "Indeed, the veteran who resided in New Mexico as an infant long ago would immediately qualify for the exemption upon settling in the State at any time in the future regardless of where he resided before, during, or after military service."

Justice Stevens dissented, joined by Justices Rehnquist and O'Connor. He argued that even if there were some instances where the statute produces an arbitrary result, the Equal Protection Clause did not require exactitude. Justice Powell did not participate.

(7) *Tax Exemption for Local Public Utilities.* In *General Motors Corporation v. Tracy*, 519 U.S. 278 (1997), the Court upheld against an equal protection challenge an exemption from a sales tax that applied to regulated public utilities, but not to other sellers of natural gas. The Court also rejected a dormant commerce clause challenge to the exemption. Ohio levied a 5% sales and use tax on goods, including gas, bought or to be used in Ohio. " 'Local distribution companies,' " (LDCs), were exempted by statute because they provided core energy services to Ohio citizens. LDCs are primarily public

utilities, operating in a noncompetitive arena, charging regulated rates, and providing a largely residential clientele dependent on gas for essential uses with various "bundled" services of gas delivery and various protections for continued supply. The Ohio Supreme Court determined that independent producers and marketers, such as those with whom the General Motors Corporation (GMC) did business, were not LDCs and consequently, were not afforded the exemption. GMC consumed "unbundled" gas, choosing the services they desired from a competitive market. Writing for the Court, Justice Souter stated that the key to the exemption was not where the companies operated, but what kind of services they provided. "Out-of-state public utilities may therefore qualify for Ohio's sales and use tax exemption." The tax did not discriminate against out-of-staters, but "between regulated local gas utilities and unregulated marketers." The Court held Ohio could offer a better tax rate to LDCs, who provided Ohio citizens with core services, unlike GMC's supplier. The tax differences rested on "a rational basis for Ohio's distinction between these two kinds of entities." Justice Scalia wrote a concurring opinion and Justice Stevens dissented.

VACCO v. QUILL, 521 U.S. 793 (1997). In *Vacco*, the Court held that New York did not violate the Equal Protection Clause through its prohibition on assisted suicide. Like most states, New York allowed patients to decline lifesaving medical care, but made it a crime to assist another in committing or attempting suicide. In this case, three physicians practicing in New York asserted that, like competent patients who may refuse life-sustaining medical treatment, terminally ill patients should have the right, under the Equal Protection Clause, to lethal medication from their physicians, despite the New York law forbidding physician-assisted suicide.

Writing for the majority, Chief Justice Rehnquist recognized that, although New York's laws prohibiting assisting suicide significantly affected all of its citizens, they "neither infringe fundamental rights nor involve suspect classifications." Thus, these statutes receive " 'a strong presumption of validity.' "

"On their faces, neither New York's ban on assisted suicide nor its statutes permitting patients to refuse medical treatment treat anyone differently than anyone else or draw any distinctions between persons. Everyone, regardless of physical condition, is entitled, if competent, to refuse unwanted lifesaving medical treatment; no one is permitted to assist a suicide." "[T]he distinction between assisting suicide and withdrawing life-sustaining treatment, a distinction widely recognized and endorsed in the medical profession[16] and in our legal traditions, is both important and logical; it is certainly rational."

This basic difference "comports with fundamental legal principles of causation and intent." For instance, when a patient declines life-saving treatment, the underlying disease causes death. However, when a patient takes lethal medication prescribed by a physician, the medication causes death. Moreover, when a physician withdraws life-support or obeys a patient's request not to administer such treatment, the physician may only intend to honor the patient's wish to discontinue ineffectual or degrading treatment when little or no hope exists that the patient will receive any benefit. On the other hand, a physician who assists a suicide " 'must, necessarily and indubitably, intend primarily that the patient be made dead.' " Likewise, a patient committing suicide with a physician's aid "has the specific intent to end his or her own life, while a patient who refuses or discontinues treatment might not." In light of these distinctions,

---

[16] The American Medical Association finds a " 'fundamental difference between refusing life-sustaining treatment and demanding a life-ending treatment' " because assisted suicide " 'is contrary to the prohibition against using the tools of medicine to cause a patient's death.' " Of course, this suit itself demonstrates the difference of opinions throughout the medical profession regarding this subject

many courts, including New York courts, have crafted a scrupulous distinction between assisted suicide and the refusal of life-saving treatment.

Moreover, the majority of state legislatures have "carefully distinguished between refusing life-sustaining treatment from suicide."[17] New York is among the states that has "reaffirmed the line between 'killing' and 'letting die.'" Chief Justice Rehnquist found that this distinction is also consistent with the difference between physician-assisted suicide and "'terminal sedation,'" such as "'inducing barbiturate coma and then starving the person to death.'" A state may allow "palliative care," which may carry the expected but unintended "'double effect' of hastening the patient's death."

Substantial public concerns, including "prohibiting intentional killing and preserving life; preventing suicide; maintaining physicians' role as their patients' healers; protecting vulnerable people from indifference, prejudice, and psychological and financial pressure to end their lives; and avoiding a possible slide towards euthanasia," validated New York's ban on assisted suicide. These significant public interests fulfilled the constitutional requirement that the statutes rationally relate to a legitimate interest.[18]

Justice O'Connor wrote a concurring opinion, which Justice Ginsburg joined and which Justice Breyer joined, except where it joined the majority opinion. Justice O'Connor agreed with the majority that there exists no "generalized right to 'commit suicide.'" In this facial challenge to the New York statute, however, she found it unnecessary to address the specific issue raised by respondents "whether a mentally competent person who is experiencing great suffering has a constitutionally cognizable interest in controlling the circumstances of his or her imminent death." Justice O'Connor had "no reason to think the democratic process will not strike the proper balance between the interests of terminally ill, mentally competent individuals who would seek to end their suffering and the State's interests in protecting those who might seek to end life mistakenly or under pressure." Justice O'Connor noted: "There is no dispute that dying patients in Washington and New York can obtain palliative care, even when doing so would hasten their deaths. The difficulty in defining terminal illness and the risk that a dying patient's request for assistance in ending his or her life might not be truly voluntary justifies the prohibitions on assisted suicide we uphold here."

Justice Stevens concurred in the judgment. "The morality, legality, and practicality of capital punishment have been the subject of debate for many years." Yet, when the state legislatures "sufficiently narrowed the category of lives that the State could terminate, and had enacted special procedures to ensure that the defendant belonged in that limited category," the Court upheld capital punishment statutes against facial challenges. The Court, however, has subsequently held some applications of capital punishment statutes unconstitutional. In this case, since the three terminally ill patients died before the case reached the Supreme Court, the Court could not consider the statute as it applied to these individuals. Instead, the Court could only address a facial challenge, which is the most difficult challenge to raise successfully since it requires that the challenger prove that no circumstance would render the statute valid.[19]

---

[17] In *Cruzan v Director, Mo. Dept. of Health, supra* § 7.04[4], the Court noted that most states impose criminal penalties on those who assist suicides.

[18] In his concurrence, Justice Stevens noted that the Court's holding does not preclude the New York statute from constituting an "'intolerable intrusion on the patient's freedom'" in some instances. However, to succeed in proving that the New York ban on assisted suicide is unconstitutional, an individual plaintiff would have to present substantially different and stronger arguments than those presented in this case.

[19] Justice Stevens remarked that the Court has never "actually applied such a strict standard."

Justice Stevens continued: "[h]istory and tradition" support the Court's refusal to recognize an unrestricted constitutional right to commit suicide. "The value to others of a person's life is far too precious to allow the individual to claim a constitutional entitlement to complete autonomy in making a decision to end that life." There are some circumstances, however, that would require constitutional protection for an individual's "interest in hastening death."

Justice Stevens agreed with the majority that the State's distinction between allowing the underlying disease to cause death and administering lethal medication to prematurely induce death justified upholding the statute. However, Justice Stevens did not believe that the intent of the physicians, the patients, and the families substantially differs in these two situations.[20] The AMA approves terminal sedation, administering pain-killing medication to terminally ill patients to reduce intolerable pain even though such drugs will hasten death.

Justice Souter also concurred in the judgment, stating that "the distinction between assistance to suicide, which is banned, and practices such as termination of artificial life support and death-hastening pain medication, which are permitted" is not arbitrary. His analysis was predicated exclusively on the Due Process Clause: "The doctors also rely on the Equal Protection Clause, but that source of law does essentially nothing in a case like this that the Due Process Clause cannot do on its own."

Justice Breyer concurred in the judgment and emphasized the importance of the "'right to die with dignity.'" Justice Breyer expressed a concern for protecting "personal control over the manner of death, professional medical assistance, and the avoidance of unnecessary and severe physical suffering — combined."

CONCLUDING NOTE

For some comparative perspectives on equal protection theory, see, e.g., Osakwe, *Equal Protection of Law in Soviet Constitutional Law and Theory — A Comparative Analysis*, 59 Tul. L. Rev. 974 (1985); Williams, *Aspects of Equal Protection in the United Kingdom*, 59 Tul. L. Rev. 959 (1985). Professor Peter Westen has argued that equality is a concept largely devoid of normative content. *See* Westen, *The Empty Idea of Equality*, 95 Harv L. Rev. 537 (1982). This argument has generated a good deal of discussion. *See, e.g.*, Chemerinsky, *In Defense of Equality: A Reply to Professor Westen*, 81 Mich. L. Rev. 575 (1983); Cohen, *Is Equality Like Oakland? Equality as a Surrogate for Other Rights*, 59 Tul. L. Rev. 884 (1985); D'Amato, *Is Equality a Totally Empty Idea?*, 81 Mich. L. Rev. 600 (1983); Greenwalt, *How Empty Is the Idea of Equality?* 83 Colum. L. Rev. 1167 (1983); Westen, *To Lure the Tarantula From its Hole: A Response*, 83 Colum. L. Rev. 1186 (1983); Westen, *The Meaning of Equality in Law, Science, Math and Morals: A Reply*, 81 Mich. L. Rev. 604 (1983); Westen, *On "Confusing Ideas" Reply*, 91 Yale L.J. 1153 (1982). Is Professor Westen right? Does equality have any independent normative content, or must reference be made to other values to give it meaning? What meaning has the Supreme Court given to equality in its equal protection jurisprudence?

---

[20] A survey of Oregon doctors showed that "60% of the responding doctors supported legalizing assisted suicide for terminally ill patients." In another study, 12 percent of Washington physicians stated that they had been asked by terminally ill patients for lethal medication to hasten death and that, in the year before the study, 24 percent of those physicians had prescribed such medication. A survey of Michigan oncologists also reported that 18 percent of the responding oncologists actively participated in assisted suicide.

Chapter XII
POLITICAL SPEECH AND ASSOCIATION

§ 12.01 OVERVIEW

Introductory Note. No provision of the Constitution imposes restrictions on government with more certainty and clarity than does the First Amendment with its unqualified admonition: "Congress shall make no law respecting an establishment of religion, or prohibiting the free exercise thereof; or abridging the freedom of speech, or of the press; or the right of the people peaceably to assemble, and to petition the Government for a redress of grievances." Nevertheless, the Amendment, particularly its free speech and press clause, ranks with the due process and equal protection clauses in having spawned an enormous and complex body of decisions, as courts have tried to define terms and balance interests.

The ideal of freedom of expression has also spawned an extensive body of scholarly commentary. *See, e.g.,* C. EDWIN BAKER, HUMAN LIBERTY AND FREEDOM OF SPEECH (1989); ZECHARIAH CHAFFEE, FREE SPEECH IN THE UNITED STATES (1941); MELVILLE NIMMER, NIMMER ON FREEDOM OF SPEECH: A TREATISE ON THE FIRST AMENDMENT (1984); WILLIAM VAN ALSTYNE, INTERPRETATIONS OF THE FIRST AMENDMENT (1984); Robert Bork, *Neutral Principles and Some First Amendment Problems,* 47 IND. L.J. 1 (1971); Michael J. Perry, *Freedom of Expression: An Essay on Theory and Doctrine,* 78 NW. U. L. REV. 1137 (1983).

The two scholars who have exerted the most influence are Alexander Meiklejohn and Thomas Emerson. *See, e.g.,* THOMAS EMERSON, THE SYSTEM OF FREEDOM OF EXPRESSION (1970); ALEXANDER MEIKLEJOHN, FREEDOM OF SPEECH AND ITS RELATION TO SELF-GOVERNMENT (1948); Thomas Emerson, *Legal Foundations of the Right to Know,* 1977 WASH. U. L.Q. 1; Alexander Meiklejohn, *The First Amendment is an Absolute,* 1961 SUP. CT. REV. 245. *See also* William Brennan, *The Supreme Court and the Meiklejohn Interpretation of the First Amendment,* 79 HARV. L. REV. 1 (1965). Professor Meiklejohn justified strong protection for freedom of speech because it advances democracy. In contrast, Professor Emerson argued for strong protection for freedom of speech because it fosters individual self-fulfillment or self-actualization, the advancement of knowledge or truth, the democratic process and constructing the entire culture, and political dissent and social change. In line with their justifications for protecting free speech, Professor Meiklejohn emphasized the audience's right to know, whereas Professor Emerson emphasized the speaker's right to speak. Both favored very strong protection for freedom of expression. For another analysis surveying various reasons offered for protecting freedom of expression, see Kent Greenawalt, *Free Speech Justifications,* 89 COLUM. L. REV. 119 (1989).

The case law in the free speech area is of surprisingly recent vintage. One reason is that arguably greater pressures on freedom of expression have resulted from foreign and domestic events since the beginning of World War I. These years have seen the fear of internal subversion (the domestic reaction to this country's emergence as a world power with real, and perceived, threats to the national interest), the growth of urbanization (resulting in competing pressures for the use of the public facilities which only a city can provide), the expansion of government at all levels with the inevitable pressures to stifle criticism, the growth of the media both in power and technology, the civil rights and anti-Vietnam War protest movements, the tensions resulting from dissatisfaction of large segments of the population with their economic status, and the changing social mores accompanied by different standards of literary and artistic expression. All of these historical developments, and many more, have been reflected in rapidly changing free speech law.

By its terms, of course, the First Amendment restricts only Congress, although there has never been serious doubt about the Amendment's applicability to all branches of the Federal Government. The case of *Barron v. Baltimore*, 7 Pet. 243 (1833), held that the Bill of Rights did not restrict the states, see § 7.01. In *Gitlow v. New York*, 268 U.S. 652 (1925), the rights of freedom of speech and press were "assume[d]" by the Court to be among the " 'liberties' " protected against state infringement by the Due Process Clause of the Fourteenth Amendment.

Courts draw few distinctions between the federal government and the states in the areas of free expression, although, of course, the differing interests of these governments in such areas as national security, or regulating traffic, are readily apparent.

Perhaps the most fundamental free speech question that a democracy faces is the extent to which individuals should be free to speak on behalf of an objective that is assumed to be unlawful, particularly when the message urges the overthrow of the same institutions which the speaker invokes for protection. Since these questions will often surface during periods when society appears threatened, it is not surprising that the leading cases in the United States grew out of the events of the two World Wars.

Section 12.02 reviews the development of protection for subversive speech. While the focus is on this specific category of speech, the theories discussed in these cases have exerted broad influence on First Amendment free speech jurisprudence. Turning to political association, § 12.03 explores the extent to which government can sanction persons for membership in political groups. Like § 12.02, many of the cases also involve groups that government has deemed subversive. The cases in § 12.04 move beyond formal sanctions to consider the extent to which governmental investigations of organizations may abridge associational rights. Continuing with the theme of freedom of association, § 12.05 explores associational rights in other contexts such as an economic boycott by the N.A.A.C.P., and discrimination by private clubs. Shifting gears a bit, § 12.06 considers the free speech rights of government employees. With regard to government employees, separate subsections treat patronage, political campaigning, and criticizing the government.

§ 12.02 ADVOCACY OF UNLAWFUL OBJECTIVES

SCHENCK v. UNITED STATES
249 U.S. 47, 39 S. Ct. 247, 63 L. Ed. 470 (1919)

[Section 3. Title I of the Espionage Act of 1917 provided:

SEC. 3. Whoever, when the United States is at war, shall willfully make or convey false reports or false statements with intent to interfere with the operation or success of the military or naval forces of the United States or to promote the success of its enemies and whoever, when the United States is at war, shall willfully cause or attempt to cause insubordination, disloyalty, mutiny, or refusal of duty, in the military or naval forces of the United States, or shall willfully obstruct the recruiting or enlistment service of the United States, to the injury of the service or of the United States, shall be punished by a fine of not more than $10,000 or imprisonment for not more than twenty years, or both.]

JUSTICE HOLMES delivered the opinion of the Court.

This is an indictment in three counts. The first charges a conspiracy to violate the Espionage Act of June 15, 1917 . . . by causing and attempting to cause insubordination, in the military and naval forces of the United States, and to obstruct the recruiting and enlistment service of the United States, when the United States was at war with the German Empire, to-wit, that the defendant willfully conspired to have printed and circulated to men who had been called and accepted for military service . . . a document set forth and alleged to be calculated to cause such insubordination and obstruction. The count alleges overt acts in pursuance of the conspiracy, ending in the distribution of the document set forth. The second count alleges a conspiracy to commit an offense against the United States, to-wit, to use the mails for the transmission of matter declared to be non-mailable by . . . the Act. . . . The third count charges an unlawful use of the mails for the transmission of the same matter. . . . The defendants were found guilty on all the counts. . . .

. . . According to the testimony Schenck said he was general secretary of the Socialist party and had charge of the Socialist headquarters from which the documents were sent. He identified a book found there as the minutes of the Executive Committee of the party. The book showed a resolution of August 13, 1917, that 15,000 leaflets should be printed on the other side of one of them in use, to be mailed to men who had passed exemption boards, and for distribution. Schenck personally attended to the printing. . . .

The document in question upon its first printed side recited the first section of the Thirteenth Amendment, said that the idea embodied in it was violated by the conscription act and that a conscript is little better than a convict. In impassioned language it intimated that conscription was despotism in its worst form and a monstrous wrong against humanity in the interest of Wall Street's chosen few. It said, "Do not submit to intimidation," but in form at least confined itself to peaceful measures such as a petition for the repeal of the act. The other and later printed side of the sheet was headed "Assert Your Rights." It stated reasons for alleging that any one violated the Constitution when he refused to recognize "your right to assert your opposition to the draft," and went on, "If you do not assert and support your rights, you are helping to deny or disparage rights which it is the solemn duty of all citizens and residents of the United States to retain." It described the arguments on the other side as coming from cunning politicians and a mercenary capitalist press, and even silent consent to the conscription law as helping to support an infamous conspiracy. It denied the power to send our citizens away to foreign shores to shoot up the people of other lands, and added that words could not express the condemnation such cold-blooded ruthlessness deserves, winding up, "You must do your share to maintain, support and uphold the rights of the people of this country." Of course the document would not have been sent unless it had been intended to have some effect, and we do not see what effect it could be expected to have upon persons subject to the draft except to influence them to obstruct the carrying of it out. . . .

But it is said, suppose that that was the tendency of this circular, it is protected by the First Amendment to the Constitution. . . . It well may be that the prohibition of laws abridging the freedom of speech is not confined to previous restraints, although to prevent them may have been the main purpose. . . . We admit that in many places and in ordinary times the defendants in saying all that was said in the circular would have been within their constitutional rights. But the character of every act depends upon the circumstances in which it is done. . . . The most stringent protection of free speech would not protect a man in falsely shouting fire in a theatre and causing a panic. It does not even protect a man from an injunction against uttering words that may have all the effect of force. The question in every case is whether the words used are used in such circumstances and are of such a nature as to create a clear and present danger that they will bring about the substantive evils that Congress has a right to prevent. It is a question of proximity and degree. When a nation is at war many things that might be said in time of peace are such a hindrance to its effort that their utterance will not be endured so long as men fight and that no Court could regard them as protected by any constitutional right. . . .   The statute of 1917 in section 4 punishes conspiracies to obstruct as well as actual obstruction. If the act, (speaking, or circulating a paper,) its tendency and the intent with which it is done are the same, we perceive no ground for saying that success alone warrants making the act a crime. . . .

DEBS v. UNITED STATES
249 U.S. 211, 39 S. Ct. 252, 63 L. Ed. 566 (1919)

JUSTICE HOLMES delivered the opinion of the court.

This is an indictment under the Espionage Act of June 15, 1917, c. 30, § 3. . . .   It has been cut down to two counts. . . .   The former of these alleges that on or about June 16, 1918, at Canton, Ohio, the defendant caused and incited and attempted to cause and incite insubordination, disloyalty, mutiny and refusal of duty in the military and naval forces of the United States and with intent so to do delivered, to an assembly of people, a public speech, set forth. The fourth count alleges that he obstructed and attempted to obstruct the recruiting and enlistment service of the United States and to that end and with that intent delivered the same speech, again set forth. There was a demurrer to the indictment on the ground that the statute is unconstitutional as interfering with free speech, contrary to the First Amendment. . . .   The defendant was found guilty and was sentenced to ten years' imprisonment on each of the two counts, the punishment to run concurrently on both.

The main theme of the speech was socialism, its growth, and a prophecy of its ultimate success. With that we have nothing to do, but if a part or the manifest intent of the more general utterances was to encourage those present to obstruct the recruiting service and if in passages such encouragement was directly given, the immunity of the general theme may not be enough to protect the speech. The speaker began by saying that he had just returned from a visit to the workhouse in the neighborhood where three of their most loyal comrades were paying the penalty for their devotion to the working class — these being Wagenknecht, Baker and Ruthenberg, who had been convicted of aiding and abetting another in failing to register for the draft. . . .   He said that he had to be prudent and might not be able to say all that he thought, thus intimating to his hearers that they might infer that he meant more, but he did say that those persons were paying the penalty for standing erect and for seeking to pave the way to better conditions for all mankind. Later he added further eulogies and said that he was proud of them. He then expressed opposition to Prussian militarism in a way that naturally might have been thought to be intended to include the mode of proceeding in the United States.

After considerable discourse that it is unnecessary to follow, he took up the case of Kate Richards O'Hare, convicted of obstructing the enlistment service, praised her for her loyalty to socialism and otherwise, and said that she was convicted on false testimony, under a ruling that would seem incredible to him if he had not had some experience with a Federal Court. We mention this passage simply for its connection with evidence put in at the trial. The defendant spoke of other cases, and then, after dealing with Russia, said that the master class has always declared the war and the subject class has always fought the battles-that the subject class has had nothing to gain and all to lose, including their lives; that the working class, who furnish the corpses, have never yet had a voice in declaring war and have never yet had a voice in declaring peace. . . .   The defendant next mentioned Rose Pastor Stokes, convicted of attempting to cause insubordination and refusal of duty in the military forces of the United States and obstructing the recruiting service. He said that she went out to render her service to the cause in this day of crises, and they sent her to the penitentiary for ten years; that she had said no more than the speaker had said that afternoon; that if she was guilty so was he, and that he would not be cowardly enough to plead his innocence. . . .

There followed personal experiences and illustrations of the growth of socialism, a glorification of minorities, and a prophecy of the success of the international socialist crusade, with the interjection that "you need to know that you are fit for something better than slavery and cannon fodder." The rest of the discourse had only the indirect though not necessarily ineffective bearing on the offenses alleged that is to be found in the usual contrasts between capitalists and laboring men, sneers at the advice to cultivate war gardens, attribution to plutocrats of the high price of coal . . . and a final exhortation "Don't worry about the charge of treason to your masters; but be concerned about the treason that involves yourselves." The defendant addressed the jury himself, and while contending that his speech did not warrant the charges said: "I have been accused of obstructing the war. I admit it. Gentlemen, I abhor war. I would oppose the war if I stood alone." The statement was not necessary to warrant the jury in finding that one purpose of the speech, whether incidental or not does not matter, was to oppose not only war in general but this war, and that the opposition was so expressed that its natural and intended effect would be to obstruct recruiting. If that was intended and if, in all the circumstances, that would be its probable effect, it would not be protected by reason of its being part of a general program and expressions of a general and conscientious belief.

The chief defenses upon which the defendant seemed willing to rely were the denial that we have dealt with and that based upon the First Amendment to the Constitution, disposed of in *Schenck v. United States*. . . .

There was introduced also an "Anti-war Proclamation and Program" adopted at St. Louis in April, 1917, coupled with testimony that about an hour before his speech the defendant had stated that he approved of that platform in spirit and in substance. The defendant referred to it in his address to the jury, seemingly with satisfaction and willingness that it should be considered in evidence. But his counsel objected and has argued against its admissibility, at some length. . . . It said "We brand the declaration of war by our Government as a crime against the people of the United States and against the nations of the world. In all modern history there has been no war more unjustifiable than the war in which we are about to engage." Its first recommendation was, "continuous, active, and public opposition to the war, through demonstrations, mass petitions, and all other means within our power." Evidence that the defendant accepted this view and this declaration of his duties at the time that he made his speech is evidence that if in that speech he used words tending to obstruct the recruiting service he meant that they should have that effect. The principle is too well established and too manifestly good sense to need citation of the books. We should add that the jury were most carefully instructed that they could not find the defendant guilty for advocacy of any of his opinions unless the words used had as their natural tendency and reasonably probable effect to obstruct the recruiting service, and unless the defendant had the specific intent to do so in his mind.

Without going into further particulars we are of opinion that the verdict on the fourth count, for obstructing and attempting to obstruct the recruiting service of the United States, must be sustained. Therefore it is less important to consider whether that upon the third count, for causing and attempting to cause insubordination, in the military and naval forces, is equally impregnable. . . .

ABRAMS v. UNITED STATES, 250 U.S. 616 (1919). The Espionage Act was broadened to make unlawful the use of language intended to "incite, provoke or encourage resistance to the United States' in the war, or with intent to hinder the United States war effort, to urge that war production be curtailed." . . . [A] group of socialists and anarchists were convicted under these amendments. They had printed and distributed circulars condemning the American intervention in the Russian Civil War, and calling for a general strike. Writing for the Court, Justice Clarke described the circulars as follows:

> The first of the two articles attached to the indictment is conspicuously headed, "The Hypocrisy of the United States and her Allies." After denouncing President Wilson as a hypocrite and a coward because troops were sent into Russia, it proceeds to assail our government in general, saying:
>
> "His [the President's] shameful, cowardly silence about the intervention in Russia reveals the hypocrisy of the Plutocratic gang in Washington and vicinity."
>
> It continues:
>
> "He (the President) is too much of a coward to come out openly and say: 'We capitalistic nations cannot afford to have a proletarian republic in Russia.' "
>
> Among the capitalistic nations Abrams testified the United States was included.
>
> Growing more inflammatory as it proceeds, the circular culminates in:
>
> "The Russian Revolution cries: Workers of the World! Awake! Rise! Put down your enemy and mine!"
>
> "Yes, friends, there is only one enemy of the workers of the world and that is CAPITALISM."
>
> This is clearly an appeal to the "workers" of this country to arise and put down by force the government of the United States, which they characterize as their "hypocritical," "cowardly," and "capitalistic" enemy.
>
> It concludes:
>
> "Awake! Awake, you Workers of the World!"
>
> "REVOLUTIONISTS."
>
> The second of the articles was printed in the Yiddish language and in the translation is headed, "Workers — Wake up." After referring to "his Majesty, Mr. Wilson, and the rest of the gang; dogs of all colors!" it continues:
>
> "Workers, Russian emigrants, you who had the least belief in the honesty of *our* Government, '"which defendants admitted referred to the United States government,' "
>
> "must now throw away all confidence, must spit in the face the false, hypocritic, military propaganda which has fooled you so relentlessly. . . . "
>
> It goes on:
>
> . . . "*Workers in the ammunition factories, you are producing bullets, bayonets, cannon, to murder not only the Germans, but also your dearest, best, who are in Russia and are fighting for freedom. . . .* "
>
> Again, the spirit becomes more bitter as it proceeds to declare that —
>
> "America and her Allies have betrayed (the Workers.) . . . The destruction of the Russian Revolution, that is the politics of the march to Russia."
>
> "*Workers, our reply to the barbaric intervention has to be a general strike! An open challenge* only will let the government know that not only the Russian Worker fights for freedom, but also *here in America lives the spirit of Revolution. . . .* "

"Do not let the government scare you with their wild punishment in prisons, hanging, and shooting. We must not and will not betray the splendid fighters of Russia. *Workers, up to fight.*"

After more of the same kind, the circular concludes:

"Woe unto those who will be in the way of progress. Let solidarity live!"

It is signed, "The Rebels."

Relying on *Schenk*, Justice Clarke . . . summarily dismissed a constitutional challenge to the conviction. Responding to the argument that the intent of the defendants was not to hinder the war effort as such, but only to promote the Bolshevik cause, Justice Clarke had applied the "probable effects" test. The general strike advocated by the defendants "necessarily involved, before it could be realized, defeat of the war program of United States" against Germany.

JUSTICE HOLMES, joined by JUSTICE BRANDEIS, . . . dissented:

This indictment is founded wholly upon the publication of two leaflets. . . . The first count charges a conspiracy pending the war with Germany to publish abusive language about the form of government of the United States, laying the preparation and publishing of the first leaflet as overt acts. The second count charges a conspiracy pending the war to publish language intended to bring the form of government into contempt, laying the preparation and publishing of the two leaflets as overt acts. The third count alleges a conspiracy to encourage resistance to the United States in the same war, and to attempt to effectuate the purpose by publishing the same leaflets. The fourth count lays a conspiracy to incite curtailment of production of things necessary to the prosecution of the war, and to attempt to accomplish it by publishing the second leaflet to which I have referred. . . .

No argument seems to me necessary to show that these pronunciamentos in no way attack the form of government of the United States, or that they do not support either of the first two counts. What little I have to say about the third count may be postponed until I have considered the fourth. With regard to that it seems too plain to be denied that the suggestion to workers in the ammunition factories that they are producing bullets to murder their dearest, and the further advocacy of a general strike, both in the second leaflet, do urge curtailment of production of things necessary to the prosecution of the war within the meaning of the Act of May 16, 1918. . . . But to make the conduct criminal, that statute requires that it should be 'with intent by such curtailment to cripple or hinder the United States in the prosecution of the war.' It seems to me that no such intent is proved.

I am aware, of course, that the word "intent" as vaguely used in ordinary legal discussion means no more than knowledge at the time of the act that the consequences said to be intended will ensue. Even less than that will satisfy the general principle of civil and criminal liability. A man may have to pay damages, may be sent to prison, at common law might be hanged, if at the time of his act he knew facts from which common experience showed that the consequences would follow, whether he individually could foresee them or not. But, when words are used exactly, a deed is not done with intent to produce a consequence unless that consequence is the aim of the deed. It may be obvious, and obvious to the actor, that the consequence will follow, and he may be liable for it even if he regrets it, but he does not do the act with intent to produce it unless the aim to produce it is the proximate motive of the specific act, although there may be some deeper motive behind.

. . . A patriot might think that we were wasting money on aeroplanes, or making more cannon of a certain kind than we needed, and might advocate curtailment with success; yet, even if it turned out that the curtailment hindered and was thought by other minds to have been obviously likely to hinder the United States in the prosecution of the war, no one would hold such conduct a crime. I admit that my illustration does not answer all that might be said, but it is enough to show what I think and to let me pass to a more important aspect of the case. I refer to the 1st Amendment to the Constitution that Congress shall make no law abridging the freedom of speech.

I never have seen any reason to doubt that the questions of law that alone were before this court in the cases of *Schenck*, *Frohwerk* [*v. United States*, 249 U.S. 204 (1919)], and *Debs*, were rightly decided. I do not doubt for a moment that by the same reasoning that would justify punishing persuasion to murder, the United States constitutionally may punish speech that produces or is intended to produce a clear and imminent danger that it will bring about forthwith certain substantive evils that the United States constitutionally may seek to prevent. The power undoubtedly is greater in time of war than in time of peace because war opens dangers that do not exist at other times.

But, as against dangers peculiar to war, as against others, the principle of the right to free speech is always the same. It is only the present danger of immediate evil or an intent to bring it about that warrants Congress in setting a limit to the expression of opinion where private rights are not concerned. Congress certainly cannot forbid all effort to change the mind of the country. Now nobody can suppose that the surreptitious publishing of a silly leaflet by an unknown man, without more, would present any immediate danger that its opinions would hinder the success of the government arms or have any appreciable tendency to do so. Publishing those opinions for the very purpose of obstructing, however, might indicate a greater danger, and at any rate would have the quality of an attempt. . . .

I do not see how anyone can find the intent required by the statute in any of the defendants' words. The second leaflet is the only one that affords even a foundation for the charge, and there, without invoking the hatred of German militarism expressed in the former one, it is evident from the beginning to the end that the only object of the paper is to help Russia and stop American intervention there against the popular government, not to impede the United States in the war that it was carrying on. . . .

I return for a moment to the third count. That charges an intent to provoke resistance to the United States in its war with Germany. Taking the clause in the statute that deals with that in connection with the other elaborate provisions of the act, I think that resistance to the United States means some forcible act of opposition to some proceeding of the United States in pursuance of the war. I think the intent must be the specific intent that I have described, and for the reasons that I have given I think that no such intent was proved or existed in fact. I also think that there is no hint at resistance to the United States, as I construe the phrase.

In this case sentences of twenty years' imprisonment have been imposed for the publishing of two leaflets that I believe the defendants had as much right to publish as the government has to publish the Constitution of the United States. . . . I will add, even if what I think the necessary intent were shown, — the most nominal punishment seems to me all that possibly could be inflicted, unless the defendants are to be made to suffer not for what the indictment alleges, but for the creed that they avow, — a creed that I believe to be the creed of ignorance and immaturity . . . but which, although made the subject of examination at the trial, no one has a right even to consider in dealing with the charges before the court.

Persecution for the expression of opinions seems to me perfectly logical. If you have no doubt of your premises or your power and want a certain result with all your heart you naturally express your wishes in law and sweep away all opposition. . . . But when men have realized that time has upset many fighting faiths, they may come to believe even more than they believe the very foundations of their own conduct that the ultimate good desired is better reached by free trade in ideas, — that the best test of truth is the power of the thought to get itself accepted in the competition of the market; and that truth is the only ground upon which their wishes safely can be carried out. That, at any rate, is the theory of our Constitution. It is an experiment, as all life is an experiment. Every year, if not every day, we have to wager our salvation upon some prophecy based upon imperfect knowledge. While that experiment is part of our system I think that we should be eternally vigilant against attempts to check the expression of opinions that we loathe and believe to be fraught with death, unless they so imminently threaten immediate interference with the lawful and pressing purposes of the law that an immediate check is required to save the country. I wholly disagree with the argument of the government that the 1st Amendment left the common law as to seditious libel in force. . . . I had conceived that the United States through many years had shown its repentance for the Sedition Act of July 14, 1798 by repaying fines that it imposed. Only the emergency that makes it immediately dangerous to leave the correction of evil counsels to time warrants making any exception to the sweeping command, "Congress shall make no law abridging the freedom of speech. . . . "

GITLOW v. NEW YORK, 268 U.S. 652 (1925). Benjamin Gitlow was convicted and imprisoned under New York's "Criminal Anarchy" provision. The provision punished as a felony, advising or teaching "the duty, necessity or propriety of overthrowing or overturning organized government by force or violence," or by any other unlawful means. It was also a felony to print or publish writings which propagated such a doctrine.

Gitlow was a member of an extremist faction of the Socialist Party. He was convicted for having published "The Left Wing Manifesto," a document advocating the violent overthrow of organized government: " 'The proletariat revolution and the Communist reconstruction of society — *the struggle for these* — is now indispensable. . . . The Communist International calls the proletariat of the world to the final struggle!' "

For the first time, the Court spoke of First Amendment rights as being incorporated in the Fourteenth Amendment: "For present purposes we may and do assume that freedom of speech and of the press — which are protected by the First Amendment from abridgement by Congress — are among the fundamental personal rights and 'liberties' protected by the due process clause of the Fourteenth Amendment from impairment by the States."

Nevertheless, Justice Sanford, writing for the majority, upheld Gitlow's conviction under New York's Criminal Anarchy Law: "The statute does not penalize the utterance or publication of abstract 'doctrine' or academic discussion having no quality of incitement to any concrete action. It is not aimed against mere historical or philosophical essays." Defendant's writing, far from being a philosophical treatise, constituted a direct incitement to violent action. The State was acting well within its police power when it penalized such expression: "[A] State may punish utterances endangering the foundations of organized government and threatening its overthrow by unlawful means. These imperil its own existence as a Constitutional State. . . . [I]n short [freedom of speech] does not deprive a State of the primary and essential right of self preservation. . . . [U]tterances inciting to the overthrow of organized government by unlawful means. . . . threaten breaches of the peace and ultimate revolution. And the immediate danger is none the less real and substantial, because the effect of a given utterance cannot be accurately foreseen. . . . A single revolutionary spark may kindle a fire that, smoldering for a time, may burst into a sweeping and destructive conflagration. It cannot be said that the State is acting arbitrarily or unreasonably when in the exercise of its judgment as to the measures necessary to protect the public peace and safety, it seeks to extinguish the spark without waiting until it has enkindled the flame or blazed into the conflagration. It cannot reasonably be required to defer the adoption of measures for its own peace and safety until the revolutionary utterances lead to actual disturbances of the public peace or imminent and immediate danger of its own destruction. . . .

"[W]hen the legislative body has determined generally, in the constitutional exercise of its discretion, that utterances of a certain kind involve such danger of substantive evil that they may be punished, the question whether any specific utterance coming within the prohibited class is likely, in and of itself, to bring about the substantive evil, is not open to consideration. It is sufficient that the statute itself be constitutional and that the use of the language comes within its prohibition."

Given the legislative pre-determination that mere advocacy of the specified action entailed substantive evil, the clear and present danger test set out in *Schenck* was inapplicable in the *Gitlow* case. The latter test was intended to apply only to cases where the controlling statute did not proscribe speech as such, but conduct. In such cases, the clear and present danger test was applicable to determine whether mere speech could be said to constitute a criminal attempt to incite the prohibited behavior.

Justice Holmes, joined by Justice Brandeis, filed the following dissent:

The general principle of free speech, it seems to me, must be taken to be included in the Fourteenth Amendment, in view of the scope that has been given to the word "liberty". . . . If I am right then I think that the criterion sanctioned by the full Court in *Schenck v. United States*, applies:

The question in every case is whether the words used are used in such circumstances and are of such a nature as to create a clear and present danger that they will bring about the substantive evils that [the State] has a right to prevent.

It is true that in my opinion this criterion was departed from in *Abrams v. United States*. . . . If what I think the correct test is applied it is manifest that there was no present danger of an attempt to overthrow the government by force on the part of the admittedly small minority who shared the defendant's views. It is said that this manifesto was more than a theory, that it was an incitement. Every idea is an incitement. It offers itself for belief and if believed it is acted on unless some other belief outweighs it or some failure of energy stifles the movement at its birth. The only difference between the expression of an opinion and an incitement in the narrower sense is the speaker's enthusiasm for the result. Eloquence may set fire to reason. But whatever may be thought of the redundant discourse before us it had no chance of starting a present conflagration. If in the long run the beliefs expressed in proletarian dictatorship are destined to be accepted by the dominant forces of the community, the only meaning of free speech is that they should be given their chance and have their way.

If the publication of this document had been laid as an attempt to induce an uprising against government at once and not at some indefinite time in the future it would have presented a different question. The object would have been one with which the law might deal, subject to the doubt whether there was any danger that the publication could produce any result, or in other words, whether it was not futile and too remote from possible consequences. But the indictment alleges the publication and nothing more.

NOTES

(1) For an interesting argument that correspondence with a young Judge Learned Hand helped to account for the reason why Justice Holmes wrote the majority opinions in *Schenck* and *Debs*, but dissented in *Abrams* and *Gitlow*, see GERALD GUNTHER, LEARNED HAND: THE MAN AND THE JUDGE (1994), and Gerald Gunther, *Learned Hand and the Origins of Modern First Amendment Doctrine: Some Fragments of History*, 27 STAN. L. REV. 719 (1975). On the other hand, Professor Bernard Schwartz has argued that the Holmes clear and present danger test "has been the foundation of our law's protection of First Amendment rights during the present century." *See* Bernard Schwartz, *Holmes Versus Hand: Clear and Present Danger or Advocacy of Unlawful Action?*, 1994 SUP. CT. REV. 209, 210 (1994).

(2) For an interesting explanation of why free speech protection has developed during the twentieth century, see G. Edward White, *The First Amendment Comes of Age: The Emergence of Free Speech in Twentieth-Century America*, 95 MICH. L. REV. 299, 301 (1996) ("the most complete and satisfactory account of the twentieth-century jurisprudential and cultural emergence of the First Amendment and the idea of freedom of speech is one that associates the elevation of speech to special status with the emergence, in the early years of the twentieth century, of a 'modernist' consciousness. This modernist consciousness bore a distinctive relationship to democracy and capitalism, the two prominent political and economic models of what I call 'modernity.' ").

(3) For a critique of the marketplace of ideas, see Stanley Ingber, *The Marketplace of Ideas: A Legitimizing Myth*, 1984 DUKE L.J. 1 ("[W]e must pierce the myth of the neutral marketplace of ideas and expose the flawed market model assumption of objective truth and the power of rationality. . . . Other than assuring dominance of national perspectives, the marketplace of ideas encourages only fine-tuning among established groups."). *See also* C. Edwin Baker, *The Media That Citizens Need*, 147 U. PA. L. REV. 317, 408 (1998) ("Complex democracy recognizes that the market could be failing, either by providing a media too homogeneous or too pluralistic, or by corrupting the available versions of either or both. These possibilities suggest that the Press Clause should be read to allow the government to promote a press that, in its best judgment, democracy needs but that the market fails to provide.").

WHITNEY v. CALIFORNIA, 274 U.S. 357 (1927). Under California's Criminal Syndicalism Act, it was a felony to be a member of any organization which advocated "criminal syndicalism." The statute defined criminal syndicalism as including any doctrine advocating crimes or unlawful violent acts as a means of bringing about political change. Writing for the majority, Justice Sanford noted that the Communist Labor Party, of which Anita Whitney was a member, espoused a "revolutionary class struggle to conquer the capitalist state." She had supported a resolution seeking to move the party away from a strongly militant line and emphasizing the need for participation in the electoral process. She had, however, remained a member of the party after the resolution had been rejected in favor of a more militant program.

Justice Sanford, citing *Gitlow*, rejected the contention that the Syndicalism Act, as applied in the case, violated the Fourteenth Amendment as a restraint on the rights of free speech, assembly, and association: "The . . . offence . . . partakes of the nature of a criminal conspiracy. . . . That such united and joint action involves even greater danger to the public peace and security than the isolated utterances and acts of individuals is clear. We cannot hold that, as here applied, the Act is an unreasonable or arbitrary exercise of the police power of the State, unwarrantably infringing any right of free speech, assembly or association."

Justice Brandeis, joined by Justice Holmes, concurred because Whitney failed to raise the proper constitutional objection below. Instead of alleging the lack of the requisite clear and present danger, Whitney contended that she lacked the intent to accomplish the unlawful objectives of the Communist labor party. The majority, and the concurring Justices considered this merely an objection to the sufficiency of the evidence. Although he concurred, Justice Brandeis took the opportunity to deliver the following opinion:

> Despite arguments to the contrary which had seemed to me persuasive, it is settled that the due process clause of the Fourteenth Amendment applies to matters of substantive law as well as to matters of procedure. Thus all fundamental rights comprised within the term liberty are protected by the federal Constitution from invasion by the states. . . . But, although the rights of free speech and assembly are fundamental, they are not in their nature absolute. Their exercise is subject to restriction, if the particular restriction proposed is required in order to protect the state from destruction or from serious injury, political, economic or moral. That the necessity which is essential to a valid restriction does not exist unless speech would produce, or is intended to produce, a clear and imminent danger of some substantive evil which the state constitutionally may seek to prevent has been settled. *See Schenck v. United States*, [249 U.S. 47 (1919), *supra*]. . . .

> This court has not yet fixed the standard by which to determine when a danger shall be deemed clear; how remote the danger may be and yet be deemed present; and what degree of evil shall be deemed sufficiently substantial to justify resort to abridgement of free speech and assembly as the means of protection. . . .

> Those who won our independence believed that the final end of the state was to make men free to develop their faculties, and that in its government the deliberative forces should prevail over the arbitrary. They valued liberty both as an end and as a means. They believed liberty to be the secret of happiness and courage to be the secret of liberty. They believed that freedom to think as you will and to speak as you think are means indispensable to the discovery and spread of political truth; that without free speech and assembly discussion would be futile; that with them, discussion affords ordinarily adequate protection against the dissemination of noxious doctrine; that the greatest menace to freedom is an inert people; that public discussion is a political duty; and that this should be a fundamental principle of the American government. They recognized the risks to which all human institutions are subject. But they knew that order cannot be secured merely through fear of punishment for its infraction; that it is hazardous to discourage thought, hope and imagination; that fear breeds repression; that repression breeds hate; that hate menaces stable government; that the path of safety lies in the opportunity to discuss freely supposed grievances and proposed remedies; and that the fitting remedy for evil

counsels is good ones. Believing in the power of reason as applied through public discussion, they eschewed silence coerced by law — the argument of force in its worst form. Recognizing the occasional tyrannies of governing majorities, they amended the Constitution so that free speech and assembly should be guaranteed.

Fear of serious injury cannot alone justify suppression of free speech and assembly. Men feared witches and burnt women. It is the function of speech to free men from the bondage of irrational fears. To justify suppression of free speech there must be reasonable ground to fear that serious evil will result if free speech is practiced. There must be reasonable ground to believe that the danger apprehended is imminent. There must be reasonable ground to believe that the evil to be prevented is a serious one. . . . But even advocacy of violation, however reprehensible morally, is not a justification for denying free speech where the advocacy falls short of incitement and there is nothing to indicate that the advocacy would be immediately acted on. The wide difference between advocacy and incitement, between preparation and attempt, between assembling and conspiracy, must be borne in mind. In order to support a finding of clear and present danger it must be shown either that immediate serious violence was to be expected or was advocated, or that the past conduct furnished reason to believe that such advocacy was then contemplated.

Those who won our independence by revolution were not cowards. They did not fear political change. They did not exalt order at the cost of liberty. To courageous, self-reliant men, with confidence in the power of free and fearless reasoning applied through the processes of popular government, no danger flowing from speech can be deemed clear and present, unless the incidence of the evil apprehended is so imminent that it may befall before there is opportunity for full discussion. If there be time to expose through discussion the falsehood and fallacies, to avert the evil by the processes of education, the remedy to be applied is more speech, not enforced silence. Only an emergency can justify repression. Such must be the rule if authority is to be reconciled with freedom. . . .

Moreover, even imminent danger cannot justify resort to prohibition of these functions essential to effective democracy, unless the evil apprehended is relatively serious. . . . The fact that speech is likely to result in some violence or in destruction of property is not enough to justify its suppression. There must be the probability of serious injury to the State. . . .

NOTES

(1) *Ruthenberg Dissent.* For an interesting discussion of Justice Brandeis' concurrence in *Whitney*, see Robert Cover, *The Left, the Right and the First Amendment 1918-1928:*, 40 Md. L. Rev. 349 (1981). This article revealed that Brandeis did not originally pen the concurrence to uphold the conviction of Anita Whitney who was a relatively minor figure in a relatively moderate faction of the Communist Labor Party. Instead, Justice Brandeis wrote the opinion to reverse the conviction of a man named Ruthenberg who had been the first national secretary of the Communist Party and had advocated "extra-parliamentary means of achieving power," including "the use of armed force." While pending before the Supreme Court, the *Ruthenberg* case was mooted by Ruthenberg's death.

(2) *The 1930s and 1940s.* As propounded by Justice Brandeis in his *Whitney* concurring opinion, the "clear and present danger" test was a far more speech-protective standard than that originally expounded by Justice Holmes in *Schenck* and

Debs. During the 1930s and 1940s the Brandeis "clear and present danger" test appeared to be more in line with the Court's approach to free speech issues. (*see* cases cited in the *Dennis* opinion below.) Thus, a test which initially was employed to justify the suppression of speech emerged as more of a shield for First Amendment rights, although often in contexts quite different from the subversive advocacy situations in *Schenck* and *Whitney*. During this time, the Court used the test to invalidate a number of government actions as abridging freedom of speech. *See Cantwell v. Connecticut*, 310 U.S. 296 (1940) ("breach of the peace" law applied to a member of Jehovah's Witness playing phonograph on street); *Herndon v. Lowry*, 301 U.S. 242 (1937) ("attempt to incite insurrection" applied to Communist Party organizer); *Bridges v. California*, 314 U.S. 252 (1941) (contempt of court because of newspaper comments on pending litigation); *Thornhill v. Alabama*, 310 U.S. 88 (1940) (ban on peaceful picketing); *Thomas v. Collins*, 323 U.S. 516 (1945) (law requiring union organizer to register with state). At the same time criticism of the "clear and present danger" doctrine was developing from civil libertarian sources, most notably in Alexander Meiklejohn's book, FREE SPEECH AND ITS RELATION TO SELF-GOVERNMENT (1948).

DENNIS v. UNITED STATES, 341 U.S. 494 (1951). Petitioners in *Dennis* were indicted under the conspiracy provisions of the Smith Act.[1] "The indictment charged the petitioners with willfully and knowingly conspiring (1) to organize as the Communist Party of the United States of America a society, group and assembly of persons who teach and advocate the overthrow and destruction of the Government of the United States by force and violence, and (2) knowingly and willfully to advocate and teach the duty and necessity of overthrowing and destroying the Government of the United States by force and violence. The indictment further alleged that § 2 of the Smith Act proscribes these acts and that any conspiracy to take such action is a violation of § 3 of the Act."

The Court granted certiorari to determine whether § 2 or § 3 of the Smith Act was unconstitutional on its face or as construed and applied in this case.

"The trial of the case extended over nine months, six of which were devoted to the taking of evidence, resulting in a record of 16,000 pages."

Writing for a plurality of four, Chief Justice Vinson began by noting that the "obvious purpose of the statute is to protect existing Government, not from change by peaceable, lawful and constitutional means, but from change by violence, revolution and terrorism." The plurality rejected "any principle of governmental helplessness in the face of preparation for revolution, which principle, carried to its logical conclusion, must lead to anarchy." Congress clearly has the power "to prohibit acts intended to

---

[1] Sections 2 and 3 of the Smith Act provide as follows:

Sec. 2 (a) It shall be unlawful for any person —

(1) to knowingly or willfully advocate, abet, advise, or teach the duty, necessity, desirability, or propriety of overthrowing or destroying any government in the United States by force or violence, or by the assassination of any officer of any such government;

(2) with intent to cause the overthrow or destruction of any government in the United States, to print, publish, edit, issue, circulate, sell, distribute, or publicly display any written or printed matter advocating, advising, or teaching the duty, necessity, desirability, or propriety of overthrowing or destroying any government in the United States by force or violence;

(3) to organize or help to organize any society, group, or assembly of persons who teach, advocate, or encourage the overthrow or destruction of any government in the United States by force or violence; or to be or become a member of, or affiliate with, any such society, group, or assembly of persons, knowing the purposes thereof. . . .

Sec. 3. It shall be unlawful for any person to attempt to commit, or to conspire to commit, any of the acts prohibited by the provisions of . . . this title.

overthrow the Government by force and violence. The question with which we are concerned here is not whether Congress has such *power*, but whether the *means* it has employed conflict with the First and Fifth Amendments to the Constitution."

Defendants contend that the statute is facially invalid "on the grounds that by its terms it prohibits academic discussion of the merits of Marxism-Leninism, that it stifles ideas and is contrary to all concepts of a free speech and a free press."

The language of the Smith Act negates defendants' interpretation. The Act "is directed at advocacy, not discussion. Thus, the trial judge properly charged the jury that they could not convict if they found that petitioners did 'no more than pursue peaceful studies and discussions or teaching and advocacy in the realm of ideas.' He further charged that it was not unlawful 'to conduct in an American college and university a course explaining the philosophical theories set forth in the books which have been placed in evidence.' " This charge strictly conformed with the language of the statute.

"No important case involving free speech was decided by this Court prior to *Schenck v. United* States." In that unanimous decision, "Justice Holmes stated that the 'question in every case is whether the words used are used in such circumstances and are of such a nature as to create a clear and present danger that they will bring about the substantive evils that Congress has a right to prevent.' " He and Justice Brandeis dissented in *Abrams, Schaefer,* and *Pierce*. These dissents argued insufficient evidence and "did not mark a change in principle. The dissenters doubted only the probable effectiveness of the puny efforts toward subversion."

While the Court has never expressly overruled the majority opinions in *Gitlow* and *Whitney*, "there is little doubt that subsequent opinions have inclined toward the Holmes-Brandeis rationale." This "Holmes-Brandeis philosophy insisted that where there was a direct restriction upon speech, a 'clear and present danger' that the substantive evil would be caused was necessary before the statute in question could be constitutionally applied."

Government overthrow "by force and violence is certainly a substantial enough interest for the Government to limit speech. Indeed, this is the ultimate value of any society, for if a society cannot protect its very structure from armed internal attack, it must follow that no subordinate value can be protected. . . ."

"Obviously, [a 'clear and present danger'] cannot mean that before the Government may act, it must wait until the *putsch* is about to be executed." Even an attempted government overthrow by force "doomed from the outset because of inadequate numbers or power of the revolutionists, is a sufficient evil for Congress to prevent. The damage which such attempts create both physically and politically to a nation makes it impossible to measure the validity in terms of the probability of success, or the immediacy of a successful attempt."

The *Gitlow* case involved "a comparatively isolated event, bearing little relation in their minds to any substantial threat to the safety of the community." Justices Holmes and Brandeis "were not confronted with any situation comparable to the instant one-the development of an apparatus designed and dedicated to the overthrow of the Government, in the context of world crisis after crisis."

The plurality adopted the construction of the clear and present danger test formulated by Chief Judge Learned Hand for the majority below. "In each case [courts] must ask whether the gravity of the 'evil,' discounted by its improbability, justifies such invasion of free speech as is necessary to avoid the danger."

The plurality also affirmed the trial court and the Court of Appeals in "finding that the requisite danger existed. The mere fact that from the period 1945 to 1948 petitioners' activities did not result in an attempt to overthrow the Government by force and violence is of course no answer to the fact that there was a group that was ready to make the attempt. The formation by petitioners of such a highly organized conspiracy, with rigidly disciplined members subject to call when the leader, these petitioners, felt that the time had come for action, coupled with the inflammable nature of world conditions, similar uprisings in other countries, and the touch-and-go nature of our relations with countries with whom petitioners were in the very least ideologically attuned, convince us that their convictions were justified on this score. And this analysis disposes of the contention that a conspiracy to advocate, as distinguished from the advocacy itself, cannot be constitutionally restrained, because it comprises only the preparation. It is the existence of the conspiracy which creates the danger."

The Court concluded with the finding that sufficient danger existed to apply the statute to the defendants, and proceeded to examine the trial judge's charge to the jury. The jury only had to determine whether defendant violated the statute. The trial judge decided whether sufficient danger existed to submit the question of defendant's guilt or innocence to the jury. "We hold that the statute may be applied where there is a 'clear and present danger' of the substantive evil which the legislature had the right to prevent. Bearing, as it does, the marks of a 'question of law,' the issue is properly one for the judge to decide."

Justice Frankfurter concurred in the affirmance of the judgment. Those who would find in the Constitution a "wholly unfettered right of expression," he stated, view the words of the Constitution "as though they were found on a piece of outworn parchment instead of being words that have called into being a nation with a past to be preserved for the future."

Justice Frankfurter summarized the Court's First Amendment decisions into "six different types of cases" in which the Court "recognized and resolved conflicts between speech and competing interests." Drawing upon that history, the decisions expressed three values that helped resolve the issues in *Dennis*.

"*First.* . . . [W]e are not legislators. . . . How best to reconcile competing interests is the business of legislatures, and the balance they strike is a judgment not to be displaced by ours, but to be respected unless outside the pale of fair judgment."

"*Second.* . . . [C]areful weighing of. . . . [t]he complex issues presented by regulation of speech in public places, by picketing, and by legislation prohibiting advocacy of crime have been resolved by scrutiny of many factors besides the imminence and gravity of the evil threatened."

Recalling "that Justice Holmes regarded questions under the First Amendment as questions of 'proximity and degree,' it would be a distortion, indeed a mockery, of his reasoning to compare the 'puny anonymities,' to which he was addressing himself in the *Abrams* case in 1919 or the publication that was 'futile and too remote from possible consequences,' in the *Gitlow* case in 1925 with the setting of events" in this 1950 case.

"*Third.* Not every type of speech occupies the same position on the scale of values. There is no substantial public interest in permitting certain kinds of utterances. . . . "

The defendants' conviction is for "conspiring to organize a party of persons who advocate the overthrow of the Government by force and violence." The value of such speech is low.

"Congress has determined that the danger created by advocacy of overthrow justifies the ensuing restriction on freedom of speech. The determination was made after due deliberation."

"To make validity of legislation depend on judicial reading of events still in the womb of time — a forecast, that is, of the outcome of forces at best appreciated only with knowledge of the topmost secrets of nation — is to charge the judiciary with duties beyond its equipment."

Justice Jackson concurred in the judgment. "If we must decide that this Act and its application are constitutional only if we are convinced that petitioner's conduct creates a 'clear and present danger' of violent overthrow, we must appraise imponderables, including intentional and national phenomena which baffle the best informed foreign offices and our most experienced politicians. We would have to foresee and predict the effectiveness of Communist propaganda, opportunities for infiltration, whether, and when, a time will come that they consider propitious for action, and whether and how fast our existing government will deteriorate. And we will have to speculate as to whether an approaching Communist *coup* would not be anticipated by a nationalistic fascist movement." The statute, indictment and conviction in this case all involve conspiracy. As conspiracies necessarily require communications "by letters, conversations, speeches, and documents" free speech doctrine cannot render the government powerless to defend itself against conspiracies to overthrow it.

Justice Black dissented. "These petitioners were not charged with an attempt to overthrow the Government. They were not charged with overt acts of any kind designed to overthrow the Government. They were not even charged with saying anything or writing anything designed to overthrow the Government. The charge was that they agreed to assemble and to talk and publish certain ideas at a later date: The indictment is that they conspired to organize the Communist Party and to use speech or newspapers and other publications in the future to teach and advocate the forcible overthrow of the Government. No matter how it is worded, this is a virulent form of prior censorship of speech and press, which I believe the First Amendment forbids. I would hold § 3 of the Smith Act authorizing this prior restraint unconstitutional on its face and as applied." To affirm the convictions, the opinions that form the majority in this case directly or indirectly repudiate the clear and present danger test.

Justice Douglas also dissented. "If this were a case where those who claimed protection under the First Amendment were teaching the techniques of sabotage, the assassination of the President, the filching of documents from public files, the planting of bombs, the art of street warfare, and the like, I would have no doubts. The freedom to speak is not absolute; the teaching of methods of terror and other seditious conduct should be beyond the pale along with obscenity and immorality."

Justice Douglas noted that petitioners "were not charged with a 'conspiracy to overthrow the Government,'" but only with "a conspiracy to form a party and groups and assemblies of people who teach and advocate the overthrow of our Government by force or violence and with a conspiracy to advocate and teach its overthrow by force and violence."

Justice Douglas stated that "never until today has anyone seriously thought that the ancient law of conspiracy could constitutionally be used to turn speech into seditious conduct." Speech should be suppressed only when no time exists to avoid the evil threatened in the speech. "Otherwise, free speech which is the strength of the Nation will be the cause of its destruction."

While Communism is a serious threat in other parts of the world, "Communism has been so thoroughly exposed in this country that it has been crippled as a political force. Free speech has destroyed it as an effective political party." During "days of trouble and confusion, when bread lines were long, when the unemployed walked the streets, when people were starving, the advocates of a short-cut by revolution might have a chance to gain adherents. But today there are no such conditions. . . . [T]he doctrine of Soviet revolution is exposed in all of its ugliness and the American people want none of it. How it can be said that there is a clear and present danger that this advocacy will succeed is, therefore, a mystery." On the other hand, "nations less resilient than the United States, where illiteracy is high and where democratic traditions are only budding, might have to take drastic steps and jail these men for merely speaking their creed. But in America they are miserable merchants of unwanted ideas; their wares remain unsold."

Justice Douglas concluded with a 1938 quote from Vishinsky's *The Law of the Soviet State*: "In our state, naturally, there is and can be no place for freedom of speech, press, and so on for the foes of socialism." Such a standard is unacceptable in the United States.

BRANDENBURG v. OHIO
395 U.S. 444, 89 S. Ct. 1827, 23 L. Ed. 2d 430 (1969)

PER CURIAM.

The appellant, a leader of a Ku Klux Klan group, was convicted under the Ohio Criminal Syndicalism statute for "advocat[ing] . . . the duty, necessity, or propriety of crime, sabotage, violence, or unlawful methods of terrorism as a means of accomplishing industrial or political reform" and for "voluntarily assembl[ing] with any society, group, or assemblage of persons formed to teach or advocate the doctrines of criminal syndicalism." OHIO REV. CODE ANN. § 2923.13. He was fined $1,000 and sentenced to one to 10 years' imprisonment. . . . We reverse.

The record shows that a man, identified at trial as the appellant, telephoned an announcer-reporter on the staff of a Cincinnati television station and invited him to come to a Ku Klux Klan "rally". . . . With the cooperation of the organizers, the reporter and a cameraman attended the meeting and filmed the events. Portions of the films were later broadcast on the local station and on a national network.

The prosecution's case rested on the films and on testimony identifying the appellant as the person who communicated with the reporter and who spoke at the rally. The State also introduced into evidence several articles appearing in the film, including a pistol, a rifle, a shotgun, ammunition, a Bible, and a red hood worn by the speaker in the films.

One film showed 12 hooded figures, some of whom carried firearms. They were gathered around a large wooden cross, which they burned. No one was present other than the participants and the newsmen who made the film. Most of the words uttered during the scene were incomprehensible when the film was projected, but scattered phrases could be understood that were derogatory of Negroes and, in one instance, of Jews. Another scene on the same film showed the appellant, in Klan regalia, making a speech. . . .

> . . . [W]e have hundreds, hundreds of members throughout the State of Ohio. . . . The Klan has more members in the State of Ohio than does any other organization. We're not a revengent organization, but if our President, our Congress, our Supreme Court, continues to suppress the white, Caucasian race, it's possible that there might have to be some revengance taken.
>
> We are marching on Congress July the Fourth, four hundred thousand strong. From there we are dividing into two groups, one group to march on St. Augustine, Florida, the other group to march into Mississippi. Thank you.

The second film showed six hooded figures one of whom, later identified as the appellant, repeated a speech very similar to that recorded on the first film. The reference to the possibility of "revengance" was omitted, and one sentence was added: "Personally, I believe the nigger should be returned to Africa, the Jew returned to Israel." Though some of the figures in the films carried weapons, the speaker did not.

The Ohio Criminal Syndicalism Statute was enacted in 1919. From 1917 to 1920, identical or quite similar laws were adopted by 20 States and two territories. E. DOWELL, A HISTORY OF CRIMINAL SYNDICALISM LEGISLATION IN THE UNITED STATES 21 (1939). In 1927, this Court sustained the constitutionality of California's Criminal Syndicalism Act, the text of which is quite similar to that of the laws of Ohio. *Whitney v. California.* . . . But *Whitney* has been thoroughly discredited by later decisions. These later decisions have fashioned the principle that the constitutional guarantees of free speech and free press do not permit a State to forbid or proscribe advocacy of the use of force or of law violation except where such advocacy is directed to inciting or producing imminent lawless action and is likely to incite or produce such action. As we said in *Noto v. United States*, 367 U.S. 290, 297–98 (1961), "the mere abstract teaching . . . of the moral propriety or even moral necessity for a resort to force and violence, is not the same as preparing a group for violent action and steeling it to such action." . . .

Measured by this test, Ohio's Criminal Syndicalism Act cannot be sustained. The Act punishes persons who "advocate or teach the duty, necessity, or propriety" of violence "as a means of accomplishing industrial or political reform;" or who publish or circulate or display any book or paper containing such advocacy; or who "justify" the commission of violent acts "with intent to exemplify, spread or advocate the propriety of the doctrines of criminal syndicalism; or who "voluntarily assemble" with a group formed "to teach or advocate the doctrines of criminal syndicalism." Neither the indictment nor the trial judge's instructions to the jury in any way refined the statute's bald definition of the crime in terms of mere advocacy not distinguished from incitement to imminent lawless action.

Accordingly, we are here confronted with a statute which, by its own words and as applied, purports to punish mere advocacy and to forbid, on pain of criminal punishment, assembly with others merely to advocate the described type of action. Such a statute falls within the condemnation of the First and Fourteenth Amendments. . . . *Whitney v. California* . . . is therefore overruled. . . .

JUSTICE BLACK, concurring.

I agree with the views expressed by Justice Douglas in his concurring opinion in this case that the "clear and present danger" doctrine should have no place in the interpretation of the First Amendment. . . .

JUSTICE DOUGLAS, concurring. . . .

The "clear and present danger" test was adumbrated by Justice Holmes in a case arising during World War I. . . .

. . . Though I doubt if the "clear and present danger" test is congenial to the First Amendment in time of a declared war, I am certain it is not reconcilable with the First Amendment in days of peace. . . .

My own view is quite different. I see no place in the regime of the First Amendment for any "clear and present danger" test, whether strict and tight as some would make it, or free-wheeling as the Court in *Dennis* rephrased it.

When one reads the opinions closely and sees when and how the "clear and present danger" test has been applied, great misgivings are aroused. First, the threats were often loud but always puny and made serious only by judges so wedded to the *status quo* that critical analysis made them nervous. Second, the test was so twisted and perverted in *Dennis* as to make the trial of those teachers of Marxism an all-out political trial which was part and parcel of the cold war that has eroded substantial parts of the First Amendment. . . .

The line between what is permissible and not subject to control and what may be made impermissible and subject to regulation is the line between ideas and overt acts.

The example usually given by those who would punish speech is the case of one who falsely shouts fire in a crowded theatre.

This is, however, a classic case where speech is brigaded with action. . . . [A] prosecution can be launched for the overt acts actually caused. Apart from rare instances of that kind, speech is, I think, immune from prosecution. Certainly there is no constitutional line between advocacy of abstract ideas . . . and advocacy of political action. . . .

NOTES

(1) *Suppression of Alleged Communist Sympathizers.* The *Brandenburg* case was the culmination of a series of cases in which the Court sharply restricted the techniques which had been created in the post-World War II (Cold War) period to penalize alleged left-wing sympathizers and their organizations. The legal arsenal was formidable, including the Smith Act, congressional investigations, loyalty-security programs at all levels of government, and dismissals from employment for invoking the privilege against self-incrimination. The activity extended into the private sector, with "black lists" against authors and actors, and with the publication (without hearings) of lists of organizations deemed subversive whose members were then barred from political positions or from jobs in industry or academia. Cases in this section show both the development of these techniques for restricting speech and association in the name of national security, and the manner in which the Court ultimately asserted First Amendment values. *Cf.* David M. Rabben, *Free Speech in Progressive Social Thought*, 74 TEX. L. REV. 951, 953 (1996) ("In an attempt to demonstrate the political neutrality of its free speech principles, the liberal Supreme Court might have deliberately chosen *Brandenburg*, a case that overturned the conviction of a Ku Klux Klan leader, as the vehicle for its most protective interpretation of the First Amendment.").

For a broad historical perspective of the impact of the Cold War period on civil liberties, see DANIEL CAUTE, THE GREAT FEAR: THE ANTI-COMMUNIST PURGE UNDER TRUMAN AND EISENHOWER (1978); VICTOR NAVASKY, NAMING NAMES (1980). For additional discussion of the development of strong protection for freedom of speech, see LEE BOLLINGER, THE TOLERANT SOCIETY: FREEDOM OF SPEECH AND EXTREMIST SPEECH IN AMERICA (1986); NAT HENTOFF, THE FIRST FREEDOM: THE TUMULTUOUS HISTORY OF FREE SPEECH IN AMERCIA (1988); Frank R. Strong, *Fifty Years of "Clear and Present Danger": From Schenck to Brandenburg-And Beyond*, 1969 SUP. CT. REV. 41.

(2) *Applying Brandenburg.* The Court applied *Brandenburg* in *Hess v. Indiana*, 414 U.S. 105, 105 (1973), in which it overturned the conviction of a student for disorderly conduct during an antiwar demonstration. "The events leading to Hess' conviction began with an antiwar demonstration on the campus of Indiana University. In the course of the demonstration, approximately 100 to 150 of the demonstrators moved onto a public street and blocked the passage of vehicles. When the demonstrators did not respond to verbal directions from the sheriff to clear the street, the sheriff and his deputies began walking up the street, and the demonstrators in their path moved to the curbs on either side, joining a large number of spectators who had gathered. Hess was standing off the street as the sheriff passed him. The sheriff heard Hess utter the word 'fuck' in what he later described as a loud voice and immediately arrested him on the disorderly conduct charge. It was later stipulated that what appellant had said was 'We'll take the fucking street later,' or 'We'll take the fucking street again.' Two witnesses who were in the immediate vicinity testified, apparently without contradiction, that they heard Hess' words and witnessed his arrest. They indicated that Hess did not appear to be exhorting the crowd to go back into the street, that he was facing the crowd and not the street when he uttered the statement, that his

statement did not appear to be addressed to any particular person or group, and that his tone, although loud, was no louder than that of the other people in the area."

In a per curiam opinion, the Court took issue with the state court's characterization of the appellant's speech as both intended and likely to incite lawless action. The Court contended that the appellant's statement was not addressed to anyone or any group in particular, nor was it said in a voice markedly louder than the clamor of appellant's immediate surroundings. "[At] best, [appellant's] statement could be taken as counsel for present moderation; at worst, it amounted to nothing more than advocacy of illegal action at some indefinite future time." The appellant was not "advocating, in the normal sense, any action." There was no evidence that the words were "intended to produce, and likely to produce, imminent disorder." Justice Rehnquist wrote a dissent, in which he was joined by Chief Justice Burger and Justice Blackmun.

(3) *Threatened Retaliation Against Boycott Violators.* *Brandenburg's* protective free speech standard was reaffirmed by the Court in *N.A.A.C.P. v. Claiborne Hardware Co.*, 458 U.S. 886 (1982), where the Court unanimously overturned an award of damages by the Mississippi Supreme Court against the N.A.A.C.P. and a group of individuals for organizing and participating in a boycott by black citizens against white merchants to achieve civil rights goals. An important issue in the case was whether remarks contained in a speech by Charles Evers, one of the leaders of the boycott, could justify an award of damages against him and the N.A.A.C.P. The Court in *Claiborne* seemed to focus on whether violence in fact occurred after speech in determining whether the *Brandenburg* test was met. Justice Rehnquist concurred in the result and Justice Marshall did not participate. The *Claiborne Hardware* case is at § 12.05.

(4) *Clear and present danger test.* The Court clearly shunned the "clear and present danger" test in *Brandenburg* and has rarely invoked it since. The test may have survived in the area of threats to the administration of justice, where the Court has invalidated attempts to restrain, or punish, comments about judicial proceedings. *See Wood v. Georgia*, 370 U.S. 375 (1962), *Nebraska Press Ass'n. v. Stuart*, 427 U.S. 539 (1976), *infra* § 13.02, and the cases discussed therein. In *Landmark Communications v. Virginia*, 435 U.S. 829 (1978), the Court eschewed the test in reversing the conviction of a newspaper publisher for printing reports of a quasi-judicial proceeding. Moreover, the Court criticized the Virginia Supreme Court's broad interpretation of the test. (*See Richmond Newspaper, Inc. v. Virginia, infra* § 13.03.)

(5) *"Propaganda" labels.* In *Meese v. Keene*, 481 U.S. 465 (1987), the Court upheld the constitutionality of a provision of the Foreign Agents Registration Act of 1938 that required agents of foreign countries to follow certain procedures in the dissemination of material the statute defined as " 'political propaganda.' " The material must be labeled as having been " 'prepared, edited, issued or circulated' " by the agent of the foreign government. The label also advises the recipient that the agent has filed dissemination reports with the Department of Justice. The statute was challenged by a member of the California State Senate who wanted to exhibit three Canadian motion pictures, dealing with nuclear war and acid rain, that had been disseminated by the National Film Board of Canada, a registered agent of a foreign government. Under the Act, the films had been identified as " 'foreign propaganda.' "

Writing for a 5-3 majority, Justice Stevens held that the designation " 'political propaganda' " in the statute "has no pejorative connotation" and that the disclosures required by Congress place "no burden on protected expression." The additional disclosures "would better enable the public to evaluate the import of the propaganda. . . . The statute does not prohibit appellee from advising his audience that the films have not been officially censured in any way." Over the nearly forty-year history of the statutory designation, no evidence has come forth that the law has had an adverse impact on the distribution of foreign advocacy materials.

Justice Blackmun dissented, joined by Justices Brennan and Marshall. Film distributors may not want to be "associated with materials officially classified as propaganda." This designation impairs credibility.

McINTYRE v. OHIO ELECTIONS COMMISSION, 514 U.S. 334 (1995). In *McIntyre*, the Court held that § 3599.09(A) of the Ohio Code, prohibiting the distribution of anonymous campaign literature, violated the First Amendment. McIntyre distributed leaflets at a public meeting at an Ohio middle school opposing an impending referendum on a proposed school tax levy. Some of the pamphlets identified her as the author, while others professed to express the views of "CONCERNED PARENTS AND TAX PAYERS." Her activities violated the requirement imposed by the Ohio law that campaign literature contain the name and address of the person distributing it. The Ohio Supreme Court upheld the fine assessed on McIntyre by the Ohio Election Commission. The leaflets at issue did not contain false, misleading, or libelous statements.

Writing for a 7-2 majority, Justice Stevens invalidated the statute. "The decision in favor of anonymity may be motivated by fear of economic or official retaliation, by concern about social ostracism, or merely by a desire to preserve as much of one's privacy as possible. Whatever the motivation may be, at least in the field of literary endeavor, the interest in having anonymous works enter the marketplace of ideas unquestionably outweighs any public interest in requiring disclosure as a condition of entry." Justice Stevens likened anonymous handbills to such democratic mainstays as the Federalist Papers, which were published under pseudonyms, and the secret ballot.

Talley v. California, 362 U.S. 60 (1960), invalidated a city ordinance prohibiting the distribution of anonymous handbills advocating an economic boycott.

As the Ohio statute was a content-based limitation on political "pure speech," it had to be "narrowly tailored to serve an overriding state interest." Ohio argued that its important and legitimate state interest in preventing fraudulent and libelous statements and its interest in providing the electorate with relevant information were sufficiently compelling to justify the prohibition of anonymous handbills. Rejecting the interest in providing the electorate with information, the "identity of the speaker is no different from other components of the document's content that the author is free to include or exclude." While the author's identity is helpful to the reader in evaluating the speaker's message, the reader can take a document's anonymity into account in deciding "what is 'responsible,' what is valuable, and what is truth." In any event, for a "handbill written by a private citizen who is not known to the recipient, the name and address of the author adds little, if anything, to the reader's ability to evaluate the document's message."

The Court did accept Ohio's asserted interest in preventing election fraud because electoral misrepresentations "may have serious adverse consequences for the public at large." However, this interest is insufficient to justify the statute's "extremely broad prohibition" because other portions of the Ohio Election Code include separate "detailed and specific prohibitions against making or disseminating false statements during political campaigns." Moreover, the regulation at issue "encompasses documents that are not even arguably false or misleading. It applies not only to the activities of candidates and their organized supporters, but also to individuals acting independently and using only their own modest resources." Those publishing false electoral information can negate any enforcement utility that an anonymity ban may have by simply using false names. "[A] State's enforcement interest might justify a more limited identification requirement."

In contrast to the Ohio statute, the disclosure requirement upheld in *Buckley v. Valeo*, 424 U.S. 1 (1976), *infra* § 15.02, required that those expending money in support of a political candidate, beyond a certain threshold level, report the amount and use of such funds to the Federal Election Commission. *Buckley* permitted a narrowly drawn disclosure requirement to promote powerful state interests in avoiding corruption including contributions "as a quid pro quo for special treatment." Moreover, the Federal Election Campaign Act of 1971 upheld in *Buckley* may not be constitutional in all applications.

Anonymous pamphleteering has "an honorable tradition of advocacy and dissent. Anonymity is a shield from the tyranny of the majority." While anonymity may sometimes protect fraudulent conduct, "in general, our society accords greater weight to the value of free speech than to the dangers of its misuse."

Concurring, Justice Ginsburg stated that the Ohio statute applied even to an individual leafletter operating in her local community. Justice Ginsburg stressed that the majority opinion did not forbid a state from imposing disclosure requirements in "other, larger circumstances."

Justice Thomas concurred in the judgment. "Instead of asking whether 'an honorable tradition' of anonymous speech has existed throughout American history, or what the 'value' of anonymous speech might be, [the Court] should determine whether the phrase 'freedom of speech, or of the press,' as originally understood, protected anonymous political leafletting."

The anonymous publication of the Federalist Papers during the ratification of the Constitution was only one example indicating that the Framers opposed government disclosure requirements. "The practice of publishing one's thoughts anonymously or under pseudonym was so widespread that only two major Federalist or Anti-Federalist pieces appear to have been signed by their true authors." The practice of anonymous publication extended beyond the Ratification to the first federal elections, in which "anonymous political pamphlets and newspaper articles remained the favorite medium for expressing views on candidates" and also on issues.

In a dissent joined by Chief Justice Rehnquist, Justice Scalia attacked the majority for relying on "a hitherto unknown right-to-be-unknown while engaging in electoral politics." For Justice Scalia, "the Constitution bears its original meaning and is unchanging. Under that view, 'on every question of construction, [we should] carry ourselves back to the time when the Constitution was adopted; recollect the spirit manifested in the debates; and instead of trying [to find] what meaning may be squeezed out of the text, or invented against it, conform to the probable one in which it was passed.'" While anonymous electioneering was common when the Bill of Rights and the Fourteenth Amendment were adopted, little historical evidence exists as to whether the Framers of those documents regarded anonymous electioneering to be a constitutional right. When a practice cannot clearly be attributed to constitutional principles, the Court must exercise its judgment.

"A governmental practice that has become general throughout the United States, and particularly one that has the validation of long, accepted usage, bears a strong presumption of constitutionality." Justice Scalia noted that every state except California has a law similar to the Ohio statute struck down by the majority, and that 24 states had such laws since just after World War I. "Such a universal and long established American legislative practice must be given precedence, I think, over historical and academic speculation regarding a restriction that assuredly does not go to the heart of free speech."[2]

The "right to anonymity" is not "such a prominent value in our constitutional system that even protection of the electoral process" can "be purchased at its expense," particularly as the record contains no "threats, harassment, or reprisals."

Justice Scalia noted that the majority and Justice Ginsburg's concurrence state that disclosure laws may be constitutional in some instances. "It may take decades to work out the shape of this newly expanded right-to-speak-incognito." He cited several examples of activities which are now arguably subject to debate. "Must a parade permit, for example, be issued to a group that refuses to provide its identity, or that agrees to do so only under assurance that the identity will not be made public? Must a municipally owned theater that is leased for private productions book anonymously sponsored presentations? Must a governmental periodical that has a 'letters to the editor' column disavow the policy that most newspapers have against the publication of anonymous letters?"

NOTE

Ideological Message on License Plate. In *Wooley v. Maynard*, 430 U.S. 705 (1977), the Court ruled that two Jehovah's Witnesses could not constitutionally be subject to criminal sanctions for having covered over a license plate motto " 'Live Free or Die' " which they found repugnant to their religious and moral beliefs. Skirting the religious nature of appellee's objection, the Court based its decision on broad freedom of expression grounds. "We begin with the proposition that the right of freedom of thought protected by the First Amendment against state action includes both the right to speak freely and the right to refrain from speaking at all. *See Board of Education v. Barnette*, 319 U.S. 624 (1943). A system which secures the right to proselytize religious, political, and ideological causes must also guarantee the concomitant right to decline to foster such concepts. The right to speak and the right to refrain from speaking are complementary components of the broader concept of 'individual freedom of mind.' "

The *Barnette* Court stuck down "a state statute which required public school students to participate in daily public ceremonies by honoring the flag both with words and traditional salute gestures. . . . Compelling the affirmative act of a flag salute involved a more serious infringement upon personal liberties than the passive act of carrying the state motto on a license plate, but the difference is essentially one of degree. Here, as in *Barnette*, we are faced with a state measure which forces an individual, as part of his daily life — indeed constantly while his automobile is in public view — to be an instrument for fostering public adherence to an ideological point of view he finds unacceptable."

Justice Rehnquist dissented, joined by Justice Blackmun. He argued that people would not assume that a license plate conveyed the view of the person displaying it. There was, moreover, nothing to stop appellees from, for example, displaying a bumper sticker emphatically indicating their dissent from the sentiments reflected on their license tags.

---

[2] "[P]ostadoption tradition formed after the adoption of the Constitution cannot alter the core meaning of a constitutional guarantee."

§ 12.03 MEMBERSHIP IN POLITICAL ORGANIZATIONS AS A BASIS FOR GOVERNMENT SANCTIONS

KEYISHIAN v. BOARD OF REGENTS, 385 U.S. 589 (1967). In *Keyishian*, the Court held overbroad and vague a New York plan to prevent the appointment or retention of "subversive" persons in state employment. The teachers, faculty members of the State University of New York at Buffalo, had been told to sign a statement saying that they were not Communists and that if they ever had been, they had informed the President of the University accordingly. If they refused to sign, they would be dismissed. The whole plan was governed by the Feinberg Law, which charged the State Board of Regents with drawing up a list of "subversive" organizations. Membership in such organizations would be prima facie evidence of disqualification from employment in public schools.

Writing for a narrow majority, Justice Brennan found the significant parts of both statutes unconstitutional. The term "seditious," as used in the Education Law, was unconstitutionally vague: "The teacher cannot know the extent, if any, to which a 'seditious' utterance must transcend mere statements about abstract doctrine, the extent to which it must be intended to and tend to indoctrinate or incite to action in furtherance of the defined doctrine." Several provisions of the Civil Service Act were also unconstitutionally vague.

Academic freedom was "of transcendent value." The First Amendment did not "tolerate laws that cast a pall of orthodoxy over the classroom." Where government regulation abridged freedom of speech in places where that freedom was absolutely central, regulations had to be drawn with narrow specificity. "New York's complicated and intricate scheme plainly violates [the applicable] standard. [T]he danger of [a] chilling effect upon the exercise of vital First Amendment rights must be guarded against by sensitive tools which clearly inform teachers what is being proscribed."

The Court held that "[m]ere knowing membership without a specific intent to further the unlawful aims of an organization, [was] not a constitutionally adequate basis for exclusion from such positions as those held by appellants." In the light of these new standards, the statutes were overbroad as they penalized both forms of membership that could legitimately be proscribed and forms that could not.

Justice Clark dissented, joined by Justices Harlan, Stewart, and White: "[T]he majority has by its broadside swept away one of our most precious rights, namely, the right of self-preservation."

NOTES

(1) *Overbreadth*. The attack on the Feinberg Law in *Keyishian* was based on the doctrine of "overbreadth." The Court's use of that technique to invalidate the law on its face, rather than as applied, is perhaps one reason why it is difficult to define precisely the Court's reasons for invalidity. For further discussion of the "overbreadth" doctrine in First Amendment cases, see Note, *The First Amendment Overbreadth Doctrine*, 83 HARV. L. REV. 844 (1970). See the discussion of the doctrine in *Broadrick v. Oklahoma*, 413 U.S. 601 (1973) (§ 12.06[2]). *See also* the use of overbreadth in *United States v. Robel* and *Aptheker v. Secretary of State*, discussed in below in Note 2; *Erznoznik v. City of Jacksonville*, 422 U.S. 205 (1975).

(2) *Vagueness*. The *Keyishian* majority opinion demonstrated another technique for the invalidation of statutes — "void for vagueness" — which has special significance in First Amendment cases, although it is applied in other areas as well. A statute is "void for vagueness" if it proscribes certain activity in terms that are so vague that a person

does not have the requisite notice that he or she is violating its provisions. It is, therefore, a due process concept. Overbreadth, on the other hand, deals with the problem where the statute covers some activities that are constitutionally protected, and some that are not. An overbroad statute may not be vague. It may apply, as in *Robel* and *Aptheker*, specifically to membership in the Communist Party, but be overbroad because it covers both active and inactive membership. In the free speech area, it is likely that a vague statute will also be overbroad. An overbroad statute will not necessarily be vague, but sometimes is, as in *Keyishian. See* Anthony Amsterdam, *The Void-for-Vagueness Doctrine in the Supreme Court*, 109 U. PA. L. REV. 67 (1960).

(3) *Defense Plants.* Similarly, in *United States v. Robel*, 389 U.S. 258 (1967), the Court again used overbreadth to invalidate a statutory prohibition against a member of a Communist-action organization being employed in a defense plant, as the prohibition violated the First Amendment's right of association. "It is precisely because that statute sweeps indiscriminately across all types of association with Communist-action groups, without regard to the quality and degree of membership, that it runs afoul of the First Amendment." Chief Justice Warren's majority (6-2) opinion emphasized that "nothing we hold today should be read to deny Congress the power under narrowly drawn legislation to keep from sensitive positions in defense facilities those who would use their positions to disrupt the Nation's production facilities." Justice Brennan's concurring opinion suggested that, under a proper statutory delegation of authority to the Secretary of Defense, Congress could exclude any Communist Party member from employment in certain sensitive defense facilities.

(4) *Oath Denying Membership in the Communist Party.* In light of the *Keyishian* case, can a public employer require an employee, as a condition of employment, to sign an oath swearing that the employee is not, and will not become, a member of the Communist Party or any other organization which has, as one of its purposes, the violent overthrow of the government? Could an employee who signed such an oath be dismissed for membership in such an organization, if it should be shown that the employee knew of the unlawful objectives? Must there be active membership and intent to bring about the unlawful objective? *See Elfbrandt v. Russell*, 384 U.S. 11 (1966) ("law which applies to membership without the 'specific intent' to further the illegal aims of the organization infringes unnecessarily on protected freedoms"). *See also Baggett v. Bullitt*, 377 U.S. 360 (1964).

(5) *Oath Opposing Violent Overthrow.* What about an oath "to support the Constitution of the United States" or "to oppose the overthrow of the government of the United States by force, violence, or any illegal or unconstitutional method?" *See Cole v. Richardson*, 405 U.S. 676 (1972), and *Knight v. Board of Regents*, 269 F. Supp. 339 (S.D.N.Y. 1967), *aff'd, per curiam*, 390 U.S. 36 (1968) (oaths with similar language upheld in both cases).

(6) In *Dawson v. Delaware*, 503 U.S. 159 (1992), the Supreme Court denied the admissibility, at a capital sentencing hearing, of evidence of defendant's membership in the Aryan Brotherhood, "because the evidence proved nothing more than Dawson's abstract beliefs." In an 8-1 decision, the Court vacated a capital sentence imposed because a Delaware trial court improperly admitted, at the sentencing hearing, a stipulation noting Dawson's membership in the Aryan Brotherhood which the trial court described as a "white racist prison gang." Because the prosecution failed to present any evidence that Dawson's membership in the organization indicated anything more than abstract beliefs, the stipulation was not relevant evidence as to Dawson's character. Admission of the evidence, therefore, violated Dawson's right of association. In dissent, Justice Thomas characterized the stipulation as merely relevant bad character evidence, admissible to rebut the mitigating character evidence submitted by the defense in the capital sentencing proceedings.

ILLINOIS EX REL. MADIGAN v. TELEMARKETING ASS'N, 538 U.S. 600 (2003). In *Madigan*, the Court concluded that the First Amendment does not protect for-profit organizations from fraudulent misrepresentations that they make concerning the percentage of proceeds that will go to charity. VietNow is a nonprofit organization working to "advance the welfare of Vietnam veterans." VietNow contracted a professional fund-raiser, "Telemarketers," to collect donations. As a part of the contract, Telemarketers would retain 85 percent of the proceeds, with 15 percent going to VietNow. The Attorney General of Illinois filed a complaint in state court for fraud and breach of fiduciary duty, alleging that Telemarketers misrepresented the amount of funds collected that would go to VietNow. The trial court dismissed the complaint on First Amendment grounds.

Writing for a unanimous Court, Justice Ginsburg reversed. While a mere failure to disclose to potential donors the percentage of proceeds that will go directly to the charity does not establish fraud, "when nondisclosure is accompanied by intentionally misleading statements designed to deceive the listener, the *First Amendment* leaves room for a fraud claim." In response to a question concerning the percentage of contributions that would be used for fundraising expenses, one affiant " 'was told 90% or more goes to the vets.' Another affiant stated she was told her donation would not be used for 'labor expenses' because 'all members were volunteers.' " While the First Amendment protects charitable solicitation, this protection does not extend to fraud. An " 'intentional lie' is 'no essential part of any exposition of ideas.' " Similar to "other forms of public deception, fraudulent charitable solicitation is unprotected speech."

Schaumburg v. Citizens for a Better Env't, 444 U.S. 620 (1980), invalidated on overbreadth grounds an ordinance requiring charitable organizations to use at least 75 percent of contributions directly for the " 'charitable purpose of the organization.' " *Sec'y of State of Md. v. Joseph H. Munson Co.*, 467 U.S. 947 (1984), invalidated a law with the same 25 percent limit except " 'where [it] would effectively prevent the charitable organization from raising contributions.' " *Riley v. Nat'l Fed'n of Blind of N.C., Inc.*, 487 U.S. 781 (1988), struck down a law establishing a rebuttable presumption of unreasonableness if charities paid fundraising fees greater than 35 percent of the donations. The law at issue in *Riley* also required the fundraisers to inform potential donors the percentage of donations that they had actually turned over to charity during the previous year. This " 'unduly burdensome' prophylactic rule," incorrectly assumed that charities derived no benefit from the information disseminated through the solicitation process itself.

In the present case, the complaint and affidavits relate not only what Telemarketers failed to disclose, but what they " 'misleadingly represented.' " Interpreting all evidence in favor of the Attorney General, the First Amendment does not protect such misrepresentations.

To prove fraud, Illinois requires the plaintiff to show by clear and convincing evidence that the defendant "made a false representation of a material fact knowing that the representation was false," and that the defendant "made the representation with the intent to mislead the listener, and succeeded in doing so." As a further protection "responsive to *First Amendment* concerns, an appellate court could independently review the trial court's findings."

Justice Scalia wrote a concurring opinion joined by Justice Thomas. *Riley* and *Munson* teach that the large differences in legitimate charitable fundraising expenses render impossible establishing "a maximum percentage that is reasonable" for those expenses. The judgment in this case, however, "rests upon a 'solid core' of misrepresentations that go well beyond" the issue of the percentage of funds committed to charitable purposes.

§ 12.04 COMPULSORY DISCLOSURE OF POLITICAL AFFILIATIONS OR MEMBERSHIP

COMMUNIST PARTY OF THE UNITED STATES v. SUBVERSIVE ACTIVITIES CONTROL BOARD, 367 U.S. 1 (1961). In this case, the Court, after ten years of litigation, narrowly upheld an SACB order that the Communist Party register as a "Communist-Action organization." Under terms of the Subversive Activities Control Act, a "Communist-Action organization," included any organization "substantially directed, dominated, or controlled by the foreign government or foreign organization controlling the world Communist movement" and which operated primarily to advance the objectives of the movement. At the time of registration, the organization was compelled to submit, *inter alia*, a list of the names of all of its members. Once ordered by the board to register, the organization and its members became subject to a variety of special regulations and restrictions, including the requirement that items sent through the mails by the organization be stamped as being disseminated by "'a Communist organization.'" Once registered, members of such organizations suffered a number of deprivations. For example, they could not hold public non-elective office, or otherwise be employed by the government. Moreover, they could not work in defense plants, become officers or employees of unions, or apply for passports.

Writing for the majority, Justice Frankfurter narrowed the issues presented to the registration requirement itself. He refused to consider any of the penalties resulting from registration. As these penalties had not yet been imposed, they were not ripe for adjudication. "The claim that the registration order created a present harm by deterring membership and financial support was also considered too hypothetical and involved only abstract 'assertions of possible future injury.'"

Justice Frankfurter acknowledged that "a governmental regulation which requires registration as a condition upon the exercise of speech may in some circumstances affront the constitutional guarantee of free expression." However, "[t]he present statute does not, of course, attach the registration requirement to the incident of speech, but to the incidents of foreign domination and of operation to advance the objectives of the world Communist movement-operation which, the Board has found here, includes extensive, long-continuing organizational, as well as 'speech' activity." The Court acknowledged that the compulsory disclosure of the names of members of organizations may in certain instances infringe constitutionally protected rights of association.

After noting that the Subversive Activities Control Act was the product of extensive legislative investigation and findings, Justice Frankfurter concluded that, in this instance, judicial deference to the legislature was appropriate. "[W]here the problems of accommodating the exigencies of self-preservation and the values of liberty are as complex and intricate as they are in the situation described in the findings of § 2 of the Subversive Activities Control Act when existing government is menaced by a world-wide integrated movement which employs every combination of possible means . . . to destroy the government itself — the legislative judgment as to how that threat may best be met consistently with the safeguarding of personal freedom is not to be set aside merely because the judgment of judges would, in the first instance, have chosen other methods."

Justice Frankfurter acknowledged that, in a highly charged political atmosphere, the listing of individuals as Communists might entail consequences for freedom of speech. But as against this danger, there had to be weighed the overriding national interest.

Resisting the charge that the Court's action would empower Congress to "impose similar requirements upon any group which pursues unpopular political ideology,"

Justice Frankfurter opined: "The Subversive Activities Control Act applies only to *foreign-dominated* organizations which work primarily to advance the objectives of a world movement controlled by the government of a *foreign* country. It applies only to organizations directed, dominated, or controlled by a particular foreign country, the leader of a movement which, Congress has found, is 'in its origins, its development, and its present practice, . . . a world-wide revolutionary movement whose purpose it is, by treachery, deceit, infiltration into other groups . . ., espionage, sabotage, terrorism, and any other means deemed necessary, to establish a Communist totalitarian dictatorship in the countries throughout the world through the medium of a world-wide Communist Organization.' This is the full purported reach of the statute, and its fullest effect."

Chief Justice Warren and Justices Black, Douglas, and Brennan each wrote dissenting opinions, but only Justice Black found the Act violative of the First Amendment. In the only case during the "Cold War" era in which Justices Black and Douglas parted company on a First Amendment issue, Justice Douglas opined: "When an organization is used by a foreign power to make advances here, questions of security are raised beyond the ken of disputations and debate between the people resident here. . . . [T]he bare requirement that the Communist Party register and disclose the names of its officers and directors is in line with the most exacting adjudications touching first amendment activities."

Justice Black's dissent began, "I do not believe that it can be too often repeated that the freedoms of speech, press, petition and assembly guaranteed by the First Amendment must be accorded to the ideas we hate or sooner or later they will be denied to the ideas we cherish." He criticized the majority's refusal to consider as not ripe for adjudication the constitutionality of the burdens that would affect the Party immediately after registration. These burdens amounted to the effective "outlawry" of the organization.

Justice Black continued: "Talk about the desirability of revolutions has a long and honorable history, not only in other parts of the world, but also in our own country." If the talk is "used at the wrong time and for the wrong purpose," the remedy must be "education and contrary argument."

He analogized the Subversive Activities Control Act to an earlier episode in American history, when Congress passed the Alien and Sedition Acts, but declined to go further in suppressing dissent: "All the fervor and all the eloquence and all the emotionalism and all the prejudice and all the parades of horrors about letting the people hear arguments for themselves were not sufficient in 1798 to persuade the members of Congress to pass a law which would directly and unequivocally outlaw the party of Jefferson, at which the law was undoubtedly aimed. The same arguments were made then about the 'Jacobins,' meaning the Jeffersonians, with regard to their alleged subservience to France, that are made today about the Communists with regard to their subservience to Russia. The Jacobins were 'trained, officered, regimented and formed to subordination, in a manner that our militia have never yet equalled'; and 'it is as certain as any future event can be, that they [the Jeffersonians] will take arms against the laws as soon as they dare.' "

NOTES

(1) *Self-incrimination.* Although the Registration Order was upheld in the above case, subsequent attempts to enforce the Subversive Activities Control Act encountered constitutional obstacles which Justice Frankfurter's majority opinion had declined to consider. The Court of Appeals for the District of Columbia reversed, on self-incrimination grounds, the Party's conviction for failing to register. *Communist Party v. United States*, 331 F.2d 807 (D.C. Cir. 1963). An order of the Subversive Activities Control Board directing two Party members to register was held to violate the

member's Fifth Amendment privilege. *Albertson v. Subversive Activities Control Bd.*, 382 U.S. 70 (1965) (unanimous opinion). For further use of the protection against self-incrimination in this context, see Note (3), *infra* after *Gibson v. Florida Legislative Investigation Committee.*

(2) In *Barenblatt v. United States*, 360 U.S. 109 (1959), the Court upheld a conviction for contempt of Congress which arose out of defendant's refusal to answer questions asked of him by a Subcommittee of the House Committee on Un-American activities.[3]

Expressly declining to rely on the Fifth Amendment, the defendant justified his refusal to answer questions as to his past or present affiliation with the Communist Party on the First Amendment. As Barenblatt was an academic, his First Amendment objections prominently featured considerations of academic freedom. Writing for the five-to-four majority, Justice Harlan rejected this claim: "In the last analysis this power rests on the right of self preservation, 'the ultimate value of any society,' [*Dennis*]."

Justice Black, joined by Chief Justice Warren and Justice Douglas, dissented. Justice Black reiterated his objections to the use of the balancing test to uphold laws directly abridging First Amendment freedoms.

GIBSON v. FLORIDA LEGISLATIVE INVESTIGATION COMM., 372 U.S. 539 (1963). In *Gibson*, the Court considered the legitimacy of a legislative inquiry into alleged Communist Party affiliation of members of the Miami branch of the National Association for the Advancement of Colored People (N.A.A.C.P.). The Court concluded that the legislative committee had not established an adequate nexus between the groups to allow the infringement of the associational rights of the N.A.A.C.P.

The Florida's Legislative Investigation Committee ordered the defendant, then president of the Miami branch of the N.A.A.C.P., to appear before it and to bring the group's records identifying members and contributors. Defendant appeared before the Committee but refused to disclose the records. While defendant was the custodian of such records, he stated that he had not brought them and would not make them available in the future. He did offer to answer questions based on his personal knowledge. The Committee showed defendant fourteen photographs of persons previously associated with the Communist party; however, he was not able to link any of them to the N.A.A.C.P. A state tribunal found defendant in contempt of the committee and sentenced him to six months in prison and a $1,200 fine, or if the fine could not be paid, an additional six months in prison. The Florida Supreme Court affirmed.

Justice Goldberg wrote for the Court. "[I]t is an essential prerequisite to the validity of an investigation which intrudes into the area of constitutionally protected rights of speech, press, association and petition that the State convincingly show a substantial relation between the information sought and a subject of overriding and compelling state interest." Indeed, there was no evidence or indication that the Miami branch of the N.A.A.C.P. was itself or was in any way tied to a subversive group. Moreover, there was no indication that the Communist party influenced or dominated the N.A.A.C.P.

---

[3] The Court noted that the House Un-American Activities Committee "was principally a consequence of concern over the activities of the German-American Bund, whose members were suspected of allegiance to Hitler Germany, and of the Communist Party, supposed by many to be under the domination of the Soviet Union." From its creation in 1938, "the Committee has devoted a major part of its energies to the investigation of Communist activities. More particularly, in 1947 the Committee announced a wide-range program in this field, pursuant to which during the years 1948 to 1952 it conducted diverse inquiries into such alleged activities as espionage; efforts to learn atom bomb secrets; infiltration into labor, farmer, veteran, professional, youth, and motion picture groups; and in addition held a number of hearings on various legislative proposals to curb Communist activities."

Rather, the record established that the group has been against Communist participation and has excluded Communists from membership.

Other cases requiring the production of Communist Party membership information due to a compelling state interest were not dispositive when the inquiry concerns "an admittedly lawful organization." Moreover, "the record in this case is insufficient to show a substantial connection between the Miami branch of the N.A.A.C.P. and Communist *activities* which the respondent Committee itself concedes is an essential prerequisite to demonstrating the immediate, substantial, and subordinating state interest necessary to sustain its right of inquiry into the membership lists of the association."

An investigator for the Committee named fourteen individuals who "either were or had been Communists or members of Communist 'front' or 'affiliated' organizations. His description of their connection with the association was simply that 'each of them has been a member of and/or participated in the meetings and other affairs of the N.A.A.C.P. in Dade County, Florida.'" The fourteen named individuals could have simply attended one or two public meetings of the N.A.A.C.P. — perhaps many years prior to the investigation at issue.

"The respondent Committee has laid no adequate foundation for its direct demands upon the officers and records of a wholly legitimate organization for disclosure of its membership; the Committee has neither demonstrated nor pointed out any threat to the State by virtue of the existence of the N.A.A.C.P. or the pursuit of its activities or minimal associational ties of the 14 asserted Communists. The strong associational interest in maintaining the privacy of membership lists of groups engaged in the constitutionally protected free trade in ideas and beliefs may not be substantially infringed upon such a slender showing as here made by the respondent."

Justice Black argued for reversal due to "a direct abridgment of the right of association of the National Association for the Advancement of Colored People and its members." However, as the Court assumed in this case that First Amendment freedoms had not been directly violated, Justice Black concurred in the opinion.

Justice Douglas also concurred. "Government can interfere only when belief, thought, or expression moves into the realm of action that is inimical to society."

Justice Harlan dissented, joined by Justices Clark, Stewart, and White. Essential facts overlooked by the Court included the Committee's information that fourteen past or present residents of Dade County, who at some point had been "members of the Communist Party or connected organizations, were or had been members or had 'participated in meetings and other affairs' of this local branch of the N.A.A.C.P." Moreover, upon being shown photographs of these fourteen individuals, defendant was unable to provide any information and claimed no knowledge of the individuals. The Committee requested the defendant to utilize the membership records to aid his memory, and earlier the Committee made clear that it did not wish to look at the records itself. Justice Harlan could not identify any infringement of associational rights. "In effect what we are asked to hold here is that the petitioner had a constitutional right to give only partial or inaccurate testimony, and that indeed seems to me the true effect of the Court's holding today."

Justice White, dissenting separately, argued that the Court's decision "insulate[s] from effective legislative inquiry and preventive legislation the time-proven skills of the Communist Party in subverting and eventually controlling legitimate organizations. Until such group, chosen as an object of Communist Party action, has been effectively reduced to vassalage, legislative bodies may seek no information from the organization under attack by duty-bound Communists. When the job has been done and the legislative committee can prove it, it then has the hollow privilege of recording another victory for the Communist Party."

NOTES

(1) *Narrowing Investigatory Authority.* Two cases involving the N.A.A.C.P., decided during the period when the Court was dealing with the "subversion" cases, established the principle that the First Amendment provides some protection against the compulsory disclosure of an organization's membership lists. *See N.A.A.C.P. v. Alabama,* 357 U.S. 449 (1958), and *Bates v. Little Rock,* 361 U.S. 516 (1960). *See also Shelton v. Tucker,* 364 U.S. 479 (1960) (invalidating an Arkansas statute requiring every schoolteacher to disclose the name of every organization to which the teacher had belonged for a five-year period).

These cases, however, did not act as an effective barrier against governmental power to compel disclosure about political affiliation and belief when the disclosure involved Communist or "subversive" organizations, as the *S.A.C.B.* and *Barenblatt* cases make clear. Nevertheless, the same trends which were leading toward the result in *Keyishian* (limiting the power of government to penalize membership in such organizations) were also operating in the area of compulsory disclosures of organizational membership and activities.

In *Gibson,* it was a question of establishing a "nexus" between Communist activities and the branch of the N.A.A.C.P. Other cases insisted that the witness be informed of the subject of the inquiry and the pertinence of the questions to such subject. Moreover, the indictment had to identify the subject of the inquiry, and the government was required to meet the burden of proving the pertinence of the questions. These were non-constitutional cases, decided as a matter of interpreting 2 U.S.C. 192, which imposed criminal sanctions for a refusal to answer questions "pertinent to the question under inquiry." *See Watkins v. United States,* 354 U.S. 178 (1957); *Deutch v. United States,* 367 U.S. 456 (1961); *Russell v. United States,* 369 U.S. 749 (1962).

In *DeGregory v. New Hampshire,* 383 U.S. 825 (1966), the Court applied the principles of "prior cases" and concluded that the state had failed to show a compelling interest in obtaining information, in 1964, about Communist Party activities prior to 1964. Thus, by the mid-1960s the Court, by whatever route, had moved away from its position in *Barenblatt* and was far more sympathetic to individual and organizational resistance to compulsory disclosure of political activities or beliefs.

(2) *Admission to the Bar.* Another line of cases relating to a person's refusal to reveal Communist Party membership involved applicants for admission to the bar. In two cases, *Konigsberg v. California,* 366 U.S. 36 (1961), and *In re Anastaplo,* 366 U.S. 82 (1961), the Court sustained state refusals to admit bar applicants who had refused to answer questions concerning membership in the Communist Party. The majority and dissenting opinions of Justices Harlan and Black provide a stirring debate on First Amendment principles and the role of the Court.

(3) *Self-incrimination.* While the First Amendment proved to be a weak reed as a defense for the right to refuse to disclose political associations and beliefs, the privilege against self-incrimination has proved far more effective. In light of the arsenal of laws penalizing Communist Party members, their refusals to answer questions with regard to such associations were clearly protected by the privilege. The major constitutional issue arising out of the claim of the privilege during the Cold War period was whether a government employer could discharge an employee because the employee had invoked the privilege. Although the issue came to the forefront as a result of inquiries into political associations, it is obviously relevant in investigations of corruption and other conduct relating to the employee's performance of his or her duties. *See Gardner*

v. Broderick, 392 U.S. 273 (1968), and *Lefkowitz v. Cunningham*, 431 U.S. 801 (1977). *Cf. Selective Serv. Sys. v. Minn. Pub. Interest Research Group*, 468 U.S. 841 (1984). This last case rejected a self-incrimination challenge to a statute that denied federal financial aid to those who had not registered for the draft even though it forced students to choose between forgoing financial aid and admitting to the crime of late registration.

(4) *Socialist Party*. Disclosure of political associations has come before the Court in connection with campaign finance laws requiring disclosure of the names and addresses of campaign contributors and recipients of campaign disbursements. In *Buckley v. Valeo*, § 15.02, the Court, while generally upholding disclosure provisions of the federal statute, held that the First Amendment barred compulsory disclosure by a minor party which could show a "reasonable probability" that disclosures would subject identified persons to "threats, harassment, or reprisals." In *Brown v. Socialist Workers 74 Campaign Comm.*, 459 U.S. 87 (1983), involving the Ohio Campaign Expense Reporting law, the Court held that the *Buckley* test rendered the disclosure provisions of the Ohio law invalid as applied to the Socialist Workers Party. Justice Marshall wrote the majority opinion, while Justice O'Connor partially dissented, joined by Justices Rehnquist and Stevens, arguing that the Ohio statute should have been upheld as applied to recipients of disbursements. For additional discussion of *Brown*, see § 15.02, Note (5).

§ 12.05 ASSOCIATIONAL RIGHTS IN OTHER CONTEXTS

EU v. SAN FRANCISCO COUNTY DEMOCRATIC CENTRAL COMMITTEE, 489 U.S. 214 (1989). A unanimous Court invalidated sections of the California Election Code that regulated the internal workings of ballot-qualified political parties in the state, and also prohibited their governing bodies from endorsing or opposing a candidate in a partisan primary election. Writing for the Court, Justice Marshall ruled that these restrictions deprived the parties and their members of freedom of speech and association.

Section 11702 of the California Election Code forbade the "official governing bodies" of political parties from endorsing or opposing candidates in partisan primary elections.[4] A related section made it a misdemeanor for a candidate in a primary to claim such an endorsement.

Other sections of the code regulated the internal organization and composition of the parties' official governing bodies. For example, the code "dictate[d] the size and composition of the state central committees; set forth rules governing the selection and removal of committee members; fix[ed] the maximum term of office for the chair of the state central committee; require[d] that the chair rotate between residents of northern and southern California; specif[ied] the time and place of committee meetings; and limit[ed] the dues parties may impose on members."

With regard to the prohibition on primary endorsements, the Court found that this ban "directly affects speech which 'is at the core of our electoral process and of the First Amendment freedoms.'" For Justice Marshall, "California's ban on primary endorsements, however, prevents party governing bodies from stating whether a candidate adheres to the tenets of the party or whether party officials believe that the candidate is qualified for the position sought. This prohibition directly hampers the ability of a party to spread its message and hamstrings voters seeking to inform themselves about

---

[4] The Code defined a party's "official governing bodies" as its "state convention," "state central committee," and "county central committee."

the candidates and the campaign issues." Banning political speech between a political party and its members was "particularly egregious."

The restrictions on endorsements were also invalid because they violated freedom of association. "Freedom of association means not only that an individual voter has the right to associate with the political party of her choice, but also that a political party has a right to 'identify the people who constitute the association,' and to select a 'standard bearer who best represents the party's ideologies and preferences.'"

The interests advanced by the State to justify the election laws were "stable government and protecting voters from confusion and undue influence." While Justice Marshall accepted these interests as compelling, he held that California had failed to establish that the endorsement prohibition was necessary to promote them. With respect to stable government, the State claims "that its compelling interest in stable government embraces a similar interest in party stability." However, the Court rejected the notion that "'a State may enact election laws to mitigate intraparty factionalism.'" Indeed, the Court specifically stated that "[a] primary is not hostile to intraparty feuds; rather it is an ideal forum in which to resolve them." Justice Marshall also rejected California's proffered interest in avoiding voter confusion and undue influence. "While a State may regulate the flow of information between political associations and their members when necessary to prevent fraud and corruption, *see Buckley v. Valeo*, there is no evidence that California's ban on party primary endorsements serves that purpose." The endorsement prohibition burdened both the freedoms of speech and association of California's political parties, without advancing a compelling state interest.

Turning to the statutory regulations of the parties and their committees' internal workings, "[t]hese laws directly implicate the associational rights of political parties and their members." These structural restrictions burden associational rights in a number of ways. "By requiring parties to establish official governing bodies at the county level, California prevents the political parties from governing themselves with the structure they think best. And by specifying who shall be the members of the parties' official governing bodies, California interferes with the parties' choice of leaders."

Again, Justice Marshall concluded that these burdens on associational rights were not necessary to serve a compelling state interest. "A State indisputably has a compelling interest in preserving the integrity of its election process. *Rosario v. Rockefeller*, 410 U.S. 752, 761 (1973). Toward that end, a State may enact laws that interfere with a party's internal affairs when necessary to ensure that elections are fair and honest. For example, a State may impose certain eligibility requirements for voters in the general election even though they limit parties' ability to garner support and members. *See, e.g., Dunn v. Blumstein*, 405 U.S. [330, 343–344 (1972)] (residence requirement); *Oregon v. Mitchell*, 400 U.S. [112, 118 (1970)] (age minimum); *Kramer v. Union Free School Dist.*, No. 15, 395 U.S. [621, 625 (1969)] (citizenship requirement). We have also recognized that a State may impose restrictions that promote the integrity of primary elections. *See, e.g., Am. Party of Tex. v. White*, 415 U.S. [767, 779–780 (1974)] (requirement that major political parties nominate candidates through a primary and that minor parties nominate candidates through conventions); *id.*, at 785–786, (limitation on voters' participation to one primary and bar on voters both voting in a party primary and signing a petition supporting an independent candidate); *Rosario v. Rockefeller, supra* (waiting periods before voters may change party registration and participate in another party's primary); *Bullock v. Carter*, 405 U.S. [134, 145 (1972)] (reasonable filing fees as a condition of placement on the ballot). None of these restrictions, however, involved direct regulation of a party's leaders. Rather, the infringement on the associational rights of the parties and their members was the indirect consequence of laws necessary to the successful completion of a party's external responsibilities in ensuring the order and fairness of elections."

The Court held that "a State cannot substitute its judgment for that of the party as to the desirability of a particular internal party structure, any more than it can tell a party that its proposed communication to party members is unwise."

Justice Stevens filed a concurring opinion in which he repeated a criticism that Justice Blackmun had made in an earlier case concerning the Court's excessive dependence on short-hand phrases like "compelling state interest."

NOTES

(1) *Primaries.* A 1984 rule of the Republican Party of Connecticut permitted independent voters (registered voters not affiliated with any political party) to vote in Republican primaries. This rule conflicted with a Connecticut statute, enacted in 1955, that required voters in a party primary to be registered members of the party. In *Tashjian v. Republican Party of Conn.*, 479 U.S. 408 (1987), the Court (5-4) struck down the statute as an unconstitutional infringement on the First Amendment associational rights of the Republican Party. Justice Marshall's majority opinion emphasized that this was not a case where the state was taking action to prevent disruption of the parties from those not in the party structure. Here the statute prevents the parties from "taking internal steps affecting their own process for the selection for candidates."

Justices Stevens and Scalia dissented, arguing that the Qualifications Clauses empower states to determine voter qualifications here. Justice Scalia, joined by Chief Justice Rehnquist and Justice O'Connor, rejected the First Amendment associational freedom challenge.

(2) For further discussion of *EU and Tashian,* see Daniel Lowenstein, *Associational Rights of Major Political Parties: A Skeptical Inquiry,* 71 Tex. L. Rev. 1741, 1792 (1993) ("The Supreme Court displayed great restraint in its major party cases in the 1970s. In *Tashijian v. Republican Party of Conn.,* and *Eu,* it stepped backward. In those cases, it sought to force intraparty disputes into the mold of an autonomous government's interference with the freedom of association of a typical private organization. Whatever one may think of the results the Court reached, its mode of analysis detached the Court from realistic discernment of the controversies that were before it.").

(3) *Signatures for New Parties.* In *Norman v. Reed,* 502 U.S. 279 (1992), the Court (7-1) struck down an Illinois requirement that to run candidates for county office from any district, a new political party must collect 25,000 signatures from each district in the county. On the other hand, the Court upheld a requirement that a new party collect 25,000 signatures from a particular district to run candidates from that district.

Writing for the majority, Justice Souter reaffirmed that "any severe restriction" must be "narrowly drawn to advance a state interest of compelling importance."

Justice Souter also invalidated another provision which appeared to prohibit any candidates from a party established in one subdivision of the State from using the party's name in any other subdivision of the State. Essentially, the statute would preclude "the development of any political party lacking the resources to run a statewide campaign."

Justice Scalia dissented. "It is reasonable to require a purported 'party,' which presumably has policy plans for the political subdivision, to run candidates in all the districts that elect the multimember board governing the subdivision." Justice Thomas did not participate in this case.

(4) *Appearing on More than One Ballot.* In *Timmons v. Twin Cities Area New Party*, 520 U.S. 351 (1997), the Court upheld Minnesota's ban on candidates appearing on the ballot under more than one political party. Few states currently allow this practice called " 'fusion,' " which is also known as " 'cross-filing' " or " 'multiple party nomination.' "

Writing for the majority (6-3), Chief Justice Rehnquist affirmed a political party's right to choose its candidates. "The New Party remains free to endorse whom it likes, to ally itself with others, to nominate candidates for office, and to spread its message to all who will listen." However, the Court concluded that "the burdens Minnesota's fusion ban imposes on the New Party's associational rights are justified by 'correspondingly weighty' valid state interests in ballot integrity and political stability."

Justice Stevens wrote a dissenting opinion in which Justices Ginsburg and Souter joined. Justice Stevens viewed the ballot as expressive of "a standard bearer who best represents the party's ideologies and preferences." He also said that legislation that "discriminates against minor political parties cannot survive simply because it benefits the two major parties." Justice Souter wrote a separate dissent.

(5) *Petitions for Ballot Initiatives.* In *Buckley v. Am. Constitutional Law Found.*, 525 U.S. 182 (1999), the Court invalidated Colorado requirements for ballot initiatives that petition circulators be registered voters, that they wear identification nametags, and that their compensation be disclosed. Colorado's badge requirement was more onerous than Ohio's ban on anonymous speech struck down in *McIntyre v. Ohio Elections Comm'n*, § 12.02. Consequently, this requirement failed " 'exacting scrutiny.' " Justice Ginsburg also invalidated the requirement of revealing the identities of and amounts earned by paid circulators. In contrast, it upheld, under *Buckley v. Valeo*, 424 U.S. 1 (1976), § 15.02, disclosing the identities of and amounts paid by those who compensate circulators.

Justice Thomas concurred in the judgment, arguing that the Court should have applied "strict scrutiny" as the law "directly regulates core political speech." Chief Justice Rehnquist dissented. Justice O'Connor, joined by Justice Breyer, concurred with the judgment in part and dissented in part.

(6) *Blanket Primaries.* In *Cal. Democratic Party v. Jones*, 530 U.S. 567 (2000), the Court found blanket primaries violate freedom of association. Proposition 198 allowed voters in California primaries to choose candidates regardless of the party affiliation of the voter or the candidate.

Writing for the majority, Justice Scalia stressed that along with the right to associate comes "the right not to associate." A blanket primary may select a candidate whom party members did not want; it can also cause candidates to take more centrist views in order to ensure his or her position as the party candidate. Moreover, since Proposition 198 was implemented, the vote totals received by some smaller parties more than double their total membership. Neither were the interests asserted by the State compelling, nor was a blanket primary necessary to serve the State's interest. The Court did not decide the constitutionality of the open primary where a voter may only vote on one party's ballot.

Justice Kennedy concurred. Justice Stevens dissented, joined by Justice Ginsburg in his free speech analysis. The power of the State to control the election process is "a quintessential attribute of sovereignty." The Court has struck down statutory limitations on who can vote, but never a statute enabling "additional citizens to participate" in the voting process.

(7) *Semi-closed Primaries.* In *Clingman v. Beaver*, 544 U.S. 581 (2005), the Court upheld an Oklahoma semi-closed primary election system that allows voters registered

to a particular political party to vote only in that party's primary election. The Libertarian Party of Oklahoma (LPO) wanted to open its primary to all registered voters. While the state opened the LPO's primary to independents, it would not allow voters who were registered with other parties to vote in the LPO's primary. Writing for the majority, Justice Thomas stated that "the Constitution grants States 'broad power to prescribe the "Time, Places and Manner of holding Elections for Senators and Representatives." ' " In this case, voters can easily switch their party registration to the LPO or change to independent status by filling out a form at the county election board. However, the individuals who brought this lawsuit have not taken this simple step, indicating that they "do not want to associate with the LPO" formally. "When a state electoral provision places no heavy burden on associational rights, 'a State's important regulatory interests will usually be enough to justify reasonable, nondiscriminatory restrictions.' " Here, Oklahoma's primary system ensures that primary elections reflect the views of party members; helps parties' "electioneering and party-building efforts"; and prevents individuals and other parties from manipulating the outcome of the parties' primaries by, for example, switching blocs of voters in an organized way.

Justice O'Connor, joined in part by Justice Breyer, concurred in part and concurred in the judgment. Had the issue been timely raised, the Court should have considered the "*cumulative* burdens" of a state's election laws. A State's justifications for its regulations would receive greater scrutiny if that State's laws "imposed a weighty or discriminatory restriction on voters' ability to participate in" a party's primary. Justice Stevens dissented, joined by Justice Ginsburg and in part by Justice Souter. Justice Stevens argued that Oklahoma "denies a party the right to invite willing voters to participate in its primary elections." The case implicates not only the right of voters to associate, but also their right to vote. With the Democrats and Republicans increasingly gerrymandering "safe districts," primary elections are replacing general elections "as the most common method of actually determining the composition of our legislative bodies."

N.A.A.C.P. v. CLAIBORNE HARDWARE CO., 458 U.S. 886 (1982). In March of 1966, African American citizens of Port Gibson, Mississippi, and other areas of Claiborne County demanded racial equality and integration by presenting white elected officials with a list of 19 specific items for change. For example, they sought to end the condescending way blacks were addressed. Titles like " 'Mr.,' 'Mrs.,' or 'Miss' " were to replace names like " 'boy,' 'girl,' 'shine,' 'uncle' " and other offensive terms. Socially and politically, blacks demanded equality as well. Among other demands were fully integrated public schools, facilities, and bus stations; public improvements in black residential areas; black jury members; and an end to verbal abuse by law enforcement officers. On March 23, two more items were added. One stated that black clerks and cashiers must be employed by every store. The supplement also required a response by April 1.

When an unsatisfactory response was received, the N.A.A.C.P. (National Association for the Advancement of Colored People) acted. In a local chapter meeting at the First Baptist Church, several hundred black persons voted to boycott white merchants in the area. On April 1, 1966, Charles Evers gave a speech at a meeting initiating the boycott in which the chancellor found that "Evers told his audience that they would be watched and that blacks who traded with white merchants would be *answerable to him*." One sheriff who observed the speech testified that, "Evers told the assembled black people that any 'uncle toms' who broke the boycott would 'have their necks broken' by their own people." The speech was not recorded.

On April 18, 1969, Roosevelt Jackson — a young black man — "was shot and killed during an encounter with two Port Gibson police officers." This created strong public response and "[t]ension in the community neared a breaking point." The city responded by "plac[ing] a dawn-to-dusk curfew into effect."

The next day, Charles Evers spoke at the church and "led a march to the courthouse" demanding that the dismissal of the entire police force. The boycott was imposed once again "[w]hen the demand was refused." In one of his recorded speeches, Evers stated that boycott violators would be " 'disciplined' by their own people, and warned that the Sheriff could not sleep with boycott violators at night."

In another unrecorded boycott speech on April 21, the trial court "found that Evers stated: 'If we catch any of you going in any of them racist stores, we're gonna break your damn neck.' "

Several of the white merchants answered the boycott by filing suit in state court on October 31, 1969. The complaint named several defendants including the N.A.A.C.P.; Charles Evers, Field Secretary of the N.A.A.C.P. in Mississippi; and 144 other individuals who participated in the boycott. The merchants "sought injunctive relief and an attachment of property, as well as damages." The chancery court entered judgment against defendants of $1,250,699. The court found the defendants "liable for the tort of malicious interference with plaintiffs' businesses" and in "violation of Mississippi's antitrust statute" for having diverted black patrons away from the plaintiffs. The court also enjoined defendants "from stationing 'store watchers' at the respondents' business premises; from 'persuading' any person to withhold his patronage from respondents; from 'using demeaning and obscene language to or about any person' because that person continued to patronize the respondents; from 'picketing or patroling' the premises of any of the respondents; and from using violence against any person or inflicting damage to any real or personal property."

The court noted that a number of practices used to encourage people to boycott were entirely peaceful and orderly. " 'Store watchers' " called " 'Black Hats' " revealed who violated the boycotts. Violators' names were read aloud at Claiborne County N.A.A.C.P. meetings and published in the " 'Black Times.' " Violators were called demeaning names and socially ostracized.

The court found there were no incidents of violence after the suit was filed. However, years earlier, there were several incidents of boycott-related violence.[5] Specifically, the court "identified 10 incidents that 'strikingly' revealed the 'atmosphere of fear that prevailed among blacks from 1966 until 1970.' " Five of these occurred in 1966 and the others were not dated. In April 1966, shots were fired into the home of a black boycott violator named Cox. Another boycott violator had his tires slashed on Christmas Eve of 1966. Another received a threatening phone call and a personal warning that he would receive a whipping. Another had a whiskey bottle pulled from his hands. Four men beat up another boycott violator, and hearsay testimony indicated that several young black males pulled down the pants of another boycott violator and spanked him.

Under *United States v. O'Brien*, government can regulate in certain areas, such as the economy, even though that regulation incidentally affects speech. For example, government can prohibit business associations to curtail competition. "Unfair trade practices may be restricted. Secondary boycotts and picketing by labor unions may be prohibited, as part of 'Congress' striking of the delicate balance between union freedom of expression and the ability of neutral employers, employees, and consumers to remain

---

[5] On August 22, 1966, birdshot was fired into a boycott violator's home. In June of 1966, a brick was thrown through the car windshield of another boycott violator. "In November, 1966, shotgun pellets were fired into the wall of his mother's home" after she received threatening telephone calls for boycott violations. These activities were a result of the two patronizing white merchants. A young black male testified that he damaged an old black woman's flower garden for violating the boycott.

free from coerced participation in industrial strife.' "[6]

Defendants "sought to vindicate rights of equality and of freedom that lie at the heart of the Fourteenth Amendment itself." Nevertheless, the First Amendment does not protect violence, and "acts of violence occurred. No federal rule of law restricts a State from imposing tort liability for business losses that are caused by violence and by threats of violence." Compensation may not be awarded for the consequences of non-violent, conduct protected by the First Amendment, but only for "losses proximately caused by unlawful conduct."

The First Amendment does not tolerate a " 'blanket prohibition of association with a group having both legal and illegal aims.' " Moreover, liability may not be imposed merely because an individual belonged to a group, some members of which committed acts of violence. For liability to be imposed by reason of a valid association alone, it is necessary to establish that the group "itself possessed unlawful goals and that individual held specific intent to further those illegal aims."

The Mississippi Supreme Court wholly failed to show that business losses suffered in 1972 — three years after suit was filed — were proximately caused by the isolated acts of violence found in 1966. Furthermore, that court "relied on isolated acts of violence during a limited period to uphold [plaintiffs'] recovery of all business losses sustained over a seven-year span," and did not attribute any losses "to the voluntary participation of individuals determined to receive 'justice and equal opportunity.' "

As to liability for Evers' speech itself, "references to the possibility that necks would be broken and to the fact that the chief of police could not sleep with boycott violators at night implicitly conveyed a sterner 'form of discipline than social ostracism.' " "In the passionate atmosphere, in which the speeches were delivered, they might have been understood as inviting an unlawful form of discipline or at least as intending to create a fear of violence." *Brandenburg v. Ohio* states that "mere *advocacy* of the use of force or of law violation does not remove speech from the protection of the First Amendment." Evers' speech contained strong language. "If that language had been followed by acts of violence, a substantial question would have been presented whether Evers could be held liable for the consequences of that unlawful conduct."

"In this case, however — with the possible exception of the Cox incident — the acts of violence identified in 1966 occurred weeks or months after the April 1, 1966 speech; the chancellor made no finding of any violence after the challenged 1969 speech. Strong and effective extemporaneous rhetoric cannot be nicely channeled in purely dulcet phrases. An advocate must be free to stimulate his audience with spontaneous and emotional appeals for unity and action in a common cause. When such appeals do not incite lawless action, they must be regarded as protected speech." Had there been "other evidence of his authorization of wrongful conduct, the references to discipline in the speeches could be used to corroborate that evidence. Here there is no evidence — apart from the speeches themselves — that Evers authorized, ratified, or directly threatened acts of violence."

The N.A.A.C.P., like other organizations, may be liable for the actions of its agents. In this case, the N.A.A.C.P.'s liability derived solely from any liability of Charles Evers. Since he is not liable, neither is the principal. "To impose liability without a finding that the N.A.A.C.P. authorized — either actually or apparently — or ratified unlawful

---

[6] "We need not decide in this case the extent to which a narrowly tailored statute designed to prohibit certain forms of anticompetitive conduct or certain types of secondary pressure may restrict protected First Amendment activity. . . . Nor are we presented with a boycott designed to secure aims that are themselves prohibited by a valid state law."

conduct would impermissibly burden the rights of political association that are protected by the First Amendment."

Individuals who committed acts of violence may be held individually liable. "The burden of demonstrating that it colored the entire collective effort, however, is not satisfied by evidence that violence occurred or even that violence contributed to the success of the boycott. A massive and prolonged effort to change the social, political, and economic structure of a local environment cannot be characterized as a violent conspiracy simply by reference to the ephemeral consequences of relatively few violent acts. Such a characterization must be supported by findings that adequately disclose the evidentiary basis for concluding that specific parties agreed to use unlawful means, that carefully identify the impact of such unlawful conduct, and that recognize the importance of avoiding the imposition of punishment for constitutionally protected activity. The burden of demonstrating that fear rather than protected conduct was the dominant force in the movement is heavy." The lower court findings are "insufficient to support the judgment that all petitioners are liable for all losses resulting from the boycott." Justice Rehnquist concurred in the result. Justice Marshall did not participate in considering this case.

NOTES

(1) *Political Association.* The right to associate with others to pursue political, social, economic, educational, religious and cultural ends is a form of free speech, e.g., in *N.A.A.C.P. v. Alabama*, 357 U.S. 449 (1958).

(2) *Civic Organizations.* In *Roberts v. United States Jaycees*, 468 U.S. 609 (1984), the Court considered whether the State of Minnesota could enforce its Human Rights Act to compel the all-male Jaycees to admit women. Justice Brennan's opinion recognized that a law that forces the Jaycees to admit those it would not otherwise accept implicates the right to associate. Moreover, "freedom of association . . . plainly presupposes a freedom not to associate."

However, the right to associate is not absolute. Minnesota's interest in eradicating discrimination against women was a compelling interest. Nothing in the record indicated why the admission of women would impede the organization's ability to engage in protected associational activities. It was only vague speculation to assume that the positions taken on various issues by the Jaycees were based on the male composition of its membership. "[E]ven if enforcement of the Act causes some incidental abridgment of the Jaycees' protected speech, that effect is no greater than is necessary to accomplish the State's legitimate purposes."

Justices O'Connor and Rehnquist concurred, and the Chief Justice and Justice Blackmun did not participate. *See also Bd. of Dirs. of Rotary Int'l v. Rotary Club of Duarte*, 481 U.S. 537 (1987) (unanimously upholding a state law requiring the Rotary Club to stop excluding women from membership). In Justice Powell's opinion the admission of women would not affect, "in any significant way" the ability of the club to carry out its purposes, and that even if a burden on association could be shown, the state has a compelling interest in assuring to women equal access to business contacts and the acquisition of leadership skills.

(3) *Intimate Association.* In *Roberts*, the Court also rejected the claims of the Jaycees that the state laws abridged their rights of "intimate association" guaranteed by the Due Process Clause of the Fourteenth Amendment. This aspect of the case is discussed at § 7.04[5].

(4) *Private Clubs.* In *New York State Club Ass'n v. City of New York*, 487 U.S. 1 (1988), the Court unanimously rejected a facial challenge to a New York City Law that prohibited discrimination in certain private clubs. A club is subject to the law, if it has

more than four hundred members, provides regular meal service, receives payment for dues, the use of its facilities, or for meals and beverages "for or on behalf of nonmembers for the furtherance of trade or business." Although the law was part of the city's over-all Human Rights Law and was, therefore, applicable to discrimination against minorities as well as women, the principal opposition to the law came from clubs that barred women from membership.

Relying on the *Rotary* and *Roberts* decisions, the Court held that a facial challenge could not be sustained since the law "certainly could be constitutionally applied at least to some of the large clubs." Justice White's majority opinion recognized that there might conceivably be some clubs with the characteristics specified in the law that might be able to assert claims of "intimate" or "expressive" association. We could hardly hold otherwise on the record before us, which contains no specific evidence on the characteristics of any club covered by the Law." The Court also rejected an "overbreadth" challenge, since there was no evidence that a substantial number of clubs existed to which the law could not be constitutionally applied. Justices O'Connor, Kennedy, and Scalia concurred.

(5) *Institutional Academic Freedom, Discovery, and Tenure.* In *Univ. of Pennsylvania v. EEOC*, 493 U.S. 182 (1990), the Court held that the First Amendment provides universities with no special privileges against disclosing relevant "peer review materials" used in tenure decisions when charges of race or gender discrimination are pending. When an associate professor at the University of Pennsylvania was denied tenure, she filed race and gender discrimination charges with the Equal Employment Opportunity Commission (EEOC). The University refused to satisfy a subpoena request by the EEOC for "peer review materials" used in the tenure decision-making process, protesting that forced disclosure of all materials would violate the First Amendment privilege of academic freedom.

Justice Blackmun, writing for a unanimous Court, recognized the need for academic freedom, but found the University's reliance on the principle somewhat "misplaced." In contrast to cases like *Keyishian v. Bd. of Regents*, 385 U.S. 589 (1967), § 12.03, the government was not attempting to regulate "content" of university speech through selection of faculty. Instead, the government was merely attempting to prevent the selection of faculty by the University on grounds prohibited by Title VII. This decision did not affect the Court's respect for *"legitimate* academic decisionmaking." Nevertheless, Justice Blackmun did not consider academic freedom to have been violated in this case as the burden here on the University was "extremely attenuated" and "speculative." Because the subpoena issued by the EEOC did not infringe any special First Amendment right of the University, the EEOC "need not demonstrate any special justification" for the subpoenaed materials. *Cf.* J. Peter Byrne, *Academic Freedom: A "Special Concern of the First Amendment,"* 99 YALE L.J. 251, 312 (1989) ("judicial protection of institutional autonomy is the appropriate concern for constitutional academic freedom.").

BOY SCOUTS OF AM. & MONMOUTH COUNCIL v. DALE, 530 U.S. 640 (2000). In *Boy Scouts of Am.,* the Court held that a New Jersey public accommodations laws violated the Boy Scouts' right of expressive association. James Dale, a former Eagle Scout, sued the Boy Scouts for revoking his adult membership based on his being an "avowed homosexual and gay rights activist." The New Jersey Supreme Court held that the State's public accommodations law prohibited the Boy Scouts from discriminating based on Dale's sexual orientation.

Chief Justice Rehnquist's majority opinion focused on the right of expressive association which applies to groups engaged in public and private speech. "The Boy Scouts asserts that it 'teach[es] that homosexual conduct is not morally straight.'"

Moreover, "it does 'not want to promote homosexual conduct as a legitimate form of behavior.'" The Court accepted the written evidence in the record of these positions as establishing "the sincerity of the professed beliefs," and stated that further inquiry "to determine the nature of the Boy Scouts' expression" was unnecessary. "As we give deference to an association's assertions regarding the nature of its expression, we must also give deference to an association's view of what would impair its expression."

The Chief Justice compared the case to *Hurley v. Irish-Am. Gay, Lesbian and Bisexual Group of Boston, Inc.*, § 14.02: Dale's presence as an assistant scoutmaster would infringe "the Boy Scout's choice not to propound a point of view contrary to its beliefs." Similarly, the presence of the Irish-American Gay, Lesbian, and Bisexual group of Boston in "Boston's St. Patrick's Day parade would have interfered with the parade organizers' choice not to propound a particular point of view."[7] "The fact that the organization does not trumpet its views from the housetops" and "tolerates dissent within its ranks" on its homosexuality policy does not extinguish the Boy Scouts' ability to assert the right of expressive association.

The Court distinguished *Roberts v. United States Jaycees*, 468 U.S. 609 (1984), and *Rotary Int'l v. Rotary Club of Duarte*, 481 U.S. 537 (1987). The *Roberts* Court held "'the Jaycees [had] failed to demonstrate . . . any serious burden on the male members' freedom of expressive association.'" In contrast, "a state requirement that the Boy Scouts retain Dale as an assistant scoutmaster would significantly burden the organization's right to oppose or disfavor homosexual conduct."

Justice Stevens dissented, joined by Justices Souter, Ginsburg, and Breyer. Justice Stevens found that neither "'morally straight'" nor "'clean' — says the slightest thing about homosexuality." Instead these terms fail to convey "any position whatsoever on sexual matters." The Boy Scouts' own statements advise Scouts "to seek guidance on sexual matters from their religious leaders (and Scoutmasters are told to refer Scouts to them)." The Boy Scouts must be "aware that some religions do not teach that homosexuality is wrong."

Indeed, the Boy Scouts never "establish[ed] any clear, consistent, and unequivocal position on homosexuality." While an organization may "adopt the message of it choice," the Court must "inquire whether the group is, in fact, expressing a message (whatever it may be)." The Court must use *"independent* analysis, rather than deference to a group's litigating posture." This case is distinguishable from *Hurley* because Dale's membership in the Boy Scouts conveyed "no cognizable message" with his presence. He did not "carry a banner or a sign; he did not distribute any fact sheet; and he expressed no intent to send any message."

Justice Souter also wrote a dissent joined by Justices Ginsburg and Breyer. Justice Souter stressed that to "claim a right of expressive association," a group must identify "a clear position to be advocated over time in an unequivocal way." Otherwise, "to allow exemption from a public accommodations statute based on any individual's difference from an alleged group ideal, however expressed and however inconsistently claimed,

---

[7] Anticipating the result in this case, the *Hurley* Court stated "'GLIB could nonetheless be refused admission as an expressive contingent with its own message just as readily as a private club could exclude an applicant whose manifest views were at odds with a position taken by the club's existing members.'"

would convert the right of expressive association into an easy trump of any antidiscrimination law."

NOTE

Rumsfeld v. Forum for Academic & Institutional Rights ("Fair"), 547 U.S. 47 (2006) (rejecting the argument that the Solomon Amendment violated the law school's "right of expressive association" since military recruiters are not a part of the schools they visit and law schools' recruiting services merely assist them.) This case is reproduced at § 15.03.

§ 12.06   FREE SPEECH PROBLEMS OF GOVERNMENT EMPLOYEES

Section Note. Some issues concerning the First Amendment rights of government employees have already been considered in the context of whether the government may impose sanctions on an individual because of his political affiliations (*Keyishian*, § 12.03) and whether the government may compel the disclosure of membership in political groups [*Barenblatt* and *Gibson*, § 12.04]. Here we consider restrictions on First Amendment rights which would clearly be invalid if imposed by government on private individuals, but where the government asserts the public employee's special status as justification for a different result.

[1]   Patronage Dismissals

BRANTI v. FINKEL
445 U.S. 507 (1980), 100 S. Ct. 1287, 61 L. Ed. 2d 574 (1980)

JUSTICE STEVENS delivered the opinion of the Court.

The question presented is whether the First and Fourteenth Amendments to the Constitution protect an assistant public defender who is satisfactorily performing his job from discharge solely because of his political beliefs.

Respondents, Aaron Finkel and Alan Tabakman, commenced this action in the United States District Court for the Southern District of New York in order to preserve their positions as assistant public defenders in Rockland County, New York. . . .

The critical facts can be summarized briefly. The Rockland County Public Defender is appointed by the County Legislature for a term of six years. He in turn appoints nine assistants who serve at his pleasure. The two respondents have served as assistants since their respective appointments in March 1971 and September 1975; they are both Republicans.

Petitioner Branti's predecessor, a Republican, was appointed in 1972 by a Republican-dominated County Legislature. By 1977, control of the legislature had shifted to the Democrats and petitioner, also a Democrat, was appointed to replace the incumbent when his term expired. As soon as petitioner was formally appointed on January 3, 1978, he began executing termination notices for six of the nine assistants then in office. Respondents were among those who were to be terminated. With one possible exception, the nine who were to be appointed or retained were all Democrats and were all selected by Democratic legislators or Democratic town chairmen on a basis that had been determined by the Democratic caucus.

The District Court found that Finkel and Tabakman had been selected for termination solely because they were Republicans and thus did not have the necessary

Democratic sponsors. . . . Noting that both Branti and his predecessor had described respondents as "competent attorneys," the District Court expressly found that both had "been satisfactorily performing their jobs as Assistant Public Defenders."

. . . [T]he District Court held that those discharges would be permissible under this Court's decision in *Elrod v. Burns*, 427 U.S. 347, only if assistant public defenders are the type of policymaking, confidential employees who may be discharged solely on the basis of their political affiliations. He concluded that respondents clearly did not fall within that category. . . . They did not "act as advisors or formulate plans for the implementation of the broad goals of the office" and, although they made decisions in the context of specific cases, "they do not make decisions about the orientation and operation of the office in which they work."

The District Court also rejected the argument that the confidential character of respondent's work justified conditioning their employment on political grounds. He found that they did not occupy any confidential relationship to the policymaking process, and did not have access to confidential documents that influenced policymaking deliberations. Rather, the only confidential information to which they had access was the product of their attorney-client relationships with the office's clients. . . .

I

In *Elrod v. Burns* the Court held that the newly elected Democratic sheriff of Cook County, Ill., had violated the constitutional rights of certain non-civil service employees by discharging them "because they did not support and were not members of the Democratic Party and had failed to obtain the sponsorship of one of its leaders." 427 U.S., at 351. That holding was supported by two separate opinions.

Writing for the plurality, Justice Brennan identified two separate but interrelated reasons supporting the conclusions that the discharges were prohibited by the First and Fourteenth Amendments. First, he analyzed the impact of a political patronage system on freedom of belief and association. Noting that in order to retain their jobs the sheriff's employees were required to pledge their allegiance to the Democratic party, work for or contribute to the party's candidates, or obtain a Democratic sponsor, he concluded that the inevitable tendency of such a system was to coerce employees into compromising their true beliefs. That conclusion, in his opinion, brought the practice within the rule of cases like *Bd. of Educ. v. Barnette*, 319 U.S. 624, condemning the use of governmental power to prescribe what the citizenry must accept as orthodox opinion.

Second, . . . Justice Brennan, also stated that the practice had the effect of imposing an unconstitutional condition on the receipt of a public benefit and therefore came within the rule of cases like *Perry v. Sindermann*, 408 U.S. 593. In support of the holding in *Perry* that even an employee with no contractual right to retain his job cannot be dismissed for engaging in constitutionally protected speech, the Court had stated:

> For at least a quarter-century, this Court has made clear that even though a person has no "right" to a valuable governmental benefit and even though the government may deny him the benefit for any number of reasons, there are some reasons upon which the government may not rely. It may not deny a benefit to a person on a basis that infringes his constitutionally protected interests — especially his interest in freedom of speech. . . . This would allow the government to "produce a result which [it] could not command directly." *Speiser v. Randall*, 357 U.S. 513, 526. . . .

If the First Amendment protects a public employee from discharge based on what he has said, it must also protect him from discharge based on what he believes.[8]

Under this line of analysis, unless the Government can demonstrate "an overriding interest," 427 U.S., at 368, "of vital importance," *id.*, at 362, requiring that a person's private beliefs conform to those of the hiring authority, his beliefs cannot be the sole basis for depriving him of continued public employment. . . .

[T]here is no requirement that dismissed employees prove that they, or other employees, have been coerced into changing, either actually or ostensibly, their political, allegiance. To prevail in this type of action, it was sufficient, as *Elrod* holds, for respondents to prove that they were discharged "solely for the reason that they were not affiliated with or sponsored by the Democratic Party." *Id.* at 350.

II

[P]arty affiliation may be an acceptable requirement for some types of government employment. Thus, if an employee's private political beliefs would interfere with the discharge of his public duties, his First Amendment rights may be required to yield to the State's vital interest in maintaining governmental effectiveness and efficiency. 427 U.S. at 366. . . .

Under some circumstances a position may be appropriately considered political even though it is neither confidential nor policymaking in character. As one obvious example, if a State's election laws require that precincts be supervised by two election judges of different parties, a Republican judge could be legitimately discharged solely for changing his party registration. That conclusion would not depend on any finding that the job involved participation in policy decisions or access to confidential information. Rather, it would simply rest on the fact that the party membership was essential to the discharge of the employee's governmental responsibilities.

It is equally clear that party affiliation is not necessarily relevant to every policy-making or confidential position. The coach of a state university's football team formulates policy, but no one could seriously claim that Republicans make better coaches than Democrats, or vice versa. . . .   On the other hand, it is equally clear that the governor of a state may appropriately believe that the official duties of various assistants who help him write speeches, explain his views to the press, or communicate with the legislature cannot be performed effectively unless those persons share his political beliefs and party commitments. In sum, the ultimate inquiry is not whether the label "policymaker" or "confidential" fits a particular position; rather, the question is whether the hiring authority can demonstrate that party affiliation is an appropriate requirement for the effective performance of the public office involved.

Having thus framed the issue, it is manifest that the continued employment of an assistant public defender cannot properly be conditioned upon his allegiance to the political party in control of the county government. The primary, if not the only, responsibility of an assistant public defender is to represent individual citizens in controversies with the State. . . .   [9]

---

[8] [Court's footnote 10] "The Court recognized in *United Public Workers v. Mitchell*, 330 U.S. 75, 100 (1947), that 'Congress may not "enact a regulation providing that no Republican, Jew or Negro shall be appointed to federal office. . .'" This principle was reaffirmed in *Wieman v. Updegraff*, 344 U.S. 183 (1952), which held that a State could not require its employees to establish their loyalty by extracting an oath denying past affiliation with Communists. And in *Cafeteria Workers v. McElroy*, 367 U.S. 886, 898 (1961), the Court recognized again that the government could not deny employment because of previous membership in a particular party." 427 U.S., at 357–58.

[9] [Court's footnote 13] This is in contrast to the broader public responsibilities of an official such as a

Thus, whatever policymaking occurs in the public defender's office must relate to the needs of individual clients and not to any partisan political interests. Similarly, although an assistant is bound to obtain access to confidential information arising out of various attorney-client relationships, that information has no bearing whatsoever on partisan political concerns. Under these circumstances, it would undermine, rather than promote, the effective performance of an assistant public defender's office to make his tenure dependent on his allegiance to the dominant political party. . . .

JUSTICE STEWART dissenting. . . .

[[T]he employees in the *Elrod* case were three process servers and a juvenile court bailiff and security guard]. The respondents in the present case are . . . those of assistants in the office of the Rockland County Public Defender. The analogy to a firm of lawyers in the private sector is a close one, and I can think of few occupational relationships more instinct with the necessity of mutual confidence and trust than that kind of professional association. . . .

JUSTICE POWELL, with whom JUSTICE REHNQUIST joins and with whom JUSTICE STEWART joins as to Part I, dissenting.

The Court today continues the evisceration of patronage practices begun in *Elrod v. Burns*. With scarcely a glance at almost 200 years of American political tradition, the Court further limits the relevance of political affiliation to the selection and retention of public employees. Many public positions previously filled on the basis of membership in national political parties now must be staffed in accordance with a constitutionalized civil service standard that will affect the employment practices of federal, state, and local governments. Governmental hiring practices long thought to be a matter of legislative and executive discretion now will be subjected to judicial oversight. . . .

I

. . . Patronage is a long-accepted practice that never has been eliminated totally by civil service laws and regulations. The flaw in the Court's opinion lies not only in its application of First Amendment principles, *see* parts II-IV *infra*, but also in its promulgation of a new, and substantially expanded, standard for determining which governmental employees may be retained or dismissed on the basis of political affiliation. . . .

The standard articulated by the Court is framed in vague and sweeping language certain to create vast uncertainty. Elected and appointed officials at all levels who now receive guidance from civil service laws, no longer will know when political affiliation is an appropriate consideration in filling a position. Legislative bodies will not be certain whether they have the final authority to make the delicate line-drawing decisions embodied in the civil service laws. Prudent individuals requested to accept a public appointment must consider whether their predecessors will threaten to oust them through legal action.

II

. . . The Court . . . relies upon the decisions in *Perry v. Sindermann*, 408 U.S. 593 (1972), and *Keyishian v. Bd. of Regents*.

Both *Keyishian* and *Perry* involved faculty members who were dismissed from state educational institutions because of their political views. . . . In neither case did the

---

prosecutor. We express no opinion as to whether the deputy of such an official could be dismissed on grounds of political party affiliation or loyalty. *Cf. Newcomb v. Brennan*, 558 F.2d 825 (7th Cir. 1977), *cert. denied*, 434 U.S. 968 (dismissal of deputy city attorney).

State suggest that the governmental positions traditionally had been regarded as patronage positions. . . .

III

Patronage appointments help build stable political parties by offering rewards to persons who assume the tasks necessary to the continued functioning of political organizations. . . .   Many, if not most, of the jobs filled by patronage at the local level may not involve policymaking functions. The use of patronage to fill such positions builds party loyalty and avoids "splintered parties and unrestrained factionalism [that might] do significant damage to the fabric of government." *Storer v. Brown*, 415 U.S. 724, 736 (1974).

. . . Political parties, dependent in many ways upon patronage, serve a variety of substantial governmental interests. A party organization allows political candidates to muster donations of time and money necessary to capture the attention of the electorate. Particularly in a time of growing reliance upon expensive television advertisements, a candidate who is neither independently wealthy nor capable of attracting substantial contributions must rely upon party workers to bring his message to the voters. In contests for less visible offices, a candidate may have no efficient method of appealing to the voters unless he enlists the efforts of persons who seek reward through the patronage system. Insofar as the Court's decision today limits the ability of candidates to present their views to the electorate, our democratic process surely is weakened.

Strong political parties also aid effective governance after election campaigns end. Elected officials depend upon appointees who hold similar views to carry out their policies and administer their programs. Patronage — the right to select key personnel and to reward the party "faithful" — serves the public interest by facilitating the implementation of policies endorsed by the electorate. . . .

. . . This decision comes at a time when an increasing number of observers question whether our national political parties can continue to operate effectively. Broad-based political parties supply an essential coherence and flexibility to the American political scene. They serve as coalitions of different interests that combine to seek national goals. The decline of party strength inevitably will enhance the influence of special interest groups whose only concern all too often is how a political candidate votes on a single issue. . . .

IV

The facts of this case also demonstrate that the Court's decision may well impair the right of local voters to structure their government. . . .

. . . Among the responsibilities that the voters give to the legislature is the selection of a County Public Defender. . . .   In 1976, the voters elected a majority of Democrats to the legislature. The Democratic majority in turn, selected a Democratic Public Defender who replaced both respondents with assistant public defenders approved by the Democratic legislators.

. . . The voters' choice of public officials on the basis of political affiliation is not yet viewed as an inhibition of speech; it is democracy. . . .

V

. . . The decision to place certain governmental positions within a civil service system is a sensitive political judgment that should be left to the voters and to elected representatives of the people. . . .   In my view, the First Amendment does not incorporate a national civil service system. . . .

NOTES

(1) *Non-Civil Service Employees. Elrod v. Burns*, 427 U.S. 347 (1976), discussed at length in *Branti v. Finkel*, involved the dismissal of non-civil-service employees of the Cook County Sheriff's office because they were not affiliated with or sponsored by the Democratic Party, whose candidate had been elected Sheriff. Justice Brennan's plurality opinion (joined by Justices White and Marshall) was a broad attack on the patronage system as infringing First Amendment rights, and appeared to confine valid patronage dismissals to "policymaking positions." Justice Stewart wrote a brief concurrence, joined by Justice Blackmun, stating that "[t]he single substantive question involved in this case is whether a non-policymaking, non-confidential government employee can be discharged or threatened with discharge from a job that he is satisfactorily performing upon the sole ground of his political beliefs. I agreed with the plurality that he cannot." *See* Justice Stewart's dissent in *Branti*.

Chief Justice Burger wrote a brief, but sharp, dissent in *Elrod*, arguing that the decision impaired the ability of cities and states to govern themselves. For additional discussion of *Branti* and *Elrod* see Note, *An Objective and Practical Test for Adjudicating Political Patronage Dismissals*, 35 CLEV. ST. L. REV. 277 (1987) (arguing that the *Branti* and *Elrod* tests are vague, making it difficult for lower courts to determine to which governmental employees the standard applies).

(2) *Unconstitutional Conditions.* For additional discussion of the unconstitutional conditions aspect of *Branti*, see Kathleen Sullivan, *Unconstitutional Conditions*, 102 HARV. L. REV. 1413, 1421 (1989) ("Unconstitutional conditions implicate three distributive concerns. The first is the boundary between the public and the private realms, which government can shift through the allocation of benefits as readily as through the use or threat of force. Whatever the reason to preserve a realm of private autonomy from government encroachment, unconstitutional conditions present the same structural threat to that realm: they permit circumvention of existing constitutional restraints on direct regulation. The second distributive concern of unconstitutional conditions doctrine is the maintenance of government neutrality or evenhandedness among rightholders. The third is the prevention of constitutional caste: discrimination among rightholders who would otherwise make the same constitutional choice, on the basis of their relative dependency on a government benefit."); Cass Sunstein, *Why the Unconstitutional Conditions Doctrine is an Anachronism (With Particular Reference to Religion, Speech, and Abortion)*, 70 B.U. L. REV. 593, 595 (1990) ("Instead of a general unconstitutional conditions doctrine asking where there has been 'coercion' or 'penalty,' what is necessary is a highly particular, constitutionally-centered model of reasons: an approach that asks whether, under the provision at issue, the government has constitutionally sufficient justifications for affecting constitutionally protected interests.").

RUTAN v. REPUBLICAN PARTY OF ILLINOIS, 497 U.S. 62 (1990). In *Rutan*, the Court held that party patronage practices may not affect "promotion, transfer, recall and hiring decisions involving low-level public employees." In 1980, the Governor of Illinois issued an executive order declaring a "hiring freeze" whereby no state official "subject to his control" could hire new employees, fill vacancies, or create new positions without his "express permission after submission of appropriate requests to [his] office." The order affected "60,000 state positions," 5,000 of which "become available each year." Plaintiffs alleged that the Governor has been using the freeze "to operate a political patronage system to limit state employment and beneficial employment-related decisions to those who are supported by the Republican Party." They alleged that the

Governor's office considered such criteria as voting in the Republican primaries, past "financial or other support" of the Republican Party, promised future involvement with the Republican Party, and support by various Republican officials. A rehabilitation counselor and a road equipment operator were denied promotions because they had not "worked for or supported" or been supported by the Republican Party. The equipment operator further contended that he had also been denied a transfer closer to his home for similar reasons. A third plaintiff alleged that he "had repeatedly been denied employment as a prison guard" because he was not backed by Republican officials. The two remaining plaintiffs, a state garage worker and a mental health department dietary manager, had not been recalled after layoffs allegedly because of their party affiliations.[10]

Writing for a 5-4 majority, Justice Brennan began with the claims of the "four current or former employees." The defendants sought to distinguish *Elrod v. Burns*, and *Branti v. Finkel* on the grounds that plaintiffs had no right to recall, promotion, or transfer. Justice Brennan responded that although there is "no legal entitlement" to a "valuable governmental benefit" such as employment, the government cannot withhold such benefits for reasons that infringe on *constitutionally protected interests — especially . . . freedom of speech."*

These denials of recalls, promotions, and transfers are "significant penalties and are imposed for the exercise of rights guaranteed by the First Amendment." Such patronage practices must be "narrowly tailored to further vital government interests" to pass constitutional muster. "A government's interest in securing effective employees can be met by discharging, demoting or transferring staff members whose work is deficient. A government's interest in securing employees who will loyally implement its policies can be adequately served by choosing or dismissing certain high-level employees on the basis of their political views."

The " 'preservation of the democratic process' is no more furthered by the patronage promotions, transfers, and rehires at issue here than it is by patronage dismissals." First, political parties "have already survived the substantial decline in patronage employment practices in this century." They have other means of sustaining themselves. Second, these practices inhibit "the elective process by discouraging free political expression by public employees." The Court held that these various employment practices "based on political affiliation or support" violate the First Amendment. While the First Amendment does not guarantee these employment benefits, it forbids the government, "except in the most compelling circumstances," from conditioning such benefits on particular beliefs and associations. The Court remanded the actual disposition of these promotion, transfer and recall cases to the district courts.

Turning to the hiring claim, Justice Brennan rejected the defendants' argument that denial of the job did not exact a burden "of constitutional magnitude." This contention was inconsistent with *Keyishian v. Bd. of Regents of State Univ. of New York* [§ 12.06[3]] and *Elfbrandt v. Russell*, which struck down laws conditioning the appointment to public employment on political belief and association.

Justice Stevens filed a concurring opinion. He responded to three arguments advanced in Justice Scalia's dissent. First, Justice Stevens rejected the assertion that the Court was constitutionalizing a civil service system. He analogized the difference between a Civil Service Code and the Court's patronage restrictions to the difference between "the grant of tenure to an employee — a right which cannot be conferred by

---

[10] The dietary manager eventually was given a lower paid position after he solicited the favor of the local Republican Party chairman.

judicial fiat — and the prohibition of a discharge for a particular impermissible reason." Second, he disputed the proposition that the long tradition of patronage practices should save them from being struck down by the Court. Third, Justice Stevens rejected the assertion that *Elrod* and *Branti* had departed from precedent. For example, the Court had prohibited excluding members of the Communist Party from government employment.

Patronage practices have caused various kinds of "financial corruption" and government inefficiency. Patronage practices effectively allow government resources, such as employment opportunities, "to subsidize partisan activities." Finally, with respect to the problem of deciding which positions do or do not require political affiliation, the difficulty of "deciding borderline cases does not justify imposition of a loyalty oath in the vast category of positions in which it is irrelevant."

Justice Scalia dissented, joined by Chief Justice Rehnquist, and Justice Kennedy, and in part, by Justice O'Connor. In the part of his opinion joined only by Chief Justice Rehnquist and Justice Kennedy, Justice Scalia suggested that the government job least appropriate for a requirement of party affiliation was that of judge. "It is, however, rare that a federal administration of one party will appoint a judge from another party." Ironically, then, the majority's rule "will be enforced by a corps of judges (the Members of this Court included) who overwhelmingly owe their office to its violation." As the party machines "have faded into history, we find that political leaders at all levels increasingly complain of the helplessness of elected government, unprotected by 'party discipline' before the demands of small and cohesive interest-groups." Particularly against this backdrop, "the choice between the desirable mix of merit and patronage principles in widely varying federal, state, and local political contexts is not so clear that I would be prepared, as an original matter, to chisel a single, inflexible prescription into the Constitution." Differentiating between government's roles as "lawmaker" and as "employer," Justice Scalia argued that the latter require less in the way of constitutional restrictions on governmental authority when a governmental practice, like patronage, is not "expressly prohibited by the text of the Bill of Rights" and "bears the endorsement of a long tradition of open, widespread, and unchallenged use that dates back to the beginning of the Republic."

Justice Scalia was joined by Justice O'Connor, as well as Chief Justice Rehnquist and Justice Kennedy, in the remainder of his opinion. Justice Scalia refused to apply the majority's "strict-scrutiny" test to the government's role as employer. Quoting *Connick v. Myers* [§ 12.06[3]], he maintained that "government offices could not function if every government employment decision became a constitutional matter." Instead of strict scrutiny then, Justice Scalia applied the following test: "Can the governmental advantages of this employment practice reasonably be deemed to outweigh its 'coercive' effects?"

As to the advantages, patronage "stabilizes political parties and prevents excessive political fragmentation." Money and the media have not supplanted personal contacts in political campaigns; to the extent they have, the political process has suffered. "Increased reliance on money-intensive campaign techniques tends to entrench those in power much more effectively than patronage — but without the attendant benefit of strengthening the party system. A challenger can more easily obtain the support of party-workers (who can expect to be rewarded even if the candidate loses — if not this year, then the next) than the financial support of political action committees (which will generally support incumbents, who are likely to prevail)."

Justice Scalia was also less sanguine about the well-being of political parties 14 years after *Elrod*. During that period, the Congress has generally been controlled by one political party and the Executive Branch by the other, and in the last federal election,

98% of the incumbents were re-elected. Patronage also promotes a two-party system in which each party moderates its views in an attempt to appeal to more people. *"Elrod* and *Branti,* by contributing to the decline of party strength, have also contributed to the growth in interest-group politics in the last decade." The patronage system has also helped racial and ethnic groups to achieve "economic and social advancement."

Patronage also has disadvantages such as helping to foster financial corruption and less qualified workers. Justice Scalia did not use this balancing test to assert that patronage was "always and everywhere arguably desirable," but only that it was "sometimes a reasonable choice."

Finally, he argued that the *Elrod* and *Branti* test is "unworkable."[11] He concluded that both *Branti* and *Elrod* should be overruled, or at the very least confined to their facts.

The following case could usefully be read in conjunction with *Bd. of Comm'rs v. Umbehr,* § 12.06[3].

O'HARE TRUCK SERV. v. CITY OF NORTHLAKE, 518 U.S. 712 (1996). In *O'Hare,* the Court held that *Elrod v. Burns,* and *Branti v. Finkel* extend First Amendment scrutiny to government retaliation "against a contractor or a regular provider of services, for the exercise of rights of political association or the expression of political allegiance."

Plaintiff, the owner of O'Hare Truck Service (O'Hare), performed towing services in Cook and DuPage Counties in Illinois. The city of Northlake maintains a rotation list of all companies available to provide towing services. O'Hare was removed from this list shortly after its owner had refused to contribute to the Mayor of Northlake's reelection campaign, and instead openly supported the Mayor's opponent.

As the case came up on a Rule 12(b)(6) dismissal, the Court assumed the facts alleged in the complaint were true and that the removal of O'Hare from the list was in retaliation for refusing to support the Mayor's campaign.

Writing for the majority (7-2), Justice Kennedy distinguished this case from those in which "a government employer takes adverse action on account of an employee or service provider's right of free speech. There, we apply the balancing test from *Pickering v. Bd. of Educ.,* 391 U.S. 563 (1968). *See generally Bd. of Comm'rs v. Umbehr,"* § 12.06[3]. This case instead follows *Elrod* and *Branti,* in which the "raw test of political affiliation sufficed to show a constitutional violation, without the necessity of an inquiry more detailed than asking whether the requirement was appropriate for the employment in question. There is an advantage in so confining the inquiry where political affiliation alone is concerned, for one's beliefs and allegiances ought not to be subject to probing or testing by the government." The test is to determine whether the political "affiliation requirement is a reasonable one, so it is inevitable that some case-by-case adjudication will be required even when political affiliation is a test the government has imposed. A reasonableness analysis will also accommodate those many

---

[11] "A few examples will illustrate the shambles *Branti* has produced. A city cannot fire a deputy sheriff because of his political affiliation, but then again perhaps it can, especially if he is called the 'police captain.' A county cannot fire on that basis its attorney for the department of social services, nor its assistant attorney for family court, but a city can fire its solicitor and his assistants, or its assistant city attorney, or its assistant state's attorney, or its corporation counsel. A city cannot discharge its deputy court clerk for his political affiliation, but it can fire its legal assistant to the clerk on that basis. Firing a juvenile court bailiff seems impermissible, but it may be permissible if he is assigned permanently to a single judge. A city cannot fire on partisan grounds its director of roads, but it can fire the second in command of the water department. A government cannot discharge for political reasons the senior vice president of its development bank, but it can discharge the regional director of its rural housing administration."

cases, perhaps including the one before us, where specific instances of the employee's speech or expression, which require balancing in the *Pickering* context, are intermixed with a political affiliation requirement. . . . This case-by-case process will allow the courts to consider the necessity of according to the government the discretion it requires in the administration and awarding of contracts over the whole range of public works and the delivery of governmental services."

Justice Kennedy rejected the city's argument that *Elrod* and *Branti* should not apply to independent contractors.[12] "A rigid rule 'giving the government carte blanche to terminate independent contractors for exercising First Amendment rights . . . would leave [those] rights unduly dependent on whether state law labels a government service provider's contract as a contract of employment or a contract for services, a distinction which is at best a very poor proxy for the interests at stake.' *Bd. of Comm'rs v. Umbehr*."

O'Hare alleged a substantial loss of income due to its removal from the city's rotation list. "Perhaps some contractors are so independent from government support that the threat of losing business would be ineffective to coerce them to abandon political activities." However, some government employees "might find work elsewhere if they lost their government jobs. If results were to turn on these sorts of distinctions, courts would have to inquire into the extent to which the government dominates various job markets as employer or as contractor," a task for which courts are ill-suited.

"The Constitution accords government officials a large measure of freedom as they exercise the discretion inherent" in awarding contracts for goods and services. "Interests of economy may lead a governmental entity to retain existing contractors or terminate them in favor of new ones without the costs and complexities of competitive bidding. A government official might offer a satisfactory justification, unrelated to the suppression of speech or associational rights, for either course of action. The first may allow the government to maintain stability, reward good performance, deal with known and reliable persons, or ensure the uninterrupted supply of goods or services; the second may help to stimulate competition, encourage experimentation with new contractors, or avoid the appearance of favoritism." Governments should not be prohibited from making these types of decisions "provided of course the asserted justifications are not the pretext for some improper practice." If the government terminates an independent contractor "for reasons unrelated to political association, as, for example, where the provider is unreliable, or if the service provider's political 'affiliation is an appropriate requirement for the effective performance' of the task in question, there will be no First Amendment violation."

The Court concluded that the lower courts "on remand should decide whether the case is governed by the *Elrod-Branti* rule or by the *Pickering* rule."

Justice Scalia dissented, joined by Justice Thomas, filing the same dissenting opinion in this case as in *Umbehr*. In *Rutan v. Republican Party of Illinois*, the Court extended *Elrod* and *Branti* to protect applicants for government jobs from rejection "on the basis of their political affiliation." As *Rutan* was a 5-4 decision, Justice Scalia found "inconceivable" the further extension of this principle to independent contractors six years later. "[W]hen a practice not expressly prohibited by the text of the Bill of Rights bears the endorsement of a long tradition of open, widespread, and unchallenged use

---

[12] The Court found nothing to distinguish the city's action in this case "from the coercion exercised in our other unconstitutional conditions cases. *See, e.g., Keyishian v. Bd. of Regents*, 385 U.S. 589 (1967)." Furthermore, if the Mayor had "solicited the contribution as a quid pro quo for not terminating O'Hare's arrangement with the city, they might well have violated criminal bribery statutes."

that dates back to the beginning of the Republic, we have no proper basis for striking it down."

In *Umbehr*, the Court at least adopted the *Pickering* balancing test; however, the Court did not apply this test in *O'Hare*. In fact, the majority determined that "it 'need not inquire' into any government interests that patronage contracting may serve — even generally, much less in the particular case at hand — for *Elrod* and *Branti* establish that patronage does not justify the coercion of a person's political beliefs and associations.' " This "assertion obviously contradicts the need for 'balancing' announced in the companion *Umbehr* decision."

NOTE

For further discussion of patronage, see Cynthia Grant Bowan, *"We Don't Want Anybody Sent": The Death of Patronage Hiring in Chicago*, 86 Nw. U. L. REV. 57, 95 (1991) ("Rather than bringing new groups into the political process, patronage parties have historically used patronage to perpetuate their own power and have relied upon selective mobilization of the vote instead of encouraging political participation in general. . . . In Chicago, for example, patronage was used to consolidate the political power of groups whose interests were directly opposed to those of the emerging Black near-majority."); *The Supreme Court, 1989 Term, Political Patronage in Promotion, Hiring, Transfer, and Recall Decisions*, 104 HARV. L. REV. 227, 237 (1990) ("Political patronage sacrifices public values and public interests to private ambitions and selfish goals."); Bryan A. Schneider, *Do Not Go Gentle into that Good Night: The Unquiet Death of Political Patronage*, 1992 WIS. L. REV. 511, 514 (1992) ("patronage nevertheless continues to survive because of the lower courts' perversion of the Supreme Court's patronage doctrine").

[2] Restraints on Political Activity

BROADRICK v. OKLAHOMA

413 U.S. 601, 93 S. Ct. 2908, 37 L. Ed. 2d 830 (1973)

JUSTICE WHITE delivered the opinion of the Court.

Section 818 of Oklahoma's Merit System of Personnel Administration Act, restricts the political activities of the State's classified civil servants in much the same manner that the Hatch Act proscribes partisan political activities of federal employees. Three employees of the Oklahoma Corporation Commission who are subject to the proscriptions of § 818 seek to have two of its paragraphs declared unconstitutional on their face and enjoined because of asserted vagueness and overbreadth. After a hearing, the District Court upheld the provisions and denied relief. 338 F. Supp. 711. . . . We affirm the judgment of the District Court.

Section 818 was enacted in 1959 when the State first established its Merit System of Personnel Administration. The section serves roughly the same function as the analogous provisions of the other 49 States, and is patterned on § 9(a) of the Hatch Act. Without question, a broad range of political activities and conduct is proscribed by the section. Paragraph six, one of the contested portions, provides that "[n]o employee in the classified service . . . shall, directly or indirectly, solicit, receive, or in any manner be concerned in soliciting or receiving any assessment . . . or contribution for any political organization, candidacy or other political purpose." Paragraph seven, the other challenged paragraph, provides that no such employee "shall be a member of any national, state or local committee of a political party, or an officer or member of a committee of a partisan political club, or a candidate for nomination or election to any paid public office." That paragraph further prohibits such employees from "tak[ing] part in the management or affairs of any political party or in any political campaign, except to exercise his right as a citizen privately to express his opinion and to cast his vote." As a complementary proscription (not challenged in this lawsuit) the first paragraph prohibits any person from "in any way" being "favored or discriminated against with respect to employment in the classified service because of his political . . . opinions or affiliations. . . . " Violation of § 818 results in dismissal from employment and possible criminal sanctions and limited state employment ineligibility. . . .

Appellants do not question Oklahoma's right to place even-handed restrictions on the partisan political conduct of state employees. Appellants freely concede that such restrictions serve valid and important state interests, particularly with respect to attracting greater numbers of qualified people by insuring their job security, free from the vicissitudes of the elective process, and by protecting them from "political extortion." *See United Public Workers of America v. Mitchell*, 330 U.S. 75 (1947). Rather, appellants maintain that however permissible, even commendable, the goals of § 818 may be, its language is unconstitutionally vague, and its prohibitions too broad in their sweep, failing to distinguish between conduct that may be proscribed and conduct that must be permitted. . . .

. . . Whatever other problems there are with § 818, it is all but frivolous to suggest that the section fails to give adequate warning of what activities it proscribes or fails to set out "explicit standards". . . . In the plainest language, it prohibits any state classified employee from being "an officer or member" [of a committee] of a "partisan political club" or a candidate for "any paid public office." . . . Words inevitably contain germs of uncertainty and, as with the Hatch Act, there may be disputes over the meaning of such terms in § 818 as "partisan," or "take part in," or "affairs of" political parties. But what was said in *Letter Carriers, supra*, 413 U.S. at 578–79 is applicable here: "there are limitations in the English language with respect to being both specific and manageably brief, and it seems to us that although the prohibition may not satisfy those intent on finding fault at any cost, they are set out in terms that the ordinary person exercising ordinary common sense can sufficiently understand and comply with. . . . Moreover, even if the outermost boundaries of § 818 may be imprecise, any such uncertainty has little relevance here, where appellants' conduct falls squarely within the "hard core" of the statute's proscriptions and appellants concede as much. . . .

Appellants assert that § 818 has been construed as applying to such allegedly protected political expression as the wearing of political buttons or the displaying of bumper stickers. But appellants did not engage in any such activity. They are charged with actively engaging in partisan political activities — including the solicitation of money — among their coworkers for the benefit of their superior. Appellants concede — and correctly so, *see Letter Carriers, supra*, that § 818 would be constitutional as applied to this type of conduct. They nevertheless maintain that the statute is overbroad and purports to reach protected, as well as unprotected conduct, and must therefore be struck down on its face and held to be inescapable of any constitutional application. We do not believe that the overbreadth doctrine may appropriately be invoked in this manner here.

Embedded in the traditional rules governing constitutional adjudication is the principle that a person to whom a statute may constitutionally be applied will not be heard to challenge that statute on the ground that it may conceivably be applied unconstitutionally to others, in other situations not before the Court. . . . A closely related principle is that constitutional rights are personal and may not be asserted vicariously. . . . These principles . . . reflect the conviction that under our constitutional system courts are not roving commissions assigned to pass judgment on the validity of the Nation's laws. . . .

It has long been recognized that the First Amendment needs breathing space. . . . The Court has altered its traditional rules of standing to permit — in the First Amendment area — "attacks on overly broad statutes with no requirement that the person making the attack demonstrate that his own conduct could not be regulated by a statute drawn with the requisite narrow specificity." *Dombrowski v. Pfister*, 380 U.S., at 486. Litigants, therefore, are permitted to challenge a statute not because their own rights of free expression are violated, but because of a judicial prediction or assumption that the statute's very existence may cause others not before the court to refrain from constitutionally protected speech or expression.

Such claims of facial overbreadth have been entertained in cases involving statutes which, by their terms, seek to regulate "only spoken words." . . . In such cases, it has been the judgment of this Court that the possible harm to society in permitting some unprotected speech to go unpunished is outweighed by the possibility that protected speech of others may be muted and perceived grievances left to fester because of the possible inhibitory effects of overly broad statutes. Overbreadth attacks have also been allowed where the Court thought rights of association were ensnared in statutes which, by their broad sweep, might result in burdening innocent associations. *See Keyishian v. Bd. of Regents*; *United States v. Robel*; *Aptheker v. Sec'y of State*. . . . Facial overbreadth claims have also been entertained where statutes, by their terms, purport to regulate the time, place and manner of expressive or communicative conduct . . . and where such conduct has required official approval under laws that delegated standardless discretionary power to local functionaries, resulting in virtually unreviewable prior restraints on First Amendment rights. . . .

The consequence of our departure from traditional rules of standing in the First Amendment area is that any enforcement of a statute thus placed at issue is totally forbidden until and unless a limiting construction or partial invalidation so narrows it as to remove the seeming threat or deterrence to constitutionally protected expression. Application of the overbreadth doctrine in this manner is, manifestly, strong medicine. It has been employed by the Court sparingly, and only as a last resort. Facial overbreadth has not been invoked when a limiting construction has been or could be placed on the challenged statute. . . . Equally important, overbreadth claims, if entertained at all, have been curtailed when invoked against ordinary criminal laws that are sought to be applied to protected conduct. [*Cantwell v. Connecticut*, 310 U.S. 296, (1940).] The Court did not hold that the offense "known as breach of the peace" must fall *in toto* because it was capable of some unconstitutional applications *Id.*, at 308. . . .

[F]acial overbreadth adjudication is an exception to our traditional rules of practice and that its function, a limited one at the outset, attenuates as the otherwise unprotected behavior that it forbids the State to sanction moves from "pure speech" toward conduct and that conduct — even if expressive — falls within the scope of otherwise valid criminal laws that reflect legitimate state interests in maintaining comprehensive controls over harmful, constitutionally unprotected conduct. . . . To put the matter another way, particularly where conduct and not merely speech is involved, we believe that the overbreadth of a statute must not only be real, but substantial as well, judged in relation to the statute's plainly legitimate sweep. It is our view that § 818 is not substantially overbroad and that whatever overbreadth may exist should be cured through case-by-case analysis of the fact situations to which its sanctions, assertedly, may not be applied.

Unlike ordinary breach-of-the-peace statutes or other broad regulatory acts, § 818 is directed, by its terms, at political expression which if engaged in by private persons would plainly be protected by the First and Fourteenth Amendments. But at the same time, § 818 is not a censorial statute, directed at particular groups or viewpoints. *Cf. Keyishian v. Bd. of Regents.* The statute, rather, seeks to regulate political activity in an even-handed and neutral manner. . . . Moreover, the fact remains that § 818 regulates a substantial spectrum of conduct that is as manifestly subject to state regulation as the public peace or criminal trespass. . . . Under the decision in *Letter Carriers,* there is no question that § 818 is valid at least insofar as it forbids classified employees from: soliciting contributions for partisan candidates, political parties, or other partisan political purposes; becoming members of national, state, or local committees of political parties, or officers or committee members in partisan political clubs or candidates for any paid public office; taking part in the management or affairs of any political party's partisan political campaign; serving as delegates or alternates to caucuses or conventions of political parties; addressing or taking an active part in partisan political rallies or meetings; soliciting votes or assisting voters at the polls or helping in a partisan effort to get voters to the polls; participating in the distribution of partisan campaign literature; initiating or circulating partisan nominating petitions; or riding in caravans for any political party or partisan political candidate.

. . . Without question, the conduct appellants have been charged with falls squarely within these proscriptions.

. . . The State Personnel Board . . . has construed § 818's explicit approval of "private" political expression to include virtually any expression not within the context of active partisan political campaigning, and the State's Attorney General, in plain terms, has interpreted § 818 as prohibiting "clearly partisan political activity" only. Surely a court cannot be expected to ignore these authoritative pronouncements in determining the breadth of a statute. . . . Appellants further point to the Board's interpretive rules purporting to restrict such allegedly protected activities as the wearing of political buttons or the use of bumper stickers. It may be that such restrictions are impermissible and that § 818 may be susceptible of some other improper applications. But, as presently construed, we do not believe that § 818 must be discarded in toto because some persons' arguably protected conduct may or may not be caught or chilled by the statute. Section 818 is not substantially overbroad and is not, therefore, unconstitutional on its face.

JUSTICE DOUGLAS, dissenting. . . .

I do not see how government can deprive its employees of the right to speak, write, assemble, or petition once the office is closed and the employee is home on his own. . . .

I would not allow the bureaucracy in the State or Federal government to be deprived of First Amendment rights. . . .

JUSTICE BRENNAN, with whom JUSTICE STEWART and JUSTICE MARSHALL join, dissenting. . . .

[T]he Court . . . does assume not only that the ban on the wearing of badges and buttons may be "impermissible," but also that the Act "may be susceptible of some other improper applications. . . . "

. . . [T]he Court makes no effort to define what it means by "substantial overbreadth. . . ."

NOTES

(1) *Hatch Act.* In a companion case to *Broadrick*, United *States Civil Serv. Comm'n v. Letter Carriers, AFL-CIO*, 413 U.S. 548 (1973), the Court (6-3) upheld provisions of the Hatch Act which prohibited Federal employees from taking "an active part in political campaigns." The statute delegated to the Civil Service Commission the job of defining the statutory proscription. The Commission's regulations prohibited only partisan political conduct, e.g., organizing a political club, managing a campaign, soliciting funds, which the First Amendment did not protect in light of the strong governmental interest in maintaining the non-partisan character of the federal civil service. The specificity of the regulations precluded a successful challenge on either overbreadth or vagueness grounds. Justices Douglas, Brennan and Marshall dissented, re-stating some of the arguments in the *Broadrick* dissents.

(2) *Ballot Access. Broadrick v. Oklahoma* was a principal basis for a 1982 decision (5-4) narrowly upholding two provisions of the Texas Constitution which limited the ability of designated public officials in Texas to run for other public offices, either (in some cases) by prohibiting them from running for the legislature until their present term of office has expired, or (in other cases) by treating the announcement of a candidacy as an automatic resignation from the candidate's present office. *Clements v. Fashing*, 457 U.S. 957 (1982). Justice Rehnquist's majority opinion rejected a First Amendment challenge, asserting that these restrictions "are in reality no different than the provisions we upheld in *Mitchell, Letter Carriers, and Broadrick*, which required dismissal of any civil servant who became a political candidate."

(3) *Sexual Performances by Children.* The "substantial overbreadth" analysis in *Broadrick* was employed by the Court in rejecting an overbreadth challenge to New York State's law which prohibits a person from promoting "sexual performances" by children under 16 through the distribution of material depicting such performances. *See New York v. Ferber*, 458 U.S. 747, (1982), in § 15.05, Obscenity. *See also Vill. of Schaumburg v. Citizens for a Better Env't*, 444 U.S. 620 (1980); *Erznoznik v. City of Jacksonville*, 422 U.S. 205 (1975) (allowing facial challenge of an ordinance prohibiting exhibition of non-obscene films visible from public streets).

(4) *Overbreadth and Standing.* The Court has sometimes been reluctant to allow the overbreadth doctrine to supply a litigant standing to pursue the claims of third parties, who are not parties to the litigation.

(a) Several Supreme Court decisions made in the 1990s may narrow the applicability of the overbreadth doctrine in cases of third-party standing. In *Madsen v. Women's Health Ctr.*, 512 U.S. 753 (1994), the Court refused to use the overbreadth doctrine to extend plaintiffs' standing to challenge portions of an injunction that did not affect them. Plaintiffs successfully challenged part of an ordinance which enjoined persons acting "in concert" with abortion clinic protestors. However, since Madsen was an actual protestor and not a person acting "in concert" with such protestors, Madsen needed her standing extended in order to challenge this portion of the ordinance. The Court declined to use the overbreadth doctrine to extend her standing because it might cause "an abstract controversy."

In *United States v. Nat'l Treasury Employees Union*, 513 U.S. 454 (1995), the Court again declined use of overbreadth to extend a party's standing to challenge portions of an injunction that did not affect them. In this case, government employees rated GS-16 and below challenged a ban on honoraria. These employees asked that the statute be held facially unconstitutional even as it applies to government employees rated above

GS-16. Although the Court did enjoin the statute as applied to GS-16 employees and below, it refused to use the overbreadth doctrine to afford plaintiffs standing to challenge the law's application to government employees above GS-16: "we neither want nor need to provide relief to nonparties when a narrower remedy will fully protect the litigants." For additional discussion of this case, *see* internet.

(5) *Abortion Protests.* In *Hill v. Colorado*, 530 U.S. 703 (2000), the Court rejected overbreadth and vagueness challenges to a statute that prohibits, within 100 feet of a health care facility, "knowingly" approaching "within eight feet of" a person without consent, "passing a leaflet or handbill to, displaying a sign to, or engaging in oral protest, education, or counseling." For more extensive treatment, see § 14.04.

In *Schenck v. Pro-Choice Network*, 519 U.S. 357 (1997), the Court rejected overbreadth and vagueness challenges to provisions of a district court injunction that imposed a "fixed buffer zone" restricting demonstrations within 15 feet of an entrance to an abortion clinic. However, the Court struck down the injunction's "floating buffer zone" which prohibited demonstrating "within fifteen feet of any person or vehicle seeking access to or leaving" an abortion clinic. Once an individual indicated that she did not want counseling, the two counselors permitted in the buffer zone had to stop counseling, retreat 15 feet from the people having been counseled, and remain outside the buffer zone. For more extensive treatment, see § 12.02.

(6) *"Interrupting" a Police Officer.* In *City of Houston v. Hill*, 482 U.S. 451 (1987), a Houston, Texas law provided that it "shall be unlawful for any person to assault, strike or in any manner oppose, molest, abuse or interrupt any policeman in the execution of his duty, or any person summoned to aid in making an arrest." Justice Brennan's opinion (joined by Justices White, Marshall, Blackmun, and Stevens) concluded that the law was "substantially overbroad" because it "criminalizes a substantial amount of constitutionally protected speech, and accords the police unconstitutional discretion in enforcement." Justice Powell appeared to disagree with the overbreadth analysis, concluding instead that the Houston statute was unconstitutionally vague. Justice Scalia agreed with Justice Powell's vagueness approach. Chief Justice Rehnquist dissented.

(7) *Speech in Airports.* In *Bd. of Airport Comm'rs of Los Angeles v. Jews for Jesus*, 482 U.S. 569 (1987), the Court held that a regulation of the Los Angeles Commissioners banning all "First Amendment activities" at the Airport was facially overbroad since it banned "the universe of expressive activity. . . . The regulation does not merely regulate expressive activity in the Central Terminal Area that might create problems such as congestion or the disruption of activities of those who use the [terminal]." For further discussion of this case, see § 14.04[4].

(8) *"Decency"/"respect."* In *Nat'l Endowment for the Arts v. Finley*, 524 U.S. 569 (1998) (the Court rejected a facial challenge to a provision of the National Foundation on the Arts and Humanities Act, upholding the requirements of "decency" and "respect" in considering applications for funding. These requirements neither infringe on artists' speech rights in creating artwork, nor are they unconstitutionally vague. For a further discussion of *Finley*, see § 15.03.)

(9) For further discussion on the impact of an overbreadth ruling, *see* Richard H. Fallon, Jr., *Making Sense of Overbreadth*, 100 YALE L.J. 853, 854, 907 (1991) ("Even a Supreme Court determination that a state statute is void for overbreadth lacks the strong medicinal effects often ascribed to such a pronouncement. The Supreme Court has no authority to excise a law from state's statute books. Nor can the Supreme Court bar a state court from providing a narrowing construction of an 'invalidated' statute to ensure that it operates within constitutional bounds. What an 'invalidated' statute means is a state law question; and whether the state court can and should change its

interpretation in light of a Supreme Court overbreadth holding is also a state law question. . . . [P]rophylactic overbreadth is a judge-made doctrine aimed at eliminating the chilling effect of overbroad statutes and, even more importantly, at inducing state legislatures to craft statutes narrowly and state courts to furnish narrowing constructions.").

(10) *Private Roads.* In *Virginia v. Hicks*, 539 U.S. 113 (2003), Justice Scalia, writing for a unanimous Court, rejected an overbreadth challenge to the trespass policy imposed by Richmond Redevelopment and Housing Authority (RRHA). The city of Richmond conveyed public streets to RRHA, which were "closed to public use and travel." RRHA's trespass policy prohibited anyone other than a resident or employee from entering the streets without "*a legitimate business or social purpose* for being on the premises." Any such person found on the premises would be notified that she was barred and subject to arrest if she came back. The respondent was convicted of trespassing and challenged the policy on overbreadth grounds.

To be overbroad, a law must apply a substantial amount of protected speech "not only in an absolute sense, but also relative to the scope of the law's plainly legitimate applications." Whether or not the Virginia courts should have allowed the overbreadth challenge to be presented is a state law issue as the Case or Controversy clause of the United States Constitution only limits federal courts. The rules at issue extend to all persons seeking to enter these private streets regardless of whether they "seek to engage in expression." Overbreadth challenges rarely "succeed against a law or regulation that is not specifically addressed to speech or to conduct necessarily associated with speech (such as picketing or demonstrating.)" Alleged First Amendment violations caused by this law can be addressed through as-applied challenges. Justice Souter filed a concurring opinion, joined by Justice Breyer.

[3] Employee's Right to Criticize Government

CONNICK v. MYERS
461 U.S. 138, 103 S. Ct. 1684, 75 L. Ed. 2d. 708 (1983)

JUSTICE WHITE delivered the opinion of the Court.

In *Pickering v. Bd. of Educ.*, 391 U.S. 563 (1968), we stated that a public employee does not relinquish First Amendment rights to comment on matters of public interest by virtue of government employment. . . . The problem, we thought, was arriving "at a balance between the interests of the [employee], as a citizen, in commenting upon matters of public concern and the interest of the State, as an employer, in promoting the efficiency of the public services it performs through its employees." *Id.* We return to this problem today and consider whether the First and Fourteenth Amendments prevent the discharge of a state employee for circulating a questionnaire concerning internal office affairs.

I

The respondent, Sheila Myers, was employed as an Assistant District Attorney in New Orleans for five and a half years. She served at the pleasure of petitioner Harry Connick, the District Attorney for Orleans Parish. During this period Myers competently performed her responsibilities of trying criminal cases.

In the early part of October, 1980, Myers was informed that she would be transferred to prosecute cases in a different section of the criminal court. Myers was strongly opposed to the proposed transfer and expressed her view to several of her supervisors, including Connick. Despite her objections, on October 6 Myers was notified that she was being transferred. Myers again spoke with Dennis Waldron, one of the first assistant district attorneys, expressing her reluctance to accept the transfer. A number of other office matters were discussed and Myers later testified that, in response to Waldron's suggestion that her concerns were not shared by others in the office, she informed him that she would do some research on the matter.

That night Myers prepared a questionnaire soliciting the views of her fellow staff members concerning office transfer policy, office morale, the need for a grievance committee, the level of confidence in supervisors, and whether employees felt pressured to work in political campaigns. . . . Myers then distributed the questionnaire to 15 assistant district attorneys. Shortly after noon, Dennis Waldron learned that Myers was distributing the survey. He immediately phoned Connick and informed him that Myers was creating a "mini-insurrection" within the office. Connick returned to the office and told Myers that she was being terminated because of her refusal to accept the transfer. She was also told that her distribution of the questionnaire was considered an act of insubordination. Connick particularly objected to the question which inquired whether employees "had confidence in and would rely on the word" of various superiors in the office, and to a question concerning pressure to work in political campaigns which he felt would be damaging if discovered by the press.

Myers filed suit under 42 U.S.C. § 1983, contending that her employment was wrongfully terminated because she had exercised her constitutionally-protected right of free speech. . . .

II

. . . *Pickering v. Bd. of Educ.* . . . held impermissible under the First Amendment the dismissal of a high school teacher for openly criticizing the Board of Education on its allocation of school funds between athletics and education and its methods of informing taxpayers about the need for additional revenue. *Pickering's* subject was "a matter of legitimate public concern" upon which "free and open debate is vital to informed decision-making by the electorate." 391 U.S. at 571–72.

Our cases following *Pickering* also involved safeguarding speech on matters of public concern. . . .

Pickering, its antecedents and progeny, lead us to conclude that if Myers' questionnaire cannot be fairly characterized as constituting speech on a matter of public concern, it is unnecessary for us to scrutinize the reasons for her discharge. When employee expression cannot be fairly considered as relating to any matter of political, social, or other concern to the community, government officials should enjoy wide latitude in managing their offices, without intrusive oversight by the judiciary in the name of the First Amendment. Perhaps the government employer's dismissal of the worker may not be fair, but ordinary dismissals from government service which violate no fixed tenure or applicable statute or regulation are not subject to judicial review even if the reasons for the dismissal are alleged to be mistaken or unreasonable. . . .

We do not suggest, however, that Myers' speech, even if not touching upon a matter of public concern, is totally beyond the protection of the First Amendment. . . . For example, an employee's false criticism of his employer on grounds not of public concern may be cause for his discharge but would be entitled to the same protection in a libel action accorded an identical statement made by a man on the street. We hold only that when a public employee speaks not as a citizen upon matters of public concern, but instead as an employee upon matters only of personal interest, absent the most unusual circumstances, a federal court is not the appropriate forum in which to review the wisdom of a personnel decision taken by a public agency allegedly in reaction to the employee's behavior.

Whether an employee's speech addresses a matter of public concern must be determined by the content, form, and context of a given statement, as revealed by the whole record. In this case, with but one exception, the questions posed by Myers to her coworkers do not fall under the rubric of matters of "public concern." We view the questions pertaining to the confidence and trust that Myers' coworkers possess in various supervisors, the level of office morale, and the need for a grievance committee as mere extensions of Myers' dispute over her transfer to another section of the criminal court. . . .   Myers did not seek to inform the public that the District Attorney's office was not discharging its governmental responsibilities in the investigation and prosecution of criminal cases. Nor did Myers seek to bring to light actual or potential wrongdoing or breach of public trust on the part of Connick and others. . . .   While discipline and morale in the workplace are related to an agency's efficient performance of its duties, the focus of Myers' questions is not to evaluate the performance of the office but rather to gather ammunition for another round of controversy with her superiors. . . . [13]

One question in Myers' questionnaire, however, does touch upon a matter of public concern. Question 11 inquires if assistant district attorneys "ever feel pressured to work in political campaigns on behalf of office supported candidates. . . . "

B

Because one of the questions in Myers' survey touched upon a matter of public concern, and contributed to her discharge we must determine whether Connick was justified in discharging Myers. . . .   *Pickering* unmistakably states, and respondent agrees, that the state's burden in justifying a particular discharge varies depending upon the nature of the employee's expression. . . .

C

The *Pickering* balance requires full consideration of the government's interest in the effective and efficient fulfillment of its responsibilities to the public. . . .

We agree with the District Court that there is no demonstration here that the questionnaire impeded Myers' ability to perform her responsibilities. The District Court was also correct to recognize that "it is important to the efficient and successful operation of the District Attorney's office for Assistants to maintain close working relationships with their superiors." 507 F. Supp., at 759. . . .   When close working relationships are essential to fulfilling public responsibilities, a wide degree of deference to the employer's judgment is appropriate. Furthermore, we do not see the necessity for an employer to allow events to unfold to the extent that the disruption of the office and the destruction of working relationships is manifest before taking action. We caution that a stronger showing may be necessary if the employee's speech more substantially involved matters of public concern. . . .

Also relevant is the manner, time, and place in which the questionnaire was distributed. . . .   Although some latitude in when official work is performed is to be allowed when professional employees are involved, and Myers did not violate

---

[13] [Court's footnote 8] This is not a case like *Givhan*, where an employee speaks out as a citizen on a matter of general concern, not tied to a personal employment dispute, but arranges to do so privately. Mrs. Givhan's right to protest racial discrimination — a matter inherently of public concern — is not forfeited by her choice of a private forum. . . .

announced office policy, the fact that Myers, unlike Pickering, exercised her rights to speech at the office supports Connick's fears that the functioning of his office was endangered.

Finally, the context in which the dispute arose is also significant. This is not a case where an employee, out of purely academic interest, circulated a questionnaire so as to obtain useful research. Myers acknowledges that it is no coincidence that the questionnaire followed upon the heels of the transfer notice. When employee speech concerning office policy arises from an employment dispute concerning the very application of that policy to the speaker, additional weight must be given to the supervisor's view that the employee has threatened the authority of the employer to run the office. . . .

III

Myers' questionnaire touched upon matters of public concern in only a most limited sense. . . . The limited First Amendment interest involved here does not require that Connick tolerate action which he reasonably believed would disrupt the office, undermine his authority, and destroy close working relationships. . . . We reiterate, however, the caveat we expressed in *Pickering*, *supra*, at 569: "Because of the enormous variety of fact situations in which critical statements by . . . public employees may be thought by their superiors . . . to furnish grounds for dismissal, we do not deem it either appropriate or feasible to lay down a general standard against which all such statements may be judged."

[I]t would indeed be a Pyrrhic victory for the great principles of free expression if the Amendment's safeguarding of a public employee's right, as a citizen, to participate in discussions concerning public affairs were confused with the attempt to constitutionalize the employee grievance that we see presented here. . . .

JUSTICE BRENNAN, with whom JUSTICE MARSHALL, JUSTICE BLACKMUN, and JUSTICE STEVENS join, dissenting. . . .

I . . .

The Court's decision today is flawed in three respects. First, the Court distorts the balancing analysis required under *Pickering* by suggesting that one factor, the context in which a statement is made, is to be weighed *twice* — first in determining whether an employee's speech addresses a matter of public concern and then in deciding whether the statement adversely affected the government's interest as an employer. Second, in concluding that the effect of respondent's personnel policies on employee morale and the work performance of the District Attorney's Office is not a matter of public concern, the Court impermissibly narrows the class of subjects on which public employees may speak out without fear of retaliatory dismissal. Third, the Court misapplies the *Pickering* balancing test in holding that Myers could constitutionally be dismissed for circulating a questionnaire addressed to at least one subject that *was* "a matter of interest to the community," in the absence of evidence that her conduct disrupted the efficient functioning of the District Attorney's Office.

II

. . . I would hold that Myers' questionnaire addressed matters of public concern because it discussed subjects that could reasonably be expected to be of interest to persons seeking to develop informed opinions about the manner in which the Orleans Parish District Attorney, an elected official charged with managing a vital governmental agency, discharges his responsibilities. . . . It is beyond doubt that personnel decisions that adversely affect discipline and morale may ultimately impair an agency's efficient performance of its duties. . . .

. . . [T]he Court misapplies the *Pickering* test and holds — against our previous authorities — that a public employer's mere apprehension that speech will be disruptive justifies suppression of that speech when all the objective evidence suggests that those fears are essentially unfounded. . . .

The Court's decision today inevitably will deter public employees from making critical statements about the manner in which government agencies are operated for fear that doing so will provoke their dismissal. As a result, the public will be deprived of valuable information with which to evaluate the performance of elected officials. . . .

NOTES

(1) *Employee's Speech on Matters of Public Concern.* In *Rankin v. McPherson*, 483 U.S. 378 (1987), a 19-year-old probationary clerical worker was fired because, after hearing about the attempted assassination of President Reagan on March 30, 1981, she remarked to her co-worker and boyfriend, in what she thought was a purely private conversation, "If they go for him again, I hope they get him." The remark was overheard by another employee who reported it to the County Constable who promptly fired the employee. Although the discharged employee was designated a "deputy constable," all employees of the constable's office, regardless of actual duties, had this title. According to Justice Marshall's majority opinion which held the discharge unconstitutional, "[the employee] was not a commissioned peace officer, did not wear a uniform, and was not authorized to make arrests or permitted to carry a gun. . . . Her job was to type data from court papers into a computer that maintained an automated record of the status of civil process in the county."

The majority (Justice Marshall, joined by Justices Brennan, Blackmun, Powell, and Stevens), applied the *Connick v. Myers* analysis and concluded that the speech "plainly dealt with a matter of public concern" and "there is no evidence that it interfered with the efficient functioning of the office." Nor had the employee "discredited the office by making her statement in public," and, since she served no policymaking or public contact role, she could not be said to have undermined the mission of her public employer or interfered with the agency's successful functioning.

Justice Scalia's vigorous dissent, joined by Chief Justice Rehnquist, and Justices White and O'Connor, concluded: "In sum . . . Constable Rankin's interest in maintaining both an esprit de corps and a public image consistent with his office's law enforcement duties outweighs any interest his employees may have in expressing on the job a desire that the President be killed."

(2) *Speech Unrelated to a Matter of Public Concern.* In *City of San Diego, California v. Roe*, 543 U.S. 77 (2004), the Court, in a unanimous per curiam opinion, held that a police officer's sexually explicit videos were not protected government employee speech. In a video that he sold on eBay, the officer, wearing a police uniform, issued a ticket but revoked it after masturbating. The San Diego Police Department ordered the officer to stop distributing sexually explicit material, and after he failed to remove the description and price of the videos from his eBay profile, the Department terminated the officer.

The First Amendment protects the right of government employees to "speak on matters of public concern, typically matters concerning government policies that are of interest to the public at large." Moreover, under *United States v. Treasury Employees*, 513 U.S. 454 (1995), they may "speak or write on their own time on topics unrelated to their employment" unless the government has a "justification 'far stronger than mere speculation' in regulating it." Neither of these theories protect the police officer's speech in this case.

As the speech at issue was not a matter of public concern under *Connick v. Meyers*, 461 U.S. 138 (1983), *supra*, the *Pickering v. Board of Education* balancing test does not even apply to this case. Connick "directs courts to examine the 'content, form and context of a given statement, as revealed by the whole record' in assessing whether an employee's speech addresses a matter of public concern." This standard is the same as that for an invasion of privacy action at common law. Matters of public concern include subjects "of legitimate news interest." They can also include "certain private remarks, such as negative comments about the President." However, "this is not a close case," as the police officer's activities neither involved political news nor public information about the police department's functioning. Instead, the officer's speech was "designed to exploit his employer's image" and harmed its "mission and functions."

(3) *Employee's Right to Confer with Employer on Employment-Related Matters*. In *Minnesota State Bd. for Cmty. Colls. v. Knight*, 465 U.S. 271 (1984), a state statute defining the rights of bargaining agents and their members required public employers to "meet and negotiate" with the exclusive bargaining agent of public employees on terms and conditions of employment. Professional employees, such as college faculty members, were given the right to "meet and confer" with their employers on employment-related matters outside the scope of mandatory collective bargaining. However, if professional employees have selected an exclusive bargaining agent, the employer may not meet and confer with any member of the bargaining unit except through the exclusive representative.

The Court (6-3) rejected the nonunion faculty members' claim of constitutional entitlement to a particular form of a government audience to communicate views to their employers. Justice O'Connor's opinion stressed that nonunion members were free both to communicate their views and to associate for purposes of advocating them. They are not, however, entitled to a government audience.

In his dissent, Justice Stevens found the breadth of communication prohibited by this statute to be "remarkable." Justice Stevens also suggested that the Minnesota statute violated public employees' First Amendment right *not* to associate since it totally curtailed the ability of nonunion faculty members to communicate effectively with public policy-making bodies. Justices Brennan and Powell also dissented while Justice Marshall concurred in the judgment, but objected to some of the sweeping language in the Court's opinion concerning the rights of employees or citizens to have their views heard.

(4) *Private Criticism of Government*. In *Givhan v. W. Line Consol. Sch. Dist.*, 439 U.S. 410 (1979), the Court unanimously rejected a Court of Appeal's conclusion that a school teacher's communication to her school principal lacked constitutional protection because it was private in nature. During meetings with the principal in the principal's office, petitioner had used strong language to convey her dissatisfaction with allegedly discriminatory school policies. Writing for the Court, Justice Rehnquist insisted that freedom of speech was not forfeited just because a public employee chose to communicate with her employer in private rather than in public.

(5) *Employee's Right to Reinstatement after Unconstitutional Discharge*. The *Givhan* case, *supra*, also discussed the employee's remedy following a discharge for the exercise of a constitutional right. While *Givhan* was pending at the Court of Appeals, the Supreme Court had handed down its decision in *Mt. Healthy City Sch. Dist. v. Doyle*, 429 U.S. 274 (1977). In that case, the Court had rejected the view that a public employee must be reinstated if constitutionally protected conduct is found to have played a substantial part in the decision to dismiss. In his *Givhan* opinion, Justice

Rehnquist noted that such a rule would have the absurd result that it would "require reinstatement of employees that the public employer would have dismissed even if the constitutionally protected conduct had not occurred and consequently 'could place an employee in a better position as a result of the exercise of constitutionally protected conduct than he would have occupied had he done nothing.'" Thus, the Court in *Givhan* held that once the employee has shown that his constitutionally protected conduct played a 'substantial role' in the employer's decision not to rehire him, the employer is entitled to show 'by a preponderance of the evidence that it would have reached the same decision as to [the employee's] reemployment even in the absence of the protected conduct.'"

(6) *See* Note, *Politics and the Non-Civil Service Public Employee: A Categorical Approach to First Amendment Protection*, 85 Colum. L. Rev. 558 (1985) (describing the analysis in speech discharge cases as "ad hoc balancing").

WATERS v. CHURCHILL, 511 U.S. 661 (1994). In *Waters*, the Court held that a public employer who intends to discharge an employee for alleged insubordinate remarks must conduct a reasonable investigation of the incident and must believe the results of such inquiry to be true. The case arose out of a conversation between nurses Cheryl Churchill and Melanie Perkins-Graham during a dinner break at a public hospital. Churchill allegedly made inappropriate, negative remarks denigrating the hospital and her supervisors. Churchill insisted that her statements were primarily limited to criticism of hospital policy which she believed threatened patient care and exacerbated staff shortages. After several interviews with those who overheard the conversation as well as Churchill herself, the hospital fired Churchill.

Churchill sued under 42 U.S.C § 1983, claiming that she had been discharged for speech that involved a matter of public concern under the analysis set forth in *Connick v. Myers*, 461 U.S. 138 (1983), *supra*.

Writing for a plurality of four, Justice O'Connor stated that what procedural safeguards the First Amendment mandates must be decided on a case-by-case basis. Rather than following some general rule, "the propriety of a proposed procedure must turn on the particular context in which the question arises — on the cost of the procedure and the relative magnitude and constitutional significance of the risks" at stake. The Court has afforded the government greater latitude in its role as employer than in its role as sovereign.

The practical realities of the employer-employee relationship require that the government maintain greater power to restrict the speech of its employees than the speech of other citizens. For example, government employees do not enjoy First Amendment protection for offensive speech, false speech, political campaigning, or, for high-ranking executive officers, criticizing the government. Different procedural safeguards also obtain for speech by government employees. For instance, restrictions on speech may be vague, such as, do not be "'rude to customers.'" Procedurally, the Court has given "substantial weight to government employers' reasonable predictions of disruption, even when the speech involved is on a matter of public concern."

Government employees, like all citizens, may have a legitimate interest in voicing their opinions on public matters. Moreover, government employees are in a unique position to identify the weaknesses of their respective agencies. Of course, the government can extend additional protections to its employees beyond what the First Amendment requires.[14]

---

[14] For example, the government may protect certain kinds of disruptive activity like whistleblowing. *See* Whistleblower Protection Act of 1989, 5 U.S.C.A. § 1201 (1994). . . .

The government's interest in efficiently and effectively carrying out its goals as employer increases its power in this area. In determining facts, the government employers need not adhere to the boundaries of evidentiary rules. Employers, both public and private, rely on hearsay, personal knowledge, and other indicative factors in investigating matters. For example, a government manager may discipline an employee based on accusations of a co-worker or complaints by patrons that the employee is rude-even if these are reported by someone else as hearsay.

If "a reasonable supervisor would recognize that there is a substantial likelihood" that the speech actually uttered by the employee is protected, then the supervisor must treat with additional care. The discharge cannot be based on no evidence of what was said or based "on extremely weak evidence when strong evidence is clearly available." This care need not reach the level necessitated by trial procedure; however, it should "be the care that a reasonable manager would use before making an employment decision-discharge, suspension, reprimand, or whatever else-of the sort involved in the particular case." There may indeed be instances in which reasonable employers would disagree as to the extent of investigation and as to who is to be believed. In such cases, "many different courses of action will necessarily be reasonable. Only procedures outside the range of what a reasonable manager would use may be condemned as unreasonable."

The inquiry conducted by the hospital supported the reasonable belief that Churchill had made disruptive comments. The manager making the determination had "the word of two trusted employees, the endorsement of those employees' reliability by three hospital managers, and the benefit of a face-to-face meeting with the employee he fired." Furthermore, under the *Connick* test, Churchill's speech, as reported by several others, was unprotected. Even if Churchill's criticism of the cross-training policy "was speech on a matter of public concern-something we need not decide-the potential disruptiveness of the speech as reported was enough to outweigh whatever First Amendment value it might have had." Discouraging an employee from working for a department, undermining management's authority to another employee, and saying that the employee could not "wipe the slate clean" with the supervisor were, as a matter of law, unprotected statements.

Nor was Churchill protected from discharge by having made other nondisruptive remarks which addressed matters of public concern. "An employee who makes an unprotected statement is not immunized from discipline by the fact that this statement is surrounded by protected statements." The crucial inquiry is whether she was fired solely for her unprotected statements that were disruptive or unrelated to a matter of public concern. The *Connick* test is applicable only to statements for which the individual was discharged.

Since the case had come up on summary judgment, the Court remanded it as, on the record, reasonable factfinders might differ on whether Churchill was actually fired because of her disruptive statements or because of her nondisruptive statements concerning hospital policy.

Although Justice Souter joined Justice O'Connor's plurality opinion, he wrote separately, concurring in the judgment, "to emphasize that, in order to avoid liability, the public employer must not only reasonably investigate the third-party report, but must also actually believe it." A court must examine both the objective reasonableness of the employer's investigation and his actual, subjective beliefs.

Justice Scalia, joined by Justices Kennedy and Thomas, wrote a separate concurrence criticizing the requirement of a reasonable investigation as effectively instituting a new First Amendment procedural right. Justice Scalia said that employers would have difficulty ascertaining what procedures will satisfy the plurality's standard.

A pretext analysis, ferreting out government intent, was adequate in other areas.

Justice Stevens, joined by Justice Blackmun, dissented. Justice Stevens would have the trier of fact make findings as to what the employee actually said rather than simply the reasonableness of management's inquiry. The reasonableness of a government employer's decision in violating a First Amendment right went to the issue of damages, not to the existence of the violation.

GARCETTI v. CEBALLOS, 546 U.S. 410 (2006). In *Garcetti*, the Court held "that when public employees make statements pursuant to their official duties, the employees are not speaking as citizens for First Amendment purposes, and the Constitution does not insulate their communications from employer discipline."

Defense counsel alleged that an affidavit used to obtain a search warrant contained certain "inaccuracies" that prompted him to challenge the warrant. In his supervisory capacity as deputy district attorney, Ceballos investigated. After conducting an investigation, plaintiff thought that the affidavit contained several material inaccuracies. After speaking "on the telephone to the warrant affiant, a deputy sheriff," plaintiff communicated his concerns to his supervisors and prepared "a disposition memorandum" which "recommended dismissal of the case." Plaintiff later submitted a second memo to his supervisor "describing a second telephone conversation between Ceballos and the warrant affiant." Ceballos' actions led to a meeting between all interested parties which "allegedly became heated" and the prosecution continued "[d]espite Ceballos' concerns." Ceballos claims that he suffered "retaliatory employment actions" in response to the above events.

Ceballos sued under 42 U.S.C. § 1983, claiming that the retaliatory actions violated his First Amendment rights.

Justice Kennedy wrote for a 5-4 majority. It is well-established that a public employee has a right, "in certain circumstances, to speak as a citizen" on matters of public concern. However, a government entity has broad "discretion to restrict speech when it acts in its role as employer, but the restrictions it imposes must be directed at speech that has some potential to affect the entity's operations." A citizen who works for the government "by necessity must accept certain limitations on his or her freedom." The government, like any employer, must ensure that services are rendered efficiently. When a public employee, who is often in a position of trust, expresses her views, this speech might "contravene governmental policies or impair the proper performance of governmental functions."

At the same time, "the Court has recognized that a citizen who works for the government is nonetheless a citizen." As established in *Connick v. Myers, supra,* if "employees are speaking as citizens about matters of public concern, they must face only those speech restrictions that are necessary for their employers to operate efficiently and effectively." There is value in "promoting the public's interest in receiving the well-informed views of government employees engaging in civic discussion;" however, this protection value does not go so far as to " 'constitutionalize the employee grievance.' "

The case at hand does not turn on Ceballos' having "expressed his views inside his office, rather than publicly." Second, that the speech in the memo concerned the speaker's job is also "nondispositive." Instead, the "controlling factor" is that plaintiff's "expressions were made pursuant to his duties as a calendar deputy." Restriction of speech involves "employer control over what the employer itself has commissioned or created." Ceballos was not acting as a citizen when he wrote the memo; he was acting as a government employee. Ceballos' duties leading to the memo included activities such as "supervising attorneys, investigating charges, and preparing filings." Consequently, if his "supervisors thought his memo was inflammatory or misguided, they had the authority to take proper corrective action."

Consistent "with the sound principles of federalism and the separation of powers," established precedents forbid "judicial supervision" overriding "managerial discretion" in supervision of government employees. Public employees maintain some protection for public speech unrelated to their employment responsibilities as this activity resembles that of a private citizen. The analogy to a private citizen evaporates if "a public employee speaks pursuant to employment responsibilities." Public employers cannot restrict "employees' rights by creating excessively broad job descriptions." As job descriptions are rarely accurate representations of an employee's true responsibilities, "the listing of a given task in an employee's written job description is neither necessary nor sufficient to demonstrate that conducting the task is within the scope of the employee's professional duties for First Amendment purposes." Moreover, Justice Kennedy stated that the Court is not deciding if this analysis "would apply in the same manner to a case involving speech related to scholarship or teaching." The typical governmental employer-employee relationship does not fully account for the constitutional interest in academic freedom.

Finally, when government employees seek to excuse "inefficiency and misconduct," they have a "powerful network of legislative enactments-such as whistle-blower protection laws and labor codes."

In his dissent, Justice Stevens rejected "a categorical difference between speaking as a citizen and speaking in the course of one's employment." In *Givhan v. W. Line Consol. Sch. Dist.*, 439 U.S. 410 (1979), the Court did not consider whether the teacher's speech was related to her employment responsibilities. The Court has not hinged "constitutional protection for exactly the same words . . . on whether they fall within a job description."

Justice Souter also dissented, joined by Justice Stevens and Justice Ginsberg. Justice Souter would "hold that private and public interests in addressing official wrongdoing and threats to health and safety can outweigh the government's stake in the efficient implementation of policy," and when they do, "public employees who speak on these matters in the course of their duties should be eligible to claim First Amendment protection." Justice Souter maintains "that the individual and public value of such speech is no less, and may well be greater, when the employee speaks pursuant to his duties in addressing a subject he knows intimately for the very reason that it falls within his duties." The public's interest in such speech is high "when, for example, a public auditor speaks on his discovery of embezzlement of public funds, when a building inspector makes an obligatory report of an attempt to bribe him, or when a law enforcement officer expressly balks at a superior's order to violate constitutional rights he is sworn to protect." The decision also threatens "First Amendment protection of academic freedom in public colleges and universities, whose teachers necessarily speak and write 'pursuant to official duties.' " For example, a teacher's job responsibilities could be broadened to "invest them with a general obligation to ensure sound administration of the school."

The majority's rule encourages government to define the job duties of public employees expansively to diminish First Amendment protection. So, for example, "the First Amendment gives Ceballos no protection, even if his judgment in this case was sound and appropriately expressed." The majority's caution that job duties be interpreted practically will only engender litigation. Finally, "state and national statutes protecting government whistleblowers from vindictive bosses" do not undercut the need for First Amendment protection as these vary dramatically.

In a separate dissent, Justice Breyer argued that the majority's rule is "too absolute" as it never protects a public employee who speaks "in the course of his ordinary duties." On the other hand, Justice Souter's standard "fails to give sufficient weight to the serious managerial and administrative concerns" of government employers. Justice Breyer concludes "that the First Amendment sometimes does authorize judicial actions based upon a government employee's speech that both (1) involves a matter of public concern and also (2) takes place in the course of ordinary job-related duties. But it does so only in the presence of augmented need for constitutional protection and diminished risk of undue judicial interference with governmental management of the public's affairs." As these conditions were met in this case, he applied the *Pickering* balancing test here.

BD. OF COMM'RS v. UMBEHR, 518 U.S. 668 (1996). In *Umbehr*, the Court held that "the First Amendment protects independent contractors from the termination of at-will government contracts in retaliation for their exercise of the freedom of speech."

The plaintiff, Umbehr, had an exclusive contract with Wabaunsee County, Kansas (County) to haul trash for six cities in the county from 1985 to 1991. As negotiated, the contract was "automatically renewed annually unless either party terminated it by giving notice at least 60 days before the end of the year or a renegotiation was instituted on 90 days' notice." During this time, "Umbehr was an outspoken critic of" the Board of County Commissioners, speaking out at meetings of the Board and writing letters and editorials in the local newspapers. He accused the Board of violating the Kansas Open Meetings Act, allegations which were later vindicated, and ran for a position on the Board himself, but lost. The Board terminated Umbehr's contract with the County in 1991, and Umbehr brought this action.

Justice O'Connor, writing for a 7-2 majority in which Chief Justice Rehnquist joined in all but one part of the opinion, began by pointing out the similarities between government employees and contractors. Both employees and independent contractors receive financial benefits, "the threat of the loss of which in retaliation for speech may chill speech on matters of public concern by those who, because of their dealings with the government, 'are often in the best position to know what ails the agencies for which they work.'"

The Court found "no reason to believe that proper application of the *Pickering* balancing test cannot accommodate the differences between employees and independent contractors. There is ample reason to believe that such a nuanced approach, which recognizes the variety of interests that may arise in independent contractor cases, is superior to a brightline rule distinguishing independent contractors from employees." The Court's "unconstitutional conditions precedents span a spectrum from government employees, whose close relationship with the government requires a balancing of important free speech and government interests, to claimants for tax exemptions, users of public facilities, and recipients of small government subsidies who are much less dependent on the government but more like ordinary citizens whose viewpoints on matters of public concern the government has no legitimate interest in repressing." The status of independent contractors seems "to lie somewhere between" employees and persons having less close relationships with the government.

In the part of her opinion in which Chief Justice Rehnquist did not join, Justice O'Connor rejected the "dissent's fears of excessive litigation" as a justification for "a special exception to our unconstitutional conditions precedent to deprive independent government contractors of protection."

The Court concluded that independent contractors and government employees are similar "in most relevant respects," even though "both the speaker's and the government's interests are typically-though not always-somewhat less strong in the independent contractor case." Therefore, "the same form of balancing analysis should apply to each."

The Court remanded to apply the balancing test. "To prevail, Umbehr must show that the termination of his contract was motivated by his speech on a matter of public concern, an initial showing that requires him to prove more than the mere fact that he criticized the Board members before they terminated him. If he can make that showing, the Board will have a valid defense if it can show, by a preponderance of the evidence, that, in light of their knowledge, perception and policies at the time of the termination, the Board members would have terminated the contract regardless of his speech. The Board will also prevail if it can persuade the District Court that the County's legitimate interests as contractor, deferentially viewed, outweigh the free speech interests at stake. And, if Umbehr prevails, evidence that the Board members discovered facts after termination that would have led to a later termination anyway, and evidence of mitigation of his loss by means of his subsequent contracts with the cities, would be relevant in assessing what remedy is appropriate."

Finally, the Court emphasized that since "Umbehr's suit concerns the termination of a pre-existing commercial relationship with the government, we need not address the possibility of suits by bidders or applicants for new government contracts who cannot rely on such a relationship."

Justice Scalia's dissenting opinion, in which Justice Thomas joined, was identical to his dissent in a companion case, *O'Hare Truck Serv. v. City of Northlake. See* § 12.01[1]. *Elrod* and *Branti* conflict with the long-standing American political tradition of "rewarding one's allies" and "refusing to reward one's opponents." But even if one agrees with *Elrod* and *Branti*, their principles should not be extended to independent contractors. Public employees are always individuals, to whom "the termination or denial of a public job is the termination or denial of a livelihood. A public contractor, on the other hand, is usually a corporation; and the contract it loses is rarely its entire business, or even an indispensable part of its entire business."

Extending speech and political affiliation protection to independent contractors will greatly increase the volume of litigation in the field of government contracting. The majority's decision means "that all government entities, no matter how small, are at risk of § 1983 lawsuits for violation of constitutional rights, unless they adopt (at great cost in money and efficiency) the detailed and cumbersome procedures that make a claim of political favoritism (and a § 1983 lawsuit) easily defended against."

To illustrate some of the difficulties that the decision may cause, Justice Scalia gives "an uncomfortable example from real life: An organization (I shall call it the White Aryan Supremacist Party, though that was not the organization involved in the actual incident I have in mind) is undoubtedly entitled, under the Constitution, to maintain and propagate racist and antisemitic views. But when the Department of Housing and Urban Development lets out contracts to private security forces to maintain law and order in units of public housing, must it really treat this bidder the same as all others?" Many state and local regulations "require that a contract be awarded not to the lowest bidder but to the 'lowest responsible bidder.'" However, the Court's decision will, "presumably," allow this type of consideration "only if the disfavored moral views of the bidder have never been verbalized, for otherwise the First Amendment will produce entitlement to the contract, or at least guarantee a lawsuit."

At least when there is alleged retaliation for speech as against party affiliation, the *Umbehr* majority follows the *Pickering* balancing test, rather than the compelling state interest test. *O'Hare* contradicted *Umbehr* by not applying the balancing test. To reconcile *O'Hare* with *Umbehr*, the Court divided "'freedom of speech'" into two different categories: "(1) the 'right of free speech,' where 'we apply the balancing test from *Pickering*,' and . . . (2) 'political affiliation,' where we apply the rigid rule of *Elrod* and *Branti*." Even if "facts involving the 'right of free speech' and facts involving 'political affiliation' can actually be segregated into separate categories, there arises, of course, the problem of what to do when both are involved. One would expect the more rigid test (*Elrod* nonbalancing) to prevail." Instead, where " 'specific instances of the employee's speech or expression, which require balancing in the *Pickering* context, are intermixed with a political affiliation requirement,' balancing rather than categorical liability will be the result."

Finally, Justice Scalia predicted that the principles of both cases easily extend to contract bidders, despite the majority's assertion that it was not deciding that case.

[4]   Special Protection for Legislators and other Government Employees

HUTCHINSON v. PROXMIRE, 443 U.S. 111 (1979). One of the issues considered by the Court in this case was whether the Speech and Debate Clause of the Constitution (Art. 1, § 6) affords members of Congress immunity against defamation suits based upon their statements in press releases and newsletters. A research behavioral scientist had instituted action against Senator Proxmire, after the Senator had awarded his "Golden Fleece" award, for the most egregious waste of public money, to the Federal agency that had sponsored the petitioner's research. Senator Proxmire's speech in the Senate, in which he announced the award, was quoted in a widely circulated press release. It was also publicized in newsletters subsequently distributed by the Senator's office.

Writing for the Court, Chief Justice Burger observed that, literally read, the Speech and Debate Clause would protect only speech in either of the two Houses of Congress. Prior Supreme Court precedents did not, however, so restrict the immunity afforded by the Clause. For example, committee hearings were covered by the Clause, even if they were held outside the chambers. Still, this broad reading of the Clause had not gone beyond the objective of protecting only legislative activities. Nor was there any precedent for treating the Clause as protective of all speech and conduct outside the House which was in some way related to the legislative process. " 'Legislative acts are not all-encompassing. The heart of the Clause is speech or debate in either House. Insofar as the Clause is construed to reach other matters, *they must be an integral part of the deliberative and communicative processes by which Members participate in committee and House proceedings* with respect to the consideration and passage or rejection of proposed legislation or with respect to other matters which the Constitution places within the jurisdiction of either House . . .' *Gravel v. United States*, *supra*, 408 U.S. at 625 (emphasis added)."

NOTES

(1) *Legislative Privileges*. A privilege similar to that in the Speech and Debate Clause exists, either by common law, statute, or constitution, in virtually all states. In *Tenney v. Brandhove*, 341 U.S. 367 (1951), the Court, relying in part on the widespread recognition of the privilege at the federal and state levels, held that state legislators were immune from suit under the federal civil rights laws, specifically 42 U.S.C. 1983, if they were acting in their legislative capacities. The Court also has held, however, that a state legislator has no privilege to bar the introduction of evidence of legislative acts in federal criminal proceedings. *United States v. Gillock*, 445 U.S. 360 (1980).

(2) *Executive Privileges*. In *Barr v. Matteo*, 360 U.S. 564 (1959), the Court extended a privilege against defamation actions to federal executive officials. It is an absolute privilege as long as the utterance is within "the outer perimeter" of the official's duties. Many states have fashioned similar privileges to state executive officials. The broad

protection for freedom of speech of government officials should be compared with the more limited protection which is accorded to private citizens who criticize public officials. *See New York Times v. Sullivan*, 376 U.S. 245 (1964), § 13.08[1].

In *Harlow v. Fitzgerald*, 457 U.S. 800 (1982), the Court held that executive officials of the Federal Government are generally entitled only to qualified, or good-faith, immunity in damage suits alleging unlawful conduct. It is not clear whether the absolute privilege upheld in *Barr v. Matteo* for common law defamation suits survives *Harlow v. Fitzgerald*, but the one reference to *Barr* in the latter case would appear to indicate that the Court did not intend to alter the absolute privilege rule.

[5] Judicial Electioneering

REPUBLICAN PARTY OF MINNESOTA v. WHITE, 536 U.S. 765 (2002). In *White*, the Court considered "whether the First Amendment permits the Minnesota Supreme Court to prohibit candidates for judicial election in that State from announcing their views on disputed legal and political issues."

Since 1912, Minnesota has selected all of its judges through nonpartisan election. Such elections have subsequently been subject to a legal restriction based largely on "Canon 7(B) of the 1972 American Bar Association (ABA) Model Code of Judicial Conduct," which states "that a 'candidate for a judicial office, including an incumbent judge,' shall not 'announce his or her views on disputed legal or political issues.'" Judges who violate this "announce clause" risk "discipline, including removal, censure, civil penalties, and suspension without pay." Lawyers who are candidates "for judicial office must also comply with the announce clause," or be "subject to, *inter alia*, disbarment, suspension, and probation."

While campaigning for associate justice of the Minnesota Supreme Court, one of the petitioners "distributed literature criticizing several Minnesota Supreme Court decisions on issues such as crime, welfare, and abortion."

Writing for the majority, Justice Scalia concluded that the "canon of judicial conduct prohibiting candidates for judicial election from announcing their views on disputed legal and political issues violates the First Amendment." The announce clause covered "much more than *promising* to decide an issue a particular way," extending "to the candidate's mere statement of his current position, even if he does not bind himself to maintain that position after election." This is so, because the Minnesota Code also "contains a so-called 'pledges or promises' clause, which *separately* prohibits judicial candidates from making 'pledges or promises of conduct in office other than the faithful and impartial performance of the duties of the office.'" The announce clause does not cover criticism of past decisions, reaching "only disputed issues that are likely to come before the candidate if he is elected judge," and allowing "general discussions of case law and judicial philosophy."

Despite these limitations, Justice Scalia stated that "the announce clause prohibits a judicial candidate from stating his views on any specific nonfanciful legal question within the province of the court for which he is running, except in the context of discussing past decisions — and in the latter context as well, if he expresses the view that he is not bound by *stare decisis*." Nor did the limiting constructions narrow the scope of the announce clause to the ABA's 1990 canon, which "prohibits a judicial candidate from making 'statements that commit or appear to commit the candidate with respect to cases, controversies or issues that are likely to come before the court.'" Unlike other jurisdictions, Minnesota did not adopt the new ABA canon. The Court limited its decision to the announce clause (as interpreted by state authorities) rather than the 1990 ABA canon.

Respondents also claimed that the announce clause did allow discussion of "a candidate's 'character,' 'education,' 'work habits,' and 'how [he] would handle administrative duties if elected.'" Moreover, "the Judicial Board has printed a list of preapproved questions which judicial candidates are allowed to answer." Such questions include "how the candidate feels about cameras in the courtroom, how he would go about reducing the caseload, how the costs of judicial administration can be reduced, and how he proposes to ensure that minorities and women are treated more fairly by the court system."

Respondents had the "burden to prove that the announce clause is (1) narrowly tailored, to serve (2) a compelling state interest." Respondents set forth two interests to justify the announce clause: "preserving the impartiality of the state judiciary and preserving the appearance of the impartiality of the state judiciary."

Justice Scalia, however, found the respondents' concept of impartiality vague. "'[I]mpartiality' in the judicial context — and of course its root meaning — is the lack of bias for or against either *party* to the proceeding." In this sense, the announce clause "is barely tailored to serve that interest *at all*, inasmuch as it does not restrict speech for or against particular *parties*, but rather speech for or against particular *issues*. To be sure, when a case arises that turns on a legal issue on which the judge (as a candidate) had taken a particular stand, the party taking the opposite stand is likely to lose. But not because of any bias against that party, or favoritism toward the other party. *Any* party taking that position is just as likely to lose. The judge is applying the law (as he sees it) evenhandedly."

Impartiality could also "mean lack of preconception in favor of or against a particular *legal view*." Such impartiality "would be concerned, not with guaranteeing litigants equal application of the law, but rather with guaranteeing them an equal chance to persuade the court on the legal points in their case." This type of impartiality does not comprise a compelling state interest. "For one thing, it is virtually impossible to find a judge who does not have preconceptions about the law." Even assuming the possibility of selecting "judges who did not have preconceived views on legal issues, it would hardly be desirable to do so." As "avoiding judicial preconceptions on legal issues is neither possible nor desirable, pretending otherwise by attempting to preserve the 'appearance' of that type of impartiality can hardly be a compelling state interest either."

The "third possible meaning of 'impartiality'" is "openmindedness," which "seeks to guarantee each litigant, not an *equal* chance to win the legal points in the case, but at least *some* chance of doing so." Respondents argue that the announce clause "relieves a judge from pressure to rule a certain way in order to maintain consistency with statements the judge has previously made." However, Justice Scalia doubted "that a mere statement of position enunciated during the pendency of an election will be regarded by a judge as more binding — or as more likely to subject him to popular disfavor if reconsidered — than a carefully considered holding that the judge set forth in an earlier opinion denying some individual's claim to justice."

Arguing "that the special context of electioneering justifies an *abridgement* of the right to speak out on disputed issues sets our First Amendment jurisprudence on its head. '[D]ebate on the qualifications of candidates' is 'at the core of our electoral process and of the First Amendment freedoms.'" The Court has "never allowed the government to prohibit candidates from communicating relevant information to voters during an election."

The Court neither asserted nor implied "that the First Amendment requires campaigns for judicial office to sound the same as those for legislative office." Rather, "the announce clause still fails strict scrutiny because it is woefully underinclusive, prohibiting announcements by judges (and would-be judges) only at certain times and in certain forms."

Justice Scalia maintained that Justice Ginsburg's dissent "greatly exaggerates the difference between judicial and legislative elections." Such "complete separation of the judiciary from the enterprise of 'representative government' might have some truth in those countries where judges neither make law themselves nor set aside the laws enacted by the legislature. It is not a true picture of the American system. Not only do state-court judges possess the power to 'make' common law, but they have the immense power to shape the States' constitutions as well."

While "a 'universal and long-established' tradition of prohibiting certain conduct creates 'a strong presumption' that the prohibition is constitutional," "prohibiting speech by judicial candidates on disputed issues . . . is neither long nor universal." By the "Civil War, the great majority of States elected their judges." Moreover, the Court knew of "no restrictions upon statements that could be made by judicial candidates (including judges) throughout the 19th and the first quarter of the 20th century." In fact, "judicial elections were generally partisan during this period." "[T]he movement toward nonpartisan judicial elections" did not even begin "until the 1870s." Justice Scalia concluded: "There is an obvious tension between the article of Minnesota's popularly approved Constitution which provides that judges shall be elected, and the Minnesota Supreme Court's announce clause which places most subjects of interest to the voters off limits."

Justice O'Connor's concurrence expressed "concerns about judicial elections generally," in particular, that "the very practice of electing judges undermines" the State's "compelling governmental interes[t] in an actual and perceived . . . impartial judiciary." Obviously, "contested elections generally entail campaigning," which generally "requires judicial candidates to engage in fundraising. Yet relying on campaign donations may leave judges feeling indebted to certain parties or interest groups." Even assuming that "judges were able to refrain from favoring donors, the mere possibility that judges' decisions may be motivated by the desire to repay campaign contributors is likely to undermine the public's confidence in the judiciary." "Despite these significant problems, 39 States currently employ some form of judicial elections for their appellate courts, general jurisdiction trial courts, or both." Others have adopted the Missouri Plan, in which "judges are appointed by a high elected official, generally from a list of nominees put together by a nonpartisan nominating commission, and then subsequently stand for unopposed retention elections in which voters are asked whether the judges should be recalled." This approach "reduces threats to judicial impartiality, even if it does not eliminate all popular pressure on judges." Nevertheless, "Minnesota has chosen to select its judges through contested popular elections instead of through an appointment system or a combined appointment and retention election system along the lines of the Missouri Plan. Any problem with judicial impartiality is largely one the State brought upon itself by continuing the practice of popularly electing judges."

Justice Kennedy concurred. For him, "content-based speech restrictions that do not fall within any traditional exception should be invalidated without inquiry into narrow tailoring or compelling government interests." Political speech by candidates "does not come within any of the exceptions to the First Amendment recognized by the Court."

Justice Stevens dissented, joined by Justices Souter, Ginsburg, and Breyer. "There is a critical difference between the work of the judge and the work of other public officials. In a democracy, issues of policy are properly decided by majority vote; it is the business of legislators and executives to be popular. But in litigation, issues of law or fact should not be determined by popular vote; it is the business of judges to be indifferent to unpopularity." Moreover, statements made regarding one's views "when one is running for an intermediate or trial court" office "mislead the voters by giving them the false impression that a candidate for the trial court will be able to and should decide cases based on his personal views rather than precedent." Justice Stevens continued: "By recognizing a conflict between the demands of electoral politics and the distinct characteristics of the judiciary, we do not have to put States to an all or nothing choice of abandoning judicial elections or having elections in which anything goes." In conclusion, "the judicial reputation for impartiality and openmindedness is compromised by electioneering that emphasizes the candidate's personal predilections rather than his qualifications for judicial office."

Justice Ginsburg dissented, joined by Justices Stevens, Souter, and Breyer. "Legislative and executive officials act on behalf of the voters who placed them in office; 'judge[s] represen[t] the Law.' " Those who framed "the Federal Constitution sought to advance the judicial function through the structural protections of Article III, which provide for the selection of judges by the President on the advice and consent of the Senate, generally for lifetime terms." This case examines "whether the First Amendment stops Minnesota from furthering its interest in judicial integrity through this precisely targeted speech restriction." Justice Ginsburg "would differentiate elections for political offices, in which the First Amendment holds full sway, from elections designed to select those whose office it is to administer justice without respect to persons." Those who stand for political office, "in keeping with their representative role, must be left free to inform the electorate of their positions on specific issues." In contrast, judges "are not political actors. They do not sit as representatives of particular persons, communities, or parties; they serve no faction or constituency." Instead, they "act only in the context of individual cases, the outcome of which cannot depend on the will of the public." Therefore, "the rationale underlying unconstrained speech in elections for political office — that representative government depends on the public's ability to chose agents who will act at its behest — does not carry over to campaigns for the bench."

For Justice Ginsburg, "the Court ignores a crucial limiting construction placed on the Announce Clause by the courts below. The provision does not bar a candidate from generally 'stating [her] views' on legal questions; it prevents her from 'publicly making known how [she] would *decide*' disputed issues." Moreover, the Announce Clause "does not prohibit candidates from discussing appellate court decisions." Thus, the Clause is "more tightly bounded, and campaigns conducted under that provision more robust, than the Court acknowledges."

Moreover, the type of impartiality guaranteed by due process advances a core principle: "[N]o man is permitted to try cases where he has an interest in the outcome." "[A] litigant is deprived of due process where the judge who hears his case has a 'direct, personal, substantial, and pecuniary' interest in ruling against him." That interest could affect maintenance of judicial office. Finally, "due process does not require a showing that the judge is actually biased as a result of his self-interest. Rather, our cases have 'always endeavored to prevent even the probability of unfairness.' "

Beyond the compelling state interests in safeguarding due process, "the pledges or promises clause advances another compelling state interest: preserving the public's confidence in the integrity and impartiality of its judiciary." By focusing on "statements that do not technically constitute pledges or promises but nevertheless 'publicly mak[e] known how [the candidate] would decide' legal issues, the Announce Clause prevents this end run around the letter and spirit of its companion provision." At bottom, "the Announce Clause is an indispensable part of Minnesota's effort to maintain the health of its judiciary."

Chapter XIII

GOVERNMENT AND THE MEDIA: PRINT AND ELECTRONIC

Introductory Note. In addition to protecting freedom of speech, the First Amendment also explicitly mentions freedom of the press. This perhaps demonstrates the Framers' appreciation for the importance of a free press. As the cases in this Chapter discuss, both the government and individual citizens have asserted a variety of interests that they maintain are constricted by a free and often powerful press. Among these are national security, unequal access to the marketplace of ideas, harm to reputation, and privacy. The media have, in turn, asserted a number of interests buttressing their liberty. These include ferreting out corruption and maintaining an informed citizenry, which is crucial to democracy.

While freedom of speech and freedom of the press are separately specified in the First Amendment, the cases in this Chapter indicate that the Court treats both of these freedoms in the same way. Still, certain doctrines in First Amendment jurisprudence have evolved to respond to the needs of the media and consequently have particular applicability to the press. Section 13.01 begins with one such doctrine, the prohibition against prior restraints. Over time, the Court has taken a particularly dim view of any attempt by government to suppress speech before it has even had the chance to be introduced into the marketplace of ideas. Section 13.02 treats the related subject of impediments to reporting on government affairs. Section 13.03 moves one step back in the reporting process to discuss the issue of press access to learn about the workings of government.

The cases in Section 13.04 discuss protection of media sources and other aspects of the newsgathering process. Sections 13.05, 13.06, and 13.07 consider a variety of questions involving restrictions on the press. Focusing on governmental regulation, Section 13.05 treats problems of public access to speak in the media. Section 13.06 considers taxation and Section 13.07 focuses on the special problems of electronic media. Finally, Section 13.08 identifies the constitutional issues that defamation and privacy actions pose for press freedoms.

§ 13.01 THE DOCTRINE AGAINST PRIOR RESTRAINTS

NEAR v. MINNESOTA, 283 U.S. 697 (1931). A Minnesota law provided that a newspaper, magazine or other periodical could be enjoined as a nuisance if a court determined that it was in the business of publishing material that was "malicious, scandalous, and defamatory."

The suit to enjoin publication was filed after *The Saturday Press*, a Minneapolis newspaper, published a series of articles accusing a number of highly placed public officials of corruption and dereliction of duties. The trial court found that the disputed articles were a nuisance as defined in the statute and granted a permanent injunction against the newspaper. The Minnesota Supreme Court affirmed.

Chief Justice Hughes' majority (5-4) opinion reversed. Under the statute, "public authorities may bring the owner or publisher of a newspaper or periodical before a judge upon a charge of conducting a business of publishing scandalous and defamatory matter — in particular that the matter consists of charges against public officers of official dereliction — and, unless the owner or publisher is able and disposed to bring competent evidence to satisfy the judge that the charges are true and are published with good motives for justifiable ends, his newspaper or periodical is suppressed and further publication is made punishable as a contempt. This is the essence of censorship."

While the protections against prior restraints are strong, they are not "absolutely unlimited." Specifically, the Court outlined several examples of exceptional circumstances permitting government to issue a prior restraint: " 'When a nation is at war many things that might be said in time of peace are such a hindrance to its effort that their utterance will not be endured so long as men fight . . .' *Schenck v. United States*[, 249 U.S. 47 (1919)]. No one would question that a government might prevent actual obstruction to its recruiting service or the publication of the sailing dates of transports or the number and location of troops. On similar grounds, the primary requirements of decency may be enforced against obscene publications. The security of the community life may be protected against incitements to acts of violence and the overthrow by force of orderly government. The constitutional guaranty of free speech does not 'protect a man from an injunction against uttering words that may have all the effect of force.' " As these exceptions were inapplicable in the present case, the proper remedy for the maligned public officials was to seek punishment or other appropriate remedies after the abuse had occurred.

The Court rejected the arguments advanced by the state to justify the restraint at issue in this case: "In attempted justification of the statute, it is said that it deals not with publication per se, but with the 'business' of publishing defamation. . . . [C]haracterizing the publication as a business, and the business as a nuisance, does not permit an invasion of the constitutional immunity against restraint. Similarly, it does not matter that the newspaper or periodical is found to be 'largely' or 'chiefly' devoted to the publication of such derelictions." Chief Justice Hughes also noted that the truth or falsity of the accusations made against the officials was not relevant to the Court's considerations.

Justice Butler dissented. He maintained that the defendants were in the business of publishing material that was chiefly false and malicious, that the existing libel laws provided inadequate protection against defamatory comments, and that the Court's decision was an unprecedented restriction of a State's abilities to prevent the publishing of defamatory matter. Basically, the Minnesota statute did not operate as a proper prior restraint at all, as the law enjoined only publications and persons duly judged by a court to constitute a nuisance.

NEW YORK TIMES CO. v. UNITED STATES
403 U.S. 713, 91 S. Ct. 2140, 29 L. Ed. 2d 822 (1971)

[Shortly after the *New York Times* and *Washington Post* began publishing the Pentagon Papers in June of 1971, the Attorney-General of the United States sued to enjoin publication. The Southern District of New York rendered judgment for the New York Times Co. The Court of Appeals for the Second Circuit, *en banc*, remanded the case to the District Court for a hearing to determine whether the disclosure of certain items, specified by the United States, would irreparably endanger the security of the United States. The District Court for the District of Columbia refused to enjoin publication by the Post and, there, the Court of Appeals affirmed. Temporary restraining orders in both circuits prevented publication pending the decision by the Supreme Court.]

Per Curiam.

. . . [I]n these cases . . . the United States seeks to enjoin the New York Times and the Washington Post from publishing the contents of a classified study entitled "History of U.S. Decision-Making Process on Vietnam Policy."

"Any system of prior restraints of expression comes to this Court bearing a heavy presumption against its constitutional validity." *Bantam Books, Inc. v. Sullivan*, 372 U.S. 58, 70 (1963); *see also Near v. Minnesota ex rel. Olson.* The Government "thus carries a heavy burden of showing justification for the imposition of such a restraint." *Organization for a Better Austin v. Keefe*, 402 U.S. 415, 419 (1971). The District Court for the Southern District of New York in the New York Times case, 328 F. Supp. 324, and the District Court for the District of Columbia and the Court of Appeals for the District of Columbia Circuit, 446 F.2d 1327, in the Washington Post case held that the Government had not met that burden. We agree.

The judgment of the Court of Appeals for the District of Columbia Circuit is therefore affirmed. The order of the Court of Appeals for the Second Circuit is reversed, 444 F.2d 544, and the case is remanded with directions to enter a judgment affirming the judgment of the District Court for the Southern District of New York. The stays entered June 25, 1971, by the Court are vacated. . . .

JUSTICE BLACK, with whom JUSTICE DOUGLAS joins, concurring.

I adhere to the view that the Government's case against the Washington Post should have been dismissed and that the injunction against the New York Times should have been vacated without oral argument when the cases were first presented to this Court. I believe that every moment's continuance of the injunctions against these newspapers amounts to a flagrant, indefensible, and continuing violation of the First Amendment. . . .

. . . Madison proposed what later became the First Amendment in three parts, two of which are set out below, and one of which proclaimed: "The people shall not be deprived or abridged of their right to speak, to write, or to publish their sentiments; *and the freedom of the press, as one of the great bulwarks of liberty, shall be inviolable.*" The amendments were offered to curtail and restrict the general powers granted to the Executive, Legislative, and Judicial Branches two years before in the original Constitution. . . . Yet the Solicitor General argues and some members of the Court appear to agree that the general powers of the Government adopted in the original Constitution should be interpreted to limit and restrict the specific and emphatic guarantees of the Bill of Rights adopted later. I can imagine no greater perversion of history. Madison and the other Framers of the First Amendment, able men that they were, wrote in language they earnestly believed could never be misunderstood: "Congress shall make no law . . . abridging the freedom of the press. . . . " Both the history and language of the First Amendment support the view that the press must be left free to publish news, whatever the source, without censorship, injunctions, or prior restraints.

. . . The press was protected so that it could bare the secrets of government and inform the people. Only a free and unrestrained press can effectively expose deception in government. And paramount among the responsibilities of a free press is the duty to prevent any part of the government from deceiving the people and sending them off to distant lands to die of foreign fevers and foreign shot and shell. . . . In revealing the workings of government that led to the Vietnam war, the newspapers nobly did precisely that which the Founders hoped and trusted they would do.

. . . [T]he Government argues in its brief that in spite of the First Amendment, "the authority of the Executive Department to protect the nation against publication of information whose disclosure would endanger the national security stems from two interrelated sources: the constitutional power of the President over the conduct of foreign affairs and his authority as Commander-in-Chief."

. . . The Government does not even attempt to rely on any act of Congress. . . .

. . . To find that the President has "inherent power" to halt the publication of news by resort to the courts would wipe out the First Amendment and destroy the fundamental liberty and security of the very people the Government hopes to make "secure." . . .

The word "security" is a broad, vague generality whose contours should not be invoked to abrogate the fundamental law embodied in the First Amendment. The guarding of military and diplomatic secrets at the expense of informed representative government provides no real security for our Republic. . . .

"The greater the importance of safeguarding the community from incitements to the overthrow of our institutions by force and violence, the more imperative is the need to preserve inviolate the constitutional rights of free speech, free press and free assembly in order to maintain the opportunity for free political discussion, to the end that government may be responsive to the will of the people and that changes, if desired, may be obtained by peaceful means. Therein lies the security of the Republic, the very foundation of constitutional government."[1]

JUSTICE DOUGLAS, with whom JUSTICE BLACK joins, concurring. . . .

. . . [T]he First Amendment . . . leaves, in my view, no room for governmental restraint on the press.

There is, moreover, no statute barring the publication by the press of the material which the Times and the Post seek to use. . . .

So any power that the Government possesses must come from its "inherent power."

. . . The Constitution by Art. I, § 8, gives Congress, not the President, power "to declare War." . . . We need not decide therefore what leveling effect the war power of Congress might have. . . .

. . . It is common knowledge that the First Amendment was adopted against the widespread use of the common law of seditious libel to punish the dissemination of material that is embarrassing to the powers-that-be. . . . A debate of large proportions goes on in the Nation over our posture in Vietnam. That debate antedated the disclosure of the contents of the present documents. The latter are highly relevant to the debate in progress.

Secrecy in government is fundamentally anti-democratic, perpetuating bureaucratic errors. Open debate and discussion of public issues are vital to our national health. . . .

The stays is these cases that have been in effect for more than a week constitute a flouting of the principles of the First Amendment as interpreted in *Near v. Minnesota* [, 283 U.S. 697 (1931)].

JUSTICE BRENNAN, concurring.

. . . So far as I can determine, never before has the United States sought to enjoin a newspaper from publishing information in its possession. . . .

The error that has pervaded these cases from the outset was the granting of any injunctive relief whatsoever, interim or otherwise. The entire thrust of the Government's claim throughout these cases has been that publication of the material sought to be enjoined "could," or "might," or "may" prejudice the national interest in various ways. But the First Amendment tolerates absolutely no prior judicial restraints of the press predicated upon surmise or conjecture that untoward consequences may result. Our cases, it is true, have indicated that there is a single, extremely narrow class of cases in which the First Amendment's ban on prior judicial restraint may be overridden. Our cases have thus far indicated that such cases may arise only when the

---

[1] [Court's footnote 6] *DeJonge v. Oregon*, 299 U.S. 353, 365 [(1937)].

Nation "is at war," *Schneck v. United States* (1919), during which times "no one would question but that a government might prevent actual obstruction to its recruiting service or the publication of the sailing dates of transports or the number and location of troops." *Near v. Minnesota ex rel. Olson*, 283 U.S. 697, 716. Even if the present world situation were assumed to be tantamount to a time of war, or if the power of presently available armaments would justify even in peacetime the suppression of information that would set in motion a nuclear holocaust, in neither of these actions has the Government presented or even alleged that publication of items from or based upon the material at issue would cause the happening of an event of that nature. . . . Thus, only governmental allegation and proof that publication must inevitably, directly, and immediately cause the occurrence of an event kindred to imperiling the safety of a transport already at sea can support even the issuance of an interim restraining order. In no event may mere conclusions be sufficient: for if the Executive Branch seeks judicial aid in preventing publication, it must inevitably submit the basis upon which that aid is sought to scrutiny by the judiciary. . . .

JUSTICE STEWART, with whom JUSTICE WHITE joins, concurring.

In the governmental structure created by our Constitution, the Executive is endowed with enormous power in the two related areas of national defense and international relations. This power, largely unchecked by the Legislative and Judicial branches, has been pressed to the very hilt since the advent of the nuclear missile age. . . .

In the absence of the governmental checks and balances present in other areas of our national life, the only effective restraint upon executive policy and power in the areas of national defense and international affairs may lie in an enlightened citizenry — in an informed and critical public opinion which alone can here protect the values of democratic government. . . . [W]ithout an informed and free press there cannot be an enlightened people.

Yet it is elementary that the successful conduct of international diplomacy and the maintenance of an effective national defense require both confidentiality and secrecy. Other nations can hardly deal with this Nation in an atmosphere of mutual trust unless they can be assured that their confidences will be kept. And within our own executive departments, the development of considered and intelligent international policies would be impossible if those charged with their formulation could not communicate with each other freely, frankly, and in confidence. In the area of basic national defense the frequent need for absolute secrecy is, of course, self-evident.

. . . The responsibility must be where the power is. If the Constitution gives the Executive a large degree of unshared power in the conduct of foreign affairs and the maintenance of our national defense, then under the Constitution the Executive must have the largely unshared duty to determine and preserve the degree of internal security necessary to exercise that power successfully. . . .

This is not to say that Congress and the courts have no role to play. Undoubtedly Congress has the power to enact specific and appropriate criminal laws to protect government property and preserve government secrets. Congress has passed such laws, and several of them are of very colorable relevance to the apparent circumstances of these cases. . . . Moreover, if Congress should pass a specific law authorizing civil proceedings in this field, the courts would likewise have the duty to decide the constitutionality of such a law as well as its applicability to the facts proved.

But in the cases before us we are asked . . ., quite simply, to prevent the publication by two newspapers of material that the Executive Branch insists should not, in the national interest, be published. I am convinced that the Executive is correct with respect to some of the documents involved. But I cannot say that disclosure of any of them will surely result in direct, immediate, and irreparable damage to our Nation or its people. . . .

JUSTICE WHITE, with whom JUSTICE STEWART joins, concurring.

. . . I do not say that in no circumstances would the First Amendment permit an injunction against publishing information about government plans or operations. Nor, after examining the materials the Government characterizes as the most sensitive and destructive, can I deny that revelation of these documents will do substantial damage to public interests. Indeed, I am confident that their disclosure will have that result. But I nevertheless agree that the United States has not satisfied the very heavy burden that it must meet to warrant an injunction against publication in these cases, at least in the absence of express and appropriately limited congressional authorization for prior restraints in circumstances such as these. . . .

At least in the absence of legislation by Congress, . . . I am quite unable to agree that the inherent powers of the Executive and the courts reach so far as to authorize remedies having such sweeping potential for inhibiting publications by the press. Much of the difficulty inheres in the "grave and irreparable danger" standard suggested by the United States. If the United States were to have judgment under such a standard in these cases, our decision would be of little guidance to other courts in other cases, for the material at issue here would not be available from the Court's opinion or from public records, nor would it be published by the press. Indeed, even today where we hold that the United States has not met its burden, the material remains sealed in court records and it is properly not discussed in today's opinions. Moreover, because the material poses substantial dangers to national interests and because of the hazards of criminal sanctions, a responsible press may choose never to publish the more sensitive materials. To sustain the Government in these cases would start the courts down a long and hazardous road that I am not willing to travel, at least without congressional guidance and direction.

. . . That the Government mistakenly chose to proceed by injunction does not mean that it could not successfully proceed in another way. . . .

The Criminal Code contains numerous provisions potentially relevant to these cases. Section 797 makes it a crime to publish certain photographs or drawings of military installations. Section 798, also in precise language, proscribes knowing and willful publication of any classified information concerning the cryptographic systems or communication intelligence activities of the United States as well as any information obtained from communication intelligence operations. If any of the material here at issue is of this nature, the newspapers are presumably now on full notice of the position of the United States and must face the consequences if they publish. I would have no difficulty in sustaining convictions under these sections on facts that would not justify the intervention of equity and the imposition of a prior restraint.

The same would be true under those sections of the Criminal Code casting a wider net to protect the national defense. Section 793(e) makes it a criminal act for any unauthorized possessor of a document "relating to the national defense" either (1) willfully to communicate or cause to be communicated that document to any person not entitled to receive it or (2) willfully to retain the document and fail to deliver it to an officer of the United States entitled to receive it. . . .

It is thus clear that Congress has addressed itself to the problems of protecting the security of the country and the national defense from unauthorized disclosure of potentially damaging information. . . . It has not, however, authorized the injunctive remedy against threatened publication. . . . I am not, of course, saying that either of these newspapers has yet committed a crime or that either would commit a crime if it published all the material now in its possession. . . .

JUSTICE MARSHALL, concurring.

. . . In these cases there is no problem concerning the President's power to classify information as "secret" or "top secret." Congress has specifically recognized Presidential authority, which has been formally exercised in Exec. Order 10501 (1953), to classify documents and information. . . . Nor is there any issue here regarding the President's power as Chief Executive and Commander in Chief to protect national security by disciplining employees who disclose information and by taking precautions to prevent leaks.

. . . [I]n some situations it may be that under whatever inherent powers the Government may have, as well as the implicit authority derived from the President's mandate to conduct foreign affairs and to act as Commander in Chief, there is a basis for the invocation of the equity jurisdiction of this Court as an aid to prevent the publication of material damaging to "national security," however that term may be defined. . . .

In these cases we are not faced with a situation where Congress has failed to provide the Executive with broad power to protect the Nation from disclosure of damaging state secrets. Congress has on several occasions given extensive consideration to the problem of protecting the military and strategic secrets of the United States. This consideration has resulted in the enactment of statutes making it a crime to receive, disclose, communicate, withhold, and publish certain documents, photographs, instruments, appliances, and information. . . .

. . . Congress has specifically rejected passing legislation that would have clearly given the President the power he seeks here and made the current activity of the newspapers unlawful. . . .

CHIEF JUSTICE BURGER, dissenting.

. . . We do not know the facts of the cases. No District Judge knew all the facts. No Court of Appeals Judge knew all the facts. No member of this Court knows all the facts. . . .

I suggest we are in this posture because these cases have been conducted in unseemly haste. . . .

. . . An issue of this importance should be tried and heard in a judicial atmosphere conducive to thoughtful, reflective deliberation, especially when haste, in terms of hours, is unwarranted in light of the long period the Times, by its own choice, deferred publication.[2]

It is not disputed that the Times has had unauthorized possession of the documents for three to four months, during which it has had its expert analysts studying them. . . . During all of this time, the Times, presumably in its capacity as trustee of the public's "right to know," has held up publication for purposes it considered proper and thus public knowledge was delayed. No doubt this was for a good reason; the analysis of 7,000 pages of complex material drawn from a vastly greater volume of material would inevitably take time. . . . But why should the United States Government, from whom this information was illegally acquired by someone, along with

---

[2] [Court's footnote 1] As noted elsewhere the Times conducted its analysis of the 47 volumes of Government documents over a period of several months and did so with a degree of security that a government might envy. . . . Meanwhile the Times has copyrighted its material and there were strong intimations in the oral argument that the Times contemplated enjoining its use by any other publisher in violation of its copyright. Paradoxically this would afford it a protection, analogous to prior restraint, against all others — a protection the Times denied the Government of the United States.

all the counsel, trial judges, and appellate judges be placed under needless pressure?
. . .

Would it have been unreasonable, since the newspaper could anticipate the Government's objections to release of secret material, to give the Government an opportunity to review the entire collection and determine whether agreement could be reached on publication? Stolen or not, if security was not in fact jeopardized, much of the material could no doubt have been declassified, since it spans a period ending in 1968. With such an approach — one that great newspapers have in the past practiced and stated editorially to be the duty of an honorable press — the newspapers and Government might well have narrowed the area of disagreement as to what was and was not publishable, leaving the remainder to be resolved in orderly litigation, if necessary. To me it is hardly believable that a newspaper long regarded as a great institution in American life would fail to perform one of the basic and simple duties of every citizen with respect to the discovery or possession of stolen property or secret government documents. That duty, I had thought — perhaps naively — was to report forthwith, to responsible public officers. . . . [3]

. . . It is interesting to note that counsel, on both sides, in oral argument before this Court, were frequently unable to respond to questions on factual points. . . . I agree generally with Justice Harlan and Justice Blackmun but I am not prepared to reach the merits.[4]

I would affirm the Court of Appeals for the Second Circuit and allow the District Court to complete the trial aborted by our grant of certiorari, meanwhile preserving the status quo in the *Post* case. I would direct that the District Court on remand give priority to the *Times* case to the exclusion of all other business of that court but I would not set arbitrary deadlines. . . .

JUSTICE HARLAN, with whom THE CHIEF JUSTICE and JUSTICE BLACKMUN join, dissenting.

. . . With all respect, I consider that the Court has been almost irresponsibly feverish in dealing with these cases.

Both the Court of Appeals for the Second Circuit and the Court of Appeals for the District of Columbia Circuit rendered judgment on June 23. The New York Times' petition for certiorari, its motion for accelerated consideration thereof, and its application for interim relief were filed in this Court on June 24 at about 11 a.m. The application of the United States for interim relief in the *Post* case was also filed here on June 24 at about 7:15 p.m. This Court's order setting a hearing before us on June 26 at 11 a.m., a course which I joined only to avoid the possibility of even more peremptory action by the Court, was issued less than 24 hours before. The record in the *Post* case was filed with the Clerk shortly before 1 p.m. on June 25; the record in the *Times* case did not arrive until 7 or 8 o'clock that same night. The briefs of the parties were received less than two hours before argument on June 26.

This frenzied train of events took place in the name of the presumption against prior restraints created by the First Amendment. . . . In order to decide the merits of

---

[3] [Court's footnote 2] Interestingly the Times explained its refusal to allow the Government to examine its own purloined documents by saying in substance this might compromise its sources and informants! . . .

[4] [Court's footnote 3] With respect to the question of inherent power of the Executive to classify papers, records, and documents as secret, . . . [n]o statute gives this Court express power to establish and enforce the utmost security measures for the secrecy of our deliberations and records. Yet I have little doubt as to the inherent power of the Court to protect the confidentiality of its internal operations by whatever judicial measures may be required.

these cases properly, some or all of the following questions should have been faced:

1. Whether the Attorney General is authorized to bring these suits in the name of the United States. . . .

2. Whether the First Amendment permits the federal courts to enjoin publication of stories which would present a serious threat to national security. *See Near v. Minnesota.*

3. Whether the threat to publish highly secret documents is of itself a sufficient implication of national security to justify an injunction on the theory that regardless of the contents of the documents harm enough results simply from the demonstration of such a breach of secrecy.

4. Whether the unauthorized disclosure of any of these particular documents would seriously impair the national security.

5. What weight should be given to the opinion of high officers in the Executive Branch of the Government with respect to questions 3 and 4.

6. Whether the newspapers are entitled to retain and use the documents notwithstanding the seemingly uncontested facts that the documents, or the originals of which they are duplicates, were purloined from the Government's possession and that the newspapers received them with knowledge that they had been feloniously acquired. . . .

7. Whether the threatened harm to the national security or the Government's possessory interest in the documents justifies the issuance of an injunction against publication in light of —

a. The strong First Amendment policy against prior restraints on publication;

b. The doctrine against enjoining conduct in violation of criminal statutes; and

c. The extent to which the materials at issue have apparently already been otherwise disseminated.

These are difficult questions of fact, of law, and of judgment; the potential consequences of erroneous decision are enormous. . . .

. . . It is plain to me that the scope of the judicial function in passing upon the activities of the Executive Branch of the Government in the field of foreign affairs is very narrowly restricted. . . .

I agree that, in performance of its duty to protect the values of the First Amendment against political pressures, the judiciary must review the initial Executive determination to the point of satisfying itself that the subject matter of the dispute does lie within the proper compass of the President's foreign relations power. . . . Moreover the judiciary may properly insist that the determination that disclosure of the subject matter would irreparably impair the national security be made by the head of the Executive Department concerned — here the Secretary of State or the Secretary of Defense — after actual personal consideration by that officer. This safeguard is required in the analogous area of executive claims of privilege for secrets of state. . . .

But in my judgment the judiciary may not properly go beyond these two inquiries and redetermine for itself the probable impact of disclosure on the national security. . . .

Even if there is some room for the judiciary to override the executive determination, it is plain that the scope of review must be exceedingly narrow. I can see no indication in the opinions of either the District Court or the Court of Appeals in the *Post* litigation that the conclusions of the Executive were given even the deference owing to an administrative agency, much less that owing to a co-equal branch of the Government operating within the field of its constitutional prerogative. . . .

Pending further hearings in each case conducted under the appropriate ground rules, I would continue the restraints on publication. I cannot believe that the doctrine prohibiting prior restraints reaches to the point of preventing courts from maintaining the *status quo* long enough to act responsibly in matters of such national importance as those involved here.

[JUSTICE BLACKMUN's dissenting opinion is omitted.]

NOTES

(1) *Classified CIA Information.* May the United States enforce an agreement with an employee of the Central Intelligence Agency not to publish classified information? *See United States v. Marchetti*, 466 F.2d 1309 (4th Cir.), *cert. denied*, 409 U.S. 1063 (1972) (agreement upheld). What if the employee violates an agreement to submit all writings to the Agency for prepublication review? In *Snepp v. United States*, 444 U.S. 507 (1980), the Court, in a *per curiam* summary decision based on the Government's cross-petition for certiorari, rejected the Court of Appeals' remedy of punitive damages and imposed a "constructive trust" on the author's profits. Unlike *Marchetti*, where the Court of Appeals enforced the agreement relating to publication of classified material, the action against *Snepp*, and the remedy, were based on the failure to submit the material in advance, regardless of whether the material was classified.

(2) *Obscene Materials.* May a film distributor be required to submit a film in advance of its showing? *See Times Film Corp. v. Chicago*, 365 U.S. 436 (1961). *See also Kingsley Books v. Brown*, 354 U.S. 436 (1957), upholding a New York procedure that permitted law enforcement officials to obtain *ex parte* restraining orders against the display of allegedly obscene booklets. The procedures that the "rule" against prior restraints requires in the motion picture censorship situation are discussed in the section on obscenity, § 15.05.

(3) *Demonstration Permits.* The prior restraint issue arises when one applies for a permit to parade or demonstrate in public places. *See Cox v. New Hampshire*, 312 U.S. 569 (1941), § 14.02, and the note following the case.

(4) *Abortion Protestors.* In *Madsen v. Women's Health Center*, 512 U.S. 753 (1994), the Court declined to apply prior restraint analysis to a broad ranging injunction issued by a Florida court against abortion protestors and instead inquired whether the injunction burdened no more speech than necessary to serve a significant government interest. Using this test, the Court upheld the part of the injunction that restricted noise during certain times of the day as well as a 36-foot buffer zone around an abortion clinic's entrances and driveway. It also used the test to invalidate other parts of the injunction, including a 36-foot buffer zone that applied to the private property adjacent to the clinic, a proscription on "images observable" from the clinic, a prohibition on physically approaching potential patients within 300-feet of the clinic, and a prohibition on picketing within 300-feet of the residence of a clinic employee.

Chief Justice Rehnquist wrote for the majority. "Prior restraints do often take the form of injunctions. Not all injunctions which may incidentally affect expression, however, are 'prior restraints' in the sense that the term was used in *New York Times Co.*" The protestors would not be "prevented from expressing their message in any one of several different ways; they are simply prohibited from expressing it within the 36-foot buffer zone." Moreover, the injunction at issue in *Madsen* "was not issued because of the content of petitioners' expression, as was the case in *New York Times Co.*, but because of their prior unlawful conduct." For further discussion of *Madsen*, see § 14.04[1].

Schenck v. Pro-Choice Network of Western New York, 519 U.S. 357 (1997), upheld that part of a District Court injunction that imposed "fixed buffer zone" restrictions on demonstrations outside abortion clinics. The Court, however, struck down the injunction's "floating buffer zone" restrictions as violating the First Amendment. For further discussion of *Schenck*, see § 14.04[1].

In *Hill v. Colorado*, 530 U.S. 703 (2000), the Court rejected a prior restraint challenge to a statute that prohibits, within 100 feet of a health care facility, "knowingly" approaching "within eight feet of" a person without consent, "passing a leaflet or handbill to, displaying a sign to, or engaging in oral protest, education, or counseling." For more extensive treatment, see § 14.04[1].

For additional discussion, see Stephen Carter, *Book Review: Abortion, Absolutism, and Compromise*, 100 YALE L.J. 2747, 2766 (1991) ("[I]in a world in which moral absolutists, many in number, are not content with the results of the political process, there are few alternatives to litigation or civil war. We tried civil war once already, and if hundreds of thousands died, at least the viciously repressive system of chattel slavery was eradicated. In the abortion debate, the most firmly committed activists on both sides seem to think that every bit as much is at stake now as was then, which suggests that until there is some sign of political consensus, it may turn out that in this democracy, litigation and protest are all we have.").

(5) *Plaintiff's Death and Mootness.* In *Tory v. Cochran*, 544 U.S. 734 (2005), the Court in a 7-2 decision declined to address "whether a permanent injunction as a remedy in a defamation action, preventing all future speech about an admitted public figure, violates the First Amendment," but instead invalidated it as an overly broad prior restraint. The lower court had found that the defendant engaged in a continuous pattern of defamatory activity, including picketing, aimed at forcing plaintiff to pay him to stop. The injunction prohibited the defendant "from 'picketing,' from 'displaying signs, placards or other written or printed material,' and from 'orally uttering statements' " about plaintiff or his law firm "in any public forum."

Writing for a 7-2 majority, Justice Breyer held that despite plaintiff Johnnie Cochran's death, the case was not moot. Plaintiffs could point to nothing in California law suggesting that plaintiff's death nullified the injunction. However, because plaintiff had died, the picketing and other speech prohibited by the injunction could no longer move plaintiff to pay "tribute" to stop it. Consequently, the reason for the injunction was "much diminished" or had "disappeared" entirely. As a result, the injunction was "an overly broad prior restraint upon speech," without "plausible justification." The Court left open the possibility that another appropriate party might still request injunctive relief.

Justice Thomas dissented, joined by Justice Scalia, stating that he "would dismiss the writ of certiorari as improvidently granted."

(6) For historical perspective on *New York Times v. United States*, see BERNARD SCHWARTZ, THE ASCENT OF PRAGMATISM 159 (1990). In discussing the case, Justice Black once remarked, "Well, I never did see how it hurts national security for someone to tell the American people that their government lied to them."

For additional discussion of prior restraints, see Stephen Barnett, *The Puzzle of Prior Restraint*, 29 STAN. L. REV. 539 (1977); Ariel L. Bendor, *Prior Restraint, Incommensurability, and the Constitutionalism of Means*, 68 FORDHAM L. REV. 289, 291–292 (1999) (Challenging "the possibility, the propriety, and the morality of enforcing incommensurable 'anti-speech entitlements'; such as the individual rights to good reputation and privacy, and the right of the state to national security, with ex post criminal sanctions or civil penalties. The negative externalities that the prior regime generates pose a collateral difficulty. In essence, the system allows the public to enjoy benefits at the expense of particular individuals. Because the harms suffered by individuals from unrestrainable speech are incommensurable, a liability rule system cannot provide full compensation for them. . . .   Moreover, a reliance on the prohibition against prior restraints assumes incorrectly that subsequently imposed penalties will always be less burdensome on speech than prior restraints."); John Jeffries, *Rethinking Prior Restraint*, 92 YALE L.J. 409 (1983); Symposium: *Near v. Minnesota, 50th Anniversary*, 66 MINN. L. REV. l (1981).

ELDRED v. ASHCROFT, 537 U.S. 186 (2003). In *Eldred*, the Court held that Congress did not violate either the Copyright Clause of the Constitution or the First Amendment when they extended the length of protection for a copyright. The Copyright Term Extension Act (CTEA) in 1998 increased copyright protection from 50 to 70 years following the death of the author. This protection applies "to all works not published by January 1, 1978."[5]

Plaintiffs dealt with products or services that "build on copyrighted works that have gone into the public domain." They objected to Congress' "enlarging the term for published works with existing copyrights."

In a 7-2 decision, Justice Ginsburg noted the 1993 European Union (EU) "directive instructing EU members to establish a copyright term of life plus 70 years." The EU directive denied this longer protection to the works of any non-member nation that did not afford the same protection. The CTEA secured for American authors the same copyright protection in Europe that their European counterparts would receive. Justice Ginsburg found the CTEA "rational." Moreover, its extension treating existing and future copyrights the same followed "unbroken congressional practice."

The Court also rejected the argument that the CTEA should receive heightened scrutiny under the First Amendment. As the Copyright Clause and the First Amendment were adopted close in time, it appears that the Framers viewed "copyright's limited monopolies" as "compatible with free speech principles. Indeed, copyright's purpose is to *promote* the creation and publication of free expression." Copyright laws accommodate First Amendment interests. They distinguish between ideas and expressions, and they allow only for the protection of the latter. As such, the ideas, theories, and facts that appear in a copyrighted work are not protected. They are "instantly available for public exploitation at the moment of publication." Even the expression of facts and ideas contained in a copyrighted work are available for " 'fair use.' " Under certain circumstances, " '[t]he fair use of a copyrighted work, including such use by reproduction in copies . . . for purposes such as criticism, comment, news reporting, teaching (including multiple copies for classroom use), scholarship, or research, is not an infringement of copyright.' "[6] The Court would not second guess Congress' judgment on copyright policy.

Justices Stevens and Breyer each filed a dissent. For Justice Stevens, the policy concerns underlying the Constitution's prohibition of ex post facto laws and laws impairing the obligation of contracts invalidate the CTEA's retroactive changes.

---

[5] For materials that copyrighted prior to January 1, 1978, that still retained a valid copyright at the time of the CTEA, the protection was extended to a term of 95 years from the date of publication. The CTEA granted anonymous works, pseudonymous works, and works made for hire a copyright with a term of 95 years from publication or 120 years from creation, whichever came first.

[6] The CTEA itself incorporated certain First Amendment safeguards. It allows "libraries, archives, and similar institutions to 'reproduce' and 'distribute, display, or perform in facsimile or digital form' copies of certain published works 'during the last 20 years of any term of copyright . . . for purposes of preservation, scholarship, or research' if the work is not already being exploited commercially and further copies are unavailable at a reasonable price." The CTEA also allows "small businesses, restaurants, and like entities" to play music from a "licensed radio, television, and similar facilities" without having to pay performance royalties.

Retroactively extending a copyright or patent changes "the public's bargain" with that author or inventor and amounts to a taking requiring just compensation. Persons intending to use an invention or copyrighted work when it enters the public domain should be protected against such "retroactive modification."

In dissent, Justice Breyer stated that the Copyright Clause and the First Amendment each encourages the "creation and dissemination of information." When a statute exceeds the proper bounds of the Copyright Clause, however, it "may set Clause and Amendment at cross-purposes, thereby depriving the public of the speech-related benefits that the Founders, through both, have promised." He "would review plausible claims that a copyright statute seriously, and unjustifiably, restricts the dissemination of speech somewhat more carefully than reference to this Court's traditional Commerce Clause jurisprudence might suggest" — although he refused to characterize this review as " 'intermediate scrutiny.' "

Justice Breyer also said that the costs of this extension on education, learning, and research will multiply as "children become ever more dependent for the content of their knowledge upon computer-accessible databases." The costs of this extension outweigh the benefits as the extension will not act as "an economic spur encouraging authors to create new works."

§ 13.02 THE RIGHT TO REPORT GOVERNMENTAL AFFAIRS

NEBRASKA PRESS ASSOCIATION v. STUART, 427 U.S. 539 (1976). Erwin Charles Simants was indicted for the October 18, 1975, murder of a family of six in Sutherland, Nebraska, a town of about 850 people. The Court's unanimous decision invalidated a Nebraska Supreme Court order to delay, until a jury was impaneled, the publication and broadcast of specific facts in the Simants case.

Originally, the County Attorney and Simants' attorney requested a restrictive order from the County Court relating to " 'matters that may or may not be publicly reported or disclosed to the public,' because of the 'mass coverage by news media' and the 'reasonable likelihood of prejudicial news which would make difficult, if not impossible, the impaneling of an impartial jury and tend to prevent a fair trial.' " Two days later, the State District Court granted a motion by the petitioners for leave to intervene. The trial judge also issued an order prohibiting pretrial reporting of certain information about the Simants case.

The Nebraska Supreme Court modified the District Court's order "to accommodate the defendant's right to a fair trial and the petitioners' interest in reporting pretrial events." The modified order postponed the reporting of: "(a) the existence and nature of any confessions or admissions made by the defendant to law enforcement officers, (b) any confessions or admissions made to any third parties, except members of the press, and (c) other facts 'strongly implicative' of the accused."

Chief Justice Burger delivered the opinion of the Court, which examined the tension a sensational criminal case like Simants creates between rights of the press and the public under the First Amendment, and the Sixth Amendment guarantee of a "trial . . . by an impartial jury." While pretrial publicity seldom impairs Sixth Amendment rights, " 'sensational' " cases generate "tensions" between these rights.

The Chief Justice argued that the trial court could have employed a number of alternative measures to protect Simants' rights without prior restraints on news reports:

> [W]here there is a reasonable likelihood that prejudicial news prior to trial
> will prevent a fair trial, the judge should continue the case until the threat

abates, *or transfer it* to another county not so permeated with publicity. In addition, *sequestration of the jury* was something the judge should have raised *sua sponte* with counsel. If publicity during the proceedings threatens the fairness of the trial, a new trial should be ordered. But we must remember that reversals are but palliative; the cure lies in those remedial measures that will prevent the prejudice at its inception. . . . *Neither prosecutors, counsel for defense, the accused, witnesses, court staff nor enforcement officers coming under the jurisdiction of the court should be permitted to frustrate its function.* Collaboration between counsel and the press as to information affecting the fairness of a criminal trial is not only subject to regulation, but is highly censurable and worthy of disciplinary measures.

Sheppard v. Maxwell, 384 U.S. 333, at 362–363 (emphasis added).

"[P]rior restraints on speech and publication are the most serious and the least tolerable infringement on First Amendment rights. A criminal penalty or a judgment in a defamation case is subject to the whole panoply of protections afforded by deferring the impact of the judgment until all avenues of appellate review have been exhausted. . . . A prior restraint, by contrast and by definition, has an immediate and irreversible sanction. If it can be said that a threat of criminal or civil sanctions after publication 'chills' speech, prior restraint 'freezes' it at least for the time."

The Court noted the particularly severe damage that prior restraints inflict on "communication of news and commentary on current events." In turn, these "extraordinary protections of the First Amendment carry with them something in the nature of a fiduciary duty to exercise the protected rights responsibly — a duty widely acknowledged but not always observed by editors and publishers."

Chief Justice Burger characterized the defendant's argument as ranking Sixth Amendment rights over First Amendment rights; however, the Framers did not rank these rights. Instead, the Court examined "the evidence before the trial judge when the order was entered to determine (a) the nature and extent of pretrial news coverage; (b) whether other measures would be likely to mitigate the effects of unrestrained pretrial publicity; and (c) how effectively a restraining order would operate to prevent the threatened danger. The precise terms of the restraining order are also important."

On the first issue, the Court found "that the trial judge was justified in concluding that there would be intense and pervasive pretrial publicity concerning [the Simants] case." The Court also observed that "[the judge's] prediction of the impact on prospective jurors was of necessity speculative." Turning to the second inquiry, the Court noted the lack of a "finding that alternative measures would not have protected Simants' rights."

In analyzing the third issue, the Chief Justice addressed the difficulties that arise in "managing and enforcing pretrial restraining orders." He wrote: "The territorial jurisdiction of the issuing court is limited by concepts of sovereignty. . . . The need for in personam jurisdiction also presents an obstacle to a restraining order that applies to publication at large as distinguished from restraining publication within a given jurisdiction." He also observed that the swift flow of rumors in a community of 850 people "could well be more damaging than reasonably accurate news accounts."

In summary, the Court asserted: "on the record now before us, it is not clear that further publicity, unchecked, would so distort the views of potential jurors that 12 could not be found who would, under proper instructions, fulfill their sworn duty to render a just verdict exclusively on the evidence presented in open court." The record did not indicate that alternatives to a prior restraint "would not have sufficiently mitigated the adverse effects of pretrial publicity so as to make prior restraints unnecessary. Nor can we conclude that the restraining order actually entered would serve its intended purpose."

Chief Justice Burger left open the possibility that a "threat to fair trial rights" may "possess the requisite degree of certainty to justify restraint" on publication and broadcast.

Justice White concurred in the opinion, but expressed "grave doubt" whether the kind of prior restraint issued in this case "would ever be justifiable."

Justice Powell also concurred in the opinion. To obtain a prior restraint in a case like this one, Justice Powell required that: "(i) there is a clear threat to the fairness of trial, (ii) such a threat is posed by actual publicity to be restrained, and (iii) no less restrictive alternatives are available. Notwithstanding such a showing, a restraint may not issue unless it also is shown that previous publicity or publicity from unrestrained sources will not render the restraint inefficacious."

Justices Stewart and Marshall joined Justice Brennan's opinion concurring in the judgment, in which he argued that the rule against prior restraints protects "any information pertaining to the criminal justice system, even if derived from nonpublic sources and regardless of the means employed by the press in its acquisition." He cited the " 'military security' situation, addressed in *New York Times Co. v. United States*," as the "only exception" to the rule against prior restraints established to that point.

Justice Brennan also noted that much of the information guarded by the restraining order at issue was already in the public domain. He concluded that "at least in the context of prior restraints on publication, the decision of what, when, and how to publish is for editors, not judges."[7]

In an opinion concurring in the judgment, Justice Stevens said: "Whether the same absolute protection would apply no matter how shabby or illegal the means by which the information is obtained, no matter how serious an intrusion on privacy might be involved, no matter how demonstrably false the information might be, no matter how prejudicial it might be to the interests of innocent persons, and no matter how perverse the motivation for publishing it, is a question I would not answer without further argument." He also conceded that he was likely to follow Justice Brennan's ultimate conclusion "if ever required to face [these] issues squarely."

NOTES

(1) *Gag Orders.* For further discussion of *Nebraska Press*, see Note, *A Prior Restraint by Any Other Name: The Judicial Response to Media Challenges of Gag Orders Directed at Trial Participants*, 88 MICH. L. REV. 1171, 1206 (1990) ("[F]ollowing *Nebraska Press Association v. Stuart*'s virtual ban of prior restraints directed at the media, courts began to achieve the same communication restriction by directing gag orders at the trial participants. When the media has challenged these orders, many courts have responded by applying a communicator-oriented prior restraint standard that is unable to accommodate claims based on receivers' rights.").

(2) *Reports on Judicial Ethics Proceedings.* In *Landmark Communications, Inc. v. Virginia*, 435 U.S. 829 (1978), the Court invalidated a statute that imposed criminal sanctions for disclosing truthful information about a judicial misconduct inquiry. The *Virginia Pilot*, a Landmark Communications newspaper, published an article accurately reporting a pending inquiry by the Virginia Judicial Inquiry and Review

---

[7] While "there may in some instances be tension between uninhibited and robust reporting by the press and fair trials for criminal defendants, judges possess adequate tools short of injunctions against reporting for relieving that tension."

Commission. The article identified the state judge under investigation. The Virginia Circuit Court convicted Landmark Communications of violating a Virginia statute that imposed criminal sanctions for breaching the confidentiality of proceedings before the commission.

Writing for the Court, Chief Justice Burger stated that the question confronted is not "any constitutional challenge to a State's power to keep the Commission's proceedings confidential or to punish participants for breach of this mandate. . . . [N]or does Landmark argue for any constitutionally compelled right of access for the press to those proceedings." The Chief Justice acknowledged that the state did have legitimate interests in maintaining the confidentially of the proceedings, such as the protection of a judge's reputation, maintenance of confidence in the judicial system, and protection of complainants and witnesses. These interests, however, did not outweigh First Amendment considerations. The article published by Landmark furnished "accurate factual information about a legislatively-authorized inquiry pending before the Judicial Inquiry and Review Commission."

The Court rejected the state's claim stating that much of the risk "can be eliminated through careful internal procedures to protect the confidentiality of the Commission proceedings."

(3) *Juvenile Offenders*. In *Smith v. Daily Mail Publishing Co.*, 443 U.S. 97 (1979), the Court invalidated a West Virginia statute that prohibited the publication in a newspaper of the name of a person charged as a juvenile offender, without the written approval of the juvenile court. Chief Justice Burger's opinion concluded that the law was unconstitutional regardless of whether it was classified as a prior restraint. "If a newspaper lawfully obtains truthful information about a matter of public significance then state officials may not constitutionally punish publication of the information, absent a need to further a state interest of the highest order."

(4) *Rape Victims*. Cox Communications Corp. v. Cohn, 420 U.S. 469 (1975), held that a state could not permit recovery in a tort action for invasion of privacy against a television station that had broadcast the name of a rape victim who had been murdered in the attack. Justice White's opinion relied on the fact that the name was a public record. "At the very least," he wrote, "the First and Fourteenth Amendments will not allow exposing the press to liability for truthfully publishing information released to the public in official court records." Justice Rehnquist dissented.

(5) *The Nixon tTapes*. During the Watergate cover-up trial, 22 hours of White House tapes were played to the public and the jury in the courtroom. In *Nixon v. Warner Communications*, 435 U.S. 589 (1978), the Court held that *Cox Communications Corp. v. Cohn* had simply guaranteed the press the right to "publish accurately information contained in court records open to the public," but did not give the press a right to physical access, since the general public had no such right. Since Congress had created statutory procedures for custody and ultimate public access to the tapes, the Court concluded that it was not necessary to weigh the competing claims of former President Nixon against the "general right to inspect and copy public records and documents. . . . The presence of an alternative means of public access tips the scales in favor of denying release." Justices White, Brennan, Marshall, and Stevens dissented, but not on constitutional grounds.

(6) *Broadcasting Attorney-Client Direct Communication*. In *Cable News Network v. Noriega* 498 U.S. 976 (1990), the Court (7-2) denied certiorari and refused to stay the district court's order enjoining the Cable News Network (CNN) from broadcasting taped communications between Manuel Noriega, a defendant in a pending criminal proceeding, and his attorney. CNN refused to make the tapes available to the judge. Without the tapes and without making a determination that suppression of the

broadcast was necessary to protect Noriega's right to a fair trial, the district court judge temporarily enjoined CNN until he could review the tapes to determine whether a permanent injunction should issue.

Justice Marshall, joined by Justice O'Connor, dissented from the denial of certiorari. "Our precedents make unmistakably clear that '[a]ny prior restrain[t] of expression comes to this Court bearing a heavy presumption against its constitutional validity,' and that the proponent of this drastic remedy 'carries a heavy burden of showing justification for [its] imposition.'" *Nebraska Press Ass'n v. Stuart*, 427 U.S. 539, 558 (1976); *accord, New York Times Co. v. United States.*

(7) *Discovery Protective Orders.* In *Seattle Times Co. v. Rhinehart*, 467 U.S. 20 (1984), a unanimous Court upheld a protective order prohibiting the defendant newspaper from publishing information acquired through pre-trial discovery. A religious group sued a newspaper for defamation and invasion of privacy. In the course of discovery, the newspaper sought detailed financial and membership information about the religious group. In response, the group sought a protective order prohibiting the newspaper from publishing this information about the group, which was obtained through the discovery process. The religious group sought the protective order under a state discovery rule modeled on Rule 26(c) of the Federal Rules of Civil Procedure.

Upholding the protective order issued by the trial court, Justice Powell said that the protective order was "not the kind of classic prior restraint that requires exacting First Amendment scrutiny" because it did not prohibit publishing information obtained though other means. In enabling parties to obtain information relevant to litigation, "Rule 26(c) furthers a substantial government interest unrelated to the suppression of expression." Moreover, as the information was obtained through pre-trial discovery, the government also has a substantial interest in preventing abuse of that judicial process. As the trial judge "is in the best position to weigh fairly the competing needs and interests of parties affected by discovery," Rule 26 (c) properly afforded the trial court broad discretion in issuing protective orders. Justice Brennan wrote a concurring opinion joined by Justice Marshall.

GENTILE v. STATE BAR OF NEVADA, 501 U.S. 1030 (1991). In *Gentile*, the Court considered the First Amendment protections afforded to an attorney who made statements regarding a pending case in which he represented one of the parties. Gentile, a criminal defense attorney, made statements at a press conference the day after his client, Sanders, was indicted. Gentile called a press conference to refute allegations made by the police department concerning Sanders' involvement in the theft of money and drugs from a safety deposit box kept by the Las Vegas Metropolitan Police Department. The State Bar of Nevada filed a complaint against Gentile for making these statements at the press conference in violation of Nevada Supreme Court Rule 177 "that prohibits an attorney from making extra-judicial statements to the press which he knows or reasonably should know will have a 'substantial likelihood of materially prejudicing' an adjudicative proceeding." A subsection of Rule 177 listed a "safe harbor" for an attorney by providing a list of "a number of statements that can be made without fear of discipline."

Parts III and IV of Justice Kennedy's opinion were joined by Justices Marshall, Blackmun, Stevens, and O'Connor. This 5-4 majority struck down Rule 177 as vague. Justice Kennedy, in the "void for vagueness" portion of his opinion commanding a majority, opined that the safe harbor provision "misled petitioner into thinking that he could give his press conference without fear of discipline. Rule 177(3)(a) provides that a lawyer 'may state without elaboration . . . the general nature of the . . . defense.'" Determining when one is protected by the safe harbor provision is difficult: "The right to explain the 'general' nature of the defense without 'elaboration' provides insufficient guidance because 'general' and 'elaboration' are both classic terms of degree. In the context before us, these terms have no settled usage or tradition of interpretation in the law."

Chief Justice Rehnquist, joined by Justices White, O'Connor, Scalia, and Souter, wrote for a different majority, holding that the " 'substantial likelihood of material prejudice' standard applied by Nevada . . . satisfies the First Amendment." Chief Justice Rehnquist disagreed, however, that the Nevada rule was "void for vagueness" and therefore dissented from this holding in an opinion joined by Justices White, Scalia and Souter. Justice O'Connor provided the crucial swing vote for both majorities. In her concurrence, she agreed with Justice Kennedy that Rule 177 was "void for vagueness," while concurring with Chief Justice Rehnquist that the substantial likelihood standard satisfied the First Amendment. Chief Justice Rehnquist opined that the criminal justice system operates in the context of a government of the people who need information about the workings of the system in order to implement necessary changes. "The First Amendment protections of speech and press have been held . . . to require a showing of 'clear and present danger' that a malfunction in the criminal justice system will be caused before a State may prohibit media speech or publication about a particular pending trial."

While an attorney does enjoy the freedom to "castigate the courts in their administration of justice," he cannot do so in a pending criminal case in which he is an officer of the court. "The courts must take such steps by rule and regulation that will protect their processes from prejudicial outside interferences. Neither prosecutors, counsel for defense, the accused, witnesses, court staff nor enforcement officers coming under the jurisdiction of the court should be permitted to frustrate its function. *Collaboration between counsel and the press as to information affecting the fairness of a criminal trial is not only subject to regulation, but is highly censurable and worth of disciplinary measures.*"

The Chief Justice continued: "When a state regulation implicates First Amendment rights, the Court must balance those interests against the State's legitimate interest in regulating the activity in question. . . . The 'substantial likelihood' test embodied in Rule 177 is constitutional under this analysis, for it is designed to protect the integrity and fairness of a state's judicial system and it imposes only narrow and necessary limitations on lawyer's speech. The limitations are aimed at two principal evils: (1) comments that are likely to influence the actual outcome of the trial, and (2) comments that are likely to prejudice the jury venire, even if an untainted panel can ultimately be found."

The regulation at issue was "narrowly tailored" to serve the state's objectives. The Court found the appropriate balance between the state's interest in a fair trial and low court costs both "important" and "substantial." The restraint on speech under the "substantial likelihood test" is "narrowly tailored to achieve those objectives" since the rule merely postpones the speech in question.

§ 13.03   ACCESS BY THE MEDIA TO GOVERNMENT ACTIVITY

HOUCHINS v. K.Q.E.D., INC.
438 U.S. 1, 98 S. Ct. 2588, 57 L. Ed. 2d 553 (1978)

CHIEF JUSTICE BURGER announced the judgment of the Court and delivered an opinion, in which JUSTICE WHITE and JUSTICE REHNQUIST joined.

The question presented is whether the news media have a constitutional right of access to a county jail, over and above that of other persons, to interview inmates and make sound recordings, films, and photographs for publication and broadcasting by newspapers, radio and television.

Petitioner Houchins, as Sheriff of Alameda County, Cal., controls all access to the Alameda County Jail at Santa Rita. Respondent KQED operates licensed television and radio broadcasting stations. . . . On March 31, 1975, KQED reported the suicide of a prisoner in the Greystone portion of the Santa Rita Jail. . . .

KQED requested permission to inspect and take pictures within the Greystone facility. After permission was refused, KQED and the Alameda and Oakland Branches of the National Association for the Advancement of Colored People (NAACP) filed suit under 42 U.S.C. § 1983. . . .

On June 17, 1975, when the complaint was filed, there appears to have been no formal policy regarding public access to the Santa Rita Jail. However, according to petitioner, he had been in the process of planning a program of regular monthly tours since he took office six months earlier. On July 8, 1975, he announced the program and invited all interested persons to make arrangements for the regular public tours. News media were given notice in advance of the public and presumably could have made early reservations.

Six monthly tours were planned and funded by the County at an estimated cost of $1,800. . . .

Each tour was limited to 25 persons and permitted only limited access to the jail. The tours did not include the disciplinary cells or the portions of the jail known as "little Greystone," the scene of alleged rapes, beatings, and adverse physical conditions. Photographs of some parts of the jail were made available, but no cameras or tape recorders were allowed on the tours. Those on the tours were not permitted to interview inmates and inmates were generally removed from view. . . .

After considering the testimony, affidavits, and documentary evidence presented by the parties, the District Court preliminarily enjoined petitioner from denying KQED news personnel and "responsible representatives" of the news media access to the Santa Rita facilities, including Greystone, "at reasonable times and hours" and "from preventing KQED news personnel and responsible representatives of the news media from utilizing photographic and sound equipment or from utilizing inmate interviews in providing full and accurate coverage of the Santa Rita facilities." . . .

. . . This Court has never intimated a First Amendment guarantee of a right of access to all sources of information within government control. . . .

The respondents' argument is flawed, not only because it lacks precedential support and is contrary to statements in this Court's opinions, but also because it invites the Court to involve itself in what is clearly a legislative task which the Constitution has left to the political processes. . . .

A number of alternatives are available to prevent problems in penal facilities from escaping public attention. . . . Citizen task forces and prison visitation committees continue to play an important role in keeping the public informed on deficiencies of prison systems and need for reforms. Grand juries, with the potent subpoena power — not available to the media — traditionally concern themselves with conditions in public institutions; a prosecutor or judge may initiate similar inquiries and the legislative power embraces an arsenal of weapons for inquiry relating to tax supported institutions. In each case, these public bodies are generally compelled to publish their findings. But the choice as to the most effective and appropriate method is a policy decision to be resolved by legislative decision. . . .

. . . Public bodies and public officers . . . may be coerced by public opinion to disclose what they might prefer to conceal. . . .

There is no discernable basis for a constitutional duty to disclose, or for standards governing disclosure of or access to information. . . . We, therefore, reject the . . . assertion that the public and the media have a First Amendment right to government information regarding the conditions of jails and their inmates and presumably all other public facilities such as hospitals and mental institutions. . . .

. . . Respondents have a First Amendment right to receive letters from inmates criticizing jail officials and reporting on conditions. *Procunier v. Martinez*, [416 U.S. 396 (1974)] 413–418. Respondents are free to interview those who render the legal assistance to which inmates are entitled. They are also free to seek out former inmates, visitors to the prison, public officials, and institutional personnel, as they sought out the complaining psychiatrist here.

Moreover, California statutes currently provide for a prison Board of Corrections that has the authority to inspect jails and prisons and must provide a public report at regular intervals. Health inspectors are required to inspect prisons and provide reports to a number of officials, including the State Attorney General and the Board of Corrections. Fire officials are also required to inspect prisons. Following the reports of the suicide at the jail involved here, the County Board of Supervisors called for a report from the County Supervisor, held a public hearing on the report, which was open to the media. . . .

Neither the First Amendment nor Fourteenth Amendment mandates a right of access to government information or sources of information within the government's control. . . . [U]ntil the political branches decree otherwise, as they are free to do, the media have no special right of access to the Alameda County Jail different from or greater than that accorded the public generally. . . .

Justice Marshall and Justice Blackmun took no part in the consideration or decision of this case.

Justice Stewart, concurring in the judgment. . . .

The First and Fourteenth Amendments do not guarantee the public a right of access to information generated or controlled by government, nor do they guarantee the press any basic right of access superior to that of the public generally. The Constitution does no more than assure the public and the press equal access once government has opened its doors. Accordingly, I agree substantially with what the opinion of The Chief Justice has to say on that score.

. . . [H]owever, . . . [w]hereas he appears to view "equal access" as meaning access that is identical in all respects, I believe that the concept of equal access must be accorded more flexibility in order to accommodate the practical distinctions between the press and the general public. . . .

That the First Amendment speaks separately of freedom of speech and freedom of the press is no constitutional accident, but an acknowledgement of the critical role played by the press in American society. The Constitution requires sensitivity to that role, and to the special needs of the press in performing it effectively. . . . [I]f a television reporter is to convey the jail's sights and sounds to those who cannot personally visit the place, he must use cameras and sound equipment. In short, terms of access that are reasonably imposed on individual members of the public may, if they impede effective reporting without sufficient justification, be unreasonable as applied to journalists. . . .

The District Court found that the press required access to the jail on a more flexible and frequent basis than scheduled monthly tours if it was to keep the public informed. By leaving the "specific methods of implementing such a policy . . . [to] Sheriff

Houchins," the Court concluded that the press could be allowed access to the jail "at reasonable times and" without causing undue disruption. The District Court also found that the media required cameras and recording equipment for effective presentation to the viewing public of the conditions at the jail seen by individual visitors, and that their use could be kept consistent with institutional needs. These elements of the Court's order were both sanctioned by the Constitution and amply supported by the record.

In two respects, however, the District Court's preliminary injunction was overbroad. It ordered the Sheriff to permit reporters into the Little Greystone facility and it required him to let them interview randomly encountered inmates. In both these respects, the injunction gave the press access to areas and sources of information from which persons on the public tours had been excluded. . . .

. . . In my view, the availability and scope of future permanent injunctive relief must depend upon the extent of access then permitted the public, and the decree must be framed to accommodate equitably the constitutional role of the press and the institutional requirements of the jail.

JUSTICE STEVENS, with whom JUSTICE BRENNAN and JUSTICE POWELL join, dissenting. . . .

. . . The public and the press had consistently been denied any access to those portions of the Santa Rita facility where inmates were confined and there had been excessive censorship of inmate correspondence. . . .

. . . Our system of self-government assumes the existence of an informed citizenry. . . . It is not sufficient, therefore, that the channels of communication be free of governmental restraints. Without some protection for the acquisition of information about the operation of public institutions such as prisons by the public at large, the process of self-governance . . . would be stripped of its substance. . . .

. . . The question is whether petitioner's policies, which cut off the flow of information at its source, abridged the public's right to be informed about those conditions.

The answer to that question does not depend upon the degree of public disclosure which should attend the operation of most governmental activity. Such matters involve questions of policy which generally must be resolved by the political branches of government. Moreover, there are unquestionably occasions when governmental activity may properly be carried on in complete secrecy. For example, the public and the press are commonly excluded from "grand jury proceedings, our own conferences, [and] the meetings of other official bodies gathering in executive session. . . . " *Branzburg v. Hayes*, 408 U.S. [665 (1972)] at 684. In addition, some functions of government — essential to the protection of the public and indeed our country's vital interests — necessarily require a large measure of secrecy, subject to appropriate legislative oversight. . . . [8]

In this case, however, "[respondents] do not assert a right to force disclosure of confidential information or to invade in any way the decisionmaking processes of governmental officials." . . . While prison officials have an interest in the time and manner of public acquisition of information about the institutions they administer, there is no legitimate, penological justification for concealing from citizens the conditions in

---

[8] [Court's footnote 27] In *United States v. Nixon*, 418 U.S. 683, we also recognized the valid need for protection of communications between high Government officials and those who advise and assist them in the performance of their manifold duties. . . . [T]hose who expect public dissemination of their remarks may well temper candor with a concern for appearances and for their own interests to the detriment of the decisionmaking process." *Id.* at 705.

which their fellow citizens are being confined.

. . . Not only are [prisons] public institutions, financed with public funds and administered by public servants; they are an integral component of the criminal justice system. . . . [An inmate] retains constitutional protections against cruel and unusual punishment, a protection which may derive more practical support from access to information about prisons by the public than by occasional litigation in a busy court.

. . . Though the public and the press have an equal right to receive information and ideas, different methods of remedying a violation of that right may sometimes be needed to accommodate the special concerns of the one or the other. . . .

RICHMOND NEWSPAPERS, INC. v. VIRGINIA, 448 U.S. 555 (1980). The "narrow question presented in this case" was "whether the right of the public and press to attend criminal trials is guaranteed by the United States Constitution." A man was convicted of second-degree murder in his first trial, and his second and third trials were both declared mistrials.[9] The last mistrial may have resulted from a prospective juror reading about the case in the newspaper and telling "other prospective jurors about it before the retrial began." Under a Virginia statute, defense counsel in the fourth trial "moved that it be closed to the public." No objections were raised by the prosecutor or by appellants, who were reporters.

The question of first impression for the Court was "whether a criminal trial itself may be closed to the public upon the unopposed request of a defendant, without any demonstration that closure is required to protect the defendant's superior right to a fair trial, or that some other overriding consideration requires closure." Chief Justice Burger, in the majority opinion, observed that "criminal trials both here and in England had long been presumptively open," in order to ensure fair proceedings and to discourage perjury, participant misconduct and biased decisions. Furthermore, "the means used to achieve justice must have the support derived from public acceptance of both the process and its results. When a shocking crime occurs" in a community, people naturally feel a need for justice, and even for retribution. In an open criminal trial "there is at least an opportunity borh for understanding the system in general and its workings in a particular case."

However, the state argued that "neither the Constitution nor the Bill of Rights contains any provision . . . guarantee[ing] . . . the right to attend criminal trials." Chief Justice Burger noted that "the First Amendment guarantees of speech and press, standing alone, prohibit the government from summarily closing courtroom doors which had long been open to the public at the time that amendment was adopted." Citing *Branzburg v. Hayes*, he asserted that whether the right to attend trials was characterized "as a 'right of access' or a 'right to gather information'" was not important "for we have recognized that 'without some protection for seeking out the news, freedom of the press could be eviscerated.'" The relationship between the First Amendment guarantees of speech and press and the right of assembly was relevant to the Court's decision.[10]

"[T]he Constitution's draftsmen [expressed concern] that some important rights

---

[9] [Courts footnote 1] "A newspaper account published" the day after the second trial reported that "'a bloodstained shirt [was] obtained from Stevenson's wife soon after the killing. The Virginia Supreme Court, however, ruled that the shirt was entered into evidence improperly.'"

[10] Turning again to history, the Chief Justice asserted that "[f]rom the outset, the right of assembly was regarded not only as an independent right but also as a catalyst to augment the free exercise of the other First Amendment rights."

might be thought disparaged because not specifically guaranteed."[11] The Court has acknowledged certain implicit rights within the enumerated guarantees of the Constitution and the Bill of Rights.[12] In this case, the majority held that the right to attend a criminal trial was guaranteed by the First and the Fourteenth Amendments.

Chief Justice Burger next turned to the issue of whether the closure order was proper. "Despite the fact that this was the fourth trial of the accused, the trial judge made no findings to support closure; no inquiry was made as to whether alternative solutions would have met the need to ensure fairness; there was no recognition of any right under the Constitution for the public or press to attend the trial."[13] Reversing the judgment below, the majority held that "[a]bsent an overriding interest articulated in findings, the trial of a criminal case must be open to the public."[14] After reviewing the findings of the trial judge, the Chief Justice concluded that problem witnesses could have been excluded or sequestered during the trial, and that sequestration of the jury could have protected the jurors from improper influences. Thus, no overriding interest justified closure.

Justice White and Justice Stevens concurred. Specifically, Justice Stevens noted that "[t]his is a watershed case." While "the dissemination of information" has always received "virtually absolute protection," the Court has not "squarely held that the acquisition of newsworthy matter is entitled to any constitutional protection whatsoever." Justice Stevens found it ironic that the Court was more willing to recognize a right of access where the most powerful voices in the community proposed an exception to the tradition of open criminal trials than it was in *Houchins v. K.Q.E.D., Inc.*, in which the weakest segment of society, prisoners, challenged secrecy.

Justice Marshall joined Justice Brennan's concurrence. Justice Brennan focused on the structural function of the First Amendment in maintaining a republican system of self-government.[15] "[C]ountervailing interests" that might compel reversal of the "presumption of openness" were irrelevant in this case since "trial closures at the unfettered discretion of the judge and parties" were authorized by statute.

In a separate concurrence, Justice Stewart emphasized that the right of public and press to attend criminal trials is not absolute. He distinguished the courtroom from other places, observing the need for quiet and order during a trial as well as the limited space inside a courtroom.[16]

---

[11] Madison told Congress that a constitutional "saving clause" was necessary to prevent the implication that the inclusion of expressly defined rights in the Constitution or Bill of Rights, excluded those not mentioned. Madison's efforts resulted in the Ninth Amendment to the Constitution.

[12] The "rights of association and of privacy, the right to be presumed innocent and the right to be judged by a standard of proof beyond a reasonable doubt in a criminal trial, as well as the right to travel." To clarify the right at issue in the case, the Court added, "[w]hether the public has a right to attend trials of civil cases is a question not raised by this case, but we note that historically both civil and criminal trials have been presumptively open."

[13] The Court previously had "made clear [in *Gannett Co., Inc. v. DePasquale*] that although the Sixth Amendment guarantees the accused a right to a public trial, it does not give a right to a private trial."

[14] The First Amendment rights of the press and public might be limited under different circumstances. It further noted the need for "a quiet and orderly setting" for trial and the limited seating capacity of courtrooms as factors that potentially could create a need to limit courtroom access.

[15] "A conceptually separate, yet related, question is whether the media should enjoy greater access rights than the general public."

[16] Justice Stewart noted that the public might be excluded from part of a civil trial to protect a trade secret or from a rape trial during the testimony of a young witness, as long as the defendant's Sixth Amendment right to a public trial was preserved.

Justice Rehnquist dissented because he believed that the Court improperly had used its constitutional powers to "rein in . . . the ultimate decisionmaking power" of federal and individual state courts over the administration of justice. The Court should not apply an "ever-broadening use of the Supremacy Clause" to "smother a healthy pluralism which would ordinarily exist in a national government embracing 50 States."

NOTES

(1) *Testimony of Rape Victim. Richmond Newspapers* was the basis for the Court's decision in *Globe Newspapers Co. v. Superior Court,* 457 U.S. 596 (1982). In that case, the Court overturned a Massachusetts statute that, as construed by the Massachusetts Supreme Judicial Court, required trial judges, "at trials for specified sexual offenses involving a victim under the age of 18, to exclude the press and general public from the courtroom during the testimony of that victim." *Globe* involved a rape trial in which the victim was under 18. Justice Brennan's majority (6-3) opinion recognized the importance of the state's interest in "safeguarding the physical and psychological well-being of a minor," but concluded that the compelling nature of that interest did not justify the mandatory closure rule in all specified cases. The Court also rejected the second proffered justification for the statute — that it would encourage victims of such crimes to come forward and offer testimony. Justice Brennan noted that there was no empirical evidence to support the state's position and that the media was free, despite the statute, to publicize the name of the victim and all aspects of the testimony through reference to the transcript.

In a dissent joined by Justice Rehnquist, Chief Justice Burger pointed out the long history of excluding the public from trials involving sexual assaults. Since the state had not denied the public the right to receive information about the trial, the statute should be governed by a reasonableness standard in order to determine whether "the interests of the Commonwealth override the very limited incidental effects of the law on First Amendment rights." Justice Stevens dissented on grounds of mootness.

(2) *Televised Trials.* In *Chandler v. Florida,* 449 U.S. 560 (1981), the Court (8-0, Justice Stevens not participating) upheld a Florida Supreme Court rule that permitted the televising of criminal trials over the objection of the defendant. The Court said that televising a criminal defendant's trial, without her consent, is not inherently a denial of due process. Chief Justice Burger concluded that the defendants (two Miami police officers convicted of burglarizing a restaurant) had failed to show that their own trial had been tainted or that televised trials generally would deprive defendants of fair trials. The decision was framed in terms of a defendant's right to a fair trial and did not create any First Amendment right of access to the courts for broadcast journalists. The question of whether a state may constitutionally prohibit broadcast media from trial coverage while admitting print journalists remains open.

(3) *Voir Dire.* In *Press-Enterprise Co. v. Superior Court of California,* 464 U.S. 501 (1984), the Court, without dissent, extended the holding in *Richmond Newspapers* to *voir dire. Press-Enterprise* involved a rape-murder trial in which the prosecution opposed the newspaper's motion to be present at *voir dire* on grounds that if the press were present, the jurors' responses "would lack the candor necessary to assure a fair trial." Both the prosecution and defense opposed a release of the *voir dire* transcript on grounds that release would violate the juror's right to privacy. Chief Justice Burger's opinion concluded that there has been a presumption of open trials "back to the days before the Norman Conquest" and that, at least since the Sixteenth Century, the jury selection process has been public. "The presumption of openness may be overcome only by an overriding interest based on findings that closure is essential to preserve higher values and is narrowly tailored to serve that interest. The interest is to be articulated

along with findings specific enough that a reviewing court can determine whether the closure order was properly entered."

In this case, three days of *voir dire* were open and six weeks were closed. The Court recognized that the accused's right to a fair trial would justify closure but found nothing in the record to indicate why prolonged closure was necessary to protect this interest. Nor did the record indicate how the jurors' privacy interests were protected by closure or by the refusal to release the testimony. Moreover, unless the trial court considers alternative measures to protect the interests of the defendant and jurors, neither closure nor the sealing of the *voir dire* testimony is permitted. "Assuming that some jurors had protectible privacy interests in some of their answers, the trial judge provided no explanation why his broad order denying access to information at the *voir dire* was not limited to information that was actually sensitive and deserving of privacy protection. Nor did he consider whether he could disclose the substance of the sensitive answers while preserving the anonymity of the jurors involved."

(4) *Suppression Hearing.* In *Waller v. Georgia*, 467 U.S. 39 (1984), the defendant objected to closure of a suppression hearing and asserted a Sixth Amendment right to an open trial. Justice Powell, writing for a unanimous Court in *Waller*, ruled that the accused's right to a public trial encompasses the suppression hearing and that the same standard that was applicable to the public under the First Amendment, as articulated in *Richmond Newspapers* and *Press-Enterprise*, would govern public trial claims by the defendant under the Sixth Amendment.

"[T]he explicit Sixth Amendment right of the accused is no less protective of a public trial than the implicit First Amendment right to the press and public." Since the test in *Waller* under the Sixth Amendment is the same as under the First Amendment, it is clear that the defendant's Sixth Amendment claim will result in the equivalent degree of access for the press and public as would be achieved if the latter's First Amendment right of access were recognized at suppression hearings.

(5) *"Of the Press."* The view that the words "of the press" in the First Amendment have special significance relating to the press as an institution are discussed (from different perspectives) in Justice Stewart's article, *Or of the Press*, 26 Hastings L.J. 631 (1975), and in Chief Justice Burger's concurring opinion in *First National Bank of Boston v. Bellotti*, 435 U.S. 765 (1978), § 15.02. *See also* Justice Brennan's emphasis on the "structural" role of the press, in his *Richmond Newspapers* concurrence and in *Address*, 32 Rutgers L. Rev. 173 (1979).

PRESS ENTERPRISE COMPANY v. SUPERIOR COURT OF CALIFORNIA, 478 U.S. 1 (1986) (*"Press Enterprise II"*). In *Press Enterprise II*, the Court held that the First Amendment right of access to criminal trials applied to preliminary hearings. A California state court closed the preliminary hearing of a murder trial under a state statute that allowed such proceedings to be closed to protect defendant's right to a fair trial. The defendant nurse was accused of murdering 12 patients with drug overdoses. The case had attracted national publicity. At the end of the 41-day hearing, the judge refused Press Enterprise's request that the transcripts be released.

Chief Justice Burger reversed the judgment and extended the right of access in criminal trials to preliminary hearings. First, in contrast to grand jury proceedings, there "has been a tradition of public access to preliminary hearings of the type conducted in California."

Second, public access to preliminary hearings plays a crucial role in the proper functioning of the criminal justice system. "In California, to bring a felon to trial, the prosecutor has a choice of securing a grand jury indictment or a finding of probable cause following a preliminary hearing. Even when the accused has been indicted by a grand jury, however, he has an absolute right to an elaborate preliminary hearing before a neutral magistrate. The accused has the right to personally appear at the hearing, to be represented by counsel, to cross-examine hostile witnesses, to present exculpatory evidence, and to exclude illegally obtained evidence. If the magistrate determines that probable cause exists, the accused is bound over for trial; such a finding leads to a guilty plea in the majority of cases." Moreover, "the absence of a jury long recognized as an 'inestimable safeguard against the corrupt or overzealous prosecutor and against the compliant, biased, or eccentric judge,' makes the importance of public access to a preliminary hearing even more significant."

In defining this right of access, the Court quoted from its earlier opinion in *Press Enterprise I*, that since a qualified First Amendment right of access applied to preliminary hearings, the proceedings could not be closed unless "specific, on the record findings are made demonstrating that . . . 'closure is essential to preserve higher values and is narrowly tailored to serve that interest. If the interest asserted is the right of the accused to a fair trial' . . . the preliminary hearing shall be closed only if specific findings are made demonstrating that first, there is a substantial probability that the defendant's right to a fair trial will be prejudiced by publicity that closure would prevent, and second, reasonable alternatives to closure cannot adequately protect the defendant's free trial rights." California had failed to apply this standard and to consider alternatives to ferreting out juror prejudice like *voir dire*. The Chief Justice cautioned that "even if closure were justified for the hearings on a motion to suppress, closure of an entire 41-day proceeding would rarely be warranted."

Justice Stevens dissented. He emphasized that the right to obtain information is "far narrower" than the right to disseminate it. "In this case, the risk of prejudice to the defendant's right to a fair trial is perfectly obvious. For me, the risk is far more significant than the countervailing interest in publishing the transcript of the preliminary hearing sooner rather than later."

Justice Rehnquist joined in the remainder of Justice Stevens' dissenting opinion. The "compelling governmental interest/least restrictive means" test failed to properly account for prejudice to defendant.

§ 13.04   PROTECTING THE NEWSGATHERING PROCESS

BRANZBURG v. HAYES
408 U.S. 665, 92 S. Ct. 2646, 33 L. Ed. 2d 626 (1972)

Opinion of the Court by JUSTICE WHITE, announced by THE CHIEF JUSTICE.

The issue in these cases is whether requiring newsmen to appear and testify before state or federal grand juries abridges the freedom of speech and press guaranteed by the First Amendment. We hold that it does not.

I

On November 15, 1969, the [Louisville] Courier-Journal carried a story under petitioner's by-line describing in detail his observations of two young residents of Jefferson County synthesizing hashish from marihuana . . . The article included a photograph of a pair of hands working above a laboratory table on which was a substance identified by the caption as hashish. The article stated that petitioner had promised not to reveal the identity of the two hashish makers. Petitioner was shortly subpoenaed by the Jefferson County grand jury; he appeared, but refused to identify the individuals he had seen possessing marihuana or the persons he had seen making hashish from marihuana. . . .

The second case involving petitioner Branzburg arose out of his later story published on January 10, 1971, which described in detail the use of drugs in Frankfort, Kentucky. The article reported that in order to provide a comprehensive survey of the "drug scene" in Frankfort, petitioner had "spent two weeks interviewing several dozen drug users in the capital city" and had seen some of them smoking marihuana. A number of conversations with and observations of several unnamed drug users were recounted. Subpoenaed to appear before a Franklin County grand jury "to testify in the matter of violation of statutes concerning use and sale of drugs," petitioner Branzburg moved to quash the summons; the motion was denied, although an order was issued protecting Branzburg from revealing "confidential associations, sources or information" but requiring that he "answer any questions which concern or pertain to any criminal act, the commission of which was actually observed by [him]." Prior to the time he was slated to appear before the grand jury, petitioner sought mandamus and prohibition from the Kentucky Court of Appeals. . . .

In addition to the *Branzburg* case, two other cases, *In re Pappas* and *Caldwell v. United States*, were heard and decided together. *Pappas* involved the refusal of a television newsman- photographer to answer questions before a grand jury relating to what had taken place inside Black Panther headquarters. . . .

United States v. Caldwell involved the refusal of a New York Times reporter to testify, and to bring notes and tape recordings, relating to conversations with Black Panther Party leaders. The grand jury was investigating possible violations of federal criminal statutes. Although the District Court ruled that Caldwell need not divulge confidential sources, he was ordered to appear and reveal information he had gathered. A contempt order, issued after he refused to appear, was reversed by the Court of Appeals, 434 F.2d 1081 (9th Cir. 1970). . . .

II

. . . The use of confidential sources by the press is not forbidden or restricted. . . . No attempt is made to require the press to publish its sources of information or indiscriminately to disclose them on request.

The sole issue before us is the obligation of reporters to respond to grand jury subpoenas as other citizens do and to answer questions relevant to an investigation into the commission of crime. . . .

. . . Under prior cases, otherwise valid laws serving substantial public interests may be enforced against the press as against others, despite the possible burden that may be imposed. . . . Likewise, a newspaper may be subjected to nondiscriminatory forms of general taxation. . . .

Despite the fact that news gathering may be hampered, the press is regularly excluded from grand jury proceedings, our own conferences, the meetings of other official bodies gathered in executive session, and the meetings of private organizations. Newsmen have no constitutional right of access to the scenes of crime or disaster when the general public is excluded. . . .

It is, thus, not surprising that the great weight of authority is that newsmen are not exempt from the normal duty of appearing before a grand jury and answering questions relevant to a criminal investigation. At common law, courts consistently refused to recognize the existence of any privilege authorizing a newsman to refuse to reveal confidential information to a grand jury. . . .

A number of States have provided newsmen a statutory privilege of varying breadth, but the majority have not done so, and none has been provided by federal statute. . . . On the records now before us, we perceive no basis for holding that the public interest in law enforcement and in ensuring effective grand jury proceedings is insufficient to override the consequential, but uncertain, burden on news gathering that is said to result from insisting that reporters, like other citizens, respond to relevant questions put to them in the course of a valid grand jury investigation or criminal trial.

. . . Only where news sources themselves are implicated in crime or possess information relevant to the grand jury's task need they or the reporter be concerned about grand jury subpoenas. Nothing before us indicates that a large number or percentage of all confidential news sources falls into either category and would in any way be deterred by our holding that the Constitution does not, as it never has, exempt the newsman from performing the citizen's normal duty of appearing and furnishing information relevant to the grand jury's task.

The preference for anonymity of those confidential informants involved in actual criminal conduct is presumably a product of their desire to escape criminal prosecution, and this preference, while understandable, is hardly deserving of constitutional protection. . . .

There remain those situations where a source is not engaged in criminal conduct but has information suggesting illegal conduct by others. . . . Such informants presumably desire anonymity in order to avoid being entangled as a witness in a criminal trial or grand jury investigation. They may fear that disclosure will threaten their job security or personal safety or that it will simply result in dishonor or embarrassment.

The argument that the flow of news will be diminished by compelling reporters to aid the grand jury in a criminal investigation is not irrational, nor are the records before us silent on the matter. But we remain unclear how often and to what extent informers are actually deterred from furnishing information when newsmen are forced to testify before a grand jury. . . .

Accepting the fact, however, that an undetermined number of informants not themselves implicated in crime will nevertheless, for whatever reason, refuse to talk to newsmen if they fear identification by a reporter in an official investigation, we cannot accept the argument that the public interest in possible future news about crime from undisclosed, unverified sources must take precedence over the public interest in pursuing and prosecuting those crimes reported to the press by informants and in thus deterring the commission of such crimes in the future.

We note first that the privilege claimed is that of the reporter, not the informant, and that if the authorities independently identify the informant, neither his own reluctance to testify nor the objection of the newsman would shield him from grand jury inquiry. . . . More important, it is obvious that agreements to conceal information relevant to commission of crime have very little to recommend them from the standpoint of public policy. . . .

. . . From the beginning of our country the press has operated without constitutional protection for press informants, and the press has flourished. . . .

It is said that currently press subpoenas have multiplied, that mutual distrust and tension between press and officialdom have increased, that reporting styles have changed, and that there is now more need for confidential sources, particularly where the press seeks news about minority cultural and political groups or dissident organizations suspicious of the law and public officials. These developments, even if true, are treacherous grounds for a far-reaching interpretation of the First Amendment fastening a nationwide rule on courts, grand juries, and prosecuting officials everywhere. . . .

. . . The administration of a constitutional newsman's privilege would present practical and conceptual difficulties of a high order. Sooner or later, it would be necessary to define those categories of newsmen who qualified for the privilege, a questionable procedure in light of the traditional doctrine that liberty of the press is the right of the lonely pamphleteer who uses carbon paper or a mimeograph just as much as of the large metropolitan publisher who utilizes the latest photocomposition methods. . . . The informative function asserted by representatives of the organized press in the present cases is also performed by lecturers, political pollsters, novelists, academic researchers, and dramatists. Almost any author may quite accurately assert that he is contributing to the flow of information to the public, that he relies on confidential sources of information, and that these sources will be silenced if he is forced to make disclosures before a grand jury.

In each instance where a reporter is subpoenaed to testify, the courts would also be embroiled in preliminary factual and legal determinations with respect to whether the proper predicate had been laid for the reporter's appearance: Is there probable cause to believe a crime has been committed? Is it likely that the reporter has useful information gained in confidence? Could the grand jury obtain the information elsewhere? Is the official interest sufficient to outweigh the claimed privilege?

Thus, in the end, by considering whether enforcement of a particular law served a "compelling" governmental interest, the courts would be inextricably involved in distinguishing between the value of enforcing different criminal laws. . . .

At the federal level, Congress has freedom to determine whether a statutory newsman's privilege is necessary and desirable and to fashion standards and rules as narrow or broad as deemed necessary to deal with the evil discerned and, equally important, to refashion those rules as experience from time to time may dictate. There is also merit in leaving state legislatures free, within First Amendment limits, to fashion their own standards in light of the conditions and problems with respect to the relations between law enforcement officials and press in their own areas. It goes without saying, of course, that we are powerless to bar state courts from responding in their own way and construing their own constitutions so as to recognize a newsman's privilege, either qualified or absolute.

In addition, there is much force in the pragmatic view that the press has at its disposal powerful mechanisms of communication and is far from helpless to protect itself from harassment or substantial harm. Furthermore, if what the newsmen urged in these cases is true — that law enforcement cannot hope to gain and may suffer from subpoenaing newsmen before grand juries — prosecutors will be loath to risk so much for so little. . . .

Finally, as we have earlier indicated, news gathering is not without its First Amendment protections, and grand jury investigations if instituted or conducted other than in good faith, would pose wholly different issues for resolution under the First Amendment. Official harassment of the press undertaken not for purposes of law enforcement but to disrupt a reporter's relationship with his news sources would have no jurisdiction. Grand juries are subject to judicial control and subpoenas to motions to quash. . . .

III

We turn, therefore, to the disposition of the cases before us. From what we have said, it necessarily follows that the decision in *United States v. Caldwell* must be reversed. If there is no First Amendment privilege to refuse to answer the relevant and material questions asked during a good-faith grand jury investigation, then it is a *fortiori* true that there is no privilege to refuse to appear before such a grand jury until the Government demonstrates some "compelling need" for a newsman's testimony. . . .

The decisions in *Branzburg v. Hayes* and *Branzburg v. Meigs* must be affirmed. . . . In both cases, if what petitioner wrote was true, he had direct information to provide the grand jury concerning the commission of serious crimes.

The only question presented at the present time in *In re Pappas* is whether petitioner Pappas must appear before the grand jury to testify pursuant to subpoena. . . . We affirm the decision of the Massachusetts Supreme Judicial Court and hold that petitioner must appear before the grand jury to answer the questions put to him, subject, of course, to the supervision of the presiding judge as to "the propriety, purposes, and scope of the grand jury inquiry and the pertinence of the probable testimony." 358 Mass., at 614.

JUSTICE POWELL, concurring.

. . . As indicated in the concluding portion of the opinion, the Court states that no harassment of newsmen will be tolerated. If a newsman believes that the grand jury investigation is not being conducted in good faith he is not without remedy. Indeed, if the newsman is called upon to give information bearing only a remote and tenuous relationship to the subject of the investigation, or if he has some other reason to believe that his testimony implicates confidential source relationships without a legitimate need for law enforcement, he will have access to the court on a motion to quash and an appropriate protective order may be entered. The asserted claim to privilege should be judged on its facts by the striking of a proper balance between freedom of the press and the obligation of all citizens to give relevant testimony with respect to criminal conduct. The balancing of these vital constitutional and societal interests on a case-by-case basis accords with the tried and traditional way of adjudicating such questions. . . .

JUSTICE DOUGLAS, dissenting in *United States v. Caldwell.*

It is my view that there is no "compelling need" that can be shown which qualifies the reporter's immunity from appearing or testifying before a grand jury, unless the reporter himself is implicated in a crime. His immunity in my view is therefore quite complete, for, absent his involvement in a crime, the First Amendment protects him against an appearance before a grand jury and if he is involved in a crime, the Fifth Amendment stands as a barrier. Since in my view there is no area of inquiry not protected by a privilege, the reporter need not appear for the futile purpose of invoking one to each question. And, since in my view a newsman has an absolute right not to appear before a grand jury, it follows for me that a journalist who voluntarily appears before that body may invoke his First Amendment privilege to specific questions. . . .

. . . Fear of exposure will cause dissidents to communicate less openly to trusted reporters. . . .

JUSTICE STEWART, with whom JUSTICE BRENNAN and JUSTICE MARSHALL join, dissenting. . . .

A corollary of the right to publish must be the right to gather news. . . .

The right to gather news implies, in turn, a right to a confidential relationship between a reporter and his source. . . .

. . . Moreover, the vices of vagueness and overbreadth that legislative investigations may manifest are also exhibited by grand jury inquiries, since grand jury investigations are not limited in scope to specific criminal acts . . . and since standards of materiality and relevance are greatly relaxed. . . .

Accordingly, when a reporter is asked to appear before a grand jury and reveal confidences, I would hold that the government must (1) show that there is probable cause to believe that the newsman has information that is clearly relevant to a specific probable violation of law; (2) demonstrate that the information sought cannot be obtained by alternative means less destructive of First Amendment rights; and (3) demonstrate a compelling and overriding interest in the information.

This is not to say that a grand jury could not issue a subpoena until such a showing were made, and it is not to say that a newsman would be in any way privileged to ignore any subpoena that was issued. Obviously, before the government's burden to make such a showing were triggered, the reporter would have to move to quash the subpoena, asserting the basis on which he considered the particular relationship a confidential one.

. . . The sad paradox of the Court's position is that when a grand jury may exercise an unbridled subpoena power, and sources involved in sensitive matters become fearful of disclosing information, the newsman will not only cease to be a useful grand jury witness; he will cease to investigate and publish information about issues of public import. . . .

NOTES

(1) *Recognizing a Reporter's Privilege.* Many federal and state courts have recognized an absolute or qualified reporter's privilege in civil or criminal proceedings other than grand jury investigations. *See* Paul Marcus, *The Reporter's Privilege: An Analysis of the Common Law,* Branzburg v. Hayes, *and Recent Statutory Developments,* 25 ARIZ. L. REV. 815 (1983); Note, Disclosure of Confidential Sources in International Reporting, 61 S. CAL. L. REV. 1631 (1988); Note, *In re Jury Matter, Gronowicz: Qualified Newsperson's Privilege Does Not Extend to Authors,* 61 NOTRE DAME L. REV. 245, 251, n.41 (1986).

For a discussion of the necessity of protecting the newsgathering process in the wake of *Branzburg v. Hayes,* see Timothy Dyk, *Newsgathering, Press Access, and the First Amendment,* 44 STAN. L. REV. 927, 930 (1992): "[T]he press should enjoy a presumptive right of access, greater than that of the general public, in three specific situations: first, when the government discriminates in granting access, either between the press and the public or among press organizations; second, when the government denies press access in situations where it has been traditionally allowed (a standard similar in concept to the test for public and press access in *Richmond Newspapers*); and third, when the government grants access selectively and arbitrarily (for example, when the government admits the press one day and excludes it the next). This presumption of press access is essential for preserving the press' function as a check on government abuses."

(2) *Promissory Estoppel.* In *Cohen v. Cowles Media Co.,* 501 U.S. 663 (1991), the Court stated that the First Amendment did not bar a newspaper source from recovering, under state promissory estoppel law, from a newspaper for breaching a promise of confidentiality. Cohen, an advisor in a gubernatorial campaign, gave court records concerning another party's candidate to newspaper reporters. The reporters promised to keep confidential his identity. Nevertheless, Cohen's name was reported, and he was subsequently fired from his job.

Writing for the (5-4) majority, Justice White relied on *New York Times Co. v. Sullivan* to find that judicial enforcement of damages recovered under state promissory estoppel law constitutes state action. Justice White relied on cases holding that "generally applicable laws do not offend the First Amendment simply because their enforcement against the press has incidental effects on its ability to gather and report the news." For example, "the truthful information sought to be published must have been lawfully acquired. The press may not with impunity break and enter an office or dwelling to gather news." Moreover, the First Amendment does not shield a reporter from revealing confidential sources in a grand jury investigation; the press may only publish in accordance with the copyright laws, the National Labor Relations Act, the

Fair Labor Standards Act and antitrust laws; and the press "must pay nondiscriminatory taxes."

The parties themselves are defining "the scope of their legal obligation and any restrictions which may be placed on the publication of truthful information." The promissory estoppel cause of action does not "target or single out the press," but applies to all state citizens. Therefore, its enforcement against the press is "not subject to stricter scrutiny than would be applied to enforcement against other persons or organizations."

Justice Blackmun wrote a dissenting opinion, joined by Justices Marshall and Souter. Justice Blackmun argued that the Court should have applied the compelling state interest test. Justice Souter filed a separate dissenting opinion, in which Justices Marshall, Blackmun and O'Connor joined. He asserted that the proper approach would be a balancing of interests, giving great weight to the public's interest in the publication of information.

(3) *Book Proceeds.* In *Simon & Schuster, Inc. v. New York State Crime Victims Board*, 502 U.S. 105 (1992), the Court (6-2-0) struck down a New York statute that applied to persons convicted of a crime or who acknowledged in writing the commission of a crime. It required that the income of such persons derived from works describing the crime be deposited in an escrow account for five years. Funds from the account were made available to the victims of the crime and to the criminal's other creditors.

Analogizing to the discriminatory tax struck down in *Arkansas Writers' Project v. Ragland*, 481 U.S. 221 (1987), Justice O'Connor found that the law "establishes a financial disincentive to create or publish works with a particular content." Such content-based discrimination must be "necessary to serve a compelling state interest and is narrowly drawn to achieve that end." Justice O'Connor accepted as compelling the state's proffered interests in "compensating victims from the fruits of the crime." Nevertheless, the law was overinclusive in covering any work in which the author mentioned his or her crime. The statute would have applied to *The Autobiography of Malcolm X* and *The Confessions of St. Augustine*, had they been written today. The statute applied to any work in which an author mentioned a crime, even if he never had been convicted or accused of it or had committed it years earlier.

Justice O'Connor narrowed the decision to the New York statute at issue, not addressing the validity of other state and federal statutes of this kind. For a list of such statutes, Note, *Simon and Shuster, Inc. v. Fischetti: Can New York's Son of Sam Law Survive First Amendment Challenge?*, 66 NOTRE DAME L. REV. 1075, 1075 n. 6 (1991). Justice Blackmun and Justice Kennedy each filed separate concurring opinions; Justice Thomas took no part in the decision.

(4) *Search Warrants.* In *Zurcher v. The Stanford Daily*, 436 U.S. 547 (1978), the Court held that the search of a newspaper office conducted pursuant to a properly issued warrant did not violate the First, Fourth, or Fourteenth Amendments, even if the newspaper was not implicated in any crime. This case arose when a staff member of Stanford University's student newspaper photographed a student assault on police. The police, having probable cause to believe that the newspaper offices contained photographs that could identify the demonstrators, obtained a warrant to search the office. A search of the *Daily's* darkrooms, filing cabinets, computer disks, and waste baskets gave the police the opportunity to read notes and correspondence, although the police did not open locked doors or rooms.

Writing for the majority, Justice White held that the standards for issuing warrants are the same irrespective of whether the place to be searched is possessed by a person suspected of criminal activity or is possessed by an innocent third party. He reasoned that, if properly satisfied, the requirements for a search warrant of reasonableness, specificity and probable cause provided sufficient constitutional protection. When the third party is a newspaper and First Amendment issues are at stake, the requirements of the Fourth Amendment must be applied with "scrupulous exactitude." The majority did not believe that its decision would give the authorities license to "rummage at large in newspaper files or to intrude into or to deter normal editorial and publication decisions." Where presumptively protected materials are sought to be seized, the warrant requirement should be administered to leave as little as possible to the discretion of the officer in the field.

In any event, Justice White predicted that prosecutors would generally opt for the easier course of obtaining a subpoena. They would likely only pursue a search warrant "when necessary to secure or to avoid the destruction of evidence."

Justice Stewart dissented, joined by Justice Marshall. Justice Stevens dissented separately, and Justice Brennan did not participate.

(5) *Subpoenas.* In response to the criticism of the *Zurcher* case, the Carter Administration proposed legislation that would require subpoenas, in both federal and state proceedings, in most instances when evidence is sought from a person preparing material for publication, if the person is not a suspect. Some criticized the proposal as not going far enough in that the files of lawyers, doctors, accountants and other non-suspects, who may be in possession of evidence, could be searched under the *Zurcher* decision. In October 1980, P.L. 96-440, 94 Stat. 1879, entitled the Privacy Protection Act of 1980, was enacted into law to protect the work product of persons "reasonably believed to have a purpose to disseminate to the public a form of public communication." The law severely limited the use of search warrants to obtain material in the possession of the media, requiring law enforcement officials to rely primarily on subpoenas.

(6) *Media Ride Along.* In *Wilson v. Layne*, 526 U.S. 603 (1999), the Court found that a " 'media ride along' " violated the Fourth Amendment. A photographer and a reporter from the *Washington Post* had entered the home of a fugitive's parents with police officers who attempted to execute an arrest warrant and mistakenly restrained the fugitive's father. Chief Justice Rehnquist held that, while the warrant need not specify every action taken by police during the arrest of a suspect, the presence of the media inside the home "was not related to the objectives of the authorized intrusion." The Fourth Amendment does not permit "police to bring members of the media or other third parties into a home during the execution of a warrant when the presence of the third parties in the home was not in aid of the execution of the warrant." Because this Fourth Amendment violation was not established at the time of the incident and the officers had no way to know that inviting the media along would be illegal, the officers enjoyed qualified immunity from a suit for damages. *Accord Hanlon v. Berger*, 526 U.S. 808 (1999) (companion case).

(7) For an interesting perspective on liability for the process of investigative journalism, see Erwin Chemerinsky, *Protect the Press: A First Amendment Standard for Safeguarding Aggressive Newsgathering*, 33 U. RICH. L. REV. 1143, 1144 (2000) ("The consensus, though, appears to be that the media is liable when it commits torts such as intrusion and invasion of privacy, even when its actions are necessary to expose serious threats to the public's health and safety. . . . In this article, I challenge that consensus and argue for greater First Amendment protection for newsgathering by the media."); C. Thomas Dienes, *Protecting Investigative Journalism*, 67 GEO. WASH. L. REV. 1139, 1140 (1999) ("[T]he First Amendment constraints, which protect press publication against claims for libel, disclosure of private facts, and intentional infliction of emotional distress, will be circumvented by use of . . . newsgathering tort and contract actions. Plaintiffs who cannot successfully sue the press for the content of what

they say instead sue based on the methods used to gather the information. Plaintiffs then seek to recover damages resulting from the publication as consequential damages."); Rodney A. Smolla, *Qualified Intimacy, Celebrity, and the Case for a Newsgathering Privilege*, 33 U. RICH. L. REV. 1233, 1251 (2000) ("At least in cases in which the plaintiff has been caught in serious wrongdoing and no palpable interests in protecting confidential communications, intimacy, or proprietary information are advanced, the journalist who has pursued a story of high public interest on the basis of genuine probable cause deserves a privilege against liability."); Diane Leenheer Zimmerman, *I Spy: The Newsgatherer Under Cover*, 33 U. RICH. L. REV. 1185, 1187 (2000) ("[T]he reporting methods of the press have been attacked as trespass, fraud, violation of eavesdropping statutes, physical harassment, theft of information, RICO claims, theft of images, violation of wiretapping laws, violations of federal civil rights laws, violation of copyright, and the theft of trade secrets. . .").

§ 13.05   REGULATION AND TAXATION

RED LION BROADCASTING CO. v. F.C.C.
395 U.S. 367, 89 S. Ct. 1947, 23 L. Ed. 2d 371 (1969)

JUSTICE WHITE delivered the opinion of the Court.

The Federal Communications Commission has for many years imposed on radio and television broadcasters the requirement that discussion of public issues be presented on broadcast stations, and that each side of those issues must be given fair coverage. This is known as the fairness doctrine, which originated very early in the history of broadcasting and has maintained its present outlines for some time. It is an obligation whose content has been defined in a long series of FCC rulings in particular cases, and which is distinct from the statutory requirement of § 315 of the Communications Act that equal time be allotted all qualified candidates for public office. Two aspects of the fairness doctrine, relating to personal attacks in the context of controversial public issues and to political editorializing, were codified more precisely in the form of FCC regulations in 1967. . . .

The Red Lion Broadcasting Company is licensed to operate a Pennsylvania radio station, WGCB. On November 27, 1964, WGCB carried a 15-minute broadcast by the Reverend Billy James Hargis as part of a "Christian Crusade" series. A book by Fred J. Cook entitled "Goldwater — Extremist on the Right" was discussed by Hargis, who said that Cook had been fired by a newspaper for making false charges against city officials; that Cook had then worked for a Communist-affiliated publication; that he had defended Alger Hiss and attacked J. Edgar Hoover and the Central Intelligence Agency; and that he had now written a "book to smear and destroy Barry Goldwater." When Cook heard of the broadcast he concluded that he had been personally attacked and demanded free reply time, which the station refused. After an exchange of letters among Cook, Red Lion, and the FCC, the FCC declared that the Hargis broadcast constituted a personal attack on Cook; that Red Lion had failed to meet its obligation under the fairness doctrine . . . to send a tape, transcript, or summary of the broadcast to Cook and offer him reply time; and that the station must provide reply time whether or not Cook would pay for it. . . .

The broadcasters challenge the fairness doctrine and its specific manifestations in the personal attack and political editorial rules . . ., alleging that the rules abridge their freedom of speech and press. Their contention is that the First Amendment protects their desire to use their allotted frequencies continuously to broadcast whatever they choose, and to exclude whomever they choose from ever using that frequency. No man may be prevented from saying or publishing what he thinks, or from refusing in his speech or other utterances to give equal weight to the views of his opponents. This right, they say, applies equally to broadcasters.

Although broadcasting is clearly a medium affected by a First Amendment interest, . . . differences in the characteristics of new media justify differences in the First Amendment standards applied to them. . . .

Just as the Government may limit the use of sound-amplifying equipment potentially so noisy that it drowns out civilized private speech, so may the Government limit the use of broadcast equipment. The right of free speech of a broadcaster, the user of a sound truck, or any other individual does not embrace a right to snuff out the free speech of others. . . .

When two people converse face to face, both should not speak at once if either is to be clearly understood. But the range of the human voice is so limited that there could be meaningful communications if half the people in the United States were talking and the other half listening. . . . But the reach of radio signals is incomparably greater than the range of the human voice and the problem of interference is a massive reality. The lack of know-how and equipment may keep many from the air, but only a tiny fraction of those with resources and intelligence can hope to communicate by radio at the same time if intelligible communication is to be had, even if the entire radio spectrum is utilized in the present state of commercially acceptable technology.

. . . It was this reality which at the very least necessitated first the division of the radio spectrum into portions reserved respectively for public broadcasting and for other important radio uses such as amateur operation, aircraft, police, defense, and navigation; and then the subdivision of each portion, and assignment of specific frequencies to individual users or groups of users. . . .

. . . It would be strange if the First Amendment, aimed at protecting and furthering communications, prevented the Government from making radio communication possible by requiring licenses to broadcast and by limiting the number of licenses so as not to overcrowd the spectrum.

. . . No one has a First Amendment right to a license or to monopolize a radio frequency; to deny a station license because "the public interest" requires it "is not a denial of free speech." *National Broadcasting Co. v. United States*, 319 U.S. 190, 227 [(1943)].

. . . There is nothing in the First Amendment which prevents the Government from requiring a licensee to share his frequency with others and to conduct himself as a proxy or fiduciary with obligations to present those views and voices which are representative of his community and which would otherwise, by necessity, be barred from the airwaves. . . . It is the right of the viewers and listeners, not the right of the broadcasters, which is paramount. . . . It is the purpose of the First Amendment to preserve an uninhibited marketplace of ideas in which truth will ultimately prevail, rather than to countenance monopolization of that market, whether it be by the Government itself or a private licensee. . . . It is the right of the public to receive suitable access to social, political, aesthetic, moral, and other ideas and experiences which is crucial here. That right may not constitutionally be abridged either by Congress or by the FCC.

Rather than confer frequency monopolies on a relatively small number of licensees, in a Nation of 200,000,000, the Government could surely have decreed that each frequency should be shared among all or some of those who wish to use it, each being assigned a portion of the broadcast day or the broadcast week. The ruling and regulations at issue here do not go quite so far. They assert that under specified circumstances, a licensee must offer to make available a reasonable amount of broadcast time to those who have a view different from that which has already been expressed on his station. The expression of a political endorsement, or of a personal attack while dealing with a controversial public issue, simply triggers this time sharing. As we have said, the First Amendment confers no right on licensees to prevent others from broadcasting on "their" frequencies and no right to an unconditional monopoly of a scarce resource which the Government has denied others the right to use. . . .

Nor can we say that it is inconsistent with the First Amendment goal of producing an informed public capable of conducting its own affairs to require a broadcaster to permit answers to personal attacks occurring in the course of discussing controversial issues, or to require that the political opponents of those endorsed by the station be given a chance to communicate with the public. Otherwise, station owners and a few networks would have unfettered power to make time available only to the highest bidders, to communicate only their own views on public issues, people and candidates, and to permit on the air only those with whom they agreed. There is no sanctuary in the First Amendment for unlimited private censorship operating in a medium not open to all. . . .

It is strenuously argued, however, that if political editorials or personal attacks will trigger an obligation in broadcasters to afford the opportunity for expression to speakers who need not pay for time and whose views are unpalatable to the licensees, then broadcasters will be irresistibly forced to self-censorship and their coverage of controversial public issues will be eliminated or at least rendered wholly ineffective. . . .

At this point, however, as the Federal Communications Commission has indicated, that possibility is at best speculative. The communications industry, and in particular the networks, have taken pains to present controversial issues in the past, and even now they do not assert that they intend to abandon their efforts in this regard. . . . [I]f experience with the administration of those doctrines indicates that they have the net effect of reducing rather than enhancing the volume and quality of coverage, there will be time enough to reconsider the constitutional implications. The fairness doctrine in the past has had no such overall effect.

. . . [I]f present licensees should suddenly prove timorous, the Commission is not powerless to insist that they give adequate and fair attention to public issues. It does not violate the First Amendment to treat licensees given the privilege of using scarce radio frequencies as proxies for the entire community, obligated to give suitable time and attention to matters of great public concern. To condition the granting or renewal of licenses on a willingness to present representative community views on controversial issues is consistent with the ends and purposes of those constitutional provisions forbidding the abridgment of freedom of speech and freedom of the press. . . .

We need not and do not now ratify every past and future decision by the FCC with regard to programming. There is no question here of the Commission's refusal to permit the broadcaster to carry a particular program or to publish his own views; of a discriminatory refusal to require the licensee to broadcast certain views which have been denied access to the airwaves; of government censorship of a particular program contrary to § 326; or of the official government view dominating public broadcasting. Such questions would raise more serious First Amendment issues. But we do hold that the Congress and the Commission do not violate the First Amendment when they require a radio or television station to give reply time to answer personal attacks and political editorials.

It is argued that even if at one time the lack of available frequencies for all who wished to use them justified the Government's choice of those who would best serve the public interest by acting as proxy for those who would present differing views, or by giving the latter access directly to broadcast facilities, this condition no longer prevails so that continuing control is not justified. To this there are several answers.

Scarcity is not entirely a thing of the past. Advances in technology, such as microwave transmission, have led to more efficient utilization of the frequency spectrum, but uses for that spectrum have also grown apace. . . . Among the various uses for radio frequency space, including marine, aviation, amateur, military, and common carrier users, there are easily enough claimants to permit use of the whole with an even smaller allocation to broadcast radio and television uses than now exists.

Comparative hearings between competing applicants for broadcast spectrum space are by no means a thing of the past. The radio spectrum has become so congested that at times it has been necessary to suspend new applications. The very high frequency television spectrum is, in the country's major markets, almost entirely occupied, although space reserved for ultra high frequency television transmission, which is a relatively recent development as a commercially viable alternative, has not yet been completely filled. . . .

Even where there are gaps in spectrum utilization, the fact remains that existing broadcasters have often attained their present position because of their initial government selection in competition with others before new technological advances opened new opportunities for further uses. Long experience in broadcasting, confirmed habits of listeners and viewers, network affiliation, and other advantages in program procurement give existing broadcasters a substantial advantage over new entrants, even where new entry is technologically possible. These advantages are the fruit of a preferred position conferred by the Government. Some present possibility for new entry by competing stations is not enough, in itself, to render unconstitutional the Government's effort to assure that a broadcaster's programming ranges widely enough to serve the public interest.

In view of the scarcity of broadcast frequencies, the Government's role in allocating those frequencies, and the legitimate claims of those unable without governmental assistance to gain access to those frequencies for expression of their views, we hold the regulations and ruling at issue here are both authorized by statute and constitutional. . . . [17] Not having heard oral argument in these cases, Justice Douglas took no part in the Court's decision.

NOTES

(1) *Abolition of Fairness Doctrine.* On August 4, 1987, the Federal Communications Commission abolished the Fairness Doctrine. Fairness Alternatives Report, 2 FCC RECORD 5272 (1987). Since this time, there have been Congressional efforts and litigation to revise the doctrine. The First Amendment analysis propounded in *Red Lion*, of course, is not altered by the FCC's decision.

(2) *Political Editorials. Federal Communications Commission v. League of Women Voters of California*, 468 U.S. 364 (1984), held that the federal government could not

---

[17] [Court's footnote 28] We need not deal with the argument that even if there is no longer a technological scarcity of frequencies limiting the number of broadcasters, there nevertheless is an economic scarcity in the sense that the Commission could or does limit entry to the broadcasting market on economic grounds and license no more stations than the market will support. Hence, it is said, the fairness doctrine or its equivalent is essential to satisfy the claims of those excluded and of the public generally. A related argument, which we also put aside, is that quite apart from the scarcity of frequencies, technological or economic, Congress does not abridge freedom of speech or press by legislation directly or indirectly multiplying the voices and views presented to the public through time sharing, fairness doctrines, or other devices which limit or dissipate the power of those who sit astride the channels of communication with the general public. . . .

forbid public radio and television stations from editorializing as a condition of receiving government subsidies. This case contains important comments about *Red Lion*. The case required that regulations imposed on the broadcast media be narrowly tailored to further a substantial governmental interest. For additional discussion of this case, see § 13.07[1].

(3) For further discussion of *Red Lion*, see R. Randall Rainey, *The Public's Interest in Public Affairs Discourse, Democratic Governance, and Fairness in Broadcasting: A Critical Review of the Public Interest Duties of the Electronic Media*, 82 Geo. L.J. 269, 369 (1993) ("Although their efforts were sustained by the Supreme Court in *Red Lion* and in almost every subsequent case reviewing the public interest duties of the electronic media, recent federal regulatory policy is conceptually flawed because it uncritically accepts the commercial marketplace as an appropriate structure for mediating public affairs discourse and overstates the First Amendment liberty of FCC licensees."); Johnathan Weinberg, *Broadcasting and Speech*, 81 Cal. L. Rev. 1101, 1109-10 (1993) ("[O]ur system of broadcast regulation can be seen as reflecting a competing worldview. That worldview emphasizes the community rather than the individual. It stresses that government plays a pervasive role in the so-called 'private' sphere. Because, under this approach, values are objective or communally determined, government paternalism is often appropriate.").

COLUMBIA BROADCASTING SYSTEM v. DEMOCRATIC NATIONAL COMMITTEE, 412 U.S. 94 (1973). In *CBS v. DNC*, the Court upheld an order of the FCC permitting a licensee to exclude all editorial advertisements. A business executives group opposed to American involvement in Vietnam sought to purchase a series of one-minute spot announcements, and the Democratic National Committee wanted to buy time "to present the views of the Democratic Party and to solicit funds." Chief Justice Burger wrote an opinion, joined by Justices Stewart and Rehnquist, which was also the opinion of the Court because it was joined, in its major parts, by Justices Stewart, Powell, Blackmun, and White, who also wrote concurring opinions. The Chief Justice held that the First Amendment does not mandate a private right of access to the broadcast media.

Chief Justice Burger's opinion argued that providing access for editorial advertising would weight the system "in favor of the financially affluent, or those with access to wealth." Moreover, in order to satisfy the Fairness Doctrine, a broadcaster might have to "make regular programming time available to those holding a view different from that expressed in an editorial advertisement," thus causing a "further erosion of the journalistic discretion of broadcasters in the coverage of public issues." A suspension of the Fairness Doctrine "to alleviate these problems" would threaten the balanced discussion of public issues.

A right of access to paid editorial advertising would tend to draw the FCC into a "continuing case-by-case determination of who should be heard and when." This might lead to relaxation of "accepted constitutional principles against control of speech content."

Justice Stewart concurred. Referring to *Red Lion*, Justice Stewart wrote, "Rightly or wrongly, we there decided that broadcasters' First Amendment rights were 'abridgeable.' But surely this does not mean that those rights are nonexistent."

Justice Douglas concurred saying he did not participate in *Red Lion* and "would not support it. The Fairness Doctrine has no place in our First Amendment regime. . . . [I]t is anathema to the First Amendment to allow Government any role or censorship over newspapers, magazines, books, art, music, TV, radio or any aspect of the press."

Justices White, Powell, and Blackmun agreed in brief concurrences that the First Amendment does not require right of access for editorial advertising.

Justice Brennan dissented, joined by Justice Marshall, arguing that the First Amendment protects not only the broadcasters but also the public, which has "strong First Amendment interests in the reception of a full spectrum of views . . . on controversial issues of public importance."

Describing the broadcast frequencies as "forums" that are even more dedicated to the expression of ideas than such traditional public forums as streets and parks, Justice Brennan concluded that citizens could not be denied access to the broadcast "forum," just as they could not be totally excluded from other places of public expression. A limited right of access would still leave the FCC with wide latitude "to develop reasonable regulations to govern the availability of editorial advertising."

NOTES

(1) *Candidate Air Time.* In *CBS, Inc. v. Federal Communications Commission*, 453 U.S. 367 (1981), the Court held that the Communications Act gave legally qualified candidates the right to purchase air time on a reasonable basis. Chief Justice Burger's majority (6-3) opinion, based primarily on statutory grounds, concluded that such a "*limited* right to 'reasonable' access . . . properly balances the First Amendment rights of federal candidates, the public, and broadcasters." The Court was not approving a general right of access to the media.

(2) *Cable Access.* In *F.C.C. v. Midwest Video Corp.*, 440 U.S. 689 (1979), the Court held that the Commission lacked statutory authority to require cable systems to provide public-access channels. In *Turner Broadcasting, Inc. v. FCC*, 512 U.S. 622 (1994), § 13.07[2], the Court, in upholding the constitutionality of a 1992 statute's must-carry provisions, noted some important distinctions between the broadcast media and cable television.

(3) *Cable Television.* In *Denver Area Educ. Tele-Communications Consortium, Inc. v. Federal Communications Commission*, 518 U.S. 727 (1996), the Court struck down § 10(b) of the Television Consumer Protections and Competition Act of 1992 ("Act") which required cable companies to restrict the availability, on leased channels, of patently offensive material, as well as § 10(c) which empowered cable companies to regulate public access channels for similar programming.

Comparing the case to *F.C.C. v. Pacifica Foundation*, 438 U.S. 726 (1978), the plurality upheld § 10(a) of the Act, which gave cable companies the discretion to change schedules in order to make the material available at times when children would not generally have access to it. Justice Breyer noted that allowing the cable companies to change telecast times likely restricted speech less than the ban at issue in *Pacifica*.

Section 10(b) required cable companies to block leased channels showing sexual material that was deemed patently offensive. The section failed a " 'least restrictive alternative' " test because it was not designed narrowly enough to protect children while making it more difficult for adult viewers to access the materials.

In Part IV of his opinion, Justice Breyer, joined by Justices Stevens and Souter, invalidated § 10(c) of the Act, even though it allowed the cable companies to regulate public access channels in the same manner they could regulate leased channels under § 10(a). Unlike leased channels, cable companies have not historically exercised editorial control over public access channels. Moreover, public access channels, which receive some public funds, are supervised by local boards that could minimize or eliminate programming that could be deemed offensive to children. Various other Justices filed opinions. For further discussions of the case, see § 13.07[2].

(4) *Internet.* In *Reno v. American Civil Liberties Union*, 521 U.S. 844 (1997), the Court struck down the government's attempt to restrict speech on the Internet through

the Communications Decency Act of 1996 ("CDA"). The Court contrasted the CDA with its decision in *Pacifica.*

In *Pacifica*, the question was not whether the monologue ("Seven Dirty Words" by George Carlin) could be played, but when. Unlike the FCC, there is no expert regulatory agency for the Internet, and the ban imposed by the CDA is not limited to any particular time. While the order in *Pacifica* was not punitive, the CDA provides for rather harsh criminal penalties. Finally, the Court noted that radio had " 'received the most limited First Amendment protection,' " because there is no effective way to warn all listeners about what they might hear. The Internet has no history of limited First Amendment protection. Also, unlike the radio listener, there is little chance that an Internet user will unintentionally encounter indecent material, as usually there are a number of steps one must take in order to access such material.

MIAMI HERALD PUBLISHING COMPANY v. TORNILLO, 418 U.S. 241 (1974). In *Tornillo*, the Court struck down a state statute that required newspapers printing editorials critical of political candidates to publish the candidates' replies. The *Miami Herald* published two editorials criticizing a candidate for the Florida House of Representatives. After the newspaper refused to print the candidate's response to the editorial, he sued based on a Florida "right of reply" statute that afforded a candidate for nomination or election to public office who was criticized in a newspaper article, free newspaper space on demand and in a conspicuous place to respond to the article.

The Supreme Court unanimously struck down the statute as a violation of the First Amendment. Writing for the majority, Chief Justice Burger discussed the legitimate intent of the statute, which was "to ensure that a variety of views reach the public" in an economic environment in which "[c]hains of newspapers, national newspapers, national wire and news services, and one-newspaper towns, are the dominant features of a press that has become noncompetitive and enormously powerful and influential in its capacity to manipulate popular opinion and change the course of events." Moreover, in many cities the same interests that own a television and a radio station also own the newspaper. High entry costs render "almost impossible" the addition of other competitors. "The First Amendment interest of the public in being informed is said to be in peril because 'the marketplace of ideas' is today a monopoly controlled by the owners of the market."

Nevertheless, the Court held the statute unconstitutional. "However much validity may be found in these arguments, at each point the implementation of a remedy such as an enforceable right of access necessarily calls for some mechanism, either governmental or consensual." Compelling a newspaper "to publish that which 'reason' tells them should not be published" is unconstitutional. "The Florida statute exacts a penalty on the basis of the content of the newspaper. The first phase of the penalty resulting from the compelled printing of a reply is exacted in terms of the cost in printing and composing time and materials and in taking up space that could be devoted to other material the newspaper may have preferred to print." While a newspaper does not have the "finite technological limitations of time that confront a broadcaster," it does face economic constraints.

Even if a newspaper did not incur additional costs or was not required to forego printing other material, the statute also intruded "into the function of editors. A newspaper is more than a passive receptacle or conduit for news, comment, and advertising. The choice of material to go into a newspaper and the decisions made as to limitations on the size and content of the paper, and treatment of public issues and public officials — whether fair or unfair — constitute the exercise of editorial control and judgment."

In a concurring opinion, Justice Brennan emphasized that the decision "implies no view upon the constitutionality of 'retraction' statutes affording plaintiffs able to prove defamatory falsehoods a statutory action to require publication of a retraction."

Justice White, in another concurring opinion, affirmed the Court's holding and asserted that the individual's redress from published criticisms should be in actions for libel. He lamented, however, the "emaciated" form in which *Gertz v. Welch*, 418 U.S. 323 (1974), § 13.08[1], which was decided that same day, left libel actions.

NOTES

(1) For an interesting perspective on media regulation, see RICHARD W. MCCHESNEY, RICH MEDIA, POOR DEMOCRACY (1999).

(2) For additional discussion of a First Amendment right to access to the media, see ITHIEL DE LA SOLA POOL, TECHNOLOGIES OF FREEDOM (1983); Jerome A. Barron, *Structural Regulation of the Media and the Diversity Rationale*, 52 FED. COMM. L.J. 555, 560 (2000) ("For a democratic society, the justice of rules designed to make sure that a few people or a few entities do not run away with the opinion process should not be suspect. If diversification of ownership policies have no more justification than limiting such domination, then the case for their validity is established."); Jerome Barron, *Access to the Press — A New First Amendment Right*, 80 HARV. L. REV. 1641 (1967); Lee Bollinger, *Freedom of the Press and Public Access: Toward a Theory of Partial Regulation of the Mass Media*, 75 MICH. L. REV. 1 (1976); Donald Lively, *The Information Superhighway: A First Amendment Roadmap*, 35 B.C. L. REV. 1067, 1079 (1994) ("Print media functions in a constitutional order that prioritizes editorial autonomy. The prioritized First Amendment status of newspapers and other nonelectronic textual media seems to reflect a heavy factoring of historical tradition. As digitalized satellite and fiber-optic systems allow the transmission of electronic newspapers, magazines and books, and publishers enter into strategic alliances for electronic delivery of their product, any logic in the Court's tradition-based rationale further diminishes.").

§ 13.06   TAXATION

MINNEAPOLIS STAR AND TRIBUNE v. MINNESOTA COMMISSIONER OF REVENUE, 460 U.S. 575 (1983). In *Minneapolis Star*, the Court held that a state's special tax on newspapers violated the First Amendment. Minnesota enacted a general sales tax on all retail sales. On all property to which the sales tax did not apply, the legislature imposed a use tax for the " 'privilege of using, storing or consuming in Minnesota tangible personal property.' " When originally enacted in 1967, Minnesota exempted periodicals from both the sales and use taxes. In 1971, the legislature modified the scheme. It continued the sales tax exemption on periodicals, but enacted a use tax on the cost of paper and ink products used in producing periodicals. The first $100,000 spent for paper and ink was exempt from this tax. Within the small group that paid the tax during the first two years, the *"Star Tribune"* contributed almost two-thirds of the total.

In *Grosjean v. American Press Co.*, 297 U.S. 233 (1936), the Court had invalidated a Louisiana state license tax that was imposed in addition to the general tax. The tax took two percent of the gross receipts from the sale of advertising from newspapers with weekly circulations of more than 20,000. The tax was "bad because, in the light of its history and of its present setting, it is seen to be a deliberate and calculated device in the guise of a tax to limit the circulation of information."

The *Minneapolis Star* Court interpreted *Grosjean* as turning on legislative "intent to penalize a selected group of news." Since there was no legislative history and no indication apart from the structure of the tax itself of any impermissible or censorial motive by the Minnesota legislature, *Grosjean* was not controlling.

Nevertheless, the Court held the statute unconstitutional. "When the State singles out the press, . . . the political constraints that prevent a legislature from passing crippling taxes of general applicability are weakened, and the threat of burdensome taxes becomes acute. That threat can operate as effectively as a censor to check critical comment by the press. Differential treatment of the press could not be tolerated unless the state asserted a "counterbalancing interest of compelling importance" that could not be accomplished without the differential taxation.

The state's revenue goal did not justify the different tax treatment of the press. Alternative means such as taxing businesses generally would produce the same results without raising First Amendment problems. The Court rejected the State's rationale that taxing the inexpensive papers under a general sales tax would be impractical. The Court cautioned against different methods of taxation for the press, regardless of whether they were lighter or more burdensome than general taxation. First, future changes in the law may render the tax more burdensome. Second, the possibility that the Court may not correctly perceive the true nature of the burden poses "too great a threat to concerns at the heart of the First Amendment."

The $100,000 tax exemption presented a greater threat because it focused on a small part of the press. Only a few papers had to pay any significant amount. Because it carries great possibilities for abuse, "[a] tax that singles out the press, or that targets individual publications within the press, places a heavy burden on the State to justify its action," which Minnesota failed to do.

Justice White concurred in part and dissented in part. He agreed with the Court's decision because the exemption limited the burden to a few newspapers. Unlike the majority, however, he would allow the state to impose alternative methods of taxation that did not impose a greater burden on the press.

Justice Rehnquist dissented. While the First Amendment forbade schemes that singled out newspapers for heavier taxation, it did not prevent legislatures from imposing less burdensome taxes. Had the newspapers been forced to pay the general tax, the *"Star Tribune"* would have been taxed at three times the rate of the use tax. Justice Rehnquist also rejected the majority's opinion that the tax exemption for the first $100,000 violated the First Amendment. The exemption was made without any improper legislative motive and only benefited the exempted newspapers. Imposing the general four-percent state tax on such an inexpensive item as a newspaper would be impractical; the tax on ink and paper presented a reasonable alternative.

NOTES

(1) *Selective Exemptions for Certain Publications*. Relying on *Minneapolis Star & Tribune Company v. Minnesota Commissioner of Revenue*, the Court (7-2) in *Arkansas Writers Project v. Ragland*, 481 U.S. 221 (1987), overturned a state sales tax that taxed "general interest" magazines but exempted newspapers and religious, professional, trade, and sports journals. It appeared that only one or two magazines published within Arkansas were subject to the tax. "Because the Arkansas tax scheme treats some magazines less favorably than others, it suffers from the several types of discrimination identified in *Minnesota Star*." Moreover, the tax suffered from the additional defect of discrimination based on content of the publication. Scrutiny of a magazine's content as a basis for imposition of the tax is "entirely incompatible with the First Amendment's guarantee of freedom of the press." None of the State's asserted interests — raising revenues, helping "fledgling publications," or fostering

communication — satisfies the "heavy burden" necessary to justify the selective exemption from the tax.

Justice Scalia and Chief Justice Rehnquist dissented, arguing that the classification was rationally related to the objective of encouraging small publishers "with limited audiences and advertising revenues." The differential tax was just another form of selective subsidy.

(2) *Discrimination Aamong Media.* In *Leathers v. Medlock*, 499 U.S. 439 (1991), the Court upheld Arkansas' extension of its sales tax to cable television and satellite services, while exempting certain print media. The Arkansas Gross Receipt Act (AGRA) imposed a sales tax on all personal property and specified services; however, the AGRA exempted receipts from newspaper and magazine subscription sales and over-the-counter newspaper sales.

Writing for the majority, Justice O'Connor stated that *Grosjean v. American Press Co.*, 297 U.S. 233 (1936), struck down a state tax that fell only on 13 newspapers. *Arkansas Writers' Project* struck down a state tax exempting receipts from "religious, professional, trade and sports magazines. "A tax will always need a compelling justification if it "single[s] out the press" or "targets a small group of speakers" or "discriminates on the basis of the content of taxpayer speech." However, "there is no indication in this case that Arkansas has targeted cable television in a purposeful attempt to interfere with its First Amendment activities." The statute does not refer "to the content of mass media communications. Moreover, the record establishes that cable television offers subscribers a variety of programming that presents a mixture of news, information, and entertainment. It contains no evidence, nor is it contended, that this material differs systematically in its message from that communicated by satellite broadcast programming, newspapers, or magazines." In contrast to *Grosjean*, *Minneapolis Star* and *Arkansas Writers'*, the Arkansas legislature has chosen simply to exclude or exempt certain media from a generally applicable tax.

Justice Marshall, joined by Justice Blackmun, dissented. He said that the differential tax "distorts consumer preferences for particular information formats and thereby impaired 'the widest possible dissemination of information from diverse and antagonistic sources.'"

§ 13.07   ELECTRONIC MEDIA

[1]   Broadcast Media

FEDERAL COMMUNICATIONS COMMISSION v. LEAGUE OF WOMEN VOTERS OF CALIFORNIA, 468 U.S. 364 (1984). In *League of Women Voters*, the Court invalidated § 399 of the Public Broadcasting Act, which forbade any public broadcasting stations that received a government grant to engage in editorializing. Justice Brennan asserted that any such ban in the print media would have to undergo "the most exacting scrutiny." Nevertheless, due to their unique nature as limited resources, radio and television must operate under restraints not placed upon the other media. "The fundamental principles that guide our evaluation of the broadcast media are now well established." First, in regulating this "scarce and valuable national resource," Congress can ensure "that only those who satisfy the public interest, convenience, and necessity are granted a license to use radio and television broadcast frequencies." Second, Congress could seek a balanced presentation of information on matters "of public importance that otherwise might not be addressed if control of the medium were left entirely in the hands of those who own and operate broadcasting stations."

Although broadcasters must operate under considerable restrictions, "the First Amendment must inform and give shape to the manner in which Congress exercises its regulatory power in this area." As a result, restrictions on broadcasters would be upheld only if they were "narrowly tailored to further a substantial governmental interest, such as ensuring adequate and balanced coverage of public issues, e.g., *Red Lion*. Making that judgment requires a critical examination of the interests of the public and broadcasters in light of the particular circumstances of each case."

In assessing whether the restraints imposed by § 399 met the test, the Court first examined "two central features of the ban against editorializing." First, the law restrained the expression of editorial opinion, a form of speech considered sacred to the First Amendment. The editorial has traditionally played an important role in maintaining good government by informing the public and criticizing governmental incompetence. Second, the restriction was based solely on the content of the suppressed speech. It "singles out non-commercial broadcasters, and denies them the right to address their chosen audience on matters of public importance." In doing this, Congress attempted to "limit discussion of controversial topics and thus to shape the agenda of public debate."

Against this backdrop, the Court scrutinized the two purposes of the statute. First, the statute served to protect noncommercial educational broadcasting stations from being coerced, as a result of federal financing, into becoming vehicles for government propagandizing or the objects of governmental influence. Second, it kept these stations from becoming convenient targets for capture by private interest groups wishing to express their own partisan viewpoints.

With respect to preventing government propagandizing, the Court found that other aspects of the statutory scheme insulate local stations from government interference.[18]

"Furthermore, the manifest imprecision of the ban imposed by § 399 reveals that its proscription is not sufficiently tailored to the harms it seeks to prevent to justify its substantial interference with broadcasters' speech. Section 399 includes within its grip a potentially infinite variety of speech, most of which would not be related in any way to governmental affairs, political candidacies or elections. Indeed, the breadth of editorial commentary is as wide as human imagination permits."

The Court also rejected the government's contention that the statute was indispensable in preventing private interest groups from using public broadcasting for their own ends. "The patent over and underinclusiveness of § 399's ban 'undermines the likelihood of a genuine (governmental) interest' in preventing private groups from propagating their own views via public broadcasting. If it is true, as the government contends, that noncommercial stations remain free, despite § 399, to broadcast a wide variety of controversial views through their power to control program selection, to select which persons will be interviewed, and to determine how news reports will be presented, then it seems doubtful that § 399 can fairly be said to advance any genuinely substantial governmental interest in keeping controversial or partisan opinions from being aired by noncommercial stations." On the other hand, protections like the fairness doctrine, which apply to both commercial and noncommercial broadcasters, would "ensure that such editorializing would maintain a reasonably balanced and fair presentation of controversial issues." The way to secure balance in editorializing was *"more speech"* rather than suppression.

---

[18] Safeguards included a private, bipartisan management structure for the Corporation for Public Broadcasting. Congress funded the Corporation on a long-term rather than an annual basis. Moreover, the Corporation could neither own nor operate any of the hundreds of stations across the nation that comprise the public broadcasting system.

Finally, Justice Brennan distinguished *Regan v. Taxation with Representation of Washington*, 461 U.S. 540 (1983), in which it held "that Congress could, in the exercise of its spending power, reasonably refuse to subsidize the lobbying activities of tax-exempt charitable organizations by prohibiting such organizations from using tax-deductible contributions to support their lobbying efforts." Unlike the organization in *Regan*, a noncommercial educational station that received only a small fraction of its income from government grants was totally barred from editorializing and could not limit federal funds to noneditorial activities.

"In conclusion, we emphasize that our disposition of this case rests upon a narrow proposition. We do not hold that the Congress or the FCC are without power to regulate the content, timing, or character of speech by noncommercial educational broadcasting stations. Rather, we hold only that the specific interests sought to be advanced by § 399's ban on editorializing are not served in a sufficiently limited manner to justify the substantial abridgment of important journalistic freedoms which the First Amendment jealously protects."

Justice Rehnquist dissented, joined by Chief Justice Burger and Justice White. "Here, in my view, Congress has rationally concluded that the bulk of taxpayers whose monies provide the funds for grants by the CPB would prefer not to see the management of public stations engage in editorializing or the endorsing or opposing of political candidates. . . . Congress' decision to enact § 399 is a rational exercise of its spending powers and strictly neutral."

Justice Stevens also dissented. He cautioned against the use of government funds for editorializing. "By enacting the statutory provision that the Court invalidates today, a sophisticated group of legislators expressed a concern about the potential impact of government funds on pervasive and powerful organs of mass communication. One need not have heard the raucous voice of Adolph Hitler over Radio Berlin to appreciate the importance of that concern. . . . The quality of the interest in maintaining government neutrality in the free market of ideas — of avoiding subtle forms of censorship and propaganda — outweigh the impact on expression that results from this statute."

NOTE

In *Arkansas Educational Television Commission v. Forbes*, 523 U.S. 666 (1998), the Court held a public broadcaster's exclusion on of a candidate from a televised debate was viewpoint-neutral and reasonable. Forbes, an independent candidate, was excluded from the planned debate, according to Arkansas Educational Television Commission (AETC) staff, because he lacked substantial public interest and was not considered a serious candidate by the news media covering the election. The jury found the decision was not based on the broadcaster's opposition to his views.

Writing for the Court, Justice Kennedy noted that both public and private broadcasters normally must utilize editorial discretion to meet programming obligations. The broadcaster, as a state-owned facility, is subject to constitutional constraints that a private broadcaster is not. Nevertheless, the Court placed the debate into the nonpublic forum category of public fora. This category only required the decision to exclude Forbes to be reasonable and viewpoint-neutral, which it was.

Justice Stevens dissented, joined by Justices Souter and Ginsburg, arguing that AETC's regulations afforded it standardless discretion to exclude candidates from the debate. For discussion of this case, see § 14.04[1].

[2] Cable Television

TURNER BROADCASTING SYSTEM, INC. v. FEDERAL COMMUNICATIONS COMMISSION
512 U.S. 622, 114 S. Ct. 2445, 129 L. Ed. 497 (1994)

JUSTICE KENNEDY announced the judgment of the Court and delivered the opinion of the Court, except as to Part III-B.

Sections 4 and 5 of the Cable Television Consumer Protection and Competition Act of 1992 require cable television systems to devote a portion of their channels to the transmission of local broadcast television stations. This case presents the question whether these provisions abridge the freedom of speech or of the press, in violation of the First Amendment.

The United States District Court for the District of Columbia granted summary judgment for the United States . . . Because issues of material fact remain unresolved in the record as developed thus far, we vacate the District Court's judgment and remand the case for further proceedings.

I

A

. . . Cable systems . . . rely upon a physical, point-to-point connection between a transmission facility and the television sets of individual subscribers. Cable systems make this connection much like telephone companies, using cable or optical fibers strung aboveground or buried in ducts to reach the homes or businesses of subscribers. . . . As a result, the cable medium may depend for its very existence upon express permission from local governing authorities. . . . Cable technology affords two principal benefits over broadcast. First, it eliminates the signal interference sometimes encountered in over-the-air broadcasting and thus gives viewers undistorted reception of broadcast stations. Second, it is capable of transmitting many more channels than are available through broadcasting. . . .

B

At issue in this case is the constitutionality of the so-called must-carry provisions, contained in §§ 4 and 5 of the Act, which require cable operators to carry the signals of a specified number of local broadcast television stations. Section 4 requires carriage of "local commercial television stations." . . . Taken together §§ 4 and 5 subject all but the smallest cable systems nationwide to must-carry obligations, and confer must-carry privileges on all full power broadcasters operating within the same television market as a qualified cable system. . . .

C

Congress found that the physical characteristics of cable transmission, compounded by the increasing concentration of economic power in the cable industry, are endangering the ability of over-the-air broadcast television stations to compete for a viewing audience and thus for necessary operating revenues. Congress determined that regulation of the market for video programming was necessary to correct this competitive imbalance. In particular, Congress found that over 60 percent of the households with television sets subscribe to cable and for these households cable has replaced over-the-air broadcast television as the primary provider of video programming. . . .

According to Congress, this market position gives cable operators the power and the incentive to harm broadcast competitors. . . . By refusing carriage of broadcasters' signals, cable operators, as a practical matter, can reduce the number of households that have access to the broadcasters' programming, and thereby capture advertising dollars that would otherwise go to broadcast stations. § 2(a)(15).

Congress found, in addition, that increased vertical integration in the cable industry is making it even harder for broadcasters to secure carriage on cable systems, because cable operators have a financial incentive to favor their affiliated programmers. . . . Congress also determined that the cable industry is characterized by horizontal concentration, with many cable operators sharing common ownership. This has resulted in greater "barriers to entry for new programmers and a reduction in the number of media voices available to consumers." § 2(a)(4). . . .

II

. . . By requiring cable systems to set aside a portion of their channels for local broadcasters, the must-carry rules regulate cable speech in two respects: The rules reduce the number of channels over which cable operators exercise unfettered control, and they render it more difficult for cable programmers to compete for carriage on the limited channels remaining. Nevertheless, because not every interference with speech triggers the same degree of scrutiny under the First Amendment, we must decide at the outset the level of scrutiny applicable to the must-carry provisions.

A

We address first the Government's contention that regulation of cable television should be analyzed under the same First Amendment standard that applies to regulation of broadcast television. . . . [T]he rationale for applying a less rigorous standard of First Amendment scrutiny to broadcast regulation, whatever its validity in the cases elaborating it, does not apply in the context of cable regulation. The justification for our distinct approach to broadcast regulation rests upon the unique physical limitations of the broadcast medium. *See FCC v. League of Women Voters of Cal.*, 468 U.S. 364, 377 (1984). . . . The scarcity of broadcast frequencies . . . required the establishment of some regulatory mechanism to divide the electromagnetic spectrum and assign specific frequencies to particular broadcasters. . . . In addition, the inherent physical limitation on the number of speakers who may use the broadcast medium has been thought to require some adjustment in traditional First Amendment analysis to permit the Government to place limited content restraints, and impose certain affirmative obligations, on broadcast licensees. *Red Lion Broadcasting Co. v. FCC*, 395 U.S. 367, 390 (1969). . . .

Although courts and commentators have criticized the scarcity rationale since its inception, we have declined to question its continuing validity as support for our broadcast jurisprudence, *see FCC v. League of Women Voters*, and see no reason to do so here. The broadcast cases are inapposite in the present context because cable television does not suffer from the inherent limitations that characterize the broadcast medium. Indeed, given the rapid advances in fiber optics and digital compression technology, soon there may be no practical limitation on the number of speakers who may use the cable medium. Nor is there any danger of physical interference between two cable speakers attempting to share the same channel. In light of these fundamental technological differences between broadcast and cable transmission, application of the more relaxed standard of scrutiny adopted in *Red Lion* and the other broadcast cases is inapt when determining the First Amendment validity of cable regulation. . . .

This is not to say that the unique physical characteristics of cable transmission should be ignored when determining the constitutionality of regulations affecting cable speech. . . .

Although the Government acknowledges the substantial technological differences between broadcast and cable . . . it advances a second argument for application of the *Red Lion* framework to cable regulation. It asserts that the foundation of our broadcast jurisprudence is not the physical limitations of the electromagnetic spectrum, but rather the "market dysfunction" that characterizes the broadcast market. Because the cable market is beset by a similar dysfunction, the Government maintains, the *Red Lion* standard of review should also apply to cable. While we agree that the cable market suffers certain structural impediments, the Government's argument is flawed in two respects. First, as discussed above, the special physical characteristics of broadcast transmission, not the economic characteristics of the broadcast market, are what underlies our broadcast jurisprudence. . . . Second, the mere assertion of dysfunction or failure in a speech market, without more, is not sufficient to shield a speech regulation from the First Amendment standards applicable to nonbroadcast media. . . .

Because the must-carry provisions impose special obligations upon cable operators and special burdens upon cable programmers, some measure of heightened First Amendment scrutiny is demanded. *See Minneapolis Star & Tribune Co. v. Minnesota Comm'r of Revenue*, 460 U.S. 575 (1983).

B

. . . Our precedents thus apply the most exacting scrutiny to regulations that suppress, disadvantage, or impose differential burdens upon speech because of its content. . . . In contrast, regulations that are unrelated to the content of speech are subject to an intermediate level of scrutiny . . . because in most cases they pose a less substantial risk of excising certain ideas or viewpoints from the public dialogue. . . .

C

Insofar as they pertain to the carriage of full power broadcasters, the must-carry rules, on their face, impose burdens and confer benefits without reference to the content of speech. Although the provisions interfere with cable operators' editorial discretion by compelling them to offer carriage to a certain minimum number of broadcast stations, the extent of the interference does not depend upon the content of the cable operators' programming. . . .

. . . [E]ven a regulation neutral on its face may be content-based if its manifest purpose is to regulate speech because of the message it conveys. . . .

The design and operation of the challenged provisions confirm that the purposes underlying the enactment of the must-carry scheme are unrelated to the content of speech. The rules, as mentioned, confer must-carry rights on all full power broadcasters, irrespective of the content of their programming. They do not require or prohibit the carriage of particular ideas or points of view. They do not penalize cable operators or programmers because of the content of their programming. They do not compel cable operators to affirm points of view with which they disagree. They do not produce any net decrease in the amount of available speech. And they leave cable operators free to carry whatever programming they wish on all channels not subject to must-carry requirements.

Appellants and the dissent make much of the fact that, in the course of describing the purposes behind the Act, Congress referred to the value of broadcast programming. . . . That Congress acknowledged the local orientation of broadcast programming and the role that noncommercial stations have played in educating the public does not indicate that Congress regarded broadcast programming as more valuable than cable programming. Rather, it reflects nothing more than the recognition that the services provided by broadcast television have some intrinsic value and, thus, are worth preserving against the threats posed by cable. . . .

The scope and operation of the challenged provisions make clear, in our view, that Congress designed the must-carry provisions not to promote speech of a particular content, but to prevent cable operators from exploiting their economic power to the detriment of broadcasters, and thereby to ensure that all Americans, especially those unable to subscribe to cable, have access to free television programming — whatever its content. . . .

D

Appellants advance three additional arguments to support their view that the must-carry provisions warrant strict scrutiny. In brief, appellants contend that the provisions (1) compel speech by cable operators, (2) favor broadcast programmers over cable programmers, and (3) single out certain members of the press for disfavored treatment. None of these arguments suffices to require strict scrutiny in the present case.

1

. . . Relying principally on *Miami Herald Publishing Co. v. Tornillo*, 418 U.S. 241 (1974), appellants say this intrusion on the editorial control of cable operators amounts to forced speech which, if not per se invalid, can be justified only if narrowly tailored to a compelling government interest.

Tornillo affirmed an essential proposition: The First Amendment protects the editorial independence of the press. The right of reply statute at issue in *Tornillo* required any newspaper that assailed a political candidate's character to print, upon request by the candidate and without cost, the candidate's reply in equal space and prominence. . . . Because the right of access at issue in *Tornillo* was triggered only when a newspaper elected to print matter critical of political candidates, it "exacted a penalty on the basis of . . . content." 418 U.S., at 256. . . .

. . . Moreover, by affording mandatory access to speakers with which the newspaper disagreed, the law induced the newspaper to respond to the candidates' replies when it might have preferred to remain silent.

The same principles led us to invalidate a similar content-based access regulation in *Pacific Gas & Electric v. Public Utilities Comm'n of Cal.*, 455 U.S. 1 (1986). At issue was a rule requiring a privately-owned utility, on a quarterly basis, to include with its monthly bills an editorial newsletter published by a consumer group critical of the utility's ratemaking practices. . . . Like the statute in *Tornillo*, the regulation conferred benefits to speakers based on viewpoint, giving access only to a consumer group opposing the utility's practices. . . .

. . . [U]nlike the access rules struck down in those cases, the must-carry rules . . . are not activated by any particular message spoken by cable operators and thus exact no content-based penalty. . . . Likewise, they do not grant access to broadcasters on the ground that the content of broadcast programming will counterbalance the messages of cable operators. . . .

Finally, the asserted analogy to *Tornillo* ignores an important technological difference between newspapers and cable television. Although a daily newspaper and a cable operator both may enjoy monopoly status in a given locale, the cable operator exercises far greater control over access to the relevant medium. A daily newspaper, no matter how secure its local monopoly, does not possess the power to obstruct readers' access to other competing publications — whether they be weekly local newspapers, or daily newspapers published in other cities. . . .

The First Amendment's command that government not impede the freedom of speech does not disable the government from taking steps to ensure that private interests not restrict, through physical control of a critical pathway of communication, the free flow of information and ideas. . . .

2

Second, appellants urge us to apply strict scrutiny because the must-carry provisions favor one set of speakers (broadcast programmers) over another (cable programmers). Appellants maintain that as a consequence of this speaker preference, some cable programmers who would have secured carriage in the absence of must-carry may now be dropped. Relying on language in *Buckley v. Valeo*, 424 U.S. 1 (1976), appellants contend that such a regulation is presumed invalid under the First Amendment because the government may not "restrict the speech of some elements of our society in order to enhance the relative voice of others." *Id.* at 48–49. . . .

Our holding in *Buckley* does not support appellants' broad assertion that all speaker-partial laws are presumed invalid. Rather, it stands for the proposition that speaker-based laws demand strict scrutiny when they reflect the Government's preference for the substance of what the favored speakers have to say (or aversion to what the disfavored speakers have to say). . . . The question here is whether Congress preferred broadcasters over cable programmers based on the content of programming each group offers. The answer . . . is no. . . .

3

Finally, appellants maintain that strict scrutiny applies because the must-carry provisions single out certain members of the press — here, cable operators — for disfavored treatment. . . . In support, appellants point out that Congress has required cable operators to provide carriage to broadcast stations, but has not imposed like burdens on analogous video delivery systems, such as multichannel multipoint distribution (MMDS) systems and satellite master antenna television (SMATV) systems. . . . Regulations that discriminate among media, or among different speakers within a single medium, often present serious First Amendment concerns. *See Minneapolis Star.* . . .

It would be error to conclude, however, that the First Amendment mandates strict scrutiny for any speech regulation that applies to one medium (or a subset thereof) but not others. In *Leathers v. Medlock*, for example, we upheld against First Amendment challenge the application of a general state tax to cable television services, even though the print media and scrambled satellite broadcast television services were exempted from taxation. . . . [H]eightened scrutiny is unwarranted when the differential treatment is "justified by some special characteristic of" the particular medium being regulated.

. . . Appellants do not argue, nor does it appear, that other media — in particular, media that transmit video programming such as MMDS and SMATV — are subject to bottleneck monopoly control, or pose a demonstrable threat to the survival of broadcast television. . . .

III

A

In sum, the must-carry provisions do not pose such inherent dangers to free expression, or present such potential for censorship or manipulation, as to justify application of the most exacting level of First Amendment scrutiny. We agree with the District Court that the appropriate standard by which to evaluate the constitutionality of must-carry is the intermediate level of scrutiny applicable to content-neutral restrictions that impose an incidental burden on speech. *See Ward v. Rock Against Racism*, 491 U.S. 781 (1989); *United States v. O'Brien*, 391 U.S. 367 (1968).

Under *O'Brien*, a content-neutral regulation will be sustained if "it furthers an important or substantial governmental interest; if the governmental interest is unrelated to the suppression of free expression; and if the incidental restriction on alleged First Amendment freedoms is no greater than is essential to the furtherance of that interest." *Id.* at 377. To satisfy this standard, a regulation need not be the least speech-restrictive means of advancing the Government's interests. "Rather, the requirement of narrow tailoring is satisfied 'so long as the . . . regulation promotes a substantial government interest that would be achieved less effectively absent the regulation.'" *Ward*, at 799. . . . Narrow tailoring in this context requires, in other words, that the means chosen do not "burden substantially more speech than is necessary to further the government's legitimate interests." *Ward*, at 799.

Congress declared that the must-carry provisions serve three interrelated interests: (1) preserving the benefits of free, over-the-air local broadcast television, (2) promoting the widespread dissemination of information from a multiplicity of sources, and (3) promoting fair competition in the market for television programming. . . . None of these interests is related to the "suppression of free expression," *O'Brien*, 391 U.S., at 377, or to the content of any speakers' messages. And viewed in the abstract, we have no difficulty concluding that each of them is an important governmental interest. . . . [T]he importance of local broadcasting outlets "can scarcely be exaggerated, for broadcasting is demonstrably a principal source of information and entertainment for a great part of the Nation's population." *Id.* at 177.

Likewise, assuring that the public has access to a multiplicity of information sources is a governmental purpose of the highest order, for it promotes values central to the First Amendment. . . . Government's interest in eliminating restraints on fair competition is always substantial, even when the individuals or entities subject to particular regulations are engaged in expressive activity protected by the First Amendment. . . .

B

That the Government's asserted interests are important in the abstract does not mean, however, that the must-carry rules will in fact advance those interests. . . . [T]he Government. . . . must demonstrate that the recited harms are real, not merely conjectural, and that the regulation will in fact alleviate these harms in a direct and material way. . . .

Thus, in applying *O'Brien* scrutiny we must ask first whether the Government has adequately shown that the economic health of local broadcasting is in genuine jeopardy and in need of the protections afforded by must-carry. Assuming an affirmative answer to the foregoing question, the Government still bears the burden of showing that the remedy it has adopted does not "burden substantially more speech than is necessary to further the government's legitimate interests." *Ward*, 491 U.S., at 799. On the state of the record developed thus far, and in the absence of findings of fact from the District Court, we are unable to conclude that the Government has satisfied either inquiry.

In defending the factual necessity for must-carry, the Government relies in principal part on Congress' legislative finding that, absent mandatory carriage rules, the continued viability of local broadcast television would be "seriously jeopardized." § 2(a)(16). . . .

We agree that courts must accord substantial deference to the predictive judgments of Congress. . . .

. . . [W]e have stressed in First Amendment cases that the deference afforded to legislative findings does "not foreclose our independent judgment of the facts bearing on an issue of constitutional law." *Sable Communications of Cal., Inc. v. FCC*, 492 U.S. 115, 129 (1989). . . . This obligation to exercise independent judgment when First Amendment rights are implicated is not a license to reweigh the evidence de novo, or to replace Congress' factual predictions with our own. Rather, it is to assure that, in formulating its judgments, Congress has drawn reasonable inferences based on substantial evidence. . . .

The Government's assertion that the must-carry rules are necessary to protect the viability of broadcast television rests on two essential propositions: (1) that unless cable operators are compelled to carry broadcast stations, significant numbers of broadcast stations will be refused carriage on cable systems; and (2) that the broadcast stations denied carriage will either deteriorate to a substantial degree or fail altogether.

As support for the first proposition, the Government relies upon a 1988 FCC study showing, at a time when no must-carry rules were in effect, that approximately 20 percent of cable systems reported dropping or refusing carriage to one or more local broadcast stations on at least one occasion. See *Cable System Broadcast Signal Carriage Survey*, Staff Report by the Policy and Rules Division, Mass Media Bureau, p. 10, Table 2 (Sept. 1, 1988), cited in S. Rep. No. 102–92, at 42–43. The record does not indicate, however, the time frame within which these drops occurred, or how many of these stations were dropped for only a temporary period and then restored to carriage. The same FCC study indicates that about 23 percent of the cable operators reported shifting the channel positions of one or more local broadcast stations, and that, in most cases, the repositioning was done for "marketing" rather than "technical" reasons.

The parties disagree about the significance of these statistics. But even if one accepts them as evidence that a large number of broadcast stations would be dropped or repositioned in the absence of must-carry, the Government must further demonstrate that broadcasters so affected would suffer financial difficulties as a result. . . . We think it significant, for instance, that the parties have not presented any evidence that local broadcast stations have fallen into bankruptcy, turned in their broadcast licenses, curtailed their broadcast operations, or suffered a serious reduction in operating revenues as a result of their being dropped from, or otherwise disadvantaged by, cable systems. . . .

Also lacking are any findings concerning the actual effects of must-carry on the speech of cable operators and cable programmers — i.e., the extent to which cable operators will, in fact, be forced to make changes in their current or anticipated programming selections; the degree to which cable programmers will be dropped from cable systems to make room for local broadcasters; and the extent to which cable operators can satisfy their must-carry obligations by devoting previously unused channel capacity to the carriage of local broadcasters. The answers to these and perhaps other questions are critical to the narrow tailoring step of the *O'Brien* analysis, for unless we know the extent to which the must-carry provisions in fact interfere with protected speech, we cannot say whether they suppress "substantially more speech than . . . necessary" to ensure the viability of broadcast television. *Ward*, 491 U.S., at 799. Finally, the record fails to provide any judicial findings concerning the availability and efficacy of "constitutionally acceptable less restrictive means" of achieving the Government's asserted interests. See *Sable Communications*, 492 U.S., at 129.

In sum, because there are genuine issues of material fact still to be resolved on this record, we hold that the District Court erred in granting summary judgment in favor of the Government. . . .

The judgment below is vacated, and the case is remanded for further proceedings consistent with this opinion.

JUSTICE BLACKMUN, concurring. . . .

I write to emphasize the paramount importance of according substantial deference to the predictive judgments of Congress . . . particularly where, as here, that legislative body has compiled an extensive record in the course of reaching its judgment. Nonetheless, the standard for summary judgment is high, and no less so when First Amendment values are at stake. . . .

JUSTICE STEVENS, concurring in part and concurring in the judgment.

. . . I agree with most of Justice Kennedy's reasoning, and join Parts I, II(C), II(D), and III(A) of his opinion. . . .

On its face, that scheme is rationally calculated to redress the dangers that Congress discerned after its lengthy investigation of the relationship between the cable and broadcasting industries.

It is, thus, my view that we should affirm the judgment of the District Court. Were I to vote to affirm, however, no disposition of this appeal would command the support of a majority of the Court. An accommodation is therefore necessary. . . . Accordingly, because I am in substantial agreement with Justice Kennedy's analysis of the case, I concur in the judgment vacating and remanding for further proceedings.

JUSTICE O'CONNOR, with whom JUSTICE SCALIA and JUSTICE GINSBURG join, and with whom JUSTICE THOMAS joins as to Parts I and III, concurring in part and dissenting in part.

There are only so many channels that any cable system can carry. . . . By reserving a little over one-third of the channels on a cable system for broadcasters, [Congress] ensured that in most cases it will be a cable programmer who is dropped and a broadcaster who is retained. . . .

I

A

The 1992 Cable Act implicates the First Amendment rights of two classes of speakers. First, it tells cable operators which programmers they must carry, and keeps cable operators from carrying others that they might prefer. . . .

Second, the Act deprives a certain class of video programmers — those who operate cable channels rather than broadcast stations — of access to over one-third of an entire medium. . . . As the Court explains in Parts I, II-A and II-B of its opinion, which I join, cable programmers and operators stand in the same position under the First Amendment as do the more traditional media.

Under the First Amendment, it is normally not within the government's power to decide who may speak and who may not, at least on private property or in traditional public fora. . . . [L]ooking at the statute at issue, I cannot avoid the conclusion that its preference for broadcasters over cable programmers is justified with reference to content. . . .

Preferences for diversity of viewpoints, for localism, for educational programming, and for news and public affairs all make reference to content. . . . The First Amendment. . .generally prohibits the government from excepting certain kinds of speech from regulation because it thinks the speech is especially valuable. . . . The interest in ensuring access to a multiplicity of diverse and antagonistic sources of information, no matter how praiseworthy, is directly tied to the content of what the speakers will likely say. . . .

B

. . . Of course, the mere possibility that a statute might be justified with reference to content is not enough to make the statute content based, and neither is evidence that some legislators voted for the statute for content-based reasons. But when a content-based justification appears on the statute's face, we cannot ignore it because another, content-neutral justification is present.

C

Content-based speech restrictions are generally unconstitutional unless they are narrowly tailored to a compelling state interest. . . .

The interest in localism, either in the dissemination of opinions held by the listeners' neighbors or in the reporting of events that have to do with the local community, cannot be described as "compelling." . . .

Finally, my conclusion that the must-carry rules are content based leads me to conclude that they are an impermissible restraint on the cable operators' editorial discretion as well as on the cable programmers' speech. . . .

II

. . . The must-carry provisions are fatally overbroad, even under a content-neutral analysis: They disadvantage cable programmers even if the operator has no anticompetitive motives, and even if the broadcaster that would have to be dropped to make room for the cable programmer would survive without cable access. . . .

III

I have no doubt that there is danger in having a single cable operator decide what millions of subscribers can or cannot watch. And I have no doubt that Congress can act to relieve this danger. In other provisions of the Act, Congress has already taken steps to foster competition among cable systems. Congress can encourage the creation of new media, such as inexpensive satellite broadcasting, or fiber-optic networks with virtually unlimited channels, or even simple devices that would let people easily switch from cable to over-the-air broadcasting. And of course Congress can subsidize broadcasters that it thinks provide especially valuable programming.

Congress may also be able to act in more mandatory ways. If Congress finds that cable operators are leaving some channels empty — perhaps for ease of future expansion — it can compel the operators to make the free channels available to programmers who otherwise would not get carriage. . . . Congress might also conceivably obligate cable operators to act as common carriers for some of their channels, with those channels being open to all through some sort of lottery system or timesharing arrangement. . . .

[JUSTICE GINSBURG concurred in part and dissented in part.]

TURNER BROADCASTING SYSTEM, INC. v. FEDERAL COMMUNICATIONS COMMISSION (*"Turner II"*), 520 U.S. 180 (1997). In *Turner II*, the Court addressed "the two questions left open during the first appeal: First, whether the record as it now stands supports Congress' predictive judgment that the must-carry provisions further important governmental interests; and second, whether the provisions do not burden substantially more speech than necessary to further those interests."[19]

On remand, the three-judge District Court, in a divided opinion, upheld Congress' must-carry provisions, noting that cable providers refrained from dropping broadcast stations while the litigation was pending. The District Court stated that the noncarriage problem would be magnified without the must-carry requirement because of cable providers "increasing incentives to use their growing economic power to capture broadcasters' advertising revenues and promote affiliated cable programmers. The court concluded 'substantial evidence before Congress supported the predictive judgment that a local broadcaster denied carriage would suffer financial harm and possible ruin.' " The District Court held that must-carry was narrowly tailored to advance the government's legitimate interests, citing the minimal effects on cable operators.

Writing for a majority in all but one small portion of the opinion, Justice Kennedy again applied *United States v. O'Brien* [391 U.S. 367 (1968)]. " '[I]ncreasing the number of outlets for community self-expression' " furthered an important government interest; it "represents a 'long-established regulatory goa[l] in the field of television broadcasting.' " Consistent with this objective, the Cable Act's findings reflect a concern that congressional action was necessary to prevent 'a reduction in the number of media voices available to consumers.' " Justice Kennedy also noted that broadcast television is "an essential part of the national discourse" on a wide variety of subject matter. "Congress has an independent interest in preserving a multiplicity of broadcasters to ensure that all households have access to information and entertainment on an equal footing with those who subscribe to cable."

In Part II-A-1 of his opinion, Justice Kennedy wrote only for a plurality of four, to the extent he relied on an anticompetitive rationale.

Justice Kennedy noted that horizontal concentration[20] and vertical integration[21] were increasing both the incentives and ability of cable operators to drop local broadcasters. Indeed, before Congress passed the Cable Act, cable operators dropped 1,261 broadcast stations for at least a year.

"The issue before us is whether, given conflicting views of the probable development of the television industry, Congress had substantial evidence for making the judgment that it did. We need not put our imprimatur on Congress' economic theory in order to validate the reasonableness of its judgment." Obviously, the must-carry rules advance the Federal Government's interests " 'in a direct and effective way.' Must-carry ensures that a number of local broadcasters retain cable carriage, with the concomitant

---

[19] "The District Court oversaw another 18 months of factual development on remand yielding a record of tens of thousands of pages of evidence, comprised of materials acquired during Congress' three years of pre-enactment hearings, as well as additional expert submissions, sworn declarations and testimony, and industry documents obtained on remand."

[20] "By 1994, the 10 largest MSO's [Multiple System Operators] controlled 63 percent of cable systems, a figure projected to have risen to 85 percent by the end of 1996."

[21] "The vertical integration of the cable industry also continued, so by 1994, MSO's serving about 70 percent of the Nation's cable subscribers held equity interests in cable programmers."

audience access and advertising revenues needed to support a multiplicity of stations."

Writing again for a majority, Justice Kennedy stated that the must-carry provisions do not burden substantially more speech than necessary to further governmental interests. "Under intermediate scrutiny, the Government may employ the means of its choosing 'so long as the . . . regulation promotes a substantial governmental interest that would be achieved less effectively absent the regulation,' and does not 'burden substantially more speech that is necessary to further' that interest." Concluding that the burden was not great, Justice Kennedy stated that "94.5 percent of the 11,628 cable systems nationwide have not had to drop any programming in order to fulfill their must-carry obligations; the remaining 5.5 percent have had to drop an average of only 1.22 services from their programming, and cable operators nationwide carry 99.8 percent of the programming they carried before enactment of must-carry." Moreover, the current burden of must-carry will only diminish as cable channel capacity increases. "The 5,880 channels occupied by added broadcasters represent the actual burden of the regulatory scheme." Cable operators would drop most of those stations absent must-carry. "Because the burden imposed by must-carry is congruent to the benefits it affords," it is "narrowly tailored to preserve a multiplicity of broadcast stations for the 40 percent of American households without cable."

Finally, Justice Kennedy stated that it is the task of Congress to reconcile the competing economic interests in the "fast-changing field of television." Courts should not displace content-neutral congressional rules if congressional "policy is grounded on reasonable factual findings supported by evidence that is substantial for a legislative determination."

Justice Stevens wrote a brief concurrence. "If this statute regulated the content of speech rather than the structure of the market, our task would be quite different."

Justice Breyer, concurred in all of the majority opinion except insofar as Part-II-A-1 relied on an anticompetitive rationale. His conclusion to uphold must-carry rested not upon its effort to " 'promot[e] fair competition,' " but upon the statute's goals of " '(1) preserving the benefits of free, over-the-air local broadcast television,' " and " '(2) promoting the widespread dissemination of information from a multiplicity of sources.' " Must-carry suppresses speech by hindering cable providers in selecting their own programming and by blocking cable subscribers from watching programs that they would have preferred.

However, for the shrinking population who do not subscribe to cable, the statute averts "too precipitous a decline in the quality and quantity" of programming choices. This rationale comports with long-standing national communications policy requiring " 'the widest possible dissemination of information from diverse and antagonistic sources.' "

When important First Amendment interests reside on both sides of the debate, the "key question becomes one of proper fit." Justice Breyer agreed with the majority opinion that Congress could not have achieved its objectives using less restrictive means and that the statute struck a "reasonable balance between potentially speech-restricting and speech-enhancing consequences."

Justice O'Connor dissented, joined by Justices Scalia, Thomas and Ginsburg. The Court "adopted the wrong analytic framework in the prior phase of this case." Must-carry is not content-neutral and therefore should not have been subject to intermediate scrutiny. The FCC's "characterization of must-carry as a means of protecting these stations, and the Court's explicit concern for promoting " 'community self-expression' " and the " 'local origination of broadcasting programming,' " reveal a content-based preference for broadcast programming."

Moreover, Justice O'Connor argued that must-carry "is not a measured response to congressional concerns about monopoly power." In this connection, she cited evidence of 263 new broadcasting stations having been established before Congress enacted must-carry.

Finally, Justice O'Connor criticized the majority for extreme deference toward Congress. The Court failed to explain the inadequacy of less restrictive means, like forced leased access at regulated rates accompanied by government subsidies for poorer broadcast stations.

DENVER AREA EDUCATIONAL TELE-COMMUNICATIONS CONSORTIUM, INC. v. FEDERAL COMMUNICATIONS COMMISSION, 518 U.S. 727 (1996). In *Tele-Communications Consortium*, a sharply divided Court invalidated two provisions of the Television Consumer Protection and Competition Act of 1992 which required cable operators to restrict the availability of "patently offensive" programming on leased access channels and empowered cable operator programming on public access channels. A different majority upheld another section of the act, which allowed operators discretion to restrict " 'patently offensive' " programming on leased access channels. Justice Breyer delivered a plurality opinion joined in its entirety only by Justices Stevens and Souter.

The Court upheld against a First Amendment challenge the "first provision-that permits the operator to decide whether or not to broadcast such programs on leased access channels." However, the "second provision, that requires leased channel operators to segregate and to block that programming, and the third provision, applicable to public, educational, and governmental channels, violate the First Amendment, for they are not appropriately tailored to achieve the basic, legitimate objective of protecting children from exposure to 'patently offensive' material."

In Part I of his opinion, Justice Breyer was joined by Justices Stevens, O'Connor, and Souter. In Part I, Justice Breyer discussed the history and specifics of the three provisions. The 1992 Act affected two types of federally regulated cable channels. "A 'leased channel' is a channel that federal law requires a cable system operator to reserve for commercial lease by unaffiliated third parties. About 10 to 15 percent of a cable system's channels would typically fall into this category. 'Public, educational, or governmental channels' (which we shall call 'public access' channels) are channels that, over the years, local governments have required cable system operators to set aside for public, educational, or governmental purposes as part of the consideration an operator gives in return for permission to install cables under city streets and to use public rights-of-way. Between 1984 and 1992 federal law prohibited cable system operators from exercising any editorial control over the content of any program broadcast over either leased or public access channels."

In 1992, Congress sought to change the federal regulatory law by enacting the three provisions at issue. The first provision, § 10(a), allows "a cable operator to enforce prospectively a written and published policy of prohibiting programming that the cable operator reasonably believes describes or depicts sexual or excretory activities or organs in a patently offensive manner as measured by contemporary community standards."

"The second provision," § 10(b), "applicable only to leased channels requires cable operators to segregate and to block similar programming if they decide to permit, rather than to prohibit, its broadcast. The provision tells the Federal Communications Commission (FCC or Commission) to promulgate regulations that will (a) require 'programmers to inform cable operators if the programming would be indecent as defined by Commission regulations'; (b) require 'cable operators to place such material on a single channel'; and (c) require 'cable operators to block such single channel unless the subscriber requests access to such channel in writing.' "

§ 10(c) is similar to § 10(a), but applies only to public access facility for " 'any programming which contains obscene material, sexually explicit conduct, or material soliciting or promoting unlawful conduct.' "

Justices Stevens, O'Connor, and Souter joined Part II of Justice Breyer's opinion which upheld the constitutionality of § 10(a). Justice Breyer declined to employ "categorical standards" that the Court has developed "in other contexts" of First Amendment analysis. "No definitive choice among competing analogies (broadcast, common carrier, bookstore) allows us to declare a rigid single standard, good for now and for all future media and purposes." Instead, "aware as we are of the changes taking place in the law, the technology, and the industrial structure, related to telecommunications, we believe it unwise and unnecessary definitely to pick one analogy or one specific set of words now."

Justice Breyer closely scrutinized § 10(a), and concluded that it was "a sufficiently tailored response to an extraordinarily important problem." First, § 10(a) has "an extremely important justification" which the "Court has often found compelling — the need to protect children from patently offensive sex-related material."

"Second, the provision arises in a very particular context-congressional permission for cable operators to regulate programming that, but for a previous Act of Congress, would have had no path of access to cable channels free of an operator's control."

Third, the current problem and its solution are similar to *FCC v. Pacifica Foundation, supra* § 13.05, Note (3) after *Columbia Broadcasting System.* "Cable television broadcasting, including access channel broadcasting, is as 'accessible to children' as over-the-air broadcasting, if not more so." Material on cable television "can 'confront the citizen' in the 'privacy of the home.' "

Fourth, "the permissive nature of § 10(a)" contains "a flexibility that allows cable operators," sometimes to ban broadcasts, but also "to rearrange broadcast times, better to fit the desires of adult audiences while lessening the risks of harm to children."

The plurality concluded "that the permissive nature of [§ 10(a)], coupled with its viewpoint-neutral application, is a constitutionally permissible way to protect children from the type of sexual material that concerned Congress, while accommodating both the First Amendment interests served by the access requirements and those served in restoring to cable operators a degree of the editorial control that Congress removed in 1984."

Petitioners and Justice Kennedy maintained that *Sable Communications of Cal., Inc. v. FCC,* 492 U.S. 114 (1989), prompted a different conclusion. In *Sable,* the "Court found unconstitutional a statute that banned 'indecent' telephone messages." However, the ban "was not only a total governmentally imposed ban on a category of communications, but also involved a communications medium, telephone service, that was significantly less likely to expose children to the banned material, was less intrusive, and allowed for significantly more control over what comes into the home than either broadcasting or the cable transmission system before us."

Petitioners also argued that the public forum doctrine applied to leased access channels. Justice Breyer thought that it was "unnecessary, indeed, unwise" to decide if this doctrine applied. "First, while it may be that content-based exclusions from the right to use common carriers could violate the First Amendment, it is not at all clear that the public forum doctrine should be imported wholesale into the area of common carriage regulation. As we discussed above, we are wary of the notion that a partial analogy in one context, for which we have developed doctrines, can compel a full range of decisions in such a new and changing area. Second, it is plain from this Court's cases that a public forum 'may be created for a limited purpose.' Our cases have not yet determined, however, that the Government's decision to dedicate a public forum to one type of content or another is necessarily subject to the highest level of scrutiny. Must a local government, for example, show a compelling state interest if it builds a band shell in the park and dedicates it solely to classical music (but not to jazz)? The answer is not obvious. But, at a minimum, this case does not require us to answer it."

Lastly, petitioners "argue that the definition of the materials subject to the challenged provisions is too vague, thereby granting cable system operators too broad a program-screening authority." However, the language of § 10(a) "is similar to language adopted by this Court in *Miller v. California*, [413 U.S. 9, 15 (1973),] as a 'guideline' for identifying materials that states may constitutionally regulate as obscene." Moreover, *Pacifica* noted that "what is 'patently offensive' depends on context (the kind of program on which it appears), degree (not 'an occasional expletive'), and time of broadcast." There is little likelihood of "overly broad application" of § 10(a) or unfair discrimination because the provision "permits cable system operators to screen programs only pursuant to 'a written and published policy.'"

In Part III, Justice Breyer wrote for a majority comprised of Justices Stevens, O'Connor, Kennedy, Souter, and Ginsburg. The Court discussed the constitutionality of § 10(b), which directed "cable system operators to restrict speech by segregating and blocking 'patently offensive' sex-related material appearing on leased channels (but not on other channels)." The provision required cable system operators "to unblock the channel within 30 days of a subscriber's written request for access; and to reblock the channel within 30 days of a subscriber's request for reblocking." These various "up-to-30-day delays, along with single channel segregation, mean that a subscriber cannot decide to watch a single program without considerable advance planning and without letting the 'patently offensive' channel in its entirety invade his household for days, perhaps weeks, at a time." In addition, "the written notice 'requirement will further restrict viewing by subscribers who fear for their reputations should the operator, advertently or inadvertently, disclose the list of those who wish to watch the patently offensive' channel." Also, "the added costs and burdens that these requirements impose upon a cable system operator may encourage that operator to ban" the programming entirely.

While the "protection of children is a 'compelling interest,'" § 10(b) "is not a 'least restrictive alternative,' and is not 'narrowly tailored' to meet its legitimate objective." In addition, it "seems considerably 'more extensive than necessary.' That is to say, it fails to satisfy this Court's formulations of the First Amendment's 'strictest,' as well as its somewhat less 'strict,' requirements." The Telecommunications Act of 1996 "requires cable operators to 'scramble or . . . block' such programming on any (unleased) channel 'primarily dedicated to sexually-oriented programming.' In addition, cable operators must honor a subscriber's request to block any, or all, programs on any channel to which he or she does not wish to subscribe. And manufacturers, in the future, will have to make television sets with a so-called 'V-chip' — a device that will be able automatically to identify and block sexually explicit or violent programs."

While "we cannot, and do not, decide whether the new provisions are themselves lawful . . ., we note that they are significantly less restrictive than the provision here at issue." If such devices adequately protect children from patently offensive material on ordinary channels, they should protect children from leased channels.

Moreover, the subscriber has a statutory right to request a "'lockbox,'" which blocks all cable at the subscriber's will. This device also helps to protect children and undercuts the need for § 10(b).

In Part IV of his opinion, joined only by Justices Stevens and Souter, Justice Breyer assessed the constitutionality of § 10(c). This "provision, as implemented by FCC regulation, is similar to" § 10(a), as it also "permits a cable operator to prevent transmission of 'patently offensive' programming, in this case on public access channels. But there are four important differences."

Whereas leased channels arrangements allow the lessee to have "total control of programming during the leased time slot," public "[a]ccess channel activity and management are partly financed with public funds," and are supervised by a local supervisory board.

Lastly, "public non-profit programming control systems now in place would normally avoid, minimize, or eliminate any child-related problems concerning patently offensive programming." At bottom, § 10(c) "could radically change present programming-related relationships among local community and nonprofit supervising boards and access managers, which relationships are established through municipal law, regulation, and contract."

In Part V, Justice Breyer was joined by Justices Stevens, O'Connor, and Souter. The plurality found that "legislative intent" suggested § 10(a) was "severable from the two other provisions." The "Act's 'severability' intention" was evident "in its structure and purpose." Section 10(a), "capable of functioning on its own, still helps to achieve" the Act's basic objective.

Only Justices Stevens and Souter joined Part VI of Justice Breyer's opinion upholding § 10(a) and invalidating §§ 10(b) and 10(c).

Justice Stevens concurred "to emphasize the difference between" § 10(a) and § 10(c) "and to endorse the analysis in Part III-B of Justice Kennedy's opinion even though" he did "not think it necessary to characterize the public access channels as public fora."

Section 10(a) does not establish "a public forum. Unlike sidewalks and parks, the Federal Government created leased access channels in the course of its legitimate regulation of the communications industry. In so doing, it did not establish an entirely open forum, but rather restricted access to certain speakers, namely unaffiliated programmers able to lease the air time."

When it opens channels "that would otherwise be left entirely in private hands," the Federal Government "deserves more deference than a rigid application of the public forum doctrine would allow. At this early stage in the regulation of this developing industry, Congress should not be put to an all or nothing-at-all choice in deciding whether to open certain cable channels to programmers who would otherwise lack the resources to participate in the marketplace of ideas." Justice Stevens believed: "If the Government had a reasonable basis for concluding that there were already enough classical musical programs or cartoons being telecast — or, perhaps, even enough political debate — I would find no First Amendment objection to an open access requirement that was extended on an impartial basis to all but those particular subjects."

Justice Souter's concurrence rejected "categorical analysis" because cable is "presently in a state of technological and regulatory flux." As "broadcast, cable, and the cyber-technology of the Internet and the World Wide Web approach the day of using a common receiver, we can hardly assume that standards for judging the regulation of one of them will not have immense, but now unknown and unknowable, effects on the others."

Justice O'Connor dissented in part. "I agree that § 10(a) is constitutional and that § 10(b) is unconstitutional, and I join Parts I, II, III, and V, and the judgment in part." However, the "asserted 'important differences' between §§ 10(a) and 10(c) are" insufficient "to justify striking down § 10(c)." Like § 10(a), § 10(c) furthers "the well-established compelling interest of protecting children from exposure to indecent material," supported by *Pacifica*.

Justice Kennedy, joined by Justice Ginsburg, joined "Part III of the opinion (there for the Court) striking down § 10(b) of the Act," concurred "in the judgment that § 10(c) is unconstitutional," and dissented "from the remainder." Precedent required the Court "to hold § 10(a) invalid." The "most disturbing aspect of the plurality opinion" was its failure to apply "any clear legal standard in deciding this case." Also troubling was "the plurality's approach" suggesting "that Congress has more leeway than usual to enact restrictions on speech where emerging technologies are concerned, because we are unsure what standard should be used to assess them."

Justice Kennedy maintained that public access channels comprised public forums by designation. They are "created by local or state governments in the cable franchise" agreement. "[I]n return for granting cable operators easements to use public rights-of-way for their cable lines, local governments have bargained for a right to use cable line for public access channels." By enacting § 10(c), "the Federal Government at the same time ratified the public-forum character of public access channels but discriminated against certain speech based on its content."

In Justice Kennedy's view, "strict scrutiny also applies to § 10(a)'s authorization to cable operators to exclude indecent programming from" leased accessed channels, which are creatures of Federal law. Strict scrutiny applied because the FCC designated cable operators as § 10(a) common carriers. Under § 10(a), cable operators may "ban indecent programming on leased access channels." *Sable Communications* holds "that a law precluding a common carrier from transmitting protected speech is subject to strict scrutiny."

To avoid strict scrutiny the Government relies on *Pacifica*. However, *Pacifica* did not create "a special standard for indecent broadcasting." Rather, the Court applied "a context-specific analysis of the FCC's restriction on indecent programming during daytime hours." The *Pacifica* Court relied on the lesser protection afforded to broadcasting, a standard which the *Turner* Court rejected for cable television. Finally, the broadcaster in *Pacifica* wanted to air the speech at issue; here, the cable operator does not.

While Congress does have "a compelling interest in protecting children from indecent speech," neither § 10(a) nor § 10(c) is "narrowly tailored to protect" that interest. "A block-and-segregate requirement similar to § 10(b), but without its constitutional infirmity of requiring persons to place themselves on a list to receive programming protects children with far less intrusion on the liberties of programmers and adult viewers than allowing cable operators to ban indecent programming from access channels altogether."

Justice Thomas, joined by the Chief Justice Rehnquist and Justice Scalia, concurred in the judgment in part and dissented in part. "I agree with the plurality's conclusion that § 10(a) is constitutionally permissible, but I disagree with its conclusion that §§ 10(b) and (c) violate the First Amendment.

The Court's "First Amendment distinctions between media, dubious from their infancy, placed cable in a doctrinal wasteland in which regulators and cable operators alike could not be sure whether cable was entitled to the substantial First Amendment protections afforded the print media or was subject to the more onerous obligations shouldered by the broadcast media." However, *Turner* adopted much of the print paradigm and rejected *Red Lion*.

Justice Thomas contended that "leased and public access are a type of forced speech," which *Turner* subjects to heightened scrutiny. As "the access provisions are part of a scheme that restricts the free speech rights of cable operators, and expands the speaking opportunities of access programmers, who have no underlying constitutional right to speak through the cable medium, I do not believe that access programmers can challenge the scheme, or a particular part of it, as an abridgment of their 'freedom of speech.' " Sections "10(a) and (c) do not burden a programmer's right to seek access for its indecent programming on an operator's system. Rather, they merely restore part of the editorial discretion an operator would have absent government regulation without burdening the programmer's underlying speech rights."

Justice Thomas disagreed with plaintiffs' claim that a public access channel is a public forum. "Cable systems are not public property."

Justice Thomas also argued that § 10(b) should be upheld as constitutional. "Unlike §§ 10(a) and (c), § 10(b) clearly implicates petitioners' free speech rights." As "§ 10(b) is narrowly tailored to achieve that well-established compelling interest" of " 'protecting the physical and psychological well-being of minors,' " Justice Thomas would uphold it.

Evidence suggests that "indecent programming on leased access channels is 'especially likely to be shown randomly or intermittently between non-indecent programs,' " necessitating constantly reprogramming the lockbox.

NOTES

(1) For additional discussion of the Court's application of current First Amendment doctrine to government regulation of mass media, see Ashutosh Bhagwat, *Of Markets and Media: The First Amendment, The New Mass Media, and The Political Components of Culture*, 74 N.C. L. Rev. 141, 217 (1995) ("[A]t least in the mass media context, governmental or majoritarian manipulation of cultural formation should be the primary evil against which First Amendment policy is directed. . . . [A] general preference for market mechanisms and structural methods of regulating speech are the most effective ways to guard against this danger.").

(2) For further discussion of *Turner Broadcasting*, see Cass Sunstein, *The First Amendment in Cyberspace*, 104 Yale L.J. 1757, 1765 (1995) ("*Turner* involved two highly distinctive problems: (a) the peculiar 'bottleneck' produced by the current system of cable television, in which cable owners can control access to programming; and (b) the possible risk to free television programming created by the rise of pay television. These problems turned out to be central to the outcome in the case. For this reason, *Turner* is quite different from imaginable future cases involving new information technologies, including the Internet, which includes no bottleneck problem.").

[3]   The Internet

RENO v. AMERICAN CIVIL LIBERTIES UNION
521 U.S. 844, 117 S. Ct. 2329, 138 L. Ed. 2d 874, 65 (1997)

Justice Stevens delivered the opinion of the Court.

At issue is the constitutionality of two statutory provisions enacted to protect minors from "indecent" and "patently offensive" communications on the Internet. Notwithstanding the legitimacy and importance of the congressional goal of protecting children from harmful materials, we agree with the three-judge District Court that the statute abridges "the freedom of speech" protected by the First Amendment.

I

The District Court made extensive findings of fact, most of which were based on a detailed stipulation prepared by the parties. *See* 929 F. Supp. 824, 830–849 (ED Pa. 1996). . . . [22]

The Internet

The Internet is an international network of interconnected computers. It is the outgrowth of what began in 1969 as a military program called "ARPANET."[23] . . . The Internet is "a unique and wholly new medium of worldwide human communication." The number of "host" computers — those that store information and relay communications — increased from about 300 in 1981 to approximately 9,400,000 by the time of the trial in 1996. Roughly 60% of these hosts are located in the United States. About 40 million people used the Internet at the time of trial. . . .

Individuals can obtain access to the Internet from many different sources, generally hosts themselves or entities with a host affiliation. . . . [C]ommercial online services had almost 12 million individual subscribers at the time of trial.

Anyone with access to the Internet may take advantage of a wide variety of communication and information retrieval methods. These methods are constantly evolving and difficult to categorize precisely. . . . All of these methods can be used to transmit text; most can transmit sound, pictures, and moving video images. Taken together, these tools constitute a unique medium — known to its users as "cyberspace" — located in no particular geographical location but available to anyone, anywhere in the world, with access to the Internet.

E-mail enables an individual to send an electronic message — generally akin to a note or letter — to another individual or to a group of addressees. . . . A mail exploder is a sort of e-mail group. Subscribers can send messages to a common e-mail address, which then forwards the message to the group's other subscribers. Newsgroups also serve groups of regular participants, but these postings may be read by others as well. . . .

The best known category of communication over the Internet is the World Wide Web, which allows users to search for and retrieve information stored in remote computers, as well as, in some cases, to communicate back to designated sites. In concrete terms, the Web consists of a vast number of documents stored in different computers all over the world. . . .

Navigating the Web is relatively straightforward. A user may either type the address of a known page or enter one or more keywords into a commercial "search engine" in an effort to locate sites on a subject of interest. . . . Access to most Web pages is freely available, but some allow access only to those who have purchased the right from a commercial provider. The Web is thus comparable, from the readers' viewpoint, to both a vast library including millions of readily available and indexed publications and a sprawling mall offering goods and services.

From the publishers' point of view, it constitutes a vast platform from which to address and hear from a world-wide audience of millions of readers, viewers, researchers, and buyers. Any person or organization with a computer connected to the

---

[22] [Court's footnote 2] The Court made 410 findings, including 356 paragraphs of the parties' stipulation and 54 findings based on evidence received in open court.

[23] [Court's footnote 3] An acronym for the network developed by the Advanced Research Project Agency.

Internet can "publish" information. Publishers include government agencies, educational institutions, commercial entities, advocacy groups, and individuals.[24]

Publishers may either make their material available to the entire pool of Internet users, or confine access to a selected group, such as those willing to pay for the privilege. "No single organization controls any membership in the Web, nor is there any centralized point from which individual Web sites or services can be blocked from the Web."

Sexually Explicit Material

Sexually explicit material on the Internet includes text, pictures, and chat and "extends from the modestly titillating to the hardest-core." These files are created, named, and posted in the same manner as material that is not sexually explicit, and may be accessed either deliberately or unintentionally during the course of an imprecise search. "Once a provider posts its content on the Internet, it cannot prevent that content from entering any community." Thus, for example, "when the UCR/California Museum of Photography posts to its Web site nudes by Edward Weston and Robert Mapplethorpe to announce that its new exhibit will travel to Baltimore and New York City, those images are available not only in Los Angeles, Baltimore, and New York City, but also in Cincinnati, Mobile, or Beijing — wherever Internet users live. . . . Some of the communications over the Internet that originate in foreign countries are also sexually explicit." . . .

. . . "A child requires some sophistication and some ability to read to retrieve material and thereby to use the Internet unattended." . . .

Age Verification

The problem of age verification differs for different uses of the Internet. The District Court categorically determined that there "is no effective way to determine the identity or the age of a user who is accessing material through e-mail, mail exploders, newsgroups or chat rooms."[25]

. . . [E]ven if it were technologically feasible to block minors' access to newsgroups and chat rooms containing discussions of art, politics or other subjects that potentially elicit "indecent" or "patently offensive" contributions, it would not be possible to block their access to that material and "still allow them access to the remaining content, even if the overwhelming majority of that content was not indecent."

. . . Credit card verification is only feasible . . . either in connection with a commercial transaction in which the card is used, or by payment to a verification agency. . . .

. . . Even if passwords are effective for commercial purveyors of indecent material, the District Court found that an adult password requirement would impose significant burdens on noncommercial sites, both because they would discourage users from

---

[24] [Court's footnote 9] "Web publishing is simple enough that thousands of individual users and small community organizations are using the Web to publish their own personal 'home pages,' the equivalent of individualized newsletters about the person or organization." . . .

[25] [Court's footnote 20] "An e-mail address provides no authoritative information about the addressee, who may use an e-mail 'alias' or an anonymous remailer. . . . The difficulty of e-mail age verification is compounded for mail exploders such as listservs, which automatically send information to all e-mail addresses on a sender's list. . . .

accessing their sites and because the cost of creating and maintaining such screening systems would be "beyond their reach."[26]

In sum, the District Court found:

"Even if credit card verification or adult password verification were implemented, the Government presented no testimony as to how such systems could ensure that the user of the password or credit card is in fact over 18. The burdens imposed by credit card verification and adult password verification systems make them effectively unavailable to a substantial number of Internet content providers."

II

The Telecommunications Act of 1996, Pub. L. 104-104, 110 Stat. 56, was an unusually important legislative enactment. . . . The major components of the statute have nothing to do with the Internet; they were designed to promote competition in the local telephone service market, the multichannel video market, and the market for over-the-air broadcasting. The Act includes seven Titles, six of which are the product of extensive committee hearings and the subject of discussion in Reports prepared by Committees of the Senate and the House of Representatives. By contrast, Title V — known as the "Communications Decency Act of 1996" (CDA) — contains provisions that were either added in executive committee after the hearings were concluded or as amendments offered during floor debate on the legislation. An amendment offered in the Senate was the source of the two statutory provisions challenged in this case.

They are informally described as the "indecent transmission" provision and the "patently offensive display" provision.

The first, 47 U.S.C. A. § 223(a) (Supp. 1997), prohibits the knowing transmission of obscene or indecent messages to any recipient under 18 years of age. It provides in pertinent part:

"(a) Whoever —

"(1) in interstate or foreign communications —

"(B) by means of a telecommunications device knowingly —

"(i) makes, creates, or solicits,

"(ii) initiates the transmission of,

"any comment, request, suggestion, proposal, image, or other communication which is obscene or indecent, knowing that the recipient of the communication is under 18 years of age, regardless of whether the maker of such communication placed the call or initiated the communication;

"(2) knowingly permits any telecommunications facility under his control to be used for any activity prohibited by paragraph (1) with the intent that it be used for such activity, not more than two years, or both."

The second provision, § 223(d), prohibits the knowing sending or displaying of patently offensive messages in a manner that is available to a person under 18 years of age. It provides:

"(d) Whoever

---

[26] [Court's footnote 23] "'. . . There is evidence suggesting that adult users, particularly casual Web browsers, would be discouraged from retrieving information that required use of a credit card or password. There is concern by commercial content providers that age verification requirements would decrease advertising and revenue because advertisers depend on a demonstration that the sites are widely available and frequently visited.'"

"(1) in interstate or foreign communications knowingly —

"(A) uses an interactive computer service to send to a specific person or persons under 18 years of age,

"(B) uses any interactive computer service to display in a manner available to a person under 18 years of age,

"any comment, request, suggestion, proposal, image, or other communication that, in context, depicts or describes, in terms patently offensive as measured by contemporary community standards, sexual or excretory activities or organs, regardless of whether the user of such service placed the call or initiated the communication; or

"(2) knowingly permits any telecommunications facility under such person's control to be used for an activity prohibited by paragraph (1) with the intent that it be used for such activity, shall be fined under Title 18, or imprisoned not more than two years, or both."

The breadth of these prohibitions is qualified by two affirmative defenses. One covers those who take "good faith, reasonable, effective, and appropriate actions" to restrict access by minors to the prohibited communications. § 223(e)(5)(A). The other covers those who restrict access to covered material by requiring certain designated forms of age proof, such as a verified credit card or an adult identification number or code. § 223(e)(5)(B).

III

. . . After an evidentiary hearing, [a three-judge District Court] entered a preliminary injunction against enforcement of both of the challenged provisions. . . .

. . . In its appeal, the Government argues that the District Court erred in holding that the CDA violated both the First Amendment because it is overbroad and the Fifth Amendment because it is vague. While we discuss the vagueness of the CDA because of its relevance to the First Amendment overbreadth inquiry, we conclude that the judgment should be affirmed without reaching the Fifth Amendment issue. . . .

IV

In arguing for reversal, the Government contends that the CDA is plainly constitutional under three of our prior decisions: (1) *Ginsberg v. New York*, 390 U.S. 629 (1968); (2) *FCC v. Pacifica Foundation*, 438 U.S. 726 (1978); and (3) *Renton v. Playtime Theatres, Inc.*, 475 U.S. 41 (1986).

In *Ginsberg*, we upheld the constitutionality of a New York statute that prohibited selling to minors under 17 years of age material that was considered obscene as to them even if not obscene as to adults. . . . [W]e relied not only on the State's independent interest in the well-being of its youth, but also on our consistent recognition of the principle that "the parents' claim to authority in their own household to direct the rearing of their children is basic in the structure of our society." In four important respects, the statute upheld in *Ginsberg* was narrower than the CDA. First, we noted in *Ginsberg* that "the prohibition against sales to minors does not bar parents who so desire from purchasing the magazines for their children." *Id.* at 639. Under the CDA, by contrast, neither the parents' consent — nor even their participation — in the communication would avoid the application of the statute.

Second, the New York statute applied only to commercial transactions, whereas the CDA contains no such limitation. Third, the New York statute cabined its definition of material that is harmful to minors with the requirement that it be "utterly without redeeming social importance for minors." *Id.* at 646. The CDA fails to provide us with any definition of the term "indecent" as used in § 223(a)(1) and, importantly, omits any requirement that the "patently offensive" material covered by § 223(d) lack serious literary, artistic, political, or scientific value. Fourth, the New York statute defined a minor as a person under the age of 17, whereas the CDA, in applying to all those under 18 years, includes an additional year of those nearest majority.

In *Pacifica*, we upheld a declaratory order of the Federal Communications Commission, holding that the broadcast of a recording of a 12-minute monologue entitled "Filthy Words" that had previously been delivered to a live audience "could have been the subject of administrative sanctions." (internal quotations omitted). The Commission had found that the repetitive use of certain words referring to excretory or sexual activities or organs "in an afternoon broadcast when children are in the audience was patently offensive" and concluded that the monologue was indecent "as broadcast". . . . In the portion of the lead opinion not joined by Justices Powell and Blackmun, the plurality stated that the First Amendment does not prohibit all governmental regulation that depends on the content of speech. Accordingly, the availability of constitutional protection for a vulgar and offensive monologue that was not obscene depended on the context of the broadcast. . . .

As with the New York statute at issue in *Ginsberg*, there are significant differences between the order upheld in *Pacifica* and the CDA. First, the order in *Pacifica*, issued by an agency that had been regulating radio stations for decades, targeted a specific broadcast that represented a rather dramatic departure from traditional program content in order to designate when — rather than whether — it would be permissible to air such a program in that particular medium. The CDA's broad categorical prohibitions are not limited to particular times and are not dependent on any evaluation by an agency familiar with the unique characteristics of the Internet. Second, unlike the CDA, the Commission's declaratory order was not punitive. . . . Finally, the Commission's order applied to a medium which as a matter of history had "received the most limited First Amendment protection," *id.* at 748, in large part because warnings could not adequately protect the listener from unexpected program content. The Internet, however, has no comparable history. Moreover, the District Court found that the risk of encountering indecent material by accident is remote because a series of affirmative steps is required to access specific material.

In *Renton*, we upheld a zoning ordinance that kept adult movie theatres out of residential neighborhoods. The ordinance was aimed, not at the content of the films shown in the theaters, but rather at the "secondary effects" — such as crime and deteriorating property values — that these theaters fostered. . . . According to the Government, the CDA is constitutional because it constitutes a sort of "cyberzoning" on the Internet. But the CDA applies broadly to the entire universe of cyberspace. And the purpose of the CDA is to protect children from the primary effects of "indecent" and "patently offensive" speech, rather than any "secondary" effect of such speech. . . .

These precedents, then, surely do not require us to uphold the CDA and are fully consistent with the application of the most stringent review of its provisions.

V

In *Southeastern Promotions, Ltd. v. Conrad*, 420 U.S. 546, 557 (1975), we observed that "each medium of expression . . . may present its own problems." Thus, some of our cases have recognized special justifications for regulation of the broadcast media that are not applicable to other speakers, *see Red Lion Broadcasting Co. v. FCC*, 395 U.S. 367 (1969); *FCC v. Pacifica Foundation*, 438 U.S. 726 (1978). In these cases, the Court relied on the history of extensive government regulation of the broadcast medium, see, e.g., *Red Lion*, 395 U.S., at 399–400; the scarcity of available frequencies at its inception, see, e.g., *Turner Broadcasting System, Inc. v. FCC*, 512 U.S. 622, 637–638 (1994); and its "invasive" nature, *see Sable Communications of Cal., Inc. v. FCC*, 492 U.S. 114, 128 (1989).

Those factors are not present in cyberspace. Neither before nor after the enactment of the CDA have the vast democratic fora of the Internet been subject to the type of government supervision and regulation that has attended the broadcast industry.[27]

Moreover, the Internet is not as "invasive" as radio or television. The District Court specifically found that "communications over the Internet do not 'invade' an individual's home or appear on one's computer screen unbidden. Users seldom encounter content 'by accident.' " It also found that "almost all sexually explicit images are preceded by warnings as to the content," and cited testimony that " 'odds are slim' that a user would come across a sexually explicit sight by accident."

Finally, unlike the conditions that prevailed when Congress first authorized regulation of the broadcast spectrum, the Internet can hardly be considered a "scarce" expressive commodity. It provides relatively unlimited, low-cost capacity for communication of all kinds. The Government estimates that "as many as 40 million people use the Internet today, and that figure is expected to grow to 200 million by 1999." This dynamic, multifaceted category of communication includes not only traditional print and news services, but also audio, video, and still images, as well as interactive, real-time dialogue. Through the use of chat rooms, any person with a phone line can become a town crier with a voice that resonates farther than it could from any soapbox. Through the use of Web pages, mail exploders, and newsgroups, the same individual can become a pamphleteer. . . . [O]ur cases provide no basis for qualifying the level of First Amendment scrutiny that should be applied to this medium.

VI

Regardless of whether the CDA is so vague that it violates the Fifth Amendment, the many ambiguities concerning the scope of its coverage render it problematic for purposes of the First Amendment. For instance, each of the two parts of the CDA uses a different linguistic form. The first uses the word "indecent," 47 U.S.C. A. § 223(a) (Supp. 1997), while the second speaks of material that "in context, depicts or describes, in terms patently offensive as measured by contemporary community standards, sexual or excretory activities or organs," § 223(d). Given the absence of a definition of either term, this difference in language will provoke uncertainty among speakers about how the two standards relate to each other and just what they mean.[28]

Could a speaker confidently assume that a serious discussion about birth control practices, homosexuality, the First Amendment issues raised by the Appendix to our *Pacifica* opinion, or the consequences of prison rape would not violate the CDA? This uncertainty undermines the likelihood that the CDA has been carefully tailored to the congressional goal of protecting minors from potentially harmful materials.

---

[27] [Court's footnote 33] When *Pacifica* was decided, given that radio stations were allowed to operate only pursuant to federal license, and that Congress had enacted legislation prohibiting licensees from broadcasting indecent speech, there was a risk that members of the radio audience might infer some sort of official or societal approval of whatever was heard over the radio. No such risk attends messages received through the Internet, which is not supervised by any federal agency.

[28] [Court's footnote 37] The statute does not indicate whether the "patently offensive" and "indecent" determinations should be made with respect to minors or the population as a whole. The Government asserts that the appropriate standard is "what is suitable material for minors." But the Conferees expressly rejected amendments that would have imposed such a "harmful to minors" standard. . . .

The vagueness of the CDA is a matter of special concern for two reasons. First, the . . . vagueness of such a regulation raises special First Amendment concerns because of its obvious chilling effect on free speech. . . . Second, . . . the CDA threatens violators with penalties including up to two years in prison for each act of violation. The severity of criminal sanctions may well cause speakers to remain silent rather than communicate even arguably unlawful words, ideas, and images.

VII

We are persuaded that the CDA lacks the precision that the First Amendment requires when a statute regulates the content of speech. In order to deny minors access to potentially harmful speech, the CDA effectively suppresses a large amount of speech that adults have a constitutional right to receive and to address to one another. That burden on adult speech is unacceptable if less restrictive alternatives would be at least as effective in achieving the legitimate purpose that the statute was enacted to serve.

In arguing that the CDA does not so diminish adult communication, the Government relies on the incorrect factual premise that prohibiting a transmission whenever it is known that one of its recipients is a minor would not interfere with adult-to-adult communication. The findings of the District Court make clear that this premise is untenable. Given the size of the potential audience for most messages, in the absence of a viable age verification process, the sender must be charged with knowing that one or more minors will likely view it. . . .

The District Court found that at the time of trial existing technology did not include any effective method for a sender to prevent minors from obtaining access to its communications on the Internet without also denying access to adults. . . . As a practical matter, the Court also found that it would be prohibitively expensive for noncommercial — as well as some commercial — speakers who have Web sites to verify that their users are adults.

. . . By contrast, the District Court found that "despite its limitations, currently available user-based software suggests that a reasonably effective method by which parents can prevent their children from accessing sexually explicit and other material which parents may believe is inappropriate for their children will soon be widely available."

The breadth of the CDA's coverage is wholly unprecedented. Unlike the regulations upheld in *Ginsberg* and *Pacifica*, the scope of the CDA is not limited to commercial speech or commercial entities. Its open-ended prohibitions embrace all nonprofit entities and individuals posting indecent messages or displaying them on their own computers in the presence of minors. The general, undefined terms "indecent" and "patently offensive" cover large amounts of nonpornographic material with serious educational or other value.[29]

Moreover, the "community standards" criterion as applied to the Internet means that any communication available to a nation-wide audience will be judged by the standards of the community most likely to be offended by the message.

The regulated subject matter includes any of the seven "dirty words" used in the *Pacifica* monologue, the use of which the Government's expert acknowledged could constitute a felony. It may also extend to discussions about prison rape or safe sexual

---

[29] [Court's footnote 44] . . . In fact, when Congress was considering the CDA, the Government expressed its view that the law was unnecessary because existing laws already authorized its ongoing efforts to prosecute obscenity, child pornography, and child solicitation. See 141 Cong. Rec. S8342 (June 14, 1995) (letter from Kent Markus, Acting Assistant Attorney General, U.S. Department of Justice, to Sen. Leahy).

practices, artistic images that include nude subjects, and arguably the card catalogue of the Carnegie Library.

For the purposes of our decision, we need neither accept nor reject the Government's submission that the First Amendment does not forbid a blanket prohibition on all "indecent" and "patently offensive" messages communicated to a 17-year old — no matter how much value the message may contain and regardless of parental approval. . . . Under the CDA, a parent allowing her 17-year-old to use the family computer to obtain information on the Internet that she, in her parental judgment, deems appropriate could face a lengthy prison term. Similarly, a parent who sent his 17-year-old college freshman information on birth control via e-mail could be incarcerated even though neither he, his child, nor anyone in their home community, found the material "indecent" or "patently offensive," if the college town's community thought otherwise.

The breadth of this content-based restriction of speech imposes an especially heavy burden on the Government to explain why a less restrictive provision would not be as effective as the CDA. It has not done so. The arguments in this Court have referred to possible alternatives such as requiring that indecent material be "tagged" in a way that facilitates parental control of material coming into their homes, making exceptions for messages with artistic or educational value, providing some tolerance for parental choice, and regulating some portions of the Internet — such as commercial web sites — differently than others, such as chat rooms. Particularly in the light of the absence of any detailed findings by the Congress, or even hearings addressing the special problems of the CDA, we are persuaded that the CDA is not narrowly tailored if that requirement has any meaning at all.

VIII

. . . The Government . . . asserts that the "knowledge" requirement of both §§ 223(a) and (d), especially when coupled with the "specific child" element found in § 223(d), saves the CDA from overbreadth. . . . This argument ignores the fact that most Internet fora — including chat rooms, newsgroups, mail exploders, and the Web — are open to all comers. The Government's assertion that the knowledge requirement somehow protects the communications of adults is therefore untenable. Even the strongest reading of the "specific person" requirement of § 223(d) cannot save the statute. It would confer broad powers of censorship, in the form of a "heckler's veto," upon any opponent of indecent speech who might simply log on and inform the would-be discoursers that his 17-year-old child . . . would be present.

IX

The Government's three remaining arguments focus on the defenses provided in § 223(e)(5). First, relying on the "good faith, reasonable, effective, and appropriate actions" provision, the Government suggests that "tagging" provides a defense that saves the constitutionality of the Act. The suggestion assumes that transmitters may encode their indecent communications in a way that would indicate their contents, thus permitting recipients to block their reception with appropriate software. It is the requirement that the good faith action must be "effective" that makes this defense illusory. The Government recognizes that its proposed screening software does not currently exist. Even if it did, . . . [w]ithout the impossible knowledge that every guardian in America is screening for the "tag," the transmitter could not reasonably rely on its action to be "effective."

For its second and third arguments concerning defenses — which we can consider together — the Government relies on the latter half of § 223(e)(5), which applies when the transmitter has restricted access by requiring use of a verified credit card or adult identification. Such verification is not only technologically available but actually is used by commercial providers of sexually explicit material. These providers, therefore, would be protected by the defense. Under the findings of the District Court, however, it is not economically feasible for most noncommercial speakers to employ such verification. . . .

X

At oral argument, the Government relied heavily on its ultimate fall-back position: If this Court should conclude that the CDA is insufficiently tailored, it urged, we should save the statute's constitutionality by honoring the severability clause, and construing nonseverable terms narrowly. In only one respect is this argument acceptable.

A severability clause requires textual provisions that can be severed. We will follow § 608's guidance by leaving constitutional textual elements of the statute intact in the one place where they are, in fact, severable. The "indecency" provision, 47 U.S.C. A. § 223(a), applies to "any comment, request, suggestion, proposal, image, or other communication which is *obscene or indecent*." (Emphasis added.) Appellees do not challenge the application of the statute to obscene speech, which, they acknowledge, can be banned totally because it enjoys no First Amendment protection. [*Miller v. California*, 413 U.S. 9, 15 (1973)]. As set forth by the statute, the restriction of "obscene" material enjoys a textual manifestation separate from that for "indecent" material, which we have held unconstitutional. Therefore, we will sever the term "or indecent" from the statute, leaving the rest of § 223(a) standing. In no other respect, however, can § 223(a) or § 223(d) be saved by such a textual surgery. . . .

Justice O'connor, with whom The Chief Justice joins, concurring in the judgment in part and dissenting in part.

I write separately to explain why I view the Communications Decency Act of 1996 (CDA) as little more than an attempt by Congress to create "adult zones" on the Internet. . . . Despite the soundness of its purpose, however, portions of the CDA are unconstitutional because they stray from the blueprint our prior cases have developed for constructing a "zoning law" that passes constitutional muster.

Appellees bring a facial challenge to three provisions of the CDA. The first, which the Court describes as the "indecency transmission" provision, makes it a crime to knowingly transmit an obscene or indecent message or image to a person the sender knows is under 18 years old. What the Court classifies as a single " 'patently offensive display' " provision, is in reality two separate provisions. The first of these makes it a crime to knowingly send a patently offensive message or image to a specific person under the age of 18 ("specific person" provision). § 223(d)(1)(A). The second criminalizes the display of patently offensive messages or images "in any manner available" to minors ("display" provision). § 223(d)(1)(B). . . . Thus, the undeniable purpose of the CDA is to segregate indecent material on the Internet into certain areas that minors cannot access. . . .

I

. . . A minor can see an adult dance show only if he enters an establishment that provides such entertainment. And should he attempt to do so, the minor will not be able to conceal completely his identity (or, consequently, his age). Thus, the twin characteristics of geography and identity enable the establishment's proprietor to prevent children from entering the establishment, but to let adults inside.

. . . [C]yberspace allows speakers and listeners to mask their identities. . . .

. . . Internet speakers (users who post material on the Internet) have begun to zone cyberspace itself through the use of "gateway" technology. Such technology requires Internet users to enter information about themselves — perhaps an adult identification number or a credit card number — before they can access certain areas of cyberspace. . . .

. . . Gateway technology is not ubiquitous in cyberspace, and because without it "there is no means of age verification," cyberspace still remains largely unzoned — and unzoneable. . . .

Although the prospects for the eventual zoning of the Internet appear promising, I agree with the Court that we must evaluate the constitutionality of the CDA as it applies to the Internet as it exists today. Given the present state of cyberspace, I agree with the Court that the "display" provision cannot pass muster. Until gateway technology is available throughout cyberspace, and it is not in 1997, a speaker cannot be reasonably assured that the speech he displays will reach only adults because it is impossible to confine speech to an "adult zone." Thus, the only way for a speaker to avoid liability under the CDA is to refrain completely from using indecent speech. But this forced silence impinges on the First Amendment right of adults. . . .

The "indecency transmission" and "specific person" provisions present a closer issue, for they are not unconstitutional in all of their applications. As discussed above, the "indecency transmission" provision makes it a crime to transmit knowingly an indecent message to a person the sender knows is under 18 years of age. 47 U.S.C.A. § 223(a)(1)(B). The "specific person" provision proscribes the same conduct, although it does not as explicitly require the sender to know that the intended recipient of his indecent message is a minor. § 223(d)(1)(A). Appellant urges the Court to construe the provision to impose such a knowledge requirement and I would do so. . . .

So construed, both provisions are constitutional as applied to a conversation involving only an adult and one or more minors — e.g., when an adult speaker sends an e-mail knowing the addressee is a minor, or when an adult and minor converse by themselves or with other minors in a chat room. In this context, these provisions are no different from the law we sustained in *Ginsberg*. . . .

The analogy to *Ginsberg* breaks down, however, when more than one adult is a party to the conversation. If a minor enters a chat room otherwise occupied by adults, the CDA effectively requires the adults in the room to stop using indecent speech. . . . [T]he absence of any means of excluding minors from chat rooms in cyberspace restricts the rights of adults to engage in indecent speech in those rooms. The "indecency transmission" and "specific person" provisions share this defect.

. . . I agree with the Court that the provisions are overbroad in that they cover any and all communications between adults and minors, regardless of how many adults might be part of the audience to the communication.

This conclusion does not end the matter, however. Where, as here, "the parties challenging the statute are those who desire to engage in protected speech that the overbroad statute purports to punish . . . the statute may forthwith be declared invalid to the extent that it reaches too far, but otherwise left intact." *Brockett v. Spokane Arcades, Inc.*, 472 U.S. 491, 504 (1985). . . . I would therefore sustain the "indecency transmission" and "specific person" provisions to the extent they apply to the transmission of Internet communications where the party initiating the communication knows that all of the recipients are minors.

II

. . . [T]he CDA could ban some speech that is "indecent" (i.e., "patently offensive") but that is not obscene as to minors.

I do not deny this possibility, but to prevail in a facial challenge, it is not enough for a plaintiff to show "some" overbreadth. Our cases require a proof of "real" and "substantial" overbreadth, *Broadrick v. Oklahoma*, 413 U.S. 601, 615 (1973), and appellees have not carried their burden in this case. . . .

NOTES

(1) For a view of the internet analogizing the media to a public forum, see David J. Goldstone, *The Public Forum Doctrine in the Age of the Information Superhighway (Where Are the Public Forums on the Information Superhighway?)*, 46 HASTINGS L.J. 335, 337, 402 (1995) ("Rather than drawing an analogy to a traditional public forum, like a park, or to a non-public forum, like an airport terminal, this article argues that the NII [National Information Infrastructure] should be conceptualized on a broader scale as an entity, like a city, that includes an abundance of both public forums and nonpublic forums . . . some landmarks on the Information Superhighway should have constitutional significance . . . government-owned or government-controlled forums that are operated on a nonprofit basis and have unrestricted access to message recipients and viewpoint-neutral access to a reasonably large number of message senders. . . . [F]our sets of issues . . . will surely be raised: topic dedication, forum membership, forum costs, and forum closure.").

(2) For an interesting analysis of the limitations of the new media, see Cass R. Sunstein, *The First Amendment in Cyberspace*, 104 YALE L.J. 1757, 1785 (1995) ("The American polity is a republic, not a direct democracy, and for legitimate reasons; direct democracy is unlikely to provide successful governance, for it is too likely to be free from deliberation and unduly subject to short-time reactions and sheer manipulation . . . . In the current period, there is thus a serious risk that low-cost or costless communications will increase government's responsiveness to myopic or poorly considered public outcries, or to sensationalistic or sentimental anecdotes that are a poor basis for governance.").

(3) For an interesting critique of these cases, see Catherine J. Ross, *Anything Goes: Examining the State's Interest in Protecting Children from Controversial Speech*, 53 VAND. L. REV. 427, 430–31 (2000) ("Over the last decade, the Supreme Court has ruled on three other cases involving the constitutionality of federal efforts to regulate speech in order to shelter children from content: *Sable Communications, Inc. v. FCC* (492 U.S. 115 (1989)), *Denver Area Educational Telecommunications Consortium, Inc. v. FCC* (518 U.S. 727 (1996)); and *Reno v. ACLU* ("ACLU I") (521 U.S. 844, 864 (1997)). In each instance, the Court rejected the State's argument that the goal of shielding children justified significant intrusions on constitutionally protected speech, and in each instance, the Supreme Court overturned all or part of the statute at issue.").

(4) For a note of caution in cyberspace, see Cass R. Sunstein, *Constitutional Caution*, 1996 U. CHI. LEGAL F. 361, 374 (1996) ("When values and institutions are in flux, it is appropriate for the court to proceed casuistically and to avoid broad rulings. The constitutional issues raised by cyberspace will turn on issues that cannot be fully resolved in 1995, 1996, or even 1999.").

(5) *Community or National Standard for Internet pPornography?* In *Ashcroft v. The Free Speech Coalition*, a deeply divided court rejected a facial challenge to a statute imposing a community standard on Internet pornography viewed by minors. A majority of Justices appear to suggest that a national standard may eventually be

necessary. For additional discussion of this case, see § 15,05[1].

(6) *Morphed Child Pornography*. In *Ashcroft v. ACLU*, the Court extended First Amendment protection to computer-generated images of child pornography. The standards for pornography using actual children did not apply, as no real children were used. For further discussion of this case, see § 15.05[1], Note (10) after *Arcara*.

(7) *Library Pornography*. In *United States v. Am. Library Ass'n*, the Court upheld the Children's Internet Protection Act (CIPA) which required a library to install Internet filtering software in order to receive federal funding. Adults could request the librarian to disable the filter or unblock a specific site. For further discussion of this case, see § 15.03, Note after *NEA v. Finlay*.

(8) *Obscene for Minors*. In *Ashcroft v. ACLU*, 542 U.S. 656 (2004), the Court in a 6-3 decision upheld an injunction enjoining enforcement of the Child Online Protection Act (COPA). COPA was a second attempt by Congress to "protect minors from exposure to sexually explicit materials on the Internet" after the Communications Decency Act of 1996 was invalidated. COPA criminalized "the knowing posting, for 'commercial purposes,' internet "content that is 'harmful to minors.' "[30] Writing for the majority, Justice Kennedy upheld the preliminary injunction: "respondents must be deemed likely to prevail unless the Government has shown that respondents' proposed less restrictive alternatives are less effective than COPA. . . . That conclusion was not an abuse of discretion, because on this record there are a number of plausible, less restrictive alternatives to the statute."

For example, "[f]ilters may well be more effective than COPA." The Court also questioned the effectiveness of COPA as "40% of harmful-to-minors content comes from overseas." Moreover, "the District Court found that verification systems may be subject to evasion and circumvention, for example by minors who have their own credit cards." Finally, filters could be applied to email communication available via the World Wide Web. The Court did not foreclose a later holding by the District Court that COPA is constitutional, holding only that the injunction should remain in place until trial on the merits. In his concurrence, joined by Justice Ginsburg, Justice Stevens emphasized that violations of COPA carry a potential fine of "as much as $50,000 and a term of imprisonment as long as six months, for each offense"; moreover, "intentional" violators may be subject to "a fine of up to $50,000 for each day of the violation."

In dissent, Justice Scalia stated that the Court "err[ed], however, in subjecting COPA to strict scrutiny." The Court has previously held that " 'pandering' by 'deliberately emphasizing the sexually provocative aspects . . . in order to catch the salaciously disposed' " was constitutionally unprotected behavior. Joined in his dissent by Justices Rehnquist and O'Connor, Justice Breyer emphasized that "the parties agreed that a Web site could store card numbers or passwords at between 15 and 20 cents per number," a nominal financial burden. Filters are not an effective alternative. "[I]n the absence of words, the software alone cannot distinguish between the most obscene pictorial images and the Venus de Milo."

---

[30] The statute define " 'harmful to minors' . . . as" Internet content that is " 'obscene or that' " " 'appeal[s] to . . . the prurient interest,' " " 'depicts' " explicitly sexual acts, and " 'lacks . . . value for minors.' "

§ 13.08   DEFAMATION AND PRIVACY

[1]   Public Figures versus Private Individuals

NEW YORK TIMES COMPANY v. SULLIVAN
376 U.S. 254, 84 S. Ct. 710, 11 L. Ed. 2d 686 (1964)

JUSTICE BRENNAN delivered the opinion of the Court. . . .

Respondent L. B. Sullivan is one of the three elected Commissioners of the City of Montgomery, Alabama. He testified that he was "Commissioner of Public Affairs and the duties are supervision of the Police Department, Fire Department, Department of Cemetery and Department of Scales." He brought this civil libel action against the four individual petitioners, who are Negroes and Alabama clergymen, and against petitioner the New York Times Company. . . .   A jury in the Circuit Court of Montgomery County awarded him damages of $500,000, the full amount claimed, against all the petitioners, and the Supreme Court of Alabama affirmed.

Respondent's complaint alleged that he had been libeled by statements in a full-page advertisement that was carried in the New York Times on March 29, 1960. Entitled "Heed Their Rising Voices," the advertisement began by stating that "As the whole world knows by now, thousands of Southern Negro students are engaged in widespread non-violent demonstrations in positive affirmation of the right to live in human dignity as guaranteed by the U.S. Constitution and the Bill of Rights." It went on to charge that "in their efforts to uphold these guarantees, they are being met by an unprecedented wave of terror by those who would deny and negate that document which the whole world looks upon as setting the pattern for modern freedom. . . . " Succeeding paragraphs purported to illustrate the "wave of terror" by describing certain alleged events. The text concluded with an appeal for funds. . . .

The text appeared over the names of 64 persons, many widely known for their activities in public affairs, religion, trade unions, and the performing arts. Below these names, and under a line reading "We in the south who are struggling daily for dignity and freedom warmly endorse this appeal," appeared the names of the four individual petitioners and of 16 other persons, all but two of whom were identified as clergymen in various Southern cities. The advertisement was signed at the bottom of the page by the "Committee to Defend Martin Luther King and the Struggle for Freedom in the South," and the officers of the Committee were listed.

Of the 10 paragraphs of text in the advertisement, the third and a portion of the sixth were the basis of respondent's claim of libel. They read as follows:

Third paragraph:

In Montgomery, Alabama, after students sang "My Country, 'Tis of Thee" on the State Capitol steps, their leaders were expelled from school, and truckloads of police armed with shotguns and tear-gas ringed the Alabama State College Campus. When the entire student body protested to state authorities by refusing to re-register, their dining hall was padlocked in an attempt to starve them into submission.

Sixth paragraph:

Again and again the Southern violators have answered Dr. King's peaceful protests with intimidation and violence. They have bombed his home almost killing his wife and child. They have assaulted his person. They have arrested him seven times — for "speeding," "loitering" and similar "offenses." And now they have charged him with "perjury" — a *felony* under which they could imprison him for *ten years*. . . .

Although neither of these statements mentions respondent by name, he contended that the word "police" in the third paragraph referred to him as the Montgomery Commissioner who supervised the Police Department. . . .

It is uncontroverted that some of the statements contained in the two paragraphs were not accurate descriptions. . . . Although Negro students staged a demonstration on the State Capital steps, they sang the National Anthem and not "My Country, 'Tis of Thee." Although nine students were expelled by the State Board of Education, this was not for leading the demonstration at the Capitol, but for demanding service at a lunch counter in the Montgomery County Courthouse on another day. Not the entire student body, but most of it, had protested the expulsion, not by refusing to register, but by boycotting classes on a single day; virtually all the students did register for the ensuing semester. The campus dining hall was not padlocked on any occasion, and the only students who may have been barred from eating there were the few who had neither signed a preregistration application nor requested temporary meal tickets. Although the police were deployed near the campus in large numbers on three occasions, they did not at any time "ring" the campus, and they were not called to the campus in connection with the demonstration on the State Capitol steps, as the third paragraph implied. Dr. King had not been arrested seven times, but only four; and although he claimed to have been assaulted some years earlier in connection with his arrest for loitering outside a courtroom, one of the officers who made the arrest denied that there was such an assault.

On the premise that the charges in the sixth paragraph could be read as referring to him, respondent was allowed to prove that he had not participated in the events described. Although Dr. King's home had in fact been bombed twice when his wife and child were there, both of these occasions antedated respondent's tenure as Commissioner, and the police were not only not implicated in the bombings, but had made every effort to apprehend those who were. Three of Dr. King's four arrests took place before respondent became Commissioner. Although Dr. King had in fact been indicted (he was subsequently acquitted) on two counts of perjury, each of which carried a possible five-year sentence, respondent had nothing to do with procuring the indictment. . . .

[An advertising] agency submitted the advertisement with a letter from A. Philip Randolph, Chairman of the Committee, certifying that the persons whose names appeared on the advertisement had given their permission. . . . Each of the individual petitioners testified that he had not authorized the use of his name, and that he had been unaware of its use until receipt of respondent's demand for a retraction. The manager of the Advertising Acceptability Department testified that he had approved the advertisement for publication because he knew nothing to cause him to believe that anything in it was false, and because it bore the endorsement of "a number of people who are well known and whose reputation" he "had no reason to question." Neither he nor anyone else at the Times made an effort to confirm the accuracy of the advertisement, either by checking it against recent Times news stories relating to some of the described events or by any other means. . . .

I

We may dispose at the outset of two grounds asserted to insulate the judgment of the Alabama courts from constitutional scrutiny. The first is the proposition relied on by the State Supreme Court — that "The Fourteenth Amendment is directed against State action and not private action." . . . Although this is a civil lawsuit between private parties, the Alabama courts have applied a state rule of law which petitioners claim to impose invalid restrictions on their constitutional freedoms of speech and press. It matters not that that law has been applied in a civil action and that it is common law only, though supplemented by statute. . . . The test is not the form in which state power has been applied but, whatever the form, whether such power has in fact been exercised. . . .

The second contention is that the constitutional guarantees of freedom of speech and of the press are inapplicable here, at least so far as the Times is concerned, because the allegedly libelous statements were published as part of a paid, "commercial" advertisement. . . .

The publication here was not a "commercial" advertisement. . . . It communicated information, expressed opinion, recited grievances, protested claimed abuses, and sought financial support on behalf of a movement whose existence and objectives are matters of the highest public interest and concern. . . . That the Times was paid for publishing the advertisement is as immaterial in this connection as is the fact that newspapers and books are sold. . . . Any other conclusion . . . might shut off an important outlet for the promulgation of information and ideas by persons who do not themselves have access to publishing facilities. . . . To avoid placing such a handicap upon the freedoms of expression, we hold that if the allegedly libelous statements would otherwise be constitutionally protected from the present judgment, they do not forfeit that protection because they were published in the form of a paid advertisement.

II

Under Alabama law as applied in this case, a publication is "libelous per se" if the words "tend to injure a person . . . in his reputation" or to "bring [him] into public contempt." . . . Once "libel per se" has been established, the defendant has no defense as to stated facts unless he can persuade the jury that they were true in all their particulars. . . . Unless he can discharge the burden of proving truth, general damages are presumed, and may be awarded without proof of pecuniary injury. . . .

Respondent relies heavily, as did the Alabama courts, on statements of this Court to the effect that the Constitution does not protect libelous publications. . . . In deciding the question now, we are compelled by neither precedent nor policy to give any more weight to the epithet "libel" than we have to other "mere labels" of state law. . . . Like insurrection, contempt, advocacy of unlawful acts, breach of the peace, obscenity, solicitation of legal business, and the various other formulae for the repression of expression that have been challenged in this Court, libel can claim no talismanic immunity from constitutional limitations. It must be measured by standards that satisfy the First Amendment. . . .

Thus we consider this case against the background of a profound national commitment to the principle that debate on public issues should be uninhibited, robust, and wide-open, and that it may well include vehement, caustic, and sometimes unpleasantly sharp attacks on government and public officials. . . . The present advertisement, as an expression of grievance and protest on one of the major public issues of our time, would seem clearly to qualify for the constitutional protection. . . .

If neither factual error nor defamatory content suffices to remove the constitutional shield from criticism of official conduct, the combination of the two elements is no less inadequate. This is the lesson to be drawn from the great controversy over the Sedition Act of 1798, 1 Stat. 596, which first crystallized a national awareness of the central meaning of the First Amendment. . . . That statute made it a crime, punishable by a $5,000 fine and five years in prison, "if any person shall write, print, utter or publish . . . any false, scandalous and malicious writing or writings against the government of the United States, or either house of the Congress . . ., or the President

. . ., with intent to defame . . . or to bring them, or either of them, into contempt or disrepute; or to excite against them, or either or any of them, the hatred of the good people of the United States." The Act allowed the defendant the defense of truth, and provided that the jury were to be judges both of the law and the facts. Despite these qualifications, the Act was vigorously condemned as unconstitutional in an attack joined in by Jefferson and Madison. . . .

Although the Sedition Act was never tested in this Court,[31] the attack upon its validity has carried the day in the court of history. Fines levied in its prosecution were repaid by Act of Congress on the ground that it was unconstitutional. . . . Jefferson, as President, pardoned those who had been convicted and sentenced under the Act and remitted their fines. . . .

What a State may not constitutionally bring about by means of a criminal statute is likewise beyond the reach of its civil law of libel. The fear of damage awards under a rule such as that invoked by the Alabama courts here may be markedly more inhibiting than the fear of prosecution under a criminal statute. . . . The judgment awarded in this case — without the need for any proof of actual pecuniary loss — was one thousand times greater than the maximum fine provided by the Alabama criminal statute, and one hundred times greater than that provided by the Sedition Act. . . . Whether or not a newspaper can survive a succession of such judgments, the pall of fear and timidity imposed upon those who would give voice to public criticism is an atmosphere in which the First Amendment freedoms cannot survive. . . .

The state rule of law is not saved by its allowance of the defense of truth. . . . Under such a rule, would-be critics of official conduct may be deterred from voicing their criticism, even though it is believed to be true and even though it is in fact true, because of doubt whether it can be proved in court or fear of the expense of having to do so. . . .

The constitutional guarantees require, we think, a federal rule that prohibits a public official from recovering damages for a defamatory falsehood relating to his official conduct unless he proves that the statement was made with "actual malice" — that is, with knowledge that it was false or with reckless disregard of whether it was false or not. . . .

Such a privilege for criticism of official conduct[32] is appropriately analogous to the protection accorded a public official when he is sued for libel by a private citizen. In *Barr v. Matteo*, 360 U.S. 564, 575, this Court held the utterance of a federal official to be absolutely privileged if made "within the outer perimeter" of his duties. The States accord the same immunity to statements of their highest officers, although some differentiate their lesser officials and qualify the privilege they enjoy. But all hold that all officials are protected unless actual malice can be proved. The reason for the official privilege is said to be that the threat of damage suits would otherwise "inhibit the fearless, vigorous, and effective administration of policies of government." . . . *Barr v. Matteo, supra*, 360 U.S., at 571. Analogous considerations support the privilege for the citizen-critic of government. It is as much his duty to criticize as it is the official's duty to administer. . . .

---

[31] [Court's footnote 16] The Act expired by its terms in 1801.

[32] [Court's footnote 21] The privilege immunizing honest misstatements of fact is often referred to as a "conditional" privilege to distinguish it from the "absolute" privilege recognized in judicial, legislative, administrative and executive proceedings. *See, e.g.*, Prosser, Torts (2d ed., 1955), § 95.

III

We hold today that the Constitution delimits a State's power to award damages for libel in actions brought by public officials against critics of their official conduct. Since this is such an action,[33] the rule requiring proof of actual malice is applicable. . . .

Since respondent may seek a new trial, we deem that considerations of effective judicial administration require us to review the evidence in the present record to determine whether it could constitutionally support a judgment for respondent. . . . We must "make an independent examination of the whole record," *Edwards v. South Carolina*, 372 U.S. 229, 235, so as to assure ourselves that the judgment does not constitute a forbidden intrusion on the field of free expression.[34]

Applying these standards, we consider that the proof presented to show actual malice lacks the convincing clarity which the constitutional standard demands. . . . The case of the individual petitioners requires little discussion. Even assuming that they could constitutionally be found to have authorized the use of their names on the advertisement, there was no evidence whatever that they were aware of any erroneous statements or were in any way reckless in that regard. . . .

As to the Times, we similarly conclude that the facts do not support a finding of actual malice. The statement by the Times' Secretary that, apart from the padlocking allegation, he thought the advertisement was "substantially correct," . . . the statement does not indicate malice at the time of the publication; even if the advertisement was not "substantially correct" — although respondent's own proofs tend to show that it was — that opinion was at least a reasonable one, and there was no evidence to impeach the witness' good faith in holding it. . . .

Finally, there is evidence that the Times published the advertisement without checking its accuracy against the news stories in the Times' own files. The mere presence of the stories in the files does not, of course, establish that the Times "knew" the advertisement was false, since the state of mind required for actual malice would have to be brought home to the persons in the Times' organization having responsibility for the publication of the advertisement. With respect to the failure of those persons to make the check, the record shows that they relied upon their knowledge of the good reputation of many of those whose names were listed as sponsors of the advertisement, and upon the letter from A. Philip Randolph, known to them as a responsible individual, certifying that the use of the names was authorized. . . . We think the evidence against the Times supports at most a finding of negligence in failing to discover the misstatements, and is constitutionally insufficient to show the recklessness that is required for a finding of actual malice. . . .

JUSTICE BLACK, with whom JUSTICE DOUGLAS joins (concurring). . . .

"Malice," even as defined by the Court, is an elusive, abstract concept, hard to prove

---

[33] [Court's footnote 23] We have no occasion here to determine how far down into the lower ranks of government employees the "public official" designation would extend for purposes of this rule, or otherwise to specify categories of persons who would or would not be included. Nor need we here determine the boundaries of the "official conduct" concept. It is enough for the present case that respondent's position as an elected city commissioner clearly made him a public official, and that the allegations in the advertisement concerned what was allegedly his official conduct as Commissioner in charge of the Police Department. . . .

[34] [Court's footnote 26] The Seventh Amendment does not, as respondent contends, preclude such an examination by this Court. That Amendment, providing that "no fact tried by a jury, shall be otherwise reexamined in any Court of the United States, than according to the rules of the common law," is applicable to state cases coming here. . . . But its ban on re-examination of facts does not preclude us from determining whether governing rules of federal law have been properly applied to the facts. . . .

and hard to disprove. . . .   Unlike the Court, therefore, I vote to reverse exclusively on the ground that the Times and the individual defendants had an absolute, unconditional constitutional right to publish in the Times advertisement their criticisms of the Montgomery agencies and officials. . . .

The half-million-dollar verdict does give dramatic proof, however, that state libel laws threaten the very existence of an American press virile enough to publish unpopular views. . . .   Moreover, a second half-million-dollar libel verdict against the Times based on the same advertisement has already been awarded to another Commissioner. . . . In fact, briefs before us show that in Alabama there are now pending eleven libel suits by local and state officials against the Times seeking $5,600,000, and five such suits against the Columbia Broadcasting System seeking $1,700,000. . . .

JUSTICE GOLDBERG, with whom JUSTICE DOUGLAS joins (concurring in the result). . . .

. . . Government is not an abstraction; it is made up of individuals — of governors responsible to the governed. . . .   If the rule that libel on government has no place in our Constitution is to have real meaning, then libel on the official conduct of the governors likewise can have no place in our Constitution. . . .

This is not to say that the Constitution protects defamatory statements directed against the private conduct of a public official or private citizen. . . .   Purely private defamation has little to do with the political ends of a self-governing society. The imposition of liability for private defamation does not abridge the freedom of public speech or any other freedom protected by the First Amendment.

The conclusion that the Constitution affords the citizen and the press an absolute privilege for criticism of official conduct does not leave the public official without defenses against unsubstantiated opinions or deliberate misstatements. "Under our system of government, counterargument and education are the weapons available to expose these matters, not abridgement . . . of free speech. . . . " *Wood v. Georgia*, 370 U.S. 375, 389. The public official certainly has equal if not greater access than most private citizens to media of communication. . . .   As Justice Brandeis correctly observed, "sunlight is the most powerful of all disinfectants."[35]

NOTES

(1) *Reckless Disregard.* In *St. Amant v. Thompson*, 390 U.S. 727 (1968), the Court clarified the actual knowledge/reckless disregard standard articulated in *New York Times*. The case arose from a televised political speech in which defendant St. Amant read the answers of a union leader, Albin, to a series of questions. One of the answers he read falsely charged a sheriff named Thompson with criminal activities. "St. Amant had no personal knowledge of Thompson's activities; he relied solely on Albin's affidavit although the record was silent as to Albin's reputation for veracity; he failed to verify the information with those in the union office who might have known the facts; he gave no consideration as to whether or not the statements defamed Thompson and went ahead heedless of the consequences; and he mistakenly believed he had no responsibility for the broadcast because he was merely quoting Albin's words."

In holding that publication under these circumstances did not meet the *New York Times* standard, the Court clarified the standard: "These cases are clear that reckless conduct is not measured by whether a reasonably prudent man would have published or would have investigated before publishing. There must be sufficient evidence to permit the conclusion that the defendant in fact entertained serious doubts as to the truth of his publication." This is a subjective test. Writing for the Court, Justice White gave

---

[35] [Court's footnote 7] *See* FREUND, THE SUPREME COURT OF THE UNITED STATES 61 (1949).

examples of conduct that would and would not satisfy the test: "The finder of fact must determine whether the publication was indeed made in good faith. Professions of good faith will be unlikely to prove persuasive, for example, where a story is fabricated by the defendant, is the product of his imagination, or is based wholly on an unverified anonymous telephone call. Nor will they be likely to prevail when the publisher's allegations are so inherently improbable that only a reckless man would have put them in circulation. Likewise, recklessness may be found where there are obvious reasons to doubt the veracity of the informant or the accuracy of his reports."

(2) *Discovery.* In *Herbert v. Lando*, 441 U.S. 153 (1979), the Court allowed pre-trial discovery to depose the defendants (producers, editors, and narrators of the *60 Minutes* TV show) about a wide range of editorial decisions leading to the presentation of the allegedly defamatory program. The purpose of the questions was to establish the actual knowledge/reckless disregard standard of *New York Times v. Sullivan.* The Court held that such court-approved questioning of the editorial judgments of the media did not violate the First Amendment. Justices Brennan, Stewart, and Marshall dissented.

(3) *Official Conduct.* The applicability of the *New York Times* standard to governmental officials hinges on who is a public official and what comprises official conduct. In *Monitor Patriot Co. v. Roy*, 401 U.S. 265 (1971), the Court made clear that official conduct included anything that might relate to an official's fitness for office including past events. *Monitor* applied the *New York Times* standard to the charge that a candidate for the United States Senate had been a "small-time bootlegger during Prohibition."

Justice Stewart opined: "[W]hatever vitality the 'official conduct' concept may retain with regard to occupants for public office, it is clearly of little applicability in the context of an election campaign. . . . Given the realities of our political life, it is by no means easy to see what statements about a candidate might be altogether without relevance to his fitness for the office he seeks."

(4) *Public Official.* In *Rosenblatt v. Baer*, 383 U.S. 75 (1966), the Court held that the supervisor of a county recreation area was a public official for purposes of applying the *New York Times* standard. The test for determining whether a particular plaintiff was a public official was whether "the position in government has such apparent importance that the public has an independent interest in the qualifications and importance of the person who holds it beyond the general public interest in the performance of all governmental employees." The Court also said that such an official should "appear to [have] substantial responsibility for or control over the conduct of governmental affairs."

Hutchinson v. Proxmire, 443 U.S. 111 (1979), *supra* § 12.06[4], made clear that not all governmental employees were public officials for purposes of applying the *New York Times* standard.

(5) *Intentional Infliction of Emotional Distress.* In *Hustler Magazine v. Falwell*, 485 U.S. 46 (1988), a unanimous Court (Justice Kennedy not participating) extended First Amendment protection to a "parody" of an advertisement that featured Jerry Falwell, the nationally known minister. Parodying an ad for Campari Liqueur, the display contained a picture of Falwell and was entitled " 'Jerry Falwell talks about his first time.' " The ad featured a fictional interview of Jerry Falwell. "This parody was modeled after actual Campari ads that included interviews with various celebrities about their 'first times.' " Although it was apparent by the end of each interview that this meant the first time they sampled Campari, the ads clearly played on the sexual double entendre of the general subject of "first times." In the Hustler interview, "Falwell states that his 'first time' was a drunken incestuous rendezvous with his

mother in an outhouse. . . . In small print at the bottom of the page, the ad contains the disclaimer, 'ad parody — not to be taken seriously.' The magazine's table of contents also lists the ad as 'Fiction; Ad and Personality Parody.' "

The trial court ruled against Falwell on the libel action because, as a parody, the article was not intended to be understood as depicting actual facts and, therefore, was not false. Both the trial court and the Fourth Circuit Court of Appeals, however, allowed Falwell to recover on a claim for "intentional infliction of emotional distress."

Writing for the Court, Chief Justice Rehnquist rejected the Circuit Court's analysis of the emotional distress claim. The Chief Justice cited the long history of parody, and political cartoons, as important forms of political expression. He reasoned that the First Amendment's protection for the expression of political ideas precluded recovery for intentional infliction of emotional harm based on a subjective standard evaluating the "outrageous" quality of the statement. "We conclude that public figures and public officials may not recover for the tort of intentional infliction of emotional distress by reason of publications such as the one here at issue without showing in addition that the publication contains a false statement of fact which was made with 'actual malice,' i.e., with knowledge that the statement was false or with reckless disregard as to whether or not it was true."

(6) For a discussion of the seminal importance of *New York Times v. Sullivan* in departing from the two-tiered model of protecting only some speech and generally expanding protection for freedom of speech, see Harry Kalven, *The New York Times Case: A Note on the Central Meaning of the First Amendment*, 1964 SUP. CT. REV. 191; Frederick Schauer, *Uncoupling Free Speech*, 92 COLUM. L. REV. 1321, 1322–23 (1992) ("existing understandings of the First Amendment are based on the assumption that, because a price must be paid for free speech, it must be the victims of harmful speech who are to pay it. . . . [A]lthough much of modern law reform, especially in torts, has reflected attempts to reallocate costs towards those best able to bear them and to adjust incentives in order to achieve optimal patterns of behavior, this trend has as yet failed to influence our understanding of constitutional rights in general and free speech rights in particular.").

GERTZ v. WELCH, INC.
418 U.S. 323, 94 S. Ct. 2997, 41 L. Ed. 2d 789 (1974)

JUSTICE POWELL delivered the opinion of the Court.

This Court has struggled for nearly a decade to define the proper accommodation between the law of defamation and the freedoms of speech and press protected by the First Amendment. . . .

I

In 1968, a Chicago policeman named Nuccio shot and killed a youth named Nelson. The state authorities prosecuted Nuccio for the homicide and ultimately obtained a conviction for murder in the second degree. The Nelson family retained petitioner Elmer Gertz, a reputable attorney, to represent them in civil litigation against Nuccio.

Respondent publishes American Opinion, a monthly outlet for the views of the John Birch Society. Early in the 1960's the magazine began to warn of a nationwide conspiracy to discredit local law enforcement agencies and create in their stead a national police force capable of supporting a Communist dictatorship. As part of the continuing effort to alert the public to this assumed danger, the managing editor of American Opinion commissioned an article on the murder trial of Officer Nuccio. For this purpose he engaged a regular contributor to the magazine. In March 1969 respondent published the resulting article under the title "FRAME-UP: Richard Nuccio And The War On Police." The article purports to demonstrate that the testimony against Nuccio at his criminal trial was false and that his prosecution was part of the Communist campaign against the police.

In his capacity as counsel for the Nelson family in the civil litigation, petitioner attended the coroner's inquest into the boy's death and initiated actions for damages, but he neither discussed Officer Nuccio with the press nor played any part in the criminal proceeding. Notwithstanding petitioner's remote connection with the prosecution of Nuccio, respondent's magazine portrayed him as an architect of the "frame-up." According to the article, the police file on petitioner took "a big, Irish cop to lift." The article stated that petitioner had been an official of the "Marxist League for Industrial Democracy, originally known as the Intercollegiate Socialist Society, which has advocated the violent seizure of our government." It labeled Gertz a "Leninist" and a "Communist-frontier." It also stated that Gertz had been an officer of the National Lawyers Guild, described as a Communist organization that "probably did more than any other outfit to plan the Communist attack on the Chicago police during the 1968 Democratic Convention."

These statements contained serious inaccuracies. The implication that petitioner had a criminal record was false. Petitioner had been a member and officer of the National Lawyers Guild some 15 years earlier, but there was no evidence that he or that organization had taken any part in planning the 1968 demonstrations in Chicago. There was also no basis for the charge that petitioner was a "Leninist" or a "Communist-frontier." And he had never been a member of the "Marxist League for Industrial Democracy" or the "Intercollegiate Socialist Society."

The managing editor of American Opinion made no effort to verify or substantiate the charges against petitioner. Instead, he appended an editorial introduction stating that the author had "conducted extensive research into the Richard Nuccio Case." And he included in the article a photograph of petitioner and wrote the caption that appeared under it: "Elmer Gertz of Red Guild harasses Nuccio." Respondent placed the issue of American Opinion containing the article on sale at newsstands throughout the country and distributed reprints of the article on the streets of Chicago. . . .

II

The principal issue in this case is whether a newspaper or broadcaster that publishes defamatory falsehoods about an individual who is neither a public official nor a public figure may claim a constitutional privilege against liability for the injury inflicted by those statements. . . .

Three years after *New York Times*, a majority of the Court agreed to extend the constitutional privilege to defamatory criticism of "public figures." This extension was announced in *Curtis Publishing Co. v. Butts* and its companion, *Associated Press v. Walker*, 388 U.S. 130. The first case involved the Saturday Evening Post's charge that Coach Wally Butts of the University of Georgia had conspired with Coach "Bear" Bryant of the University of Alabama to fix a football game between their respective schools. *Walker* involved an erroneous Associated Press account of former Major General Edwin Walker's participation in a University of Mississippi campus riot. Because Butts was paid by a private alumni association and Walker had resigned from the Army, neither could be classified as a "public official" under *New York Times*. The Court extended the constitutional privilege announced in that case to protect defamatory criticism of nonpublic persons who "are nevertheless intimately involved in the resolution of important public questions or, by reason of their fame, shape events in areas of concern to society at large."

In his opinion for the plurality in *Rosenbloom v. Metromedia, Inc.*, [403 U.S. 29 (1971),] Justice Brennan took the *New York Times* privilege one step further. He concluded that its protection should extend to defamatory falsehoods relating to private persons if the statements concerned matters of general or public interest. . . .

Justice Harlan dissented. . . .

Justice Marshall [also] dissented . . . in an opinion joined by Justice Stewart. . . . [He] reached the conclusion, also reached by Justice Harlan, that the States should be "essentially free to continue the evolution of the common law of defamation and to articulate whatever fault standard best suits the State's need," so long as the States did not impose liability without fault. . . .

III

We begin with the common ground. Under the First Amendment there is no such thing as a false idea. However pernicious an opinion may seem, we depend for its correction not on the conscience of judges and juries but on the competition of other ideas. But there is no constitutional value in false statements of fact. Neither the intentional lie nor the careless error materially advances society's interest in "uninhibited, robust, and wide-open" debate on public issues. *New York Times Co. v. Sullivan.* . . .

Although the erroneous statement of fact is not worthy of constitutional protection, it is nevertheless inevitable in free debate. . . . And punishment of error runs the risk of inducing a cautious and restrictive exercise of the constitutionally guaranteed freedoms of speech and press. . . .

The need to avoid self-censorship by the news media is, however, not the only societal value at issue. . . .

The legitimate state interest underlying the law of libel is the compensation of individuals for the harm inflicted on them by defamatory falsehood. . . .

The *New York Times* standard defines the level of constitutional protection appropriate to the context of defamation of a public person. Those who, by reason of the notoriety of their achievements or the vigor and success with which they seek the public's attention, are properly classed as public figures and those who hold governmental office may recover for injury to reputation only on clear and convincing proof that the defamatory falsehood was made with knowledge of its falsity or with reckless disregard for the truth. . . .

. . . Public officials and public figures usually enjoy significantly greater access to the channels of effective communication and hence have a more realistic opportunity to counteract false statements than private individuals normally enjoy. . . .

. . . An individual who decides to seek governmental office must accept certain necessary consequences of that involvement in public affairs. He runs the risk of closer public scrutiny than might otherwise be the case. . . .

Those classed as public figures stand in a similar position. Hypothetically, it may be possible for someone to become a public figure through no purposeful action of his own, but the instances of truly involuntary public figures must be exceedingly rare. . . . Some occupy positions of such persuasive power and influence that they are deemed public figures for all purposes. More commonly, those classed as public figures have thrust themselves to the forefront of particular public controversies in order to influence the resolution of the issues involved. In either event, they invite attention and comment.

. . . [A] private individual . . . has not accepted public office or assumed an "influential role in ordering society." *Curtis Publishing Co. v. Butts*, 388 U.S. at 164. . . . Thus, private individuals are not only more vulnerable to injury than public officials and public figures; they are also more deserving of recovery.

For these reasons we conclude that the States should retain substantial latitude in their efforts to enforce a legal remedy for defamatory falsehood injurious to the reputation of a private individual. The extension of the *New York Times* test proposed by the *Rosenbloom* plurality would abridge this legitimate state interest to a degree that we find unacceptable. And it would occasion the additional difficulty of forcing state and federal judges to decide on an *ad hoc* basis which publications address issues of "general or public interest." . . .

We hold that, so long as they do not impose liability without fault, the States may define for themselves the appropriate standard of liability for a publisher or broadcaster of defamatory falsehood injurious to a private individual. This approach . . . recognizes the strength of the legitimate state interest in compensating private individuals for wrongful injury to reputation, yet shields the press and broadcast media from the rigors of strict liability for defamation. At least this conclusion obtains where, as here, the substance of the defamatory statement "makes substantial danger to reputation apparent." This phrase places in perspective the conclusion we announce today. Our inquiry would involve considerations somewhat different from those discussed above if a State purported to condition civil liability on a factual misstatement whose content did not warn a reasonably prudent editor or broadcaster of its defamatory potential. . . . Such a case is not now before us, and we intimate no view as to its proper resolution.

IV

. . . [W]e endorse this approach in recognition of the strong and legitimate state interest in compensating private individuals for injury to reputation. But this countervailing state interest extends no further than compensation for actual injury. For the reasons stated below, we hold that the States may not permit recovery of presumed or punitive damages, at least when liability is not based on a showing of knowledge of falsity or reckless disregard for the truth.

The common law of defamation is an oddity of tort law, . . . the existence of injury is presumed from the fact of publication. Juries may award substantial sums as compensation for supposed damage to reputation without any proof that such harm actually occurred. The largely uncontrolled discretion . . . of presumed damages invites juries to punish unpopular opinion rather than to compensate individuals for injury sustained. . . .

. . . It is necessary to restrict defamation plaintiffs who do not prove knowledge of falsity or reckless disregard for the truth to compensation for actual injury. We need not define "actual injury," as trial courts have wide experience in framing appropriate jury instructions in tort actions. Suffice it to say that actual injury is not limited to out-of-pocket loss. Indeed, the more customary types of actual harm inflicted by defamatory falsehood include impairment of reputation and standing in the community, personal humiliation, and mental anguish and suffering. Of course, juries must be limited by appropriate instructions, and all awards must be supported by competent evidence concerning the injury, although there need be no evidence which assigns an actual dollar value to the injury.

. . . Like the doctrine of presumed damages, jury discretion to award punitive damages unnecessarily exacerbates the danger of media self-censorship, but, unlike the former rule, punitive damages are wholly irrelevant to the state interest that justifies a negligence standard for private defamation actions. They are not compensation for injury. Instead, they are private fines levied by civil juries to punish reprehensible conduct and to deter its future occurrence. In short, the private defamation plaintiff who establishes liability under a less demanding standard than that stated by *New York Times* may recover only such damages as are sufficient to compensate him for actual injury.

V

Notwithstanding our refusal to extend the *New York Times* privilege to defamation of private individuals, respondent contends that we should affirm the judgment below on the ground that petitioner is either a public official or a public figure. There is little basis for the former assertion. Several years prior to the present incident, petitioner had served briefly on housing committees appointed by the mayor of Chicago, but at the time of publication he had never held any remunerative governmental position. Respondent admits this but argues that petitioner's appearance at the coroner's inquest rendered him a de facto public official. Our cases recognize no such concept. Respondent's suggestion would sweep all lawyers under the *New York Times* rule as officers of the court and distort the plain meaning of the public official category beyond all recognition. We decline to follow it.

Respondent's characterization of petitioner as a public figure raises a different question. . . .

That designation may rest on either of two alternative bases. In some instances an individual may achieve such pervasive fame or notoriety that he becomes a public figure for all purposes and in all contexts. More commonly, an individual voluntarily injects himself or is drawn into a particular public controversy and thereby becomes a public figure for a limited range of issues. In either case such persons assume special prominence in the resolution of public questions.

Petitioner has long been active in community and professional affairs. He has served as an officer of local civic groups and of various professional organizations, and he has published several books and articles on legal subjects. Although petitioner was consequently well known in some circles, he had achieved no general fame or notoriety in the community. . . . We would not lightly assume that a citizen's participation in community and professional affairs rendered him a public figure for all purposes. Absent clear evidence of general fame or notoriety in the community, and pervasive involvement in the affairs of society, an individual should not be deemed a public personality for all aspects of his life. It is preferable to reduce the public-figure question to a more meaningful context by looking to the nature and extent of an individual's participation in the particular controversy giving rise to the defamation.

In this context it is plain that petitioner was not a public figure. He played a minimal role at the coroner's inquest, and his participation related solely to his representation of a private client. He took no part in the criminal prosecution of Officer Nuccio. Moreover, he never discussed either the criminal or civil litigation with the press and was never quoted as having done so. He plainly did not thrust himself into the vortex of this public issue, nor did he engage the public's attention in an attempt to influence its outcome. We are persuaded that the trial court did not err in refusing to characterize petitioner as a public figure for the purpose of this litigation. . . .

[JUSTICE BLACKMUN filed a concurring opinion and CHIEF JUSTICE BURGER filed a dissent.]

JUSTICE DOUGLAS, dissenting. . . .

. . . The standard announced today leaves the States free to "define for themselves the appropriate standard of liability for a publisher or broadcaster" in the circumstances of this case. This of course leaves the simple negligence standard as an option. . . . I fear that it may well be the reasonable man who refrains from speaking. . . .

JUSTICE BRENNAN, dissenting.

. . . Under a reasonable-care regime, publishers and broadcasters will have to make prepublication judgments about juror assessment of such diverse considerations as the size, operating procedures, and financial condition of the newsgathering system, as well as the relative costs and benefits of instituting less frequent and more costly reporting at a higher level of accuracy. . . . Moreover, in contrast to proof by clear and convincing evidence required under the *New York Times* test, the burden of proof for reasonable care will doubtless be the preponderance of the evidence. . . .

. . . Moreover, the Court's broad-ranging examples of "actual injury," including impairment of reputation and standing in the community, as well as personal humiliation, and mental anguish and suffering, inevitably allow a jury bent on punishing expression of unpopular views a formidable weapon for doing so.

JUSTICE WHITE, dissenting.

For some 200 years — from the very founding of the Nation — the law of defamation and right of the ordinary citizen to recover for false publication injurious to his reputation have been almost exclusively the business of state courts and legislatures. Under the typical state defamation law, the defamed citizen had to prove only a false publication that would subject him to hatred, contempt, or ridicule. Given such publication, general damage to reputation was presumed, while punitive damages required proof of additional facts. The law governing the defamation of private citizens remained untouched by the First Amendment because until relatively recently, the consistent view of the Court was that libelous words constitute a class of speech wholly unprotected by the First Amendment, subject only to limited exceptions carved out since 1964. . . .

II

. . . Scant, if any, evidence exists that the First Amendment was intended to abolish the common law of libel, at least to the extent of depriving ordinary citizens of meaningful redress against their defamers. . . .

The central meaning of *New York Times*, and for me the First Amendment as it relates to libel laws, is that . . . the citizen has the privilege of criticizing his government and its officials. . . .

III

. . . The press today is vigorous and robust. To me, it is quite incredible to suggest that threats of libel suits from private citizens are causing the press to refrain from publishing the truth. I know of no hard facts to support that proposition, and the Court furnishes none.

The communications industry has increasingly become concentrated in a few powerful hands operating very lucrative businesses reaching across the Nation and into almost every home. Neither the industry as a whole nor its individual components are easily intimidated. . . . Requiring them to pay for the occasional damage they do to private reputation will play no substantial part in their future performance or their existence.

In any event, if the Court's principal concern is to protect the communications industry from large libel judgments, it would appear that its new requirements with respect to general and punitive damages would be ample protection. Why it also feels compelled to escalate the threshold standard of liability I cannot fathom, particularly when this will eliminate in many instances the plaintiff's possibility of securing a judicial determination that the damaging publication was indeed false, whether or not he is entitled to recover money damages. . . .

. . . [S]uch statements serve no purpose whatsoever in furthering the public interest or the search for truth but, on the contrary, may frustrate that search and at the same time inflict great injury on the defenseless individual. The owners of the press and the stockholders of the communications enterprises can much better bear the burden. And if they cannot, the public at large should somehow pay for what is essentially a public benefit derived at private expense.

IV

Not content with escalating the threshold requirements of establishing liability, the Court abolishes the ordinary damages rule. . . .

[D]amage to reputation is recurringly difficult to prove and . . . requiring actual proof would repeatedly destroy any chance for adequate compensation. . . .

With a flourish of the pen, the Court also discards the prevailing rule in libel and slander actions that punitive damages may be awarded on the classic grounds of common-law malice, that is, " '[a]ctual malice' in the sense of ill will or fraud or reckless indifference to consequences." C. McCormick, Law of Damages § 118, p. 431 (1935). . . .

. . . For almost 200 years, punitive damages and the First Amendment have peacefully coexisted. . . .

V

I fail to see how the quality or quantity of public debate will be promoted by further emasculation of state libel laws for the benefit of the news media. If anything, this trend may provoke a new and radical imbalance in the communications process. . . .

NOTES

(1) *Public Figures.* In a series of cases since *Gertz v. Welch*, the Court has continued the trend, started in *Gertz*, of narrowing the category of persons who will be considered public figures.

(a) In *Time Inc. v. Firestone*, 424 U.S. 448 (1976), the wife of "the scion of one of America's wealthier industrial families" was divorced by her husband after a well-publicized trial. The court granted the divorce because "neither of the parties has shown the least susceptibility to domestication," but it found much of the testimony about the "extramarital escapades" of both partners to be "unreliable." *Time Magazine*, however, reported that the divorce had been granted on grounds of "extreme cruelty and adultery," and that led to Mrs. Firestone's libel action. Writing for the Court, Justice Rehnquist ruled that she was not a public figure: "Respondent did not assume any role of especial prominence in the affairs of society, other than perhaps Palm Beach society, and she did not thrust herself to the forefront of any particular public controversy in order to influence the resolution of the issues involved in it." The Court rejected the argument that she had become a public figure because the divorce was a "cause celebre." That approach would have extended the *New York Times* rule to all public controversies. The case was remanded because the record "afford[ed] no basis" for a conclusion that a factfinder had made a determination of fault to satisfy *Gertz*.

Justice Brennan dissented, urging outright reversal on grounds that *Gertz v. Welch* should not have been extended to reporting of judicial proceedings but that the "actual-malice standard of *New York Times*" should apply. Justice White would have upheld the verdict for plaintiff because, under his *Gertz* dissent, the First Amendment does not require a fault standard and, "in any event, fault was properly found below." Justice Marshall dissented because he considered the respondent a public figure. Justice Powell, joined by Justice Stewart, concurred, but wrote separately emphasizing the absence of fault by *Time Magazine*.

For additional discussion of *Firestone* and the privilege of neutral reportage as applied to both private individuals and the government, see Katheryn Sowle, *Defamation and the First Amendment: The Case for a Constitutional Privilege of Fair Report*, 54 N.Y.U. L. Rev. 469 (1979).

(b) In *Hutchinson v. Proxmire*, 443 U.S. 111 (1979), (discussed at § 13.08[1], Note (4), in connection with the Speech or Debate Clause), the plaintiff, who had been designated by Senator Proxmire to receive the "Golden Fleece Award," was not a public figure. Writing for the majority, Chief Justice Burger opined: "On this record, Hutchinson's activities and public profile are much like those of countless members of his profession. His published writings reach a relatively small category of professionals concerned with research in human behavior. To the extent the subject of his published writings became a matter of controversy, it was a consequence of the Golden Fleece Award. Clearly those charged with defamation cannot, by their own conduct, create their own defense by making the claimant a public figure." Justice Brennan dissented.

(c) In *Wolston v. Reader's Digest, Inc.*, 443 U.S. 157 (1979), the plaintiff sued because a book, published in 1974, described him as a "Soviet agent." He had been convicted of criminal contempt in 1958 for failing to appear before a grand jury investigating alleged Soviet espionage. Justice Rehnquist's majority opinion rejected the argument that Wolston's 1958 conviction made him a public figure with regard to comment on espionage activities during an earlier period. Justice Rehnquist emphasized the fact that Wolston had not thrust himself into public controversy. If conviction rendered someone a public figure, writers would have an "open season" to defame those convicted of crimes.

Justice Blackmun, joined by Justice Marshall, concurred on grounds that, even if Wolston was a public figure in 1958, he no longer had that status in 1974. While this analysis might leave historians subject to a greater risk of liability than contemporary journalists, a historian has more time for reflection and for checking the accuracy of sources. Justice Brennan, in dissent, argued that Wolston remained a public figure in 1974.

(2) For a discussion of libel law after *Gertz*, see David Anderson, *Is Libel Law Worth Reforming?*, 140 U. Pa. L. Rev. 487, 488 (1991) ("The remnants of American libel law provide little protection for reputation. The actual malice rule of *New York Times v. Sullivan* does not adequately protect the press, so courts have imposed many other constitutional limitations on the libel action. Cumulatively, these make the remedy largely illusory. Most victims of defamation cannot meet the actual malice requirement and many who can are thwarted by other constitutional obstacles.").

[2] Opinions

MILKOVICH v. LORAIN JOURNAL CO., 497 U.S. 1 (1990). In *Milkovich*, the Court held that no "additional separate constitutional privilege for 'opinion' is required to ensure the freedom of expression guaranteed by the First Amendment." Plaintiff Milkovich was a high school wrestling coach. He was accused of encouraging a fight that broke out at a wrestling match. After a hearing, the Ohio High School Athletic Association (OHSAA) disciplined plaintiff and placed his team on probation. Parents and wrestlers challenged the OHSAA hearing in federal district court, which overturned the results of the hearing on due process grounds. The day after the court's decision, an article by Thomas Diadiun appeared in a local newspaper owned by Lorain Journal Co.

Milkovich sued both the Lorain Journal Co. and Diadiun for defamation, alleging that the article implied that he had perjured himself in the District Court action. The Ohio trial court dismissed Milkovich's defamation on summary judgment and its decision was affirmed on appeal.

Writing for a 7-2 majority, Chief Justice Rehnquist stated that certain kinds of speech "may not be the subject of defamation actions" — for example, "rhetorical hyperbole." The First Amendment, however, did not protect all defamatory statements that are "categorized as 'opinion' as opposed to 'fact.'" Chief Justice Rehnquist said the statement in *Gertz v. Welch* that "there is no such thing as a false idea" does not "create a wholesale defamation exemption for anything that might be labeled 'opinion.'"

Chief Justice Rehnquist noted "that expressions of 'opinion' may often imply an assertion of objective fact." Many statements of opinion can imply defamatory facts. "Even if the speaker states the facts upon which he bases his opinion, if those facts are either incorrect or incomplete, or if his assessment of them is erroneous, the statement may still imply a false assertion of fact." Nor can the use of prefatory phrases eliminate liability for statements that are defamatory. Saying "[i]n my opinion, Jones is a liar," can be as destructive to reputation as saying "Jones is a liar." Similarly, the use of the words, "I think," do not insulate the speaker from liability.

The Court found that the article had implied that Milkovich had committed perjury. "This is not the sort of loose, figurative or hyperbolic language which would negate the impression that the writer was seriously maintaining petitioner committed the crime of perjury. Nor does the general tenor of the article negate this impression."

Justice Brennan, joined by Justice Marshall, dissented. Agreeing that the Court does not afford special protection for statements of opinion that implied underlying facts, Justice Brennan argued that "the challenged statements cannot reasonably be interpreted as either stating or implying defamatory facts about" Milkovich. Instead, he found that the article makes clear that the author was "simply guessing." It was riddled with cautionary words like "seemed," "probably," and "apparently." Moreover, "the tone and format of the piece notify readers to expect speculation and personal judgment. The tone is pointed, exaggerated and heavily laden with emotional rhetoric and outrage." In format, the article "is a signed editorial column with a photograph of the columnist and the logo 'TD Says.'" The article amounted to a statement of "conjecture" and conjecture cannot be actionable for defamation.

Justice Brennan gave some examples of conjecture: "Did NASA officials ignore sound warnings that the Challenger Space Shuttle would explode? Did Cuban-American leaders arrange for John Fitzgerald Kennedy's assassination? Was Kurt Waldheim a Nazi officer? Such questions are matters of public concern long before all the facts are unearthed, if they ever are. Conjecture is a means of fueling a national discourse on such questions and stimulating public pressure for answers from those who know more."

[3] Quoted Material

MASSON v. NEW YORKER MAGAZINE, INC., 501 U.S. 496 (1991). In *Masson*, the Court considered the applicability of the actual knowledge/reckless disregard standard of *New York Times v. Sullivan* to allegedly altered quotations that the defendant, *The New Yorker* magazine, attributed to the plaintiff, Jeffrey Masson. In 1980, Jeffrey Masson, a psychoanalyst, was appointed Projects Director of the Sigmund Freud Archives in New Haven, Connecticut. Soon after, Masson became disillusioned with Freudian psychology and, in 1981, was terminated as a result of his public advancement of his theories.

In 1983 and 1984, *The New Yorker* published an article based on an interview with Masson about his relationship with the Archives. The reporter who had conducted the interview taped the conversation with Masson. The printed article contained lengthy quotations attributed to Masson. Masson then brought a libel action based on these altered passages, proving the alterations with the reporter's tapes of the interview. The parties had agreed that Masson was a public figure and had to demonstrate that a reasonable finder of fact could find that the article was published with actual knowledge of falsity or reckless disregard as to whether the information was true or false.

Writing for the majority, Justice Kennedy indicated that quotations can cause harm by attribution of, "an untrue factual assertion to the speaker" — for example, a fabricated admission of a conviction. Alternatively, quotations regardless of their factual accuracy can cause harm, "the attribution may result in injury to reputation because the manner of expression or even the fact that the statement was made indicates a negative personal trait or an attitude the speaker does not hold." For example, John Lennon of the Beatles was once quoted as saying, "[w]e're more popular than Jesus Christ now." Quotations have peculiar force because they are essentially admissions. Justice Kennedy rejected Masson's argument that knowledge of the alteration alone demonstrated actual malice.[36] Justice Kennedy explained that the common law of libel makes exceptions for errors of grammar or syntax, "overlooks minor inaccuracies and concentrates upon substantial truth." The Court held that error could not make a document false "so long as the substance, the gist, the sting, of the libelous charge be justified." Put differently, the Court does not consider a statement false unless it "would have a different effect on the mind of the reader from that which the pleaded truth would have produced." Even a deliberate alteration would not make a statement false unless the alteration effected a "material change in the meaning conveyed by the statement."

As the appeal came up on summary judgment granted in favor of the defendant, the Court drew "all justifiable inferences" in favor of the non-moving party. Accordingly, the Court assumed, except as otherwise indicated by the taped transcripts, that Masson

---

[36] In a footnote, Justice Kennedy explained:

The existence of both a speaker and a reporter; the translation between two media, speech and the printed word; the addition of punctuation; and the practical necessity to edit and make intelligible a speaker's perhaps rambling comments, all make it misleading to suggest that a quotation will be reconstructed with complete accuracy. The use or absence of punctuation may distort a speaker's meaning, for example, where that meaning turns upon a speaker's emphasis of a particular word. In other cases, if a speaker makes an obvious misstatement, for example by unconscious substitution of one name for another, a journalist might alter the speaker's words but preserve his intended meaning. And conversely, an exact quotation out of context can distort meaning, although the speaker did use each reported word.

was "correct in denying that he made the statements attributed to him by" the reporter. The Court further assumed that the alterations were made with actual knowledge of falsity or reckless disregard.

Considering each alleged altered passage separately, the Court found that in five out of six of them, a jury could find material differences. In one passage concerning his intentions for a house he was planning to occupy, the article quoted Masson as stating he wanted to have " 'sex, women, and fun.' " The tape revealed that Masson had actually stated that he wanted to have great parties. The article also incorrectly quoted Masson as saying that he was an " 'intellectual gigolo,' " which he had never said. One other quotation had Masson stating his intention to " 'pass women on to each other' " in a context that the Court found "may not even refer to Freud house activities." As a matter of law, the Court held that this change could be found to have materially altered the quoted material.

In another passage in which Masson described his reasons for adopting his abandoned family name "Moussaieff," the article quoted Masson as making the change because " 'it sounded better.' " On tape Masson said he " 'just liked' " the other name. In contrast to the other passages at issue, the Court found that, as a matter of law, this alteration did not materially alter the meaning of Masson's statement.

Another passage in the article concern a conversation between Masson and the head of the Sigmund Freud Archives in which the latter pleaded for Masson to keep a "stoic silence." The tapes revealed that Masson had actually "described himself as willing to undergo a scandal in order to shine the light of publicity upon the actions of the Freud Archives," not as the " 'wrong man' to do 'the honorable thing' " which the article reported. The Court held that a trier of fact could find this alteration material.

Justice White wrote an opinion concurring in part and dissenting in part, in which Justice Scalia joined. Justice White agreed with the application of the reckless disregard standard to quotations but disagreed that it only applied to material alterations. In effect, "the reporter may lie a little, but not too much."

[4] Jurisdictional and Other Procedural Rules

BOSE CORPORATION v. CONSUMERS UNION OF UNITED STATES, INC., 466 U.S. 485 (1984). In *Bose*, the Court (6-3) significantly extended the media's First Amendment protection by ruling that a district court's finding of malice is not subject to the deferential "clearly erroneous" standard accorded findings of fact by Rule 52(a) of the Federal Rules of Civil Procedure. Instead, courts of appeal must make an independent examination of the entire record to determine "whether the evidence in the record is sufficient to cross the constitutional threshold that bars the entry of any judgment that is not supported by clear and convincing proof of 'actual malice.' " The case grew out of an article in the magazine *Consumer Reports* that had disparaged a loudspeaker system manufactured by Bose Corporation.[37] The District Court found that defendant reported that the sound transmitted by the speakers "tended to wander along the wall, 'rather than about the room.' " The District Court also found that the "about the room" statement had been made with knowledge that it was false or with reckless disregard of its truth or falsity. A key issue in the District Court's finding of malice was the state of mind of an engineer employed by Consumers Union, and Justice

---

[37] Significantly, the District Court ruled that Bose Corporation was a "public figure" for purposes of a product disparagement suit. Because the District Court determined the Corporation to be a public figure, it applied the reckless disregard standard of *New York Times v. Sullivan*. See *Bose v. Consumers Union of United States, Inc.*, 508 F. Supp. 1249 (D. Mass. 1981). The Corporation's public figure status was not contested before the Supreme Court.

Stevens' majority opinion acknowledged that it "surely does not stretch the language of [Rule 52(a)] to characterize an inquiry into what a person knew at a given point in time as a question of fact."

The majority opinion recalled that *New York Times v. Sullivan* held that an appellate court had an obligation to review the record independently to determine whether the judgment constituted an infringement of First Amendment rights. While *New York Times* arose from a state court, "surely it would pervert the concept of federalism for this Court to . . . review . . . state-court judgments [more extensively] than . . . the judgments of intermediate federal courts."

Justice Stevens' majority opinion tried to reconcile the apparent inconsistency between its holding and Rule 52(a), pointing out that the rule does not forbid an independent examination of the record and that there are some cases in which the presumption of correctness is stronger than others. Three characteristics of the *New York Times* "actual malice" rule support an independent review of the record by an appellate court: "First, the common law heritage of the rule itself assigns an especially broad role to the judge in applying it to specific factual situations. Second, the content of the rule is not revealed simply by its literal test, but rather is given meaning through the evolutionary process of common law adjudication; though the source of the rule is found in the Constitution, it is nevertheless largely a judge-made rule of law. Finally, the constitutional values protected by the rule make it imperative that judges — and in some cases judges of this Court — make sure that it is correctly applied."

The Court went on to emphasize that there are some categories of speech that have been held to be outside the protection of the First Amendment, particularly "fighting words," incitements to riot, obscenity, child pornography, and certain forms of libelous speech. "In such cases, the Court has regularly conducted an independent review of the record both to be sure that the speech in question actually falls within the unprotected category . . . in an effort to ensure that protected expression will not be inhibited."

Justice Stevens concluded that the statement by the witness that the sound moved "about the room" was "the sort of inaccuracy that is commonplace in the forum of robust debate" and that the Court of Appeals was correct in concluding, notwithstanding the findings of the District Court, that "the difference between hearing violin sounds move around the room and hearing them wander back and forth fits easily within the breathing space that gives life to the First Amendment."

Justice Rehnquist, joined by Justice O'Connor, dissented on ground that "actual knowledge" of falsity is a "pure question of fact" and not the kind of mixed question of fact and law involved in a determination as to whether, for example, material appeals to the "prurient interest" or is "patently offensive." While issues of "falsity" and "actual malice" may be close in this case, Justice Rehnquist concluded that he could not "join the majority's sanctioning of factual second guessing by appellate courts." Justice White also dissented in a separate opinion.

NOTES

(1) *Appellate Review of Factual Findings. Harte-Hanks Communications, Inc. v. Connaughton*, 491 U.S. 657 (1989), applied the *Bose* rule to a jury trial to review whether the record supported findings of actual malice, rather than subsidiary facts.

(2) *Personal Jurisdiction.* In *Keeton v. Hustler Magazine, Inc.*, 465 U.S. 770 (1984), the Court unanimously ruled that *Hustler's* monthly sale of 10–15,000 magazines in New Hampshire constituted sufficient "minimum contacts" to support an assertion of personal jurisdiction over a nonresident defendant magazine. Moreover, the New York plaintiff's lack of residence and other contacts with New Hampshire could not defeat this jurisdiction which was based on defendant's minimum contacts. Justice Rehnquist's

opinion also rejected the lower court's argument that the defendant's liability for nationwide damages under New Hampshire's "single publication" rule, together with New Hampshire's uniquely long statute of limitations, resulted in an unfair assertion of jurisdiction over a nonresident defendant.

The Court reached a similar result in the companion case of *Calder v. Jones*, 465 U.S. 783 (1984). In *Calder*, the plaintiff sued the *National Enquirer* and its distributor in a libel suit in California. Neither the magazine nor the distributor objected to California jurisdiction. The Court also allowed plaintiff to draw into California the writer of the article and editor of the paper, both of whom were Florida residents. The Court concluded that "intentional, and allegedly tortious, actions were expressly aimed at California," as plaintiff lived and worked there. Such acts created sufficient contacts with the forum state. First Amendment concerns would not defeat the otherwise valid jurisdiction.

(3) *Summary Judgment.* In *Anderson v. Liberty Lobby*, 477 U.S. 242 (1986), the Court outlined the standard to be applied when the defendant moves for summary judgment on the issue of malice. The plaintiffs, Liberty Lobby, Inc., had moved for summary judgment, relying on evidence of inaccuracies and the failure of the defendants to check out allegedly unreliable sources. The defendant had asserted that the author had thoroughly researched the articles and relied on numerous sources. Relying on the "preponderance of evidence" standard, the Court of Appeals had ruled that the motion for summary judgment should be denied, as a jury could or could not have reasonably found malice. Justice White's majority (6-3) opinion concluded: "When determining if a genuine factual issue as to actual malice exists in a libel suit brought by a public figure, the trial judge must bear in mind the actual quantum and quality of proof necessary to support liability under *New York Times*." Consequently, "where the factual dispute concerns actual malice, clearly a material issue in a *New York Times* case, the appropriate summary judgment question will be whether the evidence in the record could support a reasonable jury finding either that the plaintiff has shown actual malice by clear and convincing evidence or that the plaintiff has not." A judge must evaluate a motion for summary judgment or directed verdict "through the prism of the substantive evidentiary burden. The question here is whether a jury could reasonably find either that the plaintiff proved his case by the quality and quantity of evidence required by the governing law or that he did not." The case was remanded for a determination by the trial judge as to whether, applying the *New York Times* standard, the jury could have found for either side.

Justice Brennan's dissent was based on his concern that the majority's opinion could lead to trial judges' deciding factual issues that properly belong to the jury. Justice Rehnquist's dissent, joined by Chief Justice Burger, questioned the practical significance of the decision and the difficulty of applying it to concrete cases.

(4) *Communications Concerning Candidates for Government Posts.* In *McDonald v. Smith*, 472 U.S. 479 (1985), a unanimous Court rejected the claim that the Petition Clause of the First Amendment provides absolute immunity to a defendant who expresses libelous falsehoods in a letter to the President of the United States. The case arose from two letters written to President Reagan containing allegedly false and damaging statements about a person being considered for federal office. In a subsequent libel action, the defendant asserted an absolute immunity under the First Amendment's Petition Clause. Chief Justice Burger's opinion concluded, however, that the Petition Clause provided no greater rights to a libel defendant than did Speech and Press Clauses. As plaintiff was an applicant for the post of United States Attorney, his defamation action would have to meet the *New York Times v. Sullivan* actual knowledge/reckless disregard standard. Justice Brennan concurred in an opinion joined by Justices Marshall and Blackmun.

[5]　Matters of Public Concern

DUN & BRADSTREET v. GREENMOSS BUILDERS, INC., 472 U.S. 749 (1985). In *Dun & Bradstreet*, the Court held that the First Amendment failed to restrict the damages that a private individual could obtain from a publisher for a libel that did not involve a matter of public concern. The Court concluded that the *Gertz v. Welch* decision did not control. Rather, plaintiff could recover presumed and punitive damages without a showing of "actual malice," as the defamatory statements did not involve a matter of public concern.

Defendant Dun & Bradstreet was a credit reporting agency which provided subscribers with detailed financial information of certain businesses. The reported information was strictly confidential; all subscribers agreed not to reveal the information to anyone. On July 26, 1976, defendant provided a report to five subscribers, indicating that respondent construction company had filed for bankruptcy. "This report was false and grossly misrepresented respondent's assets and liabilities."

Greenmoss brought a defamation action in state court. At trial, it was established that the error in the report was made by a seventeen-year-old high school student who had inadvertently attributed to Greenmoss a bankruptcy petition filed by its employee. Although defendant routinely verified its information with the business being examined before reporting, it did not follow its practice in this case. The jury awarded plaintiff $50,000 in presumed damages and $300,000 in punitive damages.

Justice Powell, writing for a plurality of three, stated that the cases establishing constitutional protection for defamatory speech involving public officials and public figures all involved public issues. In *Gertz*, the Court balanced the stronger state interest in compensating private individuals for injuries to reputation against the same First Amendment interest at stake in *New York Times v. Sullivan*. The result was that a state was prohibited from allowing recovery of presumed and punitive damages absent a showing of actual malice.

The Court had never considered the applicability of the *Gertz* balancing test when the defamatory statement does not involve a matter of public concern. The First Amendment interest in statements concerning non-public issues, however, is of less importance than the interest at stake in *Gertz*. Indeed, the Court has "long recognized that not all speech is of equal First Amendment importance."[38]

According to *Connick v. Meyers*, to determine whether a public concern is involved the Court must look to the "content, form, and context . . . as revealed by the whole record." Considering the report as a whole, it did not concern a public issue. The speech was "solely in the individual interest of the speaker and its specific business audience. This particular interest warrants no special protection when — as in this case — the speech is wholly false and clearly damaging to the victim's business reputation." Moreover, as the report was revealed to only five subscribers who were bound to a confidentiality agreement, it was not integral to the flow of commercial information. "There is simply no credible argument that this type of credit reporting requires

---

[38] On many occasions the Court has recognized that certain speech is less integral to the First Amendment. For example, obscene remarks and "fighting words" have no First Amendment protection. Commercial speech affords the best example of reduced constitutional protection. In *Ohralik v. Ohio State Bar Ass'n*, 436 U.S. 447 (1978) the Court stated that there are " '[n]umerous examples . . . of communications that are regulated without offending the First Amendment, such as the exchange of information about securities, corporate proxy statements, the exchange of price and production information among competitors, and employers' threats of retaliation for the labor activities of employees.' " On the other hand, political speech is given the highest First Amendment protection.

special protection to ensure that 'debate on public issues [will] be uninhibited, robust, and wide-open.' "

Like advertising, the speech at issue is solely motivated by profit and, therefore, less likely to be deterred by state regulation. "Arguably, the reporting here was also more objectively verifiable than speech deserving of greater constitutional protection." The plurality concluded "that permitting recovery of presumed and punitive damages in defamation cases absent a showing of 'actual malice' does not violate the First Amendment when the defamatory statements do not involve matters of public concern."

Chief Justice Burger concurred in the judgment. He agreed with the plurality that the *Gertz* decision is limited to cases involving statements of public concern, and that the statement involved in the instant case involved a matter of private concern. "I continue to believe, however, that *Gertz* was ill-conceived, and therefore agree with Justice White that *Gertz* should be overruled." The Chief Justice also agreed with Justice White that *New York Times v. Sullivan* should be reexamined.

Justice White also concurred in the judgment. He opined that "First Amendment values are not at all served by circulating false statements of facts about public officials." *New York Times* requires that a complaint by a public official must be dismissed unless he establishes a knowing or reckless falsehood. With this high standard, not only will the lie remain but also the plaintiff can rarely get his case to a jury. Even when a plaintiff wins before a jury, appellate courts often overturn the verdict for inadequate proof of this standard. If the case does go to a jury, "the jury will likely return a general verdict" and if the verdict goes against the plaintiff, no judgment will exist "that the publication was false, even though it was without foundation in reality."[38]

The *New York Times* decision could have achieved the necessary goals of protecting the press from oppressive liability by limiting recoverable damages rather than escalating plaintiff's burden of proof. "At the very least, the public official should not have been required to satisfy the actual malice standard where he sought no damages but only to clear his name." The burdens imposed by *Gertz* and *New York Times* engendered expensive discovery and litigation on the workings of the press, how a news story is developed, and the state of mind of the reporter and publisher. Justice White suspected "that the press would be no worse off financially if the common-law rules were to apply and if the judiciary was careful to insist that damages awards be kept within bounds."

Justice Brennan dissented, joined by Justices Marshall, Blackmun and Stevens. Justice Brennan found that the report produced by Dun & Bradstreet involved a matter of public concern, despite the commercial nature of the report. "Time and again we have made clear that speech loses none of its constitutional protection even though it is carried in a form that is 'sold for profit.' " Moreover, information about a company's bankruptcy would greatly interest people in the community in which the company is located and information about bankruptcy informs the citizenry's decisions about economic regulation.

NOTES

(1) *Plaintiff Must Prove Falsity.* In *Philadelphia Newspapers, Inc. v. Hepps,* 475 U.S. 767 (1986), the Court held that private figures alleging defamation by media defendants must bear the burden of proving the falsity of the statements in matters of

---

[38] The jury may be instructed to return separate verdicts on falsity and "actual malice." Thus, there could be a verdict returned for plaintiff on falsity, but against him on "actual malice." Although there would not be a judgment in his favor, the verdict of falsity would set the public record straight.

public concern. The principal stockholder of a chain of convenience stores and his franchisees brought a defamation suit in Pennsylvania state court against the *Philadelphia Inquirer*. The *Inquirer* had published a series of articles accusing the principal plaintiff of having links to the underworld and using those links "to influence the state's governmental processes, both legislative and administrative." Pennsylvania law at the time was consistent with *Gertz v. Welch*, which required a private figure plaintiff bringing a defamation suit against a media defendant to bear the burden of proving negligence or malice. It followed the common law, however, in that the private figure plaintiff did not have to prove the falsity of the media defendant's statements. If the defendant wished to invoke the truth as a defense, it bore the burden of proof.

Writing for the majority, Justice O'Connor held that the private figure plaintiff had the responsibility of proving the falsity of the media defendant's statements. The Court did not consider the standards to be applied to a non-media defendant. Justice O'Connor discussed the Court's prior holdings that dealt with the issue of fault and the important distinctions that could be gleaned from them. First to be considered is whether the plaintiff is a public official or figure, or a private person; second, whether the matter is of public interest or private concern. Relying on *Gertz*, the Court concluded that there was "constitutional requirement that the plaintiff bear the burden of showing falsity, as well as fault, before recovering damages."

Justice Brennan concurred, joined by Justice Blackmun. While the majority reserved the question of whether its holding should apply to nonmedia defendants, Justice Brennan asserted instead that the value of speech did not depend on whether the source was a newspaper or private individual.

Justice Stevens dissented, joined by Chief Justice Burger and Justices White and Rehnquist. The Court had incorrectly looked to its own precedents involving public figures, which legitimately place the burden of persuasion on the plaintiff. "In libel suits brought by private individuals, in contrast, 'the state interest in compensating injury to the reputation of private individuals requires that a different rule should obtain.'"

(2) For additional discussion of constitutional protection against defamation actions, see Arlen Langvardt, *Media Defendants, Public Concerns, and Public Plaintiffs: Toward Fashioning Order from Confusion in Defamation Law*, 49 U. Pitt. L. Rev. 91 (1987); Rodney Smolla, *Dun & Bradstreet, Hepps, and Liberty Lobby: A New Analytic Primer on the Future Course of Defamation*, 75 Geo. L.J. 1519 (1987). For some provocative discussion of the appropriate approach to constitutional protection in this area, see Rodney Smolla, Suing the Press (1986); Symposium, *New Perspectives in the Law of Defamation*, 74 Cal. L. Rev. 677 (1986); Marc Franklin, *Constitutional Libel Law: The Role of Content*, 34 UCLA L. Rev. 1657 (1987); Peter Tiersma, *The Language of Defamation*, 66 Tex. L. Rev. 303 (1987). For comparative perspectives on these issues, see Press Law in Modern Democracies: a Comparative Study (Pnina Lahav, ed., 1986).

[6]　Invasions of Privacy

ZACCHINI v. SCRIPPS-HOWARD, 433 U.S. 562 (1977). In *Zacchini*, the Court (5-4) held that the press did not have a constitutional privilege under the First and Fourteenth Amendments to broadcast matters of public interest that were commercial in nature. State law could grant such a privilege to the press.

This case involved a performer of a "human cannonball" act who brought suit against a local television company. The television station broadcast the performer's entire fifteen-second act during its news program, despite his timely request that the station not film the act.

Writing for the majority, Justice White distinguished *Zacchini* from *Time, Inc. v. Hill.* In *Time,* the Court held that the plaintiff could not recover after being placed in a "false light" for a matter of public interest unless it was done with knowledge of falsity or reckless disregard for the truth. While *Time* involved a "false light" privacy statute, *Zacchini* was an "appropriation" case. " 'The interest protected' in permitting recovery for placing the plaintiff in a false light 'is clearly that of reputation, with the same overtones of mental distress as in defamation.' " In "contrast, the State's interest in permitting a 'right of publicity' is in protecting the proprietary interest of the individual in his act in part to encourage such Entertainment."

Moreover, unlike *Time* and defamation cases previously decided by the Court, *Zacchini* involved "an attempt to broadcast or publish an entire act for which the performer ordinarily gets paid. It is evident, and there is no claim here to the contrary, that petitioner's state-law right of publicity would not serve to prevent respondent from reporting the newsworthy facts about petitioner's act. Wherever the line in particular situations is to be drawn between media reports that are protected and those that are not, we are quite sure that the First and Fourteenth Amendments do not immunize the media when they broadcast a performer's entire act without his consent."

The First Amendment did not immunize such broadcasts any more than it would "privilege respondent to film and broadcast a copyrighted dramatic work without liability to the copyright owner . . . or to film and broadcast a prize fight or a baseball game," if seeing the performance for free on television would render people less inclined to pay to see the act in person. This result went "to the heart of petitioner's ability to earn a living." It also lessened the performer's incentive to make the effort to produce something that was of public interest. There was no First Amendment barrier to Ohio's encouraging such individual effort by protecting it.

Justice Powell dissented, joined by Justices Brennan and Marshall. "I do not view respondent's action as comparable to unauthorized commercial broadcasts of sporting events, theatrical performances, and the like where the broadcaster keeps the profits. There is no suggestion here that respondent made any such use of the film. Instead, it simply reported on what petitioner concedes to be a newsworthy event." News editors may decline to cover events that might be considered an entire performance. Since Zacchini made his performance newsworthy, he should not complain when he cannot now seek to regulate the "means and manner" of such coverage.

Instead of the majority's "quantitative analysis of the performer's behavior — is this or is this not his entire act?," Justice Powell would substitute another approach. "When a film is used, as here, for a routine portion of a regular news program, I would hold that the First Amendment protects the station from a 'right of publicity' or 'appropriation' suit, absent a strong showing by the plaintiff that the news broadcast was a subterfuge or cover for private or commercial exploitation."

NOTES

(1) *False Light Privacy.* In *Time Inc. v. Hill,* 385 U.S. 374 (1967), which was distinguished in the *Zacchini* case, the Court (6-3) applied the *New York Times v. Sullivan* standard to an action brought against a magazine under the New York "right of privacy" statute. The New York Court of Appeals had previously construed the statute to provide an absolute defense if the defendant truthfully reported newsworthy events. Thus, *Time Inc. v. Hill* did not involve a pure invasion of privacy action but was based on a claim that a national magazine had portrayed the plaintiff in a false light by describing, in an allegedly fictitious manner, the entry into plaintiff's home by a group of escaped convicts and the holding of his family as hostages. "We hold," wrote Justice Brennan, "that the constitutional protections for speech and press preclude the

application of the New York statute to redress false reports of matters of public interest in the absence of proof that the defendant published the report with knowledge of its falsity or in reckless disregard for the truth."

Time, Inc. v. Hill was decided shortly before *New York Times v. Sullivan* had been extended to public figures in *Curtis Publishing Co. v. Butts* and *Associated Press v. Walker*. In view of *Gertz v. Welch*, which refused to extend the *New York Times'* rule in defamation cases to private persons involved in matters of public concern, is there any justification for the decision in *Time, Inc. v. Hill*, which involved a private plaintiff claiming damages for invasion of privacy resulting from a fictitious portrayal of an event in his life? *But cf.* W. PAGE KEETON, DAN DOBBS, ROBERT KEETON & DAVID OWEN, PROSSER AND KEETON ON TORTS 866 (5th ed. 1984) (arguing that tort law itself imposes a reckless disregard requirement for a false light privacy action).

(2) *True Privacy Actions.* New York, as noted above, construed its privacy statute to permit the defense of truthful reporting of newsworthy events. Does the First Amendment require such a construction, or could a state make such truthful reporting actionable if it invaded plaintiff's privacy? In *Cox Broadcasting Corp. v. Cohn*, 420 U.S. 469 (1975), discussed at § 14.02, in connection with the reporting of governmental affairs, the Court held that a broadcaster could not be held liable for reporting official court records about a rape case. Because the case reported about was already a matter of public record, it was not necessary to decide whether a privacy statute could ever be held applicable to the truthful reporting of newsworthy events.

FLORIDA STAR v. B.J.F., 491 U.S. 524 (1989). In *Florida Star*, the Court reversed on constitutional grounds a Florida decision holding a newspaper liable for truthfully reporting the name of a rape victim, which was lawfully obtained from a police report. The *Florida Star* is a weekly newspaper published in Jacksonville, Florida; it carries a regular feature called "Police Reports." On October 20, 1983, B.J.F. reported to the county police department that she had been raped and robbed. The department prepared a report and left it in the press room. In violation of internal police department policy, the police report inadvertently included the full name of the rape victim. A "reporter-trainee" copied the report verbatim. Based on this copy of the report, a one-paragraph entry of the incident, which included the victim's full name, ran in the "robberies" subsection in the "Police Reports" column on October 29, 1983. The newspaper had a policy of not reporting the names of rape victims.

Section 794.03 of the Florida Code made it a crime to "print, publish, or broadcast" the name of a rape victim. B.J.F. sued the newspaper, claiming it negligently violated this law.[39] She testified "that she had heard about the article from fellow workers and acquaintances; that her mother had received several threatening phone calls from a man who stated that he would rape B.J.F. again; and that these events forced B.J.F. to change her phone number and residence, to seek police protection, and to obtain mental health counseling." The trial judge directed a verdict against the *Florida Star* on the issue of negligence, finding the *Florida Star* negligent *per se* for violation of the nondisclosure law.

Writing for a 6-3 majority, Justice Marshall initially noted that this case followed a "trilogy of cases" that had tested the balance between the media's First Amendment right to report the news truthfully and the individual's right to privacy. The trilogy consisted of *Cox Broadcasting Corp. v. Cohn, Smith v. Daily Mail Publishing Co.* and *Oklahoma Publishing Co. v. District Court.*[40] After noting this case's similarity to *Cox Broadcasting*, Justice Marshall opined "that case cannot be fairly read as controlling

---

[39] B.J.F. settled her suit with the police department.

[40] *Cox Broadcasting* and *Daily Mail* are described in § 14.02. In *Oklahoma Publishing*, the Court struck

here" because *Cox Broadcasting* involved court records and this case did not. However, Justice Marshall did state that this case fit into a principle established in *Daily Mail*: "[I]f a newspaper lawfully obtains truthful information about a matter of public significance then state officials may not constitutionally punish publication of the information, absent a need to further a state interest of the highest order."

The Court held that there were "three separate considerations" for such "ample protection" of the media. "First, because the *Daily Mail* formulation only protects the publication of information which a newspaper has 'lawfully obtain[ed],' the government retains ample means of safeguarding significant interests upon which publication may impinge, including protecting a rape victim's anonymity. To the extent sensitive information rests in private hands, the government may under some circumstances forbid its nonconsensual acquisition, thereby bringing outside of the *Daily Mail* principle the publication of any information so acquired. To the extent sensitive information is in the government's custody, it has even greater power to forestall or mitigate the injury caused by its release. The government may classify certain information, establish and enforce procedures ensuring its redacted release, and extend a damages remedy against the government or its officials where the government's mishandling of sensitive information leads to its dissemination. Where information is entrusted to the government, a less drastic means than punishing truthful publication almost always exists for guarding against the dissemination of private facts." Second, "punishing the press for its dissemination of information which is already publicly available is relatively unlikely to advance the interests in the service of which the State seeks to act." The information already rests in the public domain; moreover, the appropriate party to sanction is the government which made the information available in the first place. A third difficulty averted by the *Daily Mail* rule is the "timidity and self-censorship" which another rule may produce. "A contrary rule, depriving protection to those who rely on the government's implied representations of the lawfulness of dissemination, would force upon the media the onerous obligation of sifting through government press releases, reports, and pronouncements to prune out material arguably unlawful for publication."

Applying the *Daily Mail* standard to the facts of this case, Justice Marshall first found that the Florida Star "lawfully obtain[ed] truthful information about a matter of public significance."[41] The Court proceeded to consider whether protecting the identity of B.J.F. "serves 'a need to further a state interest of the highest order.' " B.J.F. claimed that there were three such interests: "the privacy of victims of sexual offenses; the physical safety of such victims, who may be targeted for retaliation if their names become known to their assailants; and the goal of encouraging victims of such crimes to report these crimes without fear of exposure." Justice Marshall recognized these as "highly significant interests" and did not rule out permitting liability in some future case of "overwhelming necessity." Nevertheless, he listed three reasons why imposing liability "under the circumstances of this case is too precipitous a means of advancing these interests." First, the government had given the newspaper the information in a news release. Second, the Court worried that "the broad sweep of the negligence per se standard" fails to consider the facts of a particular case.[42] Third, Justice Marshall felt

---

down a state court's injunction preventing the media from publishing the name or photograph of an 11-year-old boy involved in a juvenile hearing at which reporters were lawfully present.

[41] While the Florida code outlawed dissemination of such information, it did not proscribe its receipt — even assuming such a proscription would be constitutional.

[42] For example, the victim's identity might already be "known throughout the community"; or the victim's identity may have "otherwise become a reasonable subject of public concern — because, perhaps, questions have arisen whether the victim fabricated an assault by a particular person."

that the "facial underinclusiveness" of the statute "raises doubts about whether Florida is in fact serving, with this statute, the significant interests" which B.J.F. advanced. Specifically, the statute only proscribed information being disseminated by an "instrument of mass communication," and not by a malicious individual. Justice Marshall concluded: "Our holding today is limited. We do not hold that truthful publication is automatically constitutionally protected, or that there is no zone of personal privacy within which the State may protect the individual from intrusion by the press, or even that a State may never punish publication of the name of a victim of a sexual offense. We hold only that where a newspaper publishes truthful information which it has lawfully obtained, punishment may lawfully be imposed, if at all, only when narrowly tailored to a state interest of the highest order, and that no such interest is satisfactorily served by imposing liability under § 794.03 to appellant under the facts of this case."

Justice Scalia wrote an opinion concurring in part and in the judgment that relied solely on the "facial underinclusiveness" of the law in not applying to all disseminators.

Justice White wrote a dissenting opinion in which Chief Justice Rehnquist and Justice O'Connor joined. Justice White disagreed with the applicability of the "trilogy" of precedents cited by the majority, detailing how none of them presented the issue currently before the Court. He contended that the closest case in point, *Cox Broadcasting*, did not control as court records at issue in that case historically had been open to the public and were open by state law in *Cox Broadcasting*. Florida had followed the recommendations that the *Cox Broadcasting* Court itself suggested to keep sensitive information private. "[I]t is not too much to ask the press, in instances such as this, to respect simple standards of decency and restrain from publishing a victim's name, address, and/or phone number."

Justice White also maintained that the newspaper had hardly been blameless: "As the Star's own reporter conceded at trial, the crime incident report that inadvertently included B.J.F.'s name was posted in a room that contained signs making it clear that the names of rape victims were not matters of public record, and were not to be published. The Star's reporter indicated that she understood that she '[was not] allowed to take down that information' (i.e., B.J.F.'s name) and that she '[was] not supposed to take the information' from the police department."

Justice White predicted that the decision would have broad-ranging implications: "At issue in this case is whether there is any information about people, which — though true — may not be published in the press. By holding that only 'a state interest of the highest order' permits the States to penalize the publication of truthful information, and by holding that protecting a rape victim's right to privacy is not among those state interests of the highest order, the Court accepts appellant's invitation to obliterate one of the most noteworthy legal inventions of the 20th Century: the tort of the publication of private facts. Even if the Court's opinion does not say as much today, such obliteration will follow inevitably from the Court's conclusion here. If the First Amendment prohibits wholly private persons (such as B.J.F.) from recovering for the publication of the fact that she was raped, I doubt there remain any 'private facts' which persons may assume will not be published in the newspapers, or broadcast on television."

BARTNICKI v. VOPPER, 532 U.S, 514 (2001). In *Bartnicki*, the Court invalidated a federal and state wiretapping statute that imposed liability for knowing disclosure of unlawfully obtained electronic communications. Since 1992, a teacher's union had been engaged in heated negotiations with the school board. In May 1993, the union's head negotiator, Bartnicki, used her cellular phone to call the union's president, Kane, to discuss the progress of the negotiations. "An unidentified person intercepted and recorded that call."[43] Soon after, Jack Yocum, "the head of a local taxpayers' organization that had opposed the union's demands throughout the negotiations," found the taped conversation in his mailbox. After listening to it, Defendant Yocum delivered the tape to Defendant Vopper, a radio personality with a public affairs talk show. Defendant Vopper aired the tape on his show, as did other members of the media.

Plaintiffs Bartnicki and Kane filed suit against Vopper, Yocum, and media representatives, alleging that the repeated disclosures of their illegally intercepted conversation violated Title 18 U.S.C. § 2511(1)(c) and an almost identical Pennsylvania Act, under which they were entitled to recover actual, statutory, and punitive damages, as well as attorney's fees and costs. Vopper claimed the First Amendment protected the disclosures: and even if the conversation had been illegally intercepted, he had received the tape lawfully.

Writing for the Court, Justice Stevens accepted that the unknown person had intercepted the phone conversation intentionally.[44] The Court also recognized three factual differences from previous cases. First, the other defendants "played no part in the illegal interception. . . . Second, their access to the information on the tapes was obtained lawfully. . . . Third, the subject matter of the conversation was a matter of public concern." Both statutes at issue were content-neutral. In particular, § 2511 "does not distinguish based on the content of the intercepted conversations, nor is it justified by reference to the content of those conversations." Instead, it focuses on communications that have been "illegally intercepted." At bottom, § 2511(1)(c)'s "naked prohibition against disclosures is fairly characterized as a regulation of pure speech."

While this case is a matter of first impression, "[a]s a general matter, 'state action to punish the publication of truthful information seldom can satisfy constitutional standards.' " For example, *New York Times Co. v. United States*, protects the press' right "to publish information of great public concern obtained from documents stolen by a third party." However, neither *New York Times*, nor *Landmark Communications, Inc. v. Virginia*, resolved the issue of whether government could punish the media or a source for " 'not only the unlawful acquisition, but the ensuing publication as well.' " The issue in this case was even narrower:

" 'Where the punished publisher of information has obtained the information in question in a manner lawful in itself but from a source who has obtained it unlawfully, may the government punish the ensuing publication of that information based on the defect in a chain?' " More broadly, the Court has repeatedly declined to "answer categorically whether truthful publication may ever be punished consistent with the First Amendment."

The Government asserted that § 2511(1)(c) served two interests: "removing an incentive for parties to intercept private conversations," and "minimizing the harm to persons whose conversations have been illegally intercepted." While these interests may justify prohibiting the interceptor's using the information, "punishing disclosures of lawfully obtained information of public interest by one not involved in the illegality is [not] an acceptable means of serving those ends."

In contrast to the case at hand, identified persons have violated § 2511 (1)(c) "motivated by either financial gain or domestic disputes." While this may be the

---

[43] Although parts of the phone conversation were undecipherable, the union's president could be heard threatening to go to the board members' homes: " 'to blow off their front porches.' " The recording also revealed Kane saying, " 'we'll have to do some work on some of those guys . . . because this is, you know, this is bad news.' "

[44] The Court also assumed for purposes of the interlocutory appeal that the defendants at least " 'had reason to know' " the tape was obtained unlawfully.

"exceptional case" where an unidentified person "will risk criminal prosecution by passing on information without any expectation of financial reward or public praise," the Court was still unconvinced that punishing the publisher of that information would "deter the unidentified scanner from continuing to engage in surreptitious interceptions. Unusual cases fall far short of a showing that there is a 'need of the highest order' for a rule supplementing the traditional means of deterring antisocial conduct." Justice Stevens stressed that this holding "does not apply to punishing parties for obtaining the relevant information unlawfully."

While the Government's interest in protecting privacy was more persuasive, "important interests . . . on *both* sides of the constitutional calculus" must be balanced. Although privacy of communication is important, and "the fear of public disclosure" may chill private speech, this case does not involve "disclosures of trade secrets or domestic gossip or other information of purely private concern. *Cf. Time, Inc. v. Hill.*" This interest was not strong enough to justify "impos[ing] sanctions on the publication of truthful information of public concern." At bottom, "a stranger's illegal conduct does not suffice to remove the First Amendment shield from speech about a matter of public concern."

Concurring, Justice Breyer, joined by Justice O'Connor, emphasized the narrowness of the holding as "the radio broadcasters acted lawfully (up to the time of final public disclosure)" and as "the information publicized involved a matter of unusual public concern, namely a threat of potential physical harm to others." Justice Breyer focused on "whether the statutes strike a reasonable balance between their speech-restricting and speech-enhancing consequences. Or do they instead impose restrictions on speech that are disproportionate when measured against their corresponding privacy and speech-related benefits, taking into account the kind, the importance, and the extent of these benefits, as well as the need for the restrictions in order to secure those benefits? What this Court has called 'strict scrutiny' — with its strong presumption against constitutionality — is normally out of place where, as here, important competing constitutional interests are implicated."

Still the statutes at issue "disproportionately interfere with media freedom." Moreover, plaintiffs "had little or no *legitimate* interest" in keeping private phone discussions about " 'blowing off . . . front porches' and 'doing some work on some of these guys.' " When "publication of private information constitutes a wrongful act, the law recognizes a privilege allowing the reporting of threats to public safety . . . [e]ven where the danger may have passed by the time of publication." In any event, plaintiffs were " 'limited public figures' " acting on behalf of the teacher's union. Although the Constitution does not require "public figures to give up entirely the right to private communication, i.e., communications free from telephone taps or interceptions," the disclosed information was a matter of public concern.

Concerned that the decision may discourage legislatures from regulating emerging technologies, Justice Breyer emphasized that "the Constitution permits legislatures to respond flexibly to the challenges future technology may pose to the individual's interest in basic personal privacy." Eavesdropping on cellular telephones used on the street differs from, "eavesdropping on encrypted cellular phone conversations or those carried on in the bedroom." Legislatures may even better tailor statutes like the one at issue to encourage "more effective privacy-protecting technologies."

Chief Justice Rehnquist dissented, joined by Justices Scalia and Thomas. Today, "[w]e are placed in the uncomfortable position of not knowing who might have access to our personal and business e-mails, our medical and financial records, or our cordless and cellular telephone conversations." As a result, "the United States, the District of Columbia, and 40 States have enacted laws prohibiting the intentional interception and knowing disclosure of electronic communications." By negating these statutes, the Court chills the speech of those who rely on these devices.

The majority incorrectly "subjects these laws to the strict scrutiny normally reserved for governmental attempts to censor viewpoints or ideas." It mistakenly relies on "the *Daily Mail* string of newspaper cases," which scrutinized laws that "regulated the content or subject matter of speech." Moreover, the reporters in the *Daily Mail* cases "lawfully obtained their information through consensual interviews or public documents." As the Court explained in *Florida Star v. B.J.F.*, "three other unique factors also informed the scope of the *Daily Mail* principle." First, "the information published by the newspapers had been lawfully obtained [generally] from the government itself." Second, "the information in each case was already 'publicly available.'" Third, the cases were "concerned with the 'timidity and self-censorship' which may result from allowing the media to be punished for publishing certain truthful information." Antidisclosure provisions "allow private conversations to transpire without inhibition."

In contrast, § 2511 and the Pennsylvania Act are content neutral laws which "only regulate information that was illegally obtained; they do not restrict republication of what is already in the public domain; they impose no special burdens upon the media; they have a scienter requirement to provide fair warning; and they promote the privacy and free speech of those using cellular telephones." It was difficult to conceive of "a more narrowly tailored prohibition." Applying *Turner Broadcasting System, Inc. v. FCC.*, the Court should uphold these laws as "they further a substantial governmental interest unrelated to the suppression of free speech."

Absent a "prohibition on disclosure, an unlawful eavesdropper who wanted to disclose the conversation could anonymously launder the interception through a third party and thereby avoid detection." Without antidisclosure provisions, "[t]he law against interceptions, which the Court agrees is valid, would be utterly ineffectual." Based on similar reasoning, the Court "upheld against First Amendment challenge a law prohibiting the distribution of child pornography" in *New York v. Ferber*. There, "we did not demand, nor did Congress provide, any empirical evidence to buttress this basic syllogism" that allowing damages for publishing illegally obtained materials dries up their market. Even "[m]ore mystifying still is the Court's reliance upon the 'Pentagon Papers' case" which involved "Government controlled information" and "fell squarely under our precedents holding that prior restraints on speech bear "'a heavy presumption against . . . constitutionality.'" Indeed, "it was this presumption that caused Justices Stewart and White to join the 6-to-3 *per curiam* decision."

NOTES

(1) The classic article on privacy is Warren & Brandeis, *The Right to Privacy*, 4 Harv. L. Rev. 193 (1890). For an argument that these tort actions may have been largely preempted by the freedom of speech concerns, see Diane Zimmerman, *Requiem for a Heavyweight: A Farewell to Warren and Brandeis' Privacy Tort*, 68 Cornell L. Rev. 291 (1983). *But see* Erwin Chemerinsky, *Balancing the Rights of Privacy and the Press: A Reply to Professor Smolla*, 67 Geo. Wash. L. Rev. 1152, 1161 (1999) ("Threats to privacy have increased exponentially as a result of the development of the electronic media, the creation of technology which can facilitate intrusion, and the seemingly ever increasing cultural preoccupation with celebrity. . . . There is no doubt that freedom of speech and privacy are both values of the highest order in society. The Supreme Court never has regarded and never will regard the freedoms of speech or the press as absolutes. Therefore, the only approach must be explicit and careful balancing of these important rights."); Robert M. O'Neil, *Ride-Alongs, Paparazzi, and Other Media*

Threats To Privacy, 33 U. Rich L. Rev. 1167, 1183 (2000) ("[T]he historic role of privacy has been to protect only that which is truly not public-the physical sanctity of the home, the integrity of 'papers and effects,' and the right of citizens to withhold most information they wish not to reveal. Conversely, when a person leaves the home or enters a public place, anything and everything becomes fair game, 'private' or not. What troubles us these days is the degree to which rapidly changing technology and novel means of gathering information and images serve to blur these traditional and once clear distinctions. The use of electronic devices on public streets and sidewalks to 'invade' the private home, without any physical trespass, most acutely tests our once easy assumptions."); Rodney A. Smolla, *Privacy and the First Amendment Right to Gather News,* 67 Geo. Wash. L. Rev. 1097, 1158 (1999) ("the widespread sense of public disquiet that privacy is an endangered species, perhaps on the edge of extinction, will inevitably engender calls for legal reforms designed to retrench the right to be let alone, restoring some sense of equilibrium to modern life. . . . Information gatherers, particularly the mainstream press, must be sensitive to this growing concern. As matters stand today, strong First Amendment doctrines stand in the way of many of the most meaningful privacy reforms. But the First Amendment tradition is always evolving; like all law, it is malleable and elastic, constantly being shaped by evolving social movements and cultural sensibilities. A press with no respect for society's interests in privacy may someday find itself in a society with no respect for the press.").

For additional discussions of privacy actions, see Gavison, *Privacy and the Limits of Law,* 89 Yale L.J. 421 (1980); Felcher & Rubin, *Privacy, Publicity, and the Portrayal of Real People by the Media,* 88 Yale L.J. 1577 (1979).

(2) For an interesting contrast of the approaches to privacy under the First Amendment and under substantive due process, see Robert F. Nagel, *Privacy and Celebrity: An Essay on the Nationalization of Intimacy* 33 U. Rich L. Rev. 1121, 1123 (2000) ("What the constitutional right to privacy actually protects and what the public apparently wants is not privacy in the conventional sense of insulation or concealment, but a set of personal liberties that are thought to be especially important. These include, of course, the right to sexual freedom (because, some say, sexuality is crucial to individual identity), the right to reproductive freedom (because that freedom, say others, is crucial for preventing the government from asserting totalitarian control over people's lives), the right to refuse medical treatment (because of the importance of bodily autonomy), and so on. Once the right to privacy is understood to refer to certain favored liberties, the paradox of the populace's simultaneous commitments to privacy and publicness dissolves into a single strong commitment to personal liberty.").

Chapter XIV
SPEECH IN PUBLIC PLACES

Introductory Note. Protecting a right to speak or publish against government interference by no means guarantees access to the marketplace of ideas. For instance, those who lack monetary resources may have tremendous difficulty finding an effective forum in which to introduce their views. A speaker who has no effective forum in which to express her ideas may find her constitutional right to free speech impaired, if not illusory. To help redress these egalitarian problems of access, First Amendment jurisprudence has long extended a right to speak on certain government property held to comprise a public forum.

Still, an absolute right of access to a public forum might jeopardize enjoyment of speech rights for everyone. For example, if a number of speakers want to use the same public forum at the same time, they will drown each other out and no speaker could convey her particular message. Thus, to render practical this concept of a public forum where some or all citizens have a right to speak, the Court has permitted government to place certain restrictions on this right. Primarily, permissible regulations are content-neutral time, place, and manner restrictions. *Cf.* A. Meiklejohn, Political Freedom 24–28 (1960) (analogizing restrictions on freedom of expression to restrictions imposed to ensure orderly discussion at a town meeting).

The cases in Section 14.01 address the question of what can be said in the public forum. Specifically, the section focuses on offensive speech in public places. The remainder of the Chapter continues to be concerned with the permissible scope of content-based restrictions in the public forum; however, it also treats questions of when, where, and how one can speak; that is, permissible time, place, and manner restrictions. Section 14.02 discusses the traditional public forums: streets, parks, and sidewalks. Section 14.03 considers the pressures on the public forum catalyzed by the civil rights movement of the 1960s. Section 14.04 treats modern public forum theory. This analysis divides public forums into certain categories and restricts speech according to the particular type of public forum where it takes place. Amplifying this categorization theme, the second part of this section treats the question of what private property can acquire the characteristics of a public forum. The third and fourth parts of section 14.04 explore free speech rights in public schools and religious speech in the public forum.

§ 14.01   OFFENSIVE SPEECH IN PUBLIC PLACES

[1]   Defamation: General Principles

CHAPLINSKY v. NEW HAMPSHIRE
315 U.S. 568, 62 S. Ct. 766, 86 L. Ed. 1031 (1942)

Justice Murphy delivered the opinion of the Court.

Appellant, a member of the sect known as Jehovah's Witnesses, was convicted in the municipal court of Rochester, New Hampshire, for violation of Chapter 378, Section 2, of the Public Laws of New Hampshire: "No person shall address any offensive, derisive or annoying word to any other person who is lawfully in any street or other public place, nor call him by any offensive or derisive name, nor make any noise or exclamation in his presence and hearing with intent to deride, offend or annoy him, or to prevent him from pursuing his lawful business or occupation."

The complaint charged that appellant "with force and arms, in a certain public place in said city of Rochester, to wit, on the public sidewalk on the easterly side of Wakefield Street, near unto the entrance of the City Hall, did unlawfully repeat, the words following, addressed to the complainant, that is to say, 'You are a God damned racketeer' and 'a damned Fascist and the whole government of Rochester are Fascists or agents of Fascists' the same being offensive, derisive and annoying words and names." . . .

There is no substantial dispute over the facts. Chaplinsky was distributing the literature of his sect on the streets of Rochester on a busy Saturday afternoon. Members of the local citizenry complained to the City Marshal, Bowering, that Chaplinsky was denouncing all religion as a "racket." Bowering told them that Chaplinsky was lawfully engaged, and then warned Chaplinsky that the crowd was getting restless. Some time later a disturbance occurred and the traffic officer on duty at the busy intersection started with Chaplinsky for the police station, but did not inform him that he was under arrest or that he was going to be arrested. On the way they encountered Marshal Bowering who had been advised that a riot was under way and was therefore hurrying to the scene. Bowering repeated his earlier warning to Chaplinsky who then addressed to Bowering the words set forth in the complaint.

Chaplinsky's version of the affair was slightly different. He testified that when he met Bowering, he asked him to arrest the ones responsible for the disturbance. In reply Bowering cursed him and told him to come along. Appellant admitted that he said the words charged in the complaint with the exception of the name of the Deity. . . .

Allowing the broadest scope to the language and purpose of the Fourteenth Amendment, it is well understood that the right of free speech is not absolute at all times and under all circumstances. There are certain well-defined and narrowly limited classes of speech, the prevention and punishment of which has never been thought to raise any Constitutional problem. These include the lewd and obscene, the profane, the libelous, and the insulting or "fighting" words — those which by their very utterance inflict injury or tend to incite an immediate breach of the peace. It has been well observed that such utterances are no essential part of any exposition of ideas, and are of such slight social value as a step to truth that any benefit that may be derived from them is clearly outweighed by the social interest in order and morality. "Resort to epithets or personal abuse is not in any proper sense communication of information or opinion safe-guarded by the Constitution, and its punishment as a criminal act would raise no question under that instrument." *Cantwell v. Connecticut*, 310 U.S. 296, 309-10 [(1940)]. . . .

On the authority of its earlier decisions, the state court declared that the statute's purpose was to preserve the public peace, no words being "forbidden except such as have a direct tendency to cause acts of violence by the person to whom, individually, the remark is addressed." It was further said:

> The word "offensive" is not to be defined in terms of what a particular addressee thinks. . . . The test is what men of common intelligence would understand would be words likely to cause an average addressee to fight-. . . . The English language has a number of words and expressions which by general consent are "fighting words" when said without a disarming smile. . . . Such words, as ordinary men know, are likely to cause a fight. So are threatening, profane or obscene revillings. Derisive and annoying words can be taken as coming within the purview of the statute as heretofore interpreted only when they have this characteristic of plainly tending to excite the addressee to a breach of the peace. . . . The statute, as construed, does no

more than prohibit the face-to-face words plainly likely to cause a breach of the peace by the addressee, words whose speaking constitute a breach of the peace by the speaker — including "classical fighting words," words in current use less "classical" but equally likely to cause violence, and other disorderly words, including profanity, obscenity and threats.

We are unable to say that the limited scope of the statute as thus construed contravenes the constitutional right of free expression. It is a statute narrowly drawn and limited to define and punish specific conduct lying within the domain of state power, the use in a public place of words likely to cause a breach of the peace. . . . This conclusion necessarily disposes of appellant's contention that the statute is so vague and indefinite as to render a conviction thereunder a violation of due process. . . .

Argument is unnecessary to demonstrate that the appellations "damn racketeer" and "damn Fascist" are epithets likely to provoke the average person to retaliation, and thereby cause a breach of the peace. . . .

NOTES

(1) *Offensive Speech.* In *Cohen v. California,* 403 U.S. 15 (1971), defendant was arrested in a courthouse for wearing a jacket with "Fuck the Draft" printed on it. He was convicted for violating a California statute that prohibited individuals from "maliciously and willfully disturb[ing] the peace or quiet of any neighborhood or person . . . by . . . offensive conduct."

Justice Harlan's majority opinion concluded that "the statute was not a reasonable manner restriction" and the words were not obscene. The Court also held that the fighting words exception did not apply, as no one "actually or likely to be present could reasonably have regarded the words on the appellant's jacket as a direct personal insult." The State also could not suppress speech that was offensive in some generic sense. While the words may be "distasteful," often "one man's vulgarity is another's lyric."

Justice Blackmun dissented, joined by Chief Justice Burger and Justice Black. Justice Blackmun argued that the epithet was "mainly conduct and little 'speech' and thus fell within the 'fighting words' doctrine."

(2) *Overbreadth and "Fighting Words."* After *Cohen,* other cases may also indicate a narrowing of the fighting words doctrine. *See, e.g., Gooding v. Wilson,* 415 U.S. 519 (1972), and *Lewis v. City of New Orleans,* 415 U.S. 130 (1974). In *Gooding,* an antiwar protestor said to a policeman during a scuffle: "White son of a bitch I'll kill you! You son of a bitch, I'll choke you to death." In *Lewis,* a mother who thought that a policeman had arrested her son said "you goddamn motherfucking police," while threatening to complain to the superintendent. Convictions in both cases stem from an individual's violation of a local or state law prohibiting the use of offensive language in public. In both instances, the Supreme Court overturned the convictions, declaring the applicable laws overbroad and facially invalid. The overbreadth holdings leave somewhat ambiguous precisely how these cases may modify the fighting words doctrine.

See also Mannheimer, *The Fighting Words Doctrine,* 93 Colum. L. Rev. 1527, 1528 (1993) ("Although some have suggested that the Supreme Court abandon the fighting words doctrine, this prospect appears unlikely, as the Court has recently reaffirmed the doctrine by assuming its continuing validity. The Court has recognized that the doctrine, properly narrowed, still serves a useful function: preventing breaches of the peace that are both imminent and likely to occur.").

(3) *Hostile Audiences.* Justice Harlan's majority opinion in the *Cohen* case cited the Court's decision in *Feiner v. New York,* 340 U.S. 315 (1951), as an example of how the

State's police power may be used "to prevent a speaker from intentionally provoking a given group to hostile reaction." Generally, the question of whether there has been provocation will be judged in terms of the words of the speaker. Thus, a speaker who is not provoking violence by his or her words cannot be arrested for breach of the peace because of the reaction of a hostile crowd. *See Terminiello v. Chicago*, 337 U.S. 1 (1949); *see also National Socialist Party v. Skokie, infra.* Governments may have the power, under narrowly drawn statutes, to halt a speech if the best efforts of the police cannot maintain order because of the divergent views of those who may be exercising their rights of free speech and assembly in public places. See the concurring opinion of Justice Black, joined by Justice Douglas, in *Gregory v. Chicago*, 394 U.S. 111 (1969).

NATIONAL SOCIALIST PARTY v. SKOKIE, 432 U.S. 43 (1977). In early 1977, the National Socialist Party of America ("NSPA") announced its intention to demonstrate in the Village of Skokie, Illinois, a suburb of Chicago. The NSPA's announcement came on the heels of recent attempts by the Chicago Park District to limit the NSPA's right to march on its home turf of Marquette Park by requiring the organization to post $250,000 in liability insurance prior to demonstrating in any Chicago park. While NSPA sought to challenge this ordinance in federal court, its leader, Frank Collins, decided to take his organization's cause to Chicago's northern suburbs, where many Jewish people resided. At the time, the Village of Skokie had a population of about 70,000, the majority of whom were Jewish. Of these, a sizeable number were survivors of the Holocaust.

In late 1976, NSPA applied for a permit to demonstrate in Skokie. The Skokie Park District, like the Chicago Park District, informed the NSPA that, in order to march, the NSPA would have to post a bond of $350,000 or provide insurance coverage in an equal amount. In response, the NSPA announced its intentions to congregate at Skokie Village Hall on May 1 to denounce the Village's denial of its application. At a meeting of local leaders, Skokie granted the NSPA a permit to march on Village Hall. As word of the impending demonstration spread throughout the community, however, resistance grew — particularly among Holocaust survivors. Large counter-demonstrations by members of Skokie's Jewish community were planned. In April 1977, Skokie obtained an injunction from the Cook County Circuit Court enjoining the NSPA from demonstrating.

In May 1977 the Village passed a series of ordinances effectively banning all forms of hate-group speech. *See, e.g.*, Downs, *Skokie Revisited: Hate Group Speech and the First Amendment*, 80 NOTRE DAME L. REV. 629 (1985). The first prohibited "[t]he dissemination of any materials within the Village of Skokie which promotes and incites hatred against persons by reason of their race, national origin, or religion, and is intended to do so." The second ordinance prohibited the wearing of "military-style uniforms" by members or advocates of political parties in demonstrations or marches. The third ordinance required that groups of 50 or more demonstrators post $350,000 in insurance bonds before a permit could be granted.

The April 1977 injunction prohibited the NSPA, within the Village of Skokie, from marching in the National Socialist uniform and displaying the swastika. The injunction further prohibited the NSPA from inciting or promoting hatred against persons of the Jewish faith or of any other faith. Thereafter, the NSPA applied for a stay of the injunction pending an appeal. This was denied by the Illinois Appellate Court. The Illinois Supreme Court, in turn, denied a stay and further denied NSPA leave for an expedited appeal.

The U.S. Supreme Court, however, granted certiorari and reversed and remanded. *Nationalist Socialist Party v. Skokie*, 432 U.S. 43 (1977). The Court held that "the outstanding injunctions . . . deprive[d] [the NSPA] of rights protected by the First

Amendment during the period of appellate review. . . . If a State seeks to impose a restraint of this kind, it must provide strict procedural safeguards, including immediate appellate review. Absent such review, the State must instead allow a stay."

Justice Rehnquist, in dissent, joined by Chief Justice Burger and Justice Stewart, "simply [did] not see how the refusal of the Supreme Court of Illinois to stay an injunction granted by an inferior court within the state system" could be described as a final judgment. Justice Rehnquist "[did] not disagree with the Court that the provisions of the injunction . . . [were] extremely broad."

On remand, the Illinois Appellate Court modified the injunction and upheld only that portion of the injunction that prevented the display of swastikas "in the course of a demonstration, march or parade." *Village of Skokie v. National Socialist Party of America*, 366 N.E.2d 347 (Ill. App. Ct. 1977). Again a stay pending an expedited review was sought and denied. Ultimately, "albeit reluctantly," the Illinois Supreme Court reversed the remaining portion of the injunction. *Village of Skokie v. National Socialist Party of America*, 373 N.E.2d 21 (Ill. 1978).

In the meantime, on June 22, the NSPA applied for and was denied a permit under the new ordinances. With the help of the ACLU, NSPA filed suit in federal District Court. Relying heavily on the "fighting-words" doctrine, the District Court declared the ordinances unconstitutional on their face, and granted the requested declaratory and injunctive relief. *Collin v. Smith*, 447 F. Supp. 676 (N.D. Ill. 1978). Approaching each ordinance individually, the District Court founded its holding on various constitutional doctrines, including prior restraint, void-for-vagueness, overbreadth, and symbolic speech.

The Seventh Circuit Court of Appeals, with one judge dissenting, affirmed. *Collin v. Smith*, 578 F.2d 1197 (7th Cir. 1978). Echoing the District Court, the Court of Appeals held that its decision was "dictated by the fundamental proposition that if these civil rights are to remain vital for all, they must protect not only those society deems acceptable, but also those whose ideas it quite justifiably rejects and despises."

The Supreme Court, without opinion, denied certiorari. *Collin v. Smith*, 439 U.S. 916 (1978). Justice Blackmun, joined by Justice White, dissented from the Supreme Court's denial of certiorari. In his brief dissent, Justice Blackmun commented:

Judge Sprecher of the Seventh Circuit observed that "each court dealing with these precise problems (the Illinois Supreme Court, the District Court and this Court) feels the need to apologize for its result."

. . . I also feel that the present case affords the Court an opportunity to consider whether, in the context of the facts that this record appears to present, there is no limit whatsoever to the exercise of free speech. There indeed may be no such limit, but when citizens assert, not casually but with deep conviction, that the proposed demonstration is scheduled at a place and in a manner that is taunting and overwhelmingly offensive to the citizens of that place, that assertion, uncomfortable though it may be for judges, deserves to be examined. It just might fall into the same category as one's "right" to cry "fire" in a crowded theater, for "the character of every act depends upon the circumstances in which it is done." *Schenk v. United States*, 249 U.S. 47, 52 (1919).

In the end, NSPA chose not to march in Skokie. Instead, as the result of a favorable verdict in a separate federal suit, they once again secured the right to demonstrate in Marquette Park.

NOTES

(1) For additional discussion of *Skokie*, see, e.g., R. BINGHAM & J. GIBSON, CIVIL LIBERTIES AND NAZIS: THE SKOKIE FREE SPEECH CONTROVERSY (1985); D. DOWNS, NAZIS IN SKOKIE: FREEDOM, COMMUNITY AND THE FIRST AMENDMENT (1985); D. HAMLIN, THE NAZI/SKOKIE CONFLICT: A CIVIL LIBERTIES BATTLE (1980); A. NEIER, DEFENDING MY ENEMY: NAZIS IN SKOKIE (1979); Downs, *Skokie Revisited: Hate Group Speech and the First Amendment*, 80 NOTRE DAME L. REV. 629 (1985).

(2) *Group Libel. Skokie* also brings up the problem of libel against a particular racial or ethnic group. In *Beauharnais v. Illinois*, 343 U.S. 250 (1952), the Court upheld a conviction under a criminal statute for the distribution of a leaflet that maligned black persons. The pamphlet provided in part: " 'If persuasion and the need to prevent the white race from becoming mongrelized by the negro will not unite us, then the aggressions . . . rapes, robberies, knives, guns and marijuana of the negro surely will.' "

The statute prohibited the distribution in a public place of any publication that " 'portrays depravity, criminality, unchastity, or lack of virtue of a class of citizens, of any race, color, creed or religion which said publication or exhibition exposes the citizens of any race, color, creed or religion to contempt, derision, or obloquy or which is productive of breach of the peace or riots.' " In upholding the conviction (5-4), the Court relied in part on the fact that certain types of speech, such as fighting words and libel, did not then receive constitutional protection. Justices Black, Reed, Douglas, and Jackson each wrote dissenting opinions.

While *Beauharnais* has never been explicitly overruled, many commentators have assumed that the case did not survive *New York Times v. Sullivan*, 376 U.S. 254 (1964), *supra* § 13.08[1]. *See* R. ROTUNDA, J. NOWAK & J. YOUNG, CONSTITUTIONAL LAW (1986). The Seventh Circuit in *Collin* has been one of several lower federal courts that has rejected group libel justifications for the suppression of speech. *See id.* at § 16.32, n.9.

(3) For further discussion of the problem of offensive speech, see, e.g., Attanasio, *Equal Justice Under Chaos: The Developing Law of Sexual Harassment*, 51 U. CIN. L. REV. 1 (1982); Delgado, *Words that Wound: A Tort Action for Racial Insults, Epithets, and Name-Calling*, 17 HARV. C.R.-C.L. L. REV. 133 (1982); Gard, *Fighting Words as Free Speech*, 58 WASH. U. L.Q. 531 (1980); Note, *First Amendment Limitations on Tort Liability for Words Intended to Inflict Severe Emotional Distress*, 85 COLUM. L. REV. 1749 (1985); Note, *A Communitarian Defense of Group Libel Laws*, 101 HARV. L. REV. 682 (1988).

(4) For a critical analysis of recent regulations of "hate-speech" or "racist-speech" on college campuses, see Linzer, *White Liberal Looks at Racist Speech*, 65 ST. JOHN'S L. REV. 187 (1991) ("The more we call out the names of the respectable people who are supporting racist speech, the more we boycott them and the racist speakers, and the more we speak out against racist speech, the more we will stop racist speech. And we, the people, should do it with as little as possible of the heavy hand of the government.").

R.A.V. v. ST. PAUL, 505 U.S. 377 (1992). Defendant and other teenagers allegedly burned a cross in the yard of a black family. The City of St. Paul charged Defendant under its Bias-Motivated Crime Ordinance.[1] Justice Scalia's majority opinion held the

---

[1] The City could have charged defendant "under any of a number of laws" — for example, those prohibiting terroristic threats, arson, and criminal damage to property.

ordinance facially unconstitutional because it prohibited otherwise permissible speech based on the subject matter that the speech addressed. First Amendment precedents from 1791 to the present allow categorical content restrictions "in a few limited areas which are 'of such slight social value as a step to truth that any benefit that may be derived from them is clearly outweighed by the social interest in order and morality.' *Chaplinsky* [*v. New Hampshire*]." Moreover, while the Court has "narrowed the scope of the traditional categorical exceptions for defamation, see *New York Times Co. v. Sullivan* [, 376 U.S. 254 (1964)]; and for obscenity, see *Miller v. California* [, 413 U.S. 15 (1973)], a limited categorical approach has remained an important part of our First Amendment jurisprudence."

Content-based regulation of obscenity, defamation and other "proscribable expression," is permissible, except when these modes of expression are "vehicles for content discrimination unrelated to their distinctively proscribable content." For example, "the government may proscribe libel, but not make the further content discrimination of proscribing only libel critical of the government." Alternatively, "a city council [cannot] enact an ordinance prohibiting only those legally obscene works that contain criticism of the city government."

Justice Scalia rejected the assertions of concurring Justices that the Court has established "a new First Amendment principle that prohibition of constitutionally proscribable speech cannot be 'underinclusive,'" Instead the First Amendment prohibits "content discrimination" limitations on expression. While "prohibition in certain media or markets would be 'underinclusive,' it would not discriminate on the basis of content." Moreover, if the grounds for content discrimination render "the entire class of speech at issue" proscribable, there cannot be "idea or viewpoint discrimination." "A State might choose to prohibit only that obscenity which is the most patently offensive in its prurience — i.e., that which involves the most lascivious displays of sexual activity. But it may not prohibit, for example, only that obscenity that includes offensive political messages. . . . [T]he Federal Government can criminalize only those threats of violence that are directed against the President, see 18 U.S.C. § 871 — since the reasons why threats of violence are outside the First Amendment have special force when applied to the person of the President." However, "the Federal Government may not criminalize only those threats against the President that mention his policy on aid to inner cities. [A] State may choose to regulate price advertising in one industry but not in others, because the risk of fraud (one of the characteristics of commercial speech that justifies depriving it of full First Amendment protection), is in its view greater there. But a State may not prohibit only that commercial advertising that depicts men in a demeaning fashion."

If a "subclass of proscribable speech" is "associated with particular secondary effects" of speech, regulation is justified "without reference to its content." For example, Justice Scalia cited "sexually derogatory 'fighting words,' [that] may produce a violation of Title VII's general prohibition against sexual discrimination in employment practices."

Justice Scalia next applied the foregoing principles to the St. Paul ordinance. First, he concluded that it applied "to 'fighting words' that insult, or provoke violence, 'on the basis of race, color, creed, religion or gender.'" Also, "displays containing abusive invective, no matter how vicious or severe, are permissible unless they are addressed to one of the specified disfavored topics." Notably, he asserted that the ordinance does not cover "fighting words" used "to express hostility" related to the idea of homosexuality, for example. He further concluded that the ordinance operated to permit "actual viewpoint discrimination."

In Justice Scalia's analysis, the ordinance proscribed all "fighting words that communicate messages of racial, gender, or religious intolerance," and thus, it was possible the city "[sought] to handicap the expression of particular ideas." St. Paul argued that the ordinance was within the exception from *Renton v. Playtime Theatres, Inc.*, 475 U.S. 41 (1986), "that allows content discrimination aimed only at the 'secondary effects' of the speech," and that its intention was to protect members of groups who were historically victims of discrimination. However, Justice Scalia noted: "The emotive impact of speech on its audience is not a secondary effect." *Id.*[2]

Justice Scalia asserted that the "basic human rights" of those historically subject to discrimination are "compelling interests," therefore, the issue in the case was "whether content discrimination [was] reasonably necessary to achieve St. Pau's compelling interests." He believed that St. Paul's ordinance unnecessarily allowed content discrimination that violated the First Amendment by "displaying the city council's special hostility towards the particular biases thus singled out. The politicians of St. Paul are entitled to express that hostility — but not through the means of imposing unique limitations upon speakers who (however benightedly) disagree." Although "burning a cross in someone's front yard is reprehensible," St. Paul could "prevent such behavior without adding the First Amendment to the fire."

Justice White, joined by Justices Blackmun, O'Connor and Stevens (except as to Part I-A), concurred in the judgment. Justice White agreed with Petitioner's argument that "the St. Paul ordinance is fatally overbroad because it criminalizes not only unprotected expression but expression protected by the First Amendment." He maintained that the majority "seriously depart[ed]" from the Court's First Amendment precedents. In Part I-A Justice White's concurrence stated: the majority inconsistently held "that the government may proscribe an entire category of speech because the content of that speech is evil," when "it may not treat a subset of that category differently without violating the First Amendment." Justice White argued that this inconsistency "necessarily signals that expressions of violence, such as the message of intimidation and racial hatred conveyed by burning a cross on someone's lawn, are of sufficient value to outweigh the social interest in order and morality that has traditionally placed such fighting words outside the First Amendment." The majority "characteriz[ed] fighting words as a form of 'debate,'" thereby "legitimat[ing] hate speech."

Part II of Justice White's opinion concluded: "Although the ordinance reaches conduct that is unprotected, it also makes criminal expressive conduct that causes only hurt feelings, offense, or resentment, and is protected by the First Amendment."

Justice Blackmun's concurrence construed the Court's holding as "seem[ing] to abandon the categorical approach, and inevitably to relax the level of scrutiny applicable to content-based laws." He agreed with Justice White's position that "this weakens the traditional protections of speech. If all expressive activity must be accorded the same protection, that protection will be scant."

Justice Blackmun speculated "that this case will not significantly alter First Amendment jurisprudence, but, instead, will be regarded as an aberration." While the government of St. Paul may punish "race-based fighting words," he "agree[d] with Justice White that this particular ordinance reaches beyond fighting words to speech protected by the First Amendment."

Justices White and Blackmun also joined in Part I of a concurrence by Justice Stevens. Justice Stevens agreed that "the St. Paul ordinance was unconstitutionally overbroad, for the reasons stated in Part II of Justice White's opinion," but he "[wrote]

---

[2] [Court's Footnote 7] . . . [T]he St. Paul ordinance regulates on the basis of the "primary" effect of the speech — i.e., its persuasive (or repellant) force.

separately to suggest how the allure of absolute principles has skewed the analysis of both the majority and concurring opinions."

"Our entire First Amendment jurisprudence creates a regime based on the content of speech. Although the First Amendment broadly protects 'speech,' it does not protect the right to 'fix prices, breach contracts, make false warranties, place bets with bookies, threaten, [or] extort.' Whether an agreement among competitors is a violation of the Sherman Act or protected activity under the Noerr-Pennington doctrine hinges upon the content of the agreement."

VIRGINIA v. BLACK, 538 U.S. 343 (2003). In *Black*, the Court invalidated a statute that defines cross burning as prima facie evidence of intent to intimidate. Writing for a 5-4 Court, Justice O'Connor held that a state may ban "cross burning carried out with the intent to intimidate;" however, Virginia has violated the First Amendment by passing a statute that allows the act of cross burning itself to be evidence of the intent to intimidate.

In 1998, defendant Black led a Ku Klux Klan rally which 25 to 30 people attended. This rally occurred on private property with the permission of the owner. When Black burned a cross at the rally, the sheriff arrested him for violating the cross burning statute at issue.

"The *First Amendment* permits 'restrictions upon the content of speech in a few limited areas, which are "of such slight social value as a step to truth that any benefit that may be derived from them is clearly outweighed by the social interest in order and morality." ' " One such permissible restriction is upon "fighting words — 'those are personally abusive epithets which, when addressed to the ordinary citizen, are, as a matter of common knowledge, inherently likely to provoke violent reaction.' " The First Amendment also allows a State to restrict a " 'true threat.' " This type of threat consists of statements where the speaker aims to "communicate a serious expression of an intent to commit an act of unlawful violence to a particular individual or group of individuals." For a true threat to exist, a speaker need not intend to carry out the threat. Rather a prohibition on true threats " 'protects individuals from the fear of violence' and 'from the disruption that fear engenders.' " One type of true threat is constitutionally proscribable intimidation, "where a speaker directs a threat to a person or group of persons with the intent of placing the victim in fear of bodily harm or death." After reviewing the extensive history of cross burning, Justice O'Connor concluded that "the history of cross burning in this country shows that cross burning is often intimidating, intended to create a pervasive fear in victims that they are a target of violence."

In *R.A.V. v. City of St. Paul, supra*, this Court held that "it would be constitutional to ban only a particular type of threat." Consistent with this ruling, "Virginia's statute does not run afoul of the *First Amendment* insofar as it bans cross burning with intent to intimidate. Unlike the statute at issue in *R.A.V.*, the Virginia statute does not single out for opprobrium only that speech directed toward 'one of the specified disfavored topics.' It does not matter whether an individual burns a cross with intent to intimidate because of the victim's race, gender, or religion, or because of the victim's 'political affiliation, union membership, or homosexuality.' " Virginia may regulate only a "subset of intimidating messages in light of cross burning's long and pernicious history as a signal of impending violence. Thus, just as a State may regulate only that obscenity which is the most obscene due to its prurient content, so too may a State choose to prohibit only those forms of intimidation that are most likely to inspire fear of bodily harm."

The Supreme Court of Virginia has not yet interpreted the prima facie evidence part of the statute. This provision, "as interpreted by the jury instruction, renders the statute unconstitutional." The Virginia Supreme Court failed to "expressly disavow the jury instruction," which was the Model Jury Instruction. "The prima facie evidence provision permits a jury to convict in every cross burning case in which defendants exercise their constitutional right not to put on a defense. And even where a defendant like Black presents a defense, the prima facie evidence provision makes it more likely that the jury will find an intent to intimidate regardless of the particular facts of the case. The provision permits the Commonwealth to arrest, prosecute, and convict a person based solely on the fact of cross burning itself." So interpreted, this provision creates " 'an unacceptable risk of the suppression of ideas.' " This provision conflates situations in which an intent to intimidate exists with situations in which it does not. A burning of a cross at a political rally would " 'almost certainly be protected expression.' " For example, cross burnings that have appeared in movies such as Mississippi Burning are performed without an intent to intimidate.

"All we hold is that because of the interpretation of the prima facie evidence provision given by the jury instruction, the provision makes the statute facially invalid at this point. We also recognize the theoretical possibility that the court, on remand, could interpret the provision in a manner different from that so far set forth in order to avoid the constitutional objections we have described. We leave open that possibility. We also leave open the possibility that the provision is severable."

Justice Stevens filed a concurring opinion. Dissenting, Justice Thomas noted that "[i]n our culture, cross burning has almost invariably meant lawlessness and understandably instills in its victims well-grounded fear of physical violence." For Justice Thomas, "[t]his statute prohibits only conduct, not expression. And, just as one cannot burn down someone's house to make a political point and then seek refuge in the *First Amendment*, those who hate cannot terrorize and intimidate to make their point." Relying on *Wigmore*, Justice Thomas states that *"an inference, sometimes loosely referred to as a presumption of fact, does not compel a specific conclusion. An inference merely applies to the rational potency or probative value of an evidentiary fact to which the fact finder may attach whatever force or weight it deems best."*[3] In light of "the horrific effect cross burning has on its victims, it is also reasonable to presume intent to intimidate from the act itself." Justice Thomas found ironic that the Court had permitted restrictions on advice not wanted by persons seeking to obtain an abortion but not restrictions on cross burning because "one day an individual might wish to burn a cross" lacking "an intent to intimidate anyone."

Justice Scalia filed an opinion concurring in part, concurring in the judgment in part, and dissenting in part. Justice Thomas joined all parts of Justice Scalia's opinion discussed here. Justice Scalia said that cross burning intended not to intimidate but to convey ideological or artistic messages could be challenged on a case-by-case basis. In holding the prima facie evidence provision facially invalid, the plurality appears to rely on "some species of overbreadth doctrine." The class of persons who could impermissibly be convicted under this provision include individuals who: "(1) burn a cross in public view, (2) do not intend to intimidate, (3) are nonetheless charged and prosecuted, and (4) refuse to present a defense." This set of cases is not large enough "to render the statute *substantially* overbroad."

Justice Souter, joined by Justices Kennedy and Ginsburg, concurred in the judgment in part and dissented in part. The prima facie case provision brings "within the statute's prohibition some expression that is doubtfully threatening though certainly distasteful." A content-based regulation "can only survive if narrowly tailored to serve a compelling state interest, a stringent test the statute cannot pass; a content-neutral statute

---

[3] An inference does not involve the "procedural consequence of shifting the burden of production."

banning intimidation would achieve the same object without singling out particular content."

NOTES

(1) *Limiting Free Speech.* For further discussion, see Curtis, *Critics of "Free Speech" and the Uses of the Past*, 12 CONST. COMMENT. 29, 33 (1995) ("A representative government can make a decision to limit free speech or democracy. But to the extent of the departure, representative government becomes something else. If the departure from free speech is sufficiently substantial, government is no longer democratic or representative."); Massey, *Hate Speech, Cultural Diversity, and the Foundational Paradigms of Free Expression*, 40 UCLA L. REV. 103, 197 (1992) ("However well-meaning the egalitarian effort to suppress hate speech may be, the costs that would be imposed are large and fundamental. The very structure of autonomous self-governance would be threatened, for once the idea of preserving cultural diversity is accepted as reason enough to muzzle speakers in public discourse, there is no logical reason why any other cultural perspective may be denied the opportunity to suppress public discourse in the name of preservation of the desired cultural perspective."); Strossen, *Regulating Racist Speech on Campus: A Modest Proposal?*, 1990 DUKE L.J. 484, 570 ("[A] focus on the hateful message conveyed by particular speech may distort our view of fundamental neutral principles applicable to our system of free expression generally. We should not let the racist veneer in which expression is cloaked obscure our recognition of how important free expression is and of how effectively it has advanced racial equality.").

(2) *Modify Standards.* As a consequence of *R.A.V.*, one commentator has suggested that "some ordinances and campus codes must be rewritten to satisfy the standards outlined by the set of *R.A.V.* opinions. To be consistent with the current dictates of constitutional law, such codes must both be narrowly limited to 'fighting words' of the sort likely to cause immediate violence and refrain from singling out speech based on its tendency to reinforce patterns of discrimination." *See* Lupu, *Statutes Revolving in Constitutional Law Orbits*, 79 VA. L. REV. 1, 10 (1993); *see also* Shiffrin, *Racist Speech, Outsider Jurisprudence, and the Meaning of America*, 80 CORNELL L. REV. 43, 102–3 (1994) ("Speech targeted at members of historically oppressed racial groups that insults on the basis of race ought to be punished; individuals deserve redress for what is intended and felt as particularized injury even if racist speech regulations are symbolically ineffective or even counterproductive.").

For an argument of the constitutionality of university prohibitions of public expression that insults members of the academic community on account of race, see Byrne, *Racial Insults and Free Speech Within the University*, 79 GEO. L.J. 399, 400 (1991) ("On campus, general rights of free speech should be qualified by the intellectual values of academic discourse. I conclude that the protection of these academic values, which themselves enjoy constitutional protection, permits state universities lawfully to bar racially abusive speech, even if the state legislature could not constitutionally prohibit such speech throughout society at large. At the same time, however, I assert that the First Amendment renders state universities powerless to punish speakers for advocating any idea in a reasoned manner.").

(3) *Hate Crimes.* In *Wisconsin v. Mitchell*, 508 U.S. 476 (1993), the Court upheld a law authorizing sentence enhancement for certain "hate crimes." Defendant was convicted of aggravated battery, an offense that ordinarily carried a maximum sentence of two years in Wisconsin. That maximum increased to seven years because the jury found that defendant had intentionally selected his victim because of the victim's race. The judge then sentenced Mitchell to four years imprisonment. The Wisconsin statute

at issue authorized sentence enhancement for certain offenses if the defendant intentionally selected the victim based on the "race, religion, color, disability, sexual orientation, national origin or ancestry of that person or the owner or occupant of that property."

Defendant and several friends had just finished watching the movie *Mississippi Burning*, in which a white man beat a young black boy. Mitchell allegedly addressed the group and said, "Do you all feel hyped up to move on some white people?" Soon after, when the victim walked by on the other side of the street, Mitchell allegedly said, "There goes a white boy; go get him." The group then beat the boy unconscious.

Writing for a unanimous Court, Chief Justice Rehnquist found that a physical assault is not protected expressive conduct just because the actor intends thereby to express an idea. In determining a sentence, judges have traditionally considered various factors besides evidence of guilt. One important factor is the defendant's motive for the crime, as against his abstract beliefs.

The Court distinguished *Dawson v. Delaware*, 503 U.S. 159 (1992), *supra* § 12.03, Note (6) after *Keyishian v. Board of Regents*. *Dawson* invalidated the introduction of evidence at a capital sentencing hearing that the defendant was a member of a white supremacist prison gang. Such evidence proved nothing more than the defendant's "abstract beliefs." The instant case more closely resembled *Barclay v. Florida*, 463 U.S. 939 (1983) (plurality opinion), which allowed the defendant's racial animus toward his victim to be considered in a death sentence.

Using similar reasoning, Chief Justice Rehnquist distinguished *R.A.V. v. St. Paul*. The ordinance invalidated in *R.A.V.* was directed at certain expression based on content, while the one at issue here focuses on conduct, i.e., a racially biased assault. In upholding the Wisconsin "hate crime" statute, the Court emphasized that the First Amendment does not bar evidence of speech to establish the defendant's motive or intent in committing the criminal act.

[2] Sexually Offensive Speech

YOUNG v. AMERICAN MINI THEATRES, INC.
427 U.S. 50, 96 S. Ct. 2440, 49 L. Ed. 2d 310 (1976)

JUSTICE STEVENS delivered the opinion of the Court.

Zoning ordinances adopted by the city of Detroit differentiate between motion picture theaters which exhibit sexually explicit "adult" movies and those which do not. The principal question presented by this case is whether that statutory classification is unconstitutional because it is based on the content of communication protected by the First Amendment.

Effective November 2, 1972, Detroit adopted the ordinances challenged in this litigation. Instead of concentrating "adult" theaters in limited zones, these ordinances require that such theaters be dispersed. Specifically, an adult theater may not be located within 1,000 feet of any two other "regulated uses" or within 500 feet of a residential area. The term "regulated uses" includes 10 different kinds of establishments in addition to adult theaters.[4]

The classification of a theater as "adult" is expressly predicated on the character of

---

[4] [Court's footnote 3] In addition to adult motion picture theaters and "mini" theaters, which contain less than 50 seats, the regulated uses include adult bookstores; cabarets (group "D"); establishments for the sale of beer or intoxicating liquor for consumption on the premises; hotels or motels; pawnshops; pool or billiard halls; public lodging houses; secondhand stores; shoeshine parlors; and taxi dance halls.

the motion pictures which it exhibits. If the theater is used to present "material distinguished or characterized by an emphasis on matter depicting, describing or relating to 'Specified Sexual Activities' or 'Specified Anatomical Areas,' "[5] it is an adult establishment.[6]

The 1972 ordinances were amendments to an "Anti-Skid Row Ordinance" which had been adopted 10 years earlier. At that time the Detroit Common Council made a finding that some uses of property are especially injurious to a neighborhood when they are concentrated in limited areas. The decision to add adult motion picture theaters and adult book stores to the list of businesses which, apart from a special waiver, could not be located within 1,000 feet of two other "regulated uses," was, in part, a response to the significant growth in the number of such establishments. In the opinion of urban planners and real estate experts who supported the ordinances, the location of several such businesses in the same neighborhood tends to attract an undesirable quantity and quality of transients, adversely affects property values, causes an increase in crime, especially prostitution, and encourages residents and businesses to move elsewhere.

Respondents are the operators of two adult motion picture theaters. . . . Both theaters were located within 1,000 feet of two other regulated uses and [one] was less than 500 feet from a residential area.

. . . [R]espondents contend (1) that the ordinances are so vague that they violate the Due Process Clause of the Fourteenth Amendment; (2) that they are invalid under the First Amendment as prior restraints on protected communication; and (3) that the classification of theaters on the basis of the content of their exhibitions violates the Equal Protection Clause of the Fourteenth Amendment. . . .

I

There are two parts to respondents' claim that the ordinances are too vague. They do not attack the specificity of the definition of "Specified Sexual Activities" or "Specified Anatomical Areas." They argue, however, that they cannot determine how much of the described activity may be permissible before the exhibition is "characterized by an emphasis" on such matter. . . .

Because the ordinances affect communication protected by the First Amendment, respondents argue that they may raise the vagueness issue even though there is no uncertainty about the impact of the ordinances on their own rights. On several occasions we have determined that a defendant whose own speech was unprotected had standing to challenge the constitutionality of a statute which purported to prohibit protected speech, or even speech arguably protected. . . . *See Broadrick v. Oklahoma*, 413 U.S. 601, 611–14 [(1973)]. . . .

. . . Since there is surely a less vital interest in the uninhibited exhibition of material

---

[5] [Court's footnote 4] These terms are defined as follows:

"For the purpose of this section, 'Specified Sexual Activities' is defined as:

1. Human Genitals in a state of sexual stimulation or arousal;

2. Acts of human masturbation, sexual intercourse or sodomy;

3. Fondling or other erotic touching of human genitals, pubic region, buttock or female breast.

And "Specified Anatomical Areas" is defined as:

1. Less than completely and opaquely covered: (a) human genitals, pubic region, (b) buttock, and (c) female breast below a point immediately above the top of the areola; and

2. Human male genitals in a discernibly turgid state, even if completely and opaquely covered."

[6] [Court's footnote 5] There are three types of adult establishments — bookstores, motion picture theaters, and mini motion picture theaters. . . .

that is on the borderline between pornography and artistic expression than in the free dissemination of ideas of social and political significance, and since the limited amount of uncertainty in the ordinances is easily susceptible of a narrowing construction, we think this is an inappropriate case in which to adjudicate the hypothetical claims of persons not before the Court. . . .

The application of the ordinances to respondents is plain. . . .

II

Petitioners acknowledge that the ordinances prohibit theaters which are not licensed as "adult motion picture theaters" from exhibiting films which are protected by the First Amendment. Respondents argue that the ordinances are therefore invalid as prior restraints on free speech.

The ordinances are not challenged on the ground that they impose a limit on the total number of adult theaters which may operate in the city of Detroit. There is no claim that distributors or exhibitors of adult films are denied access to the market or, conversely, that the viewing public is unable to satisfy its appetite for sexually explicit fare. Viewed as an entity, the market for this commodity is essentially unrestrained.

It is true, however, that adult films may only be exhibited commercially in licensed theaters. But that is also true of all motion pictures. The city's general zoning laws require all motion picture theaters to satisfy certain locational as well as other requirements; we have no doubt that the municipality may control the location of theaters as well as the location of other commercial establishments, either by confining them to certain specified commercial zones or by requiring that they be dispersed throughout the city. . . .

Putting to one side for the moment the fact that adult motion picture theaters must satisfy a locational restriction not applicable to other theaters, we are also persuaded that the 1,000-foot restriction does not, in itself, create an impermissible restraint on protected communication. . . .

III

. . . The question whether speech is, or is not, protected by the First Amendment often depends on the content of the speech. Thus, the line between permissible advocacy and impermissible incitation to crime or violence depends, not merely on the setting in which the speech occurs, but also on exactly what the speaker had to say. Similarly, it is the content of the utterance that determines whether it is a protected epithet or an unprotected "fighting comment."[7] And in time of war "the publication of the sailing dates of transports or the number and location of troops" may unquestionably be restrained, *see Near v. Minnesota ex rel. Olson*, 283 U.S. 697, 716 [(1931)], although publication of news stories with a different content would be protected.

Even within the area of protected speech, a difference in content may require a different governmental response. In *New York Times Co. v. Sullivan*, 376 U.S. 254 (1964), we recognized that the First Amendment places limitations on the States' power to enforce their libel laws. We held that a public official may not recover damages from a critic of his official conduct without proof of "malice" as specially defined in that opinion. Implicit in the opinion is the assumption that if the content of the newspaper

---

[7] [Court's footnote 24] In *Chaplinsky v. New Hampshire*, 315 U.S. 568 (1942), we held that a statute punishing the use of "damned racketeer[s]" and "damned Fascist[s]" did not unduly impair liberty of expression.

article had been different — that is, if its subject matter had not been a public official — a lesser standard of proof would have been adequate.

. . . But that assumption did not contradict the underlying reason for the rule which is . . . the need for absolute neutrality by the government; its regulation of communication may not be affected by sympathy or hostility for the point of view being expressed by the communicator. Thus, although the content of a story must be examined to decide whether it involves a public figure or a public issue, the Court's application of the relevant rule may not depend on its favorable or unfavorable appraisal of that figure or that issue.

We have recently held that the First Amendment affords some protection to commercial speech.[8] We have also made it clear, however, that the content of a particular advertisement may determine the extent of its protection. A public rapid transit system may accept some advertisements and reject others.[9] A state statute may permit highway billboards to advertise businesses located in the neighborhood but not elsewhere,[10] and regulatory commissions may prohibit businessmen from making statements which, though literally true, are potentially deceptive. The measure of constitutional protection to be afforded commercial speech will surely be governed largely by the content of the communication.

More directly in point are opinions dealing with the question whether the First Amendment prohibits the State and Federal Governments from wholly suppressing sexually oriented materials on the basis of their "obscene character. . . . " Members of the Court who would accord the greatest protection to such materials have repeatedly indicated that the State could prohibit the distribution or exhibition of such materials to juveniles and unconsenting adults. . . . [A]ny such prohibition must rest squarely on an appraisal of the content of material. . . .

[T]he regulation of the places where sexually explicit films may be exhibited is unaffected by whatever social, political, or philosophical message a film may be intended to communicate. . . .

Moreover, even though we recognize that the First Amendment will not tolerate the total suppression of erotic materials that have some arguably artistic value, it is manifest that society's interest in protecting this type of expression is of a wholly different, and lesser, magnitude than the interest in untrammeled political debate. . . . Whether political oratory or philosophical discussion moves us to applaud or to despise what is said, every schoolchild can understand why our duty to defend the right to speak remains the same. But few of us would march our sons and daughters off to war to preserve the citizen's right to see "Specified Sexual Activities. . . . " Even though the First Amendment protects communication in this area from total suppression, we hold that the State may legitimately use the content of these materials as the basis for placing them in a different classification from other motion pictures.

The remaining question is whether the line drawn by these ordinances is justified by the city's interest in preserving the character of its neighborhoods. . . . The record disclosed a factual basis for the Common Council's conclusion that this kind of restriction will have the desired effect.[11] It is not our function to appraise the wisdom of

---

[8] [Court's footnote 28] *Virginia Pharmacy Board v. Virginia Consumer Council*, 425 U.S. 748 (1976).

[9] [Court's footnote 29] *Lehman v. City of Shaker Heights*, 418 U.S. 298 (1974) (product advertising accepted, while political cards rejected).

[10] [Court's footnote 30] *Markham Advertising Co. v. State*, 439 P.2d 248 (1968), appeal dismissed for want of a substantial federal question, 393 U.S. 316 (1969).

[11] [Court's footnote 34] The Common Council's determination was that a concentration of "adult" movie

its decision to require adult theaters to be separated rather than concentrated in the same areas. In either event, the city's interest in attempting to preserve the quality of urban life is one that must be accorded high respect. Moreover, the city must be allowed a reasonable opportunity to experiment with solutions to admittedly serious problems.

Since what is ultimately at stake is nothing more than a limitation on the place where adult films may be exhibited,[12] even though the determination of whether a particular film fits that characterization turns on the nature of its content, we conclude that the city's interest in the present and future character of its neighborhoods adequately supports its classification of motion pictures. We hold that the zoning ordinances requiring that adult motion picture theaters not be located within 1,000 feet of two other regulated uses does not violate the Equal Protection Clause of the Fourteenth Amendment. . . .

JUSTICE POWELL, concurring in the judgment and portions of the opinion.

Although I agree with much of what is said in the Court's opinion, and concur in Parts I and II, my approach to the resolution of this case is sufficiently different to prompt me to write separately.[13] I view the case as presenting an example of innovative land-use regulation, implicating First Amendment concerns only incidentally and to a limited extent. . . .

. . . [I]t is clear beyond question that the Detroit Common Council had broad regulatory power to deal with the problem that prompted enactment of the Anti-Skid Row Ordinance. . . .

. . . The constraints of the ordinance with respect to location may indeed create economic loss for some who are engaged in this business. But in this respect they are affected no differently from any other commercial enterprise that suffers economic detriment as a result of land-use regulation. . . .

The inquiry for First Amendment purposes is not concerned with economic impact; rather, it looks only to the effect of this ordinance upon freedom of expression. This prompts essentially two inquiries: (i) Does the ordinance impose any content limitation on the creators of adult movies or their ability to make them available to whom they desire, and (ii) does it restrict in any significant way the viewing of these movies by those who desire to see them? On the record in this case, these inquiries must be answered in the negative. At most the impact of the ordinance on these interests is incidental and minimal. Detroit has silenced no message, has invoked no censorship,

---

theaters causes the area to deteriorate and become a focus of crime, effects which are not attributable to theaters showing other types of films. It is this secondary effect which these zoning ordinances attempt to avoid, not the dissemination of "offensive" speech. In contrast, in *Erznoznik v. City of Jacksonville*, 422 U.S. 205 (1975), the justifications offered by the city rested primarily on the city's interest in protecting its citizens from exposure to unwanted, "offensive" speech. The only secondary effect relied on to support that ordinance was the impact on traffic — an effect which might be caused by a distracting open-air movie even if it did not exhibit nudity.

[12] [Court's footnote 35] The situation would be quite different if the ordinance had the effect of suppressing, or greatly restricting access to, lawful speech. Here, however, the District Court specifically found that "[t]he Ordinances do not affect the operation of existing establishments but only the location of new ones. There are myriad locations in the City of Detroit which must be over 1000 feet from existing regulated establishments. This burden on First Amendment rights is slight." [*Nortown Theatre Inc. v. Gribbs*,] 373 F. Supp. [363,] 370 [(E.D. Mich. 1974)]. . . .

[13] [Court's footnote 1] I do not think we need reach, nor am I inclined to agree with, the holding in Part III (and supporting discussion) that nonobscene, erotic materials may be treated differently under First Amendment principles from other forms of protected expression. I do not consider the conclusions in Part I of the opinion to depend on distinctions between protected speech.

and has imposed no limitation upon those who wish to view them. The ordinance is addressed only to the places at which this type of expression may be presented, a restriction that does not interfere with content. Nor is there any significant overall curtailment of adult movie presentations, or the opportunity for a message to reach an audience. On the basis of the District Court's finding, . . . it appears that if a sufficient market exists to support them the number of adult movie theaters in Detroit will remain approximately the same. . . . To be sure some prospective patrons may be inconvenienced by this dispersal. But other patrons, depending upon where they live or work, may find it more convenient to view an adult movie when adult theaters are not concentrated in a particular section of the city.

In these circumstances, it is appropriate to analyze the permissibility of Detroit's action under the four-part test of *United States v. O'Brien*, 391 U.S. 367, 377 (1968). Under that test, a governmental regulation is sufficiently justified, despite its incidental impact upon First Amendment interests, "if it is within the constitutional power of the Government; if it furthers an important or substantial governmental interest; if the governmental interest is unrelated to the suppression of free expression; and if the incidental restriction on . . . First Amendment freedoms is no greater than is essential to the furtherance of that interest." *Ibid.* . . .

There is, as noted earlier, no question that the ordinance was within the power of the Detroit Common Council to enact. . . . Nor is there doubt that the interests furthered by this ordinance are both important and substantial. Without stable neighborhoods, both residential and commercial, large sections of a modern city quickly can deteriorate into an urban jungle with tragic consequences to social, environmental, and economic values. . . .

The third and fourth tests of *O'Brien* also are met on this record. It is clear both from the chronology and from the facts that Detroit has not embarked on an effort to suppress free expression. The ordinance was already in existence, and its purposes clearly set out, for a full decade before adult establishments were brought under it. When this occurred, it is clear — indeed it is not seriously challenged — that the governmental interest prompting the inclusion in the ordinance of adult establishments was wholly unrelated to any suppression of free expression. Nor is there reason to question that the degree of incidental encroachment upon such expression was the minimum necessary to further the purpose of the ordinance. . . . [14]

JUSTICE STEWART, with whom JUSTICE BRENNAN, JUSTICE MARSHALL, and JUSTICE BLACKMUN join, dissenting. . . .

This case does not involve a simple zoning ordinance, or a content-neutral time, place, and manner restriction or a regulation of obscene expression or other speech that is entitled to less than the full protection of the First Amendment.

What this case does involve is the constitutional permissibility of selective interference with protected speech whose content is thought to produce distasteful effects. . . . By refusing to invalidate Detroit's ordinance the Court rides roughshod over cardinal principles of First Amendment law, which require that time, place, and manner regulations that affect protected expression be content neutral except in the limited context of a captive or juvenile audience.

I can only interpret today's decision as an aberration. . . .

---

[14] [Court's footnote 6] In my view Justice Stewart's dissent misconceives the issue in this case by insisting that it involves an impermissible time, place, and manner restriction based on the content of expression. It involves nothing of the kind. We have here merely a decision by the city to treat certain movie theaters differently because they have markedly different effects upon their surroundings. . . .

[JUSTICE BLACKMUN, joined by the three other dissenters, wrote a separate dissent based on vagueness.]

FEDERAL COMMUNICATIONS COMMISSION v. PACIFICA FOUNDATION, 438 U.S. 726 (1978). In *Pacifica*, the Court upheld a Federal Communications Commission (FCC) Declaratory Order regulating indecent broadcasts even if they were not obscene. "George Carlin recorded a 12-minute monologue entitled 'Filthy Words' " in which he repeated a variety of " 'the words that you couldn't say on the public, ah, airwaves, um, the ones you definitely wouldn't say, ever." During a Tuesday afternoon, "a New York radio station, owned by . . . Pacifica Foundation, broadcast the 'Filthy Words' monologue." A listener, while in the car with his young son, heard the monologue and complained to the FCC. Pacifica responded to the complaint by explaining that, at the beginning of the program which included the monologue, it had broadcast a disclaimer alerting listeners to the sensitive nature of the language that some might find offensive. "Pacifica characterized George Carlin as 'a significant social satirist, who, like Twain or Sahl before him, examines the language of ordinary people. . . . Carlin is not mouthing obscenities, he is merely using words to satirize as harmless and essentially silly our attitudes towards those words.' "

The FCC issued a Declaratory Order against Pacifica pursuant to its statutory authority to regulate radio broadcasting that uses "any obscene, indecent, or profane language" and to "encourage the larger and more effective use of radio in the public interest." The Declaratory Order held that Carlin's monologue was " 'patently offensive,' though not necessarily obscene." Furthermore, it was "indecent," a concept "intimately connected with the exposure of children" to patently offensive language, because it was broadcast at a time of day when children may listen. The FCC "concluded that certain words depicted sexual and excretory activities in a patently offensive manner, noted that they 'were broadcast at a time when children were undoubtedly in the audience (i.e., in the early afternoon),' and that the prerecorded language, with these offensive words 'repeated over and over,' was 'deliberately broadcast.' "

Writing for a plurality of three, Justice Stevens rejected Pacifica's argument that the FCC's order was overbroad. While the FCC's definition of indecency may deter some "broadcasting of patently offensive references to excretory and sexual organs and activities" that "may be protected, they surely lie at the periphery of First Amendment concern. . . . Invalidating any rule on the basis of its hypothetical application to situations not before the Court is 'strong medicine' to be applied 'sparingly and only as a last resort.' We decline to administer that medicine to preserve the vigor of patently offensive sexual and excretory speech."

Justice Stevens again wrote for a plurality of three on the first part of the challenge to the order as applied to Pacifica. He stated that "the question is whether the First Amendment denies government any power to restrict the public broadcast of indecent language in any circumstance."[15] Both the content and the context of the speech are crucial components in analyzing speech under the First Amendment. The Court has allowed the government to forbid fighting words and obscene speech and more stringently to regulate commercial speech and speech that defames private citizens, rather than public officials. In *Young v. American Mini Theatres*, the Court "refused to hold that a 'statutory classification is unconstitutional because it is based on the content of communication protected by the First Amendment.' " The FCC did not characterize

---

[15] "Pacifica's position would of course deprive the Commission of any power to regulate erotic telecasts unless they were obscene under *Miller v. California*, 413 U.S. 15 (1973). Anything that could be sold at a newsstand for private examination could be publicly displayed on television."

the speech as offensive because of its political or satirical content. "The monologue does present a point of view; it attempts to show that the words it uses are 'harmless' and our attitudes toward them are essentially 'silly.' The Commission objects not to this point of view, but to the way in which it is expressed." The words are offensive "for the same reason that obscenity offends."

While "these words ordinarily lack literary, political or scientific value, they are not entirely outside the protection of the First Amendment. Some uses of even the most offensive words are unquestionably protected." With the speech at issue, "both its capacity to offend and its 'social value,' to use Justice Murphy's term, vary with the circumstances."

Justice Stevens found that "the content of Pacifica's broadcast was 'vulgar,' 'offensive,' and 'shocking.' Because content of that character is not entitled to absolute constitutional protection under all circumstances, we must consider its context in order to determine whether the Commission's action was constitutionally permissible."

The last section of Justice Stevens' opinion was for a majority of five. Every medium of expression presents special First Amendment problems. "And of all forms of communication, it is broadcasting that has received the most limited First Amendment protection" for two reasons. First, broadcasting "has a uniquely pervasive presence in the lives of all Americans." Patently offensive, indecent broadcasts enter the home where "the individual's right to be let alone plainly outweighs the First Amendment rights of an intruder. Because the broadcast audience is constantly tuning in and out, prior warnings cannot completely protect the listener or viewer from unexpected program content. To say that one may avoid further offense by turning off the radio when he hears indecent language is like saying that the remedy for an assault is to run away after the first blow." The second distinguishing feature of broadcasting is its access "to children, even those too young to read." The Court has upheld regulations forbidding bookstores and movie theaters from making indecent material available to children.

In concluding, Justice Stevens emphasized the narrowness of the Court's holding.[16] "This case does not involve a two-way radio conversation between a cab driver and a dispatcher, or a telecast of an Elizabethan comedy. We have not decided that an occasional expletive in either setting would justify any sanction, or indeed, that this broadcast would justify a criminal prosecution." The Commission's decision rested entirely on a nuisance rationale under which context is all-important. The concept requires consideration of a host of variables. The time of day was emphasized by the Commission. The content of the program in which the language is used will also affect the composition of the audience, and differences between radio, television, and perhaps closed-circuit transmissions, may also be relevant.

Justice Powell, joined by Justice Blackmun, concurred in the judgment joining only the last part of Justice Stevens' opinion in which Justice Stevens wrote for a majority. Justice Powell agreed with the Court's reviewing of only the FCC's imposition of civil sanctions for a monologue that was indecent as broadcast at two o'clock in the afternoon. He noted that the monologue was not obscene in the constitutional sense and was not comprised of fighting words. Carlin could not be punished within the First Amendment for delivering the same monologue to adults who chose to attend a live performance. Moreover, an adult could read or listen to a copy of the recording of the monologue at home.

The FCC's holding does not prevent broadcasting the monologue late in the evening

---

[16] "As Justice Sutherland wrote, a 'nuisance may be merely a right thing in the wrong place-like a pig in the parlor instead of the barnyard.' "

when fewer children are listening, "nor from broadcasting discussions of the contemporary use of language at any time during the day." Moreover, neither the Commission's nor the Court's holding involve "the isolated use of a potentially offensive word" during a broadcast.

Justice Powell disagreed with the plurality that judges can determine "which speech protected by the First Amendment is most 'valuable' and hence deserving of the most protection, and which is less 'valuable' and hence deserving of less protection." In his view, the decision did not rest on the "value" of the monologue, which was a determination to be made by its listeners, not judges.[17]

"The result turns instead on the unique characteristics of the broadcast media, combined with society's right to protect its children from speech generally agreed to be inappropriate for their years, and with the interest of unwilling adults in not being assaulted by such offensive speech in their homes."

Justice Brennan dissented, joined by Justice Marshall. "Despite the Court's refusal to create a sliding scale of First Amendment protection" based on the value of the speech's content, the Court's holding accepts the FCC's sanction of the monologue as a permissible time, place, and manner regulation. In reaching this conclusion, both the plurality and Justice Powell rely on: "(1) the capacity of a radio broadcast to intrude into the unwilling listener's home, and (2) the presence of children in the listening audience."

With respect to the privacy interest, the Court "misconceives the nature of the privacy interests involved where an individual voluntarily chooses to admit radio communications into his home." The Court also "ignores the constitutionally protected interests of both those who wish to transmit and those who desire to receive broadcasts that many — including the FCC and this Court — might find offensive."

The government does have a "special interest in the well-being of children" which enables government strictly to control the communicative materials available to children. The method for such restriction is the " 'variable obscenity' " standard for material available to minors adopted in *Ginsberg v. New York*, 390 U.S. 629 (1968).

Moreover, Justice Brennan criticized both the intrusion and children rationales, which could be used as a base for censorship without "principled limits." Such justifications could censor a host of "literary works, novels, poems, and plays by the likes of Shakespeare, Joyce, Hemingway, Ben Johnson, Henry Fielding, Robert Burns and Chaucer." These rationales could also support the suppression of much political speech, such as the Nixon tapes; and even certain portions of the Bible could be restricted.

Justice Brennan also distinguished the case at bar from *Young v. American Mini Theatres*. "First the zoning ordinances in *Young* had valid goals other than the channeling of protected speech." Second, they "did not restrict the access of distributors or exhibitors to the market or impair the viewing public's access to the regulated material." Here, the FCC's order restricts both the groups wanting to send the monologue and the groups wanting to hear the monologue.

Justice Brennan concluded by stating that the Court's "acute ethnocentric myopia" would have the greatest impact on those who express themselves with words which may be regarded as offensive by the majority or those from different socioeconomic backgrounds.

Justice Stewart, joined by Justices Brennan, White, and Marshall, dissented. Since

---

[17] Justice Powell was also unwilling to predicate the use of the overbreadth doctrine on the Court's perceptions of the value of the speech. In the past, the Court has only done this in the commercial speech area.

the monologue was not "obscene" it should not have been constitutionally restricted by the FCC.

NOTES

(1) *Drive-in Theaters.* In *Erznoznik v. City of Jacksonville*, 422 U.S. 205 (1975), the Court (6-3) held invalid an ordinance that prohibited a drive-in theatre from showing films that contained nudity and were visible from a public street or other public area. Justice Powell's majority opinion said that the unwilling viewer could easily "avert his eyes," as in *Cohen v. California*, 403 U.S. 15 (1971), *supra* § 14.01[1], Note (1) after *Chaplinsky v. New Hampshire*. Likewise, Justice Powell rejected the claim that the ordinance was a reasonable means of protecting minors since it was "not directed against sexually explicit nudity, nor is it otherwise limited." Because the ordinance was not easily narrowed and had a real and substantial constraining effect on freedom of expression, it was "overbroad" and invalid on its face. Chief Justice Burger and Justices Rehnquist and White dissented.

(2) *Concentrating Theatres.* (a) In *City of Renton v. Playtime Theatres, Inc.*, 475 U.S. 41 (1986), the Court upheld a law that prohibited an "adult motion picture theatre" from locating within 1,000 feet "of any residential zone, single-or multiple-family dwelling, church, park, or school." The Court (7-2) upheld the Renton ordinance, relying primarily on *Young*. Justice Rehnquist's majority opinion concluded that the ordinance was "content-neutral" and was designed to protect the city's retail trade, preserve the quality of urban life, and maintain property values. The majority accepted the district court's finding of "predominate" intent and rejected the court of appeals' conclusion that the ordinance must fall if a motivating factor was to restrict First Amendment rights.

The *Young* case had emphasized that the Detroit ordinance did not shut off channels of communication but merely required that the adult theatres and similar establishments be dispersed throughout the city. The Renton statute, on the other hand, had the effect of limiting the location of adult theatre sites to 520 acres. The Court of Appeals had concluded that, since very little of the undeveloped land within this 520 acres was available for an adult theatre site, the Renton ordinance resulted in a substantial restriction of speech. The Supreme Court majority disagreed: "That respondents must fend for themselves in the real estate market, on an equal footing with other prospective purchasers and lessees, does not give rise to a First Amendment violation. [W]e have never suggested that the First Amendment compels the government to ensure that adult theatres, or any other kinds of speech-related businesses for that matter, will be able to obtain sites at bargain prices."

Justice Brennan's dissent, joined by Justice Marshall, was based on the lack of adequate findings to support the land-use or quality-of-life justifications for the ordinance. Moreover, the Renton ordinance effectively denied adult theaters a reasonable opportunity to operate, a factor that distinguished this case from *Young* "where there was no indication that the Detroit zoning ordinance seriously limited the locations available for adult businesses."

(b) *Separating "adult establishments."* In *City of Los Angeles v. Alameda Books, Inc.*, 535 U.S. 425 (2002), the Court upheld a Los Angeles ordinance that prohibited "more than one adult entertainment business" occupying the same building. The ordinance defines adult establishments as "an adult arcade, bookstore, cabaret, motel, theater, or massage parlor or a place for sexual encounters." Respondents, operators of two adult establishments that rent and sell sexually oriented products "in the same commercial space" in which video booths are located, alleged that the provision was unconstitutional on its face. The case came up on summary judgment for the businesses, and the Supreme Court reversed.

Writing for a plurality of four, Justice O'Connor concluded that "it is rational for the city to infer that reducing the concentration of adult operations in a neighborhood, whether within separate establishments or in one large establishment," will advance the City's interest in reducing crime. *Renton v. Playtime Theatres, Inc.*, 475 U.S. 41 (1986), allows a municipality to rely "on any evidence that is 'reasonably believed to be relevant' for demonstrating a connection between speech and a substantial, independent government interest," in this case, reducing crime. The evidence need only "fairly support" that connection. A Los Angeles study found that concentrations of adult establishments helped to increase prostitution, robbery, assaults, and thefts. This study was sufficient to overcome the summary judgment against the city. Justice O'Connor left the question of the content neutrality of the ordinance to the lower courts.

Justice Scalia filed a concurring opinion. Justice Kennedy concurred in the judgment. He required that the purpose of the ordinance must be to split adult businesses, rather than forcing their closure in a way that would not substantially diminish the amount of speech.

Justice Souter dissented, joined by Justices Stevens, Ginsburg, and Breyer. By forcing adult businesses to divide into two or more separate units, the regulations will double overheads. Accordingly, the City's purpose may well be to drive adult establishments out of business.

(3) *Dial-a-Porn.* In *Sable Communications of California, Inc. v. Federal Communications Commission*, 492 U.S. 115 (1989), a dial-a-porn vendor facially challenged a 1988 federal statute that banned indecent and obscene commercial telephone messages. Writing for a 6-3 majority, Justice White upheld the portion of the statute banning obscene commercial phone messages. A unanimous Court, however, invalidated the statute's prohibition of messages that were indecent, yet not obscene. Governmental regulation of the content of such constitutionally protected speech must comprise the "least restrictive means" of promoting a compelling state interest. The Court recognized the government's interest in protecting children from exposure to indecent dial-a-porn as compelling. The outright ban on such material, however, "was not sufficiently narrowly drawn."

In contrast to the total ban at issue in *Sable*, the government regulation in *FCC v. Pacifica* merely "sought to channel [the indecent expression] to times of day when children most likely would not be exposed to it." Moreover, unlike *Pacifica*, this case did not involve a "captive audience"; the child had to take "affirmative steps" to access the dial-a-porn message. The FCC's "credit card, access code, and scrambling rules were a satisfactory solution to the problem of keeping indecent dial-a-porn messages out of the reach of minors." For additional discussion of *Sable*, see § 15.05[1], Note (8) after *Arcara v. Cloud Books, Inc.*

(4) *Public Nudity.* In *Barnes v. Glen Theatre*, 501 U.S. 560 (1991), a plurality of the Court upheld Indiana's public indecency statute that required dancers to "wear 'pasties' and 'G-strings.' " Writing for a plurality of three, Chief Justice Rehnquist stated that "nude dancing of the kind sought to be performed here is expressive conduct within the outer perimeters of the First Amendment, though we view it as only marginally so."

The Chief Justice rejected Indiana's argument that the regulation was a valid time, place or manner restriction. This "test was developed for evaluating restrictions on expression taking place on public property which had been dedicated as a 'public forum' although we have on at least one occasion applied it to conduct occurring on private property. *See Renton v. Playtime Theatres, Inc.*" Instead, the Court applied the similar standard for scrutinizing expressive conduct that was set forth in *United States v.*

O'Brien, 391 U.S. 367 (1968), § 15.01. Under the *O'Brien* standard, government regulation of conduct that infringes incidentally on speech is justified " 'if it is within the constitutional power of the Government; if it furthers an important or substantial governmental interest; if the governmental interest is unrelated to the supervision of free expression; if the incidental restriction on alleged First Amendment freedom is no greater than is essential to the furtherance of that interest.' "

Applying the *O'Brien* test, the plurality determined that the Indiana regulation was within the State's traditional police powers. Moreover, the regulation of public nudity advances the substantial state interests of protecting "societal order" and "morality." Such regulations "are of ancient origin, and presently exist in at least 47 states."

Indiana's interest in protecting order and morality "is unrelated to the suppression of free expression."[18] Moreover, "the requirement that the dancers don pasties and G-strings does not deprive the dance of whatever erotic message it conveys; it simply makes the message slightly less graphic. The perceived evil that Indiana seeks to address is not erotic dancing, but public nudity. The appearance of people of all shapes, sizes and ages in the nude at a beach, for example, would convey little if any erotic message, yet the State still seeks to prevent it." The statute also passed the fourth prong of the *O'Brien* test: "It is without cavil that the public indecency statute is 'narrowly tailored;' Indiana's requirement that the dancers wear at least pasties and a G-string is modest, and the bare minimum necessary to achieve the State's purpose."

Concurring in the judgment, Justice Scalia believed the statute's purpose to be the enforcement of traditional moral beliefs. He concluded that the statute is a "general law" that regulates conduct and is not directed at expression.

Justice Souter filed an opinion, concurring in the judgment. Unlike Justice Scalia, Justice Souter agreed with both the plurality and the dissent that the "nude dancing at issue here is subject to a degree of First Amendment protection." While he also applied *O'Brien*, Justice Souter upheld the statute not based on defending morality but instead on its "combating the secondary effects of adult entertainment establishments."

Justice White dissented, joined by Justices Marshall, Blackmun and Stevens. "The sight of a fully clothed, or even a partially clothed, dancer generally will have a far different impact on a spectator than that of a nude dancer, even if the same dance is performed. The nudity is itself an expressive component of the dance, not merely incidental 'conduct.' "

ERIE v. PAP'S A.M., 529 U.S. 277 (2000). In *Erie*, the Court upheld a city ordinance in Erie, Pennsylvania banning public nudity. Pap's, the owner of the totally nude dancing establishment, Kandyland, contested the ordinance because it required Kandyland dancers to wear, at a minimum, " 'pasties' and a 'G-string.' " Writing for a majority of five in Section II of the opinion, Justice O'Connor rejected plaintiff's mootness claim under the theory of voluntary cessation. Even though Kandyland no longer exists, plaintiff could still open another establishment. Moreover, as plaintiff won below, the city suffers continuing injury by being barred from enforcing the statute.

Writing for a plurality of four in Section III of the opinion, Justice O'Connor relied on *United States v. O'Brien*, 391 U.S. 367 (1968), as the ban on public nudity is unrelated to the suppression of expression. The Court had analyzed a nearly identical ordinance in *Barnes v. Glen Theater*, 501 U.S. 560 (1991), *supra* Note (4); however, it was divided on the rationale for its conclusion in that case.

The terms of the Erie ordinance regulate conduct alone. The ordinance bans all

---

[18] The *O'Brien* Court stated: "We cannot accept the view that an apparently limitless variety of conduct can be labeled 'speech' whenever the person engaged in the conduct intends thereby to express an idea."

types of public nudity "regardless of whether that nudity is accompanied by expressive activity." Even though the preamble to the ordinance mentioned limiting "erotic dancing of the type performed at Kandyland," one purpose of the ordinance was " 'to combat negative secondary effects' " associated with such establishments. The "ordinance does not attempt to regulate the primary effects of the expression, i.e., the effect on the audience of watching nude erotic dancing, but rather the secondary effects, such as the impacts on public health, safety, and welfare, which we have previously recognized are 'caused by the presence of even one such' establishment."

In response to Pap's allegation that the ordinance was aimed at suppressing expression through nude dancing, the plurality said it "will not strike down an otherwise constitutional statute on the basis of an alleged illicit motive. *O'Brien*." Moreover, any effect that pasties and G-strings may have on the erotic message is *de minimis.*" As Justice Stevens stated in *Young v. American Mini Theaters, Inc*, 427 U.S. 50 (1976), *supra* § 14.01[2], " 'society's interest in protecting this type of expression is of a wholly different, and lesser, magnitude than the interest in untrammeled political debate.' "

Justice O'Connor discussed "incidental burdens" and "secondary effects" as theories that are not identical, but closely related in this case. A city may enact a general ordinance that incidentally burdens some speech, while "recognizing that one specific occurrence of public nudity — nude erotic dancing — is particularly problematic because it produces harmful secondary effects."

Again writing for a plurality of four in Section IV of the opinion, Justice O'Connor applied the four-part test of *O'Brien*. First, the government has the power to enact the legislation as "protect[ing] public health and safety are clearly within the city's police powers." Second, "regulating conduct through a public nudity ban and of combating the harmful secondary effects associated with nude dancing are undeniably important" governmental interests. "Erie could reasonably rely on the evidentiary foundation set forth in *Renton* [*v. Playtime Theaters, Inc.*] and *American Mini Theaters* indicating that secondary effects are caused by the presence of even one adult entertainment establishment in a given neighborhood."[19] Erie did use its own findings as well because the council members who passed the ordinance were likely to be familiar with the area and the effects of the nude dancing establishments.

The regulation furthers the government interest of protecting against crime and other health and safety problems. As previously stated, requiring the dancers to wear pasties and G-strings has only a minimal negative effect, if any, in furthering the government interest of protecting against secondary effects. Third, as discussed in Section III of the plurality opinion, "the government interest is unrelated to the suppression of free expression." Fourth, "the restriction is no greater than is essential" to advance the government interest. "The ordinance regulates conduct, and any incidental impact on the expressive element of nude dancing is *de minimis*."

Justice Scalia, joined by Justice Thomas, concurred in the judgment first arguing the case was moot because there is no dispute that the dancing establishment in question has been closed and sold. Reaching the merits, Justice Scalia maintained that no First Amendment issue existed. Both the Erie ordinance and the Indiana statute at issue in Barnes restrict "not merely nude dancing, but the act — irrespective of whether it is engaged in for expressive purposes — of going nude in public." Justice Scalia rejected Justice Stevens' argument that the ordinance is discriminatory because the prosecutor did not enforce it against a theatrical production in town that involved nudity. "One

---

[19] Similarly, in *Nixon v. Shrink Missouri Government PAC*, 528 U.S. 377 (2000), the majority relied on evidence of corruption caused by campaign contributions taken from another Supreme Court decision.

instance of nonenforcement — against a play already in production that prosecutorial discretion might reasonably have 'grandfathered' — does not render this ordinance discriminatory on its face."[20]

Alternatively, even if Erie had singled out nude dancing, Justice Scalia would have to be convinced that it was the "communicative character of nude dancing" that motivated the ban. The First Amendment has not eradicated the "traditional power of government to foster good morals."

Justice Souter concurred in part and dissented in part. Relying on *O'Brien*, he agreed with the plurality that the City's "interest in combating the secondary effects associated with nude dancing establishments is an interest unrelated to the suppression of expression." However, Erie did not provide a sufficient evidentiary showing to uphold the ordinance. While the City could have borrowed an evidentiary basis from the record of another government, the reliance "must be a matter of demonstrated fact, not speculative supposition." In this case, one councilman "spoke of increases in sex crimes in a way that might be construed as a reference to secondary effects." Justice Souter would vacate the decision of the lower court and remand for further proceedings.

Justice Stevens, joined by Justice Ginsburg, dissented arguing that the ordinance suppresses speech. He pointed to the fact that until now the *O'Brien* test was only used in reference to zoning regulations and the location of establishments such as Kandyland. In contrast, "the Court has now held that such effects may justify the total suppression of protected speech." Unlike the statute in *Barnes* that was not aimed at a particular form of speech, the Erie ordinance was aimed at nude dancing establishments in its scope and its enforcement. For example, the City did not enforce the ordinance to ban the nude play "Equus."[21]

§ 14.02 SPEECH IN TRADITIONAL PUBLIC FORUMS: STREETS, SIDEWALKS, PARKS

COX v. NEW HAMPSHIRE
312 U.S. 569, 61 S. Ct. 762, 85 L. Ed. 1049 (1941)

CHIEF JUSTICE HUGHES delivered the opinion of the Court.

Appellants are five "Jehovah's Witnesses" who, with sixty-three others of the same persuasion, were convicted in the municipal court of Manchester, New Hampshire, for violation of a state statute prohibiting a "parade or procession" upon a public street without a special license.

The statutory prohibition is as follows: "No theatrical or . . . dramatic representation shall be performed or exhibited, and no parade or procession upon any public street or way, and no open-air public meeting upon any ground abutting thereon, shall be permitted, unless a special license therefor shall first be obtained from the selectmen of the town, or from a licensing committee for cities hereinafter provided for. . . . "

The facts, which are conceded by the appellants to be established by the evidence, are these: The sixty-eight defendants and twenty other persons met at a hall in the City of Manchester on the evening of Saturday, July 8, 1939, "for the purpose of engaging in

---

[20]   He further stated that, "I do not think that a law contains the vice of being directed against expression if it bans all public nudity, except that public nudity that the Supreme Court has held cannot be banned because of its expressive nature."

[21]   The Court ignores the evidence of illicit motive by saying that it will not invalidate a law on this basis.

an information march." The company was divided into four or five groups, each with about fifteen to twenty persons. Each group then proceeded to a different part of the business district of the city and there "would line up in single-file formation and then proceed to march along the sidewalk, 'single-file,' that is, following one another." Each of the defendants carried a small staff with a sign reading "Religion is a Snare and a Racket" and on the reverse "Serve God and Christ the King." Some of the marchers carried placards bearing the statement "Fascism or Freedom. Hear Judge Rutherford and Face the Facts." The marchers also handed out printed leaflets announcing a meeting to be held at a later time in the hall from which they had started, where a talk on government would be given to the public free of charge. Defendants did not apply for a permit and none was issued. . . .

The sole charge against appellants was that they were "taking part in a parade or procession" on public streets without a permit as the statute required. . . .

Civil liberties, as guaranteed by the Constitution, imply the existence of an organized society maintaining public order without which liberty itself would be lost in the excesses of unrestrained abuses. The authority of a municipality to impose regulations in order to assure the safety and convenience of the people in the use of public highways has never been regarded as inconsistent with civil liberties but rather as one of the means of safeguarding the good order upon which they ultimately depend. The control of travel on the streets of cities is the most familiar illustration of this recognition of social need. . . . As regulation of the use of the streets for parades and processions is a traditional exercise of control by local government, the question in a particular case is whether that control is exerted so as not to deny or unwarrantedly abridge the right of assembly and the opportunities for the communication of thought and the discussion of public questions immemorially associated with resort to public places. . . .

In the instant case, we are aided by the opinion of the Supreme Court of the State which construed the statute and defined the limitations of the authority conferred for the granting of licenses for parades and processions. . . . Recognizing the importance of the civil liberties invoked by appellants, the court thought it significant that the statute prescribed "no measures for controlling or suppressing the publication on the highways of facts and opinions, either by speech or by writing;" that communication "by the distribution of literature or by the display of placards and signs" was in no respect regulated by the statute; that the regulation with respect to parades and processions was applicable only "to organized formations of persons using the highways;" and that "the defendants separately or collectively in groups not constituting a parade or procession," were "under no contemplation of the act. . . . "

It was with this view of the limited objective of the statute that the state court considered and defined the duty of the licensing authority and the rights of the appellants to a license for their parade, with regard only to considerations of time, place, and manner so as to conserve the public convenience. The obvious advantage of requiring application for a permit was noted as giving the public authorities notice in advance so as to afford opportunity for proper policing. And the court further observed that, in fixing time and place, the license served "to prevent confusion by overlapping parades or processions, to secure convenient use of the streets by other travelers, and to minimize the risk of disorder." But the court held that the licensing board was not vested with arbitrary power or an unfettered discretion; that its discretion must be exercised with "uniformity of method of treatment upon the facts of each application, free from improper or inappropriate considerations and from unfair discrimination. . . . " The defendants, said the court, "had a right, under the act, to a license to march when, where and as they did, if after a required investigation it was found that the convenience of the public in the use of the streets would not thereby be unduly disturbed, upon such conditions or changes in time, place, and manner as would avoid disturbance. . . . "

There remains the question of license fees which, as the court said, had a permissible range from $300 to a nominal amount. The court construed the Act as requiring "a reasonable fixing of the amount of the fee." "The charge," said the court, "for a circus parade or a celebration procession of length, each drawing crowds of observers, would take into account the greater public expense of policing the spectacle, compared with the slight expense of a less expansive and attractive parade or procession, to which the charge would be adjusted." The fee was held to be "not a revenue tax, but one to meet the expense incident to the administration of the act and to the maintenance of public order in the matter licensed." There is nothing contrary to the Constitution in the charge of a fee limited to the purpose stated. The suggestion that a flat fee should have been charged fails to take account of the difficulty of framing a fair schedule to meet all circumstances, and we perceive no constitutional ground for denying to local governments that flexibility of adjustment of fees which in the light of varying conditions would tend to conserve rather than impair the liberty sought.

There is no evidence that the statute has been administered otherwise than in the fair and non-discriminatory manner which the state court has construed it to require. . . .

The argument as to freedom of worship is also beside the point. No interference with religious worship or the practice of religion in any proper sense is shown, but only the exercise of local control over the use of streets for parades and processions. . . .

NOTES

(1) *Standardless Discretion.* In *Cantwell v. Connecticut*, 310 U.S. 296 (1940), the Court invalidated the conviction of Jehovah's witnesses for breach of the peace and for violating a Connecticut statute that prohibited the solicitation of money without approval from an administrative official. Reversing the convictions on due process grounds, the Court said that the "concept of liberty" in the Due Process Clause included the "liberties guaranteed by the First Amendment."

First analyzing the statutory permit requirement, Justice Roberts objected to the standardless discretion vested in administrative officials to determine whether the cause seeking a soliciting permit is religious. While the distinction between a discretionary and a ministerial act is not easily made, the state court did not interpret the statute as only imposing a ministerial duty. Although judicial remedies are available for abuse of discretion, "the system of licensing" still comprises a prior restraint.

To protect against "fraudulent solicitation," strangers can be made to prove who they are and for what purpose they desire to solicit funds. In addition, the State may regulate the way in which solicitation occurs and the time it occurs to protect public safety interests, community peace, comfort, or convenience. However, government cannot determine "what is a religious cause."

The Court also set aside the breach of peace violation, noting that the standard was "a common law concept of the most general and undefined nature." While government can regulate noise and interference with traffic, government cannot suppress speech. In addition, there were no findings of "truculent bearing, intentional discourtesy or personal abuse." Free speech and religion protect the free development of many beliefs and opinions and lifestyles, which is vital to a country with so many races and creeds.

(2) *Leaflets.* In *Lovell v. City of Griffin*, 303 U.S. 444 (1938), a Jehovah's witness was convicted under a city ordinance for distributing pamphlets and magazines without a permit. The Court invalidated the ordinance, holding that it was too broad and,

therefore, an unconstitutional prior restraint on freedom of speech. The ordinance applied regardless of the type of literature distributed and when, where or how distribution took place.

(3) *Park Permits.* In *Thomas v. Chicago Park District*, 534 U.S. 316 (2002), the Court unanimously decided that a permit system to use public parks did not have to incorporate the procedural safeguards of *Freedman v. Maryland*, 380 U.S. 51 (1965). The Chicago ordinance "requires a person to obtain a permit in order to 'conduct a public assembly, parade, picnic, or other event involving more than fifty individuals,' or engage in any activity such as 'creating or emitting any Amplified Sound.' " Applications must be decided within 14 days, and can only be denied in writing based on 13 grounds, which limit administrative discretion. Applicants may appeal denials to the General Superintendent of Parks, and then to a judicial court.

Finding *Freedman* inapplicable, Justice Scalia neither required the Park District to "initiate litigation every time it denies a permit," nor specify a deadline for prompt judicial review of challenges. Unlike the censorship of films at issue in *Freedman*, the ordinance in this case is a content-neutral time, place, and manner restriction. Moreover, it contains "adequate standards to guide the official's decision and render it subject to effective judicial review." Such grounds include the filing of an incomplete or materially false application, unpaid damage to a park, a prior applicant for the same time and place, unreasonable health or safety dangers, and violation of a prior permit. The Court did not reach the question of whether the *Freedman* "requirement of prompt judicial review means a prompt judicial determination or the prompt commencement of judicial proceedings."

(4) *Home Solicitation Permits.* In *Watchtower Bible and Tract Society of New York, Inc. v. Village of Stratton*, 536 U.S. 150 (2002), the Court invalidated on its face a municipal ordinance prohibiting " 'canvassers' from going on private property for the purpose of explaining or promoting any 'cause' unless they receive a permit and the residents visited have not opted for a 'no solicitation' sign." Petitioners are Jehovah's Witnesses who offer free religious literature. While they do not solicit contributions, they do accept donations. The Village has never denied an application for a permit, nor has it ever revoked a permit. Another section of the ordinance permits residents to file a "No Solicitation Registration Form" that lists a series of 19 exceptions, including Scouting Organizations, Camp Fire Girls, Jehovah's Witnesses, and Christmas Carolers, that residents can prohibit "from canvassing unless expressly exempted."

Writing for the Court, Justice Stevens stated first that freedom of speech and of the press protects the "hand distribution of religious tracts." Second, "door-to-door canvassing and pamphleteering must proceed *free and unhampered* by censorship." Third, the state has some interest in regulating these activities, particularly when soliciting money is involved. Fourth, it is "essential to the poorly financed causes of little people."

The ordinance requires a permit to go on private property to explain or promote "any 'cause.' " "Had this provision been construed to apply only to commercial activities and the solicitation of funds, arguably the ordinance would have been tailored to the Village's interest in protecting the privacy of its residents and preventing fraud." However, it applies to " 'soliciting the votes of neighbors,' or ringing doorbells to enlist support for employing a more efficient garbage collector."

In addition to its sweeping effect, Justice Stevens identified three other concerns resulting from a permit requirement. First, the permit requirement undermines anonymous speech. While prohibiting anonymity may sometimes be justified — for example, to protect "the integrity of a ballot-initiative process," or to prevent fraudulent transactions, the Village ordinance goes well beyond such interests. Second, obtaining a permit may rail against a person's political or religious views. Third, the requirement curtails spontaneous speech.

The "breadth and unprecedented nature" rendered it invalid, as did its not being tailored to the Village's interests in crime prevention and privacy. With respect to privacy, the ordinance allows posting "No Solicitation" signs, and residents can refuse to speak with visitors. With respect to crime prevention, permit requirements are unlikely to deter criminals from knocking.

Justice Breyer concurred, joined by Justices Souter and Ginsburg. Justice Scalia, joined by Justice Thomas, concurred in the judgment. Chief Justice Rehnquist dissented, indicating that he was unclear as to what test the majority applied, but that intermediate scrutiny allows a discretionless permit requirement.

(5) *Parade Fees.* In *Forsyth County v. Nationalist Movement*, 505 U.S. 123 (1992), Justice Blackmun's majority opinion held facially unconstitutional a parade and assembly fee ordinance affording broad administrative discretion. Under the ordinance, applicants paid up to $1,000 a day for a permit. The county administrator charged the Nationalist Movement a $100 fee for 10 hours of the city administrator's time in processing the organization's permit to demonstrate on Martin Luther King's birthday.

The ordinance granted the administrator broad discretion to set the amount to be paid for the expense to administer the ordinance and to maintain public order for the particular event. He also determined whether "the fee would include any or all of the county's administrative and security expenses."

In this case, the administrator chose not to include clerical or security expenses, and "deliberately kept the fee low by undervaluing the time he spent processing the application." On some other occasions, he kept the fee even lower. The county had not articulated fee standards in the ordinance or in practice. "The administrator is not required to rely on objective factors. He need not provide any explanation for his decision, and that decision is not reviewable."

In assessing the fee for event security costs, the county administrator inevitably projected "the amount of hostility likely to be created by the speech based on its content." Justice Blackmun found "irrelevant" the amount of the fee at issue, but focused on the unbridled administrative discretion.

Chief Justice Rehnquist dissented, joined by Justices White, Scalia, and Thomas. The Chief Justice contended that the discretion afforded by the Forsyth ordinance parallels that afforded by the ordinance in *Cox v. New Hampshire*. Moreover, there was no evidence that the administrator had abused his discretion in applying this relatively new statute.

(6) *Sound Trucks.* The "sound truck" cases raised not only the usual problems of adjusting competing claims to the use of public streets and parks but also the issue of whether noise in city streets invaded the privacy expectations of urban residents. In *Saia v. New York*, 334 U.S. 558 (1948), the Court struck down a Lockport, New York, law that prohibited the use of "sound amplification devices except with the permission of the Chief of Police." The Court (5-4) held that giving broad discretion to the police chief constituted a prior restraint. Justice Douglas' majority opinion emphasized: "There are no standards prescribed for the exercise of his discretion. The statute is not narrowly drawn to regulate the hours or places of use of loudspeakers, or the volume of sound (the decibels) to which they must be adjusted."

Justice Frankfurter, in dissent, argued that the State could authorize local officials to protect the peace and quiet of those "who sought quiet and other pleasures that a park affords." In a separate dissent, Justice Jackson saw no reason why property which was set aside for recreational purposes had to be made available for the propagation of religion.

In *Kovacs v. Cooper*, 336 U.S. 77 (1949), the Court (5-4) upheld a conviction under a Trenton, New Jersey law that barred the use of an amplifying device on public streets which "emits . . . loud and raucous noises."

Justice Frankfurter's concurrence in *Kovacs v. Cooper* provided an opportunity for him to expound his view that the phrase "the preferred position of freedom of speech" in constitutional law was a deceptive oversimplification of a complex range of value judgments. Justice Rutledge concluded that First Amendment guarantees do occupy a preferred position in the Bill of Rights and "also in the repeated decisions of this Court."

(7) *Discretion in Applying Volume Standards.* In *Ward v. Rock Against Racism*, 491 U.S. 781 (1989), the Court upheld, against a facial challenge, New York City "Use Guidelines" requiring that performers in a city park use sound equipment and a sound technician provided by the City.

Writing for a 6-3 majority, Justice Kennedy upheld the guidelines as valid time, place, and manner restrictions. For additional discussion of mandated use of the city's equipment and technician, see § 14.04[1].

Justice Kennedy rejected the argument that the regulations placed unfettered discretion "in the hands of city officials." "[R]espondent does not suggest that City officials enjoy unfettered discretion to deny Bandshell permits altogether."

The City's guideline states that its goals are to "provide the best sound for all events" and to "insure appropriate sound quality balanced with respect for nearby residential neighbors and the mayorally decreed quiet zone of [the] Sheep Meadow." While these standards are "undoubtedly flexible, and the officials implementing them will exercise considerable discretion, perfect clarity and precise guidance have never been required even of regulations that restrict expressive activity."

In rejecting the facial challenge, the Court also found highly relevant the City's interpretation, which provides "additional guidance to the officials charged with its enforcement. The District Court expressly found that the City's policy is to defer to the sponsor's desires concerning sound quality. With respect to sound volume, the City retains ultimate control, but City officials 'mak[e] it a practice to confer with the sponsor if any questions of excessive sound arise, before taking any corrective action.' The City's goal of ensuring that the 'sound amplification [is] sufficient to reach all listeners within the defined concert ground,' serves to limit further the discretion of the officials on the scene."

Justice Blackmun concurred in the result. Justice Marshall filed a dissenting opinion in which Justices Brennan and Stevens joined. "With neither prompt judicial review nor detailed and neutral standards fettering the city's discretion to restrict protected speech, the Guidelines constitute a quintessential, and unconstitutional, prior restraint."

(8) *Abortion Clinics.* In *Madsen v. Women's Health Center, Inc.*, 512 U.S. 753 (1994), the Court upheld part of a Florida court injunction which, among other things, prohibited "singing, chanting, whistling, shouting, yelling, use of bullhorns, auto horns, sound amplification equipment or other sounds or images observable to or within earshot of the patients inside" an abortion clinic "from 7:30 until noon, on Monday through Saturdays, during surgical procedures and recovery periods." Writing for the majority, Chief Justice Rehnquist stated that, in determining whether regulations burden speech more than is necessary, courts must consider the place where the regulations apply. "Noise control is particularly important around hospitals and medical

facilities during surgery and recovery periods." The noise restrictions in the injunction at issue did not burden any more speech than necessary to protect patient well-being. "The First Amendment does not demand that patients at a medical facility undertake Herculean efforts to escape the cacophony of political protests." For further discussion of *Madsen*, see § 14.04[1].

(9) *Mailbox*. In *U.S. Postal Service v. Greenburgh Civic Ass'n.*, 453 U.S. 114 (1981), the Court upheld a federal regulation prohibiting the insertion of unstamped political material in mailboxes made to government specification and used for the receipt of mail in private residences. The Court reversed a lower court ruling and held that such boxes could not be regarded as public forums. Justice Marshall's dissent emphasized the interest in an effective means of free communication. Justice Stevens filed a separate dissent.

(10) *Newsracks*. In *City of Lakewood v. Plain Dealer Publishing Co.*, 486 U.S. 750 (1988), the Court addressed the constitutionality of a Lakewood City ordinance regulating the placement of newsracks on public property. The ordinance granted "the Mayor the authority to grant or deny applications for annual newsrack permits." For each denial of a newsrack permit, the ordinance required that the mayor "stat[e] the reasons for such denial."

Before addressing the merits of the challenge, Justice Brennan, writing for a narrow (4–3) majority, addressed whether the Lakewood ordinance was susceptible to a facial challenge by the *Plain Dealer*. He found "that when a licensing statute allegedly vests unbridled discretion in a government official over whether to permit or deny expressive activity, one who is subject to the law may challenge it facially without the necessity of . . . being denied a license."

Justice Brennan then proceeded to address the merits. "Nothing in the law as written requires the Mayor to do more than make the statement 'it is not in the public interest' when denying a permit application. Similarly, the Mayor could grant the application, but require the newsrack to be placed in an inaccessible location without providing any explanation." These " 'illusory constraints' " were not standards.

Justice White dissented, joined by Justices Stevens and O'Connor. While conceding that the *Plain Dealer* had a constitutional right to distribute its newspapers, Justice White contended that it did not have the right to "distribute [its newspapers] where, when and how [it] chooses." Specifically, "[t]here is no constitutional right to place news racks on city sidewalks over the objections of the city." Justice White concluded that the Court should reject the newspaper's facial challenge and take an as-applied approach in this case.

Neither Chief Justice Rehnquist nor Justice Kennedy participated in the decision.

(11) *Complying with Government Procedures*. Lakewood, Madsen, and other cases in these notes raise the issue of what procedural steps protestors must undertake to resist even unconstitutional statutory requirements or court orders. In *Lakewood*, the speaker did not apply for a permit under the City's amended permit procedure before challenging it in the court. A related issue raised by *Lovell v. Griffin* and *Cox v. New Hampshire* is whether a speaker who does not apply for a permit, or who does not challenge a denial of the permit in court, may ignore the permit requirement and speak or demonstrate without one. *Lovell v. Griffin* and *Saia v. New York* are cases in which the permit requirement was alleged to be invalid on its face.

People generally cannot ignore a permit requirement unless it is invalid on its face. In claims where there has been an invalid application of a valid permit requirement, the cases impose limitations on the right of a speaker to ignore the requirement procedures or judicial restraints on the ability to assemble. Speakers must comply with a valid permit requirement before filing suit. Nevertheless, state review procedures must be protective of First Amendment rights. Most importantly, a valid permit requirement must provide the opportunity for prompt judicial review of the denial of the permit, and for prompt consideration of merits of the First Amendment claim if a temporary injunction has been issued. *See Shuttlesworth v. Birmingham*, 394 U.S. 147 (1969); *Carroll v. President and Comm'rs of Princess Anne*, 393 U.S. 175 (1968); *Walker v. City of Birmingham*, 388 U.S. 307 (1967); *Freedman v. Maryland*, 380 U.S. 51 (1965); and *Poulos v. New Hampshire*, 345 U.S. 395 (1953). A scheme that does not comport with these requirements is invalid on its face. Similarly, speakers may not simply ignore a judicial restraint on speech unless it is transparently invalid or frivolous, but instead must petition to have the restraint set aside on appeal. *Walker v. City of Birmingham*, *supra*.

Similar issues are raised under those laws requiring applications for licenses for films or for permission to use municipal auditoriums. *See* § 14.05. On parade permits, see generally Baker, *Unreasoned Reasonableness: Mandatory Parade Permits and Time, Place, and Manner Regulations*, 78 Nw. U. L. Rev. 937 (1983).

HURLEY v. IRISH-AMERICAN GAY, LESBIAN, AND BISEXUAL GROUP OF BOSTON, 515 U.S. 557 (1995). In *Hurley*, the Court invalidated the application of a Massachusetts public accommodations law that required a private organization to include the Irish-American Gay, Lesbian, and Bisexual Group of Boston (GLIB) in its parade. The South Boston Allied War Veterans Council organizes and conducts the annual St. Patrick's Day-Evacuation Day Parade. A state court ordered GLIB's participation, finding the parade a place of public accommodation on which the law prohibited discrimination based on sexual orientation.

Writing for a unanimous Court, Justice Souter rejected the trial court's finding of fact that the parade was not an expressive activity.[22] The First Amendment not only protects the "banners and songs" of a parade, but treats the parade itself as a symbolic means of expression.

The Council's general lenience in including participants in the parade did not alter its freedom to exclude participants. The Court analogized the protection afforded to the Council in conducting the parade to that afforded cable operators in selecting the material to be displayed on their channels and to newspaper publishers in selecting which advertisements or op-ed pieces to print.

GLIB's own participation in the parade was expressive. GLIB's purpose was to participate in the parade and to "celebrate its members' identity as openly gay, lesbian, and bisexual descendants of the Irish immigrants" within the Boston community.

The Council did not exclude any openly homosexual or bisexual belonging to any organization that was allowed to participate. Instead, the violation of the public accommodations law concerned its exclusion of GLIB participating as a group. Requiring the Council to include GLIB in the parade would have forced the Council to communicate a message that it did not desire to express. Outside the commercial speech context, a speaker's "right to tailor the speech applies not only to expressions of value, opinion, or endorsement, but equally to statements of fact that the speaker would rather avoid."

The Court rejected GLIB's argument based on *Turner Broadcasting System, Inc. v. FCC*, 512 U.S. 622 (1994). GLIB asserted that the Council, like the cable operator in

---

[22] When a conclusion of law regarding a federal right hinges on a finding of fact made by a state or federal court, the Supreme Court is "obliged to make a fresh examination of crucial facts," and will not defer to trial court findings of fact based on witness credibility.

Turner Broadcasting, "is merely 'a conduit' for the speech of participants." The Court, however, determined that "GLIB's participation would likely be perceived as having resulted from the Council's customary determination about a unit admitted to the parade," suggesting that the Council thought "that its message was worthy of presentation and quite possibly of support as well." Instead, the Court likened the parade to a newspaper, which is " 'more than a passive receptacle or conduit' " because " 'the choice of material . . . and the decisions made as to limitations on the size and content . . . and treatment of public issues . . . — whether fair or unfair — constitute the exercise of editorial control and judgment' upon which the State cannot intrude." In contrast, " 'given cable's long history of serving as a conduit for broadcast signals, there appears little risk that cable viewers would assume that the broadcast stations carried on a cable system convey ideas or messages endorsed by the cable operator.' " Broadcasters regularly disclaim any identity of viewpoint between the management and the speakers who use the broadcast facility. Unlike cable viewers, however, spectators may not understand parades to be "neutrally presented."

Additionally, the Court recognized that in *Turner Broadcasting*, the cable operators enjoyed a "monopolistic opportunity to shut out some speakers." The federal regulations at issue in *Turner Broadcasting* allowed "broadcasters who might otherwise be silenced and consequently destroyed" to have a voice. Here, however, there is no such monopoly based on the mere fact that the council's parade enjoys success and has a large viewing audience; GLIB is free to organize its own parade.

The broader goal of the State's public accommodations law "of forbidding acts of discrimination toward certain classes" in hopes of producing "a society free of the corresponding biases" itself violates the First Amendment. The State may not regulate noncommercial speech "to produce thoughts and statements acceptable to some groups or, indeed, all people" because that "amounts to nothing less than a proposal to limit speech in the service of orthodox expressions."

Finally, the Court contrasted this case with its holding in *New York State Club Ass'n., Inc. v. City of New York*, 487 U.S. 1 (1988). In that case, the Court upheld the application of an antidiscriminatory public accommodations statute to a private club. Although the Court rejected the club's expressive association challenge, it "recognized that the State did not prohibit exclusion of those whose views were at odds with positions espoused by the general club memberships."

NOTES

(1) *Residential Picketing Targeted on Particular Houses.* (a) *Content-based bans on residential picketing.* In *Carey v. Brown*, 447 U.S. 455 (1980), the Court struck down an Illinois statute prohibiting the picketing of all residences, except under certain circumstances. The statute read: " 'It is unlawful to picket before or about the residence or dwelling of any person, except when the residence or dwelling is used as a place of business. However, this Article does not apply to a person peacefully picketing his own residence or dwelling and does not prohibit the peaceful picketing of a place of employment involved in a labor dispute or the place of holding a meeting or assembly on premises commonly used to discuss subjects of general public interest.' " Relying on *Police Dep't of Chicago v. Mosley*, 408 U.S. 92 (1972), Justice Brennan invalidated the statute under the Equal Protection Clause and the First Amendment because it afforded "preferential treatment to the expression of views on one particular subject." Specifically, the ordinance preferred disseminating information about labor disputes over other issues.

Justice Rehnquist, joined by Chief Justice Burger and Justice Blackmun, dissented. Justice Rehnquist believed that the State had a valid interest in protecting residential privacy. Justice Rehnquist argued that the exceptions were based on the character of the residence, not on the substance of the speech.

(b) *Content-neutral bans on residential picketing.* In *Organization for a Better Austin v. Keefe*, 402 U.S. 415 (1971), the Court (8-1) ruled that an organization could not be enjoined from picketing the home of a real estate broker who had engaged in "blockbusting" or "panic selling" tactics. The picketers were members of an organization seeking to stabilize a racially integrated neighborhood in Chicago. They distributed leaflets in the hometown of the broker, several miles from the area affected by his practices.

Despite *Keefe*, the *Carey* court explicitly left open the question of whether a content-neutral ban on residential picketing would be constitutional. However, in *Frisby v. Schultz*, 487 U.S. 474 (1988), the Court upheld a local Brookfield, Wisconsin, law that banned picketing "before or about" a residence. While reaffirming the conclusions in *Carey v. Brown* concerning the right to picket on public streets in residential neighborhoods, Justice O'Connor's majority (6-3) opinion upheld the law by construing it to prohibit "only focused picketing taking place solely in front of a particular residence." As so construed, the law could validly prohibit the picketing by abortion opponents outside the home of a physician who performed abortions. Thus, the majority opinion viewed the law as a content-neutral "time, place, and manner" restriction subject only to the test that it be "narrowly tailored to serve a significant government interest, and leave open ample alternative channels of communication."

Justice O'Connor held that protection of residential privacy was a "significant government interest," and ample alternative means of communication were available. The Court distinguished *Keefe* on the grounds that the picketing in that case was designed to inform the community of the allegedly discriminatory business practices of a real estate broker. In contrast, the picketing at issue "is narrowly directed at the household, not the public. The type of picketers banned by the Brookfield ordinance generally do not seek to disseminate a message to the general public, but to intrude upon the targeted resident, and to do so in an especially offensive way. Moreover, even if some such picketers have a broader communicative purpose, their activity nonetheless inherently and offensively intrudes on residential privacy.

Justice Brennan's dissent, joined by Justice Marshall, argued that the speech involved here did not implicate a residential privacy interest. Relying on *Keefe*, Justice Brennan wrote: "[S]o long as the speech remains outside the home and does not unduly coerce the occupant, the government's heightened interest in protecting residential privacy is not implicated." Justice White wrote a separate concurring opinion, and Justice Stevens wrote a separate dissent.

(c) *General residential picketing.* In *Madsen v. Women's Health Center, Inc.*, 512 U.S. 753 (1994), the Court struck down as unconstitutional the part of an injunction that prohibited picketing, demonstrating or using sound amplification equipment within 300 feet of the residences of any of an abortion clinic's employees, staff, owners, or agents.

Chief Justice Rehnquist rejected the argument that the injunction in question was content-based. The abortion protestors contended that because the ordinance restricted only the speech of anti-abortion protestors, it was necessarily content-based and should be subject to the strictest standard of scrutiny. The Court stated, however, that to classify this injunction as content-based "would be to classify virtually every injunction as content or viewpoint based. An injunction, by its very nature, applies only to a particular group (or individuals) and regulates the activities, and perhaps the speech, of that group." The lack of any such orders issued to "those demonstrating in favor of abortion is justly attributable to the lack of any similar demonstrations by" those groups.

Nevertheless, the Court invalidated that part of the injunction restricting residential picketing for lack of sufficient justification. The ordinance upheld in *Frisby v. Schultz*, was limited to "focused picketing taking place solely in front of a particular residence." In contrast, the injunction in *Madsen* banned "general marching through residential neighborhoods, or even walking a route in front of an entire block of houses." Without sufficient justification, a ban this broad could not be sustained. Chief Justice Rehnquist found that "a limitation of the time, duration of picketing, and number of pickets outside a smaller zone could have accomplished the desired result." *Madsen* is reproduced at § 14.04[1].

(2) *Residential Signs.* In *City of Ladue v. Gilleo*, 512 U.S. 753 (1994), the Court held that signs on residential property are constitutionally protected. The majority assumed *arguendo* that the law was free of content discrimination even though this was arguably not the case. The Court struck down the law because it prohibited an entire means of communication. For further discussion of *Ladue*, see § 14.01[1].

(3) *Permissible Content-Based Restrictions.* As we have seen in the cases involving sexually offensive material in public areas, *supra*, the Court has upheld regulations based on content. Similarly, the extension of First Amendment protection to commercial speech (*see* § 15.04), has left certain types of commercial speech, e.g., false or misleading advertising, still subject to government regulation, based on content. And, as the cases in the following section indicate, a speaker's right to use a particular forum depends on the appropriateness of the speaker's message in relation to the forum.

(4) For additional discussion of *Hurley*, see Darren Lenard Hutchinson, *Accommodating Outness: Hurley, Free Speech, and Gay and Lesbian Equality*, 1 J. CONST. L. 85, 125 (1998) ("As *Hurley* indicates, litigation involving claims of discrimination against gays and lesbians is deeply political. Three justices of the Supreme Court believe that elected officials should enjoy a seemingly boundless ability to discriminate against gays and lesbians. All nine Justices fail to appreciate or understand the importance of outness in the struggle for gay and lesbian equality.").

§ 14.03 THE CIVIL RIGHTS MOVEMENT, MASS DEMONSTRATIONS, AND NEW RULES FOR NEW PUBLIC FORUMS

COX v. LOUISIANA
(NO. 24 — COX I)
379 U.S. 536, 85 S. Ct. 453, 13 L. Ed. 2d 471 (1965)

JUSTICE GOLDBERG delivered the opinion of the court.

Appellant, the Reverend Mr. B. Elton Cox, the leader of a civil rights demonstration, was arrested and charged with four offenses under Louisiana law — criminal conspiracy, disturbing the peace, obstructing public passages and picketing before a courthouse. In a consolidated trial before a judge without a jury, and on the same set of facts, he was acquitted of criminal conspiracy but convicted of the other three offenses. He was sentenced to serve four months in jail and pay a $200 fine for disturbing the peace, to serve five months in jail and pay a $500 fine for obstructing public passages, and to serve one year in jail and pay a $5,000 fine for picketing before a courthouse. The sentences were cumulative. . . .

I

THE FACTS

On December 14, 1961, 23 students from Southern University, a Negro college, were arrested in downtown Baton Rouge, Louisiana, for picketing stores that maintained segregated lunch counters. This picketing, urging a boycott of those stores, was part of a general protest movement against racial segregation, directed by the local chapter of the Congress of Racial Equality [CORE], a civil rights organization. The appellant, an ordained Congregational minister, the Reverend Mr. B. Elton Cox, a Field Secretary of CORE, was an advisor to this movement. On the evening of December 14, appellant and Ronnie Moore, student president of the local CORE chapter, spoke at a mass meeting at the college. The students resolved to demonstrate the next day in front of the courthouse in protest of segregation and the arrest and imprisonment of the picketers who were being held in the parish jail located on the upper floor of the courthouse building.

The next morning about 2,000 students left the campus, which was located approximately five miles from downtown Baton Rouge. . . .

When Cox arrived, 1,500 of the 2,000 students were assembling at the site of the old State Capitol building, two and one-half blocks from the courthouse. Cox walked up and down cautioning the students to keep to one side of the sidewalk while getting ready for their march to the courthouse. The students circled the block in a file two or three abreast occupying about half of the sidewalk. . . . Captain Font of the City Police Department and Chief Kling of the Sheriff's office, two high-ranking subordinate officials, approached the group and spoke to Cox at the northeast corner of the capitol grounds. Cox identified himself as the group's leader. . . . Kling asked Cox to disband the group and "take them back from whence they came." Cox did not acquiesce in this request but told the officers that they would march by the courthouse, say prayers, sing hymns, and conduct a peaceful program of protest. The officer repeated his request to disband, and Cox again refused. . . . [S]tudents, led by Cox, began their walk toward the courthouse.

They walked in an orderly and peaceful file, two or three abreast, one block east. . . .

As Cox, still at the head of the group, approached the vicinity of the courthouse, he was stopped by Captain Font and Inspector Trigg and brought to Police Chief Wingate White, who was standing in the middle of St. Louis Street. The Chief then inquired as to the purpose of the demonstration. Cox, reading from a prepared paper, outlined his program to White, stating that it would include a singing of the Star Spangled Banner and a "freedom song," recitation of the Lord's Prayer and the Pledge of Allegiance, and a short speech. White testified that he told Cox that "he must confine" the demonstration "to the west side of the street." White added, "This, of course, was not — I didn't mean it in the import that I was giving him any permission to do it, but I was presented with a situation that was accomplished, and I had to make a decision." Cox testified that the officials agreed to permit the meeting. James Erwin, news director of radio station WIBR, a witness for the State, was present and overheard the conversation. He testified that "My understanding was that they would be allowed to demonstrate if they stayed on the west side of the street and stayed within the recognized time," and that this was "agreed to" by White.

The students were then directed by Cox to the west sidewalk, across the street from the courthouse, 101 feet from its steps. . . . The group did not obstruct the street. It was close to noon and, being lunch time, a small crowd of 100 to 300 curious white people, mostly courthouse personnel, gathered on the east sidewalk and courthouse steps, about 100 feet from the demonstrators. Seventy-five to eighty policemen, including city and state patrolmen and members of the Sheriff's staff, as well as members of the fire department and a fire truck were stationed in the street between the two groups. . . .

Several of the students took from beneath their coats picket signs similar to those which had been used the day before. These signs bore legends such as "Don't buy discrimination for Christmas," "Sacrifice for Christ, don't buy," and named the stores which were proclaimed "unfair." They then sang "God Bless America," pledged allegiance to the flag, prayed briefly, and sang one or two hymns, including "We Shall Overcome." The 23 students, who were locked in jail cells in the courthouse building out of the sight of the demonstrators, responded by themselves singing; this in turn was greeted with cheers and applause by the demonstrators. Appellant gave a speech, described by a State's witness as follows:

He said that in effect that it was a protest against the illegal arrest of some of their members and that other people were allowed to picket . . . and he said that they were not going to commit any violence, that if anyone spit on them, they would not spit back on the person that did it.

Cox then said:

> All right. It's lunch time. Let's go eat. There are twelve stores we are protesting. A number of these stores have twenty counters; they accept your money from nineteen. They won't accept it from the twentieth counter. This is an act of racial discrimination. These stores are open to the public. You are members of the public. We pay taxes to the Federal Government and you who live here pay taxes to the State.

In apparent reaction to these last remarks, there was what state witnesses described as "muttering" and "grumbling" by the white onlookers.

The Sheriff, deeming, as he testified, Cox's appeal to the students to sit in at the lunch counters to be "inflammatory," then took a power microphone and said, "Now, you have been allowed to demonstrate. Up until now your demonstration has been more or less peaceful, but what you are doing now is a direct violation of the law, a disturbance of the peace, and it has got to be broken up immediately." The testimony as to what then happened is disputed. Some of the State's witnesses testified that Cox said, "don't move;" others stated that he made a "gesture of defiance." It is clear from the record, however, that Cox and the demonstrators did not then and there break up the demonstration. Two of the Sheriff's deputies immediately started across the street and told the group, "You have heard what the Sheriff said, now, do what he said." A state witness testified that they put their hands on the shoulders of some of the students "as though to shove them away."

Almost immediately thereafter — within a time estimated variously at two to five minutes — one of the policemen exploded a tear gas shell at the crowd. This was followed by several other shells. The demonstrators quickly dispersed, running back towards the State Capitol and the downtown area; Cox tried to calm them as they ran and was himself one of the last to leave.

. . . The next day appellant was arrested and charged with the four offenses above described.

II

The Breach of the Peace Conviction

Appellant was convicted of violating a Louisiana "disturbing the peace" statute. . . . It is clear to us that on the facts of this case, which are strikingly similar to those present in *Edwards v. South Carolina*, 372 U.S. 229 [(1963)], . . . Louisiana infringed appellant's rights of free speech and free assembly by convicting him under this statute. . . . We hold that Louisiana may not constitutionally punish appellant under this statute for engaging in the type of conduct which this record reveals, and also that the statute as authoritatively interpreted by the Louisiana Supreme Court is unconstitutionally broad in scope.

The Louisiana courts have held that appellant's conduct constituted a breach of the peace under state law . . . but our independent examination of the record, which we are required to make,[23] shows no conduct which the State had a right to prohibit as a breach of the peace. . . .

Finally, the State contends that the conviction should be sustained because of fear expressed by some of the state witnesses that "violence was about to erupt" because of the demonstration. It is virtually undisputed, however, that the students themselves were not violent and threatened no violence. The fear of violence seems to have been based upon the reaction of the group of white citizens looking on from across the street. One state witness testified that "he felt the situation was getting out of hand" as on the courthouse side of St. Louis Street "were small knots or groups of white citizens who were muttering words, who seemed a little bit agitated." A police officer stated that the reaction of the white crowd was not violent, but "was rumblings." Others felt the atmosphere became "tense" because of "mutterings," "grumbling," and "jeering" from the white group. There is no indication, however, that any member of the white group threatened violence. . . .

Here again, as in *Edwards*, this evidence "showed no more than that the opinions which [the students] were peaceably expressing were sufficiently opposed to the views of the majority of the community to attract a crowd and necessitate police protection." *Edwards v. South Carolina, supra*, 372 U.S. at 237. . . .

There is an additional reason why this conviction cannot be sustained. The statute at issue in this case, as authoritatively interpreted by the Louisiana Supreme Court, is unconstitutionally vague in its overly broad scope. The statutory crime consists of two elements: (1) congregating with others "with intent to provoke a breach of the peace, or under circumstances such that a breach of the peace may be occasioned," and (2) a refusal to move on after having been ordered to do so by a law enforcement officer. While the second part of this offense is narrow and specific, the first element is not. The Louisiana Supreme Court in this case defined the term "breach of the peace" as "to agitate, to arouse from a state of repose, to molest, to interrupt, to hinder, to disquiet." 156 So. 2d [448,] 455 [(La. 1963)]. In *Edwards*, defendants had been convicted of a common-law crime similarly defined by the South Carolina Supreme Court. Both

---

[23] [Court's footnote 8] Because a claim of constitutionally protected right is involved, it "remains our duty in a case such as this to make an independent examination of the whole record." *Edwards v. South Carolina*, 372 U.S. 229, 235. . . . In the area of First Amendment freedoms as well as areas involving other constitutionally protected rights, "we cannot avoid our responsibilities by permitting ourselves to be 'completely bound by state court determination of any issue essential to decision of a claim of federal right, else federal law could be frustrated by distorted fact finding.'" *Haynes v. State of Washington*, 373 U.S. 503, 515–516 [(1963)]. . . .

definitions would allow persons to be punished merely for peacefully expressing unpopular views. . . . [T]he conviction under this statute must be reversed as the statute is unconstitutional in that it sweeps within its broad scope activities that are constitutionally protected free speech and assembly. . . .

III

THE OBSTRUCTING PUBLIC PASSAGES CONVICTION

We now turn to the issue of the validity of appellant's conviction for violating the Louisiana statute, LSA-Rev. Stat. § 14:100.1 (Cum. Supp.1962), which provides:

Obstructing Public Passages

No person shall wilfully obstruct the free, convenient and normal use of any public sidewalk, street, highway, bridge, alley, road, or other passageway, or the entrance, corridor or passage of any public building, structure, watercraft or ferry, by impeding, hindering, stifling, retarding or restraining traffic or passage thereon or therein. . . .

Appellant was convicted under this statute, not for leading the march to the vicinity of the courthouse . . . but for leading the meeting on the sidewalk across the street from the courthouse. . . . There is no doubt from the record in this case that this far sidewalk was obstructed, and thus, as so construed, appellant violated the statute. . . .

. . . Although the statute here involved on its face precludes all street assemblies and parades . . . it appears that the authorities in Baton Rouge permit or prohibit parades or street meetings in their completely uncontrolled discretion. . . .

This Court has recognized that the lodging of such broad discretion in a public official allows him to determine which expressions of view will be permitted and which will not. This . . . permits the official to act as a censor. . . .

. . . It follows, therefore, that appellant's conviction for violating the statute as so applied and enforced must be reversed. . . .

COX v. LOUISIANA, (No. 49–Cox II), 379 U.S. 559 (1965). In a companion case to *Cox I*, the Supreme Court set aside the appellant's conviction for picketing in front of a courthouse. Writing for the majority, Justice Goldberg first rejected the contention that the Louisiana statute was invalid on its face. The Court emphasized that this was a narrowly drawn statute sharply contrasting with the ones at issue in *Cox I*. "There can be no question that a State has a legitimate interest in protecting its judicial system from the pressures which picketing near a courthouse might create." The prohibitions on picketing and parading involved "conduct subject to regulation so as to vindicate important interests of society and the fact that free speech is intermingled with such conduct does not bring it constitutional protection." The Court also rejected the appellant's contention that the statute was unconstitutional as applied. The state was simply protecting judges from being consciously or unconsciously influenced. The state was also protecting the integrity of the judicial process in the minds of the public.

The Court, however, held that the conviction violated due process. The statute under which Cox was convicted permitted an arrest for picketing not only "in," but also "near" the courthouse. The appellant was specifically given permission to picket across the street from the courthouse, and the Chief of Police instructed him that they could not assemble within 101 feet of the courthouse steps. "In effect, [the] appellant was advised that a demonstration at the place it was held would not be one 'near' the courthouse within the terms of the statute." Thus, appellant was convicted for being in a place where the police specifically advised him he could be.

Justices Clark and Black concurred in *Cox I* and dissented in *Cox II*. Justice White concurred in the reversal of the breach of the peace conviction in *Cox I*, but dissented from the reversal of the obstructing public passageways conviction in that case. He also dissented from the reversal of the conviction in *Cox II*. Justice Black concurred in the Court's judgment reversing the breach of the peace and obstructing public passageways convictions, but for different reasons than those stated by the Court. Because he did not view parades as speech, Justice Black would uphold the conviction in *Cox II*.

NOTES

(1) *State Capitols.* As the *Cox* cases demonstrate, the Court had some difficulty in applying to mass civil rights demonstrations those doctrines developed in cases involving the distribution of leaflets or the utterances of a few speakers on street corners or in parks. In *Edwards v. South Carolina*, 372 U.S. 229 (1963), which was relied on by the majority in *Cox I*, a breach of the peace statute was enforced against civil rights demonstrators on the state house grounds. The Court (8-1) (Justice Clark dissenting) held that a breach of the peace statute could not be used to convict demonstrators for what the Court described as "an exercise of these basic constitutional rights in their most pristine and classic form." The majority opinion did not make clear whether the convictions were being reversed because the statute was unconstitutionally vague or overbroad, or because the statute was being unconstitutionally applied. Justice Goldberg's opinion in *Cox I* appears to draw all of these conclusions from *Edwards* as authority for reversing the breach of the peace convictions.

(2) *New Pressures on the Public Forum.* Because civil rights demonstrations often took the form of obstructing sidewalks or congregating near courthouses and other public places, such as statehouse grounds, or areas in front of jails, or in libraries and other public buildings, demonstrators were charged with trespassing or the violation of statutes and laws such as those involved in *Cox I* (obstructing public passages) and *Cox II* (picketing or parading near a courthouse). Here, the Court had more difficulty than with breach of the peace statutes such as those in *Edwards* and *Cox I*. Justice Goldberg's opinions in *Cox I* and *Cox II* may be seen as an effort to protect this new form of expression (mass demonstrations) without striking down statutes that dealt with conduct that the state had a clear right to regulate, i.e., trespassing and obstructing sidewalks. *Cf. United States v. Grace*, 461 U.S. 171 (1983), *infra* § 14.04[1], Note (3) after *Cornelius. v. N.A.A.C.P.* (enforcing a constitutional right of expressive activity on the sidewalk surrounding the United States Supreme Court).

While *Edwards*, *Cox I*, and *Cox II* involved forms of speech that differed from the single-speaker or small-group forms of expression in *Cantwell*, *Lovell*, *Saia*, and *Feiner*, the forums (statehouse grounds and sidewalks) were similar to those in earlier cases. When the civil rights and antiwar movements took their message to other public facilities, however, it became more difficult to reconcile governmental and free speech interests.

(3) *Public Library.* In *Brown v. Louisiana*, 383 U.S. 131 (1966), five black men staged a peaceful and quiet sit-in demonstration in a reading room of a public library to protest the racial policies of the library, which served schools in the parish through the use of "bookmobiles" operated on a racially segregated basis. The demonstrators were asked to leave, and when they refused, they were arrested and charged with violating the same breach of the peace statute that was held unconstitutionally vague and overbroad in *Cox I*. Justice Fortas, in an opinion joined by Chief Justice Warren and Justice Douglas, did not rely on overbreadth, but concluded that the demonstrators had

not engaged in conduct that could be considered a breach of the peace and, "even if the accused action were within the scope of the statutory instrument, we would be required to assess the constitutional impact of its application, and we would have to hold that the statute cannot constitutionally be applied to punish petitioners' actions in the circumstances of this case."

Justice Brennan concurred on grounds of the overbreadth ruling in *Cox I*, concluding that "it is wholly unnecessary to reach, let alone rest reversal, as the prevailing opinion seems to do, on the proposition that even a narrowly drawn statute cannot constitutionally be applied to punish petitioner's actions in the circumstances of this case." Justice White filed a separate concurring opinion.

Justice Black dissented, joined by Justices Clark, Harlan, and Stewart. "The part of the statute involved here which makes it an offense to congregate in a public building and refuse to leave it when asked to do so by an authorized person, does not affect or threaten in any way an exercise of the rights of free speech."

(4) *Jails*. A hint of the Court's present "public forum" analysis can be found in *Adderley v. State of Florida*, 385 U.S. 39 (1966). In *Adderley*, the petitioners were charged and convicted for trespassing with "malicious and mischievous" intent when they demonstrated on the grounds of the Leon County, Florida jail. The petitioners, students at Florida A&M University, demonstrated to protest the earlier jailing of fellow students and, more generally, to protest racial segregation. Writing for a narrow majority, Justice Black upheld the convictions, resting the Court's decision largely on the location of the demonstration.

The Court first rejected vagueness and overbreadth challenges to the statute. It then held that the trespassing conviction did not deprive petitioners of their rights of freedom of speech, press, assembly or petition. The Court determined that the sheriff did not exercise his power "because [he] objected to what was being sung or said by the demonstrators or because he disagreed with the objectives of their protest. The record reveals that he objected only to their presence on that part of the jail grounds reserved for jail uses. The United States Constitution does not forbid a State to control the use of its own property for its own lawful nondiscriminatory purpose."

Justice Douglas dissented, joined by Chief Justice Warren, Justice Brennan, and Justice Fortas. "The jailhouse, like an executive mansion, a legislative chamber, a courthouse, or the statehouse itself (*Edwards v. South Carolina*) is one of the seats of government whether it be the Tower of London, the Bastille, or a small county jail."

§ 14.04   THE MODERN APPROACH: LIMITING SPEECH ACCORDING TO THE CHARACTER OF THE PROPERTY

[1]   Public Property

GREER v. SPOCK, 424 U.S. 828 (1976). In *Greer*, the Court upheld two regulations at the Fort Dix Military Reservation in rural New Jersey. The Federal Government exercises exclusive jurisdiction over the entire reservation, including roads that pass through it. Civilian vehicular and pedestrian traffic was permitted on both roads and footpaths. The two regulations banned speeches and demonstrations of a partisan political nature and further banned distribution of any literature without prior written approval of the base commander.

The respondents,[24] minor party candidates for the offices of President and Vice-President of the United States, wrote a letter to the commanding officer at Fort Dix, informing him of their intention to enter the base for the purpose of distributing campaign literature and holding a meeting to discuss election issues with service personnel. The base commander rejected their request, relying on the two regulations that governed political campaigning and the distribution of literature.

Justice Stewart, writing for the majority, stated that the appellate court was mistaken "in thinking that whenever members of the public are permitted freely to visit a place owned or operated by the Government, then that place becomes a 'public forum' for purposes of the First Amendment. Such a principle of constitutional law never existed, and does not exist now." Justice Stewart noted that the military authorities had never abandoned any claim in regulating political activities.

The purpose of a military base is to "train soldiers, not to provide a public forum." The regulations against political speech were also justified by the "American constitutional tradition of a politically neutral military establishment under civilian control."

Justice Brennan dissented, joined by Justice Marshall.

Justice Brennan argued that even where a governmental facility was not a "public forum" at all, expressive activity should be permitted on it as long as the activity was compatible with the activities occurring there. Respondents "indicated in unequivocal terms their willingness to confine the rally to such times and places as might reasonably be designated by petitioners" and "sought only to distribute leaflets in unrestricted areas. . . . Respondents . . . distinguish between a military base considered as a whole and those portions of a military base open to the public. . . . "

"It bears special note that the notion of 'public forum' has never been the touchstone of public expression, for a contrary approach blinds the Court to any possible accommodations to First Amendment values in this case. In *Brown v. Louisiana*, for example, the First Amendment protected the use of a public library as a site for a silent and peaceful protest by five young black men against discrimination. There was no finding by the Court that the library was a public forum. Similarly, in *Edwards v. South Carolina*, the First Amendment protected a demonstration on the grounds of a State Capitol building. Again, the Court never expressly determined that those grounds constituted a public forum. . . . Moreover, none of the opinions that have expressly characterized locales as public forums has really gone that far, for a careful reading of those opinions reveals that their characterizations were always qualified, indicating that not every conceivable form of public expression would be protected. . . . "

"Those cases permitting public expression without characterizing the locale involved as a public forum, together with those cases recognizing the existence of a public forum, albeit qualifiedly, evidence the desirability of a flexible approach to determining when public expression should be protected. Realizing that the permissibility of a certain form of public expression at a given locale may differ depending on whether it is asked if the locale is a public forum or if the form of expression is compatible with the activities occurring at the locale, it becomes apparent that there is need for a flexible approach. Otherwise, with the rigid characterization of a given locale as not a public forum, there is the danger that certain forms of public speech at the locale may be suppressed, even though they are basically compatible with the activities otherwise occurring at the locale."

----

[24] Two of the respondents were candidates for the People's Party, and the other two respondents were the candidates for the Socialist Workers Party.

Justice Brennan argued that the respondents should be permitted to distribute their literature "in those streets and lots unrestricted to civilian traffic," since those areas did not "differ in their nature and use from city streets and lots where open speech long has been protected." Further, the time and location of rallies could be carefully regulated so as to prevent disruption of military training.

PERRY EDUCATION ASS'N v. PERRY LOCAL EDUCATORS' ASS'N
460 U.S. 37, 103 S. Ct. 948 74 L. Ed. 2d 794 (1983)

JUSTICE WHITE delivered the opinion of the Court. . . .

I

The Metropolitan School District of Perry Township, Ind. operates a public school system of 13 separate schools. Each school building contains a set of mailboxes for the teachers. Interschool delivery by school employees permits messages to be delivered rapidly to teachers in the District. The primary function of this internal mail system is to transmit official messages among the teachers and the school administration. In addition, teachers use the system to send personal messages, and individual school building principals have allowed delivery of messages from various private organizations.[25]

Prior to 1977, both the Perry Education Association (PEA) and the Perry Local Educators' Association (PLEA) represented teachers in the School District and apparently had equal access to the interschool mail system. In 1977, PLEA challenged PEA's status as de facto bargaining representative for the Perry Township teachers by filing an election petition with the Indiana Education Employment Relations Board (Board). PEA won the election and was certified as the exclusive representative, as provided by Indiana law.

The Board permits a school district to provide access to communication facilities to the union selected for the discharge of the exclusive representative duties of representing the bargaining unit and its individual members without having to provide equal access to rival unions. Following the election, PEA and the School District negotiated a labor contract in which the School Board gave PEA "access to teachers' mailboxes in which to insert material" and the right to use the interschool mail delivery system to the extent that the School District incurred no extra expense by such use. The labor agreement noted that these access rights were being accorded to PEA "acting as the representative of the teachers" and went on to stipulate that these access rights shall not be granted to any other "school employee organization. . . . "

The exclusive-access policy applies only to use of the mailboxes and school mail system. PLEA is not prevented from using other school facilities to communicate with teachers. PLEA may post notices on school bulletin boards; may hold meetings on school property after school hours; and may, with approval of the building principals, make announcements on the public address system. . . .

III

The primary question presented is whether the First Amendment, applicable to the State by virtue of the Fourteenth Amendment, is violated when a union that has been

---

[25] [Court's footnote 2] Local parochial schools, church groups, YMCA's, and Cub Scout units have used the system. The record does not indicate whether any requests for use have been denied, nor does it reveal whether permission must separately be sought for every message that a group wishes delivered to the teachers.

elected by public school teachers as their exclusive bargaining representative is granted access to certain means of communication, while such access is denied to a rival union. There is no question that constitutional interests are implicated by denying PLEA use of the interschool mail system. . . . The First Amendment's guarantee of free speech applies to teacher's mailboxes as surely as it does elsewhere within the school. . . . But this is not to say that the First Amendment requires equivalent access to all parts of a school building in which some form of communicative activity occurs. . . . The existence of a right of access to public property and the standard by which limitations upon such a right must be evaluated differ depending on the character of the property at issue.

A

In places which by long tradition or by government fiat have been devoted to assembly and debate, the rights of the State to limit expressive activity are sharply circumscribed. At one end of the spectrum are streets and parks which "have immemorially been held in trust for the use of the public and, time out of mind, have been used for purposes of assembly, communicating thoughts between citizens, and discussing public questions." *Hague v. CIO*, 307 U.S. 496, 515 (1939). In these quintessential public forums, the government may not prohibit all communicative activity. For the State to enforce a content-based exclusion it must show that its regulation is necessary to serve a compelling state interest and that it is narrowly drawn to achieve that end. *Carey v. Brown*, 447 U.S. 455, 461 (1980). The State may also enforce regulations of the time, place, and manner of expression which are content-neutral, are narrowly tailored to serve a significant government interest, and leave open ample alternative channels of communication.

A second category consists of public property which the State has opened for use by the public as a place for expressive activity. The Constitution forbids a State to enforce certain exclusions from a forum generally open to the public even if it was not required to create the forum in the first place. *Widmar v. Vincent*, 454 U.S. 263 (1981) (university meeting facilities); *City of Madison Joint School Dist. v. Wisconsin Employment Relations Comm'n.*, 429 U.S. 167 (1976) (school board meeting); *Southeastern Promotions, Ltd. v. Conrad*, 420 U.S. 546 (1975) (municipal theater).[26] Although a State is not required to indefinitely retain the open character of the facility, as long as it does so it is bound by the same standards as apply in a traditional public forum. Reasonable time, place, and manner regulations are permissible, and a content-based prohibition must be narrowly drawn to effectuate a compelling state interest.

Public property which is not by tradition or designation a forum for public communication is governed by different standards. . . . In addition to time, place, and manner regulations, the State may reserve the forum for its intended purposes, communicative or otherwise, as long as the regulation on speech is reasonable and not an effort to suppress expression merely because public officials oppose the speaker's view. As we have stated on several occasions, "[t]he State, no less than a private owner of property, has power to preserve the property under its control for the use to which it is lawfully dedicated." [*United States Postal Serv. v. Greenbaugh,*] 453 U.S. [119, 129–130 (1981)].

The school mail facilities at issue here fall within this third category. The Court of Appeals recognized that Perry School District's interschool mail system is not a

---

[26] [Court's footnote 7] A public forum may be created for a limited purpose such as use by certain groups, e.g., *Widmar v. Vincent* (student groups) or for the discussion of certain subjects, e.g., *City of Madison Joint School Dist. v. Wisconsin Pub. Employment Relations Comm'n* (school board business).

traditional public forum. . . . The internal mail system, at least by policy, is not held open to the general public. It is instead PLEA's position that the school mail facilities have become a "limited public forum" from which it may not be excluded because of the periodic use of the system by private non-school-connected groups, and PLEA's own unrestricted access to the system prior to PEA's certification as exclusive representative.

. . . In the Court of Appeals' view . . . the access policy adopted by the Perry school favors a particular viewpoint, that of PEA, on labor relations and consequently must be strictly scrutinized regardless of whether a public forum is involved. There is, however, no indication that the School Board intended to discourage one viewpoint and advance another. We believe it is more accurate to characterize the access policy as based on the status of the respective unions rather than their views. Implicit in the concept of the nonpublic forum is the right to make distinctions in access on the basis of subject matter and speaker identity. These distinctions may be impermissible in a public forum but are inherent and inescapable in the process of limiting a nonpublic forum to activities compatible with the intended purpose of the property. The touchstone for evaluating these distinctions is whether they are reasonable in light of the purpose which the forum at issue serves.[27]

B

The differential access provided PEA and PLEA is reasonable because it is wholly consistent with the District's legitimate interest in "preserv[ing] the property . . . for the use to which it is lawfully dedicated." *United States Postal Serv., supra,* 453 U.S. at 129–130. Use of school mail facilities enables PEA to perform effectively its obligations as exclusive representative of all Perry Township teachers.

Conversely, PLEA does not have any official responsibility in connection with the School District and need not be entitled to the same rights of access to school mailboxes. We observe that providing exclusive access to recognized bargaining representatives is a permissible labor practice in the public sector. . . . [E]xclusion of the rival union may reasonably be considered a means of insuring labor peace within the schools. The policy "serves to prevent the District's schools from becoming a battlefield for inter-union squabbles. . . . "

Finally, the reasonableness of the limitations on PLEA's access to the school mail system is also supported by the substantial alternative channels that remain open for union-teacher communication to take place. These means range from bulletin boards to meeting facilities to the United States' mail. During election periods, PLEA is assured of equal access to all modes of communication. There is no showing here that PLEA's ability to communicate with teachers is seriously impinged by the restricted access to the internal mail system. . . .

IV

The Court of Appeals also held that the differential access provided the rival unions constituted impermissible content discrimination in violation of the Equal Protection

---

[27] [Court's footnote 9] . . . Justice Brennan . . . insists that the Perry access policy is a forbidden exercise of viewpoint discrimination. . . . [W]e disagree with this conclusion. The access policy applies not only to PLEA but also to all unions other than the recognized bargaining representative, and there is no indication in the record that the policy was motivated by a desire to suppress PLEA's views. . . . Although his viewpoint-discrimination thesis might indicate otherwise, Justice Brennan apparently would not forbid the School District to close the mail system to all outsiders for the purpose of discussing labor matters while permitting such discussion by administrators and teachers. . . .

Clause of the Fourteenth Amendment. We have rejected this contention when cast as a First Amendment argument, and it fares no better in equal protection garb. . . .

[O]n government property that has not been made a public forum, not all speech is equally situated, and the State may draw distinctions which relate to the special purpose for which the property is used. As we have explained above, for a school mail facility, the difference in status between the exclusive bargaining representative and its rival is such a distinction.

JUSTICE BRENNAN, with whom JUSTICE MARSHALL, JUSTICE POWELL, and JUSTICE STEVENS join, dissenting.

I

. . . This case does not involve an "absolute access" claim. It involves an "equal access" claim. As such it does not turn on whether the internal school mail system is a "public forum. . . . "

A

. . . Viewpoint discrimination is censorship in its purest form and government regulation that discriminates among viewpoints threatens the continued vitality of "free speech."

B

. . . By focusing on whether the interschool mail system is a public forum, the Court disregards the independent First Amendment protection afforded by the prohibition against viewpoint discrimination. . . .

II

. . . The Court responds to the allegation of viewpoint discrimination by suggesting that there is no indication that the Board intended to discriminate and that the exclusive-access policy is based on the parties' status rather than on their views. . . .

On a practical level, the only reason for the petitioner to seek an exclusive-access policy is to deny its rivals access to an effective channel of communication. . . . No other group is explicitly denied access to the mail system. In fact, as the Court points out, many other groups have been granted access to the system. . . . The very argument the petitioner advances in support of the policy, the need to preserve labor peace, also indicates that the access policy is not viewpoint-neutral. . . .

III

. . . In light of the fact that viewpoint discrimination implicates core First Amendment values, the exclusive-access policy can be sustained "only if the government can show that the regulation is a precisely drawn means of serving a compelling state interest." *Consolidated Edison Co. v. Public Serv. Comm'n*, 447 U.S. 530, 540 (1980).

A

. . . As the Court of Appeals pointed out, the exclusive-access policy is both "overinclusive and underinclusive" as a means of serving the State's interest in the efficient discharge of the petitioner's legal duties to the teachers. The policy is overinclusive because it does not strictly limit the petitioner's use of the mail system to performance of its special legal duties and underinclusive because the Board permits outside organizations with no special duties to the teachers, or to the students, to use the system. . . .

NOTE

For further discussion, see Stanley Ingber, *Rediscovering the Communal Worth of Individual Rights: The First Amendment in Institutional Contexts*, 69 Tex. L. Rev. 1, 107–8 (1990) ("[C]lassifying a medium of communication as a public forum may cause legitimate governmental interests to be thoughtlessly brushed aside. Even more likely, classifying it as something else may lead courts to ignore the incompatibility of the challenged regulations with first-amendment values.").

CORNELIUS v. N.A.A.C.P. LEGAL DEFENSE & EDUCATIONAL FUND
473 U.S. 788, 105 S. Ct. 3439, 87 L. Ed. 2d 567 (1985)

JUSTICE O'CONNOR delivered the opinion of the Court.

This case requires us to decide whether the Federal Government violates the First Amendment when it excludes legal defense and political advocacy organizations from participation in the Combined Federal Campaign (CFC or Campaign), a charity drive aimed at federal employees. . . .

I

The CFC is an annual charitable fund-raising drive conducted in the federal workplace during working hours largely through the voluntary efforts of federal employees. At all times relevant to this litigation, participating organizations confined their fund-raising activities to a 30-word statement submitted by them for inclusion in the Campaign literature. . . . Contributions may take the form of either a payroll deduction or a lump sum payment made to a designated agency or to the general Campaign fund. Undesignated contributions are distributed on the local level by a private umbrella organization to certain participating organizations. . . .

The CFC was designed to lessen the Government's burden in meeting human health and welfare needs by providing a convenient, nondisruptive channel for Federal employees to contribute to non-partisan agencies that directly serve those needs. The Order [Executive Order No. 12404] limited participation to "voluntary, charitable, health and welfare agencies that provide or support direct health and welfare services to individuals or their families," and specifically excluded those "[a]gencies that seek to influence the outcomes of elections or the determination of public policy through political activity or advocacy, lobbying, or litigation on behalf of parties other than themselves. . . ."

II

The issue presented is whether the respondents have a First Amendment right to solicit contributions that was violated by their exclusion from the CFC. To resolve this issue we must first decide whether solicitation in the context of the CFC is speech protected by the First Amendment, for, if it is not, we need go no further. Assuming that such solicitation is protected speech, we must identify the nature of the forum, because the extent to which the Government may limit access depends on whether the forum is public or nonpublic. Finally, we must assess whether the justifications for exclusion from the relevant forum satisfy the requisite standard. Applying this analysis, we find that respondents' solicitation is protected speech occurring in the context of a nonpublic forum and that the Government's reasons for excluding respondents from the

CFC appear, at least facially, to satisfy the reasonableness standard. We express no opinion on the question whether petitioner's explanation is merely a pretext for viewpoint discrimination. Accordingly, we reverse and remand for further proceedings consistent with this opinion.

A

Charitable solicitation of funds has been recognized by this Court as a form of protected speech. . . .

In *Village of Schaumburg v. Citizens for a Better Env't*, 444 U.S. 620 (1980), the Court struck down a local ordinance prohibiting solicitation in a public forum by charitable organizations that expended less than 75 percent of the receipts collected for charitable purposes. The plaintiff in that case was a public advocacy group that employed canvassers to distribute literature and answer questions about the group's goals and activities as well as to solicit contributions. The Court found that "charitable appeals for funds, on the street or door to door, involve a variety of speech interests — communication of information, the dissemination and propagation of views and ideas, and the advocacy of causes — that are within the protection of the First Amendment." 444 U.S. at 632. . . .

Notwithstanding the significant distinctions between in-person solicitation and solicitation in the abbreviated context of the CFC, we find that the latter deserves First Amendment protection. The brief statements in the CFC literature directly advance the speaker's interest in informing readers about its existence and its goals. Moreover, an employee's contribution in response to a request for funds functions as a general expression of support for the recipient and its views. *See Buckley v. Valeo*, 424 U.S. 1, 21 (1976). Although the CFC does not entail direct discourse between the solicitor and the donor, the CFC literature facilitates the dissemination of views and ideas by directing employees to the soliciting agency to obtain more extensive information. Finally, without the funds obtained from solicitation in various fora, the organization's continuing ability to communicate its ideas and goals may be jeopardized. . . . Although government restrictions on the length and content of the request are relevant to ascertaining the Government's intent as to the nature of the forum created, they do not negate the finding that the request implicates interests protected by the First Amendment.

B

The conclusion that the solicitation which occurs in the CFC is protected speech merely begins our inquiry. . . . [T]he Court has adopted a forum analysis as a means of determining when the Government's interest in limiting the use of its property to its intended purpose outweighs the interest of those wishing to use the property for other purposes. . . .

Petitioner contends that a First Amendment forum necessarily consists of tangible government property. Because the only "property" involved here is the federal workplace, in petitioner's view the workplace constitutes the relevant forum. Under this analysis, the CFC is merely an activity that takes place in the federal workplace. Respondents, in contrast, argue that the forum should be defined in terms of the access sought by the speaker. . . . Because respondents seek access only to the CFC and do not claim a general right to engage in face-to-face solicitation in the federal workplace, they contend that the relevant forum is the CFC and its attendant literature.

We agree with respondents that the relevant forum for our purposes is the

CFC. . . . [I]n defining the forum we have focused on the access sought by the speaker. . . .

. . . *Perry Educ. Ass'n.* . . . identified three types of fora: the traditional public forum, the public forum created by government designation, and the nonpublic forum. Traditional public fora are those places which "by long tradition or by government fiat have been devoted to assembly and debate." 460 U.S. at 45. Public streets and parks fall into this category. In addition to traditional public fora, a public forum may be created by government designation of a place or channel of communication for use by the public at large for assembly and speech, for use by certain speakers, or for the discussion of certain subjects.

The government does not create a public forum by inaction or by permitting limited discourse, but only by intentionally opening a non-traditional forum for public discourse. Accordingly, the Court has looked to the policy and practice of the government to ascertain whether it intended to designate a place not traditionally open to assembly and debate as a public forum. The Court has also examined the nature of the property and its compatibility with expressive activity to discern the government's intent. For example, in *Widmar v. Vincent*, 454 U.S. 263 (1981), we found that a state university that had an express policy of making its meeting facilities available to registered student groups had created a public forum for their use. The policy evidenced a clear intent to create a public forum. . . . Additionally, we noted that a university campus, at least as to its students, possesses many of the characteristics of a traditional public forum.

Not every instrumentality used for communication, however, is a traditional public forum or a public forum by designation. . . . We will not find that a public forum has been created in the face of clear evidence of a contrary intent, nor will we infer that the Government intended to create a public forum when the nature of the property is inconsistent with expressive activity. In *Perry Educ. Ass'n.*, we found that the School District's internal mail system was not a public forum. In contrast to the general access policy in *Widmar*, school board policy did not grant general access to the school mail system. The practice was to require permission from the individual school principal before access to the system to communicate with teachers was granted. Similarly, the evidence in *Lehman v. City of Shaker Heights*, 418 U.S. 298 (1974), revealed that the City intended to limit access to the advertising spaces on City transit buses. It had done so for 26 years, and its management contract required the managing company to exercise control over the subject matter of the displays. Additionally, the Court found that the City's use of the property as a commercial enterprise was inconsistent with an intent to designate the car cards as a public forum. In cases where the principal function of the property would be disrupted by expressive activity, the Court is particularly reluctant to hold that the Government intended to designate a public forum. Accordingly, we have held that military reservations, *Greer v. Spock*, and jailhouse grounds, *Adderley v. Florida*, do not constitute public fora.

Here the . . . Government contends, and we agree, that neither its practice nor its policy is consistent with an intent to designate the CFC as a public forum open to all tax-exempt organizations. In 1980, an estimated 850,000 organizations qualified for tax-exempt status. The Government's consistent policy has been to limit participation in the CFC to "appropriate" voluntary agencies and to require agencies seeking admission to obtain permission from federal and local Campaign officials. Although the record does not show how many organizations have been denied permission throughout the 24-year history of the CFC, there is no evidence suggesting that the granting of the requisite permission is merely ministerial.

Nor does the history of the CFC support a finding that the Government was motivated by an affirmative desire to provide an open forum for charitable solicitation in the federal workplace. . . . The decision of the Government to limit access to the CFC is not dispositive in itself; instead, it is relevant for what it suggests about the Government's intent in creating the forum. The Government did not create the CFC for purposes of providing a forum for expressive activity. That such activity occurs in the context of the forum created does not imply that the forum thereby becomes a public forum for First Amendment purposes.

An examination of the nature of the government property involved strengthens the conclusion that the CFC is a nonpublic forum. The federal workplace, like any place of employment, exists to accomplish the business of the employer. It follows that the Government has the right to exercise control over access to the federal workplace in order to avoid interruptions to the performance of the duties of its employees. In light of the Government policy in creating the CFC and its practice in limiting access, we conclude that the CFC is a nonpublic forum.

C

. . . Although a speaker may be excluded from a nonpublic forum if he wishes to address a topic not encompassed within the purpose of the forum or if he is not a member of the class of speakers for whose especial benefit the forum was created, the Government violates the First Amendment when it denies access to a speaker solely to suppress the point of view he espouses on an otherwise includible subject. . . .

. . . The Government's decision to restrict access to a nonpublic forum need only be *reasonable*; it need not be the most reasonable or the only reasonable limitation. In contrast to a public forum, a finding of strict incompatibility between the nature of the speech or the identity of the speaker and the functioning of the nonpublic forum is not mandated. Even if some incompatibility with general expressive activity were required, the CFC would meet the requirement because it would be administratively unmanageable if access could not be curtailed in a reasonable manner. . . . The First Amendment does not demand unrestricted access to a nonpublic forum merely because use of that forum may be the most efficient means of delivering the speaker's message. Here, as in *Perry Educ. Ass'n.*, the speakers have access to alternative channels, including direct mail and in-person solicitation outside the workplace, to solicit contributions from federal employees.

The reasonableness of the government's restriction of access to a nonpublic forum must be assessed in the light of the purpose of the forum and all the surrounding circumstances. Here the President could reasonably conclude that a dollar directly spent on providing food or shelter to the needy is more beneficial than a dollar spent on litigation that might or might not result in aid to the needy. Moreover, avoiding the appearance of political favoritism is a valid justification for limiting speech in a nonpublic forum. . . .

Finally, the record amply supports an inference that respondents' participation in the CFC jeopardized the success of the Campaign. OPM submitted a number of letters from Federal employees and managers, as well as from Chairmen of local Federal Coordinating Committees and members of Congress expressing concern about the inclusion of groups termed "political" or "nontraditional" in the CFC. More than 80 percent of this correspondence related requests that the CFC be restricted to "non-political," "non-advocacy," or "traditional" charitable organizations. . . . Many Campaign workers indicated that extra effort was required to persuade disgruntled employees to contribute. The evidence indicated that the number of contributors had declined in some areas. . . . Although the avoidance of controversy is not a valid ground for restricting speech in a public forum, a nonpublic forum by definition is not dedicated to general debate or the free exchange of ideas. The First Amendment does not forbid a viewpoint-neutral exclusion of speakers who would disrupt a nonpublic forum and hinder its effectiveness for its intended purpose.

D

On this record, the Government's posited justifications for denying respondents access to the CFC appear to be reasonable in light of the purpose of the CFC. The existence of reasonable grounds for limiting access to a nonpublic forum, however, will not save a regulation that is in reality a facade for viewpoint-based discrimination. . . .

The Government contends that controversial groups must be eliminated from the CFC to avoid disruption and ensure the success of the Campaign. As noted *supra*, we agree that these are facially neutral and valid justifications for exclusion from the nonpublic forum created by the CFC. Nonetheless, the purported concern to avoid controversy excited by particular groups may conceal a bias against the viewpoint advanced by the excluded speakers. . . . Organizations that do not provide direct health and welfare services, such as the World Wildlife Fund, the Wilderness Society, and the United States Olympic Committee, have been permitted to participate in the CFC. Although there is no requirement that regulations limiting access to a nonpublic forum must be precisely tailored, the issue whether the Government excluded respondents because it disagreed with their viewpoints was neither decided below nor fully briefed before this Court. We decline to decide in the first instance whether the exclusion of respondents was impermissibly motivated by a desire to suppress a particular point of view. Respondents are free to pursue this contention on remand.

III

We conclude that the Government does not violate the First Amendment when it limits participation in the CFC in order to minimize disruption to the federal workplace, to ensure the success of the fund-raising effort, or to avoid the appearance of political favoritism without regard to the viewpoint of the excluded groups. . . .

JUSTICE MARSHALL took no part in the consideration or decision of this case. JUSTICE POWELL took no part in the decision of this case.

JUSTICE BLACKMUN, with whom JUSTICE BRENNAN joins, dissenting.

I agree with the Court that the Combined Federal Campaign (CFC) is not a traditional public forum. I also agree with the Court that our precedents indicate that the Government may create a "forum by designation" (or, to use the term our cases have adopted, a "limited public forum") by allowing public property that traditionally has not been available for assembly and debate to be used as a place for expressive activity by certain speakers or about certain subjects. I cannot accept, however, the Court's circular reasoning that the CFC is not a limited public forum because the Government intended to limit the forum to a particular class of speakers. Nor can I agree with the Court's conclusion that distinctions the Government makes between speakers in defining the limits of a forum need not be narrowly tailored and necessary to achieve a compelling governmental interest. Finally, I would hold that the exclusion of the several respondents from the CFC was, on its face, viewpoint-based discrimination. Accordingly, I dissent.

I

. . . In essence, the Court today holds that the First Amendment's guarantee of free speech and assembly . . . reduces to this: when the Government acts as the holder of public property other than streets, parks, and similar places, the Government may do whatever it reasonably intends to do, so long as it does not intend to suppress a particular viewpoint.

The Court's analysis . . . empties the limited public forum concept of all its meaning.

A

. . . [I]n answering the question whether a person has a right to engage in expressive activity on government property, the Court has recognized that the person's right to speak and the interests that such speech serves for society as a whole must be balanced against the "other interests inhering in the uses to which the public property is normally put." *Adderley v. Florida*, 385 U.S. 39, 54 (1966) (dissenting opinion).

The result of such balancing will depend, of course, upon the nature and strength of the various interests, which in turn depend upon such factors as the nature of the property, the relationship between the property and the message the speaker wishes to convey, and any special features of the forum that make it especially desirable or undesirable for the particular expressive activity. Broad generalizations about the proper balance are, for the most part, impossible. The Court has stated one firm guideline, however: the First Amendment does not guarantee that one may engage in expressive activity on governmental property when the expressive activity would be incompatible with important purposes of the property. . . .

The line between limited public forums and nonpublic forums "may blur at the edges," and is really more in the nature of a continuum than a definite demarcation. . . . The Government may invite speakers to a nonpublic forum to an extent that the forum comes to be a limited public forum because it becomes obvious that some types of expressive activity are not incompatible with the forum. . . .

Further, the . . . categories are not exclusive. There are instances in which property has not traditionally been used for a particular form of expressive activity, and the Government has not acquiesced, but the Court's examination of the nature of the forum and the nature of the expressive activity led it to conclude that the activity was compatible with normal uses of the property and was to be allowed. *See, e.g., Brown v. Louisiana*, 383 U.S. 131, 142 (1966) (plurality opinion). . . .

Nor should tradition or governmental "designation" be completely determinative of the rights of a citizen to speak on public property. Many places that are natural sites for expressive activity have no long tradition of use for expressive activity. Airports, for example, are a relatively recent phenomenon, as are government-sponsored shopping centers. . . .

C

. . . The Court makes it virtually impossible to prove that a forum restricted to a particular class of speakers is a limited public forum. If the Government does not create a limited public forum unless it intends to provide an "open forum" for expressive activity, and if the exclusion of some speakers is evidence that the Government did not intend to create such a forum, no speaker challenging denial of access will ever be able to prove that the forum is a limited public forum. . . .

II

A

. . . If the Government draws the line at a point which excludes speech that would be compatible with the intended uses of the property . . . then the Government must explain how its exclusion of compatible speech is necessary to serve, and is narrowly tailored to serve, some compelling governmental interest other than preserving the property for its intended uses.

B

. . . [T]he fact that the President or his advisers may believe the money is best "directly spent on providing food or shelter to the needy" starkly fails to explain why respondents are excluded from the CFC while other groups that do not spend money to provide food or shelter directly to the needy are allowed to be included.

Nor is the Government's "interest in avoiding controversy" a compelling state interest that would justify the exclusion of respondents. . . .

III

Even if I were to agree with the Court's determination that the CFC is a nonpublic forum, or even if I thought that the Government's exclusion of respondents from the CFC was necessary and narrowly tailored to serve a compelling governmental interest, I still would disagree with the Court's disposition, because I think the eligibility criteria, which exclude charities that "seek to influence . . . the determination of public policy," is on its face viewpoint-based. . . .

By devoting its resources to a particular activity, a charity expresses a view about the manner in which charitable goals can best be achieved. . . .

[Justice Stevens filed a separate dissenting opinion.]

NOTES

(1) *Placards Inside Buses.* In *Lehman v. City of Shaker Heights*, 418 U.S. 298 (1974), a candidate for the Ohio General Assembly "sought to promote his candidacy by purchasing car card space on the Shaker Heights Rapid Transit System." In its 26 years of operation, the Shaker Heights transit system had never permitted "any political or public issue advertising on its vehicles."

The Court characterized the City's car card space as "part of a commercial venture." Justice Blackmun opined: "No First Amendment forum is here to be found. The city consciously has limited access to its transit system advertising space in order to minimize chances of abuse, the appearance of favoritism, and the risk of imposing upon a captive audience. These are reasonable legislative objectives advanced by the city in a propriety capacity."

Justice Douglas wrote a separate concurring opinion in which he emphasized the rights of commuters as a captive audience.

Justice Brennan dissented, joined by Justices Stewart, Marshall and Powell. "Once such messages have been accepted and displayed, the existence of a forum for communication cannot be gainsaid. To hold otherwise, and thus sanction the city's preference for bland commercialism and noncontroversial public service messages over 'uninhibited, robust, and wide-open' debate on public issues, would reverse the traditional priorities of the First Amendment."

(2) *Utility Poles. Members of City Council of the City of Los Angeles v. Taxpayers for Vincent*, 466 U.S. 789 (1984), upheld a Los Angeles ordinance that prohibited posters on utility poles and other places.[28] The poster at issue read: " 'Ronald Vincent — City Council.' " After "an extensive" review of the overbreadth doctrine, the Court determined that the respondents had "failed to demonstrate a realistic danger that the ordinance [would] significantly compromise recognized First Amendment protections of individuals not before the Court." In a 6-3 decision written by Justice Stevens, the Court upheld the law. Since the ordinance was "viewpoint neutral," the Court used the test set forth in *United States v. O'Brien*, 391 U.S. 367 (1968), 391 U.S. 367 (1968), § 15.01. The City's proffered interest in aesthetics was "basically unrelated to the suppression of ideas." Moreover, the ordinance advanced a "substantial" state interest and did "no more than eliminate the exact source of evil it sought to remedy."

Utility poles were not a public forum, as there was no "traditional right of access" to them. "Public property which is not by tradition or designation a forum for public communication may be reserved by the State 'for its intended purposes, communicative or otherwise, as long as the regulation on speech is reasonable and not an effort to suppress expression merely because public officials oppose the speaker's view.' Given our analysis of the legitimate interest served by the ordinance, its viewpoint neutrality, and the availability of alternative channels of communication, the ordinance is certainly constitutional as applied to appellees under this standard."

Justice Brennan dissented, joined by Justices Marshall and Blackmun. He argued that the City failed to show "that its interest in eliminating 'visual clutter' justifies its restriction of appellees' ability to communicate" with voters. Costing even less than handbills, "signs posted on public property are doubtless 'essential to the poorly financed causes of little people.' "

(3) *Sidewalk Surrounding the Supreme Court*. In *United States v. Grace*, 461 U.S. 171 (1983), the Court invalidated a prohibition on the display of " 'any flag, banner, or device designed or adapted to bring into public notice any party organization, or movement' " in the building or on the grounds of the U.S. Supreme Court, as applied to the public sidewalks around the Supreme Court building. Writing for the majority, Justice White did not decide whether the Supreme Court buildings and grounds were public forums. "Sidewalks, of course, are among those areas of public property that traditionally have been held open to the public for expressive activities and are clearly within those areas of public property that may be considered, generally without further inquiry, to be public forum property."

The total ban on expressive activity in 40 U.S.C. § 13k was an unreasonable time, place or manner restriction because it was not required as a means to maintain order or decorum, or to secure access to the Supreme Court. The Court also rejected the argument that the public might infer that the Court was subject to improper influences if signs and banners were displayed, since these sidewalks are no different from other public sidewalks.

Justices Marshall and Justice Stevens filed seperate opinions concurring in part and dissenting in part.

---

[28] As quoted by the Court, the Los Angeles ordinance read as follows: " 'Sec. 28.04. Hand-bill, signs — public places and objects:

(a) No person shall paint, mark or write on, or post or otherwise affix, any hand-bill or sign to or upon any sidewalk, crosswalk, curb, curbstone, street lamp post, hydrant, tree, shrub, tree stake or guard, railroad trestle, electric light or power or telephone or telegraph or trolley wire pole, or wire appurtenance thereof or upon any fixture of the fire alarm or police telegraph system or upon any lighting system, public bridge, drinking fountain, life buoy, life preserver, life boat or other life saving equipment, street sign or traffic sign.' "

(4) *Sidewalks Near Foreign Embassies.* In *Boos v. Barry*, 485 U.S. 312 (1988), the Court struck down a District of Columbia law that made it "unlawful to display any flag, banner, placard, or device designed . . . to intimidate, coerce, or bring into public odium any foreign government, party, or organization, or any officer or officers thereof, or to bring into public dispute political, social, or economic acts, views, or purposes of any foreign government, party or organization within 500 feet of a building used by a foreign government or representative for official purposes." Justice O'Connor's majority (5-3) opinion invalidated the law as a "content-based restriction on political speech in a public forum." The Court rejected the argument that the "secondary effects" of the speech warranted the regulation. Where the "secondary effect" consists of the impact on the audience, it "presents a different situation" from cases where, for example, the desire to prevent crime might justify preventing the concentration of adult films, as in *City of Renton v. Playtime Theatres*, 475 U.S. 41 (1986). The "secondary effect" in *Renton* related only to the category of speech (sexually explicit films) and was content-neutral. In contrast, the asserted justification for the Washington, D.C., law was that the content of the speech was critical of a foreign government.

Writing for a unanimous Court, Justice O'Connor did uphold, against facial challenges, a separate clause allowing police to disperse congregations that are directed at the embassy and that police reasonably believe threaten its "security or peace." The law made it unlawful to "congregate within 500 feet of [a building used by a foreign government as an embassy, legation or consulate] . . . and refuse to disperse after having been ordered to do so by the police."

Justice Brennan, joined by Justice Marshall, concurred but took issue with Justice O'Connor's assumption that *City of Renton* "applies not only outside the context of business purveying sexually explicit materials but even to political speech." Chief Justice Rehnquist, joined by Justices White and Blackmun, dissented. He maintained that the ordinance was narrowly tailored to serve the compelling interest of fulfilling the country's obligations under international law to protect the "dignity of foreign diplomatic personnel." Justice Kennedy did not participate.

(5) For further discussion of public forum doctrine, see Daniel A. Farber & John E. Nowak, *The Misleading Nature of Public Forum Analysis: Content and Context in First Amendment Adjudication*, 70 VA. L. REV. 1219 (1984). Professors Farber and Nowak argue that the concept of a public forum is comparatively new. At the time they wrote their article, they found only 32 Supreme Court cases in which the phrase had appeared. "Only two of these decisions were rendered prior to 1970 and thirteen of the thirty-two have been rendered in the eighties." The authors argue that public forum analysis permits the government to engage in content discrimination: "The crux of the problem is the government's power to differentiate among speakers or types of speech based on their impact on a given environment. Notwithstanding the arguments made for content neutrality in some judicial opinions and scholarly analyses, it is clear today that content regulation is not absolutely impermissible." For a classic early discussion of the concept of the public forum, see Harry Kalven, Jr., *The Concept of the Public Forum: Cox v. Louisiana*, 1965 SUP. CT. REV. 1.

WARD v. ROCK AGAINST RACISM, 491 U.S. 781 (1989). In *Ward*, the Court upheld New York City's " 'Use Guidelines' " requiring that performances in Naumberg Acoustic Bandshell in Central Park use the city's sound equipment and sound technician. The " 'Use Guidelines' " provided that the city's sound technician, in consultation with the event's sponsors, control volume and sound mix through the mixing board. The guidelines were partly in reaction to noise complaints against concerts by Rock Against Racism (RAR). RAR filed suit, challenging the guidelines as facially invalid because of their burden on free speech.

Writing for a 6-3 majority, Justice Kennedy stated that music is "a form of expression and communication" protected by the First Amendment and that "the Bandshell is a public forum for performances."

The " 'Use Guidelines' " were valid time, place, and manner restrictions. The Court first examined whether the guidelines were content neutral. "The principal inquiry in determining content neutrality, in speech cases generally and in time, place, or manner cases in particular, is whether the government has adopted a regulation of speech because of disagreement with the message it conveys. The government's purpose is the controlling consideration. A regulation that serves purposes unrelated to the content of the expression is deemed neutral, even if it has an incidental effect on some speakers or messages but not others." The City's purpose in promulgating the guidelines, the quiet enjoyment of adjacent areas in the park and nearby residences is content-neutral. The City also seeks to ensure "the quality of sound at Bandshell events." The Court held that "the city's concern with sound quality extends only to the content-neutral goals of ensuring adequate sound amplification and avoiding the volume problems associated with inadequate sound mix."

Justice Kennedy recognized "that government ha[s] a substantial interest in protecting its citizens from unwelcome noise" which extends to protecting "even such traditional public forums as city streets and parks from excessive noise." A time, place, or manner restriction "must be narrowly tailored to serve the government's legitimate content-neutral interests but . . . it need not be the least-restrictive or least-intrusive means of doing so. Instead, the requirement of narrow tailoring is satisfied 'so long as the . . . regulation promotes a substantial government interest that would be achieved less effectively absent the regulation.' " The Court continued: "So long as the means chosen are not substantially broader than necessary to achieve the government's interest, however, the regulation will not be invalid simply because a court concludes that the government's interest could be adequately served by some less-speech-restrictive alternative. The validity of [time, place, or manner] regulations does not turn on a judge's agreement with the responsible decisionmaker concerning the most appropriate method for promoting significant government interests or the degree to which those interests should be promoted."

In applying this analysis, the Court found that "the city's substantial interest in limiting sound volume is served in a direct and effective way by the requirement that the city's sound technician control the mixing board during performances." Justice Kennedy afforded the city considerable discretion to make this determination. "The Court of Appeals erred in failing to defer to the city's reasonable determination that its interest in controlling volume would be best served by requiring Bandshell performers to utilize the city's sound technician." The guidelines also served the other city interest of ensuring adequate sound. "Here, the regulation's effectiveness must be judged by considering all the varied groups that use the Bandshell, and it is valid so long as the city could reasonably have determined that its interests overall would be served less effectively without the sound amplification guideline than with it." In sum, "it is apparent that the guideline directly furthers the city's legitimate governmental interests and that those interests would have been less well served in the absence of the sound-amplification guideline."

Finally, the "requirement, that the guideline leave open ample alternative channels of communication, is easily met." The guidelines did not attempt to ban protected speech and "ha[ve] no effect on the quantity or content of that expression beyond regulating the extent of amplification. That the city's limitations on volume may reduce to some degree the potential audience for respondent's speech is of no consequence, for there has been no showing that the remaining avenues of communication are inadequate."

Justice Blackmun concurred in the result. Justice Marshall wrote a dissenting opinion that Justices Stevens and Brennan joined. The majority altered the Court's traditional construction of the words "narrowly tailored" replacing "constitutional scrutiny with mandatory deference." The Court "requires only that government show that its interest cannot be served as effectively without the challenged restriction. The aspect of the case dealing with the discretion given to city officials in applying the sound quality and volume guidelines is discussed at § 14.02, Note (7) after *Cox v. New Hampshire*.

UNITED STATES v. KOKINDA, 497 U.S. 720 (1990). In *Kokinda*, the Court held that the United States Postal Service may prohibit solicitation on a sidewalk that "lies entirely on Postal Service property" without violating the First Amendment. Two volunteers for the National Democratic Policy Committee, who had been arrested for soliciting bypassers on Postal Service property, filed the suit. The post office is a "freestanding building" that is surrounded by its own parking lot and faces a highway with a sidewalk running along the highway's edge. Defendants had set up a table on a sidewalk that runs "adjacent to the building itself, separating the parking lot from the building." Customers must use this sidewalk to enter the post office. In the several hours defendants had been soliciting, the post office "received between 40 and 50 complaints regarding their presence."

Justice O'Connor, joined by Chief Justice Rehnquist and Justices White and Scalia, found the regulation "valid as applied." The plurality distinguished the "postal sidewalk" at issue that runs adjacent to the post office from the "municipal sidewalk" running parallel to the edge of the highway. Remarking that "mere physical characteristics of the property cannot dictate forum analysis," the plurality characterized a municipal sidewalk as "a public passageway." In contrast, the postal sidewalk "is not such a thoroughfare. Rather it leads only from the parking area to the front door of the post office" and "was constructed solely to provide for the passage of individuals engaged in postal business." According to Justice O'Connor, "individuals or groups have been permitted to leaflet, speak, and picket on postal premises, but a regulation prohibiting disruption, and a practice of allowing some speech activities on postal property do not add up to the dedication of postal property to speech activities." In *Cornelius v. N.A.A.C.P.*, the Court held that "[t]he government does not create a public forum by . . . permitting limited discourse, but only by intentionally opening a nontraditional forum for public discourse." Restriction on "access to a nonpublic forum can be based on subject matter and speaker identity so long as the distinctions drawn are reasonable in light of the purpose served by the forum and are viewpoint neutral."

Justice O'Connor agreed that "solicitation is inherently disruptive of the postal service's business of efficiently delivering the mail." That the Postal Service "permits other types of potentially disruptive speech on a case-by-case basis" does not render the government's actions unreasonable. "That claim, however, is more properly addressed under the equal protection component of the Fifth Amendment . . .The Service's generous accommodation of some types of speech testifies to its willingness to provide as broad a forum as possible, consistent with its postal mission." Compelling government to treat all categories of speech equally in a nonpublic forum would "create, in the name of the First Amendment, a disincentive for the Government to dedicate its property to any speech activities at all." Confrontation by a person asking for money disrupts passage and is more intrusive and intimidating than an encounter with a person giving out information.

Justice Kennedy concurred in the judgment. "There remains a powerful argument that, because of the wide range of activities that the Government permits to take place on this postal sidewalk, it is more than a nonpublic forum . . . If our public forum jurisprudence is to retain vitality, we must recognize that certain objective characteristics of Government property and its customary use by the public may control the case."

Whether the sidewalk is a "public or nonpublic forum," Justice Kennedy found that "the postal regulation at issue meets the traditional standards we have applied to time, place, and manner restrictions." Individuals may still "distribute literature soliciting support" if "there is no in-person solicitation for payments on the premises."

Justice Brennan dissented, joined by Justices Marshall and Stevens, and joined in Part I of his dissent by Justice Blackmun. The plurality's assertion that this sidewalk, as opposed to public sidewalks in general, is not a public forum is "strained and formalistic." Even if the sidewalk was not a " 'traditional' public forum," then it was at least a " 'limited purpose' forum." Justice Brennan also disagreed with Justice Kennedy's characterization of the restriction as "content-neutral." "If a person on postal premises says to members of the public, 'Please support my political advocacy group,' he cannot be punished. If he says, 'Please contribute $10,' he is subject to criminal prosecution."

In contrast to a "narrowly tailored" time, place or manner restriction, the prohibition on solicitation is an absolute ban.

Justice Brennan was joined only by Justices Marshall and Stevens in the second and third portions of his opinion. Even if the sidewalk was a nonpublic forum, the regulation is not "reasonable as applied" to the defendants because under the regulation a political rally could draw thousands of persons to the area right outside a post office. Rather, Justice Brennan would rely on " 'the general disturbance and obstruction rules' contained in other postal regulations."

SOCIETY FOR KRISHNA CONSCIOUSNESS v. LEE, 505 U.S. 672 (1992). In *Lee*, one majority (Chief Justice Rehnquist, and Justices White, O'Connor, Scalia, and Thomas, with Justice Kennedy concurring in the judgment) upheld a restriction prohibiting the repetitive solicitation of money at three airport terminals owned and operated by the Port Authority of New York and New Jersey. The restriction prohibited the International Society for Krishna Consciousness (ISKCON) from performing a ritual known as sankirtan, which requires members to go to public places to distribute religious literature and solicit funds. Upholding the solicitation ban, the Chief Justice opined: "Considering the lateness with which the modern air terminal has made its appearance, it hardly qualifies for the description of [a traditional public forum] having immemorially . . . 'time out of mind' been held in the public trust and used for purposes of expressive activity." Moreover, the terminals could not be considered designated public forums because they were not "intentionally opened by their operators to such activity."

The Chief Justice rejected ISKCON's argument that airport terminals were similar to "rail stations, bus stations and wharves," because bus and rail terminals traditionally have had private ownership. Moreover, "when new methods of transportation develop, new methods for accommodating that transportation are also likely to be needed" and not all transportation necessities are compatible with all kinds of expressive activity. Airports are commercial enterprises designed for the purpose of facilitating passenger air travel, not for the promotion of expression. As airports have expanded their functions "beyond merely contributing to efficient air travel, few have included among their purposes the designation of a forum for solicitation and distribution activities."

Airline passengers, who cannot easily avoid face-to-face solicitation, are on tight schedules. "The inconveniences to passengers and the burdens on Port Authority officials flowing from solicitation activity may seem small, but viewed against the fact that 'pedestrian congestion is one of the greatest problems facing the three terminals,' the Port Authority could reasonably worry that even such incremental effects would prove quite disruptive."

Justice Kennedy filed an opinion concurring in the judgment. Justices Blackmun, Stevens and Souter joined in the first part of Justice Kennedy's opinion holding that the terminals are public forums and consequently that the ban on leafleting is unconstitutional. They did not join the part of Justice Kennedy's opinion upholding the ban on solicitation. Justice Kennedy argued that the Court's analysis "leaves the government with almost unlimited authority to restrict speech on its property by doing nothing more than articulating a non-speech-related purpose for the area, and it leaves almost no scope for the development of new public forums absent the rare approval of government." Finding that airport terminals are public forums, Justice Kennedy invalidated the prohibition on distributing literature. He upheld the ban on solicitation, however, as "a narrow and valid regulation of the time, place, and manner of protected speech" or as a "valid regulation of the nonspeech elements of expressive conduct."

Justice O'Connor concurred with the Chief Justice in the parts of his opinion that characterized airports as nonpublic forums and upheld the ban on solicitation. She pointed out that, while it was true that the airport's stated purpose was to facilitate air travel, "the Port Authority is operating a shopping mall as well as an airport." Thus, the proper inquiry is whether the restrictions on speech are "reasonably related to maintaining the multipurpose environment that the Port Authority has deliberately created." Applying this standard, Justice O'Connor found that the ban on face-to-face solicitation was reasonable, but that the prohibition on leafleting was not reasonable.

Justice Souter, joined by Justices Blackmun and Stevens, concurred in striking down the ban on leafleting, but dissented from the Court's holding on solicitation. He encouraged case-specific inquiry into whether the forum in question shares fundamental characteristics with fora traditionally viewed as public. Justice Souter, like Justice Kennedy, stated that whether a forum is categorized as a traditional place for public expression should not dispose of the public forum issue. Instead, the Court "should classify as a public forum any piece of public property that is 'suitable for discourse' in its physical character, where expressive activity is 'compatible' with the use to which it has actually been put."

Justice Souter formed part of the majority that struck down the leafleting ban, but also would have struck down the solicitation ban. In dissent, he asserted that the state's purported interest in preventing coercion that might result from aggressive solicitation failed to rise to the level of significance required by precedent. Lastly, Justice Souter did "not think the Port Authority's solicitation ban leaves open the 'ample' channels of communication required of a valid content-neutral time, place, and manner restriction. . . . [It] shuts off a uniquely powerful avenue of communication."

NOTE

Government Intent and the Public Forum Doctrine. One commentator has suggested that "[a]fter *Kokinda*, and as confirmed by the *Lee* decision, the government's intent will even control the determination of a traditional forum, except for 'public streets.' This approach completely reverses the thrust of the traditional public forum concept. In short, the problem is that the Court's application of the modern forum doctrine blindly trusts the intentions of governmental officials. This is a fatal flaw. For that reason alone, the modern forum doctrine should be abandoned." David S. Day, *The End of the Public Forum Doctrine*, 78 Iowa L. Rev. 143, 202 (1992).

CITY OF LADUE v. GILLEO, 512 U.S. 43 (1994). In *Ladue*, the Court held that a city ordinance banning all residential signs, with narrowly-tailored exemptions, violated a homeowner's right to free speech. In 1990, Margaret Gilleo, a homeowner in Ladue,

Missouri placed a sign reading "Say No to War in the Persian Gulf, Call Congress Now" on her front lawn. The first sign was stolen; then its replacement was knocked to the ground. On registering a complaint to the City, Gilleo was informed that Ladue prohibited such signs. After a court issued a preliminary injunction against enforcing the ordinance, Gilleo posted a small sign in the second story window of her home stating, "For Peace in the Gulf." The Ladue City Council responded by enacting a new ordinance broadly prohibiting "signs" except those which fell within one of ten exceptions.[29]

Writing for a unanimous Court, Justice Stevens said that government may "regulate the physical characteristics of signs" as they can "obstruct views, distract motorists, displace alternative uses of land, and pose other problems that legitimately call for regulation." In *Metromedia Inc. v. San Diego*, 453 U.S. 490 (1981), § 15.04[1], Note (2) after *Cent. Hudson Gas & Elec. Corp. v. Pub. Serv. Comm'n of N.Y.*, the Court struck down an ordinance imposing substantial prohibitions on outdoor signs. The *Metromedia* Court invalidated the ordinance on two different grounds. One plurality stated that the city engaged in impermissible content discrimination by permitting commercial signs on the site of the business they describe while prohibiting off-site non-commercial signs. A different plurality voted to strike down the ordinance on the ground that it worked "To eliminate the billboard as an effective medium of communication."[30]

Metromedia and other decisions establish two analytically distinct strands by which the constitutionality of municipal sign prohibitions is tested. The first rests on the restriction of too little speech by discriminating based on content classifications; the other strand simply invalidates laws that restrict too much speech. Under the content discrimination rationale utilized by the Court of Appeals, the ordinance could theoretically pass constitutional muster by merely eliminating all exceptions. If, however, the Ladue ordinance was vulnerable due to its prohibition of too much speech, such a solution by the City would be unavailing. Consequently, the Court first assumed, *arguendo*, that the ordinance did not discriminate based on content.

"Ladue's sign ordinance is supported principally by the City's interest in minimizing the visual clutter associated with signs, an interest that is concededly valid." The comprehensive nature of Ladue's virtually complete ban on residential signs exacerbated its detrimental impact on the free communication of political, religious, and personal messages by residents. Furthermore, signs are a most effective medium for initiating and responding to community change.

The Court has invalidated complete bans on pamphlet distributions in *Lovell v. Griffin*, 303 U.S. 444, 451-52 (1938), on door-to-door literature distributions in *Martin v. Struthers*, 319 U.S. 141, 145–49 (1943), and on live nude entertainment in *Schad v. Mount Ephraim*, 452 U.S. 61, 75-76 (1981). Ladue contended that its ordinance merely regulated the "time, place, or manner" of speech. The Court rejected as inadequate the City's alternatives of "hand-held signs, letters, handbills, flyers, telephone calls, newspaper advertisements, bumper stickers, speeches, and neighborhood or community meetings."

The restriction at issue "foreclosed a venerable means of communication that is both unique and important." Residential signs are both inexpensive and convenient; persons

[29] Generally, exceptions were allowed for real estate signs, road and safety hazard signs, municipal signs, health inspection signs, public transportation stops, school and church signs, on-site gasoline station signs, and commercial signs in districts zoned commercial or industrial. . . .

[30] While *City Council of Los Angeles v. Vincent*, 466 U.S. 789 (1984), upheld a ban on public utility pole signs as advancing the City's interest in aesthetics, a " 'private citizen's interest in controlling the use of his own property justifies' not extending the ban to private property. "

of modest means may have no viable alternatives. Moreover, a yard or window sign may be the best way of reaching one's neighbors. "A special respect for individual liberty in the home has long been part of our culture and our law; that principle has special resonance when the government seeks to constrain a person's ability to speak there."

Other considerations might apply in a case, for example, where residents displayed political or other signs for a fee or residential signs advertising off-site commercial enterprises. A resident's self-interest in maintaining her own private property in and of itself acts as a deterrent to the "unlimited" proliferation of signs.

Justice O'Connor filed a concurring opinion. She found it unusual that the Court, confronted by a regulation which on its face made content distinctions, would assume *arguendo* that such exemptions were free of discrimination. "The normal inquiry that our doctrine dictates is, first, to determine whether a regulation is content-based or content-neutral, and then, based on the answer to that question, to apply the proper level of scrutiny." Nevertheless, Justice O'Connor agreed with the conclusion of the Court that even if the restriction was content-neutral, it would still be invalid.

NOTES

(1) For further discussion, see Alan Howard, *City of Ladue v. Gilleo: Content Discrimination and the Right to Participate in Public Debate*, 14 ST. LOUIS U. PUB. L. REV. 349 (1995) (stating that "the Court appeared to make clear that the Citizen Participation Principle is no less important than the Content Discrimination Principle, and that it will be enforced no less rigorously").

(2) *Permissible Content-Based Restrictions.* In *Burson v. Freeman*, 504 U.S. 191 (1992), the Court upheld a Tennessee statute that prohibited the solicitation of votes and the display or distribution of campaign materials within 100 feet of the entrance to a polling place. A plurality of four found that, although the statute contained a content-based restriction on political speech in a public forum, it was narrowly tailored to serve a compelling government interest.

In the election-day "campaign-free" zone "the display of campaign posters, signs or other campaign materials, distribution of campaign materials, and solicitation of votes for or against any person or position on a question are prohibited."

Justice Blackmun found that the speech prohibited by the statute "obviously is political speech." Political speech "is the essence of self-government," and "the First Amendment 'has its fullest and most urgent application' to speech uttered during a campaign for political office." The statute "bars speech in quintessential public forums." However, the statute "is not facially content-neutral."

In order to survive strict scrutiny, "the accommodation of the right to engage in political discourse" must be reconciled "with the right to vote." The Court found Tennessee's interests "to vote freely" and "in an election conducted with integrity and reliability" compelling.

The evolution of election reform demonstrated "the necessity of restricted areas in or around polling places" in order to fight "a persistent battle against two evils: voter intimidation and election fraud."

In addition, Justice Blackmun found a restrictive area around polling places essential to "preserve the secrecy of the ballot." The issue of "whether the 100-foot boundary line could be somewhat tighter" is not "a question of 'constitutional dimension,' [but] a difference only in degree, not a less restrictive alternative in kind."

According to Justice Blackmun, "restrictions on speech around polling places on election day are as venerable a part of the American tradition as the secret ballot." Justice Blackmun found the statute "constitutional because it is a reasonable, viewpoint neutral regulation of a nonpublic forum."

Justice Stevens dissented, joined by Justices O'Connor and Souter. Justice Stevens noted that statutes, which cordon off large areas, often intend "censorship of election-day campaigning." The statute "bars the simple 'display of campaign posters, signs, or other campaign materials.' Bumper stickers on parked cars and lapel buttons on pedestrians are taboo."

Moreover, the statute selectively prohibits "speech based on content." It "silences all campaign-related expression, but allows expression on any other subject." In addition, the statute does not prohibit exit polling.

ARKANSAS EDUCATIONAL TELEVISION COMMISSION v. FORBES, 523 U.S. 666 (1998). In a 6 to 3 decision, Justice Kennedy determined that a state owned public television station was a nonpublic forum and that the station's decision to exclude a candidate from a televised debate was a "reasonable, viewpoint neutral exercise of journalistic discretion." The Arkansas Educational Television Commission (AETC) excluded congressional candidate Forbes from its televised debates.

First Amendment jurisprudence has never afforded broad rights of access to television broadcasts as such access "would be antithetical, as a general rule, to the discretion that stations and their editorial staff must exercise to fulfill their journalistic purpose and statutory obligations." As the Court stated in *Columbia Broad. Sys., Inc. v. Democratic Nat'l Comm.*, 412 U.S. 94 (1973), § 13.05[1], "Congress has rejected the argument that 'broadcast facilities should be open on a nonselective basis to all persons wishing to talk about public issues.'" However, the First Amendment does not "bar the legislative imposition of neutral rules for access to public broadcasting."

Generally, "the nature of editorial discretion counsels against subjecting broadcasters to claims of viewpoint discrimination. Programming decisions would be particularly vulnerable to claims of this type because even principled exclusions rooted in sound journalistic judgment can often be characterized as viewpoint-based."[31]

While public forum doctrine generally is not applied to public broadcasting, "the narrow exception to the rule" is candidate debates. Debates are different from general broadcasting, first, because a debate is "by design a forum for political speech by the candidates" and it is clear that the candidates are presenting their own views not those of the broadcaster.

Second, "candidate debates are of exceptional significance." They typically offer the "'only occasion during a campaign when the attention of a large portion of the American public is focused on the election.'"

Applying the Court's public forum analysis, both parties agreed "the AETC debate was not a traditional public forum." Even if the Court were to go beyond the historic guidelines of the traditional public forum, the "unfettered access of a traditional public forum would be incompatible with the programming dictates a television broadcaster must follow."

Nor was the debate a designated public forum, which requires that government intend to make "its property generally available to a certain class of speakers, as the university made its facilities generally available to student groups in *Widmar*. On the other hand, the government does not create a designated public forum when it does no more than reserve eligibility for access to the forum to a particular class of speakers, whose members must then, as individuals, 'obtain permission,'" to use it. In this case,

---

[31] "Much like a university selecting a commencement speaker, a public institution selecting speakers for a lecture series, or a public school prescribing its curriculum, a broadcaster by its nature will facilitate the expression of some viewpoints instead of others."

"just as the Government in *Cornelius* made agency-by-agency determinations as to which of the eligible agencies would participate in the CFC, AETC made candidate-by-candidate determinations as to which of the eligible candidates would participate in the debate."

Classifying the debate as a public forum by designation would open it to all eligible candidates, which "would place a severe burden upon public broadcasters who air candidates' views. In each of the 1988, 1992, and 1996 Presidential elections, for example, no fewer than 22 candidates appeared on the ballot in at least one State. In the 1996 congressional elections, it was common for 6 to 11 candidates to qualify for the ballot for a particular seat." Faced with the choice of airing all of the eligible candidates' views or suffering "First Amendment liability . . . a public television broadcaster might choose not to air candidates' views at all."

The record showed that Forbes was excluded not because of his viewpoint but because he generated no appreciable public interest. Consequently, the "decision to exclude him was reasonable."[32] "Justice Stevens dissented, joined by Justices Souter and Ginsburg. Forbes had been "a serious contender for the Republican nomination for Lieutenant Governor" in 1986 and 1990. In the 1990 primary he "received 46.88% of the statewide vote and had carried 15 of the 16 counties" within his congressional district by "absolute majorities." As AETC is a public broadcaster "owned by the State, deference to its interest in making ad hoc decisions about the political content of its programs necessarily increases the risk of government censorship and propaganda in a way that protection of privately owned broadcasters does not."[33]

Ironically, the Court uses AETC's standardless decision to exclude Forbes to conclude that the debate was a nonpublic forum rather than a limited public forum. Under the majority's reasoning, if AETC invited "either the entire class of 'viable' or " 'newsworthy' candidates" (as it claims it did) "it created a designated public forum." Access to political debates operated by state-owned organizations should be governed by "pre-established, objective criteria."

MADSEN v. WOMEN'S HEALTH CENTER, INC.
512 U.S. 753, 114 S. Ct. 2516, 129 L. Ed. 593 (1994)

CHIEF JUSTICE REHNQUIST delivered the opinion of the Court.

Petitioners challenge the constitutionality of an injunction entered by a Florida state court which prohibits antiabortion protestors from demonstrating in certain places and in various ways outside of a health clinic that performs abortions. We hold that the establishment of a 36-foot buffer zone on a public street from which demonstrators are excluded passes muster under the First Amendment, but that several other provisions of the injunction do not.

---

[32] "Forbes was excluded because (1) 'the Arkansas voters did not consider him a serious candidate'; (2) 'the news organizations also did not consider him a serious candidate'; (3) 'the Associated Press and a national election result reporting service did not plan to run his name in results on election night'; (4) Forbes 'apparently had little, if any, financial support, failing to report campaign finances to the Secretary of State's office or to the Federal Elections Commission'; and (5) 'there [was] no "Forbes for Congress" campaign headquarters other than his house' (citation omitted). Forbes himself described his campaign organization as 'bedlam' and the media coverage of his campaign as 'zilch.' *Cf. Perry Educ. Ass'n v. Perry Local Educators' Ass'n*, 460 U.S. 37, 49 (1983) (exclusion from nonpublic forum 'based on the status' rather than the views of the speaker is permissible) (emphasis in original)."

[33] Incongruously, AETC did "invite a major-party candidate with even less financial support than Forbes."

I

Respondents operate abortion clinics throughout central Florida. Petitioners and other groups and individuals are engaged in activities near the site of one such clinic in Melbourne, Florida. They picketed and demonstrated where the public street gives access to the clinic. In September 1992, a Florida state court permanently enjoined petitioners from blocking or interfering with public access to the clinic, and from physically abusing persons entering or leaving the clinic. Six months later, respondents sought to broaden the injunction, complaining that access to the clinic was still impeded by petitioners' activities and that such activities had also discouraged some potential patients from entering the clinic, and had deleterious physical effects on others. The trial court thereupon issued a broader injunction, which is challenged here.

The court found that, despite the initial injunction, protesters continued to impede access to the clinic by congregating on the paved portion of the street — Dixie Way — leading up to the clinic, and by marching in front of the clinic's driveways. It found that as vehicles heading toward the clinic slowed to allow the protesters to move out of the way, "sidewalk counselors" would approach and attempt to give the vehicle's occupants antiabortion literature. The number of people congregating varied from a handful to 400, and the noise varied from singing and chanting to the use of loudspeakers and bullhorns.

The protests, the court found, took their toll on the clinic's patients. A clinic doctor testified that, as a result of having to run such a gauntlet to enter the clinic, the patients "manifested a higher level of anxiety and hypertension causing those patients to need a higher level of sedation to undergo the surgical procedures, thereby increasing the risk associated with such procedures." The noise produced by the protestors could be heard within the clinic, causing stress in the patients both during surgical procedures and while recuperating in the recovery rooms. And those patients who turned away because of the crowd to return at a later date, the doctor testified, increased their health risks by reason of the delay.

Doctors and clinic workers, in turn, were not immune even in their homes. Petitioners picketed in front of clinic employees' residences; shouted at passersby; rang the doorbells of neighbors and provided literature identifying the particular clinic employee as a "baby killer." Occasionally, the protestors would confront minor children of clinic employees who were home alone. This and similar testimony led the state court to conclude that its original injunction had proved insufficient. . . . The amended injunction prohibits petitioners from engaging in the following acts:[34]

"(1) At all times on all days, from entering the premises and property of the Aware Woman Center for Choice [the Melbourne clinic]. . . . "

"(2) At all times on all days, from blocking, impeding, inhibiting, or in any other manner obstructing or interfering with access to, ingress into and egress from any building or parking lot of the Clinic."

"(3) At all times on all days, from congregating, picketing, patrolling, demonstrating or entering that portion of public right-of-way or private property within [36] feet of the property line of the Clinic. . . . "

"(4) During the hours of 7:30 a.m. through noon, on Mondays through Saturdays, during surgical procedures and recovery periods, from singing, chanting, whistling,

---

[34] [Court's footnote 1] In addition to petitioners, the state court's order was directed at "Operation Rescue, Operation Rescue America, Operation Goliath, their officers, agents, members, employees and servants, and . . . Bruce Cadle, Pat Mahoney, Randall Terry . . . and all persons acting in concert or participation with them, or on their behalf. . . . "

shouting, yelling, use of bullhorns, auto horns, sound amplification equipment or other sounds or images observable to or within earshot of the patients inside the Clinic."

"(5) At all times on all days, in an area within [300] feet of the Clinic, from physically approaching any person seeking the services of the Clinic unless such person indicates a desire to communicate by approaching or by inquiring of the [petitioners]. . . . "

"(6) At all times on all days, from approaching, congregating, picketing, patrolling, demonstrating or using bullhorns or other sound amplification equipment within [300] feet of the residence of any of the [respondents'] employees, staff, owners or agents, or blocking or attempting to block, barricade, or in any other manner, temporarily or otherwise, obstruct the entrances, exits or driveways of the residences of any of the [respondents'] employees, staff, owners or agents. The [petitioners] and those acting in concert with them are prohibited from inhibiting or impeding or attempting to impede, temporarily or otherwise, the free ingress or egress of persons to any street that provides the sole access to the street on which those residences are located."

"(7) At all times on all days, from physically abusing, grabbing, intimidating, harassing, touching, pushing, shoving, crowding or assaulting persons entering or leaving, working at or using services at the [respondents'] Clinic or trying to gain access to, or leave, any of the homes of owners, staff or patients of the Clinic."

"(8) At all times on all days, from harassing, intimidating or physically abusing, assaulting or threatening any present or former doctor, health care professional, or other staff member, employee or volunteer who assists in providing services at the [respondents'] Clinic."

"(9) At all times on all days, from encouraging, inciting, or securing other persons to commit any of the prohibited acts listed herein."

Operation Rescue v. Women's Health Center, Inc., 626 So. 2d 664, 679–80 (Fla. 1993).

The Florida Supreme Court upheld the constitutionality of the trial court's amended injunction.

Shortly before the Florida Supreme Court's opinion was announced, the Eleventh Circuit struck down the injunction, characterizing the dispute as a clash "between an actual prohibition of speech and a potential hinderance to the free exercise of abortion rights." *Cheffer v. McGregor*, 6 F.3d 705, 711 (1993).

II

We begin by addressing petitioners' contention that the state court's order, because it is an injunction that restricts only the speech of antiabortion protesters, is necessarily content or viewpoint based. . . . We disagree. To accept petitioners' claim would be to classify virtually every injunction as content or viewpoint based. An injunction, by its very nature, applies only to a particular group (or individuals) and regulates the activities, and perhaps the speech, of that group. It does so, however, because of the group's past actions in the context of a specific dispute between real parties. . . .

The fact that the injunction in the present case did not prohibit activities of those demonstrating in favor of abortion is justly attributable to the lack of any similar demonstrations by those in favor of abortion, and of any consequent request that their demonstrations be regulated by injunction. . . . [N]one of the restrictions imposed by the court were directed at the contents of petitioner's message. . . .

We thus look to the government's purpose as the threshold consideration. Here, the state court imposed restrictions on petitioners incidental to their antiabortion message because they repeatedly violated the court's original order.[35]. . .

III

If this were a content-neutral, generally applicable statute, instead of an injunctive order — we would determine whether the time, place, and manner regulations were "narrowly tailored to serve a significant governmental interest." *Ward*, 491 U.S. at 791.

There are obvious differences between an injunction and a generally applicable ordinance. Ordinances represent a legislative choice regarding the promotion of particular societal interests. Injunctions, by contrast, are remedies imposed for violations (or threatened violations) of a legislative or judicial decree. Injunctions also carry greater risks of censorship and discriminatory application than do general ordinances. "There is no more effective practical guaranty against arbitrary and unreasonable government than to require that the principles of law which officials would impose upon a minority must be imposed generally." *Ry. Express Agency, Inc. v. New York*, 336 U.S. 106 (1949). Injunctions, of course, have some advantages over generally applicable statutes in that they can be tailored by a trial judge to afford more precise relief than a statute where a violation of the law has already occurred.

Accordingly, when evaluating a content-neutral injunction, we must ask whether the challenged provisions of the injunction burden no more speech than necessary to serve a significant government interest.

The Florida Supreme Court concluded that numerous significant government interests are protected by the injunction. It noted that the State has a strong interest in protecting a woman's freedom to seek lawful medical or counseling services in connection with her pregnancy. *See Roe v. Wade.* The State also has a strong interest in ensuring the public safety and order, in promoting the free flow of traffic on public streets and sidewalks, and in protecting the property rights of all its citizens. In addition, the court believed that the State's strong interest in residential privacy, acknowledged in *Frisby v. Schultz*, 487 U.S. 474 (1988), applied by analogy to medical privacy. The court observed that while targeted picketing of the home threatens the psychological well-being of the "captive" resident, targeted picketing of a hospital or clinic threatens not only the psychological, but the physical well-being of the patient held "captive" by medical circumstance. We agree with the Supreme Court of Florida that the combination of these governmental interests is quite sufficient to justify an appropriately tailored injunction to protect them. We now examine each contested provision of the injunction to see if it burdens more speech than necessary to accomplish its goal.[36]

---

[35] [Court's footnote 2] We also decline to adopt the prior restraint analysis urged by petitioners. Prior restraints do often take the form of injunctions. *See, e.g., New York Times Co. v. United States*, 403 U.S. 713 (1971) (refusing to enjoin publications of the "Pentagon Papers"). Not all injunctions which may incidentally affect expression, however, are "prior restraints" in the sense that that term was used in *New York Times Co.* Here petitioners are not prevented from expressing their message in any one of several different ways; they are simply prohibited from expressing it within the 36-foot buffer zone. Moreover, the injunction was issued not because of the content of petitioners' expression, as was the case in *New York Times Co.*, but because of their prior unlawful conduct.

[36] [Court's footnote 5] Petitioners do not challenge the first two provisions of the state court's 1993 order. The provisions composed what had been the state court's 1992 permanent injunction and they chiefly addressed blocking, impeding, and inhibiting access to the clinic and its parking lot. Nor do petitioners challenge the restrictions in paragraphs 7, 8, and 9, which prohibit them from harassing and physically abusing clinic doctors, staff, and patients trying to gain access to the clinic or their homes. . . .

A

1

We begin with the 36-foot buffer zone. The state court prohibited petitioners from "congregating, picketing, patrolling, demonstrating or entering" any portion of the public right-of-way or private property within 36 feet of the property line of the clinic as a way of ensuring access to the clinic. This speech-free buffer zone requires that petitioners move to the other side of Dixie Way and away from the driveway of the clinic, where the state court found that they repeatedly had interfered with the free access of patients and staff. . . .

We have noted a distinction between the type of focused picketing banned from the buffer zone and the type of generally disseminated communication that cannot be completely banned in public places, such as handbilling and solicitation. Here the picketing is directed primarily at patients and staff of the clinic.

The 36-foot buffer zone protecting the entrances to the clinic and the parking lot is a means of protecting unfettered ingress to and egress from the clinic, and ensuring that petitioners do not block traffic on Dixie Way. The state court seems to have had few other options to protect access given the narrow confines around the clinic. . . . Dixie Way is only 21 feet wide in the area of the clinic.

The need for a complete buffer zone near the clinic entrances and driveway may be debatable, but some deference must be given to the state court's familiarity with the facts and the background of the dispute between the parties even under our heightened review. Moreover, one of petitioners' witnesses during the evidentiary hearing before the state court conceded that the buffer zone was narrow enough to place petitioners at a distance of no greater than 10 to 12 feet from cars approaching and leaving the clinic. Protesters standing across the narrow street from the clinic can still be seen and heard from the clinic parking lots. We also bear in mind the fact that the state court originally issued a much narrower injunction, providing no buffer zone, and that this order did not succeed in protecting access to the clinic. The failure of the first order to accomplish its purpose may be taken into consideration in evaluating the constitutionality of the broader order. On balance, we hold that the 36-foot buffer zone around the clinic entrances and driveway burdens no more speech than necessary to accomplish the governmental interest at stake.

Justice Scalia's dissent argues that a videotape made of demonstrations at the clinic represents "what one must presume to be the worst of the activity justifying the injunction." This seems to us a gratuitous assumption. [W]itnesses also testified as to relevant facts in a 3-day evidentiary hearing. Indeed, petitioners themselves studiously refrained from challenging the factual basis for the injunction both in the state courts and here. Petitioners argued against including the factual record as an appendix in the Florida Supreme Court, and never certified a full record. We must therefore judge this case on the assumption that the evidence and testimony presented to the state court supported its findings that the presence of protesters standing, marching, and demonstrating near the clinic's entrance interfered with ingress to and egress from the clinic despite the issuance of the earlier injunction.

2

The inclusion of private property on the back and side of the clinic in the 36-foot buffer zone raises different concerns. The accepted purpose of the buffer zone is to protect access to the clinic and to facilitate the orderly flow of traffic on Dixie Way. Absent evidence that petitioners standing on the private property have obstructed access to the clinic, blocked vehicular traffic, or otherwise unlawfully interfered with the clinic's operation, this portion of the buffer zone fails to serve the significant government interests relied on by the Florida Supreme Court. We hold that on the record before us the 36-foot buffer zone as applied to the private property to the north and west of the clinic burdens more speech than necessary to protect access to the clinic.

B

In response to high noise levels outside the clinic, the state court restrained the petitioners from "singing, chanting, whistling, shouting, yelling, use of bullhorns, auto horns, sound amplification equipment or other sounds or images observable to or within earshot of the patients inside the clinic" during the hours of 7:30 a.m. through noon on Mondays through Saturdays. We must, of course, take account of the place to which the regulations apply in determining whether these restrictions burden more speech than necessary. We have upheld similar noise restrictions in the past, and as we noted in upholding a local noise ordinance around public schools, "the nature of a place, 'the pattern of its normal activities, dictate the kinds of regulations that are reasonable.'" *Grayned v. City of Rockford*, 408 U.S. 104, 116 (1972). Noise control is particularly important around hospitals and medical facilities during surgery and recovery periods.

We hold that the limited noise restrictions imposed by the state court order burden no more speech than necessary to ensure the health and well-being of the patients at the clinic. . . .

C

The same, however, cannot be said for the "images observable" provision of the state court's order. Clearly, threats to patients or their families, however communicated, are proscribable under the First Amendment. This broad prohibition on all "images observable" burdens more speech than necessary to achieve the purpose of limiting threats to clinic patients or their families. Similarly, if the blanket ban on "images observable" was intended to reduce the level of anxiety and hypertension suffered by the patients inside the clinic, it would still fail. . . . [I]t is much easier for the clinic to pull its curtains than for a patient to stop up her ears. . . .

D

The state court ordered that petitioners refrain from physically approaching any person seeking services of the clinic "unless such person indicates a desire to communicate" in an area within 300 feet of the clinic. The state court was attempting to prevent clinic patients and staff from being "stalked" or "shadowed" by the petitioners as they approached the clinic. [I]t is difficult, indeed, to justify a prohibition on all uninvited approaches of persons seeking the services of the clinic, regardless of how peaceful the contact may be, without burdening more speech than necessary to prevent intimidation and to ensure access to the clinic. Absent evidence that the protesters' speech is independently proscribable (i.e., "fighting words" or threats), or is so infused with violence as to be indistinguishable from a threat of physical harm this provision cannot stand. The "consent" requirement alone invalidates this provision; it burdens more speech than is necessary to prevent intimidation and to ensure access to the clinic.[37]

---

[37] [Court's footnote 6] We need not decide whether the "images observable" and "no-approach" provisions are content based. . . .

E

The final substantive regulation challenged by petitioners relates to a prohibition against picketing, demonstrating, or using sound amplification equipment within 300 feet of the residences of clinic staff. The prohibition also covers impeding access to streets that provide the sole access to streets on which those residences are located. The same analysis applies to the use of sound amplification equipment here as that discussed above: the government may simply demand that petitioners turn down the volume if the protests overwhelm the neighborhood. . . .

[T]he 300-foot zone around the residences in this case is much larger than the zone provided for in the ordinance which we approved in *Frisby*. The ordinance at issue there . . . was limited to "focused picketing taking place solely in front of a particular residence." *Id.* at 483. By contrast, the 300-foot zone would ban "general marching through residential neighborhoods, or even walking a route in front of an entire block of houses." *Id.* The record before us does not contain sufficient justification for this broad a ban on picketing; it appears that a limitation on the time, duration of picketing, and number of pickets outside a smaller zone could have accomplished the desired result.

IV

Petitioners also challenge the state court's order as being vague and overbroad. They object to the portion of the injunction making it applicable to those acting "in concert" with the named parties. But petitioners themselves are named parties in the order, and they therefore lack standing to challenge a portion of the order applying to persons who are not parties. Nor is that phrase subject, at the behest of petitioners, to a challenge for "overbreadth;" the phrase itself does not prohibit any conduct, but is simply directed at unnamed parties who might later be found to be acting "in concert" with the named parties. . . .

Petitioners also contend that the "in concert" provision of the injunction impermissibly limits their freedom of association guaranteed by the First Amendment. . . . The freedom of association protected by the First Amendment does not extend to joining with others for the purpose of depriving third parties of their lawful rights.

V

In sum, we uphold the noise restrictions and the 36-foot buffer zone around the clinic entrances and driveway because they burden no more speech than necessary to eliminate the unlawful conduct targeted by the state court's injunction. We strike down as unconstitutional the 36-foot buffer zone as applied to the private property to the north and west of the clinic, the "images observable" provision, the 300-foot no-approach zone around the clinic, and the 300-foot buffer zone around the residences, because these provisions sweep more broadly than necessary to accomplish the permissible goals of the injunction. . . .

[JUSTICE SOUTER concurred in a brief opinion.]

JUSTICE STEVENS, concurring in part and dissenting in part.

. . . The Court correctly and unequivocally rejects petitioners' argument that the injunction is a "content-based restriction on free speech," as well as their challenge to the injunction on the basis that it applies to persons acting "in concert" with them. I therefore join Parts II and IV of the Court's opinion. . . .

II

. . . [Paragraph 5 of the injunction] does not purport to prohibit speech; it prohibits a species of conduct. . . .

The "physically approaching" prohibition entered by the trial court is no broader than the protection necessary to provide relief for the violations it found. . . .

Justice Scalia, with whom Justice Kennedy and Justice Thomas join, concurring in the judgment in part and dissenting in part. . . .

The entire injunction in this case departs so far from the established course of our jurisprudence that in any other context it would have been regarded as a candidate for summary reversal. But the context here is abortion. . . .

I

The record of this case contains a videotape, with running caption of time and date, displaying what one must presume to be the worst of the activity justifying the injunction. . . . The tape was shot by employees of, or volunteers at, the Aware Woman Clinic. . . . Anyone . . . who is familiar with run-of-the-mine labor picketing, not to mention some other social protests, will be aghast at what it shows we have today permitted an individual judge to do. . . .

. . . What the videotape, the rest of the record, and the trial court's findings do not contain is any suggestion of violence near the clinic, nor do they establish any attempt to prevent entry or exit.

II

A

. . . [T]his public sidewalk area is a "public forum," where citizens generally have a First Amendment right to speak. . . . Petitioners claimed the benefit of so-called "strict scrutiny," the standard applied to content-based restrictions. . . . Respondents, on the other hand, contended for what has come to be known as "intermediate scrutiny" . . . applicable to so-called "time, place, and manner regulations" of speech. . . . The Court adopts neither of these, but creates, brand-new for this abortion-related case, an additional standard that is (supposedly) "somewhat more stringent," than intermediate scrutiny. . . . [W]hereas intermediate scrutiny requires that the restriction be "narrowly tailored to serve a significant government interest," the new standard requires that the restriction "burden no more speech than necessary to serve a significant government interest. . . . "

. . . [A] restriction upon speech imposed by injunction (whether nominally content based or nominally content neutral) is at least as deserving of strict scrutiny as a statutory, content based restriction. . . . When a judge, on the motion of an employer, enjoins picketing at the site of a labor dispute, he enjoins (and he knows he is enjoining) the expression of pro-union views. Such targeting of one or the other side of an ideological dispute cannot readily be achieved in speech-restricting general legislation . . . it is achieved in speech-restricting injunctions almost invariably. . . .

The second reason speech-restricting injunctions are at least as deserving of strict scrutiny is obvious enough: they are the product of individual judges rather than of legislatures — and often of judges who have been chagrined by prior disobedience of their orders. . . . And the third reason is that the injunction is a much more powerful weapon than a statute, and so should be subjected to greater safeguards. Normally, when injunctions are enforced through contempt proceedings, only the defense of factual innocence is available. The collateral bar rule of *Walker v. Birmingham*, 388 U.S. 307 (1967), eliminates the defense that the injunction itself was unconstitutional. Thus, persons subject to a speech-restricting injunction who have not the money or not the time to lodge an immediate appeal . . . must remain silent, since if they speak their First Amendment rights are no defense in subsequent contempt proceedings. . . .

Finally, though I believe speech-restricting injunctions are dangerous enough to warrant strict scrutiny even when they are not technically content based, I think the injunction in the present case was content based (indeed, viewpoint based) to boot. . . .

B

[A]n injunction against speech is the very prototype of the greatest threat to First Amendment values, the prior restraint. . . . [38]

At oral argument neither respondents nor the Solicitor General, appearing as amicus for respondents, could identify a single speech-injunction case applying mere intermediate scrutiny. . . . In *Youngdahl v. Rainfair, Inc.*, 355 U.S. 131 (1957), we refused to allow a blanket ban on picketing when, even though there had been scattered violence, it could not be shown that "a pattern of violence was established which would inevitably reappear in the event picketing were later resumed." . . .

III

A

. . . *N.A.A.C.P. v. Claiborne Hardware Co.* involved, like this case, protest demonstrations against private citizens mingling political speech with (what I will assume for the time being existed here) significant illegal behavior. . . .

. . . [B]oycott leader Charles Evers told a group that boycott violators would be disciplined by their own people and warned that the Sheriff "could not sleep with boycott violators at night." He stated at a second gathering that "If we catch any of you going in any of them racist stores, we're gonna break your damn neck." *Id.* In connection with the boycott, there were marches and picketing (often by small children). "Store watchers" were posted outside boycotted stores to identify those who traded, and their names were read aloud at meetings of the Claiborne County N.A.A.C.P. and published in a mimeographed paper. The chancellor found that those persons were branded traitors, called demeaning names, and socially ostracized. Some had shots fired at their houses, a brick was thrown through a windshield and a garden damaged. Other evidence showed that persons refusing to observe the boycott were beaten, robbed and publicly humiliated (by spanking). . . .

We said . . . that any characterization of a political protest movement as a violent conspiracy "must be supported by findings that adequately disclose the evidentiary basis for concluding that specific parties agreed to use unlawful means, that carefully identify the impact of such unlawful conduct, and that recognize the importance of avoiding the imposition of punishment for constitutionally protected activity." 458 U.S.

---

[38] [Court's footnote 3] [T]oday's opinion . . . says . . . that injunctions are not prior restraints (or at least not the nasty kind) if they only restrain speech in a certain area, or if the basis for their issuance is not content but prior unlawful conduct. This distinction has no antecedent in our cases. . . .

at 933–934. Because this careful procedure had not been followed by the Mississippi courts, we set aside the entire judgment, including the injunction.

B

. . . [T]he only findings and conclusions of the court that could conceivably be considered relate to a violation of the original injunction. They all concern behavior by the protestors causing traffic on the street in front of the abortion clinic to slow down, and causing vehicles crossing the pedestrian right-of-way, between the street and the clinic's parking lot, to slow down or even, occasionally, to stop momentarily while pedestrians got out of the way. . . . There is no factual finding that petitioners engaged in any intentional or purposeful obstruction. . . .

If the original injunction is read as it must be, there is nothing in the trial court's findings to suggest that it was violated. The Court today speaks of "the failure of the first injunction to protect access." But the first injunction did not broadly "protect access." It forbade particular acts that impeded access, to-wit, intentionally "blocking, impeding or obstructing." The trial court's findings identify none of these acts, but only a mild interference with access that is the incidental by-product of leafletting and picketing. . . .

I almost forgot to address the facts showing prior violation of law (including judicial order) with respect to the other portion of the injunction the Court upholds: the no-noise-within-earshot-of-patients provision. That is perhaps because, amazingly, neither the Florida courts nor this Court makes the slightest attempt to link that provision to prior violations of law. . . .

The First Amendment . . . reels in disbelief. . . .

C

Finally, I turn to the Court's application of the second part of its test: whether the provisions of the injunction "burden no more speech than necessary" to serve the significant interest protected. . . .

With regard to the 36-foot speech-free zone . . . the test which the Court sets for itself has not been met. Assuming a "significant state interest" of the sort cognizable for injunction purposes (i.e., one protected by a law that has been or is threatened to be violated) in both (1) keeping pedestrians off the paved portion of Dixie Way, and (2) enabling cars to cross the public sidewalk at the clinic's driveways without having to slow down or come to even a "momentary" stop, there are surely a number of ways to protect those interests short of banishing the entire protest demonstration from the 36-foot zone. For starters, the Court could have (for the first time) ordered the demonstrators to stay out of the street (the original injunction did not remotely require that). It could have limited the number of demonstrators permitted on the clinic side of Dixie Way. . . .

But I need not engage in such precise analysis, since the Court itself admits that the requirement is not to be taken seriously. "The need for a complete buffer zone," it says, "*may be debatable*, but some deference must be given to the state court's familiarity with the facts and the background of the dispute between the parties even under our heightened review. . . ."

The proposition that injunctions against speech are subject to a standard indistinguishable from (unless perhaps more lenient in its application than) the "intermediate scrutiny" standard we have used for "time, place, and manner" legislative restrictions; the notion that injunctions against speech need not be closely tied to any violation of law, but may simply implement sound social policy; and the practice of accepting trial-court conclusions permitting injunctions without considering whether those conclusions are supported by any findings of fact — these latest by-products of our abortion jurisprudence ought to give all friends of liberty great concern. . . .

SCHENCK v. PRO-CHOICE NETWORK OF WESTERN NEW YORK, 519 U.S. 357 (1997). In *Schenck*, the Court upheld provisions of a District Court injunction that imposed "fixed buffer zone" restrictions on demonstrations outside abortion clinics. The Court, however, struck down the injunction's "floating buffer zone" restrictions as violating the First Amendment.

Three doctors and four medical clinics filed a complaint against the defendants alleging various federal and state causes of action.

Defendant protesters would form "large-scale blockades" by marching, standing, kneeling, sitting, or lying in the parking lot entrances and doorways of the clinics. In addition, protesters trespassed on clinic parking lots and buildings; crowded around cars, doorways and parking lot driveways; and threw themselves on the top of cars entering clinic parking lots. They also handed out literature in attempts to dissuade women from having abortions. Sometimes, protesters used more aggressive methods, including getting very near the women trying to enter the clinics and jostling, grabbing, pushing, or shoving them. Protesters also grabbed or spat on clinic volunteers escorting patients into the clinics. "On the sidewalks outside the clinics, protesters called 'sidewalk counselors' used similar methods."

Plaintiffs filed their complaint four days prior to a scheduled large-scale blockade by defendants. The District Court issued a temporary restraining order (TRO) that enjoined defendants from "physically blockading the clinics, physically abusing or tortiously harassing anyone entering or leaving the clinics, and 'demonstrating within 15 feet of any person' entering or leaving the clinics." However, the "TRO allowed two sidewalk counselors to have 'a conversation of a nonthreatening nature' with individuals entering or leaving the clinic." Once an individual indicated that she did not want counseling, the counselors had to stop counseling and retreat 15 feet away from that individual. While defendants complied with the TRO's ban on physical blockades, they continued to demonstrate and harass patients and staff around clinic entrances. The District Court then issued a preliminary injunction against the defendants. The injunction banned 'demonstrating within fifteen feet from either side or edge of, or in front of, doorways or doorway entrances, parking lot entrances, driveways and driveway entrances of such facilities' ('fixed buffer zones'), or 'within fifteen feet of any person or vehicle seeking access to or leaving such facilities' ('floating buffer zones')."

Moreover, once sidewalk counselors, who could enter the buffer zones, had to stop counseling; they not only had to retreat 15 feet from the people whom they had been counseling but also had "to remain outside the boundaries of the buffer zones." Defendants challenged the fixed and floating buffer zones and the requirement that counseling cease and desist under certain circumstances.

Applying *Madsen v. Women's Health Center, supra,* Chief Justice Rehnquist inquired whether the injunction provisions at issue "burden more speech than is necessary to serve the relevant governmental interests." As in *Madsen*, the Court accepted the governmental interests of "ensuring public safety and order, promoting the free flow of traffic on streets and sidewalks, protecting property rights, and protecting a woman's freedom to seek pregnancy-related services." These "in combination are certainly significant enough to justify an appropriately tailored injunction to secure unimpeded physical access to the clinics."

The Court invalidated "the floating buffer zones around people entering and leaving the clinics because they burden more speech than is necessary to serve the relevant governmental interests." Excepting the two sidewalk counselors, the floating buffer zones completely prevented defendants "from communicating a message from a normal conversational distance or handing leaflets to people entering or leaving the clinics who are walking on the public sidewalks." Distributing leaflets and "commenting on matters of public concern are classic forms of speech that lie at the heart of the First Amendment, and speech in public areas is at its most protected on public sidewalks, a prototypical example of a traditional public forum." Unless an individual entering or leaving one clinic walked a straight line alongside the outer edge of the 17-foot-wide sidewalk, protesters who want to convey their message would have to walk in the street.[39] The uncertainties accompanying floating buffer zones would lead to "a substantial risk that much more speech will be burdened than the injunction forbids."

The Court also struck down a 15-foot floating buffer zone around vehicles. These zones burdened "more speech than necessary to serve the relevant governmental interests" because they "would restrict the speech of those who simply line the sidewalk or curb in an effort to chant, shout, or hold signs peacefully."

In contrast, the Court upheld the fixed buffer zones around the doorways and driveways as necessary to allow people and vehicles to enter or exit.

As in *Madsen*, the record shows that protesters purposefully or effectively blockaded or hindered people from entering and exiting the clinics.

Moreover, protesters' harassment of local police made it uncertain that they could quietly counteract threats to patients or employees.[40] Following *Madsen*, the Chief Justice afforded the District Court some deference in setting the boundaries of the fixed zone at 15 feet. *Madsen* did not require the district court to issue a " 'non-speech-restrictive' " injunction first. The failure to issue such an initial injunction was only a factor for a court to consider in determining the constitutionality of a speech-restrictive injunction. Moreover, as the defendants' conduct was extraordinary, the Court upheld the district court's conclusion "that keeping defendants away from the entrances was necessary to ensure access" to the clinics.

The Court also upheld the " 'cease and desist' " provisions aimed at sidewalk counselors as ensuring physical access. The exception for sidewalk counselors was part of the district court's effort "to enhance [defendant's] speech rights."

Finally, the Court rejected the argument that the " 'cease and desist' " provision was content-based for allowing "a clinic patient to terminate a protester's right to speak based on, among other reasons, the patient's disagreement with the message being conveyed." The *Madsen* injunction was not content-based, "even though it was directed only at abortion protesters, because it was only abortion protesters who had done the acts which were being enjoined."

Justice Scalia, joined by Justices Kennedy and Thomas, concurred in part and dissented in part. Justice Scalia argued that the majority postulated reasons that "*might*" have justified the injunction rather than analyzing the reasons articulated by the District Court. The dissent agreed with "the most important holding" of the majority: "There is no right to be free of unwelcome speech on the public streets while seeking entrance to or exit from abortion clinics." The District Court, however, shaped its injunction around "a right to be free of unwanted speech." The fixed buffer zones were founded in part on the right to be left alone. Moreover, the sole basis of the cease-

---

[39] While a protester could walk 15 feet, either in back, or in front of the individual while walking backwards, the protesters would be unable to see others approaching the clinic in the opposite direction to the targeted individual.

[40] Allowing the sidewalk counselors, who were subject to the " 'cease and desist' " into the fixed buffer zones "was an effort to bend over backwards to 'accommodate' defendants' speech rights."

and-desist provision was "the supposed right to be left alone, and not the right of unobstructed access to clinics."

Justice Scalia concluded that the majority's opinion made a destructive inroad upon First Amendment law in holding that the validity of an injunction against speech is to be determined by an appellate court on the basis of what the issuing court might reasonably have found as to necessity, rather than on the basis of what it in fact found.

The Court could have upheld the fixed buffer zone without including the cease-and-desist provision since the District Court concluded, with appropriate factual support, that "limiting the protesters to two was necessary to prevent repetition of the obstruction of access." Such a limited fixed buffer zone would still have been invalid, as the district court only found a cause of action for trespass not for obstruction of access.[41]

Justice Breyer concurred in upholding the fixed buffer zone; however, he dissented from the invalidation of the floating buffer zone. The words of the injunction do not necessarily create floating buffer zones. As the issue of floating buffer zones first arose during an *en banc* argument before the Court of Appeals, the district judge should have the opportunity to interpret the language of the preliminary injunction before an appellate court could pass on the question.

HILL v. COLORADO, 530 U.S. 703 (2000). In *Hill*, the Court upheld a Colorado statute "that regulates speech-related conduct within 100 feet of the entrance to any health care facility." The statute made "it unlawful within the regulated areas for any person to 'knowingly approach' within eight feet of another person, without that person's consent, 'for the purpose of passing a leaflet or handbill to, displaying a sign to, or engaging in oral protest, education, or counseling with such other person.'" The statute "does not require a standing speaker to move away from anyone passing by" nor does it restrict content of the message "either inside, or outside the regulated areas."

Supporters and opponents of the clinics testified "that demonstrations in front of abortion clinics impeded access to those clinics and were often confrontational." Some clinics even offered "escorts for persons entering and leaving the clinics both to ensure their access and to provide protection from aggressive counselors who sometimes used strong and abusive language in face-to-face encounters. There was also evidence that emotional confrontations may adversely affect a patient's medical care. There was no evidence, however, that the 'sidewalk counseling' conducted by the petitioners in this case was ever abusive or confrontational."

Justice Stevens wrote for the majority. Free speech "may not be curtailed simply because the speaker's message may be offensive to his audience." However, the "recognizable privacy interest in avoiding unwanted communication varies widely in different settings." If an offer of speech is "declined, as it may rightfully be, then persistence, importunity, following and dogging, become unjustifiable annoyance and obstruction which is likely soon to savor of intimidation." Disagreeing with the dissent, Justice Stevens stated that "whether there is a 'right' to avoid unwelcome expression is not before us in this case." The purpose of the statute is "to protect those who seek medical treatment from the potential physical and emotional harm suffered when an unwelcome individual delivers a message."

Courts commonly "examine the content of a communication to determine the speaker's purpose. Whether a particular statement constitutes a threat, blackmail, an

---

[41] The Executive Branch, which generally is charged with protecting public safety, did not initiate any action. Consequently, for the courts to interfere on their own, constitutes a separation of powers violation.

agreement to fix prices, a copyright violation, a public offering of securities, or an offer to sell goods often depends on the precise content of the statement. We have never held, or suggested, that it is improper to look at the content of an oral or written statement in order to determine whether a rule of law applies to a course of conduct. With respect to the conduct that is the focus of the Colorado statute, it is unlikely that there would often be any need to know exactly what words were spoken in order to determine whether 'sidewalk counselors' are engaging in 'oral protest, education, or counseling' rather than pure social or random conversation."

The Colorado statute is "content neutral." It seeks to protect "those who enter a health care facility from the harassment, the nuisance, the persistent importuning, the following, the dogging, and the implied threat of physical touching that can accompany an unwelcome approach within eight feet of a patient."

The majority found the statute a "valid time, place, and manner regulation." Its restrictions are "content neutral" and "'narrowly tailored'" to serve "governmental interests that are significant and legitimate." It also "leaves open ample alternative channels for communication."

The statute regulates "display of signs, leafletting, and oral speech." The 8-foot buffer "should not have any adverse impact on the readers' ability to read signs." Turning to oral communication, the "statute places no limitation on the number of speakers or the noise level, including the use of amplification equipment," even though prior cases such as *Madsen v. Women's Health Center*, *supra*, have upheld such restrictions. In contrast to *Schenck v. United States*, *supra*, an 8-foot zone, rather than 15-feet, "allows the speaker to communicate at a 'normal conversational distance.'" Moreover, the speaker may "remain in one place, and other individuals can pass within eight feet of the protester without causing the protester to violate the statute." The knowledge requirement protects the speaker who mistakenly did not keep the requisite distance. While, the 8-foot buffer does, to an extent, hinder the ability to distribute handbills, it does not prohibit the protester from "standing near the path of oncoming pedestrians" to distribute leaflets.

Justice Stevens noted that the buffer restriction applies "only within 100 feet of a health care facility." Prior cases have taken into consideration the "unique concerns" affecting hospitals.

Justice Stevens rejected plaintiff's overbreadth argument stating that, "the comprehensiveness of the statute is a virtue, not a vice, because it is evidence against there being a discriminatory governmental motive." In addition, "'particularly where conduct and not merely speech is involved,'" overbreadth must be substantial.

The statute is not "impermissibly vague" because, the statute "contains a scienter requirement. The statute only applies to a person who 'knowingly' approaches within eight feet of another, without that person's consent, for the purpose of engaging in oral protest, education, or counseling. The likelihood that anyone would not understand any of those common words seems quite remote." Words cannot achieve "'mathematical certainty.'" Even more importantly, "speculation about possible vagueness in hypothetical situations" cannot "support a facial attack." The statute holds an "even lesser prior restraint concern than those at issue in *Schenck* and *Madsen* where particular speakers were at times completely banned within certain zones." The Colorado statute at issue would "only apply if the pedestrian does not consent to the approach."

Justice Souter concurred, joined by Justices O'Connor, Ginsburg, and Breyer. The "right to express unpopular views does not necessarily immunize a speaker from liability for resorting to otherwise impermissible behavior meant to shock members of the speaker's audience, *see United States v. O'Brien*," 391 U.S. 367 (1968), § 15.01. He considered the injunction a reasonable time, place, and manner restriction which does not remove a subject or a viewpoint from effective discourse.

Justice Souter found a content-based restriction entails government disagreement with the message the speech conveys not regulation of "offensive behavior identified with its delivery."

Justice Scalia dissented, joined by Justice Thomas, stating that the statute at issue "enjoys the benefit of the 'ad hoc nullification machine' that the Court has set in motion to push aside whatever doctrines of constitutional law stand in the way of that highly favored practice" of abortion. This statute is "content-based. A speaker wishing to approach another for the purpose of communicating *any* message except one of protest, education, or counseling may do so without first securing the other's consent." The regulation "depends entirely on *what he intends to say*." The dissent sees the Colorado legislators as "taking aim at" the " 'right to protest or counsel *against* certain medical procedures.' " The State has "restricted certain categories of speech — protest, counseling, and education." In addition, this is "the first case in which, in order to sustain a statute, the Court has relied upon a governmental interest not only unasserted by the State, but positively repudiated." " 'Outside the home, the burden is generally on the observer or listener to avert his eyes or plug his ears.' "

Justice Scalia also maintained the "labor movement, in particular, has good cause for alarm." Modern free speech jurisprudence does not allow the " 'right to be free' from 'persistent, importunity, following and dogging.' " Even if it did, the law is not narrowly tailored as it goes far beyond this behavior to restrict "all speakers who wish to protest, educate, or counsel."

In contrast to subsection (3) of the statute which is at issue, subsection (2) is "narrowly tailored" to advance the real State interest: "in unimpeded access to health care facilities." It imposes criminal and civil liability on any person who " 'knowingly obstructs, detains, hinders, impedes, or blocks another person's entry to or exit from a health care facility' " thus rendering subsection (3) unnecessary.

The burden on speech is "substantial." An amplification system will not help a "woman who hopes to forge, in the last moments before another of her sex is to have an abortion, a bond of concern and intimacy that might enable her to persuade the woman to change her mind and heart." Moreover, "leafletting will be rendered utterly ineffectual by" requiring "permission to approach" unless from a "stationary post."

Criticizing the majority's rejection of the overbreadth challenge, Justice Scalia stated that the Court "acknowledged — indeed, boasted — that the statute 'takes a prophylactic approach.' "

Justice Kennedy dissented, agreeing with Justice Scalia's analysis of the First Amendment. The statute is a "textbook example" of a content based law. The violations are judged by the "substance" of the message. The statute also "applies only to a special class of locations" and the "entrances to medical facilities concern a narrow range of topics — indeed, one topic in particular." If faced with a statute "regulating 'oral protest, education, or counseling' within 100 feet of the entrance to any lunch counter, our predecessors would not have hesitated to hold it was content based or viewpoint based."

Justice Kennedy stated that the statute restricts "discussion on one of the most basic moral and political issues in all of contemporary discourse." Its "purpose and design" are "to restrict speakers on one side of the debate: those who protest abortions."

The law is "more vague and overly broad than any criminal statute the Court has sustained as a permissible regulation of speech." For example, " 'protest,' " " 'counseling,' " and " 'education' " are all "imprecise" words. "Scienter cannot save so vague a statute as this." The majority flips precedent "on its head, stating the statute's overbreadth is 'a virtue, not a vice.'" A narrowly tailored statute would have focused on "pinching or shoving or hitting" which can carry criminal and tort liability.

[2] Private Property as a Public Forum: Shopping Centers and Company Towns

HUDGENS v. N.L.R.B.
424 U.S. 507, 96 S. Ct. 1029, 47 L. Ed. 2d 196 (1976)

JUSTICE STEWART delivered the opinion of the Court. . . .

I

The petitioner, Scott Hudgens, is the owner of the North DeKalb Shopping Center, located in suburban Atlanta, Ga. The center consists of a single large building with an enclosed mall. Surrounding the building is a parking area which can accommodate 2,640 automobiles. The shopping center houses 60 retail stores leased to various businesses. One of the lessees is the Butler Shoe Co. Most of the stores, including Butler's, can be entered only from the interior mall.

In January 1971, warehouse employees of the Butler Shoe Store Co. went on strike to protest the company's failure to agree to demands made by their union in contract negotiations. The strikers decided to picket not only Butler's warehouse but its nine retail stores in the Atlanta area as well, including the store in the North DeKalb Shopping Center. On January 22, 1971, four of the striking warehouse employees entered the center's enclosed mall carrying placards which read: "Butler Shoe Warehouse on Strike, AFL-CIO, Local 315." The general manager of the shopping center informed the employees that they could not picket within the mall or on the parking lot and threatened them with arrest if they did not leave. The employees departed but returned a short time later and began picketing in an area of the mall immediately adjacent to the entrances of the Butler store. After the picketing had continued for approximately 30 minutes, the shopping center manager again informed the pickets that if they did not leave they would be arrested for trespassing. The pickets departed. . . .

II

. . . It is, of course, a commonplace that the constitutional guarantee of free speech is a guarantee only against abridgment by government, federal or state. . . . Thus, while statutory or common law may in some situations extend protection or provide redress against a private corporation or person who seeks to abridge the free expression of others, no such protection or redress is provided by the Constitution itself.

This elementary proposition is little more than a truism. But even truisms are not always unexceptionably true, and an exception to this one was recognized almost 30 years ago in *Marsh v. Alabama*, 326 U.S. 501 (1946). In *Marsh*, a Jehovah's Witness who had distributed literature without a license on a sidewalk in Chickasaw, Ala., was convicted of criminal trespass. Chickasaw was a so-called company town, wholly owned by the Gulf Shipbuilding Corp. . . .

The Court pointed out that if the "title" to Chickasaw had "belonged not to a private but to a municipal corporation and had appellant been arrested for violating a municipal ordinance rather than a ruling by those appointed by the corporation to manage a company town it would have been clear that appellant's conviction must be reversed." *Id.* at 504. Concluding that . . . Chickasaw . . . did "not function differently from any other town," *Id.* at 506–508, the Court invoked the First and Fourteenth Amendments to reverse the appellant's conviction.

It was the *Marsh* case that in 1968 provided the foundation for the Court's decision in *Amalgamated Food Employees Union v. Logan Valley Plaza*, 391 U.S. 308 (1968). That case involved peaceful picketing within a large shopping center near Altoona, Pa. One of the tenants of the shopping center was a retail store that employed a wholly nonunion staff. Members of a local union picketed the store, carrying signs proclaiming that it was nonunion and that its employees were not receiving union wages or other union benefits. The picketing took place on the shopping center's property in the immediate vicinity of the store. . . . [T]he *Marsh* case required . . . that the First and Fourteenth Amendments would clearly have protected the picketing if it had taken place on a public sidewalk. . . .

The Court's opinion then reviewed the *Marsh* case in detail, emphasized the similarities between the business block in Chickasaw, Ala., and the Logan Valley shopping center and unambiguously concluded:

"The shopping center here is clearly the functional equivalent of the business district of Chickasaw involved in *Marsh*." 391 U.S. at 318. . . .

There were three dissenting opinions in the *Logan Valley* case, one of them by the author of the Court's opinion in *Marsh*, Justice Black. His disagreement with the Court's reasoning was total:

. . . *Marsh* was never intended to apply to this kind of situation. *Marsh* dealt with the very special situation of a company-owned town, complete with streets, alleys, sewers, stores, residences, and everything else that goes to make a town. . . . I can find very little resemblance between the shopping center involved in this case and Chickasaw, Alabama. . . .

Four years later the Court had occasion to reconsider the *Logan Valley* doctrine in *Lloyd Corp. v. Tanner*. That case involved a shopping center covering some 50 acres in downtown Portland, Ore. On a November day in 1968 five young people entered the mall of the shopping center and distributed handbills protesting the then ongoing American military operations in Vietnam. Security guards told them to leave, and they did so, "to avoid arrest. . . . "

The Court in its *Lloyd* opinion did not say that it was overruling the *Logan Valley* decision. Indeed a substantial portion of the Court's opinion in *Lloyd* was devoted to pointing out the differences between the two cases, noting particularly that, in contrast to the hand-billing in *Lloyd*, the picketing in *Logan Valley* had been specifically directed to a store in the shopping center and the pickets had had no other reasonable opportunity to reach their intended audience. But the fact is that the reasoning of the Court's opinion in *Lloyd* cannot be squared with the reasoning of the Court's opinion in *Logan Valley*. . . .

If a large self-contained shopping center is the functional equivalent of a municipality, as *Logan Valley* held, then the First and Fourteenth Amendments would not permit control of speech within such a center to depend upon the speech's content. . . . [I]f the respondents in the *Lloyd* case did not have a First Amendment right to enter that shopping center to distribute handbills concerning Vietnam, then the pickets in the present case did not have a First Amendment right to enter this shopping center for the purpose of advertising their strike against the Butler Shoe Co.

We conclude, in short, that under the present state of the law the constitutional guarantee of free expression has no part to play in a case such as this. . . .

Justice Stevens took no part in the consideration or decision of this case.

Justice Powell, with whom The Chief Justice joins, concurring.

Although I agree with Justice White's view concurring in the result that *Lloyd Corp. v. Tanner*, did not overrule *Food Employees v. Logan Valley Plaza*, and that the present case can be distinguished narrowly from *Logan Valley*, I nevertheless have joined the opinion of the Court today.

The law in this area, particularly with respect to whether First Amendment or labor law principles are applicable, has been less than clear since *Logan Valley* analogized a shopping center to the "company town" in *Marsh v. Alabama*. . . . I now agree with Justice Black that the opinions in these cases cannot be harmonized in a principled way. Upon more mature thought, I have concluded that we would have been wiser in *Lloyd Corp.* to have confronted this disharmony rather than draw distinctions based upon rather attenuated factual differences. . . . [42]

Justice White, concurring in the result.

While I concur in the result reached by the Court, I find it unnecessary to inter *Food Employees v. Logan Valley Plaza*, and therefore do not join the Court's opinion. I agree that "the constitutional guarantee of free expression has no part to play in a case such as this," but *Lloyd Corp. v. Tanner*, did not overrule *Logan Valley*, either expressly or implicitly, and I would not, somewhat after the fact, say that it did.

One need go no further than *Logan Valley* itself, for the First Amendment protection established by *Logan Valley* was expressly limited to the picketing of a specific store for the purpose of conveying information with respect to the operation in the shopping center of that store. . . .

. . . The pickets of the Butler Shoe Co. store in the North DeKalb Shopping Center were not purporting to convey information about the "manner in which that particular [store] was being operated" but rather about the operation of a warehouse not located on the center's premises. The picketing was thus not "directly related in its purpose to the use to which the shopping center property was being put. . . . "

Justice Marshall, with whom Justice Brennan joins, dissenting.

. . . *Marsh v. State of Alabama*, which the Court purports to leave untouched, made clear that in applying those cases granting a right of access to streets, sidewalks, and other public places, courts ought not let the formalities of title put an end to analysis. . . .

. . . The underlying concern in *Marsh* was that traditional public channels of communication remain free, regardless of the incidence of ownership. Given that concern, the crucial fact in *Marsh* was that the company owned the traditional forums essential for effective communication; it was immaterial that the company also owned a sewer system and that its property in other respects resembled a town.

In *Logan Valley* we recognized what the Court today refuses to recognize — that the owner of the modern shopping center complex, by dedicating his property to public use as a business district, to some extent displaces the "State" from control of historical First Amendment forums, and may acquire a virtual monopoly of places suitable for effective communication. The roadways, parking lots, and walkways of the modern shopping center may be as essential for effective speech as the streets and sidewalks in the municipal or company-owned town. . . .

. . . Lloyd retained the availability of First Amendment protection when the

---

[42] [Court's footnote 2] The editorial "we" above is directed primarily to myself as the author of the Court's opinion in *Lloyd Corp.*

picketing is related to the function of the shopping center, and when there is no other reasonable opportunity to convey the message to the intended audience. Preserving *Logan Valley* subject to Lloyd's two related criteria guaranteed that the First Amendment would have application in those situations in which the shopping center owner had most clearly monopolized the forums essential for effective communication. . . .

. . . [T]he cases cited by the Court to the effect that government may not "restrict expression because of its message, its ideas, its subject matter, or its content," *Police Dept. of Chicago v. Mosley*, 408 U.S. 92 (1972), are simply inapposite. . . . The shopping center cases are quite different. . . . The very question in these cases is whether, and under what circumstances, the First Amendment has any application at all. The answer to that question, under the view of *Marsh* described above, depends to some extent on the subject of the speech the private entity seeks to regulate, because the degree to which the private entity monopolizes the effective channels of communication may depend upon what subject is involved. . . .

The interest of members of the public in communicating with one another on subjects relating to the businesses that occupy a modern shopping center is substantial. Not only employees with a labor dispute, but also consumers with complaints against business establishments, may look to the location of a retail store as the only reasonable avenue for effective communication with the public. . . .

NOTES

(1) *State of Access.* (a) *Shopping centers.* In *Pruneyard Shopping Center v. Robins*, 447 U.S. 74 (1980), the Supreme Court reviewed a decision of the California Supreme Court, which had applied the free speech provision of the California Constitution to uphold the right of students to solicit petition signatures on the premises of a privately owned shopping center. Thus, the California court had adopted the position of the dissent in *Lloyd v. Tanner* as a matter of state constitutional law. The federal issue considered by the U.S. Supreme Court was whether the ruling of the California Supreme Court deprived the property owner of property rights under the Fifth Amendment, and privacy or free expression rights under the First Amendment. In an opinion written by Justice Rehnquist, the Court unanimously held that, while a speaker had no First Amendment right to use the shopping center as a forum, this did not prevent the states from recognizing such a right under their own constitutions. The interests of the property owners did not rise to the level of federal constitutional protection.

(b) *Utility bill envelopes.* In *Pacific Gas & Electric Company v. Pub. Utils. Comm'n of California*, 475 U.S. 1 (1986), the Court invalidated an order of the California Public Utilities Commission requiring that a public utility make space available in its billing envelopes for the mailing pieces of a ratepayers' organization. Justice Powell's opinion (joined by Chief Justice Burger and by Justices Brennan and O'Connor), and Justice Marshall's concurrence, thought that the *Pruneyard* case was inapplicable. The shopping center owner in *Pruneyard* was not claiming, as was the utility, that his own right to speak was affected by the petition-gatherers. The owner "did not even allege that he objected to the content of the pamphlets; nor was the access-right content based."

Concurring in the judgment, Justice Marshall emphasized that the shopping center in *Pruneyard* was open to the public. At the owner's invitation, people were engaged in a wide variety of activities. "Adding speech to the list of these activities," wrote Justice Marshall, "did not in any great way change the complexion of the property."

Justice Rehnquist dissented, joined by Justices White and Stevens. The utility, like the shopping center owner, could disclaim identification with the views of outside organizations. Moreover, the corporate entity should not be viewed as possessing a "mind" or "conscience" that would be oppressed by being compelled to transmit opposing points of view. For further discussion of this case, see § 15.04[1], Note (4) after *Central Hudson Gas.*

(2) For a critique of the Court's treatment of the clash between rights to speak and ownership of property, see Norman Dorsen & Joel Gora, *Free Speech, Property, and the Burger Court: Old Values, New Balances*, 1982 SUP. CT. REV. 195 (arguing that the Burger Court often exalted property rights over competing rights to freedom of speech). For a general critique of the Court's public forum decisions, see Steven G. Gey, *Reopening the Public Forum — From Sidewalks to Cyberspace*, 58 OHIO L.J. 1535, 1634 (1998)("I have suggested that existing public forum doctrine is inadequate in three major respects: First, because it limits the key reference point of the traditional public forum to antiquated public spaces that have a decreasing impact on the everyday communicative lives of modern citizens. Second, because the Supreme Court has created a mutated middle category of 'limited' public forums that are defined tautologically in terms of the government's intent as to whether speech may take place in the forum. And third, with the exception of the *Rosenberger* decision, the Court has been reluctant to extend the application of the public forum doctrine beyond the context of physical forums — which limits the doctrine's usefulness in an era when an increasing proportion of public debate occurs electronically between conversants who are separated geographically by great distances.").

(3) For application of the Court's public forum decisions to the context of beggings see Robert C. Ellickson, *Controlling Chronic Misconduct in City Spaces: Of Panhandlers, Skid Rows, and Public Zoning*, 105 YALE L.J. 1165, 1171–72) (1996) (". . . [A] city's code of conduct should be allowed to vary spatially — from street to street, from park to park, from sidewalk to sidewalk. Just as some system of "zoning" may be sensible for private lands, so may it be for public lands.") and Helen Hershkoff & Adam S. Cohen, *Begging to Differ: The First Amendment and the Right to Beg*, 104 HARV. L. REV. 896, 913 (1991) ("Begging disturbs the listener not only in its content, but also in its presentation. The beggar's appeal attempts to build a human relationship with an individual listener. The beggar does not merely mount a soapbox and declaim abstractly about her outcast status; she speaks directly to her listeners and attempts to evoke a human response.").

[3]　Speech in Public Schools

TINKER v. DES MOINES INDEPENDENT SCHOOL DISTRICT, 393 U.S. 503 (1969). Writing for the majority, Justice Fortas upheld the rights of students to wear black armbands to school in protest of the violence in Vietnam. In *Tinker*, a group of students and adults attended a meeting in December 1965 at which they decided to demonstrate their objections to the conflict in Vietnam and their support of peace by wearing black armbands throughout the holidays and by fasting on December 16 and New Year's Eve. Upon learning of the plan, the principals of the Des Moines schools met on December 14, 1965, and created a policy that students who wore armbands to school and refused to remove them would be suspended until they removed them. Fully aware of this policy, the petitioners wore black armbands to school and were suspended until they would return without the armbands. The petitioners did not return until after New Year's Day.

Writing for the Court, Justice Fortas first established that students and teachers do not lose their constitutional rights to freedom of speech and expression "at the schoolhouse gate." It recognized that this case concerned the pure speech rights of the

First Amendment rather than disruptive demonstrations. Since no evidence showed that the petitioners' actions interfered with the other students' rights to "be secure and to be let alone," the case did not involve speech or action that hindered the school's work or the students' rights. If no evidence demonstrated that the students' actions would " 'materially and substantially interfere with the requirements of appropriate discipline in the operation of the school,' " the petitioners must prevail.

Next, the Court focused on the school officials' failure to forbid "the wearing of all symbols of political or controversial significance." While some students wore political buttons and Nazi paraphernalia, the ban did not extend to these examples but, instead, singled out the black armbands. The Court concluded that the schools could not prohibit the expression of one opinion without evidence that such exclusion was necessary to preserve the integrity of the schoolwork or discipline. In fact, schools should encourage the exchange of ideas among students. "This is not only an inevitable part of the process of attending school; it is also an important part of the educational process."

Justices Stewart and White concurred. Justice Black dissented, arguing that the evidence showed that the "armbands caused comments, warnings by other students, [and] the poking of fun at them." The students' armbands disrupted classes and the learning process. Justice Black contended that schools were designed to provide education and not to encourage political speech by actual or symbolic speech. Because discipline is so vital to raising children, if they are allowed to bring actions for damages and injunctions against their teachers, they will soon "believe it is their right to control the schools." Justice Harlan wrote a dissent and stated that the students must prove that the school officials were not motivated by "legitimate school concerns" but by, for instance, a desire to suppress minority opinions while allowing the expression of the majority opinion.

HAZELWOOD SCHOOL DISTRICT v. KUHLMEIER
484 U.S. 260, 108 S. Ct. 562, 98 L. Ed. 2d 592 (1988)

Justice White delivered the opinion of the Court.

This case concerns the extent to which educators may exercise editorial control over the contents of a high school newspaper produced as part of the school's journalism curriculum.

I

. . . Respondents are three former Hazelwood East students who were staff members of Spectrum, the school newspaper. They contend that school officials violated their First Amendment rights by deleting two pages of articles from the May 13, 1983, issue of Spectrum.

Spectrum was written and edited by the Journalism II class at Hazelwood East. . . .

The Board of Education allocated funds from its annual budget for the printing of Spectrum. These funds were supplemented by proceeds from sales of the newspaper. . . .

The practice at Hazelwood East during the spring 1983 semester was for the journalism teacher to submit page proofs of each Spectrum issue to Principal Reynolds for his review prior to publication. On May 10, Emerson delivered the proofs of the May 13 edition to Reynolds, who objected to two of the articles scheduled to appear in that edition. One of the stories described three Hazelwood East students' experiences with pregnancy; the other discussed the impact of divorce on students at the school. . . .

Reynolds believed that there was no time to make the necessary changes in the stories before the scheduled press run and that the newspaper would not appear before the end of the school year if printing were delayed to any significant extent. . . . Accordingly, he directed Emerson to withhold from publication the two pages containing the stories on pregnancy and divorce. . . . [43]

II

Students in the public schools . . . cannot be punished merely for expressing their personal views on the school premises — whether "in the cafeteria, or on the playing field, or on the campus during the authorized hours," [*Tinker v. Des Moines Indep. Comty. School Dist.*, 393 U.S. 503,] 512–13 [1969], — unless school authorities have reason to believe that such expression will "substantially interfere with the work of the school or impinge upon the rights of other students. . . . "

We have nonetheless recognized that the First Amendment rights of students in the public schools "are not automatically coextensive with the rights of adults in other settings," *Bethel School Dist. No. 403 v. Fraser*, 478 U.S. 675, 682, (1986), and must be "applied in light of the special characteristics of the school environment." *Tinker, supra*, 393 U.S. at 506. A school need not tolerate student speech that is inconsistent with its "basic educational mission," *Fraser, supra*, 478 U.S. at 685 even though the government could not censor similar speech outside the school. . . . We [have] recognized that "[t]he determination of what manner of speech in the classroom or in school assembly is inappropriate properly rests with the school board," *Id.* at 682 rather than with the federal courts. . . .

A

We deal first with the question whether Spectrum may appropriately be characterized as a forum for public expression. . . . [S]chool facilities may be deemed to be public forums only if school authorities have "by policy or by practice" opened those facilities "for indiscriminate use by the general public," *Perry Educ. Ass'n v. Perry Local Educators' Ass'n*, 460 U.S. 37, 47 (1983), or by some segment of the public, such as student organizations. If the facilities have instead been reserved for other intended purposes, "communicative or otherwise," then no public forum has been created, and school officials may impose reasonable restrictions on the speech of students, teachers, and other members of the school community. . . .

Hazelwood . . . Board Policy 348.51 provided that "[s]chool sponsored publications are developed within the adopted curriculum and its educational implications in regular classroom activities." The Hazelwood East Curriculum Guide described the Journalism II course as a "laboratory situation in which the students publish the school newspaper applying skills they have learned in Journalism I. . . . " Journalism II was taught by a faculty member during regular class hours. . . .

School officials did not deviate in practice from their policy that production of Spectrum was to be part of the educational curriculum and a "regular classroom activit[y]." The District Court found that Robert Stergos, the journalism teacher during most of the 1982–1983 school year, "both had the authority to exercise and in fact exercised a great deal of control over Spectrum." For example, Stergos selected the

---

[43] [Court's footnote 1] The two pages deleted from the newspaper also contained articles on teenage marriage, runaways, and juvenile delinquents, as well as a general article on teenage pregnancy. Reynolds testified that he had no objection to these articles and that they were deleted only because they appeared on the same pages as the two objectionable articles.

editors of the newspaper, scheduled publication dates, decided the number of pages for each issue, assigned story ideas to class members, advised students on the development of their stories, reviewed the use of quotations, edited stories, selected and edited the letters to the editor, and dealt with the printing company. Many of these decisions were made without consultation with the Journalism II students. The District Court thus found it "clear that Mr. Stergos was the final authority with respect to almost every aspect of the production and publication of Spectrum, including its content." Moreover, after each Spectrum issue had been finally approved by Stergos or his successor, the issue still had to be reviewed by Principal Reynolds prior to publication. . . .

The evidence relied upon by the Court of Appeals in finding Spectrum to be a public forum, is equivocal at best. For example, Board Policy 348.51, which stated in part that

> "[s]chool sponsored student publications will not restrict free expression or diverse viewpoints within the rules of responsible journalism," also stated that such publications were "developed within the adopted curriculum and its educational implications." One might reasonably infer from the full text of Policy 348.51 that school officials retained ultimate control over what constituted "responsible journalism" in a school-sponsored newspaper. . . .

B

The question whether the First Amendment requires a school to tolerate particular student speech — the question that we addressed in *Tinker* — is different from the question whether the First Amendment requires a school affirmatively to promote particular student speech. The former question addresses educators' ability to silence a student's personal expression that happens to occur on the school premises. The latter question concerns educators' authority over school-sponsored publications, theatrical productions, and other expressive activities that students, parents, and members of the public might reasonably perceive to bear the imprimatur of the school. These activities may fairly be characterized as part of the school curriculum, whether or not they occur in a traditional classroom setting, so long as they are supervised by faculty members and designed to impart particular knowledge or skills to student participants and audiences.

Educators are entitled to exercise greater control over this second form of student expression to assure that participants learn whatever lessons the activity is designed to teach, that readers or listeners are not exposed to material that may be inappropriate for their level of maturity, and that the views of the individual speaker are not erroneously attributed to the school. Hence, a school may in its capacity as publisher of a school newspaper or producer of a school play "disassociate itself," *Fraser*, 478 U.S. at 685, not only from speech that would "substantially interfere with [its] work . . . or impinge upon the rights of other students," *Tinker*, 393 U.S. at 509, but also from speech that is, for example, ungrammatical, poorly written, inadequately researched, biased or prejudiced, vulgar or profane, or unsuitable for immature audiences. A school must be able to set high standards for the student speech that is disseminated under its auspices — standards that may be higher than those demanded by some newspaper publishers or theatrical producers in the "real" world — and may refuse to disseminate student speech that does not meet those standards. In addition, a school must be able to take into account the emotional maturity of the intended audience in determining whether to disseminate student speech on potentially sensitive topics, which might range from the existence of Santa Claus in an elementary school setting to the particulars of teenage sexual activity in a high school setting. A school must also retain the authority to refuse to sponsor student speech that might reasonably be perceived to advocate drug or alcohol use, irresponsible sex, or conduct otherwise inconsistent with "the shared values of a civilized social order," *Fraser*, *supra*, 478 U.S. at 685, or to associate the school with any position other than neutrality on matters of political controversy. Otherwise, the schools would be unduly constrained from fulfilling their role as "a principal instrument in awakening the child to cultural values, in preparing him for later professional training, and in helping him to adjust normally to his environment." *Brown v. Board of Education*, 347 U.S. 483, 493 (1954).

Accordingly, we conclude that the standard articulated in *Tinker* for determining when a school may punish student expression need not also be the standard for determining when a school may refuse to lend its name and resources to the dissemination of student expression. Instead, we hold that educators do not offend the First Amendment by exercising editorial control over the style and content of student speech in school-sponsored expressive activities so long as their actions are reasonably related to legitimate pedagogical concerns.[44]

. . . It is only when the decision to censor a school-sponsored publication, theatrical production, or other vehicle of student expression has no valid educational purpose that the First Amendment is so "directly and sharply implicate[d]," *ibid.*, as to require judicial intervention to protect students' constitutional rights.[45]

II

We also conclude that Principal Reynolds acted reasonably in requiring the deletion from the May 13 issue of Spectrum of the pregnancy article, the divorce article, and the remaining articles that were to appear on the same pages of the newspaper.

The initial paragraph of the pregnancy article declared that "[a]ll names have been changed to keep the identity of these girls a secret." The principal concluded that the students' anonymity was not adequately protected, however, given the other identifying information in the article and the small number of pregnant students at the school. Indeed, a teacher at the school credibly testified that she could positively identify at least one of the girls and possibly all three. . . . The article did not contain graphic accounts of sexual activity. The girls did comment in the article, however, concerning their sexual histories and their use or nonuse of birth control. It was not unreasonable for the principal to have concluded that such frank talk was inappropriate in a school-sponsored publication distributed to 14-year-old freshmen and presumably taken home to be read by students' even younger brothers and sisters.

The student who was quoted by name in the version of the divorce article seen by Principal Reynolds made comments sharply critical of her father. The principal could reasonably have concluded that an individual publicly identified as an inattentive parent — indeed, as one who chose "playing cards with the guys" over home and family — was entitled to an opportunity to defend himself as a matter of journalistic fairness. These concerns were shared by both of the Spectrum's faculty advisers for the 1982–1983 school year, who testified that they would not have allowed the article to be printed without deletion of the student's name.

Principal Reynolds testified credibly at trial that, at the time that he reviewed the proofs of the May 13 issue during an extended telephone conversation with Emerson, he

---

[44] [Court's footnote 6] We reject respondents' suggestion that school officials be permitted to exercise prepublication control over school-sponsored publications only pursuant to specific written regulations. To require such regulations in the context of a curricular activity could unduly constrain the ability of educators to educate. We need not now decide whether such regulations are required before school officials may censor publications not sponsored by the school that students seek to distribute on school grounds. . . .

[45] [Court's footnote 7] . . . We need not now decide whether the same degree of deference is appropriate with respect to school sponsored expressive activities at the college and university level.

believed that there was no time to make any changes in the articles, and that the newspaper had to be printed immediately or not at all. . . . Emerson did not volunteer the information that printing could be delayed until the changes were made. We nonetheless agree with the District Court that the decision to excise the two pages containing the problematic articles was reasonable given the particular circumstances of this case. These circumstances included the very recent replacement of Stergos by Emerson, who may not have been entirely familiar with Spectrum editorial and production procedures, and the pressure felt by Reynolds to make an immediate decision so that students would not be deprived of the newspaper altogether.

In sum, . . . Reynolds could reasonably have concluded that the students who had written and edited these articles had not sufficiently mastered those portions of the Journalism II curriculum that pertained to the treatment of controversial issues and personal attacks, the need to protect the privacy of individuals whose most intimate concerns are to be revealed in the newspaper, and "the legal, moral, and ethical restrictions imposed upon journalists within [a] school community" that includes adolescent subjects and readers. Finally, we conclude that the principal's decision to delete two pages of Spectrum, rather than to delete only the offending articles or to require that they be modified, was reasonable under the circumstances as he understood them. . . . [46]

JUSTICE BRENNAN, with whom JUSTICE MARSHALL and JUSTICE BLACKMUN join, dissenting.

. . . Spectrum . . . "was a . . . forum established to give students an opportunity to express their views. . . . " 795 F.2d 1368, 1373 (8th Cir. 1986) "School sponsored student publications," [the School Board] vowed, "will not restrict free expression or diverse viewpoints within the rules of responsible journalism. . . . "

I

. . . In *Tinker* . . . [w]e held that official censorship of student expression . . . is unconstitutional unless the speech "materially disrupts classwork or involves substantial disorder or invasion of the rights of others. . . . " *Tinker*, 393 U.S. at 513.

. . . The Court today casts no doubt on *Tinker's* vitality. Instead it erects a taxonomy of school censorship, concluding that *Tinker* applies to one category and not another. . . .

II

Even if we were writing on a clean slate, I would reject the Court's rationale for abandoning *Tinker* in this case. The Court offers no more than an obscure tangle of three excuses to afford educators "greater control" over school-sponsored speech than the *Tinker* test would permit; the public educator's prerogative to control curriculum; the pedagogical interest in shielding the high school audience from objectionable viewpoints and sensitive topics; and the school's need to dissociate itself from student expression. None of the excuses, once disentangled, supports the distinction that the Court draws. *Tinker* fully addressed the first concern; the second is illegitimate; and the third is readily achievable through less oppressive means.

---

[46] [Court's footnote 9] . . . The dissent correctly acknowledges "[t]he State's prerogative to dissolve the student newspaper entirely." It is likely that many public schools would do just that rather than open their newspapers to all student expression that does not threaten "materia[l] disrup[tion of] classwork" or violation of "rights that are protected by law," regardless of how sexually explicit, racially intemperate, or personally insulting that expression otherwise might be.

A

. . . [T]he principal never consulted the students before censoring their work. . . . The Court's supposition that the principal intended (or the protesters understood) those generalities as a lesson on the nuances of journalistic responsibility is utterly incredible. . . .

NOTES

(1) *School Assembly*. In *Bethel School Dist. No. 408 v. Fraser*, 478 U.S. 675 (1986), the Court upheld the suspension of a student for giving a sexually explicit speech to an audience that included 14-year-old students. After being warned by two teachers, the respondent gave a speech nominating a fellow classmate for student government.

As quoted in Justice Brennan's concurrence, the speech read:

> I know a man who is firm — he's firm in his pants, he's firm in his shirt, his character is firm — but most . . . of all, his belief in you, the students of Bethel, is firm.
>
> Jeff Kuhlman is a man who takes his point and pounds it in. If necessary, he'll take an issue and nail it to the wall. He doesn't attack things in spurts — he drives hard, pushing and pushing until finally — he succeeds.
>
> Jeff is a man who will go to the very end — even the climax, for each and every one of you.
>
> So vote for Jeff for A.S.B. vice-president — he'll never come between you and the best our high school can be.

For giving his speech, the respondent was suspended for three days under a school disciplinary rule prohibiting "conduct which interferes with [the] educational process, including the use of obscene, profane language or gestures." Moreover, he was no longer a candidate to speak at graduation.

The Court repeatedly spoke of the role of public education in inculcating "fundamental values necessary to the maintenance of a democratic system." These values must include "tolerance of divergent political and religious views, even when the views expressed may be unpopular." Nevertheless, the "*freedom* to advocate unpopular and controversial views in schools and classrooms must be balanced against society's countervailing interest in teaching the boundaries of socially appropriate behavior." Chief Justice Rehnquist emphasized the role of the school *in loco parentis*. In pursuing its mission to install the virtues of "clean" public discourse, a school need not afford children the same latitude as adults in permitting the use of offensive language. Moreover, children are given special protection from sexually explicit and vulgar language.

Chief Justice Rehnquist concluded: "Unlike the sanctions imposed on the students wearing armbands in *Tinker*, the penalties imposed in this case were unrelated to any political viewpoint. The First Amendment does not prevent the school officials from determining that to permit a vulgar and lewd speech such as respondent's would undermine the school's basic educational mission."

Justice Brennan concurred in the judgment. His concurrence, however, did not rest on the offensiveness of the respondent's language, but rather on the disruption of "the school's educational mission." Justice Blackmun concurred in the result without opinion.

In dissent, Justice Marshall said that the school district "failed to demonstrate that [the] respondent's remarks were indeed disruptive." Justice Stevens dissented on inadequate notice grounds.

(2) For further discussion, see Susan H. Bitensky, *A Contemporary Proposal for Reconciling the Free Speech Clause with Curricular Values Inculcation in the Public Schools*, 70 NOTRE DAME L. REV. 769, 843 (1995) ("[I]n *Fraser* . . . and *Kuhlmeier*, the Justices put the public schools on notice that the Free Speech Clause permits the inculcation of values that enable the preservation of a democratic political system and civilized social order. The Court's assumption is that, at a minimum, moral education must enable, not simply the moral individual, but the moral society as well."). *See also* William Buss, *School Newspapers, Public Forum, and the First Amendment*, 74 IOWA L. REV. 505, 542–43 (1989) ("Only Chicken Little would see the sky falling from *Hazelwood*, but only Dr. Pangloss would fail to wonder whether it has sent a few stones rolling down the hill.").

[4]   Religious Speech in Public Places

WIDMAR v. VINCENT, 454 U.S. 263 (1981). In *Widmar*, the Court required a state university that allowed student organizations to use its facilities to open those facilities to a student religious organization. *See* § 16.03 *infra*, which deals with government support of religious practices. The University of Missouri at Kansas City (UMKC) "provides facilities for the meetings of registered organizations." A registered group of evangelical Christian students named Cornerstone used University facilities for its meetings from 1973 until it was denied access in 1977. These meetings typically "included prayer, hymns, Bible commentary, and discussion of religious views and experiences."

Writing for the Court, Justice Powell stated: "Through its policy of accommodating [their] meetings, the University has created a forum generally open for use by student groups." Moreover, the First Amendment protects "religious worship and discussion [as] forms of speech and association."

As the exclusion of Cornerstone from university facilities discriminated against certain speech based on the religious content, UMKC had to prove "that its regulation [is] necessary to serve a compelling state interest and that it [is] narrowly drawn to achieve that end." Under the Establishment Clause, the university asserted a "compelling interest" in "strict separation of church and State." Although this interest is "compelling," "an 'equal access' policy" does not by itself violate the clause. Relying solely on freedom of speech and association, Justice Powell found no need to address whether the regulation infringed on the Free Exercise Clause or whether "State accommodation of Free Exercise and Free Speech rights [would], in a particular case, conflict with the prohibitions of the Establishment Clause."

"[A]n open forum in a public university does not confer any imprimatur of State approval on religious sects or practices." University students are "young adults" and therefore "less impressionable than younger students" about religion. "Second, the forum is available to a broad class of non-religious as well as religious speakers; there are over 100 recognized student groups at UMKC."

The university argued that the Missouri Constitution requires more stringent separation of church and state than the Federal Constitution. The Court replied that the Federal Constitution's Free Exercise and Free Speech Clauses limit the state's interest "in achieving greater separation of church and State than is already ensured under the Establishment Clause." Consequently, this interest was not "sufficiently 'compelling' to justify content-based discrimination against respondents' religious speech."

Concurring in the judgment, Justice Stevens stated that it was "both necessary and appropriate" for university officials to "evaluate the content of a proposed student activity." Limited resources "routinely" require decisions on using school facilities for extracurricular activities. Such decisions "should be made by academicians, not by federal judges."

Justice White dissented. While "[a] state university may permit its property to be used for purely religious services" neither the Speech Clause nor the Free Exercise Clause required the university to open its facilities to this religious group.

NOTES

(1) In *Board of Educ. v. Mergens*, 496 U.S. 226 (1990), the Court upheld the Equal Access Act against an Establishment challenge. The Act required high schools to give " 'student religious groups including prayer groups, permission to meet on school premises during noninstructional time.' "

(2) *Fairgrounds*. In *Heffron v. Int'l Soc'y for Krishna Consciousness, Inc.*, 452 U.S. 640 (1981), the Supreme Court upheld a Minnesota State Fair regulation that provided that the sale or distribution of "any merchandise, including printed or written material" was prohibited unless from "a duly licensed location" in the fairgrounds. Justice White's opinion justified the regulation as a valid "time, place, and manner" regulation that served the significant governmental interest of crowd control. Justice White also described the Fair as a "limited public forum" where the booth arrangement was an adequate means to sell and solicit, leaving other available channels for protected speech that did not involve the distribution or sale of materials on the fairgrounds.

On the issue of the sale of literature and the solicitation of funds, the Court was unanimous, although Justices Brennan, Marshall, and Stevens relied on protection against fraud as a justification. They and Justice Blackmun, dissented from that portion of the opinion dealing with the distribution of literature. The dissenters argued, in opinions by Justices Brennan and Blackmun, that crowd control was an insufficient justification for the sweeping ban on the distribution of literature in a place like a state fairground.

CAPITOL SQUARE REVIEW BD. v. PINETTE, 515 U.S. 753 (1995). In *Pinette*, the Court held that a private, unattended display of a cross on Capitol Square in Columbus, Ohio, a traditional public forum, did not violate the Establishment Clause. The Capitol Square Review and Advisory Board receives applications from private groups and permits them to use the grounds of Capitol Square as long as the group meets certain content-neutral criteria. The board allows " 'a broad range of speakers and other gatherings of people to conduct events on the Capitol Square' including homosexual rights organizations, the Ku Klux Klan and the United Way. The Board has also permitted a variety of unattended displays on Capitol Square: a state-sponsored lighted tree during the Christmas season, a privately sponsored menorah during Chanukah, [and] a display showing the progress of a United Way fundraising campaign, and booths and exhibits during an arts festival."

In December 1993, after permitting the display of a Christmas tree and menorah on Capitol Square, the board rejected an application from the Ku Klux Klan to erect an unattended cross on the grounds from December 8, 1993 to December 24, 1993.

Justice Scalia wrote for the Court (7-2) as to Parts I, II and III of the decision. As Capitol Square is a "traditional public forum," the State may only restrict protected expression "if such a restriction is necessary, and narrowly drawn, to serve a compelling state interest." The State rejected the Klan's application to avoid an "official endorsement of Christianity," as prohibited by the Establishment Clause. The Court agreed that "compliance with the Establishment Clause is a state interest sufficiently compelling to justify content-based restrictions on speech."

In *Lamb's Chapel v. Center Moriches Union Free School Dist.*, 508 U.S. 384 (1993), *infra* Note (1), the Court held that the school district could not invoke an Establishment Clause defense in denying a private group's use of a school's facilities for religious purposes because the facilities were open to the public's use. The determinative factors in *Lamb's Chapel* and *Widmar v. Vincent* also controlled this case: Capitol Square is open to the public; the proposed activity is not sponsored by the state; and all groups seeking to use the grounds have the same application process and terms.

Only Chief Justice Rehnquist and Justices Kennedy and Thomas joined Part IV of Justice Scalia's opinion. The state tried to distinguish *Widmar* and *Lamb's Chapel* based on the forum's proximity to the seat of government, which could "produce the perception that the cross bears the State's approval." Affording all displays equal access to a public forum would not indicate that the "government 'promotes' or 'favors' a religious display."

Justice Scalia differentiated "between government speech endorsing religion, which the Establishment Clause forbids, and private speech endorsing religion, which the Free Speech and Free Exercise Clauses protect." The State would have violated the Establishment Clause — as well as the Speech Clause through content discrimination — had it given preferential treatment to the religious displays over other forms of private expression. The plurality stated that private religious speech should receive the same treatment as any other speech in the public forum. Denying equal access to religious speech — as Justices Stevens, O'Connor and Souter suggest in their opinions — relegates religious expression to the level of protection of "sexually explicit displays and commercial speech."

Justice Scalia suggested that the State could require disclaimers that these were private displays, as content-neutral "manner" restrictions discouraging any public misperceptions of government endorsement of the religious expression.

The plurality concluded, "Religious expression cannot violate the Establishment Clause where it (1) is purely private and (2) occurs in a traditional or designated public forum, publicly announced and open to all on equal terms."

Justice Thomas concurred. No one should "think that a cross erected by the Ku Klux Klan is a purely religious symbol." The Klan uses the cross primarily as a political "symbol of hate."

Justice O'Connor, joined by Justices Souter and Breyer, concurred with Parts I, II and III of the opinion. Justice O'Connor concurred in the judgment as to Part IV. In this case, there was "no realistic danger that the community would think that the State was endorsing religion." Justice O'Connor stressed that "the endorsement test necessarily focuses upon the perception of a reasonable, informed observer." The endorsement test requires the Court to ask "whether the challenged governmental practice either has the purpose or effect of 'endorsing' religion."

Justice O'Connor disagreed with the plurality that the endorsement test is limited to "direct government speech or outright favoritism." Moreover, going beyond the plurality's suggestion of a disclaimer, Justice O'Connor would require the government itself to post "a sign disclaiming government sponsorship or endorsement, which would make the State's role clear to the community."

Disagreeing with Justice Scalia, Justice O'Connor stated that a neutral law should be invalidated if a reasonable observer misperceives a private display to understand that the State endorses religion. If a display in a public forum controlled by the government "has the effect of endorsing religion," it violates the Establishment Clause. For example, "a private religious group may so dominate a public forum that a formal policy of equal access is transformed into a demonstration of approval." Domination by a religious group may also result from "the fortuity of geography, the nature of the particular public space, or the character of the religious speech at issue."

Determining whether a certain governmental practice endorses religion "requires courts to examine the history and administration" of the practice. Courts must determine at what point the government "becomes responsible, whether due to favoritism toward or disregard for the evident effect of religious speech, for the injection of religion into the political life of the citizenry." According to Justice O'Connor, "proper application of the endorsement test requires that the reasonable observer be deemed more informed than the casual passerby." This does not mean, however, that the endorsement test prefers the "perceptions of the majority over those of a 'reasonable non-adherent.'" This observer "must be deemed aware of the history and context of the community and forum in which the religious display appears." In this case, the reasonable observer should be aware that "the cross is a religious symbol, that Capitol Square is owned by the State, and that the large building nearby is the seat of state government." The observer should also know the general history of Capitol Square as a public forum. Justice O'Connor concluded that permitting a private group to display an unattended cross with an adequate disclaimer on Capitol Square would not communicate government endorsement of religion.

Justice Souter, with whom Justices O'Connor and Breyer joined, concurred in part and concurred in the judgment. Although "the Capitol lawn has been the site of public protests and gatherings," the State could still prohibit all private, unattended displays. Justice Souter upheld the right to display the cross largely because of the possibility of attaching a disclaimer to the display.

He disagreed with the plurality because an "intelligent observer may mistake private, unattended religious displays in a public forum for government speech endorsing religion." While an observer may reasonably assume that someone who speaks in the public forum is presenting her own views, an observer may also reasonably assume that an unattended display belongs to — and communicates the message of — whoever owns the land on which it sits. In each case, the Court must make "a contextual judgment taking account of the circumstances of the specific case."

Justice Souter also noted that the board had other alternatives to rejecting outright the Klan's application. The Klan was willing to label the cross to express private sponsorship, the wording of which the Klan was willing to negotiate with the board. Fearing any perception of endorsement, then, the board could have required the sign to be noticeable enough to the public to prevent any misperception of government support. Moreover, the board could have assigned all private, unattended displays to a specific area within the square displaying a single disclaimer of government endorsement.[47]

In his dissent, Justice Stevens interpreted the Establishment Clause "to create a strong presumption against the installation of unattended religious symbols on public property." In a footnote, Justice Stevens criticized Justice O'Connor's reasonable observer as being a "well-schooled jurist," who "knows and understands much more than meets the eye." This reasonable person standard "strips of constitutional protection every reasonable person whose knowledge happens to fall below some 'ideal' standard." He would prohibit displays that some reasonable, as opposed to ideal, viewers would likely perceive as endorsing religion.

The display of a cross in front of a statehouse is a powerful symbol implying "official

---

[47] Justice Souter noted, however, that a disclaimer does not entirely eliminate the possibility of an Establishment Clause violation if "other indicia of endorsement outweigh the mitigating effect of the disclaimer." Examples might include "government invitation of the religious display or other indications that government intended to endorse religion. . . . "

recognition and reinforcement of its message," which no disclaimer could negate. Justice Stevens would also extend the right of the government to prohibit other forms of expression, like "erotic exhibits, commercial advertising, and perhaps campaign posters as well without violating the Free Speech Clause."

Justice Ginsburg also dissented. She rejected Justice Souter's suggestions of a disclaimer or a separate area for such displays. In ordering the board to permit the display, the District Court did not order a disclaimer to accompany it. In fact, the disclaimer that was ultimately attached "was unsturdy: it did not identify the Klan as sponsor; it failed to state unequivocally that Ohio did not endorse the display's message; and it was not shown to be legible from a distance." Consequently, the District Court order violated the Establishment Clause. Justice Ginsburg did not decide the more difficult question of the constitutionality of a "court order allowing display of a cross, but demanding a sturdier disclaimer."

NOTES

(1) *Nonstudent Groups.* In *Lamb's Chapel v. Center Moriches Union Free School Dist.*, 508 U.S. 384 (1993), the Court held that denying a church's applications to use school property to present a film series on religious grounds violates the Freedom of Speech Clause. Section 414 of the New York Education Law enables local school boards to adopt reasonable regulations authorizing the after-hours use of school property for 10 specified purposes. Pursuant to § 414, Center Moriches Union Free School District (District) allowed social, civic and recreational uses (Rule 10), and use by political organizations secured in compliance with § 414 (Rule 8). Rule 7, however, prohibited the use of school premises "by any group for religious purposes." Lamb's Chapel, an evangelical church, filed two applications for permission to use school facilities to exhibit a film series about child-rearing and family values "from the Christian perspective." The series featured lectures by a prominent psychologist who advocated a return to Christian values.

Writing for the majority, Justice White did not decide whether the school board had created a limited public forum that included religious uses. Terming this classification "a close question," he did acknowledge that the school board had opened school premises to several groups that could be called religious, including a lecture series by a New Age religious group.

Treating the school premises as a nonpublic forum, Justice White struck down the ban because it was not "viewpoint neutral." The film series at issue dealt with family issues and child-rearing, subjects otherwise permissible under Rule 10, and its exhibition was denied solely on the basis of the film's religious viewpoint.

Relying on *Widmar v. Vincent*, Justice White rejected the argument that the Establishment Clause justified the District's discrimination against religious speech. He noted that exhibition of the films "would not have been during school hours, would not have been sponsored by the school, and would have been open to the public." As in *Widmar*, Justice White applied the *Lemon v. Kurtzman*, 403 U.S. 602 (1971), test to determine that allowing the film's exhibition had a secular purpose, did not have the primary effect of advancing or inhibiting religion, and did not foster an excessive entanglement with religion.

Moreover, Justice White saw no danger that the community would believe that the District was "endorsing religion" by allowing the film's exhibition and viewed any benefit to Lamb's Chapel resulting from the exhibition as incidental.

Justice Scalia filed a concurring opinion in which Justice Thomas joined. Justice Kennedy filed a separate concurrence. *Lamb's Chapel* is also discussed at § 16.03[1], Note (3) after *Good News Club v. Milford Central School.*

(2) *Funding Christian Student Newspapers.* In *Rosenberger v. Univ. of Virginia,* 515 U.S. 819 (1995), the Court (5-4) held that the University of Virginia violated the Freedom of Speech Clause when it refused to fund a student-run newspaper published from a Christian viewpoint. The University allowed student "Contracted Independent Organizations" to receive funding from the Student Activities Fund for printing costs. Writing for the Court, Justice Kennedy held that the denial of funding was unconstitutional viewpoint discrimination. "It is as objectionable to exclude both a theistic and an atheistic perspective in the debate as it is to exclude one, the other, or yet another political, economic, or social viewpoint." Having established a public forum in which it encouraged diversity of student views, the University could not engage in viewpoint discrimination. Providing funds to print a student newspaper that was not a religious organization was no different than providing the funds necessary for funding the meeting space in *Widmar.* Moreover, the money went directly to the printer, not to the student newspaper.

Justices O'Connor and Thomas filed concurring opinions. Justice Souter dissented, joined by Justices Stevens, Ginsburg, and Breyer. This case is reproduced on § 15.03. For further discussion of the Establishment Clause aspects of *Rosenberger,* see § 15.03.

GOOD NEWS CLUB v. MILFORD CENTRAL SCHOOL, 533 U.S. 98 (2001). In *Good News,* the Court reversed a grant for summary judgment that allowed Milford Central School (Milford) to exclude a religious club from using the school's premises for afterschool activities. In 1992, defendant Milford adopted a "community use policy," in accordance with New York Education Law § 414, allowing its facilities to be used for afterschool activities, subject to the school district's approval.[48] Plaintiff Good News Club is "a private Christian organization for children ages 6 to 12," which sought to hold weekly meetings in Milford's cafeteria. The Club described its meetings as children having "'a fun time of singing songs, hearing a Bible lesson and memorizing scripture.'" The school district described these activities as "'religious worship.'" Since Milford's policy prohibited use "'by an individual or organization for religious purposes,'" the school district denied the Club's request.

Writing for a 6-3 majority, Justice Thomas first noted both parties "have agreed that Milford created a limited public forum" by opening up the school's premises. In the context of a limited public forum, the State does not have to permit all types of speech. However, any state-imposed restriction "must not discriminate against speech on the basis of viewpoint, and . . . must be 'reasonable in light of the purpose served by the forum.'" By Milford's own admission, its policy allowed for "discussions of subjects such as child rearing, and of 'the development of character and morals from a religious perspective,'" which included using "Aesop's Fables to teach children moral values." And "it is clear that the Club teaches morals and character development to children."

Justice Thomas analogized this case to *Lamb's Chapel v. Center Moriches Union Free School Dist.,* 508 U.S. 384 (1993). "The only apparent difference" between the two groups is that "Lamb's Chapel taught lessons through films" whereas the Club teaches children through "live storytelling."[49] Excluding the Good News Club "constitutes impermissible viewpoint discrimination."

---

[48] The community use policy enumerated several purposes for which school district residents could use the school's facilities, including "'instruction in any branch of education, learning or the arts[,]' and 'social, civic and recreational meetings and entertainment events, and other uses pertaining to the welfare of the community, provided that such uses shall be nonexclusive and shall be opened to the general public.'"

[49] The majority also relied on *Rosenberger v. Rector & Visitors of Univ. of Virginia,* 515 U.S. 819 (1995), in which the University of Virginia unconstitutionally "denied funding for printing expenses" to a Christian student publication.

The Court rejected Milford's argument that the restriction was necessary to avoid violating the Establishment Clause. Even though "a state interest in avoiding an Establishment Clause violation 'may be characterized as compelling,' and therefore may justify content-based discrimination," it is unclear whether such an interest "would justify viewpoint discrimination." However, the Court did not "confront the issue" as plaintiff had "no valid Establishment Clause interest." Like the activities in *Lamb's Chapel*, "the Club's meetings were held after school hours, not sponsored by the school, and open to any student who obtained parental consent, not just to Club members. As in *Widmar [v. Vincent]*, Milford made its forum available to other organizations." Milford sought to distinguish these cases as neither involves elementary school children.

One of the key factors in deciding whether to uphold "'governmental programs in the face of an Establishment Clause attack is their *neutrality* towards religion.'" In this connection, "allowing the Club to speak on school grounds would ensure neutrality, not threaten it." Also relevant is "whether the community would feel coercive pressure to engage in the Club's activities." In this case, the "community would be the parents," as children must receive parental consent to attend the Club's meetings. Milford argued that elementary school children would automatically believe the school was endorsing religion simply because the Club meets on school grounds. The Court, however, rejected such a categorical rule and also rejected the existence of endorsement on the facts of this case.

Club meetings took place after school hours "in a combined high school resource room and middle school special education room, not in an elementary school classroom." Moreover, "the instructors are not schoolteachers. And the children in the group are not all the same age as in the normal classroom setting; their ages range from 6 to 12.[50] In sum, these circumstances simply do not support the theory that small children would perceive endorsement here."

Justice Thomas stated that "the danger that children would misperceive the endorsement of religion" was not "any greater than the danger that they would perceive a hostility toward the religious viewpoint if the Club were excluded from the public forum." The "'endorsement inquiry is *not about the perceptions of particular individuals*.'" Instead, "'the reasonable observer in the endorsement inquiry must be deemed aware of the history and context of the community and forum in which the religious [speech]'" occurs.

Justice Scalia concurred. The Club may not "independently discuss the religious premise on which its views are based — that God exists and His assistance is necessary to morality." In contrast to other organizations, the Club cannot defend the premise on which it exists. "This is blatant viewpoint discrimination."

Concurring in part, Justice Breyer wrote separately to assert three points. First, neutrality is only one of the significant factors determining if a school's community use policy violates the Establishment Clause. Second, "endorsement of religion" may be the crucial Establishment Clause issue in this case. "The time of day, the age of the children, the nature of the meetings, and other specific circumstances are relevant in helping to determine, whether, in fact, the Club 'so dominate[s]' the 'forum' that, in the children's minds, 'a formal policy of equal access is transformed into a demonstration of approval.'" However, the case was not in the "procedural posture" to decide the Establishment Clause issue. For Justice Breyer, the Court's holding simply meant "the

---

[50] [Court's footnote 8] Although Milford "relies on the Equal Access Act as evidence that Congress recognized the vulnerability of elementary school children to misperceiving endorsement of religion," the Act "applies only to public secondary schools and makes no mention of elementary schools."

school was not entitled to summary judgment, either in respect to the Free Speech or the Establishment Clause issue."

Justice Stevens dissented. Government "may not generally exclude even religious worship from an open public forum." However, in a limited public forum, Milford could allow speech about a topic from a religious perspective while disallowing both worship and proselytizing.

Justice Souter, joined by Justice Ginsburg, also dissented. "It is beyond question that Good News intends to use the public school premises not for the mere discussion of a subject from a particular, Christian point of view, but for an evangelical service of worship calling children to commit themselves in an act of Christian conversion."

In the *Widmar* case, "the nature of the university campus and the sheer number of activities offered precluded the reasonable college observer from seeing government endorsement in any one of them, and so did the time and variety of community use in the *Lamb's Chapel* case." As one of only four groups which meets in Milford's facilities, the Club is "seemingly, the only one whose instruction follows immediately on the conclusion of the official school day." Indeed, "there is a good case that Good News's exercises blur the line between public classroom instruction and private religious indoctrination."

Chapter XV

SPECIAL DOCTRINES IN THE SYSTEM OF FREEDOM OF EXPRESSION

Introductory Note. In *Chaplinsky v. New Hampshire*, *supra* § 14.01[1], the Court sketched a two-tiered approach to protect freedom of expression. The Court divided speech into two general categories, that which received constitutional protection and that which did not. *New York Times v. Sullivan*, 376 U.S. 254 (1964), altered the basic method of First Amendment analysis by suggesting that at least some judicial scrutiny extend to all governmental infringements on expressive behavior. *See generally* Harry Kalven, Jr., *The New York Times Case: A Note on the Central Meaning of the First Amendment*, 1964 SUP. CT. REV. 191. In many ways, *New York Times* invited an analytical transition from the comparatively narrow scope of First Amendment protection to a more diffuse and creative application of guarantees for freedom of expression. Predictably, attorneys sought constitutional protection for such diverse areas as symbolic expression, funding of political campaigns, commercial advertising, and obscenity. The Supreme Court addressed these issues using the intellectual paradigm fashioned in *New York Times v. Sullivan*. Rather than classify these areas as protected or unprotected speech, the Court fashioned tests tailored to each of these areas which protected a considerable amount of expressive behavior.

Section 15.01 considers the question of constitutional protection for what commentators have called expressive conduct or symbolic speech. Many of the cases derive from the anti-war, civil rights, and other movements of the 1960s. Section 15.02 examines constitutional protection for contributions to, and expenditures by, political campaigns. Extending constitutional protection to some of these activities has helped to bolster political action committees and otherwise deeply influence our political process. Section 15.03 examines a different sort of monetary issue, i.e., government funding of speech. Section 15.04 turns to the question of constitutional protection for commercial advertising, an area which had traditionally not received First Amendment protection. Finally, Section 15.05 explores the Court's struggle with the degree of constitutional protection for sexually explicit materials. While the Court rhetorically has steadfastly refused to afford constitutional protection to materials that are actually obscene, it has wavered on the extent of protection for sexually explicit materials. At one time, it afforded *de facto* nearly absolute protection and more recently allowing some government regulation.

§ 15.01 EXPRESSIVE CONDUCT

UNITED STATES v. O'BRIEN
391 U.S. 367, 88 S. Ct. 1673, 20 L. Ed. 2d 672 (1968)

CHIEF JUSTICE WARREN delivered the opinion of the Court.

On the morning of March 31, 1966, David Paul O'Brien and three companions burned their Selective Service registration certificates on the steps of the South Boston Courthouse. . . . Immediately after the burning, members of the crowd began attacking O'Brien and his companions. An FBI agent ushered O'Brien to safety inside the courthouse. After he was advised of his right to counsel and to silence, O'Brien stated to FBI agents that he had burned his registration certificate because of his beliefs, knowing that he was violating federal law. . . .

He stated in argument to the jury that he burned the certificate publicly to influence others to adopt his anti-war beliefs. . . .

The indictment upon which he was tried charged that he "willfully and knowingly did mutilate, destroy, and change by burning . . . [his] Registration Certificate. . . ."

I

When a male reaches the age of 18, he is required by the Universal Military Training and Service Act to register with a local draft board. He is assigned a Selective Service number, and within five days he is issued a registration certificate. . . .

Both the registration and classification certificates are small white cards, approximately 2 by 3 inches. The registration certificate specifies the name of the registrant, the date of registration, and the number and address of the local board with which he is registered. Also inscribed upon it are the date and place of registrant's birth, his residence at registration, his physical description, his signature, and his Selective Service number. The Selective Service number itself indicates his State of registration, his local board, his year of birth, and his chronological position in the local board's classification record.

The classification certificate shows the registrant's name, Selective Service number, signature, and eligibility classification. It specifies whether he was so classified by his local board, an appeal board, or the President. It contains the address of his local board and the date the certificate was mailed.

Both the registration and classification certificates bear notices that the registrant must notify his local board in writing of every change in address, physical condition, and occupational, marital, family, dependency, and military status, and of any other fact which might change his classification. Both also contain a notice that the registrant's Selective Service number should appear on all communications to his local board.

. . . Under §§ 12(b)(1)–(5) of the 1948 Act, it was unlawful (1) to transfer a certificate to aid a person in making false identification; (2) to possess a certificate not duly issued with the intent of using it for false identification; (3) to forge, alter, "or in any manner" change a certificate or any notation validly inscribed thereon; (4) to photograph or make an imitation of a certificate for the purpose of false identification; and (5) to possess a counterfeited or altered certificate. 62 Stat. 622. In addition, as previously mentioned, regulations of the Selective Service System required registrants to keep both their registration and classification certificates in their personal possession at all times. . . .

By the 1965 Amendment, Congress added to § 12(b)(3) of the 1948 Act the provision here at issue, subjecting to criminal liability not only one who "forges, alters, or in any manner changes" but also one who "knowingly destroys, [or] knowingly mutilates" a certificate. . . . Amended § 12(b)(3) on its face deals with conduct having no connection with speech. It prohibits the knowing destruction of certificates issued by the Selective Service System, and there is nothing necessarily expressive about such conduct. The Amendment does not distinguish between public and private destruction, and it does not punish only destruction engaged in for the purpose of expressing views. . . . A law prohibiting destruction of Selective Service certificates no more abridges free speech on its face than a motor vehicle law prohibiting the destruction of drivers' licenses, or a tax law prohibiting the destruction of books and records. . . .

II

O'Brien first argues that the 1965 Amendment is unconstitutional as applied to him because his act of burning his registration certificate was protected "symbolic speech" within the First Amendment. . . .

We cannot accept the view that an apparently limitless variety of conduct can be labeled "speech" whenever the person engaging in the conduct intends thereby to express an idea. However, even on the assumption that the alleged communicative element in O'Brien's conduct is sufficient to bring into play the First Amendment, it does not necessarily follow that the destruction of a registration certificate is constitutionally protected activity. This Court has held that when "speech" and "nonspeech" elements are combined in the same course of conduct, a sufficiently important governmental interest in regulating the nonspeech element can justify incidental limitations on First Amendment freedoms. . . . [W]e think it clear that a government regulation is sufficiently justified if it is within the constitutional power of the Government; if it furthers an important or substantial governmental interest; if the governmental interest is unrelated to the suppression of free expression; and if the incidental restriction on alleged First Amendment freedoms is no greater than is essential to the furtherance of that interest. We find that the 1965 Amendment to § 12(b)(3) of the Universal Military Training and Service Act meets all of these requirements, and consequently that O'Brien can be constitutionally convicted for violating it.

The constitutional power of Congress to raise and support armies and to make all laws necessary and proper to that end is broad and sweeping. . . . Pursuant to this power, Congress may establish a system of registration for individuals liable for training and service, and may require such individuals within reason to cooperate in the registration system. The issuance of certificates indicating the registration and eligibility classification of individuals is a legitimate and substantial administrative aid in the functioning of this system. And legislation to insure the continuing availability of issued certificates serves a legitimate and substantial purpose in the system's administration.

. . . We agree that the registration certificate contains much information of which the registrant needs no notification. This circumstance, however, does not lead to the conclusion that the certificate serves no purpose, but that, like the classification certificate, it serves purposes in addition to initial notification. . . . Among these are:

1. The registration certificate serves as proof that the individual described thereon has registered for the draft. The classification certificate shows the eligibility classification of a named but undescribed individual. Voluntarily displaying the two certificates is an easy and painless way for a young man to dispel a question as to whether he might be delinquent in his Selective Service obligations. . . . [I]t is in the interest of the just and efficient administration of the system that they be continually available, in the event, for example, of a mix-up in the registrant's file. Additionally, in a time of national crisis, reasonable availability to each registrant of the two small cards assures a rapid and uncomplicated means for determining his fitness for immediate induction, no matter how distant in our mobile society he may be from his local board.

2. The information supplied on the certificates facilitates communication between registrants and local boards, simplifying the system and benefiting all concerned. . . .

3. Both certificates carry continual reminders that the registrant must notify his local board of any change of address, and other specified changes in his status. . . .

4. The regulatory scheme involving Selective Service certificates includes clearly valid prohibitions against the alteration, forgery, or similar deceptive misuse of certificates. The destruction or mutilation of certificates obviously increases the difficulty of detecting and tracing abuses such as these. . . .

The many functions performed by Selective Service certificates establish beyond doubt that Congress has a legitimate and substantial interest in preventing their wanton and unrestrained destruction. . . . And we are unpersuaded that the preexistence of the nonpossession regulations in any way negates this interest. . . .

. . . We perceive no alternative means that would more precisely and narrowly assure the continuing availability of issued Selective Service certificates than a law which prohibits their wilful mutilation or destruction. . . . [B]oth the governmental interest and the operation of the 1965 Amendment are limited to the noncommunicative aspect of O'Brien's conduct. The governmental interest and the scope of the 1965 Amendment are limited to preventing harm to the smooth and efficient functioning of the Selective Service System. When O'Brien deliberately rendered unavailable his registration certificate, he willfully frustrated this governmental interest. For this noncommunicative impact of his conduct, and for nothing else, he was convicted. . . .

In conclusion, we find that because of the Government's substantial interest in assuring the continuing availability of issued Selective Service certificates, because amended § 462(b) is an appropriately narrow means of protecting this interest and condemns only the independent noncommunicative impact of conduct within its reach, and because the noncommunicative impact of O'Brien's act of burning his registration certificate frustrated the Government's interest, a sufficient governmental interest has been shown to justify O'Brien's conviction.

III

O'Brien finally argues that the 1965 Amendment is unconstitutional as enacted because what he calls the "purpose" of Congress was "to suppress freedom of speech." We reject this argument because under settled principles the purpose of Congress, as O'Brien uses that term, is not a basis for declaring this legislation unconstitutional. . . .

Inquiries into congressional motives or purposes are a hazardous matter. When the issue is simply the interpretation of legislation, the Court will look to statements by legislators for guidance as to the purpose of the legislature, because the benefit to sound decision-making in this circumstance is thought sufficient to risk the possibility of misreading Congress' purpose. It is entirely a different matter when we are asked to void a statute that is, under well-settled criteria, constitutional on its face, on the basis of what fewer than a handful of Congressmen said about it. What motivates one legislator to make a speech about a statute is not necessarily what motivates scores of others to enact it, and the stakes are sufficiently high for us to eschew guesswork. . . .

JUSTICE HARLAN, concurring

I wish to make explicit my understanding that [the Court's opinion] does not foreclose consideration of First Amendment claims in those rare instances when an "incidental" restriction upon expression, imposed by a regulation which furthers an "important or substantial" governmental interest and satisfies the Court's other criteria, in practice has the effect of entirely preventing a "speaker" from reaching a significant audience with whom he could not otherwise lawfully communicate. This is not such a case, since O'Brien manifestly could have conveyed his message in many ways other than by burning his draft card.

JUSTICE DOUGLAS, dissenting.

The underlying and basic problem in this case, however, is whether conscription is permissible in the absence of a declaration of war. That question has not been briefed nor was it presented in oral argument; but it is, I submit, a question upon which the litigants and the country are entitled to a ruling. . . .

NOTES

(1) *Expression or Intent.* In *Street v. New York*, 394 U.S. 676 (1969), the Court reversed a conviction for burning a flag while uttering words of protest. "Street was protesting the shooting of James Meredith (the first person to attend the University of Mississippi)," stating that " '[i]f they did that to Meredith, we don't need an American flag.' " Writing for a 5-4 majority, Justice Harlan found "this record insufficient to eliminate the possibility either that appellant's words were the sole basis of his conviction or that appellant was convicted for both his words and his deed."

Writing the dissent, Chief Justice Warren stated that the words simply established intent to desecrate the Flag, a necessary element of the State's case. The Chief Justice predicted that the Court would " 'protect the flag from acts of desecration and disgrace' " if squarely faced with the issue of flag burning. Justices Black, White, and Fortas wrote separate dissents, substantially agreeing with Chief Justice Warren.

(2) *Symbols on Flags.* In *Spence v. Washington*, 418 U.S. 405 (1974), the Court reversed a conviction for taping a peace symbol to a flag. To protest the invasion of Cambodia and the killings at Kent State University, a college student attached "a peace symbol (i.e., a circle enclosing a trident) made of removable black tape" to his U.S. flag and hung it upside down from the window of his apartment on private property. The peace symbol covered "roughly half of the surface," front and back, of his flag. The student told Seattle police officers that he would take the flag down, but they seized it and arrested him. Subsequently, he was convicted under Washington's " 'improper use' " statute. In a *per curiam* opinion, the Court held the statute was unconstitutional "as applied to appellant's activity."

The Court predicated its decision on several factors. First, the flag was "privately owned." In contrast, "the State or National Governments constitutionally may forbid anyone from mishandling in any manner a flag that is public property." Second, defendant displayed his flag on private property upon which "he engaged in no trespass or disorderly conduct." Third, the record contained no evidence "of any risk of breach of the peace."

The Court treated the student's use of the flag in protest as "a form of communication." Thus, it was "necessary to determine whether his activity was sufficiently imbued with elements of communication" to attract First Amendment protection. In this case, "the nature of appellant's activity, combined with the factual context and environment in which it was undertaken, lead to the conclusion that he engaged in a form of protected expression."

Moreover, defendant's use of the flag and the peace sign was intended "to convey a particularized message . . . and in the surrounding circumstances the likelihood was great that the message would be understood by those who viewed it."

Washington asserted an "interest in preserving the national flag as an unalloyed symbol of our country" — an interest not defined by the state court. The Court assumed that the state's interest might have been to prevent "association of the symbol with a particular product or viewpoint, [which] might be taken erroneously as evidence of governmental endorsement," or alternatively, to preserve "the uniquely universal character of the national flag as a symbol."

The majority assumed that the display would not be mistaken as endorsed by the government. Moreover, defendant displayed his flag "in a way closely analogous to the manner in which flags have always been used to convey ideas."

Chief Justice Burger's dissent asserted that "it should be left to each State and ultimately the common sense of its people to decide how the flag, as a symbol of national unity, should be protected." Justice Rehnquist also wrote a dissenting opinion, joined by Chief Justice Burger and Justice White. The enforcement of Washington's "'improper use'" statute "does not depend upon whether the flag is used for communicative or non-communicative purposes; upon whether a particular message is deemed commercial or political; or upon whether the use of the flag is respectful or contemptuous; or upon whether any particular segment of the state's citizenry might applaud or oppose the intended message." Instead, "it simply withdraws a unique national symbol from the roster of materials that may be used as a background for communications."

(3) *Black Armbands.* In *Tinker v. Des Moines Ind. Community School District*, 393 U.S. 503 (1969), the Court upheld the right of students to protest the Vietnam War by wearing black armbands to school. *Tinker* is reproduced at § 14.04[3].

(4) *Offensive Speech.* In *Cohen v. California*, 403 U.S. 15 (1971), defendant was arrested in a courthouse for wearing a jacket with "'Fuck the Draft'" printed on it. He was convicted for violating a California statute that prohibited individuals from "maliciously and willfully disturb[ing] the peace or quiet of any neighborhood or person . . . by . . . offensive conduct."

Justice Harlan's majority opinion concluded that "the statute was not a reasonable manner restriction" and the words were not obscene. The Court also held that the fighting words exception did not apply as no one "actually or likely to be present could reasonably have regarded the words on the appellant's jacket as a direct personal insult." The State also could not suppress speech that was offensive in some generic sense. While the words may be "distasteful," often "one man's vulgarity is another's lyric."

Justice Blackmun dissented, joined by Chief Justice Burger and Justice Black. Justice Blackmun argued that the epithet was "mainly conduct . . . and thus fell within the 'fighting words' doctrine."

(5) For further discussion of problems in symbolic speech, see Dean Alfange, Jr., *Free Speech and Symbolic Conduct: The Draft Card Burning Case*, 1968 Sup. Ct. Rev. 1; Melville B. Nimmer, *The Meaning of Symbolic Speech Under the First Amendment*, 21 UCLA. L. Rev. 29 (1973). *See also* Peter Meijes Tiersma, *Nonverbal Communication and the Freedom of "Speech,"* 1993 Wis. L. Rev. 1525, 1588 (1993) ("For nonverbal behavior to constitute communication in this sense, it must both have meaning and must be performed with an intent to communicate.").

TEXAS v. JOHNSON
491 U.S. 397, 109 S. Ct. 2533, 105 L. Ed. 2d 342 (1989)

Justice Brennan delivered the opinion of the Court. . . .

I

While the Republican National Convention was taking place in Dallas in 1984, respondent Johnson participated in a political demonstration dubbed the "Republican War Chest Tour." As explained in literature distributed by the demonstrators and in speeches made by them, the purpose of this event was to protest the policies of the Reagan administration and of certain Dallas-based corporations. The demonstrators marched through the Dallas streets, chanting political slogans and stopping at several corporate locations to stage "die-ins" intended to dramatize the consequences of nuclear war. On several occasions they spray-painted the walls of buildings and overturned potted plants, but Johnson himself took no part in such activities. He did, however, accept an American flag handed to him by a fellow protestor who had taken it from a flag pole outside one of the targeted buildings.

The demonstration ended in front of Dallas City Hall, where Johnson unfurled the American flag, doused it with kerosene, and set it on fire. While the flag burned, the protestors chanted, "America, the red, white, and blue, we spit on you." . . . No one was physically injured or threatened with injury, though several witnesses testified that they had been seriously offended by the flag-burning.

Of the approximately 100 demonstrators, Johnson alone was charged with a crime. The only criminal offense with which he was charged was the desecration of a venerated object in violation of Tex. Penal Code Ann. § 42.09(a)(3)(1989).[1]

After a trial, he was convicted, sentenced to one year in prison, and fined $2,000. . . . [T]he Texas Court of Criminal Appeals reversed, 755 S.W.2d 92 (1988), holding that the State could not, consistent with the First Amendment, punish Johnson for burning the flag in these circumstances. . . .

. . . We granted certiorari and now affirm.

II

Johnson was convicted of flag desecration for burning the flag rather than for uttering insulting words.[2]

This fact somewhat complicates our consideration of his conviction under the First Amendment. We must first determine whether Johnson's burning of the flag constituted expressive conduct, permitting him to invoke the First Amendment in challenging his conviction. *See, e.g., Spence v. Washington*, 418 U.S. 405, 409–411 (1974). If his conduct was expressive, we next decide whether the State's regulation is related to the suppression of free expression. *See, e.g., United States v. O'Brien*, 391 U.S. 367, 377 (1968). If the State's regulation is not related to expression, then the less stringent standard we announced in *United States v. O'Brien* for regulations of noncommunicative conduct controls. If it is, then we are outside of *O'Brien's* test, and we must ask whether this interest justifies Johnson's conviction under a more demanding standard.[3]

---

[1] Tex. Penal Code Ann. § 42.09 (1989) provides in full:

§ 42.09. Desecration of Venerated Object

(a) A person commits an offense if he intentionally or knowingly desecrates:

(1) a public monument;

(2) a place of worship or burial; or

(3) a state or national flag.

(b) For purposes of this section, "desecrate" means deface, damage, or otherwise physically mistreat in a way that the actor knows will seriously offend one or more persons likely to observe or discover his action.

(c) An offense under this section is a "Class A misdemeanor."

[2] Unlike the law we faced in *Street* [*v. New York*, 394 U.S. 576, 578 (1969)], . . . the Texas flag-desecration statute does not on its face permit conviction for remarks critical of the flag. . . .

[3] Although Johnson has raised a facial challenge to Texas' flag-desecration statute, we choose to resolve this case on the basis of his claim that the statute as applied to him violates the First Amendment. Section 42.09 regulates only physical conduct with respect to the flag, not the written or spoken word, and although one violates the statute only if one "knows" that one's physical treatment of the flag "will seriously offend one or more persons likely to observe or discover his action," Tex. Penal Code Ann. § 42.09(b) (1989), this fact does not necessarily mean that the statute applies only to *expressive* conduct protected by the First Amendment. . . . A tired person might, for example, drag a flag through the mud, knowing that this conduct is likely

Especially pertinent to this case are our decisions recognizing the communicative nature of conduct relating to flags. . . .

We have not automatically concluded, however, that any action taken with respect to our flag is expressive. Instead, in characterizing such action for First Amendment purposes, we have considered the context in which it occurred. . . .

The State of Texas conceded for purposes of its oral argument in this case that Johnson's conduct was expressive conduct. . . . At his trial, Johnson explained his reasons for burning the flag as follows: "The American Flag was burned as Ronald Reagan was being renominated as President. . . . "

III

. . . [W]e have limited the applicability of O'Brien's relatively lenient standard to those cases in which "the governmental interest is unrelated to the suppression of free expression." [*O'Brien, supra,*] at 377. In stating, moreover, that *O'Brien's* test "in the last analysis is little, if any, different from the standard applied to time, place, or manner restrictions," *Clark* [*v. Community for Creative Non-Violence,* 468 U.S. 288,] 298 [(1984)], we have highlighted the requirement that the governmental interest in question be unconnected to expression. . . .

The State offers two separate interests to justify this conviction: preventing breaches of the peace, and preserving the flag as a symbol of nationhood and national unity. We hold that the first interest is not implicated on this record and that the second is related to the suppression of expression.

A

. . . [N]o disturbance of the peace actually occurred or threatened to occur because of Johnson's burning of the flag. . . . [A] principal "function of free speech under our system of government is to invite dispute. It may indeed best serve its high purpose when it induces a condition of unrest, creates dissatisfaction with conditions as they are, or even stirs people to anger." *Terminiello v. Chicago,* 337 U.S. 1, 4 (1949). . . .

Thus, we have not permitted the Government to assume that every expression of a provocative idea will incite a riot, but have instead required careful consideration of the actual circumstances surrounding such expression, asking whether the expression "is directed to inciting or producing imminent lawless action and is likely to incite or produce such action." *Brandenburg v. Ohio,* 395 U.S. 444, 447 (1969). . . . To accept Texas' arguments that it need only demonstrate "the potential for a breach of the peace," and that every flag-burning necessarily possesses that potential, would be to eviscerate our holding in *Brandenburg.* . . .

Nor does Johnson's expressive conduct fall within that small class of "fighting words." . . . *Chaplinsky v. New Hampshire,* 315 U.S. 568, 574 (1942). No reasonable onlooker would have regarded Johnson's generalized expression of dissatisfaction with the policies of the Federal Government as a direct personal insult or an invitation to exchange fisticuffs. . . .

---

to offend others, and yet have no thought of expressing any idea. . . .

. . .While we have rejected "the view that an apparently limitless variety of conduct can be labeled 'speech' whenever the person engaging in the conduct intends thereby to express an idea," *United States v. O'Brien, supra,* at 376, we have acknowledged that conduct may be "sufficiently imbued with elements of communication to fall within the scope of the First and Fourteenth Amendments." *Spence, supra,* at 409. . . .

B

The State also asserts an interest in preserving the flag as a symbol of nationhood and national unity. In *Spence*, we acknowledged that the Government's interest in preserving the flag's special symbolic value "is directly related to expression in the context of activity" such as affixing a peace symbol to a flag. We are equally persuaded that this interest is related to expression in the case of Johnson's burning of the flag. . . . We are thus outside of *O'Brien's* test altogether.

IV

. . . Johnson . . . was prosecuted for his expression of dissatisfaction with the policies of this country, expression situated at the core of our First Amendment values.

Moreover, Johnson was prosecuted because he knew that his politically charged expression would cause "serious offense." If he had burned the flag as a means of disposing of it because it was dirty or torn, he would not have been convicted of flag desecration under this Texas law: federal law designates burning as the preferred means of disposing of a flag "when it is in such condition that it is no longer a fitting emblem for display," 36 U.S.C. § 176(k), and Texas has no quarrel with this means of disposal. The Texas law is thus not aimed at protecting the physical integrity of the flag in all circumstances, but is designed instead to protect it only against impairments that would cause serious offense to others. Texas concedes as much.". . .

. . . Johnson's political expression was restricted because of the content of the message he conveyed. We must therefore subject the State's asserted interest in preserving the special symbolic character of the flag to "the most exacting scrutiny." *Boos v. Barry*, 485 U.S. 321 (1988).[4]

Texas argues that its interest in preserving the flag as a symbol of nationhood and national unity survives this close analysis. Quoting extensively from the writings of this Court chronicling the flag's historic and symbolic role in our society, the State emphasizes the "special place" reserved for the flag in our Nation. . . . [T]he State's claim is that it has an interest in preserving the flag as a symbol of *nationhood* and *national unity*, a symbol with a determinate range of meanings. . . . [5]

If there is a bedrock principle underlying the First Amendment, it is that the Government may not prohibit the expression of an idea simply because society finds the idea itself offensive or disagreeable. . . .

. . . In *Street v. New York*, we held that a State may not criminally punish a person for uttering words critical of the flag. . . . Nor may the Government, we have held, compel conduct that would evince respect for the flag. "To sustain the compulsory flag salute we are required to say that a Bill of Rights which guards the individual's right to speak his own mind, left it open to public authorities to compel him to utter what is not in his mind." [*Barnette*, 319 U.S.] at 634.

. . . "If there is any fixed star in our constitutional constellation, it is that no official, high or petty, can prescribe what shall be orthodox in politics, nationalism, religion, or other matters of opinion or force citizens to confess by word or act their faith therein." *Id.* at 642. In *Spence*, we held that the same interest asserted by Texas here was

---

[4] [Court's footnote 8] . . . [N]othing in our opinion should be taken to suggest that one is free to steal a flag so long as one later uses it to communicate an idea. We also emphasize that Johnson was prosecuted *only* for flag desecration — not for trespass, disorderly conduct, or arson.

[5] [Court's footnote 9] . . . [I]f Texas means to argue that its interest does not prefer *any* viewpoint over another, it is mistaken; surely one's attitude towards the flag and its referents is a viewpoint.

insufficient to support a criminal conviction under a flag-misuse statute for the taping of a peace sign to an American flag. . . . [6]

. . . [T]hat the Government may not prohibit expression simply because it disagrees with its message, is not dependent on the particular mode in which one chooses to express an idea.[7] . . .

. . . To conclude that the Government may permit designated symbols to be used to communicate only a limited set of messages would be to enter territory having no discernible or defensible boundaries. Could the Government, on this theory, prohibit the burning of state flags? Of copies of the Presidential seal? Of the Constitution? In evaluating these choices under the First Amendment, how would we decide which symbols were sufficiently special to warrant this unique status? To do so, we would be forced to consult our own political preferences, and impose them on the citizenry. . . .

There is, moreover, no indication — either in the text of the Constitution or in our cases interpreting it — that a separate juridical category exists for the American flag alone. . . .

It is not the State's ends, but its means, to which we object. It cannot be gainsaid that there is a special place reserved for the flag in this Nation, and thus we do not doubt that the Government has a legitimate interest in making efforts to "preserv[e] the national flag as an unalloyed symbol of our country." *Spence*, 418 U.S. at 412. . . . "National unity as an end which officials may foster by persuasion and example is not in question. The problem is whether under our Constitution compulsion as here employed is a permissible means for its achievement." *Barnette*, 319 U.S. at 640. . . .

We are tempted to say, in fact, that the flag's deservedly cherished place in our community will be strengthened, not weakened, by our holding today. Our decision is a reaffirmation of the principles of freedom and inclusiveness that the flag best reflects, and of the conviction that our toleration of criticism such as Johnson's is a sign and source of our strength. . . .

The way to preserve the flag's special role is not to punish those who feel differently about these matters. It is to persuade them that they are wrong. . . . We can imagine no more appropriate response to burning a flag than waving one's own, no better way to counter a flag-burner's message than by saluting the flag that burns, no surer means of preserving the dignity even of the flag that burned than by — as one witness here did — according its remains a respectful burial. We do not consecrate the flag by punishing its desecration, for in doing so we dilute the freedom that this cherished emblem represents. . . .

JUSTICE KENNEDY, concurring . . . .

. . . It is poignant but fundamental that the flag protects those who hold it in contempt. . . .

---

[6] [Court's footnote 10] . . . Nor does *San Francisco Arts & Athletics v. Olympic Committee*, 348 U.S. 522, 524 (1987), addressing the validity of Congress' decision to "authoriz[e] the United States Olympic Committee to prohibit certain commercial and promotional uses of the word 'Olympic,' " relied upon by the dissent even begin to tell us whether the Government may criminally punish physical conduct towards the flag engaged in as a means of political protest.

[7] [Court's footnote 11] The dissent appears to believe that Johnson's conduct may be prohibited and, indeed, criminally sanctioned, because "his act . . . conveyed nothing that could not have been conveyed and was not conveyed just as forcefully in a dozen different ways." Not only does this assertion sit uneasily next to the dissent's quite correct reminder that the flag occupies a unique position in our society — which demonstrates that messages conveyed without use of the flag are not "just as forcefu[l]" as those conveyed with it — but it also ignores the fact that, in *Spence, supra*, we "rejected summarily" this very claim.

CHIEF JUSTICE REHNQUIST, with whom JUSTICE WHITE and JUSTICE O'CONNOR join, dissenting.

. . . For more than 200 years, the American flag has occupied a unique position as the symbol of our Nation, a uniqueness that justifies a governmental prohibition against flag burning in the way respondent Johnson did here. . . .

[The Chief Justice proceeded to review in some detail the history of the flag as a uniquely revered national symbol.]

. . . Until 1967, Congress left the regulation of misuse of the flag up to the States. Now, however, Title 18 U.S.C. § 700(a), provides that:

Whoever knowingly casts contempt upon any flag of the United States by publicly mutilating, defacing, defiling, burning, or trampling upon it shall be fined not more than $1,000 or imprisoned for not more than one year, or both.

. . . With the exception of Alaska and Wyoming, all of the States now have statutes prohibiting the burning of the flag. . . .

. . . The flag is not simply another "idea" or "point of view" competing for recognition in the marketplace of ideas. Millions and millions of Americans regard it with an almost mystical reverence regardless of what sort of social, political, or philosophical beliefs they may have. . . .

Only two Terms ago, in *San Francisco Arts & Athletics, Inc. v. United States Olympic Committee*, 483 U.S. 522 (1987), the Court held that Congress could grant exclusive use of the word "Olympic" to the United States Olympic Committee. The Court thought that this "restrictio[n] on expressive speech properly [was] characterized as incidental to the primary congressional purpose of encouraging and rewarding the USOC's activities." *Id.* at 536. As the Court stated, "when a word [or symbol] acquires value 'as the result of organization and the expenditure of labor, skill, and money' by an entity, that entity constitutionally may obtain a limited property right in the word [or symbol]." *Id.* at 532 . . . Surely Congress or the States may recognize a similar interest in the flag.

. . . In *Chaplinsky v. New Hampshire*, a unanimous Court said:

. . . There are certain well-defined and narrowly limited classes of speech . . . that . . . are no essential part of any exposition of ideas, and are of such slight social value as a step to truth that any benefit that may be derived from them is clearly outweighed by the social interest in order and morality. *Id.* at 571–572 (footnotes omitted). . . .

Here it may equally well be said that the public burning of the American flag by Johnson was no essential part of any exposition of ideas, and at the same time it had a tendency to incite a breach of the peace. Johnson was free to make any verbal denunciation of the flag that he wished; indeed, he was free to burn the flag in private. He could publicly burn other symbols of the Government or effigies of political leaders. He did lead a march through the streets of Dallas, and conducted a rally in front of the Dallas City Hall. He engaged in a "die-in" to protest nuclear weapons. He shouted out various slogans during the march. . . . For none of these acts was he arrested or prosecuted. . . .

. . . It was Johnson's use of this particular symbol, and not the idea that he sought to convey by it or by his many other expressions, for which he was punished. . . .

. . . The government may conscript men into the Armed Forces where they must fight and perhaps die for the flag, but the government may not prohibit the public burning of the banner under which they fight. . . .

JUSTICE STEVENS, dissenting. . . .

A country's flag is a symbol of more than "nationhood and national unity." It also signifies the ideas that characterize the society that has chosen that emblem as well as the special history that has animated the growth and power of those ideas. . . .

So it is with the American flag. It is more than a proud symbol of the courage, the determination, and the gifts of nature that transformed 13 fledgling Colonies into a world power. It is a symbol of freedom, of equal opportunity, of religious tolerance, and of goodwill for other peoples who share our aspirations. . . .

The Court is . . . quite wrong in blandly asserting that respondent "was prosecuted for his expression of dissatisfaction with the policies of this country, expression situated at the core of our First Amendment values." Respondent was prosecuted because of the method he chose to express his dissatisfaction with those policies. Had he chosen to spray paint — or perhaps convey with a motion picture projector — his message of dissatisfaction on the facade of the Lincoln Memorial, there would be no question about the power of the Government to prohibit his means of expression. The prohibition would be supported by the legitimate interest in preserving the quality of an important national asset. Though the asset at stake in this case is intangible, given its unique value, the same interest supports a prohibition on the desecration of the American flag. . . . [8]

NOTES

(1) For additional discussion of the lessons in the Court's holding in *Texas v. Johnson*, see Sheldon Nahmod, *The Sacred Flag and the First Amendment*, 66 IND. L.J. 511, 514 (1991) ("*Johnson's* lessons include: a deep understanding of what the American flag as patriotic symbol represents; the triumph of reason and, therefore, of the Enlightenment; and, finally, important insights about symbols, their manufacture and manipulation by those in positions of power, and the difference between symbols and truth. Thus, I defend *Johnson* for its educational functions even though I find patriotic symbols important to the sense of political community in the United States.").

(2) *Federal Statute.* In *United States v. Eichmann*, 497 U.S. 310 (1990), the Court struck down the federal Flag Protection Act of 1989. Congress had passed the Act in response to *Texas v. Johnson*, hoping that removal of "explicit content-based limitations on the scope of prohibited conduct" would eliminate the First Amendment problems. In relevant part, the Act provided:

> (a)(1) Whoever knowingly mutilates, defaces, physically defiles, burns, maintains on the floor or ground, or tramples upon any flag of the United States shall be fined under this title or imprisoned for not more than one year, or both.

> (2) This subsection does not prohibit any conduct consisting of the disposal of a flag when it has become worn or soiled.

> (b) As used in this section, the term "flag of the United States" means any flag of the United States, or any part thereof, made of any substance, of any size, in a form that is commonly displayed.

18 U.S.C.A. § 700 (Supp. 1990).

Writing for a 5–4 majority, Justice Brennan found *Texas v. Johnson* controlling. The

---

[8] The Court suggests that a prohibition against flag desecration is not content-neutral because this form of symbolic speech is only used by persons who are critical of the flag or the ideas it represents. In making this suggestion the Court does not pause to consider the far-reaching consequences of its introduction of disparate impact analysis into our First Amendment jurisprudence. It seems obvious that a prohibition against the desecration of a gravesite is content-neutral even if it denies some protesters the right to make a symbolic statement by extinguishing the flame in Arlington Cemetery where John F. Kennedy is buried while permitting others to salute the flame by bowing their heads. . . .

government maintained that flag burning was expressive conduct. However, it sought to distinguish *Texas v. Johnson* as the Act prohibited "conduct (other than disposal) that damages or mistreats a flag without regard to the actor's motive, his intended message, or the likely effects of his conduct on onlookers." Justice Brennan stated that the government's asserted interest in safeguarding the flag's identity "as the unique and unalloyed symbol of the Nation" is directed at suppressing free expression, thus rendering the *O'Brien* test inapplicable.

Nearly all of the terms used in the Act — "knowingly mutilates, defaces, physically defiles," etc. — suggest disrespect towards the flag and impairment of its symbolic value. This focus required "the most exacting scrutiny." Although the government could advance its interest in national symbols by promoting respect for the flag, it could not "criminally proscrib[e] expressive conduct because of its likely communicative impact."

In a footnote, the Court stated that the Government has an interest in protecting the flag "as incident of sovereignty" and expressed no view on regulating behavior that might threaten that function, such as, commercial appropriation of the flag. However, flag-burning does not interfere with the association between flag and nation; "indeed, the flag-burner's message depends in part on the viewer's ability to make this very association."

Justice Stevens, joined by Chief Justice Rehnquist, and Justices White and O'Connor, dissented. Justice Stevens argued that the ban on flag-burning was unrelated to the content of speech because the government wanted to protect the flag as a symbol of national unity regardless of the particular ideas advocated by the flag burner.

CLARK v. COMMUNITY FOR CREATIVE NON-VIOLENCE, 468 U.S. 288 (1984). A federal regulation prohibited camping in certain National Parks, two of which were Lafayette Park, "a roughly seven-acre square located across Pennsylvania Avenue from the White House," and the Mall, an area two miles away, lying between the Capitol and the Lincoln Memorial. However, the National Park Service did grant groups permits for the purpose of holding demonstrations. In 1982, the Park Service issued the Community for Creative Non-Violence (CCNV) a permit to hold a "wintertime demonstration in Lafayette Park and the Mall for the purpose of demonstrating the plight of the homeless. The permit authorized the erection of two symbolic tent cities" of 20 tents in Lafayette Park and 40 tents in the Mall. However, the Service "specifically denied CCNV's request that demonstrators be permitted to sleep in the symbolic tents." CCNV brought an action to enjoin the anti-camping prohibitions from applying to its demonstration, alleging that the regulations violated its free speech rights.

Writing for the Court, Justice White assumed *arguendo*, without deciding, that sleeping in the tents, coupled with the demonstration, was expressive conduct afforded some protection under the First Amendment. Oral, written, or symbolic expression is "subject to reasonable time, place, and manner restrictions." Such restrictions must be content neutral, "narrowly tailored to serve a significant governmental interest," and "leave open ample alternative channels for communication of the information."

Under *Spence v. Washington*, conduct can be communicative if it is "intended to be communicative and that, in context, would reasonably be understood by the viewer to be communicative." Under *United States v. O'Brien*, symbolic speech can be restricted if the regulation is "narrowly drawn to further a substantial governmental interest, and if the interest is unrelated to the suppression of free speech."

The Court found that the anti-sleeping regulation was content neutral and did not prohibit the demonstrators from communicating the plight of the homeless. Moreover, the regulation was narrowly tailored to further a substantial governmental interest in "maintaining the parks in the heart of our capital in an attractive and intact condition." In advancing this interest, "if the parks would be more exposed to harm without the sleeping prohibition than with it, the ban" was valid "as a reasonable regulation on the manner in which a demonstration may be carried out."

For these reasons, the anti-sleeping restrictions constituted a reasonable time, place, and manner restriction. The parks can be damaged by demonstrators as well as non-demonstrators. Park regulations must be observed just as they "must observe the traffic laws, sanitation regulations, and laws to preserve the public peace."

The above analysis also applies to sustain the restriction under the four-part test of *United States v. O'Brien*, which "is little, if any, different from the standard applied to time, place, and manner restrictions." Government certainly has constitutional power to prohibit camping. As outlined above, the sleeping ban "plainly serve[s]" a substantial governmental interest. Limiting the "wear and tear on park properties" is not related to suppressing expression. "[T]he judiciary" lacks "the authority to replace the Park Service as the manager of the Nation's parks or endow the judiciary with the competence to judge how much protection of park lands is wise and how that level of conservation is to be attained."

Concurring, Chief Justice Burger characterized camping as conduct, "a form of 'picketing,' " and not protected speech.

Justice Marshall, joined by Justice Brennan, dissented. Because sleeping was an essential part of the demonstration, it was symbolic speech afforded the protection of the First Amendment. However, the regulation failed to satisfy the time, place, and manner restriction standard. The government interest in preserving the parks was not satisfied because the Government failed to evidence how sleeping "will cause substantial wear and tear on park property."

The majority applied minimal scrutiny to the regulation because the ban was facially content neutral. "[T]he Court has seemingly overlooked the fact that content-neutral restrictions are also capable of unnecessarily restricting protected expressive activity." While silencing "all may fulfill the dictates of an even-handed content-neutrality," such a result would offend the "profound national commitment" that public debate "be uninhibited, robust, and wide-open." Moreover, the majority's deference to government officials overlooked the incentives and tendency of these officials "to overregulate even in the absence of an intent to censor particular views." Officials were more likely to accommodate the interests of the general public over those few who want to demonstrate in the park.

§ 15.02 EXPENDITURES OF MONEY IN THE POLITICAL ARENA

BUCKLEY v. VALEO
424 U.S. 1, 96 S. Ct. 612, 46 L. Ed. 2d 659 (1976)

PER CURIAM.

These appeals present constitutional challenges to the key provisions of the Federal Election Campaign Act of 1971 (Act), and related provisions of the Internal Revenue Code of 1954, all as amended in 1974.

. . . The statutes at issue summarized in broad terms, contain the following provisions: (a) individual political contributions are limited to $1,000 to any single candidate per election, with an overall annual limitation of $25,000 by any contributor; independent expenditures by individuals and groups "relative to a clearly identified candidate" are limited to $1,000 a year; campaign spending by candidates for various federal offices and spending for national conventions by political parties are subject to prescribed limits; (b) contributions and expenditures above certain threshold levels must be reported and publicly disclosed; (c) a system for public funding of Presidential campaign activities is established by Subtitle H of the Internal Revenue Code; and (d) a Federal Election Commission is established to administer and enforce the legislation. . . .

This suit was originally filed by appellants in the United States District Court for the District of Columbia. . . . On plenary review, a majority of the Court of Appeals rejected, for the most part, appellants' constitutional attacks. The Court found "a clear and compelling interest," 519 F.2d 821, 841 (D.C. Cir. 1975), in preserving the integrity of the electoral process. . . .

I

CONTRIBUTION AND EXPENDITURE LIMITATIONS

The intricate statutory scheme adopted by Congress to regulate federal election campaigns includes restrictions on political contributions and expenditures that apply broadly to all phases of and all participants in the election process. The major contribution and expenditure limitations in the Act prohibit individuals from contributing more than $25,000 in a single year or more than $1,000 to any single candidate for an election campaign[9] and from spending more than $1,000 a year "relative to a clearly identified candidate." Other provisions restrict a candidate's use of personal and family resources in his campaign and limit the overall amount that can be spent by a candidate in campaigning for federal office. . . .

A. *General Principles*

The Act's contribution and expenditure limitations operate in an area of the most fundamental First Amendment activities. . . .

In upholding the constitutional validity of the Act's contribution and expenditure provisions on the ground that those provisions should be viewed as regulating conduct, not speech, the Court of Appeals relied upon *United States v. O'Brien*, 391 U.S. 367 (1968). . . .

We cannot share the view that the present Act's contribution and expenditure limitations are comparable to the restrictions on conduct upheld in *O'Brien*. . . .

Even if the categorization of the expenditure of money as conduct were accepted, . . . the interest in regulating the alleged "conduct" of giving or spending money "arises in some measure because the communication allegedly integral to the conduct is itself thought to be harmful." 391 U.S. at 382.

Nor can the Act's contribution and expenditure limitations be sustained. . . . [C]ontribution and expenditure limitations impose direct quantity restrictions on political communication and association by persons, groups, candidates, and political parties in addition to any reasonable time, place, and manner regulations otherwise imposed.[10]

---

[9] [Court's footnote 12]. . . . An organization registered as a political committee for not less than six months which has received contributions from at least 50 persons and made contributions to at least five candidates may give up to $5,000 to any candidate for any election. . . . Other groups are limited to making contributions of $1,000 per candidate per election.

[10] [Court's footnote 17] The nongovernmental appellees argue that just as the decibels emitted by a sound truck can be regulated consistently with the First Amendment, *Kovacs v. Cooper*, 336 U.S. 77 (1949), the Act may restrict the volume of dollars in political campaigns without impermissibly restricting freedom of

A restriction on the amount of money a person or group can spend on political communication during a campaign necessarily reduces the quantity of expression by restricting the number of issues discussed, the depth of their exploration, and the size of the audience reached.[11]

This is because virtually every means of communicating ideas in today's mass society requires the expenditure of money. . . . The electorate's increasing dependence on television, radio, and other mass media for news and information has made these expensive modes of communication indispensable. . . .

. . . [T]hey would have required restrictions in the scope of a number of past congressional and Presidential campaigns and would operate to constrain campaigning by candidates who raise sums in excess of the spending ceiling.

By contrast with a limitation upon expenditures for political expression, a limitation upon the amount that any one person or group may contribute to a candidate or political committee entails only a marginal restriction upon the contributor's ability to engage in free communication. A contribution serves as a general expression of support for the candidate and his views, but does not communicate the underlying basis for the support. The quantity of communication by the contributor does not increase perceptibly with the size of his contribution, since the expression rests solely on the undifferentiated, symbolic act of contributing. At most, the size of the contribution provides a very rough index of the intensity of the contributor's support for the candidate. A limitation on the amount of money a person may give to a candidate or campaign organization thus involves little direct restraint on his political communication, for it permits the symbolic expression of support evidenced by a contribution but does not in any way infringe the contributor's freedom to discuss candidates and issues. . . .

Given the important role of contributions in financing political campaigns, contribution restrictions could have a severe impact on political dialogue if the limitations prevented candidates and political committees from amassing the resources necessary for effective advocacy. There is no indication, however, that the contribution limitations imposed by the Act would have any dramatic adverse effect on the funding of campaigns and political associations. The overall effect of the Act's contribution ceilings is merely to require candidates and political committees to raise funds from a greater number of persons and to compel people who would otherwise contribute amounts greater than the statutory limits to expend such funds on direct political expression, rather than to reduce the total amount of money potentially available to promote political expression.

The Act's contribution and expenditure limitations also impinge on protected associational freedoms. Making a contribution, like joining a political party, serves to affiliate a person with a candidate. In addition, it enables like-minded persons to pool their resources in furtherance of common political goals. The Act's contribution ceilings thus limit one important means of associating with a candidate or committee, but leave the contributor free to become a member of any political association and to assist personally in the association's efforts on behalf of candidates. And the Act's contribution limitations permit associations and candidates to aggregate large sums of

---

speech. . . . The decibel restriction upheld in *Kovacs* limited the *manner* of operating a soundtruck but not the *extent* of its proper use. By contrast, the Act's dollar ceilings restrict the extent of the reasonable use of virtually every means of communicating information. . . .

[11] [Court's footnote 18] Being free to engage in unlimited political expression subject to a ceiling on expenditures is like being free to drive an automobile as far and as often as one desires on a single tank of gasoline.

money to promote effective advocacy. By contrast, the Act's $1,000 limitation on independent expenditures "relative to a clearly identified candidate" precludes most associations from effectively amplifying the voice of their adherents, the original basis for the recognition of First Amendment protection of the freedom of association. . . .

In sum, although the Act's contribution and expenditure limitations both implicate fundamental First Amendment interests, its expenditure ceilings impose significantly more severe restrictions on protected freedoms of political expression and association than do its limitations on financial contributions.

B. *Contribution Limitations*

The $1,000 Limitation on Contributions by Individuals and Groups

to Candidates and Authorized Campaign Committees

Section 608(b) provides, with certain limited exceptions, that "no person shall make contributions to any candidate with respect to any election for Federal office which, in the aggregate, exceed $1,000." . . .

. . . Even a " 'significant interference' with protected rights of political association" may be sustained if the State demonstrates a sufficiently important interest and employs means closely drawn to avoid unnecessary abridgment of associational freedoms. . . .

It is unnecessary to look beyond the Act's primary purpose — to limit the actuality and appearance of corruption resulting from large individual financial contributions — in order to find a constitutionally sufficient justification for the $1,000 contribution limitation. . . . To the extent that large contributions are given to secure a political *quid pro quo* from current and potential office holders, the integrity of our system of representative democracy is undermined. Although the scope of such pernicious practices can never be reliably ascertained, the deeply disturbing examples surfacing after the 1972 election demonstrate that the problem is not an illusory one.

Of almost equal concern . . . is the impact of the appearance of corruption stemming from public awareness of the opportunities for abuse inherent in a regime of large individual financial contributions. . . .

Appellants contend that the contribution limitations must be invalidated because bribery laws and narrowly drawn disclosure requirements constitute a less restrictive means of dealing with "proven and suspected *quid pro quo* arrangements." But laws making criminal the giving and taking of bribes deal with only the most blatant and specific attempts of those with money to influence governmental action. And while disclosure requirements serve the many salutary purposes discussed elsewhere in this opinion, Congress was surely entitled to conclude that disclosure was only a partial measure. . . .

The Act's $1,000 contribution limitation focuses precisely on the problem of large campaign contributions — the narrow aspect of political association where the actuality and potential for corruption have been identified — while leaving persons free to engage in independent political expression, to associate actively through volunteering their services, and to assist to a limited but nonetheless substantial extent in supporting candidates and committees with financial resources.[12]

---

[12] [Court's footnote 31] . . . While providing significant limitations on the ability of all individuals and groups to contribute large amounts of money to candidates, the Act's contribution ceilings do not foreclose the making of substantial contributions to candidates by some major special-interest groups through the combined

The $25,000 Limitation on Total Contributions During Any Calendar Year

In addition to the $1,000 limitation on the nonexempt contributions that an individual may make to a particular candidate for any single election, the Act contains an overall $25,000 limitation on total contributions by an individual during any calendar year. . . . [This] quite modest restraint upon protected political activity serves to prevent evasion of the $1,000 contribution limitation by a person who might otherwise contribute massive amounts of money to a particular candidate through the use of unearmarked contributions to political committees likely to contribute to that candidate, or huge contributions to the candidate's political party. . . .

C. *Expenditure Limitations*

The $1,000 Limitation on Expenditures "Relative to a

Clearly Identified Candidate"

Section 608(e)(1) provides that . . . all individuals, who are neither candidates nor owners of institutional press facilities, and all groups, except political parties and campaign organizations, from voicing their views "relative to a clearly identified candidate" through means that entail aggregate expenditures of more than $1,000 during a calendar year. The provision, for example, would make it a federal criminal offense for a person or association to place a single one-quarter page advertisement "relative to a clearly identified candidate" in a major metropolitan newspaper. . . .

. . . The markedly greater burden on basic freedoms caused by § 608(e)(1) thus cannot be sustained simply by invoking the interest in maximizing the effectiveness of the less intrusive contribution limitations. Rather, the constitutionality of § 608(e)(1) turns on whether the governmental interests advanced in its support satisfy the exacting scrutiny applicable to limitations on core First Amendment rights of political expression.

. . . First, assuming, *arguendo*, that large independent expenditures pose the same dangers of actual or apparent *quid pro quo* arrangements as do large contributions, § 608(e)(1) does not provide an answer that sufficiently relates to the elimination of those dangers. Unlike the contribution limitations' total ban on the giving of large amounts of money to candidates, § 608(e)(1) prevents only some large expenditures. So long as persons and groups eschew expenditures that in express terms advocate the election or defeat of a clearly identified candidate, they are free to spend as much as they want to promote the candidate and his views. The exacting interpretation of the statutory language necessary to avoid unconstitutional vagueness thus undermines the limitation's effectiveness as a loophole-closing provision by facilitating circumvention by those seeking to exert improper influence upon a candidate or office-holder. . . .

Second, quite apart from the shortcomings of § 608(e)(1) in preventing any abuses generated by large independent expenditures, the independent advocacy restricted by

---

effect of individual contributions from adherents or the proliferations of political funds each authorized under the Act to contribute to candidates. As a prime example, § 610 permits corporations and labor unions to establish segregated funds to solicit voluntary contributions to be utilized for political purposes. Corporate and union resources without limitation may be employed to administer these funds and to solicit contributions from employees, stockholders, and union members. Each separate fund may contribute up to $5,000 per candidate per election. . . .

The act places no limit on the number of funds that may be formed through the use of subsidiaries or divisions of corporations, or of local and regional units of a national labor union. . . .

the provision does not presently appear to pose dangers of real or apparent corruption comparable to those identified with large campaign contributions. . . . Section 608(b)'s contribution ceilings rather than § 608(e)(1)'s independent expenditure limitation prevent attempts to circumvent the Act through prearranged or coordinated expenditures amounting to disguised contributions. By contrast, § 608(e)(1) limits expenditures for express advocacy of candidates made totally independently of the candidate and his campaign. . . . The absence of prearrangement and coordination of an expenditure with the candidate or his agent not only undermines the value of the expenditure to the candidate, but also alleviates the danger that expenditures will be given as a *quid pro quo* for improper commitments from the candidate. . . .

It is argued, however, that the ancillary governmental interest in equalizing the relative ability of individuals and groups to influence the outcome of elections serves to justify the limitation on express advocacy of the election or defeat of candidates imposed by § 608(e)(1)'s expenditure ceiling. But the concept that government may restrict the speech of some elements of our society in order to enhance the relative voice of others is wholly foreign to the First Amendment, which was designed "to secure 'the widest possible dissemination of information from diverse and antagonistic sources.' " . . .

Limitation on Expenditures by Candidates from Personal or Family Resources

The Act also sets limits on expenditures by a candidate "from his personal funds, or the personal funds of his immediate family, in connection with his campaigns during any calendar year." § 608(a)(1). These ceilings vary from $50,000 for Presidential or Vice Presidential candidates to $35,000 for senatorial candidates, and $25,000 for most candidates for the House of Representatives.

The ceiling on personal expenditures by candidates on their own behalf, like the limitations on independent expenditures contained in § 608(e)(1), imposes a substantial restraint on the ability of persons to engage in protected First Amendment expression. The candidate, no less than any other person, has a First Amendment right to engage in the discussion of public issues and vigorously and tirelessly to advocate his own election and the election of other candidates. Indeed, it is of particular importance that candidates have the unfettered opportunity to make their views known so that the electorate may intelligently evaluate the candidates. . . .

The primary governmental interest served by the Act — the prevention of actual and apparent corruption of the political process — does not support the limitation on the candidate's expenditure of his own personal funds. . . . Indeed, the use of personal funds reduces the candidate's dependence on outside contributions and thereby counteracts the coercive pressures and attendant risks of abuse to which the Act's contribution limitations are directed.

The ancillary interest in equalizing the relative financial resources of candidates competing for elective office, therefore, provides the sole relevant rationale for § 608(a)'s expenditure ceiling. . . . [T]he First Amendment simply cannot tolerate § 608(a)'s restriction upon the freedom of a candidate to speak without legislative limit on behalf of his own candidacy. . . .

Limitations on Campaign Expenditures

Section 608(c) places limitations on overall campaign expenditures by candidates seeking nomination for election and election to federal office. Presidential candidates may spend $10,000,000 in seeking nomination for office and an additional $20,000,000 in the general election campaign. The ceiling on senatorial campaigns is pegged to the size of the voting-age population of the State with minimum dollar amounts applicable to campaigns in States with small populations. In senatorial primary elections, the limit is the greater of eight cents multiplied by the voting-age population or $100,000, and in the general election the limit is increased to 12 cents multiplied by the voting-age population or $150,000. The Act imposes blanket $70,000 limitations on both primary campaigns and general election campaigns for the House of Representatives. . . . These ceilings are to be adjusted upwards at the beginning of each calendar year by the average percentage rise in the consumer price index for the 12 preceding months. § 608(d).

No governmental interest that has been suggested is sufficient to justify the restriction on the quantity of political expression imposed by § 608(c)'s campaign expenditure limitations. . . .

The interest in equalizing the financial resources of candidates competing for federal office is no more convincing a justification for restricting the scope of federal election campaigns. Given the limitation on the size of outside contributions, the financial resources available to a candidate's campaign, like the number of volunteers recruited, will normally vary with the size and intensity of the candidate's support. . . . Moreover, the equalization of permissible campaign expenditures might serve not to equalize the opportunities of all candidates, but to handicap a candidate who lacked substantial name recognition or exposure of his views before the start of the campaign.

The campaign expenditure ceilings appear to be designed primarily to serve the governmental interests in reducing the allegedly skyrocketing costs of political campaigns. . . . The First Amendment denies government the power to determine that spending to promote one's political views is wasteful, excessive, or unwise. . . . [13]

In sum, . . . contribution ceilings thus serve the basic governmental interest in safeguarding the integrity of the electoral process without directly impinging upon the rights of individual citizens and candidates to engage in political debate and discussion. By contrast, the First Amendment requires the invalidation of the Act's independent expenditure ceiling, § 608(e)(1), its limitation on a candidate's expenditures from his own personal funds, § 608(a), and its ceilings on overall campaign expenditures, § 608(c). These provisions place substantial and direct restrictions on the ability of candidates, citizens, and associations to engage in protected political expression. . . .

II

REPORTING AND DISCLOSURE REQUIREMENTS . . . .

A. *General Principles*

 . . . [W]e have repeatedly found that compelled disclosure, in itself, can seriously infringe on privacy of association and belief guaranteed by the First Amendment. *See, e.g., Gibson v. Florida Legislative Comm.*, 372 U.S. 539 (1963). . . .

Since *N.A.A.C.P. v. Alabama* [, 357 U.S. 449, 463 (1958)] we have required that the subordinating interests of the State must survive exacting scrutiny. We also have insisted that there be a "relevant correlation" or "substantial relation" between the

---

[13] [Court's footnote 65] For the reasons discussed in Part III, *infra*, Congress may engage in public financing of election campaigns and may condition acceptance of public funds on an agreement by the candidate to abide by specified expenditure limitations. . . .

governmental interest and the information required to be disclosed. . . .

The governmental interests sought to be vindicated by the disclosure requirements . . . fall into three categories. First, disclosure provides the electorate with information "as to where political campaign money comes from and how it is spent by the candidate" in order to aid the voters in evaluating those who seek federal office. It allows voters to place each candidate in the political spectrum more precisely than is often possible solely on the basis of party labels and campaign speeches. The sources of a candidate's financial support also alert the voter to the interests to which a candidate is most likely to be responsive and thus facilitate predictions of future performance in office.

Second, disclosure requirements deter actual corruption and avoid the appearance of corruption by exposing large contributions and expenditures to the light of publicity. A public armed with information about a candidate's most generous supporters is better able to detect any post-election special favors that may be given in return. . . .

Third, and not least significant, record-keeping, reporting, and disclosure requirements are an essential means of gathering the data necessary to detect violations of the contribution limitations described above. . . .

It is undoubtedly true that public disclosure of contributions to candidates and political parties will deter some individuals who otherwise might contribute. In some instances, disclosure may even expose contributors to harassment or retaliation. . . . [W]e note and agree with appellants' concession that disclosure requirements — certainly in most applications — appear to be the least restrictive means of curbing the evils of campaign ignorance and corruption that Congress found to exist. . . .

B. *Application to Minor Parties and Independents*

. . . We are not unmindful that the damage done by disclosure to the associational interests of the minor parties and their members and to supporters of independents could be significant. . . . In some instances fears of reprisal may deter contributions to the point where the movement cannot survive. . . .

. . . Minor parties must be allowed sufficient flexibility in the proof of injury to assure a fair consideration of their claim. The evidence offered need show only a probability that the compelled disclosure of a party's contributors' names will subject them to threats, harassment, or reprisals from either Government officials or private parties. The proof may include, for example, specific evidence of past or present harassment of members due to their associational ties, or of harassment directed against the organization itself. A pattern of threats or specific manifestations of public hostility may be sufficient. New parties that have no history upon which to draw may be able to offer evidence of reprisals and threats directed against individuals or organizations holding similar views. . . .

C. *Section 434(e)*

Section 434(e) requires "[e]very person (other than a political committee or candidate) who makes contributions or expenditures" aggregating over $100 in a calendar year "other than by contribution to a political committee or candidate" to file a statement with the Commission. Unlike the other disclosure provisions, this section does not seek the contribution list of any association. Instead, it requires direct disclosure of what an individual or group contributes or spends. . . .

Section 434(e) is part of Congress' effort to achieve "total disclosure" by reaching "every kind of political activity" in order to insure that the voters are fully informed and to achieve through publicity the maximum deterrence to corruption and undue influence possible. The provision is responsive to the legitimate fear that efforts would be made, as they had been in the past, to avoid the disclosure requirements by routing financial support of candidates through avenues not explicitly covered by the general provisions of the Act. . . .

D. *Thresholds*

[Another] contention, based on alleged overbreadth, is that the monetary thresholds in the record-keeping and reporting provisions . . . are too low . . . to . . . have a corrupting influence. . . .

The $10 and $100 thresholds are indeed low. . . . We cannot say, on this bare record, that the limits designated are wholly without rationality. . . .

The $10 recordkeeping threshold . . . facilitates the enforcement of the disclosure provisions by making it relatively difficult to aggregate secret contributions in amounts that surpass the $100 limit. We agree with the Court of Appeals that there is no warrant for assuming that public disclosure of contributions between $10 and $100 is authorized by the Act. Accordingly, we do not reach the question whether information concerning gifts of this size can be made available to the public without trespassing impermissibly on First Amendment rights. . . .

In summary, we find no constitutional infirmities in the recordkeeping reporting, and disclosure provisions of the Act.

III

PUBLIC FINANCING OF PRESIDENT ELECTION CAMPAIGNS

A. *Summary of Subtitle H*

Section 9006 [of the Internal Revenue Code] establishes a Presidential Election Campaign Fund (Fund), financed from general revenues in the aggregate amount designated by individual taxpayers, under § 6096, who on their income tax returns may authorize payment to the Fund of one dollar of their tax liability. . . .

Chapter 95 of Title 26, which concerns financing of party nominating conventions and general election campaigns, distinguishes among "major," "minor," and "new" parties. A major party is defined as a party whose candidate for President in the most recent election received 25% or more of the popular vote. A minor party is defined as a party whose candidate received at least 5% but less than 25% of the vote at the most recent election. All other parties are new parties, including both newly created parties and those receiving less than 5% of the vote in the last election.

For expenses in the general election campaign, § 9004(a)(1) entitles each major-party candidate to $20,000,000. This amount is also adjusted for inflation. To be eligible for funds the candidate must pledge not to incur expenses in excess of the entitlement under § 9004(a)(1) and not to accept private contributions except to the extent that the fund is insufficient to provide the full entitlement. Minor-party candidates are also entitled to funding, again based on the ratio of the vote received by the party's candidate in the preceding election to the average of the major-party candidates. Minor-party candidates must certify that they will not incur campaign expenses in excess of the major-party entitlement and that they will accept private contributions only to the extent needed to make up the difference between that amount and the public funding grant. New-party candidates receive no money prior to the general election, but any candidate receiving 5% or more of the popular vote in the election is entitled to post-election payments according to the formula applicable to minor-party candidates. . . .

. . . [T]he Presidential Primary Matching Payment Account . . . is intended to aid campaigns by candidates seeking Presidential nomination "by a political party" in "primary elections." . . .

B. *Constitutionality of Subtitle H*

Appellants argue that Subtitle H is invalid . . . because Subtitle H invidiously discriminates against certain interests in violation of the . . . Due Process Clause of the Fifth Amendment. We find no merit in these contentions. . . .

. . . [T]he principle has been developed that restrictions on access to the electoral process must survive exacting scrutiny. . . .   Subtitle H does not prevent any candidate from getting on the ballot or any voter from casting a vote for the candidate of his choice; the inability, if any, of minor-party candidates to wage effective campaigns will derive not from lack of public funding but from their inability to raise private contributions. . . .   But eligible candidates suffer a countervailing denial. . . . [A]cceptance of public financing entails voluntary acceptance of an expenditure ceiling. Noneligible candidates are not subject to that limitation. . . .

It cannot be gainsaid that public financing as a means of eliminating the improper influence of large private contributions furthers a significant governmental interest. In addition, the limits on contributions necessarily increase the burden of fundraising, and Congress properly regarded public financing as an appropriate means of relieving major-party Presidential candidates from the rigors of soliciting private contributions. . . .   Congress' interest in not funding hopeless candidacies with large sums of public money, necessarily justifies the withholding of public assistance from candidates without significant public support. . . .

Furthermore, appellants have made no showing that the election funding plan disadvantages nonmajor parties by operating to reduce their strength below that attained without any public financing. First, such parties are free to raise money from private sources, and by our holding today new parties are freed from any expenditure limits, although admittedly those limits may be a largely academic matter to them. . . .   The relative position of minor parties that do qualify to receive some public funds because they received 5% of the vote in the previous Presidential election is also enhanced. Public funding for candidates for major parties is intended as a substitute for private contributions; but for minor-party candidates such assistance may be viewed as a supplement to private contributions since these candidates may continue to solicit private funds up to the applicable spending limit. Thus, we conclude that the general election funding system does not work an invidious discrimination against candidates of nonmajor parties. . . .   Identical treatment of all parties. . . . "would not only make it easy to raid the United States Treasury, it would also artificially foster the proliferation of splinter parties." 519 F.2d at 881. . . .

IV.

The Federal Election Commission

[This portion of the Court's opinion is discussed *supra*.] As summarized by the Court, it was held that "most of the powers conferred by the Act upon the Federal Election Commission can be exercised only by 'Officers of the United States,' appointed in conformity with Art. II, § 2, cl. 2, of the Constitution, and therefore cannot be exercised by the Commission as presently constituted," because they were appointed by Congressional leaders. 424 U.S. at 142. Subsequent legislation corrected the method of appointment by having all members appointed by the President subject to legislative confirmation.]

CHIEF JUSTICE BURGER, concurring in part and dissenting in part.

For reasons set forth more fully later, I dissent from those parts of the Court's holding sustaining the statutory provisions (a) for disclosure of small contributions, (b) for limitations on contributions, and (c) for public financing of Presidential campaigns. . . .

(1)

DISCLOSURE PROVISIONS

. . . Rank-and-file union members or rising junior executives may now think twice before making even modest contributions to a candidate who is disfavored by the union or management hierarchy. Similarly, potential contributors may well decline to take the obvious risks entailed in making a reportable contribution to the opponent of a well-entrenched incumbent. . . .

. . . [S]ecrecy and privacy as to political preferences and convictions are fundamental in a free society. . . .

In saying that the lines drawn by Congress are "not wholly without rationality," the Court plainly fails to apply the traditional test. . . .

Finally, no legitimate public interest has been shown in forcing the disclosure of modest contributions that are the prime support of new, unpopular, or unfashionable political causes. . . .

I would therefore hold unconstitutional the provisions requiring reporting of contributions of more than $10 and to make a public record of the name, address, and occupation of a contributor of more than $100.

(2)

CONTRIBUTION AND EXPENDITURE LIMITS

. . . For me contributions and expenditures are two sides of the same First Amendment coin. . . .

. . . We do little but engage in word games unless we recognize that people — candidates and contributors — spend money on political activity because the wish to communicate ideas, and their constitutional interest in doing so is precisely the same whether they or someone else utters the words. . . .

. . . [I]t seems clear to me that in approving these limitations on contributions the Court must rest upon the proposition that "pooling" money is fundamentally different from other forms of associational or joint activity. . . .

(3)

PUBLIC FINANCING

. . . [T]he inappropriateness of subsidizing, from general revenues, the actual political dialogue of the people — the process which begets the Government itself — is as basic to our national tradition as the separation of church and state. . . .

I [also] agree with Justice Rehnquist that the scheme approved by the Court today invidiously discriminates against minor parties. . . . The fact that there have been few drastic realignments in our basic two-party structure in 200 years is no constitutional justification for freezing the status quo of the present major parties . . . in legislation, enacted by incumbents of the major political parties. . . .

(4)

. . . [W]hen central segments, key operative provisions, of this Act are stricken, can what remains function in anything like the way Congress intended? . . . All candidates can now spend freely; affluent candidates, after today, can spend their own money without limit; yet, contributions for the ordinary candidate are severely restricted in amount — and small contributors are deterred. I cannot believe that Congress would have enacted a statutory scheme containing such incongruous and inequitable provisions. . . .

JUSTICE WHITE, concurring in part and dissenting in part.

. . . I agree with the Court's conclusion and much of its opinion with respect to sustaining the disclosure provisions. I am also in agreement with the Court's judgment upholding the limitations on contributions. I dissent, however, from the Court's view that the expenditure limitations of 18 U.S.C. § 608(c) and (e) violate the First Amendment.

. . . [T]he Court strikes down the provision, strangely enough claiming more insight as to what may improperly influence candidates than is possessed by the majority of Congress that passed this bill and the President who signed it. Those supporting the bill undeniably included many seasoned professionals who have been deeply involved in elective processes and who have viewed them at close range over many years.

It would make little sense to me, and apparently made none to Congress, to limit the amounts an individual may give to a candidate or spend with his approval but fail to limit the amounts that could be spent on his behalf. . . .

Proceeding from the maxim that "money talks," the Court finds that the expenditure limitations will seriously curtail political expression by candidates and interfere substantially with their chances for election. The Court concludes that the Constitution denies Congress the power to limit campaign expenses; federal candidates — and I would suppose state candidates, too — are to have the constitutional right to raise and spend unlimited amounts of money in quest of their own election. . . .

As an initial matter, the argument that money is speech and that limiting the flow of money to the speaker violates the First Amendment proves entirely too much. Compulsory bargaining and the right to strike, both provided for or protected by federal law, inevitably have increased the labor costs of those who publish newspapers, which are in turn an important factor in the recent disappearance of many daily papers. Federal and state taxation directly removes from company coffers large amounts of money that might be spent on larger and better newspapers. The anti-trust laws are aimed at preventing monopoly profits and price fixing, which gouge the consumer. . . . But it has not been suggested, nor could it be successfully, that these laws, and many others, are invalid because they siphon off or prevent the accumulation of large sums that would otherwise be available for communicative activities.

. . . The record before us no more supports the conclusion that the communicative efforts of congressional and Presidential candidates will be crippled by the expenditure limitations than it supports the contrary. The judgment of Congress was that reasonably effective campaigns could be conducted within the limits established by the Act. . . .

. . . Without limits on total expenditures, campaign costs will inevitably and endlessly escalate. Pressure to raise funds will constantly build and with it the temptation to resort in "emergencies" to those sources of large sums, who, history shows, are sufficiently confident of not being caught to risk flouting contribution limits. . . .

I also disagree with the Court's judgment that § 608(a), which limits the amount of money that a candidate or his family may spend on his campaign, violates the Constitution. . . . By limiting the importance of personal wealth, § 608(a) helps to assure that only individuals with a modicum of support from others will be viable candidates. This in turn would tend to discourage any notion that the outcome of elections is primarily a function of money. Similarly, § 608(a) tends to equalize access to the political arena, encouraging the less wealthy, unable to bankroll their own campaigns, to run for political office. . . .

JUSTICE MARSHALL, concurring in part and dissenting in part.

I join in all of the Court's opinion except Part I-C-2, which deals with 18 U.S.C. § 608(a). That section limits the amount a candidate may spend from his personal funds, or family funds under his control, in connection with his campaigns during any calendar year. . . .

. . . Section 608(a) imposes no overall limit on the amount a candidate can spend; it simply limits the "contribution" a candidate may make to his own campaign. . . .

The concern that candidacy for public office not become, or appear to become, the exclusive province of the wealthy assumes heightened significance when one considers the impact of § 608(b) [contribution limits], which the Court today upholds. . . . In short, the limitations on contributions put a premium on a candidate's personal wealth. . . .

. . . Regardless of whether the goal of equalizing access would justify a legislative limit on personal candidate expenditures standing by itself, I think it clear that that goal justifies § 608(a)'s limits when they are considered in conjunction with the remainder of the Act. . . .

[JUSTICE BLACKMUN, concurred in part and dissented in part.]

JUSTICE REHNQUIST, concurring in part and dissenting in part. . .

. . . [I] join in all of the Court's opinion except Part III-B-1, which sustains, against appellants' First and Fifth Amendment challenges, the disparities found in the congressional plan for financing general Presidential elections between the two major parties, on the one hand, and minor parties and candidacies on the other. . . .

. . . Congress in this legislation . . . has enshrined the Republican and Democratic Parties in a permanently preferred position, and has established requirements for funding minor-party and independent candidates to which the two major parties are not subject. . . .

NOTES

(1) Some commentators have critiqued *Buckley v. Valeo* on egalitarian grounds. *See, e.g.*, JOHN RAWLS, LIBERTY, EQUALITY, AND THE LAW (1987) (criticizing the decision as not comporting with the Rawlsian concept of equal liberty); C. Edwin Baker, *Campaign Expenditures and Free Speech*, 33 HARV. C.R.-C.L. L. REV. 1, 3 (1998) (". . . much legislation regulating campaign finance and campaign expenditures is constitutionally acceptable. Regulations are justified as long as they aim at increasing the democratic

quality of the institutionalized process of choosing public officials or making binding legal decisions."); Jeffrey M. Blum, *The Divisible First Amendment: A Critical Functionalist Approach to Freedom of Speech and Electoral Campaign Spending*, 58 N.Y.U. L. REV. 1273 (1983) (warning that *Buckley* could skew the First Amendment structure by allowing the wealthy to drown out the ideas of others). *Cf.* Cass R. Sunstein, *Lochner's Legacy*, 87 COLUM. L. REV. 873 (1987) (discussing that regardless of whether *Buckley* was rightly decided, "*Buckley*, like *Lochner*, grew out of an understanding that for constitutional purposes, the existing distribution of wealth must be taken simply as 'there,' and that efforts to change that distribution are impermissible"). *But see* Lillian R. Bevier, *Money and Politics: A Perspective on the First Amendment and Campaign Finance Reform*, 73 CAL. L. REV. 1045 (1985) (arguing that "political giving and spending directly implicate fundamental first amendment freedom" and that compromising these liberties for egalitarian ends would have caused a loss of political liberty); Bradley A. Smith, *Money Talks: Speech, Corruption, Equality, and Campaign Finance*, 86 GEO. L.J. 45, 98–99 (1997) (". . . [T]he governmental interest in preventing corruption, which the Supreme Court has used to uphold significant infringements on First Amendment rights, is in fact not sufficient to justify such burdens and should be revisited by the Court.").

For some empirical studies of the tremendous influence that money has had on political campaigns since *Buckley v. Valeo*, see HERBERT E. ALEXANDER, FINANCING THE 1980 CONGRESSIONAL ELECTION (1983); ELIZABETH DREW, POLITICS AND MONEY (1983); GARY C. JACOBSON, MONEY IN CONGRESSIONAL ELECTIONS (1980). For an historical and philosophical analysis of the relationship between money and influence, see JOHN T. NOONAN, BRIBES (1984); Daniel Hays Lowenstein, *Political Bribery and the Intermediate Theory of Politics*, 32 UCLA L. REV. 784 (1985). For an argument that campaign speech should be distinguished from political speech, see C. Edwin Baker, *Campaign Expenditures and Free Speech*, 33 HARV. C.R.-C.L. L. REV. 1, 3 (1998) ("[M]uch legislation regulating campaign finance and campaign expenditures is constitutionally acceptable. Regulations are justified as long as they aim at increasing the democratic quality of the institutionalized process of choosing public officials or making binding legal decisions.").

(2) *Contributions for Referenda.* In *Citizens Against Rent Control v. Berkeley*, 454 U.S. 290 (1981), the Court, with only Justice White dissenting, relied on *Buckley v. Valeo* to invalidate a municipal ordinance that placed a $250 limit on contributions to committees or groups formed to support or oppose measures placed on the ballot for popular approval or disapproval. Chief Justice Burger wrote: "*Buckley* identified a single narrow exception to the rule that limits on political activity were contrary to the First Amendment. The exception relates to the perception of undue influence of large contributors to a *candidate*. . . . Contributions by individuals to support concerted action by a committee advocating a position on a ballot measure is beyond question a very significant form of political expression." The Court rejected the justification of the governmental interest in retaining public confidence in the electoral process. The Berkeley ordinance impermissibly restricted both freedom of association and expression. Justices Marshall and Blackmun wrote concurring opinions.

(3) *Limitations on Contributions to PACs.* In *California Medical Association (CMA) v. Federal Election Commission (FEC)*, 453 U.S. 182 (1981), the Court upheld the section of the Federal Election Campaign Act that prohibited individuals and unincorporated associations from contributing more than $5,000 to any multi-candidate political committee in a calendar year. CMA, a not-for-profit unincorporated association of 25,000 California doctors, formed the California Medical Political Action Committee (CALPAC).

With respect to CMA's First Amendment challenge, Justice Marshall wrote for four members of the Court. Justice Marshall rejected claims that these contributions deserved full protection: " 'speech by proxy' that CMA seeks to achieve through its contributions to CALPAC is not the sort of political advocacy that this Court in *Buckley* found entitled to full First Amendment protection." *Buckley* upheld ceilings on contributions that individuals and multi-candidate political committees could make to candidates in a calendar year. "If the First Amendment rights of a contributor are not infringed by limitations on the amount he may contribute to a campaign organization which advocates the views and candidacy of a particular candidate, the rights of a contributor are similarly not impaired by the limits on the amount he may give to a multi-candidate political committee, such as CALPAC, which advocates the views and candidacies of candidates."

Writing for a majority of five, Justice Marshall also rejected an equal protection challenge to the law. The equal protection challenge rested on the grounds that Congress did not limit contributions to PACs made by corporations or labor unions so long as the corporation or labor union made the contribution from a separate, segregated fund. This disparate treatment reflected "a judgment by Congress that these entities have differing structures and purposes, and that they therefore may require different forms of regulation in order to protect the integrity of the electoral process."

Justice Blackmun concurred on the equal protection challenge, and concurred in the judgment on the First Amendment challenge. Unlike the plurality, he thought that political contributions were "entitled to full First Amendment protection." Nevertheless, he thought that the contributions limitation was a narrowly drawn means to advance the important state interest of preventing corruption.

Justice Stewart, joined by Chief Justice Burger, and Justices Powell and Rehnquist, dissented on procedural grounds.

(4) *Contributors of PACs. In Federal Election Commission v. National Conservative Political Action Committee, ("NCPAC")* 470 U.S. 480 (1985), the Court enforced the right of PACs to make "independent expenditures to influence elections for public office." If a Presidential candidate accepted matching funds under the Presidential Election Campaign Act ("Fund Act") 26 U.S.C. § 9001 *et-seq.*, the Fund Act made it a crime for independent political committees "to expend more than $1,000 for that candidate's election." NCPAC made independent expenditures to promote the election campaigns of conservative candidates, not done at the request of any candidate.

Writing for the majority, Justice Rehnquist viewed these organizations as means by which the less wealthy could pool their political clout. That the members of the NCPAC could not control the use of these funds did not change the result. Thus, PAC speech was fully protected political speech.

Following *Buckley*, the Court protected the role of independent expenditures: "Unlike contributions, such independent expenditures may well provide little assistance to the candidates' campaign and indeed prove counterproductive. The absence of a prearrangement and coordination of an expenditure with the candidate or his agent not only undermines the value of the expenditure to the candidate, but also alleviates the danger that expenditures will be given as a *quid pro quo* for improper commitments from the candidate."

Justice White, joined by Justices Brennan and Marshall, dissented on the grounds that *Buckley* was wrongly decided. Even if *Buckley* was rightly decided, the Fund Act should be upheld as "part of an integrated and complex system" of funding Presidential campaigns.

(5) *Minority Parties.* The disclosure provisions of an Ohio campaign disclosure law

were held invalid as applied both to the contributors and to the recipients of expenditures of the Socialist Workers Party. *See Brown v. Socialist Workers '74 Campaign Committee*, 459 U.S. 87 (1982). In *Buckley v. Valeo*, 424 U.S. 1 (1976), *supra*, the Court had indicated that minor parties must be permitted to offer evidence that the disclosure provisions would raise "a probability that the compelled disclosures of a party's contributors' names will subject them to threats, harassments or reprisals from either government officials or private parties." For a fuller discussion of the *Socialist Workers* case, see § 12.04.

(6) *Campaign Promises.* In *Brown v. Harlage*, 456 U.S. 45 (1982), the Court invalidated the Kentucky Corrupt Practices Act, which made it unlawful for a candidate to promise "money or other things of value . . . in consideration of the vote or financial or moral support of that person." The Kentucky Court of Appeals had construed the Act to prevent a candidate from promising to reduce the salary of the part-time position for which he was running. Justice Brennan's majority opinion recognized that some types of promises by candidates can be prohibited even though they take the form of words. But the First Amendment does not permit a state to limit a candidate's right to promise voters that they will benefit financially if the candidate is elected. This type of promise is different from a solicitation to enter into an unlawful commercial transaction which the government can regulate or ban altogether. The Chief Justice and Justice Rehnquist concurred.

(7) *Independent Expenditures by Political Parties.* In *Colorado Republican Fed. Campaign Comm. v. Federal Election Comm'n*, 518 U.S. 604 (1996), the Court held that the application of the Federal Election Campaign Act of 1971 (FECA) to an independent expenditure made by a political party violated the First Amendment. The Colorado Republican Federal Campaign Commission (Colorado Party) challenged the application of the Party Expenditure Provision of the FECA to its purchase of radio advertisements attacking the likely senatorial candidate for the Democratic Party.

Under the FECA, a contribution made by an individual "to a candidate 'with respect to any election' " is limited to $1,000, and a contribution made by a " 'multicandidate political committee' " is limited to $5,000 a year. Expenditures made in coordination with a candidate are considered indirect contributions and are subject to these limitations. Therefore, under these provisions, a coordinated expenditure made by a political party cannot exceed the $5,000 limit. However, an exception allows the expenditures of political parties made during a senatorial election campaign to equal "the greater of $20,000 or '2 cents multiplied by the voting age population of the State.' " Accordingly, the limit on the amount a Colorado party could spend in connection with the 1986 election was approximately $103,000.

Justice Breyer, joined by Justices O'Connor and Souter concluded that the Constitution protects the Colorado Party's expenditure for the radio advertisements as "an 'independent' expenditure." The Colorado Party presented direct evidence that the Party itself developed the advertisements independently of any candidate.

The plurality remanded the question of coordinated expenditures by political parties.

Justice Thomas concurred in the judgment.

In his dissent, Justice Stevens, joined by Justice Ginsburg, would allow Congress "special deference" to limit all senatorial campaign expenditures made by a political party as contributions. This limitation prevented corruption, the circumvention of the Act's other spending limitations, such as the limit on individual contributions to a candidate, and leveled "the electoral playing field" by reducing federal campaign costs.

Justice Kennedy, joined by Chief Justice Rehnquist and Justice Scalia, concurred in the judgment and dissented in part. He would not remand the case as he would hold unconstitutional any limitation on expenditures made by political parties, including coordinated expenditures. For Justice Kennedy, party spending on a candidate's campaign is indistinguishable from a candidate spending on her own campaign, which is constitutionally protected.

Chief Justice Rehnquist and Justice Scalia joined Justice Thomas in Parts I and III of his concurrence. Coordinating efforts to achieve common goals is a traditional part of the relationship between political parties and their candidates. Moreover, the *Buckley* anti-corruption rationale for the regulation of contributions does not apply to political party expenditures.

FEDERAL ELECTION COMM'N v. COLORADO REPUBLICAN FEDERAL CAMPAIGN COMM., 533 U.S. 431 (2001). In *Colorado*, the Court upheld a restriction in the Federal Campaign Act of 1971 limiting a political party's coordinated expenditures with its candidate. In 1996, the Court struck down a similar limitation as applied to independent spending by a political party in *Colorado Republican Federal Campaign Comm. v. Federal Election Comm'n*, 518 U.S. 604 (1996) (*Colorado I*) but remanded the issue of the constitutionality of the claim that any restrictions on congressional campaign expenditures coordinated by a political party were unconstitutional.

Writing for the majority, Justice Souter explained the general differences between contributions and expenditures. The Court agreed with the Act's treatment of coordinated expenditures as contributions.[14] As such, Justice Souter refused to apply the higher level of scrutiny afforded independent expenditures. Under the Court's precedents, "limits on political expenditures deserve closer scrutiny than restrictions on political contributions" since "[r]estraints on expenditures generally curb more expressive and associational activity than limits on contributions do." Moreover, "limits on contributions are more clearly justified by a link to political corruption," giving the government a legitimate interest in regulating them.[15]

When individuals or Political Action Committees (PACs) spend money "according to an arrangement with a candidate," classification grows difficult. Consequently, "Congress drew a functional . . . line" providing that "coordinated expenditures by individuals and nonparty groups" fall under the Act's contribution limitations. The Party argued that "its coordinated spending, like its independent spending, should be left free from restriction under the *Buckley* [v. Valeo] line of cases." Unlike individuals or nonparty groups, political parties express themselves by electing candidates, who in turn express the party's views. Thus, "any limit on party support for a candidate imposes a unique First Amendment burden."

For Justice Souter, the Party's assertion that "coordinated spending is essential" appeared weak in the face of "decades of limitation on coordinated spending" not rendering parties useless. Instead, they "continue to organize to elect candidates, and also function for the benefit of donors whose object is to place candidates under obligation." In fact, this very power to elect candidates makes parties an effective channel "for circumventing contribution and coordinated spending limits binding on other political players." Accordingly, the Court applied "the same scrutiny we have applied to other political actors, that is, scrutiny appropriate for a contribution limit, enquiring whether the restriction is 'closely drawn' to match what we have recognized

---

[14] The Act defines contributions as "'expenditures made by any person in cooperation, consultation, or concert, with, or at the request or suggestion of, a candidate, his authorized political committees, or their agents.'"

[15] Corruption is not only understood as *quid pro quo* agreements, but also as undue influence on an officeholder's judgment, and the appearance of such influence."

as the 'sufficiently important' government interest in combating political corruption."[16]

The evidence demonstrated that "unlimited coordinated spending by a party raises the risk of corruption . . . through circumvention of valid contribution limits." The Act limits a donor to a $2,000 contribution to a single candidate per election cycle. However, "the same donor may give as much as another $20,000 each year to a national party committee supporting the candidate," often with the silent understanding that "the favored candidate will benefit." The incentive to circumvent the contribution limitation would, therefore, "almost certainly intensify" if "suddenly every dollar of spending could be coordinated with the candidate." Indeed, "the record shows that even under present law substantial donations turn the parties into matchmakers whose special meetings and receptions give the donors the chance to get their points across to the candidates."

The Court rejected allegedly more narrow alternatives like the earmarking provision, which treats contributions that " 'are in any way earmarked or otherwise directed . . . to [a] candidate' " as direct contributions. This "would reach only the most clumsy attempts to pass contributions through to candidates."

The Court also rejected the alternative of curbing circumvention by limiting contributions to parties. The choice here was not "between a limit on pure contributions and pure expenditures," as it was in *Buckley* and *Colorado I*. Rather, "[t]he choice is between limiting contributions and limiting expenditures whose special value as expenditures is also the source of their power to corrupt. Congress is entitled to its choice."

Justice Thomas dissented, joined by Justices Scalia and Kennedy, and by Chief Justice Rehnquist as to Part II. He would have invalidated the restriction because it "sweeps too broadly, interferes with the party-candidate relationship, and has not been proven necessary to combat corruption." In Part 1, Justice Thomas reiterated his position that *"Buckley v. Valeo* should be overruled." He maintained that the Court "has extended the most generous First Amendment safeguards to filing lawsuits, wearing profane jackets, and exhibiting drive-in movies with nudity, but has only offered tepid protection to the core speech and associational rights that our Founders sought to defend."

Even without overruling *Buckley* and without applying strict scrutiny, the dissent believed the restriction was unconstitutional. Chief Justice Rehnquist joined this part of the analysis. "In practice, *Buckley* scrutiny has meant that restrictions on contributions by individuals and political committees do not violate the First Amendment so long as they are 'closely drawn' to match a 'sufficiently important' government interest, but that restrictions on independent expenditures are constitutionally invalid." The Court has drawn two "flawed" conclusions: "coordinated expenditures are no different from contributions, and political parties are no different from individuals and political committees." The Act's definition of a coordinated expenditure "covers a broad array of conduct, some of which is akin to independent expenditure." Take "a situation in which the party develops a television advertising campaign touting a candidate's record on education, and the party simply 'consults' with the candidate on which time slot the

---

[16] [Court's footnote 17] The Court did not determine "[w]hether a different characterization, and hence a different type of scrutiny, could be appropriate in the context of an as-applied challenge focused on the application of the limit to specific expenditures." The Party argued that "the limitation is facially invalid because of its potential application to expenditures that involve more of the party's own speech" — and not just those amounting to "payment of the candidate's bills." However, the Party failed to show "what proportion of the spending falls in one category or the other." Consequently, it did not "lay the groundwork for its facial overbreadth claim."

advertisement should run." There is "no constitutional difference between this expenditure and a purely independent one."

Even ignoring "the breadth of the statutory text," Justice Thomas would still strike down the restriction since "[p]olitical parties and their candidates are 'inextricably intertwined' in the conduct of an election." Indeed, "a party's public image is largely defined by what its candidates say and do." Breaking "this link between the party and its candidates would impose 'additional costs and burdens to promote the party message.'"

Justice Thomas would also invalidate the statute even if coordinated expenditures by political parties were analogous to contributions by individuals or PACs. The Government has not shown that "the restriction is 'closely drawn' to curb . . . corruption." Specifically, it has not presented any evidence "of corruption or the perception of corruption." The lack of evidence stems from "the unique relationship between a political party and its candidates: 'The very aim of a political party is to influence its candidate's stance on issues and, if the candidate takes office'" how he votes.

The majority also "relies upon an alternative theory of corruption" — circumvention — even though the District Court's findings and the "overwhelming evidence" discredit this theory. *Colorado I* determined that the opportunity for corruption through circumvention "was 'at best, attenuated.'"

More narrowly "tailored alternatives for addressing the corruption" include enforcing the prohibition on earmarking contributions to a particular candidate or reducing the maximum contribution to a party.

RANDALL v. SORRELL, 538 U.S. 230 (2006). In *Randall*, the Court invalidated both the expenditure and contribution limits of Vermont's campaign finance statute. "Well-established precedent makes clear that the expenditure limits violate the First Amendment. The contribution limits are unconstitutional because in their specific details (involving low maximum levels and other restrictions) they fail to satisfy the First Amendment's requirement of careful tailoring."

Vermont's campaign finance statute ("Act 64") "imposes mandatory expenditure limits on the total amount a candidate for state office can spend during a 'two-year general election cycle.'" Incumbent candidates running for "statewide office may spend no more than 85%" of the expenditure limit, "and incumbents seeking reelection to the State Senate or House may spend no more the 90%." The limits apply to "the primary plus the general election, in approximately the following amounts: governor, $300,000; lieutenant governor, $100,000; other statewide offices, $45,000; state senator, $4,000 (plus an additional $2,500 for each additional seat in the district); state representative (two-member district), $3,000; and state representative (single member district), $2,000." The law permits these expenditure limits to be adjusted for inflation. The limitations also apply to an expenditure by a political party "that is coordinated with the campaign and benefits the candidate."

On the contributions side, the Act limits how much "any single individual can contribute to the campaign of a candidate for state office during a 'two-year general election cycle.'" Contributions are "limited as follows: governor, lieutenant governor, and other statewide offices, $400; state senator, $300; and state representative, $200." These same limits apply to political committees and political parties. Moreover, the statute "imposes a limit of $2,000 upon the amount any individual can give to a political party during a 2-year general election cycle."

Justice Breyer delivered the judgment of the Court and delivered an opinion which was joined in part by Chief Justice Roberts and by Justice Alito. Justice Breyer relied on *Buckley v. Valeo*, *supra*, to determine the constitutionality of the Act's expenditure limits. He wrote alone of general views on *stare decisis*. "The Court has often recognized the 'fundamental importance' of *stare decisis*" because it "avoids the instability and unfairness that accompany disruption of settled legal expectations." The Court may only depart from established precedent under "exceptional" circumstances that require " 'special justification.' " This principle "is especially true where, as here, the principle has become settled through iteration and reiteration over a long period of time."

In a part of the opinion joined only by Chief Justice Roberts, Justice Breyer found no "special justification" that *Buckley* be overruled. "Subsequent case law has not made *Buckley* a legal anomaly or otherwise undermined its basic legal principles." Moreover, there is no "demonstration that circumstances have changed so radically as to undermine *Buckley's* critical factual assumptions." Lastly, legislators rely on *"Buckley* when drafting campaign finance laws." No "strong justification . . . warrant[ed] overruling so well established a precedent."

Justice Alito joined the remainder of Justice Breyer's opinion. Writing for a plurality of three, Justice Breyer discussed the "more complex question" of the Vermont Act's "contribution limits." Typically, the Court will defer to the legislature's " 'particular expertise' " to determine appropriate campaign costs unless contribution limits are so harmfully low that they put challengers at "a significant disadvantage" in "mounting effective campaigns against incumbent officeholders thereby reducing democratic accountability." If there is "strong indication" of such risks, "courts, including appellate courts, must review the record independently and carefully with an eye toward assessing the statute's 'tailoring,' that is, toward assessing the proportionality of the restrictions."

The plurality believed that the Vermont statute's "limits are sufficiently low as to generate suspicion that they are not closely drawn" in comparison to limits the Court has previously upheld and comparable limits "in other States." When adapted "to reflect its value in 1976 (the year *Buckley* was decided), Vermont's contribution limit on campaigns for statewide office (including governor) amounts to $113.91 per 2-year election cycle, or roughly $57 per election, as compared to the $1,000 per election limit on individual contributions at issue in *Buckley*. (The adjusted value of Act 64's limit on contributions from political parties to candidates for statewide office, again $200 per candidate per election, is just over one one-hundredth of the comparable limit before the Court in *Buckley*, $5,000 per election.) Yet, Vermont's gubernatorial district-the entire State-is no smaller than the House districts to which *Buckley's* limits applied." Indeed, "considered as a whole, Vermont's contribution limits are the lowest in the Nation."

Moreover, "Vermont's limit is well below the lowest limit this Court has previously upheld, the limit of $1,075 per election (adjusted for inflation every two years) for candidates for Missouri state auditor." *See Nixon v. Shrink*, *infra* Note: Small Contributions. Adjusted for population, *"per citizen*, Vermont's limit is slightly more generous." Nevertheless, campaigning "for state auditor is likely to be less costly than a campaign for governor." These and other "danger signs" prompted the plurality to "examine the record independently and carefully to determine" if the "limits are 'closely drawn.' "

Examination convinced the plurality that the "contribution limits are too restrictive" based on the combination of five factors. *First*, there is evidence that the "contribution limits will significantly restrict the amount of funding available for challengers to run competitive campaigns."[17] For example, the challenger's "expert witnesses" presented evidence that "Vermont political parties (particularly the Republican Party) 'target' their contributions to candidates in competitive races, that those contributions represent a significant amount of total candidate funding in such races, and that the contribution limits will cut the parties' contributions to competitive races dramatically" by as much as "85% (for the legislature on average) and 99% (for governor)."

Still, "the critical question concerns not simply the *average* effect of contribution limits on fundraising but, more importantly, the ability of a candidate running against an incumbent officeholder to mount an effective *challenge*." The challenger's studies together with the "low *average* Vermont campaign expenditures and the typically higher costs that a challenger must bear to overcome the name-recognition advantage enjoyed by an incumbent, raise a reasonable inference that the contribution limits are so low that they may pose a significant obstacle to candidates in competitive elections."

Second, the contribution limit's application to political parties threatens "the right to associate in a political party." The Act's individual limits of $200 to $400 are applied "to virtually all affiliates of a political party taken together as if they were a single contributor." The Act not only has a "negative effect on "amassing funds" but it "would severely limit the ability of a party to assist its candidates' campaigns by engaging in coordinated spending on advertising, candidate events," and the like. Furthermore, the Act would prevent parties from distributing collected funds to what it considers key competitive races because the amount would likely exceed the limit. "Thus . . . preventing a political party from using contributions by small donors to provide meaningful assistance to any individual candidate." The plurality agreed with the District Court's determination that "contribution limits 'would reduce the voice of political parties' in Vermont to a "whisper."

Third, while "the Act excludes from its definition of 'contribution' all 'services provided without compensation by individuals volunteering their time on behalf of a candidate,' " there is no exception for a volunteer's expenses "such as travel expenses." The lack of an exception may be significant when "contribution limits are very low" but not when "a limit . . . is reasonably high."

Fourth, the "contribution limits are not adjusted for inflation."

Fifth, no "special justification" legitimates these low contribution limits. Small contributions are unlikely "to prove a corruptive force." The plurality determined that the "five sets of considerations, taken together, lead" to a conclusion that the "contribution limits are not narrowly tailored." Instead, the Act "disproportionately burdens numerous First Amendment interests."

It is not "possible to sever some of the Act's contribution limit provisions from others that might remain fully operative." This "would require us to write words into the statute (inflation indexing), or leave gaping loopholes (no limits on party contributions), or to foresee which of many different possible ways the legislature might respond to the constitutional objections we have found. Given these difficulties, we believe the Vermont Legislature would have intended us to set aside the statute's contribution limits, leaving the legislature free to rewrite these provisions in light of the constitutional objections we have identified."

Justice Alito concurred except in that portion of Justice Breyer's opinion which discusses the importance of adhering to *Buckley*. "Whether or not a case can be made

---

[17] For instance, the challenger's expert "concluded that Act 64's contribution limits would have reduced the funds available in 1998 to Republican challengers in competitive races in amounts ranging from 18% to 53% of their total campaign income."

for reexamining *Buckley* in whole or in part, what matters is that respondents do not do so here."

Justice Kennedy concurred in the judgment. "Vermont's contributions . . . are even more stifling than the ones that survived [the] unduly lenient review [of *Nixon v. Shrink Missouri Government PAC*, 528 U.S. 377 (2000)]." He expressed "skepticism" about a system that "requires us to explain why $200 is too restrictive a limit while $1,500 is not."

Justice Thomas, joined by Justice Scalia, concurred in the judgment. Justice Thomas reiterated his view that he "would overrule *Buckley* and subject both the contribution and expenditure restrictions of Act 64 to strict scrutiny, which they would fail." The plurality opinion establishes a "multifactor test," which is "unclear" and puts the "Court in the position of addressing the propriety of regulations of political speech based upon little more than its *impression* of the appropriate limits." Violations of First Amendment rights are not contingent on the size of the infringement.

Justice Stevens dissented. "*Buckley's* holding on expenditure limits is wrong, and that the time has come to overrule it." *Buckley* itself changed precedent. "For the preceding 65 years, congressional races had been subject to statutory limits on both expenditures and contributions." In his *Buckley* dissent, "Justice White recognized" that "it is quite wrong to equate money and speech." For Justice Stevens, "these limits on expenditures are far more akin to time, place, and manner restrictions than to restriction on the content of speech."

Justice Souter also filed a dissenting opinion joined by Justice Ginsberg and in part by Justice Stevens. Justice Souter "would adhere to the Court of Appeal's decision to remand for further enquiry bearing on the limitations on candidates' expenditures." He thought that "the contribution limits satisfy controlling precedent." In some instances, "aggregated donations simply could not sustain effective campaigns." However in this case, the Court should defer to the Vermont Legislature, which "evidently tried to account for the realities of campaigning in Vermont" in which campaign costs are on the "low side."

NOTE

Small Contributions. In *Nixon v. Shrink Missouri Government PAC*, 528 U.S. 377 (2000), the Court upheld a Missouri statute placing limits on campaign contributions to candidates running for state office. The statute placed limits ranging from $250 for offices involving populations fewer than 100,000; and $1000 for offices involving populations of more than 250,000. Under this system, Fredman, a candidate for Missouri State Auditor, had an inflation adjusted contribution cap of $1,075. Joined by the Shrink Missouri Government PAC ("Shrink"), Fredman challenged the contribution limits.

Writing for the majority, Justice Souter stated that the amount of "empirical evidence needed to satisfy heightened judicial scrutiny of legislative judgments will vary up or down with the novelty and plausibility of the justification raised." The Missouri Legislature shared concerns about corruption similar to those that had motivated Congress in *Buckley*. Moreover, the $1,000 contribution limit upheld in *Buckley* was not "a constitutional minimum below which legislatures could not regulate."

The District Court found that despite contributions limits, candidates for state-wide office remained " 'quite able to raise funds sufficient to run effective campaigns.' " Contribution limits were too low if they impeded candidates' raising " 'the resources necessary for effective advocacy.' "

Concurring, Justice Stevens said "money is property, it is not speech."

Justice Breyer, joined by Justice Ginsburg, concurred. The $1,075 limit may unfairly favor incumbents by amplifying their existing media and reputational advantages. However, "the type of election at issue; the record of adequate candidate financing post-reform; and the fact that the statute indexes the amount for inflation" shows that the statute "does not work disproportionate harm" to candidates such as Fredman.

The line that *Buckley* draws between contributions and expenditures may need to be less absolute. For example, the expenditures of independently wealthy candidates "might be considered contributions to their own campaigns." If *Buckley* "denies the political branches sufficient leeway to enact comprehensive solutions to the problems posed by campaign finance," then the Court should re-examine *Buckley*.

Dissenting, Justice Kennedy would also reevaluate *Buckley*. He substantially agreed with Justice Thomas' dissent that government may not be able to limit campaign contributions or expenditures. However, he would "leave open the possibility" of "some limits on both expenditures and contributions, thus permitting officeholders to concentrate their time and efforts on official duties rather than on fundraising."

Justice Thomas, joined by Justice Scalia, dissented, arguing that *Buckley* should be overruled. He would place campaign contributions under strict scrutiny and hold the Missouri statute unconstitutional. As Fredman does not benefit from incumbency, name recognition, or substantial personal wealth, the statute inhibits his ability to run a successful campaign, and forbids his message from reaching the public.

FIRST NATIONAL BANK v. BELLOTTI, 435 U.S. 765 (1978). In *Bellotti*, the Court struck down a Massachusetts criminal statute that prohibited business corporations from using corporate funds to influence voters on issues that did not pertain to that corporation's property, business, or assets. The corporations challenging the law wanted to use corporate funds to make the public aware of their stand regarding "a proposed constitutional amendment that was to be submitted to the voters" for adoption of a graduated personal income tax.

Writing for the Court, Justice Powell stated that the speech at issue "is at the heart of the First Amendment's protection." Government would attempt to stop an individual from making these statements. "It is the type of speech indispensable to decisionmaking in a democracy, and this is no less true because the speech comes from a corporation rather than an individual. The inherent worth of the speech in terms of its capacity for informing the public does not depend upon the identity of the source, whether corporation, association, union, or individual." The Court did not address whether natural persons and corporations have coextensive First Amendment rights.

The press has far-reaching First Amendment protection regardless of whether it operates in the corporate form. Moreover, commercial speech jurisprudence reinforces the notion that the First Amendment protects information conveyed by corporations. Legislatures cannot "dictat[e] the subjects about which persons may speak and the speakers who may address a public issue. *Police Dept. of Chicago v. Mosley*, 408 U.S. 92, 96 (1972). If a legislature may direct business corporations to 'stick to business' it also may limit other corporations — religious, charitable, or civic — to their respective 'business' when addressing the public."

Justice Powell rejected "the State's interest in sustaining the active role of individual citizens in the electoral process and thereby preventing diminution of the citizen's confidence in government." He noted that "if . . . corporate advocacy threatened imminently to undermine the the democratic processes, thereby denigrating rather than serving First Amendment interests, these arguments would merit our consideration. But there has been no showing that the relative voice of corporations has been overwhelming or even significant in influencing referenda in Massachusetts, or that there has been any threat to the confidence of the citizenry in government." Furthermore, "[t]he risk of corruption perceived in cases involving candidate elections simply is not present in a popular vote on a public issue." In any event, " 'the concept that government may restrict the speech of some elements of our society in order to enhance the relative voice of others is wholly foreign to the First Amendment.' "

Justice Powell also rejected the State's second asserted interest in protecting minority shareholders as underinclusive for a number of reasons. Among the reasons was that the State did not prohibit other corporate activity which might offend minority shareholders such as lobbying. At the same time, the regulation was overinclusive as it even prohibited corporate speech about referenda which all shareholders supported. Justice Powell reasoned that shareholders could protect their interests through intracorporate remedies, as well as judicial remedies such as shareholder derivative suits.

Chief Justice Burger concurred. Justice White dissented, joined by Justices Brennan and Marshall. Justice White argued that the First Amendment permitted a state to restrict a corporation's ability to circulate fact and opinion irrelevant to their businesses. In this context, "what some have considered to be the principal function of the First Amendment, the use of communication as a means of self-expression, self-realization, and self-fulfillment, is not at all furthered by corporate speech." Of course, "there are some corporations formed for the express purpose of advancing certain ideological causes shared by all their members, or, as in the case of the press, of disseminating information and ideas. Under such circumstances, association in a corporate form may be viewed as merely a means of achieving effective self-expression. But this is hardly the case generally with corporations operated for the purpose of making profits."

The First Amendment does protect advertising and information "for employees, customers, and shareholders . . . about matters relating to the functioning of the corporation." Restrictions on such data might shrink the marketplace of ideas. In contrast, "it is unlikely that any significant communication would be lost by such [the Massachusetts] prohibition. These individuals would remain perfectly free to communicate any ideas which could be conveyed by means of the corporate form."

The state interest in restricting corporate political activity is in preventing corporations "which have been permitted to amass wealth as a result of special advantages extended by the State for certain economic purposes from using that wealth to acquire an unfair advantage in the political process, especially where, as here, the issue involved has no material connection with the business of the corporation. The State need not permit its own creation to consume it."

Finally, Justice White found "an additional overriding interest" in preventing corporate management from forcing its views on shareholders. Justice Rehnquist filed a separate dissent.

NOTES

(1) *Expenditures by Advocacy Corporations.* In *Fed. Election Comm'n v. Mass. Citizen for Life, Inc.*, 479 U.S. 238 (1986), MCFL was a nonprofit, nonstock corporation organized under Massachusetts law. Its purpose was " '[t]o foster respect for life and to defend the right to life of all human beings, born and unborn.' " In 1978, MCFL published a " 'Special Edition' " newsletter prior to the primary elections in Massachusetts entitled " 'EVERYTHING YOU NEED TO KNOW TO VOTE PRO-LIFE.' " The newsletter provided pro-life voting records of the candidates. The Federal Election Commission (FEC) filed a complaint alleging violation of the Federal Election

Campaign Act (2 U.S.C. § 441b) which prohibits corporations' spending corporate treasury funds " 'in connection with any election' " to public office. The law, however, did permit expenditures " 'financed by voluntary contributions to a separate segregated fund.' "

Writing for the Court, Justice Brennan stated that the prohibition "limit[ed] the ability of such organizations to engage in core political speech." Justice Brennan emphasized that MCFL was not a " 'traditional corporation organized for economic gain.' "

There were three characteristics of MCFL that made § 441b unconstitutional as it applied to the organization. First, it was expressly designed to promote political ideas. "This ensures that political resources reflect political support." Second, no shareholders or other individuals could claim ownership over MCFL's assets or earnings. "This ensures that persons connected with the organization will have no economic disincentive for disassociating with it if they disagree with its political activity." Third, it was not formed by either a business corporation or a labor union and does not accept contributions from such entities. "This prevents such corporations from serving as conduits for the type of direct spending that creates a threat to the political marketplace."

Chief Justice Rehnquist, joined by Justices White, Blackmun and Stevens, dissented. The Chief Justice considered any difference among corporations to be " 'distinctions in degree' " which fall short of " 'differences in kind.' " Consequently, he would have afforded the legislature substantial deference in determining the need for prophylactic measures to combat corporate corruption.

(2) *Contributions by Advocacy Corporations.* In *Fed. Election Comm'n v. Beaumont*, 539 U.S. 146 (2003), Justice Souter, upheld (7-2) a 1907 federal law that prohibits nonprofit advocacy corporations from "contributing directly to candidates for federal office." The statute allows corporations to form and control PACs which can solicit contributions from corporate employees and shareholders. These PACs may in turn contribute to candidates for federal office.

Buckley v. Valeo, supra, afforded campaign contributions less deference than campaign expenditures. *"Within the realm of contributions generally, corporate contributions are furthest from the core of political expression, since corporations' First Amendment speech and association interests are derived largely from those of their members."* Individual members of North Carolina Right to Life, Inc. could still make their own independent contributions. *Fed. Election Comm'n v. Nat'l Right to Work Comm.*, 459 U.S. 197 (1982), approved limiting even advocacy corporations to making campaign contributions "only through its PAC and subject to a PAC's administrative burdens."

Justice Kennedy, concurring in the judgment, stated that he might have joined Justice Thomas in dissent had the Court been comprehensively reviewing the different scrutiny for campaign contributions and expenditures. Justice Thomas, joined by Justice Scalia, dissented. Strict scrutiny is the appropriate standard of review for all campaign finance laws.

AUSTIN v. MICHIGAN CHAMBER OF COMMERCE, 494 U.S. 652 (1990). The Court upheld a Michigan statute prohibiting corporations from contributing out of their general funds to support or oppose a candidate running for state office. The statute did allow corporations to contribute funds from a segregated account.

The Michigan Chamber of Commerce is a nonprofit organization with both political and nonpolitical purposes. It wished to use its general funds to finance an advertisement in support of a candidate for State office. Under § 54 (1) of the Michigan

Campaign Finance Act, this expenditure was a felony. The Chamber sought a declaratory judgment that the statute was unconstitutional.

The 6-3 majority, written by Justice Marshall, relied on *Buckley v. Valeo* to find that expenditures on political campaigns constitute political speech thereby upholding the statute. The Court found that the Act's limitations on corporate campaign spending burdened political speech. Michigan, however, argued that its statute would prevent corruption and unfair political advantages created by such preferences as "limited liability, perpetual life, and favorable treatment of the accumulation and distribution of assets" that "enable corporations to amass large amounts of wealth."

Justice Marshall found that the "Act does not attempt 'to equalize the relative influence of speakers on elections;' rather, it ensures that expenditures reflect actual public support for the political ideas espoused by corporations." This rationale was "sufficiently compelling" to uphold the Act. The Act was "sufficiently narrow tailored to achieve its goal" of eliminating "the distortion caused by corporate spending while also allowing corporations to express their political views." Requiring that corporations use a segregated fund for campaign expenditures ensures that these expenditures will reflect the political views of those who contribute to that separate fund.

Moreover, the Court rejected the Chamber's argument that the Act is "overinclusive, because it includes within its scope closely held corporations that do not possess vast reservoirs of capital." The Act restricts corporations due to the preferences afforded them by the state that increase their ability to distort the political process, not on the corporations' amount of capital.

The Chamber does not meet the three distinctions outlined in *Fed. Election Comm'n v. Massachusetts Citizens for Life, Inc.*, 479 U.S. 238 (1986) (*MCFL*). First, the Chamber is not purely political, unlike MCFL. Therefore, its resources do not clearly reflect the support of its members. Second, while neither the Chamber nor MCFL have shareholders, Chamber members have strong nonpolitical reasons for their affiliation with the Chamber, which will deter their terminating membership for disagreement with the Chamber's political views. Third, the Chamber is subject to the influence of business corporations, unlike MCFL, which did not even accept contributions from business corporations. "In striking contrast, more than three-quarters of the Chamber's members are business corporations, whose political contributions and expenditures can constitutionally be regulated by the State."

The Chamber also argued against § 54(1), claiming it is "underinclusive because it does not regulate the independent expenditures of unincorporated labor unions." While "unincorporated unions, and indeed individuals, may be able to amass large treasuries, they do so without the significant state-conferred advantages of the corporate structure." Moreover, a union may not compel those employees to support financially "union activities beyond those germane to collective bargaining, contract administration, and grievance adjustment."

The Chamber also contended that the Act violated the Equal Protection Clause because it excepted the independent expenditures of corporations engaged in the media business. Michigan included the exception because it anticipated that the "Act's definition of 'expenditure' conceivably could be interpreted to encompass election-related news stories and editorials." While "the press' unique societal role may not entitle the press greater protection under the Constitution, it does provide a compelling reason for the State to exempt media corporations from the scope of political expenditure limitations."

Concurring, Justice Brennan stated: "The Michigan law at issue is not an across-the-board prohibition on political participation by corporations or even a complete ban on corporate political expenditures." Justice Brennan disagreed with Justice Kennedy's claim that the limitation on independent expenditures applied to groups like the Sierra Club and the American Civil Liberties Union. Such situations could be resolved with as-applied challenges under *MCFL*.

In his separate concurrence, Justice Stevens suggested that "the distinctions between individual expenditures and individual contributions that the Court identified in *Buckley v. Valeo*, should have little, if any, weight" here as the corporate context increased the risk of actual or perceived "*quid pro quo* relationships."

Justice Scalia began his dissent: "Attention all citizens. To assure the fairness of elections by preventing disproportionate expression of the views of any single powerful group, your Government has decided that the following associations of persons shall be prohibited from speaking or writing in support of any candidate." Justice Scalia describe the majority opinion as an "Orwellian" abbreviation of "the absolutely central truth of the First Amendment: that government cannot be trusted to assure, through censorship the 'fairness' of political debate." By requiring separate funds, "the corporation as a corporation is prohibited from speaking."

In considering the privileged position of the corporation, Justice Scalia asserted that "the State cannot exact as the price of those special advantages the forfeiture of First Amendment rights." He also rejected the association of wealth with corruption.

Justice Kennedy, joined by Justices Scalia and O'Connor, filed a separate dissenting opinion. The majority's opinion validates two kinds of censorship. First, "the Court upholds a direct restriction on the independent expenditure of funds for political speech for the first time in history." Second, the Court is creating through its decision a "value-laden, content-based speech suppression that permits some nonprofit corporate groups but not others to engage in political speech."

No compelling state interest justifies the Act's distinctions based both on the subject of the speech (candidate elections), and on the identity of the speakers (corporations). The majority's decision abandons the distinctions "between payments to candidates ('contributions') and payments to express one's own vices ('independent expenditures')." The "corrosive and distorting effects of immense aggregations of wealth" outline an ambiguous definition of corruption, far removed from the *quid pro quo* variety. "While it is questionable whether such imprecision would suffice to justify restricting political speech by for-profit corporations, it is certain that it does not apply to nonprofit entities." Both *Buckley* and *Bellotti* "rejected the argument that the expenditure of money to increase the quantity of political speech somehow fosters corruption."

The statute is "overinclusive because it covers all groups which use the corporate form, including all nonprofit corporations." It also "assumes that the government has a legitimate interest in equalizing the relative influence of the speakers."

The statute suggested alternatives for political speech that are far less advantageous. One suggested alternative, the political action committee, consumes from 25 to 50 percent of its resources for administration.

Likewise, the practice of insulating views inconsistent with the corporations was rejected by *Bellotti*. Members harboring conflicting views may "seek change from within, withhold financial support, cease to associate with the group or form a rival group of their own." By prohibiting corporations from announcing their views on candidates for office, the "Court . . . now becomes itself the censor."

NOTE

For discussions of the constitutional legal rights afforded to corporations, see Daniel J. H. Greenwood, *Essential Speech: Why Corporate Speech Is Not Free*, 83 IOWA L. REV. 995, 1070 (1998) ("Ford, the man, must decide whether to pursue his class interests, narrowly defined, or to pursue the public interest as he or others see it; Ford, the corporation, is directed by law and market not to make that choice or consider the consequences of that decision."); Charles D. Watts, Jr., *Corporate Legal Theory Under the First Amendment: Bellotti and Austin*, 46 U. MIAMI L. REV. 317, 377 (1991) ("[E]xplicit consideration of the appropriate societal role for corporations is important today, and promises to become more so as national borders recede in the face of global economic competition. Controversies over the constitutional rights of corporations generally, and their First Amendment rights more specifically, provide an opportunity for defining the societal role of corporations.").

One commentator observed that, pre-*Austin*, "the Court committed itself to two propositions" regarding campaign finance. "First, neither political equality nor enhancement of democratic dialogue is a permissible legislative goal under the First Amendment, at least if the pursuit of either entails 'restricting the speech of some elements of our society in order to enhance the relative voice of others,' or requires a serious incursion into editorial autonomy. . . . Second, the Court's rulings suggested that the only permissible purpose of limiting campaign contributions is to prevent the reality and the appearance of corruption, corruption being narrowly defined as a 'quid pro quo' exchange of money for the political favor of office holders or candidates. However, by accepting an expansive corruption-prevention rationale for the challenged restriction on independent expenditures by corporations in *Austin*, the Court itself cast doubt on the continuing validity of this second proposition." *See* Lillian R. Bevier, *Campaign Finance Reform: Specious Arguments, Intractable Dilemmas*, 94 COLUM. L. REV. 1258, 1258 (1994).

McCONNELL v. FEDERAL ELECTION COMMISSION
540 U.S. 93, 124 S. Ct. 619, 157 L. Ed. 2d 491 (2003)

JUSTICE STEVENS and JUSTICE O'CONNOR delivered the opinion of the Court with respect to BCRA Titles I and II.[18]

The Bipartisan Campaign Reform Act of 2002 (BCRA), contains a series of amendments to the Federal Election Campaign Act of 1971 (FECA), 2 U.S.C.A. § 431, et seq., the Communications Act of 1934, 48 Stat. 1088, as amended, 47 U.S.C.A. § 315, and other portions of the United States Code, 18 U.S.C.A. § 607, 36 U.S.C.A. §§ 510-511, that are challenged in these cases. In this opinion we discuss Titles I and II of BCRA. The opinion of the Court delivered by The Chief Justice, discusses Titles III and IV, and the opinion of the Court delivered by Justice Breyer, discusses Title V.

I

More than a century ago the "sober-minded Elihu Root" advocated legislation that would prohibit political contributions by corporations in order to prevent " 'the great aggregations of wealth, from using their corporate funds, directly or indirectly,' " to elect legislators who would " 'vote for their protection and the advancement of their interests as against those of the public.' " *United States v. Automobile Workers*, 352 U.S. 567, 571 (1957) (quoting E. Root, Addresses on Government and Citizenship 143 (R. Bacon & J. Scott eds. 1916)). . . . The Congress of the United States has repeatedly enacted legislation endorsing Root's judgment.

BCRA is the most recent federal enactment designed "to purge national politics of what was conceived to be the pernicious influence of 'big money' campaign contributions." *Id.* at 572. . . .

---

[18] [Court's footnote *] JUSTICE SOUTER, JUSTICE GINSBURG, and JUSTICE BREYER join this opinion in its entirety.

Our opinion in *Buckley* [*v. Valeo*] addressed issues that primarily related to contributions and expenditures by individuals, since none of the parties challenged the prohibition on contributions by corporations and labor unions. . . .

Three important developments in the years after our decision in Buckley persuaded Congress that further legislation was necessary to regulate the role that corporations, unions, and wealthy contributors play in the electoral process. . . .

Soft Money

. . . [P]rior to the enactment of BCRA, federal law permitted corporations and unions, as well as individuals who had already made the maximum permissible contributions to federal candidates, to contribute "nonfederal money" — also known as "soft money" — to political parties for activities intended to influence state or local elections.

Shortly after *Buckley* was decided, . . . the FEC ruled that political parties could fund mixed-purpose activities — including get-out-the-vote drives and generic party advertising — in part with soft money. In 1995 the FEC concluded that the parties could also use soft money to defray the costs of "legislative advocacy media advertisements," even if the ads mentioned the name of a federal candidate, so long as they did not expressly advocate the candidate's election or defeat. FEC Advisory Op. 1995-25.

As the permissible uses of soft money expanded, the amount of soft money raised and spent by the national political parties increased exponentially. Of the two major parties' total spending, soft money accounted for 5% ($21.6 million) in 1984, 11% ($45 million) in 1988, 16% ($80 million) in 1992, 30% ($272 million) in 1996, and 42% ($498 million) in 2000. The national parties transferred large amounts of their soft money to the state parties, which were allowed to use a larger percentage of soft money to finance mixed-purpose activities under FEC rules. In the year 2000, for example, the national parties diverted $280 million — more than half of their soft money — to state parties.

Many contributions of soft money were dramatically larger than the contributions of hard money permitted by FECA. . . . In the most recent election cycle the political parties raised almost $300 million — 60% of their total softmoney fundraising — from just 800 donors, each of which contributed a minimum of $120,000. . . .

Not only were such softmoney contributions often designed to gain access to federal candidates, but they were in many cases solicited by the candidates themselves. . . . [19]

Issue Advertising

In *Buckley* we construed FECA's disclosure and reporting requirements, as well as its expenditure limitations, "to reach only funds used for communications that expressly advocate the election or defeat of a clearly identified candidate." 424 U.S. at 80 (footnote omitted). As a result of that strict reading of the statute, the use or omission of "magic words" such as "Elect John Smith" or "Vote Against Jane Doe" marked a bright statutory line separating "express advocacy" from "issue advocacy." *See id.* at 44,

---

[19] [Court's footnote 15] . . . One former party official explained to the District Court: " 'Once you've helped a federal candidate by contributing hard money to his or her campaign, you are sometimes asked to do more for the candidate by making donations of hard and/or soft money to the national party committees, the relevant state party (assuming it can accept corporate contributions), or an outside group that is planning on doing an independent expenditure or issue advertisement to help the candidate's campaign.' " [*McConnell v. Fed. Election Comm'n,*] 251 F. Supp. 2d [176,] 479 [(D.D.C. 2003)] (Kollar-Kotelly, J.).

n.52. . . . So-called issue ads, on the other hand, not only could be financed with soft money, but could be aired without disclosing the identity of, or any other information about, their sponsors. . . .

. . . Corporations and unions spent hundreds of millions of dollars of their general funds to pay for these ads,[20] and those expenditures, like softmoney donations to the political parties, were unregulated under FECA. . . .

Senate Committee Investigation

In 1998 the Senate Committee on Governmental Affairs issued a six volume report summarizing the results of an extensive investigation into the campaign practices in the 1996 federal elections. . . .

The report . . . concluded that both parties promised and provided special access to candidates and senior Government officials in exchange for large softmoney contributions. . . .

In 1996 both parties began to use large amounts of soft money to pay for issue advertising designed to influence federal elections. The Committee found such ads highly problematic for two reasons. Since they accomplished the same purposes as express advocacy (which could lawfully be funded only with hard money), the ads enabled unions, corporations, and wealthy contributors to circumvent protections that FECA was intended to provide. Moreover, though ostensibly independent of the candidates, the ads were often actually coordinated with, and controlled by, the campaigns. The ads thus provided a means for evading FECA's candidate contribution limits.

The report also emphasized the role of state and local parties. While the FEC's allocation regime permitted national parties to use soft money to pay for up to 40% of the costs of both generic voter activities and issue advertising, they allowed state and local parties to use larger percentages of soft money for those purposes. For that reason, national parties often made substantial transfers of soft money to "state and local political parties for 'generic voter activities' that in fact ultimately benefit[ed] federal candidates because the funds for all practical purposes remain[ed] under the control of the national committees." . . .

II

In BCRA, Congress enacted many of the committee's proposed reforms. BCRA's central provisions are designed to address Congress' concerns about the increasing use of soft money and issue advertising to influence federal elections. Title I regulates the use of soft money by political parties, officeholders, and candidates. Title II primarily prohibits corporations and labor unions from using general treasury funds for communications that are intended to, or have the effect of, influencing the outcome of federal elections. . . .

---

[20] [Court's footnote 20] . . . In the 1996 election cycle, $135 to $150 million was spent on multiple broadcasts of about 100 ads. In the next cycle (1997-1998), 77 organizations aired 423 ads at a total cost between $270 and $340 million. By the 2000 election, 130 groups spent over an estimated $500 million on more than 1,100 different ads. Two out of every three dollars spent on issue ads in the 2000 cycle were attributable to the two major parties and six major interest groups.

III

Title I is Congress' effort to plug the softmoney loophole. The cornerstone of Title I is new FECA § 323(a), which prohibits national party committees and their agents from soliciting, receiving, directing, or spending any soft money. In short, § 323(a) takes national parties out of the softmoney business.

The remaining provisions of new FECA § 323 largely reinforce the restrictions in § 323(a). New FECA § 323(b) prevents the wholesale shift of softmoney influence from national to state party committees by prohibiting state and local party committees from using such funds for activities that affect federal elections. . . . New FECA § 323(d) reinforces these softmoney restrictions by prohibiting political parties from soliciting and donating funds to tax-exempt organizations that engage in electioneering activities. New FECA § 323(e) restricts federal candidates and officeholders from receiving, spending, or soliciting soft money in connection with federal elections and limits their ability to do so in connection with state and local elections. Finally, new FECA § 323(f) prevents circumvention of the restrictions on national, state, and local party committees by prohibiting state and local candidates from raising and spending soft money to fund advertisements and other public communications that promote or attack federal candidates.

Plaintiffs mount a facial First Amendment challenge to new FECA § 323, as well as challenges based on the Elections Clause, U.S. Const., Art. I, § 4, principles of federalism, and the equal protection component of the Due Process Clause. We address these challenges in turn.

A

In *Buckley* and subsequent cases, we have subjected restrictions on campaign expenditures to closer scrutiny than limits on campaign contributions. . . .

We have recognized that contribution limits may bear "more heavily on the associational right than on freedom to speak," *Shrink Missouri, supra*, at 388, since contributions serve "to affiliate a person with a candidate" and "enabl[e] like-minded persons to pool their resources," *Buckley*, 424 U.S. at 22. Unlike expenditure limits, however, which "preclud[e] most associations from effectively amplifying the voice of their adherents," contribution limits both "leave the contributor free to become a member of any political association and to assist personally in the association's efforts on behalf of candidates," and allow associations "to aggregate large sums of money to promote effective advocacy." *Id.* The "overall effect" of dollar limits on contributions is "merely to require candidates and political committees to raise funds from a greater number of persons." *Id.* at 21-22. Thus, a contribution limit involving even " 'significant interference' " with associational rights is nevertheless valid if it satisfies the "lesser demand" of being " 'closely drawn' " to match a " 'sufficiently important interest.' " *Beaumont*, 539 U.S. 146, at 162 (quoting *Shrink Missouri, supra*, at 387-388).

Our treatment of contribution restrictions . . . reflects the importance of the interests that underlie contribution limits — interests in preventing "both the actual corruption threatened by large financial contributions and the eroding of public confidence in the electoral process through the appearance of corruption." *National Right to Work*, 459 U.S. at 208. . . . It also provides Congress with sufficient room to anticipate and respond to concerns about circumvention of regulations designed to protect the integrity of the political process.

. . . Complex as its provisions may be, § 323, in the main, does little more than regulate the ability of wealthy individuals, corporations, and unions to contribute large sums of money to influence federal elections, federal candidates, and federal officeholders.

Plaintiffs contend that we must apply strict scrutiny to § 323 because many of its provisions restrict not only contributions but also the spending and solicitation of funds raised outside of FECA's contribution limits. But for purposes of determining the level of scrutiny, it is irrelevant that Congress chose in § 323 to regulate contributions on the demand rather than the supply side. *See, e.g., National Right to Work, supra,* at 206-21 (upholding a provision restricting PACs' ability to solicit funds). The relevant inquiry is whether the mechanism adopted to implement the contribution limit, or to prevent circumvention of that limit, burdens speech in a way that a direct restriction on the contribution itself would not. That is not the case here.

. . . The fact that party committees and federal candidates and officeholders must now ask only for limited dollar amounts or request that a corporation or union contribute money through its PAC in no way alters or impairs the political message "intertwined" with the solicitation. . . . And rather than chill such solicitations . . . the restriction here tends to increase the dissemination of information by forcing parties, candidates, and officeholders to solicit from a wider array of potential donors. As with direct limits on contributions, therefore, § 323's spending and solicitation restrictions have only a marginal impact on political speech.

. . . Section 323 merely subjects a greater percentage of contributions to parties and candidates to FECA's source and amount limitations. . . . [21]

New FECA § 323(a)'s Restrictions on National Party Committees

The core of Title I is new FECA § 323(a). . . .

The main goal of § 323(a) is modest. In large part, it simply effects a return to the scheme that was approved in *Buckley* and that was subverted by the creation of the FEC's allocation regime, which permitted the political parties to fund federal electioneering efforts with a combination of hard and soft money. . . .

1. *Governmental Interests Underlying New FECA § 323(a)*

. . . "The quantum of empirical evidence needed to satisfy heightened judicial scrutiny of legislative judgments will vary up or down with the novelty or the plausibility of the justification raised." *Shrink Missouri, supra,* at 391. The idea that large contributions to a national party can corrupt or, at the very least, create the appearance of corruption of federal candidates and officeholders is neither novel nor implausible. . . .

. . . Parties kept tallies of the amounts of soft money raised by each officeholder, and "the amount of money a Member of Congress raise[d] for the national political committees often affect[ed] the amount the committees g[a]ve to assist the Member's campaign." 251 F. Supp. 2d at 474-475 (Kollar-Kotelly, J.). Donors often asked that their contributions be credited to particular candidates, and the parties obliged, irrespective of whether the funds were hard or soft. *Id.* at 477-478 (Kollar-Kotelly, J.); *id.* at 824, 847 (Leon, J.). National party committees often teamed with individual candidates' campaign committees to create joint fundraising committees. . . . [22]

---

[21] [Court's footnote 43] Justice Kennedy is no doubt correct that the associational burdens imposed by a particular piece of campaign-finance regulation may at times be so severe as to warrant strict scrutiny. *Id.* In light of our interpretation of § 323(a), however, § 323 does not present such a case. . . .

[22] [Court's footnote 46] . . . Particularly telling is the fact that, in 1996 and 2000, more than half of the top

. . . The evidence connects soft money to manipulations of the legislative calendar, leading to Congress' failure to enact, among other things, generic drug legislation, tort reform, and tobacco legislation. . . .

More importantly, plaintiffs conceive of corruption too narrowly. . . . Many of the "deeply disturbing examples" of corruption cited by this Court in *Buckley*, 424 U.S. at 27, to justify FECA's contribution limits were not episodes of vote buying, but evidence that various corporate interests had given substantial donations to gain access to high-level government officials. . . .

The record in the present case is replete with similar examples of national party committees peddling access to federal candidates and officeholders in exchange for large softmoney donations. . . .

. . . Justice Kennedy would limit Congress' regulatory interest only to the prevention of the actual or apparent *quid pro quo* corruption "inherent in" contributions made directly to, contributions made at the express behest of, and expenditures made in coordination with, a federal officeholder or candidate. . . .

. . . Just as troubling to a functioning democracy as classic *quid pro quo* corruption is the danger that officeholders will decide issues not on the merits or the desires of their constituencies, but according to the wishes of those who have made large financial contributions valued by the officeholder. . . .

2. *New FECA § 323(a)'s Restriction on Spending and Receiving Soft Money*

Plaintiffs and the Chief Justice contend that § 323(a) is impermissibly overbroad because it subjects all funds raised and spent by national parties to FECA's hard-money source and amount limits, including, for example, funds spent on purely state and local elections in which no federal office is at stake. . . .

. . . The national committees of the two major parties are both run by, and largely composed of, federal officeholders and candidates. . . .

Given this close connection and alignment of interests, large softmoney contributions to national parties are likely to create actual or apparent indebtedness on the part of federal officeholders, regardless of how those funds are ultimately used.

. . . Access to federal officeholders is the most valuable favor the national party committees are able to give in exchange for large donations. The fact that officeholders comply by donating their valuable time indicates either that officeholders place substantial value on the softmoney contribution themselves, without regard to their end use, or that national committees are able to exert considerable control over federal officeholders. . . . The Government's strong interests in preventing corruption, and in particular the appearance of corruption, are thus sufficient to justify subjecting all donations to national parties to the source, amount, and disclosure limitations of FECA.

3. *New FECA § 323(a)'s Restriction on Soliciting or Directing Soft Money*

Plaintiffs also contend that § 323(a)'s prohibition on national parties' soliciting or directing softmoney contributions is substantially overbroad. The reach of the solicitation prohibition, however, is limited. It bars only solicitations of soft money by national party committees and by party officers in their official capacities. The committees remain free to solicit hard money on their own behalf, as well as to solicit

---

50 softmoney donors gave substantial sums to both major national parties, leaving room for no other conclusion but that these donors were seeking influence, or avoiding retaliation, rather than promoting any particular ideology. . . .

hard money on behalf of state committees and state and local candidates.[23] They also can contribute hard money to state committees and to candidates. In accordance with FEC regulations, furthermore, officers of national parties are free to solicit soft money in their individual capacities, or, if they are also officials of state parties, in that capacity. . . .

4. *New FECA § 323(a)'s Application to Minor Parties*

The McConnell and political party plaintiffs contend that § 323(a) is substantially overbroad and must be stricken on its face because it impermissibly infringes the speech and associational rights of minor parties such as the Libertarian National Committee, which, owing to their slim prospects for electoral success and the fact that they receive few large soft- money contributions from corporate sources, pose no threat of corruption comparable to that posed by the RNC and DNC. In *Buckley*, we rejected a similar argument concerning limits on contributions to minor-party candidates. . . . We have thus recognized that the relevance of the interest in avoiding actual or apparent corruption is not a function of the number of legislators a given party manages to elect. . . . It is therefore reasonable to require that all parties and all candidates follow the same set of rules designed to protect the integrity of the electoral process.

We add that nothing in § 323(a) prevents individuals from pooling resources to start a new national party. Only when an organization has gained official status, which carries with it significant benefits for its members, will the proscriptions of § 323(a) apply. Even then, a nascent or struggling minor party can bring an as-applied challenge if § 323(a) prevents it from "amassing the resources necessary for effective advocacy." *Buckley, supra,* at 21.

5. *New FECA § 323(a)'s Associational Burdens*

Finally, plaintiffs assert that § 323(a) is unconstitutional because it impermissibly interferes with the ability of national committees to associate with state and local committees. . . .

. . . As long as the national party officer does not personally spend, receive, direct, or solicit soft money, § 323(a) permits a wide range of joint planning and electioneering activity. Intervenor-defendants, the principal drafters and proponents of the legislation, concede as much. . . .

. . . Moreover, § 323(a) leaves national party committee officers entirely free to participate, in their official capacities, with state and local parties and candidates in soliciting and spending hard money; party officials may also solicit soft money in their unofficial capacities. . . .

Accordingly, we reject the plaintiffs' First Amendment challenge to new FECA § 323(a).

---

[23] [Court's footnote 52] Plaintiffs claim that the option of soliciting hard money for state and local candidates is an illusory one, since several States prohibit state and local candidates from establishing multiple campaign accounts, which would preclude them from establishing separate accounts for federal funds. . . . But the challenge we are considering is a facial one, and on its face § 323(a) permits solicitations. The fact that a handful of States might interfere with the mechanism Congress has chosen for such solicitations is an argument that may be addressed in an as-applied challenge.

New FECA § 323(b)'s Restrictions on State and Local Party Committees

. . . Section 323(b) is designed to foreclose wholesale evasion of § 323(a)'s anticorruption measures by sharply curbing state committees' ability to use large softmoney contributions to influence federal elections. . . .

Section 323(b)(2), the so-called Levin Amendment. . . allows state and local party committees to pay for certain types of federal election activity with an allocated ratio of hard money and "Levin funds" — that is, funds raised within an annual limit of $10,000 per person. . . .

. . . [S]tate and local parties can use Levin money to fund only activities that fall within categories (1) and (2) of the statute's definition of federal election activity — namely, voter registration activity, voter identification drives, [Get Out the Vote] drives, and generic campaign activities [promoting a party rather than a particular candidate]. . . .

1. *Governmental Interests Underlying New FECA § 323(b)*

. . .We "must accord substantial deference to the predictive judgments of Congress," *Turner Broadcasting System, Inc. v. FCC*, 512 U.S. 622, 665 (1994), particularly when, as here, those predictions are so firmly rooted in relevant history and common sense. Preventing corrupting activity from shifting wholesale to state committees and thereby eviscerating FECA clearly qualifies as an important governmental interest.

2. *New FECA § 323(b)'s Tailoring*

Plaintiffs argue that even if some legitimate interest might be served by § 323(b) . . . the provision is substantially overbroad because it federalizes activities that pose no conceivable risk of corrupting or appearing to corrupt federal officeholders. . .

a. *§ 323(b)'s Application to Federal Election Activity* . . .

. . . § 323(b) is narrowly focused on regulating contributions that pose the greatest risk of . . . corruption: those contributions to state and local parties that can be used to benefit federal candidates directly. . . . We conclude that § 323(b) is a closely-drawn means of countering both corruption and the appearance of corruption. . . . [24]

b. *Associational Burdens Imposed by the Levin Amendment*

Plaintiffs also contend that § 323(b) is unconstitutional because the Levin Amendment unjustifiably burdens association among party committees by forbidding transfers of Levin funds among state parties, transfers of hard money to fund the allocable federal portion of Levin expenditures, and joint fundraising of Levin funds by state parties. . . .

. . . Without the ban on transfers of Levin funds among state committees, donors could readily circumvent the $10,000 limit on contributions to a committee's Levin account by making multiple $10,000 donations to various committees that could then transfer the donations to the committee of choice. . . .

---

[24] [Court's footnote 64] We likewise reject the argument that § 301(20)(A)(iii) is unconstitutionally vague. . . .

c. *New FECA § 323(b)'s Impact on Parties' Ability to Engage in Effective Advocacy*

Finally, plaintiffs contend that § 323(b) is unconstitutional because its restrictions on softmoney contributions to state and local party committees will prevent them from engaging in effective advocacy. . . . If the history of campaign finance regulation discussed above proves anything, it is that political parties are extraordinarily flexible in adapting to new restrictions on their fundraising abilities. . . . The question is not whether § 323(b) reduces the amount of funds available over previous election cycles, but whether it is "so radical in effect as to . . . drive the sound of [the recipient's] voice below the level of notice." *Shrink Missouri*, 528 U.S. at 397. If indeed state or local parties can make such a showing, as-applied challenges remain available.

We accordingly conclude that § 323(b), on its face, is closely drawn to match the important governmental interests of preventing corruption and the appearance of corruption.

New FECA § 323(d)'s Restrictions on Parties' Solicitations for, and Donations to, Tax-Exempt Organizations

Section 323(d) prohibits national, state, and local party committees, and their agents or subsidiaries, from "solicit[ing] any funds for, or mak[ing] or direct[ing] any donations" to, any organization established under § 501(c) of the Internal Revenue Code[25] that makes expenditures in connection with an election for federal office, and any political organizations established under § 527 "other than a political committee, a State, district, or local committee of a political party, or the authorized campaign committee of a candidate for State or local office." 2 U.S.C.A. § 441i(d). . . .

1. *New FECA § 323(d)'s Regulation of Solicitations*

The Government defends § 323(d)'s ban on solicitations to tax-exempt organizations engaged in political activity as preventing circumvention of Title I's limits on contributions of soft money to national, state, and local party committees. That justification is entirely reasonable. . . . Absent the solicitation provision, national, state, and local party committees would have significant incentives to mobilize their formidable fundraising apparatuses, including the peddling of access to federal officeholders, into the service of like-minded tax-exempt organizations that conduct activities benefiting their candidates. . . .

Section 323(d)'s solicitation restriction is closely drawn to prevent political parties from using tax-exempt organizations as softmoney surrogates. . . .

2. *New FECA § 323(d)'s Regulation of Donations*

Section 323(d) also prohibits national, state, and local party committees from making or directing "any donatio[n]" to qualifying § 501(c) or § 527 organizations. 2 U.S.C.A. § 441i(d) (Supp. 2003). The Government again defends the restriction as an anticircumvention measure. We agree insofar as it prohibits the donation of soft money. . . . We will not disturb Congress' reasonable decision to close that loophole. . . .

---

[25] [Court's footnote 66] Section 501(c) organizations are groups generally exempted from taxation under the Internal Revenue Code. 26 U.S.C. § 501(a). These include § 501(c)(3) charitable and educational organizations, as well as § 501(c)(4) social welfare groups.

The prohibition does raise overbreadth concerns if read to restrict donations from a party's federal account — i.e., funds that have already been raised in compliance with FECA's source, amount, and disclosure limitations. Parties have many valid reasons for giving to tax-exempt organizations, not the least of which is to associate themselves with certain causes and, in so doing, to demonstrate the values espoused by the party. . . .

New FECA § 323(e)'s Restrictions on Federal Candidates and Officeholders

New FECA § 323(e) . . . prohibits federal candidates and officeholders from "solicit[ing], receiv[ing], direct[ing], transfer[ing], or spend[ing]" any soft money in connection with federal elections. § 441i(e)(1)(A). It also limits the ability of federal candidates and officeholders to solicit, receive, direct, transfer, or spend soft money in connection with state and local elections. . . .

No party seriously questions the constitutionality of § 323(e)'s general ban on donations of soft money made directly to federal candidates and officeholders, their agents, or entities established or controlled by them. Even on the narrowest reading of *Buckley*, a regulation restricting donations to a federal candidate, regardless of the ends to which those funds are ultimately put, qualifies as a contribution limit subject to less rigorous scrutiny. . . .

. . . Rather than place an outright ban on solicitations to tax-exempt organizations, § 323(e)(4) permits limited solicitations of soft money. . . .   Similarly, §§ 323(e)(1)(B) and 323(e)(3) preserve the traditional fundraising role of federal officeholders by providing limited opportunities for federal candidates and officeholders to associate with their state and local colleagues through joint fundraising activities. . . .

New FECA § 323(f)'s Restrictions on State Candidates and Officeholders

. . . Section 323(f) generally prohibits candidates for state or local office, or state or local officeholders, from spending soft money to fund "public communications" as defined in § 301(20)(A)(iii) — i.e., a communication that "refers to a clearly identified candidate for Federal office . . . and that promotes or supports a candidate for that office, or attacks or opposes a candidate for that office." 2 U.S.C.A. § 441i(f)(1); § 431(20)(A)(iii). . . .

Section 323(f) places no cap on the amount of money that state or local candidates can spend on any activity. Rather, like §§ 323(a) and 323(b), it limits only the source and amount of contributions that state and local candidates can draw on to fund expenditures that directly impact federal elections. And, by regulating only contributions used to fund "public communications," § 323(f) focuses narrowly on those softmoney donations with the greatest potential to corrupt or give rise to the appearance of corruption of federal candidates and officeholders. . . .

B

[The Court rejected federalism challenges against the Act, noting that it only regulates private individuals whom Congress could regulate under its Election Clause power.]

C

Finally, plaintiffs argue that Title I violates the equal protection component of the Due Process Clause of the Fifth Amendment because it discriminates against political parties in favor of special interest groups such as the National Rifle Association (NRA),

American Civil Liberties Union (ACLU), and Sierra Club. . . .

. . . Interest groups do not select slates of candidates for elections. Interest groups do not determine who will serve on legislative committees, elect congressional leadership, or organize legislative caucuses. Political parties have influence and power in the legislature that vastly exceeds that of any interest group. . . .

IV. . .

BCRA § 201's Definition of "Electioneering Communication"

The first section of Title II, § 201 . . . coins a new term, "electioneering communication," to replace the narrowing construction of FECA's disclosure provisions adopted by this Court in *Buckley*. As discussed further below, that construction limited the coverage of FECA's disclosure requirement to communications expressly advocating the election or defeat of particular candidates. By contrast, the term "electioneering communication" is not so limited, but is defined to encompass any "broadcast, cable, or satellite communication" that "(I) refers to a clearly identified candidate for Federal office. . . . "

. . . BCRA's use of this new term is not, however, limited to the disclosure context: A later section of the Act (BCRA § 203 . . .) restricts corporations' and labor unions' funding of electioneering communications. Plaintiffs challenge the constitutionality of the new term as it applies in both the disclosure and the expenditure contexts.

The major premise of plaintiffs' challenge to BCRA's use of the term "electioneering communication" is that *Buckley* drew a constitutionally mandated line between express advocacy and so-called issue advocacy, and that speakers possess an inviolable First Amendment right to engage in the latter category of speech. . . .

That position misapprehends our prior decisions, for the express advocacy restriction was an endpoint of statutory interpretation, not a first principle of constitutional law. In *Buckley* we . . . provided examples of words of express advocacy, such as " 'vote for,' 'elect,' 'support,' . . . 'defeat,' [and] 'reject,' " *id.* at 44, n.52, and those examples eventually gave rise to what is now known as the "magic words" requirement. . . .

. . . In narrowly reading the FECA provisions in *Buckley* to avoid problems of vagueness and overbreadth, we nowhere suggested that a statute that was neither vague nor overbroad would be required to toe the same express advocacy line. . . .

BCRA § 201's Disclosure Requirements

. . . [W]e turn to . . . § 304's disclosure provisions. . . .

We agree with the District Court that the important state interests that prompted the *Buckley* Court to uphold FECA's disclosure requirements — providing the electorate with information, deterring actual corruption and avoiding any appearance thereof, and gathering the data necessary to enforce more substantive electioneering restrictions — apply in full to BCRA. Accordingly, *Buckley* amply supports application of FECA § 304's disclosure requirements to the entire range of "electioneering communications." . . .

The District Court was also correct that *Buckley* forecloses a facial attack on the new provision in § 304 that requires disclosure of the names of persons contributing $1,000 or more to segregated funds or individuals that spend more than $10,000 in a calendar year on electioneering communications. . . .

". . . Minor parties must be allowed sufficient flexibility in the proof of injury to assure a fair consideration of their claim. The evidence offered need show only a reasonable probability that the compelled disclosure of a party's contributors' names will subject them to threats, harassment, or reprisals from either Government officials or private parties." *Id.* at 74. . . .

In this litigation the District Court applied *Buckley's* evidentiary standard and found . . . that the evidence did not establish the requisite "reasonable probability" of harm to any plaintiff group or its members. . . .

We also are unpersuaded by plaintiffs' challenge to new FECA § 304(f)(5), which requires disclosure of executory contracts for electioneering communications. . . .

As the District Court observed . . . the required disclosures " 'would not have to reveal the specific content of the advertisements, yet they would perform an important function in informing the public about various candidates' supporters *before* election day.' " 251 F. Supp. 2d at 241. . . .

BCRA § 202's Treatment of "Coordinated Communications" as Contributions

Section 202 . . . provide[s] that disbursements for "electioneering communication[s]" that are coordinated with a candidate or party will be treated as contributions to, and expenditures by, that candidate or party. . . . [T]here is no reason why Congress may not treat coordinated disbursements for electioneering communications in the same way it treats all other coordinated expenditures. . . .

BCRA § 203's Prohibition of Corporate and Labor Disbursements for Electioneering Communications

Since our decision in *Buckley*, Congress' power to prohibit corporations and unions from using funds in their treasuries to finance advertisements expressly advocating the election or defeat of candidates in federal elections has been firmly embedded in our law. . . .

Section 203 of BCRA . . . extend[s] this rule . . . to all "electioneering communications". . . . Thus, under BCRA, corporations and unions may not use their general treasury funds to finance electioneering communications, but they remain free to organize and administer segregated funds, or PACs, for that purpose. . . .

. . . [P]laintiffs . . . challenge the expanded regulation on the grounds that it is both overbroad and underinclusive. . . .

. . . Even if we assumed that BCRA will inhibit some constitutionally protected corporate and union speech, that assumption would not "justify prohibiting all enforcement" of the law unless its application to protected speech is substantial, "not only in an absolute sense, but also relative to the scope of the law's plainly legitimate applications." *Virginia v. Hicks*, 539 U.S. 113 (2003). . . .

Plaintiffs also argue that FECA § 316(b)(2)'s segregated-fund requirement for electioneering communications is underinclusive because it does not apply to advertising in the print media or on the Internet. The records developed in this litigation and by the Senate Committee adequately explain the reasons for this legislative choice. . . . As we held in *Buckley*, "reform may take one step at a time. . . . " 424 U.S. at 105. . . .

In addition to arguing that [the] segregated-fund requirement is underinclusive, some plaintiffs contend that it unconstitutionally discriminates in favor of media companies. . . . Plaintiffs argue this provision gives free rein to media companies to engage in speech without resort to PAC money. . . . "A valid distinction . . . exists between corporations that are part of the media industry and other corporations that are not involved in the regular business of imparting news to the public." *Austin*, 494 U.S. at 668. . . .

BCRA § 204's Application to Nonprofit Corporations

Section 204 of BCRA . . . applies the prohibition on the use of general treasury funds to pay for electioneering communications to not-for-profit corporations. . . .

Because our decision in the [*Fed. Election Comm'n v. Massachusetts Citizens For Life*, 479 U.S. 146 (2003)] case was on the books for many years before BCRA was enacted, we presume that the legislators who drafted § 316(c)(6) were fully aware that the provision could not validly apply to MCFL-type entities. . . .

BCRA § 213's Requirement that Political Parties Choose Between Coordinated and Independent Expenditures After Nominating a Candidate

Section 213 of BCRA amends FECA § 315(d)(4) to impose certain limits on party spending during the postnomination, preelection period. . . .

. . . A party that wishes to spend more than $5,000 in coordination with its nominee is forced to forgo only the narrow category of independent expenditures that make use of magic words. . . . To survive constitutional scrutiny, a provision that has such consequences must be supported by a meaningful governmental interest.

The interest in requiring political parties to avoid the use of magic words is not such an interest. We held in *Buckley* that a $1,000 cap on expenditures that applied only to express advocacy could not be justified as a means of avoiding circumvention of contribution limits or preventing corruption and the appearance of corruption. . . .

BCRA § 214's Changes in FECA's Provisions Covering Coordinated Expenditures

Ever since our decision in *Buckley*, it has been settled that expenditures by a noncandidate that are "controlled by or coordinated with the candidate and his campaign" may be treated as indirect contributions subject to FECA's source and amount limitations. 424 U.S. at 46. . . . Section 214(a) of BCRA . . . applies the same rule to expenditures coordinated with "a national, State, or local committee of a political party." 2 U.S.C.A. § 441a(a)(7)(B)(ii). . . . Subsection (c) provides that the new "regulations shall not require agreement or formal collaboration to establish coordination." 2 U.S.C.A. § 441a(a) note.

Plaintiffs do not dispute that Congress may apply the same coordination rules to parties as to candidates. They argue instead that new FECA § 315(a)(7)(B)(ii) and its implementing regulations are overbroad and unconstitutionally vague because they permit a finding of coordination even in the absence of an agreement. . . .

. . . By contrast, expenditures made after a "wink or nod" often will be "as useful to the candidate as cash." *Id.* at 442, 446. . . . Therefore, we cannot agree with the submission that new FECA § 315(a)(7)(B)(ii) is overbroad. . . .

V

Many years ago we observed that "[t]o say that Congress is without power to pass appropriate legislation to safeguard . . . an election from the improper use of money to influence the result is to deny to the nation in a vital particular the power of self protection." *Burroughs v. United States*, 290 U.S. at 545. We abide by that conviction in considering Congress' most recent effort to confine the ill effects of aggregated wealth on our political system. . . . In the main we uphold BCRA's two principal, complementary features: the control of soft money and the regulation of electioneering communications. . . .

CHIEF JUSTICE REHNQUIST delivered the opinion of the Court with respect to BCRA Titles III and IV. . . . [26]

BCRA § 311

FECA § 318 requires that certain communications "authorized" by a candidate or his political committee clearly identify the candidate or committee or, if not so authorized, identify the payor and announce the lack of authorization. 2 U.S.C.A. § 441d. . . .

. . . We think BCRA § 311's inclusion of electioneering communications in the FECA § 318 disclosure regime bears a sufficient relationship to the important governmental interest of "shed[ding] the light of publicity" on campaign financing. *Buckley*, 424 U.S. at 81. . . .

BCRA § 318

BCRA § 318. . . prohibits individuals "17 years old or younger" from making contributions to candidates and contributions or donations to political parties. 2 U.S.C.A. § 441k. . . .

Minors enjoy the protection of the First Amendment. *See, e.g., Tinker v. Des Moines Independent Community School Dist.*, 393 U.S. 503, 511–513 (1969). . . . When the Government burdens the right to contribute, we . . . ask whether there is a "sufficiently important interest" and whether the statute is "closely drawn" to avoid unnecessary abridgment of First Amendment freedoms. The Government asserts that the provision protects against corruption by conduit; that is, donations by parents through their minor children to circumvent contribution limits applicable to the parents. . . .

Even assuming, *arguendo*, the Government advances an important interest, the provision is overinclusive. The States have adopted a variety of more tailored approaches — e.g., counting contributions by minors against the total permitted for a parent or family unit, imposing a lower cap on contributions by minors, and prohibiting contributions by very young children. Without deciding whether any of these alternatives is sufficiently tailored, we hold that the provision here sweeps too broadly. . . .

JUSTICE BREYER delivered the opinion of the Court with respect to BCRA Title V.[27]

We consider here the constitutionality of § 504 [which] requires broadcasters to keep publicly available records of politically related broadcasting requests. . . .

---

[26] [Court's footnote *] JUSTICE O'CONNOR, JUSTICE SCALIA, JUSTICE KENNEDY, and JUSTICE SOUTER join this opinion in its entirety. JUSTICE STEVENS, JUSTICE GINSBURG, and JUSTICE BREYER join this opinion, except with respect to BCRA § 305. JUSTICE THOMAS joins this opinion with respect to BCRA §§ 304, 305, 307, 316, and 319. . . .

[27] [Court's footnote *] JUSTICE STEVENS, JUSTICE O'CONNOR, JUSTICE SOUTER, and JUSTICE GINSBURG join this opinion in its entirety.

II

BCRA § 504's "candidate request" requirements are virtually identical to those contained in a regulation that the Federal Communications Commission (FCC) promulgated as early as 1938. . . .

In its current form the FCC regulation requires broadcast licensees to "keep" a publicly available file "of all requests for broadcast time made by or on behalf of a candidate for public office," along with a notation showing whether the request was granted, and (if granted) a history that includes "classes of time," "rates charged," and when the "spots actually aired." 47 CFR § 73.1943(a) (2002); § 76.1701(a) (same for cable systems). . . .

The McConnell plaintiffs argue that these requirements are "intolerabl[y]" "burdensome and invasive." But we do not see how that could be so. The FCC has consistently estimated that its "candidate request" regulation imposes upon each licensee an additional administrative burden of six to seven hours of work per year. . . .

. . . The FCC has pointed out that "[t]hese records are necessary to permit political candidates and others to verify that licensees have complied with their obligations relating to use of their facilities by candidates for political office" pursuant to the "equal time" provision of 47 U.S.C. § 315(a). 63 Fed.Reg. 49493 (1998). . . . They will help make the public aware of how much money candidates may be prepared to spend on broadcast messages. And they will provide an independently compiled set of data for purposes of verifying candidates' compliance with the disclosure requirements and source limitations of BCRA and the Federal Election Campaign Act of 1971. . . .

III

BCRA § 504's "election message request" requirements call for broadcasters to keep records of requests (made by any member of the public) to broadcast a "message" about "a legally qualified candidate" or "any election to Federal office." 47 U.S.C.A. §§ 315(e)(1)(B)(i), (ii) (Supp. 2003). Although these requirements are somewhat broader than the "candidate request" requirement, they serve much the same purposes. . . .

IV

The "issue request" requirements call for broadcasters to keep records of requests (made by any member of the public) to broadcast "message[s]" about "a national legislative issue of public importance" or "any political matter of national importance." 47 U.S.C.A. §§ 315(e)(1)(B), (e)(1)(B)(iii) (Supp. 2003). These recordkeeping requirements seem likely to help the FCC determine whether broadcasters are carrying out their "obligations to afford reasonable opportunity for the discussion of conflicting views on issues of public importance," 47 CFR § 73.1910 (2002), and whether broadcasters are too heavily favoring entertainment, and discriminating against broadcasts devoted to public affairs, *see id.*; 47 U.S.C. § 315(a); *Red Lion [Broadcasting Co. v. F.C.C.]*, 395 U.S. [367,] 380 [(1969)]. . . .

Whether these requirements impose disproportionate administrative burdens is . . . difficult to say. . . .

The regulatory burden, in practice, will depend on how the FCC interprets and applies this provision. The FCC has adequate legal authority to write regulations that may limit, and make more specific, the provision's potential linguistic reach. . . .

The McConnell plaintiffs and The Chief Justice . . . say that the "issue request" requirement will force them to disclose information that will reveal their political strategies to opponents, perhaps prior to a broadcast. . . . [T]he "strategy disclosure" argument does not show that BCRA § 504 is unconstitutional on its face, but the plaintiffs remain free to raise this argument when § 504 is applied. . . .

JUSTICE SCALIA, concurring with respect to BCRA Titles III and IV, dissenting with respect to BCRA Titles I and V, and concurring in the judgment in part and dissenting in part with respect to BCRA Title II.

With respect to Titles I, II, and V: I join in full the dissent of The Chief Justice; I join the opinion of Justice Kennedy, except to the extent it upholds new § 323(e) of the Federal Election Campaign Act of 1971 (FECA) and § 202 of the Bipartisan Campaign Reform Act of 2002 (BCRA) in part; and because I continue to believe that *Buckley v. Valeo*, 424 U.S. 1 (1976) (*per curiam*), was wrongly decided, I also join Parts I, II-A, and II-B of the opinion of Justice Thomas. With respect to Titles III and IV, I join The Chief Justice's opinion for the Court. . . .

This is a sad day for the freedom of speech. . . . We are governed by Congress, and this legislation prohibits the criticism of Members of Congress by those entities most capable of giving such criticism loud voice: national political parties and corporations, both of the commercial and the not-for-profit sort. It forbids pre-election criticism of incumbents by corporations, even not-for- profit corporations, by use of their general funds; and forbids national-party use of "soft" money to fund "issue ads" that incumbents find so offensive.

To be sure, the legislation is evenhanded. . . . But . . . if incumbents and challengers are limited to the same quantity of electioneering, incumbents are favored. . . .

Beyond that, however, the present legislation *targets* for prohibition certain categories of campaign speech that are particularly harmful to incumbents. Is it accidental, do you think, that incumbents raise about three times as much "hard money" — the sort of funding generally *not* restricted by this legislation — as do their challengers? . . . And is it mere happenstance, do you estimate, that national-party funding, which is severely limited by the Act, is more likely to assist cash-strapped challengers than flush-with-hard-money incumbents? . . . Was it unintended, by any chance, that incumbents are free personally to receive some soft money and even to solicit it for other organizations, while national parties are not? . . .

(a) *Money is Not Speech*

. . . [T]oday's cavalier attitude toward regulating the financing of speech (the "exacting scrutiny" test of *Buckley, see id.*, is not uttered in any majority opinion, and is not observed in the ones from which I dissent) frustrates the fundamental purpose of the First Amendment. . . .

. . . The right to speak would be largely ineffective if it did not include the right to engage in financial transactions that are the incidents of its exercise. . . .

[A] law limiting the amount a person can spend to broadcast his political views is a direct restriction on speech. That is no different from a law limiting the amount a newspaper can pay its editorial staff or the amount a charity can pay its leafletters. It is equally clear that a limit on the amount a candidate can raise from any one individual for the purpose of speaking is also a direct limitation on speech. . . .

(b) *Pooling Money is Not Speech*

Another proposition which could explain at least some of the results of today's opinion is that the First Amendment right to spend money for speech does not include the right to combine with others in spending money for speech. . . . The freedom to associate with others for the dissemination of ideas - . . . by pooling financial resources for expressive purposes — is part of the freedom of speech. . . .

(c) *Speech by Corporations Can Be Abridged*

But what about the danger to the political system posed by "amassed wealth"? The most direct threat from that source comes in the form of undisclosed favors and payoffs to elected officials — which have already been criminalized, and will be rendered no more discoverable by the legislation at issue here. The use of corporate wealth (like individual wealth) to speak to the electorate is unlikely to "distort" elections — *especially* if disclosure requirements *tell* the people where the speech is coming from. . . .

. . . It cannot be denied, however, that corporate (like noncorporate) allies will have greater access to the officeholder, and that he will tend to favor the same causes as those who support him (which is usually *why* they supported him). That is the nature of politics — if not indeed human nature. . . .

But let us not be deceived. While the Government's briefs and arguments before this Court focused on the horrible "appearance of corruption," the most passionate floor statements during the debates on this legislation pertained to so-called attack ads, which the Constitution surely protects, but which Members of Congress analogized to "crack cocaine," 144 Cong. Rec. S868 (Feb. 24, 1998) (remarks of Sen. Daschle). . . .

Another theme prominent in the legislative debates was the notion that there is too much money spent on elections. . . .

And what exactly are these outrageous sums frittered away in determining who will govern us? A report prepared for Congress concluded that the total amount, in hard and soft money, spent on the 2000 federal elections was between $2.4 and $2.5 billion. . . . *All* campaign spending in the United States, including state elections, ballot initiatives, and judicial elections, has been estimated at $3.9 billion for 2000, Nelson, Spending in the 2000 Elections, in Financing the 2000 Election 24, Tbl. 2-1 (D. Magleby ed. 2002), which was a year that "shattered spending and contribution records," *id.* at 22. Even taking this last, larger figure as the benchmark, it means that Americans spent about half as much electing all their Nation's officials, state and federal, as they spent on movie tickets ($7.8 billion); about a fifth as much as they spent on cosmetics and perfume ($18.8 billion). . . .

JUSTICE THOMAS, concurring with respect to BCRA Titles III and IV, except for BCRA 311 and 318, concurring in the result with respect to BCRA 318, concurring in the judgment in part and dissenting in part with respect to BCRA Title II, and dissenting with respect to BCRA Titles I, V, and 311.[28]

. . . [T]he Court today upholds what can only be described as the most significant abridgment of the freedoms of speech and association since the Civil War. With breathtaking scope, the Bipartisan Campaign Reform Act of 2002 (BCRA), directly targets and constricts core political speech. . . .

. . . Apparently, the marketplace of ideas is to be fully open only to defamers, nude dancers, pornographers, flag burners, and cross burners.

Because I cannot agree with the treatment given by Justice Stevens' and Justice O'Connor's opinion (hereinafter joint opinion) to speech . . . I respectfully dissent. I also dissent from Justice Breyer's opinion upholding BCRA § 504. I join The Chief

---

[28] [Court's footnote *] JUSTICE SCALIA joins Parts I, II-A, and II-B of this opinion.

Justice's opinion in regards to BCRA §§ 304, 305, 307, 316, 319, and 403(b); concur in the result as to § 318; and dissent from the opinion as to § 311. I also fully agree with Justice Kennedy's discussion of § 213 and join that portion of his opinion.

I

A

. . . [A]s I have previously noted, it is unclear why "[b]ribery laws [that] bar precisely the *quid pro quo* arrangements that are targeted here" and "disclosure laws" are not "less restrictive means of addressing [the Government's] interest in curtailing corruption." *Shrink Missouri, supra,* at 428.

The joint opinion not only continues the errors of *Buckley v. Valeo,* by applying a low level of scrutiny to contribution ceilings, but also builds upon these errors by expanding the anticircumvention rationale beyond reason. . . .

II

. . . Today's holding continues a disturbing trend: the steady decrease in the level of scrutiny applied to restrictions on core political speech. . . . Although this trend is most obvious in the review of contribution limits, it has now reached what even this Court today would presumably recognize as a direct restriction on core political speech: limitations on independent expenditures.

A

. . . The particular language used, "expenditures made by any person . . . in cooperation, consultation, or concert with, or at the request or suggestion of, a national, State, or local committee of a political party," BCRA § 214(a)(2), captures expenditures with "no constitutional difference" from "a purely independent one." [*Fed. Election Comm'n v. Colorado Republican Fed. Campaign Committee,* 533 U.S. 431,] at 468 [(2001)] (Thomas, J., dissenting).[29] . . .

C

I must now address an issue on which I differ from all of my colleagues: the disclosure provisions in BCRA § 201, now contained in new FECA § 304(f). The "historical evidence indicates that Founding-era Americans opposed attempts to require that anonymous authors reveal their identities on the ground that forced disclosure violated the 'freedom of the press.'" *McIntyre v. Ohio Elections Comm'n,* 514 U.S. 334, 361 (1995) (Thomas, J., concurring). Indeed, this Court has explicitly recognized . . . that "an author's decision to remain anonymous . . . is an aspect of the freedom of speech protected by the First Amendment." *Id.* at 342. The Court now backs away from this principle, allowing the established right to anonymous speech to be stripped away based on the flimsiest of justifications.

The right to anonymous speech cannot be abridged based on the interests asserted by the defendants. I would thus hold that the disclosure requirements of BCRA § 201 are unconstitutional. Because of this conclusion, the so- called advance disclosure

---

[29] [Court's footnote 7] This is doubly so now that the Court has decided that there is no constitutional need for the showing even of an "agreement" in order to transform an expenditure into a "coordinated expenditur[e]" and hence into a contribution for FECA purposes.

requirement of § 201 necessarily falls as well.

D

. . . [I]t is, or at least was, clear that any regulation of political speech beyond communications using words of express advocacy is unconstitutional. Hence, even under the joint opinion's framework, most of Title II is unconstitutional, as both the "primary definition" and "backup definition" of "electioneering communications" cover a significant number of communications that do not use words of express advocacy. . . .

JUSTICE KENNEDY, concurring in the judgment in part and dissenting in part with respect to BCRA Titles I and II.[30]

The First Amendment guarantees our citizens the right to judge for themselves the most effective means for the expression of political views and to decide for themselves which entities to trust as reliable speakers. Significant portions of Titles I and II of the Bipartisan Campaign Reform Act of 2002 (BCRA or Act) constrain that freedom. These new laws force speakers to abandon their own preference for speaking through parties and organizations. . . .

. . . To reach today's decision, the Court surpasses *Buckley's* limits and expands Congress' regulatory power. . . .

A few examples show how BCRA reorders speech rights and codifies the Government's own preferences for certain speakers. BCRA would have imposed felony punishment on Ross Perot's 1996 efforts to build the Reform Party. *Compare* Federal Election Campaign Act of 1971 (FECA) §§ 309(d)(1)(A), 315(a)(1)(B), and 323(a)(1) (prohibiting, by up to five years' imprisonment, any individual from giving over $25,000 annually to a national party), *with Spending By Perot*, The Houston Chronicle, Dec. 13, 1996, p. 43 (reporting Perot's $8 million founding contribution to the Reform Party). BCRA makes it a felony for an environmental group to broadcast an ad, within 60 days of an election, exhorting the public to protest a Congressman's impending vote to permit logging in national forests. *See* BCRA § 203. BCRA escalates Congress' discrimination in favor of the speech rights of giant media corporations and against the speech rights of other corporations, both profit and nonprofit. . . .

Our precedents teach, above all, that Government cannot be trusted to moderate its own rules for suppression of speech. . . .

With respect, I dissent from the majority opinion upholding BCRA Titles I and II. I concur in the judgment as to BCRA § 213 and new FECA § 323(e) and concur in the judgment in part and dissent in part as to BCRA §§ 201, 202, and 214.

I. TITLE I AND COORDINATION PROVISIONS

Title I principally bans the solicitation, receipt, transfer and spending of soft money by the national parties (new FECA § 323(a), 2 U.S.C.A. § 441i(a) (Supp. 2003)). It also bans certain uses of soft money by state parties (new FECA § 323(b)); the transfer of soft money from national parties to nonprofit groups (new FECA § 323(d)); the solicitation, receipt, transfer, and spending of soft money by federal candidates and officeholders (new FECA § 323(e)); and certain uses of soft money by state candidates (new FECA § 323(f)). . . . Even a cursory review of the speech and association

---

[30] [Court's footnote *] THE CHIEF JUSTICE joins this opinion in its entirety. JUSTICE SCALIA joins this opinion except to the extent it upholds new FECA § 323(e) and BCRA § 202. JUSTICE THOMAS joins this opinion with respect to BCRA § 213.

burdens these laws create makes their First Amendment infirmities obvious:

> Title I bars individuals with shared beliefs from pooling their money above limits set by Congress to form a new third party. *See* new FECA § 323(a). Title I bars national party officials from soliciting or directing soft money to state parties for use on a state ballot initiative. This is true even if no federal office appears on the same ballot as the state initiative. *See* new FECA § 323(a).

> A national party's mere involvement in the strategic planning of fundraising for a state ballot initiative risks a determination that the national party is exercising "indirect control" of the state party. If that determination is made, the state party must abide by federal regulations. . . . *See* new FECA § 323(a).

> Title I compels speech. Party officials who want to engage in activity such as fundraising must now speak magic words to ensure the solicitation cannot be interpreted as anything other than a solicitation for hard, not soft, money. *See id.*

> Title I prohibits the national parties from giving any sort of funds to nonprofit entities, even federally regulated hard money, and even if the party hoped to sponsor the interest group's exploration of a particular issue in advance of the party's addition of it to their platform. *See* new FECA § 323(d).

> By express terms, Title I imposes multiple different forms of spending caps on parties, candidates, and their agents. *See* new FECA §§ 323(a), (e), and (f). . . .

Until today's consolidated cases, the Court has accepted but two principles to use in determining the validity of campaign finance restrictions. First is the anticorruption rationale. . . . Second, the Court . . . has said that the willing adoption of the entity form by corporations and unions justifies regulating them differently. . . .

A. *Constitutionally Sufficient Interest*

. . . The Court . . . interprets the anticorruption rationale to allow regulation not just of "actual or apparent *quid pro quo* arrangements," *id.*, but of any conduct that wins goodwill from or influences a Member of Congress. . . . The Court . . . concludes that access, without more, proves influence is undue. . . .

The generic favoritism or influence theory articulated by the Court is at odds with standard First Amendment analyses because it is unbounded and susceptible to no limiting principle. . . .

. . . Democracy is premised on responsiveness. . . .

. . . Under *Buckley's* holding . . . the Court asked whether the Government had proved that the regulated conduct, the expenditures, posed inherent *quid pro quo* corruption potential. . . .

1. *New FECA §§ 323(a), (b), (d), and (f)*

Sections 323(a), (b), (d), and (f), 2 U.S.C.A. §§ 441i(a), (b), (d), and (f) (Supp. 2003), cannot stand because they do not add regulation to conduct that poses a demonstrable *quid pro quo* danger. . . .

Section 323(a) . . . only adds regulation to soft money party donations not solicited by, or spent in coordination with, a candidate or officeholder.

These donations (noncandidate or officeholder solicited soft money party donations that are independently spent) do not pose the *quid pro quo* dangers that provide the basis for restricting protected speech. . . .

Even § 323(b)'s narrowest regulation, which bans state party soft money funded ads that (1) refer to a clearly identified federal candidate, and (2) either support or attack any candidate for the office of the clearly mentioned federal candidate fails the constitutional test. . . .

Section 323(d), which governs relationships between the national parties and non-profit groups, fails for similar reasons. . . .

When one recognizes that §§ 323(a), (b), (d), and (f) do not serve the interest the anticorruption rationale contemplates, Title I's entirety begins to look very much like an incumbency protection plan. . . That impression is worsened by the fact that Congress exempted its officeholders from the more stringent prohibitions imposed on party officials. . . .

2. *New FECA § 323(e)*

Ultimately, only one of the challenged Title I provisions satisfies *Buckley's* anticorruption rationale and the First Amendment's guarantee. It is § 323(e). . . . These provisions . . . limit candidates' and their agents' solicitation of soft money. . . .

. . . The making of a solicited gift is a *quid*. . . .

B. *Standard of Review*

. . . In *Buckley*, we applied "closely drawn" scrutiny to contribution limitations and strict scrutiny to expenditure limitations. . . .

Title I's provisions prohibit the receipt of funds; and in most instances, but not all, this can be defined as a contribution limit. They prohibit the spending of funds; and in most instances this can be defined as an expenditure limit. They prohibit the giving of funds to nonprofit groups; and this falls within neither definition as we have ever defined it. Finally, they prohibit fundraising activity. . . .

. . . *Buckley's* application of a less exacting review to contribution limits must be confined to the narrow category of money gifts that are directed, in some manner, to a candidate or officeholder. Any broader definition of the category contradicts *Buckley's quid pro quo* rationale and overlooks *Buckley's* language . . . .

The majority makes *Buckley's* already awkward and imprecise test all but meaningless in its application. If one is viewing BCRA through *Buckley's* lens, as the majority purports to do, one must conclude the Act creates markedly greater associational burdens than the significant burden created by contribution limitations and, unlike contribution limitations, also creates significant burdens on speech itself. While BCRA contains federal contribution limitations, which significantly burden association, it goes even further. The Act entirely reorders the nature of relations between national political parties and their candidates, between national political parties and state and local parties, and between national political parties and nonprofit organizations. . . .

II. TITLE II PROVISIONS

A. *Disclosure Provisions*

. . . Section 201's advance disclosure requirement . . . imposes real burdens on political speech that *post hoc* disclosure does not. It forces disclosure of political strategy by revealing where ads are to be run and what their content is likely to be (based on who is running the ad). It also provides an opportunity for the ad buyer's opponents to dissuade broadcasters from running ads. . . .

B. *BCRA § 203*

The majority permits a new and serious intrusion on speech when it upholds § 203, the key provision in Title II that prohibits corporations and labor unions from using money from their general treasury to fund electioneering communications. . . .

1.

The majority's holding cannot be reconciled with *First Nat. Bank of Boston v. Bellotti*, 435 U.S. 765 (1978), which invalidated a Massachusetts law prohibiting banks and business corporations from making expenditures "for the purpose of" influencing referendum votes on issues that do not "materially affect" their business interests. *Id.* at 767. . . .

Austin [*v. Michigan Chamber of Commerce*, 494 U.S. 652 (1990),] was the first and, until now, the only time our Court had allowed the Government to exercise the power to censor political speech based on the speaker's corporate identity. . . .

To be sure, *Bellotti* concerns issue advocacy, whereas *Austin* is about express advocacy. . . .

Austin was based on a faulty assumption. . . . [T]here is a general recognition now that discussions of candidates and issues are quite often intertwined in practical terms. . . .

2.

Even under *Austin*, BCRA § 203 could not stand. . . .

The Government is unwilling to characterize § 203 as a ban, citing the possibility of funding electioneering communications out of a separate segregated fund. This option, though, does not alter the categorical nature of the prohibition on the corporation. . . .

The majority can articulate no compelling justification for imposing this scheme of compulsory ventriloquism. . . .

. . . Never before in our history has the Court upheld a law that suppresses speech to this extent. . . .

Conclusion

. . . The First Amendment . . . cannot be read to allow Congress to provide for the imprisonment of those who attempt to establish new political parties and alter the civic discourse. . . .

Chief Justice Rehnquist, dissenting with respect to BCRA Titles I and V.[31]

Although I join Justice Kennedy's opinion in full, I write separately to highlight my disagreement with the Court on Title I of the Bipartisan Campaign Reform Act of 2002 (BCRA), 116 Stat. 81, and to dissent from the Court's opinion upholding § 504 of Title V.

I

The issue presented by Title I is . . . whether Congress can permissibly regulate much speech that has no plausible connection to candidate contributions or corruption to achieve those goals. . . .

The lynchpin of Title I, new FECA § 323(a) . . . does not regulate only donations

---

[31] [Court's footnote *] Justice Scalia and Justice Kennedy join this opinion in its entirety.

given to influence a particular federal election; it regulates *all donations* to national political committees, no matter the use to which the funds are put. . . .

. . . [T]he means chosen by Congress, restricting all donations to national parties no matter the purpose for which they are given or are used, are not "closely drawn to avoid unnecessary abridgment of associational freedoms," *Buckley*, at 25.

BCRA's overinclusiveness is not limited to national political parties. . . . For example, new FECA § 323(b) . . . prohibits state parties from using nonfederal funds for general partybuilding activities such as voter registration, voter identification, and get out the vote for state candidates even if federal candidates are not mentioned. New FECA § 323(d) prohibits state and local political party committees, like their national counterparts, from soliciting and donating "any funds" to nonprofit organizations such as the National Rifle Association or the National Association for the Advancement of Colored People (NAACP). . . .

II

BCRA § 504 . . . differs from other BCRA disclosure sections because it requires broadcast licensees to disclose *requests* to purchase broadcast time rather than requiring *purchasers* to disclose their *disbursements* for broadcast time.

This section is deficient because of the absence of a sufficient governmental interest to justify disclosure of mere requests to purchase broadcast time, as well as purchases themselves. The Court approaches § 504 almost exclusively from the perspective of the broadcast licensees, ignoring the interests of candidates and other purchasers, whose speech and association rights are affected by § 504. . . .

Justice Stevens, dissenting with respect to § 305.[32]

. . . I would entertain plaintiffs' challenge to § 305 on the merits and uphold the section. Like BCRA §§ 201, 212, and 311, § 305 serves an important — and constitutionally sufficient — informational purpose. . . .

Finally, I do not regard § 305 as a constitutionally suspect "viewpoint-based regulation." . . . Although the section reaches only ads that mention opposing candidates, it applies equally to all such ads. . . .

FED. ELECTION COMM'N v. WISCONSIN RIGHT TO LIFE, INC., 127 S. Ct. 2652 (2007). In *Fed. Election Comm'n v. Wisconsin Right To Life, Inc.* (WRTL), the Court declared Section 203 of the Bipartisan Campaign Reform Act of 2002 (BCRA) unconstitutional as applied to the corporate advertisements at issue because they were "not the 'functional equivalent' of express campaign speech." BCRA § 203 restricts corporate broadcasts shortly before an election that name a federal candidate for elected office and target the electorate. During this time, it is a federal crime for any labor union or incorporated entity to "pay for any 'electioneering communication' " from general treasury funds. Prohibited communications include "broadcast, cable or satellite communication that refers to a candidate for federal office and that is aired within 30 days of a federal primary election or 60 days of a federal general election in the jurisdiction in which that candidate is running for office."

As part of a lobbying campaign, WRTL aired three commercials prior to the 2004 federal primary election that referred to Washington Senators by name. The commercials encouraged citizens to contact these Senators to request that they oppose a federal judicial nominee filibuster. BCRA § 203 prevented WRTL from broadcasting these commercials less than 30 days prior to the primary election. Believing this provision was

---

[32] [Court's footnote *] Justice Ginsburg and Justice Breyer join this opinion in its entirety.

unconstitutional as applied to their broadcasts, WRTL sought declaratory and injunctive relief against the Federal Election Commission requesting to air these commercials.

Chief Justice Roberts delivered the judgment of the Court and the opinion of the Court with respect to Parts I and II. In *McConnell v. Fed. Election Comm'n, supra,* the Court rejected a facial challenge to BCRA § 203. *McConnell* concluded that those raising the facial challenge "failed to carry their 'heavy burden' of establishing that all enforcement of the law should therefore be prohibited." *McConnell* itself recognized that the justifications for regulating campaign speech and its " 'functional equivalent' 'might not apply' " when regulating issue advocacy. When distinguishing issue advocacy from campaign speech or express advocacy of a particular candidate, "the First Amendment requires [the Court] to err on the side of protecting political speech rather than suppressing it."

Chief Justice Roberts first held that the speech at issue was "not the 'functional equivalent' of express campaign speech." Second, the Court found that the interests justifying campaign speech regulation did not justify issue advocacy restrictions. Therefore, the Court held "that BCRA § 203 is unconstitutional as applied to the advertisements at issue."

Only Justice Alito joined Parts III and IV of the Chief Justice's opinion. In Part III, the Chief Justice subjected BCRA to strict scrutiny as it "burdens political speech." Government has the burden to "prove that applying BCRA to WRTL's ads furthers a compelling interest and is narrowly tailored to achieve that interest." However, *McConnell* holds that "BCRA survives strict scrutiny to the extent it regulates express advocacy or its functional equivalent." The BCRA's definition of "Electioneering Communications" targets *"ads that have the purpose or effect of supporting candidates for election to office."*

Relying on *Buckley v. Valeo, supra,* and *McConnell,* the Chief Justice rejected tests based on "amorphous considerations of intent and effect." Instead, "a court should find that an ad is the functional equivalent of express advocacy only if the ad is susceptible of no reasonable interpretation other than as an appeal to vote for or against a specific candidate." WRTL's ads did not meet this test for two reasons. "First, their content [was] consistent with that of a genuine issue ad." The ads focused on issue promotion and advocated contacting public officials to take a position on the particular legislative issue. "Second, their content lack[ed] indicia of express advocacy." They "do not mention an election, candidacy, political party, or challenger; and they do not take a position on a candidates' character, qualifications or fitness for office."

The Chief Justice also addressed Justice Scalia's criticism that his *"no reasonable interpretation"* test is vague. The Chief Justice agreed that this area requires "clarity" and responded to Justice Scalia's concerns by emphasizing "that (1) there can be no free-ranging intent-and-effect test; (2) there generally should be no discovery or inquiry into. . .'contextual' factors. . .; (3) discussion of issues cannot be banned merely because the issues might be relevant to an election; and (4) in a debatable case, the tie is resolved in favor of protecting speech." Further, Chief Justice Roberts stressed that "this test is only triggered if the speech meets the brightline requirements of BCRA § 203 in the first place." As the "ads may reasonably be interpreted as something other than as an appeal to vote for or against a specific candidate, we hold they are not the functional equivalent of express advocacy, and therefore fall outside the scope of *McConnell's* holding."

Again writing for a plurality, in Part IV, the Chief Justice rejected two compelling state interest arguments. First, the government argued "that an expansive definition of 'functional equivalent' " is necessary to prevent issue advocacy from circumventing "the rule against express advocacy." They argued this could in turn promote "circumvention

of the rule against contributions." However, " '[t]he desire for a bright-line rule-
. . . hardly constitutes the *compelling* state interest necessary to justify any infringement on First Amendment freedom.' " Second, the Court acknowledged that the state
has a compelling interest in addressing " 'the corrosive and distorting effects of immense
aggregations of wealth that are accumulated with the help of the corporate form.' "
However, the Court held "that the interest recognized in *Austin* [*v. Michigan Chamber
of Commerce, supra*] as justifying regulation of corporate campaign speech" does not
apply "to issue advocacy."

In conclusion, Chief Justice Roberts distinguished the Court's holding from that in
McConnell and confirmed that its precedent was undisturbed. "*McConnell* held that
express advocacy of a candidate or his opponent by a corporation shortly before an
election may be prohibited, along with the functional equivalent of such express
advocacy." However, when the issue is "what speech qualifies" as express advocacy, the
Court will "give the benefit of the doubt to speech, not censorship."

Justice Alito's concurrence predicted that if the Court's test as laid out "impermissibly chills political speech," then the Court would "be asked in a future case to
reconsider the holding in *McConnell*, that § 203 is facially constitutional."

Justice Scalia, joined by Justices Kennedy and Thomas, concurred in part and in the
judgment. Concluding that *McConnell* should be revisited, he explained that no test for
distinguishing between express and issue advocacy "can both (1) comport with the
requirement of clarity that unchilled freedom of political speech demands, and (2) be
compatible with the facial validity of § 203 (as pronounced in *McConnell*)." He would
reconsider *McConnell* as it forces the Court to make "issue-speech from election-speech
with no clear criterion." The Chief Justice's test was "impermissibly vague" as "the line
between electoral advocacy and issue advocacy dissolves in practice."

Because the rationale of *Austin* was weak and "the clarity of *Buckley's* express-
advocacy line" has long been accepted, Justice Scalia concluded that "it was adventurous
for *McConnell* to extend *Austin* beyond corporate speech constituting express advocacy." The attempt to apply *McConnell* to the cases at bar made it "apparent" that
"*McConnell's* holding concerning § 203 was wrong."

Justice Souter dissented, joined by Justices Stevens, Ginsburg, and Breyer. Justice
Souter listed three reasons he found the decision significant: "the demand for campaign
money in huge amounts from large contributors, whose power has produced a cynical
electorate; the congressional recognition of the ensuing threat to democratic integrity as
reflected in a century of legislation restricting the electoral leverage of concentrations of
money in corporate and union treasuries; and *McConnell*, declaring the facial validity of
the most recent Act of Congress in that tradition, a decision that is effectively, and
unjustifiably, overruled today."

For Justice Souter, "[d]evoting concentrations of money in self-interested hands to
the support of political campaigning . . . threatens the capacity of this democracy to
represent its constituents and the confidence of its citizens in their capacity to govern
themselves. These are the elements summed up in the notion of political integrity, giving
it a value second to none in a free society."

Justice Souter emphasized the reasonableness of § 203's limited restrictions. Quoting
McConnell, he noted that " 'corporations can still fund electioneering communications
with PAC money.' " He concluded that the Court's judgment effectively overruled
McConnell. Because an ad is only found the equivalent of express advocacy if it is
" 'susceptible of no reasonable interpretation other than as an appeal to vote for or
against a specific candidate,' " the opinion's test "is flatly contrary to *McConnell*." The
Chief Justice's test "wrongly jettisons our conclusions about the constitutionality of
regulating ads with electioneering purpose."

Justice Souter disagreed with the Chief Justice's conclusion that an " 'electioneering purpose' " would "be objectively apparent from those ads' content and context." Today's decision renders § 203's ban on corporate and union contributions "open to easy circumvention." Companies and unions can now simply run " 'issue ads' without express advocacy, or by funneling the money through an independent corporation like WRTL."

§ 15.03 GOVERNMENT FUNDING OF SPEECH-RELATED ACTIVITIES

RUST v. SULLIVAN
500 U.S. 173, 111 S. Ct. 1759, 114 L. Ed. 2d. 233 (1991)

CHIEF JUSTICE REHNQUIST delivered the opinion of the Court, in which JUSTICES WHITE, KENNEDY, SCALIA, and Souter, JJ., joined.

These cases concern a facial challenge to Department of Health and Human Services (HHS) regulations which limit the ability of Title X fund recipients to engage in abortion-related activities. . . .

I

A

In 1970, Congress enacted Title X of the Public Health Service Act (Act), 42 U.S.C. §§ 300–300a-41, which provides federal funding for family-planning services. The Act authorizes the Secretary to "make grants to and enter into contracts with public or nonprofit private entities to assist in the establishment and operation of voluntary family planning projects which shall offer a broad range of acceptable and effective family planning methods and services." 42 U.S.C. § 300(a). . . . Section 1008 of the Act, however, provides that "none of the funds appropriated under this subchapter shall be used in programs where abortion is a method of family planning." 42 U.S.C. § 300a-6. That restriction was intended to ensure that Title X funds would "be used only to support preventive family planning services, population research, infertility services, and other related medical, informational, and educational activities." H.R. Conf. Rep. No. 91-1667, p. 8 (1970).

In 1988, the Secretary promulgated new regulations designed to provide " 'clear and operational guidance' to grantees about how to preserve the distinction between Title X programs and abortion as a method of family planning." 53 Fed. Reg. 2923–2924 (1988). The regulations clarify . . . that Congress intended Title X funds "to be used only to support *preventive* family planning services." H.R. Conf. Rep. No. 91-1667, p. 8 (emphasis added). Accordingly, Title X services are limited to "preconceptual counseling, education, and general reproductive health care," and expressly exclude "pregnancy care (including obstetric or prenatal care)." 42 CFR § 59.2 (1989).

The regulations attach three principal conditions on the grant of federal funds for Title X projects. First, . . . a "Title X project may not provide counseling concerning the use of abortion as a method of family planning or provide referral for abortion as a method of family planning." 42 CFR 59.8(a)(1) (1989). . . . Title X projects must refer every pregnant client "for appropriate prenatal and/or social services by furnishing a list of available providers that promote the welfare of the mother and the unborn child." *Id.* . . . The Title X project is expressly prohibited from referring a pregnant woman to an abortion provider, even upon specific request. One permissible response to such an inquiry is that "the project does not consider abortion an appropriate method of family planning and therefore does not counsel or refer for abortion." § 59.8(b)(5).

Second, the regulations broadly prohibit a Title X project from engaging in activities that "encourage, promote or advocate abortion as a method of family planning." § 59.10(a). Forbidden activities include lobbying for legislation that would increase the availability of abortion as a method of family planning, developing or disseminating materials advocating abortion as a method of family planning, providing speakers to promote abortion as a method of family planning, using legal action to make abortion available in any way as a method of family planning, and paying dues to any group that advocates abortion as a method of family planning as a substantial part of its activities. *Id.*

Third, the regulations require that Title X projects be organized so that they are "physically and financially separate" from prohibited abortion activities. § 59.9. . . . The regulations provide a list of nonexclusive factors . . . to consider in conducting a case-by-case determination of objective integrity and independence, such as the existence of separate accounting records and separate personnel, and the degree of physical separation of the project from facilities for prohibited activities. *Id.*

B

Petitioners are Title X grantees and doctors who supervise Title X funds suing on behalf of themselves and their patients. Respondent is the Secretary of the Department of Health and Human Services. After the regulations had been promulgated, but before they had been applied, petitioners filed two separate actions, later consolidated, challenging the *facial* validity of the regulations and seeking declaratory and injunctive relief to prevent implementation of the regulations.

II

. . . Petitioners face a heavy burden in seeking to have the regulations invalidated as facially unconstitutional. . . .

III

Petitioners contend that the regulations violate the First Amendment by impermissibly discriminating based on viewpoint because they prohibit "all discussion about abortion as a lawful option — including counseling, referral, and the provision of neutral and accurate information about ending a pregnancy — while compelling the clinic or counselor to provide information that promotes continuing a pregnancy to term." . . . [P]etitioners also assert that while the Government may place certain conditions on the receipt of federal subsidies, it may not "discriminate invidiously in its subsidies in such a way as to 'aim at the suppression of dangerous ideas.' " *Regan [v. Taxation With Representation of Wash.*, 461 U.S. 540,] 548 [(1983)].

There is no question but that the statutory prohibition contained in § 1008 is constitutional. In *Maher v. Roe*, 432 U.S. 464 (1997) we upheld a state welfare regulation under which Medicaid recipients received payments for services related to childbirth, but not for nontherapeutic abortions. . . . Here the Government is exercising the authority it possesses under *Maher and Harris v. McRae*, 448 U.S. 297 (1980) to subsidize family planning services which will lead to conception and child birth, and declining to "promote or encourage abortion." The Government can, without violating the Constitution, selectively fund a program to encourage certain activities it believes to be in the public interest, without at the same time funding an alternate program which seeks to deal with the problem in another way. In so doing, the Government has not discriminated on the basis of viewpoint; it has merely chosen to fund one activity to the exclusion of the other. . . .   "There is a basic difference between direct state interference with a protected activity and state encouragement of an alternative activity consonant with legislative policy." *Maher*, 432 U.S. at 475.

. . . This is not a case of the Government "suppressing a dangerous idea," but of a prohibition on a project grantee or its employees from engaging in activities outside of its scope.

To hold that the Government unconstitutionally discriminates on the basis of viewpoint when it chooses to fund a program dedicated to advance certain permissible goals, because the program in advancing those goals necessarily discourages alternate goals, would render numerous government programs constitutionally suspect. When Congress established a National Endowment for Democracy to encourage other countries to adopt democratic principles, 22 U.S.C. § 4411(b), it was not constitutionally required to fund a program to encourage competing lines of political philosophy such as Communism and Fascism. . . .

Petitioners rely heavily on their claim that the regulations would not, in the circumstance of a medical emergency, permit a Title X project to refer a woman whose pregnancy places her life in imminent peril to a provider of abortions or abortion-related services. . . . On their face, we do not read the regulations to bar abortion referral or counseling in such circumstances. . . . [A]nd it does not seem that a medically necessitated abortion . . . would be the equivalent of its use as a "method of family planning". . . . Moreover, the regulations themselves contemplate that a Title X project would be permitted to engage in otherwise prohibited abortion-related activity in such circumstances. Section 59.8(a)(2) provides a specific exemption for emergency care and requires Title X recipients "to refer the client immediately to an appropriate provider of emergency medical services." . . .

Petitioners' reliance on these cases is unavailing, however, because here the government is not denying a benefit to anyone, but is instead simply insisting that public funds be spent for the purposes for which they were authorized. . . . The Title X grantee can continue to perform abortions, provide abortion-related services, and engage in abortion advocacy; it simply is required to conduct those activities through programs that are separate and independent from the project that receives Title X funds.

In contrast, our "unconstitutional conditions" cases involve situations in which the government has placed a condition on the *recipient* of the subsidy rather than on a particular program or service, thus effectively prohibiting the recipient from engaging in the protected conduct outside the scope of the federally funded program. In *FCC v. League of Women Voters of Cal.*, [468 U.S. 364 (1984),] we invalidated a federal law providing that noncommercial television and radio stations that receive federal grants may not "engage in editorializing." . . . We expressly recognized, however, that were Congress to permit the recipient stations to "establish 'affiliate' organizations which could then use the station's facilities to editorialize with nonfederal funds, such a statutory mechanism would plainly be valid." *Id.* . . .

Similarly, in *Regan* we held that Congress could, in the exercise of its spending power, reasonably refuse to subsidize the lobbying activities of tax-exempt charitable organizations by prohibiting such organizations from using tax-deductible contributions to support their lobbying efforts. . . . [A] charitable organization could create, under § 501(c)(3) of the Internal Revenue Code of 1954, 26 U.S.C. § 501(c)(3), an affiliate to conduct its nonlobbying activities using tax-deductible contributions, and at the same time establish, under § 501(c)(4), a separate affiliate to pursue its lobbying efforts without such contributions. . . .

The same principles apply to petitioners' claim that the regulations abridge the free speech rights of the grantee's staff. . . . The regulations, which govern solely the scope of the Title X project's activities, do not in any way restrict the activities of those persons acting as private individuals. The employees' freedom of expression is limited during the time that they actually work for the project; but this limitation is a consequence of their decision to accept employment in a project, the scope of which is permissibly restricted by the funding authority.

This is not to suggest that funding by the Government, even when coupled with the freedom of the fund recipients to speak outside the scope of the Government-funded project, is invariably sufficient to justify government control over the content of expression. For example . . . we have recognized that the university is a traditional sphere of free expression so fundamental to the functioning of our society that the Government's ability to control speech within that sphere by means of conditions attached to the expenditure of Government funds is restricted by the vagueness and overbreadth doctrines of the First Amendment, *Keyishian v. Board of Regents*, 385 U.S. 589, 603, 605–606 (1967). It could be argued by analogy that traditional relationships such as that between doctor and patient should enjoy protection under the First Amendment from government regulation, even when subsidized by the Government. We need not resolve that question here, however, because the Title X program regulations do not significantly impinge upon the doctor-patient relationship. Nothing in them requires a doctor to represent as his own any opinion that he does not in fact hold. Nor is the doctor-patient relationship established by the Title X program sufficiently all-encompassing so as to justify an expectation on the part of the patient of comprehensive medical advice. . . . The doctor is always free to make clear that advice regarding abortion is simply beyond the scope of the program. In these circumstances, the general rule that the Government may choose not to subsidize speech applies with full force.

IV

. . . That the regulations do not impermissibly burden a woman's Fifth Amendment rights is evident from the line of cases beginning with *Maher* and *McRae* and culminating in our most recent decision in *Webster* [*v. Reproductive Health Services*, 492 U.S. 490 (1989)]. . . . Congress' refusal to fund abortion counseling and advocacy leaves a pregnant woman with the same choices as if the government had chosen not to fund family-planning services at all. . . .

Petitioners contend, however, that most Title X clients are effectively precluded by indigency and poverty from seeing a health care provider who will provide abortion-related services. But . . . "[t]he financial constraints that restrict an indigent woman's ability to enjoy the full range of constitutionally protected freedom of choice are the product not of governmental restrictions on access to abortion, but rather of her indigency." *McRae, supra*, at 316. . . .

JUSTICE BLACKMUN with whom JUSTICE MARSHALL joins, with whom JUSTICE STEVENS joins as to Parts II and III, and with whom JUSTICE O'CONNOR joins as to Part I, dissenting.

. . . [T]he Secretary's regulation of referral, advocacy, and counseling activities exceeds his statutory authority, and, also, that the Regulations violate the First and Fifth Amendments of our Constitution. . . .

I

The majority does not dispute that "federal statutes are to be so construed as to avoid serious doubt of their constitutionality." . . . *Machinists v. Street*, 367 U.S. 740, 749 (1961). . . . Whether or not one believes that these Regulations are valid, it avoids reality to contend that they do not give rise to serious constitutional questions. . . .

As is discussed in Parts II and III, *infra*, the Regulations impose viewpoint-based restrictions upon protected speech and are aimed at a woman's decision whether to continue or terminate her pregnancy. In both respects, they implicate core constitutional values. . . .

. . . [T]he language of § 1008 easily sustains a constitutionally trouble-free interpretation.[33]

II

I also, strongly disagree with the majority's disposition of petitioners' constitutional claims. . . .

A

Until today, the Court never has upheld viewpoint-based suppression of speech simply because that suppression was a condition upon the acceptance of public funds. . . .

It cannot seriously be disputed that the counseling and referral provisions at issue in the present cases constitute content-based regulation of speech. Title X grantees may provide counseling and referral regarding any of a wide range of family planning and other topics, save abortion. . . .

The Regulations are also clearly viewpoint-based. While suppressing speech favorable to abortion with one hand, the secretary compels anti-abortion speech with the other. . . .

Moreover, the Regulations command that a project refer for prenatal care each woman diagnosed as pregnant, irrespective of the woman's expressed desire to continue or terminate her pregnancy. . . . If a client asks directly about abortion, a Title X physician or counselor is required to say, in essence, that the project does not consider abortion to be an appropriate method of family planning. . . . Both requirements are antithetical to the First Amendment. *See Wooley v. Maynard*, 430 U.S. 705, 714 (1977).

The Regulations pertaining to "advocacy" are even more explicitly viewpoint-based. These provide: "A Title X project may not *encourage, promote or advocate* abortion as a method of family planning." § 59.10 (emphasis added). . . . The Regulations do not, however, proscribe or even regulate anti-abortion advocacy. . . .

. . . Clearly, there are some bases upon which government may not rest its decision to fund or not to fund. For example, the Members of the majority surely would agree that government may not base its decision to support an activity upon considerations of race. *See, e.g., Yick Wo v. Hopkins*, 118 U.S. 356 (1886). As demonstrated above, our cases make clear that ideological viewpoint is a similarly repugnant ground upon which to base funding decisions. . . .

---

[33] [Court's footnote 1] . . . Were the Court to read § 1008 to prohibit only the actual performance of abortions with Title X funds — as, indeed, the Secretary did until February 2, 1988, *see* 53 Fed. Reg. 2923 (1988) — the provision would fall within the category of restrictions that the Court upheld in *Harris v. MacRae*, 448 U.S. 297 (1980), and *Maher v. Roe*, 432 U.S. 464 (1977). By interpreting the statute to authorize the regulation of abortion-related speech between physician and patient, however, the Secretary, and now the court, have rejected a constitutionally sound construction in favor of one that is by no means clearly constitutional.

B

The Court concludes that the challenged Regulations do not violate the First Amendment rights of Title X staff members because any limitation of the employees' freedom of expression is simply a consequence of their decision to accept employment at a federally funded project. But it has never been sufficient to justify an otherwise unconstitutional condition upon public employment that the employee may escape the condition by relinquishing his or her job. . . .

. . . Under the majority's reasoning, the First Amendment could be read to tolerate *any* governmental restriction upon an employee's speech so long as that restriction is limited to the funded workplace. . . .

. . . When a client becomes pregnant, the full range of therapeutic alternatives includes the abortion option, and Title X counselors' interest in providing this information is compelling.

The Government's articulated interest in distorting the doctor/patient dialogue — ensuring that federal funds are not spent for a purpose outside the scope of the program — falls far short of that necessary to justify the suppression of truthful information and professional medical opinion regarding constitutionally protected conduct. . . .

C

III

. . . *Roe v. Wade*, 410 U.S. 113 (1973), and its progeny are not so much about a medical procedure as they are about a woman's fundamental right to self-determination. . . .

The undeniable message conveyed by this forced speech, and the one that the Title X client will draw from it, is that abortion nearly always is an improper medical option. . . . Others, delayed by the Regulations' mandatory prenatal referral, will be prevented from acquiring abortions during the period in which the process is medically sound and constitutionally protected. . . .

The substantial obstacles to bodily self-determination that the Regulations impose are doubly offensive because they are effected by manipulating the very words spoken by physicians and counselors to their patients. . . .

JUSTICE STEVENS, dissenting.

In contrast to the statutory emphasis on making relevant information readily available to the public, the statute contains no suggestion that Congress intended to authorize the suppression or censorship of any information by any Government employee or by any grant recipient. . . .

JUSTICE O'CONNOR, dissenting.

"[W]here an otherwise acceptable construction of a statute would raise serious constitutional problems, the Court will construe the statute to avoid such problems unless such construction is plainly contrary to the intent of Congress." *Edward J. DeBartolo Corp. v. Florida Gulf Coast Building & Construction Trades Council*, 485 U.S. 568, 575 (1988). Justice Blackmun has explained well why this long-standing canon of statutory construction applies in this case, and I join Part I of his dissent. . . .

. . . I do not join Part II of the dissent, however, for the same reason that I do not join Part III, in which Justice Blackmun concludes that the regulations are unconstitutional under the Fifth Amendment. The canon of construction that Justice

Blackmun correctly applies here is grounded in large part upon our time-honored practice of not reaching constitutional questions unnecessarily. . . .

. . . It is enough in this case to conclude that neither the language nor the history of § 1008 compels the Secretary's interpretation, and that the interpretation raises serious First Amendment concerns. . . .

NOTE

See David Cole, *Beyond Unconstitutional Conditions: Charting Spheres of Neutrality in Government-Funded Speech*, 67 N.Y.U. L. Rev. 675, 747 (1992) ("The confusion demonstrated by the *Rust* decision reflects a fundamental and inescapable paradox. Government-funded speech is at once a necessary and valuable part of the marketplace of ideas and an ever-present threat to an autonomous citizenry and free public debate.").

One commentator has suggested that "we must recognize that the process of awarding subsidies to support the arts is unique among government functions, in that it involves allocating finite resources among projects that are by their very nature expressive speech under the First Amendment. The inevitable result is that some protected speech will be promoted at the expense of other protected speech. Moreover, the theoretically impartial standard imposed on this process — artistic merit — necessarily requires the consideration of content, or its component parts." *See* Amy Sabrin, *Thinking About Content: Can it Play an Appropriate Role in Government Funding of the Arts?*, 102 Yale L.J. 1209, 1233 (1993).

ROSENBERGER v. UNIV. OF VA., 515 U.S. 819 (1995). In *Rosenberger v. Virginia*, the Court struck down a University of Virginia regulation that provided funding to diverse student organizations, but denied funding to religious organizations. The University maintained that funding religious organizations would violate the Establishment Clause. Although the University generally funded media groups, it denied funding to Wide Awake Productions which published a magazine styled *Wide Awake: A Christian Perspective at the University of Virginia.*

The student organization challenged the denial of funding as a violation of their free speech rights. Writing for the Court, Justice Kennedy opined:

> When the government disburses public funds to private entities to convey a governmental message, it may take legitimate and appropriate steps to ensure that its message is neither garbled nor distorted by the grantee.

> It does not follow, however, . . . that viewpoint-based restrictions are proper when the University does not itself speak or subsidize transmittal of a message it favors but instead expends funds to encourage a diversity of views from private speakers. A holding that the University may not discriminate based on the viewpoint of private persons whose speech it facilitates does not restrict the University's own speech, which is controlled by different principles. . . .

> The distinction between the University's own favored message and the private speech of students is evident in the case before us. The University itself has taken steps to ensure the distinction in the agreement each CIO must sign. The University declares that the student groups eligible for SAF support are not the University's agents, are not subject to its control, and are not its responsibility. . . .

> Vital First Amendment speech principles are at stake here. The first danger to liberty lies in granting the State the power to examine publications to determine whether or not they are based on some ultimate idea and if so for the State to classify them. The second, and corollary, danger is to speech from the

chilling of individual thought and expression. That danger is especially real in the University setting, where the State acts against a background and tradition of thought and experiment that is at the center of our intellectual and philosophic tradition. . . .

. . . The prohibition on funding on behalf of publications that "primarily promote or manifest a particular belief in or about a deity or an ultimate reality," in its ordinary and commonsense meaning, has a vast potential reach. . . . Were the prohibition applied with much vigor at all, it would bar funding of essays by hypothetical student contributors named Plato, Spinoza, and Descartes. And if the regulation covers, as the University says it does, those student journalistic efforts which primarily manifest or promote a belief that there is no deity and no ultimate reality, then undergraduates named Karl Marx, Bertrand Russell, and Jean-Paul Sartre would likewise have some of their major essays excluded from student publications. . . .

Based on the principles we have discussed, we hold that the regulation invoked to deny SAF support, both in its terms and in its application to these petitioners, is a denial of their right of free speech guaranteed by the First Amendment. . . .

Justice O'Connor concurred, rejecting the Establishment Clause challenge. Justice Thomas concurred, arguing that the dissent discriminated against religion. Justice Souter dissented, joined by Justices Stevens, Ginsburg, and Breyer. Also relying on the Establishment Clause, Justice Stevens said that this is the first time that the government "approved direct funding of core religious functions." The Establishment problems obviated any free speech, public forum concerns.

NOTES

(1) *Tax Deductions for Lobbying.* In *Regan v. Taxation with Representation of Washington,* ("TWR"), 461 U.S. 540 (1983), the Court unanimously rejected the First Amendment and equal protection claims of an organization which was denied tax exemption under Section 501(c)(3) of the Internal Revenue Code because it engaged in substantial lobbying activities. As a result of this denial, contributions to the organization were not tax deductible. The Internal Revenue Code allowed TWR and other non-profit organizations to obtain tax exemption by creating an affiliate organization, under Section 501(c)(4). The Code, however, denied tax deduction status for contributions to the 501(c)(4) affiliate organizations.

Writing for the Court, Justice Rehnquist stated that government is under no obligation to subsidize lobbying or any other First Amendment activities. For this conclusion, he relied heavily on *Cammarano v. United States,* 358 U.S. 498 (1959), which held that the government is not obligated to provide "business expense deductions for lobbying activities."

The equal protection claim arose from another provision of the Code which allows deductions for contributions to veterans' organizations even if they engage in lobbying. Justice Rehnquist's opinion gave short shrift to the equal protection-free speech contention. The deduction for veterans' organizations was not an effort to suppress or control ideas based on their content. "It is not irrational for Congress to decide that, even though it will not subsidize substantial lobbying by charities generally, it will subsidize lobbying by veterans organizations."

A concurring opinion by Justice Blackmun, joined by Justices Brennan and Marshall, emphasized that the difference in tax deduction status between contributions to veterans organizations and charitable organizations was not based on the content of speech.

(2) *Student Activity Fees.* In *Board of Regents of the University of Wisconsin System v. Southworth*, 529 U.S. 217 (2000), the Court upheld a viewpoint neutral student activity fee. Writing for the majority, Justice Kennedy stated that this speech "springs from the initiative of the students, who alone give it purpose and content in the course of their extracurricular endeavors." A different case may have been presented had the University officials been the speakers or had the speech been funded by tuition dollars.

The complaining students argued that, under *Keller v. State Bar of California*, 496 U.S. 1, the University could not require a student to pay the portion of an activities fee that was allocated to groups advocating political or ideological positions with which the student does not agree. *Keller* allowed the California Bar to require lawyers admitted to practice in the State to join the Bar and to fund activities that were germane to the purpose of the Association. However, the Bar could not require that lawyers fund the promotion of its political activities that were not germane to the Association. The Court refused to apply the *Keller* standard of germaneness to a university setting. Requiring a university to dictate what speech is germane would be counter to its broad, exploratory mission.

Relying on *Rosenberger v. Rector and Visitors of University of Virginia, supra*, the majority required that the University be viewpoint neutral in allocating funds to student organizations. As the parties had stipulated that two of the three methods of fee allocation at issue in this case were viewpoint neutral, the Court upheld the methods. Justice Kennedy remanded for further findings about a third method of allocation requiring a student referendum.

Justice Souter concurred in the opinion, joined by Justices Stevens and Breyer. Justice Souter criticized strict application of the viewpoint neutral standard. Instead, he asserted that the allocation of activities fees is integral to the implementation of the University's educational mission and therefore was protected by academic freedom. As tuition may be used to fund an academic course on certain topics but not others which may offend some students, a university may use student activities fees to fund certain activities.

(3) For additional discussion of unconstitutional conditions, see *Unconstitutional Conditions Symposium*, 26 San Diego L. Rev. 175 (1991) (articles by Larry Alexander, Richard Epstein, John Garvey, Seth Kreimer, William Marshall, Michael McConnell, Albert Rosenthal, Kenneth Simmons, Kathleen Sullivan, and Cass Sunstein).

(4) *Consent to Use Funds.* In *Davenport v. Wash. Educ. Ass'n*, 127 S. Ct. 2372 (2007), a series of cases restricted the ability of unions to use fees collected from objecting nonmembers for ideological purposes unrelated to the union's collective bargaining agreement. Such use violates the Free Speech rights of nonmembers. *Abood v. Detroit Bd. of Educ.*, 431 U.S. 209 (1977); *see also Keller v. State Bar of Cal.*, 496 U.S. 1 (1990) (using bar association dues for purposes to which bar members object). However, the fees could be used for purposes related to collective bargaining because nonmembers benefit from the resultant collective bargaining agreements. The Court's precedents require that the government allow nonunion members the opportunity to object to the union's using their dues for ideological purposes outside the scope of the collective bargaining process. *Davenport* allows the government to exceed the constitutional minimum required by *Abood* by not merely affording the nonunion member the opportunity to object, but by requiring the union to obtain affirmative consent from the nonunion member for such ideological use of funds.

NATIONAL ENDOWMENT FOR THE ARTS v. FINLEY, 524 U.S. 569 (1998). In *National Endowment for the Arts*, the Court rejected a facial challenge to a provision of the National Foundation on the Arts and Humanities Act that required "the

Chairperson of the National Endowment for the Arts (NEA) to ensure that 'artistic excellence and artistic merit are the criteria by which [grant] applications are judged, taking into consideration general standards of decency and respect for the diverse beliefs and values of the American public.' " The Court of Appeals had invalidated the provision based on viewpoint discrimination and vagueness.

Writing for the majority, Justice O'Connor set out the legislative history surrounding the statute, including Congress' rejection of the Crane Amendment "which would have virtually eliminated the NEA" and the Rohrbacher Amendment which would have prohibited a grant from the NEA that "could be used to 'promote, distribute, disseminate, or produce matter that has the purpose or effect of denigrating the beliefs, tenets, or objects of a particular religion' or 'of denigrating an individual, or group of individuals, on the basis of race, sex, handicap, or national origin.' " The statute at issue countered both proposals and required judges of grant applications "to 'take into consideration general standards of decency' " when considering an application's artistic merit. "Facial invalidation 'is, manifestly, strong medicine' that 'has been employed by the Court sparingly and only as a last resort.' *Broadrick v. Oklahoma*, 413 U.S. 601, 613 (1973)." The facial challenge here may be challenging the criteria in the statute as "sufficiently subjective that the agency could utilize them to engage in viewpoint discrimination. Given the varied interpretations of the criteria and the vague exhortation to 'take them into consideration,' it seems unlikely that this provision will introduce any greater element of selectivity than the determination of 'artistic excellence' itself." The Court will not strike down legislation based on assumptions.

"Any content-based considerations that may be taken into account in the grant-making process are a consequence of the nature of arts funding." With limited resources "it would be 'impossible to have a highly selective grant program without denying money to a large amount of constitutionally protected expression.' " The NEA's decisions on applicants have an "inherently content-based 'excellence' threshold."

The case would be different had the NEA penalized certain viewpoints. "[E]ven in the provision of subsidies, the Government may not 'aim at the suppression of dangerous ideas.' "

In a portion of the opinion not joined by Justice Ginsburg, the Court acknowledged that the "Government may allocate competitive funding according to criteria that would be impermissible were direct regulation of speech or a criminal penalty at stake. So long as legislation does not infringe on other constitutionally protected rights, Congress has wide latitude to set spending priorities." *Rust v. Sullivan* held that "Congress may 'selectively fund a program to encourage certain activities it believes to be in the public interest.' "

Refusing to hold the statute unconstitutionally vague, Justice O'Connor stated that "when the Government is acting as patron rather than as sovereign, the consequences of imprecision are not constitutionally severe." When dealing with "selective subsidies, it is not always feasible for Congress to legislate with clarity. Indeed, if this statute is unconstitutionally vague, then so too are all government programs awarding scholarships and grants on the basis of subjective criteria such as 'excellence' " as would be many other government programs.

Justice Scalia concurred, joined by Justice Thomas. He criticized the majority for "gutting" the statute. The statute, Justice Scalia said "establishes content-and viewpoint-based criteria upon which grant applications are to be evaluated," which is "perfectly constitutional."

The concurrence questioned the majority's speculation that the statute was "merely 'advisory.'" Instead, the statute required "the decency and respect factors to be" part of the evaluation process. "A reviewer may, of course, give varying weight to the factors."

Justice Scalia pointed out that the statute was created in response to the NEA's funding of "such offensive productions as Serrano's 'Piss Christ,' the portrayal of a crucifix immersed in urine, and Mapplethorpe's show of lurid homoerotic photographs." *Rust v. Sullivan* allowed government to '"selectively fund a program to encourage certain activities it believes to be in the public interest, without at the same time funding an alternative program.'"

Justice Souter dissented. "'If there is a bedrock principle underlying the First Amendment, it is that the government may not prohibit the expression of an idea simply because society finds the idea itself offensive or disagreeable.'" Justice Souter explained that "Congress has no obligation to support artistic enterprises that many people detest." However, in choosing to fund programs like the NEA, Congress "may not discriminate by viewpoint in deciding who gets the money."

The statute's "'general standards of decency,' are quintessentially viewpoint based: they require discrimination on the basis of conformity with mainstream mores." Specifically, "a statute disfavoring speech that fails to respect America's 'diverse beliefs and values' is the very model of viewpoint discrimination."

In its roles as speaker and buyer, the government may utilize viewpoint discrimination. However, in its association with the NEA, "the Government acts as a patron, financially underwriting the production of art by private artists and impresarios for independent consumption." In this role, it cannot engage in viewpoint discrimination. Finally, Justice Souter distinguished criteria of general decency from excellence: the latter was a merit-based criterion that did not necessarily discriminate based on viewpoint.

NOTE

Library Pornography. In *United States v. Am. Library Ass'n*, 539 U.S. 194 (2003), Chief Justice Rehnquist upheld (6-3) a statute that withholds funding from public libraries unless they install computer software that prevents viewing pornography. Congress worried that its programs subsidizing Internet access by public libraries "were facilitating access to illegal and harmful pornography." The Children's Internet Protection Act (CIPA) provides that a public library will not be eligible for federal funding to provide Internet access without first having installed "software to block images that constitute obscenity or child pornography, and to prevent minors from obtaining access to material that is harmful to them."

"Public library staffs necessarily consider content in making collection decisions and enjoy broad discretion in making them." Internet access does not qualify as a public forum, either traditional or designated. Libraries have always been charged with deciding what material is suitable for their collections. This liberty extends to deciding on Internet material. When filtering software sometimes blocks access to constitutionally protected speech for adults, adult users may simply ask the librarian to disable the filter or unblock a specific site.

The Court also rejected the unconstitutional condition challenge. *Rust v. Sullivan*, *supra* § 15.03, affords the government broad discretion to limit the use of public funds. Traditionally, libraries have not included pornographic material in their collections. CIPA only restricts libraries from allowing unfiltered access with federal funding. Libraries are able to offer this without the federal assistance.

Concurring in the judgment, Justice Kennedy said that if a library is unable to unblock a particular site, or if an adult patron's right to view protected material is substantially burdened, these can be dealt with by as-applied challenges. Concurring in the judgment, Justice Breyer would neither apply a rational basis test nor strict scrutiny level of review. "Given the comparatively small burden that the Act imposes upon the library patron seeking legitimate Internet materials, I cannot say that any speech-related harm that the Act may cause is disproportionate when considered in relation to the Act's legitimate objectives."

Dissenting, Justice Stevens argued that the filtering software underblocks because it limits access to sites based on text, not images. At the same time, these programs will restrict access to a large number of sites that, while harmless, contain a word that triggers the filter.

Justice Souter dissented, and Justice Ginsburg joined. Libraries have evolved away from the plurality's conception allowing any adult "access to any of its holdings."

LEGAL SERVICES CORP. v. VELAZQUEZ, 531 U.S. 533 (2001). In *Velazquez*, the Court invalidated a Congressional restriction on using Legal Services Corporation (LSC) funds to bring claims challenging existing welfare laws. The Legal Services Corporation Act distributes "funds appropriated by Congress to eligible local grantee organizations." The recipient organizations hire and oversee attorneys who provide legal services to indigent clients, including litigation concerning welfare benefits.

From the time it created the LSC program, Congress has restricted the use of its funds — for example, proscribing funds for litigation involving nontherapeutic abortions, secondary school desegregation, military desertion, or violations of the Selective Service statute." Grantees are also prohibited "from bringing class-action suits unless express approval is obtained from LSC."

In 1996, Congress imposed additional funding restrictions prohibiting funding of any organization " 'that initiates legal representation or participates in any other way, in litigation, lobbying, or rulemaking, involving an effort to reform a Federal or State welfare system, except that this paragraph shall not be construed to preclude a recipient from representing an individual eligible client who is seeking specific relief from a welfare agency if such relief does not involve an effort to amend or otherwise challenge existing law.' "

Writing for a 5-4 majority, Justice Kennedy opined: "We have said that viewpoint-based funding decisions can be sustained in instances in which the government is itself the speaker, *see Board of Regents of Univ. of Wis. System v. Southworth*, or instances, like *Rust* [*v. Sullivan*], in which the government 'used private speakers to transmit information pertaining to its own program.' *Rosenberger v. Rector & Visitors of Univ. of Va.*"[34] When sending its own message, the government is " 'accountable to the electorate.' "

In contrast, viewpoint-based restrictions may not be " 'proper when the [government] does not itself speak or subsidize transmittal of a message it favors but instead expends funds to encourage a diversity of views from private speakers.' " LSC "was designed to facilitate private speech, not to promote a governmental message." Specifically, "an LSC-funded attorney speaks on the behalf of the client in a claim against the government for welfare benefits."

Resembling the prohibition of editorializing by public broadcasting invalidated in *FCC v. League of Women Voters of Cal.*, "the Government seeks to use an existing

---

[34] *Rosenberger* said that when private organizations receive governmental funds with the purpose of conveying a " 'governmental message,' " the government may take certain " 'steps to ensure that its message is neither garbled nor distorted by the grantee.' "

medium of expression and to control it, in a class of cases, in ways which distort its usual functioning." Restrictions on advising clients and on arguing in court "distor[t] the legal system by altering the traditional role of the attorneys."[35] Government "may not design a subsidy to effect this serious and fundamental restriction on advocacy of attorneys and the functioning of the judiciary."

When "a question of statutory validity is present in any anticipated or pending case or controversy, the LSC-funded attorney must cease the representation at once," regardless of "whether the validity issue becomes apparent during initial attorney-client consultations or in the midst of litigation proceedings."[36] At bottom, the statute interferes with the duty of the courts to interpret the law as articulated in *Marbury v. Madison*, 1 Cranch 137, 177 (1803). "An informed, independent judiciary presumes an informed, independent bar." Instead, the restriction prohibits "expression upon which courts must depend for the proper exercise of the judicial power." In effect, it "sifts out cases presenting constitutional challenges in order to insulate the Government's laws from judicial inquiry" which is "inconsistent with accepted separation-of-powers principles."

That the LSC attorney could withdraw from a case did not cure the problem. The Act attempts to limit the LSC program "to arguments and theories Congress finds" acceptable. Even worse, these welfare clients are "unlikely to find other counsel." In *Rust*, "a patient could receive the approved Title X family planning counseling funded by the Government and later could consult an affiliate or independent organization to receive abortion counseling." In contrast, since the restriction at issue requires an LSC attorney to "withdraw whenever a question of a welfare statute's validity arises, an individual could not obtain joint representation" allowing for the non-LSC funded attorney to advance constitutional arguments while the LSC-funded attorney continued to pursue other claims.

Moreover, the restriction conveys "no programmatic message of the kind recognized in *Rust* and which sufficed there to allow the Government to specify the advice deemed necessary for its legitimate objectives." While Congress can limit what types of legal relationships and representation it will support,[37] Congress cannot "insulate its own laws from legitimate judicial challenge."

The Court invalidated the funding restriction at issue "leaving the balance of the statute operative and in place." However, the Court did not address severability and the Second Circuit's decision to strike out only a portion of the statute, as neither party raised this issue before it.

Justice Scalia, joined by Chief Justice Rehnquist, and Justices O'Connor and Thomas, dissented. When LSC lawyers must withdraw from a case, they "*must* explain to the client why they cannot represent him. They are also free to express their views of the legality of the welfare law to the client, and they may refer the client to another attorney who can accept the representation."

Importantly, LSC is a subsidy program. "Regulations directly restrict speech; subsidies do not. Subsidies, it is true, may *indirectly* abridge speech, but only if the funding scheme is 'manipulated' to have a 'coercive effect' on those who do not hold the subsidized position. *National Endowment for Arts v. Finley*, 524 U.S. 569, 587 (1998)."

---

[35] The restriction at issue even prohibits Supremacy Clause challenges against state statutes for inconsistency with federal law.

[36] "[I]f, during litigation, a judge were to ask an LSC attorney whether there was a constitutional concern, the LSC attorney simply could not answer."

[37] Indeed, Congress was not required to fund legal representation for the poor at all.

Only once, in *Rosenberger*, has the Court found "such selective spending unconstitutionally coercive" because government spending created a public forum in which government funding discriminated based on viewpoint. "When the limited spending program does not create a public forum, proving coercion is virtually impossible, because simply denying a subsidy 'does not "coerce" belief.' "

Like the statute upheld in *Rust*, the LSC Act "does not create a public forum." Further, the majority's attempt to distinguish "*Rust* because the welfare funding restriction 'seeks to use an existing medium of expression and to control it . . . in ways which distort its usual functioning' " is "wrong on both the facts and the law." No precedent limits government funding that " 'distorts an existing medium of expression.' " The majority's " 'nondistortion' principle is also wrong on the facts." Courts can consider only those questions "*that are presented by litigants*, and if the Government chooses not to subsidize the presentation of some such questions, that in no way 'distorts' the courts' role." In any event, the majority's concern that the client will not find another attorney to represent him if the LSC-funded attorney withdraws "is surely irrelevant, since it leaves the welfare recipient in no *worse* condition than he would have been in had the LSC program never been enacted."

In any event, the majority's concern that the client will not find another attorney to represent him if the LSC-funded attorney withdraws "is surely irrelevant, since it leaves the welfare recipient in no *worse* condition than he would have been in had the LSC program never been enacted."

For Justice Scalia, the only plausible way to distinguish this case from *Rust* is that in the latter "even patients who wished to receive abortion counseling could receive the nonabortion services that the Government-funded clinic offered, whereas" LSC lawyers cannot represent clients whose "cases raise a reform claim that an LSC lawyer may not present. This difference, of course, is required by the same ethical canons that the Court elsewhere does not wish to distort. Rather than sponsor 'truncated representation,' Congress chose to subsidize only those cases in which the attorneys it subsidized could work freely."

The dissenting justices also disagreed with the failure to address the severability issue. The dissent believed Congress would not have agreed to fund welfare litigation "without the restriction that the Court today invalidates." By lifting these restrictions on welfare reform litigation, the majority eliminates "a significant *quid pro quo* of the legislative compromise." Essentially, the majority "permits to stand a judgment that awards general litigation funding that the statute does not contain."

RUMSFELD v. FORUM FOR ACADEMIC & INSTITUTIONAL RIGHTS ("FAIR"), 547 U.S. 47 (2006). In *Rumsfeld v. Forum for Academic & Institutional Rights*, the Court held that the Solomon Amendment does not violate the First Amendment rights of law schools. Congress enacted the Solomon Amendment in response to law schools' restricting "the access of military recruiters to their students because of disagreement with the Government's policy on homosexuals in the military."[38] The Solomon Amendment provides "that if any part of an institution of higher education denies military recruiters access equal to that provided other recruiters, the entire institution" loses certain federal funds. A group of law schools and faculties (FAIR) claim that the Solomon Amendment abridged their freedoms of speech and association by forcing them "to choose between exercising their First Amendment right to decide whether to disseminate or accommodate a military recruiter's message,

---

[38] "Under this policy, a person generally may not serve in the Armed Forces if he has engaged in homosexual acts, stated that he is a homosexual, or married a person of the same sex. Respondents do not challenge that policy in this litigation."

and ensuring the availability of federal funding for their universities."

Writing for a unanimous court,[39] Chief Justice Roberts held that the Solomon Amendment did not violate the First Amendment rights of law schools.[40]

Chief Justice Roberts considered whether the Solomon Amendment constituted an unconstitutional condition on the receipt of federal funds. Relying on *Rostker v. Goldberg*, § 9.01, Chief Justice Roberts noted that " 'judicial deference . . . is at its apogee' when Congress legislates under its authority to raise and support armies." Rather than invoke its military powers, however, Congress used its spending power. The use of the spending power "does not reduce the deference given to Congress in the area of military affairs. Congress' choice to promote its goal by creating a funding condition deserves at least as deferential treatment as if Congress had imposed a mandate on universities." Congress did not impose an unconstitutional condition on Free Speech "[b]ecause the First Amendment would not prevent Congress from directly imposing the Solomon Amendment's access requirement."

Under the Solomon Amendment, law schools remain free "to express whatever views they may have on the military's congressionally mandated employment policy." At bottom, "[t]he Solomon Amendment regulates conduct, not speech."

The First Amendment prohibits the government from telling people what to say. For example, *West Virginia Board of Education v. Barnette*, 319 U.S. 624 (1943), prohibits states from "requiring schoolchildren to recite the Pledge of Allegiance and to salute the flag." *Wooley v. Maryland*, 430 U.S. 705 (1977), invalidated a law requiring motorists "to display the state motto-'Live Free or Die'-on their license plates." In contrast, "[t]he Solomon Amendment does not require any similar expression by law schools. Nonetheless, recruiting assistance provided by the schools often includes elements of speech. For example, schools may send e-mails or post notices on bulletin boards on an employer's behalf. Law schools offering such services to other recruiters must also send e-mails and post notices on behalf of the military to comply with the Solomon Amendment." Such services are "a far cry from the compelled speech" in these other cases. "The Solomon Amendment, unlike the laws at issue in those cases, does not dictate the content of the speech at all." Chief Justice Roberts found the alleged compelled speech to be "plainly incidental to the Solomon Amendment's regulation of conduct." Requiring "a law school that sends scheduling e-mails for other recruiters to send one for a military recruiter is simply not the same as forcing a student to pledge allegiance, or forcing a Jehovah's Witness to display the motto 'Live Free or Die,' and it trivializes the freedom protected" by those cases "to suggest that it is."

Of course, "compelled speech cases are not limited to the situation in which an individual must personally speak the government's message," and can also entail hosting or accommodating another speaker's message. "*See Hurley v. Irish-American Gay, Lesbian and Bisexual Group of Boston, Inc.*, § 14.02, (state law cannot require a parade to include a group whose message the parade's organizer does not wish to send)."[41] However, requiring the law schools to provide access to military recruiters

---

[39] Justice Alito did not take part in the decision.

[40] "It is insufficient for a law school to treat the military as it treats all other employers who violate its nondiscrimination policy. Under the statute, military recruiters must be given the same access as recruiters who comply with the policy."

[41] The Court also relied on "*Pacific Gas & Elec. Co. v. Public Util. Comm'n of Cal.*, 475 U.S. 1, 20-21 (1986) (plurality opinion); accord, *id.*, at 25 (Marshall, J., concurring in judgment) (state agency cannot require a utility company to include a third-party newsletter in its billing envelope); *Miami Herald Publishing Co. v. Tornillo*, 418 U.S. 241, (1974) (right-of-reply statute violates editors' right to determine the content of their newspapers)."

does not constitute compelled speech. "Law schools facilitate recruiting to assist their students in obtaining jobs. A law school's recruiting services lack the expressive quality of a parade, newsletter, or the editorial page of a newspaper."

The Court also refused to characterize these activities as expressive conduct. The Court has "extended First Amendment protection only to conduct that is inherently expressive," such as flag burning. "[T]he conduct regulated by the Solomon Amendment is not inherently expressive." Were combining speech with conduct "enough to create expressive conduct, a regulated party could always transform conduct into 'speech' simply by talking about it."

Even if the Solomon Amendment did interfere with expressive conduct, *United States v. O'Brien*, § 15.01, permits incidental burdens on speech " 'so long as the neutral regulation promotes a substantial government interest that would be achieved less effectively absent the regulation.' " Chief Justice Roberts stated: "Military recruiting promotes the substantial Government interest in raising and supporting the Armed Forces-an objective that would be achieved less effectively if the military were forced to recruit on less favorable terms than other employers."

The Chief Justice also found that the Solomon Amendment did not violate the law school's " 'right of expressive association.' " In *Boy Scouts of America v. Dale*, § 12.05, a New Jersey law violated this freedom by requiring the Boy Scouts "to accept a homosexual as a scoutmaster." Law schools merely assist them. "Unlike the public accommodations law in *Dale*, the Solomon Amendment does not force a law school 'to accept members it does not desire.' "

Freedom of association also protects anonymity of membership and prohibits the government from imposing penalties "based on membership in a disfavored group." The Solomon Amendment has no such impact. "Students and faculty are free to associate to voice their disapproval of the military's message; nothing about the statute affects the composition of the group by making group membership less desirable." Simple "presence on campus does not violate a law school's right to associate, regardless of how repugnant the law school considers the recruiter's message."

§ 15.04 COMMERCIAL SPEECH

[1] Protection for Commercial Speech: General Principles

VIRGINIA STATE BD. OF PHARMACY v. VIRGINIA CITIZENS CONSUMER COUNCIL, INC.
425 U.S. 748, 96 S. Ct. 1817, 48 L. Ed. 2d 346 (1976)

JUSTICE BLACKMUN delivered the opinion of the Court.

The plaintiff-appellees in this case attack, as violative of the First and Fourteenth Amendments, that portion of § 54-524.35 of Va. Code Ann. (1974), which provides that a pharmacist licensed in Virginia is guilty of unprofessional conduct if he "(3) publishes, advertises or promotes, directly or indirectly, in any manner whatsoever, any amount, price, fee, premium, discount, rebate or credit terms . . . for any drugs which may be dispensed only by prescription." . . .

I

. . . The "practice of pharmacy" [in Virginia] . . . is subject to extensive regulation aimed at preserving high professional standards. The regulatory body is the appellant Virginia State Board of Pharmacy. The Board is broadly charged by statute with various responsibilities, including the "[m]aintenance of the equality, quantity, integrity, safety and efficacy of drugs or devices distributed, dispensed or administered." § 54-524.16(a). . . .

The Board is also the licensing authority. . . .

Once licensed, a pharmacist is subject to a civil monetary penalty, or to revocation or suspension of his license, if the Board finds that he "is not of good moral character," or has violated any of a number of stated professional standards [including] . . . advertising . . . the price for any prescription drug. . . .

Inasmuch as only a licensed pharmacist may dispense prescription drugs in Virginia, advertising or other affirmative dissemination of prescription drug price information is effectively forbidden in the State. . . . The prohibition does not extend to nonprescription drugs, but neither is it confined to prescriptions that the pharmacist compounds himself. Indeed, about 95% of all prescriptions now are filled with dosage forms prepared by the pharmaceutical manufacturer.

II

. . . The present . . . attack on the statute is . . . made . . . by prescription drug consumers who claim that they would greatly benefit if the prohibition were lifted and advertising freely allowed. The plaintiffs are an individual Virginia resident who suffers from diseases that require her to take prescription drugs on a daily basis, and two nonprofit organizations. Their claim is that the First Amendment entitles the user of prescription drugs to receive information that pharmacists wish to communicate to them through advertising and other promotional means, concerning the prices of such drugs. . . .

III

The question first arises whether, even assuming that First Amendment protection attaches to the flow of drug price information, it is a protection enjoyed by the appellees as recipients of the information, and not solely, if at all, by the advertisers themselves who seek to disseminate that information.

Freedom of speech presupposes a willing speaker. But where a speaker exists, as is the case here, the protection afforded is to the communication, to its source and to its recipients both. . . . If there is a right to advertise, there is a reciprocal right to receive the advertising, and it may be asserted by these appellees.

IV

. . . There can be no question that in past decisions the Court has given some indication that commercial speech is unprotected. . . . *Valentine v. Chrestensen*, [316 U.S. 52 (1942)] . . .

. . . [I]n *Pittsburgh Press Co. v. Human Relations Comm'n*, 413 U.S. 376 (1973), . . . the Court upheld an ordinance prohibiting newspapers from listing employment advertisements in columns according to whether male or female employees were sought to be hired. The Court, to be sure, characterized the advertisements as "classic examples of commercial speech," *Id.* at 385. . . . The Court, however, upheld the ordinance on the ground that the restriction it imposed was permissible because the discriminatory hirings proposed by the advertisements, and by their newspaper layout, were themselves illegal.

Last Term, in *Bigelow v. Virginia*, 421 U.S. 809 (1975), [w]e reversed a conviction for violation of a Virginia statute that made the circulation of any publication to encourage or promote the processing of an abortion in Virginia a misdemeanor. The defendant had published in his newspaper the availability of abortions in New York. . . .

. . . We noted that . . . the advertisement "did more than simply propose a commercial transaction. It contained factual material of clear 'public interest.' " *Id.* at 822. And, of course, the advertisement related to activity with which, at least in some respects, the State could not interfere. *See Roe v. Wade*, 410 U.S. 113 (1973). . . .

Here, in contrast, the question whether there is a First Amendment exception for "commercial speech" is squarely before us. . . . Our pharmacist does not wish to editorialize on any subject, cultural, philosophical, or political. He does not wish to report any particular newsworthy fact, or to make generalized observations even about commercial matters. The "idea" he wishes to communicate is simply this: "I will sell you the X prescription drug at the Y price." Our question, then, is whether this communication is wholly outside the protection of the First Amendment.

V

We begin with several propositions that already are settled or beyond serious dispute. It is clear, for example, that speech does not lose its First Amendment protection because money is spent to project it, as in a paid advertisement of one form or another. . . . Speech likewise is protected even though it is carried in a form that is "sold" for profit. . . . *Joseph Burstyn, Inc. v. Wilson*, 343 U.S. 495 (1952) (motion pictures) . . . and even though it may involve a solicitation to purchase or otherwise pay or contribute money. *Cantwell v. Connecticut*, 310 U.S. 296, 306–307 (1940). . . .

Focusing first on the individual parties to the transaction that is proposed in the commercial advertisement, we may assume that the advertiser's interest is a purely economic one. That hardly disqualifies him from protection under the First Amendment. . . .

As to the particular consumer's interest in the free flow of commercial information, interest may be as keen, if not keener by far, than his interest in the day's most urgent political debate. . . . Those whom the suppression of a prescription drug price information hits the hardest are the poor, sick and particularly the aged. . . .

Generalizing, society also may have a strong interest in the free flow of commercial information. Even an individual advertisement, though entirely "commercial," may be of general public interest. . . .

Moreover, there is another consideration that suggests that no line between publicly "interesting" or "important" commercial advertising and the opposite kind could ever be drawn. Advertising, however tasteless and excessive it sometimes may seem, is nonetheless dissemination of information as to who is producing and selling what product, for what reason, and at what price. So long as we preserve a predominantly free enterprise economy, the allocation of our resources in large measure will be made through numerous private economic decisions. It is a matter of public interest that those decisions, in the aggregate, be intelligent and well informed. To this end, the free flow of commercial information is indispensable. . . . And if it is indispensable to the proper allocation of resources in a free enterprise system, it is also indispensable to the formation of intelligent opinions as to how that system ought to be regulated or altered. . . .

Arrayed against these substantial individual and societal interests are a number of justifications for the advertising ban. These have to do principally with maintaining a high degree of professionalism on the part of licensed pharmacists.[42]

Indisputably, the State has a strong interest in maintaining that professionalism. . . . [E]ven with respect to manufacturer-prepared compounds, there is room for the pharmacist to serve his customer well or badly. . . . He may know of a particular antagonism between the prescribed drug and another that the customer is or might be taking, or with an allergy the customer may suffer. . . . A pharmacist who has a continuous relationship with his customer is in the best position, of course, to exert professional skill for the customer's protection.

Price advertising, it is argued, will place in jeopardy the pharmacist's expertise and, with it, the customer's health. It is claimed that the aggressive price competition that will result from unlimited advertising will make it impossible for the pharmacist to supply professional services in the compounding, handling, and dispensing of prescription drugs. Such services are time consuming and expensive; if competitors who economize by eliminating them are permitted to advertise their resulting lower prices, the more painstaking and conscientious pharmacist will be forced either to follow suit or to go out of business. It is also claimed that prices might not necessarily fall as a result of advertising. If one pharmacist advertises, others must, and the resulting expense will inflate the cost of drugs. It is further claimed that advertising will lead people to shop for their prescription drugs among the various pharmacists who offer the lowest prices, and the loss of stable pharmacist-customer relationships will make individual attention — and certainly the practice of monitoring — impossible. Finally, it is argued that damage will be done to the professional image of the pharmacist. This image, that of a skilled and specialized craftsman, attracts talent to the profession and reinforces the better habits of those who are in it. Price advertising, it is said, will reduce the pharmacist's status to that of a mere retailer.

The strength of these proffered justifications is greatly undermined by the fact that high professional standards, to a substantial extent, are guaranteed by the close regulation to which pharmacists in Virginia are subject. . . . Surely, any pharmacist guilty of professional dereliction that actually endangers his customer will promptly lose his license. At the same time, we cannot discount the Board's justifications entirely. . . .

. . . [T]he State's protectiveness of its citizens rests in large measure on the advantages of their being kept in ignorance. . . . The advertising ban does not directly affect professional standards one way or the other. . . . There is no claim that the advertising ban in any way prevents the cutting of corners by the pharmacist who is so inclined. That pharmacist is likely to cut corners in any event. The only effect the advertising ban has on him is to insulate him from price competition and to open the way for him to make a substantial, and perhaps even excessive, profit in addition to providing an inferior service. The more painstaking pharmacist is also protected but, again, it is a protection based in large part on public ignorance.

It appears to be feared that if the pharmacist who wishes to provide low cost, and assertedly low quality, services is permitted to advertise, he will be taken up on his offer by too many unwitting customers. They will choose the low-cost, low-quality service and drive the "professional" pharmacist out of business. . . .

There is, of course, an alternative to this highly paternalistic approach. That alternative is to assume that this information is not in itself harmful, that people will

---

[42] [Court's footnote 21] An argument not advanced by the Board, . . . but which on occasion has been made to other courts, is that the advertisement of low drug prices will result in overconsumption and in abuse of the advertised drugs. The argument prudently has been omitted. By definition, the drugs at issue here may be sold only on a physician's prescription. . . .

perceive their own best interests if only they are well enough informed, and that the best means to that end is to open the channels of communication rather than to close them. . . . It is precisely this kind of choice, between the dangers of suppressing information, and the dangers of its misuse if it is freely available, that the First Amendment makes for us. Virginia is free to require whatever professional standards it wishes of its pharmacists; it may subsidize them or protect them from competition in other ways. . . . [T]he justifications Virginia has offered for suppressing the flow of prescription drug price information, far from persuading us that the flow is not protected by the First Amendment, have reinforced our view that it is. We so hold.

VI

In concluding that commercial speech, like other varieties, is protected, we of course do not hold that it can never be regulated in any way. Some forms of commercial speech regulation are surely permissible. We mention a few only to make clear that they are not before us and therefore are not foreclosed by this case.

There is no claim, for example, that the prohibition on prescription drug price advertising is a mere time, place, and manner restriction. We have often approved restrictions of that kind provided that they are justified without reference to the content of the regulated speech, that they serve a significant governmental interest, and that in so doing they leave open ample alternative channels for communication of the information. . . . Whatever may be the proper bounds of time, place, and manner restrictions on commercial speech, they are plainly exceeded by this Virginia statute, which singles out speech of a particular content and seeks to prevent its dissemination completely.

Nor is there any claim that prescription drug price advertisements are forbidden because they are false or misleading in any way. Untruthful speech, commercial or otherwise, has never been protected for its own sake. *Gertz v. Robert Welch, Inc.*, 418 U.S. 323, 340 (1974). . . . Obviously, much commercial speech is not probably false, or even wholly false, but only deceptive or misleading. We foresee no obstacle to a State's dealing effectively with this problem.[43]

The First Amendment as we construe it today, does not prohibit the State from insuring that the stream of commercial information flow cleanly as well as freely.

Also, there is no claim that the transactions proposed in the forbidden advertisements are themselves illegal in any way. . . . Finally, the special problems of the electronic broadcast media are likewise not in this case. . . .

---

[43] [Court's footnote 24] . . . There are commonsense differences between speech that does "no more than propose a commercial transaction," *Pittsburgh Press Co. v. Human Relations Comm'n*, 413 U.S. at 385, and other varieties. Even if the differences do not justify the conclusion that commercial speech is valueless, and thus subject to complete suppression by the State, they nonetheless suggest that a different degree of protection is necessary to insure that the flow of truthful and legitimate commercial information is unimpaired. The truth of commercial speech, for example, may be more easily verifiable by its disseminator than, let us say, news reporting or political commentary, in that ordinarily the advertiser seeks to disseminate information about a specific product or service that he himself provides and presumably knows more about than anyone else. Also, commercial speech may be more durable than other kinds. Since advertising is the sine qua non of commercial profits, there is little likelihood of its being chilled by proper regulation and forgone entirely.

Attributes such as these, the greater objectivity and hardiness of commercial speech, may make it less necessary to tolerate inaccurate statements for fear of silencing the speaker. . . . They may also make it appropriate to require that a commercial message appear in such a form, or include such additional information, warnings, and disclaimers, as are necessary to prevent its being deceptive. . . . They may also make inapplicable the prohibition against prior restraints. . . .

What is at issue is whether a State may completely suppress the dissemination of concededly truthful information about entirely lawful activity, fearful of that information's effect upon its disseminators and its recipients. Reserving other questions,[44] we conclude that the answer to this one is in the negative.

JUSTICE STEVENS took no part in the consideration or decision of this case.

CHIEF JUSTICE BURGER, concurring.

The Court notes that roughly 95% of all prescriptions are filled with dosage units already prepared by the manufacturer and sold to the pharmacy in that form. . . . As the Court notes, quite different factors would govern were we face with a law regulating or even prohibiting advertising by the traditional learned professions of medicine or law. . . . Attorneys and physicians are engaged *primarily* in providing services in which professional judgment is a large component, a matter very different from the retail *sale* of labeled drugs already prepared by others. . . .

I doubt that we know enough about evaluating the quality of medical and legal services to know which claims of superiority are "misleading" and which are justifiable. Nor am I sure that even advertising the price of certain professional services is not inherently misleading, since what the professional must do will vary greatly in individual cases. It is important to note that the Court wisely leaves these issues to another day.

JUSTICE STEWART, concurring. . . .

[S]ince it is a cardinal principle of the First Amendment that "government has no power to restrict expression because of its message, its ideas, its subject matter, or its content," the Court's decision calls into immediate question the constitutional legitimacy of every state and federal law regulating false or deceptive advertising. I write separately to explain why I think today's decision does not preclude such governmental regulation. . . .

. . . Since the factual claims contained in commercial price or product advertisements relate to tangible goods or services, they may be tested empirically. . . . Indeed, the elimination of false and deceptive claims serves to promote the one facet of commercial price and product advertising that warrants First Amendment protection — its contribution to the flow of accurate and reliable information relevant to public and private decisionmaking.

JUSTICE REHNQUIST, dissenting. . . .

. . . While there is again much to be said for the Court's observation as a matter of desirable public policy, there is certainly nothing in the United States Constitution which requires the Virginia Legislature to hew to the teachings of Adam Smith in its legislative decisions regulating the pharmacy profession. . . .

The Court concedes that legislatures may prohibit false and misleading advertisements, and may likewise prohibit advertisements seeking to induce transactions which are themselves illegal. In the final footnote the opinion tosses a bone to the traditionalists in the legal and medical professions by suggesting that because they sell services rather than drugs the holding of this case is not automatically applicable to advertising in those professions. But if the sole limitation on permissible state proscription of advertising is that it may not be false or misleading, surely the

---

[44] [Court's footnote 25] . . . Although we express no opinion as to other professions, the distinctions, historical and functional, between professions, may require consideration of quite different factors. Physicians and lawyers, for example, do not dispense standardized products; they render professional services of almost infinite variety and nature, with the consequent enhanced possibility for confusion and deception if they were to undertake certain kinds of advertising.

difference between pharmacists' advertising and lawyers' and doctors' advertising can be only one of degree and not of kind. . . .

. . . In this case, . . . the Court has unfortunately substituted for the wavering line previously thought to exist between commercial speech and protected speech a no more satisfactory line of its own — that between "truthful" commercial speech, on the one hand, and that which is "false and misleading" on the other. . . .

The Court insists that the rule it lays down is consistent even with the view that the First Amendment is "primarily an instrument to enlighten public decisionmaking in a democracy." I had understood this view to relate to public decisionmaking as to political, social, and other public issues, rather than the decision of a particular individual as to whether to purchase one or another kind of shampoo. It is undoubtedly arguable that many people in the country regard the choice of shampoo as just as important as who may be elected to local, state, or national political office, but that does not automatically bring information about competing shampoos within the protection of the First Amendment. . . .

. . . [W]hile prescription drugs are a necessary and vital part of medical care and treatment, there are sufficient dangers attending their widespread use that they simply may not be promoted in the same manner as hair creams, deodorants, and toothpaste. The very real dangers that general advertising for such drugs might create in terms of encouraging, even though not sanctioning, illicit use of them by individuals for whom they have not been prescribed, or by generating patient pressure upon physicians to prescribe them, are simply not dealt with in the Court's opinion. . . . Nothing we know about the acquisitive instincts of those who inhabit every business and profession to a greater or lesser extent gives any reason to think that such persons will not do everything they can to generate demand for these products in much the same manner and to much the same degree as demand for other commodities has been generated.

Both Congress and state legislatures have by law sharply limited the permissible dissemination of information about some commodities because of the potential harm resulting from those commodities, even though they were not thought to be sufficiently demonstrably harmful to warrant outright prohibition of their sale. Current prohibitions on television advertising of liquor and cigarettes are prominent in this category, but apparently under the Court's holding so long as the advertisements are not deceptive they may no longer be prohibited. . . .

BOLGER v. YOUNGS DRUG PRODUCTS CORP., 463 U.S. 60 (1983). *Bolger* invalidated a federal law that prohibited the mailing of any "unsolicited advertisement of matter which is designed, adapted or intended for preventing conception." At issue were "multi-page, multi-item flyers promoting a large variety of products available at a drugstore, including prophylactics; flyers exclusively or substantially devoted to promoting prophylactics; [and] informational pamphlets discussing the desirability and availability of prophylactics in general or Young's products in particular." Justice Marshall's opinion held that all of the material was entitled to the "qualified but nonetheless substantial protection accorded to commercial speech." The material was neither false, deceptive, or misleading; nor was it related to illegal behavior. The government argued that the prohibition protects recipients from offensive material and helps parents control the methods by which they will inform their children about birth control. As for the claim of offensiveness, the Court concluded that advertising for contraceptives involved substantial individual and societal interests in the free flow of information and relates to activity which is protected from unwarranted state interference. The fact that the information was coming into the home did not create a "captive audience" problem, since the material could easily be moved "from mailbox to trash can." Moreover, one's name can be removed from the company's mailing list.

The Court also had little difficulty disposing of the claim that the prohibition helped parents in their efforts to discuss birth control with their children. Parents can exercise considerable control over the disposition of incoming mail, and already have to cope "with the multitude of external stimuli that color their children's perception of sensitive subjects."

The Court also commented on some difficult definitional problems of commercial speech: "Most of appellee's mailings fall within the core of commercial speech . . . Youngs' informational pamphlets, however, cannot be characterized merely as proposals to engage in commercial transactions. . . . The mere fact that these pamphlets are conceded to be advertisements does not compel the conclusion that they are commercial speech. Similarly, the reference to a specific product does not by itself render the pamphlets commercial speech. Finally, the fact that Youngs has an economic motivation for mailing the pamphlets would clearly be insufficient by itself to turn the material into commercial speech.

"The combination of *all* these characteristics, however, provide strong support for the District Court's conclusion that the information pamphlets are properly characterized as commercial speech. The mailings constitute commercial speech notwithstanding the fact that they contain discussions of important public issues such as venereal disease and family planning. We have made clear that advertising which links a product to a current public debate is not thereby entitled to the constitutional protection afforded noncommercial speech. Advertisers should not be permitted to immunize false or misleading product information from government regulation simply by including references to public issues."

Justice Rehnquist filed an opinion concurring in the judgment in which Justice O'Connor joined. Justice Stevens also filed an opinion concurring in the judgment. Justice Brennan did not participate.

NOTE

For additional discussion, see Martin H. Redish, *Product Health Claims and the First Amendment: Scientific Expression and the Twilight Zone of Commercial Speech*, 43 VAND. L. REV. 1433, 1460–1 (1990) ("The level of public interest in communication and information concerning the health implications of everyday products is no less when that information comes from the manufacturer of those products than when the same information comes from an objective scientific or medical expert.").

CENT. HUDSON GAS & ELEC. CORP. v. PUB. SERV. COMM'N OF N.Y., 447 U.S. 557 (1980). In *Central Hudson*, the Court invalidated a regulation of the New York Public Service Commission which in 1973 prohibited electric utilities in the State from advertising to promote the use of electricity. "The order was based on the Commission's finding that 'the inter-connected utility system in New York State does not have sufficient fuel stocks or sources of supply to continue furnishing all customer demands for the 1973–1974 winter.'"

After the energy crisis causing the fuel shortage had eased, the Commission extended the ban for three additional years. Central Hudson objected to the extension of the ban.

In the Policy Statement extending the ban, the Commission divided utility advertising into promotional advertising which was designed to stimulate the purchase of utility services, and institutional or informational advertising which was not designed to promote sales. The Commission banned promotional advertising as "contrary to the national policy of conserving energy" and to curb " 'unnecessary growth' in energy consumption." However, the Commission allowed institutional or informational advertising, including " 'informational' advertising designed to encourage '*shifts* of consumption' from peak demand times to periods of low electricity demand."

Writing for the Court, Justice Powell stated that the "Commission's order restricts only commercial speech, that is, expression related solely to the economic interests of the speaker and its audience."[45]

Noting that the Constitution "accords lesser protection to commercial speech than to other constitutionally guaranteed expression," the Court posited the following four-part test. First, commercial speech "must concern lawful activity and not be misleading. Next, we ask whether the asserted government interest is substantial. If both inquiries yield positive answers, we must determine whether the regulation directly advances the governmental interest asserted, and whether it is not more extensive than is necessary to serve that interest."

As to the first step of the inquiry, the Commission did not claim that the expression at issue was misleading or related to an unlawful activity. Instead, the New York Court of Appeals rejected protection for commercial speech in a monopolized utility as "advertising in a 'non-competitive market' could not improve the decisionmaking of consumers." Rejecting this argument, Justice Powell noted that electricity competes with natural gas and fuel oil in some markets such as home heating. In these markets, advertising helps consumer decision-making.[46]

The Court accepted that the state's asserted interest in energy conservation was substantial. Moreover, the Commission's order "directly advances" the State's interest in energy conservation. "There is an immediate connection between advertising and demand for electricity."

Nevertheless, the complete ban on this promotional advertising was "more extensive than necessary to further the State's interest in energy conservation." The energy conservation rationale would not justify preventing Central Hudson "from promoting electric services that would reduce energy use by diverting demand from less efficient sources, or that would consume roughly the same amount of energy as do alternative sources of energy." "The Commission also has not demonstrated that its interest in conservation cannot be protected adequately by more limited regulation of [Central Hudson's] commercial expression." Permissible regulations might even require limited warnings or disclaimers.

Finally, in a footnote at the end of the opinion, the Court indicated that the Commission could consider "previewing" advertising for compliance with the conservation policy. Justice Powell noted that the Court had allowed a "prescreening arrangement" in other areas such as obscenity "if it includes adequate procedural safeguards."[47]

Justice Brennan wrote a separate opinion concurring in the judgment. Justice Blackmun also filed an opinion concurring in the judgment, joined by Justice Brennan. In his view, government could not conserve energy by suppressing information but

---

[45] The majority took issue with the broader definition of commercial speech advanced in the concurring opinion of Justice Stevens. That opinion suggested that promotional advertising comprehending questions commonly discussed by political leaders be afforded full First Amendment protection. For example, advertising promoting electricity for environmental reasons should be given such protection. Rejecting this position, Justice Powell noted that such discussions still receive full First Amendment protection when they occur outside the advertising context.

[46] In a footnote, the Court indicated that it carefully scrutinized blanket bans on commercial speech designed to advance some "non-speech related policy." The Court had only approved such blanket bans on commercial speech that was "deceptive or related to unlawful activity."

[47] While the order initially responded to a fuel shortage, the Commission did not claim that one still exists.

instead must use more direct methods such as "prohibiting air conditioning or regulating thermostat levels."

Justice Stevens concurred in the judgment, joined by Justice Brennan. Justice Stevens believed that the ban prohibited more commercial speech as it encompassed "a great deal more than mere proposals to engage in certain kinds of commercial transactions." For example, it suppressed advocacy of using electricity — even for environmental reasons.

Justice Rehnquist dissented. "When the source of the speech is a state-created monopoly such as this, traditional First Amendment concerns, if they come into play at all, certainly do not justify the broad interventionist role adopted by the Court." Moreover, by failing to sufficiently subordinate the position of commercial speech, the majority's opinion harkened back to *Lochner v. New York*, 198 U.S. 45 (1905). "I doubt there would be any question as to the constitutionality of New York's conservation effort if the Public Service Commission had chosen to raise the price of electricity; to condition its sale on specified terms; or to restrict its production. In terms of constitutional values, I think that such controls are virtually indistinguishable from the State's ban on promotional advertising."

Criticizing the Court's *laissez-faire* view, he said that there is no evidence "that the marketplace of ideas is free from market imperfections any more than there is to believe that the invisible hand will always lead to optimum economic decisions in the commercial market."

NOTES

(1) *Real Estate Signs and "White Flight."* In *Linmark Associates Inc. v. Township of Willingboro*, 431 U.S. 85 (1977), the Court (8-0) invalidated a municipal ordinance that prohibited the posting of real estate "For Sale" and "Sold" signs insofar as the ordinance impaired "the flow of truthful and legitimately commercial information." The township asserted that it had enacted the ordinance in order to stem perceived "white flight" from an integrated community. The Court found that neither speakers nor listeners — those desiring to sell their homes or would-be purchasers — differed from the parties in *Bigelow and Virginia Pharmacy* simply because the commercial information focused on realty rather than abortions or drugs.

The Court found the ordinance an unconstitutional content regulation. "The record here demonstrates that respondents failed to establish that this ordinance is needed to assure that Willingboro remains an integrated community." More importantly, the Township Council "acted to prevent its residents from obtaining certain information. That information, which pertains to sales activity in Willingboro, is of vital interest to Willingboro residences, since it may bear on one of the important decisions they have a right to make: 'where to live and raise their families.' "

(2) *Selective Ban on Billboards.* In *Metromedia, Inc. v. San Diego*, 453 U.S. 490 (1981), a majority of the Court appeared to be willing to sustain a law banning all commercial outdoor advertising signs except for so-called "on-site" signs used to advertise the business of the owner or occupant of the premises. Nevertheless, a majority held that the San Diego law was invalid, primarily because of its sweeping prohibition of non-commercial outdoor advertising. The plurality opinion of Justice White, joined by Justices Stewart, Marshall and Powell, agreed that a ban on off-site commercial advertising was justified by the City's interest in traffic safety and aesthetics. The exception for on-site commercial advertising was a legitimate recognition by the City that some commercial interests outweighed the City's interest. Justice Stevens' dissent agreed with this portion of the plurality's opinion, as did the dissents of Chief Justice Burger and Justice Rehnquist, which would have sustained the

San Diego ordinance in its entirety. Thus, there were seven votes for this position of allowing the ban on off-site commercial signs.

Sharp differences emerged, however, with regard to non-commercial advertising, which resulted in a judgment holding the law invalid. The plurality objected to allowing on-site, commercial advertising but prohibiting on-site, non-commercial advertising. Barring the latter "inverts" the judgment that non-commercial speech must be accorded greater protection than commercial speech. Moreover, the plurality objected to content discrimination in permitting only non-commercial speech (e.g., temporary political campaign signs, signs carrying news items, religious symbols) whether on-site or off-site. If San Diego allows some non-commercial messages, "San Diego must similarly allow billboards conveying other non-commercial messages throughout those zones."

In a footnote (n. 20), Justice White's opinion rejected such an implication: "Because a total prohibition of outdoor advertising is not before us, we do not indicate whether such a ban would be inconsistent with the First Amendment." The same footnote, however, cited *Schad v. Borough of Mount Ephraim*, 452 U.S. 61 (1981), in which the Court invalidated a complete ban on live entertainment in a commercial zone.

Having concluded that the ban on non-commercial speech reached "too far into the realm of protected speech," the plurality held the law unconstitutional on its face. The necessary majority for a holding of facial invalidity was provided by the concurrence of Justice Brennan, joined by Justice Blackmun. Justice Brennan treated the San Diego law as a complete ban on outdoor advertising as a means of expression. He concluded that the City had not met the burden of demonstrating that its interest in traffic safety or aesthetics justified this broad restriction on First Amendment rights. Moveover, Justice Brennan objected to the commercial/non-commercial distinction because of the discretion that it afforded local officials to decide what types of messages could be conveyed.

Justice Stevens agreed with the plurality that the City could draw a distinction between off-site and on-site commercial advertising. But he would have held that "a wholly impartial total ban on billboards would be permissible," a conclusion which Chief Justice Burger and Justice Rehnquist both appeared to accept in their separate dissenting opinions. Chief Justice Burger's dissent defended the exceptions that San Diego made to its broad prohibition on non-commercial outdoor advertising. These exceptions represented, in his view, a sensitivity to the free speech aspects of non-commercial advertising.

(3) *Complete Ban of Signs on Public Property.* In *Los Angeles City Council v. Taxpayers for Vincent*, 466 U.S. 789 (1984), the Court relied in part on the reasoning of the several opinions in *Metromedia, Inc. v. San Diego, supra,* in upholding a Los Angeles statute prohibiting the posting of all signs on public property. Referring to the earlier case, the Court in *Vincent* said: "There the Court considered the city's interest in avoiding visual clutter, and seven Justices explicitly concluded that this interest was sufficient to justify a prohibition of billboards. . . . We reaffirm the conclusion of the majority in *Metromedia.*" For additional discussion of *Vincent*, see § 14.04[1], Note (2).

(4) *Access to Public Utility Billing. Consolidated Edison Co. v. Public Service Comm'n*, 447 U.S. 530 (1980), invalidated an order of the New York State Public Service Commission prohibiting "utilities from using bill inserts to discuss political matters including the desirablility of future development of nuclear power." In *Pacific Gas and Electric Company v. Public Utilities Commission of California*, 475 U.S. 1 (1986), the Court sustained a public utility's right to include its own material in its billing envelopes. The California Commission ordered the utility to allow an outside organization, representing rate-payers, to include its mailings in the billing envelopes

four times a year for two years. The Court compared the Commission's ruling to the Florida law (invalidated in *Miami Herald v. Tornillo*, 418 U.S. 241 (1974)) which had accorded political candidates the right to reply to a personal character attack. The majority in *Pacific Gas and Electric* ruled that the Commission's order deterred the utility from expressing its own views and forced the utility to disseminate views with which it disagreed. The plurality opinion of Justice Powell, and the concurrences of Chief Justice Burger and Justice Marshall, extended to business corporations the right not to be compelled to be a forum for the dissemination of views they opposed. This right had previously been recognized for newspapers and individuals in *Tornillo* and in *Wooley v. Maynard* (*see infra*). For additional discussion of *Pacific Gas and Electric Company*, see § 14.04[2], Note 1(b).

(5) *Promotional Newsracks.* In *City of Cincinnati v. Discovery Network, Inc.*, 507 U.S. 410 (1993), the Court applied the "reasonable fit" standard, to strike down a city ordinance prohibiting the distribution of promotional materials through newsracks placed on public property. In 1989, the City of Cincinnati authorized Discovery Network, Inc. and Harmon Publishing Company, Inc. to place a total of 62 newsracks on public property. Discovery Network used its 38 newsracks to dispense free magazines promoting the company's educational, recreational, and social programs. A portion of its magazine was also devoted to "current events of general interest." Harmon Publishing used its 24 newsracks to distribute magazines devoted in part to real estate advertising and in part to providing information about "interest rates, market trends, and other real estate matters." One year later, the city revoked the permits authorizing use of the newsracks, citing a preexisting ordinance which prohibited the distribution of "commercial handbills" on public property. The City did not similarly restrict other newsracks dispensing newspapers, which numbered some 1,500–2,000.

Writing for the Court, Justice Stevens discussed the difficulty of drawing lines between commercial and noncommercial speech. Newspapers contain much commercial advertising, while respondents' publications contained much material that was not "core commercial speech." The blurry distinction between the two is a matter of degree. Assuming that the speech at issue was commercial speech, Justice Stevens nevertheless struck down the city's ordinance: "Not only does Cincinnati's categorical ban on commercial newsracks place too much importance on the distinction between commercial and noncommercial speech, but in this case, the distinction bears no relationship *whatsoever* to the particular interests the City has asserted." The few newsracks banned under the ordinance posed no greater burden on the City's asserted interest in aesthetics than did the many newspaper racks permitted under the ordinance. The Court concluded further that the ordinance was not a valid time, place, or manner restriction as it was content-based. Chief Justice Rehnquist dissented, joined by Justices White and Thomas.

(6) *Lottery Advertising.* In *United States v. Edge Broadcasting Co.*, 509 U.S. 418 (1993), the Court upheld, against an "as applied" challenge, a federal statute prohibiting the broadcasting of lottery advertisements, except those for state-run lotteries aired by stations licensed in states that conduct lotteries. Edge Broadcasting Company (Edge) owned a radio station licensed by North Carolina. Because North Carolina is a nonlottery state, the statute prohibited the station from broadcasting lottery advertisements. More than 90% of the station's listeners and revenue came from across the border in Virginia, which did sponsor lotteries.

Justice White's majority opinion focused on the third and fourth factors of the test set out in *Central Hudson Gas & Electric Corp. v. Public Service Commission of New York*. With regard to the third factor, the appropriate inquiry is not whether the ban as applied to a single broadcaster directly advances the government's interest. Instead, the Court evaluated this third factor in light of the statute's general applicability to broadcasters throughout North Carolina. In this context, the general ban on lottery advertisements by all North Carolina stations directly advanced the substantial interest of respecting state policies on lotteries.

The ban also met the fourth *Central Hudson* factor, as it was "more extensive than is necessary to serve the governmental interest." Applying the ban to Edge was reasonable to prevent Virginia from controlling what advertisements North Carolina stations may broadcast. Moreover, that North Carolina residents could hear the lottery advertisements of Virginia stations did not undercut the fit.

Justice Souter filed a separate opinion concurring in part, in which Justice Kennedy joined. Justice Stevens filed a dissenting opinion in which Justice Blackmun joined. He would have held that banning truthful speech about the legal lottery in Virginia "is a patently unconstitutional means of effectuating the Government's interest in protecting the policies of nonlottery States."

(7) *Alcohol Content on Labels*. In *Rubin v. Coors Brewing Co.*, 514 U.S. 476 (1995), the Court invalidated a provision of the Federal Alcohol Administration Act that prohibited disclosing on labels the alcohol content of beer and descriptive words implying high alcohol content such as "strong" or "extra strength."

Writing for the Court, Justice Thomas applied the *Central Hudson* test. Both parties agreed that the information prohibited was not misleading. The Government's interest in protecting its citizens from strength wars "which could lead to greater alcoholism and its attendant social costs" was substantial. Nevertheless, the "overall irrationality" of the Act prevented the ban from "directly and materially" promoting this substantial interest. For example, the Act permitted disclosing alcohol content in advertising — but not on labels — in states that permit such advertisements. Further evidencing a failure to advance the Government's interest, other provisions permitted disclosing alcohol content on wines and spirits and the term "malt liquor" to indicate greater strength malt beverages.

Finally, the Government could have advanced its interest without infringing on First Amendment rights by "directly limiting the alcohol content of beers," or "limiting the labeling ban to malt liquors, which is the segment of the market that allegedly is threatened with a strength war." Consequently the regulation was "more extensive than necessary." Concurring in the judgment, Justice Stevens would not have treated the alcohol content message as commercial speech but instead, would have afforded that message full First Amendment protection.

(8) For an interesting perspective on commercial speech, see, e.g., Alex Kozinski & Stuart Banner, *Who's Afraid of Commercial Speech?*, 76 VA. L. REV. 627, 653 (1990) ("The commercial speech doctrine, like all other shortcuts in the law, is not cost free. It gives government a powerful weapon to suppress or control speech by classifying it as merely commercial. If you think carefully enough, you can find a commercial aspect to almost any First Amendment case."); Alan Howard, *The Constitutionality of Deceptive Speech Regulations: Replacing the Commercial Speech Doctrine with a Tort-Based Relational Framework*, 41 CASE W. RES. L. REV. 1093, 1176 (1991) ("The Commercial Speech Doctrine should be abandoned primarily for two reasons. First, the Commercial Speech Doctrine turns on an amorphous definition of commercial speech that has yet to coalesce into a coherent category. Second, the Commercial Speech Doctrine justifies diminished First Amendment protection by according commercial speech less value, cutting against the policy of content neutrality that lies at the heart of the First Amendment.").

44 LIQUORMART, INC. v. RHODE ISLAND, 517 U.S. 484 (1996). In this case, the Court invalidated two Rhode Island statutes prohibiting the advertisement of retail prices of alcoholic beverages. Although the decision to strike down the price advertising ban was unanimous, Justice Stevens wrote for a majority of the Court (six) only in Parts I, II, and VII of the opinion. In other parts of his opinion, Justice Stevens wrote for only three or four Justices. Part I described the two Rhode Island statutes. The first prohibited in-state vendors and out-of-state manufacturers, wholesalers, and shippers from " 'advertising in any manner whatsoever' " the price of any alcoholic beverage sold in the state, except it allowed price tags or signs displayed with the merchandise that were not visible from the street. The second statute prohibited publication or broadcast of any advertisements that referred "to the price of any alcoholic beverages."

Justice Stevens again wrote for a majority of six in Part II of his opinion, which described the facts and procedural history of the case. The 44 Liquormart, Inc. ran an ad in a Rhode Island newspaper. Noting that " 'State law prohibits advertising liquor prices,' " the ad stated the low prices at which snack foods and drink mixers could be purchased, identified various brands of liquor, and pictured rum and vodka bottles with the word " 'WOW' " next to them. Rhode Island concluded that the ad implied bargain liquor prices.

Joined by Justices Kennedy, Souter, and Ginsburg in Part III of his opinion, Justice Stevens construed key commercial speech precedents, including *Central Hudson Gas & Elec. Corp. v. Public Serv. Comm'n of N.Y.*, *supra*, as prohibiting blanket bans on commercial speech that was neither deceptive nor related to unlawful activity. In Part IV of the opinion, again joined only by Justices Kennedy and Ginsburg, Justice Stevens explained that "neither the 'greater objectivity' nor the 'greater hardiness' of truthful, nonmisleading commercial speech justifies reviewing its complete suppression with added deference." Bans on "truthful, nonmisleading commercial messages rarely protect consumers." Instead, "they usually rest solely on the offensive assumption that the public will respond 'irrationally' to the truth."

Justice Stevens was joined by Justices Kennedy, Souter and Ginsburg in Part V of his opinion. Under *Central Hudson*, a restriction of commercial speech " 'may not be sustained if it provides only ineffective or remote support for the government's purpose.' " Relying on *Edenfield v. Fane*, *infra*, § 15.04[2], Note (1)(f), the plurality required the State to show "not merely that its regulation will advance its interest, but also that it will do so 'to a material degree.' " As the case involves a complete ban of truthful, nonmisleading information, the State must show that the price advertising ban would "*significantly* reduce alcohol consumption." Without any findings of fact or evidentiary support, the speech prohibition did not significantly advance the State's interest in promoting temperance.

The restriction was also "more extensive than necessary." Other regulations "that would not involve any restriction on speech would be more likely to achieve the State's goal of promoting temperance." Such alternatives included increasing regulation or taxation which will increase prices, or educating people about the problems caused by drinking.

Justice Stevens, joined by Justices Kennedy, Thomas, and Ginsburg in Part VI of his opinion, rejected Rhode Island's argument that *Posadas de Puerto Rico Associates v. Tourism Co. of P.R.* — which upheld ads about legal casino gambling — allowed reduction of alcohol consumption by suppressing advertising rather than by a less speech-restrictive alternative. The plurality of four termed the *Posadas* Court analysis "paternalistic." The plurality also rejected the argument derived from the *Posadas* majority which held that " 'the greater power to completely ban casino gambling necessarily includes the lesser power to ban advertising of casino gambling.' "

The plurality also rejected the State's argument that its regulations were valid because they targeted commercial speech relating to a " 'vice' activity," *citing Rubin v.*

Coors Brewing Co., supra § 15.04[1], Note (7).

In Part VII, a majority of six held that the Twenty-first Amendment did not shield the regulation at issue from First Amendment scrutiny. The Court held that the Twenty-first Amendment, which repealed prohibition and delegated to the states "the power to prohibit commerce in, or the use of, alcoholic beverages," does not limit other constitutional provisions. Finally, in Part VIII of Justice Stevens' opinion, a majority of five held that the Rhode Island statutes violated the First Amendment.

Justice Scalia concurred in the judgment, as well as in Parts I, II, VII, and VIII of Justice Stevens' opinion. Justice Scalia shared Justice Thomas' discomfort with the *Central Hudson* test. While he shared "Justice Stevens' aversion towards paternalistic governmental policies," it is also "paternalism for us to prevent the people of the States from enacting laws that we consider paternalistic, unless we have good reason to believe that the Constitution itself forbids them." As the text of the First Amendment was "indeterminate" and "the core offense of suppressing particular political ideas is not at issue," Justice Scalia would be guided by the "long accepted practices of the American people." These would include views, and more importantly state legislative practices, with regard to regulating commercial speech at the time the First Amendment was adopted. Perhaps more relevant still are such state legislative practices at the time the Fourteenth Amendment was adopted. Also relevant was "any national consensus that had formed regarding state regulation of advertising *after* the Fourteenth Amendment, and before this Court's entry into the field. The parties and their *amici* provide no evidence on these points." Consequently he was "not disposed to develop new law, or reinforce old, on this issue," and simply concurred in the judgment.

Justice Thomas concurred in Parts I, II, VI, and VII and concurred in the judgment. He would simply strike down the regulations under *Virginia Bd. of Pharmacy v. Virginia Citizens Consumer Council, Inc., supra* § 15.04[1]. "In cases such as this, in which the government's asserted interest is to keep legal users of a product or service ignorant in order to manipulate their choices in the marketplace, the balancing test adopted in *Central Hudson Gas & Elec. Corp. v. Public Serv. Comm'n of N.Y.*, should not" inhere. "Rather, such an 'interest' is per se illegitimate and can no more justify regulation of 'commercial' speech than it can justify regulation of 'noncommercial' speech."

Justice O'Connor concurred in the judgment, and wrote a separate opinion in which Chief Justice Rehnquist, Justice Souter, and Justice Breyer joined. Justice O'Connor maintained the Court should have applied the established *Central Hudson* test. Even assuming that the regulation satisfied the first three prongs, it would fail the fourth prong, since, as the State's own expert conceded, "the objective of lowering consumption of alcohol by banning price advertising could be accomplished by establishing minimum prices and/or by increasing sales taxes on alcoholic beverages." Consequently, the fit between the State's means and ends was not "'narrowly tailored.'" Relying on the decision in the previous term in *Florida Bar v. Went For It, Inc., infra* § 15.04[2], Note 1(e), Justice O'Connor observed that "the scope of the restriction on speech must be reasonably, though it need not be perfectly, targeted to address the harm intended to be regulated." In *City of Cincinnati v. Discovery Network, Inc., supra* § 15.04[1], Note (5), the Court required that the state regulation "indicate a carefu[l] calculat[ion of] the costs and benefits associated with the burden on speech imposed by its prohibition. The availability of less burdensome alternatives to reach the stated goal signals that the fit between the legislature's ends and the means chosen to accomplish those ends may be too imprecise to withstand First Amendment scrutiny. *See Rubin v. Coors Brewing Co.* If alternative channels permit communication of the restricted speech, the regulation is more likely to be considered reasonable."

As the State failed to show a "reasonable fit" between its ban on price advertising and its goal of temperance, the Court need only apply *Central Hudson*. Consequently, the four concurring Justices did not address the question of whether "the test we have employed since *Central Hudson* should be displaced."

NOTES

(1) *Compelled Subsidization of Advertising*. (a) *Trade Associations*. In *Glickman v. Wileman Bros. & Elliott, Inc.*, 521 U.S. 457 (1997), the Court upheld a Department of Agriculture marketing order which required the producers of certain fruits to finance a "generic advertising" campaign.

The Agricultural Marketing Agreement Act of 1937 (AMAA) enacted a comprehensive regulatory scheme in order to ensure "orderly marketing conditions and fair prices for agricultural commodities." The basic message of the generic advertising at issue was that " 'California Summer Fruits' are wholesome, delicious, and attractive to discerning shoppers." Wileman Bros. & Elliott, Inc. owed the Department of Agriculture $3.1 million in back assessments for its share of the advertising.

Writing for the majority, Justice Stevens emphasized the regulation was part of a statutory scheme which broadly limited the activities of the producers and handlers. The orders do not impinge on the "freedom of any producer to communicate any message to any audience;" they do not force anyone to "engage in any actual or symbolic speech" and they do not force "producers to endorse or to finance any political or ideological views." Consequently, the Court did not view the regulation with any stricter scrutiny than that normally applicable to "other anticompetitive features of the marketing orders." The financial burden also did not attract heightened scrutiny.

The Court also rejected applying its compelled speech jurisprudence to the regulatory scheme because the assessments did not "require respondents to repeat an objectionable message out of their own mouths." The advertising was "unquestionably germane to the purposes of the marketing orders and, in any event, the assessments are not used to fund ideological activities."

Justice Souter dissented, joined by the Chief Justice and Justices Scalia and Thomas. "[P]rotected speech may not be made the subject of coercion to speak or coercion to subsidize speech." In a separate dissent, joined by Justice Scalia, Justice Thomas criticized the "discounted weight given to commercial speech" afforded by the *Central Hudson* test.

(b) *Generic advertising associations*. In *United States v. United Foods, Inc.*, 533 U.S. 405 (2001), the Court invalidated a mandatory assessment imposed on fresh mushroom producers used to fund generic advertisements promoting mushroom sales. Congress enacted the Mushroom Promotion, Research, and Consumer Information Act. Under the Act, the Secretary of Agriculture established a Mushroom Council which assessed mushroom handlers largely for generic advertising. United Foods refused to pay.

Writing for a 6-3 majority, Justice Kennedy distinguished *Glickman v. Wileman Brothers & Elliot, Inc.* "In *Glickman*, the mandated assessments for speech were ancillary to a more comprehensive program restricting marketing autonomy." In this context, "the compelled contributions were nothing more than additional economic regulation." In contrast, the main objective of the mushroom program was advertising without a larger regulatory scheme. Even requiring United Foods "to support speech by others" is "contrary to the First Amendment principles set forth in cases" like *Abood v. Detroit Bd. of Ed.*, 431 U.S. 209 (1977), and *Keller v. State Bar of Cal.*, 496 U.S. 1 (1990). *Keller* rejected compelled "speech subsidies for matters not germane to the larger regulatory purpose which justified the required association."

Concurring, Justice Stevens rejected as insufficient the interest in "making one entrepreneur finance advertising for the benefit of his competitors."

Concurring, Justice Thomas would subject to strict scrutiny any regulation mandating "the funding of advertising."

Justice Breyer wrote a three part dissent. Joined by Justices Ginsburg and O'Connor in Parts I and III, Justice Breyer found the program indistinguishable from the economic program upheld in *Glickman* which did not restrain "any producer to communicate any message to any audience," did not compel any producer "to engage in any actual or symbolic speech," and did not require any producer "to finance any political or ideological views." The compelled contributions invalidated in *Abood* and *Keller* were "subsidiary activities of the organization" which were also "political activities that might 'conflict with one's freedom of belief.' "

(c) *Generic advertising and government speech.* In *Johanns v. Livestock Marketing Association*, 544 U.S. 550 (2005), the Court rejected a facial challenge to a generic Beef advertising campaign, funded by a $1 assessment per head of cattle ("checkoff") imposed by the Secretary of Agriculture, as it funded the government's own speech. Plaintiffs, who were subject to the checkoff, sued.

Writing for the majority, Justice Scalia noted that compelled speech challenges fell into two categories. First, the Court has invalidated cases of "true 'compelled speech' " in which government compels an individual to express a message he disagrees with. *See West Virginia Board of Education v. Barnette*, 319 U.S. 624 (1943), (invalidating a law compelling school children to recite the pledge of allegiance). Second, in "compelled subsidy" cases, such as *United Foods*, the Court has stopped government from imposing fees on an individual to subsidize a message with which he disagrees. However, the Court has allowed such mandatory fees if they are part of a "broader regulatory scheme." Moreover, a compelled subsidy of government's own speech does not necessarily violate the First Amendment, as compelled support of the government is constitutional and it is inevitable that some funds raised by the government will be spent on speech to advocate its own positions.

Despite the prominent role of the Beef Board, which is not a government entity, in the advertising campaign, "when, as here, the government sets the overall message to be communicated and approves every word that is disseminated, it is not precluded from relying on the government-speech doctrine merely because is solicits assistance from nongovernmental sources in developing specific messages." The advertisements were government speech despite their being funded by a targeted assessment rather than general tax revenues. There is "no *First Amendment* right not to fund government speech." Finally, the Court rejected a facial challenge on the basis that crediting the advertisements to "America's Beef Producers" impermissibly implies that plaintiffs endorse a message with which they do not agree. This theory may support an as-applied challenge if the producers establish that beef advertisements were actually attributed to them.

Justices Thomas and Breyer each wrote concurring opinions. Justice Thomas stated that an as-applied challenge would exist if the advertisements "associated" their generic message with the plaintiffs. Justice Ginsburg, concurring in judgment, would uphold the assessments "as permissible economic regulation."

Justice Souter dissented, joined by Justices Stevens and Kennedy. He argued that this case was indistinguishable from *United Foods*, as the speech regulation was not "incidental" to a "comprehensive regulatory scheme." Moreover, the advertisements are not government speech because government was not required to signal that it is providing the advertisements.

(2) *Gambling*. In *Greater New Orleans Broadcasting Association, Inc. v. United States*, 527 U.S. 173 (1999), the Court invalidated the application of a Federal prohibition of "broadcast advertising of lotteries and casino gambling" to Louisiana where the advertised gambling was legal. The Court applied the test established in *Central Hudson Gas & Elec. Corp. v. Public Serv. Comm'n of N.Y.*, saying that each of the four prongs of this test is interconnected, and may affect the answer to one of the other three questions.

Under the second prong, the Court found " 'substantial' " the government interests in reducing the social costs related to gambling and helping states that make gambling illegal. The Court did question these interests in light of the many statutory exceptions, such as, gambling run by American Indian tribes and State-sponsored gambling.

To meet the third prong the government cannot simply speculate that "the speech restriction directly and materially advances the asserted governmental interest," but instead "must demonstrate that the harms it recites are real and that its restriction will in fact alleviate them to a material degree." The fourth prong does not require that the Government utilize the "least restrictive means conceivable," but the "costs and benefits" imposed on free speech must be "carefully calculated," and the solution chosen must be "one whose scope is in proportion to the interest served."

The Court found that the implementation of § 1304 "is so pierced with exemptions and inconsistencies that the Government cannot hope to exonerate it." The government presented no good reason for distinguishing tribal and State-sponsored gambling enterprises from privately owned ones. The government bans accurate product information based on the identity of the speaker. Rather than restricting advertising, the government could directly limit abuses by imposing betting limits or admissions restrictions. Chief Justice Rehnquist filed a concurring opinion. Justice Thomas concurred only in the judgment.

LORILLARD TOBACCO CO. v. REILLY, 533 U.S. 525 (2001). In *Lorillard*, the Court invalidated several restrictions primarily focused on signs advertising tobacco products and upheld certain others primarily focused on sales behind the counter.[48] Promulgated by the Massachusetts Attorney General (Attorney General) in 1999, one regulation barred outdoor advertising of these products, " 'including advertising in enclosed stadiums and advertising from within a retail establishment that is directed toward or visible from the outside of the establishment . . . within a 1,000 foot radius of any public playground, playground area in a public park, elementary school or secondary school.' " Another prohibited retailers from using "self-service displays" of cigars, cigarettes, and smokeless tobacco products and also mandated them to place these products in areas only accessible to employees. The Attorney General also imposed restrictions on "point-of-sale advertising," proscribing retailers from placing these products "lower than five feet from the floor." Finally, the regulations prohibited the "sampling of cigars or little cigars."

The restrictions were designed to prevent children from using tobacco products. The cigar regulations were also designed to heighten awareness of the health risks associated with cigar smoking. The District Court had granted summary judgment, upholding all of the regulations except the point-of-sale restriction.

Writing for a majority of six Justices, Justice O'Connor applied the four-part test from *Central Hudson Gas & Elec. Corp. v. Public Serv. Comm'n of New York*. On the second prong of *Central Hudson*, the tobacco companies conceded the importance of

---

[48] The Court also ruled that the Federal Cigarette Labeling and Advertising Act (FCLAA) preempted certain parts of the Massachusetts law. Accordingly, the Court's First Amendment analysis only applied to parts not preempted.

the state interest in preventing children from using tobacco products. Under part three of *Central Hudson*, the Court focused on the relationship between the harm and the means employed to dispel it. Specifically, the State must establish " 'that the harms it recites are real and that its restriction will in fact alleviate them to a material degree.' " To prove this, the government can refer "to studies and anecdotes pertaining to different locales altogether, or even, in a case applying strict scrutiny, to justify restrictions based solely on history, consensus, and 'simple common sense.' "

The 1,000-foot outdoor advertising regulations survived the third part of *Central Hudson*. Justice O'Connor stated that some evidence showed that preventing "targeted campaigns and limiting youth exposure to advertising will decrease underage use of smokeless tobacco and cigars." Moreover, the Court could not conclude that "the Attorney General's decision to regulate advertising of smokeless tobacco and cigars in an effort to combat the use of tobacco products by minors was based on mere 'speculation [and] conjecture.' "

Turning to the fourth part of the test, the Court asked whether there was "a reasonable 'fit between the legislature's ends and the means chosen to accomplish those ends, . . . a means narrowly tailored to achieve the desired objective.' " Justice O'Connor opined: "The broad sweep of the regulations indicates that the Attorney General did not 'carefully calculate the costs and benefits associated with the burden on speech imposed' by the regulations." Consequently, the 1000-foot restriction was invalid. "The breadth and scope of the regulations, and the process by which the Attorney General adopted the regulations, do not demonstrate a careful calculation of the speech interests involved." For example, "the effect of the Attorney General's speech regulations will vary based on whether a locale is rural, suburban, or urban. The uniformly broad sweep of the geographical limitation demonstrates a lack of tailoring."

The Court also found "the range of communications restricted seems unduly broad." For example, "a retailer is unable to answer inquiries about its tobacco products if that communication occurs outdoors. Similarly, a ban on all signs of any size seems ill suited to target the problem of highly visible billboards, as opposed to smaller signs." Narrow tailoring would instead target advertising and practices that studies have indicated appeal to youth while allowing other advertising. In addition, a retailer may have "no means of communicating to [a] passerby on the street that it sells tobacco products." Moreover, the prohibition on "any indoor advertising that is visible from the outside also presents problems in establishments like convenience stores, which have unique security concerns that counsel in favor of full visibility of the store." Invalidating the outdoor advertising regulations, Justice O'Connor explained that "[a] careful calculation of the costs of a speech regulation does not mean that a State must demonstrate that there is no incursion on legitimate speech interests, but a speech regulation cannot unduly impinge on the speaker's ability to propose a commercial transaction and the adult listener's opportunity to obtain information about products."

The Court also invalidated the indoor, point-of-sale restriction requiring retailers located within a 1,000 feet of any school or playground to place smokeless tobacco and cigar advertisements at least five feet above the floor. This restriction failed the third and fourth parts of the *Central Hudson* test. Even in light of the State's interest to dissuade children from using tobacco products, the five-foot rule did not appear to further that objective. First, "[n]ot all children are less that 5 feet tall, and those who are certainly have the ability to look up and take in their surroundings." Second, the restriction cannot be scrutinized under *United States v. O'Brien* "as a mere regulation of conduct," as the regulation was related to expression in attempting "to regulate directly the communicative impact of indoor advertising." The Court distinguished between the State targeting "tobacco advertisements and displays that entice children, much like the floor-level candy displays in a convenience store" from imposing a "blanket height restriction [that] does not constitute a reasonable fit."

Upholding the regulations that "bar the use of self-service displays and require that tobacco products be placed out of the reach of all consumers in a location accessible only to salespersons," the Court stated, consistent with the *O'Brien* test, that the State was regulating "the placement of tobacco products for reasons unrelated to the communication of ideas." Massachusetts chose means that "are narrowly tailored to prevent access to tobacco products by minors, are unrelated to expression, and leave open alternative avenues for vendors to convey information about products and for would-be consumers to inspect products before purchase."

Justice Kennedy concurred in part and concurred in the judgment, joined by Justice Scalia. He agreed that the outdoor advertising restrictions failed the fourth part of the *Central Hudson* test, but he found it unnecessary to address "whether the restrictions satisfy the third part of the test, a proposition about which there is considerable doubt." He would not have considered whether the *Central Hudson* analysis "should be retained in the face of the substantial objections that can be made to it." As the test may afford "insufficient protection to truthful, nonmisleading commercial speech," he refused to join the Court's analysis of its third prong.

Justice Thomas, concurring in part and concurring in the judgment, continued "to believe that when the government seeks to restrict truthful speech in order to suppress the ideas it conveys, strict scrutiny is appropriate," which would invalidate "all of the advertising restrictions." The State argued that "tobacco . . . is . . . so unlike any other object of regulation, that application of normal First Amendment principles should be suspended." However, upholding the regulations "would be to accept a line of reasoning that would permit restrictions on advertising for a host of other products." It is widely known that tobacco use is " 'the single leading cause of preventable death in the United States.' " Obesity is the second; alcohol ranks third. While tobacco companies openly target children, so do makers of fast food. Despite the fact that "every State prohibits the sale of alcohol to those under age 21, much alcohol advertising is viewed by children."

Justice Souter concurred with the Court on most points but dissented on the outdoor restrictions. Rather than invalidate these, he would have remanded for trial on their constitutionality.

Justice Stevens, joined by Justices Ginsburg and Breyer, concurred in part, concurred in the judgment pertaining to the sales practices regulations, and dissented in part. In Part I of his opinion, Justice Stevens dissented from the majority's holding that Congress had preempted some of the Massachusetts regulations.[49] Part II of Justice Stevens' opinion dissented from the majority's First Amendment analysis. The State's "regulations serve interests of the highest order and are, therefore, immune from any ends-based challenge, whatever level of scrutiny one chooses to employ."

With regard to the 1,000-foot rule, this "does not present a tailoring problem." To the contrary, "it is appropriate, indeed necessary, to tailor advertising restrictions to the areas where that segment of the community congregates — in this case, the area surrounding schools and playgrounds." Indeed, the 1,000-foot rule may "unduly restric[t] the ability of cigarette manufacturers to convey lawful information to adult consumers," but this is "a question of line-drawing." In trying to strike a balance between the State's interest in protecting children and adults' interest in receiving

---

[49] The regulations at issue concerned "two powers that lie at the heart of the States' traditional police power — the power to regulate land usage and the power to protect the health and safety of minors." Consequently, the Court should require a clear rather than ambiguous congressional intent to preempt. Justice Souter also joined Part I of Justice Stevens' opinion.

information, "one crucial question is whether the regulatory scheme leaves available sufficient 'alternative avenues of communication.'" However, the dissent believed that the Court lacked sufficient information to determine that question and, accordingly, would vacate the summary judgment award and remand the case for trial on that issue. For example, "the parties remain in dispute as to the percentage of these urban areas that is actually off limits to tobacco advertising." Moreover, the record contained no information about "other avenues of communication available to cigarette manufacturers and retailers," such as print advertising.

Justice Stevens also maintained "that the sales practices restrictions are best analyzed as regulating conduct, not speech." Like the majority, he would uphold the restrictions on how to display tobacco products.

Disagreeing with the majority, Justice Stevens would uphold the point-of-sale regulation "limiting tobacco advertising in certain retail establishments to the space five feet or more above the floor." This restriction was "little more than an adjunct to the other sales practice restrictions." Ultimately, Justice Stevens stated that he disagreed with the majority's "disposition or its reasoning on each of the regulations" and would have upheld all of them.

NOTE

Compounded Drugs. In *Thompson v. Western States Medical Center*, 535 U.S. 357 (2002), the Court invalidated an advertising restriction on "compounded drugs." The restriction exempted compounded drugs from the normal testing required to approve new drugs if pharmacists did not promote or advertise them. Writing for the majority of the Court, Justice O'Connor applied the *Central Hudson, supra* § 15.04[1], test. The Government has important interests both in wanting to subject new drugs to FDA approval, and in permitting compounded drugs that can tailor medications to meet particular needs of particular patients. Such specific mixtures should not have to undergo the testing process for new drugs. Consequently, "the Government needs to be able to draw a line between small-scale compounding and large-scale drug manufacturing." Nonetheless, the Government failed to demonstrate that its advertising restrictions are "not more extensive than is necessary to serve" the interests it advances. In this case, the Government could differentiate between compounding and manufacturing with lines unrelated to speech. For example, the Government could "ban the use of 'commercial scale manufacturing or testing equipment' for compounding drug products.'" It could limit compounding to "prescriptions already received." It could prohibit selling compounded drugs at wholesale prices for resale. It could cap "the amount of any particular compounded drug, either by drug volume, number of prescriptions, gross revenue, or profit."

While the dissent described another governmental interest, that of "prohibiting the sale of compounded drugs to 'patients who may not clearly need them,'" the Government did not advance this interest. Finally, the Government's ban could prevent useful advertising. For example, pharmacists could post information about compounds that make it easier for children to swallow pills or that change the flavor of a particular medication.

Justice Thomas concurred, but reaffirmed his position that the *Central Hudson* test should not apply to commercial speech restrictions, "at least when, as here, the asserted interest is one that is to be achieved through keeping would-be recipients of the speech in the dark."

Justice Breyer dissented joined by Chief Justice Rehnquist and Justices Stevens and Ginsburg. Justice Breyer maintained that "an overly rigid 'commercial speech' doctrine will transform what ought to be a legislative or regulatory decision about the best way to protect the health and safety of the American public into a constitutional decision." In light of the history of the Due Process Clause, this would be a "tragic constitutional misunderstanding."

[2] Lawyer and Other Professional Advertising

BATES v. STATE OF ARIZONA, 433 U.S. 350 (1977). During its term after the *Virginia Pharmacy* case, the Court extended First Amendment protection to advertising by lawyers. *Bates* involved a newspaper advertisement by two lawyers for a legal clinic. The ad offered "legal services at very reasonable fees" and listed fees for uncontested divorce or legal separation proceedings, uncontested non-business bankruptcies, and certain adoption proceedings. A one-week suspension for each lawyer was recommended by the Arizona State Bar and was affirmed by the Supreme Court of Arizona. The disciplinary action was based on a violation of Disciplinary Rule 2-101B of the Code of Professional Responsibility which had been adopted in Arizona by court rule and which contained a broad prohibition against lawyer advertising with very limited exceptions.

Justice Blackmun wrote the majority opinion joined by Justices Brennan, White, Marshall, and Stevens. He held that lawyers had a First Amendment right to advertise the price at which they would perform routine services. The Court specifically declined to address "the peculiar problems associated with advertising claims relating to the *quality* of legal services." Such claims "under some circumstances, might well be deceptive or misleading to the public, or even false." The Court rejected the various arguments advanced in support of the restriction on "price advertising." These were: that it has an adverse effect on professionalism; that it is inherently misleading because of the individualized nature of legal services; that advertising would adversely effect the administration of justice because it would stir up litigation; that it would increase overhead costs of lawyers; that it would lower the quality of lawyers' work by encouraging the packaging of services at set prices; and that a total ban is necessary because of the difficulty of enforcing a ban only on false or misleading advertising.

The Court declined to hold that the Disciplinary Rules prohibiting advertising were facially overbroad. The Court ruled, instead, that "advertising by attorneys may not be subject to blanket suppression, and the advertisement at issue is protected." The opinion concluded: "The constitutional issue in this case is only whether the State may prevent the publication in a newspaper of appellants' truthful advertisement concerning the availability and terms of routine legal services. We rule simply that the flow of such information may not be restrained, and we therefore hold the present application of the disciplinary rule against appellants to be violative of the First Amendment."

Chief Justice Burger dissented, as did Justice Powell (joined by Justice Stewart). They emphasized that, unlike the advertising that was constitutionally protected in *Virginia Pharmacy*, lawyer advertising would be inherently misleading, and any effort to confine it to a description of fees for routine services would present very difficult enforcement problems.

The emphasis in Justice Powell's dissent on the difficulty of defining "routine" legal services led Justice Rehnquist, in his strong dissent, to state that he could not join "the implication in [Justice Powell's] opinion that some forms of legal advertising may be constitutionally protected." In Justice Rehnquist's view, the Court started down a "slippery slope" when it abandoned its earlier position that commercial advertising is not protected. He concluded: "I am still unwilling to take even one step."

NOTES

(1) *Solicitation.* (a) *In-person solicitation for pecuniary gain.* The *Bates* case left open many questions concerning in-person and mail solicitation. Many have been resolved by the Court. In *Ohralik v. Ohio State Bar Association*, 436 U.S. 447 (1978), the Court held that a state could constitutionally discipline a lawyer for soliciting clients "for pecuniary gain, under circumstances likely to pose dangers that the State has a right to prevent." *Ohralik* involved a lawyer who had heard about an automobile accident and then visited one potential client in the hospital and another while she was recuperating at home. Justice Powell, writing for a unanimous Court, agreed that the state's interest in preventing fraud, intimidation, and undue influence justified promulgating a broad "prophylactic rule" against this type of solicitation. Justices Marshall and Rehnquist concurred. Justice Brennan did not participate.

(b) *Mailed solicitation by a civil rights group.* The Court distinguished *Ohralik* in its companion case, *In re Primus*, 436 U.S. 412 (1978) (7-1, with Justice Rehnquist dissenting and Justice Brennan not participating). In that case the Court held that a cooperating lawyer for the American Civil Liberties Union could not be disciplined for sending a letter to a woman advising her that free legal services would be made available by the organization. The proposed representation involved the woman's claim against her physician for what was believed to be an illegal sterilization performed on her. The letter followed a meeting in which the lawyer had advised those present, including the recipient of the subsequent letter, "of their legal rights and suggested the possibility of a lawsuit." Justice Powell's majority opinion held that solicitation of prospective litigants by a civil liberties organization engaged in litigation is an activity which involves constitutionally protected expression and association. *See N.A.A.C.P. v. Button*, 371 U.S. 415 (1963). There was nothing in this record to suggest that the organization or the attorney had engaged in the overreaching, misrepresentation, invasion of privacy or pressuring which was the concern of the Court in *Ohralik*.

(c) *Targeted newspaper advertisements.* In *Zauderer v. Office of Disciplinary Counsel of the Supreme Court of Ohio*, 471 U.S. 626 (1985), the Court reviewed the action of the Supreme Court of Ohio disciplining a lawyer for a newspaper advertisement offering to represent women who had suffered injuries from the use of the Dalkon Shield Intrauterine Device. The advertisement offered representation on a contingent fee basis and promised that no "legal fees" would be owing if there was no recovery.

Justice White wrote the majority opinion, joined by Justices Brennan, Marshall, Blackmun, and Stevens. Apart from the contingent fee information, the advertisements, including the illustration, were neither false nor misleading. The State's interests in restricting "in person solicitation," i.e., preventing "overreaching, invasion of privacy, the exercise of undue influence, and outright fraud" were not present in this advertisement, which contained advice about a specific legal problem. The majority also rejected the State's assertion that the restriction was necessary to prevent lawyers from "stirring-up" litigation: "That our citizens have access to their civil courts is not an evil to be regretted; rather it is an attribute of our system of justice in which we ought to take pride."

Justice O'Connor, joined by Chief Justice Burger and Justice Rehnquist, concurred in part and dissented in part. Justice O'Connor agreed, at least in the context of print media, that the task of monitoring illustrations is not so unmanageable in attorney ads as to justify Ohio's blanket ban. Justice O'Connor dissented from the majority's refusal to accept Ohio's rules on unsolicited legal advice because of the "risk of overreaching and undue influence." Justice Powell did not participate.

A different majority of Justice White, Chief Justice Burger, and Justices Blackmun, Rehnquist, Stevens, and O'Connor, sustained Ohio's imposition of discipline for failing to disclose that plaintiffs might be liable for litigation costs even if their lawsuits were ultimately unsuccessful. Justice White's opinion concluded, "an advertiser's rights are adequately protected as long as disclosure requirements are reasonably related to the State's interest in preventing deception of consumers." This majority also sustained State discipline of an advertisement that offered a contingent fee for defending drunken driving charges. Justice White upheld the State's position that the advertisement was misleading in that it failed to mention the common practice of plea bargaining in drunken driving cases and, therefore, may have deceived readers into believing that there would be no fee resulting from a bargained plea to a lesser offense. Justices Brennan and Marshall dissented from this portion of the majority's opinion, arguing that the majority's standard of "reasonableness was not sufficiently protective of First Amendment interests."

(d) *Targeted mail solicitation.* In *Shapero v. Kentucky Bar Assn.*, 486 U.S. 466 (1988), the Court protected letters sent by lawyers to potential clients known to face specific legal problems. The *Zauderer* case, *supra*, dealt with a newspaper advertisement addressed to potential clients relating to possible litigation. The rule at issue in *Shapero* was A.B.A. Model Rule 7.3 which, in effect, prohibited direct mail solicitation for pecuniary gain to persons "known to need legal services . . . in a particular matter." Justice Brennan's majority opinion concluded that targeted solicitation letters, which were addressed to potential clients against whom foreclosure suits had been filed, did not pose the danger of coercion that the presence of a lawyer would cause. The risk of false or misleading information could be minimized by requiring that letters be filed and reviewed, and by provisions for disciplining lawyers for distributing false or misleading information.

Justice O'Connor, joined by Chief Justice Rehnquist and Justice Scalia, dissented in an opinion disagreeing with the line of cases that have extended to lawyer advertising the First Amendment protection accorded to commercial speech generally.

(e) *Victim targeted solicitation.* In *Florida Bar v. Went For It, Inc.*, 515 U.S. 618 (1995), the Court limited protection of direct mail solicitation by lawyers. The Florida regulation at issue ordered that lawyers may not, directly or indirectly, contact or solicit business from accident victims or their relatives until 30 days after the date of the disaster.

Justice O'Connor, writing for the (5-4) majority, upheld the constitutionality of the regulation under the *Central Hudson* test as narrowly drawn to "directly and materially" advance a substantial government interest. States have substantial interests in sheltering their citizens from invasive breaches of privacy, and they have a "compelling" interest in upholding the integrity of all professions including law.

In passing *Central Hudson's* second prong, Justice O'Connor distinguished the case at bar from *Shapero v. Kentucky Bar Ass'n.* "First and foremost," the State did not attempt to justify its regulation on privacy grounds and "*Shapero's* treatment of privacy was casual." Second, *Shapero* involved a broad-based ban on all direct mail solicitations, whereas the Florida regulation only required a 30-day blackout period. Finally, the State in *Shapero* did not substantiate its claim with any evidence showing the harms of direct mail solicitations. In contrast, the Florida Bar commissioned a study showing egregious harms deriving from early contact with accident victims and their relatives.

Central Hudson's third prong was not a " 'least restrictive means' test." The "fit" between the interest and the regulation must only be "reasonable," not "perfect."

Respondents asserted that this ban would deprive victims and their relatives of useful and necessary legal information, without which they would fall prey to the claims of "opposing counsel and insurance adjusters." The Court said that important information could be disseminated through numerous other legal advertisements including: telephone and legal directories; radio, television and print media; signs; and recorded messages and written communications that do not solicit. The ban would be almost impossible to narrow to only people with "severe" grief and pain.

Justice Kennedy, joined by Justices Stevens, Souter, and Ginsburg, dissented, characterizing the Court's decision as a departure from *Shapero* and other commercial speech cases.

(f) *In-person solicitation by CPAs.* In *Edenfield v. Fane*, 507 U.S. 761 (1993), the Court invalidated a ban on in-person solicitation by CPAs. Respondent Scott Fane, a Florida CPA, was prohibited by regulation from soliciting potential business clients by telephone and through in-person meetings. Writing for the Court, Justice Kennedy noted that in-person solicitation enabled the seller to direct proposals to those most interested, allowed a potential buyer to evaluate the seller personally, and provided the opportunity for direct and detailed communication regarding the service offered. For "nonstandard products like the professional services offered by CPAs, these benefits are significant."

The State's ban on such solicitation failed the three-part *Central Hudson* test. Applying the first prong, the Court concluded that the State's asserted interests in protecting consumers from fraud, deception, and invasion of privacy were substantial, as were the State's interests in maintaining the fact and appearance of CPA independence. Turning to the second prong, the State must establish that the harms to be avoided are real and that the restrictions alleviate these harms to a material degree. Finding that the Board had not met this burden, the Court pointed to the absence of statistical or anecdotal evidence in the business context about the dangers of in-person solicitation by CPAs. As the restrictions lacked a "close and substantial relationship" to the proffered State interests, the Court rejected the state's claim that the regulation was a legitimate time, place, or manner restriction.

Finally, the State argued that *Ohralik v. Ohio State Bar Association* justified a prophylactic ban on in-person solicitation as such conduct is difficult to monitor. Justice Kennedy cautioned that *Ohralik* only allowed such a prophylactic rule when the situation inherently or likely posed dangers of misconduct. Unlike lawyers, CPAs are trained to be independent and objective, and are not "trained in the art of persuasion." Unlike the young accident victims in *Ohralik*, the CPA in this case sought to solicit business executives who likely already had other CPAs.

In her dissent, Justice O'Connor saw little difference between the dangers of overreaching by accountants and by lawyers.

(g) *Student recruitment for athletic programs.* In *Tennessee Secondary School Athletic Assn. v. Brentwood Academy*, 127 S. Ct. 2489 (2007), the Court held that enforcing a rule that prohibits high school coaches from recruiting middle school athletes does not violate the First Amendment. The Tennessee Secondary School Athletic Association (TSSAA) sanctioned one of its member schools, Brentwood Academy, because its football coach sent eighth-graders a letter that violated a TSSAA rule. The rule prohibited members from using "undue influence" in recruiting students for their athletic programs. Brentwood maintained that enforcement of TSSAA's rule violated its First Amendment rights. The Court rejected Brentwood's claim.

Writing for the majority, Justice Stevens pointed out that "there is a difference of constitutional dimension between rules prohibiting appeals to the public at large, and rules prohibiting direct, personalized communication in a coercive setting."

Consequently, the TSSAA's "anti-recruiting rule strikes nowhere near the heart of the First Amendment." He analogized this case to *Ohralik v. Ohio State Bar Assn.*, 436 U.S. 447 (1978). In *Ohralik*, the Court held that the First Amendment did not prohibit a state bar association from disciplining a lawyer for in-person client solicitation.

Just as the personal solicitation by the lawyer presented harm of overreaching in *Ohralik*, the high school coach's recruitment of impressionable eighth-graders poses the risk of undue influence. Such letters are not the same as general advertising of athletic programs through brochures and billboards, which TSSAA member schools remain free to do. In sum, "TSSAA's limited regulation of recruiting conduct poses no significant First Amendment concerns."

Brentwood's decision to join TSSAA and to abide by its anti-recruiting rule was voluntary. The "athletic league's interest in enforcing its rules [can] sometimes warrant curtailing the speech of its voluntary participants." Similarly, the "government's interest in running an effective workplace can in some circumstances outweigh employee speech rights." Although TSSAA does not have an "unbounded authority to condition membership on the relinquishment of any and all constitutional rights," it can impose the conditions "that are necessary to managing an efficient and effective state-sponsored high school athletic league."

Justice Kennedy concurred in part and concurred in the judgment, joined by Chief Justice Roberts and Justices Scalia and Alito. Justice Kennedy disagreed with the majority's reliance on *Ohralik*, because it "undermine[d] the argument that, in the absence of Brentwood Academy's consensual membership in the [TSSAA], the speech by the head coach would be entitled to First Amendment protection." *Edenfield v. Fane*, 507 U.S. 761 (1993), invalidated a ban on in-person solicitation of potential clients by CPAs. *Ohralik* was a narrow decision that applied only in the context of attorney-client relationship, and " 'did not hold that all personal solicitation is without First Amendment protection.' "

Justice Thomas concurred only in the judgment on the grounds that the First Amendment does not apply to this case as the TSSAA is not a state actor, but a private athletic association.

(2) *Trade Names.* In *Friedman v. Rogers*, 440 U.S. 1 (1979), a 7-2 majority upheld a Texas law that prohibited the practice of optometry under an assumed name, trade name, or corporate name. Justice Powell reasoned that a trade name has no intrinsic meaning. "It conveys no information about the price and nature of the services offered by an optometrist until it acquires meaning over a period of time by associations formed in the minds of the public between the name and some standard of price or quality." The dangers of deception included the possibility that different individuals might practice under a trade name from time-to-time, that different trade names could create the illusion of competition among different offices of the same firm, or that the trade name could give the false impression of standardized care.

Justices Blackmun and Marshall dissented on the grounds that the use of the trade name was not inherently misleading and that there were other ways for the State to deal with the possibility of deception without the complete ban on the use of trade names.

(3) *State-Prescribed Announcements.* In *In re R.M.J.*, 455 U.S. 191 (1982), the Court invalidated a Missouri rule that set forth precise language by which a lawyer could describe his or her areas of practice, required a disclaimer of certification of expertise, limited the distribution of announcement cards, and prevented the lawyer from listing the jurisdictions in which she was licensed to practice. Justice Powell, for a unanimous Court, wrote: "There is no finding that appellant's speech was misleading. Nor can we say that it was inherently misleading, or that restrictions short of an absolute

prohibition would not have sufficed to cure any possible deception."

(4) *Specialization.* In *Peel v. Attorney Registration and Disciplinary Commission of Illinois*, 496 U.S. 91 (1990), the Court held that a statement on a lawyer's letterhead claiming that the lawyer has been certified by the National Board of Trial Advocacy (NBTA) as a civil trial specialist was protected by the First Amendment. NBTA maintains an "objective and demanding" process of certifying lawyers in trial advocacy. Gary Peel, a lawyer with a great deal of trial experience, was licensed to practice in three states, and was certified by NBTA.

The Illinois Disciplinary Commission found that the letterhead displaying certification violated disciplinary rules that a lawyer may not "hold himself out as 'certified' or a 'specialist,' " or make "any false or misleading statement."

Justice Stevens delivered a plurality opinion, joined by Justices Brennan, Blackmun, and Kennedy. Relying on *In re R.M.J.*, Justice Stevens stated that "the States may not place an absolute prohibition on certain types of potentially misleading information, e.g., a listing of areas of practice, if the information also may be presented in a way that is not deceptive." He found Peel's letterhead statement "true and verifiable." Although some clients might assume from the letterhead that Peel is more qualified than the general legal practitioner, the NBTA's "rigorous requirements" justified that assumption in this case.

Illinois could not ban all lawyer claims of "certified" and "specialist" on the ground that these claims are "potentially misleading." States can impose requirements for a particular certification or could screen certifying organizations or require disclaimers "about the certifying organization or the standards of a specialty."

Justice Marshall, joined by Justice Brennan, concurred in the judgment. Justice Marshall said that total bans as such measures were only proper when commercial speech was "actually or inherently misleading." Other measures could "prevent deception or confusion."

Justice O'Connor dissented, joined by Chief Justice Rehnquist, and Justice Scalia. Justice O'Connor thought that the letterhead was "inherently misleading." Justice O'Connor also doubted the consumer's ability to determine that NTBA is not government-connected. Information about concentration of practice, which Illinois did permit, was useful but not misleading. Justice White also dissented.

(5) *Certification.* In *Ibanez v. Florida Department of Business and Professional Regulation, Board of Accountancy*, 512 U.S. 136 (1994), the Court held that the First Amendment protected a professional advertisement of a certified financial planner (CFP). Silvia Ibanez was licensed by the state of Florida as a lawyer and certified public accountant (CPA), and recognized by a private association as a CFP. She advertised these areas of expertise in the phone book, on business cards, and on letterhead. The Board of Accountancy sanctioned Ibanez on the grounds that including the CPA and CFP designations after her name was misleading.

Writing for the Court, Justice Ginsburg stated that the Board cannot restrict commercial speech simply because it is "potentially misleading." Instead, the Board must demonstrate that real injuries exist and that its remedy would "alleviate them to a material degree." Moreover, because the Board failed to rely on actual harm, the Court rejected the position of the Board that the "specialist" designation must be accompanied by a disclaimer. The Court would not, however, consider at this point whether in alternative situations "a disclaimer might serve as an appropriately tailored check against deception and confusion." The detailed disclaimer required by the Board would essentially eliminate specialist designations "on a business card or letterhead, or in a yellow pages listing." "CFP" is a designation accepted by the SEC and by universities and is a protected federal trademark.

Justice O'Connor, joined by Chief Justice Rehnquist, concurred in part and dissented in part. Justice O'Connor opined that the coupling of the CPA and CFP designations may cause consumers to believe that the State conferred both certifications.

(6) For additional discussion of lawyer advertising, *see* Lori B. Andrews, *Lawyer Advertising and the First Amendment*, 1981 Am. B. F. Res. J. 967; John B. Attanasio, *Lawyer Advertising in England and the United States*, 34 Am. J. Comp. L. 493 (1984); Fred S. McChesney, *Commercial Speech in the Professions: The Supreme Court's Unanswered Questions and Questionable Answers*, 134 U. Pa. L. Rev. 45 (1985).

§ 15.05   OBSCENITY

[1]   The Constitutional Standard

MILLER v. CALIFORNIA
413 U.S. 15, 93 S. Ct. 2607, 37 L. Ed. 2d 419 (1973)

Chief Justice Burger delivered the opinion of the Court.

This is one of a group of "obscenity-pornography" cases being reviewed by the Court in a re-examination of standards enunciated in earlier cases involving what Justice Harlan called "the intractable obscenity problem." *Interstate Circuit, Inc. v. Dallas*, 390 U.S. 676, 704 (1968) (concurring and dissenting).

Appellant conducted a mass mailing campaign to advertise the sale of illustrated books, euphemistically called "adult" material. . . . Appellant's conviction was specifically based on his conduct in causing five unsolicited advertising brochures to be sent through the mail in an envelope addressed to a restaurant in Newport Beach, California. The envelope was opened by the manager of the restaurant and his mother. They had not requested the brochures; they complained to the police.

The brochures advertise four books entitled "Intercourse," "Man-Woman," "Sex Orgies Illustrated," and "An Illustrated History of Pornography," and a film entitled "Marital Intercourse." While the brochures contain some descriptive printed material, primarily they consist of pictures and drawings very explicitly depicting men and women in groups of two or more engaging in a variety of sexual activities, with genitals often prominently displayed.

I

. . . This Court has recognized that the States have a legitimate interest in prohibiting dissemination or exhibition of obscene material when the mode of dissemination carries with it a significant danger of offending the sensibilities of unwilling recipients or of exposure to juveniles. . . .

. . . [I]t is useful for us to focus on two of the landmark cases in the somewhat tortured history of the Court's obscenity decisions. In *Roth v. United States*, 354 U.S. 476 (1957), the Court sustained a conviction under a federal statute punishing the mailing of "obscene, lewd, lascivious or filthy. . ." materials. The key to that holding was the Court's rejection of the claim that obscene materials were protected by the First Amendment. Five Justices joined in the opinion stating:

. . . [I]mplicit in the history of the First Amendment is the rejection of obscenity as utterly without redeeming social importance. . . . This is the same judgment expressed by this Court in *Chaplinsky v. New Hampshire*, 315 U.S. 568, 571–572 (1942).

". . . There are certain well-defined and narrowly limited classes of speech, the prevention and punishment of which have never been thought to raise any Constitutional problem. *These include the lewd and obscene. . . . It has been well observed that such utterances are no essential part of any exposition of ideas, and are of such slight social value as a step to truth that any benefit that may be derived from them is clearly outweighed by the social interest in order and morality. . . .* " [Emphasis by Court in *Roth* opinion.]

We hold that obscenity is not within the areas of constitutionally protected speech or press. 354 U.S. at 484–485.

Nine years later, in *Memoirs v. Massachusetts*, 383 U.S. 413 (1966), the Court veered sharply away from the *Roth* concept and, with only three Justices in the plurality opinion, articulated a new test of obscenity. The plurality held that under the *Roth* definition as elaborated in subsequent cases, three elements must coalesce: it must be established that (a) the dominant theme of the material taken as a whole appeals to a prurient interest in sex; (b) the material is patently offensive because it affronts contemporary community standards relating to the description or representation of sexual matters; and (c) the material is utterly without redeeming social value. *Id.* at 418. . . .

While *Roth* presumed "obscenity" to be "*utterly* without redeeming social importance," *Memoirs* required that to prove obscenity it must be affirmatively established that the material is "*utterly* without redeeming social value." Thus, even as they repeated the words of *Roth*, the *Memoirs* plurality produced a drastically altered test that called on the prosecution to prove a negative, i.e., that the material was "*utterly* without redeeming social value" — a burden virtually impossible to discharge under our criminal standards of proof. . . .

Apart from the initial formulation in the *Roth* case, no majority of the Court has at any given time been able to agree on a standard to determine what constitutes obscene, pornographic material subject to regulation under the States' police power. . . . [50]

This is not remarkable, for in the area of freedom of speech and press the courts must always remain sensitive to any infringement on genuinely serious literary, artistic, political, or scientific expression. This is an area in which there are few eternal verities.

The case we now review was tried on the theory that the California Penal Code § 311 approximately incorporates the three-stage *Memoirs* test. But now the *Memoirs* test has been abandoned as unworkable by its author,[51] and no Member of the Court today supports the *Memoirs* formulation.

---

[50] [Court's footnote 3] In the absence of a majority view, this Court was compelled to embark on the practice of summarily reversing convictions for the dissemination of materials that at least five members of the Court, applying their separate tests, found to be protected by the First Amendment. *Redrup v. New York*, 386 U.S. 767 (1967). Thirty-one cases have been decided in this manner. Beyond the necessity of circumstances, however, no justification has ever been offered in support of the *Redrup* "policy." The *Redrup* procedure has cast us in the role of an unreviewable board of censorship for the 50 States, subjectively judging each piece of material brought before us.

[51] [Court's footnote 4] See the dissenting opinion of Justice Brennan in *Paris Adult Theatre I v. Slaton*, 413 U.S. 49 (1973).

II

. . . State statutes designed to regulate obscene materials must be carefully limited. . . . As a result, we now confine the permissible scope of such regulation to works which depict or describe sexual conduct. That conduct must be specifically defined by the applicable state law, as written or authoritatively construed.[52]

A state offense must also be limited to works which, taken as a whole, appeal to the prurient interest in sex, which portray sexual conduct in a patently offensive way, and which, taken as a whole, do not have serious literary, artistic, political, or scientific value.

The basic guidelines for the trier of fact must be: (a) whether "the average person, applying contemporary community standards" would find that the work, taken as a whole, appeals to the prurient interest, *Roth v. United States*, 354 U.S. at 489; (b) whether the work depicts or describes, in a patently offensive way, sexual conduct specifically defined by the applicable state law; and (c) whether the work, taken as a whole, lacks serious literary, artistic, political or scientific value. We do not adopt as a constitutional standard the "utterly without redeeming social value" test of *Memoirs v. Massachusetts*, 383 U.S. at 419; that concept has never commanded the adherence of more than three Justices at one time. If a state law that regulates obscene material is thus limited, as written or construed, the First Amendment values applicable to the States through the Fourteenth Amendment are adequately protected by the ultimate power of appellate courts to conduct an independent review of constitutional claims when necessary.

We emphasize that it is not our function to propose regulatory schemes for the States. That must await their concrete legislative efforts. It is possible, however, to give a few plain examples of what a state statute could define for regulation under part (b) of the standard announced in this opinion, *supra*:

(a) Patently offensive representations or descriptions of ultimate sexual acts, normal or perverted, actual or simulated.

(b) Patently offensive representation or descriptions of masturbation, excretory functions, and lewd exhibition of the genitals.

Sex and nudity may not be exploited without limit by films or pictures exhibited or sold in places of public accommodation any more than live sex and nudity can be exhibited or sold without limit in such public places.[53]

At a minimum, prurient, patently offensive depiction or description of sexual conduct must have serious literary, artistic, political or scientific value to merit First Amendment protection. For example, medical books for the education of physicians and related personnel necessary use graphic illustrations and descriptions of human anatomy. In resolving the inevitably sensitive questions of fact and law, we must continue to rely on the jury system, accompanied by the safeguards that judges, rules

---

[52] [Court's footnote 6] *See, e.g.*, Oregon Laws 1971, c. 743, Art. 29, §§ 255–262, and Hawaii Penal Code, Tit. 37, §§ 1210–1216, 1972 Hawaii Session Laws, Act 9, c. 12, pt. II, pp. 126–129, as examples of state laws directed at depiction of defined physical conduct, as opposed to expression. Other state formulations could be equally valid in this respect. In giving the Oregon and Hawaii statutes as examples, we do not wish to be understood as approving of them in all other respects nor as establishing their limits as the extent of state power.

[53] [Court's footnote 8] Although we are not presented here with the problem of regulating lewd public conduct itself, the States have greater power to regulate nonverbal, physical conduct than to suppress depictions or descriptions of the same behavior. . . .

of evidence, presumption of innocence, and other protective features provide. . . . [54]

Justice Brennan . . . has abandoned his former position and now maintains that no formulation of the Court, the Congress, or the States can adequately distinguish obscene material unprotected by the First Amendment from protected expression, *Paris Adult Theatre I v. Slaton.* Paradoxically, Justice Brennan indicates that suppression of unprotected obscene material is permissible to avoid exposure to unconsenting adults, as in this case, and to juveniles, although he gives no indication of how the division between protected and nonprotected materials may be drawn. . . .

Under the holdings announced today, no one will be subject to prosecution for the sale or exposure of obscene materials unless these materials depict or describe patently offensive "hard core" sexual conduct specifically defined by the regulating state law, as written or construed. . . .

III

Under a National Constitution, fundamental First Amendment limitations on the powers of the States do not vary from community to community, but this does not mean that there are, or should or can be, fixed, uniform national standards of precisely what appeals to the "prurient interest" or is "patently offensive." These are essentially questions of fact, and our Nation is simply too big and too diverse for this Court to reasonably expect that such standards could be articulated for all 50 States in a single formulation, even assuming the prerequisite consensus exists. When triers of fact are asked to decide whether "the average person, applying contemporary community standards" would consider certain materials "prurient," it would be unrealistic to require that the answer be based on some abstract formulation. The adversary system, with lay jurors as the usual ultimate fact finders in criminal prosecutions, has historically permitted triers of fact to draw on the standards of their community, guided always by limiting instructions on the law. To require a State to structure obscenity proceedings around evidence of a *national* "community standard" would be an exercise in futility.

As noted before, this case was tried on the theory that the California obscenity statute sought to incorporate the tripartite test of *Memoirs.* This, a "national" standard of First Amendment protection enumerated by a plurality of this Court, was correctly regarded at the time of trial as limiting state prosecution under the controlling case law. The jury, however, was explicitly instructed that, in determining whether the "dominant theme of the material as a whole . . . appeals to the prurient interest" and in determining whether the material "goes substantially beyond customary limits of candor and affronts contemporary community standards of decency," it was to apply "contemporary community standards of the State of California." . . .

We conclude that neither the State's alleged failure to offer evidence of "national standards," nor the trial court's charge that the jury consider state community standards, were constitutional errors. Nothing in the First Amendment requires that a jury must consider hypothetical and unascertainable "national standards" when attempting to determine whether certain materials are obscene as a matter of fact. . . .

It is neither realistic nor constitutionally sound to read the First Amendment as requiring that the people of Maine or Mississippi accept public depiction of conduct found tolerable in Las Vegas, or New York City. . . . People in different States vary

---

[54] [Court's footnote 9] The mere fact juries may reach different conclusions as to the same material does not mean that constitutional rights are abridged. . . . *Roth v. United States,* 354 U.S. at 492 n.30.

in their tastes and attitudes, and this diversity is not to be strangled by the absolutism of imposed uniformity. . . . We hold that the requirement that the jury evaluate the materials with reference to "contemporary standards of the State of California" serves this protective purpose and is constitutionally adequate.

IV

The dissenting Justices sound the alarm of repression. But, in our view, to equate the free and robust exchange of ideas and political debate with commercial exploitation of obscene material demeans the grand conception of the First Amendment. . . .

In sum, we (a) reaffirm the *Roth* holding that obscene material is not protected by the First Amendment; (b) hold that such material can be regulated by the States, subject to the specific safeguards enunciated above, without a showing that the material is "*utterly* without redeeming social value"; and (c) hold that obscenity is to be determined by applying "contemporary community standards," not "national standards." . . .

Justice Douglas, dissenting. . . .

. . . [T]here are no constitutional guidelines for deciding what is and what is not "obscene." The Court is at large because we deal with tastes and standards of literature. What shocks me may be sustenance for my neighbor. What causes one person to boil up in rage over one pamphlet or movie may reflect only his neurosis, not shared by others. We deal here with a regime of censorship which, if adopted, should be done by constitutional amendment after full debate by the people. . . .

. . . The idea that the First Amendment permits punishment for ideas that are "offensive" to the particular judge or jury sitting in judgment is astounding. No greater leveler of speech or literature has ever been designed. . . .

Justice Brennan, with whom Justice Stewart and Justice Marshall join, dissenting.

. . . I need not now decide whether a statute might be drawn to impose, within the requirements of the First Amendment, criminal penalties for the precise conduct at issue here. For it is clear that under my dissent in *Paris Adult Theatre I*, the statute under which the prosecution was brought is unconstitutionally overbroad, and therefore invalid on its face. . . .

PARIS ADULT THEATER I v. SLATON, 413 U.S. 49 (1973). In *Paris Adult*, the Court upheld the Georgia Supreme Court's ruling that "the sale and delivery of obscene material to willing adults is not protected under the First Amendment" and, therefore, could be enjoined. The injunction operated against two allegedly obscene films displayed in an adult theater. The films depicted simulated fellatio, cunnilingus, and group sex intercourse.[55]

Writing for the Court, Chief Justice Burger "remanded the case for reconsideration in light of" *Miller v. California*, decided the same day. The Court reaffirmed the critically important state interests "in regulating the exposure of obscene materials to juveniles and unconsenting adults." The Chief Justice also listed other legitimate state interests in stemming the tide of commercialized obscenity, including "the interest of the public in the quality of life and the total community environment, the tone of commerce in the great city centers, and, possibly, the public safety itself." Moreover, the Georgia legislature could reasonably find a possible or actual connection between

---

[55] There was no evidence of minors having entered the theater although there was also no evidence of any systematic policy barring minors beyond a sign requiring those entering "be 21 and able to prove it."

antisocial behavior and obscene material, even without conclusive proof. The Court refused to analogize this case to *Stanley v. Georgia*, 394 U.S. 557 (1969), which guaranteed a constitutional right to view obscene materials in the privacy of one's home.

Additionally, the Court rejected the argument that conduct that only involves "consenting adults" can never be regulated by the state.[56]

"Commercial exploitation of depictions, descriptions, or exhibitions of obscene conduct on commercial premises open to the adult public falls within a State's broad power to regulate commerce and protect the public environment."

Justice Douglas filed a dissenting opinion arguing that government should not determine the individual's "tastes, beliefs, and ideas."

Justice Brennan, joined by Justices Stewart and Marshall, dissented. Justice Brennan criticized the departure from the centrally important third part of the test in *Memoirs v. Massachusetts*. While that test required that the material be "utterly lacking in social values" the Court now requires that obscene materials merely lack "serious literary, artistic, social or scientific value." Justice Brennan would hold "that at least in the absence of distribution to juveniles or obtrusive exposure to unconsenting adults, the First and Fourteenth Amendments prohibit the State and Federal Governments from attempting wholly to suppress sexually oriented materials on the basis of their allegedly 'obscene' contents."

ARCARA v. CLOUD BOOKS, INC., 478 U.S. 697 (1986). In *Arcara*, the Court addressed the issue whether "the First Amendment bars enforcement of a statute authorizing closure of a premises found to be used for prostitution and lewdness because the premises are also used as adult bookstore."

Cloud Books owned and operated an adult bookstore. A police officer observed instances of solicitation and "of masturbation, fondling, and fellatio by patrons on the premises of the store, all within the observation of the proprietor." The New York Public Health Law provided that any "building, erection, or place, or the ground itself, in or upon which any lewdness, assignation, or prostitution is conducted, permitted, or carried on, continued, or exists . . . are hereby declared to be a nuisance and shall be enjoined and abated." The City sought closure for the mandatory one-year period provided by the statute.

Chief Justice Burger, writing for the majority, reasoned that the *O'Brien* test did not apply to this closure. "[U]nlike the symbolic draft card burning in *O'Brien*, the sexual activity carried on in this case manifests absolutely no element of protected expression." The Chief Justice offered this illustration of his reasoning: "If the city imposed closure penalties for demonstrated Fire Code violations or health hazards from inadequate sewage treatment, the First Amendment would not aid the owner of premises who had knowingly allowed such violations to persist." In analyzing the closure sanction, the majority concluded that First Amendment scrutiny under the least restrictive means test was warranted only when "conduct with a significant expressive element . . . drew the legal remedy in the first place, as in *O'Brien*, or where a statute based on a nonexpressive activity has the inevitable effect of singling

---

[56] "The state statute books are replete with constitutionally unchallenged laws against prostitution, suicide, voluntary self-mutilation, brutalizing 'bare fist' prize fights, and duels, although these crimes may only directly involve 'consenting adults.' Statutes making bigamy a crime surely cut into an individual's freedom to associate, but few today seriously claim such statutes violate the First Amendment or any other constitutional provision."

out those engaged in expressive activity." The Chief Justice said that this case involved neither situation.[57]

Justice O'Connor, joined by Justice Stevens, concurred. The concurrence stated that the New York Court of Appeals erred in using a First Amendment standard of review where "the government is regulating neither speech nor an incidental, non-expressive effect of speech. Any other conclusion would lead to the absurd result that any government action that had some conceivable speech-inhibiting consequences, such as the arrest of a newscaster for a traffic violation, would require analysis under the First Amendment."

Justice Blackmun's dissent, joined by Justices Brennan and Marshall, complained that the Court's decision allowed a state "to suppress speech as much as it likes, without justification, so long as it does so through generally applicable regulations that have 'nothing to do with any expressive conduct.' "

NOTES

(1) " 'Hard Core' Sexual Conduct." In Jenkins v. Georgia, 418 U.S. 153 (1974), decided only one year after the Miller case, the Court reversed a conviction for the showing of the film "Carnal Knowledge." The State based its conviction on the pre-Miller test established in the Court's opinion in Memoirs v. Massachusetts, 383 U.S. 413 (1966). The Supreme Court, however, found that "Carnal Knowledge" was not obscene even under the new Miller standard. Justice Rehnquist's majority opinion made it clear that the Miller case, with its emphasis on "community standards," was not intended to relieve courts of the responsibility of reviewing individual films, or possibly books, to determine whether the individual work was entitled to First Amendment protection. "Not only did we there say that the First Amendment values . . . are adequately protected by the ultimate power of appellate courts to conduct an independent review of constitutional claims, . . . but we made it plain that under the holding no one will be subject to prosecution for the sale or exposure of obscene materials unless these materials depict or describe patently offensive 'hard core' sexual conduct."

(2) The Search for a "Community Standard." The Court has found it necessary to interpret certain aspects of the Miller test.

(a) Average person in the community. In Hamling v. United States, 418 U.S. 87 (1974), the Court provided guidance as to how a juror should apply the community standard on the elements of patent offensiveness and appeal to the prurient interest. "A juror is entitled to draw on his own knowledge of the views of the average person in the community or vicinage from which he comes for making the required determination, just as he is entitled to draw on his knowledge of the propensities of a 'reasonable' person in other areas of the law."

(b) Defining community standards under a federal statute. In Smith v. United States, 431 U.S. 291 (1977), the Court sustained a federal criminal prosecution for the mailing of obscene material even though the State where the crime occurred, Iowa, did not have an obscenity statute applicable to the defendant's conduct at the time of the mailing. The "community standards" rule in Miller was held not to be circumscribed by

---

[57] The Chief Justice also rejected the characterization of the closure as a prior restraint. "The closure order sought in this case differs from a prior restraint in two significant respects. First, the order would impose no restraint at all on the dissemination of particular materials, since respondent is free to carry on his bookselling business at another location, even if such locations are difficult to find. Second, the closure order sought would not be imposed on the basis of an advance determination that the distribution of particular materials is prohibited — indeed, the imposition of the closure order has nothing to do with any expressive conduct at all."

the State's regulatory statutes. Indeed, the Court said that state legislatures could not prescribe community standards for juries. A state might, however, "impose a geographic limit on the determination of community standards by defining the area from which the jury could be selected in an obscenity case, or by legislating with respect to the instructions that must be given to the jurors in such cases." For appeal to prurient interest and patent offensiveness, the community standard cannot "be defined legislatively."

In *Hamling v. United States, supra*, the Court approved the application of local standards in the enforcement of a federal penal statute, even if this resulted in a non-uniform interpretation of the federal law throughout the country.

(3) *The Standard for "Literary, Artistic, Political, or Scientific Value": Community or National?* In *Smith v. United States, supra*, the Court held that juries should apply the first two parts of the *Miller* test to reflect contemporary community standards. The third prong of the *Miller* test — that the work "lacks serious, literary, artistic, political, or scientific value" — is not judged by a community standard.

In *Pope v. Illinois*, 481 U.S. 479 (1987), Justice White stated that the value of the work "cannot vary from community to community based on the degree of local acceptance it has won. The proper inquiry is not whether an ordinary member of any given community would find serious literary, artistic, political, or scientific value in allegedly obscene material, but whether a reasonable person would find such value in the material, taken as a whole."

Justice Scalia concurred in this portion of the opinion, but suggested that "it is quite impossible to come to an objective assessment of (at least) literary or artistic value."

Justice Stevens' dissent, joined by Justice Marshall, disagreed with the "reasonable person" test. "[T]here are many cases in which *some* reasonable people would find that specific sexually oriented materials have serious artistic, political, literary, or scientific value, while *other* reasonable people would conclude that they have no such value." Justice Brennan also filed a brief dissent.

(4) *Must the Statute Describe "Patently Offensive" Sexual Conduct?* In *Ward v. Illinois*, 431 U.S. 767 (1977), the Court upheld the Illinois obscenity statute even though the State "has not provided an exhaustive list" of what sexual conduct may be patently offensive. Justice White, joined by the Chief Justice and Justices Blackmun, Powell and Rehnquist, ruled that it was sufficient to adopt the explanatory examples set forth in *Miller*. Justice Stevens, joined by Justices Brennan, Stewart and Marshall, argued that the Court had abandoned part (b) of the *Miller* test. In addition, Justice Brennan filed a separate dissent.

(5) *Scienter.* Several substantive doctrines developed by the Court during the years between *Roth* and *Miller* remain applicable. In *Smith v. California*, 361 U.S. 147 (1959), the Court (8-1) held invalid a Los Angeles ordinance which "imposed a strict or absolute criminal responsibility on appellant not to have obscene books in his shop." Justice Brennan's majority opinion concluded that the elimination of the scienter requirement imposed "a severe limitation on the public's access to constitutionally protected matter." Strict liability on the bookseller would cause him "to restrict the books he sells to those he has inspected."

(6) *The Constitutional Standard for Minors.* In *Ginsberg v. New York*, 390 U.S. 629 (1968), the Court upheld a conviction under a New York statute for peddling two "so-called 'girlie magazines'" to a 16-year-old boy. The New York trial court found: "(1) that the magazines contained pictures which depicted female 'nudity' in a manner defined in [the statute] that is 'the showing of . . . female . . . buttocks with less than a full opaque covering, or the showing of the female breast with less than a fully opaque

covering of any portion thereof below the top of the nipple . . .,' and (2) that the pictures were 'harmful to minors' in that they had, within the meaning of [the New York Statute] 'that quality of . . . representation . . . of nudity . . . (which) . . . (i) predominantly appeals to the prurient, shameful or morbid interest of minors, and (ii) is patently offensive to prevailing standards in the adult community as a whole with respect to what is suitable material for minors, and (iii) is utterly without redeeming social importance for minors.'" The *Roth* test was thus re-defined in terms of applicability to minors. The Court has not however provided guidance as to how the *Miller* test might be modified for minors.

(7) *Pandering.* In *Ginzburg v. United States*, 383 U.S. 463 (1966), a sharply divided Court (5-4) held that the manner in which the material was marketed — "pandering" by the seller in material that displays the "leer of the sensualist" — could be "probative" in deciding whether the *Roth* test had been met, even though the same material would not be considered "obscene" if marketed in a different fashion. Justices Black, Douglas, Stewart, and Harlan dissented from Justice Brennan's majority opinion.

(8) *Dial-a-Porn.* In *Sable Communications v. Federal Communications Commission*, 492 U.S. 115 (1989), the Court upheld, against a facial challenge, a federal statute's ban on obscene commercial telephone messages, but struck down that part of the statute banning messages that were merely indecent.

Writing for a unanimous Court, Justice White held that as the First Amendment protected indecent speech, the government could only regulate it "in order to promote a compelling interest if it chooses the least restrictive means to further the articulated interest." The Court did recognize "that there is a compelling interest in protecting the physical and psychological well-being of minors." However, several alternatives to an outright ban were less restrictive. "The FCC, after lengthy proceedings, determined that its credit card, access code, and scrambling rules were a satisfactory solution to the problem of keeping indecent dial-a-porn messages out of the reach of minors."

In upholding that part of the statute that banned obscene dial-a-porn messages, Justice White wrote for a 6-3 majority. "The case before us today does not require us to decide what is obscene or what is indecent but rather to determine whether Congress is empowered to prohibit transmission of obscene telephonic communications." Sable also argued that the nationwide ban on obscene transmissions compelled "them to tailor all their messages to the least tolerant community." Noting that the *Miller* standard had previously been applied to federal legislation, the Court stated that "Sable is free to tailor its messages, on a selective basis, if it so chooses, to the communities it chooses to serve. . . . If Sable's audience is comprised of different communities with different local standards, Sable ultimately bears the burden of complying with the prohibition on obscene messages."

Justice Brennan wrote an opinion concurring in part and dissenting in part, which Justices Stevens and Marshall joined. While agreeing with the majority that the ban on indecent speech violated the First Amendment, Justice Brennan would have extended First Amendment protection to messages that the majority would label obscene. This case is also discussed at § 14.01[2], Note (3).

(9) *Internet.* In *Reno v. American Civil Liberties Union*, 521 U.S. 844 (1997), the Court invalidated the Communications Decency Act of 1996 ("CDA") as unconstitutionally interfering with free speech. The law was designed to protect children from "'obscene or indecent'" material on the Internet. The Court found that the obscenity standard in the CDA did not meet the *Miller* test.

While the CDA banned "'patently offensive'" material, it omitted the "critical requirement" of part (b) of the *Miller* test "that the proscribed material be 'specifically defined by the applicable state law.'" The CDA also lacked the other two prongs of the

Miller test which required that the work "appeal to the 'prurient' interest and that it lack "serious literary, artistic, political or scientific value." The CDA also bans patently offensive materials according to community standards. In contrast, the third prong of *Miller* requires that the material lacks serious literary, artistic, or scientific value according to a national standard. Since the Internet is a world wide network in which nearly every community participates, the CDA approach would result in the materials' being judged "by the standards of the community most likely to be offended by the message." The opinion is reproduced at § 13.07[3].

(10) *Community Standards for Internet?* In *Ashcroft v. American Civil Liberties Union*, 535 U.S. 564 (2002), the Court rejected a facial challenge against the Child Online Protection Act's (COPA) reliance on "'community standards' to identify 'material that is harmful to minors.'" Writing for a majority of the Court, Justice Thomas noted that following the Reno decision, Congress passed the more limited Child Online Protection Act (COPA). First, unlike the CDA which applied to all Internet communications including e-mails, COPA applies only to displays on the World Wide Web. Second, "unlike the CDA, COPA covers only communications made for 'commercial purposes.'" Finally, unlike the CDA's prohibition of "indecent" and "patently offensive" communications, COPA restricts only the narrower category of "material that is harmful to minors," as defined in *Miller v. California*, 413 U.S. 15 (1973). COPA also allows affirmative defenses, if an individual "'in good faith, has restricted access by minors to material that is harmful to minors — (A) by requiring the use of a credit card, debit account, adult access code, or adult personal identification number; (B) by accepting a digital certificate that verifies age; or (C) by any other reasonable measures that are feasible under available technology.'" Violating COPA is a crime punishable by a maximum prison sentence of 6 months or maximum fine of $50,000.

Writing for a plurality of four, Justice Thomas noted that unlike CDA, COPA only bans works that "'depict, describe, or represent, in a manner patently offensive with respect to minors,' particular sexual acts or parts of the anatomy. They must also be designed to appeal to the prurient interests of minors, and 'taken as a whole, lack serious literary, artistic, political, or scientific value for minors.'" Moreover, adopting *Miller's* approach, COPA adopts a national standard to assess serious value.

Writing for a plurality of three, Justice Thomas concluded that when a statute is sufficiently narrowed by "'serious value'" and "'prurient interest'" inquiries, both *Hamling v. United States*, 418 U.S. 87 (1974), and *Sable Communications of Cal., Inc. v. FCC*, 492 U.S. 115 (1989), hold that "requiring a speaker disseminating material to a national audience to observe varying community standards does not violate the First Amendment." The fact that Internet publishers cannot control where their materials go does not change this result. Publication over the Internet is necessarily national. When a publisher sends material to a community, it must "abide by that community's standards," even if the publisher "decides to distribute its material to every community in the Nation." If the application of community standards to the Web rendered COPA unconstitutional, federal obscenity statutes would also be unconstitutionally applied to the web. However, *Reno* suggested that "the application of the CDA to obscene speech was constitutional."

Writing for a majority, Justice Thomas held that "COPA's reliance on community standards to identify 'material that is harmful to minors' does not *by itself* render the statute substantially overbroad." The Court did not express "any view as to whether COPA suffers from substantial overbreadth for other reasons, including whether the statute is unconstitutionally vague, or whether the District Court correctly concluded that the statute likely will not survive strict scrutiny."

Concurring in part and concurring in the judgment, Justice O'Connor would adopt "a national standard for defining obscenity on the Internet." Concurring in part and concurring in the judgment, Justice Breyer also would adopt a "nationally uniform adult-based standard." Application of this standard by different local juries does not violate the First Amendment.

Justice Kennedy concurred in the judgment, joined by Justices Souter and Ginsburg. "In order to discern whether the variation creates substantial overbreadth, it is necessary to know what speech COPA regulates and what community standards it invokes." Justice Stevens dissented.

NEW YORK v. FERBER, 458 U.S. 747 (1982). In *Ferber*, the Court unanimously held that child pornography was not protected by the First Amendment. An undercover agent purchased from the proprietor of a Manhattan Bookstore two films depicting young boys masturbating. The proprietor, Ferber, was found guilty under a New York statute for knowingly distributing material that depicts a sexual performance of a child under 16.

In affirming the conviction, Justice White's majority opinion offered five reasons for permitting the states to have great leeway in the regulation of child pornography. "*First*. . . . [A] State's interest in 'safeguarding the physical and psychological well-being of a minor' is 'compelling.' . . . *Second*. The distribution of photographs and films depicting sexual activity by juveniles is intrinsically related to the sexual abuse of children in at least two ways. First, the materials produced are a permanent record of the children's participation and the harm to the child is exacerbated by their circulation. Second, the distribution network for child pornography must be closed if the production of material which requires the sexual exploitation of children is to be effectively controlled." Neither prosecuting the illegal activities involved in producing the movies nor prosecuting their distribution under the test would likely be a feasible alternative. "*Third*. The advertising and selling of child pornography provide an economic motive for and are thus an integral part of the production of such materials, an activity illegal throughout the Nation." The illegality of production was not even questioned and for First Amendment purposes, effectively proscribing production would be just as suppressive as a ban on distribution. "*Fourth*. The value of permitting live performances and photographic reproductions of children engaged in lewd sexual conduct is exceedingly modest, if not *de minimis*. We consider it unlikely that visual depictions of children performing sexual acts or lewdly exhibiting their genitals would often constitute an important and necessary part of a literary performance or scientific or educational work." Literary or artistic interests could be satisfied by using adults simulating minors. "*Fifth*. Recognizing and classifying child pornography as a category of material outside the protection of the First Amendment is not incompatible with our earlier decisions. 'The question whether speech is, or is not, protected by the First Amendment often depends on the content of the speech.' *Young v. American Mini Theatres*, 427 U.S. 50, 66 (1976) (opinion of Stevens, J., joined by Burger, C. J., and White and Rehnquist, J.J.). . . . Thus, it is not rare that a content-based classification of speech has been accepted because it may be appropriately generalized that within the confines of the given classification, the evil to be restricted so overwhelmingly outweighs the expressive interests, if any, at stake, that no process of case-by-case adjudication is required." In light of the burden on children, the balance of competing interests rendered these materials "as without the protection of the First Amendment."

"[T]he conduct to be prohibited must be adequately defined by the applicable state law, as written or authoritatively construed. Here the nature of the harm to be combatted requires that the state offense be limited to works that *visually* depict sexual conduct by children below a specified age. The category of 'sexual conduct' proscribed must also be suitably limited and described."

"The test for child pornography is separate from the obscenity standard enunciated in *Miller*, but may be compared to it for purpose of clarity. The *Miller* formulation is adjusted in the following respects: A trier of fact need not find that the material appeals to the prurient interest of the average person; it is not required that sexual conduct portrayed be done so in a patently offensive manner; and the material at issue need not be considered as a whole. We note that the distribution of descriptions or other depictions of sexual conduct, not otherwise obscene, which do not involve live performance or photographic or other visual reproduction of live performances, retains First Amendment protection. As with obscenity laws, criminal responsibility may not be imposed without some element of scienter on the part of the defendant."

Justice White also rejected an overbreadth challenge to the statute based on its potential regulation of "pictures in medical textbooks or National Geographic." Such "arguably impermissible restrictions" would not likely exceed a "tiny fraction of the statute's applications."

Justice Blackmun concurred in the result, without opinion. Justice O'Connor also concurred to stress that the Court's holding did not require New York to exempt material with serious literary, scientific or educational value from the reach of the criminal statute. "For example, a 12-year-old child photographed while masturbating surely suffers the same psychological harm whether the community labels the photograph 'edifying' or 'tasteless.' "

Justice Brennan, joined by Justice Marshall, concurred in the judgment. Agreeing with the majority, Justice Brennan stated that the materials at issue were "of exceedingly 'slight social value' and the State [had] a compelling interest in their regulation." He emphasized that materials that were a serious contribution to art or science would pose a different case.

Justice Stevens also concurred in the judgment. He opined, "on a number of occasions, I have expressed the view that the First Amendment affords some forms of speech more protection from governmental regulation than other forms of speech. Today the Court accepts this view, putting the category of speech described in the New York statute in its rightful place near the bottom of this hierarchy."

NOTES

(1) *Possession of Child Pornography in the Home.* In *Osborne v. Ohio*, 495 U.S. 103 (1990), the Court upheld an Ohio statute that prohibited private possession and viewing of child pornography. Pursuant to a valid search of Osborne's home, police had found four sexually explicit photos of a male adolescent. Writing for a 6-3 majority, Justice White relied heavily on *New York v. Ferber*, which assessed the value of child pornography as being "exceedingly modest, if not *de minimis*." Distinguishing *Stanley v. Georgia*, 394 U.S. 557 (1969), Justice White said that Ohio is not relying on "a paternalistic interest in regulating Osborne's mind" but instead is destroying "a market for the exploitative use of children." Assuming *arguendo* that some First Amendment interests were at stake, the Ohio statute advanced the compelling state interest in "safeguarding the physical and psychological well-being of a minor." The underground nature of the child pornography market justified banning possession and not only production and distribution. Other interests justifying Ohio's prohibition on possession were the permanent record that such films produced and the possibility that such films would be used as a means of seducing other children.

Again relying heavily on *Ferber*, Justice White also rejected overbreadth and vagueness challenges to the statute. For discussion of the overbreadth challenge, see § 12.06, Note (3).

Justice Blackmun filed a brief concurring opinion. Justice Brennan, joined by

Justices Stevens and Marshall, dissented. He did not agree that *Ferber* should displace the important interest protected by *Stanley* to view whatever materials one desires in the privacy of one's own home. The bans on production and distribution upheld in *Ferber* were more than adequate to satisfy Ohio's asserted interests in protection against the exploitation of minors.

(2) *"Knowing" Transportation of Child Pornography.* In *United States v. X-Citement Video, Inc.*, 513 U.S. 64 (1994), the Court upheld the Protection of Children Against Sexual Exploitation Act of 1977, against a challenge that it lacked the necessary scienter requirement. As a result of a sting operation, the owner of X-Citement Video was indicted under the Act. Defendant argued that the Act was facially unconstitutional because it lacked a scienter requirement. The Court read the term "knowingly" to modify the phrase "use of a minor" even though this was not the "most grammatical reading." The Court cited precedents supplying scienter requirements in criminal statutes that do not explicitly contain them. Rather than simply seeking the most grammatical reading, the Court tries to construe a statute constitutionally so long as its "reading is not plainly contrary to the intent of Congress." Justice Stevens filed a concurring opinion. Justice Scalia dissented, joined by Justice Thomas.

ASHCROFT v. THE FREE SPEECH COALITION, 535 U.S. 234 (2002). In *Free Speech Coalition*, the Court invalidated parts of the Child Pornography Prevention Act of 1996 (CPPA) that prohibited "sexually explicit images that appear to depict minors but were produced without using any real children."

Before 1996, Congress defined child pornography as "images made using actual minors." In addition, § 2256(8)(B) of the 1996 Act prohibits "'any visual depiction, including any photograph, film, video, picture, or computer or computer-generated image or picture' that 'is, or appears to be, of a minor engaging in sexually explicit conduct.'" Its prohibition encompasses "'virtual child pornography,' which include computer-generated images."[58] Also at issue, § 2256(8)(D) bans "any sexually explicit image that was 'advertised, promoted, presented, described, or distributed in such a manner that conveys the impression' it depicts 'a minor engaging in sexually explicit conduct.'" Under the CPPA, "[a] first offender may be imprisoned for 15 years," while a "repeat offender" may be imprisoned for 5–30 years.

Writing for the majority, Justice Kennedy found both §§ 2256(8)(B) and 2256(8)(D) "substantially overbroad." While the First Amendment does not protect "certain categories of speech, including defamation, incitement, obscenity, and pornography produced with real children," the regulations at issue involved none of these. The CPPA proscribed materials that did not meet the three-part test for obscenity set forth in *Miller v. California*, 413 U.S. 15 (1973). First, the materials "need not appeal to the prurient interest," as the CPPA banned all depictions "of sexually explicit activity, no matter how it is presented." Second, the images need not be patently offensive. For example, "[p]ictures of what appear to be 17-year-olds engaging in sexually explicit activity do not in every case contravene community standards." Additionally, the "CPPA prohibits speech despite its serious literary, artistic, political, or scientific value." Teenage sexuality "is a fact of modern society and has been a theme in art and

---

[58] "The statute also prohibits Hollywood movies, filmed without any child actors, if a jury believes an actor 'appears to be' a minor engaging in 'actual or simulated . . . sexual intercourse.'"

Section 2256(8)(C), which is not at issue, "prohibits a more common and lower tech means of creating virtual images, known as computer morphing. Rather than creating original images, pornographers can alter innocent pictures of real children so that the children appear to be engaged in sexual activity." Such images "implicate the interests of real children, and are in that sense closer to the images in" *New York v. Ferber*, 458 U.S. 747 (1982).

literature throughout the ages." Moreover, age eighteen is "higher than the legal age for marriage in many States, as well as the age at which persons may consent to sexual relations." Finally, under the First Amendment, "a single explicit scene" does not determine a work's "artistic merit." Instead, the work must be considered "as a whole." In contrast, the CPPA punishes the possessor of a film containing "a single graphic depiction of sexual activity within the statutory definition" regardless of "the work's redeeming value."

In contrast to child pornography, "the CPPA prohibits speech that records no crime and creates no victims by its production. Virtual child pornography is not 'intrinsically related' to the sexual abuse of children." In contrast to *New York v. Ferber*, 458 U.S. 747 (1982), "harm does not necessarily follow from the speech, but depends upon some unqualified potential for subsequent criminal acts."

Importantly, "*Ferber's* judgment about child pornography was based upon how it was made, not on what it communicated." Moreover, *Ferber* recognized that some child pornography "might have significant value." *Ferber* itself said, "[i]f it were necessary for literary or artistic value," a film could use "a person over the statutory age who perhaps looked younger" or a "[s]imulation." As such, § 2256(8)(B) "is inconsistent with *Miller*, and finds no support in *Ferber*."

The Government, however, sought to justify Section 2256(8)(B) in other ways. Rejecting the argument that "the CPPA is necessary because pedophiles may use virtual child pornography to seduce children," Justice Kennedy noted that "[t]here are many things innocent in themselves, such as cartoons, video games, and candy, that might be used for immoral purposes, yet we would not expect those to be prohibited because they can be misused." Second, the Government submits that "virtual child pornography whets the appetites of pedophiles and encourages them to engage in illegal conduct." However, "[t]he mere tendency of speech to encourage unlawful acts is not a sufficient reason for banning it." Third, Justice Kennedy rejected the argument that virtual images are indistinguishable from real ones. "If virtual images were identical to illegal child pornography, the illegal images would be driven from the market by the indistinguishable substitutes. Few pornographers would risk prosecution by abusing real children if fictional, computerized images would suffice."

Fourth, Justice Kennedy rejected the Government's argument that "producing images by using computer imaging makes it very difficult for it to prosecute those who produce pornography by using real children." This argument "turns the First Amendment upside down," as "Government may not suppress lawful speech as the means to suppress unlawful speech." Section 2256(8)(B) is overbroad because the First Amendment "prohibits the Government from banning unprotected speech if a substantial amount of protected speech is prohibited or chilled in the process."

Justice Kennedy also struck down § 2256(8)(D) of the CPPA. "[P]andering may be relevant, as an evidentiary matter, to the question whether particular materials are obscene." However, § 2256(8)(D) is "substantially overbroad" because it punishes "possession of material described, or pandered, as child pornography by someone earlier in the distribution chain."

Justice Thomas concurred in the judgment. He noted that "technology may evolve to the point where it becomes impossible to enforce actual child pornography laws because the Government cannot prove that certain pornographic images are of real children." At that time, "the Government may well have a compelling interest in barring or otherwise regulating some narrow category of 'lawful speech' in order to enforce effectively laws against pornography made through the abuse of real children."

Chief Justice Rehnquist, with whom Justice Scalia joined in part, dissenting, agreed with Justice O'Connor that "Congress has a compelling interest in ensuring the ability to enforce prohibitions of actual child pornography, and we should defer to its findings that rapidly advancing technology soon will make it all but impossible to do so."[59] Chief Justice Rehnquist also argued that "the CPPA can be limited so as not to reach any material that was not already unprotected before."[60] The Chief Justice would also uphold the pandering prohibition, but limit its reach to the panderer. He concluded that "while potentially impermissible applications of the CPPA may exist, I doubt that they would be 'substantial . . . in relation to the statute's plainly legitimate sweep.' " The CPPA focuses on "computer-generated images that are virtually indistinguishable from real children engaged in sexually explicit conduct. The statute need not be read to do any more than precisely this."

Justice O'Connor filed an opinion, in which she concurred in part, and dissented in part. In Part I of her opinion, Justice O'Connor agreed with the majority that the pandering ban of § 2256(8)(D) "fails strict scrutiny." In Part I, Justice O'Connor also agreed with the Court that the CPPA's ban on "pornographic images of adults that look like children" is overbroad. However, Justice O'Connor would invalidate § 2256(8)(B) "only insofar as it is applied to the class of youthful-adult pornography."

In Part II of her opinion, Justice O'Connor, joined by Chief Justice Rehnquist and Justice Scalia, disagreed that "the CPPA's prohibition of virtual-child pornography is overbroad." This ban is supported by the long-recognized "compelling interest in protecting our Nation's children." Specifically, "[s]uch images whet the appetites of child molesters . . . who may use the images to seduce young children." Justice O'Connor also believed "that defendants indicted for the production, distribution, or possession of actual-child pornography may evade liability by claiming that the images attributed to them are in fact computer-generated." Because of "rapid" advances in "computer-graphics technology, the Government's concern is reasonable."

Justice O'Connor read the statute "only to bar images that are virtually indistinguishable from actual children," which would render its ban "narrowly tailored, but would also assuage any fears that the 'appears to be . . . a minor' language is vague." Litigants challenging as overbroad a regulation, which is narrowly tailored to a compelling state interest, "bear the heavy burden of demonstrating that the regulation forbids a substantial amount of valuable or harmless speech." The challengers here "provide no examples of films or other materials that are wholly computer-generated and contain images that 'appear to be . . . of minors' engaging in indecent conduct, but that have serious value or do not facilitate child abuse. Their overbreadth challenge therefore fails."

NOTE: THE FEMINIST ATTACK ON PORNOGRAPHY

Pornography has been attacked by feminist scholars as a form of sexual subjugation of women which has demonstrably harmful consequences that justify either direct governmental restriction or private civil remedies. *See generally* Catharine A. McKinnon, *Pornography, Civil Rights, and Free Speech,* 20 Harv. C.R.-C.L. L. Rev. 1 (1985) (Professor McKinnon helped to draft the Indianapolis statute considered in the *Hudnut* case below.).

---

[59] Chief Justice Rehnquist also agreed with Justice O'Connor that "serious First Amendment concerns would arise were the Government ever to prosecute someone for simple distribution or possession of a film with literary or artistic value, such as 'Traffic' or 'American Beauty.' "

[60] "The CPPA's definition of 'sexually explicit conduct' is quite explicit in this regard. It makes clear that the statute only reaches 'visual depictions' of: 'actual or simulated . . . . sexual intercourse, including genital-genital, oral-genital, anal-genital, or oral-anal, whether between persons of the same or opposite sex; . . . bestiality; . . . masturbation; . . . sadistic or masochistic abuse; . . . or lascivious exhibition of the genitals or pubic area of any person.' "

In *American Booksellers Ass'n, Inc. v. Hudnut*, 771 F.2d 323 (7th Cir. 1985), *aff'd*, 475 U.S. 1001 (1986), the Court summarily affirmed a decision of the Seventh Circuit Court of Appeals invalidating an Indianapolis ordinance that, as described in the Court of Appeals' opinion, "contained four prohibitions. People may not 'traffic' in pornography, 'coerce' others in performing in pornographic works, or 'force' pornography on anyone. Anyone injured by someone who has seen or read pornography has a right of action against the maker or seller of the product."

"Pornography" was defined as "the graphic sexually explicit subordination of women, whether in pictures or in words, that also includes one or more of the following:

(1) Women are presented as sexual objects who enjoy pain or humiliation; or

(2) Women are presented as sexual objects who experience sexual pleasure in being raped; or

(3) Women are presented as sexual objects tied up or cut up or mutilated or bruised or physically hurt, or as dismembered or truncated or fragmented or severed into body parts; or

(4) Women are presented as being penetrated by objects or animals; or

(5) Women are presented in scenarios of degradation, injury, abasement, torture, shown as filthy or inferior, bleeding, bruised, or hurt in a context that makes these conditions sexual; or

(6) Women are presented as sexual objects for domination, conquest, violation, exploitation, possession, or use, or through postures or positions of servility or submission or display."

Judge Easterbrook's opinion concluded: "The definition of 'pornography' is unconstitutional. No construction or excision of particular terms could save it." The ordinance ". . . is not neutral with respect to viewpoint . . . and we have held the definition of 'pornography' to be defective root and branch." Chief Justice Burger and Justices Rehnquist and O'Connor would have noted probable jurisdiction and set the case for oral argument. For a critical appraisal of the statute at issue in *Hudnut*, see Edward A. Carr, *Feminism, Pornography, and the First Amendment: An Obscenity-Based Analysis of Proposed Anti-Pornography Laws*, 34 UCLA L. REV. 1265 (1987). *But see* Deana Pollard, *Regulating Violent Pornography*, 43 VAND. L. REV. 125, 126 (1990) ("Researchers, however, have shown that certain types of pornography, such as violent, sexually explicit materials, specifically harm women. The proven relationship between violent pornography and aggression of men toward women evidences a need for regulation, but constitutional barriers to censorship under First Amendment analysis are great.").

[2] Procedural Issues in Obscenity Cases — "Prior Restraints" and Seizure of Materials

SOUTHEASTERN PROMOTIONS LTD. v. CONRAD, 420 U.S. 546 (1975). In *Southeastern Promotions*, the Court held that a municipal theater's refusing to house the play "Hair" because of its content was an unlawful prior restraint. Although none of the directors had seen or read the play, the directors of the Chattanooga Memorial Auditorium rejected an application to present the play. Because the directors understood that the play contained nudity and obscenity on stage, they determined that housing the production would not be "in the best interest of the community." Justice Blackmun, writing for the majority, stated that in rejecting the application to use this public forum, the directors accomplished a prior restraint under a system lacking in constitutionally required minimal procedural safeguards.

The action was a prior restraint even though the decision did not effectively suppress any showing of "Hair" in the community.[61] The "restraint was final. It was no mere temporary bar while necessary judicial proceedings were under way."

However, merely labeling the directors' "action a prior restraint does not end the inquiry. Prior restraints are not unconstitutional *per se*." The Court has refused to find that the First Amendment affords absolute protection to exhibit all films at least once, even if it contains "the basest type of pornography, or incitement to riot or forceful overthrow of orderly government."

Reaffirming *Freedman v. Maryland*, 380 U.S. 51 (1965), Justice Blackmun stated that the Constitution requires that prior restraints have certain procedural safeguards. "*First*, the burden of instituting judicial proceedings and of proving that the material is unprotected, must rest on the censor. *Second*, any restraint prior to judicial review can be imposed only for a specified brief period and only for the purpose of preserving the status quo. *Third*, a prompt final judicial determination must be assured."

This case aptly illustrates the perils of a prior restraint "where neither the Board nor the lower courts could not have known precisely the extent of nudity or simulated sex in the musical, or even that either would appear, before the play was actually performed." Moreover, failure to observe the *Freedman* procedural requirements rendered the Board's action invalid regardless of its substantive merits. The Board provided no "procedure for prompt judicial review." Although the trial court heard the motion for preliminary injunction a few days after the Board's decision, the trial court did not review the merits of the Board's decision until five months after this hearing. Instead, the court only evaluated the "likelihood of success on the merits" and whether Southeastern "would suffer irreparable injury pending full review." Moreover, Southeastern Promotions carried the burden of obtaining a judicial proceeding and, at least during that proceeding, also carried the burden of persuasion. Irrespective of its substantive merits, the directors' action constituted an unlawful prior restraint as it lacked proper procedural safeguards.

Justice Douglas dissented in part and concurred in the judgment in part, maintaining the invalidity of any system of prior restraints regardless of procedural safeguards.

Justice White dissented, joined by Chief Justice Burger. Justice White stated that despite any deficiencies under *Freedman* in the Board's procedural safeguards, "the parties now have been to court; and, after trial, 'Hair' has been held violative of Tennessee statutes by both the District Court and the Court of Appeals." As the Court has not disturbed the substantive findings of obscenity made by the courts below, it cannot order that a play adjudicated obscene now be performed because of procedural irregularities.

Justice Rehnquist also dissented. He distinguished this case from *Freedman* by

---

[61] In a footnote, Justice Blackmun stated that a "licensing scheme need not effect total suppression of speech in order to create a prior restraint." In *Interstate Circuit v. Dallas*, 390 U.S. 676, 668 (1968), the Court held that a Texas administrative board created a prior restraint when it required movie theaters to obtain a special permit and advertise a special classification of films they deemed " 'not suitable for young persons.' " In *Bantam Books, Inc. v. Sullivan*, 372 U.S. 58 (1963), the Court held that " 'informal censorship' working by exhortation and advice sufficiently inhibited expression to constitute a prior restraint." The Court found that a government commission's persuasion, intimidation, and other informal methods created effective prior restraints.

saying that the State, in *Freedman*, prohibited an exhibitor from showing a movie in his own theater.

NOTES

(1) *Modification of Freedman.* In *FW/PBS, Inc. v. City of Dallas*, 493 U.S. 215 (1990), the Court invalidated "a licensing scheme in a comprehensive city ordinance regulating sexually oriented businesses" as a prior restraint without adequate procedural safeguards. A Dallas ordinance imposed various zoning, licensing, and inspection regulations on "sexually oriented businesses," defined as "an adult arcade, adult bookstore or adult video store, adult cabaret, adult motel, adult motion picture theater, adult theater, escort agency, nude model studio, or sexual encounter center." The ordinance also prohibited persons convicted of certain crimes from operating a sexually oriented business for a specified number of years.

Writing for a plurality, Justice O'Connor invalidated Dallas' licensing scheme as a prior restraint lacking the necessary procedural safeguards. The required inspections created an impermissible risk of delay. She allowed a facial challenge because the inspection requirement created a risk of delay for every application for a new permit or for annual renewal. Violating two procedural safeguards for prior restraints in *Freedman v. Maryland*, 380 U.S. 51 (1965), the ordinance did not effectively limit the time for making the licensing decision or provide for prompt judicial review.

However, Justice O'Connor did not impose *Freedman's* third requirement that the censor bear the burden of obtaining judicial review and the burden of proof once in court. In *Freedman*, the state reviewed and censored particular expressive material. In contrast, the Dallas ordinance simply requires a ministerial review of an applicant's general qualifications rather than discretionary review of the content of speech. Moreover, *Freedman* required the censor to carry the burdens because the censor's decision would otherwise have been final. The owners of sexually oriented businesses have much more at stake than in *Freedman*, where just one movie was censored. As a license is essential for business, the owner has a great incentive to pursue any denial of that license in court. These factual differences allowed the plurality to dispense with *Freedman's* third procedural safeguard in this case.

Writing for a majority, Justice O'Connor rejected the motel owner's contention that the 10-hour limitation on motel room rental unconstitutionally offended the right to freedom of association.

Justice Brennan concurred, joined by Justices Marshall and Blackmun. Justice Brennan contended that all three procedural safeguards outlined in *Freedman v. Maryland* should have been applied, not just two.

Justice White, joined by Chief Justice Rehnquist, concurred in part and dissented in part. Justice White argued that the ordinance did have a 30-day limitation in which the licensor must act. Moreover, all licensing decisions "are immediately appealable to a permit and license appeal board and are stayed pending that appeal." In turn, those board decisions are again immediately appealable to the courts.

Justice Scalia concurred in part and dissented in part, arguing that *Ginzburg v. United States*, 383 U.S. 463 (1966), allows government to ban and *a fortiori* regulate businesses engaged in pandering.

(2) *Prompt Judicial Review.* In *Littleton v. Z.J. Gifts*, 541 U.S. 774 (2004), the Court upheld a city ordinance requiring a license for adult businesses. The ordinance set forth "eight specific circumstances" which require "the city to deny a license." License denials may be appealed to the state district court. Rather than apply for a license, Z.J. Gifts mounted a facial challenge, claiming that the ordinance failed to provide prompt

judicial review. In response to the city's defenses of the law, the Court said that *Freedman v. Maryland* and *FW/PBS, Inc. v. City of Dallas* requires not only prompt access to judicial review, but also " 'prompt judicial *determination*' " of the validity of denying a license to an adult business. Nevertheless, the Court held that state law did provide for a "prompt judicial determination."

Writing for the majority, Justice Breyer explained that "ordinary court procedural rules and practices, in Colorado as elsewhere," allow courts to accelerate the review process to sufficiently "avoid delay-related First Amendment harm." Unlike *Freedman*, the instant ordinance is not designed to censor, but instead "applies reasonable objective, nondiscriminatory criteria."

Z.J. Gifts did not suffer any judicial delay, but merely challenged the law on its face. "Where (as here and as in *FW/PBS*) the regulation simply conditions the operation of an adult business on compliance with neutral and nondiscretionary content, an adult business is not entitled to an unusually speedy judicial decision of the *Freedman* type. Colorado's rules provide for a flexible system of review in which judges can reach a decision promptly in the ordinary case, while using their judicial power to prevent significant harm to First Amendment interests where circumstances require." Justice Breyer left open the possibility of an as applied challenge to address "special problems of undue delay." Justices Stevens and Souter each filed opinions concurring in part and concurring in the judgment. Justice Kennedy joined Justice Souter's opinion. Justice Scalia filed a separate opinion concurring in the judgment.

(3) *Prior Restraints on Displays of Pornography.* In *Times Film Corp. v. Chicago*, 365 U.S. 43 (1961), the Court, by a narrow majority, ruled that the "prior restraint" doctrine did not preclude a city from requiring a distributor of a film to submit the film to a public official for examination prior to exhibition. The Court carefully pointed out that such a requirement was not facially invalid and that the "narrow attack upon the ordinance does not require that any consideration be given to the validity of the standards set out therein. They are not challenged and are not before us."

(4) *Injunctions for Nuisance. Vance v. Universal Amusement Co.*, 445 U.S. 308 (1980), held invalid a Texas statute which authorized actions by public officials to enjoin, as a nuisance, the use of premises which engaged in the commercial distribution of obscene material. Under certain conditions the premises could be closed for one year. In a *per curiam* 5-4 decision, the Court held that the standards of *Freedman v. Maryland* had not been met. Chief Justice Burger, and Justices Powell, White, and Rehnquist dissented.

(5) *Seizure of a Copy.* In *Heller v. New York*, 413 U.S. 483 (1973), the Court held that an adversary hearing is not necessary *prior* to seizing a film for the purpose of preserving it as evidence in a criminal proceeding. The *Heller* Court was careful, however, to distinguish the procedures which New York followed from those held invalid in earlier cases where films and books had been seized to destroy them or to block their distribution.

Chief Justice Burger opined: "But seizing films to destroy them or to block their distribution or exhibition is a very different matter from seizing a single copy of a film for the bona fide purpose of preserving it as evidence in a criminal proceeding, particularly where, as here, there is no showing or pretrial claim that the seizure of the copy prevented continuing exhibition of the film. If such a seizure is pursuant to a warrant, issued after a determination of probable cause by a neutral magistrate, and, following the seizure, a prompt and judicial determination of the obscenity issue in an adversary proceeding is available at the request of any interested party, the seizure is constitutionally permissible. In addition, on a showing to the trial court that other copies of the film are not available to the exhibitor, the court should permit the seized film to be copied so that showing can be continued pending a judicial determination of the obscenity issue in an adversary proceeding. Otherwise, the film must be returned."

Although the judge had actually viewed the film in the *Heller* case before signing the warrant authorizing the seizure, the Court did not indicate that such viewing was a necessary condition for satisfying the "probable cause" requirement.

(6) *Standard to Obtain a Warrant.* In *New York v. P.J. Video, Inc.* 475 U.S. 868 (1986), the Court (6-3) addressed the issue of the proper standard of probable cause for the issuance of a warrant for the seizure of allegedly obscene video-cassettes. "[T]he standard of probable cause in the First Amendment area is no different than in other contexts." That standard, according to Justice Rehnquist's majority opinion, does not require the actual demonstration of criminal activity but only a substantial probability of the criminal activity. The affidavits presented to the judge issuing the warrant consisted primarily of descriptions of scenes that established probable cause that the films depicted specified sexual conduct in a patently offensive manner. The affidavits, however, contained no allegations concerning the predominant appeal of the film taken as a whole, or its overall literary or artistic value. Justice Rehnquist concluded: "Our review of the affidavits convinces us that the issuing justice . . . was given more than enough information to conclude that there was a 'fair probability' that the movies satisfied the first and third elements of the statutory definition, namely that the 'predominant appeal [of the movies] is to the prurient interest in sex,' and that the movies 'lac[k] serious literary, artistic, and scientific value.' "

The affidavits alleged that defendants described the films as "adult cassette movies" in their advertisements. "Each affidavit describes the numerous acts of deviate sexual intercourse and the objectification of women occurring in each film which the majority concede to be offensive. Each film is of relatively short duration. Manifestly, the acts described in each movie consume a substantial time span. Thus, the magistrate may reasonably have concluded that the described, successive acts of deviate sexual intercourse pervaded each film. When the title of each movie is considered together with its plot and setting, its general theme and serious value, if any, may reasonably be discerned."

Justice Marshall, joined by Justices Brennan and Stevens dissented on grounds that the mere listing of selected scenes does not establish probable cause of the statutory violation which must be based on the film as a whole.

(7) *Officer Purchase.* In *Maryland v. Macon,* 472 U.S. 463 (1985), the Court ruled that the purchase of allegedly obscene magazines by undercover police officers did not constitute an unreasonable search and seizure. Justice O'Connor's majority (7-2) opinion concluded that "respondent did not have any reasonable expectation of privacy in areas of the store where the public was invited to enter and to transact business." Respondent also claimed that the warrantless arrest of an attendant of the store required the exclusion of the magazine. Justice O'Connor concluded: "Again, assuming *arguendo,* that the warrantless arrest was an unreasonable seizure in violation of the Fourth Amendment — a question we do not decide — it yielded nothing of evidentiary value that was not already in the lawful possession of the police."

Justice Brennan's dissent joined by Justice Marshall argued that an "official seizure of presumptively protected books, magazines, or films is not 'reasonable' within the meaning of the Fourth Amendment unless a neutral and detached magistrate has issued a warrant particularly describing the things to be seized." The subsequent warrantless arrest was also unconstitutional because of First Amendment considerations.

(8) *Entrapment.* In *Jacobson v. United States,* 503 U.S. 540 (1992) (5-4), the Court reversed the defendant's conviction for violating the Child Protection Act on the

grounds that he was entrapped. After obtaining the defendant's name through a mailing list created before receipt of child pornography materials became illegal, government agents began repeatedly soliciting the defendant to order child pornography materials through the mail. They sent him sexual preference questionnaires, catalogs, correspondence from a government-manufactured "pen pal," and, in particular, pressured him to order these materials "as part of a fight against censorship and the infringement of individual rights." Writing for the majority, Justice White held that the government had gone beyond merely providing an "opportunity," and had failed to establish beyond a reasonable doubt that the defendant was independently predisposed to violate the law. Justice O'Connor, joined by Chief Justice Rehnquist and Justice Kennedy, dissented. Justice Scalia joined in part of Justice O'Connor's dissent.

(9) For diverging views on constitutional protection for erotic materials, see, e.g., ANDREA DWORKIN, PORNOGRAPHY: MEN POSSESSING WOMEN (1981); FREDERICK SHAUER, THE LAW OF OBSCENITY (1976); TAKE BACK THE NIGHT: WOMEN ON PORNOGRAPHY (L. Ledered ed., 1980); LOUIS A. ZURCHER & R. GEORGE KIRPATRICK, CITIZENS FOR DECENCY (1976); *The Convergence of Feminist and Civil Liberties Principles in the Pornography Debate*, in WOMEN AGAINST RACISM (V. Burstyn ed., 1985); Paul Brest & Ann Vandenberg, *Politics, Feminism, and the Constitution: The Anti-Pornography Movement in Minneapolis*, 39 STAN. L. REV. 607 (1987); Louis Henkin, *Morals and the Constitution: The Sin of Obscenity*, 63 COLUM. L. REV. 391 (1963); Eric Hoffman, *Feminism, Pornography, and Law*, 133 U. PA. L. REV. 497 (1985); Harry Kalven, Jr., *The Metaphysics of the Law of Obscenity*, 1960 SUP. CT. REV. 1; Catharine A. McKinnon, *Pornography, Civil Rights, and Speech*, 20 HARV. C.R.-C.L. L. REV. 1 (1985); Cass R. Sunstein, *Pornography and the First Amendment*, 1986 DUKE L.J. 589.

FORT WAYNE BOOKS, INC. v. INDIANA and SAPPENFIELD v. INDIANA,

489 U.S. 46 (1989). These two cases concerned the prosecution of adult bookstores using various aspects of Indiana's Racketeer Influenced and Corrupt Organization Act (RICO). A RICO violation consists of a "pattern of racketeering activity" evidenced by at least two predicate offenses. The types of crimes that constitute predicate offenses are described by the particular RICO statute. A RICO violation is a crime distinct from its predicate offenses, carrying separate civil and criminal sanctions.[62]

In *Sappenfield*, the Court held that the use of obscenity as a predicate offense was not unconstitutionally vague. Moreover, the Court rejected the claim that the "draconian" sanctions imposed by RICO were unconstitutional when applied in the First Amendment area. In *Fort Wayne Books*, however, the Court held unconstitutional a pretrial seizure in a civil RICO action of the contents of three adult bookstores.

In *Sappenfield*, the owner of an adult bookstore was charged with six misdemeanor counts of distributing obscene material. These six misdemeanor counts led to prosecutors filing two additional felony counts of RICO violations. *Sappenfield* challenged as unconstitutionally vague only the two RICO charges.

In *Fort Wayne Books*, the State filed a civil action against owners of three separate adult bookstores. Citing to 39 previous obscenity convictions, the State charged the bookstore owners with violating Indiana's RICO law. Prior to trial on the RICO complaint, the State sought an injunction to prevent the store owners from continuing their alleged racketeering activities for pretrial seizure of material that would be

---

[62] "The Federal RICO statute also permits prosecutions for a pattern of obscenity violations, in a manner quite similar to the Indiana law under review here."

subject to forfeiture under the Civil Remedies for Racketeering Act (CRRA)[63] if the
State prevailed in the civil RICO action. Pretrial seizure of materials subject to CRRA
forfeiture was authorized by Indiana statute "upon a showing of probable cause to
believe that a violation of [the State's RICO law] involving the property in question has
occurred." After an *ex parte* hearing, the court authorized the pretrial seizure. The
three bookstores were immediately padlocked, and several days later, trucks hauled
away all the property inside.

In *Sappenfield*, Justice White wrote for a 5-4 majority. Sappenfield had argued that
the "'inherent vagueness' of the [obscenity] standards established by *Miller v.
California*" precluded the use of obscenity as a predicate act for a RICO violation. As
the Indiana obscenity law closely followed the *Miller* standard, the Court found "no
merit in petitioner's claim that the Indiana RICO law is unconstitutionally vague as
applied to obscenity predicate offenses. Given that the RICO statute totally
encompasses the obscenity law, if the latter is not unconstitutionally vague, the former
cannot be vague either."

Justice White next addressed Sappenfield's argument that the "draconian" sanctions
that RICO imposed created "an improper chilling effect on First Amendment
freedoms." The Court recognized that the sanctions for the RICO violation, which was
a Class C felony, were greater than those for the obscenity charges, which was a Class
A misdemeanor. "Specifically, if petitioner is found guilty of the two RICO counts
against him, he faces a maximum sentence of 10 years in prison and a $20,000 fine; if
petitioner were convicted instead of only the six predicate obscenity offenses charged in
the indictments, the maximum punishment he could face would be six years in jail and
$30,000 in fines."

For Justice White the difference in penalties did not have significance. "The mere
assertion of some possible self-censorship resulting from a statute is not enough to
render an anti-obscenity law unconstitutional under our precedents."

Justice White also rejected Sappenfield's arguments that the predicate acts for
RICO violations relating to obscenity must be from the same jurisdiction, even though
the predicate acts could be based on different community standards under the *Miller*
test.

In *Fort Wayne Books*, Justice White, writing for a unanimous Court, held
unconstitutional the pretrial seizure of expressive materials protected by the First
Amendment based only on a showing of probable cause that a RICO violation had
occurred. "[W]hile the general rule under the Fourth Amendment is that any and all
contraband, instrumentalities, and evidence of crimes may be seized on probable cause,
(and even without a warrant in various cases), it is otherwise when materials
presumptively protected by the First Amendment are involved." The government
claimed that their purpose was not to focus on expressive materials but to seize all
"assets used and acquired in the course of racketeering activity" to facilitate eventual
disgorgement under the CRRA. Even assuming without deciding that these expressive
materials would eventually be subject to forfeiture, the Court objected to the prior
restraint on expressive material. "While a single copy of a book or film may be seized
and retained for evidentiary purposes based on a finding of probable cause, the
publication may not be taken out of circulation completely until there has been a
determination of obscenity after an adversary hearing."

Writing now for a majority of six, Justice White did not decide whether, after a
successful RICO prosecution, "bookstores and their contents are forfeitable (like other

[63] The Civil Remedies for Racketeering Activity (CRRA) statute allowed for post-trial forfeiture of
property used, derived from, or realized through racketeering activity.

property such as a bank account or a yacht) when it is proved that these items are property actually used in, or derived from, a pattern of violations of the State's obscenity laws." The cases before the Court did not present this question.

Justice O'Connor wrote an opinion concurring in *Fort Wayne Books*, but dissenting in *Sappenfield* on jurisdictional grounds. Justice Blackmun wrote an opinion agreeing with Justice O'Connor's jurisdictional objections in *Sappenfield*, but nevertheless concurring in all other aspects of Justice White's opinion.

Justice Stevens, joined by Justices Brennan and Marshall, wrote an opinion dissenting in *Sappenfield*, and concurring in part and dissenting in part in *Fort Wayne Books*. Justice Stevens agreed with the Court that the pretrial seizures in *Fort Wayne Books* could not stand. He disagreed with the Court in two critical respects. First, Justice Stevens would have upheld the vagueness challenge.

Second, the Court should have considered the RICO and CRRA statutes together. He expressed his misgivings that "even if only a small fraction of the activities of the enterprise is unlawful, the State may close the entire business, seize its inventory, and bar its owner from engaging in his or her chosen line of work." Even though the majority did not reach this question, the "RICO/CRRA scheme," and its broad forfeiture provisions should not be extended to a business like a bookstore.

ALEXANDER v. UNITED STATES, 509 U.S. 544 (1993). In *Alexander*, the Court held that requiring the convicted seller of obscene materials to forfeit his entire wholesale and retail businesses under the Racketeer Influenced and Corrupt Organizations Act (RICO) does not constitute a prior restraint. The case was remanded to determine whether the forfeiture, considered in addition to the owner's prison term and fine, constituted an excessive fine under the Eighth Amendment.

Defendant owned over one dozen retail stores which sold pornographic magazines and movies, as well as sexual paraphernalia. In 1989, Defendant was charged with selling obscene materials and violating RICO. Defendant was convicted on seventeen counts of obscenity and three counts of violating RICO.

The RICO counts were predicated on the obscenity counts. The conviction was based on the jury's determination that defendant had distributed throughout his "adult entertainment empire" multiple copies of three obscene video tapes and four obscene magazines. Defendant was sentenced to six years in prison and fined $100,000. At a subsequent forfeiture proceeding, the same jury found that defendant had used ten tracts of real estate and thirty-one businesses to further his racketeering activities. The District Court ordered defendant to forfeit his entire retail and wholesale businesses, their assets, and almost $9 million in cash under RICO forfeiture provisions. The Court of Appeals affirmed.

Alexander argued that the effect of the RICO forfeiture was indistinguishable from the permanent injunction prohibiting publication of expressive materials found to be a prior restraint in *Near v. Minnesota ex rel. Olson*, 283 U.S. 697 (1931). Writing for the majority, Chief Justice Rehnquist said that *Near* involved an injunction that permanently restrained future speech. The RICO forfeiture, however, merely deprived Alexander "of specific assets that were found to be related to his previous racketeering violations." Under the forfeiture order, Alexander would still be "perfectly free to open an adult bookstore or otherwise engage in the production and distribution of erotic materials; he just cannot finance these enterprises with assets derived from his prior racketeering offenses." Moreover, in contrast to prior restraint precedents involving obscenity, the assets in this case were not "forfeited because they were believed to be obscene, but because they were directly related to petitioner's past racketeering violations." The RICO forfeiture provisions are "oblivious to the expressive or nonexpressive nature of the assets forfeited." Also unlike previous cases, defendant was afforded the procedural safeguard of a full criminal trial which connected the forfeited assets to racketeering offenses. Finding prior restraint in the case at bar would "blur the line separating prior restraints from subsequent punishments to such a degree that it would be impossible to determine with any certainty whether a particular measure is a prior restraint or not."

Chief Justice Rehnquist also rejected defendant's overbreadth argument, noting that RICO "does not criminalize constitutionally protected speech." Defendant's "real complaint" was not overbreadth, but that the statute may serve to chill and deter future protected expression. Relying on *Fort Wayne Books, Inc. v. Indiana, supra,* the Court said that "the threat of forfeiture has no more of a chilling effect on free expression than the threat of a prison term or a large fine." As the First Amendment permits both "stiff criminal penalties for obscenity offenses" and "forfeiture of expressive materials for criminal conduct," it would be "counter-intuitive" to hold impermissible the combination of the two.

Finally, the Court remanded the case to consider whether the forfeiture, combined with defendant's six-year prison term and $100,000 fine, was an excessive fine under the Eighth Amendment. The forfeiture was "clearly a form of monetary punishment no different, for Eighth Amendment purposes, from a traditional 'fine.'" Whether the forfeiture is "excessive" must be evaluated "in light of the extensive criminal activities which petitioner apparently conducted though his racketeering enterprise over a substantial period of time."

Justice Souter, concurring in the judgment in part and dissenting in part, agreed that the case did not involve a prior restraint and that it should be remanded on the Eighth Amendment issue. However, he agreed with the dissent that the First Amendment forbids the forfeiture of those materials that were not first judged obscene.

Justice Kennedy dissented, joined by Justices Blackmun and Stevens. He criticized the majority for finding "no affront to the First Amendment in the Government's destruction of a book and film business and its entire inventory of legitimate expression as punishment for a single past speech offense." While the Court has "upheld stringent fines and jail terms" as permissible sanctions for obscenity violations, these have "little to do with the destruction of protected titles and the facilities for their distribution or publication." The majority's distinction between prior restraints and subsequent punishments was inadequate to justify "the destruction of a speech business as a punishment for past expression." While the forfeiture lacked "the form of a traditional prior restraint," it raised the same policy concerns of state censorship and chilling protected speech. In *Near*, for example, the nuisance statute struck down by the Court was aimed at suppressing the offending publication. Similarly, the purpose of RICO is "to destroy or incapacitate the offending enterprise." In this case, books and films are destroyed under RICO "not for their own content, but for the content of their owner's prior speech." Apart from the forfeiture's incongruence with the Court's prior restraint cases, the destruction of books not adjudicated obscene is without precedent. This remedy constitutes a "stark new threat to all speech enterprises."

Chapter XVI
RELIGIOUS FREEDOM

Introductory Note. That the religion clauses mark the beginning of the Bill of Rights may emphasize both the central role of freedom of religion in our society and the aspirations of our citizens, many of whom came here to escape religious persecution. The clauses endeavor to safeguard the sanctity of a human being's most cherished principles, the right to believe or not to believe as one's conscience dictates. *Cf.* Robert M. Cover, *Foreword: Nomos and Narrative*, 97 HARV. L. REV. 4 (1983) (we all inhabit a nomos or normative universe in which law occupies but a small part). The religion clauses serve as a bulwark against governmental efforts to coerce individuals' consciences. At some level, the clauses articulate a noble aspiration that human beings should be free to choose their beliefs without interference from government.

The lofty principles are stated in the First Amendment's succinct imperative: "Congress shall make no law respecting an establishment of religion or prohibiting the free exercise thereof." Unfortunately, this ideal of noninterference has proven complex to achieve. Some think that these clauses are mutually sustaining; others emphasize that they stand in tension with each other. That these competing views exist is not hard to understand. After all, one might argue that the most effective way to safeguard freedom of conscience is to guard against state involvement in the affairs of religion. On the other hand, a welfare state that is involved in so many aspects of people's lives might effectively suppress religion by stringently excluding it from all areas of governmental activity.

This Chapter explores the complex and often confusing jurisprudence that has emerged from the Court's interpretation of the Establishment and Free Exercise Clauses. Section 16.01 focuses on the competing approaches or strategies that have developed for protecting freedom of religion, i.e., accommodation and wall of separation. Section 16.02 focuses on Establishment Clause cases involving aid to religious institutions. Most of the decisions concern aid to religious schools. Section 16.03 treats another major area of establishment jurisprudence, government involvement in practices relating to religion. Many of the cases focus on prayer in the public schools. Section 16.04 considers the establishment concerns raised by religious groups becoming involved in governmental decision-making processes. Finally, Section 16.05 focuses on cases involving governmental infringement on the free exercise of religion.

Dividing the Chapter along these lines engages the Court's approach to these cases, which often emphasizes one clause or the other. Nevertheless, the division is somewhat artificial, as even the Court discusses both clauses in many cases in which it may stress one or the other. To mitigate this difficulty, Section 16.01 highlights two cases that reveal some of the Court's thinking about how these two clauses interrelate.

There has been much writing on the religion clauses. For some notable contributions, see STEPHEN L. CARTER, THE CULTURE OF DISBELIEF (1993); JESSE H. CHOPER, PRINCIPLES FOR JUICIAL ITERPRETATION OF THE RELIGION CLAUSES (1995); PHILIP V. KURLAND, RELIGION AND LAW (1962); LEONARD W. LEVY, THE ESTABLISHMENT CLAUSE (1986); JOHN T. NOONAN, THE BELIEVER AND THE POWERS THAT ARE (1987); LEO PFEFFER, RELIGION, STATE, AND THE BURGER COURT (1984); LEO PFEFFER, CHURCH, STATE, AND FREEDOM (2d. ed. 1967); Mary Ann Glendon & Raul F. Yanes, *Structural Free Exercise*, 90 MICH. L. REV. 477 (1991); Kent Greenawalt, *Symposium, The Religion Clauses*, 72 CAL. L. REV. 753 (1984); Norman Redlich, *Separation of Church: The Burger Court's Tortuous Journey*, 60 NOTRE DAME L. REV. 1094 (1985); Michael E. Smith, *The Special Place of Religion in the Constitution*, 1983 SUP. CT. REV. 83. For an interesting contextualization of the cases, see Douglas Laycock, *Continuity and Change in the Threat to Religious Liberty: The*

Reformation Era and the Late Twentieth Century, 80 MINN. L. REV. 1047, 1097 (1996) ("Government burdens on religious exercise arise as incidents of secular regulation or from eligibility requirements of benefit programs, and rarely from one religion trying to suppress another. Illustrative issues include whether the State must pay unemployment compensation to a conscientious objector who quit his job in a defense plant, whether historical landmark laws can control the architecture of churches, or whether Catholic teaching hospitals must perform and teach the techniques of abortion. Establishment Clause controversies arise from private religious exercise in public places, or from religious participation in the distribution of government social services, and only occasionally from direct government attempts to support religion."). For a critique of the Court's jurisprudence, see George W. Dent, Jr., *Secularism and the Supreme Court*, 1 BYU L. REV. 1, 73 (1999) ("For two centuries religion was widely disparaged by Western intellectuals. In the 1960s disdain for religion triumphed in the Supreme Court, which proceeded to transmogrify the religion clauses of the First Amendment. Because of changes in the main Western religions and problems with secularist theories, intellectual respect for religion has revived. The Supreme Court's secularist majority has passed on, but its ghost still haunts; the Court has not yet fashioned a new, coherent treatment of religion but has careened through inconsistent decisions and incoherent opinions."). For a comparative perspective on some of these issues, see Symposium, *Law & Religion*, 35 AM. J. COMP. L. 1 (1987).

§ 16.01 COMPETING APPROACHES: WALL OF SEPARATION VERSUS ACCOMMODATION

Section Note. This first section of the Chapter focuses on the Establishment Clause, which the Court itself has stressed in its religion jurisprudence. The cases in the first section consider not only the Establishment Clause, but also its interaction with the Free Exercise Clause. Specifically, the Section considers two general themes that emerged early in the Court's interpretation of the religion clauses. These are the wall of separation metaphor adopted and developed by Justice Black in *Everson v. Board of Education*, and the accommodationist stance articulated in *Zorach v. Clauson*. These competing paradigms have dominated the Court's thinking about the religion clauses.

[*Everson* specifically concerns aid to parochial education and might also be considered at the beginning of subsection two of this Chapter.]

EVERSON v. BOARD OF EDUCATION
330 U.S. 1, 67 S. Ct. 504, 91 L. Ed. 711 (1947)

JUSTICE BLACK delivered the opinion of the Court.

A New Jersey statute authorizes its local school districts to make rules and contracts for the transportation of children to and from schools. The appellee, a township board of education, acting pursuant to this statute, authorized reimbursement to parents of money expended by them for the bus transportation of their children on regular buses operated by the public transportation system. Part of this money was for the payment of transportation of some children in the community to Catholic parochial schools. . . .

A large proportion of the early settlers of this country came here from Europe to escape the bondage of laws which compelled them to support and attend government favored churches. The centuries immediately before and contemporaneous with the colonization of America had been filled with turmoil, civil strife, and persecutions, generated in large part by established sects determined to maintain their absolute political and religious supremacy. With the power of government supporting them, at various times and places, Catholics had persecuted Protestants, Protestants had persecuted Catholics, Protestant sects had persecuted other Protestant sects, Catholics of one shade of belief had persecuted Catholics of another shade of belief, and all of these had from time to time persecuted Jews. In efforts to force loyalty to whatever religious group happened to be on top and in league with the government of a particular time and place, men and women had been fined, cast in jail, cruelly tortured, and killed. Among the offenses for which these punishments had been inflicted were such things as speaking disrespectfully of the views of ministers of government-established churches, non-attendance at those churches, expressions of non-belief in their doctrines, and failure to pay taxes and tithes to support them.

These practices of the old world were transplanted to and began to thrive in the soil of the new America. The very charters granted by the English crown to the individuals and companies designated to make the laws which would control the destinies of the colonials authorized these individuals and companies to erect religious establishments which all, whether believers or nonbelievers, would be required to support and attend. An exercise of this authority was accompanied by a repetition of many of the old-world practices and persecutions. Catholics found themselves hounded and proscribed because of their faith; Quakers who followed their conscience were sent to jail; Baptists were peculiarly obnoxious to certain dominant Protestant sects; men and women of varied faiths who happened to be in a minority in a particular locality were persecuted because they steadfastly persisted in worshiping God only as their own conscience dictated. And all of these dissenters were compelled to pay tithes and taxes to support government-sponsored churches whose ministers preached inflammatory sermons designed to strengthen and consolidate the established faith by generating a burning hatred against dissenters. . . .

The movement toward this end reached its dramatic climax in Virginia in 1785-86 when the Virginia legislative body was about to renew Virginia's tax levy for the support of the established church. Thomas Jefferson and James Madison led the fight against the tax. Madison wrote his great Memorial and Remonstrance against the law. In it, he eloquently argued that a true religion did not need the support of law; that no person, either believer or non-believer, should be taxed to support a religious institution of any kind; that the best interest of a society required that the minds of men always be wholly free; and that cruel persecutions were the inevitable result of government-established religions. Madison's Remonstrance received strong support throughout Virginia, and . . . the proposed tax measure . . . not only died in committee, but the Assembly enacted the famous "Virginia Bill for Religious Liberty" originally written by Thomas Jefferson. The preamble to that Bill stated among other things that

> Almighty God hath created the mind free; that all attempts to influence it by temporal punishments or burthens, or by civil incapacitations tend only to beget the habits of hypocrisy and meanness, and are a departure from the plan of the Holy author of our religion, who being Lord both of body and mind, yet chose not to propagate it by coercions on either . . . that to compel a man to furnish contributions of money for the propagation of opinions which he disbelieves, is sinful and tyrannical; that even the forcing him to support this or that teacher of his own religious persuasion, is depriving him of the comfortable liberty of giving his contributions to the particular pastor, whose morals he would make his pattern. . . .

And the statute itself enacted

> That no man shall be compelled to frequent or support any religious worship, place, or ministry whatsoever, nor shall be enforced, restrained, molested, or burthened in his body or goods, nor shall otherwise suffer on account of his religious opinions or belief. . . .

This Court has previously recognized that the provisions of the First Amendment, in the drafting and adoption of which Madison and Jefferson played such leading roles, had the same objective and were intended to provide the same protection against governmental intrusions on religious liberty as the Virginia statute. . . . *Reynolds v. United States*, 98 U.S. [145,] 164 [(1878)]. . . .

The "establishment of religion" clause of the First Amendment means at least this: Neither a state nor the Federal Government can set up a church. Neither can pass laws which aid one religion and all religions, or prefer one religion over another. Neither can force nor influence a person to go to or to remain away from church against his will or force him to profess a belief or disbelief in any religion. No person can be punished for entertaining or professing religious beliefs or disbeliefs, for church attendance or non-attendance. No tax in any amount, large or small, can be levied to support any religious activities or institutions, whatever they may be called, or whatever form they may adopt to teach or practice religion. Neither a state nor the Federal Government can, openly or secretly, participate in the affairs of any religious organization or groups and vice versa. In the words of Jefferson, the clause against establishment of religion by law was intended to erect "a wall of separation between Church and State." *Reynolds v. United States*, 98 U.S. at 164.

. . . New Jersey cannot consistently with the "establishment of religion" clause of the First Amendment contribute tax-raised funds to the support of an institution which teaches the tenets and faith of any church. On the other hand, other language of the amendment commands that New Jersey cannot hamper its citizens in the free exercise of their own religion. Consequently, it cannot exclude individual Catholics, Lutherans, Muhammadans, Baptists, Jews, Methodists, Non-believers, Presbyterians, or the members of any other faith *because of their faith, or lack of it*, from receiving the benefits of public welfare legislation. While we do not mean to intimate that a state could not provide transportation only to children attending public schools, we must be careful, in protecting the citizens of New Jersey against state-established churches, to be sure that we do not inadvertently prohibit New Jersey from extending its general state law benefits to all its citizens without regard to their religious belief. . . .

Measured by these standards, we cannot say that the First Amendment prohibits New Jersey from spending tax-raised funds to pay the bus fares of parochial school pupils as a part of a general program under which it pays the fares of pupils attending public and other schools. It is undoubtedly true that children are helped to get to church schools. There is even a possibility that some of the children might not be sent to the church schools if the parents were compelled to pay their children going to and from church pockets when transportation to a public school would have been paid for by the State. The same possibility exists where the state requires a local transit company to provide reduced fares to school children including those attending parochial schools, or where a municipally owned transportation system undertakes to carry all school children free of charge. Moreover, state-paid policemen, detailed to protect children going to and from church schools from the very real hazards of traffic, would serve much the same purpose and accomplish much the same result as state provisions intended to guarantee free transportation of a kind which the state deems to be best for the school children's welfare. And parents might refuse to risk their children to the serious danger of traffic accidents going to and from parochial schools, the approaches to which were not protected by policemen. Similarly, parents might be reluctant to permit their children to attend schools which the state had cut off from such general government services as ordinary police and fire protection, connections for sewage disposal, public highways and sidewalks. Of course, cutting off church schools from these services, so separate and so indisputably marked off from the religious function, would make it far more difficult for the schools to operate. But such is obviously not the purpose of the

First Amendment. That Amendment requires the state to be a neutral in its relations with groups of religious believers and non-believers; it does not require the state to be their adversary. State power is no more to be used so as to handicap religions than it is to favor them.

This Court has said that parents may, in the discharge of their duty under state compulsory education laws, send their children to a religious rather than a public school if the school meets the secular educational requirements which the state has power to impose. *See Pierce v. Society of Sisters*, 268 U.S. 510 (1925). It appears that these parochial schools meet New Jersey's requirements. The State contributes no money to the schools. It does not support them. Its legislation, as applied, does no more than provide a general program to help parents get their children, safely and expeditiously to and from accredited schools.

The First Amendment has erected a wall between church and state. That wall must be kept high and impregnable. We could not approve the slightest breach. New Jersey has not breached it here.

JUSTICE JACKSON, dissenting.

. . . [T]he undertones of the opinion, advocating complete and uncompromising separation of Church from State, seem utterly discordant with its conclusion yielding support to their commingling in educational matters. . . .

It is no exaggeration to say that the whole historic conflict in temporal policy between the Catholic Church and non-Catholics comes to a focus in their respective school policies. The Roman Catholic Church, counseled by experience in many ages and many lands and with all sorts and conditions of men, takes what, from the viewpoint of its own progress and the success of its mission, is a wise estimate of the importance of education to religion. It does not leave the individual to pick up religion by chance. It relies on early and indelible indoctrination in the faith and order of the Church by the word and example of persons consecrated to the task.

Our public school, if not a product of Protestantism, at least is more consistent with it than with the Catholic culture and scheme of values. It is a relatively recent development dating from about 1840. It is organized on the premises that secular education can be isolated from all religious teaching so that the school can inculcate all needed temporal knowledge and also maintain a strict and lofty neutrality as to religion. . . .

I should be surprised if any Catholic would deny that the parochial school is a vital, if not the most vital, part of the Roman Catholic Church. If put to the choice, that venerable institution, I should expect, would forego its whole service for mature persons before it would give up education of the young, and it would be a wise choice. . . .

. . . If these principles seem harsh in prohibiting aid to Catholic education, it must not be forgotten that it is the same Constitution that alone assures Catholics the right to maintain these schools at all when predominant local sentiment would forbid them. [*See*] *Pierce v. Society of Sisters*, 268 U.S. 510 (1925). Nor should I think that those who have done so well without this aid would want to see this separation between Church and State broken down. If the state may aid these religious schools, it may therefore regulate them. . . .

JUSTICE FRANKFURTER joins in this opinion.

JUSTICE RUTLEDGE, with whom JUSTICE FRANKFURTER, JUSTICE JACKSON and JUSTICE BURTON agree, dissenting. . . .

I

Not simply an established church, but any law respecting an establishment of religion is forbidden. . . .

The Amendment's purpose was not to strike merely at the official establishment of a single sect, creed or religion, outlawing only a formal relation such as had prevailed in England and some of the colonies. . . . It was to create a complete and permanent separation of the spheres of religious activity and civil authority by comprehensively forbidding every form of public aid or support for religion. . . .

. . . [D]aily religious education commingled with secular is "religion" within the guaranty's comprehensive scope. So are religious training and teaching in whatever form. . . .

II

No provision of the Constitution is more closely tied to or given content by its generating history than the religious clause of the First Amendment. . . .

For Madison, as also for Jefferson, religious freedom was the crux of the struggle for freedom in general. . . .

The climax came in the legislative struggle of 1784-1785 over the Assessment Bill. This was nothing more nor less than a taxing measure for the support of religion, designed to revive the payment of tithes suspended since 1777. . . .

[Madison's Memorial and] Remonstrance, stirring up a storm of popular protest, killed the Assessment Bill. . . . With this, the way was cleared at last for enactment of Jefferson's Bill for Establishing Religious Freedom. . . .

. . . Within a little more than three years from his legislative victory at home he had proposed and secured the submission and ratification of the First Amendment as the first article of our Bill of Rights.

All the great instruments of the Virginia struggle for religious liberty thus became warp and woof of our constitutional tradition, not simply by the course of history, but by the common unifying force of Madison's life, thought and sponsorship. . . .

As the Remonstrance discloses throughout, Madison opposed every form and degree of official relation between religion and civil authority. For him religion was a wholly private matter beyond the scope of civil power either to restrain or to support. . . .

In no phrase was he more unrelentingly absolute than in opposing state support or aid by taxation. . . .

III

. . . New Jersey's action . . . exactly fits the type of exaction and the kind of evil at which Madison and Jefferson struck. . . . It is precisely because the instruction is religious and relates to a particular faith, whether one or another, that parents send their children to religious schools under the *Pierce* doctrine. And the very purpose of the state's contribution is to defray the cost of conveying the pupil to the place where he will receive not simply secular, but also and primarily religious, teaching and guidance. . . .

V

No one conscious of religious values can be unsympathetic toward the burden which our constitutional separation puts on parents who desire religious instruction mixed with secular for their children. They pay taxes for others' children's education, at the same time the added cost of instruction for their own. Nor can one happily see benefits denied to children which others receive, because in conscience they or their parents for them desire a different kind of training others do not demand.

. . . No more unjust or discriminatory in fact is it to deny attendants at religious schools the cost of their transportation than it is to deny them tuitions, sustenance for their teachers, or any other educational expense which others receive at public cost. . . .

Of course discrimination in the legal sense does not exist. The child attending the religious school has the same right as any other to attend the public school. But he forgoes exercising it because the same guaranty which assures this freedom forbids the public school or any agency of the state to give or aid him in securing the religious instruction he seeks. . . .

The problem then cannot be cast in terms of legal discrimination or its absence. This would be true, even though the state in giving aid should treat all religious instruction alike. . . . For then the adherent of one creed still would pay for the support of another, the childless taxpayer with others more fortunate. . . .

Two great drives are constantly in motion to abridge, in the name of education, the complete division of religion and civil authority which our forefathers made. One is to introduce religious education and observances into the public schools. The other, to obtain public funds for the aid and support of various private religious schools. . . . In my opinion both avenues were closed by the Constitution. . . .

NOTE

For further discussion of *Everson*, see Mary Ann Glendon & Raul Yanes, *Structural Free Exercise*, 90 MICH. L. REV. 477, 485–86 (1991) ("In sum, *Everson* committed the Court to a cluster of problematic positions. The only disagreement was on how vigorously the Court should pursue the separationist program. With little or no support from text, history, or tradition, the members of the *Everson* Court braided into the Religion Clause the notions that the establishment provision was meant to create a 'wall of separation' between religion and the government, that it was to be broadly construed to prohibit all government aid to religion, and that government was required to be strictly neutral as between religion and nonreligion. The Court thus lent its prestige and sponsorship to a controversial secularizing program without even acknowledging what in hindsight seem like obvious and serious interpretive problems: What is a religion? What does it mean to 'prohibit' religious exercise? Is there one Religion Clause or two? Does the establishment language embody a value in tension with that of free exercise, or is the ban on establishment of religion to be interpreted so as to promote free exercise? Is language that was intended to protect state arrangements regarding religion from federal intervention a proper subject for 'incorporation' at all?"); Ira C. Lupu, *Reconstructing the Establishment Clause: The Case Against Discretionary Accommodation of Religion*, 140 U. PA. L. REV. 555, 556 (1991) ("The idea of separation of church and state thus presents an image untrue to both life and law. In this respect, it may be headed for a fate similar to that which befell its cousin from the field of race law — the doctrine of separate but equal.").

One commentator has suggested drawing "on the Court's existing Establishment Clause jurisprudence to require that every government action . . . have a primarily amoral purpose and effect." *See* Steven G. Gey, *Is Moral Relativism a Constitutional Command?*, 70 IND. L.J. 331, 404 (1995) ("Under this proposal, the government would be allowed to regulate morality only to the extent necessary to protect the moral freedom of other individuals in society. Moral motivations would not be entirely excised from the law, but political control of purportedly immoral beliefs, expression, and behavior would be permitted only if the immorality threatens some direct and particularized harm to others. Despite the superficially nihilistic overtones of this proposal, it may actually produce a more moral society than that which currently exists. A constitutional command of moral relativism would produce a structure of values that is protected from the distortions imposed by the heavy hand of government coercion and punishment. Paradoxically, collective moral relativism is the only way to ensure that a system of individual morality lives up to its claims.").

McCollum and *Zorach* both involve constitutional restrictions on government activities that aid religious practices, specifically the use of public school facilities for religious training. Both also might usefully be considered at the beginning of § 16.03.

ILLINOIS EX REL. MCCOLLUM v. BOARD OF EDUCATION, 333 U.S. 203 (1948). In *McCollum*, the Court invalidated an Illinois program that allowed Catholic priests, Protestant teachers, and a Jewish rabbi to give religious lessons in school buildings during regular school hours. "Students who did not choose to take religious instruction were not released from public school duties; they were required to leave their classrooms and go to some other place in the school building for the pursuit of the secular studies. On the other hand, students who were released from the secular study for the religious instructions were required to be at the religious classes. Reports of their presence or absence were to be made to the secular teachers."

Invoking once again the "wall of separation" metaphor, Justice Black found that the scheme violated the Establishment Clause: "Pupils compelled by law to go to school for secular education are released in part from their legal duty upon the condition that they attend the religious classes. This is beyond all question a utilization of the tax-established and tax-supported public school system to aid religious groups to spread their faith. And it falls squarely under the ban of the First Amendment . . . as we interpreted it in *Everson v. Board of Education*, 330 U.S. 1 [(1947)]. . . . Here not only are the State's tax-supported public school buildings used for the dissemination of religious doctrines. The State also affords sectarian groups an invaluable aid in that it helps to provide pupils for their religious classes through the use of the State's compulsory public school machinery."

Justice Black did not think that prohibiting the use of the public school system by religious sects would amount to governmental hostility to religion, which would have been incompatible with the First Amendment's guarantee of the free exercise of religion.

In a concurring opinion joined by three other Justices, Justice Frankfurter traced in some detail the development of public education in the United States removed from sectarian influences.

He referred approvingly to a program in operation in Gary, Indiana. Under that scheme, children left their schools and moved to church premises for religious instruction during a time in which they would otherwise have had a play-period in their school. In contrast, religious education conducted during school time and on school property was "patently woven into the working scheme of the school."

Justice Reed dissented. He first discussed the Founders' position on the Establishment Clause. Thomas Jefferson — who had coined the "wall of separation" metaphor — had, as one of the founders of the University of Virginia, required students to worship at the churches of their faith situated on or near the grounds of the

University. Madison, a Visitor of the University, had approved Jefferson's view.

Everson had established that the government could not "aid" any or all religions: "But 'aid' must be understood as a purposeful assistance directly to the church itself or to some religious work of such a character that it may fairly be said to be performing ecclesiastical functions. . . . It seems clear that the 'aid' referred to by the court in the Everson case could not have been those incidental advantages that religious bodies, with other groups similarly situated, obtain as a by-product of organized society. This explains the well-known fact that all churches receive 'aid' from government in the form of freedom from taxation." For Justice Reed, federal practice offered numerous examples of this kind of "aid" given by the state to religion. The Congress had a chaplain for each House, classes in District of Columbia schools opened daily with the Lord's prayer, and Sunday attendance at church services was compulsory at both the United States Military Academy and the United States Naval Academy. "Devotion to the great principle of religious liberty should not lead us into a rigid interpretation of the constitutional guarantee that conflicts with accepted habits of our people."

ZORACH v. CLAUSON
343 U.S. 306, 72 S. Ct. 679, 96 L. Ed. 954 (1952)

JUSTICE DOUGLAS delivered the opinion of the Court.

New York City has a program which permits its public schools to release students during the school day so that they may leave the school buildings and school grounds and go to religious centers for religious instruction or devotional exercises. A student is released on written request of his parents. Those not released stay in the classrooms. The churches make weekly reports to the schools, sending a list of children who have been released from public school but who have not reported for religious instruction. . . .

Appellants, who are taxpayers and residents of New York City and whose children attend its public schools, challenge the present law, contending it is in essence not different from the one involved in the *McCollum* case. Their argument . . . reduces itself to this: the weight and influence of the school is put behind a program for religious instruction; public school teachers police it, keeping tab on students who are released; the classroom activities come to a halt while the students who are released for religious instruction are on leave; the school is a crutch on which the churches are leaning for support in their religious training; without the cooperation of the schools this "released time" program, like the one in the *McCollum* case, would be futile and ineffective. . . .

It takes obtuse reasoning to inject any issue of the "free exercise" of religion into the present case. No one is forced to go to the religious classroom and no religious exercise or instruction is brought to the classrooms of the public schools. A student need not take religious instruction. He is left to his own desires as to the manner or time of his religious devotions, if any.

There is a suggestion that the system involves the use of coercion to get public school students into religious classrooms. There is no evidence in the record before us that supports that conclusion. . . . If in fact coercion were used, if it were established that any one or more teachers were using their office to persuade or force students to take the religious instruction, a wholly different case would be presented. Hence we put aside that claim of coercion both as respects the "free exercise" of religion and "an establishment of religion" within the meaning of the First Amendment.

. . . [T]he First Amendment reflects the philosophy that Church and State should be separated. And so far as interference with the "free exercise" of religion and an "establishment" of religion is concerned, the separation must be complete and unequivocal. The First Amendment within the scope of its coverage permits no exception; the prohibition is absolute. The First Amendment, however, does not say that in every and all respects there shall be a separation of Church and State. Rather, it studiously defines the manner, the specific ways, in which there shall be no concert or union or dependency one on the other. That is the common sense of the matter. Otherwise the state and religion would be aliens to each other — hostile, suspicious, and even unfriendly. Churches could not be required to pay even property taxes. Municipalities would not be permitted to render police or fire protection to religious groups. Policemen who helped parishioners into their places of worship would violate the Constitution. Prayers in our legislative halls; the appeals to the Almighty in the messages of the Chief Executive; the proclamations making Thanksgiving Day a holiday; "so help me God" in our courtroom oaths — these and all other references to the Almighty that run through our laws, our public rituals, our ceremonies would be flouting the First Amendment. A fastidious atheist or agnostic could even object to the supplication with which the Court opens each session: "God save the United States and this Honorable Court."

We would have to press the concept of separation of Church and State to these extremes to condemn the present law on constitutional grounds. The nullification of this law would have wide and profound effects. A Catholic student applies to his teacher for permission to leave the school during hours on a Holy Day of Obligation to attend a mass. A Jewish student asks his teacher for permission to be excused for Yom Kippur. A Protestant wants the afternoon off for a family baptismal ceremony. In each case the teacher requires parental consent in writing. In each case the teacher, in order to make sure the student is not a truant, goes further and requires a report from the priest, rabbi, or the minister. The teacher in other words cooperates in a religious program to the extent of making it possible for her students to participate in it. . . .

We are a religious people whose institutions presuppose a Supreme Being. We guarantee the freedom to worship as one chooses. . . . When the state encourages religious instruction or cooperates with religious authorities by adjusting the schedule of public events to sectarian needs, it follows the best of our traditions. For it then respects the religious nature of our people and accommodates the public service to their spiritual needs. To hold that it may not would be to find in the Constitution a requirement that the government show a callous indifference to religious groups. That would be preferring those who believe in no religion over those who do believe. . . . The government must be neutral when it comes to competition between sects. It may not thrust any sect on any person. It may not make a religious observance compulsory. It may not coerce anyone to attend church, to observe a religious holiday, or to take religious instruction. But it can close its doors or suspend its operation as to those who want to repair to their religious sanctuary for worship or instruction. No more than that is undertaken here. . . .

In the *McCollum* case the classrooms were used for religious instruction and the force of the public school was used to promote that instruction. Here, as we have said, the public schools do no more than accommodate their schedules to a program of outside religious instruction. We follow the *McCollum* case. But we cannot expand it to cover the present released time program unless separation of Church and State means that public institutions can make no adjustments of their schedules to accommodate the religious needs of the people. We cannot read into the Bill of Rights such a philosophy of hostility to religion.

JUSTICE BLACK, dissenting. . . .

I see no significant difference between the invalid Illinois system [in *McCollum*] and that of New York here sustained. Except for the use of the school buildings in Illinois, there is no difference between the systems which I consider even worthy of mention. In the New York program, as in that of Illinois, the school authorities release some of the children on the condition that they attend the religious classes, get reports on whether they attend, and hold the other children in the school building until the religious hour is over. . . .

. . . Here the sole question is whether New York can use its compulsory education laws to help religious sects get attendants presumably too unenthusiastic to go unless moved to do so by the pressure of this state machinery. . . . Any use of such coercive power by the state to help or hinder some religious sects or to prefer all religious sects over nonbelievers or vice versa is just what I think the First Amendment forbids. In considering whether a state has entered this forbidden field the question is not whether it has entered too far but whether it has entered at all. . . .

Under our system of religious freedom, people have gone to their religious sanctuaries not because they feared the law but because they loved their God. . . . The spiritual mind of man has thus been free to believe, disbelieve, or doubt, without repression, great or small, by the heavy hand of government. . . . Before today, our judicial opinions have refrained from drawing invidious distinctions between those who believe in no religion and those who believe. . . .

State help to religion injects political and party prejudices into a holy field. . . .

[JUSTICE FRANKFURTER's dissenting opinion is omitted.]

JUSTICE JACKSON, dissenting. . . .

If public education were taking so much of the pupils' time as to injure the public or the students' welfare by encroaching upon their religious opportunity, simply shortening everyone's school day would facilitate voluntary and optional attendance at Church classes. But that suggestion is rejected upon the ground that if they are made free many students will not go to the Church. . . .

The greater effectiveness of this system over voluntary attendance after school hours is due to the truant officer who, if the youngster fails to go to the Church school, dogs him back to the public schoolroom. Here schooling is more or less suspended during the "released time" so the nonreligious attendants will not forge ahead of the churchgoing absentees. But it serves as a temporary jail for a pupil who will not go to Church. . . .

As one whose children, as a matter of free choice, have been sent to privately supported Church schools, I may challenge the Court's suggestion that opposition to this plan can only be antireligious, atheistic, or agnostic. My evangelistic brethren confuse an objection to compulsion with an objection to religion. . . .

NOTE

A number of commentators have discussed the relationship between the Establishment and Free Exercise Clauses. *See* Ira C. Lupu, *Reconstructing the Establishment Clause: The Case Against Discretionary Accommodation of Religion*, 140 U. PA. L. REV. 555, 558 (1991) ("My view is not so much against the idea of accommodation as it is for the idea of balance in our understandings of the religion clauses. Taken together, the clauses are most persuasively construed as mandating a regime of equal religious liberty. Under such a regime, every person may pursue religious freedom to the extent it is fully compatible with the equal pursuit of religious freedom by others."); Ira C. Lupu, *The Trouble With Accommodation*, 60 GEO. WASH. L. REV. 743, 748 (1992) ("The Establishment Clause, like the Free Exercise Clause, must be given its due. The accommodationists are reluctant to accept that statement, just as committed secularists and separationists may be uncomfortable with the converse proposition. The case against accommodation is at bottom an Establishment

Clause case."); Michael W. McConnell, *Religious Freedom at a Crossroads*, 59 U. Chi. L. Rev. 115, 194 (1992) ("[T]he Free Exercise and Establishment Clauses should protect against government-induced uniformity in matters of religion. In the modern welfare-regulatory state, this means that the state must not favor religion over nonreligion, nonreligion over religion, or one religion over another in distributing financial resources; that the state must create exceptions to laws of general applicability when these laws threaten the religious convictions or practices of religious institutions or individuals; and that the state should eschew both religious favoritism and secular bias in its own participation in the formation of public culture. This interpretation will tolerate a more prominent place for religion in the public sphere, but will simultaneously guarantee religious freedom for faiths both large and small.").

See also Scott J. Ward, Note, *Reconceptualizing Establishment Clause Cases as Free Exercise Class Actions*, 98 Yale L.J. 1739, 1739–40 (1989) ("Courts should analogize the establishment clause to a 'class action' aggregation of free exercise claims in its protection of religious liberty. Because individual religious liberty interests are generally smaller in establishment clause cases than in free exercise cases, the establishment clause protects free exercise interests that tend to be undervindicated by the use of a simple bipolar litigation model, where the incentive for any individual to bring suit is diminished. On the other hand, establishment clause claims, as currently adjudicated, tend to overstate the extent of the constitutional violation and resulting harm."); John Witte, Jr., *The Essential Rights and Liberties of Religion in the American Constitutional Experiment*, 71 Notre Dame L. Rev. 371, 444 (1996) ("In its early establishment clause cases, the Court was almost single-minded in its devotion to the principle of separationism-yielding secularist dicta that seemed anomalous to a nation so widely devoted to a public religion and a religious public.").

§ 16.02 THE ESTABLISHMENT CLAUSE AND AID TO RELIGIOUS INSTITUTIONS

NOTE

Property Tax Exemption. In *Walz v. Tax Commission*, 397 U.S. 664 (1970), the Court held that the exemption from State property tax of property used solely for religious worship did not consitute "establishment" of religion. Chief Justice Burger applied the "purpose" and "effect" test laid out by the court seven years earlier in *Abington School District v. Schempp*, 374 U.S. 203 (1963), and suggested a third criterion — that of "entanglement" between Church and State. "The Court has struggled to find a neutral course between the two Religion Clauses, both of which are cast in absolute terms, and either of which, if expanded to a logical extreme, would tend to clash with the other."

Applying this general principle, the Court found that the purpose behind the tax exemption on religious property was not to establish religion. The tax "has not singled out one particular church or religious group or even churches as such; rather, it has granted exemption to all houses of religious worship within a broad class of property owned by non-profit, quasi-public corporations which include hospitals, libraries, playgrounds, scientific, professional, historical, and patriotic groups. The State has an affirmative policy that considers these groups as beneficial and stabilizing influences." The purpose of the particular exemption at issue was simply to spare the exercise of religion the burden of the property taxation imposed on private profit-making institutions.

Turning to the exemption's effect, the Court observed that both taxing churches and exempting churches from taxation entailed a degree of governmental involvement with religion. The exemption, however, was preferable since "[e]limination of the exemption would tend to expand the involvement of government by giving rise to tax valuation of church property, tax liens, tax foreclosures, and the direct confrontations and conflicts that follow in the train of those legal processes."

The indirect benefits flowing from the exemption were less objectionable than a direct subsidy accompanied by surveillance. Such ongoing administration would constitute an excessive entanglement of church and state.

In his dissent, Justice Douglas asserted that the tax exemption amounted to a subsidy favoring believers over nonbelievers.

[1] Aid to Religious Schools

LEMON v. KURTZMAN, 403 U.S. 602 (1971). This case invalidated Pennsylvania and Rhode Island laws that provided state aid to church-related elementary and secondary schools as violating establishment and free exercise clauses. The Pennsylvania statute provided reimbursement to nonpublic schools for teacher salaries, textbooks and instructional materials in specific secular subjects. The Rhode Island statute authorized a state-funded 15% pay supplement for teachers in nonpublic elementary schools. The Court found both statutes unconstitutional.

The Rhode Island Salary Supplement Act authorized state officials to pay teachers of secular subjects in nonpublic elementary schools a supplement not to exceed 15% of the teachers' annual salary. A nonpublic school teacher's supplemented salary, however, could not exceed that of a public school teacher. Supplement recipients were also required to teach only subjects offered in public schools and to agree in writing not to teach a religion course during the supplement period. In Rhode Island, 25% of elementary school pupils attended nonpublic schools and 95% of these schools were affiliated with the Roman Catholic church. All 250 of the state's supplement applicants were employed by Roman Catholic schools.

The Pennsylvania Nonpublic Elementary and Secondary Education Act was the State's solution to a crisis caused by the impact of rapid cost increases on nonpublic schools. The statute authorized " 'contracts' " under which the State reimbursed nonpublic schools for the cost of teachers' salaries, textbooks and instructional materials approved by the state superintendent. The statute allowed reimbursement for "mathematics, modern foreign languages, physical science, and physical education," but prohibited reimbursement for "any course that contains 'any subject matter expressing religious teaching, or the morals or forms of worship of any sect.' " In Pennsylvania at the time, 20% of all pupils attended nonpublic schools and 96% of these schools were church-related, most affiliated with the Roman Catholic church.

In his majority opinion, Chief Justice Burger found that the stated purpose of both statutes was to enhance the quality of secular education in all schools, which is consistent with each State's "legitimate concern for maintaining minimum standards in all schools it allows to operate." The majority did not decide "whether these legislative precautions restrict the principal or primary effect of the programs to the point where they do not offend the Religion Clause," but held that "the cumulative impact of the entire relationship arising under the statutes in each State involves excessive entanglement between government and religion."

Total separation of church and state "is not possible in an absolute sense." For example, "fire inspections, building and zoning regulations and state requirements under compulsory school-attendance laws are necessary and permissible contacts" between government and religious organizations. The Court's test for excessive entanglement between government and religion requires examination of "the character and purposes of the institutions that are benefited, the nature of the aid that the State provides, and the resulting relationship between the government and the religious authority."

The schools in the Rhode Island Program were located close to parish churches. Religious symbols, including crosses, crucifixes and religious paintings decorated the school buildings. Church school students received 30 minutes of "direct religious instruction" each day, and "religiously oriented extracurricular activities were offered to them." At parochial schools, two-thirds of the teachers were nuns. Thus, the District Court had found that parochial schools are "an integral part of the religious mission of the Catholic Church," and "[transmit] the Catholic faith to the next generation." These findings and the "impressionable age" of the students led the Court to conclude that parochial schools have "substantial religious activity and purpose."

The Rhode Island legislature's concern that religious values would enter into secular courses resulted in "careful government controls and surveillance" of schools receiving state aid. The Court's decisions, from *Everson* to *Bd. Of Educ. v. Allen*, 392 U.S. 236 (1968), provide that supplying students with "bus transportation, school lunches, public health services, and secular textbooks" does not offend the Establishment Clause. Here, Chief Justice Burger was more concerned about teachers than textbooks. He saw teachers "under religious control and discipline" as a greater threat than textbooks to maintaining separation of religious and secular content.

Rhode Island parochial schools were supervised by a Bishop and his appointed representative. All but two school principals were nuns, and teachers' contracts were signed by the parish priest. The standards that governed the schools stated that " 'religious formation is not confined to formal courses,' " and teachers were advised to "stimulate interest in religious vocations and missionary work."

The Court concluded that the Rhode Island program presented "potential if not actual hazards." The Chief Justice clarified that the Court made no assumption "of bad faith or any conscious design to evade" the law, but simply saw the inevitability that teachers would "experience great difficulty in remaining religiously neutral." Furthermore, the contacts necessary for the "comprehensive, discriminating and continuing state surveillance" required to ensure teacher compliance would "involve excessive and enduring entanglement between state and church." Excessive entanglement could also arise from a government inspection of school records, which was mandated by the statute if the total expenditures on secular education by a nonpublic school exceeded the norm for public schools.

The Pennsylvania statute, like the Rhode Island statute, created entanglement problems due to "the very restrictions and surveillance necessary to ensure that teachers play a strictly non-ideological role." Moreover, the Pennsylvania statute impermissibly "provid[ed] state financial aid directly to the church-related schools," distinguishing the instant case from *Everson* and *Allen*, in which aid went to students and parents rather than schools. "The history of government grants of continuing cash subsidy indicates that such programs have almost always been accompanied by varying measures of control and surveillance." Thus, the Court predicted that the Pennsylvania and Rhode Island programs would produce "comprehensive measures of surveillance and controls."

The Chief Justice noted that the maintenance of parochial schools "by the gifts of faithful adherents" has saved taxpayers "vast sums."

Justice Douglas, joined by Justice Black, concurred in the judgment. He characterized the parochial school as "an organism living on one budget," with taxpayer money funding the teaching of humanities or science, without proselytizing, and school funds supporting religious training. Justice Brennan wrote a separate concurrence.

NOTES

(1) *Government Aid to Church-Related Colleges and Universities.* (a) *Construction grants.* The same three-part *Lemon* test that was used in the pre-college cases — "purpose," "primary effect" and "excessive entanglement" — has been more easily satisfied in the higher education cases. *Tilton v. Richardson*, 403 U.S. 672 (1971), involved federal construction grants to church-colleges for facilities devoted exclusively to secular educational purposes. In upholding the grants, Chief Justice Burger's plurality opinion noted that religious indoctrination was not a substantial purpose of these colleges and that college students were not as susceptible to religious teachings. Moreover, the very nature of a college curriculum would tend to curb sectarian influence and reduce the risk that the primary effect of these grants would be to encourage or support religious activities. Because the inspection necessary to determine that the facilities were devoted to secular education would be "minimal," the entanglement of church and state was not excessive.

(b) *State-issued bonds.* Two years after *Tilton*, Justice Powell (6-3) upheld a construction aid program that permitted all colleges, regardless of religious affiliation, to borrow funds at low interest rates by using state-issued revenue bonds. In *Hunt v. McNair*, 413 U.S. 734 (1973), Justice Brennan, joined by Justices Douglas and Marshall, dissented on the ground of excessive entanglement arguing that the State would have to police college affairs at least for the life of the bonds.

(c) *Annual grants.* In *Roemer v. Maryland*, 426 U.S. 736 (1976), the Court upheld a program of annual, non-categorical grants to private colleges — irrespective of church affiliation — as long as the funds were not used for sectarian purposes. Ensuring that government grants were used only for secular purposes raised a more serious entanglement problem than single, one-time aid presented. Justice Blackmun's plurality opinion noted the greater supervision required to police such grants. Chief Justice Burger and Justice Powell joined Justice Blackmun's opinion. Justice White wrote a separate concurrence joined by Justice Rehnquist. Justices Brennan, Marshall and Stevens dissented.

(d) *Cf. Bowen v. Kendrick*, 487 U.S. 589 (1988). In upholding the availability of federal grants to religious organizations that educated and counselled adolescents on the values of sexual responsibility and adoption, the Court relied heavily on *Tilton* and *Hunt*. *See* notes (1)(a) and (b), *supra*.

(2) *Testing. P.E.A.R.L. v. Regan*, 444 U.S. 646 (1980), upheld a New York statute that provided reimbursement to nonpublic schools for the actual costs of administering mandatory, state-prepared examinations and keeping certain required records. The new statute did not reimburse the costs of teacher-prepared tests, a provision held invalid in *Levitt*. Moreover, the new statute, unlike the earlier version, provided for audits of school records to ensure that only actual costs incurred in providing the secular services were reimbursed. Despite differences between the New York statute and the testing provisions approved in *Wolman*, the Court found that decision controlling. Even though the New York law, unlike the Ohio statute, provided for grading by the sectarian school personnel with state reimbursement for the administration and grading costs, these differences were not of constitutional dimension. The audit procedures assured reimbursement only for permissible secular functions in a straightforward and routine method, which did not raise the problem of excessive entanglement.

Justice Blackmun dissented, joined by Justices Brennan and Marshall. Justice Blackmun argued that the direct financial assistance had the impermissible effect of advancing religion because it comprised a significant amount of the school's personnel budget. Moreover, Justice Blackmun concluded that the audit and review procedures prescribed in the statute would constitute an excessive entanglement. In a separate dissent, Justice Stevens deplored the "largely ad hoc decisions" that attempted to distinguish between impermissible and constitutionally valid aid to nonpublic schools.

(3) *Exemptions from Regulation.* In *NLRB v. Catholic Bishop of Chicago*, 440 U.S. 490 (1979), the Court dealt with the question of whether the National Labor Relations Act covered lay teachers in parochial schools. Church groups argued that permitting these teachers to unionize under the Act would violate the separation of church and state. In a 5–4 decision, the Court decided the case on statutory grounds, finding that the NLRB lacked jurisdiction over these teachers. The dissenters accused the majority of evading the difficult constitutional question presented. *See also St. Martin Evangelical Lutheran Church v. South Dakota*, 451 U.S. 772 (1981) (exempting church-affiliated academy from the Federal Unemployment Tax Act as a matter of statutory construction); *Corporation of the Presiding Bishop of the Church of Jesus Christ of the Latter Day Saints v. Amos*, § 16.03 (upheld against establishment challenge exemption from Title VII's prohibition against religious discrimination).

(4) *Discrimination Among Religions.* In *Larson v. Valente*, 456 U.S. 228 (1982), the Court invalidated a Minnesota law that imposed registration and reporting requirements on charitable organizations, but exempted from regulation those religions that received less than half of their contributions from nonmembers. The Unification Church successfully argued that the law established a governmental preference in favor of those religions that did not rely on nonmembers for principal financial support. Justice Brennan's majority opinion applied a "compelling governmental interest" test and rejected the justifications proffered by the State. Justice Brennan also invoked the three-part test of *Lemon v. Kurtzman*, even though it was intended to apply to laws affording a uniform benefit to all religions. "We view the third [element (non-entanglement)] of those tests as most directly implicated in the present case. . . . The distinctions drawn . . . engender a risk of politicizing religion — a risk, indeed that has already been substantially realized." In dissent, Justice White, joined by Justice Rehnquist, argued that the record was not adequate to support the finding of religious preference. Four Justices (Chief Justice Burger and Justices White, Rehnquist, and O'Connor) dissented on the ground of lack of standing.

MUELLER v. ALLEN
463 U.S. 388, 103 S. Ct. 3062, 77 L. Ed. 2d 721 (1983)

JUSTICE REHNQUIST delivered the opinion of the Court.

Minnesota allows taxpayers, in computing their state income tax, to deduct certain expenses incurred in providing for the education of their children. . . .

Minnesota, like every other state, provides its citizens with free elementary and secondary schooling. It seems to be agreed that about 820,000 students attended this school system in the most recent school year. During the same year, approximately 91,000 elementary and secondary students attended some 500 privately supported schools located in Minnesota, and about 95% of these students attended schools considering themselves to be sectarian.

Minnesota . . . permits state taxpayers to claim a deduction from gross income for certain expenses incurred in educating their children. The deduction is limited to actual expenses incurred for the "tuition, textbooks and transportation" of dependents attending elementary or secondary schools. A deduction may not exceed $500 per dependent in grades K through six and $700 per dependent in grades seven through twelve. Minn. Stat. § 290.09.[1] . . .

. . . In this case we are asked to decide whether Minnesota's tax deduction bears greater resemblance to those types of assistance to parochial schools we have approved, or to those we have struck down. Petitioners place particular reliance on our decision in *Committee for Public Education v. Nyquist*, where we held invalid a New York statute providing public funds for the maintenance and repair of the physical facilities of private schools and granting thinly disguised "tax benefits," actually amounting to tuition grants, to the parents of children attending private schools. As explained below, we conclude that § 290.09(22) bears less resemblance to the arrangement struck down in *Nyquist* than it does to assistance programs upheld in our prior decisions and those discussed with approval in *Nyquist*.

The general nature of our inquiry in this area has been guided, since the decision in *Lemon v. Kurtzman*, by the "three part" test laid down in that case:

> First, the statute must have a secular legislative purpose; second, its principal or primary effect must be one that neither advances nor inhibits religion . . . finally, the statute must not foster "an excessive government entanglement with religion."

Id. at 612–613.

Little time need be spent on the question of whether the Minnesota tax deduction has a secular purpose. . . . This reflects, at least in part, our reluctance to attribute

---

[1] [Court's footnote 2] Both lower courts found that the statute permits deduction of a range of education expenses. The District Court found that deductible expenses include:

"1. Tuition in the ordinary sense.

2. Tuition to public school students who attend public schools outside their residence school districts.

3. Certain summer school tuition.

4. Tuition charged by a school for slow learner private tutoring services.

5. Tuition for instruction provided by an elementary or secondary school to students who are physically unable to attend classes at such school.

6. Tuition charged by a private tutor or by a school that is not an elementary or secondary school if the instruction is acceptable for credit in an elementary or secondary school.

7. Montessori School tuition for grades K through 12.

8. Tuition for driver education when it is part of the school curriculum." 514 F. Supp at 1000.

The Court of Appeals concurred in this finding.

In addition, the District Court found that statutory deduction for "textbooks" included not only "secular textbooks" but also:

"1. Cost of tennis shoes and sweatsuits for physical education.

2. Camera rental fees paid to the school for photography classes.

3. Ice skates rental fee paid to the school.

4. Rental fee paid to the school for calculators for mathematics classes.

5. Costs of home economics materials needed to meet minimum requirements.

6. Costs of special metal or wood needed to meet minimum requirements of shop classes.

7. Costs of supplies needed to meet minimum requirements of art classes.

8. Rental fees paid to the school for musical instruments.

9. Cost of pencils and special notebooks required for class." [*Id*].

The Court of Appeals accepted this finding.

unconstitutional motives to the states, particularly when a plausible secular purpose for the state's program may be discerned from the face of the statute.

A state's decision to defray the cost of educational expenses incurred by parents — regardless of the type of schools their children attend — evidences a purpose that is both secular and understandable. An educated populace is essential to the political and economic health of any community, and a state's efforts to assist parents in meeting the rising cost of educational expenses plainly serves this secular purpose. . . . Similarly, Minnesota, like other states, could conclude that there is a strong public interest in assuring the continued financial health of private schools, both sectarian and non-sectarian. By educating a substantial number of students such schools relieve public schools of a correspondingly great burden — to the benefit of all taxpayers. In addition, private schools may serve as a benchmark for public schools, in a manner analogous to the "TVA yardstick" for private power companies. . . .

We turn therefore to the more difficult but related question whether the Minnesota statute has "the primary effect of advancing the sectarian aims of the nonpublic schools.". . . In concluding that it does not, we find several features of the Minnesota tax deduction particularly significant. First, an essential feature of Minnesota's arrangement is the fact that § 290.09(22) is only one among many deductions — such as those for medical expenses and charitable contributions, available under the Minnesota tax laws. Our decisions consistently have recognized that traditionally "[l]egislatures have especially broad latitude in creating classifications and distinctions in tax statutes," *Regan v. Taxation with Representation*, [461 U.S. 540, 547 (1983)]. . . . Under our prior decisions, the Minnesota legislature's judgment that a deduction for educational expenses fairly equalizes the tax burden of its citizens and encourages desirable expenditures for educational purposes is entitled to substantial deference.[2]

Other characteristics of § 290.09(22) argue equally strongly for the provision's constitutionality. Most importantly, . . . [u]nlike the assistance at issue in *Nyquist*, § 290.09(22) permits all parents — whether their children attend public school or private — to deduct their childrens' educational expenses. . . . [A] program, like § 290.09(22), that neutrally provides state assistance to a broad spectrum of citizens is not readily subject to challenge under the Establishment Clause.

We also agree with the Court of Appeals that, by channeling whatever assistance it may provide to parochial schools through individual parents, Minnesota has reduced the Establishment Clause objections to which its action is subject. It is true, of course, that financial assistance provided to parents ultimately has an economic effect comparable to that of aid given directly to the schools attended by their children. It is also true, however, that under Minnesota's arrangement public funds become available only as a

---

[2] [Court's footnote 6] Our decision in *Nyquist* is not to the contrary on this point. We expressed considerable doubt that the "tax benefits" provided by New York law properly could be regarded as parts of a genuine system of tax laws. Plainly, the outright grants to low-income parents did not take the form of ordinary tax benefits. As to the benefits provided to middle-income parents, the Court said:

> The amount of the deduction is unrelated to the amount of money actually expended by any parent on tuition, but is calculated on the basis of a formula contained in the statute. The formula is apparently the product of a legislative attempt to assure that each family would receive a carefully estimated net benefit, and that the tax benefit would be comparable to, and compatible with, the tuition grant for lower income families.

Indeed, the question whether a program having the elements of a "genuine tax deduction" would be constitutionally acceptable was expressly reserved in *Nyquist*, 413 U.S. at 790 n.49. While the economic consequences of the program in *Nyquist* and that in this case may be difficult to distinguish, . . . the Minnesota plan embodies a "genuine tax deduction" . . . of some relevance, especially given the traditional rule of deference accorded legislative classifications in tax statutes.

result of numerous, private choices of individual parents of school-age children. . . . It is noteworthy that all but one of our recent cases invalidating state aid to parochial schools have involved the direct transmission of assistance from the state to the schools themselves. The exception, of course, was *Nyquist*, which, as discussed previously, is distinguishable from this case on other grounds. Where, as here, aid to parochial schools is available only as a result of decisions of individual parents, no "imprimatur of State approval," *Widmar* [*v. Vincent*, 454 U.S. 263 (1981)] can be deemed to have been conferred on any particular religion, or on religion generally. . . .

We do not think, however, that . . . [the Establishment Clause's] historic purposes . . . encompass the sort of attenuated financial benefit, ultimately controlled by the private choices of individual parents, that eventually flows to parochial schools from the neutrally available tax benefit at issue in this case.

Petitioners argue that, notwithstanding the facial neutrality of § 290.09(22), in application the statute primarily benefits religious institutions. Petitioners rely, as they did below, on a statistical analysis of the type of persons claiming the tax deduction. They contend that most parents of public school children incur no tuition expenses, and that other expenses deductible under § 290.09(22) are negligible in value; moreover, they claim that 96% of the children in private schools in 1978-1979 attended religiously-affiliated institutions. Because of all this, they reason, the bulk of deductions taken under § 290.09(22) will be claimed by parents of children in sectarian schools. Respondents reply that petitioners have failed to consider the impact of deductions for items such as transportation, summer school tuition, tuition paid by parents whose children attended schools outside the school districts in which they resided, rental or purchase costs for a variety of equipment, and tuition for certain types of instruction not ordinarily provided in public schools.

We need not consider these contentions in detail. We would be loath to adopt a rule grounding the constitutionality of a facially neutral law on annual reports reciting the extent to which various classes of private citizens claimed benefits under the law. . . .

Finally, private educational institutions, and parents paying for their children to attend these schools, make special contributions to the areas in which they operate. "Parochial schools, quite apart from their sectarian purpose, have provided an educational alternative for millions of young Americans; they often afford wholesome competition with our public schools; and in some States they relieve substantially the tax burden incident to the operation of public schools." *Wolman*, 433 U.S. at 262 (Powell, J., concurring and dissenting). If parents of children in private schools choose to take especial advantage of the relief provided by § 290.09, subd. 22, it is no doubt due to the fact that they bear a particularly great financial burden in educating their children. More fundamentally, whatever unequal effect may be attributed to the statutory classification can fairly be regarded as a rough return for the benefits, discussed above, provided to the state and all taxpayers by parents sending their children to parochial schools. . . .

Thus, we hold that the Minnesota tax deduction for educational expenses satisfies the primary effect inquiry of our Establishment Clause cases.

Turning to the third part of the *Lemon* inquiry, we have no difficulty in concluding that the Minnesota statute does not "excessively entangle" the state in religion. The only plausible source of the "comprehensive, discriminating, and continuing state surveillance," 403 U.S. at 619, necessary to run afoul of this standard would lie in the fact that state officials must determine whether particular textbooks qualify for a deduction. In making this decision, state officials must disallow deductions taken from "instructional books and materials used in the teaching of religious tenets, doctrines or worship, the purpose of which is to inculcate such tenets, doctrines or worship." Minn. Stat.

§ 290.09(22). Making decisions such as this does not differ substantially from making the types of decisions approved in earlier opinions of this Court. In *Board of Education v. Allen*, 392 U.S. 236 (1968), for example, the Court upheld the loan of secular textbooks to parents or children attending nonpublic schools; though state officials were required to determine whether particular books were or were not secular, the system was held not to violate the Establishment Clause. . . .

JUSTICE MARSHALL, with whom JUSTICE BRENNAN, JUSTICE BLACKMUN and JUSTICE STEVENS join, dissenting.

I

. . . The Minnesota tax statute violates the Establishment Clause for precisely the same reason as the statute struck down in *Nyquist*: it has a direct and immediate effect of advancing religion.

A

. . . Although this tax benefit is available to any parents whose children attend schools which charge tuition, the vast majority of the taxpayers who are eligible to receive the benefit are parents whose children attend religious schools. . . . Although the statute also allows a deduction for the tuition expenses of children attending public schools, Minnesota public schools are generally prohibited by law from charging tuition. . . . Public schools may assess tuition charges only for students accepted from outside the district. . . . In the 1978–1979 school year, only 79 public school students fell into this category. The parents of the remaining 815,000 students who attended public schools were ineligible to receive this tax benefit. . . .

B

The majority attempts to distinguish *Nyquist* by pointing to two differences between the Minnesota tuition-assistance program and the program struck down in *Nyquist*. Neither of these distinctions can withstand scrutiny.

1

. . . That the Minnesota statute makes some small benefit available to all parents cannot alter the fact that the most substantial benefit provided by the statute is available only to those parents who send their children to schools that charge tuition.

. . . Of the total number of taxpayers who are eligible for the tuition deduction, approximately 96% send their children to religious schools.

. . . Parents who send their children to free public schools are simply ineligible to obtain the full benefit of the deduction except in the unlikely event that they buy $700 worth of pencils, notebooks, and bus rides for their school-age children. . . .

2

The majority also asserts that the Minnesota statute is distinguishable from the statute struck down in *Nyquist* in another respect: the tax benefit available under Minnesota law is a "genuine tax deduction," whereas the New York law provided a benefit which, while nominally a deduction, also had features of a "tax credit." Under the Minnesota law, the amount of the tax benefit varies directly with the amount of the expenditure. Under the New York law, the amount of deduction was not dependent upon the amount actually paid for tuition but was a predetermined amount which depended on the tax bracket of each taxpayer. The deduction was designed to yield roughly the same amount of tax "forgiveness" for each taxpayer.

. . . Our prior decisions have rejected the relevance of the majority's formalistic distinction between tax deductions and the tax benefit at issue in *Nyquist*.[3] . . . Like the tax benefit held impermissible in *Nyquist*, the tax deduction at issue here concededly was designed to "encourag[e] desirable expenditures for educational purposes.". . .

C

. . . [T]he Minnesota tuition tax deduction . . . is not restricted, and cannot be restricted, to the secular functions of those schools.

II

In my view, Minnesota's tax deduction for the cost of textbooks and other instructional materials is also constitutionally infirm. . . .

. . . [T]he Minnesota statute does not limit the tax deduction to those books which the State has approved for use in public schools. Rather, it permits a deduction for books that are chosen by the parochial schools themselves. . . .

NOTES

(1) *"Community Education" Programs.* In *Grand Rapids School District v. Ball*, 473 U.S. 373 (1985), the Court struck down a "Community Education" program. The Community Education program offered nonpublic school students academic and non-academic courses taught by private school teachers employed part-time by the State at the end of the regular school day. The State leased classrooms "at a rate of $6 per classroom per week." Whenever a classroom is used for the program, a sign was posted designating the particular room a "public school classroom." The State inspected these classrooms to ensure that they were free of religious symbols; it also adjusted the schedules of these programs to accommodate religious holidays.

Writing for the Court, Justice Brennan found that the program violated the primary effect prong of the *Lemon* test. "First, the state-paid instructors, influenced by the pervasively sectarian nature of the religious schools in which they work, may subtly or overtly indoctrinate the students in particular religious tenets at public expense. Second, the symbolic union of church and state inherent in the provision of secular state-provided instruction in the religious school buildings threatens to convey a message of state support for religion to students and to the general public.

Justice O'Connor concurred in striking down the Community Education program, emphasizing the fact that many of the teachers in the program were full-time teachers at the very parochial schools where the courses were taught. Justices Rehnquist and White filed separate dissenting opinions to uphold the program.

(2) *College Vouchers.* In *Witters v. Washington Dept. of Services for Blind*, 474 U.S. 481 (1986), the Court unanimously held that a Washington rehabilitation program could

---

[3] [Dissent's footnote 5] . . . The deduction at issue in this case does differ from the tax benefits in *Nyquist* and our other prior cases in one respect: by its very nature the deduction embodies an inherent limit on the extent to which a State may subsidize religious education. Unlike a tax credit, which may wholly subsidize the cost of religious education if the size of the credit is sufficiently large, or a tax deduction of an arbitrary sum, a deduction of tuition payments from adjusted gross income can never "provide a basis for . . . *complete subsidization* of . . . religious schools." *Nyquist, supra*, at 782 n.38 (emphasis in original). *See also id.* at 779, 787 n.44. *Nyquist* made clear, however, that absolutely no subsidization is permissible unless it is restricted to the purely secular functions of those schools.

assist a visually handicapped person who was attending a Christian college and preparing to be a pastor, missionary, or youth director. "Any aid provided under Washington's program that ultimately flows to religious institutions does so only as a result of the genuinely independent and private choices of aid recipients." Justice Marshall also noted that the program was not likely to afford any substantial subsidy to sectarian education.

Justice Powell, joined by Chief Justice Burger and Justice Rehnquist, concurred. He chided the Court for failing to mention the decision in *Mueller v. Allen*, which "strongly supports the result we will reach today." In separate concurring opinions, Justices White and O'Connor agreed with Justice Powell's conclusion that *Mueller* buttressed the Court's decision. *But cf. Locke v. Davey*, 540 U.S. 712 (2004) (denying a free exercise right to funding for degrees in devotional theology even though the state provides such funding for non-devotional theology degree programs).

(3) *Individuals with Disabilities Education Act.* In *Zobrest v. Catalina Foothills School District*, 509 U.S. 1 (1993), the Court held that the Establishment Clause did not prevent a public school district from providing a deaf pupil at a sectarian school with a sign language interpreter to assist him in his education pursuant to the Individuals with Disabilities Education Act (IDEA). Writing for the majority, Chief Justice Rehnquist categorized IDEA as a neutral "social welfare program," providing benefits "to a broad class of citizens defined without reference to religion." The Establishment Clause does not prohibit such programs merely because religious institutions may receive an incidental benefit.

In upholding the program, the Court relied heavily on *Mueller v. Allen* and *Witters v. Washington Dept. of Services for the Blind*. As in *Witters*, parents had no financial incentive to choose a sectarian school. In fact, unlike *Witters* or *Mueller*, none of the funds supplied by the state "ever find their way into the sectarian school's coffers." The Court also rejected the argument that this case was distinguishable from *Witters* and *Mueller* because the interpreter was a public employee.

Unlike a teacher or a counselor, the interpreter would simply "transmit everything that is said in exactly the same way it was intended." Finally, "the Establishment Clause lays down no absolute bar to the placing of a public employee in a sectarian school."

Justice Blackmun wrote a dissenting opinion. In a part of the dissent, which Justices Stevens, O'Connor, and Souter joined, Justice Blackmun would remand the case to ascertain whether it could have been decided on statutory grounds. A part of Justice Blackmun's dissent, joined only by Justice Souter, objected that public employees would be interpreting religious instruction, Catholic Mass, and communication of secular subjects from a religious perspective.

(4) For further discussion, see Michael W. McConnell & Richard A. Posner, *An Economic Approach to Issues of Religious Freedom*, 56 U. CHI. L. REV. 1, 60 (1989) ("Since religion is a market (albeit a 'deregulated' one) with close and unbreakable connections to many other markets in which government intervention is commonplace, absolute separation — the religious equivalent of the libertarian dream of the nightwatchman state — is therefore not a serious alternative. A comprehensive form of neutrality — of identifying and eliminating subsidies and taxes, disproportionate burdens and benefits — is the more promising route for protecting religous freedom, and economics a helpful guide.").

AGOSTINI v. FELTON, 521 U.S. 203 (1997). In *Agostini*, the Court allowed public school teachers to offer remedial classes in parochial schools. Writing for a 5-4 majority, Justice O'Connor explicitly overruled *Aguilar v. Felton* 473 U.S. 402 (1985) and parts of *Grand Rapids School District v. Ball*, 473 U.S. 373 (1985), by approving a "shared time" program that those cases had held violated the Establishment Clause.

In *Aguilar*, the "Court held that the Establishment Clause of the First Amendment barred the city of New York from sending public school teachers into parochial schools to provide remedial education to disadvantaged children pursuant to a congressionally mandated program." On remand, the District Court entered a permanent injunction which effectuated the Supreme Court's ruling. "Twelve years later, petitioners — the parties bound by that injunction — seek relief from its operation." The Court held that *Aguilar* was no longer consistent with its "subsequent Establishment Clause decisions" and therefore petitioners deserve relief from the injunction.

Through the Elementary and Secondary Education Act of 1965, Congress "channels federal funds, through the States, to 'local educational agencies' (LEA's)." These "LEA's spend these funds to provide remedial educational, guidance, and job counseling to eligible students. (LEA's must use funds to 'help participating children meet State student performance standards')." An eligible student must reside in a low income area and must be "failing, or [be] at risk of failing, the State's student performance standards."

The petitioner, the Board of Education of the City of New York, an LEA, applied for funding. Ten percent of the eligible students to whom the LEA wanted to provide services attended private schools. "Recognizing that more than 90% of the private schools within the Board's jurisdiction are sectarian, the Board initially arranged to transport children to public schools for after-school Title I instruction." However, this attempt failed. A subsequent program sent public school teachers onto private school campuses after school. When this program garnered "mixed results," the Board implemented the program the Court considered in *Aguilar*. This program allowed public school teachers to go to the private schools to teach the students on the private campuses.[4]

After the Court struck down this program in *Aguilar*, the Board returned to the original practice of providing alternative classroom sites, such as public schools, leased space, and vans converted into mobile classrooms parked near the private school campuses. When *Aguilar* was decided, "it was estimated that some 20,000 economically disadvantaged children in the city" and about 183,000 children across the nation would experience a decline in services because of the new expenses required to comply with *Aguilar*.

Ten years after *Aguilar*, petitioners sought relief from the *Aguilar* injunction under Federal Rule of Civil Procedure 60(b)(5), claiming a change in the law made the injunction unjust.[5]

The Court found that more recent cases have undercut the assumptions on which *Aguilar* and *Ball* rested. The general principles used to evaluate "whether government

---

[4] Before public teachers were allowed to go to the schools, they were trained by the city. The teachers were reminded that: (i) they were public school employees, accountable only to public school supervisors; (ii) they could only select and teach students from a population eligible for the Title I program; (iii) materials and equipment used were only to be used for the Title I program; (iv) they could not engage in cooperative instruction with private school teachers; (v) they were not to involve themselves in any way with religious instruction in the school. Moreover, religious symbols were removed from the classrooms used, the teachers could only consult with the private school teachers to assess the needs of students, and a publicly employed supervisor would make at least one unannounced visit to each teacher's classroom every month to insure there was no religious instruction occurring.

[5] Fed. R. Civ. P. 60(b)(5) states " 'On motion and upon such terms as are just, the court may relieve a party . . . from a final judgment [or] order . . . [when] it is no longer equitable that the judgment should have prospective application.' "

aid violates the Establishment Clause" have not changed since *Aguilar*, as the Court continues to inquire whether or not the government acted "with the purpose of advancing or inhibiting religion." The Court also shall consider whether the funding "has the 'effect' of advancing or inhibiting religion." Since *Aguilar* and *Ball*, the Court has a new understanding of the criteria used to determine whether there is such an "impermissible effect."

First, the Court abandoned the presumption that the "placement of public employees on parochial school grounds inevitably results in the impermissible effect of state-sponsored indoctrination or constitutes a symbolic union between government and religion." In *Zobrest v. Catalina Foothills School Dist.*, 509 U.S. 1 (1993), *supra* § 16.02[1], Note (3), the Court rejected the presumption that a public employee on private property would impart religion to students or that the employee's presence created "an impermissible 'symbolic link' between government and religion." The sign-language interpreter in *Zobrest* "had the same opportunity to inculcate religion in the performance of her duties as do Title I employees."

Second, the Court acknowledged that it has departed from the rule it announced in *Ball* that no government funds directly benefit the "educational function" of religious institutions. In *Witters v. Washington Dept. Of Servs. for Blind*, 474 U.S. 481 (1986),*supra* § 16.02[1], Note (2), the Court upheld a state vocational tuition grant that allowed a blind person to use the grant for religious training because the tuition grants were made available without consideration of whether the institution receiving the grant money was public, private, religious, or nonreligious. In both *Zobrest* and *Witters*, "any money that ultimately went to religious institutions did so 'only as a result of the genuinely independent and private choices of' individuals.' " Title I funds "are instead distributed to a public agency (an LEA) that dispenses services directly to the eligible students within its boundaries, no matter where they choose to attend school."

In this case, "no evidence has ever shown that any New York City Title I instructor teaching on parochial school premises attempted to inculcate religion in students." The Court rejected the respondent's argument that the Court must presume Title I instructors to be " 'uncontrollable and sometimes very unprofessional.' " The Court also rejected the notion that the presence of public school teachers in parochial schools alone created "the impression of a 'symbolic union' between church and state."

The Court also dismissed the dissent's concern that the funding relieved sectarian schools of services they would otherwise have had to provide. No evidence exists that Title I supplants the services provided by the parochial schools. Instead, it provides supplements for children in need. The Court also refused to consider the number of sectarian students benefiting from a program as a criterion for deciding the program's constitutionality. At bottom, the Court refused to treat New York's program as subsidizing religion simply because it moved from mobile classrooms parked on the curb outside of the parochial school into the school itself.

The Court next held that Title I did not have the impermissible effect of promoting religion, as it clearly allocates services "on the basis of criteria that neither favor nor disfavor religion. The services are available to all children who meet the Act's eligibility requirements, no matter what their religious beliefs or where they go to school."

The Court also rejected *Aguilar's* conclusion that the program produced excessive entanglement between church and state. Using the *Lemon* test, the Court looked at " 'the character and purposes of the institutions that are benefited, the nature of the aid that the State provides, and the resulting relationship between the government and religious authority.' " The Court also assessed "a law's 'effect' by examining the character of the institutions benefited and the nature of the aid that the State provided." The Court analyzed entanglement as "an aspect of the inquiry into a statute's effect." Not all entanglements violate the Establishment Clause. Indeed, some interaction between church and state is to be expected. The Establishment Clause invalidates only " 'excessive' " entanglements.

In *Aguilar*, the "Court's finding of 'excessive' entanglement" rested on three grounds: "(i) the program would require 'pervasive monitoring by public authorities' to ensure that Title I employees did not inculcate religion; (ii) the program required 'administrative cooperation' between the Board and parochial schools; and (iii) the program might increase the dangers of 'political divisiveness.' " However, these "last two considerations are insufficient by themselves to create an excessive entanglement." The Court has "not found excessive entanglement in cases in which States imposed far more onerous burdens on religious institutions than the monitoring system" of "unannounced monthly visits of public supervisors."

In summary, "New York City's Title I program does not run afoul of any of three primary criteria we currently use to evaluate whether government aid has the effect of advancing religion: it does not result in governmental indoctrination; define its recipients by reference to religion; or create an excessive entanglement. We therefore hold that a federally funded program providing supplemental, remedial instruction to disadvantaged children on a neutral basis is not invalid under the Establishment Clause when such instruction is given on the premises of sectarian schools by government employees pursuant to a program containing safeguards such as those present here. The same considerations that justify this holding require us to conclude that this carefully constrained program also cannot reasonably be viewed as an endorsement of religion."

Finally, stare decisis does "not preclude us from recognizing the change in our law and overruling *Aguilar* and those portions of *Ball* inconsistent with our more recent decisions." While stare decisis often "reflects a policy judgment that 'in most matters it is more important that the applicable rule of law be settled than that it be settled right,' " this policy "is at its weakest when [the Court] interpret[s] the Constitution because our interpretation can be altered only by constitutional amendment or by overruling our prior decisions."

Justice Souter dissented, joined by Justices Stevens and Ginsburg. Believing *Aguilar* was correctly decided, Justice Souter argued that placing public school teachers in private schools would tempt them into reflecting on the school's religious beliefs, leading to a need for monitoring "and the certainty of entanglement." More importantly, the Title I program acts as a subsidy for the private schools, relieving them of some of their duties to teach such subjects as remedial math and reading, thereby allowing them to concentrate funds on other areas of education, including religious ones. "If a State may constitutionally enter the schools to teach in the manner in question, it must in constitutional principle be free to assume, or assume payment for, the entire cost of instruction provided in any ostensibly secular subject in any religious school." Moreover, the sharing of teaching burdens between private and public teachers creates the impression of state approval of religious education.

Justice Souter also disputed the majority's reading of *Zobrest*. A sign-language interpreter " 'could be seen as more like a hearing aid than a teacher.' " Justice Souter further distinguished *Zobrest* and *Witters* from the program at issue on the grounds that the aid went to isolated, individual handicapped students. In contrast, Title I programs fund core, remedial skill areas "(remedial reading, reading skills, remedial mathematics, English as a second language);" it also funded guidance services. In *Zobrest* and *Witters*, individuals applied for "benefits on a scale that could not amount to a systematic supplement."

Justice Souter also criticized the majority's excessive reliance on the apparent neutrality of the Title I program. While being evenhanded is necessary, even a neutral program may violate the Establishment Clause if it supports or endorses religion.

Justice Ginsburg also dissented, joined by Justices Stevens, Souter, and Breyer. Justice Ginsburg focused on the application of Federal Rule of Civil Procedure 60(b)(5). First, in order to rehear a case, the petition must be "filed within 25 days of the entry of the judgment in question." Justice Ginsburg would have waited for a more appropriate case to come up to revisit the rule in *Aguilar*.

MITCHELL v. HELMS
530 U.S. 793, 120 S. Ct. 2530, 147 L. Ed. 2d 660 (2000)

JUSTICE THOMAS delivered an opinion, in which THE CHIEF JUSTICE, JUSTICE SCALIA, and JUSTICE KENNEDY join.

As part of a longstanding school aid program known as Chapter 2, the Federal Government distributes funds to state and local governmental agencies, which in turn lend educational materials and equipment to public and private schools, with the enrollment of each participating school determining the amount of aid that it receives. The question is whether Chapter 2, as applied in Jefferson Parish, Louisiana, is a law respecting an establishment of religion, because many of the private schools receiving Chapter 2 aid in that parish are religiously affiliated. We hold that Chapter 2 is not such a law.

I

A

Chapter 2 of the Education Consolidation and Improvement Act of 1981, 20 U.S.C. §§ 7301–7373, . . . is a close cousin of the provision of the ESEA that we recently considered in *Agostini v. Felton*. Like the provision at issue in *Agostini*, Chapter 2 channels federal funds to local educational agencies (LEA's), which are usually public school districts, via state educational agencies (SEA's), to implement programs to assist children in elementary and secondary schools. . . .

LEA's and SEA's must offer assistance to both public and private schools (although any private school must be nonprofit). . . .

Several restrictions apply to aid to private schools. Most significantly, the "services, materials, and equipment" provided to private schools must be "secular, neutral, and nonideological." § 7372(a)(1). In addition, private schools may not acquire control of Chapter 2 funds or title to Chapter 2 materials, equipment, or property. A private school receives the materials and equipment . . . by submitting to the LEA an application detailing which items the school seeks and how it will use them; the LEA, if it approves the application, purchases those items from the school's allocation of funds, and then lends them to that school.

In Jefferson Parish (the Louisiana governmental unit at issue in this case), as in Louisiana as a whole, private schools have primarily used their allocations for nonrecurring expenses, usually materials and equipment. Among the materials and equipment provided have been library books, computers, and computer software, and also slide and movie projectors, overhead projectors, television sets, tape recorders, VCR's, projection screens, laboratory equipment, maps, globes, filmstrips, slides, and cassette recordings.

It appears that, in an average year, about 30% of Chapter 2 funds spent in Jefferson Parish are allocated for private schools. For the 1985–1986 fiscal year, 41 private schools participated in Chapter 2. For the following year, 46 participated, and the participation level has remained relatively constant since then. Of these 46, 34 were Roman Catholic; 7 were otherwise religiously affiliated; and 5 were not religiously affiliated. . . .

II

. . . Whereas in *Lemon* [*v. Kurtzman*, 403 U.S. 602 (1971)], we had considered whether a statute (1) has a secular purpose, (2) has a primary effect of advancing or inhibiting religion, or (3) creates an excessive entanglement between government and religion, in *Agostini* we modified *Lemon* for purposes of evaluating aid to schools and examined only the first and second factors. We acknowledged that our cases discussing excessive entanglement had applied many of the same considerations as had our cases discussing primary effect, and we therefore recast *Lemon's* entanglement inquiry as simply one criterion relevant to determining a statute's effect. We also acknowledged that our cases had pared somewhat the factors that could justify a finding of excessive entanglement. We then set out revised criteria for determining the effect of a statute:

"To summarize, New York City's Title I program does not run afoul of any of three primary criteria we currently use to evaluate whether government aid has the effect of advancing religion: It does not result in governmental indoctrination; define its recipients by reference to religion; or create an excessive entanglement." 521 U.S. at 234.

In this case, our inquiry under *Agostini's* purpose and effect test is a narrow one. Because respondents do not challenge the District Court's holding that Chapter 2 has a secular purpose, . . . we will consider only Chapter 2's effect. Further, in determining that effect, we will consider only the first two *Agostini* criteria, since neither respondents nor the Fifth Circuit has questioned the District Court's holding that Chapter 2 does not create an excessive entanglement. Considering Chapter 2 in light of our more recent case law, we conclude that it neither results in religious indoctrination by the government nor defines its recipients by reference to religion. . . . *Meek* [*v. Pittenger*, 421 U.S. 349 (1975)] and *Wolman* [*v. Walter*, 433 U.S. 229 (1977)] . . . are no longer good law.

A

As we indicated in *Agostini*, and have indicated elsewhere, the question whether governmental aid to religious schools results in governmental indoctrination is ultimately a question whether any religious indoctrination that occurs in those schools could reasonably be attributed to governmental action. . . . We have also indicated that the answer to the question of indoctrination will resolve the question whether a program of educational aid "subsidizes" religion, as our religion cases use that term. *See Agostini*, 521 U.S. at 230–231.

In distinguishing between indoctrination that is attributable to the State and indoctrination that is not, we have consistently turned to the principle of neutrality, upholding aid that is offered to a broad range of groups or persons without regard to their religion. . . . If the government is offering assistance to recipients who provide, so to speak, a broad range of indoctrination, the government itself is not thought responsible for any particular indoctrination. To put the point differently, if the government, seeking to further some legitimate secular purpose, offers aid on the same terms, without regard to religion, to all who adequately further that purpose, . . . then it is fair to say that any aid going to a religious recipient only has the effect of furthering that secular purpose. . . .

As a way of assuring neutrality, we have repeatedly . . . viewed as significant whether the "private choices of individual parents," as opposed to the "unmediated" will of government, [*School Dist. Of City of Grand Rapids v. Ball*, 473 U.S. 373, 395, n. 13 (1985)], determine what schools ultimately benefit from the governmental aid, and how much. For if numerous private choices, rather than the single choice of a government, determine the distribution of aid pursuant to neutral eligibility criteria, then a government cannot, or at least cannot easily, grant special favors that might lead to a religious establishment. . . .

The principles of neutrality and private choice, and their relationship to each other, were prominent not only in *Agostini*, . . . but also in *Zobrest* [*v. Catalina Foothills School Dist.*, 509 U.S. 1 (1993)], *Witters* [*v. Washington Dept. of Servs. For Blind*, 474 U.S. 481 (1986)], and *Mueller* [*v. Allen*, 463 U.S.388 (1983)]. . . .

Agostini's second primary criterion . . . requires a court to consider whether an aid program "defines its recipients by reference to religion." 521 U.S. at 234. As we briefly explained in *Agostini*, this second criterion looks to the same set of facts as does our focus, under the first criterion, on neutrality, but the second criterion uses those facts to answer a somewhat different question — whether the criteria for allocating the aid "create a financial incentive to undertake religious indoctrination." *Id.* at 231. In *Agostini* we set out the following rule for answering this question:

"This incentive is not present, however, where the aid is allocated on the basis of neutral, secular criteria that neither favor nor disfavor religion, and is made available to both religious and secular beneficiaries on a nondiscriminatory basis. Under such circumstances, the aid is less likely to have the effect of advancing religion." *Ibid.* . . .

. . . [S]imply because an aid program offers private schools, and thus religious schools, a benefit that they did not previously receive does not mean that the program, by reducing the cost of securing a religious education, creates, under *Agostini's* second criterion, an "incentive" for parents to choose such an education for their children. For any aid will have some such effect.

B

Respondents . . . offer two rules that they contend should govern our determination of whether Chapter 2 has the effect of advancing religion. They argue first, and chiefly, that "direct, nonincidental" aid to the primary educational mission of religious schools is always impermissible. Second, they argue that provision to religious schools of aid that is divertible to religious use is similarly impermissible.[6] Respondents' arguments are inconsistent with our more recent case law, in particular *Agostini* and *Zobrest*, and we therefore reject them.

1

Although some of our earlier cases, particularly *Ball*, did emphasize the distinction between direct and indirect aid, the purpose of this distinction was merely to prevent "subsidization" of religion. . . . Although the presence of private choice is easier to see when aid literally passes through the hands of individuals — which is why we have mentioned directness in the same breath with private choice — there is no reason why the Establishment Clause requires such a form. . . .

---

[6] [Court's footnote 7] Respondents also contend that Chapter 2 aid supplants, rather than supplements, the core educational function of parochial schools and therefore has the effect of furthering religion. Our case law does provide some indication that this distinction may be relevant to determining whether aid results in governmental indoctrination, but we have never delineated the distinction's contours or held that it is constitutionally required.

Of course, we have seen "special Establishment Clause dangers," *Rosenberger* [*v. University of Virginia*, 515 U.S. 819, 842 (1995)], when money is given to religious schools or entities directly rather than, as in *Witters* and *Mueller*, indirectly.

2

Respondents also contend that the Establishment Clause requires that aid to religious schools not be impermissibly religious in nature or be divertible to religious use. We agree with the first part of this argument but not the second. Respondents' "no divertibility" rule is inconsistent with our more recent case law and is unworkable. . . .

The issue is not divertibility of aid but rather whether the aid itself has an impermissible content. Where the aid would be suitable for use in a public school, it is also suitable for use in any private school. . . .

In *Agostini* itself, we approved the provision of public employees to teach secular remedial classes in private schools partly because we concluded that there was no reason to suspect that indoctrinating content would be part of such governmental aid. . . .

. . . In fact, the risk of improper attribution is *less* when the aid lacks content, for there is no risk (as there is with books), of the government inadvertently providing improper content. . . . Finally, *any* aid, with or without content, is "divertible" in the sense that it allows schools to "divert" resources. Yet we have " 'not accepted the recurrent argument that all aid is forbidden because aid to one aspect of an institution frees it to spend its other resources on religious ends.' [*Committee for Public Education and Religious Liberty, et al. v. Regan*, 444 U.S. 646, 658 (1980)]. . . . "

C

The dissent serves up a smorgasbord of 11 factors that . . . could be relevant to the constitutionality of a school-aid program. . . .

One of the dissent's factors deserves special mention: whether a school that receives aid (or whose students receive aid) is pervasively sectarian. . . .

There are numerous reasons to formally dispense with this factor. First, its relevance in our precedents is in sharp decline. . . . [W]e upheld aid programs to children who attended schools that were not only pervasively sectarian but also were primary and secondary. . . .

Second, the religious nature of a recipient should not matter to the constitutional analysis, so long as the recipient adequately furthers the government's secular purpose. If a program offers permissible aid to the religious (including the pervasively sectarian), the areligious, and the irreligious, it is a mystery which view of religion the government has established. . . . The pervasively sectarian recipient has not received any special favor, and it is most bizarre that the Court would, as the dissent seemingly does, reserve special hostility for those who take their religion seriously. . . .

Third, the inquiry into the recipient's religious views required by a focus on whether a school is pervasively sectarian is not only unnecessary but also offensive. It is well established, in numerous other contexts, that courts should refrain from trolling through a person's or institution's religious beliefs. . . .

Finally, hostility to aid to pervasively sectarian schools has a shameful pedigree that we do not hesitate to disavow. . . . Opposition to aid to "sectarian" schools acquired prominence in the 1870s with Congress's consideration (and near passage) of the Blaine Amendment, which would have amended the Constitution to bar any aid to sectarian institutions. Consideration of the amendment arose at a time of pervasive hostility to the Catholic Church and to Catholics in general, and it was an open secret that "sectarian" was code for "Catholic." *See generally* Green, *The Blaine Amendment Reconsidered*, 36 Am. J. Legal Hist. 38 (1992). . . .

. . . This doctrine, born of bigotry, should be buried now.

III

Applying the two relevant *Agostini* criteria, we see no basis for concluding that Jefferson Parish's Chapter 2 program "has the effect of advancing religion." *Agostini, supra,* at 234. Chapter 2 does not result in governmental indoctrination, because it determines eligibility for aid neutrally, allocates that aid based on the private choices of the parents of schoolchildren, and does not provide aid that has an impermissible content. Nor does Chapter 2 define its recipients by reference to religion.

Taking the second criterion first, it is clear that Chapter 2 aid "is allocated on the basis of neutral, secular criteria that neither favor nor disfavor religion, and is made available to both religious and secular beneficiaries on a nondiscriminatory basis." *Agostini, supra,* at 231. Aid is allocated based on enrollment. . . . Chapter 2 does, by statute, deviate from a pure per capita basis for allocating aid to LEA's, increasing the per-pupil allocation based on the number of children within an LEA who are from poor families, reside in poor areas, or reside in rural areas. . . .

Chapter 2 also satisfies the first *Agostini* criterion. The program makes a broad array of schools eligible for aid without regard to their religious affiliations or lack thereof. We therefore have no difficulty concluding that Chapter 2 is neutral with regard to religion. Chapter 2 aid also, like the aid in *Agostini, Zobrest,* and *Witters,* reaches participating schools only "as a consequence of private decisionmaking." *Agostini, supra,* at 222. . . .

. . . Nor, . . . is it of constitutional significance that the schools themselves, rather than the students, are the bailees of the Chapter 2 aid. The ultimate beneficiaries of Chapter 2 aid are the students who attend the schools that receive that aid. . . .

Finally, Chapter 2 satisfies the first *Agostini* criterion because it does not provide to religious schools aid that has an impermissible content. The statute explicitly bars anything of the sort, providing that all Chapter 2 aid for the benefit of children in private schools shall be "secular, neutral, and nonideological," § 7372(a)(1), and the record indicates that the Louisiana SEA and the Jefferson Parish LEA have faithfully enforced this requirement. . . .

There is evidence that equipment has been, or at least easily could be, diverted for use in religious classes. Justice O'Connor, however, finds the safeguards against diversion adequate to prevent and detect actual diversion. The safeguards on which she relies reduce to three: (1) signed assurances that Chapter 2 aid will be used only for secular, neutral, and nonideological purposes, (2) monitoring visits, and (3) the requirement that equipment be labeled as belonging to Chapter 2. As to the first, Justice O'Connor rightly places little reliance on it. As to the second, monitoring by SEA and LEA officials is highly unlikely to prevent or catch diversion. As to the third, compliance with the labeling requirement is haphazard and, even if the requirement were followed, we fail to see how a label prevents diversion. In addition, we agree with the dissent that there is evidence of actual diversion and that, were the safeguards anything other than anemic, there would almost certainly be more such evidence.[7] In

---

[7] [Court's footnote 17] Justice O'Connor dismisses as *de minimis* the evidence of actual diversion. That may be, but it is good to realize just what she considers *de minimis*. There is persuasive evidence that Chapter

any event, for reasons we discussed in Part II-B-2, the evidence of actual diversion and the weakness of the safeguards against actual diversion are not relevant to the constitutional inquiry. . . .

Respondents do, however, point to some religious books that the LEA improperly allowed to be loaned to several religious schools. . . . There were approximately 191 improper book requests over three years (the 1982–1983 through 1984–1985 school years); these requests came from fewer than half of the 40 private schools then participating; and the cost of the 191 books amounted to "less than one percent of the total allocation over all those years."

. . . We are unwilling to elevate scattered *de minimis* statutory violations, discovered and remedied by the relevant authorities themselves prior to any litigation, to such a level as to convert an otherwise unobjectionable parishwide program into a law that has the effect of advancing religion.

IV

In short, Chapter 2 satisfies both the first and second primary criteria of *Agostini*. It therefore does not have the effect of advancing religion. For the same reason, Chapter 2 also "cannot reasonably be viewed as an endorsement of religion," *Agostini, supra*, at 235. . . . [8]

JUSTICE O'CONNOR, with whom JUSTICE BREYER joins, concurring in the judgment.

. . . I believe that *Agostini* [*v. Felton*] . . . controls the constitutional inquiry. . . . To the extent our decisions in *Meek v. Pittenger* and *Wolman v. Walter* are inconsistent with the Court's judgment today, I agree that those decisions should be overruled. . . .

I

I write separately because, in my view, the plurality announces a rule of unprecedented breadth for the evaluation of Establishment Clause challenges to government school-aid programs. Reduced to its essentials, the plurality's rule states that government aid to religious schools does not have the effect of advancing religion so long as the aid is offered on a neutral basis and the aid is secular in content. The plurality also rejects the distinction between direct and indirect aid, and holds that the actual diversion of secular aid by a religious school to the advancement of its religious mission is permissible. Although the expansive scope of the plurality's rule is troubling, two specific aspects of the opinion compel me to write separately. First, the plurality's treatment of neutrality comes close to assigning that factor singular importance in the future adjudication of Establishment Clause challenges to government school-aid programs. Second, the plurality's approval of actual diversion of government aid to religious indoctrination is in tension with our precedents and, in any event, unnecessary to decide the instant case. . . .

I do not quarrel with the plurality's recognition that neutrality is an important reason for upholding government-aid programs against Establishment Clause challenges. . . . Nevertheless, we have never held that a government-aid program

---

2 audiovisual equipment was used in a Catholic school's theology department. . . . The diversion occurred over seven consecutive school years, and the use of the equipment in the theology department was massive in each of those years, outstripping in every year use in other departments such as science, math, and foreign language. In addition, the dissent has documented likely diversion of computers.

8 [Court's footnote 19] Indeed, as petitioners observe, to require exclusion of religious schools from such a program would raise serious questions under the Free Exercise Clause. . . .

passes constitutional muster *solely* because of the neutral criteria it employs as a basis for distributing aid. . . .

I also disagree with the plurality's conclusion that actual diversion of government aid to religious indoctrination is consistent with the Establishment Clause. . . .

. . . I do not believe that we should treat a per-capita-aid program the same as the true private-choice programs considered in *Witters* and *Zobrest*. First, when the government provides aid directly to the student beneficiary . . . [t]he fact that aid flows to the religious school and is used for the advancement of religion is . . . *wholly* dependent on the student's private decision. . . .

Second, . . . if the religious school uses the aid to inculcate religion in its students, it is reasonable to say that the government has communicated a message of endorsement. Because the religious indoctrination is supported by government assistance, the reasonable observer would naturally perceive the aid program as *government* support for the advancement of religion. . . .

Finally, the distinction between a per-capita-aid program and a true private-choice program is important when considering aid that consists of direct monetary subsidies. . . . If, as the plurality contends, a per-capita-aid program is identical in relevant constitutional respects to a true private-choice program, then there is no reason that, under the plurality's reasoning, the government should be precluded from providing direct money payments to religious organizations (including churches) based on the number of persons belonging to each organization. And, because actual diversion is permissible under the plurality's holding, the participating religious organizations (including churches) could use that aid to support religious indoctrination. . . .

II

. . . Respondents neither question the secular purpose of the Chapter 2 (Title II) program nor contend that it creates an excessive entanglement. . . . Accordingly, for purposes of deciding whether Chapter 2, as applied in Jefferson Parish, Louisiana, violates the Establishment Clause, we need ask only whether the program results in governmental indoctrination or defines its recipients by reference to religion.

Taking the second inquiry first, it is clear that Chapter 2 does not define aid recipients by reference to religion. . . . The statute . . . specifically mandates that all LEA expenditures on behalf of children enrolled in private schools "be equal (consistent with the number of children to be served) to expenditures for programs . . . for children enrolled in the public schools of the [LEA]." . . . As a result, it creates no financial incentive to undertake religious indoctrination.

Agostini next requires us to ask whether Chapter 2 "results in governmental indoctrination." 521 U.S. at 234. . . .

The Chapter 2 program at issue here bears the same hallmarks of the New York City Title I program that we found important in *Agostini*. First, as explained above, Chapter 2 aid is distributed on the basis of neutral, secular criteria. The aid is available to assist students regardless of whether they attend public or private nonprofit religious schools. Second, the statute requires participating SEA's and LEA's to use and allocate Chapter 2 funds only to supplement the funds otherwise available to a religious school. Chapter 2 funds must in no case be used to supplant funds from non-Federal sources. Third, no Chapter 2 funds ever reach the coffers of a religious school. . . . The LEA's purchase instructional and educational materials and then lend those materials to public and private schools. . . . Finally, the statute provides that all Chapter 2 materials and equipment must be "secular, neutral, and nonideological." That restriction is reinforced by a further statutory prohibition on "the making of any payment . . . for religious worship or instruction." Although respondents claim that Chapter 2 aid has been diverted to religious instruction, that evidence is *de minimis*. . . .

III

. . . [T]he theory does not provide a logical distinction between the lending of textbooks and the lending of instructional materials and equipment. An educator can use virtually any instructional tool, whether it has ascertainable content or not, to teach a religious message. In this respect, I agree with the plurality. . . .

IV

. . . To establish a First Amendment violation, plaintiffs must prove that the aid in question actually is, or has been, used for religious purposes. . . . [P]resumptions of religious indoctrination are normally inappropriate when evaluating neutral school-aid programs under the Establishment Clause. . . .

V

Respondents do not rest, however, on their divertibility argument alone. Rather, they also contend that the evidence respecting the actual administration of Chapter 2 in Jefferson Parish demonstrates that the program violated the Establishment Clause. . . .

. . . To find that actual diversion will flourish, one must presume bad faith on the part of the religious school officials who report to the [Jefferson Parish Public School System (JPPSS)] monitors regarding the use of Chapter 2 aid. I disagree with the plurality and Justice Souter on this point and believe that it is entirely proper to presume that these school officials will act in good faith. That presumption is especially appropriate in this case, since there is no proof that religious school officials have breached their schools' assurances or failed to tell government officials the truth. . . .

The evidence proffered by respondents, and relied on by the plurality and Justice Souter, concerning actual diversion of Chapter 2 aid in Jefferson Parish is *de minimis*. . . . At most, it proves the possibility that, out of the more than 40 nonpublic schools in Jefferson Parish participating in Chapter 2, aid may have been diverted in one school's second-grade class and another school's theology department. . . .

. . . Over three years, Jefferson Parish religious schools ordered approximately 191 religious library books through Chapter 2. . . . I agree with the plurality that, like the above evidence of actual diversion, the borrowing of the religious library books constitutes only *de minimis* evidence.

. . . .

. . . As in *Agostini*, the Chapter 2 aid is allocated on the basis of neutral, secular criteria; the aid must be supplementary and cannot supplant non-Federal funds; no Chapter 2 funds ever reach the coffers of religious schools; the aid must be secular; any evidence of actual diversion is *de minimis*; and the program includes adequate safeguards. Regardless of whether these factors are constitutional requirements, they are surely sufficient to find that the program at issue here does not have the impermissible effect of advancing religion. For the same reasons, "this carefully constrained program also cannot reasonably be viewed as an endorsement of religion." *Agostini*, 521 U.S. at 235. . . .

JUSTICE SOUTER, with whom JUSTICE STEVENS and JUSTICE GINSBURG join, dissenting.

. . . [T]he plurality opinion . . . espouses a new conception of neutrality as a practically sufficient test of constitutionality that would, if adopted by the Court, eliminate enquiry into a law's effects. . . .

II

A

. . . [N]eutrality is not alone sufficient to qualify the aid as constitutional. . . .

. . . [I]f we looked no further than evenhandedness, and failed to ask what activities the aid might support, or in fact did support, religious schools could be blessed with government funding as massive as expenditures made for the benefit of their public school counterparts, and religious missions would thrive on public money. . . .

At least three main lines of enquiry addressed particularly to school aid have emerged to complement evenhandedness neutrality. First, we have noted that two types of aid recipients heighten Establishment Clause concern: pervasively religious schools and primary and secondary religious schools. Second, we have identified two important characteristics of the method of distributing aid: directness or indirectness of distribution and distribution by genuinely independent choice. Third, we have found relevance in at least five characteristics of the aid itself: its religious content; its cash form; its divertibility or actually diversion to religious support; its supplantation of traditional items of religious school expense; and its substantiality.

1

Two types of school aid recipients have raised special concern. First, we have recognized the fact that the overriding religious mission of certain schools, those sometimes called "pervasively sectarian," is not confined to a discrete element of the curriculum.[9] . . . Based on record evidence and long experience, we have concluded that religious teaching in such schools is at the core of the instructors' individual and personal obligations, *cf.* Canon 803, § 2, Text & Commentary 568 ("It is necessary that the formation and education given in a Catholic school be based upon the principles of Catholic doctrine; teachers are to be outstanding for their correct doctrine and integrity of life"). . . . [10]

2

We have also evaluated the portent of support to an organization's religious mission that may be inherent in the method by which aid is granted. . . . [11]

---

[9] [Court's footnote 6] In fact, religious education in Roman Catholic schools is defined as part of required religious practice; aiding it is thus akin to aiding a church service. *See* 1983 Code of Canon Law, Canon 798, reprinted in The Code of Canon Law: A Text and Commentary 566 (1985) (hereinafter Text & Commentary) (directing parents to entrust children to Roman Catholic schools or otherwise provide for Roman Catholic education). . . .

[10] [Court's Footnote 7] Although the Court no longer assumes that public school teachers assigned to religious schools for limited purposes will teach religiously, *see Agostini v. Felton*, we have never abandoned the presumption that religious teachers will teach just that way. . . .

[11] [Court's footnote 8] . . . Until today, this Court has never permitted aid to go directly to schools on a school-wide basis. . . .

C

. . . Evenhandedness neutrality is one, nondispositive pointer toward an intent and (to a lesser degree) probable effect on the permissible side of the line between forbidden aid and general public welfare benefit. Other pointers are facts about the religious mission and education level of benefited schools and their pupils, the pathway by which a benefit travels from public treasury to educational effect, the form and content of the aid, its adaptability to religious ends, and its effects on school budgets. The object of all enquiries into such matters is the same whatever the particular circumstances: is the benefit intended to aid in providing the religious element of the education and is it likely to do so? . . .

III

A

. . . [A]t least three of its mistaken assumptions will show the degree to which the plurality's proposal would replace the principle of no aid with a formula for generous religious support.

First, the plurality treats an external observer's attribution of religious support to the government as the sole impermissible effect of a government aid scheme. . . .

Second, the plurality apparently assumes as a fact that equal amounts of aid to religious and nonreligious schools will have exclusively secular and equal effects, on both external perception and on incentives to attend different schools. . . .

Third, the plurality assumes that per capita distribution rules safeguard the same principles as independent, private choices. . . .

B

The plurality's conception of evenhandedness does not, however, control the case. . . . [E]ven the thin record before us reveals that actual diversion occurred.

. . . The videocassette players, overhead projectors, and other instructional aids were of the sort that we have found can easily be used by religious teachers for religious purposes. The same was true of the computers. . . . Although library books, like textbooks, have fixed content, religious teachers can assign secular library books for religious critique, and books for libraries may be religious. . . .

. . . Requests for specific items under Chapter 2 came not from secular officials, but from officials of the religious schools. . . .

. . . [T]he record indicates that nothing in the Jefferson Parish program stood in the way of giving the Chapter 2 property outright to the religious schools when it became older. . . . [12]

. . . [N]onpublic schools requested and the government purchased at least 191 religious books with taxpayer funds . . . such as *A Child's Book of Prayers*, and *The Illustrated Life of Jesus*. . . .

. . . [C]omputers lent with Chapter 2 funds were joined in a network with other non-Chapter 2 computers in some schools, and that religious officials and teachers were

---

[12] [Court's footnote 28] [U]nconstitutional supplantation [likely] occurred as well. The record demonstrates that Chapter 2 aid impermissibly relieved religious schools of some costs that they otherwise would have borne. . . .

allowed to develop their own unregulated software for use on this network. . . .
[F]ilm projectors and videotape machines purchased with public funds were [likely]
used in religious indoctrination over a period of at least seven years. . . .

IV

. . . The plurality is candid in pointing out the extent of actual diversion of Chapter
2 aid to religious use in the case before us . . . and equally candid in saying it does not
matter. . . .

ZELMAN v. SIMMONS-HARRIS
536 U.S. 639, 122 S. Ct. 2460, 153 L. Ed. 2d 604 (2002)

CHIEF JUSTICE REHNQUIST delivered the opinion of the Court.

The State of Ohio has established a pilot program designed to provide educational
choices to families with children who reside in the Cleveland City School District. The
question presented is whether this program offends the Establishment Clause of the
United States Constitution. We hold that it does not.

There are more than 75,000 children enrolled in the Cleveland City School District.
The majority of these children are from low-income and minority families. Few of these
families enjoy the means to send their children to any school other than an inner-city
public school. For more than a generation, however, Cleveland's public schools have
been among the worst performing public schools in the Nation. In 1995, a Federal
District Court declared a "crisis of magnitude" and placed the entire Cleveland school
district under state control. *See Reed v. Rhodes*, 1 F. Supp. 2d 705 (N.D. Ohio 1995).
Shortly thereafter, the state auditor found that Cleveland's public schools were in the
midst of a "crisis that is perhaps unprecedented in the history of American education."
Cleveland City School District Performance Audit 2-1 (Mar. 1996). The district had
failed to meet any of the 18 state standards for minimal acceptable performance. . . .
More than two-thirds of high school students either dropped or failed out before
graduation. Of those students who managed to reach their senior year, one of every
four still failed to graduate. Of those students who did graduate, few could read, write,
or compute at levels comparable to their counterparts in other cities.

It is against this backdrop that Ohio enacted, among other initiatives, its Pilot
Project Scholarship Program, Ohio Rev. Code Ann. §§ 3313.974-3313.979 (Anderson
1999 and Supp. 2000) (program). The program provides financial assistance to families
in any Ohio school district that is or has been "under federal court order requiring
supervision and operational management of the district by the state superintendent."
Cleveland is the only Ohio school district to fall within that category.

The program provides two basic kinds of assistance to parents of children in a
covered district. First, the program provides tuition aid for students in kindergarten
through third grade, expanding each year through eighth grade, to attend a
participating public or private school of their parent's choosing. Second, the program
provides tutorial aid for students who choose to remain enrolled in public school.

The tuition aid portion of the program is designed to provide educational choices to
parents who reside in a covered district. Any private school, whether religious or
nonreligious, may participate in the program and accept program students so long as
the school is located within the boundaries of a covered district and meets statewide
educational standards. Participating private schools must agree not to discriminate on
the basis of race, religion, or ethnic background, or to "advocate or foster unlawful
behavior or teach hatred of any person or group on the basis of race, ethnicity, national
origin, or religion." Any public school located in a school district adjacent to the covered

district may also participate in the program. Adjacent public schools are eligible to receive a $2,250 tuition grant for each program student accepted in addition to the full amount of per-pupil state funding attributable to each additional student. All participating schools, whether public or private, are required to accept students in accordance with rules and procedures established by the state superintendent.

Tuition aid is distributed to parents according to financial need. Families with incomes below 200% of the poverty line are given priority and are eligible to receive 90% of private school tuition up to $2,250. For these lowest-income families, participating private schools may not charge a parental co-payment greater than $250. For all other families, the program pays 75% of tuition costs, up to $1,875, with no co-payment cap. These families receive tuition aid only if the number of available scholarships exceeds the number of low-income children who choose to participate. . . . If parents choose a private school, checks are made payable to the parents who then endorse the checks over to the chosen school.

The tutorial aid portion of the program provides tutorial assistance through grants to any student in a covered district who chooses to remain in public school. Parents arrange for registered tutors to provide assistance to their children and then submit bills for those services to the State for payment. Students from low-income families receive 90% of the amount charged for such assistance up to $360. All other students receive 75% of that amount. The number of tutorial assistance grants offered to students in a covered district must equal the number of tuition aid scholarships provided to students enrolled at participating private or adjacent public schools.

The program has been in operation within the Cleveland City School District since the 1996-1997 school year. In the 1999-2000 school year, 56 private schools participated in the program, 46 (or 82%) of which had a religious affiliation. None of the public schools in districts adjacent to Cleveland have elected to participate. More than 3,700 students participated in the scholarship program, most of whom (96%) enrolled in religiously affiliated schools. Sixty percent of these students were from families at or below the poverty line. In the 1998-1999 school year, approximately 1,400 Cleveland public school students received tutorial aid. This number was expected to double during the 1999-2000 school year.

The program is part of a broader undertaking by the State to enhance the educational options of Cleveland's schoolchildren in response to the 1995 takeover. That undertaking includes programs governing community and magnet schools. Community schools are funded under state law but are run by their own school boards, not by local school districts. These schools enjoy academic independence to hire their own teachers and to determine their own curriculum. They can have no religious affiliation and are required to accept students by lottery. During the 1999-2000 school year, there were 10 start-up community schools in the Cleveland City School District with more than 1,900 students enrolled. For each child enrolled in a community school, the school receives state funding of $4,518, twice the funding a participating program school may receive.

Magnet schools are public schools operated by a local school board that emphasize a particular subject area, teaching method, or service to students. For each student enrolled in a magnet school, the school district receives $7,746, including state funding of $4,167, the same amount received per student enrolled at a traditional public school. As of 1999, parents in Cleveland were able to choose from among 23 magnet schools, which together enrolled more than 13,000 students in kindergarten through eighth grade. . . .

The Establishment Clause of the First Amendment, applied to the States through the Fourteenth Amendment, prevents a State from enacting laws that have the "purpose" or "effect" of advancing or inhibiting religion. *Agostini v. Felton*, 521 U.S.

203 (1997). . . . There is no dispute that the program challenged here was enacted for the valid secular purpose of providing educational assistance to poor children in a demonstrably failing public school system. Thus, the question presented is whether the Ohio program nonetheless has the forbidden "effect" of advancing or inhibiting religion.

To answer that question, our decisions have drawn a consistent distinction between government programs that provide aid directly to religious schools and programs of true private choice, in which government aid reaches religious schools only as a result of the genuine and independent choices of private individuals. . . .

. . . *Mueller*, *Witters*, and *Zobrest* . . . make clear that where a government aid program is neutral with respect to religion, and provides assistance directly to a broad class of citizens who, in turn, direct government aid to religious schools wholly as a result of their own genuine and independent private choice, the program is not readily subject to challenge under the Establishment Clause. A program that shares these features permits government aid to reach religious institutions only by way of the deliberate choices of numerous individual recipients. The incidental advancement of a religious mission, or the perceived endorsement of a religious message, is reasonably attributable to the individual recipient, not to the government, whose role ends with the disbursement of benefits. . . .

We believe that the program challenged here is a program of true private choice, consistent with *Mueller*, *Witters*, and *Zobrest*, and thus constitutional. As was true in those cases, the Ohio program is neutral in all respects toward religion. It is part of a general and multifaceted undertaking by the State of Ohio to provide educational opportunities to the children of a failed school district. It confers educational assistance directly to a broad class of individuals defined without reference to religion. . . . The program permits the participation of *all* schools within the district, religious or nonreligious. Adjacent public schools also may participate and have a financial incentive to do so. . . .

There are no "financial incentives" that "skew" the program toward religious schools. *Witters*, *supra*, at 487-488. . . . The program here in fact creates financial *dis*incentives for religious schools, with private schools receiving only half the government assistance given to community schools and one-third the assistance given to magnet schools. Adjacent public schools, should any choose to accept program students, are also eligible to receive two to three times the state funding of a private religious school. Families too have a financial disincentive to choose a private religious school over other schools. Parents that choose to participate in the scholarship program and then to enroll their children in a private school (religious or nonreligious) must copay a portion of the school's tuition. Families that choose a community school, magnet school, or traditional public school pay nothing. Although such features of the program are not necessary to its constitutionality, they clearly dispel the claim that the program "creates . . . financial incentives for parents to choose a sectarian school." *Zobrest*, 509 U.S. at 10.

Respondents suggest that even without a financial incentive for parents to choose a religious school, the program creates a "public perception that the State is endorsing religious practices and beliefs." But we have repeatedly recognized that no reasonable observer would think a neutral program of private choice, where state aid reaches religious schools solely as a result of the numerous independent decisions of private individuals, carries with it the *imprimatur* of government endorsement. . . . Any objective observer familiar with the full history and context of the Ohio program would reasonably view it as one aspect of a broader undertaking to assist poor children in failed schools, not as an endorsement of religious schooling in general. . . .

Justice Souter speculates that because more private religious schools currently participate in the program, the program itself must somehow discourage the participation of private nonreligious schools.[13] But Cleveland's preponderance of religiously affiliated private schools certainly did not arise as a result of the program; it is a phenomenon common to many American cities. . . . It is true that 82% of Cleveland's participating private schools are religious schools, but it is also true that 81% of private schools in Ohio are religious schools. . . .

Respondents and Justice Souter claim that even if we do not focus on the number of participating schools that are religious schools, we should attach constitutional significance to the fact that 96% of scholarship recipients have enrolled in religious schools. . . . We need not consider this argument in detail, since it was flatly rejected in *Mueller*, where we found it irrelevant that 96% of parents taking deductions for tuition expenses paid tuition at religious schools. Indeed, we have recently found it irrelevant even to the constitutionality of a direct aid program that a vast majority of program benefits went to religious schools. *See Agostini.* . . . The constitutionality of a neutral educational aid program simply does not turn on whether and why, in a particular area, at a particular time, most private schools are run by religious organizations, or most recipients choose to use the aid at a religious school. . . .

This point is aptly illustrated here. The 96% figure upon which respondents and Justice Souter rely discounts entirely (1) the more than 1,900 Cleveland children enrolled in alternative community schools, (2) the more than 13,000 children enrolled in alternative magnet schools, and (3) the more than 1,400 children enrolled in traditional public schools with tutorial assistance. Including some or all of these children in the denominator of children enrolled in nontraditional schools during the 1999-2000 school year drops the percentage enrolled in religious schools from 96% to under 20%. *See also* J. Greene, *The Racial, Economic, and Religious Context of Parental Choice in Cleveland 11*, Table 4 (Oct. 8, 1999), App. 217a (reporting that only 16.5% of nontraditional schoolchildren in Cleveland choose religious schools). . . .

Respondents finally claim that we should look to *Committee for Public Ed. & Religious Liberty v. Nyquist*, 413 U.S. 756 (1973), to decide these cases. We disagree for two reasons. First, . . . *Nyquist* involved a New York program that gave a package of benefits exclusively to private schools and the parents of private school enrollees. . . .

Second, . . . we expressly reserved judgment with respect to "a case involving some form of public assistance (e.g., scholarships) made available generally without regard to the sectarian-nonsectarian, or public-nonpublic nature of the institution benefitted." . . . To the extent the scope of *Nyquist* has remained an open question in light of these later decisions, we now hold that *Nyquist* does not govern neutral educational assistance programs that, like the program here, offer aid directly to a broad class of individual recipients defined without regard to religion.[14]

In sum, the Ohio program is entirely neutral with respect to religion. It provides benefits directly to a wide spectrum of individuals, defined only by financial need and residence in a particular school district. It permits such individuals to exercise genuine choice among options public and private, secular and religious. . . .

---

[13] [Court's footnote 4] . . . [T]he actual operation of the program refutes Justice Souter's argument that few but religious schools can afford to participate: Ten secular private schools operated within the Cleveland City School District when the program was adopted. . . . And while no religious schools have been created in response to the program, several *nonreligious* schools have been created. . . .

[14] [Court's footnote 7] Justice Breyer would raise the invisible specters of "divisiveness" and "religious strife" to find the program unconstitutional. . . . We quite rightly have rejected the claim that some speculative potential for divisiveness bears on the constitutionality of educational aid programs. . . .

JUSTICE O'CONNOR, concurring. . . .

III

. . . Justice Souter rejects the Court's notion of neutrality, proposing that the neutrality of a program should be gauged not by the opportunities it presents but rather by its effects. . . . But Justice Souter's notion of neutrality is inconsistent with that in our case law. As we put it in *Agostini*, government aid must be "made available to both religious and secular beneficiaries on a nondiscriminatory basis." 521 U.S. at 231 . . . .

To support his hunch about the effect of the cap on tuition under the voucher program, Justice Souter cites national data to suggest that, on average, Catholic schools have a cost advantage over other types of schools. Even if national statistics were relevant for evaluating the Cleveland program, Justice Souter ignores evidence which suggests that, at a national level, nonreligious private schools may target a market for different, if not higher, quality of education. . . .

JUSTICE THOMAS, concurring.

Frederick Douglass once said that "education . . . means emancipation. It means light and liberty. . . . Despite this Court's observation nearly 50 years ago in *Brown v. Board of Education*, that "it is doubtful that any child may reasonably be expected to succeed in life if he is denied the opportunity of an education," 347 U.S. 483, 493 (1954), urban children have been forced into a system that continually fails them. . . . Besieged by escalating financial problems and declining academic achievement, the Cleveland City School District was in the midst of an academic emergency when Ohio enacted its scholarship program.

I

. . . The Establishment Clause originally protected States, and by extension their citizens, from the imposition of an established religion by the Federal Government. Whether and how this Clause should constrain state action under the Fourteenth Amendment is a more difficult question.

The Fourteenth Amendment fundamentally restructured the relationship between individuals and the States. . . .

Consequently, in the context of the Establishment Clause, it may well be that state action should be evaluated on different terms than similar action by the Federal Government. "States, while bound to observe strict neutrality, should be freer to experiment with involvement [in religion] — on a neutral basis — than the Federal Government." *Walz v. Tax Comm'n of City of New York*, 397 U.S. 664, 699 (1970) (Harlan, J., concurring). Thus, while the Federal Government may "make no law respecting an establishment of religion," the States may pass laws that include or touch on religious matters so long as these laws do not impede free exercise rights or any other individual religious liberty interest.

II

. . . [T]he students at Cleveland's Catholic schools score significantly higher on Ohio proficiency tests than students at Cleveland public schools. Of Cleveland eighth graders taking the 1999 Ohio proficiency test, 95 percent in Catholic schools passed the reading test, whereas only 57 percent in public schools passed. And 75 percent of Catholic school students passed the math proficiency test, compared to only 22 percent of public school students. But the success of religious and private schools is in the end beside the point, because the State has a constitutional right to experiment with a variety of different programs to promote educational opportunity. . . .

. . . [T]he promise of public school education has failed poor inner-city blacks. . . . [M]any blacks and other minorities now support school choice programs because they provide the greatest educational opportunities for their children in struggling communities. . . .

While the romanticized ideal of universal public education resonates with the cognoscenti who oppose vouchers, poor urban families just want the best education for their children, who will certainly need it to function in our high-tech and advanced society. . . . For instance, a black high school dropout earns just over $13,500, but with a high school degree the average income is almost $21,000. Blacks with a bachelor's degree have an average annual income of about $37,500, and $75,500 with a professional degree. . . . [15] The failure to provide education to poor urban children perpetuates a vicious cycle of poverty, dependence, criminality, and alienation that continues for the remainder of their lives. If society cannot end racial discrimination, at least it can arm minorities with the education to defend themselves from some of discrimination's effects. . . .

JUSTICE STEVENS, dissenting.

. . . [T]he severe educational crisis that confronted the Cleveland City School District when Ohio enacted its voucher program is not a matter that should affect our appraisal of its constitutionality. . . .

Second, the wide range of choices that have been made available to students *within the public school system* has no bearing on the question whether the State may pay the tuition for students who wish . . . to attend . . . a sectarian education. . . .

Third, the voluntary character of the private choice to prefer a parochial education over an education in the public school system seems to me quite irrelevant to the question whether the government's choice to pay for religious indoctrination is constitutionally permissible. . . .

. . . [T]he Court's decision is profoundly misguided. Admittedly, in reaching that conclusion I have been influenced by my understanding of the impact of religious strife on the decisions of our forbears to migrate to this continent, and on the decisions of neighbors in the Balkans, Northern Ireland, and the Middle East to mistrust one another. Whenever we remove a brick from the wall that was designed to separate religion and government, we increase the risk of religious strife and weaken the foundation of our democracy. . . .

JUSTICE SOUTER, with whom JUSTICE STEVENS, JUSTICE GINSBURG, and JUSTICE BREYER join, dissenting. . . .

Today . . . the majority holds that the Establishment Clause is not offended by Ohio's Pilot Project Scholarship Program, under which students may be eligible to receive as much as $2,250 in the form of tuition vouchers transferable to religious schools. . . . The money will thus pay for eligible students' instruction not only in secular subjects but in religion as well, in schools that can fairly be characterized as founded to teach religious doctrine and to imbue teaching in all subjects with a religious dimension. . . .

---

[15] [Court's footnote 8] In 1997, approximately 68 percent of prisoners in state correctional institutions did not have a high school degree.

I

The majority's statements of Establishment Clause doctrine cannot be appreciated without some historical perspective on the Court's announced limitations on government aid to religious education, and its repeated repudiation of limits previously set. . . .

Viewed with the necessary generality, the cases can be categorized in three groups. In the period from 1947 to 1968, the basic principle of no aid to religion through school benefits was unquestioned. Thereafter for some 15 years, the Court termed its efforts as attempts to draw a line against aid that would be divertible to support the religious, as distinct from the secular, activity of an institutional beneficiary. Then, starting in 1983, concern with divertibility was gradually lost in favor of approving aid in amounts unlikely to afford substantial benefits to religious schools, when offered evenhandedly without regard to a recipient's religious character, and when channeled to a religious institution only by the genuinely free choice of some private individual. Now, the three stages are succeeded by a fourth, in which the substantial character of government aid is held to have no constitutional significance, and the espoused criteria of neutrality in offering aid, and private choice in directing it, are shown to be nothing but examples of verbal formalism. . . .

C

Like all criteria requiring judicial assessment of risk, divertibility is an invitation to argument, but the object of the arguments provoked has always been a realistic assessment of facts aimed at respecting the principle of no aid. . . . *Mueller v. Allen,* 463 U.S. 388 (1983), however, . . . started down the road from realism to formalism. . . .

. . . [T]oday . . . substantiality of aid has clearly been rejected as irrelevant by a majority of this Court, just as it has not been until today that a majority, not a plurality, has held purely formal criteria to suffice for scrutinizing aid that ends up in the coffers of religious schools. . . .

II

Although it has taken half a century since *Everson* to reach the majority's twin standards of neutrality and free choice, the facts show that, in the majority's hands, even these criteria cannot convincingly legitimize the Ohio scheme.

A

. . . In order to apply the neutrality test, . . . [t]he majority looks not to the provisions for tuition vouchers, but to every provision for educational opportunity. . . .

B

The majority addresses the issue of choice the same way it addresses neutrality, by asking whether recipients or potential recipients of voucher aid have a choice of public schools among secular alternatives to religious schools. . . . The majority now has transformed this question about private choice in channeling aid into a question about selecting from examples of state spending (on education) including direct spending on magnet and community public schools that goes through no private hands and could never reach a religious school under any circumstance. . . .

. . . If "choice" is present whenever there is any educational alternative to the religious school to which vouchers can be endorsed, then there will always be a choice and the voucher can always be constitutional. . . .

56 private schools in the district participating in the voucher program (only 53 of which accepted voucher students in 1999-2000), 46 of them are religious; 96.6% of all voucher recipients go to religious schools, only 3.4% to nonreligious ones. . . .

. . . [E]ven if all existing nonreligious private schools in Cleveland were willing to accept large numbers of voucher students, only a few more than the 129 currently enrolled in such schools would be able to attend, as the total enrollment at all nonreligious private schools in Cleveland for kindergarten through eighth grade is only 510 children, and there is no indication that these schools have many open seats. Second, the $2,500 cap that the program places on tuition for participating low-income pupils has the effect of curtailing the participation of nonreligious schools: "nonreligious schools with higher tuition (about $4,000) stated that they could afford to accommodate just a few voucher students." By comparison, the average tuition at participating Catholic schools in Cleveland in 1999-2000 was $1,592, almost $1,000 below the cap.

Of course, the obvious fix would be to increase the value of vouchers so that existing nonreligious private and non-Catholic religious schools would be able to enroll more voucher students, and to provide incentives for educators to create new such schools given that few presently exist. . . . And to get to that hypothetical point would require that such massive financial support be made available to religion as to disserve every objective of the Establishment Clause even more than the present scheme does.

And contrary to the majority's assertion, public schools in adjacent districts hardly have a financial incentive to participate in the Ohio voucher program, and none has.[16]

III

A

. . . The scale of the aid to religious schools approved today is unprecedented. . . .

B

. . . [E]very objective underlying the prohibition of religious establishment is betrayed by this scheme, . . . the first being respect for freedom of conscience. Jefferson described it as the idea that no one "shall be compelled to . . . support any religious worship, place, or ministry whatsoever," A Bill for Establishing Religious Freedom, in 5 The Founders' Constitution 84 (P. Kurland & R. Lerner eds. 1987), even a "teacher of his own religious persuasion," id. . . .

As for the second objective, to save religion from its own corruption. . . .

. . . [A] condition of receiving government money under the program is that participating religious schools may not "discriminate on the basis of . . . religion," Ohio Rev. Code Ann. § 3313.976(A)(4) (West Supp. 2002), which means the school may not give admission preferences to children who are members of the patron faith;

---

[16] [Court's footnote 17] As the Court points out, an out-of-district public school that participates will receive a $2,250 voucher for each Cleveland student on top of its normal state funding. The basic state funding, though, is a drop in the bucket as compared to the cost of educating that student, as much of the cost (at least in relatively affluent areas with presumptively better academic standards) is paid by local income and property taxes. . . .

children of a parish are generally consigned to the same admission lotteries as non-believers. . . .

. . . [I]s there reason to wonder when dependence will become great enough to give the State of Ohio an effective veto over basic decisions on the content of curriculums? A day will come when religious schools will learn what political leverage can do, just as Ohio's politicians are now getting a lesson in the leverage exercised by religion.

Increased voucher spending is not, however, the sole portent of growing regulation of religious practice in the school, for state mandates to moderate religious teaching may well be the most obvious response to the third concern behind the ban on establishment, its inextricable link with social conflict. As appropriations for religious subsidy rise, competition for the money will tap sectarian religion's capacity for discord. . . .

. . . [E]very major religion currently espouses social positions that provoke intense opposition. Not all taxpaying Protestant citizens, for example, will be content to underwrite the teaching of the Roman Catholic Church condemning the death penalty. Nor will all of America's Muslims acquiesce in paying for the endorsement of the religious Zionism taught in many religious Jewish schools, which combines "a nationalistic sentiment" in support of Israel with a "deeply religious" element. Nor will every secular taxpayer be content to support Muslim views on differential treatment of the sexes, or, for that matter, to fund the espousal of a wife's obligation of obedience to her husband, presumably taught in any schools adopting the articles of faith of the Southern Baptist Convention. . . .

JUSTICE BREYER, with whom JUSTICE STEVENS and JUSTICE SOUTER join, dissenting.

I write separately to emphasize the risk that publicly financed voucher programs pose in terms of religiously based social conflict. I do so because I believe that the Establishment Clause concern for protecting the Nation's social fabric from religious conflict poses an overriding obstacle to the implementation of this well-intentioned school voucher program. . . .

I

"The history of governmentally established religion, both in England and in this country, showed that whenever government had allied itself with one particular form of religion, the inevitable result had been that it had incurred the hatred, disrespect and even contempt of those who held contrary beliefs." [*Engel v. Vitale*, 370 U.S. 421 (1962)]. . . .

When it decided . . . 20th century Establishment Clause cases, the Court did not deny that an earlier American society might have found a less clear-cut church/state separation compatible with social tranquility. Indeed, historians point out that during the early years of the Republic, American schools — including the first public schools — were Protestant in character. Their students recited Protestant prayers, read the King James version of the Bible, and learned Protestant religious ideals. . . .

The 20th century Court was fully aware, however, that immigration and growth had changed American society dramatically since its early years. . . .

. . . Catholics sought equal government support for the education of their children in the form of aid for private Catholic schools. But the "Protestant position" on this matter, scholars report, "was that public schools must be 'nonsectarian' (which was usually understood to allow Bible reading and other Protestant observances) and public money must not support 'sectarian' schools (which in practical terms meant Catholic)." [John C. Jeffries, Jr. & James E. Ryan, *A Political History of the Establishment Clause*, 100 MICH. L. REV. 279, 301 (2001)] . . . .

The upshot is the development of constitutional doctrine that reads the Establishment Clause as avoiding religious strife, not by providing every religion with an equal opportunity (say, to secure state funding or to pray in the public schools), but by drawing fairly clear lines of separation between church and state — at least where the heartland of religious belief, such as primary religious education, is at issue.

II

The principle underlying these cases — avoiding religiously based social conflict — remains of great concern. As religiously diverse as America had become when the Court decided its major 20th century Establishment Clause cases, we are exponentially more diverse today. . . .

. . . Why will different religions not become concerned about, and seek to influence, the criteria used to channel this money to religious schools? . . .

III

. . . School voucher programs differ . . . in both *kind* and *degree* from aid programs upheld in the past. They differ in kind because they direct financing to a core function of the church: the teaching of religious truths to young children. . . .

Vouchers also differ in *degree*. The aid programs recently upheld by the Court involved limited amounts of aid to religion. But the majority's analysis here appears to permit a considerable shift of taxpayer dollars from public secular schools to private religious schools. . . .

IV

. . . Parental choice cannot help the taxpayer who does not want to finance the religious education of children. It will not always help the parent who may see little real choice between inadequate nonsectarian public education and adequate education at a school whose religious teachings are contrary to his own. . . .

[2] Governmental Funds to Religious Institutions in Contexts Other Than Parochial Education

BOWEN v. KENDRICK, 487 U.S. 589 (1988). *Bowen* upheld the Adolescent Family Life Act (AFLA or Act), which provides "grants to public or nonprofit private organizations" to care for pregnant adolescents and to prevent premarital sexual relations among adolescents. The Supreme Court rejected the facial challenge and remanded the as-applied challenge on specific grants for further proceedings in the district court.

Writing for the majority, Chief Justice Rehnquist analyzed the facial challenge under the three-part test in *Lemon v. Kurtzman*.

As to the first factor, "the face of the statute clearly indicated that the AFLA was motivated primarily, if not entirely, by a legitimate secular purpose-the elimination or reduction of social and economic problems caused by teenage sexuality, pregnancy, and parenthood."

As to the second *Lemon* factor, the Court stated that "there are two ways in which the statute, considered 'on its face,' might be said to have the impermissible primary effect of advancing religion. First, it can be argued that the AFLA advances religion by expressly recognizing that 'religious organizations have a role to play' in addressing the problems associated with teenage sexuality." Rejecting this argument, the Chief Justice stated that the AFLA "reflects at most Congress' considered judgment that religious organizations can help solve the problems to which the provisions of the AFLA are addressed. Nothing in our previous cases prevents Congress . . . from recognizing the important part that religion or religious organizations may play in resolving certain secular problems." Whatever effect the statute has of advancing religion, it "is at most 'incidental and remote.'" Indeed, the statute's inclusion of charitable and other private organizations reflects its neutrality between religion and nonreligion.

Second, the AFLA might have the primary effect of advancing religion by allowing religious institutions to receive federal funds.

Even when a statute is neutral on its face, government aid can still have the primary effect of advancing religion if government aid flows "to pervasively sectarian institutions." However, "the contention that there is a substantial risk of such direct aid is undercut by the AFLA's facially neutral grant requirements, the wide spectrum of public and private organizations which are capable of meeting the AFLA's requirements, and the fact that, of the eligible religious institutions, many will not deserve the label of 'pervasively sectarian.'"

The Court also found unpersuasive the District Court's conclusion "that the AFLA is invalid because it authorizes 'teaching' by religious grant recipients on 'matters [that] are fundamental elements of religious doctrine,' such as the harm of premarital sex and the reasons for choosing adoption over abortion." The Court held that "the possibility or even the likelihood that some of the religious institutions who receive AFLA funding will agree with the message that Congress intended to deliver to adolescents through the AFLA is insufficient to warrant a finding that the statute on its face has the primary effect of advancing religion."

Chief Justice Rehnquist also disagreed that the AFLA would advance religion by creating a "'crucial symbolic link' between government and religion." Noting that this argument would not support a facial challenge, Chief Justice Rehnquist stated that it would also "jeopardize government aid to religiously affiliated hospitals."

Turning to the third prong of the *Lemon* test, the Court also found that the AFLA would not lead to "excessive government entanglement with religion." For the Chief Justice, "this case presents us with yet another 'Catch-22' argument: the very supervision of the aid to assure that it does not further religion renders the statute invalid." This and other problems have prompted considerable criticism of the entanglement prong of the *Lemon* test over the years.

In this case "there is no reason to assume that the religious organizations which may receive grants are 'pervasively sectarian' in the same sense as the Court has held parochial schools to be. Unquestionably, the Secretary will review the programs set up and run by the AFLA grantees, and undoubtedly this will involve a review of, for example, the educational materials that a grantee proposes to use. The Secretary may also wish to have government employees visit the clinics or offices where AFLA programs are being carried out. But in our view, this type of grant monitoring does not amount to 'excessive entanglement,' at least in the context of a statute authorizing grants to religiously affiliated organizations that are not necessarily 'pervasively sectarian.'"

"We also disagree with the District Court's conclusion that the AFLA is invalid because it is likely to create political division along religious lines."

The Court reversed and remanded the as-applied challenge. On remand, plaintiffs must show that AFLA grants are going to "pervasively sectarian" institutions analogous to parochial schools. The grant recipient cannot simply be "affiliated with a religious institution" or "religiously inspired." On remand, the District Court should also consider whether, in specific instances, AFLA aid has funded "specifically religious activities," including whether grantees have used "materials that have an explicitly religious content or are designed to inculcate the views of a particular religious faith."

Justice O'Connor wrote a concurring opinion in which she sought to emphasize two points. "First, *any* use of public funds to promote religious doctrines violates the Establishment Clause. Second, *extensive* violations — if they can be proved in this case — will be highly relevant in shaping an appropriate remedy that ends such abuse. For that reason, appellee may yet prevail on remand."

Justice Kennedy, joined by Justice Scalia, also wrote a concurring opinion. For Justice Kennedy, when a program that is facially constitutional distributes benefits "in a neutral fashion to religious and nonreligious" organizations, it is not unconstitutional as applied solely by reason of the religious character of the specific recipient. The question in an as-applied challenge is not whether the entity is of a religious character, but how it spends its grant.

Justice Blackmun dissented, joined by Justices Brennan, Marshall and Stevens. Justice Blackmun maintained that the AFLA's "primary effect is the advancement of religion."[17]

The undisputed factual record reveals "the systematically unconstitutional operation of a statute" as revealed by "thousands of pages of depositions, affidavits, and documentary evidence." The Court has recognized that the Constitution does not prohibit the government from supporting secular social-welfare services solely because they are provided by a religiously affiliated organization. "The risk of advancing religion at public expense, and of creating an appearance that the government is endorsing the medium and the message, is much greater when the religious organization is directly engaged in pedagogy, with the express intent of shaping belief and changing behavior, than where it is neutrally dispensing medication, food, or shelter."

Moreover, nothing in the statute prevented AFLA funds from going to pervasively sectarian institutions. Indeed, "the District Court expressly found that funds have gone to pervasively sectarian institutions" — including for teaching religion.

Preventing any advancement of religion will require an "unprecedented degree of entanglement between Church and State."[18]

NOTES

(1) *Commentary.* For additional discussion, see Richard S. Myers, *The Supreme Court and the Privatization of Religion*, 41 Cath. U. L. Rev. 19, 25 (1991) ("Religious institutions, if they choose to be, ought to be full participants in public programs such as education or child care. Allowing these institutions to preserve their religious identities

---

[17] Justice Blackmun opined that Congress had not intended to pay for the following instruction:

"You want to know the church teachings on sexuality. . . . You are the church. You people sitting here are the body of Christ. The teachings of you and the things you value are, in fact, the values of the Catholic Church."

Or the curricula that taught:

"The Church has always taught that the marriage act, or intercourse, seals the union of husband and wife, (and is a representation of their union on all levels). Christ commits Himself to us when we come to ask for the sacrament of marriage. We ask Him to be active in our life. God is love. We ask Him to share His love in ours, and God procreates with us. He enters into our physical union with Him, and we begin new life."

[18] Justice Blackmun also noted the Court's rejection of Justice Kennedy's suggestion that aid can flow to a pervasively sectarian institution.

is particularly important as the government continues to increase its role in areas that traditionally have been the province of mediating institutions."); David E. Steinberg, *Religious Exemptions as Affirmative Action*, 40 EMORY L.J. 77, 138 (1991) ("The affirmative action approach suggested in this Article attempts to resolve this dilemma by advocating the use of religious exemptions only to accommodate minority religions. Popular religions, on the other hand, could reform burdensome secular rules by resorting to the democratic process.").

(2) *Religion in Public Life.* "The privatization theory — that religion is a private affair that should not play a role in public life — has had considerable support on the Court. Justices Brennan, Marshall, Blackmun, and Stevens have consistently supported this theory. Thus, these Justices have typically denied the constitutionality of both aid to religious institutions and the constitutionality of legislation that embodies religiously-influenced moral principles. These Justices are not necessarily hostile to religion and do not invariably vote against either religious entities or individuals. Instead, these Justices are hostile to religion when it takes a public role. As the free-exercise cases illustrate, when religion is used to 'dissent' from some standard of public order, these Justices are quite supportive. Despite several enthusiastic supporters on the Court, the privatization theory is losing influence among the Justices. The conservatives on the Court — Chief Justice Rehnquist and Justices Kennedy, O'Connor, Scalia, and White — reject the privatization theory, as revealed by their positions on the Establishment Clause and substantive due process. These Justices accept the constitutionality of both the inclusion of religious institutions in publicly funded programs and legislation that embodies religiously-influenced moral principles." Richard S. Myers, *The Supreme Court and the Privatization of Religion*, 41 CATH. U. L. REV. 19, 79 (1991).

TEXAS MONTHLY, INC. v. BULLOCK, 489 U.S. 1 (1989). In *Texas Monthly*, the Court invalidated a Texas law exempting publishers of religious magazines and books from paying a state sales and use tax. Justice Brennan delivered an opinion in which Justices Marshall and Stevens joined. Just as "government may not be overtly hostile to religion," government "may not place its prestige, coercive authority, or resources behind a single religious faith or behind religious belief in general."

Justice Brennan found that Texas' sales tax exemption "lacks sufficient breadth to pass scrutiny under the Establishment Clause." Every tax exemption constitutes a subsidy that affects nonqualifying taxpayers, forcing them to become "indirect and vicarious 'donors.'" Insofar as that subsidy is conferred upon a wide array of nonsectarian groups as well as religious organizations in pursuit of some legitimate secular end, the fact that religious groups benefit incidentally does not deprive the subsidy of the secular purpose and primary effect mandated by the Establishment Clause. Government cannot, however, direct a subsidy exclusively to religious organizations that either burdens nonbeneficiaries markedly or cannot reasonably be seen as removing a significant state-imposed deterrent to the free exercise: it "provide[s] unjustifiable awards of assistance to religious organizations" and cannot but "convey[y] a message of endorsement" to slighted members of the community.

"If the State chose to subsidize, by means of a tax exemption, all groups that contribute to the community's cultural, intellectual, and moral betterment, then the exemption for religious publications could be retained, provided that the exemption swept as widely as the property tax exemption we upheld in *Walz*. By contrast, if Texas sought to promote reflection and discussion about questions of ultimate value and the contours of a good and meaningful life, then a tax exemption would have to be available to an extended range of associations whose publications were substantially devoted to such matters; the exemption could not be reserved for publications dealing solely with religious issues."

Texas argued that its exemption served the compelling state interests of avoiding violations of both the Establishment Clause and the Free Exercise Clause. Rejecting the free exercise defense, the plurality did not think that "the payment of a sales tax by subscribers to religious periodicals or purchasers of religious books would offend their religious beliefs or inhibit religious activity."

"The sales tax that Texas imposes is not an occupation tax levied on religious missionaries." Nor is it a flat tax that "restrains in advance" the free exercise of religion. On the contrary, because the tax is equal to a small fraction of the value of each sale and payable by the buyer, it poses little danger of stamping out missionary work involving the sale of religious publications and, because of its generality, it can hardly be viewed as a covert attempt to curtail religious activity.

Concurring in the judgment, Justice White argued that the exemption was based on the content of the publication, which was "plainly forbidden by the Press Clause of the First Amendment. *Arkansas Writers' [sic] Project v. Ragland.*" *See supra* § 13.06, Note (1). The plurality said that it did not have to deal with this argument in light of its Establishment Clause holding.

Justice Blackmun, joined by Justice O'Connor, also concurred in the judgment.

The plurality "would resolve the tension between the Free Exercise and Establishment Clause values simply by subordinating the Free Exercise value. However, Justice Blackmun also felt that Justice Scalia's "opinion, conversely, would subordinate the Establishment Clause value. This position, it seems to me, runs afoul of the previously settled notion that government may not favor religious belief over disbelief."

Justice Blackmun suggested that a carefully drawn exemption may be "consistent with both values: for example, a state statute might exempt the sale not only of religious literature distributed by a religious organization but also of philosophical literature distributed by nonreligious organizations devoted to such matters of conscience as life and death, good and evil, being and nonbeing, right and wrong."

He would simply hold that "a tax exemption *limited* to the sale of religious literature by religious organizations violates the Establishment Clause," and not have reached the free exercise issues addressed in Justice Brennan's opinion.

Justice Scalia, joined by Chief Justice Rehnquist and Justice Kennedy, dissented. Justice Scalia argued that the Court's reasoning could be extended "to sales taxes on items other than publications and to other types of taxes such as property, income, amusement, and motor vehicle taxes." In this connection, at minimum 45 state codes contain exemptions for religious groups without analogous exemptions for other types of nonprofit institutions. For over half a century the federal Internal Revenue Code has allowed "minister[s] of the gospel" (a term interpreted broadly enough to include cantors and rabbis) to exclude from gross income the rental value of their parsonages. "Where accommodation of religion is the justification, by definition religion is being singled out."

§ 16.03 GOVERNMENT SUPPORT FOR RELIGIOUS PRACTICES

[1] Prayer in Public Schools

ENGEL v. VITALE
370 U.S. 421, 82 S. Ct. 1261, 8 L. Ed. 2d 601 (1962)

JUSTICE BLACK delivered the opinion of the Court.

The respondent Board of Education of Union Free School District No. 9, New Hyde Park, New York, acting in its official capacity under state law, directed the School District's principal to cause the following prayer to be said aloud by each class in the presence of a teacher at the beginning of each school day:

Almighty God, we acknowledge our dependence upon Thee, and we beg Thy blessings upon us, our parents, our teachers and our Country.

This daily procedure was adopted on the recommendation of the State Board of Regents, a governmental agency created by the State Constitution to which the New York Legislature has granted broad supervisory, executive, and legislative powers over the State's public school system. These state officials composed the prayer which they recommended and published as a part of their "Statement on Moral and Spiritual Training in the Schools," saying: "We believe that this Statement will be subscribed to by all men and women of good will, and we call upon all of them to aid in giving life to our program.". . .

. . . [W]e think that the constitutional prohibition against laws respecting an establishment of religion must at least mean that in this country it is no part of the business of government to compose official prayers for any group of the American people to recite as a part of a religious program carried on by a government.

It is a matter of history that this very practice of establishing governmentally composed prayers for religious services was one of the reasons which caused many of our early colonists to leave England and seek religious freedom in America. The Book of Common Prayer, which was created under governmental direction and which was approved by Acts of Parliament in 1548 and 1549, set out in minute detail the accepted form and content of prayer and other religious ceremonies to be used in the established, tax-supported Church of England. The controversies over the Book and what should be its content repeatedly threatened to disrupt the peace of that country as the accepted forms of prayer in the established church changed with the views of the particular ruler that happened to be in control at the time. Powerful groups representing some of the varying religious views of the people struggled among themselves to impress their particular views upon the Government and obtain amendments of the Book. . . . Other groups, lacking the necessary political power to influence the Government on the matter, decided to leave England and its established church and seek freedom in America from England's governmentally ordained and supported religion.

It is an unfortunate fact of history that when some of the very groups which had most strenuously opposed the established Church of England found themselves sufficiently in control of colonial governments in this country to write their own prayers into law, they passed laws making their own religion the official religion of their respective colonies. Indeed, as late as the time of the Revolutionary War, there were established churches in at least eight of the thirteen former colonies and established religions in at least four of the other five. But the successful Revolution against English domination was shortly followed by intense opposition to the practice of establishing religion by law. This opposition crystallized rapidly into an effective political force in Virginia where the minority religious groups such as Presbyterians, Lutherans, Quakers and Baptists had gained such strength that the adherents to the established Episcopal Church were actually a minority themselves. In 1785–1786, those opposed to the established Church, led by James Madison and Thomas Jefferson, who, though themselves not members of any of those dissenting religious groups, opposed all religious establishments by law on grounds of principle, obtained the enactment of the famous "Virginia Bill for Religious Liberty" by which all religious groups were placed on an equal footing so far as the State was concerned. Similar though less far-reaching legislation was being considered and passed in other States.

By the time of the adoption of the Constitution our history shows that there was a widespread awareness among many Americans of the dangers of a union of Church and State. These people knew, some of them from bitter personal experience, that one of the greatest dangers to the freedom of the individual to worship in his own way lay in the Government's placing its official stamp of approval upon one particular kind of prayer or one particular form of religious services. . . . The First Amendment was added to the Constitution to stand as a guarantee that neither the power nor the prestige of the Federal Government would be used to control, support or influence the kinds of prayer the American people can say. . . .

. . . Neither the fact that the prayer may be denominationally neutral nor the fact that its observance on the part of the students is voluntary can serve to free it from the limitations of the Establishment Clause, as it might from the Free Exercise Clause. . . . Although these two clauses may in certain instances overlap, they forbid two quite different kinds of governmental encroachment upon religious freedom. The Establishment Clause, unlike the Free Exercise Clause, does not depend upon any showing of direct governmental compulsion and is violated by the enactment of laws which establish an official religion whether those laws operate directly to coerce nonobserving individuals or not. This is not to say, of course, that laws officially prescribing a particular form of religious worship do not involve coercion of such individuals. When the power, prestige and financial support of government is placed behind a particular religious belief, the indirect coercive pressure upon religious minorities to conform to the prevailing officially approved religion is plain. But the purposes underlying the Establishment Clause go much further than that. Its first and most immediate purpose rested on the belief that a union of government and religion tends to destroy governmentally-established religion, both in England and in this country. . . . That same history showed that many people had lost their respect for any religion that had relied upon the support of government to spread its faith. The Establishment Clause thus stands as an expression of principle on the part of the Founders of our Constitution that religion is too personal, too sacred, too holy, to permit its "unhallowed perversion" by a civil magistrate. Another purpose of the Establishment Clause rested upon an awareness of the historical fact that governmentally established religions and religious persecutions go hand in hand. . . .

It has been argued that to apply the Constitution in such a way as to prohibit state laws respecting an establishment of religious services in public schools is to indicate a hostility toward religion or toward prayer. Nothing, of course, could be more wrong. The history of man is inseparable from the history of religion. . . . [T]here grew up a sentiment that caused men to leave the cross-currents of officially established state religions and religious persecution in Europe and come to this country filled with the hope that they could find a place in which they could pray when they pleased to the God of their faith in the language they chose. . . .

. . . To those who may subscribe to the view that because the Regents' official prayer is so brief and general there can be no danger to religious freedom in its governmental establishment, however, it may be appropriate to say in the words of James Madison, the author of the First Amendment:

> [I]t is proper to take alarm at the first experiment on our liberties. . . . Who does not see that the same authority which can establish Christianity, in exclusion of all other Religions, may establish with the same ease any particular sect of Christians, in exclusion of all other Sects? . . .[19]

JUSTICE FRANKFURTER took no part in the decision of this case.

JUSTICE WHITE took no part in the consideration or decision of this case.

JUSTICE DOUGLAS, concurring.

. . . The point for decision is whether the Government can constitutionally finance a religious exercise. Our system at the federal and state levels is presently honeycombed with such financing.[20] Nevertheless, I think it is an unconstitutional undertaking, whatever form it takes. . . .

What New York does on the opening of its public schools is what we do when we open court. Our Crier has from the beginning announced the convening of the Court and then added "God save the United States and this Honorable Court." That utterance is a supplication, a prayer in which we, the judges, are free to join, but which we need not recite any more than the students need recite the New York prayer.

What New York does on the opening of its public schools is what each House of Congress does at the opening of each day's business. . . .

. . . [O]nce government finances a religious exercise it inserts a divisive influence into our communities. . . .

JUSTICE STEWART, dissenting. . . .

. . . I cannot see how an "official religion" is established by letting those who want to say a prayer say it. On the contrary, I think that to deny the wish of these school children to join in reciting this prayer is to deny them the opportunity of sharing in the spiritual heritage of our Nation.

The Court's historical review of the quarrels over the Book of Common Prayer in England throws no light for me on the issue before us in this case. England had then and has now an established church. Equally unenlightening, I think, is the history of the early establishment and later rejection of an official church in our own States. For we

---

[19] [Court's footnote 22] Memorial and Remonstrance against Religious Assessments, II Writings of Madison, 183, at 185–186.

[20] [Concurrence's footnote 1]. . . "To mention but a few at the federal level, one might begin by observing that the very First Congress which wrote the First Amendment provided for chaplains in both Houses and in the armed services. There is compulsory chapel at the service academies, and religious services are held in federal hospitals and prisons. The President issues religious proclamations. The Bible is used for the administration of oaths. N.Y.A. and W.P.A. funds were available to parochial schools during the depression. Veterans receiving money under the 'G.I.' Bill of 1944 could attend denominational schools, to which payments were made directly by the government. During World War II, federal money was contributed to denominational schools for the training of nurses. The benefits of the National School Lunch Act are available to students in private as well as public schools. The Hospital Survey and Construction Act of 1946 specifically made money available to non-public hospitals. The slogan 'In God We Trust' is used by the Treasury Department, and Congress recently added God to the pledge of allegiance. . . . Religious organizations are exempt from the federal income tax and are granted postal privileges. Up to defined limits — 15 per cent of the adjusted gross income of individuals and 5 per cent of the net income of corporations — contributions to religious organizations are deductible for federal income tax purposes. There are no limits to the deductibility of gifts and bequests to religious institutions made under the federal gift and estate tax laws. . . . " [DAVID] FELDMAN, THE LIMITS OF FREEDOM 40-41 (1959).

deal here not with the establishment of a state church, which would, of course, be constitutionally impermissible, but with whether school children who want to begin their day by joining in prayer must be prohibited from doing so. Moreover, I think that the Court's task, in this as in all areas of constitutional adjudication, is not responsibly aided by the uncritical invocation of metaphors like the "wall of separation," a phrase nowhere to be found in the Constitution. What is relevant to the issue here is not the history of an established church in sixteenth century England or in eighteenth century America, but the history of the religious traditions of our people, reflected in countless practices of the institutions and officials of our government.

At the opening of each day's Session of this Court we stand, while one of our officials invokes the protection of God. Since the days of John Marshall our Crier has said, "God save the United States and this Honorable Court." Both the Senate and the House of Representatives open their daily Sessions with prayer. Each of our Presidents, from George Washington to John F. Kennedy, has upon assuming his office asked the protection and help of God. . . .

One of the stanzas of "The Star-Spangled Banner," made our National Anthem by Act of Congress in 1931, contains these verses:

> Blest with victory and peace, may the heav'n rescued land Praise the Pow'r that hath made and preserved us a nation! Then conquer we must, when our cause it is just, And this be our motto "In God is our Trust."

In 1954 Congress added a phrase to the Pledge of Allegiance to the Flag so that it now contains the words "one Nation under God indivisible, with liberty and justice for all." In 1952 Congress enacted legislation calling upon the President each year to proclaim a National Day of Prayer. Since 1865 the words "IN GOD WE TRUST" have been impressed on our coins. . . .

. . . It was all summed up by this Court just ten years ago in a single sentence: "We are a religious people whose institutions presuppose a Supreme Being." *Zorach v. Clauson*, 343 U.S. 306, 313 [(1952)]. . . .

NOTES

(1) *Bible Reading and the Lord's Prayer.* One year after *Engel v. Vitale*, the Court struck down a state law which required Bible reading and recitation of the Lord's Prayer at the beginning of the school day. *Abington School Dist. v. Schempp*, 374 U.S. 203 (1963). The Court found that such a statute breached the "wholesome neutrality" of church-state relations required by both the Free Exercise and the Establishment Clauses. Justice Clark, writing for the majority, noted that, although the two Clauses overlap, they are distinct in that "the Establishment Clause unlike the Free Exercise Clause, does not depend upon any showing of direct governmental compulsion and is violated by the enactment of laws which establish an official religion whether those laws operate directly to coerce non-observing individuals or not." Consequently, the statute's provision permitting students to be excused from the exercises upon a written request from a parent could not save it from invalidation.

Justice Brennan's concurrence discussed some problems with using original intent with reference to education. "A too literal quest for the advice of the Founding Fathers upon the issue of these cases seems to me futile and misguided for several reasons: First, on our precise problems the historical record is at best ambiguous, and statements can readily be found to support either side of the proposition. . . . Second, the structure of American education has greatly changed since the First Amendment was adopted. . . . Third, our religious composition makes us vastly more diverse people than were our forefathers. . . . Fourth, the American experiment in free public education available to all children has been guided in large measure by the dramatic evolution of the religious diversity among the population which our public schools serve."

Justice Stewart, the only dissenter, maintained that any dogmatic and mechanical interpretation of the Establishment Clause would lead inevitably to a conflict with that core value of free exercise. Unless governmental coercion was involved, the program did not rise to the level of governmental support of religion prohibited by the Establishment Clause.

(2) *Ten Commandments*. In *Stone v. Graham*, 449 U.S. 39 (1980), the Court, by summary reversal, invalidated a Kentucky statute that required public school superintendents to post a copy of the Ten Commandments, purchased with private contributions, in every public classroom. Each plaque bore a notation explaining the purpose of the display as demonstrating secular application of the Ten Commandments "in its adoption as the fundamental legal code of Western civilization and the common law of the United States." Notwithstanding this avowed secular purpose, the Court's *per curiam* opinion concluded that the statute served no secular legislative purpose and was, therefore, unconstitutional under the Court's three-part test for determining whether a state statute violates the Establishment Clause. "The Ten Commandments is undeniably a sacred text in the Jewish and Christian faiths, and no legislative recitation of a supposed secular purpose can blind us to that fact." The Court distinguished the objective study of the Bible in the school curriculum from the mere posting of Biblical texts, which "serves no such educational function." Justice Rehnquist, in dissent, objected to the majority's summary rejection of the secular purpose expressly articulated by the Kentucky legislature. Chief Justice Burger, Justice Blackmun, and Justice Stewart also dissented from the Court's summary reversal.

(3) *Prayers in Legislatures*. In *Marsh v. Chambers*, 463 U.S. 783 (1983), the Court (6–3) upheld the payment of legislative chaplains by the State of Nebraska, and the practice of opening each state legislative session with a prayer, against the Establishment Clause challenge. Chief Justice Burger's majority opinion was based almost entirely on an historical analysis, emphasizing that the practices challenged were identical to those adopted by the very Congress that approved the First Amendment in 1789. Moreover, the issue of legislative chaplains was actually considered by the Framers and apparently not viewed as the type of evil that the Establishment Clause was designed to prevent. The Court paid little attention to the fact that the same chaplain had been employed for sixteen years.

Although the Chief Justice's opinion was based almost entirely on history, it also described the Nebraska practice as "simply a tolerable acknowledgment of beliefs widely-held among people of this country."

Justice Brennan's dissent, joined by Justice Marshall, questioned the emphasis on the intent of the members of the First Congress, arguing that the Constitution "is not a static document" and that " 'practices which may have been objectionable to no one in the time of Jefferson and Madison may today be highly offensive to many persons, the deeply devout and the non-believers alike.' " He would approve some expressions in public life such as "In God We Trust" because "they have lost any true religious significance."

Justice Stevens' dissent focused on the 16-year tenure of the Chaplain, which evidenced the legislature's preference for a particular religion.

LEE v. WEISMAN, 505 U.S. 577 (1992). In *Lee*, the Court held (5–4) that the Establishment Clause prohibits prayers, conducted by invited clergy, at official public school graduation ceremonies. Every year, school officials in Providence, Rhode Island, permitted middle and high school principals to invite clergy to participate in graduation exercises. Participating clergy were provided with a pamphlet prepared by the National

Conference of Christians and Jews entitled "Guidelines for Civic Occasions." The pamphlet recommended "that public prayers at nonsectarian civic ceremonies be composed with inclusiveness and sensitivity."

In June of 1989, Deborah Weisman graduated from Nathan Bishop Middle School, a school that customarily invited clergy to address the graduates and their families. That year, her principal invited Rabbi Leslie Gutterman to give the invocation and the benediction.[21] Deborah Weisman's graduation ceremony, like most middle school commencement exercises in Providence, was held on school grounds.[22] Justice Kennedy opined that the State's "involvement with religious activity in this case is pervasive, to the point of creating a state-sponsored and state-directed religious exercise in a public school. Conducting this formal religious observance conflicts with settled rules pertaining to prayer exercises for students, and that suffices to determine the question before us."

"The principle that government may accommodate the free exercise of religion does not supersede the fundamental limitations imposed by the Establishment Clause." At the very least, "government may not coerce anyone to support or participate in religion or its exercise, or otherwise act in a way which establishes a [state] religion or religious faith, or tends to do so." The principal's decisions to have a convocation and benediction and his selection of Rabbi Gutterman were decisions attributable to the state. Moreover, the principal controlled the content of the prayer by furnishing the rabbi with the " 'Guidelines for Civic Occasions' and advised him that his prayers should be nonsectarian."

Justice Kennedy also said that the process of selecting a particular member of the clergy could cause divisiveness. "[T]he student had no real alternative which would have allowed her to avoid the fact or appearance of participation."

For many students at the graduation, "the act of standing or remaining silent was an expression of participation in the Rabbi's prayer." The brevity of the exercise did not render its impact *de minimis*. Nor was the constitutionality of the prayer saved by the formal voluntariness of attendance at the graduation ceremony.

Justice Kennedy recognized that "there must be a place in the student's life for precepts of a morality higher even than the law we today enforce. We express no hostility to those aspirations, nor would our oath permit us to do so. A relentless and all-pervasive attempt to exclude religion from every aspect of public life could itself become inconsistent with the Constitution. We recognize that, at graduation time and

---

[21] The prayers were as follows: INVOCATION. "God of the Free, Hope of the Brave: For the legacy of America where diversity is celebrated and the rights of minorities are protected, we thank You. May these young men and women grow up to enrich it. For the liberty of America, we thank You. May these new graduates grow up to guard it. For the political process of America in which all its citizens may participate, for its court system where all may seek justice we thank You. May those we honor this morning always turn to it in trust. For the destiny of America we thank You. May the graduates of Nathan Bishop Middle School so live that they might help to share it. May our aspirations for our country and for these young people, who are our hope for the future, be richly fulfilled. AMEN."

BENEDICTION. "O God, we are grateful to You for having endowed us with the capacity for learning which we have celebrated on this joyous commencement. Happy families give thanks for seeing their children achieve an important milestone. Send Your blessings upon the teachers and administrators who helped prepare them. The graduates now need strength and guidance for the future, help them to understand that we are not complete with academic knowledge alone. We must each strive to fulfill what You require of us all: To do justly, to love mercy, to walk humbly. We give thanks to You, Lord, for keeping us alive, sustaining us and allowing us to reach this special, happy occasion. AMEN."

[22] Most high school graduation ceremonies in the Providence school system are conducted away from the school.

throughout the course of the educational process, there will be instances when religious values, religious practices, and religious persons will have some interaction with the public schools and their students. But these matters, often questions of accommodation of religion, are not before us. . . . No holding by this Court suggests that a school can persuade or compel a student to participate in a religious exercise."

Justice Blackmun concurred, joined by Justices Stevens and O'Connor. While "proof of government coercion is not necessary to prove an Establishment Clause violation," it is sufficient. Government pressure to participate in a religious activity is an obvious indication that the government is endorsing or promoting religion.

Justice Souter filed a concurring opinion in which Justices Stevens and O'Connor joined. In defining the scope of permissible religious accommodation under the Establishment Clause, "one requirement is clear: accommodation must lift a discernible burden on the free exercise of religion." Government-sponsored graduation prayers "crossed the line from permissible accommodation to unconstitutional establishment."

Justice Scalia wrote a dissent in which Chief Justice Rehnquist, Justice White, and Justice Thomas joined. He began by describing the rich tradition of prayer at public ceremonies in general and at public school productions in particular. "In addition to this general tradition of prayer at public ceremonies, there exists a more specific tradition of invocations and benedictions at public-school graduation exercises."

The Court "claims only that students are psychologically coerced 'to stand . . . or, at least, maintain respectful silence.' " Students stood for the Pledge of Allegiance that immediately preceded the rabbi's invocation. Moreover, since the Pledge of Allegiance includes the phrase 'under God,' recital of the Pledge would appear to raise the same Establishment Clause issue as the invocation and benediction."

Graduating seniors are not susceptible to the psychological coercion the Court fears. Many high school students are old enough to vote.

There was nothing in the record to suggest that any school official "ever drafted, edited, screened or censored graduation prayers, or that Rabbi Gutterman was a mouthpiece of the school officials."

Justice Scalia would not expand "the concept of coercion beyond acts backed by threat of penalty." The Framers sponsored nonsectarian prayer in public events. They understood that "speech is not coercive; the listener may do as he likes."

Schools could avoid the decision. "All that is seemingly needed is an announcement, or perhaps a written insertion at the beginning of the graduation program, to the effect that, while all are asked to rise for the invocation and benediction, none is compelled to join in them, nor will be assumed, by rising, to have done so."

NOTES

(1) For further discussion of the "coercion" theory, see Stephen G. Gey, *Religious Coercion and the Establishment Clause*, 1994 U. ILL. L. REV. 463, 533 ("[T]he concept of 'psychological coercion' is just as susceptible to manipulation and debate as the three components of the *Lemon* standard. Moreover, even these versions of coercion theory would permit the government to serve as the agent of the majority's faith. A substantial increase in government funding of religious education would be the most immediate consequence, but the subtle effects of majoritarianism would also be evident in other areas of church-state relations. Under such a weak Establishment Clause regime, many government policies and symbolic acts of religious 'acknowledgement' would reflect the widely held, but fundamentally wrongheaded, notion that this is a Christian nation."); Michael Stokes Paulsen, *Lemon is Dead*, 43 CASE W. RES. L. REV. 795, 798–99 (1993) ("[I]t must be made clear that the forbidden coercion is government coercion — state

action, not private action, lest the Establishment Clause be perverted into a sword of suppression of private religious expression and evangelism that occurs on public property and lest private expression generally be deprived of constitutional protection whenever it occurs in a forum maintained or sanctioned by the state.").

(2) In *Santa Fe Independent School District v. Doe*, 530 U.S. 290 (2000), the Court held that a School District policy allowing prayer at varsity football games violated the Establishment Clause. The policy stated that the student council would conduct a student body election by secret ballot to determine whether students wanted a " 'brief invocation,' " which " 'must be nonsectarian and nonproselytizing,' " at home varsity football games " 'to solemnize the event.' " A student elected from a list of volunteers would present the invocation.

Following *Lee v. Weisman*, Justice Stevens found that a student election would not protect individuals with minority views. Indeed, such a vote may even heighten the offense to those in the minority. The school's selection process "by its terms, invites and encourages religious messages." As a football game is a "school-sponsored function conducted on school property," an " 'objective observer acquainted with the text, legislative history, and implementation' " of the policy would perceive it as endorsing prayer. Even if attendance at the game was totally voluntary, the pre-game invocation would effectively *coerce* everyone in attendance to be involved in a religious activity.

Justice Stevens allowed a facial challenge to the policy as it lacked " 'a secular legislative purpose.' " The plain language of the policy expressed a clear preference for a "traditional religious 'invocation.' " Moreover, the district promulgated its football game invocation policy in the context of having enacted other prayer-related policies "that unquestionably violated the Establishment Clause."

Chief Justice Rehnquist's dissent, joined by Justices Scalia and Thomas, emphasized that this challenge came before the district's policy went into effect. Moreover, in *Lee* the "graduation prayer given by a rabbi was 'directed and controlled' by a school official."

GOOD NEWS CLUB v. MILFORD CENTRAL SCHOOL, 533 U.S. 98 (2001). In *Good News*, the Court reversed a grant for summary judgment that had allowed Milford Central School (Milford) to exclude a religious club from using the school's premises for afterschool activities. In 1992, defendant Milford adopted a "community use policy," in accordance with New York Education Law § 414, allowing its facilities to be used for afterschool activities, subject to the school district's approval.[23] Plaintiff Good News Club is "a private Christian organization for children ages 6 to 12," which sought to hold weekly meetings in Milford's cafeteria. The Club described its meetings as children having " 'a fun time of singing songs, hearing a Bible lesson and memorizing scripture.' " The school district described these activities as " 'religious worship.' " Since Milford's policy prohibited use " 'by an individual or organization for religious purposes,' " the school district denied the Club's request.

Writing for a 6-3 majority, Justice Thomas first noted both parties "have agreed that Milford created a limited public forum" by opening up the school's premises. In a limited public forum, the State does not have to permit all types of speech. However, any state-imposed restriction "must not discriminate against speech on the basis of viewpoint, and . . . must be 'reasonable in light of the purpose served by the forum.' " By Milford's own admission, its policy allowed for "discussions of subjects such as child

---

[23] The community use policy enumerated several purposes for which school district residents could use the school's facilities, including " 'instruction in any branch of education, learning or the arts[,]' " and " 'social, civic and recreational meetings and entertainment events, and other uses pertaining to the welfare of the community, provided that such uses shall be nonexclusive and shall be opened to the general public.' "

rearing, and of 'the development of character and morals from a religious perspective,' " which included using "Aesop's Fables to teach children moral values." And "the Club teaches morals and character development to children."

Justice Thomas analogized this case to *Lamb's Chapel v. Center Moriches Union Free School Dist.*, 508 U.S. 384 (1993). "The only apparent difference" between the two groups is that "Lamb's Chapel taught lessons through films" whereas the Club teaches children through "live storytelling." Excluding the Good News Club "constitutes impermissible viewpoint discrimination."

Even though "a state interest in avoiding an Establishment Clause violation 'may be characterized as compelling,' and therefore may justify content-based discrimination," it is unclear whether such an interest "would justify viewpoint discrimination." However, the Court did not "confront the issue" as plaintiff had "no valid Establishment Clause interest." Like the activities in *Lamb's Chapel*, "the Club's meetings were held after school hours, not sponsored by the school, and open to any student who obtained parental consent, not just to Club members. As in *Widmar* [v. *Vincent*], Milford made its forum available to other organizations." Plaintiff sought to distinguish these cases as neither involves elementary school children.

One of the key factors in upholding governmental programs against an establishment challenge " 'is their *neutrality* towards religion.' " Permitting "the Club to speak on school grounds would ensure neutrality, not threaten it." Also relevant is "whether the community would feel coercive pressure to engage in the Club's activities." In this case, the "community would be the parents," as children must receive parental consent to attend the Club's meetings. Milford argued that elementary school children would automatically believe the school was endorsing religion simply because the Club meets on school grounds. The Court, however, rejected such a categorical rule and also rejected the existence of endorsement on the facts of this case.

Club meetings took place after school hours "in a combined high school resource room and middle school special education room, not in an elementary school classroom." Moreover, "the instructors are not schoolteachers. And the children in the group are not all the same age as in the normal classroom setting; their ages range from 6 to 12.[24] In sum, these circumstances simply do not support the theory that small children would perceive endorsement here."

Justice Thomas stated that "the danger that children would misperceive the endorsement of religion" was not "any greater than the danger that they would perceive a hostility toward the religious viewpoint if the Club were excluded from the public forum." The " 'endorsement inquiry is *not about the perceptions of particular individuals*.' " Instead, " 'the reasonable observer in the endorsement inquiry must be deemed aware of the history and context of the community and forum in which the religious [speech]' " occurs.

Concurring, Justice Scalia compared the Club's activities to those of the Boy Scouts of America. While the Scouts may advocate living " 'morally straight' " and " 'clean' lives", the Club "may only discuss morals and character, and cannot give *its* reasons why they should be fostered." In contrast to other organizations, the Club may not "independently discuss the religious premise on which its views are based — that God exists and His assistance is necessary to morality." This distinction "is blatant viewpoint discrimination."

---

[24] [Court's footnote 8] Although Milford "relies on the Equal Access Act as evidence that Congress recognized the vulnerability of elementary school children to misperceiving endorsement of religion," the Act "applies only to public secondary schools and makes no mention of elementary schools."

Justice Breyer concurred in part. First, neutrality is only one significant factor in determining if a school's community use policy violates the Establishment Clause. Second, endorsement may be the crucial issue here. "The time of day, the age of the children, the nature of the meetings, and other specific circumstances are relevant in helping to determine, whether, in fact, the Club 'so dominate[s]' the 'forum' that, in the children's minds, 'a formal policy of equal access is transformed into a demonstration of approval.'" However, because of the "procedural posture", the Court's holding simply meant "the school was not entitled to summary judgment, either in respect to the Free Speech or the Establishment Clause issue."

In dissent, Justice Stevens distinguished between various types of religious speech to conclude that Milford could exclude the Club. "First, there is religious speech that is simply speech about a particular topic from a religious point of view." Second, there is worship. Third, in between, there is "proselytizing or inculcating belief in a particular religious faith." Government "may not generally exclude even religious worship from an open public forum." However, a limited public forum, like Milford created, can allow "the first type of religious speech without allowing the other two," so "long as this is done in an even handed manner."

Justice Souter, joined by Justice Ginsburg, also dissented. "It is beyond question that Good News intends to use the public school premises not for the mere discussion of a subject from a particular, Christian point of view, but for an evangelical service of worship calling children to commit themselves in an act of Christian conversion."

In the *Widmar* case, "the nature of the university campus and the sheer number of activities offered precluded the reasonable college observer from seeing government endorsement in any one of them, and so did the time and variety of community use in the *Lamb's Chapel* case." By their "timing and format," the "Good News's gatherings, on the other hand, may well affirmatively suggest the *imprimatur* of officialdom in the minds of the young children." As one of only four groups which meets in Milford's facilities, the Club is "seemingly, the only one whose instruction follows immediately on the conclusion of the official school day."

NOTES

(1) *Public University Grounds.* In *Widmar v. Vincent*, 454 U.S. 263 (1981), § 14.04[4], the Court held unconstitutional a regulation of the University of Missouri that prevented student religious groups from using University facilities. Even though the activities to be conducted included religious discussion and worship, the majority held that the exclusion of religious groups would constitute a discriminatory regulation based on content and, therefore, violate the First Amendment's free speech guarantee. In reaching this conclusion, the Court also determined that allowing religious groups to share the limited public forum that the University made available to all student groups would not constitute an establishment of religion.

(2) *Equal Access Act.* In *Board of Education v. Mergens*, 496 U.S. 226 (1990), the Court upheld the Equal Access Act against an establishment challenge, thereby extending the holding of *Widmar* to the secondary school level. Under the Equal Access Act, "a public secondary school with a 'limited open forum'" is prohibited from discriminating against students who wish to conduct a meeting within that forum on the basis of the "religious, political, philosophical or other content of the speech at such meetings." In a majority opinion penned by Justice O'Connor, the Court held that a public secondary school's official recognition of certain student organizations but not of a religious club violated the act, despite the fact that the school allowed the group to meet informally on school grounds. Paralleling the analysis of *Widmar*, the Court held that the Equal Access Act did not violate the Establishment Clause. The act had the

secular purpose of preventing content discrimination against speech. Moreover, the act did not have the primary effect of advancing religion, as secondary school students were mature enough to understand that the school was not endorsing religion. Finally, the act did not foster "excessive entanglement between government and religion." As the Court's decision was based on statutory grounds, the Court declined to address any free speech issues involving public forum doctrine.

Justice Kennedy, joined by Justice Scalia, concurred in those parts of the decision concerning interpretation of the statute and the Establishment Clause issue. However, Justice Kennedy utilized his two-part coercion test from *County of Allegheny v. American Civil Liberties Union* to find that the Act did not violate the Establishment Clause. First, the act did not "give direct benefits to religion in such a degree that it in fact 'establishes a [state] religion or religious faith, or tends to do so.' " Second, the act did not "coerce any students to participate in a religious activity." Justice Marshall, joined by Justice Brennan, concurred in the judgment. Justice Marshall was concerned that the school's general posture toward its clubs could be construed as endorsement rather than toleration. Justice Stevens' dissent disputed the majority's construction of the act.

(3) *Films.* In *Lamb's Chapel v. Center Moriches Union Free School District*, 508 U.S. 384 (1993), the Court held that allowing a religious group to display Christian films on public school property would not constitute an establishment of religion. The majority used the *Lemon* test in its analysis. Writing for the majority, Justice White also concluded that this practice would not offend the endorsement test. Concurring in the judgment, Justice Scalia, joined by Justice Thomas, forcefully argued that he thought that Lemon had been effectively overruled in *County of Allegheny v. American Civil Liberties Union*. Concurring in part and concurring in judgment in part, Justice Kennedy found the Court's use of *Lemon* unsettling and also criticized its use of the endorsement test. *See supra* § 14.04[4], Note (1), for a discussion of the free speech aspects of *Lamb's Chapel*, and the interplay between the free speech rights of the religious groups and the *Lemon* test.

(4) *Teaching Creationism in Public Schools.* In *Edwards v. Aguillard*, 482 U.S. 578 (1987), the Court held that Louisiana's "Balanced Treatment for Creation-Science and Evolution-Science in Public School Instruction" Act violated the Establishment Clause. The Act prohibited public schools from teaching the theory of evolution unless they also taught creation science. While Louisiana did not require public schools to teach either evolution or creation science, if a school chose to teach one of these sciences, the Act required the school to also teach the other.

Writing for the Court, Justice Brennan applied the *Lemon* test and found that Louisiana had "identified no clear secular purpose" for the Act. While the Court frequently defers to government's asserted secular purpose, this stated purpose must be genuine and not merely a mask for an ulterior motive. Examining the Act's legislative history, Justice Brennan found that the purpose of the Act was not to promote academic freedom but to "narrow the science curriculum." Before the Act, Louisiana allowed public school teachers to teach any theory about the origins of life; the Act restricted this freedom.

During the legislative hearings on the Act, its sponsor explained "that his disdain for the theory of evolution resulted from the support that evolution supplied to views contrary to his own religious beliefs." The Court found that "the purpose of the Creationism Act was to restructure the science curriculum to conform with a particular religious viewpoint." While the introduction of many scientific theories may have had the secular purpose of "enhancing the effectiveness of science instruction," the Act's primary purpose of endorsing a particular religious belief violated the Establishment Clause.

Finally, the Supreme Court rejected Louisiana's claim that because there was a genuine issue of material fact, the District Court erred in granting summary judgment. Summary judgment was appropriate based upon various factors including the language of the Act and the legislative history leading to the passage of the Act. Affidavits asserting the scientific merits of creation science did not create a factual issue regarding the legislative purpose in passing the Act.

Concurring, Justice Powell emphasized "that nothing in the Court's opinion diminishes the traditionally broad discretion accorded state and local school officials in the selection of the public school curriculum." Justice White filed an opinion concurring in the judgment. Justice Scalia filed a dissenting opinion in which Chief Justice Rehnquist joined. Justice Scalia believed that enough witnesses testified before the legislature about the academic validity of creationism as to create a factual dispute as to whether the legislature had secular as well as religious motives, which would be sufficient to pass the secular purpose prong of the *Lemon* test.

[2]   Religious Displays

LYNCH v. DONNELLY

465 U.S. 668, 104 S. Ct. 1355, 79 L. Ed. 2d 604 (1984)

The Chief Justice delivered the opinion of the Court. . . .

I

Each year, in cooperation with the downtown retail merchants' association, the City of Pawtucket, Rhode Island, erects a Christmas display as part of its observance of the Christmas holiday season. The display is situated in a park owned by a nonprofit organization and located in the heart of the shopping district. The display is essentially like those to be found in hundreds of towns or cities across the Nation — often on public grounds — during the Christmas season. The Pawtucket display comprises many of the figures and decorations traditionally associated with Christmas, including, among other things, a Santa Claus house, reindeer pulling Santa's sleigh, candy-striped poles, a Christmas tree, carolers, cutout figures representing such characters as a clown, an elephant, and a teddy bear, hundreds of colored lights, a large banner that reads "SEASONS GREETINGS," and the crèche at issue here. All components of this display are owned by the City.

The crèche, which has been included in the display for 40 or more years, consists of the traditional figures, including the Infant Jesus, Mary and Joseph, angels, shepherds, kings, and animals, all ranging in height from 5″ to 5′. In 1973, when the present crèche was acquired, it cost the City $1365; it now is valued at $200. The erection and dismantling of the crèche costs the City about $20 per year; nominal expenses are incurred in lighting the crèche. No money has been expended on its maintenance for the past 10 years. . . .

The District Court held that the City's inclusion of the crèche in the display violates the Establishment Clause. . . . The City was permanently enjoined from including the crèche in the display.

A divided panel of the Court of Appeals for the First Circuit affirmed. We granted certiorari . . . and we reverse.

II

A

This Court has explained that the purpose of the Establishment and Free Exercise Clauses of the First Amendment is to prevent, as far as possible, the intrusion of either [the church or the state] into the precincts of the other. *Lemon v. Kurtzman.*

At the same time, however, the Court has recognized that

> "total separation is not possible in an absolute sense. Some relationship between government and religious organizations is inevitable."

In every Establishment Clause case, we must reconcile the inescapable tension between the objective of preventing unnecessary intrusion of either the church or the state upon the other, and the reality that, as the Court has so often noted, total separation of the two is not possible.

The Court has sometimes described the Religion Clauses as erecting a "wall" between church and state. . . . The metaphor has served as a reminder that the Establishment Clause forbids an established church or anything approaching it. But the metaphor itself is not a wholly accurate description of the practical aspects of the relationship that in fact exists between church and state.

No significant segment of our society and no institution within it can exist in a vacuum or in total or absolute isolation from all the other parts, much less from government. . . . Nor does the Constitution require complete separation of church and state; it affirmatively mandates accommodation, not merely tolerance, of all religions, and forbids hostility toward any. . . . Indeed, we have observed, such hostility would bring us into "war with our national tradition as embodied in the First Amendment's guaranty of the free exercise of religion." *McCollum,* 333 U.S. at 211–212.

B

. . . In the very week that Congress approved the Establishment Clause as part of the Bill of Rights for submission to the states, it enacted legislation providing for paid chaplains for the House and Senate. . . .

It would be difficult to identify a more striking example of the accommodation of religious belief intended by the Framers.

C

. . . Beginning in the early colonial period long before Independence, a day of Thanksgiving was celebrated as a religious holiday to give thanks for the bounties of Nature as gifts from God. President Washington and his successors proclaimed Thanksgiving, with all its religious overtones, a day of national celebration and Congress made it a National Holiday more than a century ago. That holiday has not lost its theme of expressing thanks for Divine aid any more than has Christmas lost is religious significance.

Executive Orders and other official announcements of Presidents and of the Congress have proclaimed both Christmas and Thanksgiving National Holidays in religious terms. And, by Acts of Congress, it has long been the practice that federal employees are released from duties on these National Holidays. . . .

Other examples of reference to our religious heritage are found in the statutorily prescribed national motto "In God We Trust," 36 U.S.C. § 186, which Congress and the President mandated for our currency, and in the language "One nation under God," as part of the Pledge of Allegiance to the American flag. . . .

Art galleries supported by public revenues display religious paintings of the 15th and 16th centuries, predominantly inspired by one religious faith. The National Gallery in Washington, maintained with Government support, for example, has long exhibited masterpieces with religious messages, notably the Last Supper, and paintings depicting the Birth of Christ, the Crucifixion, and the Resurrection, among many others with explicit Christian themes and messages.[25] The very chamber in which oral arguments on this case were heard is decorated with a notable and permanent — not seasonal — symbol of religion: Moses with Ten Commandments. Congress has long provided chapels in the Capitol for religious worship and meditation.

. . . Congress has directed the President to proclaim a National Day of Prayer each year "on which [day] the people of the United States may turn to God in prayer and meditation at churches, in groups, and as individuals." Our Presidents have repeatedly issued such Proclamations. Presidential Proclamations and messages have also issued to commemorate Jewish Heritage Week, and the Jewish High Holy Days. . . .

III

. . . In our modern, complex society, whose traditions and constitutional underpinnings rest on and encourage diversity and pluralism in all areas, an absolutist approach in applying the Establishment Clause is simplistic and has been uniformly rejected by the Court.

. . . Joseph Story wrote a century and a half ago:

> The real object of the [First] Amendment was . . . to prevent any national ecclesiastical establishment, which should give to an hierarchy the exclusive patronage of the national government. 3 Story, *Commentaries on the Constitution of the United States*, 728 (1833). . . .

In the line-drawing process we have often found it useful to inquire whether the challenged law or conduct has a secular purpose, whether its principal or primary effect is to advance or inhibit religion, and whether it creates an excessive entanglement of government with religion. But, we have repeatedly emphasized our unwillingness to be confined to any single test or criterion in this sensitive area. . . .

In this case, the focus of our inquiry must be on the crèche in the context of the Christmas season. . . .

. . . The District Court plainly erred by focusing almost exclusively on the crèche. When viewed in the proper context of the Christmas Holiday season, it is apparent that, on this record, there is insufficient evidence to establish that the inclusion of the crèche is a purposeful or surreptitious effort to express some kind of subtle governmental advocacy of a particular religious message. In a pluralistic society a variety of motives and purposes are implicated. The City, like the Congresses and Presidents, however, has principally taken note of a significant historical religious event long celebrated in the Western World. . . .

The narrow question is whether there is a secular purpose for Pawtucket's display of the crèche. The display is sponsored by the City to celebrate the Holiday and to depict the origins of that Holiday. These are legitimate secular purposes.[26] The District Court's inference, drawn from the religious nature of the crèche, that the City has no secular

---

[25] [Court's footnote 4] The National Gallery regularly exhibits more than 200 similar religious paintings.

[26] [Court's footnote 6] The City contends that the purposes of the display are "exclusively secular." We hold only that Pawtucket has a secular purpose for its display, which is all that *Lemon* requires. . . .

purpose was, on this record, clearly erroneous.

The District Court found that the primary effect of including the crèche is to confer a substantial and impermissible benefit on religion in general and on the Christian faith in particular. Comparisons of the relative benefits to religion of different forms of governmental support are elusive and difficult to make. But to conclude that the primary effect of including the crèche is to advance religion in violation of the Establishment Clause would require that we view it as more beneficial to and more an endorsement of religion, for example, than expenditure of large sums of public money for textbooks supplied throughout the country to students attending church-sponsored schools, *Board of Education v. Allen*, expenditure of public funds for transportation of students to church-sponsored schools, *Everson v. Board of Education*, federal grants for college buildings of church-sponsored institutions of higher education combining secular and religious education, *Tilton*, noncategorical grants to church-sponsored colleges and universities, *Roemer v. Board of Public Works*, 426 U.S. 736 (1976); and the tax exemptions for church properties sanctioned in *Walz*. It would also require that we view it as more of an endorsement of religion than the Sunday Closing Laws upheld in *McGowan v. Maryland*, 366 U.S. 420 (1961); the release time program for religious training in *Zorach*, and the legislative prayers upheld in *Marsh*. . . .

. . . Here, whatever benefit to one faith or religion or to all religions, is indirect, remote and incidental; display of the crèche is no more an advancement or endorsement of religion than the Congressional and Executive recognition of the origins of the Holiday itself as "Christ's Mass," or the exhibition of literally hundreds of religious paintings in governmentally supported museums.

The District Court found that there had been no administrative entanglement between religion and state resulting from the City's ownership and use of the crèche. But it went on to hold that some political divisiveness was engendered by this litigation. . . . The Court of Appeals expressly declined to accept the District Court's finding that inclusion of the crèche has caused political divisiveness along religious lines. . . .

Entanglement is a question of kind and degree. In this case, however, there is no reason to disturb the District Court's finding on the absence of administrative entanglement. There is no evidence of contact with church authorities concerning the content or design of the exhibit prior to or since Pawtucket's purchase of the crèche. No expenditures for maintenance of the crèche have been necessary; and since the City owns the crèche, now valued at $200, the tangible material it contributes is *de minimis*. In many respects the display requires far less ongoing, day-to-day interaction between church and state than religious paintings in public galleries. . . .

IV

Justice Brennan describes the crèche as a "re-creation of an event that lies at the heart of Christian faith." The crèche, like a painting, is passive; admittedly it is a reminder of the origins of Christmas. Even the traditional, purely secular displays extant at Christmas, with or without a crèche, would inevitably recall the religious nature of the Holiday. . . .

. . . It would be ironic, however, if the inclusion of a single symbol of a particular historic religious event, as part of a celebration acknowledged in the Western World for 20 centuries, and in this country by the people, by the Executive Branch, by the Congress, and the courts for two centuries, would so "taint" the City's exhibit as to render it violative of the Establishment Clause. To forbid the use of this one passive symbol — the crèche — at the very time people are taking note of the season with Christmas hymns and carols in public schools and other public places, and while the

Congress and Legislatures open sessions with prayers by paid chaplains would be a stilted over-reaction contrary to our history and to our holdings. If the presence of the crèche in this display violates the Establishment Clause, a host of other forms of taking official note of Christmas, and of our religious heritage, are equally offensive to the Constitution. . . .

JUSTICE O'CONNOR, concurring.

I concur in the opinion of the Court. I write separately to suggest a clarification of our Establishment Clause doctrine. The suggested approach leads to the same result in this case as that taken by the Court, and the Court's opinion, as I read it, is consistent with my analysis.

I

The Establishment Clause prohibits government from making adherence to a religion relevant in any way to a person's standing in the political community. . . .

. . . Focusing on institutional entanglement and on endorsement or disapproval of religion clarifies the *Lemon* test as an analytical device.

II

. . . Political divisiveness is admittedly an evil addressed by the Establishment Clause. Its existence may be evidence that institutional entanglement is excessive or that a government practice is perceived as an endorsement of religion. But the constitutional inquiry should focus ultimately on the character of the government activity that might cause such divisiveness, not on the divisiveness itself. . . .

III

The central issue in this case is whether Pawtucket has endorsed Christianity by its display of the crèche. To answer that question, we must examine both what Pawtucket intended to communicate in displaying the crèche and what message the City's display actually conveyed. . . .

. . . Examination of both the subjective and the objective components of the message communicated by a government action is . . . necessary to determine whether the action carries a forbidden meaning. . . .   The effect prong asks whether, irrespective of government's actual purpose, the practice under review in fact conveys a message of endorsement or disapproval. An affirmative answer to either question should render the challenged practice invalid.

A

The purpose prong of the *Lemon* test requires that a government activity have a secular purpose. That requirement is not satisfied, however, by the mere existence of some secular purpose, however dominated by religious purposes. . . .

Applying that formulation to this case, I would find that Pawtucket did not intend to convey any message of endorsement of Christianity or disapproval of nonChristian religions. . . .   Celebration of public holidays, which have cultural significance even if they also have religious aspects, is a legitimate secular purpose. . . .

B

Focusing on the evil of government endorsement or disapproval of religion makes clear that the effect prong of the *Lemon* test is properly interpreted not to require invalidation of a government practice merely because it in fact causes, even as a primary effect, advancement or inhibition of religion. . . . What is crucial is that a government practice not have the effect of communicating a message of government endorsement or disapproval of religion. It is only practices having that effect, whether intentionally or unintentionally, that make religion relevant, in reality or public perception, to status in the political community.

. . . Although the religious and indeed sectarian significance of the crèche, as the district court found, is not neutralized by the setting, the overall holiday setting changes what viewers may fairly understand to be the purpose of the display — as a typical museum setting, though not neutralizing the religious content of a religious painting, negates any message of endorsement of that content. The display celebrates a public holiday, and no one contends that declaration of that holiday is understood to be an endorsement of religion. The holiday itself has very strong secular components and traditions. . . .

These features combine to make the government's display of the crèche in this particular physical setting no more an endorsement of religion than such governmental "acknowledgments" of religion as legislative prayers of the type approved in *Marsh v. Chambers*, 463 U.S. 783 (1983), government declaration of Thanksgiving as a public holiday, printing of "In God We Trust" on coins, and opening court sessions with "God save the United States and this honorable court." Those government acknowledgments of religion serve, in the only ways reasonably possible in our culture, the legitimate secular purposes of solemnizing public occasions, expressing confidence in the future, and encouraging the recognition of what is worthy of appreciation in society. . . . It is significant in this regard that the crèche display apparently caused no political divisiveness prior to the filing of this lawsuit, although Pawtucket had incorporated the crèche in its annual Christmas display for some years. For these reasons, I conclude that Pawtucket's display of the crèche does not have the effect of communicating endorsement of Christianity.

. . . [T]he question is, like the question whether racial or sex-based classifications communicate an invidious message, in large part a legal question to be answered on the basis of judicial interpretation of social facts. The District Court's conclusion concerning the effect of Pawtucket's display of its crèche was in error as a matter of law.

IV

Every government practice must be judged in its unique circumstances to determine whether it constitutes an endorsement or disapproval of religion. . . . Government practices that purport to celebrate or acknowledge events with religious significance must be subjected to careful judicial scrutiny. . . .

Justice Brennan, with whom Justice Marshall, Justice Blackmun and Justice Stevens join, dissenting.

. . . [T]he Court reaches an essentially narrow result which turns largely upon the particular holiday context in which the City of Pawtucket's nativity scene appeared. The Court's decision implicitly leaves open questions concerning the constitutionality of the public display on public property of a crèche standing alone, or the public display of other distinctively religious symbols such as a cross.[27] . . .

I

A

. . . To be found constitutional, Pawtucket's seasonal celebration must at least be non-denominational and not serve to promote religion. The inclusion of a distinctively religious element like the crèche, however, demonstrates that a narrower sectarian purpose lay behind the decision to include a nativity scene. . . .

The "primary effect" of including a nativity scene in the City's display is, as the District Court found, to place the government's imprimatur of approval on the particular religious beliefs exemplified by the crèche. . . . The effect on minority religious groups, as well as on those who may reject all religion, is to convey the message that their views are not similarly worthy of public recognition nor entitled to public support. . . .

B

The Court advances two principal arguments to support its conclusion that the Pawtucket crèche satisfies the *Lemon* test. Neither is persuasive.

First. The Court, by focusing on the holiday "context" in which the nativity scene appeared, seeks to explain away the clear religious import of the crèche and the findings of the District Court that most observers understood the crèche as both a symbol of Christian beliefs and a symbol of the City's support for those beliefs. . . .

When government decides to recognize Christmas day as a public holiday, it does no more than accommodate the calendar of public activities to the plain fact that many Americans will expect on that day to spend time visiting with their families, attending religious services, and perhaps enjoying some respite from pre-holiday activities. The Free Exercise Clause, of course, does not necessarily compel the government to provide this accommodation, but neither is the Establishment Clause offended by such a step. *Cf. Zorach v. Clauson*, 343 U.S. 306 (1952). Because it is clear that the celebration of Christmas has both secular and sectarian elements, it may well be that by taking note of the holiday, the government is simply seeking to serve the same kinds of wholly secular goals — for instance, promoting goodwill and a common day of rest — that were found to justify Sunday Closing laws in *McGowan*. If public officials go further and participate in the secular celebration of Christmas — by, for example, decorating public places with such secular images as wreaths, garlands or Santa Claus figures — they move closer to the limits of their constitutional power but nevertheless remain within the boundaries set by the Establishment Clause. But when those officials participate in or appear to endorse the distinctively religious elements of this otherwise secular event,

---

[27] [Dissent's footnote 1] For instance, nothing in the Court's opinion suggests that the Court of Appeals for the Third Circuit erred when it found that a city-financed platform and cross used by Pope John Paul II to celebrate mass and deliver a sermon during his 1979 visit to Philadelphia was an unconstitutional expenditure of city funds. *Gilfillan v. City of Philadelphia*, 637 F.2d 924 (3d Cir. 1980). Nor does the Court provide any basis for disputing the holding of the Court of Appeals for the Eleventh Circuit that the erection and maintenance of an illuminated Latin cross on state park property violates the Establishment Clause. *American Civil Liberties Union of Georgia v. Rabun County Chamber of Commerce, Inc.*, 698 F.2d 1098 (11th Cir. 1983). And given the Court's focus upon the otherwise secular setting of the Pawtucket crèche, it remains uncertain whether absent such secular symbols as Santa Claus' house, a talking wishing well, and cut-out clowns and bears, a similar nativity scene would pass muster under the Court's standard. . . .

they encroach upon First Amendment freedoms. . . .

. . . It would be another matter if the crèche were displayed in a museum setting, in the company of other religiously-inspired artifacts, as an example, among many, of the symbolic representation of religious myths. In that setting, we would have objective guarantees that the crèche could not suggest that a particular faith had been singled out for public favor and recognition. . . .

II

. . . Invoking the celebration of Thanksgiving as a public holiday, the legend "In God We Trust" on our coins, and the proclamation "God save the United States and this Honorable Court" at the opening of judicial sessions, the Court asserts, without explanation, that Pawtucket's inclusion of a crèche in its annual Christmas display poses no more of a threat to Establishment Clause values than these other official "acknowl-edgments" of religion. . . .

. . . [T]he Court has never comprehensively addressed the extent to which govern-ment may acknowledge religion by, for example, incorporating religious references into public ceremonies and proclamations, and I do not presume to offer a comprehensive approach. Nevertheless, it appears from our prior decisions that at least three principles — tracing the narrow channels which government acknowledgments must follow to satisfy the Establishment Clause — may be identified. First, although the government may not be compelled to do so by the Free Exercise Clause, it may, consistently with the Establishment Clause, act to accommodate to some extent the opportunities of individuals to practice their religion. . . .

Second, our cases recognize that while a particular governmental practice may have derived from religious motivations and retain certain religious connotations, it is nonetheless permissible for the government to pursue the practice when it is continued today solely for secular reasons. As this Court noted with reference to Sunday Closing Laws in *McGowan v. Maryland*, the mere fact that a governmental practice coincides to some extent with certain religious beliefs does not render it unconstitutional. . . .

Finally, we have noted that government cannot be completely prohibited from recognizing in its public actions the religious beliefs and practices of the American people as an aspect of our national history and culture. . . . While I remain uncertain about these questions, I would suggest that such practices as the designation of "In God We Trust" as our national motto, or the references to God contained in the Pledge of Allegiance can best be understood, in Dean Rostow's apt phrase, as a form a "ceremonial deism," protected from Establishment Clause scrutiny chiefly because they have lost through rote repetition any significant religious content. . . . Moreover, these refer-ences are uniquely suited to serve such wholly secular purposes as solemnizing public occasions, or inspiring commitment to meet some national challenge in a manner that simply could not be fully served in our culture if government were limited to purely non-religious phrases. The practices by which the government has long acknowledged religion are therefore probably necessary to serve certain secular functions, and that necessity, coupled with their long history, gives those practices an essentially secular meaning.

The crèche fits none of these categories. Inclusion of the crèche is not necessary to accommodate individual religious expression. . . . The religious works on display at the National Gallery, Presidential references to God during an Inaugural Address, or the national motto present no risk of establishing religion. To be sure, our understand-ing of these expressions may begin in contemplation of some religious element, but it does not end there. Their message is dominantly secular. In contrast, the message of the crèche begins and ends with reverence for a particular image of the divine. . . .

III

. . . The intent of the Framers with respect to the public display of nativity scenes is virtually impossible to discern primarily because the widespread celebration of Christmas did not emerge in its present form until well into the nineteenth century. . . .

. . . The Puritans, and later the Presbyterians, Baptists and Methodists, generally associated the celebration of Christmas with the elaborate and, in their view, sacrilegious celebration of the holiday by the Church of England, and also with, for them, the more sinister theology of "Popery." . . .

JUSTICE BLACKMUN, with whom JUSTICE STEVENS joins, dissenting. . . .

. . . [I]ronically, the majority does an injustice to the crèche and the message it manifests. While certain persons, including the Mayor of Pawtucket, undertook a crusade to "keep Christ in Christmas," the Court today has declared that presence virtually irrelevant. . . . The city has its victory — but it is a Pyrrhic one indeed. . . .

NOTES

(1) *Lynch v. Donnelly* was mentioned prominently by the Second Circuit Court of Appeals when it ruled that the City of Scarsdale could not bar the display of a privately-financed nativity scene in a public park. To counter the claim that it was discriminating against religious speech in a park that had been used as a public forum, Scarsdale argued that a quasi-permanent crèche would constitute an endorsement of religion and that the City has the right to avoid Establishment Clause problems. The Second Circuit held that *Lynch v. Donnelly* had resolved the Establishment Clause concerns. The Supreme Court affirmed by a divided court. *See McCreary v. Village of Scarsdale*, 739 F.2d 716 (2d Cir.1984), *aff'd* by an equally divided Court, 471 U.S. 83 (1985).

(2) For further discussion of *Lynch*, see David M. Cobin, *Crèches, Christmas Trees and Menorahs: Weeds Growing in Roger Williams' Garden*, 1990 WIS. L. REV. 1597, 1597 ("Roger Williams, Puritan religious leader and the founder of Rhode Island, understood that governmental involvement with religion weakens religion. To Williams, the church was a garden in the wilderness; but when government enters the realm of religion this garden becomes a wilderness. The Supreme Court has recognized that Williams' views have been incorporated into the first amendment, yet has ignored these concerns when ruling on governmental display of religious objects. By ruling that such display is permissible so long as the holiday's secular nature is emphasized, the Court has encouraged the state to plant weeds in Roger Williams' garden."); Ira C. Lupu, *The Lingering Death of Separationism*, 62 GEO. WASH. L. REV. 230, 279 (1993) ("[S]trong separationism itself may well have favored irreligion, because it lined up state power with secular rationality. One of the powerful lessons of the past twenty years of American law and history is that an ideology of secular rationality is not objective or neutral but is partial to a particular set of institutions (most notably science and the markets). Nor is secular rationality particularly conducive to the life of the spirit, without which it may not be possible for a nation to thrive.").

For additional discussion on Justice Brennan's dissents in *Lynch* and *Marsh*, see Arlin M. Adams, *Justice Brennan and the Religion Clauses: The Concept of a "Living Constitution"*, 139 U. PA. L. REV. 1319, 1327 (1991) ("A reading of Justice Brennan's dissenting opinions in *Marsh* and *Lynch* reveals his commitment to protect religious pluralism in America. He recognized that in determining the constitutionality of contemporary practices under the establishment clause, the Court must not look solely to the historical background of the first amendment, but instead it must recognize the importance of America's increasing religious diversity.").

COUNTY OF ALLEGHENY v. AMERICAN CIVIL LIBERTIES UNION,

GREATER PITTSBURGH, 492 U.S. 573 (1989). In *County of Allegheny*, the Court considered the constitutionality of two holiday displays — a crèche on the courthouse steps and a menorah displayed outside a public administrative building — annually erected on public property. Different majorities of the Court invalidated the display of the crèche but allowed the display of the menorah.

Only Justices Stevens and O'Connor joined the following portion of Justice Blackmun's opinion. The County Courthouse, owned by Allegheny County, constituted the seat of government. For almost a decade, the county permitted a Roman Catholic organization to erect a crèche on the Grand Staircase of the courthouse for the duration of the Christmas season. The crèche included figures from the Christian depiction of Jesus' birth at the manger in Bethlehem: Mary, Joseph, the infant Jesus, the wise men, and, at the crest of the manger, an angel bearing a banner reading " 'Gloria in Excelsis Deo!' " During the 1986-1987 holiday season, a placard was added which stated: " 'This Display Donated by the Holy Name Society.' " In addition, the county placed poinsettia plants and two evergreen trees decorated with red bows outside the fence. The county also placed two large wreaths with red ribbons in the windows behind the Grand Staircase and small evergreen trees next to a sign indicating the location of county offices. For much of the month of December, the county used the crèche for its Christmas program to which it invited high school choirs and other musical groups to perform. While a "gallery forum" lay next to the Grand Staircase, it was not part of the crèche display.

The City-County building, owned jointly by the City of Pittsburgh and the County of Allegheny, is a block from the courthouse; this building houses the Mayor's office. The city maintains responsibility for the Grand Street entrance which features three rounded archways. For years, the city has placed and decorated a 45-foot Christmas tree under the center arch. In 1986, the city placed a sign at the foot of the Christmas tree displaying the Mayor's name and titled "Salute to Liberty." Below this title, the sign stated: "During this holiday season, the City of Pittsburgh salutes liberty. Let these festive lights remind us that we are the keepers of the flame of liberty and our legacy of freedom."

Since 1982, the city expanded its holiday display by including "a symbolic representation of Chanukah, an 8-day Jewish holiday that begins on the 25th day of the Jewish lunar month of Kislev." Jewish authorities explain that the lighting of Chanukah candles is a symbolic celebration of a miracle. During the 1986 holiday season, the city placed in the Grand Street entrance an 18-foot Chanukah menorah next to the 45-foot Christmas tree. Although the menorah was owned by a Jewish organization, the city took responsibility for storing, erecting, and dismantling the menorah each year.

The dispute began in 1986 when the Greater Pittsburgh Chapter of the American Civil Liberties Union sought a permanent injunction on the display of the crèche by the county and the menorah by the city as violations of the Establishment Clause of the First Amendment.[28]

Writing for a majority, Justice Blackmun reviewed the Court's three-part establishment test in *Lemon v. Kurtzman*. The Establishment Clause, at the very least, prohibits government from appearing to take a position on questions of religious belief or from "making adherence to a religion relevant in any way to a person's standing in the political community."

In a portion of his opinion joined only by Justice Stevens, Justice Blackmun opined: since the holding in *Lynch* the Court has evaluated governmental actions under the

---

[28] The ACLU did not claim that the city's Christmas tree or the county's choral program violated the Establishment Clause.

Establishment Clause by inquiring whether "the challenged governmental action is sufficiently likely to be perceived by adherents of the controlling denominations as an endorsement, and by the nonadherents as a disapproval, of their individual religious choices." Therefore, in determining the constitutionality of the display of the crèche and the menorah, the Court must determine whether, in their physical settings, the displays effect an impression of endorsing or disapproving particular religious beliefs.

Again writing for a majority, Justice Blackmun noted the many distinguishing characteristics between the present crèche display and the one upheld in *Lynch*. The *Lynch* display contained many other holiday symbols — Santa's house, reindeer, and a "talking" wishing well — each of which was "a center of attention separate from the crèche. Here, in contrast, the crèche stands alone: it is the single element of the display on the Grand Staircase." Moreover, the floral decorations surrounding the crèche in this case are not equivalent to the holiday symbols in *Lynch*. "The floral frame, like all good frames, serves only to draw one's attention to the message inside the frame." Also, the Christmas carol program did not diminish the crèche's religious meaning. The 1986 carol program lasted at most two hours a day from December 3 to December 23. Moreover, as many of the songs were religious in nature, they were "more likely to augment the religious quality of the scene than to secularize it." Finally, the crèche sits in the main part of the seat of county government.

Justice Blackmun disagreed with Justice Kennedy's dissent which concluded that the crèche was consistent with the Establishment Clause. Unfortunately, this Nation has on numerous occasions explicitly accepted official acts endorsing Christianity. The Court has rejected the Framers' positions displaying favoritism toward Christianity. "The clearest command of the Establishment Clause is that one religious denomination cannot be officially preferred over another."

Moreover, Justice Blackmun found that Justice Kennedy's efforts to replace an endorsement test with his "proselytization" test is simply an attempt to reduce judicial scrutiny under the Establishment Clause. "Although Justice Kennedy repeatedly accuses the Court of harboring a 'latent hostility' or 'callous indifference' toward religion, nothing could be further from the truth, and the accusations could be said to be as offensive as they are absurd." A secular state is not analogous to an atheistic or antireligious state but instead promotes respect for religious diversity as required by the Constitution.

Turning to the constitutionality of the menorah, Justice Blackmun wrote only for himself in this portion of the opinion. He began by noting that its "message is not exclusively religious. The menorah is the primary visual symbol for the holiday that, like Christmas, has both religious and secular dimensions." As the city may recognize Christmas as a secular holiday, it may similarly acknowledge Chanukah as such. To hold otherwise would be to promote discrimination against Jews.

Accordingly, "[t]he relevant question for Establishment Clause purposes is whether the combined display of the tree, the sign, and the menorah has the effect of endorsing both Christian and Jewish faiths, or rather simply recognizes that both Christmas and Chanukah are part of the same winter-holiday season, which has attained a secular status in our society." Although the Christmas tree at one time represented religious ideals, it — unlike the menorah — is now considered a secular holiday symbol. The 45-foot Christmas tree constituted "the predominant element" in the city's display. It was placed in front of the middle of the archway, with the 18-foot menorah set to one side. "Given this configuration, it is much more sensible to interpret the meaning of the menorah in light of the tree, rather than *vice versa*."

The city lacked "reasonable alternatives that are less religious in nature." Failure to use an available secular alternative does not constitute an Establishment Clause violation, but is a factor to consider in determining whether the religious symbol amounts to religious endorsement. "It is difficult to imagine a predominantly secular symbol of Chanukah that the city could place next to its Christmas tree. An 18-foot dreidel would look out of place, and might be interpreted by some as mocking the celebration of Chanukah." The Mayor's sign, stating the city's wishes to salute liberty, further diminished any threat that the menorah and Christmas tree would be viewed as official endorsement of Christianity and Judaism.

The display's effect must be considered according to a standard of a "reasonable observer."[29] Justice Blackmun and a majority of the Court concluded that the menorah did not have the effect of endorsing religion. However, the case must be remanded to determine whether the menorah might violate the "purpose" or "entanglement" prongs of the *Lemon* test.

Concurring in part and concurring in the judgment, Justice O'Connor found the crèche in the present case distinguishable from the one at issue in *Lynch*. The crèche in *Lynch* was part of a larger Christmas display containing many secular symbols erected in a private park. The crèche at issue in the present controversy stood alone in the county courthouse. In the part of her opinion joined by Justices Brennan and Stevens, Justice O'Connor highlighted the fact that, under the endorsement test, the "history and ubiquity" of a practice "is relevant because it provides part of the context in which a reasonable observer evaluates whether a challenged governmental practice conveys a message of endorsement of religion. It is the combination of the longstanding existence of practices such as opening legislative sessions with legislative prayers or opening Court session with 'God save the United States and this honorable Court,' as well as their nonsectarian nature, that lead me to the conclusion that those particular practices, despite their religious roots, do not convey a message of endorsement of particular religious beliefs. Similarly, the celebration of Thanksgiving as a public holiday, despite its religious origins, is now generally understood as a celebration of patriotic values rather than particular religious beliefs. The question under endorsement analysis, in short, is whether a reasonable observer would view such longstanding practices as a disapproval of their particular religious choices, in light of the fact that they serve a secular purpose rather than a sectarian one and have largely lost their religious significance over time."

The endorsement test requires "careful and often difficult balancing and is highly content-specific." Government may accommodate religious practices and indeed, the Free Exercise Clause often requires it to do so. The crèche display cannot reasonably be viewed as an accommodation of any government-imposed burdens interfering with the free exercise of religion; Christians may display crèches at home or in church.

In displaying the menorah in combination with the secular symbol of a Christmas tree and a sign saluting liberty, "the city did not endorse Judaism or religion in general, but rather conveyed a message of pluralism and freedom of belief during the holiday season." Quoting from the *Lynch* decision, Justice O'Connor noted that the physical setting of a display "changes what viewers may fairly understand to be the purpose of the display — as a typical museum setting, though not neutralizing the religious content of a religious painting, negates any message of endorsement of that content."

---

[29] Justice Blackmun refused to validate the combined display of a Christmas tree and a menorah on all government property, specifically expressing concern about such a display in a public school.

Moreover, the menorah display might constitute an impermissible endorsement on different facts. For example, although this issue was not brought before the Court, some evidence suggested that "in the past Chabad lit the menorah in front of the City-County building in a religious ceremony that included the recitation of religious blessings."

Finally, Justice O'Connor criticized "Justice Blackmun's new rule, that an inference of endorsement arises every time government uses a symbol with religious meaning if a 'more secular alternative' is available." This "is too blunt an instrument for Establishment Clause analysis, which depends on sensitivity to the context and circumstances presented by each case."[30]

Concurring in part and dissenting in part, Justice Brennan, in an opinion joined by Justices Marshall and Stevens, would have struck down both displays on Establishment Clause grounds. Justice Brennan took issue with Justice Blackmun's position that the Christmas tree rendered the message of the menorah more secular. Instead, Justice Brennan thought that placing the Christmas tree next to a menorah amplified the religious significance of the tree. This conclusion was particularly surprising for Justice Brennan in light of Justice Blackmun's quick dismissal of the suggestion that the floral display around the crèche would dilute its religious significance. Perhaps the distinction relates to the size of the tree which was 2 1/2 times taller than the menorah. "And, though Justice Blackmun shunts the point to a footnote at the end of his opinion, it is highly relevant that the menorah was lit during a religious ceremony complete with traditional religious blessings."

Finally, Justice Brennan opined that "Justice Blackmun, in his acceptance of the city's message of 'diversity,' and, even more so, Justice O'Connor, in her approval of the 'message of pluralism and freedom to choose one's own beliefs,' appear to believe that, where seasonal displays are concerned, more is better." The Establishment Clause does not permit that "governmental promotion of religion is acceptable so long as one religion is not favored. We have, on the contrary, interpreted that Clause to require neutrality, not just among religions, but between religion and nonreligion." The idea of religious diversity may itself be offensive to some.

In a partial concurrence and partial dissent joined by Justices Brennan and Marshall, Justice Stevens warned that religious displays on public property could cause societal foment.[31]

Concurring in part and dissenting in part, Justice Kennedy wrote an opinion joined by Chief Justice Rehnquist, Justice White, and Justice Scalia. Justice Kennedy would have upheld the display of both the crèche and the menorah. The majority held that the crèche display violated the Establishment Clause because it failed the "primary effect" test of *Lemon*. "This view of the Establishment Clause reflects an unjustified hostility toward religion, a hostility inconsistent with our history and our precedents."

Justice Kennedy expressed his disapproval of the continuing use of the *Lemon* test in Establishment Clause cases. "A categorical approach would install federal courts as jealous guardians of an absolute 'wall of separation,' sending a clear message of disapproval." Instead, acknowledging and accommodating religion "in a society with a pervasive public sector requires diligent observance of the border between accommodation and establishment. Our cases disclose two limiting principles: government may not coerce anyone to support or participate in any religion or its exercise; and it may not, in the guise of avoiding hostility or callous indifference, give direct benefits to religion in such a degree that it in fact 'establishes a [state] religion or

---

[30] Justice Blackmun's own concession that the dreidel is a more secular symbol of Chanukah demonstrates the necessity for context sensitivity.

[31] "This case illustrates the danger that governmental displays of religious symbols may give rise to unintended divisiveness, for the net result of the Court's disposition is to disallow the display of the crèche but to allow the display of the menorah. Laypersons unfamiliar with the intricacies of Establishment Clause jurisprudence may reach the wholly unjustified conclusion that the Court itself is preferring one faith over another."

religious faith, or tends to do so.' " The definition of "coercion" need not be solely a "direct tax" in support of religion; the word also encompasses a symbolic recognition of religion in extreme cases. For instance, "the Clause forbids a city to permit the permanent erection of a large Latin cross on the roof of city hall." Thus, Justice Kennedy suggested the following test: "Non-coercive government action within the realm of flexible accommodation or passive acknowledgement of existing symbols does not violate the Establishment Clause unless it benefits religion in a way more direct and more substantial than practices that are accepted in our national heritage."

Applying this test to the case at hand, the city and county were merely "celebrat[ing] the season," and acknowledging the history and the religious together with the secular nature of the holidays of Christmas and Chanukah. "If government is to participate in its citizens' celebration of a holiday that contains both a secular and a religious component, enforced recognition of only the secular aspect would signify . . . callous indifference toward religious faith . . . ; for by commemorating the holiday only as it is celebrated by nonadherents, the government would be refusing to acknowledge the plain fact, and the historical reality, that many of its citizens celebrate its religious aspects as well." A judicial denial of the city's recognition of its citizens beliefs "would signal not neutrality but a pervasive intent to insulate government from all things religious."

Justice Kennedy could not comprehend why "the placement of a government-owned crèche on private land is lawful while placement of a privately owned crèche on public land is not. If anything, I should have thought government ownership of a religious symbol presented the more difficult question under the Establishment Clause."

Any test that the Court applies in the establishment area must respect the historical "practices and understandings" of the citizenry. For example, the United States Code has long recognized the President's power to set aside a National Day of Prayer. Moreover, the Pledge of Allegiance describes our nation as "one Nation under God." Beyond "disregarding precedent and historical fact," the majority "embraces a jurisprudence of minutiae. A reviewing court must consider whether the city has included Santas, talking wishing wells, reindeer, or other secular symbols as 'a center of attention separate from the crèche.' " A court must also weigh "the prominence of the setting in which the display is placed. In this case, the Grand Staircase of the county courthouse proved too resplendent.

Justice Kennedy also criticized the "least-religious means" analysis that Justice Blackmun fashioned to uphold the display of the menorah. "First, . . . there are innumerable secular symbols of Christmas, and that there will always be a more secular alternative available in place of a crèche. Second, the test as applied by Justice Blackmun is unworkable, for it requires not only that the Court engage in the unfamiliar task of deciding whether a particular alternative symbol is more or less religious, but also whether the alternative would 'look out of place.' "

For Justice Kennedy, the results in this case illustrate the inherent problems with the endorsement test: its focus on how a "reasonable observer" looks to the minority or majority status of a religion. "If there be such a person as the 'reasonable observer,' I am quite certain that he or she will take away a salient message from our holding in this case: the Supreme Court of the United States has concluded that the First Amendment creates classes of religions based on the relative numbers of their adherents. Those religions enjoying the largest following must be consigned to the status of least-favored faiths so as to avoid any possible risk of offending members of minority religions."

NOTES

(1) *Religious Displays in Public Forums.* In *Capitol Sq. Review Bd. v. Pinette*, 515 U.S. 753 (1995), the Court (7–2) held that allowing a private group to display an unattended cross on Capitol Square near the Statehouse in Columbus, Ohio, would not violate the Establishment Clause. In December, 1993, after allowing private displays of a Christmas tree and a menorah on Capitol Square, the Review and Advisory Board denied the Ku Klux Klan's application to display an unattended cross. Finding that Capitol Square was a traditional public forum, open to various forms of private expression, the Court held that a state may only restrict protected expression "if such a restriction is necessary, and narrowly drawn, to serve a compelling state interest." While avoiding an Establishment Clause violation is a compelling state interest, the Court relied heavily on *Widmar v. Vincent* and *Lamb's Chapel v. Center Moriches Union Free School Dist.* in denying the existence of such a violation. Capitol Square is a public forum equally accessible to all groups in the community.

None of the five separate opinions applied the *Lemon* test. In part of his opinion, Justice Scalia refused to apply the "so-called 'endorsement test,' " as there was no governmental "expression or demonstration of approval or support." Only Chief Justice Rehnquist and Justices Kennedy and Thomas joined Justice Scalia. Restricting religious expression simply because of its proximity to a governmental body would result in a " 'transferred endorsement' test relying on the misperceptions of a hypothetical reasonable observer. Justice Scalia suggested disclaimers to discourage any public misperceptions of government endorsement."

Concurring in part and concurring in the judgment, Justice O'Connor, with whom Justices Souter and Breyer joined, disagreed with the plurality that this case presented "an exception to the endorsement test for the public forum context." She stressed that the "endorsement test necessarily focuses upon the perception of a reasonable, informed observer," and requires the Court to ask "whether the challenged governmental practice either has the purpose or effect of 'endorsing' religion." To eliminate these effects, Justice O'Connor would require the government to display a disclaimer of any government endorsement in addition to any signs posted by the private group.

The test is not what the "casual passerby" observes, but rather, an observer "deemed aware of history and context of the community and forum in which the religious display appears." Because an observer in this case would realize that Capitol Square has traditionally been a public forum, Justice O'Connor concluded that an unattended cross accompanied by a disclaimer would not violate the Establishment Clause.

Justice Souter, with whom Justices O'Connor and Breyer joined, concurred in part and concurred in the judgment. Justice Souter disagreed with the plurality that only purposeful government endorsement violates the Establishment Clause. Instead, the Establishment Clause requires the Court to look at the circumstances of a particular case to decide if an "intelligent observer" perceives a religious display, on government property, as government endorsement of religion. Rather than reject the application, the State could have required the sign specifying private sponsorship to be easily recognizable to the public, or placed all unattended displays in one area with a general disclaimer of government endorsement for the area.

Dissenting, Justice Stevens maintained that the Establishment Clause creates "a strong presumption against the installation of unattended religious symbols on public property."

Justice Ginsburg dissented because the District Court had not ordered a disclaimer, and the disclaimer that ultimately was attached was inadequate.

(2) For a discussion of religious displays in public fora, see Daniel Parish, *Comment, Private Religious Displays in Public Fora*, 61 U. CHI. L. REV. 253, 289 (1994) ("At first glance, banning every religious display from the public forum may not seem all that horrible. After all, no one is prohibited from practicing his own religion on private grounds, and we would thereby wholly avoid the risk of apparent government endorsement of religion. But such a suggestion would be practically unworkable in this very religious nation, while the Free Exercise and Free Speech Clauses would seem to require permitting religious expression to have some voice in the public forum. At the same time, giving religious displays a free run of the public forum would be politically unacceptable as well. It would also tend to eviscerate the Establishment Clause. Allowing the displays while requiring real and effective disclaimers strikes a balance between these competing concerns.").

For further discussion, see Steven D. Smith, *The Rise and Fall of Religious Freedom in Constitutional Discourse*, 140 U. PA. L. REV. 149, 149 (1991) ("[R]eligious freedom, at least as it has come to be understood, forbids governmental reliance upon religious justifications as a basis for public policies or decisions. Therein lies the paradox — our constitutional commitment to religious freedom undermines its own foundation; it cancels itself out by precluding government from recognizing and acting upon the principal justification supporting that commitment.").

VAN ORDEN v. PERRY
545 U.S. 677, 125 S. Ct. 2854, 162 L. Ed. 2d 607 (2005)

CHIEF JUSTICE REHNQUIST delivered the opinion of the Court.

The question here is whether the Establishment Clause of the First Amendment allows the display of a monument inscribed with the Ten Commandments on the Texas State Capitol grounds. We hold that it does.

The 22 acres surrounding the Texas State Capitol contain 17 monuments and 21 historical markers commemorating the "people, ideals, and events that compose Texan identity." Tex. H. Con. Res. 38, 77th Leg. (2001).[32] The monolith challenged here stands 6-feet high and 3-feet wide. It is located to the north of the Capitol building, between the Capitol and the Supreme Court building. Its primary content is the text of the Ten Commandments. An eagle grasping the American flag, an eye inside of a pyramid, and two small tablets with what appears to be an ancient script are carved above the text of the Ten Commandments. Below the text are two Stars of David and the superimposed Greek letters Chi and Rho, which represent Christ. The bottom of the monument bears the inscription "PRESENTED TO THE PEOPLE AND YOUTH OF TEXAS BY THE FRATERNAL ORDER OF EAGLES OF TEXAS 1961."

The legislative record surrounding the State's acceptance of the monument from the Eagles — a national social, civic, and patriotic organization — is limited to legislative journal entries. After the monument was accepted, the State selected a site for the monument based on the recommendation of the state organization responsible for maintaining the Capitol grounds. The Eagles paid the cost of erecting the monument, the dedication of which was presided over by two state legislators.

---

[32] [Court's footnote 1] The monuments are: Heroes of the Alamo, Hood's Brigade, Confederate Soldiers, Volunteer Fireman, Terry's Texas Rangers, Texas Cowboy, Spanish-American War, Texas National Guard, Ten Commandments, Tribute to Texas School Children, Texas Pioneer Woman, The Boy Scouts' Statue of Liberty Replica, Pearl Harbor Veterans, Korean War Veterans, Soldiers of World War I, Disabled Veterans, and Texas Peace Officers.

Petitioner Thomas Van Orden is a native Texan and a resident of Austin. . . .

Forty years after the monument's erection and six years after Van Orden began to encounter the monument frequently, he sued numerous state officials in their official capacities under 42 U.S.C. § 1983, seeking both a declaration that the monument's placement violates the Establishment Clause and an injunction requiring its removal. . . .

Our cases, Januslike, point in two directions in applying the Establishment Clause. One face looks toward the strong role played by religion and religious traditions throughout our Nation's history. . . .

The other face looks toward the principle that governmental intervention in religious matters can itself endanger religious freedom.

This case, like all Establishment Clause challenges, presents us with the difficulty of respecting both faces. Our institutions presuppose a Supreme Being, yet these institutions must not press religious observances upon their citizens. One face looks to the past in acknowledgment of our Nation's heritage, while the other looks to the present in demanding a separation between church and state. Reconciling these two faces requires that we neither abdicate our responsibility to maintain a division between church and state nor evince a hostility to religion by disabling the government from in some ways recognizing our religious heritage[.] . . .

These two faces are evident in representative cases both upholding and invalidating laws under the Establishment Clause. Over the last 25 years, we have sometimes pointed to *Lemon v. Kurtzman*, 403 U.S. 602 (1971), as providing the governing test in Establishment Clause challenges. . . . Yet, just two years after *Lemon* was decided, we noted that the factors identified in Lemon serve as "no more than helpful signposts." *Hunt v. McNair*, 413 U.S. 734, 741 (1973). Many of our recent cases simply have not applied the *Lemon* test. Others have applied it only after concluding that the challenged practice was invalid under a different Establishment Clause test.

Whatever may be the fate of the *Lemon* test in the larger scheme of Establishment Clause jurisprudence, we think it not useful in dealing with the sort of passive monument that Texas has erected on its Capitol grounds. Instead, our analysis is driven both by the nature of the monument and by our Nation's history.

As we explained in *Lynch v. Donnelly*, 465 U.S. 668 (1984): "There is an unbroken history of official acknowledgment by all three branches of government of the role of religion in American life from at least 1789." *Id.*, at 674. For example, both Houses passed resolutions in 1789 asking President George Washington to issue a Thanksgiving Day Proclamation to "recommend to the people of the United States a day of public thanksgiving and prayer, to be observed by acknowledging, with grateful hearts, the many and signal favors of Almighty God." President Washington's proclamation directly attributed to the Supreme Being the foundations and successes of our young Nation[.] . . .

In this case we are faced with a display of the Ten Commandments on government property outside the Texas State Capitol. Such acknowledgments of the role played by the Ten Commandments in our Nation's heritage are common throughout America. We need only look within our own Courtroom. Since 1935, Moses has stood, holding two tablets that reveal portions of the Ten Commandments written in Hebrew, among other lawgivers in the south frieze. Representations of the Ten Commandments adorn the metal gates lining the north and south sides of the Courtroom as well as the doors leading into the Courtroom. Moses also sits on the exterior east facade of the building holding the Ten Commandments tablets.

Similar acknowledgments can be seen throughout a visitor's tour of our Nation's

Capital. For example, a large statue of Moses holding the Ten Commandments, alongside a statue of the Apostle Paul, has overlooked the rotunda of the Library of Congress' Jefferson Building since 1897. And the Jefferson Building's Great Reading Room contains a sculpture of a woman beside the Ten Commandments with a quote above her from the Old Testament (Micah 6:8). A medallion with two tablets depicting the Ten Commandments decorates the floor of the National Archives. Inside the Department of Justice, a statue entitled "The Spirit of Law" has two tablets representing the Ten Commandments lying at its feet. In front of the Ronald Reagan Building is another sculpture that includes a depiction of the Ten Commandments. So too a 24-foot-tall sculpture, depicting, among other things, the Ten Commandments and a cross, stands outside the federal courthouse that houses both the Court of Appeals and the District Court for the District of Columbia. Moses is also prominently featured in the Chamber of the United States House of Representatives.[33]

. . . The Executive and Legislative Branches have also acknowledged the historical role of the Ten Commandments. . . .

Of course, the Ten Commandments are religious — they were so viewed at their inception and so remain. The monument, therefore, has religious significance. According to Judeo-Christian belief, the Ten Commandments were given to Moses by God on Mt. Sinai. But Moses was a lawgiver as well as a religious leader. And the Ten Commandments have an undeniable historical meaning, as the foregoing examples demonstrate. Simply having religious content or promoting a message consistent with a religious doctrine does not run afoul of the Establishment Clause.

There are, of course, limits to the display of religious messages or symbols. For example, we held unconstitutional a Kentucky statute requiring the posting of the Ten Commandments in every public schoolroom. *Stone v. Graham*, 449 U.S. 39 (1980) *(per curiam)*. . . . [W]e have "been particularly vigilant in monitoring compliance with the Establishment Clause in elementary and secondary schools" *Edwards v. Aguillard*, 482 U.S. 578, 583-584 (1987). . . . [34]

. . . Texas has treated her Capitol grounds monuments as representing the several strands in the State's political and legal history. The inclusion of the Ten Commandments monument in this group has a dual significance, partaking of both religion and government. . . .

JUSTICE SCALIA, concurring.

I join the opinion of The Chief Justice because I think it accurately reflects our current Establishment Clause jurisprudence — or at least the Establishment Clause jurisprudence we currently apply some of the time. I would prefer to reach the same result by adopting an Establishment Clause jurisprudence that is in accord with our Nation's past and present practices, and that can be consistently applied — the central relevant feature of which is that there is nothing unconstitutional in a State's favoring religion generally, honoring God through public prayer and acknowledgment, or, in a nonproselytizing manner, venerating the Ten Commandments.

JUSTICE THOMAS, concurring. . . .

---

[33] [Court's footnote 9] Other examples of monuments and buildings reflecting the prominent role of religion abound. For example, the Washington, Jefferson, and Lincoln Memorials all contain explicit invocations of God's importance. . . .

[34] [Court's footnote 11] Nor does anything suggest that *Stone* would extend to displays of the Ten Commandments that lack a "plainly religious," "pre-eminent purpose," [*Stone v. Graham*, 449 U.S. 39 (1980).] . . . Indeed, we need not decide in this case the extent to which a primarily religious purpose would affect our analysis because it is clear from the record that there is no evidence of such a purpose in this case.

This case would be easy if the Court were willing to abandon the inconsistent guideposts it has adopted for addressing Establishment Clause challenges, and return to the original meaning of the Clause. I have previously suggested that the Clause's text and history "resist incorporation" against the States. If the Establishment Clause does not restrain the States, then it has no application here, where only state action is at issue.

Even if the Clause is incorporated . . . our task would be far simpler if we returned to the original meaning of the word "establishment" than it is under the various approaches this Court now uses. The Framers understood an establishment "necessarily [to] involve actual legal coercion." [*Elk Grove Unified School Dist. v.*] *Newdow*, [542 U.S. 1,] 52 [(2004)] (Thomas, J., concurring in judgment). . . . "In other words, establishment at the founding involved, for eample, mandatory observance or mandatory payment of taxes supporting ministers." *Cutter* [*v. Wilkinson*, 544 U.S. 709, 729 (2005)] (Thomas, J., concurring). . . .

. . . In no sense does Texas compel petitioner Van Orden to do anything. . . .

. . . All told, this Court's jurisprudence leaves courts, governments, and believers and nonbelievers alike confused. . . .

First, this Court's precedent permits even the slightest public recognition of religion to constitute an establishment of religion. For example, . . . a park ranger has claimed that a cross erected to honor World War I veterans on a rock in the Mojave Desert Preserve violated the Establishment Clause, and won. *See Buono v. Norton*, 212 F. Supp. 2d 1202 (CD Cal. 2002). If a cross in the middle of a desert establishes a religion, then no religious observance is safe from challenge. . . .

Second, in a seeming attempt to balance out its willingness to consider almost any acknowledgment of religion an establishment, in other cases Members of this Court have concluded that the term or symbol at issue has no religious meaning by virtue of its ubiquity or rote ceremonial invocation. But words such as "God" have religious significance. For example, just last Term this Court had before it a challenge to the recitation of the Pledge of Allegiance, which includes the phrase "one Nation under God." . . .

Finally, the very "flexibility" of this Court's Establishment Clause precedent leaves it incapable of consistent application. . . . The inconsistency between the decisions the Court reaches today in this case and in *McCreary County v. American Civil Liberties Union of Ky.*, [545 U.S. 844 (2005)], only compounds the confusion. . . .

Much, if not all, of this would be avoided if the Court would return to the views of the Framers and adopt coercion as the touchstone for our Establishment Clause inquiry. . . .

JUSTICE BREYER, concurring in the judgment. . . .

If the relation between government and religion is one of separation, but not of mutual hostility and suspicion, one will inevitably find difficult borderline cases. And in such cases, I see no test-related substitute for the exercise of legal judgment. . . .

The case before us is a borderline case. . . . On the one hand, the Commandments' text undeniably has a religious message, invoking, indeed emphasizing, the Diety. On the other hand, focusing on the text of the Commandments alone cannot conclusively resolve this case. Rather, to determine the message that the text here conveys, we must examine how the text is *used*. And that inquiry requires us to consider the context of the display.

In certain contexts, a display of the tablets of the Ten Commandments can convey not simply a religious message but also a secular moral message (about proper standards of social conduct). And in certain contexts, a display of the tablets can also convey a historical message (about a historic relation between those standards and the law) — a fact that helps to explain the display of those tablets in dozens of courthouses throughout the Nation, including the Supreme Court of the United States.

Here the tablets have been used as part of a display that communicates not simply a religious message, but a secular message as well. The circumstances surrounding the display's placement on the capitol grounds and its physical setting suggest that the State itself intended the latter, nonreligious aspects of the tablets' message to predominate. . . .

The group that donated the monument, the Fraternal Order of Eagles, a private civic (and primarily secular) organization, while interested in the religious aspect of the Ten Commandments, sought to highlight the Commandments' role in shaping civic morality as part of that organization's efforts to combat juvenile delinquency. The Eagles' consultation with a committee composed of members of several faiths in order to find a nonsectarian text underscores the group's ethics-based motives. The tablets, as displayed on the monument, prominently acknowledge that the Eagles donated the display, a factor which, though not sufficient, thereby further distances the State itself from the religious aspect of the Commandments' message.

The physical setting of the monument, moreover, suggests little or nothing of the sacred. The monument sits in a large park containing 17 monuments and 21 historical markers, all designed to illustrate the "ideals" of those who settled in Texas and of those who have lived there since that time. The setting does not readily lend itself to meditation or any other religious activity. But it does provide a context of history and moral ideals. . . . [T]he context suggests that the State intended the display's moral message — an illustrative message reflecting the historical "ideals" of Texans — to predominate.

. . . [A] further factor is determinative here. As far as I can tell, 40 years passed in which the presence of this monument, legally speaking, went unchallenged (until the single legal objection raised by petitioner). . . . Those 40 years suggest that the public visiting the capitol grounds has considered the religious aspect of the tablets' message as part of what is a broader moral and historical message reflective of a cultural heritage.

. . . The display is not on the grounds of a public school, where, given the impressionability of the young, government must exercise particular care in separating church and state. This case also differs from *McCreary County*, where the short (and stormy) history of the courthouse Commandments' displays demonstrates the substantially religious objectives of those who mounted them, and the effect of this readily apparent objective upon those who view them. . . . And, in today's world, in a Nation of so many different religious and comparable nonreligious fundamental beliefs, a more contemporary state effort to focus attention upon a religious text is certainly likely to prove divisive in a way that this longstanding, pre-existing monument has not.

For these reasons, I believe that the Texas display — serving a mixed but primarily nonreligious purpose, not primarily "advancing" or "inhibiting religion," and not creating an "excessive government entanglement with religion," — might satisfy this Court's more formal Establishment Clause tests. *Lemon*, 403 U.S., at 612-613. But, . . . I rely less upon a literal application of any particular test than upon consideration of the basic purposes of the First Amendment's Religion Clauses themselves. This display has stood apparently uncontested for nearly two generations. That experience helps us understand that as a practical matter of *degree* this display is unlikely to prove divisive. And this matter of degree is, I believe, critical in a borderline case such as this one.

At the same time, to reach a contrary conclusion here, based primarily upon on the religious nature of the tablets' text would, I fear, lead the law to exhibit a hostility toward religion that has no place in our Establishment Clause traditions. Such a holding might well encourage disputes concerning the removal of longstanding depictions of the Ten Commandments from public buildings across the Nation. And it could thereby create the very kind of religiously based divisiveness that the Establishment Clause seeks to avoid. . . .

In light of these considerations, I cannot agree with today's plurality's analysis. Nor can I agree with Justice Scalia's dissent in *McCreary County*. I do agree with Justice O'Connor's statement of principles in *McCreary County*, though I disagree with her evaluation of the evidence as it bears on the application of those principles to this case. . . .

JUSTICE STEVENS, with whom JUSTICE GINSBURG joins, dissenting.

. . . This State endorses the divine code of the "Judeo-Christian" God. . . .

I

In my judgment, at the very least, the Establishment Clause has created a strong presumption against the display of religious symbols on public property. . . .

. . . The wall that separates the church from the State does not prohibit the government from acknowledging the religious beliefs and practices of the American people, nor does it require governments to hide works of art or historic memorabilia from public view just because they also have religious significance. . . . [35]

. . . This Nation's resolute commitment to neutrality with respect to religion is flatly inconsistent with the plurality's wholehearted validation of an official state endorsement of the message that there is one, and only one, God. . . .

II

Though the State of Texas may genuinely wish to combat juvenile delinquency, and may rightly want to honor the Eagles for their efforts, it cannot effectuate these admirable purposes through an explicitly religious medium. . . .

. . . For many followers, the Commandments represent the literal word of God as spoken to Moses and repeated to his followers after descending from Mount Sinai. The message conveyed by the Ten Commandments thus cannot be analogized to an appendage to a common article of commerce ("In God we Trust") or an incidental part of a familiar recital ("God save the United States and this honorable Court"). . . .

Even if . . . the message of the monument . . . fairly could be said to represent the belief system of all Judeo-Christians, it would still run afoul of the Establishment Clause by prescribing a compelled code of conduct from . . . a Judeo-Christian God. . . .

. . . [A]llowing the seat of government to serve as a stage for the propagation of an unmistakably Judeo-Christian message of piety would have the tendency to make nonmonotheists and nonbelievers "feel like [outsiders] in matters of faith, and [strangers] in the political community." [*Capitol Square Review & Advisory Board v.*] *Pinette*, 515 U.S., at 799 (Stevens, J., dissenting). . . .

---

[35] [Court's footnote 9] Though this Court has subscribed to the view that the Ten Commandments influenced the development of Western legal thought, . . . the District Court categorically rejected respondent's suggestion that the State's actual purpose in displaying the Decalogue was to signify its influence on secular law and Texas institutions.

III

. . . [A]lthough Thanksgiving Day proclamations and inaugural speeches undoubtedly seem official, in most circumstances they will not constitute the sort of governmental endorsement of religion at which the separation of church and state is aimed. . . .

. . . [F]or nearly a century after the Founding, many accepted the idea that America was not just a *religious* nation, but "a Christian nation." *Church of Holy Trinity v. United States*, 143 U.S. 457, 471 (1892).

The original understanding of the type of "religion" that qualified for constitutional protection under the Establishment Clause likely did not include those followers of Judaism and Islam who are among the preferred "monotheistic" religions Justice Scalia has embraced in his *McCreary County* opinion. . . .

It is our duty . . . to interpret the First Amendment . . . not by merely asking what those words meant to observers at the time of the founding, but instead by deriving from the Clause's text and history the broad principles that remain valid today. . . . [W]e have construed the Equal Protection Clause of the Fourteenth Amendment to prohibit segregated schools even though those who drafted that Amendment evidently thought that separate was not unequal. . . .

. . . We serve our constitutional mandate by expounding the meaning of constitutional provisions with one eye towards our Nation's history and the other fixed on its democratic aspirations. . . .

. . . Fortunately, we are not bound by the Framers' expectations — we are bound by the legal principles they enshrined in our Constitution. . . .

IV

The judgment of the Court in this case stands for the proposition that the Constitution permits governmental displays of sacred religious texts. This makes a mockery of the constitutional ideal that government must remain neutral between religion and irreligion. If a State may endorse a particular deity's command to "have no other gods before me," it is difficult to conceive of any textual display that would run afoul of the Establishment Clause. . . .

JUSTICE O'CONNOR, dissenting.

For essentially the reasons given by Justice Souter, as well as the reasons given in my concurrence in *McCreary County v. American Civil Liberties Union of Ky.*, I respectfully dissent.

JUSTICE SOUTER, with whom JUSTICE STEVENS and JUSTICE GINSBURG join, dissenting.

Although the First Amendment's Religion Clauses have not been read to mandate absolute governmental neutrality toward religion, the Establishment Clause requires neutrality as a general rule. . . .

. . . [A] pedestrian happening upon the monument at issue here needs no training in religious doctrine to realize that the statement of the Commandments, quoting God himself, proclaims that the will of the divine being is the source of obligation to obey the rules, including the facially secular ones. . . . [T]he most eye-catching segment of the quotation is the declaration "I AM the LORD thy God." What follows, of course, are the rules against other gods, graven images, vain swearing, and Sabbath breaking. . . .

To drive the religious point home, and identify the message as religious to any viewer who failed to read the text, the engraved quotation is framed by religious symbols: two tablets with what appears to be ancient script on them, two Stars of

David, and the superimposed Greek letters Chi and Rho as the familiar monogram of Christ. Nothing on the monument, in fact, detracts from its religious nature,[36] *see* [*County of Allegheny v. American Civil Liberties Union, Greater Pittsburgh Chapter*, 492 U.S. 573, 598 (1989)] ("Here, unlike in *Lynch* [*v. Donnelly*, 465 U.S. 668 (1984)], nothing in the context of the display detracts from the crèche's religious message"). . . .

The monument's presentation of the Commandments with religious text emphasized and enhanced stands in contrast to any number of perfectly constitutional depictions of them, the frieze of our own Courtroom providing a good example, where the figure of Moses stands among history's great lawgivers. While Moses holds the tablets of the Commandments showing some Hebrew text, no one looking at the lines of figures in marble relief is likely to see a religious purpose behind the assemblage or take away a religious message from it. Only one other depiction represents a religious leader, and the historical personages are mixed with symbols of moral and intellectual abstractions like Equity and Authority. . . . Moses enjoys no especial prominence on the frieze, viewers can readily take him to be there as a lawgiver in the company of other lawgivers. . . . [A] display of the Commandments accompanied by an exposition of how they have influenced modern law would most likely be constitutionally unobjectionable.[37] And the Decalogue could, as *Stone* [*v. Graham*, 449 U.S. 39 (1980)] suggested, be integrated constitutionally into a course of study in public schools. *Stone*, 449 U.S., at 42.

Texas . . . argues that its monument . . . ought to be viewed as only 1 among 17 placed on the 22 acres surrounding the state capitol. . . .

But 17 monuments with no common appearance, history, or esthetic role scattered over 22 acres is not a museum, and anyone strolling around the lawn would surely take each memorial on its own terms. . . . One monument expresses admiration for pioneer women. One pays respect to the fighters of World War II. And one quotes the God of Abraham whose command is the sanction for moral law. . . . In like circumstances, we rejected an argument similar to the State's, noting in *County of*

---

[36] [Dissent's footnote 2] That the monument also surrounds the text of the Commandments with various American symbols (notably the U.S. flag and a bald eagle) only underscores the impermissibility of Texas's actions: by juxtaposing these patriotic symbols with the Commandments and other religious signs, the monument sends the message that being American means being religious (and not just being religious but also subscribing to the Commandments, i.e., practicing a monotheistic religion).

[37] [Dissent's footnote 4] For similar reasons, the other displays of the Commandments that the plurality mentions do not run afoul of the Establishment Clause. The statues of Moses and St. Paul in the Main Reading Room of the Library of Congress are 2 of 16 set in close proximity, statues that "represent men illustrious in the various forms of thought and activity. . . . " Moses and St. Paul represent religion, while the other 14 (a group that includes Beethoven, Shakespeare, Michelangelo, Columbus, and Plato) represent the nonreligious categories of philosophy, art, history, commerce, science, law, and poetry. Similarly, the sculpture of the woman beside the Decalogue in the Main Reading Room is one of 8 such figures "representing eight characteristic features of civilized life and thought," the same 8 features (7 of them nonreligious) that Moses, St. Paul, and the rest of the 16 statues represent. The inlay on the floor of the National Archives Building is one of four such discs, the collective theme of which is not religious. Rather, the discs "symbolize the various types of Government records that were to come into the National Archive." (. . . Each disc is paired with a winged figure; the disc containing the depiction of the Commandments, a depiction that, notably, omits the Commandments' text, is paired with a figure representing legislation.) As for Moses's "prominent featuring in the Chamber of the United States House of Representatives," Moses is actually 1 of 23 portraits encircling the House Chamber, each approximately the same size, having no religious theme. The portraits depict "men noted in history for the part they played in the evolution of what has become American law." More importantly for purposes of this case, each portrait consists only of the subject's face; the Ten Commandments appear nowhere in Moses's portrait.

Allegheny that "the presence of Santas or other Christmas decorations elsewhere in the . . . courthouse, and of the nearby gallery forum, fail to negate the [crèche's] endorsement effect." . . .

. . . The monument in this case sits on the grounds of the Texas State Capitol. . . . [I]t is the civic home of every one of the State's citizens. If neutrality in religion means something, any citizen should be able to visit that civic home without having to confront religious expressions clearly meant to convey an official religious position. . . .

Finally, though this too is a point on which judgment will vary, I do not see a persuasive argument for constitutionality in the plurality's observation that Van Orden's lawsuit comes "forty years after the monument's erection." . . . I doubt that a slow walk to the courthouse, even one that took 40 years, is much evidentiary help in applying the Establishment Clause. . . .

McCREARY COUNTY v. AMERICAN CIVIL LIBERTIES UNION OF KENTUCKY, 545 U.S. 844 (2005). In *McCreary County*, the Court declared unconstitutional a display of the Ten Commandments in certain courthouses. The Court held "that the counties' manifest objective may be dispositive of the constitutional enquiry, and that the development of the presentation should be considered when determining its purpose." Two counties had first hung in their courthouses "large, gold-framed copies of an abridged text of the King James version of the Ten Commandments, including a citation to the Book of Exodus." Shortly after the American Civil Liberties Union of Kentucky sued, the counties authorized "a second, expanded display" stating that "the Ten Commandments are 'the precedent legal code upon which the civil and criminal codes of . . . Kentucky are founded.' "[38] The second version of the displays added "copies of the resolution" authorizing the displays and "eight other documents in smaller frames, each either having a religious theme or excerpted to highlight a religious element."[39] The final display, "the third within a year," contained "nine framed documents of equal size" with the Ten Commandments being "quoted at greater length than before."[40] This third display included the words: " 'The Ten Commandments provide the moral background of the Declaration of Independence and the foundation of our legal tradition.' "

Writing for a 5-4 majority, Justice Souter began by discussing the Court's decision 25 years ago in *Stone v. Graham*, 449 U.S. 39 (1980), *supra* § 16.03[1], Note (2). *Stone* stated that "that the Commandments 'are undeniably a sacred text in the Jewish and Christian faiths' and held that their display in public classrooms violated" the

---

[38] In support of this assertion, the counties referred to the fact that in 1993, the state House of Representatives "voted unanimously . . . to adjourn . . . 'in remembrance and honor of Jesus Christ, the Prince of Ethics,' " and also claimed "that the 'Founding Fathers [had an] explicit understanding of the duty of elected officials to publicly acknowledge God as the source of America's strength and direction.' "

[39] The other documents on display included "the 'endowed by their Creator' passage from the Declaration of Independence; the Preamble to the Constitution of Kentucky; the national motto, 'In God We Trust'; a page from the Congressional Record of February 2, 1983, proclaiming the Year of the Bible and including a statement of the Ten Commandments; a proclamation by President Abraham Lincoln designating April 30, 1863, a National Day of Prayer and Humiliation; an excerpt from President Lincoln's 'Reply to Loyal Colored People of Baltimore upon Presentation of a Bible,' reading that 'the Bible is the best gift God has ever given to man'; a proclamation by President Reagan marking 1983 the Year of the Bible; and the *Mayflower Compact*."

[40] The documents in the third display, "entitled 'The Foundations of American Law and Government Display' " included "copies of the Magna Carta, the Declaration of Independence, the Bill of Rights, the lyrics of the Star Spangled Banner, the Mayflower Compact, the National Motto, the Preamble to the Kentucky Constitution, and a picture of Lady Justice" in addition to the Ten Commandments. Each document was accompanied by "a statement about its historical and legal significance."

Establishment Clause. "The touchstone" for the majority's analysis was "governmental neutrality between religion and religion, and between religion and nonreligion." Relying on Justice O'Connor's concurrence in *Santa Fe Independent School Dist. v. Doe*, 530 U.S. 290 (2000), Justice Souter stated: "The eyes that look to purpose belong to an 'objective observer,' one who takes account of the traditional external signs that show up in the 'text, legislative history, and implementation of the statute,' or comparable official act."

Lemon v. Kurtzman, 403 U.S. 602 (1971), "said that government action must have 'a secular . . . purpose' " and cases since then have shown "that although a legislature's stated reasons will generally get deference, the secular purpose required has to be genuine, not a sham, and not merely secondary to a religious objective." When "in those unusual cases where the claim was an apparent sham, or the secular purpose secondary the unsurprising results have been findings of no adequate secular object, as against a predominantly religious one."[41] The determination takes "historical context" into consideration: "reasonable observers have reasonable memories, and our precedents sensibly forbid an observer 'to turn a blind eye to the context in which [the] policy arose.' " Consequently, "the same government action may be constitutional if taken in the first instance and unconstitutional if it has a sectarian heritage."

Because this case came "on appeal from a preliminary injunction," the Court reviewed "the District Court's legal rulings *de novo*, and its ultimate conclusion for abuse of discretion." While *Stone* is "the initial legal benchmark," that case did not determine "the constitutionality of every possible way the Commandments might be set out," and with "the Establishment Clause detail is key." Therefore, "we look to the record of evidence showing the progression leading up to the third display of the Commandments."[42] At the county "ceremony for posting the framed Commandments" a pastor proclaimed "the certainty of the existence of God." After being sued, the second display included "the statement of the government's purpose expressly set out in the county resolutions, and underscored it by juxtaposing the Commandments to other documents with highlighted references to God as their sole common element." Understandably, "the Counties make no attempt to defend their undeniable objective" in the second display "but the reasonable observer could not forget it." The third exhibit, entitled "Foundations of American Law and Government," displayed "the Commandments in the company of other documents the Counties thought especially significant in the historical foundation of American government." However, neither the District Court of Appeals "found legitimizing secular purpose in this third version of the display." " 'When both courts [that have already passed on this case] are unable to discern an arguably valid secular purpose, this Court normally should hesitate to find one.' " But even though "repeal of the earlier county authorizations would not have erased them from the record of evidence bearing on current purpose, the extraordinary resolutions for the second display passed just months earlier were not repealed." In fact, the third exhibit, "which quoted more of the purely religious language of the Commandments than the first two displays had done," enhanced "the sectarian spirit" of the resolution common to the second and third displays.

The Court did "not decide that the Counties' past actions forever taint any effort on their part to deal with the subject matter. We hold only that purpose needs to be taken seriously under the Establishment Clause and needs to be understood in light of

---

[41] The dissent maintains "that the purpose test is satisfied" by "any secular purpose for the government action," however this "would leave the purpose test with no real bite."

[42] Displaying the text of the Commandments is "different from a symbolic depiction, like tablets with 10 roman numerals, which could be seen as alluding to a general notion of law, not a sectarian conception of faith."

context." If conditions changed in a "constitutionally significant" manner, the "district courts are fully capable of adjusting preliminary relief." The Court did not "hold that a sacred text can never be integrated constitutionally into a governmental display on the subject of law, or American history." Indeed, the courtroom in which the Supreme Court hears oral argument itself displays "the figure of Moses holding tablets exhibiting a portion of the Hebrew text of the later, secularly phrased Commandments," alongside "17 other lawgivers, most of them secular."

In responding to the dissent, Justice Souter admitted that the "two clauses tied to 'religion'" sometimes "compete: spending government money on the clergy looks like establishing religion, but if the government cannot pay for military chaplains a good many soldiers and sailors would be kept from the opportunity to exercise their chosen religions. At other times, limits on governmental action that might make sense as a way to avoid establishment could arguably limit freedom of speech when the speaking is done under government auspices." Because of these difficulties, "the principle of neutrality has provided a good sense of direction: the government may not favor one religion over another, or religion over irreligion." This allows "not only to protect the integrity of individual conscience in religious matters, but to guard against the civic divisiveness that follows when the Government weighs in on one side of the religious debate."

Reviewing the drafts of the Establishment Clause, "the final language" specifically "extended [the] prohibition to state support for "religion" in general." Indeed, Thomas Jefferson "refused to issue Thanksgiving Proclamations because he believed that they violated the Constitution." In light of this information, "the dissent fails to show a consistent original understanding from which to argue that the neutrality principle should be rejected," but "does manage to deliver a surprise" by proposing "that the deity the Framers had in mind was the God of monotheism." This "apparently means that government should be free to approve the core beliefs of a favored religion over the tenets of others."[43]

Justice O'Connor concurred. "Free people are entitled to free and diverse thoughts, which government ought neither to constrain nor to direct." Current world events evidence "the violent consequences of the assumption of religious authority by government," but our "constitutional boundaries" have enabled "private religious exercise to flourish."[44] Justice O'Connor continued: "Those who would renegotiate the boundaries between church and state must therefore answer a difficult question: Why would we trade a system that has served us so well for one that has served others so poorly?" To join "secular and religious authority together poses risks to both." Considering "the history of this particular display of the Ten Commandments" it violates the Establishment Clause as "it conveys an unmistakable message of endorsement to the reasonable observer."

Justice Scalia dissented, joined by the Chief Justice and Justices Kennedy and Thomas. France exemplifies "one model of the relationship between church and state," whose Constitution begins "'France is [a] . . . secular . . . Republic.'" America did

---

[43] Quoting Justice Story as probably reflecting "the thinking of the framing generation," Justice Souter noted, "that the purpose of the Clause was 'not to countenance, much less to advance, Mahometanism, or Judaism, or infidelity, by prostrating Christianity; but to exclude all rivalry among Christian sects.'" The majority argued that "the Framers would, therefore, almost certainly object to the dissent's unstated reasoning that because Christianity was a monotheistic "religion," monotheism with Mosaic antecedents should be a touchstone of establishment interpretation."

[44] The statement made in *Zorach v. Clauson*, "'we are a religious people,' has proved true. Americans attend their places of worship more often than do citizens of other developed nations."

not follow this example.[45] Today "the views of our people on" religion have not "significantly changed."[46] Considering the evidence, "how can the Court *possibly* assert that 'the First Amendment mandates governmental neutrality between . . . religion and nonreligion?' " This proposition is unsupported except by "the Court's own say-so, citing as support only the unsubstantiated say-so of earlier Courts going back no farther than the mid-20th century." Notably, "a majority of the Justices on the current Court (including at least one Member of today's majority) have, in separate opinions, repudiated the brain-spun '*Lemon* test' that embodies the supposed principle of neutrality between religion and irreligion." Furthermore, the test "is discredited because the Court has not had the courage (or the foolhardiness) to apply the neutrality principle consistently." For example, "when the government relieves churches from the obligation to pay property taxes, when it allows students to absent themselves from public school to take religious classes, and when it exempts religious organizations from generally applicable prohibitions of religious discrimination, it surely means to bestow a benefit on religious practice," and the Court has approved all of this.

"Our Nation's historical practices" make clear "that the Establishment Clause permits this disregard of polytheists and believers in unconcerned deities, just as it permits the disregard of devout atheists. The Thanksgiving Proclamation issued by George Washington at the instance of the First Congress was scrupulously nondenominational — but it was monotheistic." Significantly, "Christianity, Judaism, and Islam — which combined account for 97.7% of all believers — are monotheistic" and each believes "that the Ten Commandments were given by God to Moses." Unlike the majority, who relied on "mere 'proclamations and statements' of the Founders," Justice Scalia maintained that he "relied primarily upon official acts and official proclamations of the United States or of the component branches of its Government." This position did not violate the rights of nonmonotheists "because governmental invocation of God is not an establishment."

The Court's decision "modifies *Lemon* to ratchet up the Court's hostility to religion." In relying on the "objective observer," the "inquiry focuses not on the *actual purpose* of government action, but the 'purpose apparent from government action.' " The decision also "replaces *Lemon's* requirement that the government have 'a secular . . . purpose' with the heightened requirement that the secular purpose 'predominate.' " Even so, "the displays at issue here were constitutional." Styled "The Foundations of American Law and Government Display," the Ten Commandments were "the same size and had the same appearance" as the eight accompanying government documents in the display.[47]

"The frequency of these displays testifies to the popular understanding that the Ten Commandments are a foundation of the rule of law, and a symbol of the role that

---

[45] For instance, "George Washington added to the form of Presidential oath" the "words 'so help me God;' " the Marshall Court "opened its sessions with the prayer, 'God save the United States and this Honorable Court;' " and "the First Congress" opened "its legislative sessions with a prayer." Additionally, the very "week that Congress submitted the Establishment Clause as part of the Bill of Rights for ratification" they also provided for "paid chaplains in the House and Senate" and "the day after the First Amendment was proposed, the same Congress" asked "the President to proclaim 'a day of public thanksgiving and prayer, to be observed.' " The First Congress also included in the Northwest Territory Ordinance language about " 'religion, morality, and knowledge, being necessary to good government.' "

[46] "Presidents continue to conclude the Presidential oath with the words 'so help me God,' " and "this Court" continues "to open with . . . prayer." Likewise, "our coinage bears the motto 'IN GOD WE TRUST,' " and the "Pledge of Allegiance contains" the words "under God."

[47] The exhibit also included "a document that informs passersby that it 'contains documents that played a significant role in the foundation of our system of law and government.' "

religion played, and continues to play, in our system of government."[48] The problem for the majority lay in "the Counties' *purpose* in erecting the Foundations Displays, not the displays themselves." The result is that "[d]isplays erected in silence (and under the direction of good legal advice) are permissible, while those hung after discussion and debate are deemed unconstitutional." Finally, "it is unlikely that a reasonable observer *would even have been aware* of the resolutions, so there would be nothing to 'cast off.' "

The dissent summed up: "[t]he first displays did not necessarily evidence an intent to further religious practice; nor did the second displays, or the resolutions authorizing them; and there is in any event no basis for attributing whatever intent motivated the first and second displays to the third." The majority "may well be correct in identifying the third displays as the fruit of a desire to display the Ten Commandments, but neither our cases nor our history support its assertion that such a desire renders the fruit poisonous."

[3]   Moment of Silence

WALLACE v. JAFFREE
472 U.S. 38, 105 S. Ct. 2479, 86 L. Ed. 2d 29 (1985)

JUSTICE STEVENS delivered the opinion of the Court.

At an early stage of this litigation, the constitutionality of three Alabama statutes was questioned: (1) § 16-1-20, enacted in 1978, which authorized a one-minute period of silence in all public schools "for meditation";[49] (2) § 16-1-20.1, enacted in 1981, which authorized a period of silence "for meditation or voluntary prayer";[50] and (3) § 16-1-20.2, enacted in 1982, which authorized teachers to lead "willing students" in a prescribed prayer to "Almighty God . . . the Creator and Supreme Judge of the world."[51]

At the preliminary-injunction stage of this case, the District Court distinguished § 16-1-20 from the other two statutes. It then held that there was "nothing wrong" with § 16-1-20, but that § 16-1-20.1 and 16-1-20.2 were both invalid because the sole purpose

---

[48] The dissent emphasized the many displays of the Ten Commandments in the Supreme Court and other buildings around the nation's capital.

[49] Alabama Code § 16-1-20 (Supp. 1984) reads as follows:

At the commencement of the first class each day in the first through the sixth grades in all public schools, the teacher in charge of the room in which each such class is held shall announce that a period of silence, not to exceed one minute in duration, shall be observed for meditation, and during any such period silence shall be maintained and no activities engaged in.

Appellees have abandoned any claim that § 16-1-20 is unconstitutional.

[50] Alabama Code § 16-1-20.1 (Supp. 1984) provides:

At the commencement of the first class of each day in all grades in all public schools the teacher in charge of the room in which each class is held may announce that a period of silence not to exceed one minute in duration shall be observed for meditation or voluntary prayer, and during any such period no other activities shall be engaged in.

[51] Alabama Code § 16-1-20.2 (Supp. 1984) provides:

From henceforth, any teacher or professor in any public educational institution within the state of Alabama, recognizing that the Lord God is one, at the beginning of any homeroom or any class, may pray, may lead willing students in prayer, or may lead the willing students in the following prayer to God:

Almighty God, You alone are our God. We acknowledge You as the Creator and Supreme Judge of the world. May Your justice, Your truth, and Your peace abound this day in the hearts of our countrymen, in the counsels of our government, in the sanctity of our homes and in the classrooms of our schools in the name of our Lord. Amen.

of both was "an effort on the part of the State of Alabama to encourage religious activity." . . .

The Court of Appeals agreed with the District Court's initial interpretation of the purpose of both §§ 16-1-20.1 and 16-1-20.2, and held them both unconstitutional. We have already affirmed the Court of Appeals' holding with respect to § 16-1-20.2.[52] Moreover, appellees have not questioned the holding that § 16-1-20 is valid. Thus, the narrow question for decision is whether § 16-1-20.1, which authorizes a period of silence for "meditation or voluntary prayer," is a law respecting the establishment of religion within the meaning of the First Amendment.

I

Appellee Ishmael Jaffree is a resident of Mobile County, Alabama. On May 28, 1982, he filed a complaint on behalf of three of his minor children; two of them were second-grade students and the third was then in kindergarten. The complaint named members of the Mobile County School Board, various school officials, and the minor plaintiffs' three teachers as defendants. The complaint alleged that the appellees brought the action "seeking principally a declaratory judgment and an injunction restraining the Defendants and each of them from maintaining or allowing the maintenance of regular religious prayer services or other forms of religious observances in the Mobile County Public Schools. . . . " The complaint further alleged that two of the children had been subjected to various acts of religious indoctrination "from the beginning of the school year in September, 1981"; that the defendant teachers had "on a daily basis" led their classes in saying certain prayers in unison; that the minor children were exposed to ostracism from their peer group class members if they did not participate; and that Ishmael Jaffree had repeatedly but unsuccessfully requested that the devotional services be stopped. . . . [53]

II

. . . If there is any fixed star in our constitutional constellation, it is that no official, high or petty, can prescribe what shall be orthodox in politics, nationalism, religion, or other matters of opinion or force citizens to confess by word or act their faith therein. . . .

---

[52] [Court's footnote 8] *Wallace v. Jaffree*, 466 U.S. 924 (1984).

[53] [Court's footnote 23] The District Court wrote:

Defendant Boyd, as early as September 16, 1981, led her class at E.R. Dickson in singing the following phrase:

" 'God is great, God is good,

Let us thank him for our food,

bow our heads we all are fed,

Give us Lord our daily bread.

Amen!' "

Defendant Pixie Alexander has led her class at Craighead in reciting the following phrase:

" 'God is great, God is good,

Let us thank him for our food.' "

Further, defendant Pixie Alexander had her class recite . . . the Lord's Prayer. . . .

The recitation of these phrases continued on a daily basis throughout the 1981–82 school year. . . .

III

. . . [I]n *Lemon v. Kurtzman*, 403 U.S. 602, 612–613 (1971), we wrote:

. . . First, the statute must have a secular legislative purpose; second, its principal or primary effect must be one that neither advances nor inhibits religion, *Board of Education v. Allen*, 392 U.S. 236, 243 (1968); finally, the statute must not foster "an excessive government entanglement with religion."

Walz [*v. Tax Commission*, 397 U.S. 664, 674 (1970)]. It is the first of these three criteria that is most plainly implicated by this case. . . . [N]o consideration of the second or third criteria is necessary if a statute does not have a clearly secular purpose. For even though a statute that is motivated in part by a religious purpose may satisfy the first criterion, . . . the First Amendment requires that a statute must be invalidated if it is entirely motivated by a purpose to advance religion.

In applying the purpose test, it is appropriate to ask "whether government's actual purpose is to endorse or disapprove of religion."[54] In this case, the answer to that question is dispositive. For the record not only provides us with an unambiguous affirmative answer, but it also reveals that the enactment of § 16-1-20.1 was not motivated by any clearly secular purpose — indeed, the statute had no secular purpose.

IV

The sponsor of the bill that became § 16-1-20.1, Senator Donald Holmes, inserted into the legislative record — apparently without dissent — a statement indicating that the legislation was an "effort to return voluntary prayer" to the public schools. Later Senator Holmes confirmed this purpose before the District Court. In response to the question whether he had any purpose for the legislation other than returning voluntary prayer to public schools, he stated, "No, I did not have no other purpose in mind." The State did not present evidence of any secular purpose.

The unrebutted evidence of legislative intent contained in the legislative record and in the testimony of the sponsor of § 16-1-20.1 is confirmed by a consideration of the relationship between this statute and the two other measures that were considered in this case. The District Court found that the 1981 statute and its 1982 sequel had a common, nonsecular purpose. The wholly religious character of the later enactment is plainly evident from its text. When the differences between § 16-1-20.1 and its 1978 predecessor, § 16-1-20, are examined, it is equally clear that the 1981 statute has the same wholly religious character. . . .

[T]he only significant textual difference is the addition of the words "or voluntary prayer." . . .

The legislative intent to return prayer to the public school is, of course, quite different from merely protecting every student's right to engage in voluntary prayer during an appropriate moment of silence during the school day. The 1978 statute already protected that right. . . .

We must, therefore, conclude that the Alabama Legislature intended to change existing law and that it was motivated by the same purpose that the Governor's Answer to the Second Amended Complaint expressly admitted; that the statement inserted in the legislative history revealed; and that Senator Holmes' testimony frankly described. The Legislature enacted § 16-1-20.1 despite the existence of § 16-1-20 for the sole purpose of expressing the State's endorsement of prayer activities for one minute at the beginning of each school day. The addition of "or voluntary prayer" indicates that the

---

[54] [Court's footnote 42] *Lynch v. Donnelly*, 465 U.S. at 690 (O'Connor, J., concurring). . . .

State intended to characterize prayer as a favored practice. Such an endorsement is not consistent with the established principle that the Government must pursue a course of complete neutrality toward religion. . . .

. . . The well-supported concurrent findings of the District Court and the Court of Appeals — that § 16-1-20.1 was intended to convey a message of State-approval of prayer activities in the public schools — make it unnecessary, and indeed inappropriate, to evaluate the practical significance of the addition of the words "or voluntary prayer" to the statute. . . .

JUSTICE POWELL, concurring.

I concur in the Court's opinion and judgment that Ala. Code § 16-1 — 20.1 violates the Establishment Clause. . . . I agree fully with Justice O'Connor's assertion that some moment-of-silence statutes may be constitutional, a suggestion set forth in the Court's opinion as well. . . .

The record before us . . . makes clear that Alabama's purpose was solely religious in character. . . . I agree with Justice O'Connor that a single legislator's statement, particularly if made following enactment, is not necessarily sufficient to establish purpose. But, as noted in the Court's opinion, the religious purpose of § 16-1-20.1 is manifested in other evidence, including the sequence and history of the three Alabama statutes. . . .

I would vote to uphold the Alabama statute if it also had a clear secular purpose. . . .

Although we do not reach the other two prongs of the *Lemon* test, I note that the "effect" of a straightforward moment-of-silence statute is unlikely to "advanc[e] or inhibi[t] religion." See *Board of Education v. Allen*, 392 U.S. 236, 243 (1968). Nor would such a statute "foster 'an excessive government entanglement with religion.'" . . .

JUSTICE O'CONNOR, concurring in the judgment.

Nothing in the United States Constitution as interpreted by this Court or in the laws of the State of Alabama prohibits public school students from voluntarily praying at any time before, during, or after the school day. Alabama has facilitated voluntary silent prayers of students who are so inclined by enacting Ala. Code § 16-1-20, which provides a moment of silence in appellees' schools each day. The parties to these proceedings concede the validity of this enactment. . . . I write separately to identify the peculiar features of the Alabama law that render it invalid, and to explain why moment of silence laws in other States do not necessarily manifest the same infirmity. I also write to explain why neither history *nor* the Free Exercise Clause of the First Amendment validate the Alabama law struck down by the Court today.

I

The religious clauses of the First Amendment, coupled with the Fourteenth Amendment's guaranty of ordered liberty, preclude both the Nation and the States from making any law respecting an establishment of religion or prohibiting the free exercise thereof. . . . Although a distinct jurisprudence has enveloped each of these clauses, their common purpose is to secure religious liberty. On these principles the Court has been and remains unanimous.

. . . Last Term, I proposed a refinement of the *Lemon* test. . . . *Lynch v. Donnelly* (concurring opinion).

The endorsement test is useful because of the analytic content it gives to the *Lemon*-mandated inquiry into legislative purpose and effect. . . . A statute that ostensibly promotes a secular interest often has an incidental or even a primary effect of helping or hindering a sectarian belief. Chaos would ensue if every such statute were invalid under the Establishment Clause. For example, the State could not criminalize murder for fear that it would thereby promote the Biblical command against killing. . . .

The endorsement test does not preclude government from acknowledging religion or from taking religion into account in making law and policy. It does preclude government from conveying or attempting to convey a message that religion or a particular religious belief is favored or preferred. . . .

A

Twenty-five states permit or require public school teachers to have students observe a moment of silence in their classrooms. . . . The typical statute . . . calls for a moment of silence at the beginning of the school day during which students may meditate, pray, or reflect on the activities of the day. . . .

A state sponsored moment of silence in the public schools is different from state sponsored vocal prayer or Bible reading. First, a moment of silence is not inherently religious. . . . Second, a pupil who participates in a moment of silence . . . is left to his or her own thoughts, and is not compelled to listen to the prayers or thoughts of others. . . . Scholars and at least one member of this Court have recognized the distinction and suggested that a moment of silence in public schools would be constitutional. See Abington, 374 U.S. at 281 (Brennan, J., concurring) ("[T]he observance of a moment of reverent silence at the opening of class" may serve "the solely secular purposes of the devotional activities without jeopardizing either the religious liberties of any members of the community or the proper degree of separation between the spheres of religion and government.") . . .

By mandating a moment of silence, a State does not necessarily endorse any activity that might occur during the period. . . . Even if a statute specifies that a student may choose to pray silently during a quiet moment, the State has not thereby encouraged prayer over other specified alternatives. Nonetheless, it is also possible that a moment of silence statute, either as drafted or as actually implemented, could effectively favor the child who prays over the child who does not. For example, the message of endorsement would seem inescapable if the teacher exhorts children to use the designated time to pray. Similarly, . . . [t]he crucial question is whether the State has conveyed or attempted to convey the message that children should use the moment of silence for prayer. This question cannot be answered in the abstract, but instead requires courts to examine the history, language, and administration of a particular statute to determine whether it operates as an endorsement of religion. . . .

. . . If a legislature expresses a plausible secular purpose for a moment of silence statute in either the text or the legislative history, or if the statute disclaims an intent to encourage prayer over alternatives during a moment of silence, then courts should generally defer to that stated intent. It is particularly troublesome to denigrate an expressed secular purpose due to post-enactment testimony by particular legislators or by interested persons who witnessed the drafting of the statute. Even if the text and official history of a statute express no secular purpose, the statute should be held to have an improper purpose only if it is beyond purview that endorsement of religion or a religious belief "was and is the law's reason for existence." Epperson v. Arkansas, 393 U.S. 97, 108 (1968). Since there is arguably a secular pedagogical value to a moment of silence in public schools, courts should find an improper purpose behind such a statute only if the statute on its face, in its official legislative history, or in its interpretation by a responsible administrative agency suggests it has the primary purpose of endorsing prayer. . . .

. . . [T]he Lynch concurrence suggested that the effect of a moment of silence law is not entirely a question of fact. . . . The relevant issue is whether an objective observer, acquainted with the text, legislative history, and implementation of the statute, would perceive it as a state endorsement of prayer in public schools. A moment of silence law that is clearly drafted and implemented so as to permit prayer, meditation, and reflection within the prescribed period, without endorsing one alternative over the others, should pass this test.

B

. . . However deferentially one examines its text and legislative history, however objectively one views the message attempted to be conveyed to the public, the conclusion is unavoidable that the purpose of the statute is to endorse prayer in public schools. . . .

II

. . . Justice Holmes once observed, "[i]f a thing has been practiced for two hundred years by common consent, it will need a strong case for the Fourteenth Amendment to affect it." *Jackman v. Rosenbaum Co.*, 260 U.S. 22, 31 (1922). . . .

When the intent of the Framers is unclear, I believe we must employ both history and reason in our analysis. The primary issue raised by Justice Rehnquist's dissent is whether the historical fact that our Presidents have long called for public prayers of Thanks should be dispositive on the constitutionality of prayer in public schools.[55] I think not. At the very least, Presidential proclamations are distinguishable from school prayer in that they are received in a non-coercive setting and are primarily directed at adults, who presumably are not readily susceptible to unwilling religious indoctrination. . . .

. . . Our cases have interpreted the Free Exercise Clause to compel the Government to exempt persons from some generally applicable government requirements so as to permit those persons to freely exercise their religion. Even where the Free Exercise Clause does not compel the Government to grant an exemption, the Court has suggested that the Government in some circumstances may voluntarily choose to exempt religious observers without violating the Establishment Clause. . . .

It is obvious that either of the two Religion Clauses, "if expanded to a logical extreme, would tend to clash with the other." *Walz*, 397 U.S. at 668–669. . . .

The solution to the conflict between the religion clauses lies not in "neutrality," but rather in identifying workable limits to the Government's license to promote the free exercise of religion. . . . It is disingenuous to look for a purely secular purpose when the manifest objective of a statute is to facilitate the free exercise of religion by lifting a government-imposed burden. Instead, the Court should simply acknowledge that the religious purpose of such a statute is legitimated by the Free Exercise Clause. I would also go further. In assessing the effect of such a statute — that is, in determining whether the statute conveys the message of endorsement of religion or a particular religious belief — courts should assume that the "objective observer" is acquainted with the Free Exercise Clause and the values it promotes. Thus individual perceptions, or resentment that a religious observer is exempted from a particular government

---

[55] [Court's footnote 6] Even assuming a taxpayer could establish standing to challenge such a practice, *see Valley Forge Christian College v. Americans United for Separation of Church and State, Inc.*, 454 U.S. 464 (1982), these Presidential proclamations would probably withstand Establishment Clause scrutiny given their long history. *See Marsh v. Chambers*, 463 U.S. 783 (1983).

requirement, would be entitled to little weight if the Free Exercise Clause strongly supported the exemption.

While this "accommodation" analysis would help reconcile our Free Exercise and Establishment Clause standards, it would not save Alabama's moment of silence law. If we assume that the religious activity that Alabama seeks to protect is silent prayer, then it is difficult to discern any state-imposed burden on that activity that is lifted by Alabama Code § 16-1-20.1. No law prevents a student who is so inclined from praying silently in public schools. Moreover, state law already provided a moment of silence to these appellees. . . .

CHIEF JUSTICE BURGER, dissenting.

. . . [Some] will say that all this controversy is "much ado about nothing," since no power on earth — including this Court and Congress — can stop any teacher from opening the school day with a moment of silence for pupils to meditate, to plan their day — or to pray if they voluntarily elect to do so.

I make several points about today's curious holding.

(a) It makes no sense to say that Alabama has "endorsed prayer" by merely enacting a new statute "to specify expressly that voluntary prayer is *one* of the authorized activities during a moment of silence," (O'Connor, J., concurring in the judgment) (emphasis added). To suggest that a moment-of-silence statute that includes the word "prayer" unconstitutionally endorses religion, while one that simply provides for a moment of silence does not, manifests not neutrality but hostility toward religion. . . .

Rather than determining legislative purpose from the face of the statute as a whole,[56] the opinions rely on three factors in concluding that the Alabama legislature had a "wholly religious" purpose for enacting the statute under review, Ala. Code § 16-1-20.1 (Supp. 1984): (i) statements of the statute's sponsor, (ii) admissions in Governor James' Answer to the Second Amended Complaint, and (iii) the difference between § 16-1-20.1 and its predecessor statute.

Curiously, the opinions do not mention that all of the sponsor's statements relied upon — including the statement "inserted" into the Senate Journal — were made after the legislature had passed the statute; indeed, the testimony that the Court finds critical was given well over a year after the statute was enacted. As even the appellees concede, there is not a shred of evidence that the legislature as a whole shared the sponsor's motive or that a majority in either house was even aware of the sponsor's view of the bill when it was passed. . . . No case in the 195-year history of this Court supports the disconcerting idea that post-enactment statements by individual legislators are relevant in determining the constitutionality of legislation.

Even if an individual legislator's after-the-fact statements could rationally be considered relevant, all of the opinions fail to mention that the sponsor also testified that one of his purposes in drafting and sponsoring the moment-of-silence bill was to clear up a widespread misunderstanding that a schoolchild is legally *prohibited* from engaging in silent, individual prayer once he steps inside a public school building. . . .

(c) The Court's extended treatment of the "test" of *Lemon v. Kurtzman* suggests a naive preoccupation with an easy, bright-line approach for addressing constitutional issues. We have repeatedly cautioned that *Lemon* did not establish a rigid caliper

---

[56] [Dissent's footnote 1] The foregoing opinions likewise completely ignore the statement of purpose that accompanied the moment-of-silence bill throughout the legislative process: "To permit a period of silence to be observed *for the purpose* of meditation *or* voluntary prayer at the commencement of the first class of each day in all public schools." 1981 Ala. Senate J. 14 (emphasis added).

capable of resolving every Establishment Clause issue, but that it sought only to provide "signposts." . . .

(d) The notion that the Alabama statute is a step toward creating an established church borders on, if it does not trespass into, the ridiculous. . . . The statute "endorses" only the view that the religious observances of others should be tolerated and, where possible, accommodated. . . .

Justice White, dissenting.

. . . As I read the filed opinions, a majority of the Court would approve statutes that provided for a moment of silence but did not mention prayer. But if a student asked whether he could pray during that moment, it is difficult to believe that the teacher could not answer in the affirmative. If that is the case, I would not invalidate a statute that at the outset provided the legislative answer to the question "May I pray?" . . .

Justice Rehnquist, dissenting.

Thirty-eight years ago this Court, in *Everson v. Board of Education*, [330 U.S. 1, 16 (1947)], summarized its exegesis of Establishment Clause doctrine thus:

> In the words of Jefferson, the clause against establishment of religion by law was intended to erect "a wall of separation between church and State." *Reynolds v. United States*, [98 U.S. 145, 164 (1879)]. . . . [57]

Thomas Jefferson was of course in France at the time the constitutional amendments known as the Bill of Rights were passed by Congress and ratified by the states. . . .

Jefferson's fellow Virginian James Madison, with whom he was joined in the battle for the enactment of the Virginia Statute of Religious Liberty of 1786, did play as large a part as anyone in the drafting of the Bill of Rights. . . . But when we turn to the record of the proceedings in the First Congress leading up to the adoption of the Establishment Clause of the Constitution, including Madison's significant contributions thereto, we see a far different picture of its purpose than the highly simplified "wall of separation between church and State." . . .

The language Madison proposed for what ultimately became the Religion Clauses of the First Amendment was this:

> The civil rights of none shall be abridged on account of religious belief or worship, nor shall any national religion be established, nor shall the full and equal rights of conscience be in any manner, or on any pretext, infringed. . . .

It seems indisputable from . . . glimpses of Madison's thinking, as reflected by actions on the floor of the House in 1789, that he saw the amendment as designed to prohibit the establishment of a national religion, and perhaps to prevent discrimination among sects. He did not see it as requiring neutrality on the part of government between religion and irreligion. Thus the Court's opinion in *Everson* — while correct in bracketing Madison and Jefferson together in their exertions in their home state leading to the enactment of the Virginia Statute of Religious Liberty — is totally incorrect in suggesting that Madison carried these views onto the floor of the United States House of Representatives when he proposed the language which would ultimately become the Bill of Rights. . . .

None of the other Members of Congress who spoke during the August 15th debate expressed the slightest indication that they thought the language before them from the Select Committee, or the evil to be aimed at, would require that the Government be

---

[57] [Dissent's footnote 1] *Reynolds* is the only authority cited as direct precedent for the "wall of separation theory." [330 U.S. at 16]. *Reynolds* is truly inapt; it dealt with a Mormon's Free Exercise Clause challenge to a federal polygamy law.

absolutely neutral as between religion and irreligion. The evil to be aimed at . . . was definitely not concerned about whether the Government might aid all religions even-handedly. . . .

. . . The "wall of separation between church and State" is a metaphor based on bad history, a metaphor which has proved useless as a guide to judging. It should be frankly and explicitly abandoned.

The Court has more recently attempted to add some mortar to *Everson's* wall through the three-part test of *Lemon v. Kurtzman.* . . .

The results from our school services cases show the difficulty we have encountered in making the *Lemon* test yield principled results. . . .

. . . Given the "incorporation" of the Establishment Clause as against the States via the Fourteenth Amendment in *Everson*, States are prohibited as well from establishing a religion or discriminating between sects. As its history abundantly shows, however, nothing in the Establishment Clause requires government to be strictly neutral between religion and irreligion, nor does that Clause prohibit Congress or the States from pursuing legitimate secular ends through nondiscriminatory sectarian means. . . .

[4] Exemptions From Statutory Requirements

A question raised in the "school prayer" cases, and in *Lynch v. Donnelly*, is the extent to which government may accommodate the religious beliefs of individuals and organizations. As Justice O'Connor pointed out in her *Wallace v. Jaffree* concurrence, such accommodation may often be necessary under the Free Exercise Clause to lift a burden imposed by the government itself. But there may be times when the government exempts individuals and organizations from government-imposed burdens that are not free exercise violations; or the exemption may go beyond that which the Free Exercise Clause requires; or the government requires private parties to give favored treatment to employees in order to accommodate their religious beliefs. At some point the "accommodation" may cross the line and become an "establishment of religion." Consider *Estate of Thornton v. Caldor*, 472 U.S. 703 (1985). In that case, the Court held that the Establishment Clause prevented the State from compelling a private employer to give its employee the absolute right not to work on the employee's chosen weekly day of worship. Chief Justice Burger's majority (8–1) opinion stressed that the Connecticut law made no allowance for the convenience or interests — religious, or otherwise — of the employer or other employees.

Justice O'Connor's concurrence stressed that the majority opinion did not cast doubt on the validity of the provisions of Title VII of the 1964 Civil Rights Act which requires employers to make "reasonable" accommodations to an employee's religious practices, unless such accommodation would cause undue hardship to the employer's business. Justice Rehnquist dissented without opinion. For additional discussion of *Caldor*, see *infra* § 16.05, Note (2)(b) after *Sherbert*.

CORPORATION OF THE PRESIDING BISHOP OF THE CHURCH OF JESUS CHRIST OF LATTER-DAY SAINTS v. AMOS, 483 U.S. 327 (1987). In *Amos*, the Court upheld an exemption for a religious organization against an Establishment Clause claim. The Court unanimously upheld the application of Title VII's exemption of religious organizations from religious discrimination in employment to a nonprofit activity (the Desert Gymnasium) operated by the Mormon Church. The Court unanimously upheld the exemption. Justice White's majority opinion — joined by Chief Justice Rehnquist and Justices Powell, Stevens and Scalia — concluded that the first prong of the *Lemon* test was met because of the permissible purpose to "alleviate significant governmental interference with the ability of religious institutions to define and carry out their religious missions." In applying the second prong of the *Lemon* test, Justice White drew a distinction between advancing religion that results from the actions of the state, and the assistance provided when the government allows a church to engage in activities. "A law is not unconstitutional simply because it allows churches to advance religion which is their very purpose."

The Court dismissed any contention that Title VII's religious exemption impermissibly entangles church and state. On the contrary, "the statute effectuates a more complete separation of the two and avoids the kind of intrusive inquiry into religious belief that the District Court engaged in this case."

Justice Brennan wrote a concurring opinion, joined by Justice Marshall. In Justice Brennan's view, the exemption for religious institutions in the pursuit of their religious mission enables churches to define themselves. "The authority to engage in this process of self-definition," Justice Brennan wrote, "inevitably involves what we normally regard as infringement on Free Exercise rights, since a religious organization is able to condition employment in certain activities on subscription to particular religious tenets. . . . This rationale suggests that, ideally, religious organizations should be able to discriminate on the basis of religion *only* with respect to religious activities . . . because the infringement on religious liberty that results from conditioning performance of secular activity upon religious belief cannot be defended as necessary for the community's self-definition." Nevertheless, Justice Brennan supported the categorical exemption for nonprofit activities of religious organizations because "[n]onprofit activities . . . are most likely to present cases in which characterization of the activity as religious or secular will be a close question. . . . Such an exemption demarcates a sphere of deference with respect to those activities most likely to be religious. . . . Concern for the autonomy of religious organizations demands that we avoid the entanglement and the chill on religious expression that a case-by-case determination would produce."

Justice O'Connor concurred in the opinion as did Justice Blackmun in a separate opinion. This case involves a government decision to lift from a nonprofit activity of a religious organization the burden of demonstrating that the particular nonprofit activity is religious as well as the burden of refraining from discriminating on the basis of religion. Because there is a probability that a nonprofit activity of a religious organization will itself be involved in the organization's religious mission, in my view the objective observer should perceive the government action as an accommodation of the exercise of religion rather than as an endorsement of religion."

§ 16.04 ESTABLISHMENT OF RELIGION THROUGH RELIGIOUS INSTITUTIONS BECOMING INVOLVED IN GOVERNMENTAL DECISIONS

LARKIN v. GRENDEL'S DEN, INC., 459 U.S. 116 (1983). In *Larkin,* the Court voted 8–1 to strike down a statute that had been interpreted to allow churches the power to veto government decisions. A Massachusetts General Law provided that: "Premises . . . located within a radius of five hundred feet of a church or school shall not be licensed for the sale of alcoholic beverages if the governing body of such church or school files written objections thereto." Citing the receipt of such an objection from Holy Cross Church in Harvard Square, a License Commission denied appellee's application for a liquor license for premises located adjacent to the church.

Writing for the Court, Chief Justice Burger noted that deference was normally due to legislative zoning judgments. Nevertheless, where as in this case, a veto power had been delegated to a nongovernmental religious body, such deference was not warranted.

Applying the familiar *Lemon* test, Chief Justice Burger readily found that the law served a valid secular purpose of protecting "spiritual, cultural, and educational centers from the 'hurly-burly' associated with liquor outlets. . . . However, these valid secular objectives can be readily accomplished by other means — either through an absolute legislative ban on liquor outlets within reasonable prescribed distances from churches, schools, hospitals and like institutions, or by ensuring a hearing for the views of affected institutions at licensing proceedings where, without question, such views would be entitled to substantial weight."

Chief Justice Burger noted that there was no guarantee that "the churches' power would be used in a religiously neutral way." Moreover, "the mere appearance of a joint exercise of legislative authority by Church and State provides significant symbolic benefit to religion." Consequently, the statute had "a 'primary' and 'principle' effect of advancing religion."

The statute also fell foul of the third prong of the *Lemon* test. The Court concluded that "few entanglements could be more offensive to the spirit of the Constitution."

Alone in dissent, Justice Rehnquist argued that the Court had misapplied the second prong of the *Lemon* test. The statute did not "encourage, much less compel anyone to participate in religious activities or to support religious institutions." Moreover, as the State could ban the grant of liquor licenses to establishments in the vicinity of churches, the Court should have afforded it the less sweeping alternative offered by Massachusetts.

BOARD OF EDUCATION OF KIRYAS JOEL VILLAGE SCHOOL DISTRICT v. GRUMET, 512 U.S. 687 (1994). In *Grumet*, the Court invalidated a New York law that created a separate school district along the boundaries of an exclusively religious community. The Satmar Hasidic Sect formed the 320 acre village of Kiryas Joel. As non-Satmar neighbors did not want to be in the village, it was owned and inhabited entirely by Satmars. The members of the sect strictly adhere to Jewish law and customs, avoiding assimilation into the modern world.

After *Aguilar v. Felton*, 473 U.S. 402 (1985), and *School District of Grand Rapids v. Ball*, 473 U.S. 373 (1985), prohibited states from providing publicly-funded classes on religious school premises, the handicapped children of Kiryas Joel were forced to attend programs in the public school system outside the village. Parents of these children found this arrangement unacceptable as the children would suffer trauma from being placed in these public schools outside the community.[58] The New York legislature responded by enacting Chapter 748 which made Kiryas Joel a separate school district. Despite its plenary power over elementary and secondary education, the village school district only operated a special education program for disabled children. Two-thirds of the 40 full-time students came from several neighboring districts. If any child in the village sought a public school education, the district would pay for a program in a nearby district.

Writing for the Court, Justice Souter began by saying, "A proper respect for both the Free Exercise and the Establishment Clauses compels the State to pursue a course of 'neutrality toward religion,' favoring neither one religion over others nor religious adherents collectively over nonadherents." The New York law deviated from this command by relinquishing the State's discretionary power over public education "to a group defined by its character as a religious community," while offering "no assurance that governmental power has been or will be exercised neutrally."

---

[58] Consequently, only one handicapped child from the village actually attended public school; the rest received privately-funded education or none at all.

Justice Souter compared this case to *Larkin v. Grendel's Den, Inc.*, 459 U.S. 116 (1985), *supra*.

While free exercise mandates that religious people cannot be denied the rights of citizens simply because of their religious affiliations, the ability of religious people to participate in public affairs "does not mean that a state may deliberately delegate discretionary power to an individual, institution, or community on the ground of religious identity." The Court recognized that where, as here, "fusion" is at issue, the relevant distinction is "between a government's purposeful delegation on the basis of religion and a delegation on principles neutral to religion, to individuals whose religious identities are incidental to their receipt of civic authority."

Chapter 748 effectively identified the "recipients of governmental authority by reference to doctrinal adherence, even though it does not do so expressly." When New York created the Kiryas Joel School District, it was well aware that the district contained only members of the Satmar sect. Carving out this small district ran counter to the longstanding trend in New York of consolidating smaller school districts. Creating the district by a special legislative act was also "exceptional to the point of singularity, as the only district coming to our notice that the legislature carved from a single existing district to serve local residents." The State had defined "a political subdivision and hence the qualification for its franchise by a religious test, resulting in a purposeful and forbidden 'fusion of governmental and religious functions.' "[59]

Beyond placing religion in a governmental role, the creation of the district also conferred an unusual benefit by favoring the Satmar community over religious and nonreligious groups. That the aid involves a single, small religious sect does not render it less problematical than government aid to larger religious groups or to religion as a whole.

As an alternative to the program at issue, Justice Souter suggested that New York enact better bilingual and bicultural programs. As another accommodation, the Monroe-Woodbury Central School District, from which the new district was carved, could offer such services at its facilities or at a neutral site near the village's parochial schools.

In conclusion, the New York statute violated the neutrality principle in delegating a power which " 'ranks at the very apex of the function of a State,' to an electorate defined by common religious belief and practice, in a manner that fails to foreclose religious favoritism." This "crosses the line from permissible accommodation to impermissible establishment."

Concurring, Justice Blackmun emphasized that the majority opinion in no way departed from the Court's decision in *Lemon v. Kurtzman*.

Justice Stevens, joined by Justices Blackmun and Ginsburg, submitted a concurring opinion. He noted that the State could have taken alternative steps to meet the concerns of the Satmar parents. For example, children in the public schools could be taught to respect Satmar customs as a means of promoting and understanding cultural diversity. Moreover, it was revealing that a large number of the full-time students at the school were Hasidic handicapped children from outside the village. The school thus served a population defined by religion rather than geography.

Justice O'Connor, concurring in part and concurring in the judgment, emphasized equal treatment irrespective of religious or nonreligious beliefs. The "Religion Clauses

---

[59] "Because it is the unusual circumstances of this district's creation that persuade us the State has employed a religious criterion for delegating political power, this conclusion does not imply" that the Court would invalidate a district with boundaries derived from "neutral historic and geographic criteria, but whose population happens to" consist of individuals who share religious beliefs.

— the Free Exercise Clause, the Establishment Clause, the Religious Test Clause, Art. VI, cl. 3, and the Equal Protection Clause as applied to religion — all speak with one voice on this point: Absent the most unusual circumstances, one's religion ought not affect one's legal rights or duties or benefits."

While accommodations may justify different treatment for persons who share a particular belief, "they do not justify discrimination based on sect." For example, the government may exempt sacramental wine from an alcohol consumption proscription, but it cannot extend this exemption to Catholics but not to Jews.

In the instant case, New York could have enacted a general law allowing all villages to operate their own school districts. Alternatively, the Court could allow the State to revive the kind of public programs on parochial school grounds that were invalidated in *School District of Grand Rapids v. Ball* and *Aguilar v. Felton*. The Court should, in a proper case, be prepared to reconsider *Aguilar*.

Finally, Justice O'Connor also noted that in *Lee v. Weisman, Zobrest v. Catalina Foothills School District, Larson v. Valente*, and this case, the Court did not focus on the three-part Establishment test in *Lemon v. Kurtzman*. The *Lemon* test has gone the way of many traditional theories, becoming so broad and amorphous as to be a futile guide. In place of the rigid *Lemon* test, the Court has substituted a number of tests, each covering a narrower, more homogeneous range of issues.

Justice Kennedy concurred in the judgment. He rejected the implication of the Court's decision that accommodation of a particular religious group is invalid because the legislature might not confer the same accommodation on a like group. This approach needlessly restricts "the legislature's ability to respond to the unique problems of a particular religious group. The real vice of the school district, in my estimation, is that New York created it by drawing political boundaries on the basis of religion."

Justice Kennedy compared the formation of the Kiryas Joel Village to that of the Kiryas Joel School District. The village was created under "a religion-neutral self-incorporation scheme." In contrast, the school district was created under the discretionary power of the state legislature. Finally, Justice Kennedy agreed with Justice O'Connor that the decisions in *Grand Rapids* and *Aguilar* may require judicial reconsideration in light of the instant case.

Justice Scalia, joined by Chief Justice Rehnquist and Justice Thomas, dissented. Justice Scalia charged that the majority treated tolerance of a religious group's special needs as an impermissible establishment of religion. The Kiryas Joel school for handicapped students included all of the notable characteristics of any public school. While the village's religious schools were segregated by sex, the public school was co-ed and the curriculum secular. Furthermore, teachers and administrators lived outside Kiryas Joel. "The only thing distinctive about the school is that all the students share the same religion."

The law was not motivated by religion but extended similar educational benefits to a group of children who were impeded by differences in dress, culture, and language. The Court would not have questioned the secular humanitarian purposes of the legislation had the law helped an isolated group of, for example, gypsies or American Indians. Even if the legislature had been religiously motivated, the law advanced the best traditions of accommodation, particularly as it aided a small minority sect.

Justice Scalia also said that the Court no longer followed the *Lemon* test. In its place, he would rely on "the longstanding traditions of our people."

NOTES

(1) *Funding Religious College Newspaper.* In *Rosenberger v. University of Virginia,* 515 U.S. 819 (1995), the Court (5–4) held that funding the printing costs for a student-run newspaper with a religious viewpoint did not violate the Establishment Clause. The University of Virginia allows "Contracted Independent Organizations" (CIOs) to receive funding from a mandatory Students Activities Fund (SAF) to pay for third-party costs. One CIO, Wide Awake Productions (WAP) is a student-run organization that publishes a newspaper. While the newspaper has a Christian viewpoint, the University did not consider the group to be a "religious activity," which "primarily promotes or manifests a particular belief in or about a deity or an ultimate reality." Instead, WAP was classified as "student news," qualifying for funding because of its role in the University community as an information source. WAP requested funding from the SAF to pay its printing costs. The SAF, however, denied the request on Establishment Clause grounds.

Writing for the Court, Justice Kennedy found that the University violated WAP's free speech rights. Funding the Christian newspaper would have exhibited neutrality toward religion, as the SAF program is otherwise content-neutral in disbursing funds to CIOs. The Court distinguished the fees University students pay for SAF funding from "a tax levied for the direct support of a church" because the SAF is a "special fund from which any group of students with CIO status can draw." Moreover, the University required CIOs to "include in dealings with third parties and in all written materials a disclaimer, stating that the CIO is independent of the University and that the University is not responsible for the CIO." Not funding such an organization would exhibit bias rather than neutrality against religious speech.

The Court distinguished this case from the government unconstitutionally giving money to a religious institution. The student newspaper was not a religious institution, and the SAF made payments directly to the third-party contractors. Moreover, the Court found no difference between the University providing a printing or other facility and paying an outsider to provide the same service. Any benefit received by WAP was merely incidental.

Justices O'Connor and Thomas filed concurring opinions. Justice Souter filed a dissent in which Justices Stevens, Ginsburg, and Breyer joined. For further discussion of the public forum aspects of *Rosenberger,* see § 15.03.

(2) For further discussion, see Carl H. Esbeck, *The Establishment Clause as a Structural Restaint on Governmental Power,* 84 Iowa L. Rev. 1, 112 (1998) ("[I]f the Court's government-religion boundary is to have staying power it has to be defended not because it is neutral or noncontroversial, but because it is good. Indeed, it is a three-fold good: it maximizes individual religious choice, protects the institutional integrity of the *ekklesia,* and minimizes government-induced religious factionalism within the civitas."); Kent Greenawalt, *Religious Law and Civil Law: Using Secular Law To Assure Observance Of Practices With Religious Significance,* 71 S. Cal. L. Rev. 781, 781 (1998) ("Many states enforce *kosher* requirements, to which Orthodox and some Conservative Jews adhere. The laws, which penalize fraud in the labeling of products as *kosher,* serve the secular interest in preventing deception of consumers. However, the laws also force the state to decide when religious regulations have been violated."). *See also* Thomas R. McCoy, *A Coherent Methodology for First Amendment Speech and Religion Clause Cases,* 48 Vand. L. Rev. 1335, 1384 (1995) ("Unfortunately, in apparently rejecting the *Lemon* rhetoric without articulating a substitute, the Court has moved establishment clause jurisprudence further in the direction of unrestrained,

ad hoc decision-making — not exactly what one would view as doctrinal progress."); Steven D. Smith, *The Restoration of Tolerance*, 78 Cal. L. Rev. 305, 355 (1990) (stating that the "establishment clause threatens free exercise exemptions only because it has been construed to commit government to neutrality in matters of religion").

§ 16.05 FREE EXERCISE OF RELIGION

SHERBERT v. VERNER
374 U.S. 398, 83 S. Ct. 1790, 10 L. Ed. 2d 965 (1963)

Justice brennan delivered the opinion of the Court.

Appellant, a member of the Seventh-day Adventist Church, was discharged by her South Carolina employer because she would not work on Saturday, the Sabbath Day of her faith. When she was unable to obtain other employment because from conscientious scruples she would not take Saturday work, she filed a claim for unemployment compensation benefits under the South Carolina Unemployment Compensation Act. . . . The South Carolina Supreme Court . . . rejected appellant's contention that, as applied to her, the disqualifying provisions of the South Carolina statute abridged her right to the free exercise of her religion secured under the Free Exercise Clause of the First Amendment through the Fourteenth Amendment. . . . We reverse. . . .

I

The door of the Free Exercise Clause stands tightly closed against any governmental regulation of religious *beliefs* as such, *Cantwell v. Connecticut*, 310 U.S. 296 (1940). Government may neither compel affirmation of a repugnant belief . . . nor penalize or discriminate against individuals or groups because they hold religious views abhorrent to the authorities . . . nor employ the taxing power to inhibit the dissemination of particular religious views. . . . On the other hand, the Court has rejected challenges under the Free Exercise Clause to governmental regulation of certain overt acts prompted by religious beliefs or principles, for "even when the action is in accord with one's religious convictions, [it] is not totally free from legislative restrictions." *Braunfeld v. Brown*, 366 U.S. 599, 603 [(1961) (Sunday closing laws)]. The conduct or actions so regulated have invariably posed some substantial threat to public safety, peace or order. . . .

Plainly enough, appellant's conscientious objection to Saturday work constitutes no conduct prompted by religious principles of a kind within the reach of state legislation. If, therefore, the decision of the South Carolina Supreme Court is to withstand appellant's constitutional challenge, it must be either because her disqualification as a beneficiary represents no infringement by the State of her constitutional rights of free exercise, or because any incidental burden on the free exercise of appellant's religion may be justified by a "compelling state interest in the regulation of a subject within the State's constitutional power to regulate." . . . *NAACP v. Button*, 371 U.S. 415, 438 (1963).

II

We turn first to the question whether the disqualification for benefits imposes any burden on the free exercise of appellant's religion. We think it is clear that it does. . . . For "[i]f the purpose or effect of a law is to impede the observance of one or all religions or is to discriminate invidiously between religions, that law is constitutionally invalid even though the burden may be characterized as being only indirect." *Braunfeld v. Brown, supra*, 366 U.S. at 607. . . . The ruling forces her to choose between following the precepts of her religion and forfeiting benefits, on the one hand, and abandoning one of the precepts of her religion in order to accept work, on the other hand. Governmental imposition of such a choice puts the same kind of burden upon the free exercise of religion as would a fine imposed against appellant for her Saturday worship.

Nor may the South Carolina court's construction of the statute be saved from constitutional infirmity on the ground that unemployment compensation benefits are not appellant's "right" but merely a "privilege." It is too late in the day to doubt that the liberties of religion and expression may be infringed by the denial of or placing of conditions upon a benefit or privilege. . . .

III

We must next consider whether some compelling state interest enforced in the eligibility provisions of the South Carolina statute justifies the substantial infringement of appellant's First Amendment right. . . . The appellees suggest no more than a possibility that the filing of fraudulent claims by unscrupulous claimants feigning religious objections to Saturday work might not only dilute the unemployment compensation fund but also hinder the scheduling by employers of necessary Saturday work. . . . [E]ven if the possibility of spurious claims did threaten to dilute the fund and disrupt the scheduling of work, it would plainly be incumbent upon the appellees to demonstrate that no alternative forms of regulation would combat such abuses without infringing First Amendment rights.

In these respects, then, the state interest asserted in the present case is wholly dissimilar to the interests which were found to justify the less direct burden upon religious practices in *Braunfeld v. Brown*. The Court recognized that the Sunday closing law which that decision sustained undoubtedly served "to make the practice of [the Orthodox Jewish merchants'] . . . religious beliefs more expensive," 366 U.S. at 605. But the statute was nevertheless saved by a countervailing factor which finds no equivalent in the instant case — a strong state interest in providing one uniform day of rest for all workers. That secular objective could be achieved, the Court found, only by declaring Sunday to be that day of rest. Requiring exemptions for Sabbatarians, while theoretically possible, appeared to present an administrative problem of such magnitude, or to afford the exempted class so great a competitive advantage, that such a requirement would have rendered the entire statutory scheme unworkable. . . .

IV

. . . [T]he extension of unemployment benefits to Sabbatarians in common with Sunday worshipers reflects nothing more than the governmental obligation of neutrality in the face of religious differences, and does not represent that involvement of religious with secular institutions which it is the object of the Establishment Clause to forestall. Nor does the recognition of the appellant's right to unemployment benefits under the state statute serve to abridge any other person's religious liberties. Nor do we, by our decision today, declare the existence of a constitutional right to unemployment benefits on the part of all persons whose religious convictions are the cause of their unemployment. This is not a case in which an employee's religious convictions serve to make him a nonproductive member of society. . . .

[JUSTICE DOUGLAS's concurring opinion is omitted.]

JUSTICE STEWART, concurring in the result. . . .

I

. . . [O]n occasion, and specifically in *Braunfeld v. Brown*, the Court has shown what has seemed to me a distressing insensitivity to the appropriate demands of this constitutional guarantee. By contrast I think that the Court's approach to the Establishment Clause has on occasion, and specifically in *Engel*, *Schempp* and *Murray*, been not only insensitive, but positively wooden, and that the Court has accorded to the Establishment Clause a meaning which neither the words, the history, nor the intention of the authors of that specific constitutional provision even remotely suggests. . . .

[T]he Establishment Clause as construed by this Court not only permits but affirmatively requires South Carolina . . . to deny the appellant's claim for unemployment compensation when her refusal to work on Saturdays is based upon her religious creed. . . .

To require South Carolina to so administer its laws as to pay public money to the appellant under the circumstances of this case is thus clearly to require the State to violate the Establishment Clause as construed by this Court. This poses no problem for me. . . . I think that the guarantee of religious liberty embodied in the Free Exercise Clause affirmatively requires government to create an atmosphere of hospitality and accommodation to individual belief or disbelief. . . .

II

My second difference with the Court's opinion is that I cannot agree that today's decision can stand consistently with *Braunfeld v. Brown*. . . . The *Braunfeld* Case involved a state criminal statute. The undisputed effect of that statute, as pointed out by Justice Brennan in his dissenting opinion in that case, was that "Plaintiff, Abraham Braunfeld, will be unable to continue in his business if he may not stay open on Sunday and he will thereby lose his capital investment." . . .

The impact upon the appellant's religious freedom in the present case is considerably less onerous. . . . Even upon the unlikely assumption that the appellant could not find suitable non-Saturday employment, the appellant at the worst would be denied a maximum of 22 weeks of compensation payments. . . . I think the *Braunfeld* case was wrongly decided and should be overruled. . . .

JUSTICE HARLAN, whom JUSTICE WHITE joins, dissenting. . . .

First, despite the Court's protestations to the contrary, the decision necessarily overrules *Braunfeld v. Brown*. . . . [T]he indirect financial burden of the present law is far less than that involved in *Braunfeld*. Forcing a store owner to close his business on Sunday may well have the effect of depriving him of a satisfactory livelihood if his religious convictions require him to close on Saturday as well. Here we are dealing only with temporary benefits, amounting to a fraction of regular weekly wages and running for not more than 22 weeks. . . .

Second, . . . at least under the circumstances of this case it would be a permissible accommodation of religion for the State, if it *chose* to do so, to create an exception to its eligibility requirements for persons like the appellant. The constitutional obligation of "neutrality," is not so narrow a channel that the slightest deviation from an absolutely straight course leads to condemnation. . . . I believe [there is] enough flexibility in the Constitution to permit a legislative judgment accommodating an unemployment compensation law to the exercise of religious beliefs such as appellant's.

. . . Those situations in which the Constitution may require special treatment on account of religion are, in my view, few and far between. . . . Such compulsion in the present case is particularly inappropriate in light of the indirect, remote, and insubstantial effect of the decision below on the exercise of appellant's religion and in light of the direct financial assistance to religion that today's decision requires. . . .

NOTES

(1) *Commentary.* For further discussion, see Kathleen M. Sullivan, *Religion and Liberal Democracy*, 59 U. CHI. L. REV. 195, 222 (1992) ("[T]he Court undervalue[s] the Establishment Clause, and in particular, its affirmative implications. Just as the free exercise of religion implies the free exercise of non-religion, so the ban on establishment of religion establishes a civil public order, which ends the war of all sects against all. The price of this truce is the banishment of religion from the public square, but the reward should be allowing religious subcultures to withdraw from regulation insofar as compatible with peaceful diarchic coexistence.").

(2) *Religious Days of Worship.* (a) *Sunday closing laws.* In *McGowan v. Maryland*, 366 U.S. 420 (1961), the Court denied an establishment challenge to Maryland's Sunday Closing Law. Writing for the majority, Chief Justice Warren conceded that the Sunday labor laws were originally motivated by religious beliefs. He concluded, however, that "presently they bear no relationship to establishment of religion." Instead, the "present purpose and effect of most of them is to provide a uniform day of rest for all citizens." Because the statute's primary purpose and effect were secular, the Chief Justice rejected the claim that the statute impermissibly advanced Christianity by making other religions economically disadvantageous.

In the major companion case to *McGowan*, *Braunfeld v. Brown*, 366 U.S. 599 (1961), the majority rejected the free exercise challenge of orthodox Jewish merchants who contended that their economic well-being would be impaired by the statute because their own religious beliefs banned work on Saturdays. Chief Justice Warren's plurality opinion pointed out that the law did not prohibit any religious practice per se but simply resulted in making the appellants' religious beliefs more expensive. He refused to find that such an indirect burden on appellants' religion rose to the level of a violation of their free exercise rights. Moreover, providing an exception from the statute for those whose religious convictions recognized a day other than Sunday as a day of rest would impose too great an administrative burden on the state. Justice Douglas dissented on both establishment and free exercise grounds. Justice Brennan felt the statute forced an individual to choose between his religion and his business, and therefore violated his free exercise rights. Justice Stewart also dissented.

(b) *Individual exemptions from working on the Sabbath.* Although the Court concluded that an exemption from the statute was not constitutionally required, the Sunday Closing Law cases implicitly recognized that even when state action does not violate the Free Exercise Clause, a state may accommodate individual religious beliefs without contravening the Establishment Clause. Indeed, Justice Brennan pointed out in *Braunfeld* that 21 of the 34 states which had Sunday closing laws actually provided such religious exemptions. Many governmental actions, such as housing of military personnel on bases or ships, inhibit religion, but do not constitute a violation of the Free Exercise Clause. Permitting a state to alleviate such inhibitory effects (e.g., by constructing chapels on military bases), without offending the Establishment Clause, serves to relieve the tension between the two clauses. Such state accommodations ensure that the two clauses remain co-guarantors of the religious liberty provided by the First Amendment.

In *Estate of Thornton v. Caldor*, 472 U.S. 703 (1985), the Court held that a state law giving private employees the absolute right not to work on his or her chosen Sabbath violated the Establishment Clause. The employee claiming the exemption in *Caldor* was a Sunday worshiper who had been forced to work 31 Sundays during 1977 and 1978.

The Court stressed that the Connecticut law made no allowance for the interests — religious or otherwise — of the employer or other employees. Compare with Justice Brennan's observation in *Braunfeld v. Brown*, that it would be permissible for a state to grant exemptions to Sunday closing laws to those whose religious beliefs involve the observance of a Sabbath other than Sunday.

(c) *Religious converts. Sherbert v. Verner* was followed in the case of *Hobbie v. Unemployment Appeals Commission of Florida*, 480 U.S. 136 (1987), involving the discharge of an assistant manager of a jewelry store when she converted to the Seventh Day Adventist Church and advised her employer that she could no longer work on Saturday. She was denied unemployment benefits because the employer and the state viewed her discharge as having been based on misconduct. Justice Brennan's majority opinion refused to accept the argument that *Sherbert* was inapplicable because Hobbie had converted to the Seventh Day Adventist faith after her employment commenced. The Court also rejected an Establishment Clause challenge: "This Court has long recognized that the government may (and sometimes must) accommodate religious practices and that it may do so without violating the Establishment Clause." Chief Justice Rehnquist dissented.

(d) *Non-organized religion.* In *Frazee v. Illinois Department of Employment Security*, 489 U.S. 829 (1989), the Court held that Illinois' refusal to grant unemployment compensation benefits to a Christian who was avowedly religious but not a member of a particular sect, violated the Free Exercise Clause. The petitioner had refused a temporary job because it required him to work on Sundays. For further discussion of this case, see *infra* Note: What is a Religion?

(3) *Conscientious Objectors.* The potential clash between free exercise claims and establishment concerns came sharply into focus during the Vietnam War. Conscientious objector exemptions dramatically raised the question of whether the government's accommodation of an individual's religious beliefs becomes, in essence, an establishment of religion. The Court has never squarely considered that question, although this is undoubtedly the type of accommodation which the Establishment Clause does not preclude. The draft cases were decided, for the most part, on statutory interpretations of the Universal Military Training and Service Act of 1948. *See Gillette v. United States*, 401 U.S. 437 (1971) (selective conscientious objection to a particular war); *Welsh v. United States*, 398 U.S. 333 (1970); *United States v. Seeger*, 380 U.S. 163 (1965). *See generally* Theodore Hochstadt, *The Right to Exemption from Military Service of a Conscientious Objector to a Particular War*, 3 HARV. C.R.-C.L. L. REV. 1 (1967); Norman Redlich & Kenneth R. Feinberg, *Individual Conscience and the Selective Conscientious Objector: the Right Not to Kill*, 44 N.Y.U. L. REV. 875 (1969).

WISCONSIN v. YODER, 406 U.S. 205 (1972). In *Wisconsin v. Yoder*, the Court set aside the conviction of members of the Amish community who had failed to enroll their fourteen and fifteen year old children in high school after they had completed the eighth grade. Respondent's conviction was under a law requiring parents to enroll their children in state-certified schools until the age of sixteen.

Chief Justice Burger first considered whether the Amish's withholding of their children from school was in fact part of a " 'religious' belief or 'practice.' " In this connection, he found that the record showed that the Old Order Amish communities were "characterized by a fundamental belief that salvation requires life in a church community separate and apart from the world and worldly influences." Chief Justice Burger held that this system of belief deserved protection under the Free Exercise Clause; the Chief Justice contrasted it with the decision made by Henry David Thoreau to withdraw from society and live on Walden Pond. "Thus, if the Amish asserted their claims because of their subjective evaluation and rejection of the contemporary secular values accepted by the majority, much as Thoreau rejected the social values of his time and isolated himself at Walden Pond, their claims would not rest on a religious basis. Thoreau's choice was personal and philosophical, and such belief does not rise to the demands of the Religion Clauses." The Amish way of life was based upon "not a matter of personal preference but one of deep religious conviction, shared by an organized group, and intimately related to daily living."

Quoting from St. Paul's Epistle to the Romans "be not conformed to this world," the Chief Justice concluded that the parents' decision had its source in Biblical interpretation. The parents' refusal to send their children to high school beyond the eighth grade arose directly out of these religious beliefs, since "secondary schooling, by exposing Amish children to worldly influences . . . contravenes the basic religious tenets and practice of the Amish faith." In the long term, what was at stake here was the continued existence of the Amish faith.

Chief Justice Burger did not accept the argument that a well-established religious practice had to bow to the State's compelling interest in its system of universal compulsory education. The argument was based on the State's erroneous assumption that, but for their enrollment in a formal education system, the Amish children would go utterly untutored. In fact, the record showed that the Amish administered an elaborate system of informal vocational education. The Free Exercise Clause required that "only those interests of the highest order and those not otherwise served can overbalance legitimate claims to the free exercise of religion."

The State had failed to show "how its admittedly strong interest in compulsory education would be adversely affected by granting an exemption to the Amish." The Court was persuaded by the evidence that "an additional one or two years of formal high school for Amish children in place of their long-established program of informal vocational education" would do little to serve the interests relied upon by the State. Moreover, for children beyond the eighth grade level, the Amish themselves "continue to provide what has been characterized by expert educators as an 'ideal' vocational education for their children in the adolescent years."

The Court also rejected the argument that the right of the children themselves to a secondary education demanded that no exemption be granted to Amish parents. There was no indication that the children in fact wished to attend school, and it was in any event the free exercise rights of the parents, who had a right to direct the religious upbringing of their children, that were at stake.

Justice Stewart wrote a concurring opinion joined by Justice Brennan, and Justice White wrote a separate concurring opinion joined by Justices Brennan and Stewart. Justices Powell and Rehnquist did not take part in the decision.

Justice Douglas wrote a separate opinion dissenting in part. He argued that the free exercise interests of the young adults, which were separate from their parents, had not been adequately elicited in the proceedings below. "[I]f an Amish child desires to attend high school, and is mature enough to have that desire respected, the State may well be able to override the parents' religiously motivated objections." Justice Douglas would have remanded the case to ascertain the views of "the two children in question."

THOMAS v. REVIEW BOARD OF THE INDIANA EMPLOYMENT SECURITY DIVISION
450 U.S. 707, 101 S. Ct. 1425, 67 L. Ed. 2d 624 (1981)

CHIEF JUSTICE BURGER delivered the opinion of the Court.

We granted certiorari to consider whether the State's denial of unemployment compensation benefits to the petitioner, a Jehovah's Witness who terminated his job because his religious beliefs forbade participation in the production of armaments, constituted a violation of his First Amendment right to free exercise of religion.

I

Thomas terminated his employment in the Blaw-Knox Foundry & Machinery Co. when he was transferred from the roll foundry to a department that produced turrets for military tanks. He claimed his religious beliefs prevented him from participating in the production of war materials. The respondent Review Board denied him unemployment compensation benefits by applying disqualifying provisions of the Indiana Employment Security Act.

Thomas, a Jehovah's Witness, was hired initially to work in the roll foundry at Blaw-Knox. The function of that department was to fabricate sheet steel for a variety of industrial uses. On his application form, he listed his membership in the Jehovah's Witnesses, and noted that his hobbies were Bible study and Bible reading. However, he placed no conditions on his employment; and he did not describe his religious tenets in any detail on the form.

Approximately a year later, the roll foundry closed, and Blaw-Knox transferred Thomas to a department that fabricated turrets for military tanks. On his first day at this new job, Thomas realized that the work he was doing was weapons related. He checked the bulletin board where in-plant openings were listed, and discovered that all of the remaining departments at Blaw-Knox were engaged directly in the production of weapons. Since no transfer to another department would resolve his problem, he asked for a layoff. When that request was denied, he quit, asserting that he could not work on weapons without violating the principles of his religion. . . .

Upon leaving Blaw-Knox, Thomas applied for unemployment compensation benefits under the Indiana Employment Security Act. At an administrative hearing where he was not represented by counsel, he testified that he believed that contributing to the production of arms violated his religion. He said that when he realized that his work on the tank turret line involved producing weapons for war, he consulted another Blaw-Knox employee — a friend and fellow Jehovah's Witness. The friend advised him that working on weapons parts at Blaw-Knox was not "unscriptural." Thomas was not able to "rest with" this view, however. He concluded that his friend's view was based upon a less strict reading of Witnesses' principles than his own. . . .

The hearing referee found that Thomas' religious beliefs specifically precluded him from producing or directly aiding in the manufacture of items used in warfare. He also found that Thomas had terminated his employment because of these religious convictions. . . . The referee concluded nonetheless that Thomas' termination was not based upon a "good cause [arising] in connection with [his] work," as required by the Indiana unemployment compensation statute. Accordingly, he was held not entitled to benefits. . . .

II

. . . The determination of what is a "religious" belief or practice is more often than not a difficult and delicate task, as the division in the Indiana Supreme Court attest[s]. However, the resolution of that question is not to turn upon a judicial perception of the particular belief or practice in question; religious beliefs need not be acceptable, logical, consistent, or comprehensible to others in order to merit First Amendment protection. . . .

. . . Based upon [Thomas'] testimony, the referee held that Thomas "quit due to his religious convictions." . . .

The Indiana Supreme Court apparently took a different view of the record. . . . "
[R]easons for quitting were described as religious, it was unclear what his belief was,
and what the religious basis of his belief was." In that court's view, Thomas had made
a merely "personal philosophical choice rather than a religious choice."

In reaching its conclusion, the Indiana court seems to have placed considerable
reliance on the facts that Thomas was "struggling" with his beliefs and that he was not
able to "articulate" his belief precisely. . . .

But, Thomas' statements reveal no more than that he found work in the roll foundry
sufficiently insulated from producing weapons of war. We see, therefore, that Thomas
drew a line, and it is not for us to say that the line he drew was an unreasonable one.
Courts should not undertake to dissect religious beliefs because the believer admits
that he is "struggling" with his position or because his beliefs are not articulated with
the clarity and precision that a more sophisticated person might employ.

The Indiana court also appears to have given significant weight to the fact that
another Jehovah's Witness had no scruples about working on tank turrets; for that
other Witness, at least, such work was "scripturally" acceptable. . . . One can, of
course, imagine an asserted claim so bizarre, so clearly nonreligious in motivation, as
not to be entitled to protection under the Free Exercise Clause; but that is not the case
here, and the guarantee of free exercise is not limited to beliefs which are shared by all
of the members of a religious sect. Particularly in this sensitive area, it is not within the
judicial function and judicial competence to inquire whether the petitioner or his fellow
worker more correctly perceived the commands of their common faith. Courts are not
arbiters of scriptural interpretation.

The narrow function of a reviewing court in this context is to determine whether
there was an appropriate finding that petitioner terminated his work because of an
honest conviction that such work was forbidden by his religion. . . .

III

A

. . . It is true, however, that, as in *Sherbert*, the Indiana law does not *compel* a
violation of conscience. But, "this is only the beginning, not the end, of our inquiry." In
a variety of ways we have said that "[a] regulation neutral on its face may, in its
application, nonetheless offend the constitutional requirement for governmental
neutrality if it unduly burdens the free exercise of religion." *Wisconsin v. Yoder*, 406
U.S. at 220.

Here, as in *Sherbert*, the employee was put to a choice between fidelity to religious
belief or cessation of work; the coercive impact on Thomas is indistinguishable from
Sherbert. . . . Where the state conditions receipt of an important benefit upon
conduct proscribed by a religious faith, or where it denies such a benefit because of
conduct mandated by religious belief, thereby putting substantial pressure on an
adherent to modify his behavior and to violate his beliefs, a burden upon religion exists.
While the compulsion may be indirect, the infringement upon free exercise is
nonetheless substantial. . . .

B

. . . [O]nly those interests of the highest order . . . can overbalance legitimate
claims to the free exercise of religion." *Wisconsin v. Yoder, supra*, at 215.

The purposes urged to sustain the disqualifying provision of the Indiana unemployment compensation scheme are twofold: (1) to avoid the widespread unemployment and the consequent burden on the fund resulting if people were permitted to leave jobs for "personal" reasons; and (2) to avoid a detailed probing by employers into the job applicants' religious beliefs. . . .

There is no evidence in the record to indicate that the number of people who find themselves in the predicament of choosing between benefits and religious beliefs is large enough to create "widespread unemployment," or even to seriously affect unemployment — and no such claim was advanced by the Review Board.

. . . Nor is there any reason to believe that the number of people terminating employment for religious reasons will be so great as to motivate employers to make such inquiries.

Neither of the interests advanced is sufficiently compelling to justify the burden upon Thomas' religious liberty.

Accordingly, Thomas is entitled to receive benefits unless, as the respondents contend and the Indiana court held, such payment would violate the Establishment Clause.

IV

The respondents contend that to compel benefit payments to Thomas involves the State in fostering a religious faith. There is, in a sense, a "benefit" to Thomas deriving from his religious beliefs, but this manifests no more than the tension between the two Religious Clauses which the Court resolved in *Sherbert*. . . .

JUSTICE BLACKMUN joins Parts I, II, and III of the Court's opinion. As to Part IV thereof, he concurs in the result.

JUSTICE REHNQUIST, dissenting.

I

The Court correctly acknowledges that there is a "tension" between the Free Exercise and Establishment Clauses. . . . The causes of tension, it seems to me, are threefold. First, the growth of social welfare legislation during the latter part of the 20th century has greatly magnified the potential for conflict between the two Clauses, since such legislation touches the individual at so many points in his life. Second, the decision by this Court that the First Amendment was "incorporated" into the Fourteenth Amendment and thereby made applicable against the States, similarly multiplied the number of instances in which the "tension" might arise. The third, and perhaps most important, cause of the tension is our overly expansive interpretation of *both* Clauses. . . .

. . . Because those who drafted and adopted the First Amendment could not have foreseen either the growth of social welfare legislation or the incorporation of the First Amendment into the Fourteenth Amendment, we simply do not know how they would view the scope of the two Clauses.

II

. . . Just as it did in *Sherbert v. Verner*, the Court today reads the Free Exercise Clause more broadly than is warranted. . . . I believe that although a State could choose to grant exemptions to religious persons from state unemployment regulations, a State is not constitutionally compelled to do so. . . .

NOTE: WHAT IS A RELIGION?

The *Thomas* and *Yoder* cases devote some attention to the question of "what is a religious practice" that should receive protection under the Free Exercise Clause. A separate and even more basic question is what is a religion for purposes of receiving free exercise protection. For example, should certain cult groups receive protection under this Clause?

The Court has occasionally given some guidance on this issue. In *Torcaso v. Watkins*, 367 U.S. 488 (1961), the Court invalidated a state-imposed religious test for office requiring the profession of a belief in God. In invalidating the test, Justice Black stated that the state cannot "aid those religions based on a belief in the existence of God as against those religions founded on different beliefs." In a footnote Justice Black expanded on this passage: "Among religions in this country which do not teach what would generally be considered a belief in the existence of God are Buddhism, Taoism, Ethical Culture, Secular Humanism and others."

The Court has also given further guidance in the conscientious objector cases discussed *supra*, § 16.05, Note (3), after *Sherbert*. While those cases ostensibly involved questions of statutory interpretation rather than constitutional issues, many commentators think that the statutory construction had constitutional dimensions. For example, in *Welsh* the Court stated that conscientious objector status should not "exclude those whose . . . objection to participation in all wars is founded to a substantial extent upon considerations of public policy." Those who might be excluded from the exemption were persons "whose beliefs were not deeply held and those whose objection to war does not rest at all upon moral, ethical, or religious principle but instead rests solely upon considerations of policy, pragmatism, or expediency." *See also United States v. Seeger*, 380 U.S. 163, 176 (1965) ("A sincere and meaningful belief which occupies in the life of its possessor a place parallel to that filled by the God of those qualifying for the exemption comes within the statutory definition.").

In *Frazee v. Illinois Department of Employment Security*, 489 U.S. 829 (1989), the Court unanimously held unconstitutional Illinois' denial of unemployment benefits to petitioner, who had refused to work on Sunday. William Frazee had refused a temporary job because it required him to work on Sundays, and he could not work on "the Lord's day." Frazee claimed to be a Christian, but not a member of a particular sect. When Frazee applied for unemployment benefits claiming that there was "good cause" for his refusal to work on Sunday, the Illinois Department of Employment Security denied his application.

Justice White wrote for the Court. In reviewing the holdings of *Sherbert*, *Thomas*, and *Hobbie*, he noted that "none of those decisions turned on that consideration or on any tenet of the sect involved that forbade the work the claimant refused to perform. Our judgments in those cases rested on the fact that each of the claimants had a sincere belief that religion required him or her to refrain from the work in question."

The Court again stated that general philosophical convictions do not come within the protection of the Free Exercise Clause. "There is no doubt that '[o]nly beliefs rooted in religion are protected by the Free Exercise Clause.' Purely secular views do not suffice. Nor do we underestimate the difficulty of distinguishing between religious and secular convictions and in determining whether a professed belief is sincerely held." Problems of the sincerity or the religious nature of the belief were not at issue in this case: the State had denied benefits only because Frazee had not predicated his claim on the teachings of a particular religious sect or denomination.

For further discussion of these questions, see LAURENCE H. TRIBE, AMERICAN

CONSTITUTIONAL LAW, 1179–88 (2d. ed. 1988); Jesse H. Choper, *Defining "Religion" in the First Amendment*, 1982 U. ILL. L. REV. 579; George C. Freeman, *The Misguided Search for the Constitutional Definition of "Religion"*, 71 GEO. L.J. 1519 (1983); Kent Greenawalt, *Religion as a Concept in Constitutional Law*, 72 CAL. L. REV. 753 (1984); Stanley Ingber, *Religion or Ideology: A Needed Clarification of the Religion Clauses*, 41 STAN. L. REV. 233 (1989); Note, *Toward a Constitutional Definition of Religion*, 91 HARV. L. REV. 1056 (1978).

For a discussion of "religion" versus "ideology," see Stanley Ingber, *Religion or Ideology: A Needed Clarification of the Religon Clauses*, 41 STAN. L. REV. 233, 332 (1989) ("[C]onfusion [in religion clause jurisprudence] is due to a lack of a legally functional definition of religion that recognizes the important distinction between religion and ideology. In fact, by expanding the constitutional definition of religion to emulate developments in theology, courts and commentators often have neglected the every element of religion that makes it unique for legal purposes. Religion acknowledges the existence of a sacred or transcendent reality from which basic human obligations emanate.").

NOTES

(1) *Tax Exemptions and Racial Discrimination.* In *Bob Jones University v. United States* and *Goldsboro Christian School v. United States*, 461 U.S. 574 (1983), the Court stated that the Internal Revenue Service had the authority to deny tax exemptions to two educational institutions because of their racially discriminatory policies. This aspect of the cases is discussed at § 8.03[1], Note (7) after *Korematsu*.

The Court also upheld the Service's policy as applied "to schools that engage in racial discrimination on the basis of sincerely-held religious beliefs." Relying on the "belief/conduct" distinction, the Court held that while the First Amendment created an absolute prohibition against regulation of religious beliefs, "[on] occasion, this Court has found certain governmental interests so compelling as to allow even regulations prohibiting religiously-based conduct."

The Court concluded that the government has "a fundamental, overriding interest in eradicating racial discrimination in education" which "substantially outweighs whatever burden denial of tax benefits places on petitioners' exercise of their religious beliefs." While denial of tax exemption "may have a substantial impact on the operation of private religious schools," it will "not prevent those schools from observing their religious tenets." And, unlike the situation where the state seeks to deny unemployment compensation because of a person's refusal to work on Saturday, or in a factory producing weapons, in violation of his or her religious beliefs, there are no "less restrictive means" available for achieving the state's objective. Finally, the Court was careful to point out, in a footnote, that the case only involved "religious schools — not . . . churches or other purely religious institutions." Justice Powell filed a concurring opinion and Justice Rehnquist dissented.

(2) *Minimum Wage.* In *Tony & Susan Alamo Foundation v. Sec'y of Labor*, 471 U.S. 290 (1985), a unanimous Court rejected a Free Exercise Clause claim raised by a nonprofit religious organization that objected to the enforcement of the Fair Labor Standards Act with regard to employees of various commercial businesses operated by the Foundation. The Alamo Foundation derived its income from businesses staffed by former drug addicts, derelicts, or criminals who had been converted by the Foundation. The employees received no cash salaries, but the Foundation provided food, shelter, clothes and other benefits. Justice White's opinion observed that since the employees were being paid (albeit in noncash form), and the religious objection did not relate to the amount of compensation, compliance with the Act would not interfere with religious

belief. Nor would the record-keeping requirements constitute an "excessive government entanglement" in violation of the Establishment Clause. Religious organizations are not exempt from government regulation with regard to their secular, commercial activities.

GOLDMAN v. WEINBERGER, 475 U.S. 503 (1986). In *Goldman*, the Court ruled that the Free Exercise Clause permitted the Air Force to forbid an Orthodox Jew from wearing his yarmulke while on duty. Writing for the Court, Justice Rehnquist emphasized the extraordinary deference in reviewing military regulations. In this instance, the Court deferred to the "considered professional judgment of the Air Force . . . that the traditional outfitting of personnel in standardized uniforms encourages the subordination of personal preferences and identities in favor of the overall group mission."

Justice Rehnquist stressed the stringent uniformity of regulations pertaining to the Air Force uniform. Regulations "authorize a few individual options with respect to certain pieces of jewelry and hair style, but even these are subject to severe limitations." The regulations with respect to headgear were particularly stringent. "The Air Force has drawn the line essentially between religious apparel which is visible and that which is not, and we hold that those portions of the regulations challenged here reasonable and evenhandedly regulate dress in the interest of the military's perceived need for uniformity."

Justice Stevens, joined by Justices White and Powell, concurred. The yarmulke is "a familiar and accepted sight" and "Captain Goldman's military duties [as a clinical psychologist in a California base] are performed in a setting in which a modest departure from the uniform regulation creates almost no danger of impairment of the Air Force's military mission." Nevertheless, Justice Stevens recognized a "legitimate and rational" interest in the uniformity of military garb.

Even more important "is the interest in uniform treatment for the members of all religious faiths" — for example Sikhs or Rastafarians.

Justice Brennan, joined by Justice Marshall, dissented. He would have required that the regulation "be a narrowly tailored means of promoting important military interests." That military discipline would be undermined as a result of Orthodox Jews wearing their yarmulkes was utterly implausible.

As to the distinguishability of a Rastafarian wearing dreadlocks, dress and grooming rules "that have a *reasoned* basis in, for example, functional utility, health and safety considerations" would impinge less on the free exercise of rights than the blanket test sanctioned by the Court: "The visibility test permits *only* individuals whose outer garments and grooming are indistinguishable from those of mainstream Christians to fulfill their religious duties. In my view, the Constitution requires the selection of criteria that permit the greatest possible number of persons to practice their faiths freely."

Justice Blackmun also dissented. "If, in the future, the Air Force is besieged with requests for religious exemptions from the dress code, and the requests cannot be distinguished on functional grounds from Goldman's, the service may be able to argue credibly that circumstances warrant a flat rule against any visible religious apparel."

In a dissent joined by Justice Marshall, Justice O'Connor concluded that military discipline was "especially important," but the government had not demonstrated that this interest would be substantially harmed by an exception for Captain Goldman.

LYNG v. NORTHWEST INDIAN CEMETERY PROTECTIVE ASS'N, 485 U.S. 439 (1988). In *Lyng*, a 5-3 majority upheld the decision of the United States Forest

Service to construct a road through, and allow timber harvesting in a portion of a national forest that had been used for religious purposes by three American Indian tribes. A study commissioned by the Service had concluded that the road "would cause serious and irreparable damage to the sacred areas which are an integral and necessary part of the belief system and lifeway of Northwest California Indian peoples." Justice O'Connor's opinion said that the burden on religious practice was not heavy enough to attract strict scrutiny.

Crucial to the majority's holding was the distinction that it drew between the free exercise burden caused by the decision of the Forest Service and the burdens involved in *Sherbert v. Verner, Thomas v. Review Board, Wisconsin v. Yoder*, and *Hobbie v. Unemployment Comm'n*: "It is true that this Court has repeatedly held that indirect coercion or penalties on the free exercise of religion, not just outright prohibitions, are subject to scrutiny under the First Amendment. . . . This does not and cannot imply that incidental effects of government programs, which may make it more difficult to practice certain religions but which have no tendency to coerce individuals into acting contrary to their religious beliefs, require the government to bring forward a compelling justification for its otherwise lawful actions. The crucial word in the constitutional text is 'prohibit.' "

Justice O'Connor's opinion also suggested that the legislature, not the judiciary is responsible to review public works that may offend some religious beliefs. "Even if we assume that we should accept the Ninth Circuit's prediction, according to which the G-O road will 'virtually destroy the Indians' ability to practice their religion,' the Constitution simply does not provide a principle that could justify upholding respondents' legal claims. However much we might wish that it were otherwise, government simply could not operate if it were required to satisfy every citizen's religious needs and desires. A broad range of government activities — from social welfare programs to foreign aid to conservation projects — will always be considered essential to the spiritual well-being of some citizens, often on the basis of sincerely held religious beliefs. Others will find the very same activities deeply offensive, and perhaps incompatible with their own search for spiritual fulfillment and with the tenets of their religion. The First Amendment must apply to all citizens alike, and it can give to none of them a veto over public programs that do not prohibit the free exercise of religion. The Constitution does not, and courts cannot, offer to reconcile the various competing demands on government, many of them rooted in sincere religious belief, that inevitably arise in so diverse a society as ours. That task, to the extent that it is feasible, is for the legislatures and other institutions. *Cf.* THE FEDERALIST No. 10 (Alexander Hamilton) (suggesting that the effects of religious factionalism are best restrained through competition among a multiplicity of religious sects)."

Justice Brennan dissented, joined by Justices Marshall and Blackmun. The Constitution prohibits any form of governmental action that frustrates or inhibits religious practice. His opinion criticized the failure of the majority's analysis to consider the relative importance of the government's interest in the road and timber project as compared to the burden it placed on the Indians' religious practice caused by the destructive effect on this specific religious site.

"Today, the Court holds that a federal land-use decision that promises to destroy an entire religion does not burden the practice of that faith in a manner recognized by the Free Exercise Clause. Having thus stripped respondents and all other Native Americans of any constitutional protection against perhaps the most serious threat to their age-old religious practices, and indeed to their entire way of life, the Court assures us that nothing in its decision 'should be read to encourage governmental insensitivity to the religious needs of any citizen.' I find it difficult, however, to imagine conduct more insensitive to religious needs than the Government's determination to build a marginally useful road in the face of uncontradicted evidence that the road will render the practice of respondents' religion impossible." Justice Kennedy did not participate.

EMPLOYMENT DIVISION, DEPARTMENT OF HUMAN RESOURCES OF OREGON v. SMITH
494 U.S. 872, 110 S. Ct. 1595, 108 L. Ed. 2d 876 (1990)

JUSTICE SCALIA delivered the opinion of the Court.

This case requires us to decide whether the Free Exercise Clause of the First Amendment permits the State of Oregon to include religiously inspired peyote use within the reach of its general criminal prohibition on use of that drug, and thus permits the State to deny unemployment benefits to persons dismissed from their jobs because of such religiously inspired use.

I

Oregon law prohibits the knowing or intentional possession of a "controlled substance" unless the substance has been prescribed by a medical practitioner. . . . Persons who violate this provision by possessing a controlled substance listed on Schedule I are "guilty of a Class B felony." As compiled by the State Board of Pharmacy under its statutory authority . . . Schedule I contains the drug peyote. . . .

Respondents Alfred Smith and Galen Black were fired from their jobs with a private drug rehabilitation organization because they ingested peyote for sacramental purposes at a ceremony of the Native American Church, of which both are members. When respondents applied to petitioner Employment Division for unemployment compensation, they were determined to be ineligible for benefits because they had been discharged for work-related "misconduct.". . .

II

Respondents' claim for relief rests on our decisions in *Sherbert v. Verner*, [374 U.S. 398 (1963)], *Thomas v. Review Board, Indiana Employment Security Div.*, [450 U.S. 707 (1981)], and *Hobbie v. Unemployment Appeals Comm'n of Florida*, 480 U.S. 136 (1987), in which we held that a State could not condition the availability of unemployment insurance on an individual's willingness to forgo conduct required by his religion. . . . [H]owever, the conduct at issue in those cases was not prohibited by law. . . .

A

. . . The government may not compel affirmation of religious belief, punish the expression of religious doctrines it believes to be false, impose special disabilities on the basis of religious views or religious status, or lend its power to one or the other side in controversies over religious authority or dogma.

But the "exercise of religion" often involves not only belief and profession but the performance of (or abstention from) physical acts: assembling with others for a worship service, participating in sacramental use of bread and wine, proselytizing, abstaining from certain foods or certain modes of transportation. It would be true, we think (though no case of ours has involved the point), that a state would be "prohibiting the free exercise [of religion]" if it sought to ban such acts or abstentions only when they are engaged in for religious reasons, or only because of the religious belief that they display. . . .

We have never held that an individual's religious beliefs excuse him from compliance with an otherwise valid law prohibiting conduct that the State is free to regulate. On the contrary, the record of more than a century of our free exercise jurisprudence contradicts that proposition. . . . We first had occasion to assert that principle in *Reynolds v. United States*, 98 U.S. 145 (1879), where we rejected the claim that criminal laws against polygamy could not be constitutionally applied to those whose religion commanded the practice. . . . Subsequent decisions have consistently held that the right of free exercise does not relieve an individual of the obligation to comply with a "valid and neutral law of general applicability on the ground that the law proscribes (or prescribes) conduct that his religion prescribes (or proscribes)." *United States v. Lee*, 455 U.S. 252, 263 n. 3 (1982) (Stevens, J., concurring in judgment). In *Prince v. Massachusetts*, 321 U.S. 158 (1944), we held that a mother could be prosecuted under the child labor laws for using her children to dispense literature in the streets, her religious motivation notwithstanding. . . . In *Braunfield v. Brown*, 366 U.S. 599 (1961) (plurality opinion), we upheld Sunday-closing laws against the claim that they burdened the religious practices of persons whose religions compelled them to refrain from work on other days. In *Gillette v. United States*, 401 U.S. 437, 461 (1971), we sustained the military selective service system against the claim that it violated free exercise by conscripting persons who opposed a particular war on religious grounds.

Our most recent decision involving a neutral, generally applicable regulatory law that compelled activity forbidden by an individual's religion was *United States v. Lee*, 455 U.S. at 258–261. There, an Amish employer, on behalf of himself and his employees, sought exemption from collection and payment of Social Security taxes on the ground that the Amish faith prohibited participation in governmental support programs. We rejected the claim that an exemption was constitutionally required. . . .

The only decisions in which we have held that the First Amendment bars application of a neutral, generally applicable law to religiously motivated action have involved not the Free Exercise Clause alone, but the Free Exercise Clause in conjunction with other constitutional protections, such as freedom of speech and of the press . . . or the right of parents, acknowledged in *Pierce v. Society of Sisters*, 268 U.S. 510 (1925), to direct the education of their children. Some of our cases prohibiting compelled expression, decided exclusively upon free speech grounds, have also involved freedom of religion. . . .

The present case does not present such a hybrid situation, but a free exercise claim unconnected with any communicative activity or parental right. Respondents urge us to hold, quite simply, that when otherwise prohibitable conduct is accompanied by religious convictions, not only the convictions but the conduct itself must be free from governmental regulation. We have never held that, and decline to do so now. There being no contention that Oregon's drug law represents an attempt to regulate religious beliefs, the communication of religious beliefs, or the raising of one's children in those beliefs, the rule to which we have adhered ever since *Reynolds* plainly controls. . . .

B

Respondents argue that even though exemption from generally applicable criminal laws need not automatically be extended to religiously motivated actors, at least the claim for a religious exemption must be evaluated under the balancing test set forth in *Sherbert v. Verner*. Under the *Sherbert* test, governmental actions that substantially burden a religious practice must be justified by a compelling governmental interest. . . . Applying that test we have, on three occasions, invalidated state unemployment compensation rules that conditioned the availability of benefits upon an applicant's willingness to work under conditions forbidden by his religion. We have never invalidated any governmental action on the basis of the *Sherbert* test except the denial of unemployment compensation. Although we have sometimes purported to apply the *Sherbert* test in contexts other than that, we have always found the test satisfied. In recent years we have abstained from applying the *Sherbert* test (outside the unemployment compensation field) at all. In *Bowen v. Roy*, 476 U.S. 693 (1986), we declined to apply *Sherbert* analysis to a federal statutory scheme that required benefit applicants and recipients to provide their Social Security numbers. The plaintiffs in that case asserted that it would violate their religious beliefs to obtain and provide a Social Security number for their daughter. . . . In *Lyng v. Northwest Indian Cemetery Protective Ass'n*, 485 U.S. 439 (1988), we declined to apply *Sherbert* analysis to the Government's logging and road construction activities on lands used for religious purposes by several Native American Tribes, even though it was undisputed that the activities "could have devastating effects on traditional Indian religious practices," 485 U.S. at 451. In *Goldman v. Weinberger*, 475 U.S. 503 (1986), we rejected application of the *Sherbert* test to military dress regulations that forbade the wearing of yarmulkes. In *O'Lone v. Estate of Shabazz*, 482 U.S. 342 (1987), we sustained, without mentioning the *Sherbert* test, a prison's refusal to excuse inmates from work requirements to attend worship services.

Even if we were inclined to breathe into *Sherbert* some life beyond the unemployment compensation field, we would not apply it to require exemptions from a generally applicable criminal law. . . .

. . . To make an individual's obligation to obey such a law contingent upon the law's coincidence with his religious beliefs, except where the State's interest is "compelling" — permitting him, by virtue of his beliefs, "to become a law unto himself," *Reynolds v. United States*, 98 U.S. at 167 — contradicts both constitutional tradition and common sense. . . .

The "compelling government interest" requirement seems benign. . . . [W]hat it would produce here — a private right to ignore generally applicable laws — is a constitutional anomaly.[60]

Nor is it possible to limit the impact of respondents' proposal by requiring a "compelling state interest" only when the conduct prohibited is "central" to the individual's religion. It is no more appropriate for judges to determine the "centrality" of religious beliefs before applying a "compelling interest" test in the free exercise field, than it would be for them to determine the "importance" of ideas before applying the "compelling interest" test in the free speech field. . . . Repeatedly and in many different contexts, we have warned that courts must not presume to determine the place of a particular belief in a religion or the plausibility of a religious claim.[61]

. . . [I]f "compelling interest" really means what it says (and watering it down here would subvert its rigor in the other fields where it is applied), many laws will not meet the test. . . . Precisely because "we are a cosmopolitan nation made up of people of almost every conceivable religious preference," *Braunfield v. Brown*, 366 U.S. at 606,

---

[60] [W]e have held that race-neutral laws that have the effect of disproportionately disadvantaging a particular racial group do not thereby become subject to compelling-interest analysis under the Equal Protection Clause. . . . Our conclusion that generally applicable, religion-neutral laws that have the effect of burdening a particular religious practice need not be justified by a compelling governmental interest is the only approach compatible with these precedents.

[61] . . . As Justice Blackmun's opinion proceeds to make clear, inquiry into "severe impact" is no different from inquiry into centrality. . . .

and precisely because we value and protect that religious divergence, we cannot afford the luxury of deeming *presumptively invalid*, as applied to the religious objector, every regulation of conduct that does not protect an interest of the highest order. The rule respondents favor would open the prospect of constitutionally required religious exemptions from civic obligations of almost every conceivable kind — ranging from compulsory military service, to the payment of taxes, to health and safety regulation such as manslaughter and child neglect laws, compulsory vaccination laws, drug laws, and traffic laws, to social welfare legislation such as minimum wage laws, child labor laws, animal cruelty laws, environmental protection laws, and laws providing for equality of opportunity for the races. The First Amendment's protection of religious liberty does not require this.

. . . [A] number of States have made an exception to their drug laws for sacramental peyote use. But to say that a nondiscriminatory religious-practice exemption is permitted, or even that it is desirable, is not to say that it is constitutionally required, and that the appropriate occasions for its creation can be discerned by the courts. It may fairly be said that leaving accommodation to the political process will place at a relative disadvantage those religious practices that are not widely engaged in; but that unavoidable consequence of democratic government must be preferred to a system in which each conscience is a law unto itself or in which judges weight the social importance of all laws against the centrality of all religious beliefs. . . .

JUSTICE O'CONNOR, with whom JUSTICE BRENNAN, JUSTICE MARSHALL, and JUSTICE BLACKMUN join as to Parts I and II, concurring in the judgment.[62]

Although I agree with the result the Court reaches in this case, I cannot join its opinion. In my view, today's holding dramatically departs from well-settled First Amendment jurisprudence, appears unnecessary to resolve the question presented, and is incompatible with our Nation's fundamental commitment to individual religious liberty. . . .

II

. . . [T]he Court holds that where the law is a generally applicable criminal prohibition, our usual free exercise jurisprudence does not even apply. . . .

A

. . . Because the First Amendment does not distinguish between religious belief and religious conduct, conduct motivated by sincere religious belief, like the belief itself, must therefore be at least presumptively protected by the Free Exercise Clause.

The Court today, however, interprets the Clause to permit the government to prohibit, without justification, conduct mandated by an individual's religious beliefs, so long as that prohibition is generally applicable. . . . A person who is barred from engaging in religiously motivated conduct is barred from freely exercising his religion. Moreover, that person is barred from freely exercising his religion regardless of whether the law prohibits the conduct only when engaged in for religious reasons, only by members of that religion, or by all persons. . . .

The First Amendment . . . does not distinguish between laws that are generally applicable and laws that target particular religious practices. . . .

---

[62] Although JUSTICE BRENNAN, JUSTICE MARSHALL, and JUSTICE BLACKMUN join Parts I and II of this opinion, they do not concur in the judgment.

The Court endeavors to escape from our decisions in Cantwell and Yoder by labeling them "hybrid" decisions, but there is no denying that both cases expressly relied on the Free Exercise Clause and that we have consistently regarded those cases as part of the mainstream of our free exercise jurisprudence. . . .

B

. . . [W]e have never distinguished between cases in which a State conditions receipt of a benefit on conduct prohibited by religious beliefs and cases in which a State affirmatively prohibits such conduct. The *Sherbert* compelling interest test applies in both kinds of cases. . . .

. . . [W]e have . . . "rejected" or "declined to apply" the compelling interest test in our recent cases. . . .

The Free Exercise Clause simply cannot be understood to require the Government to conduct its own internal affairs in ways that comport with the religious beliefs of particular citizens." *Roy, supra*, at 699. . . .

Similarly, the other cases cited by the Court for the proposition that we have rejected application of the *Sherbert* test outside the unemployment compensation field are distinguishable because they arose in the narrow, specialized contexts in which we have not traditionally required the government to justify a burden on religious conduct by articulating a compelling interest. *See Goldman v. Weinberger*, 475 U.S. 503, 507 (1986) ("Our review of military regulations challenged on First Amendment grounds is far more deferential than constitutional review of similar laws or regulations designed for civilian society"). . . .

Finally, the Court today suggests that the disfavoring of minority religions is an "unavoidable consequence" under our system of government and that accommodation of such religions must be left to the political process. In my view, however, the First Amendment was enacted precisely to protect the rights of those whose religious practices are not shared by the majority and may be viewed with hostility. . . .

III

. . . I would reach the same result applying our established free exercise jurisprudence. . . .

B

. . . Although the question is close, I would conclude that uniform application of Oregon's criminal prohibition is "essential to accomplish," its overriding interest in preventing the physical harm caused by the use of a Schedule I controlled substance. . . . Because the health effects caused by the use of controlled substances exist regardless of the motivation of the user, the use of such substances, even for religious purposes, violates the very purpose of the laws that prohibit them. . . .

Justice Blackmun, with whom Justice Brennan and Justice Marshall join, dissenting.

. . . [A] state statute that burdens the free exercise of religion . . . may stand only if the law in general, and the State's refusal to allow a religious exemption in particular, are justified by a compelling interest that cannot be served by less restrictive means. . . .

I

The State proclaims an interest in protecting the health and safety of its citizens from the dangers of unlawful drugs. It offers, however, no evidence that the religious use of peyote has ever harmed anyone. . . .

The carefully circumscribed ritual context in which respondents used peyote is far removed from the irresponsible and unrestricted recreational use of unlawful drugs.[63]

Moreover, just as in *Yoder*, the values and interests of those seeking a religious exemption in this case are congruent, to a great degree, with those the State seeks to promote through its drug laws. . . . Not only does the Church's doctrine forbid nonreligious use of peyote; it also generally advocates self-reliance, familial responsibility, and abstinence from alcohol. . . . [64]

The State also seeks to support its refusal to make an exception for religious use of peyote by invoking its interest in abolishing drug trafficking. There is, however, practically no illegal traffic in peyote. . . .

Finally, the State argues that granting an exception for religious peyote use would erode its interest in the uniform, fair, and certain enforcement of its drug laws. . . . [65]

The State's apprehension of a flood of other religious claims is purely speculative. Almost half the States, and the Federal Government, have maintained an exemption for religious peyote use for many years, and apparently have not found themselves overwhelmed by claims to other religious exemptions.[66] Allowing an exemption for religious peyote use would not necessarily oblige the State to grant a similar exemption to other religious groups. . . . Though the State must treat all religions equally, and not favor one over another, this obligation is fulfilled by the uniform application of the "compelling interest" *test* to all free exercise claims, not by reaching uniform *results* as to all claims. . . .

III

Finally, although I agree with Justice O'Connor that courts should refrain from delving into questions of whether, as a matter of religious doctrine, a particular practice is "central" to the religion, I do not think this means that the courts must turn a blind eye to the severe impact of a State's restrictions on the adherents of a minority religion. . . .

Respondents believe, and their sincerity has *never* been at issue, that the peyote plant embodies their deity, and eating it is an act of worship and communion. Without

---

[63] The Native American Church's internal restrictions on, and supervision of, its members' use of peyote substantially obviate the State's health and safety concerns.

[64] [Court's footnote 6] In this respect, respondents' use of peyote seems closely analogous to the sacramental use of wine by the Roman Catholic Church. During Prohibition, the Federal Government exempted such use of wine from its general ban on possession and use of alcohol. . . .

[65] [Court's footnote 7] The use of peyote is, to some degree, self-limiting. The peyote plant is extremely bitter, and eating it is an unpleasant experience. . . . *See State v. Whittingham*, 19 Ariz. App. 27, 30, 504 P.2d 950, 953 (1973) ("peyote can cause vomiting by reason of its bitter taste"). . . .

[66] [Court's footnote 8] Over the years, various sects have raised free exercise claims regarding drug use. In no reported case, except those involving claims of religious peyote use, has the claimant prevailed.

peyote, they could not enact the essential ritual of their religion. . . .

NOTES

(1) For further discussion of *Employment Division, Department of Human Resources of Oregon v. Smith*, see Christopher L. Eisgruber & Lawrence G. Sager, *The Vulnerability of Conscience: The Constitutional Basis for Protecting Religious Conduct*, 61 U. CHI. L. REV. 1245, 1248 (1994) ("What properly motivates constitutional solicitude for religious practices is their distinct vulnerability to discrimination, not their distinct value; and what is called for, in turn, is protection against discrimination, not privilege against legitimate governmental concerns."); Frederick Mark Gedicks, *The Normalized Free Exercise Clause: Three Abnormalities*, 75 IND. L.J. 77, 120 (2000) ("[I]t is precisely the fundamentality of the free exercise of religion, its status as a preferred constitutional right, that the Smith doctrine repudiates. By applying minimal or no scrutiny to incidental burdens on religious exercise under the Rational Basis Rule, the Court is not treating free exercise rights like speech rights."); Michael W. McConnell, *The Origins and Historical Understanding of Free Exercise of Religion*, 103 HARV. L. REV. 1409, 1415 (1990) (concluding that "exemptions from generally applicable laws . . . ha[ve] posed the most important interpretive issue. The conclusions of this analysis are (1) that exemptions were seen as a constitutionally permissible means for protecting religious freedom, (2) that constitutionally compelled exemptions were within the contemplation of the framers and ratifiers as a possible interpretation of the free exercise clause, and (3) that exemptions were consonant with the popular American understanding of the interrelation between the claims of a limited government and a sovereign God. While the historical evidence may not be unequivocal (it seldom is), it does, on balance, support *Sherbert's* interpretation of the free exercise clause."); Richard K. Sherwin, *Rhetorical Pluralism and the Discourse Ideal: Countering Division of Employment v. Smith, A Parable of Pagans, Politics, and Majoritarian Rule*, 85 N.W. U. L. REV. 388, 440–41 (1991) ("The majority's unexplained and unjustified de-elevation (to the realm of political bargaining) of the individual's right freely to exercise his religion, and the concurring opinion's equally unexplained and unjustified 'balancing' in favor of a preferred state interest in the 'war against drugs,' again at the expense of the plaintiff's free exercise right, illustrate two separate discursive dysfunctions to which the judiciary is prone."); David E. Steinberg, *Rejecting the Case Against the Free Exercise Exemption: A Critical Assessment*, 75 B. U. L. REV. 241, 318 (1995) ("Taken at face value, the argument that free exercise exemptions endorse religion suggests that the First Amendment itself improperly implies religious endorsement. . . . The endorsement concern leads to the bizarre conclusion that the First Amendment is itself unconstitutional.").

(2) *Animal Sacrifice*. In *Church of the Lukumi Babaluaye, Inc. v. City of Hialeah*, 508 U.S. 520 (1993), the Court held that ordinances enacted to prevent members of the Santeria faith from performing animal sacrifices, a principal tenet of their religion, violated the Free Exercise Clause. In response to the imminent founding of a Santeria church in Hialeah, Florida, the city council passed various ordinances prohibiting religious, ritual animal sacrifice, with certain exceptions.

Justice Kennedy wrote for the majority in all but one section of the opinion. Relying on *Oregon v. Smith*, the Court scrutinized the neutrality and general applicability of the ordinances at issue. While Justice Kennedy treated these as separate requirements, he noted that failure to satisfy one requirement typically indicates a failure to satisfy the other.

An ordinance's language or context can indicate lack of facial neutrality. Although the ordinances at issue mention "sacrifice" and "ritual," these terms did not conclusively impair facial neutrality as they have secular as well as religious meanings. Nonetheless, the ordinances represented masked hostility against the Santeria religion as their object was to suppress that religion.

While adverse impact will not always establish "an impermissible targeting," Santeria rituals were nearly the only conduct affected by the ordinances. The ordinances had many exceptions, including Kosher slaughter, hunting, and fishing. In fact, the ordinances allowed ritualistic animal killing, so long as the animal was raised and killed for food purposes and the slaughter occurred on properly zoned and licensed property. Individualized exceptions without one being made for "religious hardship" demonstrate a lack of neutrality that government must justify with compelling reasons.

Undercutting its purported interest in public health, the City conceded that the ordinances would prohibit Santeria sacrifices even if performed in properly zoned and licensed slaughterhouses. The interest in preventing animal cruelty could have been achieved by narrower restrictions, on the treatment and slaughter of animals, to prevent cruelty.

In addition to invalidating the ordinances that were not narrowly tailored, the Court also invalidated one ordinance that was narrowly tailored because it functioned with the others to suppress Santeria worship.

In a part of the opinion joined only by Justice Stevens, Justice Kennedy concluded that the legislative history revealed that the primary object of the ordinances was to suppress Santeria animal sacrifice.

Again writing for the majority, Justice Kennedy held that the ordinances were substantially underinclusive instead of generally applicable. Rather than generally promoting the city's purported interest in preventing cruelty to animals, the ordinances prohibited few slaughters except those performed during Santeria worship. Undercutting the city's public health concerns, they did not address improper disposal after nonreligious animal killings. The ordinances did not subject commercial and recreational animal slaughters to government inspection.

Regulations that are not neutral or not generally applicable have to be narrowly tailored to advance a compelling state interest. For reasons previously stated, the ordinances were not narrowly tailored as they were both substantially overbroad and underinclusive. The city impaired the compelling nature of its asserted interests by impermissibly restricting only protected religious conduct and failing to restrict secular conduct resulting in similar harm.

Concurring in part and concurring in the judgment, Justice Scalia, joined by Chief Justice Rehnquist, criticized the examination of the legislature's subjective motivations in enacting the ordinances. Concurring in part and concurring in the judgment, Justice Souter called for a reexamination of *Oregon v. Smith*. Concurring in the judgment, Justice Blackmun, joined by Justice O'Connor, also expressed dissatisfaction with the *Smith* rule.

For further discussion of *Lukumi*, see Kenneth L. Karst, *Religious Freedom and Equal Citizenship: Reflections on Lukumi*, 69 TUL. L. REV. 335, 372 (1994) ("What makes *Lukumi* important is the example Justice Kennedy set for judges — and Justices — to use in future cases. He thoroughly explored the surrounding circumstances that gave meaning to the claimants' assertions about the burden on their religion, and to the city's assertions in justification of its ordinance.").

CITY OF BOERNE v. FLORES, 521 U.S. 507 (1997). In *City of Boerne*, the Court (6-3), in an opinion written by Justice Kennedy, invalidated the Religious Freedom Restoration Act of 1993 (RFRA) because it exceeded Congressional authority. Zoning authorities denied a Roman Catholic Archdiocese permission to enlarge one of its churches, citing a historic landmark preservation ordinance. Archbishop Flores challenged the decision, relying in part on RFRA.

Congress passed RFRA in reaction to *Employment Div., Dep't Of Human Resources of Ore. v. Smith*. In *Smith*, the Court refused to apply the balancing test of *Sherbert v. Verner*, as such application would have created, "a constitutional right to ignore neutral laws of general applicability." The Court refused "to question the centrality of particular beliefs or practices to a faith, or the validity of particular litigant's interpretations of those creeds.' "

Only in "cases in which other constitutional protections were at stake" was a law that was applicable to all held unconstitutional. For example, *Wisconsin v. Yoder* involved both "the right to the free exercise of religion" as well as "the right of parents to control their children's education."

Under *Smith*, a state can apply neutral laws "to religious practices even when not supported by a compelling governmental interest." Congress enacted RFRA to prohibit federal and state governments from " 'substantially burdening' " the free exercise of religion through laws of general application unless the government could show that this burden: (1) furthered a compelling governmental interest; and (2) is the least restrictive alternative available to further that interest.

The Court found that RFRA altered the meaning of the Free Exercise Clause — "changing what the right is" rather than enforcing the Clause. While preventative measures are sometimes appropriate as remedial measures, the "appropriateness of remedial measures must be considered in light of the evil presented." Unlike the record in the Voting Rights Act cases, the legislative history of RFRA failed to demonstrate "examples of modern instances of generally applicable law passed because of religious bigotry." Instead of responding to or preventing unconstitutional behavior, RFRA itself unconstitutionally changes substantive "constitutional protections." The act opens up to a potential constitutional challenge nearly every rule of general application in the United States.

The least restrictive means test did not apply to free exercise cases even prior to *Smith*. In the modern regulatory state, "numerous state laws, such as the zoning regulations at issue here, impose a substantial burden on a large class of individuals."

In his concurrence, Justice Stevens maintained that RFRA violates the Establishment Clause, by providing "the Church with a legal weapon that no atheist or agnostic can obtain."

In his concurrence joined by Justice Stevens, Justice Scalia responded to Justice O'Connor's historical critique of *Smith*. None of the dissent's historical evidence undermines the conclusion that legislatures, not courts, ought to fashion exemptions to generally applicable laws to advance religious freedom.

Justice O'Connor dissented, joined by Justices Souter and Breyer. Justice O'Connor agreed with the Court that RFRA is not a proper exercise of Congress' power to enforce § 5 of the Fourteenth Amendment. However, she concluded that *Smith* was decided wrongly.

Justice O'Connor argued that the Founding Fathers viewed the Free Exercise Clause as a guarantee that government would not unduly interfere with religious practice — "a position consistent with our pre-*Smith* jurisprudence." All but one of the thirteen colonies had passed a Religious Freedom Act by the late eighteenth century. James Madison objected to the first drafts of Virginia's statement of religious liberty.[67]

---

[67] While protections of religious liberty were made by legislatures, this was partly due to the fact that judicial review had not yet been established.

He was critical of George Mason's "use of the term 'toleration,' contending that the word implied that the right to practice one's religion was a governmental favor, rather than an inalienable liberty."

By the time the Bill of Rights was adopted, it was commonly accepted that the government should accommodate religious practice. In his "Memorial and Remonstrance Against Religious Assessments," Madison argued that religion held a higher priority than civil law. As President in 1808, Thomas Jefferson believed that the Constitution prohibited the United States government from interfering with "the doctrines, disciplines, or exercises" of religious institutions. In a letter to a group of Quakers, George Washington "expressly stated that he believed that government should do its utmost to accommodate religious scruples."

In a separate dissent, Justice Souter stated that he had "serious doubts about the precedential value of the *Smith* rule and its entitlement to adherence. However, Justice Souter was not prepared to support or reject the Smith rule until its merits were briefed and argued.

In a separate dissent, Justice Breyer agreed that *Smith* should be reargued. Consequently, he found it unnecessary to consider whether § 5 of the Fourteenth Amendment would authorize RFRA.

NOTES

(1) For a discussion of *Boerne*, see Jed Rubenfeld, *Antidisestablishmentarianism: Why RFRA Really was Unconstitutional*, 95 MICH. L. REV. 2347, 2350 (1997) ("[T]he First Amendment, under which Congress can "make no law respecting an establishment of religion," does not only prohibit Congress from establishing religion: it prohibits Congress from dictating to the states how to legislate religion.").

(2) For a discussion of a third common law approach to religious exemptions, see Eugene Volokh, *A Common Law Model For Religious Exemptions*, 46 UCLA L. REV. 1465, 1472 (1999) ("In the *Sherbert* regime — which the RFRA rhetoric has generally aimed at "restoring" — courts did all the heavy lifting, and what they lifted stayed in place (absent a constitutional amendment). In the *Smith* regime, the assumption was that courts played almost no role, and all the decisions were up to the legislature. But state RFRAs suggest (perhaps unexpectedly) a third model, which assigns both courts and legislatures a role in developing the law of religious exemptions. This model, I argue, will in the long run lead to a better reconciliation of religious freedom claims and countervailing private rights, just as our common-law system of tort, contract, and property law has produced better results than could have arisen under either an entirely constitutionalized or an entirely codified system of private law.").

(3) For a provocative critique of the Court's religion jurisprudence, see George W. Dent, Jr., *Secularism and the Supreme Court*, 1 BYU L. REV. 1, 73 (1999) ("For two centuries religion was widely disparaged by Western intellectuals. In the 1960s disdain for religion triumphed in the Supreme Court, which proceeded to transmogrify the religion clauses of the First Amendment. Because of changes in the main Western religions and problems with secularist theories, intellectual respect for religion has revived. The Supreme Court's secularist majority has passed on, but its ghost still haunts; the Court has not yet fashioned a new, coherent treatment of religion but has careened through inconsistent decisions and incoherent opinions.").

(4) In *Locke v. Davey*, 540 U.S. 712 (2004), the Court held that a state college scholarship program that denied funds to students majoring in devotional theology did not violate the Free Exercise Clause. The Promise Scholarship Program sought to aid the state's qualified high school graduates with college expenses through grants from the state's general fund. The grant was $1,125 and $1,542 for the academic years of 1999

and 2000, respectively. Eligibility depended on certain academic and economic criteria. However, consistent with the Washington Constitution, the funds could be used for any degree program except devotional theology. While Davey received a Promise Scholarship, Washington would not let him use it to "pursue a double major in pastoral ministries and business management / administration" at Northwest College, "a private, Christian college affiliated with the Assemblies of God denomination."

Writing for a 7-2 majority, Chief Justice Rehnquist noted that "the *Establishment Clause and the Free Exercise Clause* are frequently in tension." To alleviate this tension, the Court has "long said that 'there is room for play in the joints' between them. . . . In other words, there are some state actions permitted by the *Establishment Clause* but not required by the *Free Exercise Clause.*" Citing *Witters v. Washington Dept. Of Services for Blind*, 474 U.S. 481 (1986), *supra* § 16.02[1], Note (2), the Court noted that funding a study in devotional theology did not violate the Establishment Clause if students voluntarily chose to pursue this degree. However, the Free Exercise Clause does not require the state to fund this degree program. The program "imposes neither criminal nor civil sanctions on any type of religious service or rite. It does not deny to ministers the right to participate in the political affairs of the community. . . . And it does not require students to choose between their religious beliefs and receiving a government benefit. . . . The State has merely chosen not to fund a distinct category of instruction."

The Washington Constitution can scrutinize the establishment of religion more stringently than the United States Constitution. Washington evidences no hostility toward religion as students can use the funds to "attend pervasively religious schools," or to attend a school that requires several courses in devotional theology. "Since the founding of our country, there have been popular uprisings against procuring taxpayer funds to support church leaders." Neither the text nor the history of the Washington Constitution nor the operation of the scholarship program indicates any "animus towards religion." Such "denial of funding for vocational religious instruction alone is [not] inherently constitutionally suspect." Washington's "interest in not funding the pursuit of devotional degrees is substantial and the exclusion of such funding places a relatively minor burden on Promise Scholars."

In a dissent joined by Justice Thomas, Justice Scalia argued that the statute was unconstitutional on its face as it withheld a generally available benefit on the basis of religion. In a separate dissent, Justice Thomas noted that the program denied funding to pursue any degree in theology although he acknowledged that the parties agreed that the term " 'theology' " was limited to degrees in " 'devotional theology.' "

CUTTER v. WILKINSON, 544 U.S. 709 (2005). In *Cutter v. Wilkinson*, a unanimous Court rejected a facial challenge asserting that the Religious Land Use and Institutionalized Persons Act of 2000 (RLUIPA) violates the Establishment Clause. The plaintiffs were current and former prisoners who practiced " 'nonmainstream' religions" such as "Satanist, Wicca, and Asatru" and "the Church of Jesus Christ Christian." They brought suit alleging violation of their right to practice their religion as protected by the RLUIPA.

Writing for the Court, Justice Ginsburg said, "This Court has long recognized that the government may . . . accommodate religious practices . . . without violating the Establishment Clause, *Hobbie v. Unemployment Appeals Comm'n of Fla.*," 480 U.S. 136 (1987), *supra* § 16.05, Note (2)(c). In *Locke v. Davey*, 540 U.S. 712 (2004), *supra* § 16.05, Note (4), the Court reiterated that " 'there is room for play in the joints between' the *Free Exercise and Establishment Clauses*, allowing the government to accommodate religion beyond free exercise requirements, without offense to the *Establishment Clause.*"

After *City of Boerne v. Flores* struck down the Religious Freedom Restoration Act, on the grounds that it exceeded Congress' remedial power under § 5 of the Fourteenth Amendment, Congress responded with the more limited RLUIPA, using their Spending and Commerce powers. The Act applies to substantial burdens on religious exercise which affect institutions receiving federal funds, or interstate or international commerce. One section of the Act deals with "land-use regulation"; and the other, with "religious exercise by institutionalized persons." The section at issue prohibits government from imposing " 'a substantial burden on the religious exercise of a person residing in or confined to an institution,' unless the government shows that the burden furthers 'a compelling governmental interest' and does so by 'the least restrictive means.' "

The Court of Appeals for the Sixth Circuit had invalidated RLUIPA as violating the Establishment Clause using the analysis in *Lemon v. Kurtzman*. In reversing the Sixth Circuit, the Court declined to apply the *Lemon* test. "We resolve this case on other grounds."[68] Instead, focusing in on the Establishment Clause, the Court emphasized that " 'there is room for play in the joints' between the Clauses, some space for legislative action neither compelled by the *Free Exercise Clause* nor prohibited by the *Establishment Clause*." This Act falls within that space. Consequently, the Act is a "permissible legislative accommodation of religion that is not barred by the *Establishment Clause*."

At bottom, "RLUIPA's institutionalized-persons provision" is "compatible with the *Establishment Clause* because it alleviates exceptional government-created burdens on private religious exercise." Importantly, the Act "covers state-run institutions — mental hospitals, prisons, and the like — in which the government exerts a degree of control unparalleled in civilian society and severely disabling to private religious exercise." Proper application of the RLUIPA conforms to precedent, for "courts must take adequate account of the burdens a requested accommodation may impose on nonbeneficiaries," *Estate of Thornton v. Caldor, Inc.*, 472 U.S. 703 (1985), "and they must be satisfied that the Act's prescriptions are and will be administered neutrally among different faiths." The Court also rejected Ohio's Establishment argument that RLUIPA encourages the adoption of religious beliefs in order to gain accommodation because "Ohio already facilitates religious services for mainstream faiths."

RLUIPA does not "elevate accommodation of religious observances over an institution's need to maintain order and safety." Moreover, Justice Ginsburg had "no cause to believe that RLUIPA would not be applied in an appropriately balanced way, with particular sensitivity to security concerns." In this connection, "the federal Bureau of Prisons has managed the largest correctional system in the Nation under the same heightened scrutiny standard as RLUIPA without compromising prison security, public safety, or the constitutional rights of other prisoners."

Justice Thomas wrote a concurring opinion in which he evaluated the Establishment Clause as a "federalism provision." He acknowledged the argument advanced by Ohio that "some of the Framers may have believed that the National Government had no authority to legislate concerning religion, because no enumerated power gave it that authority." In a future case, "Ohio's Spending Clause and Commerce Clause challenges, therefore, may well have merit." However, Ohio's Establishment Clause challenge is

---

[68] Moreover, Justice Ginsburg did not consider Ohio's arguments concerning the Spending and Commerce Clauses because those arguments were not heard below.

with history, as the RLUIPA is "a law respecting religion, but not one respecting an establishment of religion."

NOTE

Controlled Substances. In *Gonzales v. O Centro Espirita Beneficente Uniao Do Vegetal* ("UDV"), 546 U.S. 418 (2006), the Court upheld a preliminary injunction prohibiting the Government from enforcing a Controlled Substances Act ban on the defendant's use of a sacramental tea, *hoasca.* Defendant used the tea as part of communion. The Government argued that the tea's use was prohibited under the Controlled Substance Act because it contains the hallucinogen DMT. Although defendant's use of the tea is "a sincere exercise of religion," the Government argued "that it has a compelling interest in the *uniform* application of the Controlled Substances Act" which precluded individualized exceptions.

However, the Religious Freedom Restoration Act of 1993 ("RFRA") requires the Government to satisfy the compelling interest test when "sincere exercise of religion is being substantially burdened." The Controlled Substances Act also supports an exemption for religious use because the Controlled Substances Act contains a provision allowing for exemptions. Congress made a religious use exemption for Indian tribes with respect to another Schedule I substance, peyote. Courts may find other exceptions. Moreover, the peyote exception undermines the Government's argument that uniform application of the Controlled Substances Act was a compelling interest. *Cutter v. Wilkinson,* 544 U.S. 709 (2005), *supra,* recently reaffirmed the case-by-case examination of religious exemptions. Indeed, Congress enacted RFRA for the very purpose of responding "to a decision denying a claimed right to sacramental use of a controlled substance."

In enacting RFRA, Congress charged the courts with striking " 'sensible balances between religious liberty and' " competing government interests. The Court affirmed the lower court's conclusion that the Government failed to meet its burden of showing a compelling interest in prohibiting "UDV's sacramental useof *hoasca.*"

APPENDIX

THE CONSTITUTION OF THE UNITED STATES OF AMERICA

PREAMBLE

We the People of the United States, in Order to form a more perfect Union, establish Justice, insure domestic Tranquility, provide for the common defence, promote the general Welfare, and secure the Blessings of Liberty to ourselves and our Posterity, do ordain and establish this Constitution for the United States of America.

ARTICLE I

SECTION 1. All legislative Powers herein granted shall be vested in a Congress of the United States, which shall consist of a Senate and House of Representatives.

SECTION 2. [1] The House of Representatives shall be composed of Members chosen every second Year by the People of the several States, and the Electors in each State shall have the Qualifications requisite for Electors of the most numerous Branch of the State Legislature.

[2] No Person shall be a Representative who shall not have attained to the Age of twenty five Years, and been seven Years a Citizen of the United States, and who shall not, when elected, be an Inhabitant of that State in which he shall be chosen.

[3] Representatives and direct Taxes shall be apportioned among the several States which may be included within this Union, according to their respective Numbers, which shall be determined by adding to the whole Number of free Persons, including those bound to Service for a Term of Years, and excluding Indians not taxed, three fifths of all other Persons. The actual Enumeration shall be made within three Years after the first Meeting of the Congress of the United States, and within every subsequent Term of ten Years, in such Manner as they shall by Law direct. The Number of Representatives shall not exceed one for every thirty Thousand, but each State shall have at Least one Representative; and until such enumeration shall be made, the State of New Hampshire shall be entitled to chuse three, Massachusetts eight, Rhode Island and Providence Plantations one, Connecticut five, New York six, New Jersey four, Pennsylvania eight, Delaware one, Maryland six, Virginia ten, North Carolina five, South Carolina five, and Georgia three.

[4] When vacancies happen in the Representation from any State, the Executive Authority thereof shall issue Writs of Election to fill such Vacancies.

[5] The House of Representatives shall chuse their Speaker and other Officers; and shall have the sole Power of Impeachment.

SECTION 3. [1] The Senate of the United States shall be composed of two Senators from each State, chosen by the Legislature thereof, for six Years; and each Senator shall have one Vote.

[2] Immediately after they shall be assembled in Consequence of the first Election, they shall be divided as equally as may be into three Classes. The Seats of the Senators of the first Class shall be vacated at the Expiration of the second Year, of the second Class at the Expiration of the fourth Year, and of the third Class at the Expiration of the sixth Year, so that one third may be chosen every second Year; and if Vacancies happen by Resignation, or otherwise, during the Recess of the Legislature of any State, the Executive thereof may make temporary Appointments until the next Meeting of the

Legislature, which shall then fill such Vacancies.

[3] No Person shall be a Senator who shall not have attained to the Age of thirty Years, and been nine Years a Citizen of the United States, and who shall not, when elected, be an Inhabitant of the State for which he shall be chosen.

[4] The Vice President of the United States shall be President of the Senate, but shall have no Vote, unless they be equally divided.

[5] The Senate shall chuse their other Officers, and also a President pro tempore, in the Absence of the Vice President, or when he shall exercise the Office of President of the United States.

[6] The Senate shall have the sole Power to try all Impeachments. When sitting for that Purpose, they shall be on Oath or Affirmation. When the President of the United States is tried the Chief Justice shall preside: And no Person shall be convicted without the Concurrence of two thirds of the Members present.

[7] Judgment in Cases of Impeachment shall not extend further than to removal from Office, and disqualification to hold and enjoy any Office of honor, Trust or Profit under the United States: but the Party convicted shall nevertheless be liable and subject to Indictment, Trial, Judgment and Punishment, according to Law.

SECTION 4. [1] The Times, Places and Manner of holding Elections for Senators and Representatives, shall be prescribed in each State by the Legislature thereof; but the Congress may at any time by Law make or alter such Regulations, except as to the Places of chusing Senators.

[2] The Congress shall assemble at least once in every Year, and such Meeting shall be on the first Monday in December, unless they shall by Law appoint a different Day.

SECTION 5. [1] Each House shall be the Judge of the Elections, Returns and Qualifications of its own Members, and a Majority of each shall constitute a Quorum to do Business; but a smaller Number may adjourn from day to day, and may be authorized to compel the Attendance of absent Members, in such Manner, and under such Penalties as each House may provide.

[2] Each House may determine the Rules of its Proceedings, punish its Members for disorderly Behaviour, and, with the Concurrence of two thirds, expel a Member.

[3] Each House shall keep a Journal of its Proceedings, and from time to time publish the same, excepting such Parts as may in their Judgment require Secrecy; and the Yeas and Nays of the Members of either House on any question shall, at the Desire of one fifth of those Present, be entered on the Journal.

[4] Neither House, during the Session of Congress, shall, without the Consent of the other, adjourn for more than three days, nor to any other Place than that in which the two Houses shall be sitting.

SECTION 6. [1] The Senators and Representatives shall receive a Compensation for their Services, to be ascertained by Law, and paid out of the Treasury of the United States. They shall in all Cases, except Treason, Felony and Breach of the Peace, be privileged from Arrest during their Attendance at the Session of their respective Houses, and in going to and returning from the same; and for any Speech or Debate in either House, they shall not be questioned in any other Place.

[2] No Senator or Representative shall, during the Time for which he was elected, be appointed to any civil Office under the Authority of the United States, which shall have been created, or the Emoluments whereof shall have been increased during such time; and no Person holding any Office under the United States, shall be a Member of either House during his Continuance in Office.

SECTION 7. [1] All Bills for raising Revenue shall originate in the House of

Representatives; but the Senate may propose or concur with amendments as on other Bills.

[2] Every Bill which shall have passed the House of Representatives and the Senate, shall, before it become a Law, be presented to the President of the United States; If he approve he shall sign it, but if not he shall return it, with his Objections to that House in which it shall have originated, who shall enter the Objections at large on their Journal, and proceed to reconsider it. If after such Reconsideration two thirds of that House shall agree to pass the Bill, it shall be sent, together with the Objections, to the other House, by which it shall likewise be reconsidered, and if approved by two thirds of that House, it shall become a Law. But in all such Cases the Votes of both Houses shall be determined by Yeas and Nays, and the Names of the Persons voting for and against the Bill shall be entered on the Journal of each House respectively. If any Bill shall not be returned by the President within ten Days (Sunday excepted) after it shall have been presented to him, the Same shall be a Law, in like Manner as if he had signed it, unless the Congress by their Adjournment prevent its Return, in which Case it shall not be a Law.

[3] Every Order, Resolution, or Vote to which the Concurrence of the Senate and House of Representatives may be necessary (except on a question of Adjournment) shall be presented to the President of the United States; and before the Same shall take Effect, shall be approved by him, or being disapproved by him, shall be repassed by two thirds of the Senate and House of Representatives, according to the Rules and Limitations prescribed in the Case of a Bill.

SECTION 8. [1] The Congress shall have Power To lay and collect Taxes, Duties, Imposts and Excises, to pay the Debts and provide for the common Defence and general Welfare of the United States; but all Duties, Imposts and Excises shall be uniform throughout the United States;

[2] To borrow Money on the credit of the United States;

[3] To regulate Commerce with foreign Nations, and among the several States, and with the Indian Tribes;

[4] To establish an uniform Rule of Naturalization, and uniform Laws on the subject of Bankruptcies throughout the United States;

[5] To coin Money, regulate the Value thereof, and of foreign Coin, and fix the Standard of Weights and Measures;

[6] To provide for the Punishment of counterfeiting the Securities and current Coin of the United States;

[7] To establish Post Offices and post Roads;

[8] To promote the Progress of Science and useful Arts, by securing for limited Times to Authors and Inventors the exclusive Rights to their respective Writings and Discoveries;

[9] To constitute Tribunals inferior to the supreme Court;

[10] To define and punish Piracies and Felonies committed on the high Seas, and Offenses against the Law of Nations;

[11] To declare War, grant Letters of Marque and Reprisal, and make Rules concerning Captures on Land and Water;

[12] To raise and support Armies, but no Appropriation of Money to that Use shall be for a longer Term than two Years;

[13] To provide and maintain a Navy;

[14] To make Rules for the Government and Regulation of the land and naval Forces;

[15] To provide for calling forth the Militia to execute the Laws of the Union, suppress Insurrections and repel Invasions;

[16] To provide for organizing, arming, and disciplining, the Militia, and for governing such Part of them as may be employed in the Service of the United States, reserving to the States respectively, the Appointment of the Officers, and the Authority of training the militia according to the discipline prescribed by Congress;

[17] To exercise exclusive Legislation in all Cases whatsoever, over such District (not exceeding ten Miles square) as may, by Cession of particular States, and the Acceptance of Congress, become the Seat of the Government of the United States, and to exercise like Authority over all Places purchased by the Consent of the Legislature of the State in which the Same shall be, for the Erection of Forts, Magazines, Arsenals, dock-Yards, and other needful Buildings;—And

[18] To make all Laws which shall be necessary and proper for carrying into Execution the foregoing Powers, and all other Powers vested by this Constitution in the Government of the United States, or in any Department or Officer thereof.

SECTION 9. [1] The Migration or Importation of such Persons as any of the States now existing shall think proper to admit, shall not be prohibited by the Congress prior to the Year one thousand eight hundred and eight, but a Tax or duty may be imposed on such Importation, not exceeding ten dollars for each Person.

[2] The Privilege of the Writ of Habeas Corpus shall not be suspended, unless when in Cases of Rebellion or Invasion the public Safety may require it.

[3] No Bill of Attainder or ex post facto Law shall be passed.

[4] No Capitation, or other direct, Tax shall be laid, unless in Proportion to the Census of Enumeration herein before directed to be taken.

[5] No Tax or Duty shall be laid on Articles exported from any State.

[6] No Preference shall be given by any Regulation of Commerce or Revenue to the Ports of one State over those of another: nor shall Vessels bound to, or from, one State, be obliged to enter, clear or pay Duties in another.

[7] No Money shall be drawn from the Treasury, but in Consequence of Appropriations made by Law; and a regular Statement and Account of the Receipts and Expenditures of all public Money shall be published from time to time.

[8] No Title of Nobility shall be granted by the United States: And no Person holding any Office of Profit or Trust under them, shall, without the Consent of the Congress, accept of any present, Emolument, Office, or Title, of any kind whatever, from any King, Prince or foreign State.

SECTION 10. [1] No State shall enter into any Treaty, Alliance, or Confederation; grant Letters of Marque and Reprisal; coin Money; emit Bills of Credit; make any Thing but gold and silver Coin a Tender in Payment of Debts; pass any Bill of Attainder, ex post facto Law, or Law impairing the Obligation of Contracts, or grant any Title of Nobility.

[2] No State shall, without the Consent of the Congress, lay any Imposts or Duties on Imports or Exports, except what may be absolutely necessary for executing [its] inspection Laws: and the net Produce of all Duties and Imposts, laid by any State on Imports or Exports, shall be for the Use of the Treasury of the United States; and all such Laws shall be subject to the Revision and Controul of the Congress.

[3] No State shall, without the Consent of Congress, lay any Duty of Tonnage, keep Troops, or Ships of War in time of Peace, enter into any Agreement or Compact with another State, or with a foreign Power, or engage in War, unless actually invaded, or in such imminent Danger as will not admit of delay.

ARTICLE II

SECTION 1. [1] The executive Power shall be vested in a President of the United States of America. He shall hold his Office during the Term of four Years, and, together with the Vice President, chosen for the same Term, be elected, as follows:

[2] Each State shall appoint, in such Manner as the Legislature thereof may direct, a Number of Electors, equal to the whole Number of Senators and Representatives to which the State may be entitled in the Congress: but no Senator or Representative, or Person holding an Office of Trust or Profit under the United States, shall be appointed an Elector.

[3] The Electors shall meet in their respective States, and vote by Ballot for two Persons, of whom one at least shall not be an Inhabitant of the same State with themselves. And they shall make a List of all the Persons voted for, and of the Number of Votes for each; which List they shall sign and certify, and transmit sealed to the Seat of the Government of the United States, directed to the President of the Senate. The President of the Senate shall, in the Presence of the Senate and House of Representatives, open all the Certificates, and the Votes shall then be counted. The Person having the greatest Number of Votes shall be the President, if such Number be a Majority of the whole Number of Electors appointed; and if there be more than one who have such Majority, and have an equal Number of Votes, then the House of Representatives shall immediately chuse by Ballot one of them for President; and if no Person have a Majority, then from the five highest on the List the said House shall in like Manner chuse the President. But in chusing the President, the Votes shall be taken by States, the Representation from each State having one Vote; a quorum for this Purpose shall consist of a Member or Members from two thirds of the States, and a Majority of all the States shall be necessary to a Choice. In every Case, after the Choice of the President, the Person having the greatest Number of Votes of the Electors shall be the Vice President. But if there should remain two or more who have equal Votes, the Senate shall chuse from them by Ballot the Vice President.

[4] The Congress may determine the Time of chusing the Electors, and the Day on which they shall give their Votes; which Day shall be the same throughout the United States.

[5] No Person except a natural born Citizen, or a Citizen of the United States, at the time of the Adoption of this Constitution, shall be eligible to the Office of President; neither shall any Person be eligible to that Office who shall not have attained to the Age of thirty five Years, and been fourteen Years a Resident within the United States.

[6] In Case of the Removal of the President from Office, or of his Death, Resignation, or Inability to discharge the Powers and Duties of the said Office, the Same shall devolve on the Vice President, and the Congress may by Law provide for the Case of Removal, Death, Resignation or Inability, both of the President and Vice President, declaring what Officer shall then act as President, and such Officer shall act accordingly, until the Disability be removed, or a President shall be elected.

[7] The President shall, at stated Times, receive for his Services, a Compensation, which shall neither be increased nor diminished during the Period for which he shall have been elected, and he shall not receive within that Period any other Emolument from the United States, or any of them.

[8] Before he enter on the Execution of his Office, he shall take the following Oath or Affirmation:—"I do solemnly swear (or affirm) that I will faithfully execute the Office of President of the United States, and will to the best of my Ability, preserve, protect and defend the Constitution of the United States."

SECTION 2. [1] The President shall be Commander in Chief of the Army and Navy of the United States, and of the Militia of the several States, when called into the actual Service of the United States; he may require the Opinion, in writing, of the principal Officer in each of the executive Departments, upon any Subject relating to the Duties of their respective Offices, and he shall have Power to grant Reprieves and Pardons for Offenses against the United States, except in Cases of Impeachment.

[2] He shall have Power, by and with the Advice and Consent of the Senate, to make Treaties, provided two thirds of the Senators present concur; and he shall nominate, and by and with the Advice and Consent of the Senate, shall appoint Ambassadors, other public Ministers and Consuls, Judges of the supreme Court, and all other Officers of the United States, whose Appointments are not herein otherwise provided for, and which shall be established by Law: but the Congress may by Law vest the Appointment of such inferior Officers, as they think proper, in the President alone, in the Courts of Law, or in the Heads of Departments.

[3] The President shall have Power to fill up all Vacancies that may happen during the recess of the Senate, by granting Commissions which shall expire at the End of their next Session.

SECTION 3. He shall from time to time give to the Congress Information of the State of the Union, and recommend to their Consideration such Measures as he shall judge necessary and expedient; he may, on extraordinary Occasions, convene both Houses, or either of them, and in Case of Disagreement between them, with Respect to the Time of Adjournment, he may adjourn them to such Time as he shall think proper; he shall receive Ambassadors and other public Ministers; he shall take Care that the Laws be faithfully executed, and shall Commission all the Officers of the United States.

SECTION 4. The President, Vice President and all Civil Officers of the United States, shall be removed from Office on Impeachment for, and Conviction of, Treason, Bribery, or other high Crimes and Misdemeanors.

ARTICLE III

SECTION 1. The judicial Power of the United States, shall be vested in one supreme Court, and in such inferior Courts as the Congress may from time to time ordain and establish. The Judges, both of the supreme and inferior Courts, shall hold their Offices during good Behaviour, and shall, at stated Times, receive for their Services, a Compensation, which shall not be diminished during their Continuance in Office.

SECTION 2. [1] The judicial Power shall extend to all Cases, in Law and Equity, arising under this Constitution, the Laws of the United States, and Treaties made, or which shall be made, under their Authority;—to all Cases affecting Ambassadors, other public Ministers and Consuls;—to all Cases of admiralty and maritime Jurisdiction;—to Controversies to which the United States shall be a Party;—to Controversies between two or more States;—between a State and Citizens of another State;—between Citizens of different States;—between Citizens of the same State claiming Lands under Grants of different States, and between a State, or the Citizens thereof, and foreign States, Citizens or Subjects.

[2] In all Cases affecting Ambassadors, other public Ministers and Consuls, and those in which a State shall be Party, the supreme Court shall have original Jurisdiction. In all the other Cases before mentioned, the supreme Court shall have appellate Jurisdiction, both as to Law and Fact, with such Exceptions, and under such Regulations as the Congress shall make.

[3] The Trial of all Crimes, except in Cases of Impeachment, shall be by Jury; and such Trial shall be held in the State where the said Crimes shall have been committed;

but when not committed within any State, the Trial shall be at such Place or Places as the Congress may by Law have directed.

SECTION 3. [1] Treason against the United States, shall consist only in levying War against them, or in adhering to their Enemies, giving them Aid and Comfort. No Person shall be convicted of Treason unless on the Testimony of two Witnesses to the same overt Act, or on Confession in open Court.

[2] The Congress shall have Power to declare the Punishment of Treason, but no Attainder of Treason shall work Corruption of Blood, or Forfeiture except during the Life of the Person attainted.

ARTICLE IV

SECTION 1. Full Faith and Credit shall be given in each State to the public Acts, Records, and judicial Proceedings of every other State. And the Congress may by general Laws prescribe the Manner in which such Acts, Records and Proceedings shall be proved, and the Effect thereof.

SECTION 2. [1] The Citizens of each State shall be entitled to all Privileges and Immunities of Citizens in the several States.

[2] A Person charged in any State with Treason, Felony, or other Crime, who shall flee from Justice, and be found in another State, shall on Demand of the executive Authority of the State from which he fled, be delivered up, to be removed to the State having Jurisdiction of the Crime.

[3] No Person held to Service or Labour in one State, under the Laws thereof, escaping into another, shall, in Consequence of any Law or Regulation therein, be discharged from such Service or Labour, but shall be delivered up on Claim of the Party to whom such Service or Labour may be due.

SECTION 3. [1] New States may be admitted by the Congress into this Union; but no new State shall be formed or erected within the Jurisdiction of any other State; nor any State be formed by the Junction of two or more States, or Parts of States, without the Consent of the Legislatures of the States concerned as well as of the Congress.

[2] The Congress shall have Power to dispose of and make all needful Rules and Regulations respecting the Territory or other Property belonging to the United States; and nothing in this Constitution shall be so construed as to Prejudice any Claims of the United States, or of any particular State.

SECTION 4. The United States shall guarantee to every State in this Union a Republican Form of Government, and shall protect each of them against Invasion; and on Application of the Legislature, or of the Executive (when the Legislature cannot be convened) against domestic Violence.

ARTICLE V

The Congress, whenever two thirds of both Houses shall deem it necessary, shall propose Amendments to this Constitution, or, on the Application of the Legislatures of two thirds of the several States, shall call a Convention for proposing Amendments, which, in either Case, shall be valid to all Intents and Purposes, as Part of this Constitution, when ratified by the Legislatures of three fourths of the several States, or by Conventions in three fourths thereof, as the one or the other Mode of Ratification may be proposed by the Congress; Provided that no Amendment which may be made prior to the Year One thousand eight hundred and eight shall in any Manner affect the first and fourth Clauses in the Ninth Section of the first Article; and that no State, without its Consent, shall be deprived of its equal Suffrage in the Senate.

ARTICLE VI

[1] All Debts contracted and Engagements entered into, before the Adoption of this Constitution, shall be as valid against the United States under this Constitution, as under the Confederation.

[2] This Constitution, and the Laws of the United States which shall be made in Pursuance thereof; and all Treaties made, or which shall be made, under the Authority of the United States, shall be the supreme Law of the Land; and the Judges in every State shall be bound thereby, any Thing in the Constitution or Laws of any State to the Contrary notwithstanding.

[3] The Senators and Representatives before mentioned, and the Members of the several State Legislatures, and all executive and judicial Officers, both of the United States and of the several States, shall be bound by Oath or Affirmation, to support this Constitution; but no religious Test shall ever be required as a Qualification to any Office or public Trust under the United States.

ARTICLE VII

The Ratification of the Conventions of nine States, shall be sufficient for the Establishment of this Constitution between the States so ratifying the Same.

ARTICLES IN ADDITION TO, AND AMENDMENT OF, THE CONSTITUTION OF THE UNITED STATES OF AMERICA, PROPOSED BY CONGRESS, AND RATIFIED BY THE SEVERAL STATES, PURSUANT TO THE FIFTH ARTICLE OF THE ORIGINAL CONSTITUTION.

AMENDMENT I [1791]

Congress shall make no law respecting an establishment of religion, or prohibiting the free exercise thereof; or abridging the freedom of speech, or of the press; or the right of the people peaceably to assemble, and to petition the Government for a redress of grievances.

AMENDMENT II [1791]

A well regulated Militia, being necessary to the security of a free State, the right of the people to keep and bear Arms, shall not be infringed.

AMENDMENT III [1791]

No Soldier shall, in time of peace be quartered in any house, without the consent of the Owner, nor in time of war, but in a manner to be prescribed by law.

AMENDMENT IV [1791]

The right of the people to be secure in their persons, houses, papers, and effects, against unreasonable searches and seizures, shall not be violated, and no Warrants shall issue, but upon probable cause, supported by Oath or affirmation, and particularly describing the place to be searched, and the persons or things to be seized.

AMENDMENT V [1791]

No person shall be held to answer for a capital, or otherwise infamous crime, unless on a presentment or indictment of a Grand Jury, except in cases arising in the land or naval forces, or in the Militia, when in actual service in time of War or public danger; nor shall any person be subject for the same offence to be twice put in jeopardy of life or limb; nor shall be compelled in any criminal case to be a witness against himself, nor be deprived of life, liberty, or property, without due process of law; nor shall private property be taken for public use, without just compensation.

AMENDMENT VI [1791]

In all criminal prosecutions, the accused shall enjoy the right to a speedy and public trial, by an impartial jury of the State and district wherein the crime shall have been committed, which district shall have been previously ascertained by law, and to be informed of the nature and cause of the accusation; to be confronted with the witnesses against him; to have compulsory process for obtaining witnesses in his favor, and to have the Assistance of Counsel for his defence.

AMENDMENT VII [1791]

In Suits at common law, where the value in controversy shall exceed twenty dollars, the right of trial by jury shall be preserved, and no fact tried by a jury, shall be otherwise re-examined in any Court of the United States, than according to the rules of the common law.

AMENDMENT VIII [1791]

Excessive bail shall not be required, nor excessive fines imposed, nor cruel and unusual punishments inflicted.

AMENDMENT IX [1791]

The enumeration in the Constitution, of certain rights, shall not be construed to deny or disparage others retained by the people.

AMENDMENT X [1791]

The powers not delegated to the United States by the Constitution, nor prohibited by it to the States, are reserved to the States respectively, or to the people.

AMENDMENT XI [1798]

The Judicial power of the United States shall not be construed to extend to any suit in law or equity, commenced or prosecuted against one of the United States by Citizens of another State, or by Citizens or Subjects of any Foreign State.

AMENDMENT XII [1804]

The Electors shall meet in their respective states and vote by ballot for President and Vice-President, one of whom, at least, shall not be an inhabitant of the same state with themselves; they shall name in their ballots the person voted for as President, and in distinct ballots the person voted for as Vice-President, and they shall make distinct lists of all persons voted for as President, and of all persons voted for as Vice-President, and of the number of votes for each, which lists they shall sign and certify, and transmit sealed to the seat of the government of the United States, directed to the President of the Senate;—The President of the Senate shall, in the presence of the Senate and House of Representatives, open all the certificates and the votes shall then be counted;—The person having the greatest number of votes for President, shall be the President, if such number be a majority of the whole number of Electors appointed; and if no person have such majority, then from the persons having the highest numbers not exceeding three on the list of those voted for as President, the House of Representatives shall choose immediately, by ballot, the President. But in choosing the President, the votes shall be taken by states, the representation from each state having one vote; a quorum for this purpose shall consist of a member or members from two-thirds of the states, and a majority of all the states shall be necessary to a choice. And if the House of Representatives shall not choose a President whenever the right of choice shall devolve upon them, before the fourth day of March next following, then the Vice-President shall act as President, as in the case of the death or other constitutional disability of the President —The person having the greatest number of votes as Vice-President, shall be the Vice-President, if such number be a majority of the whole number of Electors appointed, and if no person have a majority, then from the two highest numbers on the list, the Senate shall choose the Vice-President; a quorum for the purpose shall consist of two-thirds of the whole number of Senators, and a majority of the whole number shall be necessary to a choice. But no person constitutionally ineligible to the office of President shall be eligible to that of Vice-President of the United States.

AMENDMENT XIII [1865]

SECTION 1. Neither slavery nor involuntary servitude, except as a punishment for crime whereof the party shall have been duly convicted, shall exist within the United States, or any place subject to their jurisdiction.

SECTION 2. Congress shall have power to enforce this article by appropriate legislation.

AMENDMENT XIV [1868]

SECTION 1. All persons born or naturalized in the United States and subject to the jurisdiction thereof, are citizens of the United States and of the State wherein they reside. No State shall make or enforce any law which shall abridge the privileges or immunities of citizens of the United States; nor shall any State deprive any person of life, liberty, or property, without due process of law; nor deny to any person within its jurisdiction the equal protection of the laws.

SECTION 2. Representatives shall be apportioned among the several States according to their respective numbers, counting the whole number of persons in each State, excluding Indians not taxed. But when the right to vote at any election for the choice of electors for President and Vice President of the United States, Representatives in Congress, the Executive and Judicial officers of a State, or the members of the Legislature thereof, is denied to any of the male inhabitants of such State, being twenty-one years of age, and citizens of the United States, or in any way abridged, except for participation in rebellion, or other crime, the basis of representation therein shall be reduced in the proportion which the number of such male citizens shall bear to the whole number of male citizens twenty-one years of age in such State.

SECTION 3. No person shall be a Senator or Representative in Congress, or elector of President and Vice President, or hold any office, civil or military, under the United States, or under any State, who, having previously taken an oath, as a member of Congress, or as an officer of the United States, or as a member of any State legislature, or as an executive or judicial officer of any State, to support the Constitution of the United States, shall have engaged in insurrection or rebellion against the same, or given aid or comfort to the enemies thereof. But Congress may by a vote of two-thirds of each House, remove such disability.

SECTION 4. The validity of the public debt of the United States, authorized by law, including debts incurred for payment of pensions and bounties for services in suppressing insurrection or rebellion, shall not be questioned. But neither the United States nor any State shall assume or pay any debt or obligation incurred in aid of insurrection or rebellion against the United States, or any claim for the loss of emancipation of any slave; but all such debts, obligations and claims shall be held illegal and void.

SECTION 5. The Congress shall have power to enforce, by appropriate legislation, the provisions of this article.

AMENDMENT XV [1870]

SECTION 1. The right of citizens of the United States to vote shall not be denied or abridged by the United States or by any State on account of race, color, or previous condition of servitude.

SECTION 2. The Congress shall have power to enforce this article by appropriate legislation.

AMENDMENT XVI [1913]

The Congress shall have power to lay and collect taxes on incomes, from whatever source derived, without apportionment among the several States, and without regard to any census or enumeration.

AMENDMENT XVII [1913]

[1] The Senate of the United States shall be composed of two Senators from each State, elected by the people thereof, for six years; and each Senator shall have one vote. The electors in each State shall have the qualifications requisite for electors of the most numerous branch of the State legislatures.

[2] When vacancies happen in the representation of any State in the Senate, the executive authority of such State shall issue writs of election to fill such vacancies: *Provided*, That the legislature of any State may empower the executive thereof to make temporary appointments until the people fill the vacancies by election as the legislature may direct.

This amendment shall not be so construed as to affect the election or term of any Senator chosen before it becomes valid as part of the Constitution.

AMENDMENT XVIII [1919]

SECTION 1. After one year from the ratification of this article the manufacture, sale, or transportation of intoxicating liquors within, the importation thereof into, or the exportation thereof from the United States and all territory subject to the jurisdiction thereof for beverage purposes is hereby prohibited.

SECTION 2. The Congress and the several States shall have concurrent power to enforce this article by appropriate legislation.

SECTION 3. This article shall be inoperative unless it shall have been ratified as an amendment to the Constitution by the legislatures of the several States, as provided in the Constitution, within seven years from the date of the submission hereof to the States by the Congress.

AMENDMENT XIX [1920]

[1] The right of citizens of the United States to vote shall not be denied or abridged by the United States or by any State on account of sex.

[2] Congress shall have power to enforce this article by appropriate legislation.

AMENDMENT XX [1933]

SECTION 1. The terms of the President and Vice President shall end at noon on the 20th day of January, and the terms of Senators and Representatives at noon on the 3d day of January, of the years in which such terms would have ended if this article had not been ratified; and the terms of their successors shall then begin.

SECTION 2. The Congress shall assemble at least once in every year, and such meeting shall begin at noon on the 3d day of January, unless they shall by law appoint a different day.

SECTION 3. If, at the time fixed for the beginning of the term of the President, the President elect shall have died, the Vice President elect shall become President. If a President shall not have been chosen before the time fixed for the beginning of his term, or if the President elect shall have failed to qualify, then the Vice President elect shall act as President until a President shall have qualified; and the Congress may by law provide for the case wherein neither a President elect nor a Vice President elect shall have qualified, declaring who shall then act as President, or the manner in which one who is to act shall be selected, and such person shall act accordingly until a President or Vice President shall have qualified.

SECTION 4. The Congress may by law provide for the case of the death of any of the persons from whom the House of Representatives may choose a President whenever the right of choice shall have devolved upon them, and for the case of the death of any of the persons from whom the Senate may choose a Vice President whenever the right of choice shall have devolved upon them.

SECTION 5. Sections 1 and 2 shall take effect on the 15th day of October following the ratification of this article.

SECTION 6. This article shall be inoperative unless it shall have been ratified as an amendment to the Constitution by the legislatures of three-fourths of the several States within seven years from the date of its submission.

AMENDMENT XXI [1933]

SECTION 1. The eighteenth article of amendment to the Constitution of the United States is hereby repealed.

SECTION 2. The transportation or importation into any State, Territory, or possession of the United States for delivery or use therein of intoxicating liquors, in violation of the laws thereof, is hereby prohibited.

SECTION 3. This article shall be inoperative unless it shall have been ratified as an amendment to the Constitution by conventions in the several States, as provided in the Constitution, within seven years from the date of the submission hereof to the States by the Congress.

AMENDMENT XXII [1951]

SECTION 1. No person shall be elected to the office of the President more than twice, and no person who has held the office of President, or acted as President, for more than two years of a term to which some other person was elected President shall be elected to the office of the President more than once. But this Article shall not apply to any person holding the office of President when this Article was proposed by the Congress, and shall not prevent any person who may be holding the office of President, or acting as President, during the term within which this Article becomes operative from holding the office of President or acting as President during the remainder of such term.

SECTION 2. This article shall be inoperative unless it shall have been ratified as an amendment to the Constitution by the legislatures of three-fourths of the several States within seven years from the date of its submission to the States by the Congress.

AMENDMENT XXIII [1961]

SECTION 1. The District constituting the seat of Government of the United States shall appoint in such manner as the Congress may direct:

A number of electors of President and Vice President equal to the whole number of Senators and Representatives in Congress to which the District would be entitled if it were a State, but in no event more than the least populous State; they shall be in addition to those appointed by the States, but they shall be considered, for the purposes of the election of President and Vice President, to be electors appointed by a State; and they shall meet in the District and perform such duties as provided by the twelfth article of amendment.

SECTION 2. The Congress shall have power to enforce this article by appropriate legislation.

AMENDMENT XXIV [1964]

SECTION 1. The right of citizens of the United States to vote in any primary or other election for President or Vice President, for electors for President or Vice President, or for Senator or Representative in Congress, shall not be denied or abridged by the United States or any State by reason of failure to pay any poll tax or other tax.

SECTION 2. The Congress shall have power to enforce this article by appropriate legislation.

AMENDMENT XXV [1967]

SECTION 1. In case of the removal of the President from office or of his death or resignation, the Vice President shall become President.

SECTION 2. Whenever there is a vacancy in the office of the Vice President, the President shall nominate a Vice President who shall take office upon confirmation by a majority vote of both Houses of Congress.

SECTION 3. Whenever the President transmits to the President pro tempore of the Senate and the Speaker of the House of Representatives his written declaration that he is unable to discharge the powers and duties of his office, and until he transmits to them a written declaration to the contrary, such powers and duties shall be discharged by the Vice President as Acting President.

SECTION 4. Whenever the Vice President and a majority of either the principal officers of the executive departments or of such other body as Congress may by law provide, transmit to the President pro tempore of the Senate and the Speaker of the House of Representatives their written declaration that the President is unable to discharge the powers and duties of his office, the Vice President shall immediately assume the powers and duties of the office as Acting President.

Thereafter, when the President transmits to the President pro tempore of the Senate and the Speaker of the House of Representatives his written declaration that no inability exists, he shall resume the powers and duties of his office unless the Vice President and a majority of either the principal officers of the executive department or of such other body as Congress may by law provide, transmit within four days to the President pro tempore of the Senate and the Speaker of the House of Representatives their written declaration that the President is unable to discharge the powers and duties of his office. Thereupon Congress shall decide the issue, assembling within forty-eight hours for that purpose if not in session. If the Congress, within twenty-one days after receipt of the latter after Congress is required to assemble, determines by two-thirds vote of both Houses that the President is unable to discharge the powers and duties of his office, the Vice President shall continue to discharge the same as acting President; otherwise, the President shall resume the powers and duties of his office.

AMENDMENT XXVI [1971]

SECTION 1. The right of citizens of the United States, who are eighteen years of age or older, to vote shall not be denied or abridged by the United States or by any State on account of age.

SECTION 2. The Congress shall have power to enforce this article by appropriate legislation.

AMENDMENT XXVII [1992]

No law, varying the compensation for the services of the Senators and Representatives, shall take effect, until an election of Representatives shall have intervened.

TABLE OF CASES

[References are to pages]

TABLE OF CASES

[References are to pages]

[References are to pages]

[References are to pages]

[References are to pages]

[References are to pages]

[References are to pages]

Port Authority v. Feeney 188

Poulos v. New Hampshire. 978

Powell v. McCormack 12; 49; 56, 57; 149

Powell v. State of Alabama. 437

Powers v. Ohio 43; 611

PRESS ENTERPRISE COMPANY v. SUPERIOR COURT OF CALIFORNIA 864; 865

Primus, In re. 1145

Prince v. Massachusetts 444; 1290

PRINTZ v. UNITED STATES. 127; 131; 179

PRIZE CASES. 291

Procunier v. Martinez 860

Pruneyard Shopping Center v. Robins. 1027

Purkett v. Elem 614

Q

Quern v. Jordan 188

Quirin, Ex parte 297; 304, 305; 309; 311

R

R.A.V. v. ST. PAUL 952; 955

R.M.J, In re. .1148

Raich v. Ashcroft 121

RAILWAY EXPRESS AGENCY, INC. v. NEW YORK. 757; 1012

Raines v. Byrd 41, 42

Rainey v. United States 144

RANDALL v. SORRELL 1074

Rankin v. McPherson 827

Ray v. Atlantic Richfield Co 232

RED LION BROADCASTING CO. v. FCC. .693; 874; 887; 907, 908; 1097

Redrup v. New York. 1151

Reed v. Reed. 620, 621

REEVES, INC. v. STAKE 227

Regan v. Taxation With Representation of Wash. .1109; 1192

Regan v. Wald. 757

REGENTS OF UNIVERSITY OF CALIFORNIA REGENTS v. BAKKE . 45; 565, 566; 647; 661; 663; 665–670; 672; 679; 685; 693

Reid v. Colorado 81

Reid v. Covert. 146

Reitman v. Mulkey 592

Reno v. ACLU ("ACLU"). 902; 913

Reno v. Condon. 181

Renton v. Playtime Theatres, Inc.. . .906; 954; 967, 968; 1001

REPUBLICAN PARTY OF MINNESOTA v. WHITE. .836

REYNOLDS v. SIMS 729; 734; 740; 749

Reynolds v. United States. . . .1178; 1269; 1290, 1291

Rice v. Collins. 615

Richardson; United States v. 39

RICHMOND v. J. A. CROSON, CO. . .567; 569, 570; 599; 683

RICHMOND NEWSPAPERS, INC. v. VIRGINIA . 862

Robel; United States v. 790

Roberts v. City of Boston. 540

Roberts v. United States Jaycees. . .523; 629; 804; 806

Robertson v. Seattle Audubon Society 24

Rochin v. People of State of California. 438; 517

ROE v. WADE. 45; 442; 481; 499; 1113; 1125

Roemer v. Board of Public Works. 1238

ROGERS v. LODGE 594

Rome, City of v. United States 350; 363

ROMER v. EVANS 502; 714

Rosario v. Rockefeller. 798

ROSENBERGER v. RECTOR & VISITORS OF UNIV. OF VIRGINIA 1040; 1114; 1116; 1275

Rosenblatt v. Baer. 921

Rosenbloom v. Metromedia, Inc. 924

Ross v. Moffitt 724

ROSTKER v. GOLDBERG. 622

Roth v. United States. 1150; 1152, 1153

Rubin v. Coors Brewing Co. 1135, 1136

Ruckelshaus v. Monsanto Co. 416

RUMSFELD v. FORUM FOR ACADEMIC & INSTITUTIONAL RIGHTS ("FAIR"). . .807; 1121

RUNYON v. McCRARY 366

Russell v. United States. 796

RUST v. SULLIVAN 142; 453; 488; 1108

RUTAN v. REPUBLICAN PARTY OF ILLINOIS . 812

Ryder v. United States. 280

S

Sable Communications of Cal., Inc. v. FCC. .892, 893; 913; 968; 1159

Sabri v. United States. 143

Sacramento, County of v. Lewis 501

SAENZ v. ROE 238; 381; 753

Saia v. New York. 975

Salyer Land Co. v. Tulare Water District. 728

SAN ANTONIO SCHOOL DISTRICT v. RODRIGUEZ 655; 705; 708; 713; 720

San Diego, California, City of v. Roe 827

San Francisco Arts & Athletics, Inc. v. United States Olympic Committee 1053

Sanchez; United States v. 137

[References are to pages]

X

Y

Z

INDEX

[References are to page numbers.]

[References are to page numbers.]

[References are to page numbers.]

[References are to page numbers.]

[References are to page numbers.]

[References are to page numbers.]

[References are to page numbers.]

[References are to page numbers.]

[References are to page numbers.]

[References are to page numbers.]

[References are to page numbers.]

[References are to page numbers.]

[References are to page numbers.]

[References are to page numbers.]

R

[References are to page numbers.]

[References are to page numbers.]

[References are to page numbers.]

[References are to page numbers.]

[References are to page numbers.]

W

Z